Good Beer Guide 2008

Edited by
Roger Protz
Glenfiddich Drink Writer of the Year 1997 and 2004; short-listed 2007

Project Co-ordinator
Emma Haines

Assistant Editors
Ione Brown and Sylvia Goulding

Managing Editor
Simon Hall

CAMRA BOOKS

Campaign for Real A
230 Hatfield Road, St Alb
Hertfordshire AL1 4LW

D0277912

Contents

Editorial Assistance: Debbie Williams and Marcus Hardy

Beer Index compiled by Jeff Evans

Thanks to the following at CAMRA head office Chief Executive, Mike Benner; The Campaigns, Marketing and Website team: Georgina Rudman, Iain Loe, Tony Jerome, Jonathan Mail, Kate Foster, Owen Morris and Alison Thomas; The Administration team: Cressida Feiler, John Cottrell, Malcolm Harding, Jean Jones, Gary Fowler, Michael Green, Carwyn Davies, Caroline Clerembeaux, Gillian Dale, Liz McGlynn and Gary Ranson.

Thanks also to 87,000 CAMRA members who carried out research for the pubs; Rick Pickup and Steve Westby for advising on new breweries; the Campaign's Regional Directors, who co-ordinated the pub entries; Paul Moorhouse for assembling the beer tasting notes; Dave Gamston and Michael Slaughter for assembling and checking the National Inventory of pubs with historic interiors; and CAMRA's National Executive for their support.

Photo credits Front cover: Don Klumpp (left), Alamy (right), Banana Stock (main); back cover: Alamy; The Tenacious Ten: Blue Anchor, Square & Compass and Star Inn: Michael Slaughter; Cherry Tree: Cris Bartlett; Roscoe Head: John White; New Inn, Dave Schofield; Buckingham Arms, Queens Head, Sow & Pigs and Star Tavern, Roger Protz.

Production team Cover and colour section: Howells Design Ltd, London W13; brewery section origination: Redbus, London W4; pubs section origination: AMA Dataset, Preston, Lancs; maps by David and Morag Perrott, PerroCarto, Machnylleth, Wales. Printed by William Clowes, Beccles, Suffolk.

Published by the Campaign for Real Ale Ltd, 230 Hatfield Road, St Albans, Herts, AL1 4LW. Tel 01727 867201. Email CAMRA@CAMRA.org.uk Website www.CAMRA.org.uk

© Campaign for Real Ale Ltd 2007/2008

ISBN 978-1-85249-231-1

Now you can really enjoy your beer…

The ban on smoking offers pubs a great opportunity to attract new customers

IT IS TIMELY THAT THE 35TH EDITION of the Good Beer Guide is marked by a seismic change in pub life. All pubs – with England, Wales and Northern Ireland following Scotland – are now free from the smoke and fug created by cigarettes, pipes and cigars. When the Guide was first launched in 1973, most pubgoers smoked. Tables and bar tops were liberally sprinkled with ashtrays. Scroll forward 35 years and the situation has been turned on its head: people did not visit pubs precisely because they were smoky.

During the run-up to the introduction of the ban, the pub trade press was knee-deep in nostalgic cigarette ash. We heard the usual 'end of civilisation' arguments if smokers were driven from pubs, with thousands of hostelries closing. This argument was holed below the waterline by the not insignificant fact that thousands of pubs were closing every year *before* the ban came into place.

Pub owners eventually got the message. The ban was coming and the sensible course of action was to prepare for it by providing facilities for smokers outside pubs while improving interiors. Far from spelling doom for the British pub, the smoking ban offers a once-in-a-lifetime opportunity to recover lost business and attract new custom. The overwhelming majority of people in Britain do not smoke and their number is growing. They must be encouraged to visit pubs and pub owners need to exercise great skill in mounting a national promotion for their licensed premises. The Good Beer Guide, smoke-free and gratis, offers the following simple

Fag end of history…when the Good Beer Guide was first published in 1973, pubs (as above) were knee-deep in cigarette ash while the aroma and flavour of beer were ruined by smoke

Hurrying back to the bar

A survey by CAMRA in 2007 showed that 17% of all adults in England and Wales who visit pubs regularly are more likely to visit them more often following the ban on smoking. 97% of the group were non-smokers. 840,000 people who currently never go to pubs said they would after the ban. 93% of real ale drinkers said they were more likely to visit pubs now they are smoke-free.

CAMRA's national chairman, Paula Waters (pictured), said: 'CAMRA believes that the future for pubs lies in offering the public an experience beyond simply a place to have a drink and a smoke. Our research has shown that non-smokers will be attracted to pubs after the ban comes into force and many of them would like to find a real ale waiting for them when they get there. Striving to offer a pleasant and memorable experience for everyone who walks through the door of a pub will mean there is no reason why there should be any drop in trade in the long term.'

■ *The survey was conducted by TNS for CAMRA from a sample of 1,500 adults in England and Wales.*

slogan: 'Visit the pub and now really enjoy your beer'. The aim of the Guide for 35 years has been to extol the virtues of natural, living, cask-conditioned beer. That aim has always been made difficult by the fact that clouds of stale smoke have a detrimental effect on both the aroma and palate of good beer. The breweries section of the Guide offers carefully deliberated tasting notes for many of the beers listed. But the tempting array of beers with spicy and peppery hops aromas and citrus fruit and biscuity malt characteristics in the mouth are not helped if you attempt to sample one of these succulent brews with your nostrils full of smoke and nicotine seeping into the beer.

Now you can breathe again, smell again, taste again. Everything in the pub will be better. The pub trade – and all praise to it – has made a mighty effort in recent years to encourage customers to dine as well as drink in its hostelries. Many pubs match beers with specific dishes on their menus while beer is also used as an ingredient in cooking. The virtues of beer styles old and new – India Pale Ales, porters, stouts, golden ales and summer beers – are promoted as companions as fit for the dining table as wine.

That argument takes on greater momentum and importance now that pubs are free from cigarette smoke. Beer and food taste better, and the melding and mingling of aromas and tastes will significantly improve the pleasure of eating and drinking. During the 35 years of the Good Beer Guide, society and the pub have seen dramatic changes. New entrants to the 'leisure industry', grossly unfair price competition from supermarkets, and a campaign of vilification from some sections of the media have buffeted the pub. As always, it has survived. The smoking ban offers a new start and new opportunities. It can once again be at the heart of communities in towns, cities and villages, reaching out to a new audience of people previously deterred from visiting smoky bars. So go back to the pub. Be pleasurably surprised. Breathe freely...and enjoy your pint.

The Tenacious Ten

It is a remarkable sign of the resilience of the British pub that 10 of them have appeared in all 35 editions of the Good Beer Guide.

THESE ARE THE PUBS THAT WERE FLYING THE FLAG for cask beer in 1973 at a time when keg beers such as Watneys Red were rampant. Thanks to their commitment to real ale, they have survived. They have seen the rise and fall of keg beer, the introduction of British 'lager', government investigations of the brewing industry and the arrival of the new pub companies that now dominate the beer-drinking scene and too often restrict choice for consumers.

The owners of the featured pubs refused to bow to marketing 'wisdom' and accept keg beers and lagers. They have majored on cask ale and have prospered as a result. We salute them and wish them well for the next 35 years.

Blue Anchor, Helston, Cornwall

A granite and thatch inn, it is the oldest brewpub in the country. It dates from 1400 and started life as a monks' hospice. The pub still has its own small brewhouse where strong Spingo ales are brewed. The 'weakest' is 4.6% and locals recall a Christmas Special of around 12% that extended the holiday period by several days. Small, beamed rooms are connected by a central corridor. Flagstones cover the floor and seats have been fashioned from old beer casks.

Buckingham Arms, London SW1

A Young's house that was once handy for the Passport Office in Petty France, now the Department of Justice. The pub dates from 1780, was once a hat shop and became a pub in 1820. It has one long central bar that displays certificates and plaques won from the Good Beer Guide over the years. There is plenty of comfortable seating and an interesting collection of Royal Doulton Toby-jugs.

Cherry Tree Inn, Tintern, Gwent

This is the real meaning of a 'community pub' – the Cherry Tree not only serves excellent beer, drawn mainly from smaller independents, but also doubles as the village shop and post office. It enjoys a breathtaking location in a deep valley and an outside patio gives drinkers wonderful views of the surrounding countryside. The Cherry Tree specialises in home-cooked meals, with curries a speciality. Traditional cider is also available. The pub dates from the 1500s and has always been an inn.

New Inn, Kilmington, Devon

The most remarkable fact about the New Inn is that it suffered a dreadful fire in 2004, was rebuilt – and didn't miss a single entry in the Good Beer Guide. It dates from the 14th century when it was a farm and became an inn in 1805 – a sailor involved in the Battle of Trafalgar stopped to report that Nelson had died. The thatched building has charming gardens, an aviary and a skittle alley. It predates the Old Inn in the village as a building but its friendly rival is the elder of the two as a pub.

Queen's Head, Newton, Cambridgeshire

The pub started life as a farm in the 17th century and when the farmer gained a reputation for his home-brewed beer he turned the building into an alehouse. It stands at the junction of several roads and has bowed windows, a beamed ceiling, settles, scrubbed benches, a tiled floor and a loudly ticking clock. A corridor leads to a room where traditional pub games are played. Visitors have included the German Kaiser before WWI and the Shah of Persia. The queen on the pub sign is Anne of Cleves.

Roscoe Head, Liverpool, L1

The pub has been in the same family's hands for 20 years and a recent refurbishment has carefully and sensitively retained the original layout of four small rooms. It's named after William Roscoe (1753-1831), a local author and campaigner against the slave trade. He wrote a poem The Wrongs of Africa in 1787, denouncing the trade. The pub is quiet but friendly and welcoming, and is the meeting place of the Sunday Night Club.

Sow & Pigs, Toddington, Bedfordshire

This is what 'unspoilt pub' means: a simple and homely Victorian alehouse (though the cellars are older), made up of one long room with bare boards, open fires and wooden settles. There are many piggy artefacts as well as large collection of photos showing the history of the pub over the years, along with paintings by local artists. There is a separate room used for banquets and a patio garden at the back. Excellent home-made food is served in the bar.

Square & Compass, Worth Matravers, Dorset

Known as a 'bastion of the Purbecks', this ancient alehouse is named after the tools used by workmen to quarry the local stone. It's more than 200 years old and has been run by members of the Newman family for 100 years. There's no bar, with beer served behind a hatch straight from casks. As well as comfortable rooms for drinkers, there's a small fossils museum and, outside, breathtaking views of the Jurassic Coast and St Albans Head.

Star Inn, Netherton, Northumberland

The Star was built around the time of World War One and hasn't changed much since. It looks like a private house and visitors say it's like walking into someone's living room. It has been in the hands of the same family, the Mortons, for most of its time, and they concentrate on supplying fine ale straight from the cask and served through a hatch in the entrance hall. The main bar has benches round the walls and there are well-tended gardens outside. Food is not served: you come to drink.

Star Tavern, London SW1

It's claimed that the Great Train Robbery was planned in the upstairs bar but there's no real evidence to support this. Based in a quiet mews off Belgrave Square, the Georgian pub has a tiny front bar that opens out into a larger room at the back. The upstairs bar, reached by narrow stairs, can certainly lay claim to the fact that several editions of the Good Beer Guide have been launched there, including 2008.

It's a new golden age for real ale...

...if you live in the same world as the Good Beer Guide. It means, says **Roger Protz**, you must ignore siren voices from a parallel universe

J B PRIESTLEY, THE CELEBRATED YORKSHIRE AUTHOR and playwright, had his ashes scattered close to his favourite pub, the George Inn in Hubberholme. As well as enjoying good ale, Priestley developed a theory, used with dramatic effect in several of his plays, that past, present and future do not exist; people live in parallel universes and occasionally move between one and another.

It's a theory that will not be lost on students of the modern pub trade and brewing industry. There is one universe, in which CAMRA and the Good Beer Guide cheerfully exist, where cask beer is enjoying a spirited revival, with pubs listed in this edition of the Guide promoting real ale with enthusiasm and innovation.

There is a second universe, inhabited by global brewers, some pub owners and marketing analysts, who believe cask beer has no future and argue that pubs should concentrate solely on Britain's poor apology for lager and ice-cold 'cream-flow' keg ale.

Occasionally the two universes collide. The Good Beer Guide cannot disguise the fact that some 56 pubs a month are closing. These closures often

Now only the ancient advertisement for Gold Flake remains...this York pub, like thousands throughout the country, is witnessing a revival of cask beer sales, with help from the smoking ban

constitute a grave loss to local communities. In some cases, isolated villages can wither and die when the last pub, the hub of the community, pulls down the shutters.

But we do not accept that such closures are the result of the 'decline' in sales of real ale. It is clear from these pages that thousands of pubs are thriving precisely as a result of their commitment to cask beer. There are many examples in this edition of pubs that were threatened with closure being restored to success by keen landlords. They recognise that handpumps on the bar and a wide range of cask beers can draw customers like a magnet.

A case in point is the Wellington in Birmingham city centre. A large pub chain would have walked away from the opportunity to open a pub on Bennetts Hill. The local wisdom was that such a pub would be too close to many 'youth venues' that serve only keg beers and lagers. The area, the pundits added, already had one good cask beer outlet, Fuller's Old Joint Stock, which backs on to Bennetts Hill.

Packed pubs

But the Black Country Brewery believed otherwise and has been proved spectacularly right. Its pub has been packed from opening day. It serves more than 2,000 cask ales a year, along with imported beers and English ciders. It stages regular beer festivals and offers such a vast range of ales that they have to be listed on screens with numbers in the style of a Chinese restaurant.

The Wellington is not an isolated case. The Tynemill pub company in the East Midlands thrives on cask beer. Its 17 pubs serve more than 1,500 cask beers a year and their success ridicules the claims of bigger pub companies that there is no demand for real ale.

In the pages that follow, pub after pub shows how to survive and thrive at a time when global brewers and giant national pub companies distort the market with their devotion to big volume brands. The publicans in the Good Beer Guide are successful and worthy of their inclusion because they do not sit back and wait for custom that may never arrive. They promote themselves. They announce their commitment to cask beer. Where possible, they rotate the beers they serve and scour the country for brands not usually available in their trading areas. Many stage regular beer festivals.

Equally important, their pubs are hubs of the communities. They provide facilities for families as well as quizzes, darts, pool and other pub games. In some cases, the pubs are the unofficial pavilions for local cricket, football and rugby teams. And, increasingly, they offer good food with imaginative menus.

Growth fuelled by demand

The success of the pubs chosen for the Guide is mirrored by the continuing growth of the craft-brewing sector. More than 50 new breweries are listed in this edition. They followed 80 in 2007 and a similar number the year before. One reason for the development of the sector is the introduction of Progressive Beer Duty by the government, which reduced duty levels for breweries that produce fewer than 30,000 barrels of beer a year.

But the other reason is that demand is fuelling the growth. People do not give up regular jobs or sink savings and redundancy money in risky ventures requiring a considerable capital outlay if no one wants to drink their beers. The breweries section is dotted with success stories: production doubled, new brewing equipment installed, brand portfolios expanded, a few pubs bought. In some cases, growth has been spectacular. Ringwood in Hampshire produces more than 30,000 barrels a year and is classified as a regional rather than a micro-brewery. Its success led to

Down in Wye Valley something stirs...a new fermenter is lowered into the brewery at Stoke Lacy to enable the company to keep up with demand for its ales. Close to £1 million has been invested in new equipment

it being bought in July 2007 by Marston's.

Wye Valley in Herefordshire moved from a tiny plant in outbuildings at the Barrels pub in Hereford to the former Symonds' cider factory in Stoke Lacy. Production was boosted to 15,000 barrels a year, with a £750,000 investment in new equipment. In July 2007, Wye Valley announced it had installed two new fermenters to keep up with demand. 'We're ahead of our sales budgets – we're working flat out,' managing director Vernon Amor said.

Hawkshead in Cumbria, founded in 2002 by former BBC broadcaster Alex Brodie, now has two sites, the second with a custom-built brewhouse that can be viewed from a restaurant above. Bath Ales, Hambleton, Titanic and Woodforde's are just a few more of the smaller breweries that are making similar progress. In London, Meantime of Greenwich has carved out an entirely new route to market with a magnificent range of bottle-conditioned beers, including a proper IPA. Many of these companies brew substantially more beer a year than long-running independent family brewers. 'Micro-brewery' has become something of a misnomer.

Expansion and diversification

Among the longer established companies, Adnams has made a multi-million pound investment in a new brewhouse and warehouse complex in Suffolk. Hall & Woodhouse, of Badger Beer fame, is building a new brewery in Dorset and is number three in the packaged beer sector behind S&N and Greene King.

The combined force of Brakspear and Wychwood in Oxfordshire has not only saved the former Henley beers but also morphed into a sizeable regional company with national sales of its brands on draught and in bottle. In Yorkshire, Black Sheep is a substantial presence in the beer trade while its near neighbour Theakston, freed from the embrace of S&N, has also seen welcome growth. Cains of Liverpool, under the energetic ownership of the Dusanj brothers, has enjoyed considerable expansion of its beer brands and has now added the Honeycombe Leisure pub company, with around 100 pubs. Cains is now a major force on the beer and pub scene.

Why then, in the second universe, is there nothing but gloom? Why are pubs closing and global breweries turning their backs on cask beer? One reason is a natural decline in pub numbers. Once the pub was the main leisure outlet for millions of people. But competition from an array of new restaurants, as well as a growing tendency to drink at home in front of multi-channel television, has seen an inevitable fall in pub outlets. But the decrease has been unnaturally boosted by two factors: giant pub companies and supermarkets. For the pubcos, pubs are 'retail outlets' where volumes and profits have to be maximised. Sales that would satisfy a smaller company are of no interest to the giants. If volumes are not maintained, then pubs are either sold on or closed, with little attention given to the impact on local communities.

Supermarkets have added to pub woes with a policy of deep discounting, with scant regard for social responsibility. Curiously, those sections of the media besotted by binge drinking among a small minority of people concentrate their cameras on high street pubs and ignore the supermarkets. But it's the multiple retailers who fuel over-consumption, selling beer at almost giveaway prices. Beer is cheaper than bottled water in many stores.

Distorted figures

The other claim from the second universe – that real ale is in decline – is based on distorted facts and figures. Total sales of cask beer have fallen – but that is due to the fact that the global brewers, who account for eight out of ten pints brewed in Britain, have turned their backs on the style. Take, as a sad example, the case of Draught Bass. It was once the undisputed king of the premium cask sector, worth two million barrels a year. Today, as a result of malign neglect by successive owners, first Bass and now InBev, production has fallen to fewer than 100,000 barrels a years, overtaken by Fuller's London Pride and Marston's Pedigree.

John Smith's Bitter and Tetley Bitter are Britain's biggest-selling ale brands but they are overwhelmingly produced in keg form. As the Guide was preparing for press, there were persistent rumours that Carlsberg, the owner of Tetley, might close the historic Leeds brewery. Coors, American owner of the former Bass breweries in Burton, has stripped out all its cask beer kit and has to outsource its few draught ales to regional breweries.

The reason for the globals' declining interest in cask beer is, once again, volumes. Bigger profits can be made from dead, pasteurised keg ales and lagers, the Long Life milk of the beer world. Cask beer is fiddly, demands skill and attention and, horror of horrors, has a short shelf life. At best it's ignored, with little or no promotion, at worst consigned to the scrapheap. It's a policy the globals may live to regret. Premium lager sales are static or even declining. Stella is no longer stellar.

Back in our universe, we are full of optimism. The beer world has changed out of all recognition since the first edition of the Guide appeared in 1973. The independent sector has declined alarmingly over the ensuing 35 years. But today choice and diversity are awesome. The craft-brewing sector has abandoned the comfort blanket of mild and bitter and added a brilliant range of new beers – genuine IPAs, porters and stouts, and New Age summer, wheat, fruit and honey beers.

In our universe, cask beer is entering a new golden age. Go forth and sup – and raise a glass to the memory of J B Priestley, the sage who wanted to be commemorated next to a real ale pub.

The big beer giveaway... some pubs are struggling due to the supermarkets' policy of selling heavily discounted packaged beers. Beer is often cheaper than bottled water

Beer on the table – and at the bar

Top food writer **Fiona Beckett** says we should stop ignoring beer as a companion for food and start treating it as seriously as wine

WALK INTO ANY GOOD RESTAURANT IN THIS COUNTRY and there's only the remotest of chances that it will have a decent beer list. Go to friends for dinner and you're unlikely to find a bottle of beer on the table – unless they're members of CAMRA, of course ... The only time we seem to bring out the beer is at a barbecue or with a takeaway. When I ran a poll on my website, 25% voted for beer as a good choice for pizza compared to the miserly 3% who thought it was a good match for grilled salmon.

How on earth did it get to this in a country where beer is the national drink? Go to Belgium, Germany and even the United States and you'll find great beer anywhere you choose to eat. Maybe it's because we're in love with the cooking of southern Europe, with whose Mediterranean tradition beer hasn't traditionally been associated, but I can't help but feel that what it really comes down to is that beer still has a downmarket image.

It's also more than likely that people just haven't had the chance to taste the best the beer world has to offer. One of the things that's amazed us in the past year when my son Will and I have been working on An Appetite for Ale, our new book for CAMRA, is just how many different flavours there are in beer and how they complement food in an entirely different way from wine (and we both speak as wine-lovers, too)

Craft beer at airports

Contrast this with the situation in Belgium, where we ate at two restaurants, Belga Queen and Den Dyver, where you could try a different beer with every dish, or with almost any bar or restaurant in Munich where there's a choice of at least 12 beers to enjoy with your food. Or even with the U.S., where I was amazed to find, when I went over for the Great American Beer Festival in Denver, that a modest restaurant in the local shopping mall had a serious beer list. You could even drink craft beer at the airport.

Things are changing here, too, but painfully slowly, it seems at times. Too many pubs seem to think that turning themselves into a gastropub is an excuse to have a flashy wine list rather than a wider range of beer. Will and his business partner Huw Gott feel strongly about this. At their London, Islington pub, the Marquess Tavern, which was voted Time Out's gastropub of the year in 2006, they have a list of 40 different beers. It's encouraging to see a new generation of beer-focused restaurants such as Brew Wharf and Lowlander, and beers creeping onto the lists of top restaurants like Le Gavroche and Le Manoir aux Quat' Saisons, but it's not happening fast enough.

Vanessa Courtier

The fact is there are many dishes that taste better with beer than they do with wine. Cheese is the obvious example – how many times have you struggled to find a wine match for an oozy Epoisses or even for a really mature Cheddar? – but pickled and smoked foods, spicy foods, savoury foods with sweet, sticky glazes or marinades, pies, sausages, roasts or any other dish accompanied by a rich, meaty or onion gravy are other examples.

There are other dishes with which beer goes at least as well as wine – seafood being the prime example. Think of freshly dressed crab with a refreshing witbier, battered or fried fish and chips with a fine British bitter or the classic oysters and stout. And a strong golden ale such as Duvel is just as good with salmon as a Chardonnay (for those fainthearts who don't believe beer makes a good match for salmon!)

There are other dishes, admittedly, where beer is not such a spontaneous choice: with pasta dishes, for example, or other Italian dishes cooked with wine and tomatoes. But many of these can be adapted to make them more beer-friendly. One of the most popular dishes I came up with for the book was a smoky bacon Bolognese, cooking our adopted national dish with Leffe Blonde and giving it a smoky twist with smoked bacon (veggies can use soy mince and smoked pimenton).

Cooking – or preparing – recipes with beer can add a whole new dimension that goes way beyond the classic carbonnade and steak and ale pie, good though those dishes are. In Fingerprint in Germany we came across a wonderful weissbier sorbet that was used as a palate-cleanser between dishes but makes an equally good

13

refreshing dessert with fresh tropical fruits. You can make spectacular, brightly coloured jewel-like jellies with undiluted fruit beers. And if you've ever struggled to make a good home-baked bread, try adding real ale as part of the liquid and your dough will take off!

But the beer dish I've had most success with is that great American invention beer-can chicken, where you insert a half-full can of beer up the chicken's backside and pop it on a covered barbecue. The steam from the beer keeps the flesh tender and moist while the fat runs down the bird and bastes the skin to crispy perfection. There is no-one I've cooked this for who hasn't gone away and tried it themselves.

So maybe that's the secret of the beer and food revolution that we all want to happen but which never quite gets off the ground. Start with a dish that grabs the imagination then gradually win your friends round. Other sure-fire winners are serving a creamy, berry-topped cheesecake with a raspberry or cherry flavoured beer or a rich chocolate dessert with a cherry beer or porter.

The next plank of the strategy is to give your friends a better beer than they expect with the dishes with which they are used to drinking beer. An IPA instead of a lager with a curry; a Viennese-style lager or a Saison at a barbecue; a really good Pilsner or a Kölsch with a pizza. Start with what I tend to think of as the New British beers just as you'd start a novice wine drinker on New World wines: beers like Jaipur IPA, Harviestoun Schiehalliion or almost any of the beers from Meantime.

The biggest compliment I had recently was from some good friends who have been guineapigs for many of the recipes I have tested for the book. We went to their house where they served us beer-can chicken followed by a chocolate roulade with a chilled cherry beer. That's what we need to create a food culture around beer in this country: a quiet grass-roots revolution. Good Beer Guide readers, it's up to you . . .

Hold the wine...ales, wheat beers, fruit beers and quality imported lagers all make ideal companions for the dining table with either meat dishes (page 13) or rich desserts

■ Fiona Beckett is co-author with Will Beckett of An Appetite for Ale (CAMRA Books, £19.99) and has her own website www.matchingfoodandwine.com which includes matches with beer and other drinks.

Vanessa Courtier

Don't let your local be Dun Roamin'

If your pub is threatened with closure, don't fall off your bar stool, **Paul Ainsworth** says, but organise to save it for the community and the future

ACCORDING TO CAMRA'S RESEARCH, an average of 56 pubs call 'Last Orders' every month. Some are converted to shops, offices or houses. Others are flattened, with the land used for other purposes.

Each of these pubs served a community and was somebody's local. Particularly in towns, where there will be another pub down the road, there may be a tendency to shrug shoulders and find another bar stool but pubs under threat can be saved.

So when you hear that the owner of your local wants to shut it or convert it into something horrendous, what can you do? Intelligence gathering is your first step. Who owns the pub? Why do they want to close it? Is it genuinely because the pub isn't making money or is the prospect of making a fast buck on the property market the real reason?

By far the commonest reason given by would-be pub-closers is that the business isn't 'viable' – not only isn't it profitable now but has no hope of being so in the future. This is often a dodgy argument. A current poor state of trade often reflects the capability and commitment of the current regime more than anything else. CAMRA has developed a Public House

Under threat...the bar at the Crook Inn in Tweedsmuir could close if the owner sells the pub and hotel. But a vigorous local campaign has been launched to save the inn

Michael Slaughter

Crook Inn

There has been a vigorous, community-based campaign in the Scottish Borders to save the Crook Inn at Tweedsmuir, Scotland's first licensed coaching inn (pictured on the previous page). The inn dates from 1590, has 1920s Art Deco additions, is a listed building and is also on CAMRA's National Inventory. When the owner peremptorily closed the Crook and applied for change of use to a private dwelling, a Save the Crook Inn organisation was set up overnight. It has lobbied MPs, MSPs and MEPs, and also the local Borders planning authority, arguing that the pub and hotel provide local jobs, attract visitors and also act as a post office. The authority has told the owner it is highly unlikely it would agree to change of use for the inn. See www.savethecrook.org.uk.

Viability Test that enables claims of non-viability to be thoroughly tested.

The next big question is, what do the owners want to do with the building. It's a sad fact that a pub can be worth a lot more if converted to a private house or if the site can be released for development. Fortunately, in most cases, any change of use will need planning permission. The owners will have to persuade the local council, as planning authority, that a different use is merited. You'll have to argue that it isn't.

Now you need to mobilise support for the campaign – and the obvious place to start is with the pub's regulars. If few of them are bothered to fight the good fight then you're likely to be up against it from the outset. However, let's assume enough folk are sufficiently outraged to join the campaign.

Next, reach out into the wider community. This can be easiest in a village where you can enlist the support of the parish council. But urban areas have communities, too, and people such as local councillors ought to come on board.

Alienating the community

A common scenario involves a licensee who so alienates the local community that they increasingly stay away from the pub. The licensee then claims that the business isn't viable and tries to shut it. In this case, you need to locate the people who would use the pub if it weren't for the person currently in charge.

By now you should know the intentions of the owners and how much local support you've got, so you can begin to plan your campaign proper. Your next steps will include:

● Publicity. The local media loves a 'Save Our Pub' campaign, especially if there's a David versus Goliath element. Get your press releases out and appoint a spokesperson well-armed with juicy soundbites – 'This pub's the heart of the community', 'Old Alf has been coming here for 53 years – where will he go now?' and 'Five societies and six sports club use the pub as their HQ.'

● Explore the heritage angle. Some pub buildings are 'listed' as being of architectural or historic importance. CAMRA maintains inventories of pub interiors recognised as being of national and regional significance (see the website www.heritagepubs.org.uk and also the National Inventory listing in the Guide). Should your pub be in one or both of these categories, make the most of it: portray any loss as the squandering of a national heritage asset. If your local isn't listed but you feel the building has architectural merit, you could discuss with local planners the potential for emergency 'spot listing'. Once a building is listed, severe restraints are placed on what would-be developers can do with it, making it perhaps a less attractive proposition.

● Talk to the planners: the council's planners are key players, as final decisions will often rest with them. You must hope that the council has planning policies that aim

Dave Hallows

to protect community assets like pubs.

● Talk to the owners: though they might not want to talk to you! Is there scope, for instance, for a stay of execution while your group works with the pub and local community on ways to drum up trade and increase profits? Talk to others: you would hope to get local councillors on your side and your MP might also lend support.

● Seek help from the Community Pubs Foundation. This is an organisation set up by CAMRA specifically to help local groups fight the loss of their local by giving advice, guidance and, where appropriate, small grants to help with campaigning activity. You can visit the website at www.communitypubs.org.uk.

The Crescent, Salford

The Crescent in Salford is a Grade II listed building that seemed destined for closure in 2007 when plans were announced to turn it into student accommodation. In the 19th century, when it was called the Red Dragon, it was used by Karl Marx and Friedrich Engels when Marx visited his companion and financial supporter in Manchester. Again, a local campaign to save the pub seems to have paid off. A property developer announced he would use buildings alongside the pub for new student flats but would maintain the pub.

If planning consent is required before the pub's use can change, you now need to submit your formal objections. Stressing the community angle is important – argue that without the pub the community would lose cohesion and be a less attractive place to live. Be sure to counter any non-viability claims. If there's a history or heritage angle, exploit it.

The desired happy ending is for planning permission to be refused and for the owners to abandon their plans. Unfortunately, the grief could continue. An appeal might be lodged against the planning decision, in which case you've a further fight on you hands. Or the owners could just shut the pub and sit on the property, hoping the planners will eventually change their mind.

For situations like these, and indeed for all aspects of saving pubs, CAMRA has produced a detailed guidance document Promoting and Protecting the Pub, which can be found on its website www. CAMRA.org.uk.

One drastic step a community can take is to purchase the pub itself – and there are several examples of this being successfully accomplished. CAMRA has produced a booklet, Saving Your Local, that gives detailed advice on how to go about it, along with case studies of success stories.

■ Paul Ainsworth is a member of CAMRA's Pub Heritage Group.

Our aim is perfect pints – every time

Cask Marque celebrates a decade of improving the quality of the beer in your glass

THE CASK MARQUE TRUST IS 10 YEARS OLD in 2008 and much has been achieved since four brewers, Adnams, Marstons, Greene King and Morlands identified beer quality as a key issue for cask ale. The original survey commissioned by the brewers in 1997 showed that two out of every five pints in the pub were of poor quality. In those days, brewers had strict control on beer quality up to the brewery gate but little investment was being made in pubs to deliver the perfect pint. How times have changed.

After much campaigning by Cask Marque, a non-profit-making organisation set up to champion cask ale within the industry, a significant investment has been made in pubs in the form of cellar management training and equipment to dispense beer at cellar temperature.

The Cask Marque Award

To reward licensees who serve great beer, Cask Marque set up an accreditation sheme. To date, over 4,000 licensees now have the award. These pubs display the Cask Marque plaque and a dated framed certificate. A list of these outlets can be found on the Cask Marque website **www.cask-marque.co.uk** or by using a unique text messaging service which will identify the two nearest outlets

Mine's a pint...Tony Millington is one of over 45 Cask Marque assessors who check beer quality – and enjoy a beer after work. Right, CM's unique text messaging service.

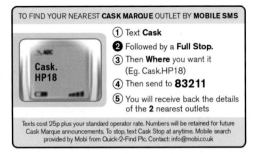

to your postcode (see instruction right). You can also download a free regional guide showing Cask Marque pubs in your area. To gain accreditation a licensee has to pass two unannounced inspections by a qualified assessor who is normally a brewer. The assessor will test up to six cask ales on sale for temperature, appearance, aroma and taste and each beer must pass otherwise the inspection has failed. In subsequent years, the licensee has two further visits, one in the summer and one in the winter. All pubs are subject to random visits at any time.

Beer temperature is frequently a reason for failure, particularly in the summer. Brewers recommend dispensing ales at cellar temperature, i.e. 11° – 13°C, and in a survey undertaken by Cask Marque last summer, 43% of non Cask Marque outlets failed on beer temperature, even allowing for a 1°C variation on the brewers recommended specification.

Cask Marque has over 45 assessors across the country who undertake over 13,000 visits a year checking beer quality. Apart from having a brewery background, assessors have to undertake an annual refresher course on beer tasting at Brewing Research International (BRI), a world authority on this subject matter, and sit an examination.

Your help

The Cask Marque award is made to the licensee and not the pub so if, as a consumer, you are unhappy with the quality of your cask ale in a Cask Marque outlet please raise the issue with the licensee. If you are not satisfied with the response do either ring, e-mail or write to Cask Marque and we will take up the matter. Our challenge in 2008 is to have 5,000 great cask ale pubs with the Cask Marque accreditation by the end of our 10th anniversary. You can help us by giving us details of pubs you consider worthy of this award.

Cask ale is a premium product and it costs more to produce than other beers, takes a great deal of professionalism in the cellar to produce the perfect pint and is a product that is unique to the British pub.

When you visit a Cask Marque pub do congratulate the licensee on his award and help us to help the continued revival in cask ale sales.

■ Cask Marque Trust, The Seedbed Centre, Severalls Park, Colchester, Essex, CO4 9HT
T:01206 752212   e-mail: info@cask-marque.co.uk
www.cask-marque.co.uk

CASK MARQUE™

For pubs which serve the perfect pint

Heroes of beer and brewing '08

The Good Beer Guide salutes companies dedicated to real ale and a greener agenda

Adnams

The independent Suffolk brewery has invested £5.8 million in a new warehouse and distribution complex in Reydon, which cuts down on delivery trucks snarling up Southwold, the seaside and fishing town where the brewery and offices are based. The complex (pictured above) uses solar power and collects rainwater for cleaning and even for staff showers. It's sited at road level and has a grass roof to blend with the surrounding countryside. In Southwold, £3.7 million has been invested in a third update to the brewery in the past decade: new vessels include a mashing regime that is environmentally-friendly and uses less energy.

Wye Valley

Vernon (left) and Peter Amor, managing director and chairman of Wye Valley Brewery in Stoke Lacy, Herefordshire, have invested close to £1 million on expanding the brewery, which is now in its third home, the former Symond's cider works. Wye

Valley has grown from a tiny micro and pub brewery to a powerful force in brewing in the English-Welsh borders region. New fermenters installed in July 2007 will enable the brewery to expand beyond its current production of 15,000 barrels a year. Wherever possible, local materials – Herefordshire hops in particular – are used to give the beers provenance and to cut down on carbon footprints.

Don Burgess and Warminster Maltings

Don Burgess of Freeminer Brewery in Gloucestershire (pictured) has supplied the Co-op for several years with bottle-conditioned organic beers. He was keen to go the extra mile and use the finest malting barley – Maris Otter – grown by identifiable farmers in cask as well as bottled beers. Following discussions with Robin Appel of Warminster Maltings in Wiltshire, a new concept of barley growing has been conceived. It's called 'From Field to Firkin' – a firkin is a nine-gallon beer cask – based on contracts with farmers. Suppliers are given a Warranty of Origin so they know which farmer grew the barley and even in which field. Warminster has developed a directory of farms with details of soil type, domain and harvesting techniques.

Westerham

Westerham Brewery in Kent, close to Sir Winston Churchill's Chartwell Estate, launched to great acclaim William Wilberforce Freedom Ale in cask and bottle-conditioned form. The beer coincided with the 200th anniversary in 2007 of Wilberforce's campaign to abolish slavery. Brewer Robert Wicks buys Maris Otter malt from Warminster Maltings (see above) and uses locally-grown Goldings and Northdown hops. The major innovation is the use of Fairtrade demerara sugar from a co-op in Malawi. Along with Freeminer's Fairplay Ale, it's one of the first Fairtrade beers available in Britain and sales of the draught version outstripped Westerham's main beer, British Bulldog.

Hoggy's never stumped for beer

England's star bowler even has an ale named in his honour...for his batting. **Roger Protz** reports.

MATTHEW HOGGARD IS NOT ONLY ONE OF THE STARS of England cricket – a member of the Ashes-winning side of 2005 – but is also a keen real ale drinker. He fronts the Marston's Pedigree promotion for the England cricket team, which has given cask beer a much higher profile in a game for too long dominated by global lager brands – remember the sacrilege of the Foster's Oval?

Marston's is also sponsoring several county sides, including Surrey and Warwickshire, and has made Pedigree widely available at grounds throughout the country. Matthew – Hoggy to friend and foe alike – should by age and background be a member of the lager-swilling brigade. But he converted to cask beer at an early age thanks to the influence of his father.

'He took me to a pub in the Yorkshire Dales,' he recalls. 'It had dozens of handpumps. There must have been 15 beers on tap. That was my introduction to real ale.

'I like it because it tastes good. Lager is fizzy and fills you up. Lager is for yobs – not cultured gents'. It's said tongue-in-cheek, for Hoggy is living proof that cricket in England is no longer dominated by

Never a sticky wicket... Matthew Hoggard enjoys cask beer for its flavour. Lager, he says, is 'fizzy and fills you up – not a cultured drink'

public school chaps. Hoggy was born in Leeds in 1976 – three years after the first Good Beer Guide was published – and had an unusual introduction to the game.

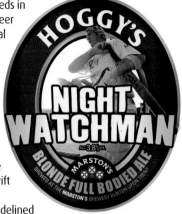

'I didn't start playing cricket until I was 11 or 12,' he says. 'I didn't play at school at all but started to play for a local club.'

Phil Carrick, the stalwart of Yorkshire CC, spotted Hoggy when he was playing club cricket and got him a trial with the county at the age of 17. His ability to swing the ball and move it dramatically off the seam soon won him a county cap and swift elevation to the national squad.

When he is not playing – and he was sidelined for the early part of the 2007 season with injury – Hoggy's favourite pub is the Acorn in Eldwick, near Shipley. It has good food and a fine pint of Pedigree.

Does he enjoy other beers? He is loyal to Yorkshire and names Dent and Black Sheep. When he is touring, finding good beer can be tough. 'In places like the Caribbean and India, it's very hot and it's mainly lager to drink. But Marston's send us supplies of Pedigree. They even sponsor Barmy Army pubs in Australia.' The Barmy Army is not, of course, the England squad but the legendary group of supporters that follow England from country to country.

I mentioned Cooper's Sparkling Ale in Adelaide, a world classic beer in my book, but Hoggy wasn't impressed. If there's no Pedigree available on tour, he sticks to Guinness.

Hoggy has acquired a reputation as a limited but trusty lower order batsman who can hang around if a wicket falls near close of play. Marston's has recognised this talent by naming a new beer in his honour – Nightwatchman.

MATTHEW HOGGARD
FACT FILE

- Born Leeds 1976

- In the great Ashes series of 2005 he took nine wickets in the Trent Bridge Test and 4-97 in the Oval Test that clinched the Ashes for England

- Along with his team mates, he was awarded the MBE and was named Wisden Cricketer of the Year 2006

BOWLING RECORD TO JUNE 2007

- 64 Tests, 240 wickets, average 30.03
- 26 ODIs, 32 wickets, average 36.00
- 154 First Class games, 545 wickets, average 27.5

- Test Match batting average: 7.40

Beer festival calendar 2008

THE CAMPAIGN FOR REAL ALE'S BEER FESTIVALS are magnificent shop windows for cask ale and they give drinkers the opportunity to sample beers from independent brewers rare to particular localities. Beer festivals are enormous fun: many offer good food and live entertainment, and – where possible – facilities for families. Some seasonal festivals specialise in spring, autumn and winter ales. Festivals range in size from small local events to large regional ones. CAMRA holds two national festivals, the National Winter Ales Festival in January, and the Great British Beer Festival in August; the latter features around 500 beers. The festivals listed are those planned for 2008. For up-to-date information, contact the CAMRA website: **www.CAMRA.org.uk** and click on 'CAMRA Near You'. By joining CAMRA – there's a form at the back of the Guide – you will receive 12 editions of the campaign's monthly newspaper What's Brewing, which lists every festival on a month-by-month basis. Dates listed are liable to change: check with the website or What's Brewing.

JANUARY

Derby Winter
Exeter Winter
Redditch
Cambridge Winter
Bent & Bongs Beer Bash, Wigan
Burton Winter
National Winter Ales, Manchester
Colchester Winter

FEBRUARY

Tewkesbury Winter
Pendle, East Lancashire
Chelmsford Winter
Magpie, Nottingham
White Cliffs Winter, Dover
Salisbury Winter
Dorchester
Chesterfield
Battersea
Liverpool
Ale & Arty, Cleveland
Luton
25th Fleetwood
Portsmouth Winter, Gosport

MARCH

Banbury
Bradford
Loughborough
Elysian, Ely
Bristol
Sussex, Hove
Leicester
Leeds
Darlington Springtime
Hitchin
Wigan
London Drinker
Walsall
Mansfield
Ascot
Oldham
Bexley

APRIL

Planet Thanet
Maldon
Doncaster
Coventry
Newcastle
Paisley
East Anglian, Bury St Edmunds
Farnham
Chippenham

MAY

Kingdom of Fife
Reading
Chester
Rugby
Stourbridge
Halifax
Newport
Newark & Notts Show

Beer on Broadway, Ealing
Ilkeston
Barrow Hill Rail Ale
Stratford Upon Avon

Yapton
Derbyshire Food & Drink
Cambridge
Lincoln
Alloa
Newark
Skipton
Northants Delapre
Wolverhampton
Stockport
Colchester
Macclesfield

JUNE

St Ives, Cornwall
Woodchurch Rare Breeds
Thurrock
Catford
Southampton Ashfield
Scottish Traditional
Braintree Real
South Downs, Lewes
Kingston
Stafford
Great Welsh, Cardiff

JULY

Derby
Bromsgrove
Woodcote Steam Fair
Kent

Cotswold, Winchcombe
Beer By The Bridge, Halton
Plymouth Pavilions
Beer on the Wye, Hereford
Ardingly
Devizes
Chelmsford

AUGUST

Great British, London
Peterborough
South Shields
Mumbles, Swansea
Worcester
Barnstaple
Clacton
Harbury

SEPTEMBER

Faversham Hop
Tamworth
Grantham Autumn
Booze on the Ouse, St Ives
Saltaire
Birmingham
Lytham
Ipswich
Rochford Cider
Redcar
Southport
Northwich

Burton
Severn Valley/Bridgnorth
Shrewsbury

OCTOBER

Barnsley
Chester Autumn
Sawbridgeworth
Potteries
Solihull

NOVEMBER

Dudley
York

DECEMBER

Pig's Ear, East London
Harwich

The big tent...
Peterborough beer festival,
held in giant marquees, is
second only to the Great
British festival in size and
draws beer lovers from all
over eastern England

Frothing with rage over short pints

Join CAMRA'S call to get full measure in the pub

DID YOU KNOW THE GOVERNMENT ALLOWS DRINKERS TO BE CHEATED out of £1.3 million every day? Getting what you pay for is a basic consumer right – but it's a right the beer drinker is denied.

Pints of beer are being served up to 10% short and this is costing drinkers £1.3 million every single day. If you buy a litre of petrol or a pint of milk, you are entitled to receive a full litre of petrol or a full pint of milk. But when you order a pint of beer at the bar, a full pint is not guaranteed. CAMRA and the Good Beer Guide believe a pint should be exactly that: a full pint. You are entitled to get what you pay for.

The government recognises that short beer measures are a growing problem. Back in 1997 during the general election campaign, the Labour Party promised to bring in legislation that would guarantee full pints for drinkers. But as a result of lobbying from brewers and pub companies, the government, when elected, broke its full pint promise.

The government's solution was to define a 'pint' of beer as being only 95% of one pint. This is outrageous: you cannot define a pint as anything less than the full measure. Imagine the outrage among car drivers if they found they were getting less than a litre of petrol but had to pay the full price.

The overwhelming majority of publicans work hard to provide their customers with a great pub environment and good value for money. Unfortunately, some big pub companies encourage their licensees to squeeze 185 pints from a cask that holds only 176 pints. The hard-pressed licensee can achieve this only by serving short measures. The industry's position is that publicans should only have to serve customers with 95% beer in a pint glass. CAMRA and the Good Beer Guide consider this is quite unacceptable and customers should have the right to a full pint.

What you can do

If you're served a short measure, ask for it to be topped up. The bar staff should do this with good grace. But if you are refused a top up with good grace or the short measure is substantial and consistent, you should complain to your local Trading Standards department. The department should then investigate. You can find your local department by visiting www.tradingstandards.gov.uk.

You can add your voice to CAMRA's demand for a full pint law by visiting www.takeittothetop.co.uk. Or write to CAMRA at 230 Hatfield Road, St Albans, Herts, AL1 4LW and ask for a petition form to be sent to you.

Or you could write direct to the Prime Minister in Downing Street and ask him to bring in legislation that will define a pint of beer as nothing less than 100% liquid and will require licensees to serve full measure every time.

Down Memory Lane

1973 WAS NOT A GREAT YEAR for the England football team – what's new? – as they were knocked out of the World Cup qualifiers by Poland and failed to get to Germany in 1974.

RACING DRIVER JACKIE STEWART reigned supreme by being crowned Formula One world champion and BBC Sports Personality of the Year. On another racetrack, Red Rum notched up his first win in the Grand National.

RAY REARDON BEAT EDDIE CHARLTON to win the professional snooker open championship, while Tom Weiskopf won the British Golf Open. On the rugby pitch the Barbarians met the All Blacks in a clash of small shorts and large sideburns and produced what many consider to be the greatest match of all time.

IN THE CINEMA THE BIG FILMS WERE LIVE AND LET DIE and The Exorcist. A vintage year for TV sitcoms saw the first episodes of Porridge and Open All Hours, Some Mothers do 'Ave 'Em, Whatever Happened to the Likely Lads, Last of the Summer Wine and Man About the House. For kids, 1973 saw the first showing of We are the Champions where schools competed against each other. Memorable TV ads from 1973 included the Martians singing 'For Mash get Smash' and Elvis Costello's dad crooning 'I'm a Secret Lemonade Drinker' for R White's. Trevor McDonald becomes the first black newsreader on British TV.

AVERAGE EARNINGS WERE £2,170 and the average house price was £9,767. A pint of milk cost 5p and the average price for a pint of beer was 13p. Drinking in the early 70s was still dominated by keg bitters such as Watneys Red, although lagers such as Harp were beginning to make an impact. Bottled pale ales such as Bass Red Triangle and Double Diamond were also popular. CAMRA, founded in 1971, was championing the cause of cask beer and sales began to rise, although they were still a minority taste.

NOTABLE DEATHS IN 1973 included Pablo Picasso, W H Auden, Lyndon B Johnson and J R R Tolkien as well as martial arts guru Bruce Lee. Ryan Giggs and Peter Andre were born.

Britain's classic beer styles

You can deepen your appreciation of cask ale and get to grips with all the beers listed in The Breweries section with this run-down on the main styles available

Mild

Mild was once the most popular style of beer but was overtaken by Bitter from the 1950s. It was developed in the 18th and 19th centuries as a less aggressively bitter style of beer than porter and stout. Early Milds were much stronger that modern interpretations, which tend to fall in the 3% to 3.5% category, though there are stronger versions, such as Gale's Festival Mild and Sarah Hughes' Dark Ruby. Mild ale is usually dark brown in colour, due to the use of well-roasted malts or roasted barley, but there are paler versions, such as Banks's Original, Timothy Taylor's Golden Best and McMullen's AK. Look for rich malty aromas and flavours with hints of dark fruit, chocolate, coffee and caramel and a gentle underpinning of hop bitterness.

Old Ale

Old Ale recalls the type of beer brewed before the Industrial Revolution, stored for months or even years in unlined wooden vessels known as tuns. The beer would pick up some lactic sourness as a result of wild yeasts, lactobacilli and tannins in the wood. The result was a beer dubbed 'stale' by drinkers: it was one of the components of the early, blended Porters. The style has re-emerged in recent years, due primarily to the fame of Theakston's Old Peculier, Gale's Prize Old Ale and Thomas Hardy's Ale, the last saved from oblivion by O'Hanlon's Brewery in Devon. Old Ales, contrary to expectation, do not have to be especially strong: they can be no more than 4% alcohol, though the Gale's and O'Hanlon's versions are considerably stronger. Neither do they have to be dark: Old Ale can be pale and burst with lush sappy malt, tart fruit and spicy hop notes. Darker versions will have a more profound malt character with powerful hints of roasted grain, dark fruit, polished leather and fresh tobacco. The hallmark of the style remains a lengthy period of maturation, often in bottle rather than bulk vessels.

Bitter

Towards the end of the 19th century, brewers built large estates of tied pubs. They moved away from vatted beers stored for many months and developed 'running beers' that could be served after a few days' storage in pub cellars. Draught Mild was a 'running beer' along with a new type that was dubbed Bitter by drinkers. Bitter grew out of Pale Ale but was generally deep bronze to copper in colour due to the use of slightly darker malts such as crystal that give the beer fullness of palate. Best is a stronger version of Bitter but there is considerable crossover. Bitter falls into the 3.4% to 3.9% band, with Best Bitter 4% upwards but a number of brewers label their ordinary Bitters 'Best'. A further development of Bitter comes in the shape of Extra or Special Strong Bitters of 5% or more: familiar examples of this style include Fuller's ESB and Greene King Abbot. With ordinary Bitter, look for a spicy, peppery and grassy hop character, a powerful bitterness, tangy fruit and juicy and nutty malt. With Best and Strong Bitters, malt and fruit character will tend to dominate but hop aroma and bitterness are still crucial to the style, often achieved by 'late hopping' in the brewery or adding hops to casks as they leave for pubs.

Golden Ales

This new style of pale, well-hopped and quenching beer developed in the 1980s as independent brewers attempted to win younger drinkers from heavily-promoted lager brands. The first in the field were Exmoor Gold and Hop Back Summer Lightning, though many micros and regionals now make their versions of the style. Strengths will range from 3.5% to 5%. The hallmark will be the biscuity and juicy malt character derived from pale malts, underscored by tart citrus fruit and peppery hops, often with the addition of hints of vanilla and sweetcorn. Above all, such beers are quenching and served cool.

IPA and Pale Ale

India Pale Ale changed the face of brewing early in the 19th century. The new technologies of the Industrial Revolution enabled brewers to use pale malts to fashion beers that were genuinely golden or pale bronze in colour. First brewed in London and Burton-on-Trent for the colonial market, IPAs were strong in alcohol and high in hops: the preservative character of the hops helped keep the beers in good condition during long sea journeys. Beers with less alcohol and hops were developed for the domestic market and were known as Pale Ale. Today Pale Ale is usually a bottled version of Bitter, though historically the styles are different. Marston's Pedigree is an example of Burton Pale Ale, not Bitter, while the same brewery's Old Empire is a fascinating interpretation of a Victorian IPA. So-called IPAs with strengths of around 3.5% are not true to style. Look for juicy malt, citrus fruit and a big spicy, peppery, bitter hop character, with strengths of 4% upwards.

Porter and Stout

Porter was a London style that turned the brewing industry upside down early in the 18th century. It was a dark brown beer – 19th-century versions became jet black – that was originally a blend of brown ale, pale ale and 'stale' or well-matured ale. It acquired the name Porter as a result of its popularity among London's street-market workers. The strongest versions of Porter were known as Stout Porter, reduced over the years to simply Stout. Such vast quantities of Porter and Stout flooded into Ireland from London and Bristol that a Dublin brewer named Arthur Guinness decided to fashion his own interpretation of the style. Guinness in Dublin blended some unmalted roasted barley and in so doing produced a style known as Dry Irish Stout. Restrictions on making roasted malts in Britain during World War One led to the demise of Porter and Stout and left the market to the Irish. In recent years, smaller craft brewers in Britain have rekindled an interest in the style, though in keeping with modern drinking habits, strengths have been reduced. Look for profound dark and roasted malt character with raisin and sultana fruit, espresso or cappuccino coffee, liquorice and molasses.

Barley Wine

Barley Wine is a style that dates from the 18th and 19th centuries when England was often at war with France and it was the duty of patriots, usually from the upper classes, to drink ale rather than Claret. Barley Wine had to be strong – often between 10% and 12% – and was stored for prodigious periods of as long at 18 months or two years. When country houses had their own small breweries, it was often the task of the butler to brew ale that was drunk from cut-glass goblets at the dining table. The biggest-selling Barley Wine for years was Whitbread's 10.9% Gold Label, now available only in cans. Bass's No 1 Barley Wine (10.5%) is occasionally brewed in Burton-on-Trent, stored in cask for 12 months and made available to CAMRA beer festivals. Fuller's Vintage Ale (8.5%) is a bottle-conditioned version of its Golden Pride and is brewed with different varieties of malts and hops every year. Many micro-brewers now produce their interpretations of the style. Expect massive sweet malt and ripe fruit of the pear drop, orange and lemon type, with darker fruits, chocolate and coffee if darker malts are used. Hop rates are generous and produce bitterness and peppery, grassy and floral notes.

Scottish Beers

Historically, Scottish beers tend to be darker, sweeter and less heavily hopped than English and Welsh ales: a cold climate demands warming beers. But many of the new craft breweries produce beers lighter in colour and with generous hop rates. The traditional, classic styles are Light, low in strength and so-called even when dark in colour, also known as 60/-, Heavy or 70/-, Export or 80/- and a strong Wee Heavy, similar to a barley wine, and also labelled 90/-. In the 19th century, beers were invoiced according to strength, using the now defunct currency of the shilling.

Choosing the pubs

Beer quality sets the pace...

THE GOOD BEER GUIDE IS UNIQUE. There are several pub guides available and in the main they concentrate on picture-postcard country pubs and food. This guide, on the other hand, starts with beer quality: hence its title. It is more than just a pub guide. The driving force of the Campaign for Real Ale is quality cask-conditioned draught beer and it has been the Guide's belief for 34 years that if a landlord keeps his beer well and pours perfect pints, then everything else in his pub – welcome, food, accommodation and family facilities – are likely to be of an equally high standard.

The heart of the guide is its pub section, offering more than 4,500 pubs throughout the country. They are all full entries. One pub guide says it offers 5,000 pubs but the editorial team only inspects 1,000 of them: the remainder are unchecked.

Every pub in the Good Beer Guide has been inspected many times by CAMRA members during the course of a year. They visit them to check that beer quality has not declined. All CAMRA members can vote for the quality of beer using the National Beer Scoring Scheme. The scheme uses a 0-5 scale for beer quality that can be submitted online to **www.beerscoring.org.uk**. For more information about the scheme, go to www. CAMRA.org.uk. The guide does not charge for entry, neither does it make do with questionnaires sent to publicans.

The Guide is unique in several ways. It has an army of 87,000 unpaid CAMRA volunteers. They choose the entries, with detailed descriptions of beer, food, history, architecture, facilities and public transport available. There is a considerable turnover of pubs from edition to edition as CAMRA members delete those that have fallen below an acceptable standard or rotate pubs in an area with a substantial number of good outlets.

And it is not a guide to country pubs alone. CAMRA has campaigned to sustain rural pubs and they feature prominently in these pages. But drinkers visit urban pubs, too, and all the major towns and cities feature in the guide with an abundance of choice.

As this is a guide to beer as well as pubs, we also offer our unique contribution to beer appreciation: the Breweries section. It is an annual snapshot of the industry, listing all the beers produced with strengths and tasting notes. It indicates breweries that have closed and new entrants to the industry. The section complements the pub listings, helping you to appreciate the beers available, and stressing the enormous choice and diversity.

■ You can keep your copy of the guide up to date by visiting the CAMRA website: www. CAMRA.org.uk . Click on 'Good Beer Guide' then 'Updates to the GBG 2008'. You will find information on brewery changes to pubs and breweries.

England

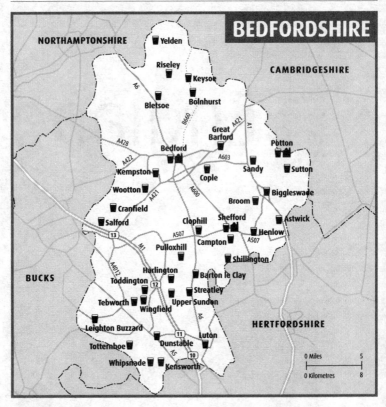

BEDFORDSHIRE

NORTHAMPTONSHIRE

Yelden

Riseley

Keysoe

CAMBRIDGESHIRE

Bletsoe

Bolnhurst

Great Barford

Potton

Bedford

Sandy

Sutton

Kempston

Cople

Wootton

Broom

Biggleswade

Cranfield

Shefford

Astwick

Salford

Clophill

Henlow

Campton

Pulloxhill

Shillington

BUCKS

Harlington

Barton le Clay

Toddington

Streatley

Tebworth

Upper Sunden

Wingfield

Leighton Buzzard

Luton

HERTFORDSHIRE

Totternhoe

Dunstable

Whipsnade

Kensworth

0 Miles 5
0 Kilometres 8

Astwick

Tudor Oaks

Taylor's Road, SG5 4AZ (on A1 northbound, 1 mile N of jct 10)
🕐 11-11; 11-4, 7-10.30 Sun
☎ (01462) 834133 🌐 tudoroakslodge.co.uk
Beer range varies Ⓗ
A 15th-century coaching inn with a covered Mediterranean-style courtyard. The inn is fully timbered, and later extensions complement the original building. Its large bar area offers up to seven real ales from breweries and micros across the country, plus real cider, perry and Belgian bottled beers. The spirits selection includes malt whiskies and a comprehensive cocktail list. The restaurant offers a wide choice of fresh food, cooked to order. ⊛🏮🍽️◑●P🚭

Barton-le-Clay

Bull

77 Bedford Road, MK45 4LL
🕐 12-2.30, 6-1am (2am Fri & Sat); 12-2.30, 6-midnight Sun
☎ (01582) 705070
Adnams Bitter; Greene King IPA; McMullen Country; Shepherd Neame Spitfire Ⓗ
Old, oak-beamed pub in the centre of the village, popular with a varied clientele. It is a rare local outlet for McMullen Country Bitter. The main dining area offers a Wednesday night two-course special; there is also a children's menu (no food Mon or Thu). The

pub has dominoes and darts teams and a pool table. For smokers there is a small outside seating area. 🏮⊛◑🚐♣P🚭

Bedford

Cricketers Arms

35 Goldington Road, MK40 3LH (on A428 E of town centre)
🕐 5 (12 Sat)-11; 6.30-10.30 Sun
☎ (01234) 303958 🌐 cricketersarms.co.uk
Adnams Bitter; guest beers Ⓗ
Small, one-bar pub opposite Bedford Blues Rugby Union ground, popular with rugby fans and busy on match days. Live internationals are shown on screens at each end of the wood-panelled bar. Rotating guest beers are from Punch Taverns' Finest Cask selection so micros are rarely represented. The cider is Addlestones Premium Cloudy. The pub opens early on Sundays for live Six Nations games. Local CAMRA Pub of the Year 2006. ⊛◑🚐●🚭

Wellington Arms

40-42 Wellington Street, MK40 2JX
🕐 12-11; 12-10.30 Sun
☎ (01234) 308033 🌐 wellingtonarms.co.uk
Adnams Bitter; B&T Two Brewers; guest beers Ⓗ
Street corner B&T pub offering a wide choice of regional and micro-brewery beers, plus real

cider and perry from 14 handpumps. Belgian and other imported beers are available on draught and bottled. Breweriana abounds throughout, and there is a courtyard outside for drinking and smoking. Filled rolls are available. A friendly clientele makes this a welcoming pub. Street parking is limited but there is a multi-storey car park near. ❀🚌●🚬

White Horse
84 Newnham Avenue, MK41 9PX
⏲ 11 (12 Sun)-11
☎ (01234) 409306
Wells Eagle IPA, Bombardier; guest beers Ⓗ
This pub does a brisk trade in good value food, with a regular Sunday roast and occasional themed evenings. There are quiz nights on Tuesday and Sunday, and live music on Monday evening. The licensees and staff have won several brewery and local business awards. ❀◑◐♿🚌P🚬

Biggleswade

Rising Sun
38 Sun Street, SG18 0BP
⏲ 4 (12 Sat)-11; 12-10.30 Sun
☎ (01767) 220088
Wells Eagle IPA, Bombardier; guest beers Ⓗ
Welcoming, traditional community local with a comfortable lounge and spacious public bar, situated at the edge of this old market town close to the railway station. Pub games include darts, pool, crib and dominoes. Major sporting events are screened on TV. The secluded garden has a covered patio area. The Kingfisher Way long distance footpath is five minutes' walk away. ❀🛏🚌♣P🚬

Wheatsheaf
5 Lawrence Road, SG18 0LS
⏲ 11-4, 7-11; 11-11 Fri & Sat; 12-10.30 Sun
☎ (01767) 222220
Greene King XX Mild, IPA, Abbot Ⓗ
A true locals' pub, standing at the end of a row of terraced cottages. This community hostelry organises activities including trips to the races and a Sunday meat raffle, and runs darts and dominoes teams. It was winner of the Mercia region 'Quality in Glass' award in 2006, recognising that the Wheatsheaf offers the best pint in over 1300 competing Greene King pubs. It is one of the few local inns to serve Greene King's excellent XX mild. ⛫❀⇌🚌♣🚬

Bletsoe

Falcon
Rushden Road, MK44 1QN (on A6)
⏲ 12-3, 6-11; 12-11 Sat; 12-10.30 Sun
☎ (01234) 781222 🌐thefalconbletsoe.co.uk
Wells Eagle IPA, Bombardier; guest beers Ⓗ
Traditional coaching inn dating from the 17th century with a variety of large and small rooms. An extensive menu of home-made pub food is available all week except Sunday evening. The large garden, overlooked by a new covered terrace, runs down to the River Great Ouse. Live jazz plays on bank holiday Monday afternoon. ⛫👶❀◑◐P🚬

Bolnhurst

Plough
Kimbolton Road, MK44 2EX (on B660 at S end of village)
⏲ 12-2, 6.30-11; closed Mon; 12-2.30 Sun
☎ (01234) 376274 🌐bolnhurst.com
Bateman XB; Potton Village Bike; guest beers Ⓗ
Relaxed and informal pub restaurant with a bar and large dining area offering high quality food. The bar has a modern fireplace and plenty of seating. Outside is a large drinking area alongside the car park. Real cider is available in summer. ⛫Q❀◑◐♿●P

Broom

Cock ☆
23 High Street, SG18 9NA
⏲ 12-3 (4 Sat), 6-11; 12-4, 7-10.30 Sun
☎ (01767) 3144411
Greene King IPA, Ruddles County, Abbot Ⓖ
Delightful village inn, full of character, with many small rooms. The pub is a listed building, as are the surrounding terraced houses. The parlour has a wood fire and skittles is played in the front room. Beer is served from the cellar, direct from the cask. Food is available during most opening hours. The car park is at the rear of the pub, and there are camping facilities. ⛫Q❀◑◐🛏🚌♣P

Campton

White Hart
Mill Lane, SG17 5NX
⏲ 7 (5 Fri; 3 Sat)-11; 12-4, 7-11 Sun
☎ (01462) 812657
Courage Directors; John Smith's Bitter; Theakston Best; guest beer Ⓗ
A Guide regular since 1976, the pub has been run by the same family for over 37 years. This 300-year old, Grade II listed free house has three bar areas. Exposed brickwork, wooden beams, quarry-tiled floors and iinglenooks feature throughout. The pub hosts a monthly quiz, has several teams including darts, crib, petanque and dominoes and runs a golf society. The large garden has a well-equipped play area. ⛫❀♣P

Clophill

Stone Jug
10 Back Street, MK45 4BY (off A6, N end of village)
⏲ 12-3, 6-11; 12-11 Fri; 11-11 Sat; 12-10.30 Sun
☎ (01525) 860526
B&T Shefford Bitter; Fuller's London Pride; Young's Bitter; guest beers Ⓗ
Popular village local created from three 17th-century stone cottages. The L-shaped bar serves two drinking areas and a function/family room leading to a rear patio garden. There are picnic benches at the front for alfresco drinking in fine weather. Excellent home-made lunches are served Monday to Saturday. Bedfordshire CAMRA Pub of the Year 2006. Q👶❀◑♣●P🚬

Cople

Five Bells
1 Northill Road, MK44 3TU
🕙 11-midnight
☎ (01234) 838289 ⊕ fivebellscople.co.uk
Greene King IPA, Abbot Ⓗ
Cosy pub in the centre of the village opposite the church. The main bar has low beams and a warming fire in winter. The lounge and dining rooms have recently been refurbished and the pub is renowned for good food, with a menu of modern British cuisine that changes according to season. No evening meals are served on Sunday. There is a small garden at the rear. ♨❀◐▶🖵P

Cranfield

Carpenters Arms
93 High Street, MK43 0DP
🕙 12-3 (not Mon), 6-11; 12-11 Sat; 12-10.30 Sun
☎ (01234) 750232
Wells Eagle IPA; guest beers Ⓗ
Situated in the middle of the village, this is a real community pub. Traditional pub games are played in the bar. Home-cooked meals are served in the lounge/dining area. There is a large car park and patio garden outside. Q❀◐🖵🚌♣P🕭

Dunstable

Globe
43 Winfield Street, LU6 1LS
🕙 12-11 (midnight Fri & Sat); 12-10.30 Sun
☎ (01582) 512300 ⊕ globe-pub.co.uk
B&T Two Brewers, Shefford Bitter, Black Dragon Dark Mild, Dragonslayer, Edwin Taylor's Extra Stout; guest beers Ⓗ
Opened in 2005, this is B&T's third tied pub. It has a clean, bright bar decorated with breweriana – no frills, just a friendly welcome and quality beer. A good pub to meet and talk or play darts, dominoes and cards and no juke box or fruit machines. With eleven beers to choose from, why not try the one-third-of-a-pint selection offer. Regular beer festivals are hosted. South Beds CAMRA Pub of the Year 2007. Q❀♣♦🕭

Victoria
69 West Street, LU6 1ST
🕙 11-12.30am (1am Fri & Sat)
☎ (01582) 662682
Beer range varies Ⓗ
A frequent CAMRA local Pub of the Year, this town centre pub usually offers four ales including a house beer, Victoria Bitter, from Tring Brewery. The ever-changing guest beers are from micro and regional breweries. Good value lunchtime meals are served. Darts and dominoes are popular and sport on TV features in the bar. Quarterly beer festivals are held. No admittance after 11pm. ❀◐♣🕭

Great Barford

Anchor Inn
High Street, MK44 3LF
🕙 12-3, 6 (5.30 Fri)-11; 12-11 Sat; 12-4, 6.30-10.30 Sun
☎ (01234) 870364

Wells Eagle IPA; guest beers Ⓗ
Busy village pub situated next to the church overlooking the River Ouse. At least two guest beers are usually available from an extensive range. Good, home-cooked food is served in the bar and restaurant as well as a fine selection of wines. ♨Q◐▶&P🕭

Harlington

Old Sun
34 Sundon Road, LU5 6LS
🕙 12-2, 5-11; 12-11 Fri-Sat & summer Sun
☎ (01525) 872417 ⊕ theoldsunharlington.co.uk
Adnams Bitter; guest beer Ⓗ
The Old Sun is situated in the heart of this pretty commuter village, and the attractive, half-timbered building dates back to the 1640s and has been a pub since 1785. There are two bar areas as well as outdoor seating and a children's play area. The guest beer is often from the local Potton Brewery. A wide range of food is served every day (not Sun eve or Mon). ❀◐≒🚌♣P🕭

Henlow

Engineers Arms
68 High Street, SG16 6AA
🕙 12-midnight (1am Fri & Sat); 12-10.30 Sun
☎ (01462) 812284
Everards Tiger; guest beers Ⓗ
Two-bar village local, this free house serves a range of up to 40 beers and ciders, mostly from micro-breweries. An annual festival is hosted in October. The pub has weekly live music, from folk and blues to rock. The interior displays sporting and brewery memorabilia. Community events and organised trips make it a hub of local life, while a friendly welcome is assured for all ages. There is a heated patio for smokers. ♨❀&🚌♣♦🕭

Kempston

Half Moon
108 High Street, MK42 7BN
🕙 12-3 (4 Sat), 6 (5 Fri, 7 Sat)-11; 12-4, 7-11 Sun
☎ (01234) 852464
Wells Eagle IPA, Bombardier Ⓗ
Situated near the Great River Ouse, this pub is well supported by the local community and has a number of pub teams in local leagues. The public bar has a skittles table and other games, and there is a comfortable lounge bar. The large garden has a children's play area and boules pitches. Meals are available at lunchtime except Sunday. ♨❀◐&🚌♣P🕭

Kensworth

Farmers Boy
216 Common Road, LU6 2PJ
🕙 12-2.30 (not Mon), 3 (5 winter)-11; 12-midnight Fri & Sat; 12-11 Sun
☎ (01582) 872207
Fuller's London Pride, ESB; guest beers Ⓗ
This village pub from the 1880s has separate areas for drinking and dining, with a garden to the rear and seating out front. Children are welcome if dining and there is a play area in the garden. Community sports and events are

supported and dogs are welcome. The licensee has a Fuller's Master Cellarman certificate and the pub was runner-up in the Outstanding Achievement category of the 2006-07 Fuller's Pub Awards.
🏨⊛🌣🍴ᵭ🛏♿♣P⌐

Keysoe

White Horse

Kimbolton Road, MK44 2JA (on B660 at Keysoe Row crossroads)
🕓 12-3, 6-11; 12-11 Sat & Sun
☎ (01234) 376363
Wells Eagle IPA; guest beers Ⓗ
One of the oldest pubs in the Charles Wells' estate, this single bar country inn has a thatched roof and low beams, a conservatory with a pool table and dartboard and a large garden with children's play area. There are normally two guest beers from the Wells & Young's list available. No food is served on Monday or on Sunday evening. 🏨⊛🌣♣P⌐

Leighton Buzzard

Hare

10 Southcott Village, Linslade, LU7 2PR
🕓 12-midnight
☎ (01525) 373941
Courage Best Bitter; Fuller's London Pride; Tring Buck Bitter; Wadworth 6X; guest beers Ⓗ
Popular local pub overlooking the village green, attracting a good mix of drinkers. Over the years the village of Linslade has expanded and it is now part of the town of Leighton Buzzard. A collection of village photographs features in the pub. An annual St George's Day beer festival is held in a marquee in the large rear garden. There is a heated smoking area outside. Two regularly changing guest beers are usually on offer. 🏨⊛🚲♣P⌐

Luton

Bricklayers Arms

16-18 High Town Road, LU2 0DD
🕓 12-3, 5-11; 12-midnight Fri & Sat; 12-10.30 Sun
☎ (01582) 611017
Everards Beacon, Tiger; guest beers Ⓗ
This somewhat quirky town centre pub has been run by the same landlady for more than 21 years. The five handpumps serve three guest beers, displayed on a notice board – on average 10 a week – sourced mainly from micro-breweries. Popular with Hatters fans, the pub's two TVs show football. Quiz night is Monday. There are three draught Belgian beers and a modest selection of beers in bottles. ⊛🍴≠♣

English Rose

46 Old Bedford Road, LU2 7PA
🕓 12-11
☎ (01582) 723889 ⊕ englishroseluton.co.uk
Beer range varies Ⓗ
Friendly town pub with a village local atmosphere. Three frequently changing beers are chosen from a range of breweries nationwide. Food is served Tuesday to Friday lunchtime and until early evening on Saturday, with a takeaway service. The quiz on Tuesday

evening is a highlight and there is a pool table. The garden accommodates both smokers and non-smokers. Local CAMRA Pub of the Year in 2006 and runner up 2007.
⊛🍴≠⌐

Globe

26 Union Street, LU1 3AN
🕓 11-11; 12-10.30 Sun
☎ (01582) 728681
Caledonian Deuchars IPA; Greene King IPA; guest beer Ⓗ
Popular one-room street corner local, just out of the town centre. The pub offers a guest ale from a micro or regional brewery and stages regular beer festivals. Sport is shown on TV. Good value food is served at lunchtime. An enclosed patio area is at the rear of the small car park. ⊛🍴♣P⌐

Potton

Old Coach House

12 Market Square, SG19 2NP
🕓 12-2.30, 5.30-11; 12-11 Sat; 12-10.30 Sun
☎ (01767) 260221
Potton Shannon; guest beers Ⓗ
Georgian inn in a prime position on Potton market. Recent renovations have upgraded the bedrooms and dining rooms, and added a new restaurant in the old stables. The pub has two interconnecting bars; the back area doubles as a dining room. Good food is served in both restaurants and the bar has a menu too. An interesting range of guest beers includes a second Potton ale and three guests from micros or regional breweries. ⊛🚃🍴🛏P

Pulloxhill

Cross Keys

13 High Street, MK45 5HB
🕓 12-3, 6-11; 12-3, 7-10.30 Sun
☎ (01525) 712442
Adnams Broadside; Wells Eagle IPA, Bombardier Ⓗ
Old, oak-beamed inn near the top of the hill in a pretty village – popular for dining due to home-made specials and a good wine list. The restaurant can be used as a function room. The pub is well known for live jazz on a Sunday night. The grounds include a children's play area next to the car park. Q⊛🍴♿🚗🛏♣P⌐

Riseley

Fox & Hounds

High Street, MK44 1DT
🕓 11-2.30, 6-11; 12-3, 7-10.30 Sun
☎ (01234) 708240
Wells Eagle IPA, Bombardier; guest beers Ⓗ
Old village inn, originally two 16th-century cottages, complete with priest's hiding hole and resident ghosts. It has a reputation for good food, with charcoal-grilled steak, sold by weight and served with salad, a speciality. The dining room can be reserved, but booking is not necessary for bar meals – relax over a pint while your food is cooked. The garden has a covered patio with heaters. Q⊛🍴🛏P⌐

Salford

Red Lion Country Hotel

Wavendon Road, MK17 8AZ (2 miles N of jct 13 on M1)

☼ 11-2.30, 6-11; 12-2.30, 7-10.30 Sun

☎ (01908) 583117

Wells Eagle IPA, Bombardier Ⓗ

Traditional country hotel serving a fine selection of home-cooked food in the bar and no-smoking restaurant. The bar, warmed by an open fire in winter, offers a selection of board games. The large garden has a covered area and secure childen s playground. Accommodation is in six rooms, some with four-poster beds. ▲Q❀✍◀❶▣❶❤P

Sandy

Queen's Head

244 Cambridge Road, SG19 1JE

☼ 11.30-11 (11.30 Fri & Sat); 12-11 Sun

☎ (01767) 681115

Greene King IPA, Abbot Ⓗ

Originally the Maidenhead, this pub was built by William Randall in 1750 and retains much of its original structure and character. A traditional, friendly, unspoilt, small town pub just off the Market Square, a roaring log fire warms the public bar on cold winter evenings. Lunchtime meals are served and the Sunday roast is always popular. Note that guest beers (from the Greene King range) are on a cask breather. ▲❀◀❤P

Shefford

Brewery Tap

14 North Bridge Street, SG17 5DH

☼ 11.30-11; 12-10.30 Sun

☎ (01462) 628448

B&T Shefford Bitter, Shefford Dark Mild, Dragonslayer; Everards Tiger; guest beer Ⓗ

A short walk from the B&T Brewery, this tap was rescued and renamed by B&T in 1996. Primarily a drinkers' pub, it offers four regular and one guest beer. The open-plan interior is served by a single bar and there is a separate family room. The patio garden and car park are through an archway next to the pub. ❧❀▣❤P⮐

Shillington

Musgrave Arms

16 Apsley End Road, SG5 3LX

☼ 12 (4.30 Mon)-11; 12-10.30 Sun

☎ (01462) 711286

Greene King IPA, Abbot; Ⓖ **guest beers** Ⓗ

Original oak beams add to the character of this splendid multi-roomed country pub, with its magnificent range of casks on view behind the bar. Home cooked meals are served, with steak night on Tuesday and senior special lunches on Thursday (no food Sun eve or Mon). Monthly quizzes are held and there is fortnightly live music on Friday. Children and dogs are welcome. Dominoes and petanque are popular. ▲Q❀◀❶▣❶Å❤P⮐❸

Streatley

Chequers

Sharpenhoe Road, LU3 3PS

☼ 12-11.30 (12.30 Fri & Sat); 12-11 Sun

☎ (01582) 882072

Greene King IPA, Morland Original, Abbot, Old Speckled Hen; guest beers Ⓗ

Village pub of Georgian origin on the green next to the church. One of the few pubs in the region to use oversized, lined pint glasses, it usually offers five real ales. A popular pub with locals and visitors alike - especially in good weather due to the large patio area. Quiz night is Tuesday and traditional jazz plays on the first Sunday afternoon of the month. ▲❀✍◀❶❶❤P⮐❸

Sutton

John O' Gaunt Inn

30 High Street, SG19 2NE

☼ 12-2.30, 7-11; 12-10.30 Sun

☎ (01767) 260377

Black Sheep Best Bitter; guest beers Ⓗ

A Guide regular, this former Greene King pub was taken over by Admiral Taverns in 2007, and now has access to over 200 real ales. The licensees have been here for more than 30 years and continue to serve excellent home-cooked food (booking is recommended). The saloon bar displays the Village Quilt assembled by local societies and village schoolchildren. The pub runs its own golf society and the local folk club. Northamptonshire skittles and petanque are played here. ▲Q❀◀❶▣❶❤P

Tebworth

Queen's Head

The Lane, LU7 9QB

☼ 12-3 (not Tue & Wed), 6-11

☎ (01525) 874101

Adnams Broadside; Ⓖ **Wells Eagle IPA,** Ⓗ **Bombardier; Young's Special** Ⓖ

Traditional two-bar village local with a public bar, popular for darts and dominoes, and a lounge, which offers a quiz on Thursday and live music on Friday evening. A large garden is at the rear. No food is served but customers are welcome to bring their own. The pub has featured in this Guide for more than 25 years under the present landlord who also has a career as an actor with appearances on stage, radio and TV. ▲❀▣❤P⮐

Toddington

Oddfellows Arms

2 Congar Lane, LU5 6BP

☼ 5-11 (midnight Fri); 12-midnight Sat; 12-11 Sun

☎ (01525) 872021

Adnams Broadside; Fuller's London Pride; guest beers Ⓗ

Attractive 15th-century pub facing the village green with a heavily-beamed and brassed bar and restaurant. There is a choice of 20 bottled Belgian beers, all served in the correct glasses. Weston's Old Rosie cider and occasional guest ciders or perries are available. The varied menu offers good food (Tue-Sat eves and Sat & Sun lunch). Festivals are held in the spring and autumn. Tables on the small patio area are popular. ♨⚙🏠🍴🐕🍺⌐

Sow & Pigs
14 Church Square, LU5 6AA
⚙ 11 (12 Sun)-midnight
☎ (01525) 873089 🌐 sowandpigs.co.uk
Greene King IPA, Abbot; guest beers Ⓗ
This 19th-century inn has featured in every edition of the Guide. Heated by open fires, the long, narrow bar is decorated with pigs, golf memorabilia and paintings of the pub by local artists. Excellent home-made food is offered daily. Restaurant meals (rare-breed pork is a speciality) are also available (book in advance). The patio garden is pleasant in summer and the pub offers comfortable and reasonably-priced accommodation.
♨Q⚙🏠🍴🚃🐕P⌐

Totternhoe

Cross Keys
201 Castle Hill Road, LU6 2DA
⚙ 11.30-3, 5.30-11; 11.30-11 Fri & Sat; 11-11 Sun
☎ (01525) 220434
Adnams Broadside; Greene King IPA, Abbot; guest beer Ⓗ
This attractive thatched Grade II listed inn dating from 1433 has undergone much refurbishment, while maintaining its character, following a serious fire a few years ago. The restaurant offers lunchtime and evening meals (not Sun eve). In the warmer months basket meals and barbecues are served in the garden, which has views over the vale of Aylesbury. Dogs are welcome in the public bar. Q⚙🍴🚃P⌐

Old Farm
16 Church Road, LU6 1RE
⚙ 12-3, 5-3am; 12-3am Fri-Sun
☎ (01525) 661294 🌐 theoldfarminn.co.uk
Fuller's Discovery, London Pride, ESB; guest beer Ⓗ
Located in the conservation area of Church End, this village local has two inglenooks. The public bar with its low-boarded ceiling is the place to enjoy good conversation and traditional pub games. The restaurant serves good value food every day except Sunday evening (unless by prior arrangement). Wheelchair access is via the restaurant. Senior citizens specials are served on Thursday lunchtime. Dogs are welcome in the public bar and there is a large child-friendly garden next to the pub. Q♿⚙🍴🚃🐕P⌐

Upper Sundon

White Hart
56 Streatley Road, LU3 3PQ
⚙ 11-11; 12-10.30 Sun
☎ (01525) 872493
Wells Eagle IPA; guest beer Ⓗ
Attractive mock Tudor, two-bar Charles Wells' pub with leaded windows, tucked away from the village centre on the old village green. Close to Sundon Hills Country Park, a site of special scientific interest, the pub is popular with walkers. A gazebo is provided for smokers. The guest beer comes from the Charles Wells' list and a selection of malt whiskies is stocked. ⚙🚃🐕P⌐

Whipsnade

Old Hunters Lodge
The Crossroads, LU6 2LN
⚙ 11.30-3, 5-11; 11-11 Sun
☎ (01582) 672228 🌐 old-hunters.com
Greene King IPA, Abbot; guest beers Ⓗ
The Old Hunters Lodge is a 15th-century inn set on the outskirts of Whipsnade village. Guest beers are sourced from micro-breweries. A large dining area provides food throughout the week (until 7pm Sun). The Lodge has six guest rooms, one a bridal suite. Close by is Whipsnade Zoo, where endangered animals are bred. ♨Q⚙🏠🍴P⌐

Wingfield

Plough
Tebworth Road, LU7 9QH
⚙ 12-midnight
☎ (01525) 873077
Fuller's London Pride, ESB, seasonal beers; guest beers Ⓗ
Thatched village inn dating from the 17th century, decorated with paintings of rural scenes. Good food is available daily except Sunday evening. There are tables outside the front; to the rear is a conservatory and prize-winning garden, illuminated at night with a gazebo for smokers. ♨⚙🍴🚃P⌐

Wootton

Chequers
Hall End, MK43 9HP OS001457
⚙ 11.30-2.30, 5.30-11; 12-10.30 Sun
☎ (01234) 768394
Wells Eagle IPA Ⓗ
Originally a farmhouse, the building was converted to a pub in the early part of the 20th century. It retains heavy wooden beams and other original features. The large garden with plenty of seating is popular in summer. An interesting range of food is served Wednesday to Sunday lunchtime and Tuesday to Saturday evening. ♨⚙🍴🚃♿🐕P⌐

Yelden

Chequers
High Street, MK44 1AW
⚙ 12-2 (not Mon & Tue), 5-11; 12-midnight Fri & Sat; 12-10.30 Sun
☎ (01933) 356383
Fuller's London Pride; Ⓗ **Greene King Abbot;** Ⓖ **Taylor Landlord; guest beers** Ⓗ
Traditional village pub offering five real ales and two ciders. Good, home-cooked pub meals are served daily, with occasional ticket-only guest chef days. A cooked breakfast is served at the weekend. The extensive rear garden hosts an annual summer beer and cider festival. The village lies on the Three Shires Way walkers' route and features the impressive remains of an abandoned Norman castle. Supervised children are welcome in the separate skittles room. ♨♿⚙🍴🚃🐕🐕P⌐

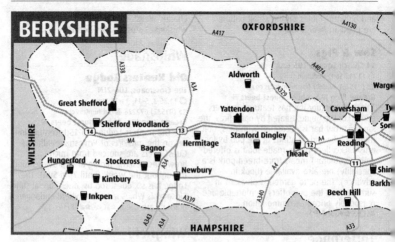

BERKSHIRE

Aldworth

Bell ☆
Bell Lane, RG8 9SE (off B4009 in centre of village)
🕐 11-3, 6-11; 12-3, 7-10.30 Sun
☎ (01635) 578272
Arkell's 3B, Kingsdown; West Berkshire Old Tyler, Maggs Mild, seasonal beers Ⓗ
Genuine, unspoilt village pub run by the same family for 200 years, close to the Ridgeway path and popular with walkers and cyclists. The pleasant garden is next to the cricket ground. West Berkshire's ever-changing monthly beers are usually available, as well as locally-produced Uptons farmhouse cider. The locals' tipple is 'Two Stroke', a 50/50 mixture of Kingsdown and 3B. Delicious filled rolls and home-made soups are recommended. CAMRA awards go back decades, including regional Pub of the Year in 2005 and 2006.
🚪Q🏠🐕♣🐾P

Bagnor

Blackbird
RG20 8AQ
🕐 11.45-2.30, 6-11; 12-3, 7-9 Sun
☎ (01635) 40638
Butts Jester, Barbus Barbus; Fuller's London Pride; guest beer Ⓟ
Situated in a picturesque village not far from Newbury, the Blackbird was built in the 1950s to replace a previous thatched pub that burned down, although the building has been an inn since the 17th century. The comfortable single bar is complemented by a small dining area. The menu features home-cooked food with ingredients from local suppliers (no meals Sun eve). Popular with horse trekkers, ramblers and cyclists, there is a pleasant, enclosed garden at the side. The famous Watermill Theatre is close by. 🚪Q🏠🐕♣🐾P⅃

Barkham

Bull at Barkham
Barkham Road, RG41 7TL (on B3349)
🕐 11-3, 5.30-11; 12-3, 7-10.30 Sun
☎ (0118) 976 0324 ⊕ thebullatbarkham.com

Adnams Bitter, Broadside; Courage Best Bitter; guest beers Ⓗ
Grade II listed building with an inglenook fireplace. The restaurant area dates back to 1728 and was a working smithy until 1982. Home-cooked meals are also available in the comfortable bar. Traditional hand-made blue cheeses, produced in Barkham by Two Hoots, are used in cooking and are available to take away, as are sausages made with Barkham Blue cheese. Bus 144 passes the door.
🚪🏠🐕🍺P

Beech Hill

Elm Tree
Beech Hill Road, RG7 2AZ
🕐 12-11; 12-10.30 Sun
☎ (0118) 988 3505 ⊕ the-elmtree.com
Adnams Bitter; Fuller's London Pride; Greene King IPA Ⓗ
West of the A33 and south of Reading, this cosy village pub offers serious food. The elm tree that stood beside the door died of dutch elm disease and supplied the massive planks that make up the bar front; where the tree was is now a heated terrace garden with views of the surrounding countryside. One room contains an interesting collection of clocks and old pictures of the village and pub. Ladies, note the must-see loo! Smoking is permitted on the verandah. 🚪Q🏠🐕P⅃

Binfield

Jack o' Newbury
Terrace Road North, RG42 5PH (north of village off B3018)
🕐 11-3, 5.30-11; 12-3, 7-10.30 Sun
☎ (01344) 454881 ⊕ jackofnewbury.co.uk
Rebellion IPA; guest beers Ⓗ
Cosy horseshoe-shaped room with fires and settle-style seating festooned with brasses, pots, guns and other paraphernalia. Family run

INDEPENDENT BREWERIES

Butts Great Shefford
West Berkshire Yattendon
Zerodegrees Reading

with a good kitchen, the pub has a homely feel. There is a skittle alley for hire in the barn. The pub is named after a 16th-century merchant who aided Henry VIII at Flodden Field in 1513. It is the current local CAMRA Pub of the Year. The 53a bus from Bracknell to Maidenhead passes the door. No evening meals on Monday. ♨⚜◑➡P

Victoria Arms

Terrace Road North, RG42 5JA
🕐 11.30-11 (midnight Fri & Sat); 12-11 Sun
☎ (01344) 483856
Fuller's Discovery, London Pride, ESB, seasonal beers Ⓗ
Separate drinking areas are served from a central bar. A vast bottled beer collection fills the rafters and a 'Hop Leaf' enamel is a reminder of previous Simonds Brewery ownership. The menu is varied with some dishes made with Fuller's beers. A safe garden and large TV for big sporting occasions make this a village pub for everyone. Observe the Bracknell town skyline from the back window, this is close enough. Bus 53a from Bracknell to Maidenhead passes the door. ♨⚜◑➡P

Bracknell

Old Manor

Church Road, Grenville Place, RG12 1BP
🕐 9-midnight (1am Fri & Sat)
☎ (01344) 304490
Greene King Abbot; Marston's Pedigree; guest beers Ⓗ
Busy Wetherspoon's by the inner ring road, half a mile from Bracknell rail and bus stations, offering a competitively priced range of guest beers, mostly regional ales. The interior has a sprawling open bar area with disabled access, adjoining low beamed snug and dining areas. Smoking is permitted in the covered, heated patio outside. The car park is pay and display, but parking refunds are available from the bar. Gets busy in the evening. ⚜◑ð≒➡P⌐

Caversham

Prince of Wales

76 Prospect Street, RG4 8JN

🕐 12-3, 6-11; 12-midnight Fri & Sat; 12-10.30 Sun
☎ (0118) 947 2267
Brakspear Bitter, Special, seasonal beers Ⓗ
Five minutes' walk up the hill from central Caversham, this large community local offers a warm welcome to all. This is a 'proper pub' with no pretensions. Games friendly, with pool, darts, crib and dominoes, it gets very busy when football is on TV. Dogs are welcome and children permitted until 7pm. Food is served weekday evenings and all day at the weekend. ⚜◑➡♣P

Cookham

Bounty

Riverside, SL8 5RG (footpath from station car park, across bridge, along towpath) OS893868
🕐 12-10.30 (winter closed Mon-Fri; 12-dusk Sat); 12-10.30 (12-dusk winter) Sun
☎ (01628) 520056
Rebellion IPA, Mutiny; guest beers Ⓗ
Fronting the river Thames, there is no road access to this inn – even the beer arrives by boat. The front room has a boat-shaped bar and is decorated with flags and other nautical paraphernalia. A large patio and garden with a children's play area make the pub popular with families. Food is served until the early evening. Limited mooring and camping are available – ask at bar. Note the winter opening times. ♨⛵⚜◑▲≒(Bourne End)♣⌐

Cookham Dean

Jolly Farmer

Church Road, SL6 9TD
🕐 11.30-11 (11.45 Fri & Sat); 12-10.30 Sun
☎ (01628) 482905 🌐 jollyfarmercookhamdean.co.uk
Brakspear Bitter; Courage Best Bitter; Young's Bitter; guest beers Ⓗ
Opposite the church, this pub is owned by the village. The terracotta-floored, low-beamed public bar is cosy with a real fire. The larger Dean Bar is popular with diners as well as drinkers. A more formal small dining room is also available (when not in use for the St George's Day or Hallowe'en beer festivals). The large garden has a children's play area. Two guest beers complement the three regular ales. No evening meals served on Sunday or Monday. ♨Q⚜◑P

Hermitage

Fox Inn

High Street, RG18 9RB
🕐 12-2.30, 5-11; 12-midnight Fri & Sat; 12-10.30 Sun
☎ (01635) 201545
Fuller's London Pride; Shepherd Neame Master Brew Bitter, Spitfire; guest beers Ⓗ
Welcoming, two-bar village pub, much improved in recent years. It has established a reputation for excellent real ales and good affordable food, ranging from bar meals, including a range of hot and cold filled baguettes, to an à la carte menu in the evening (meals finish at 7pm Sun). The regular ales are supplemented by guest beers, chosen by locals from a list displayed at the bar. Beers are served in branded glasses

wherever possible. Real cider is usually available in summer. ♨☼☺◐⊟⊞▲⊠⊟(9)♣♠P⌐

Hungerford

Downgate

13 Down View, Park Street, RG17 0ED (edge of Hungerford Common)
☼ 11 (12 Sun)-11
☎ (01488) 682708 ⊕ the-downgate.co.uk
Arkell's 2B, 3B, seasonal beers ⊞
Cosy, relaxing pub divided into three areas, one with a real fire. Situated on the eastern edge of this market town, the pub overlooks Hungerford Common and the outdoor tables have pleasant views. Award-winning hanging baskets adorn the pub in summer. Displays of former brewers' barrel bushes, past currencies and photographs of old Hungerford decorate the interior. Old blow lamps and model aircraft are suspended from the ceiling. The good value, traditional pub food includes Sunday roasts. ♨☼☺◐≈⊟(13)♣

Hurley

Dew Drop

Batts Green, Honey Lane, SL6 6RB (1 mile S of A4130) OS824815
☼ 11.30-3, 5.30-11 (midnight Fri); 12-11 Sun
☎ (01628) 824327 ⊕ thedewdropinn.co.uk
Brakspear Bitter, Special, seasonal beers ⊞
Off the beaten track between Hurley and Burchetts Green, this 17th-century pub is popular with walkers and horse riders. Dick Turpin is reputed to have drunk here once upon a time. It has a large outside seating area which is popular in the warmer weather and ideal for families. Good food is served daily (not Sun eve). Hitching posts, fresh hay and water are available for equine visitors. ♨Q☼◐♣P⌐

Inkpen

Crown & Garter

Inkpen Common, RG17 9QR (follow signs for Inkpen Common from Kintbury)
☼ 12-3 (not Mon & Tue), 5.30-11; 12-5, 7-10.30 Sun
☎ (01488) 668325 ⊕ crownandgarter.com
West Berkshire Mr Chubb's Lunchtime Bitter, Good Old Boy; guest beers ⊞
Set in an area of outstanding natural beauty, this 17th-century inn is ideally situated for country walks. It is said to have been visited by King James II, hence the name. The bar area has a huge inglenook fireplace and criss-crossed beams; alongside is a small, comfortable dining area serving excellent home-cooked meals (no food Sun eve). Local ales come from the West Berkshire brewery. Good en-suite accommodation is available. A large, tree-lined garden offers views of Combe Hill. ♨☼☺◐⊠⊟(13)♣♠P⌐

Kintbury

Dundas Arms

53 Station Road, RG17 9UT (opp station)
☼ 11-2.30, 6-11; 12-2.30 Sun
☎ (01488) 658263 ⊕ dundasarms.co.uk

Adnams Bitter; Ramsbury Gold; West Berkshire Good Old Boy; guest beer ⊞
Nestling between the Kennet and Avon Canal and the River Kennet, this classy, whitewashed inn dates back to the 18th century. There are pleasant views from the riverside seating area and Kintbury railway station is just across the canal bridge. The single bar features a counter studded with polished old pennies. Excellent food can be enjoyed either in the bar or in the quieter restaurant. No meals are served on Sundays or Monday evening. Q☼☺◐≈⊟(13)P

Knowl Hill

Bird in Hand

Bath Road, RG10 9UP (on A4 between Reading and Maidenhead)
☼ 11-3, 5-11; 11-11 Sat; 12-10.30 Sun
☎ (01628) 826622 ⊕ birdinhand.co.uk
Brakspear Bitter; guest beers ⊞
A genuine free house, well-known for its variety of regularly-changing guest ales from breweries near and far. At least one dark beer is usually available. Welcoming to both drinkers and diners, the staff are friendly and helpful. Generous portions of hearty, traditional food are served, with Sunday roasts a speciality. Large fireplaces, a wide variety of comfortable seating and music-free environment encourage conversation. A function room is available. Local CAMRA Pub of the Year 2007. ♨Q☼☺◐⊟(127)P⌐

Seven Stars

Bath Road, RG10 9UR (on A4 between Reading and Maidenhead)
☼ 11-3, 5-12; 11-1am Fri & Sat; 12-10.30 Sun
☎ (01628) 822967
Brakspear Bitter, Special ⊞
Friendly, picturesque community pub set back from the A4 in a large lay-by. This is the place to drink Brakspear's ales as they can and should be served. The function room/skittles alley hosts various meetings, including the local Folk Club on Thursday night. A variety of vehicle owners' clubs meet here – from Discovery and Aston-Martin to VW and scooter enthusiasts. Traditional pub games are kept behind the bar. ♨☍☼◐♿⊟(127)P

Littlewick Green

Cricketers

Coronation Road, SL6 3RA OS838801
☼ 11-3, 5-11; 11-11 Thu-Sat; 12-10.30 Sun
☎ (01628) 822888
Hall & Woodhouse Best, K&B Sussex, Tanglefoot, seasonal beers ⊞
Overlooking the village green, this three-bar pub has a cricketing theme, naturally. Check out the splendid old clock. Food is available at lunchtime and every evening except Sunday. Badger beers are unusual for the area. A good crowd congregates outside in summer to watch the cricket. Children are welcome. Buses run along the A4, 200 metres away. ♨☍☼☺◐⊞⊟(127)P⌐

Maidenhead

Greyhound

92-96 Queen Street, SL6 1HT
🕓 9-midnight (1am Fri & Sat)
☎ (01628) 779410
Greene King Abbot; Marston's Burton Bitter, Pedigree; guest beers Ⓗ
Large, modern Wetherspoon's near the station offering up to six guest beers, often including Loddon and Rebelllion, as well as Weston's Old Rosie cider on handpump. Now branded as a Lloyd's No.1, it has an additional room where quiet music plays. A quiz is held on Sunday evening. The original Greyhound – now a bank – was where Charles I met his children before his execution in 1649.
◑≢⊟♠

Maidenhead Conservative Club

32 York Road, SL6 1SF
🕓 10.30-2.30, 5.30-11; 10.30-11 Sat; 12-3, 7-11 Sun
☎ (01628) 620579
Fuller's Discovery, London Pride, seasonal beers; Greene King IPA; guest beers Ⓗ
Friendly real ale outlet close to the station. The club steward is a CAMRA member and this is reflected in the beer quality. Two guest brews are available, as well as bottle-conditioned beers. Monday is crib night, Tuesday and Wednesday darts. Quiz night is Sunday. The parking is very limited, but there is a public car park just 100 metres away. Show this Guide or a CAMRA membership card to get in.
と◑శ≢⊟P

Newbury

Gun

142 Andover Road, Wash Common, RG14 2NE
🕓 12-11
☎ (01635) 47292
Adnams Broadside; Courage Best Bitter; Shepherd Neame Spitfire, Bishop's Finger; Wadworth 6X; guest beer Ⓗ
There has been a pub on this site a mile uphill from the town centre since the Civil War – the First Battle of Newbury was fought nearby. Today's pub is a two-room community local, one side devoted to pool, darts and other electronic amusements, the other side a quieter lounge. There are rumours of a resident ghost. Bishop's Finger may give way to another guest ale as the licensee likes to vary his selection. No meals are served Sunday evenings. ❀◑⊟(1, 12)P

Pinkneys Green

Stag & Hounds

1 Lee Lane, SL6 6NU
🕓 12-4 7-10.30 (12-10.30 summer); 12-3, 6-11 Sat (12-11 summer); 12-10.30 Sun
☎ (01628) 630268
Beer range varies Ⓗ
After a difficult period in the early part of the decade, this rural free house has now been in steady hands for a few years and is back to its best. It offers five real ales, usually including one from Rebellion. The public bar is cosy, the lounge has a real fire and tables for dining. The large garden is popular in summer. A skittle alley in the function room can be hired.

Occasional beer festivals are hosted.
🏨Q❀◑⊟♣P♣≘

Waggon & Horses

112 Pinkneys Road, SL6 5DN
🕓 11.30-3, 5-11; 12-midnight Sat; 12-11 Sun
☎ (01628) 781001
Greene King IPA, Morland Original, Abbot, Old Speckled Hen Ⓗ
Pub of an uncertain age, surrounded by National Trust land, in a historic village just outside Maidenhead. The unfussy front bar is complemented by a pleasant back lounge. There is pinball in the corridor between the two. The large garden is popular during the summer months. Quiz night is Thursday. No food is available on Sunday. The village green opposite is the cricket ground as well as home to an annual steam fair held in May.
🏨❀◑♣P♣≘

Reading

Allied Arms

57 St Mary's Butts, RG1 2LG
🕓 11-11; closed Sun
☎ (0118) 959 0865 ⊕ allied-arms.co.uk
Fuller's London Pride; Loddon Hullabaloo; guest beer Ⓗ
Popular pub, one of the oldest in Reading, with a small bar at the front and a larger bar (with undulating ceiling) at the rear. It attracts a mixed crowd and gets lively when London Irish are playing at home. The main bar features a sports screen and a juke box with an eclectic selection of music. All are welcome at the popular quiz every other Wednesday. Two regular draught beers are frequently supplemented by a guest. ❀≢≘

Eldon Arms

19 Eldon Terrace, RG1 4DX
🕓 11-3, 5.30-11.30 (midnight Fri); 11-3, 7-midnight Sat; 12-3, 7-11.30 Sun
☎ (0118) 957 3857
Wadworth Mild, IPA, 6X, seasonal beers Ⓗ
Traditional two-room community local tucked away in a side street close to the Royal Berks Hospital. The old-fashioned and lively public bar contrasts with the cosy, smartly-decorated lounge, which features an interesting collection of knick-knacks. The entrance area retains the old 'jug & bottle' hatch, and there is a secluded garden. The long-serving hosts reputedly sell more Mild than any other pub. Food is available Monday-Saturday lunchtime only. The pub may close early in the afternoon if quiet. Q❀◑⊟⊟♣♠≘

Hobgoblin

2 Broad Street, RG1 2BH
🕓 11-11; 12-10.30 Sun
☎ (0118) 950 8119
Beer range varies Ⓗ
A strange little watering hole where it's always Hallowe'en; chaotic decor disguises cruel pubco neglect. Eight real ales (three West Berkshire and five guests) enjoy a fast turnover; dark or unconventional beers are often available, plus Weston's cider and perry and never enough cellar space. Drinking is permitted in a small area of the pedestrianised street. The handsome old

doorway offers minimal shelter, while much of the pub is technically in the adjoining building. No food, children or mobiles.
🏠🚆🖨❧

Jolly Angler

314 Kennetside, RG1 3EA
🕓 12-11 (10.30 Sun)
☎ (0118) 926 7588
Harveys Sussex Best Bitter; guest beers Ⓗ
Extensively refurbished in 2006, this riverside inn is near the confluence of the Kennet and Thames, close to the Thames Path and National Cycle Route 4. It is a rare local outlet for Harveys Sussex Best, complemented by two changing guests, often from local breweries such as Loddon and Triple fff. The pub is dominated at times by television when sporting events are shown. Pool and darts are played. There are benches on the riverside path for pleasant outdoor drinking. 🏠◑♣

Outlook

76-78 Kings Road, RG1 3BJ
🕓 12-11; closed Sun
☎ (0118) 958 6194
Greene King IPA, Abbot, Old Speckled Hen; guest beer Ⓗ
Formerly a Hogshead and now part of the Greene King empire, this is a large, modern pub on two levels. Small outdoor terraces enjoy views over an arm of the River Kennet, while the interior is all wood and flagstones with plenty of seating including comfortable sofas. Popular with the local office crowd, it is a short walk from the town centre shops. Good basic pub food is served all day. Main bus routes to east Reading pass the door. 🏠◑&🖨

Retreat

8 St John's Street, RG1 4EH
🕓 4-11; 12-11.30 Fri & Sat; 12-11 Sun
☎ (0118) 957 1593 ⊕ retreatpub.co.uk
Loddon Ferryman's Gold; Ringwood Best Bitter; guest beers Ⓗ
Unpretentious back-street boozer with six handpumps, interesting cider (and sometimes perry) and a range of bottled foreign beers. A genuine community pub, it is the meeting place for the local residents' association, while regulars can order their organic veg boxes and join the occasional 'pig club' for quality free-range meat. Live music plays on Thursday night and Sunday lunchtime often with a jazz, swing or folk feel. A piano and quality juke box complete your musical entertainment. 🖨♣❧

Three Guineas

Station Approach, RG1 1LY
🕓 10-11 (10.30 Sun)
☎ (0118) 957 2473
Greene King IPA; Young's Bitter; guest beers Ⓗ
Located in the Victorian railway station's former ticket hall and adjoining offices – the ideal place to start or end your visit to Reading. Spacious, with high ceilings, the bar area features dozens of rugby shirts from all over the world. Big screens show major sporting events; small monitors show train departure times. Eight real ales are always available. Popular with rugby fans, the bar is

very busy when London Irish are playing at home in Reading's Madejski Stadium.
🏠🚆🖨⌐

Ruscombe

Royal Oak

Ruscombe Lane, RG10 9JN
🕓 12-3, 6 (5 Fri)-11; closed Mon eve; 12-4 Sun
☎ (0118) 934 5190 ⊕ burattas.co.uk
Brakspear Bitter; Fuller's London Pride; guest beer Ⓗ
Large, relaxing pub/restaurant just outside the village of Twyford, featuring modern, tasteful decor. A variety of bistro-style food is offered. Booking is strongly advised, as this pub is very popular with local diners but it is equally welcoming to those who come just to drink. The spacious conservatory is heated and curtained for winter use. The large garden has ample seating and is home to ducks and chickens. Disabled access is via the back door. 🏛Q💲🏠◑🖨&P

St Nicholas Hurst

Wheelwrights Arms

Davis Way, RG10 0TR (off B3030)
🕓 11.30-2.30, 5.30-11; 11.30-11 Sat; 11.30-10.30 Sun
☎ (0118) 934 4100
Wadworth IPA, 6X, JCB; guest beers Ⓗ
A former farmhouse dating back to the 18th century, the building retains flagstone floors, beams and a log fire. This friendly community pub runs local bridge, gun and golf clubs. Good pub food is popular (no food Sat and Sun eve). The manager is a real ale enthusiast and there is always a mild available. Close to Winnersh station and with ample parking, the pub attracts locals and visitors, particularly nearby workers at lunchtime. The smoking area has heated umbrellas. 🏛🏠◑🚆P⌐

Shefford Woodlands

Pheasant Inn

Ermin Street, RG17 7AA (on B4000 just N of M4 jct 14)
🕓 11-12.30am (1am Fri & Sat); 11-midnight Sun
☎ (01488) 648284 ⊕ thepheasantinnlambourn.co.uk
Butts Jester; Loddon Hoppit; Wadworth 6X Ⓗ
Standing beside the old Roman road from Silchester, this rural pub has changed its character over the past few years. Purchased by members of the horseracing fraternity, racing memorabilia decorates the red-painted interior. An extension at the back adds a new restaurant, meeting room and accommodation. The pub remains a sociable haunt for drinkers, with ring-the-bull still played. The rare bottle-glass screens above the bar have been retained. Food is highly recommended. 🏛🏠🚆◑&♣P⌐

Shinfield

Magpie & Parrot

Arborfield Road, RG2 9EA
🕓 12-7 (3 Sun)
☎ (0118) 988 4130
Fuller's London Pride; guest beer Ⓗ

A pub for more than 250 years, recent changes include the opening of the formerly private sitting room to customers, replacement of the nursery greenhouses with a large marquee and the erection of a pub sign. A mellow, timber-framed locals' pub, it is packed with curios (including stuffed magpie and parrot), comfy armchairs and sofas. Dogs are worshipped, children and mobiles banished outside to the huge garden. It closes early in the evening except during two annual beer festivals. ⌂Q❀⬆️🚃(144)♣P⬱

Slough

Rose & Crown
312 High Street, SL1 1NB
🕒 11-11; 12-10.30 Sun
☎ (01753) 521114
Beer range varies Ⓗ
Situated at the eastern end of the High Street, this Grade II listed building dates back to the late 16th century. A proper pub with two small bars, it serves up to three different beers, often one from Rebellion. Real cider is sometimes available, often in summer. A beer festival is held in early July. Entertainment includes karaoke on alternate Friday nights and occasional live music. There is a large screen TV for sports. ❀≈🚃♣⬱

Wheatsheaf
15 Albert Street, SL1 2BE
🕒 12-11 (10.30 Sun)
☎ (01753) 522019
Fuller's London Pride, ESB, Gale's HSB, seasonal beers Ⓗ
Originally a bakery, this traditional local in the Upton area of Slough has been licensed since 1897. The comfortable single bar hosts a quiz on Thursday, live music twice a month and regular games nights. It has a pleasant patio garden at the back and barbecues are held in summer. The pub may stay open beyond 11pm on Friday and Saturday if busy. A smoking area outside is covered and heated. ❀◖♣⬱

Sonning

Bull Inn
High Street, RG4 6UP
🕒 11-11 (11.30 Fri & Sat); 12-10.30 Sun
☎ (0118) 969 3901
Fuller's Chiswick, Discovery, London Pride, Gale's HSB Ⓗ
Traditional English inn dating from the 16th century in a narrow street at the heart of the village, near the Thames Path. To the left is a 'proper' bar, popular with the locals, while to the right is a rambling dining area. Full of character, with exposed beams and a choice of sofas, the Bull is mentioned in the 1889 book Three Men in a Boat. Food is good; bedrooms are expensive but of a high standard. ⌂Q❀✎◖⬆️🚃P

Stanford Dingley

Bull
RG7 6LS (on Yattendon to Burnt Hill road)
🕒 12-3, 6-11; 12-3, 7-10.30 Sun

☎ (0118) 974 4409 ⊕ thebullatstanforddingley.co.uk
Brakspear Bitter; West Berkshire Skiff, Good Old Boy; guest beer Ⓗ
This 15th-century country pub, extended to create six popular letting rooms, is situated in a picturesque part of the Pang Valley. It has a saloon bar and dining room, plus a tap room with an exposed wattle and daub wall. No meals are served on Sunday evenings. Folk night is every second Wednesday and blues every fourth Friday of the month. Ring the bull is played here. The large, safe garden is ideal for families. Skiff is a beer unique to the pub. ⌂Q❀✎◖⬆️&♣P

Stockcross

Rising Sun
Ermin Street, RG20 8LG
🕒 12 (11 summer)-2.30, 6 (5.30 summer)-11; 12-3 (11-2.30 summer), 5.30-11 Fri; 12 (11 summer)-11 Sat; 12-3, 7-10.30 Sun
☎ (01488) 608131 ⊕ therisingsun-stockcross.co.uk
West Berkshire Mr Chubb's Lunchtime Bitter, Maggs Mild, Good Old Boy, seasonal beers Ⓗ
Formerly an Ushers' alehouse and premises of a coach firm, this is now West Berkshire Brewery's first tied house. The interior has been lovingly restored with a three-area layout; much of the work was done by brewery owner Dave Maggs himself. A central passageway with an engraved window divides the pub, with one area hosting regular live music evenings. The pub is also HQ of the local AJS & Matchless Motorcycle Club. No evening meals are served on Sunday. ⌂Q❀◖⬆️&🚃(4)P

Theale

Crown
2 Church Street, RG7 5BT
🕒 11 (12 Sat)-11; 12-10.30 Sun
☎ (0118) 930 2310
Adnams Broadside; Greene King IPA; West Berkshire Good Old Boy Ⓗ
Community pub in the heart of a village renowned for numerous hostelries – a legacy from its location on the old coaching route from London to Bath when the Crown was built in 1710. Although the interior has now been knocked into a single room, different areas still maintain something of the ambience of a separate public, lounge and bar. This is a popular place to enjoy a pint while waiting for a bus or train. ❀◖⬆️≈🚃(101, 103, 104)♣P

Twyford

Land's End
Land's End Lane, Charvil, RG10 0UE (jct of Land's End Lane and Park Lane)
🕒 12-3, 6-11; 11-11 Sat; 12-10.30 Sun
☎ (0118) 934 0700
Brakspear Bitter; guest beer Ⓗ
Large rural pub close to a ford over the River Loddon; take care when driving across, as it can be impassable after heavy rain. Recently refurbished, the pub still retains many original features, and has a variety of seating areas. Equally welcoming to drinkers and diners, an

eclectic menu includes simpler snacks. The pub boasts a large outdoor seating area and car park. Q🌣⌂◧&⚑⌐

Waltham St Lawrence

Bell

The Street, RG10 0JJ (next to church)
🕐 12-3, 5-11; 12-11 Sat; 12-10.30 Sun
☎ (0118) 934 1788 ⊕ thebellinn.biz
Beer range varies Ⓗ
Owned by a local charity for the poor of the parish, this friendly, lively 14th-century pub has two cosy, beamed, traditional rooms, a more modern dining room (with a view down the well), courtyard tables and a huge garden. Five real ales are stocked. No.1 is the house beer, brewed by West Berkshire – the cider is Gray's. An eclectic menu includes simple snacks. Dogs, children and walkers are all welcome. Busy Sunday lunchtimes.
♨Q☻🌣⌂◧(53A)♣●P

Wargrave

St George & Dragon

High Street, RG10 8HY
🕐 11-11 (10.30 Sun)
☎ (0118) 940 5021 ⊕ stgeorgeanddragon.co.uk
Loddon Hullabaloo; Taylor Landlord Ⓗ
Large riverside inn with stunning views over the Thames Valley, especially from the large decked patio. Alternatively, take your pint down the steps to the tables on the river bank. Indoors, exposed beams contrast with bare floorboards and bright, modern decor. The restaurant trade is important, but the drinker is always most welcome. Mooring is available for those arriving by boat. The annual Wargrave & Shiplake regatta takes place in early August. ♨🌣⌂◧&⇌◧(328)P⚑⌐☖

Windsor

Carpenters Arms

4 Market Street, SL4 1PB
🕐 11-11 (midnight Fri & Sat)
☎ (01753) 755961
Beer range varies Ⓗ
Situated on a cobbled street between the castle and Guildhall, this 16th-century pub attracts locals and tourists alike. Originally it was linked to the castle by a series of tunnels, now bricked up – you can see the evidence in the lower seating area towards the rear of the building. A recent winner of local CAMRA Pub of the Year, it offers an ever-changing selection of up to five real ales from breweries across the country.
🌣⌂◧⇌(Windsor & Eton Central)◧⌐

Duke of Connaught

165 Arthur Road, SL4 1RZ
🕐 12-midnight (1am Fri & Sat)
☎ (01753) 840748
Greene King IPA, Abbot; guest beer Ⓗ
Originally No. 1 Connaught Cottages, this pub was the home of Mr Charles Wilkins, a beer retailer in 1895. Later on the tavern was owned by the now defunct Victoria Brewing Company, Windsor. Today it is a friendly, stylish, street corner pub with a good

atmosphere. It shows sport on TV and hosts live music and occasional quiz evenings. The interior has bare floorboards and old film photographs decorate the walls. There is a covered area outside for smokers.
♨🌣⌂◧⇌(Windsor & Eton Central)◧⌐

Trooper

97 St Leonards Road, SL4 3BZ
🕐 11-11; 12-10.30 Sun
☎ (01753) 670123
Fuller's London Pride, Gale's HSB, seasonal beers Ⓗ
Situated just beyond the end of Windsor's main shopping street and opposite the Arts Centre, this former coaching inn is popular with office workers at lunchtime and locals in the evening. Two television screens in the main bar area attract sports fans. There is an additional dining room at the rear of the pub which can be hired out for private functions. There is a covered and heated area outside for smokers. 🌣⌂◧⇌(Windsor & Eton Central)⌐

Two Brewers

34 Park Street, SL4 1LB
🕐 11.30-11 (11.30 Fri & Sat); 12-10.30 Sun
☎ (01753) 855426
Courage Best Bitter; Fuller's London Pride; guest beer Ⓗ
This Grade II listed pub was once part of the Crown Estate and the interior has been decorated in keeping with its origins. Built in the 17th century, it was reputedly a brothel and drinking house on the main road from Windsor to London. The frontage was replaced after a fire in the 19th century. No food is served on Sunday evening, with a tapas menu only on Friday and Saturday evenings.
♨🌣⌂◧⇌(Windsor & Eton Central)◧

Vansittart Arms

105 Vansittart Road, SL4 5DD
🕐 12-11 (11.30 Thu; midnight Fri & Sat); 12-11 Sun
☎ (01753) 865988
Fuller's Discovery, London Pride, ESB, seasonal beers Ⓗ
Situated to the west of the town centre, the pub was once five cottages for castle workers. The two main bar areas have recesses and real fires. The large garden and patio are popular in the summer, hosting occasional barbecues and special events. Rugby is keenly followed here and the pub sponsors a local team. An outside smoking area is partially covered and heated. ♨🌣⌂◧⇌(Windsor & Eton Central)⌐

Winkfield

Old Hatchet

Hatchet Lane, SL4 2EE (on A330 NW of Ascot)
🕐 12-11 (10.30 Sun)
☎ (01344) 899911
Fuller's Discovery, London Pride, Gale's HSB, ESB Ⓗ
Comfortable country pub, full of character, now returned to a pub with food following a short spell as a restaurant with bar. It is one of the few entries in this Guide with a French landlord. The pub is built on several levels, and has beamed ceilings. Excellent home-cooked food is served at all sessions with an ever-changing specials board. Children are

welcome if dining. A guest beer sometimes replaces the Discovery, and Fuller's seasonal ales are occasionally available. ♨Q☻◐▸&P

Wokingham

Broad Street Tavern

29 Broad Street, RG40 1AU
✪ 12-11 (midnight Thu-Sat); 12-10.30 Sun
☎ (0118) 9773706 ⊕ broadstreettavern.co.uk
Wadworth IPA, 6X, JCB, seasonal beers; guest beers Ⓗ
Comfortable and welcoming town centre local. Two quiet rooms, with wood-panelled walls, complement the main bar and seating area. Traditional pub games are played and a monthly quiz is held on a Thursday evening. Superb quarterly beer festivals are hosted, offering a large range of cask and bottled ales from home and abroad. The garden has a heated and covered outside seating area. Three times winner of local CAMRA Pub of the Year. ☻◐▸≠🖫♣⸽

Crispin

45 Denmark Street, RG40 2AY
✪ 12-11 (midnight Sat & Sun)
☎ (01189) 780309
Fuller's London Pride; guest beers Ⓗ
Situated just out of the town centre, the pub has a two-room bar area with black wood beams, a U-shaped bar with more black wood and two fireplaces. One regular ale is served, accompanied by up to four guest beers. Various pump clips are displayed along the front of the bar. Darts and quizzes are regular features here, along with poker nights. Food is served all day. Dogs are welcome. ♨☻◐≠🖫⸽

Rifle Volunteer

141 Reading Rd, RG41 1HD
✪ 11-11; 12-5.30, 7-11 Sun
☎ (0118) 9784484
Courage Best Bitter; Fuller's London Pride; guest beer Ⓗ
Traditional community pub a mile outside the town centre with one bar and a small family

room. Military prints decorate the walls. The pub runs a football team, ladies' and men's darts teams, and hosts a pub quiz every Sunday evening. Two large TV screens show major football matches. One guest hand pump serves a changing beer, often from a local micro. Filled baguettes are available at lunchtime. ➷☻&🖫(190)♣P⸽

Ship Inn

104 Peach Street, RG40 1XH (next to All Saints Church)
✪ 12-11 (midnight Thu-Sat)
☎ (01189) 780389
Fuller's Discovery, London Pride, ESB, seasonal beers Ⓗ
The inn can trace its origins as an ale house back to the mid 1700s, however it wasn't until the 1800s that it became known as The Ship. Some original features from the past remain, including wood beams and open fireplaces, one of which is still in use. The small courtyard with covered tables is popular in summer. Food is available lunchtimes and evenings during the week and all day Saturday and Sunday. Awarded local CAMRA Pub of the Year in 2006. ♨☻◐≠🖫P⸽

White Horse

Easthampstead Road, RG40 3AF (south of the town)
✪ 11-2.30, 5-11; 12-11 Sat; 12-10.30 Sun
☎ (0118) 978 1025
Greene King IPA, Ruddles County, Abbot Ⓗ
Friendly locals' pub in a rural location two miles south of Wokingham, with the best-kept Greene King beers in the area. Good, honest, home-cooked food is available at all sessions, including a children's menu. The pub has recently been refurbished; music and/or TV is played at low volume throughout the pub. Live music is hosted on some Saturday evenings. Handy for Holme Grange Craft Village nearby. The Ruddles County is sometimes replaced by a Greene King seasonal beer. ☻◐♣P⸽

What is real ale?

Real ale is also known as cask-conditioned beer or simply cask beer. In the brewery, the beer is neither filtered nor pasteurised. It still contains sufficient yeast and sugar for it to continue to ferment and mature in the cask. Once it has reached the pub cellar, it has to be laid down for maturation to continue, and for yeast and protein to settle at the bottom of the cask. Some real ale also has extra hops added as the cask is filled, a process known as 'late hopping' for increased flavour and aroma. Cask beer is best served at a cellar temperature of 11-12 degrees C, although some stronger ales can benefit from being served a little warmer. Each cask has two holes, in one of which a tap is inserted and is connected to tubes or 'lines' that enable the beer to be drawn to the bar. The other hole, on top of the cask, enables some carbon dioxide produced during secondary fermentation to escape. It is vital that some gas, which gives the beer its nature sparkle or condition, is kept within the cask: the escape of gas is controlled by inserting porous wooden pegs called spiles into the spile hole. Real ale is a living product and must be consumed within three or four days of a cask being tapped as oxidation develops.

300 Beers To Try Before You Die

ROGER PROTZ

300 beers from around the world, handpicked by award-winning journalist, author and broadcaster Roger Protz to try before you die! A comprehensive portfolio of top beers from the smallest microbreweries in the United States to family-run British breweries and the world's largest brands. This book is indispensable for both beer novices and aficionados.

£14.99   ISBN 978 1 85249 213 7

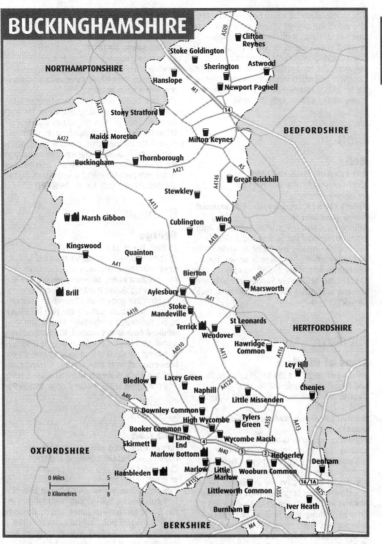

BUCKINGHAMSHIRE

NORTHAMPTONSHIRE

Clifton Reynes
Stoke Goldington
Sherington
Astwood
Hanslope
Newport Pagnell
Stony Stratford
Maids Moreton
Milton Keynes
BEDFORDSHIRE
Thornborough
Buckingham
Great Brickhill
Stewkley
Marsh Gibbon
Cublington
Wing
Kingswood
Quainton
Bierton
Brill
Aylesbury
Marsworth
Stoke Mandeville
St Leonards
Terrick
Wendover
HERTFORDSHIRE
Hawridge Common
Ley Hill
Bledlow
Lacey Green
Chenies
Naphill
Little Missenden
Downley Common
High Wycombe
Tylers Green
Booker Common
Wycombe Marsh
Skirmett
Lane End
OXFORDSHIRE
Marlow Bottom
Hedgerley
Denham
Hambleden
Marlow
Little Marlow
Wooburn Common
Littleworth Common
Iver Heath
Burnham
BERKSHIRE

0 Miles 5
0 Kilometres 8

Astwood

Old Swan

8 Main Road, MK16 9JS
☼ 11-3, 6-11 (closed Mon); 12-3.30 Sun
☎ (01234) 391351
Everards Beacon, Tiger; guest beers Ⓗ
Low, beamed 17th-century free house
halfway between Bedford and Milton Keynes,
just inside the county boundary. A large
assortment of blue and white china and an
impressive water jug collection adorn the
interior. The restaurant regularly has game
and fish dishes on the specials board, sourced
from local suppliers (bookings recommended).
ᕈQ❀♣P

Aylesbury

Hop Pole

83 Bicester Road, HP19 9AZ
☼ 12-11 (midnight Fri & Sat)

☎ (01296) 482129
Vale Best Bitter; guest beers Ⓗ
With 10 handpumps offering up to nine guest
ales including mild and porter, the pub lives
up to the boast on the sign outside:
'Aylesbury's permanent beer festival'. Vale
Brewery's sole outlet in town, it offers myriad
micro-brewery beers, plus cider in summer. A
brand new, spacious function room completes
the refurbishment of what was once a run
down old boozer. The friendly welcome as
well as the wide range of beer attracts
discerning drinkers from far and wide.
ᕈ❀₳◑➡(2, 16)♣

King's Head

Farmers Bar, Market Square, HP20 2RW
☼ 11-11; 12-10.30 Sun
☎ (01296) 718812
**Chiltern Ale, Beechwood, seasonal beers; guest
beers** Ⓗ

The oldest courtyard inn in England, situated at the top of the market square, very close to bus and rail stations. It offers a comfortable, relaxed environment in which to enjoy beers from Buckinghamshire's oldest micro-brewery. The food is freshly sourced from local suppliers and often incorporates local ales; the menu also recommends ales to complement many of the dishes. Q❀◐❶ ⅙⇌🚍

Bierton

Bell

191 Aylesbury Road, HP22 5DS
🕐 11-11 (midnight Fri & Sat); 12-11 Sun
☎ (01296) 436055
Fuller's Chiswick, London Pride, ESB, seasonal beers; guest beer Ⓗ
Village local two miles from Aylesbury with a small, traditional public bar and a slightly larger room mainly for dining. A wide choice of food at affordable prices is served from noon until 9pm daily except Sunday evening. Quizzes are held every Sunday evening and there is occasional live music (blues or rock). ◐🚻🚍(X15)♣P⅄

Bledlow

Lions of Bledlow

Church End, HP27 9PE (off B4009 between Chinnor and Princes Risborough) OS776020
🕐 11.30-3, 6-11; 12-10.30 (12-4, 7-10.30 winter) Sun
☎ (01844) 343345
Marston's Pedigree; Wadworth 6X; guest beers Ⓗ
Rambling, unspoilt, Grade II listed 16th-century free house complete with beams, inglenooks and a large log fire. Originally three shepherds' cottages, notes and pictures illustrating earlier days are displayed. There is a restaurant and large bar with wide-ranging blackboard menus. The extensive garden is busy in summer with walkers and families; tables at the front enjoy a picturesque setting at the junction of footpaths and bridleways. The pub has featured in TV series including Midsomer Murders and Miss Marple. 🅰Q❀◐P⅄

Booker Common

Live & Let Live

Limmer Lane, HP12 4QZ (minor road off the Cressex to Lane End road)
🕐 11-11; 12-10.30 Sun
☎ (01494) 520105 ⊕ theliveandletlive.co.uk
Fuller's London Pride; Rebellion IPA Ⓗ
Contemporary two-bar pub, tricky to locate down an unlit bridle path, frequented by ramblers from the adjacent common and nearby woods, close to Wycombe airpark. The traditional bar contrasts with a more modern dining area. Local cricket teams are featured in numerous pictures adorning the walls. The pub sign features a cat and mouse existing in harmony against a background of beer barrels. ❀◐🚍♣P⅄

Buckingham

Woolpack

57 Well Street, MK18 1EP
🕐 10-11 (midnight Fri); 11.30-10.30 Sun
☎ (01280) 817972 ⊕ buckinghamwoolpack.co.uk
Black Sheep Best Bitter; Caledonian Deuchars IPA; guest beers Ⓗ
This free house with a modern interior has been part of the Buckingham scene for some time. The pub makes full use of the new relaxed opening hours opening at 10am in typical old market town style. A good, varied food menu is offered. Children are welcome in the back room where there are toys to keep them entertained. Regular live bands add to the appeal of a pub for all. 🚼❀◐P

Burnham

George

20 High Street, SL1 7JH
🕐 12-11 (midnight Fri & Sat); 12-10.30 Sun
☎ (01628) 605047 ⊕ georgeinnburnham.co.uk
Courage Best Bitter, Directors; guest beers Ⓗ
This thriving Grade II listed 16th-century coaching inn goes from strength to strength. Once a magistrate's court, the pub is believed to be the oldest in the High Street. The landlord now offers around 30 guest beers a month and holds occasional beer festivals. He is a keen ale drinker and sources beers from breweries all over the country. A community feel and a warm welcome await visitors (over-21s only) and well-behaved dogs. 🅰❀🐕🚍P⅄

Chenies

Red Lion

Latimer Road, WD3 6ED (off A404 between Chorleywood and Little Chalfont) OS021980
🕐 11-2.30, 5.30-11; 12-3, 6.30-10.30 Sun
☎ (01923) 282722
Vale Best Bitter; Wadworth 6X; guest beer Ⓗ
This outstanding village pub has featured in this Guide for many decades, run by the same landlord. A real pub that happens to serve excellent food, it offers a good range of ales including house beers sourced from local breweries: Lion Pride from Rebellion and Ben's from the Vale Brewery. The tiny snug at the back and the small dining room add to the cosy atmosphere. Close to Chenies Manor and good walking country, it is well worth a visit. Q❀◐🚍(336)P⅄

Clifton Reynes

Robin Hood

Church Road, MK46 5DR OS903512
🕐 12-3, 6.30-11 (closed Mon); 12-3, 7-10.30 Sun
☎ (01234) 711574 ⊕ therobinhoodpub.co.uk
Greene King IPA, Abbot; guest beer Ⓗ

INDEPENDENT BREWERIES

Chiltern Terrick
Old Luxters Hambleden
Oxfordshire Ales Marsh Gibbon
Rebellion Marlow Bottom
Vale Brill

A true country pub with a superb atmosphere, the food is of the highest quality and prepared to order. The conservatory and lounge have tables for diners. Look for the numerous pictures of the legendary Nottingham outlaw, as well as a list of landlords going back hundreds of years. Well-behaved dogs are welcome in the public bar. Put your mobile on silent, there is a £1 fine to charity if it rings! ﷼Q❀①◗⌸&♣P

Cublington

Unicorn

High Street, LU7 0LQ

✪ 12-3, 5-11; 12-11 Sat; 12-10.30 Sun

☎ (01296) 681261

Bateman XXXB; Caledonian Deuchars IPA; Shepherd Neame Spitfire; guest beers Ⓗ

Picturesque village free house run by three local families, voted community Pub of the Year 2007 by Aylesbury Vale Council. The long, low-ceilinged bar has open fires at each end. Food is available every day (not Sun eve), either in the bar or a small dining area. The large, attractive garden hosts occasional beer festivals from the first Bank Holiday in May. Many local clubs and sports teams use the pub for meetings and socials. ﷼Q❀①🚍(65)♣P

Denham

Falcon

Village Road, UB9 5BE (off A40 near M40 jct 1)

✪ 12-3, 5-11; 12-10.30 Sun

☎ (01895) 832125 🌐 falconinn.biz

Hogs Back Bitter, Hop Garden Gold; guest beers Ⓗ

Situated in the Denham preservation area by the village green, this single bar inn is over 500 years old. Although the pub has been updated, features including timber beams and two open hearths have been retained, and much of the olde-worlde charm remains. There is a lower back room and, unusually, the toilets are upstairs. The pub has a supper licence until midnight. ﷼Q🐾❀🛏①⇌🖳⌐

Downley Common

Le de Spencer Arms

The Common, HP13 5YQ OS849959

✪ 12-3, 6-11; 12-11 Fri & Sat; 12-10.30 Sun

☎ (01494) 535317

Fuller's Chiswick, London Pride, ESB, seasonal beers; guest beers Ⓗ

Family-oriented brick and flint building remotely situated off Downley Common. It has numerous secluded areas and a small room off the bar. In summer there are barbecues and two mini beer festivals under canvas. Pub games include mole in the hole. A much-frequented pub for ramblers in the area, food is served every lunchtime plus Friday and Saturday evenings. Sunday roasts are popular. Live music is performed monthly on a Saturday. ﷼Q❀①🚍(31)♣P⌐

Great Brickhill

Old Red Lion

2 Ivy Lane, Lower Way, MK17 9AH

✪ 12-1am; 12-11 Sun

☎ (01525) 261715 🌐 oldredlion.co.uk

Greene King IPA; Tring Side Pocket for a Toad; guest beer Ⓗ

Picturesque village pub with a friendly clientele dating back in part to the 17th century, offering excellent hospitality and superb home cooking. There is a real fire in the public bar in winter. The restaurant is spacious and comfortable with a good range of food; in fact you may have difficulty choosing your meal from the large menu as all the dishes are tempting. ﷼❀◗P

Hambleden

Stag & Huntsman

RG9 6RP (opp churchyard)

✪ 11-2.30 (3 Sat), 6-11; 12-3, 7-10.30 Sun

☎ (01491) 571227 🌐 stagandhuntsman.co.uk

Rebellion IPA; Wadworth 6X; guest beers Ⓗ

Utopian, unspoilt, rural gem situated in a dreamy brick and flint National Trust village. The pub boasts three contrasting bars, a snug public, cosy front bar concealed behind a curtain and larger rear lounge. A separate dining room caters for diners and offers cuisine from a diverse menu. The ever-changing guest ale is often from a west country micro. Thatchers dry cider is available on handpump at this former local CAMRA Pub of the Year. ﷼❀🛏①◗⌸♣🖕P⌐

Hanslope

Globe

50 Hartwell Road, MK19 7BZ

✪ 12-3.30, 6-11; 12-4, 7-10.30 Sun

☎ (01908) 510336

Banks's Bitter; guest beers Ⓗ

A former CAMRA Pub of the Year, this classic village pub returns to the Guide. Situated in a mixed farming and commuter village, it has a community-oriented public bar. A quiet, comfortable lounge leads to the restaurant – food is also served in the bars. There is a pleasant garden with a children's play area. Real cider is available in summer. Q❀⌸P⌐

Hawridge Common

Full Moon

HP5 2UH (between Chesham and Tring) OS936069

✪ 12-11 (10.30 Sun)

☎ (01494) 758959

Adnams Bitter; Draught Bass; Brakspear Special; Fuller's London Pride; guest beers Ⓗ

A 16th-century pub that entices visitors with an array of six ales. It has a brick-built bar and three distinct low-beamed, flagstoned drinking areas; one set around a large open fireplace, another with an extensive display of water jugs. Part of the pub is set aside for diners but meals are also served in the bar. A pergola-covered patio is delightful in summer. Children and dogs are welcome. ﷼Q❀①&P

Rose & Crown

The Vale, HP5 2UG (2 miles from A416) OS948062

✪ 12-3, 6-11; 12-11 Sat; 12-10.30 Sun

☎ (01494) 758944 🌐 theroseandcrownhawridge.co.uk

Fuller's London Pride; Tring Side Pocket for a Toad; guest beers Ⓗ

Enter through the front door of this friendly country pub and discover a welcoming, cosy bar complete with four handpumps. The bar leads to a raised wooden-floored area, which is sometimes set for diners; a further secluded room overlooks the large enclosed garden. This pub was voted local CAMRA's Most Improved Pub in 2006. Guest beers often come from the local Tring Brewery and beer festivals are held twice a year. 🏨⌘❀◑●P

Hedgerley

White Horse

Village Lane, SL2 3UY

✪ 11-2.30, 5-11; 11-11 Sat; 12-10.30 Sun
☎ (01753) 643225

Greene King IPA; Rebellion IPA; guest beers Ⓖ

This family run free house is a proper village pub and usually offers seven real ales, including five that change constantly, from small breweries all over the country. A draught Belgian beer as well as real cider are also always available. As if that were not enough, an annual beer festival held over the Whitsun bank holiday sources over a hundred real ales. Many times local CAMRA Pub of the Year, the garden is popular. 🏨Q⌘◑Ⓔ♣●P↤

High Wycombe

Bell

Frogmore, HP13 5DQ

✪ 11-11; 12-10.30 Sun
☎ (01494) 525588 ● thebellonline.co.uk

Fuller's Discovery, London Pride, ESB, seasonal beers Ⓗ

A rare find: a traditional Grade II listed pub in the town centre, with a 16th-century frontage. The separate rooms have been opened out into one large space but the welcoming, cosy atmosphere remains. Accommodation is available in five en-suite rooms. The food is English and Thai cuisine (no meals available on Sunday). 🏨⌘◑◗≉⊞↤

Belle Vue

45 Gordon Road, HP13 6EQ (100 yards from station, platform 3 exit)

✪ 12-2.30, 5-11; 12-11 Sat; 12-10.30 Sun
☎ (01494) 524728

Beer range varies Ⓗ

Friendly, street corner, purpose-built community pub, just a short walk from the town centre. This classic pub interior is a U-shaped room with bare boards and plenty of character. Three varying guest ales are on offer, increasing to four at the weekend. Beers are selected from the Punch Taverns guest portfolio. A rear beer garden is popular in summer; handy for city commuters on their way home from work. The art of conversation is strongly encouraged. 🏨⌘≉⊞♣↤

Iver Heath

Whip & Collar

135 Swallow Street, SL0 0HU (off A4007 Slough Road)

✪ 12-3, 5-11 (12-11 summer); 12-10.30 Sun
☎ (01753) 653455

Fuller's London Pride; Theakston Best Bitter; guest beer Ⓗ

Small, cosy, friendly one-bar pub, off the main road, with a large patio to the front. The black-beamed interior is adorned with a huge collection of horse brasses and some old pistols. The lunchtime menu (served Mon-Sat) attracts employees from nearby Pinewood Film Studios, while in the evening the clientele is more local. Live music evenings are held monthly. The 58 bus stops close by. 🏨⌘◑⊞P

Kingswood

Plough & Anchor

Bicester Road, HP18 0RB

✪ 12-11 (8 Sun)
☎ (01296) 770251 ● thepna.co.uk

Fuller's London Pride; guest beer Ⓗ

Comfortable and well-appointed roadside hostelry, enlarged since last year, with a new conservatory and a bigger car park. It is more a restaurant than a pub, but drinkers are welcome. The guest beer is usually under 4% ABV. Large open fires in the bar and restaurant are fuelled by truly massive logs. Excellent food with high quality ingredients is served at lunchtime and in the evening, all day Sunday. Live jazz or blues is performed every Sunday 4.30-7.30pm. 🏨Q⌘◑⟐⊞P↤

Lacey Green

Whip

Pink Road, HP27 0PG

✪ 11-11; 12-10.30 Sun
☎ (01844) 344060 ● whipinn.co.uk

Rebellion IPA; guest beers Ⓗ

The Whip is a 150-year-old free house situated on top of the Chilterns escarpment with outstanding views; in the heart of good walking country, the Ridgeway national trail is close by. Over the last year 450 different ales have been pulled through the five handpumps, mainly from micros and local breweries. Two beer festivals are held annually, including the alternative Oktoberfest with live jazz. This real ale cornucopia has an enclosed garden and offers good food, including freshly-landed fish. 🏨Q⌘◑⊞(300)♣●↤

Lane End

Old Sun

Church Road, HP14 3HG (just off High Street towards Frieth)

✪ 12-1am
☎ (01494) 883959

Tring Ridgeway, seasonal beers Ⓗ

A fairly recent refurbishment to this former Wethered pub has transformed this village local. Bright, airy and welcoming, the interior has various drinking areas where drinkers and diners can interact, creating a pleasant, congenial atmosphere. Tring beers, rare to this part of Bucks, include one regular and one ever-changing seasonal monthly or special from the independent brewery. There is outside drinking in summer beyond the car park. 🕮🕪♿🚲♣🅿⌐

Ley Hill

Swan

Ley Hill Common, HP5 1UT (off Botley Road, B4505)

🕓 12-3.30, 5.30-11; 12-4, 6-10.30 Sun

☎ (01494) 783075 🌐 swanleyhill.com

Adnams Bitter; Brakspear Bitter; Fuller's London Pride; Taylor Landlord; guest beer Ⓗ

An amalgamation of separate cottages dating back to 1520, this country pub claims to be the oldest in Buckinghamshire and was previously the last stop-off for condemned prisoners. It later became the watering hole for Hollywood actors Clark Gable, James Stewart and jazz legend Glenn Miller. Regulars still come over from the local cricket and golf clubs, sampling the wide range of beers and enjoying jazz and food evenings. Good food is prepared by an experienced chef. 🕮Q🕪🕪♿🚲(373)🅿⌐

Little Marlow

King's Head

Church Road, SL7 3RZ (on A4155 between Marlow and Bourne End)

🕓 11-11; 12-10.30 Sun

☎ (01628) 484407

Adnams Bitter; Fuller's London Pride; St Austell Tribute; Taylor Landlord Ⓗ

Enchanting 14th-century inn in a quaint old village with a 12th-century church and a picturesque village green. This cosy, one-bar, heavily-beamed public house serves good home-cooked food from an extensive, varied menu. A commodious rear garden is pleasant for alfresco summer drinking, while a real log fire warms the cockles during the winter months. A regular in this Guide, four pumped ales are always available in this popular pub. 🕮🕪🕪♿🅿⌐

Little Missenden

Crown

HP7 0RD (off A413, between Amersham and Gt Missenden)

🕓 11-2.30, 6-11; 12-3, 7-11 Sun

☎ (01494) 862571

Adnams Bitter; Brakspear Bitter; St Austell Tribute; guest beer Ⓗ

Classic small village pub serving only good ale. A cosy, friendly, one-bar haven, it has been run by the same family for more than 90 years. Good pub food, served at lunchtime, is simple and generous. Popular with walkers, the large and attractive garden is a great place to unwind and enjoy a peaceful pint. A regular in the Good Beer Guide for over 25 years. 🕮Q🕪🕪♣🅿

Littleworth Common

Blackwood Arms

Common Lane, SL1 8PP OS936862

🕓 12-10 (midnight Fri & Sat); 12-6 Sun

☎ (01753) 642169

Brakspear Bitter, Special; Hook Norton Hooky Dark, seasonal beers Ⓗ

Secluded country pub to the north of Burnham Beeches, popular with walkers. It is the only pub in the area that always has cask mild available. The large outside seating area is deservedly popular in warmer weather and is suitable for families. Good food is available lunchtime and evening during the week and all day Saturday and Sunday. Note early close on Sunday. 🕮Q🕪🕪♿♣🅿⌐

Jolly Woodman

Littleworth Road, SL1 8PF OS935865

🕓 11-11; 12-10.30 Sun

☎ (01753) 644350 🌐 jollywoodman.co.uk

Brakspear Bitter; Hop Back Summer Lightning; St Austell Tribute; guest beers Ⓗ

Pleasant country pub, close to the northern edge of Burnham Beeches. It is popular for its range of beers and good food, as well as its live Monday night jazz sessions. The bar area features a large collection of old beer bottles as well a rowing boat in the rafters. Plenty of seating is available in the garden. 🕮🕪🕪♿♣🅿⌐

Maids Moreton

Wheatsheaf

Main Street, MK18 1QR (off A413, Buckingham to Towcester road)

🕓 12-3, 6-11 (10 Sun)

☎ (01280) 815433

Greene King Old Speckled Hen; Hook Norton Hooky Bitter; Tring Side Pocket for a Toad Ⓗ

Low beams, nooks and crannies and a sloping floor add to the character of this ancient village pub. Sympathetically extended, it has an attractive conservatory for dining where children are welcome. No food is served on Sunday evening; booking is advisable at other times. The staff will remove sparklers if requested. It is handy for the National Trust's Stowe Park and Silverstone race circuit. Q🕪🕪🚲🅿

Marlow

Duke of Cambridge

19 Queens Road, SL7 2PS (north end of High St)

🕓 11-midnight (1am Fri & Sat); 10-midnight Sun

☎ (01628) 488555

Beer range varies Ⓗ

This one-bar back-street local is now attracting the discerning real ale drinker from further afield. The ever-changing beer range is sourced from independent and micros, with local breweries regularly featured (note the display of pump clips). Tropical birds and fish are part of the fixtures and fittings. The 'Duke' is the archetypal antidote to the voguish town-centre pubs that seem to be cloned. 🕪🕪♿🚲🚲♣⌐

Three Horseshoes

Burroughs Grove Hill, SL7 3RA (on the Wycombe road between High Wycombe and Marlow)

🕓 11.30-3, 5-11; 11.30-11 Fri & Sat; 12-5, 7-10.30 Sun

☎ (01628) 483109

Rebellion Mild, IPA, Smuggler, Mutiny, seasonal beers Ⓗ

Popular, acclaimed brewery tap for the Rebellion Beer Company, showcasing six of its ales. The pub was closed and vulnerable before Rebellion took on the lease several years ago. Now it is busy daily with diners and drinkers enjoying an extensive menu (no meals Sun eve) and the brewery's award-winning beers. The interior has three distinct areas; an enclosed garden is family friendly during the summer months. Local CAMRA Pub of the Year 2005. The High Wycombe to Marlow bus stops outside. ₩Q❀◑⊟P⅄

Marsh Gibbon

Plough
Church Street, OX27 0HQ
🕐 12 (3 winter Mon-Thu)-11
☎ (01869) 278759
Greene King IPA; Oxfordshire Ales Triple B, Marshmellow Ⓗ
Situated in a quiet Domesday village near Bicester, this 16th-century pub has two bars, with food available, and a restaurant. Pool, darts, dominoes and cribbage are played throughout the year, Aunt Sally during the summer. One bar has electronic games, some sports TV and a juke box. An adventure playground for children is behind the pub. Live music features on Saturday evening. This pub is an outlet for the nearby Oxfordshire Ales brewery. ₩➣❀◑⊞🖳(16)♣P⅄

Marsworth

Angler's Retreat
Startops End, HP23 4LJ (on B489, opp Startops reservoir car park)
🕐 11-11
☎ (01442) 822250 🌐 anglersretreatpub.co.uk
Fuller's London Pride; Tring Side Pocket for a Toad; guest beers Ⓗ
Close to the Grand Union canal and in the shadow of Startops reservoir. The main bar area is adorned with taxidermic fish and has a cosy fire to one end, another has a small bar and dartboard. Beer festivals are held in spring and autumn. Dark and mild beers are a favourite with the licensees and are frequently found at the bar. A conservatory leads to a large garden with marquee, aviaries and pets' corner. Families (and dogs) are made welcome. ₩❀◑⊟P

Red Lion
90 Vicarage Road, HP23 4LU (off B489, by canal bridge)
🕐 11-3, 5 (6 Sat)-11; 12-3, 7-10.30 Sun
☎ (01296) 668366
Fuller's London Pride; Vale Best Bitter; guest beers Ⓗ
Dating from the 17th century, this three-room pub is served by a central bar. Each room has its own atmosphere: the upper room with a mixture of furnishing and selection of brewery mirrors is suited to diners, the lower public style bar with a real fire leads to the games area equipped with dartboard and bar billiards, and a small snug bar is to the front. Children are welcome in the games area. Skittles can be played by arrangement. Evening meals are served Tuesday-Saturday. ₩Q❀◑⊞🖳♣🖐P

Milton Keynes

Victoria Inn
Vicarage Road, Bradwell Village, MK13 9AQ
🕐 11-11 (midnight Fri & Sat); 12-10.30 Sun
☎ (01908) 316355
Fuller's London Pride; guest beers Ⓗ
An old village local though not far from the centre of the new city. The decor is more modern than the exterior. There are two guest ales, often from micro-breweries. The range increases for the annual August Bank Holiday beer festival. Regular quiz nights, darts and pool matches make this a true community pub. Q❀◑🖐

Wetherspoons
201 Midsummer Boulevard, MK9 1EA
🕐 9-midnight (1am Fri & Sat)
☎ (01908) 606074 🌐 jdwetherspoon.co.uk
Courage Best Bitter, Directors; Greene King Abbot; Marston's Pedigree; guest beers Ⓗ
A welcome return to the Guide for this JD Wetherspoons beer emporium. More than five guest ales are usually available, as well as real cider both draught and bottled. The pub can get very busy, particularly on food themed nights. The decor is modern and airy; there are heated outdoor umbrellas for chillier nights. Handy for the Milton Keynes central rail station. ❀◑♿≢🖐⅄

Naphill

Wheel
100 Main Road, HP14 4QA
🕐 12.30-2.30 (not Mon), 4.30-11; 12-midnight Fri & Sat; 12-10.30 Sun
☎ (01494) 562210 🌐 thewheelnaphill.com
Greene King IPA; guest beers Ⓗ
The Wheel is a community local that is also popular with walkers and ornithologists out spotting the famous Chiltern Red Kites. Parts of the pub date back to the 18th century and the interior retains a multi-roomed layout. The public bar has a bar billiards table. The pub sponsors local sports teams and host regular events such as quiz nights, live music and themed food evenings. Four beer festivals are held every year. Families enjoy the two extensive gardens. ₩❀◑⊞🖳(300)♣P⅄

Newport Pagnell

Cannon
50 High Street, MK16 8AQ
🕐 11-11 (midnight Fri & Sat); 12-11 Sun
☎ (01908) 211495
Banks's Bitter; Marston's Pedigree; guest beers Ⓗ
With 11 consecutive years in the Guide, local CAMRA Pub of the Year 2006 is situated in the centre of town. The beer prices are excellent for the area. Once the home of the Cannon Brewery, it has retained a number of the old outbuildings at the rear of the pub. Note military memorabilia, particularly the old uniform preserved in a glass case. The car park at the back can reached from Union Street. ₩QP

Quainton

George & Dragon

The Green, HP22 4AR

✪ 12-11 (midnight Fri & Sat) summer; winter hours vary; 12-11 summer, 12-2.30, 5-11 winter Sun

☎ (01296) 655436

Black Sheep Best Bitter; Fuller's London Pride; Hook Norton Hooky Bitter; guest beers Ⓗ

Two-bar local on a sloping village green overlooked by a tall windmill. The lower bar offers reasonably priced meals with vegetarian and children's options. Inexpensive lunches are offered for older people on Tuesday and bargain-priced steaks on Tuesday evening (no food Sun eve or Mon lunch). Cider is stocked in summer. Post office facilities are available in the bar Mon, Wed and Sat 9.30-11.30am. The Buckinghamshire railway centre, just outside the village, is popular with steam and railway history enthusiasts.

▲Q✪❶🍴(16)♣🏠P⬚

St Leonards

White Lion

Jenkins Lane, HP23 6NN (4 miles from Chesham on Wendover road)

✪ 11.30-midnight; 12-11.30 Sun

☎ (01494) 758387

Greene King IPA; guest beers Ⓗ

Probably the highest pub in the Chilterns and a long way from the sea, despite the wooden lifeboat out front. Close to both the Chiltern and Ridgeway walks, the pub is always popular with walkers and their dogs. The atmosphere is friendly with a single bar, three different drinking areas and a small meeting room. The real fire makes for a cosy winter haven and the garden is an ideal spot for catching the summer sun. ▲Q✪❶P

Sherington

White Hart

1 Gun Lane, MK16 9PE (off A509)

✪ 12-3, 5-11.30; 12-4, 7-10.30 Sun

☎ (01908) 611954 ⊕ whitehartsherington.com

Archers Village; guest beers Ⓗ

Previous local CAMRA Pub of the Year, the White Hart achieves the right balance between offering a range of quality real ales and serving gourmet food. The annual beer and sausage festival held over the May bank holiday is a highlight. Guest beers are varied and extensive. Good accommodation is available across the car park from the pub. Booking for food is essential. ▲Q✪🍴❶🍴♣

Skirmett

Frog

RG9 6TG (off M40 jct 5, through Ibstone to Skirmett)

✪ 11.30-3, 6-11; 12-4 (10.30 summer) Sun

☎ (01491) 638996 ⊕ thefrogskirmett.co.uk

Adnams Bitter; Rebellion IPA; guest beers Ⓗ

With fine views across the countryside, this 300-year-old free house lies in the beautiful Hambleden valley. The Frog is a family owned pub exuding warmth and tranquillity. It offers a fine restaurant and high quality accommodation. Guest beers often come from

local breweries. Snacks are available in the bar where an inviting log fire burns in winter. Food is cooked to order, specials are available daily. Themed nights are a regular feature. ▲Q✪🍴❶♣P⬚

Stewkley

Swan

Chapel Square, High Street North, LU7 0HA

✪ 12-1am (2am Fri & Sat)

☎ (01525) 240285

Courage Best Bitter; guest beers Ⓗ

Close to the village centre, the Swan is a lively local appealing to all. The 16th-century building retains many oak beams and an attractive inglenook. Guest ales are often from the Tring Brewery or other independents. Freshly-prepared food is available daily. Summer barbecues are held on Friday evening in the large garden, which also includes a children's play area. Live music is played on most Saturdays and a popular folk jam session is hosted on some Wednesdays. ✪❶♣P

Stoke Goldington

Lamb

16-20 High Street, MK16 8NR

✪ 12-3, 5-11 (midnight Sat); 12-7 Sun

☎ (01908) 551233

⊕ thelambstokegoldington.moonfruit.com

Nethergate IPA; guest beers Ⓗ

A Guide regular for a number of years, the owners strive to make this pub an asset to the community. Guest ales come from all over the UK, often featuring the Northampton Frog Island brews. The resident Weimaraner dog, Tilly, greets patrons. Rare Northamptonshire skittles can be played here. Sunday lunches are enormous and great value. Belgian beer lovers will enjoy the bottled Duvel, cider fans the Weston's Old Rosie. Ring ahead to check Sunday opening hours in winter. ▲✪❶♣🏠P

Stoke Mandeville

Bull

5 Risborough Road, HP22 5UP

✪ 12-3, 5.30-11; 12-11 Fri & Sat; 12-10.30 Sun

☎ (01296) 613632

Fuller's London Pride; Shepherd Neame Spitfire; Tetley Bitter Ⓗ

Small pub situated on a main road, well served by public transport. The front bar is popular with locals, especially sports fans who gather to watch football and horse racing on TV. The comfortable lounge bar at the back tends to be quieter and leads out to a large, secure garden behind the pub. Popular with families in summer, the garden has plenty to keep children amused. Q✪🍴🚌🚃(300)♣P

Stony Stratford

Fox & Hounds

87 High Street, MK11 1AT

✪ 12-3, 5.30-11; 12-11 Sat & Sun

☎ (01908) 563307 ⊕ foxandhounds.info

Beer range varies Ⓗ

Situated just north of the town centre, this pub has been transformed and now has a modern feel to it. There is a dining area in a small side room. The pub offers an ever-changing list of guest ales. At the heart of the local music scene, a small stage has been added. It gets busy on music nights, usually a Thursday. ❀◑⬗P

Thornborough

Two Brewers

Bridge Street, MK18 2DN (off A421, turn by Lone Tree pub)
☼ 12-3 (Wed & Sat only), 6-11; 11.30-3, 7-11 Sun
☎ (01280) 812020
Frog Island Best Bitter; guest beer Ⓗ

A real drinkers' pub off the beaten track. The landlord is a fan of Frog Island beers, which feature among the changing guest ales. This welcoming village pub does not serve food, but on Friday evening the fish & chip van visits. The pub does not open weekday lunchtimes except Wednesday. ▟Q❦⬗⬗

Tylers Green

Horse & Jockey

Church Road, HP10 8EG (turn left at church at top of Hammersley Lane)
☼ 12-3, 5-11; 12-11 Fri & Sat; 12-10.30 Sun
☎ (01494) 815963 ⊕ horseandjockeytylersgreen.co.uk
Adnams Bitter, Broadside; Brakspear Bitter; Fuller's London Pride; Greene King Abbot; guest beer Ⓗ

Converted into a pub in 1821, this cosy, traditional local is shadowed by the Tylers Green church. A popular pub, it is now a regular in the Guide and an asset to the village. The single-room bar is horseshoe shaped with a welcoming, homely atmosphere enjoyed by diners and drinkers. The six handpumped ales on offer have their tasting notes on the bar blackboard. Overflow car parking is on the other side of the road. ▟❀◑⬗よ⊟(31)♣P⬈

Wendover

Pack Horse

29 Tring Road, HP22 6NR
☼ 12-11 (midnight Fri & Sat); 12-10.30 Sun
☎ (01296) 622075
Fuller's Gale's Butser, London Pride, seasonal beers; guest beers Ⓗ

Small, friendly village pub situated at the end of a thatched terrace known as the Anne Boleyn Cottages. The pub, a free house on the Ridgeway Path, dates from 1769 and has been owned by the same family for 44 years. The wall above the bar is decorated with RAF squadron badges denoting connections with nearby RAF Halton. The pub runs men's and

women's darts teams, dominoes and cribbage. ⫘⊟(54)♣

Wing

Queen's Head

9 High Street, LU7 0NS
☼ 11-3, 5.30-11; 11.30-11 Fri & Sat; 12-10.30 Sun
☎ (01296) 688268
Fuller's London Pride; Greene King IPA; Wychwood Hobgoblin; guest beers Ⓗ

Welcoming locals' pub in the centre of the village with an increasing number of real ales. The 16th-century building features real log fires in the main bar and restaurant, where good home-made specials are served all week. The excellent adult-only snug is comfortably equipped with leather sofas; board games are available at each table. Outside is a large, attractive garden and patio area. ▟❀◑⬗⊟(X15)♣P

Wooburn Common

Royal Standard

Wooburn Common Road, HP10 0JS (follow signs to Odds farm) OS923876
☼ 12-11 (10.30 Sun)
☎ (01628) 521121
Caledonian Deuchars IPA; Ⓗ Hop Back Summer Lightning; Ⓖ guest beers Ⓗ/Ⓖ

Unmissable! Renowned, semi-rural, time-honoured public house offering 10 real ales, five on handpump, five on gravity dispense. A dark beer, usually a porter or stout, and a stronger ABV beer are among the real ales available. A popular haunt for local discerning drinkers who enjoy the lively banter and traditional values that the pub endorses; diners are also well catered for. A large real fire warms in winter. Local CAMRA Pub of the Year 2007. ▟Q❀◑よP⬈

Wycombe Marsh

General Havelock

114 King's Mead Road, Loudwater, HP11 1HZ
☼ 12-2.30, 5.30-11; 11-11 Fri & Sat; 12-10.30 Sun
☎ (01494) 520391
Fuller's Chiswick, London Pride, ESB, seasonal beers Ⓗ

Imposing building, originally a farmhouse, now situated between playing fields and a ski slope. The family-run pub has notched up 16 consecutive appearances in this Guide and welcomes customers of all ages. Lunchtime food is served daily except Saturday. Evening meals are only available on Friday. The garden is popular in summer. ▟❀◑♣P⬈

Your shout

We would like to hear from you. If you think a pub not listed in the Guide is worthy of consideration, please let us know. Send us the name, full address and phone number (if known). If a pub in the Guide has given poor service, we would also like to know. Write to Good Beer Guide, CAMRA, 230 Hatfield Road, St Albans, Herts, AL1 4LW or email **gbgeditor@camra.org.uk**

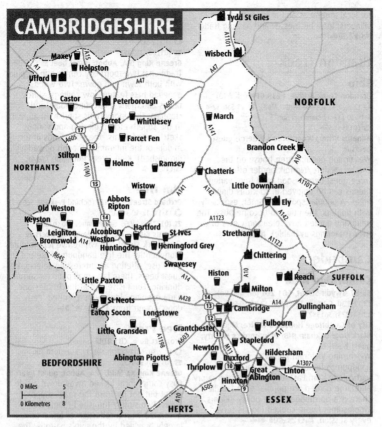

Abbots Ripton

Three Horseshoes
Moat Lane, PE28 2PA
🕑 11.30-3, 6-11; closed Mon; 12-10.30 Sun
☎ (01487) 773440 ⊕ thethreehorseshoes.com
Adnams Bitter, Broadside; Oakham JHB; guest beers Ⓗ
Part of the De Ramsey estate, this is a picturesque pub in a village of thatched cottages. The small, listed thatched building has been carefully refurbished and extended with the quarry-tiled, original oak-beamed bar area sensitively retained as a family room. Extensions include a comfortable large lounge bar, restaurant and accommodation. The menu offers varied modern cuisine.
🏚Q🍃🕏🛏️🕮P

Abington Pigotts

Pig & Abbot
High Street, SG8 0SD (off A505 through Litlington)
🕑 12-3, 6-11; 12-11 Sat; 12-10.30 Sun
☎ (01763) 853515 ⊕ pigandabbot.co.uk
Adnams Bitter; Fuller's London Pride; guest beers Ⓗ
Located in a surprisingly remote part of the south Cambridgeshire countryside, this deceptively large Queen Anne period pub offers a warm welcome. The bar has exposed oak beams and large inglenook featuring a wood-burning stove. A comfortable restaurant offers choices from traditional pub food to more exotic Thai curry. Guest beers are often from Woodforde's or Timothy Taylor.
🏚Q🕏🕮P

Alconbury Weston

White Hart
2 Vinegar Hill, PE28 4JA
🕑 12-2.30, 5.30-11; 12-4, 6.30-11 Sat; 12-5.30 Sun
☎ (01480) 890331
Adnams Bitter; Courage Directors; guest beers Ⓗ
Welcoming 16th-century coaching inn on the old Great North Road with an open-plan two-tier layout providing different drinking areas. The two regularly changing guest beers come from a wide variety of breweries. Home-cooked food is served and international dining nights feature. Live music is performed occasionally. This community pub raises funds

INDEPENDENT BREWERIES

Cambridge Moonshine Cambridge
City of Cambridge Chittering
Devil's Dyke Reach
Elgood's Wisbech
Fenland Little Downham
Hereward Ely
Milton Milton
Oakham Peterborough
Tydd Steam Tydd Saint Giles
Ufford Ufford

for local amenities and is supported by villagers, local businesses and passing trade. ❀◐&⬚♣P⅃

Brandon Creek

Ship

Brandon Creek Bridge, PE38 0PP (off A10)
◑ 12-3, 6-11 (closed winter Mon); 12-11 Sat; 12-4, 6-10.30 (12-11 summer) Sun
☎ (01353) 676228
Adnams Bitter; Woodforde's Wherry; guest beers Ⓗ
Welcoming genuine free house on the Cambridgeshire/Norfolk border offering up to three guest beers. Good food from varied menus can be enjoyed in spacious dining areas. A popular spot in summer, especially with boaters, the pub can become busy. The patio and garden have pleasing views of the river (moorings available). ⬚❀◐P⅃

Cambridge

Cambridge Blue

85-87 Gwydir Street, CB1 2LG (off Mill Rd)
◑ 12-2.30, 5.30-11; 12-11 Sat; 12-10.30 Sun
☎ (01223) 361382
City of Cambridge Hobson's Choice; Elgood's Black Dog; Oakham JHB; Woodforde's Wherry; guest beers Ⓗ
Welcoming Victorian pub with seven handpumps featuring a wide variety of beers, particularly from East Anglia. The conservatory and large garden are popular with families. There is a no mobile phone policy indoors. Wholesome, home-cooked food is served every session. ⬚Q⏃❀◐≠♣⅃

Carlton Arms

Carlton Way, Arbury, CB24 2BY
◑ 11-11; 12-10.30 Sun
☎ (01223) 355717 ⊕ thecarltonarms.co.uk
Caledonian Deuchars IPA; Taylor Landlord; guest beers Ⓗ/Ⓖ
Corking, much-improved, two-bar community pub. The lounge is comfortable and relaxing while the public bar has TV, darts, pool and skittles. Good food is on offer at reasonable prices. The patio in front of the pub is perfect for warm, sunny days. Three beer festivals are staged every year; check out the Cambridge beer festival memorabilia. A selection of unusual Belgian bottled beers is kept. Quiz night is Wednesday. Do not miss this gem of a pub, the epitome of a true community local. Q❀◐⬚&⬚♣P

Castle Inn

38 Castle Street, CB3 0AJ
◑ 12-2.30, 5 (6 Sat & Sun)-11
☎ (01223) 353194
Adnams Bitter, Explorer, Broadside; Fuller's London Pride; guest beers Ⓗ
In the shadow of the mound of the long-gone Cambridge Castle, this Adnams house (its most westerly outlet) offers a great range of its own beers plus changing guests from all over the country. Two floors offer a choice of drinking areas while the suntrap garden is a delight when it is warm. Excellent food is served every session. ⬚❀◐

Champion of the Thames

68 King Street, CB1 1LN
◑ 11 (12 Sun)-11
☎ (01223) 352043
Greene King IPA, Abbot; guest beer Ⓗ
Traditional two-room city centre pub, popular with both town and gown. Two wood-panelled bars feature low ceilings, sturdy tables and many interesting nooks and crannies. The eponymous sportsman appears in the superb etched glazing and various sketches and prints. The pub stands in the middle of the infamous (though nowadays diminished) 'King Street Run' pub crawl. ⬚Q◐⬚♣

Elm Tree

Orchard Street, CB1 1JS (behind Parkside School)
◑ 11-11; 12-10.30 Sun
☎ (01223) 363005 ⊕ theelmtreepub.co.uk
Adnams Bitter; Wells Eagle; guest beers Ⓗ
Cosy, back-street pub where live jazz features prominently. The five handpumps are put to good use, offering an interesting selection of guest beers. There is a small patio for summer drinking. Food is served at lunchtimes and early evening along with a limited 'early doors' menu from 11am. ❀◐⅃

Free Press

Prospect Row, CB1 1DU
◑ 12-2.30, 6-11; 12-11 Sat; 12-3, 7-10.30 Sun
☎ (01223) 368337
Greene King XX Mild, IPA, Abbot; guest beers Ⓗ
Cosy corner local tucked away down a side street but not far from the main shopping areas. Two simply furnished rooms are decorated with a collection of bric-a-brac largely provided by the pub's patrons. The snug is the subject of occasional capacity record attempts. A good menu offers plenty of choice with old favourites soup and pasta always popular. There is additional seating in the sheltered, walled garden. The pub has a no mobile phone policy. ⬚Q❀◐⬚♣⅃⬚

Green Dragon

5 Water Street, CB4 1NZ (off Chesterton High St)
◑ 11-11 (midnight Fri & Sat)
☎ (01223) 505035
Greene King XX Mild, IPA, Abbot Ⓗ
Formerly a coaching inn where Oliver Cromwell once stayed, with a cosy and traditional atmosphere, the bar has a huge inglenook, where a fire blazes on cold days. The pub is located just off the Millennium cycle path, within easy walking distance of the city centre along the River Cam. ⬚❀◐

Kingston Arms

33 Kingston Street, CB1 2NU (off Mill Rd)
◑ 12-2.30, 5-11; 12-midnight Fri & Sat; 12-11 Sun
☎ (01223) 319414 ⊕ kingston-arms.co.uk
Crouch Vale Brewers Gold; Elgood's Black Dog; Hop Back Entire Stout; Oakham JHB; Taylor Landlord; guest beers Ⓗ
Bustling 10-handpump pub, popular for its award-winning food (evening booking is advised). Unusually it stocks no keg beers or cider. The walled patio has canopies and heaters – children are permitted until 9pm. Free WiFi and Internet access are available. ⬚Q❀◐≠♣⅃

Live & Let Live

40 Mawson Road, CB1 2EA

⊘ 11.30-2.30, 5.30 (6 Sat)-11; 12-3, 7-11 Sun

☎ (01223) 460261

Adnams Bitter; Everards Tiger; Nethergate Umbel Ale; guest beers Ⓗ

Traditional, 19th-century back-street local appealing to a lively and mixed clientele. Wood panelling and bare wooden floors help to create a cosy, welcoming atmosphere. Seven real ales always include one dark beer. Real cider is from Cassels and there is a good selection of bottled beers and a guest on draught from Belgium. Home-cooked meals are served. Two beer festivals a year are hosted at CAMRA's Cambridgeshire Pub of the Year 2006. Q⊕⇥⊑♣♠

St Radegund

129 King Street, CB1 1LD (500m from Drummer St bus station)

⊘ 5 (12 Sat)-11; 12-2, 6.30-10.30 Sun

☎ (01223) 311794

Fuller's London Pride; guest beers Ⓗ

Named after a 5th-century Frankish queen, this is one of the smallest pubs in Cambridge. A true free house, it is a regular outlet for the local Milton Brewery beers. The plain but pleasant entrance belies the lively interior with an enjoyable, somewhat eccentric atmosphere. The pub has a Vera Lynn appreciation club, a 'wall of shame' noticeboard and hosts occasional jazz. Q⊑♠

Castor

Prince of Wales Feathers

38 Peterborough Road, PE5 7AL

⊘ 12-3 (not Tue), 5-11.30; 12-1am Fri & Sat; 12-midnight Sun

☎ (01733) 380222 ⊕ princeofwalesfeathers.co.uk

Adnams Bitter; John Smith's Bitter; guest beers Ⓗ

Refurbished village local that has retained most of its authentic charm including the original stained glass windows. The beer range regularly showcases local micros, supported by traditional cider and continental bottled beers. Excellent home-cooked food is served; live entertainment is hosted fortnightly and beer festivals in May and October. Ring the bull, shut the box and shove ha'penny can be played here. The pub is just a short walk from the steam railway and country park. ⊯⊛⊘♿⊑♣♠⊑⊓

Chatteris

Walk the Dog

34 Bridge Street, PE16 6RN

⊘ 11.30-2.30, 6-11.30; 11-11.30 Fri & Sat; 11-4, 7-11 Sun

☎ (01354) 693695

Fuller's London Pride; guest beers Ⓗ

Single room community pub with a keen real ale following. One regular and three changing guest ales are available. There are popular monthly cheese & wine and bottled beer nights. Lots of traditional games can be played including crib, darts and dominoes and Scrabble. Benches at the front of the pub catch the sun in summer. No food is served Sunday. ⊯⊘⊑♣♠⊑

Dullingham

Boot

18 Brinkley Road, CB8 9UW

⊘ 11-11 (midnight Fri & Sat)

☎ (01638) 507327

Adnams Bitter, Broadside; guest beer Ⓗ

A friendly pub with a loyal following, the clientele ranges from race horse owners to farm labourers. A modern, open plan, L-shaped bar with a low ceiling, the pub was saved from development a few years ago. The Boot boasts its own magazine containing local gossip and jokes. ⊯⊛⊘⇥P

Duxford

Plough

59 St Peters Street, CB2 4RP

⊘ 11-3, 5.30-11; 12-10.30 Sun

☎ (01223) 833170

Adnams Bitter; Everards Beacon; guest beers Ⓗ

Handy for the world-renowned air museum, this pretty thatched pub has two bars. The bar on the right, adorned with lots of airfield-related artefacts, is where the serious drinkers gather; the other bar is more food-oriented offering a wide selection of classic English dishes. Fish and chip night is Friday and curry night Saturday (eve meals Tue-Sat). The pub cat is delightful to look at but best not to touch! A quiz night is held every other Monday. ⊯Q⊛⊘P⊑

Eaton Socon

Rivermill Tavern

School Lane, PE19 8GW

⊘ 11-11 (midnight Fri); 10.30-11 Sun

☎ (01480) 219612 ⊕ rivermilltavern.co.uk

Adnams Broadside; Greene King IPA, Abbot; guest beers Ⓗ

Popular riverside pub converted from a flour mill at Eaton Socon lock on the River Great Ouse. It has a galleried area above the bar and children are well catered for in the family room. A choice of up to three guest beers is on offer from independent breweries. There is an extensive and varied food menu. Live music plays on Tuesday, Wednesday and Friday evenings, and a quiz is held on Sunday evening. The patio has splendid views of the river and marina and moorings are available. ⊱⊛⊘⊑P

Wheatsheaf

125 Great North Road, PE19 8EQ

⊘ 11 (12 Sat & Sun)-11

☎ (01480) 405942

Wells Eagle IPA; guest beer Ⓗ

This 1930s roadhouse style pub, on a well-pubbed part of the old Great North Road, is dominated by a busy public bar and games area with pool and darts. It has a cosy lounge area to one side. It is a rare outlet for cask mild – often Elgood's Black Dog. The small garden with outdoor games provides a safe area for children. ⊛⊘⊑⊑♣P⊑

Ely

Prince Albert

62 Silver Street, CB7 4JF (opp. cathedral car park)
✪ 11-3.30, 6.30 (6 Fri)-11 (11.30 Fri & Sat); 12-3.30,
7-10.30 Sun
☎ (01353) 663494
Greene King XX Mild, IPA, Abbot; guest beers Ⓗ
Proper little back-street local with a lovely
garden, a regular CAMRA local Pub of the Year.
No music or gaming machines disturb the
pleasant bar room banter. A rare outlet for XX
Mild, two guest beers are usually available,
mainly from Greene King. Food is served
Monday-Saturday. Secondhand book sales and
regular events help fundraise for local good
causes. Children are permitted in the garden
and well behaved dogs welcome. Q❀◑≠♣

Town House

60-64 Market Street, CB7 4LS (near the museum)
✪ 11-11 (1am Fri & Sat); 12-11 Sun
☎ (01353) 664338
Beer range varies Ⓗ
Near to the city centre, this Georgian town
house is now a busy pub with a modern bar
and an airy conservatory. Three changing
guest ales are usually available, sometimes
from local breweries. A DJ plays from 9pm on
Friday and Saturday nights attracting a young
crowd. The annual beer festival is held during
July in the enclosed rear garden. A popular
quiz night is held on Sunday. ಕ❀◑🖵

West End House

16 West End, CB6 3AY
✪ 12-3, 6-11; 12-midnight Fri & Sat; 12-4, 7-11 Sun
☎ (01353) 662907
**Adnams Bitter; Greene King IPA; Shepherd
Neame Spitfire; guest beers** Ⓗ
Very much a drinkers' pub, located away from
the city centre and a short distance from Oliver
Cromwell's house. Two guest beers are
available, often from local breweries. A snug
pub with low, beamed ceilings, it is split into
four distinct areas. Basic lunchtime food is
served. Well behaved children are allowed
until 8pm. An enclosed patio has a marquee
and heating for smokers. CAMRA local Pub of
the Year 2007. ▲ಕ❀◑⸺

Farcet

Black Swan

77 Main Street, PE7 3DF (off B1091)
✪ 12-2 (not Mon or winter Mon-Thu), 5-11; 12-11 Fri &
Sat; 12-10.30 Sun
☎ (01733) 240387
John Smith's Bitter; guest beers Ⓗ
Traditional village pub next to the river at the
bottom of the village, a short walk from Farcet
church bus stop. It has separate lounge and
public bars, both with real log fires and settles.
Food is served in both rooms (Fri-Sun lunch
and Tue-Sat eves). An annual charity beer
festival is held in September. Camping is
available in the extensive garden.
▲❀◑⸬▤(3)♣P⸺

Farcet Fen

Plough

Milk & Water Drove, Ramsey Road, PE7 3DR (on
B1095, S of A605)
✪ 12-11.30 (10.30 Sun)
☎ (01733) 844307 ⊕ theploughfarcet.co.uk
**Elgood's Black Dog; Fuller's London Pride;
Oakham JHB; guest beers** Ⓗ
Isolated Fenland pub with a reputation for
good food and ale, offering two guest beers.
Refurbished for structural reasons, the pub has
lost the real fire but gained a dining area. The
bar, which has a farming theme, has a
beamed ceiling and leather settees. A large
tropical fish tank divides the lounge into two
areas. Children are welcome and there is an
outdoor play area. The public bar contains a
bar billiards table. Live music plays on Friday
evening. ❀◑⸬♣♣P⸺

Fulbourn

Six Bells

9 High Street, CB1 5DH
✪ 11.30-3, 6-11.30; 12-11.30 Fri & Sat; 12-11 Sun
☎ (01223) 880244
Adnams Bitter; Greene King IPA; guest beers Ⓗ
An open log fire, the landlord s cheery
welcome and fine, home-cooked food are
three of the ingredients that make this former
coaching inn an archetypal village pub. The
three changing guest beers mean that the
customer always has something interesting to
look forward to. Food is served both in the
restaurant and bar (eve meals Tue-Sun). Other
attractions are live jazz twice a month and a
large garden. ▲Q ಕ❀◑⸬♣♣P

Grantchester

Blue Ball

57 Broadway, CB3 9NQ
✪ 12-3, 6-11 (midnight Thu-Sat); 12-10.30 Sun
☎ (01223) 840679
Adnams Bitter; guest beer Ⓗ
An authentic, traditional and relaxing
experience, this small, cosy pub is full of
friendly locals (no children or draught lagers).
Established in 1767, it holds the oldest licence
in the village and displays a full list of
landlords since then. Games such as shut the
box, ring the bull and shove-ha'penny are
played. Conversation is the main
entertainment here except on Thursday
evening when live blues is played. Local
CAMRA Pub of the Year 2002. ▲Q❀≠♣

Great Abington

Three Tuns

75 High Street, CB1 6AB
✪ 12-2.30, 6-11; 12-11 Sat; 12-10.30 Sun
☎ (01223) 891467 ⊕ thethreetuns-
greatabington.co.uk
**Greene King IPA; Nethergate seasonal beers;
guest beers** Ⓗ
Compact two-bar free house opposite the
village cricket green. There is a small dining
room and slightly larger main bar, both
featuring wood floors and panelling. An
excellent authentic Thai menu is available

Monday-Saturday, plus a roast on Sunday (booking advisable). The changing beer range includes ales from Adnams, Cottage and Woodforde's. Folk musicians visit some Sunday evenings. ▲▲❀◑▲⊟(13)P⅃

Hartford

King of the Belgians
27 Main Street, PE29 1XU
✪ 11-3.30, 5.30-11; 11-12.30am Fri & Sat; 12-11 Sun
☎ (01480) 452030
Beer range varies Ⓗ
Situated in a picturesque old village, it is believed that Oliver Cromwell used to frequent this 16th-century establishment. The pub comprises a public bar and restaurant. The ceiling in the bar displays a collection of aviation memorabilia of the Cold War era. A changing range of up to three real ales and good value pub food are highlights.
Q❀◑⊟⊟P⅃

Helpston

Blue Bell
10 Woodgate, PE6 7ED
✪ 11.30-2.30, 5-11 (midnight Fri & Sat); 12-10.30 Sun
☎ (01733) 252394
Grainstore Cooking Bitter, Ten Fifty; guest beers Ⓗ
Stone-built, 17th-century village pub with traditional values. The wood-panelled bar is popular with locals and a new extension has provided a dining area and cosy snug, both created from the old cellar. The 18th-century English poet John Clare, known as the peasant poet, was a pot boy here. Three guest beers usually include a mild. The pub runs a crib team. ▲▲Q❀◑⊟⅂⊟♣P⅃

Hemingford Grey

Cock
47 High Street, PE28 9BJ (off A14)
✪ 11.30-3, 6-11; 12-4, 6.30-10.30 Sun
☎ (01480) 463609 ⊕ cambscuisine.com/tc_index.html
Earl Soham Victoria Bitter; Woodforde's Wherry; guest beers Ⓗ
Award-winning village local with separate doors to 'pub' and 'restaurant'. The convivial bar has a bright decor and is warmed by a solid fuel stove. A range of distinctive East Anglian ales is always well presented. The larger restaurant has won many accolades. It features an extensive fish board, meat and game and a changing menu of home-made sausages. Booking is essential.
▲▲Q❀◑▲⊟P⅃

Hildersham

Pear Tree
High Street, CB21 6BU
✪ 11.45-2.30 (not Mon), 6.30-11; 11.45-2, 6-11 Fri & Sat; 11.45-2, 7-10.30 Sun
☎ (01223) 891680 ⊕ thepeartreehildersham.co.uk
Greene King IPA, Abbot; guest beer Ⓗ
Nestling in the picturesque heart of the village, opposite thatched cottages, this cosy pub is a great place to relax. The single bar is neat, comfortable and attractively decorated.

Food varies from a fixed menu of old pub favourites to an ever-changing specials board of gastro-pub style home-cooked food, with extra attention given to special dietary requirements. Old fashioned table games are played including shoot the moon. Q❀◑♣P

Hinxton

Red Lion
32 High Street, CB10 1QY
✪ 11-3.30, 6-11.30; 12-4.30, 7-11 Sun
☎ (01799) 530601 ⊕ redlionhinxton.co.uk
Adnams Bitter; Greene King IPA; Woodforde's Wherry; guest beer Ⓗ
Inviting Grade II listed free house at the heart of the village since the 16th century. It has a choice of comfortable seating areas with traditional green and cream decor and prints on the walls of old village life. The airy, spacious restaurant has a vaulted ceiling with exposed oak rafters. A locals' pub, but will the old village retainers disappear with the smoking ban? And if they do, who will tend the dovecot in the garden? The guest beer is usually from a local brewery. ▲▲Q❀◑P

Histon

Red Lion
68 High Street, CB4 4JD
✪ 10.30-2.30, 5 (4 Fri)-11; 10.30-11 Sat; 12-6, 7-10.30 Sun
☎ (01223) 564437
Elgood's Black Dog; Everards Beacon, Sunchaser, Tiger; Oakham Bishops Farewell; guest beers Ⓗ
Two-bar free house with a quiet(ish) lounge where food is served, and a more boisterous, newly extended public bar, displaying a fine collection of bottled beers. Breweriana features throughout, including old pub signs and water jugs. Two beer festivals are held annually: an Easter 'aperitif' and the main event in September with a marquee in the garden and live entertainment. An extensive range of Belgian beers includes three on draught. Popular monthly curry nights and other special events are staged. The garden has a petanque piste. ▲▲❀⊟⊟(7)●

Holme

Admiral Wells
41 Station Road, PE7 3PH (jct of B660 & Yaxley Rd)
✪ 12-2.30, 5-11; 12-11 Sat; 12-10.30 Sun
☎ (01487) 831214
Nethergate Augustinian Ale; Shepherd Neame Spitfire; Woodforde's Wherry; guest beers Ⓗ
Recently refurbished Victorian inn said to be the lowest pub in England, situated next to the East Coast mainline railway. It is named after one of the pallbearers at Nelson's funeral. Up to six real ales plus a traditional cider are served in the two drinking areas, lounge and dining room. Booking is recommended for the popular restaurant, particularly at weekends. There is a large shady garden; a function room with a skittle alley can be hired.
▲▲❀◑♣●P⅃

Huntingdon

Old Bridge Hotel

1 High Street, PE29 3TQ

⏰ 11-11; 12-10.30 Sun

☎ (01480) 424300 ⊕ huntsbridge.com/
theoldbridgehotel.php

**Adnams Bitter; City of Cambridge Hobson's
Choice; guest beers** ⊞

This handsome hotel bar is a luxurious and
relaxing place to come to enjoy a pint in peace
and quiet. Residents, diners and local beer
drinkers mix in the main bar and covered
terrace. Imaginative and high quality food and
wine are served here and in the more formal
dining room. The 18th-century building was
once a private bank and enjoys a prominent
position alongside the river Great Ouse in the
birthplace of Oliver Cromwell.
▥Q❀✍⬱⏰≢P⅃

Keyston

Pheasant

Village Loop, PE28 0RE (on B663, 1 mile S of A14)

⏰ 12-2.30, 6-11 (10.30 Sun; closed winter Sun eve)

☎ (01832) 710241

Adnams Bitter; guest beers ⊞

The Pheasant was originally a row of thatched
cottages in an idyllic setting. The village is
named after Ketil's Stone, probably an Anglo-
Saxon boundary marker. The pub offers high
quality food, fine wines and well-kept cask
ales. There is a splendid lounge bar and three
dining areas include the Garden Room in a
rear extension overlooking the herb garden.
Local micro-breweries' products usually
feature. ▥Q❀⏰P

Leighton Bromswold

Green Man

37 The Avenue, PE28 5AW (1 mile N of A14)

⏰ 12-3 (Fri-Sun only), 7-11; closed Mon; 12-3, 7-10.30
Sun

☎ (01480) 890238 ⊕ greenmanpub.org

Nethergate IPA; Young's Special; guest beers ⊞

Delightful haven in a charming village on a high
ridge (the 'Bromswold') not far from the
Northamptonshire border. The Green Man
provides a congenial focus for a small village
community and attracts visitors from a wide
area for good food and ale. An interesting,
frequently-changing beer range typically
includes three guests and British bottled real
ales. Hood skittles is a popular game here. A
real fire adds atmosphere in winter. No food is
served on Sunday evening. ▥⬱❀⏰♣P⅃

Linton

Crown

11 High Street, CB1 6HS

⏰ 12-2.30, 5.30-11; 12-8 Sun

☎ (01223) 891759

Beer range varies ⊞

Splendid community pub offering a warm
welcome to all – a popular meeting place with
a variety of comfortable seating areas. Freshly
prepared food from an eclectic menu is served
in the bar or dining room (no food Sun eve).
The friendly bar staff are well informed about

the choice of beers, usually from small
breweries. Accommodation is newly
refurbished and fairly quiet. ▥❀✍⏰⬱P⅃

Little Gransden

Chequers

71 Main Road, SG19 3DW

⏰ 12-2, 7-11; 11-11 Fri & Sat; 12-6, 7-10.30 Sun

☎ (01767) 677348

Oakham JHB, seasonal beers; guest beers ⊞/⑮

A true local at the heart of this small village,
run by the same family for the last 57 years. A
well researched and documented history
around the walls makes interesting reading.
The unspoilt public bar, with wooden bench
seating and roaring fire, buzzes with friendly
conversation. An additional lounge and dining
room add much needed space. There is always
an interesting guest beer to try here.
▥Q❀⬱⊟(18)♣P

Little Paxton

Anchor

High Street, PE19 6HA (off A1)

⏰ 12-11 (midnight Fri & Sat); 12-10.30 Sun

☎ (01480) 473199 ⊕ theanchorlittlepaxton.co.uk

Theakston Black Bull Bitter; guest beers ⊞

Built in the early 1800s, the Anchor is a
friendly pub that has recently been
extensively refurbished to create a separate
dining area and large L-shaped bar. Four real
ales are served. The pub is popular with all
age groups from the village. It has a large car
park, beer garden and patio area. Live music
plays on Saturday night. The well known
Paxton Pits nature reserve is nearby.
▥❀⏰♿♣P

Longstowe

Red House

134 Old North Road, CB3 7UT

⏰ 12-3 (not Mon), 5.30-11 (midnight Fri); 12-midnight
Sat; 12-10.30 Sun

☎ (01954) 718480 ⊕ novastream.co.uk/redhouse

Beer range varies ⊞

You can be sure of a warm welcome at this
former coaching inn on the old Great North
Road in a peaceful rural location not far from
Wimpole Hall (NT). Four handpumps offer a
changing selection of ales, often from local
breweries such as Potton. The restaurant,
recently extended into an adjoining barn, has
an enviable reputation. A local artist painted
the sporting murals and the decor features
many eccentric touches. ▥⬱❀⏰♣P

March

Rose & Crown

41 St Peters Road, PE15 9NA

⏰ 4-11 (midnight Fri); 12-midnight Sat; 12-3, 7-10.30
Sun

☎ (01354) 656705

**Fuller's London Pride; Thwaites Original;
Woodforde's Wherry; guest beers** ⊞

Friendly, independent, two-bar free house.
This pub is a true community local with a good
atmosphere, where no TV or juke box is
allowed to disturb the banter from the loyal

locals. Seven real ales are usually available, with micro-breweries well supported and an occasional mild. ⊛♿�‌♨️

Maxey

Blue Bell

37-39 High Street, PE6 9EE
🕐 5.30 (12 Sat)-midnight; 12-4.30, 7.30-11 Sun
☎ (01778) 348182
Abbeydale Absolution; Fuller's London Pride; Oakham JHB; guest beers Ⓗ
Superb village pub dating from 1645, built of local limestone. The pub has been sympathetically modernised, retaining low beams and flagstones. Six real ales are usually available and a free buffet is served on Sunday lunchtime. Friday is Hawaiian shirt night. Very much part of the village and well supported by locals, dominoes and crib are played; a golf society and birdwatchers' group meet here. Local CAMRA Pub of the Year 2006.
🅼Q⊛🅫🚲🚌♣P

Milton

Waggon & Horses

39 High Street, CB4 6DF
🕐 12-2.30, 5-11; 12-4, 6-11 Sat; 12-3, 7-10.30 Sun
☎ (01223) 860313
Elgood's Black Dog, Cambridge Bitter, Golden Newt; guest beers Ⓗ
Imposing mock Tudor, half-timbered building with a large, child-friendly garden. Meals here are good value, served at lunchtime and in the evening. Traditional pub games include skittles, shove ha-penny and cribbage. Note the impressive collection of hats. ⊛🅲♣

Newton

Queen's Head

Fowlmere Road, CB22 7PG
🕐 11.30-2.30, 6-11; 12-2.30, 7-10.30 Sun
☎ (01223) 870436
Adnams Bitter, Broadside, seasonal beers Ⓖ
Popular village establishment serving the local community, with a framed list of the 18 licensees since 1729 on display. Run by the same family for many years, the pub has appeared in every edition of this Guide. Good, simple food is available in both the public and saloon bars. The head on the pub sign is Anne of Cleves. The stuffed goose on display used to patrol the car park. 🅼Q🅲🅫🚲🚌♣♨️P

Old Weston

Swan

Main Street, PE28 5LL (on B660, N of A14)
🕐 12-2.30 (Sat), 6.30 (7 Sat)-11; 12-3.30, 7-10.30 Sun
☎ (01832) 293400
Adnams Bitter, Broadside; Greene King Abbot; guest beers Ⓗ
Dating from the 16th century, this oak-beamed village pub started life as two private houses that were later merged, and has evolved and grown over the years. There is a central bar with a large inglenook, a dining area and a games section offering hood skittles, darts and pool. On Saturday and Sunday a varied menu of traditional pub food

is available, including home-made puddings.
🅼Q⊛🅲🅫♣P

Peterborough

Brewery Tap

80 Westgate, PE1 2AA
🕐 12-11 (1.30am Fri & Sat); 12-11
☎ (01733) 358500 ⊕oakhamales.com
Oakham JHB, White Dwarf, Bishops Farewell; guest beers Ⓗ
Former labour exchange that has been converted into an airy, spacious public house. It is home to Oakham Ales but is still under threat of demolition as the North Westgate area of Peterborough is redeveloped. It has a mix of comfortable leather settees and wooden tables and chairs. When live music is performed at the weekend there may be a door charge. Excellent Thai food is all cooked by Thai chefs. The 12 real ales on offer always includes a mild; Belgian bottled beers are also sold. 🅲🚄🚌

Charters

Town Bridge, PE1 1EH
🕐 12-11 (2am Fri & Sat); 12-10.30 Sun
☎ (01733) 315700 ⊕bluesontheboat.co.uk
Oakham JHB, White Dwarf, Bishops Farewell; guest beers Ⓗ
Large Dutch barge moored near Town Bridge, owned by the same group as Oakham Ales. Twelve or more real ales are usually available on handpump or by gravity on request, including a mild as well as a stout or porter in winter. Traditional cider comes from the cellar. The pub boasts the largest beer garden in Peterborough, with a marquee where regular beer festivals are held. Monthly poetry readings – 'Pint and a Poem' – are hosted.
🅫⊛🅲🚄🚌♣♨️🚲

Coalheavers Arms

5 Park Street, Woodston, PE2 9BH
🕐 12-2 (Thu only), 5-11; 12-11 Fri & Sat; 12-10.30 Sun
☎ (01733) 565664 ⊕individualpubs.co.uk/coalheavers
Beer range varies Ⓗ
Small, single room, back-street local, where eight handpumps serve a mix of real ales from Milton Brewery plus guests, always including a mild. A real cider and Belgian bottled beers are also stocked. The large, popular garden holds two annual beer festivals on May bank holiday weekend and three weeks after the Peterborough Beer Festival in the permanent marquee that also acts as a covered smoking area. Opening hours are extended in summer.
⊛🚌♨️♨️🚲

Drapers Arms

29-31 Cowgate, PE1 1LZ
🕐 9am-midnight (1am Fri & Sat)
☎ (01733) 847570
Courage Directors; Greene King Abbot; Marston's Pedigree; guest beers Ⓗ
Spacious Wetherspoon's pub with wood-panelled walls adorned with pictures of the city in bygone days. Attracting a mixed clientele of all ages, this is one of the city's most popular pubs – winner of local CAMRA Pub of The Year 2007. Food is served all day. With the recent addition of two extra

handpumps, the beers can number up to 10, often supporting local brewers. Q◑&⟁≠⊟⌐

Goodbarns Yard

64 St Johns Street, PE1 5DD (near market)
◐ 11-midnight (1.30am Fri & Sat); 12-11 Sun
☎ (01733) 551830
Adnams Broadside; Caledonian Deuchars IPA; guest beers Ⓖ
On the edge of city centre, the pub looks modern from the outside, but inside you will find a cosy local with a good old fashioned friendly welcome. All beers are served by gravity from the cellar. A previous local CAMRA Pub of The Year, it has two quite spacious bars and a conservatory useful for meetings. Views of the cathedral can be enjoyed from the front of the pub. ⊛⊟⌐

Hand & Heart ☆

12 Highbury Street, Millfield, PE1 3BE
◐ 11-11
☎ (01733) 564653
John Smith's Bitter; guest beers Ⓗ
An unspoilt, terraced 1930s community local with two rooms accessed via an impressive black and white tiled corridor. The public bar features a war memorial. The rear room has no bar, just a serving hatch; a more ornate servery provides drinks in the corridor. A cheese club meets on the last Thursday of the month. The pub fields teams in local darts, dominoes and cribbage leagues.
ᴁQ⊛⊟♣⌐

Palmerston Arms

82 Oundle Road, PE2 9PA
◐ 4 (3 Fri; 12 Sat)-11 (midnight Fri & Sat); 12-11 Sun
☎ (01733) 565865 ⊕ palmerston-arms.co.uk
Beer range varies Ⓖ
Stone-built, 17th-century pub owned by Bateman. It offers two to four Bateman's ales plus up to 11 others and three traditional ciders and/or perries. The pub has no handpumps and the only keg beers are imported ones. Breweriana adorns the walls and jugs hang from the beams. The small, sheltered outdoor area is popular in summer. Rolls and locally made pork pies and pasties are available. Q⟿⊛⊟♣⌐

Ramsey

Jolly Sailor

43 Great Whyte, PE26 1HH
◐ 11-2 (3 Sat), 5.30 (6 Sat)-11; 12-3, 7-10.30 Sun
☎ (01487) 813388
Adnams Bitter, Broadside; Black Sheep Best Bitter; Wells Bombardier; guest beer Ⓗ
This Grade II listed building, with three linked rooms, has been a pub for over 400 years. Warm and welcoming, it attracts a good mix of ages who enjoy the beer and friendly conversation, free from background music or machines. No food is served. There is a guest beer at the weekend and the pub holds a monthly quiz. ᴁ⊛⊟♣⌐

Reach

Dyke's End

8 Fair Green, CB25 0JD

◐ 12-3 (not Mon), 6-11; 12-3, 7-10.30 Sun
☎ (01638) 743816
Beer range varies Ⓗ
By the time the Guide is published, two of the pumps here will be dispensing beers from the pub's own Devil's Dyke Brewery, with a changing guest on the third. Threatened with closure in 1999, the pub was initially bought by a group of villagers but is now privately owned and thriving. It has become a model for similar rescues nationwide. The upstairs restaurant has an excellent reputation (booking advisable); bar food is served downstairs. ᴁQ⊛◑&⊟♣⌐♠P⌐

St Ives

Oliver Cromwell

13 Wellington Street, PE27 5AZ
◐ 11-11 (12.30am Fri & Sat); 12-11 Sun
☎ (01480) 465601
Adnams Bitter, Broadside, seasonal beers; Oakham JHB; guest beers Ⓗ
Wood-panelled bar in an 18th-century row of cottages close to St Ives river quay. A brewery operated here until the 1920s and an old well has been preserved as a feature in one of the bar areas. There is a heated rear patio where smoking is permitted. Three guest beers are always available. Entertainment includes a monthly Tuesday night quiz, and live music on occasional Sunday afternoons and the first and last Thursday evenings of the month. ⊛◑⊟⌐

St Neots

Lord John Russell

25 Russell Street, PE19 1BA
◐ 12-11 (9am-midnight Sat); 11-11 Sun
☎ (01480) 406330
Bateman Mild, XB; guest beers Ⓗ/Ⓖ
Traditional, small back-street pub with a strong local following. The pub centres around the bar, with the main room a mix of pine panelling and brick. At the rear is a pool room and large conservatory, leading to a patio area. Food focuses on home-made, good value meals and snacks, with lunchtime specials. Bateman's Salem Porter and seasonal beers usually feature among the guests.
Q⟿⊛◑♣P⌐

Stapleford

Longbow

2 Church Street, CB22 5DS
◐ 11-3, 5-11.15; 11-midnight Fri; 11-3, 6-midnight Sat; 12-3, 7-11 Sun
☎ (01223) 566855
Adnams Bitter; guest beers Ⓗ
Busy community pub in a large Victorian building offering a variety of entertainment from bar games to regular live music most weekends. The Adnams Bitter is supplemented by up to four guest beers, usually from East Anglian breweries. Home-cooked food is available every session except Sunday evening. The cider is from Cassels. There is a gazebo for smokers.
⊛◑≠(Shelford)⊟♣⌐♠P⌐

Stilton

Bell Inn

Great North Road, PE7 3RA
🕐 12-2.30, 6-11 (midnight Fri & Sat); 12-3, 7-11 Sun
☎ (01733) 241066 ⊕ thebellstilton.co.uk
Fuller's London Pride; Greene King IPA, Abbot; Oakham JHB; guest beers Ⓗ
Renowned as the birthplace of Stilton cheese, the magnificent sign hanging outside this former coachhouse is an exact replica of the 16th-century original. The welcoming, stone built 'village bar' has a flagstone floor, high, beamed ceiling and large open fire. Past visitors at this historic pub include Dick Turpin, Lord Byron, Clarke Gable and Joe Lewis. Excellent accommodation. 🏠Q🌞🍴🌙&🖂P

Stretham

Red Lion

47 High Street, CB6 3JQ
🕐 11-11; (12.30am Fri); 12-10.30 Sun
☎ (01353) 648132 ⊕ redlion-stretham.co.uk
Greene King IPA; guest beers Ⓗ
Renovated 17th-century pub at the heart of the village serving up to three guest beers. It has a traditional public bar and a more relaxed saloon with extensions to the rear providing extra facilities including a pleasant restaurant in the conservatory. The rear patio garden has outside seating and a heated smoking area. Accommodation is available in 12 rooms, with breakfast also served to non-residents 7.30-9am. 🏠🛏🌞🍴🌙 ⊞&🖂♣P

Swavesey

White Horse

Market Street, CB4 5QG
🕐 12-2.30, 6-11 (12.30am Fri); 11.30-12.30am Sat; 12-11 Sun
☎ (01954) 232470
Caledonian Deuchars IPA; guest beers Ⓗ
Adjacent to the old market area in the centre of the village, at the heart of this popular social hub is the public bar, the oldest room, dating back centuries. In later years the pub expanded into adjoining buildings, creating space for a lounge bar with restaurant area to one side, a pool room and function room. The pub hosts an annual regional pinball meet and boasts its own fine old pinball machine in the corner. No food is available Sunday evening. 🏠Q🌞🌙⊞🖂♣

Thriplow

Green Man

2 Lower Street, SG8 7RJ
🕐 12-3, 6-11; closed Mon; 12-3 (closed eve) Sun
☎ (01763) 208855 ⊕ greenmanthriplow.co.uk
Beer range varies Ⓗ
Despite the name, blue is the predominant colour on the exterior of this village pub. The emphasis here is on good quality, interesting food, but drinkers are more than welcome, with beers to cater for all tastes. An ever-changing range often includes ales from local micro-breweries. The two airy rooms are a popular place for family gatherings at the weekends. Outside seating is available in front

of the pub on the green and on the rear patio.
🏠Q🌞🌙 Å🖂P

Ufford

White Hart

Main Street, PE9 3BH
🕐 12-11; 12-6 (9.30 summer) Sun
☎ (01780) 740250 ⊕ whitehartufford.co.uk
Adnams Bitter; Ufford Idle Hour, White Hart; guest beer Ⓗ
Old stone farmhouse offering ales from the on-site brewery, Ufford Ales. The guest beer may also be one of its seasonal ales. Visits to the brew house can be arranged. The main bar has some interesting artefacts and high quality food is served. At the back of the pub is a patio overlooking large gardens. En-suite accommodation is available. 🏠Q🌞🍴🌙&🖂♣P

Whittlesey

Boat

2 Ramsey Road, PE7 1DR
🕐 12-11
☎ (01733) 202488
Elgood's Black Dog, Cambridge, Golden Newt, Pageant Ale, seasonal beers; guest beers Ⓖ
Traditional local where visitors are made welcome, stocking an extensive selection of single malt whiskies. During Saturday night's live music sessions any musicians are welcome to join in. Popular with anglers, a large screen shows Premiership football matches. Note the boat-shaped bar front in the lounge. Mentioned in the Domesday Book, it offers good value accommodation.
Q🌞🍴⊞&🖂♣P

Bricklayers Arms

9 Station Road, PE7 1UA
🕐 11-5, 7-11; 11-11 Fri & Sat
☎ (01733) 202593
John Smith's Bitter; guest beers Ⓗ
Excellent local with a long, plainly furnished public bar and a cosy no-smoking lounge, attracting a mixed bunch of regulars of all ages. The large garden is popular in summer. Close to the railway station, buses and boat moorings, the pub is HQ for the Whittlesey Straw Bear Festival. A good range of guest beers always includes a mild on offer at a discounted price. 🌞⊞&⇌🖂♣P🍴

Wistow

Three Horseshoes

Mill Road, PE28 2QQ
🕐 12-3, 6-11; 12-11 Sat; 12-4 Sun
☎ (01487) 822270 ⊕ wistow-pub.co.uk
Adnams Bitter, Broadside; guest beers Ⓗ
Traditional village pub in an attractive multi-room, brick and thatch 18th-century building opposite the village church. Part of the building was originally a blacksmith's and it is thought that part was always a hostelry. The pub has a strong local following as well as attracting passing trade with its traditional pub food and at least three real ales. Woodforde's Wherry is a frequent guest beer. 🏠🌞🌙🍴P

CHESHIRE

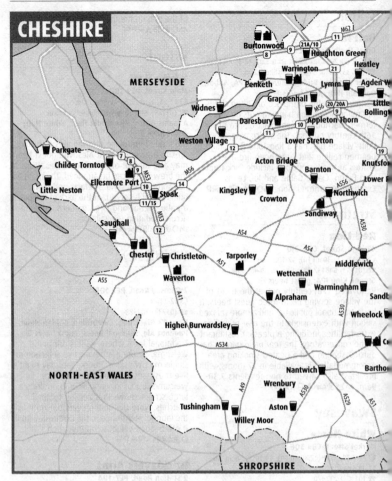

MERSEYSIDE

Burtonwood
Houghton Green
Warrington
Heatley
Penketh
Lymm
Agden W
Grappenhall
Widnes
Daresbury
Appleton Thorn
Little
Bolling
Weston Village
Lower Stretton
Parkgate
Acton Bridge
Barnton
Knutsfo
Childer Tornton
Kingsley
Northwich
Lower F
Little Neston
Ellesmere Port
Crowton
Stoak
Sandiway
Saughall
Chester
Christleton
Tarporley
Middlewich
Waverton
Wettenhall
Warmingham
Sandb
Alpraham
Wheelock
Higher Burwardsley
Cr
NORTH-EAST WALES
Nantwich
Bartho
Wrenbury
Tushingham
Aston
Willey Moor

SHROPSHIRE

Acton Bridge

Hazel Pear Inn

1 Hill Top Road, CW8 3RA (opp railway station)
☼ 12-11 (10.30 Sun)
☎ (01606) 853195
Marston's Pedigree; Taylor Landlord; Tetley Bitter; guest beer Ⓗ
Named after the hazel pear trees found in the grounds, this pub has something for everyone – a public bar with TV, pool and darts, comfortable lounge, separate dining room (although food can be eaten throughout) and upstairs function room. Outside are a bowling green, dog run and even a mini-farm with ducks, goats and chickens alongside the children's play area. Guest beers are from the Punch list. Wednesday is curry night.
ﾑ⚛️⊄Ⅾ☀️Ⓐ≒⊠(48)♣️PⅬ

Agden Wharf

Barn Owl

Warrington Lane, WA13 0SW (off the A56)
OS707872
☼ 11-11; 12-10.30 Sun
☎ (01925) 752020 ⊕ thebarnowlinn.co.uk

Marston's Burton Bitter, Pedigree; Jennings Cumberland Ale; guest beers Ⓗ
Remote, converted canal-side building with superb farmland vistas. This popular pub is well worth seeking out for the fascinating Bridgewater narrow boat activity, the thrill of taking the Little Owl ferry to the opposite towpath, duck feeding and a warm welcome to the pub itself. One large room with a conservatory accommodates individuals and club functions. The occasional live music programme is ever changing at this frequent local CAMRA award winner. ⚛️⊄Ⅾ♿️P

Alpraham

Travellers Rest ☆

Chester Road, CW6 9JA (on A51, 200m N from Bunbury Road)
☼ 6.30-11; 12-4.30, 6-11 Sat; 12-3, 7-10.30 Sun
☎ (01829) 260523
Caledonian Deuchars IPA; Tetley Bitter Ⓗ
Cheerful staff and friendly customers make visiting this community pub a rejuvenating experience. Intelligent and amusing conversation is the loudest sound around. It has been owned, and carefully preserved, by the same family for 105 years. Although the

Poynton

Wilmslow
Abberley
Great Warford

Kettleshulme

Bollington

DERBYSHIRE

Macclesfield

er Heath

Sutton

Marton

Wincle

Congleton

Smallwood

Mow Cop

STAFFORDSHIRE

| 0 Miles | 5 |
| 0 Kilometres | 8 |

Aston

Bhurtpore Inn
Wrenbury Road, CW5 8DQ
☺ 12-2.30, 6.30-11.30 (midnight Fri); 12-3,
6.30-midnight Sat; 12-11 Sun
☎ (01270) 780917 ⊕ bhurtpore.co.uk
Beer range varies Ⓗ
Friendly family-run free house renowned for
real ales, real food and good company. Ever
changing beers are mostly from micro and
small regional brewers, many of them rarely
seen in south Cheshire. A wide range of
continental bottled and draught beers is also
available. Curries are a highlight of the
extensive food menu. The annual July beer
festival attracts drinkers from far and near. The
pub is home to the Wobbly Wheels cycling
group and a keen cricket team. Worth a detour
anytime. ▲Q❀❶❹❺Ⓐ≥(Wrenbury)●P⅃

Barnton

Barnton Cricket Club
Broomsedge, Townfield Lane, CW8 4LH (200yds
from A533 via Stoneheyes Lane)
☺ 6.30-midnight (12.30am Thu & Fri); 12-12.30am Sat;
12-midnight Sun
☎ (01606) 77702 ⊕ barntoncc.co.uk
**Boddingtons Bitter; Hydes Mild, 1863; Tetley
Bitter; guest beers** Ⓗ
Established in 1880, this former CAMRA
Regional Club of the Year has evolved to a
multi-faceted sports club featuring bowls,
squash, dominoes, darts, quizzes and a golf
society as well as cricket for its 600-strong
membership. A CAMRA membership card
gains entry, and members and visitors can
choose from two guest beers (usually from
micros) in addition to the four standard
offerings. In November there is a popular beer
festival. Excellent value food is served
Thursday to Saturday evenings and Sunday
lunchtime. ❀❶❺☐♣P⅃

Barthomley

White Lion ☆
Audley Road, CW2 5PG (jct of Audley Road and
Radway Green Road)
☺ 11.30-11; 12-10.30 Sun
☎ (01270) 882242
**Jennings Sneck Lifter; Marston's Burton Bitter,
Mansfield Bitter, Pedigree; guest beer** Ⓗ
Friendly three-room, low-beamed, half-
timbered, thatched pub, popular with locals,
walkers, cyclists and bikers. The building dates
from 1614, but records show that ale was sold
here even earlier. The name derives from the
heraldic silver lion, rampant, on the coat of
arms of the Crewe family. There is an exposed
panel in the larger of the two higher level
rooms showing the original wattle and daub
wall construction. An imaginative menu is
available at lunchtime. Dogs are welcome.
▲Q❀❶P⅃

Bollington

Cock & Pheasant
15 Bollington Road, Bollington Cross, SK10 5EJ
☺ 11.30-11 (midnight Fri & Sat); 12-11 Sun

four-room family-run free house is Victorian in
origin, it has a late 1940s aura, with exposed
varnished ceiling beams, bench seating along
some of the walls and rattan cane seats. The
bowling green completes a quintessentially
English pub. Q❹☐♣P

Appleton Thorn

Appleton Thorn Village Hall
Stretton Road, WA4 4RT (on B5356)
☺ 7.30-11 Thu-Sat (closed Mon-Wed); 1-4, 7.30-10.30
Sun
☎ (01925) 261187 ⊕ atvh.org
Beer range varies Ⓗ
This thriving village hall, current CAMRA
Regional Club of the Year, now offers an ever-
changing range of seven beers from regional
and micro-breweries. Situated in the former
village school, a comfortable lounge and
larger hall accommodate drinkers, while a
pool room leads off the hall. Outside are a
bowling green and garden area. Regular
events are held, including live music sessions.
Dogs on leads are welcome. Food is served
Sunday lunchtimes (1-3pm). A former CAMRA
National Club of the Year. Q❀❶❺☐♣●❒

☎ (01625) 573289
Boddingtons Bitter; Storm Bosley Cloud;
Theakston Best Bitter Ⓗ
Celebrating its 250th anniversary in 2006, this large, popular pub is on the main road entering Bollington from Macclesfield. Low ceilings and a stone-flagged floor make for a cosy bar with ample dining areas. Outside are a patio and children's play area. An excellent pub for both beer and food, a well-balanced menu is served daily. The pub is a regular outlet for local brewer Storm. It has an active golf society and league darts and dominoes. The bus stops outside the front door.
⌘⏻⅋⏽Ⓟ⏥

Poachers Inn

95 Ingersley Road, SK10 5RE (edge of Bollington heading towards Rainow)
✪ 12-2 (not Mon), 5.30-11; 12-2, 7-midnight Sat; 12-10.30 Sun
☎ (01625) 572086 ⊕ thepoachers.org
Copper Dragon Best Bitter; Taylor Landlord;
guest beers Ⓗ
Family-run free house with a friendly atmosphere, converted from five stone-built terraced cottages. The suntrap garden is delightful in summer and a coal fire welcoming in winter. Three guest beers often support local breweries, especially Storm. Home-prepared food is available in the bar or à la carte restaurant (not Mon). Popular with ramblers and cyclists, regular quiz nights and golf days are organised. ⌘⏻⏽Ⓟ⏥

Vale Inn

29-31 Adlington Road, SK10 5JT
✪ 12-3, 5.30-11; 12-11 Sat & Sun
☎ (01625) 575147 ⊕ valeinn.co.uk
Beer range varies Ⓗ
Dating from the 1860s, this single room, stone built free house offers a selection of five guest beers, usually including a dark option. Real cider is available in summer. Regular beer festivals with live music add to the appeal of this real ale gem close to the canal and footpaths. On balmy summer evenings the garden provides the perfect place to enjoy a pint while watching the local cricket team in action. Excellent home-cooked food is served – the chips are highly recommended.
⌘⏻⏽Ⓟ

Burtonwood

Fiddle i'th Bag

Alder Lane, WA5 4BJ
✪ 12-3.15, 4.45-11; 12-11 Sat; 12-10.30 Sun
☎ (01925) 225442
Beer range varies Ⓗ
Slightly off the beaten track but well worth a visit, the Fiddle offers up to three changing guest beers and good food served at lunchtimes and evenings. The single central bar serves three dining and drinking areas. The growing range of unusual items on display includes a mechanical remote controlled deer's head and two orang-utans in fancy dress. Q⌘⏻⅋⏽Ⓟ⏥

Chester

Bear & Billet

94 Lower Bridge Street, CH1 1RU
✪ 12-11 (11.30 Wed & Thu; midnight Fri & Sat); 12-11 Sun
☎ (01244) 311886
Okells Bitter, IPA; guest beers Ⓗ
Fine historic building built in 1664 retaining much of the original woodwork on the inside and out. The wooden-floored bar is divided into three areas: the ground floor has an open fire and a plasma TV, there is a sitting/dining room on the first floor and a function room on the second floor. Outside is a small yard with tables. Up to six cask ales and an extensive selection of continental beers are available.
⏢⌘⏻⅋⏽

Cherry Orchard Inn

5 Chapel Lane, CH3 5EN (off A41 Whitchurch road out of city centre)
✪ 11.30-11.30; 12-10.30 Sun
☎ (01244) 852013
Theakston Mild, Best Bitter; guest beers Ⓗ
Friendly, popular local in the suburban area of Boughton, close to the Shropshire Union Canal and River Dee. One bar serves several open-plan areas including a darts room and a lounge area around an open fire. Quiz night is Wednesday and occasional music nights are held. Smoking is permitted in the outside heated patio and decking areas. No food is served on Sunday evening. ⏢Q⌘⏻⏽♣Ⓟ⏥

Mill Hotel

Milton Street, CH1 3NF (by canal E of inner ring road/A51/A56 jcts)
✪ 12-midnight (no entry after 11); 12-10.30 Sun
☎ (01244) 350035 ⊕ millhotel.com
Theakston XB; Weetwood Best Bitter; guest
beers Ⓗ
City centre hotel in a former corn mill dating from 1830. It's a beer festival every day here with up to 16 real ales on handpump, including a guest mild and real cider. Three plasma screens show sports. The hotel has five dining areas serving a range of food from bar snacks to full restaurant fare. It also offers real ale cruises on the adjacent Shropshire Union Canal. Alternatively, you can simply sit on the patio and watch the narrowboats pass by.
⌘⏮⏻⏽⇌♣Ⓟ⏥

Old Harkers Arms

1 Russell Street, CH3 5AL (down steps from City Road to canal)
✪ 11.30-11; 12-10.30 Sun
☎ (01244) 344525 ⊕ harkersarms-chester.co.uk

INDEPENDENT BREWERIES

Beartown Congleton
Borough Arms Crewe
Burtonwood Burtonwood
Coach House Warrington
Northern Sandiway
Spitting Feathers Waverton
Station House Ellesmere Port
Storm Macclesfield
WC Chester
Weetwood Tarporley
Woodlands Wrenbury

Thwaites Original; Wapping Bitter; Weetwood Cheshire Cat; guest beers Ⓗ

This upmarket pub was converted from the run-down basement of a former Victorian warehouse alongside the Shropshire Union Canal. Bookcases, prints and mirrors adorn the walls and wooden flooring features throughout the light and airy interior. Tasting notes help you choose one of the nine or so real ales on sale, mostly from independent micros. Food is available all day with booking recommended for busy times. Door policy is in place at weekends. Q⊕♦≠⊠♠

Ship Victory

47 George Street, CH1 3EQ (off St Oswald's Way near fire station)

🕔 11-1am (2am Fri & Sat)

☎ (01244) 3765453 ⊕ shipvictory.com

Tetley Bitter; guest beer Ⓗ

Friendly and welcoming community pub at the side of a city centre car park. With the enthusiasm of the landlord and regulars who cheerfully support the pub's games teams and charitable causes, nights without some form of entertainment are rare. Rock bands and folk music feature strongly among the live music performed here. The local Manchester City FC supporters' club meets here, and there are regular quiz nights. Guest beers are often sourced from local micros. ≠⊠♠♣

Telford's Warehouse

Tower Wharf, CH1 4EZ (turn into Canal Street from the top of Northgate Street)

🕔 12-11 (1am Wed; 12.30am Thu; 2am Fri & Sat); 12-1am Sun

☎ (01244) 390090 ⊕ telfordswarehouse.com

Taylor Landlord; Thwaites Original; Weetwood Cheshire Cat; guest beers Ⓗ

Converted warehouse with large picture windows overlooking the Shropshire Union Canal basin. An industrial crane dominates the bar area and an interesting variety of artwork adorns the walls. A further downstairs bar is open on live music evenings and for the Wednesday evening salsa sessions. A restaurant on the first floor serves high quality food. An outside drinking area is situated next to the canal. Admission charges apply after 10pm at the weekend and during some live events. ❀⊕♣P

Childer Thorton

White Lion

New Road, CH66 5PU (off A41)

🕔 11.30-11.30 (midnight Fri & Sat); 12-11.30 Sun

☎ (0151) 339 3402

Thwaites Mild, Original, Lancaster Bomber Ⓗ

Cosy country pub on the outskirts of Ellesmere Port selling probably the best Thwaites beers in the country and celebrating its 29th year in the Guide. Three small rooms cater for locals and visitors alike in a friendly, convivial atmosphere. Families are welcome in the snug at lunchtime. The pub offers excellent value meals – try the home-made chicken tikka. ▲Q❀⊕⊠P

Christleton

Plough Inn

Plough Lane, CH3 7PT (1 mile E of village centre)

🕔 12-midnight; 12-11 Sun

☎ (01244) 336096

Spitting Feathers Special Ale; Theakston Best Bitter; guest beers Ⓗ

This 18th-century red brick former farmhouse has been extended several times over recent years into a large country-style pub/restaurant. Three distinct areas – public bar, lounge and restaurant – are served from the large central bar. Up to nine real ales are available, usually including two or three from the nearby Spitting Feathers brewery. The busy, award-winning restaurant features local produce including home-grown vegetables and home-reared livestock (booking is recommended, no food Sunday evening). Q❀⊕⊡♣▲⊠♣P

Congleton

Beartown Tap

18 Willow Street, CW12 1RL (on A54 Buxton road)

🕔 12-2, 4-11; 12-11 Fri & Sat; 12-10.30 Sun

☎ (01260) 270990

Beartown Kodiak Gold, Bearskinful, Polar Eclipse, Black Bear; guest beers Ⓗ

Popular local just yards from Beartown Brewery. Opened in 1999, this was the brewery's first pub. Since then it has gained a reputation for beer quality, winning regional CAMRA Pub of the Year in 2003 and 2004. Non-regular beers are likely to include a guest beer sourced from another micro alongside an ever-changing selection from the Beartown range. The real cider changes regularly and there is always a good selection of Belgian bottled beers. Parking is on the street outside the pub. ▲Q≠⊠♣♠

Congleton Leisure Centre

Worrall Street, CW12 1DT (off A54 Mountbatten Way)

🕔 10.15-1.15 (not Mon), 7-10.30 (7-11 Mon & Thu Sept-Apr); closed Sat; 8-11 Sun

☎ (01260) 271552

Beer range varies Ⓗ

Municipal leisure centre bar that requires no membership fee and you don't even need to use the sporting facilities. Efforts have been made to create a real pub atmosphere with posters and pump clips decorating the walls. Three ever-changing real ales, usually from micro-breweries, are on offer (sometimes only two in the summer), including seasonal beers unlikely to be found elsewhere in the area. A well-attended 20 beer real ale festival is held in early March each year. Five minutes' walk from Congleton Bus Station. ♿≠⊠P

Queen's Head Hotel

Park Lane, CW12 3DE (on A527 Biddulph road, opp Congleton rail station)

🕔 11-midnight (2am Fri & Sat); 12-midnight Sun

☎ (01260) 272546 ⊕ queensheadhotel.org.uk

Courage Directors; Draught Bass; Greene King Abbot; Wells Bombardier; guest beers Ⓗ

Canalside pub with its own moorings, popular with locals and canal users. Going from strength to strength in recent years, it has twice been awarded local CAMRA Pub of the Season. Seven or eight real ales are usually available. Guest beers change regularly, often sourced from local micro-brewers including Woodlands and Titanic. Real cider is available in the summer months. Bar meals are inexpensive and include vegetarian options. The large garden includes a children's play area. ⊛🚃◑≒🖪♣♠P

Crewe

Angel

2 Victoria Centre, CW1 2PU (below street level in Victoria Centre)
✪ 10-7 (10 Sat); closed Sun
☎ (01270) 212003
Oakwell Barnsley Bitter ⊞
Friendly pub in the Victoria Centre in Crewe's main shopping area, just a few minutes from the bus station. There is one large bar downstairs with a pool table and plenty of comfortable seating. Excellent value meals, all home cooked, are available until 3pm and often later. The beers are competitively priced, rivalling the well-known chain outlet nearby. ◑≒🖪♣

Borough Arms

33 Earle Street, CW1 2BG
✪ 7 (3 Fri)-11; 12-11 Sat; 12-10.30 Sun
☎ (01270) 254999
Beer range varies ⊞
A breath of fresh air has blown into this free house with the arrival of the new landlord; the brilliant beer policy includes nine constantly-changing guest ales from brewers near and far – now served in oversize glasses. The micro-brewery on the premises usually provides two changing beers, with up to 16 Belgian/German beers also on draught. You can also choose from more than 100 bottled beers. The pub atmosphere here is excellent, with no juke box, cigarette machines or pool table. ☎⊛🖪♣🗊

Crown

25 Earle Street, CW1 2BH
✪ 11 (12 Sun)-11
☎ (01270) 257295
Robinson's Hatters, Unicorn, seasonal beers ⊞
Large red-brick Robinson's house near the town's library square, carefully refurbished a few years ago. Now open plan, it has a tile and wood floor and dark wood-panelled bar. This traditional, friendly pub has a strong local following with well-supported darts and dominoes teams. Old Tom is added to the beer range from October to March, and is popular enough to warrant its own handpump. An outdoor smoking area with canopy has been added. 🖪♣🗝

Crowton

Hare & Hounds

Station Road, CW8 2RN (on B5153)
✪ (01928); 788851
Greene King IPA; guest beers ⊞
Local CAMRA Community Pub of the Year 2007, this pub is a local hub that also offers a warm welcome to visitors from outside the area. There is a charity plastic duck race held on Easter Monday each year on the stream at the end of the garden. The parlour features a display of winning ducks over the years. The pub is renowned for food of excellent quality, particularly the daily fish specials and signature steak speciality. 🚃⊛◑🖪(48)P🗝

Daresbury

Ring O' Bells

Chester Road, WA4 4AJ
✪ 11-11 (midnight Fri & Sat summer); 12-10.30 Sun
☎ (01925) 740256
Courage Directors; Theakston Best Bitter; Wells Bombardier; guest beers ⊞
Multi-roomed pub in the heart of Daresbury dating back to the 18th century. One of the rooms was the location for the local parish court in days gone by. The extensive gardens offer a view of the local church across the way, where Lewis Carroll's father was the vicar; related memorabilia is prominently displayed, including photographs of the commemorative stained window. Food, including daily specials, is served all day. 🚃⊛◑🕭🖪P🗝

Grappenhall

Grappenhall Community Centre

Bellhouse Farm, Bellhouse Lane, WA4 2SG (200 yds off the A50)
✪ 7.30-11.30 (midnight Fri); 12-midnight Sat; 12-11 Sun
☎ (01925) 268633 ⊕ grappenhall.com
Greene King Ruddles Best; guest beers ⊞
The Bellhouse Club is a private members' club with a games room offering darts, dominoes and pool, and a large projection screen showing all Sky Sports matches. Extensively refurbished in 2004, the bar, comfortable lounge and games room are served by a central bar. An ever-changing variety of real ales is available. Your CAMRA membership card gains admission. The Bridgewater Canal is nearby. Q⊛🕭♣P

Great Warford

Stag s Head

Mill Lane, SK9 7TY (W of A535 between Alderley Edge and Chelford)
✪ 12-3, 5-11; 12-11 Sat; 12-4, 7-10.30 Sun
☎ (01565) 872350
Black Sheep Best Bitter; Boddingtons Bitter; Taylor Landlord ⊞
Set in open countryside, the stark external appearance of this building belies a comfortable and welcoming interior. The bar entrance is overlooked by the eponymous stuffed animal. Two rooms off the bar provide seating for those wishing to sample the good value menu (no food Sun eve). Summer drinking and occasional barbecues can be enjoyed in the garden overlooking fields, sometimes with grazing horses, while additional winter warmth is provided by real fires. 🚃Q⊛◑🗝

Heatley

Railway
42 Mill Lane, WA13 9SQ
🕒 12-11
☎ (01925) 752742
**Black Sheep Best Bitter; Boddingtons Bitter;
Taylor Landlord; guest beers** Ⓗ
Just like a pub should be – many rooms of
differing sizes provide a drinking experience
to suit most needs. Live music is featured
regularly with folk particularly popular.
Outside, a large grassed area provides a play
space for younger family members. The
railway is no longer next to the pub; the track
bed is now the Trans-Pennine Trail. A previous
local CAMRA Pub of the Year. ❀◖🕭🖢🖴♣P

Higher Burwardsley

Pheasant Inn
CH3 9PF (follow signs on A41 and A49 for Cheshire
Workshops)
🕒 7-9.30am, 12-midnight; 8-10.30am, 12-11.30 Sun
☎ (01829) 770434 🌐 thepheasantinn.co.uk
Weetwood Best, Eastgate; guest beers Ⓗ
With a stunning location in the Peckforton
Hills, the Pheasant is a splendid country pub
popular with walkers and visitors to the
nearby Candle Workshops. Real fires warm the
bars in winter, and in summer outside dining
and drinking areas offer breathtaking views.
The regular beers are usually complemented
by guests from other micros. Food of an
excellent standard is served and high quality
accommodation is available in 12 en-suite
rooms. ❀❀🖴◖🕭🖢P🖴

Houghton Green

Plough
Mill Lane, WA2 0SU
🕒 11.30-11 (11.30 Thu; midnight Fri; 11.30 Sat); 12-11
Sun
☎ (01925) 815409
Wells Bombardier; guest beers Ⓗ
Dating from 1774, this once rural pub has
been swallowed up by the new estates of
north Warrington. Extended in the late 1980s,
the emphasis here is on food, though up to
five guest beers are served. The pub maintains
a rural feel with its bowling green, despite the
M62 running alongside the bottom of the car
park. Two beer festivals are hosted around St
George s Day and Hallowe en. Quiz night is
Thursday. ❀◖🕭🖴P

Kettleshulme

Swan
Macclesfield Road, SK23 7QU (on B5470)
🕒 12 (5.30 Mon)-11; 12-10.30 Sun
☎ (01663) 732943 🌐 the-swan-inn-kettleshulme.co.uk
Marston's Burton Bitter; guest beers Ⓗ
Village pub saved from closure in 2005 when
it was bought by a group of locals. The 15th-
century white stone building has a small,
quaint interior with timber beams, stone
fireplaces and an open fire in winter. Two
frequently-changing guest beers from micros
are always available; a beer festival is hosted
in September. The food is of a high quality

from an interesting, regularly-changing menu
(no lunchtime meal Mon, no eve meals Sun-
Tue). Families and walkers are welcome at
this excellent inn within the Peak District
national park surrounded by good walking
country. ❀❀◖🕭🖴(60, 64)P

Kingsley

Red Bull
The Brow, WA6 8AN (50 yds from main B5153)
🕒 12-3, 5.30-midnight; 12-3, 7-11.30 Sun
☎ (01928) 788097 🌐 redbullpub.co.uk
Copper Dragon Scotts 1816; guest beers Ⓗ
Now a free-house, this enterprising pub
focuses on beers from micro-breweries,
particularly from the local area, with up to five
handpumps dedicated to an ever-changing
array of guest ales. There has been an inn on
the site since 1771, the present building built
in 1906, providing a focal point for the village.
The good value food features 'real' chips; curry
night is Wednesday. Occasional live music
plays on Saturday evening. ❀❀◖🕭🖢♣P

Knutsford

Lord Eldon
27 Tatton Street, WA16 6AD
🕒 11-11.30 (midnight Thu-Sat); 12-10.30 Sun
☎ (01565) 652261
Tetley Bitter; guest beers Ⓗ
Historic 300-year-old pub with a delightful
exterior with sundial and hanging baskets. The
cosy, rambling and attractive interior includes
three rooms plus the bar. Roaring fires, low
beams and a riot of brass and pictures provide
the background to a friendly local pub. The
pleasant, hidden away, enclosed rear garden
is well worth a visit in summer. Live
entertainment features regularly through the
year. ❀❀🖈🖴

Little Bollington

Swan with Two Nicks
Park Lane, WA14 4TJ (off A56) SJ729871
🕒 12-11 (10.30 Sun)
☎ (0161) 928 2914
Taylor Landlord; guest beers Ⓗ
Tucked away at the end of a road leading to
the River Bollin, this classic country pub is
convenient for the National Trust's Dunham
Hall and Deer Park. The cosy front rooms have
real fires, bench seating as well as tables,
beams, horse brasses and pictures of old local
scenes. Dogs are welcome. There is a spacious
restaurant at the rear and a large decked
seating area outside. The house beer Swan
With Two Nicks is from the local Coach House
brewery. There are typically three frequently-
changing guest beers. ❀Q❀◖🖴P

Little Neston

Harp
19 Quayside, CH64 0TB
🕒 12-11 (10.30 Sun)
☎ (0151) 336 6980
**Holt Bitter; Taylor Landlord; Titanic Iceberg;
guest beers** Ⓗ

A former coal miners' inn, this pub can be difficult to find along an unmade track on the edge of the Dee Marshes, but is well worth the effort to seek out. Set in a glorious location overlooking the Dee Estuary (popular with twitchers), it can be cut off at high tide. Converted from two cottages, it has a public bar and a lounge/family room. The outside drinking area is a superb spot for watching breathtaking sunsets over North Wales.
ᴁQ❦❀◁ⵧP

Lower Peover

Crown Inn
Crown Lane, WA16 9QB
✪ 11.30-3, 5.30-11; 12-10.30 Sun
☎ (01565) 722074
Caledonian Deuchars IPA; Flowers IPA; Greene King Old Speckled Hen; Taylor Landlord; Tetley Bitter; guest beers Ⓗ
Traditional country pub with an L-shaped bar dividing the stone-flagged bar from the comfortable lounge. Good home-cooked local food is available in the pub and in the small restaurant (no food Sun eve). The pub has one changing guest beer to complement the five regulars, often including a mild. Darts and dominoes are played. There is a cobbled area for outdoor drinking. ᴁQ❀◁♣P

Lower Stretton

Ring o' Bells
Northwich Road, WA4 4NZ (A559 just off jct 10 M56)
✪ 12-2.30 (not Mon), 5.30-11; 12-3, 5.30 (7 Sat)-11 Thu-Sat; 12-4, 7-10.30 Sun
☎ (01925) 815409
Fuller's London Pride; Tetley Bitter; guest beer Ⓗ
Situated on the edge of the Cheshire countryside to the south of Warrington, this popular, traditional local is an oasis in a sea of food-oriented pubs. With no juke box or fruit machine, lively conversation among the locals dominates the main bar. There are two quieter side rooms. A folk night is held on the first Tuesday of the month, and boules is played in summer. ᴁQ❀❦♣P

Lymm

Spread Eagle
47 Eagle Brow, WA13 0AG
✪ 11-11 (midnight Fri & Sat); 12-10.30 Sun
☎ (01925) 757467
Lees Bitter, seasonal beers Ⓗ
Large, traditional pub situated in the village centre, near the lower dam and Bridgewater Canal. The interior includes a lounge and restaurant area, with a small public bar and even smaller snug boasting a real fire. An upstairs function room is also available. The drinking area outside is busy in summer. A pub popular with locals and passing trade including walkers and boaters. ᴁQ❀◁ⵧ&ⵧ

Macclesfield

British Flag
42 Coare Street, SK10 1DW
✪ 5.30 (5 Sat)-11; 12-3, 7-10.30 Sun

☎ (01625) 425500
Robinson's Hatters, Unicorn, Old Tom, seasonal beers Ⓗ
Originally a ginger beer factory in the 1860s, this old fashioned and friendly town local is 10 minutes' walk from the railway station. Four rooms surround a central bar with one dedicated to pool; the tap room hosts darts and dominoes and houses the landlord's trophy cabinet full of Macclesfield Town football memorabilia. Pub games are popular including table skittles. A large-screen TV shows sport. Old Tom is only available in winter. ❧≢♣

Dolphin
76 Windmill Street, SK11 7HS (side street off main London Road)
✪ 12-2.30, 5-11; 12-10.30 Sun
☎ (01625) 616179
Robinson's Hatters, Unicorn, Old Tom; guest beers Ⓗ
Friendly pub serving the local community but also very welcoming to visitors. A central bar separates the two drinking areas, with another room providing an ideal venue for meetings and pub games fixtures. The original glass door is distinctive in this traditional style pub. Award-winning Old Tom is always available during the winter. Home-cooked food is served Monday-Saturday lunchtimes only. A previous CAMRA Pub of the Season award winner. ᴁQ◁❦≢♣

Porters Prince of Wales
33 Roe Street, SK11 6UT
✪ 11.30-11 (midnight Fri & Sat); 12-10.30 Sun
☎ (01625) 424796 ⊕ portersprinceofwales.co.uk
Caledonian Deuchars IPA; Theakston Bitter; guest beers Ⓗ
Comfortable, friendly and always busy town centre pub threatened by development but seemingly saved after a widespread campaign. One large room has quieter corners. Look out for the modern mosaics at the entrance and fish tank separating the Gents from the bar area. Games teams play in local leagues. Oysters are available at the bar on Friday evenings during the season September-April. Three constantly-changing guest beers usually come from independent breweries. ᴁ❀≢♣

Railway View
1 Byroms Lane, SK11 7JW (off the main London Road)
✪ 6 (4 Fri)-11 (7 winter); 12-11 Sat; 12-10.30 Sun
☎ (01625) 423657
Storm Head of Steam; guest beers Ⓗ
Once a regular entry in the Guide, the pub now has new family owners and is back to its best, winning local CAMRA Pub of the Season in spring 2006. Originally two rooms, it has been opened out into one, with a large chimney breast dividing it into different areas. The outside drinking area is a trainspotter's heaven, hence the name. Monday night offers reduced price beer. Regular music evenings and beer festivals are held. ᴁ❀&≢ⵧ♣❦

Waters Green Tavern
98 Waters Green, SK11 6LH
✪ 11.30-3, 5.30-11; 11-3, 7-11 Sat; 12-3, 7-10.30 Sun

☎ (01625) 422653
Greene King IPA; guest beers ⓗ
Handy for both train and bus stations, this friendly, traditional town pub has three distinct drinking areas, including a pool room at the rear. Catering for all tastes, it has thriving darts, pool and crib teams plus quiet corners to read and relax. A popular pub, it has won numerous awards from the local CAMRA branch. Beer choice regularly includes Roosters, Oakham and Phoenix, but also more diverse breweries, often including a dark beer. Good value, traditional, home cooked food is available. ♨⑩♿⛟♣🍴

Marton

Davenport
Congleton Road, SK11 9HF (on A34 4 miles N of Congleton)
✪ 11.45-3 (not Mon), 6-11; 12-11 Fri & Sat; 12-11 Sun
☎ (01260) 224269
Courage Directors; Websters Yorkshire Bitter; guest beers ⓗ
Originally a farmhouse, now a popular pub and restaurant, the Davenport has taken on a new lease of life under the current owners. Guest beers often, but not always, come from Cheshire micro-brewers such as Weetwood or Storm. The restaurant is hugely popular (booking advisable at the weekend) – all meals contain only fresh ingredients. Bar meals are also served (no food Mon). The large adjoining garden includes a children's play area. ♨⛺❀⑩♣P

Middlewich

Royal British Legion
100 Lewin Street, CW10 9AS
✪ 12-3 (4 Fri), 7-11; 12-11.30 Sat; 12-3, 7-10.30 Sun
☎ (01606) 833286
Hydes Dark Mild, Original Bitter; guest beers ⓗ
Multiple CAMRA branch Club of the Year winner with three areas: the main bar has three snooker tables and a dartboard, the end bar has a large-screen TV showing football matches, horse racing and other sport, and there is a third no-smoking room. A large function room holds the annual beer festival in October. Further function rooms are available upstairs. Show a CAMRA membership card or copy of this Guide for entry. ❀⛟♣P🔻

Mobberley

Roebuck
Mill Lane, WA16 7HX (signposted from the B5085)
✪ 12-11 (10.30 Sun)
☎ (01565) 873322 ⊕ theroebuck.com
Greene King Old Speckled Hen; Taylor Landlord; Tetley Bitter; guest beer ⓗ
Tucked away in a tranquil part of Cheshire, this fashionable restaurant/pub has a wine bar atmosphere and a clean, modern farmhouse style. The three open rooms have timber and tiled floors with scrubbed wooden tables. The emphasis is on food with an adventurous menu of home-cooked local produce, but the quality of the beer is always a priority. A private function room is available. ♨❀⑩P

Mow Cop

Crown Inn
16 Chapel Street, Mount Pleasant, ST7 4NT
✪ 4-midnight; 12-1am Fri & Sat; 12-12.30am Sun
☎ (01782) 511331
Tetley Imperial; guest beers ⓗ
Reopened in 2006 following five years closure, this exceptionally friendly free house is at the heart of the village. It is situated one mile uphill from Kent Green Wharf Marina on the Macclesfield Canal. The interior is open plan but with distinct areas – furniture ranges from leather sofas to bar stools. Catering for all ages, sport on TV is popular but does not dominate. The guest beers are sourced nationwide including unusual micros. Beer prices are very low for the area. ♨❀♣🔻

Nantwich

Black Lion
29 Welsh Row, CW5 5ED
✪ 4 (1 Sat)-11; 1-10.30 Sun
☎ (01270) 628711
Titanic White Star; Weetwood Best Bitter, Old Dog, Oasthouse Gold ⓗ
This 350-year-old building has many nooks, including a comfy lounge upstairs (the stairs are adjacent to the bar) complete with sofas, and an outdoor heated conservatory. A hub of social activity with quizzes, pub games (including chess) and live music throughout the week. Dogs welcome, as long as they don't mind sharing with the resident hounds. Q⛟❍♣P

Crown Hotel
24 High Street, CW5 5AS
✪ 11-midnight
☎ (01270) 625283 ⊕ crownhotelnantwich.com
Boddingtons Bitter; Draught Bass; guest beer ⓗ
Originally mentioned in the Domesday Book, the Crown was destroyed in the 1583 fire of Nantwich – the current building dates from 1585. The interior comprises a traditional bar, carvery and Italian restaurant. Real ale is available throughout with table service. Guest ales are mainly sourced from Salopian and Storm. With regular jazz played in the bar, the Crown enthusiastically supports Nantwich music festivals and hosts live music in the upstairs ballroom. Nantwich station is a five-minute walk away. ♨❀⛵⑩♿⛟P🔻

Rifleman
68 James Hall Street, CW5 5QE
✪ 1-midnight Mon; 2-1am Tue & Wed; 2-midnight Thu; 1-1am Fri; 11-1am Sat; 12-1am Sun
☎ (01270) 629977
Robinson's Hatters, Unicorn ⓗ
Small, friendly pub tucked away in a side street to the north of the town centre. Known locally as the Gun, the pub was voted Community Pub of the Year 2007 by South Cheshire CAMRA. Darts and dominoes teams play in local leagues and there is a pool table in a separate room. Occasional live music is hosted at weekends. Nantwich rail and bus stations are both nearby. ♨❀♿⛟♣P🔻

Northwich

Penny Black

110 Witton Street, CW9 5AB
☼ 9am-midnight (1am Fri & Sat)
☎ (01606) 42029
Greene King Abbot; Marston's Pedigree; Tetley Bitter; guest beers Ⓗ
Converted from the former town post office (hence the name), this Grade II listed black and white building designed in 1914 is the town's largest liftable building. Now a Wetherspoon's outlet, it features up to seven guest beers plus real cider from Weston's. The high roof has numerous skylights creating a bright and airy feel. The small car park is reached from Meadow Street by a sharp right turn immediately after the new Royal Mail sorting office. Q❧☼➊⅃♿≠╤◆P┖

Parkgate

Ship Hotel

The Parade, CH64 6SA
☼ 11-11; 12-10.30 Sun
☎ (0151) 336 3931
Tetley Bitter; guest beers Ⓗ
Large whitewashed hotel on the front at Parkgate, with dramatic views towards the Welsh hills. The hotel dates from 1758, when it was known as the Union Hotel, and has a through lounge (featuring historic photographs of old Parkgate) and a public bar. All cask ales are sold in the lounge. The hotel enthusiastically promotes local micro-breweries such as Spitting Feathers, Weetwood, Woodlands, Brimstage and Station House. Q❀✿➊⅃╤◆P┖

Penketh

Ferry Tavern

Station Road, WA5 2UJ
☼ 12-3, 5.30-11; 12-11.30 Sat; 12-10.30 Sun
☎ (01925) 791117 ⊕ theferrytavern.com
Boddingtons Bitter; Greene King Ruddles County, Abbot; guest beers Ⓗ
Situated on the Trans Pennine Trail between the Sankey Canal and River Mersey, the pub is popular with walkers, cyclists and locals. Dogs on leads are also welcome in the non-carpeted areas. Up to three guest ales as well as real cider and a large collection of Scotch and Irish whiskies are stocked. Meals are served on Monday to Friday lunchtimes. A large outdoor drinking area is busy in summer. ⚞Q❧☼➊⅃◆P┖

Peover Heath

Dog Inn

Wellbank Lane, WA16 8UP (off A50 at Whipping Stocks Inn and continue for 2 miles) OS792735
☼ 11.30-3, 4.30-11; 11.30-11 Sat; 12-10.30 Sun
☎ (01625) 861421 ⊕ doginn-overpeover.co.uk
Copper Dragon Scotts 1816; Hydes Bitter; Moorhouses Black Cat; Weetwood Best Bitter Ⓗ
This rambling pub, converted from a row of 18th-century cottages, has a tap room for pool and darts, a comfortable lounge bar with a real fire and an extensive restaurant (meals available all day Sunday). There is an attractive patio at the front as well as a small beer garden next to the car park. Quiz nights on Thursday and Sunday are very popular, and live music usually plays once a month on Friday. ⚞❀✿➊⅃☐♿◆P┖

Poynton

Royal British Legion

Georges Road West, SK12 1JY
☼ 12-11; 12-10.30 Sun
☎ (01625) 873120
Beer range varies Ⓗ
Extensive, comfortable and welcoming club that brings a much needed variety of real ale to Poynton. The frequently changing guest beers are invariably from micros. Beer festivals are held twice a year in spring and autumn. The club hosts regular social evenings including live music – folk nights are a highlight. The large-screen TV in one room offers regular live sporting events. Non-members can be signed in. Q❀⅃≠╤◆P

Sandbach

Cricketers

54 Crewe Road, CW11 4NN
☼ 4.30 (4 Fri, 12 Sat)-1am; 12-1am Sun
☎ (01270) 766960
Hydes Dark Mild, Original Bitter; guest beers Ⓗ
Terraced house on the edge of town, rejuvenated by the present landlords. The building has been opened out and brightened up, with a warming real fire in winter. It has a friendly atmosphere attracting a good mixture of ages, and can be lively at times, particularly when sport is shown on TV. There are three guest ales, usually from micros, and a new decked smoking area has been added outside. ⚞❀╤◆┖

Saughall

Greyhound Inn

Seahill Road, CH1 6BJ
☼ 11.30-11.30; 12-10.30 Sun
☎ (01244) 880205
Beer range varies Ⓗ
Large, friendly, historic pub in an attractive village 20 minutes by bus from the centre of Chester and close to the Chester to Shotton cycleway. The multi-roomed interior is served by a central bar, offering up to six beers. Usually at least one local beer is available and a guest cider and perry alternate. Smoking is permitted in the outside, covered, heated area. No food is served on Sunday evening. Q❀➊╤◆●P┖

Smallwood

Blue Bell

Spen Green, CW11 2XA (between A50, A534 & A34 W of Congleton) OS820607
☼ 12-3, 5-11; 12 -11 Fri & Sat; 12 -10.30 Sun
☎ (01477) 500262
Black Sheep Best Bitter; Caledonian Deuchars IPA; guest beers Ⓗ
The Blue Bell was built in 1727 as a farmstead and ale house, and nestles alongside surrounding farm buildings. The three-room

interior has low beamed ceilings, with a real fire in winter, and is free of fruit machines or music. There is a large secure garden area that provides facilities for smokers. Food may be available early evening from Tuesday to Thursday, and there is occasional live music on Wednesday. ⚌Q🏠◑🍴🖾♣P↳

Stoak

Bunbury Arms

Little Stanney Lane, CH2 4HW (signposted off A5117)
✪ 12-11 (10.30 Sun)
☎ (01244) 301665
Beer range varies Ⓗ

Built in the 16th century, this attractive red-brick pub is situated in a tiny hamlet, bordering a small wood, with moorings on the Shropshire Union Canal close by. Comprising a small public bar and smart open plan lounge, there are four handpumps regularly serving a range of guest ales from local breweries. This traditional yet food oriented pub is a hidden gem and a popular retreat for walkers and cyclists, packing the usually tranquil beer garden during the summer months.
⚌Q🏠◑ 🖾♿🖾(4)♣P↳

Sutton

Sutton Hall

Bullocks Lane, SK11 0HE (off the old London Road, between Macclesfield and Sutton)
✪ 10-midnight
☎ (01260) 253211
Hydes Original Bitter; Marston's Burton Bitter; guest beer Ⓗ

The solid beams and 16th-century woodwork are evidence of the age of this building, dating from the 1200s. Once the centre of a vast estate belonging to Richard Sutton, the building has been a pub for the last 24 years, run by the present owners throughout. Inside, beware those low beams! A suit of armour stands beside one of the huge fireplaces and a wooden elephant opposite the bar. The food here is renowned locally. The guest ale alternates between Moorhouses Blonde Witch and Pride of Pendle. ⚌Q🏠🌿◑🖾P

Tushingham

Blue Bell Inn

SY13 4QS (signed Bell' O' Th' Hill from A41)
✪ 12-3 (not Mon), 6-11 (midnight Fri & Sat); 12-3, 7-11 Sun
☎ (01948) 662172
Copper Dragon Golden Pippin; Salopian Shropshire Gold; guest beers Ⓗ

Wonderful black and white timber-framed 17th-century Cheshire pub with plenty of atmosphere just off the A41. A cobbled entrance leads to an ancient, heavy front door. The main bar is popular with friendly regulars as well as visitors. Well-behaved dogs are welcome in the bar. One of the walls in the dining area features part of the pub's original wattle and daub. ⚌Q🌿🏠◑🖾♣P

Warmingham

Bear's Paw

School Lane, CW11 3QN
✪ 5 (12 Sat & Sun)-11
☎ (01270) 526317 ⊕ thebearspaw.co.uk
Tetley Bitter; guest beers Ⓗ

A successful blend of local pub, restaurant and hotel within an impressive red brick building. To one side is an open plan bar with a raised seating area and a 'sports' bar to the rear. On the other is a stylish restaurant area. Bar snacks are also available (food is served all day at the weekends). Accommodation is offered in 12 en-suite rooms. Quality food is matched by excellent beers, frequently from local or smaller breweries. 🏠⚌◑🖾♣P↳

Warrington

Bull's Head

33 Church Street, WA1 2SS
✪ 12-11 (10.30 Sun)
☎ (01925) 635680
Cains Bitter; Wells Bombardier; guest beers Ⓗ

Though situated on the edge of the town centre, this feels more like a country pub. On one side is the bar, on the other a comfortable lounge with a low ceiling. A small snug is hidden behind the bar and an even smaller room, adorned with the history of the pub's bowling team, even more hidden to the side. The sports bar at the back, catering for larger parties, overlooks the bowling green. Runner-up CAMRA branch Community Pub of the Year. 🏠🖾≈(Central)🖾♣

Lower Angel

27 Buttermarket Street, WA1 2LY
✪ 12-7; 11-midnight Fri & Sat; closed Sun
☎ (01925) 633299
Tetley Mild, Bitter, Burton Ale; guest beer Ⓗ

Traditional, two-room, town centre pub, with a public bar and smarter lounge, unspoilt by so called modernisation. A change in the licensee has seen the return of the Walkers window in the lounge, highlighting the pub's history. It's a winner of many CAMRA local and regional awards over the past 20 years. Buses from the south and east of Warrington all stop within 100 yards of pub. 🖾≈(Central)🖾

Tavern

25 Church Street, WA1 2SS
✪ 2-11; 12-11.30 Fri & Sat; 12-11 Sun
☎ (01925) 577990
Beer range varies Ⓗ

Fortunately for Warrington drinkers, the two best pubs in town are next door to each other! This single-room pub, a genuine free house, continues to go from strength to strength, offering six beers, invariably from micro-breweries. An interesting range of bottled Belgian beers, as well as Scotch and Irish whiskies, are also available. The courtyard at the back eases some of the congestion on Rugby League match nights. Sky TV is screened. Buses from the east of town stop 100 yards from pub. 🏠≈(Central)🖾

Weston Village

Royal Oak
187 Heath Road South, WA7 4RP
⊕ 12-11.30 (11 Sun)
☎ (01928) 580908
Adnams Broadside; Cains Bitter; Highgate Mild; Wells Bombardier ⊞
Situated in the centre of Weston Village, this family-run pub caters for the local community and is welcoming to all, offering darts and dominoes in a comfortable, open plan bar. It hosts karaoke on a Friday evening and features live music on Saturday evenings on a regular basis; themed nights take place throughout the year. Outside is a large enclosed garden popular in the summer months. Food is available in the evening except Sunday. Q❀⊕⅄♣≃

Wettenhall

Little Man
Winsford Road, CW7 4DL
⊕ 12.30-4.30, 7-midnight (10.30 Sun)
☎ (01270) 528203
Beer range varies ⊞
Believed to be named after a 19th-century local character, this rural inn serves the farming and equestrian communities. One side of the pub has a public bar feel, with televised sport; the other opens out into a comfortable dining area with a welcoming fire in winter. There are usually four beers available, from the length and breadth of the country, and dogs are welcome.
🚶❀⊕⅄P≃–⊟

Wheelock

Nag's Head
504 Crewe Road, CW11 3RL (at A534/Mill Lane jct)
⊕ 12-2am
☎ (01270) 762457
Beer range varies ⊞
This attractive black and white pub offers three changing guest beers from micros, frequently Storm and Titanic. A traditional family pub, there is a public bar to the rear where sport is shown on TV. A small dining area with a real fire is at one end, adjoining a large L-shaped lounge. An outdoor covered area is provided for smokers. Live music plays at weekends in summer, and quarterly mini-beer festivals are held. 🚶❀⊕⅄⊟≃–

Widnes

Four Topped Oak
2 Hough Green Road, WA8 4PE
⊕ 12-11 (midnight Thu-Sat)
☎ (0151) 257 8030
Cains Bitter; Fuller's London Pride; guest beer ⊞
Well laid out, comfortable pub, decorated in a modern style, with a number of different areas in which to sit. A calming and relaxed atmosphere prevails, with friendly staff. Food is served until 9pm. Occasional themed beer promotions are offered. There is a large outside patio area. Children under 14 are not permitted. ❀⊕⅄P

Willey Moor

Willey Moor Lock Tavern
Tarporley Road, SY13 4HF (300m from A49)
OS534452
⊕ 12-2.30 (3 summer), 6-11; 7 (6 summer)-10.30 Sun
☎ (01948) 663274
Theakston Best Bitter; guest beers ⊞
Accessed by a footbridge over the Llangollen Canal, the Willey Moor was a former lock keeper's cottage. This genuine free house always has an esoteric range of up to five beers on offer. It is popular with canal boaters and walkers on the nearby Sandstone Trail. The interior is comfortably furnished with padded wall seats, local watercolour paintings and a collection of teapots. Real fires warm in winter and an outside terrace plus enclosed beer garden are pleasant in summer. 🚶❀⊕P

Wilmslow

Coach & Four
69-71 Alderley Road, SK9 1PA
⊕ 11.30-11 (midnight Fri); 12-midnight Sat; 12-11 Sun
☎ (01625) 525046
Hydes 1863, Original Bitter, Jekyll's Gold; guest beer ⊞
This large and comfortable Hyde's pub caters for a mixed clientele of drinkers, diners and residents. The seating area on two sides of the bar is divided by screens to give smaller secluded areas, including a snug. Travel-lodge style accommodation is attached to the pub, and a full English breakfast is served until mid-morning. Friday evening features live bands, and quiz night is Sunday. ❀⊨⅄⇌⊟P≃

Rifleman's Arms
113 Moor Road, SK9 6BY
⊕ 12-11 (10.30 Sun)
☎ (01625) 537235 ⊕ riflemansarms.co.uk
Boddingtons Bitter; Theakston Mild, Best Bitter; guest beers ⊞
Some distance from the town centre, this is a spacious pre-war roadhouse that never got its road and is now a popular locals' pub. The central bar serves both the lounge and the vault or public bar where darts and dominoes are played. Dogs are welcome here. The gardens and patio area are fully enclosed, making them safe for children. ❀⊨⅄⊟♣P

Wincle

Ship
SK11 0QE (off A54 near Danebridge) OS652962
⊕ 12-3, 6.30 (5.30 Fri)-11; closed Mon; 12-11 Sat; 12-10.30 Sun
☎ (01260) 227217
Fuller's London Pride; Moorhouses Premier; guest beers ⊞
One of the rare Fuller's outlets in the area, this attractive 16th-century sandstone inn is very popular, and can become busy on summer weekends. The drinks menu features a range of bottle-conditioned beers, with tasting notes. The pub is well known for its imaginative menu. Local CAMRA Pub of the Year 2006, it holds a beer festival on August bank holiday. The two guest ales usually include a mild. 🚶Q⊁❀⊕⅄♣P

Pubs Transport – 2008

JOURNEY PLANNING

To plan a journey involving bus, coach and rail or all three together try:
Website: www.traveline.org.uk

BUSES

National Traveline: a standard call service giving countrywide information
Telephone: 0870 608 2608
Textphone: 0870 241 2216

COACHES

For longer distance coach service timetables and planners contact:
National Express
Telephone: 08705 808080
Website: www.nationalexpress.co.uk

SCOTTISH CITYLINK

Telephone: 08705 505050
Website: www.citylink.co.uk

TRAINS

The national hotline for all train information is:
Telephone: 08457 484950
Minicom: 0845 60 50 600

ALE TRAILS

Many local authorities and some transport operators have a programme of local public-transport based Ale Trails with publicity leaflets listing timetables and pubs to visit. These help both transport and local pubs. Contact your local council for details.

Good Beer Guide Belgium
Tim Webb

Now in its 5th edition and in full colour, this book has developed a cult following among committed beer lovers and beer tourists. It is the definitive, totally independent guide to understanding and finding the best Belgian beer and an essential companion for any beer drinker visiting Belgium or seeking out Belgian beer in Britain. Includes details of the 120 breweries and over 800 beers in regular production, as well as 500 of the best hand-picked cafés in Belgium.

£12.99   ISBN: 978 1 85249 210 6

CORNWALL

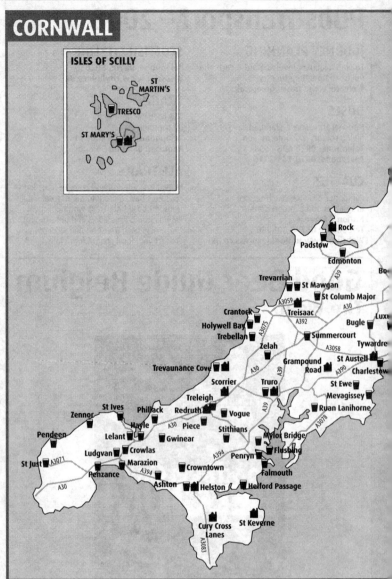

ISLES OF SCILLY

ST MARTIN'S
TRESCO
ST MARY'S

Rock
Padstow
Edmonton
Trevarrian
St Mawgan
St Columb Major
Crantock
Treisaac
Bugle
Luxu
Holywell Bay
Trebellan
Summercourt
Tywardre
Zelah
St Austell
Grampound Road
Charlestow
Trevaunance Cove
Scorrier
Truro
St Ewe
Treleigh
Mevagissey
St Ives
Phillack
Redruth
Vogue
Ruan Lanihorne
Zennor
Hayle
Piece
Stithians
Pendeen
Lelant
Gwinear
Mylor Bridge
Flushing
Ludgvan
Crowlas
Penryn
St Just
Marazion
Crowntown
Falmouth
Penzance
Ashton
Helston
Helford Passage
Cury Cross Lanes
St Keverne

Ashton

Lion & Lamb

Fore Street, TR13 9RW (on A394, Helston-Penzance road)

✪ 12-11 (11.30 Fri & Sat)

☎ (01736) 763227

Sharp's Doom Bar; Shepherd Neame Spitfire; Skinner's Betty Stogs; guest beers Ⓗ

Newly refurbished and welcoming family-run pub with a large single bar. Up to six ales in the busy summer months are reduced to four during winter; guest beers change regularly. A superb floral display adorns the seating area at the front of the pub and there is a grass area behind with more seating and space for camping. Children and dogs are welcome. Live entertainment plays on Friday evening and some Saturdays – local choirs are always popular. Bar snacks are available between main mealtimes. ❀◐▲⊞❤P⌐

Blisland

Blisland Inn

The Green, PL30 4JF

✪ 11.30-11; 12-10.30 Sun

☎ (01208) 850739

Beer range varies Ⓗ/Ⓖ

Set in an idyllic location on the green of a moorland village, this granite pub is well worth seeking out. A friendly community inn, it has a warm and welcoming atmosphere. Eclectic decor includes numerous barometers, toby jugs, beer mats and pump clips. CAMRA National Pub of the Year in 2000, it is famous

Cornish brewery. The restaurant offers freshly-cooked, locally-sourced food including daily specials and a Sunday roast. Popular with cyclists and walkers; children and dogs are also welcome. Q ♿ 🕎 ☕ ◖◗ ▲ P

Bude

Bencoolen Inn

Bencoolen Road, EX23 8PJ
⊘ 12-midnight
☎ (01288) 3546494
St Austell Tribute; Sharp's Doom Bar, Own; guest beer Ⓗ
Spacious, friendly hostelry with a huge U-shaped bar in the centre. All beers can be served by gravity on request. Named after a local ship that was wrecked in 1862, some of the timbers were used in the pub's construction. Diners can enjoy a la carte international cuisine with a Spanish flair in the restaurant; food is also available in the bar lunchtimes and evenings. There is wheelchair access to the restaurant only.
Q ♿ 🕎 ◖◗ ▲ 🖼 P ⌐

Bugle

Bugle Inn

57 Fore Street, PL26 8PB (on A391)
⊘ 11-midnight
☎ (01726) 850307
St Austell IPA, Dartmoor Best, Tribute Ⓗ
Warm and welcoming village-centre local that gets its name from the sound of the horn as the stagecoaches used to pass through. Located in the middle of Cornwall, with five en-suite B&B rooms, this family-friendly pub is a convenient base for attractions such as the Eden Project, five kilometres away. Meals are served all day, with breakfast from 8am. Entertainment includes darts, pool and the juke box, and live music most Sunday evenings. 🕎 🛏 ◖◗ ≠ 🖼 ♣ P

Charlestown

Harbourside Inn

Charlestown Road, PL25 3 NJ (on harbour front)
⊘ 11-11 (midnight Fri & Sat)
☎ (01726) 67955
Fuller's London Pride; St Austell Tribute; Sharp's Own; Skinner's Cornish Knocker; guest beer Ⓗ
Modern bar on the waterfront attached to the Pier House Hotel. A sympathetic conversion of

for the range and quality of its beers, with six or seven constantly changing real ales. The bar menu features good home-cooked food.
🖼 Q 🕎 ♿ ☕ ◖ ♣ 🖼 P ⌐

Bodmin

Bodmin Jail

Berrycoombe Road, PL31 2NR
⊘ 11-11 (midnight Sat); 12-11 Sun
☎ (01208) 76292
Brains SA; Princetown Jail Ale; St Austell Proper Job IPA; guest beer Ⓗ
Once the site of the infamous Bodmin jail, a tour of the prison museum is a must. The pub has recently been refurbished to create a comfortable lounge/dining area. The guest ale varies regularly though it is usually from a

INDEPENDENT BREWERIES

Ales of Scilly St Mary's
Atlantic Treisaac
Blackawton Saltash
Blue Anchor Helston
Coastal Redruth
Doghouse Scorrier
Driftwood Trevaunance Cove
Keltek Redruth
Lizard St Keverne
Organic Cury Cross Lanes
Sharp's Rock
Skinner's Truro
St Austell St Austell
Wooden Hand Grampound Road

an old warehouse with exposed stone and wooden flooring, it has a large glass doorway providing views over the harbour and historic tall ships often moored there. Up to seven real ales are on offer; the Sharp's and Skinner's beers may vary and the guest ale changes regularly. Cider is also available on handpump. Food is served all day. ✿◑▣🗅

Crantock

Old Albion

Langurroc Road, TR8 5RB
✪ 12 (2 winter Mon-Thu)-midnight; 12-11 Sun
☎ (01637) 830243
Courage Best Bitter; Skinner's Betty Stogs; guest beer Ⓗ
Village pub tucked away down a lane leading to the church. The pub has a history of smuggling, with secret tunnels to the beach caves and church. Up to two guest ales are usually available in summer when the pub is busy with visitors attracted by the good value meals. There is a pleasant outdoor drinking area, and sandy dunes and the beach nearby. The pub is handy for camping and caravan facilities as well as hotel and B&B accommodation. ⚐🛏🐕✿◑▲🗅🅿🚶

Cremyll

Edgecumbe Arms

PL10 1HX (on B3247)
✪ 11-11; 12-10.30 Sun
☎ (01752) 822294
St Austell Tinners, Tribute, Proper Job IPA, HSD Ⓗ
Large and comfortable 18th-century inn, easily reached by foot ferry from Plymouth. Situated at the start of the Cornish section of the south west coast path, it is also handy for Mount Edgcumbe Country Park. The wood-panelled interior has low ceilings, a slate-flagged bar and several snugs for cosier drinking. Outside tables by the river bank afford superb views across the River Tamar. ✿🛏◑♿▲🗅

Crowlas

Star Inn

TR20 8DX (on A30)
✪ 11.30-11; 12-10.30 Sun
☎ (01736) 740375
Beer range varies Ⓗ
Friendly roadside pub on the A30, Cornwall CAMRA's Pub of the Year 2007. The spacious room has a long bar sporting several handpumps dispensing ever-changing real ales, mostly from micro-breweries. A beer drinkers' local where conversation is the main entertainment, food is limited to good quality pub grub, available Thursday to Sunday in summer. A small boat hanging from the ceiling was used in the Crowlas flood of 2003. Good value B&B makes the Star an excellent base for local pub crawling. Q🛏◑⊟▲🗅🅿♣

Crowntown

Crown Inn

TR13 0AD (on B3303)
✪ 5.30-11; 7-10.30 Sun
☎ (01326) 565538 ⊕ crownlodges.co.uk

Skinner's Betty Stogs, Cornish Knocker; guest beer Ⓖ
Old granite free house, once a hunting lodge on the Trevarno estate, now a community pub where conversation dominates. Although a single bar, it has distinct drinking areas, a dining space and a pool room. Occasional live entertainment and quiz nights are hosted. The guest beers vary frequently, favouring Cornish breweries. Unusually, the ales are dispensed by gravity straight from the cellar, despite the array of four handpumps (complete with pump clips) on the bar. ✿🛏◑♿♣♠🅿

Edmonton

Quarryman Inn

PL27 7JA (just off A39 near Royal Cornwall Showground)
✪ 12-10.30 (11 Fri & Sat)
☎ (01208) 816444
Oakham JHB; guest beers Ⓗ
Real gem of a pub, well worth a visit – but beware the landlord who becomes irascible if mobile phones are not switched off. This convivial pub is full of character and conversation thrives. The interior divides into public bar and lounge/dining area, with an eclectic collection of bric-a-brac. The beer menu includes one ale from Skinner's and up to two from other micro-breweries. Buses run along the A39, 10 minutes' walk away. ⚐Q✿◑⊟▲🗅🅿

Falmouth

Oddfellows Arms

Quay Hill, TR11 3HG
✪ 12-11 (10.30 Sun)
☎ (01326) 318530 ⊕ theoddfellowsarms.co.uk
Sharp's Eden Ale, Special; Ⓗ **guest beers** Ⓖ
Small but perfectly formed, this basic, unpretentious, single bar pub tucked up a side street is a real locals' local near the town centre. The Sharp's beers are supplemented by ever-changing guest ales served straight from the cask behind the bar. Games include euchre and darts, and there is a small pool room to the rear. The pub holds an annual 'cake fest' in June, hotly contested by the locals. ≈🗅♣

Seven Stars ☆

The Moor, TR11 3QA
✪ 11-3, 6-11; 12-3, 7-10.30 Sun
☎ (01326) 312111 ⊕ sevenstarsfalmouth.co.uk
Draught Bass; Sharp's Special; Skinner's Cornish Knocker; guest beers Ⓖ
Run by a priest, this local is an unspoilt, old town-centre pub with lively narrow tap room and quiet snug at the back. The old 'bottle & jug' hatch still exists for outside drinkers. The Sharp's and Skinner's beers alternate; note the eccentrically-designed stillage. The planked bar ceiling is festooned with key fobs while the ancient bar top shows distinct signs of warping. This is Cornwall's only entry in CAMRA's National Inventory of Historic Pub Interiors. Q✿≈🗅♣

Flushing

Seven Stars

3 Trefusis Road, TR11 5TY (on waterfront)
🕙 11 (12 Sun)-11
☎ (01326) 374373

Sharp's Doom Bar; Skinner's Betty Stogs, Cornish Knocker, seasonal beer ⊞

Central village pub with tables outside overlooking the Penryn River, popular with locals and visitors. Inside is a large, well-furnished L-shaped bar and restaurant serving good, reasonably-priced food – fish is a speciality. Parking is difficult; easiest access to the pub during the daytime is via a short trip on the foot passenger ferry from Falmouth.
🏬Q🌼🕦🖵

Fowey

Galleon Inn

12 Fore Street, PL23 1AQ
🕙 11 (12 Sun)-11 (midnight summer)
☎ (01726) 833014 🌐 galleon-inn.co.uk

Draught Bass; Sharp's Cornish Coaster, Doom Bar; guest beer ⊞

Riverside pub in the town centre dating back 400 years – the only untied pub in Fowey featuring Cornish real ales. There are delightful river views throughout the modernised, wood-panelled main bar and conservatory. Outside tables are placed on the quay wall and in a sheltered courtyard with heaters. A wide range of meals is available daily. There is a pool table in the bar. Accommodation is in seven rooms, all en-suite and most with river views. 🏬Q🌼🖼🕦&🛆🖵🌼⏻

Ship Inn

3 Trafalgar Square, PL23 1AZ
🕙 10-11 (midnight Mon-Wed; 1am Thu-Sat summer);
10-11 (midnight summer) Sun
☎ (01726) 832230

St Austell Tinners, Tribute, HSD ⊞

Historic pub, once the squire's town house, patronised by many a famous name in British naval history. One block from the town quay, this comfortable single bar pub retains much of its ancient charm. It boasts a roaring log fire in winter, two snugs (one with booths, the other with overstuffed sofas) and an upstairs dining room. Excellent meals are served all day in summer, lunchtime and evenings in winter. Seven letting rooms are available, two en suite. 🏬Q🖼🕦🛆🖵

Gwinear

Royal Standard Inn

50 Churchtown, TR27 5JL
🕙 7-11 (midnight Thu); 12-midnight Fri & Sat; 12-3,
7-10.30 Sun
☎ (01736) 850080

Skinner's Cornish Knocker; guest beers ⊞

Originally a mining courthouse, now a community-oriented free house in a quiet village. The single bar is decorated with heraldic flags and ancient weaponry, with cushioned sofas adding to the quiet, comfortable atmosphere. It has a separate games area and dining room serving quality food, Thursday-Saturday evenings, and a Sunday lunchtime carvery (barbecue in

summer). Outside, a sheltered rear patio and extensive beer garden are popular. The Skinner's beer may be supplemented by another from the range. 🏬Q🌼🕦🛆🅿

Hayle

Cornish Arms

86 Commercial Road, TR27 4DJ (on B3301, between Copperhouse and Hayle)
🕙 11.30-3, 5.30-midnight; 11.30-midnight Sat & summer; 12-midnight Sun
☎ (01736) 753237

St Austell IPA, Tinners, Dartmoor Best, Tribute, HSD ⊞

Roomy and convivial locals' pub, popular with a broad mix of the community. The 'public' has a pool table; the more spacious lounge houses the dartboard. An extension to the back of the pub serves as a restaurant, and there is a beer garden beyond. It is one of the few pubs to feature most of St Austell's real ales, as the array of handpumps testifies – check both bars, as an extra seasonal brew may also be available. 🏬🌼🕦🖵🛆🗺🖵🌼🅿

Helford Passage

Ferry Boat Inn

TR11 5LB
🕙 10 (11.30 Sun)-midnight
☎ (01326) 250625

St Austell Tinners, Tribute, HSD ⊞

Large open-plan pub in an idyllic creekside position overlooking its own beach and the Helford River. The walls and beamed ceilings of the bar are festooned with an eclectic mix of nautical bric-a-brac including a wooden ship's mast. The bar itself is set into three stone arches. Wooden furniture is complemented by leather-style sofas. The patio affords good views over the water. Convenient for Trebah and Glendurgan gardens nearby. 🏬🌼🖼🕦🖵🅿

Helston

Blue Anchor

50 Coinagehall Street, TR13 8EU
🕙 10.30-midnight (11 Sun)
☎ (01326) 562821 🌐 spingoales.com

Blue Anchor Spingo Jubilee, Middle, Special, seasonal beers ⊞/🅖

Rambling, unspoilt 15th-century granite building with a thatched roof and its own brewery at the rear. It has appeared in every edition of the Guide since 1973. There are no distracting games machines or juke box – conversation flourishes in the two small bars. An indoor skittle alley with its own bar can be booked for group functions. The occasional seasonal beer may be a winter warmer or other commemorative brew – a 'bragget' or honey and herb based beer appears in summer. 🏬Q🍴🌼🖼🕦🖵🖵🌼

Holywell Bay

St Piran's Inn

TR8 5PP
🕙 5-midnight (11-11 Fri-Sat & summer); 12-3.30
(midnight summer) Sun

☎ (01637) 830205
St Austell Tribute; Shepherd Neame Spitfire; guest beer Ⓗ
Free house in a converted pair of coastguard cottages situated an easy walk away from a golden sandy beach. The beamed interior is spacious with wood furnishings, much bric-a-brac and an open fire in winter creating a homely, welcoming atmosphere. An imaginative menu of good food is available. The pub offers a range of frequently changing guest beers (up to four in summer), usually including at least one local brew. Families (and dogs) are welcome.
🏠Q🗑️🌟🕙🚃⅄🏘️P⸜

Lelant

Watermill Inn
TR27 6LQ (off A3074, on secondary St Ives road)
🕐 11-11; 12-10.30 Sun
☎ (01736) 757912
Sharp's Doom Bar; guest beers Ⓗ
Former 18th-century mill house, set in beautiful surroundings, converted to a pub downstairs, with the former mill loft upstairs open evenings as a restaurant. The bar is a single room divided into drinking and dining areas, with the business-end mechanism of the waterwheel on view inside. An extensive beer garden straddles the mill stream; families with children are welcome. An annual beer festival is held in late June. Lelant Saltings station is a short walk away. 🏠Q🌟🕙🚃⅄🚉🏘️P

Lostwithiel

Globe Inn
3 North Street, PL22 0EG (off A390)
🕐 12-2.30, 6-11; 12-2.30, 7-10.30 Sun
☎ (01208) 872501 ⊕ globeinn.com
Sharp's Doom Bar; Skinner's Betty Stogs; guest beer Ⓗ
Cosy 13th-century pub in the narrow streets of this old town, close to the medieval river bridge and station. The rambling old building has a single bar with several drinking and dining spaces, opening on to a restaurant and a sheltered sun-trap patio. Good home-cooked food is available from an extensive menu. Live music plays on Wednesday evening. The pub is named after the ship on which a member of a former owners' family was killed in a sea battle in 1813. Q🌟🚃🕙🚉⅄🚉

Ludgvan

White Hart
Churchtown, TR20 8EY (on B3309)
🕐 12-3, 5.30-11; 12-3, 7-10.30 Sun
☎ (01736) 740574
Draught Bass; Flowers IPA; Greene King Abbot; Sharp's Doom Bar Ⓖ
Popular village local, this unspoilt 14th-century inn is next to the church. Uneven floorboards reflect the pub's age and the wooden partitions, large wood-burning stoves, interesting furniture and old photographs give the alcoves and corners an authentic atmosphere. Beer is dispensed direct from casks behind the bar. The pub's menu offers generous helpings of excellent,

good value food, much of it made from local ingredients (no food Mon Oct-March). The car park is shared with the church. 🏠Q🌟🕙🚉P

Luxulyan

King's Arms
Bridges, PL30 5EF
🕐 12-midnight (11.30 Sun)
☎ (01726) 850202
St Austell Tinners, Tribute, HSD Ⓗ
Granite village pub, locally known as 'Bridges', offering a friendly, no-nonsense welcome to all, including children and dogs. Recently tastefully refurbished, the spacious single room is partially divided into lounge and bar areas. The lounge is for drinking and dining, there is a pool table in the bar. The pub can be reached via the beautiful Luxulyan Valley, where many remnants of the area's industrial past remain. It is on the Atlantic Coast Line rail ale trail. Q🌟🕙⅄🚉P

Marazion

King's Arms
The Square, TR17 0AP
🕐 11-11; 12-10.30 Sun
☎ (01736) 710291
St Austell Tribute, HSD Ⓗ
Old market-corner pub opposite the ferry quay for St Michael's Mount. A true local, although popular with tourists in the season, it is a small but comfortable family-friendly bar. Additional seating is available on the pavement outside. Local produce features on an imaginative menu. Quiz night is Tuesday. On the first Thursday evening of the month there is a musical jam session, with visitors welcome to join in. An extra ale from St Austell may appear in summer.
🏠Q🌟🕙⅄🚉🚉♣

Mevagissey

Fountain Inn
3 Cliff Street, PL26 6QH
🕐 11.30-11; 12-10.30 Sun
☎ (01726) 842320
St Austell Tinners, HSD Ⓗ
Friendly, two bar 15th-century inn with slate floors, stone walls, historic photographs and low beams – the tunnel to the side door is particularly low. You can still see signs of the pilchard press once housed in the Smugglers Bar – a glass plate in the floor covers the pit where the fish oil was caught, which doubled as a store for contraband. The meat was compressed to feed Nelson's navy. Buses serve St Austell and the Lost Gardens of Heligan. 🏠Q🚃🕙🚉

Morwenstow

Bush Inn
Cross Town, EX23 9SR (off A39 N of Kilkhampton)
🕐 11-midnight
☎ (01288) 331242 ⊕ bushinn-morwenstow.co.uk
St Austell HSD; Skinner's Betty Stogs; guest beer Ⓗ
This ancient building, once a chapel, dates in parts back to 950AD. A welcoming country inn,

log fires burn in several of the quaint old rooms. Hearty meals sourced from local produce are available all day, served in a new restaurant extension at the back. There is a covered smokers' area in the ancient courtyard at the front of the pub. The large garden offers superb views over the valley and out to sea. ♨Q❀🛏◑♿⛺🚌♣P⚡

Mylor Bridge

Lemon Arms

Lemon Hill, TR11 5NA (off A393 at Penryn)
⏲ 11-3, 6-11; 12-3, 7-11 Sun
☎ (01326) 373666
St Austell Tinners, Tribute, HSD Ⓗ
There has been an inn on this site since 1765. This friendly, one bar pub at the village centre is popular with local sports teams. Good home-cooked food is available, and families with children are made most welcome; booking is advisable for Sunday lunch. Buses run from Falmouth during the week.
♨❀◑🚌♣P

Padstow

London Inn

6-8 Lanadwell Street, PL28 8AN
⏲ 11-11.30; 12-11 Sun
☎ (01841) 532554
St Austell Tinners, Tribute, HSD Ⓗ
Popular and cosy village inn converted from cottages, frequented by locals and summer visitors. Unmodernised and unspoilt, it has a long, narrow bar divided into public and family areas, with a rear bar room used mainly for dining. The atmosphere is friendly and welcoming, sometimes boisterous; there is often spontaneous folk music. The pub is renowned for its delightful floral displays in summer. 🛏◑🍺⛺🚌

Pendeen

North Inn

TR19 7DN (on B3306)
⏲ 11-midnight (1am Fri & Sat); 12-11 Sun
☎ (01736) 788417
St Austell IPA, Tinners, Black Prince, Tribute Ⓗ
Welcoming village inn, Cornwall CAMRA's Pub of the Year 2003, serving an area rich in the tin mining tradition. The pictures and artefacts decorating the bar room walls are mostly from nearby Geevor, the last working mine in the area and now a mining museum. The inn is in an area of outstanding natural beauty, with nearby cliffs and good walking. There are two double rooms available for B&B, as well as a campsite round the back. ♨Q❀🛏◑⛺🚌P

Penryn

Seven Stars

73 The Terrace, TR10 8EL
⏲ 11 (12 Sun)-11
☎ (01326) 373573
Blue Anchor Spingo Middle; Skinner's Betty Stogs, Heligan Honey, Cornish Knocker, Figgy's Brew Ⓗ
The nearest thing that Penryn has to an ale house, this single bar town pub is run by a jovial Dutchman. The Skinner's beer range may vary. Decorated with foreign cash, postcards and beer-related clippings, the spacious bar has a raised and comfortably-furnished separate drinking annexe at the rear, dominated by a huge ship's wheel. The pub is home to the Penryn Community Theatre, which entertains here with plays and pantos. A piano is available for competent pianists and occasional live music is performed. ♨⇌🚌

Penzance

Crown Inn

Victoria Square, TR18 2EP
⏲ 12-midnight (12.30am Fri & Sat)
☎ (01736) 351070
Otter Ale; Skinner's Heligan Honey; guest beer Ⓗ
Genuine local on the corner of a Victorian residential square off the town centre. The one room interior includes a comfortable mini-snug with settees and an open fire. A good variety of food, made with ingredients sourced from local producers where possible, is available daily. The guest ale is usually from Ales of Scilly. Pub games include chess and backgammon. Quiz night is Tuesday. Bus and rail stations are close by.
♨Q☕❀◑♿⛺⇌🚌♣⚡

Pirate Inn

Alverton Road, TR18 4PS (on old A30, W of town centre)
⏲ 11-11; 12-10.30 Sun
☎ (01736) 366094 🌐pirateinn.co.uk
Sharp's Doom Bar; Skinner's Cornish Knocker; guest beers Ⓗ
Welcoming, traditional two bar local on the old main road west out of town. A converted farmhouse, it has low ceilings and an impressive stone fireplace. The spacious and pleasant garden is ideal for families – barbecues are often held in summer. There is an almost rural feel to this town pub with its plentiful trees and shrubs, and free-ranging chickens and a cockerel to greet overnight guests in the morning. Up to three varying guest ales are available.
♨Q❀🛏◑🍺⛺🚌♣P

Phillack

Bucket of Blood

14 Churchtown Road, TR27 5AE
⏲ 12-2.30 Tue (not winter)-Fri, 6-11; 11.30-3, 6-11 Sat; 12-4, 7-10.30 Sun
☎ (01736) 752378
St Austell Dartmoor Best, Proper Job IPA, HSD Ⓗ
Friendly old pub whose name is linked to a gory legend involving a customs officer and the pub's well. The notice 'Familiarity breeds contempt' serves as a warning rather than a proverb – the beams are very low! The single bar room has a cosy drinking and dining area at one end with settles and a recently-exposed old fireplace. A painted mural depicting St Ives Bay overlooks the pool table. The beer range may occasionally vary. The kitchen closes in winter. ♨❀◑⛺🚌♣P

Piece

Countryman Inn

TR16 6SG (on Four Lanes-Pool road)
☼ 11-11 (midnight Sat); 12-11 Sun
☎ (01209) 215960
Courage Best Bitter; Greene King Old Speckled Hen; Sharp's Doom Bar; Skinner's Heligan Honey, Cornish Blonde; Theakston Old Peculier Ⓗ
Lively country pub, once a miners' grocery shop, set high among the old copper mines near Carn Brea. There are two bars, the larger one hosting some form of live entertainment every night, as well as a raffle in support of local charities on Sunday lunchtime. The range of up to 10 ales includes a Sharp's house beer called No Name, as it was never given one. Guest ales may sometimes appear from various sources. Food is available all day.
🏚❀◑ⓒ♿�''P

Polkerris

Rashleigh Inn

PL24 2TL (off A3082, near Par)
☼ 11-11; 12-10.30 Sun
☎ (01726) 813991
Sharp's Doom Bar; Taylor Landlord; guest beer Ⓗ
Near the Saints' Way footpath, this excellent free house is situated beside a secluded beach. The atmospheric main bar in the 18th-century building was formerly a pilchard boathouse. Exposed stonework, beamed ceilings, open fires and attractive furnishings add character. Up to four guest beers are available. A good food selection ranges from bar snacks to an a la carte menu in the split-level restaurant. The sheltered terrace gives panoramic views over St Austell Bay and the setting sun. 🏚Q❀◑ Å P

Polperro

Blue Peter Inn

Quay Road, PL13 2QZ
☼ 11-11; 12-10.30 Sun
☎ (01503) 272743 ⊕ thebluepeterinn.co.uk
St Austell Tribute; guest beer Ⓗ
Named after the naval flag, this friendly pub is reached by a flight of steps near the quay, and boasts the only sea view from a pub in town. It offers up to four guest ales in summer. The cider comes from Cornish Orchards. On two levels, it has wooden floors, low beams and hidden corners; the eclectic decor includes foreign breweriana, unusual souvenirs and work by local artists. The pub is popular with visitors, locals, fishermen and their dogs.
🏚🐾◑Å�♣●

Crumplehorn Inn

The Old Mill, PL13 2RJ (on A387)
☼ 11-11; 12-10.30 Sun
☎ (01503) 272348 ⊕ crumplehorn-inn.co.uk
St Austell Tribute; Skinner's Betty Stogs; guest beer Ⓗ
Once an old mill and mentioned in the Domesday Book, this 14th-century inn at the top of town still has a fine waterwheel outside. Inside, the split-level inn is divided into three comfortable areas. Guest beers are usually Cornish, while good food includes dishes featuring locally caught fish. The garden has gazebos to protect customers from the sun. Accommodation is B&B or self-catering. In summer, catch a horse tram from here down to the harbour. 🏚Q❀🛏◑Å🚪▲🚗♣

Ruan Lanihorne

King's Head Inn

TR2 5NX
☼ 12-2.30, 6-11 (closed Mon, Nov-Easter)
☎ (01872) 501263 ⊕ kingsheadruan.co.uk
Skinner's Betty Stogs, Cornish Knocker Ⓗ
Delightful family-run free house nestling on the Fal estuary within the Roseland Peninsula. The homely interior, quiet and traditional in style, includes a single bar and two dining areas. Full of character, the decor reflects village history. The pub is renowned for superb food and drink (no meals Sun eve in winter). A sun terrace and quaint sunken garden provide space for alfresco drinking and dining. The house beer is Grade Ruan from Skinner's. 🏚Q❀◑ Å P

St Columb Major

Ring O' Bells

3 Bank Street, TR9 6AT
☼ 12-2 (not Wed & winter), 5-11; 12-3, 7-10.30 Sun
☎ (01637) 880259
Sharp's Doom Bar, Eden Ale; Ⓗ **guest beer** Ⓖ
A former brewhouse built to commemorate the parish church tower, this is the oldest pub in town. The narrow frontage of this charming 15th-century free house belies the capacious interior, with its three bars, open beams and slate floors. Each bar has its own character and custom. Wood-burning stoves and wooden furnishings give a traditional feel. A cosmopolitan restaurant menu is available in the converted old brewery. A guest ale is available in summer only. 🏚Q❀🛏Å🚗♣

St Ewe

Crown Inn

PL26 6EY
☼ 12-3, 5-11 (11-11 summer); 12-3, 6-10.30 (12-10.30 summer) Sun
☎ (01726) 843322
St Austell Tinners, Tribute, Proper Job IPA, seasonal beer Ⓗ
Situated in an unspoilt Cornish village not far from the Lost Gardens of Heligan, this cosy 16th-century community pub has low beams, slate flagged floors and a comfortable lounge/restaurant in an upper level extension. The former snug has been opened out but still provides a secluded drinking area. In summer there is a marquee in the garden for families. The pub sits over an old well; the stone fireplace sports an original and working iron spit. No food is served on Sunday and Monday evenings. 🏚Q❀🛏◑Å🚪P

St Ives

Castle Inn

Fore Street, TR26 1AB
☼ 11-11 (midnight Fri & Sat); 12-11 Sun
☎ (01736) 796833

Beer range varies Ⓗ
On the St Ives Bay rail ale trail, this traditional Cornish pub offers a warm welcome. The large, comfortable bar has wood-panelled walls and ceiling and a slab slate floor in typical old Cornwall fashion. Up to six varying ales are offered, including one dispensed by gravity from an upstairs cellar via a decorative cask end. The pub holds a real ale festival at Easter, and gravity-served cider is from Cornish Orchards. Food is available May to September.
Q◐▲≒⊟♣♠

Golden Lion

High Street, TR26 1RS
☼ 11 (12 Sun)-midnight
☎ (01736) 793679
Courage Best Bitter; Sharp's Eden Ale; Skinner's Cornish Knocker; guest beer Ⓗ
Busy, town-centre pub on the St Ives Bay rail ale trail, popular with locals. Formerly a coaching inn, it has two bar rooms: the small horseshoe-shaped front lounge attracts drinkers who enjoy convivial conversation, the larger and more boisterous 'public' at the rear, with a pool table, is favoured by younger drinkers. High quality food is home cooked using local produce. The Skinner's beer and the single guest ale change often.
🍴🕯❀◐♿▲≒⊟♣⚓

St Just

King's Arms

5 Market Square, TR19 7HF
☼ 11 (12 Sun)-12.30am
☎ (01736) 788545
St Austell Tinners, Tribute, seasonal beers Ⓗ
Situated in the town square, this granite building was originally three 14th-century cottages. The rambling interior reflects the building's origins – a single L-shaped bar serves the many drinking areas within. The stone flagged entrance, low exposed beams, open fire and wooden furnishings add to the traditional feel. Seating outside overlooks the town square. Food is home cooked using local produce. The pub is home to the local Cape Singers – be prepared for an impromptu singsong on Friday evening.
🍴❀⊟◐♿⊟♣

Star Inn

1 Fore Street, TR19 7LL
☼ 11-midnight (12.30am Fri & Sat)
☎ (01736) 788767
St Austell Tinners, Dartmoor Best Bitter, Tribute, HSD, seasonal beers Ⓗ
Popular 18th-century granite inn near the square. The atmospheric bar interior reflects a long connection with mining and the sea. The low beams are draped with Celtic flags. A separate snug functions as a family room. This timeless place is a proper drinkers' pub, welcoming to all, with conversation the main entertainment. Monday features a Fiddly-Dee night – a sort of Irish folk jam session – and Thursday is 'open mic' night.
🍴🐾❀♿▲⊟♣⚓

St Mary's, Isles of Scilly

Mermaid Inn

The Bank, TR21 0HY
☼ 11-11; 12-10.30 Sun
☎ (01720) 422701
Ales of Scilly Scuppered; Greene King IPA; guest beer Ⓗ
Busy, boisterous and popular with the locals and tourists alike, this old granite pub by the quay is the first one you come to when leaving the Scillonian ferry from Penzance. The main bar is crammed with maritime bric-a-brac. It has a restaurant upstairs, and a second, newly-refurbished cellar bar/restaurant downstairs called the Slip Inn which opens at mealtimes. The pub serves breakfast from 8.30am. A third ale is added in summer, normally Sharp's Doom Bar. 🍴◐▲

St Mawgan

Falcon Inn

TR8 4EP
☼ 11-3, 6-11.30 (11-11.30 summer); 12-3, 7-10.30 Sun
☎ (01637) 860225
St Austell Tinners, Tribute, HSD Ⓗ
Attractive pub in the idyllic setting of the unspoilt Lanherne Valley, not far from the bustle of Newquay and the airport. At the centre of a quiet village, the pub is closely involved in local activities. The single bar has a warm, welcoming atmosphere, with decor reflecting country life. Meals are served in the dining room where local art is displayed. The pub is family friendly, with a large award-winning garden with play area, and a games room. 🍴Q❀🐾◐▲⊟♣P

Stithians

Seven Stars Inn

Church Road, TR3 7DH
☼ 12-2.30, 5.30 (5 Fri)-11; 12-midnight Sat; 12-10.30 Sun
☎ (01209) 860003
St Austell IPA, Tribute, Proper Job IPA, HSD Ⓗ
Lively village local used by a good cross-section of the community, where euchre is enthusiastically played. The pub was originally purpose built as an extension to a farmhouse to serve the drinking needs of local tin miners at the end of the 19th century. The beers may vary within the St Austell range, including the occasional seasonal brew. The original bar and lounge areas have been joined to form a U-shaped drinking area, while a modern extension houses the pool table.
🍴Q❀◐⊟♣

Stratton

King's Arms

Howells Road, EX23 9BX
☼ 12-11
☎ (01288) 352396
Exmoor Ale; Sharp's Doom Bar; Shepherd Neame Spitfire; guest beer Ⓗ
Popular local at the heart of this ancient market town. The name of this 17th-century coaching inn reflects the town's political loyalties after the Civil War. A two-bar pub, it

retains many original features, including well-worn Delabole slate flagstone and wood floors, and a large open fireplace. A small bread oven was exposed in recent years. Draught cider and an extra guest beer are available in summer. Accommodation is in four rooms, one en-suite.
⚨Q⊛✿⍾◑Ġ💺🖾♠♥P

Summercourt

London Inn
1 School Road, TR8 5EA (off A30)
✪ 5 (6 Sat)-11; 12-2.30, 7-10.30 Sun
☎ (01872) 510281
Beer range varies Ⓗ
Lively and family-friendly free house with a large single bar room divided by wooden screens to create separate spaces for drinking or dining. Good traditional home-cooked food is available. The ales on offer come from Cornish brewers Skinner's, Sharp's and St Austell. There may be a guest beer in summer. The eclectic decor features Laurel and Hardy figurines set among wooden furnishings and coach lamp lighting. Good bus services pass close by. ⚨⊛◑ Å🖾♣P

Trebellan

Smugglers Den Inn
TR8 5PY (off Cubert road from A3075)
✪ 12-3, 6-11 (11-11 summer)
☎ (01637) 830209 ⊕ thesmugglersden.co.uk
Beer range varies Ⓗ
Rambling, former 16th-century farmhouse tucked away down a narrow, hilly lane. Once a hangout for smugglers, the atmospheric and convivial bar, original oak beams, paved courtyards and curio-filled corners add to the authentic olde-worlde charm. The range of ales features Cornish breweries, while good value meals are available in the split-level restaurant. Occasional jazz or folk evenings are hosted and a beer festival is held in May. Convenient for camping and caravan sites nearby. ⚨Q⊛◑ Å🖾♣P

Treleigh

Treleigh Arms
TR16 4AY (off old Redruth bypass)
✪ 11-3, 6 (5 Fri)-11; 12-3, 6-11 (12-11 summer) Sun
☎ (01209) 315095
Draught Bass; Sharp's Doom Bar; Skinner's Betty Stogs; guest beer Ⓗ
Traditional whitewashed cottage-style pub beside the church in a historic mining district. It has a comfortable stone-walled bar and separate dining room. A friendly service is offered by the licensees who have made this busy free house very popular over recent years for its beer, cider and good food. Conversation flourishes here without juke box, TV or gaming machines. The guest ale varies regularly. Quiz night is Tuesday. There is a petanque pitch outside. Dogs are welcome. ⚨Q⊛◑ Å🖾♣P⅃

Tresco, Isles of Scilly

New Inn
Townshill, TR24 0QG
✪ 11-3, 6 (5 Fri)-11; 12-10.30 Sun
☎ (01720) 422844 ⊕ isles-of-scilly.co.uk/new-inn-tresco.html
Ales of Scilly Scuppered; St Austell Tribute; Skinner's Betty Stogs Ⓗ
Excellent old pub near New Grimsby harbour, a haven before boarding the boat to St Mary's. Recent extensions to the garden and provision of a covered pavilion have added to the appeal of this popular real ale outlet. Beers may vary, usually within the Skinner's range, with brews from the local Ales of Scilly often making an appearance. The house beer is a Skinner s blend called Tresco Tipple. Beer festivals are held during spring and August bank holiday weekends. ⛵⊛✿⍾◑

Trevarrian

Traveller's Rest
TR8 4AQ (on B3276, coast road)
✪ 12-3, 5-11; 12-midnight Sun
☎ (01637) 860245
St Austell Tinners, Tribute, HSD Ⓗ
Comfortable 16th-century coaching inn popular with locals as well as holidaymakers. The beamed, slate-flagged bar area is comfortably furnished with several drinking corners. A large boat rudder leans against the bar pillar, and the walls are decorated with pictures of RAF aircraft old and new, reflecting the pub's proximity to the local airbase. The spacious family and games room has a TV screen. A Sunday roast carvery is offered here – the pub has a small restaurant.
⚨⛵⊛◑ Å🖾P

Trevaunance Cove

Driftwood Spars
Quay Road, TR5 0RT
✪ 11-midnight (1am Fri & Sat)
☎ (01872) 552428
Driftwood Cuckoo Ale; St Austell HSD; Sharp's Doom Bar, Own; Tetley Bitter Ⓗ
Outstanding family-run free house, popular with cliff walkers and surfers, with its own flourishing micro-brewery. A former mine warehouse and sail loft, it is built from granite and enormous ships' spars. The interior includes three comfortable bars featuring beamed ceilings, leaded windows and granite fireplaces. Steps or a lift provide access to the sun terrace and an excellent restaurant specialising in fish and game. Live music and theatre are frequently staged.
⚨Q⊛✿◑ 💺Ġ Å♥P⅃

Truro

City Inn Hotel
Pydar Street, TR1 3SP
✪ 12-11.30; 11-12.30am Fri & Sat; 12-11.30 Sun
☎ (01872) 272623
Courage Best Bitter; Sharp's Doom Bar; Skinner's Betty Stogs; guest beer Ⓗ
Community-focused, 19th-century two-bar pub, a village local although close to the city

centre. The comfortable lounge has several drinking areas and is decorated with an impressive collection of water jugs; the more functional back bar is sports-oriented. Up to five ales are available, mostly from SIBA member breweries. Regular charity events include an annual conker championship, and a beer festival is held at Easter. The beer garden is a real suntrap. Q❀🏠🚃🌑🖁🍴🚃♿🚶🐾🍺

Try Dowr
Lemon Quay, TR1 2LP
🕐 9am-midnight (1am Fri & Sat)
☎ (01872) 265840
Beer range varies Ⓗ
Overlooking the piazza on Lemon Quay, the Try Dowr (Three Rivers in Cornish) follows the standard Wetherspoon's format, although it offers up to four local ales as well as the usual national fare, and up to three real draught ciders. The spacious seating area is supplemented by a separate restaurant space. This hugely popular pub is a Lloyds No. 1 bar and tends to be noisy most evenings when the music comes on. 🌑♿🚃🖁🐾

Tywardreath
New Inn
Fore Street, PL24 2QP
🕐 12-11 (10.30 Sun)
☎ (01726) 813901
Draught Bass; Ⓖ **St Austell Dartmoor Best Bitter, Tribute, Proper Job IPA** Ⓗ
Classic village local with a large, secluded garden. The games room houses the juke box so any noise is confined to the back of the pub, allowing good conversation to flourish, and sometimes singing in the bar. Built in 1752 by local copper mine owners, the pub is the hub of village life, and many functions are held in the garden. A slotted brass plate remains in the bar where miners inserted their beer tokens. 🍴Q🚶❀🏠🅰️🚃(Par)🚃

Vogue
Star Inn
TR16 5NP
🕐 12-midnight (1am Fri & Sat); 12-11 Sun
☎ (01209) 820242
Draught Bass; Flowers IPA; guest beers Ⓗ

Close to St Day and en route to Gwennap Pit lies this lively, family-friendly community local. The homely interior includes bar, snug and dining room. The pub is the centre of village activities, particularly during feast celebrations, when a beer festival is held. The guest beers always include one varied Skinner's brew, a second chosen from another Cornish micro. There is something to entertain everyone here, from boules to live music and karaoke, quiz nights to big-screen sport. 🍴❀🌑♿🅰️🚃🐾🍺P🚶

Zelah
Hawkins Arms
High Road, TR4 9HU (off A30)
🕐 11.30-3, 6-11; 12-3, 6-10.30 Sun
☎ (01872) 540339
Butcombe Bitter; guest beers Ⓗ
Easy to find off the main A30 (look for the brown signs), this traditional village free house, full of nooks and crannies, is popular with the locals. The pub is run by enthusiastic licensees who regularly vary the guest beer: 'usually something interesting', they say. The house beer by Skinner's is a blend called Zelah Mist; a draught cider is also available. Excellent home-cooked meals promote locally-supplied produce. 🍴Q❀🌑♿🅰️🚃(586)🐾🍺P

Zennor
Tinners Arms
TR26 3BY
🕐 11-3, 6.30-11 (11-11 Sat & summer); 12-10.30 Sun
☎ (01736) 796927 ⊕ tinnersarms.com
St Austell Tinners; Sharp's Doom Bar, Special Ⓗ
Ancient village pub near the northern cliffs of the Penwith Peninsula. The Sharp's Special is badged as Zennor Mermaid; farmhouse cider is also stocked. In winter, food availability is variable – phone the pub first. The garden faces south and is sheltered from the wind, a superb place to enjoy a pint on a sunny day. The coastal path and granite moorlands are nearby, making this a popular watering hole for walkers. Ask about the legend of the choirboy and the mermaid! 🍴Q🚶❀🏠🌑🅰️🚃P

Fishing for beer

Ah! My beloved brother of the rod, do you know the taste of beer – of bitter beer – cooled in the flowing river? Take your bottle of beer, sink it deep, deep in the shady water, where the cooling springs and fishes are. Then, the day being very hot and bright, and the sun blazing on your devoted head, consider it a matter of duty to have to fish that long, wide stream. An hour or so of good hammering will bring you to the end of it, and then – let me ask you avec impressement – how about that beer? Is it cool? Is it refreshing? Does it gurgle, gurgle and 'go down glug' as they say in Devonshire? Is it heavenly? Is it Paradise and all the Peris to boot? Ah! If you have never tasted beer under these or similar circumstance, you have, believe me, never tasted it at all.

Francis Francis, By Lake and River, 16th century

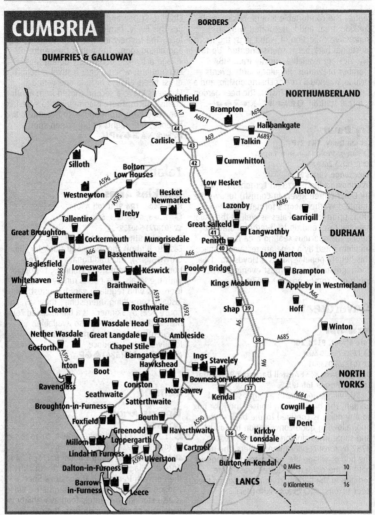

CUMBRIA

(Map showing locations including:)

BORDERS

DUMFRIES & GALLOWAY

NORTHUMBERLAND

Smithfield, Brampton, Hallbankgate, Carlisle, Talkin, Cumwhitton, Silloth, Bolton Low Houses, Low Hesket, Alston, Westnewton, Hesket Newmarket, Lazonby, Garrigill, Tallentire, Ireby, Great Salkeld, Langwathby, DURHAM, Great Broughton, Cockermouth, Mungrisedale, Penrith, Eaglesfield, Bassenthwaite, Long Marton, Whitehaven, Loweswater, Keswick, Pooley Bridge, Brampton, Braithwaite, Kings Meaburn, Appleby in Westmorland, Buttermere, Rosthwaite, Shap, Hoff, Cleator, Wasdale Head, Grasmere, Winton, Nether Wasdale, Great Langdale, Ambleside, Gosforth, Chapel Stile, Irton, Boot, Barngates, Ings, Staveley, Hawkshead, NORTH YORKS, Ravenglass, Coniston, Bowness-on-Windermere, Seathwaite, Near Sawrey, Broughton-in-Furness, Satterthwaite, Kendal, Cowgill, Foxfield, Bouth, Dent, Greenodd, Haverthwaite, Cartmel, Kirkby Lonsdale, Millom, Loppergarth, Lindal in Furness, Ulverston, Burton-in-Kendal, Dalton-in-Furness, Barrow-in-Furness, Leece, LANCS

0 Miles 10
0 Kilometres 16

Alston

Cumberland Hotel
Townfoot, CA9 3HX
🕑 12-11
☎ (01434) 381875 🌐 cumberlandhotel.co.uk
Yates Bitter; guest beer Ⓗ

Justifiably a local CAMRA Pub of the Season, the Cumberland offers an ever-changing range of at least three guest ales from around the country plus a couple of real ciders. Situated close to the centre of town, and not far away from a narrow gauge railway, and the Pennine and Cumbrian Ways, it is an ideal base for exploring the area. Cumbria's highest market town is surrounded by stunning scenery. The A686 is one of the best drives in the country. Q⊁☂✍Ⓚ♿ÅⓇ♠P↳

Ambleside

Golden Rule
Smithy Brow, LA22 9AS (100m off A591 towards Kirkstone)

🕑 11 (12 Sun)-midnight
☎ (01539) 432257
Robinson's Hatters Dark, Oldham Bitter, Hartleys XB, Cumbria Way, Unicorn, Double Hop Ⓗ

Now 'come of age' after 21 consecutive entries in the Guide, as well as a dozen since the first listing in 1974, it is the unchanging scene, the focus on good beer and the absence of pool tables, piped music and such diversions that make this pub so attractive. A Robinson's regular is sometimes replaced with a seasonal beer. There are three rooms off the central bar and a patio at the rear. Beautiful floral displays in summer have won many awards. ⚏Q☘♿Ⓡ(555, 599)♣↳

White Lion Hotel
Market Place, LA22 9DB
🕑 11-11; 12-10.30 Sun
☎ (01539) 433140
Worthington's Bitter; guest beers Ⓗ

This busy village centre inn manages to combine a brisk food operation with a drinker-friendly bar area. A major refurbishment in 2006 resulted, among other things, in a change from two permanent beers to one, but with a choice of three guests. One is usually from Hawkshead, the other two are selected from the wide choice available monthly from the M&B Cask Fresh range. The patio – with large umbrellas and heaters in winter – is an excellent spot to view the passing scene from. ⚲⊛⇔◑&🛏(555, 599)⌐

Appleby-in-Westmorland

Royal Oak Inn

Bongate, CA16 6NU

◐ 11-midnight

☎ (01768) 351463 ⊕ royaloakappleby.co.uk

Black Sheep Best Bitter; guest beers Ⓗ

Behind the attractive exterior of this former coaching inn at the edge of town are two bars with separate entrances. To the left is a traditional tap room with wood panelling and various framed group photographs. In between this and a pleasantly furnished dining room is a lounge with a small snug and bar counter. A former Cumbrian CAMRA Pub of the Year, it now has a new licensee. ⚲Q⊛⇔◑⊕🛏⇌♠P⌐

Barngates

Drunken Duck

LA12 0NG OS351013

◐ 11.30-11 (10.30 Sun)

☎ (015394) 36347 ⊕ drunkenduckinn.co.uk

Barngates range Ⓗ

Home of the Barngates Brewery, the Duck always serves four of the nine beers brewed here. Brewery tours can be arranged. The pub has been extensively renovated to create a pleasing mix of local and modern styles. Bar meals served at lunchtime and the à la carte menu available in the dining room in the evening are of an exceptionally high standard. The outside seating area at the front offers magnificent views of the fells to the north east. ⚲Q⊛⇔◑⇔♣P

Barrow in Furness

Ambrose Hotel

Duke Street, LA14 1XT

◐ 12-11

☎ (01229) 830990

Boddingtons Bitter; Caledonian Deuchars IPA; Coniston Bluebird; guest beers Ⓗ

Spacious hotel near the rugby ground offering solid home-cooked food and a wide range of guest beers, all with a real 'town pub' atmosphere. The larger front room comprises both lounge and dining areas with a central bar separating it from the rear games room. The bar can be busy, especially when hosting one of the frequent live music weekend events. ⚲⇔◑&⇌🛏♣

Bassenthwaite Lake

Pheasant ☆

CA13 9YE (S off A66, W end of lake)

◐ 12.30-2.30, 5.30-10.30 (11 Fri & Sat); 12.30-2.30, 6-10.30 Sun

☎ (017687) 76234 ⊕ the-pheasant.co.uk

Draught Bass; Jennings Cumberland Ale; Theakston Best Bitter Ⓗ

This charming 500-year-old coaching inn is now an upmarket hotel, but retains a comfortable bar open to non-residents, resplendent with varnished walls, settles and antique chairs. Situated in a picturesque location close by the lake, it is at the foot of the fell where a pair of breeding ospreys nest each year. The lounge, with its impressive open fire, is available to drinkers at lunchtime only. Q⅘⊛⇔◑&▲🛏⌐

Bolton Low Houses

Oddfellows Arms

New Street, CA7 8PA (off A595, 12 miles W of Carlisle)

◐ 12-3 (not Mon-Thu), 7 (6 Fri & Sat)-11; 12-10.30 Sun

☎ (01697) 44452

Thwaites Original; guest beers Ⓗ

Situated between Carlisle and Cockermouth, on the edge of the Lake District National Park with mountains to the south and the Solway plain to the north, the Oddfellows has two drinking areas, both served from a single L-shaped bar. Guest beers in summer alternate between beers from the Thwaites range and local micros. Food is freshly prepared, using only the best of local ingredients (served Thu-Sun). ⚲◑▲🛏♣P

Boot

Brook House Inn

CA19 1TG

◐ 9-midnight; 12-10.30 Sun

☎ (019467) 23288 ⊕ brookhouseinn.co.uk

Taylor Landlord; Theakston Best Bitter; guest beers Ⓗ

Haven of quality food and uncommon beers, right by the last station on the La'al Ratty tourist railway. It is owned and run by a dedicated group of family members spanning several generations. Set in the delightful Eskdale valley, it is popular with walkers, campers, railway enthusiasts and real ale drinkers – this is as close to heaven as it gets.

It always offers a Cumbrian beer and up to seven guests in summer. All Boot's pubs collaborate on popular, yearly beer festivals. ⌂Q✿⇌◐♿≢(Dalegarth)●P

Woolpack Inn

CA19 1TH (1 mile E of Boot) OS190010
✪ 11-11 summer; 6 (11 Sat)-11 winter; 12-10.30 Sun
☎ (019467) 23230 ⊕ woolpack.co.uk
Beer range varies Ⓗ
Surrounded by magnificent scenery, this pretty, rambling inn sits at the foot of dramatic, twisting Hardknott Pass. The owners of this friendly, highly individual inn are passionate about good local cask ales and quality food prepared from fresh ingredients. Brewing their own Hardknott beer ties in with these ideals; they also serve up to six guests from Cumbrian micros and guest ciders (including Solway). On some evenings live music is performed. It is a lovely 25-minute walk from the Dalegarth La'al Ratty terminus. ⌂Q✿⇌◐⊟▲♣●P⊓

Bouth

White Hart

LA12 8JB (off A590, 6 miles NE of Ulverston)
✪ 12-2 (Wed-Fri), 6-11; 12-11 Sat; 12-10.30 Sun
☎ (01229) 861229
Black Sheep Best Bitter; Jennings Cumberland Ale; guest beers Ⓗ
True country inn, popular for its excellent beers and food. Low, beamed ceilings, two real fires and healthy food add to its traditional rural ambience. Ahead of its time, it became the first entirely no-smoking pub in 2004. Animal lovers should be aware that a number of stuffed beasts adorn the bar area. Outside, there is a large, attractive patio. ⌂✿⇌◐▲♣P⊓

Bowness-on-Windermere

Royal Oak

Brantfell Road, LA23 3EG
✪ 11-11 (midnight Fri & Sat)
☎ (01539) 443970 ⊕ royaloak-windermere.co.uk
Coniston Bluebird; Taylor Landlord; Tetley Bitter; guest beers Ⓗ
Friendly local which, despite being just out of the village centre, is sought out by local sports clubs and ramblers on the Dales Way, which rises steeply by the side of the building. It comprises a family/dining room to the left of the bar area, raised seating to the right and an upper level with pool table and juke box. The meals here are good value, and vegetarian options are available. A framed certificate proclaims the pub as the official start/finish of the Lake-to-Lake walk, which stretches 163 miles from Windermere to Kielder in Northumberland.
⌂✿⇌◐⊟(599, 618)♣●P⊢

Braithwaite

Coledale Inn

CA12 5TN (at top of village, off Whinlatter Rd)
✪ 11-11 summer; 12-3, 6-midnight winter; 12-3, 6-11 Sun
☎ (017687) 78272 ⊕ coledale-inn.co.uk
Jennings Bitter; Yates Best Bitter; guest beers Ⓗ
This country inn looks out over the village of Braithwaite towards the Skiddaw range. Two separate bars, adorned with interesting old photographs and prints, serve a good range of beers from local and northern breweries. Guest beers are added in summer. The building dates from 1824, when it was a pencil mill. ⌂Q✿⇌◐⊟▲⊟P

Middle Ruddings Hotel

CA12 5RY (just off A66 at Braithwaite)
✪ 12-2.30, 6-11
☎ (017687) 78436 ⊕ middle-ruddings.co.uk
Beer range varies Ⓗ
This stone-built family-run hotel, dating back to 1903, lies opposite Skiddaw, making it popular with walkers. Three beers are served, mostly sourced from Cumbrian breweries and usually all of low ABV. So particular is the owner about his ales that he visits the brewery before agreeing to take the beer. The hotel is used by local groups as a community facility. Lunches and evening meals are served with the emphasis on local produce.
⌂Q✿⇌◐▲⊟P⊢

Brampton

New Inn

Near Appleby, CA16 6JS
✪ 11-11; 12-10.30 Sun
☎ (01768) 351231 ⊕ newinnbrampton.co.uk
Tirril Bewsher's Best Bitter, Brougham Ale, Old Faithful Ⓗ
Now owned by Tirril Brewery, the New Inn's bar area has wooden floors, beamed ceilings and a pool table at the rear, but no juke box, fruit machines or TV. To the left is a superb dining room with low-beamed ceiling and a working kitchen range. Home-cooked meals using produce from local farms and suppliers is the speciality here. Many footpaths criss-cross this quiet rural area, making the inn a good stop for walkers. ⌂Q✿◐♣P

Broughton-in-Furness

Manor Arms

The Square, LA20 6HY
✪ 12-11.30 (midnight Fri & Sat); 12-11 Sun
☎ (01229) 716286
Copper Dragon Golden Pippin; Hawkshead Bitter; Yates Bitter; guest beers Ⓗ
Overlooking the village square, this outstanding ale house and former regional CAMRA Pub of the Year has featured in this Guide for many years, only missing last year when there was a possibility of it being sold. Happily this did not happen and under the stewardship of the Varty family it continues to win awards. No-nonsense snacks and accommodation are available along with great craic. ⌂Q⇌⊟(X7, 511)♣●P⊓

Old Kings Head

Church Street, LA20 6HJ
✪ 12-3 (not Mon), 5-midnight (11 Mon); 12-11 Sun
☎ (01229) 716293 ⊕ oldkingshead.co.uk
Caledonian Deuchars IPA; Taylor Landlord; guest beers Ⓗ

This comfortable 400-year-old pub in the beer mecca of Broughton is popular with diners and drinkers alike, and has a large partly covered garden. The guest beers are usually from the local Beckstones Brewery. Do not miss the annual Broughton beer festival, run jointly by all the pubs in and around the village.
🏛🏠✿🛏◑◗🚃(Foxfield)🚉(X7, 511)

Burton-in-Kendal

Kings Head
Main Street, LA6 1LR
✪ 12-2, 6-11; 12-11 Sat & Sun
☎ (01524) 781409 ⊕ kingsarmsburton.co.uk
Black Sheep Best Bitter; Jennings Dark Mild; Moorhouses Premier Bitter; guest beers ⊞
A former coaching inn located beside the A6 Roman road in the centre of this attractive village a mere stone's throw from the Lancashire border, this Mitchells of Lancaster outlet is entered via a central corridor. The bar area is ahead, with a log fire and six handpumps dispensing a range of beers that has extended over recent years, making it an oasis in this southern tip of the county. The games room has a pool table and juke box; there is an extensive dining room.
🏛Q✿🛏◑◗🚻🚉(555)♣P⅃

Buttermere

Fish Hotel
CA13 9XA (off B5289 from Keswick in centre of village)
✪ 11-3, 6-11; 11-11 Sat & Sun; winter hours vary
☎ (017687) 70253 ⊕ fish-hotel.co.uk
Jennings Bitter, Sneck Lifter, seasonal beer; guest beers ⊞
Family-owned, typical Lakeland hotel in a lovely setting with views out to the Buttermere Valley. In addition to three Jennings beers there are three guests, complemented by good value bar meals. The bar is spacious and comfortable and welcomes families. The hotel is ideally located for outdoor pursuits, but check that it is open if visiting out of season. Q✿🛏◑◗🚉P

Carlisle

Carlisle Rugby Club
Warwick Road, CA1 1CW (off A69, by Carlisle United FC ground)
✪ 7 (5.30 Fri & Sat; 6 match nights)-11; 12-11 Sat (rugby season); 12-3, 7-11 Sun
☎ (01228) 521300
Theakston Best Bitter; Yates Bitter; guest beer ⊞
Recently extended and renovated following substantial damage sustained during Carlisle's 2005 flood, the worst in 100 years, this club has been extended to provide an additional room inside as well as a patio area. A guest ale is always added at weekends. It can get very crowded when Carlisle United play at home, with both home and away fans. Non members are welcome. ✿🚃🚉P⅃

Globe Inn
6 Bridge Street, CA2 5NB (W of city centre)
✪ 12-1am (2am Sat); 12-midnight Sun
☎ (07799) 608494
Beer range varies ⊞
Traditional pub for the local community including a good number of students who live in accommodation on the site of the late-lamented Carlisle State Brewery, which lies just behind the pub on the banks of the Caldew River. The Globe is situated 500m west of the ancient Carlisle Castle – use the pedestrian bridge or the underpass from the city centre. The state-of-the-art juke box has thousands of tracks, and the pub can get fairly lively later on in the evening. 🏛🚃🚉♣

Griffin
Court Square, CA1 1QX
✪ 11 (10 Sat)-11 (midnight Fri & Sat); 11-11 Sun
☎ (01228) 598941
Caledonian Deuchars IPA; guest beer ⊞
Part of the John Barras chain, the former Midland Bank building has been converted into the Griffin and features decor typical of the chain, with many old photographs adorning the walls. The large interior of the imposing building has allowed for the construction of a second floor level. A large-screen TV shows music videos and sport events, and a separate area is available for hire. ◑◗&🚃🚉⅃

King's Head
Fisher Street, CA3 8RF (behind Old Town Hall)
✪ 11 (10 Sun)-11
☎ (01228) 540100
Yates Bitter; guest beer ⊞
The King's Head is one of the older pubs in the city centre, and many pictures of Carlisle through the ages are displayed inside this local CAMRA award winner. A new covered all-weather yard boasts a large-screen TV and barbecue area. A plaque outside explains why Carlisle is not in the Domesday Book. The pub is close to the tourist area of Carlisle, with the castle, cathedral and the Lanes shopping centre nearby. ✿◑🚃🚉♣⅃

Cartmel

King's Arms
The Square, LA11 6QB
✪ 11-11; 11-10.30 Sun
☎ (015395) 36220
Barngates Tag Lag; Black Sheep Best Bitter; Hawkshead Bitter; guest beers ⊞
Surprisingly spacious village pub that has a good mix of rooms and open-plan areas. Exposed beams combine with brass and copperware to create a warm, relaxed ambience. The restaurant overlooks the ducks on the little River Eea as it passes through the village, which is always busy with tourists in summer. A drinking house has existed on this site for over 900 years. Q🏠✿◑◗&♣

Chapel Stile

Wainwrights Inn
LA22 9JH
✪ 11.30-11.30 (11.30-3, 6-11.30 Mon-Fri Feb)
☎ (01539) 438088 ⊕ langdale.co.uk/wainwrights/index.htm
Thwaites Original, Thoroughbred, Lancaster Bomber; guest beers ⊞

Originally a farmhouse, it became the gun powder works manager's house and was then transformed into the White Lion, when the pub next to the village church that previously carried this name surrendered its licence. Now part of the Langsdale Estate, it suffered a serious kitchen fire in the autumn of 2006 but reopened, phoenix-like, on Guy Fawkes Night. The refurbished large L-shaped main area is flag-floored and features an impressive fireplace, while the dining room is carpeted. Heavy ceiling beams survived, as did most of the memorabilia on the walls. The pub is surrounded by pleasant valley walks and fell views. ⚌Q❀◖▣⌖▲₪(516)♣♠P

Cleator

Brook Inn

93 Trumpet Terrace, CA23 3DX (on A5086)
🕙 11-midnight (1am Fri & Sat)
☎ (01946) 811635
Taylor Landlord; guest beers Ⓗ
Situated on the main Cleator to Egremont road, this lively village pub offers a cosy, candlelit interior. Sunday lunches are popular and music features strongly, with local bands on Friday evening and the occasional jam session on Sunday. Quiz night is Thursday. The licensee is committed to real ale and also serves Weston's cider on gravity. A runner-up local CAMRA Pub of the Year in 2006 and Pub of the Season in 2005, this is a good lunchtime watering-hole for walkers on the Coast-to-Coast route half a mile away. ⚌⌚◖▲₪♣♠

Cockermouth

Bitter End

15 Kirkgate, CA13 9PJ (off Market Place, 50m up Kirkgate)
🕙 12-3, 6-11; 11-3, 6-midnight Fri & Sat
☎ (01900) 828993 ⊕ bitterend.co.uk
Bitter End Cockermouth Pride, seasonal beers; Jennings Bitter, Cumberland Ale; guest beers Ⓗ
A favourite haunt of locals and visitors in the know, the Bitter End offers a selection of beers brewed on the premises or at the nearby Jennings Brewery, plus a range of guest beers. The pleasant surroundings, a welcoming log fire and excellent food have helped the pub to win several local CAMRA awards in recent years. Seating can be limited during dining times. ⚌Q◖▣▲₪

Bush Hotel

Main Street, CA13 9JS
🕙 11-11; 12-10.30 Sun
☎ (01900) 822064
Jennings Bitter, Cumberland Ale, Sneck Lifter; guest beer Ⓗ
Popular town centre pub comprising an atmospheric, comfortable front bar and back bar with wide-screen TV. The guest beer changes regularly. A good value lunchtime stop – try the home-made soup and baguettes or proper thick-cut sandwiches. ▣

Swan Inn

55 Kirkgate, CA13 9PH
🕙 6-11.30 (midnight Fri); 12-midnight Sat; 12-6, 7-11 (closed winter eve) Sun

☎ (01900) 822425
Jennings Dark Mild, Bitter, Cumberland Ale Ⓗ
Friendly, traditional pub, situated in a cobbled Georgian square near the centre of Cockermouth. The cosy front bar, with a stone-flagged floor and low beams, is warmed by a wood-burning stove in winter. A variety of games can be played here including darts, chess and backgammon. The pub is the watering hole for the Cockermouth Mechanics band and regularly raises funds for charity. ⚌Q♣

Coniston

Black Bull

LA21 8DU
🕙 10-11 (10.30 Sun)
☎ (015394) 41335
Coniston Bluebird, Old Man Ale, Bluebird XB Ⓗ
The tap house for the on-site Coniston Brewing Co, the Bull focuses equally on food and ale, served in the large bar and lounge areas. The outdoor seating area is a great place to relax and watch the world go by during the summer months.
⚌Q❀▱◖▲₪(X12, 505)♠P

Sun Hotel

LA21 8HQ
🕙 12-11
☎ (015394) 41248 ⊕ thesuniston.com
Coniston Bluebird; Hawkshead Bitter; guest beers Ⓗ
Pub and hotel dating back to the 16th century, situated up the hill and overlooking the village of Coniston. A typical Lakeland bar, it has a slate floor and boasts a stunning solid fuel range which is heavenly to sit and drink by in winter. In summer there is no better venue for enjoying your beer than the pleasant terrace and garden with its listed magnolia. Alongside the two regular beers are three guests, usually stronger brews.
⚌Q⌚❀▱◖▲₪(X12, 505)P⌐

Cumwhitton

Pheasant Inn

CA8 9EX (4 miles SE of A69 at Warwick Bridge)
🕙 6-11 (midnight Sat); closed Mon; 12-3, 7-11 Sun
☎ (01228) 560102 ⊕ thepheasantinncumwhitton.co.uk
Beer range varies Ⓗ
On the fringe of a tranquil village, new owners have transformed this pub into a friendly and welcoming venue with a reputation for good food and three handpumps dispensing fine ales, sourced predominantly from local micros. The stone-flagged bar and ante-room are complemented by a separate dining area and upstairs function room. Special events regularly feature on the pub's calendar. Local CAMRA Pub of The Year 2007.
⚌❀▱◖▲♣P⌐

Dalton-in-Furness

Brown Cow

The Green, LA15 8LP (just off A590)
🕙 12-11
☎ (01229) 462553
Beer range varies Ⓗ

A warm and friendly atmosphere greets visitors to this 400-year-old coaching house, which has retained many traditional features including original beams, brasses, local prints and an open fire. A winner of many awards for its five real ales, this pub also serves excellent food from a full and varied menu. Meals can be enjoyed in the large dining room or, on warmer days, the charming beer garden. Well worth a visit. ⋈Q✿✪◗≈🚆(6, 6A)P⅄☐

Dent

Sun Inn
Main Street, LA10 5QL
☺ 11-11; 12-10.30 Sun
☎ (01539) 625208
Dent Bitter, Aviator, Kamikaze; guest beers Ⓗ
Standing on an ancient cobbled street, at the centre of this popular Dales village, the Sun has an L-shaped bar with a variety of seating spaces including a darts area, a games room and an annexe which can be curtained off. While still regarded as the tap for its former owners the Dent Brewery, the George & Dragon a few yards away is now the 'official' tap. ⋈Q✿🚲◗♣●P

Eaglesfield

Black Cock
CA13 0SD (off A5086, 2 miles S of Cockermouth)
☺ 8-11; 12.30-10.30 Sun
☎ (01900) 822989
Jennings Bitter Ⓗ
This unspoilt 17th-century village pub has two rooms with low beams, stained wooden panelling and an open fire in one bar. No food is served here, but the pub oozes character. Its walls are adorned with gleaming brassware. There is so much tradition here, it feels like stepping back in time. Affectionately known locally as Annie's, this gem is well worth a detour, but note that parking is limited. ⋈Q🚆P

Foxfield

Prince of Wales
LA20 6BX (opp station)
☺ 2.45 (12 Fri & Sat)-11; 12-10.30 Sun
☎ (01229) 716238 ⊕ princeofwalesfoxfield.co.uk
Beer range varies Ⓗ
Winner of more CAMRA awards than it cares to remember, this pub offers beers from its two house breweries, Foxfield and Tigertops, always including a mild, as well as ale from all over England. On display is a fine collection of railway memorabilia, local maps and pictures which, together with comfortable furnishings and an open fire, create a welcoming atmosphere. The pub is located next to a rural railway station and a bus stop, ensuring plenty of custom for its regular beer festivals. ⋈Q✿🚲🚆(X7, 511)♣●P⅄☐

Garrigill

George & Dragon Inn
Main Street, CA9 3DS
☺ 12-2 (not Mon-Fri winter), 5-11; 12-midnight Sat; 12-10.30 Sun
☎ (01434) 381293 ⊕ garrigill-pub.co.uk
Black Sheep Best Bitter; guest beer Ⓗ
Situated high in the north Cumbrian Pennines, the George & Dragon is at the centre of the village, where it was first built as a coaching inn in the 17th century. Originally serving the local lead and zinc miners, today it is ramblers on the Pennine Way Coast-to-Coast walking routes who stop here. Over the bar is a large, hinged cover with eight glass panels displaying original drawings depicting Ritson's 'The Rights of the Dragon', with hand-written descriptions. ⋈Q✿✪◗♣

Gosforth

Gosforth Hall Hotel
CA20 1AZ
☺ 5 (12 Sat & Sun)-midnight
☎ (019467) 25322 ⊕ gosforthhallhotel.co.uk
Beer range varies Ⓗ
Full of history and character, this Grade II listed former pele tower and fortified farmhouse boasts the largest sandstone arch fireplace surviving in England. Of the three beers on offer, one is always a Cumbrian brew, and all are usually around 4% ABV. The large, landscaped garden houses a boules pitch and hosts live music on summer Sundays. Meals are available at weekend lunchtimes and every evening. Do not be surprised to come across people in medieval costume – medieval night is one of several themed events staged here. ⋈✿🚲◗▲🚆P

Grasmere

Dale Lodge Hotel (Tweedies Bar)
Langdale Road, LA22 9SW
☺ 12-midnight daily
☎ (01539) 435300 ⊕ dalelodgehotel.co.uk
Beer range varies Ⓗ
The stone floor and sturdy contemporary furniture in the bar are welcoming to walkers as well as those not wearing muddy boots. The ever-changing beers usually include a Scottish, a Taylor's and at least one from a local micro. Try a 'Tweedies Bat' of different beers in third-of-a-pint glasses; knowledgeable staff will offer advice. An imaginative menu is available in both the bar and adjoining dining room. A games room is at the rear, and there are extensive lawned grounds and full hotel facilities. ⋈✿🚲◗&🚆(555, 599)♣●P⅄

Great Broughton

Punchbowl Inn
19 Main Street, CA13 0YJ
☺ 7 (5 Fri & Sat)-11; 12-2, 7-11 Sun
☎ (01900) 824708
Jennings Bitter; guest beer Ⓗ
Traditional village pub full of character and characters. Built in the 17th century, with beams, open fire and now boasting a classic juke box, the walls are covered in tokens of local esteem and other memorabilia, all creating a welcoming atmosphere. Two well-kept ales include a Jennings and a guest, often from Archers or Copper Dragon. The car park is tiny (just two cars). ⋈Q🚆♣P

Great Langdale

Old Dungeon Ghyll Hotel

LA22 9JY

☼ 11-11; 12-10.30 Sun

☎ (01539) 437272 ⊕ odg.co.uk

Black Sheep Ale; Jennings Cumberland Ale; Theakston XB, Old Peculier; Yates Bitter; guest beers ⊞

A basic hikers' bar converted from a former shippen, it is geared up for outdoor types, with a hard floor, wooden bench seating and a kitchen range that is handy for drying wet walking gear. It offers a fine selection of quality beers, Weston's Old Rosie cider and good hearty pub grub. The patio commands stunning views of the surrounding Langdale fells. The hotel has a more sedate bar and formal dining room where pre-booked meals are served at 7.30pm. It is owned by the National Trust which also runs the campsite opposite in summer (no caravans).

🏰Q❀☎◁❶🍴🖪▲🆗(516)●▸⏃

Great Salkeld

Highland Drove

CA11 9NA (off B6412, between A686 and Lazonby)

☼ 12-3 (not Mon), 6-midnight; 12-midnight Sat & Sun

☎ (01768) 898349 ⊕ highland-drove.co.uk

John Smith's Bitter; Theakston Black Bull Bitter; guest beer ⊞

Saved from conversion into a residence in 1998, the local owners have transformed this country inn into a thriving business with an award-winning restaurant, bar, games room and a new lounge/dining area. New areas have been tastefully and sensitively designed using exposed stone brick and reclaimed timber. The warmth of the welcome and the quality of the ales have made this a deserved winner of local CAMRA Pub of the Year in 2005 and 2006. 🏰❀☎◁❶🖪🆗♣P

Greenodd

Ship Inn

Main Street, LA12 7QZ (off A590)

☼ 6-midnight (1am Sat); 12-11 Sun

☎ (07782) 655294

Beer range varies ⊞

A traditional village pub blending the old and the new, this pub is well worth a visit. Beamed ceilings contrast with leather suites, and an open fire enhances the ambience of the relaxed lounge. For those who wish to try their hand, the games room hosts a pool table, bandit and juke box. Guest beers often come from local breweries. 🏰🖪♣P🍴

Hallbankgate

Belted Will

CA8 2NJ (on A689 Alston Rd, 4 miles E of Brampton)

☼ 12-3 (Mon-Fri summer only), 5 (6 Fri)-midnight; 12-midnight Sat & Sun

☎ (01697) 746236 ⊕ beltedwill.co.uk

Beer range varies ⊞

Nestling at the foot of the northern Pennines, the warmth of the welcome here is matched by the quality of the food and the beer, with one guest usually from a local micro-brewery.

The pub's unusual name refers to William Howard of nearby Naworth Castle, who featured in one of Sir Walter Scott's poems. A host of outdoor activities are available in the area, ranging from cycling, walking and pony trekking to golf and bird-watching at a new RSPB centre just a mile away. Evening meals are available daily in summer (Sat & Sun in winter), and the pub has its own chess team. Local CAMRA Pub of the Season 2007.

🏰❀☎◁❶🖪🖪♣P

Haverthwaite

Anglers Arms

Old Barrow Road, LA12 8AJ (off A590, opp steam railway)

☼ 11.30-midnight (1am Fri & Sat)

☎ (015395) 31216

Black Sheep Best Bitter; Copper Dragon Golden Pippin; Hawkshead Bitter; Moorhouses Pride of Pendle, Pendle Witches Brew; guest beers ⊞

The bar, which features a pool table, is frequented by locals and a growing coven of witches, while the lounge serves mainly as a dining space. Delicious food is available every day at lunchtime and in the evening; booking is advisable as it is deservedly popular. You will, however, always be made welcome if you just want to try one of the many fine beers, usually numbering 10 but increasing to 20 or more during twice yearly beer festivals. You can arrive here by steam train, but take care crossing the busy A590, especially on the way back. Q❀◁❶🖪🖪(X35, 618)●

Hawkshead

King's Arms Hotel

The Square, LA22 0NZ

☼ 11-midnight

☎ (015394) 36372 ⊕ kingsarmshawkshead.co.uk

Coniston Bluebird; Hawkshead Bitter, seasonal beers; guest beer ⊞

Cosy, often busy pub, dating back to Elizabethan times, owned by the same family for more than 25 years. An unusual roof support comes in the form of a sculpture by local artist Jim Whitworth. Traditional beamed ceilings and an open fire greet the visitor to this 500-year-old listed building. A spacious dining room ensures that diners are unlikely to struggle to find a table, while additional outside seating overlooks the square. Hawkshead is ideally situated for walkers and cyclists exploring the area.

🏰❀☎◁❶🖪▲🖪♣●▸⏃

Hesket Newmarket

Old Crown

Main Street, CA7 8JG

☼ 12-2.30, 5.30-11

☎ (016974) 78288 ⊕ theoldcrownpub.co.uk

Hesket Newmarket Great Cockup Porter, Blencathra Bitter, Skiddaw Special, Doris's 90th Birthday Ale, Old Carrock Strong Ale ⊞

The pub always stocks the full range of Hesket Newmarket beers from the brewery situated in the barn at the rear. A new dining room has doubled the available seating space without detracting from the pub's atmosphere, and the new kitchen has made an expansive menu possible, using local produce. At the centre of village life, the Old Crown has received several royal visitors and won many awards. ⚠Q✿◑⊟⏚⚓♣

Hoff

New Inn
CA16 6TA (on B6260)
☺ 12 (7.30 Mon)-midnight
☎ (01768) 351317
Tirril Bewsher's Best Bitter; guest beers Ⓗ
A genuine village local where the owner is rightly proud of the display of pump clips attached to every ceiling beam and, increasingly, the walls. A cosy bar area featuring plenty of oak has a raised fireplace and a small adjoining dining area (no food Mon & Tue). Regular live music evenings – mainly folk and blues – are hosted here. It has a small, walled front patio and a car park across the road. ⚠Q✿⊯◑♣P

Ings

Watermill Inn
LA8 9PY (turn off A591 by church)
☺ 12-11
☎ (01539) 821309 ⊕ watermillinn.co.uk
Moorhouses Black Cat; Theakston Best Bitter, Old Peculier; Watermill Collie Wobbles, Wruff Night, A Bit-er Ruff; guest beers Ⓗ
Originally a water-powered wood mill, this multi-award-winning free house has been greatly extended since conversion from a simple B&B in 1990, and now includes its own brewery. The cellar and the brewery can be seen through viewing windows. Two rooms – one welcoming families, the other dogs – are used for both drinking and dining. An exceptionally wide range of real ales, quality lagers, bottled beers and cider is available and the food is also of a high standard. A relaxed atmosphere is maintained by the absence of piped music, pool, TV and games machines. Local CAMRA Pub of the Year 2006. ⚠Q✿⊯◑♿⊟(555)♣P¹⊟

Ireby

Lion
CA7 1EA
☺ 6-11 (midnight Sat); 12-3, 7-11 Sun
☎ (016973) 71460 ⊕ irebythelion.co.uk
Derwent Carlisle State Bitter; Jennings Bitter; guest beer Ⓗ
The pub sits at the centre of a quiet rural town, which is really just a village with a market cross. It features wood panelling from local churches, but the bar itself came from a pub in Leeds. The pub supplies beer for the annual folk festival in May. Four beers and a cider are usually available, mostly from local breweries. No meals are served on Monday evening. ⚠Q✿♣♿¹

Irton

Bower House
CA19 1TD
☺ 12-midnight
☎ (019467) 23244 ⊕ bowerhouseinn.co.uk
Theakston Best Bitter; guest beers Ⓗ
Attractive country pub and hotel in the picturesque Esk Valley, ideally placed for touring the western lakes and fells. Old-world ambience is conjured up by open fires in winter, oak beams, large pretty gardens with plenty of space for children to play and a warm, friendly welcome. In the spacious bar, three regularly changing guest beers are usually served and good home-cooked food can be enjoyed in the award-winning restaurant. ⚠✿✿⊯⇌P

Kendal

Burgundy's Wine Bar
19 Lowther Street, LA9 4DH
☺ 11.30-3 (not Tue & Wed), 6.30-midnight; closed Mon; 7-11 Sun
☎ (01539) 733803
Yates Fever Pitch; guest beers Ⓗ
Town-centre bar on three levels, with a games area at the rear accessible from Tanners Yard. One level above is the bar, which can be entered from Lowther Street, and higher still is an upper area with seating around a TV screen. On offer is an above-average selection of guest and bottled beers from home and abroad. The bar hosts the Cumbria Micros Beer Challenge and St George's Day celebrations each spring, and stages weekly live jazz on Thursday evening. Extensions are planned including disabled facilities and a covered, heated roof garden for smokers. ⇌♣

Castle Inn
Castle Street, LA9 7AA
☺ 11.30-midnight (1am Sat); 12-11.30 Sun
☎ (01539) 729983
Jennings Bitter; Tetley Bitter; guest beers Ⓗ
A real community pub supporting local teams and events. The central bar serves two interconnecting rooms: a lounge with an impressive fish tank set into one of the walls, and a bar with TV and raised games area. Note the framed, etched window of Duttons Brewery. Guest beers come from Cumbria and Yorkshire. Good value lunches are available; the Sunday roast is particularly popular. Catherine Parr was born in the nearby castle whose ruins form an impressive silhouette on the horizon. ✿◑⇌¹

Keswick

Square Orange
20 St John's Street, CA12 5AS (between Market Square and Alhambra cinema)
☺ 10-11 (midnight Fri & Sat)
☎ (01768) 773888
Hesket Newmarket Doris's 90th Birthday Ale; guest beer Ⓗ
Relaxed, informal café bar with a continental feel. Two Hesket Newmarket ales are offered along with a selection of bottled Belgian and continental beers. A hub of the Keswick community, it stages live music on Thursday evening and a wide selection of board games are available for winter night entertainment. Stone-baked pizzas made to authentic recipes are served at the weekend. Well-behaved dogs are welcome. ✿◑⊟♣

Kings Meaburn

White Horse

CA10 3BU NY620212

✪ 12-2 (Thu & Sat), 7 (6 Fri, Sat & summer)-11; 12-11 Sun

☎ (01931) 714256

Beer range varies ⓗ

There can be few better examples of a well run village local than this. It has just one cosy bar (even the Gents' is outside), but while small in space it is big on atmosphere. Beers are sourced countrywide and reasonably priced home-cooked meals, using local produce, are popular, especially the 'eccentric' chips (ask the landlord to explain). The White Horse hosts an August Eden Valley beer festival with live music in an adjoining field.
🏨Q🏵🎵🍴♿♣♠P⬮⬝

Kirkby Lonsdale

Sun Inn

7 Market Street, LA6 2AU

✪ 11-11

☎ (01524) 271965 ⊕ sun-inn.info

Jennings Bitter; Taylor Landlord; guest beers ⓗ

The colonnaded overhang façade of this venerable building gives a clue to the nature of the interior. The bar area at the front features exposed beams, stone walls and a wooden floor. Guest beers are usually from local micro-breweries. Further back, beyond the raised fireplace, is a wine library, a small lounge and a more formal dining room. Of particular note in this ancient market town is the view from the churchyard, made famous in a painting by Turner and much admired by Ruskin. Devils Bridge over the River Lune is a popular motorcyclists' meeting place.
🏨Q🎵🍴♿Å🚐(567)♣⬝

Langwathby

Shepherds Inn

Village Green, CA10 1LW (on A686)

✪ 12-3, 6.30-midnight; 12-midnight Sat & Sun

☎ (01768) 881335 ⊕ shepherds-inn.co.uk

Beer range varies ⓗ

Situated on the popular tourist route over Hartside and on the scenic Carlisle-Settle railway line, the pub is well frequented by locals from this thriving village and visitors to nearby attractions including an ostrich farm. The split-level interior has the bar on the lower level where two handpumps regularly dispense beers from local and Scottish micros. The inn has a substantial beer garden with a covered and heated patio for smokers. The village children's play area is nearby.
🏨🏵🎵🚐♣P⬝

Lazonby

Joiners Arms

Townfoot, CA10 1BL

✪ 12 (6 winter)-12.30am; 12-1.30am Sat & Sun

☎ (01768) 898728

Hesket Newmarket Doris's 90th Birthday Ale; guest beer ⓗ

A cottage built in the 18th century, the Joiners later became the village ale house. It has

changed little in appearance over the centuries, but various internal alterations and additions have transformed the small pub into a popular venue where good beer and food can be enjoyed. Adjacent to the bar, where two real ales from local breweries are always on offer, is a lower-level games room, while the main dining area is to the rear.
🏨🏵🎵🍴Å♿🚐♠

Leece

Copper Dog

LA12 0QP (3 miles E of Barrow-in-Furness, off A5087)

✪ 11.30-3, 5.30-11; 11.30-midnight Sat; 12-10.30 Sun

☎ (01229) 877088

Beer range varies ⓗ

Spacious village pub with a newly extended conservatory/dining room, serving freshly prepared food and offering an extensive wine list. Superb views of the surrounding countryside can be enjoyed from the panoramic conservatory; it can also be booked for private functions. An annual beer festival is held in summer; check for dates.
🏨Q🎵🏵🎵🍴♿🚐P⬝

Loppergarth

Wellington

Main Street, LA12 0JL (1 mile off A590 between Lindal and Pennington)

✪ 6-midnight (1am Fri & Sat)

☎ (01229) 582388

Beer range varies ⓗ

This local pub in the hamlet of Loppergarth has two main rooms, one for drinking and the other for games including darts and pool. Both rooms have warm and cosy open fires, wonderfully welcoming on a cold winter's night. If you are visiting the South Lakes area it is well worth seeking out this pub and meeting its friendly licensee. 🏨♣

Low Hesket

Rose & Crown

CA4 0HG (on A6 between Carlisle and Penrith)

✪ 12-3 (not Mon-Thu), 6-midnight (12.30am Fri & Sat); 12-3, 6.30-11.30 Sun

☎ (016974) 73346

Jennings Mild, Bitter, Cumberland Ale ⓗ

This recently extended pub now provides an area for dining separate from the bar. The decor has a transport theme, with old pictures and signs adorning the walls, and former coach seats for drinkers. Good local food is an added attraction. Although the M6 motorway took most of the passing trade away, the pub continues to thrive. 🏨Q🎵🍴♿P⬝

Loweswater

Kirkstile Inn

CA13 0RU (off B5289, 5 miles from Cockermouth via Lorton)

✪ 11-11 (10.30 Sun)

☎ (01900) 85219 ⊕ kirkstile.com

Coniston Bluebird; Loweswater Melbreak Bitter, Kirkstile Gold, Grasmoor Dark Ale; Yates Bitter ⓗ

This 17th-century Lakeland inn sits below Melbreak in a stunning setting 'twixt Loweswater and Crummock Water. It comprises a single bar plus two seated areas, and a restaurant serving good food. Low ceilings and stone walls add character. Home of Loweswater Brewery, four different beers are brewed, two bottled and sold at the inn. Oversized glasses are used. Local CAMRA Pub of the Year 2003 to 2005, it can get very busy at peak times. ᗰQ❀✍❶❺ᗺPᗡ

Millom

Punch Bowl

The Green, LA18 5HJ (½ mile from station)
❸ 6-11; 12-3, 6-10.30 Sun
☎ (01229) 772605
Beckstones range; guest beers ⊞
This village pub was rejuvenated when it was taken over by the Beckstones Brewery. It now offers a selection of Beckstones ales, including the award-winning Black Dog Freddy, together with guest beers from local breweries. It has a large open-plan bar area with a welcoming real fire and a separate games/TV room, all making for a convivial atmosphere. ᗰ₳(The Green)ᗺ(X7)ᗡ

Mungrisdale

Mill Inn

CA11 0XR
❸ 11-11; 12-10.30 Sun
☎ (01768) 779632 ⊕ the-millinn.co.uk
Jennings Bitter, Cumberland Ale; guest beer ⊞
The inn is situated on the north-eastern edge of the Lake District, at the base of Souther Fell and Blencathra, and perched on the banks of the Glenderamakin River. The bar is festooned with humorous cartoons around a local theme. One of the events staged here is an annual pie festival in November, but in fact pies feature large on the menu throughout the year. The food is freshly prepared from locally sourced produce. ᗰQ❀✍❶♣P�"

Near Sawrey

Tower Bank Arms

LA22 0LF (on B5285, 6 miles S of Ambleside)
OS371956
❸ 11.30-11.30; closed 3-5 Mon-Thu winter; 11.30-10.30 Sun
☎ (015394) 36334 ⊕ towerbankarms.co.uk
Barngates Tag Lag; Hawkshead Bitter; guest beers ⊞
All the features of a traditional 17th-century Lakeland inn are to be found here: slate floor, oak beams and a cooking range, all in a delightful location. Try the beer garden if the weather is clement. The pub, owned by the National Trust, is popular with Beatrix Potter fans as it stands next to her former home, Hilltop, and features in the tale of Jemima Puddleduck. Food is served in the bar and the restaurant and much of the beer is locally sourced. ᗰQ❀✍❶

Penrith

Agricultural Hotel

Castlegate, CA11 7JE (close to station)
❸ 11-midnight; 12-10.30 Sun
☎ (01768) 862622
Jennings Bitter, Cumberland Ale, Sneck Lifter, seasonal beers ⊞
This comfortable pub is situated close to Penrith Station on the West Coast Main Line and is just a few minutes' walk from the town centre. It is also a stone's throw from the ruins of Penrith Castle – a testimony to the turbulent history of the Border counties and well worth a visit. The Aggie, as it is known locally, serves good value bar meals all day. ᗰ❀✍❶❺₳ᗺPᗺ

Gloucester Arms

Great Dockray, CA11 7DE
❸ 11-11 (midnight Fri & Sat); 12-10.30 Sun
☎ (01768) 863745
Greene King Old Speckled Hen; Taylor Landlord; guest beer ⊞
The oldest pub in Penrith, this welcoming, beamed inn with a warm, cosy atmosphere claims historic links to Richard III. Traditional bar meals are served throughout the pub, and the restaurant offers excellent home-cooked food, with Sunday lunches a speciality. There is an outdoor smoking area with patio heaters. ᗰ❀❶❐₳ᗺPᗺ

Lowther Arms

3 Queen Street, CA11 7XD
❸ 11-3, 6-11 (midnight Fri & Sat); 12-3, 6-10.30 Sun
☎ (01768) 862792
Caledonian Deuchars IPA; Fuller's London Pride; guest beers ⊞
This coaching inn off the old A6 route has recently been extended, but without compromising the original building. A past winner of various awards from CAMRA and In Bloom, it can be busy at mealtimes, but is always welcoming. Drinkers are spoilt for choice, with a range of up to eight real ales usually available. ᗰQ❶₳ᗺ

Pooley Bridge

Sun Inn

CA10 2NN
❸ 12-11 (10.30 Sun)
☎ (01768) 486205
Jennings Bitter, Cumberland Ale, Sneck Lifter, seasonal beers ⊞
The split-level building comprises a wood-panelled lounge to the left of the front entrance and at the lower level a bar with an exit to the large, child-friendly garden. There is also a separate dining room. A wider choice of beers is now available here since Jennings was taken over by Marston's. It is in a handy spot for exploring the less frequented north-eastern Lake District and Lowther Park, or enjoying the Ullswater ferry cruises. ᗰQ❀✍❶❐Å❒(108)♣ᗺ

Ravenglass

Ratty Arms

CA18 1SN (through mainline station)
❸ 11 (12 Sun)-midnight

☎ (01229) 717676
Greene King Ruddles Best; Jennings Cumberland Ale; Theakston Best Bitter; guest beers ⊞
This railway-themed pub occupies the former station building at the junction of the West Coast Main Line and the popular La'al Ratty. The narrow-gauge steam railway runs deep into the striking, historic Upper Eskdale, with more real ale pubs, high fells and Roman remains to explore. Local attractions include Muncaster Castle, a Roman bathhouse and a pretty tidal inlet, rich in wildlife. Excellent, good value food is served all day and two guest beers are usually stocked in summer.
ᴹᴬQ❀◑Ⓓ&Å₹♣P

Rosthwaite

Scafell Hotel
CA12 5XB
☼ 11-11 (10.30 Sun)
☎ (017687) 77208 ⊕ scafell.co.uk
Black Sheep Best Bitter; Theakston Best Bitter, XB, Old Peculier; guest beers ⊞
Traditional country hotel in the heart of the Lake District. Real ales are served in the large Riverside Bar, which has a pool table at one end. Popular with walkers, dogs are welcome. Guest ales – two at busy times – are usually from Hesket Newmarket and Barngates. There is also a choice of more than 60 malt whiskies. Meals are served in the bar or the formal dining room in the main building.
ᴹᴬ❀⇔◑Å₪P

Satterthwaite

Eagle's Head
LA12 8LN (4 miles S of Hawkshead)
☼ 12-3.30 (not Mon), 7 (6.30 Fri & Sat)-11; 12-2.30, 7-11 Sun
☎ (01229) 860237
Beer range varies ⊞
Classic Lakeland inn, set amid Grizedale Forest. The house beers Eagle's Head Ale and Grized Ale are brewed by Moorhouses, and two guests from local companies such as Barngates or Hawkshead are also usually available. Delicious meals are served in the spacious bar/lounge area, and there is a pool room at the back. The pub sometimes closes early in the week in winter – phone to check.
ᴹᴬ❀◑ÅP⅃

Seathwaite

Newfield Inn
LA20 6ED (7 miles N of Broughton-in-Furness)
OS227950
☼ 11-11
☎ (01229) 716208
Caledonian Deuchars IPA; Jennings Cumberland Ale; Theakston Old Peculier; guest beer ⊞
A fell walkers' oasis, this free house in the tiny hamlet of Seathwaite is in the Duddon Valley, a favourite of Wordsworth's. The inn prides itself on serving both quality ales and good food – meals are served 12-9pm daily. The unspoilt pub has welcomed travellers since the 17th century and boasts a fascinating and riotous history. The spacious beer garden

affords excellent views over the fells.
ᴹᴬQ⌖❀◑ ⊞Å♣P

Shap

Greyhound Hotel
Main Street, CA10 3PW (on A6, S end of village)
☼ 11-11; 12-10.30 Sun
☎ (01931) 716474 ⊕ greyhoundshap.demon.co.uk
Jennings Bitter, Cumberland Ale; Tetley Bitter; guest beers ⊞
A Grade II listed building, this former coaching inn dating from the 1680s has been sympathetically refurbished to create a variety of comfortable drinking and dining areas as well as a games room. The guest beers are selected from far and wide, their number increasing in summer. Of particular note is the wall-mounted, large-scale copy of Wainwright's famous 1974 map of Westmorland. This is excellent walking country, with the Coast-to-Coast long distance path passing nearby.
ᴹᴬQ❀⇔◑&Å₪(106)♣P⅃

Smithfield

Robin Hood
CA6 6BP (on A6071)
☼ 12-midnight (1am Fri & Sat)
☎ (01228) 675957
Fuller's London Pride; Geltsdale Kings Forest, Tarnmonath; guest beer ⊞
Formerly the Red House, the pub sits at a crossroads where in olden days traders from Scotland, the North East and Cumberland met to buy and sell cattle and became known as Little Smithfield after the London market. Still a meeting place for farmers and residents, it also hosts travellers en route between Scotland and the North East avoiding the busier main roads. This is the most northerly outlet in England for Fuller's London Pride, supplemented by at least three local beers.
ᴹᴬ❀◑&Å♣P⅃

Staveley

Beer Hall
Mill Yard, LA8 9LR
☼ 12-6
☎ (01539) 822644 ⊕ hawksheadbrewery.co.uk
Hawkshead Bitter, Red, Lakeland Gold, Brodie's Prime; guest beers ⊞
Hawkshead Brewery's tap and visitor centre, built as a showcase for real ale, the Beer Hall looks down into the new brewery, beside the River Kent. The natural wood bar is rich in handpumps serving all the Hawkshead regular beers as well as specials, often only available here. Food and cider are supplied by local producers. Brewery tours and evening functions are a speciality; the opening hours may be extended some evenings – check the website. ◑&₹₪(555)♣P

Eagle & Child Inn
Kendal Road, LA8 9LP
☼ 11-11; 12-10.30 Sun
☎ (01539) 821320 ⊕ eaglechildinn.co.uk
Beer range varies ⊞

The U-shaped bar area displays an abundance of memorabilia and offers a variety of seating arrangements. Beers include up to two from Hawkshead, and up to five more usually sourced from northern micro-breweries. The range is further augmented by regular beer festivals held in tents in the riverside gardens across the road. Weekday lunches are a popular attraction. The upstairs function room is styled as a medieval banqueting hall and has access to the back garden. ⚒️✿☕🍴≠🖼️(555)♦P⅃

Talkin

Blacksmith's Arms
CA8 1LE
🕐 12-3, 6-11
☎ (016977) 42111 ⊕ blacksmithsarmstalkin.co.uk
Copper Dragon Bitter; Jennings Cumberland Ale; Yates Bitter; guest beer Ⓗ
One of the most popular pubs in the area, the Blackies has for many years enjoyed a reputation for good food and beer in convivial, relaxed surroundings. Originally the blacksmith's shop, the building has been altered and refurbished over the years to become the well-appointed and cosy inn it is today, comprising a restaurant, lounge, garden room and bar. Local amenities include Brampton golf course, Talkin Tarn country park and, a few miles further on, Hadrian's Wall. The pub lies on the north-western tip of the Pennines, an area of outstanding natural beauty. ⚒️✿☕🍴☕🍴&AP⅃

Tallentire

Bush Inn
CA13 0PT
🕐 7-midnight; closed Mon; 12-11 Sun
☎ (01900) 823707
Jennings Bitter; guest beers Ⓗ
A quiet country pub with a modern, minimalist interior in keeping with the simplicity of the old building and creating an uncluttered feel. The landlord has previously run other Guide-listed pubs. Jennings Bitter is a permanent feature, supported by two changing guests, usually selected from small regional breweries. Polypins of real cider are put on in summer. The restaurant serves meals Thursday to Saturday evenings, and folk music sessions are held on the last Wednesday of the month. ⚒️Q✿🍴&🖼️♦

Ulverston

Farmers Arms
Market Place, LA12 7BA
🕐 10-11 (midnight Fri & Sat); 10-10.30 Sun
☎ (01229) 584469 ⊕ farmersrestaurant-thelakes.co.uk
Beer range varies Ⓗ
Busy pub serving good quality meals and snacks, both in the upper level restaurant and the bar area. A good choice of wines and continental beers complements the six cask ales. The front terrace, complete with heaters and a canopy, overlooks the market place – an ideal spot to sit and watch the world go by. The pub stages a popular weekly quiz on Thursday. ✿🍴A≠🖼️

Swan Inn
Swan Street, LA12 7JX
🕐 3.30-11; 12-midnight Fri & Sat; 12-11 Sun
☎ (01229) 582510
Hawkshead Bitter, Lakeland Gold, Brodie's Prime; guest beers Ⓗ
This former Hawkshead Brewery pub now belongs to the Top Lock, Heapey, Chorley Group and currently offers three Hawkshead beers plus up to six ever-changing guest beers from a wide and varied range. This is a wet house like they used to be: good ale, great craic and sports-oriented. ⚒️✿&A≠🖼️♦♦🍴

Wasdale Head

Wasdale Head Inn
CA20 1EX (E off A595 at Gosforth) OS187087
🕐 11-11; 12-10.30 Sun
☎ (019467) 26229 ⊕ wasdale.com
Great Gable Burnmoor Pale, Wasd'ale, Scawfell, Illgill IPA, Yewbarrow Ⓗ
Majestically situated at the foot of England's highest mountains, including Scawfell, and well off the main roads, deep in Wasdale, past Wastwater, this famous pub is a wonderful centre for walking and climbing. It was once the abode of Will Ritson, raconteur and the World's Biggest Liar. Local CAMRA Pub of the Year in 2006, it is now the home of Great Gable Brewery and offers a comprehensive range of 10 or more of its beers. Hearty home-cooked food is based on local produce. ⚒️Q☕✿☕🍴&A♣♦P🍴

Whitehaven

Bransty Arch
Bransty Row, CA28 7XE
🕐 9am-midnight
☎ (01946) 517640
Greene King Abbot; Jennings Bitter; Marston's Pedigree; guest beers Ⓗ
This lively Wetherspoon town-centre pub has a varied mix of customers, and welcomes families in a separate area. In addition to three regular beers, up to eight guests are available, and it also serves one draught cider. Beer festivals are held throughout the year. Lying close to the attractive harbour and convenient for the station, this pub can get noisy in the evening and at weekends. 🍴&≠🖼️♦

Winton

Bay Horse Inn
CA17 4HS (off A685)
🕐 12-3 (not Mon), 6-midnight; 12-3, 6-11.30 Sun
☎ (01768) 371451
Beer range varies Ⓗ
Overlooking the green, this is a fine example of a traditional, privately owned village local. Farmhouse-style doors lead into the stone-flagged bar area and on to a raised games room at the rear. An adjoining room, with a small bar counter, is set out for dining, while a further room, featuring an unusual fireplace, provides additional space. Dogs are welcome. Apart from a regular Hawkshead ale, some 280 guest beers are served during the course of the year. Occasional beer festivals are staged here too. ⚒️Q✿☕🍴♣♦P⅃

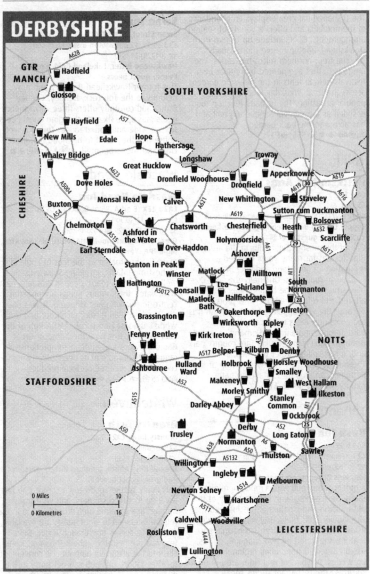

DERBYSHIRE

GTR MANCH
Hadfield
Glossop
SOUTH YORKSHIRE
Hayfield
New Mills
Edale
Hope
Whaley Bridge
Hathersage
Longshaw
Troway
Apperknowle
Great Hucklow
Dronfield Woodhouse
Dronfield
Dove Holes
Staveley
Monsal Head
Calver
New Whittington
Sutton cum Duckmanton
Buxton
Chelmorton
Ashford in the Water
Chatsworth
Chesterfield
Heath
Bolsover
Scarcliffe
Holymoorside
Earl Sterndale
Over Haddon
Ashover
Stanton in Peak
Milltown
Winster
Matlock
South Normanton
Hartington
Bonsall
Lea
Shirland
Matlock Bath
Hallfieldgate
Brassington
Oakerthorpe
Alfreton
Wirksworth
Ripley
Fenny Bentley
Kirk Ireton
Belper
Kilburn
Denby
Ashbourne
Hulland Ward
Holbrook
Horsley Woodhouse
Makeney
Smalley
West Hallam
Morley Smithy
Ilkeston
Darley Abbey
Stanley Common
Ockbrook
Trusley
Derby
Long Eaton
Normanton
Sawley
Willington
Thulston
Ingleby
Melbourne
Newton Solney
Hartshorne
Caldwell
Woodville
Rosliston
Lullington
LEICESTERSHIRE
CHESHIRE
STAFFORDSHIRE
NOTTS

0 Miles 10
0 Kilometres 16

Alfreton

Victoria Inn

80 Nottingham Road, DE55 7EL (on B600)

⚙ 1 (12 Sat)-11; 12-10.30 Sun

☎ (01773) 520156

Beer range varies Ⓗ
Extensively refurbished, busy but friendly two-roomed local served by a central bar. The lounge features an illuminated aquarium, while pump clips of previously featured beers are displayed on beams in the public bar, which has a pool table and Sky TV. Guest beers change regularly and showcase local micro-breweries; a summer beer festival is held. The outdoor terrace houses long alley skittles. Alfreton Town Football Ground is nearby. Catch the Derby-Mansfield bus or Red Arrow.
⚙🅿🚲🚆🚌♣♠

Apperknowle

Barrack Hotel

Barrack Road, S18 4AU (off main Dronfield road at Unstone) SK380781

⚙ 6-midnight; 7 (8 winter)-midnight Sat; 12-5, 7-midnight Sun

☎ (01246) 416555

Abbeydale Moonshine; Kelham Island Pale Rider; Tetley Bitter; guest beers Ⓗ
Retaining the original bar frontage on refurbishment, this 19th-century free house offers a good selection of local beers and superb home cooked food (until 8pm). Three rooms include a family room for meals only and games room. The pub enjoys spectacular views of the valley. The landlord is a keen supporter of local cricket, in particular the under 11/12 teams, and holds presentation

nights in the pub. This is a true community inn.
✿◖ᵭ◲♣️ᴾᴸ

Ashbourne

Green Man & Black's Head Royal Hotel

St Johns Street, DE6 1GH
☼ 11-11; 12-11 Sun
☎ (01335) 345783
Draught Bass; Leatherbritches seasonal beers; Marston's Pedigree; guest beers ⍚
Warmly praised by Boswell in his biography of Samuel Johnson, the Green Man still has its old gallows sign across Ashbourne's main street. A rambling 300-year-old coaching inn with stone steps from the cobbled yard, it is heated with open fires in winter. Nearby the ball is 'turned up' for the start of the Royal Shrovetide football game and mementos feature throughout. Local breweries are showcased and an August bank holiday beer festival is held. ▲Q✿✉◖ᵭ◲◱

Ashover

Old Poets' Corner

Butts Road, S45 0EW
☼ 12.30-2.30, 5-11; 12-11 Fri-Sun
☎ (01246) 590888 ⊕ oldpoets.co.uk
Ashover Light Rale; Oakham JHB; Sarah Hughes Dark Ruby; Taylor Landlord ⍚
Home of Ashover Brewery, this mock-Tudor building has open fires, hop-strewn beams and candle-lit tables creating a welcoming, relaxed atmosphere. Choose from eight handpumps, six traditional ciders, draught and bottle Belgian beers and country wines. CAMRA National Cider Pub of the Year 2006 and local CAMRA Pub of the Year 2006. Regular live music, poetry readings, a weekly quiz and at least three beer festivals a year also feature. A holiday cottage sleeping eight is available. Brewing weekends can be arranged. ▲Q✿✉◖ᵭ▲◱♣️●ᴾᴸ

Belper

Cross Keys

Market Place, DE56 1FZ
☼ 12-11 (10.30 Sun)
☎ (01773) 599191
Bateman Dark Mild, XB, XXXB, seasonal beers; Draught Bass; guest beer ⍚
This early 19th-century pub was formerly used as accommodation for visiting theatre troupes, and as a meeting place for Druids and Oddfellows; it has also witnessed at least one murder. Two-roomed, with a central bar, a real fire warms the lounge. Bar billiards and shove-ha'penny are played. The pub has enjoyed a renaissance since it was bought by Bateman – all its ales have proved popular locally and regular beer festivals are held. ▲Q✿◲ᵭ≠◱♣️●

George & Dragon

117 Bridge Street, DE56 1BA
☼ 11-11; 12-10.30 Sun
☎ (01773) 880210
Greene King Abbot; Tetley Bitter; guest beers ⍚

A fine Georgian roadside pub on the main thoroughfare featuring a prominent bay window and unusual covered pillared entrance. Formerly a coaching inn with archway, it also acted as an early post office. A deep open plan pub with different areas, it serves up a good range of changing guest ales, food and regular live entertainment. Belper Town Football Club, River Gardens and the Derwent Valley Mills World Heritage Site visitor centre are all nearby. ◖ᵭ≠◱

Queen's Head

29 Chesterfield Road, DE56 1FF
☼ 4 (12 Fri & Sat)-11; 12-10.30 Sun
☎ (01773) 825525 ⊕ derbyshirepubs.co.uk
Caledonian Deuchars IPA; Jennings Cumberland Ale; Taylor Landlord; Tetley Burton Ale; guest beers ⍚
Built during the Victorian era, this popular roadside inn comprises three rooms with a central bar, an upstairs function room and a pleasant patio area, providing panoramic views over the town and countryside. The public bar has a real fire and old photographs of Belper. Reputedly haunted, the pub hosts regular themed beer festivals, quizzes and entertainment, usually blues or folk, at the weekends. It is a short walk uphill from the market place. ▲Q✿◲♣️●

Bolsover

Blue Bell

57 High Street, S44 6HF (behind the market place, near the castle)
☼ 12-3.30, 6.30-midnight; 12-3, 7-midnight Sun
☎ (01246) 823508 ⊕ bolsover.uk.com
Jennings Bitter; guest beers ⍚
This traditional two-roomed ale house proudly holds the local CAMRA Pub of the Year 2007 title among other awards. The beer garden sits on top of a crumbling cliff face, affording panoramic views across to the Crich Lighthouse in the Peak District. The excellent

INDEPENDENT BREWERIES

Amber Ripley
Ashover Ashover
Bottle Brook Kilburn
Brunswick Derby
Danelaw Not currently brewing
Derby Derby
Derventio Trusley
Edale Edale
Falstaff Normanton
Funfair Ilkeston
Globe Glossop
Haywood Bad Ram Ashbourne
Headless Derby
Howard Town Glossop
John Thompson Ingleby
Leadmill Denby
Leatherbritches Fenny Bentley
Nutbrook West Hallam
Peak Ales Chatsworth
Spire Staveley
Thornbridge Ashford in the Water
Tollgate Woodville
Townes Staveley
Whim Hartington

range of quality guest ales often includes Jennings favourites. Look out for the 'Neglected Shed' beer festivals in the ancient stables every May. A friendly, family-run pub, the Blue Bell raises funds for local charities. Q✿◑➡♣P

Bonsall

Barley Mow
The Dale, DE4 2AY (off A5012)
✿ 6-midnight; closed Mon; 12-midnight Sat & Sun
☎ (01629) 825685 ⊕ barleymowbonsall.co.uk
Greene King Abbot; Whim Hartington Bitter ⊞
Entertainments include boules, guided walks, the World Championship Hen Race, Marrow Dressing Night and now an Art Club on Thursday. Fridays feature acoustic music sessions and there is live music on Saturday. An extensive, changing range of traditional food is created from generations-old recipes. The single room retains its 17th-century feel and appeal. Limited camping is available by request. Busy times can see guest ales on gravity from the cellar scythed into the rock behind. ▲✿◑▶ÅP

Brassington

Olde Gate Inne
Well Street, DE4 4HJ (off A5023)
✿ 12-2.30, 6-11; 12-3, 7-10.30 Sun
☎ (01629) 540448
Marston's Pedigree, seasonal beers; guest beer ⊞
Family-run, ivy-clad gem, built in 1616, now Grade II listed and reputedly haunted. Oak beams feature throughout, with gleaming copper utensils hanging around three open fireplaces. The main bar boasts pewter jugs and a black-leaded range, while a pipe rack in the snug dates from the 17th century. An extensive menu includes home-cooked dishes and game in season (no food Mon eve). No children under 10 are admitted. Boules is played here. The tourist attraction of Carsington Water is nearby. ▲Q✿◑♿Å♣P

Buxton

Beltane
8a Hall Bank, SK17 6EW
✿ 11-midnight; 12-2am Fri & Sat
☎ (01298) 26010
Beer range varies ⊞
This café bar is Buxton's newest real ale outlet, proving that it is possible to serve good-quality beer alongside wonderful locally sourced food, all in a pleasantly relaxed, smoke-free and family-friendly atmosphere. During the day, the emphasis is on food, while in the evening the Beltane becomes a popular local venue, always serving three changing beers. ◑Å⇌➡(199, T8)

George Hotel
The Square, SK17 6AZ
✿ 11-12.30am daily
☎ (01298) 24711
Kelham Island Pale Rider; guest beers ⊞
Centrally located and spacious inside, the George has an excellent range of up to five

changing guest beers. The pub gets lively, especially in the evening when live music is a regular feature. A quieter time for beer sampling is the afternoon or early evening. Good home-cooked food and the Sunday roasts are well worth trying. There is a large patio area with continental-style outdoor seating in summer. Regular beer festivals are held here. ▲✿◑Å⇌➡♣

Caldwell

Royal Oak
Main Street, DE12 6RR (near centre of village)
✿ 11-midnight (1am Fri & Sat)
☎ (01283) 761486
Marston's Pedigree; guest beers ⊞
This friendly 18th-century free house is a genuine community pub, recently renovated throughout by customers to re-create its mid-20th-century look. There is a small narrow bar with low beamed ceiling at the front and stairs leading to a smart split-level lounge with open fire and beamed ceiling at the rear. Cyclists, ramblers and dogs are welcome, as are families in the lower part of the lounge. Occasional themed food evenings are held. Locally made preserves and honey can be bought. Parking is limited. ▲✿⊞Å♣┗

Calver

Bridge Inn
Calver Bridge, S32 3XA (on A623)
✿ 11.30-3 (3.30 Sat), 5.30-11; 12-3.30, 7-10.30 Sun
☎ (01433) 630415
Greene King H&H Bitter, Abbot ⊞
Sturdy stone pub of a traditional design with central bar area separating two rooms. Both rooms are comfortably furnished, featuring a collection of local guide books, some antique fire-fighting equipment and an array of hats. The landlord has been here since Bass owned the pub in the 1980s. The pub has a pleasant garden overlooking the River Derwent and Arkwright's Calver Mill, now converted into apartments. No meals are served on Monday or winter Sunday. ▲Q✿◑♿ÅP⊡

Chelmorton

Church Inn
Main Street, SK17 9SL
✿ 12-3.30, 7-midnight (11-11 summer Sat); 12-3.30, 7-midnight (12-10.30 summer) Sun
☎ (01298) 85319
Adnams Bitter; Marston's Burton Bitter, Pedigree; guest beers ⊞
Set in beautiful surroundings opposite the church, this traditional village pub caters for walkers and locals alike. Even though the main room is laid out with dining tables, and good, home-cooked food is on offer, a cosy pub atmosphere is maintained. The low ceiling and welcoming open fire make this an excellent local, serving good beer. Parking is available on the dead-end road outside the pub. ▲Q✿◑Å

Chesterfield

Derby Tup

387 Sheffield Road, Whittington Moor, S41 8LS
SK382735

🌣 11.30-3, 5-11 Mon, Tue & Thu; 11.30-11 Wed;
11.30-midnight Fri & Sat; 12-11 Sun

☎ (01246) 454316

**Copper Dragon Golden Pippin; Taylor Landlord;
guest beers** Ⓗ

Situated on the northern outskirts of
Chesterfield, the Tup is part of the Tynemill
chain of pubs, serving up to 10 beers (one
always a stout or porter), many from local
breweries. Real cider, continental bottled
beers and a fine selection of malt whiskies
complement the beer choice. The pub has a
large main room with an open fire and two
smaller rooms. A past winner of local CAMRA
Pub of the Year. ▲Q◖🖥🖥♣👜

Industry

49 Queen Street, S40 4SF (off Newbold Road)
🌣 12-3, 5-midnight daily

☎ (01246) 554123

Beer range varies Ⓗ

Friendly community pub near the town centre,
offering three changing guest ales, usually
from local micro-breweries, and one of the
few regular outlets for Spire Brewery beers.
Good-value home-cooked food is served in a
relaxed and comfortable atmosphere. The pub
hosts weekly quiz and jam nights. A winner of
local CAMRA Pub of the Season, it has gone
from strength to strength over the past two
years. ▲❀◖🖧☿🖥🖥➷📙

Peacock

412 Chatsworth Road, Brampton, S40 3BQ (on
A619)
🌣 12-4, 5.45-11; 12-11 Fri-Sun

☎ (01246) 275115

**Adnams Broadside; Black Sheep Best Bitter;
Caledonian Deuchars IPA; Tetley Bitter; guest
beer** Ⓗ

This welcoming pub has two rooms and an
open fire. The central bar offers a good
selection of real ales and changing guest
beers. There is a large garden to the rear, ideal
for families in summer, with additional
seating at the front. Entertainment includes
league darts, dominoes, shut-the-box and a
weekly quiz night. A winner of many local
CAMRA awards, the pub has its own football
and cricket teams, giving it a friendly
community feel. ▲Q❀☿🖥♣👜⊷

Red Lion

570 Sheffield Road, Whittington Moor, S41 8LX
SK381737
🌣 12-11 (10.30 Sun)

☎ (01246) 450770

Old Mill Mild, Bitter, Bullion, seasonal beers Ⓗ

Traditional two-roomed pub served by a
central bar. There is a compact and homely
lounge area and a large, low-ceilinged main
bar featuring a large-screen TV. One of just a
few Chesterfield outlets to serve a regular
Mild, this is also the most southerly outlet for
Old Mill beers, with at least four of its beers on
sale. A true community pub, the Red Lion is
always raising money for local charities.
🖥🖥♣P

Royal Oak

1 The Shambles, S40 1PX (accessed via walkway
from Market Place)
🌣 11 (7 Mon & Tue)-11; closed Sun

☎ (01246) 237700

**Caledonian Deuchars IPA; Greene King Abbot;
Stones Bitter; guest beers** Ⓗ

Located in the Shambles area, this is said to be
the town's oldest pub, dating back to 1772.
Made up of two distinct buildings, the older
one is reputed to date back to the 16th
century. The two bars are accessible via
separate entrances, but both are served by a
central bar on two levels. The top bar has an
impressive high ceiling and exposed roof
timbers. A range of up to six cask ales is
available. ◖🖥⇌⊷

Darley Abbey

Abbey Inn

Darley Street, DE22 1DX (on riverside)
🌣 11.30-2.30, 6-11; 12-11 Sat; 12-10.30 Sun

☎ (01332) 558297

Samuel Smith OBB Ⓗ

This 15th-century former guesthouse is all that
remains of the Augustinian Abbey of St Mary
De Pratis, the most powerful abbey in Middle
England before the Dissolution. Rescued from
long neglect in 1978, it won a national award
for conversion to its present use. The upper
level bar is reached by an impressive stone
spiral staircase and boasts original church
pews for seats. This complements a lower-
level bar, with stone-flagged floor and roaring
fire. Darley Park is nearby. ▲Q❀◖🖥♣P

Derby

Alexandra Hotel

203 Siddals Road, DE1 2QE
🌣 11-11; 12-3, 7-10.30 Sun

☎ (01332) 293993

Castle Rock Harvest Pale, Elsie Mo; guest beers Ⓗ

Named after the Danish princess who married
the Prince of Wales (later Edward VII) in 1863,
the Alex was originally the Midland Coffee
House. The end wall once advertised Zacharia
Smith's Shardlow Ales, but both sign and
brewer have slipped into history. Long a
Shipstones' house, it subsequently went to
Bateman's and latterly to Tynemill; since then
it has been a strong champion of small
breweries. Two-roomed, with a central bar,
the pub was the birthplace of Derby CAMRA in
1974. ▲Q❀⟐◖🖧⇌🖥♣👜P

Babington Arms

11-13 Babington Lane, DE1 1TA (off St Peter's St)
🌣 9am-midnight (1am Fri & Sat)

☎ (01332) 383647

**Falstaff seasonal beers; Wyre Piddle seasonal
beers; guest beers** Ⓗ

Probably the best Wetherspoon's house in the
country, winning the company's prestigious
Cask Ale Pub of the Year and also local CAMRA
City Pub of the Year in 2005. Showcasing an
amazing range of beers from its 18
handpumps, it stages regular themed brewery
weekends. Originally a furniture store, now
fronted with a verandah for fair-weather
drinking, the pub stands in the former grounds

of Babington House. The first performance of Bram Stoker's Dracula was given in the neighbouring Grand Theatre in 1924. Q❀⊕&♣

Brunswick Inn

1 Railway Terrace, DE1 2RU
✪ 11-11; 12-10.30 Sun
☎ (01332) 290677
Brunswick Father Mike's, Railway Porter, Second Brew, Station Approach, Triple Hop; guest beers ⊞/Ⓖ
Originally built as the centrepiece of a railway village, the inn was closed in 1974 and fell into disrepair. Eventually rescued and restored, it opened as Derby's first multiple real ale house some 14 years later. A purpose-built brewery was added and it rapidly became one of the best-known free houses in the country before being sold to Everards in 2002. Things remain unchanged, however, and the pub was crowned local CAMRA City Pub of the Year in 2004. Q☎❀⊕&≈⊟♣♠

Falstaff

74 Silverhill Road, Normanton, DE23 6UJ (1 mile from centre)
✪ 12-11 (10.30 Sun)
☎ (01332) 342902 ● falstaffbrewery.co.uk
Falstaff Phoenix, 3-Faze, Smiling Assassin, GBD, seasonal beers; guest beers ⊞
Known locally as The Folly and reputedly haunted, this former Allied pub was originally a coaching inn before the surrounding area was built up, closing it in. Now free of ties, its on-site brewery has made it the best real ale house in Normanton. The curved bar is flanked on one side by a small lounge with Offilers Brewery memorabilia and an open fire in winter, on the other by a games room with occasional entertainment. Not posh, but a real local. ⋈Q❀♣♠♠

Flowerpot

23-25 King Street, DE1 3DZ
✪ 11-11 (midnight Fri & Sat); 12-11 Sun
☎ (01332) 204955
Headless range; Marston's Pedigree; Oakham Bishops Farewell; Whim Kaskade, Hartington IPA; guest beers ⊞/Ⓖ
Dating from the 1800s but much expanded from its original premises, the interior reaches far back from the small, roadside frontage and divides into several interlinking rooms. The furthest provides the stage for a lively ongoing gig scene and another has a glass cellar wall, revealing row upon row of stillaged firkins. The new Headless Brewery is at the rear. A showcase of real ales with more than 20 on every weekend, it was local CAMRA Pub of the Year in 2007. Q❀⊕Ⓖ&⊟♠

Olde Dolphin Inne ☆

5a Queen Street, DE1 3DL
✪ 10.30-midnight; 12-11 Sun
☎ (01332) 267711
Adnams Bitter; Black Sheep Bitter; Caledonian Deuchars IPA; Draught Bass; Greene King Abbot; guest beers ⊞
Standing below the great gothic tower of the cathedral, the timber-framed Dolphin is Derby's most picturesque and oldest surviving pub, although much restored latterly. The

beamed interior divides into bar, upper and lower lounges, snug and an upstairs steak bar, each with its own character. Reputedly haunted, regular themed evenings are supplemented by beer festivals in February and July, which spread out on to a splendid, raised rear patio. It is a real gem and not to be missed. ⋈Q❀⊕Ⓖ&P

Rowditch Inn

246 Uttoxeter New Road, DE22 3LL (1 mile from centre)
✪ 12-2 (not Mon-Fri), 7-11
☎ (01332) 343123
Marston's Pedigree; guest beers ⊞
A plain-fronted but warmly welcoming pub, its unexpectedly deep interior divides into two drinking areas and a small snug. A downstairs cellar bar opens occasionally, and the rear garden is a haven in warmer weather. Serving an ever-changing range of guest ales, the bar is adorned by a large collection of pump clips. A cheese evening is hosted each Monday, to which locals bring cheeses from far and wide. Local CAMRA City Pub of the Year 2006. ⋈❀⊟♣

Seven Stars

97 King Street, DE1 3EE
✪ 12-11 (10.30 Sun)
☎ (01332) 340169
Beer range varies ⊞
The second oldest pub in Derby, dating from 1680, this small, narrowly gabled, Grade II listed building has three rooms. Its period features include low-beamed ceilings, stone-framed fireplaces, covered wooden bench seating, low lighting and a deep well in the lounge. A rear woodpanelled snug houses the dart board. A home-brew pub until 1962, the Grade I listed St Helen's House stands directly opposite, and the Derby Crown China Works used to be to its left. ❀Ⓖ⊟♣P

Smithfield

Meadow Road, DE1 2BH (down river from market place)
✪ 11-11; 12-10.30 Sun
☎ (01332) 370429 ● thesmithfield.co.uk
Burton Bridge Top Dog Stout; Kelham Island Pale Rider; Oakham Bishops Farewell, JHB; Whim Hartington IPA; guest beers ⊞
Bow-fronted riverside pub built to serve the cattle market, which has since moved to a new site, leaving the Smithy in a bit of a backwater. A long, basic bar is flanked on one side by a games room with dartboard, and on the other by a cosy lounge with stone fireplace and old settles, overlooking a pleasant riverside patio. Exceptional beer has helped earn the pub local CAMRA's Pub of the Year award in the past. ⋈❀⊕Ⓖ♣P▯

Station Inn

12 Midland Road, DE1 2SN
✪ 11.30-2.30, 5 (7 Sat)-11; 11.30-11 Fri; 12-3, 7-10.30 Sun
☎ (01332) 608014
Draught Bass; Ⓖ Black Sheep Best Bitter; Caledonian Deuchars IPA; guest beers ⊞
This modest pub, but for its elaborate frontage and stained glass, was named after the Midland Railway's classical station nearby,

which was needlessly swept away in 1983 to be replaced by the present uninspiring edifice. A traditional bar, with panelled counter, cast-iron footrail and quarry-tiled floor, is flanked by a games area to the right and a large lounge to the rear that acts as dining area and function room. Many cellar awards attest to the skills of the licensee. ◑⊞&≠⊟♣⏢

Wardwick Tavern

15 The Wardwick, DE1 1HA (near Library)
🕓 11-11; 12-10.30 Sun
☎ (01332) 332677
Tetley Bitter; guest beers Ⓗ
This handsome, three-storied, Grade II listed, red-brick building replaces a much older stone building, the stately fireplace of which can still be seen inside. An iron plaque beside the door marks the height of the Great Flood in 1842. Alton's Wardwick Brewery, which used the Burton Union system, extended far to the rear, being taken over first by Strettons, then by Allsopps, later Ind Coope, who converted their front offices into this attractive pub with bare floorboards and wooden settles. ❀◑

Dove Holes

Queens

2 Halsteads, SK17 8BJ (on A6)
🕓 12-2.30, 7-1am; 12-1am Sat & Sun
☎ (01298) 812919
Tetley Bitter; guest beer Ⓗ
Traditional pub featuring dark beams and horse brasses, with old pictures of drays adorning the walls. Guests enter via a porch into a central room with a bar, which also serves the lounge room to the right. The dining room, which seats 20, serves good, home-cooked food, and the pub has a separate games room. There is plenty of seating throughout the rooms. Bed & breakfast is available with three en-suite rooms. ⮫❀⛺◑Å≠⊟♣P

Dronfield

Coach & Horses

Sheffield Road, S18 2GD
🕓 12-11 (midnight Fri & Sat); 12-10.30 Sun
☎ (01246) 413269
Thornbridge Jaipur; guest beers Ⓗ
Roadside pub north of the town centre, with one comfortably furnished open-plan room. Owned by Sheffield FC, the world's oldest football club founded in 1857, whose ground is adjacent, the pub is operated by Thornbridge Hall Brewery, and there are usually up to five Thornbridge beers available. Good home-made food, using locally sourced ingredients where possible, is served in a friendly, relaxed atmosphere. Evening meals served to 8.30pm. Q❀◑≠⊟♣P⏢

Dronfield Woodhouse

Jolly Farmer

Pentland Road, S18 8ZQ
🕓 12-11 (midnight Fri & Sat); 12-10.30 Sun
☎ (01246) 418018

Black Sheep Best Bitter; Caledonian Deuchars IPA; John Smith Magnet; Tetley Bitter; guest beers Ⓗ
This community pub, built in 1976 by former Nottingham Brewers Shipstones and located in a large housing estate, was turned into a themed ale house in the 1990s. The cask beers are stillaged in a glass-fronted cellar behind the bar, which is free of the usual ostentatious lager pumps. The pub is open plan, but has distinct areas including a tap room with pool table and a raised dining area. The beer range includes two guest beers, usually from small independents. A beer festival is held in November.
Q❀◑Ⓓ&⊟♣P⏢

Earl Sterndale

Quiet Woman

SK17 0BU (off B5053)
🕓 12-3.30, 7-midnight daily
☎ (01298) 83211
Jennings Dark Mild; Marston's Burton Bitter, Pedigree; guest beers Ⓗ
This unspoilt inn sits in an idyllic spot opposite the church and village green in the Peak District National Park. Warm and welcoming, it has a small bar and a real fire. On one of the low beams a collection of original Marston's pump clips from long-lost beers is displayed. For traditional pub games, there are dominoes tables in the main bar and a games room. It is popular with walkers, who stock up on local cheeses, fresh eggs and pork pies at the bar.
⮫Q⮫❀Å♣P

Fenny Bentley

Coach & Horses

DE6 1LB (on A515)
🕓 11-11; 12-10.30 Sun
☎ (01335) 350246
Marston's Pedigree; guest beers Ⓗ
This traditional 16th-century coaching inn has preserved many original features such as old flagged floors and very low beams. Coal and log burning stoves set in brick and stonework and comfortable wooden chairs and settles help create a cosy atmosphere in the bar. In the dining and garden rooms, delicious home-cooked food made from local produce is served. The outside areas make for pleasant drinking in summer when the number of guest beers increases. Many of Derbyshire's major tourist attractions are nearby.
⮫Q❀◑&ÅP

Glossop

Crown Inn

142 Victoria Street, SK13 8HY (on the Hayfield Road out of town)
🕓 5 (11.30 Fri & Sat)-11; 12-10.30 Sun
☎ (01457) 862824
Samuel Smith OBB Ⓗ
This end-of-terrace local, a few minutes' walk from the town centre, was built in 1846 and has been a Smith's house since 1977 – the only one in the entire High Peak area. An attractive curved bar serves two side snugs, each with real fires that are lit in cold weather,

and a pool/games room. Old pictures of Glossop and country prints add to a traditional feel. The beer prices are the lowest in the area. ♨Q🅿♿⚘≠🚃♣╚

Globe
144 High Street West, SK13 8HJ
🕐 5-2am; closed Tue; 1-1am Sun
☎ (01457) 852417 ⊕ globemusic.org
Beer range varies Ⓗ
The Globe Brewery, to the rear of the pub, was opened in 2006 by landlord/brewer Ron Brookes brewing solely for the pub, plus occasional specials for local beer festivals. Seven handpumps dispense Globe and guest beers. Real cider and a British bottled beer selection are also available. Live music features strongly, with an upstairs room hosting concerts on Friday and Saturday evenings. Downstairs, Monday is folk night, Wednesday a popular quiz evening and a local resident band play on Thursday. The vegetarian-only menu is great value.
Q🅿🍴♿≠🚃●╚

Old Gloveworks
Unit 1 Riverside Mill, George Street, SK13 8AY
🕐 12-midnight (1am Fri-Sat); closed Mon-Wed; 12-10.30 Sun
☎ (01457) 858432 ⊕ thegloveworksglossop.com
Beer range varies Ⓗ
This converted former mill is completely free of tie, selling six changing beers from local and regional breweries. A roof terrace and front patio afford views over Glossop Brook and Harehills Park. Thursday from 5pm is curry night, always with a vegetarian option, followed by a quiz. Friday and Saturday are disco nights, and on Sunday a live group or artist performs. An age restriction of 25 ensures a trouble-free atmosphere although children are admitted during the day at the landlord's discretion. 🍴◑≠🚃P

Star Inn Alehouse
2-4 Howard Street, SK13 7DD
🕐 2 (12 Sat)-11 (midnight Fri & Sat); 12-10.30 Sun
☎ (01457) 853072
Beer range varies Ⓗ
Highly regarded corner local, the first and last stop-off for visitors by public transport – bus stops and train station are within yards of the door. Six handpumps dispense a good range of beers. A real cider is served by jug from the cellar, and there is a popular bottled cider selection. Pictures of bygone Glossop, wooden floors and a rear tap room served by a hatch add to the atmosphere. The licensees are long-standing CAMRA members. 🚃≠🚃♣●P

Great Hucklow

Queen Anne Inn
Main Road, SK17 8RF
🕐 12-2.30 (not Tue), 6.30 (6 Fri)-11; 12-3, 6-11 Sat; 12-3, 7-10.30 Sun
☎ (01298) 871246 ⊕ thequeenanne.net
Adnams Bitter; guest beers Ⓗ
The Queen Anne was first granted a licence in 1704, although it was functioning as an ale house as early as 1577. The village thrived on lead mining in the 18th century and has a Unitarian chapel dating from this period.

Inside, the pub has low ceilings, beams and brasses, and a high-backed settle. Pets and walkers are welcome. The guest beers often come from the Storm Brewery. The pub is closed all day Monday between New Year and Easter. ♨🍴🅿⚘◑♿▲♣P🍴

Hadfield

New Lamp
12 Bankbottom, SK13 1BY (500m from railway station)
🕐 12-11.30 (10.30 Sun)
☎ (01457) 860490
Beer range varies Ⓗ
Originally called the Commercial, this late-Victorian pub earned its soubriquet 'the Red Lamp' as it was commonly used for assignations between ladies-of-the-night and navvies from the nearby Longdendale reservoirs. Recently refurbished, today it provides walkers along the Trans-Pennine Trail with a light, airy and convenient spot to sample a wide range of beers and an extensive menu. At weekend evenings, the New Lamp hosts regular music events, and has resident pool and darts teams.
♨🅿◑≠🚃♣P╚

Hallfieldgate

Shoulder of Mutton
Hallfieldgate Lane, Shirland, DE55 6AA (on B6013 crossroads)
🕐 12 (7 Tue)-11; 12-10.30 Sun
☎ (01773) 834992
John Smith Bitter; guest beer Ⓗ
This genuinely friendly and welcoming pub, with a strong community focus, is based in an attractive old stone building that was once two cottages. It is set in semi-rural surroundings, featuring a pleasant side garden with lovely views over the Amber Valley. In the small bar a juke box boasts a large and eclectic selection of tunes. The larger room has several comfortable seating areas. On offer are constantly changing guest beers (up to 10 per week), usually from micro-breweries.
🅿🚃▲♣P╚

Hartshorne

Admiral Rodney Inn
65 Main Street, DE11 7ES (on A514) SK325211
🕐 6-midnight; 12-midnight (12-3, 6-midnight winter) Sat; 12-3, 7-midnight Sun
☎ (01283) 216482
Marston's Pedigree; guest beers Ⓗ
Dating back to the early 19th century, this traditional village pub was substantially rebuilt in 1959, and more recently refurbished to provide an open-plan L-shaped drinking area. It retains the original oak beams in the former snug. A small raised area behind the bar is served through a hatch. Three guest beers are usually available. Meals are limited to themed food evenings on Wednesday and traditional Sunday lunches. The grounds include a cricket pitch, and the pub stays open during Sunday afternoon matches. ♨🅿◑♿🚃♣P

Hathersage

Little John Hotel

Station Road, S32 1DD
✪ 12-11; 12-10.30 Sun
☎ (01433) 650225
Beer range varies Ⓗ

A large stone-built pub with four seating areas – lounge, bar, family room and function area – all of which are smartly furnished. The beers come from rotating breweries, with regular appearances from Archers, Kelham Island, Slaters, Storm and Wentworth. Food is available all day on Saturday and Sunday; the pub is well known for the generous size of its meals. Folk singers sometimes perform on Saturday. Overnight guests may opt for bed & breakfast accommodation or rent a holiday cottage. ⚫🏠🕭🍴◑🍽🛏🚃🚌♣♠P

Millstone Inn

Sheffield Road, S32 1DA (east of village on A6187)
✪ 11.30-3, 6-11; 11.30-11 Fri & Sat; 12.00-10.30 Sun
☎ (01433) 650258 🌐 millstoneinn.co.uk
Black Sheep Best Bitter; Caledonian Deuchars IPA; Everards Tiger; Taylor Landlord; guest beers Ⓗ

The pub originally served the nearby millstone quarry and is now popular with walkers and climbers. Guests may choose between a large smartly decorated bar, a ballroom and extensive outdoor seating, partly under cover. Guest beers come from local breweries, and beer festivals are held in June and August. Meze-type food is a speciality. There are quizzes on Friday evening and live music on the last Sunday of the month. The landlord runs his own taxi service to the nearby station. ⚫🕭🍴◑🛏♿🚌♣♠P

Hayfield

Royal Hotel

Market Street, SK22 2EP
✪ 12-11 daily
☎ (01663) 742721 🌐 theroyalhayfield.co.uk
Hydes Bitter; guest beers Ⓗ

A former vicarage, this imposing stone pub stands near the church and cricket ground alongside the River Sett in an attractive Peak District village, which was the birth place of Arthur Lowe, the immortal Captain Mainwaring. The interior boasts original oak panels and pews that create a relaxing atmosphere, enhanced by real fires in winter. A restaurant and function room complete the facilities. An annual beer festival is staged in October. ⚫Q🕭🍴◑♿🍴🛏P

Heath

Elm Tree

Mansfield Road, S44 5SE (in village, 1 mile from M1 jct 29)
✪ 11.30-3, 5-11; 11.30-11 Sat; 12-10.30 Sun
☎ (01246) 850490 🌐 theelmtreeheath.co.uk
Beer range varies Ⓗ

Situated on the main road through the village, this pub has a large main room complemented by the smaller public bar area at the back. At least four beers are on offer at any one time. The pub is renowned for its good food – all dishes are made to order, using local produce wherever possible, and the Sunday roasts are highly recommended. For the summer, there are spacious beer gardens to the side and rear. ⚫🕭◑🍴🛏🚃P

Holbrook

Dead Poets Inn

38 Chapel Street, DE56 0TQ
✪ 12-2.30, 5-11; 12-11 Fri & Sat; 12-10.30 Sun
☎ (01332) 780301
Greene King Abbot; Marston's Pedigree; guest beers Ⓗ/Ⓖ

Built in 1800 and formerly known as the Cross Keys, the pub has undergone a remarkable transformation in recent times to create an inn with a real medieval feel. Its two rooms contain high-backed pews, stone-flagged floors, low lighting, a real fire and an inglenook. Once free, now an Everards house, it was so named because its former owner believed that many of our famous poets gained inspiration from atmospheric taverns such as this; poetry readings are held on the first Tuesday each month. ⚫Q🕭🍴◑🚌(71, 71A)♣♠P

Holymoorside

Lamb Inn

16 Loads Road, S42 7EU
✪ 5 (4 Fri)-11; 12-3, 7-11 Sat & Sun
☎ (01246) 566167
Adnams Bitter; John Smiths Bitter; guest beers Ⓗ

Cosy local in a village on the edge of the Peak District National Park where everyone is made welcome, including walkers (after removing their muddy boots) and dogs. Winner of many CAMRA awards, it can boast up to six ales on the bar, four of which are ever-changing. A roaring fire provides a focal point in winter, while the pleasant outdoor drinking area is ideal for summer evenings. Note lunchtime opening is restricted to weekends and bank holidays. ⚫Q🕭🚌(25)♣P

Hope

Cheshire Cheese

Edale Road, S33 6ZF
✪ 12-3, 6-11; 12-11 Sat; 12-10.30 Sun
☎ (01433) 620381 🌐 cheshirecheesehope.co.uk
Black Sheep Best Bitter; Robinson's Wards Best Bitter; Whim Hartington Bitter; guest beers Ⓗ

This cosy pub, dating from 1578, has three small rooms, one at a lower level which was probably originally used to house animals; nowadays it is used as a dining area (meals are served all afternoon on Sunday). The pub is ideally situated in walking country, but parking space is limited and the road outside narrow. The pub is popular with locals from nearby villages, and hosts activities including a sloe gin making competition. ⚫Q🕭🍴◑🛏AP

Horsley Woodhouse

Old Oak Inn

176 Main Street, DE7 6AW (on A609)
✪ 5 (4 Fri)-11; 12-11 Sat; 12-10.30 Sun
☎ (01332) 881299 🌐 leadmillbrewery.co.uk

Bottle Brook range; Leadmill range; guest beers Ⓗ

Once a farmhouse, the Old Oak was under threat of demolition when it was acquired and renovated by the Denby-based Leadmill Brewery in 2003. Four interconnected rooms, a courtyard and a new rear extension provide a variety of drinking spaces with real fires and hanging hops giving the pub a genuine homely atmosphere. Eight handpumps, occasional beer festivals and live music help to make it another example of a successful village local. ⚒Q❀₪(125)♣♠P⏚

Hulland Ward

Black Horse Inn

DE6 3EE (on A517)
🕓 12-2.30, 6-11; 12-3, 7-10.30 Sun
☎ (01335) 370206
Beer range varies Ⓗ

This traditional, 300-year-old country inn stands in an elevated village, in some of the most picturesque countryside outside the Peak, close to Carsington Water. Its split-level, multi-roomed drinking area, with low-beamed ceilings and quarry-tiled floors, is served by a central bar, offering rotating guest ales. An extensive bar menu is complemented by a popular Sunday carvery in the restaurant. Some guest rooms boast four-poster beds. ❀✍◑₪(109)♣P

Ilkeston

Dewdrop

24 Station Street, DE7 5TE (50 metres from A6096)
🕓 12-2.30 (4 Sat), 7-11; 12-4, 7-10.30 Sun
☎ (0115) 9329684
Oakham Bishops Farewell; Taylor Best Bitter; guest beers Ⓗ

Victorian street-corner local with rooms kept in traditional style. The lounge and snug are warmed by open fires, while the bar has a free juke box and pool table. The plaque in the original lobby commemorates the wartime stay of Barnes Wallis, the inventor of the 'bouncing bomb', who was born in nearby Ripley. The winner of local CAMRA Pub of the Year in 2004 and 2005, the licensee adds interesting guest beers at the weekend, to satisfy demand. ⚒Q❀◒₪

Ilford

93 Station Road, DE7 5LJ (on A6096)
🕓 7.30-midnight; 7-1am Fri; 2-1am Sat; 11.30-midnight Sun
☎ (0115) 9305789
Beer range varies Ⓗ

Situated by the Erewash canal, with boat moorings nearby, this former local Club of the Year champions the cause of real ale by stocking micro-brewery beers, which are sourced from near and far, often showcasing new brewers. Traditional pub games include snooker, and live music often features on Saturday evening. Given sufficient notice, the friendly landlord will open outside usual hours for visiting groups. ❀₪(27)♣⏚

Needlemakers' Arms

12 Kensington Street, DE7 5NY (10 mins walk from the town centre)
🕓 6.30-11; 12-11.30 Fri & Sat; 11-11 Sun
☎ (077651) 85788
Caledonian Deuchars IPA; guest beers Ⓗ/Ⓖ

Created by knocking two former workers' cottages into one, this popular ex-Shipstones local takes its name from the former needlemaking factory nearby. Set back from the road, it was local CAMRA Pub of the Year 2007. Inside, it has a quiet lounge area to one side of the central bar and a pool and family/function room to the rear where it has hosted beer festivals. Traditional pub games are also popular. ⛲❀₪♣P

Ingleby

John Thompson Inn

Ingleby Lane, DE73 1HW (off A514)
🕓 10.30-2.30, 5-11; 12-2, 7-10.30 Sun
☎ (01332) 862469
John Thompson JTS XXX Bitter, JTS Gold, JTS Rich Porter; Tetley Burton Ale Ⓗ

John Thompson is the former fruit grower who revived Derbyshire's brewing industry in 1977, having transformed his family home into a highly individual pub eight years earlier. Comprising a large, comfortable lounge with smaller rooms opening off, the pub is rich in local interest, displaying many prints and watercolours. Close to the banks of the River Trent, in open country just outside the village, it also has a spacious patio and large garden with the brewery housed in outbuildings. ⛲❀◑♿♣P

Kirk Ireton

Barley Mow ☆

Main Street, DE6 3JP (off B5023)
🕓 12-2, 7-11 (10.30 Sun)
☎ (01335) 370306
Hook Norton Old Hooky; Marston's Pedigree; Whim Hartington IPA; guest beers Ⓖ

Set in an olde-worlde village overlooking the Ecclesbourne Valley, this exceptionally characterful gabled Jacobean building was originally a farmhouse. Several interconnecting rooms of different size and character have low, beamed ceilings, mullioned windows, slate-topped tables, well-worn woodwork and open fires set in stone fireplaces. A small serving hatch reveals a stillage with up to six beers dispensed straight from the cask. There are not many pubs left like this rural gem. ⚒Q❀✍▲♣♠P

Lea

Jug & Glass Inn

Main Road, DE4 5GJ
🕓 12-2 (not Mon), 7-11 (10.30 Sun)
☎ (01629) 534232 ⊕jugandglass.com
Mansfield Cask Ale; Marston's Pedigree; Whim Hartington IPA; guest beers Ⓗ

Built in 1782 by Peter Nightingale (uncle of Florence), the inn formed part of a row of weavers' cottages before being converted into a pub. It was also reputedly used as a hospice by Florence. Three cosy wood-panelled rooms welcome the visitor, with bare stone walls, low-beamed ceilings, tiled and carpeted floors, traditional pew-style seating and benches outside for warmer weather. A restaurant and accommodation have also been added. Live music and beer festivals feature regularly. ⚠️Q❀🛋🕪🍴⌟🅿

Long Eaton

Hole in the Wall

6 Regent Street, NG10 1JX

🕘 10-midnight (1am Fri & Sat); 11-midnight Sun

☎ (0115) 9734920

Draught Bass; Nottingham Rock Ale Bitter, Extra Pale Ale; guest beers Ⓗ

This attractive 19th-century free house, featuring a Dutch gable, is conveniently situated for public transport and close to the Erewash Canal. A fine example of a back-street local, it offers two distinct drinking areas: a lively bar and a quiet lounge, both adorned with breweriana and featuring an old-style serving hatch. In summer you can enjoy your drink on the patio. Many local CAMRA awards have been bestowed upon the Hole, which serves an ever-changing range of mainly local micro-brewery beers.

❀🕪🅱🍴♣🍴⌐

Royal Oak

349 Tamworth Road, NG10 3LU

🕘 11 (12 Sun)-11

☎ (0115) 983 5801

Beer range varies Ⓗ

This large, friendly pub has taken advantage of the deal between SIBA and Enterprise Inns to supply guest beers to supplement regulars including Fuller's London Pride and Wadworth 6X. It benefits from a large car park and separate children's play area, while moorings on the Erewash Canal at the rear attract boaters. The bar has a pool table, darts and Sky TV and a quiz is held on Wednesday evening. Home-made food includes a vegetarian option and children's menu.

❀🕪🅱🛋🗎≋🍴♣🅿

Longshaw

Grouse Inn

S11 7TZ (on A625)

🕘 12-3, 6-11; 12-11 Sat; 12-10.30 Sun

☎ (01433) 630423

Banks's Bitter; Caledonian Deuchars IPA; Marston's Pedigree; guest beer Ⓗ

The Grouse stands in splendid isolation on bleak moorland south-west of Sheffield. A free house, which has been run by the same family since 1965, it is deservedly popular with walkers and climbers. It is adorned with some fine photographs of nearby gritstone edges, and collections of bank notes and cigarette cards are also on display. There is a lounge at the front and a smaller bar area at the rear. No meals are served on Monday evening.

⚠️Q🍴❀🕪♣🅿🗎

Lullington

Colvile Arms

Main Street, DE12 8EG

🕘 6-11; 12-3, 7-10.30 Sun

☎ (01827) 373212

Draught Bass; Marston's Pedigree; guest beer Ⓗ

Popular 18th-century free house, leased from the Lullington Estate, at the heart of an attractive hamlet at the southern tip of the county. The public bar comprises an adjoining hallway and snug, each featuring high-backed settles with wood panelling. The bar and a comfortable lounge are situated on opposite sides of a central serving area. A second lounge/function room overlooks the garden and a bowling green. Two quiz teams and the local cricket and football teams meet here.

❀🅱♣🅿

Makeney

Holly Bush Inn

Holly Bush Lane, DE56 0RX 352447

🕘 12-3, 5-11; 12-11 Fri & Sat; 12-10.30 Sun

☎ (01332) 841729

Archers Golden; Greene King Ruddles County; Ⓗ **Marston's Pedigree;** Ⓖ **Taylor Landlord; guest beers** Ⓗ

Grade II listed, and once a farmhouse with a brewery on the Strutt Estate, this late 17th-century, former Offilers' house positively oozes character. It stood on the Derby turnpike before the Strutts opened the valley route in 1818; Dick Turpin is known to have drunk here. The enclosed wooden snug is sandwiched between two bars with real fires. Regular beer festivals are staged. It's a short 10 minute walk from the Derby-Belper bus route. Local CAMRA Country Pub of the Year 2007. ⚠️Q🛏❀🅱🗎🅿

Matlock Bath

County & Station

258-260 Dale Road, DE4 3NT (on A6)

🕘 12-midnight (1am Fri & Sat)

☎ (01629) 580802 🌐 countyandstation.co.uk

Marston's Pedigree, Old Empire; Jennings Cumberland Ale; guest beer Ⓗ

This popular pub in a land-bound Derbyshire town has a seaside feel to it. Attracting both locals and visitors, the inn has an open-plan interior with a separate dining area where locally sourced British food is served (no food Sun). Live bands perform here regularly. The County & Station has ramped access for wheelchairs. Guest beers mainly come from Marston's and Jennings. 🕪≋🅱

Temple Hotel

Temple Walk, DE4 3PG (off A6) OS294575

🕘 12-2, 6.30-11 (10 Sun)

☎ (01629) 583911 🌐 templehotel.co.uk

Beer range varies Ⓗ

Historic Georgian hotel with public bar, situated above Matlock Bath and set in two acres of Derbyshire countryside with good views across Derwent Valley. Nearby are the popular cable-car rides and Gulliver's Kingdom theme park, as well as the Peak District Mining Museum for the more discerning. Past visitors enjoying a good beer here have included Lord Byron, who etched a poem on a window. Guest beers are sourced from local breweries.

Q❀🛋🕪🅱♿🗎≋🅱

Melbourne

Blue Bell
53 Church Street, DE73 1EJ
☼ 11-11; 12-10.30 Sun
☎ (01332) 865764
Shardlow Best Bitter, Golden Hop, Melbourne Mild, Reverend Eaton's Ale, seasonal beers; guest beers Ⓗ
In a prime spot close to the hall and Norman church, in a well-pubbed locality, the Blue Bell stands out as the Shardlow Brewery tap, although it is several miles from the brewery itself. The bar of this old country pub bears a sporting emphasis, while the lounge opens on to a patio with barbecue. Run on traditional lines with seasonal beers and a house mild, occasional guest beers are available, too.
🅰🛏🕙🔾🍴🖂🌳♣

Milltown

Nettle
Hard Meadow Lane, S45 0ES (on B6036)
☼ 11-2.30, 5.30-11; 11.30-10.30 Sun
☎ (01246) 590642
Bradfield Farmers Bitter, Blonde; Greene King H&H Olde Trip Ⓗ
An isolated pub near Ogston reservoir, the Nettle is a handy bar for birders and boaters. The pub's name has changed several times; originally it was known as the Greyhound, until a landlord renamed it Nettle, after his own greyhound. When the dog won a race, it became the Well Run Nettle. Under the present owners, it has reverted to the dog's name. The pub retains a public bar where games are played. It serves excellent beer and is noted locally for the quality of its food.
Q🅰🛏🔾♿🍴🚃🖂P

Monsal Head

Monsal Head Hotel
Bakewell, DE45 1NL (on B6465)
☼ 11.30-11; 12-10.30 Sun
☎ (01629) 640250 ⊕ monsalhead.com
Taylor Landlord; Theakston Best Bitter, Old Peculier; Whim Hartington Best Bitter; guest beers Ⓗ
Real ale is served mainly in the Stables Bar, behind the main hotel. This bar is what remains of an earlier inn, and retains its original stalls for horses. At weekends it can get crowded and in fine weather crowds spill out on to the ample patio. Guest beers are often local, from the likes of Abbeydale, Kelham Island and Thornbridge. The hotel is also noted for its food and wine, and meals are served all day. 🏨Q🅰🛏🔾🍴♣P

Morley Smithy

Three Horseshoes
Main Road, DE7 6DF (on A608)
☼ 11.30-11; 12-10.30 Sun
☎ (01332) 834395
Marston's Pedigree, seasonal beers; guest beers Ⓗ
An attractive, white painted, rural pub on the main Derby-Heanor road and H1 bus route. Modestly modernised inside, its long, narrow, single room is centrally divided by an archway separating the smart, food-oriented lounge from the plainer, quarry-tiled bar with open fire and fake beams. An old photo shows the original thatched inn that also served as a smithy, which was pulled down around 1910. Farm eggs can be bought at the bar.
🏨Q🅰🔾♿🖂♣P

New Mills

Pack Horse Inn
Mellor Road, SK22 4QQ
☼ 12-3, 5-11; 12-11 Sat; 12-10.30 Sun
☎ (01663) 742365 ⊕ packhorseinn.co.uk
Tetley Bitter; guest beers Ⓗ
This pub seems to grow year on year and now boasts a separate accommodation block and an elegant dining room, as well as a large stone-girt beer garden. The interior is, for the present at least, more modest in size with an open fire and stove for the winter. The landlord chooses his guest beers imaginatively so there is always the chance of a surprise. Be prepared for a brisk uphill walk from New Mills. 🏨Q🅰🛏🔾P

New Whittington

Wellington
162 High Street, S43 2AN
☼ 11-midnight (1am Fri & Sat); 12-midnight Sun
☎ (01246) 450879
Jennings Cumberland; Marston's Pedigree; guest beer Ⓗ
Within easy reach of Chesterfield and the surrounding area by bus, this is a simple but comfortable two-roomed local. Twice-weekly quizzes and weekly live music reinforce community links. Add to this good lunchtime and evening food, with great themed menu nights, and five cask ales and you are on to a winner. 🅰🔾🖂P🚃

Newton Solney

Unicorn Inn
Repton Road, DE15 0SG (on B5008) OS283257
☼ 12-midnight (1am Fri & Sat)
☎ (01283) 703324 ⊕ unicorn-inn.co.uk
Draught Bass; Marston's Pedigree; guest beers Ⓗ
This popular local was originally a farmhouse on the Ratcliffe family estate (of Bass, Ratcliffe & Gretton brewery fame), but became a pub in the late 19th century. The attractive bar area, featuring a wooden bar counter and bar stools, is linked to a cosy lounge on one side and a dining room on the other. An August beer festival is staged in the nearby village hall. The garden includes a children's play area. No food is served on Sunday evening.
🅰🛏🔾🖂♣P🚃

Oakerthorpe

Anchor Inn
DE55 7LP (on B6013)
☼ 12-3, 6.30-11; 12-11 Sat; 12-10.30 Sun
☎ (01773) 833575
Cropton Honey Gold, Monkmans Slaughter, Two Pints, seasonal beers Ⓗ

This mid 18th-century bay-fronted building can be picked out at the roadside by a huge 18ft dredger's anchor. Little of the original features remain, however, apart from a stone wall surrounding the fireplace and a few beams that are believed to originate from ship's timbers. Long and rambling inside, with four distinct areas separated by stonework archways, an unusual reverse swan-neck handpull system dispenses Cropton Brewery beers – rare in these parts. The Castle Hill Roman camp fortlet is just a short walk away. Q⍩❀◧❶◨P

Ockbrook

Royal Oak

55 Green Lane, DE72 3SE (off A52, follow Ilkeston signs)
✪ 11.30-2.30 (3 Sat), 6-11; 12-3, 7-10.30 Sun
☎ (01332) 662378
Draught Bass; guest beers Ⓗ
Set back from the road across a cobbled courtyard, this fine pub was a former CAMRA regional Pub of the Year award winner. In the same family since coronation year and little changed since then, each of the five rooms has its own distinctive character and clientele. Three ever-changing guest beers are supplemented by an annual beer festival in October. Excellent home-cooked food is served. Separate gardens cater for adults and families. Q❀◧❶◧◨(9)♣P

Over Haddon

Lathkil Hotel

DE45 1JE (off B5055, Bakewell-Monyash route)
OS207664
✪ 11-3, 6.30-11; 11.30-11 Sat & Sun
☎ (01629) 812501 ⊕ lathkil.demon.co.uk
Everards Tiger; Whim Hartington Bitter; guest beers Ⓗ
Standing above Lathkill Dale, this popular free house enjoys one of the most outstanding views of the Peak District from its front window. The traditional-styled bar, featuring an open fire and oak beams, serves a wide selection of ales. Accommodation and delicious home-cooked food are also available, and a covered beer garden invites guests for a drink outdoors in summer. Dogs are welcome in the bar, walkers are asked to remove muddy boots. ⩫⍩❀◪◧❶◧◨P⅃⍖

Ripley

Nag's Head

56 Butterley Hill, DE5 3LT
✪ 12-midnight (1am Fri & Sat)
☎ (01773) 746722
Beer range varies Ⓗ
Roadside local on the edge of town, used as the tap for Amber Ales brewery, which lies about half a mile away. The enthusiastic licensee has also introduced real cider and perry, and regular live music. It has two small rooms, one with a pool table, and skittles is played in the back garden. Sir Barnes Wallis, who invented the 'bouncing bomb', was born nearby, and the Midland Railway Centre lies just down the hill at Butterley. ❀◨♣⍖

Rosliston

Bull's Head

Burton Road, DE12 8JU
✪ 12-3, 7-11 daily
☎ (01283) 761705
Marston's Pedigree; guest beer Ⓗ
Late 19th-century brick-built free house with a comfortable public bar and smart, cosy lounge, both featuring open fires and beamed ceilings, plus a large function room in a converted stable block. A collection of china bulls is displayed behind the bar, and interesting encased models of a Burton Union brewing system can be found in both the public bar and the function room. The National Forest Forestry Centre is located about half a mile away. ⩫◧◧▲◨♣P

Sawley

Harrington Arms

392 Tamworth Road, NG10 3AU (on B6540 near River Trent and marina)
✪ 11-11 (11.30 Thu; midnight Fri & Sat)
☎ (0115) 9732614
Greene King Ruddles Best Bitter, H&H Bitter, Abbot, seasonal beers Ⓗ
A regular entry in the Guide, this former coaching inn stands near the Trent and Mersey Canal. Its spacious, beamed interior includes several drinking areas, one furnished with comfortable settees, the others have the more traditional settles. The bar has four handpulls and offers an extensive wine list. The restaurant serves a good range of dishes, complemented by a separate bar menu. There is also large, well-furnished outdoor area, complete with patio heaters.
⩫❀◧❶◪≢(Long Eaton)◨P⅃⍖

Nag's Head

1 Wilne Road, NG10 3AL (on B6540 Tamworth Rd)
✪ 11-11; 12-10.30 Sun
☎ (0115) 9732983
Marston's Burton Bitter, Pedigree; guest beers Ⓗ
A welcome return to the Guide for this popular, traditional two-roomed local, located close to the River Trent and Sawley Marina. In July 2007 the present landlord, only the fourth incumbent since World War II, completed 15 years at the Nag's Head. The pub has recently been refurbished, and additional handpumps installed. Guest beers are selected from the Marston's portfolio. Traditional pub games are played here, including long-alley skittles.
⩫Q❀◧≢(Long Eaton)◨♣P

Scarcliffe

Horse & Groom

Rotherham Road, S44 6SU (on B6417)
✪ 12-midnight (11 Sun)
☎ (01246) 823152
Black Sheep Best Bitter; Greene King Abbot; Stones Bitter; Tetley Bitter; guest beer Ⓗ
This rural free house is a gem. With a history going back 150 years, the present stone-built inn is a past Derbyshire CAMRA Pub of the Year and has won many seasonal branch awards. Free from music and games, it serves some excellent real ales, complemented by an ever-changing list of guest beers and an impressive

range of fine malts. No hot food is available. Accommodation is in three purpose-built cottages. Q༕ཙ♿☢⏱Ａ🚃(53, 81)P⌐

Shirland

Hay Inn

135 Main Road, DE55 6BA (on A61)

✪ 4.30 (6 Mon)-11.30 (midnight Fri); 12-midnight Sat; 12-11.30 Sun

☎ (01773) 835383

Fuller's London Pride; Greene King H&H Mild; guest beers Ⓗ

A former Brampton Brewery pub, dating from around 1890, this free house is a flagship real ale outlet run by long-standing, award-wining CAMRA members. Served via a central bar, this comfortable local offers a regular mild plus an interesting range of three changing guest beers, a real cider and a selection of Belgian bottled beers and country wines. Impressive attention to detail – from the decor to summer hanging baskets – a weekly quiz and annual beer festival make it well worth seeking out. Ａ🚃♣♠P

Smalley

Bell Inn

35 Main Road, DE7 6EF (on A608)

✪ 11.30-3, 5-11; 11-11 Sat; 12-10.30 Sun

☎ (01332) 880635

Adnams Broadside; Mallard Duckling; Oakham JHB; Whim Hartington Bitter, Hartington IPA; guest beers Ⓗ

This mid 19th-century inn has three rooms and a large, attractive child-friendly garden. Brewing and other memorabilia adorn the walls. Top-quality beer and food helped it become Derbyshire CAMRA Pub of the Year in 2006. Situated near Shipley Country Park, it can be reached via the Derby-Heanor H1 bus service, which stops right outside the pub. Accommodation is in three flats in a converted stable adjoining the pub. 🏨Q♿☢⏸⏱Ｅ♿🚃(H1)P

South Normanton

Clock Inn

107 Market Street, DE55 2AA (from M1 jct 28, take B6019 Mansfield Road)

✪ 4 (12 Sat & Sun)-11

☎ (01773) 811396 ⊕ theclockinn.co.uk

Jennings Bitter, Cumberland Ale; guest beers Ⓗ

Traditional free house comprising a lounge and bar, plus a beer garden at the rear, which may also be used by smokers. The number of CAMRA awards and Cask Marque certificates on display attests to the beer quality, and there is also a selection of fine malt whiskies. Q༕ཙ☢♿Ｅ(9.2)♠P⌐

Devonshire Arms

137 Market Street, DE55 2AA (from M1 jct 28, take B6019 Mansfield Road)

✪ 11-1am (2am Fri-Sat)

☎ (01773) 810748 ⊕ the-devonshire-arms.co.uk

Greene King Abbot; Sarah Hughes Dark Ruby; guest beers Ⓗ

Friendly free house comprising a restaurant, public bar and games room. Sky Sports is available in the bar and games room, and there is a digital jukebox. The restaurant serves home-made food every day, with a carvery at the weekend. It also caters for vegetarians, vegans and coeliacs and is designed to accommodate wheelchairs. Entertainment includes a quiz (Wed), live entertainment (Fri) and traditional pub games. Note: strictly no entry/re-entry after 11pm. Q༕ཙ☢⏸⏱Ｅ♿🚃(9.2)♣♠P⌐

Stanley Common

White Post Inn

237 Belper Road, DE7 6FT (on A609)

✪ 11-11; 12-10.30 Sun

☎ (0115) 930 0194

Beer range varies Ⓗ/Ⓖ

This large, white painted roadside inn on the main thoroughfare is surrounded by some fine countryside, away from the built-up sprawl. A central bar serves three interlinking rooms, with one used as a dining area where good home-cooked food is available. An interesting range of ever-changing guest beers is supplemented by occasional beer festivals, which in summer spill out on to the pleasant rear garden. 🏨Q༕ཙ☢⏸⏱Ｅ♿🚃(59)♠P

Stanton in Peak

Flying Childers

Main Road, DE4 2LW (off B6056, Bakewell-Ashbourne Rd)

✪ 12-2 (not Mon & Tue), 7-11; 12-3, 7-11 Sat & Sun

☎ (01629) 636333

Black Sheep Best Bitter; Wells Bombardier; guest beer Ⓗ

An unspoilt village pub, named after a famous 18th-century racehorse, the Childers is located near the historic Stanton moor, and attracts walkers, tourists and a diverse mix of regulars. Dogs are welcome. Friendly and welcoming, both rooms are especially cosy in winter. The beer garden, tucked away to the rear, is a pleasant spot on a summer's afternoon. There is an interesting selection of guest beers, often sourced from micros, and home-made soups and snacks are available at lunchtime. 🏨Q♿Ｅ🚃P

Staveley

Speedwell Inn

Lowgates, Chesterfield, S43 3TT

✪ 6-11 (10.30 Sun)

☎ (01246) 474665

Townes IPA, Speedwell Bitter, Staveley Cross, Staveleyan; guest beer (occasional) Ⓗ

Home of the Townes brewery since 1998, this unassuming pub has twice won the local CAMRA Pub of the Year award. Simple and comfortable surroundings provide real ale lovers with a desirable venue. Townes produces regular special brews and the pub holds an annual beer festival in early December. Occasional guest beers are also offered, as well as a small range of Belgian bottled beers. Q🚃♣

Sutton Cum Duckmanton

Arkwright Arms

Chesterfield Road, S44 5JG (on A632 between Chesterfield and Bolsover)

◷ 11-11 (10.30 Sun)

☎ (01246) 232053 ⊕ thearkers.mysite.orange.co.uk

Beer range varies Ⓗ

There is always a warm welcome at this mock-Tudor fronted free house. The public bar is separated from the lounge by a horseshoe-shaped bar; the dining room is to the rear. All three are made cosy by open fires. It stocks an excellent range of ales with ever-changing guests, normally from local micro-breweries, plus three changing ciders and two perries. Beer festivals are held on the Easter and August bank holidays, supplemented by mini-events throughout the year. Evening meals are served weekdays. Bolsover Castle is nearby. ❀◖🍴🚻🚃🏕P

Thulston

Harrington Arms

4 Grove Close, DE72 3EY (off B5010)

◷ 11.30-3 (not Mon), 6-11; 11.30-11 Sat; 12-10.30 Sun

☎ (01332) 571798

Draught Bass; guest beers Ⓗ

Formerly two cottages refronted to stand out, and brightly lit after dark, the pub has been smartly modernised, retaining low, beamed ceilings, half-timbered interior walls and open fires. Regular beer festivals are held and an adjoining restaurant serves good food. The pub features its own house beer, Earl of Harrington. Elvaston Castle Country Park, former estate of the Earls of Harrington, is nearby. Its magnificent iron entrance gates were spoils of the Napoleonic Wars from Spain. ♨❀◖🛒🚃P

Troway

Gate Inn

Main Road, S21 5RU (from B6056 turn off at minor road by Black-a-Moor pub)

◷ 12-3, 7-11 (10.30 Sun)

☎ (01246) 413280

Marston's Burton Bitter; guest beer Ⓗ

A hidden gem to be found up a narrow country lane in north Derbyshire. Relax and soak up the charm of this small, friendly pub in good walking country on the south side of the Moss Valley. Now in its 13th year under the current tenants, it has featured in this Guide for the past 12. The real ales may be enjoyed beside a log fire in winter or in the award-winning garden in summer. ♨Q❀🚃🏕P🍴

Whaley Bridge

Shepherds Arms

7 Old Road, SK23 7HR

◷ 2 (12 Sat & Sun)-midnight

☎ (01663) 732384

Marston's Burton Bitter, Pedigree; guest beer Ⓗ

This attractive, whitewashed and stone-built pub has been preserved unspoilt, conveying the feel of the farmhouse that it once was. The unchanged tap room with open fire, scrubbed tables and flagged floor is a delight – the best for miles around. There is also a comfortable lounge and a small drinking area in the garden. ♨Q❀🛒🚃🚃🏕P

Willington

Green Man

1 Canal Bridge, DE65 6BQ (by railway station)

◷ 11.30-3, 5-11; 11.30-11 Sat; 12-10.30 Sun

☎ (01283) 702377 ⊕ thegreenmanpub.co.uk

Draught Bass; Marston's Pedigree; guest beers Ⓗ

Large, attractive, whitewashed roadside pub at the heart of the village, not far from the canal. Dating back some 150 years, its two rooms feature oak beams along with traditional bench seating. A picture gallery of local landmarks decorates the lounge. A large child-friendly rear garden is complemented by tables and chairs at the front during the summer months. Good home-cooked food is served daily, and there are regular live music events. ❀◖🛒🚃🚃🏕P

Winster

Old Bowling Green

East Bank, DE4 2DS (50 metres off the main village thoroughfare)

◷ 6-11 daily (closed Mon & Tue in winter); 12-2.30, 6-11 Sun

☎ (01629) 825685 ⊕ peakparkpub.co.uk

Beer range varies Ⓗ

Multi-roomed 15th-century inn with a central bar and resident ghost. The long-term owners are rightly proud of their range of fresh home-cooked food (reservations are recommended). In the main bar area, paintings of local scenes adorn the walls alongside pictures of yesteryear and a grandfather clock. At one end is a splendid fireplace. To the rear are two smaller rooms and the beer garden. Up to four guests beers from near and far are usually available. ♨❀◖🚃P

Wirksworth

Royal Oak

North End, DE4 4FG (off B5035)

◷ 8-11; 12-3, 7.30-10.30 Sun

☎ (01629) 823000

Draught Bass; Taylor Landlord; Whim Hartington IPA; guest beers Ⓗ

Excellent little traditional local in a stone terrace near the market place, illuminated at night by fairy lights. The bar features some good breweriana and old local pictures. The Oak combines a long-standing reputation for Bass with a choice of guests. Wirksworth (or Wuzzer, as it is affectionately known) is well pubbed and the others are worthy of a visit, too. The Ecclesbourne Valley railway line is a local attraction nearby. Q🚃(6.1)♣

Beer: A high and mighty liquor
Julius Ceaser

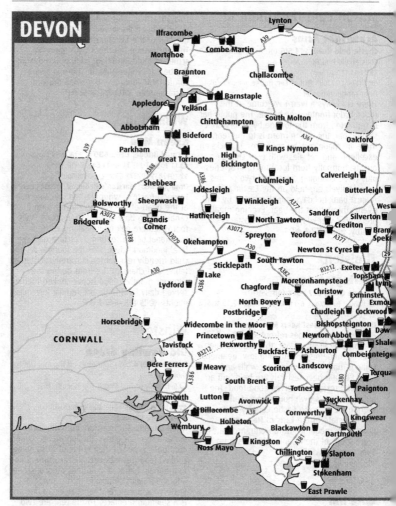

DEVON

A map of Devon showing locations including: Lynton, Ilfracombe, Combe Martin, Mortehoe, Challacombe, Braunton, Barnstaple, Appledore, Yelland, South Molton, Oakford, Abbotsham, Bideford, Chittlehampton, Parkham, Kings Nympton, Calverleigh, Great Torrington, High Bickington, Butterleigh, Shebbear, Chulmleigh, West, Holsworthy, Iddesleigh, Sheepwash, Winkleigh, Sandford, Silverton, Bridgerule, Brandis Corner, Hatherleigh, North Tawton, Crediton, Bram, Spec, Okehampton, Spreyton, Yeoford, Newton St Cyres, Sticklepath, South Tawton, Exeter, Topsham, Lake, Lydford, Chagford, Moretonhampstead, Lym, Christow, Exminster, North Bovey, Exmou, Postbridge, Chudleigh, Cockwood, Horsebridge, Widecombe in the Moor, Bishopsteignton, Daw, Princetown, Newton Abbot, Tavistock, Hexworthy, Buckfast, Ashburton, Combeinteign, Bere Ferrers, Meavy, Scoriton, Landscove, Torqu, South Brent, Totnes, Paignton, Plymouth, Lutton, Avonwick, Tuckenhay, Kingswear, Billacombe, Cornworthy, Wembury, Holbeton, Blackawton, Dartmouth, Noss Mayo, Kingston, Chillington, Slapton, Stokenham, East Prawle, CORNWALL

Appledore

Beaver Inn

2 Irsha Street, EX39 1RY OS462308
🕐 11-11 (midnight Sat); 12-10.30 Sun
☎ (01237) 474822 ⊕ beaverinn.co.uk
Beer range varies Ⓗ
Superbly located with views of the Taw and
Torridge estuary, the Beaver has a single bar
offering a choice of three handpumps plus
cider from Winkleigh. The landlord focuses on
beers from West Country brewers: Sharp's
Doom Bar is a favourite. Dogs and well-
behaved children are welcome and excellent
value food is available from the bar or
restaurant menus. ⊛➊ Å�□♣♨

Ashburton

Exeter Inn

26, West Street, TQ13 7DU
🕐 11-2.30, 5-11 (midnight Fri & Sat); 12-3, 7-10.30 Sun
☎ (01364) 652013
Badger First Gold; Greene King IPA Ⓗ
This friendly local is the oldest pub in
Ashburton, dating from 1131 with additions

from the 17th century. It was built to house
workers erecting the nearby church, and
visited by Sir Francis Drake on his journeys to
London. The main bar is L-shaped, rustic and
wood-panelled. There are two drinking areas
either side of the entrance hallway and a
further bar at the back, served through a small
hatch and counter. ⋈Q⊛➊➌□➊♣

Avonwick

Turtley Corn Mill

TQ10 9ES (off A38)
🕐 11.30-11; 12-10.30 Sun
☎ (01364) 646100 ⊕ avonwick.net
**Princetown Dartmoor IPA, Jail Ale; St Austell
Tribute; Summerskills Tamar** Ⓗ
A former roadside restaurant, standing in its
own grounds bordered by a river and with its
own lake, tastefully transformed into a prize-
winning pub. Reverting to its former name to
reflect its origins, it encompasses the ethos of
its owners by supplying local beers and locally
sourced food. Old photos of the area adorn the
walls, including a rare print of a Plymouth
Brewery now demolished. ⋈Q⊛➊⑤➔P

Greene King Abbot; Marston's Burton Bitter, Pedigree; Shepherd Neame Spitfire; Fuller's London Pride; guest beers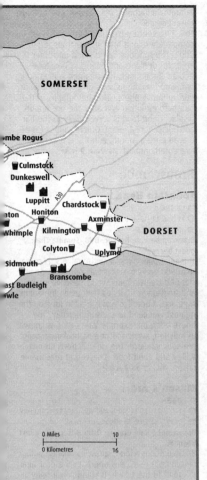
Centrally located opposite the Queen's Theatre and close to the historic Pannier Market, this popular Wetherspoon's is always buzzing. The real ale range is unrivalled in the area, with a different guest appearing almost daily, plus cider from Sheppy's and Weston's. The beer garden is a suntrap that can be covered and heated off season. An ideal place to meet, socialise and enjoy a pint along with good food from the extensive menu. Themed food days are a highlight.

Bere Ferrers

Olde Plough Inn
Fore Street, PL20 7HL (near church)
12-3, 7-11.30 (10.30 Sun); closed winter Mon
☎ (01822) 840358
Sharp's Doom Bar, Eden Ale; guest beer
This 16th-century village inn affords outstanding views over the River Tavy from the beer garden and is only a 15-minute walk from the station on the picturesque Tamar Line. Inside, visitors are greeted by exposed stonework walls, beamed ceilings, real fires and a welcoming atmosphere. Asian dishes complement a menu of traditional favourites. The guest ale changes weekly and unusual continental lagers and Sam's Poundhouse Cider are also available.

Bideford

King's Arms
7 The Quay, EX39 2HW
11-11
☎ (01237) 475196 ⊕ innonthequay.co.uk
Adnams Broadside; Butcombe Bitter; Greene King Abbot; Jollyboat Grenville's Renown; Shepherd Neame Spitfire
This 16th-century inn is situated on the main road at the centre of Bideford's historic waterfront overlooking the River Torridge and

Axminster

Lamb Inn
Lyme Road, EX13 5BE
11.30-midnight daily (2am Fri & Sat)
☎ (01297) 33922
Branscombe Vale Branoc; guest beers
A fine free house half a mile from the town centre. One big room is split into a comfortable bar area and a larger space with a pool table. Major sporting events are shown on the large-screen TV. It is home to a local football club and has a number of resident teams playing a variety of pub games. The attractive garden features two boules pistes. The new landlady has also introduced good pub food.

Barnstaple

Panniers
33/34 Boutport Street, EX31 1RX
9-midnight daily (1am Fri & Sat)
☎ (01271) 329720

INDEPENDENT BREWERIES

Barum Barnstaple
Beer Engine Newton St Cyres
Blackdown Dunkeswell
Branscombe Vale Branscombe
Clearwater Great Torrington
Combe Martin Combe Martin
Country Life Abbotsham
Exe Valley Silverton
Gargoyles Dawlish
Jollyboat Bideford
O'Hanlon's Whimple
Otter Luppitt
Princetown Princetown
Red Rock Bishopsteignton
Scattor Rock Christow
South Hams Stokenham
Summerskills Billacombe
Tarka Yelland
Teignworthy Newton Abbot
Topsham & Exminster Exminster
Union Holbeton
Warrior Exeter
Wizard Ilfracombe

the old Long Bridge. The building remains largely unaltered and a majority of the beams are original. There is one long bar with an old snug at one end and dining area at the other, with pictures on the walls depicting local history. It can get busy on Friday and Saturday evenings. No evening meals are served in winter. ♨Q🅰️◑🍴

Bishopsteignton

Bishop John de Grandisson
Clanage Street, TQ14 9QS
🕐 12-2.30 (not Mon), 6-11 (midnight Fri & Sat); 12-11 Sun
☎ (01626) 775285
Fuller's London Pride; Draught Bass; Otter Ale Ⓗ
This traditional village pub in the middle of the village has been refurbished but retains a proper pub atmosphere. The L-shaped bar preserves some original features. The small lounge has a dining area and there is a separate dining room serving home-cooked meals. The pub is well supported by locals, and fields several teams in different sports. It hosts quiz nights and other events. There is a good sized car park and an outside seating area with fine views. ♨Q❀◑🍴&♣P

Blackawton

George Inn
Main Street, TQ9 7BG (signed off A3122 Dartmouth-Halwell road) OS805509
🕐 12-3 (may vary), 6-11; 12-2, 7-10.30 Sun
☎ (01803) 712342
Princetown Jail Ale; Teignworthy Spring Tide; guest beers Ⓗ
Friendly, unspoilt village local with two bars warmed by a double-sided wood-burning stove. An impressive selection of dishes is served (no food Mon lunchtime), using ingredients from local South Hams suppliers. The pub is child friendly and has a play area at the rear; dogs are welcome. The south-facing patio and garden offer attractive rural views. Monday is curry and quiz night.
♨Q🏃❀◑🍴&♣P

Brampford Speke

Agricultural Inn
EX5 5DP
🕐 11-2.30, 6-11; closed Mon; 12-2.30 Sun
☎ (01392) 841591 ⊕ theagriculturalinn.co.uk
O'Hanlon's Yellow Hammer Ⓗ
Welcoming free house in this small village four miles north of Exeter on the Exe Valley Way. The central bar area is festooned with solid wood beams and leads to seated areas at both ends, and a large dining area upstairs. The house beer Speke Easy is brewed by nearby Beer Engine, and the food is freshly cooked using local ingredients. ♨❀◑P

Brandis Corner

Bickford Arms
EX22 7XY (on A3072 between Holsworthy and Hatherleigh) OS410039
🕐 11-11
☎ (01409) 221318 ⊕ bickfordarms.com

Princetown Dartmoor IPA; Skinner's Betty Stogs; guest beers Ⓗ
This 17th-century coaching inn was completely rebuilt after a disastrous fire in 2003. The spacious bar, divided into three areas for drinking and dining, is flagstone-floored throughout. The beamed ceiling and two wood-burning stoves give it an authentic, relaxed atmosphere. Old photographs of the pub before, during and after the fire are on display. Good food is served daily in the bar and adjacent restaurant. Quizzes and chess are played once a month, and there is occasional live entertainment. ♨❀🅰️◑&♣P

Branscombe

Fountain Head
EX12 3BG
🕐 11-3, 6-11; 12-3, 6-10.30 Sun
☎ (01297) 680359
Branscombe Vale Branoc, BVB, Summa That; guest beers Ⓗ
This neat pub, popular with walkers, is more than 500 years old, and was once a forge and cider house. It retains wood-panelled walls and flagstone floors as well as an inglenook fireplace. A beer festival is held in June on the nearest weekend to midsummer day. The house beer, Branscombe Vale's BVB, is known as Jolly Jeff, named after a particularly morose previous landlord. The cider is from Green Valley and good food is served at reasonable prices. ♨Q🏃❀◑♣P

Mason's Arms
EX12 3BH
🕐 11-3, 6-11; 11-11 Sat & mid-summer; 12-10.30 Sun
☎ (01297) 680300 ⊕ masonsarms.co.uk
Branscombe Vale Branoc; Otter Bitter, Ale; guest beers Ⓗ
Branscombe is a long, sprawling village with a pub at both ends: this one is to the east near the road to the beach. It stands on a fairly extensive site, with accommodation behind the original building. There is plenty of space outside with tables (some thatched). The bar area has an open fire which is nearly always lit; occasionally spit-roasts are cooked on it. There are separate dining rooms. The pub stages a beer festival in mid-July, and Addlestones cider is served.
♨❀🅰️◑♣♥P⌐

Braunton

Black Horse
34 Church Street, EX33 2EL OS489369
🕐 11.30-2.30, 5.30-11 (midnight Sat); 12-10.30 Sun
☎ (01272) 812386
Greene King Ruddles County, Old Speckled Hen; Sharp's Doom Bar; Shepherd Neame Spitfire; guest beers Ⓖ
Traditional 400-year-old inn, popular with locals and home to many pub league teams. The small single bar is simply furnished with separate dining areas and flat-screen TV. All real ales are served straight from the cask. Three small but popular beer festivals are held each year. Traditional pub games include skittles, pool and shove-ha'penny. Food is served Friday-Sunday only in winter, every evening in the summer, with a curry night

once a month. Regular quiz nights are also popular. ⛺❀◑◐ ▲🖵♣P⌐

Bridgerule

Bridge Inn

EX22 7EJ (W of bridge over River Tamar) OS273028
☼ 12-2.30 (not Mon-Fri), 6.30-11; 12-3.30, 6.30-10.30 Sun
☎ (01288) 381316
Fuller's London Pride; guest beers Ⓗ
Situated west of the River Tamar, but still in Devon, the Bridge is a typical community pub. Many village teams are based here and their trophies are on display in the bar. The pub is cosy, with low exposed beams and a large central, open fire lit in winter. Jam sessions take place on Monday evening and quiz nights are held fortnightly on Sunday. Sunday lunch is the only meal served, with bar snacks available at other times. 🅰Q⛺❀▲🖵♣

Buckfast

Abbey Inn

TQ11 0EA (village signed off A38)
☼ 11 (12 Sun)-11
☎ (01364) 642343
St Austell Dartmoor Best, Tribute, HSD Ⓗ
Situated in a beautiful setting on the banks of the River Dart, this large inn is within Dartmoor National Park, close to the famous Buckfast Abbey and other attractions. Its outside terrace overlooks the river, and allows glimpses of the abbey. Inside, the warm and welcoming oak-panelled bar is spacious and traditionally furnished. In the large dining room, guests can enjoy an excellent range of dishes. 🅰Q❀🛏◑◐▲🖵P

Butterleigh

Butterleigh Inn

EX15 1PN (opp church)
☼ 12-3, 6-11 (midnight Fri & Sat); 12-3, 7-10.30 Sun
☎ (01884) 855407
Cotleigh Tawny; Butcombe Bitter; Greene King Abbot; guest beer Ⓗ
An excellent country pub in a charming location, this splendid 400-year-old Devon cob building is full of character. It has a main bar and lounge with a modern, sympathetically styled dining room. The open fire in the bar and wood-burning stove in the lounge make this a warm, welcoming place in winter. In the summer guests can drink their pint outside in the attractive secluded garden and enjoy the views of the surrounding rolling hills. This fine establishment has become the focus for a vibrant community. 🅰Q❀🛏◑◐♿♣P⌐

Calverleigh

Rose & Crown

EX16 8BA (on the old Rackenford road)
☼ 11.30-midnight; 12-11.30 Sun
☎ (01884) 256301
Adnams Broadside; Butcombe Bitter; Sharp's Doom Bar Ⓗ
Traditional 17th-century country pub, not far from the town of Tiverton, with a restaurant, beer garden and skittle alley that doubles as a

function room. Excellent home-cooked food is served, made with local produce where possible. Local cider is on offer from Palmershayes across the road. ❀◑◐♣P

Chagford

Sandy Park Inn

Sandy Park, TQ13 8JW (on A382 Moretonhampstead-Whiddon Down road)
☼ 12-11
☎ (01647) 433267 ⊕ sandyparkinn.co.uk
Butcombe Bitter; St Austell Tribute; Ⓗ **guest beers** Ⓗ/Ⓖ
Thatched free house, roughly 17th century, in a small hamlet near Castle Drogo (National Trust). The main bar has a large stone open fire, ancient beams, stone flooring and pews at the tables. The snug is set around a huge table. An intimate restaurant offers mainly fresh, local produce and the specials board changes regularly. There is an extensive wine list and some bottled beers. Ales change regularly and some are on gravity; all are reasonably priced. Parking is available for 5-6 cars at the front. 🅰Q⛺❀🛏◑◐▲🖵♣♣P

Challacombe

Black Venus

EX31 4TT (on B3358 between A399 and Simonsbath) OS694411
☼ 12-3, 6-11; 12-3, 7-10.30 Sun
☎ (01598) 763251
St Austell Cousin Jack; guest beers Ⓗ
This mainly 18th-century stone-built pub nestles in a valley on the western edge of Exmoor. The single hop-strewn bar still has intact original low beams, with a pool room and dining area leading off it. An extensive menu of home-cooked dishes is available. Ideally situated for good moorland walking and cycling, a number of farm B&Bs and self-catering establishments are nearby. Guest beers are mainly from Cotleigh and Exmoor brewers. Q❀◑◐♣P

Chardstock

George Inn

Chard Street, EX13 7BX
☼ 11-2.30, 6-11; 12-3, 7-11 Sun
☎ (01460) 220241 ⊕ george-inn.co.uk
Branscombe Vale Branoc; guest beers Ⓗ
Attractive, Grade II listed 15th-century thatched church house in the heart of a rural village. The layout provides three bar areas and a games room, dining room and skittle alley. New licensees have returned the pub to its former glory, offering a varied menu using locally sourced produce and catering for all tastes. Look out for the superb linen-fold panelled screen and centuries-old graffiti. Q❀🛏◑◐♣P⌐

Chillington

Open Arms

TQ7 2LD (on A379 E of Kingsbridge)
☼ 12-2.30, 6-11; 12-3, 7-11 Sun
☎ (01548) 581171

Draught Bass; Exmoor Ale; Princetown Jail Ale; guest beer H

An unpretentious free house, this busy village local is on the narrow Kingsbridge to Dartmouth main road. Its excellent range of ales includes a well-chosen guest or there is real Devon cider. Home-cooked food is served and daily specials are chalked up including fresh fish, dependent on the catch of the day. Family friendly, the pub hosts occasional live music events. ▲Q☎✿◑▲⊞♣●⌐

Chittlehampton

Bell Inn

The Square, EX37 9QL (opp church) OS636255
☼ 11-3, 6-midnight; 11-midnight Sat; 12-11 Sun
☎ (01769) 540368 ⊕ thebellatchittlehampton.co.uk
Beer range varies H/G

Recently refurbished to provide new accommodation, this 18th-century village centre inn has real community focus. Many of the village's sports teams have historic links here as photographs and trophies around the bar testify. The focus is on beers from West Country brewers and there may be additional ales available on gravity from the cellar. The cider is Thatchers, and good food is served made with local produce. A cheap lunch is available for over 50s on Tuesday.
✿⊠◑♿▲♣●⌐

Chudleigh

Bishop Lacy

52-53 Fore Street, TQ13 0HY
☼ 12-midnight daily (1am Fri & Sat)
☎ (01626) 854585
Fuller's London Pride; O'Hanlon's Yellow Hammer; Princetown Jail Ale; guest beers H

Grade II listed, this 14th-century church house is now a bustling local. It has built up a reputation for serving a good selection of real ales. Beer festivals are a regular event at this past local and regional CAMRA Pub of the Year. The pub has two bars, both warmed by real fires in colder months. Home-cooked food is served in the restaurant area. Children and dogs are welcome. ▲Q◑⊞▲⊞♣●⌐

Chulmleigh

Old Court House

South Molton Street, EX18 7BW
☼ 11.30-midnight
☎ (01769) 580045 ⊕ oldcourthouseinn.co.uk
Cotleigh Tawny; guest beer H

'Like being in your living room – with a bar and some old friends,' was how one customer described this Grade II listed thatched inn after drinking with the cheery licensee and welcoming locals. Charles I stayed here in 1634 when he held court (hence the name), and this is commemorated with an original coat of arms in one of the bedrooms. Good food is served in the bar, dining room and cobbled courtyard garden. Thursday quiz night supports local charities.
▲✿⊠◑⊞(377)♣●⌐

Cockwood

Anchor Inn

EX6 8RA (on A379 between Starcross and Dawlish)
☼ 11-11; 12-10.30 Sun
☎ (01626) 890203
Greene King Abbot; Otter Ale; Taylor Landlord; guest beers H

Eye-catching pub in a stunning setting on an old harbour populated by small boats and swans. It boasts original old timbers, low beams and high-backed settles. Offering as good a fresh fish and shellfish menu as anywhere in the country, plus plenty of sensibly priced snacks, it fully deserves its long list of prestigious awards. At least five ales, including local brews, make this a busy pub all year round. Q✿◑▲⊞P

Colyton

Kingfisher

Dolphin Street, EX24 6NA
☼ 11-3, 6-11 (midnight Thu-Sat); 12-3, 7-10.30 Sun
☎ (01297) 552476 ⊕ kingfisherinn.co.uk
Badger First Gold; Sharp's Doom Bar; guest beers H

A traditional 16th-century stone and timber pub in the centre of this delightful small town, with a tram nearby connecting to the seaside town of Seaton. It has one very cosy bar, plus a restaurant at the rear serving well-priced meals made with locally sourced ingredients whenever possible. Quiz evenings are held and once a month there are themed food evenings (booking essential). ✿◑⊞♣

Combe Martin

Castle Inn

High Street, EX34 0HS (in front of church)
☼ 12-1am (midnight Sun)
☎ (01271) 883706 ⊕ castleinn.info
Beer range varies H/G

A proper ale house – the centrally located single bar offers four well-kept, constantly changing ales at all times, plus cider from Winkleigh. There is a small beer festival held in August during Carnival. Facilities include large-screen sports TV plus darts, pool, skittles and table football. Regular live music plays in the function room at weekends and there is a lovely rear garden. Well-behaved children and dogs are welcome. Good pub food (especially Indian dishes) is available up to 9pm, including a take-away option.
▲☎✿◑♿▲⊞♣●P⌐

Combeinteignhead

Wild Goose

TQ12 4RA (on Stoke road)
☼ 11-2.30 (3 Fri & Sat), 5.30-11 (midnight Fri & Sat); 12-3, 7-11 Sun
☎ (01626) 872241
Otter Bright; Skinner's Betty Stogs; guest beers H

A traditional village pub since 1840, this genuine free house is well-frequented by locals. The long bar has two open fires with seating areas at both ends and a dining room at the rear. Beers are selected from a comprehensive range of South West breweries from Cornwall to Wiltshire, with five brews usually available plus two Devon ciders (Martin Jenny and Suicider). The extensive menu includes vegetarian and fish dishes and uses local produce whenever possible. Live music plays on Friday night. ⚲🏠🅌🚶♣♒🅿🍴

Cornworthy

Hunter's Lodge Inn
TQ9 7ES
🕑 11.30 (12 Sun)-3, 6.30-11
☎ (01803) 732204 🌐 hunterslodgeinn.co.uk
Teignworthy Reel Ale; guest beers Ⓗ
Situated in the quiet village of Cornworthy, this pub was mentioned in the Domesday Book. This is a lively bar, popular with locals, featuring low beams and a log fire. It has an excellent reputation for home-cooked local food, and serves a good variety of well-kept beers – there are usually three available. A beer festival is held in summer, and live music and quiz nights throughout the year. The pub sponsors the local football team and is reputed to have its own resident ghost.
⚲Q🐕🏠🅌🚶♣🅿

Crediton

Crediton Inn
28A Mill Street, EX17 1EZ
🕑 11-11; 12-2, 7-10.30 Sun
☎ (01363) 772882 🌐 crediton-inn.co.uk
Fuller's London Pride; Sharp's Doom Bar; guest beers Ⓗ
Just out of the town centre, this well-established free house was local CAMRA Pub of the Year in 2005 and has maintained its high standards. A minimum of four ales is always available, plus guests usually sourced from local independent breweries. Attractive internal alterations last year have enhanced the warm, friendly interior that welcomes vistors to this pub. Good food is served on Friday and Saturday only. 🅌🚶♣🅿

Culmstock

Culm Valley Inn
EX15 3JJ
🕑 12-4, 6-11; 11-11 Sat; 12-10.30 Sun
☎ (01884) 840354
Beer range varies Ⓗ
This 300-year-old village inn is situated by the River Culm, near where it emerges from the Blackdown Hills. The car park was formerly the railway sidings of the Tiverton Light Railway, and the pub was previously called the Railway Inn. Local produce features on the menu, often organic and free-range. Bollhayes and Burrow Hill cider are served.
⚲Q🐕🛏🅌🚶♣🅿🍴

Dartmouth

Cherub Inn
13 Higher Street, TQ6 9RB
🕑 11-11; 12-10.30 Sun
☎ (01803) 832571
Summerskills Cherub Bitter; guest beers Ⓗ

Behind the beautiful Tudor façade of this Grade II listed building lies a small but cosy beamed bar. A former merchant's house in the 12th century, this is the oldest building in Dartmouth. The restaurant is up a tight, steep staircase on the first floor and is known for its local fish and seafood dishes. Meals are served in the bar at lunchtime and in the evening and three beers are available (two in winter).
Q🅌🚶

Dawlish

Smugglers' Inn
27 Teignmouth Road, EX7 0LA (on A379)
🕑 11-11; 12-10.30 Sun
☎ (01626) 862301
Draught Bass; Red Rock Back Beach; Teignworthy Reel Ale; guest beers Ⓗ
Run by its friendly owners, this large, roadside free house has superb coastal views. The bar area is heated by a wood-burning fire and the restaurant has a veranda that is popular during the summer. The beer policy is to serve one national brew and regional beers from the South West. Families are welcome and facilities for the disabled are good. There is a large car park. ⚲🅌🚶♿🅐🚂🚉🅿

East Budleigh

Sir Walter Raleigh
22 High Street, EX9 7ED (on B3170)
🕑 11.45-2.30, 6-11; 12-2.30, 7-10.30 Sun
☎ (01395) 442510
Adnams Broadside; Otter Bitter; St Austell Tribute Ⓗ
Pleasant 16th-century village pub close to Sir Walter Raleigh's birthplace of Hayes Barton, comprising a bar area and adjoining restaurant. Diners are offered a wide range of pub favourites as well as interesting a la carte choices. This is a quiet pub without piped music or gaming machines, and children are not generally welcome. There is a courtyard area at the back. Q🅌🚶🅐

East Prawle

Pig's Nose Inn
TQ7 2BY (on edge of village green) OS782365
🕑 12-2.30, 7-11 (closed all day Mon and Sun eve winter)
☎ (01548) 511209 🌐 pigsnoseinn.co.uk
Fuller's London Pride; South Hams Devon Pride; ⓖ Eddystone Ⓗ
Old three-roomed smugglers' inn set on the village green, in an area that attracts birdwatchers and coastal walkers. The beers, largely on gravity, are stored in a specially made rack behind the bar in an old alcove. Home-cooked wholesome food is served, made with local ingredients. Local CAMRA Pub of the Year 2005, children and dogs are welcome in the cluttered interior which has a maritime theme. Occasional live music is performed at weekends in a hall adjoining the pub. ⚲🐕🏠🅌🚶🅐♣🍴

119

Exeter

Brook Green Tavern

31 Well Street, EX4 6QL
✪ 4 (12 Sat and summer Fri)-11; 12-10.30 Sun
☎ (01392) 495699
Caledonian Deuchars IPA; Fuller's London Pride; Shepherd Neame Spitfire; guest beers Ⓗ
Traditonal pub situated close to St James Park football ground and St James station, and a five minute walk from the city centre. The friendly landlady always offers six different ales. Popular with students, the pub also hosts meetings of the Victorian Cricket Team and has two resident football teams. Live music plays on Sunday afternoon, and regular quiz nights are hosted. There is a small garden; parking is limited. ⌂❀✉⇌⇌(St James)🚌P⌐

City Gate Hotel

Iron Bridge, North Street, EX4 3RB
✪ 11-midnight; 12-11.30 Sun
☎ (01392) 495811 ⊕ citygatehotel.co.uk
Young's Bitter, Special; Wells Bombardier; guest beers Ⓗ
Young's has tastefully refurbished this hotel, situated a short walk from the High Street. The entrance leads into an open bar area and hotel reception. Food is served throughout the day, but restricted to snacks at off-peak times. There is a range of Young's bottled beers available to take home at favourable prices. The guest beers are mostly from the Wells and Young's list. The hotel has a large patio garden and function room.
🏰Q❀✉⏀&⇌(Central/St David's)

Double Locks Hotel

Canal Banks, EX2 6LT (road access from Marsh Barton trading estate)
✪ 11-midnight; 12-10.30 Sun
☎ (01392) 256947 ⊕ doublelocks.co.uk
O'Hanlon's Royal Oak; Otter Ale; Wells Bombardier; Young's Bitter; Ⓗ **guest beers** Ⓖ
Situated on the banks of the historic Exeter Ship Canal, this pub is popular with families, walkers, canoeists and cyclists. It has an extensive outdoor area for summer drinking and warming log fires in winter. The excellent range of ales on offer includes up to nine guests in summer, and it hosts a beer festival in May. A volleyball festival is also staged and live music plays on Saturday nights in summer. Food is available all day during the summer months. 🏰Q❀⏀&⏀P⌐

Great Western Hotel

St David's Station Approach, EX4 8NU
✪ 11-11; 12-10.30 Sun
☎ (01392) 274039 ⊕ greatwesternhotel.co.uk
Branscombe Vale Branoc, Draught Bass; Fuller's London Pride; O'Hanlon's Yellow Hammer, Royal Oak; Princetown Jail Ale; guest beers Ⓗ
Featuring the largest range of real ales in the city, this is a traditional railway hotel with a good community spirit. Twice winner of local CAMRA Pub of the Year, it holds regular beer festivals, usually at bank holidays. Meals are served in the bar and Brunel restaurant. Fairly priced home-cooked food in generous portions comes from a varied menu, with curry and steak nights and a Sunday carvery

drawing diners. Children and dogs are welcome. ❀✉⏀⇌(St David's)🚌⌐

Old Firehouse

50 New North Road, EX4 4EP
✪ 12-3 (not Sat), 5-1am; 5-midnight Sun
☎ (01392) 277279
Sharp's Doom Bar; Wychwood Hobgoblin; guest beers Ⓗ
Popular city centre pub, close to Central railway station and the bus station. Spread over three floors, the bars are on the ground and second floors. Live music plays here three nights a week. Four beers are always available (with plans to introduce two more), usually including at least one from a local brewery. Good value food is prepared on the premises, made with local ingredients.
Q❀⏀⇌(Central)🚌⌐

Well House Tavern

16-17 Cathedral Yard, EX1 1HO
✪ 11-11 (midnight Fri & Sat)
☎ (01392) 223611
Beer range varies; Ⓗ
Following a chequered history, the Well House became a pub in the 1980s, and now forms part of the Royal Clarence Hotel owned by two-star Michelin chef Michael Caines. The tavern's large windows overlook the superb 11th-century cathedral and green. The house beer, Well House Ale, is brewed by Otter, and there are regularly changing guest beers as well as occasional mini beer festivals. The cider comes from Grays. This pub is a must for any visitor to the city. ⏀⇌(Central)🚌●

Exmouth

Grove

The Esplanade, EX8 1AS
✪ 11-midnight
☎ (01395) 272101 ⊕ youngs.co.uk
Wells Bombardier; Young's Bitter, Special Ⓗ
Large Young's house at the western end of the Esplanade, 10-15 minutes' walk from the town centre, served by good bus and train links. A road train also runs from the town centre to the sea front in summer. Good food is served (12-10pm daily) in the bar or upstairs restaurant, which has panoramic views across the Exe estuary. Families are welcome and the large beer garden gets very busy in the summer. A quiz is held on Thursday evening. ❀⏀&⇌🚌

Hatherleigh

Tally Ho!

14 Market Street, EX20 3JN (opp church)
✪ 12 (11 Tue)-11 (1am Fri & Sat)
☎ (01837) 810306 ⊕ tallyhohatherleigh.co.uk
Clearwater Cavalier; guest beers Ⓗ
Single bar 15th-century inn, characterised by an olde-worlde look, with exposed beams and log fires. Tuesday is market day when selected real ales are reduced in price from 11am-3pm. Winkleigh cider is served in summer. Good value, locally sourced meals (using ingredients from the pub's own garden) may be enjoyed in the bar, restaurant or sheltered beer garden, which has a barbecue area. The

disused Okehampton-Bude railway provides good walking, and fishing is available on the nearby River Torridge. ⚲Q✿❀✪◗❑(86)●⚓—

Hexworthy

Forest Inn

PL20 6SD (off B3357)
✪ 11-2.30, 6-11
☎ (01364) 631211 ⊕ theforestinn.co.uk
Teignworthy Reel Ale, Beachcomber Ⓗ
This country inn, situated in the Dartmoor Forest, is well worth seeking out for a refreshing drink, a meal or a longer stay. All are welcome: walkers, riders, anglers, canoeists, children and dogs. Heron Valley cider is stocked and a wide range of food and accommodation is on offer, from en-suite guest rooms to a bunkhouse. The bars are furnished with Chesterfields, and there are separate dining areas. Horses can be stabled by prior arrangement. ⚲Q✿❀✐◗●P

High Bickington

Golden Lion

North Road, EX37 9BB (on B3217) OS601205
✪ 12-3 (not winter), 4.30-11; closed Tue; 12-11 Sat; 12-10.30 Sun
☎ (01769) 560213
Cotleigh Barn Owl; guest beers Ⓗ
This 17th-century free house is an inviting place to catch up with the friendly owners and locals. The bar area is festooned with local pictures, books, agricultural tools hanging from the ceiling and rows of trophies won at darts, skittles and football contests. The cider is Winkleigh's. Freshly prepared food using local produce is served. Well-behaved children and dogs are welcome. Q✿◗❑(377)♣●P

Holcombe Rogus

Prince of Wales

TA21 0PN
✪ 12-3, 6-11; 11-11 Sat; 12-10 Sun
☎ (01823) 672070
Courage Best Bitter; guest beers Ⓗ
This 17th-century country pub is situated not far from the Grand Western Canal and the Somerset border, an area popular with walkers and cyclists. Inside, the bar features unusual cash register handpumps. The dining area has recently been extended and offers home-cooked meals, including vegetarian options. A large log-burning stove warms the bar area in winter and the pool table and darts area are well used by local teams. A beer festival is held on the first weekend in September. The attractive walled garden is popular in summer. ⚲Q✿✐◗♣●P

Holsworthy

Rydon Inn

Rydon Road, EX22 7HU (½ mile W of Holsworthy on A3072 Bude road) OS331040
✪ 11.30-3, 5.30-11; closed winter Mon; 12-3, 6-10.30 (not winter eve) Sun
☎ (01409) 259444 ⊕ rydon-inn.com
Sharp's Doom Bar; St Austell Tribute Ⓗ

Spacious gastro-pub near the market town of Holsworthy, built as an old Devon longhouse. The border with Cornwall lies just a few miles away, and the beers are now supplied by two Cornish brewers. The cider is Thatchers Dry. The thatched bar area is decorated in a bright, contemporary style, with vaulted pine beams. Well-behaved children are welcome here – the pub won the North Devon Good Food award in the 'Best for Families' category. ⚲Q✿❀✪◗♿❑●P

Honiton

Holt

178 High Street, EX14 1LA
✪ 11-3, 5.30-11 (midnight Fri & Sat); 11-4 Sun
☎ (01404) 47707 ⊕ theholt-honiton.com
Otter Bitter, Bright, Ale, Head Ⓗ
Otter Brewery has a done a fine job in converting this former wine bar into its first pub. There is a good, cosy bar at street level, and a dining area upstairs, both smartly decorated with plenty of exposed wood. The kitchen is in full view and as well as restaurant food, there are usually tapas-style snacks available (no eve meals on Sun). ◗≉

Horsebridge

Royal Inn

PL19 8PJ (off A388 Tavistock to Launceston rd)
✪ 11.30-3, 6.30-11; 12-3, 7-10.30 Sun
☎ (01822) 870214 ⊕ royalinn.co.uk
Draught Bass; Sharp's Doom Bar; Ⓗ **guest beers** Ⓗ/Ⓖ
Originally built by French Benedictine monks as a nunnery in 1437, the pub overlooks an old bridge on the River Tamar, connecting Devon to Cornwall. It now features half-panelling and stone floors in the bar and lounge, both traditional in style. There is a further larger room off the lounge. The terraced gardens are suitable for children, who are welcome until 9pm. The guest beers are usually served on gravity, and the food comes highly recommended. Bar billiards is played here. ⚲Q❀◗♣P

Iddesleigh

Duke of York

EX19 8BG (off B3217 next to church) OS570083
✪ 11-11 (midnight Fri & Sat); 12-10.30 Sun
☎ (01837) 810253
Adnams Broadside; Cotleigh Tawny; guest beers Ⓖ
Ideally situated near the Tarka Trail and River Torridge, the Duke offers a homely atmosphere. Lifting the latch on the front door brings you into the simply furnished single bar, with a large log fire and rocking chair. The cider is from nearby Winkleigh and Czech Budvar lager is also available. Award-winning food (using produce from the landlord's own farm) and wines are served in the bar or separate dining areas. Well-behaved children and dogs are welcome – horses have to wait outside! ⚲❀✐◗♣●

Kilmington

New Inn

The Hill, EX13 7SF (S of A35)

⊕ 11-2.30, 7-11; 12-3, 7-10.30 Sun

☎ (01297) 33376

Palmer Copper Ale, IPA, seasonal beers Ⓗ

Cosy, thatched Devon longhouse that was rebuilt after a major fire in 2004, but retains a warm atmosphere. One benefit to have resulted from the fire is the provision of excellent toilet facilities. Secluded gardens and the landlord's aviaries are attractive outdoor features, while a well-used skittle alley is home to nine local teams. Regular quizzes and games such as crib and darts maintain this pub's position at the heart of village life. ♨Q✿❶Ⓓ➘☕♣P⅃

Kings Nympton

Grove Inn

EX37 9ST (edge of village) OS683195

⊕ 12-3 (not Mon), 6-11; 12-3, 7-10.30 Sun

☎ (01769) 580406 ⊕ thegroveinn.co.uk

Exmoor Ale; guest beers Ⓗ

A 17th-century, Grade II thatched pub situated within this picturesque village. The single bar has low beams, an interesting collection of bookmarks and an open fire for colder months. The cider is Sam's Dry from Winkleigh. The award-winning food is locally sourced, with fish and chips on Tuesday made with Exmoor Ale batter. A quiz night is held on the last Monday of the month. Well-behaved children and dogs are welcome. ♨Q✿❶Ⓓ♣♠⅃

Kingston

Dolphin Inn

TQ7 4QE (just off main lane through village, next to church)

⊕ 12-3, 6-11; 12-3, 7-10 (10.30 summer) Sun

☎ (01548) 810314

Courage Best Bitter; Sharp's Doom Bar; guest beers Ⓗ

A focal point for the local community and popular with tourists in summer, the main part of the pub is formed from three cottages dating from the 16th century. There are further buildings on the other side of the road. Open fires in winter and the pleasantly subdued lighting create a warm feel. The food is home-made, with an emphasis on locally sourced ingredients. The family room, garden and Gents' are across the road. ♨➘✿➪❶Ⓓ♣♠P⅃

Kingswear

Ship Inn

Higher Street, TQ6 0AG

⊕ 12-midnight (closed 3-6 Mon-Thu winter)

☎ (01803) 752348 ⊕ theshipinnkingswear.co.uk

Adnams Bitter; Otter Ale; Greene King IPA; guest beers Ⓗ

This popular 15th-century village pub, near the steam railway station, affords stunning views of the River Dart from its terrace and dining room. Local CAMRA Pub of the Year 2006, it has two busy bars with log fires and a welcoming ambience. The lounge has panelled walls, beams and a connecting wall to the dining room which is several metres thick. The menu features locally caught fresh fish as a speciality. In winter, quiz nights and occasional live music evenings provide entertainment. ♨Q✿❶Ⓓ➪≠

Knowle

Dog & Donkey

24 Knowle Village, EX9 6AL (on B3178)

⊕ 11.30-3, 6-11.30; 11.30-midnight Fri & Sat; 12-10.30 Sun

☎ (01395) 442021 ⊕ thedoganddonkey.co.uk

Draught Bass; Otter Ale; Ⓗ **guest beers** Ⓖ

Formerly known as the Britannia Inn (the old sign still hangs outside), this delightful pub is located in the centre of the village. There is a traditional main bar warmed by a welcoming open fire and, to the right, a smaller room with a large TV for sports enthusiasts. The tastefully refurbished restaurant has a reputation for serving excellent food, especially the very popular Sunday lunch (booking essential). The cider is Thatchers Old Rosie. ♨Q➘✿➪Ⓓ➪♣♠P⅃

Lake

Bearslake Inn

EX20 4HQ (on A386 between Okehampton and Tavistock) OS528888

⊕ 11-3, 6-11; 12-4 Sun

☎ (01837) 861334 ⊕ bearslakeinn.com

Beer range varies Ⓗ/Ⓖ

Believed to date back to the 13th century, the main building is a traditional, Grade II listed, thatched Devon longhouse, originally a working farm. The single bar offers a range of primarily West Country ales, as many as five in summer, some dispensed straight from the cask. There is a lounge area with log fires where families are welcome. Views of Dartmoor can be appreciated from the large garden. Excellent food is prepared from local ingredients when possible, with the menu changing daily. ♨Q➘✿➪❶Ⓓ➘▲➪♣P

Landscove

Live & Let Live

TQ13 7LZ (on main road through village)

⊕ 12-3, 6.30-11; closed Mon; 12-3 Sun

☎ (01803) 762663

Beer range varies Ⓗ

Small, beamed village pub with a wood-panelled L-shaped bar, a small drinking area close to the bar and two dining areas. A good choice of home-cooked meals is available at reasonable prices. One of the beers is always from Teignworthy Brewery. The bar has a large collection of miniatures on a display rail, and the large stone fireplaces make attractive focal points. There is a small, walled, decked patio area at the front of the pub. ♨Q✿Ⓓ♠P

Lutton

Mountain Inn

Old Chapel Road, PL21 9SA (off Plympton-Cornwood road) SX595594

🕏 12 (6 Tue)-11

☎ (01752) 837247

Princetown Jail Ale; guest beers 🅗

Two-roomed village pub on the edge of Dartmoor welcoming visitors, locals, horse riders, walkers and dogs. The pub's name is a corruption of a local landowner's family name, Montain. Jail Ale from Princetown is complemented by three guest ales sourced from far and wide and Winkleigh cider. The cosy bar has simple cob walls and a second room is used for dining – both rooms warmed by real fires. Simple pub food is available (not Tue). Occasional beer festivals are held.
🅰Q🕏🕘◑🖙P

Lydford

Castle Inn

EX20 4BH

🕏 11.30-11; 12-10.30 Sun

☎ (01822) 820241 ⏺castleinnlydford.co.uk

Fuller's London Pride; Otter Ale; guest beers 🅗

Comfortable and welcoming 16th-century inn featuring a public bar where dogs are welcome, a snug with settles and a lounge bar, all with low ceilings and granite floors and walls. In a perfect spot, it stands next to 12th-century Lydford Castle with St Petroc's Church and Lydford Gorge (National Trust) nearby. Dartmoor, strikingly visible, is a short walk away, and it is situated on the Devon to Devon coast-to-coast cycle route, Dartmoor Way and West Devon Way cycle/walking routes.
🅰Q🕏🖾◑🖰🖙🚃♣P⅃

Lympstone

Redwing Inn

Church Road, EX8 5JT

🕏 11.30-3, 6-11.30; 11.30-11.30 Sat; 12-10.30 Sun

☎ (01395) 222156

O'Hanlon's Royal Oak; Otter Bitter; Palmer Best Bitter; guest beer 🅗

This active village pub is a true free house, selling a range of real ales as well as draught Thatchers cider. The public bar and lounge/restaurant are separate but served by a common bar. Meals and snacks are available at all times except Sunday evening. There is a wide variety of entertainment on offer including live music, karaoke and quiz nights. The bus service drops you a mile from the pub and the station is five minutes' walk away.
Q🕏◑🖰🚈♣P

Lynton

Crown Hotel

Market Street, EX35 6AG (next to library) OS720493

🕏 11-11; 12-10.30 Sun

☎ (01598) 752253 ⏺thecrown-lynton.co.uk

Draught Bass; St Austell Tinners, Tribute, Proper Job 🅗

This 16th-century hotel is situated in a scenic North Devon coastal town in an area popular with walkers attracted by the stunning views of the rugged coastline, especially from the Valley of the Rocks and Coastal Path nearby. The bar is frequented by locals and visitors, and welcomes children and dogs. Two beer festivals are held each year in May and October. Meals can be taken in the bar, on the patio or in the restaurant. 🅰Q🕏🖾🕘◑🖙P

Meavy

Royal Oak Inn

PL20 6PJ (follow signs for Meavy from B3212 at Dousland)

🕏 11.30-3, 6-11; 11.30-11 Sat; 12-11 Sun

☎ (01822) 652944 ⏺royaloakinn.org.uk

Princetown IPA, Jail Ale; St Austell Tribute; guest beer 🅗

A classic inn at the heart of the village with a comfortable lounge bar featuring exposed beams and settles. The public bar has a flagstone floor and roaring log fire in winter. A cobbled area with bench seating in front of the pub overlooks the green where the eponymous oak tree stands. The guest beer is local, with Weston's Scrumpy cider also available. Varied lunchtime and evening meals are served (no food Sun eve). There may be impromptu live music on Wednesday evenings. 🅰Q🕏◑🖰🚈♣

Moretonhampstead

Union Inn

10 Ford Street, TQ13 8LN

🕏 11 (12 Sun)-11

☎ (01647) 440199 ⏺theunioninn.co.uk

Fuller's London Pride; guest beers 🅗

This 16th-century free house in the town centre is named after the 1801 United Kingdom Act of Union. The main bar is clad in 19th-century tongue-and-groove panelling and a corridor linking the 17th-century Linhay Bar in the former stables displays many artefacts relating to the inn's history. An ever-changing range of guest beers tends to include one lighter and one darker variety. The air-conditioned stable room offers a Sunday carvery – food is delicious and keenly priced.
🅰Q🕏🕘◑🖰🖙🚃♣P⅃🖢

Mortehoe

Chichester Arms

Chapel Hill, EX34 7DU (next to church) OS456451

🕏 12-3, 6.30-11; 12-11 Sat and summer; 12-10.30 Sun

☎ (01271) 870411

Barum Original; Cottage Somerset & Dorset Ale; Courage Directors; guest beers 🅗

This popular village free house stands in a picturesque spot, with the coastal path nearby and easy access to National Trust land at Morte Point. With the expansive beaches of Woolacombe Bay at the bottom of the hill it is very popular in summer. Gas lighting still features inside the bar where good food is served daily in summer (Wed-Sun only in winter). A games room/skittle alley and children's room are also available. There are benches at the front for drinking and dining alfresco. 🏃🕏◑🖙🚃♣P⅃

Newton Abbot

Union Inn

6 East Street, TQ12 1AF (opp magistrates court)
☼ 10-11 (midnight Fri & Sat)
☎ (01626) 354775
Draught Bass; Greene King IPA; Sharp's Doom Bar; guest beers Ⓗ
This busy town-centre pub is popular with shoppers and regulars. Guest beers usually include one local and one from further afield. Excellent breakfasts are served daily from 8.30am and good value lunches from 11.30am, using local farm produce where possible. The pub supports several darts and euchre teams and a football team. Although it has no garden, outside drinking is permitted in the pedestrianised area in front of the pub.
🏴♿◁≠🚪♣ᵇ

Wolborough Inn

55 Wolborough Street, TQ12 1JQ
☼ 12-2.30, 4.30-midnight; 12-midnight Sat; 12-11.30 Sun
☎ (01626) 334511
Beer range varies Ⓗ/Ⓖ
Real ale pub with a traditional frontage, known locally as the First and Last. It sports a refurbished interior while maintaining many original features, especially in the main L-shaped bar area: wooden floor, seating around the edge and the old Starkey Knight and Ford etched windows. There is also an open plan seating area to one side and an additional new area to the rear. The pub is very popular with locals who come to enjoy the changing ales, bottled beers and varying cider. ♿≠🚪♣♠

Newton St Cyres

Beer Engine

EX5 5AX (N of A377, next to station)
☼ 11 (12 Sun)-11
☎ (01392) 851282
Beer Engine Rail Ale, Piston Bitter, Sleeper Heavy, seasonal beers Ⓗ
Popular village pub and brewery, overlooking the Exeter to Barnstaple Tarka Line. The three ales on offer reflect the railway theme, as do the pub sign and pictures. The open-plan bar and restaurant have polished floors, a roaring log fire and ceiling beams adorned with hops, all helping to create a friendly, welcoming atmosphere. This year the pub celebrates 25 years as Devon's oldest brewery. Outside is a secluded patio and barbecue area.
🏴Q🅿◁♿≠🚪Pᵇ⏱🍴

North Bovey

Ring of Bells Inn

TQ13 8RB SX740839
☼ 11-11; 12-10.30 Sun
☎ (01647) 440375 ⊕ringofbellsinn.com
Otter Ale; St Austell Dartmoor Best; Wadworth 6X Ⓗ
Low-beamed, thatched, 13th-century inn, built to house masons while they were constructing the nearby church, nestling behind the green of this picturesque Dartmoor hamlet two miles south-west of Moretonhampstead. The pub retains many period features including a 14th-century bread oven. It is acclaimed for the good food it serves, made with local ingredients, and regular themed nights are organised. Meals can be taken in the bar or restaurant. Local Gray's farmhouse cider is available in summer. The courtyard makes a pleasant drinking area.
🏴Q🐕🅿◁🍴ᵇ

North Tawton

Railway Inn

Whiddon Down Road, EX20 2BE OS666001
☼ 12-3 (Fri and Sat only), 6 (7 Sun)-11
☎ (01837) 82789
Teignworthy Reel Ale; guest beers Ⓗ
Set in a rural location, this former local CAMRA Pub of the Year is a friendly, single-bar country pub and forms part of a working farm. It stands next to the former North Tawton Station (closed 1971), which it predates, and the bar decor features railway memorabilia and old photos of the station. The beer range is generally West Country based, likewise the cider (Gray's) stocked in summer. The dining room is popular in the evening (no food Thu); light meals are served at lunchtime.
🏴◁♣🅿

Noss Mayo

Ship Inn

PL8 1EW (off Bridgend-Stoke road)
☼ 11-11; closed winter Mon; 12-10.30 Sun
☎ (01752) 872387 ⊕nossmayo.com
Butcombe Blonde; Princetown Jail Ale; St Austell Tribute; Summerskills Tamar Ⓗ
Customers wishing to sail to the pub should ring first to ascertain the tide table and moorings, otherwise use dry land to visit this charming inn on the banks of the River Yealm. A former local CAMRA Pub of the Year, comfortable seating allows you to savour both the local beers and food prepared from locally sourced ingredients. A daytime bus service operates Monday to Saturday. 🏴Q🅿◁♿🚪P

Oakford

Red Lion

Rookery Hill, EX16 9ES
☼ 12-2.30 (not Mon), 6-11; 12-2.30 Sun
☎ (01398) 351219 ⊕theredlionhoteloakford.co.uk
Fuller's London Pride; Otter Ale; guest beer Ⓗ
Welcoming free house set in a quiet village in undulating countryside on the fringes of Exmoor. The main bar area features a large inglenook fireplace and there is a separate dining room where good value food is served. Three ales are complemented by Weston's cider. The car park and garden area are across the road. Accommodation comprises four comfortable en-suite rooms, including one with a four-poster bed. 🏴🅿🛏◁♣ᵇP

Okehampton

Plymouth Inn

26 West Street, EX20 1HH OS586951
☼ 11-midnight
☎ (01837) 53633
Beer range varies Ⓖ

Sited near the bridge over the River West Okement, this is a friendly, simply furnished pub that brings the welcoming atmosphere of a village local to an old market town. Walking and cycling groups are informally organised in summer, and two beer festivals are held (normally May and Nov), one to coincide with the Ten Tors challenge. Good pub food as well as bar snacks can be taken in the bar, restaurant and rear garden.
🛲❀◑🖂(X9, X30, 86)♣🚭

Paignton

Isaac Merritt

54-58 Torquay Road, TQ3 3AA
🕙 9-midnight
☎ (01803) 556066
Courage Directors; Greene King Abbot; Marston's Burton Bitter, Pedigree; guest beers Ⓗ
This busy, town-centre Wetherspoon's is popular with all ages. Cosy alcove seating helps to create comfortable, friendly surroundings. This splendid pub has a reputation for its ever-changing guest beers augmented by mini beer festivals on Sunday and Monday. Local CAMRA Pub of the Year 2001 and a Wetherspoon's award winner in 2004, good value meals are available all day. It is easily accessible to wheelchair users and has a designated ground-floor toilet. Fully air-conditioned. ◑♿➔🖂❀🚭

Parkham

Bell Inn

Rectory Lane, EX39 5PL (off A39 about 1½ miles S of Horns Cross) OS387212
🕙 12-3, 5.30 (5 Fri)-11; 12-3, 6-10.30 Sun
☎ (01237) 451201 ● thebellinnparkham.co.uk
Exmoor Fox; Fuller's London Pride; Greene King IPA; Sharp's Doom Bar; guest beers Ⓗ
Originally a forge and two cottages, this cosy 13th-century thatched free house has been tastefully refurbished by the current occupiers. The single bar serves two distinct areas, with a wood burner and coal fire to keep patrons warm on colder days. Food prepared from locally produced ingredients is served in the bar and the raised dining area. Senior citizens' lunch on Monday provides a main course and pudding for around £5. A popular beer festival is staged each year on the first weekend in June. 🏚❀◑♣P🚭

Plymouth

Admiral MacBride

1 The Barbican, PL1 2LR (opp Mayflower Steps Memorial)
🕙 11-11 (12-3, 6-11 winter); 11-midnight (11 winter) Sat
☎ (01752) 262054
Beer range varies Ⓗ
This popular pub is situated on Plymouth's historic Barbican, close to the site of the Mayflower Steps where the Pilgrim Fathers set sail for America in 1620. It is also close to the National Marine Aquarium, and has been attractively decorated throughout with a nautical theme. During the busy summer months up to three real ales are available.

Discos are held on Saturday nights, live music and charity quizzes feature occasionally. No food is served on Saturday or Sunday evenings. ◑🖂

Admiral Stopford Arms

172 Devonport Road, Stoke, PL1 5RE
🕙 11-11
☎ (01752) 245577
Beer range varies Ⓗ
This street-corner locals' pub attracts a broad mix of guests, and is popular with both active and armchair sports fans. Close to Plymouth Albion's rugby ground, it becomes extremely busy before home games and, if the weather is bad, sometimes during them. Ales are sourced from local, regional and national breweries, with requests for particular beers welcomed. An outside smoking area is provided in the attractive courtyard garden. Live music plays at weekends.
❀◑➔(Devonport)🖂♣🚭

Artillery Arms

6 Pound Street, Stonehouse, PL1 3RH (behind Stonehouse Barracks and military docks)
🕙 11 (10 Sat)-11; 12-10.30 Sun
☎ (01752) 262515
Draught Bass; guest beers Ⓗ
Opening at 9am for breakfast (no alcohol), this corner pub to the rear of the Brittany Ferries terminal has a single bar plus a dining area where good value, home-cooked meals are served (no food Sun). Very much a community pub, it sponsors charity fund-raising events including monkey races. A 'Beach Party' is held in February. Although not the easiest pub to locate in the back streets of Stonehouse, the effort is well rewarded with a warm and friendly welcome. 🏚◑🖂❀

Blue Peter

68 Pomphlett Road, Plymstock, PL9 7BN
🕙 11-11; 12.30-10.30 Sun
☎ (01752) 402255
Beer range varies Ⓗ/Ⓖ
In a part of Plymouth where real ale is scarce, the Blue Peter has twice been voted local CAMRA Pub of the Year. The lounge of this two-bar pub has alcove seating and is the main dining area (no food Mon & Tue); Sunday roasts are a speciality. The public bar has a large-screen TV for sports and a games area and can be used for live entertainment. Occasional beer festivals are held.
🏚Q❀◑⌖♿🖂♣P🚭

Boringdon Arms

13 Boringdon Terrace, Turnchapel, PL9 9TQ
🕙 11-midnight; 12-11 Sun
☎ (01752) 402053 ● bori.co.uk
Draught Bass; Butcombe Bitter; Otter Ale; RCH Pitchfork; Summerskills Best Bitter; guest beer Ⓗ
Recent renovations have made this local CAMRA Pub of the Year 2007 even more popular. Situated in a waterside village on the coastal footpath, Turnchapel is well served by road and water taxis from the Barbican (to Mount Batten). Beer festivals are held on the last weekend of odd-numbered months. The 'Bori' has a good reputation for home-cooked food, which may be enjoyed alfresco in the

garden planted up in a former quarry.
♨Q☾✿❀♫⊕❄♣

Britannia

1 Wolseley Road, Milehouse, PL2 3AE
🕒 9am-midnight (1am Fri & Sat)
☎ (01752) 607596
**Greene King Abbot; Marston's Burton Bitter,
Pedigree; Shepherd Neame Spitfire; guest
beers** Ⓗ
Wetherspoon's conversion from a run-down
Edwardian pub into a popular, busy local.
Home and away football supporters join a
mixed clientele on match days as it is the pub
nearest to Plymouth Argyle's ground.
However, a friendly atmosphere prevails at all
times. The guest beers include selections from
Summerskills and South West brewers, and
the cider is from Weston's.
♨Q✿❀⊕&⇌❄♠♣⚓

Dolphin Hotel

14 The Barbican, PL1 2LS
🕒 10am (9am summer)-midnight; 11-11 Sun
☎ (01752) 660876
Draught Bass Ⓖ
Take a step back in time at the Dolphin, an
unmodernised inn not be missed if you are
visiting the Barbican. This basic hostelry is
where the Tolpuddle Martyrs stayed on their
return to England. It is often quiet during the
day, but by night it can get busy and
boisterous, especially on Friday and Saturday.
Look out for the Octagon Brewery logo on the
windows. The Bass is served from large barrels
behind the bar. ♨⊕❄

Fawn Private Members Club

39 Prospect Street, Greenbank, PL4 8NY
🕒 12-11 (10.30 Sun)
☎ (01752) 660546 ⊕ thefawnclub.co.uk
Courage Best Bitter; guest beers Ⓗ
Named after the now scrapped HMS Fawn and
previously a Whitbread pub, CAMRA members
are welcomed on presentation of a current
membership card; regular visitors will be
required to join. Many of the members live
locally and are keen followers of rugby and
other televised sports, or belong to darts, pool
and euchre teams, or simply enjoy the
ambience and reasonable prices. The house
beer Fawn Ale is supplied by Sharp's; two
guest ales and real cider are also available.
✿❀⇌❄♣♥

Fisherman's Arms

31 Lambhay Street, PL1 2NN (signed from Hoe Rd
and Madeira Drive)
🕒 12 (5 winter Mon)-11; 12-10.30 Sun
☎ (01752) 661457
St Austell Tinners, Tribute, HSD; guest beer Ⓗ
Reputedly the second oldest pub in Plymouth,
hidden away behind the famous Barbican, the
Fisherman's Arms has a warm and friendly
atmosphere. Due to its location it is popular
with locals, who head for the lively public bar,
and tourists who generally settle in the
lounge. The latter has a raised area at the rear
where guests enjoy home-cooked food; the
Sunday roasts are a speciality. Three St Austell
beers are occasionally supplemented by
another from the same brewery. ⊕❄⊟❄♣

Fortescue

37 Mutley Plain, Mutley, PL4 6JQ
🕒 11-11 (midnight Thu-Sat); 12-10.30 Sun
☎ (01752) 660673
**Blue Anchor Spingo Special; Greene King Abbot;
Taylor Landlord; guest beers** Ⓗ
This lively local is frequented by a broad
section of the community, and conversation
flourishes. On Thursday the popular cellar bar
hosts an acoustic evening and at weekends
various alternative DJs play anything but chart
music. Sundays here are perfect: Sunday roast
can be washed down with Spingo beer,
followed by a brainteaser quiz. The patio is the
ideal place to spend long summer days and
draws a large crowd. Three guest beers are
usually available. ✿❀⇌❄♣

George Inn

191 Ridgeway, Plympton, PL7 2HJ
🕒 11.30-11 (midnight Fri & Sat); 12-11 Sun
☎ (01752) 342674
Courage Best Bitter; Otter Ale; guest beer Ⓗ
This 17th-century former coaching house is
situated on the old Plymouth to Exeter road. A
welcoming, friendly hostelry, it has recently
been renovated inside and out. The flower-
bedecked patio is especially popular during
fine weather. Dogs on leads are welcome in
the flagstone public bar. In the adjoining
dining area, a specials board supplements an
extensive menu (booking advisable at
weekends). Live music features on Sunday
night, with a leaning towards jazz.
♨Q✿❀⊕⊟&⊟♣♥P

Maritime Inn

19 Southside Street, Barbican, PL1 2LD
🕒 11-11; 12-10.30 Sun
☎ (01752) 664898
Beer range varies Ⓗ
Winner of Plymouth Evening Herald Pub of the
Year 2006, the Maritime is situated at Sutton
Harbour on the Barbican. It is a pub of two
distinct sections: enter from the Quay to the
bar with its slate floor, large TV and games
machines – it can get quite busy here,
especially when football matches are
screened. Or, from Southside Street, you reach
a carpeted, comfortable lounge area, suitable
for dining. Some interesting ales are offered,
particularly in winter. ✿❀⊕⊟♣

Prince Maurice

3 Church Hill, Eggbuckland, PL6 5RJ
🕒 11-3, 7-11; 11-11 Fri & Sat; 12-10.30 Sun
☎ (01752) 771515
**Adnams Broadside; Courage Best Bitter;
O'Hanlon's Royal Oak; St Austell HSD;
Summerskills Best Bitter; guest beers** Ⓗ
This four-times local CAMRA Pub of the Year
resides twixt the church and green in what
was once a village but is now a suburb of
Plymouth. It still maintains a village pub
atmosphere in both bars and continues to
offer eight beers plus Thatchers Cheddar Valley
Cider. The pub is named after the Royalist
general, the King's nephew, who had his
headquarters nearby during the Siege of
Plymouth in the Civil War. No food is served at
weekends. ♨✿❀⊕♣♥P

Sippers

18 Millbay Road, PL1 3LH
🌍 11-10.30 (11 Fri & Sat); 12-10.30 Sun
☎ (01752) 670668
Butcombe Bitter; Fuller's London Pride; Greene King Old Speckled Hen; Otter Ale; Marston's Pedigree Ⓗ
Located close to the city centre, between the Pavilions leisure centre and the ferry port, this pub is spread over four stone-floored levels, its walls bedecked with naval and other memorabilia. The unusual name refers to an old naval rum ration. Outside, the walls are adorned with hanging baskets in summer and the patio offers an alfresco drinking and dining area. A comprehensive menu is supplemented by good value lunchtime specials. ❀◑🖼🍴

Thistle Park Brewhouse

32 Commercial Road, Coxside, PL4 0LE
🌍 11-2am; 12-12.30am Sun
☎ (01752) 204890
South Hams Devon Pride, XSB, Sutton Comfort, Eddystone, seasonal beers Ⓗ
This friendly pub, situated close to the National Marine Aquarium and reached via the swing bridge from the Barbican, has recently been refurbished. It now has a new restaurant on the first floor featuring South African cuisine. New toilets have been installed downstairs. All beers, including the house beer, come from the South Hams Brewery (formerly Sutton Brewery, originally adjacent to the pub). ◑♿🖼♣●🍴

Yard Arm

159 Citadel Road, The Hoe, PL1 2HU
🌍 12-midnight
☎ (01752) 202405
Beer range varies Ⓗ
Busy street-corner pub just behind the famous Plymouth Hoe, serving home-cooked food and up to four real ales from national and local breweries. The decor features marine memorabilia and the raised, wood-panelled and naturally lit seating area and lower deck add to a nautical ambience. Within easy walking distance of the Barbican and city centre, its lively mix of guests changes throughout the day. It has a big TV screen for live sports. ❀🚆◑🍴

Postbridge

Warren House Inn

PL20 6TA (on B3212) SX674809
🌍 11-11 (11.30-5.30 Mon & Tue winter); 11-10.30 Sun
☎ (01822) 880208
Otter Ale; Summerskills Tamar; guest beers Ⓗ
Isolated and exposed at 1,425ft above sea level, the Warren House is indeed a welcome sight. The interior features exposed beams, wood panelling, rustic benches and tables and the famous fire. Guest beers vary with the seasons but usually include one strong ale. Countryman cider is available, with carry-outs. Lunch and evening menus offer home-cooked dishes made with local ingredients including Dartmoor beef, and vegetarian options. Tables outside command breathtaking views over the moors. 🏨Q🌳❀◑▲●🅿🍴

Princetown

Prince of Wales

Tavistock Road, PL20 6QF (opp Dartmoor Prison)
🌍 11-11 (midnight Fri & Sat)
☎ (01822) 890219
Princetown Dartmoor IPA, Jail Ale; guest beer (occasional) Ⓗ
Just down the road from the main square, this pub stands close to the recently enlarged Princetown Brewery, from which the two main ales are procured. There is a comfortable main bar with a small pool room leading off it. A function room provides additional dining space at busy times and also doubles as a skittle alley. Children are welcome and the food is recommended. The Yelverton-Princetown cycle path ends right behind the pub. 🏨🚆◑♣🅿

Sandford

Lamb Inn

The Square, EX17 4LW
🌍 9 (11 Sat & Sun)-11
☎ (01363) 773676 ⊕ lambinnsandford.co.uk
Beer Engine Rail Ale; Ⓗ **guest beers** Ⓗ/Ⓖ
This 16th-century former coaching inn, located in the heart of the village, is now a free house. It features up to three seasonal guest ales; the cider is from Sandford Orchards. The food is based on local ingredients, mostly seasonal, organic produce. All meals are cooked to order and guests may enjoy a coffee or light snack from 9am during the week in the garden. The skittle alley also functions as an occasional cinema and hosts open mike evenings for local bands. 🏨❀◑🖼♣●

Rose & Crown

Rose & Crown Hill, EX17 4NH
🌍 12-3, 6 (7 Sun)-11; 12-midnight Sat
☎ (01363) 772056 ⊕ roseandcrown-sandford.co.uk
Otter Bitter; guest beer Ⓗ
Traditional pub set in the delightful village of Sandford, near Crediton. Said to have been here as long ago as the 16th century, it is thought to have once been a coaching inn on the Turnpike Road to Witheridge. The original pub, built of cob and thatch, burnt down in 1896. It has a large bar and separate dining room. Sandford Orchards Farmhouse cider is available. No food is served on Monday. 🏨🌳❀◑♿🖼♣●🅿

Scoriton

Tradesman's Arms

TQ11 0JB (on Holne Road at edge of village)
🌍 12-2.30, 6-11; 12-11 Sat & Sun
☎ (01364) 631206
Princetown Dartmoor IPA; guest beers Ⓗ
A traditional country village pub, originally an ale house for tin miners in the 17th century, with a single, open-plan, L-shaped bar with additional seating for diners. The house beer, Scoriton Mystery, is brewed by Red Rock. Good food is served, prepared where possible from local produce, and special dietary needs can be catered for. There is a room that can be used by families and for meetings, and outside are gated areas for family dining in

the summer months. Well-behaved dogs are welcome. ₳Q☪☆◑P⇘

Shaldon

Clifford Arms

34 Fore Street, TQ14 0DZ
✪ 11-2.30, 5-11.30; 12-2, 7-11 Sun
☎ (01626) 872311
Greene King Abbot; Ringmore Craft Oarsome; Shepherd Neame Spitfire; guest beers Ⓗ
Village-centre pub which recently reopened after a major refit and now has a modern interior. The pub is the local outlet for Ringmore Craft Brewery, established March 2007, and guest beers are mainly from West Country breweries. There is a separate low-level restaurant (food served at all sessions except Sun eve) and outdoor decked patio. Regular events include the jazz café on Monday evening and a charity quiz on Thursday. ☆◑Å₪

Shebbear

Devil's Stone Inn

EX21 5RU (in village square) OS438092
✪ 12-3, 6-11; 12-11 Fri & Sat; 12-10.30 Sun
☎ (01409) 281210 ⊕ devilsstoneinn.com
Sharp's Special; guest beers Ⓗ
This 17th-century former coaching inn's name derives from the local tradition of turning the Devil's Stone each year on the 5th November to keep the devil away. The stone, which lies outside the church, apparently fell out of the devil's pocket on his journey from heaven to hell. The single bar interior features flagstone floors, open fireplaces and cosy armchairs. Sam's cider from Winkleigh is available in summer. There is a large garden, games room and separate dining room where a life-size talking dummy presides. ₳☆⇘◑₪◆P⇘

Sheepwash

Half Moon Inn

The Square, EX21 5NE (off A3072) OS486063
✪ 11.30-11 daily summer; 11.30-2.30, 6-11 Mon-Sat; 12-2.30, 7-10.30 Sun winter
☎ (01409) 231376 ⊕ halfmoonsheepwash.co.uk
Courage Best Bitter; Greene King Ruddles Best Bitter; guest beer Ⓗ
Originally a fishing inn, with some parts dating back to the 15th century, the pub is close to the River Torridge. A friendly, comfortable, unspoilt village local, the single bar has exposed beams and a flagstone floor plus a magnificent log fire. There is a rod room situated just off the bar area. Of the handpumps on view, three serve real ale. Good value food, prepared on the premises and using local produce, is served in both the bar and restaurant. ₳Q☆⇘◑P⇘

Sidmouth

Swan Inn

37 York Street, EX10 8BY (400m from seafront lifeboat station)
✪ 11-2.30 (3 Sat), 5.30-11; 12-3, 7-10.30 Sun
☎ (01395) 512849
Young's Bitter, Special; guest beers Ⓗ

This inn, originally cottages and a shop, was established in 1890. Situated in the winding back streets of this quaint seaside town, it is just a short walk from the seafront and main shopping area but in a quiet location. Beams and open fireplaces help create a cosy, traditional atmosphere. Dogs are welcome. There is evening parking opposite and all day public parking close by. The nearest bus stop is a four minute walk. ₳Q☆◑⊞Ġ♣

Silverton

Lamb Inn

Fore Street, EX5 4HZ
✪ 11.30-2.30, 6-11 (1am Thu; 2am Fri); 11.30-2am Sat; 12-11 Sun
☎ (01392) 860272
Exe Valley Dob's Best Bitter, Draught Bass; Ⓖ **guest beers** Ⓗ/Ⓖ
Family-run village pub with stone floors, stripped timber and old pine tables and chairs. Most of the ales are served by gravity from a temperature-controlled stillage behind the bar. A multi-purpose function room plus skittle alley and bar is well used by local teams. Good value home-cooked food is served, with a specials board including vegetarian options. ₳◑♣

Slapton

Queen's Arms

TQ7 2PN
✪ 11-3, 6-11; 12-3, 7-10.30 Sun
☎ (01548) 580800
Sharp's Doom Bar; Teignworthy Reel Ale; guest beers Ⓗ
South Devon free house with a single bar where the traditional mood is enhanced by a large open fire and old photographs depicting wartime evacuation. Two or three ales are stocked, depending on the time of year. A full menu includes a take-away service. Sunday lunchtime roasts in winter are popular (worth booking). The walled garden permits alfresco drinking. Children and dogs are welcome. ₳☆◑Å₪♣P

South Brent

Royal Oak

Station Road, TQ10 9BE (near old railway station)
✪ 12-11 (11.45 Fri & Sat)
☎ (01364) 72133 ⊕ royaloaksouthbrent.co.uk
Shepherd Neame Spitfire; Teignworthy Reel Ale, Beachcomber; guest beers Ⓗ
Busy pub in the centre of the village on the edge of Dartmoor. The main L-shaped bar is surrounded by a large open-plan area with comfortable leather settees where customers can relax. Alternatively they can sit at the wood-panelled bar and enjoy the excellent range of real ales. At the back is a restaurant/ function room based in the old skittle alley where good food is served. Beer festivals are held occasionally. Local CAMRA Pub of the Year 2007. Q◑Å

South Molton

George Hotel
1 Broad Street, EX36 3AB (in town square)
OS715258
☼ 12 (10 Thu & Sat)-3, 6 (7 Sun)-midnight
☎ (01769) 572514 ⊕ georgehotelsouthmolton.co.uk
Jollyboat Freebooter, Mainbrace; St Austell Tribute Ⓗ
Grade II listed hotel dating from the 17th-century in a historic market town. There are two main drinking areas supplied by a single partitioned bar. The Exmoor is the public bar, with a quieter drinking and dining area next door, which is where the real ale is served. Both have open fires for colder days. Local chess and fishing clubs meet here. There is frequent and varied live entertainment and films are shown in the hotel function room. ᴹᴬQ☎◑⊕ÅⱤ♣Pᵗ

South Tawton

Seven Stars
EX20 2LT OS653944
☼ 11.30-2.30, 6.30-11; 12-10.30 Sun
☎ (01837) 840292
Beer range varies Ⓗ
Traditional pub opposite the church, at the centre of the most northerly village in Dartmoor National Park. Two real ales are always available, chosen from independent brewers in Devon and Cornwall, as well as a locally produced Winkleigh cider. The Stars has a good reputation locally for the quality of its food, prepared from seasonal West Country produce. Bar meals are always available and a restaurant allows for dining in quieter surroundings. ᴹᴬ☎◑♣ᵉᵗ

Spreyton

Tom Cobley Tavern
EX17 5AL
☼ 12-3, 6.30-10.30 Mon; 6-midnight (1am Fri & Sat); 12-3, 7-11 Sun
☎ (01647) 231314
Clearwater Oliver's Nectar; Ⓖ **Cotleigh Tawny; Otter Ale; St Austell Tribute, Proper Job;** Ⓗ **guest beers** Ⓗ/Ⓖ
National CAMRA Pub of the Year 2006 and local Pub of the Year 2007, this is a true gem, serving an exceptional beer range, six on handpump and more on gravity. A warm welcome and great service are guaranteed at this 16th-century village inn, which has a homely bar and spacious dining room. This buzzing village pub is popular not just for the beers, but for its wonderful home-cooked food. Booking is advisable for all meals, particularly Sunday lunch. There are also four reasonably priced guest rooms. ᴹᴬQ☜❀⊷◑⊕♣P

Sticklepath

Taw River Inn
EX20 2NW (OS641941)
☼ 12-midnight (11 Sun)
☎ (01837) 840377 ⊕ tawriver.co.uk
Draught Bass; Greene King Abbot; Sharp's Doom Bar; St Austell Tribute Ⓗ

North Devon CAMRA Pub of the Year for 2005 and 2006, the Taw River is an active village local on the old A30, five miles east of Okehampton. The large, single bar is usually lively, as numerous sports and pub games are enjoyed by the regulars. It has a relaxed, friendly atmosphere where families and pets are more than welcome. Good pub food is available. The area is popular with walkers, and the Finch Foundry Museum (NT) is across the road. ᴹᴬ❀◑⊟(X9, X30)♣Pᵗ

Stokenham

Tradesman's Arms
TQ7 2SZ (250m from A379)
☼ 11.30-3, 6-11; 12-3, 7-10.30 Sun
☎ (01548) 580313 ⊕ thetradesmansarms.com
Brakspear Bitter; Draught Bass; South Hams Devon Pride, Eddystone; guest beers Ⓗ
Popular with locals, this pleasant free house in the South Hams is reputed to be 600 years old and features beamed ceilings and a real fire. Interconnecting rooms off the bar provide ample seating and tables. This quiet pub is the perfect place to savour the Brakspear ale and those from the local South Hams Brewery (including a guest). The landlord's previous pub was in the Chilterns, hence the Brakspear connection. An extensive food menu gives plenty of choice. ᴹᴬQ❀◑ Å⊟➌

Talaton

Talaton Inn
EX5 2RQ (from A30 follow ESCOT Park signs for 2 miles)
☼ 12-3, 7-10.30
☎ (01404) 822214
Otter Bitter; guest beers Ⓗ
An excellent example of a small village country pub, the 16th-century building has a large bar frequented by locals. There are usually three real ales on handpump, two from local breweries. The restaurant serves good value meals, with lunchtime specials and offers for senior citizens. The large skittle alley is very popular. ᴹᴬQ◑⊕⊟♣Pᵗ

Tavistock

Trout & Tipple
Parkwood Road, PL19 0JS
☼ 12-2.30 (not Tue), 6-11; 12-2.30, 6 (7 winter)-10.30 Sun
☎ (01822) 618886 ⊕ troutandtipple.co.uk
Princetown Jail Ale; guest beers Ⓗ
Just a mile north of Tavistock, this friendly hostelry features a traditional hop-draped bar and a large conservatory, games room and patio. A trout fishery is nearby. As well as seasonal beers from Teignworthy, there is a changing cider. The ceiling bears a plethora of pump clips from past guest ales. The pub stages beer festivals in February and October, with frequent single-brewery events in between. Children are welcome up to 9pm; dogs allowed. ᴹᴬQ☜❀◑ ♦P

Topsham

Bridge Inn ☆

Bridge Hill, EX3 0QQ (by River Clyst)
🕐 12-2, 6-10.30 (11 Fri & Sat); 12-2, 7-10.30 Sun
☎ (01392) 873862 ⊕ cheffers.co.uk
Beer range varies Ⓖ

An absolute gem, this is a typical 16th-century ale house, still trading on traditional ideals and with a fifth generation of family owners now being groomed to take over when the time comes. Up to nine ales, all on gravity, are served direct from the cellar, in thirds if guests fancy. Even the Queen has been to sample the hospitality – her only official pub visit in the UK. Limited bar snacks are available at lunchtimes and a hot home-made soup in winter. ⚒Q❀⇌🖾P

Exeter Inn

64 High Street, EX3 0DY
🕐 11-11 (midnight Fri & Sat); 12-10.30 Sun
☎ (01392) 873131
Teignworthy Beachcomber; guest beers Ⓗ

This unimposing, genuine free house was originally a 17th century coaching inn and has recently been taken over by real ale enthusiasts. The pub has been smartened up and now has a loyal local following from regulars who appreciate their ales – two guest beers come from all over the UK. The front area has a pool table and seating around the bar, with further seating at the rear. A large-screen TV covers major sporting events.
⚒♿⇌🖾(T, 57)♣🍴

Globe Hotel

Fore Street, EX3 0HR (towards quay from town)
🕐 11-11 (midnight Fri & Sat); 12-11 Sun
☎ (01392) 873471 ⊕ globehotel.com
Butcombe Bitter; Fuller's London Pride; St Austell Dartmoor Best; Sharp's Doom Bar; guest beers Ⓗ

A genuine free house and hotel close to the River Exe, this is a former 17th-century coaching house with a strong historic feel, enhanced by exposed beams and wood panelling. A good range of six ales is always on offer. The restaurant serves a broad range of fare, but not on Sunday when the very popular open-mike folk music evening is staged. The malthouse has a skittle alley and is available for functions. Q☎🛏❀🕐🍴⇌🖾

Torquay

Buccaneer Inn

43 Babbacombe Downs Road, TQ1 3LN
🕐 12 (11 Sat)-11 (midnight Fri & Sat summer); 12-10.30 Sun
☎ (01803) 312661 ⊕ staustellbrewery.co.uk
St Austell Tribute, HSD Ⓗ

Family-run St Austell house, overlooking the clifftop gardens and affording superb views across Lyme Bay. The single, spacious, wood-panelled bar has a separate area for pool and darts. Home-cooked food is available all year round. Children are admitted until 7pm. The forecourt provides extra space outside and there is a function room upstairs. It is a short walk from the Cliff Railway and Model Village and the steep descent to Babbacombe is

nearby. An additional house beer, Buccaneer, is brewed by St Austell. ❀🕐♿♣

Crown & Sceptre

2 Petitor Road, St Marychurch, TQ1 4QA
🕐 12-4, 5.30-11; 12-midnight Fri; 12-4, 6.30-midnight Sat; 12-4, 7-11.30 Sun
☎ (01803) 328290
Badger Tanglefoot; Courage Best Bitter; Fuller's London Pride; Greene King Old Speckled Hen; Young's Special; guest beers Ⓗ

This 200-year-old coaching inn has more than 30 consecutive years in the Guide under the stewardship of the same landlord. The interior has real character with a collection of chamberpots, pennants and an open fire; outside two small enclosed gardens are pleasant in summer. Five regular and three guest ales are on offer and food is served at lunchtime Monday to Saturday. A well supported community pub, live music plays with jazz on Tuesday evening and folk most Fridays. Dogs are very welcome.
⚒Q❀🕐🖾♣P

Hole in the Wall

6 Park Lane, TQ1 2AU
🕐 11-midnight
☎ (01803) 200755
Greene King IPA, Abbot; Sharp's Doom Bar; Shepherd Neame Spitfire; Theakston Mild; guest beers Ⓗ

Tucked away from the busy harbour, Torquay's oldest inn (circa 1540), with its beamed ceilings and cobbled floors worn smooth over the centuries, is a real ale oasis in the town centre. Its hospitality is enjoyed by seafarers, business types, locals and holidaymakers. Food is served all day in summer in the popular restaurant. Dogs on leads are welcome. The narrow passageway outside, adorned with award-winning floral displays, serves as a pleasant alfresco drinking area.
Q❀🕐🖾🍴

Totnes

Bay Horse Inn

8 Cistern Street, TQ9 5SP
🕐 12-2 (summer only), 6 (5 Thu-Sat)-11.30; 12-3, 7-11.30 Sun
☎ (01803) 862088
Everards Old Original; Otter Bitter; Princetown Jail Ale; guest beers Ⓗ

This 15th century coaching inn is rumoured to have ghosts from the same era; it was also a 19th century smugglers' haunt. Now a traditional, roomy town pub, popular with locals and visitors alike, it has an old-fashioned snug and a surprisingly spacious garden with a heated patio. Irish folk music plays on Tuesday evening and jazz on the last Sunday of the month. Good home-made food and quality B&B are available.
Q☎❀🕐🖾🍴

Tuckenhay

Maltster's Arms

Bow Creek, TQ9 7EQ
🕐 11-11
☎ (01803) 732350 ⊕ tuckenhay.com

Princetown Dartmoor IPA; guest beers ⊞
Overlooking the peaceful Bow Creek, this
lovely old pub comprises two snug rooms
linked by a long narrow bar. The pub has won
prizes for its barbecues, which are held on the
quay in summer months, and has a good
reputation for innovative pub meals. There are
boat moorings on the tidal River Dart, and
occasional live music on Friday evening. Beers
are sourced mainly from West Country
breweries, and Heron Valley cider is sold in
summer. CAMRA members receive a discount
on accommodation. ♨Q⏰❄️⚲⏰Ⓓ♿♣♠P

Uplyme

Talbot Arms

Lyme Road, DT7 3TF (on B3165)
🕐 11-2.30, 6-11; 11-midnight Fri & Sat; 12-11 Sun
☎ (01297) 443136 ⊕ talbotarms.com
Otter Bitter, Ale; guest beers ⊞
A friendly pub, named after Admiral Sir John
Talbot, with a cosy lounge and dining area,
and a games/family room downstairs which
leads to the large garden. Tuesday evening is
especially popular, with delicious take-aways
of fish and chips and pizzas on offer. Booking
is recommended for Sunday carveries. In July,
a summer beer festival is held. Do not be
confused by the address: Uplyme is in Devon.
♨⏰❄️⏰Ⓓ🚃P

Wembury

Wembury Club

99 Southland Park Road, PL9 0HH
🕐 7.30 (12 Sat & Sun)-midnight
☎ (01752) 862159 ⊕ wemburyclub.co.uk
Theakston Best Bitter; guest beers ⊞
Although a private club, CAMRA members and
their families are very welcome at this Cask
Club of Great Britain finalist, situated close to a
picturesque coastline popular with walkers. It
offers changing guest beers that are rarely
available at other local outlets, sold at uniform
prices regardless of strength. The landlord
relishes the opportunity to obtain more
unusual beers on request. It also stocks more
than 30 bottled beers, including Trappist and
Abbey. ♨Q⏰❄️⏰Ⓓ♿A🚃♣♠P⤴

Westcott

Merry Harriers

EX15 1SA (on B3181 two miles S of Cullompton)
🕐 12-3, 6-11.30 (12.30am Fri & Sat); 12-3, 6-11.30 Sun
☎ (01392) 881254
Cotleigh Tawny; O'Hanlon's Firefly, Yellow
Hammer; guest beers ⊞
This traditional pub, thought to be a former
smithy, has a friendly atmosphere. The lounge
bar is welcoming and cosy with a big fire and
beamed ceilings. The child-friendly dining
area is just through the bar, offering an
impressive menu and specials board featuring
local produce. There is seating outside and a
spacious car park plus accommodation behind
the pub. ♨Q❄️⚲⏰Ⓓ P

Whimple

New Fountain Inn

Church Road, EX5 2TA
🕐 12-3, 6.30-11; 12-3, 7-10.30 Sun
☎ (01404) 822350
O'Hanlon's Firefly; Teignworthy Reel Ale; guest
beer Ⓖ
Friendly local in a lovely village serving good-
value, home-cooked food. Do not be fooled by
the handpumps, they are for presentation only
– the ales are served directly from the barrel in
the cellar. The village heritage centre stands at
the rear of the pub's car park and is well worth
a visit. ♨Q⏰Ⓓ🚃P

Widecombe-in-the-Moor

Rugglestone Inn

TQ13 7TF (¼ mile from village centre) OS721766
🕐 11.30-3, 6.30-12.30am; 11.30-12.30am Sat;
12-11.30 Sun
☎ (01364) 621327
Butcombe Bitter; St Austell Dartmoor Best; guest
beer Ⓖ
Unspoilt, cosy pub in a splendid Dartmoor
setting. Beer is served in the small, stone-
floored bar area as well as through a hatch in
the passageway. The lounge is warmed by an
open fire and children are welcome here. The
pub is named after a local 'logan' stone.
Across the stream, a large, grassed seating
area invites drinkers on a sunny day. A wide
selection of home-cooked food is available.
♨Q⏰❄️⏰Ⓓ♿A♠P⤴

Winkleigh

King's Arms

Fore Street, EX19 8HX OS632081
🕐 11-11; 12-10.30 Sun
☎ (01837) 83384
Butcombe Bitter; Sharp's Cornish Coaster, Doom
Bar ⊞
Friendly, thatched pub, the focal point of this
picturesque village. The single bar area is
simply furnished but welcoming and warm
with a log-burning fire in colder months. On
Sunday, the price of the first two pints of each
beer pulled is donated to local charities. Cider
is from nearby Winkleigh. Excellent food made
with local produce is served both in the bar
and dining areas, which contain a covered
well and army memorabilia. ♨Q❄️⏰Ⓓ🚃♣♠

Yeoford

Mare & Foal

The Village, EX17 5JD
🕐 12-3 (not Mon), 6-11
☎ (01363) 84348 ⊕ mareandfoal.co.uk
Beer range varies ⊞
Set in beautiful countryside, this 17th-century
free house is easily accessible from the real
ale trail along the Exeter-Barnstaple Tarka line.
It offers three changing West Country ales and
an extensive menu based, as far as possible,
on locally sourced organic produce. Meals are
cooked to order and the menu changes
weekly, if not daily. Children are welcome and
dogs on leads permitted. ♨⏰❄️⏰Ⓓ🚃♠P

CAMRA's Beers of the Year

The beers listed below are CAMRA's Beers of the Year. They were short-listed for the Champion Beer of Britain competition in August 2007, and the Champion Winter Beer of Britain competition in January 2007. The August competition judged Light and Dark Milds; Bitters; Best Bitters; Strong Bitters; Golden Ales; Speciality Beers; and Real Ale in a Bottle. The winter competition judged Old Ales and Strong Milds; Porters and Stouts; and Barley Wines. Each beer was found by a panel of trained CAMRA judges to be consistently outstanding in its category and they all receive a 'full tankard' (🍺) symbol in The Breweries section.

LIGHT AND DARK MILDS
B&T Shefford Dark Mild
Bazens' Black Pig Mild
Brains Dark
Elland First Light
Harveys Sussex XX Mild
Hobson's Mild
Holden's Black Country Mild
Nottingham Rock Mild

BITTERS
Acorn Barnsley Bitter
Adnams Bitter
Bath Ales SPA
Castle Rock Harvest Pale
Durham Magus
Fyne Pipers Gold
Holden's Black Country Bitter
Matthews Brassknocker
Nethergate IPA
Peak Ales Swift Nick
Purple Moose Madog's Ale
Robinson's Oldham Bitter
Spitting Feathers Thirstquencher
Surrey Hills Ranmore Ale
Tipples Longshore
Twickenham Crane Sundancer

BEST BITTERS
Bath Ales Gem
Dorset Chesil
Elland Beyond the Pale
Fuller's London Pride
Highland Scapa Special
Nethergate Suffolk County
Nottingham Legend
Peak Ales Bakewell Best Bitter
Potton Village Bike
Purple Moose Glaslyn Ale
Robinson's Unicorn
Skinner's Betty Stogs
Station House Buzzin'
Timothy Taylor Landlord
George Wright Pipe Dream
Wye Valley Butty Bach

STRONG BITTERS
Brains SA Gold
Coach House Posthorn
Inveralmond Lia Fail
Nottingham Bullion
Thornbridge Jaipur IPA
Tipples Jack's Revenge
Uley Old Spot Prize Ale
York Centurion's Ghost

GOLDEN ALES
Facer's Landslide
Highland Orkney Best
Holden's Golden Glow
Mighty Oak Maldon Gold
Oakleaf Hole Hearted

Otley O1
Pictish Brewers Gold
York Guzzler

SPECIALITY BEERS
Beartown Ginger Bear
Cairngorm Trade Winds
Hanby Cherry Bomb
Little Valley Hebden Wheat
Malvern Hills Priessnitz Plsen
Nethergate Umbel Magna
Salopian Lemon Dream
St Peter's Grapefruit

REAL ALE IN A BOTTLE
Burton Bridge Bramble Stout
Durham Cloister
Fuller's 1845
Hobson's Town Crier
Hogs Back TEA
Hop Back Summer Lightning
Loddon Ferryman's Gold
O'Hanlon's Port Stout
Titanic Stout
Tryst Carronade IPA
Vale Black Swan Dark Mild
Wye Valley Dorothy Goodbody's Wholesome Stout

OLD ALES AND STRONG MILDS
B&T Black Dragon Mild
Harveys Old Ale
Sarah Hughes Dark Ruby
Orkney Dark Island
Rudgate Ruby Mild
West Berkshire Magg's Magnificent Mild
Winter's Tempest

PORTERS AND STOUTS
Butts Blackguard
Cairngorm Black Gold
Elland 1872 Porter
Fuller's London Porter
St Peter's Old Style Porter
Springhead Puritan's Porter
Tomos Watkin Merlin Stout

BARLEY WINES
Broughton Old Jock
Burton Bridge Thomas Sykes Ale
Durham Benedictus
Green Jack Ripper
Moor Old Freddy Walker
Orkney Skullsplitter
Robinson's Old Tom
Woodforde's Headcracker

CHAMPION WINTER BEER OF BRITAIN
Green Jack Ripper

CHAMPION BEER OF BRITAIN 2007
Hobsons Mild

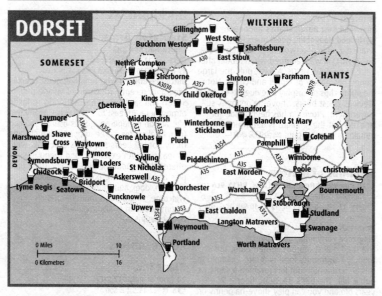

Askerswell

Spyway Inn
DT2 9EP (signed off A35, 4 miles E of Bridport)
OS529933
⏱ 12-3, 6-11
☎ (01308) 485250 ⊕ spyway-inn.co.uk
Otter Bitter, Ale; guest beers Ⓖ
Smugglers' inn dating from the 16th century perched above the village on the approach to the ancient Eggardon Hill earthwork fort. Popular with walkers and diners, this is an idyllic country pub with an exceptional garden including a children's play area. The small but charming lounge has a welcoming fire and a low-beamed ceiling. Two further rooms are mainly used for dining – the high quality food made with locally sourced ingredients is popular. The beer is from local brewers and served direct from the cask.
🏚Q🕮⚡🛌◖A P♿

Blandford

Railway
Oakfield Street, DT11 7EX
⏱ 11.30-4am
☎ (01258) 456374
Badger First Gold; Ringwood Best Bitter; guest beers Ⓗ
Popular back-street Victorian pub that dates back to when there was a railway line and station opposite. However it has embraced the 21st century with large multi-screen TVs, even at the bar. It hosts an annual beer festival in late spring. There is an outside heated and covered area for smokers. The pub makes the most of extended opening hours, remaining open until the last customer leaves.
🕮◖🛌(X8)♣♿

Bournemouth

Goat & Tricycle
27-29 West Hill Road, BH2 5PF

⏱ 12-11 (11.30 Fri & Sat)
☎ (01202) 314220
Wadworth IPA, 6X, JCB, seasonal beers; guest beers Ⓗ
Originally two neighbouring pubs, they were joined together by owners Wadworth. The full Wadworth range is complemented by a further seven handpumps offering a choice of guest beers. Look out for the collection of helmets on display. The heated patio area provides a welcome retreat at any time of year. Good value, hearty food is served at this local CAMRA Pub of the Year 2004 award winner. 🏚Q🕮◖🛌♣♿

Porterhouse
113 Poole Road, Westbourne, BH4 8BY
⏱ 10.30-11 (midnight Fri & Sat); 12-11 Sun
☎ (01202) 768586
Ringwood Best Bitter, Fortyniner, Old Thumper, seasonal beers; guest beers Ⓗ
Bournemouth's premier Ringwood Brewery pub selling its full range of award-winning beers. An ever changing choice of guests is also on handpump as well as real cider. Set in a Victorian suburb, the single bar has a welcoming, convivial atmosphere where the emphasis is on conversation and traditional table games. Full of character, it has a wooden floor, oak panelling and hops adorning the bar. A simple bar menu is supplemented by daily specials. East Dorset CAMRA Pub of the Year seven times. Q◖≠(Branksome)🛌♣♦

Royal Oak
Wimborne Road, Kinson, BH10 7BB
⏱ 10.30-11; 12-6 Sun

INDEPENDENT BREWERIES
Dorset Weymouth
Goldfinch Dorchester
Hall & Woodhouse Blandford St Mary
Isle of Purbeck Studland
Palmer Bridport
Sherborne Sherborne

133

☎ (01202) 572305
Ringwood Best Bitter; Sharp's Doom Bar; Wychwood Hobgoblin; guest beers Ⓗ
A rare example of a two-bar ex-Strongs house, the Royal Oak was renamed when rebuilt after a fire in the late 1890s. A basic pub, the large lounge has plenty of tables and chairs. Note the pump clips on display as evidence of many previous guest beers. Shove-ha'penny is still played here. Provision has been made for smokers but the landlord is determined this remains a 'proper' pub. ⚞⚵⚙⊟🖼♣P⌐

Shoulder of Mutton

1010 Ringwood Road, Bear Cross, BH11 9LA (on northbound carriageway of A348)
🕓 5-11; 12-2.30, 5-11.30 Fri; 12-11.30 Sat; 12-3.30, 7-11 Sun
☎ (01202) 573344
Ringwood Fortyniner; guest beer Ⓗ
The third oldest inn in Bournemouth, this friendly community local is a rare example in this area of a pub that has retained a separate public bar. The bar's flagstone floor is 200 years old and you can play shove-ha'penny on a century old board. The lounge is comfortable, carpeted and decorated with photographs of the local area. The pub's location on the Ringwood Road makes it an ideal place to stop off for visitors travelling into the town. Q⛵⚙&🖼(11)♣P⌐

Bridport

Greyhound

2 East Street, DT6 3LF (next to town hall)
🕓 9am-midnight (1am Fri & Sat); 9am-11 Sun
☎ (01308) 421905
Courage Best Bitter, Directors; Greene King Abbot; guest beers Ⓗ
Large, Victorian Grade II listed hotel where once guests were collected from the train station by pony and trap. It has now been refurbished by Wetherspoon and decorated in Georgian style. Inside is a large main bar with numerous adjoining rooms, making this a spacious and popular venue for a mixed clientele – weekend evenings are busy with young revellers. Families with children are welcome until 9pm. Weekly food specials include curries, steaks and Sunday roasts. Breakfast is available 9am-noon. Occasional beer festivals are hosted. Q⚙◑&▲🖼⌐

Woodman Inn

61 South Street, DT6 3NZ
🕓 11-11
☎ (01308) 456455
Branscombe Vale BVB; guest beers Ⓗ
Nestled in a town-centre terrace of tall buildings, this pub may be small but it is packed with all the features a real ale enthusiast could want. The single bar accommodates drinkers, diners and a monthly live band. There is a full-sized skittle alley at the rear and the newly refurbished garden is a peaceful drinking oasis when the sun is shining. A free quiz is hosted on Sunday evening. ⚙◑▲🖼♣

Buckhorn Weston

Stapleton Arms

Church Hill, SP8 5HS
🕓 11-3, 6-11; 11-11 Sat & Sun
☎ (01963) 370396 ⊕ thestapletonarms.co.uk
Butcombe Bitter; Taylor Landlord; guest beers Ⓗ
Imposing, recently modernised village pub. Stylish and spacious, it has a friendly, relaxed atmosphere. At least four and occasionally five ales are on handpump, guests usually sourced from local micros. Three imported draught and many bottled beers are also stocked, as well as real cider. An excellent food menu is offered throughout the pub; locally made pork pies and chutney are particularly good. Children, dogs and muddy boots are all welcome. Elegant and modern en-suite accommodation is also available.
⚞Q⚙🖼◑&♣P

Cerne Abbas

Giant Inn

24 Long Street, DT2 7JF
🕓 6-11; 12-11 Sat & Sun
☎ (01300) 341441 ⊕ thegiantinncerneabbas.co.uk
Greene King IPA; St Austell Tinners; guest beer Ⓗ
Lively, friendly village pub, formerly the Red Lion, busy with locals. Destroyed by fire in 1898 and rebuilt, all that survived was the 16th-century stone fireplace that still warms the bar today. Recently refurbished inside and out, the open-plan bar has a sitting room to the left. This popular meeting place is home to skittles and darts teams, and regularly hosts local Morris dancers. All major football, rugby and motor racing fixtures are screened. The guest beer usually comes from a local brewery. ⚞⚙♣

Chetnole

Chetnole Inn

DT9 6NU
🕓 11.30-3, 6.30-11.30; 12-3, 7-11 Sun
☎ (01935) 872337
Branscombe Vale Branoc; Butcombe Bitter; Palmer IPA; guest beer Ⓗ
Traditional village pub with flagstone floors and open fires in both bars. Tables outside overlook the church and there is a pretty garden beyond the car park. Chetnole Halt on the Weymouth to Yeovil line is a half mile walk along country lanes. Excellent Sunday lunches are popular. No food is served on Wednesday, or Sunday evening. A beer festival is held at Easter. Dogs are welcome. ⚞Q⚙🖼◑⊟&⇌🖼♣P

Chideock

Clockhouse Inn

Main Street, DT6 6JW
🕓 12-3, 6-midnight; 12-midnight July-Sept
☎ (01297) 489423
Otter Ale, Bitter; guest beers Ⓗ
Cheerful, family-owned thatched free house popular with loyal regulars and visitors to the Jurassic coast. The food menu (served all day in summer) features local produce, two-for-one deals plus a soup and a sandwich offer for

walkers. Live entertainment is hosted on Saturday night. The regular Sunday night jackpot quiz ensures two hours of fun and good company. Drivers beware the speed cameras standing sentry at either end of the village. ▲▲❀◑▶▲☒(31, X53)♣P

Child Okeford

Saxon Inn
Gold Hill, DT11 8HD
✪ 12-2.30 (4 Sat), 7-11; 12-11 Sun
☎ (01258) 860310
Butcombe Bitter; guest beers ⊞
Quaint pub hidden up an alley at the north end of the village. A popular local, it has a passing trade of walkers and horse riders. The welcoming little bar has an open fire. Note the witty remarks on brass plaques above the bar. A separate dining area offers a good range of wholesome food cooked to order including specials on a board. Fish is a speciality. Beers come from Butcombe, Ringwood and a guest. ▲▲Q❀◑P

Christchurch

Olde George Inn
2A Castle Street, BH23 1DT
✪ 11-11 (midnight Fri & Sat); 11.30-11 Sun
☎ (01202) 479383
Ringwood Fortyniner; guest beers ⊞
Dating from the 15th century, this former coaching inn has a fascinating history. Tunnels underneath run to the nearby priory and castle, and prisoners were kept here overnight in the dungeon. Two rooms are served from the main bar; two guest ales usually include one from Ringwood. Outside is a courtyard with patio heaters and extra seating. Excellent food is available all day and the barn hosts curry nights and carveries. Q❀◑▶⬛—

Thomas Tripp
10 Wick Lane, BH23 1HX
✪ 11-11; 12-10.30 Sun
☎ (01202) 490498
Ringwood Fortyniner ⊞
Lively local just off Church Street, named after a legendary local smuggler. This historic inn has a large main bar with a quieter room at the front. An excellent variety of food ranges from the full English to gourmet fresh seafood for which the pub is renowned. The large patio garden has bench seating. Local bands play on Wednesday and Sunday evenings. ▲▲❀◑⬤⬛—

Colehill

Horns Inn
Horns Inn, Burts Hill, BH21 7AA (off B3078)
OS017012
✪ 11-2.30, 6-11; 11-11 Sat; 12-10.30 Sun
☎ (01202) 883557
Badger K&B Sussex, First Gold, Tanglefoot ⊞
Rural pub with fine views over the Dorset countryside. Despite extensive refurbishment and redecoration in 2006, the attractive interior retains its original character. The lounge and dining area are cosy and the good value food popular. The village bar is homely,

ideal for a relaxing drink or to play pub games. During the spring and summer the delightful hanging baskets bring a welcome array of colour. Q❀◑▶⬤⬛♣P

Dorchester

Blue Raddle
9 Church Street, DT1 1JN
✪ 11.30-3, 6.30-11 (not Sun eve)
☎ (01305) 267762
Beer range varies ⊞
Cosy, welcoming town pub with a friendly atmosphere. Inside is a long, narrow bar, plush seating at polished tables, a real fire and a darts area. It is always a pleasure to drink here, whatever the reason – a quick after work pint, dinner with friends or family, or Friday night on the town. Reasonably priced, delicious home-cooked food and a choice of three regularly changing ales are available, with the emphasis on local micro-breweries. Superb live music includes regular Irish nights with local musicians. Local CAMRA Pub of the Year 2007. ▲▲◑≥(West)♣

East Chaldon

Sailor's Return
DT2 8DN (off A352) OS791834
✪ 11-11; 12-10.30 Sun
☎ (01305) 853847 ⊕ sailorsreturn.com
Hampshire Strong's Best Bitter; Ringwood Best Bitter; guest beers ⊞
This thatched inn on the fringe of a small hamlet provides a welcome stop for ramblers on the nearby Dorset Coastal Path. It can be very busy on summer weekends. Generous portions of excellent food are served throughout the numerous flagstone-floored rooms although the main area retains the feel of a local public bar. Up to seven beers are served in high season, usually five, as well as Westons traditional cider. A tented beer festival is held in late spring. Q❀◑⬤♣⬤P

East Morden

Cock & Bottle
BH20 7DL (on B3075, off A35 between Poole and Bere Regis)
✪ 11-2.30, 6-11; 12-3, 7-10.30 Sun
☎ (01929) 459238
Badger K&B Sussex, First Gold, Tanglefoot ⊞
Delightful village pub with friendly staff, well worth the effort to seek out. Drinkers head for the 'happy chatter' (public bar). This is a relatively unspoilt room with a large log-burning fireplace, wooden flooring and an assortment of seats, benches and settles. Award-winning food is served in the cosy dining area. The garden is pleasant for a summer pint. Disabled facilities are good with easy wheelchair access, but the pub is difficult to get to by public transport. ▲▲❀◑▶⬤♣P

East Stour

King's Arms
East Stour Common, SP8 5NB (on A30, W of Shaftesbury)
✪ 12-3, 5.30-11; 12-midnight Sat; 12-10.30 Sun

☎ (01747) 838325 ⊕ thekingsarmsdorset.co.uk
**Fuller's London Pride; Palmer Copper Ale; guest
beer** Ⓗ
Imposing, multi-roomed, single-bar country
pub alongside the A30. Beers from Palmers
feature regularly, with occasional guests
chosen by the regulars. Food here is excellent,
made with locally sourced ingredients where
possible. To ensure quality and ever changing
menus, the three chefs, an Englishman,
Scotsman and Frenchman, compete for a
monthly £100 prize. The garden room leads to
an enclosed garden and patio. Live, acoustic
music is played on the first and third Sunday of
the month. Q❀✍◑&P⬩

Farnham

Museum Inn

DT11 8DE (off A354)
◷ 12-3, 6-11; 12-3, 7-10.30 Sun
☎ (01725) 516261 ⊕ museuminn.co.uk
**Ringwood Best Bitter; Taylor Landlord; guest
beer** Ⓗ
Originally built for visitors to the local
museum, this part-thatched country inn
retains its flagstone floors and large inglenook
despite a recent extensive refurbishment. It is
always worth a visit for the changing guest
beer and well kept regulars. An extensive
menu of high quality food is available.
Situated in excellent walking country, Larmer
Tree Gardens and Cranborne Chase are nearby.
Children are permitted. ⌂Q❀✍◑&♠P⬩

Gillingham

Phoenix Inn

The Square, SP8 4AY
◷ 10-2.30 (3 Sat), 7-11 (not Mon); 12-3, 7-10.30 Sun
☎ (01747) 823277
Badger K&B Sussex, First Gold, seasonal beers Ⓗ
Charming town-centre pub built in the 15th
century, originally a coaching inn complete
with its own brewery. A cosy, one-bar pub, it
has no games machines, just occasional
background music. It is justifiably renowned
for good-value, home-cooked food, served in
the bar and a separate dining area. A small
courtyard for drinking alfresco is next to the
quaint town square. ⌂❀◑Å≈

Ibberton

Crown

Church Lane, DT11 0EN
◷ 12-3, 6-11; closed Mon; 12-3, 7-10.30 Sun
☎ (01258) 817448
Butcombe Bitter; Palmer IPA; guest beer Ⓗ
Dating from the 16th century, this rural
hideaway retains its original flagstone floor,
oak doors and inglenook fireplace. In summer
the lawned garden, with babbling brook, is a
delight. The regular beers are complemented
by guests from Palmer, White Star, Hidden and
Goddard. The village of Ibberton, mentioned in
the Domesday Book, has one of only three
churches in the country dedicated to St
Eustace. Off the beaten track, this pub is
ideally situated for walkers on the Wessex
Ridgeway. ⌂Q❀❀◑P

Kings Stag

Green Man

DT10 2AY
◷ 11-3.30, 5.30-midnight
☎ (01258) 817338
Exmoor Ale; guest beers Ⓗ
Imposing 15th-century coaching inn at the
centre of this charming village. The main bar
has four areas, mainly catering for diners, but
with plenty of room for drinkers. The interior
retains many original timbers in the ceiling
and walls. A function room caters for diners,
live music and four skittles teams. Excellent
food is available, with local game and fish the
specialities. Venison regularly features in the
carvery. Two guest beers are sourced via St
Austell Brewery, but the pub is free of tie.
⌂↘❀◑Å♣P⬩

Langton Matravers

King's Arms Hotel

27 High Street, BH19 3HA
◷ 12-3, 6-11; 12-3, 7-10.30 Sun
☎ (01929) 422979
Ringwood Best Bitter, Fortyniner; guest beer Ⓗ
Dating back to 1743, this lovely four-room pub
features the original flagstone floors. Adorning
the walls are paintings and photographs of the
local area. In the early days the front room
served as the village morgue and the rest of
the building was the inn. Outside is a large
garden with a shed housing a pool table. The
pub is ideally situated for exploring the
Purbecks. ⌂Q↘❀◑⬚(142, 143)♣⬩

Laymore

Squirrel Inn

TA20 4NT (just off B3162 towards Winsham)
OS387048
◷ 11-2.30, 6.30-late; 12-late Sun
☎ (01460) 30298 ⊕ squirrelinn.co.uk
**Branscombe Vale Best Bitter; Otter Bitter;
Sharps's Special** Ⓗ
Family friendly pub with views overlooking
the Somerset countryside. The food menu
changes constantly; all dishes are cooked to
order using local produce, with steaks
featuring on Wednesday. A beer festival is
held on the second weekend in August. The
local Ashen Faggot Festival, celebrating the 12
days of Christmas, is hosted annually on the
6th of January. The spacious garden has a
large play area for children. ⌂❀✍◑Å♣♠P

Loders

Loders Inn

DT6 3SA
◷ 11.30-3, 6-11; 12-3, 6-11 Sun (hours may vary)
☎ (01308) 422431 ⊕ lodersarms.co.uk
Palmer Copper Ale, IPA, 200, Tally Ho! Ⓗ
Charming inn in a pretty village in the River
Asker Valley. The garden overlooks medieval
field terraces carved into the surrounding hills.
Good food, made with local ingredients, is
served in the bar and restaurant. The pub is
popular with local farmers and villagers and is
home to several skittles teams. Camping is
available in a field beyond the car park.

Children (and dogs) are welcome.
🏠Q🕮🍴◑🅰🖳🆎♿P

Lyme Regis

Nag's Head

32 Silver Street, DT7 3HS
✪ 11-midnight
☎ (01297) 442312
Otter Ale; guest beers 🅗
Spacious old brick and flint coaching inn at the top of the town with magnificent views across Lyme Bay. Popular with locals and visitors alike, it has two linked bar areas and a games room with wide-screen TV for sports. Four regular ales include the house beer, Sark Lark from Otter, as well as seasonal ales. A good selection of whiskies is stocked. Live music features every Saturday night plus some Wednesdays. Bar snacks are served and occasional Sunday barbecues are hosted in summer. 🏠🕮🍴🅰🖳🆎⌐

Volunteer

31 Broad Street, DT7 3QE
✪ 11-11; 12-10.30 Sun
☎ (01297) 442214
Fuller's London Pride; guest beers 🅗
Historic, two-bar, double-fronted, olde-worlde pub in the heart of the town, a favourite haunt for locals. The house beer, Donegal – named by the long-serving landlord after his homeland – is brewed by Branscombe Vale and kept on stillage behind the bar. Two guest ales are usually from the West Country and handpumped real scrumpy is now also available. In the bar the buzz of conversation competes with background music. Excellent, wholesome pub food is served. Q🗲◑🅰🖳♿

Marshwood

Bottle Inn

DT6 5QJ (on B3162)
✪ 12-3, 6.30-11 (closed winter Mon); 12-3, 7-10.30 Sun
☎ (01297) 678254 ⊕ thebottleinn.co.uk
O'Hanlon's Royal Oak; Otter Ale, Bitter; guest beers 🅗
Fine thatched pub with commanding views across the Axe Valley into east Devon. The large garden and field behind it play host to the world famous nettle-eating contest in June, as well as an annual beer festival. The front bar concentrates on serving a wide selection of food featuring locally sourced ingredients. The back bar is a spacious facility for live music. Campers are welcome in the field. 🏠🗲🕮◑🅰♣P⌐

Middlemarsh

Hunters Moon

DT9 5QN (on A352, 7 miles S of Sherborne)
✪ 11-3, 6-11; 11-10.30 Sun
☎ (01963) 210966 ⊕ huntersmoon.co.uk
Beer range varies 🅗
Quality 400-year-old real ale country pub with a homely and welcoming atmosphere. Full of nooks and crannies, brewery memorabilia line the walls, with jugs, cups and tankards hanging from the ceiling. The menu offers something for everyone, specialising in game

from a local supplier. Sunday lunch is a carvery. The beers come from St Austell and Sharp's. Wheelchair access is good.
🏠Q🕮🍴◑♿🖳🆎P

Nether Compton

Griffins Head

DT9 4QE (1 mile N of A30, midway between Yeovil and Sherborne) OS597174
✪ 12-2.30, 7-11
☎ (01935) 812523
Beer range varies 🅗
Friendly local serving one changing real ale – Sharp's Eden, Fuller's London Pride and St Austell Tinners are all regulars. Beer stillage is out of sight in a back room. The stone-flagged saloon bar has darts and a pool table. A skittle alley is in a building beside the car park. Pub team games are hosted most weekday evenings. Quiet classical music plays in the background. A good range of food is available at all times (book ahead for Sunday lunch). ◑🖳♣

Pamphill

Vine Inn ☆

Vine Hill, BH21 4EE (off B3082)
✪ 11-3, 7-10.30 (11 Thu-Sat); 12-3, 7-10.30 Sun
☎ (01202) 882259
Beer range varies 🅗/🅖
Delightful little pub, built as a bakehouse over 200 years ago, close to the National Trust's Kingston Lacey House and Badbury Rings. Its interior is of historic interest with two small bars and a games room upstairs. The guest beer is usually from a small regional or micro-brewery. Popular with walkers and cyclists, dogs are permitted. The attractive garden has ample seating. Sandwiches and ploughman's are served at lunchtime. No bus service reaches here. Winner of numerous CAMRA awards. Q🗲🕮◑🖳♣♿⌐🖿

Piddlehinton

Thimble Inn

14 High Street, DT2 7TD
✪ 12-2.30, 7-11
☎ (01300) 348270
Badger Tanglefoot; Palmer Copper Ale, IPA; Ringwood Best Bitter, Fortyniner 🅗
Large, part-thatched village inn on the River Piddle, with cheery, welcoming staff. Five well kept ales come from local breweries, plus fruit wines and malt whiskies. The spacious low-beamed bar has two attractive brick fireplaces and plenty of nooks and crannies, with seating for cosy twosomes and larger groups. Good pub food is available. The large garden is floodlit at night, with the river running alongside. Dogs are welcome. 🏠🕮◑P

Plush

Brace of Pheasants

DT2 7RQ
✪ 12-3, 7-11; closed Mon
☎ (01300) 348357 ⊕ braceofpheasants.co.uk
Beer range varies 🅖

Cosy village pub with a friendly welcome for all (including dogs). Regularly changing ales are dispensed direct from casks kept behind the bar. The comfortable main bar area has a real fire, leading to the restaurant and on to the large, attractive garden. Renowned locally for its well-kept ales and superb food, the pub can be busy and booking is advised for meals. ⚲⚙⚏◖P

Poole

Angel

28 Market Street, BH15 1HD
⊗ 11-11 (11.30 Fri & Sat); 12-10.30 Sun
☎ (01202) 666800
Ringwood Best Bitter, Fortyniner, Old Thumper, seasonal beers; guest beers Ⓗ
Ringwood Brewery's only tied house in Poole, sitting in the shadow of the historic Guildhall. There has been an inn on this site since 1789. A large, friendly pub served by a central bar, it offers a good range of evening entertainment including a quiz night on Tuesday, live mike on Wednesday and live performances on Thursday. Popular Sunday roasts are served 12-6pm. ⚲⚙◖♿⇌🚍♣⌐

Bermuda Triangle

10 Parr Street, Lower Parkstone, BH14 0JY
⊗ 12-2.30, 5-11 (midnight Fri); 12-midnight Sat; 12-11 Sun
☎ (01202) 748087
Beer range varies Ⓗ
This gem is a mecca for real ale lovers. The wood-panelled walls are adorned with a vast array of photos, maps and marine miscellany relating to the mystery of the Bermuda Triangle. An aircraft wing is suspended from the ceiling. Four guest beers come from a variety of brewers. The small interior, divided into different areas, has a terrific atmosphere. Steps make disabled access difficult. Joint winner of East Dorset CAMRA Pub of the Year 2006. ⚙◖⇌(Parkstone)🚍⌐

Blue Boar

29 Market Close, BH15 1NE
⊗ 11-11 (10.30 Sun)
☎ (01202) 682247
Fuller's Discovery, London Pride, Gale's HSB, ESB, seasonal beers Ⓗ
Originally a merchant's house dating from 1750, situated in the old town area of Poole. Steps lead up to the nautically themed lounge bar. Downstairs is the atmospheric cellar bar where live music plays on Friday. The second floor boasts a rather plush function room with bar for private meetings or receptions. Good value Sunday lunches are served. Q⚙◖⇌🚍⌐

Brewhouse

68 High Street, BH15 1DA
⊗ 11-11; 12-10.30 Sun
☎ (01202) 685288
Milk Street Mermaid, Nick's, Beer, seasonal beers; guest beer Ⓗ
Popular town-centre pub originally belonging to the now defunct Poole Brewery, now owned by Frome's Milk Street Brewery. The split-level room is served by a single bar. The front area overlooks the High Street with benches outside; in the middle is the main bar

and TV; at the rear are pool tables and a good rock music juke box. East Dorset CAMRA Pub of the Year in 2005, it sells excellent beers, with occasional guests, at probably the cheapest prices in the area. ⇌🚍♣

Portsmouth Hoy

The Quay, BH15 1HJ
⊗ 11-3.30, 5.30-11; 11-11 Fri-Sun; extended hours in summer
☎ (01202) 673517
Badger First Gold, Tanglefoot; guest beers Ⓗ
Delightful old pub midway along the bustling quay with a small area outside for drinking and enjoying the view. Good food is available at lunchtime and until 9pm in the evening. The pub is next to the historic part of old Poole and just a short walk from the town centre, bus and rail stations. The guest beer comes from the Badger portfolio. ⚙◖♿⇌🚍

Royal Oak & Gas Tavern

25 Skinner Street, BH15 1RQ
⊗ 11 (12 Sun)-11
☎ (01202) 672022
Ringwood Best Bitter; guest beer Ⓗ
Traditional back street pub, which has occupied this site since 1798. Many original features remain – note the windows and wood-panelled walls. The front bar is now a function room and the cosy modern main bar is at the rear, accessed via a side street. Patio doors lead out to an enclosed garden where occasional barbecues are hosted. This pub is a haven of peace for locals and visitors during the busy summer season. A heated and covered area outside is available for smokers. ⚙◖⇌🚍♣⌐

Portland

Royal Portland Arms

Fortuneswell, DT5 1CZ
⊗ 11-midnight (1am Fri & Sat); 11.30-midnight Sun
☎ (01305) 862255
Beer range varies Ⓗ
Old bay-windowed town pub at the top of Fortuneswell, once visited by George III and reputed to be haunted. An excellent range of beer and cider is available, mostly from the West Country. Live music plays on many weekends and evenings, and frequent social events for the locals are hosted. Parking is in public car parks close by. Q🚍♣⚙⛶

Puncknowle

Crown

DT2 9BN
⊗ 11.30-3, 6.30-11; 12-4, 7-10.30 Sun
☎ (01308) 897711
Palmer Copper Ale, IPA, 200, Tally Ho! Ⓗ
Attractive thatched inn opposite the church in the village pronounced 'Punnel'. The two bars have log fires and books to read if you do not feel like joining in the locals' chat. Very popular for food, it has an interesting menu. There is a comfortable family room and dogs are permitted. ⚲Q⚏⚙◖♿ A🚍P

Pymore

Pymore Inn
DT6 5PN
✪ 12-3, 6 (7 Sun)-11
☎ (01308) 422625
St Austell Tribute, Tinners; guest beer Ⓗ
Attractive, creeper-clad village pub a mile
from Bridport town centre in a good area for
walking. You are sure of a warm welcome at
this cosy, cheerful bar with an open fire. Two
St Austell beers are usually on handpump, as
well as a guest in summer. The interesting
menu features local produce and includes fish
and vegetarian dishes. Children are welcome
when dining. ⚏Q❀◑Ⓓ♿ΑP‰

Seatown

Anchor Inn
DT6 6JU (half mile S of Chideock)
✪ 11-3, 6-11 (11-11 summer); 11-10.30 Sun
☎ (01297) 489215
Palmer Copper Ale, IPA, 200 Ⓗ
Dramatically situated on the edge of the
beach, nestling under the 600ft Golden Cap on
the coastal path, this comfortable pub is
predictably busy in summer. Out of season it is
quieter and a good time to take a look at the
photographs on the walls and occasional fossil
on display. Opening hours vary according to
the season and the weather conditions. Public
parking is available opposite the pub.
⚏Q❀❀◑Ⓓ⊞Α♣P‰

Shaftesbury

Crown
40 High Street, SP7 8JG
✪ 10.30 (10 Sat)-11; 12-10.30 Sun
☎ (01747) 852902
Badger K&B Sussex, First Gold, seasonal beers Ⓗ
You can access this friendly little town pub by
its old coaching arch, a reminder of its history
as a 19th-century coaching inn. Now a single
room pub, the unusual brick and wood
fireplace is reputed to be from the abbey. The
courtyard is used for summer drinking.
Convenient for the busy High Street, it is
popular with shoppers and visitors – the
famous Gold Hill and Abbey Walk are close by.
⚏❀♣‰

Mitre
23 High Street, SP7 8JE
✪ 10.30-midnight; 12-11 Sun
☎ (01747) 853002
**Young's Bitter, Special, seasonal beers; Wells
Bombardier** Ⓗ
Historic pub close to the town hall at the top of
Gold Hill. Multi roomed, it has a single bar and
an extensive terrace with grand views
overlooking the beautiful Blackmore Vale.
Popular with young drinkers but catering for
all, an extensive food menu ranges from
morning coffee to cream teas and good pub
food. The Mitre runs crib and darts teams and
hosts charity quizzes as well as occasional live
music nights. ⚏❀❀◑Ⓓ♿♣‰

Shave Cross

Shave Cross Inn
DT6 6HW (W of B3162 Bridport-Broadwindsor road)
OS415980
✪ 11-3, 6-11; closed Mon; 12-3, 7-10.30 Sun
☎ (01308) 868358
**Branscombe Vale Branoc; Dorset range; guest
beers** Ⓗ
Classic, rural award-winning pub, stone built
under a thatched roof with an idyllic garden
and steeped in history. The local owners have
rescued this remote pub from oblivion and are
sympathetically restoring it. A small
flagstoned bar with a large, welcoming
fireplace leads to the restaurant where
Caribbean food is a speciality. There is a
second bar in the skittle alley/function room.
The pub has its own Victorian pillar box.
⚏❀⇆◑Ⓓ Α♣●P

Sherborne

Digby Tap
Cooks Lane, DT9 3NS
✪ 11-2.30 (3.30 Sat), 5.30-11
☎ (01935) 813148
Beer range varies Ⓗ
Long established free house close to the
abbey, railway station and town centre. It has
four drinking areas, all with flagged floors and
cosy corners. A popular locals' pub but visitors
are made most welcome; mobile phones must
be switched off. Three or four ever-changing
beers are served, mostly from independent
brewers in the south west. Unpretentious but
wholesome pub food is served on weekday
lunchtimes. CAMRA Wessex Pub of the Year in
2006. Q❀◑◔♿⇌⊟♣●

Shroton (Iwerne Courtney)

Cricketers
Main Street, DT11 8QD (off A350)
✪ 11.30-3, 6.30-11; 12-3, 7-10.30 Sun
☎ (01258) 860421
**Greene King IPA, Abbot; Wells Bombardier;
guest beers** Ⓗ
Pleasant village local with a cricketing theme
opposite the cricket ground. The large,
comfortable public bar has a games area
including full-sized pool table. Excellent food is
served in the bar and dining room, with game
a speciality in season. The tidy garden has
plenty of seating. The bus stops right outside
the pub. ⚏❀♿⊟♣P‰

Stoborough

King's Arms
3 Corfe Road, BH20 5AB (adjacent to B3075)
✪ 11-3, 5-11; 11-11 Fri-Sun
☎ (01929) 552705
**Ringwood Best Bitter; Taylor Landlord; guest
beers** Ⓗ
This 400-year-old listed building played host
to Cromwell's troops in 1642 at the time of the
siege of Corfe Castle. A long, slim pub
renowned for its food, it has a large restaurant
and a split-level bar. The riverside dining area
is popular with families in summer. At least
two real ales are served and a cider from

Cheddar Valley. A covered and heated area outside is available for smokers.
🏰Q🍽️🕸️🕙🍴P🎵⬅️

Studland

Bankes Arms
Watery Lane, BH19 3AU
🕐 11-11
☎ (01929) 450225
Isle of Purbeck Fossil Fuel, Solar Power, Studland Bay Wrecked, IPA; guest beers ⓗ
Home of the Isle of Purbeck Brewery and situated in a picturesque village in the heart of the Purbeck heritage area, this listed old smugglers' haunt is a gem. Winner of many awards, it offers a range of nine ales and an excellent menu. The huge clifftop garden hosts an annual beer festival in August and offers spectacular views over Poole Bay and Old Harry Rocks. Local CAMRA's Rural Pub of the Year in 2006. 🏰Q🍽️🕸️🍴🕙🅰️🚃(150)🎵⬅️

Swanage

Red Lion
63 High Street, BH19 2LY
🕐 11-11; 12-10.30 Sun
☎ (01929) 423533 ⊕ redlionswanage.co.uk
Caledonian Deuchars IPA; Ringwood Best Bitter; Taylor Landlord; guest beers ⓗ
Dating from the 17th century, this hostelry retains many traditional features. It serves up to six real ales in summer, while the Westons range caters for devotees of the pressed apple. Good value meals are served from an extensive menu. Live music occasionally features. The garden is busy in summer – travel here the scenic way on an open top bus; it is handy for Swanage steam railway and the south west coastal path. Local CAMRA Pub of the Year 2005. 🏰🕸️🍴🕙🍺🚃(150)🌸🍴P

Sydling St Nicholas

Greyhound Inn
DT2 9PD
🕐 11.30-2.30 (12-3 Sat), 6-11; 12-3 Sun
☎ (01300) 342045 ⊕ thegreyhounddorset.co.uk
Palmer Tally Ho!; St Austell Tinners; Wadworth 6X ⓗ
Lovely village pub with a friendly welcome. The stone-flagged bar has a comfortable, carpeted area with a real fire and scrubbed wood tables, leading to the conservatory. The stylish restaurant offers superb food. The garden has a children's play area. B&B accommodation is available in the converted and refurbished barn. 🏰🕸️🍴🕙P

Symondsbury

Ilchester Arms
DT6 6HD
🕐 11.30-3, 6-midnight; 12-3, 6-11 Sun
☎ (01308) 422600
Palmer Copper Ale, IPA, 200, Tally Ho! ⓗ
Delightful stone and thatched village pub in a pretty village. A wood-burning stove welcomes you in winter and the garden is lovely in summer. The pub is renowned for its home-cooked food, served in the bar and

restaurant – book ahead at the weekend (no food Mon lunchtime). Real ales are complemented by Taunton Traditional cider, while local cider can also be bought from next door. Children are not allowed in the bar. A small stream with mature willow trees runs alongside the garden. 🏰Q🕸️🕙🍴♿🚃🌸🍴P

Upwey

Royal Standard
700 Dorchester Road, DT3 5LA (on A354)
🕐 12-3, 6-midnight; 12-midnight Sat; 12-11 Sun
☎ (01305) 812558
Butcombe Bitter; Hop Back GFB; Ringwood Fortyniner ⓗ
Comfortable two-room local on the outskirts of Weymouth. The wood-panelled public bar is complemented by the comfortable lounge with its homely feel. The interior is dominated by a GWR railway theme. Although customers are welcome to use the Internet facilities here, this is a welcome mobile free zone. Limited seating is available outside in summer; look for the magnificent eagle owl in the aviary outside. 🏰Q♿🍴🚃🍴P▢

Wareham

Duke of Wellington
7 East Street, BH20 4NN
🕐 11-11 (11.30 Fri & Sat); 12-11 Sun
☎ (01929) 553015
Hop Back Summer Lightning; Isle of Purbeck Fossil Fuel; Ringwood Best Bitter; guest beers ⓗ
Seven handpumps dispense a range of beers, many from local breweries, in this 400-year-old pub, close to the centre of town. Photographs of Wareham of yesteryear adorn the wood-panelled walls, while copper ornaments surround the welcoming open fireplace. The restaurant offers an extensive menu. The pleasant courtyard garden is a delightful place for a drink in the summer. 🏰🍽️🕸️🕙🚃(142, 143)⬅️

Waytown

Hare & Hounds
DT6 5LQ (off A3066 near Netherbury) OS470978
🕐 11-3, 6.30 (6 summer)-11; 12-3, 7-11 Sun
☎ (01308) 488203
Palmer Copper Ale, IPA, ⓗ Dorset Gold Ⓖ
Tucked away in a small hamlet, best reached from the Netherbury end, this unspoilt village local is set in lovely countryside with a fine view across the River Brit Valley. The single bar has a dining room on one side and children's room on the other. The extra beer, Dorset Gold (replaced by 200 in winter), is served from the cask. Taunton Traditional cider is also available. Local food features on the menu (no Sun eve meals in winter). The large garden has a play area for children. 🏰🍽️🕸️🕙♿🅰️🌸🍴P

West Stour

Ship Inn
SP8 5RP (on A30)
🕐 12-3, 6-11; 12-11 Sun
☎ (01747) 838640 ⊕ shipinn-dorset.com

Palmer Dorset Gold; Ringwood Best Bitter; guest beer Ⓗ
Imposing traditional stone coaching inn built around 1750. The main bar has a flagstone floor and low ceiling; the lounge and restaurant area are light and airy with stripped oak floorboards and farmhouse furniture. The pub affords fine views across Blackmore Vale from the front, and there is a pretty patio and large garden to the rear. This family-friendly pub is renowned for superb fresh home-cooked food. Dogs are welcome in the main bar. ▲Q❀⇄◑♣P

Weymouth

Boot Inn
High Street, DT4 8QT
🕙 11-11; 12-10.30 Sun
☎ (01305) 770327
Ringwood Best Bitter, Fortyniner, Old Thumper, seasonal beers; guest beer Ⓗ
Weymouth's oldest pub is hidden behind the fire station. The single wood-floored bar area leads to small rooms at each end with comfortable seating and warming fires. The full Ringwood beer range is supplemented by the landlord's choice of guest beer and Cheddar Valley cider. The pub's popularity can lead to a spillage of customers onto the pavement in fine weather. An old-fashioned pub where conversation dominates, it is a frequent local CAMRA Pub of the Year. ▲Q❀&⇄◹♣♠

Red Lion
33 Hope Street, DT4 8TU
🕙 11-11 (midnight Fri & Sat); 12-11 Sun
☎ (01305) 786940
Courage Best Bitter; Dorset Weymouth JD, Durdle Door, seasonal beers Ⓗ
Welcoming local in town with up to five regularly changing ales including a beer from the Dorset Brewing Company over the road from the pub in the old Devenish Brewery buildings. A historic red brick building, it has an atmospheric interior with scrubbed boards, candles on the tables and local nautical memorabilia adorning the walls and ceiling. Service is excellent and the pub food reasonably priced. A large patio with seating faces Hope Square. Popular with locals and visitors, it can be busy in the high season. ❀◑

Weatherbury Hotel
7 Carlton Road North, DT4 7PX
🕙 12-midnight
☎ (01305) 786040
Fuller's London Pride; guest beers Ⓗ
Single bar pub in a residential part of town, divided into different areas with a TV screen in each one. Well-behaved children are welcome. Alongside the London Pride there is a frequently changing range of guest beers. For outside drinking there is a patio by the front door. Q❀❀⇄◑&⇄◹P

Wellington Arms
13 St Albans Street, DT4 8PY

🕙 10-1am; 12-11 Sun
☎ (01305) 786963
Isle of Purbeck IPA; Ringwood Best Bitter; Wadworth 6X Ⓗ
Cosy, family-run, good old-fashioned town local. An interesting collection of pictures decorates the walls. Families are welcome in the quiet back room. Good value food is served daily. Traditional pub games include crib and shove-ha'penny. Note: the beer range is likely to change. Q❀◑&⇄◹♣

Wimborne

Crown & Anchor
6 Wimborne Road, Walford, BH21 1NN
🕙 11-2.30 (3 Sat), 6-11; 12-3, 6.30-10.30 Sun
☎ (01202) 841405
Badger First Gold, seasonal beers Ⓗ
On the northern outskirts of town, this comfortable one bar local has wood-panelled walls and wooden furniture including settles. Popular for its home-cooked food, the menu includes authentic Asian dishes (eve meals served Tue-Sat). There is a small garden by the River Allen and a covered and heated outdoor area for smokers. Walford Mill craft centre is nearby. ▲❀◑◹P⇄

Winterborne Stickland

Crown
North Street, DT11 0NJ (3 miles N of A354)
🕙 12-2.30, 6.30-11; 12-3, 7-10.30 Sun
☎ (01258) 880838
Ringwood Best Bitter, Fortyniner, seasonal beers; guest beer Ⓗ
In the middle of a peaceful Dorset village, this busy Ringwood owned pub is popular with locals and walkers. A two-room 18th-century Grade II listed inn, an inglenook dominates the front bar with a low-beamed dining room at the back. The garden still has the original well and a handsome thatched cottage. Good hearty home-cooked food includes a children's menu. ▲Q❀❀◑&♠♣P

Worth Matravers

Square & Compass ☆
BH19 3LF (off B3069) OS974777
🕙 12-3, 6-11; 12-11 Sat & Sun
☎ (01929) 439229
Ringwood Best Bitter; guest beers Ⓖ
Run by generations of the Newman family for more than 100 years, this 200-year-old free house has featured in every edition of this Guide. A cosy haven in winter with roaring fires and flagstone floors, 'the Square' comes alive on summer evenings. Relax in the lovely garden while enjoying the chickens, stone carvings and breathtaking views of the Jurassic coastline. This local institution has its own museum and holds cider and pumpkin festivals. It also hosts the Square Fair. Pasties are served until they run out. ▲Q❀♣♠

Well coude he know a draught of London ale – **Geoffrey Chaucer**

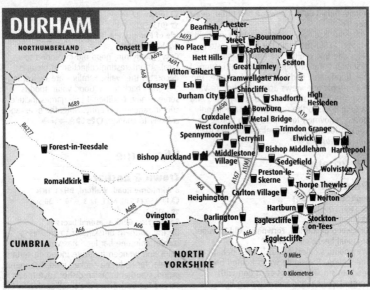

Co Durham incorporates part of the former county of Cleveland

Beamish

Sun Inn
Beamish Open Air Museum, DH9 0RG (follow signs for Beamish then catch tram)
☼ 11 (12 Sun)-3.30 (4.30 summer)
☎ (0191) 370 2908
Bull Lane BB; Theakston Old Peculier
Traditional pub formerly situated in Bishop Auckland. Step back in time in an authentic 1913 pub with sawdust on the floor and an antique till on the bar. Here you can sample Temperance drinks including sarsaparilla; Peel Walls cider is also sold. Mounted animals on display represent the taxidermist's art. Serial killer Mary Ann Cotton stayed here during her incarceration in Durham prison. The Co-op café across the road serves good food. ▲▷❀♣P

Bishop Auckland

Grand Hotel
Holdforth Crest, DL14 6DU
☼ 6 (12 Fri & Sat)-11; 12-10.30 Sun
☎ (01388) 601956 ⊕ the-grand-hotel.co.uk
Beer range varies ⊞
Imposing hotel on the edge of central Bishop Auckland, just five minutes' walk from Bishop Auckland Station. Home of Wear Valley Brewery, the pub is also a welcome purveyor of quality guest ales. A big screen shows premiership and Sky football matches. It hosts a quiz on Thursday, regular live music, a beer festival and much more. ❀⌂≠♣♠P

Pollards
104 Etherley Lane, DL14 6TU
☼ 11-11; 12-10.30 Sun
☎ (01388) 603539
Beer range varies ⊞
This comfortable community pub is a shining example of the type championed by CAMRA. It offers a range of five beers and good food served at lunchtime and in the evening. Two

roaring fires are welcoming on cold evenings. Darts and dominoes are played.
▲❀◑❒≠▣♣P

Tut 'n' Shive
68 Newgate Street, DL14 7EQ
☼ 11-midnight (1am Fri & Sat)
☎ (01388) 603252
Beer range varies ⊞
Popular with a varied clientele of all ages, this vibrant town-centre pub offers regularly changing guest ales and Weston's Old Rosie cider. Live bands are a regular and welcome feature. Close to the bus and railway stations.
≠▣♠

Bishop Middleham

Cross Keys
9 High Street, DL17 9AR (1 mile from A177)
☼ 12-11 (10.30 Sun)
☎ (01740) 651231
Theakston XB; Wells Bombardier ⊞
Busy village pub with a reputation for excellent meals. The pub is family run and offers a warm, friendly welcome. The spacious open-plan lounge bar with exposed beams is complemented by a large restaurant/function room with a full a la carte menu (booking advisable). Situated in excellent wildlife and walking countryside, a three mile circular walk starts opposite the pub. Quiz night is Tuesday. Teeside Tornados Bike Club meets on Wednesday and the pub has its own football team. ▲❀◑▣❒

Bournmoor

Dun Cow

Primrose Hill, DH4 6DY
🕑 12-11 (midnight Fri & Sat)
☎ (0191) 385 2631

Black Sheep Best Bitter; guest beers Ⓗ
Traditional northern country pub dating from
the 18th century with extensive gardens in
idyllic rural surroundings. It is reputed to be
haunted by the 'grey lady', with sightings as
recently as 2006. Home-cooked fare is
available in the bar/lounge plus a la carte in
the restaurant. A marquee can be hired for
special functions. Family friendly, there is a
bouncy castle in the garden. A beer festival is
held at the end of March. ⚑ ⏩ ✿ ◑ ▶ ⅄ ♣ P

Carlton Village

Smiths

TS21 1EA
🕑 12-2.30, 5-11; closed Mon; 12-midnight Fri & Sat;
12-10.30 Sun
☎ (01740) 630471

Caledonian Deuchars IPA; guest beer Ⓗ
Family run local at the heart of a small but
thriving village community attracting custom
from far and wide. The bustling public bar is
crowded on big match days. The newly
refurbished multi award winning restaurant,
situated in the old stables, continues to serve
good value locally sourced fresh produce
(booking advised). Sunday special prices on
food and ale continue to be an added bonus. A
popular village leek show and auction are held
annually. Q ✿ ◑ ▶ ⅄ ♣ P

Castledene

Smiths Arms

Brecon Hill, DH3 4HE
🕑 4 (12 Sat)-11; 12-10.30 Sun
☎ (0191) 385 6915

**Black Sheep Best Bitter; Courage Directors;
Taylor Landlord** Ⓗ
Despite being well tucked away, this country
pub is very popular with drinkers and diners,
particularly at weekends. Regulars gather in
the snug public bar with its real fire in winter,
where two guest ales are available. There is a
comfortable lounge with a floor that slopes
somewhat disconcertingly – it's not the drink,
honest. The games room has a pool table.
⚑ Q ▶ ⅄ ⊟ ♣ P

Chester-le-Street

Butchers Arms

DH3 3QD
🕑 11-3, 6.30-11 (midnight Fri & Sat); 12-3, 7-11.30 Sun
☎ (0191) 388 3605

Marston's Pedigree; guest beers Ⓗ
Ideal for the discerning drinker and diner, this
pub enjoys a good reputation for beer and
home-cooked food. Pies and freshly delivered
fish are specialities. Small meetings can be
accommodated with tea and coffee provided.
Note the fine array of porcelain artefacts.
⚐ ◑ ⇌

Pelaw Grange Greyhound Stadium

Drum Road, DH3 2AF (Signed from Barley Mow
roundabout on A167)
🕑 6.30 (7 Tue & Fri)-11; closed Wed; 12-4, 7-10.30 Sun
☎ (0191) 410 2141 ⊕ pelawgrange.co.uk

Black Sheep Best Bitter; guest beer Ⓗ
The Grange Club at the greyhound stadium
includes a large open bar where children are
welcome, a panoramic restaurant and a
concert room, all overlooking the track. The
club serves two cask ales. Reasonably-priced
bar meals are available. With a loyal clientele
the club has a lively atmosphere, especially on
race nights (Mon, Thu, Sat). Managed by a
CAMRA member, this is the only greyhound
stadium in Britain with real ales, an annual
beer festival and trips to local micros.
✿ ▶ ⅄ ⊟ ↳

Consett

Grey Horse

115 Sherburn Terrace, DH8 6NE
🕑 12-midnight
☎ (01207) 502585

**Consett Ale Works Steel Town Bitter, White Hot,
Red Dust; guest beers** Ⓗ
Traditional atmospheric welcoming pub with a
touch of olde-worlde charm. Home to the
Consett Ale Works, the pub dispenses its
quality beers plus guests from local and
distant brewers. Cosy and hospitable, its close
proximity to the coast-to-coast cycle route
makes this a popular stop off for weary
cyclists. Beer festivals are a regular feature.
⚑ Q ⏩ ✿ ⊟ ♣ ✦

Cornsay

Blackhorse Inn

Old Cornsay, DH7 9EL (2 miles W of B6301, Cornsay
Colliery Road)
🕑 7-11; 8-10.30 Sun
☎ (0191) 373 4211

Black Sheep Best Bitter; guest beers Ⓗ
This remote west Durham village pub
overlooking the Gladrow Valley is reckoned to
be some 200 years old, with the semi-
traditional bar separated from the former
restaurant by a partition. The earliest photo in
the bar dates back to 1890. The pub no longer
serves food except during the annual Easter
beer festival. A flagship award winner from
the Black Sheep Brewery, it has a five gallon
brew plant. Ask the landlord about the ghosts.
Q ✿ ▲ ♣ P ↳

Croxdale

Daleside Arms

Front Street, DH6 5HY (on B6288, 3 miles S of
Durham, off A167)
🕑 3 (7 Tue; 12 Sat)-midnight (11 Mon-Wed); 11-8 Sun
☎ (01388) 814165

Beer range varies Ⓗ
Situated on the main Durham to Spennymoor
road, the Daleside continues to offer
constantly changing beers plus excellent value
home-made fresh food. Micros from near and
far are well supported. A Newcastle fan,

landlord Mike's sporting memorabilia is much in evidence. Well worth the short bus ride from Durham (no 21, half hourly service), quality is key and this family-run pub excels in all it does. Are you brave enough to order the nuclear chilli spiced up? Q❀☎◑●&▬P

Darlington

Britannia

Archer Street, DL3 6LR (next to ring road, W side of town centre)

✪ 11.30-3, 5.30-11 (11.30 Fri & Sat); 12-10.30 Sun

☎ (01325) 463787

Camerons Strongarm; John Smith's Bitter; guest beers ⊞

Warm, friendly, ever popular local, close to the town centre, this CAMRA award-winning pub has sold real ale for more than 140 years. It retains the appearance and layout of the private house it once was. The bar is an enlarged living room and across the passage the parlour is used for meetings. It was the birthplace of 19th-century teetotal publisher, JM Dent. Up to four guest beers are available. Q&☀▬♣P⏢

Darlington Cricket Club

South Terrace, DL1 5JD (off Feethams South)

✪ 7.30 (7 Fri, 12 Sat)-midnight; 12-11.30 Sun

☎ (01325) 250044

Jennings Cumberland Ale; guest beer ⊞

Situated just off the ring road, this cricket pavilion overlooks the remains of Feethams football ground, once home to Darlington football club. Dating from 1906, cricket still flourishes here, and memorabilia decorates the walls in the comfortably furnished lounge. Darts, pool and snooker are also popular. A function room is available for hire. Members select the guest beer from Marston's monthly range. Show this Guide or CAMRA membership for entry. ❀☀▬♣P⏢

Darlington Snooker Club

1 Corporation Road, DL1 6AE (off North Rd)

✪ 11-11 (2am Fri & Sat); 12-10.30 Sun

☎ (01325) 241388

Beer range varies ⊞

Just out of the town centre, this first floor family-run and family-oriented private snooker club offers a warm, friendly welcome. Up to four rotating guest beers are available. There is a small, comfortable TV lounge for those not playing on one of the 10 top quality snooker tables. Twice yearly, the club plays host to a professional celebrity. CAMRA members are welcome on production of a current membership card or this Guide at CAMRA's regional Club of the Year 2004, 2005 and 2006. ☀(North Rd)▬

Number Twenty-2

22 Coniscliffe Road, DL3 7RG

✪ 12-11; closed Sun

☎ (01325) 354590

Burton Bridge Bitter; Village Brewer White Boar, Bull, Old Raby; guest beers ⊞

Town-centre ale house with a passion for cask beer; it has won many CAMRA awards since opening in 1995. Up to 13 real ales are available along with a selection of European beers on tap and bottled beers, attracting a

mixed clientele. Huge curved windows, stained glass panels and a high ceiling give it an airy spaciousness. This is the home of Village Brewer beers, commisioned from Hambleton by the licensee. Burton Bridge Festival Ale is sold here as Burton Bridge Classic Burton Ale. ◑&☀▬⏢

Old Yard Tapas Bar

98 Bondgate, DL3 7JY

✪ 10-11; 12-10.30 Sun

☎ (01325) 467385 ● tapasbar.co.uk

John Smith's Magnet; Theakston Old Peculier; guest beers ⊞

Fascinating blend of a well-stocked, popular, small bar and a Mediterranean taverna, which opened in 1995. The excellent pavement café is a sun-trap, justifiably popular in good weather. TV is for sport only. ❀◑

Quakerhouse

1-3 Mechanics Yard, DL3 7QF (off High Row)

✪ 11 (12 Sun)-midnight

☎ (07845) 666643 ● quakerhouse.net

Jarrow Rivet Catcher; Wear Valley Weardale Bitter; guest beers ⊞

Lively 10-year-old free house situated in a simple historic building tucked away in one of the old yards in the lavishly pedestrianised town centre. Up to eight regularly changing guests are mostly from micro-breweries countrywide, many rare and unusual. There is live music on Wednesday (door charge after 7.30pm). Great value lunches are popular, especially on Sunday. An upstairs function room is available for hire at this regular local CAMRA Pub of the Year winner. ◑&☀▬♠

Durham

Colpitts

Colpitts Terrace, DH1 4EG

✪ 2 (12 Thu-Sat)-11; 12-10.30 Sun

☎ (0191) 386 9913

Samuel Smith OBB ⊞

Once described as 'the most bohemian pub in Durham', this basic, street-corner local retains its reputation for sparky conversation and the cheapest cask ale in the city. The landlady maintains the character of a pub that has barely changed in 40 years. An interestingly shaped public bar is complemented by a small lounge and pool room. Less than 10 minutes' walk from rail and bus stations. ⊠Q◪☀♣

Dun Cow

37 Old Elvet, DH1 3HN

✪ 11-11; 12-10.30 Sun

☎ (0191) 386 9219

Black Sheep Best Bitter; Caledonian Deuchars IPA; Camerons Castle Eden Ale ⊞

In 995 AD, monks carrying the body of St Cuthbert following a milkmaid searching for her cow near Dun Holm (Durham) where the saint was to be buried, became the name. Part of the structure dates back to the 16th century. At the front is a comfortable and friendly snug with a larger lounge at the rear. Well known for the quality of its biggest selling ale, Castle Eden. Q◪☀▬♣⌐

Half Moon Inn

86 New Elvet, DH1 3AQ

☼ 11-11 (midnight Fri & Sat); 12-11 Sun
☎ (0191) 383 6981
Draught Bass; Taylor Landlord; guest beer ⊞
This city-centre pub, run by the same landlord for 25 years, is a favourite of locals, students and tourists alike. The CAMRA listed back bar has a large screen showing football fixtures, attracting sports fans. Popular in the summer months, the pub has a large beer garden overlooking the river. The guest beer is usually from the Durham Brewery. Q✿&

Old Elm Tree

12 Crossgate, DH1 4PS
☼ 12-11; 11-midnight Fri & Sat; 12-10.30 Sun
☎ (0191) 386 4621
Adnams Bitter; Camerons Strongarm; Greene King IPA; guest beer ⊞
Close to the bus station in North Road, this is one of Durham's oldest pubs, going back to at least 1600. It has one large L-shaped bar/lounge with a 'top' room linked by a set of stairs. A very popular pub, arrive early for the quiz on Wednesday and folk group on Monday and Tuesday. As befits its age, it is reputed to have two ghosts. The river banks and cathedral are a pleasant walk via Grape Lane. ✿(&≉⊟♣P

Queen's Head Hotel

2 Sherburn Road, Gilesgate, DH1 2JR
☼ 12-11
☎ (0191) 386 5649
Black Sheep Best Bitter; Marston's Pedigree; guest beer ⊞
Spacious and inviting family-run pub well worth the short walk or bus ride from the city centre. Home-made meals, including 'Durham's best broth' and the popular Sunday lunch, are served in the dining area. The pub has its own aviary in the large garden to the rear. Pool and TV are available in the main bar, and the pub runs a quiz night on Tuesday. ✿⊭⊞⊟♣P

Travellers Rest

1 Marshall Terrace, Gilesgate Moor, DH1 2HT
☼ 12-midnight (1am Fri & Sat)
☎ (0191) 384 7483
Fuller's London Pride ⊞
Carling drinkers pay the bills in this street corner local, but there is a growing clientele for the cask ale here. The walls are adorned with sporting memorabilia, leaving visitors in no doubt about the major topic of conversation among regulars. Particularly busy in the early evening and weekend afternoons, the pub has a thriving golf society and leek club, while exponents of the card game Crash are in full attendance on Friday evening. ⊞⊟♣

Victoria Inn ☆

86 Hallgarth Street, DH1 3AS
☼ 11.45-3, 6-11; 12-2, 7-10.30 Sun
☎ (0191) 386 5629 ⊕ victoriainn-durhamcity.co.uk
Big Lamp Bitter; guest beers ⊞
This friendliest of pubs has listed status outside and in. It has changed little over the years, with quaint decor, coal fires and a tiny snug helping to preserve the timeless atmosphere. And landlord Michael Webster's imaginative personal touches help to enhance the special character of the place. Choose from five superb ales, mainly sourced from local breweries, and a generous selection of malt and Irish whiskies. The accommodation is excellent and the historic city centre is but minutes away. ⊭Q⊭⊟≉⊟♣

Water House

65 North Road, DH1 4TM
☼ 9-midnight (1am Fri & Sat)
☎ (0191) 370 6540
Greene King Abbot; Marston's Pedigree; guest beers ⊞
Close to the bus station on Durham's lively North Road, this Wetherspoon's, the first in the town, remains popular with young and old alike. A former water board premises, the interior has been divided on split levels. The usual Wetherspoon's fare is supplemented by a cask cider and a good range of guest ales. Local micros are well represented. Q⊕⊠⊟♣

Woodman Inn

23 Gilesgate, DH1 1QW
☼ 12-midnight (11.30 Sun)
☎ (0191) 386 7500 ⊕ the-woodman-inn.co.uk
Beer range varies ⊞
A regular outlet for Durham Brewery beers, the six pumps dispense a constantly changing selection of ales. Micro-breweries continue to feature alongside the bigger regionals. Occasional festivals are held including a Germanfest. Peter and Kath have made this a friendly and comfortable retreat for visitors and locals alike. A regular in the Guide, this pub caters for many tastes, offering bingo, music or just a quiet pint. You might even get a welcome from the resident border terrier. ✿⊭≉⊟⌐

Eaglescliffe

Cleveland Bay

718 Yarm Road, TS16 0JE (jct of A67 and A135)
☼ 11-12.30am
☎ (01642) 780275
Taylor Landlord; guest beer ⊞
Whitewashed, 180-year-old former Camerons house full of character. The range of real ales continues to grow under the care of an enthusiastic licensee. The lounge is separate from the public bar, and there is a large function room to the rear. New housing now screens the historic coal drops of the Stockton and Darlington Railway. Q✿⊟&♣P⌐⊟

Egglescliffe

Pot & Glass

Church Road, TS16 9DQ
☼ 12-2, 6-11 (5.30-midnight Fri; 6-midnight Sat); 12-10.30 Sun
☎ (01642) 651009
Draught Bass; Caledonian Deuchars IPA; Jennings Cumberland Ale; guest beer ⊞
Classic village pub in a quiet cul-de-sac opposite the church. Its most striking feature is the pair of ornate bar fronts made from old country furniture by a former licensee (and cabinet maker) Charlie Abbey, whose last resting place overlooks the pub. The Pot & Glass with its two bars and a small function

room is the centre of village life, fielding darts and cricket teams. No lunches are served Monday, evening meals Tuesday-Saturday 6-8pm. ᴁQ✿◑ 㲗ᴂ♣Pᵡ

Elwick

McOrville Inn
34 The Green, TS27 3EF
☼ 12-2.30 (10-3 Sat), 5-11; 12-3, 7-10.30 Sun
☎ (01429) 273344
Beer range varies ⊞
Ancient white painted pub by the village green named after a local racehorse and winner of the 1802 St Leger. Deep damp cellars keep the three handpump beers in tip-top condition – the house beer McOrville Ale is brewed by Camerons. Locally sourced home-cooked food is available daily. A real fire warms you in winter, old village photographs adorn the walls and comfortable slippers are provided for walkers with muddy boots.
ᴁQ✿◑P

Esh

Cross Keys
Front Street, DH7 9QR (3 miles off A691 between Durham and Consett) OSNZ2044
☼ 12-3, 5.30-11; 12-10.30 Sun
☎ (0191) 373 1279
Black Sheep Best Bitter; Tetley Bitter ⊞
Pleasant, 18th-century pub in a picturesque village with a varied food menu offering vegetarian and children's choices. A comfortable locals' bar complements the lounge overlooking the Browney Valley. Delft racks display porcelain artefacts, some of which portray the old village. ◑P

Ferryhill

Surtees Arms
Chilton Lane, DL17 0DH
☼ 4 (12 Sat)-11; 12-10.30 Sun
☎ (01740) 655724
Shepherd Neame Spitfire; Taylor Landlord; guest beers ⊞
Offering the only real ale in Ferryhill, this free house continues to thrive. The nitrokeg has been removed, replaced by up to five real ales from a wide range of breweries. Themed events such as psychic nights, karaoke and 'meet the brewer' are held regularly and beer festivals hosted twice a year in spring and autumn. A function room is available for private meetings. ᴁQ✿✿◑ 㲗ᴂ♣ᵡ

Forest in Teesdale

Langdon Beck Hotel
DL12 0XP (on B6277, 8 miles NW of Middleton in Teesdale) NZ853313
☼ 11-11; 12-10.30 Sun
☎ (01833) 622267 ⊕ langdonbeckhotel.com
Black Sheep Best Bitter; Jarrow Rivet Catcher; guest beers ⊞
Situated high in the Pennines, in some of the finest countryside in England, this inn has long been a destination for walkers, fishermen and those seeking tranquility. Attracting visitors not only for the scenery, this gem offers

excellent food along with two beers, as well as up to two guests from local micro-breweries in summer. A beer festival is held in May. The spectacular High Force and Cauldron Snout waterfalls are a short walk away, while the Pennine Way passes close by.
ᴁQ✿✿ᴂ◑ 㲗ᴂᴧ♣Pᵡ

Framwellgate Moor

Tap & Spile
Front Street, DH1 5EE
☼ 6 (12 Fri)-11; 12-3, 6-11 Sat; 12-3, 7-10.30 Sun
☎ (0191) 386 5451
Beer range varies ⊞
The third pub of its type in the old Camerons chain of ale houses, now owned by Enterprise Inns. The bare stone walls of the bar and lounge are adorned with items of cellar equipment and complemented by bare wooden floors. The back room is popular with families until 9pm. Five ales are usually available, plus Westons Old Rosie cider. Popular with pubgoers young and old, no loud music means good conversation. CAMRA local Pub of the Year 2006. Q✿ᴂᴂ♣♠

Great Lumley

Old England
Front Street, DH3 4JB
☼ 11-11; 12-3, 6.30-10.30 Sun
☎ (0191) 388 5257
Beer range varies ⊞
This large family-run pub usually has three guest beers on handpump. The spacious, comfortable, split-level lounge is divided into different areas by wood and glass panels. The atmosphere is peaceful, attracting a regular clientele, including diners. The public bar can be more lively, with a pool table, dartboard, satellite and projection TV. Other entertainment includes a quiz held twice a week. ◑ 㲗ᴂᴧᴂ♣P

Hartburn

Masham Hotel
87 Hartburn Village, TS18 5DR
☼ 11-11 (midnight Fri & Sat); 12-10.30 Sun
☎ (01642) 645526
Black Sheep Best Bitter; Draught Bass; Greene King IPA; Theakston Best Bitter ⊞
For many years the Masham has been run by members of a family renowned in the area for keeping excellent real ale. Although recently refurbished inside, its origins as a 'public house' have not been lost. There is a growing emphasis on food, but many locals flock in for the real ale. Outdoor facilities are extensive and impressive, and barbecues feature regularly in warm weather. Q✿◑Pᵡ

Parkwood
64-66 Darlington Road, TS18 5ER
☼ 12-11 (midnight Fri & Sat)
☎ (01642) 587933 ⊕ theparkwoodhotel.com
Adnams Broadside; Camerons Strongarm; Greene King Abbot; guest beer ⊞
Formerly home to local ship owners and civic benefactors the Ropner family, this hotel still looks like a house from the outside and is set

in a large garden. The licensee is determined that the bar will remain separate and not become part of the restaurant. It serves good food and a wide range of real ales including some that are rare in this area. The Parkwood also offers quality en-suite accommodation. Q❀☞◑P

Hartlepool

Brewery Tap
Stockton Street, TS24 7NU (on A689 in front of Camerons Brewery)
◷ 11-4.30; closed Mon
☎ (01429) 868686 ⊕ cameronsbrewery.com/heritage_centre.htm
Camerons Strongarm, seasonal beers ⊞
It came as a surprise to the owners of Camerons Brewery to find that they owned the Stranton Inn, which had been closed for many years. With the help of various grants, it has been turned into an award-winning visitors' centre, featuring a museum, conference facilities and a bistro. It is also the start of the brewery tour. Beers from the Lion's Den micro are often available.
Q◑᪲≉P⊟

Causeway
Vicarage Gardens, Stranton, TS24 7QT (beside Stranton Church and Camerons Brewery)
◷ 11-11 (11.30 Thu; midnight Fri & Sat); 12-10.30 Sun
☎ (01429) 273954
Banks's Bitter; Camerons Strongarm; Jennings Dark Mild; Marston's Old Empire ⊞
This fine red brick Victorian watering hole sits beside Camerons Brewery in a small conservation area. Featuring an eclectic mix of live music most nights, the Causeway is something of an institution. Not many pubs in this Guide have been mentioned in Hansard. Owned by Marston's, the pub has a massive real ale turnover. The good home-cooked lunches, served Tuesday-Saturday, are popular, and there are barbecues in summer.
Q❧❀◑᪲᪲♣

Jackson's Arms
Tower Street, TS24 7HH
◷ 12-midnight (2am Fri & Sat)
☎ (01429) 862413
Beer range varies ⊞
The welcome is genuine and warm at this unassuming street-corner local, once the only Matthew Brown tied house in the area. Before that, it was offered as a prize in a raffle at £100 a ticket. Two busy bars cater for conversation at one end and pool and darts at the other. The regulars help to choose an ever-changing range of guest ales, with up to four on handpump. A new function room is now available. Q᪲≉♣

Heighington

Bay Horse
28 West Green, DL5 6PE
◷ 11-midnight; 12-10.30 Sun
☎ (01325) 312312
Black Sheep Best Bitter; John Smith's Magnet; guest beers ⊞

Picturesque, historic, 300-year-old pub overlooking the village's largest green. Its exposed beams and stone walls offer traditional surroundings, partitioned into distinct drinking and dining areas, with a large restaurant extending from the lounge. Food plays a prominent role, with excellent home-cooked meals available as well as bar snacks. The bar area gives drinkers the chance to enjoy the beer range in the evening, which includes up to three guest ales; the cider is Westons Old Rosie ᪲❀◑᪲᪲᪲♣◑P⊟

Locomotion No. One
Heighington Station, Heighington Lane, DL5 6QG
◷ 11-11; 12-10.30
☎ (01325) 320132 ⊕ locomotionone.co.uk
John Smith's Bitter; guest beers ⊞
This family-run pub occupies the former stationmaster's house at Heighington Station, next to the level crossing where the first ever locomotive to haul a passenger train was hoisted on to the track in 1825. An excellent range of real ales is enjoyed by locals and visitors alike. A terrace occupies the original platform with an additional courtyard for outdoor drinking. An extensive menu is served in the pub or upstairs restaurant (no food Sun eve). Beware, the last train leaves early.
᪲❀◑᪲≉♣P

Hett Hills

Moorings
DH2 3JU (from Chester-le-Street, B6313 under viaduct) OSNZ2451
◷ 12-11.30 (10.30 Sun)
☎ (0191) 370 1597
Black Sheep Best Bitter; Rudgate Battleaxe; Wylam Gold Tankard ⊞
Impressive pub on two levels bearing a nautical theme. The bar and bistro serve food all day with a wide choice of traditional home-cooked English fare. The upstairs restaurant overlooking the West Durham Hills offers fine food including lobster and other seafood.
❀☞◑P

High Hesleden

Ship Inn
TS27 4QD (S of B1281)
◷ 12-2 (3 Sat), 6-11; 12-9 Sun
☎ (01429) 836453
Beer range varies ⊞
Saved from dereliction in late 2001, the Ship's well-appointed bar and lounge/restaurant bear a nautical theme with models and pictures of warships. Both rooms have six handpumps for rotating ales and serve a wide range of excellent food. At the rear are seven luxury chalets, including a disabled room, with ample car parking. A marquee on the large rear lawn for functions in summer enjoys a picturesque North Sea view in clear weather.
᪲Q❀☞◑᪲᪲♣P

Metal Bridge

Old Mill Hotel
DH6 5NX (1 mile S of A1M jct 61, signed off A177)
OS303352

❂ 12-11 (10.30 Sun)
☎ (01740) 652928 🌐 theoldmill.uk.com
Beer range varies ⊞
Renowned for the quality of its service, this spacious inn, formerly a flour and wood mill, offers excellent real ale, food and accommodation. Three handpumps serve a range of beers with regular offerings from the Durham Brewery, just up the road in Bowburn. The extensive menu is freshly prepared in house with a changing list of specials. Accommodation includes en-suite facilities.
❀⇄◑♿P

Middlestone Village

Ship Inn
Low Road, DL14 8AB
❂ 4 (12 Fri & Sat)-11; 12-10.30 Sun
☎ (01388) 810904
Beer range varies ⊞
Once closed down by Vaux Brewery as unviable, this pub has outlived the Sunderland-based former owners after a vigorous local campaign to keep it open. Up to six ales from local and regional breweries are on offer. A regular winner of CAMRA awards, including Wear Valley Pub of the Year in 2007, this is a rural gem well worth seeking out.
Q❀♿🚌(7, 7A)♣P⊟

No Place

Beamish Mary Inn
DH9 0QH (off A693, Chester-le-Street to Consett road)
❂ 12-11 (10.30 Sun)
☎ (0191) 370 0237
Beer range varies ⊞
Family-run pub in a former pit village with open fires and a collection of memorabilia dating from the 1920s and 30s. A folk club is hosted on the last Wednesday of the month in the stables, Tuesday is quiz night and a beer festival is held on the last weekend in January. Winner of many CAMRA awards.
♨⇄◑♿♣●P

Norton

Unicorn
High Street, TS20 1AA
❂ 12-11 (midnight Fri & Sat)
☎ (01642) 643364
John Smith's Magnet ⊞
Set in a village conservation area and known locally as Nellie's after a previous long serving licensee, the Unicorn stands for stability in a world in which pub fashions change all the time. Many entries in this Guide feature a whole range of ales, this pub serves just one – superbly! Magnet is available on handpull and in keg form, so remember to ask for cask.
Q♨❀◐⊟♿♣

Ovington

Four Alls
The Green, DL11 7BP (2 miles S of Winston & A67)
❂ 7 (6 Fri; 3 Sat)-11; 12-10.30 Sun
☎ (01833) 627302
Tetley Bitter; guest beer ⊞
Friendly 18th-century inn opposite the green in what is known as the 'Maypole village'. Note the unusual Victorian sign denoting The Four Alls: 'I govern all (Queen), I fight for all (Soldier), I pray for all (Parson), I pay for all (Farmer)'. The pub has a bar, games room and restaurant serving excellent value food. Home of the Four Alls Brewery, its beers alternate with guests from micros countrywide; phone first if wanting to try the popular Four Alls beers as they tend not to last.
♨Q♨❀⇄◑♣P

Preston-le-Skerne

Blacksmiths Arms
Preston Lane, DL5 6JH (off A167 at Greta Green)
❂ 11.30-2, 6-11; closed Mon; 12-10.30 Sun
☎ (01325) 314873
Beer range varies ⊞
Welcoming free house known locally as the Hammers, situated in a rural location, with a long corridor separating the bar, lounge and restaurant. The beamed lounge is furnished in farmhouse style complete with Welsh dresser. It has an excellent reputation for home-cooked food and offers up to three constantly changing beers from micro-breweries countrywide. A previous local CAMRA Rural Pub of the Year, it even has a helicopter landing pad. ♨❀◑⊟♿♣P

Romaldkirk

Kirk Inn
The Green, DL12 9EN
❂ 12-3 (not Tue), 6-11; 12-3, 7-10.30 Sun
☎ (01833) 650260
Taylor Landlord; Wear Valley Weardale Bitter; guest beers ⊞
Overlooking the large village green, surrounded by many fine houses, this one-room, friendly inn is situated in an Upper Teesdale village, voted one of the most desirable in the country. The inn also serves as the village post office until noon. Guest beers are from Wear Valley Brewery. Evening meals must be booked. ♨❀◗♿🚌♣P

Seaton

Seaton Lane Inn
SR7 0LP (on B1404 W of A19)
❂ 11.30-midnight (1am Fri & Sat)
☎ (0191) 581 2038
Taylor Landlord; Theakston Best Bitter; Young's Special; guest beer ⊞
Popular roadside inn with a history as an 18th-century blacksmith's. The basic but comfortable bar with bare stone walls and pictorial history is the original part of the building. Behind this is the lounge and, three steps higher, the restaurant. At the back is a split-level decked garden and grassed area where live entertainment is performed on fine bank holidays. ♨Q❀◑⊟🚌P

Sedgefield

Ceddesfeld Hall
Sedgefield Community Association, Rectory Row, TS21 2AE (behind church)

ENGLAND

🕓 7.30-10.30; 8-11 Fri; 9-11 Sat
☎ (01740) 620341
Beer range varies H

Built in 1791 as the local parsonage, the hall comes complete with resident ghost 'the pickled parson'. Set in spacious grounds, ideal for a summer's evening, this is in fact a private club but CAMRA members are most welcome. There is a small bar, spacious lounge, function and meeting rooms. Run by volunteers from the Sedgefield Community Association, it hosts a wide variety of groups. An annual beer festival is held on the first weekend in July. Q✿♿🖳P🖥

Nag's Head

8 West End, TS21 2BS
🕓 12-2.30 (Thu-Sat only), 5-midnight; 12-2.30, 7-10.30 Sun
☎ (01740) 620234
Taylor Landlord; guest beers H

Situated in an attractive village close to Sedgefield racecourse, this free house is run as a traditional local to attract all age groups; families with well-behaved children are most welcome. There is a comfortable bar and a smaller lounge, while the restaurant serves local and international dishes prepared with fresh local produce. Meals are also served in the bar (eve meals Tue-Sat). The pub runs a thriving golf society. ✿🕪🖳♣P

Shadforth

Shadforth Plough

Southside, DU6 1LL (1 mile off A181)
🕓 12-3, 6-11; 12-11 Sat; 12-10.30 Sun
☎ (0191) 372 0375 ⊕ roseberryleisure.co.uk/shadforth
Marston's Pedigree; guest beer H

Situated in a small, quiet village, some five miles to the east of Durham city, this pub re-opened in 2005 after extensive refurbishment. The warm and welcoming stone tiled bar leads through to a carpeted lounge and the Witch Hill restaurant serving excellent quality fare (also available in the bar). Sunday is quiz night and the newly formed Plough football team also meets here. Buses 241-244 from Durham pass by the door. ♿✿🕪♿🖳♣P

Shincliffe

Seven Stars Inn

High Street North, DH1 2NU (on A177, S of Durham)
🕓 11-11 (10.30 Sun)
☎ (0191) 384 8454 ⊕ sevenstarsinn.co.uk
Black Sheep Best Bitter; Caledonian Deuchars IPA; Taylor Landlord; guest beers H

Dating from 1724, this small, cosy, beamed pub is situated on the edge of a pleasant village. Local country walks and the long distance Weardale Way pass nearby and walkers are welcome in the bar – just make sure your boots are clean. Well-behaved dogs are permitted. Meals are served in the bar and traditional restaurant. Comfortable accommodation makes the pub a good base for visiting the city and many attractions in the area. See the pub's website for details. ✿🛏🕪🖳🖳

Spennymoor

Frog & Ferret

Coulson Street, DL16 7RS
🕓 12-11 (10.30 Sun)
☎ (01388) 818312
Beer range varies H

Welcoming, family-run pub, a genuine free house offering a choice of four real ales with local micros well represented. The comfortable single room interior with brick, stone and wood claddings is based around a central three-sided bar. Darts and dominoes are played and bar snacks are available. 🚍♿♣

Penny Gill

17 Cheapside, DL16 6QE
🕓 11-11
☎ (01388) 827422
Courage Directors; guest beers H

Large, traditional, two-room pub in the town centre situated on the main bus route through Spennymoor. This free house offers some of the best value beer in the area and not surprisingly is quite popular as a result. In a keg dominated town, four handpumps serve guest beers from northern breweries. Darts and dominoes are played as well as pool. 🚍🖳🖳♣

Stockton-on-Tees

Sun Inn

Knowles Street, TS18 1SU
🕓 11-11; 12-10.30 Sun
☎ (01642) 611461
Beer range varies H

Excellent and deservedly popular traditional drinkers' pub just off the High Street, selling more Draught Bass than any other product. It supports two darts teams and a Sunday football team. Home to the Stockton Folk Club on a Monday night, it occasionally hosts other live music events in the back room. ⇌♣

Thorpe Thewles

Hamilton Russell Arms

Bank Terrace, TS21 3JU (100m off A177)
🕓 12-11.30 (10.30 Sun)
☎ (01740) 630757
Wells Bombardier; Marston's Pedigree; guest beer H

Named in celebration of the marriage of Gustavson Hamilton and Emma Maria Russell in 1928, this impressive pub was formerly part of the Marchioness of Londonderry's estate. The emphasis here is on good value, top quality food; a varied menu is served all day featuring dishes made with locally sourced produce, including many fish and vegetarian options. However, the 'Hammy' welcomes drinkers and continues to dispense fine English ales – the guest beer is usually a premium bitter. 🚍✿🕪♿P

Trimdon Grange

Dovecote Inn

Salters Lane, TS29 6EP (on B1278)
🕓 4 (7 Mon; 12 Fri-Sun)-11

☎ (01429) 880967
Beer range varies Ⓗ
The landlord of this free house hails from Charles Wells country; his twin passions are rugby union and real ale. Situated on the outskirts of a former mining village, the pub dates back to at least 1820, growing an extra storey in 1927, resulting in a distinctive tall and narrow appearance. The single large room houses a popular pool table and dartboard. There used to be a dovecote in one corner – hence the name. Quiz night is Tuesday. ♨🚌

West Cornforth

Hare & Hounds Inn

Garmondsway, DL17 9DT (1 mile S of Coxhoe on A177)
✪ 12-3, 6-11; closed Mon; 12-11 Sat & Sun
☎ (01740) 654661
Jennings Cumberland Ale; guest beers Ⓗ
Originally called the Fox Inn, the pub dates back to 1771, when it was part of a farm and coaching inn. Now owned by Enterprise Inns and run by real ale enthusiasts Stuart and Colette, it comprises a large L-shaped bar and a restaurant that doubles as a lounge; exposed beams feature throughout. It specialises in meals based on locally sourced produce, particularly beef. ♨🕼🍴🚌&P

Square & Compass

7 The Green, DL17 9JQ (off Coxhoe-W Cornforth road)
✪ 7 (11.30 Fri & Sat; 12 Sun)-midnight
☎ (01740) 653050
Beer range varies Ⓗ
Thriving local situated at the top of the green, in the oldest part of the village and quite different from the rest of 'Doggy' (the locals' name for the place). The pub comprises a large L-shaped bar/lounge and a smaller games room. This free house is popular with all ages, hosting a quiz on Thursday and entertainment on Saturday. ❀&🚌P

Witton Gilbert

Glendenning Arms

Front Street, DH7 6SY (off A691 bypass, 3 miles from Durham)
✪ 4 (3 Fri; 12 Sat)-midnight; 12-11 Sun
☎ (0191) 371 0316
Black Sheep Best Bitter; Greene King Abbot; Wells Bombardier Ⓗ
Popular village local with a lively bar and quiet, comfortable lounge. A Guide regular year after year, the bar has original 1970s Vaux red and white handpulls. The pub is the hub for local clubs and supports a darts and football team, displaying team shirts on the wall. ♨Q🕼🚌♣P

Travellers Rest

Front Street, DH7 6TQ (off A691 bypass, 3 miles from Durham)
✪ 11-11 (10.30 Sun)
☎ (0191) 371 0458
Theakston Best Bitter; guest beers Ⓗ
Typical traditional country-style inn with a large open-plan area divided into three sections with dining throughout. The latest addition to the pub is a fair sized conservatory, popular with families having meals. A wide variety of menus includes specials depending on the time of day. Quizzes are held on Tuesday and Sunday evenings. Q❀🕼🚌🍴–

Wolviston

Ship

50 High Street, TS22 5JX
✪ 12-3, 5-11.30; 12-3, 7-10.30 Sun
☎ (01740) 644420
Beer range varies Ⓗ
Comfortable 150-year-old village pub on the site of an old coaching inn – the original stables remain behind the main building. The menu offers a good range of home-cooked food (not served Sun eve). The licensee follows a vigorous real ale policy – three handpulls provide a range of frequently changing guest beers. ❀🕼♣P

Spores for thought

Yeast is a fungus, a single cell plant that can convert a sugary liquid into equal proportions of alcohol and carbon dioxide. There are two basic types of yeast used in brewing, one for ale and one for lager. (The yeasts used to make the Belgian beers known as gueuze and lambic are wild spores in the atmosphere). It is often said that ale is produced by 'top fermentation' and lager by 'bottom fermentation'. While it is true that during ale fermentation a thick blanket of yeast head and protein is created on top of the liquid while only a thin slick appears on top of fermenting lager, the descriptions are seriously misleading. Yeast works at all levels of the sugar-rich liquid in order to turn malt sugars into alcohol. If yeast worked only at the top or bottom of the liquid, a substantial proportion of sugar would not be fermented. Ale is fermented at a high temperature, lager at a much lower one. The furious speed of ale fermentation creates the yeast head and with it the rich, fruity aromas and flavours that are typical of the style. It is more accurate to describe the ale method as 'warm fermentation' and the lager one as 'cold fermentation'.

An Appetite For Ale
FIONA BECKETT/WILL BECKETT

Fiona Beckett
Will Beckett

an
Appetite
for
ALE

101 ways to enjoy beer with food

A beer and food revolution is under way in Britain and award-winning food writer Fiona Beckett and her publican son, Will, have joined forces to write the first cookbook to explore this exciting new food phenomenon that celebrates beer as a culinary tour de force. This ground-breaking collection of simple and approachable recipes has been specially created to show the versatility and fantastic flavour that ale has to offer. With sections on Snacks, Spreads and Dips, Soups, Pasta and Risotto, Seafood, Chicken and other Birds, Meat Feasts, Spicy Foods, Bread and Cheese and Sweet Treats it provides countless ideas for using beer from around the world. With an open mind, a bottle opener and a well-stocked larder, this exciting book will allow you to enjoy real food, real ale and real flavour.

£19.99   ISBN 978 1 85249 234 2

Arkesden

Axe & Compasses

Wicken Road, CB11 4EX (2 miles N of B1038)
TL483344
🕐 11.30-2.30, 6-11 (11.30 Sat); 12-3, 7-10.30 Sun
☎ (01799) 550272 ⊕ axeandcompasses.co.uk
Greene King IPA, Old Speckled Hen, Abbot Ⓗ
Partly-thatched, 17th-century village inn with
a public bar and an award-winning restaurant.
This friendly, community pub is the centre of
village life and the locals in the public bar tend
to be interested in, and talk to, strangers. The
hostelry is frequented by walkers on the
extensive footpath network in this pleasant
area where three counties meet. The
Harcamlow Way long-distance path passes
nearby. ▲Q❀◑ⓓ⌷P⌐

Ashdon

Rose & Crown

Crown Hill, CB10 2HB (5 miles NE of Saffron
Walden) TL587422
🕐 12-2, 6-11; 12-4, 7-10.30 Sun
☎ (01799) 584337
**Adnams Bitter; Black Sheep Best Bitter; Greene
King IPA, Abbot; guest beers** Ⓗ
This 16th-century, three-roomed pub reveals
many features of historical interest. Reputedly
haunted, the Cromwell Room still bears its
original decoration. Access at the front is via

steps. Evening meals are served Monday to
Saturday; the weekly fish and chips night is a
speciality. ▲Q❀◑⌷P

Ballards Gore (Stambridge)

Shepherd & Dog

Gore Road, SS4 2DA (between Rochford and
Paglesham)
🕐 12-3, 6-11; 12-4, 6-10.30 Sun
☎ (01702) 258279 ⊕ shepherdanddog.piczo.com
Beer range varies Ⓗ
Excellent family-run pub in a comfortable
cottage style – local CAMRA Pub of the Year

INDEPENDENT BREWERIES

Blanchfields Rochford
Brentwood Brentwood
Crouch Vale South Woodham Ferrers
Famous Railway Tavern Brightlingsea
Farmer's Ales Maldon
Felstar Felsted
Harwich Town Harwich
Mersea Island East Mersea
Mighty Oak Maldon
Nethergate Pentlow
Pitfield Great Horkesley
Saffron Henham
Shalford Shalford
Star Steeple

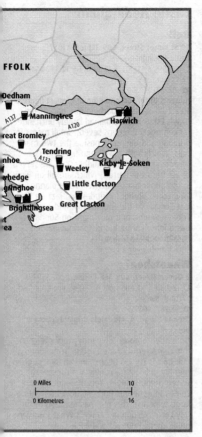

FFOLK

Dedham

Manningtree

A137

reat Bromley

A120

Harwich

nhoe

A133

Tendring

Weeley

Kirby-le-Soken

rhedge

ghinghoe

Little Clacton

Brightlingsea

Great Clacton

ea

0 Miles   10

0 Kilometres   16

2004 and winner of Rural Pub of the Year (again) in 2007. The four changing real ales generally come from micro-breweries and are often unusual for the area. Cider is stocked in summer. The restaurant serves excellent meals, and snacks are available in the bar. Walking, cycling and coach groups are welcome. A smokers' shelter is planned for outside. ✿◑❺ᕈ(60)◈P⁵⁻

Basildon

Moon on the Square

1-15 Market Square, SS14 1DF (in town centre, 300m from rail and bus stations)
🕓 9-midnight (1am Fri & Sat)
☎ (01268) 520360
Greene King Abbot; Marston's Pedigree; guest beers Ⓗ
Busy town-centre pub attracting many regulars, offering a wide range of up to six guest beers. Favourites are brought back by popular demand – Ringwood Porter especially is a frequent guest. There are mini beer festivals at Easter, in the summer and in November. Food is served all day, including roasts on Sunday, grills from 3-11pm Tuesday and curries from 3-11pm Thursday. There is a designated area for families; 'last orders' for children's meals is at 8pm. Outside is a heated area for smokers. Q◑≠ᕈ⁵⁻

Billericay

Coach & Horses

36 Chapel Street, CM12 9LU (near B1007 and Waitrose car park)
🕓 10-11; 12-10.30 Sun
☎ (01277) 622873
Adnams Bitter; Greene King IPA, Abbot; guest beers Ⓗ
A popular one-bar pub situated off the high street, with a cosy, welcoming ambience. Good quality food is served daytime and evenings from an extensive menu featuring home-made pies. The bar and food service is quick, efficient and friendly, enhancing the overall feel-good factor. Walls are adorned with prints and decorative plates, and there is a fine collection of ceramic and gleaming copper jugs behind the bar – as well as a collection of elephants. ♨✿◑≠ᕈP

Black Notley

Vine Inn

105 Witham Road, CM77 8LQ TL767208
🕓 12-2.30, 6.30-11; 12-4, 7-11 Sun
☎ (01376) 324269
Adnams Bitter; guest beers Ⓗ
The Vine is a 16th-century open-plan free house with a central bar, a lounge area to the left and a restaurant area to the right. Log-burning stoves feature at both ends. Above the lounge is a six-person mezzanine, accessible via a steep staircase. One of the two guest beers is often a second Adnams beer. Cressing railway station is a 15-minutes' walk away down country lanes. A heated, covered smoking area is provided outside. ♨Q✿◑ᕈ(21)P⁵⁻

Blackmore

Leather Bottle

Horsefayre Green, CM4 0RL TL603009
🕓 11-11; 12-10.30 Sun
☎ (01277) 821891 ⊕ theleatherbottle.net
Adnams Bitter, Broadside; Ⓗ guest beers Ⓗ/Ⓖ
Large village pub with a smallish flagstone-floored bar area. The main part is taken up by an excellent restaurant. Two guest ales are generally available on handpump, with a third on gravity at weekends (one beer is usually around 5% ABV). The cider is Weston's Old Rosie. An annexe to the bar has a pool table, dartboard and silent fruit machine. ♨✿◑❺♣◈P

Bournes Green (Great Wakering)

Rose Inn

Wakering Road, SS3 0PY (½ mile N of A13) TQ915874
🕓 11.30-11 (10.30 Sun)
☎ (01702) 588008
Adnams Broadside; Greene King IPA, Abbot; Theakston Old Peculier; guest beers Ⓗ
Big but cosy pub, warmed by an open fire during the winter. A spacious garden is inviting in the summer months and is ideal for families. There are always four ales on offer, plus one regularly-changing guest beer. Bar

food is available until 9.30pm (9pm on Sun). The number 14 bus from Southend passes nearby but times are limited.
ᴁQ⇲♿❄&⊟(14)P⚑–

Brentwood

Rising Sun

144 Ongar Road, CM15 9DJ (on A128)
✪ 3 (12 Sat)-11; 12-10.30 Sun
☎ (01277) 213749
Brakspear Bitter; Taylor Landlord; guest beers Ⓗ
This much-improved local just north of the town centre brings a good selection of real ales to an area where the choice for beer drinkers is limited. A rare but regular outlet for Brakspear, there are also two guest beers. This is a community-focused pub where local clubs meet, regular quizzes are held on a Monday evening and darts is popular. There are old prints of the local area on the walls and desk fans are fixed above the bars to keep customers cool. ᴁ❄❀⊟♣P

Brightlingsea

Railway Tavern

58 Station Road, CO7 0DT (on B1029)
✪ 12-2.30, 5-11; 12-11 Fri & Sat; 12-3, 7-10.30 Sun
☎ (01206) 302581 ⏚ geocities.com/famousrailway
Crouch Vale Crouch Best; Ⓗ **Railway Tavern Crab & Winkle Mild, Bladderwrack;** Ⓖ **guest beers** Ⓗ
All change at the famous Railway Tavern! Two well-known local brewers have assisted the landlord/brewer in extending this pub in order to add a new modern brewery in what used to be the function room. Brewing capacity has doubled, much to everyone's delight. The bar area has been knocked out and enlarged to accommodate the ever-increasing range of beers which are served either by gravity dispense or as bottle-conditioned ales. Enjoy the fire in winter and the cider festival in May. ᴁQ❀⊟♣●

Burnham-on-Crouch

Queen's Head

26 Providence, CM0 8JU (near B1010 in a one-way street, opp clock tower)
✪ 11-3, 6-11; 12-4, 6-11 Sat (hours extended in summer); 12-4, 7-10.30 Sun
☎ (01621) 784825
Adnams Bitter; Mighty Oak IPA; guest beers Ⓗ
Charming, hidden back-street gem, in walking distance from the busy, picturesque quayside. Run by an enthusiastic CAMRA landlord, this oasis of real ale has two ever-changing guest beers and hosts an annual beer festival in the pretty, enclosed courtyard garden. The bar ceiling is adorned with a variety of prints and photographs. This cosy, time-warp pub has darts and pool teams. Traditional home-cooked food can be enjoyed in a friendly, welcoming atmosphere. Popular with locals, folk nights are on the first Friday of the month. Q❀❁⇌♣●⛴

Castle Hedingham

Bell

10 St James Street, CO9 3EJ (off A1017, signed Castle Hedingham)
✪ 11.45-3, 6-11; 11.45-12.30am Fri; 12-11.30 Sat; 12-11 Sun
☎ (01787) 460350
Adnams Bitter; Greene King IPA; guest beers Ⓖ
This 15th-century coaching inn, part of the Gray's Estate, has remained largely unchanged for centuries. It retains several small rooms for drinking and dining alongside the two main bars, which both have open fires. Beers (including guests from Mighty Oak) are served direct from the barrels, which are all on view in the public bar. A beer festival is planned for July. Entertainment includes live jazz on the last Sunday of the month, folk and pop on Friday evening and quiz night on Sunday. It has a large car park and spacious garden. ᴁQ⇲❀❁⊟&⊟♣●P⚑–

Wheatsheaf

2 Queen Street, CO9 3EX (1 mile from A1017)
✪ 12-2.30, 5-11 (midnight Fri); 12-midnight Sat; 12-10.30 Sun
☎ (01787) 460555
Greene King IPA, Morlands Original; guest beers Ⓗ
Once the home of a wealthy wool merchant, this characterful Grade I listed, 16th-century pub boasts carved beams and an inglenook. A friendly pub with a convivial atmosphere, the varied menu is highly recommended and comes in generous portions, together with a large wine list. This pub has featured in the 'My Local' section in CAMRA's What's Brewing publication. ᴁQ❀❁⊟&⊟♣P⚑–

Chelmsford

Cricketers

143 Moulsham Street, CM2 0JT
✪ 11-11; 12-10.30 Sun
☎ (01245) 261157
Greene King IPA, Abbot; guest beers Ⓗ
Corner local, serving the best value decent ale in town. One or two guest beers come from small breweries, with Mighty Oak often featured. The pub has a lively public bar with juke box, pool table and Sky sports, and a quieter lounge, both featuring football and cricket memorabilia on the walls. Note the pub sign with two different sides and the mural outside. Meals are served Sunday to Friday. Q❁❀♣⚑–

Endeavour

351 Springfield Road, CM2 6AW (on B1137)
✪ 11-11; 12-10.30 Sun
☎ (01245) 257717
Greene King IPA, Abbot; Mighty Oak Maldon Gold; guest beers Ⓗ
A 15-minute walk from the town centre, this friendly pub has three rooms, one used for early evening dining on Friday and Saturday only. One of the two guest beers is Mighty Oak Oscar Wilde (from September to May). Weston's Bounds Brand cider is also stocked. Regular charity events are held, including a meat raffle on Sunday. ᴁ❁❀⊟♣●

Original Plough

28 Duke Street, CM1 1HY
🕐 11-11 (midnight Fri & Sat); 12-10.30 Sun
☎ (01245) 250145
Greene King IPA; Taylor Landlord; guest beers 🅷
Spacious, open-plan town-centre pub, attracting a varied clientele. The landlord is a keen rugby fan and the pub is home to a local rugby team, so this is the sport screened on TV in preference to others. Mild and other dark beers are often available. Evening meals are served until 7.45pm Monday to Thursday. There is an outdoor patio for drinks on milder days. 🏵️◑≠🖳⌐'

Queen's Head

30 Lower Anchor Street, CM2 0AS (near cricket ground & B1007)
🕐 12-11; 11-11.30 Fri & Sat
☎ (01245) 265181 🌐 queensheadchelmsford.co.uk
Crouch Vale Best Bitter, Brewers Gold; guest beers 🅷
Crouch Vale's only hostelry, this six-times local CAMRA Pub of the Year is Chelmsford's premier beer pub. Six constantly-changing guest ales always include a mild and a stronger dark beer. A changing cider is usually from Weston's. Good value lunches are also offered on Sunday if there is a cricket match. Live jazz plays on the last Sunday lunchtime of the month and Tuesday is quiz night. An annual beer festival is held in September. 🏚Q🏵️◑&🖳♣🖘P

United Brethren

New Writtle Street, CM2 0LF
🕐 12-11.30 (midnight Fri & Sat); closed Sun
☎ (01245) 265161 🌐 theunitedbrethren.co.uk
Fuller's London Pride; Woodforde's Wherry 🅷
This local CAMRA Most Improved Pub 2007 is named after two brothers who started selling beer in 1887 from the two cottages that now form the main part of the building. It has a large single bar and a small side annexe containing a pool table. This is Chelmsford's only permanent outlet for Wherry and the beer range expands to include Crouch Vale Brewers Gold in the summer months. Good lunchtime food is available on weekdays, prepared by an Italian chef. Note the carpet and the ceiling decorations. 🏵️◑&♣'

Woolpack

23 Mildmay Road, CM2 0DH
🕐 12-11 (midnight Fri & Sat)
☎ (01245) 259295
Greene King IPA, Ruddles Best, Abbot; guest beers 🅷
The Woolpack makes the most of the guest beers permitted by Greene King, with five ales normally on handpump. The public bar has darts and pool, while the larger lounge leads to a third room with a large-screen TV. The menu includes a weekly changing range of local speciality sausages; evening meals are served Monday to Friday. A heated outdoor patio area is provided for smokers. 🏵️◑🖳♣P'

Churchgate Street

Queen's Head

26 Churchgate Street, CM17 0JT (in centre of village, 1 mile E of Old Harlow) TL483114
🕐 11.45-3, 5-11; 12-4, 6-11 Sat; 12-4, 7-10.30 Sun
☎ (01279) 427266
Adnams Bitter, Broadside; Nethergate IPA; guest beer 🅷
Originally two cottages built in 1530, these were joined and converted to a pub in 1750. It features wooden beams throughout, with a large, warm fire in winter. The pub harmonises well with this old-style village on the edge of Harlow New Town, which maintains its non-new town character. Guest beers generally come from East Anglian micro-breweries, although Mighty Oak does tend to feature frequently. 🏚Q🏵️◑🖳(7, 59)P

Colchester

Bricklayers

27 Bergholt Road, CO4 5AA (on A134 & B1508, near North station)
🕐 11-3, 5.30-11; 11-midnight Fri; 11-11 Sat; 12-3, 7-11 Sun
☎ (01206) 852008
Adnams Bitter, Explorer, Broadside, seasonal beers; Fuller's London Pride; guest beers 🅷
The 'Brick' is a friendly, busy local with a diverse clientele. It comprises a public bar with darts and pool, lounge bar and conservatory. Run by a CAMRA award-winning landlord and family, it offers good quality home-cooked lunches (no food Sat), with the Sunday roast being particularly popular. The full range of Adnams regular and seasonal beers is served, along with at least three guest ales and Crones real cider. 🏵️◑&≠(Colchester North)🖳♣🖘P

British Grenadier

67 Military Road, CO1 2AP (opp Military church)
🕐 12 (11 Tue)-2.30, 5-11.40 (12.10am Fri); 11-12.10am Sat; 12-3, 7-11.40 Sun
☎ (01206) 500933
Adnams Bitter, Broadside, seasonal beers; guest beers 🅷
A warm welcome awaits visitors to this comfortable, friendly local, now three-times winner of local CAMRA Town Pub of the Year. It is well worth the short walk from Town station and the shops: the beer quality is excellent, and guest ales are always available, with a list of those to come displayed on a blackboard. Pump clips of those you have missed adorn the walls. Darts and pool are very popular, with pub teams active in local leagues. Sunday night's quiz is well attended. 🏵️≠(Colchester Town)🖳♣'🖵

Dragoon

82 Butt Road, CO3 3DA (on B1026, near police station)
🕐 11-midnight (1am Fri & Sat)
☎ (01206) 573464
Adnams Bitter, Explorer, Broadside, seasonal beers; guest beers 🅷
Traditional local, just outside the town centre. This single bar pub has two distinct areas: a lounge and a public bar featuring a dartboard, pool table and large-screen TV. As

well as supporting darts and pool teams, it is also popular with home and away football fans on match days, when the legendary chilli can be sampled. On other days, customers gather at the bar to indulge in the well-known art of conversation. A ghost, the 'grey lady', resides on the first floor. ❀Q✿≠(Colchester Town)❑♣╚

Fat Cat

65 Butt Road, CO3 3BZ (on B1026, near police station)
☼ 12 (11 Sat)-11 (midnight Fri & Sat)
☎ (01206) 577990 ⊕ fatcatcolchester.co.uk
Crouch Vale Brewers Gold; ⑤ Fat Cat Bitter, Honey Ale; Hop Back Summer Lightning; Ⓗ Mighty Oak Oscar Wilde; ⑤ Woodforde's Wherry; Ⓗ guest beers ⑤
Formerly the Royal, this 19th-century pub has been totally refurbished – while retaining many original features it now has a stylish, modern feel. A welcome addition is the tap room, where you will find up to 20 ales dispensed on gravity. There are three Belgian beers on handpump and a selection of bottled ales. Food is home cooked, with a Chinese night on Wednesday and roasts on Sunday (booking advisable). Local musicians provide acoustic entertainment on Sunday evening. Q❀◑&≠(Colchester Town)❑╚

Forester's Arms

1-2 Castle Road, CO1 1UW (near A1232, off Castle Rd & East Hill)
☼ 12-11 (12.30am Fri & Sat); 12-10.30 Sun
☎ (01206) 224059
Nethergate Augustinian; guest beers Ⓗ
A pleasant and comfortable back-street local, situated in a quiet area just two minutes' walk from the high street and Castle Park. A two-bar pub, it has a pleasing decor and subdued lighting. Nethergate beers are usually available, along with an ever-changing range of guest ales. There is a good and varied selection of reasonably priced meals on offer. An outside drinking area in front of the pub is ideal for refreshment on warm days. Occasional live music plays. Q❀◑❑♣╚

Fox & Fiddler

1 St John's Street, CO2 7AA (town centre, at jct with Head Street)
☼ 11-11 (midnight Fri & Sat); 12-10.30 Sun
☎ (01206) 560520
Mighty Oak IPA, English Oak; guest beers Ⓗ
Rescued from pubco obscurity five years ago, the town centre's sole free house continues to thrive. Built in 1420, the Fox's deceptively tiny frontage hides three separate dining and drinking areas, offering an ever-changing range of guest beers, often from micro-breweries. There are special offers on real ales every Monday and Tuesday. Quality pub food is served (Wed-Sun lunchtime and Wed eve); the famous steak and ale pie is made with one of the beers currently on handpump. Live music plays every Saturday night. ❀◑≠(Colchester Town)❑╚

Odd One Out

28 Mersea Road, CO2 7ET (on B1025)
☼ 4.30 (12 Fri & Sat)-11; 12-10.30 Sun

☎ (01206) 578140
Archers Best Bitter; guest beers Ⓗ
Still the best value in town, the 'Oddy' is a multiple winner of CAMRA awards, offering six ever-changing real ales, usually from micro-breweries, with dark beers well represented. Crones and two other real ciders are also available, along with a big selection of Scottish and Irish malts. The pub has a friendly atmosphere where conversation is king among its varied clientele. The unspoilt interior is reminiscent of a 1950s front room, with roaring fires in winter. Newspapers, chess, scrabble and card schools provide alternative entertainment. ▥Q❀≠(Colchester Town)❑♣●

Coxtie Green

White Horse

173 Coxtie Green Road, CM14 5PX (at jct with Mores Lane, 1 mile W of A128) TQ564959
☼ 11.30-11 (midnight Fri & Sat); 12-10.30 Sun
☎ (01277) 372410
Fuller's London Pride; guest beers Ⓗ
Excellent, small country local with a well-appointed saloon bar and a more basic public bar with a dartboard and TV. A wide-ranging clientele of all ages enjoys the relaxed and friendly atmosphere here. Six well-used handpumps feature a variety of beers, and a draught cider and perry are normally also available. Each July a beer festival is held in the large rear garden, which incorporates a children's play area. Regular golf and fishing competitions are hosted. Buses are lunchtimes only. ❀◑❑&❑♣●P

Danbury

Griffin

64 Main Road, CM3 4DH (on A414)
☼ 12-11 (10.30 Sun)
☎ (01245) 222905
Adnams Broadside; guest beers Ⓗ
The Griffin has recently changed hands from Punch to a local owner but remains food-oriented and continues to serve Broadside and two constantly-changing guest beers which are often from local brewers. Food is served all day, with specials including fresh fish dishes always available. The building, built in the 1500s, is steeped in history. One of its more illustrious visitors was Sir Walter Scott, who wrote about the pub in his first novel. ▥❀◑&❑P

Dedham

Sun Inn

High Street, CO7 6DF (on B1029, opp church)
☼ 12-11 (6 Sun)
☎ (01206) 323351 ⊕ thesuninndedham.com
Adnams Broadside; guest beers Ⓗ
This 15th-century inn has two separate bars offering Adnams and three guest ales, usually from local micro-breweries. It is renowned for high quality meals served in its spacious restaurant, and its excellent wine list. The large garden is a great attraction in warmer weather. Four en-suite guest rooms include one with a four-poster bed. Children are

welcome, and a large range of board games is available. ♨Q✿☕☎🌙🎱♣P⬤

Duton Hill

Three Horseshoes

CM6 2DX (½ mile W of B184, Dunmow-Thaxted road) TL606268

🕐 12-2.30 (not Mon-Wed; 3 Sat), 6-11; 12-3, 7-10.30 Sun

☎ (01371) 870681

Thwaites Original; guest beers Ⓗ

Cosy village local with a large garden overlooking the Chelmer Valley and open farmland. It hosts open-air theatre in July (the landlord is a former pantomime dame). Wonderful features in this unpretentious pub include a wildlife pond and millennium beacon in the garden, breweriana and a remarkable collection of Butlins memorabilia. A beer festival is held over the late spring bank holiday. The pub sign depicts a famous painting of The Blacksmith by a local resident, Sir George Clausen. ♨✿☕🚌(313)♣P

East Hanningfield

Windmill Tavern

The Tye, Main Road, CM3 8AA TL771012

🕐 11-11; 12-10.30 Sun

☎ (01245) 400315

🌐 thewindmilleasthanningfield.co.uk

Crouch Vale Brewers Gold; Greene King IPA; guest beer Ⓗ

Excellent pub on the village green with a large L-shaped bar and separate restaurant area that is also used for meetings. It offers good home-cooked food seven days a week (not Sun eve). Quiz night is Wednesday. The guest beer is usually sourced from smaller breweries. ♨✿☕🌙♣P

Eastwood

Oakwood

564 Rayleigh Road, SS9 5HX (on A1015)

🕐 11-11 (midnight Fri & Sat); 12-11 Sun

☎ (01702) 429000 🌐 theoakwood.co.uk

Beer range varies Ⓗ

Spacious, popular brick-built two-bar pub with an outside seating area and car park. It serves two ever-changing guest beers, from national as well as micro-breweries. Televised football and other sports are shown on a large screen, and there are pool tables and a dartboard at the back of the main bar. It also has a smaller, quieter bar with comfortable seating. Food is served lunchtimes and evenings (not Sun eve). Live music plays on Saturday evening. ✿🌙🚌(9, 20)♣P

Elmdon

Elmdon Dial

Heydon Lane, CB11 4NH TL461397

🕐 12-3, 6-11 (closed Mon); 12-4, 6-10.30 Sun

☎ (01763) 837386 🌐 theelmdondial.co.uk

Adnams Bitter, Broadside; Taylor Landlord; guest beer Ⓗ

A friendly, welcoming pub owned and managed by a real ale enthusiast. Dating from 1450, enlarged in 1699 and sensitively

extended in 2006, it now has a modern kitchen and restaurant. Previously the King's Head, it closed in 1998 and was used as a private house. Seven years later, after a long planning battle and a public enquiry with evidence given by villagers and CAMRA, a court-forced sale led to the present ownership. The new name and pub sign reflect a window sundial in the village church. ♨Q✿🌙🎱🚌♣P⬤

Epping

Black Lion

293 High Street, CM16 4DA (towards N end of High Street)

🕐 10-11.30 (12.30am Fri & Sat); 12-11.30 Sun

☎ (01992) 578670

Greene King IPA; guest beers Ⓗ

This 14th-century inn has remained unchanged for a long period of time, with a wonderful open wood fire. Some great old slogans adorn the walls including, in the smaller of the two bars: 'When you have lost your Inns drown your empty selves for you have lost the last of England'. The guest ales (normally two) reflect ownership by Punch Taverns; always served in perfect condition. ♨🌙🚌➔🚌(500/501)⬤P

Forest Gate

Bell Common, CM16 4DZ (near B1393, S of Epping, opp Bell Hotel) TL450011

🕐 10-2.30, 5-11; 12-3 (3.30 summer), 7-10.30 Sun

☎ (01992) 572312

Adnams Bitter, Broadside, seasonal beer; Nethergate IPA; Ⓗ **guest beers** Ⓗ/Ⓖ

Run by the same family for many years, this 17th-century pub is a genuine free house specialising in traditional real ale. On the very edge of Epping Forest, it is popular with locals and walkers alike. Snacks are usually available including the house speciality of turkey broth. Friendly dogs are welcome. The large lawn at the front of the pub is a pleasant place for summer drinking. Beers are dispensed both by handpump and gravity. ♨Q🌀✿🌙⬤P

Feering

Sun Inn

3 Feering Hill, CO5 9NH (on B1024, off A12)

🕐 12-3, 6-11 (10.30 Sun)

☎ (01376) 570442 🌐 suninnfeering.com

Beer range varies Ⓗ

Genuine free house in a village close to Kelvedon station. Three drinking areas are separated by low beams which can take their toll on the heads of the unwary. Real log fires add to the cosy atmosphere. Up to six ever-changing ales are on offer, local micro-breweries are well represented, and a dark beer is usually available. Food is served daily, ranging from traditional pub meals to exotic foreign dishes. A lovely large garden, with patio and barbecue area, is to the rear. ♨✿🌙➔(Kelvedon)🚌(71)♣P

Fingringhoe

Whalebone

Chapel Road, CO5 7BG (on B1025 towards Mersea)

❂ 11-3, 5.30-11; 11-11 Sat; 11-10.30 Sun
☎ (01206) 729307

Nethergate IPA; Woodforde's Wherry; guest beers Ⓗ

Early 1700s, Grade II listed village free house, offering two regular and two guest ales, often from local breweries. There is a large open bar and dining area, and a smaller dining room with a varied menu of good home-cooked food. The extensive garden overlooks the river valley and has a small barn which can be hired for functions. Positioned adjacent to the village green and pond, alongside a 12th-century church, this well-maintained pub is popular with locals, ramblers, dog walkers and visitors to the nearby nature reserve.
▲Q❀◐P⇌

Fyfield

Queen's Head

Queen Street, CM5 0RY (just off B184) TL570068
❂ 11-3.30, 6-11; 12-3.30, 7-10.30
☎ (01277) 899231 ∰ queensheadfyfield.co.uk

Adnams Bitter, Broadside; guest beers Ⓗ

Busy 18th-century free house in the centre of the village. It retains a cosy feel with a long, partitioned bar, oak-beamed ceiling and two inglenook fireplaces with real fires. The emphasis here is on dining and food is very popular, leading to overcrowding at times. The garden backs onto the River Roding where guests can relax and soak up the sun while feeding the ducks. The pub normally stocks at least four guest beers from micro-breweries as well as Weston's Old Rosie cider. ▲❀◐❦P

Gestingthorpe

Pheasant

Church Street, CO9 3AU (off B1058 Castle Hedingham to Sudbury road) TL813376
❂ 12-3, 6-11 (not Mon); 12-3 Sun
☎ (01787) 461196

Beer range varies Ⓗ

Set in a tiny village, this traditional pub enjoys a good reputation for its fine food, ale and cider. Recently refurbished, it has three rooms with two bars and a large garden, and enjoys a good local trade. Occasional quiz nights and music evenings make this pub an ideal venue for summer evenings as well as long winter nights. The house beer, Pleasant Pheasant, is brewed by Mauldons. ▲Q❀◐⊟➡❦P

Goldhanger

Chequers

The Square, CM9 8AS (400m from B1026) TL904088
❂ 11-11; 12-10.30 Sun
☎ (01621) 788203 ∰ thechequersgoldhanger.co.uk

Caledonian Deuchars IPA; Flowers IPA; guest beers Ⓗ

This classic country pub and restaurant was a well-deserved winner of local CAMRA Pub of the Year 2006, offering a range of up to six ever-changing ales and boasting a varied menu. Many original 15th-century features can be found in the numerous dining and drinking areas, which include a comfortable lounge bar, snug, games room and lively

public bar. Food is served lunchtimes and evenings (not Sun eve except curry night). Thursday is quiz night and there is a beer festival in March. Guest rooms are available. ▲Q❀✿⊠◐⊟▲❦P⇌

Grays

Theobald Arms

141 Argent Street, RM17 6HR (5 mins from Grays station, down Kings Walk)
❂ 11-3, 5-11; 12-1am Fri & Sat; 12-11 Sun
☎ (01375) 372253 ∰ theobaldarms.com

Courage Best Bitter; guest beers Ⓗ

Genuine, traditional pub with a public bar that has an unusual hexagonal pool table. The changing selection of three guest ales features local independent breweries. A range of unusual bottled beers is also stocked. Regular Easter and summer beer festivals are held in the old stables and on the patio; the summer festival has been running for 10 years. Meals are served at lunchtime at this popular pub.
❀◐⊟&⇌⊟(55)❦P

White Hart

Kings Walk, Argent Street, RM17 6HR (5 mins from Grays station, down Kings Walk)
❂ 12-11.30 (midnight Fri & Sat); 12-11 Sun
☎ (01375) 373319

Crouch Vale Brewers Gold; guest beers Ⓗ

Transformed and rejuvenated a little over a year ago, this traditional local just outside the town centre has views of the River Thames. Two or three guest ales usually include a mild or another dark beer. The landlord continues the success he enjoyed at his previous award-winning club, hosting regular live music events and an annual beer festival. Pool is played and a meeting/function room is available. ▲❀✿⊠⊟⇌⊟(55)❦P⇌

Great Bromley

Cross Inn

Ardleigh Road, CO7 7TL (on B1029 between Gt Bromley and Ardleigh)
❂ 12-2 (not Mon & Tue), 6.30-11; 12-3, 7-10.30 Sun
☎ (01206) 230282

Wadworth IPA; Woodforde's Wherry; guest beer Ⓖ

Quiet, cosy and warm free house with a single bar that feels like a private front room, featuring a wood burner and comfortable seating as well as fresh flowers. The landlord has run previous pubs listed in the Guide and hosts an annual beer and folk festival, usually in May. Booking is advised for meals (served Wed-Sat); occasionally there may be no food when an event takes place. Outside is a large car park and enclosed beer garden. The landlady welcomes dogs and owns two friendly huskies (close the gate!).
▲Q❀✿◐❦P

Snooty Fox

Frating Road, CO7 7JN (on B1029, 500m from A133)
❂ 12-3, 6-11; 12-11 Sun
☎ (01206) 251065

Beer range varies Ⓗ

This village inn built its reputation on its cuisine, and continues to go from strength to strength in the hands of a dedicated family. A constantly-changing range of real ales is now to be found, with the emphasis on micro-breweries and little-seen beers from around the country. The excellent value-for-money meals range from the hearty to the exotic, served in the bar and the dining room.
ÆQ❀◑P

Great Chesterford

Crown & Thistle
High Street, CB10 1PL (near B1383, close to M11/A11 jct)
✪ 12-3, 6-midnight; 12-3, 7-11 Sun
☎ (01799) 530278
Greene King IPA; Woodforde's Wherry; guest beer Ⓗ
Popular pub frequented by locals, including the cricket team. The landlord has lived in the village for 30 years. The pub, built in 1546 as the Chequers, was extended in 1603 to serve as a coaching inn and renamed at the same time. According to legend, James I stopped here on his way to London for his coronation. The magnificent inglenook in the bar is documented as the earliest example of its type in Essex. A patio has seating for outdoor drinking and dining. ÆQ❀✍◑Å⇌P⅃

Great Clacton

Plough
1 North Road, CO15 4DA (near B1032)
✪ 11-midnight (1am Fri & Sat); 12-11.30 Sun
☎ (01255) 429998
Greene King IPA; Shepherd Neame Spitfire; guest beers Ⓗ
Recently refurbished and rebuilt following a devastating fire, this cosy pub has re-established itself as a warm, friendly and lively local and quickly regained its entry in this Guide. It retains a traditional public bar together with a smart lounge. Regular karaoke is held in the public bar and also popular quiz nights. ❀◑Ð&

Great Dunmow

Saracens Head Hotel
30 High Street, CM6 1AG
✪ 12-11 (10.30 Sun)
☎ (01371) 873901 ⊕ thesaracensheadhotel.biz
Greene King IPA, Ruddles County; guest beers Ⓗ
Handy for Stansted Airport, this old coaching inn is now privately owned. Built in 1560, it incorporates an 18th-century façade with Georgian and Tudor features; the bar area has been modernised. The Dunmow Flitch, an ancient ceremony around a flitch (side) of bacon, is held every leap year opposite the hotel. Landlords here have been recorded since 1620 – one of the earliest was a Roundhead. Mighty Oak guest beers are supplemented by beers from other micro-breweries supplied by Mighty Oak.
❀✍◑⌷(33; 133)P

Great Easton

Swan
The Endway, CM6 2HG (off B184, 3 miles N of Dunmow) TL606255
✪ 12-3, 6-11; 12-3, 7-10.30 Sun
☎ (01371) 870359 ⊕ swangreateaston.co.uk
Adnams Bitter; guest beers Ⓗ
A warm welcome is assured at this 15th-century free house situated in an attractive village. A log-burning stove, exposed beams and comfortable sofas feature in the lounge; pool and darts are played in the public bar. Occasional French classes are held here. All meals are freshly prepared to order, no frozen ingredients are used and the majority are home made from local produce. The chef looks after the beers that complement the food. Accommodation is now available in three superb double rooms.
ÆQ❀✍◑⌷Å⌷(313)♣P

Great Yeldham

Waggon & Horses
High Street, CO9 4EX (on A1017)
✪ 11-11 (10.30 Sun)
☎ (01787) 237936 ⊕ waggonandhorses.net
Greene King IPA, Abbot; guest beers Ⓗ
This 16th-century inn is a busy village hostelry where everyone is made welcome. Guest beers are sourced from local brewers and Storm cider, produced locally, is always available. The friendly landlord is a long-term supporter of real ale. Food, served every day, is especially popular at weekends. Sixteen rooms in an annexe overlooking the garden provide overnight accommodation.
Æ❀✍◑♣⊛P

Halstead

Dog Inn
37 Hedingham Road, CO9 2DB (on A1124)
✪ 4 (3 Fri)-midnight; 12-1am Sat; 12-midnight Sun
☎ (01787) 477774 ⊕ innpubs.co.uk
Adnams Bitter, Broadside; guest beers Ⓗ
A classic local pub, the last remaining in a road that once held 11 hostelries. Numerous beams adorn both the public and saloon bars. A beautiful garden overlooks the town, where you can sit in summer and watch petanque being played while enjoying the barbecue. Two guest ales, often from micro-breweries, are on offer, with a mild or another dark beer usually available. En-suite bed and breakfast accommodation is offered. Æ❀✍◑⌷⌷♣P⌷

Harlow

William Aylmer
Aylmer House, Kitson Way, CM20 1DG
✪ 9-midnight (1am Fri & Sat)
☎ (01279) 620630 ⊕ jdwetherspons.co.uk
Greene King IPA; Marston's Pedigree; Shepherd Neame Spitfire; Theakston Best Bitter; guest beers Ⓗ
Situated in the centre of Harlow New Town and converted from a 1960s office building, this pub usually offers interesting guest beers, often from the local Red Squirrel Brewery. It tends to get busy at times, especially with the

night crowd warming up for local clubs at the weekend, but it never seems too crowded. The interior decor is much more appealing than the exterior would suggest. The walls feature murals and pictures relating to the history of Harlow New Town and local medical pioneer William Aylmer. ❀◖❉⬤⇌🚋⬤

Harwich

New Bell Inn

Outpart Eastward, CO12 3EN (200m from eastern end of A120)
✪ 11-3, 7-11 (midnight Sat); 12-4, 7-11 (12-11 summer) Sun
☎ (01255) 503545
Greene King IPA; guest beers Ⓗ
A warm welcome is assured at this friendly and vibrant community pub – local CAMRA Pub of the Year 2007 – which always offers a good selection of guest ales as well as a regular mild. Hearty pub fare is served at lunchtime including excellent home-made soup. The popular front bar, complete with impressive snowglobe collection, gives way to a quieter bar and dining area at the rear, then on to a modest garden. There is a newly refurbished function room upstairs.
❀◖🍴⇌(Harwich Town)🚋P

Hempstead

Bluebell Inn

High Street, CB10 2PD (on B1054, between Saffron Walden and Haverhill)
✪ 12-3, 6-11; 12-11 Fri & Sat; 12-10.30 Sun
☎ (01799) 599199
Adnams Bitter, Broadside; Woodforde's Wherry; guest beers Ⓗ
Late 16th-century village pub with 18th-century additions, reputed to be the birthplace of Dick Turpin; the walls displays posters about his life. The restaurant serves excellent meals from an extensive menu. The large bar has a log fire and ample seating is provided outside, with a children's play area at the rear. Six real ales often include a guest from Fenland or Saffron breweries. Aspall cider comes from Suffolk. Local CAMRA Pub of the Year 2005, it hosts a folk evening on Tuesday.
🏠Q❀◖🍴🚋(Saffron Walden-Haverhill)♣P╚

Heybridge

Heybridge Inn

34 The Street, CM9 4NB (on B1022, opp church, leaving Maldon towards Colchester)
✪ 11-11 (midnight Fri & Sat); 12-10.30 Sun
☎ (01621) 853545
Beer range varies Ⓗ
Friendly local where there are no strangers; only friends you haven't yet met. There has been a pub on this site since 1845. Two changing guest beers plus home-cooked food are usually available. One bar is a dedicated dining area – this is at a lower lever and not easily accessible for wheelchair users. Maldon Poets Society meets here weekly, the Golf Society monthly. Children and pets on leads are welcome. There is limited roadside parking on the main street. 🐕❀🚋♣╚

Maltsters Arms

Hall Road, CM9 4NJ (near B1022)
✪ 12-midnight (10.30 Sun)
☎ (01621) 853880
Beer range varies Ⓖ
This well-supported Gray's house is a single-bar local, where a warm welcome is extended to drinkers and their dogs. Step in straight off the pavement to enjoy the pleasant, traditional atmosphere, enhanced by a collection of bottles and copper bric-a-brac. It can be busy at lunchtimes with locals and ramblers. Two guest beers are usually available and, although no meals are served, a selection of rolls is usually on offer. The patio overlooks the old course of the tidal river.
Q❀♣╚

Horndon-on-the-Hill

Bell Inn

High Road, SS17 8LD (near B1007, opp woolmarket)
✪ 11-2.30 (3 Sat), 5.30 (6 Sat)-11; 12-4, 7-10.30 Sun
☎ (01375) 642463 🌐 bell-inn.co.uk
Draught Bass; Ⓖ **Greene King IPA; guest beers** Ⓗ
Busy 15th-century coaching inn where the bars feature beams, wood-panelling and carvings. Note the unusual hot cross bun collection – a bun is added every Good Friday. Up to five guest ales are stocked, including beers from Essex breweries. The award-winning restaurant is open at all sessions. The inn boasts five honeymoon suites. The hilltop village, now relieved by a by-pass, has a restored woolmarket.
🏠Q❀🛏◖🍴🚋(11, 374)P

Kirby-le-Soken

Red Lion

32 The Street, CO13 0EF (on B1034)
✪ 12-11.30 (12.30am Fri & Sat); 12-10.30 Sun
☎ (01255) 674832
Beer range varies Ⓗ
This perfect village pub appeals to both locals and travellers. Situated right at the heart of the old 'soke', opposite the church, the pub is steeped in history and boasts numerous beams, a priest hole and a resident ghost. An interesting and well-kept range of quality real ale is complemented by excellent value home-cooked food. The flower display in summer is spectacular. An annual beer festival takes place in the large garden in August.
🏠❀◖🚋♣P

Lamarsh

Lamarsh Lion

Bures Road, CO8 5EP (1¼ miles NW of Bures)
TL892355
✪ 12-11
☎ (01787) 227918
Greene King IPA; Nethergate Old Growler; Ⓖ
guest beers Ⓗ /Ⓖ
Late 14th-century country free house with superb views over the Stour Valley. It has a large single drinking area including log fires, plenty of oak beams and other original features, plus a games room with pool table and TV. As well as the regular ales there are

guest beers often from micro-breweries. The inn is popular with ramblers walking the Stour Valley from Manningtree to Newmarket, and a full and varied restaurant menu is available. B&B accommodation is also on offer. ♨Q☺☼✿🅰◑ 🅰♣♠P╘🖢

Langley Lower Green

Bull

CB11 4SB (off B1038 at Clavering) TL436345
☼ 12-2 (3 Sat), 6-11; 12-3, 7-10.30 Sun
☎ (01799) 777307
Greene King IPA, Abbot, seasonal beers Ⓗ
Classic Victorian village local with original cast-iron lattice windows and fireplaces. This friendly pub in beautiful, rolling countryside, two miles from the highest point in Essex, is well worth seeking out. It sits in a tiny isolated hamlet, less than a mile from the Hertfordshire border and just a bit further from Cambridgeshire. A long-distance footpath passes within a mile. The pub has a devoted band of regulars including cricket and football teams. Meals can be arranged with advance notice. ♨Q☺🅱🖢P

Layer-de-la-Haye

Donkey & Buskins

Layer Road, CO2 0HU (on B1026, S of Colchester) TL974208
☼ 11.30-3, 6-11; 11.30-11.30 Sat; 12-10.30 Sun
☎ (01206) 734774
Greene King IPA; guest beers Ⓗ
This village freehouse has established an excellent reputation for beer, wine and food, with up to three guest ales available – local micro-breweries are well supported. A friendly welcome is assured in the two comfortable bars, and in the dining areas an extensive, diverse range of home-cooked meals may be enjoyed. Sunday night's pub quiz is popular. A large, secluded garden offers peaceful summertime drinking. There are two guest rooms available. ♨Q☺☼✿🅰◑ 🅱🖢🖟P╘🖢

Leigh-on-Sea

Broker

213-217 Leigh Road, SS9 1JA
☼ 11-11 (midnight Fri & Sat); 12-11 Sun
☎ (01702) 471932 ⊕ brokerfreehouse.co.uk
Everards Tiger; Fuller's London Pride; St Austell Tribute; Shepherd Neame Spitfire; Young's Bitter; guest beers Ⓗ
Friendly, family-run free house that has featured in every edition of this Guide since 1996. It has a garden with a covered and heated area for smokers and a small pavement seating area at the front. This sporty, community pub organises local charity events including quizzes or live music on Sunday evening. Bar and restaurant meals are served at lunchtime. Children are welcome until 7.30pm in a sectioned-off area of the bar. Two guest beers are stocked.
☺◑⇌(Chalkwell)🖟♣╘

Elms

1060 London Road, SS9 3ND (on A13, approx 2½ miles W of Southend-on-Sea)

☼ 9-midnight (1am Fri & Sat)
☎ (01702) 474687
Courage Directors; Greene King Old Speckled Hen, Abbot; Marston's Pedigree; guest beers Ⓗ
Old coaching inn converted by Wetherspoon into a large, busy, traditional-style pub decorated with old photos of the local area. The restaurant area offers breakfast until noon, and main meals and snacks are served throughout the day. There are up to four constantly-changing guest ales, plus two real ciders from Weston's. Children are admitted up to 9pm. There is no music, but there are TVs and fruit machines. Outside is a paved, heated area for smokers. ☺☼◑👶🖟♣╘

Lexden

Crown Inn

235 Lexden Road, CO3 4DA (at A1124/A133 jct)
☼ 11.30-2.30, 5-midnight; 11.30-midnight Sat; 12-11 Sun
☎ (01206) 572071
Beer range varies Ⓗ
Situated on the western outskirts of Colchester, with good bus connections from the town centre, the Crown is developing a fine reputation. Up to eight ales are on offer and local micro-breweries are well represented; a good, varied food menu is also served. This three-room pub has a large public bar where pop memorabilia adorns the walls and darts and pool are played. Outside, the large, walled garden is furnished with benches. Close to Lexden Park, Colchester Caravan and Camping Park is also nearby.
☺☼◑👶🅱🖟♣P╘

Little Baddow

Rodney

North Hill, CM3 4TQ TL778080
☼ 11-11 (10.30 Sun)
☎ (01245) 222385
Greene King IPA; guest beers Ⓗ
The Rodney was built as a farmhouse circa 1650 and has been a pub since the early 1800s, also serving as a grocer's and a bakery until the early 20th century. It has a public bar with a pool table, a small snug and a compact drinking/dining area decorated with seafaring items. One of the guest beers is sometimes Rodney's, which is rebadged Morland Original, while the other ale generally comes from a smaller brewery. The food is all home-cooked and includes daily specials. Q☺☼◑🅱♣P

Little Clacton

Apple Tree

The Street, CO16 9LF
☼ 12-11.30 (2am Fri & Sat); 12-11 Sun
☎ (01255) 861026
Beer range varies Ⓖ
Little Clacton's renowned pub continues to win plaudits for the quality of its beer. Its Real Ale Club is thriving and works with the landlord to offer a good range of bitters and milds, including ales from micro-breweries such as Mighty Oak and Mauldons. Live music plays at the weekend and a pool table attracts a younger clientele. The TV screens Sky Sports.

Can you see the ghost in the picture hanging above the bar? ❀&♿♣P⁵⁻

Little Dunmow

Flitch of Bacon
The Street, CM6 3HT (850m S of B1256) TL656216
🕐 12-3 (not Mon), 5.30-11; 12-5, 7-10.30 Sun
☎ (01371) 820323
Fuller's London Pride; Greene King IPA; guest beers Ⓗ
The pub sign shows a side (or flitch) of bacon – this is the prize awarded to a married couple who have not argued for a year, in an ancient ceremony that still takes place. Note, too, the old signs advertising Bass and Worthington in bottles. The beamed bar has a large fireplace and leads to the restaurant at the rear. A good range of locally sourced food complements the well-kept beer at this traditional, rural pub. ♨Q❀♿♣◑⊟(133)

Little Thurrock

Traitor's Gate
40-42 Broadway, RM17 6EW (on A126, 1 mile E of Grays town centre)
🕐 12-11 (10.30 Sun)
☎ (01375) 372628
Beer range varies Ⓗ
Two changing guest beers are served at this friendly pub, frequented by a lively mix of people. There is an amazing collection of pump clips on display – approaching 1,500 – from ales that have featured over the years. Live music plays on Friday and Saturday, and there is an impressive collection of recorded music. Sport features on TV on most evenings. The beer garden won Thurrock in Bloom in 2004 and 2005. Home-made bar snacks are served. ❀⊟(66)♣

Little Totham

Swan
School Road, CM9 8LB (2 miles SE of B1022, between Tiptree & Maldon) TL889117
🕐 11-11; 12-10.30 Sun
☎ (01621) 892689 ⊕ theswanpublichouse.co.uk
Adnams Bitter; Crouch Vale Brewers Gold; Mighty Oak Oscar Wilde Mild, Maldon Gold; Woodforde's Wherry; guest beers Ⓖ
Archetypal 16th-century, beamed village pub; the unspoilt public bar has a dartboard, while the saloon features open fires and has an air filtration system. Twice national CAMRA Pub of the Year, it has a large garden to the front; walkers, muddy boots and dogs are all welcome. Customers may bring their own food by arrangement. The house beer Totham Parva is brewed by Mighty Oak, and several traditional ciders and perries are usually available. The summer beer festival in June is popular. Live acoustic performances and morris dancing are staged throughout the year. ♨Q❀♿&♣▲♣P⁵⁻⊟

Little Walden

Crown
High Street, CB10 1XA (on B1052, 2 miles NE of Saffron Walden)

🕐 11.30-2.30 (3 Sat), 6-11; 12-10.30 Sun
☎ (01799) 522475
Adnams Broadside; City of Cambridge Boathouse Bitter; Greene King IPA; guest beers Ⓖ
Charming, beamed country pub featuring a large walk-through fireplace. An extensive food menu is on offer with evening meals available Tuesday to Saturday. Racked cask stillage is used for dispensing an excellent range of beers. This recently extended 18th-century pub, located in a quiet hamlet, attracts customers from Saffron Walden. It is used for club meetings and hosts trad jazz on Wednesday evening. Accommodation is due for completion in 2007. ♨Q❀♿◑P

Loughton

Victoria Tavern
165 Smarts Lane, IG10 4EP (near A121)
🕐 11-3, 5-11; 12-10.30 Sun
☎ (020) 85081779
Adnams Bitter; Greene King IPA; Hancocks Bitter; Harveys Sussex Best Bitter; Taylor Landlord Ⓗ
The Victoria is a large, clean, friendly regulars' pub, given a rural feel by the photos of old Loughton that adorn the walls. It has a single horseshoe-shaped bar with a raised area for dining, but visitors are more than welcome to just pop in for a drink. There is a large, pleasant garden with a shady tree, and a spacious car park. Q❀◑Θ⊟P

Maldon

Blue Boar Hotel
Silver Street, CM9 4QE (off top end of High Street, opp All Saints Church)
🕐 11-11; 12-10.30 Sun
☎ (01621) 855888 ⊕ blueboarmaldon.co.uk
Adnams Bitter, Broadside; Crouch Vale Brewers Gold; Farmer's Nelson's Blood, Hotel Porter, Pucks Folly Ⓖ
The Blue Boar has been a hotel for more than 400 years. The two bars are original, from the oak beams to the antiques on the walls. The front bar has an inviting open fire, while the back bar houses the beers on gravity dispense. Three ales are always available from Farmer's Ales who brew in the old stables behind the hotel, and there are occasional guest beers. The upstairs function room hosts regular jazz and other music sessions as well as meetings. ♨Q❀♿◑⊟P⁵⁻

Queen's Head
The Hythe, CM9 5HN
🕐 10 (12 Sun)-11
☎ (01621) 854112
Adnams Broadside; Mighty Oak Maldon Gold, Burntwood; guest beer (occasional) Ⓗ
A pleasant pub, some 600 years old, on the quay where the sailing barges are moored. The rear bar overlooks the River Blackwater, and there is a spacious outdoor seating area on the quayside with sun umbrellas, an outside bar and barbecue. The front bar, warmed by a log fire, is a locals' meeting place. Food is served in the restaurant and bars, with seafood a speciality on the extensive menu. Children are allowed in the

restaurant. Good disabled access and WC facilities are provided. ♨⊛◑♿⌂

Swan Hotel

71/73 High Street, CM9 5EP
◐ 11-11; 12-10.30 Sun
☎ (01621) 853170
Fuller's London Pride; Mighty Oak Maldon Gold; Woodforde's Wherry; guest beers ⊞
Very popular Gray & Sons house, centrally located in the busy high street of this historic maritime town. The building dates from the 14th century and retains many period features. A good selection of well-kept real ales is available. The food menu is varied and updated daily, and there is a separate dining area. The Bewick Suite hosts live music and events, and the car park is used for the monthly farmers' market. Regular quiz nights are held, and pool and dominoes played. ⇔◑♣P

Warwick Arms

185 High Street, CM9 5BU
◐ 12-midnight (1am Fri & Sat)
☎ (01621) 850122
Mighty Oak Maldon Gold; guest beers ⊞
Dating from the late 1830s, this hostelry became the Warwick Arms in 1899. A friendly, lively pub, popular for good conversation, it offers excellent beer from local breweries including two or three changing guests. The landlord is a biking enthusiast, and there is a small display of old helmets on a shelf behind the bar. Occasionally, live music is played, usually on a Friday or Sunday. There is a bus stop right outside the pub. ♨⛽♣P

Manningtree

Red Lion

44 South Street, CO11 1BG (400m from High Street)
◐ 12-3, 5-11; 12-10.30 Sun
☎ (01206) 395052
Adnams Bitter; Caledonian Deuchars IPA; guest beers ⊞
Quaint pub split on two levels – the lower bar displays a print of Nelson accepting the surrender of a Spanish ship and the bar on the upper level has a cosy atmosphere. Crib, dominoes and darts are popular. The pub is renowned for its Tuesday night tapas evenings. The function room is ideal for meetings and hosts the expanding new CAMRA branch. Q♒⊛⊛◑≠⛽♣

Margaretting Tye

White Hart Inn

Swan Lane, CM4 9JX TL684011
◐ 11.30-3, 6-11; 11.30-midnight Sat & Sun
☎ (01277) 840478 ⊕ thewhitehart.uk.com
Adnams Bitter, Broadside; Mighty Oak IPA; ⊞ **guest beers** ⒼG
This local CAMRA Pub of the Year 2007 is based in a large building with an L-shaped bar. The original inn was built in the 16th century and a modern conservatory added recently. It is deservedly popular for its food (not served Mon eve) as well as its beer. There are usually at least six ales available, with

plenty of variety and always excellent quality. The expansive grounds include a children's play area and a pets' corner. Beer festivals are held in June and October. ♨Q♒⊛⊛◑♿♣

Mill Green

Viper ☆

Mill Green Road, CM4 0PT TL641019
◐ 12-3, 6-11; 12-11 Sat; 12-10.30 Sun
☎ (01277) 352010
Mighty Oak Oscar Wilde; guest beers ⊞
Isolated, unspoilt country pub with a lounge, public bar and wood-panelled snug. Viper ales are commissioned from Mighty Oak and Nethergate, who are also regular suppliers of the four guest beers, but guests may come from anywhere in the country. The cider is generally Weston's. A beer festival is held in September. Good home-cooked food is served at lunchtime. ♨Q⊛⊛◑⛽♣♣P

Monk Street

Farmhouse Inn

CM6 2NR (off B184, 2 miles S of Thaxted) TL614289
◐ 11-midnight
☎ (01371) 830864 ⊕ farmhouseinn.org
Greene King IPA; Mighty Oak Oscar Wilde, Maldon Gold; guest beers ⊞
Built in the 16th century, this former Dunmow Brewery pub was enlarged to incorporate a restaurant (in the old cart shed) and accommodation; the bar is in the original part of the building. Cider is sold in summer. The quiet hamlet of Monk Street overlooks the Chelmer Valley, two miles from historic Thaxted, and is convenient for Stansted Airport and the M11. A well in the pub garden is no longer used, but it did supply the hamlet with water during WWII. ⊛⇔◑⛽(313)♣P⌂

Navestock

Alma Arms

Horseman Side, CM14 5ST TQ544961
◐ 11.30-4, 5.30-11; 11.30-11 Sat; 12-10.30 Sun
☎ (01277) 372629 ⊕ almaarms.moonfruit.com
Shepherd Neame Master Brew Bitter, Spitfire or Bishops Finger; guest beer ⊞
This pleasant 16th-century country pub places its accent on food, and its conservatory extension is used as a restaurant. Shepherd Neame Spitfire and Bishops Finger alternate, and it offers one guest beer, often from a local Essex brewery such as Brentwood, Mighty Oak or Nethergate. There are plans for a marquee outside to accommodate smokers. ⊛◑P⌂

Orsett

Foxhound

18 High Road, RM16 3ER (on B188)
◐ 11-3.30, 6-11.30; 11-11.30 Fri & Sat; 12-11 Sun
☎ (01375) 891295
Courage Best Bitter; Greene King IPA; guest beer ⊞
Two-bar village local that is at the centre of social life in Orsett. It has a comfortable saloon and a basic but characterful public bar. The guest beers are usually from the Crouch Vale portfolio or other independent breweries. The

Fox's Den restaurant provides excellent meals at lunchtime and Wednesday to Saturday evenings (booking necessary); it is also available for functions and business meetings. Quiz nights are held regularly.
♔❀◑⊟♿⊟♣P⚡

Paglesham

Punch Bowl

Churchend, SS4 2DP (follow signs from Rochford to Paglesham)
⊙ 11.30-3 (2 Mon), 6.30-11; 12-3, 6.30-11 Sun
☎ (01702) 258376
Adnams Bitter; guest beers Ⓗ
South-facing, white, Essex weatherboarded pub situated in a one-street village. Dating from the 16th century, this former bakery and sailmaker's house has been an ale house since the mid-1800s, when notorious smuggler William Blyth (known as Hard Apple) drank and concealed his contraband here. The low-beamed bar displays a large collection of mugs, brassware and old pictures. It has a number of picnic tables outside at the front.
❀◑P

Radwinter

Plough

Sampford Road, CB10 2TL (B1053/B1054 jct) TL613375
⊙ 12-3, 6-11; 12-4, 7-9 Sun
☎ (01799) 599222
Archers Bitter; Greene King IPA; Saffron Pledgdon Ale; guest beer Ⓗ
Atmospheric, quiet and relaxing Grade II listed building on a country crossroads near the edge of the village, with an attractive, large garden. A 40-seat restaurant area separate from the main bar has been added, offering a large selection of wholesome meals at lunchtimes and evenings. Regularly-changing guest beers are dispensed from local breweries.
♔❀⛟◑♿♣P⚡

Rayleigh

Roebuck

138 High Street, SS6 7BU (on A129, opp police station)
⊙ 9-midnight (1am Fri & Sat)
☎ (01268) 748430
Greene King Abbot; Marston's Pedigree; Shepherd Neame Spitfire; guest beers Ⓗ
Friendly Wetherspoon pub in the High Street, close to the shops, stocking an excellent choice of guest ales and Weston's cider. Meals are served all day until 11pm and children are welcome in a sectioned-off area. It hosts well-attended beer festivals and a popular Curry Club on Thursday evening. A cordoned-off area at the front of the pub is available for alfresco drinking. Rayleigh is served by many buses and has a rail station. Q❀◑♿⇌⊟●⚡

Ridgewell

White Horse Inn

Mill Road, CO9 4SG (on A1017, between Halstead and Haverhill) TL737410
⊙ 12-3 (not Mon & Tue), 6-11; 12-10.30 Sun
☎ (01440) 785532 🌐ridgewellwh.com
Beer range varies Ⓖ
Essex CAMRA Pub of the Year 2006, the White Horse offers an ever-changing range of beers from a wide variety of local and national breweries. Ales from Mighty Oak, Mauldons and Nethergate sit alongside Caledonian or Hop Back brews, all dispensed by gravity. Real ciders come from Biddenden and Weston's. This 1860s pub has an atmosphere second to none. The excellent restaurant attracts organisations such as the Royal British Legion and CAMRA, who hold their official lunches/dinners here. Luxury en-suite accommodation is available. ♔❀⛟◑♿♣●P⚡

Rochford

Blanchfields Bar

1 Southend Road, SS4 1HA
⊙ 11-11; 12-10.30 Sun
☎ (01702) 544015 🌐blanchfields.co.uk
Beer range varies Ⓗ
A changing range of up to eight real ales from micro-breweries is on offer at this excellent bar, the tap for Blanchfields Brewery, voted SE Essex Pub of the Year in 2006 by local CAMRA members. Three ciders are also available: Double Vision is a regular, the others are changing guests. Furnished with comfortable sofas and offering excellent, good value meals, it also hosts live music events, themed evenings and regular beer festivals.
❀◑⇌⊟(7, 8)●P⊡

Golden Lion

35 North Street, SS4 1AB
⊙ 11-11 (midnight Fri & Sat)
☎ (01702) 545487
Adnams Bitter; Crouch Vale Brewers Gold; Greene King Abbot; guest beers Ⓗ
Classic, 16th-century traditional Essex weatherboarded free house with stained-glass windows and hops above the bar. A frequent local CAMRA award winner, it always serves six ales including three changing guests, one always a dark beer. Recent updates include a patio garden at the back of the pub, a fireplace with a traditional log burner and a TV showing major sporting events. Bar snacks are available Monday to Friday.
♔❀◐⇌⊟(7, 8)♣●

King's Head Inn

11 West Street, SS4 1BE (in town square)
⊙ 12-midnight
☎ (01702) 531741
Shepherd Neame Kent's Best Invicta Ale, Spitfire, Bishops Finger, seasonal beer Ⓗ
A Shepherd Neame pub, this was originally a coaching inn and it is rumoured that Henry VIII stayed here. The landlord is currently restoring the interior and has discovered much of the original woodwork. A friendly pub, it provides much-needed entertainment in Rochford in the form of regular live music.
♔⛟◐⇌⊟(7, 8)⚡

Roundbush (Purleigh)

Roundbush Inn

Fambridge Road, CM9 6NN (by B1010, Maldon-Fambridge road)

✪ 12-2.30, 5.30-11; 12-11 Sun

☎ (01621) 828354

Mighty Oak IPA; guest beers Ⓖ

Traditional, friendly roadside Gray's house with all beers on gravity dispense. The main bar has a homely, cottage feel, where conversation is the main entertainment; the second bar is more basic and has a TV. An extensive menu of good food is on offer, served in a third room used by diners. The pub also has an adjoining café where guests may enjoy an early breakfast. ▲Q❀◑◧✦P

Rowhedge

Albion

High Street, CO5 7ES (3 miles S of Colchester)

✪ 12-3 (not Mon), 5-11; 12-11 Thu-Sat; 12-10.30 Sun

☎ (01206) 728972

Beer range varies Ⓗ/Ⓖ

Village free house and well-deserved local CAMRA Pub of the Year 2007, it serves a constantly changing range of up to four beers, usually from micro-breweries, with a tantalising list of forthcoming beers displayed above the bar. The pub overlooks the River Colne, where a nearby foot passenger ferry operates in summer to Wivenhoe. Several mini beer festivals are held, including St George's Day and an event to coincide with the village regatta in June. Occasional live music plays. ❀◰(66)✦

Roxwell

Chequers

The Street, CM1 4PD

✪ 12-2.30 (Sat only), 5 (6 Sat)-11; 12-3.30, 7-10.30 Sun

☎ (01245) 248240

Greene King IPA, Abbot; Mighty Oak Maldon Gold Ⓗ

This 17th-century village inn retains several original beams in its single bar. The gentle hum of conversation dominates as background music is kept low and the TV is only occasionally pressed into service. There is a pool table in a separate room. The landlord will open on weekday lunchtimes for parties by prior arrangement. ▲◰P⅄–⊟

Saffron Walden

Old English Gentleman

11 Gold Street, CB10 1EJ (50m E of B184/B1052 jct)

✪ 11-2am (11 Sun & Mon); 11-1am Fri & Sat

☎ (01799) 523595

Adnams Bitter; Greene King IPA; guest beers Ⓗ

This 18th-century town-centre pub has log fires and a welcoming atmosphere. It serves a selection of guest ales and an extensive tapas-style lunchtime menu which changes regularly. Filled baguettes and sandwiches are available in the bar or the dining area where a variety of works of art is displayed. Saffron Walden is busy on Tuesday and Saturday

market days. The pub has a pleasant patio at the rear. ▲❀◑⅄–

Railway

Station Road, CB10 3HQ (300m SE of war memorial)

✪ 12-3, 6-11 (midnight Thu-Sat)

☎ (01799) 522208

Draught Bass; guest beers Ⓗ

Typical 19th-century town-centre railway tavern, recently refurbished to a high standard, where railway memorabilia include model trains above the bar and in the garden. The single, large bar features a mix of furniture and fittings that helps to convey a relaxed, comfortable atmosphere. An extensive menu of good meals is available lunchtimes and evenings. ❀◑◧P⅄–

Southend-on-Sea

Cornucopia

39 Marine Parade, SS1 2EN (on seafront)

✪ 10-11; 12-10.30 Sun

☎ (01702) 460770 ⊕ cornucopia.county-of-essex.com

Beer range varies Ⓗ

The smallest pub in Essex offers a big welcome to all. Two ales, supplied by Mighty Oak, are always on form, ensuring a loyal regular clientele. The pub has Sky TV and a large selection of music, with requests played. Day-tripper humour adds to the jovial atmosphere. In summer guests can sit outside and people-watch.
❀⇆≢(Southend Central)◰

Liberty Belle

10-12 Marine Parade, SS1 2EJ (on seafront)

✪ 10-11; 12-10.30 Sun

☎ (01702) 466936

Courage Best Bitter; Greene King Abbot; Hop Back Summer Lightning; guest beer Ⓗ

A regulars' pub, serving one frequently-changing guest beer – Hop Back Summer Lightning is always available. Special discounts on the beers are available to senior citizens. The bar has a pool table and juke box, and occasional live bands play. It can get busy during the summer months, but it is always pleasant sitting out front on a warm evening. Open all day, every day, the pub is easily accessible from the town centre.
❀&≢(Southend Central)◰✦–

Southminster

Station Arms

39 Station Road, CM0 7EW (near B1018/B1021)

✪ 12-2.30, 6 (5.30 Thu & Fri)-11; 2-11 Sat; 12-4, 7-10.30 Sun

☎ (01621) 772225 ⊕ thestationarms.co.uk

Adnams Bitter; Crouch Vale Brewers Gold; Dark Star Hophead; Mighty Oak Oscar Wilde; guest beers Ⓗ

This rare example of a traditional, Essex weatherboarded local continues to thrive, providing an excellent range of attractively-priced real ales and catering for the connoisseur. At least 10 guests are sold every week, with two on at any time, as well as Weston's cider. Beer festivals are hosted in the pub's tastefully restored barn. The enclosed garden is a plus and barbecues are held at festival time. The pub has won several CAMRA Pub of the Year awards. Regular live music is staged. ᴀᴀQ☀≈♣⌂♣♨⌐

Stansted Mountfitchet

Rose & Crown

31 Bentfield Green, CM24 8BX (on old A11, ½ mile W of B1383) TL507255
☼ 12-3, 6-11 (1am Fri); 12-1am Sat; 12-midnight Sun
☎ (01279) 812107
Adnams Bitter; Fuller's London Pride; guest beers ℍ
Typical Victorian pub near a duck pond on the edge of a small hamlet, now part of Stansted Mountfitchet village. This free house has been modernised to provide one large bar, but retains the atmosphere of a village local and is well used by locals. The front of the pub is brightened by floral displays. Food is basic but always excellent and good value (no eve meals Sun). ᴀᴀ☀⌁⌂(7)♣♨⌐

Stapleford Tawney

Moletrap

Tawney Common, CM16 7PU (3 miles E of Epping, 1½ miles SW of Toot Hill) TL500013
☼ 11.30-2.30, 6-11; 12-4, 6-10.30 Sun
☎ (01992) 522394
Fuller's London Pride; guest beers ℍ
Former McMullen house, now a free house, this old country pub enjoys superb views over the surrounding countryside. At least two guest beers from small independent breweries are usually on offer and good home-cooked food is served. The small bar can get crowed in summer, although the outside drinking area is delightful in good weather. Despite being just a few miles from the M25, this pub is rather remote and difficult to find, but well worth the effort. ᴀᴀ☀⌁⌂P

Stebbing

White Hart

High Street, CM6 3SQ (2 miles N of old A120 Dunmow to Braintree road)
☼ 11-3, 5-11; 11-11 Sat; 12-10.30 Sun
☎ (01371) 856383
Adnams Bitter; Greene King IPA; guest beers ℍ
Friendly 15th-century timbered inn in a picturesque village. This comfortable pub features exposed beams, an open fire, eclectic collections from chamber pots to cigarette cards, an old red post box in an interior bar wall and a section of exposed lathe and plaster wall behind a glass screen. A community pub, it is used by several local teams including badminton, indoor bowls and cricket. Good value food is served daily. Live music is performed on Sunday afternoon and occasionally on Saturday evening.
ᴀᴀQ☀⌁♣♨⌐

Stock

Hoop

High Street, CM4 9BD (by B1007)
☼ 11-11 (12.30am Fri, midnight Sat); 12-10.30 Sun
☎ (01277) 841137 ⊕ thehoop.co.uk
Adnams Bitter; ℍ **guest beers** ⒢
This recently refurbished, 15th-century weatherboarded pub has a rustic theme in its large bar area. The upstairs restaurant specialises in 'one pot' dining; bar meals are also served and all food is home-cooked. At least four guest beers are on gravity dispense and the house beer, Hoop, Stock & Barrel, is brewed for the pub by Brentwood Brewery. The large garden is the setting for the long-established spring bank holiday beer festival. Barbecues are held throughout the summer. There is a covered, heated area for smokers. Q☀⌁⌂⌁⌂(100)♣♨⌐

Stow Maries

Prince of Wales

Woodham Road, CM3 6SA (near B1012) TQ830993
☼ 11-11 (midnight Fri & Sat)
☎ (01261) 828971 ⊕ prince-stowmaries.co.uk
Beer range varies ℍ/⒢
Reopened in 1990, having sat empty for several years, this 17th-century inn was very nearly lost altogether. A gem of a pub, it has three open-plan drinking areas, all warmed by real fires. The beer range is varied and includes locals such as Farmer's, and not so local, as well as draught and bottled Belgian beers. Meals are available lunchtimes and evenings, often featuring fish or seafood specialities. In summer, drinks and food may be enjoyed outside in the garden. The annual fireworks display is famous locally.
ᴀᴀQ☞☀⌁♣⌂♣P

Tendring

Cherry Tree Inn

Crow Lane, CO16 9AD (on B1035/Crow Lane jct)
☼ 11-2, 6-11; closed Mon; 12-4 Sun
☎ (01255) 830340
Adnams Bitter; Greene King IPA; guest beers ℍ
Visitors and regulars alike are guaranteed a friendly welcome at the Cherry Tree. The tranquil bar is the perfect place to enjoy a variety of fine quality, well-kept beers. Two further areas provide a similar ambience, where diners can savour excellent food. On a warm summer evening you can take your beer outside and relax in the front garden. ☀⌁⌂P

Tollesbury

King's Head

1 High Street, CM9 8RG (on B1023, 5 miles SE of Tiptree)
☼ 12-11 (midnight Fri & Sat); 12-10.30 Sun
☎ (01621) 869203
Adnams Bitter; Greene King IPA; guest beers ℍ
Classic, lively, village free house adjacent to the church and open square, frequented by locals. The welcoming bar staff dispense three guest ales, often including a dark beer. The good-sized, beamed lounge bar has a separate area for a large-screen TV, showing live sports events. A smaller seating area is available to the rear, and the public bar has a pool table and darts. This community pub hosts regular folk nights and visits from motorcycle clubs. ᴀᴀ☀⌁⌂♣P

Warley

Brave Nelson

138 Woodman Road, CM14 5AL (½ mile E of B186)

🕐 12-4, 5-11 (11.30 Sat); 12-3.30, 7-10.30 Sun

☎ (01277) 211690

Greene King IPA; Nethergate Suffolk County Best Bitter; guest beer Ⓗ

Cosy local featuring wood-panelled bars with understated nautical memorabilia including pictures, drawings and plates. A rare, regular outlet in the area for Nethergate Suffolk County Best Bitter, the guest beer is often from Brentwood Brewery. Regular Sunday evening quizzes are well attended, starting at around 9pm. Widescreen TVs usually show sport, and darts, pool and crib are played. Live music features twice a month. No food is served on Sunday. 🏮🍴❋P🕯

Weeley

White Hart

Clacton Road, Weeley Heath, CO16 9SD

🕐 12-2.30, 4-11; 12-11 Fri-Sun

☎ (01255) 830384

Beer range varies Ⓗ

Friendly local where the landlord continues to supply a range of micro-brewed beers to satisfy the most ardent of real ale lovers. Three to four handpumps are usually in use. A thriving real ale club is able to influence the choice of beers on offer to regulars. A smoking area outside is planned. Without doubt this little gem is out in the sticks, however a regular bus service runs through the village. 🏮🚆❋P🕯

Wendens Ambo

Bell

Royston Road, CB11 4JY (on B1039, 1 mile W of B1383/old A11 jct)

🕐 11.30-3, 6-11; 11.30-12.30am Fri & Sat; 12-11.30 Sun

☎ (01799) 540382

Adnams Bitter; Woodforde's Wherry; guest beers Ⓗ

Classic country pub at the centre of a picturesque village near Saffron Walden. A past winner of local CAMRA Pub of the Year, it has an enormous garden where a beer festival is staged in the summer. Audley End station, on the Liverpool Street to Cambridge line, is five minutes' walk, and buses from Saffron Walden bring you to this welcoming hostelry. 🏮Q🏮🍴➷(Audley End)🚆P

Westcliff-on-Sea

Cricketers

225 London Road, SS0 7JG (on A13)

🕐 11-midnight daily (2am Fri & Sat)

☎ (01702) 343168

Greene King IPA, Abbot; guest beers Ⓗ

This large, street-corner pub on the edge of Southend is very popular and with its late licence gets especially busy at the weekend. A Gray & Sons pub, it serves up to five ales and two ciders, all constantly changing. An excellent music venue, Club Riga, at the back adds to the feel-good factor. Occasional beer

festivals are held. The pub is on a bus route and is also close to Southend Victoria or Westcliff rail stations. 🏮🏮🍴➷(Southend Victoria/Westcliff)🚆❋P

Wivenhoe

Horse & Groom

55 The Cross, CO7 9QL (on B1028, approx 1 mile from station)

🕐 10.30-3, 5.30 (6 Sat)-11 (midnight Fri); 12-4.30, 7-10.30 Sun

☎ (01206) 824928

Adnams Bitter, Broadside, seasonal beers; guest beers Ⓗ

Dating from the late 1700s, this pub has a plush, cosy saloon and a busy L-shaped public bar, decorated in keeping with its age, with a light, airy atmosphere. The jovial, long-serving hosts offer a dependable range of Adnams beers, and an ever-changing guest selection. Chatty locals will always welcome visitors. Food is served Monday to Saturday lunchtime. The pub has several darts teams, and offers a range of pub games. There is a small garden to the rear. Accessible by bus or a one mile walk from Wivenhoe station. 🏮🍴🚆❋P

Woodham Mortimer

Hurdlemakers Arms

Post Office Road, CM9 6ST (off A414)

🕐 12-3, 5 (6.30 Sat)-11.30; 12-11 Sun

☎ (01245) 225169

Beer range varies Ⓗ

Winner of local CAMRA Most Improved Pub in 2005, this Gray & Sons country inn has a community focus and is very popular with walkers. The energetic tenants host many special events throughout the year, while darts, crib and dominoes are played in the unspoilt public bar. The cosy lounge incorporates a dining area and overlooks the huge garden. Three guest beers change regularly and often include a dark ale. Traditional cider is also stocked. 🏮Q🏮🍴🚆❋P🕯

Writtle

Wheatsheaf

70 The Green, CM1 3DU (S of A1060)

🕐 11-3, 5-11.30; 11-midnight Fri & Sat; 12-11 Sun

☎ (01245) 420695 ⊕ wheatsheafph-writtle.co.uk

Greene King IPA, Abbot; Mighty Oak Oscar Wilde, Maldon Gold, Burntwood Ⓗ

Traditional village pub with a small public bar and an equally small lounge attracting a wide variety of customers. The atmosphere is generally quiet as the TV is only switched on for occasional sporting events. A folk night is held on the third Friday of each month. The Gray & Sons sign in the public bar was rescued from the brewery when it closed in 1974. There is a small roadside patio. Q🍴❋P🕯

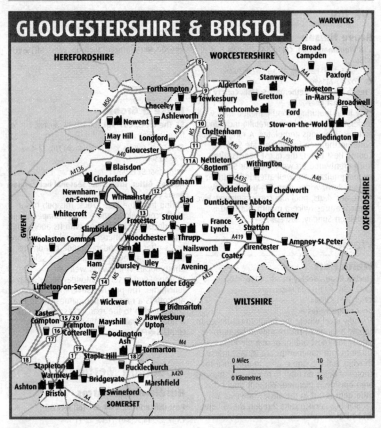

GLOUCESTERSHIRE & BRISTOL

Alderton

Gardeners Arms

Beckford Road, GL20 8NL (follow brown tourist sign from B4077)
🕐 12-2.30, 6-11 (10.30 Sun)
☎ (01242) 620257
Beer range varies Ⓗ

This listed 16th-century oak-beamed free house, at the heart of a quiet village, has an original well in the lounge. There is also a piano, and the walls are adorned with local photographs. Four handpumps serve a variety of beers changing weekly. The pub stages charity events and hosts Whitsun and Christmas mini beer festivals, which focus on local brewers. Other entertainments include a popular monthly quiz and live music performed on Friday evening. The extensive range of delicious home-cooked meals often includes fresh fish specials. The pub also serves bar meals, runs themed food nights and offers a take-away service. ♨Q♣◑ЄP

Ampney St Peter

Red Lion ☆

GL7 5SL (on A417)
🕐 12-2 (Sat only), 6-10; 12-2 Sun
☎ (01285) 851596
Hook Norton Hooky Bitter; Taylor Golden Best, Landlord Ⓗ

This superb 400-year-old pub seems caught in a time warp. Little appears to have changed since the jovial veteran landlord was a babe in arms. It has two tiny flagstone-floored rooms with open fires. There is no bar counter – the beer is served from the corner of one room. Only one beer is available most weekdays, two at weekends. This local CAMRA Pub of the Year 2007 is a rare gem where chat reigns supreme. It serves no food at all, and while it opens bank holiday lunchtimes, it is closed Sunday evening. ♨Q♣ЄⴖP

INDEPENDENT BREWERIES

Arbor Bristol: Stapleton
Bath Ales Bristol: Warmley
Battledown Cheltenham
Bristol Beer Factory Bristol: Ashton
Cotswold Spring Dodington Ash
Donnington Stow-on-the-Wold
Eagles Bush Ham
Festival Cheltenham
Freeminer Cinderford
Goff's Winchcombe
Nailsworth Nailsworth
Severn Vale Cam
Stanway Stanway
Stroud Thrupp
Uley Uley
Whittington's Newent
Wickwar Wickwar
Zerodegrees Bristol

Ashleworth

Boat Inn

The Quay, GL19 4HZ OS819251

☼ 11.30-2.30 (3 Sat; not Wed), 7 (6.30 summer)-11; closed Mon; 12-3, 7-10.30 Sun

☎ (01452) 700272 ⊕ boat-inn.co.uk

Beer range varies G

Winner of many local CAMRA awards, this unspoilt haven on the banks of the River Severn has been owned by the same family for 400 years. The beers are mainly from micro-breweries, usually including Church End, Wye Valley or RCH, and are drawn directly from the cask. The partly covered courtyard and the riverbank provide a popular outside drinking area in summer; the pub has its own mooring for boaters. Rolls and ploughmans' are available at lunchtime. ♨Q❁♣♠P

Avening

Bell

29 High Street, GL8 8ND (on B4014)

☼ 12-3, 5.30-11; closed Mon; 12-3.30 Sun

☎ (01453) 836422

Greene King IPA; St Austell Tribute; Uley Bitter H

A pleasantly refurbished old stone inn in the centre of the village, the Bell is efficiently run and comfortable. Its exposed stone walls are adorned with horse brasses and tankards, lending a traditional rustic appearance to the two rooms: one pleasant open bar with a wood-burning stove, the other a dining area. The competitively priced menu is recommended (food served until 9.30pm). ♨◑♣﹗

Blaisdon

Red Hart

GL17 0AH (off A4136, E of Longhope) OS703169

☼ 11.30-3, 6-11; 12-3.30, 6.30-10.30 Sun

☎ (01452) 830477

Hook Norton Hooky Bitter; Tetley Bitter; guest beers H

A welcoming and friendly old pub located in the middle of the beautiful village of Blaisdon on the outskirts of the Forest of Dean. Low, beamed ceilings, log fires and flagstone floors make this a cosy venue for winter dining. The large garden play area, outdoor seating and a permanent barbecue make the Red Hart a favourite destination for summer too. The menu offers a good choice, and the food is excellent. ♨Q❁◑♣♠P

Bledington

King's Head

The Green, OX7 6XQ

☼ 11-3, 6-11; 12-10.30 Sun

☎ (01608) 658365 ⊕ kingsheadinn.net

Hook Norton Hooky Bitter; guest beers H

This delightful 16th-century honey-coloured stone inn overlooks the village green with its brook and ducks. The original oak beams, inglenook with kettle and military brasses, open wood fire, flagstone floors and high-backed settles and pews create a heart-warming atmosphere. Guest ales are often from the local North Cotswold Brewery and

the regular keg lager is also brewed nearby. Good food is served in a separate dining area (booking advisable).
♨Q❁❄◑◐▯◒A⇌♠P﹗

Bridgeyate

White Harte

111 London Road, BS30 5NA (A420/A4175 jct)

☼ 11-3, 5-11; 6-11 Sat; 12-3, 7-10.30 Sun

☎ (0117) 967 3830

Bath Gem; Butcombe Bitter; Courage Best Bitter; Marston's Pedigree H

Proper traditional inn dating from 1860 and extended in 1987, with a large green in front – otherwise known as 'the Inn on the Green'. Stone and wood feature in the interior, and the unusual bar counter incorporates old spice drawers. Food is served at lunchtime only. Pub games and sporting activities are likely conversation topics, and a quiz entertains visitors on Monday evening. A limited daytime bus service passes outside, and a stiff walk takes you from the 43 route at Warmley in the evening. ♨❁◑▯♣♠P﹗

Bristol: Central

Bag o'Nails

141 St George's Road, Hotwells, BS1 5UW

☼ 12-2.30, 5.30-11; 12-11 Fri & Sat; 12-10.30 Sun

☎ (0117) 940 6776 ⊕ bagonails.org.uk

Beer range varies H

This small, friendly and gas-lit terraced free house showcases beers produced by small brewers from all over the country. Six to eight constantly changing beers are usually on offer and beer festivals are hosted twice a year, usually in April and November. A good range of British and foreign bottled beers is also available. The basic interior features wood panelling and bare floorboards. All Bristol to north Somerset buses stop nearby. Q▯

Bell

Hillgrove Street, Stokes Croft, BS2 8JT

☼ 12-2 (2.30 Fri), 5-midnight (1am Fri); 4.30-1am Sat; 1-midnight Sun

☎ (0117) 909 6612

Butcombe Bitter, Blond, Gold, seasonal beer; guest beer H

Pleasant two-roomed pub where DJs spin their discs from 10pm nightly. Friday evenings in particular attract drinkers on their way to nearby clubs. This is possibly the only Butcombe-owned pub still serving its excellent Blond bitter rather than just the cold-filtered version. The wood-panelled walls feature local art. The pub is popular with workers during the week for excellent lunches as well as for Sunday roasts (1-4.30pm). A welcome surprise is the pleasant rear garden/patio which is heated in colder weather. ❁◑▯﹗

Bridge Inn

16 Passage Street, BS2 0JF

☼ 11.30 (12 Sat)-11.30; 7-10.30 Sun

☎ (0117) 949 9967

Bath SPA, Gem, seasonal beer; guest beer H

Superbly consistent tiny pub, situated close to the station and surrounding hotels yet only a short walk from the centre. Sport is shown on its unobtrusive TV, and rock music usually plays at a sensible volume in the background. The third pump mostly features a Bath Ales seasonal beer, supplemented by guests. The Bridge is popular for its lunchtime food. Pavement seating is provided in good weather. ❀◖≋(Temple Meads)⬛

Commercial Rooms

43-45 Corn Street, BS1 1HT

✪ 8am-midnight (1am Fri & Sat); 9am-midnight Sun

☎ (0117) 927 9681

Courage Best Bitter; Greene King Abbot; Marston's Pedigree; Smiles Brigstowe; guest beers Ⓗ

Originally opened as the Bristol Rooms in 1811, this became Wetherspoon's first Bristol outlet in 1995. A palatial building with lavish Greek revival-style decor, it is decorated with numerous paintings and artefacts commemorating local celebrities. Up to seven guest beers feature on two banks of handpumps. A smaller galleried room at the rear is popular for dining, offering a refuge from the milling crowd at the bar. This was one of the first pubs to go no smoking long before the ban. Q◖◗⬛⬛❀

Cornubia

142 Temple Street, BS1 6EN

✪ 11.30 (7 Sat)-11; closed Sun

☎ (0117) 925 4415

Hidden Pint, Potential, Depths, seasonal beers; guest beers Ⓗ

This hugely loved and multi award-winning CAMRA favourite was brought back from the brink of oblivion when its was reopened by the Hidden Brewery late in 2006. Three Hidden beers, three guests from other micros and a real cider or perry can be expected here. Food is served weekdays until 7.30pm. Originally a pair of Georgian houses built in 1773, it became the Courage tasting rooms for many years. Its Grade II listed front can be admired from outdoor seating in summer. Opening hours at weekends are subject to change. Q❀◖≋(Temple Meads)⬛❀P

Hare on the Hill

41 Thomas Street West, Kingsdown, BS2 8LX

✪ 12-2.30, 5-11; 12-11.30 Fri & Sat; 12-11 Sun

☎ (0117) 908 1982

Bath SPA, Gem, Barnstormer, seasonal beer; guest beer Ⓗ

The original Bath Ales pub is a class act, stocking the full Bath range plus more than 30 malt whiskies. Good food and bar snacks are on offer as well as Sunday roasts. Wide-screen TVs show main sports events. The Hare offers something for everyone, with entertainment including a record fair on Saturday afternoon, live acoustic music most Sunday evenings (Oct-Jun), classic concerts (Jul & Aug) and silent comedy (Mon eve). ◗⬛❀

Highbury Vaults

164 St Michael's Hill, Kingsdown, BS2 8DE

✪ 12-midnight (11 Sun)

☎ (0117) 973 3203

Bath Gem; Brains SA; St Austell Tribute; Wells Bombardier; Young's Bitter, Special; guest beers Ⓗ

Long-standing Guide entry that has survived the closure of Smiles and merger of Young's and Wells, remaining a popular haunt of university students and hospital staff. Dating from the mid-19th century, its interior is dark and dingy, featuring a small front snug bar and spacious main area. A bar billiards table nestles in the corner. Good, affordable food is served lunchtime and weekday evenings. There is a large heated outdoor garden/patio. The toilets are at the bottom of steep steps. Q❀◖≋(Clifton Down)⬛(9)♣⌐

Hillgrove Porter Stores

53 Hillgrove Street North, Kingsdown, BS2 8LT

✪ 4-midnight daily

☎ (0117) 944 4780 ⊕ myspace.com/thehillgrove

Goff's Jouster; Hidden Potential; Matthews Brassknocker; guest beers Ⓗ

A stone's throw from its great friendly rival, the Hare on the Hill (above), this was the first of the Dawkins Taverns, the brainchild of a local entrepreneur. An excellent community pub, it is free of tie and usually dispenses four guest beers. All beer is available at a reduced rate on Monday, and the Ale of the Day is discounted every day until 9pm. Sunday night is quiz night. The horseshoe-shaped interior includes a wonderfully comfortable lounge area hidden behind the bar. ❀⬛♣⌐

Hope & Anchor

38 Jacobs Well Road, Clifton, BS8 1DR

✪ 12-11 (10.30 Sun)

☎ (0117) 929 2987

Beer range varies Ⓗ

Popular and friendly city local frequented by students, diners and drinkers. Up to six changing real ales are mostly from West Country micro-breweries. The pub achieves a happy balance between those who come to enjoy the excellent food (served all day) and those who just fancy a pint. Subdued lighting, candlelit tables and hop bine decoration above the bar create atmosphere. On summer days the terraced garden is very pleasant. Street parking can be hard to find but buses pass nearby in Park St and Anchor Rd. ❀◖◗⬛

King's Head ☆

60 Victoria Street, BS1 6DE

✪ 11 (7.30 Sat)-11; 12-3, 7-11 Sun

☎ (0117) 927 7860

Bath Gem; Courage Best Bitter; Sharp's Doom Bar; Wadworth 6X Ⓗ

Classic small pub dating from pre-1660, listed on CAMRA's National Inventory. The narrow area around the bar leads into the 'tramcar snug' at the rear. Numerous pictures of Old Bristol give a fascinating glimpse of the past. A resident ghost, said to be an earlier landlady, is reputed to haunt the pub. Lunchtime meals, served weekdays, are popular. A few minutes' walk from Temple Meads station, it is also well served by buses. There are tables outside in summer. Q❀◖≋⬛

Old Fishmarket

59-63 Baldwin Street, BS1 1QZ

✪ 12-11 (midnight Fri & Sat)

☎ (0117) 921 1515

Butcombe Bitter; Fuller's Discovery, London Pride, ESB, seasonal beers Ⓗ

This cracking Fuller's pub, a former fish market, has gone from strength to strength in recent years, becoming the main venue for sports fans who enjoy a great pint while watching matches on TV. It has a large front bar and an indoor side patio, plus several discrete seating booths behind the bar (for those wishing to avoid the sport). Thai and English meals are available. Just off the centre by Bristol Bridge, it is a 10-minute walk from the station. ◖▮⬤⇌▯

White Lion

Quay Head, Colston Avenue, BS1 1EB
✪ 11 (12 Sat)-11; 12-6 Sun
☎ (0117) 925 4819
Draught Bass; ℗ Wickwar Coopers WPA, BOB, Cotswold Way, seasonal beers; guest beers ⒣
This small pub has one room curled around the central bar. Wickwar's only tied house, its five handpumps always feature a selection of Wickwar beers, often accompanied by guests. Twice yearly it holds 'Bristol's smallest beer festival', when barrels on stillage appear by the bar. A five-week winter ale showcase may also be staged in January and February. Outside seating is provided all year round – great for people-watching in the busy centre. The dizzying spiral staircase to the Gents' is not for the faint-hearted or inebriated. ✿▮⬤

Zerodegrees

53 Colston Street, BS1 5BA
✪ 12-midnight (11 Sun)
☎ (0117) 925 2706 ⊕ zerodegrees.co.uk
Zerodegrees Wheat Beer, Pale Ale, Black Lager, Pilsner, seasonal beers ℗
This brew pub, winner of the national CAMRA New Build Pub Design award in 2005, has proved hugely popular with a good cross-section of local people. The high-tech brewery is on full view. All beers are served at continental style temperatures, much lower than the norm for this Guide. Mango beer is almost permanently in the range, and other seasonals may appear. The restaurant is spread over two floors with an open kitchen. Despite its size, booking is advisable at peak times. Flat-screen TVs show sport events with the sound turned off. Two balconies and a terraced patio offer escape from the omnipresent music in fair weather. ✿◖▮⬤

Bristol: East

Cross Hands

1 Staple Hill Road, Fishponds, BS16 5AA
✪ 12-3, 5-11; 12-11 Sat; 12-10.30 Sun
☎ (0117) 965 4684
Beer range varies ⒣
Transformed from a run-down and unloved pub into an exceptional venue in 2006, the Cross Hands is based in a large, imposing building. Its many cosy nooks and crannies are beautifully furnished with comfortable settees and armchairs. Twelve constantly changing real ales are dispensed, mostly from West Country micro-brewers, and changing ciders or perries feature too. The gourmet food is gaining a good reputation. Live jazz, blues or swing feature on Sunday, Tuesday and Thursday evenings in this strictly adult-only pub. Q✿◖▮♿▮(48, 49)⬤

Pied Horse

94 Summerhill Road, St George, BS5 8JS
✪ 4 (3 Fri)-midnight; 12-midnight Sat & Sun
☎ (0117) 955 1514
Beer range varies ⒣
Large, traditional community local with high ceilings and gas fires serving three changing ales from local micros and regional brewers. Originally built as a hotel in the 1890s, it has a large L-shaped bar and a function room upstairs. A large-screen TV shows sports, and football and darts teams are based here. Football memorabilia adorn the walls, and there is a pool table as well as 'Shulbac', a Dutch version of shove-ha'penny. ✿▮⬤♣⬤

Bristol: North

Duke of York

2 Jubilee Road, St Werburghs, BS2 9RS
✪ 5 (4 Sat)-11 (midnight Thu-Sat); 3.30-11 Sun
☎ (0117) 941 3677
Beer range varies ⒣
This genuine free house, saved from imminent closure, is a good old-fashioned local with an eclectic clientele. The exterior features a mural best described as an 'enchanted forest'. Best appreciated during daylight hours, it continues inside and up the stairs. At night visitors can experience the warm glow of the grotto-like, fairy light-lit interior, featuring an assortment of unusual memorabilia and 1940s newspapers. Four rooms on two levels include one of central Bristol's few remaining skittle alleys. Three handpumps offer unusual beers plus Weston's cider, and there is also a good range of bottled beers and ciders. ✿▯▮(5, 25)♣⬤

Inn on the Green

2 Filton Road, Horfield, BS7 0PA (on A38)
✪ 11-3, 5-11; 11-11 Fri & Sat; 12-11 Sun
☎ (0117) 952 1391
Butcombe Bitter, Gold; Sharp's Doom Bar; guest beers ⒣
Local CAMRA pub of the year 2006, the Inn offers an amazing 12 guest beers and four ciders. An open-plan pub divided into three areas, it caters for the local community as well as rugby and football fans from the nearby Memorial Stadium. There is a quiet, peaceful lounge area to one side, a main bar area and the former skittle alley which is used for pool, games and TV sports. Good value pub food is served, and a huge one-day beer festival is held to coincide with Bristol Rugby Club's last home game. Q✿✿◖▮♣⬤P⬤

Miners Arms

136 Mina Road, St Werburghs, BS2 9YQ
✪ 4 (2 Sat)-11 (midnight Thu-Sat); 12-11 Sun
☎ (0117) 955 6718
Butcombe Bitter; Caledonian Deuchars IPA; Fuller's London Pride; guest beers ⒣
Located close to St Werburghs City Farm and Bristol Climbing Centre, this is an excellent two-roomed street corner local. The split-level interior houses a hop-adorned bar where three or four guest beers join the regulars, and the Ale of the Day can be sampled at a big discount before 9pm. The pub dog is called Nelson and he welcomes other well-behaved

canines. Parking nearby can be tricky, so take the bus instead. The Gents', often compared to those at 1970s football grounds, is due for an upgrade soon. ⚌❀☀≢(Montpelier)🚍(5, 25)♣

Robin Hood's Retreat

197 Gloucester Road, Bishopston, BS7 8BG
✪ 12-11 (midnight Thu-Sat)
☎ (0117) 924 8639
Beer range varies Ⓗ
Elegant Victorian pub which has been transformed in the last few years into a sophisticated dining and drinking venue, with an outside decked area to the rear, offering a refuge from the bustling Gloucester Road outside. Eight handpumps offer a changing range of brews from independent outfits. A regular feature is 'brewery of the week', when a selection of beers from one brewery is offered. Good food is cooked by independent chefs at all sessions (no food Sun eve, all day Mon). Children are welcome during the daytime only. Q❀❀◑ও≢(Montpelier)🚍

Wellington

Gloucester Road, Horfield, BS7 8UR (on A38)
✪ 12-2.30, 5-11; 12-11 Fri & Sat; 12-10.30 Sun
☎ (0117) 951 3022
Bath SPA, Gem Bitter, Barnstormer, seasonal beers; guest beers Ⓗ
This large, imposing hotel at the junction of several roads has a long L-shaped bar with various drinking areas arranged around it and an extensive patio/garden. Very close to the Memorial Stadium for rugby and football fans, aside from the Bath Ales it serves a good selection of bottled beers and Czech Budvar Dark on draught. Its varied menu sometimes includes unusual specials. Q❀▱◑🚍P

Bristol: South

Coronation

18 Dean Lane, Southville, BS3 1DD
✪ 3 (12 Sat)-11; 12-10.30 Sun
☎ (0117) 940 9044
Hop Back GFB, Odyssey, Crop Circle, Summer Lightning, seasonal beer; guest beer Ⓗ
Busy street-corner local, a stone's throw from the River Avon and a 10-minute walk from the centre. Hop Back's only Bristol pub, it usually serves five Hop Back beers and the guest often comes from the associated Downton Brewery. Limited cellar space means that the range may be reduced at times. The full range of Hop Back bottle-conditioned beers and Westcroft cider are also sold here. Low-volume background music is played and the small TV is turned on only for major sports events. Monday night is quiz night. Food is limited to pizzas in the evening. ▯🚍❀

Shakespeare

1 Henry Street, Totterdown, BS3 4UD
✪ 4.30-11 (midnight Fri); 12-midnight Sat; 12-10.30 Sun
☎ (0117) 907 8818 ⊕ theshakey.co.uk
Bath Gem; Bristol Beer Factory Trail Ale; Sharp's Cornish Coaster; guest beers Ⓗ
Just a short walk uphill from Temple Meads station is this friendly street-corner pub, well-known locally for its nightly DJ. Two guest beers and a real cider complement the

permanent ales. Weekly quizzes, a pool table and other pub games provide entertainment, and the patio area hosts occasional barbecues in summer. Beer festivals featuring around 12 beers often coincide with bank holidays. ⚌❀☀≢(Temple Meads)🚍♣♠≟

Windmill

14 Windmill Hill, Bedminster, BS3 4LU
✪ 11 (12 Sat)-11 (midnight Fri & Sat); 12-10.30 Sun
☎ (0117) 963 5440 ⊕ thewindmillbristol.com
Bristol Beer Factory Red, No. 7, Sunrise Ⓗ
Completely refurbished in 2006, featuring pastel colours and wooden flooring throughout, the Windmill always sells three beers from the nearby Bristol Beer Factory, with the range changing occasionally. A few foreign bottled beers and Weston's cider are also on offer. Tasty food is served all day. The pub is on two levels, with the family room on the lower one. There is a small outside patio area to the front. If arriving by bus, alight by the railway arch and walk through. ⚌▱❀◑≢(Bedminster)🚍♠≟

Bristol: West

Eldon House

6 Lower Clifton Hill, Clifton, BS8 1BT
✪ 12-2.30, 5-11; 12-11 Fri & Sat; 12-10.30 Sun
☎ (0117) 922 1271 ⊕ theeldonhouse.co.uk
Bath SPA, Gem, seasonal beer Ⓗ
Run by the same owner as the Bridge in Passage Street, the Eldon's beer policy is much the same, but there is a greater emphasis on its food which has gained a good reputation. This end-of-terrace pub has three small rooms, the walls tastefully painted in pastel shades of green and cream, while the floorboards are bare in the main bar but carpeted to the rear. The real fire is in the smallest back bar. ⚌Q◑🚍♣

Merchants Arms

5 Merchants Road, Hotwells, BS8 4PZ
✪ 12-2.30, 5-11; 12-11 Fri & Sat; 12-10.30 Sun
☎ (0117) 904 0037
Bath SPA, Gem, Barnstormer, seasonal beer; guest beer Ⓗ
This traditional local at the end of Anchor Road, just before the Cumberland Basin, is on all the main Bristol to North Somerset bus routes. Winner of a national CAMRA award for its refurbishment a few years ago, when Bath Ales first took it on, it has two distinct drinking areas where conversation reigns supreme. Live music is hosted on some Tuesdays. The TV is hidden and only brought out to screen occasional football matches. Food is limited to bar snacks including pies and pasties. Q🚍P

Port of Call

3 York Street, Clifton, BS8 2YE (off top of Blackboy Hill)
✪ 12-2.15, 5.30-11; 12-11 Sat; 12-5 Sun
☎ (0117) 973 3600
Butcombe Blonde; Caledonian Deuchars IPA; Sharp's Cornish Coaster; Theakston Old Peculier; guest beers Ⓗ
Located up a short steep lane, a naval theme defines the decor in this pub (and the Gents' features some useful angling tips). The walls are hung with pictures of Bristol pubs. Joint

winner of local CAMRA Pub of the Year 2005, up to 12 ales are available – the beers, however, are quite pricey. A pleasant suntrap patio adds much needed space in summer. The pub gets very busy, and large groups of visitors may be turned away at weekends; mention CAMRA and you should not have a problem. This is also a popular port of call for Sunday lunch (booking strongly advised). Q✿✿❶≈(Clifton Down)🚐

Prince of Wales

84 Stoke Lane, Westbury on Trym, BS9 3SP
❸ 11-11 (midnight Fri & Sat); 12-10.30 Sun
☎ (0117) 962 3715
Bath SPA; Butcombe Bitter, Gold; Brunel IPA; Draught Bass; Fuller's London Pride; guest beers Ⓗ
Busy suburban pub owned by Butcombe but offering up to eight beers from regional or better-known breweries. Brunel IPA is available winter only. The pub offers a range of seating areas and an attractive garden. Children are welcome until 8pm. Interesting prints and sporting memorabilia adorn the walls, and fold-away TVs screen major sporting events, especially rugby. Good value lunchtime meals are popular (no food Sun). Q✿✿❶🚐(1)≗

Royal Oak

50 The Mall, Clifton, BS8 4JG
❸ 12-11 (4 Sun)
☎ (0117) 973 8846
Butcombe Bitter; Courage Best Bitter; Fuller's London Pride; Sharp's Doom Bar; guest beer Ⓗ
Busy pub in the heart of Clifton Village and a short walk from the Downs. The interior is on two levels: crowds tend to gather around the bar on the first level, while a seat can often be found in the quieter area at the back. A guest beer appears at weekends but is restricted to a single cask, with popular ales making return visits. A second guest is planned and will be dispensed by gravity. The TV is turned on for major sports events, especially rugby. Lunchtime food and a Sunday roast are offered. ❶🚐(8, 9)

Victoria

20 Chock Lane, Westbury on Trym, BS9 3EX
❸ 12-2.30 (3 Sun), 5.30-11
☎ (0117) 950 0441 ⊕ thevictoriapub.co.uk
Butcombe Bitter; Draught Bass; Wadworth IPA, 6X, seasonal beers Ⓗ
Quiet, relaxed and welcoming traditional pub, tucked away down a small lane. Wadworth owned, the beer quality is as good as you will get. The friendly pub dog enjoys a drop himself! A raised garden to the rear is a suntrap in summer. Pictures of Westbury, when it really was a village, adorn the walls. Popular home-cooked food is available at lunchtimes and early evening, with pizzas only from 8-10pm. Many social events are hosted here including quizzes, themed meals and live blues performed by the landlord himself. Q✿✿❶🚐(1)≗

Victoria

2 Southleigh Road, Clifton, BS8 2BH
❸ 4 (12 Sat)-11; 12-10.30 Sun
☎ (0117) 974 5675

Goff's Jouster; Matthews Brassknocker; guest beers Ⓗ
The third and newest Dawkins Tavern, joining the Hillgrove and Miners (see above) in this Guide, the Victoria is something of a secret gem, tucked away in a side street by an old reservoir and swimming baths, yet only 100 metres from the bustling Whiteladies Road. Eight handpumps offer a selection of beers from local and regional micro-brewers. An unobtrusive TV shows sport but this is really a place for conversation.
🏚Q≈(Clifton Down)🚐♣

Broad Campden

Bakers Arms

GL55 6UR (signed from B4081)
❸ 11.30-2.30, 4.45-11; 11.30-11 Fri-Sat & summer; 12-10.30 Sun
☎ (01386) 840515
Donnington BB; Stanway Stanney Bitter; Taylor Landlord; Wells Bombardier; guest beer Ⓗ
This genuine free house is characterised by Cotswold stone walls, exposed beams, an inglenook fireplace and an attractive bar counter. The local Stanney Bitter is a popular choice; draught cider is from Thatchers. The landlady's home-cooked meals are served in the bar and the quieter dining room. Gloucestershire CAMRA Pub of the Year 2005 and North Cotswold Sub-Branch Pub of the Year on several occasions, this is traditional Cotswold hospitality at its very best.
🏚Q✿✿❶♣🐾P≗

Broadwell

Fox Inn

The Green, GL56 0UF (off A429)
❸ 11-2.30, 6-11; 12-2.30, 7-10.30 Sun
☎ (01451) 870909 ⊕ pubs2000.com/fox_home.htm
Donnington BB, SBA Ⓗ
This attractive stone-built pub overlooking the large village green is the deserved winner of local CAMRA Pub of the Year 2007. It has an original flagstone floor in the main bar area and jugs hang from the beams. A family-run pub, this true village local serves popular Donnington beers and good home-cooked food. Aunt Sally is played in the garden; in the field behind is a caravan and camping site.
🏚Q✿✿❶🅰♣🐾P≗

Brockhampton

Craven Arms

GL54 5XQ (off A436)
❸ 11-3, 6-11; 11-11 Sat; 12-10.30 (6 winter) Sun
☎ (01242) 820410 ⊕ thecravenarms.co.uk
Hook Norton Hooky Bitter; Sharp's Craven Ale, Doom Bar; guest beer Ⓗ
This spacious 17th-century restored Cotswold pub is a true free house, set in an attractive hillside village with stunning views and lovely walks. The drinking and dining areas are separated by church-like stone windows. Bank notes from numerous countries cover the low beams. A guest beer is usually sourced from a Gloucestershire brewery, and a beer festival is held in the sizeable garden in August. It is well

situated for visits to nearby Sudeley Castle.
ᴹQ☸⊯◑&♣Pᴸ

Chaceley

Old Ferry Inn
Stock Lane, GL19 4EQ OS865928
☼ 12-2.30 (3 Sat), 6-11.30; 12-3, 7-11.30 Sun
☎ (01452) 780333
Wickwar Coopers IPA; Wye Valley Butty Bach; guest beers Ⓗ
Set on the western bank of the River Severn, the name of the pub derives from the centuries-old ferry crossing that existed here to take visitors and worshippers to the 11th-century Odda's Chapel in Deerhurst. The pub has been altered and extended over the past 200 years and now has a large, friendly public bar, comfortable lounge and a restaurant serving good value food. The pub is busy all year round, and a large fire helps draw customers in winter. ᴹ⏱☸◑⟊P

Chedworth

Seven Tuns
Queen Street, GL54 4AE OS053121
☼ 12-3.30, 6-11; 11-11 Sat & summer; 12-10.30 Sun
☎ (01285) 720242
Young's Bitter, Special, seasonal beers Ⓗ
This unspoilt, atmospheric pub, attractively located in one of England's longest villages and close to Chedworth Roman Villa, is a rare outlet for Young's beers in the county. The rooms and dining areas are tastefully furnished and display local photographs and artefacts. The upstairs skittle alley doubles as a function room and is available for hire. On a summer's day, you can sit outside and watch the water cascade from a stream opposite the pub into a stone reservoir. ᴹQ☸◑♣Pᴸ

Cheltenham

Adam & Eve
8 Townsend Street, GL51 9HD
☼ 10-2, 4-11; 10-11 Sat; 12-2, 4-10.30 Sun
☎ (01242) 690030
Arkell's 2B, 3B, seasonal beers Ⓗ
Run by the same landlady for 27 years, this friendly and unpretentious terraced local is a 15-minute walk from the town centre. Parking is limited but it is easily accessible by public transport. The pub has a skittle alley adjoining the bar and boasts resident skittles, darts and quiz teams. There is a separate lounge and the public bar has a strong community focus. A table at the end of the bar is loaded with second-hand books which are sold or lent out, the proceeds going to charity, and other charity events are regularly hosted. Q⟊♣

Bath Tavern
68 Bath Road, GL53 7JT
☼ 11-11; 12-10.30 Sun
☎ (01242) 256122
Sharp's Doom Bar; guest beers Ⓗ
This single-bar free house belonged to the Cheshire family for more than 100 years. It is now run by young owners who are keen to keep up the old pub traditions. The pub draws a mixed crowd, with younger guests actively

encouraged. Local produce is freshly cooked on the premises; Sunday lunch is especially popular. At least one of the three handpumps showcases a local beer. Music is played at background level, louder on weekend evenings. Close to Cheltenham Town Hall and the Cricket Festival at nearby Cheltenham College, this is a friendly and busy pub. ◑

Cheltenham Motor Club
Upper Park Street, GL52 6SA
☼ 12-3 (Sat only), 7-midnight; 12-2, 7-midnight Sun
☎ (01242) 522590 ∰ cheltmc.com
Donnington SBA; guest beers Ⓗ
Card-carrying CAMRA members are welcome at this friendly club situated just outside the town centre, in the former Crown pub. South West region CAMRA Club of the Year, it offers three regularly changing guest ales, mainly from micro-breweries, alongside Donnington SBA and Thatchers cider. There is also a range of bottled porters and foreign beers and often a perry. Local-league quiz, darts and pool teams are based here. Parking is limited. Q⟊🖩(B)●Pᴸ

Jolly Brewmaster
39 Painswick Road, GL50 2EZ
☼ 12-11 (10.30 Sun)
☎ (01242) 772261
Caledonian Deuchars IPA; Greene King IPA; Hook Norton Old Hooky; guest beers Ⓗ
Featured in CAMRA's Good Cider Guide, this busy pub retains the feel of an old-fashioned local. Built as a coaching inn in 1854, it has kept the distinctive etched windows and two original open fires. The unusual horseshoe-shaped bar boasts six handpumps, three offering changing guest beers. Addlestones and Cheddar Valley ciders and Weston's Perry are available on draught. Sunday lunch is excellent value, and the brick-paved courtyard provides a perfect retreat for summer evenings. Dogs are welcome. ᴹ☸●ᴸ

Royal Oak
43 The Burgage, Prestbury, GL52 3DL
☼ 11-2.30, 5.30-11; 12-10.30 Sun
☎ (01242) 522344 ∰ royal-oak-prestbury.co.uk
Taylor Landlord; guest beers Ⓗ
This Cotswold stone-built local in Prestbury village is in a handy location for the Cheltenham racecourse. The public bar features exposed oak beams, parquet flooring, equine prints and a log fire. The lounge bar serves as a dining room until 9pm, offering home-cooked dishes, with fresh fish and Cotswold game the specialities. The Pavilion, a skittle alley and function room in the garden, hosts an annual beer festival in May and a cider festival in August. Beers are listed on the website, many from the SIBA scheme.
ᴹQ☸◑🖩(A)●

Sudeley Arms
25 Prestbury Road, GL52 2PN (nr Pittville Gates)
☼ 11-11; 12-10.30 Sun
☎ (01242) 510697
Goff's Jouster; guest beers Ⓗ
Built in 1826, this friendly pub is located close to Cheltenham Town Football Club and a five-minute walk from the town centre. Visiting football fans and racegoers are always well

looked after. The pub is loosely divided into public bar, lounge and snug. Listed in CAMRA's Good Cider Guide and the Football and Real Ale Guide, five handpumps are in regular use and draught cider is always available.
Q✿❀⬛🖵(A)♠

Swan
37 High Street, GL50 1DX
🕕 12-11 (midnight Fri & Sat); 12-10.30 Sun
☎ (01242) 584929 ⊕ theswan-cheltenham.co.uk
Beer range varies ℍ
Local CAMRA Pub of the Year for the last three years, the Swan attracts a cosmopolitan clientele. Three ever-changing real ales are stocked along with Thatchers Heritage Cider. The large public car park leads directly to a spacious courtyard which also serves as an outdoor smoking area. The pub hosts a Monday quiz, themed nights and live music in addition to featuring the work of local artists. A varied menu offers excellent home-cooked meals at lunchtime and Monday-Friday evenings. ✿🕽♠🖴

Cirencester

Corinium Hotel
12 Gloucester Street, GL7 2DG (off A435)
🕕 11-11 (10.30 Sun)
☎ (01285) 659711 ⊕ coriniumhotel.co.uk
Uley Laurie Lee's Bitter, Pig's Ear; guest beers ℍ
An understated frontage conceals an agreeable two-star hotel, which was originally a wool merchant's house. The charming courtyard entrance leads to a comfortable lounge which opens out from a small flag-stoned bar. There is a separate, attractive and comfortable restaurant. For summer drinking, a well-maintained walled garden awaits, and there is ample parking. ⛺✿🛏🕽⬛♿P

Coates

Tunnel House
Tarlton Road, GL7 6PW OS965005
🕕 12-3, 6-11; 12-11 Fri & Sat; 12-10.30 Sun
☎ (01285) 770280 ⊕ tunnelhouse.com
Hook Norton Hooky Bitter; Uley Bitter; Wadworth 6X; guest beer ℍ
Lively multi-roomed pub built in the heyday of the canals beside the southern entrance to the old Severn Thames Canal tunnel. The track from the main road almost justifies the 4X4s in the car park. The pub is festooned with old advertising signs, including some for long defunct beers – note the superbly etched window advertising Bowley's Entire. Moles Black Rat cider is available in addition to the four real ales. A good range of meals is served lunchtime and evening at reasonable prices.
⛺✿🕽♿♠P

Cockleford

Green Dragon
GL53 9NW (take Elkstone turn off of A435)
🕕 11 (12 Sun)-11
☎ (01242) 870271
Butcombe Bitter; Courage Directors; Hook Norton Hooky Bitter ℍ

Delightful Cotswold stone inn dating from the 17th century. It offers a choice of two bars, both with log fires, a restaurant and a function room/skittle alley. The bar and furniture are all hand-crafted by Robert Thompson, the 'Mouse Man of Kilburn' – look out for his trademark mice carved into the furniture. Good food is available lunchtimes and evenings. The pub can get very busy at weekends. There is a large car park across the road. ⛺Q✿🛏🕽♠P🖴

Cranham

Black Horse
GL4 8HP (off A46 or B4070) OS896129
🕕 12-3, 6.30-11; closed Mon; 12-3, 8-10.30 Sun
☎ (01452) 812217
Bath Ales Gem; Butcombe Blonde; Hancock's HB; Wickwar BOB; guest beer ℍ
Delightful 17th-century free house, almost hidden up a side road in the lower half of Cranham village. The bumpy car park, low lintel above the door and the landlord's corny humour may put newcomers off, but persevere – fine ales and hearty country-style dishes amid an ambience of lively conversation more than compensate. A log fire dominates the main bar; there is a small lounge and two more rooms upstairs for dining (no food Sun eve). ⛺Q✿🕽⬛♣P

Didmarton

King's Arms
The Street, GL9 1DT (on A433) OS818875
🕕 11-11; 12-10.30 Sun
☎ (01454) 238245 ⊕ kingsarmsdidmarton.co.uk
Bath Gem; Uley Bitter; guest beer ℍ
The smart but low-key frontage belies the warm and welcoming interior of this tastefully refurbished 17th-century coaching inn. The stylishness and level of comfort of the interior, built largely from reclaimed timber, gradually increase as you progress around the central bar counter from the hop-strewn games/public bar to the excellent restaurant (food served lunchtime and evening). There is a well-maintained walled garden at the rear for the summer. ⛺✿🛏🕽⬛🖵♣P🖴

Duntisbourne Abbots

Five Mile House ☆
Old Gloucester Road, GL7 7JR (off A417)
🕕 12-3, 6 (7 Sun)-11
☎ (01285) 821432 ⊕ fivemilehouse.co.uk
Donnington BB; Taylor Landlord; Young's Bitter ℍ
Refurbishments of unspoilt pubs with Grade II listed interiors are rarely as successful as this. The tiny bar, virtually unchanged, leads to a smart dining room. To the left of the entrance is a small tap room, created by two venerable curved settles. Steps lead down to a snug and the converted old cellar. There is a wide choice of excellent, award-winning dishes and wines (food served lunchtime and evening, booking advisable). The inn is on CAMRA's National Inventory of Heritage Pubs – the fascinating building, good ales and delicious food all

combine to make a visit here a memorable experience. ▲Q❀①♣P

Dursley

Old Spot
Hill Road, GL11 4JQ (next to bus station)
◐ 11 (12 Sun)-11
☎ (01453) 542870 ⊕ oldspotinn.co.uk
Uley Old Ric; guest beers Ⓗ
This 100-year old free house, named after the Gloucestershire Old Spot pig, has been sympathetically restored by its owner, Ric. The intimate atmosphere is enhanced by log fires and brewery memorabilia. As well as Uley's Old Ric, named after the owner, it offers five guest beers, mainly from micro-brewers, served in five separate drinking areas. The wholesome menu is available 12-8pm on weekdays and 12-3pm at weekends. On the Cotswold Way, this convivial local is a popular watering hole for walkers. The secluded garden has a boules piste. This local CAMRA Pub of the Year 2007 and multi-award winner conveniently stands opposite a free car park.
▲Q❀①♣⌐

Easter Compton

Fox
Main Road, BS35 5BA (1 mile from M5 jct 17, towards Pilning)
◐ 11-2.30, 6-11; 12-4, 7-10 (12-5.30 winter) Sun
☎ (01454) 632220
Exmoor Fox; Wickwar Severn Bore; guest beer Ⓗ
Run by the same family for more than 20 years, this pub has two distinct rooms. The comfortable quiet lounge is popular for dining; home-made curries are a speciality and a children's menu is available (no food Sun eve). The livelier public bar attracts locals and darts players. A skittle alley is also available and may be booked for functions. The large garden includes a children's play area. The guest beer changes monthly.
▲Q❀①⊕⌐(624)♣P⌐

Ford

Plough Inn
Temple Guiting, GL54 5RU (on B4077, 5 miles W of Stow-on-the-Wold)
◐ 11-midnight daily
☎ (01386) 584215 ⊕ theploughinnatford.co.uk
Donnington BB, SBA Ⓗ
This thriving 16th-century stone inn is the place to sample the superb Donnington Ales. The pub has three rooms to choose from, with low, beamed ceilings, flagstone floors and inglenooks. It has gained a fine reputation for its food, which is available all day during the weekend and throughout the summer. Horse-racing chat is commonplace, which is not surprising as the racing gallops of trainer Jonjo O'Neill are just across the road. A former local CAMRA Pub of the Year, it features an extensive beer garden. ▲❀⌐⊕&Å♣♦P⌐

Forthampton

Lower Lode Inn
GL19 4RE (signed to Forthampton from A438 Tewkesbury to Ledbury road) OS878317
◐ 12-midnight (2am Fri & Sat)
☎ (01684) 293224 ⊕ lowerlodeinn.co.uk
Donnington BB; Hook Norton Old Hooky; Sharp's Doom Bar Bitter; guest beers Ⓗ
This brick-built pub, licensed since 1590, stands in three acres of lawned river frontage, looking across the River Severn to Tewksbury Abbey. It has its own moorings and a private slipway for boat owners; note that the approach roads are liable to flooding in the winter. A ferry crosses the river to the Lower Lode picnic area outside Tewkesbury from April to September. Day fishing licences can be obtained, and the pub is a licensed touring-park site. Three regular real ales are complemented by two changing guests. Lunchtime and evening meals are served, including the popular Sunday lunch carvery. En-suite accommodation is available.
▲Q❀❀⌐①&Å♣P⌐

Frampton Cotterell

Rising Sun
43 Ryecroft Road, BS36 2HN
◐ 11.30-3, 5.30-11.30; 11.30-11.30 Fri & Sat; 12-11.30 Sun
☎ (01454) 772330
Butcombe Bitter; Cotleigh Tawny Bitter; Draught Bass; Sharp's Doom Bar; Wadworth 6X; guest beer Ⓗ
Superb, family-run free house – a mainstay of this Guide for as long as anyone can remember. The pub has three rooms: the main flagstoned bar, a small raised snug and the conservatory that doubles as a restaurant. A large skittle alley is also available for functions. A former local CAMRA Pub of the Year, renowned for conversation and conviviality, children are welcome until 8.30pm. Q❀①⌐(581)♣P⌐

France Lynch

King's Head
GL6 8LT
◐ 12-3, 6-11; 12-11 Sun
☎ (01453) 882225
Otter Bitter; Sharp's Doom Bar; Young's Bitter Ⓗ
This friendly single-bar pub is hidden away at the heart of a village of winding lanes, but is well worth seeking out. The village name reveals Huguenot connections: French and Flemish weavers came to this wool-rich part of the Cotswolds in search of work. The pleasant garden has a safe play area for children. No food is served on Sunday evening. Live music, mostly jazz, blues or folk, is performed on Monday evening.
▲Q❀①♣P

Frocester

George Inn
Peter Street, GL10 3TQ
◐ 11.30-2.30, 5-11; 11-11 Fri & Sat; 12-10.30 Sun
☎ (01453) 822302 ⊕ georgeinn.co.uk

Caledonian Deuchars IPA; Sharp's Doom Bar; guest beers ⊞
This warm and friendly village inn, which was saved from extinction by the locals, is situated at the foot of Frocester Hill. It has been offering hospitality since the early 18th century when it was a coaching inn serving travellers between Gloucester and Bath. Formerly called the Royal Gloucestershire Hussars, it was renamed in 1998. It serves three regular beers with at least two changing guests, usually from local micro-brewers, plus Weston's Old Rosie cider on draught. Occasional mini beer festivals are held. The home-cooked food is based on local produce, and there are six en-suite bedrooms.
🏚Q⚙🛏◑🍺🌳♿P

Gloucester

Dick Whittington

100 Westgate Street, GL1 2PE
✪ 11-11; 12-10.30 Sun
☎ (01452) 502039
St Austell Tribute; Wells Bombardier; guest beers ⊞
The imposing 18th-century frontage of this Grade I listed building belies the true age of the structure. This was the Whittington town house from 1311 to 1546 and the four-times Mayor of London would certainly have visited it. Inside, the pub has a contemporary feel. Eight ales are on offer – among many guests Whittington's, Uley and Purple Moose are favourites. Excellent home-cooked food is served until 9pm (3pm Sun). Local CAMRA City Pub of the Year 2005 to 2007. Q⚙◑≋♣♿

Fountain Inn

53 Westgate Street, GL1 2NW
✪ 10.30-11 (midnight Fri & Sat); 12-10.30 Sun
☎ (01452) 522562
Caledonian Deuchars IPA; Fuller's London Pride; Greene King Abbot; Wickwar BOB; guest beer ⊞
The site of a pub since 1216, the present inn and name date from the 17th century. Always popular, its flower-bedecked courtyard is packed in summer. Inside, the L-shaped bar is bright and welcoming. The guest ale is usually local, the cider Weston's Old Rosie. The modernised Orange Room serves as an overflow area or a private party room, while the Long Room upstairs is ideal for meetings. Traditional home-cooked food is available until 9pm (6pm Sun). Q⚙◑&≋♿🌳

Linden Tree

73-75 Bristol Road, GL1 5SN (on A430 S of docks)
✪ 11.30-2.30, 6-11; 11.30-11 Sat; 12-11 Sun
☎ (01452) 527869
Wadworth IPA, 6X, JCB, seasonal beers; guest beers ⊞
The end property of a Grade II listed Georgian terrace, the Linden Tree is a popular community pub. The entrances, front and rear, are insignificant, but the interior matches any Cotswold inn. An open log fire, stone-faced walls, eclectic mix of furniture and unusual decorative features create a homely atmosphere. The skittles extension opens up for extra space. Eight ales are usually available, with guests coming from family brewers. The pub offers substantial home-cooked meals (no food Sat & Sun eve) and bargain accommodation. 🏚Q⚙🛏◑🍺🌳♿🍴

Pig Inn the City

121 Westgate Street, GL1 2PG
✪ 12-11 (midnight Thu-Sat); 12-11.30 Sun
☎ (01452) 421960
Brakspear Bitter; Wychwood Hobgoblin; guest beers ⊞
A listed 19th-century facade masks a much older building, which has been remodelled internally as ownership and identity have changed in recent years. The welcome and beer quality are as might be expected from Black Country hosts; the two guest ales may include one from Ma Pardoe's. Food is served until 9pm Wednesday to Saturday, and Sunday lunches in the upstairs function room are very popular. Live music on Friday and Sunday attracts a lively and friendly clientele.
⚙◑&≋♿🍴

Gretton

Royal Oak

GL54 5EP (at E end of village, 1½ miles from Winchcombe)
✪ 12-3, 6-11; 12-4, 7-10.30 Sun
☎ (01242) 604999
Donnington BB; Goff's Jouster; Stanway Stanney Bitter; guest beer ⊞
A popular Cotswold pub where a warm welcome is assured from the family owners. The regular beers come from Gloucestershire breweries and good home-cooked food is served in the conservatory, which affords magnificent views across the vale. The bar areas feature a mix of wooden and flagstone floors. The large garden hosts a beer and music festival in July and there is a hard tennis court for hire. The pub is handy for the Gloucestershire Warwickshire Steam Railway nearby. 🏚Q⚙◑♣♿🍴

Ham

Salutation

Ham Green, GL13 9QH (signed from Berkeley to Jenner Museum) OS681984
✪ 12-2.30 (not Mon), 5-11; 11-11 Sat; 12-10.30 Sun
☎ (01453) 810284
Eagles Bush Kestrel Bitter, Golden Eagle IPA; guest beers ⊞
This brew pub is situated in the Severn Valley, within walking distance of Berkeley Castle and the Jenner Museum. The popular Eagles Bush beers, which are brewed at the back of the pub, are supplemented by three guest beers from local micro-breweries. Two draught ciders come from Gwatkin and occasionally there is a perry on offer. The pub has three bar areas, including a skittle alley. The garden provides a safe play area for children. Q⚙◑🍺🌳♿P

Hawkesbury Upton

Beaufort Arms

High Street, GL9 1AU (off A46, 6 miles N of M4 jct 18)
✪ 12-11 (10.30 Sun)
☎ (01454) 238217 🌐 beaufortarms.com

Wickwar BOB; guest beers ⊞
This early 17th-century Grade II listed
Cotswold stone free house has been
extensively restored to provide separate
public and lounge bars, as well as a dining
room in the former stables (food served
lunchtimes and evenings). The skittle alley
doubles as a function room. The friendly pub is
decorated with a plethora of old brewery and
local memorabilia. Four ales on draught are
supplemented by Wickwar Screech cider. The
Beaufort, a local CAMRA award winner on
many occasions, also has an attractive garden
featuring a six-foot wood carving of a mythical
beast. ▟Q✿❀⊞&♣♠P

Fox Inn

High Street, GL9 1AU (off A46, 6 miles N of M4 jct
18)
🕐 12-3, 6-midnight; 12-midnight Sun
☎ (01454) 238219
**Cotswold Spring Codrington Royal; Uley Bitter;
guest beers** ⊞
The Fox, an 18th-century building in the centre
of the historic village, was originally a
coaching inn, but today is a typical village pub.
Comfortable and friendly, it is especially cosy
in winter, warmed by a real fire. The spacious,
enclosed garden is popular with families. Two
regular beers from local micro-breweries are
supplemented by two guest ales. Good value
food is served at lunchtimes and in the
evening. Close to the Cotswold Way, it is
located in fine walking country. Five
attractively decorated en-suite bedrooms are
available. ▟Q✿❀⊄◑♠P⅃

Littleton on Severn

White Hart

BS35 1NR (signed from B4461 at Elberton)
🕐 12-midnight (11 Sun)
☎ (01454) 412275
**Wells Bombardier; Young's Bitter, Special,
seasonal beers** ⊞
Superlative Young's pub of many rooms and
with much to explore, featuring flagstone
floors, two real fires and low wooden beams.
It was many times local CAMRA Pub of the
Year in its free house days, before Smiles,
then Young's bought it. Food is mainly sourced
from fresh local ingredients and cooked to
order. Offering something for everyone, bar
billiards and board games are played here,
and there is a family room. The pleasant and
extensive beer garden affords fine views of
the old Severn Bridge. Real cider is served
straight from the barrel and occasional guest
beers may appear. ▟Q❧✿◑♣♠P⅃

Longford

Queen's Head

84 Tewkesbury Road, GL2 9EJ (on A38, N of A40
jct)
🕐 11-3 (2.30 Mon & Tue), 5.30 (6 Sat)-11; 12-3, 7-10.30
Sun
☎ (01452) 301882
**Severn Vale Dursley Steam Bitter, Monumentale;
Sharp's Doom Bar; Taylor Landlord; Wye Valley
Butty Bach** ⊞
This partly timbered free house, dating from
the 1730s, was a blacksmith's before

becoming a pub a century ago. A mass of
flower baskets adorns the exterior in summer,
while inside the lighting is atmospheric. The
award-winning food, including the
challenging Longford Lamb, is extremely
popular (evening booking is essential). The
public bar has a stone-flagged floor and is
decorated with sporting pictures. No children
are permitted. ◑❑☐P

Marshfield

Catherine Wheel

High Street, SN14 8LR (off A420 between
Chippenham and Bristol)
🕐 12-3, 6-11; 12-11 Sat; 12-10.30 Sun
☎ (01225) 892220 ⊕ thecatherinewheel.co.uk
**Abbey Bellringer; Courage Best Bitter; guest
beers** ⊞
Beautifully restored Georgian pub on the
village high street with an attractive dining
room. The extensive main bar leads from the
original wood-panelled area, via stone-walled
rooms, to the patio area at the rear. A roaring
open fire warms guests in winter. Three guest
ales are usually available, and imaginative and
beautifully presented food is served in the bar
or garden (no meals Sun eve). Wifi Internet
access is provided. ▟Q❧✿⊄◑❑☐♠P⅃

May Hill

Glasshouse

GL17 0NN (off A40, W of Huntley) OS710213
🕐 11.30-3, 6.30-11; 12-3, 7-10.30 Sun
☎ (01452) 830529
Butcombe Bitter; Draught Bass ⒢
This delightful old pub has been
sympathetically extended using old reclaimed
timbers and stone to blend perfectly with the
original building. It is divided into three bar
areas: one with an old black-leaded range and
another with a roaring log fire. The low
beams, flagstone floors and various nooks and
crannies create a cosy atmosphere. A draught
cider is a welcome addition to the two draught
beers. A historic yew hedge with an integral
seat makes a delightful focal point to the
garden, which is enclosed and safe for
children. The food comes highly
recommended. ▟Q✿◑♣P

Mayshill

New Inn

Badminton Road, BS36 2NT (on A432 between
Coalpit Heath and Nibley)
🕐 11.45-2.30, 6-10.30 (11 Wed-Sat); 12-10 Sun
☎ (01454) 773161
Beer range varies ⊞
A 17th-century inn, with some parts much
older, the New Inn is hugely popular for its
food (booking is advised). Expect one beer
from the nearby Cotswold Spring Brewery and
three changing guests from far and wide. One
of those beers is likely to be dark – the genial
Scottish landlord's own preference. Expect
frequent outbreaks of Scottish beers too! The
main bar is warmed by a real fire in winter,
while the rear area is made over for dining.
Children are welcome until 8.45pm. A

pleasant garden awaits in summer.
⚅Q✿◑⮽P⮲

Moreton-in-Marsh

Inn on the Marsh
Stow Road, GL56 0DW (on A429, S end of town)
✪ 12-2.30, 7-11; 11-3, 6-11 Thu-Sat & summer; 12-3, 7-11 Sun
☎ (01608) 650709
Banks's Original; Marston's Bitter, Pedigree; guest beer Ⓗ

This charming pub, a rare outlet in the area for Marston's beers, always has an interesting guest ale on offer. Situated next to a duck pond, this former bakery features baskets suspended from the rafters – a reminder of Moreton's basket-weaving past. The main bar is adorned with old photographs and hanging hops and provides comfortable armchair seating. Excellent meals are served in the conservatory, with a Dutch East Indies-influence betraying the background of the landlady chef. The landlord of 10 years always extends a warm welcome.
Q✿◑ⓒⅬⅯ⮲⮽⮲P⮲

Nailsworth

George Inn
Newmarket, GL6 0RF
✪ 11-3, 6.30-11; 12-3, 7-11 Sun
☎ (01453) 833228
Moles Tap Bitter; Taylor Landlord; Uley Old Spot Ⓗ

An outstanding village local, looking south over the valley above Nailsworth, the George is a 15-minute walk from the Forest Green Rovers ground. Three chimneys confirm that this building was once three cottages. It became a pub in 1820 and was renamed in 1910 in honour of the incoming King George V. The acclaimed food can be enjoyed in the small restaurant or in the bar (booking advisable). Q✿◑P

Village Inn
The Cross, Fountain Street, GL6 0HH (on A46)
✪ 11-11 (midnight Thu-Sat); 12-10.30 Sun
☎ (01453) 835715
Nailsworth Artist's Ale, Mayor's Bitter, Town Crier, seasonal beers; guest beers Ⓗ

The Village Inn, which reopened in late 2006 as the Nailsworth Brewery's brew pub, is unrecognisable from the venue that closed in the mid-1990s – an ugly duckling reborn as a swan. An intricate warren of rooms and spaces has been created with care and flair, using salvaged furniture and fittings combined with new joinery. All it lacks is the patina of age. Note the poster for the former Nailsworth Brewery on the stairs down to the toilets and brew house. ⚅Q⮲

Nettleton Bottom

Golden Heart
GL4 8LA (on A417)
✪ 11-3, 5.30-11; 11-11 Fri & Sat; 12-10.30 Sun
☎ (01242) 870261
Otter Bitter; guest beers Ⓗ

This large 300-year-old Cotswold free house stands beside the only single carriageway section of the Swindon to Gloucester road. The small bar, which is almost hidden beyond a huge open fireplace, overlooks a stone-paved patio, garden and meadows beyond. Three guest ales are from mainly local brewers, and cider and perry come from Weston's. There are no music or games machines here – just conversation and the opportunity to enjoy award-winning dishes at reasonable prices. There are two en-suite guest bedrooms.
⚅Q✿⮲◑⮲P⮲

Newent

George
Church Street, GL18 1PU (off B4215 & B4216)
✪ 11-11 (midnight Fri & Sat); 12-10.30 Sun
☎ (01531) 820203 ⊕ georgehotel.uk.com
Hancock's HB; Whittington's Cats Whiskers; guest beers Ⓗ

This mid 17th-century hotel has had its former coach house converted into a restaurant (no food Sun eve). The bar is quiet at the front with a central serving area. The dart board, fruit machines and TV screens are located at the rear, and the games room above the restaurant has a snooker table. A beer festival is held during Newent Onion Fair in September. Local attractions include the National Birds of Prey Centre and the Shambles Museum. Accommodation has recently been refurbished: some bedrooms are en suite and there is a two-bedroom mews flat. ⚅✿⮲◑ⅬⅯ⮲P⮲

Newnham-on-Severn

Ship Inn
High Street, GL14 1BY (on A48) OS690118
✪ 5 (11 Sat)-11; 12-3, 5-10.30 Sun
☎ (01594) 516283
Sharp's Eden Pure; guest beer Ⓗ

The Ship is situated in the heart of this pretty village. It has recently been refurbished to a high standard and the atmosphere is friendly and welcoming. Both the bar and the lounge are warmed by open fires; the latter leads into a pleasant dining area (no food on Sun & Mon eve). An archway at the front of the pub takes you into the courtyard and garden – an ideal place to enjoy a drink on a summer's day.
⚅✿⮲◑⮲⮽Ⅿ⮲

North Cerney

Bathurst Arms
GL7 7BZ
✪ 12-3, 6-11; 12-3, 7-10.30 Sun
☎ (01285) 831281 ⊕ bathurstarms.co.uk
Hook Norton Hooky Bitter; Wickwar Cotswold Way; guest beer Ⓗ

This enterprising 17th-century village offers everything you would expect from a Cotswold pub. It even has a river, the Churn, running through its rear garden. The interior features flagstone flooring and a stove in an inglenook. Excellent food is served at lunchtime and in the evening both in the bar and in the smart restaurant (no food Sun eve). The kitchen also cooks the lunches for the local primary school

(Jamie Oliver would be impressed).
Accommodation is recommended.
🏨🏠🛏🍽◗🖵P

Paxford

Churchill Arms
Chipping Campden, GL55 6XH (on B4479)
✪ 11-3, 6-11; 12-3, 7-10.30 Sun
☎ (01386) 594000 🌐 thechurchillarms.com
Arkell's Moonlight; Hook Norton Hooky Bitter; guest beer Ⓗ
Although this 17th-century inn has always had a good reputation for food, it is also the perfect place to find an excellent pint, including guest ales from the nearby North Cotswold Brewery. Owned by the same couple for ten years, it has an L-shaped open-plan layout, with the bar in the middle. Timbered ceilings, an inglenook fireplace with a soot door and flag and oak flooring add to the charm. The menu is chalked up on the wall, but there are no table bookings, so arrive early. 🏨Q🏠🛏◗🍽♣🖵

Pucklechurch

Star Inn
37 Castle Road, BS16 9RF (opp playing fields)
✪ 11-11; 12-10.30 Sun
☎ (0117) 937 2391
Courage Best Bitter; Draught Bass; Wadworth 6X; guest beers Ⓖ
A real focus for the local community, the bar has up to four gravity fed beers fetched from the cellar (do not be fooled by the lack of pump clips; check out the small blackboard above the bar). There are always two ciders on handpump though, usually Thatchers Dry and Cheddar Red. Regular events are hosted including a beer festival to coincide with the village revels in June. Good food is served at reasonable prices, and the conservatory provides additional dining space.
🏠◗🖵(689)♣🚶P

Slad

Woolpack
GL6 7QA (on B4070)
✪ 12-3, 5-11.30; 12-10.30 Sun
☎ (01452) 813429
Uley Bitter, Laurie Lee's Bitter, Old Spot, Pig's Ear; guest beer Ⓗ
This popular 16th-century village inn affords superb views of the Slad Valley. It achieved fame through the late Laurie Lee, author of Cider With Rosie, who was a regular customer. The three-room building has been thoughtfully restored with wooden settles in the end room, where children are welcome. The bar extends to each room, and cider and perry are available. There is no food on Monday evening, and be sure to book in advance for Sunday lunch, which is always popular. 🏨Q🐕🏠◗🖵♣🚶P

Slimbridge

Tudor Arms
Shepherd's Patch, GL2 7BP (off A38, 1 mile beyond Slimbridge village)

✪ 11-11; 12-10.30 Sun
☎ (01453) 890306
Uley Pig's Ear; Wadworth 6X; guest beers Ⓗ
Large family-run free house, close to the famous Wildfowl and Wetlands Trust site. Recent improvements have provided two additional dining areas, an enclosed patio and a more attractive bar. The four guest ales are supplied by craft or family brewers; the cider is Moles Black Rat. A modern lodge alongside offers accommodation; a separately owned caravan and camping site is adjacent. Excellent home-cooked food is served all day, and children are welcome. Gloucester CAMRA Country Pub of the Year 2007.
🏠🛏◗🗠🏨🛏▲♣🖵P🚶

Staple Hill

Humpers Off Licence
26 Soundwell Road, BS16 4QW
✪ 12-2, 5-10.30 Mon-Fri, winter Sat & Sun; 12-10.30 summer Sat & Sun
☎ (0117) 956 5525
Butcombe Bitter; RCH Pitchfork; guest beers Ⓖ
Bristol's only specialist real ale off-licence, this long-established, independent retailer sells up to three guest beers at very reasonable prices. Cider drinkers also have up to three varying choices. There is a large range of bottled beers, too, including many bottle-conditioned ones. Bring your own containers or buy them here. A large number of different polypins can be ordered for Christmas. 🖵🚶

Red Lion
76 Broad Street, BS16 5NL
✪ 5 (12 Fri-Sun)-11
☎ (0117) 956 0230
Wadworth IPA, 6X, seasonal beers; guest beers Ⓗ
Friendly two-bar community local frequented by local sports teams. Wadworth provides its seasonal beers, but other guest beers often appear too. There are two distinct rooms: a quiet comfortable lounge decorated with Beryl Cook prints, and a more basic and lively public bar and skittle alley. A pleasant beer garden welcomes guests at the rear. The emphasis is on beer here and no food is served, but there are plenty of take-away restaurants nearby, including good curry houses on the doorstep.
🏠🗠🖵(7, 49)♣P

Stow-on-the-Wold

Queen's Head
GL54 1AB
✪ 11-11; 12-10.30 Sun
☎ (01451) 830563
Donnington BB, SBA Ⓗ
This 17th-century Cotswold town pub in the centre of the square attracts both locals and tourists. The excellent Donnington Ales can be sampled in both bar areas. The low, beamed ceilings, flagstone floors and interesting pictures and artefacts enhance an olde-worlde feel, taking you back in time. Fresh flowers adorn the dining tables. Dogs are welcome and there is plenty of car parking space in the town square. Q🏠◗🖵🚶

Stratton

Drillman's Arms

34 Gloucester Road, GL7 2JW (on old A417, just N of A435 jct)
⏰ 11-2.30, 5.30-11; 11-11 Sat; 12-4, 7-11 Sun
☎ (01285) 653892
Archers Best Bitter; Sharp's Doom Bar; guest beers Ⓗ
The low beamed ceilings, open fires, horse brasses, brewery pictures and four real ales more than compensate for the obtrusive fruit machines in the lounge in this popular old local. Reasonably priced pub fare is available at lunchtime, and evening meals can be provided if booked in advance. Tables are set outside at the front of the pub in summer, and a small beer festival is held over the August bank holiday weekend. ♨️⚫️Ⓒ◗♣P

Stroud

Queen Victoria

5 Gloucester Street, GL5 1QG
⏰ 11-11 (later Fri & Sat); 12-10.30 Sun
☎ (01453) 762396
Beer range varies Ⓗ
This imposing building formerly housed the Gloucester Street forge, and records show that it was owned by the Nailsworth Brewery in 1891. The large single bar offers a constantly changing range of at least four beers from micro-breweries. A community pub, it fields quiz, darts and pool teams in local leagues. Across the courtyard, set with tables for warm days, the spacious function room hosts a beer festival at least once a year, and provides live music on Thursday, Friday and Saturday evenings. ♨️⚫️♣♣

Swineford

Swan

Bath Road, BS30 6LN (on A431 Bristol to Bath road, 1 mile SE of Bitton)
⏰ 12-11 (midnight Fri & Sat)
☎ (0117) 932 3101
Bath SPA, Gem, Barnstormer, seasonal beer; Butcombe Bitter Ⓗ
Now under Bath Ales' ownership, the pub has been refurbished, with wood panelling helping to create a modern, uncluttered look, while retaining original features including an open fire and tiled floor in the bar area. Meals, from an interesting menu, are served throughout the pub (no children permitted in the bar area). A picnic site is nearby and walkers are welcome. A new, much needed, larger car park, courtyard garden and petanque pitch are planned.
♨️Q⚫️Ⓒ◗➡️(332, 319)♣P⅃

Tewkesbury

Berkeley Arms

8 Church Street, GL20 5PA (by the cross)
⏰ 11.30-3, 5-11; 11-11 Fri & Sat; 12-4, 7-10.30 Sun
☎ (01684) 293034
Wadworth IPA, 6X, JCB; guest beers Ⓗ
The entrance to the public bar of this superb 15th-century half-timbered Grade II listed building is from the street, while the lounge bar is accessed from one of Tewkesbury's many alleyways. The barn at the rear, which is believed to be the oldest non-ecclesiastical building in this historic town, is used for dining in summer, offering good value fare (no food Mon), and as a meeting room. The Wadworth ales are supplemented by two guests which change almost daily. Live music is performed on Saturday evening. Q◗◗⚲➡️♣

White Bear

Bredon Road, GL20 5BU (N of High St)
⏰ 10-midnight
☎ (01684) 296614
Beer range varies Ⓗ
This family-run pub on the edge of the town centre attracts a good mix of visitors and can get lively on busy evenings. The single L-shaped bar houses a dartboard and pool table. Three guest beers change often and often come from smaller and local breweries. The draught cider is from Thatchers. The pub's proximity to Tewkesbury Marina makes it popular with river users. A separate skittle alley doubles as a function room. Crib, darts, skittles and pool teams compete in local leagues. Live music is often hosted on Sunday. ⚫️♣♣P⅃

Thrupp

Waggon & Horses

London Road, GL5 2BL (on A419 between Stroud and Brimscombe)
⏰ 12-3, 5.30-11; 12-11 Sat & Sun
☎ (01453) 731686
Stroud Tom Long, Redcoat, Budding Ⓗ
This small, unpretentious roadside local serves as the notional brewery tap for the nearby Stroud Brewery. Handpumps display pump clips but all the beers are poured straight from the cask and stored in a temperature-controlled servery behind the bar. Moles Black Rat cider is available on draught. Pub games including cribbage and quoits are popular. Note the fine engraved windows of a horse and haywain – the inn sign repeats the design with the addition of a motorcycle (this is the meeting place of the Gloucestershire Branch of the Ducati Owners' Club). ⚫️Ⓒ◗➡️♣♣P

Tormarton

Major's Retreat

High Street, GL9 1HZ (off A46, 2 miles N of M4 jct 18)
⏰ 12-3, 6-11; 12-3, 7-10.30 Sun
☎ (01454) 218263
Butcombe Bitter; Otter Bitter; Uley Pig's Ear; guest beers Ⓗ
The pub has changed its name to the Major's Retreat to avoid confusion with the Portcullis in nearby Chipping Sodbury. It was built in the 1700s and remains a focal point for the village. Its modest Virginia creeper-covered frontage hides a spacious, unpretentious main bar area. The friendly landlord extends a warm welcome to all, and he is rightly proud of his fine selection of beers which are mainly from micro-breweries. The oak-panelled restaurant provides freshly-cooked meals at reasonable prices. ♨️Q⚫️⚲Ⓒ◗♣P

Uley

Old Crown

The Green, GL11 5SN (at top end of village)
✪ 12-11 daily
☎ (01453) 860502
Uley Bitter, Pig's Ear; guest beers 🅗
This attractive 17th-century whitewashed coaching inn is a free house situated on the edge of the Cotswold Way, at the top of the long village of Uley. The pub has a pleasant garden and as well as being a popular local it attracts passing walkers. The low, beamed interior features a welcoming open fire. Its beers are mainly sourced from micro-breweries, including the local Uley Brewery. Food is served at lunchtime and in the early evening. Four en-suite double bedrooms are available. ⚶Q✿✿☞◗♣⌂

Whitecroft

Miners Arms

The Bay, GL15 4PE (on B4234 near railway crossing) OS619062
✪ 12-11 (10.30 Sun)
☎ (01594) 562483
Beer range varies 🅗
A classic free house offering good value and high quality pub food including traditional Sunday lunches. It dispenses five ever-changing guest beers and a range of draught ciders. The pub was voted CAMRA Cider and Perry Pub of the Year in 2005. Its skittle alley doubles as a blues music venue once a month, and quoits is played in the bar. The garden has a boules piste, and the back garden is safe for children. ⚶❧✿✿☞◗🄶♣⌂P

Whitminster

Old Forge Inn

GL2 7NP (on A38, near M5 jct 13)
✪ 12-11 (midnight Thu-Sat); 12-10.30 Sun
☎ (01452) 741306
Brains SA; Butcombe Bitter; Greene King IPA; guest beer 🅗
Externally, the timber framework reveals the pub's age and the strange assortment of windows its chequered history. Possibly once a resting place on a drovers' route from Wales to London, it was certainly a forge in the last century. The smartly furnished interior with its aquarium, brasses and collection of commemorative spoons reflects the lively landlady's character and interests. Home-cooked food is served all day at weekends, and children are catered for. Outdoor games including chess are played on the large patio. Q✿◗⋏♣P⌂

Withington

King's Head

King's Head Lane, GL54 4BD (off Yanworth road, SE of village) OS036153
✪ 11-2.30, 6-11; 12-3, 7-10.30 Sun
☎ (01242) 890216
Hook Norton Hooky Bitter; Wickwar Cotswold Way, seasonal beers 🄶
This stone-built village pub has been run by the same family since 1912. A true free house, beer is served direct from the cask. The walls are decorated with interesting old photographs including Weston's cider prints. This unspoilt local is very popular with cyclists, walkers and visitors to nearby Chedworth Roman Villa, owned by the National Trust. Children are allowed in the lounge anteroom. Food is not usually available. ⚶Q✿✿☞♣⌂P⌂

Woodchester

Ram Inn

Station Road, GL5 5EQ (signed from A46) OS840023
✪ 11-11; 12-10.30 Sun
☎ (01453) 873329
Archers Village; Otter Ale; Uley Old Spot; guest beers 🅗
A village inn, the Ram is more than 400 years old and stands in superb walking country near Woodchester Mansion. A recently completed extension has provided wheelchair access and new toilet facilities. The pub stocks an excellent range of ales, including guests from the nearby Nailsworth and Stroud breweries. Excellent food is highly recommended. The pub is a regular venue for the Stroud morris men. Dogs are welcome. ⚶Q✿◗♿♣P

Woolaston Common

Rising Sun

GL15 6NU (1 mile off A48 at Woolaston) OS590009
✪ 12-2.30, 6.30-11; 12-3, 7-10.30 Sun
☎ (01594) 529282
Fuller's London Pride; Wye Valley Bitter 🅗
This lovely 350-year-old country pub affords spectacular views over the Forest of Dean. It features in circular pub walks of the Forest of Dean and is popular with ramblers. The landlord, who has been here for 29 years, has made sympathetic improvements over the years and the pub now comprises a large main bar and a cosy snug. Visitors are assured of a friendly welcome and a varied menu of good home-cooked food at lunchtime (no food Wed). Q✿✿⊞P

Wotton-under-Edge

Swan Hotel

16 Market Street, GL12 7AS
✪ 10-11 (midnight Fri & Sat); 12-11 Sun
☎ (01453) 843001
Uley Pig's Ear; Young's Bitter; guest beers 🅗
This 16th-century coaching inn situated at the top of the town next to the museum features an imposing exterior. The public bar has TV and gaming machines, while the comfortable lounge and restaurant are both warmed by open fires. A genuine free house, it sources the majority of its beers from local micro-breweries and also stocks a single-variety Yarlington Mill draught cider. There is also a large selection of unusual malt whiskies. A busy local, it is also popular with walkers using the Cotswold Way. ⚶Q◗⊞♣♠

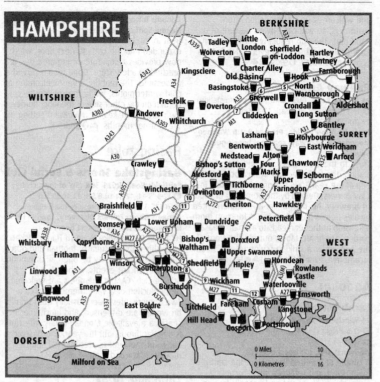

Gale's Brewery has been bought and closed by Fuller's. The beers are now brewed in London

Aldershot

White Lion

20 Lower Farnham Road, GU12 4EA (400m from A331/A323 jct)
⏲ 12-11; 11-midnight Fri & Sat; 12-10.30 Sun
☎ (01252) 323832
Triple fff Alton's Pride, Moondance, seasonal beers; guest beers Ⓗ
Delightful back-street pub, recently refurbished and opened as Triple fff's second pub – a selection of the brewery's awards is displayed around the pub. It features four Triple fff beers and two guest ales, with the names of upcoming beers displayed above the bar. This is a no-frills pub serving great real ale, reasonably priced malt whisky and snacks, but no main meals. Music is played quietly, allowing for good conversation. Traditional wooden pub games include tailor among the landlords and shove ha'penny. ⚒❀♿🚪♣💺

Alton

Eight Bells

33 Church Street, GU34 2DA
⏲ 11-11; 12-10.30 Sun
☎ (01420) 82417
Ballard's Best Bitter; Ringwood Best Bitter, seasonal beers; guest beers Ⓗ
Excellent free house, just outside the town centre on the old Alton to Odiham turnpike. The building dates from 1640 and is steeped in history. Opposite stands the ancient St

Lawrence Church, around which the Battle of Alton was fought during the Civil War. The pub has one small, oak-beamed bar with a further drinking area at the rear and a bijou garden, housing a well. Hearty, filled rolls will keep hunger pangs at bay. ⚒Q❀🌃🚪💺

King's Head

Market Street, GU34 1HA
⏲ 10 (11 Mon, Wed & Thu)-11; 12-10.30 Sun
☎ (01420) 82313
Courage Best Bitter; guest beers Ⓗ
Popular market-town free house, retaining its two-bar layout, which has been run by the same family for 20 years. The regular Courage Best – a reminder of Alton's brewing history – is complemented by a changing guest. The pub has a policy of supporting local breweries

and welcomes recommendations from customers, so you can always be sure of a good pint. The pub regularly participates in local charity and sporting events. No food is served on Sunday. Q✿◁⊕모♣⇌

Railway Arms

26 Anstey Road, GU34 2RB (400m from station)
☼ 11-11 (midnight Fri & Sat); 12-11 Sun
☎ (01420) 82218
Triple fff Alton's Pride, Pressed Rat & Warthog, Moondance, Stairway, seasonal beers; guest beers Ⓗ
Close to the Watercress Line and main line station, the U-shaped bar in this local CAMRA Pub of the Year 2006 has one side divided into cosy corners. Owned by the proprietor of Triple fff Brewery, his own beers are supplemented by ales from a host of micros. A function room extension at the rear leads to a small, pleasant garden. There are tables outside the front of the pub under a striking sculpture of a steam locomotive. ✿⇌모(X64, 64)♣●⇌

Andover

Lamb Inn

21 Winchester Street, SP10 2EA
☼ 12-midnight (1am Fri & Sat); 12-11 Sun
☎ (01264) 323961
Wadworth IPA, 6X; guest beers Ⓗ
A couple of hundred yards from the centre of town, the Lamb retains a cosy, homely atmosphere. The quiet and unspoilt lounge offers a place for conversation, while the larger public bar is where customers can enjoy pub games – the pub has numerous teams in local leagues – and the occasional live music event on Saturday. A third, smaller bar divides the two, and there is a patio for outdoor drinking. A beer festival is held over the Easter weekend. ♨Q✿◁♣⇌

Wyke Down Country Pub & Restaurant

Picket Piece, SP11 6LK (follow signs for Wyke from A303)
☼ 11-2.30, 6-11 (10.30 Sun)
☎ (01264) 352048 ⊕ wykedown.co.uk
Shepherd Neame Spitfire; Taylor Landlord; guest beer Ⓗ
This spacious country pub is based around an extended barn with exposed beams, in which many old agricultural implements are displayed. The large restaurant draws customers from afar and is also used for functions. A comfortable conservatory and adjacent games room complete the facilities in the main building. Outside there is a campsite, children's play area, golf driving range and a swimming pool. Several annual events take place in the grounds. ⋩✿◁Å♣P⇌

Arford

Crown

Arford Road, GU35 8BT (200m N of B3002)
OS826365
☼ 11-3, 6-11; 12-3, 7-10.30 Sun
☎ (01428) 712150

Adnams Bitter; Fuller's London Pride; Shepherd Neame Spitfire; guest beer Ⓗ
Built in the late 17th century, this beer house expanded into the cottage next door, which now provides a separate dining area that is reached up a few steps. Good food is served at all sessions. The real fire is very welcoming on cold winter nights, while the sunken beer garden on the other side of the lane, bordered by a stream, makes for a pleasant setting in the warmer months. ♨Q✿◁모P

Basingstoke

Basingstoke Sports & Social Club

Fairfields Road, RG21 3DR (SW of town centre)
☼ 12-3, 5-11; 12-11 Fri & Sat; 12-10.30 Sun
☎ (01256) 331646 ⊕ basingstoke-sports-club.co.uk
Adnams Bitter; Fuller's Discovery, London Pride; Ringwood Best Bitter; guest beers Ⓗ
Home to Basingstoke & North Hants Cricket Club, this club has squash, football and other sports facilities. It may be open all afternoon for major cricket events. Although it is a private club, CAMRA members are welcome on production of a valid membership card. Two or more guest beers, usually from smaller breweries, are dispensed, and lunchtime snacks are available Monday-Friday. The club is popular throughout the year, and TV screens allow for spectator appreciation of sports, mainly cricket and football. ✿◁♣P

Chineham Arms

Hanmore Road, RG24 8XA
☼ 11 (12 Sun)-11
☎ (01256) 356404
Fuller's Discovery, London Pride, ESB; guest beer Ⓗ
One of Fuller's English Inn Pubs, the Chineham Arms was built in 1989 in the northern suburb of Chineham to cater for locals as well as the staff in the modern business park that is hidden by the railway embankment. There is a large bar opening on to a restaurant (food served every day 12-9pm), and a south-facing garden in front of the pub attracts customers in summer. Sky TV allows guests to follow big matches on screen. ♨✿◁&모(1)P⇌

Maidenhead Inn

17 Winchester Street, RG21 7ED (at top of town opp old town hall)
☼ 9-midnight (1am Fri & Sat)
☎ (01256) 316030
Greene King Abbot; Marston's Pedigree; guest beers Ⓗ
This Wetherspoon pub always features an extensive menu with specials every day, and there are also at least four real ales, two or three that are constantly changing. The venue is popular at all times, especially weekends, when it can get quite crowded in the evening. Dining and drinking areas are on three levels, and there is a heated patio. ✿◁▶모

Soldier's Return

80 Upper Sherborne Road, Oakridge, RG21 5RD (near Ringway North)
☼ 11-2.30, 5.30-11; 11-11 Fri & Sat; 12-10.30 Sun
☎ (01256) 322449
Courage Best Bitter; guest beers Ⓗ

Some 150 years old, the pub is on the north side of town near the A339 ring road. A focus for the local community, the public bar can be lively at times. Even the quieter lounge bar has a long, sociable counter. Outside seating overlooks playing fields in front of the pub. Three guest beers are from micros, mainly from Loddon Brewery. Lunches are served Monday to Saturday. Q❀❀◑◐戻(5)♣P'🛏

Way Inn

Chapel Hill, RG21 5TB (near station)
✪ 12-11 (10.30 Sun)
☎ (01256) 321520 ⊕ thewayinn.org.uk
Adnams Explorer; Caledonian Deuchars IPA; Greene King Abbot; Taylor Landlord; guest beers ⊞

A short walk up the hill from the station, the Way Inn has been extensively refurbished to provide a comfortable environment for the 20+ age group. There is a large room at the rear where families are welcome, and a spacious outside drinking area. Guest beers are obtained from SIBA local brewery delivery services. There is no TV. Home-cooked traditional food, with a good vegetarian range, is available. Several buses stop outside. 🅰🐾❀◑◐⇌戻P'🛏

Bentley

Bull Inn

GU10 5JH (on A31 between Bentley and Farnham)
✪ 10-midnight; 12-10.30 Sun
☎ (01420) 22156
Courage Best Bitter; Fuller's London Pride; Ringwood Best Bitter; Young's Bitter ⊞

A fine brick building on the main Alton to Farnham road, the pub has a cosy area for drinking and dining, plus a small public bar with a huge fireplace. It is a popular resting place for walkers, after exploring the nearby Alice Holt Forest. The Bull is renowned for its food, available at all sessions. The pleasant outdoor area has a separate covered and heated space for smokers. The pub is well served by public transport: Bentley Station is a short walk on a country footpath. Oversized half-pint glasses are used. 🅰❀◑◐戻P'🛏🗍

Bentworth

Star

Church Street, GU34 5RB
✪ 12-3, 5-11; 12-11 Fri & Sat; 12-10.30 Sun
☎ (01420) 561224 ⊕ star-inn.com
Fuller's London Pride; Ringwood Best Bitter, seasonal beers; guest beers ⊞

Dating back to 1841, this friendly free house has a bar warmed by open fires and an adjacent, quiet restaurant offering freshly cooked meals. A social hub for the village community, its enthusiastic staff provide an active social calendar, including Tuesday curry evening and live music on Friday and Sunday evenings. Background music is kept to a low volume at other times. Visitors are always made welcome. 🅰❀◑◐戻(28)♣P'🛏

Bishop's Sutton

Ship Inn

Main Road, SO24 0AQ (on B3047)
✪ 12-2.30 (not Mon), 6-11; 12-3, 7-10.30 Sun
☎ (01962) 732863
Ringwood Best Bitter; guest beers ⊞

Cosy, genuine free house with a split-level bar and a real log fire providing a comfortable, relaxing atmosphere; an adjoining room acts as a restaurant and games area, while the Crow's Nest bar doubles as a family/dining room. Home-cooked food features the 'daily specials' board, and roast Sunday lunches (with a vegetarian option) are popular with the locals. A frequent bus service between Winchester and Alton stops outside, and the Watercress Line steam railway is just over a mile away at Alresford. 🅰Q🐾❀◑◐戻♣P'🛏

Bishop's Waltham

Bunch of Grapes

St Peter's Street, SO32 1AD (follow signs to church)
✪ 11-2, 6-11; 12-2, 7-10.30 Sun
☎ (01489) 892935
Courage Best Bitter; guest beer Ⓖ

The present landlord's great-grandfather took over the pub in 1911. A listed building, it has been immaculately redecorated without changing the ambience of a small village pub. The main entertainment is provided by a good chat; there is no music nor fruit machines. The guest beer changes monthly. The pub has darts and other sport teams, and the popular golfing society always has a long waiting list for membership. The face-lifted garden reopened in 2007. Q❀♣

Braishfield

Newport Inn

Newport Lane, SO51 0PL (in lane opp phone box) OS373249
✪ 12-2.30 (not Mon), 6-11; 12-2.30, 7-10.30 Sun
☎ (01794) 368225
Fuller's Gale's Butser, Gale's HSB, seasonal beers ⊞

The Newport has scarcely changed in 40 years. Values that held then still prevail today: good beer, good food (sandwiches and ploughmans) and good company. Where else would you be served by another customer while your sandwiches are being prepared? The landlady – on the piano – presides over the Saturday evening singalong, there is a folk session on Thursday, and a table is set aside for cribbage and dominoes. No wonder that this pub has a fiercely loyal troupe of regulars. 🅰❀戻♣P

Wheatsheaf

Braishfield Road, SO51 0QE
✪ 11 (12 Sun)-midnight
☎ (01794) 368372 ⊕ wheatsheafbraishfield.co.uk
Caledonian Deuchars IPA; Ringwood Best Bitter; guest beers ⊞

Warm and friendly village local, with a strong emphasis on quality food and a regularly changing selection of beers from regional and micro-breweries. Free-range chickens and a herd of rare-breed pigs, who provide most of the pork that is served in the restaurant, live in the large garden. The comfortable bar has an eclectic mix of old and new; the wooden panelling in the main seating area once formed the ends of a bed. ▲▲Q✿❀◑& P⬍

Bransgore

Three Tuns

Ringwood Road, BH23 8JH (N of A35 at Hinton)
✪ 11.30-11; 12-10.30 Sun
☎ (01425) 372232
Caledonian Deuchars IPA; Hop Back Summer Lightning; Ringwood Best Bitter, Fortyniner; Taylor Landlord ⊞
A farm in the 17th century, it was converted into this popular village pub in the early 20th century and has since been extended to its present size. The interior comprises three distinct areas: the renowned restaurant is adjacent to the lounge bar, complemented by a separate cosy public bar. Meals are served throughout from an extensive menu. Families and dogs are welcome, and the barn can be hired for private functions. There is a covered smoking area. Note no buses on Sunday and a reduced service on Saturday afternoon. ▲▲Q✿◑& ◻➠P⬍

Bursledon

Jolly Sailor

Land's End Road, SO31 8DN (signed path from station)
✪ 11-11 (midnight Fri & Sat)
☎ (023) 8040 5557
Badger K&B Sussex, First Gold, Tanglefoot, seasonal beer ⊞
The patio and covered jetty of this pub afford views of the boatyards and yachts on the busy Hamble river. Inside, the flagged and floor-boarded rooms are all served from a single bar – continuing to offer comfort and intimacy after a major overhaul. Unless you arrive by boat, there is a very steep path down to the pub; goods travel between the road and pub by funicular railway. There is little on-street parking; instead you are advised to park at the station and take a steep but brief walk to the pub. ▲▲✿◑➡◻⬍

Vine Inn

High Street, SO31 8DJ (½ mile SW of Bursledon station)
✪ 12-3 (Fri), 5.30-11; 12-4.30, 7.30-10.30 Sun
☎ (023) 8040 3836
Greene King IPA, Abbot Ⓖ
Unpretentious, single-bar pub with a welcoming atmosphere, situated in a deceptively rural area in the midst of the Solent conurbation – the surrounding maze of roads is effectively a cul-de-sac, so the inn relies on local trade. The pub is a rare outlet for gravity-dispensed Greene King beers. The single bar has several cosy nooks and crannies. Its ceiling is bedecked with copper teapots and other bric-a-brac, while the walls are adorned with pictures of Old Bursledon. ▲▲✿╬➡P

Charter Alley

White Hart

White Hart Lane, RG26 5QA (1 mile W of A340)
OS593577
✪ 12-2.30 (3 Sat), 7-11; 12-3, 7-10.30 Sun
☎ (01256) 850048 ⊕ whitehartcharteralley.com
Palmer Best Bitter; Triple fff Alton's Pride; West Berkshire Maggs Mild; guest beers ⊞
The oldest building in the village, built alongside the forge in 1819, this was the place where folk stopped to natter, hence 'chatter alley' which later became Charter Alley. A delightful rural ambience is enhanced by oak beams and log fires. The landlord has designed a beautiful terraced garden – a real suntrap, it also offers shady areas, and water features make for a lovely, peaceful drink. A cider is stocked occasionally. The pub has nine en-suite guest rooms. ▲▲Q✿❀◑╬➠Pⓗ

Chawton

Greyfriar

Winchester Road, GU34 1SB (opp Jane Austen's house)
✪ 12-11 (10.30 Sun)
☎ (01420) 83841 ⊕ thegreyfriar.co.uk
Fuller's London Pride, ESB, seasonal beers ⊞
Originally three cottages, this runner-up in Fuller's Best Country Village Pub in 2006 attracts locals and visitors alike, serving the full range of the brewery's beers. Inside, the welcoming hostelry features designated bar areas and a cosy restaurant that has gained a good reputation, offering an excellent menu that changes daily. A function room is also available. The pub benefits from a pleasant garden and a separate covered smoking area. ✿◑P⬍

Cheriton

Flower Pots

SO24 0QQ (½ mile N of A272 between Winchester and Petersfield)
✪ 12-2.30 (3 Sat), 6-11; 12-3, 7-10.30 Sun
☎ (01962) 771318
Flowerpots Bitter, Wheatsheaf Best, Gooden's Golden, seasonal beers Ⓖ
Unspoilt two-bar, red-brick pub, dating back to 1820, featuring a well in the tiled floor of the main bar. The home of the Flowerpots Brewery, it serves the brewery's full beer range, along with Weston's cider. Good home-cooked food is served daily (no food Sun eve), while an Indian chef cooks for the Wednesday curry evening. The pub is popular with walkers and cyclists. The adjacent barn provides comfortable accommodation and camping is available for customers by arrangement. ▲▲Q✿╬◑╬Å♣P

Cliddesden

Jolly Farmer

Farleigh Road, RG25 2JL (on B3046)
✪ 12-11 (midnight Thu-Sat); 12-10.30 Sun
☎ (01256) 473073
Beer range varies ⊞
Busy, listed village pub, close to Basingstoke, offering an interesting selection from the

Punch Taverns list. A cider such as Weston's Old Rosie is usually available from the cellar. The quieter second bar may be used by families when it is not reserved for functions. A large garden at the rear provides a secluded area for a peaceful drink, with several heated, covered areas for cooler evenings.
≿❀⊄▷♣☙P⅃

Copythorne

Empress of Blandings
Romsey Road, SO40 2PE (on A31 between Cadnam and Ower)
✪ 11-11; 12-10.30 Sun
☎ (023) 8081 2321
Badger First Gold, Tanglefoot, seasonal beers ⊞
Handsome modern, colonial-style building, previously a restaurant and wine bar. Inside it has a large, high-ceilinged single bar with many alcoves and two roaring log fires. The wide-ranging menu is available all day until 9pm and later on Friday and Saturday, and many dishes are available in small portions. Upstairs there is a large function room, fast becoming the haunt of various clubs.
▲❀⊄▷♿☙☴(31)P

Cosham

Churchillian
Portsdown Hill Road, PO6 3LS
✪ 11-11; 12-10.30 Sun
☎ (023) 9237 1803
Adnams Broadside; Hogs Back TEA; Ringwood Best Bitter; guest beers ⊞
In a superb location on top of Portsdown Hill, the Churchillian affords far-reaching views over Portsmouth, the south coast and the Isle of Wight. It is equally impressive inside – the walls adorned with military pictures, many featuring Winston Churchill (the D-day landings were planned not far from here). The pub is located close to several military forts that can be visited in summer. Good quality food is served from 12-9pm from an ever-changing menu featuring local ingredients; booking is advised, especially in good weather. ❀⊄▷P

Crawley

Rack & Manger
Stockbridge Road, SO21 2PH (on B3049 at Crawley/King's Somborne crossroads) OS420336
✪ 11-11 (10.30 Sun)
☎ (01962) 776281
Greene King XX Mild, IPA, Abbot, Old Speckled Hen; guest beer ⊞
At first sight a 1930s road house, the Rack is based in a late-18th to early-19th century inn which was rebuilt and extended after near-demolition by a lorry several decades ago. Inside, it has two areas: a comfortable, solidly furnished bar with adjoining pool and darts area and a light, airy restaurant. The extensive menu includes many North African specialities and often features local game as well as simple bar snacks. Booking is advised at weekends. Saturday evening entertainment is occasionally provided by a live band.
▲❀⊄▷♣P⅃

Dundridge

Hampshire Bowman
Dundridge Lane, SO32 1GD (1½ miles E of B3035) OS578185
✪ 12-11 (10.30 Sun)
☎ (01489) 892940 ⊕ hampshirebowman.com
Bowman Swift One, Quiver; Ringwood Fortyniner; Stonehenge Spire; guest beers ⓖ
This wonderful country pub has emerged enhanced after extensive alterations. The new Stable Bar provides more space, improved wheelchair access and better access to the garden, while leaving the original ('unstable') bar almost unchanged. And the beers remain on gravity. Summertime cider is Hampshire's Mr Whitehead's. The food served here is excellent and very popular. Children are allowed in the bar until 9pm if supervised. Dogs are welcome, and camping is available if arranged in advance. ▲Q❀⊄▷♿♣▲☙P⅃

East Boldre

Turfcutters' Arms
Main Road, SO42 7WL (1½ miles SW of Beaulieu, off B3054) OS374004
✪ 11-3, 6-11; 11-11 Fri & Sat; 12-10.30 Sun
☎ (01590) 612331
Ringwood Best Bitter, Fortyniner, seasonal beer; guest beer ⊞
In a tiny, timeless New Forest village, the pub is close to the Motor Museum, Abbey and Palace at Beaulieu and the 18th-century ship-building village of Buckler's Hard. Three rooms offer an unselfconsciously rustic setting in which to enjoy good ale, home-cooked food including local game (no food Sun eve) and perhaps sample one of 70 malt whiskies. Local New Forest cider is served in summer. The bookshelves offer plenty of interest to all readers. Accommodation is in an adjoining converted barn. ▲Q❀⊨⊄☴♣☙P

East Worldham

Three Horseshoes
Caker Lane, GU34 3AE (on B3004)
✪ 12-3, 6-11
☎ (01420) 83211 ⊕ theshoesworldham.com
Fuller's Chiswick, London Pride, Gale's HSB, seasonal beers ⊞
First licensed in 1834, but in parts 300 years old, the pub was purchased by Gale's (now Fuller's) in 1930. Reputedly haunted (although the upstairs bar is spook-free), the single ground-floor bar is laid out in informal areas. The attractive restaurant serves a range of daily home-cooked specials (no food Sun eve). A useful stop for walkers on the ancient Hangers Way from Alton to Selborne and beyond, the pub once provided refreshment for workers in the long-gone hop-growing district. ▲Q❀⊨⊄▷☴(13)P⅃

Emery Down

New Forest Inn
SO43 7DY (½ mile N of A35, turn at Swan Green) OS285084
✪ 11.30-3, 6-11; 11.30-11 Sat; 12-10.30 Sun
☎ (023) 8028 2329 ⊕ thenewforestinn.co.uk

Ringwood Best Bitter; guest beers Ⓗ
Grown organically from an 18th-century ale house, this inn is an architectural maze. The entrance opens into an area that resembles a hotel lobby with the bar beyond. On the left is a large space with tables which leads into an oddly shaped function room and on the right to a smaller area with a cosy snug some steps down. Dark woods abound as do many original works of art. Food from the extensive menu is available daily. Children are welcome throughout until 6pm; dogs are also permitted. There are usually four beers, frequently including Taylor's Landlord. It also boasts a covered patio and a lovely garden.
ꙮQ✿⬤P

Emsworth

Coal Exchange
21 South Street, PO10 7EG
✿ 10.30-3.30, 5.30-11; 10.30-midnight Fri & Sat; 12-11 Sun
☎ (01243) 375866
Fuller's Gale's Butser Bitter, London Pride, Gale's HSB, seasonal beers; guest beers Ⓗ
When this green-tiled pub was built in the 17th century it doubled as a pork butchery and ale house. The people of Emsworth also used it as a place to trade their produce, with coal delivered to the nearby harbour – hence the name. Commercial traffic has been replaced by pleasure boating and the harbour is now full of yachts. Award-winning food is served at lunchtime; get there early for the popular curry night on Tuesday and international evening on Thursday. ꙮ✿⬤≈⊟(700)♣

Lord Raglan
35 Queen Street, PO10 7BJ
✿ 11-3, 6-11; 12-11 Sun
☎ (01243) 372587 ⬤ thelordraglan.com
Fuller's Gale's Butser Bitter, London Pride, Gale's HSB Ⓗ
Traditional flint building alongside Slipper Mill pond and the county boundary with West Sussex. One bar has been converted into a cosy restaurant while the other surprisingly large bar hosts live music on Sunday evening. Excellent home-cooked food, served daily, represents good value. Thanks to the enthusiastic landlord this is a pleasant pub where you can enjoy traditional beer and cider, and have a lively evening out in this interesting small Hampshire town.
ꙮQ✿⬤≈⊟(700)♣

Fareham

Lord Arthur Lee
100-108 West Street, PO16 0PE
✿ 9am-midnight (1am Fri & Sat)
☎ (01329) 280447
Beer range varies Ⓗ
This Wetherspoon pub, conveniently situated near the bus station and shopping centre, is named after Viscount Lee, a former MP for Fareham who once owned the Prime Minister's country residence at Chequers. Ten handpumps dispense up to four national beers from a range of six, including a Ringwood ale, plus a further six guests, including some from overseas. The pub is popular with shoppers

and office workers on the way home.
Q✿⬤ᵹ≈⊟

Farnborough

Prince of Wales
184 Rectory Road, GU14 8AL (near North Station)
✿ 11.30-2.30, 5.30-11; 11.30-11 Fri & Sat; 12-10.30 Sun
☎ (01252) 545578
Badger Tanglefoot; Fuller's London Pride; Hogs Back TEA; Ringwood Fortyniner; Young's Bitter; guest beers Ⓗ
Popular free house which continues to set a very high standard of choice, quality and atmosphere. Separate drinking areas spread around a central bar including a pleasant snug to one side. Up to five guest beers are available, with local micros well represented. One is a low-priced session beer that changes every couple of months. Regular events are held including a celebration of mild ales in May and a beer festival in mid-October, while strong ales feature at Christmas. No food is served on Sunday. There is a small covered patio. ✿⬤≈(North)⊟P

Freefolk

Watership Down
RG28 7NJ (off B3400)
✿ 12-3, 6-11 (11.30 Fri & Sat); 12-3, 7-10.30 Sun
☎ (01256) 892254
Young's Bitter; guest beers Ⓗ
Welcoming free house with one bar but several drinking areas, including a conservatory used mostly by diners, a heated patio and large gardens with an area for children. Named after Richard Adams's book, the pub boasts an impressive collection of penny arcade machines and a table football machine. Five handpumps serve a changing range of real ales, always including a mild. Popular with walkers and cyclists, buses stop close to this local CAMRA Pub of the Year winner. ✿⬤⊟(76, 86)♣P

Fritham

Royal Oak
SO43 7HJ (1 miles S of B3078) OS232141
✿ 11.30-2.30 (11-3 summer), 6-11; 11-11 Sat; 12-10.30 Sun
☎ (023) 8081 2606
Hop Back Summer Lightning; Ringwood Best Bitter, Fortyniner; guest beers Ⓖ
Thatched gem at the end of a New Forest track. The main bar leads into several interconnecting areas served through a hatchway, with low beams and doors, colour-washed walls, log fires and board floors all adding to the charm. Guest beers are always from small local brewers. Food is simple but excellent and includes local cheeses and home-smoked sausages. The vast, tabled garden hosts barbecues, hog roasts and a mid-September beer festival. Walkers, cyclists and equestrians (facilities provided) all receive a warm welcome; dogs abound. ꙮQ✿⬤Å

Gosport

Clarence Tavern

1 Clarence Road, PO12 1BB
🕚 11 (12 Mon)-11
☎ (023) 9252 9726
Oakleaf Bitter, Hole Hearted, Blake's Gosport Bitter, seasonal beers Ⓗ

The roof covering the largest room in the Clarence came from the Isle of Wight. At one end old equipment from the former Chapel Brewery can still be seen – the brewery has now moved across the road and been renamed Oakleaf, but the Clarence is still regarded as the brewery tap. It hosts beer festivals over the Easter and August bank holiday weekends, and the local golf society meets here on Sunday. Three double rooms offer accommodation. There is a covered outdoor smoking area. ⚫🟦🏠🍽️◑🌳🚙P↕

Queen's Hotel

143 Queen's Road, PO12 1LG
🕚 11.30-2.30 (not Mon-Thu), 5-11; 11.30-11 Sat; 12-3, 7-10.30 Sun
☎ (023) 9258 2645
Ringwood Fortyniner; Rooster's Yankee; Young's Bitter; guest beers Ⓗ

Genuine back-street local free house with many CAMRA awards to its credit and more than 20 consecutive appearances in this Guide. Weekend hours can be extended by up to 30 minutes if the pub is busy. Up to three guest beers are stocked, mainly from small breweries, and a beer festival takes place in late October. Real cider is served all year round, and bar snacks are available Friday lunchtime. The main feature in the bar is an old open fireplace. ⚫🍴🌳↕

Greywell

Fox & Goose

The Street, RG29 1BY (1 mile from M3 jct 5)
🕚 11-11
☎ (01256) 702062
Courage Best Bitter; Wychwood Hobgoblin; guest beer Ⓗ

Popular 16th-century pub set in an attractive village and backed by a large field that is used for village events. In a good walking area near the Basingstoke Canal, a nearby attraction is the Greywell Tunnel with its population of bats. The pub is child-friendly, and customers may also take well-behaved dogs inside. Food is available every day and all day Saturday and Sunday. ⚫🟦◑🟦🌳🚙P

Hartley Wintney

Waggon & Horses

High Street, RG27 8NY
🕚 11-11 (midnight Fri & Sat); 12-11 Sun
☎ (01252) 842119
Courage Best Bitter; Fuller's Gale's HSB; guest beer Ⓗ

A proper village pub where the lively public bar contrasts with a quieter lounge. Tables in the High Street enable guests to watch the world go by and enjoy the atmosphere in this village, renowned for its many antique shops. At the rear of the pub is a pleasant courtyard garden. A winner of many local CAMRA

awards, the guest beer changes frequently and is always of a high quality. No food is served on Sunday. ⚫Q🟦🍴◑🟦🚙(200, 72)

Hawkley

Hawkley Inn

Pococks Lane, GU33 6NE OS747291
🕚 12-3, 5.30-11; 12-11 Sat; 12-10.30 Sun
☎ (01730) 827205
Beer range varies Ⓗ

Recently refurbished, this true free house has lost none of its character. The decor is unique: it features a moose's head which has now lost its cigarette in keeping with the times. The pub stocks up to 10 real ales, all from small independent breweries, as well as local real cider (Mr Whitehead's) and real perry. The best way to appreciate this gem is probably to stay in one of its new rooms and work up a thirst on a walk in the superb Hampshire countryside. The home-cooked food is of an equally high standard. ⚫🟦🏠◑🟦🚗🍴

Hill Head

Crofton

48 Crofton Lane, PO14 3QF
🕚 11-11; 12-10.30 Sun
☎ (01329) 314222
Adnams Broadside; Caledonian Deuchars IPA; guest beers Ⓗ

Modern estate pub in a housing area once occupied by strawberry fields. Six real ales are usually on offer – the guest beers are from Punch Taverns and Oakleaf Hole Hearted appears regularly. The function room houses a skittle alley and also hosts special events including beer festivals. Home-cooked food is served all day at weekends at this local CAMRA Pub of the Year 2006.
Q🟦🟦◑🟦🚗🟦(33, 35)🍴P↕

Hipley

Horse & Jockey

PO7 4QY (on road from Hambledon to Fareham) OS623119
🕚 11.30-11.30 (12.30am Fri & Sat); 12-11.30 Sun
☎ (023) 9263 2728
Fuller's Gale's HSB; Ringwood Best Bitter; guest beers Ⓗ

Large two-bar country pub in the pleasant Hampshire countryside just south of the village of Hipley. The main bar has a stone floor and large open fireplace, with one part converted into a dining area. The smaller back bar has a bar billiards table. The house beer is Fuller's Butser. Aside from its beers, the pub has two claims to fame: a German aircraft crashed in an adjacent field during WWII and the first horse to win two consecutive Grand Nationals was trained nearby. ⚫🟦◑🟦🟦🍴P

Holybourne

Queen's Head

20 London Road, GU34 4EG (opp Grange Hotel)
🕚 12-11 (11.30 Thu & Sat; 12.30am Fri); 12-10.30 Sun
☎ (01420) 86331
Greene King IPA, seasonal beers; guest beer Ⓗ

Reputedly of 18th-century origin but much extended, this traditional pub comprises two rooms, one a restaurant and the other a public bar. Food is based on local produce and comes in hearty portions (no eve meals Sun-Tue in winter). Regular live music events take place throughout the year, and cribbage is popular. The extensive garden features a children's play area; dogs are welcome.
&⊕⏰⇐≈(Alton)🚌(64, X64)♣P⁵⁻

White Hart

139 London Road, GU34 4EY
✪ 12-midnight (1am Fri & Sat); 12-11.30 Sun
☎ (01420) 87654
Courage Best Bitter; Greene King IPA, Old Speckled Hen; guest beer Ⓗ

Situated on the old A31 London Road, this fine building dates from the 1920s and replaced an earlier coach house. In the centre of a charming village, the pub has separate entrances to the public bar and restaurant. Each area has its own name – the Farmers was originally the off-sales room. Excellent food is served, including fish dishes. The proprietors previously ran another pub nearby that was listed in the Guide. Two double and two twin rooms are available for overnight stays.
Q♒☆⇐⊕⏰⇐♣P⁵⁻

Hook

Crooked Billet

London Road, RG27 9EH (on A30 approx 1 mile E of Hook)
✪ 11.30-3, 6-11; 6-1am Fri & Sat
☎ (01256) 762118 ∰ thecrookedbillethook.co.uk
Courage Best Bitter, Directors; guest beers Ⓗ

A spacious roadside pub that puts the emphasis on its beers. Popular with the locals, the Crooked Billet provides two guest beers usually from West Country and Lake District micro-breweries. It also stocks Thatcher's cider. There is plenty of space for drinkers and diners; food is available seven days a week. Alongside the pub runs a small river providing a relaxing feature in the pleasant garden.
🏰Q☆⊕⏰⇐🚌(200)♣P⁵⁻

Horndean

Brewers Arms

1 Five Heads Road, PO8 9NW
✪ 12-2 (Tue, Wed & Fri), 5-11 (midnight Fri); 12-4, 6-midnight Sat; 12-3, 7-11 Sun
☎ (023) 9259 1325
Courage Directors; Fuller's London Pride; Ringwood Best Bitter; guest beers Ⓗ

Pre-war pub set back from the main Portsmouth road. It is referred to by regulars as 'a proper pub' – a genuine local where people come to drink and chat. Three regular beers are supplemented by two guest ales at the weekend, usually sourced from local SIBA breweries. Pump clips adorn the bars and ceilings. Dog owners are welcome to bring their four-legged friends. Q☆⊕🚌(38, 41)♣P

Kingsclere

Swan Hotel

Swan Street, RG20 5PP

✪ 11-3, 5.30-11.30; 12-3.30, 7-11 Sun
☎ (01635) 298314 ∰ swankingsclere.co.uk
Theakston XB; Young's Bitter; guest beers Ⓗ

Traditional inn frequented by an eclectic mix of customers, serving four regularly changing handpumped beers from local micro-breweries and regionals. One of the country's oldest coaching inns dating from 1449, it has been a pub since 1600. The Grade II listed building, which retains original oak beams and fireplaces, has been associated with the Bishop of Winchester for 300 years. As befits a true inn, good food is served in the bar or dining room, and there are nine en-suite bedrooms. 🏰Q☆⇐⊕⏰🚌♣P

Langstone

Ship Inn

Langstone Road, PO9 1RD
✪ 11-11; 12-10.30 Sun
☎ (023) 9247 1719
Fuller's Gale's Butser Bitter, London Pride, Gale's HSB Ⓗ

Located on the edge of Langstone Harbour and the crossing to Hayling Island, this is an ideal base for a walk along the shore on the track of the much missed railway line to the island. The remains of the railway bridge are easily seen and explorers may locate the Roman Wade Way to Hayling and the train ferry to the Isle of Wight, which was last used in 1888. The harbour and nearby pond will be of interest to birdwatchers and nature lovers.
🏰☆⊕⏰⇐▲🚌(30, 31)P

Lasham

Royal Oak

GU34 5SJ (off A339 between Alton and Basingstoke)
✪ 12-11 (10.30 Sun)
☎ (01256) 381213 ∰ royaloak.uk.com
Hogs Back TEA; Ringwood Best Bitter; Triple fff Moondance; guest beers Ⓗ

Situated in the centre of a quiet village next to Lasham Airfield, well known for its gliding club, the Royal Oak is over 200 years old. It has two bars and food is served daily at lunchtime and in the evening, all day on Sunday. A large car park, beautiful garden and picturesque surroundings make this pub popular with ramblers and cyclists; children are welcome. 🏰Q☆⊕⏰⇐🚌(28)♣P⁵⁻

Little London

Plough Inn

Silchester Road, RG26 5EP (1 mile off A340, S of Tadley)
✪ 12-2.30, 5.30-11; 12-3, 7-10.30 Sun
☎ (01256) 850628
Ringwood Best Bitter, seasonal beers; Ⓗ **guest beers** Ⓖ

Wonderful, popular village pub with an informal atmosphere. This is a sympathetically restored cottage where in winter you can enjoy a glass of porter in front of a cheery log fire. A good range of baguettes is usually available (not Sun eve). Musicians perform popular songs on the second Tuesday of the month, and bar billiards is played. A lovely

secluded garden at the side of the pub is an added attraction. The location of this friendly hostelry is ideal for ramblers visiting the Roman ruins at nearby Silchester or Pamber Wood. CAMRA branch Pub of the Year 2007.
ᕙQ✿♣P

Long Sutton

Four Horseshoes
The Street, RG29 1TA (1 mile E of village)
OS748471
🕑 12-3 (not Mon), 6.30-11; 12-3 Sun
☎ (01256) 862488 🌐 fourhorseshoes.com
Beer range varies Ⓗ
Traditional country pub on the outskirts of the village, next to Lord Wandsworth College. Three dining areas radiate from a spacious central bar that houses a large collection of horse brasses and novelty keyrings. Scenic views can be enjoyed from the conservatory at the front of the pub. Next to the car park is a garden with a large play area for children and a boules pitch. Up to three guest beers are dispensed, predominantly from local micro-breweries. B&B accommodation is available.
ᕙQ✿🛏◑Å♣P

Lower Upham

Woodman
Winchester Road, SO32 1HA (on B2177, by B3037 jct)
🕑 12-2.30 (6 Sat & Sun), 7.15-11 (midnight Fri & Sat)
☎ (01489) 860270
Greene King IPA; guest beers Ⓗ
Dating in parts from the 17th century, the Woodman has two contrasting bars: a cosy lounge, bedecked with Toby jugs, and a public bar suited to a more gregarious clientele. Alongside its well-kept beers it offers almost 200 malt whiskies. Guest ales are from Greene King's list. In summer, fine floral displays add to the welcome and the unsuspecting visitor may be fortunate enough to stumble upon the moveable feast that is 'Sausage Saturday' (interesting contributions welcome).
ᕙ✿❄🖵(69)♣P╚🍺

Medstead

Castle of Comfort
Castle Street, GU34 5LU (2 miles N of Four Marks)
OS655373
🕑 11.30-2.30 (3 Sat), 6-11; 12-3, 6-11 Sun
☎ (01420) 562112
Courage Best Bitter; Greene King IPA; Hook Norton Hooky Best; guest beers Ⓗ
Tucked behind the church, this 17th-century village local has a public bar and a small lounge which feels more like a family living room, with a wood-burning stove set in a large fireplace. The pub is famed for its expansive floral displays throughout the summer and has a large child-friendly garden. Bar food is available at lunchtime. A perfect stopping-off place for ramblers.
ᕙQ✿◑🖵(28)♣P╚

Milford on Sea

Red Lion
32 High Street, SO41 0QD (on B3058, off A337)
🕑 11.30-2.30, 6-11; 12-3, 7-10.30 Sun
☎ (01590) 642236
Fuller's London Pride; Ringwood Best Bitter; guest beers Ⓗ
A friendly, comfortable, 18th-century village pub with a relaxed atmosphere, notable for its feature fireplace. Pool and darts are played but the pub is free from jukebox and fruit machines. The cider is Thatchers' Farmers' Tipple. The dining area can be used by drinkers after the diners have finished their delicious meals, served at competitive prices. Accommodation is in three en-suite rooms.
ᕙQ✿🛏◑&🖵♣●P

North Warnborough

Lord Derby
Bartley Heath, RG29 1HD (off A287)
🕑 11.30-3, 5.30-11 Mon & Tue; 11.30-11.30; 12-10.30 Sun
☎ (01256) 702283
Fuller's London Pride; Moorhouses Pendle Witches Brew; guest beer Ⓗ
Primarily a restaurant, the Lord Derby has a separate drinking area with a stone-flagged floor. The former main road outside has been cut off by the motorway and provides useful extra parking, except on the first Wednesday of the month during the summer (bikers' day) when it is full of expensive motorbikes. On those days, only bar food is available (also no food on Sun eve). ✿◑&🖵(200)P

Old Basing

Crown
The Street, RG24 7BW (next to Old Basing House ruins)
🕑 11-3, 5-11; 11-11.30 Fri & Sat; 11.30-10.30 Sun
☎ (01256) 321424
Fuller's London Pride; guest beers Ⓗ
The Crown sits alongside the remains of Old Basing House, which Cromwell's troops were said to have attacked from the pub. There are two bars and a cosy snug where the Pride and two regularly changing guests from independent breweries can be sampled. A wider choice of beers is on offer at the Easter beer festival. Glasses are oversized, except for the branded ones. Food is available every day.
ᕙ✿◑🖵(8)P╚

Overton

Greyhound Inn
46 Winchester Street, RG25 3HS
🕑 11-1.30, 5-11; 11-3, 5-11.30 Sat; 12-3, 7-10.30 Sun
☎ (01256) 770241 🌐 greyhound-overton.co.uk
Caledonian Deuchars IPA; Greene King IPA, Abbot; Wadworth 6X Ⓗ
A short walk from the village centre, the Greyhound retains a cosy local atmosphere while offering a genuine welcome to visitors. The single bar combines a comfortable lounge area with a games section where pool and darts are played. The licensees enthusiastically support the pub teams in all local leagues. On

most Saturday nights entertainment is laid on. The loos are presently located outside, across the rear yard. ♨⊛⊠(76, 86)♣

Ovington

Bush Inn

SO24 0RE (¾ mile N of A31) OS561319
🕐 11-3, 6-11; 12-3, 7-11 Sun
☎ (01962) 732764
Wadworth IPA, 6X, JCB Ⓗ
In this ancient 16th-century inn on the banks of the tranquil Itchen five rooms with low doors and uneven floors cluster around a central bar. The decor is dark, cool in summer, and cosy with three real fires in winter. The plethora of stuffed and cased wildlife, however, may not be to everyone's taste. This is definitely a food venue – the Bush has an extensive menu and is fairly pricy. Booking is recommended, especially in summer and at weekends. The beers occasionally include a Wadworth seasonal or guest brew, and Weston's cider is also available.
♨Q⊛◑&♠P

Petersfield

Good Intent

40-46 College Street, GU31 4AF (near old London Rd/Station Rd jct)
🕐 11-11
☎ (01730) 263838 ⊕ stuartinns.com
Adnams Bitter; Fuller's Gale's Butser, London Pride, Gale's HSB; guest beer Ⓗ
Just off the town centre, this 16th-century beamed pub is known as 'the country pub in the town'. The single bar serves a split-level room with candlelit tables and two log fires. Further rooms leading off the main area include an award-winning restaurant. The imaginative food served here includes fresh fish at the weekend, and it is renowned for its sausages. Live music is enjoyed on Sunday evening, and shut the box and shove-ha'penny are played. There is a patio at the front, and guest accommodation comprises three en-suite rooms.
♨Q⊛⋈◑⇌⊠(38)♣⌐

Portsmouth

Artillery Arms

Hester Road, PO4 8HB
🕐 12-3, 6-11; 12-11.30 Fri-Sun
☎ (023) 9273 3610
Fuller's London Pride; Ringwood Fortyniner; guest beers Ⓗ
Genuine back-street ale house with a lively public bar and a more sedate lounge, situated only a ten-minute walk from Fratton Park. Up to four constantly changing guest beers from a wide range of southern breweries are available from the handpumps. The pub gets very busy when Portsmouth plays at home. Filled rolls are available all week with superb lunches served on Sunday. ⊕▲⊠♣

Barley Mow

39 Castle Road, PO5 3DE
🕐 12 (11 Sat)-midnight; 12-11 Sun
☎ (023) 9282 3492

Fuller's London Pride, Gale's HSB; guest beers Ⓗ
This traditional Victorian street-corner pub serves excellent beer and offers outstanding service. The public bar doubles as the games room, with pool and darts, and is also the base for myriad other activities – a genuine hub for the local community. The lounge is wood-panelled with windows either side of the entrance, and the counter has an interesting leaded over-bar. The original ceiling depicted the Battle of Southsea in 1874, but this has now been removed to an art gallery and museum. ⊛◑⊟&♠⌐

Bridge Tavern

54 East Street, Old Portsmouth, PO1 2JJ
🕐 11-11; 12-10.30 Sun
☎ (023) 9275 2992
Fuller's Gale's Butser, London Pride, Gale's HSB Ⓗ
Originally a small, one-storey harbourside pub, drawing a lively mix of fishermen and locals, the Bridge was refurbished and has grown beyond recognition into an imposing edifice on two floors. Different levels, nooks and crannies add interest. This pub is well worth seeking out for the excellent ale served in pleasant surroundings by attentive and helpful staff. No meals are available Sunday evening. ◑⌐

Cellars at Eastney

56 Cromwell Road, Southsea, PO4 9PN
🕐 12-11.15 (11.30 Fri & Sat); 12-11 Sun
☎ (023) 9282 6249 ⊕ thecellars.co.uk
Ringwood Best Bitter, Fortyniner; guest beers Ⓗ
Street-corner local, situated opposite the old Royal Marine barracks and a short walk from the Royal Marines Museum. The single bar houses a small stage that hosts live music several evenings a week (see website for details). At the rear is a small conservatory. The Cellars is a rare outlet for Ringwood beers in the area and also stocks a good range of wines and Weston's Old Rosie cider. Displayed in the bar is the plate for the licensee from 1839-1969, of interest to former servicemen.
▲⊠♠

Fifth Hants Volunteer Arms

74 Albert Road, Southsea, PO5 2SL
🕐 12-midnight (1am Fri-Sun)
☎ (023) 9282 7161
Fuller's Gale's Butser, London Pride, Gale's HSB; guest beers Ⓗ
Birthplace of the local CAMRA branch, this street-corner pub is one of the few in the vicinity to retain its two bars. The lively public bar features a collection of hard hats, overcooked pizza and a chiming clock. The quieter lounge displays many certificates awarded for the pub's appearances in this Guide. It hosts a quiz on Sunday evening. This is an excellent, traditional watering hole in an area of modernised pubs. ⊕⊠(17, 18)♣

Florence Arms

18-20 Florence Road, Southsea, PO5 2NE
🕐 12-11
☎ (023) 9287 5700 ⊕ theflorencearms.com
Adnams Bitter, Broadside; Shepherd Neame Spitfire; guest beers Ⓗ

One of Southsea's hidden gems, the Florence has a genuine public bar and a quieter, more select lounge, as well as a restaurant featuring excellent home-cooked food. The guest beers come from a wide range of independent southern breweries and change several times a week. There is always a Mr Whitehead cider on sale, three in summer, and 20 wines are available by the glass. No food all day Saturday or Sunday evening. Q◑🗊 🖴🕭🔕🚻🖐

Golden Eagle

1 Delamere Road, Southsea, PO4 0JA

🕐 3-11.30; 12-midnight Fri & Sat; 12-11 Sun

☎ (023) 9282 1658

Fuller's Gale's Butser, London Pride, Gale's HSB Ⓗ

Situated a short walk from the Albert Road shops, this backstreet pub has a mixed clientele, and is home to darts and pool teams. The Eagle and its customers regularly raise funds for kidney machines. The pub also hosts a range of live music on most weekends, and it can get lively here when sports events are shown on its wide-screen TV. 🕭🖴🚄(Fratton)🖴(17, 18)

Hole in the Wall

36 Great Southsea Street, PO5 3BY

🕐 4-11; 12-2, 4-midnight Fri & Sat

☎ (023) 9229 8085

Oakleaf Hole Hearted; guest beers Ⓗ

Local CAMRA Pub of the Year 2007, this small, welcoming little pub has a good mix of customers. It offers an outstanding range of real ales including Hole Hearted, which was originally brewed especially for this pub. Alongside interesting guests, traditional cider, bottled Belgian beers and even alcoholic ginger beer are available. Simple but tasty food is served, including old favourites such as bangers and mash, and suet puddings. Monday, Tuesday and Wednesday are chilli nights. Four-pint jugs are sold at reduced prices before 9pm. No admittance after 11pm Friday and Saturday. Q🕭◑🚄🖴🔕🖐🍴

Leopold Tavern

154 Albert Road, PO4 0RT

🕐 10-11 (midnight Fri & Sat); 12-11 Sun

☎ (023) 9282 9748

Fuller's London Pride; Greene King Abbot; Hop Back Summer Lightning; Oakleaf Hole Hearted Ⓗ

Traditional street-corner Victorian public house with a long green-glazed tile exterior. The tastefully decorated interior features an island bar with several drinking areas. A dartboard, jukebox, TVs and myriad other pastimes are on offer for customers' entertainment. Often two different televised sporting events will be shown at either end of the pub. Real ale is important at the Leopold. It can get extremely busy on weekend evenings, when there may be standing room only. A real gem. 🖴(17, 18)

Old House at Home

104 Locksway Road, PO4 8JR

🕐 10-midnight (1am Fri & Sat); 12-midnight Sun

☎ (023) 9273 2606

Caledonian Deuchars IPA; Fuller's Gale's HSB; guest beers Ⓗ

A real community hostelry in every sense of the word. The pub usually stocks four real ales,

with beers coming from all over the country and seasonal guest ales too when available. Fine food is served at lunchtime and early evening – the lounge bar, which is a step back in time, doubles as a dining area at the weekend. 🚆🕭◑🖴🖴🔕🚻🖐P

Old Oyster House

291 Locksway Road, PO4 8LH (off A288, near university's Langstone site)

🕐 12 (4 Mon)-11.30; 11-10.30 Sun

☎ (023) 9282 7456

Beer range varies Ⓗ

Traditional drinkers' pub situated close to the only remaining section of the old Portsea Canal. The pub was rebuilt in 1930 next to the site of the original inn. It takes its name from the old oyster beds in Langstone Harbour, and the interior decor has a nautical theme. Four ales are supplied by small and national brewers and a scrumpy from Thatchers is always available. Well worth seeking out. 🚆🕭🖴🔕🖐

Pembroke

20 Pembroke Road, Old Portsmouth, PO1 2NR

🕐 10-midnight (11 Mon); 12-4, 7-11 Sun

☎ (023) 9282 3961

Draught Bass; Fuller's London Pride; Greene King Abbot Ⓗ

Built in 1711, this single-bar, horseshoe-shaped pub on a corner site was originally named the Little Blue Line and is mentioned in the novels of Captain Marryat. It became the Pembroke in 1900. The bar has an L-shaped servery run by friendly and efficient staff and displays all kinds of naval memorabilia. This rare haven for discerning drinkers attracts a varied clientele and offers probably the best pint of Pride in Portsmouth. 🚆◑🖴

Royal Marines Artillery Tavern

58 Cromwell Road, Southsea, PO4 9PN

🕐 6-midnight

☎ (023) 9282 0896

Fuller's Gale's Butser, London Pride, Gale's HSB; guest beers Ⓗ

Typical back-street pub frequented by local drinkers, standing right outside the main gate to the old Royal Marine barracks from which it takes its name. The beers come from Fuller's and the old Gale's portfolio. It stages live entertainment most weekends and houses the last surviving skittle alley in Portsmouth. A real fire provides a warm glow in winter. Within walking distance of the Eastney seafront, it is also convenient for the Royal Marines Museum. 🚆🕭🖴🔕

Sirloin of Beef

152 Highland Road, Southsea, PO4 9NH

🕐 11-11.30 (12.30am Fri & Sat); 12-11 Sun

☎ (023) 9282 0115

Hop Back Summer Lightning; guest beers Ⓗ

True free house where the beers are mostly sourced from southern independent breweries. It also stocks a wide range of bottle-conditioned ales. The pub has a contemporary café-style feel with a nautical theme – submarine paraphernalia is in abundance and a klaxon is used to call time. A monthly brewery evening offers beers from a featured brewery at a reduced price. 🅰🖴

Still & West Country House

2 Bath Square, Old Portsmouth, PO1 2JL
✪ 10-11; 11-10.30 Sun
☎ (023) 9282 1567
Fuller's Gale's Butser, London Pride, Gale's HSB; guest beers Ⓗ

One of the oldest pubs in Old Portsmouth, this large establishment affords stunning vistas of the harbour and the Spinnaker Tower. The downstairs bar has interesting ceilings and a diverse collection of maritime memorabilia. Excellent food is served, with fish a speciality. Well worth a visit, the pub can get crowded on sunny days in high summer, when the beer garden comes into its own.
❀◑&≉(Portsmouth Harbour)

Taswell Arms

42 Taswell Road, Southsea, PO5 2RG
✪ 12-midnight (11 Sun)
☎ (023) 9285 1301
Hop Back Summer Lightning; Shepherd Neame Spitfire; guest beer Ⓗ

This large Victorian building had other uses before becoming a typical street-corner community pub. It features outside seating front and rear, and a single split-level bar with different drinking areas. Ascend the steps and to your left is a surprisingly quiet lounge area with overstuffed settees. This pub offers myriad diversions, including table football, to its mixed clientele. The service is second to none as is the excellent real ale. Truly worth finding. ❀♣ᐧᒡ

White Horse

51 Southsea Terrace, Southsea, PO5 3AU
✪ 11-11; 12-10.30 Sun
☎ (023) 9282 8979
Fuller's London Pride, Gale's HSB, ESB; guest beer Ⓗ

Set back from the road, this large multi-roomed pub is approached through a spacious beer garden featuring many tables and illuminated at night. Directly ahead on entering is the bar; to the left lies the dining area, extended by a conservatory. All areas of the pub feature an attractive, contemporary decor. The beer is of a high standard and the food is popular too: an extensive bar menu is available 12-5pm with an equally long list of dishes to choose from in the evening until 9pm. ❀◑&ᐧᒡ

Winchester Arms

99 Winchester Road, Buckland, PO2 7PS
✪ 12 (4 Mon)-11; 12-11 Sun
☎ (023) 9266 2443
Oakleaf Hole Hearted; Shepherd Neame Spitfire; guest beers Ⓗ

Friendly two-bar local hidden among the terraced back streets. The former home of the now defunct Buckland Brewery, the brewer today plies his trade at Oakleaf in Gosport. Children and dogs are welcome. Live music plays on Sunday and there is an acoustic session on Wednesday evening, Monday is quiz night. The pub fields darts and football teams and hosts the local science fiction group's monthly meetings (second Tue). It may stay open until midnight at the weekend if busy. ᕙQ❀◲♣ᐧᒡ

Ringwood

Inn on the Furlong

Meeting House Lane, BH24 1EY
✪ 11-11 (midnight Fri & Sat)
☎ (01425) 475139
Ringwood Best Bitter, Fortyniner, Old Thumper, seasonal beers Ⓗ

Previously a private house, the cream-painted Victorian building was saved from demolition to become Ringwood's first tied house in 1985. A large, single, flag-stoned bar serves a number of linked areas including a sunny conservatory and a family area. Although a 'quiet' pub, without jukebox or games machines, it can be very busy and lively. No meals are served on Tuesday evening when there is often a live music session. The pub is situated opposite the town's main car park and bus terminus. ᕙQ❄❀◑&க♣ᐧᒡ

Romsey

Abbey Hotel

11 Church Street, SO51 8BT
✪ 11-3, 6-11; 12-3, 7-10.30 Sun
☎ (01794) 513360 ⊕ abbeyhotelromsey.co.uk
Courage Best Bitter, Directors; Young's Bitter Ⓗ

Handsome 19th-century pub, built to replace an earlier establishment which fell victim to a road-widening scheme. The interior is divided in two, with views of its ecclesiastical namesake from both parts; one side is used principally by diners. Pass beneath a lintel evincing the confidence of a former owner to enjoy a comfortable pub offering tranquillity and good conversation. The secluded garden is bordered by a stream and a medieval house. No food is served on Sunday evening.
ᕙQ❀◲◑≉◲P

Old House at Home

62 Love Lane, SO51 8DE (next to Waitrose car park)
✪ 11-3, 5-11 (11.30 Fri); 11-3, 6-11.30 Sat; 12-4, 7-10.30 Sun
☎ (01794) 513175
Fuller's Gale's Butser, London Pride, Gale's HSB, seasonal beers Ⓗ

The Old House is a well-run pub, welcoming to all. With a convenient gate from the Waitrose car park giving direct access into the pub garden, it is particularly popular with ladies at lunchtimes. Locals praise the food, which includes deeply satisfying cooked breakfasts, traditional lunches, bistro-style evening meals with fish a speciality and Sunday lunches. All the food is home-made – the kitchen has no freezer. Older locals call the pub the Spotted Cow, recalling the time when such a beast appeared behind the bar. Q❀◑≉◲P

Tudor Rose

3 The Cornmarket, SO51 8GB
✪ 10-11; 11-midnight Fri & Sat; 12-11 Sun
☎ (01794) 512126
Courage Best Bitter; Hampshire Ironside; Shepherd Neame Spitfire; guest beer Ⓗ

Small, no-frills pub with an enviable location on the Cornmarket. Market traders and their customers benefit from the early opening. The almost cubical single bar has a fine ceiling and fireplace dating from about 1450; the pub's long history includes time as a workhouse, a brothel and a guildhall. Musical entertainment of some description is staged on most weekend evenings. A courtyard provides limited outside drinking. One of the few Romsey pubs serving Hampshire Brewery beers, but note that Ironside may be badged as Totally Tudor. ▲▲&◑≠🖪♣

Rowlands Castle

Castle Inn
1 Finchdean Road, PO9 6DA
🕐 11-11 (midnight Fri & Sat)
☎ (023) 9241 2494
Fuller's Gale's Butser, London Pride, Gale's HSB; guest beers Ⓗ
Hidden behind the railway bridge and handy for both Stanstead House and Staunton Park, this traditional village inn has open hearths, wall panelling and bare boards or flagstones. Walkers and dogs are welcome in the public bar, while the lounge doubles as a restaurant (no food Sun eve). The pub is well known locally for its home-made pies, while fish and chips wrapped in newspaper is sold on Friday evening. As well as exploring the village itself, visitors can enjoy walks on the southern edge of the South Downs and the eastern end of the Forest of Bere. ▲▲&◑ ⛁&♣P⬏

Selborne

Selborne Arms
High Street, GU34 3JR (follow signs from Alton)
🕐 11-3, 6 (5.30 Fri)-11; 11-11 summer Sat; 12-11 Sun
☎ (01420) 511247
Courage Best Bitter; Oakleaf Bloomfields Suthwyck; Ringwood Fortyniner; guest beers Ⓗ
Traditional village pub in a building that dates back to the 1600s, retaining log fires and original features. It is located at the bottom of Selborne Hanger and the famous zigzag path carved by naturalist Gilbert White. The guest beers in this free house showcase local microbreweries, while the award-winning menu also features local produce. The extensive grassed garden with a children's play area and fantastic barbecue is popular in summer. ▲▲Q&◑ ⛁🖪(72, X72)♣P⬏

Shedfield

Wheatsheaf Inn
Botley Road, SO32 2JG (on A334)
🕐 12-11 (10.30 Sun)
☎ (01329) 833024
Flowerpots Bitter, Wheatsheaf Best, Gooden's Gold; Oakleaf Nuptu'ale; guest beers Ⓖ
Owned by the Flowerpots pub and brewery, this is a lively, friendly inn with comfortable public and small lounge bars. Beers, sourced from local breweries (including Flowerpots, Ringwood and Oakleaf) are served straight from casks behind the bar. On Saturday night, blues or jazz music is played here, and a beer festival is staged on the late spring bank holiday. The garden boasts a colourful display of flowers throughout the summer. Dogs on leads are welcome. Parking is across the busy main road. ▲▲Q&◑ ⛁🖪♣P

Sherfield-on-Loddon

White Hart
Reading Road, RG27 0BT (on A33)
🕐 10-midnight (11.30 Sun)
☎ (01256) 882280 ⊕ whitehartsherfield.com
Wells Bombardier; Young's Bitter, Special Ⓗ
A 17th-century country pub on the old Reading Road, opposite the village green. It used to be a staging inn and continues to cater for thirsty and hungry travellers using the A33; food is available every day. On the main fireplace stands a letter rack dating from the 1700s; it is still used at Christmas today to distribute seasonal cards. At the rear of the pub is a spacious garden for mild summer days. ▲▲&◑ &🖪(44)P⬏

Southampton

Bitter Virtue (off-licence)
70 Cambridge Road, SO14 6US (take Alma Rd from The Avenue, by church, 250m)
🕐 10.30-8.30 (not Mon); 10.30-2 Sun
☎ (023) 8055 4881 ⊕ bittervirtue.co.uk
Beer range varies Ⓖ
Gravity-dispensed draught ale, usually from smaller breweries such as Bowman, Downton, Hop Back and Loddon, complete the range of beer and cider available from this speciality shop. Celebrating 10 years in business and in this Guide, bottled beers from the UK, Belgium, Germany, USA, Australia, South America and the rest of the world will be joined in late 2007 by a Belgian microbrewery ale. A wide range of badged glasses, books and T-shirts is also stocked.

Crown
9 Highcrown Street, SO17 1QE (off Highfield Lane)
🕐 11 (12 Sun)-11
☎ (023) 8031 5033
Draught Bass; Flowers Original; Fuller's London Pride; Ringwood Best Bitter; Taylor Landlord Ⓗ
Dating from the late 19th century, when it was owned by the Scrases Star Brewery, this pub is situated near the university and attracts a mixed local and student crowd. The single bar serves five regular beers, and an extensive food menu is available at lunchtime and in the evening (booking advisable). Children are welcome on the covered, heated patio, while dogs on a lead are allowed in the pub. The car park is in Hawthorn Road. &◑P

Guide Dog
38 Earl's Road, Bevois Valley, SO14 6SF (100m W of Bevois Valley Rd)
🕐 3 (12 Fri & Sat)-11; 12-10.30 Sun
☎ (023) 8022 5642
Fuller's ESB; guest beers Ⓗ
A warm and inviting single-roomed, back-street pub, serving up to seven real ales from local and national breweries. Take-away jugs are available, and there is a good selection of continental lagers. Within walking distance of Southampton FC's ground, the pub is ideally suited for match-day drinks, and its welcoming atmosphere makes it easy to find new friends. A gypsy swing band plays here once a month, and two beer festivals are held each year. ≠(St Denys)🖪♣⬏

Humble Plumb

Commercial Street, Bitterne, SO18 6LY
🕐 11.30-2.30, 5-11; 11.30-11 Fri & Sat; 12-10.30 Sun
☎ (023) 8043 7577
Wadworth IPA, 6X, Bishop's Tipple, seasonal beers; guest beers Ⓗ

Dating from 1812, when it was the Commercial Inn, this is one of the oldest pubs in Bitterne. The friendly local has a spacious L-shaped bar featuring nine handpumps, six dispensing ever-changing seasonal and guest beers, and offers a 'try before you buy' policy. On Monday evening a popular quiz is held, and there is a meat draw on Sunday lunchtime. Food is served every lunchtime and Thursday-Saturday evenings. Dogs are welcome, and there is a covered area for smokers on the patio. ❀◑ᵭ🚃P'－

Park Inn

37 Carlisle Road, Shirley, SO16 4FN (off Romsey Rd)
🕐 11.30 (12 Sun)-midnight
☎ (023) 8078 7835
Wadworth IPA, 6X, JCB, Bishop's Tipple; guest beers Ⓗ

This friendly 19th-century Wadworth house comprises a single central bar adjoining open-plan but cosy rooms, adorned with a collection of mirrors. A true community pub, darts and cribbage are played by the regulars. The forecourt allows for outdoor drinking on milder days and has a corner for smokers. A covered area is currently being added. Dogs are welcome. ❀🚃♣'－

Platform Tavern

Town Quay, SO14 2NY
🕐 11-11 (midnight Thu-Sat)
☎ (023) 8033 7232 ⊕ platformtavern.com
Fuller's London Pride; Itchen Valley Godfathers; guest beers Ⓗ

Built in 1872, and recently expanded into the café next door, this stone-floored building incorporates parts of the old city walls. Two guest beers from local breweries feature in the bar. The café opens for breakfast at 8am (10am Sun) and specialises in fresh fish Thursday to Saturday evenings. Regular live jazz, blues and roots music draws fans, and the broad pavement area serves summer drinkers. Disabled access is via the rear (Winkle Street) door. ❀◑ᵭ🚃

Richmond Inn

108 Portswood Road, Portswood, SO17 2FW
🕐 11-11
☎ (023) 8055 4523
Greene King IPA, Abbot; guest beer Ⓗ

Well-maintained Victorian two-bar pub, with a lively public bar offering darts, jukebox and TV, as well as a quieter, comfortable lounge more suitable for conversation. Note the magnificent LSD brass till, still in use. The garden is a hidden gem, lovingly cared for and a pleasant shelter from nearby traffic. The pub has a function room available for meetings. Evening closing may be later than shown, depending on trade. ❀🖾≠(St Denys)🚃♣

South Western Arms

38-40 Adelaide Road, St Denys, SO17 2HW
(adjoins St Denys Station)

🕐 3-11; 2-midnight Fri; 12-midnight Sat; 12-11 Sun
☎ (023) 8032 4542
Caledonian Deuchars IPA; Fuller's Chiswick; Hop Back Summer Lightning; Ringwood Best Bitter; guest beers Ⓗ

Thriving community pub offering a large, changing range of ales and cider (usually Weston's or Biddenden). The pump clips of forthcoming beers are always on display. Annual beer festivals attract crowds from far and wide to this regular local CAMRA Pub of the Year. The interior has two levels with pool, darts and table football on the quieter mezzanine. It is adorned with a multitude of old inn paraphernalia – there is always something new to discover. The spacious outdoor area and the friendly pub cat help make this a popular drinking venue. ❀≠🖾♣◑P'－

Stile

163 University Road, Highfield, SO17 1TS (corner of University and Burgess roads)
🕐 12-11
☎ (023) 8058 1124
Caledonian Deuchars IPA; guest beers Ⓗ

Situated next to the university, this 1860s pub is popular with students and locals. Five of the six handpumps serve changing guest beers, although the range is sometimes reduced during university holidays. The patio has a gazebo for smokers. Food is served daily until 8pm. A selection of board games such as chess or backgammon is available on request. If trade warrants the pub may remain open until midnight. ❀◑ᵭ🚃♣'－

Waterloo Arms

101 Waterloo Road, Freemantle, SO15 3BS
🕐 12-11
☎ (023) 8022 0022
Hop Back GFB, Crop Circle, Entire Stout, Summer Lightning, seasonal beer; guest beers Ⓗ

This Hop Back tied house is a cosy one-bar local in a quiet residential area, benefiting from a secluded paved garden and a large, separate conservatory where families are welcome until 9pm. A selection of country wines is stocked and good food is served (not Sun). Dogs are permitted at this pub, just a short walk from Millbrook station and half a mile from Southampton Central station. Although not a 'sports pub', major sporting events are shown on TV in the conservatory. ⬲❀◑≠(Millbrook/Central)🚃

Wellington Arms

56 Park Road, Freemantle, SO15 3DE (Mansion Rd jct)
🕐 12-11.30 (12.30am Fri & Sat)
☎ (023) 8022 0356
Adnams Bitter; Fuller's London Pride; Greene King Abbot; Ringwood Best Bitter; Wychwood Hobgoblin; guest beers Ⓗ

Friendly, corner, two-bar local dating from the 1860s. Inside is a veritable treasure trove of Iron Duke memorabilia, and the unique bar counter is set with hundreds of old coins. The main bar features a number of settles allowing some privacy. As well as the five regular beers, there are two continually changing guest ales, and Leffe Blonde and Hoegaarden are also on draught. A paved garden caters for summer drinking, and a popular quiz is held on Thursday evening. ✿❂≉(Millbrook/Central)❂♿

Tadley

Bishopswood Golf Club

Bishopswood Lane, RG26 4AT (6 miles N of Basingstoke, off A340) OS591617

☼ 11-11 (9.30 Mon) summer; 11-6.30 (9.30 Tue & Thu; 11 Wed, Fri & Sat) winter; 12-7 Sun

☎ (0118) 981 2200

Beer range varies ⊞

A golf club is not generally a place to find any, not to mention good quality, real ale, but this one is the glorious exception to the rule. One beer is usually from Brains or West Berkshire, accompanied by another guest. A warm, friendly atmosphere pertains in the comfortable lounge (dress code applies), which features an unusual central fireplace. Snooker is also played here. Outside, a pleasant raised terrace overlooks the golf course. Local CAMRA Club of the Year four years running, visitors are welcome. ✿◑❂♿❒(2)♣P

Tichborne

Tichborne Arms

SO24 0NA OS571304

☼ 11.30-3, 6.30-11.30; 7-11 Sun

☎ (01962) 733760 ⊕ tichbornearms.com

Ringwood Best Bitter; guest beers ⒼE

This rural two-bar pub stocks locally sourced ales including Flowerpots, Ringwood and various guest ales, as well as real cider (Thatchers Traditional), all served directly from casks behind the bar. A menu of home-cooked dishes with extensive specials on the board is available every day. The large garden features a covered and heated decked terrace, and there is ample parking for visitors. Note that closing time is earlier during the winter months. Q✿◑❂♣♿P

Titchfield

Wheatsheaf

1 East Street, PO14 4AD

☼ 12-3, 6-11; 12-11 Fri & Sat; 12-10.30 Sun

☎ (01329) 842965

Flowerpots Bitter; guest beers ⊞

Situated near the centre of this ancient and picturesque village, the Wheatsheaf changed hands in 2006. Up to three guest beers are usually available, with an extra strong beer on the bar at weekends in winter. The guest beers include ales from local breweries, which may be supplemented by others from the Flowerpots range. The licensee is a qualified chef, and word of his excellent cuisine has got around (no food Sun eve and all day Mon). ᴀ✿◑❒P

Upper Farringdon

Rose & Crown Inn

Crows Lane, GU34 3ED (off A32)

☼ 12-3, 6-11, 12-11 Sat; 12-10.30 Sun

☎ (01420) 588231

Adnams Bitter; Courage Best Bitter; Greene King IPA; Triple fff Moondance; guest beers ⊞

In a village just off the beaten track, enter this friendly pub and you will find an L-shaped bar and a cosy seating area warmed by a log fire. Deeper inside is a formal dining area leading to a modern restaurant (no food Mon eve). Imaginative food is supplemented by lunchtime bar snacks. Families are welcome: in summer there is a spacious and inviting garden and in winter games can be played in the bar. The inn stages a regular Monday jazz evening. Walkers and dogs are always welcome. ᴀQ✿♿◑❂♣P♿

Waterlooville

Heroes

125 London Road, PO7 7DZ

☼ 10-11 (11.30 Tue; midnight Fri & Sat)

☎ (023) 9225 3068

Fuller's Chiswick, London Pride, Gale's HSB, ESB ⊞

This pub at the north end of Waterlooville's precinct gets busy with shoppers at lunchtime. Very much a sporting and music pub, this multi-roomed former Gale's house has many TV screens showing live sporting events. The lounge, however, is a TV-free zone. Live bands perform every Friday and Saturday, and some Sundays; Tuesday is a popular karaoke night. A pub since 1966, it was formally a doctor's house. This building replaces the previous Heroes of Waterlooville, which was demolished to make room for the shopping centre. ✿◑❂♿❒P♿

Whitchurch

Prince Regent

104 London Road, RG28 7LT (on Basingstoke road)

☼ 11-1am

☎ (01256) 892179

Hop Back Summer Lightning; Otter Bitter; Stonehenge Pigswill ⊞

This unspoilt free house is a true small-town local. Overlooking the Test Valley and the town, the single-bar pub is well worth the walk up from the centre. The friendly landlord, always ready for a lively conversation, takes great pride in the quality of his beer. Buses stop outside for the nearby towns of Winchester, Andover and Basingstoke. ✿❒(76, 86)♣P

Whitchurch Sports & Social Club

Longmeadow Sports Centre, Winchester Road, RG28 7RB (S edge of town, by football ground)

☼ 11-2.30 (Wed-Sat winter only), 7-11; 12-10.30 Sun

☎ (01256) 892493

Fuller's London Pride; Hampshire King Alfred's ⊞

Tucked away on the edge of this historic town, opposite the tranquil Millennium Meadow, it is easy to miss this fine community social club. Home to Whitchurch United FC, it also boasts an indoor bowling club whose green is viewed from the comfortable lounge, and two squash courts. Two contrasting bar areas provide a welcoming atmosphere for a wide range of events, from disco parties to beer festivals. CAMRA members can be signed in on production of a valid membership card. ❂♿❒♣P

White Hart Hotel

The Square, RG28 7DN
🕐 11 (7am for breakfast)-11; 12-10.30 Sun
☎ (01256) 892900 ⊕ whiteharthotelwhitchurch.co.uk
Arkell's 3B, Moonlight Ⓗ

Dating back to the 15th century, this impressive hotel overlooks the town square where the roads to Basingstoke, Andover, Newbury and Winchester meet. The interior is divided into separate areas, including a restaurant. The popular bar is very busy, especially at weekends when live music usually features. The emphasis here is on good service, and the staff are always friendly.
Q✿🛏◑⋒💺(76, 86)P

Whitsbury

Cartwheel

SP6 3PZ (2 miles W of Breamore) OS129189
🕐 11.30-3, 5.30-midnight; 11.30-midnight Sat; 12-10.30 Sun
☎ (01725) 518362 ⊕ cartwheelinn.co.uk
Ringwood Best Bitter, Fortyniner, Old Thumper, seasonal beer Ⓗ

A Ringwood tied house, the Cartwheel comprises a number of interconnected areas served by a central bar. Most areas have tables, but the darts section is more akin to a public bar. Meals are served daily from an extensive menu, with Tuesday billed as 'fish and chip night' and Wednesday as 'steak night'; booking is advisable on summer weekends. Children are welcome and board games as well as garden play equipment are available to keep them amused. Popular with ramblers, Rockbourne Roman Villa is just a short walk away. Dogs are welcome.
🏚Q✿◑&♣P

Wickham

Wickham Wine Bar

The Square, PO17 5JN
🕐 11.30-2, 6-11; closed Sun
☎ (01329) 832732 ⊕ wickhamwinebar.com
Bowman Swift One Ⓗ

One of the first regular outlets for Bowman ales, this wine bar and restaurant is in a listed 15th-century building featuring original vaulted oak beams and a warming open log fire. The two-storey upstairs restaurant, which extends over next door's shop, features an original 16th-century wall painting and an attractive open gallery overlooking the ground-floor bar area. The menu includes fresh fish and local game. Live jazz is staged on Wednesday evening. 🏚Q✿◑💺

Winchester

Albion

2 Stockbridge Road, SO23 7BZ (200m from station, towards city)
🕐 12-11 (midnight Sat); 12-10.30 Sun
☎ (01962) 840660
Fuller's London Pride; Taylor Landlord; Young's Bitter Ⓗ

Prominent corner pub on a busy intersection below the station. Three elevations overlook six streets, making it a great place to sit and watch the world go by. The customers are a lively mix, including commuters who fall off their trains and forget to go home. No food is served, but guests may bring in excellent fare from the sandwich bar next door, and there is also a superb Indian restaurant nearby. Background music, sometimes featuring free-form jazz, is enjoyed by music fans. The single L-shaped bar can get very busy, especially at weekends. ⇌💺

Black Boy

1 Wharf Hill, SO23 9NQ (off B3330, Chesil St)
🕐 11-3, 5-11; 12-3, 7-10.30 Sun
☎ (01962) 861754 ⊕ theblackboypub.com
Flowerpots Bitter; Hop Back Summer Lightning; Ringwood Best Bitter; guest beers Ⓗ

Centuries old, rambling building of interconnected rooms surrounding a central bar. One of these rooms is laid out as a country kitchen, with a working Aga (although the stuffed donkey seems to be out of place here), another simulates a butcher's shop, complete with papier-mâché joints of meat. Other areas are made to look like tradesmen's workshops. The entire pub resembles a folk museum. Food is typical pub fare (no food Sun eve, Mon & Tue lunchtimes). Guest beers are sourced from local breweries. Dogs are welcome.
🏚Q✿◑💺

Hyde Tavern

57 Hyde Street, SO23 7DY (on B3047)
🕐 12-2 (3 Sat), 5 (6 Sat)-11 (midnight Fri & Sat); 12-11.30 Sun
☎ (01962) 862592
Beer range varies Ⓗ

An attractive exterior leads straight into the traditional front bar with low beams and a worn, undulating floor. Conversation and laughter dominate among the customers, who are drawn from a wide range of backgrounds and age groups. The cosy back room contains a large collection of sporting memorabilia. The landlady, at the pub for 19 years, is delighted to be free to offer a changing range of beers since the pub was sold by Greene King to Admiral Taverns. Q✿◮⇌♣💺

St James Tavern

3 Romsey Road, SO22 5BE
🕐 11.30-2.30, 5.30-11; 11.30-11.30 Sat; 12-3, 6.30-10.30 Sun
☎ (01962) 890018
Butcombe Bitter; Wadworth IPA, 6X, seasonal beer Ⓗ

This handsome, end-of-terrace pub on a steep hill has an attractively rusticated ground floor with brick walls laid in Flemish bond above. The lower area of the L-shaped bar is flagged and floor-boarded; the upper is carpeted. Wood abounds and the decor is warm and relaxing. These attributes, together with the warm welcome and efficient service, make for a happy and comfortable pub in which to enjoy good ale and food, including renowned local sausages. ✿◑⇌💺

Wykeham Arms

75 Kingsgate Street, SO23 9PE (by the entrances to Cathedral Close and college)
🕐 11-11; 12-10.30 Sun
☎ (01962) 853834

Fuller's Chiswick, Gale's Butser, London Pride, Gale's HSB, seasonal beer Ⓗ
Rambling Georgian inn with many interlinked rooms, adjoining the city's ancient Kingsgate. Every available inch is filled with bric-a-brac, including (allegedly) 2,000 pewter mugs. Old school desks make convenient tables, and Nelsoniana abounds. Often busy but always civilised, it is a conversational haven away from 21st-century pressures. Seasonal beers are usually from the Gale's stable. Booking is recommended for the award-winning food (no meals Sun eve) and the accommodation is of an equally high standard. ⓆⓀ

Winsor

Compass Inn
Winsor Road, SO40 2HE (½ mile S of A31)
⌚ 11-11 (midnight Fri); 12-10.30 Sun
☎ (023) 8081 2237
Fuller's London Pride, Gale's HSB; Greene King Abbot; Ringwood Best Bitter Ⓗ
This small, traditional multi-bar pub features a welcoming lounge with polished wood furniture, fresh flowers and log-burning stove; a more sombre, panelled public bar, which is home to the pool table; and a rustic dining

room where good food is served daily. Unusually for a pub, there is an artist in residence, and his New Forest murals are a feature in the ladies' toilets. Beer festivals are held on May and August bank holidays. Dogs are welcome.

Wolverton

George & Dragon
Wolverton Townsend, RG26 5ST (1 mile E of A339, 3½ miles SW of Tadley)
⌚ 12-3, 5.30-11; 12-3, 7-10.30 Sun
☎ (01635) 298292
Brakspear Special; Fuller's London Pride; Greene King Morland Original; Wadworth IPA; West Berkshire Mr Chubb's; guest beers Ⓗ
Oak beams festooned with dried hops and a huge open hearth burning logs in winter characterise this 300-year-old inn, run by the same landlord for 22 years. It provides a superb setting in which to relish the good selection of beers, while diners sit at candlelit tables to enjoy good home-cooked cuisine in a romantic atmosphere. The large garden is set in an orchard where children can play. A function room, with bar and skittle alley, caters for parties.

In memory of three great brewers

2007 saw the deaths of three much-loved members of the brewing industry, all dedicated to cask beer.

Claude Arkell was the owner of the Donnington Brewery near Stow-on-the-Wold in the Cotswolds, described as the loveliest brewery in Britain, with its water wheel, mellow stone buildings and tree-girt lake rich in wildlife. Claude, who died aged 89, worked until his death and was a direct descendant of Thomas Arkell, who founded the brewery in 1827. The water wheel continues to provide power for the brewery, which includes the only-known example of an open-topped copper. Claude sold his delicious, uncomplicated beers in 15 delightful pubs in the Cotswolds. The brewery is now in the hands of his cousin Peter Arkell and Peter's son James, who run Arkells Brewery in Swindon. They plan to maintain production at Donnington.

George Bateman, who died aged 79, was best known as the man who saved the Wainfleet brewery and its 'Good Honest Ales' in the 1980s. When his brother and sister decided they wanted to cash in their shares, George was faced with the choice of either raising a large sum of money to buy his relatives out or see the brewery he loved disappear. After an epic struggle, during which Bateman's XXXB was named Champion Beer of Britain, George was able to buy out his relatives. Bateman's has gone from strength to strength, with additional pubs, a wide free trade and a brilliant visitor centre at Wainfleet. The brewery is now in the safe hands of his daughter Jaclyn and son Stuart.

Bill Witty, who died aged 75, was a founder of the Harrogate branch of CAMRA and creator of Daleside Brewery in Harrogate. Bill entered the licensed trade in 1986 with a small pub group called Rodent Inns, which included the Rat & Ratchet in Huddersfield and the One Eyed Rat in Ripon. In 1988 Bill founded Big End Brewery in Harrogate, using old dairy equipment. It was renamed Daleside in 1992 and Bill expanded his range of beers. They included Greengrass Old Rogue Ale, named after the TV character in Heartbeat. Bill allegedly paid Yorkshire Television £10 and got actor Bill Maynard to launch the beer. His son Craig has succeeded him at the brewery.

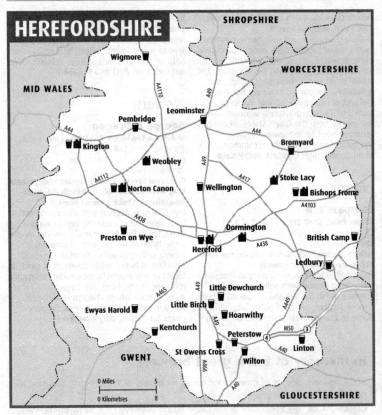

HEREFORDSHIRE

SHROPSHIRE

WORCESTERSHIRE

MID WALES

Wigmore

A4110

A49

Leominster

A44

Pembridge

A44

Kington

Bromyard

A49

Weobley

A417

Stoke Lacy

A112

Norton Canon

Wellington

Bishops Frome

A4103

A438

Dormington

Preston on Wye

British Camp

Hereford

A438

Ledbury

A465

Little Dewchurch

A449

Ewyas Harold

Little Birch

A49

Hoarwithy

M50

Kentchurch

Peterstow

4

3

Linton

GWENT

St Owens Cross

A40

Wilton

A466

A40

GLOUCESTERSHIRE

0 Miles 5

0 Kilometres 8

Bishops Frome

Green Dragon

WR6 5BP (just off B4214)

🕔 5 (4 Fri)-11; 12-11.30 Sat; 12-4, 7-10.30 Sun

☎ (01885) 490607

Taylor Golden Best, Landlord; Theakston Best Bitter; Wye Valley Butty Bach; guest beer 🅷

After a long period in the doldrums, this unspoiled 17th-century inn changed hands in 2005 and is now run with real verve and commitment. Low-beamed, it has a warren of flagstone-floored rooms, with an inglenook in the main bar. A limited menu is served (not Sun) with Scottish steaks a speciality. Draught local cider is available in summer.

Herefordshire CAMRA Country Pub of the Year 2006. ♨❀◑🖵🛏♣🐕P⅃

British Camp

Malvern Hills Hotel

Jubilee Drive, WR13 6DW (on A449)

🕔 11-11; 12-10.30 Sun

☎ (01684) 540690 ⊕ malvernhillshotel.co.uk

Malvern Hills Black Pear; Wye Valley Bitter, HPA; guest beer 🅷

Constantly improving landmark hotel located high on the Malvern Hills, near the British Camp Hill Fort. It prides itself on a genuine commitment to stocking local beers. The main wood-panelled bar is popular with locals and walkers (dry dogs and well-behaved children welcome – the latter until 4pm). Two

restaurants, one in an airy conservatory with great views, provide for good, affordable dining. Plenty of outside seating makes this an ideal venue for a fine day. ♨❀◑◑🖵🛏&♣P⅃

Bromyard

Rose & Lion

5 New Road, HR7 4AJ

🕔 11-3, 5-11; 11-midnight Fri & Sat; 12-10.30 Sun

☎ (01885) 482381

Wye Valley Bitter, HPA, Butty Bach, guest beer (occasional) 🅷

Known affectionately as the 'Rosie', this traditional three-room pub remains largely untouched. It has all the necessary ingredients: a friendly public bar, a cosy lounge, a good buzz and a pleasant garden in which to drink good ale. Located off the main street and run by Wye Valley Brewery, it enjoys a loyal following among locals, while always welcoming visitors. A folk jam session is held on Sunday evenings. Q❀🖵🛏♣P⅃

Ewyas Harold

Dog Inn

HR2 0EX (just off B4347)

☻ 10-midnight (1am Fri & Sat); 10-11 Sun

☎ (01981) 240598 ⊕ thedoginn.org.uk

Beer range varies Ⓗ

Stone-built village inn dating from the early 16th century with a main bar plus games room and restaurant. Three ever-changing beers are drawn from mainly local micro-breweries. Home-prepared and locally-sourced meals are served in the restaurant and, at lunchtime, snacks in the bar. Live music features from time to time, and a beer festival is held annually in the autumn. ♨Q❀❍Ⓓ&☐♣•᠘

Hereford

Barrels

69 St Owen Street, HR1 2JQ

☻ 11-11.30 (midnight Fri & Sat)

☎ (01432) 274968

Wye Valley Bitter, HPA, Dorothy Goodbody's Golden Ale, Wholesome Stout, seasonal beers Ⓗ

Winner of Herefordshire CAMRA Pub of the Year for the fourth time in 2006, this pub enjoys a near cult following. Popular with visitors and locals, its four distinct bars appeal to a wide clientele. A pool table occupies one bar, another has a large screen TV strictly for major sports events – otherwise banter is king. The rear courtyard, originally home to the Wye Valley Brewery, is now the venue for a major charity music and beer festival held each August Bank Holiday. ❀🅟≑☐♣•᠘

Kings Fee

49-53 Commercial Road, HR1 2BJ

☻ 9am-midnight

☎ (01432) 373240

Greene King Abbot; Marston's Pedigree; guest beers Ⓗ

Wetherspoon supermarket conversion, highly commended in the 2004 CAMRA National Pub Design Awards. The large open-plan main bar leads to an elevated family area (children welcome up to 7pm) and a courtyard. Decor is contemporary in style, and features local history panels and woodcut prints by a local artist. A welcome choice of up to eight guest ales is on offer, as well as Westons Old Rosie and Organic Vintage Cider. Good value food is served all day. Q➢❀Ⓓ&≑☐•᠘

Victory

88 St Owen Street, HR1 2QD

☻ 3 (11 summer)-11 (midnight Fri & Sat); 12-10.30 Sun

☎ (01432) 274998

Spinning Dog Hereford Organic Bitter, Owd Bull, Light Ale, Organic Oatmeal Stout, Mutley's Revenge; guest beers Ⓗ

Home of the city's only brewery, Spinning Dog, the Victory offers most of the range, plus the best selection of real cider and perry in Herefordshire including Westons and Gwatkins. The front bar is heavily timbered and the servery built in the shape of a galleon. At the rear is a skittle alley and quieter back bar. A key weekend venue for local bands, mini beer festivals are held once or twice a year. Meals are served at the weekend;

Sunday lunches a speciality. ♨⌂❀❍Ⓓ&≑☐♣•᠘

Hoarwithy

New Harp Inn

HR2 6QH OS545292

☻ 12-11 (12-3, 6-11 winter); 12-10.30 Sun

☎ (01432) 840900 ⊕ newharpinn.co.uk

Beer range varies Ⓗ

Completely refurbished, this friendly pub has one long bar with a stone floor and light, modern decor. Home-prepared food ranges from bar snacks to full à la carte, with fish night on Tuesday and frequent food events. Beers come from regional and local micro-breweries. A large selection of UK and foreign bottled beers is available plus interesting continental beers on draught. Beer festivals are held twice a year. ♨❀❍Ⓓ&☐🅟•᠘

Kentchurch

Bridge Inn

HR2 0BY (on B4347)

☻ 12-3 (not Mon & Tue), 5-11; 12-3, 7-10.30 Sun

☎ (01981) 240408

Beer range varies Ⓗ

In a beautiful location near the Welsh border on the River Monnow, the building probably dates from the 14th century. It comprises a single front bar plus a restaurant with excellent views. Attractive riverside gardens and a petanque piste are popular in summer. The freshly-prepared food ranges from bar snacks to full à la carte (not Sun eve). Guest beers come from regional and local breweries, usually including Wye Valley. Beer festivals are held on spring and August bank holidays. ♨Q❀❍Ⓓ&♣🅟

Kington

Olde Tavern

22 Victoria Road, HR5 3BX

☻ 7 (6.30 Tue-Fri)-midnight (1am Fri); 12-3, 6-1am Sat; 12-3, 7-10.30 Sun

☎ (01544) 230122

Dunn Plowman Brewhouse Bitter, Early Riser, Sting, Shirehorse Ale Ⓗ

Part of Kington's history, once the House in the Fields, then the Railway Tavern, this is a pub for the connoisseur. A two-room time warp, it is full of fascinating curios. The tap for the nearby Dunn Plowman Brewery, it offers a warm welcome from staff and locals alike. Shoehorned into an old bottle store at the rear is the diminutive Jake's Bistro, serving exceptional value English cuisine made with locally-sourced ingredients (Wed-Sat eve, booking essential). Q❀❑☐•᠘

Ledbury

Prince of Wales

Church Lane, HR8 1DL

☻ 11-11 (10.30 Sun)

☎ (01531) 632250

Banks's Bitter; Brains Rev James; Sharp's Doom Bar; guest beer Ⓗ

Timbered 16th-century pub set in a cobbled street by the church, comprising front and back bars and a side alcove. Always bustling, it holds a popular folk jam session (Wed eve) and fields pub games teams. Run with real passion, this is the pub in Ledbury for beer, cider and foreign beers. Good value, simple bar meals and Sunday roasts are popular, along with Westons perry in summer and cider. ▷❀①⊞≢🖛♣♠↦

Talbot Hotel
14 New Street, HR8 2DX
✪ 11-3, 5-11 (midnight Fri); 11-midnight Sat; 11-4, 7-11 Sun
☎ (01531) 632963 ⊕ visitledbury.co.uk/talbot
Wadworth IPA, 6X; Wye Valley Butty Bach; guest beer Ⓗ
Black and white, half-timbered hotel dating back to 1596. The heavily-beamed main bar and smaller bar area, with an island servery, offer a choice of relaxing and comfortable drinking areas. The oak-panelled dining room, with its fine carved overmantle, was once the scene of fighting between Cavaliers and Roundheads. Traditional bar snacks are available and English and continental dishes served in the restaurant, all made with local ingredients. ▲①≢🖛♣↦

Leominster

Bell Inn
39 Etnam Street, HR6 8AE
✪ 12-11.30
☎ (01568) 612818
Wye Valley Bitter, HPA, Butty Bach; guest beer Ⓗ
This friendly, modernised pub with its single U-shaped island bar has a light and airy feel. Live music features folk on Tuesday evening, a band on Thursday. Reasonably priced, home-made pub food is served at lunchtime. Guest beer comes from national breweries. It has a pleasant garden to the rear. Joint winner of Herefordshire CAMRA Pub of the Year 2005. ▲❀①≢🖛♣↦

Black Horse
74 South Street, HR6 8JF
✪ 11-2.30, 6-11; 11-11 Sat; 12-3, 7-10.30 Sun
☎ (01568) 611946
Dunn Plowman Brewhouse Bitter; Hobsons Town Crier; guest beers Ⓗ
A regular in the Guide, this old coach house was once home to the fledgling Dunn Plowman Brewery and it still keeps an excellent range of beers. It has a traditional public bar, a small, narrow lounge area, and a dining area to the rear. Bar snacks and meals are served (not Sun eve), with Sunday lunches a speciality. Games include petanque, table skittles and quoits. Q▷❀①⊞≢🖛♣↦

Chequers
63 Etnam Street, HR6 8AE
✪ 11-11; 12-10.30 Sun
☎ (01568) 612473
Banks's Bitter; Wye Valley Butty Bach; guest beer Ⓗ
Probably the oldest pub in Leominster, built in 1480. A superb timber-framed terraced building with protruding gables, the front public bar retains many original features including a splendid real fire; the refurbished lounge bar is quieter and there is a dining area

to the rear. A new outside drinking space and function room complete this community pub. Adventurous guest beers appear from micro-breweries near and far. Home-prepared lunches are served. ▲▷❀①⊞≢🖛♣♠P↦

Linton

Alma Inn
HR9 7RY (off B4221, W of M50 jct 3) OS659255
✪ 12-3 (not Mon-Fri), 6.30 (6 Fri & Sat)-11; 12-3, 7-10.30 Sun
☎ (01989) 720355 ⊕ almainnlinton.co.uk
Butcombe Bitter; Oakham JHB; RCH Pitchfork; guest beers Ⓗ
Frequent Herefordshire CAMRA Pub of the Year, the Alma proves that a well-run country pub doesn't have to sell food to be a success. This plain but thriving village pub run with real devotion and imagination, champions smaller and local breweries. The cosy lounge complements a more basic pool room and a less-used 'other room'. Visitors from afar as well as locals come to enjoy the great atmosphere. Extensive hillside gardens are the venue for a summer Blues & Ale festival. ▲Q❀♠♣P↦

Little Birch

Castle
HR2 8BB OS508321
✪ 12-3 (not Mon), 6.30 (7 Mon)-11; 12-11 Sat & Sun
☎ (01981) 540756
Otter Bitter; guest beers Ⓗ
Hidden in the lanes of a widely dispersed village, this split-level, stone-built pub can be hard to find. Refurbishment has moved the main entrance to car park level, opening into an airy, stone-floored bar. Up a short flight of stairs is the lounge/dining room where locally sourced, home-prepared food is served (not Mon). Events include regular folk, quiz, and themed food nights plus two beer festivals per year. Three guest beers come from regional breweries and Westons Scrumpy is available. ▲▷❀①⊞♣♠P↦

Little Dewchurch

Plough
HR2 6PW OS535318
✪ 11-midnight (1am Fri & Sat); 12-10.30 Sun
☎ (01432) 840542
Wye Valley Butty Bach; guest beers Ⓗ
Wayside inn on the back road from Ross to Hereford dating from the early 19th century. The single bar, simply furnished, with a pool room to one side, is being refurbished. The Ursa Major restaurant is linked to the pub and meals can be served in the pub itself. Home prepared and locally sourced, these include a large vegetarian selection. Guest beers are from micro-breweries, frequently local. ▲Q❀①⊞♣🖛♣P↦

Norton Canon

Three Horseshoes
HR4 7BH (on A480)
✪ 12-3 (Wed & Sat only), 6-11; 12-3, 7-10.30 Sun
☎ (01544) 318375

Shoes Canon Bitter, Norton Ale, Peploe's Tipple, Farriers Ale Ⓗ

Isolated roadside home of the Shoes Brewery. The largely unspoilt interior has recovered well from a major fire in 2006. A public bar leads through to a larger pool room, and there is a small, cosy lounge, comfortably furnished. The friendly landlord ensures a great atmosphere. Farriers Ale at 15.4% ABV is now available on draught as well bottled. The bus stop is half mile from the pub (Weobley Turn). ⌂Q⍩⌖⊕⊟(461, 462)♣P≞

Pembridge

New Inn
Market Square, HR6 9DZ
☼ 11-3, 6-11; 12-3, 7-10.30 Sun
☎ (01544) 388427
Black Sheep Best Bitter; Fuller's London Pride; Three Tuns XXX; guest beer Ⓗ
Imposing building of great character and charm facing the market square. Steeped in history, the public bar is resplendent with flagstone floor and inglenook; there is a lounge and downstairs restaurant. The fascinating untouched interior is decorated with hops and interesting furniture. Pub games include shove ha'penny. A wide selection of malt whiskies is available plus bottled Dunkertons Black Fox cider. ⌂Q⍩⌖⊕⊕⊟⊕♣P

Peterstow

Red Lion
Winters Cross, HR9 6LH (on A49, just NW of village)
☼ 12-2.30, 6-11.30 (12.30am Fri); closed Mon; 12-12.30am Sat; 12-11 Sun
☎ (01989) 730202
Otter Bitter; Taylor Landlord; guest beers Ⓗ
A remarkable success story; the Red Lion was delicensed in the 1970s but reverted to a pub a few years later. A single bar serves extensive drinking and dining areas, including a large, modern roadside conservatory. Home-prepared food ranges from bar snacks to full meals (booking advised). Facilities include an outdoor adventure playground for children. The regular Hereford-Ross bus stops outside. ⌂⍩⌖⊕⊕⊻⅄⊟(38)♣P≞

Preston on Wye

Yew Tree
HR2 9JT OS385414
☼ 7-midnight (1am Fri & Sat); 12-3, 7-11 Sun
☎ (01981) 500359
Beer range varies Ⓖ
Pleasantly eccentric and basic village pub, very much a drinkers' establishment. Comfortable and welcoming, it supports boules, pool and quiz teams, and is popular with fishermen and canoeists from the nearby River Wye. The beer, from local or regional breweries, is served from a cask behind the small bar. The cider is draught Thatchers Heritage. Evening meals are available in summer if ordered in advance. Live music is hosted monthly on Saturdays. ⌂Q⌖⅄♣P≞

St Owens Cross

New Inn
HR2 8LQ (A4137/B4521 jct)
☼ 11-11 (midnight Fri)
☎ (01989) 730274 ⊕ newinn.biz
Marston's Burton Bitter; guest beers Ⓗ
Black and white 16th-century inn with a timbered, split-level main bar, cosy nooks and crannies and a large inglenook. The real ales are served from a pewter beer engine rescued from a long defunct pub in Ross-on-Wye. Traditional English bar snacks and meals are served in the bar, dining room and child-friendly garden, with its Black Mountain views. Cider in summer comes from Broome Farm or Gwatkins. ⌂⊛⊕◑⅄⊟♣⊕P≞

Wellington

Wellington Inn
HR4 8AT (W of A49)
☼ 12-3 (not Mon), 6-11; 12-3, 7-10.30 Sun
☎ (01432) 830367 ⊕ wellingtonpub.co.uk
Hobsons Best Bitter; Taylor Landlord; Wye Valley Butty Bach; guest beer Ⓗ
Thriving traditional village hostelry. The public bar, where wooden benches contrast with opulent leather sofas, complements the barn-style restaurant. Food is a real speciality, with bar snacks, an elaborate menu, and Sunday carvery. Board games and newspapers are available in the bar. Guest beers are mainly from micro-breweries; Westons First Quality Cider is served. ⌂⍩⊛⊕◑⊟(492)♣⊕P≞

Wigmore

Olde Oak
HR6 9UJ (on A4110)
☼ 12-3, 6-11; 12-11 Sat; 12-10.30 (12-3, 6-10.30 winter) Sun
☎ (01568) 770247
Mayfields Crusader; Wye Valley Butty Bach; guest beer Ⓗ
Timber-framed, two-bar village pub featuring bare stone walls and beams in the comfortable public bar. The lounge leads to a conservatory restaurant. The regular beers are complemented by guests from local micros. Home-made bar and restaurant meals are served (not Sun eve). Children are welcome. ⌂Q⍩⌖⊕◑⊕⊻♣P≞

Wilton

White Lion
Wilton Lane, HR9 6AQ (just off B4260)
☼ 12-11; 12-10.30 Sun
☎ (01989) 562785 ⊕ whitelionross.co.uk
Butcombe Bitter; Wye Valley Bitter; guest beers Ⓗ
Attractive pub with gardens leading down to the River Wye offering views towards the town of Ross. The bar is open plan with exposed beams and a large stone fireplace. The restaurant was originally part of a prison house. English cuisine, freshly prepared from local ingredients, is served here and in the bar. Bottled Broome Farm Cider is stocked. A spring beer festival is held. ⌂⊛◑⅄⊟♣P≞

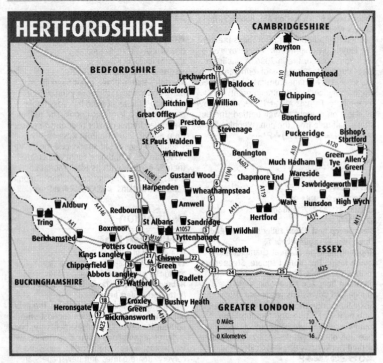

HERTFORDSHIRE

Abbots Langley

Compasses

95 Tibbs Hill Road, WD5 0LJ
🕐 11-11; 12-3.30, 7-11 Sun
☎ (01923) 262870
Courage Best Bitter; Greene King Abbot; Shepherd Neame Spitfire; guest beers ⊞
Deceptively large 18th-century suburban local run by the same family for 23 years. Sympathetically modernised a few years ago, it has two distinct bar areas that are complemented by a separate dining room, a covered decking area for smokers and a garden with children's play house. The pub holds a charity quiz fortnightly on Wednesday evening and has occasional live music on Saturday night. ✿⊭◑➡ₚ⊾

Aldbury

Valiant Trooper

Trooper Road, HP23 5RW
🕐 11.30-11; 12-10.30 Sun
☎ (01442) 851203 ⊕ valianttrooper.co.uk
Fuller's London Pride; Oakham JHB; Tring Jack O' Legs; guest beers ⊞
Ancient, rambling free house with many exposed beams, owned by the same family since 1980. A superb pub – the atmosphere is relaxing, the welcome warm. A converted stables seats 40 diners, providing excellent food from an interesting menu. Three regular and two guest beers are kept in fine condition; bar snacks are offered throughout the two main drinking areas. No meals are served on Sunday or Monday evenings. Dogs are welcome. ▲Q✿◑➡♣P

Allen's Green

Queen's Head

CM21 0LS
🕐 12-2.30 (not Mon & Tue), 5-11; 11-11 Sat; 12-10.30 Sun
☎ (01279) 723393 ⊕ shirevillageinns.co.uk
Buntingford Pargetters; ⒼFuller's London Pride; ⊞ guest beers ⊞/Ⓖ
Once threatened with closure, locals formed their own company to buy the pub, reopening it to serve the village. Still run by villagers, this is a quiet, civilised pub where a strict language code is enforced. Sales of real ale have flourished, and at least one dark beer is normally available. The third weekend of each month is a special real ale weekend, with at least 10 gravity dispensed beers on offer in a self service bar. Some beers are dispensed direct from the cask in the cellar – check the blackboard before ordering. Q✿◑P⊾

Amwell

Elephant & Castle

Amwell Lane, AL4 8EA
🕐 12-2.30, 5.30-11; 12-11 Sat; 12-10.30 Sun
☎ (01582) 832175
Greene King IPA, Morland Original, H&H Olde Trip, Abbot ⊞
Welcoming and deservedly popular 18th-century pub hidden away in a beautiful and peaceful setting. There is a 200ft well in the back bar and two real fires warm the pub in colder weather. With the added asset of two large gardens (one for adults only), this is an excellent example of a successful country pub. Lunchtime meals are served daily and evening meals Tuesday to Saturday. The pub hosts

Amwell Day – a local charity fundraising event – in June each year. ♨️❀◑🅿️🚆(304, 357)♣P

Baldock

Cock

43 High Street, SG7 6BG
🕐 5-11; 12-3.30, 7-10.30 Sun
☎ (01462) 892366
Greene King XX Mild, IPA, Old Speckled Hen, Abbot; guest beers Ⓗ
Dating from the 17th century, this appealing inn has a traditional interior and an open log fire. The beamed, split-level drinking area in this popular, friendly local enhances the pub's character. An enclosed outside drinking area is available in good weather. Greene King's XX Mild is frequently available. Market day is Wednesday when the pub is open at lunchtime. ♨️Q❀🚆♣

Benington

Lordship Arms

42 Whempstead Road, SG2 7BX
🕐 12-3, 6-11; 12-3, 7-10.30 Sun
☎ (01438) 869665
Crouch Vale Brewers Gold; Young's Bitter; guest beers Ⓗ
Excellent single bar pub decorated with telephone memorabilia – even some of the handpumps are modelled on telephones. Wednesday evening curries and Sunday roasts are always popular. The attractive garden boasts splendid floral displays in summer. Oversized glasses are used. Milds, stouts and porters regularly appear. A frequent winner of local and county CAMRA Pub of the Year awards. ♨️❀◑♣P🏵

Berkhamsted

Lamb

277 High Street, HP4 1AJ (Northchurch end of High St, A4251)
🕐 11-11; 12-10.30 Sun
☎ (01442) 862615
Adnams Bitter; Fuller's London Pride; Greene King IPA; Tring Ridgeway Ⓗ
Wonderful example of a High Street pub, sadly one of a dying breed. Two bars are joined by a small arch, each with its own door. Popular with a mixed clientele of all ages, the public bar has games and a TV area, the lounge is for dining and drinking in peace. Good, down to earth food is excellent value (not served Sun). This cosy, friendly hostelry is one of the few local outlets for Tring Ridgeway Bitter.
❀◑🍺🚆(500, 501)🚭

Rising Sun

George Street, HP4 2EG (by the Grand Union Canal towpath)
🕐 3-11 (midnight Fri); 12-midnight Sat; 12-10.30 Sun
☎ (01442) 864913
Greene King IPA; Shepherd Neame Spitfire; guest beer Ⓗ
Locals affectionately call this multi-roomed pub 'The Riser'. A former horse stables and blacksmith's built in the 1880s, it is now a canalside pub that has retained much of its original character. Set on a split-level, the bar

also serves handpumped Addlestones cider, while a TV shows sporting events. Steps lead out towards the Grand Union Canal and a garden. Its rustic charm and friendly welcome make it popular with regular customers.
❀🍺🚭🚆🍴P🚭

Bishop's Stortford

Half Moon

31 North Street, CM23 2LD (N end of North St)
🕐 11-11.30 (12.30am Wed-Sat); 12-11.30 Sun
☎ (01279) 834500
Caledonian Deuchars IPA; Fuller's London Pride; Wychwood Hobgoblin Ⓗ
Variety is the spice of the Half Moon's wide range of beers – always catering for both light and dark beer tastes. Tring Brewery ales often feature among the rotating guest beers. The 16th-century building is full of genuine character, with three bars and a large function room where regular jazz, blues and acoustic music is played, and comedy events hosted. There is a small garden outside. Westons Old Rosie cider and a large selection of malt whiskies are available. ♨️Q❀🚭🚆🍴🚭

Jolly Brewers

170 South Street, CM23 3BQ
🕐 12-1.30am (2am Fri; 1am Sat); 12-1.30am Sun
☎ (01279) 863055
Adnams Broadside; Greene King IPA; Taylor Landlord Ⓗ
Town-centre pub taking full advantage of later opening hours – although there is no admittance after midnight. Originally called the Teetotallers, this name did not last long for obvious reasons. The interior has two bars – one a quiet, relaxing saloon, the other dominated by pool, darts and a large screen TV. Bed and breakfast accommodation is due to open this year. Evening meals are served Sunday-Thursday. 🛏️◑🚭🚆(510, 333)P

Boxmoor

Post Office Arms

46 Puller Road, HP1 1QN (off St John's Rd)
🕐 12-11; 12-10.30 Sun
☎ (01442) 261235
Fuller's London Pride, ESB, seasonal beers Ⓗ
Genuine side street local occupying part of a terrace within a closely packed residential area. Known to regulars as 'The Patch' – as seen on the frosted window, the public bar has a sporting theme, dartboard and big screen. A real fire warms the saloon, where there is a small library of books. A further seating area at the back leads to a small beer garden. Wednesday is curry and a pint night. ♨️❀🍺🚭(Hemel Hempstead)🚆

INDEPENDENT BREWERIES

Alehouse St Albans
Buntingford Royston
Green Tye Green Tye
McMullen Hertford
Red Squirrel Hertford
Sawbridgeworth Sawbridgeworth
Tring Tring

Steamcoach

86 St John's Road, HP1 1NP
🕐 12-11; 12-10.30 Sun
☎ (01442) 244480
Greene King IPA, Old Speckled Hen, Abbot; guest beer ⒣

Popular roadside pub overlooking Blackbirds Moor in this village-like suburb of Hemel Hempstead. Several seating areas are spread across many levels with a mixture of upholstered and wooden furniture, served by a single bar. A large patio to the front and garden to the rear allow for fair weather drinking. The function room is available for diners or to hire. Regular quiz nights are hosted. Children are not allowed inside or out after 8pm. ✿❍▬≠(Hemel Hempstead)🚗P

Buntingford

Brambles

117 High Street, SG9 9AF
🕐 12-11; 12-10.30 Sun
☎ (01763) 271327
Fuller's London Pride, ESB; guest beers ⒣

Originally the Chequers, this pub has reopened after many years of closure. Two bars, both with real fires, offer eight handpumps dispensing the range of ales and ciders including Crones of Norfolk. Buntingford Brewery beers are usually available. The clientele is very varied, and can get exuberant at weekends. Local CAMRA Most Improved Pub 2005. ▲✿❍🚗♣P♟

Crown

17 High Street, SG9 9AB
🕐 12-3, 6-11; 12-3 Sun
☎ (01763) 271442
Everards Tiger; guest beers ⒣

This town-centre pub has a large front bar, cosy back bar and function room. Outside are a covered patio and secluded garden. Although the emphasis here is on drinking, there are regular themed speciality food nights as well as traditional fish and chips on Thursday and Friday. Crossword fans find the large collection of dictionaries and reference books useful. ▲Q✿❍▬

Bushey Heath

Black Boy

19 Windmill Street, WD23 1NB (off Windmill Lane)
🕐 12-11 (midnight Fri & Sat)
☎ (020) 8950 2230
Adnams Bitter; Draught Bass; Fuller's London Pride; Greene King Abbot; guest beer ⒣

Friendly, mid-19th century community local tucked away well off the main drag of Bushey High Road. The Black Boy has been CAMRA Watford & District branch's Pub of the Year on several occasions. Darts, dominoes and cribbage are played. Morris dancers make occasional visits to perform in the pub car park. Food is usually available during most opening hours, but it is advisable to ring first. ✿❍▬♣P♟

Chapmore End

Woodman

30 Chapmore End, SG12 0HF
🕐 12-2.30 (not Mon), 5.30-11; 12-11 Sat & Sun
☎ (01920) 463143 ⊕ woodmanpub.com
Greene King IPA, Abbot; guest beers Ⓖ

Classic, two-bar country inn in a quiet hamlet off the B158, recently sensitively updated. The pub serves gravity-dispensed real ales from cooled casks in the cellar behind the public bar. A local favourite is 'mix': half IPA and half Abbot. Winter Sunday lunchtimes feature traditional roasts, summer Sundays hog roasts. Speciality themed meal evenings are held on alternate Thursdays. The large garden at the rear where you can play petanque has a safe children's play area. ▲Q✿❍🍴▲🚗(384)♣P♟

Chipperfield

Royal Oak

1 The Street, WD4 9BH
🕐 12-3, 6-11; 12-3, 7-10.30 Sun
☎ (01923) 266537
Adnams Broadside; Wadworth 6X; Young's Bitter; guest beers ⒣

Twenty five years in the Guide, this gem is situated on the lower edge of the village. The public bar has a tiled floor and upholstered beer casks for seats, the half-panelled walls are adorned with old car photographs, local drawings and a large matchbook collection. The saloon is more spacious, furnished with horse brasses and brewery mirrors; children are welcome for meals. There is a patio area outside. No lunches are served on Sunday. ▲Q✿❍🍴🚗P

Chipping

Countryman

Ermine Street, SG9 0PG
🕐 12-11 Fri & Sat only; 12-10.30 Sun
☎ (01763) 272721
Beer range varies ⒣

Built in 1663 and a pub since 1760, the Countryman has one split-level bar. The interior boasts some well executed carvings on the bar front, an impressive fireplace and some obscure agricultural implements. Usually only one real ale is available – the beer itself will vary, but will be brown and around 4-4.5%. A second ale may be added during the summer. Note the restricted opening hours. ▲Q✿🚗P

Chiswell Green

Three Hammers

210 Watford Road, AL2 3EA TL133045
🕐 12-11 (midnight Fri & Sat)
☎ (01727) 846218
Fuller's London Pride; guest beers ⒣

An 18th-century coaching inn which has been well maintained outside. Its recently refurbished contemporary interior boasts a fireplace, leather sofas, original old oak beams and a new state of the art beer cellar. This is now a successful village pub with a large garden and car park, situated close to the National Gardens of the Rose. Meals are served daily 12-9pm. The pub has regular beer festivals and a Sunday quiz. 🏬Q❀🌢◐⌖&🖵♣P

Colney Heath

Crooked Billet

88 High Street, AL4 0NP

🕑 11-2.30, 4.30-11; 11-11 Sat; 12-10.30 Sun

☎ (01727) 822128

Tring Side Pocket for a Toad; guest beers Ⓗ

Popular and friendly cottage-style village pub dating back over 200 years with a lively public bar. A genuine free house, it stocks three to five guest beers from national, regional and micro-breweries. A wide selection of good value food is served; booking is advisable for Sunday lunches and occasional Saturday specials. This is a favourite stop off for walkers on the many local footpaths. Families are welcome in the large garden where there is play equipment. 🏬❀◐🖵🖵(304)♣P

Croxley Green

Sportsman

2 Scots Hill, WD3 3AD (on A412 at jct with the Green)

🕑 12-11 (10.30 Sun)

☎ (01923) 443360 ⊕ croxleygreen.com/sportsman

Tring Side Pocket for a Toad; Young's Special; guest beers Ⓗ

This single bar local, decorated with old sporting equipment, has become a Guide regular. It hosts spring and autumn beer festivals and a Wednesday night quiz. Live music is supported, with a blues/rock band on Saturday and monthly folk and blues jams on Sunday. A separate outbuilding, home to a diverse range of clubs, is available for private hire. It's a popular destination for dog walkers. ❀◐▲🖵♣P⅃

Great Offley

Red Lion

Kings Walden Road, SG5 3DZ

🕑 12-midnight (10.30 Sun)

☎ (01462) 768281 ⊕ redlionoffley.com

Fuller's London Pride; Young's Bitter; guest beers Ⓗ

Traditional country pub set in idyllic Hertfordshire countryside with a good reputation for food. Fresh fish on Wednesday, exceptional chips made from locally grown potatoes and the speciality Red Lion pancake are highlights of the varied menu, served in the bar or the conservatory restaurant. There is a large fire in the cosy main bar. A beer festival is held on the spring bank holiday. 🏬❀❀◐♣P

Gustard Wood

Cross Keys

Ballslough Hill, AL4 8LA (off B651)

🕑 11-3.30 (4 Sat), 5.30-11; 12-4, 7-11 Sun

☎ (01582) 832165

Adnams Bitter, Broadside; Fuller's London Pride; Greene King IPA; guest beers Ⓗ

Attractive 17th-century, country cottage style pub in a woodland setting with a wood burning inglenook fire. Collections of model cars and clocks adorn the interior (guess which one tells the right time). Reasonably priced meals are excellent; try the desserts! Home-made pizzas only are available in the evening. The large outdoor drinking area has plenty of tables and benches. Accommodation is in three en-suite rooms with antique furniture. 🏬Q❀🌢◐🖵(304)P

Harpenden

Carpenters Arms

4 Cravells Road, AL5 1BD

🕑 11-3, 5.30-11; 12-3, 7-10.30 Sun

☎ (01582) 460311

Adnams Bitter; Courage Best Bitter; Greene King Abbot; guest beer Ⓗ

Harpenden's smallest pub is cosy and comfortable with no music, juke box or fruit machines – just good beer and conversation. The new landlords continue to uphold the pub's real ale traditions. The menu has expanded and barbecues are now held on a Friday and occasional weekends in summer. The outdoor seating has been completely refurbished with stylish parasols and gazebos. Well worth a visit both in the summer and during the winter months when an open fire warms the bar. 🏬Q❀🖵(320, 321)♣P

Heronsgate

Land of Liberty, Peace & Plenty

Long Lane, WD3 5BS (close to M25 jct 17)

🕑 11-11 (midnight Fri & Sat); 12-11 Sun

☎ (01923) 282226 ⊕ landoflibertypub.com

Bateman XB; Red Squirrel Conservation Bitter; guest beers Ⓗ

Welcoming country pub with six handpumps for beers from a variety of family and micro-breweries often rare to the area. Real cider and perry are available plus a range of Belgian bottled beers. The walls display historical information about the pub, locale and breweriana. Regular events include food nights, beer tastings, quizzes, darts, pub games and live music plus beer festivals most bank holidays. There is a large garden with a boules piste where families are welcome. Local CAMRA Pub of the Year 2007. 🏬❀🖵♣●P⅂

Hertford

Black Horse

29-31 West Street, SG13 8EZ

🕑 12-2 (not Tue; 2.30 Fri), 5-11; 12-11 Sat & Sun

☎ (01992) 583630 ⊕ blackhorseherts.co.uk

Greene King IPA, Abbot, seasonal beers; guest beers Ⓗ

Timbered pub with parts dating back to 1642, with a country feel despite the town location. Situated in one of Hertford's most attractive streets, it is near the start of the Cole Green Way. Handy on match days for Hertford Town football club supporters, the Horse is renowned for its own rugby team. Good value home-made food is served lunchtime and evening (not Sat or Sun) and children are permitted until 8pm. Quiz night is Sunday. 🏬❀🖵🖵♣

Old Cross Tavern

8 St Andrew Street, SG14 1JA
● 12-11 (10.30 Sun)
☎ (01992) 583133
Fuller's London Pride; Mighty Oak IPA; Pitfield Hophead; Taylor Landlord; guest beers ⊞
Superb free house in the town offering a friendly welcome. Eight real ales – usually including a dark beer of some distinction – come from brewers large and small and there is a good choice of Belgian bottle-conditioned beers. Beer festivals are held over the spring bank holiday and in October. There is no TV or music here, just good old-fashioned conversation. In the cooler months the pub closes on Monday lunchtime, opening at 4pm – ring ahead. Filled rolls are available at the bar. ▲Q⊛⊒♣

White Horse

33 Castle Street, SG14 1HH
● 12-2.30, 5.30-11 (12-11 Fri & Sat); 12-10.30 Sun
☎ (01992) 501950 ⊕ castlestreetparty.org.uk
Adnams Bitter; Fuller's Chiswick, Discovery, London Pride, ESB; guest beers ⊞
Charming old timber-framed building with two downstairs bars and additional rooms upstairs (children welcome until 9pm). Guest beers of character come from a wide range of craft brewers. Country wines are also stocked. Beer festivals are held over the early May and August bank holiday weekends and the pub hosts a street party in July. Home-made lunches are available every day and Monday night features the Gastronomic Tour, a set menu of dishes from around the world.
▲Q⊛◑⊒⊒♣

High Wych

Rising Sun

CM21 0HZ (1 Mile W of Sawbridgeworth)
● 12-2.30, 5.30-11; 12-3.30, 6-11 Sat; 12-3.30, 7-10.30 Sun
☎ (01279) 724099
Courage Best Bitter; Mighty Oak Maldon Gold; guest beer Ⓖ
This small three-room pub is known locally as Sid's, after a former landlord. In keeping with tradition, all beers are dispensed by gravity – handpumps have never been used here. Good home-cooked food is served in the saloon Tuesday to Sunday (not Sun eve). ▲Q⊛◑

Hitchin

Half Moon

57 Queen Street, SG4 9TZ
● 12-2.30, 5-midnight; 12-11 Sun
☎ (01462) 452448
Adnams Bitter; Young's Special; guest beers ⊞
This split-level one-bar pub dates back to 1748 and was once owned by Hitchin brewer W&S Lucas. It sells two regular beers and two guests, often from local breweries. Cider and perry are available in polypins and there is a good choice of wines. Twice-yearly beer festivals are hosted. An interesting selection of home-prepared food is available (not Tue eve). Monthly quiz nights and curry nights are popular in this friendly community pub with a

loyal clientele. Local CAMRA's Most Improved Pub winner 2005. ▲⊛◑♣⬤P

Nightingale

Nightingale Road, SG5 1RL
● 12-midnight; 12-10.30 Sun
☎ (01462) 457448
Nethergate Umbel Magna; Tring Side Pocket for a Toad; Wychwood Hobgoblin; guest beers ⊞
This friendly free house is around 150 years old and reputed to have three ghosts. It was formerly owned by Fordhams of Ashwell, whose name is set into the exterior stonework. The interior is open plan but retains the layout of the original rooms, with distinct seating areas. Five beers are available from Nethergate, Tring and Wychwood, usually including a porter or a mild. Traditional entertainment includes darts, pool and board games. Sport is occasionally shown on TV.
⊛♣P

Sunrunner

24 Bancroft, SG5 1JW
● 12-3, 5-11; 12-11 Sun
☎ (01462) 440717
Draught Bass; Potton Shannon IPA; guest beers ⊞
The Sunrunner, housed in an 18th-century building, is a mini beer festival in its own right. With two regular and six ever changing guest beers, mainly from small or new micro-breweries, including stouts, porters and milds, there is always something different to try as well as cider, fruit wines and foreign beers. Home-made lunches are served. ◑⊒♣⬤

Hunsdon

Fox & Hounds

2 High Street, SG12 8NH (on B180 at S end of village)
● 12-4, 6-11; closed Mon; 12-4 Sun
☎ (01279) 843999 ⊕ foxandhoundshunsdon.co.uk
Adnams Bitter, Broadside; guest beers ⊞
This is a popular gastro pub and can be food dominated, especially at weekends. Despite this it retains a small local pub atmosphere and drinkers are welcome at the bar. A true free house, the building is an old yeoman's house and has some interesting original quirks. The toilet doors are disguised as book cases. Home-made bread is sold to take away.
▲⊛◑⊒(351)P

Ickleford

Plume of Feathers

Upper Green, SG5 3YD
● 11.30-3, 6-11.30; 11.30-midnight Fri-Sun
☎ (01462) 432729
Adnams Bitter; Flowers IPA; Wadworth 6X; guest beers ⊞
A welcoming pub run by two sisters for the last 12 years. A lively hostelry and popular with enthusiastic Rugby Union fans, it has changed little over the years. The excellent food is prepared to order (not Sun eve) and served in the restaurant. There is a pleasant secluded garden. ▲⊛◑⊒(M2)♣P

Kings Langley

Saracen's Head

47 High Street, WD4 9HU
✪ 11-2.30, 6-11; 12.30-4, 7-10.30 Sun
☎ (01923) 400144
Fuller's London Pride, ESB; Tring Ridgeway; guest beer H
This low beamed, single room pub served by one bar dates back to the early 17th century. A collection of saracens' heads, old bottled ales and antique telephones adorns the shelves around the drinking areas. An array of plates is displayed above the wood-burning fire. There are several benches outside for roadside drinking. No children are permitted.
🚶✿◑Ⓓ🚭(500)**P**

Letchworth

Three Magnets

18-20 Leys Avenue, SG6 3EW
✪ 9am-11
☎ (01462) 681093
Courage Best Bitter; Greene King Abbot; Marston's Pedigree; guest beers H
Wetherspoon's pub in a converted 1924 furniture shop. The pub chain aims to be all things to all people and this pub has something for everyone. It is a family pub during the day and early evening, a social club later, a quiet pub except during international sports events, and a restaurant with competitive prices serving food throughout all opening times. Many old photographs of early Letchworth decorate the walls. Q✿◑Ⓓ♿🚭

Much Hadham

Bull

High Street, SG10 6BU (on B1004 N end of village)
✪ 12-3, 6-11; 12-3, 7-10.30 Sun
☎ (01279) 842668
Greene King IPA; guest beers H
Food dominates at times at this village local, but the bar area is always available for drinkers who are made to feel most welcome. Popular with locals, it tends to get very busy, particularly on Sunday lunchtime. The attractive interior, on a split level, has low beams that divide the large bar into smaller areas. There are normally two guest ales on handpump. 🚶Q✿◑Ⓓ🚭(351)**P**

Nuthampstead

Woodman

Stocking Lane, SG8 8NB
✪ 11-11; 12-4, 7-10.30 Sun
☎ (01763) 848328
Adnams Bitter; Nethergate IPA; guest beer H
Free house dating from the 17th century with an L-shaped bar and wonderful open fires. The recently extended restaurant offers a la carte meals as well as house specials and snacks (no food Sun eve). Ideally located for visiting local attractions such as Duxford Imperial War Museum, during WWII the USAF 398th Bomber Group was based nearby and much memorabilia is displayed. 🚶Q✿�◑ⒹP🚭

Potters Crouch

Hollybush

Bedmond Lane, AL2 3NN (jct of Potters Crouch Lane and Ragged Hall Lane)
✪ 11.30-2.30, 6-11; 12-2.30, 6-10.30 Sun
☎ (01727) 851792
Fuller's Chiswick, London Pride, ESB, seasonal beers H
Delightful early 18th-century pub in rural surroundings with large oak tables and period chairs in three drinking areas. An immaculately kept inn, there are candles on every table. Children are welcome in the large garden only. The landlord is a regular winner of Fuller's Cellarman of the Year award.
🚶Q✿◑Ⓓ🚭(300, 301)**P⅃**

Preston

Red Lion

The Green, SG4 7UD
✪ 12-3, 5.30-11; 12-3, 7-10.30 Sun
☎ (01462) 459585
Young's Bitter; guest beers H
Attractive Georgian-style free house on the village green. It was the first community owned pub in Great Britain. The guest beers, many from micro-breweries, change constantly. The landlord and landlady continue to prepare the fresh home-made food (not served Tue eve), much of it made with ingredients sourced locally. The pub hosts the village cricket teams and fundraises for charity. A regular award winner, including CAMRA Hertfordshire Pub of the Year 2005.
🚶Q✿◑Ⓓ♿P

Puckeridge

Crown & Falcon

33 High Street, SG11 1RN
✪ 11.30-2.30, 5.30-11; 12-4.30, 7-10.30 Sun
☎ (01920) 821561 ⊕ crown-falcon.demon.co.uk
Adnams Bitter; McMullen AK; guest beers H
A public house since 1530, the Crown half of the name was taken much later from a defunct pub in the village. Changes to the interior layout can be traced on plans displayed in the bar. It is now one large open-plan room with a separate restaurant. A collection of Allied Breweries memorabilia is on display. The guest beers change weekly, often including one from Buntingford Brewery. The Falcon is mentioned in Samuel Pepys' diary of 1662 – he bought the landlord's shoes for four shillings.
🚶✿◑Ⓓ🚭♣P

White Hart

Braughing Road, SG11 1RR
✪ 12-11 (9.30 Mon; midnight Fri & Sat); 12-10.30 Sun
☎ (01920) 821309
McMullen AK, Country H
Named after the emblem of Richard II, the White Hart dates from the 14th century. The interior has many rooms; there is a huge fireplace in the dining room. Food portions are generous, with a buffet Sunday lunch every week. The large garden has children's play equipment, and there is a thatched gazebo built around a tree in the car park
🚶✿◑Ⓓ🚭🚭P

Radlett

Red Lion

78-80 Watling Street, WD7 7NP (on A5183)
🕐 11-midnight; 12-11.30 Sun
☎ (01923) 855341 ⊕ Redlionradlett.co.uk
Young's Bitter, Special; Wells Bombardier Ⓗ
This Victorian hotel opposite the railway station was once a temperance house. It now has a large, split-level bar plus a 60-seater restaurant. There are 14 guest rooms and a function room. Home-made meals are served in the bar and restaurant. A flower-bedecked patio at the front of the hotel overlooks Watling Street. 🚃🏵️⇔🕮🖩(602, 632)♣P

Redbourn

Cricketers

East Common, AL3 7ND
🕐 12-11 (midnight Fri & Sat); 12-10.30 Sun
☎ (01582) 792410
Fuller's London Pride; guest beers Ⓗ
Traditional two-bar village pub by the common dating from 1725, with a warm welcome for all. Following a change of ownership in 2004, it is now the only free house in the village. The landlord is keen on his beers, cider and perry and offers some interesting guest ales. Fresh home-made food is served and there is a function room upstairs. Parking can be tricky. The 250-year-old Redbourn cricket club is on the common over the road. Q🏵️🕮🖩♣♠P⏚

Rickmansworth

Rose & Crown

Woodcock Hill, Harefield Road, WD3 1PP
🕐 11-11; 11.30-10.30 Sun
☎ (01923) 897680 ⊕ morethanjustapub.co.uk/ theroseandcrown
Caledonian Deuchars IPA; Fuller's London Pride; guest beer Ⓗ
The focus is on quality dining at this quaint country pub, nevertheless a comfortable bar has been retained to complement the spacious, modern restaurant area. Two wood fires help to maintain a real pub feel, as well as a quiz on Thursday and board games for customers. The pub has extensive gardens with a permanent marquee for functions. A farmers' market is held on the second Saturday of the month. 🚃🏵️🕮🖩P⏚

St Albans

Boot

4 Market Place, AL3 5DG (by the Clock Tower)
🕐 12-midnight (11 Mon; 1am Fri & Sat); 12-11.30 Sun
☎ (01727) 857533
Theakston Black Bull Bitter; Young's Special; guest beers Ⓗ
Dating back to the 1400s, the Boot has been restored to a typical market town pub with low ceilings, exposed beams, a log fire and wood flooring. On Wednesday and Saturday market days it is always bustling with traders and shoppers. Live music and jam sessions are hosted on Tuesday evening. Quiz night is Monday. The landlord organises Saracens rugby club tickets and coaches to matches. The

ever-changing food menu is excellent and booking is advisable (no food Mon). 🚃🖩🖩♣♠

Farmers Boy

134 London Road, AL1 1PQ
🕐 12-midnight (2am Fri & Sat); 12-10.30 Sun
☎ (01727) 800029
Alehouse Clipper IPA, Farmers Joy; Fuller's London Pride; Taylor Landlord; guest beers Ⓗ
Cosy, cottage style pub, home of the Alehouse (formerly Verulam) Brewery which has continued to brew following a change of management. The pub has recently been tastefully refurbished. Good, home-made food is available throughout the day. Occasional guest beers are supplemented by a selection of Belgian bottled beers. Music nights are sometimes hosted. 🚃🏵️🕮🖩♣

Garibaldi

61 Albert Street, AL1 1RT
🕐 12-11 (10.30 Sun)
☎ (01727) 855046
Fuller's Chiswick, Discovery, London Pride, ESB, seasonal beers; guest beers Ⓗ
Traditional, welcoming, back-street local within walking distance of the abbey. The bar is centrally located with seating and standing room all around. The pub is named after the Italian patriot who unified Italy in the 19th century. Seasonal and guest beers are usually available. Barbecues are held in summer and a beer festival in May. Lunches are served Tuesday to Saturday. Music occasionally plays on Wednesday night. 🚃🏵️🕮🖩♣

Lower Red Lion

34-36 Fishpool Street, AL3 4RX
🕐 12-2.30, 5.30-11; 12-11 Fri & Sat; 12-10.30 Sun
☎ (01727) 855669 ⊕ lowerredlion.com
Oakham JHB; guest beers Ⓗ
Originally a coaching inn dating from the 17th century, this two-bar free house is situated in a conservation area near the abbey on the route to Roman Verulamium. The licensee also operates the Alehouse micro-brewery at the Farmers Boy and his beers often feature at this pub. Traditional continental draught and bottled beers are also available, plus a range of malt whiskies. Several beer festivals are held during the year. 🚃Q🏵️⇔🕮🖩♣♠P

Portland Arms

63 Portland Street, AL3 4RA
🕐 12-3, 5.30-11 (midnight Fri); 12-midnight Sat; 12-11 Sun
☎ (01727) 844574 ⊕ portlandarmspub.com
Fuller's Chiswick, London Pride, ESB, seasonal beers Ⓗ
Warm and welcoming back-street community pub tucked away in a residential area, handy for St Michaels and the Roman Museum. The pub serves a wide range of meals including Sunday roasts with meat supplied by a local farm. Takeaway fish and chips is also available. Sunday is music night. 🚃Q🏵️🕮🖩♣P⏚

Six Bells

16-18 St Michaels Street, AL3 4SH
🕐 12-2.30, 5-11; 12-11 Fri & Sat; 12-10.30 Sun
☎ (01727) 856945

Adnams Bitter; Caledonian Deuchars IPA; Fuller's London Pride; Greene King Abbot; guest beer ⑂
Traditional 16th-century pub situated in St Michaels parish, within walking distance of the town centre and cathedral and adjacent to Verulamium Park and Museum. The only licensed premises to lie within the walls of Roman Verulamium, four regular ales and one guest are served. The cider is from Addlestones. Food is served lunchtimes and evenings (not Sun); Monday night is fish and chip night. Quiz nights are held twice a month on Sunday and occasional live music features at this popular, friendly pub.
🏰❀◑▶🚃(300, 301)♣🍴P⌐

White Hart Tap
4 Keyfield Terrace, AL1 1QJ
🕐 12-11
☎ (01727) 860974 🌐 whiteharttap.co.uk
Caledonian Deuchars IPA; Fuller's London Pride; guest beers ⑂
Welcoming, one bar, back-street local offering three guest beers from the Punch Taverns range. Meals are served every lunchtime and Tuesday to Friday evenings with fish and chips on Friday and roasts on Sunday. Quiz night is Wednesday. Occasional live music plays on Saturday night. A public car park is opposite the pub. 🏰❀◑🚃♣

White Lion
91 Sopwell Lane, AL1 1RN (off Holywell Hill)
🕐 12 (5.30 Mon)-11; 12-11 Sun
☎ (01727) 850540 🌐 thewhitelionph.co.uk
Black Sheep Best Bitter; Young's Special; guest beers ⑂
Traditional 16th-century two-bar pub a short walk from the abbey. Six handpumps dispense two regular and four guest beers from the Punch Taverns range. The large garden has a barbecue, children's play area, petanque piste and new smokers' area. Good quality home-made food is served daily except Monday lunchtime. Listed in CAMRA's Good Pub Food, the White Lion was local Pub of the Year 2006.
🏰Q❀◑🚃♣⌐

St Pauls Walden

Strathmore Arms
London Road, SG4 8BT
🕐 12-2.30 (not Mon), 5 (6 Mon)-11; 12-11 Fri & Sat; 10-10.30 Sun
☎ (01438) 871654
Fuller's London Pride; Woodforde's Wherry; guest beers ⑂
Situated on the Bowes-Lyon estate, this pub is divided into drinking, dining and games areas. The pub does a lot of fundraising for the area. Local CAMRA Pub of the Year 2004 and Community Pub of the Year 2007, it hosts several beer festivals - obscure breweries a speciality. A ticker's paradise, it offers an ever-changing rota of guest beers as well as bottled continental beers, mainly Belgian and German. Evening meals are served Friday and Saturday. Q❀◑🍴🅰🚃(304)♣🍴P

Sandridge

Green Man
31 High Street, AL4 9DD
🕐 11-3, 5.30-11; 11-11.30 Fri & Sat; 12-11 Sun
☎ (01727) 854845 🌐 thegreenman-sandridge.co.uk
Adnams Broadside; Caledonian Deuchars IPA; Ⓖ **Greene King IPA,** ⑂ **Abbot** Ⓖ
One-bar Victorian red brick pub located in the middle of the village. This is a locals' pub that extends a warm welcome to all discerning ale drinkers, with the landlord now in his 20th year of residence. Some ales are served straight from the cask from a cellar area located nearby at floor level.
🏰Q🌳❀◑🍴🚃(304, 320)♣P

Sawbridgeworth

Gate
81 London Road, CM21 9JJ
🕐 11.30-2.30, 5.30-11; 11.30-11 Fri & Sat; 12-11 Sun
☎ (01279) 722313 🌐 the-gate-pub.co.uk
Beer range varies ⑂
The home of the Sawbridgeworth Brewery, this family-run pub is popular with a mix of young and more mature customers. One bar appeals to sports fans, the other is a quieter saloon. A beer festival is hosted in August plus several smaller festivals throughout the year. There are at least seven real ales, with beers from rare and new brewers a feature, plus the keenly-priced Sawbridgeworth ales. Real cider is also stocked. Local CAMRA Pub of the Year 2007. ❀◑&≠🚃♣🍴P

Stevenage

Our Mutual Friend
Broadwater Crescent, SG2 8EH
🕐 12-11; 12-3, 7-10.30 Sun
☎ (01438) 312282
Caledonian Deuchars IPA; guest beers ⑂
Thriving community pub brought back from the cask ale graveyard five years ago. Since then it has gone from strength to strength, now sporting six real ales, cider and perry plus a small range of Belgian bottled beers. Over a weekend there may be 12 different cask beers as they sell out so quickly! A regular beer festival brightens up January. Locals drink alongside visitors who have heard about the good beer. Winner of local CAMRA Most Improved Pub 2003 and Pub of the Year 2006 and 2007. Q❀◑🚃♣🍴P🖵

Tring

King's Arms
King Street, HP23 6BE
🕐 12 (11.30 Sat)-2.30 (3 Fri), 7-11; 12-4, 7-10.30 Sun
☎ (01442) 823318
Wadworth 6X; guest beers ⑂
A glance at the many awards that adorn the walls confirms the pedigree of this fine pub, run by the same licensees for 25 years. Five ales are available to complement the freshly home-cooked food. Children are welcome in the bar at lunchtime. Outside is a canopied patio that can be heated when necessary. Although situated in the back streets known as

the Tring Triangle, buses 61 and 500 pass close by. ⚐Q🕸🕩🚲♣💺

Robin Hood

1 Brook Street, HP23 5ED (B4635/B486 jct)
🕔 11.30-3, 5.30-11 (11.30 Fri); 12-4, 5.30-11 Sat; 12-4, 7-11 Sun
☎ (01442) 824912
Fuller's Chiswick, Discovery, London Pride, ESB; guest beer Ⓗ
Situated on the edge of town, this warm, friendly pub is popular with all ages. The cosy bar area opens out into a welcoming conservatory with a wood-burning stove, leading to the patio and garden. The paintings on the walls are supplied by a local gallery and are for sale. Freshly prepared food is available all week – seafood dishes are a speciality. ⚐🦮🕩♿🚲💺

Tyttenhanger

Plough

32 Tyttenhanger Green, AL4 0RW
🕔 12-3 (3.30 Fri & Sat), 6-11; 12-3.30, 7-10.30 Sun
☎ (01727) 857777
Fuller's London Pride, ESB; guest beers Ⓗ
Deservedly busy country free house with an ever-changing range of up to six guest beers in addition to the Fuller's staples. Excellent value food makes this a popular lunchtime destination. The large garden has children's play equipment and there is a conservatory for families. Worth visiting for the large collection of bottled beers and the idiosyncratic beer mats. ⚐Q🦮🕸🕩🚲(S7)♣P

Ware

Crooked Billet

140 Musley Hill, SG12 7NL (via New Rd from High St)
🕔 12-2.30 (Tue & Fri), 5.30-11 (midnight Fri); 12-midnight Sat; 12-11.30 Sun
☎ (01920) 462516
Greene King IPA; Theakston Mild; guest beer Ⓗ
This popular local is well worth tracking down. There are two main bars – one cosy and relaxed, the other more lively with pool and sport on TV. The landlord is a staunch Carlisle United supporter so stray Carlisle fans can expect the red carpet treatment. Acquired by Admiral Inns in 2007, this is a rare outlet for dark mild during the colder months ⚐🕸🚲(395)♣💺

Rose & Crown

65 Watton Road, SG12 0AE
🕔 12-2.30, 5-11 (midnight Thu); 12-midnight Fri & Sat; 12-11 Sun
☎ (01920) 462371
McMullen AK, Country; guest beer Ⓗ
Terrific pub with a landlord who takes great pride in his cellar, winning numerous cellarmanship awards over the years. As well as quality ale, superb home-cooked food is also served (no eve meals Sun-Tue). The pub was built with famous local hitch bricks. At the back is a colourful garden that is easy to miss from the road. There is a covered and heated conservatory, children's play area, aviary and petanque piste. ⚐🕸🕩♿🚲♣P💺

Worppell

35 Watton Road, SG12 0AD
🕔 12-2.30, 5-11; 12-midnight Fri & Sat; 12-10.30 Sun
☎ (01920) 411666
Greene King IPA, Abbot; guest beer Ⓗ
Named after the man who built the pub in the 19th century, the Worppell has been run by the same tenants for the last 24 years. A comfortable single bar local, entertainment is in the form of conversation and banter, and the locals really appreciate the quality of the beer. The occasional guest ale comes from the Greene King stable. Food is available at lunchtime Monday to Friday. 🕸🕩🚲♣

Wareside

Chequers

SG12 7QY (on B1004)
🕔 12-3, 6-11 (10.30 Sun)
☎ (01920) 467010
Greene King IPA; guest beer Ⓗ
Old, picture postcard coaching inn situated in beautiful countryside, popular with walkers and cyclists. An extensive, well-priced food menu is served in the three bars as well as the restaurant. Guest beers often come from the Red Squirrel Brewery. B&B is very popular and must be booked. ⚐Q🦮🕩♿🚲P

Watford

Southern Cross

41-43 Langley Road, WD17 4PP
🕔 11-11 (11.30 Thu-Sat); 12-10.30 Sun
☎ (01923) 256033
Caledonian Deuchars IPA; Theakston Mild; Wells Bombardier; guest beers Ⓗ
Thriving, large, open-plan bar with a central serving area. Converted from two houses, it was the home of American intelligence during WWII. Three guest beers from the Beer Seller list are usually on handpump. A regular general knowledge quiz is held on Thursday and Sunday. Board games are available. Food is served until 9pm. Children under 14 are only welcome if dining and not after 9pm. 🕸🦮🕩♿🚲P💺

West Herts Sports and Social Club

Park Avenue, WD18 7HP (south of A412, near town hall)
🕔 12-2 summer, 5-11; 12-11 Fri & Sat; 12-10.30 Sun
☎ (01923) 229239
Fuller's London Pride; Young's Bitter; guest beers Ⓗ
It is 30 years since this former CAMRA Club of the Year last appeared in the Guide. A new bar has been built; the old bar now services the function room, home of the CAMRA Watford Beer Festival for 12 years. Darts, dominoes and cribbage are played. Rolls and pies are usually available. Oversized glasses are reserved for real ale. Entry is restricted to club members, card-carrying CAMRA members, or customers carrying the current Guide. 🕸♿♣P💺🏳

Wheathampstead

Nelson

135 Marford Road, AL4 8NH

✪ 11-11
☎ (01582) 831577
Greene King IPA; McMullen AK; guest beers Ⓗ
Now restored, this 200-year-old village local has several seating and standing areas and a central real fire. Colourful hanging baskets adorn the outdoor drinking area at the front in summer where there are picnic tables. Darts is played and a regular quiz hosted. Occasional beer festivals are held. ♨✿Ⓖ➹♣♠P

Whitwell

Maiden's Head
67 High Street, SG4 8AH
✪ 12-3, 5-11; 12-4, 7-10.30 Sun
☎ (01438) 871392
McMullen AK, Country, seasonal beers Ⓗ
One of the flagship McMullen pubs, the Maiden's Head has been a regular entry in the Guide for the last 23 years. The walls are adorned with photographs, paintings and awards and there is a collection of Dinky toys. Popular with ramblers, the pub has won a community pub award and CAMRA East Anglian Pub of the Year. Evening meals are served Tuesday to Saturday. ♨Q✿Ⓓ➹Ⓖ➹♣P

Wildhill

Woodman
45 Wildhill Road, AL9 6EA (between A1000 and B158)
✪ 11.30-2.30, 5.30-11; 12-2.30, 7-10.30 Sun

☎ (01707) 642618
Greene King IPA, Abbot; McMullen AK; guest beers Ⓗ
This superb village pub offers guest beers from regional and micro-breweries from near and far, with prices some of the best in the area. Popular with office workers for lunch, it is also busy on Sunday. A favourite watering hole for sports fans – the landlord is a keen Saracens rugby supporter and the pub runs its own fantasy Formula 1 competition. A regular in the Guide, the pub has won numerous awards including local CAMRA Pub of the Year a record six times. Look out for God's Waiting Room! Q✿Ⓖ➹(200, 201)♣P

Willian

Three Horseshoes
Baldock Lane, SG6 2AE
✪ 11 (12 Sun)-11
☎ (01462) 685713
Greene King IPA, Morland Original, Old Speckled Hen, Abbot Ⓗ
Originally two 18th-century cottages, the 'Shoes' remained a two-roomed tavern until 1975 when it was converted to the cosy bar of today. It is popular with locals, home to darts, cribbage and quiz teams, and holds weekly raffles to raise funds for charity. The converted barn is well used as a function and games room. A former local CAMRA Community Pub of the Year. ♨Q✿Ⓓ➹♣P

Hops: the essential flavouring

Hops are famous for adding bitterness to beer. But this remarkable perennial climbing plant – a member of the hemp family, Cannabinaceae – also contains acids, oils and resins that impart delightful aromas and flavours to beer.

These can be detected in the form of pine, spice, sap and tart, citrus fruit. Fruit is often similar to lemon and orange, while some English hop varieties give powerful hints of apricots, blackcurrants and damsons. American hop varieties, the Cascade in particular, are famous for their grapefruit aroma and flavour.

Many British brewers now use hops from mainland Europe – such as Styrian Goldings from Slovenia and Saaz from the Czech Republic – that have been developed primarily for lager brewing. They impart a more restrained aroma and flavour, with a gentle, resinous character. Lager hops used in ale brewing are usually added late in the copper boil to give a fine aroma to the finished beer.

Kent is often thought of as the main hop-growing area of Britain but in 2004 it was overtaken by Herefordshire. The main hop varieties used in cask beer production are the Fuggle and Golding, but First Gold, introduced in the 1990s, is now a major variety. First Gold was one of the first dwarf or hedgerow hops that grow to only half the height of conventional varieties. As a result they are easier to pick, are less susceptible to disease and aphid attack, and therefore use fewer agri-chemicals. In 2004, a new hop variety called Boadicea was introduced: it is the first aphid-resistant hop and therefore needs fewer pesticides. The hop industry is working on trials of new varieties that need no pesticides or fertilisers and should gain Soil Association approval as organic hops.

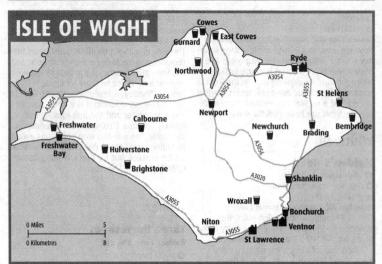

ISLE OF WIGHT

Bembridge

Olde Village Inn

61 High Street, PO35 5SF
☼ 11 (12 Sun)-11
☎ (01983) 872616
Greene King IPA, Abbot; guest beer Ⓗ
Comfortable village local with a warm and
friendly atmosphere. The one-bar interior is
expansive but has a cosy feel. Older people
are catered for Monday to Fridays with
lunchtime meals at discounted prices. Live
music is hosted on Friday.
♨✿✍◑⅁♿▯₩♣P╚

Bonchurch

Bonchurch Inn

The Chute, PO38 1NU (off Shanklin to Ventnor
road)
☼ 11-3, 6.30-11; 12-3, 7-10.30 Sun
☎ (01983) 852611 ⊕ bonchurch-inn.co.uk
Courage Best Bitter, Directors Ⓖ
Superbly preserved stone pub in a Dickensian
courtyard, formerly the stables of the adjacent
manor house. Little has changed since it
gained its licence in the 1840s, making it one
of the most unspoilt pubs on the Island. As
well as featuring in an episode of The
Detectives, the pub displays mementos from
many of the stars who have popped in when
visiting the Island. An Italian restaurant is
across the courtyard. Ruddles Best and County
are sometimes also available in the summer.
⅁✿✍◑▯♣P╚

Brading

Yarbridge Inn

Yarbridge, PO36 0AA (left at traffic lights between
Brading and Sandown)
☼ 11-11.30; 12-11 Sun; 11-3, 5-11 winter
☎ (01983) 406217 ⊕ yarbridgeinn.co.uk
Beer range varies Ⓗ
Previously known as the Anglers, this is a
pleasant, single-bar pub serving nine ever-
changing beers. The dining area offers a menu
with specials board and a choice of roasts on

Sunday. Outside is a safe play area for children
and a patio with parasols. There is plenty of
railway memorabilia, a model train and the
Brading to Sandown line at the bottom of the
garden. The pub celebrated its first CAMRA Isle
of Wight Pub of the Year award in 2006. A
beer festival is held at the end of May.
Q⅁✿◑▯₩♣P╚

Brighstone

Three Bishops

Main Road, PO30 4AH
☼ 12-11 (midnight Fri & Sat); 12-10.30 Sun
☎ (01983) 740226
Beer range varies Ⓗ
Large village centre pub with a mixed
clientele of all ages, offering something for
everyone. Recently taken over by new,
enthusiastic tenants, the pub is growing ever
more popular and successful. A selection of
four beers is usually available. The pub is
named after three past rectors of the village
church who went on to become bishops. Live
music is frequently hosted. The garden and car
park are large. A function room is available for
small parties. ✿◑♿▯(515)♣╚

Calbourne

Sun Inn

Sun Hill, PO30 4JA
☼ 11 (12 Sun)-11
☎ (01983) 531231 ⊕ sun-calbourne.co.uk
Beer range varies Ⓗ
Friendly village pub overlooking Westover
cricket ground with splendid views of
Westover and Brighstone Forest, and
Freshwater cliffs in the distance. The public bar
is traditional; there is a garden and large car
park. Good home-made food is served all day

INDEPENDENT BREWERIES

Goddards Ryde
Ventnor Ventnor
Yates' St Lawrence

including a daily roast. The choice of ales is excellent with up to four available, including an Island ale. Winkle Street is nearby. Well-behaved children are welcome.
🏮🕙🍺🍴🛉♣️P🚻

Cowes

Union Inn

Watchouse Lane, PO31 7QH
🕐 11-11; 12-10.30 Sun; 11-3, 6-11 winter
☎ (01983) 293163
Fuller's Chiswick, London Pride, Gale's HSB Ⓗ
A real gem of a pub; one three-sided bar serves the lounge, snug, dining area and airy conservatory, originally the yard. A roaring fire in winter creates a cosy atmosphere. The beer range includes a guest ale in summer from the Fuller's Gale's portfolio. An interesting collection of maritime photographs decorates the walls. Meals are served all day in summer and the specials board has some tasty offerings. 🏮🕙🍺➤🍴🚃

East Cowes

Ship & Castle

21 Castle Street, PO32 6RB
🕐 11-11; 12-late Sun
☎ (01983) 290522
Shepherd Neame Spitfire; guest beers Ⓗ
Just how street corner pubs used to be – a cosy retreat when the winds are whistling across the Red Funnel car park. Despite the small bar there are always at least three beers on offer and a weekly guest keeps the locals in suspense. Bustling on games nights – four darts teams and Sky TV keeps the sports fans happy. Easy to find – turn left off the floating bridge or once around the block if arriving from Southampton. 🛉➤🍴♣️🚻▯

Freshwater

Prince of Wales

Princes Road, PO40 9ED
🕐 11-11; 12-10.30 Sun
☎ (01983) 753535
Greene King Abbot; Hampshire King Alfred's; Wadworth 6X; Yates' Undercliff Experience; Young's Bitter Ⓗ
Fine, unspoilt town pub run by possibly the longest serving landlord on the Isle of Wight. Situated just off the main Freshwater shopping centre, there is a large garden to relax in for summer and a pleasant snug bar to sample the varied ales during the winter. A strong games section adds to the lively atmosphere. No need to phone for a taxi home – the landlord has one. Q🏮🍺🛉🍴♣️P🚻▯

Freshwater Bay

Fat Cat

Sandpipers, Coastguard Lane, PO40 9QX
🕐 11-midnight
☎ (01983) 758500 🌐 sandpipershotel.com
Beer range varies Ⓗ
A real gem within the Sandpipers Hotel, tucked away between Freshwater Bay and the Afton Nature Reserve. An ever-changing range of ales is on offer, often including beers from the more obscure breweries. This fine pub is well worth a visit, especially at the end of March/early April for the biggest real ale festival on the island with at least 100 ales to choose from. For children there is an adventure playground and cosy playroom with games and amusements. The hotel has a popular restaurant.
🏨Q🚬🏮🕙🍺🛉🍴♣️🅿️P🚻

Gurnard

Portland Inn

2 Worsley Road, PO31 8JN (opp the church)
🕐 11-11 (midnight Fri & Sat); 12-10.30 Sun
☎ (01983) 292948
Beer range varies Ⓗ
This building has been a bakery, grocer's, hardware store and a pub. Now central to the community, the present landlord has brought life back to the building. An extension into the depths of the building has created a multi-purpose area doubling as a children's room with a large TV screen; bring your own videos and see them as never before. The Gurnard Firework Charity was formed here to raise funds and support good causes. Lunches are made with local ingredients where possible. 🚬🏮🍴🚃♣️

Hulverstone

Sun Inn

Main Road, PO30 4EH
🕐 11-11; 12-10.30 Sun
☎ (01983) 852611 🌐 sun-hulverstone.com
Beer range varies Ⓗ
Six hundred year old building at the heart of rural West Wight with a charming garden and uninterrupted views to the sea. It has built up a strong following for food, served all day, with a weekly curry night and music evening. The spacious restaurant is popular and the pub caters for large wedding parties in the stunning extension. Well-behaved children are welcome. 🏨🏮🕙🍴🚃♣️P🚻

Newchurch

Pointer Inn

High Street, PO36 0NN
🕐 11.30-3, 6-11; 12-11 Sun
☎ (01983) 865202
Fuller's London Pride, Gale's HSB, seasonal beer Ⓗ
Ancient village local, family friendly, with a warm, cosy atmosphere. The main drinking area is the old public bar which has been integrated with the lounge/restaurant. Hook Norton Bitter is occasionally available. The restaurant has a fine reputation for nothing but home-cooked food prepared by a chef with 35 years' experience. The large garden has a petanque terrain. Next door is the village church with its unusual wooden steeple. 🏮🕙🍴🚃(516)♣️

Newport

Prince of Wales

36 South Street, PO30 1JE
🕐 11-11; 12-10.30 Sun

☎ (01983) 525026
Beer range varies Ⓗ
Formerly the tap to the now demolished Green Dragon, this excellent mock-Tudor, single-bar, street-corner local has established a fine reputation for its ales. Although in the centre of town, opposite the bus station and Morrisons supermarket, this is very much a locals' pub which has resisted the temptation to be 'tarted up', retaining the feel of a public bar. The three constantly changing beers are mainly from the Punch Taverns seasonal list.
♨Q◑⬛♣♠╚

Railway Medina
1 Sea Street, PO30 5BU
🕓 11-11; 12-10.30 Sun
☎ (01983) 528303
Beer range varies Ⓗ
A regular in the Guide, this unspoilt, popular and comfortable street-corner local has a pleasant, cosy atmosphere. The pub's name comes from its proximity to the now closed Newport Railway Station and the interior features many old local railway photographs and artefacts. There are always three excellent beers on offer (four in summer) in the lively public bar and cosy lounge. Under the stewardship of the latest tenants, new life has been injected into the Railway and there is now a limited range of food available. The bus station is nearby. ♨Q☀◑⬛⬛♣

Niton

White Lion
High Street, PO38 2AT
🕓 11-11 (midnight Sat)
☎ (01983) 730293 ⊕ thewhitelion.net
Wychwood Hobgoblin; Yates' Undercliff Experience; guest beers Ⓗ
Picturesque pub, full of character, in the centre of the village. The landlord has made a great impression since his arrival, overhauling the premises with a new kitchen and upgrading all the rooms. The pub has a fine reputation for food and the Sunday roast is a sell out. From the cellar comes a succession of four ever changing ales, at least one from an island brewery. A live band plays once a month. There is a covered area outside for smokers.
♨Q☀☀◑⬛⬛▲⬛P╚

Northwood

Travellers Joy
85 Pallance Road, PO31 8LS (on A3020 Yarmouth road out of Cowes)
🕓 11-2.30, 5-11; 11-midnight Fri & Sat; 12-3, 7-midnight Sun
☎ (01983) 852611 ⊕ tjoy.co.uk
Goddards Special Bitter; guest beers Ⓗ
Offering one of the best choices of cask ale on the Isle of Wight, this well renovated and extended old country inn was the island's first beer exhibition house and has been voted local CAMRA Pub of the Year on four occasions. Seven carefully chosen ales supplement the ever faithful GSB. Seasonal beers from the island's brewers are always popular – and if you can master the Northwood Nod, you may get a special from the cellar! A good range of home-cooked food is available. There is a

limited bus service to this pub.
♨♿☀◑▲⬛⬛P╚

Ryde

Simeon Arms
21 Simeon Street, PO33 1JG
🕓 11-midnight (11 Tue & Wed); 12-11.30 Sun
☎ (01983) 614954
Courage Directors; guest beers Ⓗ
Thriving gem tucked away down a Ryde back street, with a Tardis-like interior and its own annexed function hall. The pub is immensely popular with the local community, who participate in all the winter and summer pub games hosted here. There are darts, crib and pool leagues, and petanque on the enormous floodlit terrain during the summer. Food is available at lunchtime and Friday and Saturday evenings. Live music plays on Saturday night.
☀☀◑▲⬛⬛

Solent Inn
7 Monkton Street, PO33 1JW
🕓 11-11 (12.30am Thu-Sat); 12-10.30 Sun
☎ (01983) 563546
Beer range varies Ⓗ
Excellent, street-corner local with a warm, welcoming atmosphere. Live music plays at least three times a week and a friendly quiz is staged weekly. The new tenants have made a splendid impression with the locals and improvements to the interior have added to the appeal of the pub. Home-cooked food is planned. Beer quality has been maintained with an interesting range of four ales from the Punch portfolio. ☀⬛⬛⬛♣╚

St Helens

Vine Inn
Upper Green Road, PO33 1UJ
🕓 11-11 (12.30am Fri & Sat, 11.30 Sun)
☎ (01983) 872337
Fuller's London Pride; Wadworth 6X; guest beers Ⓗ
A recent refurbishment has changed the emphasis to food here. Although now a single bar, there is definitely a feel of saloon and public about this enormously successful enterprise, overlooking what is possibly the biggest village green in the kingdom, known locally as 'Goose Island'. A mixed selection of local memorabilia, from railways and hunting to breweries and marine life, decorates the walls. There is a large public car park on the green. ☀◑♿⬛⬛♣╚

Shanklin

Chine Inn
Chine Hill, PO37 6BW
🕓 11.30-midnight (12-4, 7-11 winter); 12-10.30 Sun
☎ (01983) 865880
Shepherd Neame Spitfire; Taylor Landlord; guest beers Ⓗ
This pub is a classic. The building, which has stood since 1621, must have some claim to being one of the oldest buildings with a licence on the island. Completely refurbished, it has retained plenty of the original charm for which it was well known. On a summer's day

when the sky is blue and the sun's rays are dancing on Sandown Bay, there is no finer view in England than from here. ♨ ᕼ ❀ ◑ ▸ ╚

Ventnor

Volunteer

30 Victoria Street, PO38 1ES
🕐 11-11 (midnight Fri & Sat); 12-11 Sun
☎ (01983) 853537 ⊕ volunteer-inn.co.uk
Courage Best Bitter; Greene King Abbot; Ventnor Golden Ⓗ

Built in 1866, the Volunteer is probably the smallest pub on the island. It operated as a beer house between 1869 and 1871 and retains many original features of the traditional drinkers' pub. Highly rated every year in the local CAMRA Pub of the Year awards, it achieved first place in 2003. No chips, no children, no fruit machines, no video games; this is a pure adult drinking house and one of the few places where you can still play rings. Cider is occasionally available.
Q ⊟ ♣ ● ╚

Wroxall

Four Seasons

2 Clarence Road, PO38 3BY
🕐 10-midnight; 11-11.30 Sun
☎ (01983) 854701
Fuller's Gale's HSB; Ringwood Best Bitter; Shepherd Neame Spitfire; guest beers Ⓗ

Formerly known as the Star, this pub was brought back to life after a disastrous fire, when it was threatened with closure. Now a successful village pub, it has an island-wide reputation for good food. Beers may vary but will usually include an island ale.
Q ᕼ ❀ ◑ ⊟ ▲ ⊟ ♣ P ╚

Pointer Inn, Newchurch, Isle of Wight.

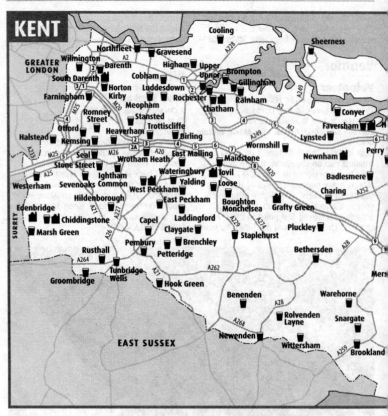

KENT

Badlesmere

Red Lion

Ashford Road, ME13 0NX (on A251)
🕐 12-3 (not Mon), 6-11; 12-midnight Fri; 11-11 Sat;
12-10.30 Sun
☎ (01233) 740320
**Fuller's London Pride; Greene King Abbot;
Shepherd Neame Master Brew Bitter; guest
beer** Ⓗ
Welcoming roadside free house dating from
1546 and retaining many exposed beams and
low ceilings. Beer festivals are held over the
Easter and August bank holiday weekends,
and live bands perform on Friday night. A
range of good food is served, including tapas
on Saturday evening (no meals Sun eve or
Mon). The large rear garden is popular in the
summer. ♨️🏵️🌢️ Ⓐ🛏️(666)♣P⁵⌐

Benenden

Bull

The Street, TN17 4DE
🕐 12-midnight
☎ (01580) 240054 🌐 thebullatbenenden.co.uk
**Harveys Sussex Best Bitter; Larkins Best; Young's
Bitter; guest beer** Ⓗ
Imposing 17th-century free house in the
centre of a pretty village. The interior is
homely and comfortable with wood flooring,
exposed beams and a real fire. Meals are
served in the bar and large conservatory (not

Sun eve); booking is essential for the popular
Sunday carvery. Families are welcome and
there is an outside area for smokers.
Biddenden Bushells cider is stocked.
♨️Q🏵️🍴️Ⓐ🛏️(297)♣🐾P⁵⌐

Bethersden

George

The Street, TN26 3AG (off A28)
🕐 12-11 (10.30 Sun)
☎ (01233) 820235
**Brakspear Bitter; Greene King Old Speckled Hen;
Harveys Sussex Best Bitter; guest beer** Ⓗ
Traditional village pub with a public bar and a
saloon. Dating from the early 18th century,
recent work has exposed the original interior
brick walls and fireplaces. A guest beer is
often available plus two ciders and a perry.
Regular beer festivals are held, including one
to celebrate St George's Day and another over
the last weekend in July. The garden has a
large children's play area. Tasty home-cooked
pub food is served. ♨️🏵️Ⓓ🛏️(400)🐾P

Birling

Nevill Bull

1 Ryarsh Road, ME19 5JW
🕐 11-3, 6.30-11; closed Mon; 12-3, 7-10.30 Sun
☎ (01732) 843193
**Adnams Bitter; Shepherd Neame Master Brew
Bitter; guest beer** Ⓗ

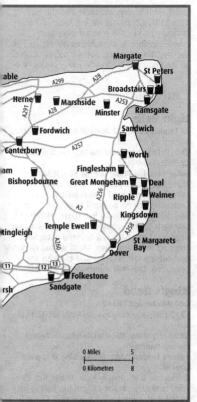

☎ (01622) 743166
Wells Bombardier; Young's Bitter, seasonal beers Ⓗ
This 600-year-old coaching inn has been in the Young's tied estate since 1999. Originally built to provide lodgings for Canterbury pilgrims, it is now an excellent country pub, offering good food and ale in spacious, welcoming surroundings. Meals are served in the bar and restaurant (no food Sun eve). Locally sourced fresh produce is used wherever possible and seafood is a speciality. ⚑Q❀◑▣🚌(59)♣P

Brenchley

Halfway House
Horsmonden Road, TN12 7AX (½ mile SE of village)
🕐 12-11.30 (10.30 Sun)
☎ (01892) 722526
Goacher's Fine Light Ale; Harveys Sussex Best Bitter; Larkins Chiddingstone; Rother Valley Smild; guest beers Ⓗ
Classic country pub with open fires, beams and interesting decorative drinking areas. All beers are served direct through an adjoining wall between the cellar and the bar. Chiddingstone cider is on draught. The large garden has a children's play area. Voted Kent CAMRA Pub of the Year 2006, its stages beer festivals twice a year on the May and August bank holidays. ⚑Q❀❀◑▣🚌(297)♣♠P⁻

Broadstairs

Brown Jug
204 Ramsgate Road, CT10 2EW
🕐 12-3, 6-11; 12-11 Sat; 12-10.30 Sun
☎ (01843) 862788
Greene King IPA; guest beers Ⓗ
Charming olde worlde pub in the Dumpton area between Broadstairs and Ramsgate. A real time warp inn, it retains a flint façade, leaded windows and outside toilets, and a wonderful collection of china jugs adorns the beams in the public bar. A selection of board games is available and the pub fields strong quiz and petanque teams. Lunchtime opening hours may vary. It is on the Thanet Loop bus route. ⚑Q❀❀🚇≠(Dumpton Park)🚌♣P

Neptune's Hall
1-3 Harbour Street, CT10 1ET
🕐 12-midnight
☎ (01843) 861400
Shepherd Neame Master Brew Bitter, Spitfire, seasonal beers Ⓗ

On a corner in the centre of the village, this pub was named after local noble Michael Nevill who was killed in WWII. It has a bar and restaurant, although the same varied menu is served throughout (no food Sun eve). Children are welcome. The decor features mock wooden beams with hanging brasses and copper. There are numerous bull-related cartoons and an interesting array of bottles on display. ⚑Q❀◑▣🚌(58)P

Bishopsbourne

Mermaid Inn
The Street, CT4 5HX (800m from A2)
🕐 12-3.30, 6 (7 Sun)-11; 12-11.30 Sat
☎ (01227) 830581
Shepherd Neame Master Brew Bitter, seasonal beers Ⓗ
Attractive community pub close to the North Downs Way. Purpose built for workers from the Prestige Estate in 1865, its name comes from the family coat of arms. It has been refurbished but retains split-level bars and a welcoming hearth. The pub is home to darts, cricket and football teams. Dogs are welcome. ⚑❀◑♿🚌(16, 17)♣⁻

Boughton Monchelsea

Cock Inn
Heath Road, ME17 4JD
🕐 11-11; 12-10.30 Sun

Busy one-bar ale house, close to the town pier. It was built in 1815 on the site of old fishermen's cottages, and was used as a hotel in the 1920s. It holds regular jamming sessions and is one of the main music venues during the town's annual folk week in August. The pub's interior was listed in 1999. 🏠◗≠♣

Prince Albert

38 High Street, CT10 1JT
🕐 9.30 (11 Sun)-11
☎ (01843) 861917
Greene King Old Speckled Hen; Harveys Sussex Best Bitter; guest beers Ⓗ
Busy, one-bar pub in the town's main thoroughfare, built in 1911 to replace the original Albert, which stood in the way of the road-widening scheme. When originally built, in line with the Victorians' objective to segregate customers, it had five bars. It is on the Thanet Loop bus route.
◗≠(Broadstairs)🚋♣

Brompton

King George V

1 Prospect Row, ME7 5AL
🕐 11.45-11; 9am-2am Fri; 9am-3am Sat; 12-10.30 Sun
☎ (01634) 842418 ⊕ kgvpub.com
Adnams Bitter; Goacher's Mild; Harveys Sussex Mild; guest beer Ⓗ
Close to Chatham Historic Dockyard, this pub is adorned with ships' crests and other memorabilia, including part of a ship's mast. The regular beers are complemented by two frequently changing guest ales plus draught and bottled Belgian beers and more than 30 malt whiskies, tasted by the pub's whisky society. There is acoustic music on the last Sunday of the month. No meals are served on Sunday or Monday evening. Q🛏◗🚋

Brookland

Woolpack

Beacon Lane, TN29 9TY (just off A259)
🕐 11-3, 6-11; 11-11 Sat; 12-10.30 Sun
☎ (01797) 344321
Shepherd Neame Master Brew Bitter, seasonal beers Ⓗ
This inn, seemingly in the middle of nowhere, is at least five centuries old. A typical timber-framed hall house, it has low ceilings and old furniture arranged in front of a large open fire. Good value home-cooked food is served in large portions. Barbecues are held on Sunday evenings in summer in the large garden, and there is often a hog roast on a bank holiday. 🏠Q🕸◗🚋🕭

Burmarsh

Shepherd & Crook

Shearway, TN29 0JJ OS102321
🕐 11-3, 7-11; 12-5, 7-11 Sat & Sun
☎ (01303) 872336
Adnams Bitter; guest beer Ⓗ
Small and friendly country pub where dogs are welcome. The bar and dining area share a single room in this family-run free house. One guest ale is always available and changes frequently. Traditional English food, all home-cooked using locally sourced ingredients where possible, is available every day except Tuesday. This pleasant, popular pub is situated on the Romney Marsh cycle route. 🏠Q🕸◗♣

Canterbury

Eight Bells

34 London Road, CT2 8LN (off A2050 roundabout, 200m from ring road)
🕐 3 (12 Sat)-11 (midnight Thu-Sat); 12-10.30 Sun
☎ (01227) 454794
Fuller's London Pride; Greene King IPA Ⓗ
There has been a pub here since 1708, but this cosy, traditional local was rebuilt in 1902. Customers are encouraged to play the piano, and there is occasional live music. Home to five darts teams, many of their trophies are on display. At the back is a covered patio with steps up to an attractive, small walled garden and outside toilets. Dogs and children are permitted. Q🕸≠(Canterbury West)🚋♣🕭

King's Head

204 Wincheap, CT1 3RY
🕐 12-2.30, 4.45-midnight; 12-midnight Sat; 12-11.30 Sun
☎ (01227) 462885 ⊕ smoothhound.co.uk/hotels/thekingshead.html
Fuller's London Pride; Greene King IPA; guest beer Ⓗ
Traditional and friendly local, worth the 15-minute walk from the city centre. Dating back to the 15th century, the building is Grade II listed. Exposed beams, hanging hops and bric-a-brac add to its charm. Bar billiards and darts are played, and bat and trap matches are held in the garden in summer. The dining room serves good value meals. Guest beers are usually sourced from micro-breweries. Parking is for residents only. 🕸🛏◗≠🚋(652)♣P🕭

Phoenix

67 Old Dover Road, CT1 3DB
🕐 11-11 (1am Fri & Sat); 12-4, 7-11 Sun
☎ (01227) 464220 ⊕ thephoenix-canterbury.co.uk
Greene King IPA; Wells Bombardier; Young's Bitter; guest beers Ⓗ
Cosy corner pub full of cricket memorabilia, handy for the cricket ground and open all day when there is a match. A changing range of guest beers comes from all over the UK and includes a mild. The pub hosts a well-attended beer festival in December, showcasing a wide range of seasonal beers. Board games are played on Monday evening. The food is good value and comes in generous portions (not Thu eve).
🕸🛏◗🚻≠(Canterbury East)🚋♣P🕭

Unicorn Inn

61 St Dunstan's Street, CT2 8BS
🕐 11-11 (midnight Fri & Sat)
☎ (01227) 463187 ⊕ unicorninn.com
Caledonian Deuchars IPA; Shepherd Neame Master Brew Bitter; guest beers Ⓗ
Comfortable 1604 pub near the historic Westgate with an attractive suntrap garden. Bar billiards can be played and a quiz, set by regular customers, is held weekly on Sunday

evening. The two guest beers often come from a Kent micro-brewery. Imaginative food ranges from pub favourites to exotic specials, and is excellent value. Buses to Whitstable pass nearby. A covered and heated area for smokers is planned.
🏰❀◑⇌(Canterbury West)🚆♣⌐

Capel

Dovecote Inn

Alders Road, TN12 6FU (½ mile W of A228 between Colts Hell and Tudeley) OS643441
🕐 12-3, 5.30-11.30; 12-11 Sun
☎ (01892) 835966
Adnams Broadside; Fuller's Gale's HSB; Gadds No 5 Ramsgate; Badger K&B Sussex Bitter; Harveys Sussex Best Bitter; guest beer Ⓖ
Welcoming, traditional pub in an idyllic rural area, popular with walkers. Up to six cask beers are served from a cooled room through a mock barrel frontage. The guest beer is chosen by popular local demand. Food is available at most sessions (not Sun eve or Mon in winter), and includes tasty Swiss rosti dishes. There is a quiz night every other Wednesday. The pleasant garden has a large children's climbing area, a patio for dining and a car park. 🏰Q❀◑P⌐

Charing

Bowl

Egg Hill Road, TN27 0HG (at Five Lanes jct) OS950154
🕐 12 (4 winter)-11.30; 12-11 Fri-Sun
☎ (01233) 712256 ⊕ bowlinn.co.uk
Fuller's London Pride; guest beers Ⓗ
Remote, award-winning pub on the crest of the North Downs overlooking the Weald of Kent. Signposts direct you to the pub from both the A20 and A251. The large garden can be used for camping (booking essential), and a beer festival is hosted in mid-July. The pub is warmed in winter by a magnificent open fire. Three guest beers are usually available, and snacks are served until 9.45pm. Note the unusual hexagonal pool table. 🏰Q❀⇌Å♣P

Chartham

Artichoke

Rattington Street, CT4 7JG (by paper mill)
🕐 11-2.30, 7-11.30 (1.30am Fri & Sat); 12-11.30 Sun
☎ (01227) 738316
Shepherd Neame Master Brew Bitter, seasonal beers Ⓗ
The quaint, half-timbered exterior hints at the age of this pub, built in the 14th century as a hall house. Half the interior is used for dining (evening meals Friday and Saturday only). Note the glass-topped well used as a table. The other half is a cosy, beamed bar with a large fireplace. Quiz and race nights are popular. Local buses pass nearby.
🏰❀◑⇌🚆P⌐

Chatham

Alexandra

43 Railway Street, ME4 4RJ
🕐 11-11; 12-10.30 Sun
☎ (01634) 830545
Shepherd Neame Master Brew Bitter, Spitfire, seasonal beers Ⓗ
Refurbished Victorian pub close to the railway station and well used by commuters and locals. It has a large U-shaped bar area and a small secluded room at the back. A wide range of meals is on offer, and occasional live music is played. The pub has won the regional most improved pub of the year award from Shepherd Neame Brewery for 2005 and 2006. Local bus services pass nearby. ◑⇌🚆

Chiddingstone Hoath

Rock

TN8 7BS (1½ miles S of Chiddingstone, via Wellers Town) OS497431
🕐 11.30-3, 6-11; closed Mon; 12-4 Sun
☎ (01892) 870296
Larkins Traditional, Chiddingstone, Best, seasonal beer Ⓗ
Attractive country pub in a remote setting on high ground to the west of Penshurst – the pub is named after one of the nearby rocky outcrops. Tied to the local Larkins Brewery, it offers its full range of beers, dispensed from a set of unusual hexagonal wooden handpumps. The main bar has a floor of well-worn brick and a beamed ceiling; a smaller, cosier saloon bar is up to the right. Bench seating runs beneath the leaded windows. A good range of food is available.
🏰Q❀◑🚱♣P

Claygate

White Hart

TN12 9PL (on B2162 between Yalding and Horsmonden)
🕐 11-11
☎ (01892) 730313 ⊕ thewhitehart.biz
Goacher's Light; Shepherd Neame Master Brew Bitter, Spitfire; guest beer Ⓗ
Popular Victorian free house set among orchards and hop gardens. The two bars, with open fires, offer a warm, welcoming atmosphere. The large adjoining restaurant serves excellent home-cooked food. A special flambé menu on Monday and theatre supper nights add variety. The large garden provides a pleasant retreat, featuring frequent barbecues and hog roasts. Children are welcome. 🏰Q❀◑🚱Å🚆(26)♣P

Cobham

Ship

14 The Street, DA12 3BN
🕐 11.30-11
☎ (01474) 814326
Courage Best Bitter; Shepherd Neame Spitfire; guest beers Ⓗ

221

Large, imposing, detached pub at the south-eastern end of the village, featuring an attractive cream-painted exterior. Parts of the building date from the 18th century, and the beams are reputed to have been salvaged from a ship that sank in the River Medway. Two rustic fireplaces are used in winter. Good meals are prepared, with steak and ale pies the speciality. A summer real ale festival is held each June. ♨Q❀❍▮🖃(416)P⅃

Conyer

Ship

Conyer Quay, ME9 9HR
✪ 12-3, 6-11; 12-midnight Sat; 12-10.30 Sun
☎ (01795) 520778
Adnams Bitter; Shepherd Neame Master Brew Bitter, Spitfire; Young's Bitter ⊞
Located in the isolated settlement of Conyer, next to a creek, this pub is popular with boat owners who moor nearby, and is a good place to take a break after a long walk through surrounding countryside. The bar has a wooden floor, and in winter there is a roaring log fire. For the summer there is pleasant outside seating. The bus from Sittingbourne runs every two hours during the day and Teynham Station is a pleasant one mile walk away. ♨❀❍🖃(344)P

Cooling

Horseshoe & Castle

The Street, ME3 8OJ
✪ 11.30 (5.30 Mon)-11 (12.30am Fri & Sat); 12-11.30 Sun
☎ (01634) 221691 ⊕ horseshoeandcastle.co.uk
Greene King IPA; Shepherd Neame Master Brew Bitter; guest beer ⊞
Nestling in the quiet village of Cooling, the pub is near a ruined castle that was once owned by Sir John Oldcastle, on whom Shakespeare's Falstaff was modelled. The local graveyard was used in the film version of Great Expectations, where young Pip was surprised by the convict Magwich. Pool, darts, petanque and bat and trap are played. Seafood is a speciality on the menu, served in the separate dining area (no food Mon). Draught Addlestones cider is available. ♨Q❀🗪❍♣♠P⅃

Darenth

Chequers

Darenth Road South, DA2 7QT
✪ 11-11; 12-10.30 Sun
☎ (01322) 224037
Courage Best Bitter; guest beers ⊞
The attractive building, dating from the 16th century, is situated in a lane cut off by construction of junction 2 of the M25/A2, two miles south of Dartford. A comfortable venue for drinkers and diners, it has retained many original features. Up to four guest ales from small breweries, including the local Millis Brewery, are available. There is a large, family-friendly garden where barbecues are held in summer. The Darent Valley footpath is nearby and walkers are welcome. Evening meals are served Wednesday to Saturday only. ❀❍🖃(414)♠P

Deal

Bohemian

47 Beach Street, CT14 6HY
✪ 11-midnight; closed Mon; 9am-midnight Sun
☎ (01304) 374843
Adnams Broadside; Woodforde's Wherry; guest beers ⊞
In a prime position on the seafront, this pub has fine views over the Downs, as the sea is confusingly known in these parts, especially from the upstairs restaurant. It has a modern yet congenial interior, and everyone's needs are catered for, with Kent beers regularly available, real Rosie's organic cider and a large range of bottled beers from Belgium and further afield. Stray 'Canaries' from Norwich are always warmly welcomed by the landlord. ❀❍🗪🍴♠⅃

Deal Hoy

16 Duke Street, CT14 6DU
✪ 12-11 (8 Sun)
☎ (01304) 363972 ⊕ dealhoy.co.uk
Shepherd Neame Master Brew Bitter, Spitfire, seasonal beers ⊞
Tucked away in a side-street terrace at the north end of town, this locals' pub is a little larger than it looks from the outside, with plenty of room to relax in the modern interior around the U-shaped bar or in comfortable armchairs. Shepherd Neame beers at their best include seasonal brews, as well as Porter and Bishops Finger. The award-winning garden is an added attraction during summer months. ❀🗪🖃⅃

Hare & Hounds

The Street, Northbourne, CT14 0LG
✪ 12-3, 6-11 (midnight Thu-Sat)
☎ (01304) 365429 ⊕ thehareandhounds.net
Adnams Bitter; Hancocks Best Bitter; Harveys Sussex Best Bitter; Wells Bombardier; guest beers ⊞
Friendly, hop-strewn country pub in a pleasant village. The menu specialises in free range and local produce with a wide range of vegetarian options. An annual beer festival is held in late summer. Monthly quizzes help to raise funds for the local cricket club and other good causes. The large enclosed garden has children's play equipment. ♨❀❍🖃P

Prince Albert

187-189 Middle Street, CT14 6LW (corner of Alfred Sq)
✪ 6 (12 Sun)-11
☎ (01304) 375425
Beer range varies ⊞
The Victorian exterior may look unassuming but inside you will find a cheerful and welcoming street-corner local with a small restaurant. Roast lunch is served on Sunday, and evening meals are available Wednesday to Saturday. Interesting beers come from a wide range of small brewers, often featuring Kentish ales. The small, sheltered garden is an added bonus in summer. The railway station

ENGLAND

and bus station are a 10-minute walk.
🏨🏾♿◗🚌

Ship

141 Middle Street, CT14 6JZ
🕐 11-11.30
☎ (01304) 372222
Caledonian Deuchars IPA; Ramsgate Gadds No 7; guest beers Ⓗ
Situated in Deal's conservation area, just off the seafront, this traditional, unspoilt, two-bar town pub is just 10 minutes' walk north of the town centre. The walls are adorned with seafaring memorabilia. A small garden is accessed through the back bar. Beers from the local Ramsgate Brewery are a feature. Without juke box or gaming machines, this is a quiet place for conversation or a peaceful read. Live music is played every Thursday. Dog-friendly, it is near Deal station and bus station.
🏨🏾≠🚌⅃

Dover

Blakes of Dover

52 Castle Street, CT16 1PJ
🕐 11.30-11; 12-5 Sun
☎ (01304) 202194 ⊕ blakesofdover.com
Goacher's Crown Imperial Stout; guest beers Ⓗ/Ⓖ
A welcome refuge from the busy thoroughfare above, this fine, cosy cellar bar has an intimate atmosphere and genial hosts. The stillage, on view behind the bar, comprises six self-tilting mounts for casks from which many of the guest beers are served on gravity. A fine range of malt whiskies is also available. Keg beer and lager are notable by their absence. Thatchers and guest ciders and perry feature at this local CAMRA Pub of the Year 2006, as well as excellent food.
Q🏾🏾◗≠🚌♦

Eagle Inn

324 London Road, CT17 0SX
🕐 12-midnight (2am Sat); 12-11 Sun
☎ (07718) 384807
Beer range varies Ⓗ
Popular local which is in its third incarnation in 10 years. The present landlord is keen on real ale and has a realistic pricing policy. The open-plan main bar is brightly decorated, with a good community atmosphere. A large games room at the rear is the venue for weekly live music entertainment. The pub is dog-friendly, and it can get busy at weekends. ♿🚌

Louis Armstrong

58 Maison Dieu Road, CT16 1RA
🕐 12-11.30; 12-2, 7-11 Sun
☎ (01304) 204759
Hopdaemon Skrimshander IPA; guest beers Ⓗ
A large town pub with L-shaped bar and stage, this free house showcases frequently-changing beers. Quiet at lunchtimes, it gets lively at the weekend when music is hosted. The walls are adorned with posters of a mix of bands, old and new. Large windows give the front part of the bar a light and airy feel. Situated on the one-way street that runs around Dover's town centre, with a large car

park opposite, it is also on local bus routes.
🏾🚌⅃

White Horse

Saint James Street, CT16 1QF
🕐 4-11; 1-10.30 Sun
☎ (01304) 242974
Taylor Landlord; guest beers Ⓗ
Do not miss this characterful tavern just a short walk from Market Square. Built in 1365, and gaining its licence in 1652, this is one of Dover's oldest and probably most unspoilt residences. Very much a beer house, it has three rooms serving up to four beers, and tends to avoid the national and regional brands. Cider usually comes from Biddenden. Frequented by cross-Channel swimmers in season and locals all year round, this is a place for good conversation.
🏾🏳≠(Dover Priory)🚌♦⅃

East Malling

King & Queen

1 New Road, ME19 6DD
🕐 10 (11 Sat & Sun)-11
☎ (01732) 842752
Beer range varies Ⓗ
A 16th-century inn at the heart of the village, opposite the church and handy for East Malling station, the King & Queen is known for its good food, available from an a la carte menu all day except Sunday, when the traditional roast lunches are popular. The beer range often includes a Kent brew. A board on the wall provides tasting notes for the real ales.
🏨🐕🏾◗≠🚌(58, 70)P⅃

Rising Sun

125 Mill Street, ME19 6BX
🕐 12-11 (10.30 Sun)
☎ (01732) 843284
Goacher's Light; Shepherd Neame Master Brew Bitter; guest beer Ⓗ
Very much a drinkers' pub, this genuine free house is popular with local football teams and darts players. Run by the same family for 17 years, the mock-Tudor interior has a horseshoe-shaped bar, with one of the three handpumps always featuring a rotating guest beer. All real ales are competitively priced, and good value bar meals are served on weekday lunchtimes. Outside is a long rear garden and a canopied passageway for smokers. Live matches are shown on Sky Sports. 🏾≠🚌♦⅃

East Peckham

Bush, Blackbird & Thrush

194 Bush Road, Peckham Bush, TN12 5LW (1 mile NE of East Peckham, via Pond Rd) OS664500
🕐 11-3 (not Mon), 6-11; 12-3, 6-10 Sun
☎ (01622) 871349
Shepherd Neame Master Brew Bitter, Spitfire, seasonal beers Ⓖ
Fine 15th-century, tile-hung Kentish building, set on the fringes of the village, with a long pub tradition. This Shepherd Neame house serves ales straight from the casks. The pub is divided into two rooms, the bar and dining

area, separated by a large brick fireplace which burns logs in winter. Good, traditional pub food is served (not Sun eve or Mon). Bat and trap and darts are played, and quiz night is Tuesday. ♨Q✿◑◐♿P

Farningham

Chequers

87 High Street, DA4 0DT
✪ 11.30 (12 Sat)-11; 12-10.30 Sun
☎ (01322) 865222
Fuller's London Pride, ESB; Taylor Landlord; guest beers Ⓗ
Situated in an attractive riverside village, this convivial, small, one-bar corner local features decorative wall murals depicting local scenes. Eight handpumps dispense regular and guest ales, many sourced from Kent micro-breweries. The pub is accessible from major roads and the Darent Valley footpath, although parking nearby is difficult. No food is served on Sunday. ◑🚌(421)♣

Faversham

Anchor

52 Abbey Street, ME13 7BP
✪ 12-11 (midnight Fri & Sat)
☎ (01795) 536471 🌐 theanchorinnfaversham.com
Shepherd Neame Master Brew Bitter, Kent's Best, Spitfire, seasonal beers Ⓗ
This 17th-century pub is located in an area of Faversham that was once part of the Abbey precinct. Built using local bricks and beams from old ships' timbers, it has a low ceiling in the bar, warmed in winter by a wood-burning stove. The adjoining dining area is spacious and dominated by a large fireplace. Regular live music plays on Sunday afternoon. It has a spacious garden for summer days.
♨Q✿◑◐🚌♣⊢

Bear Inn

3 Market Place, ME13 7AG
✪ 10.30-3, 5.30-11 (11.30 Thu); 10.30-midnight Fri & Sat; 11.30-10.30 Sun
☎ (01795) 532668
Shepherd Neame Master Brew Bitter, Kent's Best, Spitfire, seasonal beers Ⓗ
Historic market pub – one of very few that retains its early 10th-century layout with three distinct bars off a long side corridor. The busy front bar, tiny snug and larger rear lounge bar all have extensive wood panelling. It stands opposite the historic Guildhall and has outside seating in summer. Fine home-cooked lunches are served. The pub is popular with local folk musicians. ✿◑⊟≠🚌♣

Chimney Boy

59 Preston Street, ME13 8PG
✪ 11-11 (midnight Fri & Sat); 12-11 Sun
☎ (01795) 532007
Shepherd Neame Master Brew Bitter, Kent's Best Ⓗ
This 18th-century building started life as a convent then became the Limes Hotel around 1885. Shepherd Neame acquired it in the early 1930s. In the 1970s, while building work was being carried out, steps leading up the chimney in a back room were discovered and the inn renamed Chimney Boy. The upstairs function room hosts numberous societies and clubs including the Faversham Folk Club that meets on a Wednesday evening. Two large-screen TVs show sports. ♨✿◑◐≠♣P⊢

Elephant

31 The Mall, ME13 8JN
✪ 3-11.30; closed Mon; 12-midnight Sat; 12-7 Sun
☎ (01795) 590157
Beer range varies Ⓗ
Friendly, traditionally run ale house and local CAMRA Pub of the Year 2007, the Elephant places its emphasis very much on providing good beers. There are normally five ever-changing ales, usually including a mild, sourced from many local micro-breweries. The single bar has an open fireplace. A function room caters for meetings, weddings and parties. The walled garden is popular with families in summer. ♨☺✿≠🚌♣⊢

Railway Hotel

Preston Street, ME13 8PE
✪ 12-11 (10.30 Sun)
☎ (01795) 533173 🌐 railwayhotelfaversham.co.uk
Shepherd Neame Master Brew Bitter Ⓗ
In an imposing location opposite the railway station entrance, this pub has recently undergone a revival. Inside it is light and airy, and some of the original fittings have been preserved, with the promise of other features lost in the past to be restored. Patio tables are set outside in summer. The hotel dining room is open for lunches and evening meals Wednesday to Saturday, and for Sunday lunch.
Q✿⊭◑◐≠🚌♣P

Shipwright's Arms

Ham Road, Hollowshore, ME13 7TU OS017636
✪ 11-3, 6-11; closed winter Mon; 12-3, 6-10.30 Sun
☎ (01795) 590088
Goacher's Mild, Original; guest beers Ⓖ
Historic, rustic pub full of character and olde-worlde charm, overlooking the confluence of Oare and Faversham creeks, as well as extensive yacht moorings. The interior is bedecked with nautical ephemera. It has an extensive garden as well as seating at the front. Beers are sourced from Kent and Essex independent brewers, with house beer Shipwrecked brewed exclusively by Goacher's. Local CAMRA Pub of the Year 2006.
♨Q✿◑◐♣P⊢

Sun Inn

10 West Street, ME13 7JE
✪ 11-11 (11.30 Fri & Sat); 12-11 Sun
☎ (01795) 535098 🌐 sunfaversham.co.uk
Shepherd Neame Master Brew Bitter, Spitfire, seasonal beers Ⓗ
Ancient pub, originally a 15th-century hall but much altered every century since; it has recently been sympathetically extended to provide a restaurant (no eve meals Sun) and guest rooms. The main room features well-preserved oak panelling, some from the 16th century, and a beautiful old fireplace. In summer the rear garden fills up, and there are tables in the pedestrian-only street at the front. ♨✿⊭◑◐♿≠🚌⊢

Windmill Inn

Canterbury Road, ME13 8LT

☼ 12-midnight (1am Fri & Sat); 12-4, 7-11 Sun

☎ (01795) 536505

Shepherd Neame Master Brew Bitter, seasonal beers Ⓗ

This two-bar pub lies on Watling Street, the old Roman road from Chester to Dover, now the A2. Its name is derived from Preston Mill which stood close by until it was demolished in the early 1940s. The pub retains many original features including a windmill etched into the glass of the door to the front bar. Meals are available lunchtimes and evenings except Sunday evening. Dogs are permitted in the four letting rooms. ♨ⓕⓒⅅ≉⊞♣P

Finglesham

Crown

The Street, CT14 0NA

☼ 11-3, 6-11; 12-11 Sun

☎ (01304) 612555 ● thecrownatfinglesham.co.uk

Shepherd Neame Master Brew Bitter; guest beers Ⓗ

Chosen by local CAMRA as its Pub of the Year 2007, this is a friendly village local with a restaurant serving excellent home-cooked meals. Kentish micro-breweries supply regular guest ales, and bottled Biddenden ciders are available as well as occasional draught Biddenden Bushells. There is a monthly beer club and a beer festival in August. Good wines are available by the glass. Well-behaved dogs are welcome outside meal times. The pub has Caravan Club certified facilities.
♨❀ⅅΔ♣P'⌐

Folkestone

British Lion

10 The Bayle, CT20 1SG (just out of town centre)

☼ 12 (11 Sat)-4, 7-midnight; 12-4, 7-11 Sun

☎ (01303) 251478

Greene King IPA, Abbot; guest beers Ⓗ

An ale house has stood on this site since 1460. Close to all the facilities of the town centre, a comfortable, relaxed atmosphere prevails. The interior is decorated with some fine old prints from the pub's former Whitbread days, including a scene featuring the closed Chiswell Street Brewery. Two guest ales are always available. Food is served (not Tue eve). The pub fields a quiz team, and cribbage and chess are regularly played. ♨❀ⅅ♣♠

Chambers

Radnor Chambers, Cheriton Place, CT20 2BB

☼ 12-11 (midnight Fri & Sat); 7-10.30 Sun

☎ (01303) 233333

Adnams Bitter; Ringwood Old Thumper; guest beers Ⓗ

Surprisingly spacious cellar bar with a café upstairs under the same ownership. Three guest ales normally include Kentish beers, as well as some from further afield, supplemented by Biddenden and Cheddar Valley ciders. Beer festivals are held over Easter and August bank holiday weekends. The food, which includes Mexican and European choices plus daily specials, is served

every lunchtime and Sunday to Thursday evenings. ⅅ≉(Central)♣♠

Clifton Hotel

Clifton Gardens, The Leas, CT20 2EB

☼ 11.30-3, 6-midnight; 12-11.30 Sun

☎ (01303) 851231 ● thecliftonhotel.com

Beer range varies Ⓗ

Welcoming hotel bar in a premier three-star establishment, which has been a showcase for Bass for many years. Here guests may enjoy a drink in genteel tranquillity, making use of the leather armchairs to while away the time. The hotel offers spectacular views over the harbour and English Channel. Not far from local bus routes. Q❀ⓕⅅ≉(Central)⊟

East Cliff Tavern

13-15 East Cliff, CT19 6BU

☼ 4 (12 Fri; 11 Sat)-midnight; 12-midnight Sun

☎ (01303) 251132

Beer range varies Ⓗ

Back-street, two-bar, split-level pub hidden along a terraced street, on the other side of the harbour railway line. Its walls are decorated with old photos of Folkestone. One or two beers are usualy on offer, often from Kentish micro-breweries, and some from further afield. Biddenden dry cider is also stocked. The glass cabinet on the bar keeps a range of chocolates and Anadin! Q♣♠

Guildhall

42 The Bayle, CT20 1SQ (just out of town centre)

☼ 12-11 (midnight Fri & Sat); 12-10.30 Sun

☎ (01303) 251393

Draught Bass; Greene King IPA; guest beers Ⓗ

Welcoming and traditional pub close to the town centre, with a single bar that offers two guest beers. Large windows give the pub a light, airy feel. The Bayle is an attractive old area of town, where Charles Dickens once lived and started working on Little Dorrit. The pub is in a handy spot for the shops and cinema. ❀ⅅ♣P

Fordwich

Fordwich Arms

King Street, CT2 0DB

☼ 11-midnight (1am Fri & Sat)

☎ (01227) 710444

Flowers Original; Shepherd Neame Master Brew Bitter; Wadworth 6X; guest beers Ⓗ

Based in a classic 1930s building listed in Kent CAMRA's Regional Inventory, this attractive local has a large bar with a superb fireplace and woodblock floor, and a dining room. Excellent meals are served in both areas (not Sun eve). The garden and terrace overlook the River Stour and the pub is ideal for ramblers following the Stour Valley Walk. It hosts regular themed evenings and there is live folk music every second and fourth Sunday.
♨❀ⅅ≉(Sturry)⊟(4, 6)P'⌐

Gillingham

Barge

63 Layfield Road, ME7 2QY

☼ 7 (4 Fri)-11; 12-11 Sat & Sun

☎ (01634) 850485
Draught Bass; guest beers Ⓗ
Popular town pub down a dead end road with
a decked area outside offering fine views over
the Medway. The atmospheric bar is candle-lit
in the evening. Five handpumps dispense a
range of beers, sometimes from micro-
brewers including the local Nelson Brewery.
Folk night is Monday, the second and third
Wednesday of the month are Music Plus, and
the second Thursday is jazz and blues. ✿♣

Frog & Toad

Burnt Oak Terrace, ME7 2QY
🕐 11-11; 12-10.30 Sun
☎ (01634) 852231 ⊕ thefrogandtoad.com
Fuller's London Pride; guest beers Ⓗ
Three times winner of local CAMRA Pub of the
Year, this single-bar, no-nonsense, back-street
pub underwent a managerial change last year.
However, it continues to offer handpumped
ales, Biddenden Bushells cider in cask and
around 25 bottled Belgian beers poured in
their own badged glasses. It also hosts two to
three beer festivals a year on bank holidays.
Food is served Monday to Thursday until 7pm.
◑≈ᕒ♣☀‐

Upper Gillingham Conservative Club

541 Canterbury Street, ME7 5LF
🕐 11-2, 7-11; 11-11 Sat; 12-10.30 Sun
☎ (01634) 851403
**Shepherd Neame Master Brew Bitter; guest
beers** Ⓗ
The superb condition of the ales makes this
friendly and welcoming club well worth a visit
– take a copy of this Guide or a CAMRA
membership card to gain entry. A single U-
shaped bar features three handpumps offering
ales up to 4.5% ABV. The club has a snooker
room with two tables and a large-screen TV
showing Sky Sports. ᕒᕒ♣

Will Adams

73 Saxton Street, ME7 5EG
🕐 7-11; 12.30-4, 7-11 Sat; 12-4, 8-11 Sun
☎ (01634) 575902
Hop Back Summer Lightning; guest beers Ⓗ
This thriving locals' local offers a wide choice
of well-kept ales plus good value food, and is
home to darts and cards teams. The owners of
this small single bar pub have been in charge
for 14 years. The interior is painted with
scenes depicting the life and times of Will
Adams, the famous navigator. It opens at
11.30am on Saturdays when Gillingham FC
play at home. Local CAMRA Pub of the Year in
2006. ✿≈ᕒ♣☀‐

Gravesend

Crown & Thistle

44 The Terrace, DA12 2BJ
🕐 12-11 (10.30 Sun)
☎ (01474) 326049 ⊕ crownandthistle.org.uk
Daleside Shrimpers; guest beers Ⓗ
National CAMRA Pub of the Year in 2003, this
small, terraced inn is between the town
centre and river promenade. It supplies four
ever-changing guest beers and Weston's First
Quality cider on handpump. Pub food is

limited to rolls, but an oriental take-away can
be ordered at the bar to eat on the premises.
Background music is not intrusive and there
are no games machines to disturb the
conversation. In summer, barbecues and
occasional live music feature. The station and
bus services are nearby. ✿≈ᕒ☀‐

Jolly Drayman

1 Love Lane, Wellington Street, DA12 1JA
🕐 12-11.30 (midnight Fri & Sat); 12-10.30 Sun
☎ (01474) 352355 ⊕ jollydrayman.com
**Caledonian Deuchars IPA; Shepherd Neame
Spitfire; guest beers** Ⓗ
Town-centre pub and small hotel on the site of
the former Walker's Brewery. Guest beers
usually come from Punch Taverns' regularly
changing lists. The characterful low-ceilinged
bar is due to be joined by a lounge bar which,
together with the hotel bedrooms, forms part
of the defunct brewery outbuildings. The pub
hosts three darts teams and occasional live
music. Evening meals are available 6-9pm
Monday to Friday. ✿✿◑ᕒᕒ♣P‐

Great Mongeham

Three Horseshoes

139 Mongeham Road, CT14 9LL
🕐 12-midnight (1am Fri & Sat); 12-10.30 Sun
☎ (01304) 375812
Greene King IPA; Ramsgate Gadds No 5 Ⓗ
Small and welcoming one-room pub where
the friendly bar staff serve a consistently
excellent pint from the local Ramsgate
Brewery. Reasonably priced food is available
most lunchtimes and Thursday evening (no
food Tue). This is a genuine community pub,
supporting local charities throughout the year
with quiz nights, raffles and other activities.
There is live music on Friday evening. The pub
has pool and darts teams and a large child-
friendly garden. ✿◑ᕒ(14)P‐

Groombridge

Crown

TN3 9QH (A264 from Tunbridge Wells, then B2110)
🕐 11-3, 6-11; 11-11 Sat; 12-5 (10.30 summer) Sun
☎ (01892) 864742 ⊕ thecrowngroombridge.co.uk
**Greene King IPA; Harveys Hadlow Bitter; Larkins
Traditional, seasonal beers** Ⓗ
Celebrities, film crews and English Heritage
know this lovely inn, one of Britain's oldest,
dating back to 1585. With its low beams and
an inglenook fireplace, to visit is to step back
in time. A free house, it offers Greene King
and Harveys as well as Larkins which is
brewed not far away. Home cooking is
popular. The garden overlooks the picturesque
village and has a covered area for smokers.
Groombridge station on the Spa Valley
Railway is nearby. ⨝Q✿✿◑≈ᕒP‐

Halstead

Rose & Crown

Otford Lane, TN14 7EA OS489611
🕐 12-11
☎ (01959) 533120

Larkins Traditional; Whitstable East India Pale
Ale; guest beers H

Two-bar, flint-faced free house from the
1860s, formerly part of the Fox & Sons
Brewery estate and later Style & Winch. The
bars display pictures of the pub and village in
earlier times. Local CAMRA Pub of the Year
runner-up in 2006, it has featured in this Guide
for 13 consecutive years. Four regularly-
changing guest ales come from smaller
breweries. A menu of home-made food is
offered with a take-away option; booking for
Sunday lunch is advised.
▲Q ♥ ★ ◑ & ⊟ (402) ♣ P ⁵⁻

Hastingleigh

Bowl

The Street, TN25 5UU TR096449
☼ 5-midnight; closed Mon; 12-late Sat & Sun
☎ (01233) 750354 ⊕ thebowlonline.co.uk
Adnams Bitter; Fuller's London Pride; Harveys
Sussex Best Bitter; guest beer H

Lovingly restored village pub, this listed
building retains many period features
including a tap room, now used for playing
pool, and is free from juke box and game
machines. Quiz night is Tuesday. The lovely
large garden has a cricket pitch to the rear
where matches are played most Sundays in
summer. Beer festivals are held on May and
August bank holidays, featuring hog roasts.
Excellent sandwiches are usually available.
Biddenden cider is also served.
▲Q ♥ ★ ◑ ⊟ (620) ♣ ♠ P ⁵⁻

Heaverham

Chequers

Watery Lane, TN15 6NP (1½ miles N of A25,
follow signs to Chaucer Business Pk)
☼ 12-11; closed winter Mon; 12-10.30 (9 winter) Sun
☎ (01732) 763968 ⊕ heaverham.com
Shepherd Neame Master Brew Bitter, Kent's
Best, seasonal beers H

Attractive 17th-century country pub in a small
hamlet near Kemsing. It has a traditional
public bar, a pleasant saloon and a restaurant
in the adjoining 'haunted' barn. An
experienced chef, renowned for top quality
meals, prepares the food here (no food Mon &
Sun eve). The large beer garden has a
children's play area and hosts bat & trap
matches on Tuesday summer evenings. A
league quiz is held on Tuesday, and a friendly
quiz night on the last Thursday of the month.
Traditional pub games are played on
Wednesday evening, including cribbage,
shove-ha'penny and dominoes.
▲Q ★ ◑ ⊑ ≠ (Kemsing) ⊟ (433) ♣ P

Herne

Butcher's Arms

29a Herne Street, CT6 7HL (opp church)
☼ 12-1.30, 6-9 (or later); closed Sun & Mon
☎ (01227) 371000 ⊕ micropub.co.uk
Dark Star Hophead; Fuller's London Pride, ESB;
guest beers G

The smallest pub in Kent, with room for about
12 people, it contains the original chopping
tables, plus hooks and other butcher's
implements. At least four beers are dispensed
straight from the cask and there is an ever-
changing variety of guest beers. A take-away
service is offered. A real ale drinker's delight,
the landlord operates a voting system
allowing his customers to decide which beers
he should stock. The confined space ensures
that lively chat flourishes. There is a car park
nearby. Opening hours vary so telephone first.
Q ⊟ (4, 6)

First & Last

Herne Common, CT6 7JU (on A291, ½ mile outside
village)
☼ 11-11; closed Mon; 12-10.30 Sun
☎ (01227) 364465
Fuller's London Pride; Harveys Sussex Best
Bitter H

Comfortable village pub, partly dating from
1690, first licensed as an ale house in 1835.
The pub has always been known as First &
Last, which refers to its proximity to the area
boundary. Many changes have obscured the
original structure and there is now a large
single bar, a restaurant (no food served Sun
eve) and a large, popular function room. The
wood-panelled interior is decorated with
pictures and heated by two wood-burning
stoves. A covered, heated area is planned for
smokers. ▲ ★ ◑ & ⊟ (4, 6) P ⁵⁻

Smugglers Inn

1 School Lane, CT6 7AN (opp church)
☼ 11-11 (1am Fri & Sat)
☎ (01227) 741395
Shepherd Neame Master Brew Bitter, Spitfire,
seasonal beers H

Quaint village local with a smuggling history,
situated just inland from Herne Bay. Parts of
the pub are 400 years old. The saloon bar has
a low ceiling decorated with hanging hops, as
well as wood panelling and a ship's binnacle.
The public bar is more modern, with a pool
table and dartboard. The garden has a bat and
trap pitch, used in summer months.
Q ★ ◑ & ⊟ ♣

Hernhill

Three Horseshoes

46 Staple Street, ME13 9UA OS080601
☼ 12-3, 6-11; 11-11 Fri & Sat; 12-3, 7-10.30 Sun
☎ (01227) 750842 ⊕ 3shoes.co.uk
Shepherd Neame Master Brew Bitter, G Spitfire,
seasonal beers H

A traditional country pub, over 300 years old,
set in a small hamlet among fruit orchards and
hop gardens and located close to Mount
Ephraim Gardens and Farming World. This is a
friendly, mobile phone-free village local with
a growing reputation for good home-cooked
food (no food Sun eve or bank holidays). Live
music, mainly blues or jazz, is played most
weekends. In mid-July the 'Shoes holds an
annual wheelie bin grand prix.
▲Q ★ ◑ ▲ ⊟ (638) ♣ P

227

Higham

Stonehorse

Dillywood Lane, ME3 8EN (off B2000 Cliffe Road)
⏲ 12-11 (10.30 Sun)
☎ (01634) 722046
Courage Best Bitter; guest beers Ⓗ
A country pub with a large garden on the edge of Strood, surrounded by fields and handy for walkers. The unspoiled public bar sports a wood-burning range, darts and a rare bar billiard table. Good value meals are served in the restaurant at the rear (not Mon) – book ahead for Sunday lunch. The pub is dog friendly, but no children are allowed in the bar. ♨Q❀◑⊟♣P⊱

Hildenborough

Cock Horse

London Road, TN11 8NH (on B245 between Sevenoaks and Tonbridge) OS553449
⏲ 12 (11 Tue-Fri)-3, 5.30-8; 12-3, 6-midnight Sat; 12-4 Sun
☎ (01732) 833232
Shepherd Neame Master Brew Bitter, Spitfire Ⓗ
Friendly 16th-century coaching inn in an attractive countryside location but only minutes from the A21. Glyn and Janice extend a warm welcome to customers in the comfortable bar, large restaurant (please phone for reservations) or decking area outside. It has a lawned garden and ample parking; Hildenborough station is about a mile away. ♨Q❀◑⊟♿🚌(402)P⊱

Hook Green

Elephant's Head

Furnace Lane, TN3 8LJ
⏲ 12-3, 4.30-11; 12-11 Sat; 12-10.30 Sun
☎ (01892) 890279
Harveys Hadlow Bitter, Sussex Best Bitter, Armada Ale, seasonal beers Ⓗ
Built in 1489 in a rural spot near Bayham Abbey and Scotney Castle, this building has been a pub since 1768 – you can read the interesting history on one wall. The well-preserved interior includes an inglenook fireplace, burning logs in winter and oak beams hung with hop bines. There is a conservatory and a play area for children outside. A Harveys pub, it serves four real ales and a variety of meals (not Mon or Sun eve) including traditional English fish dishes and a children's menu. ♨Q☺❀◑🚌(256)♣P

Horton Kirby

Bull

3 Lombard Street, DA4 9DF
⏲ 12 (4 Mon)-11 (midnight Fri & Sat); 12-10.30 Sun
☎ (01322) 862274 🌐thebullpub.co.uk
Beer range varies Ⓗ
Recently refurbished and modernised one-bar village pub with a large, landscaped garden offering superb views across the Darent Valley. Good food is served at lunchtime (not Mon) and in the evening (Thu-Sat). The landlord selects a wide range of beers from enterprising micro-breweries, as well as a house beer, Horton Kirby's Finest, from Cottage Brewery. A range of ciders is served on gravity. Quiz night is Monday and a successful cribbage league team plays on Tuesday. There is a heated, covered area for smokers. ❀◑♿🚌(414)♣♦⊱

Ightham Common

Old House ☆

Redwell Lane, TN15 9EE (½ mile SW of Ightham Village, between A25 & A227) OS590559
⏲ 12-3 (Sat only), 7-11 (9 Tue); 12-3, 7-10.30 Sun
☎ (01732) 822383
Daleside Shrimpers; Ⓖ **Flowers IPA;** Ⓗ **Oakham JHB; guest beers** Ⓖ
Hidden away down a steep narrow lane, and without a pub sign, this brick and tile-hung cottage is a classic pub that time forgot. It is difficult to find, but not to be missed. The building dates from the 17th century and the larger, busier room boasts a Victorian wood-panelled bar and a vast inglenook fireplace. The smaller room is an old-fashioned parlour. Beers are served from a gravity stillage in a room behind the bar. ♨Q⊟♣P

Kemsing

Rising Sun

Cotmans Ash Lane, TN15 6XD OS563599
⏲ 11-3, 6-11; 12-3, 7-10.30 Sun
☎ (01959) 522683
Beer range varies Ⓗ
Hard to find, isolated hilltop pub dating in parts from the 16th century. A former hunting lodge, it features a flint exterior and oak beams inside. Situated in scenic downland countryside near several local footpaths, it offers a warm welcome to walkers, cyclists, accompanied children and owners of well-behaved dogs. An ancient African Grey parrot resides beside the large, open fireplace. Up to five ales from local and regional micro-breweries are served. ♨Q❀▲♣P⊡

Kingsdown

King's Head

Upper Street, CT14 8BJ
⏲ 12-3 (Sat only), 5.30 (6 Sat)-11.30; 12-10.30 Sun
☎ (01304) 373915
Fuller's London Pride; Greene King IPA; guest beer Ⓗ
Situated next to the village shops, halfway along the main street as it runs down to the sea, this is a welcoming, comfortable, multi-room pub, set around a central bar. Beer clips adorn the ceiling of the public bar. Note the frosted glass door bearing the name of the former local brewing company, Thompsons of Walmer. Good home-cooked food is served, and children and dogs are welcome. There is a skittle alley in the enclosed garden. ♨☺❀◑⊟🚌(84)♣⊱

Laddingford

Chequers Inn

Lees Road, ME18 6BP
✪ 12-3, 5-11; 12-11 Sat; 12-10.30 Sun
☎ (01622) 871266
Adnams Bitter; Fuller's London Pride; guest beers ⊞

Attractive, community-spirited, oak-beamed pub dating from the 15th-century in the heart of the village. During the summer, the frontage is adorned with colourful window boxes and hanging baskets. A warm welcome is assured in the simply furnished bar and split-level dining area. A beer festival is held in late April, showcasing around 30 ales. The food is excellent, with a variety of daily specials and themed nights.
⋈Q✿☎◀❶➡(26)P

Loose

Walnut Tree

657 Loose Road, ME15 9UX (on A229, S of Maidstone)
✪ 11.30-3.30 (4 Fri & Sat), 6.30-midnight (1.30am Fri & Sat); 12-4.30, 7-midnight Sun
☎ (01622) 743493
Shepherd Neame Master Brew Bitter, Spitfire, seasonal beers ⊞

The landlord has been at this popular pub for more than 20 years. Inside, it features an amazing array of cigarette cards, chamber pots, water jugs, shaving mugs, horse brasses and other equestrian bits and pieces, as well as pictures of WWII aircraft. Bar snacks and hot meals, including vegetarian dishes, are available all week except Sunday evening. Petanque is played in the garden.
✿◀❶➡♣P⅃

Luddesdown

Cock Inn

Henley Street, DA13 0XB (1 mile SE of Sole St station) OS664672
✪ 12-11 (10.30 Sun)
☎ (01474) 814208
Adnams Bitter, Broadside; Goacher's Mild; Harveys Sussex Best Bitter; Shepherd Neame Master Brew Bitter; guest beers ⊞

Enterprising, independently owned free house in a pleasant rural setting. This quintessentially English traditional public house is a regular local CAMRA award winner, always offering at least seven real ales. The landlord devises and hosts a popular open quiz on Tuesday evening. Excellent quality food is served until early evening. Function rooms are available to hire. Petanque is played in the garden, which now includes a large covered and heated area for smokers.
⋈Q✿☎◀❶⬁♣P⅃

Lynsted

Black Lion

Lynsted Lane, ME9 0RJ
✪ 11-3, 7-11; 11-11 Sat; 12-3, 7-10.30 Sun
☎ (01795) 521229

Goacher's Mild, Light, Dark, Crown Imperial Stout ⊞

A friendly pub sought out by drinkers, the interior is warmed by a roaring fire at both ends of the main room during the winter months. The public bar houses a bar billiards table and dartboard. Wooden floors throughout the pub add to its traditional character. There is a large garden at the side of the pub. ⋈Q✿◀❶➡(345)P

Maidstone

Druid's Arms

24 Earl Street, ME14 1PP (opp Hazlitt Theatre)
✪ 11-11 (midnight Thu-Sat); 12-11 Sun
☎ (01622) 758516
Greene King IPA, Abbot, Old Speckled Hen; guest beers ⊞

This town-centre pub was the original Hogshead. It is situated next to the Fremlins Walk shopping centre which replaced the old Fremlins Brewery. A mixed clientele enjoys live music on Thursday and Saturday in the heated, covered courtyard, which also caters for smokers. Upbeat piped music is played in the split-level bar, which hosts a quiz on Monday night. The landlord offers changing guest ales and stages regular beer festivals. Meals are served until 6.30pm daily. Local bus routes pass nearby.
⋈✿☎&⇌(Maidstone East)➡⅃

Pilot

23-25 Upper Stopne Street, ME15 6EU (on A229 towards Hastings)
✪ 12-3, 6-11 (midnight Fri); 12-3, 7-midnight Sat; 12-midnight (12-5, 7-midnight winter) Sun
☎ (01622) 691162
Harveys Sussex Best Bitter, Armada Ale, seasonal beers ⊞

Grade II listed building dating from the 17th-century on a busy road not far from either of the stations in Maidstone. This is Harveys' only tied house in the town, and has the feel of a country inn. There is live music at weekends, and a petanque pitch behind the pub for mild days. Log fires enhance the warm welcome in winter. The lunch menu is available Tuesday to Friday only. A mild is always served, either Harveys XX or a seasonal brew.
⋈Q➄✿☎◀⇌➡⅃

Rifle Volunteer

28 Wyatt Street, ME14 1EU
✪ 11-3, 6 (7 Sat)-11; 12-3, 7-10.30 Sun
☎ (01622) 758891
Goacher's Mild, Light, Crown Imperial Stout ⊞

A regular in the Guide, this simple pub is one of only two Goacher's tied houses, serving three of its characterful beers, always in excellent condition. Situated a short walk from Maidstone's main shopping district and railway stations, this single-bar pub is an oasis of calm where conversation can be enjoyed unhindered by music or fruit machines. Good value food is served at lunchtime.
Q◀⇌(Maidstone East)♣

Swan

2 County Road, ME14 1UY (150 yds N of Maidstone E Station, near County Hall)

✪ 12-3, 5-11; 12-11 Fri & Sat; 12-11 Sun
☎ (01622) 751264
Shepherd Neame Master Brew Bitter, Kent's Best, seasonal beers Ⓗ
A cosy, traditional pub, close to Maidstone's town centre, not far from the station and local bus services. Alongside the beer it serves speciality tea or coffee and freshly cut sandwiches at lunchtime, and stages occasional themed food nights. Darts, quiz nights, wide-screen TV, monthly karaoke and jam nights are all on offer here, and secondhand books and Kent's finest honey are for sale. Disabled access is good. There are plans for a smoking area outside.
✪❀◖♿⇌🖪♣⌐

Margate

Northern Belle
4 Mansion Street, CT9 1HE
✪ 11 (12 Sun)-midnight
☎ (07810) 088347
Shepherd Neame Master Brew Bitter; guest beer Ⓗ
This seafarers' tavern takes pride of place as the oldest standing pub in Margate. Situated up a tiny lane opposite the town's pier, this hostelry has made few concessions to modernity. Originally two fishermen's cottages, built about 1680, which stood right on the water's edge, it is named after an American merchant ship that ran aground off nearby North Foreland in 1857. A second Shepherd Neame beer regularly rotates alongside the Master Brew. ⌐⇌♣

Orb Inn
243 Ramsgate Road, CT9 4EU (on A254 Margate-Ramsgate road)
✪ 11.45 (12 Sun)-midnight
☎ (01843) 220663
Shepherd Neame Master Brew Bitter, Spitfire Ⓗ
Old wayside local situated on the edge of town, close to the QEQM Hospital. It features two real fires, making this a homely place in winter. Lunches are only available on Sunday. The Thanet Loop bus service passes this pub.
❀🖪♣P

Marsh Green

Wheatsheaf Inn
Main Road, TN8 5QL
✪ 11-11; 12-10.30 Sun
☎ (01732) 864091 ⊕ thewheatsheaf.net
Harveys Sussex Best Bitter; guest beers Ⓗ
Situated in a picturesque village, this spacious pub, with several drinking and dining areas, has been an ale house for some 100 years. Up to eight frequently-changing real ales, including a mild and local brews, are stocked, and Biddenden cider is also available. The landlord has served up to 2,500 different beers during his 15 years at the pub. A beer festival is held in summer, offering about 30 real ales and a hog roast. Home-cooked food is served daily. ❀Q☼❄◖⌐⇌🖪♣⊕P

Marshside

Gate Inn
Boyden Gate, CT3 4EB (off A28 at Upstreet)
✪ 11-2.30 (4 Sat), 6-11; 12-4, 7-10.30 Sun
☎ (01227) 860498
Shepherd Neame Master Brew Bitter, Spitfire, seasonal beers Ⓖ
The Gate has featured in this Guide for the past 32 years under the same landlord. A traditional village pub, close to the Saxon Shore Way, Wantsum Walk and Reculver Towers, it is a focal point for the community, hosting fund-raising events and traditional entertainments such as mummers' plays, hoodeners and morris dancing. The bars feature tiled floors and a log fire, and are decorated with hanging hops. In the garden there is a stream complete with ducks, and apple trees. Excellent, good value food is served daily (not Mon eve & winter Tue).
❀Q☼❄◖♣⌐P

Meopham

George
Wrotham Road, DA12 0AH (on A227 near church)
✪ 11-11; 12-10.30 Sun
☎ (01474) 814198
Shepherd Neame Master Brew Bitter, Spitfire, Bishops Finger, seasonal beers Ⓗ
Well-presented former coaching inn, partly 15th century, located on the main road near the parish church of reputedly the longest village in England. The Kentish weatherboarded exterior fronts two bars in pleasantly contrasting styles and a restaurant serving good quality food until 9pm every day. Outside is a paved, heated courtyard, a large garden and a floodlit petanque pitch.
❀☼◖⇌🖪(308, 306)♣P⌐

Mersham

Royal Oak
The Street, TN25 6NA
✪ 11-3, 6-midnight; 11-1am Fri & Sat; 12-midnight Sun
☎ (01233) 502218
Shepherd Neame Master Brew Bitter Ⓗ
Traditional three-bar village pub with a separate restaurant. The hop-decked oak beams, log fires, horse brasses and stone floors create a vintage feel. Lively and welcoming, this pub has lots of local characters who usually gather in the middle bar. A good selection of home-cooked meals and bar snacks is available (not Mon all day and Sun-Tue eve). Quizzes and darts matches are hosted. A seasonal beer may be on a cask breather. ❀☼◖⌐⇌🖪(10, 525)P⌐

Minster

New Inn
2 Tothill Street, CT12 4AG
✪ 11-midnight; 12-10.30 Sun
☎ (01843) 821294
Greene King Abbot, IPA; guest beer Ⓗ

Welcoming village local near Minster station, built in 1837 as a replacement for the original hostelry. The pub retains its old Cobbs brewery windows, and a sympathetic extension has added a dining area and space for live music. No food is served on Sunday evening or Monday. ✿✪◗≢♣P

Newenden

White Hart
Rye Road, TN18 5AN
✪ 11-11; 12-10.30 Sun
☎ (01797) 252166
Fuller's London Pride; Harveys Sussex Best Bitter; Rother Valley Level Best; guest beers ⊞
Reputedly haunted, this 500-year-old free house stands right on the Sussex border. The atmospheric interior is dominated by a magnificent inglenook fireplace. Up to two guest beers are given marks for quality by the regular customers. Seasonal cider is available occasionally. Excellent food is served and there are six guest bedrooms. Convenient for Northiam station on the KESR light railway. 﨑Q✿⌂◗▲≢♣♠P

Northfleet

Campbell Arms
1 Campbell Road, DA11 0JZ
✪ 12-11; 12-10.30 Sun
☎ (01474) 320488
Courage Best Bitter; Daleside Shrimpers; guest beers ⊞
Friendly one-bar back-street corner local, situated among Edwardian terraced housing on the border of Northfleet and Gravesend, serving a choice of four real ales which usually includes a mild. The two guest beers are competitively priced. This community pub hosts darts, football and pool teams. Note the Mann, Crossman & Paulin mirror behind the bar. ✿≢(Gravesend)🚐♣

Earl Grey
177 Vale Road, DA11 8BP (off Perry St)
✪ 12-11 (10.30 Sun)
☎ (01474) 365240
Shepherd Neame Master Brew Bitter, Spitfire, seasonal beers ⊞
Distinctive, late 18th-century cottage-style building, partly dating from 1610. The pub has a Kentish brick and flint exterior, rarely seen in this area. The L-shaped bar has a raised seating area at one end and offers a homely, convivial atmosphere. Situated near the Cygnet Leisure Centre in Perry Street, several buses pass during the day and the 499 runs late in the evening. ✿🚐♣P♠

Otford

Bull
High Street, TN14 5PG
✪ 11-11; 12-10.30 Sun
☎ (01959) 523198
Fuller's London Pride; guest beers ⊞
A Victorian exterior fronts the original timber-framed Tudor building containing 17th-century wood panelling and two large stone fireplaces, brought here from the ruined Otford Palace. Good food is served all day, with chalkboards displaying the menu; fresh fish dishes are the speciality. Three guest beers come from a large list of independent regional brewers. One handpump, labelled Dudley's Choice, features the current recommendation of the cellarman. Outside is a heated, covered area for smokers. 﨑Q✿◗≢🚐(421, 432)P♠

Pembury

Black Horse
12 High Street, TN2 4NY (on main street next to the green)
✪ 11-11; 12-10.30 Sun
☎ (01892) 822141 ⊕ blackhorsepembury.co.uk
Adnams Broadside; Courage Best Bitter; Fuller's London Pride; Greene King Old Speckled Hen ⊞
The original 16th-century building has been extended at the back several times and is now linked to the restaurant. The serving bar is in the centre of the oldest part of the pub, to the left as you enter, retaining original beams and a huge inglenook. There is a smaller carpeted bar to the right, and a larger lounge area at the back. The food menu is extensive and the restaurant is always busy – booking is advisable. 﨑Q✿◗♿🚐♣♠

Perry Wood

Rose & Crown
ME13 9RY OS042552
✪ 11-3, 6.30-11; 12-3, 7-10.30 Sun
☎ (01227) 752214
Adnams Bitter; Goacher's Mild; Harveys Sussex Best Bitter; guest beer ⊞
Historic free house located in the middle of Perry Wood near east Kent's highest point. Popular with walkers and cyclists, it is well regarded for its excellent food and, of course, beer. The bar area is dominated by a large fireplace. The interior is decorated with old woodcutting tools and corn dollies. There is a separate dining area down a few steps in converted cottages adjoining the pub. The large garden has a children's play area and heated patio. 﨑Q✿◗P

Petteridge

Hop Bine
Petteridge Lane, TN12 7NE (½ mile down lane just to the E of Brenchley) OS667413
✪ 12-2.30, 6-11; 12-3, 7-10.30 Sun
☎ (01892) 722561
Badger K&B Sussex Bitter, First Gold, seasonal beer ⊞
Mike, the landlord, is celebrating his 20th year as landlord of this cosy village local – a typical Kentish white weatherboarded, tile-hung hostelry. The L-shaped bar serves both the main room and a smaller area for diners who can choose from a genuine home-cooked menu (no food Wed lunchtime). A real fire, plenty of beams and an outside men's toilet add to the traditional ambience. There is an

enclosed garden and a covered area for smokers. Morris dancers pay the occasional visit. ᴁQ✿⬤🅙&♣♠P⊑—

Pluckley

Dering Arms
Station Road, TN27 0RR
⬤ 11.30-3, 6-11; closed Mon; 12-3 Sun
☎ (01233) 840371
Goacher's Gold Star Ⓗ
This attractive pub is easy to find, opposite Pluckley station. Built in the 1840s as a hunting lodge for the Dering estate, it was designed as a small replica of the main manor house. It features distinctive windows and stone-flagged floors. The regular house beer, Dering Ale, is brewed by Goacher's. Look out for the strong Old Ale in winter. The pub is renowned for its fine food, especially fish dishes, and holds regular gourmet evenings. ᴁQ✿🛏🅙⊯P

Rainham

Angel
Station Road, ME8 7HU
⬤ 12.30 (12 Sat)-11; 12-10.30 Sun
☎ (01634) 360219
Adnams Bitter; guest beers Ⓗ
A true local pub in a semi-rural location on the edge of Rainham, not far from the station. It has an L-shaped bar area serving Adnams, plus ever-changing guest beers, some of which are rarely seen. An excellent stop for dogs and thirsty owners. Winner of local CAMRA Pub of the Year in 2004, 2005 and again in 2007. ᴁ✿≒♣

Ramsgate

Artillery Arms
36 Westcliff Road, CT11 9JS
⬤ 12-11
☎ (01843) 853282
Beer range varies Ⓗ
Making a welcome return to the Guide, this friendly, unpretentious, small street-corner pub offers a permanent mini beer festival, featuring an ever-changing rota of at least five real ales. On alternating Wednesday nights the Malaysian landlord cooks South-East Asian noodle dishes and curries, all at very reasonable prices. The front of the pub has leaded bow windows depicting soldiers, artillery and Napoleonic memorabilia. On the Thanet Loop, the bus stops outside. ▲🖫(9)♠

Churchill Tavern
19-22 The Paragon, CT11 9JX
⬤ 11.30-11 (midnight Fri & Sat); 12-10.30 Sun
☎ (01843) 853282 ⊕ churchilltavern.co.uk
Fuller's London Pride; Ringwood Old Thumper; Wells Bombardier; guest beers Ⓗ
Rebuilt in 1986 as an English country pub in town, the Churchill combines a brasserie-style restaurant with a traditional pub atmosphere. This is a large corner-house, affording superb views across the English Channel and the busy harbour. The bar was built from 19th-century oak church pews. ᴁ🅙🅙

Foy Boat
8 Sion Hill, CT11 9HZ
⬤ 11-11; 12-10.30 Sun
☎ (01843) 591198
Greene King IPA, Abbot; Ramsgate Gadds No 5; Young's Bitter Ⓗ
Reputedly the model for the Channel Packet referred to in Ian Fleming's Goldfinger, the current building is a 1940s replacement for the old Foy Boat Tavern, a Thomson & Wotton house that was bombed in 1941. It offers superb views of Ramsgate's picturesque harbour. Good value food is available, including the popular Sunday roast which is served until 6pm. ᴁ🛏🅙

Montefiore Arms
1 Trinity Place, CT11 7HJ
⬤ 12-2.30, 7-11; 12-3, 7-10.30 Sun
☎ (01843) 593265
Beer range varies Ⓗ
Welcoming, friendly side-street local, named after Sir Moses Montefiore, a philanthropist and benefactor of the town of Ramsgate, who is buried nearby. The pub gives strong support to Mild Month and other CAMRA initiatives, and regularly comes in the top two or three in the local Pub of the Year competition. A local cider is usually available. This pub is on the Thanet Loop bus route. ≒🖫♣♠

Sir Stanley Gray
Pegwell Bay Hotel, 81 Pegwell Road, CT11 0NJ
⬤ 11-midnight; 12-10.30 Sun
☎ (01843) 599590 ⊕ pegwellbayhotel.co.uk
Beer range varies Ⓗ
Linked to the Pegwell Bay Hotel opposite by a tunnel under the road, the Sir Stanley Gray is situated on a cliff top affording spectacular views over Pegwell Bay and the English Channel. Formerly known as the Moonlighters, it is part of the Thorley Tavern chain, and the beer range often features Gadds and other small independent breweries. No food is served on Sunday evening. ᴁ🛏🅙▲♣P

Ripple

Plough Inn
Church Lane, CT14 8JH
⬤ 11.30-11 (10.30 Sun)
☎ (01304) 360209
Adnams Broadside; Fuller's ESB; Shepherd Neame Master Brew Bitter; Taylor Landlord; guest beer Ⓗ
A typical, out-of-the-way country pub, run by a landlord who is keen to get the best out of his beers, and visited by customers who appreciate his efforts. The attractive, beamed interior and single bar provide the setting for a friendly meeting place. Good food and a warm welcome are offered to regulars and visitors alike. ✿🛏🅙P

Rochester

Britannia Bar Café
376 High Street, ME1 1DJ

🕓 10-11 (2am Fri & Sat); 12-11 Sun
☎ (01634) 815204 ⊕ britannia-bar-cafe.co.uk
Beer range varies Ⓗ
Busy at lunchtimes, mainly attracting a
business clientele, the pub serves an
extensive and popular daily menu, including
breakfast (10am-noon), evening meals
Monday-Thursday and traditional Sunday
lunch. A stylish bar leads out into a small
walled garden that is a suntrap in summer.
Occasional live music is performed and a
monthly quiz is staged. Q⊛⑪◗≒⊑🛈

Good Intent

83 John Street, ME1 1YL (5 mins' walk from
Rochester High St)
🕓 12-midnight
☎ (01634) 843118
Beer range varies Ⓖ
This two-bar ale house is for real beer
enthusiasts. An invaluable local asset, it caters
for traditional and contemporary drinkers.
There is bar billiards, large-screen sport, live
music and a south-facing garden. The beer, on
the eight-barrel stillage, is sourced from
regional and national micro-breweries. A fine
range of traditional and fruit wines is also kept
in stock. Good beer, good people, good fun,
that is the Good Intent. It has Wifi computer
access. Q⊛⊛⑪&≒⊑(155)♣P🛈

Man of Kent

6-8 John Street, ME1 1YN (200m off A2)
🕓 12-11 (midnight Fri & Sat)
☎ (01634) 818771 ⊕ manofkent.org.uk
**Goacher's Gold Star; Whitstable East India Pale
Ale; guest beers** Ⓗ
Small back-street ale house with a single L-
shaped bar showcasing the largest selection of
Kentish micro-brewery cask ales in the county.
The real ales are complemented by three
Belgian and three German draught biers.
Some 30-plus bottled, conditioned beers, local
ciders, wines and soft drinks add yet more
choice. Biddenden cider is available on top
pressure. The pub hosts three regular music
nights a week. The rare tiled exterior
advertises Maidstone's former Style & Winch
Brewery. ⋒⊛≒⊑🛈

Rolvenden Layne

Ewe & Lamb

26 Maytham Road, TN17 4LN (1 mile E of
Rolvenden on Whitstable road)
🕓 11-11; 12-4 Sun
☎ (01580) 241837
**Adnams Bitter; Draught Bass; Harveys Sussex
Best Bitter** Ⓗ
Situated on the High Weald Landscape Trail,
this friendly local inn provides a pleasant
environment to relax with a pint of real ale
and excellent food. The restored interior is
warmed by a log fire, and has a dining area at
the rear. Dogs are welcome. The pub is a mile
walk from Wittersham Road train station on
the Kent & Sussex Railway, and Rolvenden is
served by several buses. ⋒Q⊛⑪P

Romney Street

Fox & Hounds

Knatts Valley, TN15 6XR OS563599
🕓 12-midnight
☎ (01959) 525428 ⊕ foxnhounds.co.uk
Beer range varies Ⓗ
Old country pub in a remote downland
location close to several footpaths, offering a
friendly welcome to all including hikers. There
is live music on the last Saturday and third
Sunday of every month. No meals are served
on Monday or Sunday evenings, while themed
food events feature occasionally. A large
secluded garden welcomes children.
Traditional games include shove-ha'penny and
shut the box. Weston's cider is served. A ramp
can be provided for wheelchair users but the
door is narrow. ⋒⊛⑪&♣⊛P

Rusthall

Beacon

Tea Garden Lane, TN3 9JH (400m off A264, opp
cricket pitch) OS563392
🕓 11-11; 12-10.30 Sun
☎ (01892) 524252 ⊕ the-beacon.co.uk
**Harveys Sussex Best Bitter; Larkins Traditional;
Taylor Landlord** Ⓗ
Sited on an outcrop of sandstone on the edge
of Happy Valley, the view from the decked
area is spectacular. There is a relaxing bar with
a magnificent fireplace and four separate
dining areas. Locally sourced ingredients are
used wherever possible and seafood features
as the speciality. A function room downstairs
is licensed for weddings. Camping and fishing
by permit are available in the 17-acre
grounds. Q⊛≒⑪ Å⊑(281)♣P🛈

St Margaret's Bay

Coastguard

CT15 6DY
🕓 11-11; 12-10.30 Sun
☎ (01304) 853176 ⊕ thecoastguard.co.uk
Beer range varies Ⓗ
If you like your food, this is the pub for you.
Located down a winding road, on the beach at
the foot of the White Cliffs, this modern-style
pub has won several food awards, including
Best Cheese Board and Best Pie. Drinkers will
appreciate the ever-changing array of real
ales, often from local breweries. Also available
is a good selection of continental beers and a
real cider. A large terrace and garden overlook
the Dover Strait. Dogs and children are
welcome. ⊛⑪♣P

St Peters

White Swan

17 Reading Street, CT10 3AZ
🕓 11-2.30, 7-11; 12-3, 7-10.30 Sun
☎ (01843) 863051
Beer range varies Ⓗ
A former Thomson & Wotton house with
origins in the 17th century, the White Swan is
situated in a quiet backwater in the Isle of

Thanet. It has an ever-changing roster of six real ales. The price differential between public and saloon bars is maintained, along with several pieces of T&W and Fremlins memorabilia. Q❶◗⊞

Sandgate

Ship
65 High Street, CT20 3AH (on A259)
✪ 11-11.45 (1am Fri & Sat)
☎ (01303) 248525
Greene King IPA, Abbot; Hop Back Summer Lightning; guest beers ⊞
Genuine community pub with a long-established landlord and landlady offering quality real ales. Guest beers often include Greene King seasonal beers and Hopdaemon Incubus. The holiday season sees the beer range rise to 12, and a regular beer festival takes place over the August bank holiday weekend. The two ciders are Biddenden Medium and Dry. There are plans to improve the facilities at the pub. ❀✿◗❶◗⬆↺❤

Sandwich

Fleur de Lis
6-8 Delf Street, CT13 9BZ
✪ 7 (8 Sat)-11; 8-10.30 Sun
☎ (01304) 611131 ⊕ thefleur-sandwich.co.uk
Greene King IPA; Wadworth 6X; guest beer ⊞
Town-centre pub offering a selection of beers including a regular guest from local micro-breweries such as Ramsgate and Hopdaemon, as well as from further afield, for example Archers. Dating from 1642, the interior is divided into a number of drinking and dining areas, including a splendid wood-panelled dining room with a painted cupola ceiling. An interesting menu is available daily, and live music plays on Friday. A friendly and popular local. ⬛◗❶⬆▲⇌⊟

Seal

Crown Seal
16 High Street, TN15 0AJ
✪ 12-11
☎ (01732) 761023 ⊕ thecrownseal.co.uk
Harveys Sussex Best Bitter; Westerham Finchcocks Original; Young's Bitter ⊞
The Crown is a pub right in the heart of the community. With three fine ales available and small beer festivals held during the year, it is well worth seeking out. Check the website for special food events; Sunday roasts are particularly recommended. The inglenook fireplace is a comfortable place to sit and appreciate a good ale. Many local sports and games, including petanque, are played here. ⬛✿◗❶⬆⊟❤P

Sevenoaks

Anchor
32 London Road, TN13 1AS
✪ 11-3, 6-11.30; 10-4, 6-midnight Fri; 10.30-4, 7-midnight Sat; 12-5, 7-11 Sun

☎ (01732) 454898
Harveys Sussex Best Bitter; guest beer ⊞
Friendly town-centre pub, popular with all ages. The guest beer frequently comes from a smaller brewery and is often unusual for the area. Excellent food is served Monday to Friday lunchtimes, with a smaller choice at other times. Christmas lunch is highly recommended. Live blues is performed on the first Wednesday of the month. The landlord is the longest-serving in the area, enjoying a reputation for maintaining consistently high quality beers. A heated and covered area for smokers is planned. ◗❶⊟❤↺

Halfway House
London Road, TN13 2JB (5 mins walk from Sevenoaks Station)
✪ 12-3, 5-11 (midnight Fri); 12-midnight Sat; 12-10.30 Sun
☎ (01732) 457108
Greene King Old Speckled Hen; guest beers ⊞
Traditional, two-bar pub, with parts dating back to the 17th century, located halfway between Sevenoaks and Riverhead, which is believed to be the origin of its name. Three football and darts teams are based here, and an open quiz is held most Saturday evenings. The food is mostly home-cooked (no food Sun eve). A small selection of real ales is sold in the bottle. The pub may close on Saturday afternoon outside the football season.
⬛✿◗⇌⊟(401, 402)P

Oak Tree
135 High Street, TN13 1XA
✪ 11-11.30 (midnight Fri & Sat); 11-10.30 Sun
☎ (01732) 742615
Courage Best Bitter; Westerham British Bulldog; guest beer ⊞
This town-centre pub regularly stocks a beer from the Westerham Brewery and the guest beer is frequently also from Westerham. The pub is used by all ages, but draws a predominantly young crowd at the weekend and in the evening. The building was originally a farmhouse and the front elevation has changed little since the early part of the last century, while the majority of the interior is of a modern construction. Food is served daily until 9pm. A heated, covered area for smokers is planned. ◗⊟❤↺

Sheerness

Red Lion
61 High Street, Blue Town, ME12 1RW (10 mins' walk from station)
✪ 11 (12 Sun)-11
☎ (01795) 664354
Beer range varies ⊞
Set facing the old naval dockyard wall, this pub is the only one left in the historic Blue Town area of Sheerness, where the High Street still has cobbles. Inside, it features a collection of photographs and maritime memorabilia associated with the former naval dockyard opposite. There are usually three ever-changing beers from micro- and regional breweries on offer. Although no meals are served, a free buffet is available all day Sunday. ⬛✿⇌⊟❤↺

Snargate

Red Lion ☆
TN29 9UQ (on B2080, 1 mile W of Brencett)
✪ 12-3, 7-10.30 daily
☎ (01897) 344648
Goacher's Light, Mild; guest beers Ⓗ
Beautiful, unspoilt, award-winning pub on the remote Walland Marsh. The interior is decorated with WWII and Women's Land Army posters and features in CAMRA's National Inventory of pubs with interiors of outstanding historical interest. A haven for good conversation, it is also a friendly place to play one of many traditional pub games on offer. Several beer festivals are hosted annually; the main festival is in June. ▲Q❀⊟♣●P

Stansted

Black Horse
Tumblefield Road, TN15 7PR (1 mile N of A20 jct 2) OS606621
✪ 11-11; 12-10.30 Sun
☎ (01732) 822355
Larkins Traditional; guest beers Ⓗ
Long-standing entry in this Guide, this imposing Victorian building is the focus of local community life and a haven for hikers and cyclists. The emphasis here is on home-cooked food, local real ales and ciders. There is a large rambling garden suitable for families. The family-run Thai restaurant is open in the evening (Tue-Sat) and Sunday lunches are recommended. ▲Q❀✿⊞◑Ⓓ&▲●P

Staplehurst

Lord Raglan
Chart Hill Road, TN12 0DE (½ mile N of A229) OS786472
✪ 12-3, 6.30-11.30; closed Sun
☎ (01622) 843747
Goacher's Light; Harveys Sussex Best Bitter; guest beer Ⓗ
Popular and unspoiled free house with the atmosphere of a country pub from bygone days. The bar is hung with hops and warmed by two log fires, and the large orchard garden catches the early evening sun. Excellent snacks and full meals are always available. The guest beer changes frequently and local Double Vision cider is sold. Well-behaved children and dogs are welcome. The pub has no distractions, thus restoring the art of lively conversation. Bus route 5 stops half a mile away at Cross-at-Hand. ▲Q❀◑⊟●P

Stone Street

Padwell Arms
TN15 0LO
✪ 12-3, 6-11.30; 12-3, 7-11 Sun
☎ (01732) 761532
Badger First Gold; Harveys Sussex Best Bitter; Hook Norton Old Hooky; Larkins Traditional; guest beer Ⓗ
A real haven for walkers where batteries can be recharged over a fine pint of real ale.

Outside seating is provided, affording fine views of the lovely countryside. Discerning drinkers will appreciate the regularly updated menu board of guest and regular ales. There is also a daily menu of good food, with a roast meal available every day. A separate dining area is provided but customers may also dine in the cosy bar. ▲❀◑ ⊟&♣●P⊟

Temple Ewell

Fox
14 High Street, CT16 3DU
✪ 11-3.30, 6-11; 12-4, 7-11 Sun
☎ (01304) 823598
Caledonian Deuchars IPA; Greene King Abbot; guest beers Ⓗ
Situated on the edge of Dover in the Dour Valley, with the chalk downs rising behind, a side-stream from the river flows alongside the pub garden. Four real ales are available and food is served at lunchtimes and evenings (not Sun eve). The pub has a wide appeal, attracting custom from the village, Dover and further afield. Traditional pastimes include darts, skittles and dominoes, as well as a big-screen TV for sporting fixtures. A regular pub quiz is staged on Tuesday evening. ▲❀&≠(Kearsney)⊟♣P⊑

Trottiscliffe

Plough
Taylor's Lane, ME19 5DR
✪ 11.30-3, 6 (6.30 Sat)-11; 12-3 Sun
☎ (01732) 822233
Adnams Bitter, Broadside; Harveys Sussex Best Bitter Ⓗ
Weatherboarded pub situated just below the Pilgrims' Way on the North Downs, providing a welcome stop for all, including walkers, families and dogs. The village, pronounced locally as 'Trosley', is noted for the Coldrum Stones, a neolithic burial chamber. Beams with horse brasses reflect the 1483 origin of this pub, and there are rumours of a friendly ghost called Alice. Several drinking areas are available, at differing levels, as well as a small patio. A separate restaurant offers good quality, home-cooked food with special mid-week deals (no food Mon eve). ▲Q❀◑⊟(58)♣P

Tunbridge Wells

Grove Tavern
19 Berkley Road, TN1 1YR
✪ 12-midnight (10.30 Sun)
☎ (01892) 526549
Harveys Sussex Best Bitter; Taylor Landlord; guest beer Ⓗ
One of the last traditional wooden-floored pubs remaining in the area, the Grove is also one of the oldest buildings in the village near Mount Sion. Customers are a friendly local crowd from young to old, enjoying a regular game of pool, darts, cribbage and other traditional pub activities. Although no food is served, families and dogs are welcome. The

landlord takes great pride in his real ale.
🏠≠♣

Sankeys

39 Mount Ephraim, TN4 8AA
🕐 10.30-11 (midnight Fri & Sat); 12-midnight Sun
☎ (01892) 511422 ⊕ sankeys.co.uk
Harveys Sussex Best Bitter; Larkins Traditional; guest beer Ⓗ
Kentish-brewed Larkins, as well as guest beers, are well looked after and always available here, alongside 16 continental or fruit beers on handpump. This old, familiar, family-run establishment has an excellent restaurant and plays live music on Sunday.
🏠❀🕐❤♿≠🖵

Upper Upnor

King's Arms

2 High Street, ME2 4XG
🕐 11 (12 Sun)-11
☎ (01634) 717490
Millis Kentish Red; guest beers Ⓗ
This village local has two bars, mainly for drinking, and a further room that serves as a restaurant. The pub has a good local reputation for food and the menu provides plenty of choice. Meals are served lunchtimes and evenings except Sunday and Monday evening. There is a large garden that becomes lively in the summer with plenty of activity from sailing boats on the local river. From the village there is a good view across the old dockyard at Chatham. 🏠Q�│❀🕐🍴♿♣

Tudor Rose

29 High Street, ME2 4XG
🕐 11 (12 Sun)-11
☎ (01634) 715035
Shepherd Neame Master Brew Bitter, Kent's Best, Spitfire, Bishops Finger, seasonal beers Ⓗ
Situated at the bottom of the cobbled High Street, this inn stands next to the historic Upnor Castle and very near the River Medway. It is a multi-roomed pub with a large, 17th-century, partly walled garden at the rear, ideal for children in summer. Meals are served at all times apart from Monday evening. Use the village car park. 🏠Q�│❀🕐🍴♣

Walmer

Berry

23 Canada Road, CT14 7EQ
🕐 11.30-2.30 (not Tue or Thu), 5.30-11 (midnight Fri); 11-midnight Sat; 11.30-11 Sun
☎ (01304) 362411
Harveys Sussex Best Bitter; guest beers Ⓗ
Congenial but with no frills, this local is well worth the short detour inland from Walmer Green and the seafront. Darts, pool, football and quiz teams keep it busy, and euchre is sometimes played on Sunday morning. The pub is also popular with rugby players on Sunday. An interesting range of beers comes from various regional breweries. An outside drinking area at the rear is a pleasant attraction in summer. Deal railway station is 20 minutes' walk. ❀♿≠(Deal)🖵♣P

Warehorne

Woolpack

Church Road, TN26 2LL
🕐 11.30 (not Mon)-3, 6-11; 12-4, 7-10.30 Sun
☎ (01233) 733888
Harveys Sussex Best Bitter; guest beer Ⓗ
Rural 16th-century free house opposite the church. The bar features beams, hops and a large inglenook and the lounge is warmed by a log- burning stove. The menu offers home-cooked food, weekly specials and a popular Wednesday carvery. The guest beer usually comes from a Kent or Sussex brewer and the house beer is from Goacher's. There are tables outside in summer and barbecues hosted on Sunday, hog roasts on bank holidays.
🏠❀🕐P🍴

Wateringbury

North Pole Inn

434 Red Hill, ME18 5BJ (¾ mile N of village)
OS549696
🕐 11-11; 12-10.30 Sun
☎ (01622) 812392 ⊕ thenorthpolepub.co.uk
Fuller's London Pride; Greene King IPA, Old Speckled Hen; Wells Bombardier; guest beer Ⓗ
Built in 1826 as a private venture, together with adjacent cottages and stabling, it was later acquired by Whitbread, as can be seen from the etched bay windows. The large, enclosed garden is reached via a staircase. The restaurant features subdued lighting and displays pictures for sale by a local artist. Traditional pub food, using fresh local produce wherever possible, is available all week except Sunday. There is a weekly quiz, and shut the box can be played. ❀🕐♣P

West Peckham

Swan on the Green

The Green, ME18 5JW (1 mile W of B2016 at Mereworth)
🕐 11-3 (4 Sat), 6-11 (8 Mon); 12-9 (5 winter) Sun
☎ (01622) 812271 ⊕ swan-on-the-green.co.uk
Swan Fuggles, Trumpeter, Cygnet, Bewick, seasonal beers Ⓗ
At the end of a no-through road (follow the sign to the church), the Swan enjoys an enviable position by the village green where cricket is played. Although licensed since 1658, the interior is quite modern, with a wooden floor and a light, airy atmosphere. A mecca for diners and drinkers alike, it offers up to six beers brewed behind the pub, as well as good food during all sessions apart from Sunday and Monday evenings. Walkers often take a break here and sit on the green in summer, undisturbed by traffic. 🏠Q🕐P

Westerham

General Wolfe

High Street, TN16 1RQ
🕐 12-11 (midnight Fri & Sat); 12-10.30 Sun
☎ (01959) 562104
Greene King Abbot, Old Speckled Hen Ⓗ

This traditional weatherboarded pub takes its name from one of the famous residents of the town, General Wolfe of Quebec (the other famous resident was Sir Winston Churchill). Adjacent to the old Black Eagle Brewery site, the interior comprises a long slim room divided into a number of areas, with a welcoming log fire in winter. The pub serves reasonably priced food (not Sun eve). Note the good range of malt whiskies. A quiz night is held on Wednesday. ⚫Q◖◗➡P

Whitstable

Four Horseshoes
62 Borstal Hill, CT5 4NA (on A290 on edge of town)
☼ 12-11 (10.30 Sun)
☎ (01227) 273876
Shepherd Neame Master Brew Bitter, Kent's Best, seasonal beers Ⓗ
Traditional small local pub, originally built as a forge in 1636, and licensed since 1801. Situated on a hillside, it has an unusual three-bar layout including a low middle bar. Traditional pub games include darts and board games, and it has a Kentish bat & trap pitch. Take-away meals can be delivered to the pub; the landlady will supply plates and cutlery. A popular meeting place for locals and visitors, it is well worth a visit. The piano is played occasionally. ⚫❀✇♿➡(4, 6)♣P⸚

New Inn
20 Woodlawn Street, CT5 1HG (near harbour)
☼ 11-11; 12-4, 7.30-11 Sun
☎ (01227) 264746
Shepherd Neame Master Brew Bitter Ⓗ
Back-street corner pub, part of Whitstable's heritage. The long, narrow bar was originally divided into tiny drinking areas, still discernible from the etched glass windows, and there is a small snug room that can be used by families. The licensees of 11 years' standing maintain a strong community spirit; visitors can join in with pool or darts in the games area or take part in the conversation at the bar. The Chinese take-away opposite will deliver food to the pub. Q➤➡♣⸚

Rose in Bloom
69 Joy Lane, CT5 4DD
☼ 11 (12 Sun)-11
☎ (01227) 276502
Adnams Bitter; Shepherd Neame Master Brew Bitter; guest beer Ⓗ
Situated in a residential area on the outskirts of town, the Rose in Bloom has an open-plan bar area and a large conservatory restaurant, where a varied menu of good meals is served. A large garden overlooks the sea; from here you can enjoy Whitstable's famous sunsets. The Saxon Shore Way runs close to the pub. ❀◖◗➡(5, 638)P⸚

Ship Centurion
111 High Street, CT5 1AY
☼ 11-11; 12-7 Sun
☎ (01227) 264740
Adnams Bitter; Elgood's Black Dog; guest beers Ⓗ

Voted local CAMRA Pub of the Year in 2007, this is the only pub in town that always serves a mild. A busy, centrally located free house, it is festooned with colourful hanging baskets in summer. Fascinating photographs of old Whitstable hang in the bar. There is live entertainment on Thursday evening (except in January). Home-cooked bar food often features authentic German produce: the only meal on Saturday is schnitzel. A public car park is close by in Middle Wall. ➤◖♿➡

Wilmington

Cressy Arms
1 Hawley Road, DA1 1NP (on A225)
☼ 12-11 (10.30 Sun)
☎ (01322) 287772
Courage Best Bitter; guest beers Ⓗ
Small corner pub with a truncated V-shaped bar, decorated with pictures of old Dartford on one wall and display cabinets of model Ford cars on the other. The landlord passed away in October 2006, but his widow continues to run an excellent and friendly establishment. Two rotating guest beers supplement the regular beer. Several buses run past, and there is a public car park opposite. ❀➡(477)♣⸚

Wittersham

Swan Inn
1 Swan Street, TN30 7PH (on B2080 between Rye & Tenterden)
☼ 11-midnight (1am Fri & Sat); 12-2am Sun
☎ (01797) 270913
Goacher's Light; Harveys Sussex Best Bitter; Rother Valley Smild; guest beers Ⓗ/Ⓖ
A regular local CAMRA Pub of the Year winner, the inn was extensively altered in 2007. It retains its two-bar character but has added extra comfort for its varied clientele. Seven beers are on offer, including a mild, some on gravity dispense, and two draught ciders. There are summer and winter beer festivals and regular live music. Good value food is available and a superb welcome is assured at all times. Well-behaved dogs are permitted. ⚫Q❀◖◗✇♿➡(312)♣P

Wormshill

Blacksmiths Arms
The Street, ME9 0TU
☼ 7.30-11; closed Mon; 12-3 Sun
☎ (01622) 884386
Beer range varies Ⓗ
Small, 17th-century village pub with a brick-floor bar, warmed by an open log fire in winter. The cosy bar is lit by candles and oil lamps, and there is a separate candle-lit restaurant serving Sunday lunch and evening meals. Frequently-changing beers come from all over the country. The pub's rural location makes it a popular destination for walkers and cyclists, and in summer the garden and outside patio area are inviting for alfresco drinking. Note the restricted opening hours. ⚫❀◖◗P

Worth

St Crispin Inn
The Street, CT14 0DF
🕐 12-2.30 (3 Sat), 6-11; 12-11 (5 winter) Sun
☎ (01304) 612081 ⊕ stcrispininn.com
Harveys Sussex Best Bitter; guest beers Ⓗ
Cosy village local, popular with the country set and town folk alike. Warm, welcoming and unspoilt, it is renowned for serving hearty food. The dining area is air-conditioned and the pub has a proper bar area for drinkers, as well as a family area. En-suite accommodation is available. ⏣🛏🎲🕿◑🚋(13)P�╚

Wrotham Heath

Moat
London Road, TN15 7RR (on A20)
🕐 12-11 (midnight Fri & Sat); 12-10.30 Sun
☎ (01732) 882263
Badger K&B Sussex Bitter, First Gold, Tanglefoot, seasonal beers Ⓗ
Large roadhouse on the A20, recently acquired and modernised by Hall & Woodhouse (Badger). The Moat pub and restaurant encompass a brand-new style while retaining some original features. Food is served every day, and all day at weekends. There is a quiz night on Thursday. Badger seasonal beers are served in special glasses. The outdoor smoking area has umbrellas and heated lamps.
⏣Q🎲◑⏣&♣P╚

Yalding

Walnut Tree
Yalding Hill, ME18 6JB
🕐 11.45-3, 6-11; 11.45-11 Fri & Sat; 12-10.30 Sun
☎ (01622) 814266 ⊕ walnuttreeyalding.co.uk
Adnams Explorer; Fuller's London Pride; Harveys Sussex Best Bitter; guest beer Ⓗ
Originally an oak-beamed Kentish yeoman's house, built around 1492, the red brick walls were added later, as was the extension that is now the restaurant. The bar has an inglenook fireplace in the small upper area, with steps down to a lower bar. Hops, brassware and pictures on the wall create a cosy atmosphere. Good food is served in the bar and a la carte meals and specials in the restaurant, all made from local produce wherever possible.
⏣◑🚋(23, 26)P

Come on in the water's lovely

The importance of water to the brewing process is often overlooked. Most people know that barley malt and hops are the main ingredients used in beer making and that yeast turns malt sugars into alcohol. But 93% of even the strongest beer is made up of water – and the quality of the water is essential to the taste and character of the finished product.

Brewers call the water they use in the brewing process 'liquor' to distinguish it from cleaning water. Brewing liquor, whether it comes from natural wells or the public supply, will be filtered and cleaned to ensure its absolute purity. Care will be taken, however, to ensure that vital salts and irons are not removed during the filtering process, as they are essential to the production of cask beer.

The benchmark for brewing liquor is Burton-on-Trent in the English Midlands. The natural spring waters of the Trent Valley have rich deposits of calcium and magnesium sulphates – also known as gypsum and Epsom salts. Salt is a flavour-enhancer and the sulphates in Burton liquor bring out the finest flavours from malts and hops. Since the 19th century, ale brewers throughout Britain and other countries have added salts to 'Burtonise' their liquor.

It's fascinating to compare the levels of salts in the water of three famous brewing locations: Burton, London and Pilsen. Pilsen is the home of the first golden lager beer, Pilsner. Brewers of genuine lager beers want comparatively soft brewing liquor to balance the toasted malt and gentle, spicy hop nature of their beers. Pilsen water has total salts of 30 parts per milligram, with minute amounts of calcium and magnesium.

London, once celebrated as a dark beer region, famous for mild, porter and stout, has 463 total salts per milligram, with high levels of sodium and carbonate. (Dublin, another dark beer city, has similar water to London's). Burton liquor has an astonishing level of total salts of 1,226 per milligram. If this figure is further broken down, Burton liquor is rich in magnesium, calcium, other sulphates and carbonate.

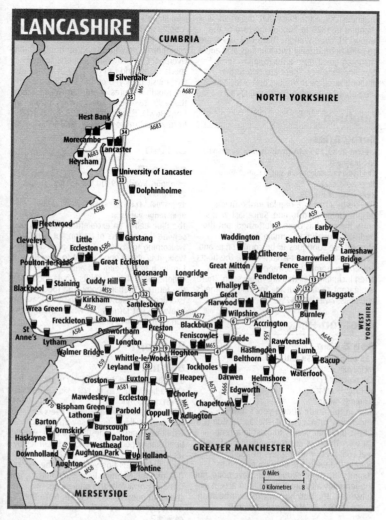

Accrington

Peel Park Hotel

Turkey Street, BB5 6EW (200m from A679, adj to Peel Park school)

🕐 12-11.30

☎ (01254) 235830

Tetley Bitter; guest beers Ⓗ

A true free house that just gets better and better. A number of teams represent the pub in darts, dominoes, pool and football leagues; the football team plays on the old Accrington Stanley ground opposite. A popular quiz is held each Thursday night, and two beer festivals are hosted annually, at spring bank holiday and in November. Cider and perry from Weston's are available all year round. The disabled access is to the rear and may be locked (please call in advance).

🏚❀◁♿(23, 263)♣♠P

Adlington

Spinners Arms

23 Church Street, PR7 4EX (on A6)

🕐 12-11; 12-2, 5-11 Tue

☎ (01257) 483331

Coniston Bluebird; guest beers Ⓗ

There are two Spinners Arms in Adlington – this one is the 'bottom' Spinner's. Dating from 1838, the interior comprises three spacious areas with plenty of seating. There are no pool tables or slot machines. The emphasis is on good beer, with a mild, stout and real cider always available. Draught Belgian fruit beer and wheat beers have recently been introduced, and six-litre carry-outs of Bluebird can be ordered. Pump clips of past guest beers are on display, as well as a CAMRA Pub of the Season award. Quiz night is Tuesday.

❀Å⇌♿♠P↳

Altham

Walton Arms

Burnley Road, BB5 5UL

🕐 11.30-3, 5.30-11; 11.30-11 Sun

☎ (01254) 774444 🌐 waltonarms-altham.co.uk

Jennings Bitter, Cumberland Ale; guest beer Ⓗ

Originally called the Black Bull, the name was changed in 1820 to honour the Lord of the Manor, RT Wroe Walton. Three cask beers are on offer here, usually two Jennings ales and a changing guest from a micro, often the Bowland Brewery. There are two further drinking areas near the bar and a restaurant separated by wooden partitions. Q◑P

Aughton

Derby Arms

Prescot Road, L39 6TA (midway between Kirkby and Maghull)
☼ 11.30-11 (midnight Fri & Sat); 11.30-10.30 Sun
☎ (01695) 422237
Beer range varies Ⓗ
The Derby Arms is a regular in the Guide despite being hard to find. Since last year's entry the pub has been refurbished, but the traditional small bars remain and the atmosphere continues to be comfortable and friendly, with an old-fashioned feel. The beers are drawn from a wide range of breweries, often including ales that are rarely seen. There is pleasant seating outside for mild summer's evenings. ⚶❀◑ ⊟✦P

Aughton Park

Dog & Gun

233 Long Lane, L39 5BU (nr Aughton Park Merseyrail station)
☼ 12-midnight (12.30am Sat & Sun)
☎ (01695) 423303
Jennings range Ⓗ
Back in the Guide after a year's absence and under new management, the Dog & Gun is a classic pub that seems to exist in a time capsule. The bars are cosy and unspoilt with real coal fires, with displays of paintings around the walls the only concession to change. The Burtonwood beers have gone, but the Jennings ales are a more than acceptable substitute. The pub has an excellent bowling green. ⚶❀♿≠(Merseyrail Station)P

Bacup

Crown Inn

19 Greave Road, OL13 9HQ (off Todmorden Rd, ½ mile from Bacup Centre)
☼ 5-midnight; 12-1am Sat; 12-midnight Sun
☎ (01706) 873982 ⊕ crowninnbacup.co.uk
Pictish Brewers Gold, Crown IPA; guest beer Ⓗ
Fascinating stone pub, built in traditional mid-Pennines style. The welcoming, cosy atmosphere is just right for a quiet social evening – no children or dogs are admitted. Bar skittles can be played. Superb sandwiches are on offer and an extensive coffee menu. Bottle-conditioned strong beers of ABV 9-11% from the Bare Arts Brewery are often available. ⚶Q❀◑♿⊟✦P⅃

Barrowford

George & Dragon

217 Gisburn Road, BB9 6JD (on A682)
☼ 3 (12 Thu)-midnight; 12-1am Fri & Sat; 12-midnight Sun
☎ (01282) 612929

John Smith's Bitter; guest beers Ⓗ
A popular village local near Barrowford Park and the Pendle Heritage Centre, and a short walk from Barrowford Locks on the Leeds and Liverpool Canal. The pub supports several sports teams and can get busy at weekends. Live music is played on the last Thursday of the month. Pictures of old Barrowford adorn the walls. Two guest beers always include one from Bowland and another usually sourced from a local micro-brewery. ❀⊟✦P⅃

Barton

Blue Bell

Southport Road, L39 7JU (on A5147)
☼ 11-midnight
☎ (01704) 841406 ⊕ thebluebellhotel.co.uk
Beer range varies Ⓗ
The Blue Bell is an excellent community pub, serving the villagers of Barton but equally welcoming to visitors. A great place to end a walk, it is also a good venue to take the family: it has a delightful animal farm for children with sheep, rabbits, goats and (star of the farm) a Shetland pony. The food is excellent too, and children will be pleased to know the pet farm is not where the meat comes from. ⚶➤❀◑⊟⊟✦P

Belthorn

Dog Inn

61 Belthorn Road, BB1 2NN OS716248
☼ 12-2 (not Mon), 5.30-11; 12-11 Sat; 12-10.30 Sun
☎ (01254) 690794
Caledonian Deuchars IPA; guest beers Ⓗ
Traditional village inn on several levels, featuring a partly stone-flagged floor, wooden beams and open stonework, and warmed by a real fire. The restaurant serves home-cooked food and affords fine views over the moors. One of originally nine beer & ale houses, only three are now left; this one serves two ever-changing guests plus a regular. Note the display case between the stairs to the toilets. ⚶❀◑P

Pack Horse

Haslingden Road, BB1 2PL
☼ 12-2 (Sat only), 6.30-1am; 3.30-1am Sun
☎ (01254) 53480
Three B's Bobbin's Bitter; guest beers Ⓗ
One-room bar with a separate lounge to the right when you enter. Beyond the bar is the restaurant, which specialises in Italian food.

INDEPENDENT BREWERIES	
Bowland Clitheroe	
Bryson's Morecombe	
Fuzzy Duck Poulton-le-Fylde	
Grindleton Clitheroe	
Hart Little Eccleston	
Hopstar Darwen	
Lancaster Lancaster	
Moonstone Burnley	
Moorhouses Burnley	
Porter Haslingden	
Red Rose Great Harwood	
Three B's Feniscowles	
Thwaites Blackburn	

There are always two of Three B's beers on the bar. The village is probably the highest in Lancashire, and excellent views can be enjoyed towards Pendle Hill. Q🏠P

Bispham Green

Eagle & Child
Maltkiln Lane, L40 3SG (off B5246)
🕐 12-3, 5.30-11; 12-10.30 Sun
☎ (01257) 462297
Thwaites Original; guest beers Ⓗ
Outstanding 16th-century local with stone-flagged floors and antique furniture. Renowned for its food, it features occasional themed menu evenings (booking advised). An annual beer festival is held in a marque on the lawn behind the pub on the first May bank holiday. Tables are set around the bowling green, affording wonderful views of the surrounding countryside. The front of the pub overlooks the village green. Aside from the Thwaites, it offers seven guest beers, always including a mild. A cider is also available, often Saxon Cross. ▲Q🏠◑&🍴P

Blackpool

Churchills
83-85 Topping Street, FY1 3AF (near Winter Gardens)
🕐 10-11 (1am Fri & Sat); 11-midnight Sun
☎ (01253) 622036
Bateman XXXB; Greene King Old Speckled Hen; Shepherd Neame Spitfire; Wells Bombardier Ⓗ
Busy town centre pub with two distinct personalities: at lunchtime it is a relaxing place to chat and in the evening and through the weekend there is live entertainment from the small stage, including cabaret and karaoke. There is also a quiz and bingo on Tuesday evening. Assorted Victoriana, old photos of Blackpool and Guinness memorabillia are displayed throughout the pub. ◑&≢(Blackpool North)🚌(2, 15)♣

Dunes
561 Lytham Road, FY4 1RD (500m from airport)
🕐 11-11 (midnight Thu-Sat); 12-11 Sun
☎ (01253) 403854
Boddingtons Bitter; Greene King IPA; Theakston Bitter; Wells Bombardier; guest beers Ⓗ
A local community pub that still has a separate vault and hosts quiz nights on Thursday and Sunday. At the front of the pub a heated, flower-decked patio allows for outdoor summer drinking. The meals served here are basic pub fare and finish at 7.30pm.
❀◑🍴&🚌(11, 68)♣P⅃

Highlands
206 Queens Promenade, Bispham, FY2 9JS (opp Bispham tram stop, Red Bank Road)
🕐 12-midnight
☎ (01253) 354877 ⊕thehighlandslodge.co.uk
Thwaites Original, Lancaster Bomber Ⓗ
Impressive seafront pub, wonderfully placed for the Illuminations, and popular with locals and visitors alike. Families are welcome in the dining area where an excellent choice of award-winning meals is served including lunchtime specials, two-for-one and an à la

carte menu. The tasteful decor extends to the superb accommodation. The pub has a separate games room and fields its own teams. From the outdoor seating area, the Prom and Irish Sea can be viewed.
❀🛏◑&⊖🚌🍴P⅃

New Road Inn
244 Talbot Road, FY1 3HL
🕐 10.30-11.30 (often midnight); 11-11.30 Sun
☎ (01253) 628872
Jennings Dark Mild, Cumberland Ale, Sneck Lifter; guest beers Ⓗ
Friendly and unassuming, the New Road Inn attracts a wide range of customers. A previous winner of a local CAMRA Pub of the Season award, this 1930s local is comfortably furnished and has Art Deco features. There is entertainment several nights a week and a games room, and dogs are welcome. Guest ales are always available, sometimes from the Jennings range. ❀◑≢⊖(North Pier)🚌♣P⅃

Old Bridge House
124 Lytham Road, FY1 6DZ (near Bloomfield Rd jct)
🕐 11-11 (midnight Fri & Sat)
☎ (01253) 341998
Theakston Mild; Wells Bombardier; guest beers Ⓗ
An easy stroll from the Prom and Blackpool FC stadium, this is a real community pub, popular with locals and visitors alike. There are usually two guest beers and food is served daily until 7pm except Tuesday. Families with children are welcome in the large cabaret bar at the rear until 6pm. There is a front forecourt with benches for outdoor drinking.
🐾❀◑&⊖(Barton Avenue)🚌♣

Pump & Truncheon
Bonny Street, FY1 5AR (opp police station)
🕐 10.30-11 (midnight Fri-Sun)
☎ (01253) 751176 ⊕pumpandtruncheon.co.uk
Boddingtons Bitter; guest beers Ⓗ
Large single-roomed pub with wooden floorboards and brick walls. A popular watering hole and the winner of several local CAMRA awards, it always has eight ales to choose from, and hosts a beer festival in June. There is live entertainment on Saturday and Sunday evenings, when it is licensed to open until midnight. Victorian police photographs plus other bric-a-brac decorate the walls. An extensive food menu is on offer plus a large-screen TV for sports fans. ▲◑⊖🚌♣

Saddle Inn
286 Whitegate Drive, FY3 9PH (at Preston Old Road jct)
🕐 12-11 (midnight Fri & Sat)
☎ (01253) 607921
Draught Bass; Thwaites Original; guest beers Ⓗ
Blackpool's oldest pub, established in 1770, and local CAMRA Pub of the Year 2007, the Saddle comprises a main bar and two side rooms, plus a large patio for outside drinking in summer. This excellent, friendly pub usually has four guest beers on offer. A good food menu includes daily specials. ▲Q❀◑&🚌P

ENGLAND

Shovels

260 Common Edge Road, FY1 5DH (on B5261, ½ mile from A5230 jct)

✪ 11.30-11 (midnight Thu-Sat); 12-11 Sun

☎ (01253) 762702

Beer range varies ℍ

Large award-winning pub, twice local CAMRA Pub of the Year. It offers six ever-changing beers, usually from small micro-breweries. The pub holds an annual week-long beer festival at the end of October. It is home to a number of sports teams. An extensive food menu is available with daily specials, served daily noon-9.30pm. ᛤ✿◑♿🚲(14)♣P

Burnley

Bridge Bier Huis

2 Bank Parade, BB11 1UH (behind shoppping centre)

✪ 12-midnight Wed & Thu; 12-2am Fri & Sat; 12-midnight Sun

☎ (01282) 411304 ⊕ thebridgebierhuis.co.uk

Hydes Original Bitter; guest beers ℍ

This smart bar caters for beer connoisseurs. Five guest handpumps usually offer micro-breweries' ales, and there are five draught foreign beers plus 40 bottled beers from around the world. No slot machines or juke box disturb the conversation, although live music sometimes plays, and an open mike session is hosted once a month. Bands entertain throughout the Easter blues festival. The pub will open its doors on a Tuesday if Burnley FC are at home. Q◑≢(Central)♣

Coal Clough

41 Coal Clough Lane, BB11 4PG

✪ 12-midnight

☎ (01282) 423226 ⊕ coalcloughpub.co.uk

Cains Traditional Bitter; Worthington's Bitter; guest beers ℍ

A true end-of-terrace pub that is always busy. Dominoes and darts are played in the games room while the main bar hosts live entertainment on Tuesday and Thursday evenings. The Massey's Traditional Bitter is brewed to an old recipe from the sadly defunct Burnley Brewery. Two guest beers are generally sourced from micro-breweries. ≢(Barracks)🚌(111, 112)♣

Gannow Wharf

Gannow Lane, BB12 6QH

✪ 6 (12 Fri-Sun)-12.15am

☎ (01282) 421908

Courage Directors; Wychwood Hobgoblin; guest beer ℍ

This friendly canalside pub hosts regular live music plus jam sessions on Wednesday evenings. A pool room to the rear, with an unusual barge-shaped bar extension, caters for games players, while a large drop-down screen entertains sports fans. Two unusual permanent beers are complemented by a stronger-than-normal guest beer. This is a biker-friendly pub. ✿≢(Rosegrove)♣

Ministry of Ale

9 Trafalgar Street, BB11 1TQ

✪ 12.30 (12 Fri-Sun)-midnight; closed Mon & Tue

☎ (01282) 830909 ⊕ ministryofale.co.uk

Moonstone Black Star; guest beers ℍ

A warm welcome is the order of the day here, and good beer and conversation are guaranteed in Burnley's only brew pub (the brewery can be seen in the front room). Another Moonstone beer plus two guests and two foreign ales complement the Black Star. A selection of foreign bottled beers is also available. Regular art exhibitions are an added attraction. Open on Tuesday if Burnley FC are at home. Q≢(Manchester Road)♣

Burscough

Slipway

48 Crabtree Lane, L40 0RN (off A59, by canal)

✪ 12-11.30 (10.30 Sun)

☎ (01704) 897767

Thwaites Original, Lancaster Bomber ℍ

The Slipway is a delightful canalside pub, situated next to a swing bridge. It has an extensive child-friendly garden for the summer and is spacious and comfortable inside in winter. The decoration is inevitably nautically themed, but the boat connection is not merely ornamental – the pub has its own slipway for trailer boats. Q✿◑♿≢(New Lane)♣P

Chapeltown

Chetham Arms

83 High Street, BL7 0EW (on B6391) OS734157

✪ 5 (12 Wed)-11; 12-1am Thu-Sat; 12-11 Sun

☎ (01204) 852279

Caledonian Deuchars IPA; guest beers ℍ

Dating from the 18th-century, this village inn has been considerably extended to provide a separate room and lounge for dining, with a long bar and a hide-away games room. A meeting place for locals, visitors and walkers, regular live music is staged – mainly folk nights – and parties can be catered for. Nearby is Turton Towers, originally a medieval pele tower set in nine acres of woodland gardens. ✿◑♣P▯

Chorley

Potters Arms

42 Brooke Street, PR7 3BY (next to Morrisons)

✪ 3-11.30 (midnight Fri); 12-4, 7-midnight Sat; 12-5, 7-11 Sun

☎ (01257) 267954

Moorhouses Premier; Tetley Bitter; Three B's Doff Cocker ℍ

Small, friendly free house named after the owners, Mr and Mrs Potter, situated at the bottom of Brooke Street, alongside the railway bridge. The central bar serves two games areas, while two comfortable lounges are popular with locals and visitors alike. The pub displays a fine selection of photographs from the world of music, as well as vintage local scenes. Regular darts and dominoes nights are well attended and the chip butties go down a treat! ᛤ≢🚌♣P

Prince of Wales

9-11 Cowling Brow, PR6 0QE (off B6228)

✪ 12 (11 Sat)-11; 12-10.30 Sun

☎ (01257) 413239

Jennings Bitter, Cumberland Ale, seasonal beers; guest beers ⊞
Stone-terraced pub situated in the south-eastern part of town, not far from the Leeds-Liverpool Canal. Its unspoilt interior incorporates a traditional tap room, games room, large lounge and comfortable snug complete with real fire. There is photographic evidence of the licencee's love of jazz, and collections of brewery artefacts and saucy seaside postcards are also on display. You will find a large selection of malt whiskies behind the bar and sandwiches are served on request. ⚒❀⊕🖳♣╘🖤

Swan With Two Necks

Hollinshead Street, PR7 1ER (behind parish church, off Park Rd)
✪ 12-1am (2am Fri & Sat); 12-midnight Sun
☎ (01257) 263021
Moorhouses Black Cat, Premier, Pride of Pendle, Blond Witch, Pendle Witches Brew ⊞
Converted from a doctor's surgery to a pub in the early 1980s, this lively inn is located just outside the town centre behind the parish church. It is a local outlet for Moorhouses beers, usually offering a choice of ales including a mild on five handpumps. ❀≢P

Cleveleys

Royal Venue

North Promenade, FY5 1LW (approx ¼ mile from bus station on promenade)
✪ 12-midnight
☎ (01253) 852143 ⊕ theroyalvenue.co.uk
Theakston Best Bitter; guest beers ⊞
The Royal Venue is a recently modernised public house with comfortable lounge seating and a grill room featuring a substantial menu. This and the upstairs Mezzaluna restaurant (open from 5pm daily) are award winners. The pub has a snooker/pool room and is also home to the Enigma nightclub which has a late licence. Live music plays every Friday and Saturday night – check the website for further details. ♿P╘

Clitheroe

New Inn

Parson Lane, BB7 2ZT
✪ 11-11 (10.30 Sun)
☎ (01200) 443653
Coach House Gunpowder Mild, ESB; Moorhouses Premier; Taylor Landlord; guest beers ⊞
Located in the centre of Clitheroe, just below the castle, the New Inn is at the heart of the local community; a number of clubs and associations meet here each week and the pub is never empty. Several small rooms are served by the central bar, which usually has up to eight handpumps in action. Beers come from a huge range of breweries, including Coach House, Taylor and Moorhouses, along with several micro-breweries. Live music events are a regular feature. ⚒Q❀≢🖳

Coppull

Red Herring

Mill Lane, PR7 5AN (off B5251, next to Coppull Mill)
✪ 12-11 (11.30 Fri & Sat)
☎ (01257) 470130
Beer range varies ⊞
In a village dominated by keg outlets, this real ale oasis, formerly the offices of the imposing mill next door, was coverted to a pub some years ago. The bar serves a large single room with an extension, usually offering three beers from micro-breweries. TV sports fans are catered for, as are anglers who use the mill pond opposite. The pub hosts regular music nights and barbecues. Handy for trainspotters, it stands by the West Coast Main Line. The first floor has a large function room. ❀♿🅰🖳♣P╘

Croston

Grapes

67 Town Road, PR26 9RA
✪ 12-11 (midnight Fri & Sat)
☎ (01772) 600225
Greene King IPA; guest beers ⊞
Old whitewashed pub situated close to the historic parish church in the heart of the village. The Grapes has been an inn since at least 1799; the building has also been used as a custom house and a magistrates' court in the past. A small bar serves a compact lounge, and there are two rooms at the front plus a restaurant at the back. Five guest beers from national and regional brewers are stocked, including occasional ales from local micros. ⛵❀⊕🖳♿≢🖳(7, 112)P

Wheatsheaf

25-27 Town Road, PR26 9RA
✪ 12-11 (10.30 Sun)
☎ (01772) 600370
Shepherd Neame Spitfire; Taylor Landlord; guest beers ⊞
Converted from a barn around 150 years ago, this local inn specialises in gastro-food. Situated next to the village green, it has open beams and wooden floors, with a romantic red room off the main bar area with real fires. Two guest beers often include ales from Southport Brewery and real cider is also available. Live music features on alternate Fridays. There is an attractive heated outside drinking area with a pergola at the front, and car parks front and rear. ⚒Q❀⊕🖳♿≢🖳(C7, 112)♣P

Cuddy Hill

Plough at Eaves

Eaves Lane, PR4 0BJ (1 mile off B5269)
✪ 12-3 (not Mon), 5.30-11; 12-midnight Sat; 12-10.30 Sun
☎ (01772) 690233
Thwaites Original, Lancaster Bomber ⊞
Near the site of a Civil War battle where Scottish Royalist forces were defeated in 1648, the whitewashed Plough is both one of the Fylde's oldest pubs and one of the hardest to find. It now has a family room, restaurant and newly added conservatory and piano room. Do not miss the old bar with its low beams and

flagstone floor, decorated with brasses and ornamental plates and warmed by a roaring fire in winter. Food is served all day.
🏚️Q🛏️🕳️🕓🛆&P

Dalton

Beacon

3 Beacon Lane, WN8 7RR
🕐 12 (4 Mon)-11 (11.30 Wed); 12-midnight Fri & Sat; 12-10.30 Sun
☎ (01695) 632323 ⊕ beaconinn.co.uk
Jennings Cumberland Ale; guest beers Ⓗ
Country pub close to Ashurst Beacon, a local beauty spot, and therefore popular with walkers. The pub has a strong role in the community and is home to a cricket club and youth football team. Quiz night on Wednesday and karaoke on Friday are popular with the locals. The choice of guest beers comes from Marston's range. The restaurant specialises in steaks and hosts regular themed nights, including Chinese banquets. Bar food is also available. The garden has a children's play area. 🕓🕳️&P

Darwen

Black Horse

72 Redearth Road, BB3 2AF (near Sainsbury's)
🕐 12-midnight
☎ (01254) 873040 ⊕ theblackun.co.uk
Three B's Stoker's Slake; guest beers Ⓗ
Lively community local, which runs four major festivals a year, showcasing over 30 beers, plus end-of-the-month mini festivals themed mainly around new and rare ales, drawing visitors from far and wide. Cider is available on request. Meal deals are offered at festivals and on Sunday afternoon. The pub also hosts a popular Thursday music night with jam sessions or live bands. There is a large paved drinking area at the back. 🕓&≠♣♠💺

Dolphinholme

Fleece

Bay Horse, LA2 9AQ (on crossroads W of village)
🕐 11-11 (10.30 Sun)
☎ (01524) 791233 ⊕ fleeceinn.co.uk
Black Sheep Best Bitter; Everards Beacon; Thwaites Lancaster Bomber; guest beers Ⓗ
A former farmhouse, now a community pub, all visitors are made more than welcome here. It has a bar and dining room, which is very popular for the good food it serves. Outside is a permanent marquee for functions, and in the summer months it even has an ice-cream van. This all-round excellent pub offers something for everyone, from families to drinkers looking for peace and quiet. However, it is not easily accessible by public transport. 🏚️🛏️🕓🕳️♣💺

Downholland

Scarisbrick Arms

2 Black-a-Moor Lane, L39 7HX (at A5147 jct)
🕐 12-2.30, 5-11; 12-11 Sat & Sun
☎ (0151) 526 1120
Beer range varies Ⓗ

If the Scarisbrick Arms was any more isolated, search parties would be necessary. But despite having no community to speak of around it, the pub continues to thrive, offering an adventurous range of beers, often including an ale from the local Southport Brewery. The food is excellent, too. Positioned in a picturesque spot, the pub is a great place to break a walk or end a country bike ride. In the winter, a warming fire welcomes guests.
🏚️Q🛏️🕓🕳️🍴🍺P

Earby

Red Lion

70 Red Lion Street, BB18 6RD (follow signs for youth hostel from Earby centre)
🕐 12-3, 5-11; 12-11 Sat & Sun
☎ (01282) 843395
Copper Dragon Best Bitter; Phoenix Monkeytown Mild; Taylor Landlord; Tetley Bitter; Theakston Best Bitter; guest beers Ⓗ
Village pub situated next to the youth hostel and popular with walkers, just a short walk from the village centre and bus terminus. Inside it has a separate public bar and lounge. Children are welcome, and there is secure parking for cyclists. Home-made pies are a speciality. Two changing guest ales are always available, with Barngates a popular choice, possibly because its beers are named after dogs. Q🕓🕳️🍴🛆🍺P

Eccleston

Original Farmers Arms

Towngate, PR7 5QS (on B5250)
🕐 11.30-12.30am (1am Fri & Sat); 11-midnight Sun
☎ (01257) 451594
Boddingtons Bitter; Phoenix Arizona; Taylor Landlord; Tetley Bitter; guest beers Ⓗ
This white-painted village pub has expanded over the years into the cottages next door, adding a substantial dining area. However, the original part of the pub is still used mainly for drinking. Two or three guest ales are changed frequently. Meals are available throughout the day, seven days a week, and there is accommodation in four good-value guest rooms. 🕓🍴🕳️🍺(113, 347)P

Edgworth

Black Bull

167 Bolton Road, BL7 0AF
🕐 11.30-midnight (1am Fri & Sat); 12-11 Sun
☎ (01204) 852811
Lees Bitter; Tetley Bitter; guest beers Ⓗ
Traditional village pub, originally two cottages which have now been joined together. Until 1995, only the front rooms were licensed (but not for spirits) and no women were admitted – they had to use the 'nanny-pen' kitchen at the back, now the lounge. These days the bar unites both areas, with handpumps at either side. Guest beers change regularly. The restaurant is in an extended back room and provides excellent meals daily. A weekly quiz night is staged at this dog-friendly pub. 🕓🕳️🍺🛆P

Euxton

Euxton Mills

Wigan Road, PR7 6JD (at A581 jct)
⏲ 11.30-3, 5-11.30; 11.30-11.30 Fri & Sat; 12-11 Sun
☎ (01257) 264002
Jennings Bitter; guest beers ⊞
This village inn has been the recipient of several Best Kept Pub awards. It is particularly attractive in the summer months, with numerous hanging baskets full of flowers outside. Low ceilings and doors help to create a cosy atmosphere inside. The pub has long enjoyed a widespread reputation for good food. Two or three guest beers are always available, and three times a year the pub hosts a beer festival.
❀◑⇌(Balshaw Lane)🚌P

Talbot

10 Balshaw Lane, PR7 6HX
⏲ 12-11 (midnight Fri & Sat); 3-11 Tue winter
☎ (01257) 411531
Theakston Mild, Best Bitter; guest beers ⊞
Large, modern pub, comfortably furnished throughout. The lounge is on two levels, with a raised area providing a refuge from the busier space near the bar. The public bar is accessed through an open doorway. This pub has steadily built up a good reputation, and in 2006 was the winner of a Best Kept Cellar award. Two guest beers are usually available.
❀◑⊟⇌(Balshaw Lane)🚌♣P

Fence

Old Sparrowhawk

152 Wheatley Lane Road, BB12 9QG (½ mile from A6068)
⏲ 12-11 (midnight Fri & Sat); 12-10.30 Sun
☎ (01282) 603034 🌐 yeoldsparrowhawk.co.uk
Black Sheep Best Bitter; Draught Bass; Moorhouses Pride of Pendle, Blond Witch; Tetley Bitter; Thwaites Original ⊞
A former Bass Vintage Inn, this friendly, hospitable country pub has a fine reputation for its locally sourced home-cooked food (served lunchtimes and evenings, all day at the weekend). The bar area features an unusual stained-glass dome which was reputedly paid for by local mill owners. The garden area to the front is the perfect place to relax on a balmy summer evening, overlooking the rolling countryside.
⌂Q❀◑♿P⍁

Feniscowles

Feildens Arms

673 Preston Old Road, BB2 5ER (at A674/A6062 jct)
⏲ 12-midnight (1am Fri & Sat)
☎ (01254) 200988
Black Sheep Best Bitter; Flowers IPA; guest beers ⊞
Welcoming, largely stone-built pub at a busy road junction, about three miles west of Blackburn. The guest beers come from small breweries and there is always a mild available. Brews from the local breweries Three B's and Moorhouses of Burnley often appear. Live football is shown regularly. The Leeds-Liverpool Canal is a short walk away.
⌂❀⇌(Pleasington)🚌♣P

Fleetwood

Steamer

1-2 Queens Terrace, FY7 6BT (next to market)
⏲ 10-midnight (1am Fri & Sat); 12-midnight Sun
☎ (01253) 771756
Caledonian Deuchars IPA; Wells Bombardier; guest beers ⊞
This former Matthew Brown outlet was built opposite the terminal for the London-Scotland ferry which sailed from Fleetwood to Ardrossan. Children are welcome until 7pm. Winner of the local CAMRA Pub of the Season award, snooker, pool, darts and dominoes can be played. There is an old blacksmith's workshop at the rear, dating from the time when the yard was used to stable police horses. ⛴❀◐⊖(Ferry Terminal)🚌♣

Thomas Drummond

London Street, FY7 6JY (between Lord St and Dock St)
⏲ 9-midnight (1am Fri & Sat)
☎ (01253) 775020
Greene King Abbot; Marston's Pedigree; Shepherd Neame Spitfire; guest beers ⊞
Situated in the town centre, this former church hall and furniture warehouse is named after a builder who helped to construct the town. A past winner of the local CAMRA silver award and Pub of the Season, it has on display details of the founders of Fleetwood, Sir Peter Hesketh Fleetwood and architect Decimus Burton. Children are welcome until 6pm. Food is served until 11pm daily (last orders for children's food is 5pm).
⛴❀◑♿⊖(London Street)🚌🍎

Wyre Lounge Bar

Marine Hall, The Esplanade, FY7 6HF (250m from pier)
⏲ 12-3.30 (4 Fri, Sat & summer), 7-11; 12-4, 7-10.30 Sun
☎ (01253) 771141 🌐 marinehall.co.uk
Courage Directors; Moorhouses Pendle Witches Brew; Phoenix Navvy; guest beers ⊞
Situated within the Marine Hall complex on the seafront, this pub is well known for its selection of beers from breweries both local and further afield, and has twice been a winner of local CAMRA Pub of the Year. The outdoor drinking area is popular in summer due to its proximity to the beach. There are great views over Morecambe Bay to the Lakeland fells. Crazy golf, pitch and putt and crown green bowls can be played in nearby gardens. ❀♿⊖(Ferry Terminal)🚌P

Freckleton

Coach & Horses

6 Preston Old Road, PR4 1PD
⏲ 11-midnight (1am Fri & Sat)
☎ (01772) 632284
Boddingtons Bitter; guest beers ⊞
Sensitively refurbished three years ago, this village local has retained its cosy character. At the centre of village life, it is home to Freckleton's award-winning brass band; an

impressive collection of trophies is proudly displayed in a cabinet in the pub. A special place is reserved for mementoes of the US Eighth Air Force. There are two guest ales usually available, from the Punch Taverns list. ⊛◐&▲🖳P'⊷

Garstang

Wheatsheaf
Park Hill Road, PR3 1EL
☼ 10-midnight (1am Fri & Sat); 11.30-11.30 Sun
☎ (01995) 603398
Courage Directors; Jennings Cumberland Ale; Theakston Best; guest beers Ⓗ
Built as a farmhouse in the late 18th century, this is now a Grade II listed building and was greatly extended in 2002. A disco is held every Sunday, and live music is staged monthly on a Monday. The pub serves breakfast, lunch and supper, and there is a covered outdoor smoking area. ⊛◐&🖳♣P'⊷

Goosnargh

Grapes
Church Lane, PR3 2BH (off B5269, at post office)
☼ 12 (3 Mon)-midnight
☎ (01772) 865234
Black Sheep Best Bitter; Greene King Abbot; Tetley Dark Mild; guest beers Ⓗ
Situated next to the historic church and Bushells House, established 300 years ago to cater for distressed gentlefolk, this village inn has a country pub atmosphere and is popular with locals and diners. Food is served six days a week, with themed nights including curries on Wednesday and Italian food on Friday. There is a separate drinkers' area and a games room. Two guest beers come from the Punch Taverns list. Outside, there is a bowling green and paved patio. ⨺⊛◐⊟🖳(44)♣P'⊷

Stag's Head
990 Whittingham Lane, PR3 2AU
☼ 12-11 (10.30 Sun)
☎ (01772) 864071 ⊕ thestagshead.co.uk
Theakston Best Bitter, Old Peculier; guest beers Ⓗ
Large roadside pub situated close to the haunted Chingle Hall. It has four drinking areas, a large beer garden with a heated area for smokers, and a restaurant. All food is sourced from local producers and home-made pickles and chutneys are available to take away. Guest beers come from the S&N Cellarman's Reserve list. Monthly live music events and regular beer festivals are popular, and the pub has a late licence for special events. A refurb is planned for 2007 which will add B&B facilities. ⨺⊛◐&🖳(4)P'⊷

Great Harwood

Royal Hotel
Station Road, BB6 7BE
☼ 4-11; 12-midnight Fri & Sat; 12-10.30 Sun
☎ (01254) 883541
Beer range varies Ⓗ
Brewery tap for the nearby Red Rose Brewery. Eight beers are on offer, including ales from the brewery and guests from near and far.

There are always at least two dark ales as well as a good selection of bottled beers. A beer festival is held over the May bank holiday. Music lovers enjoy regular free entertainment in the concert room. Well served by public transport from Accrington, Blackburn and Manchester, the Royal is a handy stop for visitors to the Ribble Valley and Pendle Witch country. ⊛⇔▲🖳♣🖵

Victoria ☆
St John's Street, BB6 7EP
☼ 4-midnight; 3-1am Fri; 12-1am Sat; 12-midnight Sun
☎ (01254) 885210
Beer range varies Ⓗ
Built in 1905 by Alfred Nuttall and known locally as Butcher Brig, the pub features a wealth of original features. The lobby has floor-to-ceiling glazed tiling and there is dark wood throughout the five rooms. On the horseshoe-shaped bar are eight handpumps dispensing beers sourced from small breweries across northern England and Scotland. Bowland, Copper Dragon and Durham beers often feature. The pub sits on a cycle way. Q♿⊛▲♣◆

Great Mitton

Aspinall Arms
Mitton Road, BB7 9PQ (on B6246, between Whalley and Clitheroe)
☼ 12-3, 6-11.30; 12-11 Sat; 12-10.30 Sun
☎ (01254) 826223 ⊕ aspinallarms.co.uk
Beer range varies Ⓗ
Despite the imposing new pub sign sponsored by Copper Dragon, this pub remains a free house. Parts of it date back to the 17th century, when a ferry crossed the River Ribble. Three handpumps feature beers from a range of breweries from Wychwood and Salamander to Bowland and Phoenix. Food is good value, with a choice of vegetarian options available. Sunday lunch is always popular (book in advance). Live music is hosted on the second Thursday of the month, quiz night on alternate Tuesdays. ⨺⊛⇔◐P

Grimsargh

Plough
187 Preston Road, PR2 5JR (on B6243)
☼ 11 (12 Sun)-midnight
☎ (01772) 652235 ⊕ theplough-grimsargh.co.uk
Taylor Landlord; guest beers Ⓗ
A focal point of village life, this award-winning country pub dates from 1785. It retains many original features including oak beams and open fires. Free from tie, the guest beers on offer often come from local breweries. Excellent home-cooked food is served, featuring local ingredients whenever possible. There is a bowling green and an outdoor drinking area, and regular quizzes, theme nights and social events add to the entertainment. ⨺⊛◐&⊟(2, 2A)♣P'⊷

Guide

King Edward VII
321 Haslingden Road, BB1 2WG (on A6177, nr M65 jct 5)

✪ 5-11.30; 3-12.30am Fri; 12-12.30am Sat & Sun
☎ (01254) 54261
Jennings Cumberland, seasonal beers Ⓗ
This prominent corner pub in Guide has
retained its original tiled interior and an
outside Gents. Traditional pub games are
played here during the week. The beers on
handpump are Jennings Cumberland and
seasonal beers. There is parking at the front of
the pub. ♨♣P

Haggate

Sun Inn
1 Burnley Road, BB10 2JJ (off A6114, 3½ miles NE
of Burnley centre)
✪ 1-midnight; 12-1am Fri & Sat; 12-midnight Sun
☎ (01282) 428785
Moorhouses Premier; guest beers Ⓗ
Busy village pub on the north-eastern edge of
Burnley, next to moorland and farmland. It
actively supports local sports teams. Guest
beers are often sourced from the Moorhouses
Brewery. A regular quiz night is popular, and
there is live entertainment on alternate
Saturday evenings. A pleasant outdoor
drinking area is superb for summer days.
♨❀&▲♣P

Haskayne

Kings Arms Hotel
Delf Lane, L39 7JJ (on A5147 at bridge)
✪ 12-midnight (1am Fri & Sat)
☎ (01704) 840245
Beer range varies Ⓗ
The Kings Arms is a picturesque pub that has
returned to the Guide after an absence of
some years. A lovely pub to visit in winter,
with snug bars and real fires, it is also a
pleasant place for refreshment in the
summertime, attracting canal walkers from
the towpath a few minutes' walk away. Guest
beers are drawn from smaller breweries, with
George Wright beers featuring frequently on
the beer menu. ♨Q✆❀⊄➡P

Heapey

Top Lock
Copthurst Lane, PR6 8LS (alongside canal at
Johnson's Hillock)
✪ 11-11; 12-10.30 Sun
☎ (01257) 263376
**Black Sheep Best Bitter; Coniston Bluebird; guest
beers** Ⓗ
Fine country pub on the Leeds-Liverpool Canal,
at the top of the series of locks known as
Johnson's Hillock. There are eight real ales in
winter, nine in summer, including a cask mild
and a real stout or porter, mostly from micro-
breweries. In October, an annual beer festival
is held in a marquee in the garden. Ciders
vary, with one available in winter, three in
summer. It has a single bar downstairs and an
upstairs dining room, serving 100 per cent
home-made dishes, English and Indian,
cooked by an Indian chef. Thursday is music
night. ❀⊄&♣P

Helmshore

Robin Hood
280 Holcombe Road, BB4 4NP
✪ 4 -11 (midnight Fri); 2-midnight Sat; 2-10.30 Sun
☎ (01706) 213180
Tetley Bitter; guest beers Ⓗ
This is a small pub, opened out but retaining
the inner walls. The handpumps are on the
wall behind the bar. As well as the regular
Tetley bitter there are always two beers from
micros, usually alternating between
Moorhouses, Phoenix and George Wright,
though other beers do appear. The pub is
situated close to the Helmshore Textile
Museum. Note the Glen Top brewery
windows. Dogs are welcome. ♨➡♣⌐

Hest Bank

Hest Bank Hotel
2 Hest Bank Lane, LA2 6DN
✪ 11.30-11
☎ (01524) 824339
**Black Sheep Best Bitter; Boddingtons Bitter;
Caledonian Deuchars IPA; Taylor Landlord; guest
beers** Ⓗ
An historic canalside pub dating from 1554,
the building was a former coaching inn for the
route across Morecambe Bay to Grange-over-
Sands. The pub was greatly extended in the
1980s, giving it a surprisingly large interior. It
has kept the two older rooms, which helps it
to retain an old-fashioned local pub
atmosphere. Food is served from an award-
winning menu daily until 9pm.
♨Q❀⊄◗⊄&➡♣P⌐

Heysham

Royal Hotel
7 Main Street, LA3 2RN
✪ 11.30-11 (midnight Fri & Sat); 12-10.30 Sun
☎ (01524) 859298 ⊕ heyshamonline.co.uk/royal/
royal.html
**Everards Beacon; Thwaites Lancaster Bomber;
guest beers** Ⓗ
Situated in the oldest part of Heysham, the
pub is close to the 11th-century St Peter's
church and the ruins of St Patrick's chapel with
its rock-hewn graves. Inside the pub, roaring
log fires warm guests in the winter months. At
the rear is a large, landscaped beer garden.
Children are welcome in both pub and garden.
♨Q❀⊄◗P⌐

Hoghton

Royal Oak
Blackburn Old Road, Riley Green, PR5 0SL (at
A675/A674 jct)
✪ 11.30-11; 12-10.30 Sun
☎ (01254) 201445
**Thwaites Dark Mild, Original, Lancaster Bomber,
seasonal beers** Ⓗ
Stone-built pub on the old road between
Preston and Blackburn, near the Riley Green
Basin on the Leeds-Liverpool Canal. The Royal
Oak is popular with diners and drinkers.
Rooms, including a dining room, and alcoves
radiate from the central bar. Low, beamed
ceilings and horse brasses give the pub a rustic

feel. This Thwaites tied house is a regular award winner and acts as an outlet for its seasonal beers. Hoghton Tower is nearby, steeped in history and worth visiting.
♨Q☮◑⌦P

Sirloin

Station Road, PR5 0DD (off A675, near level crossing)
☀ 4-11; 12-midnight Fri & Sat; 12-11 Sun
☎ (01254) 852293
Beer range varies Ⓗ
Even the ghosts are friendly in this small, 250-year-old, family-run country inn. It stands near Hoghton Tower, where King James I knighted a loin of beef, and his coat of arms hangs over the fireplace. Sirloin steak is, of course, the speciality on the menu, served in the pub and adjoining restaurant. Three handpumps dispense a choice of beers, often from Lancashire breweries – a dark beer, either mild or porter, is usually available. ♨☮◑᠗⌦♣P↳

Kirkham

Black Horse

29 Preston Street, PR4 2YA
☀ 12-midnight
☎ (01772) 671209
Greene King Old Speckled Hen; guest beers Ⓗ
First opened in the 13th century, this friendly, traditional, two-roomed local on the main street through Kirkham attracts a wide range of customers. The public bar boasts a pool table, while the large-screen TV in the spacious lounge shows major matches but is otherwise unobtrusive. The pub is built above ancient monastic tunnels and is said to be haunted by a family who died when a roof collapsed; strange noises are often heard!
☮◑᠗≢⌦♣P↳

Lancaster

Borough

Dalton Square, LA1 1PP (near town hall)
☀ 12-12.30am (11.30 Sun)
☎ (01524) 64170
Black Sheep Best Bitter; Bowland Hen Harrier; Thwaites range; guest beers Ⓗ
Originally a town house built in 1824, it became a social club in the last century. Previously part of a large pub chain, the pub has been converted and carefully refurbished to appeal to food and ale lovers alike. Deli boards are served outside restaurant hours. The patio garden is sheltered and always busy in summer. The relaxed, friendly atmosphere appeals to a varied clientele of all ages.
☮◑᠖≢⌦♣↳

Collegian Club

Gage Street, LA1 1UH
☀ 11 (11.30 Mon; 12 Tue)-3 (not Wed), 7-11; 11-11 Sat; 12-3, 6.30-10.30 Sun
☎ (01524) 65329 ⊕hometown.aol.co.uk/collegianclub
Jennings Cumberland Ale; guest beers Ⓗ
A working men's club offering an excellent beer range. It was founded in 1933, but the decor and fittings are of 1960s vintage. The bar is dominated by a pool table, and upstairs

is a function room which has no real ale. On the pumps there is Cumberland Ale or another Jennings beer, as well as a choice of guest cask ales. CIU affiliated – people carrying this Guide are welcome. ≢♣

Golden Lion

33 Moor Lane, LA1 1QD (next to Dukes Theatre)
☀ 12-midnight
☎ (01524) 842198
Caledonian Deuchars IPA; Theakston Best Bitter; guest beers Ⓗ
The pub is reputed to have been the last drinking place of the Pendle Witches in 1612. The present building is a mere 200 years old, but it is included in the Pendle Trail. An open mike night is held every Tuesday, which is very popular with local wannabe artistes. Pie and peas are served at weekends, and the pub may stay open later if busy. ≢⌦♣

John O' Gaunt

53 Market Street, LA1 1JG
☀ 11-11
☎ (01524) 65356
Boddingtons Bitter; Caledonian Deuchars IPA; guest beers Ⓗ
An original and handsome bow-windowed frontage hides this narrow pub from the hustle and bustle of the main thoroughfare. The walls are crammed with masses of beer and music memorabilia. It offers seven sessions of live music a week, and is renowned in the city for jazz music. Home-made food is available at lunchtimes. Games include backgammon, chess and Scrabble are played here. The cider is Symonds Scrumpy Jack. ☮◑᠗≢⌦♣♦↳

Sun Hotel & Bar

63-65 Church Street, LA1 1ET
☀ 10-midnight (12.30am Fri & Sat); 10-11.30 Sun
☎ (01524) 66006 ⊕thesunhotelandbar.co.uk
Lancaster Duchy, Blonde, Flaming Nora, seasonal beers; guest beers Ⓗ
Housed in a former slave exchange house, this sympathetically updated pub features exposed stonework and bare floors of wood and slate. Various original features have been left on view, including five fireplaces and an old door. The bar is supplemented by a larger space where local artists exhibit their work. Wifi internet access is available. Breakfast is served from 7.30am, and cheese boards are available until 9pm. ☮⌖◑᠖≢⌦↳

Three Mariners

Bridge Lane, LA1 1EE (near Parksafe car park)
☀ 12-midnight (1am Fri & Sat)
☎ (01524) 388957
Black Sheep Best Bitter; Everards Beacon; Jennings Cumberland Ale; guest beers Ⓗ
Considered to be the oldest pub in Lancaster, the Three Mariners has undergone some mid 20th-century renovation. Situated at the base of Castle Hill, it is unusual in having a first-floor cellar. The cobbled remains of what was once a street (Bridge Lane) form the beer garden. The pub has a thriving local clientele, and with its welcoming atmosphere and exceptional beer quality has won many awards, including local CAMRA Pub of the Year 2007.
♨☮◑᠖≢⌦♣P↳

White Cross

Quarry Road, LA1 4XT (on canalside)
🕐 11.30-11 (12.30am Fri & Sat); 12-11 Sun
☎ (01524) 33999
Boddingtons Bitter; Caledonian Deuchars IPA; Tirril Old Faithful; guest beers 🖽
A modern conversion of an old canalside warehouse with an open-plan interior and a light, airy feel. Extensive canalside seating makes this a popular venue on summer evenings. The pub's vigorous guest beer policy concentrates on local breweries, including Tirril and Dent. Meals are served throughout the week, with roast dinners available on Sunday. It hosts a quiz every Tuesday.
🅰🕽🕭🚻🖴🏵🍴🅿🏃

Yorkshire House

2 Parliament Street, LA1 1DB (S end of Greyhound Bridge)
🕐 7-midnight (1am Thu-Fri); 2-1am Sat; 2-11.30 Sun
☎ (01524) 64679 🌐 yorkshirehouse.enta.net
Everards Tiger; Moorhouses Premier; guest beers 🖽
Unusual in this area, the pub hosts a vibrant live music scene in the upstairs venue, hosting performances from all over the world. Formerly a coaching inn, this single-room bar is one of the few places in the city to serve guest cider on handpump. A welcoming atmosphere ensures that this is always a busy, thriving haven for the night-time drinker.
🅰🏵🚻🖴🏵🍴🏃

Laneshawbridge

Black Lane Ends

Skipton Old Road, Colne, BB8 7EP (on old road from Skipton to Colne)
🕐 12-midnight (1am Fri-Sun)
☎ (01282) 863070
Copper Dragon Black Gold, Best Bitter, Golden Pippin, Scotts 1816, Challenger IPA; guest beer 🖽
Unspoilt country pub on the Pennines where families are welcome. Popular with walkers, it even provides boot-washing facilities. Log fires burn in winter, and superb views can be enjoyed from here over the Lancashire hills. Food is available all day, and there is a barbecue outside in summer. It always has one guest beer on offer, alongside the full range of Copper Dragon ales. 🅰Q🏵🕽🍴🅿

Lathom

Ship

4 Wheat Lane, L40 4BX (off A5209, by Leeds-Liverpool Canal)
🕐 11.30-11; 11-midnight Sat; 12-10.30 Sun
☎ (01704) 893117
Moorhouses Black Cat, Pride of Pendle, Pendle Witches Brew; Theakston Best Bitter; Wells Bombardier; guest beers 🖽
This 200-year-old pub in an attractive canalside position used to serve the canal traffic and now caters for anyone who enjoys good beer and food. The guest beers vary, but often include a Phoenix ale, and occasionally a real cider is on offer. A regular in the Guide, the Ship has retained its small bars and cosy snugs and is surprisingly unspoilt for such a popular country pub with a strong food trade.
Q🏃🕽🏵🕽🖴🍴🅿

Lea Town

Smith's Arms

Lea Lane, PR4 0RP
🕐 12-midnight (1am Thu-Sat)
☎ (01772) 601555
Thwaites Dark Mild, Original, Thoroughbred, Lancaster Bomber, seasonal beers 🖽
Despite undergoing a huge refurbishment recently, the Smith's still feels like a country pub. Recent winner of a Food Caterer of the Year award, the licencees have also collected CAMRA awards with their previous pub. In a handy spot for the Preston-Lancaster Canal, and adjacent to an atomic fuel factory, it is also known as the Slip Inn, from the days when Fylde farmers would walk their cattle to Preston and 'slip in' for a drink. Home to darts and dominoes teams, it stages occasional live acts for special occasions such as St Patrick's Day. 🅰🏃🏵🕽🖴🍴🏃

Leyland

Eagle & Child

30 Church Road, PR25 3AA
🕐 11.45-11 (11.30 Thu-Sat); 12-11 Sun
☎ (01772) 433531
Banks's Bitter; Marston's Pedigree; guest beers 🖽
This old whitewashed building, a pub since the 15th century, nestles alongside the 1000-year-old parish church of St Andrew and the South Ribble Museum, formerly the old grammar school. Located in an area dominated by keg-only pubs, this hostelry features two guest beers from the Marston's list alongside its regulars. The pub caters for all ages. The crown green bowling green is across the road, behind the car park. 🏵🕽🖴🍴🅿🏃

Little Eccleston

Cartford Hotel

Cartford Lane, PR3 0YP (by toll bridge)
🕐 12-3, 6.30-11; 12-10.30 Sun
☎ (01995) 670166
Beer range varies 🖽
Numerous CAMRA awards adorn the walls of the bar in this 17th-century former farmhouse. The pub stand by the toll bridge across the River Wyre, and hotel guests can make use of its extensive riverbank fishing rights. The Hart Brewery, located in an outbuilding at the rear, supplies one of the eight ever-changing cask ales. Real cider is available in the summer, when the pub is busy with cyclists and campers. Food is served all day from an extensive, international menu.
🅰🏃🏵🚗🕽🅰🍴🅿

Longridge

Corporation Arms

Lower Road, PR3 2YJ (near B6243/B6245 jct)
🕐 11-11 (midnight Fri & Sat); 12-10.30 Sun
☎ (01772) 782644 🌐 corporationarms.co.uk
Beer range varies 🖽

Constructed in 1750 on the site of an older building, this family-run country inn was renamed when the Preston Corporation built the nearby reservoirs. Comfortable and relaxing, it often serves beers from local breweries, and its excellent meals contain locally-sourced ingredients where possible. Look outside for the old horse trough, now used as a planter, which was reputably used by Oliver Cromwell to water his horse on his way to the Battle of Preston. Accommodation is comfortable and of a good standard. ﾊ֍⬤⬤⬤⬤⬤A⬤P⬤⬤

Forrest Arms
1 Derby Road, PR3 3JR
✪ 4-midnight; 12-1am Fri & Sat; 12-11.30 Sun
☎ (01772) 786210
Beer range varies Ⓗ
Behind this pub's traditional stone façade is a bright, modern interior decorated in light colours and displaying both modern art and football memorabilia. It has a central bar, unusual for Lancashire, with three handpumps. The regular house beer, Thyme, is brewed by Bank Top and badged for the pub. Frequent live music nights are hosted and the pub holds twice-yearly beer festivals. Good value food is served, often using locally sourced ingredients. ֍⬤⬤⬤⬤⬤

Longton

Dolphin
Marsh Lane, PR4 5SJ (down Marsh Lane 1 mile, take right fork)
✪ 12-2.30am; 10.30-midnight Sun
☎ (01772) 612032
Beer range varies Ⓗ
Isolated country pub on the edge of the Marshes by the Ribble Way, comprising a main bar (where no children are permitted), a family room, a conservatory and a function room. A local CAMRA award winner, it stages an annual beer festival in August. Food is served until 11pm daily. Outside there is a play area with equipment for children. The range of four or five ales on offer always includes a mild; real cider is stocked in summer. A free mini bus service from local villages can be booked. An outside smoking area is planned. ﾊ⬤֍⬤⬤⬤⬤⬤P

Lumb

Hargreaves Arms
910 Burnley Road East, BB4 9PQ (on B6238)
✪ 12-3 (not Mon & Tue), 5-midnight; 12-1am Fri & Sat; 12-midnight Sun
☎ (01706) 215523
Theakston Best Bitter; guest beers Ⓗ
The pub stages a beer festival at Easter, as well as regular theme nights and wine tastings throughout the year. A restaurant menu is available in the evening Monday to Saturday, and all day Sunday, with bar meals on offer at all times. Hikers and bikers are welcome. ﾊ֍⬤⬤⬤⬤P

Lytham

Hastings
26 Hastings Place, FY8 5LZ (close to station)
✪ 12-midnight
☎ (01253) 732839
Archers Village; Moorhouses Pride of Pendle, Pendle Witches Brew; guest beers Ⓗ
Elegant and modern, the Hastings was 2006 national CAMRA Club of the Year. Up to nine real ales are on sale, and a good selection of bottled beers from around the world is stocked in the upstairs Orangery bar. Excellent home-cooked meals complement the choice of ales. Regular entertainment and themed nights are highly recommended. The Hastings is a members-only club; join at the bar, or show a CAMRA membership card or your copy of this Guide to sign in. ֍⬤⬤⬤⬤⬤⬤

Queens Hotel
Central Beach, FY8 5LB
✪ 12-11 (midnight Fri & Sat)
☎ (01253) 737316
Boddingtons Bitter; Greene King Old Speckled Hen; Theakston Best Bitter Ⓗ
This lively pub attracts younger customers but maintains its appeal to all ages, offering a quieter room towards the rear of the building. The inviting beer garden at the front affords fine views across the Ribble Estuary to Southport, and is popular in summer. Lunchtime food is freshly prepared to a very high standard, and portions are generous. Guest ales are available in the summer. ֍⬤⬤⬤⬤⬤

Taps
Henry Street, FY8 5LE
✪ 11-11 (midnight Fri & Sat)
☎ (01253) 736226 ⬤ thetaps.net
Greene King IPA; guest beers Ⓗ
Landlord Ian Rigg is a legend in the business and his pub continues to excel. Whether it is turf throughout the pub during the golf open, 'meet the brewer' evenings, or Mr Rigg's famous horizontal Christmas tree, there is always something special happening at the Taps. A small ex-Hogshead house, it retains the trademark bare boards and brickwork. There are eight beers on offer, always including a cask mild; the house beer, Taps Bitter, is brewed by Titanic. Children are admitted until 7pm. ﾊQ֍⬤⬤A⬤⬤⬤⬤⬤

Mawdesley

Black Bull
Hall Lane, L40 2QY (off B5246)
✪ 12-11 (midnight Fri & Sat); 12-10.30 Sun
☎ (01704) 822202
Black Sheep Best Bitter; Jennings Cumberland Ale; Lees Bitter; Taylor Landlord; guest beers Ⓗ
A pub since 1610, this low-ceilinged stone building boasts some magnificent oak beams. Older village residents know the pub as 'Ell 'Ob' – a reference to a coal-fired cooking range. Certificates on display record the pub's success in Lancashire's Best Kept Village competition, and it has also earned awards for its numerous hanging baskets. In the summer, the well-kept beer garden is popular with both drinkers and diners. ﾊ֍⬤⬤⬤(347)⬤P

Robin Hood

Bluestone Lane, L40 2QY (off B5250)

☼ 11.30-11; 12-10.30 Sun

☎ (01704) 822275 ⊕ robinhoodinn.co.uk

Caledonian Deuchars IPA; Jennings Cumberland Ale; Taylor Landlord; guest beers Ⓗ

Charming, white-painted inn, at the crossroads between the three old villages of Mawdesley, Croston and Eccleston. The 15th-century building was substantially altered in the 19th century. Run by the same family for more than 30 years, it enjoys a reputation for good food. The recently renovated Wilsons restaurant upstairs is open Tuesday to Sunday evenings. Bar food is served all day at the weekend. It still finds room for those who have come for a drink only, offering three guest ales. ৬✿⊕⊒(347)P

Morecambe

Ranch House

Marine Road West, LA4 4DG

☼ 11-11

☎ (01524) 851531

Beer range varies Ⓗ

A large open-plan seaside pub with adjoining amusement arcade, the Ranch House was built in 1930 as part of the 'Frontierland' amusement park. It still features the Wild West theme in its façade. Situated near major public transport links and close to the beach, it is popular with locals, day trippers and holiday-makers alike. Four ever-changing beers are available. ৬✿&⊈≢⊒♣

Smugglers Den

56 Poulton Road, LA4 5HB

☼ 12-midnight (11.30 Sun)

☎ (01524) 421684 ⊕ thesmugglersden.com

Beer range varies Ⓗ

At the heart of the old fishing village of Poulton, the Smugglers Den is the oldest pub in Morecambe, however the current name and decor date from 1960. Maritime memorabilia adorn the walls, ceiling and the space above the huge copper-canopied fireplace. A good all-round locals' pub, strangers are also made to feel at home, despite rumours of a ghost. Cask marque accredited, the pub offers a discount to card-carrying CAMRA members. ₩Q✿⊕⊈≢⊒♣●P'-

Ormskirk

Yew Tree

Grimshaw Lane, L39 1PD (off A59)

☼ 11.30-3, 6-11; 12-11 Sat; 12-4, 7-10.30 Sun

☎ (01695) 572261

Beer range varies Ⓗ

The Yew Tree epitomises the essential community pub. Serving a housing estate on the outskirts of Ormskirk, it has never wavered from its purpose of providing a comfortable meeting place with top quality beers, which usually include selections from Cains and Robinson's breweries. A regular in the Guide, the Yew Tree has been a local CAMRA Pub of the Year. Q✿⊕�⅄&⊒♣P

Parbold

Windmill

3 Mill Lane, WN8 7NW (off A5209 Wigan-Ormskirk road)

☼ 12-3, 5.30-11; 12-8.30 Sun

☎ (01257) 462935

Tetley Bitter; Wells Bombardier Ⓗ

Close to the village centre, next to an old windmill, the pub was built on a hill and access is via a set of stone steps. The main part of the building dates back to 1794, when it was used as a grain store. The multi-roomed interior is mock-Tudor, decorated with brass ornaments. Look out for the original 'Mousey' Thompson pew ends in the lounge. A warm welcome is extended to drinkers, diners, bargees and walkers. Q৬✿⊕≢⊒P'-

Pendleton

Swan With Two Necks

Main Street, BB7 1PT (just off A59)

☼ 12-3 (not Mon), 7 (6 Fri)-11; 12-2.30, 6-11 Sat; 12-10.30 Sun

☎ (01200) 423112

Beer range varies Ⓗ

Run by two CAMRA members, the Swan is one of the best real ale pubs in the Ribble Valley, handy for walkers and cyclists in this superb area of countryside. There are usually three to four beers on sale, one often from Phoenix. Other breweries featuring frequently include Copper Dragon, Tom Wood or Dark Star. Details of beers are written on a chalkboard behind the bar. Food is good value for money. Look out for the teapot collection and the white cat. ₩✿⊕P

Penwortham

Black Bull

83 Pope Lane, PR1 9BA

☼ 11-11 (11.30 Fri); 12-10.30 Sun

☎ (01772) 752953

Greenalls Bitter; Theakston Mild Ale, Best Bitter; guest beers Ⓗ

Attractive, cottage-style pub that has managed to retain a village pub atmosphere despite its location in a well-populated area. On entering, a narrow passageway leads through to a central bar, serving a number of drinking areas. An ex-Greenalls tied house, this pub has continued to serve a real mild, and is now a rare outlet for Greenalls Bitter. At least two guest beers are always available. ⊈⊒♣P

Preston

Bitter Suite

53 Fylde Road, PR1 2XQ

☼ 12-3, 6-11 (midnight Fri); 12-midnight Sat; 12-11 Sun

☎ (01772) 827007 ⊕ bittersuitepreston.co.uk

Goose Eye Bronte Bitter; guest beers Ⓗ

This single-room bar was converted from a keg-only club less than two years ago, in the hands of a landlady with 17 years of experience at another Guide entry in town. It is completely free of tie and the five guest beers from micro-breweries change almost hourly. Bronte is badged as Bitter Suite. The entrance is at the side of the Mad Ferret bar. Singers' night is Wednesday, and live music is played in the upstairs function room which serves real ale. Although surrounded by university buildings, it is not primarily a student bar. ⊛◁🖳P⌐

Finney's Sports Bar

1 East View, Deepdale Road, PR1 5AS
🕐 2-midnight; 12-midnight Sat & Sun
☎ (01772) 250490
Thwaites Original; guest beers Ⓗ
Sports-themed pub near the prison, with multiple TV screens showing different sporting channels. Over 70 sports shirts adorn the walls; look for the piece of Preston North End's plastic pitch. Two guest beers from small breweries are usually stocked. Tables outside at the front of the pub attract summer drinkers, and karaoke is popular on Friday. No track suits are permitted on Friday or Saturday nights. On match days, only PNE fans, CAMRA members and holders of this Guide are admitted. ⊛🖳♣⌐

Fox & Grapes

15 Fox Street, PR1 2AB (off Fishergate near Lloyds bank)
🕐 12-11 (midnight Fri & Sat); 12-10.30 Sun
☎ (01772) 561149
Beer range varies Ⓗ
The Fox & Grapes is a small, friendly and deservedly popular oasis near the bustling shopping centre. Six handpumps dispense a changing range of ales and the occasional cider. An impressive collection of beer mats adorns the walls and bar ceiling. Also on display are motorcycle memorabilia together with framed articles on old Preston pubs, many now long gone. The pub hosts monthly comedy nights and occasional live music; chess is available for those who enjoy quieter persuits. ≠🖳♣

Market Tavern

33-35 Market Street, PR1 2ES
🕐 10.30-9 (11 Thu; midnight Fri & Sat); 12-9 Sun
☎ (01772) 254425
Beer range varies Ⓗ
Popular city centre local overlooking the Victorian covered outdoor market. Four handpumps serve an ever-changing range of guest beers, usually from micros all over the UK. A superb selection of imported bottled beers is also on offer, plus German weisse and French blonde on draught. Outside seating is available in summer. There is no juke box, and the TV only shows rare live events. Otherwise conversation dominates this former local CAMRA Pub of the Year. No food is served, but you are welcome to bring your own. ⊛≠🖳

New Britannia

6 Heatley Street, PR1 2XB
🕐 11-11 (midnight Wed, Fri & Sat); 12-11 Sun
☎ (01772) 253424
Goose Eye Bronte Bitter; Boddingtons Bitter; guest beers Ⓗ
Single-bar city centre pub attracting real ale enthusiasts from far and wide with the quality and choice of its beers. Four guest ales, usually from micros or small independents, plus either Castle Eden Ale or Marston's Pedigree are

usually on offer. The cider range varies. Tasty home-cooked meals are served at lunchtime (not Sat), representing good value. Live music is staged on Wednesday evening, and there are occasional beer festivals. The pub can get very crowded but the service is swift. There is a small patio for smokers. ◁≠♣🌑⌐

Old Black Bull

35 Friargate, PR1 2AT
🕐 10.30-11 (midnight Fri & Sat); 12-10.30 Sun
☎ (01772) 823397
Boddingtons Bitter; Cains Traditional Bitter; guest beers Ⓗ
Mock-Tudor fronted city centre pub. A small front vault, a main bar with distinctive black and white floor tiles, two comfortable lounge areas and a pool table combine to make this a popular venue. An electronic retractable roof covers the patio to the rear. Live music is played on Saturday evening, and Sky Sports is screened. Up to seven guest beers are usually sourced from micros or small independents. Twice winner of local CAMRA Pub of the Year, it also serves a good range of meals at competitive prices. ⊛◁🖳≠🖳♣⌐

Old Vic

78 Fishergate, PR1 2UH
🕐 11.30 (12 Sun)-midnight
☎ (01772) 254690
Caledonian Deuchars IPA; Courage Directors; Marston's Pedigree; Theakston Best Bitter; guest beers Ⓗ
Situated opposite the railway station, the Old Vic attracts a mixed crowd. The handpumps are to the right on the bar as you enter, usually dispensing at least six cask ales, featuring north-west micros on at least one pump. Big screens show sports events, and a large pool table and pinball keep customers amused. The pub hosts a keen darts team and a popular quiz night on Sunday. Meals are served 12-5pm. The car park at the rear is available weekends and evenings. The pub is due for refurbishment in 2007 to create an area for smokers. ⊛◁≠🖳♣P⌐

Olde Dog & Partridge

44 Friargate, PR1 2AT
🕐 11-11.30 (12.30am Fri & Sat); 12-11.30 Sun
☎ (01772) 252217
Fuller's London Pride; Taylor Landlord; Tetley Dark Mild; guest beers Ⓗ
Renowned rock music venue with an ever-increasing reputation for real ale. Busy most nights, it features a quiz on Thursday, open mike on Monday, Students' Union Rock Society on Tuesday/Wednesday and a long-serving DJ on Sunday. Superb value meals are served at lunchtime (not Sun). Decorated with a military theme, it has a much-admired large print of a long-gone Preston pub, the Port Admiral. A Punch Taverns house, it excels with its range of guest ales. If you fail to say 'please', however, you may not be served – you have been warned! ⊛◁≠🖳♣⌐

Waterfront

Navigation Way, PR2 2YP (on Preston Marina)
🕐 9-11 (12.30am Thu; 1am Fri & Sat)
☎ (01772) 721108

Boddingtons Bitter; Taylor Landlord; guest
beers Ⓗ
Popular pub, situated close to the steam
railway. It serves good value, home-cooked
meals until 9pm (8pm Sun), including freshly
made pizzas and a Sunday carvery. The garden
overlooks the Marina and gets busy in
summer, especially during the Riversway
Festival. Thursday is quiz night and TV sports
fans are well catered for. Two guest beers
come from Fuller's, Black Sheep and other
regionals. ⚘◑♿▤(75, 88c)P

Rawtenstall

Craven Heifer
246 Burnley Road, BB4 8LA (on A682, ½ mile
from town centre)
🕒 6 (11 Sat)-11; 12-11 Sun
☎ (01706) 214757
**Moorhouses Black Cat, Premier, Pride of Pendle,
Blond Witch, Pendle Witches Brew; guest
beers** Ⓗ
This is Moorhouse's only tied pub in
Rossendale, offering the opportunity to
sample the brewery's full range of ales. The
comfortable lounge extends across the river,
and the bar area has a large TV showing sports
events. ▤▤(X43, X44)♣

St Anne's-on-the-Sea

Trawl Boat
36-38 Wood Street, FY8 1QL
🕒 9-midnight (1am Fri & Sat)
☎ (01253) 783080
**Courage Directors; Greene King Abbot; Marston's
Pedigree** Ⓗ
Smart and spacious Wetherspoon conversion
featuring an attractive patio drinking area at
the front. Light and airy by day, it attracts a
mixed clientele; by night it becomes busier
and can get lively at weekends. Families are
welcome until 9pm – play facilities are
provided for younger children. Guest ales
regularly include a cask mild.
▲Q⚘◑♿⇌▤●⌐

Salterforth

Anchor Inn
Salterforth Lane, BB18 5TT (200m from main road,
follow brown signs)
🕒 12-11
☎ (01282) 813186
**Caledonian Deuchars IPA; Courage Directors;
John Smith's Bitter; guest beers** Ⓗ
Old, traditional pub on the banks of the Leeds-
Liverpool Canal – follow the brown tourist
signs from the main road and bus stop in
Salterforth. If the pub is not busy, ask for a tour
of the cellar where you can admire the
stalactites. Food is served at all times, and
there is a separate games room. The spacious
garden is ideal for families and has plenty of
seating. ▲⛵⚘

Samlesbury

New Hall Tavern
Cuerdale Lane, PR5 0XA (at B6230 jct)
🕒 12-11 (midnight Thu-Sat); 12-10.30 Sun

☎ (01772) 877217
Shepherd Neame Spitfire; guest beers Ⓗ
Making a welcome return to the Guide after a
year's absence, following a change of
licencee, this pub is at a rural crossroads near
to InBev's 'mega-keggery'. It is an attractive
pub with a large car park and a heated outside
drinking area to the rear. Inside, the bar has a
single room with areas separated off for
dining. The excellent range of up to four guest
beers complements the good home-cooked
food, often prepared with local ingredients.
▲⚘◑♿♣♠P⌐

Silverdale

Woodlands
Woodlands Drive, LA5 0RU
🕒 7-11; 12-11.30 Sat & Sun
☎ (01524) 701655
Beer range varies Ⓗ
Formerly a large country house and set into the
hillside overlooking the village, this pub
boasts spectacular views of Morecambe Bay. A
constantly changing beer menu includes
brews from all over the country. The pub is
situated a good distance from the village
railway station, but a regular shuttle bus
between the station and the village centre
makes it more accessible. ▲Q⛵⚘▤♣●P☗

Staining

Plough
Chain Lane, FY3 0XB (off B5266)
🕒 12-11 (1am Fri & Sat)
☎ (01253) 883585
**Greene King Ruddles Best Bitter; Young's Bitter;
guest beers** Ⓗ
Vibrant village local featuring exposed brick
walls and fake oak beams. Informal music is
played every Tuesday night, a quiz night is
held on Wednesday and karaoke on Friday
night. Good food is served at all times. An
unusual collection of knots and slings
decorates the pub walls, and there is a display
of poachers' snares. It also boasts several
pictures of 19th-century Blackpool.
⛵⚘◑♿▲▤(15)♣P⌐

Tockholes

Royal Arms
Tockholes Road, BB3 0AP OS665215
🕒 12-11 (10.30 Sun); closed Mon
☎ (01254) 705373 ⊕ theroyalarms.co.uk
**Moorhouses Tockholes, Treacle; Three B's
Bobbin's Bitter; guest beers** Ⓗ
This village pub was originally two cottages
that have now been knocked into one, and
comprises four cosy rooms featuring back-to-
back fireplaces with wood fires. Some original
stone walls have been retained, and there are
flagged and wood floors. The nearest pub to
Darwen Tower and Moor, and featuring on
Roddlesworth country walks, it happily caters
for walkers with dogs. It has deservedly won
awards for its service and cuisine, as well as
the beer from local micros. ▲◑P

Tontine

Delph Tavern

Sefton Road, WN5 8JU (off B5206)

✪ 11.30-midnight (1am Fri & Sat); 12-11.30 Sun

☎ (01695) 622239

Beer range varies Ⓗ

Local CAMRA Pub of the Season in autumn 2006, the Delph has a friendly atmosphere and a warm welcome for all. Although opened out it retains a separate vault with a pool table. Good value meals are complemented by a choice of three reasonably-priced guest ales. Children are welcome, except in the vault area. Darts and dominoes teams compete in local leagues.

⑆❀❍❺⇌(Orrell)♣P

University of Lancaster

Graduate Bar

Alexandra Park, LA2 0PF (SW of main campus, signed Alexandra Park)

✪ 7 (6 Fri)-11; 8-11 Sun

☎ (01524) 592824 ⏀ gradbar.co.uk

Beer range varies Ⓗ

Modern student bar, more like a pub than most and, as the name suggests, the clientele is slightly older than at most campus bars. Between two and eight beers are stocked. Hawkshead, Copper Dragon, Acorn and Barngates feature regularly. Do not miss the major beer festival at the end of June.

❀❑♣❦

Up Holland

Old Dog

6 Alma Hill, WN8 0NW (off A557, near parish church)

✪ 5-midnight (1am Fri & Sat); 5-11.30 Sun

☎ (01695) 632487

Banks's Bitter; guest beers Ⓗ

This stone pub has historic connections with the local highwayman George Lyon. Unusually, the pub's four heavily beamed rooms are on different levels, with the rear rooms affording superb views towards the Pennines. Sensitive refurbishment has retained many original features, including etched windows and a small bar area. It only serves cask ales, and the pump clips from many past guest beers are on display. It also possesses a fine collection of ornamental dogs, and has a resident wine-tasting group and quiz team. Q❀❑

Waddington

Waddington Arms

West View, BB7 3HP (on B6478)

✪ 11-midnight (1am Fri & Sat); 11-11 Sun

☎ (01200) 423262

Bowland Sawley Tempted; Moorhouses Premier; Taylor Landlord; Theakston Best Bitter; guest beers Ⓗ

Large stone-flagged pub, right in the centre of the village, very popular with the locals. There are usually five handpumps in action, one ale always from the Bowland Brewery a few miles away. The food is excellent, with a large selection on the specials board. A wood-burning stove dominates one end of the pub, and candles throughout create an intimate atmosphere. Many of the paintings on display are for sale. Bedrooms are comfortable, but the village church clock can be intrusive.

❀⇌❍❍❺P

Walmer Bridge

Walmer Bridge Inn

65 Liverpool Old Road, PR4 5QE

✪ 4 (12 Sat)-midnight; 12-10.30 Sun

☎ (01772) 612296

Robinson's Unicorn; guest beers Ⓗ

Village local, comprising a lower-level vault and a comfortable lounge. Pictures of bygone Walmer Bridge and Longton, including the long-gone Pyes/Wilkins Breweries, are displayed on the walls. The two guest beers come from the pub group list. A local CAMRA award winner, it occasionally serves a cider in summer and a mild as a guest beer. The garden has a play area for children. There are plans for an outside smoking area.

❀❑❑♣❦P

Waterfoot

Jolly Sailor

Booth Road, BB4 9BD (200m off B6238, Burnley road)

✪ 12-midnight (1am Fri & Sat)

☎ (01706) 226340

Caledonian Deuchars IPA; Jennings Cumberland Ale; Taylor Landlord; Tetley Dark Mild; guest beer Ⓗ

Spacious, traditional pub, serving four regular real ales and one guest beer. A friendly local, good conversation is the norm here. Popular with students, it stages live music including jam sessions every two weeks and a weekly quiz. A varied pub food menu is available. It is two miles from the East Lancashire Steam Railway and the M66 motorway to Manchester. ❦❀❍❺❑♣

Westhead

Prince Albert

109 Wigan Road, L40 6HY (on A577) OS438078

✪ 12-midnight (10.30 Sun)

☎ (01695) 573656

Tetley Mild, Bitter; guest beers Ⓗ

The Prince Albert is a well-kept country pub halfway between Ormskirk and Skelmersdale. Inside, it has a small central bar and snug little rooms on three sides, ideal for quiet conversation. Neither refurbishment nor changes of licencee over the years have affected the unpretentious, comfortable feel of the place or the quality of the beer on offer. ❦❀⇌❍❺❆❑♣P

Whalley

Dog Inn

55 King Street, BB7 9SP (on B6246)

✪ 11-11; 12-10.30 Sun

☎ (01254) 823009

Beer range varies Ⓗ

The Dog usually has between four and six beers on dispense at any one time, all at reasonable prices for the Ribble Valley area. They are sourced from across the UK, with recent offerings from breweries such as Titanic, Mordue, Harviestown, Young's, St Austell and Okells. The bar has a pool/games room at one end. Sporting prints and memorabilia line the walls. The picturesque ruins of Whalley Abbey are just a few minutes' walk away. ◖&≠⊟(225)

Whittle-le-Woods

Royal Oak
216 Chorley Old Road, PR6 7NA (off A6)
◷ 3-11 (midnight Fri); 1-midnight Sat; 1-10.30 Sun
☎ (01257) 276485
Black Sheep Best Bitter; Caledonian Deuchars IPA; guest beers ⊞
Small, terraced village local built in 1820 to serve workers and shippers on the adjacent branch of the Leeds-Liverpool Canal extension (now filled in). A regular local CAMRA award winner, it has been in this Guide for more than 30 years. Long and narrow, the interior comprises a small bar/lounge and a games room. Very much a community pub, it caters for a mixed clientele, including TV sports enthusiasts. Note the etched windows from the long-gone Nuttalls Brewery from nearby Blackburn. ▲֎&⊟♣⌐

Wilpshire

Rising Sun
797 Whalley New Road, BB1 9BE (on A666, about ½ mile N of A6119 jct)
◷ 1.30-11.30 (midnight Fri); 12-midnight Sat; 12-11.30 Sun
☎ (01254) 247379
Theakston Best Bitter; guest beers ⊞
Compact, characterful pub, just over two miles north of Blackburn, on the road leading to the Ribble Valley. One real ale is served in each bar and each pump displays the choice of brews. The parlour is a good place for a chat. On the wall are old photos of Blackburn Rovers, while the lounge features pictures of former Blackburn breweries, a piano and old transport scenes. Note the 'Nuttall & Co Double Stout' window at the rear. ▲⊟≠⊟(2, 225)

Wrea Green

Villa
Moss Side Lane, PR4 2PE (¼ mile outside village, on B5259)
◷ 12-11 (midnight Fri & Sat); 12-10.30 Sun
☎ (01772) 684347
Copper Dragon Scotts 1816; Jennings Cumberland Ale; guest beer ⊞
The Villa hotel, with a sweeping drive and imposing frontage, has been sympathetically developed from a former 19th-century gentleman's residence. Visitors can expect a warm welcome from the friendly staff, and enjoy the luxury of the impressive leather sofas in front of the real fire in the oak-panelled area facing the bar. Bar snacks are excellent, and served to the same high standard as the restaurant meals. A jazz night features on some Fridays. ▲֎♿◖&⊟P

In memory of John White

There is a cryptic credit on the contents page for a photo of the Roscoe Head pub in Liverpool. It says simply John White. Behind the name lies an iconic figure in beer writing circles. John, who died tragically aged just 62 in July 2007, was a long-standing and stalwart member of the Grimsby branch of CAMRA, and helped to organise beer festivals in the town. His passion for real ale developed into a love for the beers of Belgium and Germany, too. When he took early retirement from his engineering job in the oil industry, he started to organise trips for fellow beer lovers to Belgium and Germany. From these trips he developed John White Beer Travels with its own website **(www.whitebeertravels.com)**.

The website was a blog before the name was invented. John recorded his travels in meticulous detail. The site became a 'must read' for beer drinkers and writers throughout the world. He was generous with his research and encouraged other writers to make use of it free of charge. He also organised bespoke trips for individual writers, and many of my books and articles in recent years were made possible by John.

He was a good companion, a generous colleague and a stickler for accuracy. He was best known for the regular trips he ran to Bamberg in the Franconia region of Germany, a small city famous for its smoked or 'Rauch' beers. He died of a massive heart attack two days after his home in Grimsby was flooded and he lost many valuable items collected from his trips. He will be missed by a legion of friends. It is hoped his website will be maintained by his family with the support of the British Guild of Beer Writers.

Roger Protz

LEICESTERSHIRE & RUTLAND

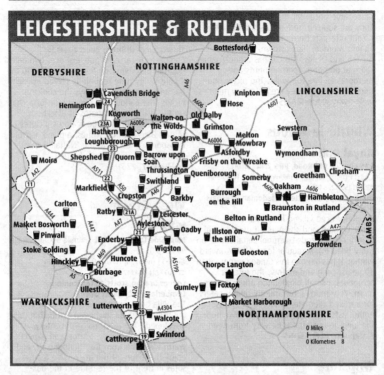

LEICESTERSHIRE
Asfordby

Horseshoes

128 Main Street, LE14 35A
⏰ 12 (11 Tue & Sat)-3, 7-11; 12-3, 7-10.30 Sun
☎ (01644) 813392
Bateman XB; Tetley Bitter; guest beers Ⓗ
Friendly locals' pub in the centre of the village.
This Bateman's house serves three regular real
ales including a mild. Buses from Leicester and
Melton Mowbray stop outside the pub door,
with an hourly service in the evenings and
Sunday. The pub has a garden and a function
room. ⏚🍷❄🏠⏚

Aylestone

Black Horse

65 Narrow Lane, LE2 8NA
⏰ 12-2.30, 5-11; 12-midnight Fri & Sat; 12-11 Sun
☎ (0116) 2832811 ⊕ philspub.co.uk
**Everards Beacon, Sunchaser, Tiger, Original;
guest beers** Ⓗ
The Black Horse is situated in an area with a
village feel, close to fields, the Grand Union
canal and Great Central Way, yet only two
miles from the city centre. This Victorian pub
has three rooms including a comfortable
lounge and a cosy snug. In winter log fires
warm the bars. There is a children's play area
in the large garden. An upstairs function room
is available to hire and skittles may be played.
Occasional beer festivals are held.
Q❄◁⏚🏠♣⏚

Barkby

Brookside

35 Brookside, LE7 3QO (off Barkby Holt Lane)
⏰ 12-2 (not Tue), 5.30-11(midnight Fri & Sat); 12-4,
7-10.30 Sun
☎ (0116) 260 0092
**Jennings Dark Mild, Cumberland Ale; Marston's
Pedigree; guest beer** Ⓗ
Cheery and welcoming pub with the air of a
country local. Two roomed with a traditional
bar and comfy lounge, log fires blaze on cold
winter nights. A restaurant leads from the
lounge (no meals Sat lunch or Sun eve). The
pub has a picturesque setting with a brook at
the front and plenty of ducks. Dogs and horses
are welcome. Guest beers are from the
Marston's list. ⏚❄◁▷⏚P⏚

Barrow upon Soar

Hunting Lodge

38 South Street, LE12 8LZ
⏰ 11.30-11; 12-10.30 Sun
☎ (01509) 412337
⊕ thehuntinglodgebarrowonsoar.co.uk
**Greene King Old Speckled Hen; Marston's
Pedigree; Taylor Landlord; guest beer** Ⓗ
Spacious bar with contemporary design. There
are large comfortable leather chairs to relax
in, wooden floors and open log fires. The
Lodge also has a restaurant offering good
home-cooked food and accommodation. Each
of the six bedrooms has a unique design,
ranging from ethnic to the more traditional.
The large garden is delightful in summer.
⏚❄🛏◁🅿&♿⏚≈P

Bottesford

Red Lion

5 Grantham Road, NG13 0DF
☼ 12-midnight; 11-1am Fri & Sat
☎ (01949) 842218
Greene King H&H Bitter, Abbot; guest beers Ⓗ
One of three excellent pubs in a village well served by public transport. The Red Lion has a small bar with dartboard and real fire, and a comfortable lounge leading to the dining area. A full menu featuring local produce is offered at lunchtime (not Mon) and evenings (not Sun). This popular pub sits neatly in the shadow of the church, notable for having the tallest spire of any village church in England.
ᴹQ❀◑ ⑤↧≠♣P

Burbage

Anchor

63 Church Street, LE10 2DA
☼ 12-11 (midnight Fri; 11.30 Sat); 12-11 Sun
☎ (01455) 636107
Marston's Burton Bitter, Pedigree; guest beers Ⓗ
Typical two-room local in the centre of the village – no food, no juke box, no pool. One or two guest beers come from the Marston's range. There is a dartboard and bar billiards table. Dogs are welcome, children tolerated. Note the centre pillar adorned with photographs of locals under the heading, 'Where's your Anchor lighter been?'
Q❀&⑤♣╘

Carlton

Gate Hangs Well

Barton Road, CV13 0DB
☼ 12-3, 6-11(midnight Fri & Sat); 7-10.30 Sun
☎ (01455) 291845
Draught Bass; Greene King Abbot; Marston's Bitter, Pedigree Ⓗ
Welcoming, traditional village inn near Market Bosworth, convenient for Bosworth battlefield and the preserved railway line. Recently refurbished seating areas are served by a central bar. Sandwiches and rolls are made to order. Singers provide entertainment on Wednesday and Saturday evenings. Popular with walkers and cyclists, there is a pleasant garden for the summer and a conservatory where families and children are welcome until mid-evening. A consistently good free house.
ᴹQ❀⑤♣P

Cavendish Bridge

Old Crown

DE72 2HL
☼ 11-midnight (1am Fri & Sat); 12-midnight Sun
☎ (01332) 792392
Jennings Cocker Hoop; Marston's Pedigree, Old Empire; guest beers Ⓗ
Coaching inn dating from the 17th century with the original oak-beamed ceiling displaying an extensive collection of old jugs. The walls are covered with pub mirrors, brewery signs and railway memorabilia which even extend into the toilets. The cosy open-plan interior is divided into two areas; a large inglenook is on the right. ᴹ❀╼◑⑤P╘

Cropston

Bradgate Arms

15 Station Road, LE7 7HG
☼ 11.30-11; 12-10.30 Sun
☎ (0116) 234 0336
Banks's Bitter; Marston's Pedigree Ⓗ
Comfortable village pub, popular with locals and tourists. Though extended to the rear in the early 1990s it retains many original features. Five drinking areas and a dining room are on two levels. Food is served all day. Darts and long alley skittles are played. The pub is handy for the Great Central Railway (Rothley) and Bradgate Country Park.
ᴥ❀◑⑤♣P

Enderby

New Inn

51 High Street, LE19 4AG
☼ 12-2.30 (3 Sat; not Mon), 7 (5.30 Fri)-11; 12-3, 7-10.30 Sun
☎ (0116) 286 3126
Everards Beacon, Tiger, Original, seasonal beers; guest beers Ⓗ
Everards' first tied house, dating from 1549, this friendly, thatched village local is tucked away at the top of High Street. It has three rooms with a central servery, plus outdoor drinking areas. Long alley skittles and a snooker room are to the rear. The pub is well know locally for the quality of its beer and you will often find Everards' brewery staff drinking here. Plentiful and imaginative lunches are served. ᴹQ❀◑⑤♣P╘

Foxton

Foxton Locks Inn

Bottom Lock, Gumley Road, LE16 7RA
☼ 11-11
☎ (0116) 279 1515
Caledonian Deuchars IPA; Courage Directors; Greene King Old Speckled Hen; Theakston Best Bitter, Old Peculier; guest beer Ⓗ
This refurbished canalside inn sits at the foot of Foxton Locks, a major attraction on the Grand Union Canal. The canal director's office, once upstairs, has been recreated at the rear of the pub, complete with a collection of original share certificates on display. Outdoor seating runs down to the canal bank where boats may be moored. Families are welcome inside the pub. Blankets are available for outdoor drinkers. ᴥ❀◑&▲♣P╘

Frisby on the Wreake

Bell Inn

2 Main Street, LE14 2NJ

✪ 12-2.30 (not Wed), 6 (7 Sat)-11; 12-3, 7-10.30 (not winter) Sun

☎ (01644) 434237

Beer range varies Ⓗ

Welcoming village local dating back to 1759, situated in a small village to the south of the river Wreake. The comfortable lounge bar features oak beams, flagstone floors and an open fire. There is a family room and a restaurant (no evening meals Sun). Changing guest ales often come from far afield. An hourly weekday daytime bus from Melton Mowbray and Leicester stops in the village. ⚲Q☎❀◑⊟P

Glooston

Old Barn

Andrews Lane, Main Street, LE16 7ST

✪ 12-3, 6-11.30; 12-11 Sun

☎ (01858) 545215

Greene King IPA, Abbot; guest beers Ⓗ

A coaching inn dating from the 16th century, this out-of-the-way pub is now divided in two. The warm and welcoming bar at the back is complemented by the restaurant, decorated in contemporary style and offering world fusion cuisine prepared under the supervision of a chef trained in Australia. Meals are also served in the bar. Guest ales can be found in summer. ⚲❀◑P⅃

Grimston

Black Horse

Main Street, LE14 3BZ

✪ 12-3, 6-11; 2-6 Sun

☎ (01644) 812358

Adnams Bitter; Belvoir Star Mild; Marston's Pedigree; guest beer Ⓗ

Popular pub overlooking the village green, very busy at lunchtimes. It has a large open-plan bar on two levels. Real cider usually replaces one beer in summer. A wide range of food is available (no eve meals Sun). It has a petanque court and is home to several local teams. The bus from Melton Mowbray stops outside the pub. ⚲Q❀◑⊟(23)♣♠⅃

Gumley

Bell Inn

2 Main Street, LE16 7RU

✪ 11-3, 6-11; 12-3 (closed eve) Sun

☎ (0116) 279 2476

Bateman XB; Greene King IPA; Taylor Landlord; guest beers Ⓗ

Early 19th-century free house, popular with locals as well a commuting urban clientele. Cricketing memorabilia adorns the entrance hall and fox hunting scenes decorate the walls of the bar and dining room. The beamed interior has an L-shaped bar and dining room serving an extensive menu. The pub has a large patio garden but children and dogs are not permitted here. ⚲Q❀◑♣♠⅃

Hathern

Dew Drop

49 Loughborough Road, LE12 5HY

✪ 12-3, 6-midnight (7-1am Fri-Sun)

☎ (01509) 842438

Greene King H&H Mild, H&H Bitter, seasonal beers Ⓗ

Traditional two room local with a large bar and comfortable small lounge with real fires. Don't miss a visit to the totally unspoilt toilets with their tiled walls and original features. A large range of malt whiskies is kept. Cobs are available at lunchtimes. ⚲Q❀❀⊟⊟♣P

Hemington

Jolly Sailor

Main Street, DE74 2RB

✪ 11.30-2.30, 4.30-11; 11-11 Sat; 12-10.30 Sun

☎ (01332) 810448

Draught Bass; Greene King Abbot; Kelham Island Gold; guest beers Ⓗ

This 17th-century building is thought to have originally been a weaver's cottage. A pub since the 19th century, it retains many original features including old timbers, open fires and beamed ceiling – a convenient place to hang the collection of blow lamps and beer mugs. The restaurant is also available for functions and meetings. Cider on gravity is available. Evening meals are served Friday and Saturday, no food Sunday. It was voted Loughborough and North Leicestershire CAMRA Pub of the Year 2006 and 2007. ⚲Q❀◑&♣♠P

Hinckley

Ashby Road Sports Club

Hangmans Lane, LE10 30A

✪ 7 (12 Sat, 5 Fri)-11; 12-10.30 Sun

☎ (01455) 615159

Worthington Bitter; guest beers Ⓗ

CAMRA members are always most welcome at this private sports and social club. The club house was built in 1957 in six acres of grounds, with a good assortment of facilities for various team activities. Separate function and meeting rooms are available. A family-friendly bar area hosts traditional pub games. Guest beers change weekly, available from Thursday evening. Caravan rallies are occasionally held. ☎❀&▲⊟♣P

New Plough Inn

24 Leicester Road, Hinckley, LE10 1LS

✪ 12-2.30 Sat only, 5-11; 12-2.30, 6-10.30 Sun

☎ (01455) 615037

Marston's Burton Bitter, Pedigree Ⓗ

Built in 1900, this traditional roadside pub has a comfortable lounge with original wooden settles. The walls are adorned with local rugby memorabilia and the exterior features shields of local rugby clubs. Table skittles is played and the pub runs its own team. There is an outdoor area for drinking in summer. Dogs are welcome. ❀♣

Hose

Black Horse

21 Bolton Lane, LE14 4JE

✪ 12-2 Fri & Sat only, 7-midnight; 12-4, 7-10.30 Sun
☎ (01949) 860336

Adnams Bitter; Castle Rock Harvest Pale; Fuller's London Pride; guest beers ⊞

Traditional pub with a lounge featuring wooden beams and a brass-ornamented brick fireplace. Blackboard menus for food and drink surround the wooden corner bar. The unspoilt public bar, decorated with pictures and mirrors, has a tiled floor, wooden furniture and a brick fireplace. The rustic restaurant serves good food using local produce (eve meals Tue-Sat). ᗰQ✿❶①⊟ᕼ♣P

Huncote

Red Lion
Main Street, LE9 3AU
✪ 12-2.30 (not Mon or Sat), 5 (4 Sat)-11; 12-10.30 Sun
☎ (0116) 286 2233 ⊕ red-lion.biz

Everards Beacon, Tiger; guest beers ⊞

Built in 1892, the Red Lion is a friendly local with a warm welcome. With beamed ceilings throughout, it has a cosy lounge with a wooden fireplace and log fire. The bar has an adjoining dining area and a pool room. The sizeable garden has picnic tables and a children's play area. The pub serves good value, home-cooked lunches. Skittles can be played by prior arrangement. ᗰ✿❶⊟♣P⅄

Illston on the Hill

Fox & Goose
Main Street, LE7 9EG
✪ 12-2 (not Mon or Tue), 5.30 (7 Mon)-11; 12-3, 7-11 Sun
☎ (0116) 259 6430

Everards Beacon, Tiger, Original; guest beers ⊞

Cosy, unspoilt pub with a timeless feel, tucked away in the village and well worth seeking out. A fascinating collection of local mementos and hunting memorabilia is on display, including original Mclaughlan cartoons. Popular events include conkers and onion growing championships and a fundraising auction for local charities. ᗰQ✿❶⊟♣

Kegworth

Red Lion
24 High Street, DE74 2DA
✪ 11.30-11; 12-10.30 Sun
☎ (01509) 672466

Adnams Bitter; Banks's Original; Courage Directors; Greene King Abbot; guest beers ⊞

Georgian building standing on the 19th-century route of the London to Glasgow road (A6). It has three small bars and a restaurant (eve meals Mon-Fri). Various flavoured Polish and Ukrainian vodkas and a good selection of malt whiskies as well as up to four guest beers are available. There is a skittle alley and petanque courts. Outside there is a large secure children's play area. Local CAMRA Pub of the Year 2005.
ᗰQ✿❶①⊟⊟(TB5)♣♠P⅄

Knipton

Manners Arms
Croxton Road, Knipton, NG32 1RH

✪ 11-11; 12-10.30 Sun
☎ (01476) 879222 ⊕ mannersarms.com

Belvoir Beaver Bitter; guest beers ⊞

Impressive Georgian hunting lodge beautifully renovated by the Duke and Duchess of Rutland, with furniture and prints taken from Belvoir Castle. The lounge and bar room share one long bar, divided by a wall housing a huge open fireplace. Large bookshelves surround comfortable seating in the lounge. Light bar dishes are available plus a wide range of interesting food made with local produce in the spacious restaurant. There is a live music programme on Thursday evening.
ᗰQ✿❶①ᕼP

Leicester

Ale Wagon
27 Rutland Street, LE1 1RE
✪ 11-11, 12-3; 7-10.30 Sun
☎ (0116) 262 3330 ⊕ alewagon.co.uk

Hoskins Hob Best Mild, Brigadier, Bitter, EXS; guest beers ⊞

Run by the Hoskins family, this city-centre pub, with 1930s interior including an original oak staircase, has two rooms with tiled and parquet floors and a central bar. There is always a selection of Hoskins Brothers ales and guests available. The pub is popular with visiting rugby fans and real ale drinkers. Local CAMRA Pub of the Year 2004. ᗰ⊟≠⊟♣

Barley Mow
149 Granby Street, LE1 6FE
✪ 11-11; 12-6 Sun
☎ (0116) 254 4663

Everards Beacon, Sunchaser, Tiger, Original, Guest beers ⊞

Spacious open-plan pub with one long bar and an open staircase up to a coffee loft which serves excellent breakfasts. It has all the atmosphere of a country pub with the convenience of the city centre and offers a warm welcome to regulars and visitors alike. Popular on football and rugby match days when the pub can be quite busy, it is reputed to be haunted, but the only spirits you will see are in the optics. ✿❶≠⊟♣

Black Horse
1 Foxon Street, LE3 5LT
✪ 3-11 (midnight Tue-Fri); 12-midnight Sat; 7-midnight Sun
☎ (0116) 254 0030

Everards Beacon, Tiger; guest beers ⊞

Small, cosy, street corner pub, the only traditional pub left on Braunstone Gate, now surrounded by wine and café bars. With all the character of a lively local, it has two rooms and a central servery. Up to five guest beers from the Everards Old English Ale Club are available as well as many malt whiskies and fruit wines. There is a general knowledge quiz on Wednesday and Sunday, the longest-running in Leicester. Acoustic music sessions are held on Monday, Tuesday and Thursday evening. ⊟⊟♠

Criterion
44 Millstone Lane, LE1 5JN
✪ 12-11; 12-10.30 Sun
☎ (0116) 262 5418

Oakham JHB; Bishops Farewell; guest beers Ⓗ
Two room, 1960s city-centre pub, formerly an
M&B house, then Hardys & Hansons. The walls
are adorned with international breweriana
and real ale pump clips. Guest ales come from
micro and regional breweries. Four real ale
festivals a year add another dozen beers; a
traditional cider festival is held in summer.
Live music plays on Saturday and Thursday.
Traditional pub food is served Sunday and
Monday, Italian-style home-baked pizza
Tuesday to Saturday. The pub is busy on
football and rugby home matches – away
supporters are welcome at Leicester CAMRA
Pub of the Year 2007. ❀◑▶♣♠🏠

Globe

43 Silver Street, LE1 5EU
🕐 11-11 (1am Fri); 12-10.30 Sun
☎ (0116) 262 9819
**Everards Beacon, Tiger, Original, seasonal beers;
guest beers Ⓗ**
Thirty years ago this city-centre pub was
hailed as Everards' first pub to return to a full
real ale range after seven years as keg only.
Major renovations in 2000 moved the beer to
the centre of the pub interior. There is a snug
and gas lighting throughout (electric too). An
upstairs room is available for meetings.
Leicester CAMRA held its first meeting here in
1974 as well as its 25th anniversary bash. A
friendly welcome awaits all. ◑🍴&≠🚃

Leicester Gateway

52 Gateway Street, LE2 7DP
🕐 12-11 (10.30 Sun)
☎ (0116) 255 7319
**Castle Rock Harvest Pale; Everards Tiger; guest
beers Ⓗ**
A warm welcome greets visitors to this
friendly free house in a converted hosiery
factory. Six real ales are usually available with
up to nine at busy times. Imported bottled
beers are also stocked. Home-made food is
served all day and the Sunday lunchtime
carvery is always popular. Quiz night is
Sunday. Close to both Leicester City football
and Tigers' rugby grounds, the pub is busy on
match days. ◑▶🚃♣♠

Out of the Vaults

24 King Street, LE1 6RL
🕐 12-11 (10.30 Sun) ● outofthevaults.com
**Millstone Tiger Rut; Oakham Bishops Farewell;
guest beers Ⓗ**
Friendly city-centre free house showcasing
real ales from micro-breweries. Regular beer
festivals keep an eclectic mix of regulars and
visitors happy. Close to the grounds, the pub is
popular with rugby and football enthusiasts;
away supporters are especially welcome. A
regular haunt of Leicester Morris dancers,
occasional live music plays on Saturday night
as well as weekly Sunday afternoon acoustic
sessions. Food is available most lunchtimes.
Traditional pub games are available from the
bar. ≠🚃

Shakespeare's Head

Southgates, LE1 5SH
🕐 12-midnight (1am Fri & Sat); 12-11 Sun
☎ (0116) 262 4378
Oakwell Old Tom Mild, Barnsley Bitter Ⓗ

This two-roomed local was built alongside the
underpass in the 1960s and has changed little
since then. It retains all the charm of a typical
town pub of its era. Two large glass doors lead
to an off-sales area with a bar to the left and
lounge to the right. Formerly a Shipstones
pub, it now sells Oakwell beers at reasonable
prices. A selection of hot food is served daily –
jacket potatoes, baguettes, etc – and Sunday
lunch is popular. ◑🍴&🚃♣

Swan & Rushes

19 Infirmary Square, LE1 5WR
🕐 12-2.45, 5-11 (midnight Thu); 12-midnight Fri & Sat;
12-11.30 Sun
☎ (0116) 233 9167 ● swanandrushes.co.uk
**Bateman XB, XXXB; Oakham JHB; Bishops
Farewell, seasonal beers; guest beers Ⓗ**
Comfortable, triangular, two-roomed pub in
the city centre with a relaxed atmosphere,
breweriana and framed photos on the wall. Up
to nine real ales (no nationals) are available, or
you can choose from the bottled beer menu
featuring more than 100 international classics
(including loads of lambics). Several food-
linked beer festivals are held each year, plus a
cider and cheese event. The Thursday night
quiz and Saturday night live blues gigs are
well supported. Good value home-cooked
food is served (Wed-Sun lunch, Wed, Fri and
Sat eves). ❀◑🍴🚃♣♠💺—🏠

Tudor

100 Tudor Road, LE3 5HT
🕐 12-2.30, 5-11; 11-11 Thu; 11-11.30 Fri & Sat;
12-10.30 Sun
☎ (0116) 262 0087
Everards Beacon, Tiger Ⓗ
Friendly community pub situated on the
corner of a terraced area with a Victorian
exterior. Inside are two rooms – bar and
lounge. A function room upstairs has table
skittles. Darts and pool are played in the bar.
There is a covered, heated area outside for
smokers. 🚃♣💺—

Loughborough

Albion Inn

Canal Bank, LE11 1QA
🕐 11-3 (4 Sat), 6-11; 12-3, 7-10.30 Sun
☎ (01509) 213952
Archers Best Bitter; Brains Dark; guest beers Ⓗ
This canalside pub was built in the late 18th
century at the same time as the
Loughborough Canal. It has a bar, darts room
and quiet lounge. Outside there is a patio with
an aviary. The house beer, Albion Special, is
brewed specially for the pub by the local
Wicked Hathern Brewery. Care should be
taken if driving to the pub along the narrow
tow path. ♨Q❀◑≠♣P

Plough Inn

28 Thorpe Acre Road, LE11 4LF
🕐 12-11 (midnight Fri & Sat)
☎ (01509) 214101
**Draught Bass; Bateman XB; M&B Mild; guest
beers Ⓗ**
Probably an early 19th-century building, part
of the original Thorpe Acre village, now
surrounded by modern houses. The unusual
look of the pub is due to a change in road

layout which has resulted in the back of the pub adjoining the road. To the front of the pub there are gardens and a children's play area. The pub is split level with the bar and front entrance lower than the lounge, which is accessed via steps leading from the road. There is live entertainment most weekends. The only food available are cobs.
🏨❀⬛️❹➕👄P💺

Swan in the Rushes

21 The Rushes, LE11 5BE
✪ 11-11 (midnight Fri & Sat); 12-10.30 Sun
☎ (01509) 217014 ⊕ tynemill.co.uk
Adnams Bitter; Archers Golden; Castle Rock Rushes Gold, Harvest Pale; guest beers ℍ
Traditional three room Tynemill pub comprising two quiet, comfortable rooms and the Charnwood Vaults – a lively room with a juke box and wooden bench seating. There is a constantly changing range of up to six guest beers, always including a mild, as well as real cider and perry, a limited range of continental bottled and draught beers and a good range of malt whiskies and country wines. Upstairs there is a skittle alley/function room which hosts live music and twice yearly beer festivals. 🏨Q➰❀❹⬦⬛️❹⬥🚆➕👄P💺

Tap & Mallet

36 Nottingham Road, LE11 1EU
✪ 5-11; 11.30-11 Sat; 12-10.30 Sun
☎ (01509) 210028
Church End Gravediggers; Courage Best Bitter; guest beers ℍ
Genuine free house conveniently situated on a direct route from the railway station to the town centre. The five guest ales are from micro-breweries, often from the east or north-east midlands, and usually beers not commonly see in the Loughborough area. The pub has a single room split into two drinking areas, one with a pool table. The lounge can be partitioned off for private functions. Outside there is a secluded walled garden with children's play equipment and a pets' corner. Cobs are available all day.
🏨❀🚆⬛️➕👄

White Horse

32 Bedford Street, LE11 2DS
✪ 12-midnight (11 Sun)
☎ (01509) 269247
Bateman XXXB; White Horse Bitter; guest beers ℍ
Reopened with its original name following a protracted refurbishment, this pub has become a firm favourite with a wide range of customers of all ages. It offers a varying range of Bateman and White Horse beers, continental beers and whiskies. The contemporary style is complemented by the virtual fish tank over the fireplace. At the rear is a noodle bar serving Chinese and Vietnamese dishes – ideal fast food to complement the beer. 🏨⬦❶🚆⬛️👄

Lutterworth

Fox Inn

34 Rugby Road, LE17 4BN (off M1 jct 20 on A426 or M6 jct 1)
✪ 12-3,5-11; 12-11 Sat; 12-3, 7-10.30 Sun

☎ (01455) 552677
Adnams Bitter; Draught Bass; Taylor Landlord; guest beers ℍ
Warm and welcoming pub with an L-shaped, open-plan interior. Divided into two, one area is furnished in traditional pub style, the other is more contemporary with soft furnishings. Both areas have real log fires. The pub is richly adorned with motor racing and rallying memorabilia and rugby footballs. RAF and other aircraft photographs decorate the walls. The car park is small but there is plenty of local parking. A good menu plus a specials board are available daily (eve meals Sun-Thu).
🏨❀❶P

Unicorn Inn

27 Church Street, LE17 4AE (on one way system near church)
✪ 10.30-11 (midnight Sat); 12-11.30 Sun
☎ (01455) 552486
Draught Bass; Greene King IPA; M&B Brew XI; Robinson's Unicorn ℍ
Busy and friendly, traditional town-centre corner pub run by the same landlord for 25 years. The large public bar is well supported by local teams playing darts and skittles. Football and rugby matches are shown on large screen TVs. The quieter lounge has its own bar decorated with many photographs of old Lutterworth. Inexpensive lunchtime snacks and meals are served throughout the week.
🏨❀🛏️❶⬛️➕P

Market Bosworth

Old Red Lion Hotel

1 Park Street, CV13 0LL
✪ 11 (10 Wed)-2.30, 5.30-11; 10-11.30 Fri & Sat; 11-10.30 Sun
☎ (01455) 291713
⊕ yeolderedlionmarketbosworth.com
Banks's Bitter; Camerons Bitter; Greene King Abbot; Marston's Pedigree; Theakston Old Peculier; guest beers ℍ
Popular with all ages, this hotel is situated near the old Market Square. It has a large beamed bar and dining area with an open fire in winter. The range of beers includes two guests. A varied menu offers good food at sensible prices (no eve meals Sun or Mon). Accommodation includes rooms with four-poster beds. 🏨Q❀🛏️❶⬛️➕P

Market Harborough

Cherry Tree

Church Walk, Kettering Road, Little Bowden, LE16 8AE
✪ 12.30-2.30, 5.30-11; 12-11.30 Fri & Sat; 12-11 Sun
☎ (01858) 463525
Everards Beacon, Sunchaser, Tiger, Original; guest beers ℍ
Although this pub is situated in Little Bowden it is very much part of the Market Harborough community. A spacious building, with low beams and a thatched roof, drinkers and diners can choose from many alcoves and seating areas. A beer festival is held over the August bank holiday. Guest beers come from Everards Old English Ale Club. ❀❶🚆⬛️➕P💺

Markfield

Bull's Head

23 Forest Road, LE67 9UN
🕐 3 (11 Sat)-11.30 (2am Fri); 12-10.30 Sun
☎ (01530) 242541
Banks's Original; Marston's Bitter, Pedigree ⊞
Long-established two-room local tucked away in the corner of the village, offering a friendly welcome to all. A typical village inn full of character, darts and dominoes are played here. Q🕮🅿🖴🛆♣🅿🍴

Melton Mowbray

Anne of Cleves

12 Burton Street, LE13 1AE
🕐 11-11; 12-4, 7-10.30 Sun
☎ (01644) 481336
Everards Tiger, Original; guest beers ⊞
One of Everards' most historic pubs and a centrepiece of the town. Part of the property dates back to 1327 when it was home to monks. The house was gifted to Anne of Cleves by Henry VIII in her divorce settlement. It is now a popular and busy pub following a sympathetic restoration and conversion of the building, with stone-flagged floors, exposed timber roof beams and wall tapestries. The building is said to be haunted and psychic research evenings feature regularly. Evening meals are served Tuesday-Saturday. Up to three guest ales are available.
🅰Q🕮🕽⇌🖴🅿🍴

Crown Inn

10 Burton Street, LE13 1AE
🕐 11-3, 7-11; 11-11 Sat; 12-4, 7-10.30 Sun
☎ (01644) 564682
Everards Beacon, Tiger; guest beers ⊞
Sociable, two-bar pub run by a long serving landlord. Right in the centre of town, it is popular with shoppers and workers at lunchtime. Owned by Everards, the pub has two guests or seasonal ales at most times. Evening meals are served Tuesday-Thursday (lunches Tue-Sun). Access by bus from Leicester is easy, and there are hourly weekday buses from Grantham, Loughborough and Nottingham. 🅰Q🕽🅿🖴⇌🖴

Harboro' Hotel

49 Burton Street, LE13 1AF
🕐 11-11 (midnight Fri & Sat); 12-11 sun
☎ (01644) 560121 🌐 harborohotel.co.uk
Tetley Bitter; guest beers ⊞
An 18th-century coaching inn conveniently located between the town centre and railway station. The open-plan bar has comfortable seating. The hotel is often busy and can be a little noisy. Guest beers vary, cider is usually available and a range of draught and bottled Belgian and German beers are always on offer. An Easter beer festival is held. Snacks are served in the bar. 🕽🕮🕽🛆⇌🖴♣🅿🍴

Moira

Woodman

Shortheath Road, DE12 6AL
🕐 12-11 (midnight Fri & Sat); 12-10.30 Sun
☎ (01283) 218316

Greene King Abbot; Marston's Pedigree; Wells Bombardier; guest beer ⊞
Formerly called the Rawdon Arms after the local mine which closed in the 1980s, the pub has a large L-shaped single room with comfortable seating. The walls are covered with commemorative plates depicting local coal mines, the last one closing in 1990. There is a separate pool and games room which can be converted to a dining area or meeting room. It was voted local CAMRA Most Improved Pub in 2004. 🅰Q🕽🕮♣🅿🍴

Oadby

Cow & Plough

Stoughton Farm Park, LE2 2FB
🕐 12-3, 5-11 (12-11 summer)
☎ (0116) 2720852 🌐 steamin-billy.co.uk
Fuller's London Pride; Jennings Dark Mild; Steamin' Billy Bitter, Skydiver; guest beers ⊞
Situated in a converted farm building with a conservatory, this pub is decked out with breweriana. It is home to Steamin' Billy beers, named after the owner's Jack Russell featured on the logo and pump clips. The beers are brewed at Grainstore Brewery. A large restaurant has been added in the former Farmworld buildings. A guest mild and Westons cider are always available. Twice CAMRA East Midlands Pub of the Year, it was Leicester CAMRA Pub of the Year 2007.
Q🕽🕮🕽🛆🅿♣🍴🅿🍴

Wheel Inn

99 London Road, LE2 5DP
🕐 11.30 (11 Sat)-midnight; 12-10.30
☎ (0116) 271 2231 🌐 wheelinn.biz
Draught Bass; Marston's Pedigree ⊞
Sports-oriented community local where there is always something going on. As well as the pub's darts, dominoes and skittles teams there are football, cricket, golf and fishing matches, casino nights, jazz evenings, train trips, cycle rides and anything else the landlord and customers can think of. Tasty home-cooked food and an extensive selection of wines and spirits add to the appeal. The Leicester bus stops outside. No food Monday. 🕮🅿🖴♣🅿🍴

Pinwall

Red Lion

Main Road, CV9 3NB (1 mile from B4116)
🕐 12-11
☎ (01827) 712223 🌐 redlionpinwall.co.uk
Draught Bass; Greene King IPA; Marston's Pedigree; Taylor Landlord; guest beers ⊞
This cosy, rural locals' pub is one of only five or six buildings that make up Pinwall, a village that does not appear on most maps. The Red Lion, with six guest rooms, offers a la carte and bar meals. Usually two guest beers are available on handpump. Sunday meals are served from 2 to 6pm. 🅰Q🕮🕽🕽🖴🅿

Queniborough

Britannia

47 Main Street, LE7 3DB
🕐 12-2.30, 6-11; 12-11 Sun
☎ (0116) 260 5675

M&B Brew XI; Marston's Pedigree; Taylor Landlord; guest beers Ⓗ
Two-roomed, comfortable village local with a traditional bar and restaurant leading off the lounge. Both rooms have an open fire providing welcome warmth on cold winter evenings. Food is available seven days a week. Old pictures of the village are on the lounge wall. Guest beers are from the Punch list. ▲⚞⛊⟨⟩ ⛤⊟♣P⅃

Quorn

Manor House
Woodhouse Road, LE12 8AL
✪ 12-11 (midnight Thu-Sat); 12-10 Sun
☎ (01509) 413416 ⊕ themanorhouseatquorn.co.uk
Adnams Bitter; Draught Bass; Black Sheep Best Bitter; Marston's Pedigree; Taylor Landlord; Wells Bombardier Ⓗ
Reopened following a massive refurbishment, there are now up to six real ales on offer here, where once there was none. The interior has been opened out to provide comfortable drinking and dining areas. Since opening the pub has received a number of awards for the quality of its beer and food. Outside there is a large decked area where you can sit and enjoy a drink while watching the Great Central Railway's steam trains go by. Q⚞⛊▲⇌⊟♣P⅃

Ratby

Railway Inn
191 Station Road, LE6 0JR
✪ 11-11; 12-4, 6-11 Sun
☎ (0116) 239 2493
Everards Beacon, Tiger, Original, seasonal beers; guest beers Ⓗ
Traditional, family-run, drinkers' pub built to serve the long-gone Leicester and Swannington railway – now a bridle path. Originally called the Wharf and doubling as a ticket office, it was renamed in 1862. It has a large L-shaped bar and a cosy snug named Leander Lounge after the steam locomotive – see the memorabilia adorning its walls. The pub has a darts team; dominoes and cribbage are played. Friday is a sing-song night with a pianist. No food is served Sunday. ⚞⟨⟩⛤⊟♣

Seagrave

White Horse
6 Church Street, LE12 7LT
✪ 12-2.30, 5.30-11; 12-11 Sat; 12-10.30 Sun
☎ (01509) 814715
Greene King IPA, Abbot; guest beer Ⓗ
Cosy, two-roomed pub with open fires and a piano in the lounge where local groups and enthusiasts meet for a folk night on Thursday. The bar is popular with the local darts and dominoes team. Prints of horse racing adorn the walls, along with plates depicting hunting scenes. ▲⚞⟨⟩⛤⊟♣P

Sewstern

Blue Dog
Main Street, NG33 5RQ
✪ 11-11; 12-10.30 Sun
☎ (01476) 860097

Greene King IPA; guest beers Ⓗ
Friendly and welcoming pub at the west end of the village, handy for walkers on the Viking Way. This 300-year-old pub was once a war hospital and is said to be haunted by a drummer boy called Albert. It gets its name from the blue tokens that were once paid to local farm workers on the Tollemache estate. The guest ales often come from local breweries. A beer festival is held in late May. A special fish and chip menu is available on Wednesday evening. ▲Q⚞⛊⟨⟩▲⊟♣P⅃

Shepshed

Richmond Arms
Forest Street, LE12 9DA
✪ 12-3, 7-11
☎ (01509) 503309
Fuller's London Pride; M&B Mild; Taylor Landlord Ⓗ
The building dates back to 1725 and has been a pub for more than 100 years. Open plan with a central bar, furnishings are simple wood clad walls and formica tables, which, along with the old jukebox, give the impression that you have stepped back in time 30 years. The present landlord and landlady are Leicestershire's longest serving, having clocked up over 37 years. ⊟♣

Somerby

Stilton Cheese
Main Street, LE14 2PZ
✪ 12-3, 6-11; 12-3, 7-10.30 Sun
☎ (01644) 454394
Grainstore Ten Fifty; Marston's Pedigree; Tetley Bitter; guest beers Ⓗ
Like most of the buildings in the village, this late 16th-century pub is built in local ironstone. Tall customers in particular will note the wide range of pump clips on the low beams (mind your head!). There are two rooms and a function room. A popular pub, booking is advised for food.
▲Q⚞⛊⟨⟩⊟(113)♠

Three Crowns Inn
39 High Street, LE14 2PZ
✪ 12-2.30, 6.30 (5.30 Fri)-11; closed Mon; 12-10.30 Sun
☎ (01644) 454777
Draught Bass; Parish Special Bitter; guest beer Ⓗ
Traditional pub on the main street in the village. The 15th-century building was given by Sir Richard Sutton to Brasenose College, Oxford in 1508. The cosy inn has a large fireplace and plenty of character. Local Parish beers are featured and there is an annual beer festival during May. Occasional live music plays on Saturday night.
▲Q⚞⛊⟨⟩⛤▲⊟(113)♣P

Stoke Golding

White Swan
High Street, CV13 6HE
✪ 6.30-midnight; 12-4, 7-midnight Sun
☎ (01455) 212313
Adnams Bitter, Broadside; Everards Tiger, Original; guest beers Ⓗ

Situated close to the site where Henry VII was crowned after the battle of Bosworth, the Swan was originally built for the navvies employed on the construction of the nearby Ashby canal more than 200 years ago. A typical, unspoilt, two-room village local, it is known for raising money for village charities. Food here is good value, home made where possible (no meals Sun eve). Q⊛①▶♣P⁴

Swinford

Chequers
High Street, LE17 6BL
🕐 12-2.30 (not Mon), 6 (7 Mon)-11; 12-3, 7-11.30 Sun
☎ (01788) 860318
Adnams Bitter; guest beers 🖰
Family run, friendly and welcoming, open-plan pub offering frequently changing guest ales to complement the regular Adnams offering. Popular with locals and visitors to nearby Stanford Hall, good food including vegetarian and weekly specials are available most opening times. Many events are hosted throughout the year, including quiz nights and an annual beer festival in mid July.
🚲Q⊛①▲🖳♣P⁴

Swithland

Griffin Inn
174 Main Street, LE12 8TJ
🕐 11-11; 12-10.30 Sun
☎ (01509) 890535
Everards Beacon, Tiger, Original; guest beers 🖰
Friendly and welcoming local with three comfortable rooms. Set in the heart of Charnwood Forest, there are many walking and cycling routes nearby. Swithland Reservoir, Bradgate Park and the preserved Great Central Railway are also close by. Light snacks are available every afternoon, including Melton Mowbray pork pies. Guest beers are chosen from Everards Old English Ale Club. 🚲Q⊛①♣♣P⁴

Thrussington

Blue Lion
5 Rearsby Road, LE7 4UD
🕐 12-2.30 (not Wed), 5.30-11; 12-3, 6-11 Sat; 12-3, 7-10.30 Sun
☎ (01664) 424266
Marston's Burton Bitter, Pedigree, seasonal beers; guest beer 🖰
Late 18th-century rural pub, originally two cottages. It has a comfortable lounge where you can enjoy good value pub grub made with meat from a local butcher. The bar is the heart of the inn, where locals meet to challenge each other to high pressure darts and dominoes matches, watched over by licensees Mandy and Bob. Look out for the extensive collection of teapots, numbering over 160.
🚲Q⊛①🖳▲🖳(128)♣P

Walcote

Black Horse
25 Lutterworth Road, LE17 4JU
🕐 12-2.30, 5-midnight; 12-midnight Fri-Sun
☎ (01455) 552684

Beer range varies 🖰/🗗
In 2006 this long-standing Guide entry was demolished and rebuilt six feet back from the road to a similar floor plan. The range of real ales was then increased to nine on handpump and up to eight served on gravity from a glass-fronted cool room. Ales are sourced from regional and micro-breweries. Good traditional pub food is served at lunchtime as well as Thai dishes on Friday lunchtime and every evening. 🚲⊛①▶🖳♣P⁴

Walton-on-the-Wolds

Anchor Inn
2 Loughborough Road, LE12 8HT
🕐 12-3 (not Mon), 7-11; 12-3, 7-10.30 Sun
☎ (01509) 880018
Adnams Bitter; Taylor Landlord; Marston's Pedigree; guest beer 🖰
Situated in an elevated position in the centre of the village, the pub has an open-plan, comfortable L-shaped lounge with an open fire. Prints and photographs of classic cars and village scenes adorn the walls. One corner is given over to sporting memorabilia and trophies. Good quality food is served Tuesday to Saturday and a roast on Sunday lunchtime. Accommodation is self catering or B&B.
🚲Q⊛🛏①▶🖳P⁴

Whitwick

Three Horseshoes ☆
11 Leicester Road, LE67 5GN
🕐 11-3, 6.30-11; 12-2, 7-10.30 Sun
☎ (01530) 83731
Draught Bass; M&B Mild; Marston's Pedigree 🖰
Listed on CAMRA's National Inventory of unspoilt pubs, the nickname of 'Polly's' refers to a former landlady, Polly Burton. The pub was originally two separate buildings, possibly joined in 1882. To the left is a long bar with quarry-tiled floor and open fires, wooden bench seating and pre-war fittings. To the right is a similarly furnished small snug. There is no till, only pint pots full of coins on a shelf behind the bar. The outside toilets are still in use. 🚲Q🖳🖳♣

Wigston

Star & Garter
114 Leicester Road, LE18 1DS
🕐 11-3, 5-11; 11-11 Thu; 11-midnight Fri & Sat; 12-11 Sun
☎ (0116) 288 2450
Everards Beacon, Tiger; guest beers 🖰
This pub retains the original two rooms and a central bar. Very much a locals' pub, it offers a warm welcome to all members of the community. Skittles can be played by prior arrangement. Thursday is curry night.
⊛🖳♣P⁴

Wymondham

Berkeley Arms
59 Main Street, LE14 2AG
🕐 12-3 (not Mon), 6-11; 12-3,7-10.30 Sun
☎ (01572) 787587

Greene King IPA; Marston's Pedigree; guest beer H

An award-winning pub in the centre of the village at the foot of the road to Wymondham windmill. The two room interior has been modernised but retains much of the character of the building. This local at the heart of the village is also popular with diners from the surrounding area. The RF2 bus connects with Melton Mowbray and Oakham. ▲Q❀☀⊕🖿P⤚

RUTLAND
Barrowden

Exeter Arms
28 Main Street, LE15 8EQ (1 mile S of A47)
☼ 12-2.30 (3.30 Sat, not Mon), 6-11; 12-4, 7-10.30 (12-5 winter) Sun
☎ (01572) 747247 ⊕ exeterarms.com
Barrowden Beach, Hop Gear, seasonal beers; Greene King IPA; guest beers H
Collyweston stone-built, one-room hostelry overlooking the village green and duckpond. Food is highly regarded here, served in the dining area at one end (no meals Sun eve or Mon). The use of mobile phones is forbidden. The Barrowden Brewery is housed in the barn at the end of the garden. The terraced drinking area outside has extensive views across the Welland Valley. Petanque is played in the summer, dominoes in winter. Folk music plays on alternate Mondays. ▲Q❀☀⊕(I)&≈♣P

Belton in Rutland

Sun Inn
24 Main Street, LE15 9LB
☼ 12-1.30, 6-11; 12-10.30 Sun
☎ (01572) 717227
Banks's Bitter; guest beers H
Cosy, unspoilt pub tucked away in a small, quiet village, well worth a detour off the nearby A47. It was originally a Phipps pub. Set on three floors, it has a separate games room. Guest beers are available between March and November. It has an unusual washer-on-nail system for recording drinks left in by locals. ▲Q❀🖿♣

Braunston in Rutland

Old Plough Inn
2 Church Street, LE15 8QY
☼ 11-11 (midnight Sat); 12-10.30 Sun
☎ (01572) 722714
Grainstore Cooking, Ten Fifty; guest beers H
One of just a few pubs owned by the Grainstore Brewery, this popular inn has a bar and comfortable low-beamed lounge, conservatory/restaurant and patio garden. Two guest beers or Grainstore seasonal beers are on handpump. ▲Q❀⊕(I)🖥♣P⤚

Clipsham

Olive Branch
Main Street, LE15 7SH
☼ 12-3, 6-11; 12-11 Sat; 12-10.30 Sun
☎ (01780) 410355 ⊕ theolivebranchpub.com
Beer range varies H
Created from three farm cottages over 100 years ago, the pub retains the original floor plan. French monastery pews and English settles add to the charm of this award-winning dining pub. The large mature garden is popular in summer. A selection of continental bottled and local fruit beers complements the comprehensive wine list. Real cider is available in summer. ▲Q❀🖛⊕(I)&♠

Greetham

Plough
23 Main Street, LE15 7NJ
☼ 11-3, 5-11; 11-11 Thu-Sat & summer; 12-10.30 Sun
☎ (01572) 813613
Beer range varies H
Stone-built pub with a comfortable carpeted L-shaped bar with beams, horse brasses and books. A mild is always available as well as traditional cider. Fruit beers come from Melbourne Brewery. A wide range of fresh food comes from local suppliers; pie nights are Sunday and Monday. The Plough fields quiz, petanque and darts teams, hosts the Greetham reading circle and provides community Internet facilities. Traditional games include devil among the tailors, dominoes and cribbage. ▲Q❀☀⊕(I)&▲🖥♣♠P⤚

Hambleton

Finch's Arms
Oakham Road, LE15 8TL
☼ 10-11; 12-10.30 Sun
☎ (01572) 756575
Beer range varies H
Situated on the banks of Rutland Water in a tiny hamlet, the first sighting of the pub is the unusual sign outside depicting a door into a garden. The stone building has three drinking and dining areas, including one with splendid views over the reservoir waters. Three beers are on offer, normally including Taylor Landlord. The food is of very high quality and the pub is popular with walkers and cyclists throughout the year. ▲Q❀🖛⊕(I)&▲🖥P⤚

Oakham

Grainstore
Station Approach, LE15 6RE
☼ 11-11 (midnight Fri & Sat)
☎ (01572) 770065
Grainstore Rutland Panther, Cooking, Triple B, Ten Fifty; guest beers H
Named after the former Victorian grain store the pub and brewery now occupy, the bar is an ideal waiting room for the sparse railway station nearby. Wooden flooring and steel pillars support the upper part of the brewery; the lower part can be seen through the glass panel in the large bar. Additional seasonal beers from the brewery plus the odd guest ale are also on offer, as well as a selection of Belgian bottled beers. Wooden tables and chairs on a patio area at the front are popular with summertime drinkers. Q❀⊕&≈🖿P

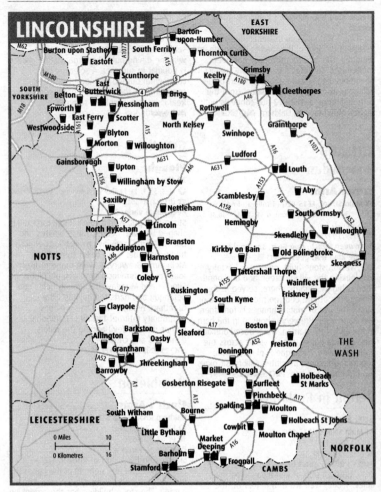

LINCOLNSHIRE

Aby

Railway Tavern

Main Road, LN13 0DR (off A16 via S Thoresby)
🕐 12-12.30am; closed winter Tue
☎ (01507) 480676

Bateman XB; Everards Tiger; guest beer Ⓗ
Cosy village pub off the beaten track, close to
Claythorpe Watermill, offering good food, with
an excellent Sunday lunch, and a guest beer
that changes often. Inside, open fires and a
fine display of railway memorabilia, including
the original Aby platform sign, greet visitors.
The pub holds a quiz night on Wednesday, and
is known for its excellent themed nights and
games in support of local charities. With good
local walks and fishing nearby, dogs are
welcome. ♨Q🏠◑&♣P

Allington

Welby Arms

The Green, NG32 2EA (1 mile from A1 Gonerby
Moor roundabout)
🕐 12-3, 6-11; 12-10.30 Sun
☎ (01400) 281361

**John Smith's Bitter; Taylor Landlord; Wells
Bombardier; Young's Bitter; guest beer** Ⓗ
A truly picturesque village inn, ideally placed
for visits to Belvoir Castle, Isaac Newton's
birthplace and the historic town of Stamford. It
provides comfortable en-suite
accommodation, and there is a large car park.
Superb home-cooked food attracts customers
from as far as Grantham and Nottingham, as
well as from local areas. The six ales are
always in excellent condition, cared for by an
enthusiastic landlord who is also a CAMRA
member. The monthly quiz is reckoned to be
the best in the area. ♨Q🏠🐕◑&P

Barholm

Five Horseshoes

Main Street, PE9 4RA
🕐 5 (12 Sat)-11; 12-10.30 Sun
☎ (01778) 560238

Oakham JHB; Adnams Bitter; guest beers Ⓗ
Pleasant, friendly, 18th-century, multi-roomed
pub situated in a quiet hamlet. Constructed
from locally quarried Barnack stone, with a
creeper-covered patio and large attractive
gardens, open fires greet visitors on chilly

evenings. This rustic pub concentrates on its real ales and always has four guests on offer. It actively supports micro-breweries, with a strong beer often available. ⚲❀🅿

Barkston

Stag Inn

Church Street, NG32 2NB (off A607)
🕒 11-2.30, 5-11; 12-3, 6-10.30 Sun
☎ (01400) 250363 ⊕ the-stag.com
Everards Beacon, Tiger; Brains SA Gold; guest beer Ⓗ

Everard's village local situated on the main Grantham to Lincoln bus route, within a mile of Belton House. The comfortable, modern bar area features traditional flagstone flooring. It hosts pub games and has a small TV in one corner. As well as the two house beers, it also offers a rotating guest, usually from Brains. Food is served in the main restaurant and in a conservatory overlooking the large beer garden, which gets very busy during the summer. ❀◑❒♣🅿

Barrowby

White Swan

High Road, NG32 1HN (off A1 and A52)
🕒 11.30-midnight (1am Fri & Sat)
☎ (01476) 562375
Adnams Bitter, Broadside; Greene King IPA; guest beer Ⓗ

Cosy two-roomed stone cottage-style pub situated just off the village green and popular with locals, especially when Barrowby holds its annual gala at the end of June. Good home-cooked food is served at lunchtime during the week. The traditional bar divides into two separate areas; games and a jukebox feature in one while the other is for relaxation and conversation with friends. Regular Sunday night quizzes are hosted in a small, cosy lounge. Outside, a well-maintained beer garden is set back from the car park, a perfect place to unwind during long summer evenings. Q❀◑❒♣🅿

Barton-upon-Humber

Sloop Inn

81 Waterside Road, DN18 5BA (follow Humber Bridge viewing signs)
🕒 11-11; 12-10.30 Sun
☎ (01652) 637287 ⊕ sloopinn.net
Tom Wood Shepherds Delight, Bomber County; guest beer Ⓗ

Welcoming pub situated away from the town centre, decorated on a nautical theme, with different areas named after parts of a ship. The central bar serves a games section with a pool table and darts, plus a drinking/dining area and two more rooms along one side. Three real ales come from Tom Wood's Highwood Brewery, one a rotating guest (two in summer). Excellent home-cooked food is available, including a varied specials menu. Far Ings Nature Reserve, Waterside Visitor Centre and the Humber Bridge are all nearby. ❀◑♿▲≢♣

Belton

Crown

Church Lane, Churchtown, DN9 1PA (off A161)
🕒 4 (12 Sat)-11; 12-10.30 Sun
☎ (01427) 872834
John Smith's Bitter; Theakston Best Bitter; guest beers Ⓗ

Difficult to find, situated behind All Saints' Church, but well worth the effort, this friendly local dating back 200 years is a haven for the discerning beer drinker. No smooth beers are kept and no food is served. Cask ales from the nearby Glentworth and Tom Wood breweries are served on a rotating basis. A games room is situated at the back of the pub. ⚲❀♣🅿

Billingborough

Fortescue Arms

27 High Street, NG34 0QB
🕒 12-3, 5.30-11; 12-11 Sat & Sun
☎ (01529) 240228
Greene King IPA; Taylor Landlord; Tetley Burton Ale; guest beers Ⓗ

Grade II listed, fine country inn set in a village with spring wells. The oak-beamed bar and lounge have that country feel, and a warming fireplace is set between the lounge and dining room. Nearby is the site of Sempringham Abbey with a monument to Gwenllian, daughter of the Prince of Wales, who was confined to the priory in the 12th century. Stone from the abbey was used to build parts of the inn. ⚲Q❀◑❒🅿≢

Blyton

Black Horse

93 High Street, DN21 3JX
🕒 12-2.30, 5-midnight; closed Mon; 12-midnight Fri-Sun
☎ (01427) 628277
Greene King IPA; guest beers Ⓗ

A newly refurbished and extended free house, maintaining the character of the old pub. There are three drinking areas, including the original public bar, all served from a new central bar. A fourth room is set aside for diners. Guest beers often come from Lincolnshire micro-breweries, including Fugelestou and Oldershaw. Traditional, home-cooked fare is served. Darts and quiz nights feature among the entertainment. Further

INDEPENDENT BREWERIES

Bateman Wainfleet
Blue Bell Holbeach St Marks
Blue Cow South Witham
Brewsters Grantham
DarkTribe East Butterwick
Fen Spalding
Fugelestou Louth
Highwood/Tom Wood Grimsby
Hopshackle Market Deeping
Melbourn Stamford
Newby Wyke Little Bytham
Oldershaw Grantham
Poachers North Hykeham
Riverside Wainfleet
Willy's Cleethorpes

work will provide a new games room and guest rooms by 2008. ᛘQ❀◑❶⬛◖🗐♣P

Boston

Ball House

Wainfleet Road, PE21 9RL (on A52, 2 miles from town centre)

◗ 11.30-3, 6.30-11; 12-3, 7-10.30 Sun

☎ (01205) 364478 ⊕ bateman.co.uk/tenancy/ball_house.htm

Bateman XB, XXXB; Draught Bass; guest beers ⊞

A cheery welcome greets customers old and new at this early 13th-century, mock-Tudor pub that stands on the site of an old Cannonball store. Stunning award-winning floral displays can be enjoyed during the summer. There is a play area and plenty of seating in the pleasant gardens. A varied menu offers excellent home-cooked meals, using home-grown produce; small portions are always available. Monthly theme nights are hosted from January-July. ᛘQ❦❀◑❶♣P

Coach & Horses

86 Main Ridge, PE21 6SY (100m E of John Adams Way)

◗ 5 (6 Fri)-11; 11-3, 7-11 Sat; 12-3, 7-10.30 Sun

☎ (01205) 362301

Bateman XB, XXXB ⊞

This one-roomed hostelry fields thriving pool, dominoes and darts teams. In a handy spot for Boston United home fixtures, you need to get here early on match days. It is well worth the walk from the town centre to try the XXXB. No food is served, but the popular Eagles fish and chip café and takeaway is nearby. ᛘ❀🗐♣🗓

Cowbridge

Horncastle Road, PE22 7AX (on B1183, N of town)

◗ 11-3, 6-11; 12-4, 7-10.30 Sun

☎ (01205) 362597

Greene King Old Speckled Hen; Theakston Mild, Best Bitter; guest beers ⊞

Just out of town, this pub is popular with drinkers and diners. It divides into three main areas: the public bar is a no-nonsense drinking and darts environment with a large array of football scarves; the smaller lounge is warm and cosy, with a welcoming open fire, and adorned with a collection of baseball caps; beyond is the restaurant serving excellent, freshly cooked food. The pub is frequented by members of Boston Golf Club, which is just up the road. ᛘQ❀◑❶⬛♣P🗓

Eagle

144 West Street, PE21 8RE (300m from station)

◗ 11 (11.30 Thu)-11 (midnight Fri & Sat)

☎ (01205) 361116

Banks's Bitter; Castle Rock Harvest Pale; Taylor Landlord; guest beers ⊞

Part of the Tynemill chain, the Eagle is known as the real ale pub of Boston. This two-roomed, friendly pub has an L-shaped bar with a large TV screen for live sports events. The small, cosy lounge has an open fire. It stocks an ever-changing range of guest ales, usually including at least one from Castle Rock, and at least one cider. A function room upstairs is home to Boston Folk Club on Monday. Thursday is quiz night – allegedly the hardest in town. ᛘQ❀⬛≷🗐♣🍺🗓

Hammer & Pincers

Swineshead Road, PE21 7JE

◗ 11-11 (midnight Sat); 12-10.30 Sun

☎ (01205) 361323

Bateman XB; Courage Directors; Fuller's London Pride; guest beer ⊞

Located on the eastern fringes of Boston, on the busy A52, this welcoming pub is popular with visitors and locals. The pub is divided into a lively public bar with gaming machines and pool table, and a quieter, comfortable lounge adorned with old local maps and brassware. A large conservatory creates a bright and airy dining area, offering a varied range of reasonably priced home-cooked meals. ᛘQ❀◑❶⬛🍴P🗓

Moon under Water

6 High Street, PE21 8SH

◗ 9am-midnight (1am Fri & Sat)

☎ (01205) 311911

Bateman XXXB; Greene King Abbot; Marston's Burton Bitter, Pedigree; Wells Bombardier; guest beers ⊞

Large, lively, town-centre pub near the tidal section of the River Witham. It features the usual mix of drinking and dining areas associated with a Wetherspoon conversion, with an imposing central staircase leading from the central lounge up to the toilets. There are two dining areas, one set aside for families. A bright and airy conservatory leads to a small outdoor patio. Local history around the walls highlights the characters associated with Boston. ᛘ❀◑❶⬛♿

Bourne

Smith's

25 North Street, PE10 9AE

◗ 10-11 (midnight Fri & Sat); 12-11 Sun

☎ (01778) 426819

Fuller's London Pride; Oakham JHB; guest beers ⊞

Winner of the national CAMRA/English Heritage Conversion to Pub Use award, this former grocer's, in a three-storey listed Georgian building, is now a fine contemporary pub. Two bars are on the ground floor and there are several further comfortable and attractively designed drinking areas throughout the building. Outside is a large, well-equipped patio and garden. The pub usually offers four guest beers. If you miss lunch, a cheeseboard is available until 7pm. ᛘ❦❀◑❶⬛🗐🍺

Branston

Waggon & Horses

High Street, LN4 1NB

◗ 12-2, 5 (4 Fri)-1am; 12-1am Sat (& Fri in summer); 12-midnight Sun

☎ (01522) 791356

Draught Bass; John Smith's Bitter; Taylor Landlord; guest beer ⊞

Unpretentious, brick-built, roadhouse-style pub at the centre of a commuter village. The Waggon was built in the 1950s to replace a Warwicks Brewery pub on the same site, as can be seen from photographs in the comfortable lounge bar. The lounge hosts a

quiz night on Monday, live music on Tuesday and Thursday, and further entertainment on Saturday. The lively public bar offers pub games including pool and sports TV. A guest beer appears on Thursday for the weekend.
❀◖◗⊟⊟♣P⚍

Brigg

Black Bull

3 Wrawby Street, DN20 8JH

⌚ 11-3 (4 Thu), 7-11.30 (11 Wed); 11-midnight Fri & Sat; 12-3, 7-11 Sun

☎ (01652) 652153

John Smith's Bitter; Tom Wood Harvest Bitter; guest beer ⊞

Popular, friendly, town-centre pub that gets busy on market days (Thu and Sat). The pub is centrally situated in the main shopping street. One of the regular beers comes from local brewer Tom Wood, and there is a changing guest beer in addition to the John Smith's. Horse racing features regularly on TV on Saturday. Brigg can be reached by bus from Scunthorpe and Barton, and by train on a Saturday on the Sheffield-Cleethorpes line.
❀◖⇌⊟♣P⚍

White Horse

Wrawby Street, DN20 8JR (close to station at E end of Wrawby St)

⌚ 12 (5.30 Mon)-midnight; 12-10.30 Sun

☎ (01652) 652242

Black Sheep Best Bitter; Shepherd Neame Spitfire ⊞

The pub is situated at the end of the main shopping street, with a large patio area to the front. The interior comprises two rooms: a traditional public bar and a lounge/dining room. Both rooms are decorated with photographs of old Brigg and the horse fair that has been held in the town for more than 700 years. A wide range of meals is served daily. Sunday is quiz night.
♨❀◖◗♿⇌⊟♣P⚍

Yarborough Hunt

49 Bridge Street, DN20 8NF (across bridge from market place)

⌚ 11-11 (midnight Fri); 10-midnight Thu & Sat

☎ (01652) 658333

Greene King IPA; Tom Wood Best Bitter; guest beers ⊞

Recipient of the CAMRA/English Heritage Joe Goodwin award in 2006, this former Sergeants Brewery tap has been carefully restored. Built in the early 1700s, the pub retains original features and its four rooms are simply furnished. Four rotating guest beers and Weston's Old Rosie cider are supplemented by Belgian beers and a wide selection of malt whiskies. A wood-burning range and original Hewitts and Sergeants brewery signs feature in one of the four simply furnished rooms.
♨Q❀♿⇌⊟♣●⚍

Burton-upon-Stather

Ferry House

Stather Road, DN15 9DJ (follow campsite signs through village)

⌚ 5-midnight summer; 7-11 winter; 12-midnight Sat & Sun

☎ (01724) 721504

Beer range varies ⊞

Friendly village local at the bottom of a hill next to the River Trent. It has a large open-plan room with a brick-fronted bar, and a separate lounge overlooking the river. Nautical artefacts are displayed throughout. One or two real ales are offered on a rotating basis, plus draught foreign beers and lagers, and Weston's Old Rosie cider. The Cask Marque awarded pub stages regular beer festivals and wine tasting evenings throughout the year. It is also renowned for good value Sunday lunches. There are facilities nearby for tents and caravans. ❀◖♿▲⊟(60)●P

Claypole

Five Bells

95 Main Street, NG23 5BJ

⌚ 11-3 (not Mon), 6-11; 11-1am Sat; 12-10.30 Sun

☎ (01636) 626561

Beer range varies ⊞

Winner of local CAMRA Pub of the Year in 2007, this busy, popular free house has a central bar serving the long, beamed public bar and restaurant. It offers a choice of four beers, usually from local micros, that changes every few days. A mild, usually Tetley's, is often available. Regulars enjoy a quiz night on Wednesday and play pool and darts, with various trophies on display. The pub offers comfortable accommodation.
❀⛟◖◗⊟⊟(68, 602)♣P

Cleethorpes

Crows Nest

Balmoral Road, DN35 9ND

⌚ 11-3, 6-11; 11-11 Sat; 12-4, 7-10.30 Sun

☎ (01472) 698867

Samuel Smith OBB ⊞

A genuine local, the Crows is the only pub in the area selling Sam Smith beers. The pub is a wonderful example of 1950s styling and retains many original features. The interior is complemented by an outdoor area to the front and a large garden at the rear.
Q❀⛟⊟⊟(7, 14)♣P⚍

No. 2 Refreshment Room

Station Approach, DN35 8AX

⌚ 9am-1am; 10-midnight Sun

☎ (07905) 375587

Greene King H&H Olde Trip; Hancock's Bitter; M&B Mild; Worthington's Bitter; guest beers ⊞

This three-times winner of local CAMRA Pub of the Year has recently undergone refurbishment that included the replacement of the pine benches with plush, upholstered seating and a new carpet. Four regular beers including the mild are complemented by two changing guest beers, often sourced from local breweries. With a mix of young and not-so-young regulars, this small, clean, cosy pub is always welcoming. ❀♿⇌♣⚍

Willy's

17 Highcliff Road, DN35 8RQ

⌚ 11-11 (2am Fri & Sat); 12-11 Sun

☎ (01472) 602145
Bateman XB; Willy's Original; guest beers Ⓗ
A long-established entry in the Guide, Willy's maintains a policy of offering beers from mainly micro-breweries. Good value, home-cooked food is available at lunchtime and also Monday, Tuesday and Thursday evenings. The on-site micro-brewery has been supplying the pub since 1989. An upstairs bar, affording spectacular views, is available for private hire.
◑≒₪(9)'–

Coleby

Bell Inn
3 Far Lane, LN5 0AH
✪ 11-3, 5.30-11; 12-10.30 Sun
☎ (01522) 810240 ⊕ thebellinncoleby.co.uk
Beer range varies Ⓗ
Tucked away behind the church in a picturesque cliff village, the Bell is on the edge of the Viking Way. An ever-changing selection of guest beers is dispensed from three handpumps. The interior has distinct areas for drinking only, and for private events. The main bar is small but cosy, with a real fire on winter evenings. There is a separate restaurant and the pub has an excellent reputation for the quality of its home-cooked food.
⚹Q♒❀❀◑₪P

Cowbit

Olde Dun Cow
164 Barrier Bank, PE12 6AL (on A1073 between Crowland & Spalding)
✪ 12-3, 6-11; 12-4, 7-10.30 Sun
☎ (01406) 380543
Beer range varies Ⓗ
A thriving, revitalised village pub, this recent local CAMRA award winner supports both regional and micro-breweries, offering four well-kept cask ales. Delicious bar meals are available, as well as a la carte meals in the comfortable, separate restaurant, with exotic meat dishes including ostrich and zebra the house speciality. The pub also offers a good wine list and a selection of more than 50 malt whiskies. There is a resident darts team, and a fine collection of bygone Fenland life memorabilia is on display. ⚹❀◑⚹₪➧P'–

Donington

Black Bull
7 Market Place, PE11 4ST
✪ 11-midnight; 11.30-11.30 Sun
☎ (01775) 822228
John Smith's Bitter; Wells Bombardier; guest beers Ⓗ
Old coaching inn dating back to the 16th century with oak beams and an open fire in the bar. Situated in the market place, it is opposite a statue of Matthew Flinders who discovered south Australia and was born in the village. The restaurant, offering good home cooking, leads off the cosy bar. The guest beers change constantly in this popular village local. ⚹Q❀◑⚹₪➧P'–

East Butterwick

Dog & Gun
High Street, DN17 3AJ (off A18 at Keadby Bridge)
✪ 5 (12 Sat)-11; 12-11 Sun
☎ (01724) 782324
DarkTribe Galleon; John Smith's Bitter; guest beers Ⓗ
Home to the DarkTribe Brewery, this small but busy village pub serves two from its own range of tasty brews as well as quality guest ales. Its traditional, cheerful atmosphere attracts locals as well as visitors from nearby villages, who come for the welcoming real fire in winter or a pleasant pint on the river bank in summer, where views of the Trent Aegir are a possibility. ⚹Q❀❀₪♣P

East Ferry

House Inn
High Street, DN21 3DZ
✪ 5-11 (midnight Sat); 12-11 Sun
☎ (01427) 628822 ⊕ thehouseinn.co.uk
Greene King IPA; guest beer Ⓗ
Friendly village local with an enthusiastic landlord keen to promote the pub within the community. The guest ale changes twice weekly and some rare beers for the area are featured. Good home-cooked food is served in the evening (not Thu and Sun) and Sunday lunchtime. The wooden furniture in the bar is unusual and the beer garden extends to the bank of the River Trent. Pool and bar billiards are played, and live music is performed on Saturday night. Daisy, the African grey parrot, is always available for a chat. ⚹❀◑⚹♣P'–

Eastoft

River Don Tavern
Sampson Street, DN17 4PQ (on A161 Goole-Gainsborough road)
✪ 7.30 (5 Wed-Fri; 12 Sat)-11; 12-10.30 Sun
☎ (01724) 798040
John Smith's Bitter; guest beers Ⓗ
Comfortable village local in the Isle of Axholme. The open-plan interior with an L-shaped bar offers discrete areas for dining and drinking. In summer you can take your drink into the orchard at the rear. Dark beams, agricultural implements and black and white photographs of country pursuits give a distinctly rural ambience. It offers three guest beers (two in winter). Good value food includes a weekend carvery. An annual beer festival is staged in summer. ⚹❀◑♣P

Epworth

Queen's Head
19 Queen Street, DN9 1HG (off A161, near town centre)
✪ 12 (11.30 Sat)-midnight
☎ (01427) 872306
John Smith's Bitter; guest beers Ⓗ
A 'locals' local' in a busy tourist destination, the Queen's Head caters for a mixed age clientele. The recent decision by the long-serving licensee to introduce two rotating guest beers has proved highly popular. Quizzes and pub games are a regular feature

of this community inn, a meeting place for local societies. A spacious, open-plan pub, it won an Epworth in Bloom award in 2006.
🌸🍴♣P🚼

Freiston

King's Head
Church Road, PE22 0NT
🕐 11-2.30, 6.30-11; 11-11.30 Sat; 12-10.30 Sun
☎ (01205) 760368
Bateman Dark Mild, XB Ⓗ
This welcoming village local is a regular finalist in Bateman's floral display competition, and it looks a treat in summer. Good, home-cooked food is excellent value and ideal for those with a hearty appetite. Pub games are played and local teams compete in darts and dominoes leagues. Located on the Wash banks, it is ideal for angling and bird watching. 🏨Q🌸🕐▲♣P🚼

Friskney

Barley Mow
Sea Lane, PE22 8SD (on A52, between Boston & Skegness)
🕐 7 (12 Wed-Sat)-11; 12-10.30 Sun
☎ (01754) 820883
Bateman Dark Mild, XB; guest beers Ⓗ
Situated on the busy Boston-Skegness road, this 300-year-old hostelry is known locally as the Barley Mow (pronounced Cow). Frequented by locals and visitors alike, it is especially popular in the summer months. A wide selection of home-cooked meals features on an imaginative menu. A conservatory and large garden adds to the atmosphere at this gem of a pub.
Q🌸🕐🍴🚲≠♣●🚼

Frognall

Goat
155 Spalding Road, PE6 8SA
🕐 11.30-3, 6-11; 12-10.30 Sun
☎ (01778) 347629
Beer range varies Ⓗ
Friendly, cosy pub with comfortable surroundings including a bar and two dining areas. Real fires welcome visitors on chilly evenings. A changing selection of guest beers, often from small and brand-new micro-breweries, is supplemented by a growing range of Belgian beers and 50-plus malt whiskies. In July the pub hosts its annual beer festival with over 25 real ales to choose from. It also offers hot and cold home-cooked meals. 🏨Q🛏🌸🕐🍴●P🚼🚽

Gainsborough

Eight Jolly Brewers
Ship Court, Silver Street, DN21 2DW (behind market place)
🕐 11-midnight
☎ (07767) 638806
Beer range varies Ⓗ
Gainsborough's premier real ale venue and winner of local CAMRA Pub of the Year 2006-07. This pleasant, town-centre pub is near the River Trent, based in a former carpenter's workshop, with a downstairs bar and quieter lounge upstairs. Eight draught beers include ales from Bateman and Glentworth. There is usually one heavily discounted beer as well as Belgian Leffe on draught and a wide selection of bottled beers and fruit wines. Live music plays on Thursday evening. Q🌸🍴🚲●P

Elm Cottage
139 Church Street, DN21 2JU (100m W of Trinity football ground)
🕐 11.30-3, 6-midnight; 11.30-midnight Fri-Sun
☎ (01427) 615474
Jennings Cumberland Ale; John Smith's Bitter; guest beer Ⓗ
Local CAMRA Gainsborough Pub of the Season 2006-07, there has been a pub on this site since 1850. It has one room with a central bar and dining area featuring two bay windows with seating. Pictures of old Gainsborough and views of the River Trent decorate the walls. The pub is home to two darts teams, two football teams and two cricket teams, and stages quiz nights on alternate Tuesdays. Live entertainment features on the last Saturday of the month. 🌸🕐🍴♣P

Gosberton Risegate

Duke of York
105 Risegate Road, PE11 4EY
🕐 12 (6.30 Mon)-11; 12-3.30, 7-10.30 Sun
☎ (01775) 840193
Bateman XB; Black Sheep Best Bitter; guest beers Ⓗ
Excellent pub with an established and well-deserved reputation for good value beer and food. In addition to the regular beers, guests generally come from independent brewers. The pub plays a large part in the local community, supporting charities, sports teams and other social activities. There is a large garden and children's play area, with goats and other animals an added attraction for families. The arch above the public bar indicates that the pub was previously owned by Bateman. 🏨🌸🕐🍴🚲♣P

Grainthorpe

Blackhorse Inn
Mill Lane, LN11 7HU (off A1031, signed to pub)
🕐 7-11.30 Mon & Tue; 12-3, 5.30-midnight Wed-Fri; 12-midnight Sat & Sun
☎ (01472) 388229
Fuller's London Pride; Tom Wood Best Bitter; guest beers Ⓗ
A two-room pub off the main road, the interior is adorned with old local pictures and lots of horse brasses, and features open fires in winter. It is renowned locally for its Sunday lunches. The pub competes in local games leagues for dominoes, darts and pool. There are beaches nearby, with good walking and fishing, as well as a colony of grey seals that come here to pup in winter.
🏨Q🛏🌸🕐🚲♣P

Grantham

Blue Bull
64 Westgate, NG31 6LA

🕑 11 (12 Sun)-midnight
☎ (01476) 570929
Beer range varies 🅗
Three-roomed local, popular with all ages, situated at the west end of the market place and only five minutes' walk from the rail and bus stations. A busy bar contrasts with a quiet lounge that is available for private functions; the games room has pool and darts. There is a decked drinking area outside at the rear, and tables and chairs are put out on the pavement in summer. Beers are mainly supplied by Abbeydale, Newby Wyke and Oldershaw breweries. Occasional live music is hosted at the weekend. ✿≉P

Blue Pig

9 Vine Sreet, NG31 6RQ (opp St Wulframs church)
🕑 11 (10.30 Sat)-11 (1.30am Fri & Sat); 12-11 Sun
☎ (01476) 563704
Caledonian Deuchars IPA; Taylor Landlord; Wells Bombardier; guest beers 🅗
One of four Tudor buildings to survive fires in 1660 but surprisingly not the oldest building in Grantham, the Pig was once a lodging house for stonemasons who were building St Wulframs church around 1160. 'Blue' refers to the Manners political family along with other 'Blue' pubs in town, while 'Pig' is a reference to the drovers who used to take pigs to the medieval church market along Swinegate. A good range of meals is served in this traditionally furnished hostelry. Mind the steps leading from one area to another. Quiz night is Monday. ♨Q◖▣≉ㄴ

Chequers

25 Market Place, NG31 6LR (on a narrow side street between Market Place and High St)
🕑 12-midnight
☎ (01476) 570149
Beer range varies 🅗
Tucked away in a narrow side street at the east end of the market place, this is a contemporary single-room bar divided into smaller drinking areas. Furnished with leather sofas, it is quiet and cosy during the week, becoming more lively at weekends. A true free house, the ever-changing range of interesting beers is sourced from micros throughout the UK and supplemented with an excellent wine list. Freshly filled paninis and wraps are served at lunchtime (not Sun). ◖

Lord Harrowby

65 Dudley Road, NG31 9AB (½ mile E of town centre, near crematorium)
🕑 4 (11 Sat)-midnight; 12-11 Sun
☎ (01476) 563515
Tom Wood Best Bitter; Wadworth 6X; guest beer 🅗
A back-street gem, this small, friendly, two-roomed traditional pub is situated on the edge of the town centre. A lounge on the right is furnished in typical 1960s style and features a real coal fire in winter. The walls are decorated with pictures of aeroplanes, some from WWII, highlighting the importance of Lincolnshire during that period when Bomber Command plotted the raids on the German dams. Darts, crib and pool teams play here, and regular live jazz bands visit once a month.

The large beer garden has a smoking area. ♨✿◖♣ㄴ

Tollemache Inn

28 St Catherine's Road, NG31 6QF (jct of St Peter's Hill & St Catherine's Rd)
🕑 9am-midnight (1am Fri & Sat)
☎ (01476) 594696
Greene King Abbot; Marston's Burton Bitter, Pedigree; guest beers 🅗
The Tollemache Inn is a tasteful Wetherspoon conversion of an old Co-op store and mortuary named after Frederick Tollemache, a former Liberal MP whose statue stands outside the front door. The ever-changing guest beers are supplied predominantly by local micros. A series of themed beer festivals is held throughout the year. ✿◖&

Grimsby

Hope & Anchor

148 Victoria Street, DN31 1NX
🕑 12-midnight (2am Fri & Sat)
☎ (01472) 500706
Tetley Bitter; guest beers 🅗
Spacious open-plan pub with a central bar that divides the room into smaller areas. Situated just away from the town centre, it is quiet in the week but more lively at weekends. Good food is served Monday to Friday lunchtime, with an interesting menu at pub prices. Handily placed for the bus station and Freshney Place shopping centre, there is a patio outside for summer drinking. ✿◖≉🚍♣

Royal Oak

190 Victoria Street, DN31 1NX
🕑 11-11 (1am Fri & Sat); 12-11 Sun
☎ (01472) 317312
Black Sheep Best Bitter; Greene King IPA, Old Speckled Hen; Theakston Mild, Old Peculier 🅗
Traditional two-roomed, friendly town-centre pub, with a Tudor-style frontage, within easy reach of the shops, bus and railway stations. The lively bar with its pool table, darts and dominoes attracts regulars, some who have been coming here for years. The cosy lounge has a mixed clientele of all ages. The real ales are those that have proved popular with the regulars. Sunday is quiz night. ▣≉🚍♣ㄴ

Rutland Arms

26-30 Rutland Street, DN31 3AF (behind Ramsden's Superstore)
🕑 11-11 (midnight Fri & Sat); 12-10.30 Sun
☎ (01472) 268732
Old Mill Mild, Bitter, Bullion, seasonal beers 🅗
A welcome return to this Guide after a few years' absence, this once run-down social club is now a well-appointed one-room local, catering mainly for the immediate vicinity. It is the only pub for miles around serving real ale and the only Old Mill tied house in the region. There is a resident pool and soccer team, and Grimsby Town FC performs its weekly shenanigans at Blundell Park, a 10-minute walk from here. ✿≉(New Clee)🚍♣P

Swigs

21 Osborne Street, DN31 1EY
🕑 11-midnight; 12-11 Sun
☎ (01472) 354773

Tom Wood Shepherd's Delight; Willy's Original; guest beers ⒣
Swigs, the second Willy's in Grimsby, is a long-term regular in this Guide and provides a welcome alternative to the usual town centre chain and circuit pubs. The beers are usually sourced from micro-breweries. A unique atmosphere and a warm welcome make this an ideal lunch stop or evening meeting place. A wide and varied food menu offers good-value home-cooked food. ◖≠⌷

Tap & Spile

Haven Mill, Garth Lane, DN31 3AF (behind Freshney Place shopping precinct)
☼ 12 (3 Mon)-11; 12-10.30 Sun
☎ (01472) 357493

Brakspear Bitter; Wychwood Hobgoblin; guest beers ⒣
Spacious, open-plan pub where old stone, brick and cast-iron floor supports have been retained, as well as remnants of a former flour mill. An area towards the rear has games facilities and access to a balcony overlooking the river Freshney. Food is served Tuesday to Saturday. Two regular ales are supplemented by four guests. All main bus routes call at the nearby town centre bus station. ⑳◖≠⌷♣ʟ

Yarborough Hotel

9 Bethlehem Street, DN31 1JN (next to station)
☼ 9am-midnight (1am Fri & Sat)
☎ (01472) 268283

Bateman Mild; Greene King Abbot; Marston's Pedigree; Shepherd Neame Spitfire; guest beers ⒣
Twice local CAMRA Pub of the Year, this spacious Wetherspoon pub, centrally situated for shops and transport, takes up the ground floor of an imposing Victorian former railway hotel. There are two large bar areas. Well-patronised thanks to its late opening hours, it is popular with all groups and particularly busy at weekends. The house beer is Highwood Yarborough Gold, and good value meals are served all day. ⦾⑳◖&≠⌷♣ʟ

Harmston

Thorold Arms

High Street, LN5 9SN (off A607)
☼ 12-3 (not Mon & Tue), 6-11; 12-11 Sun
☎ (01522) 720358 ⊕ thoroldarms.co.uk

Beer range varies ⒣
Current local CAMRA Pub of the Year, it specialises in micro-brewery beers – some 230 different ales were sold in 2006. A beer and music festival is held on August bank holiday. The 17th-century building has a comfortable bar area with an open fire. Home-cooked food is served in the dining room or bar. Quiz nights are hosted every Thursday, and black-tie bashes are organised for special occasions such as St George's Day. Opening hours may vary. ⚞Q⑳◖&⌷♣Pʟ

Hemingby

Coach & Horses

Church Lane, LN9 5QF (1 mile from A158)
☼ 12-2 (not Mon & Tue), 7 (6 Wed-Fri)-11; 12-3, 7-10.30 Sun

☎ (01507) 578280
⊕ coachandhorses.mysite.wanadoo-members.co.uk

Bateman Mild; Riverside Dixon's Major; guest beers ⒣
Whitewashed community pub in a small village on the edge of the picturesque Lincolnshire Wolds, an area of outstanding natural beauty. Beware the low beams! A central open hearth separates the main bar from the pool area. Guest beers come from all corners of the country. Home-cooked meals are available and the pub has won many local awards for its food. Overnight camping is available. ⚞Q⑳◖▲⌷♣Pʟ

Holbeach St Johns

Plough

1 Jekils Bank, PE12 8RF (4 miles S of Holbeach on B1168)
☼ 12-midnight (1am Thu-Sun)
☎ (01406) 540654

Adnams Bitter; Oakham Bishops Farewell; guest beer ⒣
A real ale oasis in a small community in Holbeach Fen. The landlord is a supporter of local breweries – Oakham and Fen ales are often on the pumps. The pub has a pool table and TV for the big match, and a skittle alley can be readily set up when required to cater for the sporting fraternity. The absence of muzak means the pub is quiet enough for conversation, a joke and a laugh. ⑳▲♣P

Keelby

Nag's Head

8 Manor Street, DN41 8EF
☼ 12-midnight
☎ (01469) 560660

John Smith's Bitter; Theakston Mild; Tom Wood Best Bitter; guest beer ⒣
Two-roomed free house in an 18th-century building with a wood-beamed interior opposite the village green, just off the A18. Outside, it has a beer garden and children are welcome in the play area. The guest beer often comes from a micro-brewery. Live music is hosted three times a month on Friday and Saturday, and the pub hosts a quiz night on Tuesday. It also participates in an Aunt Sally league. ⑳⌷♣Pʟ

Kirkby on Bain

Ebrington Arms

Main Street, LN10 6YT
☼ 12-3, 6-midnight; 12-11 Sun
☎ (01526) 354560

Bateman XB; Greene King Abbot; Woodforde's Wherry; guest beers ⒣
This delightful country hostelry is situated close to the River Bain and quiet countryside, making it an ideal place to start or finish a pleasant walk. The pub was used by airmen during WWII; coins still slotted into the ceiling beams were intended to pay for a beer when they returned from their missions. The popular restaurant offers good food made with local produce (booking advised). The garden has an awning to protect outside drinkers if the weather turns cool, and there is a Caravan

Club site within a mile of the pub.
♨Q❀◑♿♣▲✦P⅞

Lincoln

Dog & Bone

10 John Street, LN2 5BH (off Monks Rd)
🕒 12-3 (not Mon), 7-11
☎ (01522) 522403
Bateman XB, Valiant, seasonal beers; guest beers Ⓗ
This friendly community inn is a surprising oasis among east Lincoln's dense Victorian terraces. Winter and summer beer festivals, weekly cribbage and darts nights all add to the warm, sociable ambience at this traditional, comfortable town pub with a village feel. Visitors are warmed by two real fires and the lounge is lined with bookcases – the pub runs an excellent book exchange scheme.
♨❀≑🖼P

Golden Eagle

21 High Street, LN5 8BD (1 mile S of city centre)
🕒 11-11 (11.30 Fri & Sat); 12-10.30 Sun
☎ (01522) 521058 ⊕ goldeneagle.org.uk
Bateman Valiant; Castle Rock Harvest Pale; Everards Beacon; guest beers Ⓗ
Once a Georgian coaching inn, this popular traditional Tynemill pub serves three regular beers, up to six guests and Old Rosie cider. Beyond the rear car park is a large garden with a heated marquee and petanque pitch. Children are welcome up to 9pm. Among the entertainments are live music on most Sunday nights, open mike every other Tuesday and a quiz on Friday. There is a function room upstairs, and a walking club and war games group meet here. Q❀◑🖼♣✦P

Jolly Brewer

27 Broadgate, LN2 5AQ
🕒 12-11 (midnight Wed & Thu); 1am Fri & Sat)
☎ (01522) 528583 ⊕ thejollybrewer.co.uk
Taylor Landlord; Young's Bitter; guest beers Ⓗ
Popular city-centre pub, just a short walk north of bus and rail stations. The single long bar is splendidly decorated in Art Deco style. It has a darts area, adjacent corridor and an outdoor drinking space. Guest beers are usually sourced from Lincolnshire breweries and Weston's perry is available on draught in addition to the varying guest ciders. Saturday night is music time with live bands. An open mike evening is held every Wednesday.
♨❀≑🖼♣✦P⅞

Morning Star

11 Greetwell Gate, LN2 4AW (200 yds E of cathedral)
🕒 11-midnight; 12-11 Sun
☎ (01522) 527079
Caledonian Deuchars IPA; Draught Bass; Greene King Ruddles Best Bitter, Abbot; Tetley Bitter; Wells Bombardier Ⓗ
Conversation is the principal entertainment in this busy pub, situated in the uphill area close to the cathedral. Reputed to have become an inn in the 18th century, the building has since been extended into an adjacent cottage. The bar is at the front of the pub, with a smaller lounge at the rear. Live music features

occasionally throughout the year and regularly in the garden in summer. Q❀◑🖼♣P

Peacock Hotel

23 Wragby Road, LN2 5SH (400m E of Minster)
🕒 11.30 (12 Sun)-11
☎ (01522) 524703
Greene King IPA, H&H Bitter, Old Speckled Hen, Abbot; guest beers Ⓗ
A prominent corner pub with distinct bar and restaurant areas, the Peacock is situated on the edge of Lincoln's uphill tourist area, close to the Minster, the hospital and the prison. Guest beers come from the Greene King stable. Food is available noon to 8.30pm daily. A painting in the bar depicts the Roaring Meg, named after a large Civil War cannon and part of Lincoln's colourful pub history. ❀◑🖼P

Sippers

26 Melville Street, LN5 7HW
🕒 11-11; 12-3, 7-11 Sun
☎ (01522) 527612
Hop Back Odyssey, Crop Circle, Summer Lightning; John Smith's Bitter; guest beers Ⓗ
Friendly, comfortable, city centre free house with three distinct drinking areas, located close to bus and rail stations. The majority of the beer range comes from Hop Back, including its bottle-conditioned beers. The pub is busy on weekday lunchtimes, when food is served Monday to Saturday, and tends to be quieter in the evening. Monthly quiz nights benefit local charities. Competitive darts is played by the pub's three teams. ◑≑🖼♣

Strugglers Inn

83 Westgate, LN1 7HW (under NW corner of castle)
🕒 11-11 (midnight Thu-Sat); 12-10.30 Sun
☎ (01522) 527612
Black Sheep Best Bitter; Draught Bass; Fuller's London Pride; Greene King Abbot; Taylor Landlord; Tetley Mild Ⓗ
A regular in the Guide, this small and cosy city centre pub is in the ancient Bail area near the cathedral and castle. The bustling bar contrasts with a quieter snug. A small garden is used in summer and hosts occasional barbecues, while in winter an all-over marquee and garden heaters create additional outdoor drinking space. Lunchtime food is highly recommended. Q❀◑

Tap & Spile

21 Hungate, LN1 1ES (100 yds E of police station)
🕒 12-11.15 (12.30am Fri & Sat); 4-11.15 Sun
☎ (01522) 534015 ⊕ tapandspilelincoln.co.uk
Black Sheep Best Bitter; Caledonian Deuchars IPA; Greene King Abbot; Wells Bombardier; Wychwood Hobgoblin; guest beers Ⓗ
Quaint pub, just off Lincoln's busy High Street, with a warm and welcoming atmosphere. It features rugged walls adorned with pictures of blues musicians as well as old advertising posters. A varying range of up to eight cask-conditioned ales is on offer, including beers from local breweries as well as the big names. Live bands play on Friday and a jam night is hosted on Sunday. Other entertainments include circular chess on Thursday, a weekly general knowledge quiz on Sunday and a music quiz on the second Wednesday of each month. ◑≑♣✦⅞

Treaty of Commerce

173 High Street, LN5 7AF
🕔 11-11; 12-10.30 Sun
☎ (01522) 541943
Bateman XB, Valiant, XXXB; guest beers 🍺
Built in 1788, this is one of Lincoln's oldest pubs. Uniquely named, it sits unobtrusively amid high-street shops, just south of the infamous level crossing. The pub was rescued and restored by Bateman's, and now offers three of its beers and up to three guests. The interior has three separate and distinct drinking areas, including an unusual wooden barrel-vaulted ceiling at the far end of the single long bar. Good value food is served at lunchtime. 🕸◗≈🚌

Victoria

6 Union Road, LN1 3BJ (by W gate of Lincoln Castle)
🕔 11-11 (11.30 Fri & Sat); 12-11 Sun
☎ (01522) 536048
Bateman XB, XXXB; Castle Rock Harvest Pale, Elsie Mo; Taylor Landlord; guest beers 🍺
Now a Bateman's pub – a rarity for Lincoln – the Victoria retains the qualities that have ensured its perennial inclusion in this Guide. Ten or more real ales including a mild are dispensed here, complemented by a range of bottled continental beers, Biddendens real cider and good food at lunchtime. During the warmer months, tables are put out on the south-facing plaza next to the castle's west gate, a lunchtime suntrap. Q🕸◗🍴♣⌐

Louth

Boar's Head

12 Newmarket, LN11 9HH (next to cattle market)
🕔 5 (12 Wed)-11; 9.30am-11 Thu; 12-11 Fri-Sun
☎ (01507) 603561
Bateman XB, Valiant; guest beers 🍺
A Bateman's pub with ever-changing guest beers, situated next to the cattle market a short distance from the town centre. There are two main rooms plus the old snug, which is now the games room. Warmed by real fires in winter, it always provides a friendly welcome. Pub games include darts, shove-ha'penny and dominoes. Thursday is cattle market day, which is reflected in the opening times. A council-controlled car park is next door. 🏚Q⌐◗🍴♣⌐

Masons Arms Hotel

Cornmarket, LN11 9PY
🕔 10-11 (midnight Fri & Sat); 12-11 Sun
☎ (01507) 609525 🌐 themasons.co.uk
Bateman XB, XXXB; Kelham Island Pale Rider; Marston's Pedigree; guest beers 🍺
This early 18th-century Grade II listed building, with its balcony and canted bays to the ground floor, is a commanding presence on the town's bustling market place. Once one of Louth's principal posting inns and home to the Masonic Lodge, today the Masons is a thriving family-run hotel serving excellent home-cooked meals featuring local produce, and ever-changing guest beers. Local CAMRA Pub of the Year 2006 and 2007, it hosts the Louth beer festival. Quiz night is Thursday. ⌐◗🍴&🚌

Newmarket Inn

133 Newmarket, LN11 9EG
🕔 7 (6 Wed & Fri)-11; 12-3, 7-10.30 Sun
☎ (01507) 605146
Adnams Bitter; Young's Bitter 🍺
This former Hewitts pub, now a free house, has been in the same family for more than 30 years. Closed lunchtimes except Sunday, it is a laid-back, friendly place to enjoy a pint. Food is served in both the bar and separate bistro (Wed-Sat eves and Sun lunchtime); booking is advisable. 🕸◗P

Wheatsheaf Inn

62 Westgate, LN11 9YD (close to St James' church)
🕔 11-3, 5-11; 11-11 Sat; 12-4, 7-10.30 Sun
☎ (01507) 606262
Beer range varies 🍺
Attractive, traditional inn, dating back to 1625, situated in a Georgian terrace close to St James' Church, which boasts the tallest spire of any parish church in England. Three rooms are all warmed by coal fires in winter. Well-behaved dogs are welcome in the outside drinking area. Daily home-cooked specials are offered on the menu, and a beer-and-bangers festival is held annually at the end of May. 🏚🕸◗P

Woolpack Inn

Riverhead Road, LN11 0DA (1 mile E of town centre)
🕔 11-3 (not Mon), 5-midnight; 11-midnight Sat; 11.45-midnight Sun
☎ (01507) 606568
Bateman Mild, XB, XXXB; Greene King IPA, Abbot; guest beers 🍺
Occupying a former wool merchant's house and a pub since 1770, the Woolpack stands at the head of the Louth Navigation. The interior comprises two L-shaped bars and a separate restaurant. Meals are home-cooked using local produce (no food Sun eve & Mon). There are open fires in winter and a warm welcome all year round. The large beer garden is ideal for families. 🏚Q🕸◗⌐&♣P

Ludford

White Hart Inn

Magna Mile, LN8 6AD
🕔 12-2 (not Mon-Wed), 5.30-11; 12-3, 6-11 Sat; 12-4, 7-11 Sun
☎ (01507) 313489
Fugelestou Marsh Mild; guest beers 🍺
Thought to have first been used as a public house in 1742, this two-roomed rural village pub, close to the Viking Way, is very popular with hikers and ramblers. It always offers four changing guest beers; the licensees pride themselves on serving real ale from micro-breweries. All food served here is home-cooked, using ingredients from local suppliers. The guest accommodation is separate from the pub. Well-behaved dogs are welcome. 🏚Q🕸⌐◗♣P

Market Deeping

Vine

19 Church Street, PE6 8AN
🕔 12-3, 5-11; 12-11 Thu-Sat; 12-10.30 Sun

☎ (01778) 344699 🌐 inn-the-vine.co.uk
Wells Eagle IPA, Bombardier; guest beer 🅗
Friendly local close to the centre of Market Deeping. This attractive building of local limestone was originally a Victorian preparatory school. Inside, a low-ceilinged front bar extends along the full length of the building, and there is a cosy snug at the rear. Recently refurbished, the pub now has a new courtyard plus a garden with a children's play area. Guest beers are mostly from local breweries. Snacks are served at lunchtimes. Disabled access is via the rear of the pub, and there is a large canopy outside for smokers.
🏚Q🕮🛇Φ🅗占🖳🖳🛱P🔚🗝

Messingham

Bird in the Barley
Northfield Road, DN17 3SQ (on A159, Gainsborough road)
🕚 11.30-3.30, 5.30-11.30 (midnight Fri & Sat); closed Mon; 11.30-3, 5.30-10.30 Sun
☎ (01724) 764744
Jennings Sneck Lifter; Marston's Pedigree; guest beers 🅗
Traditionally styled village inn featuring wooden beams, bare bricks and rural artefacts. Recently refurbished, the pub now has a large conservatory dining area. A relaxed, friendly atmosphere prevails, with the emphasis on dining. Real ale is also promoted with tasting notes and a try-before-you-buy policy. The two guest beers rotate. This is an excellent place to drink and dine, and booking is advisable for weekend evening meals and Sunday lunch. 🏚🕮Φ🅗占🖳P🔚

Horn Inn
61 High Street, DN17 3NU
🕚 11-11 (midnight Fri & Sat)
☎ (01724) 762426
John Smith's Bitter; guest beers 🅗
Friendly, family-run pub that attracts regulars and passing trade. Two guest ales are sourced through the SIBA scheme, with a discount on all beers between 5-7pm daily. There are three drinking areas, all comfortably furnished and warmed by real fires in winter. A plasma-screen TV has recently been added, but is used sparingly for big sporting occasions only, and does not distract from the main pastime of chatting over a pint. Excellent, home-cooked lunches are served (booking advised for Sun). Entertainment includes live music on Wednesday and most Saturdays, and a quiz on Monday. 🏚Q🕮Φ🅗占🖳🛱P

Morton

Crooked Billet
1 Crooked Billet Street, DN21 3AG
🕚 12-midnight (1am Fri & Sat)
☎ (01427) 612584
Beer range varies 🅗
Large Victorian pub with a central bar serving three rooms. The games room houses a pool table, juke box and Sky TV, and hosts occasional live music. The old smoke room features a display of local pre-war photos, while the middle room is used for bingo and quizzes. The pub is home to several local

sports teams, including a fishing club. Beers come from a variety of breweries. 🏚Q🕮🛱🖳

Moulton

Swan
13 High Street, PE12 6QB
🕚 11 (12 Sun)-11.30
☎ (01406) 370349
Adnams Bitter; Tetley Bitter; Wells Bombardier; guest beer 🅗
Family-run pub opposite the church and the windmill at the heart of this thriving Fenland village. Renowned locally for its food, a wide choice of home-cooked meals is on offer, including game dishes. Produce is sourced locally whenever possible, enabling the pub to display the Taste of Lincolnshire logo. A pleasant garden with a bouncy castle is popular with families in summer, and a cheerful open fire welcomes guests in winter. A 24-hour licence is held although last entry is 11.30pm. 🏚🕮Φ🅗占🛱🖳(505)🛱👶🖳P🔚

Moulton Chapel

Wheatsheaf
4 Fengate, PE12 0XL
🕚 12-3 (not Mon), 5.30-11; 12-3, 7-11 Sat; 12-3, 7-10.30 Sun
☎ (01406) 380525
Beer range varies 🅗
Without TV, muzak or games machines, the only sounds in this Fenland gem are the crackling of logs on the old range and the chat and laughter of the locals in the quarry-tiled bar. One ale at a time is stocked, often from a micro, ensuring a quality pint. Guests may dine in style in either of the distinctive dining rooms, one featuring a log-burning stove and the other an original Victorian fireplace.
🏚Q🕮🛇Φ🅗🛱🖳👶P

Nettleham

Plough
1 The Green, LN2 2NR
🕚 12-11
☎ (01522) 750275
Bateman XB, XXXB; guest beers 🅗
Picturesque stone-built village centre pub, situated on the green. Inside, this engaging and well-presented Bateman's pub features an open-plan layout, with a low ceiling, exposed beams and stone columns. The walls are decorated with paintings of local interest; the fireplaces with brassware. There is an extensive bar menu, and weekday lunchtime specials are on offer for senior citizens. Meals can be taken in the separate mock-Tudor dining room, which is open evenings and Sunday lunchtime (booking essential).
🛇Φ🅗🛱🖳👶🔚

North Kelsey

Butcher's Arms
Middle Street, LN7 6EH
🕚 4-midnight (1.30am Fri); 12-1.30am Sat; 12-midnight Sun
☎ (01652) 678002

Tom Wood Best Bitter, Harvest Bitter; guest beer Ⓗ
Traditional village pub with an open-plan layout, decorated in rural fashion with hop bines, rustic furnishings and beer memorabilia. The cosy feel is enhanced by small, discrete drinking areas. The attractive garden is framed by mature trees. Owned by the local Highwood Brewery, it regularly features two of its beers plus a rotating guest; at busy times a third Tom Wood beer may be added. Table skittles is played here. A disabled toilet is provided. ⩩❀♿♣P

Oasby

Houblon Arms

Village Street, NG32 3NB (between A52 and B6403)
⌚ 12-2 (3 Sun), 7-11; closed Mon
☎ (01529) 455215
Everards Tiger; guest beers Ⓗ
An old establishment in a quiet village where time slips gently by. The traditional flagstone floor and a large inglenook are notable features. The dining room serves excellent home-cooked food, expertly presented, that tastes as good as it looks (no food Sun eve). Quiz night is Sunday. A real gem of a pub, worth finding if in the Grantham area. B&B accommodation is provided in four cottages. ⩩Q⇔◐P

Old Bolingbroke

Black Horse Inn

Moat Lane, PE23 4HH
⌚ 12-midnight summer (hours vary in winter)
☎ (01790) 763388
Bateman Mild; Young's Bitter; guest beers Ⓗ
A warm welcome is assured at this old country inn, with history on its doorstep – the village features castle remains and the roses of Henry IV and the Duke of Lancaster, dating from 1366. The pub stages regular beer festivals. Excellent food is prepared from local organic produce; Friday is Grimsby fish night, and Saturday is speciality night (booking advisable). Ploughman's lunches are available at the weekend. Ring to check opening times and food availability. ⩩Q❀◗⊟♿♣P

Pinchbeck

Bull Inn

1 Knight Street, PE11 3RA (on B1356)
⌚ 12-2.30, 5.30-midnight; 12-midnight Sat; 12-11 Sun
☎ (01775) 723022
Greene King Old Speckled Hen; John Smith's Bitter; guest beers Ⓗ
Prominently situated in the middle of the village, the Bull has two comfortable bars. The lounge is mainly used for dining while the public bar has a real fire and features bull horn decorations. The bar itself has a carved bull's head on the front, with the bar rail representing its horns. The pub has a reputation for good food: both bar snacks and meals are popular. An outside patio area is available in summer. ⩩❀◐⊟♿⊞P⌐

Rothwell

Blacksmith's Arms

Hill Rise, LN7 6AZ
⌚ 12-3, 5-midnight; 12-midnight Sat; 12-11 Sun
☎ (01472) 371300
Bateman Salem Porter; Black Sheep Best Bitter; Tom Wood Shepherd's Delight; guest beers Ⓗ
Low beamed ceilings and a real fire in the winter months help to give this pub a cosy, traditional feel. The dining room doubles as a function room, holding up to 120 people with ease. Ideally situated for walks in the Lincolnshire Wolds and Viking Way nearby, this is the perfect place for a relaxing pint and excellent food afterwards. ⩩Q❀◐♿♣P⌐

Ruskington

Potters

3 Chestnut Street, NG34 9DL
⌚ 11.30-3 (not Mon), 5-11; 12-3, 7-10.30 Sun
☎ (01526) 832777
Bateman XB; Black Sheep Best Bitter; guest beers Ⓗ
Set in a quiet part of the village, this comfortable and modern pub is housed in a building that was once a car sales showroom. It first opened as a snooker club (hence the name), but quickly evolved and is now a convivial and popular venue for all ages and its reputation for beer and food continues to grow. ◐⇌⊞P

Saxilby

Anglers

65 High Street, LN1 2HA
⌚ 11.30-2.30, 6 (5 Fri)-12.30am; 11.30-12.30am Sat; 12-midnight Sun
☎ (01522) 702200
Greene King IPA; Theakston Best Bitter; guest beers Ⓗ
A true village local, with resident darts, crib, dominoes and pool teams. The bar has a large TV screen for soccer fans – the landlord is a keen Lincoln City supporter. The lounge is home to the local history group and drama society and is adorned with pictures of old Saxilby. The village is on the Fossdyke navigation, providing moorings five minutes away. Not far from the station, the pub was formerly known as the Railway. ❀⊟⇌⊞♣P⌐

Scamblesby

Green Man

Old Main Road, LN11 9XG (off A153, Horncastle to Louth road)
⌚ 12-2.30, 5-midnight; 12-midnight Thu-Sun
☎ (01507) 343282
Black Sheep Best Bitter; Young's Bitter; guest beers Ⓗ
Set in an area of outstanding natural beauty, this 200-year-old pub is ideally situated for walkers and bike fans – Cadwell Park race circuit is at the top of the hill. The main bar includes a games area while the lounge is quiet and has a rocking chair. Many pictures of motorcycles adorn the walls. Meals are

available until 8.30pm. The pub's dog is Harry. ♔Q❀⇄◑♿⛺♣P

Scotter

White Swan

9 The Green, DN21 3UD (off A159)
✪ 11-2, 6-midnight; 11-midnight Fri-Sun
☎ (01724) 762342 ⊕ whiteswanscotter.co.uk
Black Sheep Best Bitter; John Smith's Bitter; Tom Wood Bomber County; guest beers Ⓗ
Olde-worlde 19th-century beamed country-style inn with later extensions for dining and functions. It has two bars on different levels: a traditional lounge and a cocktail bar with a more modern decor. The raised dining area has views over the river and the beer garden backs onto the river, with picnic tables. Two guest beers are usually available, generally from independent breweries. Q❀⇄◑♿🚌P

Scunthorpe

Berkeley Hotel

Doncaster Road, DN15 7DS (on A18)
✪ 11.30-2.30, 5-11; 11.30-11 Fri & Sat; 12-10.30 Sun
☎ (01724) 842333
Samuel Smith OBB Ⓗ
Large 1930s Samuel Smith's house, recently redecorated in period style, a 30-minute walk from the town centre. It has a dining room, function room and lounge, plus a public bar at the rear of building with a separate entrance. The attractive landscaped area at the front has picnic tables in summer. The hotel may close on football match days. ♔Q❀⇄⊟♿🚌♣P

Blue Bell Inn

1-7 Oswald Road, DN15 7PU (on town centre crossroads, ½ mile from bus and train stations)
✪ 9am-midnight (1am Fri & Sat)
☎ (01724) 863921
Greene King Abbot; Marston's Burton Bitter, Pedigree; guest beers Ⓗ
Recently refurbished Wetherspoon pub with an open-plan layout on two levels. The lower bar has wooden floors, with high and low tables and chairs, the upper level is a designated family area with a guarded fire at one end. Meals are served until an hour before closing time. The pub hosts regular beer festivals and themed evenings such as Burns Night, Valentine's and Halloween. There is a patio area with picnic tables to the rear of the pub. Q❀◑♿⇌🚌●

Malt Shovel

219 Ashby High Street, DN16 2JP (Ashby Broadway shopping area)
✪ 11-11 (midnight Fri & Sat)
☎ (01724) 843318
Castle Rock Harvest Pale; Courage Directors Bitter; John Smith's Bitter; guest beers Ⓗ
Beer choice and quality at this pub have been revitalised by enthusiastic new management. Three constantly-changing guest ales plus permanent real cider or perry are now available. The pub can get busy at lunchtime and early evening thanks to the excellent food. At other times a quiet drink can be enjoyed in the spacious and comfortably furnished lounge. Newspapers and magazines are provided. Quiz nights are Tuesday and Thursday. The pub has separate snooker facilities. Mini beer and food festivals are in the pipeline. The location is handy for the shops, but with beer this good who cares? ❀◑🚌●

Skegness

Red Lion

Lumley Road, PE25 2DU
✪ 9-midnight (1am Fri & Sat)
☎ (01754) 612567
Greene King Abbot; Marston's Burton Bitter, Pedigree; guest beers Ⓗ
Large open-plan pub catering for all ages, popular with holidaymakers during the summer months. The food and beer are well priced and the ever-changing real ales have created an oasis in a rather dry area for good beer. The pub is adorned with interesting facts about locals who have shot to fame. ❀◑♿⇌🚌⊢

Skendleby

Blacksmith Arms

Main Road, PE23 4QE
✪ 12-3, 6-midnight
☎ (01754) 890662
Bateman XB; Tom Wood Shepherd's Delight, Bomber County Ⓗ
Built in the 1750s, this country pub in a quiet Wolds village has recently reopened. The snug, with its low, beamed ceiling, low doors and roaring fire provides a warm welcome. The main bar has stone floors, settles and a period fireplace. The cellar can be viewed through a glass wall behind the bar. Two dining rooms offer pleasant outlooks and one has a well. ♔Q❀◑⊟P⊢

Sleaford

Barge & Bottle

Carre Street, NG34 7TR
✪ 11-11 (11.30 Thu-Sat); 12-10.30 Sun
☎ (01529) 303303 ⊕ thebargeandbottle.co.uk
Greene King IPA, Abbot; Tetley Bitter; Theakston Old Peculier; guest beers Ⓗ
Modern, open-plan pub with a separate dining area providing a wide range of reasonably priced meals. Independently owned, it offers a choice of nine real ales. The conservatory is available for private functions and the large patio area adjacent to the small river Slea is inviting in summer. A footbridge leads to the Hub regional arts and crafts centre which holds national exhibitions. A popular pub, it can get busy at weekends. ❀◑♿⇌⊢

South Ferriby

Nelthorpe Arms

School Lane, DN18 6HW (off A1077 Scunthorpe-Barton road)
✪ 12 (3 Mon)-midnight
☎ (01652) 635235
Tetley Bitter; guest beer Ⓗ
Two-roomed village local featuring a public bar with pool and darts and a separate dining room and lounge, serving popular home-

cooked meals. The bar is basic but welcoming, featuring Tetley's Bitter and a single rotating guest, often one of Naylors Brewery's excellent ales. Live music is played on Saturday evening, ranging from folk to rock, and Thursdays are set aside for open mike nights. Accommodation is available in four en-suite rooms. ⚲✿🏠◗🚲🏃🚃(350, 450)🏸P⅃

South Kyme

Hume Arms
High Street, LN4 4AD
🕘 11.30-2.30, 6-11; 12-3, 6-11 Fri & Sat; 12-3, 7-10.30 Sun
☎ (01526) 869143
Greene King IPA, Abbot; guest beers Ⓗ

This country pub, situated in a quiet village, was recently reopened after being closed for 18 months. Previously known as the Simon de Kyme, the pub escaped conversion into residential property thanks to the efforts of local groups. The interior has been tastefully refurbished, with the emphasis on natural wood. It is situated by the river Slea, known locally as the Kyme Eau, which is busy with narrowboats, especially on the May bank holiday. ⚲Q✿🏠◗🚃P⅃

South Ormsby

Massingberd Arms
Brinkhill Road, LN11 8QS (1½ miles from A16)
🕘 12-3 (not Mon), 6-11; 12-5, 7-10.30 Sun
☎ (01507) 480492
Beer range varies Ⓗ

Named after the lord of the manor, this is a quiet gem of a pub, winner of local CAMRA Pub of the Year on several occasions. It is well worth seeking out for the superb views, delicious home-cooked food and frequently changing beer range. No meals are served on Sunday evening. Guide dogs only are admitted. ⚲Q✿◗🏸P

Spalding

Olde White Horse
Churchgate, PE11 2RA
🕘 11.30-11; 12-10.30 Sun
☎ (01775) 766740
Samuel Smith OBB Ⓗ

Thatched coaching inn situated on the river Welland next to High Bridge. Originally built as a dwelling using bricks from Spalding Priory, this 450-year-old building is very much part of the historic town. Popular with drinkers and diners of all ages, it offers something for everyone, with several bars and a separate dining room. Excellent value ale is complemented by a wide range of snacks, meals and all-day Sunday roasts.
Q✿◗🚲🏃P⅃

Red Lion Hotel
Market Place, PE11 1SU
🕘 10 (12 Sun)-midnight
☎ (01775) 722869 🌐 redlionhotel-spalding.co.uk
Draught Bass; Fuller's London Pride; Greene King Abbot; Marston's Pedigree Ⓗ

This cosy and welcoming hotel bar in the Market Place is very popular with locals and

visitors alike. Well-kept cask ales and tasty bar meals make it an ideal place to take a break if you are visiting the town or the many attractions in the area. The Spalding Blues Club meets here on alternate Sundays. A separate dining room is open every evening except Sunday. ⚲Q✿🏠◗🏃🚌

Stamford

Green Man
29 Scotgate, PE9 2YQ
🕘 11 (12 Sun)-midnight
☎ (01780) 753598
Caledonian Deuchars IPA; guest beers Ⓗ

Stone-built former coaching inn dating from 1796, featuring a split-level, L-shaped bar. Beer festivals are held each Easter and September on the secluded patio. Most of the guest ales come from micro-breweries, and a good range of European bottled beers and seven traditional ciders are also stocked. No food is served on Sunday. It has a covered area for smokers. ⚲🏫✿🏠◗🚌🏃🏸🐕⅃🍺

Periwig
7 All Saints Place, PE9 2AG (in Red Lion Sq)
🕘 10-11 (midnight Wed & Thu; 1am Fri & Sat); 12-10.30 Sun
☎ (01780) 762169
Adnams Bitter; guest beer Ⓗ

This old town centre pub has been refitted and now extends over three floors with a modern interior. It attracts a mixed clientele of all ages. The large plasma TV screens have been replaced by smaller screens showing live sports. The guest beer is always from Ufford Ales. ◗🚃

Surfleet

Crown Inn
6 Gosberton Road, PE11 4AB (on B1356, opp church)
🕘 5 (12 Sat & Sun)-11
☎ (01775) 680466
Taylor Landlord Ⓗ

Situated opposite the church with its 600-year-old leaning tower, this pleasant, welcoming village pub has a large open-plan lounge bar with a log fire. Furnished with interesting pieces of furniture including a grand piano, armchairs and comfortable sofas are arranged around small tables. There is a pool table in a separate area. The pub is close to the River Glen, offering pleasant walks and boat trips in summer. ⚲🚃P

Ship Inn
154 Reservoir Road, PE11 4DH (off A16, S of A152 jct, follow brown signs)
🕘 11-3 (not Mon Nov-Apr), 6-midnight; 12-11 Sun
☎ (01775) 680547 🌐 shipinnsurfleet.com
Beer range varies Ⓗ

The original Ship was demolished in 2004 and only some flagstones in the entrance and a model on the bar bring to mind the old pub. The larger, new inn now has four guest bedrooms. On the banks of the River Glen, where it becomes tidal and joins the Welland, the area is popular with dinghy sailors. The McMillan Way footpath passes the pub. Bar meals are served daily and the upstairs restaurant affords views over the river. ⛺Q✉🕙🍴👦P

Swinhope

Click'em Inn

LN8 6BS (on B1203, 2 miles N of Binbrook)
🕐 12-3 (not Mon), 7-11; 12-11.30 Fri & Sat; 12-10.30 Sun
☎ (01472) 398253
Greene King Abbot; Shepherd Neame Spitfire; guest beers Ⓗ
Country pub set in the picturesque Lincolnshire Wolds. The unusual name originates from the counting of sheep through a nearby clicking gate. It is popular with both locals and diners thanks to the good, home-cooked food served in the bar and conservatory. The pub offers a house beer called Click'em Bitter, as well as changing guest ales and a real cider. Winner of local CAMRA Country Pub of the Year for the last five years. Q☀🕙🍴♣👦P

Tattershall Thorpe

Blue Bell Inn

Thorpe Road, LN4 4PE
🕐 12-3, 7-11 (10.30 Sun)
☎ (01526) 342206
Greene King IPA; Taylor Landlord; Tom Wood Bomber County Ⓗ
Delightful inn – one of the oldest in Lincolnshire, dating back to the 13th century – complete with beamed ceilings and a wealth of historical charm. This pub was a watering hole for the famous Dambusters 617 Squadron during WWII; the walls are adorned with numerous photos and the low ceiling is signed by many service personnel. Food is served in the bar and dining room. Three ales are usually on offer plus ever-changing guest ales. A gem of a pub in a delightful location. ⛺Q☀🕙👦🍴♣P

Thornton Curtis

Thornton Hunt Inn

DN39 6XW (on A1077, between Wooton & Barton)
🕐 12-3, 6.30-11
☎ (01469) 531252 ⊕ thornton-inn.co.uk
Taylor Landlord; Tom Wood Best Bitter, Shepherd's Delight Ⓗ
Comfortable, rustic village local, one mile from the ruins of Thornton Abbey. It has an open-plan bar, lounge and dining room open seven nights a week. Decorated in country-inn style, it is adorned with polished wood fittings, Toby jugs and hunting scenes. A strong emphasis is placed on food here, with home-cooked meals served every lunchtime and evening. Three real ales are stocked, two from the local Highwood brewery. Accommodation is in six en-suite rooms. Q☀✉🕙👦P

Threekingham

Three Kings Inn

Saltersway, NG34 0AU (just off A52)
🕐 12-3 (not Tue), 6-11; closed Mon; 12-3, 6-10.30 Sun
☎ (01529) 240249 ⊕ threekingsinn.co.uk
Draught Bass; Taylor Landlord; guest beers Ⓗ

Attractive former coaching inn with a convivial and comfortable atmosphere. The lounge contains some attractive rural prints relating to the village and its surroundings. Food is home cooked and locally sourced where possible. The village is situated near the crossroads of the Roman Mareham Lane and the even older Salters' Way which linked Droitwich's salt production to the Wash. ⛺☀🕙👦♣

Upton

Rose & Crown

30 High Street, DN21 5NQ (opp church)
🕐 4 (12 Sat & Sun)-11
☎ (01427) 838216
Tetley Bitter; guest beers Ⓗ
Busy village pub, originally built by the local Hewitts Brewery for American servicemen in the 1950s, with a large bar with lounge and an adjoining function room. Food is served Friday and Saturday evening and Sunday lunch. Outside, there is a covered patio beer garden and a children's play area. Children are also welcome in the function room, while dogs are allowed in the bar. The pub is home to football, cricket, pool and darts teams. Regular themed nights are hosted and Thursday night quizzes for local organisations and charities. ☀😋♣P⬚🛢

Waddington

Three Horseshoes

Old High Street, LN5 9RF (off A607)
🕐 12-3 (11 Wed & Thu; midnight Fri & Sat); 12-10.30 Sun
☎ (01522) 720448
John Smith's Bitter; guest beers Ⓗ
This popular village local always sells a wide range of guest beers, nearly all from micro-breweries. In 2006, nearly 300 different beers were sold here from 55 different breweries. The pub has an excellent reputation for pub games and is the headquarters for the village football and cricket teams. The bustling bar area is supplemented by a small but quieter side bar. ⛺☀😋🚃♣P

Wainfleet

Bateman's Visitor Centre

Salem Bridge Brewery, Mill Lane, PE24 4JE
🕐 11.30-3.30 (not winter Mon or Tue), evenings by appointment
☎ (01754) 880317 ⊕ bateman.co.uk
Bateman Dark Mild, XB, Salem Porter, XXXB, seasonal beers Ⓗ
A chance to sample a comprehensive range of those 'good honest ales' at source. The brewery's core brands, as well as seasonal beers, are always available. The circular Mill Bar is on the ground floor of the famous windmill landmark, next to the Brewery Experience exhibition, with its many interesting displays. A unique place to enjoy a pint, it offers indoor and outdoor games and a good selection of Lincolnshire food specialities too. Q☀🕙👦🍴Å⬚🚃♣P🛢

Westwoodside

Carpenters Arms

Newbigg, DN9 2AT (on B1396 in centre of village)
🕐 2 (12 Sun)-midnight
☎ (01427) 752416

John Smith's Bitter; Taylor Landlord; Wells Bombardier; guest beers Ⓗ

A popular village local, there has been an inn on this site since 1861. The lounge is spread over two levels and there are plans to extend the pub further. Increasing the range of beers on offer has proved popular with locals and real ale enthusiasts from a wider area. Winner of the 2007 Haxey Hood Trophy – a quirky, traditional game that dates from the 14th century – the 'Carps' is at the hub of the local community. ❀🏠🖪♣Ⓟ🚬

Willingham by Stow

Half Moon

23 High Street, DN21 5JZ
🕐 12-2 (not Mon-Wed), 5-11; 12-11 Sat & Sun
☎ (01427) 788340

Caledonian Deuchars IPA; Wells Bombardier; guest beers Ⓗ

Well-patronised and cosy village pub, always offering two real ales and a frequently changing guest on handpump. The home-cooked meals are a must, especially the renowned fish and chip suppers (served Thu-Sat eves and Fri & Sat lunchtimes). Home to the local football team, it also hosts a beer festival in summer. The landlord is waiting for consent to build and run his own micro-brewery. 🏕Q❀🕽🖪♣🚬

Willoughby

Willougby Arms

Church Lane, LN13 9SU (on Alford-Skegness road)
🕐 12-2 (not Mon; 3 Sat), 7-11; 12-3, 7-10.30 Sun
☎ (01507) 462387

Bateman XB; guest beers Ⓗ

The pub is proud to celebrate the tercentenary of its links with Captain John Smith, of Pocahontas fame – the bell from his ship hangs above the coal fire in the lounge. The bar has an L-shaped drinking area, dispensing guest beers that often reflect seasonal or calendar events. The restaurant menu changes on a weekly basis and booking is essential. Well-behaved dogs are welcome. The pub gets very busy with locals on Saturday evening. 🏕❀🕽♣Ⓟ

Willoughton

Stirrup Inn

1 Templefield Road, DN21 5RZ
🕐 5 (12 Sat)-11; 12-11 Sun
☎ (01427) 668270

John Smith's Bitter; guest beers Ⓗ

Built from local Lincolnshire limestone, this hidden gem in an out of the way location is well worth seeking out. The enthusiastic landlord keeps two constantly-changing guest ales to complement the regular beer. The pub attracts locals from the village as well as visitors from further afield, and offers a warm welcome to CAMRA members. Pub quizzes are always popular. ❀🖪🖪♣

Thorold Arms, Harmston, Lincolnshire.

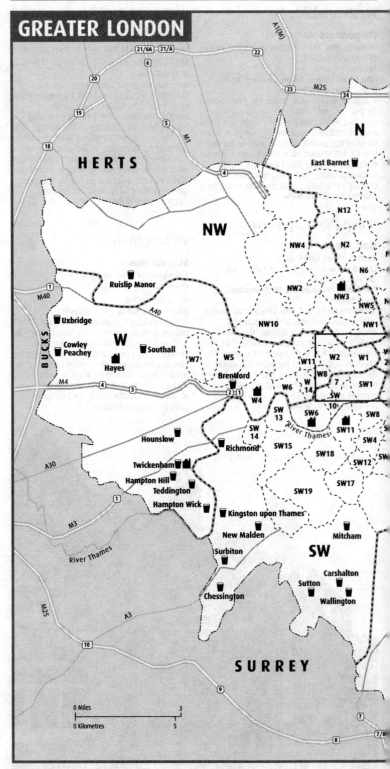

GREATER LONDON

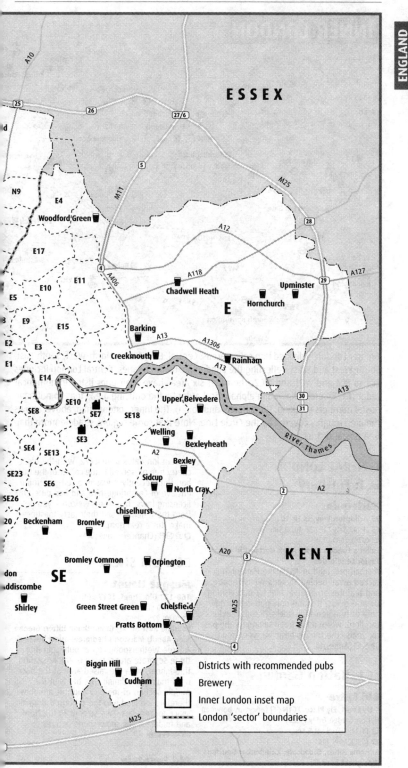

ESSEX

A10

25

26

27/6

5

M11

M25

N9

E4

Woodford Green

28

A12

E17

A406

4

A118

A127

29

Chadwell Heath

Upminster

E5

E10

E11

Hornchurch

E

E9

E15

Barking

A13

A1306

E2

E3

Creekmouth

A13

Rainham

E1

E14

30

A13

31

SE10

Upper Belvedere

SE8

SE7

SE18

River Thames

SE3

Welling

SE4

SE13

Bexleyheath

SE23

A2

Bexley

SE6

Sidcup

2

A2

SE26

North Cray

Chiselhurst

Beckenham

Bromley

20

A20

KENT

Bromley Common

Orpington

3

SE

don

ddiscombe

Green Street Green

Chelsfield

Shirley

M25

Pratts Bottom

4

M20

Biggin Hill

Cudham

Districts with recommended pubs	
Brewery	
Inner London inset map	
London 'sector' boundaries	

M25

INNER LONDON

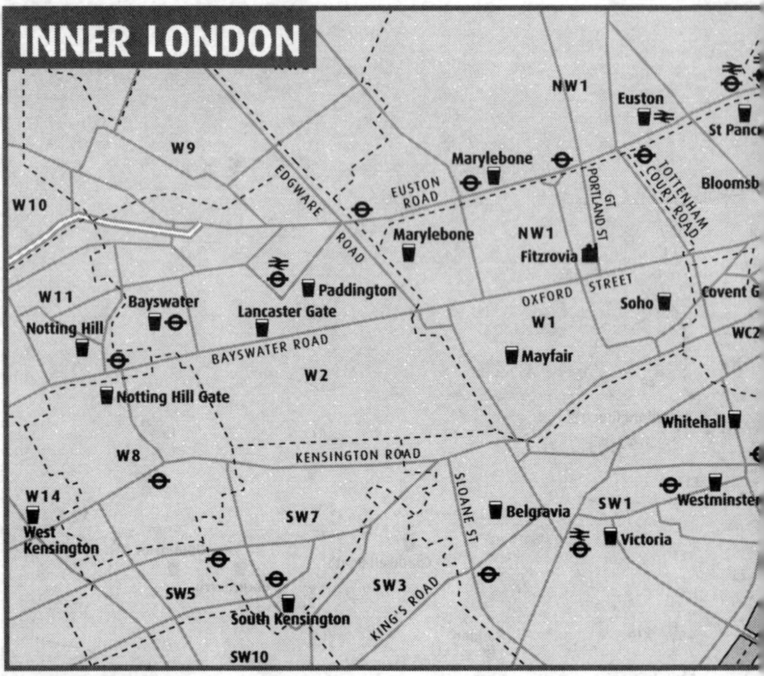

Greater London is divided into seven areas: Central, East, North, North-West, South-East, South-West and West, reflecting the London postal boundaries. Central London includes EC1 to EC4 and WC1 and WC2. The other six areas have their pubs listed in numerical order (E1, E4 etc) followed in alphabetical order by the outlying areas that do not have postal numbers (Barking, Hornchurch, and so on). The Inner London map, above, shows the area roughly covered by the Circle Line. Note that some regions straddle more than one postal district

CENTRAL LONDON

EC1: Finsbury

Harlequin

27 Arlington Way, EC1R 1UY

11 (12 Sat)-11; 7.30-10.30 Sun

☎ (020) 7689 0736

Fuller's London Pride; Hook Norton Old Hooky; Taylor Landlord Ⓗ

A small pub built in 1823, the Harlequin is tucked away behind Sadler's Wells Theatre, and features an interval bell for pub-visiting theatre-goers. It is the only pub in this quiet area of Islington that stocks Timothy Taylor's Landlord, which it has been selling for the past six years. The food is basic but very good.

◑♿⊖(Angel)🚌

EC1: Hatton Garden

Old Mitre ☆

1 Ely Court, Ely Place, EC1N 6SJ (alleyway between Hatton Garden & Ely Place)

11-11; closed Sat & Sun

☎ (020) 7405 4751

Adnams Bitter, Broadside; Caledonian Deuchars IPA; guest beer Ⓗ

One of London's most historic pubs, the original tavern was built by Bishop Goodrich in 1546 to serve the Bishop of Ely Palace. The present inn dates from 1772, with the old cherry tree preserved in the corner of the front bar. Until recently it was in a self-governing enclave of Cambridgeshire and had different licensing laws. The warm welcome you get from the tenants – and their tasty toasties – make this a real gem.

Q❀⊖(Chancery Lane)🚌

EC1: Old Street

Masque Haunt

168-172 Old Street, EC1V 9PB

9-11.30 (1am Fri & Sat)

☎ (020) 7251 4195

Courage Best Bitter; Grand Union Bitter; Greene King Abbot; Marston's Pedigree; guest beers Ⓗ

A large Wetherspoon corner pub, split into three separate areas, there is ample seating throughout, with the raised area at the back used mainly for dining. The bar is in the middle section of the pub and this area has therefore evolved into the preferred drinking space for regulars. Two screens in the front and middle areas show sports fixtures.

◑⇌⊖🚌●

Old Fountain

3 Baldwin Street, EC1V 9NU

11-11; closed Sat & Sun

☎ (020) 7253 2970

Islington N1
Hoxton
E2
Finsbury
Old Street OLD ST.
EC1
Spitalfields
E1
Moorgate Liverpool Street
Hatton-Garden
ry Lane EC2 Bishopsgate Aldgate
City
Fleet EC4 EC3
Street Tower Hill
ad
Bankside Borough London Bridge
BLACKFRIARS ROAD
Southwark Borough
SE1 Tower Bridge

- 🍺 Areas with recommended pubs
- 🏭 Brewery
- ⊖ Circle Line station
- ⇌ Rail connections
- ---- Postal District

17th century, the frontage and interior are resplendently Victorian – all seasoned wood panels and chairs and curtains in deep red. Its name recalls Dr William Butler, the doctor-entrepreneur who sold his 'medicinal ale' for tummy problems at taverns displaying the sign of his head. Today's medicinal ales are the full Shepherd Neame range. Lunch snacks are popular and the Chop House English restaurant is renowned among city diners.
◖⇌(Liverpool St) ⊖(Liverpool St)

EC3: City

Cock & Woolpack
6 Finch Lane, EC3V 3NA
🕒 11-11; closed Sat & Sun
☎ (020) 7626 4799
Shepherd Neame Master Brew, Spitfire, Bishop's Finger Ⓗ
Behind the Royal Exchange in one of the city's many age-old small alleyways, between Cornhill and Threadneedle Street, this inn dates from the late 19th-century. There is one small long and narrow bar on the ground floor, now entirely wood-panelled and sparkling with many mirrors. The toilets are downstairs. At lunchtime and early evening it can be filled to capacity with local office workers. Once owned by Bass Charrington, it is now in the Shepherd Neame stable.
Q◖⇌(Cannon St/Liverpool St) ⊖(Bank/Monument)🚌

Crosse Keys
7 Gracechurch Street, EC3Y 0DR
🕒 9-midnight (1am Fri; 7pm Sat); closed Sun
Fuller's London Pride; Greene King Abbot; Marston's Pedigree; Shepherd Neame Spitfire; guest beers Ⓗ
A typical Wetherspoon pub stocking up to 10 guest ales, nearly always including one from the Grand Union Brewery. It was originally the Hong Kong and Shanghai Bank, hence the oriental clock and ninja-style figures above the bar. The pub is large and airy, with plenty of seating, and a large-screen TV (with the sound turned off) shows mainly big sporting fixtures. Rooms are available for meetings and private functions.
◖♿⇌(Liverpool St) ⊖(Bank/Monument)🚌⇴

East India Arms
67 Fenchurch Street, EC3M 4BR
🕒 11.30-9 (10 Wed & Thu; 11 Fri); closed Sat & Sun
☎ (020) 7265 5121
Shepherd Neame Master Brew, Kent's Best, Spitfire, Bishop's Finger Ⓗ
Now a Shepherd Neame pub, serving its full range, this small one-roomed pub can get busy at lunchtime and in the early evening, but in summer there are also tables and chairs outside. The circular back bar is decorated with fascinating bric-a-brac and conceals a spiral staircase for staff use. The bar is unusually low, with wooden half-panels. The walls are adorned by a large Bass mirror and old photographs of the pub – look for those showing the pub with some of its old names.
⇌(Fenchurch St) ⊖(Aldgate/Tower Hill)🚌

Lamb Tavern
10-12 Leadenhall Market, EC3V 1LR

Fuller's Discovery, London Pride; guest beers Ⓗ
Traditional and unspoilt pub, dating back to the 1780s, with two separate street entrances. There is a single bar on two levels, with the upper level featuring a large aquarium. The Old Fountain has been run by the same family for more than 40 years and has its own full-time cellarman. Food is served daily; salt beef sandwiches are a speciality. A popular pub for visitors and business people in the area.
🕏◖⇌⊖

EC2: Bishopsgate

Magpie
12 New Street, EC2M 4TP
🕒 11-11; closed Sat & Sun
☎ (020) 7929 3889
Fuller's London Pride; Greene King IPA; Taylor Landlord Ⓗ
This city pub, hidden behind Bishopsgate police station, sells between 10 and 18 barrels of Timothy Taylor Landlord in a five-day week – the manager is fanatical about this beer. Bar meals are served lunchtimes and evenings, and the upstairs restaurant features an excellent menu majoring on pies.
◖⇌(Liverpool St) ⊖(Liverpool St)🚌

EC2: Moorgate

Old Doctor Butler's Head
2 Masons Avenue, EC2V 5BT (in alleyway between Basinghall St & Coleman St)
🕒 11-11; closed Sat & Sun
☎ (020) 7606 3504
Shepherd Neame Master Brew, Kentish Best, Spitfire, Bishop's Finger, seasonal beers Ⓗ
A hidden gem near Guildhall, this inn is always welcoming and busy. Originally built in the

✪ 11-11; closed Sat & Sun
☎ (020) 7626 2454 ⊕ thelambtavern.com
Young's Bitter, Special, seasonal beers Ⓗ
Situated in the picturesque Leadenhall Market, this Grade II listed building has an impressive Victorian frosted glass and pillar frontage. The interior is equally splendid and includes a tiled cellar bar, a mezzanine area in the main bar and a tiled scene depicting Sir Christopher Wren in the side entrance. Extremely popular with city workers, the Lamb is usually busy and drinkers overflow into the market area where tables are provided.
◖≉(Fenchurch St)⊖(Bank/Monument)

Swan

Ship Tavern Passage, 78 Gracechurch Street, EC3V 1LY
✪ 11-9; closed Sat & Sun
☎ (020) 7626 2454
Fuller's Chiswick Bitter, London Pride; guest beer Ⓗ
Just off Leadenhall Market, this traditional Fuller's house comprises a small galley-style downstairs bar with a spiral stairway leading to a larger upstairs room with its own service area. A mirrored wall in the upper bar gives a feeling of space. Look out for the huge Victorian coin on the stairway to the staff area. The guest ale comes from the Fuller's portfolio.
≉(Fenchurch St)⊖(Bank/Monument)⸜

EC3: Tower Hill

Peacock

41 Minories, EC3N 1DT
✪ 12-midnight; closed Sat & Sun
☎ (020) 7488 3630
Black Sheep Ale; Taylor Landlord; guest beer Ⓗ
Positioned in the lower left corner of Ibex House, an impressive, Grade I listed building, this pub is popular with city workers. The building was reputedly earmarked by Hitler as a Gestapo HQ had things gone differently. Nowadays there's more of a sporting emphasis, with a large-screen TV broadcasting various fixtures, especially rugby. Darts and pool are played in the upstairs area, and a selection of pub games are on offer from the bar.
◖≉(Fenchurch St)⊖(Tower Hill/Tower Gateway DLR)🚃

EC4: Fleet Street

Old Bank of England

194 Fleet Street, EC4A 2LT
✪ 11-11; closed Sat & Sun
☎ (020) 7430 2255
Fuller's Chiswick, Discovery, London Pride, ESB, seasonal beers Ⓗ
Built in 1888 as the Royal Courts of Justice branch of the Bank of England, the building was taken over by Fuller's who converted it into an atmospheric pub in 1994. The cellars are rumoured to have been used by Sweeney Todd, the demon barber. The elaborate exterior features towers at the corners, marble pillars and lots of granite. Inside, coffered ceilings, large chandeliers, high windows and tall bar fitting create a wonderful ambience. Prints and maps line the walls.

Q❀❦◖▮≉(Blackfriars)⊖(Temple/Chancery Lane)🚃⸜

WC1: Bloomsbury

Calthorpe Arms

252 Gray's Inn Road, WC1X 8JR
✪ 11-11.30; 12-10.30 Sun
☎ (020) 7278 4732
Wells Bombardier; Young's Bitter, Special, seasonal beers Ⓗ
The small traditional double doors at the corner of this one-bar pub give a clear hint of what to expect inside. The dark wooden bar has high bar stools, comfortable seating around the walls and heavy wooden/metal tables, with a warmly welcoming atmosphere. A silent TV in the corner usually screens sport. The upstairs room doubles as a restaurant and as a meeting room in the evening. An outdoor covered smoking area is available.
❀◖▮⊖(Russell Sq/Chancery Lane)⸜

Rugby Tavern

19 Great James Street, WC1N 3ES
✪ 11-11; closed Sat & Sun
☎ (020) 7405 1384
Shepherd Neame Master Brew, Spitfire, seasonal beer Ⓗ
This Georgian-style building, in a pedestrianised area off Theobalds Road, takes its name from Rugby School, on whose land it stands. There is a single ground-level room with an island bar. The windows and fittings are 1930s in style, including cast-iron table supports and a marble fireplace. Stairs at the rear lead to a function room. There are eight tables on the patio. The pub caters mainly for local office and hospital workers, and is popular at lunchtime and in the early evening, when bar food including daily specials is served. ❀◖▮⊖(Russell Sq)🚃♣

WC1: Holborn

Cittie of Yorke ☆

22 High Holborn, WC1V 6BS
✪ 11.30 (12 Sat)-11; closed Sun
☎ (020) 7242 7670
Samuel Smith OBB Ⓗ
Close to the Holborn Bars, the historic entrance to London, a pub has stood on this site since 1430. Rebuilt in 1695 as the Gray's Inn Coffee House, it is now a three-bar pub, the cellar bar being part of the 17th-century structure. Grade II listed, it boasts a hugely impressive interior with the real splendour lying in the rear bar, with its vaulted ceiling, long bar, handsome

INDEPENDENT BREWERIES	
Battersea SW11	
Brew Wharf SE1	
Bunker WC2	
Cock & Hen SW6	
Fuller's W4	
Grand Union Hayes	
Horseshoe NW6	
Mash W1	
Meantime SE7	
Twickenham Twickenham	
Zerodegrees SE3	

screenwork, private compartments and massive mounted vats. A rare triangular stove is still in use, with an underfloor chimney.
🏛Q🕒👌♿⇌(Farringdon)⊖(Chancery Lane)🚃

Penderel's Oak

283-288 High Holborn, WC1V 7HJ
🕒 9-1am daily
☎ (020) 7242 5669
Courage Best Bitter, Directors; Greene King Abbot; Marston's Pedigree; guest beers ⊞
Occupying the ground floor and basement of a modern office building, this pub has a very large L-shaped room with wood panelling, many nooks and interesting ceiling decorations. French windows face out to the street, and benches are placed outside in summer. Four guest beers from a very long list feature regularly. The noisy cellar bar, screening sport on TV, can be hired. This lively Wetherspoon's pub counts tourists and office workers among its customers.
🅿🕒👌⊖(Chancery Lane)🚃

WC1: St Pancras

Mabel's Tavern

9 Mabledon Place, WC1H 9AZ
🕒 10-11 (10.30 Sun)
☎ (020) 7387 7739
Shepherd Neame Master Brew, Kent's Best, Spitfire, Bishop's Finger, seasonal beers ⊞
Situated just off Euston Road, halfway between Euston and King's Cross stations, this bright and comfortable pub provides a range of five beers (three at weekends). Office staff at lunchtime and tourists and locals in the evening enjoy good pub food and ales. Inside, a long bar separates a raised, more intimate area on the left from the right-hand area, which is warmed by a coal-effect fire in winter. A small number of tables are placed outside in summer. 🅿🕒⇌⊖

Skinners Arms

114 Judd Street, WC1H 9NT
🕒 12-11; closed Sat & Sun
☎ (020) 7837 6521
Greene King IPA, Abbot; Taylor Landlord; guest beer ⊞
The 'Arms' in question belong to the Skinners company, founded in 1327 as one of the 'great twelve' livery companies. The street is named after Andrew Judd, master of the Skinners company, Lord Mayor and founder of Tonbridge School. The pub's mock-Victorian look extends to the curtains, bar counter, mirrored pillars, stained glass and flocked wallpaper. There is a raised seating area to the left and a more private one at the rear. A covered and heated smoking area is provided.
🅿🕒⇌⊖🚃└

WC2: Chancery Lane

Seven Stars

53 Carey Street, WC2A 2JB
🕒 11 (12 Sat)-11; 12-10.30 Sun
☎ (020) 7242 8521
Adnams Bitter, Broadside; Harveys Sussex Best; guest beers ⊞

Located near Chancery Lane, the pub's clientele typically includes barristers during the week and church musicians on Sunday. The central bar has two drinking areas on either side. Until the 1980s the Seven Stars was the only pub in London without a public convenience. Ladies were invited to use the landlord's private facilities, while gentlemen made do with a nearby pissoir! Tom Payne is the resident black cat with a white collar and big, sad eyes. Q🕒⊖🚃

WC2: Covent Garden

Freemasons Arms

81-82 Long Acre, WC2E 9NG
🕒 12-11 (11.30 Fri & Sat); 12-10.30 Sun
☎ (020) 7836 3115
Shepherd Neame Master Brew, Spitfire, seasonal beers ⊞
Originally owned by Charringtons, then Sam Smith, followed by Greene King and finally Shepherd Neame in 2003, this smartly furnished lounge bar has two raised seating areas front and rear. On the first floor, there are two function rooms and a restaurant first licensed in 1704. The 1896 pub frontage displays masonic symbols. Inside, it asserts that the football association was formed here – in fact the FA was formed at the larger Freemasons' Tavern in Great Queens Street nearby.
🏛🕒👌⇌(Charing Cross)⊖(Charing Cross/Leicester Square)└

Harp

47 Chandos Place, WC2N 4HS
🕒 10.30-11 (11.30 Fri); 12-10.30 Sun
☎ (020) 7836 0291 🌐 harpbarcoventgarden.com
Black Sheep Bitter; Harveys Sussex Best; Taylor Landlord; guest beers ⊞
Local CAMRA Pub of the Year 2006, the award certificate is dramatically displayed behind the bar at this bustling thespian pub, popular with musicians and stage hands from the nearby Coliseum. The walls are covered with items from the licensee's personal art collection, a tribute to the National Portrait Gallery nearby. Welsh harps are etched into the bar mirrors and the window panes at the front. At the far end of the long, narrow bar, a winding staircase leads to additional seating.
Q🕒⇌(Charing Cross)⊖(Leicester Sq)🚃♠

WC2: Strand

Edgar Wallace

40 Essex Street, WC2R 3JF
🕒 11-11; closed Sat & Sun
☎ (020) 7353 3120 🌐 edgarwallacepub.com
Adnams Bitter; guest beers ⊞
Named after the writer who inspired many 1960s B-movies, this is a one-room pub which can get crowded with lawyers from the nearby Temple. There is a function room upstairs which can accommodate any overflow. Six handpumps feature a good selection of constantly changing beers. Up to two beer festivals and other events are held a year; check the website for details.
🕒⊖(Temple)

Ship & Shovell

1-3 Craven Passage, WC2N 5PH
⏰ 11-11; closed Sun
☎ (020) 7839 1311
Badger K&B Sussex, Tanglefoot, seasonal beers H

Named after Admiral Sir Cloudesley Shovell, who was nearly drowned and subsequently murdered when his fleet ran into the Scilly Isles in 1707, this is a unique pub, situated on both sides of Craven Passage underneath the arches of Charing Cross station. The south side, available for private parties, has an intimate snug and upstairs room. The north side contains some magnificent etched mirrors. The walls are adorned with prints and photographs of London and naval scenes, as well as the Admiral's portrait.
⟨⇌(Charing Cross)⊖(Charing Cross/ Embankment)🚆

EAST LONDON
E1: Aldgate

Dispensary

19A Leman Street, E1 8EN
⏰ 12-11; closed Sat & Sun
☎ (020) 7265 0006
Adnams Broadside; Harveys Sussex Best Bitter H

The large, imposing cream frontage of this former hospital building leads to an opulent, smart interior. The double-height bar has a mezzanine floor and a function room, which is available for hire. The emphasis is on fine dining with a full menu and an extensive wine list, but there is also a bar menu for a more traditional alternative (meals served lunchtime and evening daily). Look out for the ghost: this pub is supposedly haunted!
⟨▶⊖(Aldgate East)

E1: Liverpool Street

Shooting Star

125-129 Middlesex Street, E1 7JF
⏰ 12-11; closed Sat & Sun
☎ (020) 7929 6818
Fuller's Chiswick, Discovery, London Pride, ESB, seasonal beers H

Large Fuller's house, tucked just round the corner from Liverpool Street station. The Shooting Star has a spacious interior with plenty of seating. Due to its location it can get extremely busy during the lunch hour and after work. The complete Fuller's range of ales is sold, including seasonals. Food is served until 9pm daily. The pub has particularly good disabled access.
⟨▶♿⇌(Liverpool St)⊖(Liverpool St)🚆—

E1: Spitalfields

Pride of Spitalfields

3 Heneage Street, E1 5LJ
⏰ 11-11 (2am Fri & Sat)
☎ (020) 7247 8933
Crouch Vale Brewers Gold; Fuller's London Pride, ESB; guest beer H

Situated just off the famous Brick Lane, this pub is ideal for a pre- (or post-!) curry pint. Due to its popularity it can get crowded, and in the summer months drinkers spill out onto the pavement where benches are provided. The guest beer is often Sharp's Doom Bar, which may well become a permanent fixture, leading to a fifth handpump dispensing the guest. ❀◀⊖(Aldgate East)

E2: Bethnal Green

Camel

277 Globe Road, E2 0JD
⏰ 4 (1 Thu & Fri)-11; 12-11 Sat; 12-10.30 Sun
☎ (020) 8983 9888 ⊕ thecamele2.co.uk
Adnams Bitter, Broadside H

Rejuvenated after a long period of closure, this pub is instantly recognisable by its dark-tiled exterior. Inside, a cosy atmosphere is created by subdued lighting, wood-panelling and attractive print wallpaper. Historical photos are mounted on the walls including some of this very pub when it was a meeting point for away-days. Gourmet pies are sold all day and their aroma permeates the air, making them hard to resist. Occasional piano players further add to the convivial ambience.
❀◀▶⇌(Bethnal Green/Cambridge Heath) ⊖(Bethnal Green)

E3: Bow

Coborn Arms

8 Coborn Road, E3 2DA
⏰ 11-11 (11.30 Wed & Thu; midnight Fri & Sat); 12-11 Sun
☎ (020) 8980 3793 ⊕ youngs.co.uk
Young's Bitter, Special, seasonal beers H

Friendly local just off the Mile End Road with a central bar serving three distinctly different areas. To the right of the entrance is a raised area for darts; the middle section, served by the bar, is a comfortable drinking area; towards the back of the pub is an area mainly reserved for dining, with plenty of tables. Outside at the front is a patio with heaters.
❀◀♿⇌(Bow Church DLR)⊖(Mile End/Bow Road)🚆♣P

Palm Tree

127 Grove Road, E3 5RP
⏰ 12.30-midnight
Beer range varies H

This hidden gem used to be a street-corner pub, but due to extensive local redevelopment it now finds itself standing alone between an ecology park and the Regent's Canal. The unspoilt interior has been used as a film set on many occasions, most recently for a TV trailer. The vintage gilt wallpaper is a particular talking point. Live music at weekends leads to enthusiastic sing-a-longs. Two guests are usually available.
❀⇌(Bethnal Green)

E4: Chingford

Royal Oak

219 Kings Head Hill, E4 7PP
⏰ 11-11 (1am Fri & Sat); 12-11 Sun
☎ (020) 8529 1492
McMullens AK, Country, seasonal beers H

Two-bar pub with a public bar featuring bar billiards (rare in this area) and large TV screens for sport. The lounge is comfortably furnished and has a raised dining area to the rear. Background music is not obtrusive. The pub is fully accessible to wheelchairs. Food is served 12-9pm daily, and children are allowed until 9.30pm. Quiz night is Sunday. Outside is a large car park and garden. ✿◖❶❦✿▲🛏♣P🔌

E5: Clapton

Anchor & Hope

15 High Hill Ferry, E5 9HS (800m N of Lea Bridge Road along river)
🌞 11 (1 winter)-11; 11-midnight Sat; 12-10.30 Sun
☎ (020) 8806 1730
Fuller's London Pride, ESB; guest beer Ⓗ
Spectacular views over the open marshes and River Lea are among this traditional boozer's attractions, a regular destination for many walkers and cyclists. A community spirit gladdens the cosy single bar and it is a treasured gathering place for locals. Fuller's beers and a guest ale are now complemented by soup and pies served until 5pm. Darts matches and watching rowers on the river add to the fun. ⚌✿≹(Clapton)🚌(393)♣

Eclipse

57 Elderfield Road, E5 0LF (off Chatsworth Rd)
🌞 4-11 (midnight Thu & Fri); 10.30-midnight Sat; 10.30-11 Sun
☎ (020) 8986 1591
Adnams Broadside; Fuller's London Pride; Harveys Sussex Best Bitter; Taylor Landlord Ⓗ
A gem of a pub, selling four real ales, tucked away in a back street off the Chatsworth Road. The Eclipse has been taken over by Punch Taverns, and the landlord has worked hard to increase trade and bring real ale to this area of Hackney. ⚌❦≹(Homerton)🚌(308)♣🔌

E8: Hackney

Pembury Tavern

90 Amhurst Road, E8 1JH
🌞 12-11
☎ (020) 8986 8597 🌐 individualpubs.co.uk/pembury
Milton Minotaur, Jupiter, Pegasus, Scarta, Nero, Colossus Ⓗ
Since opening in 2006 this pub has gone from strength to strength. It sells the full range of Milton beers as well as guest ales, which are swapped with guest micros. The Pembury stages three beer festivals a year, in March, July and November. It also sells a large selection of German and Belgian bottled beers. The menu features good food which is served lunchtime and evening, all day on Sunday. Q◖❶≹(Hackney Downs)🚌♣👶🔌🍴

E9: Homerton

Chesham Arms

15 Mehetabel Road, E9 6DU (end of Isabella Rd, off Homerton High St)
🌞 12-11
☎ (020) 8985 2919
St Austell Tribute; Wells Bombardier; guest beers Ⓗ
The Chesham Arms is a small back-street free house of a type that is becoming rare in East London. The single bar is furnished with sofas

and high tables. Guest beers can include just about any ale, and the landlady will try to obtain beers requested by her customers. Home-cooked meals are available, and a pool table and TV provide the entertainment. There is a heated canopy in the garden for smokers. ✿◖❶≹(Hackney Central)♣🔌

E10: Leyton

Leyton Orient Supporters Club

Matchroom Stadium, Oliver Road, E10 5NF (10 mins walk from Leyton underground)
🌞 matchdays 2 hrs before KO-11pm
☎ (020) 8988 8288
Beer range varies Ⓗ
The club moved into the new West Stand in August 2005. Established for more than 30 years, real ale was introduced about 12 years ago. A bright, air-conditioned club with adequate seating, it has has won several CAMRA awards. Beer festivals are held twice a year. Located opposite Waltham Forest Community Centre and the five-a-side pitches, it opens on matchdays and for some televised England and cup games. ❦⊖(Leyton)🚌🔌

E11: Wanstead

Nightingale

51 Nightingale Lane, E11 2EY (10 mins walk from Snaresbrook station)
🌞 11 (12 Sun)-midnight
☎ (020) 8530 4540
Courage Best Bitter; Fuller's London Pride; Greene King IPA; guest beers Ⓗ
Located by the green, this pub has a country look and feel. Six ales, 60 malt whiskies, 12 vodkas and approximately 10 bourbons are always available. A central bar serves the connecting rooms, with a hatch service at the rear. Among the delicious food options are seafood dishes and main meals including scallops wrapped in bacon, grilled sea bass, lamb shanks and Thai green curry. Breakfast is also served here, and there is a special vegetarian menu. ◖⊖🚌(W12)

E14: Limehouse

Grapes

76 Narrow Street, E14 8BP
🌞 12-3, 5.30-11; 12-11 Sat; 12-10.30 Sun
☎ (020) 7987 4396
Adnams Bitter; Marston's Pedigree; Taylor Landlord Ⓗ
This is a pub with a rich history – there has been an inn of some description on this site since 1585 and it was mentioned by Dickens in Our Mutual Friend. The entrance is on Narrow Street (in bygone days guests would have arrived by river). It opens onto the small bar, a walk-through to the back bar. The French doors at the rear open onto a small gantry overlooking the Thames. Upstairs is a restaurant which serves excellent fish meals. Q✿◖❶⊖(Limehouse/West Ferry DLR)♣🔌

E15: Stratford

King Edward VII

47 Broadway, E15 4BQ (through Stratford Mall from railway and bus station)
✪ 12-11 (midnight Thu-Sat); 12-11.30 Sun
☎ (020) 8534 2313 ⊕ kingeddie.co.uk
Caledonian Deuchars IPA; guest beers Ⓗ
This two-bar pub on the busy Stratford Broadway has a front bar with low ceilings. The larger rear bar is approached via a tiled passageway and steps. The three guest beers sold here are sourced through SIBA. Delicious food is available from a changing menu. Live music is performed on Thursday night and Sunday is quiz night. ⊛⊕≡⊖🍴

E17: Walthamstow Village

Nags Head

9 Orford Road, E17 9LP (10 mins walk from Walthamstow Central)
✪ 2 (12 Sat)-11; 12-10.30 Sun
☎ (020) 8520 9709
Adnams Broadside; Fuller's London Pride; Mighty Oak Oscar Wilde; guest beers Ⓗ
Situated in Walthamstow's historic quarter, this former Victorian coaching inn now has a more modern feel. There are tea-lights and table cloths, and black & white photos of legendary film stars adorn the walls. Live jazz draws the crowds on Sunday afternoon. The five handpumps always include a mild, and a range of Belgian bottled beers is available. The garden and heated marquee provide refuge for smokers. A regular customer is the village's most famous resident, Tetley the cat!
⊛≡(Walthamstow Central)⊖(Walthamstow Central)🚌(W12)🍴

Barking

Britannia

1 Church Road, IG11 8PR
✪ 11-3, 5-11; 12-11 Fri-Sun
☎ (020) 8594 1305
Wells Bombardier; Young's Bitter, Special, seasonal beers Ⓗ
When you approach this friendly local you can see evidence of Barking's nautical past: it once boasted England's largest fishing fleet. The area has been extensively rebuilt, replacing unloved flats, and the usually quiet saloon bar offers a friendly home from home. The public bar features bare floorboards, darts, pool and a jukebox. Hearty, good value food is offered at lunchtime and roasts are popular on Sunday (booking advisable).
Q⊛⊕≡⊖(Barking)🚌♣P🍴

Chadwell Heath

Eva Hart

1128 High Road, RM6 4AH
✪ 9-midnight
☎ (020) 8597 1069
Courage Best Bitter, Directors; Greene King Abbot; Marston's Pedigree; guest beers Ⓗ
This large and comfortable house, previously the old police station, is something of a pearl in a locality where real ale is pretty hard to find. Three or four guest beers are usually

available, and sometimes Weston's Old Rosie cider. Children are welcome in the balcony seating area until 9pm. There are many mementos of the eponymous Eva Hart, who was a local singer and music teacher and one of the oldest Titanic survivors. Breakfast is served until noon, and main meals and snacks until 10pm. ⊛⊕🚫≡🚌P🍴

Creekmouth

Crooked Billet

113 River Road, IG11 0EG (1½ miles S of A13)
✪ 11-midnight; 12-11 Sun
☎ (020) 8507 0126
Fuller's London Pride Ⓗ
Pleasant, traditional pub in an industrial area, featuring three bars: a public bar with pool table, a saloon bar where food is served at lunchtime and a small wood-panelled bar known as the 'middle bar'. The garden is open during the summer. The pub is the base for the Creekmouth Preservation Society. Bus route 387 terminates about half a mile from here but extends to pass the pub four times during peak periods (Mon-Fri).
🚐⊛⊕≡🚌(387)P

Hornchurch

Chequers

121 North Street, RM11 1ST
✪ 12-11 (midnight Fri); 11-midnight Sat; 12-10.30 Sun
☎ (01708) 442094
Greene King IPA; Wadworth 6X; Young's Bitter Ⓗ
This Victorian pub stands proudly in the middle of a traffic island, undisturbed by the world around it. Size restrictions have enabled it to remain a traditional local, and changes in ownership have not affected the commitment to real ale. It is popular for sporting events, transmitted on big screens, and displays an impressive array of darts trophies. Limited bar snacks, hot and cold, are available at the weekend. ≡(Emerson Pk)🚌♣P

JJ Moons

Unit 3, 46-62 High Street, RM12 4UN
✪ 9-midnight (12.30am Fri & Sat); 9-11.30 Sun
☎ (01708) 478410
Greene King IPA, Morland Original, Old Speckled Hen, Abbot; guest beers Ⓗ
An impressive range of guest beers greets you in this busy Wetherspoon pub on the edge of the High Street. In addition to the beers there are usually three real ciders served on gravity on the bar. The collection of old local photographs and information includes a feature on John Cornwall, the boy hero of the Battle of Jutland. Breakfast is served to noon and main meals to 11pm; the family area is open until 6pm. Q⊕🚫🚌♣

Rainham

Phoenix

Broadway, RM13 9YW (on B1335 near Clock Tower)
✪ 11-11; 12-3, 7-10.30 Sun
☎ (01708) 553700
Courage Directors; Greene King IPA; John Smith's Bitter; Wadworth 6X; guest beer Ⓗ

Busy, spacious town pub, close to Rainham station and in a convenient spot for Rainham Marshes. It has two bars: a public bar with dartboard and a saloon for dining (no food Sun). Quizzes and live entertainment/music alternate on Thursdays, as well as every Saturday. The large garden has five aviaries and a barbecue area. Family fun days are held on bank holiday Mondays. Accommodation is offered in seven twin and one single room.
🏠🛏️◁🕐⏰🍴🚃🚭🏠♣

Woodford Green

Cricketers
299-301 High Road, IG8 9HG
🕐 11-11 (midnight Fri); 12-11 Sun
☎ (020) 8504 2734
McMullen AK, Country; guest beer Ⓗ
Pleasant local with a warm and comfortable saloon bar and a more basic public bar with a dartboard. The saloon displays insignia plaques for all 18 first-class cricket counties, as well as photographs of Sir Winston Churchill who was for many years the local MP and whose statue stands on the green nearby. The guest beer changes monthly and the food served is hearty and good value (Mon-Sat lunchtimes only). There is a petanque pitch in the garden. 🏠◁🕐♿🚃(179, W13)**P**

Traveller's Friend
496-498 High Road, IG8 0PN
🕐 12-11
☎ (020) 8504 2435
Adnams Broadside; Courage Best Bitter; Greene King Abbot; Young's Bitter; guest beer Ⓗ
An absolute gem of a local situated on a slip road off the busy main road. This is a friendly and comfortable pub featuring oak-panelled walls and rare original snob screens. The friendly Welsh couple who have run the pub superbly for many years make all comers feel welcome and always serve their beer in tip-top condition. At least one guest beer is always available, and beer festivals are held in April and September. Lunches are served Monday to Saturday. Q🏠◁🕐♿🚃**P**

NORTH LONDON
N1: Hoxton

Prince Arthur
49 Brunswick Place, N1 6EB
🕐 11-midnight; 12-6.30 Sun
☎ (020) 7253 3187
Shepherd Neame Master Brew Bitter, Kent's Best, Spitfire Ⓗ
This friendly one-bar back-street local has been run by the same landlord for 28 years. An oasis tucked away from the bustle of nearby City Road, it has two distinct areas, with seating at tables to the front and a busy lower darts/games area to the rear. The decor is sports-themed, with pictures of racehorses and photographs of the landlord's boxing days. Unobtrusive background music plays. Light snacks are always available, and there is seating outside during clement weather. Sunday hours may be extended if busy.
🏠🚃(Old St)🚇(Old St)♣

Wenlock Arms
26 Wenlock Road, N1 7TA
🕐 12-midnight (1am Fri & Sat)
☎ (020) 7608 3406 🌐 wenlock-arms.co.uk
Adnams Bitter; Harveys Hadlow Bitter; guest beers Ⓗ
Now in its 12th year in this Guide, and four times local CAMRA Pub of the Year, the pub stands close to the former Wenlock Brewery. A choice of eight real ales is available, plus a cider or perry and a selection of continental bottled beers; check the website for regional beer festivals. Regular live jazz sessions are hosted. Community groups such as Camden Canal's Narrowboat Association meet upstairs, and the pub has its own cricket team. Snacks are substantial, including legendary salt beef sandwiches. 🚃🚇(Old St)🚃♣🍺

N1: Islington

Charles Lamb
16 Elia Street, N1 8DE
🕐 4 (12 Thu-Sat)-11; 12-10.30 Sun
☎ (020) 7837 5040 🌐 thecharleslambpub.com
Fuller's Chiswick; Taylor Landlord; guest beers Ⓗ
Saved from closure and redevelopment, the current owners relaunched the pub in 2005. A small, two-bar arrangement with a central island bar, this back-street pub sits in a quiet residential area close to the Regent's Canal off Upper Street. Nominated for a Best Gastropub award in 2007, its food is distinctly innovative and not unreasonably priced, with French and English specials changing daily. It serves a traditional Sunday roast, and has a good wine list (the pub has its own wine club). Atmosphere and service are traditional, and the cask ale range is excellent.
Q◁🕐🚇(Angel)🚃🍺

Compton Arms
4 Compton Avenue, N1 2XD
🕐 12-11 (10.30 Sun)
☎ (020) 7359 6883
Greene King IPA, Abbot; guest beers Ⓗ
This single-bar gem, tucked away around the back of busy Upper Street near the Union Chapel, is based in a striking cottage-style building. Inside, the compact dimensions and beams heighten the country pub atmosphere. The main area is bare-boarded, with bottle glass panelled windows. There is a cosy seating area to the rear of the bar, and a lower lounge leads out to a pleasant patio courtyard. The guest beer adds variety and the food is excellent. It can get crowded when Arsenal play at home.
🏠◁🚃(Highbury & Islington/Essex Rd) 🚇(Highbury & Islington)🍺

Crown
116 Cloudesley Road, N1 0EB
🕐 12-11 (10.30 Sun)
☎ (020) 7837 7107
Fuller's London Pride, ESB, seasonal beers Ⓗ
This 1820s pub, Grade II listed and on CAMRA's Regional Inventory, was originally at least four bars, which have been opened up around the surviving island bar. A fine assortment of screens and glasswork complement the ceiling decoration. A vibrant, modern English

menu is offered, all day at weekends. A real fire warms during winter months, while an outdoor patio drinking area is tempting in summer. ❀◁▯❸(Angel)

Island Queen

87 Noel Road, N1 8HD
✪ 11-midnight; 12-10.30 Sun
☎ (020) 7704 7631
Adnams Bitter, Broadside; Fuller's London Pride; guest beers Ⓗ
Gorgeous architecturally, the pub is listed on CAMRA's Regional Inventory. Built in 1851, it retains many original features including full-height timber and glass screens and impressive cut and etched glasswork. The upstairs lounge has an interesting mosaic. The large front windows overlook a patio area. Belgian bottled and draught beers are stocked, and a wide-ranging menu of traditional English and innovative modern dishes is available, including Sunday roasts. Prices are reasonable – although not a 'gastro' pub, the food is distinctly high quality. ◁▯❸(Angel)🖾

Narrow Boat

119 St Peters Street, N1 8PZ
✪ 11-midnight
☎ (020) 7288 0572
Adnams Bitter, Broadside; Fuller's London Pride; guest beers Ⓗ
Sitting above the towpath of the Regent's Canal, this long split-level pub has a boating theme, with the lower room extending alongside the towpath and the upper room providing a vista of the canal. Both have bars, but the upper one at street level is the main focus. The exterior retains some Victorian features but a recent refurbishment has created a light, airy and spacious pub. There are large but unobtrusive sports screens. Food is traditional, with daily specials.
Q◁▯❸(Angel)

N2: East Finchley

Old White Lion

121 Great North Road, N2 0NW
✪ 12-11 (midnight Thu; 1am Fri & Sat); 12-11 Sun
☎ (020) 8365 4861
Caledonian Deuchars IPA; Young's Bitter; guest beers Ⓗ
Situated next to East Finchley tube station, under the bridge, this is a busy pub with a young, cosmopolitan clientele. It offers an impressive array of foreign beers on draught, as well as five handpumps dispensing real ale. Look out for the interesting pictures of past pop artists on the walls. Quiz night is Tuesday. ◁▯❸(East Finchley)P

N4: Harringay

Salisbury Hotel ☆

1 Grand Parade, Green Lanes, N4 1JX
✪ 5-midnight (1am Thu; 2am Fri); 12-2am Sat; 12-11.30 Sun
☎ (020) 8800 9617
Fuller's Discovery, London Pride, ESB; guest beer Ⓗ
This Grade II listed building is an architectural gem retaining many original 19th-century

fittings – a framed magazine article from 1899 confirms how little has changed. Food is served from 6pm on weekdays and all day at weekends, and there is a separate dining area. Live music is staged at the weekend, jazz on occasional Sundays, a quiz night on Monday. This pub is also the meeting place of the Harringay Conservation Society. Handy for Finsbury Park, families and dogs are welcome. Q◁▯❸🖾≠(Harringay/Harringay Green Lanes)🖾♣

N6: Highgate

Flask

77 Highgate West Hill, N6 6BU
✪ 12-11 (10.30 Sun)
☎ (020) 8348 7346
Adnams Broadside; Taylor Landlord; guest beers Ⓗ
Built in the 17th century, the original bar is still evident among a variety of rooms. Brick fireplaces, old prints and a quirky collection of furniture set the tone. Regular and guest ales plus cider are backed up by foreign bottled and draught beers. The varied menu ranges from superb roasts to stews and vegetarian options, served all day at weekends. A large, heated and partially covered outdoor area eases the lack of interior space.
🏚Q❀◁▯🖾♣♦⌐

Gatehouse

1 North Road, N6 4BD (2 mins from A1)
✪ 9-11.30 (midnight Fri & Sat); 9-10.30 Sun
☎ (020) 8340 8054
Courage Best Bitter; Fuller's London Pride; Greene King Abbot; Marston's Pedigree; Shepherd Neame Spitfire; guest beers Ⓗ
A Wetherspoon house since 1993, and the site of a pub for centuries, the name reflects the area's historic significance as an entry point to the capital. Up to six guest beers are available, including at least one from the Red Squirrel Brewery of Hertford. The cider is from Weston's. Food is served all day and breakfast at weekends. Grill night on Tuesday and curry on Thursday are popular, and Sunday roasts are a highlight. Upstairs is a theatre, said to be the highest in Britain. Q❀◁▯🖾♦⌐

Wrestlers

98 North Road, N6 4AA
✪ 4.30 (12 Sat)-midnight (1am Fri & Sat); 12-11 Sun
☎ (020) 8340 4297
Fuller's London Pride; Greene King IPA, Abbot; Young's Bitter Ⓗ
This 16th-century pub was substantially rebuilt in the 1920s, but the fireplace is thought to be original. The landlord (whose father runs fellow Guide entry Rose & Crown in N16), clocks up 10 years in charge in October 2007. The pub has strong local traditions, notably the 'swearing on the horns' ceremony which commits guests to merriment and debauchery. Outdoor drinking space is provided at the front and rear of the pub. Popular events include Sunday roasts and a twice-yearly oyster and champagne night. 🏚Q❀❸(Highgate)⌐

N7: Holloway

Coronet

338-346 Holloway Road, N7 6NJ
☼ 9am-11.30
☎ (020) 7609 5014

Courage Directors; Greene King Abbot; Marston's Burton Bitter, Pedigree; Theakston Best; guest beers Ⓗ

A former cinema converted 10 years ago by Wetherspoon's, this pub is one of only two selling real ale on the Holloway Road. There are never fewer than eight beers at any time, and during regular festivals all 12 pumps dispense a different ale. It retains the style of a 1940s cinema, with an old projector in the centre of the dining area where good value food is served daily until 10.30pm.
Q❄️☺️🅳♿️≢(Drayton Pk)⊖(Holloway Rd)🚻

N8: Crouch End

Harringay Arms

153 Crouch Hill, N8 9HX
☼ 12-midnight (1am Fri & Sat)
☎ (020) 8340 4243

Adnams Broadside; Caledonian Deuchars IPA; Courage Best; Wells Bombardier Ⓗ

Small, wood-panelled pub at the foot of Crouch Hill. Old prints and maps show the development of this suburb. A rare urban gem, this is very much a pub for conversation and quiet enjoyment of a pint, but sports events are screened at a sensible volume. Up to three of the four listed beers are on offer at any time, and filled rolls are sold lunchtime and early evening. There is a small outside courtyard, and chess sets are available on request. ❄️🚻♣️

N8: Hornsey

Three Compasses

62 High Street, N8 7NX
☼ 11-11 (midnight Fri & Sat); 12-11 Sun
☎ (020) 8340 2729

Caledonian Deuchars IPA; Fuller's London Pride; Taylor Landlord; guest beers Ⓗ

A lively pub, deservedly popular with all age groups, the Compasses was CAMRA National Community Pub of 2006. The bar is L-shaped with a bright front room that is opened out at the front in summer. The rear area has a pool table under a skylight. Three regular ales are complemented by three constantly changing guest beers. A wide range of games is available, with a popular quiz night hosted on Monday. Good pub food is served all day, every day. 🅳≢(Hornsey)🚻♣️🍴

N9: Edmonton

Beehive

24 Little Bury Street, N9 9JZ
☼ 12-midnight (1am Fri & Sat); 12-11 Sun
☎ (020) 8360 4358 🌐 beehiveedmonton.co.uk

Draught Bass; Greene King IPA; guest beer Ⓗ

Cosy pub with an area for darts and pool. Dominoes and chess are also played. Food specials are pie & mash on Monday, steak on Tuesday, curry on Thursday, fish on Friday and a themed gastro night once a month: check

the website for details. Two TV screens show major sports events.
❄️🅳≢(Bush Hill Pk)🚻(W8, 192)♣️P

N12: North Finchley

Elephant Inn

283 Ballards Lane, N12 8NR
☼ 11-11 (midnight Fri & Sat); 12-10.30 Sun
☎ (020) 8343 6110

Fuller's Discovery, London Pride, ESB Ⓗ

This is a popular pub with a loyal clientele. It has a sports bar with a wide-screen TV and a quieter, more comfortable lounge warmed by a real fire in winter. Pictures of old Finchley adorn the walls. The friendly landlady organises weekly quizzes, a bridge club and darts tournaments. Thai food is served in the restaurant upstairs. 🚆❄️🅳♣️🍴

N16: Stoke Newington

Daniel Defoe

102 Stoke Newington Church Street, N16 0LA
☼ 1 (12 Sun)-1am
☎ (020) 7254 2906 🌐 thedanieldefoe.com

Greene King Abbot; St Austell Tribute; Wells Bombardier; Young's Bitter Ⓗ

Thriving traditional one-bar Victorian corner local – its name acknowledges the rich literary history of this trendy district. Young's move to Bedford is a gain for the pub with Young's Bitter now offered. Awaiting a post smoking ban facelift in late 2007, the intention is to create disabled access toilets, improve facilities for the burgeoning food trade and add two handpumps: in short to build on the pub's reputation for convivial drinking and dining. ❄️🅳≢🚻🍴

Rose & Crown

199 Stoke Newington Church Street, N16 9ES
☼ 11.30-11; 12-10.30 Sun
☎ (020) 7254 7497

Adnams Bitter; Marston's Pedigree; guest beer Ⓗ

An inter-war gem, retaining extensive original features from its Truman's of Brick Lane origins including inlaid wood panelling with the names of long-gone beers and bevelled, etched mirrors. A sweeping corner pub with unusual bottle-end curved windows, it is situated close to Clissold Park and House and both St Mary's churches. 🚆🅳🚻

N21: Winchmore Hill

Dog & Duck

74 Hoppers Road, N21 3LH
☼ 12-11 (10.30 Sun)
☎ (020) 8886 1987

Greene King IPA; Taylor Landlord; Wadworth 6X; guest beer Ⓗ

A quintessential community pub where the landlord's Irish charm soon seduces guests while the former landlady of many years is fondly remembered in the many fascinating photos on the walls – look for the pictures of the pub in the 1950s. Now open plan with a TV screening most sports, this small pub has great character, with some original features and a superb Victorian garden. Don't watch the pendulum on the clock after too many pints! ❀≠🚌(W9)♣

Orange Tree

18 Highfield Road, N21 3HA
⏲ 12-midnight (1am Fri & Sat)
☎ (020) 8360 4853
Greene King IPA; Ruddles County; guest beer 🄷
Separated from busy Green Lanes by the New River, this is a real community pub with a large garden containing a well-equipped children's play area and a covered patio. The guest beer changes regularly and good value food is served. The friendly hosts have received many awards from local CAMRA including Pub of the Year and also Enfield in Bloom for their magnificent floral displays. Sports fans enjoy pool and darts, as well as a large-screen TV. Last admission 11pm.
❀◖≠(Winchmore Hill)🚌(329)♣P

Winchmore Hill Cricket Club

The Paulin Ground, Fords Grove, N21 3ER
⏲ 7 (12 Sat)-11; 12-10.30 (6 winter) Sun
☎ (020) 8360 1271 🌐 winchmorehill.org
Greene King IPA; guest beers 🄷
A regular winner of local CAMRA Club of the Year, non-members are admitted on production of this Guide or a CAMRA membership card. At least three guest beers are always available, and a beer festival is staged during cricket week in August. This sports club is home to cricket, football, tennis and hockey and, for the slightly less active, there is table football and darts, plus a large-screen TV. Food is served at weekends only.
❀◖◗≠🚌(125, 329)♣P⁄–

East Barnet

Prince of Wales

2 Church Hill Road, EN4 8TB
⏲ 11-11 (midnight Fri & Sat); 12-11 Sun
☎ (020) 8275 5821
Adnams Bitter; Fuller's London Pride; guest beer 🄷
Located in the centre of East Barnet village, beer and food (served until 8pm daily) are competitively priced for the area. The guest beer is selected from a list which changes on a monthly basis, so an unusual or seasonal ale may be available. Disabled access to the pub is from the rear, through the car park. Nearby is St Mary's church, about 400 years old – the oldest church in the borough. It is open for viewing on Saturday morning.
❀◖◗♿≠(Oakleigh Pk)🚌(184, 307)P

Enfield

King & Tinker

Whitewebbs Lane, EN2 9HJ (¾ mile from A10/A1055 jct) TQ331998
⏲ 12-11 (10.30 Sun)
☎ (020) 8363 6411 🌐 kingandtinker.co.uk
Greene King IPA; guest beers 🄷
Despite its location within Greater London and the M25, this pub is in a very rural spot beside White Webbs Country Park, and it has an adjacent bridleway with a horse-hitching post. Parts of the pub date from the 16th century and there are records of brewing on this site since the 10th century. The name derives from the chance informal meeting at the pub by James I and a tinker – ask for details at the bar. The flower displays often win local awards.
⛫❀◖⊡P⁄–

Wonder

1 Batley Road, EN2 0JG
⏲ 11-11; 12-10.30 Sun
☎ (020) 8393 0202
McMullen AK, Country; guest beer 🄷
Equidistant between historic Enfield and open countryside close to the London Link walk, this Victorian house has a traditional public bar with open fire, where live entertainment includes piano playing and sing-alongs reminiscent of yesteryear. This is a pub where Christmas can extend spectacularly into mid-January. Facilities for those with disabilities are good and those with special needs are warmly welcomed. An outdoor heated and covered smoking area is available.
⛫❀⊡♿≠(Gordon Hill)🚌(191, W8)♣P⁄–

NORTH-WEST LONDON

NW1: Camden Town

Quinns

65 Kentish Town Road, NW1 8NY
⏲ 11-midnight (2am Thu-Sat); 12-midnight Sun
☎ (020) 7267 8240
Greene King IPA, Abbot; guest beers 🄷
Quinns is a family pub catering for the local community and weekend visitors to Camden Town. The mixed clientele is attracted by a friendly atmosphere, varied music and sports coverage on three TV screens. Seating is comfortable and well-spaced, and the food menu is diverse and reasonably priced. However, the main attraction is the beer – more than 100 Belgian, Dutch and German bottled beers are on offer as well as wonderful guest ales from micros on draught.
❀◖◗≠⊖🚌⁄–

NW1: Euston

Bree Louise

69 Cobourg Street, NW1 2HH
⏲ 11.30-11.30 (midnight Sat); 12-midnight Sun
☎ (020) 7681 4930
Caledonian Deuchars IPA; Greene King IPA; Taylor Landlord; Thwaites Original; 🄷 **guest beers** 🄷/🄶
A one-room pub with comfortable seating, named after the landlord's daughter. Eight real ales are served, three on gravity, and CAMRA literature is all around. Of the meals on offer, the pies are particularly highly recommended. The walls are decorated with the national flags of England, Scotland and Ireland as well as framed photos, including a lovely image of Dublin inns. The pub is frequented by hotel workers and commuters from Euston. ❀◖◗≠(Euston)⊖(Euston Sq)🚌

Doric Arch

1 Eversholt Street, NW1 1DN
⏲ 11-11; 12-10.30 Sun
☎ (020) 7383 3359

ENGLAND

Bateman's Mild; Fuller's Chiswick, Discovery, London Pride, ESB; Hop Back Summer Lightning; guest beers H
Located east of the bus station and in front of the railway station, the pub's single bar on the first floor is reached by two entrances. Following its refurbishment in 2006, Fuller's continues to promote a range of guest beers from the likes of Archers, Cottage, Castle Rock and Dark Star, with a mild often available, as well as two Weston's ciders and seasonal perries. It displays an impressive collection of railway artefacts. ◑≢⊖🗐♠

NW1: Marylebone

Metropolitan
7 Station Approach, NW1 5LA
🕐 9-midnight
☎ (020) 7486 3489
Courage Best; Greene King Abbot, Old Speckled Hen; Marston's Pedigree; guest beers H
Right outside Baker Street station, this Wetherspoon pub makes a handy watering hole. The entrance, which is more reminiscent of a cinema than a pub, has some seating and stairs leading to the cavernous hall where a very long bar runs down the right-hand side. A number of heraldic crests belonging to railway companies reflect the building's earlier transport links. Food is served daily until 10pm. Q◑⊖(Baker St)♠

NW1: Primrose Hill

Princess of Wales
22 Chalcot Road, NW1 8LL
🕐 11-11.30 (midnight Thu-Sat); 11-10.30 Sun
☎ (020) 7722 0354
Adnams Bitter; Fuller's London Pride; guest beer H
Delightful, traditional corner pub in an inner suburban backwater, not too far from the bustle of Camden market and the Regents Canal, and the finally reopened Roundhouse. The Princess has the feel of a pub that has cheerfully ignored all passing fads and resolved to stick to the traditions of old it knows so well. Comfortable seating is set in characterful decor with lots of old prints. ◑⊖(Chalk Farm)🗐(31, 168)

NW1: St Pancras

Euston Flyer
83 Euston Road, NW1 2QD
🕐 11-11 (midnight Tue-Sat); 11.30-11 Sun
☎ (020) 7383 0856
Fuller's Discovery, London Pride, ESB, seasonal beers; guest beers H
This pub opened 10 years ago in a former sewing machine shop. Despite its name, it is actually sited in St Pancras station, opposite the nearby British Library and new Eurostar railway station. The Flyer usually offers two guest ales, often hailing from Cottage Brewery. Customers here are mainly local office workers and commuters. A one-room bar with raised seating, it has TV screens for major sporting events. Food is served daily until 9pm. ◑👌≢⊖🗐

NW2: Cricklewood

Beaten Docket
50-56 Cricklewood Broadway, NW2 3DT
🕐 9-11 (12.30am Fri & Sat)
☎ (020) 8450 2972
Courage Directors; Greene King Old Speckled Hen, Abbot; Marston's Pedigree; guest beer H
Thanks to a long period under the same management, this typical Wetherspoon conversion of retail premises has become a beacon for real ale. A series of well-defined drinking areas disguises the vastness of the place. The pub's name refers to a losing betting slip; plenty of prints and paraphernalia reinforce the theme. Benches are outside all year. A local CAMRA Pub of the Season winner, it offers a family dining area and children's menu options (last orders 5pm). Q🕷◑👌≢🗐♠

NW3: Hampstead

Duke of Hamilton
23-25 New End, NW3 1JD
🕐 12-11 (10.30 Sun)
☎ (020) 7794 0258
Fuller's London Pride, ESB, guest ales H
Well-established and very popular, this true local, with a long-serving licensee and winner of several local CAMRA awards, has featured in the Guide for more than 15 years. This prominent site has been home to an inn since 1721, and the current pub goes back 200 years with parts of the cellar stemming from the original building. German lager and wheat beer are stocked alongside the excellent real ales. Bar snacks are available. Q🕷≢(Hampstead Heath)⊖🗐♣♠

Holly Bush
22 Holly Mount, NW3 1HE
🕐 12-11 (10.30 Sun)
☎ (020) 7435 2892 ⊕ thehollybushpub.com
Adnams Bitter, Broadside; Fuller's London Pride; Harveys Sussex Best; guest beers H
Celebrating its 200th anniversary, Hampstead's best-hidden pub, situated in a quiet residential area, is Grade II listed and steeped in history. Listed in CAMRA's Regional Inventory and very much a community pub, it has immense character, comprising several small rooms plus an upstairs dining room which is available for private hire. Real fires and a frequently sighted ghost add to the character of the pub. Organic British food and award-winning well-kept ales are enhanced by excellent service. ⚠Q🕷🕷◑⊖🗐♣♠🍴

Spaniards Inn
Spaniards Road, NW3 7JJ
🕐 11 (10 Sat & Sun)-11
☎ (020) 8731 6571
Adnams Bitter; Fuller's London Pride; Harveys Sussex Best; Marston's Old Empire; guest beers H
Multi-roomed pub close to the Heath and Kenwood House, with a colourful history dating back to 1585. The interior features wooden beams and settles. Two seasonal guest beers, a mild in winter and a wheat in summer, are offered, and four themed beer festivals draw the crowds each year. Food is

served all day, including weekend breakfast, and the menu lists suitable accompanying beers for each meal. A large outdoor area has its own bar. The pub has strong literary connections and hosts a weekly poetry group. Children are welcome. ﹗Q✿☺①⊡(210)P↳

NW4: Hendon

Greyhound
52 Church End, NW4 4JT
✪ 12-midnight (1am Fri & Sat)
☎ (020) 8457 9730
Wells Bombardier; Young's Bitter, Special, seasonal beer ⊞
Situated in the old village part of Hendon, this country-style inn sits between the fascinating Charles II-period Church Farmhouse Museum and the picturesque 18th-century church, both well worth visiting. The pub has friendly staff and attracts a mixed clientele including students from nearby Middlesex University, cadets from the police college and even local rock musicians – all out to enjoy themselves. You might even see a couple of greyhounds. ﹗✿①⊡♣P

NW5: Dartmouth Park

Dartmouth Arms
35 York Rise, NW5 1SP
✪ 11-11 (10.30 Sat); 10.30-10.30 Sun
☎ (020) 7485 3267 ⊕ dartmoutharms.co.uk
Adnams Bitter; guest beers ⊞
A two-room pub in a residential area, this hostelry can get very noisy when Arsenal are playing, as fans flock to the TV screens. The pub's entertainment schedule includes many different themed nights: quizzes and comedy nights are staged on a fortnightly rota. Food is served daily, and specials include steak and mussels. The Dartmouth also offers eight bottled ciders for lovers of the apple. ﹗✿☺①≠(Gospel Oak)⊖(Tufnell Pk)⊡(4)♣

NW5: Kentish Town

Junction Tavern
101 Fortess Road, NW5 9AG
✪ 12-11 (10.30 Sun)
☎ (020) 7485 9400 ⊕ junctiontavern.co.uk
Caledonian Deuchars IPA; guest beers ⊞
A regular entry in the Guide, the Junction is a well-established venue known for the real ales at the bar and its annual August beer festival, featuring a wide range of cask-conditioned ales. The building is of a classic Victorian design and includes many period features, most notably extensive woodwork. An open-plan kitchen and dining area complement the main bar, along with a conservatory and heated beer garden. Q✿☺①≠⊖⊡↳

Oxford
256 Kentish Town Road, NW5 2AA
✪ 12-11 (midnight Fri & Sat); 12-10.30 Sun
☎ (020) 7485 3521
Beer range varies ⊞
A welcome addition to Kentish Town, the refurbished Oxford, owned by Real Pubs, has quickly established itself in the area. The

management team takes great pride in the constantly changing selection of three real ales. Built in 1886, the large ground floor bar includes a dining area to the rear with an open-plan kitchen. The interior showcases many period features such as mosaic tiles and restored wooden flooring. A large first-floor function room hosts jazz, comedy and quiz nights. ✿①&≠⊖⊡↳

NW10: Harlesden

Grand Junction Arms
Acton Lane, NW10 7AD
✪ 11-midnight; 12-10 Sun
☎ (020) 8965 5670
Wells Bombardier; Young's Bitter ⊞
Imposing pub alongside the Grand Union Canal (moorings available), offering three contrasting bars together with extensive gardens, a patio and children's amusements. The front bar has pool tables and a large-screen TV for sport. The middle bar is more intimate and regularly features sports on a smaller TV. The beamed back bar opens onto the canal. Children are permitted until 7.30pm if dining (food served 12-9pm daily). Live free jazz plays on Sunday 2-4pm.
Q✿☺①⊕&≠⊖⊡(226, 260)♣P↳

Ruislip Manor

JJ Moons
12 Victoria Road, HA4 0AA
✪ 9-midnight (1am Fri & Sat)
☎ (01895) 622373
Courage Best Bitter; Fuller's London Pride; Greene King Abbot; Marston's Pedigree; guest beers ⊞
Traditional and reliable Wetherspoon's outlet, run by one of the chain's longest-serving and well-respected managers, who has been here since the pub was converted from a convenience store more than 16 years ago. The Moons is very popular with both young and old, especially on Thursday to Saturday evenings. There is an area at the rear reserved for diners, and in good weather tables are put outside at the front. ①&⊖⊡

SOUTH-EAST LONDON
SE1: Bankside

Founders Arms
52 Hopton Street, SE1 9JH (next to Tate Modern, on riverside path)
✪ 10-11 (midnight Fri); 9-midnight Sat; 9-11 Sun
☎ (020) 7928 1899 ⊕ foundersarms.co.uk
Wells Bombardier; Young's Bitter, Special, seasonal beers ⊞
Large, modern pub with a patio on the Thames Riverside, affording superb views of St Paul's Cathedral, the Millennium Bridge and the City of London. The pub is often busy with art lovers who have visited the Tate Modern next door. An unusual feature is the separate coffee bar, serving hot drinks and ice creams. Q✿☺①&≠(Blackfriars)⊖(Blackfriars/Southwark)⊡(RV1)↳

SE1: Borough

Market Porter

9 Stoney Street, SE1 9AA
✪ 6-8.30am, 11-11; 12-11 Sat; 12-10.30 Sun
☎ (020) 7407 2495
Harveys Sussex Best Bitter; guest beers Ⓗ
Very popular pub in Borough Market that opens early for market workers. It has recently extended to provide extra space, and is particularly busy on Friday and Saturday when the farmers' market attracts large crowds of shoppers. Nine guest beers are always available, and in an average week 50 different beers will be dispensed. Upstairs is a restaurant and the room can be hired for private functions. No food Sunday evening.
◖▯≷(London Bridge)⊖(London Bridge)🚃♦

Royal Oak

44 Tabard Street, SE1 4JU
✪ 11 (6 Sat)-11; 12-6 Sun
☎ (020) 7357 7173
Harveys Pale, Sussex XX Mild, Sussex Best Bitter, seasonal beers Ⓗ
Harvey's only tied house in London. Although very much a traditional local, this popular pub is patronised by a good mix of guests from all over the country. It has two rooms: a side lobby (former off sales counter), central bar and an attractive function room available for hire. The original Tabard Inn, made famous in Chaucer's Canturbury Tales, was not in Tabard Street but in Talbot Yard, adjacent to Guy's Hospital. The Tabard's name was changed to the Talbot when it was rebuilt following Southwark's own great fire of 1676, and demolished in 1873.
Q◖▯≷(London Bridge)⊖🚃(21)

SE1: London Bridge

Barrow Boy & Banker

6-8 Borough High Street, SE1 9QQ
✪ 11-11; 12-4 Sat; closed Sun
☎ (020) 7403 5415
Fuller's Chiswick, Discovery, London Pride, ESB; guest beer Ⓗ
Very impressive Fuller's Ale & Pie House, originally the first branch of the Nat West Bank. Much of the interior of the former banking hall has been retained, including an original fireplace (sadly no longer used). The walls are adorned with historic paintings and three large friezes. Handy for visiting Southwark Cathedral and Borough Market (Fri & Sat mornings). Food is served weekdays 12-9pm. Q◖▯≷⊖🚃

Horniman at Hays

Unit 26, Hay's Galleria, Battlesbridge Lane, Tooley Street, SE1 2HD
✪ 11-11 (midnight Thu-Sat); 12-10.30 Sun
☎ (020) 7407 1991
Adnams Broadside; Taylor Landlord; guest beers Ⓗ
Large bankside premises at Hay's Galleria, worth a visit for its mock-Victorian splendour. Part of Nicholson's estate, its ornate ceiling, chandeliers, mural walls, carved wood bar back, gilt mirrors and tiled flooring are a pleasure to behold. It also sports a lounge cellar area and mezzanine bar. A range of

bottled German beers is available and there are tasting notes on the handpumps (sampling is actively encouraged). Both bars are available for hire. ◖▯≷⊖🚃

SE1: Southwark

Charles Dickens

160 Union Street, SE1 0LH
✪ 11.30-11; 12-8 Sun
☎ (020) 7401 3744 ⊕ thecharlesdickens.co.uk
Adnams Bitter; guest beers Ⓗ
A popular air-conditioned free house enjoying a cosy atmosphere. One changing beer from Adnams is complemented by a range of five real ales from other independent breweries. Wednesday is quiz night. Good pub food is on offer at most times. A large-screen TV shows sporting events.
◖▯&≷(Waterloo East)⊖(Southwark/Borough)🚃(344)

SE1: Tower Bridge

Bridge House

218 Tower Bridge Road, SE1 2UP
✪ 11.30-11.30 (midnight Thu-Sat)
☎ (020) 7407 5818
Adnams Bitter, Explorer, Broadside, seasonal beer Ⓗ
Adnams' only tied house in London, the Bridge House enjoys a splendid location around 10 metres from Tower Bridge. It is noted for its stylish decor, with an intimate dining room downstairs and a function room upstairs, available for hire. An excellent wine list from Adnams' well-reputed cellars partners the contemporary food, with the emphasis on British fare. Even the nibbles are great!
◖▯≷(London Bridge)⊖(Tower Hill/London Bridge)🚃

Pommelers Rest

196-198 Tower Bridge Road, SE1 2UN
✪ 9-midnight (1am Fri & Sat)
☎ (020) 7378 1399
Courage Best Bitter; Greene King Abbot; Itchen Valley Tower Bridge Bitter; Marston's Pedigree; guest beers Ⓗ
A popular, very comfortable, long-time no-smoking Wetherspoon's pub, the Pommelers is located close to Tower Bridge and many other London attractions. Free Wifi Internet connection is available to customers. The Itchen Valley Brewery in Hampshire provides the aptly named Tower Bridge Bitter and the usual Wetherspoon's food is served all day.
Q◖▯≷(London Bridge)⊖(Tower Hill/London Bridge)🚃

SE4: Brockley

Brockley Barge

184 Brockley Road, SE4 2RR
✪ 9-midnight (1am Fri & Sat)
☎ (020) 8694 7690
Courage Directors; Greene King Abbot; Marston's Pedigree; guest beers Ⓗ
A rarity for a Wetherspoon's, this is a conversion from an existing pub and sports a bright, stylish, modern decor. Its layout provides a number of different drinking areas,

including a patio outside. The pub's name is a reference to the canal that ran close by. A popular local, it has a mixed clientele of all ages. Q🚫🐕♿❄️🚆🚍

SE6: Catford

Catford Ram
9 Winslade Way, SE6 4JU
🕐 11-11; 12-10.30 Sun
☎ (020) 8690 6206
Young's Bitter, Special, seasonal beer Ⓗ
This well-established market-side pub is located at the Broadway entrance to Catford Mews, a stone's throw from Catford Broadway market. It has a comfortable, large, raised seating area and a spacious standing area. Sporting events are shown on two large-screen TVs. Lunches are available Monday to Saturday. ♿🐕🚆(Catford/Catford Bridge)🚍

SE8: Deptford

Dog & Bell
116 Prince Street, SE8 3JD
🕐 12-11 (10.30 Sun)
☎ (020) 8692 5664 🌐 thedogandbell.com
Fuller's London Pride, ESB; guest beers Ⓗ
A tucked-away gem of a pub popular with locals and beer lovers. The main bar in this former local CAMRA Pub of the Year has an 80-year-old bar billiard table and leads to another room with ample seating for diners and drinkers. An imaginative range of meals is served. Ocasional curry nights are popular, and an annual pickle festival is hosted in November. Belgian beers and Scotch whiskies complement the changing cask beer range. Free Wifi is available. 📶Q🚫🐕🚆🚍♣

SE10: Greenwich

Ashburnham Arms
25 Ashburnham Grove, SE10 8UH
🕐 11-11; 12-10.30 Sun
☎ (020) 8692 2007
Shepherd Neame Master Brew, Kent's Best Invicta Ale, Spitfire, Bishop's Finger, seasonal beers Ⓗ
Take a short walk from Greenwich town centre and you would do well to disappear into the Ashburnham triangle. At the social heart of this conservation area is this wonderfully calm and coolly decorated pub, serving the Shepherd Neame range and a delicious choice of pizzas (no food Mon). The comfortable sofas offer respite from the bustling streets around the Cutty Sark. A huge painted map of London is a reminder of the location of this excellent oasis. 🚫🐕🚆⊖(DLR)🚍♣'—

Cutty Sark
4-7 Ballast Quay, SE10 9PD
🕐 11-11; 12-10.30 Sun
☎ (020) 8858 3146
Adnams Broadside; Black Sheep Best Bitter; Fuller's London Pride; St Austell Tribute Ⓗ
Tucked away from the main tourist trail in Greenwich, this large riverside pub affords superb views of the Dome and Canary Wharf. The character of the rooms adds to the charm of this pub, where the seats are made from wooden casks. The bar is behind the curving staircase leading upstairs. In good weather, the outdoor seats at the front of the pub are popular. 🚫🐕🚆(Maze Hill)⊖(Cutty Sark DLR)

Plume of Feathers
19 Park Vista, SE10 9LZ
🕐 11-11 Mon,Tue & Thu; 10-midnight Wed, Fri & Sat; 12-11 Sun
☎ (020) 8858 1661
Adnams Bitter; Fuller's London Pride; guest beers Ⓗ
A long-established (1691) pub, frequently busy with locals who know where to look. A good range of beers is served and there is a lovely restaurant facing the courtyard. The fireplace and maritime curios are a reminder of Greenwich's history. This pub provides a welcome stopping point between the park with its world-famous observatory and the National Maritime Museum. Decent pub food (no eve meals Sun & Mon) and a children's playroom add appeal for family days out. Q🚫🐕🚆(Maze Hill)⊖(Cutty Sark DLR)🚍'—

Richard I (Tolly's)
52-54 Royal Hill, SE10 8RT
🕐 11-11 (midnight Fri & Sat); 12-10.30 Sun
☎ (020) 8692 2996 🌐 youngs.co.uk
Wells Bombardier; Young's Bitter, Special, seasonal beers Ⓗ
Away from the bustle of touristy Greenwich, this one-time beer and sweet shop offers solid, old-fashioned comfort, from the bay window seating near the entrance to a fair-sized beer garden at the rear. Guests can now enjoy a decent pint of Wells Bombardier here, alongside the usual Young's beers, thanks to the merger of the two breweries. 🚫🐕🚆⊖(DLR)🚍'—

SE13: Lewisham

Jolly Farmers
354 Lewisham High Street, SE13 6LE
🕐 11-11.30; 12-11 Sun
☎ (020) 8690 2054
Beer range varies Ⓗ/Ⓖ
This great little pub is unique in the area thanks to its constantly changing ales, generally including at least one from Cornwall, as well as its delicious home-cooked food that is also great value for money. It has a loyalty card scheme for meals: dining here is rewarded with a discount after several visits (no food Mon or Sat). The bar area has a TV set for major sporting events but it is easy to escape. 🚫🐕🚆(Ladywell)🚍'—

SE15: Peckham

Gowlett
62 Gowlett Road, SE15 4HY
🕐 12-midnight (1am Fri & Sat); 12-10.30 Sun
☎ (020) 7635 7048 🌐 thegowlett.com
Beer range varies Ⓗ
Tucked away on the corner of a residential street, this former local CAMRA Pub of the Year serves four guest ales. A relaxing place, it plays smoochy jazz during the day and mellow tunes by the DJ at weekends. Stone-baked pizzas are a speciality, served whole, or by the

slice for lunch and take-away. There is a heated, covered patio, a pool table (Tue night is competition night), and for children there are high chairs and toys. Local art adorns the walls. Monday is quiz night.
❀◑≉(E Dulwich/Peckham Rye)🚌↙

SE18: Plumstead Common

Old Mill

1 Old Mill Road, SE18 1QG
🕓 11.30-11.30 (12.30am Fri); 12-10.30 Sun
☎ (020) 8244 8592
Beer range varies Ⓗ
A popular, friendly local, the pub is built around a corn mill that dates back to the 17th century. Beer has been served here since 1848. Today it offers six ever-changing ales, and holds an annual beer festival in early July. Free bar snacks are provided on Sunday, and food is served lunchtimes Monday-Saturday. Occasionally it stages live music, and many calendar dates are celebrated including St George's Day and Halloween. The large garden has an aviary. ❀◑🚌↙

SE18: Woolwich

Prince Albert (Rose's Free House)

49 Hare Street, SE18 6NE
🕓 11-11; 12-3 Sun
☎ (020) 8854 1538
Beer range varies Ⓗ
A fine old London free house, this pub serves a constantly changing range of up to six real ales as well as a selection of Belgian beers. A large collection of pub memorabilia adorns the walls and bar. The lunchtime rolls are, to say the least, 'well-filled' and inexpensive. The pub hosts events for special-interest groups such as steam railway enthusiasts, and actively participates in many CAMRA events including Community Pubs Week and Mild month. Q◪≉(Woolwich Arsenal)🚌♣

SE20: Penge

Moon & Stars

164-166 High Street, SE20 7QS
🕓 9am-11 (10.30 Sun)
☎ (020) 8776 5680
Courage Directors; Greene King Abbot; Shepherd Neame Spitfire; Theakston Old Peculier; guest beers Ⓗ
Unlike some of the more recent Wetherspoon's venues, this still has the feel of a traditional pub, perhaps thanks to the wood panelling on the walls and a number of cosy booths (17, in fact!), which are separated from one another by wood and glass partitions. There is even an open fireplace. A good range of real ales is always available.
Q❀◑♿≉(Kent House)⊖(Beckenham Rd Tramlink)🚌↙

SE22: East Dulwich

Clock House

196A Peckham Rye, SE22 9QA
🕓 11-midnight
☎ (020) 8693 2901

Young's Bitter, Special, seasonal beers Ⓗ
Opposite Peckham Rye, this local landmark is a popular choice with the more discerning residents of East Dulwich. The pub is filled with timepieces and neither gentrified nor gastro. A selection of salads and jacket potatoes is served from a buffet bar, supplemented by a daily changing board of specials in the upper dining area. A main bar and back area is fitted with a skylight dome, done out in green and featuring stuffed birds and fish. ❀◑🚌↙

Herne Tavern

2 Forest Hill Road, SE22 0RR
🕓 12-11 (1am Sat); 12-10.30 Sun
☎ (020) 8299 9521 ⊕ theherne.net
Caledonian Deuchars IPA; Fuller's London Pride; Taylor Landlord; guest beers Ⓗ
This CAMRA Regional Inventory pub has recently been renovated. It has a bright, modern style, while retaining its three rooms featuring wood panelling and stained-glass windows, plus a conservatory. It caters for a mixed clientele and, with its large, imaginatively landscaped garden and children's play area, is popular with families. The menu is contemporary, with a good and expanding wine list. ❀◑♿🚌

SE23: Forest Hill

Blythe Hill Tavern

319 Stanstead Road, SE23 1JB
🕓 11-midnight
☎ (020) 8690 5176
Adnams Broadside; Courage Best Bitter; Fuller's London Pride; Westerham Black Eagle Ⓗ
The most authentic pub in SE23, this remains a traditional corner boozer with three distinct and cosy rooms, all fitted with traditional pub furniture (small tables designed for drinking, not dining) and each with its own character. Sporting and brewery memorabilia adorn the walls. Entering the wonderful public bar is like stepping back in time. Quite properly, meals are not served: this is a place to drink and chat. Let's hope this excellent pub never changes.
Q❀♿≉(Catford/Catford Bridge)🚌(171, 185)↙

Capitol

11-21 London Road, SE23 3TW
🕓 9-midnight (1am Fri & Sat)
☎ (020) 8291 8920
Courage Best Bitter; Greene King Old Speckled Hen, Abbot; Marston's Pedigree; Shepherd Neame Spitfire; guest beers Ⓗ
A magnificent Wetherspoon's conversion of a Grade II listed cinema, retaining many original features. It is spacious and set on a number of levels, with a patio around the side and back providing an outdoor drinking area. Popular with a mixed crowd, it caters well for families. Live football is shown on big screens and TVs, and can attract crowds. A recent addition of a separate coffee shop inside the front door has been well received. The staff run occasional ghost walks into the upper circle.
❀◑♿≉🚌↙

SE26: Sydenham

Dulwich Wood House
39 Sydenham Hill, SE26 6RS
✪ 12-11 (midnight Thu-Sat); 12-10.30 Sun
☎ (020) 8693 5666
Young's Bitter, Special, seasonal beers Ⓗ
The inn's name refers to the ancient Dulwich Woode, loved by Byron when attending school in the area. The pub was designed and built a century ago by Joseph Paxton, who was responsible for the Crystal Palace which stood down the road until the fire of 1936. A sturdy, much-loved hostelry, it has a clutch of wood-panelled rooms inside and a fine garden with an expanse of lawn and children's play area. The food menu offers reasonably-priced standard pub dishes and daily changing specials. Q✪Ⓓ&≥(Sydenham Hill)🚌P♿

Addiscombe

Claret Free House
5a Bingham Corner, Lower Addiscombe Road, CR0 7AA
✪ 11.30-11; 12-10.30 Sun
☎ (020) 8656 7452
Dark Star Hophead; Palmer IPA; Sharp's Atlantic IPA; guest beers Ⓗ
Small family-run real ale bar, attracting a mixed, friendly clientele. Six ales are always on handpump, plus a further 18 announced on the noticeboard as coming soon. There is no food during the week but sandwiches are available on Saturday and bar snacks and newspapers on Sunday. There is a variety of seating, and in summer the place is air-conditioned. Two TVs screen major sporting events. Well-behaved pets are welcome. The pub has a sister bar in Cheam. &⊖(Addiscombe Tramlink)🚌♣

Cricketers
47 Shirley Road, CR0 7ER (on A215 opp Bingham Rd)
✪ 12-midnight (11.30 Sun)
☎ (020) 8655 3507
Harveys Sussex Best; Ⓗ **guest beers** Ⓗ/Ⓖ
Robust local with a mock-Tudor exterior. The keen landlord promotes real ale brewery nights, when additional guest ales are available on gravity. It has just started serving Westerham ales by gravity, and tries to obtain micro-brewery beers whenever possible. This is very much a sportsman's pub, featuring two pool tables and a dartboard as well as televised sport. Evening meals are served until 7pm. The pleasant garden is a real sun-trap in decent weather. Two outdoor smoking areas are planned.
🚶✪Ⓓ⊖(Blackhorse Lane Tramlink)🚌(367)♣♿P♿

Beckenham

Jolly Woodman
9 Chancery Lane, BR3 6NR
✪ 12 (4 Mon)-11 (midnight Fri & Sat); 12-11 Sun
☎ (020) 8663 1031
Adnams Bitter; Caledonian Deuchars IPA; Harveys Sussex Best Bitter; Taylor Landlord; Ⓗ **guest beers** Ⓗ/Ⓖ

This urban, back-street establishment has the feel of a small country local. Tucked away, it would be easy to miss. Rebuilt around 1840, reputedly close to a prison and workhouse, the present management has restored the single bar to some of its original charm. Very much a community pub, it has darts and shove-ha'penny teams. It frequently serves a guest beer on gravity, and also has a good range of whiskies, including 25 malts.
✪Ⓓ≥(Beckenham Jct)⊖(Beckenham Jct Tramlink)🚌♣♿

Bexley

Black Horse
63 Albert Road, DA5 1NJ
✪ 11.30-11 (midnight Fri); 12-11.30 Sat; 12-11 Sun
☎ (01322) 523371
Courage Best Bitter; guest beers Ⓗ
Friendly back-street local offering good value lunches in comfortable, uncrowded surroundings. The open-plan bar is split into two: to the left is an open space with a dartboard, while to the right is a smaller, more intimate area and bar, leading to the garden. The pub supports a golf society. The publican aims to put on a different beer every time one of his two guest ales runs out.
✪Ⓓ≥🚌(B15, 132)♣♿

King's Head
65 Bexley High Street, DA5 1AA
✪ 11-11
☎ (01322) 553137
Greene King IPA, Morland Original, Abbot Ⓗ
This popular pub is particularly busy at lunchtime as well as in the early evening with commuters from nearby Bexley station. Dating from the 16th century, it is one of the oldest buildings in historic Bexley village and has been a pub for at least 300 years. Its weatherboarded exterior makes it a local landmark, and the interior features many original oak beams (and a few replacements following Victorian alterations). Sunday lunch is served in the function room. ✪Ⓓ≥🚌P♿

Old Wick
9 Vicarage Road, DA5 2AL
✪ 12-11.30 (12.30am Fri & Sat)
☎ (01322) 524185
Shepherd Neame Best, Kent Best, Spitfire, seasonal beer Ⓗ
This excellent pub on the road from Bexley to Dartford Heath changed its name from the Rising Sun in 1996. The welcoming, cosy interior is enhanced by subdued lighting and the friendly staff make everyone feel welcome. It benefits from a regular, local clientele, but has a 'no dogs' rule. Porter is served in season. Accommodation and camping are available off-site.
🚶✪Ⓓ⚓≥🚌(492, B15)♣♿

Bexleyheath

Prince Albert
2 Broadway, DA6 7LE (jct Erith Rd & Watling St)
✪ 11-2.30, 4.30-11; 11-midnight Fri & Sat; 12-11 Sun
☎ (020) 8303 6309

Shepherd Neame Kent's Best, Spitfire, Bishops Finger, seasonal beers ⓗ
Cosy corner local that has been knocked through but retains a two-bar atmosphere and can get noisy at times. Upstairs is a highly rated restaurant. The bars are bedecked with a wide range of brass ephemera. At least three Shepherd Neame beers are available at any time. ◑⊜P

Robin Hood & Little John

78 Lion Road, DA6 8PF
🕓 11-3, 5.30 (7 Sat)-11; 12-4, 7-10.30 Sun
☎ (020) 8303 1128
Adnams Bitter, Broadside; Brains Rev James; Brakspear Bitter; Fuller's London Pride; Harveys Best Bitter; guest beers ⓗ
Dating from the 1830s when it sat amidst fields and farms, this delightful little back-street pub is well worth a visit. It was voted local CAMRA Pub of the Year 2000 to 2007, and London winner three times. Run by the same family since 1980, it offers eight well-kept real ales and has a deserved reputation for its home-cooked lunchtime meals (no food Sun), featuring themed specials and Italian favourites. The meals are taken at tables made of old Singer sewing machines. Over 21s only are admitted. ❀◑

Rose

179 Broadway, DA6 7ES (opp Christ Church)
🕓 11-11 (midnight Fri & Sat); 12-11.30 Sun
☎ (020) 8303 3846
Adnams Broadside; Greene King IPA; Harveys Best Bitter; Young's Bitter ⓗ
Attractive, double bay-windowed pub, in a handy location for the local shops. A horseshoe-shaped bar helps to create a cosy atmosphere. The bar benefits from comfortable seating, and the music is kept at a reasonable level. There is a small drinking area in front of the pub and a patio at the rear. Lunchtime meals are served Monday to Saturday. ❀◑⊜

Royal Oak (Polly Clean Stairs)

Mount Road, DA6 8JS
🕓 11-3, 6-11; 11-11 Sat; 12-3, 7-10.30 Sun
☎ (020) 8303 4454
Courage Best Bitter; Fuller's London Pride; guest beer ⓗ
Once the village store, this attractive brick and weatherboarded pub manages to keep its rural character, despite being surrounded by 1930s housing. Inside, the country charm continues with cosy seating areas, and plates and tankards adorning the walls and ceiling. The nickname derives from a house-proud landlady who used to wash the front steps every day. It has been run by the same licensee since 1958. Lunchtime snacks are prepared to order (not served Sun). Children are allowed in the garden. Q❀⊜(B13)P

Biggin Hill

Old Jail

Jail Lane, TN16 3AX (1 mile from A233)
🕓 11.30-3, 6-11; 12-11 Sun; 12-10.30 Sun
☎ (01959) 572979
Greene King IPA; Harveys Best Bitter; guest beer ⓗ

Although a little out of the way, this great country pub is well worth the detour and is popular with ramblers and cyclists. Decorated in a traditional style, it features exposed beams at one end and memorabilia showcases the history of the Spitfire and Biggin Hill Airport. If aviation is your thing, the garden it is an excellent place to be for the Air Show (but get there early to find a space). ₳Q❀❀◑ ⊟⊜(R8)♣P¹⊢

Bromley

Anglesea Arms

90 Palace Road, BR1 3JX
🕓 11-11 (11.30 Fri & Sat); 12-11 Sun
☎ (020) 8460 1985
Shepherd Neame Master Brew, Spitfire, seasonal beers ⓗ
This traditional back-street pub with a horseshoe-shaped, wood-panelled bar has been recently renovated, creating a bustling community feel. Monday quiz night is popular, and other entertainment is provided by Sky TV, live music events and themed food and drink nights. There is a secluded patio and beer garden as well as a drinking area at the front, and a heated, covered area outside for smokers. Lunches are served daily. No dogs are allowed inside the pub.
❀◑♿⇌(Bromley North)⊢

Bitter End Off Licence

139 Masons Hill, BR2 9HW
🕓 5-9 Mon; 12-3, 5-10 Tue-Fri; 11-10 Sat; 12-2, 7-9 Sun
☎ (020) 8466 6083 ⊕ thebitterend.biz
Beer range varies ⓖ
Ideal for those occasions when you fancy a couple of pints at home or are planning a party or larger function, this off-licence stocks a good selection of beers and ciders. Given a little notice, polypins and firkins can be obtained from a range of more than 500 beers. There is also an interesting choice of British and imported bottled beers (some bottle-conditioned). Glasses and equipment can be hired or loaned.
⇌(Bromley South)⊜♠

Bricklayers Arms

141-143 Masons Hill, BR2 9HW
🕓 11-3.30, 5.30 (7 Sat)-11; 12-3.30, 7-10.30 Sun
☎ (020) 8460 4552
Shepherd Neame Master Brew, Spitfire, Bishops Finger, seasonal beers ⓗ
The same couple have run this pub for 37 years, picking up Pub of the Year and Lifetime Achievement awards from Shepherd Neame along the way. Recently refurbished, the Bricks is light and airy with a modern and comfortable feel. The R.O. James sign once belonged to the former hardware shop which was taken over when the pub expanded some years ago. The Wurlitzer juke box with its 50s hits is only decorative. Pam's Sunday lunches are a highlight. Q◑⇌(Bromley South)⊜

Bromley Labour Club

HG Wells Centre, St Marks Road, BR2 9HG (behind new Bromley police station)
🕓 11-11 (midnight Fri & Sat); 12-10.30 Sun
☎ (020) 8460 7409
Shepherd Neame Master Brew; guest beer ⓗ

A former local CAMRA Club of the Year, this friendly, comfortable club is a good place to escape the hubbub of the many shops in the area. Situated in a quiet side street off the main road, it has a pool table and shows football and other sports on a large-screen TV. The club is open to card-carrying CAMRA members. ❀≹⇌(Bromley South)🚌♣

Partridge

194 Bromley High Street, BR1 1HE
🕐 11-11; 12-10.30 Sun
☎ (020) 8464 7656
Fuller's London Pride, ESB, seasonal beers Ⓗ
An excellent conversion of a grand traditional National Westminster bank, the pub retains many features from its banking days: the manager's office is now a nice little snug while the bar is where the original service counter stood. There is a separate dining area where delicious meals can be enjoyed in peace and quiet. A good range of Fuller's bottled beers is stocked.
❀◑ᴥ≹⇌(Bromley North)🚌

Red Lion

10 North Road, BR1 3LG
🕐 11 (12 Sun)-11
☎ (020) 8460 2691
Greene King IPA, Abbot; Harveys Best Bitter; guest beers Ⓗ
The landlord at this friendly, locally listed pub is passionate about the quality of his beer. A blackboard behind the bar announces forthcoming guest beers, and the huge collection of pump clips reflects the number of beers that have featured in the past. Shelves full of books and newspapers provide plenty to read, and the food is excellent value (served 12-7pm Mon-Sat). The pleasant outdoor patio at the front features well-tended flower displays all year round. Although Bromley town is only a short walk away, this pub retains a pleasant village feel.
Q❀◑≹(Bromley North)🚌ᴸ

Bromley Common

Two Doves

37 Oakley Road, BR2 8HD
🕐 12-3, 5.30 (5 Fri)-11; 12-11 Sat; 12-10.30 Sun
☎ (020) 8462 1627
Wells Bombardier; Young's Bitter, Special, seasonal beers Ⓗ
This traditional Young's house attracts a more mature local clientele. It has a cheerful, well-lit façade with superb leaded light windows and a quiet conservatory at the rear, which can be booked for functions. Sporting events are shown on TV and occasionally quiz nights are hosted. A lovely garden with mature shrubs and flowers invites for outdoor drinking. Q❀◑🚌(320)ᴸ

Chelsfield

Five Bells

Church Road, BR6 7RE
🕐 11-11 (midnight Fri & Sat); 12-10.30 Sun
☎ (01689) 821044

Adnams Bitter; Courage Best Bitter; Greene King Old Speckled Hen; Harveys Sussex Best Bitter; guest beers Ⓗ
This statutory-listed, weatherboarded village pub, dating from around the 18th century, has a separate public bar and dining room and a beamed saloon bar. Children and dogs are welcome. There is plenty of regular entertainment, from Tuesday quiz night, darts games and live music to fund-raising events and themed nights in the restaurant. There is an outdoor area for drinking, and limited parking at the front of the pub.
Q❀◑▯⇖🚌(R3)♣

Chislehurst

Bulls Head

Royal Parade, BR7 6NR
🕐 11-11 (midnight Fri & Sat); 12-11 Sun
☎ (020) 8467 1727 ⊕ thebullsheadhotel.co.uk
Young's Bitter, Special, seasonal beers Ⓗ
This creeper-clad inn has been a Young's pub since 1931. A large, multi-roomed hotel with a country house feel, it is attractively decorated and has a spacious saloon bar, which gets very busy at weekends. The lounge bar has the atmosphere of a gentleman's club, furnished with leather wing-back chairs. A large ballroom is available for hire.
Q♿❀⇖◑⇖🚌Pᴸ

Ramblers Rest

Mill Place, BR7 5ND (15 mins walk from Chislehurst station)
🕐 11-11; 12-10.30 Sun
☎ (020) 8467 1734
Adnams Bitter; Brakspear Bitter; Courage Best Bitter; Fuller's London Pride; Wells Bombardier Ⓗ
In a picturesque location on the fringe of the Common, near the Chislehurst Caves, this timber-fronted pub dates back to 1800 and is locally listed. The wood-panelled interior provides a cosy public bar that leads downstairs to a spacious lounge. There is a pretty garden to the rear. A good range of beers is always available. Lunches are served Monday-Saturday and free bar snacks tempt on Sunday. Quiz night is the first Wednesday of the month; cribbage is often played here. The pub is well-known for its fundraising events. Children are welcome.
Q❀◑⇖≹🚌(269, 162)♣ᴸ

Tigers Head

Watts Lane, BR7 5PJ TQ445698
🕐 12-11 (10.30 Sun)
☎ (020) 8467 3070
Adnams Bitter; Fuller's London Pride; Greene King Old Speckled Hen; guest beer Ⓗ
This large pub with a traditional exterior is open-plan inside, featuring several cosy areas furnished in a country style with scrubbed wood tables. The main emphasis is on the excellent food that can be enjoyed at candlelit tables. Advance booking is not possible, so you are advised to arrive early at weekend evenings. There is table service for food and drinks; food is served until one hour before closing. ⚐Q❀◑▯🚌(162, 269)

Croydon

Beer Circus

282 High Street, CRO 1NG
✪ 5 (12 Fri; 2 Sat)-midnight; closed Sun
☎ (07910) 095945
Dark Star Hophead; guest beers Ⓗ
This corner bar at the south end of the High Street is only a short walk from the town centre. Two guest beers are sourced from micro-breweries, often including another Dark Star ale. Many Belgian and German bottled beers are also stocked: see the beer menu on the bar. A cider or perry is also usually available. Local CAMRA Pub of the Year in 2005, the Circus contrasts pleasantly with the chain and theme bars in the centre of Croydon. Q�

Dog & Bull

24 Surrey Street, CRO 1RG
✪ 11-11 (midnight Thu-Sat); 12-10.30 Sun
☎ (020) 8667 9718
Wells Bombardier; Young's Bitter, Special, seasonal beers Ⓗ
This bustling old market pub is Grade II listed and was leased to Young & Bainbridge in 1832; the freehold was bought in 1899. Very much a venue for drinking and a chat, the bare wooden floors, pictures of old Croydon and jugs hanging from the ceiling at the rear enhance the atmosphere. A doorway at the back of the bar leads to a spacious, attractive garden where barbecues are available in summer. Lunches are served Monday-Saturday.
Q❀Ⓓ⇌(East/West Croydon)⊖(George St Tramlink)🚃端

Lion

182 Pawsons Road, CRO 2QD
✪ 12-11 (10.30 Sun)
☎ (020) 8683 0021
Hepworth Iron Horse; Shepherd Neame Kents Best, Spitfire Ⓗ
The Lion, although only a mile from the town centre, stands in splendid isolation opposite a cemetery. The pub has a resident cribbage team, and darts and pool are also played. The beers usually include two from Hepworth and three from Shepherd Neame. Food is served all day Monday to Friday and until 5pm at the weekend. ❀Ⓓ🚃端

Princess Royal

22 Longley Road, CRO 3LH
✪ 12-11
☎ (07915) 249724
Banks's Original; Fuller's London Pride; Greene King IPA Ⓗ
Street-corner local tucked away just off the London Road at Broad Green. Its nickname, Glue Pot, refers to a former factory nearby. Step inside and find yourself in a 'beams, horse brasses and real fire' country pub; outside is a secluded garden. Home to several darts teams, including a highly successful youth team, it also hosts charity quiz nights every Tuesday. Food is served to 6pm Monday-Saturday with roast lunches on Sunday to 4pm.
🚌❀Ⓓ⇌(West Croydon)⊖(West Croydon Tramlink)🚃端

Royal Standard

1 Sheldon Street, CRO 1SS
✪ 12-midnight (11 Sun)
☎ (020) 8688 9749
Fuller's Chiswick, Discovery, London Pride, ESB, seasonal beers Ⓗ
A regular Guide entry for many years, this popular corner local is situated only five minutes' walk from the main shopping area. The pub was tastefully extended in the 1990s, adding to the original 1860s building. Its garden is neatly tucked under the Croydon Old Town flyover, across the road from the main entrance.
Q❀Ⓓ⇌(East/West Croydon)⊖(George St Tramlink)🚃端

Skylark

34-36 South End, CRO 1DP
✪ 9am-midnight
☎ (020) 8649 9909
Courage Best Bitter; Greene King Abbot; Marston's Pedigree; Shepherd Neame Spitfire; guest beers Ⓗ
Spacious Wetherspoon's pub, formerly a gym and health club. Plasma TV screens and music are confined to the upstairs bar. Real ale and cider are only sold in the quieter downstairs bar – four guest beers are usually available. Pictures of old Croydon and the former airport adorn the walls. Meals are served until 11pm. Children are welcome if dining until 8pm. The outside garden area is strictly no-smoking.
Q❀Ⓓ♿⇌(South Croydon)🚃端

Spreadeagle

39 High Street, CRO 1NX
✪ 11-11 (midnight Fri & Sat); 12-10.30 Sun
☎ (020) 8781 1134
Fuller's Chiswick, Discovery, London Pride, ESB, seasonal beers; Gales HSB; guest beer Ⓗ
Smart town-centre pub, sympathetically converted by Fuller's from former bank premises into one of its Ale and Pie houses. It sells the full range of Fuller's ales as well as occasional guests. There is a large function room with its own bar plus a large-screen TV for sports events upstairs. Situated close to the historic Surrey Street market, local history prints adorn the walls. Canopies and chairs will be provided for smokers by the town hall entrance. Immaculate toilets are in the old bank vaults.
Ⓓ♿⇌(East/West Croydon)⊖(George St Tramlink)🚃端

Cudham

Blacksmiths Arms

Cudham Lane South, TN14 7QB (opp New Barn Lane) TQ446598
✪ 11-11 (11.30 Fri & Sat); 12-10.30 Sun
☎ (01959) 572678
Adnams Bitter; Courage Best Bitter; guest beers Ⓗ
This friendly, spacious country pub with a large garden and paved patio area, perched above the steep Cudham Valley, makes a welcome return to the Guide, thanks to the licensee's commitment to real ale. Four well-kept beers are available including two guests. No food is served on Sunday or Monday evening. Dogs

are allowed in the bar area nearest the entrance. ᴀᴀQ☺◑▯☷(R5)P

Green Street Green

Rose & Crown

Farnborough Way, BR6 6BT

☼ 11-11 (midnight Fri & Sat); 12-11 Sun

☎ (01689) 850095

Courage Best Bitter; Shepherd Neame Spitfire; guest beer ℍ

Large roadside pub on the edge of the green belt, handy for High Elms Country Park and golf course. The pub has been in the same family for many years. Its new manager is especially enthusiastic about real ale, hence the quality and choice of beers available. The garden has a children's play area, and food is served all day. ☺◑▯☷P⟟—

North Cray

White Cross

146 North Cray Road, DA14 5EL

☼ 11-11; 12-10.30 Sun

☎ (020) 8300 2590

Courage Best Bitter, Directors; guest beers ℍ

Although situated on a dual carriageway, this pleasant pub's setting remains rural, alongside surviving village buildings. The front part of the bar is popular with locals, while the rest of the pub is comfortable for both drinking and dining. It is renowned locally for its food, served all day, every day. The changing guest beer often comes from a micro-brewery. Q☺◑▯☷(492)P

Orpington

Cricketers

93 Chislehurst Road, BR6 0DQ

☼ 12-3, 5-11; 12-11 Sat; 12-10.30 Sun

☎ (01689) 812648

Adnams Bitter, Broadside; Wadworth 6X; guest beer ℍ

A well-run local pub that has served good quality ale for many years, the Cricketers offers a homely atmosphere to those who want to get away from the busy high street and shops. Conveniently situated for Bromhill Common, it features a pleasant wisteria-covered patio and garden. Major sporting events are screened on TV. ⇖☺▯☷(61)♣⟟—

Pratt's Bottom

Bulls Head

Rushmore Hill, BR6 7NQ TQ497614

☼ 11-11; 12-10.30 Sun

☎ (01689) 852553

Courage Best Bitter; guest beers ℍ

Traditional family-run village pub, about one mile walk via a footpath from Knockholt Station. Regular special events held throughout the year include an annual beer festival in October, and major sporting events are shown on TV. Diners can enjoy a meal in the pub or in the adjacent restaurant (food served until 8.30pm Mon-Sat, 5pm Sun). ᴀᴀQ⇖☺◑▯☷(R5)♣P

Shirley

Orchard

116 Orchard Way, CR0 7NN OS364670

☼ 12-11 (10.30 Sun)

☎ (020) 8777 9011

Fuller's London Pride; Harveys Sussex Best Bitter; guest beer ℍ

Modern, well-hidden pub in the Monks Orchard area of Shirley. It comprises two bars, one has alcoves adorned with Jack Vettriano prints. Sports TV competes with traditional darts and cribbage. Friendly and popular with locals, there are two darts teams, and the pub hosts a local football side. Bar snacks are available weekday lunchtimes (not Sun). Guest beers feature occasionally at weekends. ◑☷(367)♣P

Sidcup

Alma

10 Alma Road, DA14 4EA

☼ 11-3, 5.30-11; 11-midnight Fri; 11-4, 6-midnight Sat; 12-3, 7-11 Sun

☎ (020) 8300 3208

Courage Best Bitter; Fuller's London Pride ℍ

Back-street local near Sidcup station, popular with commuters. The pub dates from 1868 when it was called the Railway Tavern. The Alma serves well-kept beers in a traditional pub atmosphere, and provides lunches on weekdays. It has a grassed garden that offers a pleasant place to drink in summer. Parking is limited. Q☺◑☷♣P

Portrait

7-8 Elm Parade, Main Road, DA14 6NF

☼ 11-11; 12-10.30 Sun

☎ (020) 8302 8757

Archers Lover Boy; Greene King IPA, Old Speckled Hen; Westerham Grasshopper ℍ

This town-centre pub has been converted from a shop. It has a drinking area on two levels, providing a choice of open-plan spaces or more intimate booths. It keeps three guest beers that change frequently, always including ones from Archers and Westerham. Increasingly popular with diners at lunchtime, food is served all day until 9pm. Evening customers are mostly young. ◑▯☷—

Upper Belvedere

Victoria

2 Victoria Street, DA17 5LN

☼ 11-11 (midnight Fri & Sat); 12-11 Sun

☎ (01322) 433773

Adnams Bitter; Shepherd Neame Spitfire ℍ

Pleasant back-street local run in a traditional manner. A cosy horseshoe-shaped bar displays sporting memorabilia on one side and old local photos on the other. An attractive outside drinking area is ideal for summer evenings. Lunches are served weekdays. You can play shove-ha'penny, backgammon, cribbage and other games here including darts. There is entertainment on most Saturday evenings. ᴀᴀ☺◑☷(401)♣—

Welling

New Cross Turnpike

55 Bellegrove Road, DA16 3PB

🌑 9am-11 (10.30 Sun)

☎ (020) 8304 1660

Courage Best Bitter; Greene King Abbot; Marston's Pedigree; Shepherd Neame Spitfire; guest beers Ⓗ

A typical Wetherspoon's pub, the New Cross Turnpike has plenty of local charm, which is enhanced by fairly intimate decor. Varied guest ales are served by helpful staff. Seating is on four levels, including a gallery and two patios. Disabled facilities include a wheelchair lift. Note the Monday Club special offers.
🌑🍺&≠⬛♣

SOUTH-WEST LONDON
SW1: Belgravia

Horse & Groom

7 Groom Place, SW1X 7BA

🌑 11-12.30am (1am Fri)

☎ (020) 7235 6980

Shepherd Neame Master Brew, Spitfire, seasonal beers Ⓗ

Well-hidden mews pub, first licensed as a beer house in 1846. Small, wood-panelled and cosy, there is a plasma TV in one corner. The upstairs room can be used by families and the whole pub is available for private hire on Saturday and Sunday. It also hosts popular bingo nights.
🍺🌑≠⊖(Hyde Pk Corner)⬛♣⌐

Star Tavern

6 Belgrave Mews West, SW1X 8HT

🌑 11-11; 12-10.30 Sun

☎ (020) 7235 3019

Fuller's Chiswick, Discovery, London Pride, ESB, seasonal beers Ⓗ

A Grade II listed building built in 1848, the Star is well known for its award-winning ales and excellent food, and has featured in every edition of this Guide. The pub was reputedly used by members of the Great Train Robbery, and it is also associated with the notorious Lord Lucan. Located in a quiet, residential mews, the German Embassy is next door.
Q🍺⊖(Knightsbridge)♣

SW1: Victoria

Jugged Hare

172 Vauxhall Bridge Road, SW1V 1DX

🌑 11.30-11.30; 12-11 Sun

☎ (020) 7828 1543 ⊕ juggedhare.co.uk

Fuller's Chiswick, Discovery, London Pride, ESB, seasonal beers Ⓗ

A Fuller's Ale & Pie house conversion of a former Nat West bank, decorated in mock-Victorian style with chandelier and an upstairs balcony which can be hired for functions. This pub is located on the busy Vauxhall Bridge Road which is a free route between the two congestion charge areas. However, the area is mainly residential and business, and the pub attracts a mixed clientele. The manager has won awards for the quality and cellarmanship of his beers. A TV shows sporting news, usually with the volume turned down.
🌑🍺⬛≠(Victoria)⊖(Victoria)⌐

SW1: Westminster

Adam & Eve

81 Petty France, SW1H 9EX

🌑 11-11; closed Sat & Sun

☎ (020) 7222 4575

Adnams Bitter; Fuller's London Pride; Young's Bitter; guest beers Ⓗ

Corner pub built in the 1880s and close to government buildings, this venue is popular with civil servants and personnel from the nearby Wellington barracks. The premises are open plan with central high stools and a glass partition that dominates the pub. Regular drink promotions take place, and pie and sausage of the day are food specials. The alcove drinking area at the back can be booked for functions and occasional weekend openings may take place between spring and autumn. 🍺⊖(St James's Pk)

Buckingham Arms

62 Petty France, SW1H 9EU

🌑 11-11 (5.30 Sat); 12-5.30 Sun

☎ (020) 7222 3386

Wells Bombardier; Young's Bitter, Special, seasonal beers Ⓗ

Located opposite the Wellington barracks and formerly a hat shop, this Grade II listed building became a pub in 1840. It has a curved mirrored bar and a drinking corridor used by the local working class during Victorian times. Office workers and tourists frequent the pub now, which has appeared in every edition of the Guide since 1974 and is a firm favourite of most real ale aficionados. There is a TV in the corner but this is mainly turned off unless there is ground-breaking news.
Q🍺⊖(St James's Pk)

Cask & Glass

39-41 Palace Street, SW1E 5HN

🌑 11-11; 12-8 Sat; closed Sun

☎ (020) 7834 7630

Shepherd Neame Master Brew, Kent's Best, Spitfire, Bishops Finger Ⓗ

First licensed in 1862 as the Duke of Cambridge, it did not change name until 1962. The smallest pub in Westminster, it used to serve only half pints until it was taken over by the Shepherd Neame brewery. During recent refurbishment, a wood carving of tulips was found and is displayed in a glass case. The pub is frequented by local office workers and passing tourists visiting nearby Buckingham Palace. During the weekend, it may close early when quiet; it opens occasionally on Sunday in summer to attract the tourist trade. Lunchtime meals are served daily.
🍺≠(Victoria)⊖(Victoria)⌐

Royal Oak

2 Regency Street, SW1P 4BZ

🌑 11-11; 12-4 Sun

☎ (020) 7834 7046

Wells Bombardier; Young's Bitter, seasonal beers Ⓗ

Dating from 1831, this pub was saved from redevelopment in the 1990s by a determined campaign by locals and CAMRA members.

Occupying a corner position, the building has a distinctive triangular shape. Large windows create a spacious and open feeling, while half wood panelling and wooden floors add character to the single bar. A collection of drink-related bric-a-brac is displayed above the bar. Lunches are served daily.
◗⇌(Victoria)⊖(St James's Pk)🚐

Speaker

46 Great Peter Street, SW1P 2HA

✪ 12-11; closed Sat; 12-4 Sun

☎ (020) 7222 1749

Shepherd Neame Spitfire; Young's Bitter; guest beers Ⓗ

Close to the Houses of Parliament, the Speaker is a 'real' bar, devoid of music, TV or fruit machines. Political cartoons decorate the walls. Light, airy and recently refurbished, there are clay pipes on display and cards on the tables. Could the sticks of dynamite have been confiscated from Guy Fawkes and his team? Q◗⊖(St James's Pk)

SW1: Whitehall

Lord Moon of the Mall

16-18 Whitehall, SW1A 2DY

✪ 9-11.30 (midnight Fri & Sat); 9-11 Sun

☎ (020) 7839 7701

Fuller's London Pride; Greene King Abbot; Marston's Pedigree; Shepherd Neame Spitfire; guest beers Ⓗ

This listed building was built in 1872 and refitted in 1992. Originally a banking hall, the spacious and comfortably furnished interior is decorated with oil paintings, statuettes, shelves full of books and ornate alcoves. Popular with tourists, the excellent range of beers provides the perfect introduction to British real ale. Staff, who are all cellar-trained, will assist beginners in their selection. Q◗◖⇌(Charing Cross)⊖(Charing Cross)🚐♣

SW2: Streatham Hill

Crown & Sceptre

2A Streatham Hill, SW2 4AH

✪ 9-11 (midnight Fri & Sat)

☎ (020) 8671 0843

Courage Best Bitter; Greene King Old Speckled Hen, Abbot; Shepherd Neame Spitfire; guest beers Ⓗ

This large Wetherspoon's was a Truman's tied house, hence the unusual fascia which was restored at the request of the local history society. Different levels and distinct areas give this a much better atmosphere than many in the chain. This was the first of the conversions in the area and is now back to its best following a time in the doldrums. Draught beer sales are high and there are always some interesting guest ales. Q✿◗◖⇌🚐♣⏚

SW4: Clapham

Manor Arms

128 Clapham Manor Street, SW4 6ED

✪ 1-11.30; 12-midnight Fri & Sat; 12-11 Sun

☎ (020) 7622 2894

Black Sheep Best Bitter; Everards Tiger; Taylor Landlord; guest beers Ⓗ

Subdued lighting and restrained decor give this back-street local a mellow, almost continental feel. Nevertheless, the atmosphere can be lively when sporting events are shown on the three TV screens. For those who like them, board games are available. The drinking area outside the front of the pub is the place to watch the world go by. A marquee at the back is used for private functions, rugby on the big screen and charity fundraising events, often in support of London Hibs Football Club.
✿⇌(Clapham High St)⊖(Clapham North)🚐⏚

SW6: Parsons Green

White Horse

1-3 Parsons Green, SW6 4UL

✪ 11-11.30 (10.30 Sun)

☎ (020) 7736 2115 🌐 whitehorsesw6.com

Adnams Broadside; Harveys Sussex Best Bitter; Oakham JHB; Rooster's Yankee; guest beers Ⓗ

Excellent gastro-pub, offering a large selection of cask ales and Belgian beers on handpump. The decor is a combination of leather furniture and old wooden tables and benches. The menu contains exotic items such as wild boar and garam masala mussels, each dish with a recommendation for an accompanying beer. Be prepared for nouveau cuisine, jodhpurs and mobile phones. 🏨✿◗🚐(22, 424)⏚

SW7: South Kensington

Anglesea Arms

15 Selwood Terrace, SW7 3QG

✪ 11-11; 12-10.30 Sun

☎ (020) 7373 7960 🌐 capitalpubcompany.com/anglesea

Adnams Bitter, Broadside; Brakspear Special; Fuller's London Pride; Hogs Back Hair of Hog; guest beers Ⓗ

One of the few free houses in London to sell real ale in CAMRA's early days, the Anglesea Arms was built in 1827 and licensed in 1829. Later tied to Meux for more than 100 years, it was acquired by Capital Pub Group in 2002. Inside it has a bare wooden floor and dark mahogany panelling, adorned with oil paintings and photographs. Lunches and evening meals are served from an extensive menu which changes daily. Q✿◗⊖🚐⏚

SW8: South Lambeth

Priory Arms

83 Lansdowne Way, SW8 2PB

✪ 11-11; 12-10.30 Sun

☎ (020) 7622 1884

Adnams Bitter; Harveys Sussex Best; Hop Back Summer Lightning; guest beers Ⓗ

Multi award winning free house, the Priory Arms has showcased quality real ales for many years, a tradition maintained by the current owners. Two rotating guest beers change regularly; more than 4,200 beers have been offered over the years. It also stocks a wide selection of bottled German beers, 25 malt whiskies and a choice of wines. Sunday roasts (served until 6pm) are recommended, and vegetarians are also catered for. The exterior

frontage is listed.
&◧◑➻(Vauxhall)⊖(Stockwell)🚐🌢ᵉ—

Surprise
16 Southville, SW8 2PP
🕑 11-11; 12-10.30 Sun
☎ (020) 7622 4623
Young's Bitter, Special, seasonal beers Ⓗ
The surprise is that such a great, unspoilt, back-street local serving excellent ale is here at all. It has two separate drinking areas with a public bar at the front and a snug/lounge at the rear, featuring amusing depictions of current and past locals, who have always raised large sums for local charities. Entertainment includes occasional live music events, rugby on Sky TV and a regular quiz. A dog-friendly guv'nor completes the picture; not quite – the Surprise has its own boules pitch nearby.
🏙&◧◑◨➻(Vauxhall)⊖(Stockwell)🚐♣🌢ᵉ—

SW9: Brixton

Trinity Arms
45 Trinity Gardens, SW9 7DG
🕑 11-11 (midnight Fri & Sat); 12-10.30 Sun
☎ (020) 7274 4544
Wells Bombardier; Young's Bitter, Special, seasonal beers Ⓗ
A glorious, real London local with ales always in excellent condition, usually busy with office and town hall workers by day and with the pre-concert/club crowd later on. It was built in 1850 and named after Trinity Asylum, founded by Thomas Bailey in nearby Acre Lane. An outside garden area at the front makes the Trinity, voted local CAMRA Pub of the Year in 2004, a perfect summer evening drinking location. Lunches are served daily except Saturday, and early evening meals Monday to Friday. ◑➻⊖🌢ᵉ—

SW10: Chelsea

Chelsea Ram
32 Burnaby Street, SW10 0PL
🕑 11-11; 12-10.30 Sun
☎ (020) 7351 4008
Wells Bombardier; Young's Bitter, Special Ⓗ
A warm, welcoming pub providing a rural touch in the very centre of Chelsea. Inside, an attractive fireplace adds to the rustic ambience. Paintings on the walls are available for purchase. Guests can enjoy a major football match, rugby tournament or Wimbledon on the big screen. Popular for afternoon food over the weekend, 'gastrofication' has not ruined the pub. The function room can be hired. &◑◗—

SW11: Battersea

Beehive
197 St John's Hill, SW11 1TH
🕑 11-11 (midnight Fri & Sat); 12-11 Sun
☎ (020) 7564 1897
Fuller's London Pride, ESB; guest beer Ⓗ
The only Fuller's tied house in Battersea or Wandsworth, this small, friendly one-room local has a public bar feel to it, sporting a cream and green decor, light wooden tables

and chairs. The guest beer changes every week or two. This is a pub for everyone, and children are welcome. Unobtrusive background music makes way for live performances on Thursday and Sunday quiz night. Wholesome weekday lunches are served Monday to Friday. ◑🚐ᵉ—

Castle
115 Battersea High Street, SW11 3HS
🕑 11-11 (midnight Fri & Sat); 11.30-11 Sun
☎ (020) 7228 8181
Young's Bitter, Special Ⓗ
Popular, modern pub near the centre of old Battersea, which successfully combines a drinking venue with an excellent restaurant, serving a varied range of dishes. An open fire warms guests in winter. This 1960s building replaced the original Castle, a coaching inn dating from around 1600 and first leased by Young's in 1843. The outside marquee is heated. 🏙◑➻(Clapham Jct)🚐

Eagle Ale House
104 Chatham Road, SW11 6HG
🕑 12-11 (10.30 Sun)
☎ (020) 7228 2328
Adnams Bitter; Shepherd Neame Spitfire; Westerham IPA; guest beers Ⓗ
A real ale haven, away from the trendy bars of Northcote Road, the Eagle is unspoilt, with a somewhat chaotic interior featuring big leather sofas, old carpets and dusty books. It has a loyal clientele representing a wide social mix, and is always welcoming to visitors. The large-screen TV shows only major sporting events. The garden is covered by a heated marquee.
🏙&◧◑&➻(Clapham Jct)🚐(319, G1)♣🌢ᵉ—

SW12: Balham

Nightingale
97 Nightingale Lane, SW12 8NY
🕑 11-midnight; 12-11 Sun
☎ (020) 8673 1637
Wells Bombardier; Young's Bitter, Special, seasonal beers Ⓗ
Easily the best place in the area for beer and retaining a country local atmosphere, this pub attracts regulars and visitors in large numbers. A small conservatory acts as a family room while the garden is a real suntrap in summer. A full menu is served daily from 12-10pm. The pub is dog friendly, providing water bowls and biscuits. Local CAMRA Pub of the Year finalist and deservedly so.
🏙Q⛱&◧◑&➻(Wandsworth Common)⊖(Clapham S)🚐(G1)♣—

SW13: Barnes

Coach & Horses
27 Barnes High Street, SW13 9LW
🕑 11 (12 Sun)-midnight
☎ (020) 8876 2695
Wells Bombardier; Young's Bitter, Special, seasonal beers Ⓗ
A historic coaching inn, dating at least from 1776, this is now a single-bar pub and retains some dark wood panelling and leaded and stained-glass windows. The pub itself is not

very large, but its award-winning garden is, with a selection of seating areas, a well-equipped children's play area and even room for petanque. The former skittle alley at the back is now a function room. Summer weekend barbecues are very popular; at other times meals and snacks are available. 🏮🍺≠(Barnes Bridge)🚆ᴸ

Red Lion

2 Castelnau, SW13 9RU
🕐 11-11; 12-10.30 Sun
☎ (020) 8748 2984
Fuller's Discovery, London Pride, ESB, seasonal beers Ⓗ

A large Georgian landmark pub, standing at the entrance to the Wetland Centre, the Red Lion has been opened out in recent years, although the rear room still has a more exclusive feel. From here, guests reach a decked patio area and the spacious garden. Excellent food is always available from a varied, modern menu, and children are welcome in the daytime. 🏮🍺🚆ᴸ

SW14: East Sheen

Hare & Hounds

216 Upper Richmond Road West, SW14 8AH
🕐 11-11 (midnight Fri & Sat); 12-10.30 Sun
☎ (020) 8876 4304
Wells Bombardier; Young's Bitter, Special, seasonal beers Ⓗ

Situated prominently on the main South Circular, this large former coaching inn has in recent years become Sheen's landmark pub. A recent refurbishment retained the public bar and converted the snooker room into a comfortable, more secluded, boothed dining and drinking area. Regular music, quizzes and summer barbecues attract a varied clientele and there is always a good atmosphere. The spacious garden is family friendly. Good food is served throughout the day (light menu only 3-6pm). 🏮🍺≠(Mortlake)🚆ᴸ

SW15: Putney

Bricklayers Arms

32 Waterman Street, SW15 1DD
🕐 12-11 (10.30 Sun)
☎ (020) 8780 1155 🌐 bricklayers-arms.com
Taylor Dark Mild, Golden Best, Best Bitter, Landlord, Ram Tam; guest beers Ⓗ

A great back-street local in the heart of Putney, this friendly, family-run community pub may be unique (in London) in stocking the full range of Timothy Taylor beers, plus two guests from micro-breweries. A wood fire burns in winter. Children are welcome until 9pm. This is a remarkable story of a pub saved from residential development. Worthy winner of Wandsworth Business Awards Best Pub of 2006/07 and local CAMRA Pub of the Year 2006, it gets especially busy when Fulham FC are at home. 🏮🍺≠(Putney Bridge)🚆♣ᴸ

Whistle & Flute

46 Putney High Street, SW15 1SQ
🕐 11-11.30 (midnight Fri & Sat); 12-10.30 Sun
☎ (020) 8780 5437

Fuller's London Pride, ESB, seasonal beers Ⓗ

Former bank premises converted to a pub in the 1990s, this is a modern, welcoming pub serving excellent beer. Furnished with a mixture of sofas and chairs round tables, both downstairs drinking areas show Sky sports. Daily newspapers are provided. There is a function room up a few steps at the rear, available for parties and meetings. 🍺≠Ө(Putney Bridge/E Putney)🚆

SW15: Roehampton

Angel

11 Roehampton High Street, SW15 4HL
🕐 11-11; 12-10.30 Sun
☎ (020) 8788 1997
Wells Bombardier; Young's Bitter, Special, seasonal beer Ⓗ

An increasingly rare example of a traditional two-bar community pub in South-West London, the Angel is home to golf and angling clubs, reflecting a sporting interest. The TV shows only sporting events, mainly football. The menu is basic but good value (food is served lunchtimes and evenings, all day Sun). The pub is due to be refurbished but, thankfully, no major changes are planned. 🏮🍺♣ᴸ

SW17: Summerstown

Leather Bottle

538 Garratt Lane, SW17 0NY
🕐 11-11 (midnight Thu-Sat); 12-10.30 Sun
☎ (020) 8946 2309
Wells Bombardier; Young's Bitter, Special, seasonal beers Ⓗ

A split-level pub dating from the 17th century, with a distinctive Dutch-style roof, the Leather Bottle was refurbished in 2004. The pub now has a separate dining area (food served all day) and a heated marquee between the building and the large garden, which features a boules pitch. It is particularly popular with the 20-40 age group. 🏮🍺≠(Earlsfield)🚆Pᴸ

SW17: Tooting

Castle

38 Tooting High Street, SW17 0RG
🕐 11-11 (midnight Fri & Sat); 12-11 Sun
☎ (020) 8672 7018
Wells Bombardier; Young's Bitter, Special, seasonal beers Ⓗ

At the heart of Tooting's busy town centre, this spacious pub is used by a wide cross-section of the local community. Some panelling survives from the pub's construction between the wars and helps give a mellow ambience. A large Bass mirror presides over a raised area away from the street, and large-screen TV prevails elsewhere. 🏮🍺Ө(Tooting Broadway)🚆Pᴸ

SW18: Battersea

Freemasons

2 North Side, Wandsworth Common, SW18 2SS
🕐 11-11; 12-10.30 Sun
☎ (020) 7326 8580 🌐 freemasonspub.com

Everards Tiger; Taylor Landlord ⚠
One of the more popular of several gastro-pubs in the area, this Victorian building has an ornate entrance lobby and a semi-circular frontage that overlooks one of the main rail lines into Clapham Junction. The pub has unusual handpumps, where the beer passes through glass canisters. It attracts a fairly young, affluent clientele (beer prices reflect this) and has a regularly changing menu.
🕸🍺🍴♿

SW18: Wandsworth

Alma
499 Old York Road, SW18 1TF
🕐 11-midnight; 12-11 Sun
☎ (020) 8870 2537 🌐 almawandsworth.com
Wells Bombardier; Young's Bitter, Special, seasonal beers ⚠
This lively pub, located in an affluent area, has seen many changes over the years but retains its attractive, green-tiled facade and some interior features, most remarkably painted mirrors (hence its inclusion on CAMRA's London Regional Inventory). Directly opposite Wandsworth Town station, it can get busy when rugby matches are shown on the big screen. It is also popular for its excellent food; booking is advisable for the restaurant area, particularly for Sunday lunch.
🏨🍺♿🚂(Wandsworth Town)🚌(28, 44)**P**

Grapes
39 Fairfield Street, SW18 1DX
🕐 12-11 (midnight Fri & Sat); 12-10.30 Sun
☎ (020) 8874 3414
Wells Bombardier; Young's Bitter, Special ⚠
Small, traditional, friendly local pub with a mixed clientele, a stone's throw from the now defunct Young's Brewery. The Grapes was originally built in 1833 as a beer shop, licensed to sell beer only, not spirits. In summer guests may enjoy the delightful garden, a London oasis. Well-behaved children are welcome. Sport is occasionally shown on TV. Local CAMRA Pub of the Year 2005, this local is not one to pass by.
🕸🍺🚂(Wandsworth Town)🚌♣

Spread Eagle
71 Wandsworth High Street, SW18 4LB
🕐 11-11 (midnight Fri & Sat); 12-11 Sun
☎ (020) 8877 9809
Wells Bombardier; Young's Bitter, Special, seasonal beers ⚠
Large pub in the centre of Wandsworth with beautiful Victorian etched glass and an external canopy. On CAMRA's Regional Inventory of Historic Pub Interiors, it is well worth a visit for the architecture as much as for the beer. There are several distinct drinking areas: the public bar has a pool table and large TV screen, and the quieter room at the back is available for meetings and functions. Food is served on weekdays.
🏨Q🍺🍴🚂(Wandsworth Town)🚌

Wheatsheaf
30 Putney Bridge Road, SW18 1HS
🕐 11-midnight; 12-11 Sun
☎ (020) 8874 5753
Young's Bitter, Special, seasonal beers ⚠
For many years the 'forgotten' Young's pub in Wandsworth town centre, the Wheatsheaf now takes a bow as a great little unspoilt local, as others nearby gentrify and concentrate on food. Dispensing well-kept ales, this little gem is family and dog-friendly, has Sky Sports on TV and customers can buy their own food from local take-aways and eat it in the pub. This cosy pub is well worth seeking out. 🕸🚂(Wandsworth Town)🚌♣♿

SW19: South Wimbledon

Princess of Wales
98 Morden Road, SW19 3BP
🕐 11-11 (midnight Fri); 12-11 Sun
☎ (020) 8542 0573
Young's Bitter, Special, seasonal beers ⚠
A Young's pub since 1876, with unchanged mid 19th-century frontage, the former Prince of Wales was under threat of disposal before successful campaigning and the change of name in 1997 heralded a new lease of life. Inside is the former public bar area with dartboard and TV, and a quiet, spacious main saloon that extends to the enclosed patio at the back. Twinned with the Horse Brass Pub in Portland, Oregon, this is a popular local, especially with local cricket teams. Meals are served lunchtime daily and in the evening Monday-Friday.
🏨Q🕸🍺⊖(Morden Rd Tramlink)🚌♣**P**♿

Sultan
78 Norman Road, SW19 1BT
🕐 12-11 (midnight Fri & Sat)
☎ (020) 8544 9323
Hop Back GFB, Entire Stout, Summer Lightning; guest beer ⚠
The long-serving tenant has maintained this pub's quiet, friendly atmosphere, much appreciated by loyal regulars and visitors who continue to arrive in large numbers. The smaller bar, which features the dartboard, opens in the evening. Wednesday is beer club night (6-9pm), when discounted cask beers are on offer. Quiz night on Tuesday is very popular, and a weekend beer festival is held in September.
Q🕸🍴♿⊖(Colliers Wood)🚌♣♿

Trafalgar
23 High Path, SW19 2JY (jct of Pincott Rd and High Path)
🕐 12 (11 Wed-Fri)-11
☎ (020) 8542 5342 🌐 thetraf.com
Gale's HSB; Taylor Golden Best; guest beers ⚠
A truly excellent back-street local dating from the 1860s, with much Nelson memorabilia. Although a small pub, there are three distinct drinking areas and six handpumps that carry four constantly changing guest ales from micros such as Downton, Sharp's and Dark Star. Mild ales are featured in May. Good lunches are served on weekdays. Sky Sports is shown on HDTV, Wifi facilities cater for computer addicts. This local CAMRA Pub of the Year 2006 runner-up is well worth a trip down the Northern Line.
🏨🕸🍺🚂⊖(S Wimbledon)🚌♣♿

SW19: Wimbledon

Crooked Billet
15 Crooked Billet, SW19 4RQ
☼ 11-11.30 (midnight Fri & Sat); 12-10.30 Sun
☎ (020) 8946 4942
Young's Bitter; Wells Bombardier; Young's Special Ⓗ
A late 18th-century pub on the edge of Wimbledon Common, bought by Young's in 1888 and extended in 1969 into an adjoining cottage. Real fires and exposed beams add to the warm welcome of this busy, friendly pub with its separate, intimate restaurant room at the rear. The main bar is usually quiet; the TV is seldom turned on. Drink, relax and enjoy a meal. ♨⊛◑ᵜ

Hand in Hand
6 Crooked Billet, SW19 4RQ
☼ 11-11 (midnight Fri & Sat); 12-10.30 Sun
☎ (020) 8946 5720
Wells Bombardier; Young's Bitter, Special, seasonal beers Ⓗ
Originally a bakehouse in buildings owned by Daniel Watney, whose grandson founded that brewery, this award-winning pub was a beer house belonging to the Holland family until Young's bought it in 1974. Much altered and extended since, it retains an intimate feel in the drinking areas around the central bar, a separate family room and suntrap patio. Opposite, the grass triangle provides a summer drinking, picnic and play area well used by customers of this pub and the Crooked Billet. ♨♿⊛◑♣

Carshalton

Greyhound Hotel
2 High Street, SM5 3PE
☼ 11-midnight; 12-11.30 Sun
☎ (020) 8647 1511
Wells Bombardier; Young's Bitter, Special Ⓗ
Large pub, originally two adjoining buildings, facing Carshalton's pond. Inside, it has several bars, a restaurant and accommodation. The Swan bar at the front with views over the pond is quieter than some of the other drinking areas. Note the greyhound mosaic floor as you enter the Swan bar. There is a small area with tables out front.
♨Q⊛⇌◑Ⓓ♿⇌🚃Pᵜ

Racehorse
17 West Street, SM5 3EU
☼ 11 (12 Sun)-11
☎ (020) 8647 6818 ⊛racehorseinns.co.uk
Courage Best Bitter; Greene King IPA; guest beers Ⓗ
Established in the 1870s, the Racehorse caters for both diners and drinkers in traditional English pub/restaurant surroundings. A separate public bar (with piped music and TV) complements the quiet lounge, which is mainly used as a dining area. The pub serves a good selection of guest beers, mainly from micros. It provides meals from an extensive, contemporary menu as well as bar snacks, and boasts a good wine cellar too. Occasional jazz or blues nights are staged in the lounge. Children are not permitted. Q◑Ⓓ⇌🚃P

Railway Tavern
47 North Street, SM5 2HG
☼ 12-2.30, 5-11; 12-11 Sat; 12-10.30 Sun
☎ (020) 8669 8016
Fuller's London Pride, ESB Ⓗ
This small, spotless street-corner pub near Carshalton station is run by Fuller's Master Cellarman from 2002-05. The walls are adorned with awards, pictures and memorabilia from the steam era. The patio garden is ablaze with colour, as are the hanging baskets out front in summer. Traditional pub games are played, including dominoes and cribbage. Bar snacks are served Monday-Friday lunchtimes. ⊛◑⇌🚃♣ᵜ

Windsor Castle
378 Carshalton Road, SM5 3PT (on A232)
☼ 11-11 (11.30 Fri & Sat); 12-11 Sun
☎ (020) 8669 1191
Hancock's HB; Fuller's London Pride; guest beers Ⓗ
This large, one-bar pub near the ponds and station has six pumps serving beer mainly from regional brewers. The restaurant provides an à la carte menu and chef's specials including a Sunday lunchtime roast, and sandwiches are available Monday to Saturday. Across the small courtyard is the garden and a function room with its own bar. The annual beer festival held over the Mayday weekend is not to be missed. Thursday is quiz night, Saturday features live jazz.
⊛◑⇌(Carshalton Beeches)🚃♣Pᵜ

Chessington

Lucky Rover
312 Hook Road, KT9 1NY (on A243)
☼ 11-midnight
☎ (020) 8397 3227
Courage Best Bitter; Harveys Sussex Best Bitter Ⓗ
Small, busy pub situated at the north end of Hook Parade. This popular local has two separate bar areas; the larger one to the right often screens football on TV. A weekly quiz night raises funds for charity, and music nights are also staged. The garden at the rear is popular in summer. No food is served at weekends. ⊛◑⇌(Chessington N)🚃

North Star
271 Hook Road, KT9 1EQ (on A243)
☼ 12-11 (midnight Fri & Sat)
☎ (020) 8391 9811
Adnams Bitter; Caledonian Deuchars IPA; guest beers Ⓗ
This pub, dating back over 150 years, serves good food all day with snacks available until last orders. The cellarman has been looking after the beers since 1970. It has a resident golf society and hosts popular quizzes twice a week. Conversation competes with background music in some areas of the pub. The North Star participates in all the Ember Inns' beer festivals. ♨⊛◑♿🚃Pᵜ

Kingston upon Thames

Canbury Arms
49 Canbury Park Road, KT2 6LQ

☼ 9am-11; 12-10.30 Sun
☎ (020) 8255 9129 ⊕ thecanburyarms.com
Gale's HSB; Harveys Sussex Best Bitter; Hook Norton Old Hooky; Taylor Landlord; guest beer ⒣
Recently modernised, this pub is strongly food-oriented, but the landlord is also very keen on real ale. One bar is open plan, with a permanent heated marquee attached with family and smoking areas. Movie stills adorn the walls. The guest beer changes monthly, and food is served all day. Backgammon and chess are both played here and background music underlines the conversation. It stages occasional quiz nights, and the local five-a-side teams and the golf society meet here.
⑁❀◑&⇌⊞(K5)♣P⅃

Owl & Pussycat

144 Richmond Road, KT2 5HA (on A307)
☼ 11.30-11.30 (12.30am Thu-Sat); 12-11 Sun
☎ (020) 8546 9162
Adnams Bitter, Broadside; Greene King IPA; guest beer ⒣
Originally the Queen's Head, a large Victorian street-corner local, the Owl & Pussycat has been opened out into a single space. The interior features an open fire and comfortable seating. There is a pool table off to one side and a dartboard. Traditional pub food is available until 9pm (6pm Sun), and ales in handle jugs are served on request. Monday is quiz night and live bands play occasionally. It is family friendly, but has no separate family room. ⚞❀◑&⇌⊞(65)♣P⅃□

Park Tavern

19 New Road, KT2 6AP (off B351)
☼ 11-11; 12-10.30 Sun
Fuller's London Pride; Taylor Landlord; Young's Bitter; guest beers ⒣
Originally two cottages, the Park Tavern has been a pub now for more than 150 years. It attracts a lively mix of locals and those seeking refreshment after exercising in nearby Richmond Park. The three guest beers often come from small brewers. The front patio is covered by a trellis. Filled rolls are available lunchtimes Monday-Saturday, and later if there are any left. Dogs are welcome and may even get a treat. ⚞❀⊞(371)♣⅃

Willoughby Arms

47 Willoughby Road, KT2 6LN
☼ 10.30 (12 Sun)-midnight
☎ (020) 8546 4236 ⊕ thewilloughbyarms.com
Caledonian Deuchars IPA; Fuller's London Pride; Taylor Landlord; Wells Bombardier; guest beers ⒣
Welcoming Victorian back-street pub with an enterprising landlord. The pub is divided into a sports bar, with pub games and a large-screen TV, and a quieter lounge area. An upstairs function room hosts occasional live music and was used by the Yardbirds for rehearsals in the 1960s. Beer festivals are held for St George's Day and Halloween. Three guest beers come from a variety of breweries, large and small, including local ones. The large garden is used for barbecues in summer.
❀⊟&⊞(371, K5)♣♨⅃

Wych Elm

93 Elm Road, KT2 6HT

☼ 11-3.30, 5-midnight; 11-midnight Sat; 11-11 Sun
☎ (020) 8546 3271
Fuller's Chiswick, Discovery, London Pride, ESB; guest beers ⒣
A great back-street local, very welcoming and friendly, the Wych Elm has been run by its charismatic Spanish landlord for 24 years. It has a smart saloon bar with glass partition, and a basic but tidy public bar with dartboard. Local CAMRA Pub of the Year 2005, its splendid award-winning flower display out front attracts custom in summer, as does the well-kept garden at the rear. Good quality home-cooked lunches are served Monday-Saturday. ❀◑⊟⇌⊞(K5)⅃

Mitcham

Queen's Head

70 Cricket Green, CR4 4LA
☼ 11-midnight (1am Fri & Sat); 11-11 Sun
☎ (020) 8648 3382
Shepherd Neame Master Brew Bitter, Spitfire, seasonal beers ⒣
An early 20th-century pub on the edge of Mitcham's historic cricket green, the Queen's Head has two rooms, with the smaller, public bar offering TV sports, games machines and a dartboard. Excellent food is served at lunchtime, and on Friday there is fish & chips to eat inside or take away. The pub hosts several darts teams and often holds charity events. A friendly, traditional local, it is an easy walk from Mitcham Tramlink or bus stops along the London Road.
❀◑⊟⊖(Mitcham Tramlink)⊟♣P

New Malden

Woodies

Thetford Road, KT3 5DX
☼ 11-11; 12-10.30 Sun
☎ (020) 8949 5824 ⊕ woodiesfreehouse.co.uk
Adnams Broadside; Fuller's London Pride, ESB; Young's Bitter; guest beers ⒣
Once a cricket pavilion, then a club house, now a free house, Woodies can be difficult to find down a track off the Thetford Road. Its walls and ceiling are adorned with sports programmes and other memorabilia. Local CAMRA Pub of the Year 2006 and 2007, it features three guest beers, sourced mainly from micros, to complement the four regulars. The pub is building a reputation for its beer festival, held in August. There is only one room, partly separated from the dining and family area. In summer the patio is very popular. ⚞❀◑⊟P⅃

Richmond

Old Ship

3 King Street, TW9 1ND
☼ 11-11.30 (midnight Fri & Sat); 11-11 Sun
☎ (020) 8940 3461
Wells Bombardier; Young's Bitter, Special, seasonal beers ⒣
Dating back to 1735 and a Young's house since 1869, this town-centre pub by the House of Fraser store can be seen at the end of the main street. Recently refurbished with two ground-floor bars, an upstairs drinking area

and a heated, covered courtyard garden, it features ships' equipment and memorabilia with an engine-room telegraph built into a bannister. Consistently good pub food is available all day, and a Sunday night music quiz is held. ⋈Q⚹①ⓓ&≈⊖⊟

Orange Tree

45 Kew Road, TW9 2NQ
☉ 11-11 (midnight Fri & Sat)
☎ (020) 8940 0944 ⊕ orangetreerichmond.co.uk
Wells Bombardier; Young's Bitter, Special, seasonal beers Ⓗ

Close to Richmond station, this pub has recently been refurbished to a high, contemporary standard. The large bar at ground level is complemented by a cellar bar and a heated outdoor drinking area. The renowned Orange Tree Theatre is across the road. Good food is served all day; the dining area has a hanging indoor garden under the skylights. ⚹①≈⊖⊟

Red Cow

59 Sheen Road, TW9 1YJ
☉ 11-11.30 (midnight Fri & Sat); 11-11 Sun
☎ (020) 8940 2511 ⊕ redcowpub.com
Wells Bombardier; Young's Bitter, Special, seasonal beers Ⓗ

Sympathetically restored, this popular local is a few minutes' walk from Richmond's shops and station. There are three distinct drinking areas where rugs on bare floorboards and period furniture create a traditional atmosphere. Good lunches are served daily and evening meals Monday-Thursday until 9pm. Tuesday is quiz night and live music is performed regularly. The first floor has four en-suite bedrooms. ⋈⚹⌂①≈⊖⊟

Roebuck

130 Richmond Hill, TW10 6RN
☉ 12-11; 11-midnight Fri & Sat; 12-10.30 Sun
☎ (020) 8948 2329
Beer range varies Ⓗ

Overlooking the World Heritage Site of Petersham Meadows and the Thames, this 200-year-old, reputedly haunted pub is close to Richmond Park Gate. Patrons are welcome on the terrace opposite to enjoy the view cherished by their forebears and highwaymen for 500 years. A recent refurbishment has opened up three drinking areas on the first floor. Four handpumps offer regularly changing beers, and an updated menu offers great choice (food served until late). ⋈⚹①

Waterman's Arms

12 Water Lane, TW9 1TJ
☉ 11 (12 Sun)-11
☎ (020) 8940 2893
Wells Bombardier; Young's Bitter, Special, seasonal beers Ⓗ

Historic pub, one of the oldest in Richmond (rebuilt 1898), retaining its Victorian two-bar layout. In a lane leading to the river, generations of watermen have drunk here and some, along with others in riparian occupations, still do. In the 1950s it was a lunchtime stop for the Swan Uppers en route from Blackfriars to Henley. Full of character, it has a truly local feel. Good food is served until late. The pub hosts a Monday music club upstairs. ⋈Q⚹①≈⊖

White Cross

Riverside, Water Lane, TW9 1TJ
☉ 11-11; 12-10.30 Sun
☎ (020) 8940 6844
Wells Bombardier; Young's Bitter, Special, seasonal beers Ⓗ

A prominent feature on Richmond's waterfront, the pub dates from 1835, and a stained-glass panel is a reminder that it stands on the site of a former convent of the Observant Friars, whose insignia was a white cross. It is reached by steps for good reason: the river often floods here. An island bar serves two side rooms (one a mezzanine); an unusual feature is the working fireplace beneath a window. A ground-level patio bar opens at busy times. ⋈Q⚹①≈⊖

Surbiton

Cap in Hand

174 Hook Rise North, KT6 5DE (on A3/A243 jct)
☉ 9 (12 Sun)-midnight
☎ (020) 8397 3790
Greene King Abbot; Courage Best Bitter; Fuller's London Pride; Marston's Pedigree; guest beers Ⓗ

Popular road-house style pub at the 'Ace of Spades' junction. The building dates from 1934, when it was built to replace an earlier Southborough Arms, which still stands around the corner. Open plan in layout, it is divided into different areas with tables and chairs or booths. The large conservatory at the front is the designated family area until 8pm. Guest beers are sourced from local brewers including Itchen Valley. Tuesday is steak night and Thursday curry (food served all day until 11pm). Q⚹①&⊟♠P⎸

Coronation Hall

St Marks Hill, KT6 4LQ (on B3370)
☉ 9-1am
☎ (020) 8390 6164
Courage Best Bitter; Greene King Abbot; Marston's Pedigree; Shepherd Neame Spitfire; guest beers Ⓗ

Opened 10 years ago, this is a splendid conversion of a former music hall that has also seen life as a cinema, bingo hall and nudist health club. The interior has a movie theme with pictures of film stars and old cinema artefacts on display. There is seating at the front where you can sit and watch the world go by, or up the steps is a long bar with booths to the right. An upstairs balcony overlooks the bar. TV screens show the News and major sporting events. Food is served daily until 11pm. Q①&≈⊟

Sutton

Little Windsor

13 Greyhound Road, SM1 4BY
☉ 12-midnight (11.30 Sun)
☎ (020) 8643 2574
Fuller's Discovery, London Pride, ESB, seasonal beers; guest beers Ⓗ

Cosy, popular street-corner local in the New Town area. It became a pub in 1890, to replace a beer house up the road, and was originally named the Windsor Castle. It was acquired by Fuller's as part of a pub swap with Charringtons. There is a good-sized extension at the rear, plus a garden and decked area. Discounts are offered on four-pint jugs. Local CAMRA Pub of the Year 2002 and 2003, it is a real community pub with an active social programme and a quiz night on Thursday. No food is served on Sunday.
⊛◑⇌🚃(407, 154)♣🏃

Robin Hood
52 West Street, SM1 1SH (off B2230, jct with Robin Hood Lane)
🕐 11-11; 12-10.30 Sun
☎ (020) 8643 7584
Young's Bitter, Special, seasonal beers Ⓗ
Large, popular, comfortable one-bar pub, close to the St Nicholas shopping centre. Inside is a spacious L-shaped bar, and there is a small rear courtyard as well as some seating on the pavement. The upstairs function room is available for hire. Local CAMRA Pub of the Year 2006, it holds a regular quiz night on Monday evening to raise funds for charity. In addition to the draught regulars, an impressive range of Young's bottled beers is stocked here.
🏨⊛◑⇌🚃♣🏃

Wallington

Whispering Moon
25 Ross Parade, SM6 8QF
🕐 9am-midnight (1am Fri & Sat)
☎ (020) 8647 7020
Courage Best Bitter; Greene King Old Speckled Hen, Abbot; Marston's Pedigree; guest beers Ⓗ
Modest-sized Wetherspoon's pub which pre-dates their 'bigger is better' era; in this case occupying former small cinema premises. One long bar serves an L-shaped lounge which includes an elevated drinking area. Floor to ceiling glazing gives a light and airy impression. Nearby is Wallington Hall, home of the local CAMRA branch's October beer and cider festival. Guest ales are usually sourced from micro-breweries. Q🛏◑ᓵ⇌🚃🏃

WEST LONDON
W1: Marylebone

Carpenters Arms
12 Seymour Place, W1H 7NE
🕐 11-11; 12-10.30 Sun
☎ (020) 7723 1050
Adnams Broadside; Hogs Back TEA; guest beers Ⓗ
The Carpenters Arms was first licensed in 1776 and rebuilt by Mieux in 1872. Note the impressive tiling near the front door, its distinctive large windows and the side door to the mews. The pub attracts support from two main sources: real ale enthusiasts and sports fans. Drinkers can select from a changing range of ales from micro and regional breweries served from the conspicuous semi-circular bar. The pub can get busy when sporting events are shown on the TV screens.
⊛◑Θ(Marble Arch)🚃♣🏃

Wargrave Arms
40-42 Brendon Street, W1H 5HE
🕐 11-11; 12-10.30 Sun
☎ (020) 7723 0559 ⊕thewargrave.com
Young's Bitter, Special; Wells Bombardier; guest beers Ⓗ
Attractive, comfortable inn, dating from 1866, the Wargrave Arms was acquired by Young's in the 1980s. A friendly pub, it hosts chess contests on Tuesdays and bridge games on Thursdays (all comers welcome). A traditional menu is served and the food is cooked on site (lunchtimes daily, evenings Mon-Fri). Rugby frequently features on the large-screen TV.
◑⇌(Paddington)Θ(Edgware Rd)🚃♣🏃

W1: Mayfair

Coach & Horses
5 Bruton Street, W1J 6PT
🕐 11-11; 12-8 Sat; closed Sun
☎ (020) 7629 4123
Fuller's London Pride; Greene King IPA, Old Speckled Hen; guest beer Ⓗ
This listed wood-panelled building featuring a Tudor-style exterior has been a pub since 1736. It was rebuilt in 1933 for Youngers by architect John T Quilter. Queen Elizabeth II was born down the road at number 17. The tiny bar is regularly packed, mostly with business people. Pump clips are displayed all around, showcasing the hundreds of beers that have featured here. Meals are served until 9pm.
◑Θ(Oxford Circus)🚃

Coach & Horses
5 Hill Street, W1J 5LD
🕐 12-11; closed Sat & Sun
☎ (020) 7355 0300
Shepherd Neame Kent's Best, Spitfire, seasonal beer Ⓗ
The oldest surviving pub in Mayfair, dating from 1744, this former Bass pub was recently bought by Shepherd Neame. It has been refurbished and redecorated with a warming red and green colour scheme. The clientele has evolved over the years since the 1960s and 70s from croupiers, who worked at the nearby casino, to mostly office workers. The times they are a changing: this was once the meeting place of the Bob Dylan Association.
◑Θ(Bond St)

W1: Soho

Dog & Duck ☆
18 Bateman Street, W1D 3AJ
🕐 11-11 (11.30 Fri & Sat); 12-10.30 Sun
☎ (020) 7494 0697
Fuller's London Pride; Taylor Landlord; guest beers Ⓗ
Originally dating from 1734, the present pub was built in 1897. Located in the heart of Soho, it has a fascinating late-Victorian interior. There are wonderful glazed tiles and advertising mirrors for tobacco and mineral water. The rear snug has a more intimate atmosphere, warmed by a fire and featuring an antique postage stamp machine. The upstairs Orwell Bar, with its leather seating, is a good place to while away an afternoon watching the world go by from the bay

windows. Meals are served all day.
◑▶≈(Charing Cross)⊖(Leicester Sq/
Tottenham Ct Rd)⊞

Pillars of Hercules

7 Greek Street, W1D 4DF
◷ 11-11; 12-10.30 Sun
☎ (020) 7437 1179
Young's Bitter; guest beers ⊞

This pub features an impressive mock-Tudor
frontage and adjoining archway, with the
building extending above it. There has been a
pub here since the 17th century. Inside there
is a prominent bar back with clock and spiral-
carved columns. Drinkers can choose from up
to six ales, drawn from a changing monthly
selection. The clientele is diverse and the
environment welcoming. Meals are served
until 6pm daily. ◑▶⊖(Tottenham Ct Rd)⊞

Ship

116 Wardour Street, W1F 0TT
◷ 11-11; closed Sun
☎ (020) 7437 8446
**Fuller's Discovery, London Pride, ESB, seasonal
beers** ⊞

Once a rare Fuller's outlet in the West End, this
pub has some wonderful etched and leaded
glass, decorative mirrors and an ornate bar
back. The story goes that the building was
damaged by a gas explosion during WWII,
then rebuilt using the original 1895 fittings. It
was named the Ship in Distress in 1780. Now
a famous music venue, it specialises in its own
collection of Indie music. Meals are served at
lunchtime. ◑⊖(Tottenham Ct Rd)

W2: Bayswater

Kings Head

33 Moscow Road, W2 4AH
◷ 11-11; 12-10.30 Sun
☎ (020) 7229 4233
**Adnams Broadside; Fuller's London Pride;
Greene King IPA, Old Speckled Hen; Young's
Bitter; guest beers** ⊞

Traditional community pub, hosting regular
theme nights and charity events. Wooden
beams and panelling create a comfortable and
spacious feel. This is the ideal place to wind
down after shopping in busy, cosmopolitan
Queensway. There is a good range of foreign
beers on offer and branded glasses are used
whenever possible. Meals are served
throughout the day.
❀◑▶⊖(Queensway)⊞♣↳

Prince Edward

73 Princes Square, W2 4NY
◷ 11-11; 12-10.30 Sun
☎ (020) 7727 2221
**Badger K&B Sussex Bitter, Tanglefoot, seasonal
beers** ⊞

Mid 19th-century, listed building on the west
side of a leafy Victorian square, the Prince
Edward has a smartly furnished lounge with
comfortable leather armchairs, plenty of
tables and chairs and a central island bar.
Many interesting 19th-century photos of
London and old prints, etched glass mirrors
and coloured glass panels adorn the interior.
An interesting menu is offered at lunchtime

and in the evening.
❀◑▶⊖(Notting Hill Gate)↳

W2: Lancaster Gate

Mitre

24 Craven Terrace, W2 3QH
◷ 11-11 (midnight Fri & Sat); 12-10.30 Sun
☎ (020) 7262 5240
**Fuller's London Pride; Wells Bombardier; guest
beers** ⊞

A heart-shaped wooden bar divides the pub
into two main drinking areas, one with rough
wooden flooring and the other with carpet
and leather wing-back chairs. Decorative
features include rich wood panelling, ornate
etched mirrors and wooden partitions with
frosted glass inserts. Light fixtures around the
bar are suspended by chains. The scene of BBC
dramas, a Woody Allen film and a new 1960s
gangster movie, the Mitre is also known for its
good background music and occasional
acoustic nights. Two upstairs function rooms
are available for hire. ▲Q☞❀◑▶⊖⊞

W2: Paddington

Mad Bishop & Bear

**First Floor, The Lawn, Paddington Station,
W2 1HB**
◷ 8am-11 (11.30 Thu & Fri); 10-10.30 Sun
☎ (020) 7402 2441
**Fuller's Chiswick, Discovery, London Pride, ESB,
seasonal beers; guest beers** ⊞

Located on the first floor above Paddington
Station concourse, this is the perfect place to
wait for a train. Spacious and comfortable, the
interior features wood panelling and wood-
framed mirrors, and an elevated section at the
rear. A tile motif is embedded within the
polished wood floor. Mood lighting completes
the ambience. A conveniently located but
unobtrusive platform indicator keeps drinkers
informed. Meals are served until 9pm.
◑▶&≈⊖⊞

Victoria

10A Strathearn Place, W2 2NH
◷ 11-11; 12-10.30 Sun
☎ (020) 7724 1191
**Fuller's Discovery, London Pride, ESB, seasonal
beer** ⊞

There is plenty to admire in this mid-Victorian
pub, including the ornately gilded mirrors
above a crescent-shaped bar. As well as
numerous portraits of Queen Victoria at
various stages of her life, the walls are
adorned with cartoons, paperweights and a
Silver Jubilee plate. Wall niches bear painted
tiles. A recessed area at the back is furnished
with a leather bench seat. The upstairs,
reached via a spiral staircase, has a library and
theatre bar available for public use. Tuesday is
quiz night. ▲Q☞❀◑▶≈⊖⊞↳

W4: Chiswick

George & Devonshire

8 Burlington Lane, W4 2QE
◷ 12-11 (10.30 Sun)
☎ (020) 8994 1859 ⊕georgeanddevonshire.co.uk

Fuller's Chiswick, London Pride, ESB, seasonal beers ⊞
This 1790s pub, situated near the Fuller's Brewery at the Hogarth roundabout, retains its original low-key grandeur. Shakespearean plays were performed here and punters have included Elizabeth Taylor and Tom Jones. The pub was originally called the George, after the former king; it added the Devonshire after the fourth Duke who owned much of the land around here, including Chiswick House and grounds. Monthly live music and art exhibitions feature the work of eminent local artists such as Suz Hartman. ▲❀◐ ⊞♣P↝

Mawson Arms
110 Chiswick Lane South, W4 2QA
🕙 11-8; closed Sat & Sun
☎ (020) 8994 2936
Fuller's Chiswick, Discovery, London Pride, ESB, seasonal beers ⊞
This pub is the official brewery tap for the Fuller's Brewery next door. Formerly two pubs, it now has a central bar that separates the Mawson Arms side, which loosely resembles a public bar, from the Fox & Hounds side, where brewery tour groups generally assemble. Brewing first began here in 1671, and the history of the site is detailed around the pub. Portraits of the three founder family members of Fuller, Smith and Turner, who started the brewery in 1845, can also be admired. This is the official meeting point for brewery tours (information from the pub).
Q◖⊖(Turnham Green)

Old Pack Horse
434 Chiswick High Road, W4 5TF
🕙 11-11 (midnight Fri & Sat); 11-10.30 Sun
☎ (020) 8994 2872
Fuller's London Pride, ESB, seasonal beers ⊞
Located near Chiswick station, the pub is easy to spot thanks to its fine Edwardian frontage. Inside it has a U-shaped bar and a Thai restaurant to the rear. The walls feature impressively ornate woodwork and are adorned with extensive theatre memorabilia. An outdoor paved area provides seating in summer, while the snug at the rear is warmed by a real fire in winter. The late Tommy Cooper was a regular here.
Q❀◐ ⊖(Chiswick Pk)

W5: Ealing

Questors (Grapevine Bar)
Mattock Lane, W5 5BQ
🕙 7-11; 12-2.30, 7-10.30 Sun
☎ (020) 8567 0071 ⊕questors.org.uk/grapevine
Fuller's London Pride; guest beers ⊞
This friendly theatre bar once again reached the last four of the National CAMRA Club of the Year awards. The staff are all volunteers and real ale fans, which shows in the quality of the beer they serve. Four handpumps are available, but usually only three are in use. The fourth dispenses ale during the annual beer festival in October and at special events throughout the year.
Q❀去≠(Ealing Broadway)⊖(Ealing Broadway)P↝

W6: Hammersmith

Andover Arms
57 Aldensley Road, W6 0DL
🕙 12-11 (11.30 Fri & Sat); 12-3.30, 7-10.30 Sun
☎ (020) 8741 9794
Fuller's Chiswick, London Pride, ESB, seasonal beers ⊞
Small, popular back-street local, tucked away in the side streets of Hammersmith. A regular entry in this Guide, the pub holds regular quiz nights and occasional beer festivals. Its Thai restaurant serves delicious food at reasonable prices (no food Sun). The larger of the two bars has a TV for occasional sporting events.
Q◐⊖(Ravenscourt Pk)🚌

Brook Green Hotel
170 Shepherds Bush Road, W6 7PB
🕙 11 (breakfast 7am Mon-Fri; 8am Sat)-11; 12 (breakfast 8am)-10.30 Sun
☎ (020) 7603 2516
Wells Bombardier; Young's Bitter, Special, seasonal beers ⊞
Large pub and hotel dating back to 1886, overlooking Brook Green, with many striking features including huge windows, high ceilings and chandeliers, ornate mirrors and an impressive fireplace. TV screens show major live sporting events. Overnight accommodation is competitively priced.
▲❀♣◐去⊖(Hammersmith/Goldhawk Rd)🚌

Dove
19 Upper Mall, W6 9TA
🕙 11-11; 12-10.30 Sun
☎ (020) 8748 9474
Fuller's Discovery, London Pride, ESB, seasonal beers ⊞
Famous Grade II listed riverside tavern, licensed in 1740 as the Dove's coffee house and bought by the brewery in 1796. A list of names on one of the walls is evidence of the host of celebrities who have visited over the years. James Thompson composed 'Rule Britannia' in an upstairs room. The main bar area is on a raised level with the tiny public bar at the front. The rear conservatory, where a fruit-bearing vine grows, leads to a terrace overlooking the Thames.
Q❀◐ ⊞⊖(Ravenscourt Pk)↝

Plough & Harrow
120-124 King Street, W6 0QU
🕙 10 (7am breakfast)-11.30; 12 (7am breakfast)-10.30 Sun
☎ (020) 8735 6020
Courage Best Bitter, Directors; Fuller's London Pride; Greene King Abbot; Marston's Pedigree; guest beers ⊞
This pub opened in 2002 in the former car showroom that had occupied the site since the 1959 demise of the original Plough & Harrow. The spacious interior is modern in style with an Art Deco touch. The floors are largely tiled; a rear carpeted area is reserved for families and diners. There is a smaller enclosed lounge at the back; the upper floors are occupied by a Holiday Inn. ⇌◐⊖🚌

Salutation
154 King Street, W6 0QU

315

✪ 11-11; 12-12.30am Sat; 12-10.30 Sun
☎ (020) 8748 3668
Fuller's Discovery, London Pride, ESB, seasonal beers Ⓗ
With marble fireplaces, period lighting and checkerboard tiles on the floors surrounding the bar, guests could be forgiven for thinking they had been transported back to their grandparents' time. Candlelight and mirrors on the mantelpiece add to the ambience. However Spandau Ballet on the music system brings you gently back to the present day. Comfortable leather sofas lead to a conservatory which opens out to a huge paved patio. Occasional karaoke nights are held. ⊛◑⊖⊟⌐

W7: Hanwell

Fox
Green Lane, W7 2PJ
✪ 11-11 (10.30 Sun)
☎ (020) 8567 3912 ⊕ thefoxpub.co.uk
Fuller's London Pride; Taylor Landlord; guest beers Ⓗ
Tucked away on the junction of the Grand Union Canal and the River Brent, this family owned and run free house is always very welcoming, especially to families and dogs. There is a well-attended (range of ales and drinkers) annual beer festival at Easter, and during the summer months barbecues are held in the garden. Sunday roast lunches are a must, although the pub gets very busy, and evening meals are also available (Thu-Sat winter, Tue-Sat summer). ⚌⊛◑⊜⇌⊟(E8)P⌐

W8: Notting Hill Gate

Churchill Arms
119 Kensington Church Street, W8 7LN
✪ 11-11.30 (12.30am Thu-Sat); 12-11 Sun
☎ (020) 7727 4242
Fuller's Chiswick, Discovery, London Pride, ESB Ⓗ
More than 200 years old, the pub was renamed the Churchill Arms because Winston's parents drank here when he was a child. Sir Winston's birthday is celebrated every year with wartime costumes, music and decorations. Recently his granddaughter joined in the festivities. A bizarre collection of paraphernalia is suspended from the ceiling, including several vintage bedpans. Two suicidal ghosts live here – one was a former employee who hung himself on the dray doors, the other took his own life in the barman's bedroom. ⚌◑⊖⊟⌐⊟

Uxbridge Arms
13 Uxbridge Street, W8 7TQ
✪ 12-11 (10.30 Sun)
☎ (020) 7727 7326
Fuller's London Pride; guest beers Ⓗ
Traditional 19th-century, music-free pub, much loved by its regulars both young and old; loyal customers even send text messages to the landlady from abroad to say they are on their way for a pint! Sunday is quiz night, beginning around 6pm, winner takes all. Note the intriguing prints along the wood-panelled walls. This pub's fame spreads far and wide: it was featured in Norway's '100 Best Pubs in London'. Q⊛⊖⊟♣⌐

W11: Notting Hill

Cock & Bottle
17 Needham Road, W11 2RP
✪ 11-11; 12-10.30 Sun
☎ (020) 7229 1550
Fuller's London Pride; Hogs Back TEA Ⓗ
This pub dates from 1851 when it was named the White Swan, later renamed the Swan. A popular back-street local, its interior features a bar with high ceilings, exceptionally ornate pillars, glass panels and a snob screen. It still has three distinct drinking areas. Quiz night is Tuesday.
Q⊛⊛⊖(Notting Hill Gt/Bayswater)♣⌐

W14: West Kensington

Crown & Sceptre
34 Holland Road, W14 8BA
✪ 11-11
☎ (020) 7802 1866
Beer range varies Ⓗ
Named Napoleon III when it first opened in 1856, this pub soon acquired its current name. Formerly a run-down sports bar with a split-level layout, the interior now has a strong Mexican theme with a decor of orange and red pastel. Dishes from the kitchen reflect the Aztec atmosphere. The two real ales on offer are normally from micro-breweries. Quiz night is Tuesday. ◑&⇌(Olympia)⊖(Olympia)♣⌐

Brentford

Brewery Tap
47 Catherine Wheel Road, TW8 8BD
✪ 12-midnight
☎ (020) 8560 5200
Fuller's Chiswick, Discovery, London Pride, seasonal beers; guest beer Ⓗ
Originally the tap for the William Gomm Brewery, it was acquired by Fuller's in 1909. The Victorian pub is reached by steps as the river used to flood here. Renowned for regular jazz on Tuesday and Thursday evenings, it also stages other live music nightly except Monday which is quiz night and Wednesday which is quiet. Meals are served weekdays until 7.30pm and lunches are popular (booking recommended for Sunday). There are patios to the front and rear, where well-behaved dogs are welcome. ⊛◑⇌⊟♣⌐

Express Tavern
56 Kew Bridge Road, TW8 0EU
✪ 11.30-3, 5.30-11 (midnight Thu & Fri); 11.30-3, 6.30-midnight Sat; 12-10.30 Sun
☎ (020) 8560 8484
Draught Bass; Young's Bitter; guest beers Ⓗ
More than 200 years old, this friendly local at the northern end of Kew Bridge has too much history to detail, but it has played a part in the beginnings of Brentford FC, the former Brentford Market, the 'Buffalos' and, indeed, CAMRA. It is noted locally for its Bass and Young's Bitter (still known here as Pale Ale), now supplemented by two guest beers. Its two bars, quiet mock-manorial lounge and garden provide a haven from the busy road. Q⊛◑&⇌(Kew Bridge)⊟

Magpie & Crown

128 High Street, TW8 8EW
✪ 11-midnight (1am Thu-Sat); 12-midnight Sun
☎ (020) 8560 5658
Beer range varies Ⓗ
Mock-Tudor pub, set back from the High Street, with outside tables at the front and a rear patio (equipped with a cycle rack). Four changing ales (nearly 1,700 served in 11 years) have made it a magnet for beer lovers. Up to three varying ciders (and occasionally perry) are also offered, plus draught Budvar, Fruli and Paulaner, and a range of continental bottled beers. This local CAMRA Pub of the Year for 1999 and 2000 also offers Thai food (Tue-Sat eve), bar billiards and other games. ❀◗≠⊟♣●

O'Brien's

11 London Road, TW8 8JB (near canal bridge at W end of High St)
✪ 11-11; 12-10.30 Sun
☎ (020) 8560 0506
Fuller's London Pride; guest beers Ⓗ
Formerly the Northumberland Arms, this compact pub on the main road through Brentford features an ever-changing range of beers, frequently from local Twickenham and Grand Union breweries, as well as some Belgian specialities. An acoustic session is held on Tuesday evening and a quiz night on Wednesday. TV coverage of sporting events provides regular entertainment. ❀◖◗≠⊟⌐

Cowley Peachey

Paddington Packet Boat

High Road, UB8 2HT (on High Rd Cowley, on corner of Packet Boat Lane)
✪ 12-11 (midnight Fri & Sat); 12-10.30 Sun
☎ (01895) 442392
Fuller's London Pride, ESB, seasonal beers Ⓗ
More than 200 years old, this spacious pub has been completely modernised but retains some old fittings. Mirrors and other memorabilia relate to the old packet boat service to Paddington. A good mix of passing trade plus locals and workers from the Grand Union Canal frequents the pub, which hosts a quiz on Tuesday and live music at the weekend. No evening meals are served on Sunday. ❀⇆◖◗♿⊟(222)P⌐

Hampton Hill

Roebuck

72 Hampton Road, TW12 1JN
✪ 11-11 (midnight Fri & Sat); 12-4, 7-10.30 Sun
☎ (020) 8255 8133
Badger First Gold, Tanglefoot; Young's Bitter; guest beers Ⓗ
The overwhelming impression on entering this pub is that there is no room for any more bric-a-brac, but still the eclectic collection grows. It is probably the only pub in West London with a Harley Davidson hanging from the ceiling. The traffic lights on the wall change to indicate last orders and time. Despite the clutter, the pub remains comfortable; likewise the compact, award-winning garden. There is a summer house for cooler evenings. Lunches are served Monday to Friday.
♨❀⇆◖≠(Fulwell)⊟♣⌐

Hampton Wick

White Hart

1 High Street, KT1 4DA (at W end of Kingston Bridge)
✪ 11-11 (midnight Fri & Sat); 12-11 Sun
☎ (020) 8977 1786
Fuller's London Pride, ESB, seasonal beers Ⓗ
Stylish hotel conversion featuring an intimate, flagstone-floored bar and a comfortable lounge area. The building is classic brewers' Tudor, half-timbered and with leaded windows. It faces Kingston Bridge, and features a large outdoor area at the front behind railings. Food to a high standard is served to accompany the Fuller's beers in immaculate surroundings. ♨Q❀◖◗≠⊟P

Hounslow

Moon under Water

84-86 Staines Road, TW3 3LF (at W end of High St)
✪ 10 (12 Sun)-11
☎ (020) 8572 7506
Courage Best Bitter, Directors; Greene King Abbot; Marston's Pedigree; guest beers Ⓗ
Early Wetherspoon's shop conversion, since enlarged, in typical style and still displaying a few local history panels and photos. Very popular, it serves a mixed crowd including regulars from nearby and those who come from further afield. There are usually three guest ales, many more at festival times. Children are welcome until 8.30pm; the rear is considered the family area, with a patio leading off it. Q❀◖◗♿⊖(Hounslow Central)⊟

Southall

Conservative & Unionist Club

Fairlawn, High Street, UB1 3HB
✪ 11.30-2.30 (3 Fri & Sat), 7 (6 Fri & Sat)-11; 12-3, 7-10.30 Sun
☎ (020) 8574 0261
Rebellion IPA, seasonal beers; guest beers (occasional) Ⓗ
Almost the last place in Southall to sell real ale, this gem is hidden down an alley adjacent to the fire station. Weekday lunches are reasonably priced (no food Sat & Sun). There are four snooker tables and on the last Saturday of each month live music is played. ❀◖≠♣P

Teddington

Lion

27 Wick Road, TW11 9DN (off Kingston Rd, opp Langdon Pk housing development)
✪ 11-11 (11.30 Wed-Thu; midnight Fri & Sat); 12-10.30 Sun
☎ (020) 8977 3199 🌐 thelionpub.co.uk
Caledonian Deuchars IPA; Fuller's London Pride; guest beers Ⓗ
This Victorian street-corner local has been recently extended and modernised, but the old public bar area with pool table remains largely untouched. The menu ranges from traditional to contemporary English (no food

Sun eve). Live music, mainly blues, plays in the bar on Saturday evening, and Wednesday is quiz night. The function room in the large garden is home to the Bluescene Club and is available for private functions. Local CAMRA Pub of the Year 2005 and 2006, and London Pub of the Year 2006, it also stages two beer festivals a year.
🏚⌂🕽🌮⇌(Hampton Wick)🚌(281, 285)🚽

Tide End Cottage

8 Ferry Road, TW11 9NN
☼ 11-11 (12.30am Fri; midnight Sat); 12-11 Sun
☎ (020) 8977 7762
Greene King IPA, Ruddles County, Old Speckled Hen, Abbot; guest beer 🅷

Built in a terrace by Teddington Lock, this pub has a deceptively small frontage but goes back a long way. It has recently been completely refurbished internally with a substantial amount of the seating now upholstered in leather. One wall pays homage to Hendrix, the Stones, Quo and other rock legends. The guest beer is often from outside the Greene King range. For alfresco drinking there is a terrace at the front and a secluded rear garden. Food is served until 9.30pm (3.30pm on Sun).
🏚Q⌂🕽🌮⇌🚌🚽

Twickenham

Fox

39 Church Street, TW1 3NR
☼ 11-11 (12.30am Thu-Sat); 12-10.30 Sun
☎ (020) 8892 1535
Caledonian Deuchars IPA; Fuller's London Pride; Twickenham Crane Sundancer, Original, seasonal beers; guest beers 🅷

Twickenham's oldest pub, dating from around 1670, was originally known as the Bell but changed its name to the Fox in the early 1700s. It is a local favourite in this attractive area. The street outside is now some 18 inches higher than when the pub was first built, so visitors must step down into the small bar where a good selection of real ales awaits them. Its function room was built as the Assembly Rooms around 1900. 🏚⌂🕽⇌🚌🚽

Old Anchor

71 Richmond Road, TW1 3AW
☼ 12-11 (midnight Fri & Sat); 12-10.30 Sun
☎ (020) 8892 2181
Young's Bitter, Special, seasonal beers 🅷

Originally built in the 1830s as the Anchor and rebuilt in the early 20th century, this pub makes much use of pale wood in the bar, panelling, furniture and floor, creating a bright and attractive interior. Sunday lunches, made with locally-sourced organic ingredients, are recommended, as are the 'serious' sandwiches available at all times. In summer, the ample paved garden is busy. Thursday is quiz night. This is a popular pub with both regular locals and passing custom.
⌂🕽🌮⇌🚌🚽

Prince Albert

30 Hampton Road, TW2 5QB (on A311)
☼ 11-11 (midnight Fri & Sat)

☎ (020) 8894 3963
Fuller's Chiswick, Discovery, London Pride, ESB, seasonal beers; guest beers (occasional) 🅷

Originally opened as the Star Brewery in 1840, the pub was later unofficially known as 'Wiffen's' as it was run by three generations of the same family whose name is still displayed behind the bar. Nowadays the Albert is popular for its excellent beer, convivial atmosphere and delicious Thai food. It has a TV screen for sports fans, live music plays on Saturday evening and beer festivals are held featuring small brewers. In summer the attractive garden and patio are popular.
🏚Q⌂🕽🌮⇌(Strawberry Hill)🚌🚽

Prince of Wales

136 Hampton Road, TW2 5QR (on A311)
☼ 12 (4 Mon)-11
☎ (020) 8894 5054
Adnams Bitter; St Austell Tribute; Twickenham Crane Sundancer, seasonal beers; guest beers (occasional) 🅷

An inn has existed on this site for more than 150 years, serving as the final staging post on the Windsor to London stagecoach route. The original stables survive and are now listed. An unspoilt community pub with an attractive garden, it is the unofficial tap for the nearby Twickenham Fine Ales Brewery. Beer festivals featuring micro-breweries are held twice a year. Thursday is quiz night.
🏚Q🌮⇌(Strawberry Hill/Fulwell)🚌🚽

Turk's Head

28 Winchester Road, St Margarets, TW1 1LF
☼ 12-11 (11.30 Thu; midnight Fri & Sat); 12-10.30 Sun
☎ (020) 8892 1972
Fuller's Discovery, London Pride, ESB, seasonal beers 🅷

Built in 1902, this is still a genuine local corner pub, offering fine beers and food, and hosting live R&B on Friday. Beatles fans flock here to see the location for a scene in A Hard Day's Night, and the Bearcat Comedy Club has been inviting top comedians to the function room every Saturday night for more than 20 years. Rugby fans form human pyramids on match days and try to stick stamps on the high ceiling. 🏚⌂🕽🌮⇌(St Margaret's)🚌🚽

Uxbridge

Load of Hay

33 Villier Street, UB8 2PU (near Brunel University)
☼ 11 (12 Sun)-11.30
☎ (01895) 234676
Fuller's London Pride; guest beers 🅷

Originally the officers' mess of the Elthorne Light Militia, this building became a pub in the 1870s. A genuine free house, it sells a changing range of beers, usually including three guest ales. The pub hosts darts matches and other entertainment including karaoke on Thursday and Sunday, bingo on Wednesday, a quiz each Tuesday and live music on Saturday. Parking is limited. ⌂🕽🌮🚌(U3)🅿🚽

Beer, Bed & Breakfast

JILL ADAM & SUSAN NOWAK

A unique and comprehensive guide to more than 500 of the UK's real ale pubs that also offer great accommodation, from tiny inns with a couple of rooms upstairs to luxury gastro-pubs with country-house style bedrooms. All entries include contact details, type and extent of accommodation, beers served, meal types and times, and an easy-to-understand price guide to help plan your budget. This year why not stay somewhere with a comfortable bed, a decent breakfast and a well-kept pint of beer, providing a home from home wherever you are in the country.

£14.99   ISBN 978 1 85249 230 4

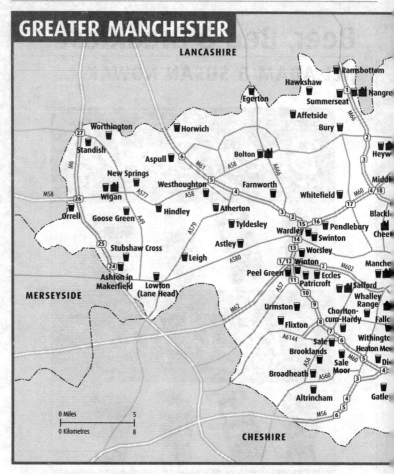

GREATER MANCHESTER

Affetside

Pack Horse

52 Watling Street, BL8 3QW (approx 2 miles NW of Walshaw) OS755136

⏰ 12-3, 6-11; 12-midnight Sat & Sun

☎ (01204) 883802

Hydes Owd Oak, Original Bitter, seasonal beers Ⓗ

This country pub benefits from superb panoramic views thanks to its situation high up on a Roman road. The bar area and cosy lounge (with real fire) are part of the original pub, dating from the 15th century. It has a function and a pool room, while the Hightop bar is used as a family room. Many a tale is told about the ghost of the local man whose skull is on view behind the bar.

🏛️Q🛏️🍴🕸️🌾◑🚶▲🅿️🚲

Altrincham

Malt Shovels

68 Stamford Street, WA14 1EY

⏰ 12-11; 12-4.30, 8-10.30 Sun

☎ (0161) 928 2053

Samuel Smith OBB Ⓗ

Town-centre pub, only five minutes from bust/train/tram interchange, serving the best-value pint in town. It stands between the former sites of Altrincham's only brewery (Richardson and Goodall) and the maltings. Meals are served at lunchtimes Tuesday to Saturday. The upstairs function room is

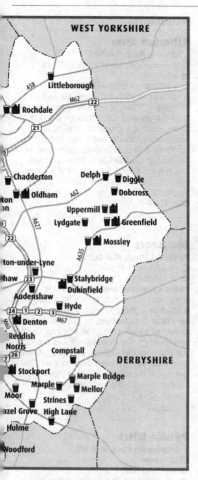

WEST YORKSHIRE

Littleborough

Rochdale

Chadderton Delph Diggle
Oldham Dobcross
Uppermill
Lydgate Greenfield
Mossley

ton-under-Lyne
haw Stalybridge
Dukinfield
Audenshaw Hyde
Denton
Reddish
Norris Compstall
DERBYSHIRE
Stockport
Marple Bridge
Marple Mellor
Moor Strines
azel Grove High Lane
Hulme
Woodford

normally used for pool and darts. Children are welcome until 8pm. Q⛽🕮♿⟲⊖🚆♣

Old Market Tavern

Old Market Place, WA14 4DN (on A56)
🕐 10-11 (midnight Wed-Sat); 12-11 Sun
☎ (0161) 927 7062 ⏣ oldmarkettavern.com
Bank Top Volunteer, Trotter's Tipple, Smokestack Lightning; Caledonian Deuchars IPA; guest beers Ⓗ
A welcome return for a regular in the Guide, now refurbished and under new management. This prominent black and white former coaching inn is divided into separate drinking areas around a central bar. Up to seven guest beers come from micros near and far. Live heavy rock/blues music on Saturday and Sunday nights is popular with drinkers of all ages. Wednesday night is quiz night with a free buffet. Children are welcome up to 7pm.
🕮⛽🕮⟲⊖🚆♣🐕P

Ashton-in-Makerfield

Jubilee Club

167-169 Wigan Road, WN4 9ST (near Bryn station heading towards Ashton)
🕐 8 (7.30 Fri & Sat)-midnight
☎ (01942) 727781 ⏣ jubileeclubashton.co.uk

Beer range varies Ⓗ
Non-members are allowed into this warm and friendly social club subject to certain constraints (frequency of visits; payment of a nominal admission charge). The main function room features occasional live entertainment. There is a games room at the rear with a small lobby bar area, and a small function room upstairs. At least one changing cask ale of consistently good quality is served, at a competitive price. The Jubilee Club actively raises money for charity. ⇌(Bryn)♣P🍴

Sir Thomas Gerrard

2 Gerrard Street, WN4 9AN (on A58)
🕐 9am-midnight (1am Fri & Sat)
☎ (01942) 713519

Greene King Abbot; Marston's Pedigree; guest beers Ⓗ
Known locally as the Tom & Jerry, this former supermarket belongs to the Wetherspoon chain of pubs. It has a number of interesting features including a tiled mural depicting aspects of Ashton-in-Makerfield's history. There are two raised areas away from the busy main floor and small booths to the rear are good for a cosy drink. The pub gets crowded at weekends and on race days as it is within walking distance of Haydock race park.
🕮⛽🕮♿🚆🐕P

Ashton-under-Lyne

Dog & Pheasant

528 Oldham Road, Waterloo, OL7 6PQ
🕐 12-11 (11.30 Fri & Sat)
☎ (0161) 330 4849

Bank's Original; Marston's Burton Bitter, Pedigree; guest beers Ⓗ
Nicknamed the Top Dog, this popular, friendly local near the Medlock Valley Country Park has a large bar serving three areas, plus another room at the front. A long menu of good value food includes vegetarian options (not served Sun eve). On Tuesday and Thursday evenings a quiz is hosted. The pub is home to a local hiking group known as the Bog Trotters. Marston's Old Empire regularly features as a guest beer. 🕮⛽🕮🚆(409)P🍴🍴

Junction Inn

Mossley Road, Hazelhurst, OL6 9BX
🕐 12-3 (not Mon), 5-midnight; 12-midnight Sat & Sun
☎ (0161) 343 1611

Robinson's Hatters, Unicorn Ⓗ
Small pub of great character that has remained little changed since the 19th century. Built of local stone, close to Ashton golf course and open country, it is the first building out of town that is not of brick construction. The small cosy rooms make it welcoming, and the unpretentious tap room is traditional in every respect. The famous home-made rag puddings, a Lancashire speciality, are available at lunchtime Tuesday to Saturday. Q⛽🕮🍴🚆♣P

Oddfellows Arms

1-7 Alderley Street, Hurst, OL6 9LJ
🕐 11-1am
☎ (0161) 330 6356

Robinson's Hatters, Unicorn, seasonal beers Ⓗ

On a corner terrace, the 'Oddies' has been in the same family since 1914. A small hatch and screen lead to the polished bar with its stained glass and nooks and crannies. A cosy tap room and vestry are to the left. Adjoining the lounge is Tom's Room, named after the late landlord. There is a walled patio to the side, used for free barbecues in the summer, and a Koi carp pool. Q✿❄✦➤☷(38, 39)¹ⁿ

Aspull

New Inn
Radcliffe Road, WN2 1YE (off B5329)
✪ 12 (7 winter)-midnight; 12 (7 winter)-12.30am Fri & Sat; 12-11.30 Sun
☎ (01942) 832109
Jennings Cocker Hoop; guest beers Ⓗ
Located on a side road, the pub has recently been refurbished and opened out but the pool room remains separate. A community pub, it stages local darts, dominoes and pool league matches, and holds a popular quiz on Tuesday and bingo on Sunday. A TV in the lounge shows sporting events. Sunday lunches are very popular. There is a beer garden to the rear and picnic tables at the front. Guest beers are from the Marston's range.
🚶✿❄☷(609)♣ⁿ

Victoria
50 Haigh Road, WN2 1YA (on B5239)
✪ 12-11.30 (12.30am Fri & Sat)
☎ (01942) 830869
Allgates Young Pretender, Napoleon's Retreat; guest beers Ⓗ
This traditional two-room local has enjoyed a new lease of life after becoming Wigan's Allgates Brewery's first pub. The smart yet intimate lounge displays photographs depicting the history of Aspull and Haigh. Two plasma TV screens cater for sports fans, although the one in the lounge is usually switched off. The pub is well located for Haigh Hall Country Park, and halfway between Bolton Wanderers and Wigan Athletic football grounds. Guest beers come from Allgates or other microbreweries. ❄☷♣P

Astley

Cart & Horses
221 Manchester Road, M29 7SD
✪ 12-11 (1am Fri & Sat); 12-10.30 Sun
☎ (01942) 870751
Holt Mild, Bitter Ⓗ
Popular community pub sporting a classic front complete with cobbled pavement, etched windows, roof sign and central door. It is in a handy spot for Astley golf range and Astley Green Colliery Museum. The interior has an open-plan lounge with a raised area leading to the patio and the garden. The bar serves a separate tap room, which is the meeting place for local societies including the Leigh Premier Cycling Club. The pub hosts regular quiz nights and the pub team has featured on TV.
✿❄❄P¹ⁿ

Atherton

Atherton Arms
6 Tyldesley Road, M46 9DD
✪ 11.30-midnight (1am Fri & Sat); 12-11 Sun
☎ (01942) 882885
Holt Mild, Bitter, seasonal beer Ⓗ
A spacious town centre local, the main entrance is accessed via a long ramp or steps onto the veranda. Once through the double doors, there is a choice of drinking areas: a comfortable hallway, the large lounge or the tap room with pool, snooker tables and TV. At the rear of the building is a concert room which hosts a local version of the X Factor. Practice sessions take place in the lounge at weekends. The function room is available for hire. ❄&♣P

Old Isaacs
48 Market Street, M46 0EQ
✪ 11-midnight; 12-11 Sun
☎ (01942) 895229
Phoenix seasonal beers; guest beers Ⓗ
Busy town centre pub, handy for a cuppa and a snack or a pint and a meal while shopping. Two large front lounges are popular, one used mostly as a dining area, the other for chatting and drinking. The main lounge has a central bar and from the standing area you can watch your meal being cooked through a window at the rear of the bar. This is also a meeting place for the Round Table and the Nuts Poker League. Q❄

Pendle Witch
2-4 Warburton Place, M46 0EQ
✪ 10-midnight
☎ (01942) 884537
Moorhouses Black Cat, Premier Bitter, Pendle Witches Brew, seasonal beers; guest beers Ⓗ
After years of planning frustration the Pendle has finally had its major refurbishment. The main bar area has been extended and a games room with pool table and big screen added. The front now has a conservatory for dining, with good food coming from the new kitchen. Toilets are now on the ground floor. Outside, even the garden has had a makeover. Keep an eye out for regular beer festivals. ❄❄&♣ⁿ

Audenshaw (Guide Bridge)

Boundary
2 Audenshaw Road, M34 5HD
✪ 11-midnight; 12-11 Sun
☎ (0161) 330 1679
Beer range varies Ⓗ
This pub is located on the banks of the Ashton Canal and thus handy for boaters. It has had a conservatory and dining room added to an already extensive frontage, providing greater capacity in the spacious interior, which is evenly split between a lounge and a tap. Good value meals are served all day until 9pm. The large car park is the venue for an annual beer festival in June. ❄❄✦✦♣P

Blackley

Golden Lion

47 Old Market Street, M19 8DX (off Rochdale Road)

🕐 11-11 (midnight Fri & Sat)

☎ (0161) 740 1944

Holt Mild, Bitter Ⓗ

Already renowned locally for its fine real ales and friendly service, this community pub aims to gain recognition for its music events. Every last Thursday of the month it hosts live music, and there is an open mike session every second Thursday. The pub features a comfortable vault, serving cask mild, a large lounge with French windows leading on to a veranda with a small quiet side lounge. A second, covered veranda is planned on the sun patio by the bowling green as a smoking shelter. ✿⬛🖳♣P⌐

Bolton

Ainsworth Arms

606 Halliwell Road, BL1 8BY (jct A58/A6099)

🕐 11.30-2 (not Tue-Thu), 5-11 (midnight Fri); 11.30-midnight Sat; 12-10.30 Sun

☎ (01204) 840671

Taylor Landlord; Tetley Mild, Bitter; guest beers Ⓗ

Near Smithills Hall, a Grade I listed building, this dog-friendly local comprises several areas. There is a raised space with alcoves and a basic tap room, complete with bell pushes that were in use until 1981. The pub has a long association with football, and is the meeting place for many local sports teams. The juke box is only switched on by request. Lunches are served Friday to Sunday, and breakfasts are excellent. Guest beers come from small, independent breweries. Q✿①♣

Barrister's Bar

7 Bradshawgate, BL1 1HJ (on A575, near Market Cross)

🕐 12-1am (2am Fri & Sat)

☎ (01204) 365174

Moorhouses Black Cat, Pride of Pendle, Blond Witch, Pendle Witches Brew; guest beers Ⓗ

The Barrister's Bar is part of the Sawn Hotel, a listed building dating from 1845. Formerly the Malt & Hops, it was closed for many years until a change of ownership in 2004. The wood-panelled interior has been retained and tastefully decorated to create the atmosphere of a traditional pub. The regular range of real ales is supplemented by guest beers primarily from local independent brewers. ✿≉(Bolton)⌐

Bob's Smithy Inn

1448 Chorley Old Road, BL1 7PX (on B6226 uphill from A58 ring road)

🕐 4.30 (12 Sat)-11 (midnight Fri & Sat); 12-11 Sun

☎ (01204) 842622

Bank Top Flat Cap; Taylor Best Bitter; Tetley Bitter; guest beers Ⓗ

This intimate, stone-built hostelry on the edge of the Moors is handy for walkers and visitors to the Reebok stadium. The inn is about 200 years old and is named after a blacksmith who allegedly spent more time here than he did at his smithy across the road. This is a genuine free house, usually offering beers from small independent breweries. Dogs are welcome. ▲✿🖳(125, 126)P⌐

Brooklyn

Green Lane, Great Lever, BL3 2EF (1½ miles from town centre, off B6536)

🕐 12-11 (11.30 Thu; midnight Fri & Sat)

Holt Mild, Bitter, seasonal beers Ⓗ

This imposing Victorian brick building, boasting a notable mansard roof and ornamental chimneys, was built in 1859 and licensed in 1926. The central bar serves a comfortable tap room and several more large rooms with elaborately moulded plasterwork on the ceilings and walls. The extensive grounds include a bowling green, outside drinking area, woodland and a car park. On Sunday meals are served until 6pm; Wednesday curry evenings are popular. ✿①▣⬛P

Hope & Anchor

747 Chorley Old Road, BL1 5QH (on B6226, downhill from A58 ring road)

🕐 12-midnight (1am Fri & Sat)

☎ (01204) 842650

Lees Bitter; Taylor Landlord; Tetley Bitter Ⓗ

Situated less than two miles from Bolton town centre, just near Doffcocker Lodge, a well-known nature reserve, this traditional local dating from the late Victorian era attracts walkers and bird watchers. A central bar serves two distinct snugs used for different functions (quiz nights, family gatherings etc). Locals call the pub the Little Cocker, to distinguish it from the big Doffcocker Inn across the road. Q⬛✿♿🖳(125, 126)♣P⌐

King's Head

52-54 Junction Road, Deane, BL3 4NA (off A676)

🕐 3.30 (12 Sat & Sun)-11

Moorhouses Pride of Pendle Ⓗ

This 300-year-old Grade II listed pub near the Deane Clough Nature Trail has three distinct drinking areas, the largest featuring a stone floor and authentic-looking range. A popular crown bowling green adjoins the children's playground and outdoor seating area. The pub welcomes children until 7pm and permits dogs. It hosts a weekly quiz on Wednesday and monthly acoustic music sessions. Piped music and TV underline the buzz of conversation. ✿♣P⌐

Lodge Bank Tavern

260 Bridgeman Street, BL3 6SA

🕐 2-midnight; 12-2am Fri & Sat; 12-midnight Sun

☎ (01204) 531946

Lees Bitter Ⓗ

Welcoming local, near Bobby Heywood's Park (with free use of floodlit pitches). The main room is divided into three smaller areas, and there is a pool room at the back of the bar. Karaoke sessions take place on Friday and Saturday evenings, and these are well attended and quite noisy. The only Lees pub in town, it was the last pub to change its ale house status to that of a full license. ✿≉♣P

Spinning Mule

Unit 2, Nelson Square, BL1 1JT

🕐 9-midnight (1am Fri & Sat)

☎ (01204) 533339

Courage Directors; Greene King Abbot; Marston's Pedigree; Shepherd Neame Spitfire; guest beers Ⓗ
Newly built in 1998, this town-centre pub, just off Bradshawgate, is an open-plan split-level building with a comfortable dining area in a modern Wetherspoon style. It is named after Samuel Crompton's Mule, a revolutionary invention in cotton spinning that made Bolton famous throughout the world. The original device may be seen in the town's museum, and Crompton himself is immortalised by the statue in the square. The Mule supports local breweries. Q◑也≠

Sweet Green Tavern

127 Crook Street, BL3 6DD (opp Sainsbury's, off A579)
✪ 11-11; 12-10.30 Sun
☎ (01204) 392258
Adnams Broadside; Fuller's London Pride; Tetley Bitter; guest beers Ⓗ
This friendly local is situated on the edge of the town centre, close to the bus/rail interchange. It comprises four small rooms served by a long bar. Its name reflects the original character of the area – 'a place of fragrant gardens' – prior to 19th-century industrial development which has, in turn, been replaced by a supermarket. The guest beers usually include at least two from Bank Top, and up to 10 beers are always available.
🚪❀☀≠♣P⅃

Broadheath

Railway ☆

153 Manchester Road, WA14 5NT (on A56)
✪ 11-11 (midnight Fri & Sat); 11-10.30 Sun
☎ (0161) 941 3383
Holt Mild, Bitter Ⓗ
A small and often boisterous three-roomed pub built in the angle of a long-gone railway viaduct, the Railway was saved from demolition in the 1990s by a campaign involving CAMRA and local people. The surrounding area has been extensively redeveloped. The car park behind does not belong to the pub and is locked up outside shopping hours. The snug little rooms are named after Manchester's railway stations (and the toilet after one of London's). Children are welcome until 6pm.
🚪❀☀≠(Navigation Rd)⊖(Navigation Rd)🚃♣⅃

Brooklands

Belmore Hotel

143 Brooklands Road, Sale, M33 4QN
✪ 11.30-11 (midnight Fri & Sat); 12-10.30 Sun
☎ (0161) 973 2538
Lees Bitter, seasonal beers Ⓗ
Sitting on a corner plot in spacious grounds, this medium-sized hotel has a largish car park and outside drinking area. Inside there is a light, airy feel to the elegant bar area, with big sash windows, high ceilings and chandelier-style light fittings. Bar meals are served throughout (as well as outside); more substantial meals from a changing menu are available in the small restaurant area.
Q❀☀◑也⊖🚃P⅃

Bury

Brown Cow

Burrs Country Park, BL8 1DA (off B6214 about 1 mile from town centre)
✪ 11-11 (midnight Fri; 12.30am Sat); 12-10.30 Sun
☎ (0161) 764 3386
Beer range varies Ⓗ
Dating back to the mid 18th century, and originally two millworkers' cottages, this is a true free house and one of the oldest pubs in Bury. Ideally positioned in the heart of a country park yet only a short distance from Bury town centre, it is a homely pub benefiting from three distinct outdoor seating areas. The large rear garden is especially popular with families. Well-sourced beers change regularly and food from the extensive menu comes highly recommended.
❀◑也⊼🚃(475, 477)♣P

Trackside

East Lancashire Railway, Bolton Street Station, BL9 0EY
✪ 12-midnight (11 Sun)
☎ (0161) 764 6461
Beer range varies Ⓗ
This free house boasts nine handpumps and also sells various ciders and perries direct from the cellar, as well as a range of foreign beers. Simple wooden tables and chairs impart a traditional railway buffet feel. The vast array of pump clips on display showcases the many beers that have been sold in the past. Quiet during the day, it can be busy at weekends when the ELR hosts special events. Tables and chairs on the platform are inviting in summer.
Q◑也≠(Bolton Street)⊖🚃♣P

Chadderton

Horton Arms

19 Streetbridge Road, OL1 2SZ (beneath motorway bridge on B6195)
✪ 11.30-midnight; 12-10.30 Sun
☎ (0161) 624 7793
Lees GB Mild, Bitter Ⓗ
A neat and attractive Lees tied house, conveniently situated on the main Middleton to Royton road. The interior is open plan but neatly divided into discrete drinking areas. A side room provides a refuge for sports fans, with major events shown live on TV. Home-cooked food is a major attraction, available at lunchtime (not Sat) and on Friday from 4.30-7pm. There is a beer garden to the rear and benches out front for good weather. The bus stop is directly outside. ❀◑🚃(412)P

Cheadle Hulme

Cheadle Hulme

47 Station Road, SU8 7AA (on A5149)
✪ 11.30-11 (midnight Fri & Sat); 12-10.30 Sun
☎ (0161) 485 4706
Holt Mild, Bitter, seasonal beers Ⓗ
Despite its prominent location in this affluent area, and its stylish interior, the Cheadle Hulme retains the friendly, bustling atmosphere of a traditional community local, attracting customers of all ages. Regular events include the 'free and easy' open mike session on a Tuesday evening, and the quiz

night on Thursday. The popular food menu is served from noon daily (until 4pm Mon-Wed, 9pm Thu-Sat and 6pm Sun). ⊛⊕◗⊟⇔≠⊟P╘

Church

90 Ravenoak Road, SK8 7EG (jct A5149/B5095)
◔ 11-11 (midnight Fri & Sat); 12-10.30 Sun
☎ (0161) 485 1897

Robinson's Hatters, Unicorn, seasonal beers Ⓗ
This pub has all the charm and character of a country inn, low and cottagey, partly hidden by a well-tended hedgerow and garden, yet in an urban setting. All of the elements of comfort are here – low ceilings, real fires, wood panelling, brass plates, and a popular restaurant – Edwardo's (open until 9.30pm Mon-Sat). A busy three-roomer, remaining ever popular with its customers.
⋈Q⊛◗⊕⊟(157, 313)♣P╘

Chorlton-cum-Hardy

Marble Beer House

57 Manchester Road, M21 0PW
◔ 12-11 (midnight Thu-Sat); 12-11.30 Sun
☎ (0161) 881 9206 ⊕ marblebeers.co.uk

Marble GSB, Manchester Bitter, Ginger, Lagonda, seasonal beers; guest beers Ⓗ
Seven handpumps offer organic and vegan beers from Manchester's Marble Brewery, whose ingredients are sourced from non-intensive agriculture, plus a couple of guest beers from other micros. Seasonal ales from Marble include the wonderful Chocolate Heavy and Port Stout during winter. This modern but laid-back bar also carries a range of guest ales and a selection of Belgian bottled beers. A mixed clientele includes folk musicians, workers and readers borrowing books.
Q⊛⊟♣◉╘

Compstall

Andrew Arms

George Street, SK6 5JD
◔ 11-11
☎ (0161) 484 5392

Robinson's Hatters, Unicorn Ⓗ
Detached stone pub in a quiet village off the main road, close to Etherow Country Park, which has wildlife and river valley walks. The pub features a comfortable lounge and a small, traditional games room, as well as a dining room. A true local, popular with all ages, it is the centre for many social activities.
⋈◗⊕⊟♣P

Delph

Royal Oak (Th' Heights)

Broad Lane, Heights, OL3 5TX OS982090
◔ 7-11; 12-5, 7-10.30 Sun
☎ (01457) 874460

Black Sheep Best Bitter; guest beers Ⓗ
Isolated, 250-year-old stone pub on a packhorse route overlooking the Tame Valley. In a popular walking area, it benefits from outstanding views. The pub comprises a cosy bar and three rooms, each with an open fire. The refurbished side room boasts a hand-carved stone fireplace while the comfortable snug rear has exposed beams and old photos

of the inn. Good home-cooked food (served eve Fri-Sun) often features game. The house beer is brewed by Moorhouses and guests include a beer from Millstone. ⋈Q⊛◗P

Didsbury

Fletcher Moss

1 William Street, M20 6RQ (off Wilmslow Rd, A5145)
◔ 12-11 (midnight Fri & Sat); 12-10.30 Sun
☎ (0161) 438 0073

Hydes Owd Oak, Bitter, Jekylls Gold, Craft Ales Ⓗ
One of the last pubs in the village to retain a strong local identity, it does not pander to the large student population that packs other venues in the village. The pub, as well as the nearby park, is named after Alderman Fletcher Moss who built the local library. The interior comprises several comfortable areas including a conservatory at the back. It can get busy on Friday and Saturday nights when entry may be restricted due to crowding. Q⊛◉≠⊟P

Nelson

3 Barlow Moor Road, M20 6TN (on A5145)
◔ 12-midnight (11 Sun)
☎ (0161) 434 5118

Jennings Cumberland Ale; Moorhouses Black Cat Ⓗ
Single-roomed pub in the centre of the village that tends to attract locals rather than students. Live music (often Irish) every Thursday and karaoke with a DJ feature at weekends. All the main sporting events are shown on TV. Catering more for workmen than business people, the pub is very friendly, offering probably the keenest prices available in an otherwise affluent village. ≠⊟♣

Diggle

Diggle Hotel

Station Houses, OL3 5JZ (½ mile off A670) OS011081
◔ 12-3, 5-midnight (1am Fri); 12-1am Sat; 12-midnight Sun
☎ (01457) 872741

Black Sheep Best Bitter; Naylor's Sparkey's Monday Night Mild; Taylor Golden Best, Landlord; guest beer Ⓗ
Stone pub in a pleasant hamlet close to the Standedge Canal Tunnel under the Pennines. Built as a merchant's house in 1789, it became an ale house and general store on the construction of the railway tunnel in 1834. Affording fine views of the Saddleworth countryside, this makes a convenient base in a popular walking area. Comprising a bar area and two rooms, the accent is on home-cooked food (served all day Sat and Sun). Brass bands play on alternate summer Sundays and the pub holds occasional mini beer festivals.
⊛⊷◗⊟(184)P╘

Dobcross

Navigation Inn

21-23 Wool Road, OL3 5NS (on A670)
◔ 12-2.30, 5-11; 12-11 Sat; 12-10.30 Sun
☎ (01457) 872418

**Greenfield Dobcross Bitter; Lees Bitter;
Moorhouses Pendle Witches Brew; Wells
Bombardier; guest beers** Ⓗ

Next to the Huddersfield narrow canal, this
stone pub was built in 1806 to slake the thirst
of the navvies cutting the Standedge Tunnel. It
comprises an open-plan bar and L-shaped
interior. Live brass band concerts are staged
on alternate Sundays in summer, and it is the
venue for annual events such as the beer walk
(spring) and the Rushcart Festival (August).
The guest ale often comes from a local micro-
brewery. Home-cooked meals including
special offer weekday lunches are popular (no
food Sun eve). Q✿◑🖾(184)P🏃

Swan Inn (Top House)

The Square, OL3 5AA

✪ 12-3, 5-11 (midnight Thu-Sat); 12-4, 7-11 Sun

☎ (01457) 873451

**Jennings Mild, Bitter, Cumberland Ale, Cocker
Hoop; guest beers** Ⓗ

Built in 1765 for the Wrigley family of chewing
gum fame, part of the building was later used
as a police court and cells. Overlooking the
attractive village square, the pub has been
well renovated, with flagged floors and three
rooms, plus a fine function room that caters
for 80 people. It gets busy during the Whit
Friday brass band contest, and the August
Rushcart Festival. Imaginative home-cooked
food features dishes from around the world
(booking advisable). ▲Q✿◑🖾🏃

Eccles

Albert Edward

142 Church Street, M30 0LS (A57 opp library)

✪ 12-11; 12.30-10.30 Sun

☎ (0161) 707 1045

Samuel Smith OBB Ⓗ

A street-corner community local with a small
tap room, which was the original pub, and
three other rooms that have been added over
the years. A basic vault-like room to the right
is complemented by a snug and upholstered
lounge to the rear. The flag floor and tiling
were uncovered during refurbishment in 2004
and have been sympathetically restored. The
walls are adorned with old local historical
photographs and there is a cosy outside
drinking area in the backyard.
▲Q✿&⇌⊖🖾♣

Eccles Cross

13 Regent Street, M30 0BP (on A57 opp tram
terminus)

✪ 9am-midnight (1am Fri & Sat)

☎ (0161) 788 0414

**Greene King Abbot; Marston's Pedigree; guest
beers** Ⓗ

The ornate facade of this pre-WWII cinema
matches that of Holt's Lamb Hotel next door.
The high balusters are identical, albeit in
yellow stone rather than red brick. These sit
either side of a lofty oeil-de-boeuf window.
The interior, more intimate than most large
Wetherspoon pubs, has four levels, with a
raised corner, balcony and several 'drinking
pits'. Two-tone blue decor around the bar is
balanced with maroon and gold elsewhere,
including a giant Celtic cross in the back
corner. ⬗✿◑&⇌⊖🖾♣🏃

Lamb Hotel ☆

33 Regent Street, M30 0BP (opp tram terminus)

✪ 11.30-11 (11.30 Fri & Sat); 12-11 Sun

☎ (0161) 787 7297

Holt Mild, Bitter Ⓗ

Situated across the road from the tram
terminus, this classic Edwardian red-brick
building is enhanced internally with ornate
carved wood and etched glass. There are two
comfortably furnished lounges and a more
basic vault with photographs of early 20th-
century Eccles on the walls. The large back
room contains a full-sized snooker table. There
is decorative tiling on the staircase and also in
the lobby, where there are shelves for vertical
drinkers to rest their glasses. Q🕀⇌⊖🖾♣🏃

Egerton

Masons Arms

156-158 Blackburn Road, BL7 9SB (A666,
northern outskirts of Bolton)

✪ 4 (3 Fri) -11 (midnight Thu & Fri); 12-midnight Sat;
12-11 Sun

☎ (01204) 303517

**Greene King Ruddles Best Bitter; Theakston
Bitter; guest beers** Ⓗ

Situated around three miles from Bolton, this
inviting pub dates from late Victorian times.
Good value, well-kept beers are dispensed
from four handpumps on an imposing bar,
which is the main interior feature. There is a
small beer garden at the back, and in summer
hanging baskets and window boxes enhance
the attractive brick and stone facade. This is a
pub for those who like a genuine local.
✿🖾(225)♣🏃

Fallowfield

Friendship

353 Wilmslow Road, MI4 6XS (on B5093)

✪ 12-11 (midnight Fri & Sat)

☎ (0161) 224 5758

**Hydes 1863, Original Bitter, Jekyll's Gold,
seasonal beers; guest beers** Ⓗ

This large and lively south Manchester pub is
located in a busy student area. Its many
drinking areas are served by a well-staffed,
horseshoe-shaped bar. Football is popular with
locals and students who can choose from
eight large-screen TVs. The Hydes regulars are
served along with its seasonal ales and two
guests. There are plans for an outdoor bar to
serve the massive beer garden that surrounds
the pub and to provide a smokers' retreat.
Quiz night is Thursday. ✿◑&🖾P🏃

Farnworth

Britannia

34 King Street, BL4 7AF (opp bus station, off
A6053)

✪ 11-11; 12-10.30 Sun

☎ (01204) 571629

Moorhouses Premier Ⓗ

Thriving local next to the market and bus
station with a basic but spacious vault and a
smaller lounge, both served by a central bar.
The pub offers reasonably priced Moorhouses
Premier and occasionally another beer from
the brewery as well as inexpensive home-

cooked lunches every day. Mini outdoor beer festivals held on May and August bank holidays are well attended. Behind the pub is a free car park. Children are welcome until 4.30pm. ⚘◑⊕≢≉♣

Flixton

Church Inn

34 Church Road, M41 6HS
◐ 11-11 (11.30 Thu; midnight Fri & Sat); 12-11 Sun
☎ (0161) 748 2158
Taylor Landlord; Theakston Black Bull; guest beers Ⓗ
Back in the Guide after a change of management, this comfortable, village-style pub stands next to the Norman/Georgian church, just a short walk from the railway station. The bar serves three seating areas including a section on the left of the main entrance used for traditional games such as darts and cribbage. As popular for its food as its ales, it offers reasonably priced meals every day. The outside seating area overlooks the churchyard. ⚏⚘◑≢⊡♣P

Gatley

Prince of Wales

Gatley Green, SK8 4NF (off Church Rd)
◐ 11.30-11 (11.30 Fri & Sat); 12-11 Sun
☎ (0161) 491 5854
Hydes Mild, Original Bitter, seasonal beers Ⓗ
Situated in the Gatley Green conservation area, this pub has been sensitively refurbished but maintains the feel of a country pub. The two-room layout includes a small room on the left with a dartboard and a larger lounge on the right; a bar in the centre serves both areas. There is a fenced patio for outdoor drinking in summer, with views across the green.
⚘◑≢♣♠

Goose Green

Bull's Head

356 Warrington Road, WN3 6QA (on A49)
◐ 5-11; 2-midnight Thu; 12-midnight Fri & Sat; 12-11 Sun
☎ (01942) 234945 ⊕ bullsheadwigan.co.uk
Beer range varies Ⓗ
The Bull's Head has an L-shaped lounge and a separate vault with dartboard and pool table, with a TV in both rooms. The friendly staff will allow guests to taste any of the draught beers and continental lagers. Guest ales change weekly, often coming from micros such as Allgates and Mayflower. An extensive range of bottled continental beers is also available. To the rear is a large beer garden. The pub stages regular beer festivals, and has live music some weekends. Hot food and sandwiches are available on Friday and Saturday. ⚘◑⊕⊡(601, 602)♣P♠

Gorton

Vale Cottage

Kirk Street, M18 8UE (off Hyde Road A57 by Gorton Butterfly Garden)
◐ 12-3, 5 (7 Sat)-11; 12-4, 7-11 Sun
☎ (0161) 223 2477

Taylor Landlord; Theakston Black Bull; guest beers Ⓗ
Tucked away in the Gore Brook conservation area, screened by trees, this local CAMRA Pub of the Year 2006 feels like a country inn. Low-beamed ceilings reveal parts of the building dating back to the 17th century. Despite rumours of a resident ghost, the atmosphere is relaxed, with quiet background music. The general knowledge quiz on Tuesday and music quiz on Thursday are popular. Live music is performed here on the last Wednesday of the month. Home-cooked lunches are served (not Sat). Q⚘◑⊡P♠

Great Moor

Crown

416 Buxton Road, SK2 7TQ (on A6)
◐ 11-11 (midnight Fri & Sat); 12-11 Sun
☎ (0161) 483 4913
Robinson's Hatters, Unicorn, Double Hop, seasonal beers Ⓗ
This large, three-gabled Robinson's house is located just north of Stepping Hill Hospital on the busy A6. Inside it is divided into several drinking areas with a double-sided bar in the middle. An interesting collection of drawings depicting old Stockport are displayed throughout. At the rear is a room for pool and darts, and behind the car park is a bowling green with an outdoor drinking area to the side – a great place for the summer.
⚘≢(Woodsmoor)⊡♣P♠

Greenfield

King William IV

134 Chew Valley Road, OL3 7DD (on A669 in centre of village)
◐ 12-midnight
☎ (01457) 873933
Caledonian Deuchars IPA; Lees Bitter; Tetley Bitter; guest beers Ⓗ
Detached stone pub at the village centre, comprising a central bar area and two rooms. A cobbled forecourt with benches allows for outdoor drinking. It offers two or three changing guest beers, often including a mild. Food is served Wednesday to Sunday until 7pm. Handy for walks over the moors, the pub is the centre of village life, participating in the annual beer walk and Rushcart Festival (Aug) and hosting a Whit Friday brass band contest.
⚘◑≢⊡(180)♣P

Railway

11 Shaw Hall Bank Road, OL3 7JZ (opp station)
◐ 12-midnight (1am Thu-Sat)
☎ (01457) 872307 ⊕ railway-greenfield.co.uk
Caledonian Deuchars IPA; Millstone True Grit; John Smith's Bitter; Taylor Landlord; Wells Bombardier; guest beer Ⓗ
Unspoilt pub where the central bar and games area draw a good mix of old and young. The tap room has a log fire and old Saddleworth photos. In a picturesque area, it provides a fine base for various outdoor pursuits and affords beautiful views across Chew Valley. The venue for live Cajun, R&B, jazz and pop music on Thursday, Friday ('Unplugged' night) and Sunday, it also hosts top-class entertainment every month including a comedy club.

Weston's cider is served on gravity.
🏮⛽♿🛏🍴👤♨🚗🅿♨

Hawkshaw

Red Lion

81 Ramsbottom Road, BL8 4JS (on A676)
🕓 12-3, 6-11; 12-11 Sat; 12-10.30 Sun
☎ (01204) 856600
Jennings Bitter, Cumberland Ale; guest beers ⓗ
Attractive stone pub nestling in a picturesque village. Inside you will find a single, large room that is a favourite with locals. The excellent menu of freshly prepared dishes has made the inn popular with diners, too, who can opt to eat in the pub or the adjacent restaurant. Meals are served all day Saturday and Sunday. Guest beers often come from Bank Top or Phoenix. 🛏🍴🚗🅿

Hazel Grove

Grapes

196 London Road, SK7 4DQ (on A6)
🕓 11.30-11; 11-midnight Fri & Sat; 12-10.30 Sun
☎ (0161) 483 4479
Robinson's Hatters, Unicorn ⓗ
This very old building retains its classic urban pub layout. The central bar separates a large vault on the left from the comfortable three-roomed lounge which features some original woodwork. The back room has images of old Hazel Grove, while pictures of local sports teams dominate the rest of the pub. To the rear is a small beer garden with well-kept floral tubs. Ask the landlady about her Tina Turner impersonation. 🏮⛽♿🍴♨🅿♨

Heaton Mersey

Griffin

552 Didsbury Road, SK4 3AJ (on A5145)
🕓 12-11 (midnight Fri & Sat)
☎ (0161) 443 2077
Holt Mild, Bitter, seasonal beers ⓗ
Four-square red-brick pub dating from 1831, with a sympathetic modern extension. The interior has a number of cosy, comfortable rooms around a magnificent carved-wood and etched-glass servery. One of the few pubs still to have beer delivered in 54-gallon hogsheads, it is very popular with customers of all age groups. Good value lunchtime food is served seven days a week. At the rear is an attractive and surprisingly secluded garden.
🏮⛽♿🍴♨🅿♨

Heaton Norris

Nursery ☆

258 Green Lane, SK4 2NA (off A6, by Stratstone Jaguar garage)
🕓 11.30-11 (midnight Fri & Sat); 12-11.30 Sun
☎ (0161) 432 2044
Hydes Mild, Original Bitter, Jekyll's Gold, seasonal beers ⓗ
CAMRA's national pub of the year 2001 and a Guide regular, the Nursery is a classic unspoilt 1930s pub, hidden away in a pleasant suburb. The multi-roomed interior includes a traditional vault with its own entrance and a spacious wood-panelled lounge, used by

diners at lunchtime. The home-made food draws customers from miles around; childen are welcome if dining. The pub's immaculate bowling green – an increasingly rare feature – is well used by local league teams.
🏮⛽🚗🅿♨

Heywood

Wishing Well

89 York Street, OL10 4NS (on A58 towards Rochdale)
🕓 12-11; 11-midnight Thu-Sat; 12-11.30 Sun
☎ (01706) 620923
Black Sheep Best Bitter; Moorhouses Pride of Pendle; Phoenix White Monk; Taylor Landlord; guest beers ⓗ
Justifiably popular free house on the Rochdale side of the town centre. A basic bar area is complemented by two other comfortable rooms and a small games room with a pool table. Guest beers (up to four at a time) are often from local breweries. The house beer is brewed by Phoenix. All beers can be served in the adjacent restaurant. Jam sessions take place each Thursday and a live band plays on Saturday. 🚍(471)♨

High Lane

Royal Oak

Buxton Road, SK6 8AY
🕓 12-3, 5-11; 12-10.30 Sun
☎ (01663) 762380
Jennings Bitter; Marston's Burton Bitter, seasonal beers ⓗ
A well-appointed pub with a pleasing exterior. Although it has an open-plan layout, there are three distinct drinking areas, one used for games. Live entertainment is hosted most Fridays, and an innovative menu is served at all sessions. The garden and play area make this a good summer and family pub. The beer choice is mostly from the Marston's range.
Q🏮⛽♿🚗🅿🍴

Hindley

Edington Arms

186 Ladies Lane, WN2 2QJ (off A58)
🕓 12-11.30 (12.30am Fri & Sat)
☎ (01942) 259229
Holt Mild, Bitter, seasonal beers ⓗ
Also known as the Top Ale House, the Edington is a cosy, welcoming pub. The single bar is centrally situated in the front lounge. There is also a games room with pool table that leads out to the beer garden at the rear. Standing next to the Liverpool to Manchester rail line, it is ideally situated for a 'rail ale crawl' into Wigan or Manchester. 🏮♿♨🅿♨

Horwich

Crown

1 Chorley New Road, BL6 7QJ (jct A673/B6226)
🕓 11-11 (midnight Fri & Sat); 12-11 Sun
☎ (01204) 690926
Holt Mild, Bitter ⓗ
Spacious pub on the edge of town, handy for the Reebok stadium (visiting away fans welcome), Rivington Pike and the West

Pennine Moors. Mainly open plan, it comprises a well-furnished drinking area, a vault and a games room at the rear. This friendly pub serves good value lunches. Sunday evenings are busy, when locals take part in sing-alongs. Wednesday is quiz night. A popular pub, it welcomes children when dining, and dogs in the tap room. Q❀❶❹&≉(Blackrod)➡♣P↳

Original Bay Horse

206 Lee Lane, BL6 7JF (on B6226, 200m from A673)

🕓 1-11.30; 12-12.30am Fri & Sat; 12-11.30 Sun

☎ (01204) 696231

Lees Bitter; Taylor Landlord; guest beers Ⓗ

Dating back to 1777, this stone pub with small windows has been run by the same family for many years. The little bar is usually busy with local drinkers. A small independent brewery beer is always available, as is Weston's Old Rosie Cider. The low ceilings add to the ambience. Live sports coverage on TV attracts crowds, and a well-designed beer garden invites for outdoor drinking in fine weather. Q❀❹♣♦P↳

Hyde

Cheshire Ring

72 Manchester Road, SK14 2BJ

🕓 2 (1 Thu-Sat)-11; 1-10.30 Sun

☎ (0161) 366 1840 🌐 cheshirering.com

Beartown Kodiak Gold, Bearskinful, seasonal beers; guest beers Ⓗ

A warm welcome is assured in this friendly pub, one of the oldest in Hyde and comprehensively overhauled by Beartown. Its seven handpumps offer a range of Beartown and other brews, as well as continental beers plus three ciders/perries (only one will be on display). It also stocks a range of bottled beers, and beer festivals periodically offer additional drinking choice. Gentle background music plays.

᠅❀❹≉(Hyde Central/Flowery Field)➡♦P

Queen's Hotel

23 Clarendon Place, SK14 2ND

🕓 11-11; 12-10.30 Sun

☎ (0161) 368 2230

Holt Mild, Bitter, seasonal beers Ⓗ

A well-appointed town centre pub with four distinct rooms/areas, furnished in different styles to offer variety to customers. The Queen's is a thriving community centre, serving as a base for various clubs and teams with a loyal local following. A sizeable function room is a popular choice for weddings and birthday parties. Late opening for special occasions is licensed.

❹&≉(Hyde Central/Newton for Hyde)➡♣

Sportsman

57 Mottram Road, SK14 2NN (adjacent to Morrisons exit)

🕓 11-11; 12-10.30 Sun

☎ (0161) 368 5000

Moorhouses Black Cat; Phoenix Bantam; Pictish Brewers Gold; Plassey Bitter; Taylor Landlord; Whim Hartington Bitter Ⓗ

True free house, serving six regular beers and two guests in addition to a range of continental beers. This pub is at the heart of the local community; it has a pool team and hosts the local chess club. There is a full-sized snooker table upstairs for hire. A former CAMRA Pub of the Region, it attracts a loyal and mixed group of regulars.

᠅❀≉(Hyde Central/Newton for Hyde)➡P

Leigh

Musketeer

15 Lord Street, WN7 1AB

🕓 12-midnight (1am Fri & Sat); 12-11 Sun

☎ (01942) 701143

Jennings Cumberland Ale; guest beers Ⓗ

Popular local – the last real two-roomed pub in Leigh town centre. The lounge is divided into two areas with a comfortable snug to the right of the bar. The tap room (with its own street entrance) is also divided into two, with various pictures of local sporting heroes decorating the walls. The pub is busy on match days for Leigh Centurions Rugby League, and when occasional live bands play. ❹❶♣

Waggon & Horses

68 Wigan Road, WN7 5AY (1 mile from town centre)

🕓 7 (4 Fri)-midnight; 12-1am Sat; 12-11 Sun

☎ (01942) 673069

Hydes Light Mild, Dark Mild, Original Bitter Ⓗ

Friendly community local that attracts regulars of all ages. Inside, there is a large, comfortable lounge with TV screens for sports fans and a quiet snug served from the main bar. The front room is dedicated to pub games, and is well used by the pub's resident teams. Children are welcome until 8pm. Parking is restricted to local side streets. ❀♣↳

Littleborough

Moorcock

Halifax Road, OL15 0LD (A58 from Littleborough centre to Halifax)

🕓 11.30-midnight (11.30 Sun)

☎ (01706) 378156

Taylor Landlord; guest beers Ⓗ

Built as a farmhouse in 1641 and first licensed in 1840, this gem nestling in the Pennine foothills is worth a visit for the view alone. Although featuring a fine 80-seat restaurant, the pub section is kept apart by clever use of floor space. Three guest beers are served in convivial surroundings. As it is near the Pennine Way, ramblers and equestrians (tethers provided for horses) join the varied clientele. Six rooms are available for overnight guests. ᠅Q❀⇤❶❹&▲P↳

White House

Blackstone Edge, OL15 0LB (A58, top of hill)

🕓 12-3, 6.30-midnight; 12.30-10.30 Sun

☎ (01706) 378456 🌐 thewhitehousepub.co.uk

Black Sheep Best Bitter, Ale; Theakston Bitter; guest beers Ⓗ

The Pennine Way passes this popular 17th-century coaching house, situated 1,300 feet above sea level. It is a landmark that benefits from panoramic views of the surrounding moors and Hollingworth Lake way below. A family-run inn extending a warm, friendly welcome, it has two bars, both with log fires.

Local guest ales, continental beers and a good range of wines complement the excellent menu and daily specials board. Food is served throughout this spacious inn (available all day Sunday). ♨Q☞❀◐❶➾P

Lowton

Travellers' Rest

443 Newton Road, WA3 1NX (on A572 between Lane Head and Newton)
✪ 12-11 (midnight Fri & Sat)
☎ (01925) 224391
Marston's Pedigree; guest beers Ⓗ
This comfortable roadside local has been serving the people of Lowton and those passing between Leigh and Newton-le-Willows for a number of years. The bar has various cosy nooks and crannies, inviting guests for a pint and a chat. The restaurant dishes up a wide range of meals, with a leaning towards Greek food. Outside is a large beer garden with plenty of seating. ❀◐P

Lowton (Lane Head)

Red Lion

324 Newton Road, WA3 1ME
✪ 12-11 (midnight Thu-Sat)
☎ (01942) 671429
Tetley Dark Mild, Bitter; guest beers Ⓗ
This pub, including the kitchen, was thoroughly refurbished at the end of 2006. It retains separate areas for dining, socialising, games and watching sport, but in different places from its previous incarnation. The new decor is minimal and bright, with carpets in the main lounge areas and a wooden floor leading to the bar. There is also a new patio in the garden. The Lion retains its great local ambience and the bowling green, but has lost the etched Wilderspool windows. Its senior citizens' club offers a discount on meals.
❀◐&♣P⚊

Lydgate

White Hart

51 Stockport Road, OL4 4JJ (close to A669/A6050 jct)
✪ 12-midnight (11 Sun)
☎ (01457) 872566 ⊕ thewhitehart.co.uk
Black Sheep Best Bitter; Lees Bitter; Taylor Golden Best, Landlord; Tetley Bitter; guest beers Ⓗ
Detached stone free house dating from 1788, commanding impressive views over the hills above Oldham. Adjoining the village church and school, the pub has four rooms, two used for dining. The small snug has its own servery and the main bar has eight handpumps. An extension, with bar, is used for weddings and gourmet meals prepared by the award-winning chef. The pub makes an excellent base for visiting Saddleworth's villages and moors. Eighteen en-suite rooms are available.
♨Q❀➡◐&🚌(180, 184)P

Manchester City Centre

Bar Fringe

8 Swan Street, M4 5JN (50m from A665/A62 jct)

✪ 11 (12 Sat)-11 (midnight Thu, 12.30am Fri & Sat); 12-11 Sun
☎ (0161) 835 3815
Beer range varies Ⓗ
Manchester City's original and best Belgian-style bar, this wonderful pub comprises a single long room with a bar on one side and a beer garden outside. Five handpumps serve an ever-changing range of beers mainly from local micro-breweries. A fine range of draught and bottled continental beers plus Thatchers draught and various bottled ciders complete the selection. An eclectic mix of rats, bats, cartoons and breweriana adorn the walls, adding to the ambience.
❀◐♿≠(Victoria)⊖(Shudehill)🚌♣⚊

Britons Protection ☆

50 Great Bridgewater Street, M1 5LE (opp Bridgewater Hall)
✪ 11-11; 12-10.30 Sun
☎ (0161) 236 5895
Jennings Cumberland; Robinson's Unicorn; Tetley Bitter; guest beers Ⓗ
This historic pub, dating from 1811 and Grade II listed, was reputed to have been a recruiting post for those who fought at the Battle of Waterloo. Now it is famous for its splendid multi-roomed interior, real fires, fine tile work and superb ceiling. Besides the five regular beers, it also stocks a selection of malt whiskies and a fine choice of champagnes. Lunches are served weekdays. It tends to close early when there is a big football match on.
♨Q❀◐&≠(Oxford Rd)⊖(G-Mex)🚌♣⚊

Castle Hotel

66 Oldham Street, M4 1QE (off Piccadilly Gardens)
✪ 11-11; 12-8 Sun
☎ (0796) 961 8357 ⊕ castlepub.co.uk
Robinson's range, seasonal beers Ⓗ
This Grade II listed hostelry comprises a bar, lobby and parlour, with a homely and lived in decor. The only city-centre outlet for Robinson's, the Castle now features up to 11 handpumps, enabling it to serve all of the Stockport brewery's beers (subject to availability) plus seasonals. The pub suffered the untimely death of its popular landlady, Kath Smethurst, and is now run by son Damien, who is regenerating the pub with real ales and live music in the back room and on the Internet. ≠(Victoria)⊖(Market St)🚌⚊

City Arms

46-48 Kennedy Street, M2 4BQ (near town hall)
✪ 11 (12 Sat)-11; 12-8 Sun
☎ (0161) 236 4610
Tetley Dark Mild, Bitter; guest beers Ⓗ
Busy little two-roomed pub situated behind the Waterhouse. It received a local CAMRA award in 2006 and has been in this Guide for 13 consecutive years. Lunchtimes can be hectic with office workers who come for the good food. The early evening can again be busy, then it settles down and gives way to a quieter period with a 'local' mood. Five guest beers are served and there is a 'guess the mystery ale' competition on Friday.
◐≠(Oxford Rd)⊖(St Peter's Sq)🚌

Crown & Kettle

2 Oldham Road, M4 5FE

☻ 11-11 (midnight Fri & Sat); 12-10.30 Sun
☎ (0161) 236 2923 ⊕crownandkettle.com
Beer range varies Ⓗ
This historic pub, prominently sited on the corner of Oldham Road and Great Ancoats Street in Manchester's northern district, reopened in late 2005 after 16 years of closure. The three-room layout incorporates many interesting architectural features including a mahogany bar and a magnificent ceiling. A diverse clientele enjoys up to four real ales from smaller (often local) breweries and a choice of real ciders. Good value food is served until 8pm weekdays, 6pm weekends.
🏠◑&≷(Victoria)⊖(Shudehill)🚌♦

Dutton Hotel

37 Park Street, M3 1EU (200m from A665/A6042 jct)
☻ 11.30-11; 12-11 Sun
☎ (0161) 234 4508
Hydes Original Bitter, Jekyll's Gold, seasonal beer Ⓗ
Tucked away behind the former Boddington Brewery, but very close to Victoria Rail Station and the MEN arena, the Dutton is in the best tradition of the small, basic, street corner boozer. Oddly shaped, there are three rooms decorated with a couple of large, genuine anvils (the Hydes Brewery trademark) and an extensive collection of blowlamps and other brass artefacts. The second bar is occasionally not available. Closing time may be extended at the licensee's discretion.
❀≷(Victoria)⊖(Victoria)🚌♣⌐

Font Bar

7 New Wakefield Street, M1 5NP (off Oxford Rd by railway viaduct)
☻ 12-1am (12.30am Sun)
☎ (0161) 236 0944
Beer range varies Ⓗ
The antithesis of the traditional pub, Font offers two cask beers, usually from local micros. A café-bar during the day, it becomes a thriving student venue by night, with loud music and dim lighting. The main bar is up a few stairs; a secondary bar downstairs. Bottled beers include interesting examples of German, Belgian and British brewing. Home-cooked food at bargain prices is available every day until 8pm. Live music plays on Sunday night.
◑&≷(Oxford Rd)⊖(St Peter's Sq)🚌

Jolly Angler

47 Ducie Street, M1 2JW (behind Piccadilly)
☻ 12-3, 5.30-11; 12-4, 8-10.30 Sun
☎ (0161) 236 5307
Hydes Bitter, seasonal beer Ⓗ
Beer journalist Michael Jackson recommends this much-loved Irish back-street hostelry to visitors from the USA. The Reynolds Family have run the basic and friendly two-roomed pub for more than 22 years. Frequented by session drinkers and travellers from Piccadilly station, as well as Man City supporters on match days, the pub now has cask marque status. Live folk and Irish music is hosted on Thursday, Saturday and Sunday evenings. Seasonal beers are sometimes available.
🏠≷(Piccadilly)⊖(Piccadilly)🚌♣⌐

Knott

374 Deansgate, M3 4LY (under railway viaduct)
☻ 12-11.30 (midnight Thu; 12.30am Fri & Sat)
☎ (0161) 839 9229
Marble Manchester Bitter, Ginger Marble; guest beers Ⓗ
Built into a railway arch in historic Castlefield, the Knott has established itself as a pub for good beer lovers from all walks of life. Its unusual layout with upstairs balcony (best tried in summer) adds to the atmosphere. Three guest beers usually come from local micros. Real cider is available, as well as bottled beers from Belgium and Germany. Imaginative home-cooked food including vegetarian options is served until 8pm daily.
❀◑≷(Deansgate)⊖(G-Mex)🚌♣♦⌐

Lass O'Gowrie

36 Charles Street, M1 7DB
☻ 12-11 (midnight Thu-Sat); 12-10.30 Sun
☎ (0161) 273 6932 ⊕thelass.co.uk
Black Sheep Best Bitter, Greene King IPA, Abbot, Old Speckled Hen; guest beers Ⓗ
Beer is no longer brewed here, but there remains plenty to attract the beer lover behind the impressive tiled façade of this famous Manchester pub. Four guest beers (one from the GK list, three independent) complement the regulars. The house beer, Lass Ale, is brewed by Titanic. The food is highly regarded and fairly priced. Often busy, the pub attracts a mixed crowd of media people from the nearby BBC offices, as well as students and staff from the university. The rear snug (a reminder of a long-gone multi-roomed interior) offers a welcome refuge. ◑≷(Oxford Rd)🚌⌐

Marble Arch ☆

73 Rochdale Road, M4 4HY
☻ 11.30 (12 Sat)-11 (midnight Fri & Sat); 12-10.30 Sun
☎ (0161) 832 5914 ⊕marblebeers.com
Marble GSB, Manchester Bitter, Ginger Marble, Lagonda IPA, seasonal beers; guest beers Ⓗ
Listed brew pub on a corner site now surrounded by new luxury apartments, the Marble Arch's impressive main room has a green-tiled sloping floor with a decorative drinks frieze, which the brave can attempt to 'drink their way round'. A smaller back room beyond the bar enjoys views of the Soil Association-accredited Marble Brewery. A selection of the brewery's organic beers is served, complemented by varied guests and a changing cider. Excellent food is available until 8pm (6pm Sun).
🏠❀◑≷(Victoria)⊖(Shudehill)🚌♦⌐

Sand Bar

120 Grosvenor Street, All Saints, M1 7HL (off Oxford Rd A34/B5117 jct)
☻ 12 (2 Sat)-midnight; 6-10.30 Sun
☎ (0161) 273 3141
Phoenix All Saints; guest beers Ⓗ
This characterful conversion of two old Georgian town houses serves a loyal crowd of students, university staff and beer enthusiasts attracted by the eclectic range of British and European beers. The house beer is complemented by two changing guests from micro-breweries. Local artists often exhibit, adding to the bohemian atmosphere. The original and inventive lunchtime food (with

good veggie options) is available Monday to Friday only. Worth a special journey.
⊕🖥🖺(42, 50)♠

Smithfield Hotel & Bar
37 Swan Street, M4 5JZ
⊕ 12-11 (10.30 Sun)
☎ (0161) 839 4424
Robinson's Hatters Dark; guest beers Ⓗ
The main attraction in this hotel bar are the handpumps, which dispense a changing selection of six unusual beers from far and wide. Occasional beer festivals have near legendary status in the 'ticking' community. The competitively priced house bitter is brewed by Phoenix. A popular pool table is sited towards the front of the narrow single room, while a TV dominates the rear. Good value accommodation is recommended.
🛏🕿(Victoria)❸(Shudehill)🖺♣

Waterhouse
69-71 Princess Street, M2 4EG
⊕ 9am-midnight (1am Fri & Sat)
☎ (0161) 200 5380
Greene King Abbot; Marston's Pedigree; guest beers Ⓗ
This Wetherspoon's claims to have been Manchester's first completely no-smoking pub. Converted from three 18th-century town houses, it was a post office and a solicitor's office in previous lives. A six-roomed pub, the Waterhouse offers a different atmosphere in each room. Food is available all day, including breakfast, at reasonable prices. Two real ciders are always stocked.
🕿⊕ᶜ🕿(Oxford Rd)❸(St Peter's Sq)🖺♣⌐

Marple

Hatters Arms
81 Church Lane, SK6 7AW
⊕ 12-11 (10.30 Sun)
☎ (0161) 427 1529 ⊕hattersmarple.co.uk
Robinson's Hatters, Unicorn, Old Tom, seasonal beers Ⓗ
At the end of a row of hatters' cottages, this small stone pub is everyone's idea of a local, replete with small rooms and wooden panelling. Service bells are still nominally in use and the pub pursues an active social life.
🕿⊕ᶜᵍ🖺♣

Railway
223 Stockport Road, SK6 3EN
⊕ 12-11 (11.30 Fri & Sat)
☎ (0161) 427 2146
Robinson's Hatters, Unicorn Ⓗ
This impressive pub opened in 1878 alongside Rose Hill station and Manchester rail commuters still number among its customers. The pub is little changed externally and is in a handy spot for walkers and cyclists on the nearby Middlewood Way. There are two open plan, airy and relaxing rooms and an outside drinking area. It is deservedly popular.
🕿⊕ᶜᵍ🕿(Rose Hill)🖺P

Marple Bridge

Lane Ends
Glossop Road, SK6 5DD

⊕ 12-2.30 (not Mon), 4-11; 12-11 Fri & Sat; 12-10.30 Sun
☎ (0161) 427 5226
Caledonian Deuchars IPA; guest beer Ⓗ
It is a long uphill walk here from Marple Bridge but the 394 Glossop to Hazel Grove bus passes the door. This stone pub borders on some lovely countryside and benefits from delightful views at the front. The interior is now open plan but its window spaces and two levels with some secluded seating give it a fairly intimate feel. Take time to look at the old local photos. Home-cooked food is served and the garden has a children's play area.
🏚🕿⊕🖺(394)P

Mellor

Oddfellows Arms
73 Moor End Road, SK6 5PT
⊕ 12-3, 5.30-11; closed Mon; 12-6 Sun
☎ (0161) 449 7826
Adnams Bitter; Marston's Burton Bitter; Phoenix Arizona; guest beer Ⓗ
A change in ownership has made no difference to this pub's focus on high quality food, and the beer receives just as much tender loving care. A delightful three-storied stone building, it has a tiny garden patio in front, and features low beams and flagging inside. The 375 bus from Stockport deigns to visit every Preston Guild. There is a challenging quarry car park opposite.
🏚Q🕿⊕ᶜ🖺P

Middleton

Tandle Hill Tavern
14 Thornham Lane, Slattocks, M24 2HB (1 mile along unmetalled road off A664 or A627) OS898091
⊕ 5 (12 Sat & Sun)-midnight
☎ (01706) 345297
Lees GB Mild, Bitter, seasonal beers Ⓗ
Situated in Tandle Hill Country Park, this delightful hidden gem is reached along a pot-holed country lane. Nestled in the midst of a cluster of farms and rolling fields, the pub comprises two cosy rooms decorated with bric-a-brac and local photos. The enthusiastic landlady welcomes all – her guests include farmers, locals and visitors. Dogs are permitted too. Meals are available until 8pm, cooked from fresh ingredients. No frozen chips! Check opening times in summer.
🏚🕿⊕

Mossley

Church Inn
82 Stockport Road, OL5 0RF
⊕ 12-midnight (1am Fri & Sat)
☎ (01457) 832021
Thwaites Original, Lancaster Bomber, seasonal beers Ⓗ
Mossley has three parish churches and the Church Inn is located close to St John the Baptist's which stands in what was once Yorkshire. Note the splendid tile work depicting a church in the pub's foyer. Traditional in appearance as well as clientele, this former Oldham Brewery house is owned by Thwaites. It is the home of Mossley Morris

Men and Pistons, the local motorcycle club, which meets here every Thursday.
❀➌⬗⇌🚇(353)♣P

Rising Sun

235 Stockport Road, OL5 0RQ
🕑 5 (2 Sun)-midnight
☎ (01457) 834436 ⊕ risingsunmossley.co.uk
Archers Village; Black Sheep Best Bitter; Shaws Golden Globe; guest beers Ⓗ
High out on Mossley's bracing northern limits, and nearly a mile from the station, the Rising Sun has excellent views eastwards (hence the name) over the Tame Valley towards Saddleworth Moor. The pub is a true free house. Local micro-breweries' beers are often stocked together with a good range of malts and vodkas. The local Blue Grass Boys meet here on Tuesday evening and there is a folk club every other Wednesday. ⚒❀➌🚇(353)♣P

Tollemache Arms

415 Manchester Road, OL5 9BG
🕑 12-midnight (1am Fri & Sat)
☎ (01457) 834555
Robinson's Old Stockport, Unicorn, Ⓗ **Old Tom** Ⓖ
An excellent example of a northern end-of-terrace local, the Tolley, as it is known locally, stands on the valley floor just over a mile from the station, tucked between the canal and Manchester Road. Prior to the canal's restoration it was the regular haunt of the Huddersfield Canal Society. The pub's patio can be accessed directly from the towpath.
❀➌▲🚇(354)♣P

Woodend Tavern

Manchester Road, OL5 9AY
🕑 12-9 (11 Thu-Sat)
☎ (01457) 833133
Beer range varies Ⓗ
The Woodend was once a working men's club, but has been a pub for the past 13 years and was recently saved from demolition. It stands in its own grounds and has a sizeable garden for outdoor dining and drinking. The interior is open plan, more akin to a hotel lounge. A genuine free house, it serves beers only from local micro-breweries and specialises in home-cooked food. ❀➊⇌🚇(354)P

Nangreaves

Lord Raglan

Mount Pleasant, BL9 6SP
🕑 12-2.30, 7 (5 Fri)-11; 12-11 Sat; 12-10.30 Sun
☎ (0161) 764 6680
Leyden Nanny Flyer, Light Brigade, Raglan Sleeve, seasonal beers Ⓗ
A country inn at the end of a cobbled lane with open views of the surrounding hills, this is the home of the Leyden Brewery, and an impressive selection of its beers always features on the bar. The Leyden family has run this friendly pub for half a century. Good food is served in both restaurant and bar, prepared by the chef who is also the head brewer. The interior is decorated with antique glass and pottery, and old photographs. Q❀➊P

New Springs

Colliers Arms

192 Wigan Road, WN2 1DU (on B5238 between Wigan and Aspull)
🕑 1.30-5.30 (Mon, Tue & Fri), 7.30-11; Sat 1.30-11; 1.30-5, 7.30-11.30 Sun
☎ (01942) 831171
Jennings Bitter Ⓗ
A welcome return to the Guide for this popular, two-roomed local, dating from 1700 and known locally as the Stone. The lounge contains many authentic example of colliery life such as pit helmets, clogs and coalboard tokens. In the vault, there are books on many different subjects, as well as board games such as Battleships and Connect 4. Quiz night is Sunday. ⚒❀➌♣P

Oldham

Ashton Arms

28-30 Clegg Street, OL1 1PL (rear of town square shopping centre)
🕑 11.30-11 (11.30 Fri & Sat); 11.30-10.30 Sun
☎ (0161) 630 9709
Beer range varies Ⓗ
A friendly welcome awaits you in this traditional mid-terraced, split-level pub. Situated in the town centre conservation area, opposite the old town hall, this genuine free house provides up to six real ales plus a permanent cider and numerous continental beers. A seat by the 200-year-old stone fireplace makes a welcome change from the trendy outlets nearby. Local micro-breweries are showcased in an array of guest beers. Meals are served weekdays until 6pm (3pm Fri). ⚒➊⇌(Mumps)♣🍴

Gardener's Arms

18 Dunham Street, Waterhead, OL4 3NH (just off A62 about 2 miles from town centre)
🕑 12-midnight (1am Fri & Sat)
☎ (0161) 624 0242
Robinson's Hatters, OB, Unicorn Ⓗ
There has been a pub on this site since 1800, but the present building dates from 1926 when it was purchased by Robinson's. Many original features remain from this rebuild, including tiled fireplaces, stained glass and woodwork. The pleasing multi-roomed layout includes bar space, two lounges and a games room. The pub hosts quizzes, games nights and live music on Saturday evening. ❀➊🚇♣🍴

Royal Oak

172 Manchester Road, Werneth, OL9 7BN (on A62 opp Werneth Park)
🕑 2-midnight; 12-11 Sun
Robinson's Hatters, OB, Unicorn Ⓗ
Traditional pub, retaining separate rooms around a central bar. This popular community local features wood panelling, old-fashioned cast-iron radiators and an antique Gledhill cash register which is still in use as a till. Regular bus services (Manchester to Oldham) stop nearby, and Werneth station is about 15 minutes' walk. The pub is in a restricted parking zone, but a small car park is nearby. Q♿🚇(82, 83)♣

Openshaw

Legh Arms

741 Ashton Old Road, M11 2HD (on A635)
🕔 11 (12 Sun)-11
☎ (0161) 223 4317
**Moorhouses Black Cat, Pendle Witches Brew;
guest beers** Ⓗ

An oasis in a real ale desert, the Legh Arms' licencee is as passionate about his beer as he is about nearby Manchester City FC. MCFC fans should not miss the house beer, brewed by Moorhouses – Blue! Originally multi-roomed, it has now been opened out, yet retains quiet nooks and crannies. Pool and darts (with an unusual log-end board) are played, and there is an enclosed beer garden at the rear, complete with barbecue and bouncy castle.
✿❧≠(Ashburys)🚇♣💪

Railway

2 Manshaw Road, M11 1HS (off A635 by Manchester/Tameside boundary)
🕔 11 (12 Sun)-11
Holt Mild, Bitter Ⓗ

Friendly community pub with an imposing Victorian frontage featuring a large lamp over the door, originally gas powered. Inside, note the glass door etched with the words News Room that leads to the games room; this was once the officers' mess for a nearby WWI camp, but today cards and darts are played here. The enthusiastic darts team competes in Manchester's log-end league. A second room is reserved for quiet drinking, and a third has a large-screen TV showing major sporting events. ✿❧≠(Fairfield)🚇♣P

Orrell

Robin Hood

117 Sandy Lane, WN5 7AZ (near rail station)
🕔 2-midnight; 12-1am Fri & Sat; 12-11 Sun
☎ (01695) 627429
Beer range varies Ⓗ

A small sandstone pub tucked away in a residential area, but well worth seeking out. Not surprisingly, the decor plays on the Robin Hood theme. The pub has a reputation for serving good, home-cooked food (Thu-Sun only, booking advisable). Beers dispensed from the three handpumps often include Caledonian Deuchars IPA, Old Speckled Hen and Taylor Landlord. A quiz night is staged here on Wednesday. ✿❶≠♣P

Patricroft

Stanley Arms ☆

295 Liverpool Road, M30 0QN (corner of Liverpool Rd and Eliza Ann St, opp fire station)
🕔 12-midnight (11 Sun)
☎ (0161) 788 8801
Holt Mild, Bitter Ⓗ

A proper pub, this small street-corner local has a solid core of local revellers who are keen to draw you into their conversation. A small bar serves the vault, and a corridor leads from here to the best room and a tiny third room. Interesting local photographs adorn the walls of this well-run and cared-for pub. 🏠≠🚇⅃

Peel Green

Grapes Hotel ☆

439 Liverpool Road, M30 7HD (on A57 near M60 jct 11)
🕔 11-11 (midnight Fri & Sat); 12-11 Sun
☎ (0161) 789 6971
Holt Mild, Bitter Ⓗ

A typical Holt Edwardian monumental red-brick inn, dating from 1903 and with many original features, the Grapes is a busy and friendly pub. There are five rooms in total, including a family room (until 7pm) and one that used to be the billiards room, but since the 1970s has only offered pool. Occasionally customers are restricted to this area, while a film crew and actors take over the rest of the pub – its photogenic mahogany, etched glass and tiling forming an ideal back-drop for many a TV drama. 🏮♿✿❧≠(Patricroft)🚇♣P⅃

Pendlebury

Lord Nelson

653 Bolton Road, M27 4EJ (A666 Bolton-Manchester Rd)
🕔 11-11 (11.30 Fri); 12-11 Sun
☎ (0161) 794 3648
Holt Mild, Bitter Ⓗ

A 1960s pub comprising a vault and a lounge with a small stage and snug-like side lounge, the Nelson is frequented by mature drinkers, and both Holt Bitter and Mild flow freely. The lounge is typically northern working-class, and has no doubt been the scene of many a knees-up in the past. Live music is staged on Sunday night and a quiz on Thursday. This is a pub where the 'flat caps' still go in the vault and the 'suits' sit in the lounge.
≠(Swinton)🚇(8)♣P⅃

Ramsbottom

Good Samaritan

13 Peel Brow, BL0 0AA (just out of centre over river bridge)
🕔 10-midnight (10.30 Sun)
☎ (01706) 823225
Copper Dragon Golden Pippin; Lees Bitter; guest beers Ⓗ

Traditional stone-built, multi-roomed local, close to the river and railway. As well as the two regular beers there are three changing guests, one always either a mild or a stout. The enthusiastic licencees, Roger and Debbie, host two or three beer festivals a year and always offer a warm welcome in this pleasant, well-run pub. ✿≠🚇(472, 474)♣P⅃

Hare & Hounds

400 Bolton Road West, Holcombe Brook, BL0 9RY
🕔 12-11 (midnight Thu-Sat)
☎ (01706) 822107
Beer range varies Ⓗ

A very large, one-roomed structure, split into several distinct drinking areas by a central bar. Now in the safe hands of the original Guide-listed landlord, the pub is once again an oasis for local drinkers seeking choice and good service. Ten handpumps dispense a wide selection of beers, often including ales from Rooster's and Phoenix. The abundance of screens testifies to the importance of sport here; all major events are covered. Food is served all day. 🚶🕭🕪🌙&🖳(472, 474)P⁻

Major

158-160 Bolton Street, BL0 9JA
🕭 5 (12 Fri-Sun)-midnight
☎ (01706) 826777
Moorhouses Pride of Pendle; Taylor Landlord; guest beers Ⓗ
Traditional stone pub comprising three Lancashire terraces. The decor includes many historical photos of picturesque Ramsbottom and surroundings. There is a choice of bar or lounge, with a central bar dispensing good beers and food. The menu lists old favourites as well as contemporary dishes, including home-made cheese and onion pie, enormous gammon steaks, Sunday lunches and real chips. Outside there is a decked area with heating and seating for smokers and non-smokers. A car park is available for those unlucky drivers. 🕪🖳♣P⁻

Rochdale

Albion

600 Whitworth Road, OL12 0SW (on A671)
🕭 12-2.30, 5-midnight (1am Fri & Sat); 12-midnight Sun
☎ (01706) 648540
Lees Bitter; Taylor Best Bitter, Golden Best, Landlord; guest beers Ⓗ
This multi-roomed traditional local is situated on the main road about two miles north of the town towards Bacup and Burnley. Recent tasteful renovation has made this a popular local venue for dining, from bar snacks to meals in the attached bistro, which serves some African specials. A good selection of regular and guest beers together with an extensive wine list are more good reasons to visit. Q🕭🕪🖳(446, 464)⁻

Baum

33-37 Toad Lane, OL12 0NU (follow the signs for the Co-op Museum)
🕭 11.30-11 (midnight Fri & Sat)
☎ (01706) 352186 🌐 thebaum.co.uk
Boddingtons Bitter; Flowers IPA; guest beers Ⓗ
Delightful, friendly, traditional pub in a conservation area, next to the world's first Co-op store. Facing the splendid St Mary's Church, the Baum stocks three guest ales and a variety of continental bottled beers. A split-level inn, it has an upstairs function room. Outside is a large area to sit and drink. Excellent meals, including vegetarian options, are served daily, and a tapas menu is available at weekends. 🕭🕪≢🖳

Cemetery Hotel ☆

470 Bury Road, OL11 5EU (B6222 about 1 mile from town centre)
🕭 12-midnight (1am Sat); 12-10.30 Sun
☎ (01706) 645635
Adnams Bitter; Black Sheep Best Bitter; Courage Best Bitter; Greene King IPA; Taylor Landlord; guest beers Ⓗ
Rochdale's original free house in the early 1970s, this pub features an interior listed in CAMRA's National Inventory because of the many original features it retaines in its multi-roomed layout. Upstairs is a newly refurbished restaurant noted for its traditional Lancashire

fare (meals served 6-9.30pm Wed-Sat, 12-6pm Sun). Well worth a visit, the hotel can get busy with Rochdale AFC supporters on match days. 🚶🕭🕪🌙🖳P

Flying Horse Hotel

37 Packer Street, OL16 1NJ (opp town hall)
🕭 11 (12 Sun)-midnight
☎ (01706) 646412 🌐 theflyinghorsehotel.co.uk
Lees Bitter; Taylor Best Bitter, Landlord; guest beer Ⓗ
Impressive stone building by the side of an equally impressive town hall, the Flying Horse was built as a hotel in the early 20th century. The warm, friendly atmosphere attracts a mixed clientele. One guest beer, usually Phoenix, is served in the large, attractively decorated open-plan lounge. Centrally located and close to all the town's amenities, it is convenient for public transport. 🛏🕪≢🖳P⁻

Healey Hotel

172 Shawclough Road, OL12 6LW (on B6377)
🕭 3 (12 Sat)-midnight; 1-11.30 Sun
☎ (01706) 645453
Robinson's Unicorn, Hatters Mild, OB, Old Tom Ⓗ
Three-roomed terrace pub situated near the local nature reserve at Healey Dell. This busy local retains many of its original features including the bar, part of the tiled walls in the main bar area and oak doors to the side rooms. The large rear garden has well-kept flower beds and features a popular petanque piste. Q🕭♣⁻

Merry Monk

234 College Road, OL12 6AF (at A6060/B6222 jct)
🕭 12-11; 12-5, 7-10.30 Sun
☎ (01706) 646919
Hydes Owd Oak, Original Bitter, Jekyll's Gold, seasonal beer; guest beer Ⓗ
This detached Victorian brick local was first licensed in 1850. Its history can be glimpsed in the fine pair of Phoenix of Heywood tile sets in the entrance. The pub passed to Bass via Cornbrook and was purchased as a free house in 1984. There are always one or two guest ales on handpump. The open-plan pub is home to strong darts and quiz teams. Ring the Bull and other games are played, and outside there are two international-standard petanque pistes. 🕭♣

Regal Moon

The Butts, OL16 1HB (next to central bus station)
🕭 9-midnight (1am Fri & Sat)
☎ (01706) 657434
Boddingtons Bitter; Greene King Abbot; Marston's Pedigree; Shepherd Neame Spitfire; guest beers Ⓗ
The Regal Moon faces the town hall square and stands next to the central bus station. Formerly an Art Deco Regal cinema, it was sympathetically converted by Wetherspoon and retains original features including ornamental pillars with uplights. A tail-coated mannequin sits at an organ over the bar, while many pictures of Rochdale's notables and old film stars adorn the walls. There is a raised family area. Up to 10 cask ales are regularly on handpump. Breakfast is served 9am-noon. 🕭🕪&≢🖳⁻

Sale

Railway

35 Chapel Road, M33 7FD (behind town hall)
🕑 12-midnight (1am Thu-Sat)
Robinson's Unicorn, Double Hop, seasonal beers H
Small Robinson's hostelry, located just out of the town centre, easy to spot with its unusual white cladding. The interior has benefited from a recent make-over, rendering it more attractive to regulars and to those visiting the newly built Sale Waterside theatre complex. The pub is also a meeting place for local quiz teams, jazz enthusiasts and a ramblers' club. A DJ plays on Friday and Sunday, and there is karaoke on Thursday. Wheelchair access is via the rear door. ⌘♿⊖⊟P⌐

Sale Moor

Legh Arms

178 Northenden Road, M33 2SR (at A6144/B5166 jct)
🕑 11.30-11 (11.30 Thu, midnight Fri & Sat); 12-10.30 Sun
☎ (0161) 973 7491
Holt Mild, Bitter, seasonal beers H
Situated in the centre of Sale Moor village and less than 15 minutes' walk from the Metrolink stations at Sale and Brooklands, this prominent terracotta-tiled pub has a traditional multi-roomed layout. The hub of the community, it stages regular quizzes, karaoke sessions and live entertainment. Two large TV screens show sporting events but there is a separate room for those wanting a quiet drink. Lunches are served Wednesday to Sunday. Q✿◑●⊟P

Salford

Crescent

19-21 Crescent, M5 4PF (on A6 by Salford University)
🕑 11-midnight (1am Fri & Sat); 12-midnight Sun
☎ (0161) 736 5600 ⊕ beer-festival.com/crescent
Bazens' Black Pig Mild; Hydes Original Bitter; Phoenix Thirsty Moon; Rooster's Special; guest beers H
Ten handpumps continue to dispense an excellent range of beers to a mixed clientele of students, university staff, regulars and beer buffs. The main room features an iron range and a low bar, with a new games room and a vault off it, and a beer garden at the rear. Beer festivals are hosted each year, and continental ales plus a cider are also available on draught and bottled. The food is high quality and good value, with a curry night on Wednesday (5-8pm). No entry after 11pm Friday-Sunday.
⌘◑●⇌(Crescent)⊟♣●P⌐-⊟

King's Arms

11 Bloom Street, M3 6AN (off A6 Chapel St)
🕑 12-11 (midnight Fri & Sat); 12-6 Sun
☎ (0161) 832 3605
Bazens' Pacific Bitter; Caledonian Deuchars IPA; Moorhouses Blond Witch; guest beers H
The 1874 building has an oval-shaped main room and snug which can be reserved for meetings and functions. There is a domed upstairs room with a stage for theatre and live music performances. It is also a meeting place for local arts groups whose paintings are regularly displayed. Beers from local micro-breweries often feature among the three guest ales and a good choice of food is served from lunchtime through to 6.30pm.
Q✿◑⇌(Central)⊟P⌐

New Oxford

11 Bexley Square, M3 6DB (off A6 near old town hall)
🕑 11 (12 Sun)-11
☎ (0161) 832 7082
Beer range varies H
Built in the 1830s, the New Oxford has had a chequered history of name changes and closures. Reopened in 2005 in its present guise, the brick exterior remains pretty much unaltered but inside there are now two main rooms around a central bar. The decor is modern with café-style wooden furniture and laminated wood flooring. The regular beer is a house special, New Oxford, brewed by Northern. Guest ales are usually sourced from local micros. There is also a regularly-changing guest cider. Q✿◑♿⇌(Central)⊟●⌐

Racecourse Hotel

Littleton Road, Lower Kersal, M7 3SE (off Cromwell Rd, by Castle Irwell)
🕑 12-11
☎ (0161) 792 1420
Oakwell Barnsley Bitter H
Magnificent, imposing Tudor building reopened some years ago by Oakwell's of Barnsley and winner of the CAMRA/English Heritage Pub Refurbishment award in 2005. Built in 1930, it served the former racecourse, and horse racing mementoes adorn the interior. Original oak panelling and wooden floors have been retained in the vast lounge and bar, separate smaller vault and side rooms. There is a large beer garden at the back, with a smoking shelter. Old Tom Mild is occasionally available.
Q⭐◑⊟⊟(93, 95)♣P⌐

Star Inn

2 Back Hope Street, Higher Broughton, M7 2FR (off Great Clowes St)
🕑 1.30-11.30 (11.45 Sat); 1.30-10.30 Sun
☎ (0161) 792 4184
Robinson's Unicorn H
Publicans Jim and Cath Crank have made this hidden gem, tucked away in the Cliff district of Salford, into a fine local, known for its excellent ales and good cheer. It is also noted for the tiny vault with bar. Orginal 19th-century features remain in the saloon and games room. A smoking shelter is provided on the popular sun patio in the yard. The late and lively Sunday quiz is great fun. ✿⊟(98)♣⌐

Union Tavern

105 Liverpool Street, M5 4LG (near M602; between B5228 and A5186)
🕑 12-midnight
☎ (0161) 736 2885
Holt Mild, Bitter H
An outstanding example of a well-run traditional local that has escaped the fate of other local pubs – demolition or change of use. The bar is situated in the front vault, while

most of the seating is in the side room where twin green-tiled fireplaces indicate an earlier two-roomed layout. The pub is smart yet has a comfortable 'lived-in' feel. A small pool room at the back now has a new door leading to the covered and heated smoking area.
⊞🍺(69)♣P⅃

Welcome

Robert Hall Street, Ordsall, M5 3LT (near jct of B5461, off A5066)
🕐 12-11; 12-3, 7.30-10.30 Sun
☎ (0161) 872 6040
Lees Mild, Bitter Ⓐ

Built as a Wilson's pub in the 1970s, this later became a J W Lees inn and took the name from the original Welcome that stood close by. A popular community pub in an area that has seen a great transformation over the last 12 years, visitors are made to feel most welcome here. The lounge is on the left with the vault on the right. The pub is well-appointed, with many old pictures of local interest.
🏵⊞≉(Crescent)⊖(Salford Quays/Exchange Quay)🍺(69)♣P⅃

Stalybridge

Stalybridge Station Refreshment Rooms (Buffet Bar) ☆

Rassbottom Street, SK15 1RF (Platform 1)
🕐 9.30 (alcohol from 11)-11; 11-10.30 Sun
☎ (0161) 303 0007 🌐 buffetbar.freewebspace.com
Boddingtons Bitter; Flowers IPA; guest beers Ⓗ

Nobody ever minds delayed trains at Stalybridge. This institution for educated drinkers serves an ever-changing range of up to nine cask beers, usually from micros, and often rare brews. These can be enjoyed in convivial Victorian splendour while enjoying a cup of black peas or a simple home-cooked meal by the roaring fire or perched outside watching the world (and the trains) go by. Foreign bottled beers are also available, and a folk club plays on Saturday. Regular beer festivals are held. ⌘Q🏵◑⊞≉🍺♣P

Stamford Arms

815 Huddersfield Road, Heyheads, SK15 3PY
🕐 12-midnight (1am Fri & Sat)
☎ (01457) 832133 🌐 stamfordarms.co.uk
Thwaites Original, Lancaster Bomber, seasonal beers Ⓗ

This listed building is Stalybridge's most northerly pub, standing metres from the pre-1974 Cheshire/Lancashire border and less than a mile and a half from Mossley station. A sporty pub, it hosts a football team, two netball teams and a golf society; furthermore, it overlooks the fairways of Stamford Golf Club. There is live entertainment on Saturday evening and a quiz night on Tuesday.
🏵◑🍺♣P

Standish

Dog & Partridge

33 School Lane, WN6 0TG (off the A49 towards M6)
🕐 1 (12 Sat)-11.30 (midnight Fri & Sat); 12-11 Sun
☎ (01257) 401218
Tetley Mild, Bitter; guest beers Ⓗ

On entering the pub, you come to a central bar area where you will find a choice of four guest beers, mostly from micro-breweries. An area to one side is popular with sports fans watching TV, while the other side is quieter. Fresh flowers add a friendly touch. Outside is a heated patio. The pub holds an annual beer festival with all proceeds going to a local charity. 🏵🍺(362)♣P⅃

Stockport

Arden Arms ☆

23 Millgate, SK1 2LX (corner of Millgate and Corporation St)
🕐 12-11
☎ (0161) 480 2185 🌐 ardenarms.com
Robinson's Hatters, Unicorn, Double Hop, Old Tom, seasonal beers Ⓗ

Grade II listed and on CAMRA's National Inventory, the Arden's distinctive curved, glazed bar and hidden snug, chandeliers and grandfather clock magic up a Victorian ambience. Gourmet lunches, quiz nights and wine tastings, however, add a contemporary touch. Conveniently close to Stockport's historic market place and the Peel Centre shops, this pub is buzzing at lunchtime but more intimate in the evening. The cellars retain body niches in the walls, testament to the building's former use as a mortuary.
⌘⌂🏵◑🍺♣P⅃

Armoury

31 Shaw Heath, SK3 8BD (on B5465)
🕐 10.30-midnight (2am Fri & Sat); 11-midnight Sun
☎ (0161) 477 3711
Robinson's Hatters, Unicorn, Old Tom Ⓗ

Thriving community local that retains three separate rooms despite some alterations, comprising a bright, comfortable lounge, a splendid vault and a back room often given over to darts. The upstairs club room is available for small functions. Convenient for Edgeley Park, the home of Sale Sharks and Stockport County, this is a fine example of a traditional pub, not to be missed. Look for the superb original Old Bells Brewery internal glasswork. Q🏵⊞≉🍺♣⅃

Blossoms

2 Buxton Road, Heaviley, SK2 6NU (at A6/A5102 jct)
🕐 12-3, 5-11; 12-11 Sat; 12-10.30 Sun
☎ (0161) 477 2397
Robinson's Hatters, Unicorn, Ⓗ **Old Tom** Ⓖ

This early Victorian multi-roomed gem still retains its original layout of lobby bar and three rooms. The rear 'smoke' room has an elegant carved fireplace surround as well as unusual stained-glass windows. Two lodges of the Royal Antedeluvian Order of Buffaloes meet here. The emphasis is on quality beer, and in winter a cask of Old Tom sits on the bar. Lunchtime choices include excellent pies, some homemade and others from a local butcher. Q◑⊞≉(Davenport)🍺♣P

Crown

154 Heaton Lane, Heaton Norris, SK4 1AR (under viaduct)
🕐 12-11 (10.30 Sun)
☎ (0161) 429 0549 🌐 thecrowninn.uk.com

Beer range varies 🄷
Situated on the main junction, the Crown is a busy pub with a choice of 14 beers and one cider on draught. The ever-changing ale range usually features at least one brew from Bank Top, Pictish and Copper Dragon breweries. Off the bar there are several rooms, one with a pool table. The large beer garden behind the pub affords an impressive view of Stockport's famous railway viaduct. On Tuesday evening there is a folk and acoustic club. ♨❀≹🚌🍎⌐

Olde Vic

1 Chatham Street, Edgeley, SK3 9ED (corner of King St West)
✪ 5 (7 Sat)-11; 7-10.30 Sun
☎ (0161) 480 2410
Beer range varies 🄷
One-roomed character pub with an old factory clocking-in machine to the left of the door as you enter and an open log fire at the far end. The strict no-swearing rule belies the easy-going, friendly atmosphere. The pub is particularly busy when Sale Sharks have a home game. Five handpump dispensers provide an ever-changing range of guest beers, usually from micro-breweries, and one handpump is reserved for draught ciders. Note that the pub is only open in the evenings.
♨❀≹🚌🍎⌐

Railway

1 Avenue Street, SK1 2BZ (corner of Avenue St and Gt Portwood St, A560)
✪ 12-11 (10.30 Sun)
☎ (0161) 429 6062
Porter Mild, Floral Dance, Sunshine, seasonal beers; guest beers 🄷
This single-roomed street corner pub is a showcase for the Porter Brewery. No fewer than 11 handpumps dispense the full Porter range, including seasonal and one-off brews, plus three guest beers at weekends. Real cider is also stocked, plus a wide range of Belgian and German bottled beers. Home-made lunches are served Monday to Saturday. Local CAMRA Pub of the Year 2007, it remains under long-term threat of demolition for redevelopment, so get there while you can.
❀◐🚌♣🍎⌐

Thatched House

74 Churchgate, SK1 1YJ
✪ closed Mon & Tue; 8-11 Wed; 8-1am Thu; 7-2am Fri; 3-2am Sat; 3-midnight Sun
☎ (0161) 335 1910 🌐thatched-live.co.uk
Black Sheep Best Bitter; Kelham Island Easy Rider; guest beers 🄷
The Thatched House is the premier live music venue in Stockport – hosting mostly hard rock, metal and punk bands (Thu, Fri & Sat) – so it is not a quiet pub. Architectural details of note are the etched windows and the mosaic in the porch. The stage is on your right as you enter, the bar is on the left. A door leads out to the beer garden which has a barbecue. Two guest ales are available along with two real ciders, 26 bottled beers and two bottled ciders.
❀🚌🍎⌐

Three Shires

32 Great Underbank, SK1 1NB
✪ 11-11 (9 Mon & Tue); 12-9 Sun
☎ (0161) 477 4579
Beer range varies 🄷
One of Stockport's oldest buildings, dating back to c1580, the Shires is now a rising star for cask ale drinkers. It was transformed over three years from a wine bar to a real ale pub and won its first Guide listing last year. Ex-manager, now owner Simon Parry takes great pride in offering beers from smaller and micro-breweries, and the range of four ales always features at least one from Copper Dragon. A varied and freshly prepared choice of meals is also on offer. ◐◑🚌

Strines

Sportsman's Arms

105 Strines Road, SK6 7GE
✪ 12-3, 5-11; 12-11 Sat; 12-10.30 Sun
☎ (0161) 427 2888 🌐sportsmans-arms.co.uk
Boddingtons Bitter; Cains Bitter; guest beers 🄷
A superb picture window view of the Goyt Valley unfolds from this pub, with the interior dominated by a monumental fireplace. The pub is largely open plan, with comfortable seating, but it has kept a snug tap room for the active darts fraternity. On the 358 bus route to Stockport, the last bus is after midnight. Some Manchester trains stop at nearby Strines station.
♨Q❀◐◑⊟♿⛺🚌(358)♣P

Stubshaw Cross

Cross Keys

76 Golborne Road, WN4 8XA (from Ashton Centre follow A58, turn right on B5207)
✪ 6 (4 Tue-Thu)-midnight; 12-1am Fri & Sat; 12-11.30 Sun
☎ (01942) 727965
Jennings Cumberland; guest beers 🄷
Dating from 1893, this is the only pub in Stubshaw Cross. An old-fashioned inn and winner of local CAMRA New Cask Outlet award in 2003, the bar is situated in the main room. There is a back lounge and a small games room; pub teams play in local darts, pool and dominoes leagues. A range of Sky sports is shown on TV. Snacks are available on request, and for special occasions a buffet can be ordered in advance. ❀♿🚌(600, 601)♣

Summerseat

Footballers Inn

28 Higher Summerseat, BL0 9UG OS788145
✪ 2 (12 Sat)-11.30 (midnight Fri & Sat); 12-11 Sun
☎ (01204) 883363 🌐footballersinn.co.uk
Caledonian Deuchars IPA; Hydes Original Bitter; Taylor Landlord; guest beers 🄷
This friendly, family-run pub in the quiet village of Summerseat caters for all. One large room is divided into several separate drinking areas. The bar boasts six cask beers, offering a wide selection of ales. Enjoy the excellent views from the rear garden where you can play petanque, or even practise your golf swing on the covered driving range. The pub runs numerous social events including a very popular quiz evening. It is dog friendly and also a Wi-Fi hot spot.
❀≹(E Lancs Steam Railway)♣P⌐

Swinton

White Horse

384 Worsley Road, M27 0FH (A572, opp Lime Avenue)
12-11 (midnight Fri & Sat)
☎ (0161) 794 2404
Boddingtons Bitter; Theakston XB; guest beers Ⓗ
Large whitewashed pub set back slightly from the main road. Although opened out, the interior maintains four distinct areas all served by the bar to the right of the front entrance. Handpumps are spread around the bar, but a list is usually chalked on a beam above and behind the bar in a central spot. A frequently busy pub with a good mix of customers, live football is shown on a large screen.
❀◐♿🚌P⅟

White Swan

186 Worsley Road, M27 5SN (close to jct A572/A580, East Lancs Rd)
12-11 (10.30 Sun)
☎ (0161) 794 1504
Holt Mild, Bitter Ⓗ
Traditional and very popular Holt outlet, built in the 1920s. The multi-roomed interior features a lounge with wood panelling and an attractive stained-glass window, and a popular vault where traditional pub games are played. At the rear is a large function room for familes, TV matches or darts. Two smaller rooms were transformed into one large space when the dividing wall was removed. All rooms are decorated with interesting pictures and artefacts, adding to the ambience of this fine pub. ❀🚌(12, 26)♣P⅟

Tyldesley

Half Moon

115-117 Elliot Street, M29 8FL
11-4, 7-midnight; 12-11 Sun
☎ (01942) 873206
Boddingtons Bitter; Holt Bitter Ⓗ
A long-established Holt hostelry, this popular and friendly local free house caters for all ages. The main lounge has various seating areas around the walls and features interesting display cabinets. There is also a second lounge, while in summer the patio offers splendid views of Winter Hill and the Pennines. ❀♣

Mort Arms

235-237 Elliot Street, M29 8FL
12-midnight (1am Sat); 12-11 Sun
☎ (01942) 883481
Holt Mild, Bitter Ⓗ
Excellent 1930s pub that has undergone little alteration through the years and remains popular with all ages. The main entrance is split between the bright, lively tap room and the lounge, adorned with wood panelling and etched glass. Dividing the lounge is the remains of a supporting wall with a fireplace on one side and a piano on the other. The pub is often used by Tyldesley Brass Band after practice. ♣

Uppermill

Cross Keys

OL3 6LW (off A670 up Church Rd)
12-midnight (11 Sun)
☎ (01457) 874268
Lees Bitter, Moonraker, seasonal beers Ⓗ
Overlooking Saddleworth Church, this attractive, 18th-century stone building has exposed beams throughout. The public bar also features a stone-flagged floor and Yorkshire range. The centre for many activities including Mountain Rescue, Garland Girls and Saddleworth Runners, it is especially busy during annual events such as the Folk Festival (July), the Road and Fell Race and the Rushcart Festival (both in Aug). It also hosts folk nights (Wed & Sun) in the barn. Food is served until 7.30pm (8pm Sat); children are welcome.
Q❀◐♣P⅟

Waggon Inn

34 High Street, OL3 6HR
11.30-11 (midnight Fri & Sat); 12-10.30 Sun
☎ (01457) 872376 thewaggoninn.co.uk
Robinson's OB, Unicorn, Ⓗ **Old Tom,** Ⓖ **seasonal beers** Ⓗ
This mid-19th century stone pub stands in a picturesque village opposite Saddleworth Museum and the Huddersfield narrow canal. With a central bar, three rooms and a restaurant, it also offers high quality en-suite B&B. The venue for many annual events, it takes part in the Whit Friday brass band contest, the July folk festival, and in August the Yanks weekend and Rushcart Festival. Good home-cooked food is available, including senior and early bird specials, as well as themed events (no eve meals Sun or Mon).
Q❀◐Å⇌(Greenfield)🚌(184, 350)
♣P⅟

Urmston

Urmston

Stretford Road, M41 9WE
12-11 (11.30 Fri & Sat)
☎ (0161) 865 2568
Lees GB Mild, Bitter, seasonal beers Ⓗ
Recent refurbishment has seen the welcome return of a real fire in the quiet east corner of this big roadhouse-style pub. The main room is divided into smaller, cosier sections by a curious Wendy House arrangement. Pool and TV are available in a vault to the north side of the bar. The large car park sees occasional displays of traction engines, particularly during Urmston's May bank holiday weekend Steam Rally. ❀⇌(Humphrey Pk)🚌P

Wardley

Morning Star

520 Manchester Road, M27 9QW (on A6 near M60/61 flyover)
12-11 (midnight Fri & Sat); 12-10.30 Sun
☎ (0161) 794 4927
Holt Mild, Bitter, seasonal beer Ⓗ
An imposing roadhouse set well back from the A6, the Morning Star is a busy community pub with a lively traditional vault, once two rooms, running the full depth of the building on the left side. Similarly opened out on the other

side of the bar, a small snug area has been retained, leading to a large square lounge. Good value breakfasts and lunches are served (Tue-Fri until 1.45pm), there is a quiz every third Wednesday, while Saturday is music night. ⏳🌣◁Φ🖾≠(Moorside)🚍♣P⌐

Westhoughton

Brinsop Country Inn

584-592 Chorley Road, BL5 3NJ (on A6, 500m from A6027 roundabout)
✪ 12-3, 5.30-11; 12-11 Fri & Sat; 12-10.30 Sun
☎ (01942) 811113
Thwaites Bitter; guest beers ⊞
Genuine free house on the busy A6, midway between Westhoughton and Horwich. The main drinking area is comfortably furnished and there is a small, cosy room to the left of the bar. Five guest beers change frequently, and the restaurant serves home-cooked food and bar meals at all times. Just 20 minutes' walk from the Reebok Stadium, it is always busy on match days; visiting away fans are welcome. Q🌣◁Φ 🖾≠(Horwich Parkway)P

Whalley Range

Hillary Step

199 Upper Chorlton Road, M16 0BH
✪ 4-11.30 (12.30am Fri & Sat); 12-11.30 Sun
☎ (0161) 881 1978
Thwaites Thoroughbred; guest beers ⊞
Lively modern bar, a pub for conversation, with wonderful bar snacks but no meals. Live jazz is performed on Sunday, and broadsheet newspapers are available most of the time. Three guest beers are generally sourced from a micro-brewery, and there is also a good selection of wines and whiskies. Coffee is always available. 🌣🖾

Whitefield

Eagle & Child

Higher Lane, M45 7EY (next to Whitefield Golf Club)
✪ 12-midnight
☎ (0161) 766 3024
Holt Mild, Bitter ⊞
Large inn situated next to Whitefield Golf Club. The pub crest of the Eagle and Child, which is also the Whitefield town crest, is etched onto the windows. The outside seating area, affording a terrific view of the excellent bowling green, is due to be extended during the coming year. The pub is well used by families at weekends and during the week by the resident darts, dominoes crib and bowls teams. A gem of a pub. 🌣🖾Θ(Besses o' th' Barn)♣P

Wigan

Anvil

Dorning Street, WN1 1ND (next to bus station)
✪ 11-11; 12-10.30 Sun
☎ (01942) 239444
Hydes Mild, Bitter; guest beers ⊞
Popular town centre pub, frequent winner of local CAMRA Pub of the Year, and now Premiership Pub of the Year 2006-2007

(Football and Real Ale Guide). The Anvil has six handpumps dispensing two regular beers plus changing guests from the nearby Allgates Brewery. It also has six continental beers on draught, plus bottles. Attentive bar staff provide excellent service. Only a short distance from the JJB Stadium (home of Wigan Athletic and Wigan RLFC), it gets busy on match days. There is a beer garden to the rear. 🌣≠(Wallgate/ North Western)🚍

Berkeley

27-29 Wallgate, WN1 1LD (opp. Wallgate station)
✪ 12-11 (midnight Fri & Sat); 12-10.30 Sun
☎ (01942) 242041
Theakston Mild, Old Peculier; guest beer ⊞
With its friendly, comfortable atmosphere the Berkeley has something for everyone, and was winner of local CAMRA New Cask Outlet in 2006. Once a coaching house, the cleverly designed interior means that although open plan there is a sense of different seating areas in the bar. Regular sporting fixtures are shown on large plasma screens. Food is served daily until 8pm. The first floor function room is available for hire. There is a dress code on Saturday night – no trainers or tracksuits. ◁Φ≠(Wallgate/North Western)🚍

Bowling Green

106 Wigan Lane, WN1 2LS
✪ 3 (12 Sat)-11 (1am Fri & Sat); 12-11 Sun
☎ (01942) 519871
Caledonian Deuchars IPA; Greene King Old Speckled Hen; Tetley Mild, Bitter; guest beers ⊞
Guest ales from various breweries change frequently at this popular pub. There are two well-appointed lounges, and a large beer garden at the rear which can get very busy in summer. This is the favourite pub for local football fans on match days, and there are resident darts and dominoes teams. Daily newspapers are provided, and bands play at the weekend. A function room is available for hire. 🛏🌣🖾≠(Wallgate/North Western)🚍(362)♣⌐

Royal Oak

111-115 Wigan Lane, WN1 1XL (on A49, N of centre)
✪ 4-midnight; 12-1am Fri & Sat; 12-midnight Sun
☎ (01942) 323137 ⊕ royaloakwigan.co.uk
Mayflower seasonal beer; Tetley Bitter; guest beers ⊞
Situated just off the ring road on the edge of the town centre, this multi-roomed pub is served by a long bar dispensing a good range of real ales as well as draught and bottled foreign beers. The Royal Oak is the brewery tap for the Mayflower Brewery (located at the rear of the pub). It hosts regular beer, live music and food festivals. There is a large garden to the rear, often used for barbecues. 🌣♿≠(Wallgate/North Western)♣⌐🖵

Tudor House

New Market Street, WN1 1SE (towards Frog Lane, opp college)
✪ 11-midnight; 10.30-11.30 Sun
☎ (01942) 700296 ⊕ thetudorhouse.co.uk
Beer range varies ⊞

A former nunnery, the Tudor features an eclectic mix of original and 21st-century furnishings arranged haphazardly in its two rooms, creating a warm, homely atmosphere. A student hangout, this venue is an important part of the live music scene – it has enough space for a stage and dance floor (packed on event nights). Poetry nights are hosted on the second Thursday in the month. It has two TV screens and outside two beer gardens.
✿◑≠(Wallgate/North Western)🖾

Winton

Ellesmere Inn

26 King William Street, M30 8HZ (50m from B5211/B5229 jct, behind Egerton Arms)
🕔 11-11.30; 12-10.30 Sun
☎ (0161) 707 0385
Holt Mild, Bitter Ⓗ
Tucked away down a side street which was truncated by the M602, this friendly two-roomed pub has a vault and lounge, separated by a central bar. A well-run, friendly pub, it survives despite its location just off the main road, providing a relaxed atmosphere and a relaxing pint. The lounge is comfortable and leads to the covered smoking shelter and garden behind the pub. A good selection of old local photos adorns the walls – some of the regulars can tell you all about them.
✿◖🖾♣⌐

Withington

Victoria

438 Wilmslow Road, M20 3BW (on B5093)
🕔 11-11
☎ (0161) 448 1083
Hydes Mild, Original Bitter, Jekyll's Gold, seasonal beers Ⓗ
This traditional south Manchester local is a relaxed meeting point for students and locals. The Victoria has been a pub for more than a century and has recently won local CAMRA awards as well as brewery recognition as Hydes' 2005 Cellar of the Year (the best of 85 Hydes' pubs). The quiet beer garden is a real suntrap in summer. Football is popular and the games room has a good pool table. Quiz night is Thursday. ✿♿🖾⌐

Woodford

Davenport Arms (Thief's Neck)

550 Chester Road, SK7 1PS (on A5102)
🕔 11-3.30, 5.15-11; 11-11 Sat; 12-3, 7-10.30 Sun
☎ (0161) 439 2435
Robinson's Unicorn, Old Tom, seasonal beers, Hatters Ⓗ
Unspoilt red-brick farmhouse-style pub, beautifully adorned with floral displays in summer. The licence has been in the same family for 75 years. The cosy rooms are warmed by real fires, and children are welcome at lunchtimes in the right-hand

snug. Excellent food is mostly home cooked, with some adventurous specials. Outside, the spacious forecourt and an attractive garden, set well away from the road, are popular in the summer months. 🏨Q🐕✿◑🖾♣P⌐

Worsley

Barton Arms

2 Stablefold, M28 2ED (on B5211)
🕔 12-11
☎ (0161) 727 9321
Black Sheep Best Bitter; Fuller's London Pride; Taylor Landlord; guest beer Ⓗ
This modern Mitchells & Butler-run pub has been smoke-free for some time. It comprises no fewer than seven separate areas, with modern furniture ranging from pouffes and coffee tables to comfortable sofas. A pleasant drinking and dining environment where all are welcome, the accent is on good real ales, with a guest from a national or regional brewery, and delicious food (served until 9pm).
Q✿◑♿🖾P

Worthington

Crown Hotel

Platt Lane, WN1 2XF (off A5106 or A49)
🕔 12-11 (10.30 Sun)
☎ (0800) 068 6678 ⊕ thecrownatworthington.co.uk
Beer range varies Ⓗ
Local CAMRA Pub of the Year 2006, this country pub offers five cask ales, mainly from micro-breweries, and is a rare outlet for Mayflower beers. High quality home-cooked food is served in the bar and conservatory/restaurant. A large decked sun terrace at the rear has patio heaters. The larger of two function rooms hosts beer festivals in March and October, as well as themed evenings, especially at Christmas. Ten en-suite rooms are available for overnight stays.
✿🛏◑🖾(640)P⌐

White Crow

Chorley Road, WN1 2XL (on A5106 between Standish and Coppull)
🕔 12-3, 5.30-11; 12-11 Fri & Sat; 12-10.30 Sun
☎ (01257) 474344
Beer range varies Ⓗ
Large, roadside country pub right on the Lancashire border offering up to four guest ales. It also provides an extensive menu and has earned a deserved reputation for its excellent food. There is a large dining area and children's room, while a pool table and TV are tucked away at one end. Close to Worthington Lakes, the pub benefits from a children's play area next to the stables. There is also a large car park and disabled toilet.
🏨Q🐕✿◑♿🖾♣P⌐

Is there anywhere in this damned place where we can get a decent bottle of Bass?

Alfred, Lord Tennyson, during a pubic performance of one of his poems, **1862**

MERSEYSIDE

Southport

LANCASHIRE

GREATER MANCHESTER

Formby

Lydiate

Crosby

Rainford Junction · Kings Moss

Waterloo

Crank

Aintree

Bootle · Knowsley · St Helens

Kirkdale · Eccleston

New Brighton

Anfield · Prescot

Wallasey Village · Liverpool · Knotty Ash

Birkenhead

Wavertree · Childwall

Greasby

Mossley Hill · Woolton

Barnston · Bebington · Aigburth

CHESHIRE

Heswall · Brimstage

Raby

0 Miles 5

0 Kilometres 8

Barnston

Fox & Hounds

107 Barnston Road, Wirral, CH61 BW
☀ 11-11; 12-10.30 Sun
☎ (0151) 648 7685
Brimstage Trappers Hat; Marston's Pedigree; Theakston Best Bitter; Webster's Yorkshire Bitter; guest beers Ⓗ
Large roadside pub in picturesque Barnston Dale, built in 1911 to replace an earlier building. A lounge, converted from tea rooms, complements the original snug and traditional tiled bar. Local photographs adorn the walls and each room has a real fire in winter. The sheltered stone courtyard is a welcoming stop on the local CAMRA summer pubs walk.
ᗰQ⛄🕭⊕🛏🍴♣P↳

Bebington

Rose & Crown

57 The Village, Wirral, CH63 7PL
☀ 12-11 (midnight Fri & Sat); 12-10.30 Sun
☎ (0151) 643 1312
Thwaites Original, Lancaster Bomber Ⓗ
Former coaching inn built in 1732, now a thriving suburban pub with a bar and games room. Satellite TV is prominent. Nearby is Port Sunlight Village, founded by William Hesketh Lever in 1888 to house his soap factory workers. In the village is the Lady Lever Art Gallery, home to one of the most beautiful collections of art in the country.
🖾≠(Port Sunlight)🚋(410)♣P

Travellers Rest

169 Mount Road, CH63 8PJ
☀ 12-11 (11.30 Wed-Thu; midnight Fri & Sat)
☎ (0151) 608 2988
Caledonian Deuchars IPA; Flowers IPA; Greene King Abbot; Taylor Landlord; Wells Bombardier; guest beers Ⓗ
Former coaching inn, reputed to be over 300 years old. This popular hostelry has a country pub feel, decorated throughout with brasses and bric-a-brac. Beers are available from a central bar serving two other rooms (one no-smoking), and regularly include brews from local micros such as Brimstage. A regular winner of local CAMRA awards, the pub is a big fundraiser for local charities. It is busy with fans visiting nearby Tranmere Rovers' ground, Prenton Park. Excellent lunches are served (not Sun). Q🕭&🚋

INDEPENDENT BREWERIES

Brimstage Brimstage
Cains Liverpool
Cambrinus Knowsley
Canavans Aintree
George Wright Rainford Junction
Higson's Liverpool
Southport Southport
Wapping Liverpool

Birkenhead

Brass Balance

39-47 Argyle Street, CH41 6AB
🕐 9-midnight (1am Fri & Sat)
☎ (0151) 650 8950
Cains Bitter; Greene King Abbot; Marston's Burton Bitter, Pedigree; guest beers Ⓗ
Busy town centre Wetherspoon's in an old restaurant building. The large bar has an outside drinking area. Highly supportive of local breweries, beers from Brimstage, Station House and Spitting Feathers regularly appear. Two draught ciders from the Weston's range are on handpump. A popular meeting place for shoppers, office workers and local residents, good value food is served all day.
❀❶&≠(Conway Pk)🚍●

Stork Hotel ☆

41-43 Price Street, CH41 6JN
🕐 11.30-11; 12-10.30 Sun
☎ (0151) 647 7506
Beer range varies Ⓗ
Built in 1840, this highly ornate pub has a wonderful mosaic floor, etched glass and carved wood. It retains many original wall fittings plus a circular bar with leaded stained glass. The main bar serves two further rooms including the 'news room', still with its original bell pushes. The lunchtime food is excellent value. Winner of many local CAMRA awards, the pub is listed in CAMRA's National Inventory and is Grade II listed.
❀❶≠(Hamilton Sq/ Conway Pk)🚍

Bootle

Wild Rose

Stanley Road, The Triad Centre, L20 3ET
🕐 9-midnight
☎ (0151) 922 0828
Beer range varies Ⓗ
Popular Wetherspoon's house next to the Strand shopping centre, usually offering four or five ales. Numerous bus routes pass the door, and Bootle bus station is nearby. Well worth a visit if you are in the area.
❶&≠(New Strand)🚍

Crank

Red Cat

Red Cat Lane, WA11 8RU (take B5201 off A570)
🕐 12-11 (10.30 Sun)
☎ (01744) 882422
Flowers IPA; guest beers Ⓗ
Situated in the hamlet of Crank, between Rainford and Billinge, the Red Cat nestles in a row of traditional stone cottages. A central bar serves the lounge and dining room, with additional rooms off the bar, and cat-related curios abound. Two rotating guest beers complement the Flowers. A welcome refuge for cyclists and walkers after enduring the ascent of Crank Hill, there is seating outside on the patio. The pub has a well-deserved reputation for good food.
Q❀❶🚍(152, 356)P

Crosby

Crow's Nest

63 Victoria Road, L23 7XY
🕐 12-11 (11.30 Fri & Sat; 10.30 Sun)
☎ (0151) 924 6953
Cains Bitter; Theakston Best Bitter; guest beers Ⓗ
Popular community local in a Grade II listed building with a cosy bar, tiny snug and comfortable lounge. The interior features a tiled floor and original etched windows; the walls are adorned with photographs and advertisements of past Liverpool. Friendly staff offer a warm welcome. There is a changing guest beer during the week and two at the weekend; a board of forthcoming ales is displayed. Outside tables are available at this suburban gem.
Q❀⬛≠(Blundellsands)🚍(53, 62)P

Stamps Wine Bar

4 Crown Buildings, L23 5SR
🕐 12-11 (midnight Fri & Sat)
☎ (0151) 286 2662 🌐 stampsbar.co.uk
Beer range varies Ⓗ
This bistro/bar was once the local post office. The upper floor is a pleasant, peaceful place to spend time chatting and reading. The lower floor with bare bricks and floorboards provides a comfortable and inviting ambience. It holds a regular quiz, film night and curry night on Thursday. The pub is well known for its live music sessions and attracts a varied clientele.
❶&≠(Blundellsands)🚍

Eccleston

Griffin Inn

Church Lane, WA10 5AD (from A570 Windle take B5201 to Prescot)
🕐 12-11 (10.30 Sun)
☎ (01744) 27907 🌐 griffininn.co.uk
Cains Bitter; Marston's Pedigree; guest beer Ⓗ
Situated on the outskirts of St Helens at Eccleston, with a distinctive sandstone frontage, the pub dates from 1812. Cains Bitter and Marston's Pedigree are complemented by a rotating guest beer. Opening hours are extended until midnight when the Saints rugby team is playing at the nearby ground. A large screen TV shows sport in the lounge. Quiz night is Wednesday. There is a popular restaurant and ensuite accommodation. Outside a patio overlooks the children's play area and garden.
Q❀⛺❶⬛🚍P

Formby

Freshfield Hotel

1A Massams Lane, Freshfield, L37 7BD
🕐 12-11 (2am Fri & Sat)
☎ (01704) 874871
Caledonian Deuchars IPA; Greene King IPA, Ruddles County, Abbot; guest beers Ⓗ
An impressive array of beers is always available at the Freshfield, with guest beers usually coming from smaller breweries. A classic community pub, it has a room set aside for comedy evenings, quiz nights and social events. The pub is just a short walk from the

National Trust's red squirrel reserve.
ﾑ⌂◗≈(Freshfield)🚃♣P

Greasby

Irby Mill
Mill Lane, CH49 3NT
🕒 12-11 (midnight Fri & Sat)
☎ (0151) 604 0194
**Cains Bitter; Greene King Abbot; Jennings
Cumberland Ale; Taylor Landlord; Theakston Old
Peculier; Wells Bombardier; guest beers** 🅷
Traditional rural pub built in 1980 on an
ancient mill site. Two rooms are linked by a
narrow bar. An ale drinkers' haven with 13
handpumps, it has won many CAMRA awards.
A favourite haunt of locals and country
walkers from nearby Royden Park and Wirral
Country Park, it is also close to West Kirby and
Hoylake beaches. Always friendly and busy, it
serves excellent, good value food until
7.45pm every day, specialising in rump steaks.
ﾑQ❧⌂◑🚃(186)P

Heswall

Dee View
Dee View Road, CH60 0DH
🕒 12-11 (midnight Fri & Sat)
☎ (0151) 342 2320
**Cains Bitter; Caledonian Deuchars IPA; Marston's
Pedigree; Taylor Landlord; Tetley Bitter; guest
beers** 🅷
Homely local with a single bar, offering a
warm welcome and six handpulled beers,
many from micro-brewers. It sits on a hairpin
bend opposite the war memorial and famous
mirror. The pub has an impressive brasswork
collection throughout. Monday is curry night
and Tuesday offers a popular and entertaining
pub quiz. Excellent Sunday lunches are served
until 4pm. ⌂◑♣P

Johnny Pye
Pye Road, CH60 0DB (next to bus station)
🕒 11-11 (11.30 Thu; midnight Fri & Sat)
☎ (0151) 342 8215
**Banks's Bitter; Marston's Burton Bitter; Jennings
Cumberland Ale** 🅷
Situated on the site of the old bus depot, this
lively, modern pub is named after a local
entrepreneur. Johnny Pye is also associated
with other buildings nearby, he was
responsible for starting the local bus service.
An autographed cartoon of Gordon Banks
adorns the bar. The pub has a wide screen TV,
string football following and darts team. The
pub food is recommended (children are
welcome if eating) and the popular curry night
covers six days. ⌂◗🚃♣⌐

Kings Moss

Colliers Arms
Pimbo Road, WA11 8RD (off B5201 from A570,
follow Houghwood Golf Club signs)
🕒 12-11 (10.30 Sun)
☎ (01744) 892894
Beer ranges varies 🅷
Situated in the rural hamlet of Kings Moss at
the foot of Billinge Hill, part of a row of
traditional miners' cottages next to the former

site of the Hillside Colliery. The interior has a
central bar serving four distinct areas,
decorated with mining memorabilia and a
selection of books. Rotating guest beers
complement the Greenalls Bitter. Popular for
food, families are welcome. There is a small
enclosed children's play area to the rear.
ﾑQ⌂⊞P

Liverpool: Aigburth

Albert
66-68 Lark Lane, L17 8UU
🕒 12-11 (10.30 Sun)
☎ (0151) 726 9119
**Black Sheep Best Bitter; Fuller's London Pride;
Greene King Old Speckled Hen; Taylor Landlord;
guest beers** 🅷
Impressive corner pub located in a
conservation area and popular with locals and
students. Built in 1873 by Robert Cain, it
retains some original fittings, glass, woodwork
and a mosaic floor. It was sympathetically
refurbished in 2004 to provide disabled
facilities and added a rear courtyard garden.
The large central bar with 11 handpumps
serves three rooms. A varied food menu is
available at lunchtime and in the evening, all
day at the weekend. ⌂◑⊞≈(St Michaels)

Liverpool: Anfield

Strawberry Tavern
Breckfield Road South, L6 5DR
🕒 12-11 (1am Fri & Sat); 12-10.30 Sun
☎ (0151) 261 9364
Oakwell Barnsley Bitter, Old Tom Mild 🅷
An Oakwell house, the Strawberry continues
to serve both its beers. The interior is divided
to give a separate games area with pool table
and dartboard. Lying between Breck Road and
West Derby Road, the pub is a welcome oasis
for thirsty fans visiting Liverpool Football Club
(may open early on match days with an early
kick off). Handy for shoppers at the adjoining
ASDA. ⌂⊞🚃(14)♣⌐

Liverpool: Childwall

Childwall Abbey
Score Lane, L16 5EY
🕒 11.30-11 (midnight Fri & Sat); 12-11 Sun
☎ (0151) 722 5293
Beer range varies 🅷
This fine 17th-century inn with its turrets
resembles a castle. Mind your head when
entering the bar! Three ales are available
supplied by Wolverhampton & Dudley. The bar
area caters for drinkers, with several rooms
available for diners. Last orders for food is
9pm. Large umbrellas and tables outside
overlook the bowling green.
Q❧⌂⊞🚃♣P

Liverpool: City Centre

Augustus John
Peach Street, L3 5TX (on University of Liverpool
campus)
🕒 11 (12 Sat)-11; occasional Sun
☎ (0151) 794 5507
Beer range varies 🅷

Modern open plan pub on the university campus catering for students, staff and locals. The AJ has six handpumps with a good mix of micro-brewery beers. Look out for real cider in the cooler. The pub has a large-screen TV and opens on occasional Sundays when Sky Sports is featuring local teams. Occasional beer festivals are hosted.
❀&≠(Lime St)⊖(Central)🚋●'≒

Baltic Fleet
33 Wapping, L1 8DQ
🕘 12 (11 Sat)-11; 12-10.30 Sun
☎ (0151) 709 3116
Wapping Bitter, Summer, Stout; guest beers Ⓗ
Located near the Albert Dock, the building is Grade II listed and based on the 'flat iron' principle. The interior is tastefully decorated with a nautical theme. The beer range comes from the Wapping Brewery located in the cellar accompanied by two guest ales. Brunch is available 12-4pm at weekends with good value lunches on weekdays. Mysterious tunnels in the cellar have led to much speculation among the customers of a dark period in history involving smuggling and press gangs. ♨Q◗⊖(James St)●

Belvedere Arms ☆
8 Sugnall Street, L7 7EB
🕘 12-midnight
☎ (0151) 709 0303
Beer range varies Ⓗ
National Inventory listed pub, recently saved from conversion into an office. This 1830s building has many original fixtures and fittings including the bar, screens, windows and dividers. The quiet, small room to the left with its real fire and old fittings is a real gem. The beer range, with up to four guests, often includes ales from smaller brewers such as Copper Dragon and Spitting Feathers. Pizzas are served all day. ♨Q❀◗🚋'≒

Blackburne Arms
24 Catharine Street, L8 7NL
🕘 12-midnight (1am Sat)
☎ (0151) 707 1249
Black Sheep Best Bitter; Cains Bitter; Caledonian Deuchars; Taylor Landlord; guest beers Ⓗ
Although at the end of a Georgian terrace, this building is deceptive as the exterior only dates from the 1930s. The interior, which was gutted in the 60s or 70s, was sensitively restored in early 2006 to give it a more traditional feel and turn some of the rooms into accommodation. The traditional pub food with a gastro twist (served until 6.30pm) and Sunday roasts are always popular with diners.
❀🛏◗&🚋(86, 82)'≒

Cambridge
Mulberry St, L7 7EE
🕘 11.30-11 (midnight Fri); 4-midnight Sat; 12-11 Sun
☎ (0151) 708 7150
Marston's Burton Bitter; guest beers Ⓗ
Two-roomed pub on the university campus, popular with students. A Marston's pub, usually just one guest beer is available. Good value food is served at lunchtime. Opening time on Saturday may change.
❀◗🚋(86, 82)♣'≒

Cracke
13 Rice Street, L1 9BB (near Philharmonic Hall)
🕘 12-11 (midnight Fri & Sat; 10.30 Sun)
☎ (0151) 709 4171
Cains Bitter; Phoenix Old Oak Ale, Wobbly Bob; guest beers Ⓗ
Originally called the Ruthin Castle, this Victorian back street pub rapidly became known as the Cracke, not because of the singing (for which it was once famous) but because of its small size. Originally it was just what is now – the tiny public bar, but has been extended several times. A back room called the War Office is where people who wanted to talk about the Boer War were dispatched. Food is served until 6pm but tends to run out mid-afternoon on Sunday.
❀◗◨≠(Lime St)⊖(Central)🚋♣●

Crown Hotel ☆
43 Lime Street, L1 1JQ
🕘 11-11; 12-10.30 Sun
☎ (0151) 707 6027
Fuller's London Pride; guest beer Ⓗ
Architectural gem just a few seconds walk from Lime Street Station. The Grade II listed building boasts an Art Nouveau-style interior; the two downstairs rooms retain the original decoration. A function room is available upstairs. A small range of beers is on offer from the large bar. Reasonably priced food is served until the early evening. The friendly staff welcome a wide variety of patrons. This pub has recently celebrated its centenary.
◗◨≠(Lime St)⊖(Central)

Dispensary
87 Renshaw Street, L1 2SP
🕘 12.30-11 (midnight Fri & Sat; 10.30 Sun)
☎ (0151) 709 2180
Cains Dark Mild, IPA, Bitter, FA; guest beers Ⓗ
Opposite Rapid Hardware, this one room pub was formerly a Tetley's pub called The Grapes (the old name is still displayed above the bar). It was bought by Cains and converted to resemble a Victorian street corner local, for which it won the CAMRA/English Heritage refurbishment award. Although a Cains house, two varying guest beers are usually available. Despite being a city centre pub it has much of the feel of a community local.
≠(Lime St)⊖(Central)🚋●

Doctor Duncan's
St John's House, St John's Lane, L1 1HF (on Queen's Square)
🕘 11.30-11 (midnight Fri & Sat); 12-10.30 Sun
☎ (0151) 709 5100
Cains Dark Mild, IPA, Bitter, FA; guest beers Ⓗ
Cains' flagship managed house, usually offering the full range of its beers plus a guest on handpump. A small bar leads to back lounges and the Grade II listed tiled room, which was the original entrance to the Pearl Assurance building, designed by Alfred Waterhouse in 1896-8. Dr Duncan implemented a public health policy to combat cholera epidemics in Liverpool around 1850. This friendly pub can get busy with people enjoying a night out at the weekend.
Q❀◗≠(Lime St)⊖🚋'≒

Everyman Bistro

5-9 Hope Street, L1 9BH (beneath Everyman Theatre)

✪ 12-midnight (2am Thu & Fri); 11-2am Sat; closed Sun

☎ (0151) 708 9545 ⊕ everyman.co.uk

Beer range varies ⊞

A pub that owns a major regional theatre – many years back the theatre went bust and the basement tenant bought the entire building. The bar serves four changing session bitters from breweries including George Wright, York, Copper Dragon and Derwent. Popular, award-winning food is served in a separate room and a function room is available. There is first rate theatre upstairs matched with equally good food and drink downstairs.

Q⊕≷(Lime St)⊖(Central)₩(1, 4)♣

Fly in the Loaf

13 Hardman Street, L1 9AS

✪ 11-11 (midnight Fri & Sat)

☎ (0151) 708 0817

Okells Bitter, IPA; guest beers ⊞

The second Manx Cat inn to be opened on the mainland by the IoM brewer Okells. The previous Kirkland's bakery whose slogan was 'no flies in the loaf' was tastefully refurbished in 2004 to a Steve Holt design with ecclesiastic fittings. Usually up to seven guest beers from micro-breweries are served alongside the Okells' beers on handpump and a good selection of foreign bottled beers. This popular pub is particularly busy weekend evenings and when Sky Sports shows big fixtures.

⊕&≷(Lime St)⊖(Central)₩⌐

Globe

17 Cases Street, L1 1HW (opp Liverpool Central Station)

✪ 11-11; 12-10.30 Sun

☎ (0151) 707 0067

Cains Bitter; Jennings Cumberland Ale; Black Sheep Best Bitter; guest beers ⊞

One hundred years old, this traditional local in the city centre is handy for the shops and stations. A lively, convivial pub, it has a small, quiet back room where a plaque commemorates the inaugural meeting of the Merseyside branch of CAMRA. Beware the sloping floor. A Punch tenancy, two guest beers are usually available.

≷(Lime St)⊖(Central)₩

Head of Steam

7 Lime Street, L1 1RJ

✪ 12-11 (1am Fri & Sat)

☎ (0151) 707 9559

Beer range varies ⊞

Situated inside Lime Street Station in part of the Grade II listed Great North Western Hotel, the pub has four bars. The Grand Hall contains an impressive array of handpumps and 1840s wall panelling. Studio 58 is a large, modern bar with lots of brushed steel and light wood furniture. The Loft is up the stairs from Studio 58 on a new mezzanine floor. Note that not all of the listed drinking areas may be open.

⊕≷(Lime St)⊖(Lime St)

Lion Tavern ☆

67 Moorfields, L2 2BP

✪ 11-11; 12-10.30 Sun

☎ (0151) 236 1743

Caledonian Deuchars IPA; Lees Bitter; Young's Bitter; guest beers ⊞

The Lion is named after the locomotive that originally worked the Liverpool to Manchester railway. A Grade II listed building, the interior has undergone numerous changes. The original building was much smaller and in 1915 the adjoining licensed premises were acquired, the two buildings amalgamated and the existing corridor layout established. This National Inventory pub attracts a mixed clientele throughout the day including office staff and journalists. Bar food is available, with speciality cheeses and hand-raised pork pies recommended.

⊕₲≷(Lime St)⊖(Moorfields)

Peter Kavanagh's ☆

2-6 Egerton Street, L8 7FY (off Catharine Street)

✪ 12-midnight (1am Fri & Sat)

☎ (0151) 709 3443

Cains Bitter; Greene King Abbot; guest beers ⊞

This back-street pub features in the National Inventory. More than 150 years old, it has original stained glass windows and wooden shutters. Over the years the pub has expanded into two adjoining houses, resulting in lots of small, interestingly shaped rooms. Two snugs boast period wall paintings by Eric Robertson, and wooden benches with carved arms, said to be caricatures of Peter Kavanagh. The staff are very happy to tell visitors about the pub's history and point out its interesting features.

Q❀₩⌐

Philharmonic ☆

36 Hope Street, L1 9BX

✪ 12-midnight

☎ (0151) 707 2837

Beer range varies ⊞

Grade II listed and featuring in CAMRA's National Inventory, the Philharmonic was described by no less an authority than historic pub expert Geoff Brandwood as the finest pub of its kind. The interior is divided into several discrete drinking areas, notably the splendid and recently refurbished Grand Lounge. The upstairs room is now a restaurant. Ladies are invited to visit the amazingly ornate gentlemen's toilet, but it is polite to check with the bar staff before doing so.

Q⊕₲&≷(Lime St)⊖(Central)₩(86)

Richard John Blackler

Units 1 & 2 Charlotte Row, L1 1HU

✪ 9-1am

☎ (0151) 709 4802

Beer range varies ⊞

Located in the former Blackler's department store, this large open plan pub is a typically spacious Wetherspoon's conversion, handily placed for city centre shops, hotels and railway stations. A long bar serves a single room with an area dedicated to serving good value meals, available all day. At least two guest beers are usually on offer. The pub regularly participates in the company's national beer festivals.

⊝⊕&≷(Lime St)⊖(Central/Lime St)

Roscoe Head

24 Roscoe Street, L1 2SX

☼ 11.30 (12 Sat)-midnight; 12-11 Sun
☎ (0151) 709 4365
Jennings Bitter; Tetley Burton Ale; guest beers Ⓗ
Ever present in the Guide, this traditional pub has been run by the same family for more than 20 years. Recently refurbished, it has retained the original layout with a tiny snug, bar, front parlour and back room. There are usually two guest beers. Quiz night is Tuesday and cribbage can be played here. Roast dinner on Sunday is recommended.
♨Q◖▣�₹(Lime St)⊖(Central)🖥♣

Ship & Mitre

133 Dale Street, L2 2HU (by Birkenhead tunnel entrance)
☼ 11-11 (midnight Thu-Sat); 12-11 Sun
☎ (0151) 236 0859 ⊕ shipandmitre.com
Beer range varies Ⓗ
An Art Deco building from about 1935, the Mitre was for many years Bent's flagship pub. Unfortunately in the 1970s new owners thought it could be improved by turning it into a replica of a ship. Fortunately little damage was done to the upstairs room which has now been returned to its original Art Deco splendour. At least 12 real ales are on handpump as well as many imported bottles. Evening meals are available Thursday to Saturday.
Q◖▷≹(Lime St)⊖(Moorfields)🖥♣♦

Swan Inn

86 Wood Street, L1 4DQ
☼ 12-11 (2am Thu-Sat); 12-10.30 Sun
☎ (0151) 709 5281 ⊕ theswaninn.org
Hydes Original; Phoenix Wobbly Bob; guest beers Ⓗ
This back-street boozer used to be surrounded by derelict warehouses. However, recent developments of the FACT Cinema and Arts Centre on one side and upmarket flats on the other now make it look quite out of place. Set on three levels, only the ground floor has six guests as well as the regular beers. A fairly basic pub with wooden floors, it is renowned for its award winning rock juke box.
&≹(Lime St)⊖(Central)🖥♦

Thomas Rigby's

23-25 Dale Street,, L2 2EZ
☼ 11.30-11
☎ (0151) 236 3269
Okells Bitter; guest beers Ⓗ
Thomas Rigby was a wholesale wine and spirit dealer. The Grade II listed buildings that bear his name once comprised offices and a pub called the George. Today, you will find an extensive world beer range and up to four changing guest ales from a range of breweries. The pub has won numerous awards and accolades for its beer and food. One room has a friendly and efficient table service. Food is served daily until 7pm.
⊛◖▷▣≹(Lime St)⊖(Moorfields)

White Star

2-4 Rainford Gardens, L2 6PT
☼ 11.30-11; 12-10.30 Sun
☎ (0151) 231 6861 ⊕ thewhitestar.co.uk
Beer range varies Ⓗ
Rare traditional Victorian public house located among the more glitzy establishments of the

historic Mathew Street area. The White Star abounds with local memorabilia and pictures of White Star liners. A strong sporting theme is highlighted not only by an abundance of boxing photography but also the regular broadcasting of football matches on screens in both rooms. It is linked with bars in the Czech Republic and Norway. House beers are from the Bowland range.
◖▣≹(Lime St)⊖(Central/ Moorfields)

Liverpool: Kirkdale

Thomas Frost

177-187 Walton Road, Kirkdale, L4 4AJ (opp Aldi, Iceland and Blockbusters on A59)
☼ 9-11.30
☎ (0151) 207 8210
Beer range varies Ⓗ
This branch of Wetherspoon's occupies the ground floor of a former drapery store. Thomas Robert Frost had a single shop on the site in 1885 and later expanded to occupy the whole block. The layout is open plan, broken only by supporting pillars, with a light and airy feel. It offers a larger selection of real ales than most Wetherspoon's outlets. Handy for Goodison Park, the pub has a family area, but no children are permitted on Liverpool or Everton home match days. ♿◖▷&P느

Liverpool: Knotty Ash

Wheatsheaf

186 East Prescot Road, L14 5NG (on A57 Liverpool to Prescot road)
☼ 11-midnight (1am Fri & Sat)
☎ (0151) 228 5080
Cains Bitter Ⓗ
This multi-roomed pub still displays the etched windows of the nearby Joseph Jones brewery some 80 years after its demise. It is probably the only pub in Liverpool still offering table service in the lounge and snug. The bar shows sport on TV. Q쉎🖥P

Liverpool: Mossley Hill

Storrsdale

43-47 Storrsdale Road, L18 7JY
☼ 3-11; 2-11.30 Fri; 12-11.30 Sat; 12-11 Sun
☎ (0151) 724 3464
Jennings Cumberland Ale; Taylor Landlord; guest beers Ⓗ
Two-room local with a comfortable wood-panelled lounge and traditional stone floored bar with darts and a juke box. Leaded windows and attractive exterior tiling reflect the 1930s construction. Sky football is shown. A small yard to the side has tables and benches for outdoor drinking in summer. Live music plays on Saturday evening and Wednesday is quiz night. Hot snacks are available on request. ⊛&🖥(86)♦

Liverpool: Wavertree

Edinburgh

4 Sandown Lane, L15 8HY
☼ 12-midnight
☎ (0151) 733 3533
Cains Dark Mild, IPA, Bitter, FA, seasonal beers Ⓗ

Small community local with a lively atmosphere in the bar. This Cains managed house has the full range of its beers on handpump. A cosy side room is quieter for relaxation and conversation except on Monday night when an Irish folk session is hosted. Quiz night is Tuesday. ❀🖾(79)♣⏄

Liverpool: Woolton

Gardeners Arms
101 Vale Road, L26 7RW
✪ 4 (2 Fri)-11; 12-11 Sat & Sun
☎ (0151) 428 1443
Cains Traditional Bitter; Caledonian Deuchars IPA; guest beers Ⓗ
Small friendly side street local hidden behind flats, a short walk from the village centre. A relaxed and friendly one room community pub, it has separate drinking areas around a central bar. It is home to a number of local sports teams including golf, football and ladies' netball. Note the Titanic History of Events display on the back wall and the large collection of bottled spirits. Sky TV shows major events and a popular quiz is held on Tuesday evening. Q🖾(76, 77)

White Horse
2 Acrefield Road, L25 5JL
✪ 12-midnight
☎ (0151) 428 1862
Black Sheep Best Bitter; Cains Bitter; Caledonian Deuchars IPA; guest beers Ⓗ
This cosy local in the centre of the village dates from the time when Woolton was a separate settlement, and is something of a local institution. Three wood-panelled drinking areas are decorated with much brasswork and photographs of old Woolton. Two guest beers are available, usually from regional brewers. Good value food is served including a daily special. There is even a home delivery service for Sunday lunches. Quiz night is Wednesday and Spanish lessons are held on Monday. ❀◑

Lydiate

Scotch Piper ☆
Southport Road, L31 4HD (on A5147)
✪ 12-3, 5.30-midnight (1am Fri); 12-1am Sat; 12-midnight Sun
☎ (0151) 526 0603 ● fortunecity.com/millenium/ellerburn/53/
Banks's Bitter; guest beers Ⓗ
Thatched inn on the edge of Lydiate overlooking fields. This largely unspoilt multi-roomed pub claims to date from 1310, despite three fires in living memory. After the last fire in 1985 examination of the roof timbers dated them to the 16th century. Though the pub has an outdoor disabled toilet the building itself is not wheelchair accessible. Usually a quiet pub, it attracts a large group of bikers on Wednesday. ♨Q❀❀(300)♣P

New Brighton

Clarence Hotel
89 Albion Street, CH45 9JQ
✪ 11.30-11 (midnight Fri & Sat); 12-10.30 Sun
☎ (0151) 639 3860

Caledonian Deuchars IPA; Camerons Castle Eden Ale; guest beers Ⓗ
Friendly suburban pub with a separate bar, lounge and dining/function room, a five minute walk from New Brighton Station (Merseyrail Wirral Line). Handpumps are on the lounge side of the drinking area, dispensing a varied range of up to three guest beers. The pub holds an excellent annual beer festival in July. Good home cooked food is served Thursday to Sunday. Winner of many local CAMRA awards including Wirral Pub of the Year 2005. ⏍❀◑🖾♿&⏄⮀🖾⏄

Prescot

Sun Inn
11 Derby Street, L34 4LE (200 metres from bus station)
✪ 12-11
☎ (0151) 426 7574
Tetley Bitter; guest beers Ⓗ
Stone-clad old-style local, conveniently situated by the main road into Prescot from Liverpool. It has several rooms served by a central bar. The comfortable lounge has a large real fire and the public bar has a dart board and is decorated with drawings of the regulars. The pub maintains a traditional Edwardian feel with attractive features including old etched windows. ♨🖾🖾(10, 10A)♣

Raby

Wheatsheaf Inn
Raby Mere Road, CH63 4JH (From M53 jct 4 take B5151)
✪ 11.30-11; 12-10.30 Sun
☎ (0151) 336 3416
Brimstage Trappers Hat; Greene King Old Speckled Hen; Tetley Bitter; Theakston Best Bitter; Thwaites Original; guest beers Ⓗ
Ancient thatched pub of great character, rebuilt after a fire in 1611. Wirral's oldest pub, an inn for 350 years, it originally dates from the 13th century. It is reputed to be haunted by Charlotte, who died here. A main bar with nine handpumps serves two rooms and the dining room. The walls are decorated with photos of old Raby. The pub's antiquity is betrayed be the low beamed ceiling and doorways – mind your head! ♨Q⏍❀◑&🖾P⏄

Rainford Junction

Junction
News Lane, WA11 7JU (from A570 follow Rainford Junction signs)
✪ 12-midnight (1am Sat)
☎ (01744) 882876 ● thejunctionrainford.co.uk
Weetwood Old Dog Bitter; guest beers Ⓗ
Community local adjacent to Rainford Junction station, home to numerous clubs. Live music plays on Wednesday evening with blue grass on Sunday and folk on Thursday, as well as club sessions in the upstairs function room. Rotating beers from Weetwood of Taporley are dispensed in addition to the guest beers. Pool and darts are played in the bar. Look out for the August beerfest held in a marquee in

the rear car park. Quiz night is Monday.
❀◗❀⬤�¬⊟➡♣P

St Helens

Abbey Hotel

1 Hard Lane, Denton's Green, WA10 6TL (just off
A570, 1 mile N of town centre)
☻ 12-11 (10.30 Sun)
☎ (01744) 25649
Holt Mild, Bitter, seasonal beers ⍾

A former coaching inn, just off the A570 to the
north of the town, heading towards Rainford,
this Holt's pub has been tastefully refurbished
retaining many original features. The central
bar area serves five rooms each with its own
character. Traditional pub games including
dominoes and pool are played in the games
room. A large screen caters for most popular
sporting broadcasts. Quiz night is Thursday.
Private parties can be catered for.
Q❀◗♣P⌐

Beechams Bar

Water Street, WA10 1PZ (jct of Westfield St and
Water St)
☻ 12-11; closed Sun
☎ (01744) 623420
Beer range varies ⍾

Part of St Helens college complex, the bar is
next to the Smith Kleine Annexe. The
contemporary bar area has been extended to
fill the space vacated by the brewhouse. Soft
leather furnishings with comfortable sofas
create a relaxing enviroment. CAMRA
members and students receive a 10%
discount on production of a current
membership card or NUS card. Three rotating
guest beers are generally available to
complement Fuller's London Pride.
◗&≈(Central)⊟⍿

Glass House

5 Market Street, WA10 1NE (near parish church)
☻ 9-midnight
☎ (01744) 762310
**Greene King Abbot; Marston's Pedigree; guest
beers** ⍾

Wetherspoon's conversion named to reflect
the town's historic links with the glassmaking
industry. A former discount store, it is situated
in the main shopping area of Church Street.
Disabled access is from the rear patio area via
a lift. Bargain prices result in long waits at the
bar; busy mealtimes are best avoided as there
are rarely enough staff to cope with demand.
Large screen TVs dominate, with an extra
projection screen for major sporting events.
Children are tolerated only if dining.
❀&≈(Central)

Sutton Oak

73 Bold Road, WA9 4JG (on B5204)
☻ 4-11; 12-midnight Fri & Sat; 12-11 Sun
☎ (01744) 813442 ⊕ suttonoak.co.uk
Beer range varies ⍾

Newly refurbished, child-friendly pub close to
the station serving at least three guest beers,
usually from independent breweries, plus a
cider. A large screen TV shows sport in the bar.
Patio doors lead to an extensive garden with
children's play area where a marquee is
erected for beer festivals over the August bank

holiday, and occasional barbecues. Other beer
festivals are held throughout the year, plus an
Easter cider festival. Local CAMRA Pub of the
Year 2006. ❀⬤&≈(Junction)⊟(141)♣♠P⍿

Turks Head

49-51 Morley Street, WA10 2DQ
☻ 2 (12 Sat)-11; 12-11 sun
☎ (01704) 751289
Beer range varies ⍾

Distinctive building with its own turret
dividing into a lounge and bar adorned with a
huge collection of spirit miniatures and
medicine bottles. The Turk's Head motif is
visible on the etched glass and bar front of the
central serving area, home to a range of up to
10 rotating ales. A large screen shows sport
and there is a pool table and dart board on the
mezzanine level. Regular festivals, music
evenings and quiz nights are hosted and curry
night is Thursday. ⍲◗⬤⊟♠⍿

Southport

Ainsdale Conservative Club

630 Liverpool Road, Ainsdale, PR8 3BH
☻ 5 (12 Sat)-midnight; 12-11 Sun
☎ (01704) 578091
Beer range varies ⍾

Due to the efforts of the bar manager, a local
CAMRA member responsible for the beers at
the Southport Beer Festival for many years,
this local community club always has an
interesting choice of guest ales. Recently
decorated to a comfortable standard and with
the addition of a large screen TV, customers
settle in the large L-shaped room or
congregate at the bar at one end and shoot
the breeze. TV screens show sporting and
other major events. Occasional entertainment
is hosted including barbecues in the garden.
Q❀≈♣

Baron's Bar (Scarisbrick Hotel)

239 Lord Street, PR8 1NZ
☻ 11-11 (11.30 Fri & Sat); 12-11 Sun
☎ (01704) 543000 ⊕ scarisbrickhotel.com
Beer range varies ⍾

A flagship bar for real ale in Southport, the
Baron's Bar is the place to go if you want an
adventurous choice of ales served in excellent
condition. It is emphatically the place to go if
you enjoy real cider, with two often available.
The bar itself is decorated in baronial style, but
not pompously so. Every May there is a beer
festival and smaller festivals are held at other
times of the year too. Q❀&≈⊟♠

Berkeley Arms

19 Queens Road, PR9 9HN (off Manchester Road)
☻ 4 (12 Fri & Sat)-11; 12-10.30 Sun
☎ (01704) 500811 ⊕ berkeley-arms.com
**Adnams Bitter; Banks's Bitter; Hawkshead
Bitter; Marston's Pedigree; Moorhouses Black
Cat; Taylor Landlord** ⍾

A long-standing entry in the Guide, though
with several name changes, the Berkeley
Arms is a Victorian-style small hotel with a
spacious bar area. It is the only pub for miles
around to serve the excellent Hawkshead
Bitter. A range of pizzas is available to
accompany the beers. Q⌀❀⬤◗≈⊟♣P

Bold Arms

59-61 Botanic Road, PR9 7NE (near Botanic Gardens)
☼ 11.30-11; 12-10.30 Sun
☎ (01704) 228192
Tetley Dark Mild, Bitter; guest beers ⊞
The oldest pub in Southport and at the centre of the attractive village of Churchtown – itself the oldest and quaintest part of what is now Southport – the Bold Arms was once a coach house and is well over 300 years old. The guest ales are drawn from a wide range of smaller breweries. There are real fires in some of the rooms. ⋈⋑⊛◑⊞⋔⋤⊕P

Cheshire Lines

81 King Street, PR8 1LQ
☼ 11.30-midnight (1am Thu-Sat); 12-10.30 Sun
☎ (01704) 532178
Tetley Dark Mild, Bitter ⊞
The Cheshire Lines Tetley is proof that a beer from a global giant can be very tasty when treated well. Named after the railway line that used to terminate not far from the pub, the pub nestles among bed and breakfast hotels in a side street running parallel to Lord Street. Very much a local, and excellent for mixed grills, it offers a comfortable drinking space and homely atmosphere. ⋈⊛◑⇌⋤⊕⋔

London

14 Windsor Road, PR9 0SR
☼ 12-midnight (1am Fri & Sat); 12-11 Sun
☎ (01704) 542885
Oakwell Old Tom Mild, Barnsley Bitter ⊞
A full range of pub games is offered at the London – darts, dominoes, pool and even a bowling green are all available – and the cups and trophies of successful teams line the walls. For the less sporty beer drinker, the availability of Oakwell beers is a major draw – no other pub regularly serves them for miles. The spacious interior means there is plenty of room for relaxed conversation. ⋑⊛⇌⋤⊕P

Mason's Arms

44 Anchor Street, PR9 0UT (off London Street)
☼ 11-1am
☎ (01704) 534123
Robinson's Unicorn, seasonal beers ⊞
Tucked away in a corner dominated by estate agents, the Mason's Arms continues to be the only pub in Southport to offer Robinson's ales on a regular basis. Although only one minute from the station and next to the heart of Southport's shopping area, the pub has the feel of a community local. The small snug is especially welcoming in winter when a log fire blazes. There is a rooftop garden for the summer. ⋈⊛⇌⋤

Sir Henry Segrave

93-97 Lord Street, PR8 1RH
☼ 9-midnight
☎ (01704) 530217
Greene King Abbot; Marston's Burton Bitter; guest beers ⊞
The Sir Henry Segrave is a Wetherspoon's pub with all the characteristic virtues of the chain. Named after an early racing driver, it is housed in a building of some architectural interest that was in Victorian times a department store. The pub offers some of the lowest prices in Southport for its regular beers and its guests are drawn from a wide variety of breweries, often including ales from the George Wright range. Typical Wetherspoon's food is good value. Q⊛◑⋤⋤⊕

Windmill

12-14 Seabank Road, PR9 0EL (off Lord Street towards the sea)
☼ 11.30-11 (midnight Thu-Sat); 12-10.30 Sun
☎ (01704) 547319
Moorhouses Black Cat; Theakston Best Bitter; guest beers ⊞
The Windmill has a community pub feel despite its location close to the marina. An impressive front garden area is an ideal place to relax on a sunny day after a trip to the beach. Inside there are small seating areas designed for comfortable conversation, the walls lined with old prints. On some nights live music plays. ⊛◑⋤⋔

Wallasey Village

Cheshire Cheese

2 Wallasey Village, CH44 2DH
☼ 11.30-11 (midnight Fri & Sat); 12-11 Sun
☎ (0151) 638 3641
Theakston Mild, Best Bitter; guest beers ⊞
Excellent local transformed from a run-down boozer to a friendly community pub by the present landlord. The multi-room layout includes a public bar, lounge and snug, with handpumps in the lounge. Excellent home cooked food is served until early evening except Thursday. The pub supports darts, golf and other sports teams and stages regular quizzes and beer festivals. It has a large courtyard drinking area. Ten minutes' walk from Wallasey Village Station (Merseyrail Wirral Line). Local CAMRA Pub of the Year 2007. Q⊛◑⋤⇌⊖⋤(403)⋔⊕⋲

Farmers Arms

225 Wallasey Village, CH45 3LG
☼ 11.30-11 (11.30 Fri & Sat); 12-11 Sun
☎ (0151) 638 2110
Cains Bitter; Tetley Bitter; Theakston Mild, Best Bitter ⊞
Excellent community local, now in its 16th consecutive year in the Guide. It has a multi-room layout with public bar, snug and lounge all served from a central bar. Good value home-cooked food is available (not Fri eve-Sun). Quiz night is Tuesday. The pub also runs its own successful golf society. A short walk from Wallasey Village and Grove Road stations, the pub was CAMRA Wirral Pub of the Year in 2004. Q⊛◑⋤⇌(Grove Road)⋤

Waterloo

Brooke Hotel

51 Brooke Road West, L22 2BE
☼ 12-midnight
☎ (0151) 924 7304
Taylor Landlord; Greene King Old Speckled Hen ⊞
Large open plan pub with lounge alcoves to either side of the entrance, a pleasant dining area, outdoor decking and garden. The Brooke has a friendly atmosphere and strong

community clientele. Occasional live bands appear, usually for charity events. There is a TV in the front alcove with games machines nearby and a large pull-down screen for sports events. Unobtrusive background music plays at quieter times. ⚘◑⮝(Blundellsands/Crosby Waterloo) 🚌(53)

Stamps Too

99 South Road, L22 0LR
🕐 12-midnight (11.30 Sun)
☎ (0151) 280 0035
Beer range varies Ⓗ

A welcome addition to the real ale scene in the area, Stamps Too is a long and narrow open plan pub with café style seating, a stage for entertainment and a bar towards the rear. The frontage opens on to the street in warmer weather. A varied bistro menu is served weekdays until 6pm. Quiz night is Wednesday

and live music plays from Thursday to Sunday evening when the pub is at its busiest. Internet access is available. ◑⮝🚌(62)

Volunteer Canteen ☆

45 East Street, L22 8QR
🕐 12-11 (10.30 Sun)
☎ (0151) 928 4676
Black Sheep Best Bitter; Theakston Best Bitter; guest beer Ⓗ

Situated in an attractive side street, this cosy traditional local has a central bar serving both the public bar and lounge, with photographs of old Liverpool, Crosby and Waterloo decorating the walls. The 'Volly' provides table service, a rarity these days, and runs its own golf society and darts team. The public bar has a small TV for sports events. Beautifully maintained, the pub has a warm convivial atmosphere, offering friendly banter and the daily newspapers. Q⬚⮝🚌(53, 62)

Doctor Duncan's, Liverpool, Merseyside.

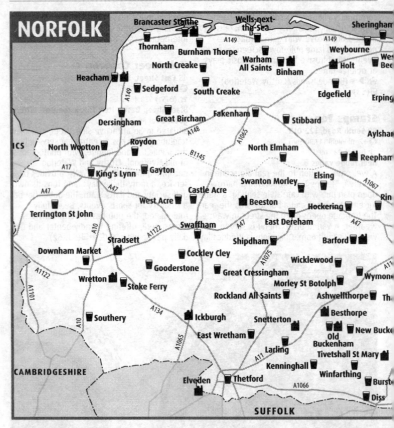

NORFOLK

Brancaster Staithe
Wells-next-the-Sea
Sheringham
Thornham
Burnham Thorpe
Warham All Saints
Weybourne
North Creake
Binham
Holt
Wes Bec
Heacham
Sedgeford
South Creake
Edgefield
Erping
Dersingham
Great Bircham
Fakenham
Stibbard
Aylsham
Roydon
North Elmham
Reepham
North Wootton
ICS
King's Lynn
Gayton
Swanton Morley
Elsing
Rin
West Acre
Castle Acre
Beeston
Hockering
Terrington St John
Swaffham
East Dereham
Stradsett
Shipdham
Barford
Downham Market
Cockley Cley
Wicklewood
Gooderstone
Great Cressingham
Wymon
Wretton
Stoke Ferry
Morley St Botolph
Rockland All Saints
Ashwellthorpe
Th
Southery
Ickburgh
Besthorpe
Snetterton
New Bucke
East Wretham
Old Buckenham
Tivetshall St Mary
Larling
CAMBRIDGESHIRE
Kenninghall
Winfarthing
Burst
Elveden
Thetford
Diss
SUFFOLK

Ashwellthorpe

Kings Head
The Turnpike, NR16 1EL (on B1113)
🕐 11-11; 12-3, 7-11 Sun
☎ (01508) 489419
Greene King Abbot; Woodforde's Wherry; guest beer H
Run by the same family for 13 years, the pub has a large L-shaped bar with a log-burning stove, darts and a pool table. The guest beer comes from a variety of breweries but is always mid-range gravity to complement the regular range. No food is served Monday lunchtime or Sunday-Tuesday evenings. Fresh eggs can be purchased at the bar, and the pub boasts a resident parrot. ♨🚫🍽️🅿️

Aylsham

Feathers
54 Cawston Road, NR11 6EB (on B1145)
🕐 12-11 (10.30 Sun)
☎ (01263) 732314
Wells Bombardier; guest beers H
This Victorian flint-and-brick built pub is a typical no-frills, friendly local town pub. The walls and ceilings in the three small bars are festooned with bric-a-brac and memorabilia including old photos of the town, brewery posters, china jugs and farm implements. There are also many books in one bar complete with reading glasses for customers

to borrow. Three guest ales usually come from local breweries. ♨🚫🍽️🅿️🔼

Barford

Cock Inn
Watton Road, NR9 4AS (on B1108)
🕐 12-3, 6 (7 Sun)-11
☎ (01603) 759266
Blue Moon Easy Life, Sea of Tranquillity, Dark Side, Hingham High H
Old 18th-century coaching inn that is home to two breweries, Blue Moon and Spectrum. All cask ales sold here come from Blue Moon Brewery. A fairly food-oriented pub, it has a number of interconnecting small rooms and a separate restaurant. A large and varied menu is available, including many specials advertised on the numerous blackboards in the pub. The garden has a bowling green. ♨Q🚫🍽️🐾🅿️

Binham

Chequers Inn
Front Street, NR21 0AL (3km S of Stiffkey)
🕐 11.30-2.30, 6-11 (11.30 Fri); 11.30-11.30 Sat; 12-2.30, 7-11 (12-11 summer) Sun
☎ (01328) 830297
Front Street Binham Cheer, Callums Ale, Unity Strong; guest beers H
This flint-stoned village pub near the medieval priory (English Heritage) has one long bar with

Runton
Walcott
Trunch
Happisburgh
rton   Dilham   Lessingham
Ingham   Horsey
on   Smallburgh   Winterton-on-Sea
tishall   Woodbastwick
Salhouse
pe St Andrew   Acle
Norwich   Lingwood
ringland   Strumpshaw   Great Yarmouth
Gorleston-on-Sea
Chedgrave   Reedham
eething   Thurlton
Broome
Geldeston
Earsham
Iburgh

0 Miles   5
0 Kilometres   8

warming open fires. It stocks a range of beers from its own brewery, Front Street, with occasional guest beers from local micros. Liefmans Kriek is on draught, and an excellent range of bottled beers is stocked, with Belgian beers featuring heavily. The chef changes the blackboard menu frequently, offering freshly cooked meals made with mostly local produce. Children are welcome. ⌂❀⏣⦿♿ẠP

Brancaster Staithe

Jolly Sailors

Main Road, PE31 8BJ
☼ 11-11; 12-10.30 Sun
☎ (01485) 210314 ⊕ jollysailors.co.uk
Brancaster IPA, Old Les; guest beer Ⓗ
Busy throughout the year with both locals and tourists, this timeless pub has three cosy drinking areas around the bar, plus a restaurant, conservatory and large beer garden. A micro-brewery on-site produces the house beers, supplemented by a guest ale. Freshly cooked food made with locally sourced ingredients is available 12-9pm. The Brancaster mussels are highly recommended.
⌂Q☄❀⦿🚃(36)♣P

White Horse

Main Road, PE31 8BY
☼ 11-11; 12-10.30 Sun
☎ (01485) 210262

Adnams Bitter; Fuller's London Pride; Woodforde's Wherry; guest beer Ⓗ
Newly refurbished, the relaxed bar area of this award-winning hotel and restaurant maintains its genuine pub feel. Bare floors and scrubbed pine furniture complement the walls, which are covered in old local photographs, and an open log fire spreads warmth and cosiness. The large terrace is a real suntrap and commands unrivalled views over the expansive salt marshes to Scolt Head Island. Bar billiards is played here, and accommodation is available in 15 en-suite rooms. ⌂❀⇆⦿♿Ạ🚃(36)♣P

Broome

Artichoke

162 Yarmouth Road, NR35 2NZ (just off A143)
TM351915
☼ 12-11 (midnight Fri & Sat); closed Mon
☎ (01986) 893325
Adnams Bitter; Elgood's Black Dog Ⓗ/Ⓖ
Built in 1805, this was once home to the brewery tap of the now defunct Crowfoot Brewery at Ditchingham. Recently renovated and sympathetically restored, the bar is on two levels and has a stone floor and bench seating with an inglenook fireplace in the upper bar. The conservatory off the lower bar doubles as a dining/function room. The tap room is visible from the bar, which offers up to four beers plus guests, usually from local breweries. Belgian beers on draught are also available. ⌂Q❀⦿Ạ🚃(580, 588)P⅃

Burnham Thorpe

Lord Nelson

Walsingham Road, PE31 8HL (off B1355)
☼ 11-3, 6-11; closed winter Mon; 12-3, 6.30-10.30 Sun
☎ (01328) 738241 ⊕ nelsonslocal.co.uk
Greene King IPA, Abbot; Woodforde's Wherry; guest beer Ⓖ
The bar of this historic pub has changed little since Nelson entertained the entire village here in 1793. Wooden settles, old pine tables and memorabilia preserve the feel of those long gone days. Real ales are dispensed direct from the tap room. Good contemporary food is served and entertainment includes Thursday music night and a monthly quiz night in winter. There is a large garden and children are made very welcome.
⌂Q❀⦿♿Ạ🚃(27, 39)♣P⅃

Burston

Crown Inn

Crown Green, IP22 5TW
☼ 12-11.30 (10.30 Sun)
☎ (01379) 741257 ⊕ burston-crown.com
Adnams Bitter; guest beers Ⓖ
This attractive 16th-century Grade II listed pub features plenty of exposed beams. Guests can relax in the deep luxury sofas and enjoy the cheery fire blazing in a huge inglenook fireplace on cold evenings, making the pub a cosy haven to enjoy the three real ales served directly from the cask. There are two bars, one with a pool table, and boules is played in the garden during the summer. A small restaurant

serves locally sourced freshly cooked food (no food Sun eve). 🛏🕮⌖◗P

Buxton

Old Crown

Crown Road, NR10 5EN (on B1534)
🕓 12-2, 5-11; 11-midnight Sat; 12-10.30 Sun
☎ (01603) 278159
Adnams Bitter, Broadside; Greene King Old Speckled Hen; Woodforde's Wherry Ⓗ
This old Dutch-gabled inn has recently been refurbished and the interior completely modernised. Once inside the pub, the exposed ceiling beams are the only reminders that this is an old building. The interior consists of three separate rooms: a main lounge with wide-screen TV, a dining room and a games room with pool table and dart board. The large south-facing terrace at the front of the pub has plenty of seats and tables for summer days.
🕮◗♣P⌐

Castle Acre

Ostrich Inn

Stocks Green, PE32 2AE (left through Bailey Gate on green)
🕓 11-11 (midnight Fri & Sat)
☎ (01760) 755398 ⊕ ostrichinn.com
Greene King IPA, Abbot, Old Speckled Hen; guest beer Ⓗ
This 16th century coaching inn has been recently refurbished to provide a traditional bar with inglenook fireplace and log burner, a cosy lounge with comfy sofas, dining room and four bedrooms. Jazz nights are a regular feature and the local folk club meets here once a month. Good food from bar meals to an a la carte menu is available in the evening, snacks and a buffet at lunchtime.
🛏Q🛌🕮⇆◗◗⊟ᴀ⊟P

Chedgrave

White Horse

5 Norwich Road, NR14 6ND
🕓 12-3, 6-11.30 (10.30 Sun)
☎ (01508) 520250
Adnams Broadside; Black Sheep Best Bitter; Caledonian Deuchars IPA; Taylor Landlord; guest beers Ⓗ/Ⓖ
This 18th-century inn has undergone much refurbishment since the present management took over in 2005 and transformed the pub. The interior comprises an L-shaped bar/lounge area with pool table and welcoming log fire at one end. A new spacious dining room has recently opened overlooking the pub's garden and the village bowling green. The doors open out onto a large beer terrace. The pub hosts jazz bands fortnightly, and has two beer festivals each year in April and November. 🛏Q🕮⇆◗◗⅄⊟ᴀ⊟♣P⌐

Cockley Cley

Twenty Churchwardens

Swaffham Road, PE37 8AN (by church)
🕓 11-3, 7-11; 12-3.30, 7-10.30 Sun
☎ (01760) 721439
Adnams Bitter Ⓗ

This historic pub was once the village school, then a Methodist chapel. In 1968 the chapel and adjoining cottages were converted into a village inn. The landlady of 22 years prides herself on keeping a fine pint and serving good wholesome food (home-made pies a speciality). The lanes and paths make this an excellent area for walking, cycling or horse riding. Close by is a reconstruction of an Iceni settlement where Queen Boudicca's followers backed the revolt against the Romans.
🛏Q🛌◗◗♣⇆♣P

Coltishall

Railway Tavern

Station Road, NR12 7JL (on B1150 Coltishall-North Walsham road) OS267203
🕓 2-11 (midnight Fri); 12-midnight Sat; 12-10.30 Sun
☎ (01603) 738316
Wolf Straw Dog; guest beers Ⓗ
A fine 19th-century flint-and-brick local, the Railway is situated at the northern end of this Broadland village, close to the narrow-gauge Bure Valley Railway. It has two distinct drinking areas: a carpeted lounge and a bar with wooden floorboards and a dartboard. There are three open fires providing cheer, while exposed beams and old sash-windows give a traditional feel to the pub. Two guest beers are available. 🛏🛌◗◗⊟♣P

Dersingham

Feathers Hotel

Manor Road, PE31 6LN
🕓 10.30-11 (midnight Fri & Sat); 10.30-10.30 Sun
☎ (01485) 540207 ⊕ thefeathershotel.co.uk
Adnams Bitter; Draught Bass; guest beers Ⓗ

INDEPENDENT BREWERIES

Beeston Beeston
Blackfriars Great Yarmouth
Blue Moon Barford
Brancaster Brancaster Staithe
Buffy's Tivetshall St Mary
Bull Box Stradsett
Chalk Hill Norwich
Elmtree Snetterton
Elveden Elveden
Fat Cat Norwich
Fox Heacham
Front Street Binham
Grain Alburgh
Humpty Dumpty Reedham
Iceni Ickburgh
Norfolk Cottage Norwich
Reepham Reepham
Spectrum Tharston
Tindall Seething
Tipples Acle
Uncle Stuarts Lingwood
Wagtail Old Buckenham
Waveney Earsham
Why Not Thorpe St Andrew
Winter's Norwich
Wissey Valley Wretton
Wolf Besthorpe
Woodforde's Woodbastwick
Yetman's Holt

This fine carrstone hotel is a former coaching house with royal connections; its proximity to Sandringham House makes it popular with tourists. There are two main bars – the saddle bar and the Sandringham bar – the latter warmed by a log fire in winter. Across from the main hotel is the stable bar, which attracts a young crowd with regular live music. Food is available in all bars and the restaurant. There is plenty of entertainment for children in the large garden. ≜Q➲❀☎◑⚊▲⊟(41)♣P⟵

Dilham

Cross Keys

The Street, NR28 9PS (off A149 Stalham-North Walsham road) TG332251

✪ 12-3, 6-11; 12-3, 7-10.30 Sun

☎ (01692) 536398

Adnams Bitter; Greene King IPA; guest beers ⊞

Attractive Broadland village inn close to the north Norfolk coast, just a short walk from quiet moorings. Keen local landlords have built a well-deserved reputation for top-quality beer. The pub is also popular for its home-cooked meals which in summer may be enjoyed on the south facing terrace overlooking the bowling green. Traditional pub games are played in a separate public bar, and the landlady's fine floral displays adorn the saloon. ≜Q❀◑⊕♣P

Diss

Cock Inn

63 Lower Denmark Street, IP22 3BE

✪ 12-11 (10.30 Sun)

☎ (01379) 643633

Adnams Bitter; guest beer ⊞

This 16th-century pub faces a large green on the outskirts of this market town. One bar serves three drinking areas furnished with a range of sofas plus wooden chairs and tables. On cold nights a large log fire welcomes customers. This is a drinkers' pub and no food is served. A large-screen TV provides entertainment in one room. During live music sessions the pub stays open later. ≜❀♣P

Downham Market

Crown Hotel

12 Bridge Street, PE38 9DH

✪ 12-3, 6-11.30; 12-11 Sat; 12-10.30 Sun

☎ (01366) 382322

Adnams Bitter; Greene King IPA, Abbot; guest beers ⊞

A refurbished 17th-century coaching inn at the heart of the old town centre, the Crown is popular with locals and visitors alike. Beer and food are served in the single bar with a beamed ceiling. Guest ales mostly come from East Anglian breweries and the food is good and varied too. Try the Crown on market day to appreciate the true flavour of a market town. ≜◑⚊⊁⊟P

Earsham

Queens Head

Station Road, NR35 2TS (just off A143)

✪ 12-3, 5-11; 12-11 Sat; 12-10.30 Sun

☎ (01986) 892623

Waveney East Coast Mild, Lightweight; guest beers ⊞

Overlooking the village green, this 17th-century pub has a comfortable olde-worlde charm. The single bar features a stone floor and wooden beams, the ceiling is decorated with pump clips of guest beers that have been served there. There is also a function room and games room with pool table. Home to the Waveney Brewing Company, which provides the regular ales, guest beers are also always available. The pub is situated in a popular walking area and dogs are welcome. ≜➲❀◑⊟(580)P⟵

East Dereham

George Hotel

Swaffham Road, NR19 2AZ (near war memorial)

✪ 10-11 (midnight Fri & Sat)

☎ (01362) 696801

Adnams Bitter, Broadside; Beeston Worth the Wait, On the Huh; Woodforde's Wherry; guest beer ⊞

This welcoming bar in a market town hotel is open to non-residents. The landlord strongly promotes local beers. It serves an excellent range of traditional bar meals and has an a la carte restaurant. The comfortable main bar features wood panelling and pictures of local historical interest. There is a fine conservatory as well as a heated outdoor patio for drinkers. The George is handy for the Mid-Norfolk Railway and has a secure car park. ≜❀☎◑⊟P⟵

East Runton

White Horse

High Street, NR27 9NX (on main A149 Cromer-Sheringham coast road)

✪ 12-11 summer; 12-3, 6-11 winter

☎ (01263) 519530

Adnams Bitter, Broadside; Greene King Old Speckled Hen ⊞

The White Horse is situated in a popular tourist area about a mile west of Cromer on the north Norfolk coast road, and is popular with visitors and locals alike. The interior has three rooms: a main bar/lounge, dining room and a small games room with a pool table. Outside there is a small beer terrace – a pleasant place to while away a summer evening. ❀◑⊟P

East Wretham

Dog & Partridge

Watton Road, IP24 1QS

✪ 12-11 (midnight Fri & Sat); 12-10.30 Sun

☎ (01953) 497014

Greene King IPA; guest beers ⊞

The countryside is fast losing the pubs that are its community hub, so it is heartening that Martin and Karen have saved this local from much-threatened closure. They have created a no-nonsense village inn serving two regular ales, with guest beers added in summer. Simple pub food is available (not Mon in winter). This venture deserves your support and encouragement. On bus route Thetford-

Watton Peddars Way Hop on-Hop off.
🏚Q☺❶◐🖳♣P

Edgefield

Pigs
Norwich Road, NR24 2RL (on B1149)
☻ 11-3, 6-11; closed Mon; 12-4 Sun
☎ (01263) 587634
Adnams Bitter, Broadside; Woodforde's Wherry; Yetman's Orange; guest beers Ⓗ
The original Pigges of 1826 became the Three Pigs, before being renamed by its new owners as the Pigs. Extensive renovation during 2007 added a new kitchen, extensions to the restaurant and on-site accommodation, as well as refurbishing the two bar areas. The tasteful decoration includes old local photographs and memorabilia. Live entertainment is sometimes staged.
Q☺❶◐🖳P⌐

Elsing

Mermaid
Church Street, NR20 3EA
☻ 12-3, 7-11; 12-10.30 Sun
☎ (01362) 637640
Adnams Broadside; Wolf Golden Jackal; Woodforde's Wherry; guest beers Ⓖ
Situated in the charming upper Wensum Valley and opposite a large 14th-century church, this pretty 17th-century country pub has a long single bar interior where pool is played at one end and a log fire blazes in winter at the other. Beers are local and gravity-dispensed. Good quality food is served in the bar and restaurant (not Mon lunchtime).
🏚Q☺❶◐&♣P

Erpingham

Spread Eagle
Eagle Lane, NR11 7QA (approx 1 mile E of A140 Aylsham-Cromer road) TG191318
☻ 11-3, 6.30-11 (midnight summer); 11-midnight Sat; 12-4, 7-11 Sun
☎ (01263) 761591
Adnams Bitter, Broadside; Woodforde's Wherry; guest beer Ⓗ
This village pub dates back to 1620 and was previously home to Woodforde's Brewery which has now moved to Woodbastwick. The long, open-plan interior features a central bar, a dining area with a fire at one end and a pool room at the other. It has recently been refurbished and there are plans for a new restaurant and accommodation. 🏚Q☺❶◐▲P

Fakenham

Star
44A Oak Street, NR21 9DY
☻ 12-2.30, 5.30-11.30 (12.30am Thu-Sat); 12-4, 7-11.30 Sun
☎ (01328) 862895
Beer range varies Ⓗ
Once the Star Manor House, owned by a priory, then a farmhouse and finally a coaching inn, this hidden gem in the town centre boasts real beams and fine panelling. Set back from the road, it is easily missed but

well worth seeking out. In the care of the same landlady for more than 20 years, beers are dispensed from a traditional cellar. Two beers are always available and guests vote for the beers they wish to sample. The large, child-friendly garden has play equipment. No food is served but a good chip shop is a few doors away. Q☺🖳♣P

Gayton

Crown
Lynn Road, PE32 1PA (on B1145)
☻ 12-3, 6-11; 11-midnight Fri & Sat; 12-11.30 Sun
☎ (01553) 636252
Greene King XX Mild, IPA, Abbot, Old Speckled Hen; guest beer Ⓗ
A true gem, voted local CAMRA Pub of the Year 2004, this is a rare outlet for the superb XX Mild. The food is excellent in both pub and dining rooms. Live music evenings and special events are well supported by locals. The pub features many wildlife pictures by a local photographer. With gardens front and back and a huge log fire in winter, this is an inn for all seasons. 🏚Q☺❶◐&▲🖳(48)♣P⌐

Geldeston

Locks Inn
Locks Lane, NR34 0HW (through village to Ellingham Mill, turn left onto track across marshes) TM391908
☻ 12-11 summer; 11-3, 6.30-11 (closed Mon & Tue) winter
☎ (01508) 518414 ⊕ geldestonlocks.co.uk
Green Jack Canary, Orange Wheat, Grasshopper, Gone Fishing; guest beers Ⓗ
A real Broadland gem, this unique and quite remote pub is gaining a good reputation locally for the live music staged in its annexe. The bar has no electricity and is lit by candles. Friday is curry night and the choice is excellent, including vegetarian options. Owned by the Green Jack Brewery, guest beers are occasionally available. The garden, which extends to the river moorings, is a lovely place to while away a summer afternoon. It holds two beer festivals each year at Easter and in September.
🏚✆☺❶♣P

Wherry
7 The Street, NR34 0LB
☻ 12-3, 7-12.30am; 12-1.30am Fri & Sat; 12-12.30am Sun
☎ (01508) 518371
Adnams Bitter, Broadside Ⓗ
The original part of the building, dating back to the 1670s, is a cosy room with a quarry-tiled floor and features a framed history of the pub on the wall. An extension was added in the 1970s. Both rooms have real fires. Phat, a traditional Norfolk pub game, is played on Monday evening – this is one of the few pubs that still plays this game regularly.
🏚Q☺❶▲♣P

Gooderstone

Swan
The Street, PE33 9BP (opp church)

✪ 12-11 (midnight Thu-Sat); 12-10.30 Sun
☎ (01366) 328365
Fuller's London Pride; Greene King IPA; guest beers ⊞
The pub has a large open-plan bar with a conservatory overlooking the garden. The beers served here are generally from large breweries, with the occasional micro brew making an appearance. A beer festival is now an annual event. A large-screen TV shows sport as well as music, and pool and darts feature, with the pub participating in leagues. Live rock and blues bands play most Fridays and every Saturday night. ♨❀◑⌖🖼🅿

Gorleston-on-Sea

Albion
87 Lowestoft Road, NR31 6SH
✪ 11 (12 Sun)-11
☎ (01493) 661035
Beer range varies ⊞
This Victorian corner local, once owned by Steward & Patteson, is situated on the south side of town. It stocks a wide and varying range of real ales, including some locals and some from further afield. The interior comprises a large L-shaped lounge and a games room. The pub can get very busy on weekend evenings. 🖼🅿

New Entertainer
80 Pier Plain, NR31 6PG
✪ 12-11
☎ (01493) 441643
Greene King IPA; guest beers ⊞
Previously known as the Suffolk Hotel, this pub dates back to the 1800s. It became the New Entertainer in 1982. Today it is a large one-room pub with a lounge area at one end and a bar area with pool table at the other. Up to six rotating guest beers are available. Care should be taken when entering and, especially, leaving this pub as it is surrounded on three sides by pavement-less streets. Q🖼♣

Great Bircham

King's Head
Lynn Road, PE31 7RJ
✪ 11-11; 12-10.30 Sun
☎ (01485) 578265 ⊕ the-kings-head-bircham.co.uk
Adnams Bitter; Fuller's London Pride; Woodforde's Wherry; guest beer ⊞
A major refurbishment of the hotel in 2004 transformed what was once the village local to a bright modern bar in a listed building. The award-winning restaurant is rated as among the best in the country. However, the pub remains very much part of the community and drinkers are welcome to pop in just for a beer. Regular quiz nights are a popular attraction. Local CAMRA Pub of the Year 2007. ❀🛏◑

Great Cressingham

Windmill Inn
Water End, IP25 6NN
✪ 11-11
☎ (01760) 756232

Adnams Bitter, Broadside; Greene King IPA; guest beers ⊞
Recently extended, this multi-roomed pub offers a different atmosphere in each drinking area, from lively to peaceful. A real drinkers' pub, the Windmill rotates its guest beers every three months or so. Good home-cooked food is available. Weekly amateur talent nights are popular. ♨Q👁❀🛏◑🚶🅰♣🅿

Great Yarmouth

Mariners Tavern
69 Howard Street South, NR30 1LN
✪ 11-midnight (1am Fri & Sat); 12-11 Sun
☎ (01493) 332299
Blackfriars Holy Smoke; Green Jack Orange Wheat; Humpty Dumpty King John; guest beers ⊞
Friendly family-run local comprising a main bar and a smaller oak-panelled lounge with a pool table. Most beers sold here come from local micros, particularly Blackfriars. The pub is currently undergoing refurbishment which will allow it to offer a broader range of ales including some continental beers. Live music sessions are held weekly.
♨Q👁❀🖼🖥♣♠🚶–☐

Red Herring
24-25 Havelock Road, NR30 3HQ
✪ 12-3, 6-1am; 11-1am Sat; 12-1am Sun
☎ (01493) 853384
Blackfriars Mild, Yarmouth Bitter; Fuller's London Pride; guest beers ⊞
Tucked away from the seafront in a residential area close to the award-winning Time & Tide Museum, this atmospheric single-bar corner local has a separate area for pool and TV. The walls are adorned with pictures of old Great Yarmouth during its long-gone herring fishing days. The pub has a loyal local clientele and welcomes visitors too. ◑🖼♣👤

St Johns Head
53 North Quay, NR30 1JB
✪ 12-12.30am (11 Sun)
☎ (01493) 843443
Elgood's Cambridge Bitter; guest beers ⊞
Situated within easy walking distance of the railway station and quayside, the pub is reputed to have been built on land confiscated from the Carmelite Order. It was acquired by Lacons Brewery in 1787. The interior consists of just one small, comfortable bar, with a pool table and wide-screen TV at one end. Four real ales are usually available, plus a real cider. ❀⇄🖼♣👤

Happisburgh

Hill House
NR12 0PN (off B1159 coast road)
✪ 12-3, 7-11.30; 12-11.30 Thu-Sun
☎ (01692) 650004
Beer range varies ⊞
Coastal hideaway, once the haunt of Sir Arthur Conan Doyle, who wrote a Sherlock Holmes novel here. The six cask ales are mainly sourced from Norfolk and Suffolk craft brewers, with Woodforde's and Nethergate frequently represented. The house beer is

brewed by Buffy's. The range of beers increases to over 40 during the annual midsummer beer festival. Hot and cold meals are served at lunchtime and in the evening. Dogs are welcome in the bar.
⚏Q☎☺🖛🕿🚻🖵(735)♣P↳

Heacham

Fox & Hounds
22 Station Road, PE31 7EX
🕒 12-11 (10.30 Sun)
☎ (01485) 570345 🌐 foxbrewery.co.uk
Adnams Broadside; guest beers Ⓗ
Home of the Fox Brewery, this pub always offers five beers, three from the Fox itself in varying strengths. There is also a good range of foreign bottled beers. The restaurant facilities have recently been upgraded, and a beer list is available for diners. Live music is staged on Tuesday evening and a quiz on Thursday. Two annual beer festivals are held, one at Easter, the other in July.
☺🕿🚻🖵(40, 41)♣P↳

Hockering

Victoria
The Street, NR20 3LH (off A47)
🕒 12-3 (not Mon or Tue), 6-11; 12-3, 6-10.30 Sun
☎ (01603) 880507
Elgood's Black Dog; guest beers Ⓗ
You can be sure of a warm welcome at this village local, which prides itself on its range of beers of all styles served from six handpumps, complemented by Belgian and other continental bottled beers. The landlord has decorated the single bar with Arsenal memorabilia and Private Eye covers. Tasty bar snacks are always available. Live music and quizzes are hosted regularly, and it has a resident darts team. ⚏☺🕿🚻🖵(X1)♣P

Horsey

Nelson Head
The Street, NR29 4AD (N of B1159 coast road)
🕒 12-11 (10.30 Sun)
☎ (01493) 393378 🌐 nelsonheadhorsey.co.uk
Woodforde's Wherry, Nelson's Revenge; guest beer Ⓗ
Traditional Broadland marshman's pub situated in a quiet rural hamlet near the famous Horsey Mill and moorings. Behind the unpretentious exterior lies a delightful bar with a timeless atmosphere. It has a fine collection of local pictures, many of them featuring Nelson, plus a number of marshman's implements including a punt gun. Popular with artists, walkers on the coastal path, visitors to the Horsey Nature Reserve, Broads boaters and regulars, a good selection of home-cooked meals using local produce is served. A ramp is available for disabled visitors on request. ⚏Q☺🕿🖵↳

Ingham

Swan Inn
Swan Corner, Sea Palling Road, NR12 9AB (1 mile NE of Stalham on B1151) TG390260
🕒 12-3, 6-11 (10.30 Sun)

☎ (01692) 581099
Woodforde's Wherry, Nelson's Revenge; guest beer Ⓗ
In a pleasant rural setting near the church and close to the north Norfolk coast and Broads, this is a delightful, thatched, flint-built pub, part of a 14th-century terrace. The interior is on a split level and features a wealth of warm brick, flint and beams. Beers come from the Woodforde's range, and a wide selection of excellent home-cooked meals made with local produce may be enjoyed in the restaurant. The secluded courtyard is a fine place to enjoy the special alfresco menu in summer. Good en-suite rooms are available in a separate block. ⚏Q🕿🖛🕿🚻P

Kenninghall

Red Lion
East Church Street, NR16 2EP (opp church)
🕒 12-3, 6.30-11; 12-11 Fri & Sat; 12-10.30 Sun
☎ (01953) 887849
Greene King IPA, Abbot; Woodforde's Wherry; guest beers Ⓗ/Ⓖ
This lovely historic pub reopened around 10 years ago after a long period of closure. It comprises three rooms: a comfortable bar, a wood-panelled snug with a pamment floor, and a restaurant. The snug features on the cover of CAMRA's Regional Inventory for East Anglia. The Abbot is dispensed directly from the cask behind the bar, and two guest beers are usually available. ⚏☺🕿🚻🖵P↳

King's Lynn

Live & Let Live
18 Windsor Road, PE30 5PL
🕒 11.30 (1 Mon)-11 (midnight Fri & Sat); 11.30-11 Sun
☎ (01553) 764990
Beer range varies Ⓗ
This thriving local, just off London Road, has a small cosy lounge bar and a larger public bar with a pool table and TV screen showing sporting events. There are always four beers available, typically two bitters, a mild (rare for the area), and something stronger, often featuring local brews. It is also one of the few outlets for Weston's cider in the area.
🕿🚋♣🍴🍽

Stuart House Hotel
35 Goodwins Road, PE30 5QX
🕒 6-11; 7-10.30 Sun
☎ (01553) 772169 🌐 stuart-house-hotel.co.uk
Beer range varies Ⓗ
The hotel is approached down a gravel drive from Goodwins Road, which is close to the football ground and Walks Park. The pleasant hotel bar has a roaring fire in winter and a beer garden in summer. Three beers are usually available, often local brews. Regular music nights are staged on a Friday, and the annual beer festival takes place around the last week in July. The bar is open evenings only except by arrangement. ☺🖛🕿P

White Horse
9 Wootton Road, PE30 4EZ
🕒 11-11 (11.30 Sat); 12-11 Sun
☎ (01553) 763258

Greene King IPA; guest beers Ⓗ
This thriving traditional local near the Gaywood clock, with separate public and lounge bars, is featured in CAMRA's East Anglian Regional Inventory of historic pub interiors. Three beers are available including two changing guests, usually a standard bitter and a strong bitter. Regulars can keep up with the football on the large-screen TV in the public bar, and traditional games such as dominoes are also popular. ⚷🚐♣P⌐🖿

Larling

Angel Inn

NR16 2QU (off A11 between Thetford & Norwich)
🕘 10-midnight
☎ (01953) 717963
Adnams Bitter; guest beers Ⓗ
A treasure just off the A11, the Angel features a superb choice of ales from micro-breweries across the country, always including a mild. There is also an excellent range of home-cooked food (booking advisable). A good mix of locals, passers-by and football supporters (the landlord is a Norwich City fan) creates an interesting atmosphere. A beer festival is held in summer with up to 60 ales and cider. ⚷🏰🐾�'⏴Ⓓ⚷Å⇌(Harling Road, limited service)P🖿

Lessingham

Star Inn

School Road, NR12 0DN (300m inland off B1159 coast road) OS284389
🕘 12-3 (not Mon), 7-midnight
☎ (01692) 580510 ⊕ thestarlessingham.co.uk
Buffy's Bitter; Greene King IPA; guest beers Ⓗ
An excellent village pub with an easy-going feel. The wood burner in the inglenook fireplace at one end of the bar is especially welcoming on cold winter days. In summer the large beer garden is a great place to relax. Home-cooked food is available (lunches Wed-Sun only). A huge display of beermats attached to the bar timbering is testimony to the many guest beers offered in the past. The cider is Weston's Old Rosie. Dogs are welcome in the bar. ⚷Q🚲🏰🐾Ⓓ Å🚐P

Morley St Botolph

Buck

Deopham Road, NR18 9AA TM075998
🕘 11-2.30 (3 Sat & Sun), 5.30-11
☎ (01953) 604483
Adnams Broadside; Greene King IPA; guest beer Ⓗ
Delightful, beamed 200-year-old single-bar country pub where two open log fires and polished horse brasses combine to provide an extremely cosy ambience. The pub supports darts, pool, cards and two football teams as well as bowls in summer. Good food is served daily (eve meals must be booked in advance). There is a beer garden and large car park. ⚷Q🏰🐾Ⓓ🦽🚐♣P

New Buckenham

King's Head

Market Place, NR16 2AN (opp. green) TG088906
🕘 12-3, 7-11 (10.30 Sun)
☎ (01953) 860487
Adnams Bitter; guest beer Ⓗ
This friendly, chatty, two-bar free house facing the village green served as a coaching inn between London and Norwich in the early part of the 16th century. A wood burner in the large inglenook warms the back bar. Traditional home-cooked food served here includes a popular Sunday lunch. Quiz night is Thursday. Close by is a 12th century Norman church and remains of a Norman castle. ⚷QⓉⓍÅ♣

North Creake

Jolly Farmers

1 Burnham Road, NR21 9JW
🕘 12-2.30, 7-11; (closed Mon & Tue); 12-3, 7-10.30 Sun
☎ (01328) 738185
Fuller's London Pride; Woodforde's Wherry; guest beer Ⓖ
Despite the ever-increasing number of village houses becoming second homes, and the proximity to upwardly mobile Burnham Market, this pub manages to retain its down-to-earth feel. Small rooms, tiled floors, stripped pine tables and real ales on gravity create a homely atmosphere. Local mussels in winter and crab and lobster in summer are complemented by a good wine and whisky selection. ⚷Q🏰ⓌⒹP⌐

North Elmham

Railway Hotel

Station Road, NR20 5HH (on B1145)
🕘 11-11
☎ (01362) 668300
Beer range varies Ⓗ/Ⓖ
Situated in the heart of this historic central Norfolk village, near the Anglo Saxon North Elmham Cathedral (English Heritage), this flint and brick built pub is a fine example of a community village local. It offers a varying range of cask ales, nearly all sourced from local micro-breweries, although a few come from further afield. Good home-cooked food is served and the pub now has a function room in an adjoining building. ⚷🏰ⒹÅP

North Wootton

House on the Green

Ling Common Road, PE30 3RE
🕘 11.30 (4 Mon)-11 (11.30 Fri & Sat); 12-11.30 Sun
☎ (01553) 631323
Adnams Broadside; Greene King IPA; Shepherd Neame Spitfire Ⓗ
This friendly pub on the outskirts of the village has a large car park and is close to the bus stop. Guest beers are available in summer. The interior comprises a public bar with music/TV and a separate lounge bar with dining room. Food is served in the restaurant as well as the bar areas (no food Sun eve and Mon). In summer, guests can enjoy the large garden with play equipment for children, excellent

seating and tables for alfresco meals. Occasional live music and charity fund-raising events are held. ⚼✿⌒◖⊞⎏⊟(43)♣P⎚

Norwich

Alexandra Tavern

16 Stafford Street, NR2 3BB

✪ 10.30-11 (midnight Thu-Sat)

☎ (01603) 627772 ⊕ alexandratavern.co.uk

Chalk Hill Tap, CHB; guest beers Ⓗ

At this friendly back-street corner local, Chalk Hill beers are supplemented by three changing guests, mainly from micro-breweries. The walls are adorned with the ex-submariner landlord's collection of nautical and Atlantic rowing memorabilia. Home-cooked meals on offer include Mexican and Mediterranean specialities. Pool, darts, crib and dominoes are played. ⚼Q✿◖⊞⎐⊟♣

Beehive

30 Leopold Road, NR4 7PJ

✪ 5-11 (midnight Fri); 12-midnight Sat; 2-3, 7-11.30 Sun

☎ (01603) 451628 ⊕ beehivepubnorwich.co.uk

Fuller's London Pride; Greene King IPA; Hop Back Summer Lightning; Wolf Golden Jackal; guest beers Ⓗ

This is a genuine local pub, frequented by customers of all ages. It supplies a fine range of beers, usually including a porter. The interior comprises two rooms: a bar and a comfortable lounge with leather sofas. There is also a function room upstairs. Home to football, golf, darts, pool and rugby clubs, it stages regular quiz nights and wine tasting evenings. The beer garden outside is popular, particularly when barbecues are held during the summer months. Q✿⊞♣P

Coach & Horses

82 Thorpe Road, NR1 1BA (400m from station)

✪ 11-midnight (1am Fri & Sat)

☎ (01603) 477077 ⊕ thecoachthorperoad.co.uk

Chalk Hill Tap, CHB, Gold, Dreadnought, Flintknapper's Mild, Old Tackle; guest beers Ⓗ

A coaching inn dating back to the early 19th century, the pub is home to the Chalk Hill Brewery and the full range of its ales is on sale here plus a number of guests. Brewery tours are available by appointment. The main bar has a large open fire. Excellent home-cooked food is available lunchtime and evenings. ⚼✿◖⇌⊞♣♥P⎚

Duke of Wellington

91-93 Waterloo Road, NR3 1EG

✪ 12-11.30 (10.30 Sun)

☎ (01603) 441182 ⊕ dukeofwellingtonnorwich.co.uk

Elgood's Black Dog; Fuller's London Pride; Wolf Golden Jackel, Straw Dog; guest beers Ⓗ/Ⓖ

Excellent, friendly, award-winning local serving a wide range of ales including up to 17 changing guest beers, as well as a selection of bottled continental lagers and beers. The Duke hosts an annual beer festival in August, as well as a regular folk evening on Tuesday. The seating area has many small nooks and crannies and a real fire, creating a cosy feel in winter. Crib, dominoes and ring-the-bell are played. Car parking space is limited but the pub can easily be reached by bus. ⚼✿⊟(9A, 16)♣P⎚

Eaton Cottage

75 Mount Pleasant, NR2 2DQ

✪ 12-11 (midnight Fri & Sat)

☎ (01603) 453048

Butler's Revenge; Caledonian Deuchars IPA; Fuller's London Pride; Wolf Golden Jackal, Straw Dog Ⓗ

This friendly community local on the south side of the city comprises a lounge and bar. The pub is currently undergoing some restoration work designed to return it to its former traditional style. Live music is hosted once a month, usually folk and blues. ✿⎐⊞♥⎚

Fat Cat

49 West End Street, NR2 4NA

✪ 12-11 (midnight Fri & Sat); 12-10.30 Sun

☎ (01603) 624364 ⊕ fatcatpub.co.uk

Adnams Bitter; Elgood's Black Dog; Fat Cat Bitter, Top Cat; Taylor Landlord; Woodforde's Wherry; guest beers Ⓗ/Ⓖ

Twice winner of CAMRA's prestigious National Pub of the Year, this hostelry offers a veritable cornucopia of real ales from around the country and its own Fat Cat Brewery. With more than 20 real ales available this is a national treasure, not to be missed. It also stocks many Belgian and other foreign beers. The interior is cosy, with many nooks and crannies, and adorned with brewery memorabilia and pictures. Cider is provided by Burnard's. A small back room can be used for meetings, as well as screening major sporting events on TV. ✿⊟♣♥

King's Arms

22 Hall Road, NR1 3HQ

✪ 11-11 (midnight Fri & Sat); 12-10.30 Sun

☎ (01603) 766361 ⊕ kingsarmsnorwich.co.uk

Adnams Bitter; Bateman Dark Mild, XB Bitter, XXXB; Wolf Coyote Bitter; guest beers Ⓗ

Friendly community local selling Bateman's ales and up to eight guests beers including a mild and a dark beer. The pub hosts quiz nights and games evenings, as well as an annual beer festival in November. It also runs its own cricket team, current holders of the Suffolk CAMRA Cup. Food is served at lunchtime and on Sunday afternoon, and you may also bring your own food. The conservatory and rear garden are popular in summer. A short walk from the football ground, the pub can be busy on match days. ✿⎐⊞♣⎚⛛

King's Head

42 Magdalen Street, NR3 1JE

✪ 12-11.30

☎ (01603) 620468

Woodforde's Nelson's Revenge; guest beers Ⓗ/Ⓖ

This CAMRA-friendly public house is a keg-free zone serving a wide range of up to 20 cask-conditioned ales from micro-breweries around East Anglia as well as an ever-changing array of foreign bottled beers and Kingfisher cider. Recently refurbished, the pub is now a welcome addition to the north side of the city and was voted local CAMRA Pub of the Year in

2006. Photos and maps of the area adorn the walls of the front bar – a timely reminder of how many pubs have been lost. Bar billiards is played in the rear bar. Q🚪🍴🕯️⌐🖥️

Nelson

122 Nelson Street, NR2 4DR

🕓 12-2, 5-midnight; 12-midnight Fri-Sun

☎ (01603) 626362 ⊕ thenelsonpubnorwich.co.uk

Badger Tanglefoot; Caledonian Deuchars IPA; Winter's Golden; Woodforde's Wherry; guest beers Ⓗ

This friendly community free house is about 15 minutes' walk to the west of the city centre. The interior comprises two bars, with a pool table in one. Good pub food is served lunchtime and evenings and the large child-friendly garden holds barbecues in summer. The pub hosts many themed nights and occasional beer festivals. 🐕🌗🚪🍴P

Reindeer

10 Dereham Road, NR2 4AY

🕓 11-11 (midnight Fri & Sat); 11-10.30 Sun

☎ (01603) 762223

Elgood's Black Dog, Cambridge, Golden Newt, Greyhound Strong; guest beers Ⓗ

L-shaped pub with a long bar and a back area that has been opened out for dining, plus a small outside deck which is pleasant in the summer. It serves Elgood's beers and guests, and a beer festival is hosted annually in March. Food is available in the evenings and Friday-Sunday lunchtimes, including an excellent carvery. Major sports events are shown on a wide-screen TV, and live music plays occasionally. 🐕🌗⅙🚪P🍴

Rosary Tavern

95 Rosary Road, NR1 4BX (5 mins from station)

🕓 12 (11.30 Sat when Norwich FC at home)-11.30; 12-11 Sun

☎ (01603) 666287

Black Sheep Best Bitter; Caledonian Deuchars IPA; Wolf Golden Jackal; guest beers Ⓗ

Very much a local pub, the Rosary has its own football team and pipe-smoking club, and hosts an annual treasure hunt as well as a bar billiards league. In addition to the regular beers, up to four changing guest beers and Kingfisher cider are available. Quiz nights and occasional live music are popular. On sunny summer days the garden is a pleasure, and regular barbecues are held. A conservatory at the rear is used for meetings and as a quiet retreat from the hustle and bustle of the front bar. 🐕🌗⇌(Thorpe)🚪🍴P🍴

Trafford Arms

61 Grove Road, NR1 3RL

🕓 11-11.30 (midnight Fri & Sat); 12-11 Sun

☎ (01603) 628466 ⊕ traffordarms.co.uk

Adnams Bitter; Tetley Bitter; Woodforde's Wherry; guest beers Ⓗ

Traditional corner local where the emphasis is on providing a service to the community. It offers nine beers including six changing guests, Kingfisher cider, fine wines and delicious food, and has hosted a regular Valentine's Beer Festival since 1994. The landlord is a loyal supporter of Norwich City football club, and live sport is shown on large screens. A former local CAMRA Pub of the

Year, the interior is divided in two, with the TV and pool table to the right and the dining area to the left. 🐕🌗🚪🖥️(9, 17)🍴🍴P

Wig & Pen

6 St Martin at Palace Plain, NR3 1RN

🕓 11.30-midnight (1am Fri & Sat); 11-6 Sun

☎ (01603) 625891 ⊕ thewigandpen.com

Adnams Bitter; Buffy's Norwich Terrier; Fuller's London Pride; guest beers Ⓗ

This compact public house has built up a good reputation for quality beer and superb food. It stocks six beers including three changing guests, and hosts an annual beer festival in early spring. There is a small function/dining room at the rear where CAMRA local branch committee meetings are held. The spacious patio comes into its own during the summer months and makes an idyllic place to while away the afternoon. A wide-screen TV shows live sports, and it has a resident chess club. ♨️🐕🌗🚪🍴

Woolpack

2 Muspole Street, NR3 1DJ (off Colgate)

🕓 11-11; 12-10 Sun

☎ (01603) 611139 ⊕ woolpack-norwich.co.uk

Beer range varies Ⓗ

Peaceful 18th-century family-run free house five minutes' walk from the market place. There is a friendly ambience about the place, which features a large fireplace and a pleasant open bar. Delicious meals can be chosen from a diverse menu. Children are allowed in a room behind the bar and in the gardens. Regular themed nights are hosted. 🚌🐕🌗🚪

Old Buckenham

Gamekeeper

The Green, NR17 1RE

🕓 11.45 (11 Sat)-11; 12-10.30 Sun

☎ (01953) 860397 ⊕ thegamekeeperfreehouse.com

Adnams Bitter; guest beers Ⓗ

This 17th-century Grade II listed free house overlooks the picturesque village green and duck pond. The interior is charmingly traditional, featuring exposed beams and bricks, and stone-flagged and wooden floors. Its many rooms include a large dining room reminiscent of a baronial hall. An extensive menu offer freshly prepared meals cooked to order – the Sunday carvery is very popular. The house bitter, produced by a local brewer, is named after the pub. A skittle alley is available for hire. ♨️Q🐕🌗🍴P🍴

Poringland

Royal Oak

The Street, NR14 7JT (on B1332)

🕓 12-3, 5-11; 12-midnight Fri & Sat; 12-11.30 Sun

☎ (01508) 493734

Adnams Bitter; Caledonian Deuchars IPA; Woodforde's Wherry; guest beers Ⓗ

Located in the centre of the village about five miles south of Norwich, this popular pub sells a range of around 12 real ales with up to nine guests. Norwich & Norfolk CAMRA Pub of the Year 2007, it has a spacious, open-plan interior with distinctive drinking areas. No food is served but there is a fish & chip shop next door. Q✿🖂🌲💠P🖵

Reedham

Ferry Inn
Ferry Road, NR13 3HA (on B1140)
🕐 11-11 summer; 10.30-3, 6.30-11 winter; 11-10.30 Sun
☎ (01493) 700429 🌐 archerstouringpark.co.uk
Adnams Bitter, Broadside; Woodforde's Wherry; guest beers 🅷
Widely regarded as Broadland's premier riverside pub, this superb 17th-century inn is situated next to the historic ferry across the River Yare, the last on the Broads. The interior features beamed ceilings, stone floors and a collection of rural tools. Guest beers are available in the summer and the food menu offers a selection of excellent home-prepared meals, with local fish, game and seafood the specialities. Themed food nights showcase dishes from around the world. A folk festival is staged during the second week in September. A caravan/camping site and extensive free moorings are available. ♨Q👁✿🕐◗ À⚓

Reepham

King's Arms
Market Place, NR10 4JJ
🕐 11.30-3, 5.30-11; 12-3, 7-10.30 Sun
☎ (01603) 870345
Adnams Bitter; Elgood's Cambridge; Greene King Abbot; Taylor Landlord; Woodforde's Wherry 🅷
This old inn, dating in parts from the 17th century, is situated in one corner of Reepham's picturesque market place, surrounded by many classic Georgian buildings. The interior of the pub is open plan, with many different drinking areas on split levels. There are plenty of exposed beams and an old well can be seen at the rear of the building. ♨Q✿🕐🖂🌲⚓

Ringland

Swan Inn
The Street, NR8 6AB OS140137
🕐 10-midnight; 12-11 Sun
☎ (01603) 868214 🌐 tasteofoz.com
Adnams Bitter; guest beers 🅷
This country inn in a small, quiet village on the banks of the picturesque River Wensum offers a unique blend of southern hemisphere and traditional English pub ambience. The single bar has recently been extended to accommodate the Taste of Oz restaurant, which features Australian-style decor and cuisine. Bar meals are also available in the traditional bar which features exposed beams and an open log fire. Quiz night is Wednesday. Outside, there is a safe grassed seating area and patio/decking overlooking the Wensum Valley. ♨✿🕐◗ ⊟&P

Rockland All Saints

White Hart
The Street, NR17 1TR (S of B1077)
🕐 11 (12 Sun)-3, 6-11; closed Mon
☎ (01953) 483361

Adnams Bitter; Fuller's London Pride; guest beer 🅷
Village local with two small dining areas, a bar area and a family/coffee room that doubles as sports TV space. The decor and furnishings throughout are contemporary and understated. Locally sourced, home-cooked food is served at reasonable prices, and the menu includes children's dishes and £5 specials. The garden has a play area and there is a covered patio for smokers. Directions are available for a rural walk starting and ending at the pub. ♨Q👁✿🕐◗P⚓

Roydon

Union Jack
30 Station Road, PE32 1AW
🕐 4 (12 Fri-Mon)-midnight
☎ (01485) 601347
Beer range varies 🅷
This is a rare village drinkers' pub that relies solely on its wet trade: food is only available on special occasions. The pub offers three guest beers, mostly around 4% ABV. Ales change frequently and are chosen in consultation with the regulars – occasional beer festivals are also held. The pub supports many sports activities including darts, dominoes, football and cribbage, and trophies abound. Live music is performed some weekends. Dogs are welcome, and a covered area is provided for smokers. ♨✿🖂(48)🌲P⚓

Salhouse

Bell Inn
Lower Street, NR13 6RW (on B1140)
🕐 12-3, 5.30-11; 12-11 Fri-Sun
☎ (01603) 721141
Buffy's Bitter; Wolf Golden Jackal; guest beers 🅷
This Broadland pub, dating back to the 1670s, is situated in the centre of the village. The public bar, where darts and pool are played, has a stone floor, beamed ceiling and an open fire. The carpeted and low-beamed lounge, also with an open fire, leads to the restaurant, which serves a good selection of tasty dishes including vegetarian options. There is a large car park to the front of the pub and a garden to the rear. ♨Q✿🕐◗ ⊟🖂P

Sedgeford

King William
Heacham Road, PE36 5LU (on B1454)
🕐 11 (6 Mon)-11; 12-10.30 Sun
☎ (01485) 571765 🌐 thekingwilliamsedgeford.co.uk
Adnams Bitter; Greene King IPA; Woodforde's Wherry; guest beers 🅷
This country village inn and restaurant is renowned locally for the quality of its food. Situated close to the Peddars Way long distance footpath and the bird reserves of north Norfolk, the King William attracts many visitors who are made very welcome. Good value accommodation is on offer.
♨Q👁✿🖂🍴🕐◗P⚓

Sheringham

Lobster

13 High Street, NR26 8JP

🕙 10-11 (1.30am Fri & Sat); 12-10.30 Sun

☎ (01263) 822716 ⊕ the-lobster.com

Adnams Bitter; Greene King Abbot; guest beers Ⓗ

Situated at the seaward end of the High Street, this is a traditional, family friendly pub. The Stables restaurant at the rear of the building serves inspired meals prepared from locally sourced fresh produce. The wood-panelled lounge has a nautical-themed ceiling and an open fire, while the public bar is open and bright. Two large beer gardens and marquees provide space for outdoor drinking in summer. Ten ales are stocked here as well as European bottled beers and a selection of fine malt whiskies. Four beer festivals are hosted a year. Q🍴🕭🌑🌓🖳🕭≠🖳🕭

Wyndham Arms

15-17 Wyndham Street, NR26 8BA

🕙 11 (12 Fri-Sun)-midnight

☎ (01263) 822609

Greene King IPA, Abbot, Old Speckled Hen; guest beers Ⓗ

Cosy pub on a narrow side street near the seafront comprising a basic but welcoming public bar, a carpeted lounge and an adjacent dining room with two outside seating areas. The food served here is all locally produced, from land and sea, and now has a distinct and authentic Greek flavour. It can be enjoyed with Greek wines or beer (Mythos/Keo) or one of three changing Norfolk guest beers. Cider from Crones is also available. The Sheringham Shantymen seem to have adopted the pub and sing here on Thursday evening. 🍴Q🍴🌑🌓🕭≠🖳🕭

Shipdham

King's Head

2 Dereham Road, IP25 7NA (on A1075)

🕙 4 (3 Fri)-11; 12-11 Sat & Sun

☎ (01362) 820861

Woodforde's Wherry, Nelson's Revenge; guest beers Ⓗ

This village pub, known as the King Billy, is run by the ever-welcoming Terry. It has one L-shaped room with a half-timbered upper floor decorated in pre-WWII style containing a pool table, piano (used infrequently), a settle and an antique sideboard. A free house, it occasionally serves guest beers. Sky Sports and background music provide non-intrusive entertainment, complemented by occasional live music. In the entrance lobby photographs are displayed and a shield that was donated to the village of Shipdham by the USAF 44th Bombardment Group (the 'Flying Eightballs'), who were stationed here. 🍴🌑🕭🖳🕭

Skeyton

Goat Inn

Long Road, NR10 5DH (on unclassified road N of RAF Coltishall) OS250244

🕙 12-3, 6-11; 6.30-11 Sun

☎ (01692) 538600

Adnams Bitter; Woodforde's Wherry; guest beers Ⓗ

This 16th-century thatched inn is set within a large garden of over seven acres, which is used for camping and caravans (the pub is registered with the Caravan Club). The interior is large and long, with a series of interconnecting dining and drinking areas featuring many exposed beams. Farm implements and old photos adorn the walls. There is a large and varied food menu offering excellent meals lunchtimes and evenings. 🌑🕭🖏🏕️🕭P

Smallburgh

Crown

North Walsham Road, NR12 9AD (on A149)

🕙 12-3 (not Mon), 5.30 (7 Sat)-11; 12-3 Sun

☎ (01692) 536314

Adnams Bitter; Greene King IPA, Abbot; guest beers Ⓗ

Welcoming, friendly and full of character, this comfortable, thatched village local is situated close to the Broads and north Norfolk coast. A locally renowned gem, it was once a 15th-century coaching inn and retains some original timbers. Two guest beers change frequently. The log fire in winter enhances the cosy atmosphere, and in summer the tranquil, tree-fringed garden beckons. A good selection of home-prepared meals, using local produce as available, is served in the bar and dining room. 🍴Q🌑🖏🕭🕭P

South Creake

Ostrich Inn

Fakenham Road, NR21 9PB (on B1355)

🕙 12-11 (10.30 Sun) summer; 12-3, 5-11 (10.30 Sun) winter

☎ (01328) 823320 ⊕ ostrichinn.co.uk

Greene King IPA, Abbot; Woodforde's Wherry; guest beer Ⓗ

Attractively modernised village inn dating from the 17th century, the Ostrich serves excellent, freshly prepared meals. In summer the garden is a perfect spot for relaxed dining, while in winter the bar is warm and cosy. A large restored barn is used for functions, and the pub offers overnight accommodation. 🍴🍴🌑🖏🕭🖏P🕭

Southery

Old White Bell

20 Upgate Street, PE38 0NA

🕙 11 (3 Wed)-11; 12-10.30 Sun

☎ (01366) 377057 ⊕ oldwhitebell.co.uk

City of Cambridge Rutherford IPA; guest beers Ⓗ

This genuine local free house, situated just off the A10 between Ely and King's Lynn, serves a lively village community, and is well worth stopping for. An open-plan pub with a small restaurant, it was voted local CAMRA Pub of the Year in 2006. Sport is much in evidence: football matches are screened live and the pub has a resident team (see website for details). Check out the collection of football shirts above the pool table too. 🌑🕭🖳(37)🖏P

Stibbard

Ordnance Arms

Guist Bottom, NR20 5PF (on A1067)
☼ 5.30-10; 12-3, 5.30-11 Sat; 12-10.30 Sun
☎ (01328) 829471 ⊕ ordnancearms.co.uk
Draught Bass; Greene King Abbot; guest beer ⊞
Enter the pub from the main entrance and you are greeted by a roaring fire in a small cosy room, while the side door takes you into a bar with a pamment-tiled floor and wood-burning stove. A further room with a pool table adjoins both bars. Attached to the pub is a Thai restaurant that opens in the evening.
🏨Q▮🚻P

Stoke Ferry

Blue Bell Country Inn

Lynn Road, PE33 9SW (off A134)
☼ 12-3, 5-11; 11-11 Fri & Sat; 12-10.30 Sun
☎ (01366) 502056
Adnams Bitter; Elgood's Pageant ⊞
Thriving village local, well worth a detour, where you can be sure of a warm welcome and a friendly face behind the bar. Although the emphasis here is firmly on good quality, home-cooked food (booking advisable, no food Sun eve), you will always find an excellent pint of ale at the Blue Bell. The pub has one large room with a full-length bar and a dining area on one side and drinking space on the other. 🏨❀◑▮P

Strumpshaw

Shoulder of Mutton

Norwich Road, NR13 4NT (S of A47)
☼ 11-11; 12-10.30 Sun
☎ (01603) 712274
Adnams Bitter, Broadside; Greene King IPA; guest beers ⊞
Close to an important local RSPB reserve with nature walks and the boating centre of Brundall, this traditional village pub is popular with locals and visitors, young and old alike. It offers an extensive choice of home-prepared meals served in the restaurant (booking advisable). Themed food evenings are a highlight. No food is served on Sunday evening, but kippers may be bought at the bar to take away. The spacious public bar has pool, darts and crib, while the large rear garden is used for petanque in summer. ❀🚻◑🍴♣P

Swaffham

Lydney House Hotel

Norwich Road, PE37 7QS
☼ 7-10.30; closed Sun
☎ (01760) 723355 ⊕ lydney-house.demon.co.uk
Woodforde's Wherry, Nelson's Revenge; guest beers Ⓖ
This small hotel is situated next to Swaffham's superb medieval church and close to the market place. Look out for the giant wind turbines for which the town has become known. The hotel continues its tradition of serving gravity ales, and its occasional guest beers are all sourced locally. Entertainment is in the form of traditional pub games played in

the bar. A basic food menu is also available.
Q❀🚻◑▮(X1)♣P

Swanton Morley

Angel Inn

Greengate, NR20 4LX TG012162
☼ 12-11 (10 winter); 12-10 Sun
☎ (01362) 637407 ⊕ theangelpub.co.uk
Hop Back Summer Lightning; Mighty Oak Oscar Wilde; Wolf Golden Jackal; guest beers ⊞
This large-fronted house built in 1610 boasts a connection with Abraham Lincoln's family. The present owners have been here for three years and are keen CAMRA members – five beers are served including two changing guest ales. The interior comprises three rooms: a main bar, a dining room which has been recently been refurbished and a games room with pool and darts. Outside there is a large garden where children are welcome.
🏨🐾❀◑▮♣P🍴

Terrington St John

Woolpack

Main Road, PE14 7RR
☼ 11-2.30, 6.30-11; 12-3, 7-10.30 Sun
☎ (01945) 881097
Greene King IPA; Tom Wood Best Bitter; guest beer ⊞
Extremely popular village pub on the old King's Lynn to Wisbech road dominated by the larger-than-life personality of its landlady. Lucille's considerable artistic talent is reflected in the decor, especially in the dining area which has a 1920s Art Deco theme. Excellent food is good value, and is so popular that booking is a must, especially at the weekend. Let Lucille know if you are celebrating a special occasion and your day may become even more memorable. 🏨❀◑▮🚻(X1)P

Thetford

Albion

93-95 Castle Street, IP24 2DN (opp Castle Hill monument)
☼ 11-11 (11.30 Thu, midnight Fri & Sat); 11-3, 6-11 Tue & Wed; 12-3, 7-11 Sun
☎ (01842) 752796
Greene King IPA, Abbot ⊞
Small flint building set among cottages in the older part of the town, with excellent views across Castle Hill Park to the ancient fortifications there. The Albion has a single bar, but a lower area caters for sportier types. While the pub is generally quiet and good for a chat, it can get busy and noisier on weekend evenings. Quiz nights are held twice a month.
🏨Q❀P

Thornham

Lifeboat

Ship Lane, PE36 6LT (signed off A149 coast road)
☼ 11-11; 12-10.30 Sun
☎ (01485) 512236 ⊕ lifeboatinn.co.uk
Adnams Bitter; Greene King IPA, Abbot; Woodforde's Wherry; guest beer ⊞
Dimly lit by oil lamps, with low doorways and cosy fires ablaze, the inn evokes its 16th-

century origins. Set on the edge of the salt marshes, it is only a short walk from the ramshackle quay. A welcoming and homely place, you can always expect to see a dog and a couple of kids competing for space on the rug in front of one of the fires. The atmospheric bar is complemented by a restaurant serving local and seasonal seafood. The cider is Weston's Old Rosie.
ꔰQ✿⇔⮂◑🚃(36)♣🚶P⸜

Thurlton

Queen's Head
Beccles Road, NR14 6RJ (1 mile N of B1136 Hales-Haddiscoe road)
🕑 5-11 (midnight Fri); 12-midnight Sat; 12-10.30 Sun
☎ (01508) 548667 ⊕ queensheadthurlton.co.uk
Fuller's London Pride; Greene King IPA; Wadworth 6X Ⓗ
Put up for sale in January 2006, the pub was bought by a syndicate of 18 local residents in April and reopened in the autumn. This is the ultimate community pub, owned and run by local residents as the hub of their village. Pleasantly and sympathetically refurbished inside, it has one main open-plan bar that leads to a patio, and a separate dining room (food served Thu-Sun eve and Sun lunch).
✿◑&P

Trunch

Crown
Front Street, NR28 0AH (opp church)
🕑 12-3 (3.30 Sat), 5.30-11; 12-3.30, 7-10.30 Sun
☎ (01263) 722341 ⊕ trunchcrown.co.uk
Bateman Dark Mild, XB Bitter, Valiant; Greene King IPA; guest beers Ⓗ
Trunch is one of north Norfolk's prettiest villages, with several very old flint cottages and larger houses. Set in the middle of the village, this is Bateman's only pub in the area, and it stocks an excellent choice of beers. The restaurant is open Wednesday to Sunday. Check the website for details of beer festivals and forthcoming events such as the monthly quiz night. Dogs are welcome in the bar.
ꔰQ✿◑🚃(5, 735)P

Walcott

Lighthouse Inn
Coast Road, NR12 0PE (on B1159)
🕑 11-11
☎ (01692) 650371 ⊕ lighthouseinn.co.uk
Adnams Bitter; Greene King IPA; guest beers Ⓗ
A large family-oriented pub situated on the Yarmouth to Cromer coast road, the Lighthouse has been under the same management since 1989. Since then a number of extensions have been added, giving the pub a spacious feel with many different drinking and dining areas. With a large garden, patio and children's play area, this pub is particularly popular with families in summer. Meals are available all day until 10.30pm.
ꔰ🍴✿◑Å♣P

Warham All Saints

Three Horseshoes ☆
Bridge Street, NR23 1NL (2 miles SE of Wells)
🕑 11.30-2.30, 6-11; 12-3, 6-10.30 Sun
☎ (01328) 710547
Greene King IPA; Woodforde's Wherry; guest beer Ⓗ/🄶
The interior of this early 18th-century pub is included in CAMRA's National Inventory. It comprises three rooms, all with stone floors and cast-iron fireplaces which have changed little since the 1930s. Unusual features include the traditional game of Norfolk twister and a 1930s one-armed bandit. Excellent home-cooked food is available at lunchtime and in the evening, using only local produce (this is a chip-free zone). There is a beer garden, and accommodation is available in an adjoining building. ꔰQ✿⇔⮂◑&♣🚶P⸜

Wells-next-the-Sea

Edinburgh Hotel
Station Road, NR23 1AE
🕑 11-11; 12-10.30 Sun
☎ (01328) 710120
Draught Bass; Hancock's HB; guest beers Ⓗ
Spacious pub centrally situated at the top end of the narrow high street in this small picturesque north Norfolk town. The interior is open plan with a traditional bar area at one end and a restaurant at the other. Bar meals are available throughout the pub lunchtimes and evenings. Beers include Draught Bass as a regular, which is a rarity these days in Norfolk.
ꔰ✿⇔◑&🚃⸜🄵

West Acre

Stag
Low Road, PE32 1TR
🕑 12-2.30 (3 summer), 7 (6.30 summer)-11; closed winter Mon; 12-2.30, 7-10.30 Sun
☎ (01760) 755395
Beer range varies Ⓗ
The pub is situated at the east end of the picturesque village of West Acre, which is famous for its summer theatre in the Priory ruins. It has been transformed over the last few years, from keg-only to providing a choice of three ever-changing real ales. Voted local CAMRA Pub of the Year in 2005, many of the beers are from local micro-breweries. Regular events are also staged here, including beer festivals. Camping (tents only) is available by prior arrangement. ꔰQ✿◑&Å♣P🄵

West Beckham

Wheatsheaf
Church Road, NR25 6NX (1 mile S of A148)
🕑 12-2.30, 6.30-11; 12-3, 7-11.30 Sun
☎ (01263) 822110
Elgood's Cambridge; Greene King IPA; Woodforde's Wherry, Nelson's Revenge; guest beers Ⓗ
Converted from an old farmhouse in the 1980s, in response to local demand, this popular pub has four rooms with authentic exposed beams and ancient brickwork, two with open log fires and all furnished in a

comfortable, rustic style. Three of the outbuildings have been converted into self-catering cottages within the pub grounds. A hearty menu of dishes is available, made with local produce where possible. The pub is conveniently situated near the attractive Sheringham Park (NT). ⚒Q⚏◁◖P⚏

Weybourne

Ship

The Street, NR25 7SZ
🌑 12-3, 6-11; closed Mon; 12-11 Sat; 12-4 Sun
☎ (01263) 588721 ⊕ shipinnweybourne.co.uk
Beer range varies Ⓗ

At the centre of the village, opposite the church and ruined priory, stands this fine Victorian brick and flint building, with Stewart & Patteson Brewery windows and a veranda. Featuring two bars and a dining area, it retains many original features, timber floors and an open fire, and is popular with visitors to the nearby military museum and heritage railway, and with walkers on the coastal path. The locally sourced food comes in generous portions from a daily changing menu. The Coasthopper bus stop is just outside.
⚒◖⚏♿▲⊟P⚏

Wicklewood

Cherry Tree

116 High Street, NR18 9QA (off B1135)
🌑 12-3, 6-11; 12-midnight Fri & Sat; 12-11 Sun
☎ (01953) 606962 ⊕ thecherrytreewicklewood.co.uk
Buffy's Bitter, Polly's Folly, Hopleaf, Norwegian Blue; guest beers Ⓗ

The open-plan interior of this pub has three distinct areas: the bar, a lounge separated from the bar by a fireplace and furnished with comfortable sofas, and a dining space. All cask ales including guests come from Buffy's Brewery. There is a patio at the front and a garden to the rear. The restaurant serves home-cooked food made with local ingredients, and themed food evenings include fish & chips on Tuesday and steak on Friday. ⚘◖P⚏

Winfarthing

Fighting Cocks

The Street, IP22 2ED (on B1077)
🌑 12-3 (not Mon), 6-11; 12-5, 7-10.30 Sun
☎ (01379) 643283
Adnams Bitter; guest beer Ⓗ

In the centre of the village, this pub has a large, heavily beamed bar with a separate pool room. The inglenook fireplace contains a roaring log fire that burns all winter. Unusually, the Adnams Bitter is available both on handpump and from a cask in the bar. The house beer, Fighting Cocks Bitter, is from Elgood's. The guest beer changes weekly. No food is served Sunday or Monday evening.
⚒⚘◖♣P

Winterton-on-Sea

Fisherman's Return

The Lane, NR29 4BN (off B1159)
🌑 11-2.30, 6-11; 11-11 Sat; 12-10.30 Sun

☎ (01493) 393305 ⊕ fishermans-return.com
Adnams Bitter, Broadside; Greene King IPA; Woodforde's Wherry, Norfolk Nog; guest beers Ⓗ

Popular traditional 17th-century brick and flint-faced pub in the centre of this attractive Norfolk coastal village. The Fisherman's Return is situated just five minutes' walk from the beach yet it is also close to the Norfolk Broads and the coastal resort of Great Yarmouth. It offers a wide range of beers, mostly from local breweries, and an extensive menu of home-prepared meals. A separate function/family room and three en-suite bedrooms are also available. ⚒⚏⚘◁◖⊟♣♠P

Woodbastwick

Fur & Feather Inn

Slad Lane, NR13 6HQ (just off B1140)
🌑 12-3, 6-11 (10 Sun)
☎ (01603) 720003 ⊕ thefurandfeatherinn.co.uk
Woodforde's Mardler's, Wherry, Sun Dew, Nelson's Revenge, Norfolk Nog, Admiral's Reserve, Headcracker Ⓗ

Converted from three cottages and opened in the early 1990s, this pub is opposite Woodforde's Brewery. Although it is independently run, it acts as the brewery tap, selling the full range of its beers. In 2005 an elegant dining/function room was added. A food-oriented pub with an extensive, upmarket menu, some of the dishes are cooked using Woodforde's beers as an ingredient. Q⚘◖P

Wymondham

Feathers Inn

13 Town Green, NR18 0PN
🌑 11-2.30, 7-11; 11-midnight Fri & Sat; 12-midnight Sun
☎ (01953) 605675
Adnams Bitter; Greene King Abbot; Marston's Pedigree; guest beers Ⓗ

This excellent market-town pub has a long, L-shaped bar and two open fires. It is traditionally furnished and the walls are adorned with memorabilia and artefacts. There is an upstairs function room, which sometimes doubles as a venue for live music events, and a large outdoor seating area. Food is served lunchtimes and evenings, and a minimum of six real ales is always available. A public car park is adjacent to the pub.
⚒Q⚘◁♿⊟P

Railway

Station Road, NR18 0JY (next to station)
🌑 11-11; 12-10.30 Sun
☎ (01953) 605202 ⊕ therailwaypub.com
Adnams Bitter; guest beers Ⓗ

This food-oriented pub is situated a short distance out of town next to the railway station. It has a large bar divided into drinking and dining areas, and two lower rooms mainly used for drinking. Food from the extensive menu is served all day and Sunday lunches are especially popular. There are usually up to six real ales available, often sourced from local brewers. Q⚘◖⇌P⊟

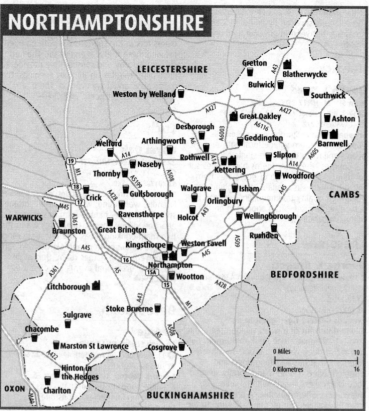

NORTHAMPTONSHIRE

Arthingworth

Bull's Head
Kelmarsh Road, LE16 8JZ (off A508)
🕐 12-3, 6-11; 12-10.30 Sun
☎ (01858) 525637
Everards Tiger, Original; Thwaites Original; guest beers Ⓗ
Large, 19th-century village pub converted from a former farmhouse with an L-shaped bar, log fires and secluded drinking areas. The dining room is separate from the main bar. An August bank holiday beer festival is held annually. Popular with walkers and cyclists, it has been awarded a three-star rating by the English Tourist Board and has eight en-suite rooms, one of them a family or disabled room. Offering three guest beers, it is a former CAMRA branch Pub of the Season.
ⓂQ⊛⇔⍟🕭&▲♣P

Ashton

Chequered Skipper
The Green, PE8 5LD
🕐 11.30-3, 6-11; 12-10.30-11 Sat; 12-10.30 Sun
☎ (01832) 273494
Oakham JHB; guest beers Ⓗ
Attractive stone and thatch pub set in the centre of the Rothschild's model village of Ashton. The modern single-bar interior has dining areas at each end. The village green to the front of the pub is the scene of the annual World Conker Championship held in October.

The food here is highly recommended – booking is advised at weekends. Q⊛🕭⍟🕭&♣

Barnwell

Montagu Arms
PE8 5PH
🕐 12-3, 6-11; 12-11 Sat; 12-10.30 Sun
☎ (01832) 273726
Adnams Bitter; guest beers Ⓗ
This 16th century inn in the centre of the village has heavy oak beams, open fires, a flagstone floor and easy access for disabled visitors. The extensive garden offers petanque and children's play areas. Following a recent change of landlord, the pub has increased the number of beers on offer from micro-breweries and has a handpump dedicated to ales from the Digfield Brewery.
ⓂQ⊛⍟🕭&▲♣♥

Braunston

Wheatsheaf
10 The Green, NN11 7HW
🕐 4-11; 12-midnight Sat; 12-10.30 Sun
☎ (01788) 890748
Flowers IPA; Greene King Abbot; guest beers Ⓗ
Friendly, open plan pub offering a frequently changing guest ale to complement the regular beers. Unusually, the pub has a Chinese takeaway operating from 5pm each evening. It hosts live music on the first and third Friday

367

of the month as well as every Saturday night. The village is serviced by an hourly Geoff Amos bus between Rugby and Banbury.
🏚🚃♣🚃

Bulwick

Queen's Head
Main Street, NN17 3DY
☼ 12-3, 6-11 (closed Mon); 12-4.30, 7-10.30 Sun
☎ (01780) 450272
Shepherd Neame Spitfire; guest beers Ⓗ
Popular, four-room village local with original beams and rustic decor. The single bar has five handpumps the other rooms have tables set for diners. A wide range of guest ales from micro-breweries is available throughout the year. High quality traditional English food is served, with game often appearing on the menu. 🏚Q🏚🕪 ⊞P

Chacombe

George & Dragon
1 Silver Street, OX17 2JR (between A361 and BB4525 near Banbury)
☼ 12-11.30
☎ (01295) 711500
Everards Beacon, Tiger; guest beers Ⓗ
Situated in front of a small village green, this smart, traditional, stone built, multi-room pub has a 26ft deep well in the bar. Sensitively refurbished, it has flagstone floors and disabled toilets. Home-made, locally sourced food is excellent, made with organic ingredients where possible. A private dining room is available for meetings. Central to the community, the inn runs pub and league quizzes and an award-winning post office.
🏚Q🏚🏚🏚🕪 ♿🚃♣🚃

Charlton

Rose & Crown
OX17 3DP (3 miles W of A43/A422 near Banbury)
☼ 12-3 (not Mon), 6-11; 12-3.30, 7-10.30 Sun
☎ (01295) 811317
Greene King IPA; guest beers Ⓗ
Delightful, recently decorated 17th-century thatched pub in a pretty village. The neat, beamed interior divides into a lounge and bar. Hops and local cricket memorabilia decorate one wall. The spacious dining room with inglenook fireplace offers an imaginative menu featuring local, freshly home-cooked dishes and traditional Sunday roasts. The grassed rear garden overlooks the Cherwell valley, and there are tables on the paved front patio. Families are welcome at this popular local, a meeting place for the Austin 10 Car Club. 🏚Q🏚🕪♿🚃♣P

Cosgrove

Navigation
Thrupp Wharf, Station Road, MK19 7BE (off A508)
☼ 12-3, 5.30-11; 12-11 Sat; 12-10.30 Sun
☎ (01908) 543156
Greene King IPA, Old Speckled Hen; guest beers Ⓗ
This popular pub is an easy stroll between the rural villages of Cosgrove and Castlethorpe

along the banks of the canal. Predominantly a food pub, good quality meals with home-made specials are available. Drinkers and diners mix in the spacious bar with an open fire and there is also a restaurant. The large garden, balcony and conservatory provide an ideal place to relax on summer evenings. Live music plays on Friday evening. There are usually two guest beers. 🏚🏚🕪P🚃

Crick

Royal Oak
22 Church Street, NN6 7TP
☼ 3.30-11; 12-10.30 Sat; 12-10.30 Sun
☎ (01788) 822340
Flowers IPA; Greene King Abbot; guest beers Ⓗ
Friendly, welcoming, wood-beamed cottage-style free house, hidden from the main A428 near the village church. Open fires warm the two main drinking areas. The guest ale range changes regularly. Northants Skittles and darts are played in the games room. Quiz nights plus other occasional events are organised.
🏚🏚🕪🚃♣

Desborough

George
79 High Street, NN14 2NB
☼ 11-midnight (1am Fri & Sat); 12-midnight Sun
☎ (01536) 760271
Everards Beacon, Tiger; guest beers Ⓗ
Situated opposite Desborough Cross, this coaching inn built in local ironstone dates from the 17th century. Over the years it has been opened up and updated, and now has a large L-shaped layout. Football, cricket, darts and pool teams are based at this community pub, with Sky TV for football fixtures. In summer the part-covered sun-trap yard comes into its own. Guest ales come from the Everards list.
🏚🏚♿🚃(19)♣P

Geddington

Star Inn
2 Bridge Street, NN14 1AZ
☼ 12-3, 6-11.30 (12.30am Fri & Sat); 12-10.30 Sun
☎ (01536) 742386 ⊕ star-inn-geddington.com
Greene King IPA; guest beers Ⓗ
The star is situated opposite one of the finest Eleanor crosses built by Edward I to mark the nightly resting places of Queen Eleanor's coffin on her last journey from Nottingham to London. The guest ales, always including at least one local brew, and home-cooked food are popular with villagers and visitors alike. A recent CAMRA local Pub of the Season.
🏚🏚🕪🚃♿♣🚃

Great Brington

Althorp Coaching Inn (Fox & Hounds)

Main Street, NN7 4EW
☻ 11-11 (11.45 Fri & Sat); 12-10.30 Sun
☎ (01604) 770651
Fuller's London Pride; Greene King IPA, Abbot, Old Speckled Hen; guest beers 🅷
This delightful stone built and thatched 'olde-worlde' pub has been serving the public since 1620. The bar is largely unspoilt with plenty of oak beams, a flagstone floor and open fireplace. The dining area has a massive inglenook. Outside there is an enclosed courtyard with tables leading to a floral garden. A good food menu is complemented by up to four guest beers. Althorp House, former home of Princess Diana, is close by.
🏚Q❀🕽P

Gretton

Bluebell

90 High Street, NN17 3DF (off A6003 on Corby Rd)
☻ 5 (4 Fri, 12.30 Sat)-midnight; 12.30-midnight Sun
☎ (01536) 770404
Greene King IPA, Abbot; guest beers 🅷
Friendly village local, once a bakery, in a row of 14th-century houses. The interior includes three connecting rooms with a slightly eccentric mix of old fashioned and modern decor. There is a real fire in the lounge. The outdoor paved drinking area at the back is put to good use during the Welland Valley beer festival in June. Meals must be pre-booked.
🏚❀♣🍺

Hatton Arms

Arnhill Road, NN17 3DN
☻ 12-2, 6 (5 Fri)-11 (closed Mon); 12-10.30 Sun
☎ (01536) 770268
Great Oakley Wot's Occurring; Marston's Pedigree; guest beers 🅷
One of the oldest pubs in Northamptonshire, dating back 700 years, this thatched stone-built country pub has two bars, a large restaurant and 'The Old Band Room' in a separate building. The public bar has a flagstone floor, solid wood beams and wooden tables and chairs. The second bar features a large stone fireplace. The brewery tap for the local Great Oakley Brewery, both bars have a small serving area with three handpumps each. During the summer the garden provides fine views of the Welland Valley. 🏚Q❀🕽➔🚲➙🚆P⅃

Guilsborough

Ward Arms

High Street, NN6 8PY
☻ 12-2.30, 5-11; 12-midnight Fri & Sat; 12-11 Sun
☎ (01604) 740265
Jennings Cumberland Ale; Nobby's Best Bitter; guest beers 🅷
This 17th-century pub is built from local ironstone with white rendering and a thatched roof. Situated opposite the old grammar school on the historic high street, it was frequented by the Duke of York who later became George VI. The late Queen Mother also put in an appearance. Handpumps take pride of place on the bar with a blackboard showing five changing guest beers as well as regular Nobby's beers. A ten-barrel plant is to be installed in the rear courtyard. Traditional home-cooked food is served.
🏚Q🕽❀🕽➔🚲➙🚆P⅃

Hinton in the Hedges

Crewe Arms

Sparrow Corner, NN13 5NF (off A43/A422)
☻ 6-11; 12-10.30 Sun
☎ (01280) 705801
Hook Norton Hooky Bitter; guest beers 🅷
Genuine free house tucked away down a lane in a village that is hard to find, especially at night time. After a two year closure the pub was a bought by two locals who have tastefully and comfortably refurbished the interior. Split up into four main areas, the pub still retains a traditional bar. Dining is very popular here and guest beers are often from local micro-breweries. 🏚❀🕽➔P

Holcot

White Swan

Main Street, NN6 9SP (Moulton to Walgrave road)
☻ 11-3, 5.30-11; 11-11 Sat; 12-10.30 Sun
☎ (01604) 781263
Batemans XB; Black Sheep Best Bitter; guest beers 🅷
White-painted stone and thatched country local with a cosy, welcoming bar displaying discreet classic vehicle memorabilia. Popular with Saints' rugby supporters, the split-level restaurant has regular themed evenings including curry night on Tuesday. Quiz and skittles nights are also held. The new landlord is a real ale enthusiast and plans occasional beers festivals. Handy for Pitsford reservoir, the Holcot Hobble and Holcot steam rally and country fair. ❀🕽➔🚆P⅃

Isham

Lilacs

39 Church Street, NN14 1HD (off A509 at church)
☻ 12-3, 5.30-1am (1.30am Fri & Sat); 12-4, 8-12.30am Sun
☎ (01536) 723948
Greene King IPA, Ruddles Best Bitter, Abbot; guest beers 🅷
Named after a breed of rabbit, this hard-to-find village pub is at the heart of the community, popular with locals, diners and those who seek out a traditional, unspoilt pub. The lounge with bay windows and a cosy snug at the front are complemented by a large games room towards the back with two pool tables, darts and Northants skittles. The guest beers are from the Greene King list.
🏚🕽❀🕽➔🚆♣P

Kettering

Alexandra Arms

39 Victoria Street, NN16 0BU
☻ 2-11 (midnight Fri & Sat); 12-11 Sun
☎ (01536) 522730
Beer range varies 🅷

Northants CAMRA Pub of the year 2005, this back street locals' pub just gets better and better. Three thousand different beers have passed through the ten handpumps in just four years. Nobby s beers are brewed in the cellar and at least one is available at all times. The front bar is covered with pump clips and the larger back bar is home to Northants skittles and pool. No under 18s are permitted at any time. If you can visit just one pub in Northants, make it this one. ⊕⬤⇙⬤⇌⊟♣↙

Piper

Windmill Avenue, NN15 6PS
☼ 11-3, 6-11; 12-10.30 Sun
☎ (01536) 513870
Hook Norton Hooky Bitter; guest beers Ⓗ
Welcoming 1950s two roomed pub close to Wicksteed Park. The lively bar/games room with Sky TV and pool is complemented by the quieter lounge. Five or six changing real ales come from the SIBA Direct Delivery scheme. Two beer festivals are held a year. Sunday is quiz night. Home-cooked food is served up to 10pm. Q⊕⬤⬤⬤♣↙⬤P

Sawyers

44 Montague Street, NN16 8RU
☼ Closed Mon; 3-11 Tue & Wed; 3-7, 8-midnight Thu-Sat; 1-11 Sun
☎ (01536) 484800 ⊕ sawyersvenue.co.uk
Oakham JHB; guest beers Ⓗ
Formerly the Swan, now named after a former landlord, this town centre pub is a major music venue and bands as famous as Dr Feelgood have played here. The pub acts as the tap for Potbelly brewery and at least two of its award-winning ales are always available. No food is served. It offers a large selection of board games. ⇌⊟⬤P

Shire Horse

18 Newland Street, NN16 8JH
☼ 11-11; 12-10.30 Sun
☎ (01536) 519078
Tetley Bitter, Burton Ale; guest beers Ⓗ
Down to earth locals' pub but very welcoming to visitors. The guest beers change regularly. Motorcycle prints cover the walls. Northants Skittles and pool are played in the open-plan bar where numerous pump clips are displayed. Shove-ha'penny is available and a wide selection of music played. The bus station is next door. ⊕⇌⊟♣⬤↙

Kingsthorpe

Queen Adelaide

50 Manor Road, NN2 6QJ (off A519)
☼ 11.30-11; 12-10.30 Sun
☎ (01604) 714524 ⊕ queenadelaide.com
Adnams Bitter, Broadside; Greene King IPA; guest beers Ⓗ
The Adelaide was originally a village pub until Kingsthorpe was swallowed up by Northampton. This friendly four-room inn has been opened out but retains quiet, intimate areas for social chat. Low beams and an uneven floor feature along with four guest ales include a locally brewed micro beer and a mild. Local CAMRA Pub of the Year runner-up in 2005. A beer festival is held on the first weekend in September. ⊕⬤⬤⬤⊟♣⬤P↙

Marston St Lawrence

Marston Inn

OX17 2DB (off A422/B4525)
☼ 12-3 (Fri & Sat), 6.30-11 (midnight Fri & Sat); 12.30-3 Sun
☎ (01295) 711906 ⊕ marstoninn.co.uk
Hook Norton Hooky Bitter; guest beer Ⓗ
You are guaranteed a lively, enthusiastic welcome from the taxi-driving magician landlord of this pub. Well worth seeking out, it has two small, friendly, linked rooms, one with a piano, and two further rooms for dining. Good quality, home-made food is recommended. A monthly quiz is held. The family-friendly pub blossoms in summer with extended hours, entertainment in the large front garden and camping facilities within the grounds. ⬤⬤▲♣P↙

Naseby

Royal Oak

Church Street, NN6 6DA
☼ 4.30 (12 Sat)-midnight; 12-7 Sun
☎ (07985) 408240
Beer range varies Ⓗ
Welcoming, traditional brick-built village pub on the outskirts of the village, close to the battlefield of Naseby, fought in 1645. The main L-shaped room is split into lounge and bar areas with open fires. It has an oak tree built into the bar. Northants skittles and darts are played in a separate games area. Adjoining barns host a popular beer festival in October and during St George's week in April. Classic car and bike meets are held in the extensive grounds. Five regularly changing beers are available. ⬤Q⊕▲♣⬤P↙

Northampton

Lamplighter

66 Overstone Road, NN1 3JS
☼ 5 (4 Fri)-11 (midnight Fri); 12-midnight Sat; 12-6 Sun
☎ (01604) 631125
Beer range varies Ⓗ
Excellent town centre traditional street corner local, well worth the short walk from the bus station. The welcoming single bar/lounge is on a split level with comfortable soft furnishings. Above the bar is a coloured canopy bearing the pub's name. Quiz nights are every Wednesday and Friday. Up to four changing guest beers are available, often including one from Timothy Taylor. ⊕⬤⊟♣↙

Malt Shovel Tavern

121 Bridge Street (opp Carlsberg factory)
☼ 11.30-3, 5-11; 12-3, 7-10.30 Sun
☎ (01604) 234212
Frog Island Natterjack; Fuller's London Pride; Great Oakley Wot's Occurring, Harpers; Tetley Bitter; guest beers Ⓗ
Popular, award-winning free house just off the town centre circuit. The Shovel is the tap for the Great Oakley Brewery, with up to four of its beers among the 13 handpumps. There is also a fine selection of draught and bottled Belgian beers, traditional farm cider, country wines and over 40 single malt whiskies. The interior is filled with breweriana. Blues bands perform every Wednesday evening and a quiz

night is hosted once a month. CAMRA regional Pub of the Year 2004. Q✿◑◔≈🖭●

Northampton Borough Club

Fish Street, NN1 2AA
✪ 12-3.30, 5-11; 1-4.30, 7-11 Sat; closed Sun
☎ (01604) 634352
Everards Beacon; guest beers Ⓗ
Town centre municipal club with a bar upstairs which has a good reputation locally for its beers. Access is via a lobby with a lift and stairs. The C-shaped bar is basic at the games end while the lounge is more plush and relaxing. A further room contains a full-sized snooker table. The weekday lunchtime menu changes daily. Show this Guide or CAMRA membership card to gain access. ➰◑&≈🖭

Racehorse

15 Abington Square, NN1 4AE
✪ 12-midnight
☎ (01604) 631997
Hampshire King Alfred's, Ironside; guest beers Ⓗ
Lively town centre pub divided into two with a large back room where live bands play. The bar on the right has what must be one of the longest seats in any pub. Regular barbecues are held in the spacious rear garden in summer. A range of six ales always includes a Hampshire brew as well as beers from local breweries. Children are welcome in the garden but not the pub. ✿🖭♣●

Romany

NN2 6JN (half mile E of Kingsthorpe)
✪ 11.30-11.30; 12-11 Sun
☎ (01604) 714647
Fuller's London Pride; Newby Wyke Bear Island; Oakham JHB; Theakston Best Bitter; guest beers Ⓗ
Large 1930s pub offering a range of nine changing ales along with real cider and perry. This two-roomed pub has an excellent games room with Northants skittles and pool. It is busy most evenings Monday is quiz night, there is live music on Thursday, Saturday and Sunday, and karaoke on Friday. The landlady offers a discount to CAMRA members on Tuesday and Wednesday evenings. A recent CAMRA branch Pub of the Season.
✿◑🖭♣●P🖳

White Elephant

Kingsley Park Terrace, NN2 7HG (on A43 opp old racecourse)
✪ 11-11; 12-10.30 Sun
☎ (01604) 711202
Greene King IPA; guest beers Ⓗ
Originally called the Kingsley Park Hotel, the pub was built in the 1860s to serve the Northampton racecourse. Due to suffragettes the racecourse closed in 1911 and the pub was renamed. The large, spacious interior has many intimate areas with soft furnishings, and an open kitchen where pizzas are a speciality. Up to four guest beers from family and established micro-breweries are stocked. A live jam night is held on Sunday and live music fortnightly on Thursdays. Quiz night is Tuesday. Q✿◑&🖭♣🖳

Wig and Pen

19 St Giles Street, NN1 1JA

✪ 12-midnight; 12-11 Sun
☎ (01604) 622178
Fenland Sparkling Wit; guest beers Ⓗ
A warm welcome to the Guide for this town centre pub recently purchased by the Fenland Brewery. Formerly a Mansfield pub, the Wig and Pen was called the Black Lion until 10 years ago. The frontage is over 300 years old; the long L-shaped bar was created with an extension 150 years ago. Up to seven guest beers are stocked from micro-breweries, including more Fenland beers. Live music plays regularly. ✿◑🖭♣●🖳

Orlingbury

Queen's Arms

11 Isham Road, NN14 1JD (off A43 S of Kettering)
✪ 11-2.30, 5.30 (5 Sat)-11; 12.30-3, 6-10.30 Sun
☎ (01933) 678258
Adnams Bitter; Caledonian Deuchars IPA; Fuller's London Pride; Taylor Landlord; Tetley Bitter; guest beers Ⓗ
Just off the village green in the direction of Isham, the Queen s Arms dates from the mid 1700s and was known as the King's Arms until 1840. The main lounge is divided into three areas and there is a separate snug. Meals may be taken in the dining room or the bar (no food Sun eve). The large garden is well equipped and hosts a popular beer festival in summer. Q➰✿◑&🖭(46)P

Ravensthorpe

Chequers

Chequers Lane, NN6 8ER (between A428 and A5199, opp. church)
✪ 12-3, 6-11; 12-11 Sat; 12-3, 7-10.30 Sun
☎ (01604) 770379
Batemans XXXB; Black Sheep Best Bitter; Greene King IPA; Jennings Bitter; guest beers Ⓗ
You are assured of a warm welcome from the lively, affable hosts at this friendly pub, popular with locals walkers and fishermen. A brick-built Grade II listed free house, guest beers come from local micros. On the beams is a collection of jugs, and the half panelled walls are festooned with bank notes. The garden has a children's adventure area and you can play Northants Skittles. The pub and restaurant serve an extensive menu of good value food. ➰✿◑&🖭♣

Rothwell

Woolpack Inn

Market Hill, NN14 6BW (off A14/B576, follow signs for Glendon)
✪ 11-11 (midnight Thu-Sat)
☎ (01536) 710284
Marston's Pedigree; guest beers Ⓗ
The pub's name is a reminder that Rothwell used to be important for its sheep markets. The long, narrow public bar leads to two further rooms. A large, comfortable lounge with a wood fire has a homely, farmhouse feel. The light, airy drinking and dining room overlooks the garden. Guest beers mainly come from local micro-breweries and change regularly to provide a choice of strength and light or dark beers. ⋈✿◑&🖭P

Rushden

Rushden Historic Transport Society

Station Approach, NN10 0AW

☼ 7.30 (12 Sat)-11; 12-3, 7-10.30 Sun

☎ (01933) 318988 ⊕ rhts.co.uk

Fuller's London Pride; guest beers Ⓗ

The LMS line from Wellingborough to Higham Ferrers closed many moons ago but the RHTS has created an oasis in this part of the county. The former ladies' waiting room is the club bar and you can drink in the coaches or outside on the platform. The warm welcome and well-kept micro-beers have made this a former CAMRA regional Club of the Year. This is a must see. Day membership is £1. ♨Q❀♣⋢

Slipton

Samuel Pepys

Slipton Lane, NN14 3AR (off A6116)

☼ 12-3, 6-11; 12-11 Sat; 12-10.30 Sun

☎ (01832) 731739 ⊕ thesamuelpepys.net

Greene King IPA; Oakham JHB; Potbelly Aisling; Ⓗ **guest beers** Ⓖ

Formerly know as the Red Cow, this stone building dates from the 1600s, now complemented by a modern conservatory. Between two and four guest beers are available on gravity all year. Good food is available in the restaurant (booking advised), the lounge or in the large garden in summer. A heated area is provided for smokers. ♨❀◑⋔P⋐

Southwick

Shuckburgh Arms

Main Street, PE8 5BL

☼ 12-2 (not Mon & Tue), 6-11; 12-10.30 Sun

☎ (01832) 274007

Fuller's London Pride; Oakham JHB; guest beer Ⓗ

Next to the village hall, this two-room pub is at the heart of the community. The main bar area dispenses beer from three handpumps; both rooms have tables set for diners. The pub can only be accessed from the rear. The large enclosed garden is behind the car park and adjacent to the village cricket pitch. Traditional pub food is popular and well priced. ♨Q❀⋔⅍Å

Stoke Bruerne

Boat Inn

Shutlanger Road, NN12 7SB (opp canal museum)

☼ 11-3, 6-11; 11-11 Fri, Sat & summer; 12-10.30 Sun

☎ (01604) 862428 ⊕ boatinn.co.uk

Banks's Bitter; Marston's Burton Bitter, Pedigree, Old Empire; guest beers Ⓗ

Situated on the banks of the Grand Union Canal, opposite the popular canal museum, the Boat has been run by the same family since 1877. For drinkers the tap bar comprises a couple of cosy rooms in the original thatched stone building. A large extension incorporates the lounge bar, restaurant and bistro, serving hearty portions. A small shop caters for canal users (from 9am summer, 10am winter). Three guest beers are available. ♨Q❀◑⋢⅍⋒♣⋐

Sulgrave

Star Inn

Manor Road, OX17 2SA (off A43 or B4525)

☼ 11-3, 6-11; 12-5 Sun

☎ (01295) 760389

Hook Norton Hooky Bitter, Old Hooky, seasonal beer Ⓗ

Delightful 300-year-old stone-built pub, set in the beautiful village of Sulgrave. Almost opposite is Sulgrave Manor, the ancestral home of the George Washington family. The front bar area is still relatively unchanged with its flagstone floor, beamed ceiling and inglenook fireplace. To the rear is a restaurant where good home-cooked food is prepared. ♨Q❀◑P

Thornby

Red Lion

Welford Road, NN6 8SJ (on A5199)

☼ 12-2.30, 5-11 (closed Mon);12-11 Sat; 12-10.30 Sun

☎ (01604) 740238

Everards Tiger; Frog Island Shoemaker; Greene King IPA; Tetley Bitter; guest beer Ⓗ

Friendly, inviting, traditional village pub that dates back over 400 years. The three-room interior features wooden beams, a stone floor in the bar area and a wood-burning open fire set half-way up the chimney breast in the cosy lounge. There is also a compact restaurant. Collections of beer steins, tankards and paintings are displayed throughout. A quiz night is held fortnightly on Tuesday. The mature garden has various seating areas. The four regular beers are supplemented by two guests. ♨❀◑Å♣P

Walgrave

Royal Oak

Zion Hill, NN6 9PN (2 miles E of A43)

☼ 12-3, 5.30-11; 12-10.30 Sun

☎ (01604) 781248

Adnams Bitter; Greene King Abbot; guest beers Ⓗ

A real gem, this old ironstone building has been a pub since the 1840s. The long front bar is split into three areas, the room to the left used for dining. There is a games room with Northants skittles and a beer garden with a children's playground. The menu is extensive, with Sunday lunch a speciality. At least two guest beers are available. ♨❀◑⋢♣♠

Welford

Wharf Inn

NN6 6JQ (off A5199 N of village)

☼ 12-11 (1am Thu-Sat)

☎ (01858) 575075 ⊕ wharfinn.co.uk

Banks's Bitter; Marston's Pedigree; guest beers Ⓗ

Brick-built inn, situated at the end of the Welford Arm of the Grand Union Canal, with a main bar and extensive dining area. Popular with barges, locals and tourists, five historic walks can be started from its landscaped garden and themed events and beer festivals are held throughout the year. Accommodation and wireless Internet access are available.

Three rotating guest beers often include one from a local micro-brewery. ⚌✿✍◑⅃&P

Wellingborough

Coach & Horses
17 Oxford Street, NN8 4HY (on A5128)
✪ 10.30-11; 12-11 Sun
☎ (01933) 441848
Fuller's ESB; Great Oakley Wot's Occurring; Okells IPA; Potbelly Pigs Do Fly; guest beers ⊞
This newly refurbished pub with eight handpumps has quickly gained a following among real ale drinkers. The landlord tries to support local micro-breweries whenever possible. Sky TV is screened. There is a large outside drinking area to the rear, covered and heated for smokers. ⚌✿🚃●≟

Locomotive
111 Finedon Road, NN8 4AL (on A510)
✪ 11-11; 12-3, 7-10.30 Sun
☎ (01933) 276600
Batemans XB; Wychwood Hobgoblin; guest beers ⊞
Friendly conversation and banter with the locals and landlord is the entertainment at this thriving community free house, originally three cottages. Genuine railway memorabilia features throughout and a train set runs permanently above the bar. Local and other micro-beers are guests. Sometimes a guest cider can be found. Good lunches are served to complement the ales. No under 18s allowed. ⚌Q✿◑⊟≟♣P

Old Grammarians Association
46 Oxford Street, NN8 4JH (on A5128)
✪ 12-2.30, 7-11; 11.30-11 Sat; 12-10.30 Sun
☎ (01933) 226188
Greene King IPA; Hook Norton Hooky Bitter, Old Hooky; guest beers ⊞
Close to the centre of town, this welcoming members club offers three or four guest beers. It has a spacious main bar, small TV lounge and games/function room. The club holds a quiz night on the first Tuesday of the month as well as regular music events. Show a CAMRA membership card or a copy of this Guide for entry – regular visitors will be asked to join. There is a large car park at the rear. ♋◑&P

Weston by Welland

Wheel & Compass
Valley Road, LE16 8HZ
✪ 12-3, 6-11; 12-11 Sat; 12-10.30 Sun
☎ (01858) 565864
Banks's Bitter; Greene King Abbot; Marston's Burton Bitter, Pedigree; guest beer ⊞
This multi-roomed village inn is as busy and popular as any city centre pub due to its well-deserved reputation for good quality food: 'We do not serve fast food, we serve good food as fast as we can.' The guest beer usually comes from a micro. The large rear garden with benches and seats plus swings and slides for children attracts families in summer. ⚌Q✿◑P

Weston Favell

Bold Dragoon
48 High Street, NN13 3JW (off A4500)
✪ 11-3, 5.30-11; 11-11 Fri & Sat; 12-10.30 Sun
☎ (01604) 401221
Fuller's London Pride; Greene King IPA; guest beers ⊞
This 1930s pub retains some of its original character. Owned by Churchill Taverns, it has 10 handpumps offering six changing guest beers from traditional breweries. Very popular for its food, dining is in the delightful conservatory or the spacious outdoor patio during clement months. The traditional tap room has a pool table and sports TV, while the lounge to the rear is decorated with hop bines. A music quiz is held on Sunday evening. Q✿✿◑⊟&🚃♣P

Woodford

Duke's Arms
83 High Street, NN14 4HE (off A14/A510)
✪ 12-11 (10.30 Sun)
☎ (01832) 732224
Greene King IPA, Abbot; Hop Back Summer Lightning; guest beers ⊞
Once known as the Lords Arms, the pub was renamed in honour of the Duke of Wellington who was a regular visitor to Woodford. Home-cooked food is served at all times except Sunday evening. To the rear of the pub there is a games room where pool, darts and Northants skittles are played. The Duke's holds a beer festival in summer and hosts regular entertainment on Thursday, Friday and Sunday evenings. ⚌♋✿◑⊟&🚃(16)♣●P≟

Wootton

Wootton Working Men's Club
High Street, NN4 6LW (off A508 near jct 15 M1)
✪ 12-2 (3 Sat; not Thu), 7 (4.30 Fri)-11 (11.30 Fri); 12-10.30 Sun
☎ (01604) 761863
Great Oakley Wot's Occurring; guest beer ⊞
Once the Red Lion, this ironstone building was rescued from closure by its regulars. Now an award-winning club, it has a bar, quiet lounge, concert room and games room featuring Northants Skittles. With six changing guest beers, the club was a previous CAMRA regional Club of the Year. Show this Guide or CAMRA membership card for admittance. Q♋

Why America was founded

For we could not now take time for further search (to land our ship) our victuals being much spent, especially our beer.
Log of the Mayflower

NORTHUMBERLAND

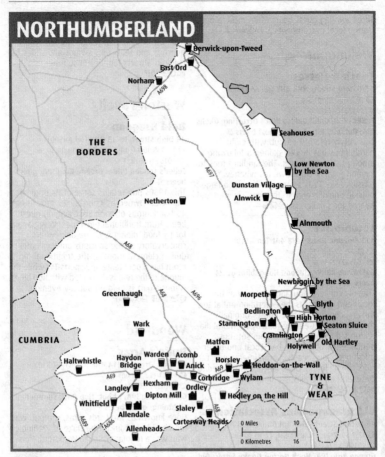

Berwick-upon-Tweed
East Ord
Norham
THE BORDERS
Seahouses
Low Newton by the Sea
Dunstan Village
Netherton
Alnwick
Alnmouth
Newbiggin by the Sea
Morpeth
Greenhaugh
Blyth
Bedlington
High Horton
Wark
Stannington
Seaton Sluice
Cramlington
Old Hartley
Matfen
Holywell
CUMBRIA
Haltwhistle
Warden
Acomb
Horsley
Heddon-on-the-Wall
Haydon Bridge
Anick
Wylam
Langley
Hexham
Corbridge
TYNE & WEAR
Ordley
Whitfield
Dipton Mill
Hedley on the Hill
Allendale
Slaley
Allenheads
Carterway Heads

0 Miles 10
0 Kilometres 16

Acomb

Miners Arms
Main Street, NE46 4PW
☼ 5 (12 Sat & Sun)-12.30am
☎ (01434) 603909 ⊕ theminersacomb.com
Black Sheep Best Bitter; Yates Bitter; guest beers Ⓗ
The inn's name is a reminder of the once prominent mining industry in this area. A central staircase divides the pub into two drinking areas: a small, cosy bar and a comfortable lounge with a real fire. Four real ales are always on handpump – the Miners is a rare outlet in the north east for Yates bitter. The dining room is to the rear.
🛏Q❀◑Ġ🚋(880, 882)♣

Allendale

Golden Lion
Market Place, NE47 9BD
☼ 12-1.30am; (2.30am Fri-Sun)
☎ (01434) 683225
Allendale Best Bitter, Golden Plover; guest beers Ⓗ
Pleasant 18th-century pub in the main square, very popular with ramblers and day trippers who wish to take advantage of excellent nearby countryside walks. Pictures of the annual new year tar barrel procession are displayed on the walls. The local choir practises here on Tuesday evening and there is live Irish music on the last day of each month. 🛏➣❀◑Ġ🚋(688)♣

Kings Head Hotel
Market Place, NE47 9BD
☼ 12-midnight
☎ (01434) 683681
Banks's Original; Jennings Cumberland Ale, Cocker Hoop Ⓗ
Welcoming inn in the market square with a traditional open log fire. Meals are served all day. This area is popular with ramblers, cyclists and day trippers. If travelling by train to Hexham ask at Newcastle for a 'plus bus' ticket which also gives unlimited bus travel for a nominal charge. Rail and bus links are good and Allendale is well worth the effort to get to. 🛏🚪◑🚋(688)

Allenheads

Allenheads Inn
NE47 9HJ
✪ 12-4, 7-11; 12-11 Fri & Sat; 12-10.30 Sun
☎ (01434) 685200 ⊕ theallenheadsinn.co.uk
Black Sheep Best Bitter; Greene King Abbot; guest beers Ⓗ
Originally the home of Sir Thomas Wentworth, this 18th-century multi-room building has a public bar with log fire, lounge, games room and dining room. It features an eclectic assembly of antiques and memorabilia throughout, with many knick-knacks hanging from the ceiling in the bar. ⚏✿◑◗➡(688)♣P

Alnmouth

Red Lion
22 Northumberland Street, NE66 2RJ
✪ 11 (12 Sun)-11
☎ (01665) 830584 ⊕ redlionalnmouth.co.uk
Black Sheep Best Bitter; guest beers Ⓗ
Built in the 18th century as a coaching inn, the cosy wood-panelled and beamed lounge bar was re-fitted in the 1950s. It is listed in CAMRA's regional inventory for the north east. Also worthy of note are the attractive coloured glass windows depicting red lions in the dining room. The raised decking in the large garden overlooking the River Aln offers superb views and is used for jazz and blues music nights. Three guest beers generally come from northern micro-breweries. Opening hours may vary in winter. ⚏✿◛◑◗➡(518)♣P'⌐

Alnwick

John Bull Inn
12 Howick Street, NE66 1UY
✪ 12-3 (Sat only), 7-11; 12-2, 7-10.30
☎ (01665) 602055 ⊕ john-bull-inn.co.uk
Beer range varies Ⓗ
Originally a beer house built circa 1830, possibly as the Alnwick Brewery tap. The landlord is a keen supporter of north east micro-breweries and offers a real cider which is rare for the area. The pub also offers the best range of Belgian bottled beers in the county. Noted for its wide selection of board games, there are no games machines or electronic music. The pub hosts the annual leek show and a beer festival to coincide with Alnwick Fair. Local CAMRA north Northumberland Pub of the Year 2007.
Q✿➡(near bus station)♣♠

Tanners Arms
Hotspur Place, NE66 1QF
✪ 12-3 (not winter Mon-Fri), 5-midnight (12.30am Fri & Sat); 12-midnight Sun
☎ (01665) 602553
Beer range varies Ⓗ
Ivy covered stone built pub just off Bondgate Without and a short distance from Alnwick Garden. The single room has a rustic interior with flagstone floor and a tree beer shelf. Regular acoustic music features. The ever changing real ales often come from north eastern micro-breweries. In summer there are also cask ales on gravity dispense in the cellar. Occasional beer festivals are held. As part of the annual fair it holds a strongman competition in the street outside. ➡♠

Anick

Rat Inn
NE46 4LN
✪ 11-11 summer (11.30-3, 6-11 winter); 12-10.30 summer (12-3, 6-10.30 winter) Sun
☎ (01434) 602814
Caledonian Deuchars IPA; Everards Beacon; guest beers Ⓗ
An outstanding country pub. The traditional old fireplace has an open log fire and more than 20 chamber pots hanging from the ceiling. An exceptional beer garden offers excellent views over Tyne Valley. Very popular with tourists and cyclists, the pub is renowned for good quality food made with ingredients from local suppliers (no eve meals Sun).
⚏⛲✿◑◗P

Berwick-upon-Tweed

Barrels Ale House
59-61 Bridge Street, TD15 1ES
✪ 11.30-midnight (3-midnight Tue-Thu winter); 11.30-1am Fri & Sat; 12-midnight Sun
☎ (01289) 308031 ⊕ thebarrels.co.uk
Harviestoun Bitter & Twisted; Shepherd Neame Spitfire, Premium Ale; Taylor Landlord; guest beers Ⓗ
This drinking emporium is part of an attractive curved stone terrace at the end of the old road bridge over the Tweed, not far from the quay. The split-level public bar features an eclectic collection of bric-a-brac: note the dentist's chair. The lounge is Victorian in style with bare boards and there is a basement used mainly by DJs and blues bands often from the USA. The pub attracts a mixed clientele of all ages. ✿◑◛➡⌐

Foxtons
26 Hyde Hill, TD15 1AB
✪ 10-11 (midnight Fri & Sat); closed Sun
☎ (01289) 303939
Caledonian Deuchars IPA, 80 Ⓗ
An unusual regular in the Guide, Foxtons looks more like a coffee shop or bistro than a pub. Alongside an extensive Mediterr??+?)P &, British and Northumbrian food menu it offers real ales, and drinkers as well as diners are welcome. Near the main shopping street it is popular with shoppers taking a break and visitors to the Maltings art centre, as well as with tourists. ✿◑◗➡⌐

Pilot
31, Low Greens, TD15 1LX
✪ 12-midnight (10.30 Sun)
☎ (01289) 304214
Caledonian Deuchars IPA; guest beers Ⓗ
Stone built end-of-terrace local dating from the 19th century. Retaining its original three-room layout and drinking corridor (an unusual feature for the region), it is listed on CAMRA's regional inventory for the north east. The wood-panelled public bar features nautical artefacts that are 100 years old. Note the fine mosaic floor at the entrance. North east and Scottish micro-breweries usually supply the

two guest beers. The pub hosts music nights and runs quoits and darts teams.
🏃🛏️🍴◖◗�"🚲(several)🍺

Blyth

Olivers Bar

60 Bridge Street, NE24 2AP
🕐 11 (2 Sat)-11; 12-10.30 Sun
☎ (01670) 540356
Greene King Ruddles County, Old Speckled Hen; Wylam Gold Ⓗ
Former newsagent's converted to a real ale oasis in a town still known for its football team heroics in the FA cup run of the 70s. Note the framed menu 'ports from the wood' which hangs on the wall in the bar. Do not be surprised to find complimentary food on the bar come Saturday teatime at this warm and friendly hostelry. A local ladies group meets on Monday evening. ♣

Carterway Heads

Manor House Inn

DH8 9LX (on A68 S of Corbridge)
🕐 12-11; 12-10.30 Sun
☎ (01207) 255268
Courage Directors; Greene King Old Speckled Hen; Theakston Best Bitter; Wells Bombardier; guest beer Ⓗ
Welcoming country inn near Derwent Reservoir enjoying views over the Derwent Valley. Guest ales from local micro-breweries can be enjoyed as well as home-cooked food served in the bar and restaurant. The cider is Weston's Old Rosie. There is even a shop selling local produce. The pub also has excellent accommodation. 🏃🛏️❀🍴◖◗🍴P

Corbridge

Angel Inn

Main Street, NE45 5LA
🕐 10 (10.30 Sun)-11
☎ (01434) 632119
Allendale Golden Plover; Durham Black Velvet Ⓗ
1726 coaching inn kept in pristine condition. Superior lounge area with comfortable sofas and traditional armchairs. Pleasant outside seating area in the summer. The bar has a reputation for a fine selection of malt whiskies. This establishment is also very popular for food
🏃Q❀🛏️◖◗&🚲(Corbridge)🚲(685)

Black Bull

Middle Street, NE45 5LE
🕐 11 (11.30 Sun)-11
☎ (01434) 632261
Greene King IPA, Ruddles County, Abbot, Old Speckled Hen Ⓗ
Beautiful stone built pub in this ancient town with strong links to the Romans. The L-shaped bar has an area for dining with a log fire. Good quality food is available all day, cooked to order by the pub's chef. This Green King pub is popular with locals, tourists and ramblers.
🏃◖◗🚲P

Cramlington

Plough

Middle Farm Buildings, NE23 9DN
🕐 11-3, 6-11; 11-11 Thu-Sat; 12-10.30 Sun
☎ (01670) 737633
Theakston XB; guest beers Ⓗ
In the centre of the ancient village of Cramlington, this pub faces the parish church. Once a farm, the old buildings were sympathetically converted some years ago. The bar is small and busy with a door leading to an outdoor seating area. The large lounge has a round 'gin gan' making it feel even more spacious. Ruddles County is served, with beers from local micros regularly appearing as guests. ❀◖◗🚂🚲P

Dipton Mill

Dipton Mill Inn

Dipton Mill Road, NE46 1YA
🕐 12-2.30, 6-11; 12-4, 7-10.30 Sun
☎ (01434) 606577
Hexhamshire Devil's Elbow, Shire Bitter, Devil's Water, Whapweasel, Old Humbug Ⓗ
The tap for Hexhamshire brewery, this small low ceilinged pub is run by a keen landlord who brews excellent beers which are sold in the pub. Great home cooked meals to complement the beers, a cosy atmosphere and a warm welcome make it well worth seeking out. The large garden has a stream running through it. 🏃Q❀◖◗P

Dunstan Village

Cottage Inn

NE66 3SZ
🕐 12-11; 12-10.30 Sun
☎ (01665) 576658
Beer range varies Ⓗ
Less than a mile from Northumbrian coastline, and suprisingly spacious, this inn has a bar, restaurant, conservatory and covered and open patios. Good food complements the excellent beer. Half a mile from Craster village, famed for its kippers, the inn is ideally located for birdwatchers, walkers, golfers and tourists. 🏃Q❀🛏️◖◗&P

East Ord

Salmon Inn

TD15 2NS
🕐 11-3, 5-11; 11-11 Fri & Sat; 12-10.30 Sun
☎ (01289) 305227
Caledonian Deuchars IPA, 80; Wells Bombardier Ⓗ
On the main street near the large village green, this single-room pub is renowned for its highly regarded locally sourced home cooked food which tempts visitors from near and far; Sunday lunches are particularly popular. In winter cask beer drinkers gather around the real fire. In summer a large marquee is installed in the garden to accommodate the weekend overflow. The pub runs a leek club and a quoits team. Regular quiz nights and barbecues are hosted.
🏃❀◖◗🍴🚲(67)♣P🍺

Greenhaugh

Hollybush Inn

NE48 1PW (1 mile N of Lanehead jct on
Bellingham-Kielder road)

☻ 5 (11 Sat)-11; 12-3, 7-10.30 Sun

☎ (01434) 240391 ⊕ hollybushinn.co.uk

High House Farm Nel's Best; guest beer ⊞

Exceptional community pub set in a row of
low stone terraced cottages in a tiny, remote
north Tyne valley hamlet. It acts as the local
community centre hosting various local groups
including mid-week adult IT courses and
received royal recognition in 2006 with a visit
from the Prince of Wales. Note the memorial
to a Wellington bomber crew which crashed
nearby during WWII. The wood-burning
cooking range warms the pub in winter.
▩Q❦❀▩⬤❶⬤♣

Haltwhistle

Black Bull

Market Square, NE49 0RL

☻ 12-11; winter closed Mon, 12-3, 6-11 Tue & Thu

☎ (01434) 320463

**Big Lamp Prince Bishop; Yates Feverpitch; guest
beers** ⊞

Warm, friendly two-room pub down a cobbled
street just off the market place with several
handpumps serving excellent ale. Also noted
for its good food, it offers an excellent menu
plus blackboard specials. An open fire, low
wood beamed ceiling and horse brasses add
to the traditional ambience.
▩Q❀❶⬤≠(Haltwhistle)⬤▩(685)

Haydon Bridge

General Havelock

9 Ratcliff Road, NE47 7HU

☻ 12-2.30, 7-10.30; closed Mon

☎ (01434) 684376

Beer range varies ⊞

This comfortable pub has a well-deserved
reputation for good food. Two handpumps
dispense ale usually from northern breweries.
The restaurant is in a small converted barn
with fine views of the River Tyne and there is
a pleasant patio area for outdoor drinking. A
popular local walk, the John Martin Trail, starts
nearby – ask at the bar for a leaflet.
▩Q❦❀❶⬤≠▩(685)♣

Hedley on the Hill

Feathers

NE43 7SW

☻ 12-3 (Sat only), 6-11; 12-3, 7-10.30 Sun

☎ (01661) 843607

Beer range varies ⊞

A cracker of a pub set in a hamlet above the
Tyne valley with views of the city and three
surrounding counties. There are two bars, both
with exposed stone walls and beams. The pub
serves high quality home-made food to
complement the four real ales. A mini beer
festival is held at Easter culminating on
Monday with the famous uphill barrel race.
▩Q❀❶⬤❶P⬤

Hexham

Tap & Spile

1 Eastgate, NE46 1BH

☻ 11-11.30 (midnight Fri & Sat); 12-11.30 Sun

☎ (01434) 602039

**Black Sheep Best Bitter; Caledonian Deuchars
IPA; guest beers** ⊞

Traditional street corner pub on the main
street oozing with character. There has been a
pub on this site for centuries and pictures on
the wall reflect its history. Folk musicians play
regularly in the rear bar. Good home-cooked
lunches are on offer (not Sun). Q⬤❶⬤♣

High Horton

Three Horseshoes

Hatherley Lane, NE24 4HF (off 189 N of
Cramlington, follow A192) OS276794

☻ 11-11; 12-10.30 Sun

☎ (01670) 822410

**Greene King Abbot, Old Speckled Hen; Tetley
Bitter; guest beers** ⊞

Extended former coaching inn at the highest
point in the Blyth Valley with views of the
Northumberland coast. The pub is open plan
with distinct bar and dining areas plus a
conservatory. Offering an extensive range of
meals and snacks, it is dedicated to real ale
with seven handpumps serving three regular
beers and a constantly changing list of guests
including ales from local micro-brewers.
Regular beer festivals. Q❦❀❶P⬤

Holywell

Olde Fat Ox Inn

Holywell Village, NE26 3TW

☻ 11-11 (midnight Fri & Sat)

☎ (0191) 237 0964

Caledonian Deuchars IPA; guest beers ⊞

Situated close to the county boundary near
Seaton Delaval, this traditional pub is in the
heart of the village. Up to three guest beers
are selected, often by popular demand by the
regulars, from the Punch Taverns fine cask list.
▩❀

Horsley

Lion & Lamb

NE15 0NS

☻ 12-11 (10.30 Sun)

☎ (01661) 832952

**Black Sheep Best Bitter; Camerons Castle Eden
Ale; Flowers IPA; Greene King IPA** ⊞

A warning to 'Mind ya heed' is a reminder of
the age of this low-ceilinged building, parts of
which date back to 1718. Traditional wooden
tables add to the ambience. Well patronised
by locals and visitors, the garden has superb
views of the Tyne Valley. Excellent food is
popular here. ▩Q❦❀❶⬤▩(685)P

Langley

Carts Bog Inn

NE47 5NW (3 miles off A69 on A686 to Alston)

☻ 12-3, 5-11; 12-11 Sat; 12-3, 7-10.30 Sun

☎ (01434) 684338

Yates Bitter; guest beers ⊞

Traditional unspoilt country pub serving a discerning local community as well as travellers on the A686. The current building dates from 1730 and is built on the site of an ancient brewery (circa 1521). The name is derived from a steeply banked corner on the old road where on wet days the horse drawn carts were invariably bogged down. A large unusual open fire divides the two rooms. Popular for Sunday lunch, you are assured of a warm welcome. The house beer is brewed by Mordue. ⚌Q❀◑P

Low Newton by the Sea

Ship Inn
Newton Square, NE66 3EL
❀ 11-3, 8 (6 Fri)-11; 11-11 Sat & summer; 12-10.30 (5 winter) Sun
☎ (01665) 576262
Black Sheep Best Bitter; guest beers ⒣
An oasis in the wilderness, set among a row of cottages around the village green and virtually on the beach. Despite its remote location the Ship can be busy most of the time, even in the winter. It is easier to get to on foot by walking along the coast than by road: cars must use the village car park and walk down the hill to the village itself. Excellent guest ales come from local micro-breweries. ⚌Q❀⇆◑

Morpeth

Joiners Arms
3 Wansbeck Street, NE61 1XZ
❀ 12 (11 Wed, Fri & Sat)-11; 12-10.30 Sun
☎ (01670) 513540
Black Sheep Best Bitter; Caledonian Deuchars IPA; guest beers ⒣
This Fitzgerald's pub is a friendly place to enjoy a good pint of real ale. Close to Carlisle Park, at the southern end of the footbridge, it has a pleasant view over the River Wansbeck from the lounge. One Mordue beer is always available. The cider is Weston's, perry is occasionally available. Q⊟⇌(Morpeth)●

Tap and Spile
23 Manchester Street, NE61 1BH
❀ 12-2.30, 4.30-11; 12-11 Fri & Sat; 12-10.30 Sun
☎ (01670) 513894
Caledonian Deuchars IPA; Everards Tiger; guest beers ⒣
An excellent local, popular with regulars and visitors alike. It has a busy front bar and quieter lounge to the rear. Eight handpumps offer a variety of ales, with local beers from High House Farm, Mordue, Northumberland and Wylam breweries often available. The cider is Weston's Old Rosie. Northumberland pipers play on Sunday lunchtime. CAMRA south east Northumberland Pub of the Year 2007. Q⊟⇢♣

Netherton

Star Inn ☆
NE65 7HD (off B634 from Rothbury)
❀ 7.30-10 (11 Fri; 10.30 Sat); closed Mon
☎ (01669) 630238
Camerons Castle Eden Ale ⒢

Entering this unspoilt gem, privately owned and unchanged for 80 years, feels like entering the living room of someone's home. The beer is served on gravity straight from the cellar at a hatch in the entrance hall. The bar area is basic with benches around the walls. This is the only pub in Northumberland to appear in every edition of the Guide and is on CAMRA's national inventory. Children are not allowed in the bar. Ring to check times. **QP**

Newbiggin by the Sea

Queens Head
7 High Street, NE64 6AT
❀ 10-12; 12-10.30 Sun
☎ (01670) 817293
John Smith's Bitter; guest beers ⒣
Traditional pub with lots of character and some unusual oval tables. The enthusiastic landlord introduced guest ales when he took over the pub four years ago. The large collection of pump clips behind the bar makes an interesting talking point. The guest ales are often from local micro-brewers and enjoyed by regulars and holidaymakers alike. Q

Norham

Masons Arms
16 West Street, TD15 2LB
❀ 12-3, 7-11 (10.30 Sun)
☎ (01289) 382326 ⊕tweed-sports.co.uk
Belhaven 80/-; Caledonian Deuchars IPA; guest beers ⒣
Traditional public bar with many century-old wooden fittings. Note the interesting iron fireplace and William Younger & Co Ltd India pale ale mirror above it. Guest beers come via Greene King. An eclectic collection of fishing tackle, joinery tools and water jugs hangs from the ceiling. A ceilidh band plays regularly so bring your whistle! The pub runs a race meeting social club. ⚌❀⇆◑⊟⊟(67)⇲

Old Hartley

Delaval Arms
NE26 4RL (jct of A193/B1325 S of Seaton Sluice)
❀ 12-11 (10.30 Sun)
☎ (0191) 2370489
Caledonian Deuchars IPA; guest beers ⒣
Grade II listed building dating from 1748 with a water storage tower in the beer garden and views up and down the coast. Guest ales are from local micros, the house beer is by Mordue. Quality, affordable meals complement the beer. To the left as you enter is a room served through a hatch from the bar and to the right a room where children are welcome. Q⟳❀◑⅋P⇲

Seahouses

Olde Ship Hotel
7-9 Main Street, NE68 7RD
❀ 11-11
☎ (01665) 720200 ⊕seahouses.co.uk
Black Sheep Best Bitter; Courage Directors; Draught Bass; Greene King Ruddles County; Hadrian & Border Farne Island; guest beers ⒣

Originally a farmhouse built in 1745 and now a hotel close to the harbour, the Olde Ship has been run by the same family since 1910. It is on north east CAMRA's regional inventory for its fascinating interior featuring a 1950s cabin bar and old maritime memorabilia including artefacts from the SS Forfarshire of Victorian heroine Grace Darling fame. It also has a rare 50-year-old Bass clock in honour of the deal to sell its beers. ▲Q✿✍❶➒⌂☐(411)♣P↳

Seaton Sluice

Melton Constable
Beresford Road, NE26 4DA
🕓 12-11 (10.30 Sun)
☎ (0191) 2377741
Adnams Broadside; Theakston XB; Wells Bombardier; guest beers ⏢
Large roadhouse facing the sea and overlooking the harbour with several drinking areas and a separate dining area. The pub is named after the southern seat of Lord Hastings, one of the local Delaval family. Guest ales come from local micros. ✿❶P

Slaley

Travellers Rest
NE46 1TT (on B6306, 1 mile N of village)
🕓 12-11 (10.30 Sun)
☎ (01434) 673231
Black Sheep Best Bitter; guest beers ⏢
Licensed for more than 150 years, this welcoming inn started life in the 16th century as a farmhouse. Living up to its name, it offers the traveller an excellent choice of guest beers, wonderful food and accommodation. The bar has a large open fire and stone walls, flag floors and comfortable furniture. An extensive choice of meals featuring local produce is served in the bar and restaurant. Children are welcome and there is a safe play area beside the pub. ▲Q✿✍❶P↳

Stannington

Ridley Arms
NE61 6EL
🕓 11.30-11 (10.30 Sun)
☎ (01670) 789216 ⊕ sjf.co.uk
Black Sheep Best Bitter; Taylor Landlord; guest beers ⏢
An excellent Fitzgerald pub with several rooms, dating back to the 18th century. Eight handpumps serve guests from the north-east as well as breweries countrywide. Known locally for its quality food made from fresh local produce, it is often busy, particularly Sunday lunchtime. Ramps and wide doors give access for the disabled. ▲Q✿❶♣P

Warden

Boatside Inn
NE46 4SQ (off A69)
🕓 11-11; 12-10.30
☎ (01434) 602233 ⊕ boatsideinn.co.uk
Beer range varies ⏢
Excellent riverside country pub nestling between the river South Tyne and the wooded slopes of Warden Hill, very popular with walkers, cyclists and tourists. Scenic woodland footpaths and bridleways surround the inn. Tasty home cooked food is served from a varied menu. B&B and self-catering cottages are available. Nearby is the world heritage site at Hadrian's Wall. ▲✿✍❶⌂☐(804)P

Wark

Battlesteads Hotel
NE48 3LS
🕓 11-11; 12-10.30
☎ (01434) 230730 ⊕ battlesteads-hotel.co.uk
Wylam Gold Tankard; guest beers ⏢
Traditional Northumberland farmhouse inn close to Hadrian's Wall and the National Park. The cosy bar has an interesting bar front converted from a 200-year-old dresser and a large inglenook fireplace. Live folk music is a regular feature. The pub's sunny, walled garden is pleasant in summer. There is excellent accommodation. ▲Q✿✍❶P

Whitfield

Elks Head
NE47 8HD
🕓 to come
☎ (01434) 345282
Beer range varies ⏢
Country pub in a fine walking area with a warm welcome for visitors and locals alike. Originally it was a private club called the Blue Black Club for Whitfield sporting estates and the estate office is next door. Excellent food made with local produce is served in the dining room. The stone-walled bar is home to darts, pool and quoits teams, and a leek club. Dogs are welcome. ▲✿✍❶♣P↳

Wylam

Black Bull
Main Street, NE41 8AB
🕓 4-11; 12-10.30 Sun
☎ (01661) 853112 ⊕ blackbull-wylam.co.uk
Beer range varies ⏢
Cheerful pub located on the main street in Wylam, very popular with locals. The landlord and staff offer a friendly welcome to all. Regular theme nights are hosted and local home cooked specialities feature in the restaurant. Two cask ales are usually available from a range of breweries. Local charity Pub of the Year in 2006. ✍▶≢(Wylam)

Boathouse
Station Road, NE41 8HR
🕓 11-11; 12-10.30 Sun
☎ (01661) 853431
Wylam Gold Tankard; guest beers ⏢
Classic two room pub next to Wylam railway station, a regular stopping off point for Whistle Stop travellers (see cannybevvy.co.uk for details). The brewery tap for Wylam, you will often find the brewers in the bar chatting to locals. Twelve handpumps also offer a wide variety of guest ales from a range of breweries. Sunday lunches are a highlight. Winner of several local CAMRA Pub of the Year awards. ▲Q✿❶☐≢(Wylam)♣P

NOTTINGHAMSHIRE

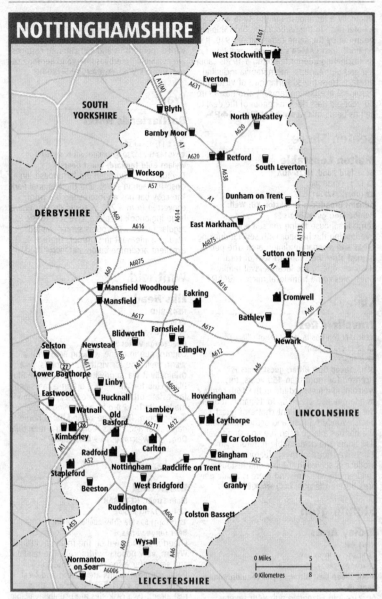

West Stockwith
Everton
Blyth
North Wheatley
Barnby Moor
SOUTH YORKSHIRE
Retford
Worksop
South Leverton
Dunham on Trent
DERBYSHIRE
East Markham
Sutton on Trent
Mansfield Woodhouse
Eakring
Mansfield
Cromwell
Bathley
Blidworth
Farnsfield
Newark
Selston
Newstead
Edingley
Lower Bagthorpe
Linby
Eastwood
Hucknall
Hoveringham
Watnall
Lambley
Old Basford
Caythorpe
LINCOLNSHIRE
Kimberley
Car Colston
Radford
Carlton
Bingham
Stapleford
Nottingham
Radcliffe on Trent
Beeston
West Bridgford
Granby
Ruddington
Colston Bassett
Wysall
Normanton on Soar
LEICESTERSHIRE

0 Miles 5
0 Kilometres 8

Barnby Moor

White Horse

Great North Road, DN22 8QS (on A638)
☼ 11 (12 Sun)-11
☎ (01777) 707721
Beer range varies Ⓗ
Attractive village pub at the side of the A638 with a large lounge bar, separate dining area and smaller public bar area. Between four and six changing cask ales are available depending on the time of the year, most coming from local micro-breweries. The walls in the lounge bar are covered with paintings, some connected to the local Grove & Rufford Hunt which has its kennels across the road and meets at the pub on Boxing Day. ♨Q❀◑▣P

Bathley

Crown

Main Street, NG23 6DA
☼ 11-3, 7-2am; 11-2am Fri-Sun
☎ (01636) 702305
Marston's Burton Bitter; Mansfield Riding Bitter; guest beer Ⓗ
Popular unspoilt, friendly village pub at the hub of the community. It hosts a charity village barbecue in August. A range of well kept beers complements the good value food. Long alley skittles is played here. The Doll Museum at Cromwell, the Workhouse at Southwell and Laxton, with its unique Medieval open-field farming system, are all close by. ♨❀◑♣P

Beeston

Malt Shovel
1 Union Street, NG9 2LU
☼ 11-11 (midnight Fri & Sat)
☎ (0115) 922 2320
Nottingham Rock Mild, Rock Bitter; guest beers Ⓗ
Just off the busy High Road, this popular pub offers a friendly welcome. The modern one room interior uses furnishings and decor to create a sense of separate drinking areas. Wooden floors, bright colours and comfortable leather sofas provide a light, airy ambience with a cosy atmosphere. There is a good value lunchtime menu (no meals Sun eve), quiz night on Wednesday and regular live music. ⚌Q✿⊕🕭☟➌P

Victoria Hotel
85 Dovecote Lane, NG9 1JG (off A6005 by station)
☼ 11 (12 Sun)-11
☎ (0115) 925 4049 ⊕ victoriabeeston.co.uk
Castle Rock Harvest Pale, Hemlock; Everards Tiger; guest beers Ⓗ
Buzzing Victorian architectural gem. This former CAMRA Pub of the Year is popular with drinkers and diners alike. The multi-roomed layout allows for a dining area, public bar and covered outside drinking. Twelve beers are served, including mild, stout and two real ciders from both regional and micro-brewers. Freshly cooked food, including a wide vegetarian choice, is available all day. Regular music festivals are held, outside in summer. ⚌Q✿⊕🕭➌➍P

Bingham

Horse & Plough
25 Long Acre, NG13 8AF
☼ 11-11 (11.30 Fri & Sat); 12-11 Sun
☎ (01949) 839313 ⊕ horseandploughbingham.com
Caledonian Deuchars IPA; Wells Bombardier; guest beers Ⓗ
Warm, friendly one-room free house with a cottage style interior and flagstone floor. Six cask ales are always available including four frequently changing guests. The pub, which has a 'try before you buy' policy, is housed in a former Methodist chapel. The first floor a la carte restaurant has a seasonal menu with good value steaks mid-week. A fresh bar menu is served weekday lunchtimes and the traditional Sunday lunch is popular. Local CAMRA Pub of the Year 2007. ⊕➍➌

Blidworth

Black Bull
Main Street, NG21 0QH
☼ 5-midnight; closed Mon; 12-2.30, 7-11.30 Sun
☎ (01623) 792291
Black Sheep Best Bitter Ⓗ
Popular with locals, this three room beamed inn is at least 400 years old. The public bar with log burning stove, lounge and snug are all served from a central bar. There is an outdoor skittles alley which is frequently used and visiting teams welcomed. Parking can be difficult, but it is well worth making an effort to visit. ⚌Q✿➌➍⚊

Blyth

Red Hart
Bawtry Road, S81 8HG
☼ 12-midnight (11.30 Sun)
☎ (01909) 591221
Beer range varies Ⓗ
Attractive village pub in the centre of Blyth – a previous winner of best-kept village. The interior has separate lounge and bar areas with a reasonably sized dining room; the walls in the lounge are decorated with photos and paintings of the local area. Regularly changing guest ales come from several micro-breweries. Restaurant quality food at pub prices is served daily. ⚌Q✿⊕➌P

Car Colston

Royal Oak
The Green, NG13 8JE (½ mile from A46)
☼ 11.30-3 (not Mon), 6-midnight; 11.30-midnight Sat & Sun
☎ (01949) 20247
Banks's Mansfield Cask; Marston's Burton Bitter; guest beer Ⓗ
This impressive country pub situated on England's largest village green has two main rooms – a lounge/restaurant on one side and a bar with comfortable seating on the other. Note the bar's interesting brickwork ceiling – a legacy from the pub's previous life as a hosiery factory. A good food menu is served lunchtime and evening – the mouthwatering range of puddings is particularly popular. Long alley skittles can be played. ⚌Q✿⊕➍▲♣P

Caythorpe

Black Horse
29 Main Street, NG14 7ED
☼ 12-2.30, 5 (6 Sat)-11; closed Mon; 12-4, 7 (8 winter)-10.30 Sun
☎ (0115) 966 3520
Caythorpe Dover Beck; guest beers Ⓗ
This 18th century free house has been in the same family for 37 years. It features a comfortable lounge, a gem of a snug bar with hatch servery, inglenook, bench seats, beams and wood panelling. A private dining room is available for dinner parties. Bar food is popular, mostly cooked to order using fresh ingredients (booking essential). Home of Caythorpe Brewery, guest beers often come from other local micro-breweries. ⚌Q✿⊕➍♣P

INDEPENDENT BREWERIES

Alcazar Old Basford
Castle Rock Nottingham
Caythorpe Caythorpe
Full Mash Stapleford
Grafton Retford
Holland Kimberley
Idle West Stockwith
Magpie Nottingham
Mallard Carlton
Maypole Eakring
Milestone Cromwell
Nottingham Radford
Springhead Sutton-on-Trent

Colston Bassett

Martins Arms
School Lane, NG12 3FD
🕛 12-3, 6-11; 12-3, 7-10.30 Sun
☎ (01949) 81361
Adnams Bitter; Draught Bass; Greene King IPA; Marston's Pedigree; Taylor Landlord; guest beers Ⓗ

Delightful country pub converted from a farmhouse, beamed and carpeted throughout with antique furnishings and hunting prints. There is a magnificent Jacobean carved wood fireplace at one end of the lounge with a brick fireplace at the other. The copper-topped bar has a wooden face and impressive carved shelves at the rear. The tap room has its own corner bar. Excellent country views can be enjoyed from the large, attractive garden. The high quality restaurant menu is excellent but pricey. ⚏Q🕸❶P

Dunham on Trent

White Swan
Main Street, NG22 0TY (on A57)
🕛 10-11 (10.30 Sun)
☎ (01777) 228307
Beer range varies Ⓗ

An attractive village pub at the side of the A57 and close to the River Trent. It has separate lounge and bar areas with a reasonably-sized dining room. The guest ales change regularly. Good value home-cooked food is served daily. The location is ideal for anyone wishing to have a day fishing on the Trent. ⚏Q🕸❶🖼P

East Markham

Queen's Hotel
High Street, NG22 0RE (½ mile from A1)
🕛 12-11 (10.30 Sun)
☎ (01777) 870288
Adnams Bitter; guest beers Ⓗ

One of two pubs in East Markham selling cask ales, this cosy hostelry has a friendly atmosphere enhanced by an open fire in winter. A single bar serves the lounge, pool room and dining area. Food, ranging from hot and cold snacks to full home-cooked meals, is available Tuesday to Sunday. There is a large garden area at the rear where you can enjoy a drink on warm summer days. North Notts CAMRA Pub of the Season 2005.
⚏Q🕸❶🖼♣P

Eastwood

Three Tuns
58 Three Tuns Road, NG16 3EJ
🕛 11-midnight (1am Fri & Sat)
☎ (01773) 713377
Black Sheep Best Bitter; Caledonian Deuchars IPA; Everards Tiger; guest beers Ⓗ

A popular addition to the local real ale scene in a town formerly dominated by Hardys & Hansons, this large pub has a modern feel but a historic past. Located in the heart of DH Lawrence country, it featured as the 'Moon & Stars' in his novel Sons and Lovers. A central bar has six handpumps dispensing beers from larger regional breweries, with occasional micro-brews. Several large screen TVs show sport and there is a pool table. 🕸❶🖼P⌐

Edingley

Old Reindeer
Main Street, NG22 8BE (off A614 towards Southwell)
🕛 12-11 (10.30 Sun)
☎ (01623) 882253
Marston's Pedigree, Old Empire; guest beers Ⓗ

Traditional 18th century village pub which has recently been modernised inside to provide a comfortable dining area and cosy bar area, without losing the essence of a country pub. Six real ales are usually on offer, always in tip-top condition. In summer the attractive beer garden attracts families. Food is top quality, and the pub offers B&B accommodation. Pub games and activities are organised.
⚏Q🕸🏠❶🖼♣P

Everton

Blacksmith's Arms
Church Street, DN10 5BQ (off the main A638 Bawtry to Gainsborough road)
🕛 10-midnight
☎ (01777) 817281 ⊕ blacksmiths-everton.co.uk
John Smith's Bitter; Theakston Old Peculier; guest beers Ⓗ

A regular winner of local CAMRA Pub of the Season awards, this 18th-century free house stands at the heart of the village. Drinking areas include the locals' bar with its original tiled floor and the games room (formerly the old smithy). The comfortable lounge area leads to a large restaurant where the emphasis is on fresh, home-cooked food (booking advisable). Outside is a Mediterranean-style garden; en-suite accommodation is available in the converted stables. ⚏Q🚬🕸❶🖼P

Farnsfield

Plough Inn
Main Street, NG22 8EA (off A614 towards Southwell)
🕛 11-3, 5.30-11; 11-11 Sat; 12-10.30 Sun
☎ (01623) 882265
Marston's Pedigree; guest beers Ⓗ

Popular with locals and visitors, this is a comfortable pub for a quiet drink. The interior includes a snug with comfy armchairs next to the fire, a bar and open plan lounge, and separate dining room. A wide range of traditional pub games is played. Parking is adequate. ⚏Q🕸❶🖼♣P⌐

Red Lion
Main Street, NG22 8EY
🕛 11-3, 6-midnight (10.30 Sun)
☎ (01623) 882304
Marston's Mansfield Cask, Pedigree; guest beers Ⓗ

Friendly, family run local with an open plan lounge divided by pillars and seating around the window area. The landlord is often found playing dominoes with the regulars. Good home cooked food is served in the restaurant.

An ever changing range of guest ales is always in first class condition. Q❄️🕐🍴♿🚃♣P

Granby

Marquis of Granby
Dragon Street, NG13 9PN
🕐 11.30-2.30 (not Mon), 5.30-midnight; 11.30-midnight Fri-Sun
☎ (01949) 859517

Brewster's Hophead, Marquis; guest beers Ⓗ
Believed to be the original Marquis of Granby, dating back to 1760 or earlier, this small, two-room pub is now the brewery tap for the award-winning Brewster's Brewery. The interior has York stone floors complementing the yew bar tops and beamed ceilings with traditional wallpaper and a welcoming open fire in the lounge in winter. Guest beers usually include a mild or stout. The pub regularly hosts live music. ♨️Q❄️🕐🍴♣

Hoveringham

Reindeer Inn
Main Street, NG14 7JR SK698468
🕐 5 (12 Sat)-1am; 12-2am Sat; 12-1am Sun
☎ (0115) 966 3629

Black Sheep Best Bitter; Castle Rock Harvest Pale; Caythorpe Stout Fellow; guest beers Ⓗ
This genuine free house is situated in a pleasant country village. It has traditional wood beams and a cosy log fire for cold winter evenings. A central servery divides the bar and restaurant. In the summer barbecues are held in the outside drinking area overlooking a cricket pitch. ♨️Q❄️≠(Thurgaton)P

Hucknall

Green Dragon
Watnall Road, NG15 7JW
🕐 12-11.30 (11 Sun)
☎ (0115) 964 0941

Beer range varies Ⓗ
Situated just out of the town centre, this traditional pub has five ever-changing hand-pulled beers. The airy open plan interior comprises a lounge with raised area for dining, games area including pool and darts and a ground floor dining room (no eve meals Sun) which can be used for parties and functions. This busy local has a quiz night on Wednesday, karaoke on Thursday, pool knockout competition on Tuesday and league darts on Monday. ❄️🕐♿≠⊖🚃P♭

Kimberley

Nelson & Railway
12 Station Road, NG16 2NR
🕐 11-midnight; 12-11 Sun
☎ (0115) 938 2177 🌐 nelsonandrailway.co.uk

Greene King H&H Bitter, H&H Olde Trip, Morland Original, Ruddles County Ⓗ
Formerly the brewery tap for Hardys & Hansons, this popular pub lies in the shadow of the defunct brewery buildings. Beers are now from the Greene King portfolio. Recently refurbished, this friendly local is renowned for its good quality food and comfortable accommodation. Unusually, the car park is to

the rear and the garden, which overlooks the main Eastwood Road, is at the front. ❄️🛏️🕐♿🚃♣P♭

Stag Inn
67 Nottingham Road, NG16 2NB
🕐 5 (1.30 Sat)-11; 12-10.30 Sun
☎ (0115) 938 3151

Adnams Bitter; Caledonian Deuchars IPA; Marston's Pedigree; Taylor Landlord; guest beer Ⓗ
Full of character, this welcoming two-room pub dates from 1537. The interior features low beams adorned by old photographs of Shipstones, the former brewery that once owned the pub. Several fairground-type, old-fashioned slot machines help to alleviate you of your small change. The spacious rear garden includes a children's play area. The pub holds an annual beer festival each late-May bank holiday weekend, raising money for charity. Q❄️♿🚃(TB1)♣P♭

Lambley

Robin Hood & Little John
82 Main Street, NG4 4PP
🕐 12-3 (not Mon), 5-11; 12-11 Fri & Sat; 12-5, 7-10.30 Sun
☎ (0115) 931 2531

Banks's Mild, Bitter; Jennings Mild; Mansfield Cask; Marston's Pedigree Ⓗ
White painted, genuine village local with a landlord dedicated to cask beer. The range never varies, with two milds quite a rarity these days. The traditional beamed public bar is deservedly popular with locals and visitors while the cosy lounge offers a peaceful retreat. Catering is limited to rolls and sandwiches. ♨️Q⌛🚃♣P

Woodlark
Church Street, NG4 4QB
🕐 12-3, 5.30-11; 12-6, 7-11 Sun
☎ (0115) 931 2535

Black Sheep Best Bitter; Fuller's London Pride; Taylor Landlord; guest beer Ⓗ
Timeless red brick village inn. The bare-brick bar is friendly and welcoming, mercifully free of electronic machines, while the comfortable lounge has a justifiable reputation for its home cooking (booking is recommended even at lunchtime). A popular downstairs steak bar is also open on Friday and Saturday evenings from 7-9pm. There is a heated patio area outside for smokers. ♨️Q⌛🕐🚃♣P♭

Linby

Horse & Groom
Main Street, NG15 8AE
🕐 12-11 (10.30 Sun)
☎ (0115) 963 2219

Theakston Mild; Greene King IPA; guest beers Ⓗ
Charming and unspoilt village pub dating back to 1800. This multi-roomed establishment is Grade II listed and boasts an inglenook in the public bar, a snug and roaring open fires. The Green Room welcomes families. There is a conservatory and the garden has a children's play area. Fine food is available at lunchtime from an extensive and varied menu. Evening

dining is on Friday and Saturday only.
🏠Q🍽☕🍴🍺🖶P⌐

Lower Bagthorpe

Dixies Arms
School Road, NG16 5HF (1½ miles from M1 jct 27)
☼ 12-11 (10.30 Sun)
☎ (01773) 810505
Greene King Abbot; Theakston Best Bitter; guest beer ⊞
Built in the late 1700s, this pub offers a friendly welcome to all. Locals and visitors alike can be found warming themselves around the real fires in the public rooms, playing darts or dominoes or gossiping in the snug. The pub's unspoilt character ensures a full house at weekends. Live music on Saturday, quiz on Sunday. Quieter on weekdays, it is a haven for real ale drinkers.
🏠☕🍴🎄🖶♣P

Shepherds Rest
Wansley Lane, NG16 5HF (2 miles from M1 jct 27)
☼ 12-11 (10.30 Sun)
☎ (01773) 811337
Caledonian Deuchars IPA; Greene King Abbot; Wells Bombardier ⊞
Dating back to the 1700s, this family run pub is reputed to be haunted. It has an extensive garden area with numerous benches and a children's play area in an idyllic countryside setting. Take your freshly prepared, home-cooked food into the garden if you wish, or enjoy the ambience of the interior with its exposed oak beams, flagstone floors and open fires. Evening meals are served Tuesday to Saturday. 🏠☕🍴🖶♣P

Mansfield

Bold Forester
Botany Avenue, NG18 5NF (on A38 ½ mile from town centre)
☼ 11-midnight (12.30 Sat)
☎ (01623) 623970
Greene King IPA, Abbot, Old Speckled Hen, Ruddles County; guest beers ⊞
Large open plan pub with split levels including a dining area, small snug and bar area with pool table. Partitions create an impression of privacy. Background music is not intrusive and the TV can be avoided. Weekly quizzes, run by the landlord, are very popular. Live music is hosted on Sunday. A beer festival is held on St George's Day. With excellent meals served all day, this has proved to be one of Mansfield's flagship real ale pubs. ☕🍴🎄≠♣P⌐

Court House
Market Place, NG18 1HX
☼ 9-midnight
☎ (01623) 412720
Greene King Abbot, Old Speckled Hen; Marston's Burton Bitter, Pedigree; guest beers ⊞
A first class conversion typical of Wetherspoon's. The building was the former town court house and retains a number of the original rooms. It keeps a good selection of reasonably priced local guest beers. Smoking is permitted outside on the forecourt. A recent

local CAMRA Pub of the Season.
Q🍽🍴🎄≠🖶♣⌐

Railway Inn
9 Station Street, NG18 1EF
☼ 10.30-11.30 (8 Tue)
☎ (01623) 623086
Bateman XB; guest beers ⊞
An 18th-century former coaching inn, the pub retains much of its original character. Under threat of closure, it was saved by the support of locals, the media and CAMRA. It now offers more guest beers and the kitchen has been extensively refurbished – excellent meals are now served in the evening as well as lunchtime. A good selection of bottled beers and ciders is always available. A genuine locals' pub, visitors are warmly welcomed.
🍴🎄🎄≠🖶♣

Widow Frost
Leeming Street, NG18 1NB
☼ 9-midnight (1am Fri & Sat)
☎ (01623) 666790
Greene King Abbot, Old Speckled Hen; Marston's Bitter, Pedigree; guest beers ⊞
Spacious Wetherspoon's conversion of two old Mansfield pubs, with ever-changing guest beers from micros and the national list. An interesting display of local history can be viewed on the walls. The reasonably priced pub menu includes an excellent breakfast, with daily specials and local dishes. WiFi connection is available free for 30 minutes to patrons. Q🍴🎄≠🖶♣

Mansfield Woodhouse

Greyhound
82 High Street, NG19 8BD
☼ 12-11 (midnight Fri & Sat); 12-10.30 Sun
☎ (01623) 464403
Greene King Abbot; Theakston Mild; Webster's Yorkshire Bitter; guest beers ⊞
This stone built pub, reputedly dating from the 17th century, has featured in the Guide for more than 15 years. Located near the old market square, the popular, friendly pub has two rooms: a lively tap room with pool table and traditional pub games, plus a quiet, comfortable lounge. Five real ales are always on offer. Quiz nights are Monday and Wednesday. Q☕🎄🎄≠🖶♣⌐

Star Inn
Warsop Road, NG19 9LE (on A6075 at crossroads)
☼ 12-3, 5-11 (10.30 Sun)
☎ (01623) 403110
Tetley Bitter; guest beers ⊞
This friendly pub is popular with locals. The cosy bar has a pool room leading off it, and both can be busy. The comfortable lounge is ideal for a quiet drink and conversation. Up to five ever-changing real ales make this a pub always worth another visit. Meals may be taken in the lounge or bar.
☕🍴🎄🎄≠🖶♣P⌐

Newark

Castle & Falcon
10 London Road, NG24 1TW

✪ 7-midnight (1am Thu); 11-3, 7-1am Fri; 12-3, 7-1am Sat; 12-3, 7-midnight Sun
☎ (01636) 703513
John Smith's Bitter; guest beers Ⓗ
Situated under the old James Hole brewery buildings, this is possibly the busiest pub in town. There is always something happening here, be it doms, darts, pool or a quiz. An easy walk from the town centre, it attracts young and old alike. With two guest beers selected from an imaginative and varied portfolio, drinkers are likely to find something different on every visit. A large and comfortable room is available for meetings and functions.
❀⊟≷(Castle)♣⌐

Crown & Mitre

53 Castlegate, NG24 1BE
✪ 11.30-3, 5-11; 11.30-1am Fri & Sat; 12-10.30 Sun
☎ (01636) 703131 ⊕ crownandmitre.co.uk
Caledonian Deuchars IPA; John Smith's Bitter; guest beer Ⓗ
Located on historic Castlegate near the castle and formerly known as the Exchange, the deeds date this pub back to 1799. Now one split level lounge bar, disabled entry is via a side door. Upstairs there is a function room and pool room. The guest beer in this Enterprise owned pub usually changes every two months. ▲⬢≷(Castle)♣P

Fox & Crown

4-6 Appletongate, NG24 1JY
✪ 10.30-11; 10.30-midnight Fri & Sat; 12-11 Sun
☎ (01636) 605820
Bateman XB; Castle Rock Nottingham Gold, Harvest Pale, Hemlock; Everards Tiger; guest beers Ⓗ
A welcome return to the Guide for this Tynemill pub. It offers a good selection of beers with two or three changing guests from local micros. Wholesome, reasonably priced food is made with local ingredients. Although open plan, the pub has separate areas, each with a different character. Bottled beers from Belgium are also available, as well as real cider and perry served from the jug, a range of flavoured vodkas and more than 60 malt whiskies. Occasional live entertainment is hosted. ⬢&≷(Castle/ Northgate)♣

Vine Hotel

117 Barnbygate, NG24 1QZ
✪ 3 (12 Fri & Sat)-11.30; 12-11.30 Sun
☎ (01636) 704333
Beer range varies Ⓗ
Good old-fashioned back-street boozer, well worth the short walk out of town. A true locals' pub, the atmosphere can be boisterous at times. The lounge has a charming painting of a market scene above the bar and a spacious function room is available upstairs. Quiz and karaoke nights feature regularly and the musical landlord is known to hold impromptu entertainment sessions. The guest beers are always sourced from micros.
❀⊟♣⌐

White Swan

50 Northgate, NG24 1HF
✪ 12-11
☎ (01636) 704700

Banks's Bitter; Jennings Sneck Lifter; guest beer Ⓗ
Small, friendly multi-roomed pub with low beamed ceilings. Full of character and characters, it is a comfortable hostelry with lots of nooks and crannies. Popular with regulars, it is home to quiz, table skittles, dominoes, darts and long-alley skittles teams. Offering a warm welcome to all, it celebrates occasional special events, notably St Patrick's Day. Q❀⬢⊟≷(Castle/Northgate)♣P⌐

Newstead

Station Hotel

Station Road, NG15 0BZ (next to station)
✪ 11-3, 5 (7 Sat)-midnight; 12-3, 7-11.30 Sun
☎ (01623) 753294
Oakwell Old Tom Mild, Barnsley Bitter Ⓗ
Enjoying a new lease of life with the advent of the Robin Hood Line from Nottingham to Worksop, this traditional railway station pub is steeped in atmosphere. Once part of a busy colliery village, it still has a community feel to it. The locals are quick to make visitors welcome, and the landlady and staff greet you as old friends. A favourite CAMRA branch meeting place, several small rooms available for private functions lead off the public bar.
▲Q❀⬢⊟≷♣⌐

Normanton-on-Soar

Plough

Main Street, LE12 5HB
✪ 11.30-11; 12-10.30 Sun
☎ (01509) 842228
⊕ probablythebestpubsintheworld.co.uk
Caledonian Deuchars IPA; Draught Bass; Greene King Abbot; guest beer Ⓗ
Set in an attractive village, the Plough is primarily a food pub, though it has a snug area with a real fire to enjoy drinks away from the main dining room and open plan bar. Although an old pub, the interior has been attractively renovated in a sympathetic contemporary style. Extensive beer gardens sweep down to the River Soar. A purpose built outside bar and barbecue draw large crowds in the summertime with occasional live entertainment. ▲❀⬢&≷P⌐

North Wheatley

Sun Inn

Low Street, DN22 9DS (just off A620)
✪ 11-3.30, 6-11; 11-11 Sat
☎ (01427) 861000
Black Sheep Best Bitter; Caledonian Deuchars IPA; Taylor Landlord Ⓗ
Spacious pub on the edge of the village with a large children's play area. It has three handpulls dispensing ale and a large restaurant serving good home-made food. The surrounding area is popular with walkers – this is an ideal stopping off point to take a well earned rest and enjoy a good pint.
▲❀⬢▲⊟⊟P

Nottingham: Central

Bell Inn

18 Angel Row, Old Market Square, NG1 6HL
✪ 10-11 (11.30 Wed; midnight Thu-Sat); 11-11 Sun
☎ (0115) 947 5241 ⊕ thebell-inn.com
Greene King IPA, Abbot, Old Speckled Hen, Ruddles County; guest beers Ⓗ
Three-roomed traditional pub in the Market Square offering a wide selection of ever-changing guest ales, many from micros. A labyrinth of Norman caves exists beneath the pub with cellar tours on Tuesday evening. Food is served daily in the Belfry Restaurant and some of the bars. A café style pavement drinking area opens during the summer months. The back bar hosts live jazz on Sunday lunchtime, and live music plays on most evenings. Occasional beer festivals are held too. Q❀✪◑🍴&≠⊖🚉⌐

Gatehouse

Toll House Hill, NG1 5FS
✪ 11-11; 12-10.30 Sun
☎ (0115) 947 3952
Jennings Cumberland Ale; Nottingham Rock Bitter; guest beers Ⓗ
In summer the front of this modern pub opens out with sliding doors onto an enclosed pavement area with further seating; there is also a heated canopy for smokers. Five handpumps dispense the beer range with local micro-breweries often showcased. Good value food is available at lunchtime and Tuesday to Friday evenings; a 'taste of the world' evening is held on the first Thursday of the month. The location is handy for both local theatres. Q❀◑&⊖(Royal Centre)🚉⌐

Kean's Head

46 St Mary's Gate, NG1 1QA (opp St Mary's Church)
✪ 10.30 (10 Sat)-midnight (12.30am Fri & Sat); 12-10.30 Sun
☎ (0115) 9474052
Bateman XB; Castle Rock Harvest Pale, Elsie Mo; guest beers Ⓗ
Named after a pub which once stood nearby, the Kean's Head was purchased by the Tynemill pub group in 2004. The name is in honour of the 19th-century actor Edmund Kean who once performed at the original Theatre Royal which stood on St Mary's Gate opposite the imposing St Mary's church in the historic Lace Market district. This one-room pub offers inventive freshly prepared food from an ever-changing menu and is awarded a star in CAMRA's Good Pub Food Guide. Occasional live music plays.
◑&≠⊖(Lace Market)⌐

Lincolnshire Poacher

161-163 Mansfield Road, NG1 3FR (on A60 500 yds N of city centre)
✪ 11-11 (midnight Thu-Sat); 12-11 Sun
☎ (0115) 941 1584
Bateman XB, Valiant; Castle Rock Poacher's Gold, Harvest Pale; guest beers Ⓗ
Two-room traditional pub with a conservatory and enclosed patio. The pub is popular with diners and the real ale fraternity doing the Mansfield Road crawl. It was probably the first pub in Nottingham to sell an ever-changing range of beers from micro-breweries and now

always offers a mild and a stout or porter as well as traditional cider on handpull. It features regular live music, often on Sunday night, and runs brewery evenings and trips to micro-breweries. ❀◑&♣🍴⌐

Newshouse

123 Canal Street, NG1 7HB
✪ 10.30-11; 12-10.30 Sun
☎ (0115) 950 2419
Everards Tiger; guest beers Ⓗ
Straightforward, friendly, two-roomed Tynemill local. At one time the national news used to be read out to customers, hence the name. Memorabilia from BBC Radio Nottingham and the local Evening Post adorn the walls. Look for the brewery names etched into ceramic wall tiles in the public bar. Sport is shown on a large screen or TV. Darts is popular here. Up to eight cask beers always include a mild. ❀◑🍴≠⊖(Station St)🚉⌐

Olde Trip to Jerusalem ☆

1 Brewhouse Yard, NG1 6AD (below castle)
✪ 10-11 (midnight Fri & Sat); 10.30-midnight Sun
☎ (0115) 947 3171 ⊕ triptojerusalem.com
Greene King H&H Mild, IPA, H&H Olde Trip, Ruddles County, Abbot, Old Speckled Hen; guest beers Ⓗ
The world famous Olde Trip to Jerusalem is reputed to date from 1189. It has a number of rooms downstairs, some cut out of the castle rock. Upstairs the Rock lounge is home to the Cursed Galleon. A museum room houses a tapestry depicting Nottingham's history. Cellar tours are run on Wednesdays in summer months or at other times by arrangement. A covered courtyard and seated pavement drinking area with waitress service are available in the summer. Winner of the English Heritage/CAMRA award 2004.
Q❀◑🍴≠⊖(Station St)🚉♣⌐

Salutation Inn

Houndsgate, Maid Marian Way, NG1 7AA
✪ 11-midnight (1am Fri & Sat); 12-midnight Sun
☎ (0115) 988 1948
Beer range varies Ⓗ
Stone-floored oak beamed 17th-century inn with a room upstairs, two snugs and haunted caves. It is a popular meeting place for various societies and hosts live rock music. A Hallowe'en beer festival is an annual highlight. Guest ales from national and micro-breweries featuring rock music and ghostly beer names are always popular. An adventurous food menu made with local produce and cooked on the premises with vegetarian options is served until the early evening. ⚶❀◑⊖(Market Sq)🚉♣⌐

Sir John Borlase Warren

1 Ilkeston Road, Canning Circus, NG7 3DG
✪ 11-11.30 (midnight Fri & Sat); 12-11 Sun
☎ (0115) 947 4247
Everards Sunchaser, Tiger; Greene King IPA; Taylor Landlord; guest beers Ⓗ
Standing proud at the junction of three major roads, this pub provides an excellent meeting place. It is immediately warm and friendly with the hubbub of conversation in the background. It has four rooms and a bar, all open plan, with original artwork on the walls

for sale. Bar snacks with daily specials all source local produce where possible and are reasonably priced. The outside seating area is on two levels, continental style, and is a real find. Q❄️⛲️◐⏣▸

Vat & Fiddle

12-14 Queen's Bridge Road, NG2 1NB
🕐 11-11 (midnight Fri & Sat); 12-11 Sun
☎ (0115) 985 0611
Castle Rock Nottingham Gold, Harvest Pale, Hemlock, Elsie Mo; guest beers Ⓗ
Deservedly popular and friendly, the Vat has a well earned reputation as a genuine drinkers' pub. The Castle Rock brewery tap, it serves four of its beers plus six guests, always including a mild. A traditional cider and a perry are also usually available. A choice of over 65 whiskies is on display together with 10 flavoured Polish vodkas and a selection of foreign bottled beers. A proposed extension will add additional rooms, incorporating a viewing area into the brewery.
Q❄️⛲️◐&⇌⊖(Station St)◗▸

Nottingham: North

Fox & Crown

33 Church Street, Basford, NG6 0GA
🕐 12-midnight
☎ (0115) 942 2002 ⊕ alcazarbrewery.co.uk
Alcazar Ale, New Dawn, Brush, Nottingham Nog, Vixens Vice, Windjammer IPA; guest beers Ⓗ
A large mural painted by a local artist on the wall outside makes this pub unmistakable. The excellent Alcazar brewery tap is a pleasant, spacious inn serving at least six Alcazar beers. Bottled ales are also available and for sale in the expanding shop nearby. A patio to the rear is a pleasant spot for outdoor drinking. The pub is renowned for its excellent Thai food.
❄️◐&⊖(Basford)🚃(69)◗P▸

Gladstone

45 Loscoe Road, Carrington, NG5 2AW (off A60 Mansfield Road)
🕐 5 (3 Fri, 12 Sat)-11 (11.30 Thu-Sat); 12-11 Sun
☎ (0115) 912 9994
Caledonian Deuchars IPA; Fuller's London Pride; Greene King Abbot; Taylor Landlord; guest beers Ⓗ
Small, friendly, two-room backstreet hostelry dating from around 1880. Sporting memorabilia is on display in the public bar and sporting events screened on TV. The lounge is home to a wide range of books for customers to read. Thursday is quiz night and the Carrington Folk Club meets in the upstairs function room on Wednesday evening. Nottingham Brewery beers can regularly be found in this community local. ❄️⊟🚃♣▸

Horse & Groom

462 Radford Road, Basford, NG7 7EA
🕐 11-11 (11.30 Fri & Sat); 12-11 Sun
☎ (0115) 970 3777 ⊕ horseandgroombasford.co.uk
Caledonian Deuchars IPA; Wells Bombardier; guest beers Ⓗ
The former Shipstone's brewery stands just a few yards south of this popular pub. Access is via steps up to the front door, although disabled access is available on request. The small bar area accommodates eight

handpumps serving mainly micro-brewery beers. The split-level pub has several distinct areas and a separate function room. There is a quiz night on Mondays.
🏚️◐⊖(Shipstone Street)🚃(NCT)

Nottingham: South

Globe

152 London Road, NG2 3BQ
🕐 11.30 (11 Sat)-11; 12-10.30 Sun
☎ (0115) 986 6881 ⊕ theglobenottingham.com
Nottingham Claytons Original, Legend; guest beers Ⓗ
Light, airy, popular pub near Nottingham's cricket, football and rugby grounds. Sporting fixtures regularly feature on several large screens. Cold snacks are only available on match days. Six handpumps serve ales mainly from micro-breweries with Nottingham beers regularly available. Seating ranges from bar stools to settees in a cosy alcove. The upstairs function room holds up to 100 people with catering facilities available. Ask about the CAMRA discount. ⇌🚃P▸

Nottingham: West

Plough

17 St Peters Street, Radford, NG7 3EN
🕐 12-midnight
☎ (0115) 970 2615
Nottingham Rock Mild, Rock Bitter, Legend, EPA, Supreme; guest beers Ⓗ
This popular back street local is the brewery tap for the Nottingham Brewery, situated at the back of the pub. A quiz night with free chilli is held on Thursday evening. The TV in the bar is turned on for sporting fixtures. Sword dancers practise in the upstairs function room and occasionally perform in the pub itself. Wireless Internet access is available.
🏚️❄️◐⊟🚃(28, 30)♣P

Radcliffe-on-Trent

Horse Chestnut

49 Main Road, NG12 2BE
🕐 11-11 (11.30 Fri & Sat); 12-11 Sun
☎ (0115) 933 1994 ⊕ horsechestnutradcliffe.com
Bateman XB; Caledonian Deuchars IPA; Fuller's London Pride; guest beers Ⓗ
Formerly the Cliffe Inn, the pub was fully refurbished in 2006 and given a smart 1920s style decor. The separate library area has sumptuous leather seating and even the toilets are worth a visit. Eight reasonably priced real ales are served including ever changing guests. An imaginative menu features home cooked food made with local ingredients. Quiz night is Monday.
❄️◐&⇌🚃P▸

Retford

Dominie Cross

Grove Street, DN22 6LA (200m from Market Square)
🕐 11-3, 5-11; 11-midnight Sat
☎ (01777) 704441
Greene King Abbot; Marston's Pedigree; Shepherd Neame Spitfire; guest beers Ⓗ

This former car showroom, garage and Netto supermarket is another JD Wetherspoon's Lloyds No 1 Bar. Attractively decorated, it makes good use of old Retford photographs. A choice of seating areas ranges from quiet little corners to a raised area overlooking the busy bar. Smoking is permitted in a heated area outside. Conveniently located, it is 200 metres from the main Retford Market Square and 50 metres from the newly refurbished bus station. ⊛◑占⊠⊱

Galway Arms

Bridgegate, DN22 7UZ (250m from Market Square)
🕙 10-1am
☎ (01777) 860788
Beer range varies Ⓗ

A fine example of a typical olde worlde English inn with a pleasant atmosphere and efficient, friendly service. Divided into three areas with two bars, the public bar has two large plasma TVs showing major sporting events. The lounge is more peaceful and there is a quaint snug with seating for just 10 people. Food is served during lunchtime and the early evening. Well worth a visit if you are in the town centre. ⚏⊛◑⊟占⊠P

Ruddington

Three Crowns

23 Easthorpe Street, NG11 6LB
🕙 12-3, 5-11; 12-11 Sat; 12-10.30 Sun
☎ (0115) 921 3226
Adnams Bitter; Nottingham EPA, Rock Mild; guest beers Ⓗ

Smart and popular single bar village local known as the 'Top House' because of the chimneys. At the rear of the pub is the well respected Luk Pra Tor Thai restaurant, open Tuesday to Saturday evenings only (booking advisable). Regular beer festivals are held, sometimes in conjunction with the White Horse. Handy for the Nottingham Heritage Centre, country park and local museums. Look for the Tuk-Tuk. ◑⊠

White Horse

60 Church Street, NG11 6HD
🕙 12-11 (10.30 Sun)
☎ (0115) 984 4550
Black Sheep Best Bitter; Wells Bombardier; guest beers Ⓗ

Excellent two-roomed 1930s pub built by Home Brewery, now a free house. Both rooms have interesting old photographs on the walls. The garden is superb in summer with patio heaters for cooler evenings. Regular beer festivals are held in the rear buildings, sometimes along with the Three Crowns. The location is handy for the village centre and the Framework Knitters Museum.
Q⊱⊛⊟占⊠(10)P⊱

Selston

Horse & Jockey

Church Lane, NG16 6FB OS464539
🕙 12-3, 5-11; 12-3, 7-10.30 Sun
☎ (01773) 781012
Draught Bass; Greene King Abbot; Taylor Landlord; Ⓖ **guest beers** Ⓗ

Friendly village local dating back to 1664, reputed to be haunted. It has a main bar, snug and lounge with iron range. Flagstone floors, open fires and low beamed ceilings give a cosy feeling throughout. You are welcome to play pool or a selection of pub games. Up to six real ales are available at any one time. Winner of several local CAMRA awards and Nottinghamshire Pub of the Year in 2004. ⚏Q⊛占⊠♣●P

South Leverton

Plough

Town Street, DN22 0BT
🕙 10-1am (midnight Sun)
☎ (01427) 880323
Greene King Ruddles County; guest beers Ⓗ

A recent winner of local CAMRA Pub of the Season, this small, friendly village pub also houses the local post office. Situated opposite the village hall, you could drive through without noticing this pub, but then you would miss out on a little gem where the locals will make you feel welcome. Some of the seating appears to be old church pews. There cannot be many pubs where you can have a pint and buy your stamps at the same time.
Q⊛▲⊠♣P

Watnall

Queens Head

40 Main Road, NG16 1HT
🕙 12-11.20
☎ (0115) 938 6774
Adnams Broadside; Everards Tiger, Original; Greene King Old Speckled Hen; Wells Bombardier; guest beers Ⓗ

A 17th-century rural gem with a lounge and dining area, small snug hidden behind the bar plus an area where the locals congregate with a grandfather clock. The fittings around the bar are original and old photographs adorn the walls creating a traditional ambience. The extensive garden has a children's play area and the pub is always busy in summer. Good, home-cooked English food is served. The pub is reputed to be haunted.
⚏Q⊛◑⊟⊠(331)P⊱

Royal Oak

25 Main Road, NG16 1HS (on B600)
🕙 12-midnight
☎ (0115) 938 3110
Greene King H&H Bitter, Abbot, Old Speckled Hen; guest beers Ⓗ

Popular roadside inn with a homely feel to it. A cosy upstairs lounge is open at weekends. The log cabin to the rear is used for occasional bands and the pub's renowned beer festivals. Pool is played in the back room and sport is shown on an unobtrusive TV. In fine weather you can sit outside at the front or rear and watch the traffic go by. Car parks are at the back of the pub and across the road.
Q⊛占⊠(331)♣P⊱

West Bridgford

Southbank Bar

1 Bridgford House, Trent Bridge, NG2 5GJ

✪ 11 (10 Sat)-midnight (11 Tue; 1am Fri & Sat);
10-midnight Sun

☎ (0115) 945 5541 ⊕ southbankbar.co.uk

**Caledonian Deuchars IPA; Fuller's London Pride;
Mallard Duck 'n' Dive; Nottingham Clayton's
Original** Ⓗ

Large, lively bar near Trent Bridge, handy for
the cricket and both football grounds. It has
comfortable seating and a patio overlooking
the Trent. Part of a small local pub group, it
always offers a beer from Mallard. The Globe,
its sister pub, is just over the bridge. A varied
and interesting selection of food is available,
including breakfast on Saturday from 10am.
Live music plays on most nights. Several TVs
show sport with two large screens for major
games. ✿◑🅰♿🖼↙

Stratford Haven

2 Stratford Road, NG2 6BA

✪ 10.30-11 (midnight Thu-Sat); 12-11 Sun

☎ (0115) 982 5981

**Adnams Broadside; Bateman XB, Valiant;
Caledonian Deuchars IPA; Castle Rock Gold,
Harvest Pale; guest beers** Ⓗ

Busy, gimmick-free Tynemill pub, tucked
away next to the Co-op, between the town
centre and Trent Bridge cricket ground. Named
as the result of a competition in the local
press, the winning entry is on display. The
beer range includes at least one mild and
Castle Rock house beers. Monthly brewery
nights offer the full range of beers from one
brewery and are usually accompanied by live
music. A good menu is available including
vegetarian options, but no chips.
Q✿◑♿🖼♣↙

West Stockwith

White Hart

Main Street, DN10 4ET

✪ 11-1am

☎ (01427) 890176

Beer range varies Ⓗ

Small country pub with a little garden
overlooking the River Trent, Chesterfield Canal
and West Stockwith Marina. One bar serves
the bar room, lounge and dining area. Beers
change frequently and come from a range of
micros, with the Idle Brewery commencing
brewing on the premises in summer 2007. The
area is especially busy during the summer due
to the volume of river traffic. West Stockwith is
where the Chesterfield Canal joins the River
Trent. Q◑♿🅰🖼♣P

Worksop

Kilton Inn

Kilton Road, DN22 6EN

✪ 11-12.30am (1.30am Fri & Sat)

☎ (01909) 473828 ⊕ kiltoninn.co.uk

**Greene King Abbot; John Smith's Bitter; Stones
Bitter** Ⓗ

Popular pub on the edge of the town centre
which has received industry awards for its
beer quality. A single bar serves a large open
plan space divided into three areas. To the left
of the bar is a quiet area with seating; the dart
board and pool table are at the other end of
the room. The pub runs active darts, dominoes

and pool teams. Three cask ales are always in
excellent condition. ≉🖼♣P

Mallard

Station Approach, S81 7AG (on railway platform)

✪ 5 (2 Fri; 12 Sat)-11; 12-4 Sun

☎ (01909) 530757

Beer range varies Ⓗ

Local CAMRA Pub of the Year in 2004 and 2005
and regular winner of Pub of the Season
awards, this welcoming pub was formerly the
Worksop station buffet. Two real ales are
always available together with a large
selection of foreign bottled beers and country
fruit wines. A room is available downstairs for
special events including the three beer
festivals the pub holds each year. Q🅰≉🖼P

Regency Hotel

Carlton Road, S81 7AG

✪ 11-2, 7-11; 12-2, 7-10.30 Sun

☎ (01909) 474108

John Smith's Magnet; guest beers Ⓗ

Large hotel with one bar and dining area
opposite Worksop railway station on the edge
of the town centre. Following its inclusion in
the 2005 Guide, the Regency has now added a
third handpull, allowing it to dispense two
guest ales as well as the permanent John
Smith's Magnet. It is popular at lunchtime due
to the good selection of reasonably priced
food on offer. Q✿◑🅰≉🖼P

Shireoaks Inn

Westgate, S80 1LT (200m from market)

✪ 11.30-4, 6-11; 11.30-11 Sat; 12-4.30, 7-10.30 Sun

☎ (01909) 472118

Beer range varies Ⓗ

Warm, friendly pub converted from cottages.
The public bar has a pool table and large
screen TV. There is a comfortable lounge bar
and separate dining area where good value,
tasty home cooked food is served. The two
handpulls dispense regularly changing guest
ales. A small outside area with tables is
available in the summer. Q✿◑🅰≉🖼♣↙

Wysall

Plough Inn

Main Street, Keyworth Road, NG12 5QQ

✪ 10.30-11; 12-10.30 Sun

☎ (01509) 880339 ⊕ ploughatwysall.co.uk

**Draught Bass; Fuller's London Pride; Greene King
Abbot; Taylor Landlord; guest beers** Ⓗ

Located in the Nottinghamshire Wolds, this
traditional, beamed 17th-century village pub
has recently been tastefully restored and
refurbished to create a distinctive interior
while retaining the character of the original
building. This is a popular, traditional drinkers'
pub drawing farmers, rugby players and other
young people from the surrounding area. The
outdoor area has tables, parasols and a red
phone box. A large car park is across the road
up a hill. Occasional special events are held
during bank holidays. ♨✿◑

OXFORDSHIRE

Abingdon

Brewery Tap

40-42 Ock Street, OX14 5BZ
🕐 11-11.30 (1am Fri & Sat); 12-11 Sun
☎ (01235) 521655 🌐 thebrewerytap.net
Greene King Morland Original, Old Speckled Hen; guest beers Ⓗ
Morland created a tap for its brewery in 1993 in an award-winning conversion of three Grade II listed town houses. The brewery was closed and its site redeveloped in 2000 following a Greene King takeover. The pub, however, run by two generations of the same family since opening, has thrived. The attractive interior features panelled walls, stone floors and an open fire. A popular lunchtime venue, it offers an innovative menu. ▲Q✿❀(◗♣P

Adderbury

Bell Inn

High Street, OX17 3LS (200m off A4260)
🕐 12-2.30, 6-11 (midnight Sat); 12-3, 7-11 Sun
☎ (01295) 810338 🌐 the-bell.com

Hook Norton Hooky Dark, Hooky Bitter, Hooky Gold, Old Hooky; guest beers Ⓗ
Charming 18th-century Hook Norton-owned pub situated in the heart of the village with old beams and open fires. Wilfred's is the newly refurbished dining room with comfy sofas and dining tables where freshly cooked meals are served including vegetarian dishes. This pub has recently been awarded the Beautiful Beer gold award by the British Beer and Pubs Association. Try the landlord's

INDEPENDENT BREWERIES

Appleford Brightwell-cum-Sotwell
Brakspear Witney
Burford Witney
Butler's Mapledurham
Cotswold Foscot
Hook Norton Hook Norton
Loddon Dunsden
Lovibonds Henley-on-Thames
Old Bog Oxford
Ridgeway South Stoke
White Horse Stanford-in-the-Vale
Wychwood Witney

'cocked ales'. Well-behaved dogs are welcome. ♨Q⚲🖾⛭◑🅿⚄🅰🖾♣⭘

Appleton

Plough

Eaton Road, OX13 5JR
🕓 12-2.30 (not Wed), 6-midnight; 12-3, 7-midnight Sun
☎ (01865) 862441
Greene King XX Mild, IPA, Morland Original; guest beers Ⓗ
Fine example of a traditional country local, dating from 1683 and serving as the social centre of this charming village. A quietly elegant and reassuring snug leads into the main bar where the landlord and landlady hold court, engaging in conversation and banter. Both bars have open fires. A separate quiet room with TV also serves as a family room. Outside Ladies and Gents add to the charm. ♨🝱🖾⛭🅱🅰♣🅿⭘

Bampton

Morris Clown

High Street, OX18 2JW
🕓 5 (12 Sat)-11; 12-10.30 Sun
☎ (01993) 850217
Courage Best Bitter; guest beers Ⓗ
Once threatened with closure by Scottish & Newcastle, this thriving village local is a fine example of how a pub can serve the local community. The pub name reflects the local 600-year-old tradition of Morris dancing. On Whit Monday the village celebrates with a beer and dancing festival. Guest beers come from local micro-breweries. ♨⚘🅰♣⭘🅿

Banbury

Bell

12 Middleton Road, Grimsbury, OX16 4QJ
🕓 1-3.30, 7-midnight; 1-midnight Fri; 12-midnight Sat; 12-6, 8-11.30 Sun
☎ (01295) 253169
Hancock's HB; Highgate Dark Mild; guest beers Ⓗ
Run by a landlord passionate about real ales with 22 years' experience, this has been a thriving community pub for 17 years. A warm, friendly drinkers' pub, some bar snacks are available. A regular in the Guide, this was voted one of the top pubs in north Oxfordshire. Within walking distance of the canal, bus and rail stations. ♨⚘🅱🖾⚄🅰♣🅿⭘

Olde Reindeer Inn

47 Parsons Street, OX16 5NA
🕓 11-11 (midnight Sat); 12-3 Sun
☎ (01295) 264031
Hook Norton Hooky Dark, Hooky Bitter, Old Hooky; guest beers Ⓗ
Traditional old English pub which first became an inn in 1570, featuring original wood panelling dating from the English Civil War. It is reported to be the location where Cromwell's men met to plan their battles. The pub features many items of interest including a large selection of pub jugs and other brewery artefacts. Food is served at lunchtime; see the blackboards for good value meals. ♨Q🝱⛭◑⚄🖾♣🅿⭘

Wool Pack at Banbury Cross

28 Horsefair, OX16 0AE
🕓 11-2.30, 5-11; 12-11 Sun
☎ (01295) 265646 🌐 banbury-cross.co.uk/woolpack
Purity Gold; guest beers Ⓗ
Despite its age this 150-year-old two room tavern has a modern feel with a bar at the front and restaurant at the back. It attracts a varied clientele at all times of the day, serving popular freshly cooked food. The excellent range of beers always includes three rare local beers and one from further afield. The pub is a regular venue for live music, quizzes and brewers' nights. Q◑🖾⚄🖾

Barford St Michael

George Inn

Lower Street, OX15 0RH (off B4031 6 miles SW of Banbury)
🕓 12-3 (Sat only), 7-11; 12-4 (plus 7-11 summer) Sun
☎ (01869) 838226
Beer range varies Ⓗ
Delightful thatched inn dating from 1672 standing in the heart of the village. A warm welcome awaits you at this free house with up to four ever changing ales usually on offer. Visitors are welcome to bring their own picnic to eat in the pub or out in the garden with its pleasant views over the countryside. The pub's chocolate labrador welcomes well-behaved dogs. ♨⚘🅰♣⭘🅿

Benson

Three Horseshoes

2 Oxford Road, OX10 6LX
🕓 11-3, 5.30-midnight; 11-midnight Sat; 12-11 Sun
☎ (01491) 838242 🌐 thethreehorseshoesbenson.co.uk
Brakspear Bitter; guest beers Ⓗ
Small, multi-roomed 17th-century inn close to the Thames with a lively local patronage. A free house, it has been under the same ownership since 1986. It has a dining room, covered patio and large enclosed garden with children's playground. The regularly changing guest beer comes from Loddon Brewery or another local micro. An extensive menu is available daily as well as a wide selection of wines. Monday is pie night with a pint or glass of wine included. Q🝱⛭◑🅿

Bloxham

Elephant & Castle

Humber Street, OX15 4LZ (off A361 4 miles W of Banbury)
🕓 10-3, 5-11; 10-11 Sat; 12-11 Sun
☎ (0845) 873 7358
Hook Norton Hooky Bitter, seasonal beer Ⓗ
Friendly 16th-century pub with a wide carriage entrance to the front doors and car park. Home cooked meals and snacks are available Monday to Saturday lunchtimes. The original bread oven remains in the restaurant area and open fires are welcoming in winter. Chas the friendly landlord has been running this Hook Norton-owned pub for 35 years. Dogs on leads are welcome if well behaved. Accommodation is available with a choice of two double bedrooms. ♨Q⚲🖾◑⚄🖾🅿

Brightwell Baldwin

Lord Nelson Inn

OX49 5NP OS653948

⏰ 12-3, 6-10.30; 12-3.30, 7-10.30 Sun

☎ (01491) 612497 ⊕ lordnelson-inn.co.uk

Brakspear Bitter; guest beers Ⓗ

This 17th-century building was a pub in Nelson's day, changing its name from Admiral Nelson to Lord Nelson when the naval hero was made a peer in 1797. Situated in a beautiful, quiet village, it is directly opposite a 14th-century church – a mixed blessing because the church had the pub closed in 1905 and it did not reopen until 1917. The pub retains its old low beams and intimate alcoves; a paved garden has been added that is popular in summer. ⚏☎♿◐P

Brize Norton

Mason's Arms

Burford Road, OX18 3NN

⏰ 12-3 (not Mon-Thu), 6.30 (5.30 Fri)-11; 12-4, 6.30-10.30 Sun

☎ (01993) 842567

Wells Bombardier; guest beers Ⓗ

Cotswold stone free house tucked away on the edge of Brize offering a homely welcome with log fires in winter and colourful gardens in summer. One long room divides into a flagstoned bar and comfortable lounge area. The friendly landlord welcomes all from games-playing locals (Aunt Sally and darts are popular) to distinguished RAF personnel. Two guest beers are always available. ⚏Q♿♿♣♥

Broughton

Saye & Sele Arms

Main Road, OX15 5ED (3 miles W of Banbury on B4035)

⏰ 11.30-2.30 (11-3 Sat), 7-11; 12-3, 7-10.30 Sun

☎ (01295) 263348

Adnams Bitter; Wadworth 6X; guest beers Ⓗ

Standing at the edge of Broughton Castle grounds and built with local Hornton stone, this is an imposing village pub, popular for its beer, food and friendly personal service. There are always two guest ales to try in the beamed and flagstoned bar and the food menu changes regularly. A huge display of water jugs provides interest. The shaded garden and patio are delightful in summer after a walk around the castle grounds. Q♿◐♿☒(480)♣P

Burford

Royal Oak

26 Witney Street, OX18 4SN (off A361)

⏰ 11-2.30 (not Tue), 6.30-11; 11-11 Sat; 11-3, 7-10.30 Sun

☎ (01993) 823278

Wadworth IPA, 6X; guest beer Ⓗ

Tucked away down a side street in a tourist town, this genuine local has a traditional pub atmosphere. The flagstoned front bar leads to a long carpeted side bar with a bar billiards table at the end. The walls of both bars are covered in interesting pictures and memorabilia. An ancient clock chimes melodiously and around 1000 tankards hang from the ceilings. The excellent home-made food features local produce. Walkers are welcome and a boot scraper provided. ⚏Q♿☎◐▲☒♣♥P

Chadlington

Tite Inn

Mill End, OX7 3NY (off A361 2 miles S of Chipping Norton)

⏰ 12-2.30, 6.30-11; closed Mon; 12-3, 7-10.30 Sun

☎ (01608) 676475 ⊕ titeinn.com

Ramsbury Bitter; Sharp's Doom Bar; guest beers Ⓗ

Family run Cotswold stone free house in the hands of the same owners for 21 years. The attractive garden has fine views with colourful shrubs lining the pathway. It has two comfortably furnished connecting bars, a restaurant and garden room in summer. Excellent freshly prepared food and six real ales are served. The pub is a focus for village activities including an annual pantomime, Great Brook rum race, Easter egg rolling and sponsored bike ride. North Oxon CAMRA Pub of the Year 2005. ⚏Q♿◐♿▲☒♣♥P

Charlbury

Rose & Crown

Market Street, OX7 3PL

⏰ 12-11 (midnight Wed & Thu; 1am Fri); 11-1am Sat; 12-11 Sun

☎ (01608) 810103 ⊕ myspace.com/theroseandcrownpub

Young's Bitter; guest beers Ⓗ

Popular, traditional, town-centre free house, 21 years in the Guide. Simply furnished, it has a split level bar with large lounge, plus a patio courtyard. On the Oxfordshire Way long distance path, walkers are welcome to bring their own picnics. A pub for the discerning drinker, seven real ales are offered, the best selection in the area. A strong supporter of micro-breweries, it has three times been North Oxon CAMRA Pub of the Year. Regular music nights feature local and touring musicians. ⚏♿▲⇄☒♥

Checkendon

Black Horse

Burncote Lane, RG8 0TE (off Uxmore Road) OS666841

⏰ 12-2, 7-11 (10.30 Sun)

☎ (01491) 680418

Butler's Oxfordshire Bitter; West Berkshire Old Father Thames, Good Old Boy Ⓖ

This 350-year-old pub has been run by generations of the same family for over a century. An unspoilt gem, it is is hidden away up a lane that at first glance appears to lead nowhere. Well worth seeking out, it is popular with walkers and horse riders from the adjoining stables. Locals and visitors are attracted by its old world charm and the promise of a good pint and friendly conversation. This is not a food pub but baguettes are usually available at lunchtime. ⚏Q♿▲P

Childrey

Hatchet Inn

Main Street, Oxon, OX12 9UF (on B4001)
☼ 12-2.30 (not Mon & Tue; 3 Sat), 7-11; 12-3.30, 7-10.30 Sun
☎ (01235) 751213
Greene King Morland Original; guest beers Ⓗ
One-room, split-level pub with a small quiet area off to one side, offering a warm welcome to all. At the centre of this small village community, it is close to the historic Uffington White Horse. Thriving and well-supported pool and quiz teams represent the pub in local leagues. Well-behaved dogs are welcome. Local CAMRA branch Pub of the Year in 2004, the Hatchet is a regular entry in the Guide.
❀♿⚐🚍(38, 67)♣P

Chinnor

Red Lion

3 High Street, OX39 4DL (on B4009)
☼ 12-3, 5-11, 12-11 Fri & Sat; 12-10.30 Sun
☎ (01844) 353468
Greene King Old Speckled Hen, IPA; Loddon Ferryman's Gold; guest beers Ⓗ
This 300-year-old friendly village local was originally three cottages. It is situated near the village centre but within easy access of the fine Chiltern countryside and a local steam railway. The outside drinking area has been refurbished and wooden decking added. Quiz nights are held monthly. Guest ales usually change three times a week. No evening meals are served on Sunday. ▲Q❀◑🍴🍺♣P⁐

Chiselhampton

Coach & Horses

Watlington Road, OX44 7UX (jct of B480 and B4015)
☼ 11.30-11; 11-3.30 Sun
☎ (01865) 890255 ⊕ coachhorsesinn.co.uk
Hook Norton Hooky Bitter; guest beers Ⓗ
Dating back to the 16th century, the Coach & Horses has a bar area and four dining areas serving good food. Plenty of beams, brickwork and open log fires create a traditional pub atmosphere. For summer drinking there is a large patio and lawn. It is not all old-fashioned nostalgia though – the pub is a Wi-Fi hotspot, free to customers. Nine chalet-style bedrooms offer quality accommodation. ▲❀🛏🍴◑♿P

Church Enstone

Crown

Mill Lane, OX7 4NN (off A44, on B4030)
☼ 12-3 (not Mon), 6-11; 12-3 (closed eve) Sun
☎ (01608) 677262
Hook Norton Hooky Bitter; guest beers Ⓗ
Dating from the 17th century, this Cotswold stone pub with an inglenook and local village photographs on the walls is a gem. The restaurant features award-winning menus of fresh fish, seafood and game (in season), made with local produce (no food Mon). The pub is popular with locals and visitors who enjoy pleasant conversation without intrusive music or games machines. It is an ideal place to visit after a walk in the surrounding countryside. Relax in the lovely rear garden or on the front patio. ▲Q❀◑🍴🚍P

Clifton

Duke of Cumberland's Head

Main Street, OX15 OPE (on B4031)
☼ 12-2.30, 6.30-10.30 (9.30 Sat); 12-2.30, 7-10 Sun
☎ (01869) 338534
Caledonian Deuchars IPA; Black Sheep Best Bitter; Hook Norton Hooky Bitter, seasonal beers; guest beers Ⓗ
Peaceful, popular pub built in 1645, situated near the Oxford Canal. It is named after Prince Rupert, the leader of the King's troops in the Battle of Edgehill in 1642. The low beamed lounge bar has a large welcoming fire. At least three beers and 30 whiskies are on offer, plus excellent food from a menu that changes monthly. The pub can be busy at weekends; well-behaved dogs are welcome.
▲Q❀🛏◑♿P⁐

Crowell

Shepherd's Crook

The Green, OX39 4RR (Off B4009 between Chinnor and M40 jct 6) OS744997
☼ 11.30-3, 5-11; 11-11 Sat; 12-10.30 Sun
☎ (01844) 351431
Black Sheep Best Bitter; guest beers Ⓗ
In the foothills of the Chilterns, this comfortable inn is renowned for its wide selection of beers; the landlord is a real ale fanatic. He is also a former fish merchant and his fresh fish comes direct from the West Country, while excellent steak and kidney pies and steaks come from the local butcher. Beers from local brewers are often available and a beer festival is held on the August bank holiday weekend. Dogs are welcome here.
▲Q❀◑♣P⁐

Eaton

Eight Bells

OX13 5PR OS448032
☼ 12-2, 6.30-11; closed Monday; 12-10.30 Sun
☎ (01865) 865389 ⊕ eight-bells.co.uk
Beer range varies Ⓗ
The no-through-road to this ancient hamlet once led to a chain ferry across the River Thames at Bablockhythe. The cream-painted brick building, originally a simple cottage, has been greatly extended. Old wooden benches and tables lend an air of rustic charm to the bar and there is a more modern dining room. The location makes this an excellent base for exploring the nearby River Thames.
▲Q❀◑🍺⚐🚍♣P

Enslow Bridge

Rock of Gibraltar

OX5 3AY (on A4095/B4027)
☼ 11 (4 Tue)-1am
☎ (01869) 331373
Beer range varies Ⓗ
Large pub by the side of the Oxford Canal dating from the 1780s. It offers a varying range of local and national beers and the restaurant serves good home-cooked food.

The landlord is Greek and Greek evenings are a popular event here. The large garden and canalside location attract a crowd in good weather. ♨☎❀①🅓 ▲P⌐

Eynsham

Queen's Head
21 Queen Street, OX29 4HH
❂ 12-2.30, 6-11; 12-midnight Fri; 12-3, 6-midnight Sat;
12-3, 7-10.30 Sun
☎ (01865) 881229
Black Sheep Best Bitter; Taylor Landlord; guest beers 🅗
Dating from the 18th century, this village inn has two bars, one quiet and cosy with a wood burning stove and a raised area for playing darts, the other larger with a pool table and sport on TV. The long standing landlord of 24 years maintains a traditional atmosphere with plenty of pub games including shove-ha'penny and Aunt Sally in the garden. Railway memorabilia on the walls reflects bygone days when Eynsham had a railway.
❀①🅗⌂🆕❀

Fernham

Woodman Inn
SN7 7NX (On B4508)
❂ 11-11; 12-10.30 Sun
☎ (01367) 820643 ⊕ thewoodmaninn.net
Beer range varies 🅖
First licensed in 1652, this delightful and spacious inn in the Vale of the White Horse caters for all. Although renowned locally for its excellent food, there is always a warm welcome for those who just want to sample a pint of one of the four ever-changing cask ales, all dispensed by gravity. Most of the building's internal walls were removed years ago but it does retain many original features including the huge roaring fire.
♨Q❀①⌂🆕❀P⌐

Fewcott

White Lion
Fritwell Road, OX27 7NZ (near jct 10 of M40)
OS346639
❂ 7 (5.30 Fri; 12 Sat)-midnight; 12-6.30 Sun
☎ (01869) 346639
Beer range varies 🅗
A true free house that offers an excellent, constantly changing choice of ales from near and far. This popular village pub is ideal for enjoying conversation or watching sport on TV, though it gets very busy on darts evenings. A quality stout or porter is often available. It has a large, quiet garden. ♨❀⌂❀P

Finstock

Plough Inn
The Bottom, OX7 3BY (off B4022)
❂ 12-3, 6-11; closed Mon; 12-6 Sun (closed eve)
☎ (01993) 868333 ⊕ theplough-inn.co.uk
Adnams Broadside; Hook Norton Hooky Bitter; guest beers 🅗
Thatched free house dating from the mid 18th century. The simply furnished flagstoned public bar features old local photos, a piano

and an old sack weighing machine; the snug bar has comfortable settees around the fireplace. The low beamed dining room offers excellent food from a small but interesting menu. Walkers (boots off), children and dogs are all welcome. The large, well kept garden is a pleasant place to relax in summer. North Oxon CAMRA cider & perry Pub of the Year 2006. ♨Q❀①🆕❀❀P

Fringford

Butchers Arms
Stratton Audley Road, OX27 8EB (off A4421)
OS604285
❂ 12-11
☎ (01869) 277363
Adnams Broadside; Caledonian Deuchars IPA; Hook Norton Hooky Bitter 🅗
Friendly and popular village inn, always cosy with comfortable seating. Very much a community pub, it hosts occasional entertainment on Saturday evening. High quality, traditional pub food served in the bar or restaurant complements the good ale. Walkers are welcome and dogs on leads permitted in the bar. ❀①⌂▲🆕❀P

Fritwell

King's Head
92 East Street, OX27 7QF (2 miles W of M40 jct 10)
❂ 12-midnight (10 Sun)
☎ (01869) 346738 ⊕ thekingsheadfritwell.co.uk
Beer range varies 🅗/🅖
Small, stone built north Oxfordshire pub with a welcoming fire to greet you on colder days. A good variety of well kept ales is often available on gravity if you ask. Food is served daily except Monday. Recently acquired by a pubco, further comforts and improvements are planned. ♨①🆕P

Fyfield

White Hart
Main Road, OX13 5LW
❂ 12-3, 6-11; 12-11 Sat; 12-10.30 Sun
☎ (01865) 390585 ⊕ whitehart-fyfield.com
Beer range varies 🅗
The White Hart was originally built in the 15th century as a chantry house and acquired after the Dissolution by St John's College, Oxford, who still owns it. Its sumptuous restaurant offers a menu prepared from local products while its more informal drinking area features an enormous log fire in winter. The four ever-changing beers usually include a Hook Norton brew. Thatcher's cider is also available. Beer festivals are held over the May and August bank holiday weekends. ♨❀①🆕(66)❀P⌐

Great Tew

Falkland Arms
19-21 The Green, OX7 4DB (off A361 and B4022)
❂ 11.30-2.30 (3 Sat), 6-11; 11.30-11 (summer Sat);
12-3, 7-10.30 (12-10.30 summer Sun)
☎ (01608) 683653 ⊕ falklandarms.org.uk
Wadworth IPA, 6X, seasonal beers; guest beers 🅗

Set in a picturesque thatched village, this award-winning pub attracts visitors who enjoy an unspoilt, relaxed atmosphere where mobile phones are banned. Simple wooden furniture rests on flagstone and bare board floors and an open inglenook fire warms you in winter. Old drinking vessels and artefacts from bygone days adorn the beams. Up to four guest ales are on offer with a range of snuffs and whiskies. High quality food is served daily except Sunday evening. Accommodation is available. ⚌Q❀≈⊷◖◗✿

Henley-on-Thames

Bird in Hand

61 Greys Road, RG9 1SB (200m SW of A4155)
🕓 11.30-2.30, 5-11; 11.30-11 Sat; 12-10.30 Sun
☎ (01491) 575775 ⊕ henleybirdinhand.co.uk

Brakspear Bitter; Fuller's London Pride; Hook Norton Hooky Dark; guest beers Ⓗ

This former Morlands pub had been a free house under the same ownership since 1993 and in the Guide for the past nine years. The only free house in Henley, this friendly one bar local is popular with regulars and visitors. The secure garden has an aviary, pond and pets. Reasonably priced lunches are served weekdays. The pub has a team in the local men's dart league and pub quizzes are held fortnightly on a Thursday. CAMRA Pub of the Year 2006. ➓❀≈Å≈♣

Hethe

Whitmore Arms

Main Street, OX27 8ES
🕓 7 (6 Fri)-midnight; 12-3, 7-midnight Sat & Sun
☎ (01869) 277654

Brakspear Bitter; Hook Norton Hooky Bitter; Ⓗ **St Austell Tribute** Ⓗ/Ⓖ

Quiet and unassuming pub, good for chatting in a relaxing atmosphere. A large fireplace in the bar and a wood-burning stove in the comfortable lounge area add to the cosy feel in winter. There is a separate room for games. Good quality ales are often available on gravity – please ask. Excellent value meals are served. ⚌❀◖◗♣P⊟

Hook Norton

Pear Tree

Scotland End, OX15 5NU (off A361 follow signs for brewery)
🕓 11.30-11.30 (1.30am Fri & Sat; midnight Sun)
☎ (01608) 737482

Hook Norton Hooky Dark, Hooky Bitter, Hooky Gold, Old Hooky, seasonal beers; guest beers Ⓗ

Small single room bar in an 18th-century brick pub featuring low beams adorned with hops and a cosy log fire. This is the brewery tap; the brewery and visitors' centre are close by. Walking sticks are for sale. Tables are outside at the front while the large garden at the rear has a children's play area. An annual beer festival is held in July. Reasonably priced home cooked bar food is on offer. Three guest rooms are available for bed and breakfast. ⚌❀≈◖◗♿≈♣P

Sun

High Street, OX15 5NH
🕓 11-3, 6-midnight; 12-3, 7-midnight Sun
☎ (01608) 737570

Hook Norton Hooky Dark, Hooky Bitter, Old Hooky, seasonal beers Ⓗ

Built of Cotswold stone, the inn has flagstone floors and a large inglenook fireplace with a wood-burning stove. Formerly two pubs, they have been combined to create roomy and comfortable drinking and dining areas, plus a skittle alley and function room. Old farm implements and harnesses hang from the beamed ceiling. A separate restaurant area offers a varied menu featuring fish and game in season. The horse-drawn brewery dray delivers on Tuesday. ⚌Q❀≈◖◗♿≈♣P

Hornton

Dun Cow

West End, OX15 6DA
🕓 6-1am; 12-11 Sat; 12-10.30 Sun
☎ (01295) 670524 ⊕ drunkenmonk.co.uk

Hook Norton Hooky Bitter; Wells Bombardier; guest beers Ⓗ

Classic, hidden-away, thatched, low beamed and flagstone-floored pub in a remote village close to the Warwickshire border. It was a butcher's slaughterhouse until 1840 and retains much of its original character. Part of the small Drunken Monk group of pubs which specialises in reproductions of historic ales, there are beer festivals organised in February and July and medieval banquets can be arranged. Bottled beers and ciders along with home cooked food are available.
⚌Q➓❀◖Ⓗ≈≈(Route 511 from Banbury) ♣✿P

Kidlington

King's Arms

4 The Moors, OX5 2AJ
🕓 11-2.30, 6-midnight; 11-midnight Fri-Sun
☎ (01865) 373004

Greene King IPA; Wells Bombardier; guest beers Ⓗ

Listed building a short walk from the centre of Old Kidlington. This traditional, friendly pub is largely dedicated to the promotion of real ales all in tip top condition to regular locals. A limited food menu is served during the week in two small bar areas; roasts are available at the weekend. The pub hosts two small beer festivals annually in the courtyard garden. Darts and Aunt Sally are played and there is a skittle alley. Say hello to Wilma the cat!
Q➓❀◖◗≈Å≈♣P⊷

Kingwood Common

Unicorn

Colmore Lane, RG9 5LX
🕓 12-3 (not Mon), 6-11; 12-3.30, 6.30-11 Sun
☎ (01491) 628452 ⊕ the-unicorn.co.uk

Brakspear Bitter, seasonal beers; Hook Norton Hooky Dark Ⓗ

First and foremost a village pub, this attractive and welcoming country inn also serves good food. Deep leather chairs next to a real fire in the bar and a well-presented dining room give

a modern yet comfortable feel. The Unicorn continues to thrive with cricket, darts and cribbage teams and now a regular Monday night quiz. A letting suite with private garden and free wireless broadband is ideal for a weekend getaway or business stopover.
⚏Q☸⌂⏃◑♣P

Lewknor

Leathern Bottle
High Street, OX49 5TW
🕑 11-2.30, 6-11; 12-3, 7-10.30 Sun
☎ (01844) 351482
Brakspear Bitter, seasonal beers Ⓗ
A 'cosy old pub' says the description of this pub in the first edition of the Guide, and it remains the same today. The Leathern Bottle has appeared in every edition of the Guide except one due to a change of landlord. This wonderful old public house has drinking and dining areas spread over three rooms. A large open fire and central servery divide the two bars and there is a family room. Consistently good ale and an extensive menu make this a public house not to be missed.
⚏Q☸⏃◑♿P

Mapledurham

Pack Saddle
Chazey Heath, RG4 7UD (on A4074)
🕑 11-3, 6-11; 11-11 Fri & Sat; 12-10.30 Sun
☎ (0118) 946 3000 ⊕ thepacksaddleinn.co.uk
Wadworth IPA, 6X, JCB, seasonal beers Ⓗ
Located between two golf courses, close to Mapledurham house, this genuine pub with a traditional feel caters for locals and visitors alike. The front bar is mainly for drinking with a huge fireplace, substantial beams and agricultural and equine paraphernalia. The food, freshly made with the emphasis on traditional English fare, is recommended for its good value and quality (booking advisable). There is an enclosed garden with children's play area, and a large paddock for beer festivals and regulars who arrive by helicopter.
⚏Q☸⏃♿♣P

Middle Assendon

Rainbow
RG9 6AU (on B480)
🕑 12-3, 6-11 (not winter Mon) Mon-Sat; 12-3, 7-10.30 Sun
☎ (01491) 574879
Brakspear Bitter Ⓗ
Compact and unspoilt pub nestling in the Stonor Valley. The cosy public bar can be packed after local field events; the lounge serves good home cooked food including locally sourced game. Popular with walkers in the Chilterns, this is also a stop for local horse drawn tours of the area. Cribbage is played every Wednesday evening in winter. The name Assendon is thought to derive from the Saxon word 'denu', meaning long, narrow, winding valley, and 'assa', meaning an ass.
Q☸◑⏃♣P

North Moreton

Bear at Home
High Street, OX11 9AT
🕑 12-3, 6-11 (midnight Thu; 1am Fri & Sat)
☎ (01235) 811311 ⊕ bear-at-home.co.uk
Taylor Landlord; guest beers Ⓗ
Originally a 15th-century coaching inn, this friendly village inn serves mostly local real ales in a beamed and bricked interior. The main bar is relaxed with sofas and an open fire, geared towards pub-goers rather than diners. Excellent food is served in the restaurant. The Bear is run by a local family who also own an antiques business and many items on display are for sale. The pub backs on to the village cricket green and Aunt Sally is played in summer. Local CAMRA Pub of the Year 2007. ⚏☸◑♣P

Oxford

Angel & Greyhound
30 St Clements Street, OX4 1AB
🕑 12-11 (midnight Fri & Sat)
☎ (01865) 242660
Wells Bombardier; Young's Bitter, Special, seasonal beers Ⓗ
Excellent, traditional local pub with friendly staff over the Magdalen Bridge in the St Clements area of Oxford. It has an open-plan single bar on two levels. Beers come from the Wells and Young's range and are consistently good. Home-made food is available at lunchtime and in the evening. The pub has bar billards, darts and plenty of board games. Outside there is a heated, covered patio for smokers. ⚏Q☸◑🖵♣⸜

Far From the Madding Crowd
10-12 Friars Entry, OX1 2BY (off Magdalen Street)
🕑 11-11.30; 11.30-midnight; 12-10.30 Sun
☎ (01865) 240900 ⊕ maddingcrowd.co.uk
Beer range varies Ⓗ
Tucked away down an alleyway in the city centre, the pub opened in 2002. It has become popular with real ale drinkers and hosts four mini ale festivals each year in March, June, September and December. The five guest ales are in constant rotation with at least one from West Berkshire or another small local brewery. It has an interesting menu with generous portions and daily specials. Live music plays occasionally and monthly special events are hosted. ◑♿🖵♣

Gardener's Arms
39 Plantation Road, OX2 6JE
🕑 12-2.30 (not Mon & Tue), 5-midnight; 12-11 Sun
☎ (01865) 559814 ⊕ thegarden-oxford.co.uk
Beer range varies Ⓗ
A favourite of students and young professionals who live in the surrounding area, the pub has a large beer garden which is very popular in summer. Four regularly changing beers are available, mainly from independent regional brewers. The food served in the Garden restaurant is entirely vegetarian, with a number of vegan options, but the imaginative menu offers a wide choice of dishes that will appeal to meat eaters as well. Q☸◑🖵

Harcourt Arms

Cranham Terrace, OX2 6DG

☼ 12-2, 5-11; 12-2, 5.30-midnight Fri & Sat; 12-2, 7-11 Sun

☎ (01865) 310630

Fuller's Chiswick, Discovery, London Pride, ESB, seasonal beers Ⓗ

Relaxed and atmospheric street corner Jericho pub with subdued lighting, background jazz and two real log fires. Patrons enjoy conversation, board games, newspapers and magazines, along with a full range of Fuller's beers, pistachio nuts by the half pint, and bar snacks (toasted sandwiches a speciality). The walls are decorated with modern art prints and an impressive collection of international bank notes. ♨☼♣

King's Arms

40 Holywell Street, OX1 3SP

☼ 10.30 (12 Sun)-midnight

☎ (01865) 242369

Wadworth 6X; Wells Bombardier; Young's Bitter, Special, seasonal beers; guest beers Ⓗ

Claiming to be the second oldest pub in Oxford, the King's Arms dates from 1607. The traditional interior is a warren of different rooms with two bars and wood panelling. The wide pavement at the front of the pub has benches and chairs – this is the only pub in Oxford city centre to be allowed pavement drinking. At least eight bottle-conditioned beers are stocked. ♨Q☼◑🚋⌐

Lamb & Flag

12 St Giles, OX1 3JS

☼ 12-11 (10.30 Sun)

☎ (01865) 515787

Palmer IPA; Shepherd Neame Spitfire; Skinner's Betty Stogs; Theakston Old Peculier; guest beers Ⓗ

St John's College owns and runs this former coaching inn on one of Oxford's most historic streets. It is hard to believe now that its future was once under threat. The rambling building has been modified but retains several distinct rooms, with some parts dating back over 600 years. The Palmer's and Skinner's beers are rare in this area, and two guest beers are always available. The house beer Lamb & Flag Gold is also a Palmer's brew. Q◑≈🚋

Mason's Arms

2 Quarry School Place, Headington Quarry, OX3 8LH os

☼ 5 (12 Sat)-11; 12-4, 7-10.30 Sun

☎ (01865) 764579 ⊕ masonsquarry.co.uk

West Berkshire Good Old Boy; Hook Norton Old Hooky; Caledonian Deuchars IPA; guest beers Ⓗ

Family run free house located in the old Quarry district of Headington. This welcoming community pub with a large garden has no food but plenty of pub games including darts, bar billards and Aunt Sally. It opened its own brewery in 2005; beers go on the bar at the weekend and are drunk quickly by the locals. Real cider is also available. A beer festival is held in September. Oxford city CAMRA Pub of the Year in 2004 and 2005. ☼♣●P⌐

Old Bookbinders

17-18 Victor Street, Jericho, OX2 6BT

☼ 12-2, 5-midnight; 12-midnight Fri & Sat; 12-11 Sun

☎ (01865) 553549 ⊕ oldbookbinders.co.uk

Greene King IPA, seasonal beers; guest beers Ⓗ

Lively and cosy back street Jericho pub decked out in ale house style, with plenty of bric-a-brac including an impressive collection of pump clips. In its Morrells days it featured in an episode of Morse but it is now part of the Greene King estate. Casks stand on a stillage behind the bar but all beers are kept in the cellar. Guest ales are a recent addition and have increased choice considerably, with four beers now usually available. ◑🚋≈♣

Rose & Crown

14 North Parade Avenue, OX2 6LX

☼ 10-midnight (1am Fri & Sat; 11 Sun)

☎ (01865) 510551 ⊕ rose-n-crown.com

Adnams Bitter, Broadside; Hook Norton Old Hooky Ⓗ

For 24 years Andrew and Debbie Hall have run this popular three-room pub, which has a large covered and heated courtyard at the rear. It is popular with a good mix of students, locals and academics who come for the warm hospitality and lively conversation – there are no gaming machines or intrusive music, and mobile phones, dogs and children are prohibited. There is no admittance after midnight and doors may close after 11pm. ♨Q☼◑🚋

Turf Tavern

7 Bath Place, OX1 3SU

☼ 11-11; 12-10.30 Sun

☎ (01865) 243235 ⊕ theturftavern.co.uk

Beer range varies Ⓗ

Tucked away between the old city walls and surrounding colleges, this famous pub with Morse connections is sought out by students, tourists and real ale drinkers. The interior has two bars with low ceilings; outside there are three flagstoned patios, one for smoking, heated in winter by coal braziers. Up to 11 varying ales plus Old Rosie cider are available. Check the pub website for popular 'meet the brewer' evenings. An annual beer festival is held in October. Q☼◑●⌐

White Horse

52 Broad Street, OX1 3AS

☼ 11-11 (midnight Fri & Sat); 11-10.30 Sun

☎ (01865) 728318

Caledonian Deuchars IPA; Taylor Landlord; guest beers Ⓗ

Sandwiched between the two entrances to Blackwell's famous book shop, this classic 16th century city centre pub has a single long and narrow bar and small snug at the back. Up to six real ales are dispensed – the guest beers frequently included brews from White Horse and Fuller's seasonal ales. This little pub can get crowded but the service is courteous and fast. The menu claims: 'The best fish and chips in Oxford'. Q◑🚋

Pishill

Crown Inn

RG9 6HH (on B480) OS724902

☼ 11.30-2.30, 6-11; 12-3, 7-10.30 Sun

☎ (01491) 638364 ⊕ crownpishill.co.uk

Brakspear Bitter; guest beers Ⓗ

The theory behind the name of Pishill is that when horses and waggons climbed out of Henley, they stopped at the inn, and while the ostlers had an ale the horses relieved themselves. This 15th-century brick and flint coaching inn has origins that may date back to the 11th century. It has a pleasant cosy interior where the focus is on dining. Though a free house, the Brakspear's is a fixture as regulars demand it and the changing guest beer is usually from West Berks. ⚲Q⚙☢⚑◑P

Ramsden

Royal Oak

High Street, OX7 3AU
☼ 11.30-3, 6.30-11; 12-3, 7-10.30 Sun
☎ (01993) 868213
Hook Norton Hooky Bitter; Young's Bitter; guest beers Ⓗ
Popular 17th century free house owned by two CAMRA members with an excellent reputation for good food and well-kept real ales. Comfortably furnished in traditional style, the main bar has an attractive inglenook fireplace and there is a small snug bar. The spacious restaurant opens onto a courtyard for summer drinking. No music, TV, fruit machines or games machines disturb the peace – this is a pub for relaxation and conversation. Always busy, children, dogs and walkers are welcome. ⚲Q⚙☢⚑◑&⚑⚲P

Satwell

Lamb

RG9 4QZ OS706834
☼ 12-11, 12-midnight Sat; 12-10.30 Sun
☎ (01491) 628482 ⊕ awtrestaurants.com
Fuller's London Pride; guest beers Ⓗ
Bought from Brakspear in 2006 by TV chef Antony Worrall Thompson, this characterful old pub with oak beams and log fire was rebuilt after a serious fire in 1992. It features two guest beers from local micro-breweries: one from Loddon, the other from Butler's or Rebellion. Food is bistro style with all meals less than £10. The garden has tables among tall pine trees and is convenient for those arriving on horseback. Look out for George, the resident ghost. ⚲⚙☢◑P

Shrivenham

Prince of Wales

High Street, SN6 8AF
☼ 12-3, 6-11 (not Sun eve)
☎ (01793) 782268 ⊕ powshriveham.co.uk
Wadworth IPA, 6X, JCB, Bishop's Tipple, seasonal beers ⒼG
Family-friendly Grade II listed former CAMRA branch Pub of the Year with a cosy atmosphere offering good home-cooked food including Sunday roasts. The landlord is a keen CAMRA member who not only organises regular trips to breweries and beer festivals for his customers but also holds his own beer festival over the spring bank holiday weekend. Quiz nights are held and board games, newspapers and wireless Internet access provided. ⚲⚙◑⚑(66)⚑⚑P⚑-

Sonning Eye

Flowing Spring

Henley Road, RG4 9RB (on A4155 near Playhatch)
☼ 11.30-11; 12-10.30 Sun
☎ (0118) 969 3207
Fuller's Chiswick, London Pride, ESB, seasonal beers Ⓗ
A destination for walkers and cyclists, this popular country local has a large riverside garden with children's swings and slide. The traditional wood panelled interior has a coal fire, dart board and balcony overlooking the garden, heated on cool sumer evenings. You may occasionally see swans swimming across the lawn after very heavy winter rain. Traditional pub food is usually served, with 'curry and a pint' specials on Monday and Tuesday evenings. Quiz night is Sunday, Autumn through to Spring. ⚲⚙◑⚑P

Stoke Lyne

Peyton Arms ☆

Main Street, OX27 8SD (off B4100 near jct 10 M40)
☼ 12-2, 5-11; closed Mon; 12-11 Sat; 12-7 Sun
☎ (01869) 345285
Hook Norton Hooky Bitter, Hooky Gold, Old Hooky; guest beers ⒼG
A welcome return to the Guide for this CAMRA inventory-listed pub, adorned with 1950s and 1960s memorabilia. Enter here for a true welcome and enjoy top quality Hook Norton ales and good conversation. This is not a pub to pass by, especially as a cheese and onion or ham roll may be available up to closing time. You can enjoy a game of Aunt Sally here. ⚲☞⚙⚑⚑

Swalcliffe

Stag's Head

The Green, OX15 5EJ (6 miles W of Banbury on B4035)
☼ 12-2.30 (not Mon), 6-11; 11.30-3, 6-11; 12-4 Sun
☎ (01295) 780232
Hook Norton Hooky Bitter; guest beers Ⓗ
Charming thatched 15th-century inn set in the heart of this pretty village, with a historic tithe barn close by. The cosy, atmospheric pub, with oak beams and an inglenook fireplace, has wooden pews and tables. Popular home-made food uses locally sourced ingredients. The guest beers change frequently, often with a northern theme. There is a delightful garden for relaxing in summer and whiling the hours away. ⚲Q⚙◑⚑(480)⚑

Thame

Falcon

1 Thame Park Road, OX9 3JA
☼ 12-11 (10.30 Sun)
☎ (01844) 212118
Hook Norton Hooky Bitter, seasonal beers; guest beers Ⓗ
This formerly struggling pub was rescued from possible oblivion by Hook Norton in 2006. It is run by two families, both newcomers to the pub trade. A small distance from the town centre, it serves as an unspoilt community local. The walls are adorned with a collection

of reproduction pub signs. Light lunches are served Monday to Saturday. ⋈Q❀◑🖳P⅃⌐

Wantage

Royal Oak Inn
Newbury Street, OX12 8DF
☼ 5.30-11; 12-2.30, 7-11 Sat; 12-2, 7-10.30 Sun
☎ (01235) 763129 ⊕ royaloakwantage.tripod.com
Wadworth 6X; ⌶/ⓖ West Berkshire Maggs Mild, ⓖ Dr Hexter's Wedding Ale, Dr Hexter's Healer; guest beers ⌶/ⓖ
The walls in this street-corner pub are adorned with photographs featuring ships bearing the pub's name, and many CAMRA awards. The bar in the lounge features a trelliswork of wrought-iron oak-leaves and acorns, largely hidden by over 200 pump clips. The smaller public bar attracts a younger crowd. The primary outlet for West Berks beers in the area, the Royal Oak remains a Mecca for the discerning drinker, with 6X served from wooden barrels. Local CAMRA Pub of the Year 2006. ⋈⬧🖳♣☙

Shoulder of Mutton
38 Wallingford Street, OX12 8AX
☼ 12-11
☎ (07836) 380543 ⊕ shoulderofmuttonwantage.com
Butts Traditional; guest beers ⌶
Corner pub renowned for its friendly atmosphere. It has a cosy snug that accommodates half-a-dozen at a pinch plus public and lounge bars with traditional decor and furnishings. The lounge has a computer with Internet access. If you prefer to stand you may also drink in the 'lay-by' in the corridor leading to a small outdoor patio which in summer is adorned with an abundance of hanging baskets. ⋈❀⬧🖳♣

Watlington

Carriers Arms
Hill Road, OX49 5AD (off B4009)
☼ 9.30-midnight; 10-11 Sun
☎ (01491) 613470
Adnams Bitter; Butler's Oxfordshire Bitter; Fuller's London Pride; guest beers ⌶
Lively village free house recently taken over by a real ale fan. This thriving local has five darts teams and hosts a quiz and a curry night on Thursday. The pub opens at 9.30am weekday mornings for a late breakfast. Situated close to the Ridgeway long distance footpath, it has a good view of the White Mark – a chalk triangle created in 1764 by a local squire who felt that the church, when viewed from his home, would appear more impressive if it looked as if it had a spire. ⋈❀◑▲♣P

Wheatley

Railway
24 Station Road, OX33 1ST os
☼ 4 (11 Tue-Sat)-11; 12-10.30 Sun
☎ (01865) 874810 ⊕ railwaywheatley.com
Fuller's London Pride, ESB ⌶
When the village still had a railway station this was the pub next door. It has a central open plan bar attractively decorated with some

railway memorabilia, a function room, several fish tanks and outside an adventure playground. A strong community pub playing Aunt Sally, pool and darts, it runs numerous teams including two football teams. Fuller's pub of the year in 2005. ❀◑⬧&🖳♣⅃⌐

Whitchurch-on-Thames

Greyhound
High Street, RG8 7EL
☼ 12-3, 6-11; 12-3, 7-10.30 Sun
☎ (0118) 984 2160
Flowers Original; Greene King IPA; Shepherd Neame Spitfire; Wells Bombardier ⌶
The small, picturesque village and conservation area of Whitchurch-on-Thames, home to around 700 residents, is just over the toll bridge from Pangbourne. The Greyhound is a cosy single L-shaped bar with plenty of low beams, wood panelling and much bric-a-brac, plus a small garden. A welcoming pub that focuses on conversation and good ale, it is an ideal stop-off for walkers exploring the surrounding Chilterns area of outstanding natural beauty. Q❀◑⇌P

Wigginton

White Swan
Pretty Bush Lane, OX15 4LE (off A361 Chipping Norton to Banbury road)
☼ 12-2.30, 6 (5 Fri)-11; 12-midnight Sat; 12-3.30, 7-midnight Sun
☎ (01608) 737669
Hook Norton Hooky Dark, Hooky Bitter, seasonal beers ⌶
An early 17th-century traditional local built of stone of the area, this pub has wonderful views across the valley. The recently refurbished bar area adds more room and maintains the building's character that features a large inglenook fireplace; a welcome sight for walkers in winter. The Hook Norton Dray delivers on Wednesday mornings, weather permitting. The rear garden is peaceful and relaxing. The menu uses locally sourced produce and is excellent value. ⋈❀◑&🖳♣P

Wootton

Killingworth Castle
Glympton Road, OX20 1EJ (on B4027 off A44)
☼ 12-3, 7-11 (midnight Wed, Fri & Sat; 10.30 Sun)
☎ (01993) 811401 ⊕ killingworthcastle.co.uk
Greene King IPA, Abbot, Morland Original ⌶
Dating from 1637, this charming coaching inn has a long beamed bar with a log-burning stove and a smaller rear bar with games including bar billiards. Simple pine furniture and timber and flagstone floors are complemented by bookcases and old rural artefacts. Popular with locals, tourists and walkers, this long-established music venue has played live music every Friday for 30 years. The garden is spacious and there is comfortable accommodation in a modern barn conversion. Excellent pub food is available. ⋈Q⌺❀⬧◑♣P

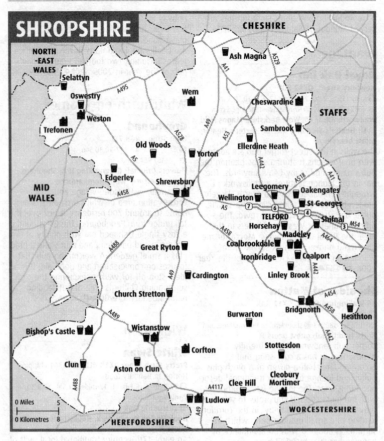

SHROPSHIRE

CHESHIRE

NORTH-EAST WALES

Ash Magna

Selattyn

Oswestry

Wem

Cheswardine

Weston

STAFFS

Trefonen

Sambrook

Old Woods

Yorton

Ellerdine Heath

MID WALES

Edgerley

Shrewsbury

Leegomery

Oakengates

Wellington

St Georges

TELFORD

Shifnal

Horsehay

Madeley

Great Ryton

Coalbrookdale

Coalport

Ironbridge

Cardington

Linley Brook

Church Stretton

Burwarton

Bridgnorth

Heathton

Bishop's Castle

Wistanstow

Stottesdon

Clun

Corfton

Aston on Clun

Cleobury Mortimer

Clee Hill

Ludlow

WORCESTERSHIRE

0 Miles 5
0 Kilometres 8

HEREFORDSHIRE

Ash Magna

White Lion

Ash Magna, SY13 4DR (off A525 2 miles from Whitchurch)

☼ 12-2 (Sat only), 6-11; 1-4, 7-10.30 Sun

☎ (01948) 663153

Draught Bass; Taylor Landlord; Worthington's Bitter; guest beers Ⓗ

At the heart of the village, this pub is the focal point of the community. The landlord and his wife have run award winning pubs in other parts of the county and their experience shows. The busy public bar displays real ale artefacts and the welcoming lounge bar, where food is served, features golf prints. The landlady is from Germany and dishes from her native country feature on the food menu. A barbecue is held every Saturday evening in summer. ⋈Q✿❀⊛◑⊟♣♠P↳⏹

Aston on Clun

Kangaroo

Clun Road, SY7 8EW (on B4368)

☼ 12-3 (not Mon and Tue), 6-11; 2-11 Fri; 12-11 Sat & Sun

☎ (01588) 660263 ⊕ kangarooinn.co.uk

Titanic Mild; Wells Bombardier; guest beers Ⓗ

Cosy village local with a small lounge, public bar, games room and dining area serving good

home-cooked food. The pub supports the annual Arbour tree redressing ceremony at the end of May, hosts summer barbecues and an annual beer festival on August bank holiday, and is part of the Clun Valley Beer Festival in October. It is also a Broadplace offering broadband access, printing facilities, web cam links and more. Outside is a large garden and patio. Dogs are welcome.
⋈Q✿❀◑▲⇌(Broome)⊟P↳⏹

Bishops Castle

Castle Hotel

Market Square, SY9 5BH

☼ 12-2.30, 6-11; 12-2.30, 7-10.30 Sun

☎ (01588) 638403

Hobsons Best Bitter, Mild; Six Bells Big Nev's; guest beers Ⓗ

Nikki and Dave, supported by their attentive staff, have lavished loving care on their 17th-century hotel for the past 18 years, with recent enhancements including sympathetic extensions and magnificent landscaped terraced gardens. Three bar areas retain much original woodwork and furnishings, providing the perfect setting to enjoy excellent home cooked food and local beer. The town's beer festival in July is actively supported by the Castle. ⋈Q✿❀◑⊟&▲⊟(553)♣P

Six Bells

Church Street, SY9 5AA

✪ 12-2.30 (not Mon), 5-11; 12-11 Sat; 12-10.30 (12-2.30, 7-10.30 winter) Sun

☎ (01588) 638930

Six Bells Big Nev's, Goldings, DA, Cloud Nine; guest beers Ⓗ

This is the Six Bells brewery tap – the adjoining Six Bells Brewery was re-established on the site of the original brewery which closed in the early 1900s. You are sure of a friendly welcome in the wood-beamed bar where you will find four real ales plus monthly specials. Excellent fresh food is served in the dining/ lounge bar (not Sun eve or Mon). The local beer festival in July is supported with up to 20 ales and real ciders plus live music in the courtyard. ⚫Q✿⚘⬤⛃Å⌷(553)♣♠⌐

Three Tuns

Salop Street, SY9 5BW

✪ 12-11 (10.30 Sun)

☎ (01588) 638797

Three Tuns Qu'Offas, Clerics Cure, Three 8, XXX, seasonal beer Ⓗ

One of the Famous Four who were still brewing in the early 1970s, this truly historic pub, together with the adjoining, but separately owned, Three Tuns Brewery, has been on this site since 1640. On one side is the dining lounge, on the other the ever popular front bar leading to the central snug and the newly added timber-framed, glass-sided dining room. As well as serving good food it hosts regular music sessions, including jazz, in the top room. ⚫Q✿⚘⬤⛃Å⌷♣♠⌐

Bridgnorth

Bell & Talbot

2 Salop Street, High Town, WV16 4QU

✪ 5-midnight; 12-2.30, 5.30-11 Sun

☎ (01746) 763233 ⊕odleyinns.co.uk

Batham Best Bitter; Hobsons Town Crier; Holden's Bitter; guest beers Ⓗ

Old coaching inn with quaint and attractive features. The larger bar has two open fires, live music on Friday and Sunday, and an unusual ceiling display of records and instruments. The small bar is home to the pub's quiz team and displays sporting equipment. Note the foliage in the rear conservatory, adorned with intriguing 'wildlife'. Guest beers, and beers for spring and autumn festivals, are selected from Shropshire and Black Country breweries within a 35 mile radius. ⚫⚰⛄≈(SVR)⌷♣

Black Horse

4 Bridge Street, Low Town, WV15 6AF

✪ 5 (12 Sat & Sun)-midnight

☎ (01746) 762415

Banks's Original, Bitter; Batham Best Bitter, Enville Ale; Hobsons Town Crier; guest beers Ⓗ

Classic, mid-1700s ale house comprising two rooms: a small front bar with an antique bar fitting and dartboard, and a larger room with a wood-panelled main bar typical of the period. Both rooms have large screen TVs, mainly for sports events. The restaurant and accommodation were refurbished a couple of years ago and are recommended. This is a popular venue for anglers after a hard day on the nearby River Severn. Guest beers include seasonal ales. ✿⚘⬤⛃⛄≈(SVR)⌷P⌐♁⌐

Friars Inn

3 St Mary's Street, High Town, WV16 4DW
(entrance in Central Court off High St or St Mary's St)

✪ 12-2, 5-11; 12-11 Sat & summer; 12-10.30 Sun

☎ (01746) 762396 ⊕virtual-shropshire.co.uk/friarsinn

Holden's Bitter, Golden Glow; guest beer Ⓗ

Tucked away in a quiet courtyard off the High Street, this is one of oldest surviving inns in Bridgnorth. First licensed in 1828 as a posting house, it has been a brewery, cider house and blacksmith's. Inside old pictures and ornaments adorn the pleasant bar and dining area. Guest beers are usually selected from local Shropshire or West Midlands breweries. In summer planters and hanging baskets decorate the courtyard seating area. Q✿⚰⬤≈(SVR)⌷

Golden Lion

83 High Street, High Town, WV16 4DS

✪ 11.30-2.30, 6-11; 11-11 (Fri & Sat); 12-10.30 Sun

☎ (01746) 762016 ⊕goldenlionbridgnorth.co.uk

Banks's Original, Bitter; Greene King IPA; Hobsons Town Crier; guest beers Ⓗ

A 17th-century coaching inn on the high street. The traditional public bar is the centre for dominoes and quiz teams, with darts and quoits also available. Historical records of the pub's sporting history are displayed on the walls of the two pleasant, quiet lounge bars. Home cooked (chip free) food is served lunchtime only. An annual beer festival is held to celebrate St George's day. There is a distracting collection of saucy seaside postcards in the Gents. Q⬤⛃⛄≈⌷♣P

Kings Head

3 Whitburn Street, High Town, WV16 4QN

✪ 11-11 (midnight Fri & Sat); 12-10.30 Sun

☎ (01746) 762141

Hobsons Best Bitter, Town Crier; guest beers Ⓗ

Sympathetically renovated Grade II listed 16th-century coaching inn retaining timber beams, roaring log fires, flagstone floors and leaded windows. Local beers are always available and there is a constantly changing selection of guest beers; Exmoor Gold is a favourite with regulars. Lunchtime and evening menus offer an interesting selection with char-grills a local produce speciality. The new Stable Bar has seven handpulls. ⚫Q✿⚘⬤⛃≈(SVR)⌷⌐⊟

INDEPENDENT BREWERIES	
Bridgnorth	Bridgnorth
Corvedale	Corfton
Dolphin	Shrewsbury
Hanby	Wem
Hobsons	Cleobury Mortimer
Lion's Tail	Cheswardine
Ludlow	Ludlow
Offa's Dyke	Trefonen
Salopian	Shrewsbury
Six Bells	Bishop's Castle
Stonehouse	Weston
Three Tuns	Bishop's Castle
Wood	Wistanstow
Worfield	Madeley

Railwayman's Arms

Hollybush Road, WV16 5DT
🕓 11.30-4, 6-11; 11-11 Sat; 12-10.30 Sun
☎ (01746) 764361 🌐 svr.co.uk
Batham Best Bitter; Hobsons Best Bitter; guest beers Ⓗ

A licensed refreshment room since 1900, owned by Severn Valley Railway, this free house attracts beer drinkers and steam buffs from around the country. The platform drinking area is perfect for soaking up the atmosphere of the steam era. The three guest beers tend to be from smaller, often local, brewers – Ma Pardoe's Bumble Hole is a popular, frequent guest – and a selection of local and European bottled beers is available. A CAMRA beer festival is held in the car park in September. 🏰Q🐕❀≉(SVR)🚃♣P⬳─🏮

Burwarton

Boyne Arms

WV16 6QH (on B4364 Bridgnorth-Ludlow road)
🕓 11-3, 6-11.30 (midnight Fri); 11-midnight Sat; 11-11 Sun
☎ (01746) 787214
Hobsons Town Crier; Taylor Landlord; Wood Shropshire Lad; guest beer Ⓗ

A large frog on a bicycle welcomes you to this 18th-century coaching inn. The impressive entrance leads to two bars and a restaurant area, all recently refurbished. Excellent meals prepared using local seasonal produce are served at lunchtime and in the evening (not Mon). The guest beer is selected from a local brewery and Weston's Scrumpy is on draught. An enclosed garden at the rear has a ROSPA certified children's area.
🏰Q🐕≏🕪🍴Ⓖ🌲P⬳─

Cardington

Royal Oak

SY6 7JZ
🕓 12-2.30, 7-midnight (1am Fri & Sat); closed Mon; 12-3, 7-midnight Sun
☎ (01694) 771266 🌐 at-the-oak.com
Hobsons Best Bitter; Wye Valley Butty Bach; guest beers Ⓗ

Reputedly the oldest continuously licensed pub in Shropshire, this free house in a conservation village dates from the 15th century. Retaining the traditional character of a country pub, the low-beamed bar has a roaring fire in winter in a vast inglenook fireplace and the dining room has exposed old beams and studwork. Guest beers are predominantly from local breweries. The food menu includes Fidget Pie made to a Shropshire recipe that has been handed down from landlord to landlord. 🏰Q🐕🕪🌲P⬳─

Church Stretton

Bucks Head

42 High Street, SY6 6RX
🕓 11-3, 7-11 winter; 11-11 Sat & summer; 12-1am Sun
☎ (01694) 722898
Hobsons Town Crier; Three Tuns XXX; Taylor Landlord; Worthington's Bitter; guest beers Ⓗ

Previously a court room and a coaching inn in the centre of this small town, parts of the building date from 1287. It has a large bar area with a games room and dining room. Weston's Old Rosie is sold in the summer and there are usually two guest beers. An annual beer festival is held in early July in conjunction with the Church Stretton Food Fair. The south Shropshire Hills offer excellent walking.
🐕🕪🛏≉🚃🌲♣P⬳─

Clee Hill

Kremlin

Clee Hill, SY8 3NB SO594755
🕓 12 (4.30 Mon)-midnight; 12-1am Fri & Sat; 12-midnight Sun
☎ (01584) 890950 🌐 thekremlin.co.uk
Hobsons Best Bitter; Sadler's Mild; guest beer Ⓗ

Set atop the Clee Hills, the Kremlin offers spectacular views over seven counties. It is the highest pub in Shropshire and possibly the second highest in England. It used to be the quarry master's house, and gets its name for a number of reasons, including its union/ communist connections and the cold war radio masts nearby. Food is served Wednesday to Sunday. Outside is a play area for children. There are numerous walks and a breeding pair of peregrine falcons in the quarry.
🏰Q🐕≏🕪🕪🍴Ⓖ🌲♣P

Clun

White Horse Inn

The Square, SY7 8JA
🕓 11-midnight (1am Fri & Sat); 12-midnight Sun
☎ (01588) 640305 🌐 whi-clun.co.uk
Hobsons Mild, Best Bitter; Salopian Shropshire Gold; Three Tuns XXX; Wye Valley Butty Bach; guest beer Ⓗ

Comfortable, 18th-century coaching inn and post house standing in the old market square at the centre of a wonderfully timeless town, described by A E Housman as 'one of the quietest places under the sun'. This friendly local, two minutes from the castle, has an L-shaped bar with low beams and adjoining dining room serving excellent, reasonably-priced home-made food. Weston's First Quality cider and a range of foreign bottled beers are stocked. Runner up local CAMRA Pub of the Year in 2007. 🏰Q🐕🕪🍴🛏🚃♣⬳─🏮

Edgerley

Royal Hill ☆

SY10 8ES
🕓 12-2, 5-midnight; 12-midnight Sat & Sun
☎ (01743) 741242
Salopian Shropshire Gold; guest beer Ⓗ

Set on a quiet road, with its garden bordering the River Severn, this delightful pub dating from the 18th century looks out over the Breidden Hills. The sympathetically extended and well-preserved building comprises a number of cosy rooms and a tiny bar where visitors are warmly welcomed. Camping is possible at the back of the pub's grounds and caravans are permitted too. Food is now served at lunchtime and in the evening, but you may wish to phone in advance.
🏰Q☾≏🐕🕪Ⓖ🛏🌲♣⬳

Ellerdine Heath

Royal Oak

TF6 6RL (midway between A53 and A442)
OS603226

☼ 12 (11 Sat)-11; 12-10.30 Sun

☎ (01939) 250300

Hobsons Best Bitter; Salopian Shropshire Gold; Wye Valley Hereford Pale Ale; guest beers Ⓗ

The Tiddly, as it is known locally, has featured in the Guide for many years. Run by hosts Barry and Rose, it ticks all the boxes: fine ale, real cider, roaring fires, children's area, disabled access to the rear, keen prices, friendly locals and good food (though not available on Mon or Tue). Cheddar Valley cider is available and a late July cider festival attracts a huge following.

ᐈQ➣❀ᕀᏧᯓ♣♠P

Great Ryton

Fox Inn

SY5 7LS (5 miles S of Shrewsbury, 1 mile E of A49 Dorrington)

☼ 12 – 2.30 (not Mon), 7-11 (midnight Sat); 12-3.30, 7-1am Sun

☎ (01743) 718499

Hobsons Best Bitter; Jennings Cumberland Ale; Salopian Shropshire Gold; Three Tuns XXX Ⓗ

Country pub nestling under the Stretton Hills. At the heart of the local community, the Fox is popular with locals and visitors from neighbouring villages. It hosts an annual beer festival and local ales are always stocked. The lunchtime bar menu is good and in the evening there is an extensive quality food menu available. Autographed football and sporting memorabilia adorns the walls.

ᐈQ❀ᕀᏧᯓᏧ♣♠P╹—▯

Heathton

Old Gate Inn

WV5 7EB (between B4176 and A458 near Halfpenny Green) OS814924

☼ 12-2.30 (not Mon), 6.30-11; 12-3, 7-10.30 Sun

☎ (01746) 710431 ⊕ oldgateinn.co.uk

Taylor Landlord; guest beers Ⓗ

A warm and friendly welcome awaits you from Jamie the landlord and his team at this 16th-century country inn, a long standing entry in the Guide. The two bars have open fires in winter months. Along with the real ale there is a quality food menu including vegetarian options and a specials board. Food is also served outside in the summer months in the garden and patio area. A recent addition is the lovingly renovated accommodation.

ᐈ❀ᖨᏧ ᎪP

Linley Brook

Pheasant Inn

WV16 4RJ (400 yds from B4373) OS680979

☼ 12-2, 7 (6.30 summer)-11; 12-3, 7 (6.30 summer)-10.30 Sun

☎ (01746) 762260 ⊕ the-pheasant-inn.co.uk

Beer range varies Ⓗ

Unspoilt pub in a rural setting with a traditional country pub feel. It has two bar rooms: the main cosy lounge housing the servery and a separate room with hatch, both with open fires. The beers are usually, but not always, from local brewers. Good locally-sourced pub food is available. The Pheasant has been in this Guide for 24 consecutive years with the same licensees and a visit is highly recommended. ᐈQ❀Ꮷ ᖨ♠P

Ludlow

Church Inn

The Buttercross, SY8 1AW

☼ 11-11 (11.30 Fri & Sat); 12-11 Sun

☎ (01584) 872174 ⊕ thechurchinn.com

Hobsons Mild, Town Crier; Ludlow Boiling Well, Gold; Weetwood Eastgate Ale; Wye Valley Bitter; guest beers Ⓗ

Situated in the centre of Ludlow, close to the castle and market square, the Church is the only free house within the town walls. The landlord, a former mayor of Ludlow, is a great advocate of real ale and also owns the Charlton Arms at Ludford Bridge. Guest ales are usually from the Salopian or Three Tuns breweries. The upstairs bar affords a wonderful view of the South Shropshire Hills and the church. Dogs are welcome.

ᐈQᏧᖨᯓ⇌▯

Nelson Inn

Rocks Green, SY8 2DS (on A4117 Kidderminster Road)

☼ 12-2.30 (not Mon), 5 (7 Tue)-midnight; 12-midnight Fri-Sun

☎ (01584) 872908

St Austell Tribute; guest beers Ⓗ

The Nelson dates back 300 years and is a fine example of a traditional beer house. The bar has a pool table, darts, quoits and a jukebox featuring 70s and 80s music. The lounge is decked out with musical instruments on the walls. Occasionally, spontaneous music events take place. It hosts a beer festival at Easter and early September in conjunction with Ludlow's Food and Drink Fair. The tasty real chips on the menu are recommended. Real cider and sometimes perry are sold. ❀Ꮷ ᖨᏧᎪᯓ♣♠╹—

Old Woods

Romping Cat

SY4 3AX

☼ 12-2.30 (not Mon, Wed & Fri), 6-11; 12-3.30, 7-11 Sat; 12-2.30, 7-10.30 Sun

☎ (01939) 290273

Draught Bass; Caledonian Deuchars IPA; Greene King Old Speckled Hen; Hobsons Best Bitter; guest beers Ⓗ

This roadside country pub is popular with locals and townsfolk alike, due in no small way to its guest beer policy in addition to the beers listed. Two are available, generally from lesser known breweries. A drinkers' pub with a cosy open coal fire, there are no distractions such as food or TV. Evidence of the pub's popularity is the many thousands raised for charity. A patio area is open in summer, enhanced by an attractive floral display.

ᐈQ❀ᖨ♣♠P▯

Oswestry

Fox Inn

Church Street, SY11 2SU
🕐 11.30-3 (not Mon), 6-midnight; 11.30-11.30 Fri & Sat;
11.30-11.30 (12-3, 6-11 winter) Sun
☎ (01691) 679669
**Jennings Dark Mild; Lakeland Bitter; guest
beers** Ⓗ
Town centre pub with timber beamed rooms
including a cosy front bar and a larger room
with a big log fire. Outside a courtyard holds
barbecues in summer. A small art gallery
features local artwork for sale. Live music is
hosted once a month. Five cask ales are
available as well as two cask ciders –
Thatcher's Heritage and Traditional. Occasional
beer festivals are held. The pub has a strict no
swearing policy. Closing time may be later in
summer. ♨Q⛄❀❀🍴🕱🚃♣🐾⛌─🖛

Sambrook

Three Horse Shoes

TF10 8AP (off A41)
🕐 12-2 (not Mon), 5 (4 summer)-11; 11-10.30 (11
summer) Sun
☎ (01952) 551133
**Banks's Original; St Austell Tribute; Salopian
Shropshire Gold; guest beers** Ⓗ
A second year in the Guide for this popular pub
with a host of regulars. People come from
near and far to drink and talk in a relaxing,
music free ambience. By popular demand Mild
is always available now, complemented by
two regulars plus varying guests. The quarry-
tiled bar is the venue for darts and dominoes
and there is a lounge and dining room.
Outside, there is a pleasant garden to enjoy in
summer. ♨Q❀🕱🕱🚃🐾♣🐾🖛─

Selattyn

Cross Keys ☆

Glyn Road, SY10 7DH (on B4579 Oswestry-Glyn
Ceiriog road)
🕐 7 (6 Fri)-1am; 12-4, 7-1am Sun
☎ (01691) 650247
Salopian Shropshire Gold; guest beers Ⓗ
A Guide regular, situated next to the church in
a small village close to the Welsh border and
Offa's Dyke. The building has been an inn
since 1840 and is CAMRA national inventory
listed. The small, cosy bar has a quarry tiled
floor and real fire. Irish music plays on
Thursday evening. Two guest beers are always
available. The pub opens at lunchtimes (Mon
to Sat) by prior arrangement. Accommodation
is available in a self-catering cottage attached
to the pub. ♨Q❀⛄❀🕱🚶♣P

Shifnal

Odfellows

Market Place, TF11 9AU
🕐 12-midnight (1am Fri & Sat)
☎ (01952) 461517 ⊕ odleyinns.co.uk
Salopian Shropshire Gold; guest beers Ⓗ
Large pub in the centre of town next to the
railway station entrance. Formerly the Star, it
was refurbished by previous owners, an
architect, teacher, plumber and draughtsman

who were known as the odfellows. There are
four handpulls and guest ales come from local
breweries. A fine example of a modern pub, it
is justifiably proud of its excellent food which
caters for all tastes and pockets. Seven en-
suite bedrooms are available.
♨Q❀⛄❀🍴🕱🕱🚃🖛─

White Hart

4 High Street, TF11 8BH
🕐 12-3, 5-11; 12-11 Fri-Sun
☎ (01952) 461161
**Adnams Broadside, Exmoor Gold; Holden's Mild,
Bitter; Wye Valley HPA; guest beers** Ⓗ
Winner of local CAMRA Pub of the Year again
in 2007, an accolade it has achieved five times
in the last six years. This listed, half-timbered
house was the first Cask Marque accredited
pub in Shropshire, and is everything a
traditional pub should be. Friendly and quiet, it
offers the best pub grub at lunchtime (not
Sun) but at night the focus is on its
outstanding ales. Q❀⛄🕱🚃♣P

Shrewsbury

Abbey Hotel

83 Monkmoor Road, SY2 5AZ
🕐 11.30-11 (midnight Fri & Sat); 12-11 Sun
☎ (01743) 264991
**Fuller's London Pride; M&B Mild, Brew XI; guest
beers** Ⓗ
The Abbey offers a choice of nine cask beers
including six guests, generally sourced from
smaller breweries. Tasting notes are
thoughtfully provided at the bar. The spacious
lounge bar has open and secluded seating
areas. Popular with groups and societies, the
pub hosts bi-weekly quiz nights in aid of
charity. Beer festivals are a regular feature.
Children under 14 years are not permitted.
Q❀⛄🚶🚃P─

Admiral Benbow

24 Swan Hill, SY1 1NF
🕐 12-2.30 (Fri only), 5-11; 12-11 Sat; 7-10.30 Sun
☎ (01743) 244423
Greene King IPA; Ludlow Gold; guest beers Ⓗ
Situated just off Shrewsbury's main square,
this spacious free house specialises in its
variety of Shropshire and Herefordshire
brewed ales; up to four are normally available
together with a selection of Belgian and
German bottled beers. Three locally-produced
ciders and a perry are also stocked in summer.
A room off the bar is available for small
functions or meetings. Children are not
catered for and under 30s are served at the
management's discretion. Outside seating is
available when the weather permits.
♨Q❀⛄🕱≋♣🐾─

Coach & Horses

Swan Hill, SY1 1NP (Near Music Hall)
🕐 11.30-midnight (12.30am Fri & Sat); 12-11.30 Sun
☎ (01743) 365661 ⊕ odleyinns.co.uk
**Phoenix Arizona; Salopian Shropshire Gold;
guest beers** Ⓗ
Set in a quiet street off the main shopping
area, the Coach & Horses provides a peaceful
haven. In summer it has magnificent floral
displays. Victorian in style, the pub has a
wood-panelled bar, a small side snug area and

a large lounge where meals are served at lunchtime and in the evening. Light snacks are available until 2.30pm. Cheddar Valley cider is also sold. Live music, electro-acoustic in the main, is hosted most Sunday evenings in the lounge/restaurant. Q❶🚼🍴♿

Nags Head
Wyle Cop, SY1 1XB
☼ 11-11 (1am Fri & Sat); 12-10.30 Sun
☎ (01743) 362455
Greene King IPA; Taylor Landlord; Wells Bombardier; guest beers Ⓗ
Situated on the historic Wyle Cop, this timber framed building is best appreciated externally, in particular the upper storey jettying and, to the rear, the timber remnants of a 14th-century hall house including a screen passage that provided protection from draughts. The old style interior has remained unaltered for many years. The pub can be very busy at times, attracting a mixed clientele. The building is reputed to be haunted and is on the Shrewsbury Ghost Trail. ⌘🚼♿

Prince of Wales
Bynner Street, Belle Vue, SY3 7NZ
☼ 12-2 (not Mon Nov-Mar), 5-midnight; 12-midnight Fri-Sun
☎ (01743) 343301 ● princeofwaleshotel.co.uk
Ansells Mild; Greene King IPA; St Austell Tribute; Salopian Golden Thread; guest beers Ⓗ
Welcoming two-roomed traditional community local with a suntrap terrace and decking area outside. Traditional pub food is served daily made with locally-sourced produce – home-made chips and mash are the house speciality. Guest chef evenings feature Indian and Italian cuisine. Charity nights are hosted and darts, bowls and dominoes are played. Two beer festivals a year are held in February and May. Awarded local CAMRA Pub of the Year 2006 and 2007, two guests accompany the regular beers and a real cider is usually available during the summer. 🏚⌘❶♿🍴🍺

Salopian Bar
Smithfield Road, SY1 1PW
☼ 5-11; closed Mon; 12-midnight Fri & Sat; 12-11 Sun
☎ (01743) 351505 ● thesalopianbar.co.uk
Salopian Shropshire Gold; Wye Valley HPA; guest beers Ⓗ
Recently refurbished, this pub has benefited from local investment. The pub has a modern, comfortable style with attractive, subtle decor. The young and dedicated management continually strives to increase the beer range and is hoping to have up to five real ales available by the end of 2007. A small selection of bottled real ale is stocked. Live acoustic music plays every Friday. Paintings by local artists are on display and for sale. Imaginative and creative food menu. ❶♿🚼🍴♿

Three Fishes
Fish Street, SY1 1UR
☼ 11.30-3, 5-11; 11.30-11.30 Fri & Sat; 12-4, 7-10.30 Sun
☎ (01743) 344793
Caledonian Deuchars IPA; Taylor Landlord; guest beers Ⓗ

This 15th-century building stands in the shadow of two churches, St Alkmond's and St Julian's, within the maze of streets and passageways in the medieval quarter of the town. Freshly-prepared food is available at lunchtime and early evening (not Sun eve). The pub offers a range of up to six local and national beers, with some dark beers featuring regularly. Local CAMRA Pub of the Year runner up in 2006. Q❶🚼🚊

Wheatsheaf
50 High Street, SY1 1ST
☼ 11-midnight; 12-11 Sun
☎ (01743) 272702
Banks's Bitter; Marston's Old Empire; guest beers Ⓗ
Comfortable town centre street corner pub with a view to St Julian's church, popular with regulars, visitors and shoppers. Three distinct bar areas are adorned with many pictures of old Shrewsbury. Food is served at lunchtime (not Sun) made from locally sourced produce. Beer festivals are held in March and October. In fine weather street seating is provided. ❶🚼🚊♿

Woodman Inn
Coton Hill
☼ 4 (12 Sun)-midnight
☎ (01743) 351007
Salopian Shropshire Gold; Weetwood Oasthouse Gold; guest beers Ⓗ
Half brick and half timbered black and white corner pub originally built in the 1800s but destroyed by fire in 1923 and rebuilt in 1925. It has a wonderful oak panelled lounge with two log fires and traditional settles, and bar with original stone-tiled flooring and listed leaded windows. The courtyard is decorated with award winning floral displays in summer. The building is reputedly haunted by an ex-landlord who died when the pub burnt down. Local CAMRA Pub of the Year runner up 2006 and 2007. 🏚Q🐕⌘❶🚼🚊♿🍴

Stottesdon

Fighting Cocks
1 High Street, DY14 8TZ
☼ 6-midnight; 5-1am Fri; 12-midnight Sat; 12-11.30 Sun
☎ (01746) 718270
Hobsons Best Bitter, Town Crier; guest beer Ⓗ
An ale house since 1830, this pub and its shop are the hub of activity for the village and local community. It has beamed ceilings, a cosy bar with log fire, two dining areas and a new function room/summer cafe. Live music plays on alternate Saturday nights and a beer festival is held in the autumn. Excellent award-winning food is served (not Sun & Mon eve) made only with fresh locally sourced produce. 🏚Q⌘❶🅿♿🅿

Telford: Coalbrookdale

Coalbrookdale Inn
12 Wellington Road, TF8 7DX
☼ 12.30-3, 5-11; 12-11 Fri & Sat; 12-midnight Sun
☎ (01952) 433953 ● coalbrookdaleinn.co.uk

Hobsons Town Crier; Three Tuns XXX; Wye Valley Hereford Pale Ale; guest beers ⊞
Built in 1831, this Grade II listed pub features memorabilia relating to the Industrial Revolution and is slowly turning itself into a Victorian experience. It has been serving the ironworkers of Coalbrookdale since the 1830s and now greets locals and visitors alike. Real ale is served from seven handpumps and freshly prepared home-cooked food is available in the bar or lounge/dining room. Extra parking space is available at the community centre up the hill on the left.
ⅧQ≈⊲◑♣P

Telford: Coalport

Shakespeare
High Street, TF8 7HT
✪ 5-11; 12-midnight Sat & Sun
☎ (01952) 580675 ⊕ shakespeare-inn.co.uk
Enville Ale; Everards Tiger; guest beers ⊞
Warm, welcoming family run pub with wonderful views of the Severn Gorge and River, ideally situated for the Coalport China and Tar Tunnel museums. Nearby is a youth hostel and the Silkin Way leading to the Blists Hill museum. A good selection of guest ales, often from local brewers, includes favourites Exmoor Gold and Three Tuns XXX. The tempting menu of excellent home-cooked dishes is always popular (Sat, Sun only, booking advised). The large three-tiered garden has a children's play area for sunnier days. Q❀≈⊲◑&♣P

Telford: Horsehay

Station Inn
Station Road, TF4 2NJ (200m from Telford Steam Railway)
✪ 6-midnight; closed Mon; 12-1am Fri & Sat; 12-midnight Sun
☎ (01952) 503006 ⊕ stationinnhorsehay.co.uk
St Austell Tribute; guest beers ⊞
Situated close to the Telford Steam Railway, this genuine family-run free house dates back to 1860. It has four handpumps, at least one dispensing a local ale, and holds beer festivals on the May bank holiday and in October. Food is home made and very good – a restaurant extension is planned. Tuesday's steak night is popular. Outside is a fenced garden and patio. Q❀◑P

Telford: Ironbridge

Robin Hood Inn
33 Waterloo Street, TF8 7HQ
✪ 10am-midnight
☎ (01952) 433100
Holden's Mild, Bitter, Golden Glow, Special; guest beers ⊞
Overlooking the River Severn opposite the free bridge, this 18th-century building is situated in the birthplace of the Industrial Revolution. Taken over by Holden's Brewery in 2004, it has five rooms with oak beamed interiors and a warm atmosphere. Known for its traditional pub grub and Holden's beers, it offers varying guests and real cider. Live Irish music plays on the first Wednesday of the

month and folk music on the second Tuesday.
Q❀≈⊲◑&♣♠P

Telford: Leegomery

Malt Shovel
Hadley Park Road, TF1 6QG (off A442)
✪ 12-2.30, 5-11; 12-11 Fri-Sun
☎ (01952) 242963
Marston's Burton Bitter, Pedigree; guest beers ⊞
Popular traditional two-roomed pub with an array of bric-a-brac adorning the walls and ceiling. The lounge is homely and comfortable while the bar with Sky TV is the hub for armchair sports fans. Excellent, reasonably-priced lunches are served during the week which attract locals and business people alike. Rolls and pies are available at other times.
ⅧQ◑⊞P

Telford: Madeley

All Nations
20 Coalport Road, TF7 5DP
✪ 12-midnight (12-3, 5-midnight Mon-Thu winter)
☎ (01952) 585747
Worfield Coalport Dodger Mild, Dabley Ale; guest beers ⊞
Re-opened in 2002, this was one of the original brew pubs in the 1973 Guide. The refurbishment revealed original beams above the plasterboard ceiling and quarry floor tiles under the lino. The Worfield Brewery now occupies a space at the back. Photographs of past local life decorate the walls. The pub is set high up off the road; across the road is a listed plate bridge leading to the Blists Hill museum. ⅧQ❀♣♠P⊟

Telford: Oakengates

Crown Inn
Market Street, TF2 6EA
✪ 12-3, 5-11 Mon & Tue; 12-11 Wed-Sun
☎ (01952) 610888 ⊕ crown.oakengates.com
Hobsons Best Bitter; guest beers ⊞
Fine example of a town pub – the original building dates from 1835. The owner is very much hands on and promotes the business with much publicity and many events. To date 6000 beers have coursed through the 14 handpulls over 12 years. Milds, stouts and porter all feature, plus continental beers, sometimes on draught. Festivals, on the first weekends of May and October, claim to be the largest of their kind in the country.
ⅧQ❀⊟&≈⊞♣♠P⅃

Station Hotel
42 Market Street, TF2 6DU
✪ 10am-11 (midnight Thu & Fri; 1am Sat); 10.30-4, 7-11 Sun
☎ (01952) 612949
Holden's Golden Glow; Salopian Shropshire Gold; guest beers ⊞
Genuine free house in a bustling environment. Facelifted in 2007 with a GWR theme, the lounge has become the Oakengates Room. Here you will find the history of the town in words and pictures. There is an ever changing and imaginative range of guest beers. Throughout the year, the landlord, holds

festivals for beer, cider and perry, and continental beers. Monster baps are on sale at most times. ▲❀❒➡♣♨

Telford: St Georges

St Georges Sports & Social Club
Church Road, TF2 9LU
✪ 7-midnight (12.30am Fri); 12-12.30am Sat & Sun
☎ (01952) 612911
Banks's Original, Bitter; guest beers Ⓗ
This club is a regular winner of CAMRA awards for enthusiastic support and promotion of real ale. CAMRA members are warmly welcomed. Beers are mainly showcased from Shropshire and Black Country breweries, but not exclusively so. The outside drinking area overlooks one of the grounds used by Shropshire Cricket Club; many other local sports teams use the club as a base. ⏱❀P

Telford: Wellington

Cock Hotel
148 Hollyhead Road, TF1 2DL
✪ 4 (12 Thu)-11.30; 12-midnight Fri & Sat; 12-4, 7-11 Sun
☎ (01952) 244954 ⊕ cockhotel.co.uk
Hobsons Best Bitter; guest beers Ⓗ
This will be 11 years of continuous entry in the Guide for the Cock. This imposing 18th-century coaching inn with a hop festooned main bar has eight handpulls dispensing constantly changing beers, always including a mild and stout or porter. Lively conversation is the norm without games machines or music to intrude. A selection of foreign beers, bottled and draught, is available. A frequent winner of local CAMRA Pub of the Year. ▲Q❀🛏❒➡❒♣♨P↳

Wistanstow

Plough Inn
SY7 8DG
✪ 12-2.30, 6.30-11.30; 12.30-3, 7-10.30 Sun
☎ (01588) 676251
Wood Parish Bitter, Shropshire Lad; guest beers Ⓗ
Traditional country pub dating from 1782 on the doorstep of the Wood Brewery. The public bar, a few steps down from the entrance, has a games area. The large lounge and dining area offer home-prepared food made with Shropshire produce wherever possible. The brewery tap for Wood, presentation packs of its beers are for sale and there is a fine display of Royal Wedding commemorative bottled beers. Handpulls are over 100 years old and have been recently renovated. ▲Q❀🛏❒➡♣P↳

Yorton

Railway Inn
SY4 3EP
✪ 12.30 (12 Sun)-4, 7-11
☎ (01939) 220240
Salopian Hop Twister; Wadworth 6X; Wood Shropshire Lad; guest beers Ⓗ
Stepping inside the Railway Inn is like going back in time. Little has changed since 1936 when the owners first moved in. Then a Southam's pub, it became a free house in 1972 when the family purchased it from Whitbread. Up until 1980 an adjacent smallholding provided milk to local dairies. The small bar is popular with locals and railway travellers with its settles and quarry-tiled floors. The cider comes from Thatchers. Snacks such as sandwiches may be available on request. ▲Q❀❒➡♣♨P

The language of beer

Nose: the aroma. Gently swirl the beer to release the aroma. You will detect malt: grainy and biscuity, often likened to crackers or Ovaltine. When darker malts are used, the nose will have powerful hints of chocolate, coffee, nuts, vanilla, liquorice, molasses and such dried fruits as raisins and sultanas. Hops add superb aromas of resins, herbs, spices, fresh-mown grass and tart citrus fruit – lemon and orange are typical, with intense grapefruit notes from some American varieties. Sulphur may also be present when waters are 'Burtonised': i.e. gypsum and magnesium salts have been added to replicate the famous spring waters of Burton-on-Trent.

Palate: the appeal in the mouth. The tongue can detect sweetness, bitterness and saltiness as the beer passes over it. The rich flavours of malt will come to the fore but hop bitterness will also make a substantial impact. The tongue will also pick out the natural saltiness from the brewing water and fruit from darker malts, yeast and hops. Citrus notes often have a major impact on the palate.

Finish: the aftertaste, as the beer goes over the tongue and down the throat. The finish is often radically different to the nose. The aroma may be dominated by malt whereas hop flavours and bitterness can govern the finish. Darker malts will make their presence felt with roast, chocolate or coffee notes; fruit character may linger. Strong beers may end on a sweet or biscuity note but in mainstream bitters, bitterness and dryness come to the fore.

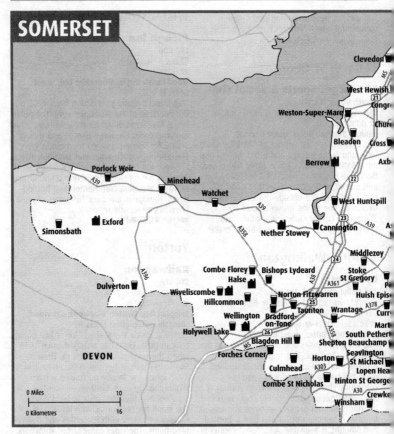

SOMERSET

Aller

Old Pound Inn

TA10 0RA (on A372 between Langport and Othery) OS400294
✪ 11-2.30, 5-midnight; 11.30-midnight Sat & Sun
☎ (01458) 250469 ⏚ oldpoundinn.co.uk
Sharp's Doom Bar; guest beers Ⓗ
Friendly village free house dating from the 16th century offering a constantly changing selection of West Country beers. The casks are kept in a controlled-temperature cellar on a sprung stillage system. As well as a large public bar, there is a family room, spacious restaurant and a function room. Extensive food and wine menus are available and over 40 malt whiskies are stocked. Dogs are welcome.
🏠Q🕏🕸⚅⏴♿⛽♣P⅃

Ashcott

Ring O' Bells

High Street, TA7 9PZ
✪ 12-2.30, 7-11 (10.30 Sun)
☎ (01458) 210232 ⏚ ringobells.com
Beer range varies Ⓗ
Village-centre pub near the church with a large single room on three levels and a function room. Award-winning food is served in the main bar and dining room. Ales often come from local breweries such as Moor and Glastonbury and local cider is stocked. A former Somerset CAMRA Pub of the Year, it

has been run by the same family for more than 20 years. 🕏🕸⏴⚅⛽♣♦P

Axbridge

Crown Inn

St Mary's Street, BS26 2BN
✪ 5-midnight; 12-1am Fri & Sat; 12-midnight Sun
☎ (01934) 732518 ⏚ axbridgecrown.co.uk
Sharp's Doom Bar; guest beers Ⓗ
Free house set just off the main square of the historic village of Axbridge. The cosy front bar has a big open fireplace. Local teams gather here for competitive games of table skittles. The back bar has a more modern feel with a pool table and games machine. The skittle alley doubles as a family room, and there is a large enclosed beer garden. Bar food is served at reasonable prices; guest beers often include the new local Cheddar Ales range.
🏠🕏🕸⏴⎔⚅⛽(126)♣♦

Barrow Gurney

Princes Motto

Barrow Street, BS48 3RY (on B3130)
✪ 10.30-11
☎ (01275) 472282
Butcombe Bitter; Draught Bass; Wadworth IPA, 6X, seasonal beers Ⓗ
Characterful, 200-year-old inn which was once three cottages. It is now split on three levels;

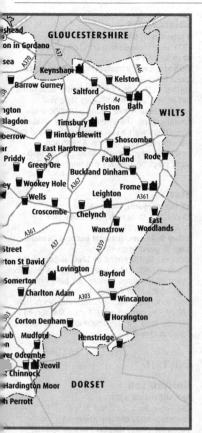

the main bar area is popular with locals, while a long side area is ideal for dining (weekday lunchtimes only). Towards the rear is a small lounge and darts area. Free-range eggs and pickled onions are sold, along with Weston's Traditional cider. There is a small garden for warmer days. Buses pass on the two main roads, but the walk to the pub is treacherous. ⁂Q✪🛈♣●P⬩⅃

Barton St David

Barton Inn
Main Street, TA11 6BZ OS541321
☼ 12-2.30, 4.30-11; 12-midnight Sat & Sun
☎ (01458) 850451
Beer range varies Ⓖ
This real country pub, full of both character and characters, where eccentricity appears to be the norm, will welcome you, your horse, your muddy dog and even your ferret if well behaved. The small bar, where the ales are racked behind the counter, and the equally small back room enhance the cosy atmosphere. Somewhat off the beaten track, those making the effort to find it are well rewarded. ⁂⛺✪🛈♿🚆♣●P⬩⅃

Bath

Bell
103 Walcot Street, BA1 5BW

☼ 11.30-11; 12-10.30 Sun
☎ (01225) 460426 ⊕ walcotstreet.com
Abbey Bellringer; Bath Gem; Hop Back Summer Lightning; Otter Bitter; RCH Pitchfork; Stonehenge Danish Dynamite Ⓗ
The Bell has a long main bar and a number of seating areas. Live bands perform on Monday and Wednesday evenings and Sunday lunchtime; posters for local gigs and other events in the Walcot area adorn the walls. The sheltered courtyard has plenty of seating. A mini-launderette and WiFi facilities have been added. ⁂🚆🛈♣●⅃

Coeur de Lion
17 Northumberland Passage, BA1 5AR
☼ 11-midnight; 12-10.30 Sun
☎ (01225) 463568 ⊕ coeur-de-lion.co.uk
Abbey Bellringer; guest beers Ⓗ
Situated in a passageway opposite the Guildhall in the centre of town, this pub claims to be the smallest in Bath. With just four tables in the single small bar, this may well be true. Traditional pub food is served at lunchtime. Seating capacity is increased in summer by placing tables outside the pub. The stained-glass window at the front is a fine example of its kind. ◖🛈🚆♣

Garrick's Head
8 St Johns Place, Sawclose, BA1 1ET
☼ 12-1am (10.30 Sun)
☎ (01225) 318368
Bath Barnstormer; Milk Street Funky Monkey; Palmer Traditional Best Bitter IPA Ⓗ
Adjoining the Theatre Royal in part of an historic house, the Garrick's Head seems more of a wine bar than a pub, but there are usually four well-kept real ales available from a variety of West Country breweries and Burrow Hill cider. Food is excellent, served in the bar and restaurant. This is the theatre pub so do not be surprised to see the odd celebrity at the bar. ⁂🛈◖🚆🛈♣●⅃

Hop Pole
Albion Buildings, Upper Bristol Road, BA1 3AR
☼ 12-11 (midnight Fri & Sat)
☎ (01225) 446327
Bath SPA, Gem, Barstormer, seasonals; guest beers Ⓗ
The Hop Pole is a friendly place situated between Victoria Park and the River Avon. An alleyway connects to the towpath, part of the Bath to Bristol cycle path. Six real ales are usually available, including four from Bath Ales. A range of bottled foreign beers and cider is also stocked. The skittle alley has been converted to a restaurant selling high quality food. No children are permitted. ⁂◖🚆♣⬩⅃

King William
36 St Thomas Street, BA1 5NN
☼ 12-3, 5-midnight; 12-midnight Sat; 12-10.30 Sun
☎ (01225) 428096 ⊕ kingwilliampub.com
Palmer Copper Ale; guest beers Ⓗ
Founded in 1827, the King William has been a pub ever since. It underwent refurbishment in 2004, transforming into a more civilised place with an emphasis on good beer and food sourced from local suppliers. The main bar is split into two areas: both are quite small and can get very crowded, a sort of Bath tradition.

The pub always features beers from Palmer and an ever-changing range of local brews.
🏚🌱⬤🍴🖪

Old Green Tree ☆

12 Green Street, BA1 2JZ
🕐 11-11; 12-10.30 Sun
☎ (01225) 448259

RCH Pitchfork; Wickwar Brand Oak Bitter; guest beers Ⓗ

Classic, unspoilt pub situated in a 300-year-old building. An atmosphere of dim cosiness pervades all three small rooms, with oak panelling dating from the 1920s. The lounge bar is decorated with pictures of World War II aircraft. During Bath's annual Fringe Festival, these are replaced by works from selected local artists. The pub can get very crowded but space can sometimes be found in the comfortable back bar. The house beer Green Tree Bitter is brewed by Blindmans. Q🌱⬤🍴🖪♣

Pulteney Arms

37 Daniel Street, BA2 6ND
🕐 12-3 (not Mon & Tue), 5-11 (midnight Fri);
12-midnight Sat; 12-10.30 Sun
☎ (01225) 463923

Bath Gem; Butcombe Bitter; Fuller's London Pride; Wadworth 6X; Young's Bitter; guest beers Ⓗ

The building dates from 1759 and is known to have been a pub as early as 1812. Gas lighting still features extensively, with five lights over the bar and four lamps outside. The cat symbol on the pub sign refers to the Pulteney coat of arms. The decor focuses on sport, particularly rugby, and the pub sponsors a number of teams, including hockey and Bath Ladies rugby. The food menu is long and deservedly popular. Q🌱🏚⬤🍴🍴🖪♣

Raven

6-7 Queen Street, BA1 1HE
🕐 11-11 (midnight Fri & Sat); 12-10.30 Sun
☎ (01225) 310324

Beer range varies Ⓗ

In a small, cobbled street near Queen Square and just off Milsom Street, this pub has been extensively refurbished, reverting to its original name after many years as Hatchetts. There is a bar and dining area upstairs; pies and sausages are a speciality. Live acoustic music is staged every other Tuesday. The pub hosts a variety of events such as storytelling evenings and the Bath Science Café. House beers Raven and Raven Gold are brewed by Blindmans. ⬤🍴

Royal Oak

Lower Bristol Road, Twerton, BA2 3BW
🕐 12-midnight
☎ (01225) 481409 🌐 theroyaloak-bath.co.uk

Beer range varies Ⓗ

This free house offers a permanent mini beer festival. Up to 10 ales from micro-breweries across the country are available, often including local brews. Beer festivals are held in February and July, and Irish music plays on Wednesday. A discount is available for CAMRA members. Evening meals are Thursday and Friday only, no food Saturday lunchtime.
🏚Q🏚⬤🍴(Oldfield Park)🖪(5)♣⬤P

Salamander

3 John Street, BA1 2JL
🕐 11.30-11 (midnight Fri & Sat); 12-10.30 Sun
☎ (01225) 428889

Bath SPA, Gem, Barnstormer, seasonal beers; guest beers Ⓗ

Former 18th-century coffee house now fitted out in the familiar Bath Ales style with wooden floorboards, wood panelling and hanging hops. The interior is subtly divided downstairs with a restaurant upstairs and can get crowded very quickly. A selection of bottled Belgian beers is available. An Irish band plays on Tuesday evening. ⬤🍴🖪

Star ☆

23 The Vineyards, BA1 5NA
🕐 12-2.30, 5.30-midnight; 12-midnight Sat & Sun
☎ (01225) 425072

Abbey Bellringer, seasonal beers; Ⓗ **Draught Bass;** Ⓖ **guest beers** Ⓗ

This pub, first licensed in 1760, is one of the oldest in Bath and is now a listed building. Its many small rooms feature oak panelling and 19th-century bar fittings. Beer festivals are held during the year and seasonal beers from Abbey Ales often appear. Bass is still served in the jug. Look for the bench known as 'Death Row'. 🏚Q🍴♣

Bayford

Unicorn Inn

BA9 9NL (on old A303)
🕐 12-2 (not Mon), 7-11; 12-2.30 Sun
☎ (01963) 32324 🌐 theunicorninnbayford.com

Butcombe Bitter; Shepherd Neame Spitfire; guest beers Ⓗ

This 270-year-old former coaching inn is accessed via the old coach arch and courtyard. The single bar is divided into three distinct areas catering for diners and drinkers. The interior has flagstone floors, beams and an open fireplace. There is also a hidden well. The beers are keenly priced; the two guests often come from local micros. Excellent value-for-money food is served at all sessions, with fish a speciality. ⚑Q✿✍✪◐&❦P

Bishops Lydeard

Lethbridge Arms

Gore Square, TA4 3BW
🕙 11-3, 6-midnight; 11-2am Fri & Sat; 12-midnight Sun
☎ (01823) 432234 ⊕ thelethbridgearms.co.uk
Cotleigh Tawny Bitter; guest beers Ⓗ
In the car park of this 16th-century coaching inn is an old fives tower which was used for playing an early form of handball and is the only surviving fives tower in Taunton Deane. The pub offers three changing guest beers and a varied menu of good food including a Sunday carvery. Barbecues are hosted in the large garden in summer.
⚑✿✍✪◐&≠(West Somerset Railway)
◱❦P⌐

Blagdon

New Inn

Church Street, BS40 7SB (100m off A368)
🕙 11-3, 6-11; 12-3, 6-10.30 Sun
☎ (01761) 462475
Wadworth IPA, 6X, seasonal beers Ⓗ
This 16th-century whitewashed inn is run by the former long-standing licensees of the Ring O' Bells at Compton Martin. Two rooms are furnished with comfortable sofas, large fireplaces, exposed beams and horse brasses. Generously portioned, reasonably priced meals are available at all sessions. The beer garden offers panoramic views across Blagdon Lake and the Mendip Hills.
⚑Q✿◐❦◱P

Blagdon Hill

Lamb & Flag

TA3 7SL (3 miles S of Taunton) OS212181
🕙 11-11 (midnight Fri); 12-10.30 Sun
☎ (01823) 421736
Otter Bitter; guest beers Ⓗ
Situated on the northern slopes of the Blackdown Hills, this 16th-century pub is frequented by locals and visitors. The main bar has the original flagstone floor and a large open fireplace separates the bar and candlelit dining area. Good food is locally sourced and home made. Four ales come from south-west micro-breweries. A skittle alley and function room are situated beyond the bar. The large garden has panoramic views from the Brendon to the Mendip Hills. ⚑✿◐◱❦P⌐

Bleadon

Queen's Arms

Celtic Way, BS24 0NF (off A370)
🕙 11.30-3, 5-11; 11-11 Fri & Sat; 12-10.30 Sun
☎ (01934) 812080
Bath Gem, Barnstormer; Butcombe Bitter, Gold, Brunel IPA; Fuller's London Pride; guest beers Ⓖ
Oldest pub of three in Bleadon, it is in the centre of the village and, bizarrely, featured in a 1980s TV ad for lager. Three rooms converge on the bar and there is a garden/patio sales hatch. From time immemorial, the ale here has only been served on gravity. Food sales

are strong but beer is a popular attraction too. Thatchers cider is sold. Expect morris dancing on May Day Monday.
⚑Q✍✿◐Æ◱(83)♣❦P⌐

Bradford-on-Tone

White Horse Inn

Regent Street, TA4 1HF (off A38 between Taunton and Wellington)
🕙 11.30-3, 5.30-11; 12-3, 7-10.30 Sun
☎ (01823) 461239 ⊕ whitehorseinn.co.uk
Cotleigh Tawny; guest beers Ⓗ
Very much a community pub at the centre of the village, it has a post office and shop in outbuildings. Two guest beers are sourced from local and national breweries. Real fires warm both bars. Excellent home-cooked food is served (booking advised) and speciality evenings are a feature. The beautiful large garden hosts barbecues in summer. The skittle alley doubles as a function room and bar billiards can be played in the main bar.
⚑✿◐◱❦P⌐

Buckland Dinham

Bell

High Street, BA11 2QT
🕙 12-3, 6-11; 12-2.30, 7-10.30 Sun
☎ (01373) 462956 ⊕ bellatbuckland.co.uk
Butcombe Bitter; Fuller's London Pride; Milk Street Funky Monkey; Wychwood Hobgoblin Ⓗ
Traditional 16th-century village pub that is the centre for many activities. A barn has been converted for various functions including a beer festival in August and there is a large field for campers. The food menu is excellent. The website was voted Best in the West 2006.
⚑✿◐&Æ◱❦P⌂

Cannington

Rose & Crown

30 High Street, TA5 2HF (off A39)
🕙 12-11 (10.30 Sun)
☎ (01278) 653190
Caledonian Deuchars IPA; Greene King IPA, Abbot, Old Speckled Hen; guest beers Ⓗ
An atmospheric, friendly pub, dating back to the 17th-century with a loyal local following. The single bar has a tiled floor and a roaring fire in winter. Original beams are covered with interesting objects donated by locals and there is a collection of clocks – a real curiosity pub. The bar has a pool table, table skittles and a collection of games hand-made by locals. The garden has won numerous Pub in Bloom awards. ⚑✿✍◱❦P

Charlton Adam

Fox & Hounds

Broadway Road, TA11 7AU (off A37)
🕙 12-3, 5.30-11; 12-3, 6.30-10.30 Sun
☎ (01458) 223466
Beer range varies Ⓗ
Friendly, stone-built pub to the east of the village. A large collection of tankards hangs from the low-beamed ceiling in the main bar and its walls are decorated with hunting scenes, Guinness prints and the original pub

sign. There is a pleasant conservatory for drinkers and diners. Good food is served – Thursday is steak night. The beers are largely from West Country breweries.
🏚🏵🌀🕹🗛♣P⌐

Cheddar

White Hart

The Bays, BS27 3QW

🕙 12-2.30, 5.30-11; 12 (11 summer)-11 Sat; 12-11 Sun
☎ (01934) 741261 ● thewhitehartcheddar.co.uk
Butcombe Bitter; Greene King Old Speckled Hen; Wychwood Hobgoblin Ⓗ

Delightfully welcoming local pub situated near Cheddar Gorge comprising a family dining room and a large main bar with an open log fireplace. Engaging photographs of regulars' day trips add interest. An excellent range of food is available all day. There are regular quiz, music and themed nights. Thatchers Cider, draught and bottled, is available. Outside is a large garden and car park.
🏚Q🌄🏵🌀🕹🚃(126)♣🍴P

Chelynch

Poachers Pocket

BA4 4PY

🕙 12-2.30, 6-11.30; 12-3, 7-11 Sun
☎ (01749) 880220 ● poachers-pocket.co.uk
Butcombe Bitter; Cotleigh Tawny; Wadworth 6X; guest beers Ⓗ

Parts of this pub date back to the 14th century. It offers a choice of three real ales and a guest, with cider from Wilkins and Addlestones. Annual beer and cider festivals are hosted and the pub supports local arts and folk music events. Live music plays on the second Sunday of the month. The skittle alley doubles as a function room. 🏚🏵🌀♣🍴P

Churchill

Crown Inn

The Batch, Skinners Lane, BS25 5PP (off A38, ¼ mile S of A368 jct)

🕙 11.30-11; 12-10.30 Sun
☎ (01934) 852995
Cotleigh range; guest beers Ⓖ

Winner of many CAMRA awards, this pub has been in the same hands for 22 years. Tucked away down a small lane yet close to the village centre, it is easily missed. There are several small rooms with stone-flagged floors warmed by two log fires. Excellent food is provided at lunchtime and in fine weather there are inspiring views from the patio gardens. Up to nine beers come straight from the cask, often from local breweries.
🏚Q🏵🌀🕀🚃(121)🍴P

Clapton in Gordano

Black Horse

Clevedon Lane, BS20 7RH (2 miles from M5 jct 19)

🕙 11-11; 12-10.30 Sun
☎ (01275) 842105 ● thekicker.co.uk
Butcombe Bitter; Shepherd Neame Spitfire; Ⓖ **Wadworth 6X; Websters Green label;** Ⓗ **guest beer** Ⓖ

Excellent 14th-century pub hidden away down a small lane. The snug was once the village lock-up. A large fireplace with a display of old rifles dominates the main bar. Beers are served from a small hatch; Thatchers Dry and Moles Black Rat cider are stocked. The games room doubles as a family room and there is a childrens' play area in the pleasant garden. Near the Gordano valley cycle route, the pub is popular with cyclists. Dogs are welcome. 🏚Q🌄🏵🌀🗛♣🍴P⌐

Clevedon

Old Inn

9 Walton Road, BS21 6AE (on Portishead road)

🕙 10-11.30 (midnight Fri & Sat); 11-11 Sun
☎ (01275) 340440 ● theoldinnclevedon.co.uk
Courage Best; Greene King Old Speckled Hen; guest beers Ⓗ

Delightful old inn with one large, beamed room that once served the carriage trade from Weston to Portishead. A wonderful community feel is sometimes enhanced by piano playing or other jollity. Two regular beers are joined by two guests, often adventurous or unusual. Excellent pub food is available at good value prices. There is a pleasant beer garden. Tynsfield, the popular National Trust attraction, is close by.
🏚Q🏵🔄🌀🚃♣🍴P

Combe Florey

Farmers Arms

TA4 3HZ (on A358 between Bishops Lydeard and Williton)

🕙 12-11 (10.30 Sun)
☎ (01823) 432267 ● farmersarmsatcombeflorey.co.uk
Cotleigh Tawny; Exmoor Ale, Gold; St Austell HSD; guest beers Ⓗ

This 16th-century, family-owned pub is situated close to the West Somerset Railway. The bar area features an inglenook fire and there is a restaurant. A games/family room is under restoration. It is justly famous for the quality of its local ales which are popular with regulars and tourists. Various ethnic food nights as well as treasure hunts are organised.
🏚🌄🏵🌀🕹🗛🚃(28)♣P⌐

Combe St Nicholas

Green Dragon

TA20 3NG OS302113

🕙 12-2.30 (not Mon), 6-midnight; 12-midnight Sat; 12-4, 7-11 Sun
☎ (01460) 63311 ● greendragon-combe.co.uk
Otter Bitter; guest beers Ⓗ

A large green dragon carved by the landlord greets visitors to this friendly free house, which has origins in the 17th century. Guest beers usually come from West Country breweries including Cottage, Exmoor and RCH, and local Burrow Hill cider is also available. A varied menu of tasty, good value, home-cooked food, using local ingredients, is served Tuesday to Sunday with a popular 'pie and a pint' on Wednesday. Carvings, some featuring regulars, adorn both bars. There is free live music on alternate Fridays.
Q🏵🌀🕀🗛♣🍴P⌐

Congresbury

Old Inn

St Pauls Causeway, BS49 5DH (off A370)
☼ 11.30-midnight (1am Fri & Sat); 12-midnight Sun
☎ (01934) 832270
Wells Bombardier; Young's Bitter, Special; guest beers Ⓗ
Popular 16th-century village local, owned by Young's. This cosy pub has a wonderful inglenook fireplace that burns chunky logs in winter. There is a main bar area and two smaller rooms, one with a TV and the other used for families. Leather straps hang from the low ceiling to steady yourself after one too many! No food is served.
ᴍQ☎🏠🚌(X1, 353)♣🐾P

Corton Denham

Queen's Arms

DT9 4LR (3 miles from A303) OS636225
☼ 11-3, 6-11; 11-11 Sat; 12-10.30 Sun
☎ (01963) 220317 ⊕ thequeensarms.com
Butcombe Bitter; Taylor Landlord; guest beers Ⓗ
Friendly village pub with a wood and flagstone floor, wooden chairs and tables and old pews. Real ale has a prominent place alongside Cheddar Valley cider, bottled beers and a good wine list. Mulled wine and occasionally mulled cider are served in winter. The Queen's Arms is in the village centre, surrounded by good walking and horse-riding country. Dogs and muddy boots are welcome. The food is excellent. ᴍQ🏠🍴🌐🐾P

Crewkerne

Old Stagecoach

Station Road, TA18 8AL (next to station)
☼ 11-2 (not Sat), 6-11; 12-2, 6-11 Sun
☎ (01460) 72972 ⊕ stagecoach-inn.co.uk
Beer range varies Ⓗ
The ideal pub to have next to a railway station, it offers accommodation, a large garden, parking and, to top it all, interesting beers and food. Opening hours are flexible if notice is given. The real ales come from West Country breweries and the extensive range of Belgian beers is probably the best in Somerset. Dishes include food cooked with beer, some with a Cajun influence, as well as more traditional fare. ᴍQ🏠🍴🌐🛏🚌♣P

Croscombe

Bull Terrier

Long Street, BA5 3QJ
☼ 12-2, 7-11 (closed Mon winter); 12-2.30, 7-11 Sun
☎ (01749) 343658
Butcombe Bitter; guest beers Ⓗ
This pub dates back to the 16th century and retains fine beams and an inglenook fireplace from that time. Two main rooms at the front are mainly used by diners. Locals gather in the common bar at the back. The pub offers up to three guest beers and Cheddar Valley cider. No food is available on Sunday in winter.
Q🏠🍴🌐🛏🐾P

George

Long Street, BA5 3QH

☼ 12 (11.45 Sat)-3, 7 (6 Fri)-11; 12-3, 7-11 Sun
☎ (01749) 342306
Butcombe Bitter; guest beers Ⓗ
This 17th-century former coaching inn was sympathetically refurbished in 2000. The house beer King George the Thirst is uniquely brewed for the pub by Blindmans and at least two guest beers are also stocked. The George hosts its own beer festivals. The interior comprises a large main bar with a smaller bar attached, plus a dining room and skittle alley. A covered terrace in the garden has been added. ᴍ🏠🍴🌐🛏♣🐾P

Cross

New Inn

Old Coach Road, BS26 2EE (by jct of A38/A361)
☼ 12-11.30
☎ (01934) 732455
Beer range varies Ⓗ
Large roadside pub offering three or four changing beers plus Thatchers cider. It is popular for its generous portions of good, home-cooked food (booking advisable at peak times), served all day. The large garden offers good views over the Somerset Levels. Seasonal beer festivals are held each year, usually on bank holiday weekends. Pool is played in the upstairs room. Children are welcome. 🏠🍴🚌(126)🐾P

White Hart

Old Coach Road, BS26 2EE (200m W of A38)
☼ 12-11.30 (midnight Thu & Fri); 12-12.30am Sat; 12-4, 8-11 Sun
☎ (01934) 732260
Black Sheep Best Bitter; Butcombe Bitter; Courage Best; Young's Special Ⓗ
This two-room 17th-century inn is on the old Bristol to Bridgwater coaching road. The pub is mentioned in the records of the 1689 Monmouth Rebellion, and much of the interior is original. Popular with locals and walkers, the bar towel moving ghost (allegedly a victim of Judge Jeffries) amuses the staff, while a resident pig entertains in the garden. The kitchen is closed Sunday evening to Tuesday lunchtime.
ᴍQ🏠🍴🛏🚌(126)♣P

Culmhead

Holman Clavel

TA3 7EA (¼ mile off B3170)
☼ 12-midnight (1am Fri & Sat); 12-3, 7-11 Sun
☎ (01823) 421432
Butcombe Bitter, Gold; guest beers Ⓗ
The only pub in England with this name, a clavel is a beam across the fireplace made from holm oak. Fresh fish and game when in season feature on the menu which has choices to suit all tastes and budgets. Guest beers come from micro-breweries and regional brewers. The pub is allegedly haunted by the ghost of a defrocked monk – but a warm welcome is assured. ᴍQ🏠🍴♣🐾P

Curry Rivel

King William IV

High Street, TA10 0EZ (on A378)

✪ 12 (7 winter Mon)-midnight; 12-11 Sun
☎ (01458) 259200
Teignworthy Reel Ale; guest beers Ⓖ
Reopened after a period of three years, this
village free house has been improved and
extended. The real ales are served straight
from the casks, which are kept on a self-tilting
stillage system. All meals are cooked on the
premises and made with locally sourced
produce where possible (no food Mon). A
glass-covered, illuminated well is a feature in
the dining area and a small snug serves as a
family room. ⚏Q☞❀◑▲🚪Pᶜ

Dulverton

Woods

4 Bank Square, TA22 9BU (near church)
✪ 11-2.30, 6-11; 12-3, 7-11 Sun
☎ (01398) 324007
Exmoor Ale; guest beer Ⓖ
Formerly a bakery, this popular bar serves
both beer-loving locals and visitors dining in
the open-plan restaurant where excellent,
locally produced food is on offer. The interior is
rustic with a wood-burning stove lit in winter,
wooden floors and bar, and country
paraphernalia. Three West Country beers are
dispensed straight from the cool room behind
the bar. Cornish Cyder Company Cloudy Rattler
and Thatchers Cheddar Valley are
stocked. Sturdy bar meals are available.
⚏❀◑▲🚪❀

East Harptree

Castle of Comfort

BA40 6DD (on jct of B3134 and two minor roads)
✪ 12-3, 6-11
☎ (01761) 221321 ⊕ castleofcomfort.com
Butcombe Bitter; guest beers Ⓗ
Splendid sprawling inn on the Mendip Hills,
not really in East Harptree at all, but within
reach of both Cheddar Gorge and Wookey Hole
Caves. The name is said to derive from the
time when it housed condemned criminals on
their last night before execution. A pub since
1684, it is popular for its locally sourced and
generously portioned food. Guest beers come
from all over the south-west and sometimes
further afield. The child-friendly garden is busy
in summer. ⚏Q❀◑♣❀P

East Woodlands

Horse & Groom

BA11 5LY (1 mile S of A361/B3092 jct)
✪ 11.30-2.30, 6.30-11; closed Mon; 12-3, 7-10.30 Sun
☎ (01373) 462802
**Blindmans Buff; Butcombe Bitter; Taylor
Landlord; guest beers** Ⓗ
A warm, welcoming pub with a large garden
on the edge of the Longleat Estate and Safari
Park at the end of a road that seems to go on
for ever. The pub boasts an open fire and
flagstone floors. The conservatory has been
turned into a restaurant offering an a la carte
menu – snacks are available in the bar. At least
one guest beer is usually available.
⚏Q❀◑🖰▲♣P

Faulkland

Tucker's Grave ☆

BA3 5XF OS752552
✪ 11.30-3, 6-11; 12-3, 7-10.30 Sun
☎ (01373) 834230
Butcombe Bitter; Draught Bass Ⓖ
This pub was built in the mid-17th century and
has changed very little since then. It was
named after Tucker who hanged himself and
was buried at the crossroads outside. All beers
and Thatchers cider are served from an alcove
rather than a bar. Shove-ha'penny is played
and there is a skittle alley. A good mix of
customers comes from all walks of life.
⚏Q☞❀♣❀P

Forches Corner

Merry Harriers

EX15 3TR (3 miles SE of Wellington) OS183171
✪ 12-3, 6.30-11; closed Mon; 12-3 Sun
☎ (01823) 421270 ⊕ merryharriers.co.uk
Beer range varies Ⓗ
Isolated but friendly old inn standing on the
county border with Devon. The bar effectively
separates the dining end of the pub from the
lounge. Three changing beers are on offer
from local micro-breweries, including Cotleigh
and Otter, as well as two ciders. Despite its
remote location, the pub has a thriving local
trade attracted by its reputation for excellent
quality food. The large, pleasant garden is
ideal for families in summer.
⚏Q☞❀◑🖰&♣❀Pᶜ

Frome

Griffin Inn

Milk Street, BA11 3DB
✪ 5-11 (1am Fri & Sat); 12-3, 6.30-10.30 Sun
☎ (01373) 467766 ⊕ milkstreetbrewery.com
Milk Street Nick's, Beer; guest beers Ⓗ
Situated in the older part of Frome and owned
by Milk Street Brewery, the small brewhouse
out the back is based in a former adult cinema.
It produces a wide range of ales, served
alongside guests and seasonal beers. The
single bar retains original features including
open fires, etched windows and wooden
floors. Live music plays on some nights. A
small garden opens in summer.
⚏❀⇆🚪Pᶜ

Green Ore

Ploughboy Inn

BA5 3ET (on crossroads of A39 and B3135)
✪ 11 (12 Sat)-2.30, 6.30 (7 Sat)-11; closed Mon;
12-2.30, 7-11 Sun
☎ (01761) 241375
**Butcombe Bitter, Brunel IPA, seasonal beers;
Otter Ale** Ⓗ
In the same safe hands for 19 years, the inside
of this pub feels like the reverse of a Tardis as
you would expect it to be much bigger based
on the impressive building and large car park.
Three real ales are subject to occasional
change. The pub is at its most busy in the early
evening but can be quiet at other times.
Reasonably priced food is popular. Note the

humorous displays: check out 'Chicken Ding' on the menu! ♨Q✿❁◐➼(376)P

Hardington Moor

Royal Oak
Moor Lane, BA22 9NW (turn left off A30 at Yeovil Court Hotel) OS520123
◉ 11.30-3.30 (not Mon), 6.30-11; 11.30-5, 6.30-10.30 Sun
☎ (01935) 862354
Branscombe Vale Branoc; Butcombe Bitter; Fuller's London Pride; guest beers Ⓖ
Sonny's, as it is locally known, is a superb village pub providing a selection of eight to ten ales on gravity. The small dining room has scrubbed wooden tables to support a fine menu which features both traditional and unusual dishes. The pool table is in a room apart. Skittles is played every weekday night in winter and there is also a popular summer league. Dogs are welcome. ♨✿◐❁➼P

Henstridge

Bird in Hand
2 Ash Walk, BA8 0RA (100m S of A30/A357 jct)
◉ 11-2.30, 5.30-11; 11-11 Sat; 12-3, 7.30-10.30 Sun
☎ (01963) 362255
Beer range varies Ⓗ
Old stone-built pub at the centre of the village. Up to three real ales are available at any one time from a continually rotating range, with favourites returning regularly. The main bar is quiet and has a well-equipped games room leading off the skittle alley at the rear. The atmosphere is warm and friendly and lunchtime snacks are particularly recommended. ♨Q✿❁◐➼P⁻

Hillcommon

Royal Oak
TA4 1DS (On B3227 Taunton-Wiveliscombe road)
◉ 12-3, 6-11; 12-4, 6-10.30 Sun
☎ (01823) 400295 ● royaloak-taunton.co.uk
Cotleigh Barn Owl; Sharp's Doom Bar; guest beers Ⓗ
Village pub on the main road frequented by local drinkers and diners. The large open-plan bar is set for diners, although there is always seating available for drinkers. Food is locally sourced, with a carvery on Tuesday, Thursday and Sunday lunchtimes (booking advisable). A beautiful large garden beckons in summer. There is also a skittle alley. ♨✿◐➼P⁻

Hinton Blewitt

Ring O' Bells
Upper Road, BS39 5AN (2 miles W of A37 at Temple Cloud) OS594570
◉ 12-3, 5-11; 12-11 Sat & Sun
☎ (01761) 452239
Butcombe Bitter, seasonal beer; guest beers Ⓗ
A welcome return to the Guide for this old favourite, now under Butcombe ownership. At the heart of village life, there is always a buzz about this pub. Entered via a small yard which contains the toilets and a few tables and chairs, you are soon in the warmth of the intimate bar. Many cricketing mementos

feature – indeed, the pub runs its own team. The food is popular and can be enjoyed in the bar and smaller snug area. ♨Q✿❁◐➼P

Hinton St George

Lord Poulett Arms
High Street, TA17 8SE OS417127
◉ 12-3, 6.30-11
☎ (01460) 73149 ● lordpoulettarms.com
Beer range varies Ⓖ
Stone-flagged floors and a bar-mounted gravity stillage provide the first impressions on entering this charming 17th-century village pub with its delightful interior. The bar has a well-stocked magazine rack and library encouraging guests to linger by the fire. Outside, you will find a Mediterranean garden with a petanque court, leading to a secluded beer garden boasting a pelotta wall dating from Napoleonic times. Burrow Hill cider is served. ♨Q✿❁➼◐❁◐➼P

Holywell Lake

Holywell Inn
TA21 0EG (1 mile N of A38 W of Wellington)
◉ 12-2.30 (not Mon), 7-11 (not winter Mon); 12-3, 7-10.30 (summer only) Sun
☎ (01823) 672770 ● theholywell.com
Cotleigh Tawny; Exmoor Ale; guest beers Ⓗ
This 15th-century inn has expanded over the years but retains the original cob walls in the main bar. Food is served in the bar and dining room. A skittle alley doubles as a function room and there is a field behind the car park for campers. A charming country pub, though not far from the main road, this inn is quiet. ♨Q◐❁▲➼P⁻

Horsington

Half Moon
BA8 0EF (200m off A357)
◉ 12-2.30 (3 Sat), 6-11; 12-3, 7-10.30 Sun
☎ (01963) 370140 ● horsington.co.uk
Wadworth 6X; guest beers Ⓗ
Real ale is a passion for the owners, with over 1,000 different beers sold over the past 10 years. Up to six ales are on handpump with the range of guests changing continuously. Apart from well-known nationals, local micros are always represented and feature prominently in the annual beer festival held in May. Friendly staff welcome locals and visitors alike. Reasonably priced food is available and there is accommodation in chalets to the rear. ♨Q⟳✿➼◐❁➼◐P

Horton

Five Dials
Goose Lane, TA19 9QH (W of Ilminster)
◉ 12 (5 Mon)-midnight (1am Fri & Sat)
☎ (01460) 55359
Beer range varies Ⓗ
A warm welcome awaits you at this roadside village pub. The real ales are often from West Country micros with Otter and Sharp's both featuring regularly. The restaurant offers a varied menu with daily specials, bar snacks and Sunday roasts (no food Sun eve or Mon).

A skittle alley/function room is available for hire. Live music plays most weekends.
🕲🍴◑🛏🧺♣P⏚

Huish Episcopi

Rose & Crown (Eli's) ☆
Wincanton Road, TA10 9QT (on A372)
🕒 11.30-2.30, 5.30-11; 11.30-11 Fri & Sat; 12-10.30 Sun
☎ (01458) 250494
Teignworthy Reel Ale; guest beers Ⓗ
This traditional thatched inn, known locally as Eli's, has been in the same family for generations. The character and unusual features remain unchanged, taking you back in time. The pub is divided into several cosy rooms and drinks are served in a flagstone tap room. Good, traditional home-cooked food is served at lunchtime and early evening. Burrow Hill cider is sold. 🐕🕲◑🛇&🛏♣🕮P⏚

Kelston

Old Crown
Bath Road, BA1 9AQ (on A431)
🕒 11-11; 12-10.30 Sun
☎ (01225) 423032
Bath Gem; Butcombe Bitter, Gold; Draught Bass; Wadworth 6X Ⓗ
Attractive, multi-roomed 18th-century coaching inn, bedecked in colourful flowers in summer, owned by Butcombe Brewery. The old beer engine in the bar, flagstone floors, open fires and settles all help to create a welcoming atmosphere. A choice of quality, imaginative food is served in the restaurant and bar areas. Barbecues are occasionally held in the large garden. In winter Butcombe's seasonal IPA, Brunel, is available.
🏛Q🕲🍴◑🛇🛏(319, 332)P⏚

Lopen Head

Poulett Arms
TA13 5JH (on former A303 E of Ilminster)
🕒 12-3, 5-midnight; 12-midnight Fri-Sun
☎ (01460) 241716
Beer range varies Ⓗ
Large family pub with games at the rear, easy to find on the former A303 between South Petherton and Ilminster. It has a double skittle alley and darts. Live music is hosted including a monthly 'jam' night. Food is available all day with a senior citizens' menu Monday to Friday lunchtime. Real cider is served in summer.
🏛◑&♣🕮P

Lower Odcombe

Masons Arms
BA22 8TX (off Yeovil to Montacute road)
🕒 12-2.30, 6-midnight daily
☎ (01935) 862591 ⊕ masonsarmsodcombe.co.uk
Odcombe No1, Spring; guest beers Ⓗ
Welcoming thatched local, a true free house in the main village street. The Odcombe Brewery operates in a small brewhouse at the rear of the pub, brewing for the Masons only. Good food using local produce is served (booking advisable for the restaurant). Regular themed food nights are held, and the first Sunday of the month is quiz night. Well-behaved

children are welcome; dogs too. Caravan hook-ups and showers are provided.
🕲🍴◑🛏&🧺♣🕮P⏚

Martock

White Hart Hotel
East Street, TA12 6JQ
🕒 12-2 (3 Sat), 5.30-midnight (2am Fri & Sat); 12-3 Sun
☎ (01935) 822005 ⊕ whiteharthotelmartock.co.uk
Otter Bitter; guest beers Ⓗ
Visitors and locals mix amiably in this family-run free house which offers at least two guest beers, typically from Sharp's, Cottage and Dorset Brewing Company. Excellent food, from snacks to an extensive restaurant menu, is prepared by the resident chef (available Tue-Sun). The large L-shaped bar has Chesterfield sofas around the fireplace.
🏛Q🕲🍴◑🛇🛏♣P

Merriott

King's Head
Church Street, TA16 5PR
🕒 12-3.30 (4 Sat), 6.30-11.30 (12.30am Fri & Sat); 12-3.30, 6-11.30 Sun
☎ (01460) 72973
Butcombe Bitter; guest beers Ⓗ
Martha, the Old English sheepdog, checks patrons and their dogs as they enter what used to be the village courthouse. For the last 310 years, however, it has been a pub and now boasts a good menu of country dishes to complement the varying selection of ales. The much-used pool table is in a separate room, and both skittles and darts have resident teams. 🏛🕲◑🛏♣P⏚

Middlezoy

George Inn
42 Main Street, TA7 0NN (just off A372)
🕒 12-3 (not Mon), 7-midnight; 12-3, 7-11.30 Sun
☎ (01823) 698215
Butcombe Bitter; guest beers Ⓗ
Dating from the 17th century, little has changed at this inn with exposed beams, a huge fireplace and stone-flagged floor. Visitors are invariably warned of the step in the middle of the bar by a chorus of locals and the booming voice of the South African landlord. An excellent selection of guest ales makes the superb home-cooked food taste even better. An annual beer festival is hosted. Local CAMRA Pub of the Year 2000. 🏛Q🕲◑🕮P⏚

Minehead

Queen's Head
Holloway Street, TA24 5NR
🕒 12-3, 5.30-11; 12-11 Sat; 12-3, 6.30-11 Sun
☎ (01643) 706000
Draught Bass; Exmoor Fox, Gold; St Austell Tribute; guest beers Ⓗ
Popular town pub situated in a side street just off The Parade selling up to eight real ales. The spacious single bar has a raised seating area for dining and families. Good value food is served – try the delicious home-made pies. There is a games room at the rear. Beer

festivals are held twice a year.
◑◐⑈♿♠⬥(West Somerset Railway)🚅♣

Mudford

Half Moon

Main Street, BA21 5TF (on A359)
☼ 12-11 (10.30 Sun)
☎ (01935) 850289 ⊕ thehalfmooninn.co.uk
RCH beer range Ⓖ
Large 17th-century inn which, although
restored, retains its character. A rare outlet in
south Somerset for RCH beers, three are
normally available from the stillage behind
the bar. A good range of meals is served all
day including bar snacks. The former skittle
alley has been converted into en-suite
bedrooms. Wheelchair access is good
throughout. ⋔✿⬥◑◐♿🚅♠P

Nailsea

Blue Flame

West End, BS48 4DE (off A370 at Chelvey)
OS449691
☼ 12-3, 6-11; 12-10.30 Sun
☎ (01275) 856910
Fuller's London Pride; RCH East Street Cream; Ⓖ
guest beers Ⓗ
Lovely rustic 19th-century free house,
unaltered for many years, comprising two
rooms, one with a bar and a snug. Coal fires
help create a cosy atmosphere in winter.
Simple, almost spartan decor and outside
toilets feature. The large rear garden is ideal
for families in summer. Camping is available
but phone first. Food is limited to filled rolls.
Live music plays on the first and third Tuesday
of the month. ⋔Q♠⬥♣♠P

North Perrott

Manor Arms

Middle Street, TA18 7SG
☼ 11-11; 12-10.30 Sun
☎ (01460) 72901 ⊕ manorarmshotel.co.uk
Butcombe Bitter; Fuller's London Pride;
O'Hanlon's Royal Oak; guest beers Ⓗ
Friendly service is the norm at this 16th-
century village inn with six to eight real ales,
mainly from West Country breweries. There is
an inglenook fireplace, flagstone floors, oak
beams, exposed stone walls and a pleasant
beer garden for summer drinking. The focus
here is on food but you will be made very
welcome if just calling in for a beer. Not to be
missed. ⋔Q✿⬥◑🚅P

Norton Fitzwarren

Cross Keys

TA2 6NR (at A358/B3227 jct W of Taunton)
☼ 11-11; 12-10.30 Sun
☎ (01823) 333062
Beer range varies Ⓗ
Large roadside pub divided into several areas
with plenty of exposed beams and knick-
knacks. The wide-ranging menu is
supplemented by daily chef's specials.
Monthly guest beers from the likes of Fuller's
and Young's are accompanied by three others
that change more frequently, mainly from

regional brewers. There is also a small
selection of bottled and German beers.
Monthly jazz evenings are a feature.
⋔☾✿◑◐⬥🚅P♮

Pitney

Halfway House

Pitney Hill, TA10 9AB (on B3153) OS451278
☼ 11.30-3.30, 5.30-11; 12-3.30, 7-11 Sun
☎ (01458) 252513 ⊕ thehalfwayhouse.co.uk
Branscombe Vale BVB Own Label; Butcombe
Bitter; Hop Back Crop Circle, Summer Lightning;
Otter Bright; Teignworthy Reel Ale; guest
beers Ⓖ
Thriving, traditional village pub, serving a
wide variety of local ales all on gravity
alongside a range of international bottled
beers. Superb home-cooked food is based on
local produce (no food Sun). There is no
jukebox or fruit machine to disturb the buzz of
conversation at this multiple national and local
award-winning pub – CAMRA's National Pub of
the Year 1996 and the current Telegraph Pub
of the Year. A real gem. ⋔Q✿◑◐⬥🚅♣♠P♮

Porlock Weir

Ship Inn

TA24 8PB (on B3225) OS864481
☼ 11-11; 12-10.30 Sun
☎ (01643) 862753 ⊕ theanchorhotelandshipinn.co.uk
Cotleigh Barn Owl, 25; Exmoor Ale; guest
beers Ⓗ
Historic pub overlooking the harbour and
beach. There is an outside covered seating
area and the long low-roofed bar caters for
both locals and tourists. An excellent base for
coastal walks to Minehead or Lynmouth, pub
food is served in the bar and there is a
restaurant in the hotel.
⋔Q☾✿⬥◑◐🚅♿⬥🚅(39)♣♠P♮

Portishead

Poacher

106 High Street, BS20 6AJ
☼ 11-2.30, 6-11; 11-11 Fri & Sat; 12-10.30 Sun
☎ (01275) 844002
Butcombe Blond; Courage Best; Sharp's Doom
Bar; guest beers Ⓗ
Originally two cottages, the Poacher dates
from the 17th century or earlier. Since then it
has been a courtroom, parish council office
and preaching room. The pub is an
increasingly rare outlet for the proper cask
version of Blond. There is a weekly quiz and
on Friday the car park becomes a
market. Smokers are provided with a shelter
at the front. No food Sunday evening and
Monday. ✿◑🚅♣P♮

Windmill Inn

58 Nore Road, BS20 6JZ (next to Municipal Golf
Course)
☼ 11-11; 12-10.30
☎ (01275) 843677
Butcombe Gold; Courage Best; Draught Bass; RCH
Pitchfork; guest beers Ⓗ
Large, split-level free house with a spacious
tiered patio to the rear. Situated on the edge
of town with panoramic views over the

Severn Estuary, both Severn bridges can be seen on clear days. A varied menu is served all day (not Mon) and is enormously popular. One large area is set aside for families. The guest ales are often locally sourced and there is an Easter beer festival. Thatchers cider is stocked. Q✿◑&🖳(359)●P

Priddy

Hunters Lodge
BA5 3AR (1 mile from A39 at Green Ore) OS549501
☼ 11.30-2.30, 6.30-11; 12-2, 7-10.30 Sun
☎ (01749) 672275
Blindmans Mine Beer; Butcombe Bitter; guest beers Ⓖ
Timeless, classic roadside inn near Priddy, the highest village in Somerset, popular with cavers and walkers. The landlord has been in charge for more than 40 years. The beer is kept in casks behind the bar. Local guest beers are growing in prominence and Wilkins cider is served. The home-cooked food is simple but excellent and exceptional value. A folk musicians' drop-in session features on Tuesday evening. There is a pleasant, secluded garden. Mobile phone use is not welcomed. ﾑQ✿◑🖭♣●P

Queen Victoria Inn
Pelting Drove, BA5 3BA (on minor road to Wookey Hole, S of village centre)
☼ 12-3, 6-11 (12-11.30 summer); 12-midnight Sat & Sun
☎ (01749) 676385
Butcombe Bitter, Gold; Wadworth 6X Ⓗ
Traditional creeper-clad pub, operating since 1851 and Butcombe-owned since 2006. It has three rooms with low ceilings, log fires and flagged floors – a wonderfully warm and relaxing haven on a cold winter night. Popular during the Priddy Folk Festival in July and the annual fair in August, children are welcome and there is a play area. Reasonably priced, mostly home-cooked food is a speciality. Cheddar Valley cider is sold. ﾑQ✿◑Å♣●P

Priston

Ring of Bells
BA2 9EE (off A367 Bath to Radstock) OS693605
☼ 11-3 (not Mon), 6-11; 12-10.30 Sun
☎ (01761) 471467 ⊕ priston.org.uk
Butcombe Bitter; Greene King IPA; Ⓗ **Otter Bright; guest beers** Ⓖ
This is a sympathetically renovated rural free house five miles from Bath, which can be reached by picturesque walks. A traditional village pub, it offers a warm welcome to all, including dogs. The pub supports local skittles and darts teams, as well as village cricket. Guest beers are served from gravity. ﾑQ✿◑&Å♣●P

Rode

Cross Keys
20 High Street, BA11 6NZ
☼ 11.30-3 (not Mon), 6-11; 12-3, 7-10.30 Sun
☎ (01373) 830900
Butcombe Bitter; guest beers Ⓗ

Reopened in 2004 after 10 years of closure, this was originally the brewery tap for the long-closed Fussell's Brewery and latterly a Bass depot. Sympathetically restored, it has succeeded in bringing back strong village trade. A passageway featuring a deep well links the two bars. There is a large restaurant. Though now owned by Butcombe, a beer from Blindmans usually features among the guests. ﾑQ✿🖾◑🖭Å🖳♣P'–

Rowberrow

Swan Inn
Rowberrow Lane, BS25 1QL (signed off A38)
☼ 12-3, 6-11; 11-11 Fri & Sat; 11-10.30 Sun
☎ (01934) 852371
Butcombe Bitter, seasonal beer; Fuller's London Pride; guest beers Ⓗ
Believed to date from around the late 17th century, this Butcombe Brewery-owned country pub enjoys an attractive setting, nestling beneath the Dolebury Iron Age Hill Fort. A convenient refreshment stop for walkers on the Mendip Hills, the emphasis is on home-cooked food but customers are welcome who just want a drink. Thatchers cider is available. There is an interesting collection of artefacts around the walls and a grandfather clock. The garden is spacious and attractive. ﾑQ✿◑●P'–

Saltford

Bird in Hand
58 High Street, BS31 3EJ
☼ 11-3 (3.30 Sat), 6-11; 12-3.30, 6-10.30 Sun
☎ (01225) 873335 ⊕ birdinhandsaltford.co.uk
Abbey Bellringer; Butcombe Bitter; Courage Best; guest beers Ⓗ
An 1869 pub, situated at the foot of the old high street in the oldest part of the village, it lies adjacent to the Bristol to Bath cycle path and the main railway line. This is a food-oriented pub and the dining area is in a recently built conservatory with fine views over the garden and hills beyond. There is a small family area at one end. A petanque pitch features in the spacious garden. Thatchers cider is sold. Q🍴✿◑&🖳♣●P'–

Seavington St Michael

Volunteer
TA19 0QE (on former A303, 2 miles E of Ilminster)
☼ 12-2.30, 6.30-11; 12-3, 7-11 Sun
☎ (01460) 240126
St Austell range; guest beers Ⓗ
Under the most recent ownership there is now a greater range of beers, and customers' suggestions are welcome. The main bar is at the front of the pub with a dining room to the left. A snug public bar with a TV is open Thursday to Sunday nights. Thatchers Gold cider is served. ﾑQ🍴✿🖾◑🖭&🖳●P'–

Shepton Beauchamp

Duke of York
North Street, TA19 0LW
☼ 12-11 (midnight Sat)
☎ (01460) 240314

SOMERSET

ENGLAND

Otter Bright; Sharp's Doom Bar; Teignworthy
Reel Ale; guest beers ⊞
Friendly village pub, popular with locals and
home to numerous darts and skittles teams.
On warmer days, the tables are placed on the
raised pavement outside, enabling patrons to
watch the world go by in rural Somerset.
There is a pool room and pleasant garden.
⚊⌂❄⌂◑⊟♣P⌐

Shoscombe

Apple Tree
BA2 8LS
❂ 12-3 (not Tue), 7-11; closed Mon; 11-11 Sat;
11-10.30 Sun
☎ (01761) 432263
Exmoor Stag; Greene King IPA; Matthews Bob
Wall ⊞
Almost literally a hidden gem, this pub is
tucked away in a valley down a series of
narrow lanes. A large sloping garden has
superb views over the rolling landscape.
Inside, the long straggling bar is a warm and
comfortable resting place after a hearty hike
through the countryside. Parking is limited.
⚊Q❄◑⌂♣P

Simonsbath

Exmoor Forest Inn
TA24 7SH (on B3224)
❂ 11.30-3 (12-2.30 winter), 6 (6.30 winter)-11; 12-3,
7-10.30 (not winter) Sun
☎ (01643) 831341 ⊕ exmoorforestinn.co.uk
Beer range varies ⊞
Elegant but non-pretentious inn situated in a
village traditionally known as the capital of
Exmoor. Inside, the walls are festooned with
antlers, stuffed animals and old prints, while a
wood-burning stove provides warmth on
winter days. The sunken bar dispenses up to
four real ales in summer (fewer in winter), all
coming from such West Country brewers as
Cotleigh, O'Hanlon's and St Austell. There is
also Budvar on draught. An easy-going and
comfortable atmosphere prevails, with familes
and dogs welcome. ⚊❄⌂◑⌂♣P

South Petherton

Brewers Arms
18 St James Street, TA13 5BW (½ mile off A303)
❂ 11.30-2.30, 6-11 (midnight Fri & Sat); 12-10.30 Sun
☎ (01460) 241887
Otter Bitter; guest beers ⊞
Situated in the centre of this beautiful
Hamstone village, the pub has an L-shaped
bar with an adjoining restaurant featuring a
stone bread oven. Two annual beer festivals
are held: one during the late May bank
holiday, the other a beer and cider fest
featuring Somerset produce on the August
bank holiday. Runner-up Somerset CAMRA Pub
of the Year 2006 and 2007, and a past winner.
A true community pub for all.
⚊❄◑Å⊟♣♣⌐

Stoke St Gregory

Royal Oak
TA3 6EH (opp church)

❂ 12-3 (not Tue & Wed), 7.30-11 (7-11.30 Thu); closed
Mon; 12-3.30, 7-midnight Fri & Sat; 12-3, 7-11 Sun
☎ (01823) 400602
St Austell Tribute; guest beers ⊞
Warm, friendly inn in the centre of the village.
Family-run since 2005, it has become a real
community pub with several skittles teams
plus darts and pool. Live music plays once a
month and is establishing a following. Ideally
positioned for taking a break when walking on
the Somerset Levels or the long-distance
Parrett Trail. ❄◑⌂⌂⊟♣♣P

Stoke sub Hamdon

Prince of Wales
Ham Hill, TA14 6RW OS479169
❂ 11-11
☎ (01935) 822848
Beer range varies Ⓖ
Set in the centre of Ham Hill Country Park,
with its panoramic views of the Somerset
wetlands on one side and far reaching views
into Dorset on the other, this is a haven for
walkers and dogs are welcome. It has a large
flagstoned bar and dining area. A good range
of ales on stillage is displayed behind the bar.
Recent longer opening hours have proved
popular. Thatchers and Burrow Hill ciders are
available. ⚊Q❄◑⌂♣P

Street

Two Brewers
38 Leigh Road, BA16 0HB
❂ 11-3, 6-11 (11.30 Fri & Sat); 11.30-2.30, 6-11 Sun
☎ (01458) 442421 ⊕ thetwobrewers.co.uk
Courage Best, Directors; Greene King Ruddles
County; guest beers ⊞
Well-kept pub on the fringe of the town centre
with ample room for drinkers and diners.
Vegetarian and children's menus are
available. The pub produces its own
newsletter, featuring a list of regular and
occasional guest beers – note the large
collection of pump clips on display in the bar.
The rear garden is attractive and has a
marked-out petanque court. Q❄◑⊟♣⌐

Taunton

Wyvern Club
Mountfields Road, TA1 3BJ
❂ 7-11; 12-3, 7-10.30 Sun
☎ (01823) 284591 ⊕ wyvernclub.co.uk
Exmoor Ale; guest beers ⊞
Large, busy sports and social club offering a
variety of West Country beers, which changes
frequently. There are usually beers from three
different breweries on offer at club prices.
Meals are available at all sessions except
Sunday evening. The club premises are
available to hire for meetings and evening
functions. Show this Guide or your CAMRA
membership card to be signed in as a guest. A
real ale festival is held in October.
❄◑⌂⊟♣P

Wanstrow

The Pub
Station Road, BA4 4SZ

419

12-2.30 (not Mon), 6 (6.30 Mon)-11; 12-3, 6-11 Fri &
Sat; 12-3, 7-10.30 Sun
☎ (01749) 850455
**Blindmans range; Draught Bass; Hop Back GFB;
guest beers** Ⓗ
An absolute gem. This friendly village local has
a lounge bar with open fire and flagstone
floors leading to a restaurant serving a small
but imaginative menu of home-made food.
The pub is a regular outlet for Blindmans beers
including seasonals, and serves up to six
guests. Games include skittles, bar billiards
and ring the bull. ⚶Q✿◑🍺♣●P

Watchet

Star Inn
Mill Lane, TA23 0BZ
12-3.30, 6.30-midnight (1am Fri & Sat); 12-4,
7-midnight Sun
☎ (01984) 631367
Beer range varies Ⓗ
Three 15th-century cottages knocked into a
single building make up this very popular pub
near the new marina on the road to Blue
Anchor. The beer range concentrates on brews
from West Country micros and there are
always beers from Cotleigh and Cottage
available. Guest beers come from the likes of
Hidden, Otter and Newmans. Home-cooked
food is available. Local CAMRA Pub of the Year
2006.
⚶🛏✿🍴◑Å≠(West Somerset Railway)
🍺♣P

Wells

City Arms
69 High Street, BA5 2AG
9-11 (midnight Thu-Sat); 11-10 Sun
☎ (01749) 673916 ⊕ thecityarmsatwells.co.uk
Butcombe Bitter; guest beers Ⓗ
In 1810 the city jail ceased its 200-year reign
as a place you would not want to visit and
became the rather more inviting City Arms.
The main bar retains the atmospheric small,
barred windows and low, vaulted ceilings of
its former existence. The Keepers Bar has been
refurbished as a patisserie and bistro and has a
modern coffee-bar feel. Up to five guest beers
are available and the cider is from Ashton
Press. 🛏✿◑♣●

West Chinnock

Muddled Man
Lower Street, TA18 7PT
11-2.30 (not winter Mon), 7-midnight; 11-midnight
Fri & Sat; 12-10.30 Sun
☎ (01935) 881235
Beer range varies Ⓗ
Friendly, welcoming, family-run pub in an
attractive Hamstone village. The good range of
beers is sourced entirely from West Country
breweries with many brews unusual for the
area. Good value, traditional meals are served
– Sunday lunch must be booked in advance.
The newly built skittle alley doubles as a
function room. Accommodation is available in
two rooms. The local cider is from Burrow Hill.
⚶✿🍴◑♣●

West Huntspill

Crossways Inn
TA9 3RA (on A38)
12-3, 5.30-11; 12-10.30 Sun
☎ (01278) 783756 ⊕ crossways-inn.com
**Flowers IPA; Fuller's London Pride; guest
beers** Ⓗ
This 17th-century inn has been in the same
hands for more than 25 years. The guest ales
change frequently. The food menu is
enhanced by specials on the blackboard,
served in the bars and dining area. There is a
skittle alley and garden seating area.
Beaujolais Nouveau Day is just one of the
popular themed events hosted by the pub. In
the summer, jazz sessions are held on some
Sunday afternoons. ⚶Q✿🍴◑🍺♣●P

Royal Artillery Arms
2 Alstone Lane, TA9 3DR (on A38)
10-midnight (1am Fri & Sat)
☎ (01278) 783553
RCH PG Steam, Double Header; guest beers Ⓗ
Real fires help to provide a warm welcome at
this cosy one-bar roadside hostelry which was
originally three cottages. Leading off from the
bar is a skittle alley that doubles as a function
room and hosts regular themed events such as
curry nights and Mexican evenings. Watch the
board outside for details of forthcoming
events. There are plans for more real ale
pumps, adding to the five already in place.
⚶Q✿◑&🍺♣●P

Weston-super-Mare

Off the Rails
Station Approach, BS23 1XY (on railway station)
7am-1am; 10-midnight Sun
☎ (01934) 415109
RCH Hewish IPA; guest beers Ⓗ
This genuine free house conveniently situated
on the railway station doubles as the station
buffet with snacks, sandwiches and
magazines available. Two guest beers come
from West Country micro-breweries with the
occasional beer from further afield. The
landlord is happy to receive suggestions from
his regulars for beers to stock. Two-pint carry-
out containers are handy for train travellers.
Thatchers and a guest cider are available.
There is a free jukebox and a quiz night on
Tuesday. ≠🍺●

Wincanton

Uncle Tom's Cabin
51 High Street, BA9 9JU
11-11 (midnight Sat); 12-11 Sun
☎ (01963) 32790
Butcombe Bitter; guest beers Ⓗ
Dating back to the 15th century in parts, the
pub is the only remaining thatched building in
the High Street. Once a shop, it became a pub
in 1861. At the rear is a courtyard drinking
area. Regular live music and karaoke evenings
are held at weekends. There is a pool table in
the upstairs room. Note the unusual tables
with old sewing machine treadles. Known
locally as a cider house, Thatchers cider is
always available. ⚶✿&🍺♣●

Winsham

Bell Inn

11 Church Street, TA20 4HU

✪ 12-2.30 (not Mon), 7-11; 12-3, 7-10.30 Sun

☎ (01460) 30677

Branscombe Vale Branoc; guest beers Ⓗ

Popular village-centre pub that comprises a large open-plan bar and a function room where darts and skittles are played. Up to three ales, mostly from the West Country, are usually available and are reasonably priced. Many village activities are hosted on the patio. Good value food is offered and the home-made pies are a speciality. Children are welcome. ♨Q❀◑➡(99)♣P

Wiveliscombe

Bear Inn

10 North Street, TA4 2JY (200m N of B3227)

✪ 11-11 (midnight Thu-Sat); 12-11 Sun

☎ (01984) 623537

Cotleigh Tawny, Golden Seahawk; Sharp's Doom Bar; guest beers Ⓗ

Lively community pub in the centre of this traditional brewing town with two rooms sharing a bar. There is a children's play area and a garden at the rear, as well as a skittle alley. This is an ideal base for exploring Exmoor and the Brendon Hills. Both Cotleigh and Exmoor breweries are just a short walk away. The pizzas are a speciality (evenings only). Somerset CAMRA Pub of the Year 2007. ♨➤❀✍◑➡♣P⁵⌐

Wookey

Burcott Inn

Wookey Road, BA5 1NJ (on B3139, 2 miles W of Wells)

✪ 11.30-2.30 (12-3 Sat), 6-11; 12-3, 7-10.30 Sun

☎ (01749) 673874

Beer range varies Ⓗ

Popular country pub featuring a copper-topped, L-shaped bar always serving two or three ales, mostly from the West Country, and sporting a real log fire. This stone-built roadside inn is characterised by low beams, pine tables and flagstone flooring. Darts and shove-ha'penny are played in the games room. The garden houses the remains of an old cider press and has superb views of the Mendip Hills. The chef's freshly prepared food including daily specials is served throughout the pub (not Sun or Mon eve) . ♨Q❀✍◑➡♣P

Wookey Hole

Wookey Hole Inn

High Street, BA5 1BP (opp Wookey Hole Caves)

✪ 12-11 (10.30 Sun)

☎ (01749) 676677 🌐 wookeyholeinn.com

Beer range varies Ⓗ

Bought by new owners in 2006, this charismatic inn has a style all of its own. All four pumps are used for changing guest beers from small brewers, often of the more unusual kind. A wide choice of continental beers also features on draught. Top quality food is served at restaurant prices, ideal for special occasions.

The large sculpted garden at the rear is great for summer days. There is also a lurid pink function-cum-overspill room and accommodation in six bedrooms. ♨❀✿✍◑➤Å➡♣P⁵⌐

Wrantage

Canal Inn

TA3 6DF (on A378, 4 miles SE of Taunton)

✪ 12-2 (not Mon), 5 (7 Sat)-11; 12-3 Sun

☎ (01823) 480210 🌐 thecanalinn.com

Beer range varies Ⓗ/Ⓖ

This roadside pub, reopened after a long campaign, has won several awards including Somerset CAMRA Pub of the Year 2005. Four ales are available, usually from local breweries. Blackdown brews the house beer, Canal Ditchwater, and a range of Belgian beers and Burrow Hill cider are also stocked. An annual beer festival is held on the second Saturday in July and a farmers' market on the last Saturday of the month. The extensive menu is supplemented by themed nights and monthly fresh fish nights. Families, boots and dogs welcome and there is a large beer garden. ♨❀✿◑Å♣♣P

Yeovil

Pall Tavern

15 Silver Street, BA20 1HW

✪ 11-11 (1am Fri & Sat); 12-11 Sun

☎ (01935) 476521

Greene King Ruddles Best, Old Speckled Hen; guest beers Ⓗ

Yeovil town centre's finest pub is actually more like a village inn in character, with a comfortable, welcoming single bar and warm-hearted locals. The pub name is pronounced 'pal', which gives an indication of its friendly nature. The music is subdued and the TV usually mute. Good value food is available (not served Mon) – Sunday lunch is exceptional. This is a safe haven in an area crowded with nightclubs. Children are welcome and well-behaved dogs permitted. ❀✍◑➡♣

Quicksilver Mail

168 Hendford Hill, BA20 2RG (at A30/A37 jct)

✪ 11-midnight (1am Fri & Sat); 12-10.30 Sun

☎ (01935) 424721

Adnams Broadside; Butcombe Bitter; guest beers Ⓗ

Friendly, well-run pub in a prominent position at a road junction. It is the only pub in the country with this name, commemorating the original Quicksilver mail coach, which attached extra horses for greater speed in dangerous areas. The original pub sign is now displayed in the bar, together with old photographs of the inn and sporting memorabilia. Good value food includes Sunday lunches. Well-behaved children are welcome and dogs allowed. The skittle alley can be booked for functions. ❀✍◑➡♣♣P⁵⌐

STAFFORDSHIRE

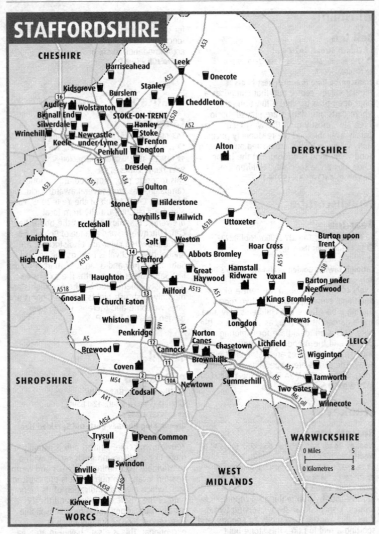

Alrewas

Crown Inn

7 Post Office Road, DE13 7BS (off Main Street)
☼ 12-2.30, 5-11; 12-11 (12-3, 5-11 winter) Sat;
12-10.30 Sun
☎ (01283) 790328
Draught Bass; Marston's Pedigree; Wells Bombardier; guest beer H
This 500-year-old former coaching inn once housed the village post office. Located near the Trent & Mersey Canal, families, boaters and walkers are all welcome. The cosy public bar and snug feature ancient, low-beamed ceilings. Meals are served in the larger, comfortable lounge (no eve meals winter Sun or Mon). Live music is performed most Monday evenings. ⚲Q✿ⓊⒹᏟᏜⵗⒷP

Barton under Needwood

Royal Oak

74 The Green, DE13 8JD (½ mile from B5016)

☼ 12-midnight (1am Fri & Sat); 12-11 Sun
☎ (01283) 713852
Marston's Pedigree; guest beers H /G
Bustling, community local situated on the southern edge of the village, home to traditional pub games and an over-40s football team. Parts of the building date back to the 16th century, but the pub has only existed since the mid-1800s. Public bar and lounge customers are served from a central sunken bar, set below the level of the rest of the ground floor. Beers are available on handpump or on gravity, direct from the cask, on request. ⚲Q☸✿ⒹᏜⵗⒷP⅃

Shoulder of Mutton

16 Main Street, DE13 8AA
☼ 12-midnight (1am Fri & Sat)
☎ (01283) 712568 ⊕ shoulderofmutton.com
Draught Bass; Marston's Pedigree; guest beer H
This 17th-century former coaching inn, with some 19th-century additions, is located at the centre of the village, opposite the church. Two rather smart Bass lanterns illuminate the

entrances. A low-beamed ceiling, wood panelling and inglenook in the lounge are in contrast to the sparsely furnished public bar. The home-cooked food includes reasonably priced specials listed on a blackboard. The small landscaped garden to the rear is popular with smokers. Live music nights are busy (see website for details). ♨Q❀☎◗⤴⊟P

Bignall End

Bignall End Cricket Club
Boon Hill, ST7 8LA (off B5500)
☼ 7-11 (12-11 Sat in cricket season); 12-4, 7-midnight Sun
☎ (01782) 720514
Beer range varies Ⓗ
Village cricket club established for well over 100 years with fantastic views across Cheshire. There is a relaxing large lounge bar and a snooker room with full-sized table, plus a large function room upstairs. The club hosts an annual beer festival and a motorcycle rally in February. CAMRA members are admitted as guests. Well worth a visit you will not be disappointed. ❀⊟P⤴

Plough
Ravens Lane, ST7 8PS (on B5500, half mile E of Audley)
☼ 12-3, 7-11 (midnight Fri & Sat); 12-10.30 Sun
☎ (01782) 720469
Banks's Bitter; guest beers Ⓗ
Award-winning family-owned free house where locally-brewed Town House beers are on sale along with Banks's Bitter and ever-changing guest ales mainly from micros, plus a selection of bottled beers. The busy public bar is complemented by a split-level lounge and dining area where excellent good value meals are served (not Sun eve). ❀◗⊟❦P

Swan
Chapel Street, ST7 8QD (just off B5500 in village centre)
☼ 12-11 (10.30 Sun)
☎ (01782) 720622
Draught Bass; guest beers Ⓗ
Small, friendly pub, known to locals as 'The Duck', with a bar and lounge, both with real fire, beer patio and outdoor smoking area. Home-cooked food is available the delicious meat and potato pie is highly recommended. As well as the five guest beers, three real ciders and a perry are on offer. Regular beer festivals are held and a real ale club has been formed to promote days out to beers festivals and other activities. ♨❀◗⊟❦♣⤴

Brewood

Swan Hotel
15 Market Place, ST19 9BS
☼ 11.45-11 (11.30 Fri & Sat); 12-11 Sun
☎ (01902) 850330
Courage Directors; Theakston Black Bull, XB; guest beers Ⓗ
A former regional CAMRA Pub of the Year, this old coaching inn has a bar area with low ceiling and two snugs either side displaying pictures of old Brewood. Seasonal log fires add to the cosy atmosphere; note the interesting

collection of witches' figures suspended from the beams. A skittle alley upstairs also hosts folk nights (www.brewoodfolk.org.uk for details). Hourly buses from Wolverhampton stop outside this village centre pub with occasional buses from Penkridge and Stafford. ♨Q♿⊟❦P

Three Stirrups
1 Engleton Lane, ST19 9DZ
☼ 11.30-11.30 (midnight Fri, 12.30 Sat); 12-11 Sun
☎ (01902) 850243
Banks's Original, Bitter; Taylor Landlord; guest beer Ⓗ
The focus of this pub is its busy public bar with pool table and dartboard. Multiple TV screens show sporting events. There is also a small snug and another large room open on Friday and Saturday evenings for live entertainment. This room is used on Sunday for carvery lunches between 12-4pm and can also be hired for private functions. ❀◗♿⊟❦P⤴

Burton upon Trent

Burton Bridge Inn
24 Bridge Street, DE14 1SY (on A511, at town end of Trent Bridge)
☼ 11.30-2.15, 5-11; 12-2, 7-10.30 Sun
☎ (01283) 536596 ∰ burtonbridgebrewery.co.uk
Burton Bridge Golden Delicious, Bitter, Porter, Festival, seasonal beer; guest beer Ⓗ
This 17th-century pub is the flagship of the Burton Bridge Brewery estate and fronts the brewery itself. Sensitively renovated and extended in 2000, it has two rooms served from a central bar. The smaller front room, with wooden pews, displays awards and brewery memorabilia; the back room features oak beams and panels. The beer range is supplemented by a fine selection of malt whiskies and fruit wines. No meals are served Sunday. A small dining/function room and a skittle alley are upstairs. ♨Q❀◗⊟❦⤴

Coopers Tavern
43 Cross Street, DE14 1EG (off Station Street)
☼ 12-3, 5-11; 12-midnight Fri & Sat; 12-3, 7-10.30 Sun
☎ (01283) 532551
Draught Bass; Tower Thomas Salt's Bitter; guest beers Ⓗ/Ⓖ

Originally the Bass Brewery bottle store, this classic, unspoilt 19th-century ale house was once the Bass Brewery tap and is now a free house. The intimate inner tap room has barrel tables and bench seats. The beer is served from a small counter, next to the cask stillage, using a mixture of gravity and handpumps. Draught cider and perry (choice varies), plus fruit wines, are also available. The more comfortable lounge sometimes hosts impromptu folk music. ⚫Q✿◑⊟≈♊♣♦⌐

Coors Visitor Centre (The Brewery Tap)

Horninglow Street, DE14 1YQ (on A511, at Guild St jct)

✪ 10am-11 (midnight Fri & Sat); 12-11 Sun

☎ (01283) 513513 ⊕ coorsvisitorcentre.com

Coors Worthington's White Shield; guest beers Ⓗ
Large, comfortable, L-shaped, single-room bar within the Visitor Centre and Museum of Brewing, accessed via the reception (to 5pm) or the rear car park. Food is served in the bar as well as in the adjacent restaurant (bookings 01283 513757; last orders 9pm), while an L-shaped conservatory (The Cloisters) overlooks the garden and children's play area. Families are welcome. Guest beers are usually from the White Shield Brewery. Entry to the museum and brewery is free to card-carrying CAMRA members. ⬈✿◑⌐♦⊟P⌐

Derby Inn

17 Derby Road, DE14 1RU (on A5121)

✪ 11.30-3, 5.30-11; 11.30-11 Thu & Sat (midnight Fri); 12-11 Sun

☎ (01283) 543674

Marston's Pedigree Ⓗ
This friendly, brick-built local, situated towards the northern edge of the town, has changed little since the 1950s. The basic bar features railway pictures and related memorabilia, plus some interesting old yellowing newspaper cuttings above the bar counter. In the smarter wood-panelled lounge the theme is horse racing. Very much a community pub, where locally produced fruit, vegetables and preserves are sold in the bar, it offers a step back in time to a more relaxed pace of life. Q⊟⌐♣P⌐

Devonshire Arms

86 Station Street, DE14 1BT

✪ 11.30-2.30, 5.30-11; 11.30-11.30 Fri & Sat; 12-3, 7-10.30 Sun

☎ (01283) 562392

Burton Bridge Golden Delicious, Bitter, Porter, Stairway to Heaven; guest beer Ⓗ
Popular old pub, dating from the 19th-century and Grade II listed; one of five Burton Bridge Brewery hostelries in the town. It comprises a small public bar at the front, and a larger, comfortable, split-level lounge to the rear. Note the 1853 map of Burton, old photographs, and unusual arched wooden ceilings. The rear patio features a fountain. A number of continental bottled beers and English fruit wines are also stocked. No meals are served Sunday. ✿◑⊟≈⌐♣P⌐

Elms Inn

36 Stapenhill Road, DE15 9AE (on A444)

✪ 12 (2 winter)-11; 12-midnight Fri & Sat; 11-10.30 Sun

☎ (01283) 535505

Draught Bass; guest beers Ⓗ
Busy free house, overlooking the River Trent. Built as a private house in the late 19th-century, this is one of Burton's original 'parlour pubs'. Recently renovated in a Victorian style, with a small public bar and snug at the front, and a larger, comfortably furnished lounge to the rear, the intimate and friendly atmosphere has been retained. Social activities include a walking club, race trips, Tuesday quiz night and summer barbecues. Guest ales normally include a Tower beer. ⚫Q✿⊟⌐♣P⌐

Burton upon Trent

Old Cottage Tavern

36 Byrkley Street, DE14 2EG (off Derby Street behind Town Hall)

✪ 12-11

☎ (01283) 511615

Old Cottage Oak Ale, Stout, Halcyon Daze; guest beers Ⓗ
This cheery and welcoming local continues to operate as the Old Cottage Brewery tap, even though it is no longer owned by the brewery. The public bar at the front and recently renovated wood-panelled lounge to the rear are served from a central bar. There is also a cosy snug to one side of the bar, plus a small restaurant beyond the lounge. Upstairs, the games/function room includes a skittle alley. ⚫✿♣⌐◑⊟≈⌐♣⌐

Cannock

Linford Arms

79 High Green, WS11 1BN

✪ 9-12 (1am Fri-Sat); 9-midnight Sun

☎ (01543) 469360

Greene King Abbot; Marston's Burton Bitter, Pedigree; guest beers Ⓗ
Typical Wetherspoon's town centre pub with a large open-plan two-storey bar, along with quieter alcoves and a separate snug room. Originally a pub some centuries ago, the Linford Arms was most recently a hardware and ironmongers shop and before that a private residence. Open all day, every day, with food served from 9am, if you find yourself in Cannock town centre this is definitely a pub worth seeking out. Q✿◑⊟≈⌐⌐

Chasetown

Uxbridge Arms

2 Church Street, WS7 8QL (opposite Spot Garage)
12-11 Sun

✪ 12-3, 5.30-11 Mon-Thu; 12-midnight Fri & Sat

☎ (01543) 674583

Draught Bass; guest beers Ⓗ
Busy corner local a short distance from Chasewater Country Park. A large public bar and lounge occupy the ground floors, with the Haycroft restaurant upstairs. Four guest beers and two real ciders are available, plus a wide choice of fruit and country wines and 50 malt whiskies. No food is served on Sunday evenings. ✿◑⊟⌐♣♦P

Cheddleton

Boat Inn

Basford Bridge Lane, ST13 7EQ (off A520 S of Leek)

☻ 12-11; 12-midnight Fri & Sat

☎ (01538) 360683 ⊕ the-boatinn.co.uk

Marston's Burton Bitter, Pedigree; guest beers ⊞
Renowned, traditional, canal-side pub in a picturesque setting with a friendly atmosphere, popular with locals and tourists. The two regular beers are supplemented by three guests. The inn has a good reputation for food with Sunday roasts a speciality. Children are welcome at mealtimes. Buses 16 and 106 stop three quarters of a mile away along the towpath; at lunchtime the 463 stops at the door. The steam railway and museum close by are worth a visit. ◑▲➡♣Ｐ⌐

Church Eaton

Royal Oak

High Street, ST20 0AJ

☻ 5 (12 Sat)-midnight Mon-Fri; 12-10.30 Sun

☎ (01785) 823078 ⊕ churcheaton.org.uk

Banks's Original, Bitter; guest beer ⊞
The only pub in the village, three years ago the Royal Oak was under threat of closure but was saved by a small consortium of local people and is now the hub of the community. It has a modern interior split into four interconnecting rooms including a bar and restaurant. One room has a pool table, another shows televised sport. Children are welcome until 7pm or later if eating in the restaurant. The ever-changing guest beers are mostly sourced from local micro-breweries. ✾◑♿Ｐ⌐

Codsall

Codsall Station

Chapel Lane, WV8 2EJ

☻ 11.30-2.30, 5-11; 11.30-11.30 Fri & Sat; 12-10.30 Sun

☎ (01902) 847061

Holden's Mild, Bitter, Golden Glow, Special, seasonal beers; guest beers ⊞
Created from the waiting room and offices of this Grade II listed former station building, the pub has won local CAMRA awards every year since 2001. The interior is divided into a bar, lounge, snug and conservatory and displays worldwide railway memorabilia. Occasional steam locomotives can be spotted from the terrace overlooking the working platforms on the Wolverhampton-Shrewsbury line. The floodlit boules piste becomes the site for the annual early September beer festival. No evening meals are served on Sunday. Q✾◑♿⇋➡Ｐ

Dayhills

Red Lion

Uttoxeter Road, ST15 8RU (4 miles E of Stone on B5027)

☻ 6-11; 4-12 Fri; 12-midnight Sat; 12-10.30 Sun

☎ (01889) 505474

Draught Bass; ⊞/Ｇ **Worthington's Bitter; guest beer** ⊞

Welcoming country pub known locally as the Romping Cat. Unspoilt and full of character, along with the adjoining farm it has been in the same family since 1920. The main room has a timeless feel with its quarry tile floor, meat hooks in the ceiling and inglenook fireplace. The atmosphere is undisturbed by music, gaming machines or TV. Draught Bass may be served straight from the cask during winter months. ▲Q♣Ｐ⌐

Eccleshall

George

Castle Street, ST21 6DF

☻ 11-11; 12-10.30 Sun

☎ (01785) 850300 ⊕ thegeorgeinn.freeserve.co.uk

Slater's Bitter, Original, Top Totty, Premium, Supreme, seasonal beer ⊞
The brewery has outgrown the extended outbuilding behind the pub, but the six handpulls serving nearly the full range of Slaters award-winning ales are still the main attraction at the George. Originally a 17th-century coaching inn, but sadly neglected for much of the last century, the George has thrived under the Slater family's ownership and now has attractive bar and lounge areas, a restaurant and 10 luxurious bedrooms. Excellent meals are served all day. ▲⇌◑➡Ｐ⌐

Enville

Cat

Bridgnorth Road, DY7 5HA (on A458)

☻ 12-2.30, 6.30 (7 Tue)-11 Wed-Fri; 12-3, 6.30-11 Sat; 12-5.30 Sun

☎ (01384) 872209 ⊕ theenvillecat.co.uk

Enville Ale; guest beers ⊞
Parts of this traditional country pub date back to the 16th century. It has four oak beamed rooms; the snug and smoke room both feature real fires. Hanging baskets adorn the garden and courtyard during summer months. Up to three guest ales are served including other beers from Enville Ales. Homemade seasonal dishes and daily specials, using local produce wherever possible, are served alongside sandwiches, baguettes and jacket potatoes. A separate menu is offered in the Malthouse restaurant. The pub is closed on Monday except bank holidays. ▲⇌✾◑▲Ｐ

Gnosall

Boat

Wharf Road, ST20 0DA (off A518 at Royal Oak)

☻ 12-midnight (1am Fri & Sat)

☎ (01785) 822208

Banks's Original, Bitter; Marston's Bitter, Pedigree; guest beers ⊞
One-room, canal-side pub popular with both locals and the boating trade. The Boat runs darts, dominoes and pool teams as well as the occasional live music night and at times can get lively. Good value food is served (no eve meals Sun). Look out for the question of the day on the blackboard by the bar and you could win your first pint for free. ▲✾◑➡♣Ｐ⌐

Royal Oak

Newport Road, ST20 0BL (On A518)
✪ 12-midnight
☎ (01785) 822362
Greene King Abbot, IPA; Highgate Dark Mild; guest beers Ⓗ

Well-run pub comprising a traditional dog-friendly bar and separate lounge. The guest beers are sourced from micro-breweries whenever possible. A wide range of home-cooked food including a good vegetarian selection is served in the lounge. The pub has an upstairs function room with a skittles alley for hire. There is a large beer garden with a climbing frame and swings. ▲▲✿❀Ⓓ♿🍴🚗♣P⅄

Great Haywood

Clifford Arms

Main Road, ST18 0SR (off A51)
✪ 12-3, 5-11.30; 12-midnight Fri & Sat; 12-11 Sun
☎ (01889) 881321
Adnams Broadside; Draught Bass; Greene King Old Speckled Hen; guest beers Ⓗ

Village-centre inn with a large bar providing plenty of seating and a restaurant adorned with past photographs of the pub. A popular local, home to darts, dominoes and quiz teams, it also attracts walkers, cyclists, boaters and visitors to the nearby Shugborough Estate (NT). The Staffordshire Way and bridge 73 of the Trent and Mersey Canal are 200 metres along Trent Lane. Dogs are welcome. ▲▲✿❀Ⓓ♿🍴🚗♣P⅄

Harriseahead

Royal Oak

High Steeet, ST7 4JT
✪ 7-11; 5-11 Fri & Sat; 12-3, 7-10.30 Sun
☎ (01782) 513262
Courage Directors; Fuller's London Pride; John Smith's Bitter; guest beers Ⓗ

A warm welcome is assured at this excellent two-room free house, popular with locals. Guest beers come from small independent and micro-brewers. An upstairs function and meeting room provides extra space for the pub's beer festivals. A good selection of Belgian bottled beers is on offer, plus a Belgian draught. Monthly quizzes are held in aid of local charities. ▲▲✿❀♿🚗♣P⅄

Haughton

Bell

Newport Road, ST18 9EX (on A518)
✪ 12-3, 6-11; 12-midnight Fri & Sat; 12-10.30 Sun
☎ (01785) 780301
Banks's Original; Marston's Burton Bitter, Pedigree; guest beers Ⓗ

Friendly, local free house with one large L-shaped room with a bar and lounge area. Sky TV is screened in the bar for football and horse racing fans. The building is over 200 years old and was originally a farm; photographs and memorabilia are on display. Two guest beers change regularly. The food here is excellent (no meals Sun eve). ✿Ⓓ♿🚗♣P⅄

High Offley

Anchor

Peggs Lane, Old Lea, ST20 0NG (by bridge 42 of Shropshire Union Canal) OS775256
✪ 12-3 (not winter Mon-Fri), 7-11 (not winter Mon-Thu); 12-3, 7-11 (not winter eve) Sun
☎ (01785) 284569
Wadworth 6X Ⓖ

On the Shropshire Union Canal, this Victorian inn is a rare example of an unspoilt country pub. It has two small bars where the cask ale and cider are served from jugs. This free house has been run by the same family since 1870 when it was called the Sebastopol. There is a large award-winning garden with a canalware gift shop at the rear. Not easily found by road, but well worth the effort to seek out. ▲▲Q✿❀♿A♣P

Hilderstone

Roebuck

Sandon Road, ST15 8SF (on B5066)
✪ 3-midnight (1am Fri); 12-1am Sat; 12-10.30 Sun
☎ (01889) 505255
Adnams Bitter; Banks's Original; guest beers Ⓗ

Friendly and comfortable pub with a cosy lounge/bar with TV showing sports and music channels and a games room with pool table. The licensee's growing collection of ornamental pigs is displayed around the rooms. Two guest beers are offered and pies and sandwiches are always available. Entertainment includes a buskers' night on Sunday and on most Saturday nights there is a live act, disco or karaoke. ▲▲✿❀♣P⅄

Hoar Cross

Meynell Ingram Arms

Abbots Bromley Road, DE13 8RB
✪ 12-11 (midnight Fri & Sat); 12-10.30 Sun
☎ (01283) 575202 ⊕ themeynell.co.uk
Marston's Pedigree; Taylor Landlord; guest beer Ⓗ

Unspoilt village pub in a pleasant rural setting. Once a farmhouse, and dating from the early 16th-century when it formed part of the Earl of Shrewsbury's estate, it has retained original beams and quarry-tiled floors. The pub was named after the Meynell family who owned nearby Hoar Cross Hall. The main bar includes a tiny snug served through a hatch, and a smaller bar leads to an intimate restaurant with an award-winning reputation for food. Outside is an attractive paved courtyard. Q✿❀Ⓓ♿♣P⅄

Keele

Keele Postgraduate Association (KPA)

Horwood Hall, University Campus, ST5 5BJ
✪ 11 (5 Sat)-midnight (not Mon); 11-1am Fri; 7-1am Sun
☎ (01782) 584228
Beer range varies Ⓗ

Founded in 1967 as Keele Research Association, it changed its name and moved to the present site in 1994, located behind the student union building. Two real ales are

always available from various independent and micro-breweries. Quiz night is Thursday. If you are looking for a peaceful pint there is a quiet room with newspapers available. Local CAMRA Club of the Year 2001, CAMRA members are welcome on production of a membership card. The bus stop is nearby.
Q◑⑪&🖳

Kidsgrove

Blue Bell

Hardingswood, ST7 1EG (off A50 near Tesco)
✪ 7.30-11, 1-4, 7-11 Sat; 12-10.30 Sun
☎ (01782) 774052 ⊕ bluebellkidsgrove.co.uk
Beer range varies ℍ

A former Staffordshire Pub of the Year, this canal-side free house is a frequent local CAMRA award winner. Six ever-changing cask beers come from a wide range of micro-breweries. Real cider and perry plus German and Czech beers provide real choice. No juke box, TV or games machines distract in this classic pub. Folk musicians perform on Sunday evening. The pub is closed on Monday except bank holidays. Dogs are welcome.
Q❀≈🖳♣P

Kinver

Constitutional Social Club

119 High Street, DY7 6HL
✪ 5-11; 4-midnight Fri; 11.30-midnight Sat; 12-10.30 Sun
☎ (01384) 872044
Banks's Original, Bitter; Greene King Abbot; Hobsons Best Bitter; Wye Valley Hereford Pale Ale; guest beers ℍ

Built in 1902 on the site of an old pub, this converted hotel has three main areas: a smart restaurant, a large snooker room and a bar dispensing up to five guest beers from myriad breweries, at reasonable prices. The club enjoys an enviable sporting reputation and hosts regular quiz and music nights. Meals are served Sunday lunchtime and Wednesday to Saturday evenings; booking advised. Card-carrying CAMRA members are welcome but must be signed in. The bus from Stourbridge stops nearby. ❀⑪&🖳♣P

Vine

1 Dunsley Road, DY7 6LJ
✪ 11.30-11; 12-10.30 Sun
☎ (01384) 877291 ⊕ vineinnkinver.co.uk
Enville Ale; Kinver Edge; guest beers ℍ

The Vine was opened in 1863 in competition with the Lock Inn that once stood opposite. Originally two converted cottages, it extended into adjacent cottages over the years and most internal walls were removed in 1980. Now a one-room pub, it retains distinct areas on different levels, with the restaurant overlooking Kinver lock on the Staffs & Worcs canal. Food is served all day in summer. The canal-side gardens are extensive. The bus from Stourbridge stops nearby. ❀⑪&🖳P

Knighton

Haberdasher's Arms

ST20 0QH (between Adbaston and Knighton)
OS753275
✪ 12.30-midnight; 7-midnight Wed & Thu; 12.30-1am Fri & Sat; 12-midnight Sun
☎ (01785) 280650
Banks's Original, Bitter; guest beer ℍ

Traditional community pub, built around 1840, offering a warm, friendly welcome. This former local CAMRA Pub of the Year has four compact rooms all served from a small bar. The large garden is used for events such as the annual Potato Club Show. It is well worth the drive through leafy country lanes to get here.
🏚Q❀🖳▲♣P⌐

Leek

Den Engel

Stanley Street, ST13 5HG
✪ 5-11; 11-11.30 Wed & Thu, 11-midnight Fri & Sat; 12-11.30 Sun
☎ (01538) 373751
Beer range varies ℍ

Just off St Edward Street is an authentic Belgian bar selling over 110 Belgian beers and four constantly-changing cask ales from micro-breweries. Entering the bar via the side door you have a choice of two rooms: the bar overlooking Stanley Street housing memorabilia of Leek Cycle Club, or a more spacious room leading onto the courtyard. Belgian cuisine is available in the restaurant.
Q❀⑪🖳⌐

Wilkes Head

St Edward Street, ST13 5DS
✪ 12 (3 Mon)-11; 12-10.30 Sun
☎ (01538) 383616
Whim Arbor Light; Hartington Bitter, seasonal beers; guest beers ℍ

Ever-popular town pub, the second oldest in Leek, dating back to the 1740s. The licensee is an enthusiastic musician and live music sessions take place on Monday evening. Quiz night is Thursday. Three music festivals a year take place and the juke box is one of the best in the area. ❀🖳P

Lichfield

Acorn

12-18 Tamworth Street, WS13 6JJ
✪ 9-midnight (1am Fri & Sat)
☎ (01543) 263400
Greene King Abbot; Marston's Burton Bitter, Pedigree; guest beers ℍ

Called the Acorn at the request of a local pub historian, the building itself originates from former retail outlets, with a large, deep interior and bar along the left-hand side. For the real ale drinker, the Acorn must be one of the best in the Wetherspoon chain; the manager is a keen supporter of local micros and sources a good range of guest ales. The local Beowulf beers appear regularly on the guest list. ⑪&≈(City)🖳♣

Duke of Wellington

Birmingham Road, WS14 9BJ
✪ 12-11; 12-10.30 Sun

☎ (01543) 263261
Black Sheep Bitter; Fuller's London Pride; Marston's Pedigree; guest beers ⊞
Deservedly popular traditional local, well worth the 20-minute walk from the city centre. The interior has been tastefully modernised with three distinct drinking areas served from a central bar. The guest ale list often includes examples from local micros. A range of wholesome bar meals is served from Monday to Saturday. Look out for occasional, mid-week themed food nights (booking essential). There is an extensive beer garden to the rear. ♨♣◑♿➡♣P'⌐

George and Dragon
28 Beacon Street, WS13 7AJ
✪ 11-11 (midnight Thu-Sat); 12-11 Sun
☎ (01543) 253667
Banks's Original, Bitter; Marston's Pedigree; guest beer ⊞
Compact, two-room pub north of the cathedral and close to Beacon Park. The walls of the lounge illustrate the story of the second siege of Lichfield in 1643, when Royalists, led by Prince Rupert, bombarded the cathedral from a mound above the pub garden. Bar snacks and a selection of teas and coffee are available. A charity quiz is held on Thursday night. ♣◐≢(City)➡♣P

King's Head
21 Bird Street, WS13 6PW
✪ 10-11 (midnight Thu-Sat)
☎ (01543) 256822
Marston's Burton Bitter; guest beers ⊞
Enthusiastically run, former coaching inn within the city's main drinking area. The King's Head is the acclaimed birthplace of the Staffordshire regiment; the walls of the front bar are covered with military paraphernalia and photographs. Music nights (free admission) are held in the covered courtyard, usually jazz on Thursday, open mic on Friday, and blues/rock on Saturday. Good value bar meals are served at lunchtime and Thursday evening. The two guest beers are from Marston's. ◐≢(City)➡'⌐

Queen's Head
4 Queen Street, WS13 6QD
✪ 12-11 (11.30 Fri & Sat); 12-3, 7-11 Sun
☎ (01543) 410932
Adnams Bitter; Marston's Pedigree; Taylor Landlord; guest beers ⊞
Long-established Guide regular, well worth the short walk from the city centre. Three regular beers are supplemented by two guests often from micro-breweries. Good-value home-cooked lunches are served Monday to Saturday, with bread, cheese and pâté available from a refrigerated counter. The pub is popular with sports people and supports two local cricket teams and Lichfield Rugby Union football club. Q◐≢(City)➡

Longdon

Swan with Two Necks
40 Brook End, WS15 4PN (just off A51)
✪ 12-3, 6-11; 12-11 Sat; 12-10.30 Sun
☎ (01543) 490251

Adnams Bitter; Caledonian Deuchars IPA; Taylor Landlord; guest beer ⊞
The pub has been in the Guide for over 27 years and plays a central role in the village and surrounding countryside community. The three regular beers are supplemented by an ever-changing micro. Meals are of a very high quality; the restaurant opens on Friday and Saturday evenings. The pub name is a reference to the two nicks on a swans beak indicating ownership. ♨Q♣◑P

Milwich

Green Man
ST18 0EG (on B5027)
✪ 12-2.30 (Thu & Fri), 5-11; 12-11 Sat; 12-10.30 Sun
☎ (01889) 505310 ⊕ greenmanmilwich.com
Adnams Bitter; Marston's Pedigree; Wells Bombardier; guest beers ⊞
A pub since 1775, this free house offers guest beers from regional and micro-breweries nationwide – see website for forthcoming guest beers. Weston's or Thatcher's cider is stocked. The current licensee is in his 17th year at the pub and a list of his predecessors, dating back to 1792, is displayed. Good food is served in a 16-seat restaurant section within the bar (lunch Thu-Sun, eve meals Tue-Sat). Local CAMRA Pub of the Year 2006 and 2007. ♨♣◑♣●P'⌐

Newcastle-under-Lyme

Arnold Machin
Ironmarket, ST5 1PB
✪ 8am-11pm (12.30am Fri & Sat)
☎ (01782) 557840
Draught Bass; Greene King Abbot; guest beers ⊞
Typical Wetherspoon outlet, with Lloyds No.1 format, sited in a converted former post office. It is named after the local sculptor who was responsible for the design of the Queen's head on British postage stamps. Situated close to the town centre and bus station, it has a patio overlooking the Queen's Gardens. ♣◑♿➡'⌐

Old Brown Jug
Bridge Street, ST5 2RY
✪ 3-midnight (1am Wed); 12-1am Fri & Sat; 12-midnight Sun
☎ (01782) 711393
Jennings seasonal beers; Marston's Pedigree; guest beers ⊞
Popular, lively town pub, just off the High Street at the north end of the town centre. The interior is open plan with wooden floors and large wooden tables. Live music features on Sunday night. Two guest beers are usually available; real cider is a speciality (Weston's a favourite), available on draught from three dedicated handpumps as well as bottled. The bus station is nearby. ♨♣●

Newtown

Ivy House
62 Stafford Road, WS6 6AZ (on A34)
✪ 12-2.30, 5-11; 12-11 Fri-Sun
☎ (01922) 476607
Banks's Original, Bitter; Marston's Pedigree; guest beers ⊞

A warm welcome is assured at this Walsall CAMRA (Staffs) 2005/2006 Pub of the Year, where the motto is 'Quality beers for quality people'. First listed as a pub in 1824, this 200-year-old building is a traditional pub with a country feel – the garden backs on to open farmland. The interior comprises three rooms on two levels plus a recently extended restaurant, serving excellent value meals. Q❀⑪&ⴲ(1, 351)P⸜

Norton Canes

Railway Tavern

63 Norton Green Lane, WS11 9PR (off Walsall Rd)
❂ 12-midnight (1am Fri & Sat)
☎ (01543) 279579
Banks's Original, Bitter; Greene King IPA; guest beers Ⓗ
Twice local CAMRA pub of the year, the Railway Tavern has been tastefully refurbished to provide a large single room with a spacious lounge/dining area. The enclosed garden contains a patio drinking area, children's play equipment and a large lawn, suitable for ball games. With entertainment every Saturday and a quiz every other Wednesday, plus real cider in summer, there is something for everyone at this friendly local pub.
❀⑪&ⴲ♣♠P⸜

Onecote

Jervis Arms

ST13 7IE (on B5053 N of A53 Leek-Ashbourne road)
❂ 12-3, 7 (6 Sat)-midnight; 12-10.30 Sun
☎ (01538) 304206
Holden's Bitter; Titanic Iceberg; guest beers Ⓗ
Family-friendly pub situated within the Peak District National Park and not far from Alton Towers. The beer range is sourced from micro-breweries across the country. Food is served daily from an extensive menu. Two beer festivals are held annually with camping available nearby. A river runs alongside the beer garden perfect on a hot summer day. A regular in the Guide, this is a real ale paradise.
⛺❀⑪♣♠P

Oulton

Brushmakers Arms

8 Kibblestone Road, ST15 8UW (500 yds W of A520, 1 mile NE of Stone)
❂ 12-3, 6-11; 12-3, 7-11
☎ (01785) 812062
Thwaites Original, Lancaster Bomber; guest beers Ⓗ
Built in 1865 and thought to be named after a local cottage industry, this pub is a fine example of a local that has retained its traditional public bar and lounge. The unspoilt bar features photos of the past and the lounge is intimate and comfortable. There are no gaming machines or juke box. Guest ales include favourites from Archers and Black Sheep. A small patio garden at the rear is popular in summer, especially at lunchtime.
⌂Q❀ⴲⴲ♠P

Penkridge

Star

Market Place, ST19 5DJ (150 yds from A449)
❂ 11-11 (11.30 Thu; midnight Fri & Sat)
☎ (01785) 712513
Banks's Original, Bitter; guest beer Ⓗ
First trading as an inn in 1827, this one-room pub is situated in the old Market Place, with a patio and seating area outside. In the early 20th century the building became a Co-op Store, then a private residence. It was restored to the licensed trade in the second half of the 20th century. Market days are Wednesday and Saturday. ❀⑪⇌ⴲP⸜

Penn Common

Barley Mow

Pennwood Lane, WV4 5JN (follow signs to Penn Golf Club from A449)
❂ 12-2.30, 6-11; 12-11 Sat; 12-10.30 Sun
☎ (01902) 333510
Caledonian Deuchars IPA; Flowers Original; Greene King Abbot; guest beers Ⓗ
Small, low-beamed pub dating from the 1600s, on the border of Wolverhampton and Staffordshire. A small extension was added in the 1990s. The 'Mow' has a well-deserved reputation for food, with meat supplied from the landlord's own award-winning butcher's shop. Next to the local golf course, the pub is a short walk over seven cornfields from Wolverhampton. Q❀⑪P

Salt

Holly Bush

ST18 0BX (off A518 opp Weston Hall)
❂ 12-11 (midnight Fri & Sat)
☎ (01889) 508234 ⊕ hollybushinn.co.uk
Adnams Bitter; Marston's Pedigree; guest beer Ⓗ
The Holly Bush is believed to be the second English inn to be granted a licence and the oldest part of the building is still thatched. With extensions and alterations over the centuries there are now three distinct areas: a bar towards the middle of the pub, a dining room and a snug, mainly occupied by diners. Food is available throughout the day. Many awards have been won for the superb yet reasonably priced meals. ⌂Q❀⑪&♠ⴲP⸜

Silverdale

Bush

High Street, ST5 6JZ
❂ 12-11 (midnight Fri & Sat); 12-10.30 Sun
☎ (01782) 713096 ⊕ the-bush.co.uk
Wells Bombardier; guest beers Ⓗ
A welcome new entry to the Guide, the Bush is an imposing building in a former mining village, with a large enclosed beer garden. Six beers on tap with five ever-changing guest ales mainly from micros and regional breweries. Good-value home-cooked food is available; Wednesday steak night and Sunday dinner are especially popular. There is entertainment on Friday and Saturday evenings and the pub hosts pool, dominoes, darts and football teams. ⌂❀⑪&ⴲ♠P⸜

Stafford

Bird in Hand

Victoria Square, ST16 2AQ
☼ 12-11 (midnight Fri & Sat); 12-10.30 Sun
☎ (01785) 252198
Courage Best Bitter; Fuller's London Pride; Wells Bombardier; guest beer Ⓗ
Described as one of Staffords most customer friendly pubs, the 'Bird' benefits greatly from retaining four separate and very different rooms: a traditional yet comfortable public bar, a quiet, cosy snug, a large lounge with TVs and a big games room that has recently been converted with a stage for live music. It stands midway between the railway station and town centre, opposite the crown court, next to St. Marys Church and not far from the famous Ancient High House. ⬥⬥⬥⬥⬥⬥⬥⬥⬥

Greyhound

12 County Road, ST16 2PU
☼ 4.30 (2 Fri; 12 Sat)-11; 12-11 Sun
☎ (01785) 222432
Beer range varies Ⓗ
The Greyhound has experienced a remarkable transformation closed and threatened with conversion to another use after failing under pub company ownership, it is now thriving as one of very few genuine free houses around Stafford. A pub since the 1830s, situated just a few minutes' walk north of the town centre, it retains the separate bar and lounge from a sensitive 2002 refurbishment. Eight hand-pulled ales are usually available, most of them from local micro-breweries but some from regional brewers. ⬥⬥⬥⬥⬥⬥⬥⬥

King's Arms

11-12 Peel Terrace, ST16 3HB (off B5066, Sandon Road)
☼ 5-11; 4-midnight Fri; 12-midnight Sat; 5-11 Sun
☎ (01785) 249872
Brains SA; Caledonian Deuchars IPA; Wells Bombardier; guest beers Ⓗ
One of several pubs now making the north end of Stafford an excellent drinking area, the Kings Arms offers five hand pumped ales, two of them guests from regional or micro-breweries. Converted long ago from two terraced houses, the pub has been further opened up in recent years but retains separate bar and snug areas. Although just a mile north of the town centre, the pub has a surprisingly large garden. Parking can be difficult. ⬥⬥⬥

Luck Penny

62 Crab Lane, ST16 1SQ
☼ 11-11 (midnight Fri & Sat); 12-11 Sun
☎ (01785) 603503
John Smith's Bitter; Marston's Pedigree; guest beer Ⓗ
Deservedly popular pub on Trinity Fields estate run by the same licensee for more than a quarter of a century, making him currently the longest serving pub landlord in the Stafford area. Built in the late 1960s at the same time as the surrounding houses, this community-based pub supports several sports and games teams. Customers can expect good service and great value food (no meals Sun eve). ⬥⬥⬥⬥⬥⬥⬥⬥⬥

Spittal Brook

106 Lichfield Road, ST17 4LP (off A34)
☼ 12-3, 5-11; 12-11 Sat; 12-4, 7-10.30 Sun
☎ (01785) 245268
Black Sheep Best Bitter; Everards Tiger; Jennings Cumberland Ale; Marston's Pedigree; guest beer Ⓗ
Formerly the Crown, the pub reverted to the original name of its locality in 1998. This thriving, traditional, two-room alehouse, adjacent to the West Coast mainline, fields darts, cribbage, water polo and netball teams and a golfing society. The premises are licensed for civil weddings. Entertainment includes a folk night on Tuesday and a quiz on Wednesday. No food is served Sunday evening. ⬥⬥⬥⬥⬥⬥⬥⬥⬥⬥

Stanley

Travellers Rest

Tompkin Lane, ST9 9LX (1 mile from B5051/A53 jct in Endon)
☼ 12-3, 6-11
☎ (01782) 502580
Marston's Burton Bitter, Pedigree; guest beers Ⓗ
'A restaurant with a bar,' is how the landlord describes this pub. A genuine free house, popular with both diners and drinkers, it has a traditional feel with beamed ceilings, highly-polished brasses and an old cash till. Guest beers are served from regional and micro-breweries from all over the country; the food menu is extensive and excellent. The large car park is accessed at the rear via an archway. ⬥⬥⬥⬥

Stoke-on-Trent: Burslem

Bull's Head

St John's Square, ST6 3AJ
☼ 3-11 (11.30 Wed & Thu); 12-midnight Fri & Sat; 12-11 Sun
☎ (01782) 834153 ⊕ titanicbrewery.co.uk/bulls
Titanic Steerage, Anchor, Iceberg, White Star; guest beers Ⓗ
The finest ale house in town, this two-room town-centre pub is 10 minutes' walk from Vale Park. The Titanic brewery tap, it boasts most of the brewerys 'fleet' and up to five seasonal or guest beers. Regular themed events keep the beer choice extensive and varied. The bar has a bar billiards table and a juke box; the altogether quieter lounge a real fire. The pub is busy at weekends and on Port Vale match days. ⬥⬥⬥⬥⬥⬥⬥⬥

Stoke-on-Trent: Dresden

Princess Royal

Carlisle Street, ST3 4HA (off Trentham Road)
☼ 12-midnight; 12-11 Sun
☎ (01782) 335488
Draught Bass; Greene King Ruddles County, Abbot; guest beer Ⓗ
Multi-room pub, full of character, in a residential area near Longton Park. The two front rooms comprise a cosy snug and tap room, the latter with an open fireplace and photographs of old Dresden and Longton on the walls. The central area has a TV screen for sports. At the rear is a pool room plus family

room with table football. The well-maintained garden is popular in summer. Dogs are welcome. ♨☆❀Qᵭ≠(Longton)🖫♣•┗

Stoke-on-Trent: Fenton

Malt 'n' Hops
King Street, ST4 3EJ
🕓 12-4, 7-11; 12-3, 7-10.30 Sun
☎ (01782) 313406
Beer range varies Ⓗ
One of the few free houses in the city, this long-established hostelry has been in the same ownership for almost two decades. Comprising a single room greatly extended over the years, the impression is of a separate traditional bar and comfortable lounge. Ever-changing guest beers from small breweries and micros make this very much a beer-oriented pub. The house beers are brewed by Tower. Belgian beers are stocked.
≠(Longton)🖫

Stoke-on-Trent: Hanley

Coachmakers Arms
Lichfield Street, ST1 3EA (off A5008 Potteries Way ring road)
🕓 12-11.30 (midnight Fri & Sat); 7-10.30 Sun
☎ (01782) 262158
Beer range varies Ⓗ
CAMRA Potteries Pub of the Year for 2006, this is a fine and rare example of a traditional Potteries town pub with four rooms and central tiled drinking corridor. The seven constantly-changing beers always include a mild and a stout or porter plus a real cider (usually Weston's). Just outside Hanley town centre and close to the bus station, it has a varied clientele attracted by the excellent beer quality and character. ♨Q✿🖫♣•┗

Unicorn
Piccadilly, ST1 1EG
🕓 12-1am (12.30am Sun)
☎ (01782) 281809 ⊕ myspace.com/theunicorninn
Fuller's London Pride; guest beers Ⓗ
A small, friendly, city centre pub based in the heart of the cultural quarter across from the Regent Theatre. Above the bar is a large collection of Toby jugs and there are numerous brasses decorating the cosy room and adjoining sitting area. Sandwiches are available at lunchtimes. Two guest beers are served in rotation. ✿🖫┗

Stoke-on-Trent: Longton

Congress
Sutherland Road, ST3 1HJ (opp police station)
🕓 12-8 Mon (11 Tue-Thu); 11-11 Fri-Sun
☎ (07790) 660845
Titanic Mild; Wychwood Hobgoblin; guest beers Ⓗ
A welcome addition to the Guide, this traditional Potteries pub has been transformed by new licensees and offers a good beer range and relaxed atmosphere. The layout allows for a pool table or entertainment. Artwork by local artists is displayed throughout. Beer is dispensed from both handpump and cask at the weekends; house beer is from Lancaster

Brewery. The staff pride themselves on their range of beers and are always happy to advise and chat. ≠🖫♣•┗

Stoke-on-Trent: Penkhull

Beehive
Honeywall, ST4 7HU
🕓 12-1am (2am Fri & Sat); 12-6, 7-11.30 Sun
☎ (01782) 846947 ⊕ beehiveinn.com
Jennings Cumberland, Cocker Hoop; Marston's Pedigree; guest beers Ⓗ
Deservedly popular local with a warm and welcoming atmosphere, run entirely by the Rowland family. Situated on the hill above Stoke, it attracts many Stoke City fans on match days and has a collection of club memorabilia. A quiz is hosted on Tuesday night, plus occasional social events. Four guest beers change weekly. ♨✿▶P┗

Stoke-on-Trent: Stoke

Wheatsheaf
Church Street, ST4 1BU
🕓 9-midnight (1am Fri & Sat)
☎ (01782) 747462
Courage Directors; Greene King Abbot; Marston's Pedigree; guest beers Ⓗ
Smallish, open-plan Wetherspoon outlet, more a traditional local than a city wine bar. Recently refurbished, it has retained its original character, with plaques on the wall featuring the local pottery industry. Separate drinking areas suit all tastes. Guest beers can number up to five with a local ale always available. ◖▷ᵭ≠🖫

Stone

Poste of Stone
1 Granville Square, ST15 8AB
🕓 9-midnight (1am Fri & Sat)
☎ (01785) 827920
Greene King Abbot; Marston's Pedigree; guest beers Ⓗ
Large, open plan Wetherspoon pub converted from the former main post office. A guest beer from Titanic or Springhead breweries is usually available. Breakfast and beer is served from 9am at this busy and friendly pub; children are welcome in the large restaurant area. Food Club nights include Tuesday steaks and Thursday curry. The pub is near the Trent and Mersey Canal and boatyards.
♨✿◖ᵭ≠🖫•┗

Swan
18 Stafford Street, ST15 8QW (on A520 by Trent and Mersey Canal)
🕓 11-midnight (1am Thu-Sat); 12-11 Sun
☎ (01785) 815570
Coach House Gunpowder Mild, John Joule Old Knotty, John Joule Old Priory, John Joule Victory; guest beers Ⓗ
This Grade II listed building was carefully renovated in 1999. It has one large L-shaped room with real fires at each end. To date beers from over 300 breweries have been served. Up to six guest beers are available. Tuesday is quiz night and live music is performed up to four nights a week. A free buffet is served

every Sunday lunchtime and snacks are available Tuesday to Saturday lunchtimes. An annual beer festival is held in the garden during the second week of July. Over 18s only are admitted. 🏠🛏️🍴&🚌🚭●⬥

Summerhill

Boat

Walsall Road, WS14 0BU

✪ 12-3, 6-11; 12-11 Sun

☎ (01543) 361692 ⊕ oddfellowsintheboat.com

Beer range varies Ⓗ

Formerly tied, this free house has been transformed into a heaven for lovers of gourmet food and real ale. Sit in the Mediterranean-style reception area and watch the chefs prepare the delectable dishes – the menu changes daily depending on what is in season. The beer may be from a local brewery or sourced nationally but there is always a wide choice and you can be assured of the quality maintained by the owners.
🏠Q🛏️🍴&P⬥

Swindon

Green Man Inn

High Street, DY3 4NR

✪ 12 (11 Sat)-11

☎ (01384) 400532

Banks's Original, Bitter; guest beer Ⓗ

Situated at the end of the High Street, this traditional hostelry has served the village since 1830. The quarry-tiled bar has a real fire and the walls are decorated with photographs of the area from a bygone era. As well as the usual pub games, quoits and Devil among the Tailors are played. In the cosy lounge home-made food such as faggots and peas and steak and kidney pie are served. One room has a pool table and gaming machines. Dogs are welcome. 🏠🛏️🍴🚌&🚌(260, 261)♣●P⬥🚃

Tamworth

Albert Hotel

32 Albert Rd, B79 7JS

✪ 12-11 (12.30am Thu-Sat); 12-10.30 Sun

☎ (01827) 64694 ⊕ tamworthhotel.co.uk

Banks's Bitter; Marston's Pedigree; guest beers Ⓗ

Friendly and popular town-centre local situated a stone's throw from Tamworth railway station, with easy access to most parts of the country. Top-quality food is served and the well-kept guest beers are from the Marston's range. There are outdoor drinking areas at the front and rear of the pub, which are popular in the summer. The well-attended quiz night is Thursday. Look out for the CAMRA heritage panel in the bar detailing the pub's history. 🛏️🍴🚌P🚃

Market Vaults

7 Market Street, B79 7LU

✪ 11-3, 6-11; 11-midnight Fri & Sat; 12-3, 7-11 Sun

☎ (01827) 69653

Banks's Original, Bitter; guest beer Ⓗ

One of the oldest buildings in Tamworth, this small pub is set in the historic market square around Thomas Guy's Town Hall. It offers a

good lunchtime food service alongside quality real ales. The pub has two levels with the lower public bar area featuring old images of the town and an upper lounge/dining area, which leads to a large garden at the rear. Guest beers are from the Marston's range. 🛏️🍴🚌🚭⬥

Sir Robert Peel

12-13 Lower Gungate, B79 7BA

✪ 11-11 (11.30 Tue, midnight Thu-Sat); 12-11.30 Sun

☎ (01827) 300910

Beer range varies Ⓗ

Popular pub in the pedestrian area of the town centre usually offering a choice of two micro-brewery beers. The landlord takes pride in choosing his ales and customers may find beers from breweries anywhere between Scotland and Cornwall. Real cider is Weston's Old Rosie. A focal point for real ale and real music in the town, the pub hosts regular live music on Tuesday and Sunday nights. 🚌🚭●

White Lion

1 Aldergate, B79 7DJ

✪ 12-11 (midnight Fri & Sat); 12-10.30 Sun

☎ (01827) 64630

Banks's Bitter; guest beers Ⓗ

Three-room pub on the edge of the town centre popular with all ages. The landlord is keen to showcase guest beers from local micro-breweries and Beowulf, Blythe, Church End and Quartz feature regularly. A large-screen TV showing sports is unobtrusive at one end of the room. Note the interesting old plan of the White Lion and its sister pub the White Horse which was demolished back in the early 1960s. The pub can be busy at weekends.
🚌🚭♣P

Trysull

Bell

Bell Lane, WV5 7JB

✪ 11.30-3, 5-11; 11.30-11 Sat; 12-10.30 Sun

☎ (01902) 892871

Batham's Best Bitter; Holden's Bitter, Golden Glow, Special, seasonal beers; guest beer Ⓗ

Standing next to the medieval church in the centre of the village, on the site of a much older pub, the current building dates from the 18th century. There are three rooms: a pleasant bar, comfortable lounge and newly refurbished restaurant. Good value meals are mostly home made – cod in Batham's batter is a favourite (no food served Sun-Tue eve). The ever-changing guest beer usually comes from a micro-brewery. Staffs & Worcs canal is a 15-minute walk away. Q🚲🛏️🍴&P🚃

Two Gates

Railway Inn

409 Watling Street, B77 5AL

✪ 12-11 (10.30 Sun)

☎ (01827) 262937

Draught Bass Ⓗ

Basic, if a little 'rough and ready', three-room traditional drinkers' pub, situated adjacent to Wilnecote railway station. The three handpumps all dispense high quality Draught Bass. All the usual pub games are played in this welcoming local which has a separate pool room. The walls in the public bar are adorned with railway memorabilia. For a more peaceful pint try the lounge, known as the clubroom. Buses from Tamworth stop close by. ₳Q☺♿❀❶➡(Wilnecote)🚲♣P

Uttoxeter

Plough
Stafford Road, ST14 8DW (on A518)
🌣 12-midnight (11 Sun)
☎ (01889) 562381
Draught Bass; Marston's Pedigree; Theakston Old Peculier; guest beers Ⓗ
This rural inn was once part of the Loxley Park Estate: a framed document on display gives details of the sale of the pub in 1918. The central bar area leads to a snug, dining room and small pool room. The clientele is drawn mainly from the local community, supplemented by passing trade visiting the local racecourse and nearby Alton Towers. Three guest beers are usually available. ❀❶🚲♣P⅃

Weston

Woolpack
The Green, ST18 0JH (off A518)
🌣 11-11 (midnight Fri & Sat); 11.30-11 Sun
☎ (01889) 270238
Banks's Original, Bitter; Marston's Pedigree; guest beer Ⓗ
Known locally as the Inn on the Green, the Woolpack is a welcoming village local with an extensive dining area. Recorded as having been owned by the Bagot family in the 1730s, four bays inside reflect the pub's origins as a row of cottages. Over the years it has been thoughtfully extended while retaining low ceilings and the original bar area. ₳❀❶❶▲🚲♣P⅃

Whiston

Swan
ST19 5QH (in Penkridge turn off A449 at George & Fox pub) OS895144
🌣 12-3 (not Mon), 5-11; 12-11 Sun
☎ (01785) 716200
Holden's Mild, Bitter; guest beer Ⓗ
Although remotely situated, high quality, well-kept ales and superb food make this a thriving pub. Built in 1593, burnt down and rebuilt in 1711, the oldest part today is the small bar housing an inglenook fireplace. The lounge features an intriguing central double-sided log fire. Six acres of grounds include a children's obstacle course, aviary and rabbits. A good food menu features seasonal specialities and vegetarian meals. ₳❀❶❶▲🚲♣P⅃

Wigginton

Old Crown
120 Main Street, B79 9DW
🌣 11.30-3, 5-11.30 (12.30 Thu-Sat); 12-3, 7-11 Sun
☎ (01827) 64588
Marston's Burton Bitter, Pedigree; guest beers Ⓗ

Splendid country pub situated just five minutes' drive from Tamworth town centre and a pleasant walk from the No 2 bus stop servicing the north of the town. Good food is served at lunchtimes and evenings, alongside a beer range that now features three regularly-changing guests (from the Marston's range) selected by the customers. The pub has an attractive garden that is popular on summer evenings and weekends. ❀❶❶🚲♣P

Wilnecote

Globe Inn
91 Watling Street, B77 5BA
🌣 11-3, 7-11; 12-10.30 Sun
☎ (01827) 280885
Marston's Pedigree Ⓗ
A real community alehouse where a warm welcome is guaranteed, this regular Guide entry is renowned locally for the quality of its Pedigree. A one-room, cosy, L-shaped pub, it supports local sports in the form of darts, dominoes and football teams. Situated on the ancient Roman road (old A5), it is a 15-minute walk from Wilnecote railway station and two other frequent Guide entries, the Bulls Head and Railway Inn. ❀♣

Wolstanton

New Smithy
Church Lane, ST5 0EH
🌣 12 (11 Sat)-11; 12-10.30 Sun
☎ (01782) 740467
Everards Beacon, Tiger; Hop Back Crop Circle; Marston's Pedigree; guest beers Ⓗ
Visitors find it hard to believe that this village pub was once threatened with demolition until a band of locals successfully fought to save it. With good management and a guest beer policy that encompasses a wide range of brewers, the pub is popular with all ages and can be busy especially at the weekend. It is the first regular outlet for the Hop Back Brewery in the area. ❀🚲♠P⅃

Wrinehill

Crown Inn
Den Lane, CW3 9BT (off A531 between Newcastle and Crewe)
🌣 12-3 (not Mon), 6-11; 12-4, 6-10.30 Sun
☎ (01270) 820472
Adnams Bitter; Jennings Bitter; Marston's Burton Bitter, Pedigree; Taylor Landlord; guest beer Ⓗ
Busy, family-owned village free house with a commitment to real ale. No pool, TV or games machines spoil the peace. The excellent, varied menu includes steaks, fresh fish, vegetarian and vegan options. There are two open fires in the comfortable lounge bar. It won the Britain in Bloom regional gold award 2003-6. Bus 85A (Newcastle-Crewe, hourly) stops nearby. ₳Q❀❶🚲P

Hand & Trumpet
Main Road, CW3 9BJ (on A531 between Newcastle and Crewe)
🌣 12-11 (10.30 Sun)
☎ (01270) 820048 ⊕ handandtrumpet-wrinehill.co.uk

Caledonian Deuchars IPA; Thwaites Original; Taylor Landlord; guest beers Ⓗ

Owned by small pubco Brunning & Price, this long-closed pub has now been splendidly refurbished. It offers three regular cask ales and three guests, usually from local independent breweries, 65 whiskies and 12 rums. The spacious, light interior is simply furnished and divides into five distinct areas including the library room and garden room. The deck area overlooks a large pond and lawn. Walkers are welcome; the pub is dog-friendly. A full menu is served all day with home-made pies and puddings and vegetarian options. ⚜Q✿ⓒ➊⬆️Ⓟ⬏

Yoxall

Golden Cup
Main Street, DE13 8NQ (on A515)

✪ 12-3, 5-midnight (1am Fri); 12-1am Sat; 12-11.30 Sun

☎ (01543) 472295 ⊕ thegoldencup.com

Marston's Pedigree; guest beer Ⓗ

Impressive family-run 300-year-old inn at the centre of the village, opposite St Peter's church, bedecked with attractive floral displays for much of the year. The smart L-shaped lounge caters for diners, with an extensive menu on offer. The public bar features aphorisms on the walls, and some colourful new murals with a classical theme enhance the men's toilet! The award-winning pub gardens stretch down to the River Swarbourn and include a camping area (for caravans and motor-homes only).

⚜✿🚲ⓒ➊Ⓖ⬆️🅿️

Marston's Old Empire, brewed in Burton upon Trent, Staffordshire.

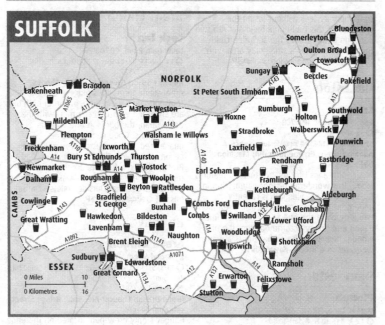

SUFFOLK

NORFOLK

Blundeston
Somerleyton
Oulton Broad
Lowestoft
Bungay • Beccles
Pakefield
Lakenheath • Brandon
St Peter South Elmham
Hoxne
Rumburgh
Southwold
Holton
Mildenhall
Flempton
Walsham le Willows
Stradbroke
Walberswick
Freckenham
Ixworth
Laxfield
Dunwich
Bury St Edmunds • Thurston
Rendham
Eastbridge
Newmarket
Tostock
Earl Soham
Dalham
Rougham
Woolpit
Cowlinge
Beyton • Rattlesden
Framlingham
Kettleburgh
Aldeburgh
Bradfield
St George
Buxhall
Combs Ford
Charsfield
Little Glemham
Great Wratting
Hawkedon
Bildeston
Combs
Swilland
Lower Ufford
Lavenham
Naughton
Woodbridge
Brent Eleigh
Ipswich
Shottisham
Sudbury • Edwardstone
Ramsholt
ESSEX
Great Cornard
Erwarton
Felixstowe
Stutton

CAMBS

0 Miles 10
0 Kilometres 16

Aldeburgh

Mill Inn

Market Cross Place, IP15 5BJ (opp Moot Hall)
🕐 11-11 (11-3, 6-11 winter); 11-11 Fri & Sat; 12-10.30 Sun
☎ (01728) 452563 🌐 themillinnaldeburgh.com
Adnams Bitter, Broadside, seasonal beers H
In a superb location across the road from the 17th century Moot Hall, close to the fishermens huts on the shingle beach, the pub is popular with locals, including members of the lifeboat crew, and tourists. After a stroll along the beach to view the controversial scallops it is the perfect place to stop for refreshments. The restaurant is a showcase for locally caught fish and offers themed food evenings. Folk music sessions are once a month on Sunday. Q❀♻♦❍▲☐♦

White Hart

222 High Street, IP15 5AJ
🕐 11.30-11; 12-10.30 Sun
☎ (01728) 453205
Adnams Bitter, Explorer, Broadside, seasonal beers H
Plenty of nautical memorabilia adorns this single room bar which used to be the public reading room. Next door to the town's renowned fish and chip shop and a few yards from the beach, it is popular with tourists and many locals. Alterations underway include the conversion of private rooms next door into an additional drinking area and access to an enclosed garden at the rear. Occasional live music is hosted on a Thursday. ♨Q❀&

Beccles

Bear & Bells

Old Market, NR34 9AP (adjacent to bus station)
🕐 11.30-3, 5.30-11; 12-3, 7-10.30 Sun
☎ (01502) 712291

Adnams Bitter; Greene King IPA; guest beers H
Comfortable Victorian pub on a site which has supported licensed premises since the 16th century and possibly earlier. Adjacent to the bus station and close to the town centre, it is also near the River Waveney, so is handy for visitors to the Broads. The central bar has a large drinking area and two separate dining areas with a good reputation for food (booking recommended). ❀♦🍴♻➜☐P

Beyton

Bear Inn

Tostock Road, IP30 9AG
🕐 12-2.30, 5-11; 12-4, 7-10.30 Sun
☎ (01359) 270249 🌐 thebearinn.net
Greene King IPA; Woodforde's Wherry; guest beers H
The Bear was rebuilt in 1900 after the original thatched inn burned down in a July thunderstorm – you can read an account of the event framed in the bar. The pub has been run by the same family since 1922; the current landlord has updated, creating a

INDEPENDENT BREWERIES

Adnams Southwold
Bartrams Rougham
Brandon Brandon
Cox & Holbrook Buxhall
Earl Soham Earl Soham
Green Dragon Bungay
Green Jack Lowestoft
Kings Head Bildeston
Mauldons Sudbury
Old Cannon Bury St Edmunds
Old Chimneys Market Weston
Oulton Oulton Broad
St Jude's Ipswich
St Peter's St Peter South Elmham

contemporary feel without losing the character of this traditional building with two bars and dining room. The secluded child-friendly garden has a small play area with climbing frame and swing. ⚌⚏⛺◻P

Bildeston

Crown
104 High Street, IP7 7EB
✪ 11-midnight
☎ (01449) 741843 ⊕ thebildestoncrown.co.uk
Adnams Bitter; Greene King IPA; Mauldons Dickens ⊞
Well worth a visit for its architectural features alone, this wonderful historic country inn in the centre of the village has recently undergone a no expenses spared restoration. While much of the building centres on fine dining and luxury accommodation, the olde-worlde, heavily timbered bar offers a warm welcome to drinkers. ⚌⛯⚏◻P

Blundeston

Plough
Market Lane, NR32 5AN
✪ 12-3, 7 (6.30 Fri & Sat)-10.30
☎ (01502) 730261
Adnams Bitter; guest beers ⊞
Charles Dickens mentioned this village inn in his book David Copperfield and not surprisingly the pub features a wealth of Dickensian memorabilia. Built in a mock-Tudor style with wood panelling and exposed beams, it has a main bar with separate dining area and pool room. The attractive garden is popular during the summer. ⚌⛯◑◻▭P

Bradfield St George

Fox & Hounds
Felsham Road, IP30 0AB
✪ 12-2.30, 6-11; closed Mon; 12-2.30, 7-10.30 Sun
☎ (01284) 386379
Beer range varies ⊞
Beautifully restored Victorian free house and country restaurant on the village outskirts, close to the historic coppiced woodland of the Suffolk Wildlife Trust. The comfortable and attractive interior is fronted by a glazed dining area. The public bar has a woodblock floor, wood-burning stove and pine seating. Service throughout is excellent. ⚌⛯⚏◑P

Brandon

Bell
48 High Street, IP27 0AQ
✪ 11-11 (1am Fri & Sat); 12-11 Sun
☎ (01842) 810465
Beer range varies ⊞
High street local with its coaching inn origins still visible. Fine blocked-in 'tax windows', of which Brandon has many, are proudly displayed. The opening of Brandon Brewery 300 metres away has resulted in increased demand for real ale and extra pumps installed on the bar – the 'local brew' is usually available. The car park is accessed from Lode Street. ⛯⇌▭♣P⌐

Brent Eleigh

Cock Inn ☆
Lavenham Road, CO10 9PB
✪ 11-4, 6-11; 12-11 Sat; 12-10.30 Sun
☎ (01787) 247371
Adnams Bitter; Greene King IPA, Abbot ⊞
An absolute gem – this pub manages to transport you back in time. In winter both bars are snug and warm; in summer, with the doors open, the bar is at one with its surroundings. Good conversation is guaranteed – sit and listen, you will soon become involved. Close to Lavenham and the Brett Valley, comfortable accommodation is recommended. The pub is CAMROT approved (Campaign for Real Outside Toilets). Do not miss it! Q⛯⚏◑◑⚏♣◻P

Bungay

Green Dragon
29 Broad Street, NR35 1EE
✪ 11-3, 5-11; 11-midnight Fri; 12-midnight Sat; 12-3, 7-11 Sun
☎ (01986) 892681
Green Dragon Chaucer Ale, Gold, Bridge Street, seasonal beer ⊞
Bungay's only brew pub, located on the edge of town with a public bar, lounge and a third quieter room that provides sanctuary when the bars are crowded. Green Dragon beers are brewed in outbuildings next to the car park at the rear. Occasional bottle-conditioned beers and strong ales are also brewed to complement the quality draught ales. ⚌⛝⛯⚏▲▭P

Bury St Edmunds

Elephant & Castle
2 Hospital Road, IP33 1JT
✪ 12-2.30, 5-11; 12-11 Sat; 12-11 Sun
☎ (01284) 755570
Greene King IPA, Abbot; guest beer ⊞
'The Trunk' is a Victorian street corner pub fronting on to Hospital Road. Access to the car park is from the main Parkway. Despite overlooking a busy junction, the two bars of this community pub have a village local feel to them. The rear bar is the hub for many games teams including football, darts, cribbage and dominoes. Outside is a large garden with children's play area. ⛯◑♣P

Old Cannon Brewery
86 Cannon Street, IP33 1JR
✪ 12-3 (not Mon), 5-11; 12-3, 7-10.30 Sun
☎ (01284) 768769 ⊕ oldcannonbrewery.co.uk
Adnams Bitter; Old Cannon Best Bitter, Gunner's Daughter, seasonal beers; guest beers ⊞
Formerly the St Edmunds Head, this excellent brew pub is on the site of the original Cannon Brewery. Now in private hands, it is a true free house. The Cannon serves good quality food (not Sun or Mon) and comfortable accommodation is available. ⚌Q⛯⚏◑◑⚏≠P⌐

Rose & Crown
48 Whiting Street, IP33 1NP
✪ 11.30-11 (11.30 Thu & Fri); 11.30-3, 7-11.30 Sat; 12-2.30, 7-11 Sun

☎ (01284) 755934
Greene King XX Mild, IPA, Abbot; guest beer ⊞
This listed red brick street corner pub with two bars and a rare off sales counter has been run by the same family for more than 30 years. Good value lunches are available Monday to Saturday in this homely hostelry. Situated in sight of Greene King's Westgate Brewery, it was Suffolk CAMRA Pub of the Year in 2005. ◖⌷⊟♣

Charsfield

Three Horseshoes
The Street, IP13 7PY
✪ 11.30-2.30 (not Thu), 7-11; 12-3, 7-10.30 Sun
☎ (01473) 737330
Adnams Bitter; guest beer ⊞
Small two-bar pub set in this pretty village which will be forever linked with the fictional village of Akenfield. The interior includes a comfortable lounge and dining area plus a livelier public bar with tiled floor, real fire and piano. Traditional food is served throughout the week. In-house darts matches and card games are played on Thursday evening. Regulars can be kept up to date with forthcoming events and guest beers by 'ale-mail' from the landlord.
🚲Q➷❀◖⊟⌷⊟♣P╘

Combs

Gardeners Arms
Moats Tye, IP14 2EY OS042550
✪ 12-2.30 (not Mon), 6-11; 12-2.30 Sun
☎ (01449) 673963
Greene King IPA; guest beers ⊞
Situated outside Combs village, this welcoming pub has one bar for drinking and the other mainly for dining, with a cheering open fire in winter. The drinking area has a homely feel, with an eclectic mix of furniture and decorative items, and a pool table. A wide menu makes this a good place to eat.
🚲❀◖♣♠P

Combs Ford

Gladstone Arms
2 Combs Ford, IP14 2AP (off Stowmarket to Needham Market road)
✪ 11-3, 5 (7 Sat)-11; 12-4, 7-10.30 Sun
☎ (01449) 612339
Adnams Bitter, Broadside; guest beer ⊞
Situated half a mile from the centre of Stowmarket, this Adnams house serves consistently good beer. The interior is divided into distinctive drinking, games and dining areas; outside the attractive beer garden beside a small stream is popular in fine weather. Good value food includes several vegetarian options; however a favourite is the steak and kidney pudding – a real filler! No food is served on Sunday or Monday evenings.
🚲❀◖⌷⊟P

Cowlinge

Three Tuns
Queens Street, CA8 9QD (left off A143 6 miles N of Haverhill)

✪ 12-11 (later Fri & Sat); 12-10.30 Sun
☎ (01440) 821847
Beer range varies ⊞
Dating from the 16th century, this gem can be hard to find but is well worth seeking out. Welcoming fires and comfortable sofas in the beamed bar, together with good conversation, make this pub a pleasure to visit. Bar snacks and more substantial meals are available. Up to four beers are on handpump, mainly sourced from independent breweries. A beer festival is held in summer, live music and quiz nights also feature. 🚲Q❀◖⌷P

Dalham

Affleck Arms
Brookside, CB8 8TG
✪ 5-11; 12-3, 6.30-11 Sat; 12-10.30 Sun
☎ (01638) 500306
Adnams Bitter; Greene King IPA; guest beers ⊞
A regular in the Guide, with a friendly atmosphere that encourages conversation, the Affleck is always well worth a visit. It offers four well-kept beers and exceptional food, home made and reasonably priced. The restaurant is recommended (booking essential) and the bar menu is excellent too. The two guest beers are usually from small breweries or micros. A rear patio and front garden overlooking the brook provide space for alfresco dining and drinking. 🚲❀⌷◖&P

Dunwich

Ship
St James Street, IP17 3DT
✪ 11-11; 12-10.30 Sun
☎ (01728) 648219 ⊕ shipinndunwich.co.uk
Adnams Bitter, Broadside; guest beer ⊞
Highly popular and characterful pub close to the beach in this historic town which has mostly been lost to the North Sea. The bar has a nautical theme while the rest of the building including the conservatory is devoted to dining. Food is traditional, locally sourced and includes fresh fish and a Sunday roast. Darts and board games are played on quieter evenings. There is seating outside and an enclosed garden at the back. Ten letting rooms are available. 🚲Q➷❀⌷◖▲⊟♣P╘

Earl Soham

Victoria
The Street, IP13 7RL (on A1120)
✪ 11.30-3, 6-11; 12-3, 7-10.30 Sun
☎ (01728) 685758
Earl Soham Victoria Bitter, Albert Ale, seasonal beers ⊞
Splendid timeless and unchanging pub set back from the road behind a small green. Simple wood furnishings, bare floorboards and an open fire create a traditional atmosphere. The excellent beer is brewed a few metres away in the village. Home made, good value meals are available from a varied menu at lunchtime and in the evening. The pub can be busy at times but is definitely worth a visit.
🚲Q➷❀◖▲⊟♣P

Eastbridge

Eel's Foot
Leiston Road, IP16 4SN (near entrance to Minsmere nature reserve)
☼ 12-3, 6-11; 11-midnight Sat; 12-10.30 Sun
☎ (01728) 830154 ⊕ theeelsfootinn.co.uk
Adnams Bitter, Explorer, Broadside, seasonal beers Ⓗ
Wonderfully cosy inn with an olde-worlde charm, popular with locals as well as walkers and birdwatchers visiting the nearby RSPB reserve at Minsmere. Local musicians play on Thursday evening and a traditional folk night is hosted on the last Sunday of the month where you are welcome to join in the chorus of an old sea shanty or two. Excellent home cooked, locally sourced food is available and there is a large garden. Everything a country pub should be! ⚲⏃❀⇦❶Ⓓ&Å♣P

Edwardstone

White Horse
Mill Green, CO10 5PX OS951429
☼ 12-3 (Sat & Sun only), 5-11
☎ (01787) 211211
Adnams Bitter; Greene King IPA; guest beers Ⓗ
Well off the beaten track, this lovely rural free house is an ideal holiday base. Camping & Caravan Club approved, it also has two self-catering chalets. Mild has long been a favourite in the bar here and one guest beer is always a dark ale. Regular beer festivals are popular locally and the pub opens late when trade demands. Recently the owner has erected a windmill to power the pub, and eventually to supply some power to the National Grid. A source of much interest! ⚲Q❀⇦Ⓓ⊟♣☞P

Erwarton

Queen's Head
IP9 1LN OS215346
☼ 11-3, 6.30-11 (10.30 Sun)
☎ (01473) 787550
Adnams Bitter; Greene King IPA; guest beer Ⓗ
Attractive two-bar pub with splendid views of the Stour estuary, popular with local ramblers. Exposed beams and woodwork can be seen in both bars and the split level lounge/restaurant area which leads to the conservatory. Interesting local pictures adorn the walls. Fresh, locally sourced food features on the menu whenever possible, as well as various specials listed on a board. The public bar is home to the local men's and women's darts teams, and crib is also played. ⚲Q⏃❀Ⓓ&ÅⓇ♣P

Felixstowe (Walton)

Half Moon
303 Walton High Street, IP11 9QL
☼ 12-2.30 (not Mon), 5-11; 12-11 Sat; 12-3, 7-10.30 Sun
☎ (01394) 216009
Adnams Bitter, Broadside; guest beer Ⓗ
Traditional community pub that retains the feel of a bygone era, when all that was needed was good ale, good company and a good landlord. This pub offers all this and more with quiz nights, darts and a selection of books for customers to read. A meeting place for local groups of all kinds, buses stop right outside the door. There are no gaming machines or music. Look for the 'word of the day' puzzle. ⚲Q❀Ⓖ⊟♣P☞

Flempton

Greyhound
The Green, IP28 6EL
☼ 11.30-3, 5-midnight; 12-4, 7-midnight Sun
☎ (01284) 728400
Greene King IPA; guest beers Ⓗ
Traditional pub on an attractive village green, neatly tucked away behind the church. Recently it has become 'ex-Greene King' so a more adventurous beer range is likely to develop. This is a quiet village so most of the trade is local or passing, but folk nights and Morris dancing in summer are popular. Close to local attractions at Lackford Lakes (RSPB) and West Stow Country Park with its replica Saxon village, the Greyhound is good for a post-visit pint. ⚲❀⇦Ⓓ⊟♣☞

Framlingham

Station
Station Road, IP13 9EE (on B1116)
☼ 12-3, 5 (7 Sun)-11
☎ (01728) 723455 ⊕ thestationhotel.net
Earl Soham Gannett Mild, Victoria Bitter, Albert Ale; guest beers Ⓗ
Friendly and cosy bar set in a former station buffet built in 1859 – the branch line closed in 1963. The room is dominated by the bar counter which features a classic set of fine Edwardian handpumps. Very popular at weekends, the pub is renowned for locally sourced, freshly prepared food and an interesting range of quality wines. A small second snug leads to an enclosed patio behind the building. Well worth a visit, especially as the town still has a reasonable bus service. ⚲Q⏃❀Ⓓ⊟P

Freckenham

Golden Boar Inn
IP28 8HZ (on B1102 from Mildenhall)
☼ 12-11 (4.30 Sun)
☎ (01638) 723000
Adnams Bitter; Taylor Landlord; guest beers Ⓗ
Superbly remodelled old coaching inn retaining many interesting original features. The bar area is spacious and a new restaurant area dominates the back of the pub. Excellent meals are served made with fresh ingredients. Three handpumps dispense ale in winter and four in summer. The guest beers normally alternate between Woodforde's Wherry and an Adnams brew. ❀⇦Ⓓ&P☞

Great Cornard

Five Bells
63 Bures Road, CO10 0HU
☼ 11-midnight (1am Sat; 11.30 Sun)
☎ (01787) 379016 ⊕ 5bells.co.uk

Greene King XX Mild, IPA, Abbot, Old Speckled Hen ⒣
Friendly community ale house near Great Cornard church (home of the five bells) on the main Sudbury to Bures road. The pub fields several teams playing traditional games including chess and backgammon plus some rarer ones such as petanque and uckers. Live music usually plays on a Friday. The landlord is Cask Marque accredited. ⌂Q⏳❀⒟⅊⎕♣P⅃

Great Wratting

Red Lion
School Road, CB9 7HA (on B1061 2 miles N of Haverhill)
🕑 11-2.30, 5-11; 11-1am Fri & Sat; 12-3, 7-10.30 Sun
☎ (01440) 783237
Adnams Bitter, Broadside, seasonal beers; guest beers ⒣
Good beer, a warm welcome and friendly conversation are the mainstay of this traditional village local, but watch out for the whale's jawbone that you pass through as you enter the front door. Take a look at the amazing collection of copper and brass while sampling the Adnams beers or an occasional guest. Good food is served in the bar and restaurant. With a huge back garden containing plenty to keep children occupied, the pub is ideal for families in summer. ⌂❀⒟P

Hawkedon

Queen's Head
Rede Road, IP29 4NN
🕑 5 (12 Sat)-11; 12-10.30 Sun
☎ (01284) 789218
Adnams Bitter; Greene King IPA; guest beers ⒣
With up to six cask ales and a strong community spirit, it is no wonder this was local CAMRA Pub of the Year 2007. The July beer festival is an event not to be missed, along with other entertainment such as live music, sporting events and theatre suppers. For summer there is a huge back garden and in winter an enormous fire blazes in the bar. The food, usually available only at weekends, is imaginative and very good. ⌂Q❀⒟⚲♣♦P⅃

Holton

Lord Nelson
Mill Road, IP19 8PP
🕑 11.30-3, 6.30-12; 12-3, 7-11 Sun
☎ (01986) 873275
Adnams Bitter; Taylor Landlord; guest beer ⒣
Traditional village local with a warm welcome for all customers, regulars and visitors. The interior is divided into two bars, one with a pool table and the other for dining and drinking. Sunday roast is a speciality – booking is advisable. Seafaring artefacts and Nelson memorabilia adorn the walls and ceiling. There is a large garden and ample parking. ❀⒟⅊♣♦P

Hoxne

Swan
Low Street, IP21 5AS
🕑 11-3, 6-11; 12-10.30 Sun
☎ (01379) 668275 ⊕ hoxneswan.co.uk
Adnams Bitter, Broadside; Woodforde's Wherry; guest beer ⒣
This 15th century pub has a colourful history – originally the home of the Bishop of Norwich and at one time a brothel. The pub is a mix of small rooms with an open fire. Outside is a large garden beside a small stream and ample car parking. An annual beer festival is held in early June (check website for details) with music from local groups. Excellent home cooked food is prepared with local produce in season. ⌂Q⏳❀⒟⎕♣P

Ipswich

Dales
216 Dales Road, IP1 4JY
🕑 11-2.30, 4.30 (6 Sat)-11; 12-2.30, 7-11 Sun
☎ (01473) 250024 ⊕ thedalespub.com
Adnams Bitter; Greene King IPA; guest beers ⒣
Modern and popular two-room estate pub serving at least four ales, always including a local interest. Black Sheep Best Bitter and Woodforde's Admiral's Reserve often feature on the guest list. A good selection of pub meals is available, some old favourites and some innovative new ideas, complemented by home-cooked specials that change daily. A comfortable garden and patio are pleasant in summer. Q❀⒟⚲⅊⎕P⅃

Dove Street Inn
St Helens Street, IP4 2LA
🕑 12-10.45
☎ (01473) 211270 ⊕ dovestreetinn.co.uk
Adnams Broadside; Crouch Vale Brewers Gold; Fuller's London Pride; Mighty Oak Oscar Wilde; Woodforde's Wherry; guest beers ⒣
Popular three-roomed pub with a tiny front room, a larger back room with oak beams and a lively and friendly main bar, plus covered seating in an outside heated area. The beer range varies with milds, seasonals, unusual beers for the area, dark porters, stouts, bitters and ciders coming from near and far. Three popular beer festivals are held annually. Food includes hot and cold snacks, pies, curries, stews and vegetarian options plus summer barbecues. CAMRA East Anglian Pub of Year 2007 and one of the runner-ups in CAMRA's national Pub of the Year competition. ⚲⅊⎕♣♦⅃⌷

Fat Cat
288 Spring Road, IP4 5NL
🕑 12-11 (1am Fri & Sat)
☎ (01473) 726524 ⊕ fatcatipswich.co.uk
Adnams Bitter; ⒣ **Crouch Vale Brewers Gold; Fuller's London Pride;** Ⓖ **Woodforde's Wherry;** ⒣ **guest beers** Ⓖ
Always a joy to visit, this pub is a superb reconstruction of a basic bareboards local, decorated with original tin advertising signs, artefacts and posters, and free of music and games machines. A wide range of keenly priced guest ales is always on offer. Ever popular, the pub is particularly busy in

summer when you can relax in the garden or on the patio. No children under 14 or dogs are allowed. Q❀≢(Derby Rd)🚍(2, 75)♠

Greyhound
9 Henley Road, IP1 3SE
☼ 11-2.30, 5-11 (midnight Fri); 12-10.30 Sun
☎ (01473) 252862 ⊕ greyhound-ipswich.com
Adnams Bitter, Broadside, Explorer, seasonal beers; guest beers Ⓗ
Popular Adnams pub, a short walk from the town centre near the museum and Christchurch park. It has a cosy front bar, comfortable long side lounge and an outside drinking area for the summer. Since the present landlord took over this pub it has been in every issue of the Guide and he is justifiably proud of the pub's reputation. Do not miss it if you are visiting the town. Q❀❸⊅🚍♣P

Lord Nelson
81 Fore Street, IP4 1JZ
☼ 11-2.30, 5-11 (midnight Fri & Sat); 12-3, 7-10.30 Sun
☎ (01473) 254072 ⊕ ipswichlordnelson.com
Adnams Bitter, Explorer, Broadside, seasonal beers; guest beers Ⓖ
Situated in a small part of what remains of the historic port area, this is one of the town's finest pubs, attracting an interesting and diverse clientele including international travellers using the rejuvenated wet dock. Dating back to the 17th century and steeped in history, it retains a half-timbered front with dormer windows. An unusual gravity dispense system is used incorporating a row of old wooden casks to good effect and guaranteeing temperature-controlled real ale. Families are welcome. ❀❸⊅ᴪ≢♣

Mannings
8 Cornhill, IP4 1DD (next to town hall)
☼ 11 (5.30 Sun)-11
☎ (01473) 254170
Adnams Bitter, Broadside; Fuller's London Pride; guest beers Ⓗ
A gem of a pub, providing an oasis of calm in the town centre, especially on Friday and Saturday nights. Outdoor tables and chairs in the summer provide the ideal place to sit and watch the world go by. The ales are excellent quality and the pub is deservedly popular with local CAMRA members and Ipswich Town fans. ❀⊅ᴪ≢🚍ᴸ

Woolpack
1 Tuddenham Road, IP4 2SH
☼ 11.30-11 (11.30-3, 5-11 winter); 11.30-12.30am Fri & Sat; 12-10.30 Sun
☎ (01473) 253059
Adnams Bitter, Broadside; Black Sheep Best Bitter; Young's Bitter; guest beers Ⓗ
Despite its location a short walk from the town centre, next to Christchurch park, the Woolpack has the feel of a country pub. It comprises a tiny snug at the front, a large lounge with a roaring fire, a larger room at the back and a small public bar. Attracting a mixed clientele, it has a friendly, welcoming atmosphere. The drinking area at the front is popular in fine weather. Excellent home-cooked food is served (not Sun and Mon eve). ᴀQ❀⊅🚍Pᴸ

Ixworth

Greyhound
High Street, IP31 2HJ
☼ 11-3, 6-11; 12-3, 7-11 Sun
☎ (01359) 230887
Greene King XX Mild, IPA, Abbot; guest beers Ⓗ
Situated in Ixworth's pretty High Street, this traditional inn has three bars including a central snug. The heart of the building dates back to Tudor times. The pub is a rare outlet for XX Mild. Good value lunches and early evening meals are served in the restaurant. Dominoes, crib, darts and pool are played in leagues and for charity. ❀⊅🚍♣Pᴸ

Kettleburgh

Chequers
IP13 7JT
☼ 12-2.30, 6 (7 Sun)-11
☎ (01728) 723760 ⊕ thechequers.net
Greene King XX Mild, IPA; guest beers Ⓗ
Substantial single-bar pub built in 1913 to replace an earlier building destroyed by fire. An unusual arrangement of branches and lights adorns the ceiling and gives the bar much character. The landlord can usually be found having a friendly chat behind the bar. The large garden leading to the River Deben is an excellent place to while away some time on sunny days. The 19th-century Deben Brewery once stood on the same site. ᴀᴄ❀⊅ᴪᴰ&ᴀ🚍♣P

Lakenheath

Brewer's Tap
54 High Street, IP27 0AU (on B1112 N of Mildenhall)
☼ 12-midnight; 12-4.30, 7-12 Sun
☎ (01842) 862328
Beer range varies Ⓗ
A good find for real ale fans, this village centre pub is full of character and a true free house. Bigger than it looks from the front, it has a patio area at the back. Two to three handpumps offer local and national beers; happy hour is 5-6pm Monday to Thursday. Good lunches including traditional Sunday roasts are popular. Crib and darts are played. A public car park is nearby. Q❀⊅♣ᴸ

Lavenham

Angel Hotel
Market Place, CO10 9QZ
☼ 11-11; 12-10.30 Sun
☎ (01787) 247388 ⊕ theangelhotel.com
Adnams Bitter, Broadside; Greene King IPA; Nethergate Bitter Ⓗ
The Angel was first licensed in 1420 and stands in the centre of this historic village. It has been owned by the same family since 1990 and is popular with locals and visitors. Four local real ales are always on handpump and these, together with a good wine list, complement the food for which the Angel is renowned. Eight well-equipped en suite bedrooms and a stunning residents' sitting room make this a comfortable place to stay. ᴀQ❀🚪⊅&♣P

Laxfield

King's Head (Low House) ☆
Gorams Mill Lane, IP13 8DW
🕐 12-11 (12-3, 6-midnight winter); 12-midnight Sun
☎ (01986) 798395
Adnams Bitter, Broadside, seasonal beer; guest beer G

Classic, timeless, multi-roomed thatched pub with an enclosed garden, always worth a visit. The main room features listed settles around a small fireplace, with beer served on gravity direct from the tap room. The dining room offers an interesting menu of locally sourced food including a Sunday roast (no food Sun eve). Accommodation in a double room is available. The pub can be difficult to find – just walk through the churchyard and exit via lower street. ♨Q☞☆♿⏰◑₪♣ᑊᒷ

Little Glemham

Lion Inn
Main Road, IP13 0BA
🕐 12-2.30, 6-11; closed Mon; 12-3, 7-10.30 Sun
☎ (01728) 746505
Adnams Bitter, Broadside; guest beer H

This large open-plan pub is an oasis on the Main Road for families making their way to the Suffolk heritage coast. Food is traditional, home cooked and invariably locally sourced, as are the guest beers. Vegetarian dishes and a children's menu are available. Tuesday is quiz night. ♨☆◑₪P

Lower Ufford

White Lion
Lower Street, IP13 6DW OS299520
🕐 11.30-2.30, 6-11; closed Mon; 12-2.30 Sun
☎ (01394) 460770
Adnams Bitter, Broadside; Wells Bombardier; guest beer G

Unspoilt 16th-century house near the River Deben, popular with walkers and families. The owners pride themselves on their fresh home-cooked fare, made with locally sourced ingredients. Beers are served direct from the cask. The pub has a full calendar of events throughout the year, many of them taking place on the meadow next to it. ♨Q☆◑P

Lowestoft

Norman Warrior
Fir Lane, NR32 2RB
🕐 10.30-midnight (12.30am Fri & Sat); 12-11.30 Sun
☎ (01502) 561982
Greene King IPA; guest beers H

Large estate pub on the outskirts of town with two contrasting bars. The public bar has Sky TV, a pool table and dart board; the lounge is more comfortable and leads through to a spacious restaurant serving good food. Weekends are very popular and booking is recommended if dining. A beer from the Wolf Brewery is usually available. ☞☆◑⏰ᐸ≠(Oulton Broad North)₪♣P

Oak Tavern
Crown Street West, NR32 1SQ
🕐 10.30-11; 12-10.30 Sun

☎ (01502) 537246
Adnams Bitter; Greene King IPA; guest beers H

On the north side of town, this lively drinkers' pub is decorated with Belgian memorabilia. The open-plan bar divides into two areas with a pool table and Sky TV (showing sporting events only) at one end, and at the other four handpumps selling real ales including a dark beer during the winter. A large range of continental brews, mainly from Belgium, is also available. ☆≠₪♣P

Triangle Tavern
29 St Peters Street, NR32 1QA
🕐 11-11 (midnight Thu, 1am Fri & Sat); 12-10.30 Sun
☎ (01502) 582711 ⊕ thetriangletavern.co.uk
Green Jack Canary, Orange Wheat, Grasshopper, Gone Fishing, seasonal beers; H **guest beers** H/G

Advertised as England's most easterly brew pub, this lively town tavern, situated on Triangle Market, is owned by the Green Jack Brewery – winner of many awards. A comfortable front bar and back bar with juke box and pool table are joined by an alleyway decorated with brewery memorabilia. The brewery is attached at the back. Live music plays on Thursday and Friday evenings. ♨⏰≠₪♣

Market Weston

Mill Inn
Bury Road, IP22 2PD
🕐 12-3 (not Mon), 5-11; 12-3, 7-11 Sun
☎ (01359) 221018
Adnams Bitter; Greene King IPA; Old Chimneys Military Mild; guest beer H

Run by the same landlady for more than 10 years, this imposing white brick and flint inn is situated on the B1111 crossroads on the outskirts of the village. The large single-bar layout has a welcoming atmosphere with a good log fire in winter. Free of tie, this is the closest outlet for Old Chimneys Brewery on the other side of the village. An interesting range of beers complements the varied menu of home-made meals (no food Mon eve). ♨Q◑♣P

Mildenhall

Queen's Arms
42 Queensway, IP28 7JY
🕐 12-2.30, 5-11.30; 12-11.30 Fri-Sun
☎ (01638) 713657
Woodforde's Wherry; guest beers H

Comfortable and homely pub used as a community centre by locals. Extremely popular with real ale drinkers since being taken over by Admiral Taverns, four handpumps are in constant use. The landlord is a real ale enthusiast and holds an annual beer festival on August bank holiday when the cycle rally comes to town. A range of alternating Belgian beers is also stocked and real cider is occasionally available. Q☆♮◑♣P

Naughton

Wheelhouse
Whatfield Road, IP7 7BS (450m off B1078)

✪ 5 (4 Fri; 6 Sat)-11; 12-10.30 Sun
☎ (01449) 740496
Beer range varies Ⓗ
Mind your head when entering this delightful rural thatched pub with low beams in the main bar. In fact the traditionally tiled floor is actually below ground level and much lower now than it used to be. The more spacious public bar is noisier and leads to a games room with a pool table and darts. There is always an interesting selection of ales available. The garden is a pleasant place to relax on sunny days. ♨Q✿❀P

Newmarket

Five Bells

15 St Mary's Square, CB8 0HZ (behind Rookery shopping centre)
✪ 11-midnight (2am Fri & Sat); 12-11 Sun
☎ (01638) 602868
Courage Directors; Woodforde's Wherry; guest beers Ⓗ
Popular town local with a much improved beer range since becoming 'ex-Greene King'. Situated away from the busy high street, it has a lively atmosphere, especially when darts and petanque teams are visiting. The large garden houses the petanque terrain and holds regular barbecues in summer. Parking in front of pub is limited but there is a public car park 300 metres away. ♨✿╤⊟♣╚

Pakefield

Ship

95 Stradbroke Road, NR33 7HW
✪ 11-11; 12-10.30 Sun
☎ (01502) 562592
Oulton Ale, Bitter, Nautilus, Gone Fishing, seasonal beers Ⓗ
This renovated and refurbished inn was a replacement for the original pub which fell victim to coastal erosion. A spacious building with a modern interior, wood panelling and floors feature throughout. It has a large central bar servicing two separate rooms with an adjoining restaurant. As well as the Oulton ales, a selection of continental beers is also available. ❶⊟P

Ramsholt

Ramsholt Arms

Dock Road, IP12 3AB (signed off B1083)
✪ 11.30-11; 12-10.30 Sun
☎ (01394) 411229
Adnams Bitter, seasonal beers; guest beers Ⓗ
An isolated Victorian pub with a scenic setting on the banks of the River Deben, popular with walkers, sailors and bird watchers. Food is mostly locally sourced and features fish and vegetarian options. The pub is child and dog friendly. Local photographs commemorate a WWII aeroplane that crashed in the river while making a flight from a nearby airfield. ♨Q✿╤❶♣P

Rattlesden

Five Bells

High Street, IP30 0RA

✪ 12-midnight; 12-11.30 Sun
☎ (01449) 737373
Beer range varies Ⓗ
Set beside the church on the high road through the village, this is a good old Suffolk drinking house – few of its kind survive. Three well chosen ales on the bar are usually sourced direct from the breweries. The cosy single room has a games room on the lower level. ♨Q✿❀

Rendham

White Horse

Bruisyard Road, IP17 2AF
✪ 12-2.30, 6-11; 12-3, 7-10.30 Sun
☎ (01728) 663497
Earl Soham Victoria Bitter; Mauldons Suffolk Pride; Taylor Landlord; guest beers Ⓗ
Attractively furnished single-bar pub divided into two comfortable seating areas with a prominent fireplace. An annual beer festival is held on August bank holiday, quiz night is the first Monday of the month and other themed evenings are hosted. A varied food menu features locally sourced produce and includes a curry night on Thursday and fish and chip takeaway on Friday. Live music plays occasionally. ♨Q✿❶▲⊟♣P╚⊟

Rumburgh

Buck

Mill Road, IP19 0NT
✪ 11.45-3, 6-11; 12-3, 7-10.30 Sun
☎ (01986) 785257
Adnams Bitter, seasonal beers; guest beers Ⓗ
Originally this inn and the parish church were part of a Benedictine priory. The historic building has been refurbished and extended to create a number of interlinked areas including dining and games rooms. A popular local at the heart of village life, it has a good reputation for food (booking advisable). Guest beers are from local micros. Outside there is a small enclosed garden with an aviary. ✿❶╜▲⊟♣P

St Peter South Elmham

St Peter's Hall

NR35 1NQ (follow sign from A144 or B1062) OS336854
✪ 11-3, 6-11; 11-11 Sat; 12-2.30 Sun
☎ (01986) 782322 ⊕ stpetersbrewery.co.uk
St Peters range Ⓗ
A 15th-century moated farmhouse conversion using architectural salvage materials. The interior is mainly from the 17th and 18th century. There are two drinking areas downstairs plus another upstairs. There is a large dining room where good organic food is served whenever possible (booking recommended). The brewery is across the courtyard in former agricultural buildings with a shop attached. ♨Q✿❶♣P

Shottisham

Sorrel Horse

Hollesley Road, IP12 3HD (in village just off B1083) OS320446

✪ 12-3, 6-11; 12-11 Sat; 12-10.30 Sun
☎ (01394) 411617 ⊕ sorrelhorseinn.co.uk
Adnams Bitter; Greene King IPA; guest beers G
Well worth seeking out, this picturesque
thatched two-bar pub dispenses its beer by
gravity, direct from the casks. Traditional food,
mostly home made including vegetarian
options, is available. Bar billiards can be
played. Accompanied dogs and horses are
welcome (there is a paddock for the latter
nearby). Quiz and folk sessions rotate during
the week. But behave yourself, there are
stocks in the garden! ▲Q✿❀①⊟⅁🖂♣P⁻

Somerleyton

Duke's Head
Slugs Lane, NR32 5QX
✪ 11-3, 6-11 (11-11 Sat & summer); 12-10.30 Sun
☎ (01502) 730281 ⊕ somerleyton.co.uk
Adnams Bitter; Greene King IPA; guest beers H
Convenient for river users, railway travellers
and ramblers, this large pub overlooks the
marshes and River Waveney. An open
fireplace separates the lounge and public bar.
The comfortable lounge and dining area lead
through to the garden room restaurant which
has a good reputation and features local
produce (booking advised). A converted barn
in the attractive grounds is used for regular
musical events featuring local artists, and
occasional beer festivals. Guest beers are
sourced from local micros. ▲✿①⊟▲≠🖂P

Southwold

Lord Nelson
42 East Street, IP18 6EJ
✪ 10.30-11; 12-10.30 Sun
☎ (01502) 722079
**Adnams Bitter, Broadside, seasonal beers; guest
beers** H
Always a busy and lively pub, popular with
both locals and visitors, next to the Sailor's
Reading Room museum. It offers three
drinking areas and children are welcome in a
side room. The main bar is flagstoned and has
an open fire during the winter months. The
pub is renowned for its good value food and
full range of Adnams beers. The nearby cliff
top enjoys fine coastal views. ▲➢✿①▲🖂

Stradbroke

Queen's Head
Queens Street, IP21 5HG
✪ 12-midnight (1am Fri & Sat)
☎ (01379) 384384
**Adnams Bitter; Greene King IPA; Woodforde's
Wherry; guest beer** H
Large timber-framed pub close to the centre
of the village. Good food is available
throughout the day, attracting local people
and walkers alike. A large jazz festival (see
festival.stradbroke.org.uk) is held annually
during the second weekend in May in
conjunction with the pub's beer festival which
offers up to 30 beers. ▲Q➢✿①🖂♣P

Stutton

Gardeners Arms
Manningtree Road, IP9 2TG
✪ 12-3.30, 6-11.30 (not Mon eve)
☎ (01473) 328868

Adnams Bitter; Mighty Oak IPA; guest beers H
Cosy two-bar pub on the edge of this small
village, close to the River Stour and historic
Flatford Mill. An interesting collection of bric-
a-brac adorns the walls including saddlery,
musical instruments, framed posters and a
huge set of bellows from a former
blacksmith's. An interesting and varied menu
of home-prepared food is available. Crib and
darts are played and there is a bridge club on
Wednesday evening. Well-behaved children
are welcome in the pub and large patio
garden. ▲Q➢✿①⅁▲🖂♣P

Sudbury

Waggon & Horses
Church Walk, Acton Square, CO10 1HJ
✪ 11-3.30, 7 (5 Wed-Fri)-11; 11-4, 7-11 Sat; 12-4,
7-10.30 Sun
☎ (01787) 312147
Greene King IPA; guest beers H
Back street local behind Market Hill. As well as
several drinking areas, there is a games area
with pool and darts and a small dining area.
Guest beers are from the Greene King list.
Food is home cooked with frequent special
menus (booking is advisable). The Phoenix
Court flats nearby are built on the site of the
defunct Phoenix Brewery, so named because
it arose from the ashes of a fire in 1890.
▲Q➢✿🛏①≠♣

Swilland

Moon & Mushroom
High Road, IP6 9LR
✪ 11.30-2.30 (not Mon), 6-11; 12-3, 7-10.30 Sun
☎ (01473) 785320
**Buffy's Norwich Terrier, Hopleaf; Crouch Vale
Brewers Gold; Nethergate Umbel Magna; Wolf
Bitter; Woodforde's Wherry; guest beer** G
Comfortable and cosy single-bar pub,
attractively decorated throughout with local
pictures, tiled floors and scrubbed tables. A
wide range of beers on gravity is always
available from the tap room. Home-cooked
food, usually including game, is served in the
bar and adjoining dining room. Occasional live
music and special themed nights are hosted.
Plenty of outdoor seating includes a small,
heated area for smokers. An hourly bus service
runs during the day. ▲➢✿①▲🖂♣P⁻

Thurston

Fox & Hounds
Barton Road, IP31 3QT
✪ 12-2.30, 5-11; 12-midnight Fri & Sat; 12-10.30 Sun
☎ (01359) 232228
Adnams Bitter; Greene King IPA; guest beers H
Now a regular in the Guide, this 1800s listed
building offers a large selection of ever
changing real ales on handpump, served by a
cheerful landlord and staff. It is situated
opposite the railway station on the Bury St

Edmunds to Ipswich line. Good home cooked food is served. The public bar has a pool table and TV and there is a quieter, more comfortable lounge. ✪🏠🍴◐🍽🅰🚭🚃♣P

Tostock

Gardeners Arms
Church Road, IP30 9PA
✪ 11.30-3, 6.30-11; 12-3.30, 7-10.30 Sun
☎ (01359) 270460
Greene King Abbot; guest beers 🅗
Situated in a charming village just two miles off the A14, this fine 14th-century building retains the original low beams and stone floor in the public bar where darts, pool and crib are played. The large lounge has a big open fireplace. Home-cooked food is served in the potting shed and tasty snacks throughout the pub. The large enclosed garden and patio are wonderful for families in the summer.
🏠✪◐🍽🚭♣P

Walberswick

Anchor
Main Street, IP18 6AU
✪ 11-4, 6-11; 11-11 Sat; 12-11 Sun
☎ (01502) 722112 🌐 anchoratwalberswick.com
Adnams Bitter, Broadside, seasonal beers 🅗
The current pub was built to replace the Blue Anchor in this idyllic coastal village. A welcoming local renowned for its food, it comprises three cosy wood-panelled rooms plus a restaurant run by the innovative chef, Sophie. The menu is committed to seasonal local produce and suggests a beer to drink with every dish. As well as the Adnams range there is an extensive real bottled beer selection from around the world. Family, walker and dog-friendly, the pub is accessible from Southwold via the footbridge.
🏠Q🚃🏠✪◐🍽🚭🅰P

Walsham-le-Willows

Blue Boar
The Street, IP31 3AA
✪ 12-2.30, 5-midnight; 12-1am Fri & Sat; 12-11.30 Sun
☎ (01359) 258533
Adnams Bitter; 🅗 **guest beers** 🅗/🅖
An ale house most of the time since 1420, this true free house offers a fine selection of ales on handpump and gravity and is a supporter of local breweries. Regular themed food nights and live music nights are hosted. A May bank holiday beer festival is held in a marquee in the garden. 🏠✪◐♣P

Woodbridge

Cherry Tree
73 Cumberland Street, IP12 4AG (on B1438)
✪ 7.30am (9am Sun)-11
☎ (01394) 384672 🌐 thecherrytreepub.co.uk
Adnams Bitter, Explorer, Broadside, seasonal beers; guest beers 🅗

Although the tree no longer remains, it can be seen in famous Suffolk painter Thomas Churchyard's picture inside the inn. Child and dog friendly, the pub offers traditional food served all day from breakfast onwards. Informal card games and quiz nights are held and family games are available to play. Mild is a permanent feature among the eight beers usually on offer and a twice-yearly beer festival is hosted. Accommodation is provided in a converted outdoor barn.
🏨✪🏠◐🚭🚃P🛏

Old Mariner
26 New Street, IP12 1DX
✪ 11-3, 5-11; 12-10.30 Sun
☎ (01394) 382679
Adnams Bitter; Black Sheep Best Bitter; Shepherd Neame Spitfire; Young's Bitter; guest beer 🅗
Traditional, lively and fairly basic bar close to the town centre, offering good food at lunchtime alongside a range of well-presented ales. The menu is based around casserole dishes, stews and occasional roasts. The front bar has scrubbed tables and a low ceiling while the rear bar is smarter and gives access to a separate seating area, garden and car park (off Castle Street). Some interesting artefacts adorn the pub walls.
🏨✪◐🚃🚭♣P🛏

Olde Bell & Steelyard
103 New Street, IP12 1DZ
✪ 12-3, 6-11.30; 12-11.30 Sat; 12-10.30 Sun
☎ (01394) 382933 🌐 yeoldbell.co.uk
Greene King IPA, Abbot, Old Speckled Hen; guest beer 🅗
Prominent, historic multi-roomed pub dating from about 1540. Recently a new bistro restaurant has been added alongside the main bar, narrow public bar and enclosed conservatory. The patio garden is popular in good weather. Live music is hosted twice a month on Saturday. The food is an eclectic mix of styles from traditional British favourites to globally inspired dishes, to suit all tastes. Outside is the listed steelyard that gave the pub its name. 🏨🚃✪◐🍽🚭🅰🚭🛏

Woolpit

Bull
The Street, IP30 9SA
✪ 11-3, 6-11 (midnight Fri); 12-4, 6-midnight Sat; 12-4, 7-10.30 Sun
☎ (01359) 240393
Adnams Bitter; guest beers 🅗
Large inn on the old Ipswich to Cambridge road through the village. A garden with a children's play area leads off the car park beside the pub. Inside, choose between the community minded front bar, hosting varied charity events throughout the year, a games room, comfortable conservatory and a spacious restaurant at the rear. Wholesome home-cooked food is served (not Sun eve).
🚃✪🏠◐🍽♣P

Bread is the staff of life, but beer is life itself.
Traditional

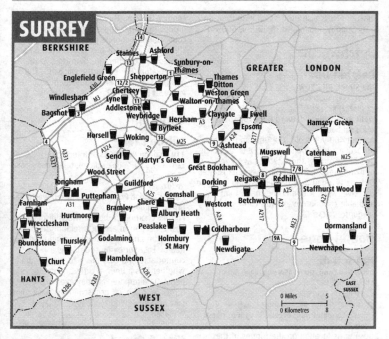

Albury Heath

William IV

Little London, GU5 9DG OS066467

🕐 11-3, 5.30-11; 12-3, 7-11 Sun

☎ (01483) 202685

**Flowers IPA; Hogs Back TEA; Surrey Hills
Ranmore Ale, Shere Drop** Ⓗ

Dating from the 16th century, this secluded pub offers beers from local micro-brewers. A wood-burning fire warms the flagstoned, wood-beamed bar in winter, while in summer there are picnic tables on the front lawn. There is a dining room up a few steps and a function room upstairs. Good value English home-made meals are served (not on Sun eve). Shove ha'penny is played here. ♨Q❀❀P

Ashford

Kings Fairway

91 Fordbridge Road, TW15 2SS (on B377)

🕐 12-11 (midnight Fri & Sat); 12-11 sun

☎ (01784) 424801

Fuller's London Pride; Young's Bitter; guest beers Ⓗ

A welcome return to the Guide for this pub after major refurbishment following a fire last year. It now feels a little larger and the six handpumps are able to offer three to four changing guests from the improved cellar. Food is now available all day. Quiz nights are Sunday and Wednesday. There is patio seating for warmer weather. Q❀❀🛏P

Ashtead

Woodman

238 Barnett Wood Lane, KT21 2DA OS180587

🕐 12-11 (midnight Thu-Sat); 12-11 Sun

☎ (01327) 274524

Fuller's London Pride; Shepherd Neame Spitfire; guest beers Ⓗ

Large, comfortable, 1930s roadhouse with newspapers and sofas, overlooking Ashtead Common. The layout is open plan with a long L-shaped bar warmed by gas fires and a real fire at the back. Regular guest ale promotions from the Ember Inns list include beers from micros. An extensive food menu is available daily. Children under 14 are not admitted. Beer gardens are front and back, with heaters for smokers. Quiz nights are Tuesday and Sunday. ♨❀❀🛏(479)P

Bagshot

Foresters Arms

173 London Road, GU19 5DH (on A30)

🕐 12-2.30, 5.30-midnight; 12-3, 7-11 Sun

☎ (01276) 472038

Courage Best Bitter; Fuller's London Pride; Hogs Back TEA; Taylor Dark Mild; guest beers Ⓗ

In every issue of the Guide for the last 10 years since the arrival of the present licensees, this traditional rural pub is renowned for its range of well-kept cask ales and good food ranging from sandwiches to roasts. The pub runs a keen golf society and has installed a two-bay practice golf net at the back. The adjoining skittle alley with its own bar is popular with skittles groups and for private functions. It is also used as an extension on busy Sunday quiz nights. ⊛◑➤(34, 500)♣P

Betchworth

Dolphin Inn
The Street, RH3 7DW
☼ 11-11; 12-10.30 Sun
☎ (01737) 842288
Wells Bombardier; Young's Bitter, Special, seasonal beers Ⓗ
Around 400 years old, the Dolphin is in an attractive setting opposite the village church and blacksmith's. The interior has three drinking areas, with open fires and flagstones. Outside is a half acre garden leading down to the River Mole. Good home-made food is available (not Sun eve), with curries a local favourite. ▲Q⊛◑P

Boundstone

Bat & Ball
Bat & Ball Lane, GU10 4SA (via Upper Bourne Lane off Sandrock Hill Rd)
☼ 11-11; 12-10.30 Sun
☎ (01252) 792108 ⊕ thebatandball.co.uk
Fuller's London Pride; Greene King IPA; guest beers Ⓗ
Despite its location on the fringes of the suburbs, there is a real country feel to this superb pub. In fact it is easier to find on foot than by car – access is via steep steps off the road, but be warned it is unlit at night. The effort to get here is always worth it, however, for the guest beers. The bar area has terracotta floor tiles, wooden furniture and an open log fire. A conservatory is used as a family room and the sunny garden has children's play equipment. ▲Q⏎⊛◑♿➤P

Bramley

Jolly Farmer
High Street, GU5 0HB (on A281)
☼ 11-11; 12-10.30 Sun
☎ (01483) 893355 ⊕ jollyfarmer.co.uk
Beer range varies Ⓗ
An 18th-century coaching inn on the route from Littlehampton to Oxford, this genuine free house is full of character. The bar area contains much local-interest memorabilia as well as beer mats from now defunct breweries and a number of stuffed animals. The front is a delight, with hanging baskets full to overflowing in season. There are up to six real ales on offer, often from local Surrey and Sussex breweries. Well worth the short bus ride from Guildford. ▲⊛◑➤P

Byfleet

Plough
104 High Road, KT14 7QT (off A245)
☼ 11-3, 5-11; 12-5, 7-10.30 Sun
☎ (01932) 353257
Courage Best Bitter; Fuller's London Pride; guest beers Ⓗ
A bastion of real ale, this is one of the best free houses for miles around with seven ever-changing guest beers. A real pub in every sense, with two magnificent fires and 18th-

century timbers. There are large tables for groups to gather and enjoy the art of conversation – mobile phones are banned. Three drinking areas are served from an L-shaped bar. Children are permitted in the conservatory (enter via the car park). The garden is a haven of tranquillity in summer. ▲Q⊛◑➤(436)♣P

Caterham

Clifton Arms
110 Chaldon Road, CR3 5PH (on B2031)
☼ 11.30-2.30, 4-11 (midnight Fri); 12-3, 5-midnight Sat; 12-11 Sun
☎ (01883) 343525
Fuller's London Pride; Young's Bitter; Westerham British Bulldog Ⓗ
Former Charrington house which displays a vast collection of artefacts relating to local history and militaria complementing the nearby East Surrey Museum. It is a comfortable and cosy place to enjoy a drink, whether it is a beer, a cider or sometimes a perry. On alternate Saturday evenings there is a rock 'n' roll band or disco in the back room. Lunches are served Monday to Friday. ⊛◑➤♣P

King & Queen
34 High Street, CR3 5UA (on B2030)
☼ 11-11; 12-10.30 Sun
☎ (01883) 345438
Fuller's Chiswick, London Pride, ESB, seasonal beers Ⓗ
A drinkers' pub, this welcoming 400-year-old red brick and flint inn has evolved since the 1840s from three former cottages. It retains three distinct areas – a front bar facing the high street, a high-ceilinged wood-beamed middle room with inglenook, and a small lower level rear area leading to a patio garden. A side room has a dart board. One of Caterham's early ale houses, its name refers to Britain's only joint monarchy, William and Mary. No meals are served on Sunday. ▲⊛◑➤♣P⏚

Chertsey

Coach & Horses
14 St Anne's Road, KT16 9DG (on B375)
☼ 12-11; 12-3, 7-10.30 Sun
☎ (01932) 563085 ⊕ coachandhorseschertsey.co.uk
Fuller's Chiswick Bitter, London Pride, ESB Ⓗ
Pleasant tile-hung pub, a regular entry in the Guide, dedicated to the enjoyment of Fuller's three long-standing bitters. The food is good value traditional English during the week, giving way to beer and conversation at the weekend when the locals 'just want it to be like a pub'. The first Thursday of the month is quiz night and there are occasional games nights. Children are permitted only if dining. ▲Q⊛⇆◑➤♣P⏚

Crown Hotel
7 London Street, KT16 8AP
☼ 10-midnight (1am Sat); 12-midnight Sun
☎ (01932) 564657 ⊕ crownchertsey.co.uk
Wells Bombardier; Young's Bitter; guest beers Ⓗ

Imposing Victorian former coaching inn. The present building dates from 1899 but there was an inn on this site at least 100 years earlier. The interior has two distinctive drinking areas which have escaped any drastic renovation and have a comfortable, lived-in feel. There is also a restaurant, conservatory and function room. Conversation is the main entertainment unless major sporting fixtures are being shown on the TV. Live jazz plays every second Tuesday. Guest beers come from the Wells & Young's list. ❧☆✍◑♦≠☷♣⌐

Churt

Crossways

Churt Road, GU10 2JE (on A287)
✪ 11-3.30, 5-11; 11-11 Fri & Sat; 12-4, 7-10.30 Sun
☎ (01428) 714323
Courage Best Bitter; Hop Back Crop Circle; Ringwood Fortyniner; Ⓗ **guest beers** Ⓖ
Situated on a busy road in good walking country, the Crossways attracts a good mix of locals, travellers and ramblers. The guest beers, usually around five at a time, are drawn straight from the cask in the cellar and four real ciders are on stillage behind the bar. Good, traditional home-cooked lunches are served Monday to Saturday. A popular beer festival is held every year offering up to 45 beers. Local CAMRA Pub of the Year for 2005 and 2006. Q☆◑♦▲☷(19)♣⌐P

Claygate

Foley Arms

106 Hare Lane, KT10 0LZ
✪ 11-midnight; 12-midnight sun
☎ (01372) 462021
Wells Bombardier; Young's Bitter, Special, seasonal beers Ⓗ
Run by a landlord with 20 years' experience and passionate about real ale, this traditional two-bar Victorian village pub was named after a family of local landowners. The buildings to the rear house a gym for Foley Boxing Club and there is also a spacious hall for hire. This is the venue for a Friday folk club which has won a BBC2 award. The large garden has a patio and children's play area. Local CAMRA Pub of the Year 2006. ⌂Q☆◑⌐☷(K3)♣⌐

Coldharbour

Plough Inn

Coldharbour Lane, RH5 6HD OS152441
✪ 11.30-11 (midnight Fri & Sat); 12-11 Sun
☎ (01306) 711793 ● ploughinn.com
Leith Hill Hoppily Ever After, Crooked Furrow, Tallywhacker; Ringwood Old Thumper; Shepherd Neame Spitfire Ⓗ
Originally on a coaching route from London to the south coast, the pub dates from the 17th century. It is home to the Leith Hill Brewery which is in an outbuilding in the garden. There is also a refurbished barn which is used as a function room and a family room at weekends and in the summer. The pub may stay open after 11pm if busy. ⌂❧☆✍◑♣⌐P

Dorking

King's Arms

45 West Street, RH4 1BU (on A25 one-way system eastbound)
✪ 11-11 (11.30 Wed; midnight Fri & Sat); 11-11 Sun
☎ (01306) 883361
Fuller's London Pride; Greene King IPA; guest beers Ⓗ
Attractive 16th-century inn situated in a street renowned for its antique shops. The split-level bar with low beams and leaded lights has a variety of drinking areas. The cosy restaurant at the back serves evening meals only (not Sun or Mon). Food is served at lunchtime in the bar. Guest beers, usually two, are mostly sourced from micro-breweries and change frequently. On Wednesday and Sunday evenings live music is played. Monday is quiz night. ☆◑≠(West)☷P⌐

Old House at Home

24 West Street, RH4 1BY (on A25 one-way system eastbound)
✪ 11-11 (1am Fri, 2am Sat); 12-11 Sun
☎ (01306) 889664
Wells Bombardier; Young's Bitter, Special, seasonal beers Ⓗ
Originally two houses, dating in parts back to the 15th century, this one-bar pub divides into four areas. The landlord is a keen Chelsea supporter and there are several flat-screen TVs showing sporting events. Live music and karaoke are sometimes hosted on Sunday and Thursday. Outside is an attractive garden with a function room. Customers must be in the pub by 11pm to make use of the extended hours. ☆◑≠(West)☷⌐

Dormansland

Old House At Home

63 West Street, RH7 6QP (signed from village, off Dormans Road) OS402422
✪ 11.30-3.30, 6-midnight; 12-4, 7-midnight Sun
☎ (01342) 832117
Shepherd Neame Master Brew Bitter, Ⓗ **Kent's Best,** Ⓖ **Spitfire, seasonal beers** Ⓗ
Traditional old pub hidden on the western side of the village, with the main bar dating back to the 16th century and the bar at the side added later. The restaurant at the back serves good quality home-made food (no food Sun eve). There is a patio for outdoor drinking. Hours may vary and last entry is around 11.30pm. Awarded Shepherd Neame Food Pub of the Year in 2007. ⌂☆◑♣P

Plough Inn

44 Plough Road, RH7 6PS (just off B2028) OS406427
✪ 12-3, 5-11; 12-midnight Fri & Sat; 12-10.30 Sun
☎ (01342) 832933
Fuller's London Pride; Harveys Sussex Best Bitter Ⓗ
Large, traditional 14th-century pub with plenty of low wood beams and an inglenook. One side of the pub is set aside for diners, with a choice of Thai or traditional English pub food. The pleasant garden is popular in summer. Conveniently situated for nearby Lingfield racecourse. ⌂Q☆◑♿☷(236, 409)P

Englefield Green

Happy Man
12 Harvest Road, TW20 0QS (off A30) OS997708
☼ 11-11 (midnight Fri & Sat); 12-10.30 Sun
☎ (01784) 433265
Hop Back Summer Lightning; guest beers Ⓗ
Popular, traditional ale house which was originally two Victorian cottages, converted around 125 years ago to a beer house to serve the labourers constructing nearby Royal Holloway College, one of the finest Victorian buildings outside London. The internal layout has barely changed and it still feels as though you are drinking in the landlord's parlour. A real back street local with an ever-changing beer range. ❀◐●⬗◲♣

Monkeys Forehead
Egham Hill, TW20 0BQ (opp Royal Holloway College)
☼ 10-11.30 (midnight Fri & Sat); 10-11 Sun
☎ (01784) 432164 ⊕ themonkeysforehead.co.uk
Beer range varies Ⓗ
The former Royal Ascot was purchased by an enterprising partnership in 2006 and is now a 'sports bar' (don't let that put you off!) free of tie. The landlord is passionate about real ale, so much so that 'smooth' beers do not even appear on the bar. Real ale tasting evenings are held to encourage local students off fizzy lager. Ideally situated for those en-route to Wentworth or Ascot races, good value food is served all day. Guest brewers might include Triple fff, Downton, Hogs Back and Hop Back. ❀◐&◲P⌐

Epsom

Barley Mow
12 Pikes Hill, KT17 4EA (off A2022, Upper High St)
☼ 12-11 (midnight Fri & Sat); 12-10.30 Sun
☎ (01372) 721044
Fuller's Discovery, London Pride, ESB, seasonal beers Ⓗ
Originally three cottages built for gravel workers, they were converted into a pub some years ago and extended more recently. Fuller's acquired the pub from Charrington in 1979 and has refurbished throughout, replacing the conservatory with a lounge that leads to the garden. The single bar has seating areas at both ends. Framed photographs of old Epsom decorate the walls. Upper High Street car park is nearby. ♨❀◐&⬗◲♣⌐

Ewell

Famous Green Man
71 High Street, KT17 1RX (off B2200)
☼ 12-11 (midnight Fri & Sat); 12-10.30 Sun
☎ (020) 8393 9719 ⊕ famousgreenman.com
Adnams Bitter; Shepherd Neame Spitfire; Wells Bombardier; guest beers Ⓗ
This pub has seen a dramatic turnaround in recent years. It is now smart, clean and vibrant, and consequently has grown in popularity. Built around 1934 to replace a previous 1890s building, it has three interconnecting rooms served by a central bar, with a separate dining area at the rear. Two guest beers come from a variety of breweries. ⏃❀◐⬗&◲P⌐

Wheatsheaf
34 Kingston Road, KT17 2AA
☼ 11-11 (midnight Fri & Sat); 12-10.30 Sun
☎ (020) 8393 2879
Wells Bombardier; Young's Bitter; guest beers Ⓗ
Well-run, traditional local pub with one bar and two drinking areas. Built in 1858, an ale house has been on this site since 1456. Behind the bar are leaded windows remembering the long-gone Isleworth Brewery. Both areas have open fires and the walls are decorated with bygone local scenes and pictures of local drinkers. The large rear garden holds occasional barbecues and the pub's frontage has impressive floral displays in summer. No meals served Sunday. ❀◐≈◲♣⌐

Farnham

Lamb
43 Abbey Street, GU9 7RJ (off A287)
☼ 11-2.30, 5-11; 11-midnight Fri & Sat; 12-10.30 Sun
☎ (01252) 714133
Shepherd Neame Kent's Best, Ⓗ **Spitfire,** Ⓖ **seasonal beers** Ⓗ/Ⓖ
Popular locals' pub in a quiet residential street between the station and town centre. It has a single bar with TV screens and a pool table at one end. Good live bands play on most Friday nights and the pub can become crowded. Outside is an attractive terrace at rooftop level. Although the pub is beer oriented, the food is excellent and great value (no food Tue eve or all day Sun). ♨❀◐≈◲♣⌐

Shepherd & Flock
22 Moor Park Lane, GU9 9JB (centre of roundabout at A31/A325 jct E of town)
☼ 11 (12 Sun)-11
☎ (01252) 716675 ⊕ shepherdandflock.com
Hogs Back TEA; Ringwood Old Thumper; guest beers Ⓗ
Situated on the largest inhabited roundabout in Europe, the interior has a long central bar, comfortable lounge and airy dining area (no food served Sun eve). The regular beers are supplemented by up to four guests including a low strength 'beer of the month', with local micros well represented. Quirky sheep knick-knacks can be spotted throughout the pub. There is a large seated area outside at the front where drinkers can watch the traffic and a more secluded garden to the rear. ♨❀◐&◲P⌐

William Cobbett
Bridge Square, GU9 7QR
☼ 11-11 (midnight Fri & Sat); 12-10.30 Sun
☎ (01252) 726281
Courage Best Bitter; Fuller's London Pride; guest beers Ⓗ
Birthplace of the 18th-century social reformer William Cobbett, the inn's flagstone floors and low beams testify to its 16th-century origins. The interior has several interlinked small areas downstairs (one with a football table) and a pool room upstairs with four tables. Although considered to be a student pub, it is in fact popular with all ages. The atmosphere is friendly and lively, particularly on music nights (live bands every Wednesday, jazz every other Tuesday) and at the weekend. ◐≈◲♣P⌐

Godalming

Jack Phillips

48-56 High Street, GU7 1DY
✪ 9-11 (midnight Thu; 1am Fri & Sat); 9-11 sun
☎ (01483) 521750
Courage Best Bitter, Directors; Hogs Back TEA; Marston's Pedigree; Shepherd Neame Spitfire; guest beers ⊞
Originally a supermarket, this pub is named after the ill-fated radio operator of the Titanic. Ten handpumps include four guest beers, with the emphasis on local breweries. The interior is narrow but deep, broken up by circular pillars, decorated in pastel shades. In summer the front opens up onto the pavement with seating out on the patio. Quiz night is Monday. ⏰❀◑≠⊟

Star

17 Church Street, GU7 1EL
✪ 11-3, 5-11; 11-1am Fri & Sat; 12-11 Sun
☎ (01483) 417717 ⊕ thestargodalming.co.uk
Greene King IPA, H&H Olde Trip; guest beers ⊞
This 400-year-old pub, situated on a delightful historic street in old Godalming, was originally a bakery. Five draught beers, three ciders and 15 Belgian beers can be enjoyed in a variety of drinking areas. The main bar is simple and traditional with low beams and a discrete alcove. Outside areas have gas heaters and there is a conservatory. The landlord hosts beer festivals at Easter and Hallowe'en in a marquee in the garden. ❀◑≠⊟◐

Gomshall

Compasses

50 Station Road, GU5 9LA (on A25)
✪ 11-11; 12-10.30 Sun
☎ (01483) 202506
Surrey Hills Ranmore Ale, Shere Drop, Gilt Complex (summer), Albury Ruby (winter); guest beers ⊞
Originally called God Encompasses, the name has contracted over time. The pub has two main areas: the bar with several small seating areas and the restaurant. Beers and ingredients for the home-made food are locally sourced. There is a large garden just the other side of the Tillingbourne river. The pub is reputed to have a friendly ghost who plays with the taps. Live music played on Friday night. ❀⇦◑≠⊟P⌐

Great Bookham

Anchor

101 Lower Road, KT23 4AH (off A246 via Eastwick Road)
✪ 11-3, 5.30-11; 12-3, 7-10.30 Sun
☎ (01372) 452429
Courage Best Bitter, Directors; guest beers ⊞
Despite additions in the 18th century, a map on the wall of the pub suggests that the Anchor dates originally from the 15th century. Grade II listed, this traditional local has beamed ceilings, exposed brick walls and wooden floors throughout, and an inglenook with a welcoming real fire in winter. The bar is adorned with hop bines. The landlord has been in residence since 1989. Good value meals are served at lunchtime Monday to

Saturday. Children are not allowed in the bar. ⌂Q❀⏰⊟(479)♣P⌐

Guildford

Keystone

3 Portsmouth Road, GU2 4BL (on A3100)
✪ 12-11 (midnight Fri & Sat); 12-7 Sun
☎ (01483) 575089 ⊕ thekeystone.co.uk
Black Sheep Best Bitter; Wadworth 6X; guest beers ⊞
Modern, comfortable over 21s town centre pub. The Keystone hosts many events throughout the year including barbecues, Morris dancing and hog roasts. Games and newspapers are available and there is a book swap on the windowsill. Excellent British food is served, featuring daily specials, all freshly made on the premises (no food Fri-Sun eve). Smoking is permitted outside in the heated and lit patio, covered by giant umbrellas. ❀◑≠⊟⌐

Three Pigeons

169 High Street, GU1 3AJ
✪ 11-11 (1am Fri & Sat); 12-10.30 Sun
☎ (01483) 374310
Draught Bass; Taylor Landlord; guest beers ⊞
Grade II listed M&B pub originally dating from 1755, rebuilt after a fire in 1906. It has a Jacobean façade and Art Nouveau ceiling in the ground floor bar. The first floor is reached by an open spiral staircase. Both bars are characteristically narrow but deep. A resident poltergeist is rumoured to frequent the building. Beers come from the Waverley range. ◑≠⊟

Varsity Bar

Egerton Road, University of Surrey, GU2 7XU
✪ 12-11 (8.30 Sat); 12-10.30 Sun
☎ (01483) 683226
Beer range varies ⊞
University sports bar open to all. The bar can be busy on match days (Wed and Sat) but quieter at other times. Three ever changing beers from near (Surrey Hills, Hogs Back) and far (Archers, Sharp's) are always available. Regular beer festivals and evenings focusing on beers from one brewery are held. Ales coming soon are displayed on a board by the bar. Sports matches are shown on the large-screen TV. Quiz night is the first Monday of the month. The food is good and burgers highly recommended. ❀◑⊟P

Hambledon

Merry Harriers

Hambledon Road, Rock Hill, GU8 4DR OS968392
✪ 11-3 (4 Sat), 6-11; 11-3, 7-10.30 Sun
☎ (01428) 682883
Greene King IPA; Hogs Back TEA; Hop Back Crop Circle; guest beers ⊞
Wonderful rural retreat in the depths of Surrey, owned by the same family for 40 years. Small, compact and unpretentious, it has a strong local community focus but warmly welcomes visitors including walkers. A collection of old chamber pots and stamped pint-measure ceramic mugs hangs from the ceiling. The traditional wooden Surrey slats have been

maintained. Food is excellent value (eve meals Fri and Sat only) and the sign outside warning of 'warm beer and lousy food' can be ignored. ⚨⏃☸⏿Ⅱ Å♣P

Hamsey Green

Good Companions

Limpsfield Road, CR6 9RH (on B269)
🕑 12-11.30 (midnight Fri & Sat); 12-11 Sun
☎ (020) 8657 6655 ⊕ thegoodcompanions.com
Westerham British Bulldog, seasonal beers Ⓗ
Dating from the 1930s, this large community establishment is split into a bar and restaurant with lounge area. Three beers come from the Westerham Brewery and food is available all day. The bar has a large-screen TV showing major sporting events and there is a pool table. Tuesday is 'open mic' night, there is live music or a disco on Saturday evening and Sunday is quiz night. See the website for forthcoming events. ☸⏿▮♿🚌(403)♣P⤙

Hersham

Royal George

130 Hersham Road, KT12 5QJ (off A244)
🕑 11-11 (midnight Fri & Sat); 12-11 Sun
☎ (01932) 220910
Wells Bombardier; Young's Bitter, Special Ⓗ
Built in 1964, this local has two spacious bars. A friendly atmosphere and a blazing fire in each bar make it a popular hostelry for all ages. The pub is named after a ship from the Napoleonic wars, which accounts for some of the pictures on the walls. A wide range of home-cooked food is available (not Sun eve). The pub raises a lot of money for charity and a quiz is held on Tuesday evening. Local CAMRA Pub of the Year 2007.
⚨Q☸⏿▮♿🚌(218)♣P⤙

Holmbury St Mary

King's Head

Pitland Street, RH5 6NP (off B2126) OS112442
🕑 12 (4 Mon)-11; 12-10.30 Sun
☎ (01306) 730282
Greene King IPA; King Horsham Best Bitter; Surrey Hills Shere Drop; guest beers Ⓗ
Tucked away in a side road, this excellent traditional local is easy to miss. The bar has several rooms and an open fireplace; hunting and shooting prints decorate the walls. A superb menu includes game (no eve meals Sun and Mon). Set in the midst of the Surrey Hills, this is a popular stop-off for walkers and mountain bikers. Beer festivals are held in late spring and August bank holiday.
⚨☸⏿🚌(21)P

Horsell

Plough

South Road, Cheapside, GU21 4JL
🕑 12-11 (midnight Fri & Sat); 12-10.30 Sun
☎ (01483) 714105 ⊕ theploughhorsell.co.uk
Wadworth 6X; guest beers Ⓗ
It is definitely worth heading out of suburbia to track down this wonderful rural retreat dating from the 1830s set among silver birch trees on the edge of Horsell Common. In good

walking territory, the friendly licensees welcome customers and their dogs. The pub has Scottish links, celebrating Burns Night and St Andrews Day, and offering a choice of more than 65 malt whiskies. Good home-made pies are a speciality. A charity fun day is hosted in August. ☸⏿🚌(73)P

Hurtmore

Squirrel

Hurtmore Road, GU7 2RN (off A3)
🕑 11-11; 12-10.30 Sun
☎ (01483) 860223 ⊕ thesquirrelinn.co.uk
Fuller's London Pride; guest beers Ⓗ
Comfortably furnished pub with two lounge areas, one with a TV showing sporting events. A varying real cider is served alongside three quality ales. There is a good choice of food ranging from bar snacks to main meals, including vegetarian dishes. Live bands play on alternate Saturdays in summer. Outside is the garden and heated patio. Hot air balloon flights are available here weather permitting.
⚨☸⏗⏿🚌(46)♣●P

Lyne

Royal Marine

Lyne Lane, KT16 0AN (off B386) OS012663
🕑 12-2.30, 5.30-11; 11-2.30, 6.30-11 Sat; 12-3 Sun
☎ (01932) 873900
Courage Best Bitter; Hogs Back TEA; guest beers Ⓗ
Comfortable, friendly village pub converted 160 years ago from two cottages. One of only six Royal Marine pubs in the country, the interior features much Marines memorabilia and a guest book for Marines past and present. The Lyne Mountain Rescue Team, a local fund-raising organisation, is based here. Guest beers are sourced from micros such as Hepworth, WJ King, Church End and Triple fff. Milds are often available during the summer. Local CAMRA Pub of the Year in 2006.
Q☸⏿🚌(P3)♣P

Martyr's Green

Black Swan

Old Lane, KT11 1NG OS089573
🕑 11-midnight (11 Sun)
☎ (01932) 862364
Adnams Bitter; Draught Bass; Surrey Hills Shere Drop; guest beers Ⓗ
Extensively rebuilt in 2006, this country pub is just two miles from the M25. The interior is modern, light and airy, open plan but divided into different areas. At the front is the informal bar area with brick fireplaces, the lounge to the left has comfy chairs and an open fire, a more formal dining area is to the rear (no eve meals Sun). Advanced booking for diners is advised. One or two guest beers often come from micros. Families are welcome.
⚨☸⏿♿P

Mugswell

Well House Inn

Chipstead Lane, CR5 3SQ OS258553
🕑 12-11 (10.30 Sun)

☎ (01737) 830640 ⊕ wellhouseinn.co.uk
Adnams Bitter; Cottage Golden Arrow; Fuller's London Pride; guest beers Ⓗ
First rate countryside pub, popular with walkers and dog friendly, with views over fields and woodland. The area gets its name from the well in the pub's garden, named St Margaret's or Mag's Well, mentioned in the Domesday Book. Inside the Grade II listed building are many curios and relics adorning the walls and ceiling. Good food is served in the restaurant and bar with generous portions (no eve meals Sun & Mon). The pub is reputed to be haunted by a monk called Harry. Quiz night is Tuesday. ▲⊛◑Ⓟ

Newchapel

Blacksmith's Head

Newchapel Road, RH7 6LE (on B2028, off A22)
🕐 11 (12 Sat)-3, 5.30 (6 Sat)-11; 12-3, 12-6 Sun
☎ (01342) 833697 ⊕ theblacksmithshead.co.uk
Fuller's London Pride; Harveys Sussex Best Bitter; guest beers Ⓗ
Built in the 1920s on the site of a former forge, this one-bar country free house has a restaurant area to the side and provides quality accommodation. Food is freshly prepared with restaurant, bar and tapas menus to choose from. Portuguese influences reflect the nationality of the licensees. Occasional quizzes are held and two regularly changing guest beers come from small independents or micros. ▲Q⊛◄◑Ⓛ▲♣Ⓟ

Newdigate

Surrey Oaks

Parkgate Road, RH5 5DZ (between Newdigate and Leigh) OS205436
🕐 11.30-2.30, 5.30-11; 11.30-3, 6-11 Sat; 12-10.30 Sun
☎ (01306) 631200 ⊕ surreyoaks.co.uk
Harveys Sussex Best Bitter; Surrey Hills Ranmore Ale; guest beers Ⓗ
A regular CAMRA award winner, the 'Soaks' continues to delight with its choice of three guest beers, mostly from micro-breweries. The central part of the bar, dating from the 16th century, has a low-beamed ceiling and flagstone floors. The dining room serves excellent home-cooked food (no eve meals Sun and Mon). Outside is a large garden and boules pitch. Beer festivals are held over the late spring and August bank holiday weekends. Local CAMRA Pub of the Year 2007. ▲Q⊛◑♣♠Ⓟ'╵

Peaslake

Hurtwood Inn

Walking Bottom, GU5 9RR OS086446
🕐 12-3, 5.30-11 (midnight Fri); 12-11 Sat & Sun
☎ (01306) 730851 ⊕ hurtwoodinnhotel.com
Hogs Back HBB, TEA; Surrey Hills Shere Drop; guest beers Ⓗ
The Hurtwood Bar at this three-star 17-bedroom hotel serves as a local for the village as well the bar for hotel guests and stop off for walkers in the beautiful surrounding countryside. Seating ranges from plush sofas to bar stools. There is a genuine 1960s Rock-Ola juke box. Food is served in the bar as well

as the restaurant. Ramblers are welcome but not muddy boots. ⊛◄◑Ⓛ(25)Ⓟ

Puttenham

Good Intent

The Street, GU3 1AR (off B3000)
🕐 11-3, 6 (5 Fri)-11; 11-11 Sat; 12-10.30 Sun
☎ (01483) 810387 ⊕ thegoodintent-puttenham.co.uk
Courage Best Bitter; Ringwood Best Bitter; guest beers Ⓗ
Traditional pub in a quiet village just off the Hogs Back. The L-shaped room, with low beams and hop bines over the bar, is dominated by a magnificent fireplace, and has dining areas at either end. Popular with walkers on the North Downs Way, dogs are permitted. Wednesday evening is fish and chips night. Welcoming to all, this atmospheric pub is well worth heading out into the countryside for. ▲Q⊛◑Ⓟ

Redhill

Garland

5 Brighton Road, RH1 6PP (on A23, S of town centre)
🕐 11-11; 12-3, 7-11 Sun
☎ (01737) 760377
Harveys Sussex XX Mild, Hadlow Bitter, Sussex Best Bitter, Armada, seasonal beers Ⓗ
An oasis of tradition in a town full of modern themed bars, this is the place to come for the best Harveys you will find anywhere. The entire range is sold along with any seasonal beers the landlord can get hold of – the record is 12 different beers on sale at one time. See if you can spot all the clowns behind the bar – there are more than 1000. Darts is popular here but does not intrude. Lunches are served Monday to Friday. ⊛◑⇌Ⓡ♣Ⓟ

Home Cottage

3 Redstone Hill, RH1 4AW (behind railway station)
🕐 11-11.30; 12-10.30 Sun
☎ (01737) 762771
Wells Bombardier; Young's Bitter, Special, seasonal beers Ⓗ
Large, mid-19th century community pub with three distinct drinking areas. The front bar has a relaxing atmosphere warmed by a real fire and offers an interesting bank of five handpumps. The back bar is the public bar. The no-smoking conservatory is a family room where children are welcome. There is also a large room available for hire. The pub hosts monthly music and comedy nights.
▲☎⊛◑⇌Ⓡ♣Ⓟ'╵

Send

New Inn

Send Road, GU23 7EN (on A247)
🕐 11-11; 12-10.30 Sun
☎ (01483) 762736
Adnams Bitter; Fuller's London Pride; Greene King Abbot; Ringwood Best Bitter; guest beers Ⓗ
As its name suggests, the New Inn replaced an older inn on the opposite side of the road. The site was originally home to a mortuary – it is claimed that the phrase 'a stiff drink' originated here. The pub is situated on the

Wey Navigation, one of Britain's oldest waterways dating from the 1660s, built to move grain and flour to the London markets. Now the pub plays hosts to recreational boaters and the pub and garden, with its barbecue, are very popular and can be crowded, particularly in summer.
Q❀◑▶🖺(462, 463)P

Shepperton

Barley Mow
67 Watersplash Road, TW17 0EE (off B376)
✪ 12-11; 12-10.30 Sun
☎ (01932) 225326
Hogs Back TEA, Summer Lightning; guest beers Ⓗ
Local CAMRA Pub of the Year in 2007, this ever popular pub attracts a friendly crowd of regulars. Five handpumps offer three constantly changing guests beers, often supplied direct from local micros. Three real ciders come from Mr Whiteheads. Quiz night is Thursday, live jazz plays on Wednesday and rock 'n' roll or blues on Saturday. Food is available lunchtimes and Wednesday evening only. There is a heated gazebo outside for smokers. ❀◑&🖺♣P᠘

Staffhurst Wood

Royal Oak
Caterfield Lane, RH8 0RR OS407485
✪ 11-11 (closed 3-5 winter Mon & Tue); 12-10.30 Sun
☎ (01883) 722207
Adnams Bitter; Harveys Sussex Best Bitter; Ⓗ guest beers Ⓗ/Ⓖ
Friendly rural free house well worth seeking out. Inside you are likely to find at least one cask of beer perched on the bar and a good selection of bottled British and Belgian beers to choose from. Guest beers come from local brewers including King, Larkins and Westerham. A couple of ciders are usually kept, too. Good-quality meals made from locally-sourced ingredients are served in the bar and restaurant (not Sun eve). Views from the garden are superb. A popular stop-off for ramblers; dogs are welcome. ⚠❀◑🖰♣♠P

Staines

Bells
124 Church Street, TW18 4YA (off B376)
✪ 12-11 (10.30 Sun)
☎ (01784) 454240
Wells Bombardier; Young's Bitter, Special Ⓗ
Quintessential 18th-century English pub in a quiet location opposite St Mary's church. This community pub with friendly bar staff serves impressive beers and food – fish dishes are a speciality. The pleasant rear garden is popular in summer. Within easy walking distance of the town centre and River Thames.
Q❀◑&🖺᠘

George
2-8 High Street, TW18 4EE (on A308)
✪ 9am-midnight (1am Fri & Sat)
☎ (01784) 462181
Courage Best Bitter; Marston's Pedigree; Shepherd Neame Spitfire; guest beers Ⓗ

Popular Wetherspoon's pub opposite the old town hall and war memorial. The large ground floor bar has several booths and a spiral staircase leading to the quieter upstairs bar. Pictures of old Staines town decorate the walls and Sky Sports is shown on TV. The constantly changing beer range features local micros. Busy with a young crowd on Friday and Saturday evenings. ◑&⚌♠🖵

Wheatsheaf & Pigeon
Penton Road, TW18 2LL (off B376)
✪ 11-11; 12-10.30 Sun
☎ (01784) 452922
Courage Best Bitter; Fuller's London Pride; guest beers Ⓗ
Splendid single bar community pub offering a warm welcome to all, from locals to Thames Path walkers. Guest beers change frequently. A wide range of food from bar snacks to curries and steaks is served, with specials and themed food evenings (no food Mon eve). The pub hosts an August bank holiday weekend beer festival and street party. ❀◑🖺(218)P

Sunbury-on-Thames

Hare & Hounds
132 Vicarage Road, TW16 7QX
✪ 11-11 (midnight Fri & Sat); 11-10.30 Sun
☎ (01932) 761478
Fuller's Chiswick, London Pride, ESB, seasonal beers Ⓗ
Comfortable roadside pub, convenient for Sunbury Cross, with a friendly landlord and staff serving an excellent range of Fuller's classic London beers. There is a growing emphasis on food with the introduction of a carvery and alfresco dining (eve meals Thu-Sun only). It has a large garden and patio area and beer festivals are planned twice a year.
❀◑&⚌🖺P᠘

Thames Ditton

George & Dragon
High Street, KT7 0RY (on B364)
✪ 11 (12 Sun)-11
☎ (020) 8398 2206
Shepherd Neame Master Brew Bitter, Kent's Best, Spitfire, seasonal beers Ⓗ
Popular village local set back from the road. The open plan interior is divided into several areas, one with TVs showing sport. Pictures of the local area adorn the wood-panelled walls. Evening meals are served Wednesday to Saturday. Local CAMRA Pub of the Year 2005.
Q❀◑&⚌🖺(514, 515)P᠘

Thursley

Three Horseshoes
Dye House Road, GU8 6QD (off A3)
✪ 12-3, 5.30-11; 12-11 Sat; 12-10.30 Sun
☎ (01252) 703268
Fuller's London Pride; Hogs Back TEA; guest beers Ⓗ
Under threat of closure and conversion into housing in 1999, the pub was purchased by 24 local supporters and reopened in 2004 after sensitive refurbishment. Just a short drive from the busy A3, it is set in open countryside

ideal for walkers. There is a restaurant but food can dominate the bar too, with many tables reserved for diners. Welcoming and friendly, the garden is popular with families. Game can be seen hanging for future consumption. ▲Q✿◗▷⑤▷P

Tongham

Hogs Back Brewery Shop

Manor Farm, GU10 1DE (off A31)
✪ 9am-8.30 (6 Sat); 10-4.30 Sun
☎ (01252) 783495 ⊕ hogsback.co.uk
Beer range varies Ⓖ
Award-winning brewery with its own off-licence selling Hogs Back beers on draught to take away, plus the brewery's full range of bottle-conditioned ales. Thousands of other bottled beers from around the world are also available including a wide selection from the UK. A 5% discount on draught beers is available to card-carrying CAMRA members.
🚃(3, 20)♣P

Walton-on-Thames

Regent

19 Church Street, KT12 2QP
✪ 9am-midnight (1am Fri & Sat); 9am-midnight Sun
☎ (01932) 243980
Courage Best Bitter; Greene King Abbot; Marston's Pedigree; guest beers Ⓗ
Wetherspoon's conversion, originally the Regent cinema in the 1920s and more recently a furniture shop. The decor reflects Walton's links to the film industry in its early years, with photographs and memorabilia. A good range of guest beer is rotated twice weekly, so there is always something different to try. Q➢◗▷⑥🚃

Westcott

Prince of Wales

Guildford Road, RH4 3QE (on A25)
✪ 11-11; 12-10.30 Sun
☎ (01306) 889699
Fuller's Chiswick Bitter, London Pride, ESB Ⓗ
A small entrance hall leads to a light and airy L-shaped bar with an area set aside for diners at one end. Good traditional pub food is served at lunchtime and in the evening, with takeaway meals also available. To the rear is a games room where pool and darts are played. Set below road level is a pleasant garden with a decked area for smokers. ✿◗▷🚃P▷

Weston Green

Marneys Village Inn

Alma Road, KT10 8JN (off A309)
✪ 11-11; 12-10.30 Sun
☎ (020) 8398 4444 ⊕ marneys.com
Courage Best Bitter; Fuller's London Pride; Wells Bombardier Ⓗ
Off the beaten track, this popular, cosy local is situated by the village pond. One bar serves two areas: one with tables set for dining, the other a more traditional bar with settles and bar stools. Good food is served at lunchtime from an extensive a la carte menu. Barbecues are held on summer Sundays 5-7pm. An

outside bar serves bottled beer. The vintage car club meets outside on the first Monday of the month. Q✿◗▷≠🚃(515)P▷

Weybridge

Jolly Farmer

41 Princes Road, KT13 9BN (off A317)
✪ 11-3, 5.30-11; 12-3, 7-11 Sun
☎ (01932) 856873
Banks's Bitter; Hop Back Summer Lightning; Marston's Pedigree; guest beers Ⓗ
Quiet, tucked away pub down a back street near the cricket green. This comfortable, friendly, mid-Victorian pub with a low-beamed ceiling has an L-shaped bar surrounded by upholstered bench seats. There are large mirrors and pictures of old Weybridge decorating the walls and a collection of Toby jugs on the high shelving. The large garden is popular in summer. Guest beers come from Marston's or Hop Back.
Q✿🚃(471)

Old Crown

83 Thames Street, KT13 8LP (off A317)
✪ 10-11; 12-10.30 Sun
☎ (01932) 842844
Courage Best Bitter, Directors; Young's Bitter; guest beer Ⓗ
Pleasant Grade II-listed, 17th-century weatherboarded pub near the River Thames. The garden runs down to the river and there is access for small boats. The interior is divided into four wood-panelled areas, each with a different feel. An interesting range of food is served at this welcoming family-run pub (no eve meals Sun-Tue). The guest beer rotates monthly. Q✿◗▷◁🚃♣P▷

Windlesham

Bee

School Road, GU20 6PD (on B386)
✪ 12-11 (10.30 Sun)
☎ (01276) 479244
Courage Best Bitter; Hop Back Summer Lightning; Young's Bitter; guest beers Ⓗ
Very much a community pub, this is a real locals' local, but visitors are always made welcome. Behind the pub is the garden, with children's play area and a barbecue, well used in summer. A range of traditional pub food is served at lunchtime. Darts is popular and the pub runs a golf society and organises clay pigeon shooting at nearby Bisley. Occasional live music evenings are hosted during the winter months. ✿◗🚃(500)♣P

Half Moon

Church Road, GU20 6BN (off B386)
✪ 11-3, 5.30-11.30; 12-4, 7-11 Sun
☎ (01276) 473329
Fuller's London Pride; Hogs Back TEA; Hop Back Summer Lightning; Taylor Landlord; Theakston Old Peculier; guest beers Ⓗ
Set in the countryside, this well-appointed pub is a true free house, offering six well-kept cask ales. Renowned for its excellent, traditional English food including game shot locally, an extension has been added to cater for diners. Ideal for families in summer, the pub has a

453

large garden with tables and benches, and children's play equipment. Disabled access is good. Q❀❂◑⛄🚆(500)P

Woking

Sovereigns

Guildford Road, GU22 7QQ (on A320)
❂ 12-11 (midnight Fri & Sat)
☎ (01483) 751426
Caledonian Deuchars IPA; guest beers Ⓗ
This large, comfortable pub decorated in typical Ember Inns style is a welcome addition to the local real ale scene. The oldest pub in Woking, circa 1840, it hosts at least four beer festivals a year. Quiz nights are Monday and Wednesday. The Caledonian beer is complemented by five changing guest ales, with samples and tasting notes available. There is outside seating at the front and rear with heaters and umbrellas. Local CAMRA Pub of the Year 2007. ᄊ❀❂◑⛄≢🚆♣P⌐

Wetherspoons

51-57 Chertsey Road, GU21 5AJ
❂ 9am-midnight (1am Fri & Sat)
☎ (01483) 722818
Courage Directors; Hogs Back TEA; Marston's Pedigree; Shepherd Neame Spitfire; guest beers Ⓗ
This pub, which was previously a Woolworths, is now an integral part of the Woking social scene, with an eclectic clientele and discerning real ale contingent who come to enjoy the four rapidly rotating guest beers. An inscrutable metallic invisble man presides over the bar and the HG Wells theme continues with a push button operated time machine clock on the ceiling. Handy for trains and buses, it is always tempting to linger for another pint in this unofficial waiting room. Q⛄❀❂◑⛄≢🚆●

Wood Street

Royal Oak

89 Oak Hill, GU3 3DA
❂ 11-3 (3.30 Sat), 5-11; 12-3.30, 7-10.30 Sun
☎ (01483) 235137
Courage Best Bitter; Hogs Back TEA; guest beers Ⓗ
This wonderful free house is well worth a visit if you are in the area. An ever-changing selection of imaginative beers is dispensed via the four guest pumps in a range of strengths, with a mild always available. Popular lunchtime food (Mon-Sat) is highly recommended – plenty of vegetables but no chips. Note the Hodgson's brewery plaque on the front wall on your way out to the garden where you will find swings and a windmill for children. Not surprisingly, this pub is a frequent winner of CAMRA awards.
❀❂🚆♣●P

Wrecclesham

Sandrock

Sandrock Hill, Boundstone, GU10 4NS (off B3384)
OS830444
❂ 12-11; 12-10.30 Sun
☎ (01252) 715865 ⊕ thesandrock.com
Batham Best Bitter; guest beers Ⓗ
A Guide entry for many years, the Sandrock offers a little bit of the Black Country in Farnham suburbia. Committed to beer variety and quality, there are eight changing real ales to choose from. This simple and unpretentious pub has three drinking areas, one dominated by a roaring fire. Award-winning home-cooked food is served daily (not Sat lunch or Sun eve). Live music plays occasionally.
ᄊQ❀❂◑🚆♣P

Surrey Oaks, Newdigate, Surrey.

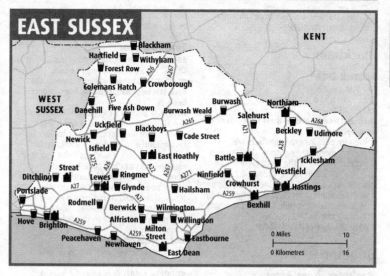

SUSSEX (EAST)

Alfriston

Smugglers Inn

Waterloo Square, BN26 5UE (by market cross)
🕐 11-2.30 (3 Sat), 6.30-11; 12-3, 7-10.30 Sun
☎ (01323) 870241
Courage Best; Harveys Sussex Best Bitter, XXXX Old Ale; Whites seasonal beers (summer) Ⓗ
Traditional 14th-century inn dominated by an impressive inglenook. Its wood beams are decorated with hops, horse race day tickets and old iron implements. Good value food helps to attract visitors to this picturesque village situated in the midst of downland on a river crossing of the South Downs Way. Q◐⑴⌐

Battle

Chequers Inn

Lower Lake, TN33 0AT (on roundabout jct of Lower Lake/Marley Lane)
🕐 11-11 (midnight Fri & Sat); 11-10.30 Sun
☎ (01424) 772088 ∰ chequersinn.eu
Adnams Broadside; Fuller's London Pride; Harveys Sussex Best Bitter; guest beers Ⓗ
This 15th-century inn south of the High Street features exposed beams and open fires. The dining/children's room boasts a large inglenook. Award-winning floral displays adorn the pub in summer. The terrace, to the rear of the pub, is pleasant and in summer hosts occasional concerts by local brass bands. The back garden overlooks the Hastings battlefield. A summer beer festival is planned. ∰▷❀✉◑⑴⇌⊟♣P

Beckley

Rose & Crown

Northiam Road, TN31 6SE (opp B2188/2165 jct)
🕐 11-12.30am; 12-11.30 Sun
☎ (01797) 252161
Fuller's ESB; Harveys Sussex Best Bitter; Taylor Landlord; guest beers Ⓗ

CAMRA's 2006 South East Sussex Pub of the Year is a well-established community pub, situated at the western end of this long village. Loyally supported by locals, it attracts a good mix of drinkers and diners. Dogs are welcome. The bar is divided into drinking and dining areas, with the wall behind the bar covered in pump clips from past guest beers. The large garden affords splendid views over the local countryside. ∰Q❀☺◑⇌(344)♣P

Berwick

Cricketers' Arms

BN26 6SP (S of A27, W of Drusilla's roundabout)
🕐 11-3, 6-11 (11-11 May-Sep); 11-10.30 Sun
☎ (01323) 870469 ∰ cricketersberwick.co.uk
Harveys Sussex Best Bitter, seasonal beers Ⓖ
Once two cottages, and a pub since the 18th century, it was extended in 1981 in keeping with its original character. Harveys beers are served straight from the cask at this pleasant village pub, which has featured in the Guide for 21 consecutive years. There is a pleasant garden, and real fires warm the bars in the winter. A popular stop for walkers on the nearby South Downs, toad in the hole can be played here. Meals are served all day at the weekend (12-9pm). ∰Q❀◑⑴♣P

Blackboys

Blackboys Inn

Lewes Road, TN22 5LG (on B2192 S of village)
🕐 11-11
☎ (01825) 890283
Harveys Hadlow Bitter, Sussex Best Bitter, seasonal beers Ⓗ
Dating from 1389, this village pub is set back from the road, right by the village pond. Inside, it has two bars and two restaurant rooms, decorated with old prints, artefacts and hop bines. Food includes good-value bar snacks as well as an interesting range of full meals. Harveys Old is served throughout the winter, and other seasonal beers feature in

455

summer. Outside are two large, pleasant garden areas. ♨☺◑P⌐

Blackham

Sussex Oak

TN3 9UA (on A264)
☼ 11-3, 6-11; 12-3, 6.30-10.30 Sun
☎ (01892) 740273
Shepherd Neame Master Brew Bitter, Kent's Best, Spitfire Ⓗ

A friendly pub, where customers are immediately made welcome, the Oak was deserved winner of the local CAMRA Pub of the Year award in 2003. The good range of home-cooked meals often includes Indian and Irish specialities, reflecting the origins of the couple who run the pub. Camping is possible at nearby Manor Court Farm.
♨Q☺◑よ▲⇌(Ashurst)🚃♣P

Brighton

Basketmakers Arms

12 Gloucester Road, BN1 4AD
☼ 11-11.30 (12.30am Thu-Sat); 12-11.30 Sun
☎ (01273) 689006
Fuller's London Pride, ESB, Gale's Butser, HSB, seasonal beers; guest beers Ⓗ

A long-term entry to the Guide, this popular street-corner local is in a convenient spot for Brighton's business and entertainment scene. Prior to takeover by Fuller's, this was a Gale's tied house, and it still stocks a selection of the Gale's range plus at least one guest beer. It also boasts a selection of fine malt whiskies. The unusual decor features old signs and metal containers. The pub is known for its good, inexpensive food, including vegetarian options. ◑⇌🚃

Battle of Trafalgar

34 Guildford Road, BN1 3LW
☼ 12-11 (midnight Fri & Sat); 10.30-11 Sun
☎ (01273) 327997
Fuller's London Pride; Harveys Sussex Best Bitter; guest beers Ⓗ

Traditional pub, situated a short walk up a steep hill from Brighton station. Inside it has a large L-shaped wood-panelled main bar area, featuring prints of sea battles and other nautical memorabilia, as well as some French Impressionist prints. Live music is sometimes staged; background music is kept at an acceptable level. Food is served between 12-5pm only at weekends. ☺◑⇌🚃

Bugle

24 St Martin's Street, BN2 3HJ
☼ 4 (3 Fri; 12 Sat)-11 (1am Fri & Sat); 12-11.30 Sun
☎ (01273) 607753
Beer range varies Ⓗ

This Irish local, decorated with pictures of Irish authors, has two drinking areas divided by an island bar. There is also a family room and a courtyard with a covered smoking area. The Bugle televises rugby matches, and has regular live music performances (Wed eve and Sun afternoon). Situated west of the busy Lewes Road, the pub attracts a mixed crowd of locals and students; children are welcome

until 8.30pm. Parking can be difficult at times. ☿☺よ⇌🚃⌐▯

Evening Star

55-56 Surrey Street, BN1 3PB (400m S of station)
☼ 12 (11.30 Sat)-11 (midnight Fri & Sat)
☎ (01273) 328931 ⊕ eveningstarbrighton.co.uk
Dark Star Hophead, seasonal beers; guest beers Ⓗ

Deserved winner of Regional CAMRA Pub of the Year 2005, free from pool tables, fruit machines or TV, this is a must for any beer-loving tourist to Brighton. Alongside Dark Star's own beers, Thatchers cider and guest ales can be sampled, together with foreign beers on draught and in bottles. Live music is performed most Sundays and occasional beer festivals are held. Filled rolls are available at lunchtime. For mild weather, there is a covered area in front of the pub. ♨☺♣⇌◔⌐

Lord Nelson

36 Trafalgar Street, BN1 4ED (near station)
☼ 11-midnight (1am Fri & Sat); 12-11 Sun
☎ (01273) 695872 ⊕ thelordnelsoninn.co.uk
Harveys Sussex XX Mild, Hadlow Bitter, Sussex Best Bitter, Armada Ale, seasonal beers Ⓗ

A Guide regular, this friendly two-bar pub is in the busy North Laine area. The left-hand bar has a pull-down screen showing major sporting events and there is a gallery at the rear which can be used for meetings. Cards, crib and dominoes are played by regulars. The Lord Nelson prides itself on stocking the entire Harveys range of beers and features regularly on the local CAMRA ale trail. ♨◑⇌🚃♣

Mitre Tavern

13 Baker Street, BN1 4JN
☼ 10.30-11; 12-10.30 Sun
☎ (01273) 683173 ⊕ mitretavern.co.uk
Harveys Sussex XX Mild, Sussex Best Bitter, Armada Ale, seasonal beers Ⓗ

Situated in a side street off one of the city's main shopping areas and close to the open market, this Harveys tied house attracts a more mature clientele. The pub dates back to Victorian times and is divided into a long narrow lounge bar and a cosy snug bar. The modern brewery etched windows do not detract from the ambience of this welcoming pub and the background music does not interrupt the flow of conversation. よ⇌🚃♣⌐

Prestonville Arms

64 Hamilton Road, BN1 5DN
☼ 5-11; 12-midnight Fri & Sat; 12-11 Sun
☎ (01273) 701007
Fuller's London Pride, Gale's Butser, HSB, seasonal beers; guest beers Ⓗ

INDEPENDENT BREWERIES

1648 East Hoathly
Beachy Head East Dean
Cuckoo Hastings
Fallen Angel Battle
FILO Hastings
Harveys Lewes
Kemptown Brighton
Rectory Streat
Rother Valley Northiam
White Bexhill-on-Sea

Street-corner local on a triangular site in a residential area; its bar is on two levels, reflecting its hilly location. There is a higher-level seating area which leads to a pleasant garden patio. It hosts a music quiz on Tuesday and a general knowledge quiz on Sunday. A good choice of well-presented, home-cooked meals is available (lunch Fri-Sun only, no eve meals Sun). ⚫🅱🌳➡🚬

Sir Charles Napier
50 Southover Street, BN2 9UE
🕐 4-11; 3-midnight Fri; 12-midnight Sat; 12-11 Sun
☎ (01273) 601413
Fuller's Discovery, London Pride, Gale's HSB, seasonal beers; guest beer Ⓗ
Traditional street-corner local in Brighton's Hanover area. This former Gale's tied house is now part of the Fuller's estate, offering a selection of beers from both ranges and a monthly guest beer. Most of the time this is a quiet pub, without loud music, but a livelier atmosphere is to be expected for the occasional themed evenings and the popular Sunday night quiz. Good-value lunches are served on Sunday. Q🌳🅰🚬

Station
1 Hampstead Road, BN1 5NG
🕐 11-midnight (1am Fri & Sat); 12-midnight Sun
☎ (01273) 501318
Courage Best; Harveys Sussex Best Bitter; guest beers Ⓗ
Back-street local overlooking Preston Park railway station, with a panoramic view across Brighton. If you are approaching from Dyke Road, it is at the bottom of a very steep hill. The pub has a large L-shaped bar with a TV screen, thankfully often with the sound turned off. A general knowledge quiz is hosted on Thursday night. Weston's Old Rosie cider is stocked, and pizza is on the menu.
🌳🅱➡(Preston Park)🍴🚬

Waggon & Horses
Church Street, BN1 2RL
🕐 11-1am (2am Fri & Sat)
☎ (01273) 602752
Adnams Broadside; Fuller's London Pride; Harveys Sussex Best Bitter Ⓗ
Well worth a visit, this pub is right by the city's main shopping area. A lively establishment with a great atmosphere, it is frequented mainly by younger pub-goers, attracted by the late Friday and Saturday nights. Although music is played, this is not a noisy pub. Weston's Vintage Organic cider is served.
🌳🅱🅰➡🚊🍴

Burwash

Rose & Crown
Ham Lane, TN19 7ER (signed from High Street)
🕐 11-3, 5-11; 11-11 Sat; 11.30-11 Sun
☎ (01435) 882600
Harveys Hadlow Bitter, Sussex Best Bitter, Armada Ale, seasonal beers Ⓗ
Village local dating from the 15th century. The main entrance takes visitors across the exposed well into the large bar, which has a beamed ceiling and an inglenook fireplace. The room is decorated with hop bines, sheet music and instruments. Meals range from bar

snacks to à la carte meals served in the restaurant (no food Sun eve). Popular live music sessions are hosted. 🏨🌳🅱🅰🍴🚬

Burwash Weald

Wheel Inn
Heathfield Road, TN19 7LA (on A265)
🕐 12-11 (10 Sun)
☎ (01435) 882758
Harveys Sussex Best Bitter; guest beers Ⓗ
Spacious, popular village pub, under new management. The main bar has a large inglenook fireplace, and there is a separate games room. The restaurant serves both snacks and full meals, and has a carvery on Sunday lunchtime. Regular events include curry nights, live music, games and quiz nights. The large garden has a climbing frame for younger visitors. 🏨🌳🅱♿🅿🚬

Cade Street

Half Moon Inn
TN21 9BS
🕐 12-11 (10.30 Sun)
☎ (01435) 868646
Harveys Sussex Best Bitter; guest beers Ⓗ
Large, friendly village pub with a long sloping south-facing garden offering uninterrupted views of the South Downs and the sea. Inside, there are open fireplaces, including an inglenook. Wood dominates the traditional decor. Alongside the Harveys Best, Fuller's and Young's beers are usually represented, complemented by a range of seasonal beers. No fried food is served, but the menu includes pizza and tapas. Shut-the-box and pool are played here. 🏨🌳🅱♣🅿

Colemans Hatch

Hatch Inn
TN7 4EJ (400m S of B2110) OS452335
🕐 11.30-2.30, 5.30-11 (11.30-11 Sat summer); 12-10.30 Sun
☎ (01342) 822363
Harveys Sussex Best Bitter; Larkins Traditional; guest beers Ⓗ
Originally three cottages dating from the 15th century, it has been a pub for the past 200 years. Inside the attractive weatherboarded exterior is a cosy bar with scrubbed tables and low beams. Convenient for Ashdown Forest (Winnie the Pooh country), the pub is much appreciated by walkers, drinkers and diners (no food Mon eve). Local breweries are well supported; this is a rare outlet for Larkins' excellent ale. 🏨Q🌳🅱🚊♣🅿

Crowborough

Coopers Arms
Coopers Lane, TN6 1SN (follow St John's Rd from Crowborough Cross) OS504317
🕐 12-2.30 (not Mon or Tue), 6 (5 Fri)-11; 12-10.30 Sun
☎ (01892) 654796
Greene King IPA, seasonal beers; guest beers Ⓗ
An out of the way classic pub with wooden floors and basic furniture, serving a good range of excellent ales including many from local Sussex breweries. Food is now served in

the evening Wednesday to Saturday. At least four beer festivals are staged each year, with the beer dispensed through additional handpumps now installed in the bar. Well worth seeking out. ♨❀◑♿▲♣P

Wheatsheaf

Mount Pleasant, Jarvis Brook, TN6 2NF
✪ 12-11; 12-10.30 Sun
☎ (01892) 663756
Harveys Sussex XX Mild, Hadlow Bitter, Sussex Best Bitter, Armada Ale, seasonal beers Ⓗ
The Wheatsheaf has three separate areas, all served from a central square bar. Wood fires in at least two areas give this pub a homely feel, with some unusual items of wooden furniture. Lunchtime meals are popular and an additional dining area is planned. All of Harveys regular ales are stocked here. Live music events are hosted on an occasional basis. ♨Q❀◑♿≠➡♣P

Crowhurst

Plough Inn

TN33 9AW (1 mile from station)
✪ 11-2.30, 6-11; 11.30-midnight Sat; 12-4, 6-11 Sun
☎ (01424) 830310
Harveys Sussex Best Bitter, Armada Ale, seasonal beers; Rother Valley Level Best Ⓗ
Excellent village local – a free house that chooses to sell Harveys ales, with an additional ale from a local micro. This pub supports local sports teams and the village. Toad in the hold, boules and pool can be played here. Live music is sometimes hosted in the bar. ♨Q❀◑♣P

Danehill

Coach & Horses

Coach and Horses Lane, RH17 7JF (off A275)
✪ 12-3 (4 Sat), 6-11; 12-4, 6-10.30 Sun
☎ (01825) 740369
Harveys Sussex Best Bitter; guest beers Ⓗ
This rural, two-bar free house boasts an award-winning restaurant (no food Sun eve). The large front garden has a children's play area, but the rear patio is reserved for adults. The guest beers change regularly and can include some unusual beers. The pub is conveniently situated for exploring Ashdown Forest, Sheffield Park Gardens and the Bluebell Railway. ♨Q❀◑◒▲➡(270)P

Ditchling

White Horse

16 West Street, BN6 8TS
✪ 11-midnight; 12-11 Sun
☎ (01273) 842006
Harveys Sussex Best Bitter; guest beers Ⓗ
Situated next to the village church, this Guide regular and winner of several awards including local CAMRA 2006 Country Pub of the Year, is a traditional family-run free house. The timber-panelled main bar area is decorated with sporting prints and engravings. Meals are served in the bar and restaurant. A dedicated games area is at the back of the pub. Weston's Organic cider is generally available on handpump. ♨❀◑➡♣♠P

East Hoathly

Kings Head

1 High Street, BN8 6DR
✪ 11-11; 12-4, 7-11 Sun
☎ (01825) 840238 ⊕ bestof.co.uk
1648 Original, Signature, seasonal beers; Harveys Sussex Best Bitter Ⓗ
Situated next to the 1648 brewery, this 17th-century pub offers the range of 1648 beers, as well as other Sussex ales. The Kings Head has a U-shaped bar and tables accommodating both drinkers and diners. Good food from an extensive menu is served, and a beer festival hosted in July. ♨Q❀◑➡P♠

Eastbourne

Buccaneer

10 Compton Street, BN21 4BW
✪ 11 (12 Sun)-11
☎ (01323) 732829
Adnams Broadside; Draught Bass; Tetley Cask Bitter; guest beers Ⓗ
Large, open pub situated at the heart of Eastbourne's theatreland; the front bar is decorated with old theatre posters of past productions. Always welcoming, it offers a choice of six real ales, including three changing guests. Good-value food is served (not Sat all day or Sun eve). Bar billiards can be played here. ◑≠➡♣

Hurst Arms

76 Willingdon Road, BN21 1TW (on A2270)
✪ 11-11; 12-10.30 Sun
☎ (01323) 721762
Harveys Sussex Best Bitter, Armada Ale, seasonal beers Ⓗ
Friendly, Victorian local with two bars: a lively public with pool, darts, a wide-screen TV and a juke box; and a homely lounge that feels like someone's front room. Harveys beers are served to an unfailing high standard, confirmed by the brewery's Cellar of the Year award. There is a quiet rear garden as well as the front patio by the road. ❀♿➡♣♠

Lamb

36 High Street, B21 1HH (on A259, next to St Mary's church)
✪ 10.30-11 (midnight Fri & Sat)
☎ (01323) 720545
Harveys Hadlow Bitter, Sussex Best Bitter, Armada Ale, seasonal beers Ⓗ
This unspoilt landmark pub is located within Eastbourne's old town area. The exact date of its construction is not known, but it is likely to have been in the 1100s. The facade has changed at least once during its lifetime. Inside it has three bars, each one with a different feel. Food is served all day every day. The Folk Club meets here on alternate Wednesdays. ♨Q◑≠➡

Victoria Hotel

27 Latimer Road, BN22 7BU (behind TAVR Centre, A259)
✪ 11-11 (1am Fri & Sat); 12-10.30 Sun
☎ (01323) 722673
Harveys Sussex Best Bitter, Armada Ale, seasonal beers Ⓗ

A return to the Guide for this friendly local, one road in from the seafront, now under new management. The large front bar has a homely feel, decorated with prints of old Eastbourne, and the smaller back room has a pool table, dartboard and TV. Behind the pub is a secluded rear garden. Home-made traditional pub food is served weekday evenings and Saturday and Sunday lunchtimes. ⌖✦◖▣♠⌐

Five Ash Down

Fireman's Arms
TN22 3AN
🕔 11-3, 6-11; 11-midnight Fri & Sat; 12-11 Sun
☎ (01825) 732191
Harveys Sussex Best Bitter; Robinsons Dark Horse; guest beers ⊞
Recently refurbished and redecorated popular two-bar village local. An extensive range of meals, representing good value and quality, is served in the dining room. There is a monthly quiz (first Tue) and open mike music sessions (last Tue). The bar is decorated with paddle steamer and railway memorabilia. Biddenden and Weston's ciders are available here.
⋈Q⌖◖⌂▣(29)♣♠⌐

Forest Row

Brambletye Hotel
The Square, Lewes Road, RH18 5EZ
🕔 11-11.30; 12-10.30 Sun
☎ (01342) 824144 ⊕ accommodating-inns.co.uk
Fuller's London Pride; Harveys Sussex Best Bitter ⊞
Prior to takeover by Fuller's, this prominent building in the centre of the village was part of the Gale's estate. It has since been tastefully refurbished, providing a large dining area. A function room is also available. The bar area features a display of old bottled beers. Aside from the regular beers, a third handpump is used for another changing beer from Fuller's. Fuller's bottled beers are also stocked, and a selection of Belgian beers. The hotel makes a good base for exploring Ashdown Forest.
⋈⌂⌖✦◖▣⌐

Glynde

Trevor Arms
The Street, BN8 6SS (over bridge from station)
🕔 11-11; 12-10.30 Sun
☎ (01273) 858208
Harveys Hadlow Bitter, Sussex Best Bitter, seasonal beers ⊞
A firm favourite with locals, walkers and music fans from nearby Glyndebourne, this Harveys tied house is a regular ale trail pub and Guide entry. Meals are served throughout the multi-roomed pub and in the garden. Located right next to Glynde station, with regular trains to Brighton and Eastbourne, this country pub is easily accessible to those without a car. Toad in the hole is played here.
Q⌖◖⌂⇄⊖▣(125)♣P

Hailsham

Grenadier
67 High Street, BN27 1AS (W of town centre)
🕔 11-11 (11.30 Fri & Sat); 12-11 Sun
☎ (01323) 842152 ⊕ thegrenny.com
Harveys Sussex XX Mild, Hadlow Bitter, Sussex Best Bitter, seasonal beers ⊞
This 200-year-old pub was used by the Grenadier Guards as a drinking house. Traditional games – toad in the hole, shove-ha'penny, table skittles and darts – are played in the public bar while the saloon has a quieter, more relaxed atmosphere. A large play area for children is provided in the garden. The pub raises money for guide dogs – with more than £5,000 raised in 18 months.
⌖◖⌐▣♠P⌐

Hartfield

Hay Waggon
High Street, TN7 4AB
🕔 11-3 (4 Sat), 6-11 (11-11 summer Sat); 12-10.30 Sun
☎ (01892) 770252 ⊕ thehaywaggon.com
Draught Bass; Harveys Sussex Best Bitter; guest beers ⊞
Attractive coaching inn dating from the 16th century. Situated in the centre of the historic village of Hartfield, it is an ideal base for exploring Ashdown Forest. Inside there are two rooms: a long bar with a low-beamed ceiling and a restaurant. The pub offers a varied menu of home-cooked food, served in the bar and restaurant. In 2007 B&B accommodation was introduced. 'Live Jazz at the Waggon' is hosted on the second Monday of the month. Q⌖✦◖⌂⅊▲▣P

Hastings

First In Last Out
14-15 High Street, Old Town, TN34 3ET (near Stables Theatre)
🕔 11-11; 12-10.30 Sun
☎ (01424) 425079 ⊕ thefilo.co.uk
FILO Crofters, Ginger Tom, seasonal beers ⊞
Home of the FILO Brewery since 1985, four beers are usually available. The large bar is heated by an attractive open log fire in the centre, and has plenty of alcove-style seating. Organic, freshly cooked food is available Tuesday-Saturday lunchtimes. The pub hosts a beer festival most bank holiday weekends.
⋈Q◖▲▣♣

White Rock Hotel
1-10 White Rock, TN34 1JU (on A259)
🕔 10-11; 12-10.30 Sun
☎ (01424) 422240 ⊕ thewhiterockhotel.co.uk
Dark Star Original; Harvey's Sussex Best Bitter; Rother Valley Boadicea; guest beers ⊞
Located next to the theatre and opposite the pier, this hotel bar offers ample seating areas and a spacious terrace. It serves beers from independent Sussex breweries, including 1648, Dark Star and White. A range of freshly prepared food is available. The hotel offers good accommodation for travellers.
Q⌖✦◖⇄▣

Hove

Downsman

189 Hangleton Way, BN3 8ES
🕓 11-4, 6-11; 12-4, 7-11 Sun
☎ (01273) 711301

Harveys Sussex Best Bitter; guest beers Ⓗ

Probably Hangleton's best kept secret, this friendly pub is situated next to the old Dyke Railway Trail, near the 'lost' village of Hangleton. Excavations during construction work in the 1950s uncovered the remains of two medieval cottages, one of which, Hangleton Cottage, has been reconstructed at Singleton Open Air Museum. The two-roomed pub has been run by the same family for the past seven years. ♨️❀◑ ⬱♿⊟♣P

Neptune

10 Victoria Terrace, Kingsway, BN3 2WB
🕓 12-1am (2am Fri & Sat); 12-midnight Sun
☎ (01273) 324870 ⊕ theneptunelivemusicbar.co.uk

Dark Star Hophead; Greene King Abbot; Harveys Sussex Best Bitter, seasonal beers; guest beers Ⓗ

The Neptune is one of the oldest pubs in Hove and one of the few remaining free houses, offering a choice of five ales. The pub is very much a traditional local and attracts a slightly older crowd. The single-room interior is plainly decorated with a long bar and a raised stage at one end. Live music plays on Friday and Sunday evenings, with rock and blues always popular. ⬱⊟🖥

Icklesham

Queen's Head

Parsonage Lane, TN36 4BL (off A259, opp village hall)
🕓 11-11; 12-10.30 Sun
☎ (01424) 814552 ⊕ queenshead.com

Beer range varies Ⓗ

This award-winning pub, tucked away at the eastern end of the village, is particularly popular at weekends. It has a large open-plan interior decorated with a fine collection of rural artefacts. Three open fires create a cosy atmosphere in winter, while the benches in the extensive gardens invite guests in the summer. A range of five or six beers, varying in strength, is always on offer. Live music is performed weekly. ♨️❀◑⊟♣♠P🖥

Isfield

Laughing Fish

Station Road, TN22 5XB (off A26 between Lewes and Uckfield) OS452172
🕓 11.30-11 daily
☎ (01825) 750349 ⊕ laughingfishonline.co.uk

Greene King IPA, Morland Original; Hardys & Hansons Old Trip; guest beers Ⓗ

A comfortable pub, the Fish has recently added a dining area, disabled access and an outdoor smoking area. A popular stop on local CAMRA's ale trail, it boasts a full calendar of interesting events, including the Easter Monday beer race. It also has a beer tent at the local village fete in July. Good food is served (not Sun and Mon eve). Popular bar games include darts, bar billiards and toad in the hole. ♨️❀◑⬱♿▲⊟(29)♣P⌐

Lewes

Brewers Arms

91 High Street, BN7 1XN
🕓 10-11; 12-10.30 Sun
☎ (01273) 475524

Harveys Sussex Best Bitter; guest beers Ⓗ

This family-run pub is a true free house, stocking an ever-changing beer range. There are two bars: a quiet comfortable saloon featuring the original architect's drawing for the building and a slightly noisier public bar at the rear. Toad in the hole, chess and darts are played here. Biddenden cider is served. Evening meals finish at 6.30pm.
Q❀◑《⬱⊟♣♠

Dorset

22 Malling Street, BN7 2RD
🕓 11-11 (10 Mon-Wed winter); 12-8 Sun
☎ (01273) 474823 ⊕ thedorsetlewes.com

Harveys Hadlow Bitter, Sussex Best Bitter, Armada Ale, seasonal beers Ⓗ

Harveys tied house, completely refurbished in 2006, with a number of drinking and dining areas including a newly created snug. The small patio is popular in summer. At least four beers are usually on handpump, and Weston's Old Rosie cider is served. The pub offers an extensive menu. Closing times may vary, especially in winter, so it is worth checking beforehand. ♨️❀♿◑⬱♿⊟♠⌐

Elephant & Castle

White Hill, BN7 2DJ (off Fisher St)
🕓 11.30-11.30 (midnight Fri & Sat); 12-11 Sun
☎ (01273) 473797

Harveys Sussex Best Bitter; guest beers Ⓗ

Built in 1838 for the long-gone Southdown and East Grinstead Brewery, this bar is popular with younger drinkers and has a lively atmosphere. The spacious bar area splits into two: one end is furnished with wooden chairs and tables, the other has a pool table and more comfortable seating. The walls are adorned with stuffed animal heads and other curiosities - look out for the Angel of Death. ♨️◑⬱⊟♣

Gardener's Arms

46 Cliffe High Street, BN7 2AN
🕓 11-11; 12-10.30 Sun
☎ (01273) 474808 ⊕ gardenersarmslewes.com

Harveys Sussex Best Bitter; guest beers Ⓗ

Genuine free house, situated in Cliffe, close to the River Ouse. Harveys Brewery is nearby and its Best Bitter is always stocked alongside five ever-changing beers and Black Rat cider. In February 2007 the landlord celebrated the pub's 2,000th draught beer with a special brew from Dark Star. The walls are adorned with photographs of the flood in Lewes and a fire at the nearby brewery shop. Pub games include toad in the hole. ⬱⊟(28, 29)♣♠

Milton Street

Sussex Ox

BN26 5RL (signed off A27) OS534041
🕓 11.30-3, 6-11; 12-3, 6-10.30 (12-5 winter) Sun
☎ (01323) 870840 ⊕ thesussexox.co.uk

Dark Star Hophead; Harveys Sussex Best Bitter; guest beers Ⓗ

Excellent country pub in the little hamlet of Milton Street, deep in the South Downs and close to the Long Man of Wilmington. At least four real ales, always in tip-top condition, are served in the small bar, which has an intimate atmosphere. Bar and restaurant meals are of a high standard and there is plenty of dining space. The pub is located on a tight bend so exercise caution when entering and exiting the car park. ♨Q❀☕❶P

Newhaven

Jolly Boatman

133-135 Lewes Road, BN9 9SJ (N of town centre)
🕓 11-11 (midnight Fri & Sat); 12-10.30 Sun
☎ (01273) 510030
Harveys Sussex Best Bitter; guest beers Ⓗ
This genuine street-corner local a short walk from the town centre is a welcome addition to the Guide in Newhaven, a largely industrial port town. The pub has a single bar on two levels. It offers an ever-changing range of guest beers, regularly including ales from Archers and WJ King. Crib and darts are among the pub games played here.
≥(Newhaven Town)➔(123)♣

Newick

Royal Oak

1 Church Road, BN8 4JU
🕓 11-11 (10.30 Sun)
☎ (01825) 722506
Fuller's London Pride; Harveys Sussex Best Bitter; guest beers Ⓗ
Friendly 16th-century local next to the green in the centre of the village. This oak-beamed pub features an exposed wattle-and-daub panel between the bars. It has a roomy public bar plus a cosy saloon area, with a large inglenook and a further dining area where a good range of home-made traditional pub meals is served. Dogs are welcome. Old Rosie cider is available during the summer.
♨Q❀❶➔➔(31, 121)♣♠ℏ

Ninfield

Blacksmiths Inn

The Green, TN33 9JL (on A269)
🕓 11-11; 12-10.30 Sun
☎ (01424) 892462
Harveys Sussex Best Bitter; guest beers Ⓗ
A welcome entry to the Guide, this friendly and popular 1930s local is now under new ownership. It has one spacious room and a separate dining area where an extensive menu of tasty home-cooked meals is on offer (no food Sun eve). The bar is adorned with a collection of old photographs depicting local characters. ❀❶♿➔♣♠ℏ

Peacehaven

Telscombe Tavern

405 South Coast Road, BN10 7AD (A259 between Rottingdean and Newhaven)
🕓 11-1am
☎ (01273) 584674 🌐 telscombetavern.com
Adnams Broadside; Greene King Old Speckled Hen; Harveys Sussex Best Bitter; guest beers Ⓗ

Gloriously situated on the cliff side of the coastal road, this spacious and welcoming two-bar pub has a restaurant area to the rear which specialises in reasonably priced, fresh local food. With its frequent live music events, ranging from the 60s to recent tunes, the pub attracts a mixed crowd of young and more mature regulars. It also hosts karaoke and disco nights. Good, affordable accommodation makes it an excellent base for exploring the South Downs and an ideal stopover for the Newhaven-Dieppe ferry. ❀🛏❶➔➔P

Portslade

Stanley Arms

47 Wolsley Road, BN41 1SS
🕓 3 (2 Fri; 12 Sat)-11; 12-10.30 Sun
☎ (01273) 430234 🌐 thestanley.com
Beer range varies Ⓗ
Genuine, family-run free house offering a varied range of beers, mainly from small and micro-breweries on four handpumps. Ten bottled Belgian beers plus Weston's perry and bottled organic cider are on sale. Beer festivals are held in February, June and September. Bar snacks are served, and in summer there are barbecues in the small garden. A large plasma TV shows sporting events. Usually a quiet pub, it does stage regular live music.
≥(Fishersgate)➔♣♠ℏ

Ringmer

Cock

Uckfield Road, BN8 5RX (on slip road off A26)
🕓 11-3, 6-11; 11-11 Sun
☎ (01273) 812040 🌐 cockpub.co.uk
Fuller's London Pride; Harveys Sussex Best Bitter, seasonal beers Ⓗ
Dating from the 16th-century, the pub is on the old Lewes to Tunbridge Wells coach road. The pub's name refers to the cock horse which used to help pull carts up a steep hill; old maps show that in the 19th century there were stables in the area of the present car park. Inside, many original features remain including exposed beams, an inglenook fireplace and stone floor in the bar area. Later extensions house dining areas, and there is extensive seating outdoors on the terrace and in the beer garden. ♨❀❶➔(29)♠P

Rodmell

Abergavenny Arms

Newhaven Road, BN7 3EZ
🕓 11-3, 5.30-11; 11-11 Sat; 12-11 Sun
☎ (01273) 472416 🌐 abergavennyarms.com
Beer range varies Ⓗ
Once a Domesday-listed Sussex barn, the oak timbers are from wrecks of the Spanish Armada. The large open fireplace also dates from the time of rebuilding. The pub has been extended over the years and the old well is now inside, in the corner. The main bar is used as a dining area, and there is a smaller public bar on the other side of the building. One of the three ales is usually from Harveys, while others are often sourced from smaller breweries. ♨Q❀❶➔♿➔(123)♣P

St Leonards

Bull
530 Bexhill Road, TN38 8AY (on A259)
☼ 12-11 (10.30 Sun)
☎ (01424) 424984 ⊕ the-bull-inn.com
Shepherd Neame Master Brew Bitter, Kent's Best, Spitfire, seasonal beers Ⓗ
Welcoming roadside pub, noted for its range of Shepherd Neame beers, voted the best pub in the Hastings area in 2006 by Observer readers. This local also offers an excellent menu (book at weekends; no food Sun eve). The car park at the rear offers much more space than appears at first. The large rear garden has barbecue facilities. The pub is convenient for the Glynde Gap shops.
▲Q✿❀◑▤&⊟♣P⅃

Horse & Groom
4 Mercatoria, TN38 0EB
☼ 11-11; 12-10.30 Sun
☎ (01424) 420612 ⊕ sussex200.com
Adnams Broadside; Greene King IPA; Harveys Sussex Best Bitter; Taylor Landlord; guest beers Ⓗ
This is St Leonards' oldest pub, built in 1829. A first-class free house, it is welcoming and comfortable, with olde-worlde charm and manners. A horseshoe-shaped bar serves two separate rooms, with a further quieter room to the rear. An adjoining restaurant offers a good selection of lunchtime food Tuesday-Saturday. The small patio is used in summer.
Q✿≹(Warrior Sq)⊟⅃

Salehurst

Salehurst Halt
TN32 5PH
☼ 12-3, 6-11; closed Mon; 12-11 Fri-Sun
☎ (01580) 880620
Harveys Sussex Best Bitter; guest beers Ⓗ
The Salehurst Halt was originally a steam railway stop on the Guinness hop-picking line. An historic, community-led, genuine free house, it was saved from redevelopment by the two local families who own and run it. The traditional single bar has low beams and an open fire, oak floors, wooden furniture and a snug with comfortable seating. In summer, the beer garden affords superb views over the Rother Valley. The menu includes dishes made from locally reared meat. ▲❀◑♣❀⅃

Uckfield

Alma
65 Framfield Road, TN22 5AJ (on B2102)
☼ 11-3, 5-11; 11-11 Sat; 12-10.30 Sun
☎ (01825) 762232
Harveys Sussex XX Mild, Sussex Best Bitter, XXXX Old Ale, Pale Ale; guest beers Ⓗ
This pleasant pub continues to serve a good selection of Harveys beers. There is a public bar where games are played, including shove-ha'penny, and a darts team is based here. The saloon is comfortable and there is a small garden next to the car park. The pub is roughly five minutes' walk from the town centre, station and bus routes. A wider range of meals is now served, with popular roast lunches on Sunday. Q✿◑&≹⊟♣P

Udimore

King's Head
Rye Road, TN31 6BG (on B2089, W of village)
☼ 11-3.30 (not Mon), 6-11; 11-3.30 Sun
☎ (01424) 882349
Harveys Sussex Best Bitter; guest beers Ⓗ
Built in 1535 and extended in the 17th century, this traditional village ale house features exposed beams, two open fires and a very long bar. The pub serves excellent, home-cooked food (lunches Tue-Sun, eve meals Mon-Sat). The owners have run this pub for 19 years and offer a warm and friendly welcome. Situated in an area of outstanding natural beauty, there are many scenic walks nearby and pleasant views over the surrounding countryside unfold from the garden. ▲Q✿❀◑ ⊟⊟♣P

Westfield

Old Courthouse
Main Road, TN35 4QE
☼ 12-11 (10.30 Sun)
☎ (01424) 751603 ⊕ oldcourthousepub.co.uk
Harveys Sussex Best Bitter; guest beers Ⓗ
The pub is central to the village and community focused. The main bar has an open fire and a low ceiling – this is where traditional games, including bar billiards, are played. There is second, smaller bar. Hot food is served all day (not Wed, or Sun eve in winter). A roast of the day is served Sunday lunchtime, and the first Friday of the month is curry night. A mini beer festival is held over the August bank holiday weekend. ▲Q✿◑ ⊟⊟♣P⅃

Willingdon

Red Lion
99 Wish Hill, BN20 9HQ (S end of Willingdon village, off A2270)
☼ 11-3, 5-11; 11-midnight Fri & Sat; 12-11 Sun
☎ (01323) 502062
Badger K&B Sussex, First Gold, Tanglefoot, seasonal beers Ⓗ
Nestling at the foot of the Downs, this friendly pub returns to the Guide under new management. Inside, its features include wood panelling, sash windows, brick fireplaces and an interesting pre-war Ordnance Survey map that shows local pubs with their earlier names. A good range of pub food is available (Mon-Tue snacks only). A popular quiz night is hosted on Wednesday, and a beer festival showcasing 18 different ales is held each August Bank Holiday weekend. ✿◑⊟♣P

Wilmington

Giant's Rest
The Street, BN26 5SQ (100m off A27)
☼ 11-3, 6-11; 11-11 Sat; 12-10.30 Sun
☎ (01323) 870207 ⊕ giantsrest.co.uk
Harveys Sussex Best Bitter; Hop Back Summer Lightning; Taylor Landlord Ⓗ
Popular Victorian free house, a short walk from the famous Long Man, a figure cut into the South Downs. An extensive menu of locally sourced dishes complements the three

regular ales, which are occasionally changed for a Harveys seasonal. The interior is mainly wood, with an airy spacious feel; there is an outdoor patio and grass area for summer. Morris men visit the pub at least once a year and dance at the foot of the giant on May Day. ⚲Q✿⌂◗&♣P

Withyham

Dorset Arms

TN17 4BD (on B2110)
✪ 11.30-3 (not Mon), 6-11; 12-3, 7-10.30 Sun
☎ (01892) 770278 ⊕ dorset-arms.co.uk
Harveys Hadlow Bitter, Sussex Best Bitter, seasonal beers Ⓗ
Popular with walkers and visitors to the nearby Ashdown Forest, this attractive village pub is set back from the road. Dating back to the 15th century, with oak floor interiors, the Dorset has a separate restaurant offering a wide-ranging menu of delicious home-cooked dishes. Extremely busy at lunchtime, booking is advisable (no food Mon lunchtime). ⚲☎✿◗➥P

SUSSEX (WEST)

Amberley

Sportsman

Crossgates, BN18 9NR (half mile E of village)
OS039134
✪ 11-3, 6-11; 12-3, 6-10.30 Sun
☎ (01798) 831787 ⊕ amberleysportsman.co.uk
Arundel Castle; Fuller's London Pride; Harveys Sussex Best Bitter; guest beers Ⓗ
Convivial 17th-century rural free house accommodating an eclectic mix of walkers, diners, locals and their dogs. There are three bars, each one with its own character, plus a conservatory restaurant and patio affording views of Amberley Wild Brooks. The pub is home to the Miserable Old Buggers Club, whose members raise money for children's charities. ⚲✿⌂◗⊞♣P

Ardingly

Oak Inn

Street Lane, RH17 6UA
✪ 11.30-midnight (1am Fri & Sat); 12-midnight Sun
☎ (01444) 892244
Harveys Sussex Best Bitter; guest beers Ⓗ
Originally a row of three 16th-century labourers' cottages, this delightful country pub's interior features an inglenook fireplace and many low beams. The walls are adorned with brass plates and horse brasses. The village (public) bar has its own entrance via the front porch, and the naturally lit restaurant overlooks the side garden. Close to the South of England Showground and the Bluebell Railway as well as Wakehurst Place, the pub is popular with walkers and business people from surrounding towns. ⚲◗⊞➥♣P⏚

Arundel

King's Arms

36 Tarrant Street, BN18 9DN
✪ 11-3, 5.30-11; 11-11 Sat; 12-10.30 Sun
☎ (01903) 882312
Fuller's London Pride; Hop Back Summer Lightning; Young's Special; guest beers Ⓗ
Arundel's only remaining true free house, the King's Arms is a friendly and welcoming local community pub. Popular with locals and visitors to Arundel alike, it offers the best pint in town. The pub displays a large selection of books, and dogs are welcome (Sultan is the resident canine). Fines imposed on customers who use their mobile phones are donated to the RNLI. ✿◗⊞Ⓐ⇌➥♣

Ashurst

Fountain

Horsham Road, BN44 3AP (on B2135)
✪ 11.30-11; 12-10.30 Sun
☎ (01403) 710219
Fuller's London Pride; Harveys Sussex Best Bitter; guest beers Ⓗ
Fine, 16th-century pub and restaurant, based in a former farmhouse with many period features including a classic rural tap room with thick oak beams and a flagstone floor. The large garden has a delightful duck pond with fountain, while the traditional wooden barn outbuilding serves as a skittle alley and function room. Guest beers include seasonals from Sussex breweries. The pub is mentioned in Hillaire Belloc's The Four Men. ⚲Q✿⌂◗&P

Bepton

Country Inn

Severals Road, GU29 0LR (1 mile SW of Midhurst)
OS870206
✪ 11.30-3, 5-midnight; 11.30-12.30am Fri & Sat; 12-midnight Sun
☎ (01730) 813466
Ballard's Midhurst Mild; Fuller's London Pride; Young's Bitter; guest beers Ⓗ
An easy walk down the lane from Midhurst, this popular local in a quiet spot offers changing guest beers from independent brewers, as well as Stowford Press cider. A single bar serves two distinct drinking areas with a log fire on one side – the dining area enjoys a busy trade (no food Sun eve). Outside at the front there are tables, while the extensive rear garden is equipped with children's play equipment. Closing may be extended on busy nights. ⚲Q✿◗➥(60)♣♣P⏚

Bosham

White Swan

Station Road, PO18 8NG (on A259 roundabout)

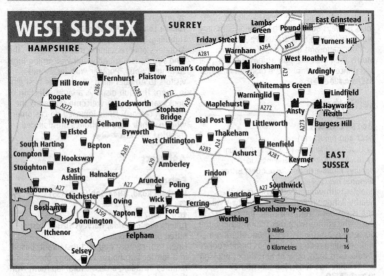

WEST SUSSEX

HAMPSHIRE
SURREY

Hill Brow · Fernhurst · Plaistow · Lambs Green · Pound Hill · East Grinstead
Friday Street · Turners Hill
Warnham · Tisman's Common · West Hoathly
Horsham · Ardingly
Rogate · Lodsworth · Warninglid · Whitemans Green · Lindfield
Nyewood · Stopham Bridge · Maplehurst · Ansty · Haywards Heath
Selham · Byworth · Dial Post · Littleworth · Burgess Hill
Elsted · West Chiltington · Thakeham
South Harting · Bepton · Ashurst · Henfield · Keymer
Compton · Hooksway · Amberley · EAST SUSSEX
Stoughton · East Ashling · Halnaker · Findon · Southwick
Westbourne · Arundel · Poling · Lancing
Bosham · Chichester · Wick · Ferring · Shoreham-by-Sea
Oving · Yapton · Ford · Worthing
Donnington
Itchenor · Felpham
Selsey

0 Miles 10
0 Kilometres 16

⏱ 12-2.30, 5-11; 12-midnight Fri-Sun
☎ (01243) 576086

**Hop Back Crop Circle, Summer Lightning;
Ringwood Best Bitter; guest beers** Ⓗ

An inn for over 300 years and parts dating
back to the 15th century, this roadside local is
spacious yet cosy, with exposed beams, bare
brick walls and two log-burning stoves. A
dining area is planned for the large P-shaped
interior. Three guest beers often include two
from Greene King or Hall and Woodhouse plus
another from a local micro, complemented by
Addlestones cider. The suntrap patio garden
will include a covered smoking area.
🏚Q⚲≠⇛(700, 56)♣♠P⌐

Burgess Hill

Watermill Inn

1 Leylands Road, RH15 0QF
⏱ 11 (12 Sun)-11
☎ (01444) 235517

**Fuller's London Pride; Greene King IPA; Young's
Bitter; guest beers** Ⓗ

Large single-bar community local in the
World's End neighbourhood of Burgess Hill. A
regular on the local CAMRA ale trail, the guest
beer is sourced from an independent southern
brewery and changes every month. Thai food
is available to eat in or take away. An
enclosed garden provides a safe area for
families in summer. Quiz night is Thursday.
⚲◑≠(Wivelsfield)⇛♣P

Byworth

Black Horse

GU28 0HL (off A283, 1 mile SE of Petworth)
⏱ 11.30-11; 12-10.30 Sun
☎ (01798) 342424

Beer range varies Ⓗ

Friendly, unspoilt, 16th-century village pub,
originally the local tannery. The front bar has a
traditional atmosphere with its large fireplace,
old flagstones and exposed beams. There are
distinct areas for diners and an old spiral
staircase leads to the function room. Next to it

is a games room with darts, pool table and
arcade machines, well away from the bar. One
of the finest pub gardens in Sussex is steeply
terraced and affords good Downs views.
🏚Q⚲⇛(1)♣P

Chichester

Bell Inn

3 Broyle Road, PO19 6AT
⏱ 11.30-3, 5-midnight; 12-3, 7-midnight Sun
☎ (01243) 783388

Adnams Bitter; guest beers Ⓗ

Attractive city local opposite the Festival
Theatre. Half-timber panelling and rustic
brickwork contribute to the homely
atmosphere. Popular with locals and
theatregoers alike, a good selection of typical
pub fare is available at all sessions except
Sunday evening. A sheltered suntrap garden
to the rear is a bonus. One guest beer is from
an independent or micro-brewery, the other is
from the Enterprise range. 🏚⚲◑⇛♣P⌐

Eastgate Inn

**4 The Hornet, PO19 7JG (500m E of Market Cross,
off Eastgate Square)**
⏱ 12 (11 Wed, 10 Sat)-11 (midnight Fri & Sat); 12-11
Sun
☎ (01243) 774877

**Fuller's London Pride; Gale's Butser Bitter, HSB,
seasonal beers** Ⓗ

A welcome return to the Guide for a fine town
pub that featured in the first edition. Dating
back to 1793, the bar is now open plan, with
an area for diners. Good value traditional pub
meals are served from the specials board at
lunchtime and summer evenings. There is a
patio garden and pool room to the rear. The
inn attracts locals, holiday-makers and
shoppers from the nearby market. A midsummer beer festival is hosted each year.
🏚⚲◑⇛♣⌐

Four Chesnuts

243 Oving Road, PO19 4EQ (E of Market Cross)
⏱ 12-11 (midnight Fri & Sat); 12-10.30 Sun

☎ (01243) 779974
**Caledonian Deuchars IPA; Oakleaf Hole Hearted;
Tetley Dark Mild; guest beers** Ⓗ
Traditional town hostelry and local CAMRA Pub
of the Year 2007, the Chesnuts has been
converted to a single bar but retains its distinct
drinking areas. The skittle alley doubles as a
dining room at busy times and occasionally
serves as a venue for successful beer festivals.
The menu of good hearty meals includes a 'pie
of the moment' (no food Mon & Sun eve). The
pub has a Saturday music night and hosts the
local folk club on Tuesday. ᴍ✿◐▤P⅃🖵

Compton

Coach & Horses
The Square, PO18 9HA (on B2146)
◷ 11.30-3 (4 Sat), 6-11; 12-10.30 Sun
☎ (02392) 631228
**Dark Star Hophead; Fuller's ESB; Triple fff
Moondance; guest beers** Ⓗ
This 16th-century pub lies in a remote but
charming village that is sometimes cut off by
downland streams. The front bar has two open
fires and a bar billiards table. The back bar,
now the restaurant (closed Sun eve and Mon),
is the oldest part of the pub, featuring plenty
of exposed beams and another open fire. Up
to five guest beers from independent
breweries are usually available. There are a
few seats outside in the village square.
ᴍQ✿◐▤(54)♣

Dial Post

Crown Inn
Worthing Road, RH13 8NH (just off A24)
◷ 11.30-3, 6-11; 12-4, 6-10.30 Sun
☎ (01403) 710902 ⊕ crowninndialpost.co.uk
**Harveys Sussex Best Bitter; King Horsham Best
Bitter, seasonal beer** Ⓗ
Attractive old coaching inn set in the peaceful
village of Dial Post featuring large wooden
pillars and beams throughout. The pub stocks
the local organic lager from Hepworth's and
sometimes a pin of seasonal ale is on the bar.
There is a comfortable sun lounge at the front
and an old dining/function room at a lower
level. The ingredients for the excellent food
are sourced locally where possible (no food
Sun eve). ᴍQ✿≠◐P⅃

Donnington

Blacksmith's Arms
Selsey Road, PO20 7PR (on B2201)
◷ 11-3, 5.30-11; 11-11 Sat; 12-10.30 Sun
☎ (01243) 783999
**Fuller's London Pride; Greene King Abbot;
Oakleaf Bitter** Ⓗ
Cosy, cottage-style, 17th-century, part Grade II
listed pub. It attracts diners and drinkers in
equal measure, and is worth seeking out for
the Oakleaf beer, which is rare for the area.
Dine in the bar or the excellent restaurant
where fresh fish is a speciality. Everything is
home made daily, using locally sourced
produce. The large, safe garden offers
activities for children. Live jazz is performed
monthly (first Thu). Umbrellas with heaters
cater for smokers. ᴍQ✿◐♣P⅃

East Ashling

Horse & Groom
PO18 9AX (on B2178)
◷ 12-3, 6-11; 12-6 Sun
☎ (01243) 575339 ⊕ horseandgroomchichester.com
**Dark Star Hophead; Harveys Hadlow Bitter; Hop
Back Summer Lightning; Young's Bitter** Ⓗ
This welcoming 17th-century inn has been
skilfully extended, using knapped Sussex
flints. The beers benefit from a deep
traditional cellar under the handpumps. The
large fireplace (once a forge) houses a fine old
range, while the flagstone floor, old settles
and half-panelled walls in the bar underpin its
character. Diners enjoy a diverse, high-quality
menu of home-made dishes in the
comfortable restaurant (no food Sun eve).
Accommodation is in oak-beamed, en-suite
rooms in a converted 17th-century flint barn.
ᴍQ✿≠◐&▲🖵(54)♣P⅃

East Grinstead

Old Mill
Dunnings Road, RH19 4AT (half mile from town
centre on road to West Hoathly)
◷ 11-11 (midnight Fri & Sat)
☎ (01342) 326341
**Harveys Hadlow Bitter, Sussex Best Bitter,
seasonal beers** Ⓗ
Formerly know as Dunnings Mill, the old
waterwheel of this large pub, dating from
1596, has been restored to working order. The
interior of the Mill is split into several areas,
and the walls are adorned with framed prints
and collectibles. An extensive range of freshly
cooked meals complements the excellent
wine list and well-kept beers. Two Harveys
seasonal ales are usually available.
ᴍ✿◐▤P⅃

Elsted

Three Horseshoes
GU29 0JY (E end of village)
◷ 11-2.30, 6-11; 12-3, 7-10.30 Sun
☎ (01730) 825746
**Ballard's Best Bitter; Fuller's London Pride;
Taylor Landlord; guest beers** Ⓗ
Former drovers' inn, ideal for cosy winter
evenings with its small, low, beamed rooms
and open fires. Or in summer, enjoy the view
of the Downs from the large garden. It serves
as the village local, with one room set aside
for dining. A good range of home-cooked
traditional country food is always available,
with game a speciality. Cider is available in
summer. ᴍQ✿◐♣P

Felpham

Fox Inn
Waterloo Road, PO22 7EN
◷ 11.30 (12 Sun)-11
☎ (01243) 865308
Young's Bitter, Special; guest beers Ⓗ
Built to replace an older pub, which was
destroyed by fire, this was the last
establishment to be built by brewers Henty &
Constable of Chichester. The comfortable
interior with its dark oak panelling exudes a

warm, clubby atmosphere; there have been few changes since it opened in 1949 (note the original Crittall steel windows). Around the walls old pictures of the pub and its predecessor can be seen. Three guest beers usually include one from Gribble, plus Harveys Best Bitter or Wadworth 6X. Q❀◑🚌P⁻

Fernhurst

Red Lion

8 The Green, GU27 3HY

☉ 11.30-3, 5-11; 11.30-11 Thu-Sat; 12-10.30 Sun

☎ (01428) 643112

Fuller's Chiswick, London Pride, ESB, seasonal beers; guest beers ⊞

Idyllically set beside the village green, the Red Lion has been a pub since 1592. Inside is a single bar with a low, timbered ceiling and two side rooms. There is a splendid inglenook fireplace with a large wood-burning stove. In mild weather customers can sit by the green or in the large rear garden. The pub is popular with locals and diners. ♨❀◑🚌(70)P⁻

Ferring

Henty Arms

2 Ferring Lane, BN12 6QY (N of level crossing)

☉ 11-3, 5.30-11; 11-11 Thu; 11-midnight Fri & Sat; 12-11 Sun

☎ (01903) 504409

Caledonian Deuchars IPA; Fuller's London Pride; Greene King Ruddles County; Young's Bitter; guest beers ⊞

Welcoming village pub, just half a mile from Goring Station along a footpath. The public bar has a TV, juke box, darts, pool and traditional games, while the spacious lounge bar is quieter. It has recently been extended by a dining area where good food is served. Dogs and well-behaved children are welcome until 9pm. On Sunday, the village cricket club team retires here after matches, and in the evening a quiz is hosted. A garden beer festival is staged in July.
♨Q❀◑⊟⇌(Goring)🚌(700)♣P⁻

Findon

Findon Manor Hotel

High Street, BN14 0TA (just S of village centre)

☉ 12-2.30, 6-11; 12-10.30 Sun

☎ (01903) 872733 🌐findonmanor.com

Black Sheep Best Bitter; Harveys Sussex Best Bitter; Wells Bombardier; guest beers ⊞

Originally the Old Rectory, dating back to 1584, this hotel is set in the lee of the South Downs, close to Cissbury Ring. The Snooty Fox bar is popular with locals, visitors and hotel guests who enjoy the log fire in winter and the attractive gardens planted with tall evergreens, splendid specimen trees and colourful shrubs in summer. Children are always welcome. The 11 bedroom suites are named after race horses that were trained in the village. ♨Q❀⇔◑🚌(1)●P

Ford

Ship & Anchor

Station Road, BN18 0BJ (400 yds S of Ford Station, down private road)

☉ 11-11 (10 Sun)

☎ (01243) 551747

Arundel seasonal beers; Ringwood Fortyniner, seasonal beers; Skinner's Betty Stogs ⊞

Set on the banks of the Arun, with views to Arundel, this congenial riverside ale house welcomes families and bikers as well as campers and boaters – there are facilities for mooring and camping, including caravans, on site. In the autumn, a conker championship and a beer festival are hosted. The food portions are generous: the mixed grill should only be tackled by the ravenous. Look out for the pub's friendly dog and three cats.
♨♉❀◑⛺⇌P

Friday Street

Royal Oak

RH12 4QA (on Rusper to Capel road, signed down side road)

☉ 11-3, 5-11; 11-11 Sat; 12-9 Sun

☎ (01293) 871393

Surrey Hill Ranmore Ale; Welton's Pride 'n' Joy; guest beers ⊞

This gem of a free house is popular with locals as well as attracting real ale lovers. Five handpumps dispense an ever-changing range of guest ales, mainly from nearby micro-breweries, and the pub also stocks JB and Thatcher's Medium Cheddar Valley ciders. Local events play a major role in the pub's agenda, and it runs special food nights offering home-cooked dishes made with local ingredients. A working area has been established with wireless internet access for business people. ♨◑♣●P

Halnaker

Anglesey Arms

Stane Street, PO18 0NQ (on A285)

☉ 11-3, 5.30-11.30; 11-11 Sat; 11-11.30 Sun

☎ (01243) 773474 🌐angleseyarms.co.uk

Adnams Bitter; Black Sheep Bitter; Dark Star Hophead; Hop Back Summer Lightning; Young's Bitter ⊞

Family-run, listed Georgian pub comprising a flagstone-floored public bar with a log fire, and a comfortable restaurant, renowned for good food using local seasonal organic produce. Wines, spirits and ciders are also organic, while steaks from Goodwood farm and fish from sustainable sources are specialities (Sun lunch booking essential). Cribbage, darts and cricket are played by pub teams. The pub has a two-acre garden and numerous flowering baskets adorn the front in summer. Weston's Old Rosie cider is sold.
♨Q❀◑⊟♿⛺🚌(55, 59)♣●P

Henfield

Plough Inn

High Street, BN5 9HP

☉ 11-11 (midnight Fri & Sat); 12-11 Sun

☎ (01273) 492280

Fuller's London Pride; Greene King Old Speckled Hen; Harveys Sussex Best Bitter; guest beer ⒣
Friendly, single-bar, former coaching inn situated in the centre of Henfield. The comfortable interior is decorated with antique firearms and horse brasses. There is a real open fire in winter. The dining area to the left of the bar features a tapas menu alongside more traditional fare. ♨❀☕◑▲🚃(17, 100)♣

Hill Brow

Jolly Drover

Hill Brow, GU33 7QL (on B2070 between Petersfield and Liphook)
☺ 11-2.30, 6-11; 12-3 Sun
☎ (01730) 893137
Fuller's London Pride; Ringwood Best Bitter; Taylor Landlord; Triple fff Alton's Pride; guest beers ⒣
Large roadside pub on the old A3, about a mile from Liss station. Large sofas offer comfortable seating in front of the fireplace with a roaring log fire in winter. Original beams and wood panelling abound, along with displays of antique items such as old weighing scales. There is an extensive range of meals on the menu. ♨Q❀☕◢◑🚃P⅃

Hooksway

Royal Oak

PO18 9JZ (off B2141) OSSU815162
☺ 11.30-2.30, 6-11; closed Mon; 12-3 Sun
☎ (01243) 535257 ⊕ royaloakhooksway.co.uk
Arundel Castle; Exmoor Beast; Fullers Gale's HSB; Hammerpot Red Hunter ⒣
Tucked away in a valley close to the South Downs Way, this 15th-century rural gem became a lunch stop for the 'guns' on West Dean estate shoots. King Edward VII was a frequent patron, but now walkers and cyclists enjoy its peaceful setting. Reasonably priced home-cooked food complements the four ales which may alter in summer but usually include a strong dark beer. Opening times/days can vary – phone if travelling far. Camping is possible behind the pub, 24 hours notice required. ♨Q☙❀☕◑▲♣P

Horsham

Beer Essentials

30A East Street, RH12 1HL
☺ 10-6 (7 Fri & Sat); closed Sun & Mon
☎ (01403) 218890 ⊕ thebeeressentials.co.uk
Arundel Sussex Gold; Dark Star Festival; guest beers ⒣
This specialist beer shop sells an extensive range of approximately 150 ever-changing bottled beers, as well as a continuously changing selection of at least six beers drawn straight from the cask. The casks come mainly from local micros while the bottles include fruit beers, porters and stouts from around the country, as well as a range of foreign beers. JB Medium cider is always stocked along with a range of bottled ciders and lagers. Minipins and polypins are available. The proprietor also runs a popular beer festival every autumn in a local hall. ♣

Black Jug

31 North Street, RH12 1RJ
☺ 12-11 (midnight Fri & Sat; 10.30 Sun)
☎ (01403) 253526 ⊕ blackjug-horsham.co.uk
Adnams Broadside; Greene King Old Speckled Hen; guest beers ⒣
Bustling town-centre pub near the station with a large conservatory leading to an outside area. In winter, real fires create a cosy feel. The pub has an excellent reputation for its food, much of it locally sourced. The house beer, Black Jug, is brewed in Horsham by Welton's, and cask-conditioned cider is also available. Friendly and efficient staff help make this an excellent place to enjoy a drink or a meal before attending a show at the nearby arts centre. ♨Q❀☕◑≹

Itchenor

Ship Inn

The Street, PO20 7AH (100m from harbour)
☺ 11.30-11; 12-10.30 Sun
☎ (01243) 512284 ⊕ theshipinn.biz
Ballard's Best Bitter; Itchen Valley Godfathers; guest beers ⒣
The pub sits a short distance from the waterfront in the village main street. Built in the 1930s, wood panelling and yachting memorabilia add character. Two rooms are dedicated to dining – a wide range of traditional meals is served, with locally caught fish a speciality. In the bar, up to four beers are available, all from small or local micro-breweries. ♨Q☙❀☕◑🚃🚃♣P

Keymer

Greyhound Inn

Keymer Road, BN6 8QT (1 mile E of Hassocks station on B2116)
☺ 11-midnight; 12-10.30 Sun
☎ (01273) 842645
Adnams Bitter; Fuller's London Pride; Harveys Sussex Best Bitter; Shepherd Neame Spitfire ⒣
Old village pub established in 1895, situated opposite the Church of St Cosmas and St Damian. It always has four beers on handpump, and the kitchen serves excellent food, making it a popular venue. A large display of beer mugs adds to the cheerful atmosphere. Well-behaved children are welcome. The Greyhound is a great place to start a walk on the South Downs between Hassocks and Ditchling. ❀☕◑🦽♣P⅃

Lambs Green

Lamb Inn

RH12 4RG (2 miles N of A264)
☺ 11.30-3, 7-10.30
☎ (01293) 871336 ⊕ thelambinn.info
Beer range varies ⒣
This delightful country pub is WJ King's only tied house. The dining area extends into a large conservatory, while drinkers are surrounded by dark oak beams and cosy nooks in the bar. Traditional home-cooked food is available daily. Biddenden's cider and mulled wine are served by the friendly staff, along with a range of King's bottled beers. ♨❀☕◑♣P

Lancing

Crabtree
140 Crabtree Lane, BN15 9NQ (W end of Crabtree)
✪ 12-11 (11.30 Fri & Sat)
☎ (01903) 875901
Fuller's London Pride; guest beers Ⓗ
Large 1930s-style suburban pub offering some of the best beer in Lancing. In the public bar drinkers may enjoy pool, darts and TV, while the comfortable saloon provides more peaceful surroundings. The large garden accommodates children and dogs. The emphasis is on good beer, and the landlord participates in the SIBA direct delivery scheme which enables him to offer three guest ales from small breweries, usually including a mild. Sunday lunches are popular. ⊛◑ ⬚≉⋈♣P

Lindfield

Stand Up Inn
47 High Street, RH16 2HN
✪ 11.30-11.30 (midnight Fri & Sat); 12-11.30 Sun
☎ (01444) 482995
Dark Star Hophead, Best, seasonal beers; guest beers Ⓗ
Vibrant and well-liked pub situated in the High Street of this picturesque village. It was built in the 1880s by Edward Durrant who constructed his ale house adjacent to his brewery. Evidence of the former Durrant's Brewery is provided by the outbuildings and the sign on the beam above the bar. Frequent beer and occasional cider festivals are held here, and two real ciders – Black Rat and Weston's Traditional – are stocked. Lunchtime bar snacks are provided. ⋈⊛⬚♣●

Littleworth

Windmill
Littleworth Lane, RH13 8EJ (off A272 W of Cowfold)
✪ 11.30-3, 5.30 (6 Sat)-11; 12-3, 7-10.30 Sun
☎ (01403) 710308
Badger K&B Sussex Bitter, Tanglefoot, seasonal beer Ⓗ
Unspoilt pleasant community local where the landlord extends a warm welcome to all. The comfortable lounge is adorned with an unusual collection of china windmills. The public bar with bar skittles has an old-fashioned rustic feel, emphasised by the agricultural tools on display. The building is fashioned in classic Sussex style and covered with wisteria, adding to the pleasure of the attractive side garden in summer. No meals Sunday evening. ⋈Q⊛◑⬚&♣●

Maplehurst

White Horse
Park Lane, RH13 6LL
✪ 12-2.30, 6-11; 12-3, 7-10.30 Sun
☎ (01403) 891208
Harveys Sussex Best Bitter; Welton's Pride 'n' Joy; guest beers Ⓗ
Delightful country pub with two small bars festooned with numerous artefacts. The conservatory doubles as a family room, leading to the pub garden where there are

activities for children. Although the pub offers a wide range of food, the emphasis is on conversation and good beer, with many guest ales sourced from small independent brewers. Local JB ciders are also stocked. Now in its 21st year in the Guide, this was local CAMRA Pub of the Year in 2006. ⋈Q⊛⬚ ⬚♣●P

Plaistow

Sun Inn
The Street, RH14 0PX
✪ 12-3 (not Mon), 7-11 (10.30 Sun)
☎ (01403) 871313
Beer range varies Ⓗ
Quiet, friendly village local comprising two small bars – a sunken corner bar to the left and a bar to the right dominated by an inglenook. A small room off this bar is mainly used for dining. Evening meals are served on Friday and Saturday, lunches on Saturday. Brick floors and exposed beams feature throughout. Opening hours may vary. ⋈Q⊛◑⬚P

Pound Hill

Tavern on the Green
Grattons Drive, RH10 3BA
✪ 10-11 (1am Fri & Sat)
☎ (01293) 882468
Harveys Sussex Best Bitter Ⓗ
Attractive, modern pub on the leafy western outskirts of Crawley, styled as a cross between a railway carriage and an airport departure lounge. The middle of the pub is dominated by a three-sided bar. This chrome-plated bar is a popular lager outlet – but real ale lovers can enjoy a well-served pint of Harveys while watching one of the four large-screen TVs, or marvelling at the collection of modern art on display. ◑⬚P

Rogate

White Horse Inn
East Street, GU31 5EA (on A272)
✪ 11-3, 6-11.30 (midnight Fri); 11-midnight Sat; 12-10.30 Sun
☎ (01730) 821333
Harveys Hadlow Bitter, Sussex Best Bitter, Old Ale, Armada Ale, seasonal beers Ⓗ
Dating from the 16th century, this old coaching inn has oak beams, flagstone floors and a huge log fire. A Harveys tied house, you can expect up to five of its beers including the seasonal brews. Half of the pub is used for dining; the large range of meals includes steaks and vegetarian choices (no food Sun eve). The car park overlooks the village sports field. ⋈Q⊛◑⬚♣P⌐

Selham

Three Moles
GU28 0PN (off A272 at Halfway Bridge)
OSSU935206
✪ 12-2, 5-11; 11.30-11 Sat; 12-10.30 Sun
☎ (01798) 861303 ⊕ thethreemoles.co.uk
Skinner's Betty Stogs; guest beers Ⓗ
Moles abound at this characterful, bijou country pub, hidden in the Rother Valley. Built in 1872 to serve Selham Station, the railway is

defunct but this welcoming free house thrives, stocking a mild plus three guest beers from small breweries. The name refers to the coat of arms of the owners, the Mitford Family. Frequently a local CAMRA Pub of the Year, it hosts a garden beer festival in June. The Worthing-Midhurst bus stops at Halfway Bridge, a pleasant mile's walk.
⚠Q❀▲🖵(1)♣♠P

Selsey

Seal
6 High Street, PO20 0JX (on B2145)
✪ 10.30-11 (midnight Fri & Sat); 12-11 Sun
☎ (01243) 602461 ⊕ the-seal.com
Dark Star Hophead; Badger First Gold, Tanglefoot; Hop Back GFB, Crop Circle, Summer Lightning; guest beers 🅗
This family-run free house, a former hotel just five-minutes' walk from the sea, has recently been refurbished to a high standard. There are three bars and a restaurant area plus a function room. At the front is a wooden decked seating area for summer drinking, while inside there is a fine display of old photographs of local historic interest. Local micro-brewery beers make occasional guest appearances. Q⭢❀🕽🖵(51)♣♠P↳

Shoreham-by-Sea

Buckingham Arms
35-39 Brunswick Road, BN43 5WA
✪ 11-11 (10.30 Sun)
☎ (01273) 453660
Greene King XX Mild, Morland Original; Harveys Sussex Best Bitter; Hop Back Summer Lightning; Taylor Landlord; guest beers 🅗
A warm welcome is guaranteed at this friendly pub opposite the station. It offers 11 beers on handpump, including a number of guests on a regular basis, plus a cider. The Buckingham Arms hosts two beer festivals a year, in February and August. Live music and a plasma TV screen attract a lively mix of customers. ❀⇌🖵♣♠P

Duke of Wellington
368 Brighton Road, BN43 6RE (on coast road)
✪ 12-11 (10.30 Sun)
☎ (01273) 389818
Dark Star Hophead, seasonal beers; guest beers 🅗
Roadside hostelry with a unique welly boot pub sign outside. Recently acquired by the owners of the Evening Star in Brighton, a programme of interior and exterior refurbishment is now almost complete. The extensive beer range hails mainly from the Dark Star brewery, complemented by guest ales. One real cider is usually available on handpump and there is a constantly changing range of continental bottled beers. Barbecues in the garden are a highlight during the summer months. ❀⇌🖵♠↳

Red Lion
Old Shoreham Road, BN43 5TE
✪ 11.30-11; 12-10.30 Sun
☎ (01273) 453171
Beer range varies 🅗

Situated opposite the old toll bridge, with pleasant views over the Downs, this ale house gets especially busy when the airshow is held at the adjacent airport in September. The ancient ale house is not designed for tall people; the top bar offers more head room. The main bar has a separate dining area. The beers come from small and micro-breweries, and the Lion hosts the Adur beer festival at Easter in a marquee in the garden.
⚠Q❀🕽🖵(2A, 9)P

South Harting

Ship
North Lane, GU31 5PZ (at B2146 jct)
✪ 11 (12 Sun)-11
☎ (01730) 825302
Ballard's Wassail; Bowman Swift One; Dark Star Hophead; Palmer IPA 🅗
Friendly 17th-century free house built using old ship's timbers. There is a small public bar and a larger lounge/restaurant where good-value meals are served (not Tue or Sun eves, Feb-Sep); booking is recommended at weekends. An enclosed garden flanks the B2146. The guest beer is always from an independent or micro-brewery, and Thatchers Gold cider is stocked.
⚠Q❀🕽🖵(54, 91)♣♠P

Southwick

Romans
Manor Hall Road, BN42 4NG
✪ 12 (11 Sat)-11; 12-10.30 Sun
☎ (01273) 592147
Beer range varies 🅗
A popular and busy local, named after a Roman building nearby, this hostelry offers a choice of at least 24 different guest beers a month. Two beer festivals are staged here every year and draw the crowds. Meals are now served all day, and in summer there are regular barbecues outside under cover. The large beer garden is a favourite with children.
⚠❀🕽🖵⇌♣♠P⊟

Stopham Bridge

White Hart
Stopham Road, RH20 1DS (1 mile W of Pulborough on A283)
✪ 10-11 daily
☎ (01798) 873321
Arundel range; Welton's range; guest beers 🅗
This 700-year old pub stands alongside a pack-horse bridge on the old toll road, a wonderful spot affording views of the river. The original bar features beams and an inglenook fireplace with a table, seat and window overlooking the lower lounge bar. The restaurant is on a lower level. Old photographs and stories of resident ghosts abound. ⚠Q❀🕽🖵(1)♣P↳

Stoughton

Hare & Hounds
The Street, PO19 9JQ (off B2146) OSSU802115
✪ 11-3, 6-11; 11-11 Fri, Sat & summer; 12-10.30 Sun
☎ (02392) 631433

Harveys Sussex Best Bitter; Itchen Valley Hampshire Rose; Taylor Landlord; guest beers Ⓗ
Traditional country pub in a beautiful downland valley, an ideal base for walking. A large dining room serves fresh local produce. The public bar, warmed by an open fire, is the locals' choice. There are three open fires which, along with stone-flagged floors, beams and simple furniture, create a cheerful rustic atmosphere. Outside is a paved drinking area at the front and a garden at the back. Guest beers include at least one from Ballard's.
ⓂQⒹ⊕♣P

Thakeham

White Lion Inn
The Street, RH20 3EP (500m from B2139)
☼ 11-11; 12-10.30 Sun
☎ (01798) 813141
Caledonian Deuchars IPA; Fuller's London Pride; Harveys Sussex Best Bitter; Hogs Back TEA Ⓗ
Traditional 18th-century village pub with three rooms around a central bar. There are wooden floors, exposed beams and wall panels as well as window seats throughout. An open fire greets visitors on chilly days. A white ornamental lion sits on the bar and an old pub sign hangs on a wall. The Gun Room, with its large hearth, is where the local gun club and running club meet every month. A good selection of quality food is served (not Sun eve). Ⓜ❀ⒹP

Tismans Common

Mucky Duck
RH12 3BW (1 mile S of A281)
☼ 11-11; 12-10.30 Sun
☎ (01403) 822300 ⊕ mucky-duck-inn.co.uk
Fuller's London Pride; King Horsham Best; guest beers Ⓗ
Excellent country free house featuring a mixture of original and new wooden beams and a long bar and counter, with an inglenook fireplace and a copper cowl at the end of the bar. The restaurant, separated from the bar area by a wall with mock-medieval windows, serves food of a high standard. Eleven luxurious rooms are available in lodges away from the main building. Ⓜ❀⇆Ⓓ♣P

Turners Hill

Red Lion
Lion Lane, RH10 4NU (off North St, B2028) OS342357
☼ 11-3, 5-11 (11.30 Fri); 11-11 Sat; 12-10.30 Sun
☎ (01342) 715416
Harveys Sussex Best Bitter, seasonal beers Ⓗ
Back in 1974 the local CAMRA branch was formed in this interesting Harveys pub. Split-level, with beams and an inglenook, it stocks many Harveys seasonals on draught and also carries a range of Harveys bottled beers. Home-cooked lunches (not Sun) are served and the pub is well used by the local community. A warm welcome is guaranteed and dogs are permitted. Ⓜ❀Ⓓ♣P⅄

Warnham

Sussex Oak
2 Church Street, RH12 3QW
☼ 11-11 (10.30 Sun)
☎ (01403) 265028 ⊕ thesussexoak.co.uk
Adnams Bitter; Fuller's London Pride; Taylor Landlord; Young's Bitter; guest beers Ⓗ
Large 16th-century pub and restaurant welcoming locals and visitors alike. It offers a range of rotating guest ales, often from local breweries, and an extensive menu of home-cooked dishes featuring local produce. The pub is gaining a reputation for its bank holiday beer festivals, and both families and dogs are welcome. The extensive pub garden is popular with customers in summer. Ⓜ❀Ⓓ⇩⇧P⅄

Warninglid

Half Moon
The Street, RH17 5TR (on B2115, 1 mile W of A23)
☼ 10.30-2.30, 5.30-11; 12-10.30 Sun
☎ (01444) 461227
Black Sheep Best Bitter; Greene King Old Speckled Hen; Harveys Sussex Best Bitter; guest beers Ⓗ
This village local continues to thrive under new owners and is much appreciated by locals. The three regular beers are well kept, and a fourth guest ale is added during the summer, usually from a local brewer. A good range of freshly prepared meals is also available (no food Sun eve). ⓂQ❀Ⓓ⇩P⅄

West Chiltington

Five Bells
Smock Alley, RH20 2QX (1 mile S of West Chiltington) OS091172
☼ 12-3, 6-11; 12-3, 7-10.30 Sun
☎ (01798) 812143 ⊕ westchiltington.com/five_bells.htm
Palmer Copper Ale, IPA; guest beers Ⓗ
Local CAMRA Pub of the Year 2007, this idyllic country free house is off the beaten track yet well worth seeking out. The licensees offer five excellent beers from independent brewers, usually including two from Palmer plus three changing guests. Additional ales and cider from Biddenden may be served from the cask at weekends. Delicious food is also served (not Sun and Mon eve). B&B accommodation is available in five double rooms. ⓂQ❀⇆Ⓓ⇩Ａ⇩(1)♣P⅄

West Hoathly

Cat Inn
Queen's Square, RH19 4PP (opp church)
☼ 11.30-3, 6-11; closed Mon; 11-11 Sat; 11.30-3.30, 7-10.30 Sun
☎ (01342) 810369
Harveys Sussex Best Bitter; guest beers Ⓗ
Village free house attracting locals as well as visitors from further afield. Reputedly the oldest building in the village, the Cat comprises a maze of cosy rooms, including one featuring a glass-covered well. One room is dominated by a real fire in winter. The restaurant serves good quality home-cooked food using local produce (snacks only Sun

eve). Harveys Old is a regular winter beer, and Hepworth's Organic Lager features on keg. No children under 14. ⚫Q⚫◐▯▭P'

Westbourne

Cricketers

Commonside, PO10 8TA

⚫ 5-11; 12-midnight Thu-Sat; 12-11 Sun

☎ (01243) 372647

Fuller's London Pride; Gribble Reg's Tipple; Hop Back Crop Circle; Ringwood Fortyniner; Suthwyk Sunshine Ale ⏢

This 300-year-old pub is a little hard to find but well worth seeking out. A genuine free house, the beer range varies between Sussex and Hampshire micro-breweries on handpump. The comfortable single L-shaped bar is partially wood-panelled, and the beer garden to the side is a veritable sun trap. No food is available. ⚫⚫♣●P'

Whitemans Green

Ship

RH15 5BY (N of Cuckfield at B2115/B2036 jct)

⚫ 12-2.30 (not Wed), 5.30-11; 12-11 Sat; 12-2.30 Sun

☎ (01444) 413219

Harveys Sussex Best Bitter; guest beers ⏢

Friendly, single-bar village local, handily placed for the Haywards Heath Rugby Club. There is an abundance of handpumps in the bar but they are not in use – all the real ales are served by gravity dispense from a cool room behind the bar. This free house is family run and has a comfortable interior with sofas around an unusual double-sided fireplace. ⚫Q⚫▱◐▲▭(271, 272)♣P

Wick

Dewdrop Inn

96 Wick Street, BN17 7JS

⚫ 10.30-3, 5.30-11; 10.30-11 Sat; 10.30-10.30 Sun

☎ (01903) 716459

Fuller's London Pride, Gale's Butser Bitter; guest beers ⏢

This friendly and welcoming Victorian local is one of the disappearing band of traditional ale houses that may be described as truly unspoilt. The small saloon bar is adorned with a variety of mirrors, copper maps and Ringwood XXXX posters. Ringwood XXXX Porter and Old Thumper feature as seasonal guests. The spacious public bar where pub games are played is plain in decor. Q▱▭♣

Worthing

George & Dragon

1 High Street, Tarring, BN14 7NN

⚫ 11-11 (midnight Fri & Sat); 12-10.30 Sun

☎ (01903) 202497

Courage Directors; Greene King Abbot; Harveys Sussex Best Bitter; Hop Back Summer Lightning; Young's Bitter; guest beers ⏢

A public house has been standing at the southern end of historic Tarring High Street since 1610. The timber-framed building houses a single bar with low exposed beams, comprising a number of separate areas for drinking and lunching. The secluded beer garden offers a peaceful retreat from the usually busy bar that attracts an eclectic mix of customers. The pub hosts annual beer festivals. ⚫◐≠(W Worthing)P

Selden Arms

41 Lyndhurst Road, BN11 2DB

⚫ 11-11 (midnight Wed, Fri & Sat); 12-10.30 Sun

Dark Star Hophead; Ringwood Fortyniner; guest beers ⏢

A most impressive community pub, tastefully refurbished by the current owners. The enthusiastic licensees offer a warm and friendly welcome to an eclectic clientele. A haven for drinkers, there are six handpumps dispensing real ales including an inspired choice of guests. Other attractions include Belgian beers, occasional live music and eagerly awaited festivals. ◐≠▭♣

Swan

79 High Street, BN11 1DN

⚫ 11-11 (midnight Fri & Sat; 10.30 Sun)

☎ (01903) 232923

Greene King Abbot; Harveys Sussex Best Bitter; Shepherd Neame Spitfire; guest beers ⏢

This 19th-century oasis bears all the hallmarks of the archetypal village local: Sussex flint walls, beams, brasses and agricultural implements. One of its fireplaces is flanked by stained-glass windows from the Kemptown Brewery, each depicting a white swan. By day the pub attracts a blend of locals and shoppers, relaxing over a drink. At night the atmosphere gets more lively. ⚫⚫◐≠

Vine

27-29 High Street, Tarring, BN14 7NN

⚫ 12-midnight (12.30am Fri & Sat); 12-11 Sun

☎ (01903) 202891

Badger K & B Sussex, Best, Hopping Hare, Tanglefoot; Hopback Summer Lightning; Wadworth 6X ⏢

One of two surviving pubs in Tarring's historic High Street, the Vine has undergone many changes over the last 20 years or so. The interior now features light wood panelling, which has brightened the place up. Old framed photos and past local adverts decorate the walls. Children are welcome in the extensive garden and play area. No evening meals Friday-Sunday.

Q⚫◐≠(W Worthing)P

Yapton

Maypole Inn

Maypole Lane, BN18 0DP (off B2132, pedestrian access from Lake Lane)

⚫ 11.30 (12 Sun)-11

☎ (01243) 551417

Arundel Sussex Mild; Skinner's Betty Stogs; Triple fff Alton's Pride; guest beers ⏢

A recent local CAMRA Pub of the Year, this small flint-built inn is hidden away from the village centre down Maypole Lane, which was cut off by the railway in 1846 leaving it in splendid isolation. The cosy lounge has a log fire and an imposing row of seven handpumps. The public bar accommodates a juke box, darts and pool; a skittle alley can be booked. Outside is a paved patio.

⚫Q⚫◐▱▲▭(66, 66A)♣●P'

Good Beer Guide Prague & The Czech Republic

EVAN RAIL

The completely independent guide to more than 100 Czech breweries, 450 different beers and over 100 great places to try them.

Good BEER Guide PRAGUE & THE CZECH REPUBLIC EVAN RAIL

Includes ideas for places to stay

CAMPAIGN FOR REAL ALE

This fully updated and expanded version of a collectible classic is the first new edition to be produced by CAMRA for 10 years! It is the definitive guide for visitors to the Czech Republic and compulsory reading for fans of great beer, featuring more than 100 Czech breweries, 400 different beers and over 100 great places to try them. It includes listings of brewery-hotels and regional attractions for planning complete vacations outside of the capital, sections on historical background, how to get there and what to expect, as well as detailed descriptions of the 12 most common Czech beer styles.

£12.99   ISBN 978 1 85249 233 5

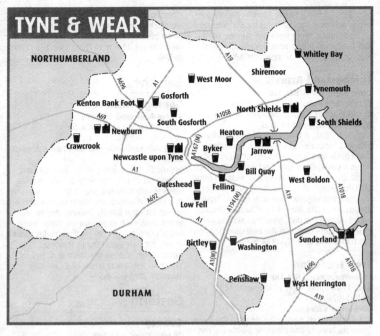

Bill Quay

Albion

10 Reay Street, NE10 0TY

🕐 4-11 (midnight Fri); 12-midnight Sat; 12-11 Sun

☎ (0191) 469 2418

Jarrow Bitter, Swinging Gibbet, Westoe IPA, seasonal beers; guest beers ⊞

One of three pubs run by the local Jarrow brewery, it stocks not just its own CAMRA award winning beers but guest beers from other highly respected micro-breweries throughout the country. The lounge bar has marvellous views across heavily industrialised Tyneside and the river. The conservatory has a pool table and the pub fields five darts teams. Live bands are hosted fortnightly plus regular buskers' nights and weekly quizzes. The Coast to Coast cycle route and Keelman's Way Walk both pass nearby. ⚒️⊖(Pelaw)🚃♣♦P

Birtley

Barley Mow Inn

Durham Road, DH3 2AG (jct Durham Road and Vigo Lane)

🕐 10-midnight

☎ (0191) 410 4504

Black Sheep Best Bitter; guest beers ⊞

Large 1930s brick-built main road suburban pub on the county boundary. Popular with local residents, it has a split level lounge plus dining area and a public bar with pool table. It runs several darts, dominoes and pool teams. The four ever-changing guest beers come from local micro-breweries as well as via the SIBA direct delivery scheme. Live music plays every weekend and a quiz is held weekly. The annual beer and music festival is a highlight. Breakfast is served from 10am daily. ✿◗🍴🚃♣P╚

Moulders Arms

Peareth Terrace, DH1 2LW

🕐 11-3, 5.30-11; 12-3, 7-10.30 Sun

☎ (0191) 410 2949

Boddingtons Bitter; Greene King Old Speckled Hen; guest beer ⊞

Although now a residential area, the pub's name reflects the town's varied industrial past. It has a large beamed public bar and split level lounge mainly for diners. The pub is noted for its dedication to raising funds for local charities over many years. It runs a popular golf society as well as darts teams and a weekly quiz. The guest beer often comes from a local micro-brewery. There is a rumour of a poltergeist here who moves things about! ✿◗🍴🚃♣♦P╚

Byker

Cluny

36 Lime Street, NE1 2PQ

🕐 11-11; 12-10.30 Sun

☎ (0191) 230 4474 ⊕ theheadofsteam.com

Beer range varies ⊞

Dating back to the 1840s, this former industrial building retains many original features. Recognised as a major live music venue, the pub attracts internationally renowned performers and their fans. Possibly the best selection of British and foreign draught and bottled beers in the area is on

INDEPENDENT BREWERIES

Big Lamp Newburn
Bull Lane Sunderland
Darwin Sunderland
Hadrian & Border Newcastle upon Tyne
Jarrow Jarrow
Mordue North Shields

offer here. It has a family friendly gallery area which acts as a showcase for locally produced art exhibitions. Work from the various artists and craftsmen in the next door studios and workshops can also be seen. ✿❶◗&✿

Cumberland Arms ☆

James Place Street, NE6 1LD
✿ 12.30 (3.30 winter)-11; 12.30-10.30 Sun
☎ (0191) 265 6151 ⊕ thecumberlandarms.co.uk
Wylam Rapper; guest beers Ⓗ
Traditional pub, a champion of independent ales and supporter of live music and dance. Live bands and comedians perform several times a week. Community activities take place in the downstairs bars every day, ranging from ukulele rehearsals to a knitting club. Winter and summer organic beer festivals are hosted and much of the annual Ouseburn Festival is based around the pub. Note that closing times may vary depending on the entertainment on the night. ⚌Q✿❷Θ(Byker)🚃✿P

Free Trade Inn

St Lawrence Road, NE6 1AP
✿ 11-11 Mon-Thurs; 11-12 Fri and Sat; 12-10.30
☎ (0191) 265 5764
Beer range varies Ⓗ
Renowned for its wonderful views of the River Tyne, its bridges and riverside buildings, this inn is a grand point from which to explore this interesting part of Newcastle. A basic but welcoming pub, it has a marvellous atmosphere. There is no TV or fruit machine, but a free juke box puts out classic sounds. An excellent selection of beers is on offer mainly from local brewers. Good value lunchtime sandwiches come from a local delicatessen. ⚌✿Θ(Byker)

Crawcrook

Rising Sun

Bank Top, NE40 4EE
✿ 11.30-11 (midnight Fri & Sat); 12-11 Sun
☎ (0191) 413 3316
Black Sheep Best Bitter; Mordue Workie Ticket; guest beers Ⓗ
This lively local offers something for everyone including the best range of beers for miles around, often sourced from local micros. Long serving licensees provide a warm welcome. It has a variety of drinking areas including quieter areas for relaxed conversation. Good value food can be enjoyed in the comfortable conservatory. A juke box and pool table provide the entertainment. ✿❶◗🚃(10, 11)♣P

Felling

Wheatsheaf

26 Carlisle Street, NE10 0HQ
✿ 5 (12 Fri & Sat)-11; 12-10.30 Sun
☎ (0191) 420 0659
Big Lamp Bitter, Sunny Daze, Prince Bishop Ale, seasonal beers Ⓗ
Traditional street corner local, now a dying breed on Tyneside. Big Lamp's first tied house still attracts a loyal following who enjoy the value-for-money beers. Darts and dominoes schools are part of the lively social scene. An 'impromptu' folk night on Tuesday is a long

standing event. Big Lamp's occasional beers are stocked including the powerful Blackout when brewed. It takes just 10 minutes on the metro to get here from Newcastle city centre. ⚌Θ♣

Gateshead

Borough Arms

82 Bensham Road, NE8 1PS
✿ 12-3, 6-11; 12-midnight Fri & Sat; 12-11 Sun
☎ (0191) 478 1323
Wells Bombardier; Wylam Gold Tankard; guest beers Ⓗ
Reputedly the oldest pub in the town and among other uses formerly a corn mill. The nearest pub with real ale to the town centre, this straightfoward one room local is also a venue for local bands, buskers' nights and music quizzes. It is popular for darts. Guest beers often come from local micro-breweries. Handy for Gateshead public transport interchange, it is on the town trail and by Windmill Hills Park, scene of a Civil War skirmish. ⚌✿Θ🚃♣P⅃

Gosforth

County

70 High Street, NE3 1HB
✿ 12 (11 Fri)-11
☎ (0191) 285 6919
Fuller's London Pride; Greene King Old Speckled Hen; Theakston Best Bitter; Wells Bombardier; guest beers Ⓗ
An impressive listed building on the southern end of the High Street. This pub was formerly a dwelling of the renowned 19th century gangland Boulmer family. The L-shaped bar serves four regular beers and up to four guests, always including a Mordue and Houston beer. A small separate room provides a quieter spot for conversation away from the bar. Food is served noon to 6pm daily. Q✿❶◗Θ(Regent Centre/South Gosforth)🚃P

Gosforth Hotel

Salters Road, NE3 1HQ
✿ 11-11.30 (12.30am Fri & Sat)
☎ (0191) 285 6617
Black Sheep Best Bitter; Fuller's London Pride; Marston's Pedigree; Shepherd Neame Spitfire; Taylor Landlord; Wells Bombardier Ⓗ
On the corner of a busy road junction, this lively pub has a mixed clientele of students, locals and business people. The front bar is furnished with tables, chairs and leather sofas – games machines and TV screens dominate here. The rear snug, only open in the evening, offers a welcome change of pace, so much so that you could be in a different pub. ◗⊟Θ(Regent Centre)🚃

Job Bulman

St Nicholas Avenue, NE3 1AA
✿ 9am-11 (10.30 Sun)
☎ (0191) 223 6320
Greene King Abbot; Marston's Pedigree; guest beers Ⓗ
A tasteful conversion from a former post office, this one room Wetherspoon's pub has a separate area for families. The choice of guest

ales at low prices is very popular with locals, but the service can sometimes be slow. There is a pleasant outdoor heated area for smokers. Buses from Newcastle stop nearby on the High Street, or it is a 10-minute walk from South Gosforth metro.

❀◑ᴗ♿⊖(Regent Centre/S Gosforth)

Heaton

Chillingham Arms
Chillingham Road, NE6 5XN (opp. metro station)
🕓 11-11 (midnight Fri & Sat); 12-10.30 Sun
☎ (0191) 265 5915
Black Sheep Best Bitter; Mordue Workie Ticket; Theakston Best Bitter, guest ales Ⓗ
A popular student venue, this large two room pub is to the east of Newcastle city centre. The bar has pool tables, darts and TV for sport. Old photos, mainly with a sporting theme, adorn the walls. The lounge is quieter with background music, decorated with prints and artwork. An upstairs function room hosts music nights. ◑❀⊟⊖(Chillingham Rd)♣♠P

Jarrow

Robin Hood
Primrose Hill, NE32 5UB
🕓 12-11 (11.30 Fri & Sat)
☎ (0191) 428 5454
Jarrow Bitter, Rivet Catcher, Joblings Swinging Gibbet, seasonal beers; guest beers Ⓗ
The Jarrow brewery adjoins this former regional CAMRA Pub of the Year, with the award winning Jarrow ales named after events in local history. It has a variety of rooms including a restaurant and brewery tap bar. Photographs of the Jarrow 1936 march for jobs adorn the walls. Two guest beers are stocked and seasonal beer festivals hosted. Buses from Jarrow and Heworth metro interchanges drop you at the door.
♨❀◑ᴗ⊟♿⊖(Fellgate)⊟♠P⅄

Kenton Bank Foot

Twin Farms
22 Main Road, NE13 8AB
🕓 11-11; 12-10.30 Sun
☎ (0191) 286 1263
Taylor Landlord; guest beers Ⓗ
Built on the site of an old farm, the interior is one large open plan room; however the clever use of alcoves gives the feel of a number of small rooms. Two real fires add to the cosy atmosphere. Food is served daily. Quiz night is Monday – the quizmaster is a colourful character! ♨Q❀◑⊖(Bank Foot)P

Low Fell

Aletaster
706 Durham Road, NE9 6JA
🕓 12-11 (midnight Fri); 11-midnight Sat
☎ (0191) 487 0770
Durham White Amarillo; Jennings Cumberland Ale; Marston's Pedigree; Theakston Best Bitter; Wychwood Hobgoblin; Wylam Gold Tankard Ⓗ
Eleven handpulls offer beers from regional and micro-breweries, often from the north east, plus a rare for the area real cider. This

alehouse features the best range of real ales for some distance and attracts discriminating drinkers from far and wide. Bare boards in the public bar contrast with the cosy snug. Note the eye-catching window in the back wall depicting George IV – the pub's former name. Live music is hosted occasionally, plus weekly quizzes and seasonal beer festivals.
❀⊟(21)♣♠⅄

Newburn

Keelman
Grange Road, NE15 8NL
🕓 11-11; 12-10.30 Sun
☎ (0191) 267 1689
Big Lamp Bitter, Sunny Daze, Summerhill Stout, Prince Bishop Ale, seasonal beers Ⓗ
Tastefully converted Grade II listed former pumping station, now home to the Big Lamp brewery and brewery tap. The full range of Big Lamp beers can be sampled in a relaxed atmosphere, served alongside good value food. The keelmen shipped coal on the River Tyne and are pictured in old photographs. The adjacent Keelman's Lodge provides quality accommodation. The Coast to Coast cycle way and Hadrian's Wall path pass close by.
❀♨◑ᴗ♿⊟(21, 22)P⅄

Newcastle upon Tyne

Bacchus
High Bridge, NE1 6BX
🕓 11.30-11; 11-midnight Fri & Sat; 7-10.30 Sun
☎ (0191) 261 1008
Harviestoun Bitter & Twisted; Mordue Five Bridge; Taylor Landlord, guest ales Ⓗ
Rebuilt several years ago, this popular pub has a comfortable seating area overlooking the street outside. There is plenty of standing room around high tables with a raised seating area at the rear and a small snug. Themed to look like the first class lounge of an ocean liner, there are photos of ships on the walls. A range of foreign bottled beers is stocked. Open Sunday lunchtime if Newcastle United are playing at home. ◑≢⊖(Monument)

Benton Ale House
Front Street, NE7 7XE
🕓 11-11 (11.30 Wed; midnight Fri & Sat); 12-11 Sun
☎ (0191) 266 1512
Banks's Bitter; Camerons Strongarm; Jennings Cumberland Ale; Marston's Pedigree, Old Empire; guest beers Ⓗ
The U-shaped bar creates distinct drinking areas with part tiled, part wooden floors and a mix of furniture adding to the traditional atmosphere. A dart board and piped music provide entertainment, plus the Wednesday quiz. Each bar has its own guest beer so check first before ordering. Food is served daily until the early evening and Sunday lunchtimes are very busy. A light, airy venue to enjoy a range of ales not regularly found in the area.
♨◑⊖(Four Lane Ends)⊟P⅄

Bodega
125 Westgate Road, NE1 4AG
🕓 11-11 (midnight Fri & Sat); 12-10.30 Sun
☎ (0191) 221 1552

Big Lamp Prince Bishop Ale; Durham Magus; Mordue Workie Ricket Ⓗ
The architectural highlight of this building is the striking original glass ceiling domes. Popular with football and music fans, the pub is next to the Tyne Theatre. The interior offers a range of standing and seating areas, with a number of brewery mirrors adorning the walls. TVs show sporting events and the bar can get busy on match days. The Bodega is a winner of a number of local CAMRA awards. ◖≆⊖(Central)♣

Bridge Hotel
Castle Garth, NE1 1RQ
◷ 11.30-11 (midnight Fri & Sat); 12-10.30 Sun
☎ (0191) 232 6400
Black Sheep Best Bitter; Caledonian Deuchars IPA; guest beers Ⓗ
Next to the high level bridge built by Stephenson and facing the castle keep, this large one room pub is divided into a number of seating and standing areas. It has fine views of the River Tyne and Gateshead Quay from the garden. Prints of old Newcastle and industrial and brewery memorabilia adorn the walls. The upstairs function room hosts music events most nights and is home to what is reputed to be one of the oldest folk clubs in the country. ❀◖≆⊖(Central)♣

Centurion Bar
Central Station, NE1 5DG (in railway station)
◷ 7am-2am; 8am-midnight Sun
☎ (0191) 261 6611 ⊕ centurion-newcastle.co.uk
Black Sheep Best Bitter; Theakston Best Bitter; guest beers Ⓗ
Located in Newcastle's central station, the Grade I listed Centurion was built in 1893 as a waiting lounge for first class passengers. It features exquisite tiling throughout, recently valued at £3.8 million. The lounge closed in the 1960s and was used as cells by the British transport police – the tiles overpainted in lurid red. Now lovingly and painstakingly restored to its former glory, it features two regular ales and two guests from local micro-breweries. ❀◖Ⅾ⊞ᕈ≆⊖(Central)⊟⸜

Cooperage
32 The Close, NE1 3RF
◷ 11-2am; 12-10.30 Sun
☎ (0191) 233 2940 ⊕ cooperagenewcastle.co.uk
Allendale Best Bitter; Mordue Geordie Pride; Wylam Gold Tankard; guest beers Ⓗ
Large four storey building near to Newcastle's famous quayside area dating back to the 14th century, reputedly haunted, and used as a coopers in the 18th century. It is now home to a small bar on the ground floor and night club and live music venue on the upper floors. A popular pub with a good reputation, the bar can be busy at times despite paying over the odds for the beers. The house ale is 1730 from Allendale. ⌂◖⊞ᕈ⊟

Crown Posada ☆
33 Side, NE1 3JE
◷ 11 (12 Sat)-11; 7-10.30 Sun
☎ (0191) 232 1269
Hadrian Gladiator; Jarrow Bitter; Taylor Landlord; guest beers Ⓗ

The one pub not to be missed in Newcastle – tiny but welcoming with stained glass windows, high ceilings and wood clad walls. A tiny snug and large lounge are decorated with old photographs of the quayside and ship building. The pub can get busy in the evenings, filled with people united mainly by their love of fine beer enjoyed in a relaxed atmosphere. Background music is provided by a record player. ♨≆⊖(Central)

Duke of Wellington
High Bridge, NE1 1EN
◷ 11-11; 12-10.30 Sun
☎ (0191) 261 8852 ⊕ dukeofwellingtonpub.co.uk
Beer range varies Ⓗ
Classic ale house, a haven for cask ale drinkers in this nightclub and pubco area of the city centre. This small, friendly pub has an L-shaped room with tiled fireplace, sparsely decorated mainly with old local pictures. Three TV screens show sport and the Monday evening quiz has a free buffet. The beers change constantly. ♨◖⊖(Monument)⊟

Fitzgeralds
60 Grey Street, NE1 6AF
◷ 11-11; 7-10.30 Sun
☎ (0191) 230 1350
Black Sheep Best Bitter; guest beers Ⓗ
On the finest street in the country, designed by John Dobson, the narrow frontage leads to a large pub well fitted and furnished. The interior is on several levels with seating around the walls. Steps lead down to the spacious bar area with plenty of standing room and high tables. The pub can be busy especially at weekends. ◖≆⊖(Monument)

Hotspur
103 Percy Street, NE1 7RY
◷ 11-11; 12-10.30 Sun
☎ (0191) 232 4352
Courage Directors; Taylor Landlord; Theakston Old Peculier; guest beers Ⓗ
Double fronted city centre pub facing the bus station. Beers from independent Scottish brewers are often on offer as guests and always prove to be popular. Regulars include weary shoppers, students from the nearby universities and staff from the local hospital. Sports fans are well catered for with large TVs dotted about. ❀◖⊖(Haymarket)

New Bridge
2-4 Argyll Street, NE1 6PF
◷ 11-11 (11.30 Thu & Fri); 12-10.30 Sun
☎ (0191) 232 1020
Beer range varies Ⓗ
Locals pub, part of the Fitzgeralds chain, on the outskirts of the town centre. It is popular with office staff at lunchtime and ale drinkers in the evening enjoying some of the best kept ales in the area. The L-shaped room is divided into bar and lounge areas with four handpumps providing a variety of ales. A cask cider is subject to availability. There are TV screens in each room plus a large screen for football fixtures. ◖⊖(Manors)⊟

Newcastle Arms
57 St Andrews Street, NE1 5SE
◷ 11-11; 12-10.30 Sun

☎ (0191) 260 2490 ⊕ newcastlearms.co.uk
Caledonian Deuchars IPA; guest beers Ⓗ
Near to Newcastle United's ground, the pub
gets very busy on match days. This one room
pub has a selection of seating areas with room
for those who like to stand and pictures of old
Newcastle on the walls. It offers an impressive
range of ales sourced throughout the country,
usually including a stout or porter with the
occasional mild and cider. CAMRA local Pub of
the Year in 2006 and 2007. ⊖(St James)♠

Strawberry
Strawberry Place, NE1 4SF
✪ 11-11
☎ (0191) 232 6865 ⊕ thestrawberrypub.co.uk
**Caledonian Deuchars IPA; Mordue No. 9; guest
beers** Ⓗ
A shrine to Newcastle United – the pub is just a
mis-kick away from the Gallowgate End of St
James' Park and gets packed out on match
days. Dating from 1859, it took its name from
the extensive strawberry gardens in the area.
The walls of this open plan one-room pub are
covered in memorabilia. Reasonably priced
food is served all day and it has a late licence.
◖▮⊖(St James)

Tilley's
105-109 Westgate Road, NE1 4AG
✪ 12-11 (midnight Fri & Sat); 12-10.30 Sun
☎ (0191) 232 0692 ⊕ theheadofsteam.com
Beer range varies Ⓗ
Enjoyable pub next door to the Tyne Theatre
and near the remains of the west side of the
old town walls. The pub is named after Vesta
Tilley, the most famous music hall male
impersonator of her day. Offering half a dozen
guest cask beers and a real cider, there is
always something interesting to try. Cider and
perry are supported during the autumn. There
is a small, comfortable sitting area away from
the main bar. ◖≈⊖(Central, St James)♠

North Shields

Oddfellows
7 Albion Road, NE30 2RJ
✪ 11-11; 12-10.30 Sun
☎ (0191) 257 4288 ⊕ oddfellowspub.co.uk
Greene King Abbot; Jarrow Bitter; guest beer Ⓗ
The walls of this small, friendly single room
lounge bar are covered with historic maps and
photographs of pre-war North Shields and
newspaper cuttings of former local boxing
heroes. The pub has strong sporting
connections and football is shown on the large
screen TV. The pub supports football, darts and
dominoes teams and raises cash for charity. A
beer festival is held in the beer garden in early
May. ✿&⊖♣╚

Porthole
11 New Quay, NE29 6LQ
✪ 11-11 (midnight Wed-Sat); 12-10.30 Sun
☎ (0191) 257 6645
Courage Directors; guest beers Ⓗ
Dating from 1834 and rebuilt around 1900, the
Porthole is situated close to the North Shields
ferry landing. It has two bars separated by a
food serving area. Local breweries are chosen
to provide the guest ales. A lunchtime jazz
club is held on Wednesday and there is live

entertainment on Friday and Sunday evenings.
✿◖⊖♣╚

Prince of Wales
2 Liddell Street, NE30 1HE
✪ 12 (3 Tue)-11; 12-10.30 Sun
☎ (0191) 296 2816
Samuel Smith OBB Ⓗ
There are records for this pub dating back to
1627 but the current building, faced with
green glazed brick, dates from 1927. The
premises lay empty for some years before
being restored in traditional style by Sam
Smith's and reopened in 1992. A rare outlet
for Sam Smith's this far north, it is well worth
a visit. Crab sandwiches and fish and chips are
served at lunch and are highly recommended.
▥Q☜✿◖▯⊖₪

Penshaw

Monument
DH4 7ER (off A183 signed Old Penshaw)
✪ 12-11 (10.30 Sun)
☎ (0191) 584 1027
Jennings Cumberland Ale Ⓗ
A popular locals' pub with a friendly
atmosphere, this traditional one room bar
overlooks the village green. It is a short walk
from Penshaw monument. The bar has old
photographs of the monument and village.
There is a beer garden for summer drinking.
Food is limited to toasties. ▥✿&₪

Shiremoor

Shiremoor House Farm
Middle Engine Lane, NE29 8DZ
✪ 11.30-11; 12-10.30 Sun
☎ (0191) 257 6302
**Mordue Workie Ticket; Taylor Landlord; guest
beers** Ⓗ
Excellent Fitzgerald's conversion of a former
farm house. It retains many original features
including the interesting 'gin-pan'. A well-
deserved reputation for the quality of its real
ales and good value food means it can get
busy at times, especially Sunday lunchtime.
Three handpulls serve two regular beers and a
guest. Q☜✿◖&P╚

South Gosforth

Victory
Killingworth Road, NE3 1SY
✪ 12-11.30 (11 Sun)
☎ (0191) 285 1254
**Caledonian Deuchars IPA; Courage Directors;
Theakston Best Bitter; Wells Bombardier; guest
beers** Ⓗ
Established on this site in 1861, the pub is
named after Nelson's flagship. Small and open
plan, the interior is divided into different
drinking areas, with low beamed ceilings,
traditional wood decor and two fireplaces. As
well as quality beers, a good whisky selection
is available. The pub can be busy at the
weekend with tables outside in summer.
▥Q✿◖⊖₪P

South Shields

Alum Ale House

River Drive, NE33 1JR

✪ 11-11; 12-10.30 Sun

☎ (0191) 427 7745

Banks's Bitter; Marston's Pedigree; guest
beers Ⓗ

Small, traditional pub adjacent to the market
place and River Tyne. The Alum is a firm
favourite with local ale drinkers as a quiet
haven for good beers. The current
management has featured over 200 different
beers in less than a year. Up to four guests are
available plus a small range of bottled beers.
☀Ⓗ⊖♣

Bamburgh

Bamburgh Avenue, NE34 6SS

✪ 10.30-11; 12-10.30 Sun

☎ (0191) 454 1899

Caledonian Deuchars IPA; Greene King Morland
Original Bitter, Ruddles County; guest beers Ⓗ

Modern, spacious pub with an open plan
layout including a central bar area, raised
dining area and a patio with splendid views
over a wide expanse of grass to the North Sea.
Four ales are kept. Very much a locals' bar
during the winter months, it is busy with
holidaymakers in warmer weather. The pub
acts as a finishing line for the Great North Run,
when thousands of runners converge on the
area in need of refreshment.
⇆☀Ⓞ⌖⊖▤(E1)P⸺

Dolly Peel

137 Commercial Road, NE33 1SH

✪ 11-11; 12-10.30 Sun

☎ (0191) 427 1441

Draught Bass; Black Sheep Best Bitter;
Caledonian Deuchars IPA; Courage Directors;
Taylor Landlord; guest beer Ⓗ

This small, compact two-room pub has been a
regular in the Guide for more than 20 years
and is a former local CAMRA Pub of the Year
winner. Quiet during the week, but at the
weekend the Dolly, on the Mill Dam real ale
circuit, comes alive. Buskers' night is
Wednesday. Q⊖(Chichester)

Maltings

Claypath Lane, NE33 4PG (off Westoe Road)

✪ 4 (11.30 Sat)-11; 12-11 Sun

☎ (0191) 427 7147

Jarrow Bitter, Rivet Catcher, Westoe IPA,
seasonal beers; guest beers Ⓗ

Sister pub and brewery to the Robin Hood in
Jarrow. On the ground floor is the Westoe
Brewery; the first floor pub is reached by a
grand staircase. The large wood panelled bar
has quiet background music. Beer festivals are
held in March and October. Q⌖⊖▤(57)♣

Riverside

3 Mill Dam, NE33 1EQ

✪ 11-11 (midnight Fri & Sat); 12-10.30 Sun

☎ (0191) 455 2328

Black Sheep Ale; Courage Directors; John Smith's
Bitter; Taylor Landlord; guest beers Ⓗ

Split level lounge-style pub a short hop from
the market place attracting a varied clientele.
Two guest beers are stocked along with
Weston's Old Rosie dispensed from the cellar.

Convenient for the Custom House theatre and
concert venue and near to Shields ferry, the
Ocean Road curry circuit is also within walking
distance. ⊖♣

Stag's Head ☆

45 Fowler Street, NE33 1NS

✪ 11-11 (midnight Fri & Sat); 12-midnight Sun

☎ (0191) 427 2911

Draught Bass; Greene King Abbot; Stones
Bitter Ⓗ

Cracking town centre pub, built in 1897, with
strong community links. The interior has
barely been touched by the ravages of time,
and the fixtures and fittings are a joy to
behold. In addition to the cosy downstairs bar
there is an upstairs lounge/function room
used regularly by various local groups. Pictures
of Old Shields adorn the walls. The bar has
three real ales always in prime condition.
Traditional pub activities – cards/darts/doms –
all feature here. Q⊖♣

Steamboat

Coronation Street, Mill Dam, NE33 1EQ

✪ 12-11 (midnight Fri & Sat); 12-11.30 Sun

☎ (0191) 454 0134

Black Sheep Best Bitter; Caledonian Deuchars
IPA; Wells Bombardier; guest beers Ⓗ

Two-room pub with a small lounge and a large
split level bar with a nautical theme. Sales of
cask beer are booming – the beer range has
increased to five since the last edition of the
Guide. A rock night is held every Thursday and
a live band on the first Thursday of the month.
Look out for the gallery of caricatures of the
locals by the pool table. Handy for the ferry
and Custom House Theatre. ◖⊖

Sunderland

Clarendon

143 High Street, SR1 2BL

✪ 12-11 (10.30 Sun)

☎ (0191) 510 3200

Bull Lane Nowtsa Matta BB, Ryhope Tug,
seasonal beers Ⓗ

Sunderland's first brew pub is located just
outside the city centre. The single room public
bar has a large rear window with panoramic
views across the River Wear. The pub is a
lively community local where the focus is
clearly on the beer. Six handpumps offer five
Bull Lane beers and a guest cider. There is live
music on Thursday. A warm welcome is
assured and the pub is well worth the walk
from the city centre. ⇌⊖▤(14, 14A)♣

Cliff

Mere Knolls Road, SR6 9LG

✪ 12-11 (midnight Fri & Sat); 12-10.30 Sun

☎ (0191) 548 6200

Beer range varies Ⓗ

Sited in a quiet residential area, the open plan
L-shaped bar feels light and airy. Popular with
sports fans, there are TVs in every corner and
even mini monitors on the beer fonts. One of
the beers often comes from a micro-brewery.
A general knowledge quiz is held weekly. ⌖

Fitzgerald's

10-12 Green Terrace, SR1 3PZ

✪ 11-11 (midnight Fri & Sat); 12-10.30 Sun

☎ (0191) 567 0852
Beer range varies ⒣
Magnificent city centre pub, a former north east CAMRA Pub of the Year. It attracts a wide clientele of all ages and is particularly busy on weekend evenings. Large screen TVs show sporting events and there is quiet background music. Ten handpumps dispense an ever-changing range of guest beers, mostly from micro-breweries, and a guest cider.
⊄⍬≉⊖(University)♠

Harbour View

Benedict Road, SR6 0NL (on coast road above north dock)
✪ 10.30-11.30 (12.30am Fri & Sat); 10.30-midnight Sun
☎ (0191) 567 1402
Caledonian Deuchars IPA; guest beers ⒣
Comfortable, modern wood-panelled restaurant and bar offering carvery lunches and impressive views over North Dock marina and harbour. A short distance from Roker beach and the football ground, it can get busy on match days. Guest beers are sourced from micro-breweries near and far. Live music plays on Thursday and quiz night is Tuesday.
⊄⊖(Stadium of Light)☷(E1)⌐

Ivy House

7 Worcester Street, SR2 7AW
✪ 11-11; 12-10.30 Sun
☎ (0191) 567 3399
Darwin Evolution, Ghost Ale; Taylor Landlord; guest beers ⒣
Tucked away down a side street near the bus and metro interchange, the Ivy is a large open plan pub popular with students and football fans. Six handpumps dispense three regular beers plus up to three guest ales. Local bands play live on Thursday and Sunday is quiz night.
⊄≉⊖(Park Lane)

King's Arms

Beech Street, Deptford, SR4 6BU (off Trimdon Street behind B&Q)
✪ 11-11 (midnight Fri & Sat); 12-10.30 Sun
☎ (0191) 567 9804
Taylor Landlord; guest beers ⒣
Local CAMRA Pub of the Year 2005 and 2006 and regional winner too in 2006. A gem of a pub with a wood panelled bar and small snug decorated with pictures of old Sunderland. Nine handpumps offer Landlord plus seven guest beers and a real cider. The guest ales are sourced from all over the country and many are rare for the area. Live music is hosted in summer in the marquee. Well worth the 10 minute' walk from the centre.
▨Q❀⊖(University/ Millfield)☷(18, 11)♠

Promenade

1 Queens Parade, SR6 8DA
✪ 11-11; 12-10.30 Sun
☎ (0191) 529 2226
Caledonian Deuchars IPA; Tetley Bitter ⒣
Seafront pub with excellent sea views from the windows. The bar itself is L-shaped with a dedicated dining area. This family-friendly pub is quiet during the day, getting busy in the evening during the summer. There are rooms available above the pub at very reasonable bed and breakfast rates. Q⇔⊄☷

Rosedene

Queen Alexandra Road, SR2 9BT
✪ 12-11 (11.30 Fri & Sat)
☎ (0191) 528 4313 ⊕ therosedene.co.uk
Greene King IPA, Abbot, Old Speckled Hen; guest beers ⒣
Once a grand Georgian mansion, built in 1830, then later pulled down and rebuilt, Rose-dene house was converted to a pub in 1964, and now belongs to Greene King. It has a spacious main room surrounded by a central bar area, restaurant, Ewardian style drawing room, large conservatory and a function room which is available for hire. Four cask ales are on offer but the emphasis here is on high quality food.
Q❀⊄₺☷(10)P⌐

Saltgrass

Hanover Place, Deptford, SR4 6BY (S of Alexander Bridge behind B&Q)
✪ 11.30-11 (midnight Fri & Sat); 12-10.30 Sun
☎ (0191) 565 7229
Black Sheep Best Bitter; Caledonian Deuchars IPA; Draught Bass; guest beers ⒣
Old style two-room pub with a friendly, warm welcome. The small bar has a real fire and beamed ceilings, decorated with wonderful old photographs from the industrial era of shipbuilding and mining. The lounge/ restaurant is popular for Sunday lunch (reservations recommended). There is an outside patio area for warmer weather. Curry night is Monday and the pub quiz is Tuesday.
▨❀⊄⊖(Millfield)☷(11)♠P

Tynemouth

Copperfields

Hotspur Street, NE30 4ER
✪ 12-11 (10.30 Sun)
☎ (0191) 293 6666 ⊕ grandhotel-uk.com
Black Sheep Best Bitter; Draught Bass; Durham Magus; guest beers ⒣
Cosy public bar on the sea front, part of the Grand Hotel. It is a short walk from the noisy and often crowded circuit pubs on Front Street but a world away in ambience. Built as a seaside home for a 19th century Duchess of Northumberland, the internal etched glasswork is based on characters from the novels of Charles Dickens. Meals are served until 8pm. ⇔⊄₺⊖P

Cumberland Arms

17 Front Street, NE30 4DX
✪ 12-11 (10.30 Sun)
☎ (0191) 257 1820 ⊕ cumberlandarms.co.uk
Courage Directors; Theakston Best Bitter; guest beers ⒣
Split level pub with two bars each dispensing six real ales. The dining area at the rear of the building serves good value meals. One of the guest ales is often a mild. The pub can become busy at the weekend when live football is shown on the large screen TV – the manager is a big football fan. ▨⊄₺⊖

Turks Head

41 Front Street, NE30 4DZ
✪ 12-11 (midnight Fri & Sat)
☎ (0191) 257 6547

Courage Directors; Theakston Best Bitter; guest beers Ⓗ

J&T Bernard pub next to the sea front and Tynemouth Priory with eight handpumps dispensing real ale. Locally known as the Stuffed Dog, if you look to your left from the front bar you will see why. Food is served in a dining area at the rear. Football fans can watch matches no matter where they are in the pub as TVs are everywhere. ◖▮⊖

Tynemouth Lodge Hotel

Tynemouth Road, NE30 4AA

✪ 11-11; 12-10.30 Sun

☎ (0191) 257 7565 ⊕ tynemouthlodgehotel.co.uk

Belhaven 80/-; Caledonian Deuchars IPA; Draught Bass; guest beers Ⓗ

This attractive externally tiled free house, built in 1799, has been in every issue of the Guide since 1984 when it was taken over by the present owner. The comfortable single room lounge is noted in the area for always having Scottish real ales on handpump and for selling reputedly the highest volume of Draught Bass on Tyneside. It is next to Northumberland Park and near the Coast To Coast cycle route. � Q❀⊖P

Washington

Courtyard

Arts Centre, Biddick Lane, Fatfield, NE38 8AB

✪ 11-11 (midnight Fri & Sat); 12-11 Sun

☎ (0191) 417 0445

Taylor Landlord; guest beers Ⓗ

Located within the council-owned Washington arts centre, this modern café style bar has a well deserved reputation for real ales, ciders and perries. Ales come from local and national independent breweries, plus a good selection of Belgian bottled beers. Beer festivals offering more than 30 beers are held twice a year. The stone flagged courtyard is ideal for chilling out on sunny days. Delicious home cooked food is served by friendly staff – curry night is Thursday. Q❀◖▮&▭♣♠P↳

Steps

Spout Lane, NE38 7HP

✪ 11-11; 12-10.30 Sun

☎ (0191) 416 7396

Beer range varies Ⓗ

A true gem, the only pub in Washington village to sell real ale is now in its 10th year in the Guide. The small, comfortable single room lounge bar is divided into two drinking areas; the walls decorated with pictures of old Washington. Three ever changing guest beers are on offer. ◖♣

West Boldon

Black Horse

Rectory Bank, NE36 0QQ

✪ 11-11; 12-10.30 Sun

☎ (0191) 536 1814

Black Sheep Best Bitter; Darwin Black Horse Ⓗ

Old fashioned bar and locally renowned restaurant with live music on Sunday night. The cosy L-shaped bar has walls adorned with bric-a-brac and candle-lit tables. There is

always a beer on handpump from the local independent Darwin Brewery. ❀◖▮▭(9, 9A)P

West Herrington

Stables

Houghton le Spring, DH4 4ND (off B1286)

✪ 3.30-11; 12-midnight Fri & Sat; 12-10.30 Sun

☎ (0191) 584 9226

Black Sheep Best Bitter; Taylor Landlord; guest beer Ⓗ

The Stables may not look much like a pub from the outside but this old barn conversion is well worth a visit. Friendly and welcoming, it retains the original beams plus wooden furnishings, with a large collection of horse-related memorabilia. A small, quieter room off the main bar has a games area. Happy 'hour' is 3.30-7pm Monday-Friday. ▮Q☜❀&▭(35)P

West Moor

George Stephenson

Great Lime Road, NE12 7NJ

✪ 12-11

☎ (0191) 268 1073

Caledonian Deuchars IPA; guest beers Ⓗ

Much altered over the last century, the pub retains two largely separate drinking areas which, when required, can become a single room by opening dividing doors. A side patio offers outside drinking in the lee of the East Coast rail line. A well established music venue, live bands are hosted on several evenings and some Sunday afternoons – phone for details. Several guest beers change regularly, often from smaller local breweries. ❀P

Whitley Bay

Briardene

71 The Links, NE26 1UE

✪ 11-11; 12-10.30 Sun

☎ (0191) 252 0926

Beer range varies Ⓗ

Every day is a beer festival at this Fitzgerald's pub, now with seven handpumps dispensing constantly changing beers from all over the country. Once a toll house, it enjoys a well earned reputation for good quality beer and fine food. The attractive lounge has coloured leaded glass above the bar and overlooks the Links, St Mary's Lighthouse and the sea. The smaller rear bar has TV, pool and darts. A former local CAMRA Pub of the Year. ❀◖▮&▲♣P↳

Rockcliffe Arms

Algernon Place, NE26 2DT

✪ 11-11 (11.15 Fri & Sat); 12-11 Sun

☎ (0191) 253 1299

Beer range varies Ⓗ

A warm welcome is assured at this outstanding backstreet Fitzgerald's pub a couple of minutes' walk from the metro station and the mayhem of the town centre at the weekend. Four constantly changing guest beers are always kept in tip-top condition. Regular darts and dominoes matches are held in the snug. Do not forget to try the famous pork pies and scotch eggs. ▭⊖▭♣

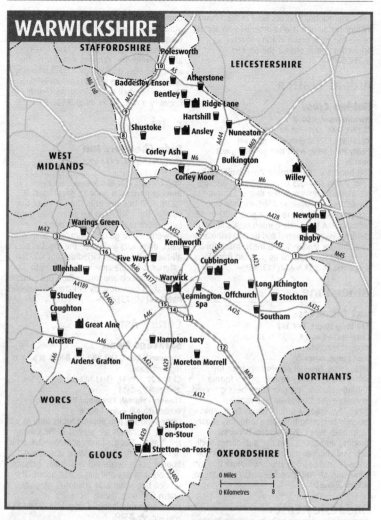

Alcester

Holly Bush
Henley Street, B49 5QX
🕐 12-11 (1am Fri & Sat; 11.30 Sun)
☎ (01789) 762482
Black Sheep Best Bitter; Greene King Abbot; Purity Pure Gold; Uley Bitter; guest beers Ⓗ
Traditional local in an historic market town. Recent improvements include restoring original features to some of the rooms within the pub. A beer festival is hosted during the Alcester Folk Festival in June and another in October. Regular folk sessions are held twice a month and there may be spontaneous music at any time. The pub is home to the White Hart Morris Men who meet regularly on Monday evening. Current CAMRA branch Pub of the Year and a previous winner on several occasions. ♨️⚙️🕕🖂♿🖂♣️🍴↨

Three Tuns
34 High Street, B49 5AB
🕐 12-11; 12-10.30 Sun
☎ (01789) 762626

Hobsons Best Bitter; guest beers Ⓗ
This local CAMRA award-winning pub is how a real pub used to be: no music, no pool and no food. Inside there is a single room with low beams, stone flagged floor and an exposed area of wattle and daub. Up to eight ales from micros and independents provide a permanent yet ever-changing mini beer festival. Q🖂♣️

Ansley

Lord Nelson Inn
Birmingham Road, CV10 9PG
🕐 12-2.30, 5.30-11; 12-11 Sat; 12-10.30 Sun
☎ (024) 76392305

Draught Bass; Tunnel Late OTT, seasonal beers; guest beers Ⓗ
Long-established large, friendly, family-run roadside pub with a nautical theme. It has two fine restaurants and a bar featuring five handpulls with up to three Tunnel beers available at any one time. The Tunnel brewery (a separate venture) can be viewed from the paved garden at the side. The brewery runs

481

beer appreciation courses held in the 90-seat Victory restaurant. It also organises an annual coach trip to Belgium visiting several breweries – look out for the posters. ❀◑⊟🚌P⅟

Ardens Grafton

Golden Cross

Wixford Road, B50 4LG
⊙ 12-3, 5-11; 12-11 Sat; 12-10.30 Sun
☎ (01789) 772420 ⊕ thegoldencross.net
Purity Pure UBU; Wells Bombardier; guest beer ⊞
This beautiful 18th-century stone-built pub has seen a few changes over the years. Outside are glorious views over the Vale of Evesham to the Cotswolds, while inside there are stone-flagged floors and a real fire plus a 40-seater restaurant. A large safe garden area is ideal for children, with a covered and heated patio area available for smokers. The fresh British food menu sources as much as possible from local suppliers. ⛺❀◑♿⛺🚌(212)●P⅟

Atherstone

Hat & Beaver

130 Long Street, CV9 1AF
⊙ 12-11 (2am Fri & Sat); 12-10.30 Sun
☎ (01827) 720082
Beer range varies ⊞
Welcoming two-bar community pub; the name is a reference to the town's former hatting industry. Just one guest beer is served to ensure good turnover and variety. Weekdays enjoy a 6-8pm happy hour – this extends to closing time on a randomly chosen night each week. Widescreen TVs draw sporting audiences, and the pub allows well-behaved children. No food is served but you are welcome to bring your own. Note that last admission on Friday and Saturday is 11.30pm. ❀⊟⇌🚌♣●P⅟

Baddesley Ensor

Red Lion

The Common, CV9 2BT
⊙ 12-3 (Sat only), 7 (4 Fri)-11; 12-3, 7-10.30 Sun
☎ (01827) 718186
Everards Tiger; Marston's Pedigree; guest beers ⊞
Traditional one room cosy free house with a warming fire in winter. Three guest beers may come from any independent brewer and a real cider is now on the bar too. A small patio at the front is pleasant on summer evenings. Well worth finding but take note of the limited opening hours. Off road parking is opposite. ⛺Q❀🚌♣●

Bentley

Horse & Jockey

Coleshill Road, CV9 2HL (on B4116)
⊙ 12-3 (not winter Mon), 5.30-11.30; 12-11.30 Fri-Sun
☎ (01827) 715236
Marston's Pedigree; Shepherd Neame Spitfire; guest beers ⊞
The weathered sign depicts a local landowner who rode in the 1952 Grand National. He came off, but the pub canters along nicely, attracting a diverse clientele. The small time-warp bar features scrubbed wooden tables, an open fire and quarry tiles. A larger, cosy lounge welcomes drinkers and diners. The attractive beer garden has a children's play area. Opposite the pub a pleasant bridleway through bluebell woods leads to Church End Brewery a mile away. ⛺❀◑⊟♣P

Bulkington

Olde Chequers Inn

Chequers Street, CV12 9NH
⊙ 12-11 (10.30 Sun)
☎ (024) 7631 2182 ⊕ oldechequersinn.com
Draught Bass; M&B Brew XI; guest beers ⊞
Renowned free house in the centre of the village. The traditional bar offers two guest beers from regional and local micro-breweries. Two games rooms are busy with darts, dominoes and pool – the regulars play in all the local leagues including football. The exterior is picturesque in summer with hanging baskets and flower tubs. Bus numbers 56 and 75 pass close by but check timetables. ⛺❀♿🚌(56, 75)♣P⅟

Corley Ash

Saracens Head

Tamworth Road, CV7 8BP (on B4098 at jct with Highfield Lane)
⊙ 12-2.30, 5.30-11; 12-11 Fri & Sat; 6-10.30 Sun
☎ (01676) 540853
Flowers Original; Ringwood Best Bitter; Wadworth 6X; guest beer ⊞
Large roadside pub popular for its food as well as real ale. Meals are served in the dining room as well as the larger split level bar which has four handpulls. The stone and wood floored bar is decorated with horse brasses and brass plates and has a dart board. The garden has a separate children's play area. A warm welcome awaits from the knowledgeable landlord who is dedicated to real ale. ❀◑🚌P

Corley Moor

Bull & Butcher

Common Lane, CV7 8AQ OS279850
⊙ 10am-midnight (1am Fri & Sat); 11-11 Sun
☎ (01676) 540241
Greene King Abbot; guest beers ⊞
Classic village community pub with an unspoilt bar. Tubs and hanging baskets adorn the front of the building throughout the year. A new restaurant has been built at the back, with fine views over the moor. Meals are good and unpretentious; the home-made pies are

INDEPENDENT BREWERIES

Atomic Rugby
Church End Ridge Lane
North Cotswold Stretton-on-Fosse
Purity Great Alne
Rugby Willey
Slaughterhouse Warwick
Tunnel Ansley
Warwickshire Cubbington

highly recommended. A child-friendly pub, the play area in the garden includes a bouncy castle. Ample car parking is available.
🚲Q❀🕙🅳🕎🅿⏚

Coughton

Throckmorton Arms
Coughton Hill, B49 5HX (on A435 between Studley and Alcester)
🕓 12-11 (10.30 Sun)
☎ (01789) 766366 ⊕ thethrockmortonarms.co.uk
Hook Norton Hooky Bitter; St Austell Tribute; guest beers Ⓗ
Large roadside hotel that is smart and comfortable at the same time. Up to two guest beers includes an ale from Purity, Wye Valley or Cottage. The hotel is popular with business people during the week and visitors on weekend breaks. The restaurant is next to a large patio overlooking fields to the west and serves food seven days a week, from snacks to full home-cooked meals. Wednesday is quiz night. Coughton Court opposite is worth a visit with its Gunpowder Plot connections.
🚲❀🕙🅳🕎🅿⏚

Cubbington

Queen's Head
20 Queen Street, CV32 7NA
🕓 12-11 (10.30 Sun)
☎ (01926) 429949
Ansells Mild, Bitter; Draught Bass; Greene King IPA; guest beers Ⓗ
Traditional Victorian village pub with a public bar, pool room and comfortable lounge. It is a real drinkers' pub – the loudest noise is usually conversation. A true community pub, it is home to darts and crib teams as well as the meeting point for many village societies and groups. A large TV screen in the bar is used for major sporting events. Guest beer changes four or five times a week.
Q❀🅳🕎🚆(68)♣🅿⏚

Five Ways

Case is Altered ☆
Case Lane, CV35 7JD (off Five Ways Road near A4141/A4177 jct)
🕓 12-2.30, 6-11; 12-2, 7-10.30 Sun
☎ (01926) 484206
Greene King IPA; Hook Norton Old Hooky; Ⓖ **guest beers** Ⓗ
Charming, 350-year-old, National Inventory listed, rural treasure comprising a bar and a snug. The entrance and facilities have been sympathetically refurbished without losing any of their charm. Memorabilia of long-gone local breweries and an old aircraft propeller decorate the bar. No machines, music or mobiles interfere with the buzz of conversation. The regular beers are dispensed straight from the cask using antique pumps; guest beers usually include one from a local brewery. The bar billiards table takes old 6d coins. 🚲Q❀🕎♣🅿

Hampton Lucy

Boar's Head
Church Street, CV35 8BE
🕓 11.30-3, 5.30-11; 11-11 Fri & Sat; 12-10.30 Sun
☎ (01789) 840533
Flowers IPA; guest beers Ⓗ
Friendly, cosy village pub dating back to the 17th century when it was built as a cider house – the present kitchen was originally a mortuary. Situated on a Sustrans route and close to the river Avon, it is frequented by cyclists, walkers and visitors to nearby Charlecote Park (NT). The sheltered rear garden is popular for Sunday afternoon barbecues in summer. Guest beers change frequently, with up to 10 served in a week, mostly from small independent brewers.
🚲❀🕙🅿

Hartshill

Anchor Inn
Mancetter Road, CV10 0RT (on A4131, where road crosses Coventry Canal)
🕓 12-2.30 (not Mon), 6-11; 12-11 Sat; 12-10.30 Sun
☎ (024) 7639 8839
Everards Tiger, Original; guest beers Ⓗ
The Anchor was thought to be a trading post and mail collection place for narrowboat workers following completion of the canal in 1790. It has a cosy feel in winter with wooden beams and open fires; in summer there are plenty of outdoor areas including a children's playground. Three restaurants and a carvery are on different levels (no eve meals Sun). Up to four guest beers complement the Everards.
🚲❀🕙🅳🕎🅿⏚

Stag & Pheasant
The Green, CV10 0SW
🕓 3 (12 Thu)-midnight; 12-12.30 Fri & Sat; 12-11.30 Sun
☎ (024) 7639 3173
Draught Bass; Flowers Original; Marston's Pedigree; guest beer Ⓗ
Two-room pub overlooking the village green, opposite Hartshill Hayes Country Park and close to the canal. The traditional Sunday lunch is popular, Monday is curry and chilli night and there is Chinese food to eat in or take away the rest of the week. Guest beers are usually from Church End. A beer festival is held in the garden in June with many one-off beers. Bus numbers 48 and 776 pass close to the pub but check timetables.
❀🕙🅳🕎🚆(48, 776)♣🅿⏚

Ilmington

Red Lion
Front Street, CV36 4LX
🕓 12-2.30, 5.30-11; 12-11 Sat; 12-10.30 Sun
☎ (01608) 682366
Hook Norton Hooky Bitter, Old Hooky, seasonal beer Ⓗ
Traditional two-bar village pub with log fires for winter evenings. Pub games include Aunt Sally, and there is a quiz night on Sunday. Meals are served throughout the day – the menu features traditional home-cooked food with regional delicacies. A large beer garden provides an ideal venue to spend a pleasant summer afternoon. The Red Lion is one of only

100 English pubs to gain the BBPA Beautiful Beer Gold award. ♨Q❀⚙①Ⓓ♿▲🚗♣P⅃

Kenilworth

Engine
8 Mill End, CV8 2HP
❂ 4 (12 Thu)-midnight; 11-1am Fri & Sat; 11-midnight Sun
☎ (01926) 853341
M&B Brew XI; guest beers Ⓗ
Tucked away from the main part of Kenilworth, this building became a pub in 1854. The traditional wood-beamed one-roomed pub is set around a central bar with a U-shaped interior. Friendly and welcoming, this is true drinkers' pub; meals are served only on Thursday afternoon, when it can be busy. Two guest beers come from the Punch Taverns list. Q🚗(X17)♣⅃

Old Bakery
12 High Street, CV8 1LZ (near A429/A452 jct)
❂ 5.30 (5 Fri & Sat)-11; 12-2, 7-10.30 Sun
☎ (01926) 864111 ⊕ theoldbakeryhotel.co.uk
Hook Norton Hooky Bitter; Taylor Landlord; guest beers Ⓗ
Attractively restored former bakery in the centre of the old town, handy for visitors to nearby Abbey Fields and Kenilworth Castle. This was the first pub in the county to be completely no smoking, for which it was awarded the National Clean Air gold award. Inside it has two rooms and outside a patio area; disabled access is from the rear car park. Main bus routes to Coventry, Warwick University and Leamington pass close by. Q❀🛏♿🚗P

Virgins & Castle
7 High Street, CV8 1LY (A429/A452 jct)
❂ 11-11.30 (11 Sun)
☎ (01926) 853737
Everards Beacon, Sunchaser, Tiger, Original; Fuller's London Pride; guest beers Ⓗ
Centuries old building that was originally two adjacent inns. It has an L-shaped bar serving the lounge and several smaller rooms with wood panelling and exposed beams. Outside is a heated terrace. The menu is an interesting mix of traditional English and Japanese and Filipino cuisine. Although parking outside is limited there is a public car park in nearby Abbey Fields. Main bus routes to Coventry, Warwick University and Leamington pass close by. ♨Q❀①Ⓓ♿🚗P⅃

Wyandotte Inn
Park Road, CV8 2GF (Jct of Park Rd/Stoneleigh Rd)
❂ 12-midnight (1am Fri); 11.30-1am Sat; 11.30-11 Sun
☎ (01926) 859076
Marston's Burton Bitter; guest beers Ⓗ
Comfortable street corner pub with a single room split-level bar. It gets its name from links to the Wyandotte Indian Tribe from Michigan and Ohio – note the large wooden North American Indian on the wall. The pub has a relaxing atmosphere in which to sample beers from Marston's guest beer list. All the major sporting events are shown on TV. Outside is a splendid large heated patio area. Bus services pass the door. ❀🚗(X17, 538)♣P⅃

Leamington Spa

Red House
113 Radford Road, CV31 1JZ
❂ 11-11 (midnight Thu-Sat)
☎ (01926) 881725
Adnams Broadside; Draught Bass; Hook Norton Hooky Bitter; guest beer Ⓗ
Small, cosy, popular and very friendly Victorian pub. Although located on the main road near the edge of town, it has the atmosphere of a village community local. The single bar has two seating areas at the front and a corridor at the back for vertical drinkers. Look for the fine collection of Guinness toucans and the unusual blue and pink handpumps. Q❀🚗

Long Itchington

Harvester Inn
6 Church Road, CV47 9PG
❂ 12-2.30, 6-11; 12-3, 7-10.30 Sun
☎ (01926) 812698 ⊕ theharvesterinn.co.uk
Hook Norton Hooky Bitter, Old Hooky; guest beer Ⓗ
A Guide regular since the Mills family took over in 1984. An unpretentious village local with a few surprises, such as Budweiser Budvar Dark on draught and a WiFi hotspot. The restaurant serves good value food, especially the steaks. Brews from Archers and Church End are regular guest beers. Five minutes' walk from the Grand Union canal, camping is by arrangement with other village pubs. Q①Ⓓ🛏▲🚗(64)P

Moreton Morrell

Black Horse
CV35 9AR
❂ 11.30-3, 5.30 (7 Sat)-11; 12-3, 7-10.30 Sun
☎ (01926) 651231
Hook Norton Hooky Bitter; guest beer Ⓗ
This village pub is a throwback to a bygone age – nothing seems to have changed since the 60s. Wooden settles are arranged around the walls of the cosy bar; music on the juke box is mostly from the Beatles era. A pool table in the back room is popular with younger folk. No meals are available but the freshly-made rolls are excellent value. The peaceful garden overlooks the Warwickshire countryside. The guest beer is usually of highish gravity and from a small independent brewery. Q❀▲🚗(277)

Newton

Stag & Pheasant
27 Main Street, CV23 0DY
❂ 12-3, 6-11.30; 12-3, 7-11 sun
☎ (01788) 860326
Banks's Original, Bitter; Jennings Cumberland; guest beer Ⓗ
Popular A-framed thatched-roofed local in a quiet village with ample parking. Inside a large single room has a traditional pub games area to one end including skittles, plus a comfortable seating area with sofas and a real fire at the other. Four ales are usually on offer including a regular guest. Home-made food is available at lunchtime during the week.

Regular quiz nights are held and occasional live music on Saturday. Dogs are welcome. 🏚️❀🍺🖰♣🚶🏠

Nuneaton

Crown Inn

10 Bond Street, CV11 4BX (Between rail & bus stations)
🕐 12-11 (midnight Fri & Sat)
☎ (024) 7637 3343
Oakham JHB; guest beers 🅗
Ten real ales and ciders are normally on offer in this split level music bar, formerly known as Lloyds. The pub holds quizzes and other social events. There is a pool table and regular live folk and blues acts on Saturday. Beer festivals are held in June and December. A function room is available for hire. ❀⇆🖰♣P🚶

Hearty Goodfellow

285 Arbury Road, CV10 7NQ
🕐 11-11; 12-10.30 Sun
☎ (024) 7638 8152
Marston's Burton Bitter, Pedigree; guest beers 🅗
Thriving sports-oriented community local. The L-shaped room is home to pool and darts teams and the Ford Sports Football Club. Several large TVs show live games. Look out for the display of sports trophies, football pennants and shirts. The atmosphere is always lively here and the locals will make you feel at home. Four handpulls dispense two regulars and two guests, usually from the Marston's group. ❀🖰♣

Offchurch

Stag's Head

Welsh Road, CV33 9AQ
🕐 12-3, 5-11; 12-11 Fri & Sat; 12-10.30 Sun
☎ (01926) 425801
Adnams Broadside; Caledonian Deuchars IPA; Jennings Cumberland Ale 🅗
A must-visit 16th century thatched pub with whitewashed walls and original features. Family friendly, it has open plan areas including a bar, lounge and conservatory with a variety of seating from settees to easy chairs. Traditional home cooked food is served. Photographs of rural scenes decorate the walls. Dogs are permitted in the bar area. The large rear garden has plenty of picnic tables. Do not be confused by the door to the lounge marked 'Toilets'. 🏚️Q❀🍴P

Polesworth

Red Lion

Bridge Street, B78 1DR (300m N of B5000)
🕐 11-midnight (11.30 Sun)
☎ (01827) 896978
Taylor Landlord; guest beer 🅗
Large village centre pub, popular with drinkers of all ages. The central bar serves a variety of drinking areas including a lounge with leather settees and a pool room. The spacious bar features maps and photographs of old Polesworth. Outside, the garden has a large patio and lawn for pleasant summer drinking. The remains of Polesworth Abbey, dating from 829AD, is nearby. ❀🍴⇆🖰♣P🚶

Ridge Lane

Church End Brewery Tap

109 Ridge Lane, CV10 0RD OS295947
🕐 6 (12 Fri & Sat)-11; closed Mon-Wed; 12-10.30
☎ (01827) 713080 🌐 churchendbrewery.co.uk
Beer range varies 🅗
Local CAMRA Pub of the Year in 2004 and 2005, the tap has eight handpumps serving ales fresh from the brewery (visible from the bar). A changing real cider and an excellent bottled Belgian beer range are also available in this light, airy bar. No food is served but you are welcome to bring your own. Dogs are permitted in the bar but children are relegated to the meadow-style garden. Q❀🅰♣🍺P🚐

Rugby

Alexandra Arms

72 James Street, CV21 2SL (Next to John Barford Multi-storey car park)
🕐 11.30-11 (midnight Fri & Sat); 12-10.30 Sun
☎ (01788) 578660 🌐 alexandraarms.co.uk
Greene King Abbot, IPA; guest beers 🅗
Seven times winner of local CAMRA Pub of the Year, the pub is home to a micro-brewery producing the Alexandra Ales and Atomic ranges. Guest beers include milds, stouts and porters, plus Addlestones cider on draught. The pub has a quiet, comfortable lounge, and a noisier games room where lively debate flourishes among the locals, featuring pool, skittles, bar billiards and a well-stocked juke box. The garden is a venue for summer beer festivals with open and covered seating. Q❀🍴🖰♿⇆(Rugby)♣🚶

Bull

33-35 Main Street, CV23 0BH
🕐 11.30-3, 5-11; 11.30-11 Fri & Sat; 11.30-11.30 Sun
☎ (01788) 552237
Fuller's London Pride; guest beers 🅗
Situated on the main road, this is a family oriented pub catering for local villagers. It has a large main bar, pool room and dining area. The extensive home-cooked food includes a Sunday roast (no food Sun eve). The Bull holds regular activities and entertainment including theme nights and quizzes. Guest ales are selected by the locals. ❀🍴♿⇆🖰🚶

Fighting Cocks

39 Cymbeline Way, CV22 6JZ (off A426 near Sainsburys)
🕐 12 (4 mon)-11; 12-midnight Fri & Sat; 12-10.30 Sun
☎ (01788) 810628
Greene King IPA; Wells Bombardier; guest beers 🅗
A friendly, convivial atmosphere awaits in this community estate pub where families and dogs are welcome. Filled rolls are always available along with up to five real ales including ever changing guest beers. Darts, skittles and pool teams play during the week. Live music is hosted on Saturday. ❀🍴♿🖰♣P

Merchants Inn

5-6 Little Church Street, CV21 3AW
🕐 12-midnight (1am Fri & Sat; midnight Sun)
☎ (01788) 571119 🌐 merchantsinn.co.uk
B&T Shefford Bitter; Everards Tiger; guest beers 🅗

Established ale house with a warm, cosy atmosphere, wooden seating, comfortable sofas, flagstone floors and an abundance of brewery memorabilia. Between eight and ten ales are offered plus traditional cider and perry and a superb selection of Belgian beers. Home-cooked food is served daily. On Tuesday evening the pub becomes a popular live music venue. A beer festival is hosted in spring and autumn, plus a annual Belgium themed evening in February. Local CAMRA Pub of the Year 2006. ◑₳⊒♣♠⁵⊥

Seven Stars

40 Albert Square, CV21 2SH (behind Rugby Citroen dealer)
✪ 12-11 (10.30 Sun)
☎ (01788) 561402
Wells Bombardier; guest beers Ⓗ
True local community pub on the edge of James Street housing development with a traditional bar area and lounge plus a conservatory. The good value food menu includes specials of the day, a Saturday 'gut buster' breakfast and Sunday lunch. The Stars has regular quiz nights and curry days, and hosts darts, dominoes, skittles and cricket teams. Guest beers usually include a brew from Young's or Courage. Q♿❀◑₳≠♣⁵⊥

Squirrel Inn

33 Church Street, CV21 3PU
✪ 12-11 (10.30 Sun)
☎ (01788) 544154
Marston's Pedigree; guest beers Ⓗ
Winner of local CAMRA Most Improved Pub award in 2006, this traditional free house features ever-changing guest ales including many local brews. Dating from the early 19th century, it is one of the oldest buildings in Rugby. Now a single room, the pub was originally three tiny rooms and the boundaries are still clearly evident. Entertainment includes live acoustic music every Wednesday and a wide selection of games such as table skittles, darts and chess. Q≠⊒♣

Victoria Inn

1 Lower Hillmorton Road, CV21 3ST
✪ 4-11; 12-1am Fri & Sat; 12-midnight Sun
☎ (01788) 544374
Atomic Bomb, Fission, Fusions, Strike; guest beers Ⓗ
Newly revitalised street corner two-room local following an acquisition by Atomic brewery owner Nick Pugh. As well as seven draught real ales it offers a wealth of Belgian bottled beers plus a draught wheat beer. The bar doubles as a games room with darts and pool. The lovely lounge is a Victorian design retaining many original features – a pleasant place to sit and appreciate the excellent ales on offer. Q◑≠⊒♣♠⁵⊥

Shipston-on-Stour

Black Horse

Station Road, CV36 4BT
✪ 11-3, 5-11; 11-midnight Sat; 12-3, 7-midnight Sun
☎ (01608) 661617
Greene King IPA, Abbot; guest beers Ⓗ
G?G??built pub for the town's discerning drinkers – the only thatched building in

Shipston. The licence dates back to 1540, and it was brewing illegally before that. The cosy and welcoming lounge has a large inglenook and real log fires. Aunt Sally is played here, as are crib, darts and doms. An informal folk musicians' session is on the first Sunday evening of the month. ₳❀◑⊒♣♠♠P

Shustoke

Griffin Inn

Church Road, B46 2LB (on B4116)
✪ 12-2.30, 7-11; 12-3, 7-10.30 Sun
☎ (01675) 481205
Banks's Original; Hook Norton Old Hooky; Marston's Pedigree; RCH Pitchfork; Theakston Old Peculier; guest beers Ⓗ
Classic rural free house which has been championing cask ale for decades. Five regular beers and five ever-changing guests attract customers from far and wide. The low central bar is framed by tree-trunk beams. Three glowing wood stoves warm the tile and stone interior in winter, while a beer terrace and meadow garden are popular for summertime drinking. Food is served Monday to Saturday lunchtime; local eggs and cheese are for sale at the bar. Children are welcome in the conservatory. ₳Q♿❀◑₳P

Southam

Bull Inn

Bull Street, CV47 1PQ
✪ 12-2.30 (summer), 5-midnight (1am Fri & Sat); 12-midnight Sun
☎ (01926) 817766
Wells Bombardier; guest beers Ⓗ
Friendly country pub in the heart of the town appealing to a mixed local clientele of all ages. The Grade II listed building retains beamed ceilings and wooden floors. In the winter sit in a cosy armchair by the log fire, in summer enjoy a pint outside on the walled patio. Regular quiz nights are held. The family-friendly pub has a small pets' corner to interest children. Well-behaved dogs are welcome. ₳❀◑⊒⊒(64)♣P⁵⊥

Stoneythorpe Hotel

10 Warwick Road, CV47 0HN
✪ 10.30-11; 12-10.30 Sun
☎ (01926) 812365 ⊕ thestoneythorpehotel.co.uk
Fuller's London Pride; guest beers Ⓗ
Originally an eye-hospital founded in 1774 by Dr Henry Lilley-Smith, the building has been an independently run hotel for 45 years. The architecture reflects the building's origins with unusual pointed arched windows. In 1823 the world's first dispensary was established here, celebrated by a nearby monument and in the naming of the hotel's bar. Relax in the comfortable, airy lounge while enjoying the wide range of ales – five guest beers are normally available. A midsummer beer festival is held in June each year. Q♿❀◑≠⊒⊒(63, 64)P⁵⊥

Stockton

Crown

8 High Street, CV47 8JZ

11-midnight (1am Fri & Sat)
(01926) 812255
Adnams Broadside; Ansells Mild, Bitter H
Popular Victorian brick built village local with a games area, attracting a mixed clientele. The clues to the landlord's origins are all around with a good collection of Guinness memorabilia, not to mention a wide range of Irish whiskeys. The restaurant serves good food and is well frequented. Unusual for the area, the pub boasts a petanque pitch which draws teams from far and wide during the summer.

Stretton-on-Fosse

Plough
GL56 9QX
11.30-2.30 (not Mon), 6-11; 12-2.30, 7-10.30 Sun
(01608) 661053
Hook Norton Hooky Bitter; Purity Pure Gold; guest beers H
Popular with villagers and visitors alike, this stone pub with flagstoned bar and restaurant area has four handpumps providing a choice from breweries near and far. Dominoes, cribbage and Aunt Sally are well supported and quizzes, folk musicians, bridge and whist are hosted on successive Sunday evenings. Delicious blackboard menu food is available (not Sun eve or Mon). On winter Sundays a roast is slowly turned over the inglenook fire by means of a windscreen wiper motor.
Q P

Studley

Little Lark
108 Alcester Road, B80 7NP (Tom's Town Lane jct)
12-3, 6-11; 12-11 Sat; 12-3, 6.30-10.30 Sun
(01527) 853105
Adnams Bitter, Broadside; Ansells Mild; guest beer H
Popular village local with three drinking areas served by a central bar. The interior has a newspaper theme, with framed front pages adorning the walls. Good quality reasonably priced meals cooked by the licensee are served seven days a week – try the Cow Pie. Traditional country wines and a selection of single malt whiskies are available. The pub hosts two cheese festivals every year.
Q

Ullenhall

Winged Spur
Main Street, B95 5PA
12-midnight
(01564) 792005 thewingedspur.com
Flowers IPA; guest beers H
An unassuming open plan village pub, with nooks and crannies making a pleasant drinking environment. The name derives from the Knight family crest – the spur was the medieval symbol of knighthood. Up to three guest beers as well as two ciders are available. Good food, including vegetarian, is served lunchtime and evenings and special dietary requirement can be catered for with notice. Sunday night is quiz night. The TV shows major events only. Q P

Warings Green

Blue Bell Cider House
Warings Green Road, B94 6BP (S of Cheswick Green, off Ilshaw Heath Road) OS127742
11.30-11; 12-10.30 Sun
(01564) 702328
Weatheroak Light Oak; guest beers H
Friendly canalside free house offering up to three real ales and five draught ciders, including a house special from Weston's. Eight temporary moorings make it a popular stop for boaters, and walking, cycling and fishing parties are catered for. The large lounge and cosy bar have real fires in winter. Reasonably priced food includes a children's menu and vegetarian options. Regular quiz nights and occasional live music are held. Some locals remember the former landlady who used to brew her own beer. Q P

Warwick

Millwright Arms
67 Coten End, CV34 4NU
12-2.30, 5.30-11 (midnight Fri & Sat)
(01926) 496955 millwrightarms.co.uk
Adnams Broadside; Black Sheep Best Bitter; Caledonian Deuchars IPA; Greene King IPA; Shepherd Neame Spitfire; guest beer H
Half-timbered 16th-century Tudor coaching inn with a multi-roomed interior featuring exposed beams and fine old settles and benches. It has a snug to the rear and dining room to the side. Home-cooked food is excellent – booking recommended. Families and well behaved dogs are welcome. An annual summer beer festival uses the outside bar in the spacious garden. The pub is open all day during the summer.
Q (X17) P

Old Fourpenny Shop
27-29 Crompton Street, CV34 6HJ (near racecourse, between A429 and A4189)
12-2.30 (3 Sat), 5.30-11; 12-11 Fri; 12-3, 6-10.30 Sun
(01926) 491360 fourpennyshophotel.co.uk
RCH Pitchfork; guest beers H
Featuring in the Guide for the last 16 years consecutively, this pub is popular with locals and visitors alike. Six handpumps provide a constantly changing selection of carefully chosen beers, with many from small breweries. The comfortable, bright and airy single bar has a contemporary decor. Good quality food is available. Twice a winner of CAMRA's Warwickshire Pub of the Year, this is a real treasure. Q P

Keep your Good Beer Guide up to date by visiting **www.camra.org.uk**, click on **Good Beer Guide** then **Updates to the GBG 2008** where you will find information about changes to pubs.

WEST MIDLANDS

STAFFORDSHIRE

M6 Toll

Brownhills

Bloxwich

Short Heath
Wednesfield
Aldridge
Willenhall
A454
Wolverhampton
Bilston
Walsall
Darlaston
Sutton Coldfield
Coseley
Wednesbury
Sedgley
Woodsetton
Tipton
Upper Gornal
West Bromwich
Lower Gornal
Dudley
Oldbury
Newtown
Pensnett
Netherton
Langley
Hockley
Nechells
Kingswinford
BIRMINGHAM
Brierley Hill
Blackheath
Digbeth
Amblecote
Cradley Heath
Highgate
Wollaston
Edgbaston
Balsall
Oldswinford
Lye
Halesowen
Heath
Stourbridge
Harborne
Moseley
Selly Oak
Solihull
Stirchley
Barst
Shirley
Knowl
WORCESTERSHIRE
Major's Green

Aldridge

Lazy Hill Tavern

196 Walsall Wood Road, WS9 8HB
☼ 6-11; 12-2.30, 6-11 Sat; 12-2.30, 7-10.30 Sun
☎ (01922) 452040
Caledonian Deuchars IPA; Courage Best; Greene King Abbot; Marston's Pedigree; Theakston Mild; guest beer Ⓗ
Large, welcoming, family-run free house run by the same licensee for 30 years. Originally a farmhouse, it became a country club, then finally a pub in 1986. Four separate rooms are all similarly and comfortably furnished with original beams exposed in the middle two. The large, 160-seater function room is used midweek by local sports organisations and can be booked for weddings. ᴹQ🖼️P

Amblecote

Maverick

Brettell Lane, DY8 4BA (on jct of A491/A461)
☼ 12-midnight (1am Wed, Fri & Sat); 12-11 Sun
☎ (01384) 824099
Jennings Cumberland Ale; guest beers Ⓗ
This friendly pub welcomes all age groups, including families. The main room has a Wild West decor and there is also a Mexican styled room. A separate bar serves the covered beer garden. Live music is a regular feature, with styles ranging from folk and blues to roots and bluegrass. Sports fans can watch their

favourite matches live on Sky TV and there is a dart board. 🌼🖼️(311)♣⚋

Robin Hood

119 Collis Street, DE8 4EQ (on A4102, off Brettell Lane)
☼ 12-3, 6-11; 12-midnight Fri-Sat; 12-11 Sun
☎ (01384) 821120
Batham Best Bitter; Enville Ale, Ginger; Salopian Shropshire Gold; guest beers Ⓗ
In the Glass Quarter and close to the canal network, this family-owned and run free house prides itself on the range and quality of its ale. It also offers an interesting bottled beer selection. The restaurant features good food that has earned the pub plaudits. En-suite accommodation is available including a family room. ᴹ🌼🛏️◑よ🖼️♣P

Swan

10 Brettel Lane, DY8 4BN (on A461 towards Dudley, ⅓ mile after A491)
☼ 12-2.30 (not Tue-Thu), 7-11; 12-11 Sat & Sun
☎ (01384) 76932
Beer range varies Ⓗ
A friendly neighbourhood free house comprising a comfortable lounge and public bar, with a TV screening popular sporting events. Many charities, such as the Air Ambulance, are supported by fund-raising regulars. Three real ales change continuously, providing plenty of variety. The popular garden is a delightful suntrap in summer. 🌼🍴🖼️♣

changing menu (no meals Sun eve).
△Q✿◐♣P↺

Bilston

Olde White Rose
20 Lichfield Street, WV14 0AG
🕑 12-11 (11.30 Fri & Sat)
☎ (01902) 498339
Beer range varies Ⓗ
The Olde White Rose offers up to 12 real ales,
a variety of foreign beers plus cider and perry
from Weston's. As well as the menu served
until 9pm Monday to Saturday, there is also a
carvery lunchtimes and evenings (until 5pm
Sun). Quiz nights are held on Tuesday and
Wednesday, with live folk music down in the
bierkeller on Thursday. Bus and metro stations
are nearby.
✿◐&⊖(Bilston Central)🚌(79)♣↺

Sir Henry Newbolt
45-47 High Street, WV14 0EP
🕑 9am-midnight (1am Fri & Sat)
☎ (01902) 404636
**Enville Ale; Greene King Abbot; Marston's
Pedigree; guest beers** Ⓗ
A typical Wetherspoon conversion of an old
cinema building, the pub opened in 2000. Its
frontage, designed to blend in with other
nearby buildings, does not mark it out as a
pub and you can easily walk past without
realising. The name commemorates a poet,
born in Bilston, who was famous for his
nautical ballads and patriotic poems. Food is
served daily until 11pm.
✿◐&⊖(Bilston Central)🚌↺

Trumpet
58 High Street, WV14 0EP
🕑 11-3.30 (4 Sat), 7.30-11.30; 11-4, 7.30-11.30 Sun
☎ (01902) 493723 ⊕trumpetjazz.org
**Holden's Mild, Bitter, Golden Glow, seasonal
beers** Ⓗ
Busy, compact and characterful one-room
local serving Holden's award-winning ales at
reasonable prices. Music and cartoons of locals
adorn the walls, while the ceiling is festooned
with musical instruments. Live jazz is
performed here seven nights a week and on
Sunday afternoon all year round; there is no
admission charge, although a collection plate
is taken round. ✿⊖(Bilston Central)🚌↺

Birmingham: Balsall Heath

Old Moseley Arms
53 Tindal Street, B12 9QU
🕑 12-11.30 (11 Sun)
☎ (0121) 440 1954
**Black Sheep Best Bitter; Enville Ale, Ginger;
Greene King Abbot; guest beer** Ⓗ
Lovely back-street pub set on the end of a
terrace. It is well tucked away, but only a few
minutes' walk from the bus stop. Live music is
staged every Sunday upstairs in the pool
room, while a popular curry night is held on
Tuesday and Thursday. Sporting events are
shown on a big screen, but the comfortable
lounge area remains sports-free. The jukebox
caters for all, including the oldies – this is a
truly multicultural establishment.
✿◐🍴🚌(50)↺

WARWICKSHIRE

0 Miles   5
0 Kilometres   8

Allesley
Coventry
Balsall Common

Balsall Common

Railway
547 Station Road, CV7 7EF (off A452, next to
Berkswell railway station)
🕑 12-midnight (11.30 Sun)
☎ (01676) 533284
**Adnams Broadside; Draught Bass; Taylor
Landlord** Ⓗ
A railside pub with plenty of character. The
long, panelled bar effectively divides the room
into two; one side hosts a pool table and the
other is a quieter area. The patio is an ideal
spot to sit and watch the trains go by on a
summer's day. △✿◐🚲🚉🚌(192, 194)♣P↺

Barston

Bull's Head
Barston Lane, B92 0JU
🕑 11-2.30, 5-11; 11-11 Sat; 12-10.30 Sun
☎ (01675) 442830 ⊕thebullsheadbarston.co.uk
**Adnams Bitter; Hook Norton Hooky Bitter; guest
beers** Ⓗ
Village local with a coaching inn history dating
back to 1490. It has three beamed rooms,
comprising two bars with real fires and an
intimate restaurant in the oldest part of the
building. Outside there is a secluded beer
garden with a covered area. The pub has
featured in this Guide for 15 consecutive
years, and was local CAMRA Pub of the Year
winner in 1998, 2000 and 2002. It offers high
quality seasonal food with a regularly

Birmingham: City Centre

Briar Rose

25 Bennetts Hill, B2 5RE
🕒 7am-1am; 8am-midnight Sun
☎ (0121) 643 8100 ⊕ jdwetherspoon.co.uk
Courage Directors; Fuller's Discovery, London Pride; Greene King Abbot; Wye Valley HPA; guest beers Ⓗ
Large, city-centre Wetherspoon's pub, located in the former Abbey House building, the first branch of the Abbey National. This comfortable and plushly decorated pub has a 40-bedroom Wetherlodge attached, plus a large function room. Children are welcome in a family area at the rear until 9pm. Breakfast is served from 7am (8am Sun) until noon, and a full menu to 11pm, offering the usual Wetherspoon's food deals. Guest beers regularly feature for a week at a time.
🛏🚭🕽&⇌(New St/ Snow Hill)⊖(Snow Hill)
♣

Bull

1 Price Street, B4 6JU (off St Chads Queensway)
🕒 12-11; closed Sun
☎ (0121) 333 6757 ⊕ thebull-pricestreet.com
Adnams Broadside; Ansells Mild; Marston's Pedigree; guest beer Ⓗ
One of the oldest pubs in Birmingham, this is a popular and friendly back-street local situated close to the Children's Hospital and Aston University. The two main rooms are served by a central bar, and there is a quieter room at the rear, with easy chairs. You cannot help but notice the vast collection of plates, cups and water jugs alongside old photos and prints of Birmingham. Also look for the etched Ansells Ales windows. The guest beer frequently changes. Q🚭🕽&⇌(Snow Hill)⊖(Snow Hill)🚇♣P⅄╌🖵

Old Fox

54 Hurst Street, B5 4TD (opp Hippodrome Theatre)
🕒 11.30-midnight (2am Thu-Sat); 12-midnight Sun
☎ (0121) 622 5080
Everards Tiger; Greene King Old Speckled Hen; Marston's Pedigree; Tetley Bitter; guest beers Ⓗ
Located on the edge of the Chinese and gay quarters and close to the Bullring shopping centre, the classic Victorian facade of the pub contrasts with the surrounding modern buildings. Charlie Chaplin reputedly drank here. Inside is a horseshoe shaped bar with bare floorboards, the walls adorned with old theatre posters. An unusual feature is the mirrored pillars. Popular with after-work drinkers, it is subject to surges of custom before and after theatre performances. There is a small family dining area that allows children. 🕽&⇌(New Street)🚇

Old Joint Stock

4 Temple Row, B2 5NY (opp St Philip's Cathedral)
🕒 11-11; closed Sun
☎ (0121) 200 1892
Fuller's Chiswick, Discovery, London Pride, ESB, seasonal beers; guest beer Ⓗ
Grade II listed building, formerly the Old Joint Stock Bank. The interior mixes neo-classical and Victorian design with Roman statuettes, a cupola and colonnades. There is a central island bar, with a quieter room at the rear. A theatre space has been created at the upper level, with regular performances. The pub attracts office workers, shoppers and real ale drinkers, and regular mini beer festivals are hosted. The changing guest is usually from Beowulf. 🚭🕽&⇌(New Street/Snow Hill)⊖(Snow Hill)🚇

Old Royal

53 Church Street, B3 2DP (off Colmore Row)
🕒 12-11
☎ (0121) 200 3841
Draught Bass; Fuller's London Pride; Taylor Landlord Ⓗ
Classic Victorian corner pub with a large single bar. Popular with local office workers, it can get busy at lunchtime and early evening. The pub boasts stained-glass windows and original tiling on the staircase leading to the upstairs function room/restaurant (no food Sun). A plaque, taken from another pub, commemorates the young Princess Victoria's visit, hence the name. A large screen in the main bar shows sports.
🕽&⇌(Snow Hill)⊖(Snow Hill)🚇

Pennyblacks

132-134 Wharfside Street, The Mailbox, B1 1XL (in Mailbox complex at canal level)
🕒 11-11 (midnight Fri & Sat); 11-10.30 Sun
☎ (0121) 632 1460 ⊕ penny-blacks.com
Hook Norton Old Hooky; St Austell Tribute; Taylor Landlord; guest beers Ⓗ
Upmarket bar benefiting from a canal-side location with some outdoor tables. It features wood and leather decor, with bar seating in front and a dining area at the rear. Food is a draw, with traditional Victorian English dishes prepared to a high standard. Note the unusual stillaging arrangement, with casks racked behind the bar area. Pennyblacks is part of a new chain with a commitment to real ale. Occasional beer evenings and mini-festivals are held, and Church End and Wye Valley are regular guests. 🚭🕽&⇌(New Street)

Prince of Wales

84 Cambridge Street, B1 2NP (behind International Convention Centre)
🕒 12-11 (10.30 Sun)
☎ (0121) 643 9460
Adnams Broadside; Ansells Mild; Everards Tiger; Taylor Landlord; Wells Bombardier; guest beers Ⓗ
Small and intimate Punch Taverns pub in the heart of Birmingham attracting a mix of locals and real-ale enthusiasts; one of the regulars even has a reserved seat with an engraved plaque. This pub is usually full, particularly after shows at the nearby NIA, ICC and Repertory Theatre. Good value food is

INDEPENDENT BREWERIES

Batham Brierley Hill
Black Country Lower Gornal
Highgate Walsall
Holden's Woodsetton
Olde Swan Netherton
Rainbow Allesley
Sarah Hughes Sedgley
Toll End Tipton
Windsor Castle Lye

available lunchtime and early afternoon, in hefty portions. Two rotating guest beers are usually available. Occasional live music sessions are hosted.
◖╤(New St/Snow Hill)⊖(Snow Hill)🚆

Queen's Arms

150 Newhall Street, B3 1RY
✪ 12-11 (10.30 Sun)
☎ (0121) 236 3710
Ansells Mild; Courage Directors; Flowers IPA; guest beers Ⓗ
Situated on the edge of the Jewellery Quarter, this recently refurbished classic Victorian corner pub has an exceptional tiled sign outside. Traditional pub food is available on weekdays until 8pm. Bar snacks only are on offer on Saturday, and the Sunday roast beef in giant Yorkshire pudding is not to be missed. Background music is played, and a quiz is held every Wednesday from 8.30pm.
🚪◖⊖(St Paul's)

Shakespeare

Lower Temple Street, B2 4JD
✪ 11-11 (midnight Fri & Sat); 12-10.30 Sun
☎ (0121) 316 7841
Fuller's London Pride; Marston's Pedigree; guest beer Ⓗ
A popular city-centre inn, the Shakespeare is one of the few pubs to have escaped redevelopment, and now offers somewhere to take a welcome break from shopping, or to unwind after work. The original M&B mosaic-tiled entranceway has been preserved. The bar area is at the front, with some plusher seating to the rear, and cafe-style tables on the pavement outside. ◖╤(New Street)🚆

Shakespeare

31 Summer Row, B3 1JJ (200m from city end of Broad St)
✪ 11 (12 Sat)-11; 12-10.30 Sun
☎ (0121) 214 5081
M&B Brew XI; guest beers Ⓗ
Extensively but tastefully restored small city centre local, near Broad Street and at the heart of the Summer Row nightclub complex. The traditional bar has a small hatch to serve the rear snug and features a superb engraved Mitchells & Butlers large mirror. It is popular with early evening office workers and students from the nearby College of Food. Regularly changing guest ales are stocked, and food is served until late (4pm on Sun). Barbecues are hosted in summer.
Q🕸◖🍴♿╤(Snow Hill)⊖(Snow Hill)🚆

Utopia

16 Church Street, B3 2NP
✪ 10 (12 Sat)-11; closed Sun
☎ (0121) 233 3666 ⊕ utopiainns.com
Hook Norton Hooky Bitter; Taylor Landlord; guest beer Ⓗ
Light background music greets you at this busy and stylish city-centre bar with a modern interior situated close to St Philip's Cathedral. It usually stocks a guest beer from a local brewery, and interesting traditional food is served from fish and chips to swordfish steak, as well as vegetarian options. Private parties can be catered for. The pub sometimes closes

early at the beginning of the week.
◖♿╤(New St/Snow Hill)⊖(Snow Hill)🚆

Wellington

37 Bennetts Hil, B2 5SN
✪ 10-midnight
☎ (0121) 200 3115 ⊕ thewellingtonrealale.co.uk
Black Country Pig on the Wall, Fireside; Wye Valley Hereford Pale Ale; guest beers Ⓗ
Birmingham CAMRA Pub of the Year 2006, you will always find a friendly atmosphere in this pub, where you can sample a wide range of ales and ciders, as well as foreign bottled beers. Over 2,500 different beers were stocked during 2006. Quarterly beer festivals along with quiz nights and cheese tasting evenings are also popular. No food is served but you can bring your own (plates and cutlery provided). New Street and Snow Hill stations are five minutes' walk.
Q╤(Snow Hill/New St)⊖(Snow Hill)🚆♣

Birmingham: Digbeth

Anchor ☆

308 Bradford Street, B5 6ET
✪ 11-midnight; 12-11 Sun
☎ (0121) 622 4516 ⊕ the-anchor-inn.fsnet.co.uk
Ansells Mild; Tetley Bitter; guest beers Ⓗ
A Grade II listed building, this pub has won local CAMRA Pub of the Year three times. The bar is split by an original three-quarter height partition. The lounge is served through a hatch, and there is a separate quiet room. A wide selection of cask ales featuring small breweries is always stocked, plus bottled foreign beers and at least one cider. It also hosts regular themed beer weekends and two annual beer festivals. Convenient for travellers using Digbeth coach station.
Q🕸◖🍴♿╤(New St/Moor St)🚆♣

White Swan ☆

276 Bradford Street, B12 0QY
✪ 12-3, 4.15-11; 11-11 Thu (1am Fri & Sat); 12-midnight Sun
☎ (0121) 622 2586
Banks's Original, Bitter; Jennings Cumberland Ale, Cocker Hoop; guest beer Ⓗ
Two-roomed Victorian pub in the Irish quarter, largely unspoilt, featuring impressive original tiling in the hallway. The bar has remained unaltered, although large TVs now feature in both rooms. The licensee has been here for 37 years, and the pub has appeared in almost every edition of the Guide. The Swan was originally built for Ansells, and is a good example of the pub architecture of the time.
🍴╤(New St/Moor St)🚆╘

Birmingham: Edgbaston

Garden House

160 Hagley Road, B16 9NX (10 mins' walk from Five Ways roundabout)
✪ 11-11; 12-10.30 Sun
☎ (0121) 454 8315
Hobsons Town Crier; Greene King Old Speckled Hen; guest beers Ⓗ
Large Chef and Brewer pub that could easily be missed from the Hagley Road. It features a fascinating, old-style interior, with both

original and mock-Tudor wooden beams, fireplaces and ornaments from stone jars to brasses. The pub is regularly busy with locals, business people and passers-by. This hostelry mainly prides itself on food, however real ale features prominently at the bar. ⛼❀♿P⁻

Birmingham: Harborne

Bell

11 Old Church Road, B17 0BB (beside St Peter's Church)
🕘 12-11 (midnight Thu-Sat)
☎ (0121) 427 0934
Caledonian Deuchars IPA; guest beer Ⓗ
In a wealthy suburb, this pub retains a rural feel, situated next to St Peter's churchyard. The main beamed room is decorated in warm colours with modern prints. There is also a panelled snug. At the rear a large patio overlooks an L-shaped bowling green, the scene of regular club matches in summer. The servery hatch in the corridor has two handpumps. The food is good value, especially Sunday lunch. ❀◑◐🚌P

Green Man

2 High Street, B17 9NE
🕘 12-11 (11.30 Wed & Thu; 1am Fri & Sat)
☎ (0121) 427 0961
M&B Brew XI; Marston's Pedigree; Taylor Landlord; guest beer Ⓗ
This Ember Inn pub on the High Street in Harborne has a long and venerable history and is decorated with old photographs on the walls. A large pub used by regulars and shoppers, it can get busy at times, especially for the popular Sunday lunches. A good value menu is served until 9pm daily. Seating is available outside on a patio area by the pavement, and at the rear of the pub beside the large car park. The weekly quiz night is Tuesday. ❀◑◐♿🚌P

White Horse

2 York Street, B17 0HG (100m off Harborne High St)
🕘 11-11 (11.30 Tue-Thu; midnight Fri & Sat); 12-11 Sun
☎ (0121) 427 6023
🌐 whitehorseharborne.homestead.com
Greene King IPA, Abbot; Marston's Pedigree; Shepherd Neame Spitfire; guest beers Ⓗ
This suburban pub is a short bus ride from the city centre, just off Harborne High Street. It features a central island bar with a snug at the front. Televised sporting events are shown on big screens in both the front and back areas, and it can get busy during major fixtures. The pub offers a good range of guest beers and a decent menu served until 6pm (3pm Sun).
❀◑◐♿🚌

Birmingham: Highgate

Lamp

257 Barford Street, B5 7EP (500m from Pershore Road)
🕘 12-5am
☎ (0121) 622 2599
Church End Gravediggers; Everards Tiger; Stanway Stanney Bitter; guest beers Ⓗ
Small, friendly back-street local, near market areas and a proposed Irish Quarter development. The only regular outlet for Stanway beers in the city, its beer range is complemented by regular and fast-changing guests, mostly from small micro-breweries. The pub can get busy at times due to the small bar area, which has seating and tables to the front of it. There is a large function room at the back that is well used by a number of societies and also serves as a venue for live acts.
♿⇌(New St)🚌⁻🀆

Birmingham: Hockley

Black Eagle

16 Factory Road, B18 5JU (in Jewellery Quarter)
🕘 12-3, 5.30-11; 12-11 Fri; 12-3, 5.30-11 Sat; 12-3 Sun
☎ (0121) 523 4008
Ansells Mild; Marston's Pedigree; Taylor Landlord; guest beers Ⓗ
Situated in a quiet backwater of inner-city Birmingham, this pub retains many original features, including Minton tiles. A four-times winner of local CAMRA Pub of the Year, the four small bar areas and à la carte restaurant provide a cosy atmosphere for drinkers and diners. Bar meals are also served. There are usually three guest beers available, and a beer festival is held in the well-tended garden in July. ❀◑◐⊟⊖(Soho Benson Rd)🚌

Church

22 Great Hampton Street, B18 6AQ
🕘 11.30-midnight (1.30am Thu-Sat); 12-11 Sun (may close early if quiet)
☎ (0121) 515 1851
Batham Bitter; guest beers Ⓗ
A warm welcome back into the Guide for a former long-standing entry. A change of landlord has seen Sunday opening introduced and curries added to the popular, extensive food menu renowned for legendary portions. Fears that the city would lose its only regular outlet for Batham beers have proved unfounded, and this backstreet local looks set to regain its place as part of the city's real ale circuit.
Q⛭◑◐♿⇌(Jewellery Quarter)⊖(St Paul's)🚌(74, 79)

Birmingham: Moseley

Prince of Wales

118 Alcester Road, B13 8EE
🕘 11-11; 12-10.30 Sun
☎ (0121) 449 8284
Adnams Bitter, Broadside; Greene King Abbot; Wells Bombardier; guest beer Ⓗ
Very much a locals' community pub, this large, multi-roomed Victorian establishment is situated on a main road in the cosmopolitan 'village' of Moseley. New proprietors are endeavouring to restore this once thriving pub to its former glory. The pub's most famous patron, JRR Tolkien, was a regular, and he met his future wife, Edith Bratt, while she was lodging here. ❀⊟🚌(50)⁻

Birmingham: Nechells

Villa Tavern ☆

307 Nechells Park Road, B7 5PD (400 yds from Aston stn off Lichfield Rd)

✪ 12-midnight (1am Fri & Sat); 12-midnight Sun
☎ (0121) 326 7466
Ansells Mild, Bitter Ⓗ
Situated a short walk from Aston Station and
Lichfield Road, the Villa is easily accessible
from the city centre. A splendid Victorian-style
pub, with intact bar, lounge and function
room, much of the original tiling and floors
have also been retained in the vestibule area.
A traditional community pub, it is well
frequented by locals, and offers darts, pool
and a regular quiz night. ◖Ⓗ≠(Aston)🚌♣P

Birmingham: Newtown

Bartons Arms ☆

144 High Street, B6 4UP (at A34/B4144 jct, opp
Newtown Baths)
✪ 12-11; 11-10.30 Sun
☎ (0121) 333 5988 ⊕ oakham-ales.co.uk
**Oakham JHB, White Dwarf, Bishops Farewell;
guest beers** Ⓗ
This classic, palatial Victorian pub is fitted
throughout with beautiful Minton tiling and
many original features are well-preserved or
restored to their previous standard. The
building is Grade II listed and is one of
Birmingham's finest in the CAMRA National
Inventory of pub interiors. An elaborate
staircase leads to two function rooms on the
first floor; the larger room often hosts events
such as quiz and comedy nights. Live music
plays in the main bar and delicious, good
value Thai food is served. ▲◖Ⓗ♿🚌♣P⏃

Birmingham: Selly Oak

Country Girl

1 Raddlebarn Road, B29 6HJ (500m from hospital;
750m from station)
✪ 12-11 (midnight Thu-Sat)
☎ (0121) 414 9921
**Greene King Old Speckled Hen; M&B Brew XI;
Marston's Pedigree; guest beer** Ⓗ
Regularly busy with locals and students, this
pub has a surprising exterior that looks out of
place in the Birmingham suburbs and is more
suited to a large village inn. The comfortable
interior features a typical Ember Inns layout,
with gas fireplace, brick pillars and ornaments.
There is an outdoor patio seating area at the
rear, and it has its own large car park with
disabled spaces. ❀◖♿🚌(11, 69)P⏃

Birmingham: Stirchley

British Oak ☆

1364 Pershore Road, B30 2XS (on main A441)
✪ 11-11 (1am Fri & Sat); 12-11 Sun
☎ (0121) 458 1758
M&B Mild; guest beers Ⓗ
This large, listed building, noted in CAMRA's
National Inventory of pub interiors, is a fine
example of a 1920s-style road house. The
varied rooms contain a wealth of original
fittings: note the fine oak panelling and
superb fireplace in the rear lounge. The public
bar can become lively at times, but the side
rooms offer peace and tranquillity. The large
rear garden is ideal for alfresco drinking and
watching bowls on a summer's evening. The

bowling club, however, is for gentlemen only.
▲☎❀◖Ⓗ♿≠(Bourneville)🚌(45, 47)♣P⏃

Blackheath

Britannia

124 Halesowen Street, B65 0EG
✪ 9-midnight (1am Fri & Sat)
☎ (0121) 559 0010 ⊕ jdwetherspoon.co.uk
Oakham JHB; guest beers Ⓗ
Unusually for a Wetherspoon conversion, this
building has always been a pub and although
open-plan it has a homely atmosphere. It
offers a frequently changing range of up to 10
guest ales and the usual Wetherspoon fare –
the far end of the pub is reserved for diners.
The pub has a strong community feel and is
well worth a visit. It is close to Rowley Regis
train station and Blackheath town centre
where a wide range of buses stop from
Dudley, Birmingham and West Bromwich.
❀◖♿≠(Rowley Regis)🚌♣P⏃

Malt Shovel

61 High Street, B65 0EH (5 mins' walk from
Blackheath centre)
✪ 11-11 (2am Fri); 10-2am Sat; 12-11 Sun
☎ (0121) 561 2321
Holden's Golden Glow; Oakham JHB Ⓗ
A small, sports-oriented locals' pub, the Malt
Shovel has a single L-shaped room with three
TV screens. There is a large garden where a
marquee is erected six to eight times a year
for special events such as live music, and a
skittle alley is available. Barbecues are held
throughout the summer, whatever the
weather. A number of buses stop outside or in
the centre of Blackheath.
☎❀♿≠(Rowley)🚌(404)♣♠

Waterfall

Waterfall Lane, B64 6RG (at top of main
Blackheath-Old Hill road)
✪ 12-2, 5-11; 12-midnight Fri & Sat; 12-10.30 Sun
☎ (0121) 5613499 ⊕ holdensbrewery.co.uk
**Batham Bitter; Holden's Black Country Bitter,
Golden Glow, Special; guest beers** Ⓗ
Acquired by Holden's a few years ago, this
characterful pub is near to Blackheath town
centre. It serves up to six guest beers, tending
towards the stronger brews. The outside
drinking area affords wonderful views during
the summer, although the elevated position
means a steep walk uphill from Old Hill
Station. Basic pub meals at reasonable prices
are served daily. It can get very crowded at
weekends. ❀◖≠(Old Hill)🚌♣P

Bloxwich

Lamp Tavern

34 High Street, WS3 2DA (by Leisure Centre)
✪ 12-11
☎ (01922) 479681
Holden's Mild, Bitter; guest beers Ⓗ
The perfect venue after a session at the
adjacent Leisure Centre, this one-roomed local
features a bar on one side and a comfortable,
quieter lounge on the other. Pleasantly
decorated, the building was formerly a farm
and stables. The pub has plentiful charm and is

a focus for the community of all ages – a genuine slice of Bloxwich life. Karaoke is popular on Friday and Sunday evenings.
⌂❀♿☗♨

Brierley Hill

Rose & Crown

161 Bank Street, DY5 3DD (B4179)
☼ 12-2, 6-11; 12-11 Fri & Sat; 12-3.30, 7-11 Sun
☎ (01384) 77825
Holden's Mild, Bitter, Special, seasonal beers; guest beer Ⓗ
This traditional side-street pub was originally two terraced properties. The lounge has a cosy relaxed atmosphere with a friendly clientele. One end of the small bar is dominated by the dartboard; a recent conservatory extension adds welcome extra space. Good value pub food is served (not Sun). The ever-changing guest beer comes from a variety of small breweries. It is five minutes' walk from Brierley Hill High Street which is served by several bus routes. ◐❀☗♣P♨☐

Vine (Bull & Bladder)

10 Delph Road, DY5 2TN
☼ 12-11 (10.30 Sun)
☎ (01384) 78293
Batham Mild, Best Bitter, XXX (winter) Ⓗ
Classic, unspoilt brewery tap with an ornately decorated façade proclaiming the Shakespearian words, 'Blessings of your heart, you brew good ale'. Nothing could be more apt for this elongated pub with a labyrinthine feel. The rooms have contrasting characters: the front bar is small and staunchly traditional, while the larger rear bar, with its own servery, houses the dartboard. On the other side of the central passageway is a homely lounge converted from former brewery offices. Good value Black Country lunches are served.
Q❀◐☗♣P♨

Brownhills

Prince of Wales

98 Watling Street, WS8 7NP (on A5)
☼ 5 (4.30 Fri)-midnight; 12-1am Sat; 11.30-midnight Sun
☎ (01543) 372551
Banks's Original; Beowulf Heroes Bitter Ⓗ
Cheerful, friendly corner local on the A5, near to Chasewater Park and the light railway. The extended single room houses a large-screen TV for sporting events. It can be busy on Wednesday evening, when a free buffet is served, and Friday and Saturday evenings are also very popular. Filled rolls are generally available. Parking can be difficult. ⌂❀♣♨

Royal Oak

68 Chester Road, WS8 6DU (on A452)
☼ 12-3, 6-11; 12-3.30, 6-midnight Sat; 12-3.30, 7-11 Sun
☎ (01543) 452089 ⊕ theroyaloakpub.co.uk
Banks's Original; Caledonian Deuchars IPA; Greene King Abbot; Tetley Bitter; guest beers Ⓗ
Known locally as the Middle Oak, this pub has gone back to its roots and is beautifully decorated in a 1930s Art Deco style. Games

are played in the traditional bar, while the comfortable lounge has a more relaxed atmosphere. There is a separate dining room and a large garden off the patio drinking area to the rear. ⌂Q❀◐☗♿☗♨P♨

Coseley

New Inn

35 Ward Street, WV14 9LQ (backs on to A4123)
☼ 4-11; 12-11.30 Sat; 12-10.30 Sun
☎ (01902) 676777
Holden's Mild, Bitter, seasonal beers Ⓗ
Cosy one-roomed local, best approached from the rear car park off Birmingham New Road. The lounge area is housed in a late 20th-century extension while the bar area is in the older, 19th-century part of the building. The two areas are separated by a modern bar-counter which is the hub of the pub. Food is served Tuesday to Saturday evenings; hot pork sandwiches are available Saturday lunchtime and on Sunday the lunches are popular. Family parties/events can be catered for.
⌂❧❀◐♿≢☗(126)♣♠P☐

Coventry

Beer Engine

35 Far Gosford Street, CV1 5DW
☼ 12-2am
☎ (024) 7626 7239 ⊕ thebeerengine.net
Black Sheep Best Bitter; guest beers Ⓗ
The walls in this single-room town pub feature film posters and pictures for sale by local artists. Five guest beers are always available. Leffe Blonde is on draught and a selection of continental bottled beers is always stocked. Meals are served Sunday lunchtime only; at other times customers are welcome to bring their own. Music plays on Saturday evening and there is an occasional beer festival. No children are admitted. Doors close at midnight. ⌂❀◐♣♨

City Arms

1 Earlsdon Street, CV5 6EP (on roundabout at centre of Earlsdon)
☼ 9-midnight (1am Fri & Sat)
☎ (024) 767 18170
Greene King Abbot; Marston's Pedigree; Rugby Twickers; guest beers Ⓗ
Typical Wetherspoon's pub, formerly known as Ma Cooper's, in the heart of Earlsdon, close to the city centre and well served by public transport. It gets busy at weekends but has a separate area for families until 8pm. Up to eight guest beers are stocked, many from micro-breweries such as Church End. Weston's Old Rosie and Organic Vintage cider are available on gravity. Food is served throughout the day until 11pm. There is a heated, covered smoking area outside.
❀◐♿☗♠P♨

Craven Arms

58 Craven Street, Chapelfields, CV5 8DW (1 mile W of city centre, off Allesley Old Road)
☼ 11 (4 Tue)-11.30 (11 Tue); 11-12.30am Fri & Sat; 12-11 Sun
☎ (024) 7671 5308

Flowers Original; Sarah Hughes Dark Ruby; guest beers Ⓗ
The enthusiastic landlord of this community corner local has increased the range of real ales from four to six; it is probably the only regular outlet for Sarah Hughes Dark Ruby mild for miles around. The pub comprises a lounge and a room in what used to be the house next door, where darts and pool are played. Quiz night is Thursday and live music plays on Sunday when it can get busy.
🏿🕏🗐♣💪

Gatehouse Tavern

46 Hill Street, CV1 4AN (adjacent to the Belgrade Plaza)
🕐 11-3, 5-11; 11-midnight Thu-Sat; 12-10.30 Sun
☎ (024) 7663 0140
Beer range varies Ⓗ
Small free house rebuilt from the remains of the gatehouse of the Leigh textile mill. Stained-glass windows depicting the Six Nations reflect the pub's sporting theme. The beers are usually a mix of local micro-breweries and bigger brands, and a selection of German and Belgian bottled beers now also features. Food is served lunchtimes and evenings (not Sun). The garden is probably the largest within the city centre. 🕏🕼🗐💪

Greyhound Inn

Sutton Stop, Hawkesbury Junction, CV6 6DF (1 mile along Blackhorse Rd from B4113 jct)
🕐 11-11; 12-10.30 Sun
☎ (024) 7636 3046 🌐 thegreyhoundinn.com
Highgate Mild; Marston's Pedigree; guest beers Ⓗ
Winner of the 2005/06 Godiva awards for best pub in Coventry and Warwickshire, this canal-side inn dates back to around 1830 and has retained many original features. The cosy restaurant serves an extensive menu created by an award-winning chef, and you can eat in the decked side garden in the summer. The pub hosts beer festivals in the spring/summer and autumn in the rear garden.
🏿Q🕏🕼🗐(C37, C47)♣P💪

Hare & Hounds

Watery Lane, Keresley End, CV7 8JA (Bennetts Rd jct)
🕐 12-11
☎ (024) 7633 2716 🌐 hareandhounds.co.uk
Adnams Broadside; Draught Bass; Greene King Abbot, Old Speckled Hen; M&B Brew XI; guest beers Ⓗ
The 150-year-old former coaching inn has a comfortably furnished L-shaped bar/lounge with two real fires. There is live music on Thursday and Sunday, and Tuesday is quiz night. Good food is available in the bar and restaurant. An adjacent pavilion caters for weddings, conferences or simply a faggot and pea supper while playing skittles on the alley. The garden has ample seating and a children's play area. Real cider is stocked in summer. 🏿Q🕏🕼🗐(36)♣💪

Nursery Tavern

38-39 Lord Street, Chapelfields, CV5 8DA (1 mile W of city centre, off Allesley Old Rd)
🕐 12-11.30; 11-midnight Fri & Sat; 12-11 Sun
☎ (024) 7667 4530

Courage Best Bitter; Fuller's London Pride; John Smith's Bitter; guest beers Ⓗ
Thriving community pub, situated in a terraced street in the historic watchmaking area. The tavern has been in the same ownership for more than a decade and is a long-standing entry in this Guide. It has two front rooms served by a central bar and a third room at the rear which is quieter and regularly hosts traditional pub games and quizzes. A mild is always stocked and beer festivals are held on the patio behind the pub in summer and winter. Q🕭🕏🕼🗐♣🕏💪

Old Windmill

22-23 Spon Street, CV1 3BA
🕐 11-11 (midnight Fri & Sat); 12-midnight Sun
☎ (024) 7625 2183
Caledonian Deuchars IPA; Greene King Old Speckled Hen; Taylor Landlord; Theakston Old Peculier; Wychwood Hobgoblin; guest beers Ⓗ
Timber-framed pub in historic Spon Street popular with students, shoppers and cinema-goers. Known locally as Ma Brown's, the remnants of the old 19th-century brewhouse can be seen in the back room. Flagstones and beams are much in evidence in the small rooms. Two guest beers, often from micro-breweries, are usually on offer. Lunchtime meals are served daily, and Weston's Old Rosie and Bounds Brand ciders are available on draught. 🏿🕼🕿🗐🕏

Rose & Woodbine

40 North Street, Stoke Heath, CV2 3FW
🕐 12-11 (11.30 Fri & Sat); 12-5, 7-11 Sun
☎ (024) 7645 1480
Banks's Original; Draught Bass; Tetley Bitter; Wells Bombardier; guest beers Ⓗ
The beer range has increased from four when this pub was first listed in the Guide to the seven now on offer. It includes Banks's Original mild, which is unusual for the area, and one beer from a local brewery. This pleasant community pub is very popular with the locals. Children are permitted until 7pm and the lunch menu caters for all ages.
🕏🕼🗐♿🗐(10)♣💪

Whitefriars Olde Ale House

114-115 Gosford Street, CV1 5DL
🕐 12-midnight (1am Fri & Sat); 12-11 Sun
☎ (024) 7625 1655 🌐 whitefriarscov.com
Beer range varies Ⓗ
The original building dates back to the 14th century, with many changes over the years including the addition of chimneys in the 16th century. In 1850 the building was combined with its 17th-century neighbour to form a butcher's shop. Many original features are still discernible today, especially upstairs. Seven frequently changing guest beers are available, and the selection of Belgian bottled beers includes Chimay and Duvel. Beer festivals are held on many public holidays and there is a covered and heated area for smokers.
🏿Q🕏🕼🗐♣P💪

Cradley Heath

Holly Bush

53 Newtown Lane, B64 5EA
🕐 7 (2 Sat & Sun)-2am

☎ (07949) 594484 ⊕ hollybushpub.net
Beer range varies Ⓗ
Two-roomed split-level corner pub, located just off the High Street. Its lower-level front bar has an open fireplace and a small raised area just inside the entrance where live music and comedy performances take place Thursday to Saturday (see website for details). A larger lounge at the rear provides an alternative quiet haven in which to enjoy the three changing guest beers. ⚲✿➊⊖🖵☙⌐

Darlaston

Prince of Wales
74 Walsall Road, WS10 9JJ
✿ 3 (12 Fri & Sat)-11; 12-10.30 Sun
☎ (0121) 526 6244
Holden's Bitter, Golden Glow; guest beers Ⓗ
Traditional Black Country pub. The small, comfortable lounge, which is family-friendly, is adorned with photographs of local swimming teams, football clubs and old town maps, while the long, narrow bar is decorated with advertising mirrors. Darts is played at one end. At the rear is a conservatory and a garden with a play area and bench seats. Occasional quiz and live music nights are hosted, and there is a covered area for smokers. ⟆✿➊⊖🖵☙⌐

Dudley

Lamp Tavern
116 High Street, DY1 1QT
✿ 12-2.30, 5-11; 12-11 Fri & Sat; 12-10.30 Sun
☎ (01384) 254129
Batham Mild, Best Bitter, XXX (winter) Ⓗ
At the very top of the High Street, across the busy junction, stands the Lamp Tavern. This lively pub has a sporty U-shaped front bar and a quieter lounge. To the rear is the former Queen's Cross brewery – its ground floor is an intimate venue for music and comedy nights, as well as doubling as a function room. Substantial bar snacks are available weekday lunchtimes. ✿➊⟓&🖵P

Halesowen

Coombs Wood Sports & Social Club
Lodgefield Road, B62 8AA (off A4099 to Blackheath)
✿ 7.30 (7 Fri)-11; 12.30-11 Sat; 12-10.30 Sun
☎ (0121) 561 1932
Beer range varies Ⓗ
For many years this former steelworks cricket club has thrived as a social centre for the community. The club is family friendly, with sports naturally featuring strongly: there is a large TV, pool and darts indoors and various sports are played outside in the extensive grounds. The enthusiastic manager at this current regional Club of the Year provides five or six regular ales which swell to 12 for the annual beer festival in January. Hot and cold snacks are served at the weekend.
🖵(247A, 248A)☙

Hawne Tavern
78 Attwood Street, B63 3UG
✿ 4.30 (12 Sat)-11; 12-10.30 Sun
☎ (0121) 602 2601
Banks's Bitter; Batham Best Bitter; guest beers Ⓗ
This busy pub, now in its tenth consecutive year in the Guide, is a fine example of a true free house, offering two regular and up to six guest beers. You can drink in the small cosy lounge or the lively bar where mounted beer mats around the serving area are testimony to some of the unusual beers served in the past, many from micro-breweries. A discreet TV shows sports results, and pool and darts are played. Sun worshippers and smokers enjoy the enclosed rear garden. Q✿➊⊖🖵(9)♣P⌐

Somers Sports & Social Club
The Grange, Grange Hill, B62 0JH (on bypass at A456/B4551 jct)
✿ 12-2.30 (3 Sat), 6-11; 12-2, 7-10.30 Sun
☎ (0121) 550 1645
Banks's Bitter; Batham Mild, Best Bitter; Olde Swan Original; guest beers Ⓗ
Three-times winner of CAMRA National Club of the Year, the club occupies a large 250-year-old house set in extensive grounds. A patio area overlooks the bowling green, tennis courts and children's play area, and the plush interior is adorned with sporting memorabilia, a fish tank and Laurel and Hardy figures. Around 10 real ales are usually on offer and snacks are available. Show your CAMRA membership card or this Guide for admission. Groups of five or more should telephone ahead. ✿🖵(9)♣P

Waggon & Horses
21 Stourbridge Road, B63 3TU (on A458, ½ mile from bus station)
✿ 12-11.30 (12.30am Fri & Sat)
☎ (0121) 550 4989
Batham Best Bitter; Nottingham Extra Pale Ale; Oakham White Dwarf; guest beers Ⓗ
Its regular beers, supplemented by 11 guests, many sourced from micros, make this pub a 'must' for enlightened drinkers. Real cider and three Belgian beers are also kept on draught. Quieter seating at both ends complements the traditional bar. Despite its national reputation, this CAMRA County Pub of the Year 2006 manages to retain a real community feel. Tasty home-made cobs are available and a charity quiz is held on alternate Wednesdays. A dog-friendly establishment. Q🖵(9)♣

Kingswinford

Bridge
110 Moss Grove, DY6 9HH (A491)
✿ 12-3, 5-11.30; 12-11.45 Fri & Sat; 12-11.30 Sun
☎ (01384) 352356
Banks's Original, Bitter; guest beers Ⓗ
Popular pub with a healthy local trade, offering a warm welcome to all visitors. The bar extends across the front of the building and there is a cosy lounge behind, warmed by an open fire in winter. In summer the well-equipped garden beckons. One or two guest beers come from the brewery list. Occasional live entertainment is staged at weekends, and

sandwiches can usually be made to order. 🏨🏵🚐♣️P⬋

Knowle

Vaults

St John's Close, B93 0JU (off High St A4141)
🕐 12-2.30, 5-11.30; 12-11.30 Fri & Sat; 12-11 Sun
☎ (01564) 773656
Ansells Mild; Greene King IPA; Tetley Bitter, Draught Burton Ale; guest beers Ⓗ
Located just off the High Street, this is a proper drinkers' pub, which has been voted local CAMRA branch Pub of the Year for four consecutive years from 2003-6. Guest beers are often from small breweries rarely seen in the area. Weston's cider is also available. The pub holds occasional beer festivals, and an annual pickled onion competition. Light lunches are served Monday to Saturday. Fishing gear on display highlights the landlord's penchant for the sport. 🚐♦️

Langley

Model

Titford Road, B69 4PZ (1 min walk from Langley High St)
🕐 11.30-11.30 (midnight Fri & Sat); 12-11 Sun
☎ (0121) 532 0090 ⊕ themodelinn.co.uk
Greene King Abbot; Taylor Landlord; guest beer Ⓗ
A true community pub in the heart of Langley, well served by passing buses and a short walk from Langley Green train station. Two cask ales and an occasional guest are offered. The U-shaped bar is divided into two distinct areas and the conservatory is used mainly for dining. Excellent value meals are served all week with chef's specials on Friday and Saturday evenings (no food Sun).
🏨🚌🏵🕐♿🚆(Langley Green)🚐(120)♣️P

Lower Gornal

Black Bear

86 Deepdale Lane, DY3 2AE
🕐 5 (4 Fri)-11; 12-11 Sat; 12-10.30 Sun
☎ (01384) 253333
Kinver Black Bear; Shepherd Neame Spitfire; guest beers Ⓗ
This charming traditional pub, originally an 18th-century farmhouse, built on the hillside with views over the south of the Black Country, is supported with massive buttresses. Inside, the L-shaped, split-level room has discrete and comfortable seating areas. Up to five guest beers are usually available, mainly from smaller breweries. The house beer Black Bear is brewed by Kinver. Ten minutes' walk from Gornal Wood bus station, this is a dog-friendly pub. 🏵♿🚐(257)♣️

Five Ways

Himley Road, DY3 2PZ (jct of B4176/4175, 3 mins from Gornal Wood bus station)
🕐 12-midnight (1am Fri & Sat); 12-10.30 Sun
☎ (01384) 252968
Batham Best Bitter Ⓗ
Warm and welcoming wayside watering hole on the western edge of the West Midlands conurbation, now with extended opening

hours. Its one crook-shaped room is just big enough to accommodate a large TV screen for football matches at one end without interrupting the civilised social discourse at the other. There is also a raised decking area overlooking the car park at the back of the pub. Good value weekday lunches are served. 🏵🕐🚐(257)♣️♦️P

Fountain

8 Temple Street, DY3 2PE (on B4157, 3 mins from Gornal Wood bus station)
🕐 12-11 (10.30 Sun)
☎ (01384) 242777
Enville Ale; Greene King IPA, Abbot; Hook Norton Old Hooky; RCH Pitchfork; guest beers Ⓗ
Twice winner of local CAMRA Pub of the Year, this excellent free house serves nine real ales accompanied by draught and bottled Belgian beers, real cider and 20 fruit wines. The busy, vibrant bar is complemented by an elevated dining area serving excellent food until 9pm Monday to Saturday and Sunday lunches until 5pm. During the summer months the rear garden is a suntrap and a pleasant area to while away an hour or two. 🚏🏵🕐♿🚐♣️♦️

Old Bull's Head

1 Redhall Road, DY3 2NU (at Temple St jct)
🕐 2 (12 Fri & Sat)-11; 12-11 Sun
☎ (01384) 231616 ⊕ oldbullshead.co.uk
Black Country Bradley's Finest Golden, Pig on the Wall, Fireside, seasonal beers; guest beers Ⓗ
This imposing late-Victorian pub has two separate rooms. The larger lounge bar is popular for pub games and there is a raised area at one end serving as a stage for varied entertainment on several evenings a week. There is also a sports lounge with pool table, dart board and large-screen TV. The Black Country Ales Brewery is at the rear and there are usually two guest beers from small breweries supplementing the regulars. Cobs are available daily. 🏨🏵🚐(541)♣️♦️P

Lye

Windsor Castle Inn

7 Stourbridge Road, DY9 7DG (at Lye Cross)
🕐 11-11
☎ (01384) 897809 ⊕ windsorcastlebrewery.com
Sadler's Green Man, Mild Ale, Worcester Sorcerer, 1900 Original Bitter, Thin Ice, IPA, seasonal beers; guest beer Ⓗ
The Windsor Castle Brewery has been revived in its new location by the descendants of the original brewer. The tap house to the side of the brewery is a new addition to the local pub scene. It features modern decor, serving good food in a separate dining area, and a wide selection of home-brewed Sadler's ales which you can enjoy in the bar area or with your food. Brewery tours are held every Monday evening (telephone first). 🕐🚆🚐(9)P

Major's Green

Drawbridge

Drawbridge Road, B90 1DD (S of Shirley, off Haslucks Green Rd)
🕐 12-11 (midnight Sat)
☎ (0121) 4745904

Marston's Pedigree; Wells Bombardier; guest beers Ⓗ
Family-oriented local, sitting alongside the distinctive drawbridge on the Stratford-upon-Avon Canal.This is a modern pub with a large, wood-panelled, L-shaped open-plan interior, where the emphasis is very much on food, served all day. The present management has put so much effort into promoting real ale that the pub was voted local CAMRA Most Improved Pub of the Year in 2006. Entertainment of some sort is laid on most evenings, from quiz nights to live music.
❀⊕&⇌♣P⌐

Netherton

Olde Swan (Ma Pardoe's) ☆
89 Halesowen Road, DY2 9PY (in centre, on A459 Dudley Old Hill)
🕙 11-11; 12-4, 7-10.30 Sun
☎ (01384) 253075
Olde Swan Original, Dark Swan, Entire, Bumblehole, seasonal beers Ⓗ
Characterful venue on CAMRA's National Inventory of historic interiors and home to the Olde Swan Brewery, the pub was also runner-up CAMRA National Pub of the Year in 2004. The front bar is an unspoilt gem with an enamelled ceiling and solid-fuel stove, and there is a cosy rear snug. The upstairs restaurant is highly regarded for its à la carte menu (booking is essential for all meals).
ቋQ❀⊕⊟&⊞P

Oldbury

Waggon & Horses ☆
17A Church Street, B69 3AD (opp Sandwell Council House)
🕙 12-11 (midnight Fri & Sat); 12-10.30 Sun
☎ (0121) 552 5467
Brains Rev James; Enville White; Oakham JHB; guest beers Ⓗ
National Inventory listed pub noted for its splendidly ornate tiled walls, copper-panelled ceiling and Holt Brewery etched windows. The pub comprises a bar, lounge and a passageway that is used as an extra drinking area. It offers a peaceful haven from the bustling town centre and is popular with office workers, locals and visitors alike. A wide variety of dishes at keen prices is served mainly at lunchtime during the week and Monday to Saturday evenings until 8pm. Monthly quizzes are held.
ቋQ☜⊕⊟&⇌(Sandwell & Dudley)⊟♣

Oldswinford

Shrubbery Cottage
28 Heath Lane, DY8 1RQ
🕙 11.30-11; 12-10.30 Sun
☎ (01384) 377598
Holden's Bitter, Golden Glow, Special, seasonal beers Ⓗ
Refurbished, welcoming pub with a single, spacious, open room and a large U-shaped bar. There is a large-screen TV at one end, often showing live golf or football matches. The pub provides full disabled access from the car park and has Wifi Internet connection. In

the garden there is a barbecue and a miniature putting green.
❀⊕&⇌(Stourbridge Jct)⊟(247)P

Pensnett

Fox & Grapes
176 High Street, DY5 4JQ (A4101)
🕙 11 (12 Fri & Sat)-11; 12-10.30 Sun
☎ (01384) 261907
Batham Mild, Best Bitter, seasonal beer Ⓗ
A former Holt, Plant and Deakin pub now acquired by Batham. Beyond the striking brick frontage a Batham-tiled passageway leads to several drinking areas around a central bar. A solid-fuel stove warms two areas at the back; the space at the front is more akin to a separate public bar. There is a garden behind the pub and a patio with tables and benches at the front. ቋ❀⊟♣P⌐

Sedgley

Beacon Hotel ☆
129 Bilston Street, DY3 1JE (on A463)
🕙 12-2.30 (3 Sat), 5.30 (6 Sat)-11; 12-3, 7-10.30 Sun
☎ (01902) 883380
Sarah Hughes Pale Amber, Surprise Bitter, Dark Ruby, seasonal beers; guest beers Ⓗ
This classic, beautifully restored Victorian tap house and brewery is the home of Sarah Hughes ales. The heart of this atmospheric, popular and dog-friendly pub is the small island servery with hatches. Off the central corridor is a traditional room with benches, a small cosy snug, a large main room and a family room with access to a well-equipped garden and play area. Cobs are available.
Q☜❀⊟(545)P

Bull's Head
27 Bilston Street, DY3 1JA (A463)
🕙 10 (11 Sun)-11.30
☎ (01902) 661676
Holden's Bitter, Golden Glow, seasonal beers Ⓗ
On the edge of Sedgley village, this pub has a community atmosphere. The front bar is lively with local chatter, pub games and a large screen showing sports. To the side is a lounge which can be curtained off to provide a small function room where children are welcome. Behind the pub is a pleasant walled yard used for outdoor drinking. Cobs are available.
ቋ❀⊟(545)♣⌐

Mount Pleasant (Stump)
144 High Street, DY3 1RH (on A459)
🕙 6-11; 12-3, 7-10.30 Sun
RCH Pitchfork, Double Header; guest beers Ⓗ
The mock-Tudor exterior of this sensitively refurbished free house fronts a friendly and cheerful interior. The good-sized front bar has a convivial feel, while the homely and warm rear lounge is split into two rooms on different levels, both with coal stoves. Eight handpumps major on ales from RCH including the house beer, Stumpy, but also provide a small selection from other breweries. Dog-friendly, the pub is five minutes' walk from Sedgley centre. ቋQ❀⊟(558)♣⌐

Shirley

Bernie's Real Ale Off-Licence
266 Cranmore Boulevard, B90 4PX
☼ 12-2 (11.30-1.30 Wed), 6-10 (5.30-9 Fri); 11-3, 5-9 Sat; 12-2, 7-9 Sun
☎ (0121) 744 2827
Beer range varies Ⓗ
This off-licence, run by local CAMRA members, has featured in the Guide for more than two decades. The beer range is interesting and varied, sourced mainly from micro- and craft-breweries the length and breadth of the country. This is a real gem and fully deserves its many loyal customers. You are encouraged to try before you buy; take-away is available for anything from a pint to a firkin. Usually three to four real ales are available at any one time, plus a good selection of British and Belgian bottled beers. 🚃

Short Heath

Duke of Cambridge
82 Coltham Road, WV12 5QD
☼ 12-3.30 (not Mon & Tue), 7-11; 12-3.30, 7-10.30 Sun
☎ (01922) 408895
Greene King Old Speckled Hen; Highgate Dark; Taylor Landlord; Worthington's Bitter; guest beers Ⓗ
Convivial family-run free house, converted from 17th-century farm cottages and licensed for nearly 200 years. The public bar is warmed by a solid-fuel stove, while the lounge, which is divided by a wall containing an aquarium, features exposed beams in the front. Both rooms display cases of model commercial vehicles. The large family room houses pool and football tables. ⚫Q☼🚃♣P

Solihull

Fieldhouse
10 Knightcote Drive, Monkspath, B91 3JU (off Monkspath Hall Rd)
☼ 12-11 (11.30 Thu; midnight Fri & Sat); 12-11.30 Sun
☎ (0121) 711 8011
Hook Norton Old Hooky; M&B Brew XI; Wells Bombardier; guest beers Ⓗ
Part of the Ember Inns chain, this large, modern pub is tastefully decorated and comfortably furnished, featuring four large fires (one real, three coal-effect) and pleasant patio areas. It usually serves two or three well-known ales changing periodically plus two or three more unusual ones, which are rotated more frequently. Often busy, it attracts a wide age range, but children must be over 14 and dining. Regular quiz nights are held on Sunday and Tuesday. ⚫☼◑Ġ➔🚃P▱

Golden Acres
Rowood Drive, Damsonwood, B92 9NG (off Damson Lane)
☼ 12-11 (midnight Fri-Sat)
☎ (0121) 704 9002
Beer range varies Ⓗ
An unusually shaped building located on a 1960s housing estate, the pub's name allegedly refers to a comment made by the local farmer who previously owned the land. Inside there is a public bar and comfortable lounge. Three beers usually include a well-

known national brand, an ale from a small brewery such as Wye Valley, and a seasonal beer. It was joint winner of local CAMRA Most Improved Pub in 2005. Chinese food can be ordered to eat in or take away. ⚫☼🚃♣●P

Stourbridge

Royal Exchange
75 Enville Street, DY8 1XW (on A458 just outside town centre)
☼ 1 (12 Sat & summer)-11; 12-10.30 Sun
☎ (01384) 396726
Batham Mild, Best Bitter, seasonal beers Ⓗ
Just a 15 minute walk from the train station (Stourbridge Town), with a bus stop outside, the pub has a lively bar, small plush lounge and an upstairs meeting room available for private hire. The bars and large patio area are all accessed from the street via a narrow passageway. There is a public car park opposite. A warm welcome is guaranteed here and, apart from the fine ales, snacks are available including occasional hot bar food. Q☼◑🚃♣

Sutton Coldfield

Bishop Vesey
63 Boldmere Road, B73 5UY
☼ 9-11
☎ (0121) 355 5077 ⊕ jdwetherspoon.co.uk
Courage Directors; Greene King Abbot; Marston's Burton Bitter, Pedigree; Shepherd Neame Spitfire; guest beers Ⓗ
Situated in a suburb of Sutton Coldfield and named after the town's benefactor, this busy and popular Wetherspoon's pub attracts local customers. It has an open-plan layout with upstairs seating and a cosy book-lined area at the end of the bar. There is an outside, heated patio for smokers. Children are allowed in a family area. Good value food is served including a breakfast menu from 9am. Themed evenings and regular mini beer festivals are staged.
☼◑Ġ⇌(Wylde Green)🚃▱

Crown
66 Walsall Road, Four Oaks, B74 4RA (on Walsall Road A454, opp Crown Lane)
☼ 12-11 (midnight Thu-Sat)
☎ (0121) 323 2715
M&B Brew XI; guest beers Ⓗ
Ember Inns comfort and good food are to be found in this spacious pub with a large car park. There are plenty of individual seating areas and a large, curving bar to accommodate all customers. The clientele is mixed but all enjoy the top quality changing guest beers which set this pub apart from other local Embers.
☼◑Ġ⇌(Butlers Lane)🚃P▱

Laurel Wines
63 Westwood Road, Banners Gate, B73 6UP (200m off A452, near Sutton Pk)
☼ 12-10
☎ (0121) 353 0399
Batham Best Bitter; Enville Ale; Laurel Four Four; Taylor Landlord; guest beers Ⓗ

Well-frequented real ale off-licence with a constantly changing range of guest ales and bottled beers, sourced nationally. Also stocking a wide range of cider, wines, spirits, soft drinks and off-licence commodities, it offers something for all. Parties are catered for, with cask ale supplied and set up, and glass hire is available. You may also use your own containers, and draught ales can be sampled before purchase. &

Tipton

Port 'n' Ale

178 Horseley Heath, DY4 7DS
✪ 12-11 (midnight Fri & Sat)
☎ (0121) 520 6572 ⊕ portnale.co.uk
Greene King Abbot; guest beers Ⓗ
This friendly pub serves up to 10 ever-changing real ales including at least one dark beer, and also usually stocks two traditional ciders. It has a large central bar area with an open-plan interior and additional beer garden and conservatory. Good food is served all day and children are welcome until 9pm. A regular quiz night takes place on Tuesday with beer festivals held in spring and autumn.
⚞⊛⌾&⇌⊟(74)♣⌾P⌐

Rising Sun

116 Horseley Road, DY4 7NH (off B4517)
✪ 12-2.30, 5-11; 12-11 Sat; 12-10.30 Sun
☎ (0121) 530 2308
Banks's Original; Oakham JHB; guest beers Ⓗ
Imposing Victorian hostelry comprising two distinct rooms: the bright bar to the right is adorned with pictures of local sporting heroes, and the comfortable lounge to the left is divided into two areas by a wooden screen, each warmed by an open fire in cold weather. In summer the back yard is open for drinking and occasional functions. Up to six guest beers complement the two regulars. ⚞⊛⌸⊟♣

Upper Gornal

Britannia (Sally's) ☆

109 Kent Street, DY3 1UX (on A459)
✪ 12-3, 7-11; 12-11 Fri-Sat; 12-10.30 Sun
☎ (01902) 883253 ⊕ bathams.co.uk
Batham Mild, Bitter, seasonal beer Ⓗ
Attractive former brewhouse on one of the main Dudley-Wolverhampton roads. It owes its National Inventory listing to the cosy tap room at the rear, named 'Sally's bar' after legendary former landlady Sally Perry. Its wall-mounted handpumps can be seen in action on Friday evening, at other times service is obtained from the main front bar, itself a very comfortable place to be. There is also a TV room and a pleasant enclosed garden.
⚞Q☼⊛⌸&⊟♣⌐

Jolly Crispin

25 Clarence Street, DY3 1UL (on A459)
✪ 4 (12 Fri & Sat)-11; 12-10.30 Sun
☎ (01902) 672220 ⊕ thejollycrispin.co.uk
Beer range varies Ⓗ
This vibrant pub, dating in parts from the 18th century, is entered down a couple of steps from street level (take care!), leading into a cosy front bar with two distinct areas. Eight

ever-changing guest beers are served – the house beer Crispy Nail is from Titanic. At the rear is a comfortable lounge with a panoramic view over the north of the Black Country. Local CAMRA branch Pub of the Year for 2007, it is deservedly popular with locals and visitors. Dogs are welcome. ⊛⌸⊟(558)P

Walsall

Arbor Lights

127-128 Lichfield Street, WS1 1SY (off A4148 ring road)
✪ 10-11 (midnight Fri & Sat); 12-11 Sun
☎ (01922) 613361 ⊕ arborlights.co.uk
Beer range varies Ⓗ
Opened in 2003, this modern, open-plan town-centre pub is popular with drinkers and diners alike. The award-winning restaurant offers good locally produced food (booking is recommended, especially at the weekend). The pub's name is derived from the nearby arboretum illuminations, which are known locally as 'The Lights', held annually in September. Three rotating guest beers are always available and Weston's Old Rosie cider is stocked in summer. ⌾&⇌⊟♣⌐

Fountain

49 Lower Forster Street, WS1 1XB (off A4148 ring road)
✪ 12-midnight
☎ (01922) 629741
Caledonian Deuchars IPA; Fuller's London Pride; guest beer Ⓗ
This friendly community pub on the edge of the town centre makes a welcome break from the circuit. Convenient for local history and leather museums, the small two-roomed Victorian local is situated in a conservation area that has been sympathetically modernised. Its decor is restrained and comfortable, featuring a display of photographs of old Walsall. Good pub food includes home-made pies and Sunday roasts. Entertainment is held on various nights.
Q⌾⌸⇌⊟♣

Lyndon House Hotel

9-10 Upper Rushall Street, WS1 2HA (at top of market)
✪ 11-11.30; 12-11 Sun
☎ (01922) 612511
Courage Directors; Greene King Abbot; Highgate Dark; Theakston Best Bitter; guest beers Ⓗ
Formerly the Royal Exchange, now a one-roomed pub with an island bar. While the woodwork and beams may not be original, this is a warm, cheerful and comfortable venue. The pub is part of a Tardis-like complex that contains a hotel, Italian restaurant and a balcony drinking area for the summer. At the top of Walsall Market, it is popular with the business community. A real slice of Walsall life, it provides a pleasant spot for a pre-dinner drink before visiting one of the many nearby restaurants. ⚞Q⊛⌸⇌⊟

Prince

239 Stafford Street, WS2 8JD
✪ 10-midnight
☎ (01922) 623607
Banks's Original, Bitter; guest beers Ⓗ

Situated near the town centre and art gallery, this pub is named after the Prussian General Blucher, who fought with Wellington at Waterloo. The facade still carries the logo of former owners North Worcester Breweries. You will find a potted history of the pub in the front bar, where traditional games are played. The spacious lounge has a pool table. There is a benched area at the rear. ⚙⊟≉⊟♣P'—

Rose & Crown

55 Old Birchills, WS2 8QH (off A34)
☼ 12-midnight (1am Fri & Sat); 11-11 Sun
☎ (01922) 720533
Black Country Pig on the Wall; guest beers Ⓗ
Grade II listed, this three-roomed corner pub dating from 1901 once belonged to Lord's Brewery, a company noted for the quality of its buildings. Guests enter into a central corridor that also serves as a drinking area. The long bar has a fine bar back and contains glazed tiling. There is live entertainment on Saturday evening and karaoke on Friday evening and Sunday afternoon. A pool table, function room and Sky sports TV are also available. ⚙⅁⊟♣

Walsall Arms

17 Bank Street, WS1 2EP (behind Royal Hotel, off A34)
☼ 12-2 (3 Fri & Sat), 6-11; 12-5, 7-10.30 Sun
☎ (01922) 626660
Banks's Mansfield Dark, Mansfield Cask Ale; Marston's Burton Bitter, Pedigree Ⓗ
A cheerful, traditional back-street locals' pub, the Walsall Arms comprises a basic saloon bar with quarry-tiled floor, a small, intimate snug and a corridor drinking area at the rear. It has a permanent skittle alley and a smart external smoking area. Images of old Walsall adorn the walls throughout. ⚙⅁⊟♣'—

Walsall Cricket Club

Gorway Road, WS1 3BE (off A34, by university campus)
☼ 8-11; 7-midnight Fri & Sat; 12-11 Sun
☎ (01922) 622094 ⊕ walsallcricketclub.com
Marston's Burton Bitter; guest beers Ⓗ
Established in 1830, the club has occupied this site since 1907. The comfortable lounge displays cricket memorabilia and the bar is staffed by members. On match days, the cricket can be viewed through panoramic windows. In good weather the lounge is opened out onto the patio. Beer festivals are staged here. Entry to the Club for non-members is by showing this Guide or a CAMRA membership card. Q⚙P⏁

White Lion

150 Sandwell Street, WS1 3EQ
☼ 12-11 (midnight Fri & Sat)
☎ (01922) 628542
Adnams Bitter; Greene King IPA; Highgate Dark; Wychwood Hobgoblin; guest beers Ⓗ
Imposing late-Victorian back-street local. The classic sloping bar, with its deep end and shallow end, is one of the best in town. A plush, comfortable lounge caters for the drinker who wants to languish. This pub is a great community melting pot, with popular acoustic nights on Tuesday and Sunday, and

bands also playing in the Band Box Room. There is an outdoor pagoda in the walled garden for smokers. ⚙✍⅁⊟♣♦'—

Wednesbury

Old Blue Ball

19 Hall End, WS10 9ED
☼ 12-3, 5-11; 12-11 Fri; 12-4.30, 7-11 Sat; 12-3.30, 7-11 Sun
☎ (0121) 556 0197
Everards Original; Taylor Landlord; guest beers Ⓗ
A traditional back-street local where cask sales are booming. The bar now boasts six hand pulls, dispensing four changing guest beers. The pub has three rooms: a small bar through a sliding door on the right, a family room where darts is keenly contested on the left and the quieter back room snug. Drinking is acceptable in the corridor which, like the snug, has a serving hatch. The large garden has plenty of seating and a children's play area. Q⅁⚙⅁⊖(Gt Western St)⊟♣'—

Wednesfield

Pyle Cock

Rookery Street, WV11 1UN (on old Wolverhampton Road)
☼ 10.30-11 (11.30 Fri & Sat); 11-11 Sun
☎ (01902) 732125
Banks's Original, Bitter; guest beers Ⓗ
A friendly welcome awaits you in this three-roomed traditional pub which dates back to the 1860s. The public bar offers wooden settles and the lounge and further rooms are reached via a corridor. With its wide mix of regulars, visitors are soon drawn into conversation. ⚙⅁⊟(559)P'—

Royal Tiger

41 High Street, WV11 1ST
☼ 9am-midnight (1am Fri & Sat)
☎ (01902) 307816
Banks's Original; Enville Ale; Greene King Abbot; Marston's Pedigree; guest beers Ⓗ
A modern, purpose-built pub which opened in 2000, this Wetherspoon's outlet offers a range of real ales, cider and a typical food menu. The patio at the rear, which is adjacent to the canal, is popular during the summer months. Theer is no car park, but the pub is easily reached by bus. ⚙⏅⅁⊟(559)♦

West Bromwich

Wheatsheaf

379 High Street, B70 9QW
☼ 11-11.30 daily (midnight Fri & Sat)
☎ (0121) 553 4221
Holden's Mild, Bitter, Golden Glow, Special, seasonal beers Ⓗ
Every high street should have at least one pub like this classic town hostelry. It has a lively, basic front bar and a plush, more genteel lounge tucked away from the hustle and bustle at the rear. It is much beloved by office workers during the week, footie fans at weekends and horse racing enthusiasts all week long. Quiz nights take place on the first Wednesday of the month. Good value food is served weekday lunchtimes and on Saturday

when the 'Baggies' are at home.
❀◁▣⊖▨(74)❀⚊

Willenhall

Falcon

77 Gomer Street West, WV13 2NR (off B4464, behind flats)
✪ 12-11; 12-10.30 Sun
☎ (01902) 633378
Greene King Abbot; Oakham JHB; Olde Swan Mild; RCH Pitchfork; guest beers Ⓗ
A two-roomed pub built in 1936, the Falcon has built up a well-deserved reputation for the quality and range of its beers. Nine ales are usually available, the regulars plus five guests including a stout or porter. With so many characters on both sides of the bar, you can expect humorous if colourful exchanges here – use the quieter lounge if easily offended. This popular venue has been local CAMRA Pub of the Year for two years running, in 2005/2006. Darts, dominoes and crib are all played. The Willenhall Lock Museum is nearby. ▨❀▣▨♣▯

Wollaston

Forresters Arms

Bridgnorth Road, DY8 3PL (on A458 towards Bridgnorth)
✪ 12-2.30, 6-midnight; 12-3, 7-11 Sun
☎ (01384) 394476
Enville Ale; Marston's Pedigree; guest beers Ⓗ
Friendly local on the outskirts of Wollaston. The L-shaped room provides a convenient dining area where good value food is served. Quizzes are held on the first and third Sunday of the month. For the more energetic, the annual local charity fun run starts from here and finishes with a barbecue in the garden. The pub has a resident golf team. ▨❀◁♣P

Unicorn

145 Bridgnorth Road, DY8 3NX (on A458 towards Bridgnorth)
✪ 12-11; 12-4, 7-10.30
☎ (01384) 394823
Batham Mild, Bitter, seasonal beers Ⓗ
This former brewhouse was purchased by Batham in the early 1990s and has earned the reputation of being one of the brewery's busiest pubs, serving one of the best pints in its estate. The remains of the old brewhouse are visible at the side of the pub and there are plans to convert them to an outdoor smoking area. The pub itself is a basic two-roomed venue, mainly for drinkers: food is limited to lunchtime sandwiches. 'Unspoilt by progress' is apt for this pub. Q❀▣⚊P⚊

Wolverhampton

Chindit

113 Merridale Road, WV3 9SE
✪ 2 (12 Sat)-11; 12-11 Sun
☎ (01902) 425582 ⊕ thechindit.co.uk
Caledonian Deuchars IPA; Enville Ale; Wye Valley Hereford Pale Ale; guest beers Ⓗ
Street-corner pub named in honour of the local men who served with the South Staffordshire Regiment, taking part in the 1944 Chindit campaign in Burma. The pub

comprises two rooms: a comfortable lounge and a bar with a pool table, both with TV screens showing live sport. Up to three guest beers are available, usually from local micro-breweries. There is live music on Friday evening and an outdoor beer festival over the May Day weekend. ❀▣▨(513, 543)P⚊

Combermere Arms

90 Chapel Ash, WV3 0TY (on A41 Tettenhall Rd)
✪ 11-3, 5.30-11; 12-11 Fri & Sat; 12-10.30 Sun
☎ (01902) 421880
Banks's Original, Bitter; guest beers Ⓗ
Small, terraced pub with intimate drinking areas including a bar, family room, corridor and covered courtyard. The beer garden is also used for summer drinking. The inn is renowned locally for the tree growing inside the gents' toilets. Named after Viscount Combermere, Wellington's cavalry commander in the Peninsular war, the pub is particularly busy at weekends and when Wolves play at home. Food is served Monday to Friday lunchtime and evening. ❀◁▣▨P

Goose in the City

32-36 Lichfield Street, WV1 1DN
✪ 10-11 (midnight Thu-Sat); 12-11 Sun
☎ (01902) 717843
Banks's Bitter; Brains SA; Marston's Pedigree; Wells Bombardier; guest beer Ⓗ
Converted from a number of old shops, as its address suggests, this M&B pub is located opposite the city's Art Gallery, a large and lively city centre location. It prides itself on serving five cask ales, and while very busy at weekends, the Goose nevertheless attempts to retain a relationship with its regulars. Daily newspapers are available and food (including breakfast) is served from opening time, including Sunday. ◁▤♿⇌⊖(St George's)▨

Great Western

Sun Street, WV10 0DJ
✪ 11-11; 12-3, 7-10.30 Sun
☎ (01902) 351090
Batham Best Bitter; Holden's Mild, Bitter, Golden Glow, Special; guest beers Ⓗ
This historic 150-year-old pub is a joy to behold. The corner house where two streets meet, the original building was extended in the 1990s. Situated opposite the former Great Western low-level railway station, which is being redeveloped, it is reached via the railway subway from the city centre. This award-winning pub is famous for its good value food at lunchtime, served at a speed that cannot be beaten. It is adorned with both railway and Wolverhampton Wanderers memorabilia. ❀◁⇌⊖(St George's)⚊

Hog's Head

186 Stafford Street, WV1 1NA
✪ 12-11 (midnight Fri & Sat); 12-10.30 Sun
☎ (01902) 717955
Caledonian Deuchars IPA; Enville White; Greene King Old Speckled Hen; Wells Bombardier; Young's Bitter; guest beers Ⓗ
Built around 1889 as the Vine, it closed in 1984 before reopening as the Hog's Head in 1998. The pub is locally listed for its excellent terracotta exterior. TV screens showing various sports, two pool tables and a bar football table

attract a younger clientele in the evening. Lunchtimes are quieter. Food is served daily until 9pm (may be earlier at the weekend). ✿◗&≅⊖◨

Moon under Water

53-55 Lichfield Street, WV1 1EQ (opp Grand Theatre)
✪ 9am-midnight (1am Fri & Sat)
☎ (01902) 422447
Banks's Original; Greene King Abbot; Marston's Pedigree; guest beers Ⓗ
Former Co-op store, converted by Wetherspoon's in 1995. The decor includes pictures showing the industrial history of Wolverhampton. The Grand Theatre is directly opposite and the pub is popular with theatre patrons; it can also get busy on weekend evenings with pre-clubbers. Beers from Enville Brewery often appear as guests along with Weston's cider. Food is served daily until 11pm. It is handy for both bus and railway stations. ◗&≅⊖(St George's)◨◆

Newhampton

19 Riches Street, WV6 0DW
✪ 11-11 (midnight Fri & Sat); 12-11 Sun
☎ (01902) 745773
Caledonian Deuchars IPA; Courage Best; Theakston Old Peculier; Wye Valley Hereford Pale Ale; guest beers; Courage Directors Ⓗ
Multi-roomed local with an unexpectedly large garden where games facilities include a bowling green and a boules piste. Its upstairs function room is a thriving venue for folk and other music. It also has a pool room and bowls pavilion. The home-cooked food includes good vegetarian options. Outside is a soft-surface play area with a slide and climbing frame for the under-eights. ♨✿◗◪♣◆◆

Posada

48 Lichfield Street, WV1 1DG (opp Art Gallery)
✪ 12-11 (midnight Wed & Thu; 1am Fri & Sat); 5-11 Sun
☎ (01902) 429011
Adnams Broadside; Caledonian Deuchars IPA; Greene King Abbot; Shepherd Neame Spitfire; guest beers Ⓗ
Built in 1884 on the site of a pub called the Noah's Ark, its distinctive frontage was added in 1907. The interior layout of the pub was altered in 1983 when it was turned into one room. It retains its original tiles, together with a superb bar back and snob screens. A narrow building, it has an outside area for drinking behind the pub. ✿◗≅⊖(St George's)◨

Shoulder of Mutton

62 Wood Road, Tettenhall Wood, WV6 8NF (up the Holloway from Compton Island A454)
✪ 11.30-2.30, 5-11 (midnight Fri & Sat); 12-2.30, 7-11 Sun
☎ (01902) 756672
Banks's Original, Bitter; guest beer Ⓗ
One-roomed, low-ceilinged pub with genuine oak beams in the Tettenhall Wood area of the city. Good value, traditional home-cooked food is available at lunchtimes only. The games room is served from a hatch and can be used by families or booked for meetings. There is a patio area where occasional barbecues are hosted. Live entertainment

takes place on some weekday evenings. The car park is large. Q✿◗&◨(510)♣P

Stile

3 Harrow Street, Whitmore Reans, WV1 4PB (off Newhampton Rd East)
✪ 10-12.30am (1am Fri & Sat)
☎ (01902) 425336
Banks's Original, Bitter; guest beer Ⓗ
A late-Victorian community pub with a bar and club room. It was built in 1900 to replace the former pub on the site – the stable block opposite the L-shaped bowling green still survives. It attracts a varied mix of customers, from locals to an influx of football fans on match days, as the pub is close to the football ground. ✿◗◪◨♣⌐

Swan (at Compton)

Bridgnorth Road, Compton, WV6 8AE (at Compton Island A454)
✪ 11-11 (11.30 Thu; midnight Fri & Sat); 12-11 Sun
☎ (01902) 754736
Banks's Original, Bitter; guest beers Ⓗ
Grade II listed inn in the Compton area of the city. This is a basic, unspoilt gem with a convivial atmosphere – the traditional bar features wooden settles, exposed beams and a faded painting of a swan dating from 1777. The bar and L-shaped snug are both supplied from a central servery. The lounge has Sky TV for sports, and doubles as a games room with a dartboard. Q✿◪◨(510)♣P

Tap & Spile

35 Princess Street, WV1 1HD
✪ 9am-11
☎ (01902) 713319
Banks's Bitter; guest beers Ⓗ
City-centre pub, comprising a narrow bar and two snugs. A large-screen TV and three further screens show major sporting events and music. It can get busy with Wolves fans on match days and it is also a popular darts pub, with four teams playing here. Beers from local micro-breweries, obtained through the SIBA direct delivery scheme, are usually available, along with Weston's Old Rosie cider. The former car park is now a smoking area. ✿&≅⊖(St George's)◨♣◆⌐

Woodsetton

Park Inn

George Street, DY1 4LW (on A457, 200m from A4123)
✪ 12-11 (10.30 Sun)
☎ (01902) 661279
Holden's Mild, Bitter, Golden Glow, Special, seasonal beers Ⓗ
Lively suburban brewery tap near the crossroads formed by the main Dudley-Wolverhampton and the Sedgley-Tipton routes. Its bright and breezy main bar has a raised dining area and a large-screen TV. There is also a conservatory and games room. Fairly priced food is served at lunchtime and in the early evening. ✿◗◨(545, 126)♣P

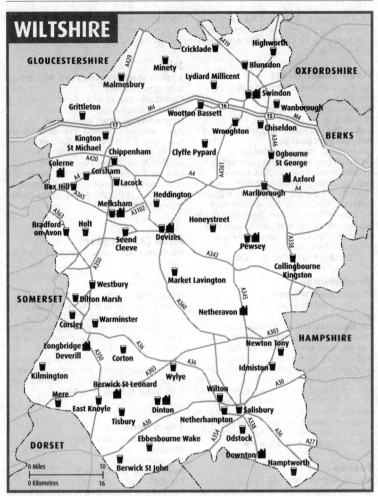

WILTSHIRE

GLOUCESTERSHIRE

OXFORDSHIRE

BERKS

SOMERSET

HAMPSHIRE

DORSET

Cricklade · Highworth · Minety · Blunsdon · Lydiard Millicent · Malmesbury · Swindon · Wanborough · Grittleton · Wootton Bassett · Chiseldon · Kington St Michael · Wroughton · Chippenham · Clyffe Pypard · Ogbourne St George · Colerne · Corsham · Axford · Box Hill · Lacock · Heddington · Marlborough · Melksham · Holt · Honeystreet · Bradford-on-Avon · Seend Cleeve · Devizes · Pewsey · Westbury · Market Lavington · Collingbourne Kingston · Dilton Marsh · Warminster · Corsley · Netheravon · Longbridge Deverill · Corton · Newton Tony · Kilmington · Wylye · Idmiston · Mere · Berwick St Leonard · Wilton · East Knoyle · Dinton · Salisbury · Tisbury · Netherhampton · Ebbesbourne Wake · Odstock · Berwick St John · Downton · Hamptworth

0 Miles 10
0 Kilometres 16

Berwick St John

Talbot

The Cross, SP7 0HA (S of A30, 5 miles E of Shaftesbury)
🕐 12-2.30, 6-11; 12-4 Sun
🕿 (01747) 828222
Draught Bass; Ringwood Best Bitter; Wadworth 6X; guest beers Ⓗ

The Talbot opened as a beer house circa 1832, despite vehement opposition from the then parson's wife. The building is predominantly stone built with a long low bar with beams and an inglenook fireplace. As well offering three regular ales the landlord is keen to promote local micros with a choice of guest ales. The more inquisitive visitor may find the cosy dining room behind the inglenook. The pub is very popular with walkers from the local downs. ♨Q🕯️🛏️◀◖🚫♣♦P

Blunsdon

Heart in Hand

43 High Street, SN2 4AG
🕐 11-3.30, 5.30-11; 5.30-midnight Fri & Sat;
12.00-3.30, 6.30-10.30 Sun

🕿 (01793) 721314
Beer range varies Ⓗ

Friendly one room pub offering a constantly changing range of beers. Very popular with locals, it is home to seven darts teams. All food is home cooked with a good choice on offer. This is a family run business with everyone helping out. 🕯️🛏️◀◖🚫♦🚲♣P

Box Hill

Quarrymans Arms

SN13 8HN (S of A4 between Corsham and Box)
OS834693
🕐 11-3, 6-11.30; 11-midnight Fri & Sat; 11.30 Sun
🕿 (01225) 743569 🌐 quarrymans-arms.co.uk
Butcombe Bitter; Moles Best Bitter; Wadworth 6X; guest beers Ⓗ

As first time visitors to the Quarrymans will be only too aware, this pub can be hard to find, but is well worth the effort (check the website or phone for directions if you need to). A 300-year-old miners' pub, it offers a friendly welcome and is renowned for high quality food and ales, served in the bar, restaurant or garden. Bed and breakfast accommodation is available. Q🕯️🛏️◀◖🚫🚲P🅿️⏎

Bradford-on-Avon

Beehive

263 Trowbridge Road, BA15 1UA
☼ 12-3, 7-11; 12-11 Fri-Sun
☎ (01225) 863620 ⊕ beehivepub.com
Butcombe Bitter; guest beers Ⓗ
Next to the Kennet & Avon Canal, this 19th-century pub continues to refresh the canal trade. Old playbills and cricket prints cover the walls. Up to five guest beers are available and good honest pub food (not Sun eve or Mon). The garden has a children's play area and boules piste. Occasional live music is hosted. Note that entrance to the car park is a test of skill and accuracy. ▲Q✿♦◐▲♠P

Bunch of Grapes

14 Silver Street, BA15
☼ 12-11 (midnight Fri & Sat); 12-10.30 Sun
☎ (01225) 863877
Wells Bombardier; Young's Bitter, Special; guest beers Ⓗ
Town centre pub easily recognised by the grapevine growing over the side. The narrow bar is divided into separate drinking areas and there is a restaurant upstairs serving good value food. The carvery on Sunday is always popular and theme nights are held once a month. The pub is quite small and gets crowded quickly. A rare outlet for Young's in this area. ✿◐≢

Rising Sun

231 Winsley Road, BA15 1QS
☼ 12-11 (10.30 Sun)
☎ (01225) 862354
⊕ therisingsunatbradfordonavon.co.uk
Beer range varies Ⓗ
On the outskirts of Bradford-on-Avon at the top of a hill, this is a popular local serving three ever-changing guest beers and Inch's cider. It has two bars: the lounge which is small and quiet with pictures of cricket pavilions on the wall and the more spacious saloon with a large TV screen. Visitors are greeted by the pub's ancient spaniel. ▲✿♣♠⊟

Chippenham

Old Road Tavern

Old Road, SN15 1JA (200m from railway station)
☼ 11-11.30 (12.30am Fri-Sat); 12-11.30 Sun
☎ (01249) 652094
Courage Best Bitter; Fuller's London Pride; Wychwood Hobgoblin; guest beers Ⓗ
Good old back street local with an eclectic mix of regulars ensuring lively and friendly conversation. Guest ales are often sourced from local and regional micro-breweries. Simple but good value food is available at lunchtime. Impromptu entertainment may come from local folk musicians and morris dancers who use the pub as their base. Live music sessions are hosted on Saturday evening and the garden is ever popular with many tables and chairs. Sport is sometimes shown on TV. ✿◐⊟≢

Chiseldon

Patriots Arms

6 New Road, SN4 0LU
☼ 12-2, 5.30-11; closed Mon; 12-11 Sat; 12-10.30 Sun
☎ (01793) 740331 ⊕ patriotsarms.co.uk
Courage Best Bitter; Wadworth 6X; West Berks Mr Chubb; guest beers Ⓗ
There is something for everyone at this multi-roomed pub which welcomes families and diners alongside casual drinkers. A large family room opens on to the secure garden where a big wooden playship is berthed. As well as the public bar and lounge there is a restaurant offering a mixture of traditional and modern dishes. Fresh meat is supplied by the local butcher. An external heated terrace has been added for family dining, functions, events and festivals. Q✿♣✿♦◐⊟▲⊟♠P⊾

Clyffe Pypard

Goddard Arms

Wood Street, SN4 7PY OS074769
☼ 12-2.30, 7-11; 12-11 Sat; 12-10.30 Sun
☎ (01793) 731386
Beer range varies Ⓗ
Cosy and friendly, historic community pub – the hub for many local activities. Beers are well-maintained and mainly from local breweries. Two small bar areas are adorned with a gallery of locally produced art and drinkers are offered a good selection of daily newspapers. The hostelry houses a YHA hostel, open all year round, with a large garden and covered area. The White Horse Trail passes nearby, making the pub a welcome pit-stop for weary cyclists, walkers and dogs. ▲Q✿♣✿◐⊟♠P

Collingbourne Kingston

Barleycorn

SN8 3SD
☼ 12-3, 7-11 (midnight Thu & Fri); 12-midnight Sat; 12-11 Sun
☎ (01264) 850368
Brakspear Bitter, Special; Wadworth IPA; Wychwood Hobgoblin; guest beers Ⓗ
Built in the early 19th century, this large roadside pub in an elevated position on the main road from Swindon to Salisbury and is popular with locals as well as travellers passing through. Good quality traditional bar food is available as well as an a la carte menu in the restaurant in the evening. Up to five real

ales are on handpump including guest brews.
🏰🌣🛏◑🖵♣P⅃

Corsham

Two Pigs
38 Pickwick, SN13 9BU
🕔 7-11; 12-2.30, 7-10.30 Sun
☎ (01249) 712515 🌐 the2pigs.info
Stonehenge Pigswill; guest beers Ⓗ
A true free house run by the owner in his own style without meals, gaming machines or pub games. Discreet jazz or blues is played as background music except on Monday when there is live music – usually blues. The interior is decorated with pig-related artefacts. Pigswill was originally a house beer but is now available elsewhere as well. Guest beers tend to be from the south-west and Wessex. There is a courtyard (known as the Sty) for outdoor drinking. 🏰🌣🖵(231)

Corsley

Cross Keys
Lye's Green, BA12 7PB (off A362 Corsley Heath roundabout) OS821462
🕔 12-3, 6.30-11; 12-4, 7-10.30 Sun
☎ (01373) 832406 🌐 crosskeyscorsley.co.uk
Wadworth IPA, 6X, JCB; guest beers Ⓗ
There is a warm, friendly ambience at this 18th century pub with a large open fire in the bar. Excellent bar food and restaurant meals are served. The landlord and staff are happy to help and a good portfolio of guest beers makes the pub always worth a visit. There is an attractive, award-winning garden for outdoor drinking, and a function room, the Oak Apple Room. Situated close to Longleat House and safari park. 🏰Q🌣◑P

Corton

Dove
BA12 0SZ (on Wylye Valley road S of Sutton Veny) OS934405
🕔 12-2.30 (3 fri & Sat), 6-11; 12-3, 7-10.30 Sun
☎ (01985) 850109
Butcombe Bitter; Hop Back GFB; Shepherd Neame Spitfire; guest beers Ⓗ
Village pub in the picturesque Wylye Valley with a candlelit conservatory and restaurant where children are welcome. Food is excellent with a varied lunchtime menu and a more sophisticated evening choice featuring local ingredients including game and fish. The guest beers vary, one in winter and two in summer, as does the real cider. Outside is a large garden and uncovered smoking area. Corton is situated on the Wiltshire cycleway.
🏰Q🌣🛏◑🖵Å♣🐾P⅃

Cricklade

Red Lion
74 High Street, SN6 6DD
🕔 12-11 (10.30 Sun)
☎ (01793) 750776
Moles Best Bitter; Ramsbury Gold; Sharp's Doombar; Wadworth 6X; guest beers Ⓗ
Friendly, 16th-century ale house serving a variety of up to nine real ales from small local breweries. Food is served in what used to be the back bar and is now the restaurant (no food Mon). A past winner of CAMRA South West Regional Pub of the Year.
🏰Q🌣🛏◑🖵♿🖵P

Devizes

British Lion
9 Estcourt Street, SN10 1LQ
🕔 11-11 (midnight Sat); 12-11 Sun
☎ (01380) 720665
Beer range varies Ⓗ
Classic working men's pub – this basic town centre free house has a friendly atmosphere, good bar staff and a dedicated landlord. The pub is a winner of many awards and a Guide regular. The choice of beers is displayed on a blackboard by the door and a further board in the bar provides tasting notes. Four handpumps dispense up to 12 beers a week, mostly from small, local breweries, often including stouts or milds. 🌣🖵♣🐾P

Hare & Hounds
Hare & Hounds Street, SN10 1LZ
🕔 11 (12 Mon)-2.30 (2 Tue; 3 Sat), 7-midnight; 12-4, 7-12 Sun
☎ (01380) 723231
Wadworth IPA, 6X, seasonal beer Ⓗ
This traditional back street local has been knocked about a few times over the years without losing any of its charm. Its community atmosphere, friendly landlady and band of loyal locals give it the feel of a village pub. A Guide regular, it provides a benchmark for what Wadworth beers should taste like.
🏰🌣◑🖵♣P

Lamb Inn
20 St John Street, SN10 1BT (behind town hall)
🕔 11-11 (1am Fri & Sat); 12-11 Sun
☎ (01380) 725426 🌐 devizeslamb.co.uk
Wadworth IPA, 6X, seasonal Ⓗ
Traditional, popular and friendly town pub with an eclectic clientele. The panelled main bar serves well-kept Wadworth's ales with a seasonal offering supplementing the regulars. Warmed in winter by a real fire, the bar is decorated with a collection of sheep-themed curios. There is also a pool room and a quiet room with a shooting tunnel. Live music events of various genres are hosted throughout the year. Children are permitted in the sheltered courtyard. Don't leave Devizes without visiting the Lamb. 🏰🌣🛏♿♣⅃

Southgate
Potterne Rd, SN10 5BY (on A360)
🕔 11-11 (1am Thu; 4am Fri & Sat); 12-11 Sun
☎ (01380) 722872
Beer range varies Ⓗ
Small, friendly and comfortable pub run by a popular Italian landlord. A range of guest ales often includes Hop Back and foreign beers complemented by a good selection of spirits. Outside is a small patio with tables and a function room that hosts occasional live music and an annual beer festival at Easter. The pub can be busy at weekends. 🏰🌣♿🖵♣🐾P

Dilton Marsh

Prince of Wales

94 High Street, BA13 4DZ

✪ 12-2.30 (not Mon & Tue), 7-11; 12-2.30,
5.30-midnight Fri; 12-3, 7-midnight Sat; 12-3, 7-11 Sun

☎ (01373) 865487

Wadworth 6X; Young's Bitter; guest beers [H]
Friendly village local with a single bar serving
two drinking areas plus a small pool table
annexe and a skittle alley. It offers a wide
variety of guests, mostly session beers. The
pub participates in local skittles, crib and pool
leagues. There is a weekly Sunday evening
quiz. Moles (not necessarily the beer) are
something of a feature at the pub. The pub
sign is factually incorrect – can you spot the
error! ❀◑ﻬ♿≠🚂♣◐P⅃

Dinton

Wyndham Arms

Hindon Rd, SP3 5EG

✪ 12-3, 5-11; 12-11 Sat & Sun

☎ (01722) 716999

Ringwood Best Bitter; guest beers [H]
Purpose built in 1934 and saved from
development a few years ago, this friendly
pub is now a focal point for the village. It has
one L-shaped room with a dining area and a
recently extended games area, home to pool
and darts teams. The two or three guest beers
change frequently. There is a large rear garden
and a patio at the front. Locals and visitors
alike are warmly welcomed. Live music is
hosted monthly. ❀❀◑♠🚂(25)♣P

East Knoyle

Seymour Arms

The Street, SP3 6AJ

✪ 12-3, 7-11 (10.30 Sun); closed Mon; 12-3, 7-10.30
Sun

☎ (01747) 830374

Wadworth IPA, 6X, JCB, seasonal beers [H]
Large ivy-covered former farmhouse in the
centre of the village where Sir Christopher
Wren was born, named after the family of
Jane Seymour, third wife of Henry VIII. Very
much at the heart of the local community, the
pub enjoys a good reputation for high quality
food (no meals Sun eve). The single bar has a
number of discrete areas. Outside there is a
pleasant garden with a children's play area.
❀Q❀🏠◑ﻬ♿P

Ebbesbourne Wake

Horseshoe Inn

The Cross, SP5 5JF (just off A30) OS993239

✪ 12-3, 6.30-11 (11.30 Fri & Sat); 12-4 Sun

☎ (01722) 780474

**Bowman Swift One; Otter Bitter; Palmer Dorset
Gold; Ringwood Best Bitter, Old Thumper** [G]
Unspoilt 18th century inn in a remote rural
setting at the foot of an old ox drove. This
friendly pub has two small bars, a restaurant
and a conservatory. The bars house an
impressive collection of old farm implements,
tools and lamps. The beers are served direct
from the casks that are stillaged behind the
bar. Service is via either the bar or the original

single serving hatch just inside the front door.
There is a pleasant garden and bed and
breakfast is offered. ❀Q❀🏠◑ﻬ⏚🚂♣P

Grittleton

Neeld Arms

The Street, SN14 6AP

✪ 12-3 (3.30 Sat), 5.30-11; 12-3.30, 7-11 Sun

☎ (01249) 782470 🌐 neeldarms.co.uk

Wadworth Henrys IPA, 6X; guest beers [H]
Cosy, comfortable 17th century inn in a
beautiful and unspoilt south Cotswold village.
The ever-changing range of guest beers
means that there is always something
interesting to try. A log fire is welcoming in
the winter. A good selection of home-made
food is offered. Popular with locals and
visitors, the pub is heavily involved with the
community. It is close to tourist attractions
including Castle Coombe, Malmesbury and
Bath. ❀Q❀❀◑P⅃

Hamptworth

Cuckoo Inn

Hamptworth Rd, SP5 2DU OS244197

✪ 11.30-2.30, 5.30-11; 11.30-11 Sat; 12-10.30 Sun

☎ (01794) 390302

**Hop Back GFB, Summer Lightning; Ringwood
Best Bitter; guest beers** [G]
Beautiful thatched pub within the New Forest
National Park. Inside are four small rooms,
three served from the same bar. Ales are
dispensed direct from the cask, racked in the
ground floor cellar. At least two guest ales and
up to six in the summer are available
alongside Frams Scrumpy cider. Pasties and
snacks are available. The large garden has a
quiet adults' only space as well as a children's
area with swings. An annual beer festival is
held in late summer. ❀Q❀❀♣◐P

Heddington

Ivy

Stockley Road, SN11 0PL (2 miles off A4 from
Calne)

✪ 12-3, 6.30-11; 12-4, 7-10.30 Sun

☎ (01380) 850276

Wadworth IPA, 6X, seasonal beers [G]
An outstanding thatched village local,
originally three 15th century cottages, the Ivy
is a focal point for the surrounding area. It has
a well deserved reputation for ample portions
of high quality food (eve meals served Thu to
Sat – restaurant booking advisable). The
village is situated at the foot of the
Marlborough Downs and there are a number
of footpaths and cycleways crossing this area
of outstanding natural beauty. ❀Q❀◑🚂P

Highworth

Cellar Bar

10 High Street, SN6 7AG OS201924

✪ 5-11 (1am Fri & Sat); 2-11 Sun

☎ (01793) 763828

Bath Gem; guest beers [G]
Unusual little cellar bar, once the kitchen for
the house above. The cellar extends under the
road and it is said that it used to be a tunnel to

the church, dating from the English Civil War. Decorated in the style of a café bar, it has light coloured wood and chrome plate throughout. A small patio area is at ground level in the side alley next to the Town Council office. Black Rat cider is usually available. ❀🕮🌢🕯

Rose & Crown

19 The Green, SN6 7DB (off A361) OS200922
🕐 12-3, 5-11 (1am Thu); 12-2am Fri; 12-1am Sat; 12-11.30 Sun
☎ (01793) 766287
Courage Best Bitter; Wadworth 6X; Wells Bombardier; guest beers 🖽
A pub since at least 1768, when it was sold for £25, the Rose & Crown has been brewery owned since 1821, passing through the hands of now-departed breweries Dixons, Bowlys, Simonds, Courage and Ushers. A wide choice of malt whiskies is stocked as well as the beer range. A friendly local, it has one of the largest gardens in Highworth. Boules is played regularly. Lunch is Sunday only, evening meals Wednesday to Saturday. 🕮❀🕦🕮🌢P🕯

Holt

Tollgate

Ham Green, BA14 6PX
🕐 12-2.30, 6-11; closed Mon; 11.30-2.30 Sun
☎ (01225) 782326 ⊕ tollgateholt.co.uk
Beer range varies 🖽
A gem of an old village pub. The range of four to five real ales, which changes weekly, is imaginative with a good selection of local beers and many from farther away. The food in both the upstairs restaurant and the bar is excellent while the rear garden overlooks a pretty valley. The pub has an upmarket atmosphere with sofas in the bar. 🕮❀🕮🕦P🕯

Honeystreet

Barge Inn

SN9 5PS (At Honeystreet drive through the timber yard)
🕐 11.30-11; 12-10.30 Sun
☎ (01672) 851705 ⊕ the-barge-inn.com
Brakspear Bitter; Butcombe Bitter; Hobgoblin Dark Ale; guest beers 🖽
Opened in 1810 when the Kennet & Avon Canal was completed, it was purchased in 1897 by T&J Usher of Bristol, and is now owned by Punch Taverns. It has a small front bar with dining area to the side; at the back is a pool room which doubles as a crop circle information centre with details, photos and dates. The large caravan and camping field is in clear sight of the White Horse of Alton Barnes. 🕮Q❀🕦🕮A🌢🕯

Idmiston

Earl of Normanton

Tidworth Rd, SP4 0AG (on A338)
🕐 11-3, 6-11; 12-3, 7-10.30 Sun
☎ (01980) 610251 ⊕ earlofnormanton.co.uk
Hop Back Summer Lightning; guest beers 🖽
This popular roadside pub boasts an enviable selection of real ales. The five handpumps feature local breweries, often including one

from Triple fff. Appetising and good value food is served and there is a small but pleasant garden, albeit a little steep. Accommodation is available separately from the pub. This was Salisbury CAMRA Pub of the Year in 2002. 🕮❀🕦🕮(63, 64)P

Kilmington

Red Lion Inn

BA12 6RP (on B3092 to Frome 3 miles N of A303 Mere)
🕐 11-2.30, 6.30-11; 12-3, 7-10.30 Sun
☎ (01985) 844263
Butcombe Bitter; Butts Jester; guest beers 🖽
Originally a farmworker's cottage, this National Trust-owned pub is more than 400 years old. It is close to Stourhead house and gardens, next to an old coach road and the South Wiltshire Downs. The single bar is mainly stone-flagged with a real fire at each end and a smaller room to one side. Excellent, value for money food is served at lunchtime only. Walkers and dogs are welcome. The large garden has direct access to the coach road. 🕮Q❀🕦🌢🕯

Kington St Michael

Jolly Huntsman

SN14 6JB
🕐 11-2.30, 6-11; 11-2.30, 6-midnight Fri & Sat; 12-3, 7-10.30 Sun
☎ (01249) 750305
Greene King IPA; Wadworth 6X; guest beers 🖽
In the heart of the village, on the high street, you will find a warm welcome and good quality ale here. Two regular beers and two changing guest ales provide plenty of choice. Excellent food is available lunchtimes and evenings. Various entertainment is held including live music and games. 🕮🕮🕦🌢P

Lacock

Bell Inn

The Wharf, Bowden Hill, SN15 2PJ
🕐 11.30-2.30, 6-11; 11.30-11 Sat; 12-10.30 Sun
☎ (01249) 730308
Bath Gem; Wadworth 6X; guest beers 🖽
Friendly and welcoming free house on the outskirts of the National Trust village of Lacock. Originally canal cottages, the building was alongside the Wilts & Berks Canal. The canal path has now been restored and forms part of the Chippenham to Melksham cycle path. The pub has a reputation for good food served daily. Beer festivals are held in January and June. Local CAMRA Pub of the Year for the last four years. ❀🕦&🌢P🕯

Rising Sun

32 Bowden Hill (1 mile E of Lacock) OS937680
🕐 12-3, 6-11(midnight Wed-Sat); 12-11 Sun
☎ (01249) 704363
Moles Tap, Best Bitter, Rucking Mole, Molecatcher, seasonal 🖽
Charming 17th-century pub full of original character with spectacular views over the Avon Valley from the spacious conservatory and large beer garden. The brewery tap for the local Melksham brewery Moles, its full

range of beers is on offer. A wide choice of pub food including daily specials is also available. Live music plays on Wednesday evening. ♨Q✿❀ⓓ&A♣♠P╚

Lydiard Millicent

Sun Inn
SN5 3LU
🕐 11.30-3, 5.30-11.30 (5-12.30am Fri; 6-11.30 Sat); 12-4, 6.30-11 Sun
☎ (01793) 770425
Wadworth 6X; guest beers Ⓗ
Traditional 18th-century village pub, the focal point of community life, offering a warm and friendly welcome to visitors and locals alike. Two separate, cosy dining areas, open fires and original wood beams throughout add to its charm. It has a well-deserved reputation for excellent food. Two ever-changing guest ales come from breweries locally and further afield. A large, sunny garden with heated patio area makes this a popular choice for the summer. ♨Q✿❀ⓓ&⊞♣♠P╚

Malmesbury

Smoking Dog
62 High Street, SN16 9AT
🕐 12-11 (midnight Fri & Sat); 12-10.30 Sun
☎ (01666) 825823
Archers Best Bitter; Brains Rev James; guest beers Ⓗ
A mixed clientele of all ages, locals and visitors, frequent this picturesque pub. It is the kind of place to relax with the newspapers or stop off after taking the dog for a walk. The bar is a listed building full of character with Cotswold stone walls, wooden floors and a fire. It has a restaurant and good-sized enclosed garden for warmer weather. The pub is famous for its annual Beer and Sausage Festival in May. A Cider Festival in August is a new event. ♨❀ⓓ⊞╚

Whole Hog
8 Market Cross, SN16 9AS
🕐 11-11; 12-10.30 Sun
☎ (01666) 825845
Archers Best Bitter; Wadworth 6X; Young's Bitter; guest beers Ⓗ
Located between the 15th century Market Cross and Abbey, the building has at various times served as a cottage hospital, gas showroom, and café/restaurant before becoming a licensed premises. With a warm friendly atmosphere, the pub is popular with locals and visitors alike. Meals can be eaten in the bar or the dining area (no food Sun eve). Cider is sold in the summer Qⓓ⊞♠

Market Lavington

Green Dragon
26 High Street, SN10 4AG
🕐 12-3.30, 5.30-midnight; 12-midnight Thu-Sun
☎ (01380) 813235
Wadworth IPA, 6X, seasonal beers Ⓗ
Traditional pub popular with locals and visitors close to the Westbury White Horse. It was the winner of Wadworth's 2006 perfect pint competition for all of its tenanted pubs. Good

food and overnight accommodation including a family room are available. The enclosed garden has a pets' corner and petanque terrain. Like most successful village pubs there is something here for everyone. ♨☕✿❀ⓓ&♣P╚

Marlborough

Sun
90 High Street, SN8 1HF
🕐 12-11.30 (midnight Fri & Sat)
☎ (01672) 515011 ⊕ thesunmarlborough.co.uk
Ramsbury Gold; Shepherd Neame Spitfire; Taylor Landlord; Wadworth 6X Ⓗ
Dating from the 15th century, this coaching inn has a homely feel, retaining many original features. The two front bars have heavily beamed ceilings and wood panelling. The back room is lined with book shelves and decorated with a collection of guitars. Real fires and uneven floors add to the period atmosphere. Five rooms are available for B&B accommodation. Lunch is available Tuesday to Sunday. ♨Q☕✿❀ⓓ⊞♣P╚

Mere

New Walnut Tree
Shaftesbury Road, BA12 6BH
🕐 10-11; 12-11 Sun
☎ (01747) 861220 ⊕ walnut-tree-inn.co.uk
Ringwood Best Bitter; guest beers Ⓗ
A true free house, recently opened and the third Walnut Tree to occupy a site here. Built in traditional style, it was designed using photographs of the original Walnut Tree as a guide. The inn features part tiled, part flagstone floors, wooden beams and rustic furniture. There is ample outdoor seating. A family oriented pub, it has a reputation for good food, including regular carveries and themed nights. Two guest beers usually include one from the local area. ❀ⓓ&P╚

Minety

Turnpike Inn
SN16 9QY (B4040 Cricklade-Malmesbury road)
🕐 12-3, 7-11; closed Mon; 7-11 Sat; 7-10.30 Sun
☎ (01666) 860746
Moles Best Bitter; Pewsey Vale Barbury Castle Ⓗ
A traditional Cotswold stone-built, single-room pub on the main road through the village. Popular with locals, it is characterised by low-beamed ceilings and a tiled floor, with a Rayburn fire to keep you warm in winter. Other than a gaming machine it is reminiscent of a bygone era, the walls decorated with horse brasses and country pictures. Structurally little has changed over the last 30 years. Moles Black Rat cider is available. ♨Q❀&♣♠P

Netherhampton

Victoria & Albert
SP2 8PU (opp. church) OS108298
🕐 11-3, 5.30-11; 12-3, 7-10.30 Sun
☎ (01722) 743174
Beer range varies Ⓗ

509

Lovely thatched country pub built in 1540 with a large covered and heated patio area and garden. Inside, a log fire welcomes you on a cold night. The four constantly changing real ales are from small independent brewers – more than 1,200 different beers have been drunk in the last three years. Food is prepared in the pub and the menu ranges from snacks to restaurant meals. Dogs are welcome. Salisbury CAMRA Pub of the Year in 2005 and 2007. ᴹᴬQ♿❀⟁◑▲🎫🐾P⅃

Newton Tony

Malet Arms

SP4 0HF (1 mile off A338) OS215403
🕐 11-3, 6-11; 12-3, 7-10.30 Sun
☎ (01980) 629279

Palmer Best Bitter; guest beers Ⓗ

Classic country pub named after a local family who are well represented in the village churchyard. There are two comfortable bars and a restaurant. The larger bar features a huge fireplace and a window reputed to have come from an old galleon. Four beers are on handpump, usually including ales from local brewers Stonehenge Ales and Ramsbury. The cider is Weston's Old Rosie. A blackboard menu based on fresh local ingredients changes daily. ᴹᴬQ❀◑🎫(63, 64)🐾P

Odstock

Yew Tree Inn

Whitsbury Rd, SP5 4JE
🕐 11-3, 6-11.30; 12-3.30, 7-10.30 Sun
☎ (01722) 329786

Ringwood Best Bitter; guest beers Ⓗ

Situated at the village crossroads, this picture postcard thatched 16th-century country inn has low beams and an inglenook fireplace. The landlord is enthusiastic about his real ale and offers two guests which change weekly. A friendly country pub and a focal point for the village, it is a popular venue for a meal out as well as an ideal place for a quiet drink. The garden provides a tranquil dining and drinking area in summer and has a covered smokers' area. ᴹᴬQ❀◑🎫P⅃

Ogbourne St George

Inn With The Well

SN8 1SQ
🕐 12-2.30 (not Mon-Thu winter), 6-11; 12-2.30 Sun
☎ (01672) 841445 ⊕ theinnwiththewell.com

Wadworth 6X; guest beers Ⓖ

The pub gets its name from the 90ft well in the dining room (the glass cover is supposed to be bullet proof). Originally a coaching inn dating from 1647, the pub is well placed for walking the Ridgeway or the Og Valley. The handpumps are just for show – the beer is served by gravity straight from the cellar. The pub now has full wireless Internet connection for anyone wishing to browse while drinking. It holds a St George's Day Beer Festival. Q❀🛏◑♿▲🎫🐾P⅃

Pewsey

Crown Inn

60 Wilcot Road, SN9 5EL
🕐 12-midnight (1am Sat & Sun)
☎ (01672) 562653

Cottage Atlantic; Ramsbury Gold; Sharp's Doombar; Three Castles Vale Ale; Wadworth 6X; guest beers Ⓗ

Away from the town centre, this inn with a bright blue exterior cannot be missed. It has a small public bar with a pool table and a large lounge with seating and darts area. The pub attracts mainly real ale drinkers who have a choice of five ales, including occasional guests from Pewsey's own brewery Three Castles. ᴹᴬ❀🚂🎫🐾P

Salisbury

Deacons

118 Fisherton Street, SP2 7QT
🕐 5-11.30; 4-1am Fri; 12-1am Sat; 12-midnight Sun
☎ (01722) 504723

Hop Back GFB, Summer Lightning; Sharp's Doom Bar; guest beers Ⓗ

This traditional, friendly drinkers' pub, popular with a mixture of locals and visitors, is convenient for the city centre and railway station. The front bar has an open gas fire in a traditional hearth and woodblock flooring. The back bar has table football. Last entry is normally around 10.40pm. ⍈🚂🎫🐾🍴

Rai d'Or

69 Brown Street, SP1 2AS
🕐 5-11; closed Sun
☎ (01722) 327137 ⊕ raidor.co.uk

Beer range varies Ⓗ

This historic free house dating from 1292 retains its original atmosphere with an open fireplace, wood floor and panelled benches. The name originated over 700 years ago when it was a brothel and tavern in the old red light district of Salisbury. The pub specialises in excellent Thai food served at all opening times. Today you will find two beers from local micro-breweries, frequently including Stonehenge or Downton, a welcoming landlord and 700 years of history. ◑🎫🐾

Royal George

17 Bedwin Street, SP1 3UT (close to Salisbury Arts Centre)
🕐 12-midnight (2am Thu-Sat)
☎ (01722) 327782

Hop Back GFB, Summer Lightning; Ringwood Best Bitter Ⓗ

Originally a 15th century inn, this Grade II listed pub is named after the sister ship of HMS Victory and features a beam said to be from that ship. The low beamed bar is decorated with pictures of ships and sea battles. The pub is well known locally for its involvement in crib, darts, pool and football leagues, and has a large garden. Food is served at lunchtime. Last entry is 11pm. ❀◑🎫P⅃

Village Freehouse

33 Wilton Road, SP2 7EF (on A36 near St Paul's roundabout)
🕐 12-midnight

☎ (01722) 329707
Downton Quadhop; Taylor Landlord; Ⓗ guest beers Ⓗ/Ⓖ
This friendly city local serves at least three changing guest beers, focusing on local micro-breweries and beers unusual for the area. Dark ale, mild, porter or stout are usually available, making this the only regular outlet for such ales in the city. Guest beer requests are welcome. Close to the station, it is popular with visitors by rail, and railway memorabilia adorns the walls. Cricket, rugby and football are shown on a small TV. Two times winner of CAMRA local Pub of the Year. ≠🖾♣

Wyndham Arms
27 Estcourt Rd, SP1 3AS
🕐 4.30-11.30; 3-1am Fri; 12-midnight Sat; 12-11.30 Sun
☎ (01722) 331026
Hop Back GFB, Crop Circle, Summer Lightning, seasonal beers; guest beers Ⓗ
The original home of the Hop Back brewery, although brewing has long since moved to nearby Downton. A carved head of Bacchus greets you as you enter the pub. A genuine local, it caters for all. Inside is a small bar and two further rooms, one that admits children. This pub is all about beer with six real ales available, usually five from Hop Back and one from Downton. There is also a selection of bottled ales including Entire Stout. ঙ🖾♣

Seend Cleeve

Brewery Inn
SN12 6PX (off A361 between Trowbridge and Devizes) OS930611
🕐 12-3, 6.30-11; 12-11 Fri & Sat; 12-3, 6-10.30 Sun
☎ (01380) 828463
Greene King IPA; Sharp's Doom Bar; guest beers Ⓗ
At the centre of the community, this friendly village pub focuses on beers and ciders. The intimate bar area is popular with locals and tourists alike; a flight of steps leads to the games room. Outside is a decked area for dining, lawned gardens and a secure fenced play area. A traditional menu of locally sourced produce is served. Sunday barbecues are held in the summer and a cider festival in June. The canal is a short walk away.
🏨Q☎❀🕮Ⓓ🕾🍴🅰🖾♣P🕯⌐

Swindon

Steam Railway
14 Newport Street, SN1 3DX
🕐 12-11; 12-10.30 Sun
☎ (01793) 538048
Fuller's London Pride; Wadworth 6X; Wells Bombardier; guest beers Ⓗ
The main part of this large pub is the covered courtyard of the former railway hotel, where discos are held and TV screens show sports events. The traditional real ale bar has a low ceiling and wood panelling; nine handpumps offer three regular and several guest beers, always including one from Adnams. The bar gets busy when major sporting events are shown on TV; at other times you can enjoy a quiet drink. 🏨☎Ⓓ🖾♣🕯⌐

Tisbury

Boot Inn
High Street, SP3 6PS
🕐 11-2.30, 7-11; 12-4 Sun
☎ (01747) 870363
Marston's Burton Bitter, Pedigree; guest beers Ⓖ
This fine village pub, built of Chilmark stone, has been licensed since 1768. The landlord has been here since 1976 and maintains a relaxed, friendly atmosphere appealing to locals and visitors alike. Three beers are served direct from the casks stillaged behind the bar. Now owned by Marston's, the guest will be from its range of regular or seasonal beers. Good food is available (pizza only on Tuesday) and there is a spacious garden.
🏨☎Ⓓ≠🖾(25, 26)♣P

Wanborough

Harrow
High Street, SN4 0AE
🕐 12-3, 6-11; 12-3, 5.30-midnight Fri & Sat; 12-3, 7-midnight Sun
☎ (01793) 790622 ⊕ theharrowinnwanborough.com
Black Sheep Best Bitter; Wadworth 6X; guest beers Ⓗ
This thatched pub dates back to 1637, making it the oldest in the village. It features two enormous fire grates and many concealed cupboards in the eaves, once used by smugglers to hide their illegal goods. Today's more law abiding visitors can enjoy good food, except on Sunday evening when there is live music. B&B is available in the newly converted accommodation block. 🏨Q☎❀🛏Ⓓ🕾🖾♣P🕯⌐

Plough
High Street, SN4 0AE
🕐 12-3, 5-11 Mon-Thu & Sat; 12-11 Fri; 12-3, 7-10.30 Sun
☎ (01793) 790523
Draught Bass; Fuller's London Pride; Wadworth 6X; guest beers Ⓗ
This thatched building is Grade II listed and has a cosy interior with low beams and large fireplaces. Note the skull behind the bar. The wide beer range is complemented by a good choice of food including many specials (no food Sun). Traditional games are popular and outside there is a small patio and a boules piste. 🏨Q☎❀Ⓓ🕾🖾♣P

Warminster

Fox & Hounds
6 Deverill Road, BA12 9QP
🕐 11-11 (midnight Sat & Sun)
☎ (01985) 216711
Ringwood Best Bitter; Wessex Warminster Warrior; guest beer Ⓗ
Friendly two-bar locals' pub just off the town centre. One of the bars is a cosy snug, the other includes a pool table and TV situated unobtrusively at the back. The two regular real ciders Rich's and Thatchers are a mainstay of the pub. The guest beer is usually sourced from a local micro. 🏨Q☎❀🕾≠🖾♣🕯⌐

Organ
49 High Street, BA12 9AQ
🕐 4 (12 Sat)-midnight; 12-11 Sun

☎ (01985) 211777 ⊕ theorganinn.co.uk
Beer range varies Ⓗ
The Organ was converted from a fish and fruit shop in July 2006. The building dates from around 1770 and was originally a public house up until 1913. The new landlords have created a welcoming pub with a traditional feel. There are three rooms including a snug and a games room with a skittles alley. The cider is usually Weston's or Bulmers and the beer range includes three guests. The brewer of Organ Bitter is a closely guarded secret.
🏚Q✿🏠♿❧🖫♣●⌐

Westbury

Horse & Groom
Alfred Street, BA13 3DY
🕔 12-2.45, 7-11 (midnight Fri); 12-midnight Sat; 12-11 Sun
☎ (01373) 822854
Beer range varies Ⓗ
This pub used to host its own brewery but its beers are now brewed by Hobden's Wessex Brewery under the Westbury name. This locals' pub has a public and lounge bar. Crib and quiz nights are held and skittles and shove ha'penny played. The food is good honest pub grub and the welcome is genuine. Just the place to stop off for refreshments after a hike up the Westbury White Horse.
🏚Q✿◑❧🖫♣P⌐

Wilton

Bear Inn
12 West Street, SP2 0DF
🕔 11-2.30, 4.30-11.30; 11-3, 4.30-12.30am Fri; 11-4, 6-1am Sat; 12-3, 6-11.30 Sun
☎ (01722) 742398
Badger First Gold, Tanglefoot Ⓗ
Dating back some 300 years, this is a homely and welcoming traditional town pub. A coal fire warms the bar in winter and outside there is a large peaceful walled garden with areas of sun and shade. Darts and rings are played and pool is popular with the pub dog joining in. Home-cooked food is available at lunchtimes and holidays are celebrated with some fun parties. Parking is available nearby in the market square. 🏚✿🖫♣P⌐

Wootton Bassett

Five Bells
Wood Street, SN4 7BD

🕔 12-3, 5-11.30; 12-midnight Fri-Sun
☎ (01793) 849422
Black Sheep Best Bitter; Fuller's London Pride; guest beers Ⓗ
Busy and cosy thatched local with a beamed ceiling. It opened before 1841 and absorbed the adjoining cottage in 1921. The bar sports five handpumps for two regular and three guest beers. Another pump serves Addlestones cider. The large blackboard displays an interesting selection of lunchtime meals. Themed food evenings are held on Wednesday. Robert Burns and St George are honoured with suppers. A fine display of summer flowers has won the Bassett in Bloom competition several times. A beer festival is hosted in August. 🏚✿🖫♣●P⌐

Wroughton

Carters Rest
High Street, SN4 9JU
🕔 12-2, 5-midnight; 12-3, 5-1am Fri; 12-1am Sat; 12-11 Sun
☎ (01793) 812288 ⊕ cartersrest.co.uk
Archers Best Bitter; Bath Gem; Cotswold Spring Old English Rose; Hop Back Crop Circle; guest beers Ⓗ
Decorated with photographs of bygone Wroughton, this large two-bar traditional pub on the High Street is very welcoming. Five frequently changing real ales are displayed on a beer board. Live music events are held twice a month and quiz night is Thursday. The pub welcomes children until early evening and allows dogs. 🏚Q✿🏠♿🖫♣P⌐

Wylye

Bell
High St, BA12 0QP
🕔 11.30-3, 6-11; 12-3, 6-10.30 Sun
☎ (01985) 248338 ⊕ thebellatwylye.com
Hidden Pint, Quest, Pleasure, seasonal Ⓗ
This former coaching Inn was built in 1373. The building has changed little over the years and offers an authentic interior with an open fire within an inglenook, flagstone floors and a wealth of old beams. The Bell was acquired by the Hidden Brewery in 2005 and is the brewery tap. A warm welcome is offered to all including children and dogs. It is a few minutes' walk from the bus stop at the Deptford interchange. 🏚✿🛏◑▣🖫P⌐

Cask breather

Where an entry states that some beers in a pub are served with the aid of cask breathers, this means that demand valves are connected to both casks and cylinders of gas; as beer is drawn off, it is replaced by applied gas (either carbon dioxide, nitrogen or both) to prevent oxidation. The method is not acceptable to CAMRA as it does not allow beer to condition and mature naturally. The Campaign believes brewers and publicans should use the size of casks best suited to the turnover of beer in order to avoid oxidation. If a pub in the Good Beer Guide uses cask breathers, we list only those beers that are free of the device.

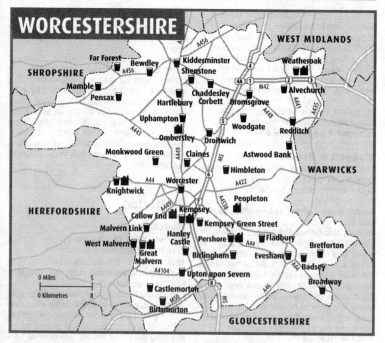

Alvechurch

Weighbridge

Scarfield Wharf, Scarfield Hill, B48 7SQ
🕐 12-3, 7-11; 12-3 (4.30 summer), 7-10.30 Sun
☎ (0121) 445 5111 ⊕ the-weighbridge.co.uk
Weatheroak Tillerman's Tipple; guest beer Ⓗ
It is hard to believe that only six years ago this popular pub (Redditch & Bromsgrove CAMRA Pub of the Year 2005) was a house and social club. Situated adjacent to the marina, it has established itself as a popular retreat for boaters and walkers. The pub has two lounges and a public bar and serves good value home-cooked food (not Tue and Wed). Two beer festivals are held, one in summer and one in the autumn. The guest beer is invariably from a micro-brewery. ⚶Q🛏️❄️⊗ⓄⒹ🚃⇌PꟐ

Astwood Bank

Oddfellows Arms

24 Foregate Street, B96 6BW
🕐 12-11.30; 12-midnight Sat; 12-11 Sun
☎ (01527) 892806
M&B Brew XI; Wye Valley Hereford Pale Ale Ⓗ
Small two-room back street pub with a friendly local atmosphere hosting various games and events throughout the week. The bar is to the front, lounge at the rear and the Outside Inn restaurant doubles as a function room. Beer festivals are held occasionally. The garden has a patio and children's play area.
⚶🛏️❄️⊗Ⓖ♿🚃(70)♣

Badsey

Round of Gras

47 Bretforton Road, WR11 7XQ (On B4035 at E end of village)
🕐 11-11; 11-11 Sun

☎ (01386) 830206 ⊕ roundofgras.co.uk
Flowers IPA; Uley Pigs Ear; guest beers Ⓗ
Open-plan roadside inn on the eastern edge of the village with an attractive beer garden. It is named in honour of the asparagus that is the speciality of this part of the Vale of Evesham: the 'gras' features prominently on the menu from April to June, and other locally sourced produce is available all the year round. Two guest beers, often from micros or independents, and Weston's Old Rosie cider complement the regular ales.
❄️ⓄⒹ♿🚃(247, 554)♣♠P

Bewdley

Black Boy

50 Wyre Hill, DY12 2UE (follow Sandy Bank from B4194 at Welch Gate)
🕐 12-3, 6-11; 12-11 Fri-Sun
☎ (01299) 403523
Banks's Original, Bitter; Marston's Pedigree; guest beer Ⓗ
Long standing Guide entry up a steep hill away from the town centre. The building dates back several hundred years and has two main rooms served from a single bar. The rewards for taking on the hill are in no doubt – take note of the many awards for cellarmanship on display. There is a small separate room that may be used by families at the landlord's discretion. Guest beers come from Banks's guest list. ⚶Q❄️⊗Ⓖ♿🅿️🚃♣♠

Mug House

5 Severnside North, DY12 2EE (150m from river bridge)
🕐 12-11 (midnight Fri); 12-11.30 Sat; 12-1am Sun
☎ (01299) 402543 ⊕ mughousebewdley.co.uk
Taylor Landlord; Wye Valley Hereford Pale Ale; guest beers Ⓗ

Situated beside the River Severn, the Mug House is not to be missed. The name originates from the time when deals were struck between trow haulers and carriers – over a mug of ale. A welcoming fire greets thirsty drinkers. Guest beers come from breweries such as RCH, Titanic, Beowulf and Wye Valley, and local English wine is stocked. The May Day weekend beer festival is a regular fixture. Fine food is served in the restaurant, including live lobster.
🏠⛺🅿️🍴◑🚲♿🅰️≢(SVR)🚃♣⬅️

Waggon & Horses

91 Kidderminster Road, DY12 1DG (on Bewdley-Kidderminster road)
🕐 12-3, 6-11; 12-midnight Fri & Sat; 12-11.30 Sun
☎ (01299) 403170
Banks's Original, Bitter; Batham Bitter; guest beer Ⓗ
Recently refurbished and extended, this locals' pub has a friendly atmosphere. The single bar serves two rooms and a third is used as a dining area complete with old kitchen range. The small snug has settles, tables and a dartboard; the larger room has a large roll-down screen for major sporting events. Food is available at lunchtime and evening with a carvery on Sunday (booking advised). Guest ales come from local independents.
⛺◑♿≢(SVR)🚃♣🅿️⬅️

Woodcolliers Arms

76 Welch Gate, DY12 2AU
🕐 12-3 (not Mon), 5-midnight; 12-midnight Sat & Sun
☎ (01299) 400589 🌐 woodcolliers.co.uk
Wye Valley Hereford Pale Ale; guest beers Ⓗ
Just a short walk from the centre of Bewdley, this friendly local pub offers a constantly changing range of guest beers usually including Sadlers, Hobsons or Wood. An old style pub with real open fires and beams, it is undergoing some changes under the Russian landlady and as well as regular fare now offers traditional Russian food and a bottled Russian beer, Baltika. Quiz night is Tuesday.
🏠Q🏠⛺◑♿🅰️≢(SVR)🚃♣⬅️

Birlingham

Swan

Church Street, WR10 3AQ
🕐 12-3, 6.30-11 (10.30 Sun)
☎ (01386) 750485 🌐 theswaninn.co.uk
Wye Valley Bitter; guest beers Ⓗ
Black and white thatched pub dating back over 500 years in a quiet village with a pleasant south-facing garden. The open bar/lounge boasts exposed beams and a wood-burning stove. Over 600 different guest beers have been served in the last two years and beer festivals are held in May and September. Traditional home-cooked food is served in the conservatory (not Sun eve). Crib, darts and dominoes are played in the bar. Laminated maps of local walks are provided and dogs are welcome. 🏠⛺◑♣⬅️🅿️

Birtsmorton

Farmers Arms

Birts Street, WR13 6AP (off B4208)

🕐 11-4, 6-11; 12-4, 7-11 Sun
☎ (01684) 833308
Hook Norton Hooky Bitter, Old Hooky; guest beer Ⓗ
Classic black and white village pub, tucked away down a quiet country lane. A large stone-flagged bar area with a splendid inglenook fireplace is complemented by a cosy lounge area with low beams. Good value, home made, traditional food is on offer every day. The guest beer usually comes from a small independent brewer, often local. The spacious, safe garden with swings provides fine views of the Malvern Hills in the distance.
🏠Q⛺◑◑🅿️P

Bretforton

Fleece Inn ☆

The Cross, WR11 7JE (near church)
🕐 11-11 (11-3, 6-11 Mon-Fri winter)
☎ (01386) 831173 🌐 thefleeceinn.co.uk
Hook Norton Hooky Bitter; Purity Pure Ubu; Uley Pigs Ear; guest beers Ⓗ
Famous old National Trust-owned village pub which re-opened in 2005 following a fire that all but gutted much of the interior. Fortunately the public area escaped almost unscathed, including the world-famous collection of 17th century pewter-ware. The restoration has been excellent and the pub remains one of the stars of CAMRA's National Inventory. Visitors may drink inside or in the orchard, which is the site of the famous asparagus auction in the (very short) season. Local CAMRA Pub of the Year 2006.
🏠Q⛺🏠◑♿♣⬤

Broadway

Crown & Trumpet

Church Street, WR12 7AE
🕐 11-11 (11-3, 5-11 Mon-Fri winter)
☎ (01386) 853202
Hook Norton Hooky Bitter; Taylor Landlord; Stanway seasonal beer; guest beer Ⓗ
Fine 17th-century Cotswold stone inn next to the village green on the road to Snowshill, complete with oak beams and log fires along with plenty of Flowers brewery memorabilia. The traditional menu offers specials made with locally grown fruit and vegetables, popular with locals, tourists and walkers alike. The pub offers an unusual range of pub games, with live music mainly on Saturday evening. The Stanway seasonal beers change with the seasons; some are brewed exclusively for the pub. 🏠⛺◑♿🅰️P

INDEPENDENT BREWERIES

Blue Bear Kempsey
Brandy Cask Pershore
Cannon Royall Ombersley
Malvern Hills Great Malvern
St George's Callow End
Teme Valley Knightwick
Weatheroak Weatheroak
Wyre Piddle Peopleton

Bromsgrove

Hop Pole

78 Birmingham Road, B61 0DF
✪ 4 (12 Thu)-11; 12-11.30 Fri & Sat; 12-11 Sun
☎ (01527) 870100 ⊕ hop-pole.com
Worfield OBJ; guest beers Ⓗ

This revitalised one room pub was Redditch & Bromsgrove CAMRA Pub of the Autumn Season in 2004. A varied lunchtime menu is served Thursday to Saturday including freshly prepared soup, salads, hot snacks and sandwiches. The inviting enclosed beer garden is sunny in the afternoon. The pub hosts local live bands of many musical styles in the evenings from Thursday to Sunday – see the website for details. On a quieter note, Monday is quiz night. ✿⊙&⊟

Ladybird

2 Finstall Road, B60 2DZ (on B4184, adjacent to railway station)
✪ 11-11; 12-10.30 Sun
☎ (01527) 878014 ⊕ ladybirdinns.co.uk
Batham Best Bitter; Hobsons Best Bitter; guest beers Ⓗ

This popular local has grown in recent years and now boasts a bar, lounge, Italian restaurant, beer garden and 45-room hotel. Next to the railway station, it is popular with visitors to the West Midlands. The lounge has polished wooden floors and a light airy feel in contrast with the busy drinkers' bar. A painting of the nearby Lickey Incline is on the wall in the bar. ✿⊙&⊟≠⊟P⌐

Red Lion

73 High Street, B61 8AQ
✪ 10.30-11 (11.30 Thu; midnight Fri & Sat); 11-3 Sun
☎ (01527) 835387
Banks's Original, Bitter; guest beers Ⓗ

Busy one-room pub in the main shopping street, famous for its slogan 'This pub will never sell smooth pour'. Seven real ales, including interesting guest beers, are complemented by fruit wines. The simple, fresh cooked bar food, available at lunchtime, is exceptional value. Monday night is curry night. Live music plays on most Thursdays, and Wednesday is quiz night. The pub has a covered patio area to the rear. Winner of many CAMRA awards, beer festivals are held regularly. ✿⊙⊟♣P⌐

Wishing Well

St John Street, B61 8QY
✪ 6 (4 Tue & Wed)-11, 12-midnight Thu-Sat; 12-11 Sun
☎ (01527) 574156 ⊕ thewishing-well.co.uk
Adnams Broadside; Greene King IPA; guest beer Ⓗ

Dating from the early 17th century, this half timber clad building stands on the site of a 14th-century ale house. Officially re-opened in 2005 by Robert Plant (of Led Zeppelin fame), rock & roll memorabilia adorns the walls. A couple of steps lead to the comfortable single room lounge bar with plenty of seating. Although a town pub, the place has the feel of a country inn. The garden features raised decking areas and caves carved into the sandstone rock face. A popular live music venue at weekends. ✿⊙&⌐

Castlemorton

Plume of Feathers

Gloucester Road, WR13 6JB (On B4208)
✪ 12-11 (10.30 Sun)
☎ (01684) 833554
Greene King Abbot; Hobsons Best Bitter; Three Tuns XXX; guest beers Ⓗ

Classic country pub on the edge of Castlemorton Common with splendid views of the Malvern Hills from the front garden – an ideal starting point for a walk across the common and onto the hills. The main bar has a wealth of beams and a real fire, a small side room has TV and darts and there is a dining room. A beer festival is held in mid summer and occasional live music hosted. A local bus passes by on Saturday only. ₳Q❀&⊙⊟P

Chaddesley Corbett

Fox Inn

Bromsgrove Road, DY10 4QN (on A448)
✪ 11.30-2.30, 5-11; 11.30-11 Sat; 12-10.30 Sun
☎ (01562) 777247 ⊕ foxinn-chaddesleycorbett.co.uk
Theakston Best Bitter; guest beers Ⓗ

Roadside pub to the south of this attractive village. The open plan L-shaped lounge has a games room to the side. Food is served throughout the pub and there is a separate restaurant. A popular, good value carvery is available at lunchtime (not Mon) and Wednesday and Friday evenings, and a comprehensive range of main meals and snacks is available daily. One of the guest beers is usually from an independent micro-brewer. An area for smokers is planned around the patio. ₳⑤❀⊙&⊟♣⦿P⌐

Swan

The Village, DY10 4DS
✪ 11-3, 6-11; 11-11 Sat; 12-3, 7-11 Sun
☎ (01562) 777302 ⊕ bathams.co.uk/pubs_swan.php
Batham Mild, Best Bitter, XXX Ⓗ

Dating from 1606, this popular pub has a traditional bar, large lounge with shuttered windows, small snug and restaurant (evening meals served Thu-Sat). Lunch is available daily, however there is no hot food available on Monday. A convenient watering hole for walkers, well-behaved dogs are welcome in the bar. Live jazz plays on Monday evening. Weston's Old Rosie cider is available. A covered and heated area is planned for smokers in the extensive garden. ₳Q❀⊙⊟♣⦿P⌐

Talbot

The Village, DY10 4SA
✪ 11-3, 5-11; 11-11 Sat summer; 12-3, 6-10.30 Sun
☎ (01562) 777388 ⊕ talbotinn.net
Banks's Original, Bitter; guest beers Ⓗ

There has been an inn standing on this site since 1600. A smart, half-timbered and historic pub with a cosy feel, it has a bar with pool table, two wood panelled lounges with hidden alcoves and a restaurant upstairs. A varied and interesting menu is served daily, offering something for everyone. The large patio is shaded by a grape vine. ₳Q⑤❀⊙⊟♣⌐

Claines

Mug House
Claines Lane, WR3 7RN
🕐 12-2.30, 5-11; 12-11 Sat & Sun
☎ (01905) 56649
Banks's Original, Bitter; guest beers Ⓗ
Picturesque village pub on the edge of
Worcester next door to Claines church. The
classic multi-room interior has a central bar
serving two rooms and a snug. The decor
reflects the historic building and the bar is
warmed by a real fire in winter. The Banks's
beers are served by electric dispense in lined
glasses with two constantly changing guest
beers on handpump. The garden attracts early
evening drinkers in summer. Occasional jazz
nights are held. ⚌Q❧❀◑⏚⏛▲🚃🍴

Droitwich

Hop Pole Inn
40 Friar Street, WR9 8ED
🕐 12-11 (10.30 Sun)
☎ (01905) 770155 ⊕ thehoppoleatdroitwich.co.uk
**Malvern Hills Black Pear; Wye Valley Hereford
Pale Ale, Butty Bach; guest beer** Ⓗ
Close to the train station, this traditional,
welcoming 300-year-old pub offers good
value food at lunchtime in an interior with oak
settles and exposed beams. There is a pool
room and darts and cards are played. In the
evening the pub is livelier with younger pub-
goers and on some nights music plays – see
website for details. An adjacent gazebo for
smokers has its own bar, and is also used for
beer festivals. ⚌❧❀◑⇋🚃(144)🍴⁵ᵇ

Evesham

Old Swanne Inne
66 High Street, WR11 4HG
🕐 9am-midnight (1am Fri & Sat)
☎ (01386) 442650
**Greene King Abbot; Marston's Pedigree; guest
beers** Ⓗ
Busy town centre Wetherspoon's pub on the
High Street, offering the widest range of beers
in Evesham. Opened in late 1998, the building
has undergone many changes since it was
built in 1586. Evesham Civic Society
commended the refurbishment which
'transformed a scruffy and derelict building
into one which is an asset to the town'.
Photographs of old Evesham adorn the walls.
It offers two guest beers, although the range
may be smaller mid-week, and hosts mini-
festivals throughout the year.
Q❧❀◑⏚⇋🚃🍴⁵ᵇ

Far Forest

Plough
Cleobury Road, DY14 9TE (half mile from A456/
B4117 jct)
🕐 12-11.30; 11-11 Sat
☎ (01299) 266237 ⊕ nostalgiainns.co.uk
**Wood Shropshire Lad, Shropshire Lass; Wye
Valley Hereford Pale Ale; guest beers** Ⓗ
Busy, popular country pub/restaurant with
open fires and rustic decor in a number of
drinking and dining areas served from the
main bar. The beer range varies with ales from
Wood, Purity, Theakston, Wye Valley and
Sadlers featuring regularly. For diners, there is
a renowned carvery and extensive menu
choice. Children are allowed in the dining
areas. Food is served all day on Sunday –
booking essential. ⚌❧❀◑⏚⏛▲🚃♣◑P⁵ᵇ

Fladbury

Anchor
Anchor Lane, WR10 2PY
🕐 11.30-3, 5-11; 11.30-11 Fri & Sat; 11.30-10 Sun
☎ (01386) 860391 ⊕ anchorfladbury.co.uk
**Batham Bitter; M&B Brew XI; Wood Shropshire
Lad; guest beers** Ⓗ
Traditional country pub with exposed beams
on the green at the heart of the picturesque
village of Fladbury. You can be sure of a warm
greeting to this welcoming local from the
friendly landlord and cat Charley. The 17th-
century pub, family owned and run, is at the
centre of the local community with a variety
of local groups meeting here. The cosy dining
room serves good home-made food and there
is a function and pool room.
⚌❀◑⏚🚃(551)♣⁵ᵇ

Great Malvern

Great Malvern Hotel
Graham Road, WR14 2HN
🕐 10-11; 11-10.30 Sun
☎ (01684) 563411 ⊕ great-malvern-hotel.co.uk
Wood Shropshire Lad; guest beers Ⓗ
Popular hotel public bar just a short walk from
the Malvern Theatres complex; an ideal venue
for pre- or post- performance refreshment.
Guest beer often comes from a local brewery
including the nearby Malvern Hills Brewery.
Meals are served (not Sun) in the bar and
brasserie area, or you can relax in the lounge
with comfortable sofas, fresh coffee and
newspapers. Free WiFi access is available. A
short walk down the hill to the rail station;
local buses stop close by. Q◑⇋🚃P

Hanley Castle

Three Kings ☆
Church End, WR8 0BL (signed off B4211) OS838420
🕐 12-3, 7-11; 12-3, 7-10.30 Sun
☎ (01684) 592686
**Butcombe Bitter; Hobsons Best Bitter; guest
beers** Ⓗ
Unspoilt 15th-century country pub on the
village green near the church, run by the same
family since 1911. A former CAMRA National
Pub of the Year, it also features in CAMRA's
National Inventory. The three room interior
comprises a small snug with large inglenook,
serving hatch and settle wall; family room (no
bar); and Nell's Lounge with inglenook and
beams. Three interesting guest ales are often
from local breweries. Regular live music
sessions are hosted and a popular beer festival
is held in November.
⚌Q❧❀◑⏚🚃(363/364)♣P

Hartlebury

Hartlebury British Legion

Millridge Way, DY11 7LD (Off A449, down a track on Waresley Court Road)

🕑 12-2 Tue only, 8 (7 Sat)-11; 12-4.30, 8-11 Sun

☎ (01299) 250252

Cannon Royall Fruiterer's Mild; guest beers Ⓗ
Friendly, welcoming club on the edge of Hartlebury with a large open-plan lounge bar with pool table and dartboard. Four guest beers are usually from micro-breweries and sold at reasonable prices, alongside two ciders. Tuesday and Saturday are bingo nights with crib played on Wednesday. Bring a copy of this guide or a CAMRA membership card to get signed in. 🏠🅱🕘🚫🍴🍺⇌🞨♣🞥P⁻🖰

Himbleton

Galton Arms

Harrow Lane, WR9 7LQ

🕑 12-2 (not Mon), 4.30-11; 11-11 Sun

☎ (01905) 391672

Banks's Bitter; Batham Bitter; Wye Valley Hereford Pale Ale; guest beer Ⓗ
Popular village local with a welcoming atmosphere. Formerly known as the Harrow Inn, the building has been a pub since the 1800s and was renamed after a local family. The main bar area has original beams and there is a separate dining room. Guest beers come from local micro-breweries. No food is served on Sunday or Monday evening. 🏠Q🏠🞨🕘🞤P

Kempsey

Walter de Cantelupe

34 Main Road, WR5 3NA

🕑 12-2.30, 7-10.30; closed Mon

☎ (01905) 820572 ⊕ walterdecantelupeinn.com

Cannon Royall Kings Shilling; Taylor Landlord; Wye Valley Dorothy Goodbody's Golden Ale; guest beer Ⓗ
Named after the 13th-century Bishop of Worcester, the pub has a bar area with large inglenook and original settle dating from the 1700s, dining area and an attractive walled garden. The menu is of a high quality, using local produce where possible – ploughmans and sandwiches made with local bread and cheeses are a speciality. Regular events throughout the year include an all day outdoor paella party in June. Three en-suite rooms are available for overnight stays. 🏠Q🞨🞤🕘🞥P🖰

Kempsey Green Street

Huntsman Inn

Green Street, WR5 3QB (take Post Office Lane off A38 at Kempsey) OS868490

🕑 12-3.30 (Sat only), 5-midnight

☎ (01905) 820336

Batham Best Bitter; Everards Beacon, Tiger Ⓗ
Originally a farmhouse, this 300-year-old exposed beamed inn welcomes visitors with a cosy and friendly atmosphere, real fires throughout adding to its character. It has a bar and lounge served by a central bar and a restaurant offering reasonably priced home-cooked food. An attractive garden is situated to the side and the impressive skittle alley has its own bar. Dogs are welcome in the bar. 🞤Q🞨🞥🕘🞥P

Kidderminster

Boar's Head

39 Worcester Street, DY10 1EW

🕑 12-11 (12.30am Thu-Sat); 7-11.30 Sun

☎ (01562) 68776 ⊕ thetaphouse.co.uk

Banks's Bitter; Marston's Bitter; guest beers Ⓗ
Popular town centre Victorian pub. The cosy lounge has wood panelling and a wood burning stove. The main bar leads to a large covered and heated courtyard where live music is staged on Thursday and Sunday evenings. There is also a tented garden area for the summer. Note the Pop Art style paintings and pumpclip collection dotted around the pub. An ever widening range of guest beers comes from Banks's list. There is a free mineral water dispenser for drivers. 🞤🞨🕙🞤⇌🞥🞥⁻

King & Castle

SVR Station, Comberton Hill, DY10 1QX

🕑 11-3, 5-11; 11-11 Sat; 12-10.30 Sun

☎ (01562) 747505

Batham Best Bitter; Wyre Piddle Royal Piddle; guest beers Ⓗ
Popular with locals and visitors to the Severn Valley Railway, and very much a Guide regular, the K&C is a recreation of a GWR refreshment room. As you would expect, there is plenty of seating and even a carpet with the GWR logo. A varied selection of guest beers is on offer, many from local independents – the Royal Piddle is brewed especially for the pub. Food is served daily with breakfast at the weekend. A wheelchair WC is available on the platform. 🞤🞨🕙🞤⇌🞥P⁻

Olde Seven Stars

13-14 Coventry Street, DY10 2BG

🕑 11-11; 11-3, 6-11 Sun

☎ (01562) 755777 ⊕ yeoldesevenstars.co.uk

Adnams Broadside; Caledonian Deuchars IPA; Enville Ale; Fuller's London Pride; guest beers Ⓗ
Kidderminster's oldest public house, close to the town centre within walking distance of the Severn Valley Railway. The large garden has an under-cover smoking area. Customers are welcome to bring in their own food to eat from local takeaways with cutlery and condiments supplied. The interior is wood panelled throughout with polished wood floorboards, an open fire place plus an inglenook. A pub not to be missed. 🞤🏠🞨🞤⇌🞥♣⁻🖰

Red Man

92 Blackwell Street, DY10 2DZ

🕑 11.30-11 (midnight Thu-Sat); 12-10.30 Sun

☎ (01562) 67555

Adnams Broadside; Black Sheep Best Bitter; Greene King Old Speckled Hen, Abbot; Taylor Landlord; guest beer Ⓗ
Popular hostelry on the outskirts of Kidderminster town centre just off the ring road. It has the feel of two pubs in one with a quiet front lounge favoured by diners and in

contrast a large back room with Sky Sports, pool tables and darts. Five regular beers are on offer plus a changing guest. A large room to the rear is ideal for children as it has no bar, and there is a garden and conservatory. ⌂❀◑❈⌂♣P⌐

Knightwick

Talbot
WR6 5PH (On B4197, 400 yards from A44 junction)
🕐 11-12; 12-10.30 Sun
☎ (01886) 821235
Hobsons Best Bitter; Teme Valley This, That, seasonal beer Ⓗ
A large pub which manages to retain an air of intimacy with several smaller drinking and dining areas, in a beautiful riverside location away from the hustle and bustle of everyday life. The restaurant serves high quality food using local ingredients, including the surplus from neighbours' gardens. The Teme Valley Brewery is located behind the hotel. A highlight in the calendar is the Green Hop Festival (early October). A farmer's market is held in front of the pub on the second Sunday of the month. ⌂Q❀◑⌂⌂(420)♣❀P

Malvern Link

Nags Head
21 Bank Street, WR14 2JG
🕐 11-11.15 (11.30 Fri & Sat); 12-11 Sun
☎ (01684) 574373
Banks's Bitter; Batham Best Bitter; Malvern Hills Black Pear; St Georges Maiden's Saviour; Sharp's Doom Bar; guest beers Ⓗ
Award-winning pub at the top of Malvern Link Common enjoying stunning views across the hills. Formerly a row of cottages, the pub has several rooms in which to enjoy a wide range of ever-changing beers. Newspapers are provided for those wanting a quiet read. At weekends and in the evening the pub has a lively atmosphere and can be busy. In winter heated marquees are erected in the gardens to allow more drinking space. The restaurant serves food until 9pm. ❀◑≠⌂♣⌐

Star
59 Cowleigh Road, WR14 1QE
🕐 4.30-11; 12-midnight Fri; 12-11 Sun
☎ (01684) 891918
Everards Tiger; Wye Valley Hereford Pale Ale; guest beers Ⓗ
Recently renovated pub specialising in high quality Chinese food. The bar is light and airy, decorated in modest Chinese style, but retaining its original splendid ornate bar back. The separate Chinese restaurant is well worth a visit and a takeaway service is available from the old snug bar. Q❀◑⌂≠⌂♣P⌐

Mamble

Sun & Slipper
DY14 9JL (signed from A456)
🕐 12-3, 6.30-midnight (1am Fri & Sat); closed Mon; 12-4, 7-midnight Sun
☎ (01299) 832018
Banks's Original; Hobsons Best Bitter; guest beers Ⓗ

In the centre of the village on the old village green, this attractive country pub has a small, cosy bar with open fire plus a dining room with log burning stove. There are old photos of village life in the hallway and in winter a blazing fire in the grate. The food is good with menus changing monthly. Two regular beers are complemented by two changing guests, often from local independents. Look out for the large, friendly dog. ⌂Q❀◑⌂♣P⌐

Monkwood Green

Fox
WR2 6NX (follow signs to Wichenford off A443)
🕐 12-2.30 (Fri only), 5-11; 12-5, 7-10.30 Sun
☎ (01886) 889123
Cannon Royall Arrowhead, Muzzle Loader; guest beer Ⓗ
Friendly rural single bar village local dating to Georgian times with good views of the Malvern Hills to the south. A rare outlet for Barkers farmhouse cider and award-winning perry, the guest beer is usually from a local micro. The centre for many local events, various pub games are played here and there is a skittle alley and indoor air rifle shooting. Music night is the last Friday of the month. Opening hours and food availability are flexible – ring ahead. ⌂Q⌂❀◑Å⌂♣❀P

Pensax

Bell
WR6 6AE (on B4202, Clows Top-Great Witley)
🕐 12-2.30 (not Mon), 5-11; 12-10.30 Sun
☎ (01299) 896677
Hobsons Best Bitter; guest beers Ⓗ
A regular winner of CAMRA local Pub of the Year, this friendly and welcoming pub offers a constantly changing range of four guest beers, often from local independents, and Weston's cider and perry. The beers, their ABV and prices are chalked on a board in the bar and in the entrance next to the serving hatch. Good food is prepared using local produce and there is a dining room and snug where children are welcome. ⌂Q⌂❀◑ⒹÅ♣P

Pershore

Brandy Cask
25 Bridge Street, WR10 1AJ
🕐 11.30-2.30 (3 Fri & Sat), 7-10.30 (11.30 Thu-Sat); 12-3, 7-11 Sun
☎ (01386) 552602
Brandy Cask Brandy Snapper, John Baker's Original, Whistling Joe; guest beers Ⓗ
Popular and lively town pub with its own brewery. Three of the home brewed ales are constantly on handpump, with seasonal brews including Ale Mary appearing regularly. Three guest beers and a real cider are also usually available. Good value food is served (not Tue in winter) in the bar and restaurant. The garden which fronts the River Avon is a joy in summer months. ⌂Q❀◑♣

Redditch

Golden Cross

Unicorn Hill, B97 4RA
☉ 11-11 (midnight Fri & Sat); 12-10.30 Sun
☎ (01527) 63711
Banks's Bitter; guest beers Ⓗ
Centrally located town pub with two rooms: a basic, old fashioned bar with a pool table, darts, TV and juke box, and a lounge with a carvery. A disco on Friday and Saturday evenings features music from the 60s, 70s and 80s. The pub has no parking but if you use the pay and display car park next door you can get a refund. ◑🕭🅑🛆⇌🅟♣🅟

Shenstone

Plough

Shenstone Village, DY10 4DL (off A450/A448)
☉ 12-3, 6-11; 12-3, 7-10.30 Sun
☎ (01562) 777340
Batham Mild Ale, Best Bitter, seasonal beer Ⓗ
Traditional country pub serving Batham's beers at reasonable prices. There is a single servery for the public and lounge bars, each with a real fire. Many pictures of the Falklands War and other memorabilia adorn the walls. No cooked food is available but there are bar snacks and delicious home-made pork pies. Children are allowed in the courtyard. Local CAMRA Pub of the Season Autumn 2006.
🏚Q🎗❀🅐🅟

Uphampton

Fruiterer's Arms

Uphampton Lane, WR9 0JW (off A449 at Reindeer pub) OS839649
☉ 12.30-3, 7-midnight; 12-5, 7-midnight Sat & Sun
☎ (01905) 620305
Cannon Royall Fruiterer's Mild, Arrowhead, Muzzle Loader, seasonal beers; John Smiths Bitter Ⓗ
Half a mile up a narrow lane, this small red brick cottage is home to the Cannon Royall Brewery. Run by the same family for generations, this gem offers its own well priced beer with seasonal specials. The quiet, cosy, wood-panelled lounge is decorated with pub history, local prints, CAMRA awards and a grandfather clock. Darts and dominoes are played in the more lively, basic bar. Walkers and cyclists enjoy the views across local farmland. Children are not permitted.
🏚Q❀🅑♣🅟⌐

Upton upon Severn

White Lion Hotel

WR8 0HJ
☉ 10am-12.30am
☎ (01684) 592551 ⊕ whitelionhotel.biz
Greene King Abbot; guest beers Ⓗ
This traditional inn dating from the 16th century is mentioned in Henry Fielding's novel Tom Jones. The owners ensure that while the facilities and service are three star, the welcome is unstuffy, warm and relaxed. Bar meals are available or you can spoil yourself in the high quality restaurant. Three guest ales often include one from a local brewery. Beer

festivals are held during the last bank holiday in May and at the same time as Upton's many riverside music festivals.
Q❀◑🍴🖪(363/364)🅟

Weatheroak

Coach & Horses

Weatheroak Hill, B48 7EA (Alvechurch to Wythall road)
☉ 11.30-11; 12-10.30 Sun
☎ (01564) 823386
Hobsons Mild; Weatheroak Light Oak, Ale, Keystone Hops; Wood Shropshire Lad; guest beers Ⓗ
A recipient of numerous local CAMRA awards, this attractive rural pub is home to the Weatheroak Brewery. It has a quarry-tiled public bar with real fire and functional seating, a comfortable split level lounge/bar and a modern restaurant with disabled access and toilets. Meals are available in the restaurant and bar daily except Sunday evening. The large, family-friendly garden and patio are popular in summer. Beer festivals, barbecues and morris dancing are frequent attractions. Children under 14 are not permitted.
🏚Q🎗❀◑🅑♣🅟

West Malvern

Brewers Arms

Lower Dingle, WR14 4BQ (off West Malvern Road)
☉ 12-3, 6-midnight; 12-midnight Sat & Sun
☎ (01684) 568147 ⊕ brewersarmswithaview.co.uk
Marston's Burton Bitter, Pedigree; guest beers Ⓗ
Now reinstated as a hub for the village community under its new licensee after several years in the doldrums, the pub is home to local groups including hillwalkers, musicians, actors, sports players and more. The view over the Black Mountains from the garden was voted Best Pub View in Britain in 2005. The bar area is quite small and can get busy at times but there is a separate building (The Armpit) for dining. Children and dogs are welcome. 🏚Q❀◑🖪(675)

Woodgate

Gate Hangs Well

Woodgate Road, B60 4HG (off Hanbury Road) SO966664
☉ 12-11.30 (midnight Fri & Sat)
☎ (01527) 821957 ⊕ thegatehangswell.co.uk
Weatheroak Scoop, Duck & Cover; guest beers Ⓗ
This inviting pub and restaurant was fully refurbished in 2004 and winner of Redditch & Bromsgrove CAMRA Pub of the Year in 2006. Log fires, snug areas, a pool table and beer garden all add to the traditional look and feel of this smart inn. The owners have created a balance between the best of fresh food, cooked to order, and quality ales. Two house beers, brewed by Weatheroak for the pub, are augmented by four changing guests, often from local breweries. 🏚🎗❀◑🛆🅐🖪♣🅟⌐

Worcester

Berkeley Arms

School Road, WR2 4HF

519

🌼 12-3.30, 5-midnight; 12-12.30am Fri & Sat; 12-3.30, 7-11 Sun

☎ (01905) 421427

Banks's Original, Bitter; guest beer Ⓗ

This compact local pub has two front rooms: one a basic public bar with a small TV used for sporting events, the other a more comfortably furnished lounge. A third room at the rear with a dartboard, pool table and TV can be used for meetings or as a family room, and outside is a patio area for warmer weather. The guest beer supplied by Marston's is usually either one of its own specials or from one of the larger independents. 🏵️◁🖳♣P⏚

Cricketers

6 Angel Street, WR1 3QT

🌼 11-11; 12-3, 7-10.30 Sun

☎ (01905) 23583

Beer range varies Ⓗ

Welcoming single-room house described by the landlady as 'a village pub in the city centre'. The four real ales are rotated regularly, with one always from Punch's Finest Cask scheme. As you would expect from the name, there is a wealth of cricketing memorabilia on the walls. Gathered over 25 years, the collection includes signed bats, photographs, paintings and cigarette cards from county and national sides. There is a function room available.

🖼️◁≷(Foregate St)🖳♦

Dragon Inn

51 The Tything, WR1 1JT (on A449, 200m N of Foregate St Station)

🌼 12-3, 4.30-11 (11.30 Fri); 12-11 Sat; 12-3, 7-10.30 Sun

☎ (01905) 25845 ⏀ thedragoninn.com

Beer range varies Ⓗ

A winner of many awards, this real ale paradise offers the widest range of beers from small independent brewers in Worcester. The walls are adorned with mementos of life in the pub – note the list of banned conversation topics. There is nearly always a stout or porter available plus an offering from a local brewery. A partially covered and heated rear seating area allows for outdoor drinking all year round. Good value lunchtime meals are available (not Sun).

Q🏵️◁≷(Foregate St)🖳♦⏚

New Inn

Ombersley Road, WR3 7DH

🌼 12-11 (midnight Fri & Sat)

☎ (01905) 452025

Banks's Original, Bitter; guest beers Ⓗ

Large, popular and friendly pub on the northern outskirts of the city, one of the more attractive examples of Marston's architecture in the area. It has a smartly decorated lounge plus no-frills bar area with dartboard and dominoes, and outside a large garden and patio with heaters. Three ever changing guest beers are from the Marston's portfolio. Good quality home produced food is served all day plus a roast on Sunday. 🏵️◁♿🖳♣P⏚

Plough

23 Fish Street (next to fire station)

🌼 12-11 (midnight Fri; 1am Sat)

☎ (01905) 21381 ⏀ theploughworcester.co.uk

Hobsons Best Bitter; Malvern Hills Black Pear; guest beers Ⓗ

A friendly pub with a good mix of drinkers of all ages, this Grade II listed pub re-opened under new management to become CAMRA Worcester Branch Pub of the Year. The selection of real ales has increased from two to six and local real cider and perry are also available. Two rooms with original features are either side of the bar. A function room upstairs has a large screen showing major sports events. Good food made with local produce is served daily.

▷🏵️◁≷(Foregate St)♣♦⏚

Postal Order

18 Foregate Street, WR1 1DN

🌼 9am-midnight (1am Fri & Sat)

☎ (01905) 22373

Greene King Abbot; Marston's Pedigree; Wyre Piddle Piddle in the Post; guest beers Ⓗ

Classic Wetherspoon's mega-pub, conveniently situated next to Foregate Street station, in what was originally Worcester's telephone exchange, decorated in Victorian style. Beers from local micros feature prominently, together with up to seven guests. Tubs of Weston's Old Rosie and Vintage Organic cider are also available. Good value food is served all day every day.

◁♿≷(Foregate St)🖳♦🅞🗍

Saracens Head

4 The Tything, WR1 1HD

🌼 12-11.30; 12-10.30 (closed 3-6pm in winter) Sun

☎ (01905) 24165

Caledonian Deuchars IPA; Greene King Old Speckled Hen; Marston's Pedigree; guest beer Ⓗ

On the edge of the city centre, this small, friendly community pub has two rooms, each divided into two areas, and seven handpumps. Access is via a cobbled yard which serves as a covered outdoor drinking area. Special celebrations are held for St George's Day. The pub has a skittle alley that doubles as a function room and is noted for its numerous sports teams.

🏵️◁◁≷(Foregate St)🖳♣⏚

Winning Post

Pope Iron Road, WR1 3HB

🌼 11 (4 Mon-Thu Jan & Feb)-midnight

☎ (01905) 21178

Cannon Royall Arrowhead; guest beers Ⓗ

Cosy back-street single-room pub to the north of city centre close to the racecourse, but at the opposite end to the winning post! Sports TV features large, but there is a well-stocked bookshelf for those who prefer a good read. Lunchtime snacks are available and guest beers rotate every six weeks. The garden has heaters for cooler evenings. 🏵️◁♣⏚

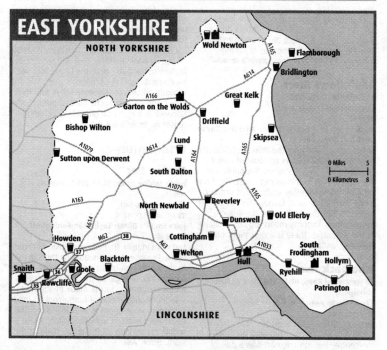

YORKSHIRE (EAST)

Beverley

Dog & Duck Inn
33 Ladygate, HU17 8BH
🕐 11-4, 7-midnight; 11-midnight Fri & Sat; 11.30-3, 7-11 Sun
☎ (01482) 862419
Caledonian Deuchars IPA; Greene King Abbot; John Smith's Bitter; guest beers Ⓗ
Just off the main Saturday market, next to the historic picture playhouse building, the Dog & Duck, built in the 1930s, has been run by the same family for over 30 years. It comprises a former tap room, with a period brick fireplace and bentwood seating, a lounge and a rear snug area; only the dividing walls have been removed. The good value, home-made lunches are popular and include pensioners' specials. Guest accommodation is in six purpose-built, self-contained rooms.
🛏🍴🚪🔌♣

Durham Ox
48 Norwood, HU17 9HJ
🕐 10.30 (12 Sun)-11
☎ (01482) 679444
John Smith's Bitter; Tetley Bitter; guest beers Ⓗ
Victorian local near the new Tesco store, on the site of the former cattle market. The two-roomed pub has been refurbished after consultation with CAMRA's local pub preservation officer. The lounge was extended to include a games area, but retains its original etched windows; the public bar has the old wooden floor, with an off-sales hatch in the entrance lobby. The pub fields five darts and two dominoes teams. Off-street parking is possible directly opposite. Meals are served weekdays and 12-5pm Fri and Sat.
🛏🍴🚪🔌♣⌐

Molescroft Inn
75 Molescroft Road, HU17 7EG (1 mile NW of town centre)
🕐 11.30-11 (midnight Fri & Sat); 12-11 Sun
☎ (01482) 862968
Jennings Sneck Lifter; Mansfield Riding Bitter; guest beers Ⓗ
A much enlarged village local dating back to the 18th century, the Molescroft was comprehensively altered in the 1980s with the loss of some small rooms to create a large L-shaped lounge/dining room with separate bar area around a central servery. A restaurant extension is planned adjacent to the large car park. Meals are served 12-8.30pm on Sunday.
🛏🍴🚪♣P⌐

Monk's Walk
19 Highgate, HU17 0DN
🕐 12-11 (10.30 Sun)
☎ (01482) 862710
Black Sheep Best Bitter; Greene King Abbot; Taylor Landlord; guest beers Ⓗ
Formerly the George & Dragon, the pub's 18th-century frontage hides two timber framed buildings separated by a former medieval street. Guest beers often come from Yorkshire micros including Copper Dragon, Wold Top and Rudgate. Folk nights are Tuesday and the first Sunday of the month. A

INDEPENDENT BREWERIES

Garton Garton on the Wolds
Great Newsome South Frodingham
Old Mill Snaith
Whalebone Hull
Wold Top Wold Newton

brick archway at the end of the bar leads to a dining room with open roof timbers and a warming log fire. There are plans to extend into the garden and renovate adjoining cottages and out-buildings. ♨✪ⓘ🍴�🚬

Oddfellows Arms
15 Eastgate, HU17 0DR
🕐 11-midnight (1am Fri & Sat)
☎ (01482) 860795
Black Sheep Best Bitter; Greene King IPA; Taylor Landlord; guest beer Ⓗ
Street corner local near the railway station and minster, the Oddfellows underwent major refurbishment in 2005 when the public bar was opened on to the games room. The front snug remains, together with a tiled entrance lobby with an unusual layout. The TVs are on non-stop, but thankfully with the volume turned down. Evening meals are not available at the weekend. There is a quiz night on Thursday. ♨✪ⓘ�♣

Woolpack Inn
37 Westwood Road, HU17 8EN (near Westwood, S of hospital)
🕐 6-11 (midnight Fri & Sat); 12-11 Sun
☎ (01482) 867095
Jennings Bitter; guest beers Ⓗ
Located in a Victorian residential street west of the centre, this inn originated as a pair of cottages in about 1830. CAMRA's East Yorkshire Town Pub of the Year 2004 and runner-up in 2006, the Woolpack was sensitively restored in 2000, retaining its cosy snug, log fire and outside toilets. It serves tasty home-made meals based on fresh produce on Friday and Saturday; Thursday is curry night. The pub hosts occasional folk music and quiz nights on Sunday evening. Children and dogs are welcome. ♨Q✪♣🚬

Bishop Wilton

Fleece Inn
Pocklington Road, YO42 1RU (1 mile from foot of Garrowby Hill, on A166)
🕐 12-3 (not Mon & Tue), 6.30-11; 12-3, 6-10.30 Sun
☎ (01759) 368251
Black Sheep Best Bitter; John Smith's Bitter; guest beers Ⓗ
This watering hole is popular with walkers exploring the dry valleys of the Yorkshire Wolds. The pub has an open-plan layout around a horseshoe-shaped bar, with a cosy games corner well away from the dining tables. A penny farthing bicycle once owned by the village's agricultural merchants hangs from the ceiling. Guest beers often come from local micro-breweries with gems from further afield; note the 'traffic light' system on the guest beer board, indicating which beers are available. No food Monday or Tuesday. ♨✪🛏ⓘ🅿&🚬♣P

Blacktoft

Hope & Anchor
Main Street, DN14 7YW (S of Gilberdyke Station)
🕐 12 (4 Mon & Tue)-11; 12-10.30 Sun
☎ (01430) 440441
Old Mill Mild; John Smith's Bitter; guest beers Ⓗ

Thriving village local, superbly located on the bank of the River Ouse, near the spot where it joins with the Trent to form the Humber. The RSPB's Blacktoft Sands bird sanctuary is visible on the far bank. Humour, past and present, is a feature of the pub – note the Laurel and Hardy memorabilia and the licensee's sharp wit. The recently added conservatory offers fine river views and popular home-cooked meals – the haddock is huge! Two guest beers change regularly. 🚬✪ⓘ&♣P

Bridlington

Marine Bar
North Marine Drive, YO15 2LS (1 mile NE of centre)
🕐 11-11 (11.30 Sat)
☎ (01262) 675347
John Smith's Bitter; Taylor Landlord; guest beers Ⓗ
Large, triangular-shaped, open-plan bar, part of the Expanse Hotel, situated on the sea front to the north east of the town. The bar attracts a good mix of regulars throughout the year and is welcoming to the influx of summer visitors. A good menu of home-cooked food (including vegetarian) is available daily. The guest beer is often from Theakston. There is ample car parking on the promenade at the front. ✪🛏ⓘ🅿🚬

Prior John
34-36 The Promenade, YO15 2QD
🕐 9am-midnight (1am Fri & Sat)
☎ (01262) 674256
Courage Directors Bitter; Greene King Abbot; Marston's Burton Bitter; guest beers Ⓗ
Large, busy Wetherspoon's pub in the town centre and close to the bus station. Modern in appearance, the interior is basically one large half-moon shape. To the left of the serving area is a first-floor gallery, reached by a sweeping metal staircase. The downstairs room is a clever mix of metal and wood with a segmented ceiling supported by steel pillars. The decor is plain and bright using mainly pastel colours. Two guest beers are always available. Q✪&🚬🅿

Cottingham

King William IV
152 Hallgate, HU16 4BD
🕐 11 (12 Sun)-11.30
☎ (01482) 847340
Marston's Pedigree; guest beers Ⓗ
The narrow, plain exterior belies a multi-roomed pub with a strongly traditional public bar and lounge. The function room at the rear started life as a brewery. The pub has a large plasma screen TV for sports fans and hosts many events including music nights featuring different types of music, a quiz night and even psychic nights. The rear garden has a pleasant terrace area. Q✪ⓘ🅿♣🚬

Driffield

Bell Hotel
46 Market Place, YO25 6AN
🕐 10-11; 12-3, 7-10.30 Sun

☎ (01377) 256661 ⊕ bw-bellhotel.co.uk/
Beer range varies ⊞
Local CAMRA Town Pub of the Year 2005, this inn has a feeling of elegance with a long wood-panelled bar with red leather seating, substantial fire places, antiques and prints. Two or three beers are kept, usually from Wold Top, Hambleton or Highwood breweries, but other micros are also represented. Over 300 malt whiskies are stocked. A covered courtyard functions as a bistro, and there is a splendid lunchtime carvery buffet (Mon-Sat); Sunday lunch must be booked. Children are welcome until 7.30pm. Q☎⌖⌖◑♿≠⌑P

Foundry

7 Market Walk, YO25 6BW (down passage off market place)
◷ 10-3 (not Wed; 4 Fri), 7-11; closed Mon; 10-11 Sat; 12-3 Sun
☎ (01377) 253874
Beer range varies ⊞
Local CAMRA Town Pub of the Year 2006, the café and bar are housed in the only building that remains of the old Victoria Foundry complex. The ground floor is divided in two: a front area with a tiled floor, comfortable bench seating, tables and chairs, and a raised rear area with sofas and low tables. The walls throughout are bare brick supported by heavy beams. Daily papers are provided, and up to five beers are available at weekends.
Q☎◑≠⌑♣⌑

Rose & Crown

North Street, YO25 6AS
◷ 12 (11 Sat)-midnight (11 Wed, 1am Thu-Sat); 12-11 Sun
☎ (01377) 253041
John Smith's Bitter; guest beers ⊞
Family-run pub opposite the town's Green Flag awarded park, comprising a main bar/lounge and pool room. Two guest beers, mostly from independents, change every few days. Table service is available Thursday-Saturday evenings, and benches are provided outside for summer drinking. Live sport is shown on TV, Thursday is quiz night and regular entertainment is staged on Saturday evening. Numerous sports teams represent the pub. The EYMS 121 Hull to Scarborough bus and other services run regularly.
⌖⌑(121)♣P

Dunswell

Ship Inn

Beverley Road, HU6 0AJ (on main Hull-Beverley road)
◷ 11-11 (11.30 Fri & Sat); 12-11 Sun
☎ (01482) 854458 ⊕ theshipsquarters.co.uk
Black Sheep Best Bitter; John Smiths's Bitter; Taylor Landlord; guest beer ⊞
This whitewashed inn fronting the old Hull-Beverley road once served traffic on the nearby River Hull, and this is reflected in its nautical memorabilia and decor. Two log fires warm the convivial interior that is partly divided to form a dining area with church pew seating. A recently converted, detached extension provides overnight accommodation, aptly named the Ship's Quarters. Meals are served daily and barbecues held occasionally in the adjoining paddock. ⌖☎⌖◑⌑⌑♣P

Flamborough

Seabirds

Tower Street, YO15 1PD
◷ 12-3, 6-midnight; closed winter Mon; 12-3, 6-11 (not winter eve) Sun
☎ (01262) 850242
John Smith's Bitter; guest beer ⊞
Originally two rooms, this pub changed hands in 2003 and has been refurbished to create a clean, contemporary look. The guest beer often comes from a local brewery. A range of home-cooked meals, with vegetarian options, is based on local produce whenever possible. There is camping nearby; the pub is popular with walkers and bird enthusiasts – the spectacular cliffs and Bempton RSPB sanctuary are close by. EYMS buses 510 and 502 from Bridlington provide an occasional service.
⌖☎◑♿⌑P

Ship Inn

Post Office Street, YO15 1JS
◷ 11-11; 12-10.30 Sun
☎ (01262) 850454
John Smith's Bitter; Wells Bombardier; guest beer ⊞
Grade II listed, former 17th-century coaching inn at the village centre, offering a warm welcome to locals and visitors alike. Dark wood abounds throughout and the original stained glass windows are intact, with external lettering identifying each room. Varied bar food includes vegetarian options and daily specials. The accommodation is reasonably priced and there is also a self-catering cottage available to let. Walkers are welcome, as are dogs.
⌖⌖◑⌑⌑⌑(510)♣P⌐

Goole

City & County

Market Square, DN14 5AT (next to clock tower)
◷ 9-midnight
☎ (01405) 722600
Exmoor Gold; Marston's Pedigree; John Smith's Bitter; Wells Bombardier; guest beers ⊞
Large, bustling town-centre pub with a welcoming sense of space thanks to its lofty ceiling and open-plan bar. Converted from a former bank by Wetherspoon's, the pub features real ales in abundance – the lengthy bar includes ten handpumps – and an extensive food menu. A heated rear courtyard provides a quiet sanctuary away from town-centre life. The pub is a short walk from bus and train stations. Q☎◑♿≠⌑⌐

Macintosh Arms

13 Aire Street, DN14 5QE
◷ 10.30-midnight (1am Tue & Thu; 2am Fri & Sat)
☎ (01405) 763850
Tetley Dark Mild, Bitter, Imperial; guest beer ⊞
This Grade II listed building near Goole docks is a gem. Left alone by town planners, it retains an olde-worlde feeling. Three rooms set around a central bar have panelled walls with pictures of old Goole. A glass ceiling in the

pool bar allows a glimpse of the original plaster ceiling from the days when the building was a magistrates court. A motorcycle club meets here; live music plays on the last Friday of the month and karaoke is hosted on Sunday night. ➾🍽♣P

Great Kelk

Chestnut Horse
Main Street, YO25 8HN
🕓 6 (5.30 Fri & Sat)-11; 12-10.30 Sun
☎ (01262) 488263
Samuel Smith OBB; guest beers ⑭
Built in 1793, this delightful Grade II listed rural community pub is situated between the Wolds and Holderness. It has a cosy bar with a real fire and a comfortable games room that doubles as a daytime family room. Darts, dominoes and chess are played. Up to three guest beers are sold alongside draught Hoegaarden and Leffe; Belgian bottled beers are served in authentic glasses. The restaurant offers fine, home-cooked meals until 8.45pm (7.30pm Sunday). 🏨Q❀⑭&♣P

Hollym

Plough Inn
Northside Road, HU19 2RS
🕓 11 (5 winter Mon)-midnight; 12-midnight Sun
☎ (01964) 612049 ⊕ theploughinnhollym.co.uk
Tetley Bitter; guest beers ⑭
This family-run, 200 years old, genuine free house of wattle and daub construction has undergone considerable refurbishment over the last two years under the new owners' stewardship. Primarily a locals' pub, it is a haven for discerning holidaymakers in summer. Imported bottled Coopers beers are often stocked. Part of the pub dates from the 16th century, while photographs in the bar show its role as a WWII ARP station. Accommodation comprises three en-suite letting rooms. 🏨❀🛏⑭▲🍽♣P☂

Howden

Barnes Wallis
Station Road, DN14 7LF (on B1228)
🕓 5-11; 12-midnight Sat; 12-10.30 Sun
☎ (01430) 430639 ⊕ barneswallisinn.com
John Smith's Bitter; Taylor Landlord; guest beers ⑭
Although it is situated at the railway station, the pub takes its name from the aeronautical designer of airships and the Wellington bomber, who worked at nearby Brough; the decor features memorabilia and pictures of these machines. The pub has been refurbished recently but retains a single-room layout. At least two guest beers often include a dark beer. Lunches are served at the weekend only. A large secluded garden is ideal for children. 🏨❀⑭&➾♣P☂

Hull

Admiral of the Humber
1 Anlaby Road, HU1 2NT
🕓 9-midnight (1am Fri & Sat)
☎ (01482) 381850

Greene King Abbot; Marston's Pedigree; guest beers ⑭
Wetherspoon's second pub in the city centre and one of very few outlets in the new town selling cask ales. A short walk from the transport interchange, the large one-roomer has a raised area for diners and booths on both sides. Up to five guest beers, as well as Weston's Old Rosie and organic vintage ciders, are stocked. The bar may be rowdy when rugby Super League matches are shown. Meals are served until 11pm.
⑭&➾(Hull Paragon)🍽♣

Falcon
60 Falkland Road, HU9 5SA
🕓 11-11.30 (midnight Thu-Sat)
☎ (01482) 713721
Lees Bitter; guest beers ⑭
Situated on an estate in the real-ale desert of deepest East Hull, this is an oasis that gives the lie to those that say 'it wouldn't work here'. Up to four guest beers are available at Hull CAMRA's runner-up Pub of the Year 2006, one of them usually a mild. A community pub, games are played in the rear room. The Hull Kingston Rovers Rugby League ground is 10 minutes' walk away, and it can be busy on match days. ❀🛏🍽(41, 42)♣P

Gardeners Arms
35 Cottingham Road, HU5 2PP (near to jct with Beverley Road)
🕓 11 (12 Sun & Mon)-midnight
☎ (01482) 342396
Black Sheep Best Bitter; Tetley's Bitter; guest beers ⑭
Situated just under a mile north of the city centre, the Gardeners is well worth a visit. The original front bar has seen many alterations, but retains the matchwood ceiling that blends with the current ale house style. This room is popular for its friendly feel as well as its choice of five guest beers. The large rear extension is comfortably furnished, housing seven pool tables and plasma TV screens. The pub sponsors local Rugby Union teams and hosts three weekly quizzes. There is a large outdoor drinking area at the front. ❀⑭&🍽♣P☂

Hole in the Wall
115 Spring Bank, HU3 1BH
🕓 1 (12 Fri & Sat)-11; 12-10.30 Sun
☎ (01482) 580354
Hop Back Summer Lightning; Old Mill Mild; Rooster's Yankee; guest beers ⑭
Once an amusement arcade, converted in 2001, the Hole offers two guest beers, mainly sourced from independents including local breweries. All real ales are reduced in price Monday to Thursday. Featuring wood floors throughout, the spacious front bar has plenty of standing room and comfortable leather upholstered bench seating. Sports enthusiasts prefer the rear bar for its large-screen TV and pool table. It is handy for the KC stadium and railway station, both 15 minutes' away. ❀🛏➾🍽☂

Olde White Harte ☆
25 Silver Street, HU1 1JG
🕓 11-midnight (1am Fri & Sat); 12-midnight Sun
☎ (01482) 326363

Caledonian Deuchars IPA, 80; Theakston Old Peculier; Wells Bombardier Ⓗ

Historic 16th-century courtyard pub at the heart of the old town's commercial centre, reputedly the residence of the governor of Hull when he resolved to deny Charles I entry to the city. An impressive staircase leads to the plotting room. The whole of the first floor is used as a restaurant on Wednesday to Saturday evenings. The ground floor comprises two distinct areas, each with a bar. Award-winning floral displays, superb dark woodwork, stained-glass windows and inglenooks feature. Q✿◐≉⊟

Pave

16-20 Princes Avenue, HU5 3QA
✪ 11 (12 Mon)-11 (11.30 Fri & Sat); 12-11 Sun
☎ (01482) 333181 ⊕ pavebar.co.uk
Caledonian Deuchars IPA; Theakston Best Bitter, XB; guest beer Ⓗ

This cosmopolitan café bar is the result of a conversion in 2002. Single-roomed, it incorporates a raised stage with an open fire. Comfortable sofas and leather seating attract a mixed crowd; it is especially popular at weekends. Live jazz is played on Sunday. A secluded rear garden and front patio are pleasant in warmer months. It stocks a varied range of European draught and bottled beers. Food is served until 8pm Monday to Wednesday and 7pm Thursday to Sunday.
🚲✿◐♿⊟(15, 115)♣

Three John Scotts

Lowgate, HU1 1XW
✪ 9-midnight (1am Fri & Sat)
☎ (01482) 381910
Greene King Abbot; Marston's Pedigree; Theakston Old Peculier; guest beers Ⓗ

Converted from an Edwardian post office and situated opposite St Mary's Church in the old town, this open-plan Wetherspoon's features modern decor and original works of art. Named after three past incumbents of the church, the clientele is mixed at lunchtime, with circuit drinkers appearing at weekends. The covered, heated rear courtyard has seating. Up to six guest beers are available, usually including one from Rooster's, plus Weston's cider and perry. Food is served until 11pm, with a steak club on Tuesday and a curry club on Thursday. ✿◐♿⊟♠‡

Wellington Inn

55 Russell Street, HU2 9AB (on edge of city centre, 50 yds N of A165)
✪ 12-11 (midnight Fri & Sat)
☎ (01482) 329486 ⊕ thewellington-hull.co.uk
Tetley Bitter; guest beers Ⓗ

Back-street free house, established in 2004 in a former Hull brewery pub dating from 1861. Refurbished to a high standard, it features a walk-in cooler stocking over 100 European bottled beers; note the impressive glass-fronted display in the back bar. Up to six guest beers are available, mainly from Yorkshire independents, and two or more draught ciders, perry and Lindisfarne fruit wines add variety. No food is available but you can bring your own sandwiches. CAMRA local Pub of the Year 2005 and 2006. ✿≉⊟♦‡

Whalebone

165 Wincolmlee, HU2 0PA (500 yds N of North Bridge on west bank of river)
✪ 11-midnight daily
☎ (01482) 226648
Highwood Best Bitter; Taylor Landlord; Whalebone Diana Mild, Neckoil Bitter, seasonal beers; guest beers Ⓗ

Built in 1796 on the site of the old Lockwood's Brewery, this pub is situated on the harbour in a former industrial area; look for the illuminated M&R ales sign. The comfortable saloon bar is adorned with photos of bygone Hull pubs and the city's sporting heritage; CAMRA awards are also displayed. The adjacent Whalebone Brewery started brewing in 2003. Two real ciders, together with European draught and bottled beers, are also stocked. Hot snacks are always available.
🚲♣●

Lund

Wellington Inn

19 The Green, YO25 9TE
✪ 12-3 (not Mon), 6.30-11 (11.30 Fri & Sat); 12-11 Sun
☎ (01377) 217294
Black Sheep Best Bitter; John Smith's Bitter; Taylor Landlord; guest beer Ⓗ

Enjoying a prime location on the green in this award-winning Wold village, most of this pub's trade comes from the local farming community. It was totally renovated by the present licensee, and features stone-flagged floors, beamed ceilings and three real fires. The multi-roomed pub includes a games room and a candlelit restaurant serving evening meals (Tue-Sat). Good food can also be enjoyed at lunchtime from the bar menu and specials board. 🚲Q❄✿◐⊟♿♣P

North Newbald

Tiger Inn

The Green, YO43 4SA
✪ 12-2 (not Mon), 4-11; 12-midnight Fri-Sun
☎ (01430) 827759
Black Sheep Best Bitter; John Smith's Bitter; Taylor Landlord; guest beers Ⓗ

Facing the village green and nestling in a hollow on the Yorkshire Wolds, this unspoilt listed country pub has a relaxed atmosphere, many a cosy corner and a warming open fire in winter. Popular with cyclists, it is also close to the Wolds Way footpath. An extensive menu offers home-cooked food including seasonal dishes. The Tiger is a community pub that attracts a wide-ranging clientele, including many local characters.
🚲❄✿◐♿⊟♣P

Old Ellerby

Blue Bell Inn

Crabtree Lane, HU11 5AJ
✪ 12-4 (Sat only), 7-11.30 (midnight Fri & Sat); 7-11.30 Sun
☎ (01964) 562364
Black Sheep Best Bitter; Tetley Bitter; guest beers Ⓗ

This 16th-century inn has an L-shaped bar and a single room split into distinct areas,

including a snug to the right and a rear pool area where children are welcome until 8.30pm. Regional CAMRA Village Pub of the Year three times and runner-up in 2006, the inn has a strong community feel. It hosts live jazz on alternate Thursday evenings. Outside is a bowling green, fish pond and play area. Three guest beers in winter increase to four in summer, plus a real cider.
🏠🚲☀️🛤️🚌(230, 240)♣👜P

Patrington

Station Hotel
Station Road, HU12 0NE
🕐 12-11 (midnight Sat)
☎ (01964) 630262
Tetley Bitter; guest beers Ⓗ
A family-owned free house on the western edge of the village, the hotel used to cater for passengers on the Hull-Withernsea railway which closed in the 1960s. The Anglo-Norwegian owners have completely refurbished this once run-down pub over the past three years, with a separate games room the most recent addition. The Station Hotel is renowned locally for its excellent food as well as its interesting guest ales sourced from far and wide. ☀️◐👥🛤️🚌♣P⅃

Rawcliffe

Jemmy Hirst at the Rose & Crown
26 Riverside, DN14 8RN
🕐 6 (5 Fri)-11; 12-11 Sat & Sun
☎ (01405) 831038
Taylor Landlord; guest beers Ⓗ
Much loved by visitors across the region, the pub was CAMRA branch Pub of the Year in 2004, 2005 and 2006. You can be sure of a warm welcome from the owners and Bruno the dog. A constantly changing array of ales suits every taste. The rustic interior with a real fire and book-lined walls provides a welcome retreat, and lazy summers can be spent on the patio or river bank. Be warned: after a few visits you may want to move in.
🏠Q☀️👥🚌♣P⅃

Ryehill

Crooked Billet
Pitt Lane, HU12 9NN (400m off A1033 E of Thorngumbald)
🕐 12-2.30 (not Mon), 4.30-midnight (4-1am Fri & Sat); 12-midnight Sun
☎ (01964) 622303
Jennings Dark Mild, Bitter, Cumberland Ale; guest beers Ⓗ
This 16th-century coaching inn features stone-flagged floors, horse brasses, upholstered bench seats and a rear dining area. Two guest beers are available and a changing Jennings beer alongside the three regulars. Good quality home-cooked food is served at all times except Monday lunch. The heart of the community, it supports the local cricket team, features traditional pub games such as bar skittles, darts and shove ha'penny, and hosts monthly jazz and pub piano nights.
🏠☀️🍴◐👄🚌(76)♣P

Skipsea

Board Inn
Back Street, YO25 8SW
🕐 6-11; 12-midnight Sat; 12-11 Sun
☎ (01262) 468342
Mansfield Cask Ale; guest beers Ⓗ
Traditional village local dating from the 17th century with distinct public and lounge bars as well as a recently extended restaurant. The public bar, with its sporting focus (especially Rugby League), hosts two darts teams, two pool teams and a dominoes team. The comfortable lounge, meanwhile, is home to the landlady's water jug collection. Home-cooked food is served daily from 6pm, and in summer attracts many holiday-makers for Sunday lunch (booking advisable). Dogs are welcome. 🏠☀️◐👄🛤️▲♣P

South Dalton

Pipe & Glass
West End, HU17 7PN
🕐 12-3, 6.30-11 (not Mon); 12-10.30 Sun
☎ (01430) 810246 🌐 pipeandglass.co.uk
John Smith's Bitter; guest beers Ⓗ
This characterful pub with exposed beams serves two regularly changing guest beers. Its kitchen focuses strongly on modern British food, served in both the bar and restaurant. Ask for the separate vegetarian menu. Children are welcome throughout. Accommodation is planned for 2008.
🏠☀️🛏️◐👄👜P

Sutton upon Derwent

St Vincent Arms
Main Street, YO41 4BN (follow B1228 beyond Elvington)
🕐 11.30-3, 6-11; 12-3, 7-10.30 Sun
☎ (01904) 608349
Fuller's London Pride, ESB; Old Mill Bitter; Taylor Landlord; Wells Bombardier; York Yorkshire Terrier; guest beers Ⓗ
This striking white building, situated on a bend in the village, was smartly re-signed courtesy of Fuller's. The L-shaped bar to the right of the entrance is popular with regulars – note the large Fuller, Smith and Turner mirror – to the left is a bar/dining room and an extensive beer garden. York CAMRA's Pub of the Year in 2002 and 2006, it is renowned for its good beer and excellent food. Q☀️◐👄▲P

Welton

Green Dragon
Cowgate, HU15 1NB
🕐 11-11 (11.30 Fri & Sat)
☎ (01482) 666700 🌐 greendragonwelton.info
Beer range varies Ⓗ
Dick Turpin lodged here and was captured in the village in 1739, before his execution in York. The pub layout is open plan, with much dark wood and comfortable leather upholstery. Three to four changing beers come from the Marston's portfolio. The menu is served until 9pm daily, and dishes incorporate local produce whenever possible. Monday is quiz night and live music plays on Friday.

Accommodation is available in the converted stable block. Q★☆☎◁◀①&🖪(155)🌢P

Wold Newton

Anvil Arms

Bridlington Road, YO25 3YL
☼ 12-midnight
☎ (01262) 470279
Black Sheep Best Bitter; John Smith's Bitter; guest beer Ⓗ

Reputedly haunted, this Grade II listed building stands opposite the pond in a picturesque village on the edge of the Wolds. Sympathetically restored, it comprises a bar, games room with pool table and a restaurant that opens Friday and Saturday evenings and for Sunday lunch (booking essential). Bar snacks are available at all times. It fields darts and dominoes teams. The guest beer is likely to come from Hambleton, Daleside or Rudgate, however locally brewed beers may also appear. ▲Q☎☆①🖪🌢P

YORKSHIRE (NORTH)

Askrigg

Crown Inn

Main Street, DL8 3HQ (1 mile off A684 at top of main street)
☼ 11-1am (midnight Sun)
☎ (01969) 650298
John Smith's Bitter; Theakston Best Bitter; guest beers Ⓗ

Set in a village that gained fame as the setting for the TV series All Creatures Great and Small, this is a friendly and busy inn, attracting locals and Dales visitors. The interior has been opened out but retains much of its traditional character and an impressive fireplace. The pub is renowned for its food and hosts a wide range of activities. ▲☎🌢🖪🌢

Aysgarth

George & Dragon

DL8 3AD
☼ 11.30 (12 Sun)-2am (closing time may vary)
☎ (01969) 663358 ⊕ georgeanddragonaysgarth.co.uk
Black Sheep Best Bitter, Ale; Theakston Best Bitter; guest beers Ⓗ

Situated within a mile of the spectacular Aysgarth Falls in the Dales, this 17th-century inn occupies a prominent position on the main A684. Well-kept local beers, good wine and excellent food are served, making this cosy country pub a welcome stop on a visit to mid-Wensleydale. Accommodation is available. ▲Q◁①Å🖪🌢P⌐

Beck Hole

Birch Hall Inn ☆

YO22 5LE (1 mile NW of Goathland) OS823022
☼ 11-3, 7.30-11 (not Mon eve; closed Tue Jan & Feb); 11-11 summer & Sun
☎ (01947) 896245 ⊕ beckhole.info
Black Sheep Best Bitter; Theakston Black Bull Bitter; guest beers Ⓗ

Unspoilt rural gem, once the provisions store for the local ironstone industry. The Birch Hall

was granted a licence in 1860 and has had just three landlords in the past 80 years. The store lives on as a sweet shop, sandwiched between the two bars. The pub serves one or two guest beers, often from local breweries. Home-made pies and substantial sandwiches are available, as well as the famous Beck Hole beer cake. Cleveland CAMRA Pub of the Season summer 2006. ▲Q☎☆&≈P

Beckwithshaw

Smith's Arms

Church Row, HG3 1QW (on B6161)
☼ 11-11; 12-10.30 Sun
☎ (01423) 504871
Courage Directors; Theakston Best Bitter; guest beers Ⓗ

Spacious and welcoming stone-built inn dating from the 19th century. Part of the building used to be the village smithy. At the centre of its local community, the pub is also popular with visitors to this attractive area close to Harrogate. The guest beer often comes from the local Daleside Brewery. It enjoys a good reputation for the quality of its food. ▲Q☎①&P

Bishop Monkton

Lamb & Flag

Boroughbridge Road, HG4 3QN (off A61)
☼ 12-2 (not Mon), 5.30-11; 12-3, 7-10.30 Sun
☎ (01765) 677332
Tetley Bitter; guest beers Ⓗ

Supporting many local clubs and societies and actively raising funds for the cricket team, this cosy country pub is at the heart of village life. Its two rooms are decorated with unusual brasses. The May bank holiday hog roast takes place on the banks of the nearby stream that is also the location for the August bank holiday plastic duck race. ▲Q☎☆◁①Å🖪🌢P

INDEPENDENT BREWERIES

Abbey Bells Hirst Courtney
Black Dog Whitby
Black Sheep Masham
Brown Cow Barlow
Captain Cook Stokesley
Copper Dragon Skipton
Cropton Cropton
Daleside Harrogate
Hambleton Melmerby
Litton Litton
Marston Moor Tockwith
Moorcock Hawes
Naylor's Crosshills
North Yorkshire Pinchinthorpe
Rooster's Knaresborough
Rudgate Tockwith
Samuel Smith Tadcaster
Selby Selby (Brewing Suspended)
Suddaby's Malton
Theakston Masham
Three Peaks Settle
Wensleydale Bellerby
Wharfedale Hetton
York York
Yorkshire Dales Askrigg

NORTH YORKSHIRE

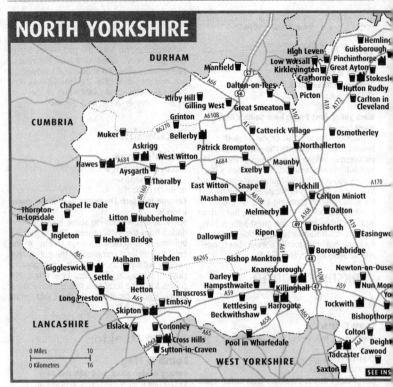

Bishopthorpe

Ebor Inn

Main Street, YO23 3RB

🕐 11 (11.30 Sun)-11

☎ (01904) 706190

Samuel Smith OBB Ⓗ

Good-sized local in a charming village close to the Archbishop's Palace. Two large rooms either side of the bar area are decorated in this local independent brewery's typical style. Good, wholesome food is freshly cooked, with fish from Whitby a speciality. In summer, the large and well-equipped garden is used for village fetes and bonfire parties. The landlord has been serving here for more than 25 years and is the only remaining tenant in the Samuel Smith estate. Q❀❍◑⬱🖵♣P⅃

Boroughbridge

Black Bull Inn

6 St James Square, YO5 9AR

🕐 11 (12 Sun)-midnight

☎ (01423) 322413

John Smith's Bitter; Taylor Best Bitter; guest beers Ⓗ

Situated in the main square, this 13th-century, Grade II listed inn is extremely popular. There are three drinking areas; the restaurant has been restored to its former glory, thanks to a complete refurbishment after suffering serious fire damage. Even the resident ghost is reported to have moved back in. The beers are good value, and an international menu is supplemented by a good choice of bar meals.

This little gem is well worth a visit; limited parking. ▲Q❀❍◑ Å♣P

Burn

Wheatsheaf

Main Road, YO8 8LJ (on A19, 3 miles S of Selby)

🕐 12-11

☎ (01757) 270614 ⊕ wheatsheafburn.co.uk

John Smith's Bitter; Taylor Landlord; guest beers Ⓗ

This genuine free house has stocked more than 600 guest beers in the last two years, all sourced from independent breweries including the local Brown Cow. Ales are always reasonably priced and wholesome, home-cooked food is served (eve meals Thu-Sat only). The interior has been opened out, while an enormous fireplace and an assortment of agricultural memorabilia preserve the rustic ambience.
▲Q❀❍◑⬱♣P⅃

Carlton Miniott

Dog & Gun

YO7 4NJ (on A61 2 miles W of Thirsk)

🕐 12-3, 5.30-midnight; 12-midnight Sat; 12-11 Sun

☎ (01845) 522150

Caledonian Deuchars IPA; John Smith's Bitter; Black Sheep Best Bitter; Theakston Best Bitter; guest beers Ⓗ

This welcoming hostelry lies on the A61, west of the market town of Thirsk. It features two regularly changing guest ales from micro-breweries. An extensive food menu is

ENGLAND

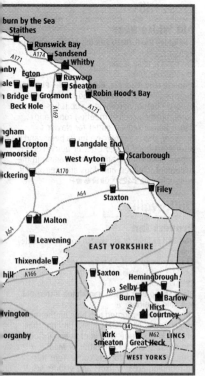

busy, friendly pub, strongly committed to beer quality. Guest ales come from the Marston's range. Q❀⏍❶♿🚃♣P🏠

Cawood

Ferry Inn

2 King Street, YO8 3TL (S side of river, near swing bridge)

🕒 12-11 (midnight Thu-Sat); 10-11 Sun
☎ (01757) 268515 ⏚ theferryinn.com
Caledonian Deuchars IPA; Taylor Landlord; Theakston Best Bitter; guest beers Ⓗ

The history of Cawood goes back to Cardinal Wolsey who resided at Cawood Castle during his time as Archbishop of York. This privately-owned village inn is dedicated to real ale, as well as fine food prepared by its French chef. If the weather permits, drinks and meals can be enjoyed on the terrace or in the garden, which overlooks the river. A marquee is set up for special events. The pub opens early on Sunday for breakfast and morning coffee.
🏚Q❀❀❶⏍ Å🚃P🏠

Chapel-le-Dale

Hill Inn

LA6 3AR (on B6255)

🕒 12-3, 6.30-11 Thu & Fri; 12-11 Sat; 12-10.30 Sun
☎ (01524) 241256
Black Sheep Best Bitter; Dent Bitter, Aviator; guest beers Ⓗ

Beloved of generations of hikers and potholers, well-worn paths run from here to Whernside (Yorkshire's highest peak) and Ingleborough (its best known). Carefully restored in 2001, it is a popular destination for diners (booking advisable). Lots of exposed wood and some stonework feature in the bar. Guest beers come from local micros. A folk evening is hosted on the last Friday of the month. The pub may close if there are no customers or bookings. 🏚Q❶ ÅP

Colton

Old Sun Inn

Main Street, LS24 8EP (1 mile S of Bilborough Services off A64) OS544448

🕒 12-2.30, 6-11 (not Mon); 12-10.30 Sun
☎ (01904) 744261 ⏚ yeoldsuninn.co.uk
John Smith's Bitter; Taylor Landlord; guest beers Ⓗ

A village pub with a small delicatessen at the rear selling local produce and home-made bread. The focus at this inn is on food, and reserving a table is advisable, especially at weekends (no meals Sun eve). Space for drinkers can be limited. For summer there are large outdoor areas, a patio, a deck and a beer garden where customers can sit and enjoy their beer. 🏚Q❀❶P🏠🍴

Cononley

New Inn

Main Street, BD20 8NR

🕒 12-2.30, 5.30-midnight; 12-1am Fri & Sat; 12-10.30 Sun
☎ (01535) 636302 ⏚ newinncononley.co.uk
Taylor Golden Best, Best Bitter, Landlord Ⓗ

---

available in the comfortable open-plan bar and in the restaurant. There is a spacious garden for outdoor drinking in summer and a sheltered patio at the front for smokers. Caravans may park beyond the garden.
🚃❀❶♿🚃♣P🏠

Carlton-in-Cleveland

Blackwell Ox

Main Street, TS9 7NU

🕒 11.30-11; 12-10.30 Sun
☎ (01642) 712287 ⏚ theblackwellox.co.uk
Black Sheep Best Bitter; Tetley Bitter; guest beers Ⓗ

Impressive village pub with smaller rooms off a central public bar. A wide selection of food is served, with Thai cuisine featuring strongly. The changing range of guest beers often includes micro-breweries' products. The garden has a children's play area and to the rear there is a camping and caravan site.
🏚Q🚃❀❶♿Å♣P

Catterick Village

Bay Horse

38 Low Green, DL10 7LP (off main street)

🕒 12-11.30
☎ (01748) 811383
Jennings Bitter, Cumberland Ale; guest beers Ⓗ

Established village local facing the picturesque green and beck, just off the main through road and convenient for the A1 and racecourse. With a largely open-plan, comfortable interior, and a restaurant in the conservatory, this is a

529

Historic inn situated in a Dales village between Keighley and Skipton, with mullioned windows and low, beamed ceilings. Always busy, this local community pub has earned a reputation for serving excellent and good value meals. Just a short walk from Cononley Station – if catching a train south, allow time to cross the level crossing.
♨Q✿❄◑❄➡(78A)♣

Crathorne

Crathorne Arms

TS15 0BA
✪ 11.30-2, 5.30-11; 11.30-11 Sat; 12-10.30 Sun
Black Sheep Best Bitter; Taylor Landlord; guest beers Ⓗ
Bypassed by the busy A19, this whitewashed gem of a village inn stands on the quiet main street, with a farm to the rear. Known to locals as Free House Farm, the new tenants extend a warm welcome to guests. The beer range has been widened, and superb food draws discerning visitors from near and far. A fine selection of historic photographs from Lord Crathorne's own collection is displayed on the walls. ♨Q✿◑&P꞊

Cray

White Lion Inn

BD23 5JB (on B6160 N of Buckden)
✪ 11-11; 12-10.30 Sun
☎ (01756) 760262 ⊕ whitelioncray.com
Moorhouses Premier; Taylor Landlord; guest beers Ⓗ
The White Lion is a former drovers' inn, built in the mid-1600s next to the cascading Cray Gill beneath Buckden Pike. This traditional Dales inn boasts stone-flagged floors, an open fire and a welcoming atmosphere. The bar is in the main drinking area with raised seating at the back. A recent local CAMRA Pub of the Season, Copper Dragon beers feature regularly. Popular with walkers and cyclists, the accommodation provides an excellent base for those enjoying outdoor pursuits. ♨Q✿▱◑▸ ▴➡♣P

Cropton

New Inn

Woolcroft, YO18 8HH (5 miles off A170, Pickering-Kirkbymoorside road) OS754888
✪ 11-11 daily
☎ (01751) 417330 ⊕ croptonbrewery.co.uk
Cropton Endeavour, Two Pints, Monkmans Slaughter; Theakston Best Bitter, seasonal beers; guest beers Ⓗ
Outstanding pub on the edge of the North Yorkshire Moors National Park, with the added attraction of the Cropton Brewery at the bottom of the garden. Seven handpumps dispense regular and seasonal beers. The top bar is ideal for drinking and casual dining; the restaurant in the lower conservatory offers wonderful food. Landscaped gardens are delightful in summer. An unmissable beer festival is held in November. Near to the North Yorkshire Moors Railway and Whitby, good value accommodation is recommended.
Q▱✿▱◑▯&▴➡♣P

Cross Hills

Old White Bear

6 Keighley Road, BD20 7RN (on A6068, close to jct with A629)
✪ 11.30-11; 12-10.30 Sun
☎ (01535) 632115
Pinnacle Mild, Pale Ale, Bitter, Blonde, Porter Ⓗ
Built in 1735, the inn has had a chequered history – before becoming a pub it has been a hotel, brothel, council meeting room and dance hall. A regular outlet for Naylor's Brewery, this is a showcase for its beers, and it also offers hand-pulled cider or perry. Food is served at lunchtime and in the evening in the restaurant. Children and dogs are welcome if well behaved. ♨➤✿◑▱♣P

Dallowgill

Drovers Inn

HG4 3RH (2 miles W of Laverton on road to Pateley Bridge) OS210720
✪ 12-3 (summer only), 7-11; closed Mon; 12-3, 6.30-11 Sat; 12-3, 6-10.30 Sun
☎ (01765) 658510
Black Sheep Best Bitter; Hambleton Bitter; Old Mill Mild or Bitter, Ⓗ
This small, one-roomed pub high on the moors above Lower Niddledale has a tiny bar that always keeps three well-kept beers, including the rarely seen Old Mill Bitter or Mild. Although most customers come from the surrounding area, walkers and visitors are always made welcome. The bell on the roof is used to communicate with shooting parties on the moors. Inside, a roaring fire warms guests in winter. ♨Q✿◑▸ ▴♣P

Dalton

Jolly Farmers Inn

Mainstreet, YO7 3HY (off A19 or A168)
✪ 12-3 (not Mon-Wed), 7 (6 Thu-Sat)-11
☎ (01845) 577359
John Smith's Bitter; Theakston Mild; guest beers Ⓗ
Popular with locals, this family-run pub, dating from the mid 1800s, is at the heart of the village, enthusiastically converting customers to real ale. Its six handpumps feature local micros and Weston's draught cider. Freshly prepared home-made dishes, using local produce, are served from the kitchen, with 'proper' chips a favourite. Booking is advisable for Sunday lunch. Three en-suite rooms make an ideal base for exploring the Dales and North Yorkshire Moors. Q✿▱◑▸♣▴P

Dalton-on-Tees

Chequers Inn

DL2 2NT
✪ 12-3, 5.30-11; 12-10.30 Sun
☎ (01325) 721213
Banks's Bitter; guest beers Ⓗ
Traditional inn dating back to the 1840s, comprising a bar, lounge and restaurant, where a warm welcome is always guaranteed. Formerly known as the Crown & Anchor, this was once part of the now-defunct Fryer's Brewery estate. The landlord is

passionate about real ale and at least two guest beers are sourced from micros countrywide. Regular gourmet evenings take place and a quiz is held every Wednesday. Q❀☎◑❖P

Danby

Duke of Wellington

2 West Lane, YO21 2LY OS708687

☼ 12-3 (not Mon), 7-11; 12-11 Fri & Sat; 12-3, 7-10.30 Sun

☎ (01287) 660351 ⊕ danby-dukeofwellington.co.uk

Daleside Bitter; Tetley Imperial; guest beers Ⓗ

Dating back to 1765, this inn at the heart of the North Yorkshire Moors overlooks the village green. The timber-beamed bars and open fire create a warm and friendly atmosphere in which to eat, drink and relax. It was used as a recruiting post during the Napoleonic War, and there is a cast iron plaque of the Duke, unearthed during restoration, above the fireplace. ᴹQ☕❀☎◑➼❖P

Darley

Wellington

HG3 2QQ (on B6451 near Harrogate)

☼ 11.30-11; 12-10.30 Sun

☎ (01423) 780363 ⊕ wellington-inn.co.uk

Caledonian Deuchars IPA; Taylor Landlord; Tetley Bitter; Theakston Best Bitter Ⓗ

Spacious, stone roadside inn, some 200 years old, nestling in a picturesque valley with views from the beer garden across Nidderdale, an area of outstanding natural beauty. The pub has high-backed bench seating and low beamed ceilings as well as an open fire. Signature dishes from the varied restaurant menu include Darley lamb and Wellington fish pie. The pub makes a good starting point for walking or cycling in the Dales. ᴹQ☕❀☎◑➼❖P

Deighton

White Swan

YO19 6HA (on A19, 5 miles S of York)

☼ 11.30-2.30, 5.30-11; 11.30-11 Sat; 12-10.30 Sun

☎ (01904) 728287

Banks's Bitter; Jennings Cumberland Ale; Marston's Pedigree; guest beers Ⓗ

Now an oasis on a busy highway, but once a drovers' inn on the road from Selby to York, the field opposite the pub is still known as the pinfold. The interior is open plan but has kept much of its original layout. Meals are served in dining areas in the front bar as well as the lounge/dining room. A comprehensive, good value menu is supplemented by daily specials and children's dishes. The tenant prepares the meals himself from fresh, local produce. Q❀◑➼❖P⅃

Dishforth

Black Swan

Main Street, YO7 3JU

☼ 12-3, 6.30 (7 Sun)-midnight

☎ (01845) 577627

Black Sheep Best Bitter; Daleside Bitter, Blonde; John Smith's Bitter Ⓗ

Traditional, friendly village inn with a single bar in the main lounge and a dining room at the rear. Seats in the bar area are made from old wooden barrels. For mild weather, there is a small outside drinking area on the cobbles at the front of the pub. Q❀◑❖P

Easingwold

George at Easingwold

Market Place, YO61 3AD

☼ 11-2.30, 5-11; 12-2.30, 5-10.30 Sun

☎ (01347) 821698 ⊕ the-george-hotel.co.uk

Black Sheep Best Bitter; Moorhouses Pride of Pendle; Tetley Bitter; guest beers Ⓗ

Overlooking Easingwold's cobbled market square opposite the market cross, this old coaching inn dates from the 18th century. Now a comfortable country inn at the hub of the local community, it offers a range of freshly-cooked food and quality accommodation. Popular with locals and visitors, its cosy rooms are served by a central bar. A rejuvenated beer range reflects the landlord's interest in matters Lancastrian. ᴹQ❀☎◑♿➼P

East Witton

Cover Bridge Inn

DL8 4SQ (half mile N of village on A6108)

☼ 11-midnight; 12-11.30 Sun

☎ (01969) 623250 ⊕ thecoverbridgeinn.co.uk

Black Sheep Best Bitter; John Smith's Bitter; Taylor Landlord; Theakston Best Bitter, Old Peculier; guest beers Ⓗ

Outstanding country inn situated at the point where the Rivers Ure and Cover meet. A CAMRA multi-award winner, it resembles a mini beer exhibition, with eight cask ales usually stocked. Fathom out the door latch (and mind your head) to enter the ancient public bar, with its splendid hearth. The tiny lounge leads to a pleasant riverside garden with a play area. An enviable reputation for food makes it popular with diners. ᴹQ☕❀☎◑ⱻ៳➼❖P☐

Egton

Wheatsheaf Inn

YO21 2TZ

☼ 11-3 (not Mon), 5.30-11; 11.30-11 Sat; 12-10.30 Sun

☎ (01947) 895271 ⊕ wheatsheafegton.com

Black Sheep Best Bitter; Caledonian Deuchars IPA; guest beer Ⓗ

Grade I listed pub at the village centre, popular with anglers and walkers. Church pew-style seats occupy the bar area, while the lounge has a fishing theme, with numerous fly rods attached to the beams. The main bar and dining room are warmed by coal fires, while a large grassed area to the front is ideal in warmer weather. Seasonal, local produce is the basis for the recommended menu. The pub has four en-suite guest rooms. ᴹ❀☎◑ⱻ៳➾P

Egton Bridge

Horseshoe Hotel

YO21 1XE (down hill from Egton Station, over bridge)
☼ 11.30-3, 6.30-11; 12-3, 7-10.30 Sun
☎ (01947) 895245
Black Sheep Best Bitter; John Smith's Bitter; guest beers Ⓗ
This hidden gem is popular with locals and visitors alike. The cosy bar, warmed by a coal fire, is furnished with old-fashioned settles. A large, raised grass area at the front makes outdoor dining a pleasure in summer, and the restaurant is also comfortably furnished. Easily reached from the station via the road or stepping stones across the Esk, it is a good start or finish point for walks on the moors or in the Esk Valley. ▲Q☎☀❄◑≋(Egton)P

Postgate

YO21 1UX
☼ 12-3, 6.30-11
☎ (01947) 895241
Black Sheep Best Bitter Ⓗ
Built in 1860, this little pub is tucked into the side of a valley. It appeared in the popular TV series Heartbeat as the 'Black Dog'. Set within the beautiful North Yorkshire Moors National Park, the inn has a warm and sociable ambience, welcoming locals and visitors. Benefitting from easy access to both the Moors and the Yorkshire coast, the inn offers five luxury bedrooms, a candlelit restaurant and a lively bar. ▲☎☀❄◑♿▲≋♣P

Elslack

Tempest Arms

BD23 3AY (off A56 Skipton-Colne road)
☼ 11-11; 12-10.30 Sun
☎ (01282) 842450 ⊕ tempestarms.co.uk
Black Sheep Best Bitter; Copper Dragon Scotts 1816; Taylor Best Bitter; Tetley Bitter; Theakston Best Bitter Ⓗ
Large, popular, up-market country pub, just off the A56, serving excellent food from an extensive menu. The decor is an attractive mixture of traditional and contemporary. A room at the back features pictures and historical items relating to the Tempest family and Broughton estate. Conference facilities and a function room are available for hire. ▲☀❄◑☐(215)P⅃

Elvington

Grey Horse

Main Street, YO41 4AG (on B1228 6 miles SE of York)
☼ 12-2.30 (not Mon or Tue), 5-11; 12-midnight Fri & Sat; 12-11 Sun
☎ (01904) 608335 ⊕ elvington.net/pub
Black Sheep Best Bitter; John Smith's Bitter; Taylor Landlord; guest beers Ⓗ
Situated opposite the village green, the pub's two rooms are served from a central bar – look out for the stool carved like the palm of a hand. In summer outdoor seating is provided at the front. The lounge displays photographs of the WWII bombers that used to fly from the nearby airfield, now the Yorkshire Air Museum. Guest beers change regularly and an

excellent menu is served (no meals Mon and Tue). ▲Q☀❄◑☐♿☐♣P⅃

Embsay

Elm Tree Inn

5 Elm Tree Square, BD23 6RB
☼ 11.30-3, 5.30-11; 12-11 (12-3, 5.30-11 winter) Sun
☎ (01756) 790717
Copper Dragon Scotts 1816; Goose Eye No-Eye Deer; Moorhouses Black Cat; Wells Bombardier, ; guest beers Ⓗ
Former coaching inn situated in the village square. Inside it has an open feel with oak beams and horse brasses. As well as the large main bar there is a smaller side room, mainly used by diners. Moorhouses Black Cat is regularly stocked. Look for the worn mounting steps outside. Well-situated for walking on the edge of the Yorkshire Dales National Park; Embsay and Bolton Abbey steam railway line is nearby. ☀❄◑☐P

Exelby

Green Dragon

High Road, DL8 2HA (signed from A1)
☼ 12-2.30, 5-midnight; 12-midnight Fri & Sat; 12-11 Sun
☎ (01677) 422233 ⊕ thegreendragonexelby.co.uk
Black Sheep Best Bitter; John Smith's Bitter; guest beers Ⓗ
This homely rambling village free house has expanded from an 1830s cottage inn to incorporate several rooms, including a lounge, bar and games room with table football. Its low beams and old kitchen range bestow plenty of character, making it hard to believe the latest parts, including the restaurant, are 1960s additions. An extensive menu, much of it locally sourced, features Tex Mex as a speciality. There are lively quizzes on Tuesday and Sunday evenings. ▲☀❄◑☐♿▲♣P⅃

Filey

Bonhommes Bar

Royal Crescent Court, The Crescent, YO14 9JH
☼ 11 (12 winter)-midnight (1am Fri & Sat); 12-midnight Sun
☎ (01723) 512034
John Smith's Bitter; guest beers Ⓗ
The bar, known from the 1950s as the American Bar, lies just off the fine Victorian Royal Crescent Hotel complex. The present name celebrates John Paul Jones, father of the American navy. His ship, the Bonhomme Richard, was involved in a battle off nearby Flamborough Head during the War of Independence. The free house serves three changing guest beers with a Yorkshire theme. Live music plays once a month and a fun quiz is held on Saturday. Lunches are provided in summer only. ◑≋☐♣

Imperial Vaults

20-22 Hope Street, YO14 9OL
☼ 12-midnight (1am Fri & Sat)
☎ (01723) 512185
John Smith's Bitter; guest beers Ⓗ
In easy reach of Filey beach and Brigg where the Cleveland Way walk ends, this is a

traditional inn, featuring plenty of wood and stone floors. There is a central bar with interconnecting rooms. Filey memorabilia adorn the walls. The pub serves one guest beer from a micro-brewery, more in season. Live music plays once a month, on Friday or Saturday. ▲☰❀♣

Giggleswick

Hart's Head Hotel

Belle Hill, BD24 0BA (on B6480 ½ mile N of Settle)
🕐 12-2.30 (not Thu), 5.30-11; 11-11 Sat; 12-10.30 Sun
☎ (01729) 822086 ⊕ hartsheadhotel.co.uk
Copper Dragon Golden Pippin, Scotts 1816; Tetley Bitter; guest beers Ⓗ
Welcoming 18th-century coaching inn, now established as a regular in this Guide. The open-plan bar retains a multi-room feel with some comfortable sofas. As well as the excellent range of beers on offer, mostly from local breweries, food features highly at this hostelry – note the enormous blackboard menu at the entrance to the dining area. The refurbished cellar houses a full-sized snooker table. ▲Q❀☡◑ ⊟➡♣P

Gilling West

White Swan Inn

51 High Street, DL10 5JG (2 miles W of Scotch Corner, off A66)
🕐 12-11 (10.30 Sun)
☎ (01748) 821123
Black Sheep Best Bitter; John Smith's Bitter; guest beers Ⓗ
Warm and friendly 17th-century country inn with an open-plan bar and a dining room offering an extensive menu. The guest beers come from local and national micro-breweries. The bar's beams are covered in bank notes, old and new, while a notable feature in the gents' toilet is the barbed-wire toilet seat! The pub fields darts and dominoes teams and has a clay-pigeon shooting club. There is live music on alternate Wednesdays. ▲Q❀◑&⊟♣

Glaisdale

Arncliffe Arms

YO21 2QL (at the bottom of the village)
🕐 12-11 summer; 12-2.30 (not Mon & Tue), 6-11 winter; 12-11 Sat & Sun
☎ (01947) 897555 ⊕ arncliffearms.co.uk
Black Sheep Best Bitter; Cropton Beggars Bridge Bitter; guest beers Ⓗ
Set in the scenic village of Glaisdale, which was an ironstone mining village in the 19th century, the Arncliffe Arms is popular with walkers and all those who come to enjoy the delights of the North Yorkshire Moors. It is recommended for its food and accommodation, as well as its beers – the Beggars Bridge Bitter, from Cropton Brewery, is exclusive to this inn. ▲Q❀☸☡◑&☰♣P

Great Ayton

Whinstone View

TS9 6QG (on B1292 ½ mile from Great Ayton)
🕐 12-11; closed Mon winter; 12-4 Sun
☎ (01642) 723285 ⊕ whinstoneview.com
Beer range varies Ⓗ
Bistro set in its own secluded grounds on the edge of the North York Moors. Beautiful and peaceful, the spacious, open-plan interior features much wood and natural materials. The changing guest beers are sourced from a wide range of breweries. A large veranda at the front overlooks the grounds and an adjacent caravan park. The Whinstone View enjoys an excellent reputation for meals. Conference facilities are upstairs. ▲Q❀☡&▲P

Great Heck

Bay Horse

Main Street, DN14 0BQ (follow signs from A19)
🕐 12-2, 5-11; 12-midnight Fri & Sat; 12-10.30 Sun
☎ (01977) 661125
Old Mill Bitter, seasonal beers Ⓗ
An outlet for the local Old Mill Brewery, the pub was converted from cottages some years ago. Although open-plan, it has distinct areas including a lounge bar and raised dining area. An open fire, exposed beams and a display of brasses add traditional character. Home-cooked meals are served throughout the pub from an extensive menu. A patio at the rear is ideal for warm weather. Thursday is quiz night, followed by a supper. ▲❀☡P

Great Smeaton

Bay Horse

Church View, DL6 2EH (on A167)
🕐 12-3 (not Mon or Tue), 5 (5.30 Mon & Tue)-midnight; 12-midnight Sat; 12-11.30 Sun
☎ (01609) 881466
Black Sheep Best Bitter; John Smith's Bitter; guest beers Ⓗ
Small 18th-century free house, set in the middle of a row of cottages in an attractive village. Comprising a beamed lounge with a central fireplace, bustling bar and games room (home to Mac, the red-bellied Macaw), it enjoys an excellent reputation for home-cooked food (not Mon). Up to two guest beers are sourced from micro-breweries countrywide. This former local CAMRA Rural Pub of the Year has an enclosed garden with a small play area. ▲Q❀☡♣P⬩⊟

Grinton

Bridge Inn

DL11 6HH (on B6270, 1 mile E of Reeth)
🕐 12-midnight (1am Fri & Sat); 12-11 Sun
☎ (01748) 884224 ⊕ bridgeinn-grinton.co.uk
Jennings Cumberland Ale, Cocker Hoop, seasonal beers; guest beers Ⓗ
On the banks of the River Swale and beneath Fremington Edge, this former coaching inn has been sensitively renovated to retain its traditional character. Inside there is a lounge with wooden panelling and beams, a restaurant to the left and games room to the right. Food prepared from seasonal produce is served daily. Families and pets are welcome, but mobile phones are not, and their use incurs a fine. Thursday is musicians' night and

mini beer festivals are hosted in March and October. ♔🍺❀⇌◑⊟⅄♣P⁵–

Grosmont

Crossing Club

Front Street, YO22 5QE (200m from station)
⊛ 7-11
☎ (01947) 895040
Beer range varies ⊞
Interesting conversion, carried out by volunteers, of the old Co-op delivery bay to a bar full of railway memorabilia, including an old crossing gate. Access is gained through a glass door (ring the bell). Well-behaved children and pets are welcome. Members are proud of their club and visitors are offered a warm welcome. In summer further guest beers are stocked, and the opening hours are extended for special steam events. Q≋♣

Station Tavern

YO22 5PA (next to station)
⊛ 7 (11 summer)-midnight; 12-midnight Sat; 12-11.30 Sun
☎ (01947) 895060 🌐 tunnelinn.co.uk
Caledonian Deuchars IPA; Camerons Stongarm; John Smith's Bitter ⊞
Welcoming family-run pub, built in 1836. In addition to the traditional bar, there is a family room where diners can eat in front of an open fire and children are always welcome. The patio and garden are pleasant in summer and quoits is played here. The owners are keen walkers and are happy to offer advice and information on the surrounding area.
♔Q🍺❀⇌◑⊟♿⅄≋♣P⁵–

Guisborough

Globe

81 Northgate, TS14 6JP (opp hospital)
⊛ 4 (2 Thu & Fri; 12 Sat)-midnight; 12-11.30 Sun
☎ (01287) 280799
Camerons Strongarm; Jennings Cumberland; guest beers ⊞
Large two-roomed community pub with a strong emphasis on live music, hosting regular music clubs throughout the week. There is a large-screen TV, usually showing sport (with the volume turned down low). The main bar is decorated with globes and sporting trophies: the silver cup won by the ladies' darts team and the wooden spoon (!) won by the men. There is a large yard at the rear for summer drinking. Q❀♿⅄●

Hampsthwaite

Joiners Arms

High Street, HG3 2EU (off A59)
⊛ 11.30-2.30, 5.30-11; 12-10.30 Sun
☎ (01423) 771673
Rudgate Viking; Tetley Bitter ⊞
Close to the A59 and Nidderdale Way, the lounge and tap room of this 200-year-old pub are connected by an unusual snug that was once the cellar and retains its original stone floor and vaulted ceiling. The lounge features an inglenook fireplace uncovered during refurbishment. The dining room displays a rare collection of gravy boats. Evening meals are served Wednesday to Saturday. Q◑⊟⊟P

Harrogate

Coach & Horses

16 West Park, HG1 1BJ (opp The Stray)
⊛ 11-11; 12-10.30 Sun
☎ (01423) 568371
Copper Dragon Best Bitter; Taylor Landlord; Tetley Bitter; guest beers ⊞
A profusion of window boxes overflowing with flowers adorns this pub in the summer, while inside it features a central bar surrounded by an assortment of snugs and alcoves, contributing to the cosy ambience. Guest beers come from Yorkshire breweries. Excellent meals are served at lunchtime, and there are frequent themed food events: curry night, 'championship pie and peas', and more. A popular quiz is held on Sunday evening. ◐≋

Hales Bar

1-3 Crescent Road, HG1 2RS
⊛ 11-midnight (1am Thu-Sat)
☎ (01423) 725570
Daleside Special Bitter; Draught Bass; Tetley Bitter; guest beers ⊞
Traditional town-centre heritage pub, on CAMRA's regional inventory. Inside there are two rooms, each with its own servery. In the tap room, wooden casks are set into the wall behind the bar. The other room features more wooden casks, a collection of stuffed birds and an ornate ceiling. Original gas lanterns and gas cigar lighters have been retained. Guest beers are from the SIBA direct delivery scheme.
⊟≋⊟

Old Bell Tavern

6 Royal Parade, HG1 2SZ (500m W of A61)
⊛ 12-11 (10.30 Sun)
☎ (01423) 507930
Black Sheep Best Bitter; guest beers ⊞
One permanent and seven changing guest beers always include a mild, as well as Rooster's and Taylor brews. Deuchars and Theakston bitter alternate on one pump. The range is complemented by an extensive choice of foreign bottled beers plus three on draught. Dating back to 1846, the inn was expanded by extending into an old Farrah's toffee shop – see the memorabilia. Top-quality food is available in the bar area, and a restaurant upstairs opens in the evening.
Q◑≋⊟

Tap & Spile

Tower Street, HG1 1HS (100m E of A61)
⊛ 11.30-11; 12-10.30 Sun (hours may vary)
☎ (01423) 526785
Fuller's London Pride; Rooster's Yankee; Theakston Old Peculier; guest beers ⊞
Well-established, quality ale house with a central bar linking the three drinking areas. Wood panelling and bare brick walls display many photographs of old Harrogate. Popular with all ages, the pub stages a folk session on Tuesday and rock on Thursday. A quiz is held on Monday evening, and darts played on alternate Tuesdays and Wednesdays. The cider is Weston's Old Rosie. Some outdoor seating is provided. ❀≋⊟♣●⁵–

Winter Gardens

4 Royal Baths, HG1 2WH
✪ 9am-midnight (1am Fri & Sat)
☎ (01423) 887010
Marston's Burton Bitter, Pedigree; guest beers Ⓗ
Magnificently recreated main hall of the Victorian Royal Baths complex, with the Harrogate Turkish Baths next door. At least five guest beers are always available at reasonable prices, and a comprehensive range of bottles beers is also stocked. Regular mini beer festivals are hosted. Good food is served from opening. Children are welcome until 9pm on weekdays. ⏳✿◑🕭&➡️🚃

Hawes

Fountain Hotel

Market Place, DL8 3RD
✪ 11.30 (12 Sun)-11.30
☎ (01969) 667206 ⊕ fountainhawes.co.uk
Black Sheep Best Bitter, Emmerdale, Ale, Riggwelter; John Smith's Bitter Ⓗ
Located in the centre of the busy market town of Hawes in Wensleydale, this large, friendly, family-run hotel serves good local beers. It is particularly busy on Tuesday, which is market day. Walkers on the Pennine Way or coast-to-coast route as well as visitors to Hardraw Falls and Semerwater also enjoy stopping by – an ideal place for a pint and a bite to eat.
🏨✿🛏◑🛆🚃♣️P⌐

Hebden

Clarendon Hotel

BD23 5DE
✪ 12-11 (winter hours vary)
☎ (01756) 752446 ⊕ theclarendonhotel.co.uk
Black Sheep Best Bitter; Taylor Best Bitter; Tetley Bitter Ⓗ
A small family-owned hotel, the Clarendon is ideally situated for exploring the surrounding fells and Dales (walkers with clean boots welcome) and for touring the many historic towns of Yorkshire. It has a comfortable lounge bar and the dining room has a reputation for good, reasonably priced food, with steaks a speciality. ✿🛏◑🚃(72)♣️P

Helwith Bridge

Helwith Bridge

BD24 0EH (off B6479, across the river) OS810695
✪ 11 (12 Sun)-midnight
☎ (01729) 860220 ⊕ helwithbridge.com
Greene King Old Speckled Hen; Webster's Bitter; Wells Bombardier; guest beers Ⓗ
Friendly, characterful, stone-flagged community pub. Backing onto the River Ribble and overlooking the Settle-Carlisle railway line, it affords good views of Pen-y-Ghent (one of the Three Peaks). The landlord's interests are reflected in the numerous paintings, photographs and railway memorabilia. A roaring fire in the main bar is guaranteed in winter. Guest beers are mainly from the Scottish Courage list. The pub is popular with members of a local caving club who meet regularly at its hostel nearby.
🏨Q✿🛏◑🛆🚃♣️☗P

Hemingbrough

Crown

Main Street, YO8 6QE (off A63, E of Selby)
✪ 3-11 (11.30 Thu); 12-midnight Fri & Sat; 12-11 Sun
☎ (01757) 638434 ⊕ thecrowninn.net
Caledonian Deuchars IPA; John Smith's Bitter Ⓗ
At the heart of the village, beneath the elegant church spire, this is an unpretentious community pub that caters for local people. A central bar serves two rooms: the front room plays host to many sports teams, especially darts enthusiasts. The rear room is used by families at the weekend and diners in the evening (not Mon), who appreciate the fresh local ingredients used in the kitchen. Lunches are also served at weekends. On Thursday evening the quiz draws a crowd.
⏳✿◑🚃♣️P⌐

Hemlington

Gables

Bluebell Cottages, TS8 9DP (on B1365)
✪ 11 (12 Sun)-11
☎ (01642) 591452 ⊕ thegablespub.co.uk
Caledonian Deuchars IPA Ⓗ
Spacious roadside inn converted from farm cottages with a warm and comfortable open-plan interior. Only one of the two handpumps is currently in use. Low ceilings and wooden beams abound, yet these only date from the 1980s. A family-run pub for the last 20 years, families are warmly welcomed here.
✿◑&♣️P

High Leven

Fox Covert

TS15 9JW (on A1044 Acklam to Richmond road)
✪ 11.30-11.30 (midnight Fri & Sat)
☎ (01642) 760033 ⊕ thefoxcovert.com
Caledonian Deuchars IPA; Theakston Old Peculier Ⓗ
Long established as an inn, this old building of traditional longhouse style is easily recognisable as the farmhouse it once was. With whitewashed walls and a pantiled roof, it dominates the crossroads. This uniquely named pub, once a Vaux house, has been run by the same family for more than 20 years. There is a strong emphasis on food, but the ales are also superbly kept. 🏨✿◑P

Hubberholme

George Inn

Kirk Gill, BD23 5JE (opp church, 1 mile NW of Buckden, off B6160) OS926782
✪ 12-3, 6-11 daily; closed Mon except Bank holidays
☎ (01756) 760223 ⊕ thegeorge-inn.co.uk
Black Sheep Special; Copper Dragon Scotts 1816; guest beer Ⓗ
Sitting snugly alongside the River Wharfe, the hamlet of Hubberholme was named after a Viking chieftain called Hubba. This remote and unspoilt 18th-century inn was reputedly the author JB Priestley's favourite watering-hole. It boasts two rooms of genuine character with heavy oak beams, the walls stripped back to the bare stone and hung with antique plates and photos. An open stove in a large fireplace

welcomes visitors to the stone-flagged bar. Wholesome bar food is available at reasonable prices. ⚞Q❀✿✍◗P

Hutton Rudby

Bay Horse

1 North Side, TS15 0DA
🕑 12-2, 6.30 (7 Sun)-11
☎ (01642) 700252 ● the-bay-horse.co.uk
Black Sheep Best Bitter; Castle Eden Ale Ⓗ
Large family-run country inn, situated close to the river Leven in a convenient spot for exploring this picturesque village and walks along the river. There is a spacious lounge area and a small bar at the side, and extensive beautifully planted gardens at the rear. Original beams and features have been retained, though some Victorian chap has scratched his name on the historic windows. Never noisy, this is a good place for a chat or dinner. Q❀◖❀⬛&♣P

Ingleton

Wheatsheaf

22 High Street, LA6 3AD
🕑 12-11
☎ (01524) 241275 ● wheatsheaf-ingleton.co.uk
Black Sheep Best Bitter, Emmerdale; Taylor Golden Best; Tetley Bitter; guest beers Ⓗ
Handy for the Waterfalls Walk, the Wheatsheaf has a good reputation for food and accommodation, as well as beer. The long, narrow bar is divided into different areas: one end has a pool table, the other leads into the restaurant, which is as large as the bar. The guest beers stocked here often come from local Dales breweries. The attractive garden has an aviary with birds of prey.
⚞❀✿◖❀⬛♣⬅

Kettlesing

Queen's Head

HG3 2LB (off A59 W of Harrogate)
🕑 11-3, 6.30-11 (10.30 Sun)
☎ (01423) 770263
Black Sheep Best Bitter; Theakston Old Peculier; guest beers Ⓗ
Located in a quiet village, the Queen's Head is noted for its good food. An entrance lobby, dominated by images of Queen Elizabeth I, leads to two bars, one decorated with cricketing memorabilia, presumably to baffle the regulars from the nearby American base. Benches are put out in front of the pub in summer and there is a large patio at the rear. ⚞Q⟿❀✍◖P

Killinghall

Travellers Rest

Otley Road, HG3 2AP (at A59/B6161 jct)
🕑 11-11 (1am Fri & Sat); 12-11 Sun
☎ (01423) 503518
Tetley Bitter; guest beers Ⓗ
Modest roadside pub with a homely atmosphere that has the feel of a real local. The main entrance to the stone building leads to a small public bar and an equally small lounge, both warmed by real fires in winter.

The guest ale is often an unusual beer from a distant part of the country. No evening meals are served on Sunday. ⚞❀◖⬛P

Kirby Hill

Shoulder of Mutton

DL11 7JH (2½ miles from A66, 4 miles NW of Richmond)
🕑 12-3 (Sat only), 6-11.30; 12-3, 6-11 Sun
☎ (01748) 822772 ● shoulderofmutton.net
Black Sheep Best Bitter; Daleside Bitter; guest beers Ⓗ
Ivy-fronted country inn in a beautiful hillside setting, overlooking Lower Teesdale and the ruins of Ravensworth Castle. Situated opposite the church, the pub has an opened-out front bar that links with the lounge and restaurant to the rear. Two guest beers are chosen by the regulars. The pub hosts live music on Monday. Popular with walkers, there are five en-suite guest bedrooms. Evening meals are served Wednesday-Sunday. ⚞Q❀✍◖&♣P⬚

Kirk Smeaton

Shoulder of Mutton

Main Street, WF8 3JY (12-2, 6-midnight winter hours vary; 12-1am Fri & Sat) 12-midnight Sun
🕑 01977; 620348
Black Sheep Best Bitter; guest beers Ⓗ
Doncaster CAMRA District Pub of the Year 2007 is a popular, traditional village inn comprising a large lounge with two open fires and a cosy, dark-panelled snug. Popular with walkers from the nearby Went Valley and Brockadale Nature Reserve, the large beer garden is inviting for summer drinking. The beer is obtained direct from mainly local independent breweries. A quiz is held on Tuesday evening. ⚞❀⬛P

Kirkbymoorside

Kings Head

5 High Market Place, YO62 6AT
🕑 10-11; 12-10.30 Sun
☎ (01751) 431340 ● kingsheadkirkbymoorside.co.uk
Jennings Cumberland Ale, Lakeland Bitter, seasonal ales; guest beers Ⓗ
Situated in a town on the edge of the North York Moors, this handsome stone coaching inn was the venue for the Duke of Cumberland's orgies in the 17th century. Nowadays there is plenty of drinking space in the roomy bar and lounge areas. A wide selection of high-quality traditional dishes is available, prepared from local ingredients. Special events include monthly themed food evenings and a beer festival in September. A large conservatory overlooks the patio and walled gardens. ⚞Q⟿❀✍◖&⬛P⬅

Kirklevington

Crown

Thirsk Road, TS15 9LT (on A67 near A19, Crathorne interchange)
🕑 12-11 (10.30 Sun)
☎ (01642) 780044
Draught Bass; John Smith's Magnet Ⓗ

Transformed by the enthusiastic licensee from a rundown Whitbread house to a thriving village pub, the Crown is beside the former South Shields to Selby trunk road. The two bar areas have blazing log fires – an environmental health officer once famously complained that he could not find the tap to turn off the gas. Meals on the small yet impressive menu are created from fresh local produce. Lunch is served on Sunday (booking essential). 🏠♿🅭🌀🛏🐾P

Knaresborough

Blind Jack's

18A Market Place, HG5 8AL
☼ 4 (5.30 Mon; 3 Fri)-11; 12-11 Sat; 12-10.30 Sun
☎ (01423) 869148 ⊕ blindjacks.villagebrewer.co.uk/
Black Sheep Best Bitter; Taylor Landlord; Village White Boar Ⓗ
Winner of CAMRA's Best New Pub award in 1993, this ale house enjoys an excellent reputation that attracts customers from afar. Inside, dark wood panelling and bare floorboards create a traditional feel. The small bar serves two downstairs rooms and two smaller rooms upstairs. One of the nine handpumps is dedicated to Rooster's beers. A mild is always available, and the pub hosts the Mild Night Run in support of CAMRA's Mild Month in May. Q🚇🚆🅭🍺

George & Dragon

9 Briggate, HG5 8BQ
☼ 5-11 (midnight Fri); 12-midnight Sat & Sun
☎ (01423) 862792
John Smith's Bitter; guest beers Ⓗ
Winner of CAMRA Pub of the Season in 2005, this bright and comfortable town pub has an open-plan interior divided by a central bar. Beers from local brewers Daleside and Rooster's are always among the four guests. Dominoes, darts and pool are played, and rugby is screened on TV during the season. The backyard adjoins the grounds of Holy Trinity Church whose tall spire can be seen for miles. Wheelchair access is via the back door. Well-behaved dogs are welcome. ♿🐾🚆🅭🚌P

So Bar

1 Silver Street, HG5 8AJ (opp bus station)
☼ 11-11 (midnight Thu-Sat)
☎ (01423) 863202
Black Sheep Best Bitter; guest beers Ⓗ
This modern continental-style bar is justly proud of the range of drinks and quality of food it offers. A long bar features three handpumps and numerous fonts. Of the guest beers, one is always from Rooster's and the other from the SIBA direct delivery scheme. A wide selection of wines and foreign beers is also stocked, including Leffe Blonde on draught. The bar area has wooden tables and chairs and there is a comfortable lounge area with sofas. 🅭🚆🚌

Langdale End

Moorcock Inn

YO13 0BN OS938913
☼ 11-2, 6.30-11; 12-3, 6.30-10.30 Sun
☎ (01723) 882268

Beer range varies Ⓗ/Ⓖ
Sympathetically restored 16 years ago, the pub is set in a picturesque hamlet near the end of the Dalby Forest Drive. The beers, usually from Daleside, Wold Top and Slaters, are served through a hatch to both bars. It can be busy in summer, especially when the village cricket team is playing. There is a grassy area for outdoor drinking. Note that in winter opening hours may vary. Bar meals prepared from local produce include a popular steak pie. 🏠Q♿🅭🌀🏕🐾P🍴

Lastingham

Blacksmith's Arms

Front Street, YO62 6TL (4 miles N of A170 between Helmsley and Pickering)
☼ 12-midnight Fri-Sun & summer; 12-2.30 (not Tue), 6-midnight
☎ (01751) 417247
Theakston Best Bitter; guest beers Ⓗ
Pretty pub in a conservation village, opposite St Mary's Church, famous for its 11th-century Saxon crypt. It was once run by the vicar's wife who had 13 children; they are gone, but Ella remains in spirit. The cosy front bar has a large range, lit in winter; the adjoining room is served by a hatch. Do not miss the secluded rear garden. Excellent food includes local game dishes. The pub is popular with walkers and twice won local CAMRA Pub of the Season. 🏠Q♿🌀🏕🅭

Leavening

Jolly Farmer

Main Street, YO17 9SA
☼ 7 (6 Fri; 12 Sat)-11; 12-10.30 Sun
☎ (01653) 658276
John Smith's Bitter; Taylor Landlord; Tetley Bitter; guest beers Ⓗ
Former York CAMRA Pub of the Year, dating from the 17th century, lying between York and Malton on the edge of the Yorkshire Wolds. Despite extensions, the cosiness of its original multi-room layout has been retained, with two small bars, plus family and dining rooms. Guest ales often include stronger beers from independent breweries. The restaurant offers a wide range of dishes and specialises in locally caught game. 🏠🛏♿🅭🐾P🍴

Long Preston

Maypole Inn

Main Street, BD23 4PH
☼ 11-2.30, 6-midnight; 11-midnight Sat; 12-11 Sun
☎ (01729) 840219 ⊕ maypole.co.uk
Moorhouses Premier; Taylor Landlord; guest beers Ⓗ
Standing by the village green, where maypole dancing is still celebrated, this welcoming local has been in the same capable hands for 24 years. The cosy lounge displays old photos of the village and surrounding area and a list of all the licensees since 1695. Dogs are permitted in the tap room, which has carved Victorian bench seating. Good, home-cooked food is also available.
🏠Q♿🛏🅭🌀🏕🚆🐾P

Low Worsall

Ship

TS15 9PH

🕐 12-midnight

☎ (01642) 780314

Taylor Landlord; guest beers Ⓗ

Busy roadside inn standing beside the old turnpike road to Richmond. The Ship takes its name from the small, disused quay that once marked the limit of navigation for commercial boats on the River Tees. The interior is warm and friendly and the garden is delightful for children, home to rabbits and guinea pigs. Food is served all day every day, and the portions are impressive. The pub is not accessible by public transport.

Q⊛❶Ⓓ🖱♣P'—

Malham

Lister Arms

Gordale Scar Road, BD23 4DB

🕐 12-11 (12-3, 7-11 winter); 12-11.30 Fri & Sat; 12-11 Sun

☎ (01729) 830330 ⊕ listerarms.co.uk

Boddingtons Bitter; Caledonian Deuchars IPA; Taylor Landlord; guest beers Ⓗ

Built in the 17th century, this coaching inn takes its name from Thomas Lister, the first Lord of Ribblesdale. The tiled entrance leads to a main bar with a large inglenook and many other original features. Up to four guest ales are supplemented by a real cider or perry and a wide choice of British and foreign bottled beers, usually served in the correct glass. Internet access is available in the bar. Look out for the magnificent resident tabby cats.

🏠⊛🖱❶Ⓓ🖱▲🖱♣P

Malton

Crown Hotel (Suddaby's)

12 Wheelgate, YO17 7HP

🕐 11-11; 12-10.45 Sun

☎ (01653) 692038 ⊕ suddabys.co.uk

Malton Double Chance, Golden Chance, Auld Bob, seasonal beers; John Smith's Bitter; guest beers Ⓗ

This Grade II listed market town-centre pub has been in the Suddaby family for 137 years. No brewing takes place on the premises now; beers are contract-brewed at Cropton and Brown Cow. It stages beer festivals at Easter, in summer and at Christmas. The on-site beer shop stocks more than 300 bottled beers mainly from micro-breweries and from Belgium, as well as wines and breweriana. Accommodation includes two en-suite family rooms. CAMRA members can claim a discount.

🏠Q🍽⊛🖱🛏🖱P'—

Manfield

Crown Inn

Vicars Lane, DL2 2RF (500m from B6275)

🕐 5 (6 winter)-11, 12-11.30 Sat; 12-11 Sun

☎ (01325) 374243 ⊕ crowninn.villagebrewer.co.uk

Village White Boar, Bull; guest beers Ⓗ

Yorkshire CAMRA Pub of the Year 2005 and a regular local award winner, this attractive 18th-century pub in a quiet village has two bars, a games room and lounge. A mix of locals and visitors creates a friendly atmosphere. Up to six guest beers come from micro-breweries countrywide; one or two ciders or perries are also stocked. Each year, the Crown Inn hosts two beer festivals and a cider festival. Dogs are welcome in this rural gem. 🏠Q⊛❶Ⓓ🖱♣♣P🍽

Masham

Black Sheep Brewery Visitors Centre

Wellgarth, HG4 4EN (follow brown tourist signs on A6108)

🕐 10-5; 11-3.30 winter; 10-11 Thu-Sat; 10.30-4.30 Sun

☎ (01765) 680100 ⊕ blacksheep.co.uk

Black Sheep Best Bitter, Special, Emmerdale, Riggwelter Ⓗ

This popular tourist attraction is housed in the spacious former maltings. As well as offering the opportunity to sample the brewery's products (plus a good range of foreign bottles beers) at the 'baaar', there is a high quality cafe/bistro serving snacks and full meals with an emphasis on local ingredients. A 'sheepy' shop stocks the bottled product and Black Sheep souvenirs. Visitors can book a 'shepherded' tour of the brewery. A small garden overlooks scenic Lower Wensleydale and the River Ure. ⊛❶Ⓓ🖱🚌(144, 159)P

White Bear

12 Crosshills, HG4 4EN (follow brown tourist signs on A6108)

🕐 12-11 (10.30 Sun)

☎ (01765) 689319

Caledonian Deuchars IPA; Theakston Best Bitter, Black Bull Bitter, XB, Old Peculier; guest beers Ⓗ

The original White Bear, situated some 100 metres away, was bombed in 1941 and the present pub was converted from brewery cottages belonging to the former Lightfoot Brewery. The impressive stone building houses two bars: a spacious lounge offering meals (not Sun eve) and occasional live music, and a more traditional public bar. Both have roaring fires in winter. The eponymous white bear stands stuffed at the back of the bar. Note the stained glass panels behind the bar depicting a cooper's shop.

🏠⊛❶Ⓓ🖱🚌(144, 159)♣P

Maunby

Buck Inn

YO7 4HD (signed from A167 at South Otterington and Kirkby Wiske)

🕐 12-2, 5-11; 12-11 Fri-Sun

☎ (01845) 587777 ⊕ buckinnmaunby.co.uk

John Smith's Bitter; guest beers Ⓗ

Slightly off the beaten track, it is well worth making the effort to find this former 18th-century dower house, with its warm, friendly atmosphere, oak beams and open fires. A thriving village local today, it has an excellent restaurant (booking recommended), which can also be booked for functions – the pub is licensed for civil wedding ceremonies. Children are welcome. 🏠Q⊛❶Ⓓ♣P'—

Muker

Farmers Arms

DL11 6QG (on B6270)
🕓 11.30-midnight daily
☎ (01748) 886297
Black Sheep Best Bitter; John Smith's Bitter; Theakston Best Bitter; guest beers Ⓗ
In the heart of beautiful Swaledale, a remote former lead-mining village, the inn attracts ramblers, cyclists and day trippers as well as locals. A recent refurbishment has preserved many original features, including the stone-flagged floor and welcoming open fire. This is a cosy pub with a warm and homely atmosphere. 🛆Q🕭🕹🕪🕩♣P

Newton on Ouse

Blacksmith's Arms

Cherry Tree Avenue, YO30 2BN
🕓 5.30-11.30; 12-3, 5.30-11 Fri & Sat; 12-10.30 Sun
☎ (01347) 848249
Cameron's Bitter; Jennings Dark Mild, Cumberland Ale; guest beers Ⓗ
Within walking distance of the National Trust Beningbrough Hall, this family-run country pub is a popular destination for cyclists and walkers. Inside it has three distinct areas: a dining and family area, bar and games room. The building used to house the Beningbrough Estate blacksmith's shop, and there are pictures of the village in bygone days, plus a collection of modern sporting items reflecting the family's connections with sport.
🛆Q🕭🕹🕪🕩♣P

Northallerton

Standard

24 High Street, DL7 8EE
🕓 12-3, 5-midnight; 12-midnight Fri-Sun
☎ (01609) 772719
Caledonian Deuchars IPA; Marston's Pedigree; John Smith's Bitter; guest beers Ⓗ
The pub is named after the Battle of Northallerton, better known as the Battle of the Standard in 1138, which was a notable defeat for the Scottish. Today, the Standard is a very welcoming pub; attractive decor with flagstone flooring, extensive wooden panelling and pictures of local scenes and aircraft help to promote a village pub feel, despite its location on the High Street. The aircraft theme is continued in the beer garden, which displays a jet. 🕭🕩🕪♣➖

Tithe Bar & Brasserie

2 Friarage Street, DL6 1DP (off High St near hospital)
🕓 12-11 (12.30am Fri & Sat)
☎ (01609) 778482 🌐 markettowntaverns.co.uk
Taylor Landlord; guest beers Ⓗ
A CAMRA award winner with the feel of a Belgian-style café bar, this member of the Market Town Taverns chain features bare floorboards and walls decorated with brewery posters. In a handy spot for the town centre, the Tithe Bar is a peaceful haven in the afternoon but gets busy most evenings. Almost a mini beer exhibition, a range of bottled beers from around the world is always available. Appetising bar meals are served

downstairs, upstairs is a brasserie.
Q🕭🕹🕭🕪🕩♦

Nun Monkton

Alice Hawthorn

The Green, YO26 8EW (off A59 York-Harrogate road)
🕓 12-2, 6-11; 12-10.30 Sun
☎ (01423) 330303 🌐 alicehawthorn.co.uk
Black Sheep Best Bitter; Caledonian Deuchars IPA; John Smith's Bitter; Taylor Landlord; guest beers Ⓗ
Isolated by the Rivers Ouse and Nidd, the village is accessible only via a remote country lane. The cosy pub, named after a racehorse famous in the 1840s, overlooks the village green complete with a maypole and duck pond. Popular with walkers, a wide range of home-cooked food is served by the convivial landlord of 25 years standing. There is a patio garden at the rear, which features a well-equipped children's playground.
🛆Q🕭🕩🕭🕹A♣P➖

Osmotherley

Golden Lion

6 West End, DL6 3AA (1 mile off A19, at A684 jct)
🕓 12-3.30, 6-11; 12-midnight Sat; 12-10.30 Sun
☎ (01609) 883526 🌐 goldenlionosmotherley.co.uk
John Smith's Bitter; Taylor Landlord; guest beers Ⓗ
On the edge of the North York Moors and close to the A19, the village and the pub are popular with visitors, especially ramblers. A CAMRA award winner, the pub has a fine reputation for its food, much of it locally sourced. It has a dining room upstairs and a small patio, with tables in the street. Drinkers enjoy the annual beer festival in November. The one-roomed bar features stone flags and whitewashed stone walls, candlelight and a plethora of mirrors, giving it a romantic atmosphere.
🛆🕭🕩A🖃

Patrick Brompton

Green Tree

DL8 1JW
🕓 12-3 (Sat only), 6 (5.15 Fri)-11; closed Tue; 12-3, 7-10.30 Sun
☎ (01677) 450262
Black Sheep Best Bitter; Taylor Landlord; guest beers Ⓗ
Nestling next to the ancient village church at the foot of Wensleydale on the Bedale to Leyburn road, this simple but welcoming Grade II listed building comprises a small but pleasant public bar with an open fire and an adjoining dining room. Motorists using the car park should beware the narrow entrance.
🛆Q🕭🕩🖃🖃♣P

Pickering

Rose

Bridge Street, YO18 8DT (opp Beck Isle Museum)
🕓 12-midnight (1am Fri & Sat)
☎ (01751) 475366
Taylor Landlord; Tetley Bitter Ⓗ

A welcoming atmosphere greets locals and steam railway enthusiasts at this multi-roomed low-ceilinged pub, situated on the banks of the attractive Pickering Beck and opposite the Beck Isle Museum of Country Life. The Pickering terminus of the North York Moors Steam Railway is also nearby. Meals are made with locally sourced produce. There is an extensive outdoor drinking area next to the Beck. Children are welcome until 8pm. The pub has flooded five times in eight years in times of torrential rain. ﴾symbols﴿

Pickhill

Nag's Head

YO7 4JG (on B6267, off A1 between Thirsk and Masham) OS346835
🕓 11-11 daily
☎ (01845) 567391 🌐 nagsheadpickhill.co.uk
Black Sheep Best Bitter; Hambleton Bitter; Theakston Best Bitter; guest beers Ⓗ
An undisputed entry in the Guide, the Nag's Head has won plenty of CAMRA awards. The owner has a policy of serving locally brewed beers and offers a very high standard of service. Food, available in the first-rate restaurant, lounge or public bar, is of an exceptionally high standard. Accommodation is superb, making this a good base for exploring the Dales and North York Moors. ﴾symbols﴿

Picton

Station Hotel

TS15 0EA (beside the level crossing on Picton to Kirklevington road)
🕓 11-4 (Sat & Sun only), 6-11
☎ (01642) 700067
John Smith's Magnet Ⓗ
This well-run village pub beside the Teesside to Northallerton railway line takes its name from the station, which closed in the 1960s. The pub, although remote, is well worth seeking out, welcoming its guests with a warm atmosphere and a good range of beers. All meals are prepared on the premises using fresh ingredients, and diners never leave hungry. ﴾symbols﴿

Pool in Wharfedale

Hunter's Inn

Harrogate Road, LS21 2PS (on A658 Harrogate-Otley road)
🕓 11-11; 12-10.30 Sun
☎ (0113) 284 1090
Tetley Bitter; Theakston Best Bitter; guest beers Ⓗ
Roadside pub with the feel of a country lodge, enhanced by a balcony furnished with tables and warmed by a roaring fire in colder months. The inn always offers seven frequently-changing guest beers from around the country. This is a very popular pub, catering for all tastes. Children are welcome until 9pm; dogs are also admitted. ﴾symbols﴿ (653, 967) ♣P

Ripon

Magdalens

26 Princess Road, HG4 1HW
🕓 12-midnight (2am Fri & Sat)
☎ (01765) 604746
John Smith's Bitter; Theakston Bitter; guest beers Ⓗ
Very much a locals pub, Magdalens supports darts, dominoes and pool teams with many sporting trophies adorning the walls. The bar runs the entire length of a comfortable lounge. The pub overlooks the River Ure and is in easy walking distance of Ripon Minster. It is also close to the old police station, which has been transformed into a fascinating police museum. ❀♣P

One-Eyed Rat

51 Allhallowgate, HG4 1LQ (near bus station)
🕓 5 (12 Fri & Sat)-11; 12-10.30 Sun
☎ (01765) 607704 🌐 oneeyedrat.com
Black Sheep Best Bitter; guest beers Ⓗ
A regular entry in the Guide for the past 12 years, this small-fronted but Tardis-like pub is tucked away in the oldest part of town. Five guest beers from small and regional breweries are always available, in addition to three continental lagers on draught and mulled and fruit wines. Nearby are the Workhouse and Courthouse Museums which give a glimpse of life in Victorian times. The Courthouse featured in the TV series Heartbeat, as Ashfordly Magistrates Court. ﴾symbols﴿

Royal Oak

36 Kirkgate, HG4 1PB
🕓 11-11 (midnight Fri & Sat); 12-10.30 Sun
☎ (01765) 602284 🌐 timothytaylor.co.uk/royaloak
Taylor Golden Best, Best Bitter, Landlord Ⓗ
The Grade II listed Royal Oak is situated just off the historic Market Square where the official hornblower has been sounding his horn for hundreds of years at nine o'clock every night. The large pub interior features beer casks and brewing memorabilia. Prince Charles has called in twice on his visits to Ripon. ﴾symbols﴿

Robin Hood's Bay

Dolphin

King Street, YO22 4SH (400m from seafront)
🕓 11 (12 winter)-11; 12-10.30 Sun
☎ (01947) 880337
Caledonian Deuchars IPA; Theakston Best Bitter, Old Peculier; Wells Bombardier Ⓗ
Friendly, old-fashioned village pub boasting an open coal fire and beamed bar. The single ground-floor room serves as a bar and dining room, decorated with old bottles and pump clips from beers sold here over the years. An upstairs room is used for families and provides further space for diners enjoying good home-made food. Friday is folk night, a quiz is staged on Sunday. Two benches at the front allow drinkers to enjoy the sea views. ﴾symbols﴿

Victoria Hotel

Station Road, YO22 4RL (at the top of the cliff)
🕓 12-11 Fri-Sun & summer; 12-2.30, 6-11
☎ (01947) 880205 🌐 thevictoriahotel.info

Banks's Bitter; Camerons Stongarm; Durham Magus; guest beers Ⓗ
An impressive hotel built in 1897 on the edge of the cliffs providing stunning views over the bay. As well as four or five real ales, the Victoria offers a menu of good-quality home-cooked fare that can be enjoyed in either the dining room or family room. The bar is light and airy with a large window at the front.
🏠Q🛏️❄️⊞◐P

Runswick Bay

Royal Hotel

TS13 5HT (off A174 at Hinderwell)
🕐 11-11 Fri-Sun & summer; 11-3, 5.30-11
☎ (01947) 840215
Black Sheep Best Bitter, Emmerdale; Tetley Bitter; guest beers Ⓗ
Old seaside hotel snuggled against the cliffs between the cottages in the village centre. There is a large front bar with an open fire, a quiet back bar, recently renovated in traditional Yorkshire style with settles, and an upstairs dining room affording good views over the bay. The patio enjoys fresh sea air, with a heater for cooler evenings. Popular with walkers along the Cleveland Way; after a few drinks the walk up the bank appears less daunting. 🏠Q❄️⊞◐ Å ♣

Ruswarp

Bridge Inn

High Street, YO21 1NJ (by bridge over River Esk)
🕐 7-midnight; 12-3, 7-1am Sat; 12-midnight Sun
☎ (01947) 602780
John Smith's Bitter; Wells Bombardier Ⓗ
Walk across the fields from Whitby, row up the Esk to the Sleights, take a trip on the Esk Valley Railway or the miniature steam trains, and drop in at the Bridge for a friendly pint. This traditional village ale house has a garden opening directly onto the river. There are two bars, entered by stepping down from the pavement, with a pool room on the right. No meals are served, but the pub is popular with folk from Ruswarp (pronounced Ruzz'p).
🏠❄️ Å ≈ ♣

Saltburn by the Sea

New Marine

Marine Parade, TS12 1DZ (on top promenade)
🕐 12-11 (10.30 Sun)
☎ (01287) 622695
Beer range varies Ⓗ
Converted from a small hotel, the bar caters for young or livelier folk with jukebox, TV and pool table, while the lounge is quiet. Both rooms are comfortably furnished and have a warm, welcoming atmosphere. An upstairs restaurant doubles as a bar and function room. The front patio affords a vista from the Durham coastline across the Tees estuary to the high cliffs of North Yorkshire. Nearby is the most northerly pier in England and a water-powered funicular rail lift to the sandy beach.
Q❄️◐ 🍴♿ Å ≈ 🖥

Saltburn Cricket, Bowls & Tennis Club

Marske Mill Lane, TS12 1HJ (by leisure centre)
🕐 8-midnight (1am Fri & Sat); 2-midnight Sat match days; 11.30-3, 8-midnight Sun
☎ (01287) 622761
Beer range varies Ⓗ
Private sports club fielding cricket, tennis and bowls teams; local divers also come here to relax. Its spacious lounge overlooks the cricket field and Tees Bay, and can be divided for private functions. A balcony overlooking the cricket pitch extends the drinking space on fine-weather days. Casual visitors are welcome without joining and may attend social events. The club normally keeps a choice of two or three real ales, sourced from Coors and S&N. ❄️♿ Å ≈ ♣ P

Sandsend

Hart Inn

East Row, YO21 3SU (on main road through village A174) OS862124
🕐 12-3, 6-11
☎ (01947) 893304
Black Sheep Best Bitter; Camerons Strongarm; guest beers Ⓗ
The monks who are reputed to have built this inn on the way to Whitby Abbey chose a lovely setting just off the beach. The inn still has its original beams and retains a traditional village pub atmosphere. The pub is popular with locals, visitors to the beach and diners. The name supposedly commemorates the hart that fell from a precipice in nearby Mulgrave Woods. 🏠❄️◐ Å ♣ P

Saxton

Greyhound

Main Street, LS24 9PY (W of A162, 5 miles S of Tadcaster)
🕐 11-3, 5.30-11; 11-11 Sat; 12-10.30 Sun
☎ (01937) 557202
Samuel Smith OBB Ⓗ
Originally a teasel barn, nestling by the village church (some occupants of the graveyard are said to still drop in for a quick one), this picturesque, Grade II listed, 13th-century, whitewashed village inn, formerly listed in CAMRA's National Inventory for pubs with outstanding interiors, is favoured by locals and walkers. A low-ceilinged, stone-flagged corridor leads to a tiny bar. Real fires blaze in two of the three rooms in winter; admire the extensive collection of colourful wall plates in two rooms. 🏠Q🛏️❄️⊞♿♣ 🍴

Scarborough

Cellars

35-37 Valley Road, YO11 2LX
🕐 12 (4 Mon & Tue winter)-11; 12-10.30 Sun
☎ (01723) 367158 🌐 scarborough-brialene.co.uk
Beer range varies Ⓗ
Family-run pub, converted from the cellars of an elegant Victorian house. The bar keeps four guest beers, including ales from Archers and Durham breweries. Excellent, good value food is served; all meals are cooked on the

premises using produce from local suppliers. The pub hosts live music on Saturday evening, majoring on blues, and an open mike night on Wednesday. Beer festivals are staged occasionally. The patio and gardens are popular for alfresco drinking, and children and dogs are welcome. ⑤❀🖾◑🅐➡🖃♣P

Indigo Alley

4 North Marine Road, YO12 7PD
◐ 4pm-2am daily
☎ (01723) 381900
Beer range varies Ⓗ

Lively, popular, one-roomed pub, offering five constantly changing real ales including a regular Rooster's brew. Belgian Leffe blonde and brown beers as well as Hoegaarden are sold on draught. Live music is performed several times a week. Local CAMRA Pub of the Year for three consecutive years, this is an absolute cracker and not to be missed. ➡

Lord Rosebery

85-87 Westborough, YO11 1JW
◐ 9-midnight (1am Fri & Sat)
☎ (01723) 361191
Greene King Abbot; Marston's Pedigree, Old Empire; guest beers Ⓗ

Located in the centre of town close to the rail station and many bus routes, this prominent Victorian building was once the Liberal Club, opened in 1895 by Lord Rosebery. Latterly it became a furniture store before conversion by Wetherspoon. The bars are on two floors, the walls adorned with pictures and displays depicting the town's history, as well as large mock seaside postcards. Up to 10 guest beers are available. Children are welcome until 9pm if dining. ◑🅓&➡🖃♦

North Riding Hotel

161-163 North Marine Road, YO12 7HU
◐ 12-midnight (1am Fri & Sat)
☎ (01723) 370004
Caledonian Deuchars IPA; Taylor Landlord; Tetley Bitter; guest beers Ⓗ

Friendly and increasingly popular pub voted local CAMRA Town Pub of the Year 2006. Located near the cricket ground on the North Bay, it has a public bar, quiet lounge and upstairs dining room serving home-cooked food. It stocks two (more in season) guest beers from micro-breweries, as well as draught Erdinger, Frambozen, Kriek and bottled Belgian beers. Seasonal beer festivals and a weekly quiz on Thursday are hosted. Q🖾◑🅑🖃♣

Old Scalby Mills

Scalby Mills Road, YO12 6RP
◐ 11 (12 winter)-11
☎ (01723) 500449
Wychwood Hobgoblin; guest beers Ⓗ

Favoured by walkers, tourists and locals, this seafront building was originally a watermill but has seen many uses over the years; old photographs and prints chart its history. Admire the superb views of the North Bay and castle from the sheltered patio or lounge. The Cleveland Way reaches the seafront here and there is a Sea Life Centre nearby. Children are welcome in the lounge until 11pm. Beers from

the local Wold Top brewery are usually stocked here. 🏚Q❀⑤❀◑🅑🅐♣ꜝ

Scholars

Somerset Terrace, YO11 2PW
◐ 12-midnight (1am Fri & Sat) summer; 4.30 (12 Sat)-midnight winter; 1 (4.30 winter)-10.30 Sun
☎ (01723) 360084
Beer range varies Ⓗ

Situated in an elegant Regency crescent and recently refurbished, the pub has a warm, friendly atmosphere in the large front bar and games room. Six handpumps dispense beers from Hambleton, Copper Dragon, Durham and Yorkshire micro-breweries. Sky TV broadcasts all major sporting events. No meals are available. &🅐➡🖃♣

Tap & Spile

94 Falsgrave Road, YO12 5AZ
◐ 11-11.30 (midnight Fri & Sat)
☎ (01723) 363837
Adnams Broadside; Caledonian Deuchars IPA; Everards Tiger; Taylor Landlord; Tetley Bitter; Wychwood Hobgoblin; guest beers Ⓗ

Sympathetically restored former coaching inn offering six permanent real ales and six rotating guests from around the country. A three-roomed local, excellent value meals are served at lunchtime, and the family-friendly enclosed patio beer garden has barbecues in summer. Children are welcome until 9pm, and dogs are permitted in the bars. There is regular live music on Thursday, Saturday and Sunday and quizzes are hosted on Monday and Wednesday. ❀◑🅐➡🖃♣♦ꜝ

Valley

51 Valley Road, YO11 2LX
◐ 12-midnight (1am Thu-Sat)
☎ (01723) 372593 ⊕ valleybar.co.uk
Theakston Best Bitter; Wold Top Mars Magic; guest beers Ⓗ

Local CAMRA Town Pub of the Year 2005 and runner-up in 2006, this family-run, multi-roomed pub has a popular cellar bar. Seven handpumps feature beers from local micros, while beer festivals during the winter months feature ales from other counties. Three to four real ciders are also available. The kitchen prepares good quality meals at reasonable prices, and there is a Sunday lunchtime carvery. Special Asian food nights are held at weekends. Children and dogs are welcome. ❀🖾◑🅐➡🖃♣♦ꜛ

Skipton

Narrow Boat

38 Victoria Street, BD23 1JE (alley off Coach St near canal bridge)
◐ 12-11
☎ (01756) 797922 ⊕ markettowntaverns.co.uk
Black Sheep Best Bitter; Caledonian Deuchars IPA; Taylor Landlord; guest beers Ⓗ

Popular free house near the canal basin. The single bar is furnished with old church pews and decorated with canal-themed murals, old brewery posters and mirrors; no juke box or gaming machines disturb the conversation. Guest ales from northern independents usually include one from the local Copper Dragon Brewery; it stocks a good selection of continental bottled beers. Monthly jazz is held on the first Tuesday and folk on alternate Sundays; Wednesday is quiz night. Children under 14 are admitted for meals; well-behaved dogs are welcome. Q❁❀❁❁❁❁❁

Snape

Castle Arms

DL8 2TB (off B6268, Bedale-Masham road)
☼ 12-3, 6-midnight (1am Thu-Sat); 12-3, 7-midnight Sun
☎ (01677) 470270
Jennings Bitter, Cumberland Ale; Marston's Pedigree; guest beers Ⓗ
Named after Snape Castle, once home of Catherine Parr, wife of Henry VIII, the Castle has an open, friendly bar with a stone-flagged floor and large fireplace. Known for its locally sourced food, the restaurant is excellent. Four-star accommodation registered with the AA and the Yorkshire Tourist Board is available in a converted barn to the rear. Quoits is played in summer. Camping and caravan facilities are available to Caravan Club members.
❁Q❁❁❁❁❁A❁P

Sneaton

Wilson Arms

Beacon Way, YO22 5HS (off B1416)
☼ 12-2 (not winter), 6.30 (7 winter)-11; 12-11 (12-4, 6.30-11 winter) Sun
☎ (01947) 602552
Black Sheep Best Bitter; John Smith's Bitter; guest beers Ⓗ
Sneaton, well-known for the ice cream produced here, is a quiet village above the River Esk. It can be reached by walking across the fields from Sleights or Robin Hood's Bay. The Wilson Arms stands near the end of the village, a half-timbered building with a single bar to the right. Popular with diners and weekend visitors, it stocks excellent beer and a fine selection of malt whiskies.
❁Q❁❁❁❁❁A❁P

Staithes

Captain Cook Inn

60 Staithes Lane, TS13 5AD (off A174)
☼ 11-11
☎ (01947) 840020 ⊕ captaincookinn.co.uk
Rudgate Viking Bitter; guest beers Ⓗ
Staithes is an olde-worlde fishing village, situated at the end of a deep, narrow valley. Overlooking the bank and affording stunning views to Boulby Cliff, England's highest at 666ft, stands the Captain Cook Inn, a former local CAMRA Pub of the Year. Dark ales (mild and porter) are usually available at the weekend, and there are regular beer festivals to celebrate St George's Day, Lifeboat Day and Guy Fawkes' Night or Halloween. There are plans to develop a restaurant.
❁Q❁❁❁❁A❁❁P

Staxton

Hare & Hounds

Main Street, YO12 4TA (on A64)
☼ 12-11.30 (10.30 Sun)
☎ (01944) 710243
John Smith's Bitter; Stones Bitter; Theakston Old Peculier; guest beers Ⓗ
Busy roadside inn, seven miles from Scarborough, which served the coaching trade during the 19th century. The bar and lounge/dining area feature low beams and open fires, and offer a peaceful oasis on the main road. Guest beers come from the local Enterprise SIBA scheme – Wold Top Mars Magic is a frequent choice. Meals are cooked on the premises. There are tables at the front and a large grassed area to the rear for summer drinking. ❁Q❁❁❁A❁❁P❁

Stokesley

White Swan

1 West End, TS9 5BL
☼ 11.30-3 (Mon, Wed & Thu), 5-11; 11.30-11 Fri & Sat; 12-3, 7-10.30 Sun
☎ (01642) 710263
Captain Cook Sunset, Slipway, seasonal beers; Tetley Imperial Ⓗ
Old-fashioned town pub, concentrating on brewing and selling quality ales – the White Swan has its own micro-brewery on site. The pub is situated in one of the prettiest parts of this fine little market town, overlooking the green. A quiz night is held on Wednesday evening. Food is only available during the annual Cheese and Ale Festival over the Easter weekend. The pub is served by buses from the surrounding villages. ❁Q❁

Sutton-in-Craven

Dog & Gun Inn

Colne Road, Malsis, BD20 8DS (on A6068 between Colne and Cross Hills)
☼ 12-2.30, 5-11; 12-11 Sat; 12-10.30 Sun
☎ (01535) 633855
Taylor Dark Mild, Golden Best, Best Bitter, Landlord, Ram Tam; guest beer Ⓗ
Formerly a farmhouse and coaching inn, the Dog & Gun is now an attractive roadside pub offering a warm welcome with a comfortable interior and friendly staff. It has several areas including a library corner, plus a working stove and fireplace. Renowned for its good-quality home-cooked food, it also features in CAMRA's Good Pub Food Guide. Very popular with families for dining, booking is advisable at peak times. ❁❁❁❁❁❁P

Tadcaster

Angel & White Horse

23 Bridge Street, LS24 9AW
☼ 11-3, 5-11; 12-4, 7-11 Sat; 12-3, 7-10.30 Sun
☎ (01937) 835470
Samuel Smith OBB Ⓗ
Samuel Smith's brewery tap in the town centre is an old coaching inn with a late-Georgian facade. At the front, large bay windows overlook the main street of this market town, while the side windows have views of the brewery yard and the stables, famous for the grey dray shire horses. Hot food is served from the carvery at lunchtime (no food Sat) in the large wood-panelled bar. The pub gets busy with drinkers enjoying the

excellent, low-priced ale from their local independent brewery. Q❀◑🖵

Thixendale

Cross Keys
YO17 9TG OS842612
✪ 12-3, 6-11; 12-3, 7-10.30 Sun
☎ (01377) 288272
Jennings Bitter; Tetley Bitter; guest beers Ⓗ
Thixendale is a picturesque village in the Yorkshire Wolds at the junction of several typical dry glacial Wolds valleys. Inhabited since the Stone Age, many tracks established in Roman times are still used today by walkers in the dramatic surrounding countryside. The hostelry is an unspoilt, unpretentious village local with a single bar, serving guest beers from independent breweries and good value, home-cooked food. Children are welcome in the garden. ⋈❀❀◑♣

Thoralby

George Inn
DL8 3SU (off A684)
✪ 12-3 (closed Mon), 6.30-11 (1am Fri & Sat); 12-3, 6.30-10.30 Sun
☎ (01969) 663256 ⊕ thegeorge.tv
Black Sheep Best Bitter; guest beers Ⓗ
The George Inn is situated in the picturesque village of Thoralby in Bishopdale, a hidden oasis in the heart of the Yorkshire Dales National Park. A changing beer from Copper Dragon is always stocked plus a guest ale. It has a cobbled area at the front for summer drinking. A bus service passes through the village three times a day. ⋈Q❀❀◑Å🖵♣P

Thorganby

Ferryboat Inn
Ferry Lane, YO19 6DD (1 mile NE of village, signed from main road) OS697426
✪ 7-11; closed Mon; 12-midnight Sat; 12-4, 7-11 Sun
☎ (01904) 448224
Acorn Barnsley Bitter; guest beers Ⓗ
Former ferryman's house at the end of a narrow lane beside the River Derwent. This remote family-run inn has one small bar and an excellent family room which leads out to the large lawn that slopes down to the tree-lined river. Families, walkers, cyclists, boaters and anglers come here to enjoy the eclectic mix of beers from Yorkshire micros and further afield. A haven of tranquillity, there is no music or gaming machines. Home to local dominoes and quiz teams. ⋈Q❀❀&Å🖵♣P▯

Thornton-in-Lonsdale

Marton Arms
LA6 3PB (quarter mile from A65/A687 jct)
✪ 11 (5 winter)-11; 11-10.30 Sun
☎ (01524) 241281 ⊕ martonarms.co.uk
Black Sheep Best Bitter; Caledonian Deuchars IPA; Moorhouses Black Cat; Taylor Landlord; Theakston Old Peculier; guest beers Ⓗ
The Marton Arms is situated in a tiny hamlet close to the inn, the village stocks and St Oswald's Church, where Sir Arthur Conan

Doyle once married. The original pub dates from the 13th century, but has been extensively modernised. It is extremely popular with visitors, attracted by the pub's reputation for its real ale dispensed from 16 handpumps and the assortment of whiskies it stocks. Walkers on the Ingleton Waterfall Walk also call in. ❀◑&♣♠P⌐

Thruscross

Stonehouse Inn
Duck Street, HG3 4AH (2 miles N of A59 at Blubberhouses) OSSE1658
✪ 12-3, 6-11; closed Mon; 12-5 Sun
☎ (01943) 880325
Black Sheep Best Bitter; guest beers Ⓗ
This rural pub, built 300 years ago, reopened in 2005 after a period of closure. The family-run inn is characterised by exposed beams, a Yorkshire stone-flagged floor, settles and a stone-fronted bar. Two snug alcoves give a feeling of partial seclusion. The pub runs a darts team, with matches on alternate Tuesdays, and hosts a weekly open dominoes competition. The menu caters for vegetarians, and breakfast can be served by arrangement. Popular with locals and walkers. ⋈❀◑P

Warthill

Agar Arms
YO19 5XW (off A166, 5 miles NE of York)
✪ 11.30-2.30, 6.30-11; 12-2.30, 7-11 Sun
☎ (01904) 488142
Samuel Smith OBB Ⓗ
On a bank overlooking the village pond, there is an air of tranquillity about this pub. A well in the floor is testament to the building's origins as a smithy. The interior is traditional, with high, dark-timbered ceilings and panelled walls. A full range of the independent brewery's merchandise is available, but it keeps only one cask-conditioned beer. Renowned for excellent food, meals are served at lunchtime and early evening. ⋈Q❧❀◑P

West Ayton

Olde Forge Valley
5 Pickering Road, YO13 9JE
✪ 11.30-11 (2am Fri & Sat; 1am Sun)
☎ (01723) 862146
Black Sheep Best Bitter; Caledonian Deuchars IPA; Tetley Bitter; guest beers Ⓗ
Attractive Tudor-style coaching inn, built around 1785 alongside John Carr's bridge over the River Derwent, situated within the North Yorkshire Moors. Inside, it has a lounge, back bar, dining room and a spectacular function room with a high, beamed ceiling, wall tapestries and real fire. Home-cooked meals including a traditional Sunday lunch are served. The pub has a large beer garden; children and dogs are welcome. Thursday is folk night and jazz plays on the last Wednesday of the month. ⋈❧❀❀◑⊟Å🖵♣P⌐

West Witton

Fox & Hounds

Main Street, DL8 4LP (on A684)

🕐 12-4, 6-midnight; 12-midnight Sat & Sun

☎ (01969) 623650 🌐 foxwitton.com

Black Sheep Best Bitter; John Smith's Bitter; guest beers Ⓗ

This CAMRA award-winning free house has been run by the same family for 11 years. A Grade II listed building dating back to 1400, the Fox & Hounds was originally a rest house for monks from Jervaulx. The welcoming bar is separated from the pool and darts area by the fireplace; the dining room boasts an inglenook and beehive oven. It offers two guest beers, often from Yorkshire micros. Good value meals are served all week, including a Sunday roast. A Friday quiz and Saturday piano session alternate fortnightly. ♨⚅🚲▲🚗🍴🐕P🗜

York

Blue Bell ☆

53 Fossgate, YO1 9TF

🕐 11-11; 12-10.30 Sun

☎ (01904) 654904

Adnams Bitter; Caledonian Deuchars IPA; Taylor Landlord; Tetley Mild; guest beers Ⓗ

Local CAMRA Pub of the Year 2007, this is a tiny pub with a big heart, twice winner of the Morning Advertiser fundraising Pub of the Year. Dating back to 1798, it has the city's only surviving perfect Edwardian interior, refurbished in 1903. The fully panelled drinking corridor, bar and snug provide a cosy retreat from the nearby hurly-burly of the tourist spots. Simple pub food is available most days until early evening. Q⚅🚗🍴

Brigantes Bar & Brasserie

114 Micklegate, YO1 6JX

🕐 12-11

☎ (01904) 675355 🌐 markettowntaverns.co.uk

Caledonians Deuchars IPA; Taylor Landlord; York Guzzler; guest beers Ⓗ

Known for quality beer and food, this listed Georgian building was the birthplace of the architect Joseph Hansom, who invented the Hansom cab in 1834. Inside, there is a large split-level room with wood panelling, with additional seating upstairs. The bar stocks a choice of eight cask beers, five changing regularly, with future ales announced on the beer board. Several European beers are on draught and the connoisseurs' beer menu features German, Belgian and other foreign bottled beers. Q⚅&🚲🚗🍴🗜

Golden Ball ☆

2 Cromwell Road, YO1 6DU

🕐 5 (4 Fri, 12 Sat)-11 (11.30 Thu-Sat); 12-11 Sun

☎ (01904) 652211 🌐 goldenball-york.co.uk

Caledonian Deuchars IPA; Everards Tiger; Marston's Pedigree; John Smith's Bitter; Wells Bombardier; guest beers Ⓗ

Excellent, late-Victorian street corner local standing on a site that has been occupied by licensed premises for more than 200 years. The impressive, glazed-brick exterior leads to a multi-roomed interior with a layout that owes much to extensive remodelling by former owners John Smith's in 1929. With its public bar, unusual bar-side snug, lounge and bar billiards/TV room, there is something here for all tastes. The well-kept garden is a delight on sunny days. Q⚅⚅▲🚲≠🚗🍴🗜

Golden Lion

9 Church Street, YO1 8BG

🕐 11-midnight (1am Fri & Sat); 12-midnight Sun

☎ (01904) 620942

Greene King IPA; John Smith's Bitter; Taylor Landlord; Theakston Old Peculier; guest beers Ⓗ

There has been a pub on this site since 1771, but the current layout was created only 20 or so years ago. The striking exterior leads to a single, two-level bar, which was recently smartly refurbished. Of particular note is the ornate wooden bar back that was salvaged from a pub in Stockton-on-Tees. The pub offers no fewer than five guest beers and often showcases the Wentworth Brewery. Food is served until 9pm. The pub may close early if quiet. ⓌⒹ🚗

Last Drop Inn

27 Colliergate, YO1 8BN

🕐 11-11 (midnight Fri & Sat); 12-11 Sun

☎ (01904) 621951

York Guzzler, Stonewall, Yorkshire Terrier, Centurion's Ghost, seasonal beers; guest beers Ⓗ

York Brewery's first tied house opened in 2000 following conversion from a solicitors' office. The single bar on two levels has large, plain glass windows, affording fine views of King's Square, a popular spot for street entertainers. The inn offers a tranquil refuge from the tourist-filled streets, without any electronic distractions. Food is served daily until 4pm; children are not admitted. Q⚅Ⓓ≠🚗

Maltings

Tanners Moat, YO1 6HU (below Lendal Bridge)

🕐 11-11; 12-10.30 Sun

☎ (01904) 655387 🌐 maltings.co.uk

Black Sheep Best Bitter; guest beers Ⓗ

Previously the Railway Tavern and Lendal Bridge, the pub has achieved renown as the Maltings following a revamp in 1992. It continues to plough its own idiosyncratic furrow in the same capable hands, and is often the first and last stop for visitors to York. A fine selection of smaller breweries' beers is complemented by good value, wholesome food in generous portions. The annual beer festival draws a cosmopolitan crowd. Ⓓ≠🚗🍴

Minster Inn

24 Marygate, YO30 7BH (off Bootham, A19, next to Museum Gardens)

🕐 2 (11 Fri & Sat)-11 daily

☎ (01904) 624499

Marston's Burton Bitter; guest beers Ⓗ

This is a proper pub like they used to be: a place to meet, enjoy a chat and relax, undisturbed by gimmicks, jukebox or gaming machines. One of the gems of the city of York, locals converge here from all over for good ale, bypassing pubs closer to home. Little changed since it was built in 1903, three rooms off a central corridor lead to an outside yard. Children and dogs are welcome. ♨Q🐾⚅⚅≠🚗🍴🗜

Rook & Gaskill

12 Lawrence Street, YO10 3WP (near Walmgate Bar)

🕐 12-11 daily (midnight Fri & Sat)

☎ (01904) 674067

Castle Rock Harvest Pale, Elsie Mo, seasonal beers; York Yorkshire Terrier; guest beers Ⓗ

A recent York CAMRA Pub of the Year, this is the most northerly outlet of the Nottingham-based Tynemill pub company. Great care is taken to ensure that the beer range – up to 12 may be available – is well-balanced with a mild and at least one stout or porter among those offered. The single bar has terrazzo flooring and comfortable bench seating, with a conservatory at the rear. No food is served Sunday. Q❀◑⊡🏠

Saddle Inn

Main Street, Fulford, YO10 4PJ (on A19, 2 miles S of York centre)

🕐 11.30-4, 6.30-midnight; 11.30-midnight Fri & Sat; 12-11 Sun

☎ (01904) 633317

Banks's Bitter; Camerons Bitter; guest beers Ⓗ

Although altered over the years, this 150-year-old pub has retained much of its original layout; the comfortable L-shaped lounge has an adjacent dining area where children are welcome. Depending on demand meals are available at lunchtime (not Mon-Wed) and in the evening. In the bar there are sports TV, darts and pool; beyond the car park the attractive garden boasts a petanque terrain – the pub's enthusiastic team welcomes visitors at open sessions. ⚲🏠❀✦◑⊡♣🏠

Sun Inn

The Green, Acomb, YO26 5LL (on B1224, York to Wetherby road)

🕐 11 (12 Sun)-11

☎ (01904) 798500

John Smith's Bitter; guest beers Ⓗ

In a suburb to the west of York, this traditional village pub next to Acomb Green has been much improved in recent times following a sensitive refurbishment. Three drinking areas create an intimate feel and views over the picturesque Green make this a popular pub for outdoor drinking in summer. Friendly management helps to attract a good mix of regulars and passers-by, and the pub has good wheelchair access. ❀◑⊠&⊡♣🏠

Tap & Spile

29 Monkgate, YO31 7PB

🕐 12-11 (midnight Thu-Sat)

☎ (01904) 656158

Rooster's Yankee; guest beers Ⓗ

Imposing, Flemish-style house dating from 1897, built by local brewers JJ Hunt of nearby Aldwark. Formerly the Black Horse, it was renamed in 1988 when it became one of the first Tap & Spiles of the chain. The spacious, split-level interior comprises a separate bar area and library-style lounge with an elegant fireplace. Four guest beers are sourced using the SIBA scheme. A regular folk night is hosted on Friday. The annual pork pie festival in September is a highlight. ❀◑♣♣🏠

Three-Legged Mare

15 High Petergate, YO1 7EN

🕐 11-11 (midnight Fri & Sat); 12-10.30 Sun

☎ (01904) 638246

York Guzzler, Stonewall, Yorkshire Terrier, Wonkey Donkey, Centurion's Ghost, seasonal beers; guest beers Ⓗ

Known locally as the Wonkey Donkey, the pub is rather ghoulishly named after a wooden device that once stood on York racecourse allowing the simultaneous hanging of three criminals; there is a replica in the garden. This York Brewery pub, a stone's throw from the Minster, is one of three tied houses, the most modern in appearance but free from electronic gimickry. There are always nine beers available. Note that the toilets are down a narrow spiral staircase. Q❀◑⊠≠⊡🏠

Yorkshire Terrier

10 Stonegate, YO1 8AS

🕐 11-11 (midnight Fri & Sat); 12-11.30 Sun

☎ (01904) 676722

York Guzzler, Stonewall, Yorkshire Terrier, Centurion's Ghost; guest beers Ⓗ

York Brewery's most recent pub in historic Stonegate won the 2005 CAMRA Pub Design award for best conversion to a pub. The frontage at this ale house, hidden in the heart of the city, is the York Brewery shop; the entrance on the left leads to a single bar with two adjoining areas. A second room and disabled toilet are upstairs, with stairlift access. At least four York beers are supplemented by several local guests, with nine handpumps in total. Occasional live music plays. Q◑&≠⊡

YORKSHIRE (SOUTH)

Auckley

Eagle & Child

24 Main Street, DN9 3HS (On B1396)

🕐 11.30-3, 5-11; 11.30-11 Sat; 12-10.30 Sun

☎ (01302) 770406 ⊕ eagleauckley.co.uk

Black Sheep Best Bitter; John Smith's Bitter; Theakston XB; guest beers Ⓗ

Attractive, traditional village gem, well supported by the local community and handy for Robin Hood airport. Guest beers are usually sourced from local micro-breweries. The excellent, varied and reasonably-priced meals on offer include a fine Sunday roast. The Eagle has received several local CAMRA awards, including Pub of the Year in 2006 and 2007. The building dates back to 1820 and is reputed to be haunted. Q❀◑⊡⊠♣P

INDEPENDENT BREWERIES

Abbeydale Sheffield
Acorn Wombwell
Bradfield High Bradfield
Concertina Mexborough
Crown & Wellington Sheffield
Frog & Parrot Brewing suspended
Glentworth Skellow
Kelham Island Sheffield
Little Ale Cart Sheffield
Oakwell Barnsley
Sheffield Sheffield
Wentworth Wentworth

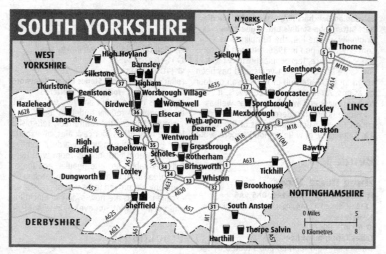

Barnsley

Gatehouse

35 Eldon Street, S70 2JJ (by rail/bus interchange)
🕐 11-11; closed Sun
☎ (01226) 282394
Acorn Barnsley Bitter; guest beers Ⓗ

Standing on one of the main routes into Barnsley, this is how the pub got its name. Opened in July 2005, it is a large open-plan venue, with one area featuring wooden floors with drinking and dining space. The other is furnished with settees plus tables and chairs. Up to six cask ales and a selection of foreign bottled beers are always available, and beer festivals are hosted at various times throughout the year. Ideally situated for public transport, it is just outside the new rail and bus interchange. ◖▶≠(Interchange)🖫⇙

George & Dragon

41-43 Summer Lane, S70 2NW (from Town End follow signs for hospital)
🕐 12-11
☎ (01226) 205609
John Smith's Bitter; guest beers Ⓗ

This busy roadside pub always seems to be full with a friendly crowd of mixed-age drinkers. Although on the edge of town it has the atmosphere of a village local. The walls show old pictures of Barnsley and changes made to the pub over the years. The open-plan lounge has comfortable seating and stand-around tables. Pool and darts are played in the games room, three steps higher than the rest of the pub. Bank holiday barbecues out on the patio are always well attended.
❀≠(Interchange)🖫(14, 43)♣P⇙🖫

Joseph Bramah

15 Market Hill, S70 2PX
🕐 9-midnight (1am Fri & Sat)
☎ (01226) 320890
Greene King Abbot; Marston's Pedigree; guest beers Ⓗ

Opened in August 2006, this Lloyds No. 1 bar is Wetherspoon's return to Barnsley town centre after selling its previous outlet to another pub company several years ago. Located in the former Orchard Brewery

premises, the long and narrow T-shaped interior is set over two floors and is dimly lit apart from the two shiny bars (one on each floor). It offers up to eight different real ales, around half usually from micro-breweries. A welcome addition to a mainly keg-dominated town centre. ❀◖▶&≠(Interchange)⇙

Keel Inn

Canal Street, S71 1LJ (off A61)
🕐 5 (7 Sat)-11; 12-11 Sun
☎ (01226) 284512
Beer range varies Ⓗ

The Keel was once at the side of the Barnsley canal (now filled in), hence its name and nautical-themed decor, despite being a long way from the sea. It is home to lively and successful darts and pool teams competing in local leagues. A concert room is available where live folk music is occasionally played. Barnsley CAMRA used to meet here in the 1970s, and the last cask of the original Barnsley Bitter was drunk here in 1977. The two beers on offer are always from local micro-breweries.
🛏🚪▶≠(Interchange)🖫(11, 59)♣P⇙🖵

Moulders Arms

49 Summer Lane, S70 2NU
🕐 4.30 (2.30 Fri; 12 Sat)-1am; 12-3.30, 7-1am Sun
☎ (01226) 215767
John Smith's Bitter; guest beers Ⓗ

Small, quiet and friendly pub with a convivial atmosphere. The bar area serves three sections all with seating. Low volume TVs and easy listening music do not distract from the flow of conversation. The garden is a pleasant place for families in summer. Darts is played here on the Yorkshire board. On Friday the small stage is open for buskers. The coffee range here is good; a welcome addition for drivers. ❀🖫(14, 43)♣P

Bawtry

Turnpike

28-30 High Street, DN10 6JE (on A638)
🕐 11-11; 12-10.30 Sun
☎ (01302) 711960

Caledonian Deuchars IPA; Greene King Ruddles
Best Bitter; John Smith's Bitter; guest beers ⊞
Originally a wine bar, the Turnpike was
converted to a pub in 1986. Situated opposite
the Market Place, this popular hostelry has had
the same licensee for 21 years, and has been
voted local CAMRA Pub of the Season on four
occasions. Arranged over three levels, it
features glass and wood panels, as well as
flagstone floors. The decor includes a county
cricket tie collection and photos of the former
RAF Finningley, now Robin Hood Airport. ⊛⊕🖛

Bentley

Three Horse Shoes

St Mary's Bridge, Town End, DN5 9AG
✪ 12 (4 winter)-11 (midnight Wed); 12-midnight Sat;
12-10.30 Sun
☎ (01302) 323571
Tetley Bitter; guest beer ⊞
Traditional multi-roomed pub situated by the
River Don, just five minutes' walk from town.
A newly created beer garden overlooks the
river. Tuesday is quiz night and there is
karaoke on Wednesday evening. A folk group
meets every Saturday evening. A private room
can be hired free of charge and freshly cooked
pizzas are available at all times. The Tetley
Bitter is one of the best in the area.
⊛⊕≠🖛♣P

Birdwell

Cock Inn

off The Walk, S70 5UD (off A61 towards Pilley)
✪ 11-3, 5.30-11; 5.30-midnight Fri; 12-midnight Sat;
12-11 Sun
☎ (01226) 742155
Black Sheep Best Bitter; John Smith's Bitter;
guest beers ⊞
Small, stone-built village pub and multiple
winner of CAMRA Pub of the Season awards.
Very welcoming with open fires, the larger of
its two rooms has a slate floor, exposed
beams, much brassware and pictures of the
old village. Home-cooked food, served daily, is
popular – Sunday lunch must be booked (no
meals Sun eve). The garden has a children's
play area. Quiz nights are held on Thursday
and Sunday, and Friday is live entertainment.
There are also occasional themed food nights
on Wednesday. ⅏Q⅍⊛⊕🖛(39)P

Blaxton

Blue Bell

Thorne Road, DN9 3AL (at A614/B1396 jct)
✪ 12 (4 Mon)-11
☎ (01302) 770424
Theakston Old Peculier; Taylor Landlord ⊞
This large yet cosy roadside inn offers a warm
welcome to all: locals, families and passing
trade, with a particular soft spot for dogs. The
bar area, with an open fire and parquet floor,
connects with a pleasant, carpeted lounge.
The restaurant offers excellent, imaginative
food (Wed-Sat eve) and a carvery every
lunchtime except Monday. The pub is
decorated with prints of the village and the
nearby airfield. It is ideally situated for Robin
Hood Airport. ⅏⊛⊕⅋♣P

Brinsworth

Phoenix Sports & Social Club

Pavilion Lane, 560 5PA (off Bawtry Road)
✪ 11-11; 12-10.30 Sun
☎ (01709) 363788
Fuller's London Pride; Stones Bitter; Wentworth
seasonal beers; Worthington's Bitter ⊞
Members of the public are very welcome at
the Phoenix. A regular outlet for local
Wentworth beers, the comfortably refurbished
lounge now offers four cask ales, all expertly
kept by the enthusiastic stewards. A family
room, TV room and snooker room with two
full-sized tables are also popular, and there
are three function rooms. A new catering
company has proved to be very successful and
excellent meals are now available lunchtimes
and evenings (not Sun eve). Q⅍⊛⊕⅋P🖛

Brookhouse

Travellers' Rest

Main Street, S25 1YA (1½ miles from Dinnington
near viaduct)
✪ 5 (12 Sat & Sun)-11
☎ (01909) 562661
Greene King XX Mild, H&H Bitter, H&H Olde
Trip ⊞
Bungalow-style pub in a farming village,
originally a house built using stone from a
watermill that stood on the site until the
1960s. In a handy location for walks to Roche
Abbey and Laughton, the pub has extensive
gardens by the brook providing seating, an old
boat, two bouncy castles and a children's ride.
Duck races take place on bank holidays. Good
value home-cooked food is served.
⊛⊕⅋⅋♣P

Chapeltown

Commercial

107 Station Road, S35 2XF
✪ 12-3, 5.30-11; 12-11 Fri & Sat; 12-10.30 Sun
☎ (0114) 2469066
Wentworth Imperial, WPA, Bumble Beer; guest
beers ⊞
Located on a main road near Asda, this pub
was built in 1890. A former Stroutts pub, it is
now a regular outlet for Wentworth beers,
including seasonals, as well as five guest ales
and a rotating cider. An island bar serves the
lounge, public/games bar and
snug. Successful beer festivals are held in May
and November. There are summer outdoor
drinking facilities to the side and rear,
bordering on to a stream at the bottom of the
garden. Children are welcome. Hot roast pork
sandwiches are available until 10pm on
Saturday (no meals Sun eve).
⅏Q⊛⊕⅋⅋≠🖛♣♠P🖛

Doncaster

Corner Pin

145 St Sepulchre Gate West, DN1 3AH (near St
James' Church)
✪ 12-midnight (1am Fri & Sat)
☎ (01302) 323159
John Smith's Bitter; guest beers ⊞

Traditional street-corner pub with a well-appointed lounge on the left and a public bar area to the right. Three frequently-changing guest beers are sourced mainly from small independent breweries via the SIBA scheme. At the rear is an attractive decked area, ideal for alfresco drinking on a warm evening. The pub fields a football team as well as the more traditional darts and dominoes. Oversized lined glasses are a welcome sight – not many outlets still use these in the Doncaster area. ❀⊟⇌⊟♣⊱⊓

Leopard

1 West Street, DN1 3AA (W of ring road near railway station)

⏲ 11-11 (11.30 Fri & Sat); 12-11 Sun

☎ (01302) 363054

John Smith's Bitter; guest beers Ⓗ

Lively street corner pub with a superb tiled frontage, a reminder of the building's origins as a Warwick and Richardson's house. A long-standing regular outlet for the local Glentworth Brewery, one of its beers is always available, along with guest ales from other independents. An eclectic mix of music is played on the juke box in both the comfortable lounge and the lively bar/games room. The upstairs room hosts regular gigs, featuring a wide range of pop and rock. ⊟⇌⊟♣P⊱

Masons' Arms

22 Market Place, DN1 1ND (near Corn Exchange)

⏲ 10.30-11

☎ (01302) 340848

Taylor Landlord; Tetley Bitter; guest beer Ⓗ

Atmospheric old ale house close to Doncaster's historic Corn Exchange building. A corridor leading to back rooms opens out around a bar counter to form a small but interesting drinking lobby. Local morris dancers often limber up here with a few pints of Landlord. Beware of annoying the pub's friendly clientele by switching on the barely used TV in the former smoke room. One regular has recently introduced a pub game for such occasions called 'tossing the telly!' Q⌂❀⊟♿⇌♣⊱

Plough ☆

8 West Laith Gate, DN1 1SF

⏲ 11-11; 12-3, 7-10.30 Sun

☎ (01302) 738310

Acorn Barnsley Bitter; Draught Bass; guest beer Ⓗ

Warm, traditional town centre pub which provides a popular escape from the bustle of the shopping area and the 'fun pub' circuit. There is a basic bright public bar and a comfortable if unusual lounge, decorated with old pictures of agricultural scenes. The Plough has won numerous CAMRA awards, including winter 2007 Pub of the Season, and features in the National Inventory with an interior that has remained unchanged since 1934. Q❀⊟⇌⊟♣

Red Lion

37-38 Market Place, DN1 1NH (SW corner of Market Place, near fish market)

⏲ 9-midnight (1am Fri & Sat)

☎ (01302) 732120

Beer range varies Ⓗ

This large, historic pub has been given a new lease of life since it was taken over by Wetherspoon. A lively front drinking area gives way to a quieter area with tables and chairs towards the rear. Although much altered over the years, it was here in 1776 that discussions took place to organise the St Leger Stakes, the oldest classic horse race. There are plaques on display commemorating the event and listing post-war winners, which include many famous jockeys. ◑♿⇌⊟●⊱

Tut 'n' Shive

6 West Laith Gate, DN1 1SF (next to Frenchgate shopping centre)

⏲ 11-11 (midnight Fri-Sun)

☎ (01302) 360300

Black Sheep Best Bitter; Greene King IPA, Abbot; guest beers Ⓗ

Up to six real ales are available at this lively town centre pub, which features a stone floor, boarded ceiling and walls decorated with pump clips from past guest beers. A DJ plays tunes on Tuesday and Sunday nights, while a juke box is in action the rest of the time. Quiz nights are on Wednesday and Sunday, and a large-screen TV shows football and other major sporting events. A relaxed but lively atmosphere ensures that all feel welcome. ◑⇌⊟

Dungworth

Royal Hotel

Main Road, S6 6HF

⏲ 6 (12 Sat)-11; 12-4, 7-10.30 Sun

☎ (0114) 2851213 🌐 royalhotel-dungworth.pwp.blueyonder.co.uk

Tetley Bitter; guest beers Ⓗ

Small, 19th-century rural pub to the north-west of Sheffield, in the vale of Bradfield, providing panoramic views over Loxley Valley. Children, walkers and well-behaved pets are welcome. One bar serves two drinking areas, with a separate room to the left. Early evening meals are available on weekdays, and all-day lunch until 8pm on Saturday and Sunday. Try the home-made pies! Sunday lunchtime carol singing from mid-November to Christmas is popular. Three en-suite rooms are available in the adjoining lodge. Q❀⇌◑⊟♣P

Edenthorpe

Beverley Inn

Thorne Road, DN3 2JE (on A18)

⏲ 12-3, 5 (6 Sat)-11; 12-3, 7-11 Sun

☎ (01302) 882724 🌐 beverleyinnandhotel.co.uk

John Smith's Bitter; guest beers Ⓗ

Welcoming family pub with a restaurant that serves mainly home-cooked food – the Sunday carvery is especially popular. Two guest ales are usually sourced from local breweries by the owner who is very knowledgeable about his beers. The comfortable lounge features Laurel and Hardy memorabilia and a clock that runs backwards. The hotel has accommodation in 14 rooms. ❀⇌◑♿⊟(87, 88)P

Eden Arms

Edenfield Road, DN3 2QR (off A18 next to Tesco)

☼ 12-11 (midnight Thu-Sat)
☎ (01302) 888682
Taylor Landlord; guest beers Ⓗ
Modern, upmarket estate pub that has been
attractively redecorated. Various seating areas
are available, and there is a patio for fine
weather. An extensive menu is served all day
until 9pm by friendly staff. Three real ales are
stocked, with two guest beers chosen from an
extensive list drawn up with the help of
customers' recommendations. A disabled
toilet is available. ⚐❀◑♿⊟P⌐

Elsecar

Market Hotel
2-4 Wentworth Road, S74 8EP (next to Heritage
Centre)
☼ 12 (11 Sat)-11
☎ (01226) 742240
Wentworth WPA; guest beers Ⓗ
A wide drinking corridor opens into many
unspoilt rooms. The large games and function
room upstairs has resident pool and football
teams, and a number of clubs and societies
meet here. Minutes from the Trans-pennine
Trail and the Dearne and Dove Canal, the pub
is well used by walkers, cyclists and runners.
Note the original stonework that offers horse
and gig for hire. Four cask ales are regularly
available featuring local breweries. There is
seating outside in the garden.
Q❀◑⇄⊟(66)♣⌐

Greasbrough

Prince Of Wales
9 Potters Hill, S61 4NU
☼ 11-4, 7-11; 12-3, 7-10.30 Sun
☎ (01709) 551358
John Smith's Bitter; guest beers Ⓗ
The Prince celebrates 13 consecutive years in
the Guide. This popular street corner pub has a
spacious, well-decorated lounge and tap
room. The friendly landlord is in his 28th year
of tenancy and provides cask beers from a
variety of breweries. The guest beer can
change up to three times a day, ensuring its
quality. In the summer, tables and chairs allow
customers to watch the world go by outside.
Q❀◑⊟♣⌐

Harley

Horseshoe Inn
9 Harley Road, S62 7UD (off A6135)
☼ 4 (2 Sat)-11; 12-10.30 Sun
☎ (01226) 742204
**John Smith's Bitter; Wentworth WPA; guest
beers** Ⓗ
A new entry to the Guide, this street-corner
village pub is situated close to the Wentworth
Brewery. It stocks one Wentworth beer as a
regular and also offers a changing guest from
the brewery. Guest beers change weekly to
ensure their quality, and the pub now serves
food. It also hosts regular quiz nights and
social functions. ▶♣

Harthill

Beehive
16 Union Street, S26 7YH (opp church on road
from Kiveton crossroads)
☼ 12-3 (not Mon), 6 (6.30 Sat)-11; 12-3, 7-11 Sun
☎ (01909) 770205
**Caledonian Deuchars IPA; Taylor Landlord; Tetley
Bitter** Ⓗ
Local CAMRA Rural Pub of the Year, this is a
welcoming village inn, close to Rother Valley
Country Park and situated on the Five Churches
Walk. It provides space for drinkers and diners,
with a full-size snooker table in the back
room. The pub is central to a number of
community activities such as morris dancing
and a folk club. There is a function room
upstairs that can be reached via a stairlift.
Children are welcome until 7pm.
Q❀◑⊟&♣P

Hazlehead

Dog & Partridge
Bord Hill, Flouch, S36 4HH (1 mile from Flouch
roundabout on A628)
☼ 12-3 (not Mon), 6-11; 11-11 Sat & Sun
☎ (01226) 763173 ⊕ dogandpartridgeinn.co.uk
Acorn Barnsley Bitter; guest beers Ⓗ
Large roadside pub and hotel on what was
once a medieval salt route, just inside the
northern section of the Peak National Park,
offering stunning moorland views. Dating back
to Elizabethan times and first licensed in 1740,
the adjoining 18th-century barn has been
converted into en-suite bedrooms, and was
adapted for the disabled. The hotel has a
restaurant and dining area for families. A vast
bar/lounge offers four quality ales. Local
CAMRA Pub of the Year 2007, it also serves
good food and features a roaring fire.
⚐Q⏟❀⇆◑&P⌐

High Hoyland

Cherry Tree
Bank End Lane, S75 4BE
☼ 12-3, 5.30-11; closed Mon; 11-11 Sat & Sun
☎ (01226) 382541
**Black Sheep Best Bitter; E&S Elland Best Bitter,
Nettlethrasher; John Smith's Bitter; Tetley
Bitter** Ⓗ
Busy pub in a rural spot. The recently
refurbished interior has two dining rooms
separated by a large central bar and drinking
area. There is a distinct emphasis on food,
with an extensive menu and daily specials
available. The pub enjoys panoramic views to
the front over Cawthorne and Barnsley.
Numerous footpaths pass close by, making it a
good starting point and a better finish for a
walk. Q◑&P⌐

Higham

Engineers Arms
Higham Common Road, S75 1PF (off A635 or
A628)
☼ 12-3, 7-11
☎ (01226) 384204
Samuel Smith's OBB Ⓗ

The split-level bar is one of the most striking features of this pub. The low level serves the lounge and games room where pictures from the TV show Last of the Summer Wine adorn the walls. The upper level is a welcoming public bar. Conversation flourished in the bar and lounge with no TV or background music. Three cricket teams play on the field outside. During match days the bar may open later, but phone to check. Q❀❁🛏(92)♣P↙

Langsett

Waggon & Horses
Manchester Road, S36 4GY (on A616)
✪ 12-3, 6.30-11; closed Mon; 12-3 Sun
☎ (01226) 763147 ⊕ langsettinn.com
Bradfield Farmers Bitter; Taylor Landlord Ⓗ
Grade II listed pub in superb countryside on the edge of the Dark Peak District. In the same family for more than 30 years, it has earned an enviable reputation for comfortable accommodation and great food. The home-cooked meat and potatoes and the bilberry pies are legendary. The pub hosts the Langsett independent film festival, which screens short films from around the world, with the audience voting for the winner. All this and great ale too – fantastic!
🛏Q❀❁◑🛏(23, 24)♣P

Loxley

Nag's Head Inn
Stacey Bank, S6 65J (on B6077 from Hillsborough)
✪ 12-1am (2am Fri & Sat); closed Mon & Tue afternoons
☎ (0114) 2851202
Greene King Ruddles County, H&H Bitter; guest beers Ⓗ
Impressive stone roadhouse, originally built as three cottages to house construction workers from the nearby Damflask Reservoir in the 19th century. Once a village, Loxley is now on the northern fringes of Sheffield. An L-shaped bar serves two distinct areas: a comfortable lounge to the right and a bar area with three quarter-sized snooker table to the left. There is another seating area popular with diners to the rear. Food is served at lunchtime and early evening (not Sun). 🛏❀◑🛏🛏♣P

Mexborough

Concertina Band Club
9A Dolcliffe Road, S64 9AZ (from flyover turn left at old library)
✪ 12-4, 7.45 (7 Fri & Sat)-11; 7-10.30 Sun
☎ (01709) 580841
Concertina Club Bitter, Bengal Tiger; John Smith's Bitter; guest beers Ⓗ
With the closure of the Federation Brewery, the Tina, as it is known, is now the only remaining club brewery. Framed photographs on the wall are a reminder of the days of the former band after which the club is named. Very much a traditional, old-fashioned establishment, it offers a warm, friendly welcome; show a CAMRA card or this Guide for admission. Occasional guest beers may be brewery specials or regular beers from independent breweries. 🛏≈🛏(222)♣🍴

Penistone

Wentworth Arms
Sheffield Road, S36 6HG
✪ 12-midnight
☎ (01226) 762494
Banks's Bitter; guest beers Ⓗ
Beside the Trans-Pennine Trail (which links Liverpool and Hornsea), this large stone pub makes an excellent watering hole, serving three quality beers. There are no frills here: simply choose between the lounge with dartboard and massive juke box to the right or a cosy bar which houses a TV high in the corner to the left. No food is served here either, but there is a chip shop next door. Conversation is the main entertainment, though there is a pool area in a room at the back. Q❀❁≈🛏(29)P↙

Rotherham

Bluecoat
The Crofts, S60 2JD
✪ 9-midnight (1am Fri & Sat)
☎ (01709) 580841
Greene King Abbot; Marston's Pedigree; guest beers Ⓗ
This converted school behind the town hall is well worth seeking out – winner of local CAMRA Pub of the Year in both 2006 and 2007. It is also Wetherspoon's Pub of the Year for 2006, and was the first in the chain to hold a music licence. Live jazz is played on Monday night. The Bluecoat offers a wide selection of beers from national breweries as well as from 15 local brewers, plus Weston's Old Rosie cider. Q❀◑&≈♣P↙

Clifton
105 Old Clifton Lane, S65 2AW (opp Rotherham rugby/cricket clubs)
✪ 4-midnight; 12-1am Fri & Sat; 12-midnight Sun
☎ (01709) 833070
Beer range varies Ⓗ
A traditional street-corner local that gets very busy when Rotherham rugby team plays at home. Local CAMRA Pub of the Season winner, it stages a popular quiz night on Thursday, and is home to darts and pool teams on Monday and Thursday. Bar food may be available during the rugby season. ❀🛏&🛏♣P↙

Hare & Hounds
52 Wellgate, S60 2LR
✪ 11.30 (11 Sat)-11; 11-10.30 Sun
☎ (01709) 821554
Greene King Abbot; guest beers Ⓗ
Situated in Rotherham town centre, the Hare & Hounds is back in the Guide by popular demand. The pub is split into three sections, all with large TV screens, and there is an upstairs function room. Greene King Abbot is always served alongside a guest beer, with both beers enjoying a quick turnover. There is a small garden, which now houses a covered smoking area, and the pub is flanked by municipal car parks. ❀♣♠↙

Scholes

Bay Horse
Scholes Lane, S61 2RQ (off A629, near M1 jct 35)

🌑 5 (12 Sat & Sun)-11.30
☎ (0114) 246 8085
Kelham Island Pale Rider; Taylor Landlord; guest beer 🅷
Traditional village pub next to the cricket club. It serves good home-cooked food including Dan's cow pie (earn a certificate if you eat everything on the plate) and popular curries. Hog roasts feature four times a year. Other regular entertainment is provided by a choir on Thursday and two weekly quizzes. Situated on the Rotherham Round Walk and the Trans-Pennine Trail, the pub is also near the local attraction of Keppel's Column. Wentworth Woodhouse Hall is a pleasant if energetic walk away. ♨Q🕭🅓♿P

Sheffield: Central

Bath Hotel ☆
66 Victoria Street, S3 7RL
🌑 12-11; 7-10.30 Sun
☎ (0114) 249 5151
Abbeydale Moonshine; Acorn Barnsley Bitter; Tetley Bitter; guest beers 🅷
Carefully restored 1930s pub with a superb two-room interior that earns it a place in CAMRA's National Inventory of heritage pubs. Discerning drinkers can choose between the clear lines of the tiled lounge and the warmth of the well-upholstered snug. Up to three guest beers from local breweries and micros from further afield are on offer, as well as an excellent choice of malt whiskies. Q◗(University)🚇

Devonshire Cat
49 Wellington Street, S1 4HG
🌑 11.30-11 (midnight Fri & Sat); 12-10.30 Sun
☎ (0114) 279 6700 🌐 devonshirecat.co.uk
Abbeydale Moonshine, Absolution; Caledonian Deuchars IPA; Theakston Old Peculier; Thornbridge Jaipur; guest beers 🅷
Showcasing what is probably the best selection of beers in the county, the Dev Cat is a great place for the discerning drinker. Twelve handpumps adorn the bar, with the house beer brewed by the local Kelham Island Brewery. Whatever time of day you visit, the clientele is a mix of beer enthusiasts, students and those in need of liquid libation. A must if you are on a short visit to the city, but be warned you may not want to leave. ◗♿(West St)🚇♣

Fagans
69 Broad Lane, S1 4BS
🌑 12-11.30 (11 Sun)
☎ (0114) 272 8430
Abbeydale Moonshine; Tetley Bitter 🅷
Away from the main drinking areas, this pub is hard to categorise, and you feel it would be more at home on a side street than on one of the city's main arteries. Well-dressed in green, red and dark wood panelling, the pub hosts folk music and a fiendish quiz on Thursday. Whether you are looking for somewhere for a quick pint or an evening's entertainment, this pub must come near the top of the list. ◗⊖(West St)🚇

Fat Cat
23 Alma Street, S3 8SA

🌑 12-midnight
☎ (0114) 249 4801
Kelham Island Bitter, Gold, Pale Rider; Taylor Landlord, seasonal beers; guest beers 🅷
Now entering its 26th year and still going strong, this is the pub that started the real ale revolution in the area. Beer from all over the country is served alongside ales from its neighbour and sister enterprise, the Kelham Island Brewery. It is also justly famed for its food, with vegetarian and gluten-free dishes featuring heavily. Do take the time to browse the number of awards that cover the walls of this pub. Q🕭🅓♿⊖(Shalesmoor)🚇♣P⬤

Harlequin
108 Nursery Street, S3 8GG
🌑 11-11; 12-10.30 Sun
☎ (0114) 275 8195
Bradfield Farmers Blonde; John Smith's Magnet; guest beers 🅷
The most recent addition to the city's 'Valley of Beer' pub crawl, the Harlequin (formerly the Manchester) takes its name from another former Wards pub round the corner, sadly now demolished. The large interior is open plan around a central bar with seating areas on two levels. As well as local brews, the eight handpumps serve beer from far and wide, with an emphasis on those from micro-breweries. There is a quiz on Wednesday and regular live music at weekends. ◗🚇♣♠

Kelham Island Tavern
62 Russell Street, S3 8RW
🌑 12-11 (midnight Fri-Sun)
☎ (0114) 272 2482 🌐 kelhamislandtavern.co.uk
Acorn Barnsley Bitter; Pictish Brewers Gold; guest beers 🅷
A true gem! Local CAMRA Pub of the Year for the past four years and a previous regional winner, this pub has an impressive 10 permanent handpumps (quite a feat given the pub's size). Two of these always dispense a mild and a stout/porter. You are sure to find something to quench your thirst. Visit in the warmer months and you can enjoy the pub's multi award-winning subtropical beer garden. Regular folk music plays on Sunday. 🕭◗♿⊖(Shalesmoor)🚇♣⬤–🚻

Museum
25 Orchard Street, S1 2GX
🌑 11-11.30; 12-10.30 Sun
☎ (0114) 275 5016
Greene King IPA, Old Speckled Hen, Abbot; guest beers 🅷
Situated within the Orchard Square shopping precinct, this pub, a former Hogshead, takes its name from the museum of the medical school that once occupied the site. Now drinkers can watch shoppers go by from the extensive outside seating area. Inside there are contrasting seating areas on three levels. On the bar the six handpumps dispense two rotating guest beers as well as four from the Greene King range. 🕭◗♿➤⊖(Cathedral)🚇

Red Deer
18 Pitt Street, S1 4DD
🌑 11.30-11; 11.30-12 Sat; 7.30-10.30
☎ (0114) 2722890 🌐 red-deer-sheffield.co.uk

Adnams Broadside; Bank's Bitter; Black Sheep Best Bitter; Caledonian Deuchars IPA; Greene King Abbot; Taylor Landlord; guest beers Ⓗ
A traditional pub in the heart of the city, hidden away behind the West Street circuit. The small frontage of the original three-roomed local leads into an open-plan pub, extended to the rear with a gallery seating area. The pub mirrors and Guinness clock sit alongside prints and watercolours of local scenes, some of which are for sale. The impressive range of nine handpulled ales includes at least one roatating guest. They also stock a selection of continental bottled beers. Evening meals are served till 7pm; no food at weekends. Q❀❀◑⊖(West St)🚋

Red Lion
109 Charles Street, S1 2ND
🕑 11.30-11.30 (midnight Fri & Sat); 7-11 Sun
☎ (0114) 272 4997
Black Sheep Best Bitter; Caledonian Deuchars IPA; Taylor Landlord; guest beers Ⓗ
A street-corner pub, now in the shadow of the ever-expanding Hallam University City Campus. A corner door leads directly into a small snug, while the main entrance opens into the lounge, with a conservatory and a raised area at the rear, once a separate concert room – comfortably furnished throughout. Its location in the cultural industries' quarter ensures a busy lunchtime and early evening crowd. Guest beers come from local brewers through the SIBA Scheme. ❀◑≉⊖(Station)🚋

Three Tuns
39 Silver Street Head, S1 2DD
🕑 11-11; 7-11.30 Sat
☎ (0114) 272 0646
Taylor Landlord; Tetley Bitter; guest beers Ⓗ
The Three Tuns is easy to miss – but make sure you don't. Once described as having 'more character than Gerard Depardieu', and at one time used as a nuns' washroom, this V-shaped pub is frequented by the 'suits' who work in nearby offices and has a buzzing atmosphere during the early evening hours. There are two handpumps on the upper level of the bar, which should not be overlooked.
◑⊖(City Hall)

Sheffield: East

Carlton
563 Attercliffe Road, S9 3RA
🕑 11-11; 7.30-10.30 Sun
☎ (0114) 244 3287
Marston's Pedigree; Wentworth WPA; guest beers Ⓗ
Built in 1862, this former Gilmours' house lies behind a deceptively small frontage. Carefully renovated in recent years, it has been transformed from a basic workmen's pub to a thriving community local. The main room around the bar is comfortably furnished in traditional style. To the rear is a newly extended games room and recently created garden. A strict no-swearing policy enhances the friendly atmosphere. Four guest beers are from local breweries as well as from further afield.
❀❀⊖(Attercliffe/Woodbourn Rd)🚋♣☞—ⴹ

Cocked Hat
75 Worksop Road, S9 3TG
🕑 11-11; 11-3, 7-11 Sat; 12-3 Sun
☎ (0114) 244 8332
Marston's Burton Bitter, Pedigree, seasonal beers; guest beers Ⓗ
This corner pub, now standing in isolation, was at the heart of the steel industry when it was built in 1840. It now lies in the shadow of the Don Valley Stadium, with players and fans providing some of the custom. The open-plan interior has a central bar with stalled seating at one end. A raised area by the entrance is occupied by a bar billiards table. This is a handy refreshment stop for walkers on the Five Weirs Walk. ⛰❀⊖(Attercliffe)🚋♣

Corner Pin
231-233 Carlisle Street, S4 7QN
🕑 11-8 (11 Fri); closed Sun
☎ (0114) 275 2334
Abbeydale Moonshine; guest beers Ⓗ
A traditional two-roomed local that once nestled among the steel works and workers' houses, but now stands in an area of light industry. After careful restoration it reopened as a free house in 2005, following a period of closure. The main bar is triangular in shape due to the angle of its street corner site. Guest beers are mainly from small Yorkshire breweries, with Osset often featured. ❀◑🚋♣

Sheffield: North

Gardeners Rest
105 Neepsend Lane, S3 8AT
🕑 3-11 (midnight Fri & Sat); 12-10.30 Sun
☎ (0114) 272 4978 ⊕ sheffieldbrewery.com
Sheffield Five Rivers, Seven Hills, Hallmark, seasonal beers; guest beers Ⓗ
The tap for Sheffield Brewery since January 2007, the pub offers up to four of its beers alongside up to eight ales from other local breweries, as well as changing guests. The interior comprises a snug and a larger main room featuring art exhibitions. Entertainments include bar billiards, weekend music, a Sunday night quiz and an annual beer festival in October. The conservatory displays information on local history, regeneration and environmental issues. The garden backs onto the River Don and the pub was damaged by flooding last June.
Q❀&⊖(Infirmary Road)🚋♣☞—ⴹ

Hillsborough Hotel
54-58 Langsett Road, S6 2UB
🕑 11-11 (midnight Fri & Sat); 12-11 Sun
☎ (0114) 232 2100 ⊕ hillsborough-hotel.com
Crown HPA, Jack the Nipper, Loxley Gold, Stannington Stout, seasonal beers; Wellington seasonal beers; guest beers Ⓗ
Family-run hotel, now with extended opening hours and serving home-cooked food. It features an ever-changing range of guest ales (40 plus per week), supplemented by beers from the house brewery in the cellar which brews under both Crown and Wellington names – tours are available. It hosts seasonal beer festivals, a popular quiz night on Tuesday with free roast potatoes, and live folk music on Sunday. The conservatory and raised

terrace at the rear have panoramic views along the upper Don Valley.
Q✿✍◑♿☻(Langsett/Primrose View) ❑♣♨

New Barrack Tavern

601 Penistone Road, S6 2GA
☼ 11-11 (midnight Fri & Sat); 12-11 Sun
☎ (0114) 234 9148 ⊕ tynemill.co.uk
Abbeydale Moonshine; Acorn Barnsley Bitter; Bateman Valiant; Castle Rock Harvest Pale, Elsie Mo; guest beers Ⓗ
An essential stop for fans travelling to nearby Hillsborough, 11 handpumps, pre-match meals and a warm welcome await. The home-cooked food is popular at all times and is served until late on Friday and Saturday. The small front bar has a dartboard. The main room features live music on Saturday and sometimes on other nights. Real ales are supplemented by a wide choice of continental beers and single malts, plus a real cider. There is an award-winning patio garden at the rear.
♨Q✿◑♿☻(Bamforth St)❑♣♨♨

Wellington

1 Henry Street, S3 7EQ
☼ 12-3 (not Mon), 5-11; 12-11 Fri & Sat; 12-4, 7-10.30 Sun
☎ (0114) 249 2295
Beer range varies Ⓗ
Formerly the Cask & Cutler, after 13 years this street-corner pub has reverted to its original name. Despite the rebadging and accompanying refurbishment, the new owner continues to champion small independent brewers on eight ever-changing handpumps. A mild, stout or porter and a real cider are always available, plus a range of continental bottled beers. The Port Mahon Brewery, adjoining the secluded garden to the rear, is set to reopen in late summer 2007.
♨Q✿☻(Shalesmoor)❑♨♨

Sheffield: South

Archer Road Beer Stop

57 Archer Road, S8 0JT
☼ 11 (10.30 Sat)-10; 5-10 Sun
☎ (0114) 255 1356
Taylor Landlord; guest beers Ⓗ
Small corner shop crowded with bottled beers, ranging from local micro-brews through to the classics from Belgium, Germany and the rest of the world. Pride of place on the shelves is given to 'CAMRA says this is real ale' bottle-conditioned beers. Four handpumps serve mainly local ales but visiting beers from further afield are sometimes showcased too. To add to previous awards, the shop now boasts a Guide ten-year certificate. ❑

Sheaf View

25 Gleadless Road, Heeley, S2 3AA
☼ 12-11.30
☎ (0114) 249 6455
Bradfield Farmers Blonde; Kelham Island Easy Rider; Wentworth WPA; guest beers Ⓗ
Historic pub dating from 1871 and enjoying a resurgence since reopening in 2000 as a genuine free house. The new owner carried out extensive refurbishment, but more significantly he supplied choice, quality and

excellent value. Five ever-changing guest beers are served in a range of gravity bands, always including a stout or porter. A large number of continental bottled beers and malt whiskies are also stocked. Excellent disabled access allows pleasant drinking for all in an atmosphere unspoilt by TV or games machines. Quiz night is Wednesday.
Q✿♿❑♣♨♨

White Lion

615 London Road, S2 4HT
☼ 12 (2 Mon & Tue)-11; 12-midnight Thu-Sat; 12-11 Sun
☎ (0114) 255 1500
Marston's Pedigree; Taylor Landlord; Tetley Dark Mild, Bitter; guest beers Ⓗ
Multi-roomed former Tetley heritage pub, situated on a busy suburban thoroughfare. Now owned by Punch, it is one of three award-winning pubs in the Just Williams group. Many original features have been retained – note the tiled corridor and Windsor Ales lettering on the windows. There are quiet drinking areas at the front, a games room and concert room at the rear. Live music, mostly rock, is played on most Thursdays, while jazz features on the first Tuesday of the month. A general knowledge quiz is hosted on Sunday. Addlestones cider is always available.
✿❑♣♨♨

Sheffield: West

Cobden View

40 Cobden View Road, Crookes, S10 1HQ
☼ 1-midnight (1am Fri); 12-1am Sat; 12-midnight Sun
☎ (0114) 266 1273
Abbeydale Moonshine; Black Sheep Best Bitter; Caledonian Deuchars IPA; Greene King IPA; Taylor Landlord; Wychwood Hobgoblin Ⓗ
Busy community pub catering for a varied clientele ranging from students to retired folk. Although opened out, the original layout is still apparent, with the bar serving a snug at the front, a games area to the rear and a lounge to the right of the front entrance. Quizzes are held on Sunday and Tuesday evenings and there is live music most Thursdays and Saturdays. The spacious garden is used for regular summer barbecues.
✿♿❑♣

Fox & Duck

227 Fulwood Road, S10 3BA
☼ 11-11.30 (midnight Fri & Sat); 12-11.30 Sun
☎ (0114) 263 1888
Abbeydale Moonshine; John Smith's Magnet; guest beers Ⓗ
Busy pub at the heart of the Broomhill shopping area. Although owned by the university Students' Union, it is popular with locals as well as students. Originally a two-roomed pub, it was converted to its present open-plan format in the 1980s and more recently extended into an adjacent shop. No food is served, but drinkers may bring in their own from the numerous nearby takeaways. The four or five guest beers are sourced from local and regional brewers. ✿❑♨

Porter Brook

565 Ecclesall Road, S11 8PR

⏱ 11-midnight (1am Fri & Sat); 12-10.30 Sun
☎ (0114) 266 5765
Greene King IPA, Ruddles County, Abbot, seasonal beers Ⓗ
This 1990s conversion of a house on the bank of the River Porter originally opened as a Hogshead. Still the leading real ale outlet on Ecclesall Road, it now offers five beers from the Greene King range. Furnished in typical ale house style, featuring bare floorboards and exposed brick work, it attracts a varied clientele, including students from the nearby campus. Meals are served throughout the afternoon every day. ⏱♿🚲

Ranmoor Inn
330 Fulwood Road, S10 3BG
⏱ 11.30-11; 12-10.30 Sun
☎ (0114) 230 1325
Abbeydale Moonshine; Black Sheep Best Bitter; Caledonian Deuchars IPA; Taylor Landlord; guest beers Ⓗ
Renovated Victorian local with original windows standing in the shadow of Ranmoor Church in the leafy suburb of Fulwood. Now open plan, the seating areas reflect the original room layout. A friendly, old-fashioned pub, it serves proper food Tuesday-Saturday. It attracts a diverse clientele from football teams to choirs; the piano is often played by an enthusiastic regular. For outdoor drinking there is a small front garden and the former stableyard which is now partly covered and heated. Q❀♿🚲♣🚃

Rising Sun
471 Fulwood Road, S10 3QA
⏱ 11 (12 Sun)-11
☎ (0114) 230 3855 ⊕ risingsunsheffield.co.uk
Abbeydale Absolution, Moonshine, Brimstone, Matins, Daily Bread; guest beers Ⓗ
Large, suburban roadhouse in the leafy western side of the city. Owned by local brewer Abbeydale, it was Sheffield's first pub to go totally no smoking when it reopened back in 2006. It has two comfortably furnished rooms, the main bar with a raised area to the rear. As well as offering a range of Abbeydale beers, there are up to five guest beers always available on the impressive bank of handpumps. Entertainment includes live music on Monday and Wednesday, and quizzes on Sunday and Tuesday. Q❀⏱♿🚲♣P🚃

Robin Hood
Greaves Lane, Little Matlock, S6 6BG (off Myers Grove Lane)
⏱ 12-3, 5-11; 12-11.30 Sat; 12-10.30 Sun
☎ (0114) 234 4565 ⊕ robin-hood-loxley.co.uk
Bradfield Farmers Blonde; guest beers Ⓗ
Large inn off the beaten track, with a central bar that serves two rooms on different levels. The public bar in this 200-year-old pub retains the original stone floor. It offers good food and accommodation; booking is advisable for the Sunday carvery. Its remote location in the Loxley Valley makes it an ideal stopping-off point for walkers in the nearby Peak District; dogs are welcome too. Q❀🛏⏱ 🍴♣P

Walkley Cottage
46 Bole Hill Road, S6 5DD
⏱ 11 (12 Sun)-11

☎ (0114) 234 4968
Black Sheep Best Bitter; Greene King Abbot; Taylor Landlord; Tetley Bitter; guest beers Ⓗ
Spacious, roadhouse-style suburban two-room local. The large tap room has a snooker table and large-screen TV, while the comfortable L-shaped lounge includes a food servery. Built for Gilmours between the wars on a large site, the extensive garden affords panoramic views across the Rivelin Valley. A lively pub, it hosts a popular quiz on Thursday. Two rotating guest beers come from a wide variety of local and regional brewers. ❀⏱ 🍴🚲♣P

Silkstone

Ring O' Bells
High Street, S75 4LN
⏱ 12-11 (midnight Sat & Sun)
☎ (01226) 790298
Greene King H&H Bitter, H&H Olde Trip, Ruddles County, Abbot Ⓗ
Set in a pretty village west of Barnsley, the Ring O' Bells has recently been swallowed up by the Greene King empire. However, the keen landlord has been trying to keep his Hardys & Hansons beers, despite pressure from the new regime. Inside, the real fire provides a homely and warming atmosphere. A flower-filled front yard has plenty of benches for alfresco drinking. The pub has won numerous local CAMRA awards. 🏚Q❀⛃🚲🚃

South Anston

Loyal Trooper
34 Sheffield Road, S25 5DT (off A57, 3 miles from M1 jct 31)
⏱ 12-3, 6-11; 12-11 Sat; 12-3, 7-10.30 Sun
☎ (01909) 562203
Adnams Bitter; Taylor Landlord; Tetley Bitter; guest beers Ⓗ
Friendly village local dating back in parts to 1690, situated on the Five Churches Walk. The pub offers a range of real ales and serves good wholesome food. The interior comprises a public bar, snug and lounge, with a function room upstairs that is used by many local groups including yoga classes, folk groups and birdwatchers. Children are welcome until 8pm. Q❀⏱ ⛃P

Sprotbrough

Boat Inn
Nursery Road, DN5 7NB
⏱ 11-11 (10.30 Sun)
☎ (01302) 858500
Black Sheep Best Bitter; John Smith's Bitter; guest beer Ⓗ
Situated near the Trans-Pennine Trail, this attractive multi-roomed riverside pub is popular with walkers, diners and the local community. Occasionally the National Trust holds outdoor activities here, and the pub has its own football team. Good value food from an extensive menu is served throughout the day. Background music is unobtrusive. Outside, there is a large courtyard area which is ideal for summer drinking. 🏚❀⏱♿P

Ivanhoe Hotel

Melton Road, DN5 7NS
✪ 11-11; 12-10.30 Sun
☎ (01302) 853130
Samuel Smith OBB ⊞
Situated by the village crossroads, this local CAMRA Pub of the Season autumn 2006 is very popular with the local community. The pub comprises a spacious lounge, a public bar with pool and snooker tables, and a conservatory where families are welcome. Good value food (not Sun eve) can be enjoyed undisturbed by background music, and the beer is one of the most competitively priced in the area. Outside there is a large beer garden adjacent to the village cricket pitch.
Q☜❀❍❶⇩♣P

Thorne

Windmill Inn

19 Queen Street, DN8 5AA (near Finkle St shopping precinct)
✪ 2-11 (midnight Fri); 12-midnight Sat; 12-11 Sun
☎ (01405) 812866 ⊕ thewindmillthorne.co.uk
Adnams Bitter; Black Sheep Best Bitter; John Smith's Bitter; Tetley Bitter ⊞
Built in the 1870s, this friendly, well-kept pub is a mere stone's throw from the old Darley Brewery Tower. Black Sheep Best Bitter and Adnams Bitter are permanent guests, kept in top condition by Nick the cellarman/barman who has worked here for 28 years. Windmill regulars include players from the Thornensians Rugby Team. This is one pub you can take your Auntie Ethel to without having to cover her ears! ❀⏣⇩⚑A⇌(Thorne North)♣P⇘

Thorpe Salvin

Parish Oven

Worksop Road, S80 3JU
✪ 12-2.30 (not Mon), 5.30-11; 12-11 Sat; 12-10.30 Sun
☎ (01909) 770685
Black Sheep Best Bitter; guest beers ⊞
The Parish Oven gets its name from its location: it is on the site of a former communal bakery. This award-winning pub is a popular venue for Sunday lunch (booking advisable) and evening meals; it offers a good variety of home-cooked dishes. There is a large outdoor play area and well-behaved dogs are welcome in the bar area. It is situated on the Five Churches Walk, and is close to the Chesterfield Canal and Rotherham Ring Walk.
❀❶⇩♣P

Thurlstone

Huntsman

136 Manchester Road, S36 9QW (on A628)
✪ 6-11; 12-10.30 Sun
☎ (01226) 764892
Black Sheep Best Bitter; Taylor Landlord; Tetley Bitter; guest beers ⊞
This comfortable roadside inn, with its exposed beams and two real fires, is the hub of the local village. Visitors can enjoy their beer and conversation in an atmosphere of warm conviviality. Quizzes and acoustic nights provide the entertainment in this TV-free pub.
🏠❀⇩🍴

Tickhill

Carpenter's Arms

Westgate, DN11 9NE
✪ 12 (4 Mon)-11; 12-midnight Fri & Sat; 12-11 Sun
☎ (01302) 742839
John Smith's Bitter; guest beer ⊞
Appealing pub that has retained a cosy front room and adjoining bar despite the alterations that have taken place over the years. A large conservatory area doubles as a family room and leads to the garden. Decking has also been installed at the front of the pub, making it ideal for warm evenings. Traditional folk music sessions are held on the first Thursday evening of the month, and music quizzes are also staged regularly.
🏠☜❀❶⇩🍴(20, 22)♣P⇘

Scarbrough Arms

Sunderland Street, DN11 9QJ (near Buttercross landmark)
✪ 12-11 (10.30 Sun)
☎ (01302) 742977
Caledonian Deuchars IPA; Courage Directors; Greene King Abbot; John Smith's Bitter; guest beers ⊞
A deserving Guide entry since 1990, this three-roomed stone pub has won several awards from CAMRA including local Pub of the Year in 1997 and 2003 and, more recently, Pub of the Season in summer 2006. Originally a farmhouse, the building dates back to the 16th century, although structural changes have inevitably taken place over the years. The snug is a delight, with its barrel-shaped tables and real fire. This is one of the few pubs in the Doncaster district using over-sized lined glasses. 🏠Q❀⇩🍴(20, 22)♣P⇘⊟

Wath upon Dearne

Church House

Montgomery Square, S63 7RZ
✪ 9-midnight (1am Fri & Sat)
☎ (01709) 879518
Marston's Pedigree; guest beers ⊞
This impressive Wetherspoon pub is set in a pedestrian square in the town centre, in a handy spot for exploring the RSPB Wetlands centre at Wombwell. It serves a wide variety of beers from around the country, as well as a number of ales from local breweries such as Wentworth and Acorn. The pub is fully air-conditioned throughout. Children are welcome for meals. 🏠Q❀❶⇩🍴

Wentworth

George & Dragon

85 Main Street, S62 7TN
✪ 10-11 (10.30 Sun)
☎ (01226) 742440
Taylor Landlord; Wentworth WPA; guest beers ⊞
One of two pubs in the picturesque village of Wentworth, it is set back from the road to allow for generous gardens. This partly 16th-century house serves a range of ales from all over the country, featuring at least two beers from the nearby Wentworth Brewery plus cask cider. Home-cooked food is served and large parties can book the private room upstairs. 🏠Q❀❶⚑A🍴(227)♣P

Rockingham Arms

8 Main Street, S62 7TL
🕐 11-11; 12-10.30 Sun
☎ (01226) 742075
Theakston Best Bitter, Old Peculier; Wentworth Needles Eye, WPA; guest beers ⓗ

Country pub situated in the grounds of the Wentworth estate near the Wentworth Brewery. An ideal stop off point for walkers, the pub offers accommodation, local entertainment, a range of home-cooked meals plus 'dogs' dinners' for canine companions at only £1. A crown green bowling green is attached. The pub is very welcoming, warmed by real fires in winter and with a patio and garden for summer drinking. ⋈Q🛏🐾♿ ⏃ ◖&▲🚌(227)P

Whiston

Chequers Inn

Pleasley Road, S60 4HB (on A618, 1½ miles from M1 jct 33)
🕐 12 (4 Mon & Tue)-11; 12-11.30 Fri & Sat; 12-11 Sun
☎ (01709) 829168
Taylor Landlord; Tetley Bitter; guest beers ⓗ

Standing next to a 13th-century thatched barn and close to the Whiston crossroads, the Chequers replaces the original pub (demolished when the road was widened in 1933). A bright, lively local, it is often busy in the evening, particularly during quiz nights. There is a lounge area with pool table, and a dining area serving home-cooked meals (not Sun eve) where children are welcome until 7pm. The large raised garden features barbecues and a bar in summer. Handy for Valley Country Park. ❀◖🚌♣P⅃

Hind

285 East Bawtry Road, S60 4ET (on M1/M18 link road, ½ mile from M1)
🕐 12-11 (midnight Thu-Sat)
☎ (01709) 704351
Taylor Landlord; Tetley Bitter; guest beers ⓗ

This large pub was built for the Mappins Brewery in 1936. Originally named King Edward VIII, it was renamed when the king abdicated. Recently it became an Ember Inn and the beer range and quality have been much improved under the current manager. Popular for its food in the daytime, it is busy with locals in the evening. The interior has been opened out, and has good disabled access. There is outdoor seating in the car park and large rear garden. Two weekly quizzes are staged, and there is a snooker table upstairs (membership required to play). Q❀◖&🚌P⅃

Worsbrough Village

Edmunds Arms

25 Worsbrough Road, S70 5LW (off A61 on to Worsbrough Road)
🕐 11.45-3 (4 Sat), 6 (7 Mon)-11; 12-4, 7-10.30 Sun
☎ (01226) 206865
Samuel Smith OBB, ⓗ

Attractive stone-built pub opposite the historic church. A range of bar meals is served daily in the tap room and lounge, while full meals can be enjoyed in the restaurant (no food Mon or Sun eve). There is a popular seating area at the front of the pub and a garden at the rear. A regular quiz night is held on Tuesday. Q❀◖ⓓ&🚌(67, 265)P

YORKSHIRE (WEST)

Ackworth

Boot & Shoe

Wakefield Road, WF7 7DF (on A638, ¼ mile N of A628 roundabout)
🕐 12-11 (10.30 Sun)
☎ (01977) 610218 🌐 thebootandshoe.co.uk
Marston's Pedigree; John Smith's Bitter; Samuel Smith OBB; Taylor Landlord ⓗ

Busy, non-food pub in the village of Ackworth, which once supplied the grindstones for Sheffield's cutlery industry. The building dates back to the late 16th century, with some original features and a delightful semi-circular vestibule. It offers a choice of cask ales and is a rare outlet for Samuel Smith in the free trade. The pub has a reputation for live music, but there is no juke box. The village cricket field is behind the pub, which also makes a good start/finish for country walks. ⋈🛏❀&🚌♣P⅃

Baildon

Junction

1 Baildon Road, BD17 6AB (on Otley road, ½ mile from Shipley Station)
🕐 11.30-midnight (1am Fri & Sat); 12-midnight Sun
☎ (01274) 582009
Fuller's ESB; Oakham JHB; Saltaire Cascade Pale Ale; Taylor Landlord; Tetley Bitter; guest beers ⓗ

Traditional pub, winner of local CAMRA Pub of the Year in 2006, with a friendly atmosphere in its three rooms. Good quality ales are sold at low prices and change regularly, as Bill and Chris listen to their customers' requests for different beers. Attractions here include a TV tuned to sports, a games room and a free juke box. Home-cooked pub lunches are served until 2pm every day. Jam sessions are staged most Sunday nights. The cider is from Saxon. ❀◖≉🚌♣♠P⅃

Berry Brow

Railway

2 School Lane, HD4 7LT (off A616, off Station Lane)
🕐 3 (12 Sat)-11; 12-10.30 Sun
☎ (01484) 318052
Old Mill Bitter; guest beers ⓗ

Built on a hillside, the pub affords excellent views across the Holme Valley from its rear windows. A village local, the Railway is home to pool, darts and dominoes teams, and is also HQ for a Sunday league football team. It comprises three distinct drinking areas: a bar lounge, a snug and a pool room complete with serving hatch. Three guest beers are usually available, from micro or family brewers. ❀≉🚌(306, 319)

557

Bingley

Brown Cow
Ireland Bridge, BD16 2QX (100m along B6429 from main street)
✪ 12-3, 5-midnight; 12-midnight Fri-Sun
☎ (01274) 564345
Taylor Golden Best, Dark Mild, Best Bitter, Landlord, Ram Tam Ⓗ
Riverside pub offering the full range of Timothy Taylor's beers and excellent food – the tiger prawns and chicken sizzler is recommended! Meal bookings are advisable, but not always necessary. Inside there are three real fires, several fish tanks and leather sofas, with plenty of tables for diners and drinkers. Dogs are welcome. Classical music is played live on Friday and Saturday evenings. Outside there is a heated, covered patio with seating, where smoking is permitted.
🚪❀◑♿🚲≢🚍(727, 616)P🖢

Myrtle Grove
Main Street, BD16 1AJ
✪ 9am-midnight
☎ (01274) 568637
Greene King IPA; Marston's Pedigree, Old Empire; guest beers Ⓗ
A smaller than usual Wetherspoon outlet, this single-room pub enjoys a prominent location in the town centre on the main through road. Winner of local CAMRA Pub of the Season in 2005, the pub regularly stocks beers from local micro-breweries, often featuring Saltaire, E&S, Goose Eye and Copper Dragon, as well as the usual Wetherspoon range. The large front windows are opened out onto the street in warm weather. This Bradford winner is handy for public transport and close to town-centre car parks. Q◑♿≢🚍

Birstall

Black Bull
5 Kirkgate, WF17 9PB (off A652, near A643)
✪ 12-11 (10.30 Sun)
☎ (01274) 873039
Boddingtons Bitter; Worthington's Bitter; guest beer Ⓗ
Grade II listed building dating in parts from the 17th-century. The prisoners' dock remains in the upstairs courtroom, now used for functions, despite the last trial being held in 1839. On the ground floor are the snug (where children are allowed) and several partly opened-out areas with dark wooden decor, creating a cosy atmosphere. The popular guest beer changes often and comes from independents from near and far. Good value lunches are available daily.
❀◑🚍(220, 283)P🖢

Bradford

Castle Hotel
20 Grattan Road, BD1 2LU (jct of Barry St & Grattan Rd)
✪ 11-11; 12-10.30 Sun
☎ (01274) 393166
Mansfield Cask Ale; Marston's Pedigree; guest beers Ⓗ
The spacious L-shaped bar gives the impression that the Castle is actually much larger than it is. This one-time Webster's house, dating from circa 1898, now sells beers from a wide range of brewers from all over the UK. A recent addition is a limited assortment of bottled Belgian beers, possibly to be extended in the future. Copper Dragon, Cottage and Ossett are frequent suppliers.
≢(Forster Sq/Interchange)🚍♣

Cock & Bottle ☆
93 Barkerend Road, BD3 9AA (jct of Shipley Airedale Rd & Barkerend Rd)
✪ 11-11
☎ (01274) 222305
Beer range varies Ⓗ
Dating from the 19th-century, this Grade II listed building was until recently home to the Greenwood Brewery. This multi-roomed pub retains many original features: note especially the mahogany bar back, etched windows and woodwork. Part of the Bradford Heritage Trail, the pub plays host to the local Topic Folk Club on Thursday. Up to five rotating guest ales, mainly from northern England micro-breweries, are usually available.
◑≢(Forster Sq/Interchange)🚍♣P

Corn Dolly
110 Bolton Road, BD1 4DE (near Cathedral)
✪ 11.30-11; 12-10.30 Sun
☎ (01274) 720219
Black Sheep Special; Draught Bass; Everards Tiger; Moorhouses Dolly Bitter; guest beers Ⓗ
White-painted stone pub, opened as the Wharf in 1834 to serve the workers on the nearby canal basin. Inside, it is open plan but has a separate games area. Winner of several local CAMRA Pub of the Year awards, the pub serves ever-changing guest beers plus a house ale from Moorhouses, as well as good value lunchtime snacks.
🚪❀◑♿≢(Forster Sq/Interchange)🚍P

Fighting Cock
21-23 Preston Street, BD7 1JE (1 mile from city centre, off Thornton Rd)
✪ 11.30-11; 12-10.30 Sun
☎ (01274) 726907
Copper Dragon Golden Pippin; Greene King Abbot; Phoenix White Monk; Taylor Landlord; Theakston Old Peculier; guest beers Ⓗ
Popular, unassuming pub, just a short walk or bus ride from the city centre. Alongside 12 real ales, this regular local CAMRA award winner serves ciders, Belgian bottled beers and fruit wines. It attracts a wide variety of customers from loyal locals to well-travelled real ale enthusiasts. Lunches are served Monday to Saturday. 🚪◑♿🚍🐾🖢

Haigy's
31 Lumb Lane, Manningham, BD8 7QU
✪ 5 (12 Fri & Sat)-2am; 12-11 Sun
☎ (01274) 731644
Tetley Bitter; guest beers Ⓗ
Friendly locals' pub, a former Bradford CAMRA Pub of the Year, on the edge of the city. It offers up to four guest ales from northern England micros including Phoenix, Newby, Wyke and Ossett. The comfortable lounge sports a fine collection of porcelain teapots. This venue is popular with Bradford City fans on match days. Pool players excel on the

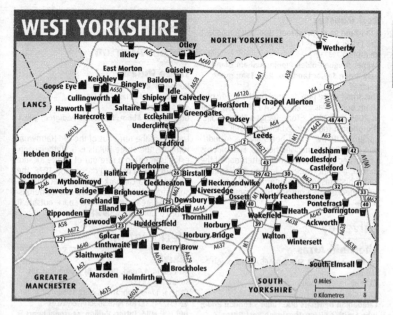

WEST YORKSHIRE

unusual hexagonal revolving pool table.
❀❅(Forster Sq/Interchange)🚆(620, 621)♣P

Prospect of Bradford

527 Bolton Road, BD3 0NW
🕑 2.30-5.30, 7-11; 2.30-11 Fri; 2-11 Sat; 12-11 Sun
☎ (01274) 727018
Taylor Golden Best; Tetley Bitter 🅷

This Victorian pub has been run by Richard and
Albina for almost 20 years. Regulars enjoy the
live entertainment and old-fashioned sing-
along evenings at the weekend – however,
this is definitely not karaoke. There is a games
room on the ground floor and a spacious
lounge area, and the first-floor function room
has its own real ale bar. Catering can be
provided for private parties.
🚶≉(Forster Sq/Interchange)🚆♣P

Sir Titus Salt

Unit B Windsor Baths, Morley Street, BD7 1AQ
(behind Alhambra Theatre)
🕑 9am-midnight (1am Fri & Sat)
☎ (01274) 732853
**Greene King Abbot; Marston's Pedigree; guest
beers** 🅷

Splendid Wetherspoon's conversion of the
original Windsor swimming baths, now named
after an eminent local industrialist and
philanthropist. An upstairs seating area
overlooks the main pub. Framed pictures
depict the educational heritage, literature and
art of the city. The pub draws a cosmopolitan
clientele including students from the
university and college, as well as
theatregoers, clubbers and diners at nearby
Indian restaurants. The location is handy for
the National Museum of the Media.
Q♿⏸♿≉(Forster Sq/Interchange)🚆♠

Brighouse

Crown

6 Lightcliffe Road, Waring Green, HD6 2DR

🕑 11-11.30 (midnight Fri & Sat); 12-11 Sun
☎ (01484) 715436
**Springhead Roaring Meg; Taylor Landlord; Tetley
Bitter; guest beer** 🅷

This welcoming, traditional pub has three
distinct seating areas and a large pool room. It
is particularly popular on Saturday nights,
when the resident pianist entertains, and
there is also a large-screen TV. The Crown is
home to the renowned Brighouse & Rastrick
Brass Band. ❀🚆♣P🍴

INDEPENDENT BREWERIES

Anglo Dutch Dewsbury
Barearts Todmorden
Bob's Ossett
Bridestone Hebden Bridge
Briscoe's Otley
Clark's Wakefield
Eastwood Elland
Elland Elland
Empire Slaithwaite
Fernandes Wakefield
Golcar Golcar
Goose Eye Keighley
Halifax Steam Hipperholme
Linfit Linthwaite
Little Valley Hebden Bridge
Old Bear Keighley
Old Spot Cullingworth
Ossett Ossett
Riverhead Marsden
Rodham's Otley
Ryburn Sowerby Bridge
Salamander Bradford
Saltaire Shipley
Summer Wine Brockholes
Tigertops Wakefield
Timothy Taylor Keighley
Turkey Goose Eye
WF6 Altofts

Red Rooster

123 Elland Road, Brookfoot, HD6 2QR (on A6025)
◆ 3 (12 Fri & Sat)-11; 12-10.30 Sun
☎ (01484) 713737
Copper Dragon Golden Pippin; Kelham Island Easy Rider; Taylor Landlord, Ram Tam; guest beers Ⓗ
This small stone pub, located on the inside of a sharp bend, was local CAMRA Pub of the Year in 2005 and 2007. Stone-flagged throughout, the original four-roomed layout is still apparent. Its five guest beers always include one from Ossett and Moorhouses. Live blues is performed on the last Sunday afternoon of the month, a charity week is held in mid-August and a beer festival in September. There is a small decked area outside for summer days. ✿⊠♣

Calverley

Thornhill Arms

18 Towngate, LS28 5NF (on A657, near parish church)
◆ 11.30-11; 12-11 Sun
☎ (0113) 256 5492
Caledonian Deuchars IPA; Fuller's London Pride; John Smith's Bitter; Theakston Best Bitter Ⓗ
A former coaching inn, there has been a building on this site since the 17th century. Built of traditional Yorkshire stone, this is a smart pub in the heart of the commuter belt between Leeds and Bradford. Good, hearty meals are available lunchtimes and evenings (not Sun eve). Note that the car park entrance is at an acute angle to a busy main road. There are plans for a covered outdoor smoking area. ✿◑&⊠♣P⅃

Castleford

Griffin

Lock Lane, WF10 2LB (off A656)
◆ 2 (12 Fri & Sat)-midnight; 12-11.30 Sun
☎ (01977) 557551
John Smith's Bitter; guest beer Ⓗ
Small, two-roomed, traditional local on the northern outskirts of the town, 100 metres from the renowned Lock Lane ARLFC and new sports centre. The landlord regularly rotates a guest beer from the Enterprise list. Lunchtime snacks are available in the summer. The pub hosts quiz nights on Wednesday and Sunday and bingo on Wednesday. A friendly greeting is provided by the pub dog. Q✿⊟⊠♣P⅃

Shoulder of Mutton

18 Methley Road, WF10 1LX (off A6032)
◆ 11 (12 Sun)-4, 7-11
☎ (01977) 736039
Tetley Dark Mild, Bitter; guest beer Ⓗ
This traditional free house started life as a farmhouse back in 1632. The landlord is an enthusiastic supporter of cask ale and is justifiably proud of the many awards he has won for his cellarmanship. Expect lively conversation and a warm welcome. The George Formby Society meets here on the last Wednesday of each month and there are open live music sessions on Sunday afternoon (when the pub may stay often all day). Traditional games including ring the bull and

nine men's morris are played here. ♨✿⊟&≢⊠♣P⅃

Chapel Allerton

Three Hulats

Harrogate Road, LS7 3NB
◆ 9am-midnight (1am Fri & Sat)
☎ (0113) 262 0524
Greene King Abbot; Marston's Pedigree; guest beers Ⓗ
Located at the terminus of the Old Harrowgate turnpike, the Three Hulats is a Wetherspoon's establishment in a rare out-of-centre location. This site was a bowling green until 1978, then turned into a car park and more recently a supermarket. Inside, this pub has numerous different areas, and there is space outside for alfresco drinking. ✿◑⬥⊠P

Cleckheaton

Marsh

28 Bradford Road, BD19 5BJ (200m S of bus station on A638)
◆ 1-11; 12-midnight Fri & Sat; 12-11 Sun
☎ (01274) 872104 ⬥ oldmillbrewery.co.uk
Old Mill Mild, Bitter, Bullion, seasonal beers Ⓗ
Furnished in the style characteristic of the Old Mill estate of 19 tied houses, this stone-built flat-iron-shaped building is a comfortable pub catering mainly for the over-30s. The Wednesday evening quiz is very popular and well-supported. The regular Old Mill beers go down a treat, and are supplemented by a rotating range of seasonal beers. Situated a short walk from the town centre, the pub is easy to find and offers a hearty welcome. ✿&⊠♣P

Darrington

Spread Eagle

Estcourt Road, WF8 3AP (off A1)
◆ 12-3, 5-11; 12-11 Sat; 12-10.30 Sun
☎ (01977) 699698
John Smith's Bitter; Tetley Bitter; guest beers Ⓗ
Pleasant, warm, friendly pub in the heart of the village. Popular with a good cross-section of the community, it is very lively in the evenings, and is rapidly building a good reputation for its delicious food. A quiz is held on Monday evening. Children are allowed in the pub until 9pm and there is a function room for hire. There are rumours of a ghost – a boy who was shot for horse rustling in 1685. Q✿◑&⊠P⅃

Dewsbury

Huntsman

Chidswell Lane, Shaw Cross, WF12 7SW (600m from A653/B6128 jct)
◆ 12-3 (not Mon), 7 (5 Thu & Fri)-11
☎ (01924) 275700
Taylor Landlord; guest beers Ⓗ
A worthy winner of the local CAMRA Pub of the Season award in spring 2006, this popular pub sits on the edge of the village and affords spectacular views over open countryside, making it a firm favourite with walkers and cyclists. Originally a pair of cottages, the

traditional Yorkshire range, horse brasses and real fires make for a homely, olde-world atmosphere. The house beer is brewed by Highwood and guest ales often come from small breweries. Lunches are served Tuesday to Saturday. ♨❀◐☕🅿♿

Leggers Inn

Robinsons Boatyard, Mill Street East, WF12 9BD
(off B649, follow brown signs to Canal Basin)
🕒 11.30 (12 Sun)-11
☎ (01924) 502846
Everards Tiger; guest beers Ⓗ
Converted from an old hayloft, the Leggers has two rooms plus a large function room, all on the first floor, overlooking a canal basin where houseboats are moored all year. Bric-a-brac on low beams (mind your head!) includes pub memorabilia and old newspaper headlines. A pool table and games machine are in one room, while the bar room has a warming fire in winter. A blackboard displays the names of the beers that are currently being dispensed on the seven handpumps and in the cellar.
♨❀◐☕♣♠🅿

Shepherd's Boy

157 Huddersfield Road, WF13 2RP
🕒 12-11 (midnight Sat)
☎ (01924) 454116 ⏺ ossett-brewery.co.uk
Ossett Pale Gold, Excelsior; Taylor Landlord; guest beers Ⓗ
A fine example of an excellent Ossett Brewery pub reconstruction, with the heart and soul of the pub reinstated and many original features emphasised, including the Webster's front door. Four separate, comfortable drinking areas are partially separated by trademark brick arches. Guest beers always include a rotating mild or stout. The house bitter Shepherds Boy is Black Bull rebadged. Quality draught and bottled international beers and a range of good wines are also available. Tuesday night is quiz night, and live music is hosted on the last Wednesday of each month. Lunches are served Monday to Saturday.
❀◐♿≠☕🅿

West Riding Licensed Refreshment Rooms

Railway Station, Wellington Road, WF13 1HF
(platform 2 Dewsbury Station)
🕒 11 (12 Mon)-11; 10-midnight Sat
☎ (01924) 459193 ⏺ imissedthetrain.com
Black Sheep Best Bitter, Riggwelter; Taylor Dark Mild, Landlord; guest beers Ⓗ
Serving a range of fine real ales from eight handpumps, including one from Dewsbury's Anglo-Dutch Brewery, this excellent, friendly, multi award-winning pub in the Grade II listed station building was one of four finalists in CAMRA's National Pub of the Year 2006 competition. It hosts annual summer and winter beer festivals and occasionally live music. Monday is quiz night, on Tuesday pie and peas are served, Wednesday is curry night. The pub is also justly famous for its good value lunches (served Mon-Sat).
♨❀◐♿≠☕🅿♠

East Morton

Busfeild Arms

Main Road, BD20 5SP
🕒 11.30-11 (midnight Fri & Sat)
☎ (01274) 550931
Taylor Landlord; Tetley Bitter; guest beers Ⓗ
Solidly built Yorkshire village pub where friendly staff offer a range of four real ales, two changing regularly. The kitchen produces a selection of good value meals. There is a separate public bar with a pool table and TV. The middle bar and lounge have been opened out, with the latter mainly used by diners.
❀◐🍴☕(727, 729)🅿

Eccleshill

Royal Oak

39 Stony Lane, BD2 2HN (on main street through village)
🕒 11-11 (11.30 Fri & Sat)
☎ (01274) 639182
Marston's Pedigree; John Smith's Bitter; Taylor Landlord; Tetley Bitter Ⓗ
Busy village local with a traditional feel, enhanced by a separate tap room and distinct drinking areas. Cellarmanship awards line the walls and reflect the landlord's skill and enthusiasm for real ale. Popular quizzes take place on Mondays and Fridays at teatime and Tuesday evening. The covered and heated rear garden attracts summer drinkers and smokers.
❀🍴☕(640, 641)♣♠

Elland

Barge & Barrel

10-20 Park Road, HX5 9HP (on A6025 over Elland Bridge)
🕒 12-midnight (1am Fri & Sat)
☎ (01422) 373623
Black Sheep Best Bitter, Special; Eastwood Best Bitter, Gold Award; Elland Bargee; Phoenix Wobbly Bob; Shepherd Neame Spitfire; guest beers Ⓗ
Large canal and roadside pub with a spacious bar area, retaining three of the original West Riding Brewery windows. The decor features breweriana and the Mitchell Eastwood Brewery is to the side of the building. Five guest ales come from micro-breweries. Beer festivals are held over the spring bank holiday weekend and in late autumn. Sunday is curry night, no food is served on Monday. In summer, there is pleasant outdoor drinking next to the canal, and a smoking shed is planned. ♨❀◐☕(537, 538)♣🅿♠

Fleece Inn

42 Westgate, HX5 0BB (on corner of Westgate & Jepson Lane)
🕒 12-midnight
☎ (01422) 373129
Jennings Sneck Lifter; Marston's Burton Bitter; guest beers Ⓗ
Originally a farmhouse dating from 1610, this stone-built pub retains many original features including the mullioned windows and large open fireplaces. The upper bar area is a quiet space where the real ale is served, while the stone-flagged lower bar has a large inglenook fireplace and a pool table. Upstairs there is

also a quiet room for meetings. The pub has resident pool and football teams, a quiz night is held on Thursday, and live bands play on Friday and Saturday. Food is served lunchtime and early evening. A smoking area is provided outside. Camping is permitted during medieval events in summer.
🏚️🏠🕸️🍴🚲(501, 503)♣P

Greengates

Albion Inn
25 New Line, BD10 9AS
🕐 12-midnight (11 Mon & Tue); 12-11.30 Sun
☎ (01274) 613211
Acorn Barnsley Bitter; John Smith's Bitter; Tetley Bitter 🅷
Busy roadside local on the Leeds-Keighley bus route. It comprises an L-shaped lounge and a rare, traditional tap room where pub games are keenly contested. Mine hosts, Steve and Bev, look after their regulars and the pub boasts a thriving social club, but strangers also receive a friendly welcome. The Albion is a rare outlet in the area for Barnsley bitter, and guest ales are occasionally available.
🕸️🍴🚲(760)♣P🗓️

Greetland

Greetland Community & Sporting Association
Rochdale Road, HX4 8JG (on B6113)
🕐 5-11; 4-midnight Fri & Sat; 12-11 Sun
☎ (01422) 370140
Taylor range; guest beers 🅷
Award-winning sports and social club, set back from the road at the top of Greetland village, with great views extending over Halifax. Current Yorkshire Club of the Year and National Club of the Year runner-up, it has now been awarded CAMRA National Club of the Year 2007. The house beer, Duckworth's Delight, is brewed by Coach House. A decked area outside is pleasant on summer days.
🏚️Q🕸️🚲♣

Guiseley

Coopers
4-6 Otley Road, LS20 8AH (opp Morrisons on A65)
🕐 12-11
☎ (01943) 878835
Black Sheep Best Bitter; Caledonian Deuchars IPA; Taylor Landlord; guest beers 🅷
This modern café-bar, decked with pre-War European posters, dispenses eight local and regional real ales, supplemented by a range of continental beers. Heavily food-oriented, the specials board features both main and dessert courses. The upstairs restaurant and function room houses a theatre and holds regular comedy and musical events, featuring mainly cover bands. A polite notice at the entrance states that no children are allowed on the premises as a 'no-child certificate' is held.
🕸️🍴🚲♿⇌

Guiseley Factory Workers Club
6 Town Street, LS20 9DT (10 mins' walk from station)
🕐 1-4 (5 Mon), 7-11; 1-11 Fri; 12-11 Sat & Sun

☎ (01943) 874793
Tetley Bitter; guest beers 🅷
This small, friendly working men's club in the old centre of Guiseley is a meeting place for local community groups and societies. A traditional three-room club, it has a lounge, snooker room (free tables on Tuesday) and a concert room, hosting Saturday night turns. The two guest beers are a mix from local micro-brewers and small regionals. Sunday is quiz night, and sports events are shown on the large-screen TV on Friday and Saturday. A beer festival is held in April. CAMRA members are welcome on production of their membership card or this Guide. 🏠🕸️♿⇌P

Ings
45A Ings Lane, LS20 9HR (off A65, near Guiseley Town FC)
🕐 11-11 (midnight Fri & Sat)
☎ (01943) 873315
Black Sheep Best Bitter; John Smith's Bitter; Taylor Landlord; Tetley Bitter 🅷
From the pub's rear windows there are scenic views of the surrounding wet marshland area from which it derives its name. The three tiled fireplaces and suspended tabletop canopy lighting highlight a memorable collection of artefacts and pictures. A music quiz on Tuesday and general knowledge quiz on Thursday provide entertainment.
🏚️Q🕸️⇌🚲(97A)P

Halifax

Big Six
10 Horsfall Street, Saville Park, HX1 3HG (off A646, Skircoat Moor Lane at King Cross)
🕐 5-11; 3.30-11.30 Fri; 12-11.30 Sat; 12-11 Sun
☎ (01422) 350169
Adnams Bitter; guest beers 🅷
Busy, friendly pub in a row of terraced houses, near the Free School Lane recreation ground. A through corridor divides two lounges from the bar, which has standing room and a cosy seating area. The decor features items relating to the pub's history as well as reminders of the Big Six Mineral Water Company that owned the premises a century ago. Guest beers on offer are chiefly from respected regional and local micro-breweries. Dog walkers are welcome. The outside area for smokers is across Horsfall Street. 🏚️Q🕸️🚲♣⇌

Three Pigeons ☆
1 Sun Fold, South Parade, HX1 2LX
🕐 3 (12 Thu-Sat)-11.30; 12-11 Sun
☎ (01422) 347001
Ossett Pale Gold, Excelsior; Taylor Landlord; guest beers 🅷
This National Inventory listed pub dates from 1932 and has had its period features restored following its acquisition by the Ossett Brewery. The central octagonal drinking area/lobby has a ceiling painting depicting the birds that give the pub its name. Three comfortable rooms radiate from this area. Guest beers include an additional Ossett brew and a dark beer. Numerous local organisations make this pub their meeting place. 🏚️Q🕸️⇌🚲♣

William IV
247 King Cross Road, HX1 3JL

✪ 11-11; 11.30-10.30 Sun
☎ (01422) 354889
Tetley Bitter Ⓗ
Popular watering hole located in the King Cross shopping street. The lounge has seating and standing space facing the bar, and behind this is a small public bar served by a hatch. To the right, additional seating is provided in a raised area created from former shop premises. Guests can enjoy lunches served Monday to Saturday, or keep up to date with sporting events on the TV screens. Picnic benches behind the pub make for pleasant outdoor drinking on milder days. There is ample parking nearby. ❀⊕🖵🖾♣

Harecroft

Station Hotel
BD15 0BP (on B6144, opp Station Rd)
✪ 4 (12 Sun)-midnight
☎ (01535) 272430
Black Sheep Best Bitter; Old Spot seasonal beer; Taylor Landlord Ⓗ
This rural pub attracts locals from the village as well as walkers and cyclists on the nearby Great Northern Trail. No trains have called here for 50 years, but visitors can catch a bus from Bingley or Cullingworth. The two good-sized rooms have open fires in winter, and a rear games room overlooks the beer garden. ⇧❀🖾(727, 729)♣P

Haworth

Black Bull Hotel
119 Main Street, BD22 8DP
✪ 11.30-11.30
☎ (01535) 642249
Caledonian Deuchars IPA; guest beers Ⓗ
Situated at the top of the cobbled main street, adjacent to Haworth Parish Church, the Black Bull is reputed to have been the favourite watering hole of Branwell Bronte. There have also been reports of ghosts and paranormal phenomena. Inside, the pub is L-shaped with low ceilings. The walls are decorated with pictures of local scenes and characters. Live Celtic music plays on Wednesday night, and 60s and 70s music on Thursday. Two guest beers often come from local micros.
⇧❀Ⓓ🅐⇌(KWLR)🖾P

Haworth Old Hall Inn
8 Sun Street, BD22 8BP (bottom of Main St)
✪ 11-11 (11.30 Thu; midnight Fri & Sat); 12-11 Sun
☎ (01535) 642709 ⊕ hawortholdhall.co.uk
Jennings Bitter, Cumberland Ale, Cocker Hoop, Sneck Lifter, seasonal beers; guest beer Ⓗ
Lovely Tudor manor house, full of charm and character, located close to the famous Main Street. On entering through the substantial, studded oak main door you will find stone floors, arches, mullioned windows, two huge fireplaces and a splendid wood-panelled bar. Good home-cooked food is served and the pub can get very busy at weekends. Quiz night is Thursday. ⇧❀🍴Ⓓ🅐⇌(KWLR)🖾P⅃

Keighley & Worth Valley Railway Buffet Car
Haworth Station, BD22 8NJ (join at any station on Worth Valley line)
✪ 11.15-5.15 Sat & Sun, Mon-Fri Jul, Aug & school hols; other dates as advertised (check timetable)
☎ (01535) 645214 ⊕ kwvr.co.uk
Beer range varies Ⓗ
Volunteer-run railway with bars on the trains serving draught real ales decanted into tea urn-style containers. The coaches have recently been refurbished. Usually one bar is in use, but up to three may be pressed into service during busy periods and for special events, subject to staff availability. Views change from industrial to rural as the train progresses between stations – see how many film and TV locations you can recognise. Please note that a ticket to travel must be purchased. Q🅐⇌🖾P

Heath

King's Arms ☆
Heath Common, WF1 5SL (off A655, Wakefield-Normanton road)
✪ 11.30-3, 5.30-11; 11.30-11 Sat; 12-11 Sun
☎ (01924) 377527
Clark's Classic Blonde; Taylor Landlord; Tetley Bitter; guest beers Ⓗ
Built in the early part of the 18th century and converted into an inn in 1841, the King's Arms is one of four pubs owned by the Clark's Brewery of Wakefield. The interior consists of three oak-panelled rooms, lit by gas lighting. It enjoys a good reputation for food, which is served all day Sunday. Children are welcome in the conservatory. There is disabled access to both pub and toilets. A quiz is staged on Tuesday. ⇧Q🌣❀Ⓓ🅕🖾♣P

Hebden Bridge

Fox & Goose
9 Heptonstall Road, HX7 6AZ (on A646)
✪ 12-11 (10.30 Sun)
☎ (01422) 842649
Castle Rock Harvest Pale; guest beers Ⓗ
This is a genuine family-owned and friendly free house. There are three rooms with a bar billiards table. A frequent finalist and several times a winner of the local CAMRA Pub of the Year competition, it holds regular beer festivals (ring for details), and its motto regarding guest ales is 'a selection of a best-un, a strong-un and a dark-un'. The family has traced the pub's history to a 12th-century ale house, run by a landlady called Margery, whose name kept appearing in the local magistrates' court register for running an illegal ale house – a 'tiddlywink' – hence the house beer's name, Margery's Tiddlywink, brewed by Millstone. Q❀⇌🖾♣♠

Moyles
4-10 New Road, HX7 8AD
✪ 7.30-11 (10.30 Sun)
☎ (01422) 845272
Pictish Brewer's Gold; guest beers Ⓗ
This bar/restaurant is primarily a food establishment, furnished in an imaginative and minimalist style. The gents' toilets are

especially well designed, making good use of a tiny space. There are four main areas divided by walls with simple fireplaces. The beer pumps are partly hidden by the bar. The outside balcony, pleasant on mild days, looks out across the canal basin. Moyles serve a fine range of bottled ales, whiskies and wines. ▲Q✿◖◗⬧≠🄱🗲

Heckmondwike

New Charnwood

4 Westgate, WF16 0EH (on A638 near green)
✪ 11-3, 5-11 (not Tue eve); closed Mon; 12-9 Sun
☎ (01924) 406512 ⊕ thenewcharnwood.co.uk
Taylor Landlord; guest beers 🄷
Built as the Oddfellows' Hall in the late 19th century, this attractive bay-windowed building has evolved from a restaurant into a bar and dining room, with an appealing front garden. Three handpulled ales usually include an Ossett beer and a dark mild or old ale. The same choice is available in the 80-seat function room upstairs. Good food is served Tuesday to Sunday lunchtimes and Wednesday to Saturday evenings. ✿◖🄿🗲

Hipperholme

Travellers Inn

53 Tanhouse Hill, HX3 8HN (on A58, back of camping centre)
✪ 12-11.30
☎ (01422) 202494
Ossett Pale Gold, Travellers Ale, Excelsior; Taylor Landlord; guest beers 🄷
Traditional stone-built local, opposite the former railway station, that has taken in adjoining cottages to create a series of distinct spaces. Children are welcome in the upper area until 7pm, where a wide selection of board games is available. Bar skittles and shove-ha'penny are also played. Dogs are welcome when the pub is not busy. There is a small south-facing drinking space outside by the road. A wide range of Belgian bottled beers, eight malt whiskies, 27 wines and traditional cider are also sometimes available. Wednesday is curry night. There is a covered yard for smokers. ▲✿🄿♣🗲

Holmfirth

Hervey's Bar

Norridge Bottom, HD9 7BB (on riverside, behind bus station)
✪ 11-12.30am summer; 4 (2 Sat)-12.30am; 2-11.30 Sun winter; closed Mon
☎ (01484) 686925 ⊕ herveys.co.uk
Black Sheep Best Bitter; Copper Dragon range; Cottage range 🄷
In the heart of 'Summer Wine' country, Hervey's is a continental-style café-bar, also offering a range of wines and freshly-brewed flavoured coffees. The licensees alternate the Copper Dragon beers between Golden Pippin, Best Bitter and Scotts 1816; and Black Sheep Best Bitter alternates with a Cottage range. The interior is split-level with bare floorboards, its café/bar feel enhanced by a large white Aga range and rustic furniture. The main bar area opens out onto a paved area outside with

tables and parasols. The pub's Mediterranean-style bar snacks (summer only) are renowned. ✿◖⬧🄿🗲

Rose & Crown (Nook)

7 Victoria Square, HD9 2DN (down alley off Hollowgate)
✪ 11.30 (12 Sun)-midnight
☎ (01484) 683960 ⊕ thenookpublichouse.co.uk
Moorhouses Black Cat Mild; Taylor Best Bitter, Landlord; Tetley Bitter; guest beers 🄷
A welcome return to the Guide for the Nook which has featured 30 times over the years. There has been a pub on this site since 1754, and for the last 33 years it has been run by the same family. Appearing small at first glance, it is deceptively spacious, and also has an outside drinking area. Attractions include monthly live music, a range of continental beers and an annual beer festival. Plans are afoot for opening a micro-brewery. ▲✿◖⬧♣🗲

Sycamore Inn

15 New Mill Road, HD9 7SH (on A635, 1 mile NE of Holmfirth)
✪ 11.30-2.30 (not Mon), 4.30-11; 11.30-11 Sat; 12-10.30 Sun
☎ (01484) 683458
Tetley Bitter; guest beers 🄷
A semi-rural pub with a long history, the Sycamore has been sympathetically regenerated in recent years. Three homely rooms, one with a wide-screen TV, provide ample relaxation and abound with atmosphere. Folk and blues nights are held once a month. The menu features many choices and food is cooked to order, including three-course Sunday lunch at a competitive price. Up to five guest beers are sourced via the SIBA network and usually come from northern breweries. ◖🄿♣P

Horbury

Boon's

6 Queen Street, WF4 6LP (off High St)
✪ 11-3, 5-11; 11-11 Fri & Sat; 12-10.30 Sun
☎ (01924) 280442
Clark's Classic Blonde; John Smith's Bitter; Taylor Landlord; guest beers 🄷
Centrally located just off the High Street, this Clark's Brewery tied house caters for all age groups and acts a real community pub. Three guest beers are always available. The pub has a sizeable outdoor drinking area where an annual beer festival is staged in summer. ▲✿◖🄿♣

Horbury Bridge

Bingley Arms

221 Bridge Road, WF4 5NL (next to River Calder)
✪ 12-midnight (10.30 Sun)
☎ (01924) 281331
Black Sheep Best Bitter; Caledonian Deuchars IPA; Tetley Bitter; guest beers 🄷
This pub is bordered by the River Calder on one side and the Aire and Calder Navigation on the other. It has its own moorings, so attracts boaters, particularly in the summer, when the large garden comes into its own.

The interior comprises two rooms, both warmed by a fire in winter. ♨Q☎❀◖♿✉♣P

Horsforth

Abbey
99 Pollard Lane, Newlay, LS13 1EQ (vehicle access via Pollard Lane) OS239368
✪ 12-11 (10.30 Sun)
☎ (0113) 258 1248 ⊕ theabbey-inn.co.uk
Old Bear Abbey Ale; Tetley Bitter; guest beers Ⓗ
Grade II listed stone building with low, beamed ceilings, situated between the Leeds-Liverpool Canal and the River Aire, with moorings nearby. The pub takes its name from 12th-century Kirkstall Abbey, just over a mile away, and is popular with walkers exploring the valley. Abbey Ale is brewed for the Abbey by the Old Bear Brewery, and the four guest beers are mainly from regional breweries including Copper Dragon, Elland, Ossett and Wharfedale. There are jam sessions on Tuesday, live music on Saturday and quiz night on Sunday. An annual weekend beer and music festival is hosted in July. ❀◖♿✉♣P⚘

Town Street Tavern
16-18 Town Street, LS18 4RJ
✪ 12-11 (10.30 Sun)
☎ (0113) 281 9996
Black Sheep Best Bitter; Caledonian Deuchars IPA; Copper Dragon Golden Pippin; Taylor Best Bitter; guest beers Ⓗ
Part of the Market Town Taverns chain and converted from a former off-licence, this pub is situated in the heart of Horsforth's main shopping area. Eight handpumps offer a multitude of ales, complemented by a range of foreign beers on draught. There is an outdoor drinking and dining area to the side of the building. Group policy forbids children, music and games machines, although traditional and modern board games are available. Dogs are welcome. Q❀◖♦✉♣P⚘

Huddersfield

Cowcliffe & Netheroyd Hill Liberal Club
181 Netheroyd Hill Road, Cowcliffe, HD2 2LZ (off A641, 2 miles from town centre)
✪ 7.30-11 (midnight Fri); 3-midnight Sat; 12-11 Sun
☎ (01484) 514706 ⊕ cowcliffelib.co.uk
Taylor Golden Best, Dark Mild, Best Bitter; guest beer Ⓗ
Winner of local CAMRA Club of the Year 2006, this popular little club is friendly and welcoming. Downstairs is a large lounge with Sky TV and a smaller committee room behind. The club members are fond of their mild (two are always available), and it is no surprise that the club has won CAMRA awards for its mild. It is home to bowling, snooker and pool teams. The upstairs snooker room opens out onto the bowling green, which affords fantastic views across the valley. Show this Guide or CAMRA membership card for entry. ✉(380, 381)♣P⚘

Grove Inn
2 Spring Grove Street, HD2 4BP
✪ 12-11 (midnight Fri & Sat)
☎ (01484) 430113 ⊕ groveinn.co.uk

Taylor Golden Best, Landlord; guest beers Ⓗ
A first time entry in the Guide for this two-roomed corner pub which offers up to nine guest ales, chosen to provide a full range of styles, including mild and stout. More than 180 bottled beers and seven foreign draughts including a guest are also available. The pub, surrounded by car parks and opposite Huddersfield bus station, has been transformed into a beer lovers' shrine. The Grove is easily reached from across the region. Folk music is played occasionally on weekday evenings. Q❀♦✉⇌✉Ⓖ

Marsh Liberal Club
31 New Hey Road, HD3 4AL (on A640, 1½ miles from town centre)
✪ 12-2, 7-11; 12-11 Sat & Sun
☎ (01484) 420152 ⊕ marshlib.co.uk
Taylor Golden Best, Best Bitter; Theakston Best Bitter; guest beers Ⓗ
This friendly club is based in an impressive Grade II listed building comprising a lounge, pool room and snooker room as well as the main bar area. Two guest beers are usually on offer, sourced from independent micros. Crown green bowling is popular outside in summer. The building has wheelchair access and a disabled WC. Show this Guide or a CAMRA membership card to be signed in. ❀♿✉♣P⚘

Rat & Ratchet
40 Chapel Hill, HD1 3EB (on A616, below ring road)
✪ 3 (12 Wed & Thu)-midnight; 12-12.30am Fri & Sat; 12-11 Sun
☎ (01484) 542400
Ossett Pale Gold, Silver King, Excelsior; Taylor Best Bitter, Landlord; guest beers Ⓗ
Traditional multi-roomed former brew-pub. The decor is enhanced by brewery adverts and music posters. The back room is heated by a welcoming stove in winter. Usually 12 beers are on sale, including four permanent ales and one rotated Ossett beer. One handpump is dedicated to mild and real cider is served. Several buses pass the pub. ❀✉♣●P

Shoulder of Mutton
11 Neale Road, Lockwood, HD1 3TN (off B6108, near A616 jct)
✪ 5 (2 Sat & Sun)-11.30
☎ (01484) 424835
Black Sheep Best Bitter; Taylor Golden Best, Landlord; Tetley Dark Mild, Bitter; guest beers Ⓗ
A good, old-fashioned back-street local, opposite the spot where the Bentley & Shaws Brewery once stood. Guests enter via a green-tiled lobby into a open lounge area with a semi-octagonal bar. Though partially opened-out, much of the original layout remains, with two wood-panelled small rooms either side of the entrance doorway. The regular Yorkshire beers are complemented by two guest ales. ❀⇌(Lockwood)✉♣P⚘

Slubbers Arms
1 Halifax Old Road, Hillhouse, HD1 6HW (off A641 Bradford Road)
✪ 12-2.30 (3 Sat), 5.30-11.30; 7-11.30 Sun
☎ (01484) 429032

Taylor Golden Best, Best Bitter, Landlord; guest beer Ⓗ

The only Timothy Taylor tied house in Huddersfield, this wedge-shaped corner terrace pub dates back 150 years to the days when the town boasted a vibrant textile industry. Situated on the edge of the town centre, it offers a warm, friendly environment. Wherever you sit in this characterful pub you are invited to admire the textile memorabilia that adorn the walls. Informal live Irish music is played most Mondays, and folk music on the first Thursday of the month. Taylor's Ram Tam and Dark Mild alternate during the winter.

🏠Q🐾🕙⇌🚋(328, 363)♣🌿

Star Inn

7 Albert Street, Lockwood, HD1 3PJ (off A616)
🕔 5 (12 Sat)-11; closed Mon; 12-10.30 Sun
☎ (01484) 545443 ⊕ thestarinn.info

Pictish Brewers Gold; Taylor Best Bitter, Landlord; guest beers Ⓗ

Back-street local enjoying deserved success since it opened a few years ago. The emphasis is on quality ale, conversation and a friendly atmosphere, without juke box, pool table or games machines. Three drinking areas surround the bar and open fire. A wide range of beers is on offer here from seven constantly-changing handpumps, one dedicated to a mild, stout or porter. Regular beer festivals (two or more a year) are staged in the garden marquee. 🏠Q🐾🕙👍🚋🌿

Station Tavern

St George's Square, HD1 1JB (in station building)
🕔 11.30-11; 12-10.30 Sun
☎ (01484) 511058 ⊕ the-station-tavern.co.uk

Beer range varies Ⓗ

Situated in the Grade I listed railway station building, the Station is an established free house that supports regional and micro-breweries by selling eight beers that are changed frequently. This friendly pub has a large, square room and stage with mosaic-tiled floors, a snug and a side room housing a TV, piano and computer. There is live music on Sunday afternoon and folk, blues and piano sing-along evenings once a month. 🏠👍⇌🚋

White Cross Inn

2 Bradley Road, Bradley, HD2 1XD (on A62)
🕔 11.45-11; 12-10.30 Sun
☎ (01484) 425728

Copper Dragon Black Gold; Taylor Golden Best; guest beers Ⓗ

Standing at the busy crossroads of Leeds and Bradley roads, this popular pub attracts both locals and passers-by, including boaters from the Huddersfield Narrow Canal and the Calder and Hebble Navigation. Past landlords are recorded going back as far as 1806. The large lounge extends on either side of the bare-boarded bar area where there are normally four guest ales available. Local CAMRA Pub of the Year 2005, it fields a pool team and hosts an annual beer festival in February.
🐾🕙👍🚋(202, 203)♣🌿

Idle

Idle Working Men's Club

23 High Street, BD10 8NB

🕔 12-4 Mon; 7.30-11 Tue-Thu; 12-4, 7-11 Fri; 12-5, 7-11.30 Sat; 12-4, 7-10.30 Sun
☎ (01274) 613602 ⊕ idle-workingmensclub.com

Tetley Bitter; guest beers Ⓗ

This club attracts members simply because of its name – souvenirs and merchandise are available! The concert room hosts live acts on weekend evenings, while the lounge offers a quieter alternative. The downstairs games room houses two full-sized snooker tables plus a large-screen TV for sports events, dartboard and cards. Show this Guide or CAMRA membership to be signed in. Parking is possible at a nearby doctor's surgery in the evenings and at the weekend. 🚋♣P🌿

Symposium Ale & Wine Bar

7 Albion Road, BD10 9PY

🕔 12-2.30 (not Mon & Tue), 5.30-11; 12-11 Fri & Sat; 12-10.30 Sun
☎ (01274) 616587

Caledonian Deuchars IPA; guest beers Ⓗ

At the heart of Idle village, this popular bar is part of the Market Town Taverns chain. A former restaurant, the food is of high quality and themed food evenings are a highlight. A single regular beer is supplemented by five guests, usually from northern England, often featuring one brewery's range at a time. It also stocks a wide range of foreign beers in bottles and on draught. The rear snug leads to a balcony which is popular in summer.
Q🐾🍽️🚋

Ilkley

Bar T'at

7 Cunliffe Road, LS29 9DZ

🕔 12-11 (11.30 Fri & Sat)
☎ (01943) 608888

Black Sheep Best Bitter; Caledonian Deuchars IPA; Taylor Landlord; guest beers Ⓗ

Popular side-street pub owned by Market Town Taverns, renowned for the quality of its beer and food. Guest ales usually include a Rooster's product and brews from Yorkshire micros. A wide choice of good foreign beers is available in bottles and on draught. Home-cooked food is on the menu every day. This three-storey building has a music-free bar area and there is a covered, heated area outdoors for smokers. It stands next to the main town-centre car park near the bus stop. Q🐾🍽️⇌🚋(963)🌿

Riverside Hotel

Riverside Gardens, Bridge Lane, LS29 9EU

🕔 10-11 (10.30 Sun)
☎ (01943) 607338

Copper Dragon Best Bitter; Samuel Smith OBB; Tetley Bitter Ⓗ

Family-run hotel with 10 bedrooms set by the River Wharfe in a popular park. The adjacent fish and chip shop and ice cream servery also run by the hotel are popular in summer. Meals are served until early evening, and the bar has a happy hour on weekdays, 4-8pm. The open fire is a welcome sight in cold weather. It is just 10 minutes' walk to the bus and train stations. 🏠🐾🛏️🍽️⇌🚋(963)P

Keighley

Boltmakers Arms

117 East Parade, BD21 5HX (200m from station)

🕐 11-11 (midnight Tue-Sat); 12-11 Sun

☎ (01535) 661936 🌐 timothy-taylor.co.uk/boltmakers

Taylor Golden Best, Best Bitter, Landlord; guest beer H

Long a Mecca for Taylor fans, this family-run pub continues to live up to its reputation. Small but warmly welcoming, the split-level pub is decorated with music memorabilia and whisky artefacts. Enjoy the quiz on Tuesday, live music on alternate Wednesdays and a smile and friendly banter at all times. The backyard serves as a tiny beer garden in summer. The guest beer and handpulled cider are from various sources, according to the licensee's whim. ▲❀⊛≢⊟♣♠

Brown Cow

5 Cross Leeds Street, BD21 2LQ

🕐 4 (12 Sat)-11; 12-10.30 Sun

☎ (01535) 602577 🌐 browncowkeighley.co.uk

Taylor Golden Best, Best Bitter, Landlord, Ram Tam; guest beers H

At the opposite end of town from the other Guide entries, this popular, friendly local is adorned with local breweriana, including the original sign from Bradford's Trough Brewery. The licensees are keen local historians and the landlord is the town's official mace-bearer and steward. Guest beers are sourced mainly from local micros, often from Brown Cow. Bad language is not tolerated at CAMRA's Pub of the Season winter 2005-06 and spring 2007. ▲❀⊟♣♠P

Cricketers Arms

Coney Lane, BD21 5JE

🕐 11.30-midnight; 12-11.30 Sun

☎ (01535) 669912

Moorhouses Premium Bitter; guest beers H

Welcoming, one-room pub on the quieter side of town, but still just 10 minutes' walk from the railway station and closer to the bus station. Serving five guest beers, real cider and a range of bottled beers alongside the Moorhouses regular, the guests showcase regional and micro-breweries rarely seen in the area. It hosts regular live music and occasional beer festivals. ❀♿≢⊟♠⫞

Ledsham

Chequers Inn

Claypit Lane, LS25 5LP

🕐 11-11; closed Sun

☎ (01977) 683135 🌐 thechequersinn.f9.co.uk

Brown Cow Bitter, seasonal beers; John Smith's Bitter; Taylor Landlord; Theakston Best Bitter H

Quintessential old English country pub in the picturesque village of Ledsham. It has two main rooms either side of the bar, plus two smaller rooms complete with oak beams, wood fires, jugs, brasses and old photographs. An extensive range of meals and sandwiches is served at all times, and there is a separate restaurant upstairs which has gained a good reputation. In the summer meals are also served in the delightful beer garden. ▲Q❀◑♿⊟P

Leeds: City

Dr Okells

159 The Headrow, LS1 5RG (opp Leeds City library)

🕐 11-11 (midnight Fri & Sat); closed Sun

☎ (0113) 242 9674

Copper Dragon Golden Pippin; Okells Bitter; guest beers H

This fine example of neo-baroque architecture has been awarded local CAMRA Pub of the Season twice in the same calendar year. It comprises a number of drinking areas, all at different levels. Four guest beers are sold, one always from Moorhouses, another from Durham, and the other two constantly changing. As well as the ales on draught, there is a good selection of draught continental lagers and bottled beers from all over the world. Two or three beer festivals are held each year. ◑♿≢⊟

North Bar

24 New Briggate, LS1 6NU

🕐 12-1am (2am Wed-Sat); 12-10.30 Sun

☎ (0113) 242 4540 🌐 northbar.com

Beer range varies H

Still going strong after 10 years, this pioneering bar is one of just a few serving handpulled beer in Leeds. Its long, narrow bar features many fonts and three handpumps, one dispensing a changing dark beer and one dedicated to Rooster's. The walls are plainly decorated but exhibit works of art at the front and a vast beer menu at the rear. The combination of real ale and beers from around the world, together with simple platters of good snacks, attracts a lively, mixed crowd. Regular beer festivals are held here. ◑▬≢⊟

Palace

Kirkgate, LS2 7DJ

🕐 11-midnight (1am Fri & Sat); 12-10.30 Sun

☎ (0113) 244 5882

Draught Bass; Tetley Bitter; guest beers H

This former festival ale house next to Leeds Parish Church was first recorded as an inn in 1841. Acquired by Melbourne's in 1926, several features of its ownership survive. A large, one-roomed pub on two levels, it has a pool table in a splendid wood-panelled corner behind the unusual large clock on a pole. There is a patio at the front and an enclosed area to the rear. The rotating guest beers, often from Yorkshire breweries, include at least one mild, stout or porter. ❀◑♠⊟⫞

Scarbrough Hotel

Bishopgate Street, LS1 5DY (opp Leeds City Station)

🕐 11-midnight; 12-10.30 Sun

☎ (0113) 243 4590

Tetley Bitter; guest beers H

This historic pub, formerly the King's Arms, was renamed in the late 1890s after the renowned theatre impresario Henry Scarbrough. This vibrant city centre pub has been opened out into one bar with several distinct drinking areas. It serves up to seven guest beers, increasing by another 10 when the second bar opens for beer festivals. Festivals include one held jointly with the Grove in the last week of January, and one to celebrate Yorkshire Day during the first week in August, when Yorkshire ales and food are showcased. Weston's Perry and Old Rosie Cider are also available. ❀◑⌂♿⇌🖂🍴

Town Hall Tavern
17 Westgate, LS1 2RA
◷ 11.30-11; closed Sun
☎ (0113) 245 3960
Taylor Golden Best, Best Bitter, Landlord, Ram Tam Ⓗ

Situated close to the civic building after which it was named, this is a pleasant open-plan pub that retains distinct drinking areas. The walls are adorned with pictures of bygone Leeds, cigarette cards and an assortment of cartoons. It attracts a mixed clientele, and is particularly popular with folk from the nearby legal chambers and general infirmary. Now part of the Taylor's estate, the pub is the only regular outlet for Taylor's beers (Landlord excepted) in Leeds city centre. Food is served weekday teatimes and from noon on Saturday.
◑♿⇌🖂🍴

Victoria Family & Commercial
28 Great George Street, LS1 3DL (at rear of town hall)
◷ 11-11 (midnight Thu-Sat); 12-6 Sun
☎ (0113) 245 1386
Acorn Barnsley Bitter; Taylor Landlord; Tetley Mild, Bitter; guest beers Ⓗ

Hidden behind Leeds Town Hall, the Victoria dates from 1865 and passed into Joshua Tetley's ownership in 1901. There are three rooms: note the swivel 'snob' windows in the main bar, although these are not original. On the bar stands a large brass Italian tea and coffee machine. The pub gets busy with office workers in the early evening and on Thursday when it stages a popular jazz night from 9.30pm. Q◑⇌🖂

Whitelocks First City Luncheon Bar ☆
Turks Head Yard, LS1 6HB (off Briggate); 11-11
☎ (12-10.30 Sun) 0113 245 3950
John Smith's Bitter; Theakston Best Bitter, Old Peculier; guest beers Ⓗ

Down an alleyway, hidden from Leeds' busiest shopping street, Whitelocks dates from 1715, when it was called the Turk's Head. Renowned for many years for its excellent beers, the pub features a marble bar and is fitted out traditionally in wood, glass and brass. Brewery mirrors adorn the walls. Drinks can be enjoyed outside in summer at barrel tables in the alley. Recent concerns for the future of the inn have led to the emergence of 'Friends of Whitelocks', dedicated to ensuring this pub's continued position as one of Leeds' finest. Lunchtime food is served. ♨Q❀◑⇌🖂

Leeds: North

Arcadia Ale & Wine Bar
34 Arndale Centre, Otley Road, Headingley, LS6 2UE
◷ 12-11
☎ (0113) 274 5599 ⊕ markettowntaverns.co.uk
Black Sheep Best Bitter; Caledonian Deuchars IPA; Taylor Landlord; guest beers Ⓗ

An award-winning conversion of a former bank, Arcadia is located at the end of the main arcade of shops in Headingley. There is a small downstairs area with a larger mezzanine floor above. Ales usually come from Yorkshire micros, and these are complemented by an extensive range of bottled and draught beers from around the world. Children are not allowed but dogs are, provided that the pub's resident canines approve. Q◑⇌🖂♣

Bricklayers Arms
8 Low Close Street, Woodhouse, LS2 9EG
◷ 12-midnight (11 Sun)
☎ (0113) 245 8277
Caledonian Deuchars IPA; John Smith's Bitter; guest beers Ⓗ

At the centre of the student heartland of Leeds and known locally as the Brickies, the management has created a true community pub that attracts a mix of locals and students. Look out for the mural depicting a builder on the gable end, opposite the entrance. The rare ceramic handpump handles display the old logo of Tadcaster's John Smith's Brewery. There are plans for a covered outdoor smoking area. ◑🖂♣🍴⟞

Pack Horse
208 Woodhouse Lane, LS2 9DX
◷ 11 (12 Sun)-11
☎ (0113) 245 3980
Tetley Bitter; guest beer Ⓗ

This pub boasts a fine interior that has been partially opened out and modernised but retains much of its Victorian multi-roomed character. The entrance hall features a mosaic. Established to serve travellers on the packhorse route between Otley and Leeds, nowadays the pub caters mainly for students from across the road. It hosts regular live bands, and at other times the upstairs room serves as a cinema. ❀◑🍴🖂

Reliance
76-78 North Street, LS2 7PN
◷ 12-11 (midnight Fri & Sat); 12-10.30 Sun
☎ (0113) 295 6060
Beer range varies Ⓗ

Opposite leafy Lovell Park and the round apartments, this bar is spacious and light, thanks to its floor-to-ceiling curvy windows. The three areas – bar, mezzanine restaurant and side room – are furnished with eclectic furniture and decorated with real works of art. The huge blackboard lists the impressive draught and bottled beer range, often served in the proper glass including dimpled tankards. Tempting food options include possibly the poshest fishfinger butty ever! ◑🍴🖂

Stables
Otley Road, LS16 5PS (in Weetwood Hall Conference Centre)
◷ 12-11 (10.30 Sun)
☎ (0113) 230 6000 ⊕ weetwood.co.uk
Black Sheep Best Bitter; Copper Dragon Golden Pippin, Scotts 1816, Challenger IPA; Taylor Landlord Ⓗ

A recent decision to concentrate on beers from Copper Dragon has given the Stables a boost, and it makes a well-deserved debut in this Guide. Not to be confused with the hotel bar, the Stables pub is in the old stable block at the rear of Weetwood Hall. The central bar serves three distinct areas including the Stable Stalls where families are welcome. There is also a large garden with children's amusements, ideal for the summer months. ⊛≠◁◑≠⇦⊞P🍴

Leeds: South

Cross Keys

107 Water Lane, The Round Foundry, Holbeck, LS11 5WD
🕐 12-11 (10.30 Sun)
☎ (0113) 243 3711 ⊕ the-crosskeys.com
Beer range varies
Under the same ownership as two city centre bars, North Bar and Reliance, the Cross Keys offers up to four real beers including a stout or porter and two changing guests. It places a strong emphasis on food although remaining drinker-friendly. Downstairs, two rooms, both warmed by wood-burning stoves, are wrapped around a central bar. Upstairs is another room and bar that can be used for functions. Exposed beams, stone flags, tiles and bare brickwork are much in evidence. Sunday meals are served until 8pm.
⊠⊛◁◑&≠⊞

Garden Gate ☆

Whitfield Place, Hunslet, LS10 2QB (behind Penny Lane shopping centre)
🕐 11-11 (10.30 Sun)
☎ (0113) 270 0379
Tetley Bitter ⊞
An architectural gem, this pub is hidden away in a modern housing estate. The exterior is tiled and the interior boasts mosaics and a tiled drinking corridor which leads to a tap room and two other rooms, all featuring mirrors and stained-glass panels. The Tetley Bitter served here is always in excellent condition. This pub is one of six public houses in Leeds that feature on the CAMRA National Inventory. ⊑⊞🍴

Grove Inn

Back Row, Holbeck, LS11 5PL
🕐 12-11 (midnight Fri & Sat); 12-10.30 Sun
☎ (0113) 243 9254
Adnams Broadside; Caledonian Deuchars IPA, 80; Moorhouses Black Cat; Wells Bombardier; guest beers ⊞
Surrounded by office blocks and next to the recently completed tallest building in Yorkshire, this winner of many local CAMRA awards in recent years is an oasis of tradition in a sea of modernity. First mentioned in a survey of Leeds in 1850, the Grove has four rooms off a traditional West Riding corridor, including a tap room and a concert room where a range of live music events is staged. Lunches are served daily except Saturday.
⊠⊛◁⊑≠⊞(1)♣🍴🍴

Leeds: West

West End House

Abbey Road, Kirkstall, LS5 3HS
🕐 11-11 (10.30 Sun)
☎ (0113) 278 6332
Beer range varies ⊞

On the road out of Leeds towards the famous Kirkstall Abbey, this stone-built pub was first recorded as an ale house in 1867. The single room interior has an impressive bay window at the front. Two cabinets feature a display of Toby jugs. Four handpumps dispense a variety of ales, usually from the north of England.
⊛◑≠(Headingley)⊞🍴

Linthwaite

Sair

139 Lane Top, HD7 5SG (top of Hoyle Ing, off A62)
OS100143
🕐 5 (12 Fri & Sat)-11; 12-10.30 Sun
☎ (01484) 842370
Linfit Dark Mild, Bitter, Swift, Autumn Gold, seasonal beers ⊞
Set on a hillside overlooking the Colne Valley, this renowned brew pub is a popular meeting place for locals and visitors alike. A central bar serves four rooms; the real fires are a welcome sight in winter. Over the years the pub has won numerous awards including National CAMRA Pub of the Year in 1997. Up to 10 beers are usually available. ⊠≠⊞♣🍴

Liversedge

Black Bull

37 Halifax Road, WF15 6JR (on A649, near A62)
🕐 12-midnight (1am Fri & Sat)
☎ (01924) 403779 ⊕ ossett-brewery.co.uk
Ossett Pale Gold, Black Bull Bitter, Excelsior; Taylor Landlord; guest beers ⊞
The first of a growing chain of Ossett brewery pubs, this 300-year-old building retains much of its original shape, despite having been partly opened out. As well as the bar snug there are four rooms in various styles, including one dubbed 'the chapel' by regulars, thanks to its handsome woodwork and stained glass. Of the nine handpulls, four are Ossett beers and one is a mild. It also stocks a good selection of wines and continental beers. Last admission is half an hour before closing time. ⊠≠⊛⊞♣P🍴

Marsden

Tunnel End Inn

Waters Road, HD7 6NF (near Standedge Visitor Centre)
🕐 12-3 (not Mon-Wed), 5 (8 Mon)-11; 12-11 Sat; 12-10.30 Sun
☎ (01484) 844636 ⊕ tunnelendinn.com
Black Sheep Best Bitter; Taylor Landlord; guest beers ⊞
Homely Pennine pub, near the Standedge tunnel the longest, highest and deepest canal tunnel in the UK. Surrounded by fine scenery, with several walking, cycling and canalside routes, the pub bears a country feel and attracts outdoor enthusiasts, while being within easy reach of the village. Patrons are assured of relaxing surroundings, good home-cooked food and the proprietors' 'personal touch'. ⊠⊛≠◁◑&⚓⊞(937)♣🍴

Mirfield

Navigation Tavern

6 Station Road, WF14 8NL (200m from Mirfield Station)
⚙ 11.30-11; 12-10.30 Sun
☎ (01924) 492476
John Smith's Bitter; Theakston Mild, Best Bitter, XB, Old Peculier, seasonal beers Ⓗ
Congenial canalside pub next to a boatyard on the Calder and Hebble Navigation near the centre of Mirfield and a stone's throw from the station. This friendly local, popular with all ages, offers a comprehensive range from Theakston and is registered as an 'Ambassador for Theakston Beer'. Good food from pub favourites to an à la carte menu is served throughout the pub and in the restaurant at lunchtime and in the evening.
⚫⚫⚫⚫⚫⚫⚫⚫⚫⚫⚫

Mytholmroyd

Shoulder of Mutton

86 New Road, HX7 5DZ (on B6138, near station)
⚙ 11.30-3, 7-11; 11.30-11 Sat; 12-11 Sun
☎ (01422) 883168
Black Sheep Best Bitter; Greene King IPA; Taylor Landlord; guest beers Ⓗ
Village inn at the lower end of the attractive, wooded Cragg Vale, tucked away between the stream and the road. It enjoys a strong local following from both drinkers and community sports teams, but it is more widely known for its excellent value food (not Mon & Tue eve). Guest beers are sourced through the SIBA scheme, and usually include one from Copper Dragon. The bar displays memorabilia relating to the Cragg Vale coiners, an infamous gang of 18th-century forgers. ⚫⚫⚫⚫⚫⚫P

North Featherstone

Bradley Arms

98 Willow Lane, WF7 6BJ (on B6128 Castleford-Featherstone rd)
⚙ 3.30-midnight; 3-1am Fri; 2-1am Sat; 12-midnight Sun
☎ (01977) 792284
Black Sheep Best Bitter; Daleside Bitter, Blonde; John Smith's Bitter Ⓗ
Lovely old ex-farm building with several rooms on different levels. The inn boasts a rich history – it was a key location in the infamous Featherstone massacre of 1893, the last occasion when British troops shot and killed British citizens on English soil. The first-ever speech on workers' rights by Cunninghame Graham was also made here. A co-founder of the Scottish Labour Party, Graham also spoke here at the time of the massacre. In these less violent times, guests may enjoy a candle-lit evening. ⚫⚫Q⚫⚫⚫⚫⚫⚫P⚫⚫

Ossett

Brewer's Pride

Low Mill Road, WF5 8ND (at bottom of Healey Rd, 1½ miles from town centre)
⚙ 12-3, 5-11; 12-11 Fri & Sat; 12-10.30 Sun
☎ (01924) 273865 🌐 brewers-pride.co.uk

Bob's Brewing Co White Lion; Ossett Pale Gold, Excelsior; guest beers Ⓗ
Genuine free house on the outskirts of Ossett, five minutes' walk from the Calder and Hebble Canal. An additional handpull has been installed, always dispensing a rotating mild. Good value lunches are served, and on Wednesday evening curries, pies or steaks feature on the menu. Monday is quiz night, while Tuesday is dedicated to bluegrass (with 'all pickers welcome'). The local folk club meets on Thursday evening, and live music is performed on the first and third Sunday of the month. A beer festival is held annually on the summer bank holiday. ⚫⚫Q⚫⚫⚫⚫⚫⚫

Otley

Junction

44 Bondgate, LS21 1AD (100 yds from bus station)
⚙ 11-11 (midnight Fri & Sat); 11-10.30 Sun
☎ (01943) 463233
Caledonian Deuchars IPA; Taylor Best Bitter, Landlord; Theakston Best Bitter, Old Peculier; guest beers Ⓗ
Vibrant stone-built pub occupying a prominent corner site on the approach from Leeds. The central stone fireplace, settles and benches add to the ambience of this fine establishment. It often hosts live entertainment on Tuesday. A regular Guide entry over the years, it has also previously won a local CAMRA Pub of the Year award. Car parks and Otley bus station are nearby. ⚫⚫⚫⚫⚫

Pontefract

Robin Hood

4 Wakefield Road, WF8 4HN (off A645, opp. traffic lights)
⚙ 12-3.30 (4.30 Fri & Sat), 7-11.30; 12-30-3.30, 7-11 Sun
☎ (01977) 702231
John Smith's Bitter; Tetley Bitter; guest beers Ⓗ
Busy local near the notorious town end traffic lights, known locally as Jenkin's Folly, with a public bar and three other drinking areas. It hosts quizzes twice weekly on Tuesday and Sunday and fields darts and dominoes teams in the local charity league. Winner of many local CAMRA awards including Pub of the Year, the Robin Hood stages a beer festival over the August bank holiday weekend.
⚫⚫⚫⚫⚫⚫(Tanshelf/Baghill)⚫⚫⚫

Pudsey

Fleece

100 Fartown, LS28 8LU
⚙ 12-11 (10.30 Sun)
☎ (0113) 236 2748
Taylor Landlord; Tetley Bitter; guest beer Ⓗ
A proper, traditional two-roomed pub that relies on good conversation and fine ale for entertainment. This well-kept local has a central bar, a comfortable tap room with dominoes and unobtrusive sport on TV, and a lounge that usually has fresh flowers and the odd pig on display. The popular guest beer pump usually dispenses a Yorkshire beer, often from Brown Cow or Ossett and, in the

cold months, sometimes a winter warmer.
❀⑤🍴P

Ripponden

Beehive Inn

48 Hob Lane, Soyland, HX6 4NX (½ mile up Royd Lane from A58) OS033199
✪ 4.30 (12 Sun)-2am
☎ (01422) 824670

Taylor Golden Best, Landlord; guest beers Ⓗ
Rural pub, a steep half mile walk up the hill from the centre of Ripponden. Dating back to 1830, the Beehive is a popular dining venue (serving evening meals and Sunday lunch). It has a large and comfortable extension to the rear, and the interior is pleasantly divided into cosy alcoves, furnished with tables and featuring traditional decorations. There is a garden and a patio for outdoor drinking in summer. ㍳❀🍴♿🍴🚃

Old Bridge Inn

Priest Lane, HX6 4DF (between A58 and B6113)
✪ 12-3, 5.30 (5 Fri)-11; 12-11 Sat; 12-10.30 Sun
☎ (01422) 822595

Taylor Golden Best, Best Bitter, Landlord; guest beers Ⓗ
Reputedly the oldest pub in Yorkshire, this timber-framed Grade II listed building dates back in parts to the 14th century. It has three rooms on two levels, the lowest featuring an astonishing cruck beam. The excellent food is a great attraction, with lunchtime buffets available Monday to Friday, and snacks on Saturday and Sunday lunchtimes. Evening meals are served on Friday and Saturday nights. The Pork Pie Appreciation Society meets here on Saturday evening and stages a pork pie competition in March or April. Live folk music is also hosted. There is a small car park over the bridge. ㍳Q❀🍴🚃

Saltaire

Victoria

192 Saltaire Road, BD18 3JF (4 mins walk from Saltaire Station)
✪ 12-midnight (11 Sun)
☎ (01274) 595090

Caledonian Deuchars IPA; Greene King Abbot; John Smith's Bitter; guest beers Ⓗ
A local community pub with a friendly atmosphere, the Victoria was awarded local CAMRA Pub of the Season in autumn 2006. A member of the SIBA scheme, the guest ales on offer change weekly; it dispensed more than 180 different ales in 2006. There are two separate rooms, one with a pool table. Live music plays on Tuesday and Thursday. The Wednesday night quiz comes with a free supper. ❀⑤♿🚃♣P🍴

Shipley

Fanny's Ale & Cider House

63 Saltaire Road, BD18 3JN (on A657, opp fire station)
✪ 12 (5 Mon)-11; 12-midnight Fri & Sat
☎ (01274) 591419

Taylor Golden Best, Landlord; Theakston Old Peculier; guest beers Ⓗ

Originally a beer shop and now a fully-licensed free house, this Guide regular has a cosy, nostalgic atmosphere, standing near the historic village of Saltaire. The walls in the gas-lit lounge are adorned with old brewery memorabilia. It stocks an excellent range of beers and also serves a number of draught ciders including Stowford Press.
㍳⇆(Saltaire)🚃(662)♠

Shipley Club

162 Bradford Road, BD18 3PD (opp A650/A6038 jct, by Northcliffe Pk)
✪ 12-4 (Wed only), 7-11; 12-11 Sat; 12-3 Sun
☎ (01274) 201842

Beer range varies Ⓗ
Established for more than a century, this thriving sports and social club is a haven for real ale, promoted by the enthusiastic steward. Up to three beers are on handpump, often from Yorkshire micros such as Litton, Saltaire and Salamander. Bowling is available, subject to club commitments, and the traditional snooker room attracts young and old alike to the green baize. Show this Guide or a CAMRA membership card to be signed in.
❀⇆🚃♣P

Shipley Pride

1 Saltaire Road, BD18 3HH (on A657, 5 mins' walk from Shipley Station)
✪ 11.30 (11 Sat)-11; 12-10.30 Sun
☎ (01274) 585341

Taylor Landlord; Tetley Bitter; guest beers Ⓗ
Formerly the Beehive Hotel, built in 1870 as a Hammond Brewery house, this friendly local now serves guests from regional brewers alongside its regular ales. Its two rooms, arranged around a central bar, both feature superb stained-glass windows. The lounge is comfortably appointed while the games room is a functional space for pool and darts fans. A quiz is held on Thursday evening.
❀⇆🚃(675, 677)♣P

South Elmsall

Barnsley Oak

Mill Lane, WF9 2DT (on B6474, off A638)
✪ 12-11.30 (10.30 Sun)
☎ (01977) 643427

John Smith's Bitter; guest beer Ⓗ
Built in 1970 and serving a former mining area, this is a fine example of a community pub. The two enthusiastic joint landlords have built a loyal following for their guest beers, which often come from Yorkshire breweries. They host quiz nights on Tuesday and Sunday, and the Barnsley Oak Golf Society meets here. Excellent value meals are served until 8pm (4.30pm Sunday), and children are welcome. Meals may be enjoyed in the conservatory, with its panoramic views of the Elms Valley.
❀🍴⑤⇆(Moorthorpe/S Elmsall)🚃(46, 496)P🍴

Sowerby Bridge

Puzzle Hall

21 Hollins Mill Lane, HX6 2RF (400m from A58)
✪ 4-11; 1-11 Sat & Sun
☎ (01422) 835547 🌐 puzzlehall.info

Taylor Landlord; guest beers H

This is a gem of a pub, nestling between the canal and the river. Opened in the 1700s, the former brew pub is dominated by the tower of the old brewery. Now a free house, it offers four guest beers every day. The pub is renowned as a venue for R&B and jazz music performances, and it stages music festivals in May and August. Beer festivals are hosted in March and September. Wednesday is quiz night. There is a heated and covered area outside for smokers. ♨♣♢▥♠♣ᴸ

Rushcart Inn

Sowerby Green, HX6 1JJ (1¼ miles from A58)
OS039232

🕓 12-11.30 (midnight Fri; 1am Sat); 10-10.30 Sun

☎ (01422) 831956

Jennings Bitter, Cumberland Ale, Cocker Hoop; guest beer H

This busy village local is a resting place for rushbearers and their carts on their annual tour of churches (and pubs), and a meeting place for various local organisations. The lounge bar features a large, old fireplace, timber boarding and a lead window depicting a rushcart. The guest beer is from the Marston's list. Limited parking is available. ♨♣♢▥♠P ᴸ

Shepherd's Rest

125 Bolton Brow, HX6 2BD (on A58)

🕓 3-11.30; 12-midnight Thu-Sun

☎ (01422) 831937

Ossett Pale Gold, Excelsior; Taylor Landlord; guest beers H

Built in 1877, this pub gets its name from an old inn that stood on the other side of Bolton Brow. It was bought by Ossett in 2005, brewers of the house beer, Shepherds Rest. Popular with locals, it also offers a warm welcome to visitors. The interior is open plan, with an arched brick fireplace and stone-flagged floor, and it displays a large butter churn. Quiz night is Monday and live music is played on the first of every month. A heated canopy is available outside for smokers. ♨♣⇌▥P ᴸ

White Horse

Burnley Road, Friendly, HX7 2UG (on A646, ¾ mile NW of centre)

🕓 12-11 (10.30 Sun)

☎ (01422) 831173

Elland Beyond the Pale; Tetley Mild, Bitter H

White-painted pub situated just back from the busy A646 on the Halifax-Todmorden bus route. In summer the prize-winning floral displays are stunning. This welcoming local has a tap room and a larger lounge bar that was originally two rooms and is still partially divided. A strong local following includes members of Friendly football club, Friendly brass band and a dominoes club. A smoking area is to be added at the rear. ❀♣▥♠P ᴸ

Works (in Progress)

12 Hollins Mill Lane, HX6 2QG (opp swimming pool)

🕓 12-11 (10.30 Sun)

☎ (01422) 834821

Taylor Golden Best, Best Bitter, Landlord; guest beers H

Formerly a joinery workshop that was only partly finished at the time – hence the name. Standing beside the Rochdale Canal, this large, open-plan pub features exposed beams and floorboards. Drinkers are spoilt for choice, with up to eight guest beers available from breweries nationwide. Home-cooked food is served daily, as well as café-style snacks such as jacket potatoes. Live blues, jazz and folk music events are staged frequently, but the music is not so loud as to prevent easy conversation. ♨Q♢♣⇌▥P ᴸ

Sowood

Dog & Partridge

Forest Hill Road, HX4 9LP (¼ mile W of B6112)
OS076183

🕓 7-11; 12-4.30, 7-10.30 Sun

☎ (01422) 374249

Black Sheep Best Bitter; Taylor Landlord; guest beer H

An increasing rarity in the 21st century, this is a no-frills rural gem. It has been run by the same family for more than 50 years. There are two rooms: a simple cosy bar and a slightly more formal separate lounge. The latter houses a piano which is sometimes pressed into service, very competently, by the landlord. Otherwise, the peace is only disturbed by the buzz of conversation, and all are welcome to join in. The landlord's own no-smoking rule has been in force since 2005. Q❀♿▥(537, 538)♣P

Thornhill

Saville Arms

12 Church Lane, WF12 0JZ (on B6117, 2½ miles S of Dewsbury)

🕓 5 (4 Fri)-11; 12-4, 7.30-11 Sat & Sun

☎ (01924) 463738

Black Sheep Best Bitter, Ale; Theakston Best Bitter H

Known as the Church House, parts of the building are 600 years old. The tap room is on consecrated ground, residing in the graveyard of the neighbouring Grade I listed Church of St Michael's. Formerly tied to Kirkstall Brewery and then Duttons, the free house features a controversial mural depicting Thornhill through the ages. Children are welcome in the large garden, which also accommodates smokers. ♨❀♣▥♣P ᴸ

Todmorden

Masons Arms

1 Bacup Road, OL14 7PN

🕓 12-midnight (1am Fri & Sat)

☎ (01706) 812180 🌐 themasonsarms.biz

Copper Dragon Best Bitter, Golden Pippin, Scotts 1816; guest beers H

This pub nestles below a railway viaduct, close to the Rochdale Canal. The brewery-owned local has an entrance corridor facing the bar, a pool room and seating to one side. Opposite is a cosy room with a large fireplace. In the 19th century, its tables were used for laying out bodies. On display are photographs and reports of the 1984 Summit Tunnel fire, including stories of long-gone customers; you can read here about the sad end of Slavering Doss. The friendly atmosphere attracts various local groups who meet here. Food is served 12-6pm. ♨Q☆◖⇌(Walsden)🖃⇌

Sportsmans Arms

Kebs Road, OL14 8SB (on Burnley old road)
🕒 7 (12 Sun)-11
☎ (01706) 813449

Taylor Landlord; Thwaites Bitter; guest beers Ⓗ
A busy pub for a sparsely populated area, overlooking the valley of Todmorden. The panelled lounge with leather sofas around the large fireplace contrasts with the adjacent light and airy art gallery. Jazz or blues plays on Saturday evening, and unusual puzzles and board games are on offer at the bar. Guest beers come from small breweries, often including a Bridestones Brewery beer, named after a rocky outcrop opposite the pub. Forty malt whiskies are also stocked. A gun club operates nearby. Evening meals are on Saturday only. ♨▷▲♣P

Top Brink Inn

Brink Top, Lumbutts, OL14 6JB (near Lumbutts Mill Activity Centre) OS956236
🕒 12-3 (not Mon & Tue), 6-11; 12-midnight Sun
☎ (01706) 812696

Boddingtons Bitter; Camerons Castle Eden Ale; Flowers Original; Taylor Landlord; guest beer Ⓗ
Large rural inn, popular with drinkers, walkers, diners and families, set in spectacularly scenic Pennine countryside. There are splendid views from the conservatory and beer garden, which is decked with fine floral displays in summer. A roomy country inn, comfortable and welcoming, it gets busy at weekends and enjoys a reputation for good value meals. The guest beer is usually sourced from a micro-brewery. ☆◖▷&▲🖃(T6, T8)P⇌

Undercliffe

Milners Arms

126 Undercliffe Road, BD2 3BN (300m from Eccleshill Library)
🕒 4-11 (11.30 Fri); 12-11.30 Sat; 12-11 Sun
☎ (01274) 639398

Beer range varies Ⓗ
Pleasant and cosy two-roomed community local with a central bar serving both the tap room and the lounge. Themed nights, taking place on the first Saturday of every month, are popular with the loyal and regular clientele. The landlord is enthusiastic about real ale and always has two available, one from a Yorkshire micro-brewery such as Rudgate, Saltaire or Salamander. ☆◖🖃(601)♣⇌

Wakefield

Alverthorpe WMC

111 Flanshaw Lane, WF2 9JG (2 miles from city)
🕒 11.30-4, 6.30-11; 11.30-11 Fri & Sat; 12-3.30, 7-11 Sun
☎ (01924) 374179

Tetley Mild, Bitter; guest beers Ⓗ
Multi-roomed, CIU-affiliated club with a cosy interior featuring unusual stained glass and an extensive collection of pot horses. It stocks a wide selection of guest beers, mostly from local micros, and holds a beer festival in October. This regular local CAMRA award winner hosts live entertainment at the weekend, while weekday amusements include snooker, darts and a wide-screen TV for armchair sports fans. It fields sports teams and outside is a floodlit bowling green. ☆◖&🖃(104, 114)♣P

Black Rock

3 Cross Square, WF1 1PQ (top of Westgate, near Bull Ring & Cathedral)
🕒 11-11 (midnight Sat); 12-10.30 Sun
☎ (01924) 375550

Tetley Bitter; guest beers Ⓗ
An arched, tiled façade leads to a traditional, compact city centre ale house, providing a hint of the comfort and elegance of a Victorian gin palace. Standing at the heart of Wakefield's drinking and clubbing centre, the Rock has recently acquired an additional handpull to double the choice of guest ales it serves. This is a real pub on the edge of the fizz-dispensing shoeboxes and blaring discos of the youth zone. ⇌(Westgate/Kirkgate)🖃

Fernandes Brewery Tap

5 Avison Yard, Kirkgate, WF1 1UA
🕒 5-11; 11-midnight Fri & Sat; 12-11 Sun
☎ (01924) 369547 ⊕ fernandes-brewery.gowyld.com

Fernandes range; guest beers Ⓗ
This pub is a regular local CAMRA award-winner and has just added Wakefield Pub of the Year 2006 to its collection. A friendly, one-room bar, it offers a constantly changing draught beer and ciders, as well as stocking a good selection of Belgian bottled beers. A real ale paradise, it also features a more unusual Belgian Genever bar.
Q⇌(Kirkgate/Westgate)🖃●

Harry's Bar

107B Westgate, WF1 1EL (opp Westgate Station)
🕒 5-11 (midnight Fri & Sat); 12-11 Sun
☎ (01924) 373773

Ossett Silver King, Excelsior; Taylor Landlord; guest beers Ⓗ
Hidden away down a narrow lane, close to the theatre and restaurants, this is a ten-year-old conversion featuring a bare brick and wooden interior. It attracts a mixed, lively clientele, creating a community pub atmosphere. For fine weather there is a sundeck and a shady yard. Live music plays on Wednesday night. The regular beers are complemented by a rotating guest beer list, as well as bottled Belgian beers. ♨☆⇌(Westgate/Kirkgate)🖃P

Henry Boon's

130 Westgate, WF2 9SR (100m below Westgate Station)
🕒 11-11 (1am Fri & Sat); 12-10.30 Sun
☎ (01924) 378126

Clark's Classic Blonde, seasonal beer; Taylor Landlord; guest beer Ⓗ
The brewery tap for Clark's Brewery, which is situated behind the pub, this friendly place recently gained top marks in Cask Marque accreditation. Situated on the 'Westgate run', it gets very busy on weekend evenings. Hogsheads are in use as tables, and the bar features a thatched roof as well as assorted breweriana. Regular live music sessions are

hosted, and two upstairs function rooms are available for hire. ≒(Westgate/Kirkgate)🚋♣

Labour Club (Red Shed)
18 Vicarage Street, WF1 1QX
🕑 12-5 (Fri only), 7-11; 11-4, 7-11 Sat; 12-4 Sun
☎ (01924) 215626 ⊕ theredshed.org.uk
Acorn Barnsley Bitter; Ossett Pale Gold; guest beers 🅗
One of a kind, the Red Shed is a former army hut that is still going strong, despite being threatened by city centre development. The Shed plays host to trade union, community and charity groups. Staffed by volunteers, it stages live music on the second and last Saturday of the month. There are three rooms, two which can be hired for functions. The space around the bar is adorned with an extensive collection of union plates and badges, as well as the numerous CAMRA awards it has won over the years. Dogs and well-behaved visitors are welcome.
≒(Westgate/Kirkgate)🚋♣P🎖

Redoubt
28 Horbury Road, WF2 8TS (corner of Horbury Rd & Westgate)
🕑 12 (11 Sat)-11.30; 11-11 Sun
☎ (01924) 377085 ⊕ theredoubt.co.uk
Taylor Landlord; Tetley Mild, Bitter 🅗
This Tetley Heritage house has four small but cosy rooms with low ceilings. Its walls are adorned with a mixture of rugby league photographs and images of old Wakefield. Known as a sporty pub, the Redoubt has its own cricket and football teams.
🏚Q❀&≒(Wakefield/Westgate)🚋♣P

Six Chimneys
41-43 Kirkgate, WF1 1HY (across road from Cathedral precinct)
🕑 9-midnight (1am Fri & Sat); 11-1am Sun
☎ (01924) 239449
Greene King Abbot; Marston's Pedigree; Theakston Old Peculier; guest beers 🅗
Typical Wetherspoon outlet converted from a former shop, catering for a wide clientele of drinkers and diners, including families in two designated areas. An interesting display features old photographs and snippets of local history. It stocks ales from many Yorkshire micro-breweries, and serves good value food all day until one hour before closing time.
Q🕭&≒(Westgate/Kirkgate)🚋

Walton

New Inn
144 Shay Lane, WF2 6LA
🕑 12-midnight
☎ (01924) 255447 ⊕ newinnwalton.co.uk
Caledonian Deuchars IPA; Jennings Cumberland Ale; John Smith's Bitter; Taylor Landlord; guest beers 🅗
Traditional, 18th-century vernacular stone building under a flagstone roof, comprising several areas including a restaurant that offers exceptionally good food (not served Mon) and a coffee shop (open from 10am Tue-Sat). One of the five handpumps at this community-focused pub is dedicated to beers from local independent breweries. It is located in an ideal spot for starting or finishing a walk along

the route of the former Barnsley Canal.
❀🕭&🚋P⅃

Wetherby

Muse Ale & Wine Bar
16 Bank Street, LS22 6NQ
🕑 12-11 (10.30 Sun)
☎ (01937) 580201
Beer range varies 🅗
Part of the excellent Market Town Taverns chain, Muse has a small drinking area next to a large fireplace filled with plants. To the rear is a larger section mainly used by diners. The bar has four handpumps, serving mainly beers brewed in Yorkshire. Some of the seating is on old church pews. The premises are free of music and games machines. Q🕭🚋P

Royal Oak
60 North Street, LS22 6NR
🕑 12-11
☎ (01937) 580508
Black Sheep Best Bitter; John Smith's Bitter; Tetley Bitter; guest beer 🅗
Friendly local situated at the north end of the town centre – the Royal Oak is the most northerly pub in the Leeds metropolitan area. It has three drinking areas arranged around an L-shaped bar. The cosy front room is adorned with a collection of china animals. The guest ale usually comes from E&S Elland's extensive range. 🏚🕭🚋♣

Wintersett

Angler's Retreat
Ferry Top Lane, WF4 2EB (between Crofton & Ryhill) OS382157
🕑 12-3, 7-11; 12-11 Sat; 12-3.30, 7-10.30 Sun
☎ (01924) 862370
Acorn Barnsley Bitter; Samuel Smith OBB; Tetley Bitter, Imperial 🅗
Locally known as the Sett, this is a fine example of an old-fashioned rural ale house. Enjoying a strong local trade, it also attracts visitors from miles around who come for the real Yorkshire welcome. Close to the Anglers Country Park and numerous footpaths, the pub has a large garden to the side and seats at the front for fine-weather drinking. 🏚Q❀🚋♣P

Woodlesford

Two Pointers
69 Church Street, LS26 8RE (400 yds from A642)
🕑 3 (12 Fri & Sat)-midnight; 12-11.30 Sun
☎ (0113) 282 3124
Black Sheep Best Bitter; John Smith's Bitter; guest beers 🅗
An oasis in an area deprived of real ale, this former coaching inn has a large, split-level lounge, bar and function room. The tap room houses a pool table, dartboard and large-screen TV. Select your chosen sporting event from the list chalked up on the tap room blackboard. The pub stages regular events to raise funds for charity. There is a half-hourly rail service from Leeds. ❀🕭&≒🚋♣P

Wales

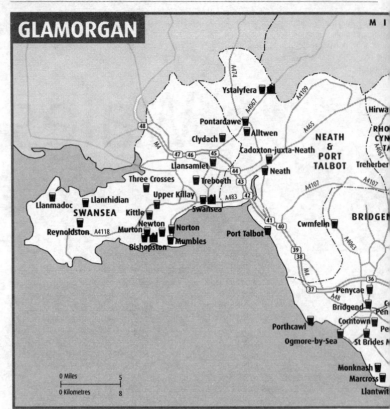

GLAMORGAN

Authority areas covered: Bridgend UA, Caerphilly UA, Cardiff UA, Merthyr Tydfil UA, Neath & Port Talbot UA, Rhondda, Cynon & Taff UA, Swansea UA, Vale of Glamorgan UA

Aberdare

Cambrian Inn
60 Seymour Street, CF44 7DL
🕒 11-5, 7-11; 11-11 Fri & Sat; 12-10.30 Sun
☎ (01685) 879120
Beer range varies Ⓗ
Welcoming town pub just a short walk from the main shopping area. The comfortable interior draws clientele from all walks of life. One beer is served, but it changes frequently and is usually sourced from a micro-brewery. The pub sign portrays a famous son of Aberdare, the conductor Griffith Rhys-Jones, or 'Caradog'. ◖⬤♣

Aberthin

Farmers Arms
Cowbridge Road, CF71 7HB (on A4222)
🕒 12-3, 6-11; 12-2, 7-10.30 Sun
☎ (01446) 773429
Wadworth 6X; guest beers Ⓗ
One mile north of Cowbridge, this comfortable two bar pub with a dining room/restaurant is renowned for value and quality. The regular beer is accompanied by a changing guest. The licensees have won CAMRA and food awards over the years. A small river runs through the grounds, making an outdoor drink in summer all the more enjoyable. There is plentiful

parking for the numerous patrons that come from near and far. ⊛◖⬤Ꮭ♿🚌(E11)♣Pᐟ

Alltwen

Butchers Arms
Alltwen Hill, SA8 3BP
🕒 12-midnight (12.30am Fri & Sat)
☎ (01792) 863100
Beer range varies Ⓗ
Traditional village pub, set off the A474 between the Neath and Swansea valleys. A beautiful open hearth, wooden floors and furniture impart a truly homely character to the pub, while artefacts add interest. The pub's restaurant has a good reputation locally and the food complements a range of up to

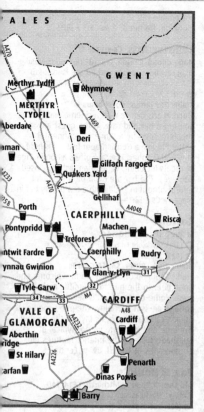

festivals are held occasionally, further extending the excellent range of ales. Cricket matches and occasional social events are organised. The 14 bus from Swansea stops outside. The car park is small – if full try 100 metres down the hill. Winner of several local CAMRA Pub of the Year awards.
ᵐQ🕮🌑🕒(14)♣P

Bridgend

Wyndham Arms
Dunraven Place, CF31 1JE
🕒 9-1am; 11-11 Sun
☎ (01656) 663608
Brains SA; Evan Evans BB; Greene King Abbot; guest beers Ⓗ
Large 18th-century coaching inn acquired and refurbished by Wetherspoon's a few years ago. The interior features various distinct areas with a history of Bridgend displayed on the walls. Friendly, helpful staff help to make the pub always busy and popular with all ages. A good range of ales is stocked with a keen pricing policy. Weston's Old Rosie is a permanent feature. Accommodation is available in this Wetherlodge.
Q🛏🕮🕒♿➔🚋♿

Brynnau Gwynion

Mountain Hare
Brynna Road, CF35 6PG (between Pencoed and Llanharan turn off A473)
🕒 12-midnight (11 Sun)
☎ (01656) 860458 🌐 mountainhare.co.uk
Bullmastiff Welsh Gold; Evan Evans BB; guest beers Ⓗ
Refurbished and extended early in 2007, this wonderful family-owned village local has retained its style, character and warmth. The two regular and two changing guest beers never disappoint. Extensive lawned outdoor areas make this a popular choice in summer. The pub hosts an annual Ales of Wales beer festival. Plenty of parking space and a regular bus service make visiting easy. 🕮🕒♿🚋♣P⌐

Cadoxton-juxta-Neath

Crown & Sceptre Inn
Main Road, SA10 8AP
🕒 11.30-11.30 (10.30 Sun)
☎ (01639) 772370
Draught Bass; Tomos Watkin OSB Ⓗ
Built in 1835 as a tap for the nearby Vale of Neath Brewery, this former coach house has a bar and lounge, the former stables a restaurant. This popular local has an excellent reputation for its ale and freshly cooked food. As well as the a la carte menus there is a wide range of bar meals – Thai chicken and fillet steak pie among the favourites. Neath Abbey is nearby. 🕮🕒♿🚋P⌐

Caerphilly

Masons Arms
Mill Road, CF83 3FE
🕒 12-11.30 (midnight Fri & Sat)
☎ (029) 208 83353
Brains Bitter; guest beers Ⓗ

three changing beers. Live music is performed on Sunday evening. ᵐ🕮🕒♿P

Barry

Castle Hotel
44 Jewel Street, CF63 3NQ
🕒 12-11.30 (midnight Fri & Sat); 12-11 Sun
☎ (01446) 408916
Brains Bitter, SA; guest beers Ⓗ
The Castle has long been the best real ale outlet in Barry and with the enthusiasm of the current landlord that is unlikely to change any time soon. A welcoming, multi-roomed late Victorian building, the pub retains the etched windows for its original tea and coffee lounges. It has strong links to the merchant navy and photos of old Barry decorate the walls. Weekly live music and quizzes are hosted. 🕮🕒➔(Barry Docks)🚋(88)⌐

Bishopston

Joiners Arms
50 Bishopston Road, SA3 3EJ
🕒 11.30-11; 12-10.30 Sun
☎ (01792) 232658
Courage Best Bitter; Marston's Pedigree; Swansea Bishopswood, Three Cliffs Gold, Original Wood; guest beers Ⓗ
Attractive stone built pub dating from the 1860s; the Swansea Brewing Company is based here. Popular with locals and always busy, the food enjoys a good reputation. Beer

Well worth the walk from Caerphilly castle and the busy town centre, this traditional local offers a friendly welcome. The public bar fronts onto the street and there is a large, comfortable lounge at the rear where meals are served. Real ales are available in both rooms, though visitors to the bar will need to ask staff what is on offer, as the handpumps are out of view. ❀◖◗⊟🚌♣P

Cardiff

Albany

105 Donald Street, CF24 4TL

⏲ 12-11.30 (midnight Fri); 11-midnight Sat; 12-11 Sun

☎ (029) 203 11075

Brains Dark, Bitter, SA, Gold, seasonal beers; guest beers Ⓗ

This traditional pub situated in a predominantly student area has become a regular fixture in the Guide in recent years and the range of guest beers grows all the time. The public bar has a lively atmosphere with a large-screen TV – the lounge is quieter. A quiz is held on Tuesday evening and there is karaoke on Saturday – added attractions are the skittle alley and large, pleasant beer garden where barbecues are held in summer. Q❀◖⊟🚌

Beverley Hotel

75-77 Cathedral Road, SF11 9PG

⏲ 10-11

☎ (029) 203 43443

Beer range varies Ⓗ

Originally two houses, this hotel was formerly the Ablisser Chrese school for young ladies until 1937 when it became the Beverley Hotel. Redevelopment in 1970 turned the building into the hotel it is today. Encouragement from local CAMRA branch members has seen the beer range, quality and consistency go from strength to strength. Three handpumps serve ales from the M&B extended range. ❀🛏◖◗♿⛺🚌P⌐

Butchers Arms

29 Llandaff Road, Canton, CF11 9NG

⏲ 11-11 (11.30 Fri & Sat); 12-10.30 sun

☎ (029) 202 27927

Brains Dark, Bitter; guest beers Ⓗ

Popular street corner locals' pub with a fairly basic public bar and more comfortable lounge. The guest ale varies and is a welcome addition to the choice of beers in the area. Two small outside drinking areas cater for bar and lounge customers. Two darts teams are based here. Dogs are welcome. Q❀⊟♿🚌♣

Cayo Arms

36 Cathedral Road, CF11 9LL

⏲ 12-11 (midnight Fri & Sat); 12-10.30 Sun

☎ (029) 203 91910

Banks's Original; Tomos Watkin OSB; guest beers Ⓗ

Busy single bar pub with a homely feel that appeals to locals, visitors and ale enthusiasts alike. Now part of the Marston's family, Tomos Watkin beers are still available, though no longer the core of the varied ale range. Conveniently situated for the Millennium Stadium and city centre, the accommodation is popular here with rooms available at reasonable rates. A well-equipped meeting room can be hired. ❀🛏◖◗♿⛺🚌P⌐

Chapter Arts Centre

Market Road, Canton, CF5 1QE (behind Cowbridge Road East between Llandaff Rd and Market Rd)

⏲ 5-11 (12.30am Fri); 1-midnight Sat; 4-10.30 Sun

☎ (029) 203 13431 🌐chapter.org

Brains Rev James; guest beers Ⓗ

Thriving arts centre with a cinema and theatre housing a bar and cafe. Three guest ales are supplemented by a range of continental bottled beers; a German beer festival is held in May and October. The café offers a good range of meals including vegetarian dishes (closed Sun eve). The bar area will be undergoing refurbishment in 2008 with a temporary bar in place. ❀◖◗♿🚌P⌐

Cottage

St Mary Street, CF10 1AA

⏲ 11-11 (midnight Fri & Sat); 11-10.30 Sun

☎ (029) 203 37195

Brains Dark, Bitter, SA, SA Gold Ⓗ

Traditional pub offering a warm welcome and good beer in the heart of Cardiff's nightclub area. Home-cooked food is served – the cottage pie is a speciality. The pub's medieval origins can be seen in its layout: the narrow frontage and long interior are typical of the burghage system. The interior features old photographs of Cardiff. ◖◗⇌(Central)

Fox & Hounds

Old Church Road, Whitchurch, CF14 1AD

⏲ 11-11; 12-10.30 Sun

☎ (029) 206 93377

Brains Dark, Bitter, SA, Rev James, SA Gold; guest beers Ⓗ

A friendly community pub not to be missed if you are in the Whitchurch area. The wood-panelled interior houses one long bar with large screens for viewing sporting events and a quiet area for dining and drinking. The pleasant garden is popular in summer with a canopy and heaters for cooler days; an extension around the corner is used for beer festivals. Helpful staff serve the full range of Brains' beer plus a changing guest. ❀◖◗♿⇌(Whitchurch/ Coryton/ Rhiwbina/ Llandaff North)🚌P⌐

Glamorgan Council Staff Club

17 Westgate Street, CF10 100

⏲ 9-11 (11.30 Fri & Sat)

☎ (029) 202 33216

Brains Bitter; guest beers Ⓗ

This historic building opposite the Millennium Stadium has been a club since 1964 and Cardiff CAMRA Club of the Year on numerous occasions. It has a public bar and a number of other bars available for functions or meetings. The club is keen to promote real ale with three guest beers regularly featuring from new breweries. Show a CAMRA membership card or this Guide for entry. On match days the club is very busy and entry is restricted to members only. ⊟⇌(Central)

Goat Major

33 High Street, CF10 1PU

⏲ 11-midnight (11 Sun)

☎ (029) 203 37161

Brains Dark, Bitter, SA, SA Gold Ⓗ
This well-appointed Brains' pub retains a traditional Victorian interior despite refurbishment, with friendly staff and a relaxing, comfortable atmosphere. The Goat Major sits in the heart of Cardiff's commercial centre and is popular with shoppers at lunchtime, serving a good selection of Welsh dishes. Beer is consistently in good form. The drinking area can become crowded in the evenings. Q⊈▮⇌(Central)🚌♣

Heathcock

58 Bridge Street, Llandaff, CF5 2EN
⏰ 12-11 (11.30 Fri & Sat); 12-10.30 Sun
☎ (029) 205 75005

Adnams Bitter, Broadside; guest beers Ⓗ
Suburban community local with public and lounge bars and a skittle alley available for hire. Regular Adnams beers are unusual for the area. The guest beer is frequently from a local micro-brewery including Vale of Glamorgan or Rhymney. Bar food includes a range of curries. The pub is handy for the historic area of Llandaff and its cathedral.
❀⊈▮🛓⇌(Danescourt/Llandaff/Fairwater)🚌♣

Mochyn Du (Black Pig)

Sophia Close, CF11 9HW
⏰ 12-11 (midnight Fri & Sat); 12-10.30 Sun
☎ (029) 203 71599

Brains Rev James, seasonal beers; guest beers Ⓗ
This free house has gone from strength to strength since leaving the Marston's fold. Close to Glamorgan county cricket ground and a leisurely 10-minute riverside walk from the city centre, the 'tafarn' is a firm favourite with local residents, visitors and students alike. The pub has become the hub of the Welsh community in west Cardiff – Welsh learners are encouraged to enjoy the 'hwyl' of a traditional Welsh pub. ❀⊈▮🛓🄰🚌🄿⌐

Old Arcade

14 Church Street, CF10 1BG
⏰ 10-midnight (1.30am Fri & Sat); 12-11 Sun
☎ (029) 202 17999

Brains Bitter, Dark, Rev James, SA; guest beers Ⓗ
Traditional pub offering good beer and a friendly atmosphere in the city centre, with two bars and a covered outdoor courtyard. The wood panelled interior features large TV screens showing sporting events and the pub can be busy during major fixtures. The full range of Brains beers is on offer here with one changing special or seasonal ale.
❀⊈▮🛓⇌(Central)🚌⌐

Pendragon

Excalibur Drive, Thornhill, CF14 9BB
⏰ 11-11 (midnight Fri & Sat); 11.30-11 Sun
☎ (029) 206 10550

Brains Dark, Bitter, SA, SA Gold Ⓗ
A regular in the Guide, this modern estate pub is reached by a long driveway. Recently refurbished, it retains three separate areas but with an increased emphasis on dining. A bonus of the increased trade is an addition to the cask ale range with SA Gold now available. The pub continues to support local charities and thousands have been raised for worthy causes. A covered patio area offers fine views

over Cardiff.
Q❀⊈▮🛓⇌(Lisvane & Thornhill)🚌(27, 28)♣🄿⌐

Vulcan

10 Adam Street, CF24 2FH
⏰ 11.30-11.30; 12-4.30 Sun
☎ (029) 204 61580

Brains Bitter, SA Ⓗ
Dating from the 1850s, this claims to be the oldest unspoilt pub in Cardiff. But situated in a redevelopment area just off city centre, regrettably the pub has little time left. It now stands alone surrounded by open space. The main bar has a spit and sawdust wooden floor, with a quieter lounge to the rear. A favourite means of escape from the hustle and bustle of nearby city centre outlets, the Vulcan has a good local following. A visit to the Gents is a must to admire the porcelain.
Q🄳⇌(Queen St/Central)♣

Clydach

Carpenters Arms

High Street, SA6 5LN (on B4603)
⏰ 11-11; 12-10.30 Sun
☎ (01792) 843333 🌐 carpentersarmsclydach.co.uk

Bullmastiff Thoroughbred; Marston's Pedigree; Wye Valley Butty Bach; guest beers Ⓗ
Popular stone fronted pub with a busy public bar and a split level lounge/restaurant serving a wide range of quality meals. Acoustic jam sessions are hosted on Thursday, and real ale festivals held on bank holidays. The pub is used by a local cycle group for meetings and events. Winner of best community pub in the HTV region in 2006, it has a patio garden and ample parking. ❀⊈▮🛓♣🄿

Corntown

Golden Mile

Corntown Road, CF35 5BA (off A48 between Cowbridge and Bridgend) OS928774
⏰ 11.45-3, 5-11; 6-11 Sat; 12-4, 7-10.30 Sun
☎ (01656) 654884

Evan Evans BB; guest beers Ⓗ
Set below road level, this fine old pub is easily overlooked, but it is well worth the effort to seek out. You can expect a warm welcome from Dave the dog in the bar, and first class food at reasonable prices in the dining room. Brassware adorns the fireplace in the cosy lounge. Pleasant views over the local countryside can be enjoyed from the patio and garden. The pub has plenty of parking space.
🛏Q❀⊈▮🛓🚌🄿

Cowbridge

Vale Of Glamorgan Inn

53 High Street, CF71 7AE
⏰ 11.30-11; 12-10.30 Sun
☎ (01446) 772252

Draught Bass; Greene King Old Speckled Hen; Hancock's HB; Vale of Glamorgan Original No 1 VoG; Wye Valley Hereford Pale Ale; guest beers Ⓗ
Situated in the heart of a busy historic market town, this small, friendly inn has extensive outdoor grounds. A regular outlet for the Vale

of Glamorgan brewery in nearby Barry, the range and quality of ales is matched by the excellent food, friendly atmosphere and convivial surroundings. The hugely popular annual beer festival, part of the town's food and drink festival, is a major attraction. Recent CAMRA Pub of the Year winner.
Q ⑤ ✿ ⊛ ⓓ ⊟ ♣ P ⅃

Craig Penllyn

Barley Mow

Craig Penllyn, CF71 7RT OS978773
✪ 12-11; 12-10.30
☎ (01446) 772555
Hancock's HB; guest beers ⏢
Old, established village inn with a strong local following and a hearty welcome for visitors, including families. Warm, cosy and comfortable, there is a great atmosphere to this hostelry. Interesting guest beers complement the bar meals and restaurant menu. A small beer garden is pleasant in summer. Ringing mobile phones are not appreciated. ⑤ ⊛ ⓓ ⊟ ⊟ ♣ P

Cwmaman

Falcon Hotel

1 Incline Row, CF44 6LU OS008998
✪ 11 (12 Sun)-11
☎ (01685) 873758 ⊕ thefalcon.co.uk
Beer range varies ⏢
Although close to the village, this rural pub feels quite isolated at the end of a lane. Popular with locals and travellers alike, especially in summer, it has an attractive riverside setting. Three beers are usually on offer, from micro-breweries and Welsh breweries especially. Well-appointed accommodation is available, with touring caravans welcome. The large bar was built with wood from a local chapel. Once visited, long remembered. ⊛ ⊭ ⓓ P

Cwmfelin

Cross Inn

Maesteg Road, CF34 9LB (on A4063)
✪ 11.45-midnight (1am Fri & Sat)
☎ (01656) 732476
Brains Bitter, seasonal beers; Wye Valley Butty Bach; guest beers ⏢
Friendly valleys local in an area of Wales where real ale is harder to find than a fire breathing dragon. Easy to reach, it stands on a main road and bus route, and is a short stroll from the railway station. A pleasant, comfortable pub, it has a bar, lounge and small back room with interesting photographs. Children are welcome until 7pm, well-behaved dogs permitted in the bar, but please ask first. ⊛ ⊟ ≠ (Garth) ⊟

Deri

Old Club

93 Bailey Street, CF81 9HX
✪ 4-midnight (2am Fri & Sat); 12-midnight Sun
☎ (01443) 830278
Beer range varies ⏢

National brands are rarely seen at the Old Club – its three guest beers are widely sourced and served with great care. Interesting foreign beers are sometimes stocked, including a selection of bottles. Easy to reach by bus from Bargoed, it is handy for Cwm Darran Country Park. Visitors are always welcome – mention the Guide on arrival. Last entry is 11pm.
⚠ ⊟ (1, 4) ♣

Dinas Powis

Star Inn

8 Station Road, CF64 4DE
✪ 11.30-11; 12-10.30 Sun
☎ (029) 205 14245
Brains Bitter, SA, Rev James, seasonal beers ⏢
Town centre local, deservedly popular with locals and visitors for the superb quality of its ales and all day food (lunchtime only Sun). Although the interior is open plan the pub retains separate and distinct drinking areas with comfortable seating. There is a patio drinking area to the rear with disabled access by wheelchair lift. The pub has plenty of car parking. ⚠ Q ⊛ ⓓ ⅍ ⊟ P ⅃

Gellihaf

Coal Hole

Bryn Road, NP12 2QE (on A4049 S of Fleur de Lys)
✪ 12-3, 6.30-11; 11-11 Fri & Sat; 12-10.30 Sun
☎ (01443) 830280
Greene King Old Speckled Hen; Hancock's HB; guest beers ⏢
Set back from the road, this friendly, comfortable one-bar pub was converted from a farm during the 19th century. The bar, which occupies the former stables, offers a regularly changing guest ale. Great food is served in the bar and restaurant every day. On Sunday the three course roast lunch is popular. Well worth a visit for the extensive views over the Rhymney Valley, warm welcome and good ale. ⓓ P

Gilfach Fargoed

Capel

Park Place, CF81 8LW
✪ 12-4, 7-11; 12-11.30 Fri & Sat; 12-10.30 Sun
☎ (01443) 830272
Brains SA; John Smith's Bitter; guest beers ⏢
Welcoming, friendly pub full of character. Mid-Glamorgan CAMRA Pub of the Year several years running, guest beers and ciders come from local and rare to the area producers. A beer festival is usually held in May. Ciders are dispensed from polycasks in a chiller cabinet and may not be on display. The local station has a limited service – check before travelling.
Q ⊛ ⓓ ≠ ⊟ (50, X38) ♣ ⓦ

Glan-y-Llyn

Fagins Ale & Chop House

8 Cardiff Road, CF15 7QD
✪ 11-midnight (1am Fri & Sat); 11-11 Sun
☎ (029) 208 11800
Otley 01; ⏢ guest beers ⏢ /Ⓖ
Choice and quality abound in this independent free house, offering the best range of beers

for miles. It features a cooled gravity stillage in addition to four handpumps and is a rare outlet for prize winning Otley brewery beers and Gwynt y Ddraig cider. Diners can choose from a comprehensive menu of home-cooked fare, served in the bar and restaurant. Beer festivals are held in April and October. Within easy reach of public transport and near the A470/M4. ▲❀◑➔⇥(26, 132)◉

Hirwaun

Glancynon Inn
Swansea Road, CF44 9PH
🕓 11-11; 12-10.30 Sun
☎ (01685) 811043
Greene King Abbot; guest beers Ⓗ
Large country pub with oak beams and a congenial atmosphere. The main outlet for real ale in the area, it is popular with drinkers and diners. Booking is essential for Sunday lunch (no meals Sun eve). The pleasant lounge is comfortable with a split level bar at the back. A little way off the main road, it is nonetheless easy to find. ❀◑ ⊟♣P

Kittle

Beaufort Arms
18 Pennard Road, SA3 3JS
🕓 11-11; 12-10.30 Sun
☎ (01792) 234521
Brains Bitter, Buckley's Best Bitter, Rev James, seasonal beers Ⓗ
Reputedly the oldest pub in Gower, the original part of the building, now the lounge, retains a beamed ceiling and old stonework. A Brains' tenanted house with three bars and a function room, it also offers outdoor seating, a covered, decked area and a well equipped children's playground. The pub has won various community and 'Gower in Bloom' awards. A quiz is held on Monday and the pub hosts the local ladies' darts team. An extensive menu is available.
⑤❀◑⊟(14)♣P

Llancarfan

Fox & Hounds
CF62 3AD
🕓 12-2.30, 6.30-11; 12-3, 7-10.30 Sun
☎ (01446) 781287
Brains Bitter, Rev James; guest beers Ⓗ
Set in an attractive part of the rural vale, this traditional village local provides a warm welcome for visitors – drinkers, diners or guests in the B&B accommodation. Cosy in winter with traditional wooden settles, the pleasant riverside garden is a joy in warmer weather. Guest beers come from near and far. Meals are excellent (not served Mon eve).
▲Q❀⇤◑⊟(V5)P⫶

Llanmadoc

Britannia Inn
Llanmadoc Gower, SA3 1DB
🕓 12-11
☎ (01792) 386624
Marston's Pedigree; guest beers Ⓗ

Ship's timbers used in the construction of this fine old two bar pub are a reminder that Llanmadoc was once a thriving port. Good food and beer await visitors to the Britannia, with families particularly well catered for. The gardens contain a virtual menagerie and offer stunning views over the estuary. The Mapsant – an ancient annual festival celebrating the patron saint of the parish – is held here in November. ▲Q❀◑ ⊟▲♣P

Llanrhidian

Greyhound Inn
Oldwalls, SA3 1HA
🕓 11-11; 12-10.30 Sun
☎ (01792) 391027
Draught Bass; Flowers IPA; Wadworth 6X; guest beers Ⓗ
Popular inn on the north Gower road welcoming locals and visitors alike. Families are well catered for in the games room and there is a function room. Winter visitors will find a real fire to relax by. The restaurant has a reputation for good quality food which is served in all the bars. The Sunday carvery is particularly popular. The pub has a large car park. ▲Q⑤❀◑ ⊟▲♣P

Llansamlet

Plough & Harrow
57 Church Road, SA7 9RL
🕓 12-11 (midnight Wed, Fri & Sat); closed winter Mon
☎ (01792) 772263
Tomos Watkin OSB, seasonal beers; guest beers Ⓗ
Former Celtic Inns pub, now part of the Marston's pub group, although still offering Tomos Watkin's OSB. Guest beers come from the Jennings range. The large bar has seating arranged in comfortable groups, with an open fire at one end. A function/dining room is upstairs and there is bench seating outside at the front for warmer days. Good disabled access and facilities are provided and family groups are welcome until 9pm. A charity quiz is run by the local vicar on Wednesday evening. ▲❀◑♿⊟(33)P

Llantwit Fardre

Bush Inn
Main Road, CF38 2EP
🕓 11-11; 12-10.30 Sun
☎ (01443) 203958
Hancock's HB; guest beers Ⓗ
Recently extended, this inn retains its village local feel. It offers some form of entertainment most evenings – darts, a quiz or live music. The guest beers are often unusual for the area, and favourite ones may be kept on by popular request. Hancock's HB is sometimes replaced by another similar strength Welsh beer. ❀♣P

Llantwit Major

Kings Head
East Street, CF61 1XY
🕓 11.30-11; 12-10.30 Sun
☎ (01446) 792697

Brains Dark, Bitter, SA; guest beer Ⓗ
Friendly town centre pub with a loyal local following offering a warm welcome to visitors. The large public bar, buzzing with banter, is complemented by a cosy, comfy lounge and dining area. The bar has a large TV screen for sporting events, Wales rugby matches are shown in the lounge and pool, darts and dominoes are played. A good sized beer garden is at the rear. The ale is second to none and the home-cooked food is excellent value. ⚫Q♿❄️🅲🅳👫🅰️➷🚌♣P↙

Old Swan Inn

Church Street, CF61 1SB
🕐 12-11; 12-10.30 Sun
☎ (01446) 792230 ⊕ oldswaninn.com
Beer range varies Ⓗ
A real gem in the old part of this historic vale town, the winner of many awards for beer and food including local CAMRA Pub of the Year. Two beers are available during the week and four at the weekend from all over the country including local breweries such as Vale of Glamorgan and Otley. The front bar attracts drinkers and diners, the back bar is popular with a younger clientele. It has a large garden and families are welcome.
⚫❄️🅲🅳👫🅰️➷🚌♣↙

Machen

White Hart

Nant-y-Ceisiad, CF83 8QQ (100 yards N of A468 at W end of village) OS203892
🕐 11.30-2.30 (not winter Mon), 6-11.30; 12-10.30 Sun
☎ (01633) 441005
Beer range varies Ⓗ
A boggling blend of old and new, this independent free house offers up to four guest beers from a wide variety of brewers. Despite its proximity to the A468, the pub has its origins in the Rhymney Tramroad, a route now revived dedicated to cycling. The interior has a maritime feel incorporating fittings from the classical liner Empress of France. Meals are served during most opening hours – booking is advised for Sunday lunch. A beer festival is usually held in November. ❄️🚄🅲🅳🚌(50)♣P

Marcross

Horseshoe Inn

CF61 1ZG
🕐 12-11 (10.30 Sun)
☎ (01656) 890568
Wye Valley Hereford Pale Ale; guest beers Ⓗ
Situated in a small village on the heritage coast, this cosy, traditional pub is close to the beach and Nash Point lighthouse. Known until recently as the Lighthouse, the pub has reverted to its original name under new ownership and to the standards set in the days when it was local CAMRA Pub of the Year. Up to six beers are available. The two bar interior has plenty of comfortable seating for eating or drinking in the interconnecting rooms.
⚫Q❄️🅲🅳🚌(145)♣P

Monknash

Plough & Harrow

CF71 7QQ (off B4265 between Wick and Marcross)
🕐 12-11 (10.30 Sun)
☎ (01656) 890209
Archers Golden; Draught Bass; Worthington's Bitter; Wye Valley Hereford Pale Ale; guest beers Ⓗ
One of the best known pubs in Wales, the current licensee has returned it to the standards that first made its reputation great. The building began as a medieval grange and has been put to many uses since then including serving as a mortuary. Visitors to the lounge note that the real ale is in the bar, as is the Weston's Old Rosie cider. Up to seven guest beers at a time come from all over the country. Unmissable.
⚫❄️🅲🅳🅰️🚌(145)♣♠P↙

Mumbles

Park Inn

23 Park Street, SA3 4AD
🕐 4 (12 Fri-Sun)-11
☎ (01792) 366738
Beer range varies Ⓗ
Swansea CAMRA Pub of the Year 2007. Five handpumps dispense an ever-changing range of beers with particular emphasis on west country and Welsh independent brews. The convivial atmosphere attracts discerning drinkers of all ages though the games room is particularly popular with younger people. Thursday is quiz night. A fine display of pump clips, pictures of old Mumbles and the Mumbles tram adorn the walls. Q🚌♣♠↙

Victoria Inn

21 Westbourne Place, SA3 4DB
🕐 12 (11.30 Sat)-11; 12-10.30 Sun
☎ (01792) 380111 ⊕ victoriainnmumbles.co.uk
Draught Bass; Greene King Old Speckled Hen; Worthington's Bitter; guest beers Ⓗ
Traditional back street corner local dating from the mid-19th century. The enthusiastic landlady has carried out refurbishments, making this a comfortable pub, but retained historical interest. A well remains in the bar – this was the water source in the days when the pub brewed its own beer. Sky Sports is popular here, particularly football and rugby. Monday is quiz night. ❄️♣↙

Murton

Plough & Harrow

88 Oldway, SA3 3DJ
🕐 11-11; 12-10.30 Sun
☎ (01792) 234459
Courage Best Bitter, Directors; guest beers Ⓗ
One of the oldest pubs in Gower, it has been enlarged and renovated in recent times, but has retained its character and local popularity. The pub combines its busy food trade with the traditions of a local. The bar has TV and pool while the comfortable lounge is quieter for conversation or a meal. Quiz night is Tuesday. Heaters are used to warm the covered decked outdoor area. A genuinely friendly pub in an attractive village. ⚫Q❄️🅲🅳🚌(14)♣P

Neath

Borough Arms

New Henry Street, SA11 1PH
☼ 4-11; 12-11 Sat; 12-3, 6-10.30 Sun
☎ (01639) 644902
Beer range varies Ⓗ
Well run traditional local just outside the town centre where a warm welcome is assured. A U-shaped central bar serves two separate areas, one with pub games. The pub has strong rugby connections with Neath RFC and the Ospreys and is busy on Six Nations match days. A good range of rotating ales is always on offer, many from outside Wales. A little off the beaten track but well worth the effort to seek out. Q❀⇌🖳♣⌐

David Protheroe

7 Windsor Road, SA11 1LS
☼ 9-midnight (1am Fri & Sat)
☎ (01639) 622130
Beer range varies Ⓗ
This large, popular, open plan Wetherspoon's outlet, opposite Neath railway station, was once the local police station and jailhouse. Beers from Welsh breweries feature regularly. The menu also contains a good selection of Welsh dishes and themed food nights are popular. There is a family dining area to the rear. Smokers are catered for in a heated outdoor area. ⌂❀⬲&⇌🖳⌐

Highlander

2 Lewis Road, SA11 1EQ
☼ 12 (4 Mon)-11
☎ (01639) 633586
Beer range varies Ⓗ
Large one-room public house with a central bar and elevated dining area serving reasonably priced meals. Two or more changing guest ales are supplied from independent breweries. A list of forthcoming beers is displayed over the side door. The front seating area has a large-screen TV but conversation is the norm. ⬲&⇌🖳

Newton

Newton Inn

New Well Lane, SA3 4SR
☼ 12-11 (10.30 Sun)
☎ (01792) 363226
Draught Bass; Fuller's London Pride; Worthington's Bitter; guest beers Ⓗ
Smart village local, open plan but with bar and lounge areas. Competitively priced meals are offered at lunchtime and early evening. The bar has a large-screen TV showing sporting events. Quiz nights are Monday and Wednesday. The draught beers can be gravity dispensed on request; the landlord regularly changes the guest beers. Roadside tables are available for outside drinking on a small patio area. ❀⬲🖳(2, 2A)

Norton

Beaufort Arms

1 Castle Road, SA3 5TE
☼ 11.30-11; 12-10.30 Sun
☎ (01792) 401319

Draught Bass; Greene King Abbot; Worthington's Bitter; guest beers Ⓗ
Village local dating from the 18th century split into a traditional bar with TV and dart board and a small, comfortable lounge. Both rooms have real fires. A pub team usually enters the Mumbles raft race each year, recorded in many photographs on the walls. Quiz night is Tuesday. A charming pub with a friendly, welcoming atmosphere. ♨Q❀⬲(2A, 3A)♣

Ogmore-by-Sea

Pelican In Her Piety

Ewenny Road, CF32 0QP
☼ 12-11 (10.30 Sun)
☎ (01656) 880049
Draught Bass; Fuller's London Pride; Greene King Old Speckled Hen; Worthington's Bitter; guest beers Ⓗ
In an attractive location opposite the ruins of Ogmore castle, this welcoming village local has a cosy log fire in winter and plentiful outdoor seating in summer. Generous helpings of good food can be washed down with equally fine ale, always served without a sparkler. Many charity fund-raising events are well supported by the locals. There is a large car parking area and a newly built covered area outside for smokers.
♨Q❀⬲▲🖳(145)P⌐

Penarth

Bear's Head

37-39 Windsor Road, CF64 1JD
☼ 10-11; 12-10.30 Sun
☎ (029) 207 06424
Brains SA; Bullmastiff Welsh Gold, Son of a Bitch; Marston's Burton Bitter; guest beers Ⓗ
Typical Wetherspoon's shop conversion offering a welcome change from the usual local outlets. Busy and popular with all ages, it has a family area upstairs with modern art on display. A welcome local outlet for Bullmastiff beers, it is frequented by the brewers themselves, ensuring the beer stays in tip top nick. Weston's cider and a good selection of foreign bottled beers are also available. The usual Wetherspoon's fare is served throughout the day. Bear's Head is the English translation of Penarth.
Q⌂⬲⇌(Dingle Rd/ Penarth)🖳♦

Windsor

93 Windsor Road, CF64 1JF
☼ 12-11 (midnight Wed & Sat)
☎ (029) 207 02821
Brains SA; Greene King Abbot; Hancock's HB; guest beers Ⓗ
The Windsor, owned by Brains, continues to offer the best beer range in town with three guest beers usually available alongside the regulars. A wall of framed pump clips displays the licensees' dedication to real ale choice. Situated on the edge of town, the pub is an ideal refuelling stop for shoppers and offers good value lunches. Regular entertainment includes live music and Morris dancers.
Q⬲⇌(Dingle Road)🖳♣

WALES

Penllyn

Red Fox

CF71 7RQ

☼ 12-3 (not Mon), 6-11; 12-10.30 Sun

☎ (01446) 772352

Hancock's HB; Tomos Watkins OSB; guest beers Ⓗ

Following the threat of closure by previous owner and former Phantom of the Opera star Peter Karrie, and saved by a high profile campaign by locals, this village pub continues to receive strong support from village residents and visitors who enjoy the good food, beer and company. The pleasant patio is popular for summertime drinking and it has a large car park. Handy for visitors to the local paintball facility. ⚑Q✿◗⅚🚃(V3)♣P

Penycae

Ancient Briton

Brecon Road, SA9 1YY (between Ystragynlais and Dan-yr-Ogof caves on A4067)

☼ 11.30-2am (1am Sun)

☎ (01639) 730273

Draught Bass; guest beers Ⓗ

Fantastic rural real ale pub offering up to six beers and one cider. Situated on the Swansea to Brecon Road, it is frequented by hikers, cavers and climbers visiting the spectacular Brecon Beacons. Built in 1835, it is sited near the historic Crayig-y-Nos Castle. Set in large grounds, it has a children's play area and beer garden. Quality home produced food is available lunchtime and evening.
⚑✿🛏◗⅚🅰🚃♣♠P⁵–🍴

Pontardawe

Pontardawe Inn

123 Herbert Street, SA8 4ED

☼ 12-midnight (1am Fri & Sat); 12-11 Sun

☎ (01792) 830791 ⊕pontardaweinn.co.uk

Banks's Original; Marston's Pedigree; guest beers Ⓗ

Known locally as the Gwachel, this 250-year-old inn has three separate rooms served by a central bar. A popular venue for musicians for many years, the pub hosts live jam sessions on Wednesday evening and live bands on Friday and Saturday. Beer festivals are held in March and August to coincide with the Pontardawe music festival. The present landlords have given the pub a new lease of life and made it a focal point for the community. Q✿◗⅚🚃P⁵

Pontneddfechan

Old White Horse Inn

12 High Street, SA11 5NP (off A465)

☼ 12-3, 6-11 (closed winter Mon); 12-11 Sat; 12-10.30 Sun

☎ (01639) 721219

Beer range varies Ⓗ

Situated in waterfall country in the Brecon Beacons national park, this inn, built around 1600, has served as a coaching house, shop and a B&B before reverting to a pub in the early 1960s. It has a cosy public bar, lounge/restaurant and a large games room. Up to three ales are stocked in winter and up to five plus a cider in summer, when the pub holds a beer festival. Popular with walkers, budget hostel accommodation is available.
⚑✿🛏◗⅚🅰🚃♣♠P

Pontypridd

Bunch of Grapes

Ynysangharad Road, CF37 4DA (off A4054, N of A470 jct)

☼ 10-midnight (1am Fri & Sat); 12-midnight Sun

☎ (01443) 402934 ⊕bunchofgrapes.org.uk

Otley O1; guest beers Ⓗ

A short walk from the town centre, this multiple award winning free house offers an eclectic range of ales (which may include other offerings from the Otley brewery) and high quality food served in the restaurant and bar. The welcoming ambience attracts customers from near and far, including travellers along the Taff Trail (Cardiff to Beacon) which passes the front door. Local CAMRA Pub of the Year 2006. ⚑✿◗⇌♣P

Llanover Arms

Bridge Street, CF37 4PE (opp entrance to Ynysangharad Park)

☼ 12-11 (midnight Sat & Sun)

☎ (01443) 403215

Brains Bitter; Felinfoel Double Dragon; guest beer Ⓗ

This free house is well sited for visitors to the town's Historical Centre and the renowned Ynysangharad Park. The three rooms are festooned with a miscellany of bric-a-brac including equine paintings, old mirrors, maps and clocks. However, the most popular feature is the constantly changing guest ale which attracts a loyal following. ✿🚃⇌♣P

Port Talbot

Lord Caradoc

69-73 Station Road, SA13 1NW

☼ 9am-midnight (1am Fri & Sat)

☎ (01639) 896007

Brains SA, Rev James; Greene King Abbot; guest beers Ⓗ

Typical Wetherspoon's situated in the centre of town a short distance from the railway station. The bar has an L-shaped layout with a raised drinking area. Children are welcome in the family area towards the rear of the pub. There is a patio area outside. The usual value for money fare is on offer including the popular steak and curry nights. ✿◗⅚⇌🚃

Porth

Rheola

Rheola Road, CF39 0LF

☼ 2-midnight; 1-1am Fri; 12-1am Sat; 12-midnight Sun

☎ (01443) 682633

Courage Directors; Draught Bass; guest beers Ⓗ

Comfortable, friendly pub with a lively bar and a cosy lounge. A guest ale is offered each weekend to supplement the two regulars. Situated at the 'Gateway to the Rhondda' and only a short distance north of the Rhondda Heritage Park, this is a pub not to be missed. Note that last entry is 10.30pm. ✿🚃⇌🚃♣P

Porthcawl

Lorelei Hotel

36-38 Esplanade Road, CF36 3YU (off the seafront)

✪ 12-2, 5-11; 11-11 Fri; 12-10.30 Sun

☎ (01656) 788342

Draught Bass; Tomos Watkin OSB; guest beers Ⓗ
In a terraced street off the seafront, this is an oasis of real ale in a desert of keg bars and mediocrity. Two guest beers and draught Budvar join the regular ales, plus a fine selection of bottled European beers and cider in summer. There are two bars and a dining room where children are welcome. Two beer festivals are held annually. The huge display of pump clips reflects the commitment to real ale that has won this popular hotel many CAMRA awards. ≿⊛🖙❄▲🖳♦

Quakers Yard

Glantaff Inn

Cardiff Road, CF46 5AH

✪ 11-4, 6-1am; 11-1am Fri & Sat; 11-midnight Sun

☎ (01443) 410822

Courage Directors; guest beers Ⓗ
Comfortable inn, adorned with a large collection of water jugs, boxing memorabilia and old photographs with a local interest. The guest ales, frequently including offerings from the local Otley and Rhymney breweries, are popular with locals, as well as walkers and cyclists travelling along the Cardiff to Brecon Taff Trail. ◑

Reynoldston

King Arthur Hotel

Higher Green, SA3 1AD

✪ 11-11; 12-10.30 Sun

☎ (01792) 390775 ∰ kingarthurhotel.co.uk

Draught Bass; Felinfoel Double Dragon; guest beers Ⓗ
Set in the heart of the beautiful Gower countryside, this splendid pub and hotel/restaurant is deservedly popular with locals and tourists. During the summer the large outside area offers idyllic surroundings and in winter a large real fire adds to the cosy and inviting atmosphere in the bar. Top quality beer and an excellent menu featuring first class local produce make this a pub not to be missed. It is reputed to be haunted by two ghosts. ≌≿⊛🖙◑🖳&♣P

Rhymney

Farmers Arms

Brewery Row, NP22 5EZ

✪ 12-11; 12-3, 7-11 Sun

☎ (01685) 840257

Brains Bitter; Fuller's London Pride; guest beers Ⓗ
Local community pub furnished in traditional style to reflect the pub's history. The walls are adorned with photographs and memorabilia from the former Rhymney Brewery and many ex-employees of the brewery frequent the pub. A quiz night is held on Thursday and a large function room is available to hire. Good

and affordable food is on offer (not Sun and Mon eve). ⊛◑≈♣P

Risca

Commercial

Commercial Street, Pontymister, NP11 6AB (on B4591 at Brookland Rd jct)

✪ 11-11.30 (midnight Fri & Sat); 12-11 Sun

☎ (01633) 612608

Beer range varies Ⓗ
Large roadside pub well served by local bus services. The open plan interior includes a games section with pool and darts, and a spacious, comfortable lounge. The guest ales on offer from small brewers attract drinkers from near and far, such is the interest in cask ales. The patio is popular in warmer weather. ⊛🖳♣ʟ

Fox & Hounds

Park Road, NP11 6PW

✪ 12-midnight (10.30 Sun)

☎ (01633) 612937

Beer range varies Ⓗ
Bustling pub near the park and local shops and handy for buses. Sports and music are popular here; the bar has a large screen TV, pool table, darts and juke box. The single guest ale is sourced from an independent brewery – demand is such that the beer changes almost daily. There is a good sized garden and additional seating at the front of the premises overlooks the park. ≌⊛🖳♣Pʟ

Rudry

Maenllwyd Inn

CF83 3EB (500m SW of village) OS201867

✪ 12-11 (10.30 Sun)

☎ (029) 208 82372

Courage Best Bitter; guest beers Ⓗ
Popular Chef & Brewer restaurant in a delightful rural setting. The old Victorian inn now serves as the entrance, leading to a modern extension at the rear. Two guest beers are stocked from regional and family brewers. A pleasant place to visit and a haven from the bustle of nearby Cardiff and Caerphilly. ≌Q⊛◑🖳P

St Brides Major

Farmers Arms

Wick Road, Pitcot, CF32 0SE

✪ 12-3, 6-11; 12-10.30 Sun

☎ (01656) 880224

Courage Best Bitter; Greene King Old Speckled Hen; Hancock's HB; Marston's Pedigree; Ushers Best Bitter Ⓗ
Extremely popular roadside pub and restaurant on the outskirts of an attractive village. Directly opposite the local pond inhabited by a family of swans, the pub attracts locals and visitors for the excellent beer and renowned food served in the bar and restaurant. A collection of china jugs hang from the beams and the porch and exterior have fine flower displays.
≌Q⊛◑🖳(145)♣P

WALES

St Hilary

Bush

CF71 7DP (off A48 E of Cowbridge)
🕐 11.30-11; 12-10.30 Sun
☎ (01446) 772745
Draught Bass; Greene King IPA, Old Speckled Hen; Hancock's HB; guest beer ⊞
A traditional gem, this beautiful, unspoilt 400-year-old thatched pub is opposite the church in a small, picturesque country village. Hops surround the fireplace in the bar. Food of excellent quality is served in one of the bars as well as the fine, locally renowned restaurant. Weston's Old Rosie is available all year round. The outdoor area is popular in summer, with plenty of parking available.
🏚Q🍴♿◑●⊟(V2)♣⌖P

Swansea

Brunswick

3 Duke Street, SA1 4HS
🕐 11-11; 12-10.30 Sun
☎ (01792) 465676
Courage Best Bitter; Theakston's XB; ⊞ **guest beer** Ⓖ
Good, well managed, side street pub, resembling a country inn in an urban setting. Wooden beams and a comfortable seating arrangement create a traditional, relaxing feel. The walls are adorned with an interesting, regularly changing display of artwork with pictures for sale. A quiz is held on Monday evening and live, acoustic music plays on Sunday, Tuesday and Thursday. A frequently changing, gravity dispensed, seasonal guest beer, occasionally from a local brewery, supplements the regular handpumped ales. ◑●♿

Eli Jenkins Ale House

24 Oxford Street, SA1 3AQ
🕐 10.30-11.30 (midnight Fri); 10-midnight Sat; 12-11 Sun
☎ (01792) 630961
Badger Tanglefoot; Brains Bitter; guest beers ⊞
City centre pub, a hundred metres from the bus station, named after a character in Under Milk Wood by Dylan Thomas. It has wooden alcoves with a mix of seating and prints of local views on the walls. Always busy, it attracts diners and drinkers throughout the day and is quieter late evening. Food is served daily until 8pm (5pm Sun). Two quality guest ales such as Fuller's ESB complement the regular range. ◑●♿

No Sign Bar

56 Wind Street, SA1 1EG (150m from Swansea Castle)
🕐 11-1am; 12-12.30am Sun
☎ (01792) 456110
Brains SA; Greene King Ruddles County; guest beers ⊞
Situated in Swansea's 'street of pubs', the No Sign has everything that is lacking from the 15 plus other pubs/restaurant bars in the road. A regular haunt of Dylan Thomas, it offers a good choice of bar meals and a full menu of delicious lunches and dinners complemented by arguably the best choice of wines and spirits in Swansea. An excellent range of ales

includes the ever popular Ruddles County.
🍴♿⊛◑●♿⊟

Queens Hotel

Gloucester Place, SA1 1TY
🕐 11-11; 12-10.30 Sun
☎ (01792) 521231
Brains Buckley's Best Bitter; Theakston XB, Old Peculier; guest beers ⊞
Vibrant free house located within the city's main nightlife area and marina, handy for the waterfront museum. The walls display many photographs depicting Swansea's maritime history. The pub enjoys strong local support and the home cooked, traditional lunches are an added attraction. Evening entertainment includes a quiz on Sunday and live music on Saturday. A good range of ales includes the rare for the area Old Peculier. Seasonal brews come from local breweries such as Tomos Watkin and Evan Evans. ⊛◑♿

Westbourne

1 Brynymor Road, SA1 4JQ
🕐 11-11.30 (midnight Thu; 12.30am Fri & Sat); 12-11 Sun
☎ (01792) 476637
Brains SA; Greene King Abbot; guest beers ⊞
Fully modernised, well known street corner establishment with a predominantly purple exterior and interior. Two regular ales feature plus two guest beers, occasionally Felinfoel Double Dragon. The bar has comfortable seating and there is an outdoor drinking area. A quiz is held on Tuesday evening and Sky Sports on TV attracts sports fans. ⊛◑♿

Three Crosses

Poundffald Inn

Tir Mynydd Road, SA4 3PB
🕐 12-11 (10.30 Sun)
☎ (01792) 873428
Brains SA; Greene King Abbot, Old Speckled Hen ⊞
Popular village local with a traditional public bar warmed by a welcoming fire. The interior features an interesting collection of horse bits and other rural implements. The lounge is mainly oriented towards food, serving good value meals based on local produce. The name Poundffald is a combination of Welsh and English – ffald is the local word for pound, meaning an enclosure. 🏚🍴⊛◑●⊟(21)P

Treboeth

King's Head

Llangyfelach Road, SA5 9EL (on B4489)
🕐 12-11 (midnight Fri, Sat & Sun)
☎ (01792) 773727
Beer range varies ⊞
Large, popular, family friendly pub in a suburb of Swansea with a split level lounge bar, restaurant and function room. Two real ales are always available which change monthly by SIBA's direct delivery system. Good value tasty meals are served all day. The patio area to the front has benches for warmer weather. Quiz nights are held twice a week on Sunday and Tuesday. Note the royal family tree in the lounge. ⊛◑♿⊟(36)P

Treforest

Otley Arms

Forest Road, CF37 1SY (near railway station)
🕐 11-midnight (1am Fri & Sat); 12-midnight Sun
☎ (01443) 402033
Otley O1, OG; guest beers Ⓗ
Tardis-like end of terrace pub catering for locals and students from the nearby university. All enjoy the ambience, the range of guest ales, which may include other beers from the Otley portfolio, and the multiple TV screens showing Sky Sports. There are disabled toilet facilities, but access to the pub is difficult for an unaccompanied wheelchair user. Note that there is no admission after 11.30pm. ◑≥≠♣

Treherbert

Baglan Hotel

30 Baglan Street, CF42 5AW
🕐 11 (3 Mon)-11; 11-1am Sat; 11-11 Sun
☎ (01443) 776111
Brains Rev James; Felinfoel Double Dragon, seasonal beers; guest beers Ⓗ
Welcoming real ale oasis owned by the same family for 60 years. Inside, the walls are adorned with photos of well known visitors and a large screen shows Sky Sports. Its location at the top of the Rhondda Valley makes the hotel an ideal base for the more active to enjoy mountain biking or hill walking. ✿≠♣

Tyla Garw

Boar's Head

Coedcae Lane, Talbot Green, CF72 9EZ OS029891
🕐 11-11; 12-4, 7-10.30 Sun
☎ (01443) 225400
Brains Rev James; RCH Pitchfork; guest beers Ⓗ
The Boar's Head has undergone substantial extension and refurbishment over the past year, but has retained its friendly country inn feel. Up to seven ales are available, always with the chance of discovering an unusual one for the area. There is a good value restaurant and a separate menu for the bar, with special deal steak and curry evenings. ♨✿◑◐⊟P

Upper Killay

Railway Inn

553 Gower Road, SA2 7DS
🕐 12-2, 4-11; 12-11 Sat; 12-10.30 Sun
☎ (01792) 203946
Swansea Deep Slade Dark, Bishopswood, Original Wood, seasonal beers; guest beers Ⓗ
Built in 1864, this is a rare gem full of character and characters. A locals' pub, visitors are warmly welcomed in the traditional public bar. At least two guest beers usually come from breweries rare to the area. Beer festivals are held in summer. The former railway track alongside is now a foot and cycle way to the seafront and part of a regional cycle network. No food is served. Children are not permitted inside. ♨✿⊞🚃(21)♣P

Ystalyfera

Wern Fawr Inn

47 Wern Road, SA9 2LX (A4067)
🕐 7 (6.30 Fri)-11; 12-3.30, 7-11 Sun
☎ (01639) 843625 ⊕ bryncelynbrewery.org.uk
Bryncelyn Buddy Marvellous, Holly Hop, Oh Boy, seasonal beers Ⓗ
Home to the Bryncelyn Brewery, this pub was CAMRA Regional Pub of the Year in 2005. The bar displays a large collection of bygone domestic and industrial curios and is heated by an old stove. There is also a comfortable lounge. The beers, named after Buddy Holly songs, are multiple award winners. 1960s music is played, and a quiz night held every other Wednesday. The pub opens all day when rugby internationals are played. Take-outs are available and polypins can be ordered. ♨Q✿⊞🚃♣⌐

Brains SA, brewed in Cardiff, Glamorgan.

GWENT

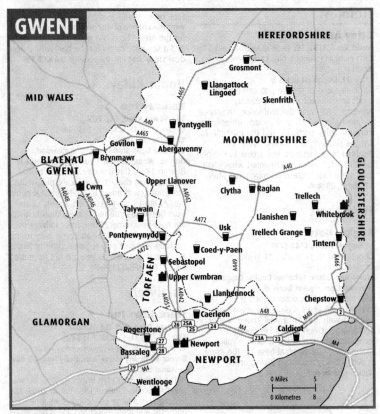

Authority areas covered: Blaenau Gwent UA, Monmouthshire UA, Newport UA, Torfaen UA

Abergavenny

Angel Hotel

15 Cross Street, NP7 5EN
☼ 10-3, 6-11 (11.30 Fri & Sat); 11-3, 6-10.30 Sun
☎ (01873) 857121 ⊕ angelhotelabergavenny.com
Brains Rev James; Fuller's London Pride; guest beers Ⓗ
This former coaching inn has undergone a gradual modernisation sympathetic with its age and style and has a pleasant, relaxed atmosphere. The Foxhunter bar has large tables and leather sofas; a quiet, comfortable lounge off the lobby displays interesting artwork. The sheltered courtyard is used for alfresco dining and drinking on warmer days, and there is a highly regarded restaurant. The hotel plays an important part in the town's annual international food and drink festival. ⊯Q❀⊯◑⊨P

Coliseum

Lion Street, NP7 5PE
☼ 9-midnight (1am Fri & Sat)
☎ (01873) 736960
Brains SA; Evan Evans Welsh Ale; Greene King Abbot; Marston's Pedigree; guest beers Ⓗ
A great success, this Wetherspoon's conversion of a former cinema is very popular, particularly at the weekend. Framed pictures are a reminder of its cinematic past while others are snapshots of local history. The bar

has a high ceiling with skylights and large windows creating a light, airy feel. The standard beer range is augmented by guest beers, sometimes from local breweries. An extensive menu served throughout the day includes dishes with a Welsh flavour. ◑&⊨➍

Grofield

Baker Street, NP7 5BB
☼ 5 (3 Sat)-midnight; 3-11 Sun
☎ (07784) 770190
Fuller's London Pride; Shepherd Neame Spitfire; guest beers Ⓗ
This side street pub has sprung back to life with new zest after a long period of closure. Fully refurbished, the attractive lounge bar has a modern style and decor that marks it out from other pubs in town. Steps lead straight to the bar counter, with comfortable seating areas on either side. Guest ales are selected from established family-owned or regional independent breweries. ❀⊨♣

INDEPENDENT BREWERIES

Cwmbran Upper Cwmbran
Dobbins & Jackson Newport
Kingstone Whitebrook
Warcop Wentlooge
Webbs Cwm

Station

37 Brecon Road, NP7 5UH

✪ 5 (1 Wed & Thu)-midnight; 12.30-1am Fri; 12-1am Sat; 11.30-11 Sun

☎ (01873) 854759

Adnams Broadside; Draught Bass; Fuller's London Pride; Greene King IPA; Rhymney Bitter; guest beers Ⓗ

It has been a long time since railway passengers alighted here at what was once the Brecon Road station to quench their thirst. A few minutes' walk from the town centre, the interior of this characterful pub remains much the same as it has for decades, retaining some reminders of its former railway connections. The small lounge is a quiet refuge; the popular public bar is the place to enjoy friendly banter and frivolity. ✿🖥🖨♣

Bassaleg

Tredegar Arms

4 Caerphilly Road, NP10 8LE (1 mile N of M4 jct 28) OS277891

✪ 12 (11 Thu & Fri)-11; 11-midnight Fri & Sat; 12-10.30 Sun

☎ (01633) 894237

Greene King IPA, Ruddles County, Abbot, Old Speckled Hen; Ⓗ **guest beers** Ⓗ/Ⓖ

Large imposing pub in a residential area to the west of Newport. Formerly a Whitbread house, it is now owned by Greene King and offers one of the largest selections of real ale in the area. It has a public bar, but the main room is where real ales are dispensed from handpump and stillage. This room has a small lounge leading to extensive dining areas. Families are welcome – there is a large garden and play area. ⇗✿◑🖥♿🖨♣P

Brynmawr

Hobby Horse Inn

30 Greenland Road, NP23 4DT (off Alma St)

✪ 12-3, 7-midnight; 11.30-midnight Sat & Sun

☎ (01495) 310996 ⊕ hobbyhorse.cjb.net

Beer range varies Ⓗ

Welcoming community free house with a distinctive Hobby Horse sign from the old Rhymney Brewery hanging outside. A front patio decked with flowers in season leads to a cosy low beamed bar displaying sports memorabilia and an array of pump clips on the ceiling. The guest beers usually come from independent brewers. Diners may eat in the bar or restaurant, choosing from an extensive menu. B&B accommodation is available. ✿🛏◑🖥♣

Caerleon

Bell Inn

Bulmore Road, NP18 1QQ (off New Road B4236)

✪ 12-3 (not Mon & Tue), 6-11; 12-11 Fri & Sat; 12-10.30 Sun

☎ (01633) 420613 ⊕ thebellatcaerleon.co.uk

Beer range varies Ⓗ

Gwent CAMRA Pub of the Year 2007. This welcoming inn has recently been revitalised and fully deserves the many accolades it has received. Beers are sourced from local micro-breweries. Four beer and cider festivals are held annually with the outside 'cwtch' used to house the ales. Events for the community are well supported. Live Celtic music features on Wednesday evening. Excellent food is based on a Welsh/Breton menu. Petanque is played in summer. ✿◑🖥♣♠P⅃

Hanbury Arms

Uskside, High Street, NP18 1AA

✪ 11.30-11 (midnight Fri & Sat); 12-10.30 Sun

☎ (01633) 420361

Brains SA, Rev James; Greene King Abbot; guest beer Ⓗ

Historic riverside pub beside an old stone bridge. A beautiful outdoor drinking area has impressive views over the River Usk which has the second highest tidal range in the world. Inside, three drinking and dining areas cater for all and good value food is served. The beer range is supplemented by an interesting guest. A good place to start or finish a tour of tourist attractions and the many local pubs. The Roman Museum, ancient amphitheatre and baths are worth visiting. ✿◑🖥P

Caldicot

Castle Inn

64 Church Road, Monmouthshire, NP26 4HN (opp St Mary's Church)

✪ 12-11 (midnight Fri & Sat)

☎ (01291) 420509

Flowers IPA; guest beers Ⓗ

Comfortable, award winning pub with a low ceiling and open plan interior warmed by a real fire on colder days. Quality food is served, with demand significantly boosted when the licensees took a gamble and became a no-smoking pub well before the national ban came into force. The pub is situated next to the impressive 12th century Caldicot Castle and its extensive grounds. ♨✿◑🅰🖥P

Chepstow

Chepstow Athletic Club

Mathern Road, NP16 5JJ (off Bulwark Rd)

✪ 7-11; 12-midnight Sat; 12-3, 7-10.30 Sun

☎ (01291) 622126

Brains SA; Flowers IPA; Rhymney Bitter; guest beers Ⓗ

This large, comfortable bar welcomes a broad cross-section of the community, attracted by ales dispensed in peak form by the long-established bar and cellar management duo. Three regular beers are complemented by three guests, usually changing at least twice a week. Sports players, fans, families, social members and visitors alike join many local clubs and societies in embracing this friendly place. Regional CAMRA Club of the Year 2007 – members are welcome (show your card for free entry). ✿🖥♣P

Coach & Horses

Welsh Street, NP16 5LN

✪ 11-11; 12-10.30 Sun

☎ (01291) 622626 ⊕ coachandhorsesinn.co.uk

Brains Buckley's Best Bitter, SA, Rev James; guest beers Ⓗ

As well as the Brains beers, this town centre inn offers three guest ales (two in summer plus a cider), usually from smaller independents. The layout of the two-level bar helps to create a relaxed, convivial atmosphere, providing a popular gathering place for locals and visitors. Chepstow's historic castle is a short downhill stroll away. In July the pub hosts a beer festival coinciding every other year with the town's own festival, a happy match of real ale with real music. ⊛☎◁◑⇌🖪♦

Clytha

Clytha Arms
NP7 9BW (on B4598 near Raglan) OS368089
🕐 12-3 (not Mon), 6-11; 12-11 Sat; 12-4, 7-10.30 Sun
☎ (01873) 840206 ⊕ clytha-arms.com
Beer range varies 🅷
Four times Gwent and twice South & Mid Wales CAMRA Pub of the Year, this is a magnificent country pub, set in lush countryside near Raglan. It holds a Welsh beer and cheese festival every year, and hosts the Welsh Cider Festival over the spring bank holiday. You can enjoy a bar meal from the interesting menu or dine in the widely-acclaimed restaurant. Oh, and the beer ain't bad either. ⋈Q⊛☎◁◑⊟♣♦P

Coed-y-Paen

Carpenters Arms
NP4 0TH (E off A4042 at crematorium then follow signs) SO334984
🕐 12-3 (not Mon), 6-11; 12-11 Sat; 12-5 Sun
☎ (01291) 672621 ⊕ thecarpenterscoedypaen.co.uk
Beer range varies 🅷
A smart and sympathetic refurbishment has maintained the feel of this interesting village local. The large beer garden has camping facilities next door. Local produce features in the restaurant, and the beer range usually includes a guest from Wye Valley Brewery. Convenient for Llandegfeth reservoir, with facilities for boating, fishing and wind-surfing, there are good walks and golf nearby. ⋈⊛◁◑ ▲P

Govilon

Bridgend Inn
Church Lane, NP7 9RP
🕐 12-3, 7-12.30am (1am Fri & Sat); 12-3, 7-10.30 Sun
☎ (01873) 830177
Beer range varies 🅷
Situated next to a stone bridge in the middle of the village, and a convenient stop if you happen to be taking an excursion along the Monmouthshire and Brecon canal, this pub is also popular with walkers and cyclists. The bar has a pool table and live music often plays on a Friday night. A small range of beers is on offer, usually from independent brewers, often including something local. Good value meals are served. ◑⊟🖪P

Grosmont

Angel Inn
NP7 8EP (off A465 at Llangua)
🕐 12-2.30 (not Mon), 6-1am (2am Fri); 12-2am Sat; 12-11 (12-2.30, 7-11 winter) Sun

☎ (01981) 240646
Wye Valley Butty Bach; guest beers 🅷
Situated in a picturesque village with a Norman castle and medieval church, this traditional pub is enjoying a new lease of life following a community takeover. A real success story, the pub starred as the hostelry The Daffodil in the film The Baker. Excellent, good value food is served at lunchtime (except Monday) and in the evening Monday to Saturday. ⋈⊛◁◑♣P

Llangattock Lingoed

Hunter's Moon
NP7 8RR (right off A465 at Llanvihangel Crucorney or left off B4251 at Llanvetherine)
🕐 12-3 (not Mon-Fri, Oct-March), 6.30-11; 12-3, 6.30-10.30 Sun
☎ (01873) 821499 ⊕ hunters-moon-inn.co.uk
Rhymney Bevan's Bitter; Wye Valley Hereford Pale Ale; guest beers 🅷
Thirteenth century inn next to an equally ancient, recently renovated church which is also well worth a visit. Situated on Offa's Dyke path, the pub provides good quality food and accommodation – popular with weary walkers. In summer the raised decking overlooking the churchyard is delightful and there is also a grassy area surrounding a natural pool with ducks. Weston's Old Rosie cider is available on draught. ⋈⊛☎◁◑♣P

Llanhennock

Wheatsheaf Inn
NP18 1LT OS352939
🕐 11-11 (closed 3-5.30 Wed winter); 12-3, 7-10.30 Sun
☎ (01633) 420468 ⊕ thewheatsheafllanhennock.co.uk
Fuller's London Pride; guest beers 🅷
With three real ales on tap, fine views all round, and close proximity to the ancient Roman town of Caerleon with its famous amphitheatre, this is an ideal place to visit for those who cherish traditional country pubs. The public bar contains unusual memorabilia and breweriana; the cosy lounge is more of a dining area. A mecca for local boules (aka petanque) players, it is home to one of the largest clubs in the area. ⋈⊛◁◑⊟♣P

Llanishen

Carpenters Arms
NP16 6QH (on B4293 between Monmouth and Devauden) SO479032
🕐 12-3 (not Tue), 5.30 (6 Tue)-11; closed Mon; 12-3, 7-10.30 Sun
☎ (01600) 860812
Wadworth 6X; guest beers 🅷
Dating back to the 17th century, this cosy and welcoming roadside pub has a large bar with a central divide and a low, beamed ceiling. On one side is a pool table and darts, the other has tables for diners. Serving a scattered community, it is close to good walks in the scenic locality, and popular with ramblers. The guest beer often comes from the local Kingstone Brewery. ⋈⊛◁◑♿⊟♣P

Newport

Godfrey Morgan

Chepstow Road, Maindee, NP19 8EG

✪ 9-midnight (1am Fri & Sat)

☎ (01633) 221928

Brains SA, SA Gold; Evan Evans Original Welsh Ale; Greene King Abbot; Marston's Pedigree; guest beers Ⓗ

This conversion of a former cinema freshened up an area already heavily populated with pubs and restaurants. It is now an established part of the Maindee circuit offering the full range of Wetherspoon's fare. The entrance area, light and airy with a high ceiling, and spacious main bar, display interesting artwork including pictures of famous stars with local connections. The pub is named after Godfrey Morgan who took part in and survived the charge of the Light Brigade. Q✿❀◑♿♻🚩♣P

John Wallace Linton

10-12 The Cambrian Centre, Cambrian Road, NP20 1GA

✪ 9-midnight (1am Fri & Sat)

☎ (01633) 251752

Brains SA, SA Gold; Evan Evans Original Welsh Ale; Greene King Abbot; Marston's Pedigree; guest beers Ⓗ

Busy Wetherspoon's near the railway station and other late night venues. After a campaign by local war veterans, it was renamed to commemorate a much decorated World War II hero, submarine commander 'Tubby' Linton VC. A popular meeting place for night clubbers and train travellers, many are happy to spend the entire evening here. Interesting guest ales are often selected from local micro-breweries and the all-day menu includes Welsh dishes. Q✿❀◑♿≠🚩♣

Old Murenger House

53 High Street, NP20 1GA

✪ 11-11; 12-10.30 Sun

☎ (01633) 263977 ⊕ murenger.com

Samuel Smith Old Brewery Bitter Ⓗ

Perennial favourite that generates its own buzz, whether on a quiet lunchtime or busy evening and weekend. It attracts a mixed clientele who come to enjoy the ambience of a real pub. Divided into different areas, the dark wood decor is easy on the eye and in keeping with the longevity of this Tudor building. The murenger was a medieval tax collector responsible for maintaining the city's defensive walls. Q◑≠🚩

Red Lion

47 Charles Street, NP20 1JH

✪ 12 (11 Wed & Thu)-midnight (1am Fri & Sat); 12-10.30 Sun

☎ (01633) 264398

Beer range varies Ⓗ

Traditional pub in the style of an ale house with a loyal following from all parts of the city. A haunt of sports fans, top rugby and soccer matches are beamed via a large TV screen. Plaques of Welsh rugby's senior clubs are displayed. Teams compete in local leagues, with shove-ha'penny a major attraction. Up to three beers are sourced from the Punch range and the pub has historic links with the local CAMRA branch. 🚶✿❀≠🚩♣⚓

St Julian Inn

Caerleon Road, NP18 1QA

✪ 11.30-11; 12-10.30 Sun

☎ (01633) 243548 ⊕ stjulian.co.uk/

John Smith's Bitter; Wells Bombardier; Young's Bitter; guest beers Ⓗ

A most consistent ale house for the last two decades. The regular beers are unusual for the area and supplemented by interesting guests. Situated just outside Caerleon, the beautiful riverside location affords excellent views of the River Usk and surrounding area, especially in summer months from the outside balcony. There are four different drinking areas each with its own atmosphere and attracting a good mix of ages. ✿❀◑♿🚩🏠♣P

Pantygelli

Crown Inn

Old Hereford Road, NP7 7HR (2 miles N of Abergavenny)

✪ 12-2.30 (not Mon), 6-11; 12-3, 6-11 Sat; 12-3, 6-10.30 Sun

☎ (01873) 853314 ⊕ thecrownatpantygelli.com

Draught Bass; Rhymney Bitter; Wye Valley Hereford Pale Ale; guest beers Ⓗ

Recent redevelopment of the dining area in the bar has not diminished the charm of this thriving, traditional pub which attracts a loyal band of regular drinkers despite its location on the outskirts of Abergavenny. The attractive patio has fine views of the Skirrid mountain and can be very popular in warm summer months. The restaurant serves a wide variety of good, freshly prepared food and booking is recommended. There is disabled access to the pub. 🚶Q✿❀◑♿♣P

Pontnewynydd

Bridgend Inn

23 Hanbury Road, NP4 6QN

✪ 12-11 (3am Fri & Sat); 12-10.30 Sun

☎ (01495) 757435

Brains SA; guest beers Ⓗ

Cosy nook entered down a wide flight of steps via a patio. The open plan bar has a TV neatly fitted into a stone fireplace at the servery end and a games section at the other with a small lounge in between. One or two interesting guest beers mainly from local Welsh or west country brewers are served. A little off the beaten track, the nearby disused railway track and hilly surrounds attract walkers. Food is by prior arrangement only. 🚶✿❀♣

Raglan

Ship Inn

High Street, Monmouthshire, NP15 2DY

✪ 11.30-11; 12-10.30 Sun

☎ (01291) 690635

Beer range varies Ⓗ

The approach to this former coach house is via a cobbled courtyard containing a disused well. Inside it has a small bar with a dining room running off it and a larger drinking area. There is also a games room with a pool table. Up to three real ales are usually on handpump. There are plans to convert the games room to

WALES

a dining area and increase the ale range.
⚲Q☆✪◑▯♣♠

Rogerstone

Tredegar Arms
157 Cefn Road, NP10 9AS OS270888
✪ 12-3, 5.30-11; 12-11 Thu-Sat; 12-4, 7-10.30 Sun
☎ (01633) 664999
Draught Bass; Courage Best Bitter; guest beers Ⓗ
Traditional pub, popular with locals and
visitors alike, with a lounge, public bar and
dining room. The pub is well known for its
good food – a large noticeboard in the lounge
displays an appetising selection of meals on
offer. Guest ales are ever changing, frequently
from micro brewers. The garden is pleasant in
summer. Q☆✪◑▯♣P

Sebastopol

Open Hearth
Wern Road, NP4 5DR
✪ 11.30-midnight; 12-11.30 Sun
☎ (01495) 763752
**Archers Golden; Caledonian Deuchars IPA;
Greene King Abbot; guest beers** Ⓗ
Family-run pub near Griffithstown Railway
Museum. Formerly the Railway Tavern, 'the
Hearth' was a popular end of shift watering
hole for local steelworkers. Entry to the public
bar is via a towpath on the Monmouthshire &
Brecon Canal and the pub has mooring and
fishing rights. The lounge is popular with
diners and there is a restaurant downstairs.
Seating outside overlooks the canal and an
extensive children's play area attracts families.
Dogs are welcome on leads. ☆◑▯♣P

Sebastopol Social Club
Wern Road, NP4 5DU
✪ 12-11.30 (12.30am Fri & Sat); 12-11 Sun
☎ (01495) 763808
Hancock's HB; guest beers Ⓗ
Award-winning former CAMRA National Club
of the Year originally know as Panteg
Comrades Club. The building was donated
after the First World War by a relative of a
current committee member. Up to seven ales,
mostly from small independent micro-
brewers, are available. The club is home to a
variety of sports teams and there is a
downstairs games room with a skittle alley. A
CAMRA membership card or copy of this Guide
will secure entry for non members. ☆◑▯♣P

Skenfrith

Bell Inn
NP7 8UH (On B4521 half way between
Abergavenny and Ross on Wye)
✪ 11-11 (not Mon, Nov-March); 12-10.30 Sun
☎ (01600) 750235 🌐skenfrith.co.uk
Freeminer Bitter; Taylor Landlord; guest beers Ⓗ
Primarily an award-winning hotel and
restaurant, the Bell has a separate stone-
flagged and oak beamed bar. The inn is
situated next to a low bridge over the river
Monnow and adjacent to an interesting
Norman castle which also acts as one leg of
the Three Castles walk from Grosmont to
Skenfrith and Whitecastle. The garden is

delightful in summer. Locally produced cider is
available. ⚲Q☆✉◑▯♠P

Talywain

Globe Inn
Commercial Road, NP4 7JH (off B4246 at
Abersychan to Talywain)
✪ 7 (12 Sat)-11; 12-10.30 Sun
☎ (01495) 772053
Brains Bitter; guest beers Ⓗ
This no frills local is very much part of the
community. From the photos on display of the
industrial past of this area, and the proximity
to the railway (long gone), it is easy to
imagine that this pub has changed little over
the years. Various teams compete in local
leagues and there is occasional live music on
Saturday. The pub offers fine views towards
the British mountain opposite, popular with
walkers. Note the distinctive pub sign.
⚲◑▯♣♠

Tintern

Cherry Tree Inn
Forge Road, NP16 6TH (off A466 at Royal George
Hotel)
✪ 12-11 (winter hours vary); 12-10.30 Sun
☎ (01291) 689292 🌐thecherry.co.uk
Hancock's HB; guest beers Ⓗ
Nestling on the steep wooded sides of the
Anghidy Valley amid scenic splendour, the
Cherry offers four real ales from smaller
independents plus cask (Bulmers Traditional)
and bottled ciders. A wide choice of home-
cooked food includes renowned curries. The
pub's ground floor is the village shop and post
office. A sheltered patio is ideal for outdoor
drinking and dining. Wales' only ever-present
entry in the Guide, this friendly pub still flies
the flag for quality and choice.
⚲Q☆✉◑▯♠P

Wye Valley Hotel
NP16 6SQ (A466, Tintern, Monmouthshire)
✪ 11-3, 6-11; 12-3, 7-10.30 Sun
☎ (01291) 689441 🌐wyevalleyhotel.co.uk
Wye Valley Bitter, Butty Bach; guest beers Ⓗ
A roadside landmark at the north end of the
village, this handsome inn built around 1930
caters for locals and the broad mix of visitors
constantly drawn to Tintern by the inspiring
scenery and rich history of the lower Wye
Valley. Inside, a two-part angled main bar
provides the stirring sight of hundreds of
commemorative beer bottles arranged around
the walls. A happy blend of pub and hotel, this
inn also provides comfort and good
conversation. Q✉◑▯♠P

Trellech

Lion Inn
NP25 4PA
✪ 12-3, 6 (7 Mon; 6,30 Sat)-11 (midnight Thu-Sat);
12-midnight Sat summer; 12-4.30 Sun
☎ (01600) 860322
Bath SPA; guest beers Ⓗ
Grade II listed award-winning pub originally
built as a brewery in 1580. Open plan, it has a
dining area to the left and a bar to the right.

Up to four constantly changing ales are available – Bath SPA is a regular visitor and beers from Kingstone Brewery in nearby Whitebrook also feature. A beer festival is held in June and a bottled beer festival in November. ♨️🏠🍴◐🏛️🚪🅿️

Trellech Grange

Fountain Inn
NP16 6QW OS503011
🕐 12-3, 6.30-11; 12-11 Sat & Sun
☎ (01291) 689303 🌐 fountaininn-tintern.com
Beer range varies Ⓗ
Two miles from Tintern, this 17th-century inn continues to flourish. A small flagstone bar leads to several dining areas. Up to three ales are on handpump, many chosen from breweries within a 50 mile radius. The owner is a chef and the emphasis here is on food, though you will be made to feel very welcome if you just want to enjoy a pint. ♨️🏠🍴◐🛏️🅿️

Upper Llanover

Goose & Cuckoo
NP7 9ER (off A4042 signed Upper Llanover)
OS292073
🕐 11.30-3, 7-11; closed Mon; 11.30-11 Fri & Sat; 12-10.30 Sun
☎ (01873) 880277 🌐 gooseandcuckoo.co.uk
Brains Rev James; Young's Bitter; guest beers Ⓗ
This traditional Grade II listed building remains unchanged from year to year, providing solace for weary walkers and cyclists. A wide range of pub games is played here including shove ha'penny. The large garden is shared with ducks and goats; from here you can enjoy glorious panoramic views out over the valley towards the Skirrid mountain and beyond. Two beer festivals are held annually at Whitsun and August bank holidays. ♨️Q🏠🍴◐🅿️

Usk

Kings Head Hotel
18 Old Market Street, NP15 1AL
🕐 11-11; 12-10.30 Sun
☎ (01291) 672963
Fuller's London Pride; Taylor Landlord Ⓗ
A long time Guide entry, the hotel's cosy lounge with its low beams has the feel of a parlour with a huge fireplace at one end.

Many items of interest are dotted around the room – can you spot the TV? Good, tasty food is served in the 'Lionel Sweet' dining room next to the lounge. There is also a restaurant and function room. The two beers are the most popular survivors from what was once a larger range. ♨️🚪◐🅿️

Nags Head Inn
Twyn Square, NP15 1BH
🕐 11-3, 5.30-11; 12-3, 5.30-10.30 Sun
☎ (01291) 672820
Brains Rev James; guest beers Ⓗ
Behind the white facade, adorned with a blaze of floral colour in season, lies a characterful old inn with dark wood decor and a plethora of artefacts and memorabilia. The inn is justifiably proud of its reputation for superb food and much emphasis is placed on dining. The rear Tack Room accommodates families with the Hoofs Coffee Shop next door. Guest beers make an occasional appearance. Q◐🚪

Royal Hotel
26 New Market Street, NP15 1AT
🕐 12-3, 7-11.30; closed Mon; 12-5 Sun
☎ (01291) 672931
Draught Bass; guest beers Ⓗ
Long-established favourite in the area renowned for its excellent food. This pub, once the home of writer Edward John Trelawny, emerged from an amalgam of two quite disparate businesses, a pot and bottle store and a funeral parlour. Steeped in tradition and character, on one side is a cosily furnished lounge and dining room, on the other an old-fashioned public bar. Bookings is advised for diners. ♨️Q🏠◐🚪🅿️

Usk Conservative Club
The Grange,, 16 Maryport Street, NP15 1AB
🕐 12-3, 7-11 (10.30 Sun)
☎ (01291) 672634
Fuller's Discovery; guest beers Ⓗ
Fine old town house tastefully converted into a comfortable private members' club. Decorated, unsurprisingly, in shades of blue, it offers pleasant surroundings including dining and games areas. At the rear is a large function room/dance hall. The beer range has gradually become more imaginative to tempt real ale drinkers, with beers from independent breweries rather than global players. Standard club entry rules apply to visitors. Evening meals are Wednesday, Friday and Saturday only. 🏠◐🚪🅿️

WALES

The soul of beer

Brewers call barley malt the 'soul of beer'. While a great deal of attention has been rightly paid to hops in recent years, the role of malt in brewing must not be ignored. Malt contains starch that is converted to a special form of sugar known as maltose during the brewing process. It is maltose that is attacked by yeast during fermentation and turned into alcohol and carbon dioxide. Other grains can be used in brewing, notably wheat. But barley malt is the preferred grain as it gives a delightful biscuit / cracker / Ovaltine note to beer. Unlike wheat, barley has a husk that works as a natural filter during the first stage of brewing, known as the mash. Cereals such as rice and corn / maize are widely used by global producers of mass-market lagers, but craft brewers avoid them.

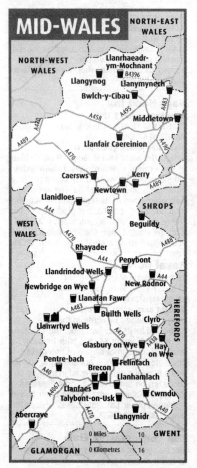

MID-WALES

NORTH-EAST WALES

NORTH-WEST WALES

Llanrhaeadr-ym-Mochnant
B4396
Llangynog
Llanymynech
Bwlch-y-Cibau
A458   A495
A489   Middletown
Llanfair Caereinion
A470   A490
Caersws   Kerry
Newtown   A489
Llanidloes   SHROPS
A44   A483
WEST WALES   Beguildy
A470   A488
Rhayader
A44   Penybont
Llandrindod Wells   A44
Newbridge on Wye   New Radnor
Llanafan Fawr
A483   Builth Wells   Clyro   HEREFORDS
Llanwrtyd Wells   A470
Glasbury on Wye   A438   Hay on Wye
Pentre-bach   Felinfach
A40   Brecon
Llanhamlach
Llanfaes   Cwmdu
Talybont-on-Usk
A4067   A470   Llangynidr   A40
Abercrave   GWENT
0 Miles   10
GLAMORGAN   0 Kilometres   16

Abercrave

Copper Beech Inn

133 Heol Tawe, SA9 1XS (off A4067 Swansea-Brecon road)
🕓 11-1.30am; 12-11 Sun
☎ (01639) 730269
Beer range varies Ⓗ
Large rural village pub built in 1876 for the Morgan family who were the local colliery owners. It is situated just off the Swansea to Brecon road on the edge of the Brecon Beacons National Park. A variety of Welsh beers is usually available. It offers accommodation and serves a wide variety of meals. A popular pub frequented by walkers, climbers, cavers and cyclists. ⋈Q❀✿⌀ Ⓗ⌀&P

Beguildy

Radnorshire Arms

LD7 1YE (on B4355)
🕓 closed Mon; 7-midnight Tue & Wed; 6-midnight Thu; 6-1am Fri & Sat; 12-3, 7-midnight Sun
☎ (01547) 510354
Fuller's London Pride; Wye Valley Beguildy Bitter; guest beers Ⓗ
This picturesque 16th-century roadside inn very close to the Wales-England border would

originally have been used by drovers. Sadly the thatched roof is no more and the exterior has also seen a number of alterations. Despite this, the building still has much charm. The guest beers are sourced from a number of breweries including Breconshire, Greene King, Six Bells, Wye Valley and Hobsons. No meals are served on Sunday evening on Monday lunchtime. ⋈❀⌀Ⓗ⌀♣P⌐

Brecon

Black Bull

86 The Struet, LD3 7LS
🕓 12-midnight (sometimes later in summer)
☎ (01874) 623900
Evan Evans BB, Cwrw, Warrior, seasonal beers Ⓗ
While still known as the Bulls Head by many, the Black Bull has become a welcoming and comfortable ale house with a friendly atmosphere. The central bar and pillars create distinctive areas for dining or drinking, but with plenty of wood and good lighting a spacious airy feel is maintained. Food is served until 8pm (6pm Sun), except Monday. ⋈Q⌀

Boar's Head

Ship Street, LD3 9AL (by bridge over River Usk)
🕓 12 (11 Tue)-midnight; 11-2am Fri & Sat; 12-1am Sun
☎ (01874) 622856
Breconshire County Ale, Welsh Pale Ale, Golden Valley, Ramblers Ruin; Fuller's London Pride; Greene King Abbot Ⓗ
The Breconshire Brewery tap is a lively and popular town centre pub, with two bars and two characters – the wood panelled front bar houses the majority of the handpumps and tends to be a little quieter than the larger back bar which holds the pool table and large screen showing sports. Both bars get very busy on match days. Regular live music events and pub quizzes are held. The patio garden boasts fine views over the River Usk and up to the Brecon Beacons. ⋈❀⌀Ⓗ⌀♣⌀P⌐

Clarence

25 The Watton, LD3 7ED
🕓 12-midnight (2am Fri & Sat)
☎ (01874) 622810
Beer range varies Ⓗ
Two room town centre community pub with a relaxed, contemporary feel and a welcoming atmosphere. The front bar tends to be frequented by locals, while the larger back bar has tables and chairs for diners and a big screen for major sporting events. Regular quiz nights are hosted. The garden is popular, especially during the Brecon jazz festival. Beers tend to be sourced from local breweries. ❀⌀Ⓗ⌀♣

Builth Wells

Greyhound Hotel

3 Garth Road, LD2 3AR
🕓 12-midnight (12-3, 6-midnight winter); 12-1am Fri & Sat; 12-11 Sun

INDEPENDENT BREWERIES

Breconshire Brecon
Heart of Wales Llanwrtyd Wells

☎ (01982) 553255 ⊕ thegreyhoundhotel.co.uk
Greene King Abbot; Wood Shropshire Lad; guest beers Ⓗ
Early 20th century hotel with open-plan bars, restaurant and a large function room. An engraved glass panel above the front door shows that a previous owner had a licence to brew, but sadly the brewery is no more. The hotel has a reputation for the high quality of its food and gets very busy, particularly at weekends, when booking is essential. The Sunday lunchtime carvery is highly recommended. Guest beers are mainly from smaller breweries including Cottage, Breconshire and RCH. ⊛⊯⊕🖾♣P

Bwlch-y-Cibau

Stumble Inn
SY22 5LL (on A490)
✿ 11-11 summer; 6-11 Mon & Tue; closed Wed; 11-11 Thu-Sat; 12-5 Sun winter
☎ (01691) 648860
Beer range varies Ⓗ
Once called the Cross Keys, this wood beamed roadside pub has a public bar, small cosy lounge and well appointed restaurant seating up to 50 people. Two changing guest beers are offered. The varied menu ranges from shark salad to wild boar terrine. The bar features a large twin blade propellor with a plaque bearing the name E.W. Alcock, which came from the Airforce Club in Manchester. ⊯⊛⊕🖾♣P

Caersws

Red Lion
Main Street, SY17 5EL (off A470)
✿ 3 (12 summer)-11; 12-11 Fri-Sun
☎ (01686) 688023
Beer range varies Ⓗ
Friendly village local with a small, cosy bar and a lounge/restaurant area. The wood beamed pub has a comfortable, relaxed feel and atttracts a varied clientele of all ages. Excellent home cooked food is served and three en-suite B&B rooms are available with a three course breakfast for just £25 per night. A summer beer festival is held and there is an attractive garden area for outdoor drinking. ⊯⊛⊯⊕🖾≒♣P

Clyro

Baskerville Arms Hotel
KR3 5RZ
✿ 10-1am (midnight Sun)
☎ (01497) 820670 ⊕ baskervillearms.co.uk
Brains Bitter; Draught Bass; Wye Valley Bitter Ⓗ
In the same village as the famous Baskerville Hall, this historic inn has an imposing wood beamed and panelled bar area featuring an impressive fireplace at the far end. One room has a pool table and there is a large function room frequently used for live music, and other regular events. Food is served every evening (curry night is Tuesday) and lunches at the weekend. A large beer garden has excellent views over to Hay Bluff. ⊯⊛⊯⊕🖾♣P

Cwmdu

Farmers Arms
NP8 1RU (on A679 between Crickhowell and Builth Wells)
✿ 12-3, 6-11; closed Mon
☎ (01874) 730464
Beer range varies Ⓗ
Exposed beams and a large fireplace containing a cast iron wood-burning cooking range dominate the main bar area of this village pub. The hop bedecked bar separates the bar and dining areas. Superb home-cooked food is served at lunchtime and in the evening; menus feature locally sourced produce, regional specialities and old favourites. Guest beers usually come from local breweries. ⊯Q⊛⊯⊕P

Felin Fach

Griffin
LD3 0UB (3 miles NE of Brecon on A470)
✿ 12-11.30
☎ (01874) 620111 ⊕ eatdrinksleep.ltd.uk.
Breconshire Golden Valley; Tomos Watkin OSB Ⓗ
'The simple things in life – done well,' claims the pub, which says it all. A welcoming country pub, restaurant and hotel, the emphasis here is on good beer and excellent food. With a multi roomed layout, it has discrete areas for dining or drinking. The huge fireplace between the main bar and dining area dominates in winter and a full sized Aga lurks in another room providing warmth throughout the pub. The large garden affords excellent views of the Brecons and Black Mountains. ⊯Q⊛⊯⊕🖾⅃

Glasbury on Wye

Hollybush
HR3 5PS (on B4350 between Glasbury and Hay)
✿ 8am-late
☎ (01497) 847371 ⊕ hollybushcamping.co.uk
Breconshire Golden Valley; Greene King Abbot; Spinning Dog Organic; guest beer Ⓗ
Welcoming and friendly pub recently refurbished and renovated. The licensees are keen supporters of self sufficiency and recycling. The main bar area has an annexe at one end and a dining room at the other. Superb home-cooked food is served all day including vegan and vegetarian dishes. Between the pub and River Wye is a camp site with a woodland walk and adventure area. The large garden has views of the Black Mountains and Begwyn Hills. Live music features regularly. ⊯Q⊛⊯⊕🖾♿▲🖾(X39 & X40)♣♣P⅃

Hay on Wye

Wine Vaults
10 Castle Street, HR3 5DF
✿ 11-11 daily
☎ (01497) 821999
Breconshire Red Dragon, Ramblers Ruin Ⓗ
Mulit-roomed cafe-bar in the centre of this famous town. The contemporary main bar has a number of black and white photos on the wall. Beyond the bar is a bright dining area,

down steps to one side is a a further seating area and access to the huge and superb garden, with its excellent views to the Black Mountains. Home-cooked food is excellent. The garden is popular with locals and tourists as an escape from the bookshops – or as a place to peruse a new purchase. Q✿❁➀▲▦✦~

Kerry

Kerry Lamb

SY16 4NP (on A489)
✿5 (12 Fri-Sun)-midnight
☎ (01686) 670226
Hobsons Best Bitter; guest beers Ⓗ
Refurbished village pub with two bars, the front one also used as a restaurant. The popular rear bar is large with a real fire creating a homely feel. A games room is off the back bar. The pub attracts a wide clientele of all ages. Guest beers are from independent breweries. The pub takes its name from a breed of sheep named after the village.
♨✿❁✦P

Llanafan Fawr

Red Lion

LD2 3PN (opp church)
✿12-3, 6-11.30; 2-3, 6-1am Fri & Sat
☎ (01597) 860204
Felinfoel Best Bitter; guest beer Ⓗ
At the centre of a historically significant area – the church opposite boasts not only the tomb of St Afan but also one of the oldest yew trees in Britain (at least 2,200 years old) – the pub (marked by a tourist sign to 'bloody good pub') claims to be the oldest in Powys, dating back to the 12th century when it was a drovers inn. The interior is a forest of beams (the building's cruck frame), with exposed stone walls and flagged floors. The pub is home of the annual world tippit championships. ♨Q✿❁➀P

Llandrindod Wells

Conservative Club

South Crescent, LD1 5DH
✿11-2, 5-11 ; 11-11.30 (Fri-Sun)
☎ (01597) 822126
Brains Bitter; Marston's Burton Bitter; guest beers Ⓗ
Quiet, comfortable haven overlooking the temple gardens. The 'Con' has a large lounge, TV room, games bar, snooker and pool tables and a small front patio. An excellent range of guest beers is available to complement the regular ales. Lunches are available Thursday-Saturday. Live entertainment is hosted occasionally in the evening. Non-members must be signed in; CAMRA members are welcomed. Q✿❁Ҁ⌇▦✦

Llanfaes

Drovers Arms

Newgate Street, LD3 8SN
✿12-midnight
☎ (01874) 623377
Breconshire Welsh Pale Ale, seasonal beers; guest beers Ⓗ

This recently refurbished community pub is a lively and friendly local. The central bar faces out into the main room which has a big screen for major sporting events. There is a small room at one end of the bar, with its own servery. A secluded and sheltered patio garden is behind the pub, offering alfresco drinking and relief to smokers. All beers are sourced from the nearby Breconshire Brewery. Closing times may be later in summer.
❁➀▦✦~

Llanfair Caereinion

Goat Hotel

High Street, SY21 0QS (on A458)
✿11-11 (midnight Fri & Sat)
☎ (01938) 810428
Beer range varies Ⓗ
Excellent beamed inn with a welcoming atmosphere. Popular with locals and tourists, the pub has a plush lounge with comfortable leather armchairs and sofas. Three real ales are available including one from the wood brewery. The lounge is dominated by a large inglenook with an open fire. There is a restaurant serving home cooked food and a games room at the rear. ♨✿⌇➀✦P

LLangynidr

Red Lion

NP8 1NT (just off B4558)
✿11.30-3 (not Mon); 6.30-midnight; 11.30-1am Fri & Sat; 11.30-midnight Sun
☎ (01874) 730223
Beer range varies Ⓗ
Lively community pub on the edge of the village. The multi-roomed interior includes a cosy main bar, games room, dining room and garden room. Food is all home-cooked using local produce where possible. Beers are sourced from the Breconshire Brewery. A beer festival is planned for the summer, with other events to follow. The pub, with its attractive garden, patio and play area, can be very popular, especially in the summer.
♨Q✾✿⌇➀▦✦✦P~

Llangynog

Tanat Valley Hotel

SY10 0EX (on B4391)
✿6-midnight; 12-11 Fri-Sun
☎ (01691) 780210
Caledonian Deuchars IPA; St Austell Tribute Ⓗ
Pleasant wooden-beamed hostelry with a stone fireplace, tiled floor and wood burning stove. The lounge has a further drinking area off it down some stairs. This lower area has a pool table. Popular village pub with a friendly, relaxed feel. ♨➀P

Llanhamlach

Old Ford

LD3 7YB (on A40 3 miles E of Brecon)
✿12-11
☎ (01874) 665220
Beer range varies Ⓗ
Much extended over the years, this 12th-century coaching inn retains all of its character

and charm. The central bar area has some unusual copper work and a collection of half pint and nip bottles from a number of British breweries. A larger room beyond the bar, mainly used for dining, provides panoramic views of the Beacons as well as excellent food. Local dishes are a speciality. Beers are usually sourced from local breweries.
🏚Q🛏🌠🍴◗🍺🕹🅿🚭

Llanidloes

Crown & Anchor Inn ☆
41 Long Bridge Street, SY18 6EF (on A470)
◷ 11-11; 12-10.30 Sun
☎ (01686) 412398
Brains Rev James; Worthington's Bitter Ⓗ
Wonderful unspoilt town centre gem with a relaxed and friendly atmosphere. The pub appears in CAMRA's National Inventory of pubs with interiors of historical interest. It has been run by the same landlady, Ruby, since 1965. Throughout that time it has remained unchanged, retaining its public bar, lounge, snug and two further rooms, one with a pool table and games machine. A central hallway separates the rooms. 🍺🕹

Red Lion Hotel
Long Bridge Street, SY18 6EE (on A470)
◷ 11-midnight (1am Fri & Sat)
☎ (01686) 412270
Beer range varies Ⓗ
Wood beamed town centre hotel with a plush lounge featuring red leather sofas. The public bar is divided into two areas – the front with an interesting wood-panelled fireplace, the rear with a pool table and games machines. Three real ales are usually available. An outside patio area is at the rear of the pub.
🏚🌠◗🍺🕹

Llanrhaeadr-ym-Mochnant

Plough Inn
SY10 0JR (on B4580)
◷ 3 (12 Sat & Sun)-midnight
☎ (01691) 780654
Brains Rev James; guest beers Ⓗ
A real community local converted from a house. The many roomed interior is wood-beamed and tile-floored, with a stone-walled public bar featuring a large open fireplace and back bar. Two guest beers are served along with the permanent Rev James. There is a games area to the rear of the pub with a pool table, table football and darts. 🏚🌠♣

Llanwrtyd Wells

Neuadd Arms
The Square, LD5 4RB
◷ to come
☎ (01591) 610236 ⏚ neuaddarmshotel.co.uk
Felinfoel Double Dragon; Hancock's HB; Neuadd Arms Welsh Gold, Heart of Wales Bitter, seasonal beers Ⓗ
Situated at the centre of Britain's smallest town, this large Victorian hotel now has its own brewery. The Bells Bar has a large fire and range, an eclectic mix of furniture and the original bells used to summon servants along

one wall. The lounge bar is a little more formal with carpets, sofas and many paintings on the walls. As well as offering a range of ales brewed in the old laundry, the hotel hosts a number of beer festivals throughout the year.
🏚Q🌠🛏◗🍺Å≈🚲🅿

Stonecroft Inn
Dolecoed Road, CD5 4RA
◷ 5-midnight; 12-1am Fri-Sun
☎ (01591) 610332 ⏚ stonecroft.co.uk
Brains Rev James; guest beers Ⓗ
Warm and friendly community pub, the hub for the town's many and varied festivities – bog snorkelling world championships, beer and food festivals, real ale rambles, to name but a few. The pub has three main areas for drinking, dining and games, plus a large riverside garden. Excellent food complements the fine range of beers. Lodge accommodation is popular with walkers and mountain bikers.
🏚🌠🛏◗Å≈🚲🅿🚭

Llanymynech

Cross Keys
North Road, SY22 6EA (on A483)
◷ 12-3 (not winter Mon & Tue), 4-12 ; 12-midnight Fri & Sat; 12-11 Sun
☎ (01691) 831585 ⏚ crosskeyshotel.info
Greene King Abbot; guest beers Ⓗ
Roadside hotel with a thriving trade in real ale. Full of character with real fires, the bar has a friendly atmosphere and a wide and varied clientele. Two changing guest beers are always available. There is a games room through an archway with a pool table and darts area. The restaurant offers good, reasonably priced food. The function room upstairs also serves real ale. 🏚🛏◗♣🅿

Middletown

Breidden Hotel
SY21 8EL (on A458)
◷ 12-2.30, 5-11; 12-midnight Sat & Sun
☎ (01938) 570250
Black Sheep Best Bitter; guest beers Ⓗ
Wooden beamed village local with a large L-shaped glass and wood framed bar and a small, cosy restaurant area. The bar has comfortable seating around the walls and a games area. Poker night is Sunday. The menu includes 99 different baguette, sandwich and jacket potato fillings. Live music plays at the weekend. 🌠◗♣🅿

New Radnor

Radnor Arms
Broad Street, LD8 2SP
◷ 12-3, 7(Fri 5)-11 (midnight Fri); 11-midnight Sat; 12-10.30 Sun
☎ (01544) 350232
Beer range varies Ⓗ
Set in the Welsh Marches and close to the English border, this cosy pub also offers accommodation, making it an ideal base for anyone looking for an away-from-it-all break. There is good walking, trekking and cycling; Offa's Dyke is nearby and Hereford 25 miles away. Food is served every day including a

popular Sunday carvery (booking advisable) and a takeaway service. Guest beers are mainly from smaller breweries including Cottage, Wood, Six Bells and Wye Valley. ▲▣Q☺☏☺◑ 🖵🖳♣♠P

Newbridge on Wye

New Inn

LD1 6HY

☺ 11-3, 5-11.30; 11-1am Fri & Sat; 11-3, 5-midnight Sun

☎ (01597) 860211 ⊕ pigsfolly.co.uk

Beer range varies ⊞

Large multi-roomed pub with a snug with small servery, many mirrors and copperwork, and main bar area with pool table and dart board. The large back bar is used for dining and there is a large function room. For the summer there is a popular, large garden. The pub also boasts its own butcher's shop selling superb home-made meat pies. Music and bingo nights are regular features, and fish and chips is available as a takeaway on Thursday. Beers usually come from local breweries. ▲▣Q☺☏☺◑ 🖵🖳🖳♣P⅃

Newtown

Bell Hotel

Commercial Street, SY16 2DE (on B4568)

☺ 4-midnight; 12-midnight Fri-Sun

☎ (01686) 625540

Beer range varies ⊞

Edge of town local with a comfortable lounge and dining area. Popular with a wide clientele, the public bar has a pool table and live music is hosted at the weekend. Three beers are available, usually including one from the Six Bells Brewery. The bar area is separated from the lounge by an archway. ☞◑♣P

Railway Tavern

Old Kerry Road, SY16 1BH (off A483)

☺ 12-2.30, 6-midnight; 11-1am Tue, Fri & Sat; 12-10.30 Sun

☎ (01686) 626156

Draught Bass; Worthington's Bitter; guest beer ⊞

Edge of town centre locals bar with exposed beams and a rear stone wall. Handy for the station, this unspoilt, compact one-bar hostelry has a good following due to its friendly atmosphere and welcoming landlord and landlady who have been at the Railway for more than 20 years. The pub has a successful darts team and match nights can be crowded. Guest beers come from a wide range of independent breweries. ☺≈🖳♣

Pentre Bach

Tafarn y Crydd (Shoemakers Arms)

LD3 8UB (follow signs to 'country pub' from Sennybridge) OS908328

☺ 11.30-3 (not Tue), 5.30-11; 12-3, 6-11 Sun

☎ (01874) 636508

Brains Rev James; guest beers ⊞

Community owned country pub on the edge of the Epynt firing ranges - the signs on the road up reassuringly declares 'the road to Pentre

Bach is always open'. The journey to this excellent pub is well worth the effort - a warm welcome, good food and well kept ales await you. The large garden area offers superb views and plentiful wildlife - a perfectly pleasant place to enjoy a pint and pass the time of day in good weather. Opening times may be extended in summer, so phoning ahead is advisable. ▲▣Q☺◑♣P

Penybont

Severn Arms

LD1 5UA

☺ 12-3, 6-midnight (1am Fri & Sat); 12-3, 7-10.30 Sun

☎ (01597) 851224

Courage Directors; Theakston Best Bitter; Wye Valley Golden Ale; guest beers ⊞

This 18th-century coaching inn celebrated its 250th anniversary in 2005. It used to be a stop-off point on the route between Hereford and Aberystwyth. The spacious bar, with its large open fireplace, leads to gardens overlooking the river Ithon, with six miles of free fishing for residents. There is a games room and a quiet, secluded restaurant - the Cheesments. The guest beers are sourced from many breweries. Trotting races take place twice yearly on a nearby course. ▲▣Q☺☏◑ 🖵🖳♣P⅃

Rhayader

Crown Inn

North Street, LD6 5BT

☺ 11-11 (midnight Fri & Sat)

☎ (01597) 811099 ⊕ thecrownrhayader.co.uk

Brains Dark, Bitter, Rev James, seasonal beers ⊞

Despite major interior changes in the 1980s this 16th-century pub retains much charm; the linen-fold bar front was saved from a demolished house. Many photographs and descriptions of local scenes and inhabitants adorn the walls of the bar and adjoining lounge. Look out of the item referring to the eccentric Major Stanscombe, a former owner. The Crown is a rare outlet in the county for cask-conditioned mild. Most guest beers are seasonal and commemorative beers from Brains. Q☺☏◑ 🖵♣♠⅃

Talybont on Usk

Star Inn

LD3 7YX (on B4558) OS114226

☺ 11-3, 6-11; 12-3, 7-11 Sun

☎ (01874) 676635

Beer range varies ⊞

Large and lively village pub set next to the Brecon and Monmouth Canal. The spacious garden tends to be extremely popular in the summer. A huge number of beers have featured in this award-winning pub; the range continues to be drawn mainly from local breweries. Local cider is also available. Quiz nights and regular live music sessions add to the mix, and the food is excellent. ▲☺☏◑ 🖵🖳♣🌢

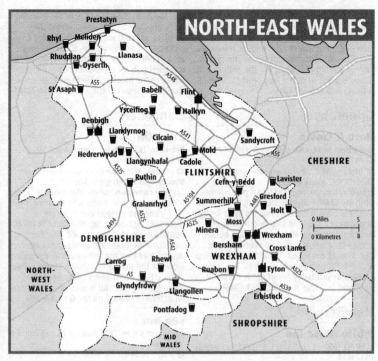

NORTH-EAST WALES

WALES

Authority areas covered: Denbighshire UA, Flintshire UA, Wrexham UA

DENBIGHSHIRE
Carrog

Grouse Inn

LL21 9AT (Jct of B5436/B5437) OS112436
☼ 12-midnight
☎ (01490) 430272 ⊕ thegrouseinn.webeden.co.uk
Lees Bitter, seasonal beers Ⓗ
Situated alongside the River Dee with
spectacular views of the Berwyn Mountains.
Close by is Carrog station, currently the
western terminus of the Llangollen Railway.
There is a campsite by the station (phone the
pub for information). The single bar serves an
open drinking area, leading to a dining room
and games room. Meals are available
throughout the day until 10pm.
Q◖◗⇌(Llangollen)P⬩

Denbigh

Railway

Ruthin Road, LL16 3EL (jct A525/B4501)
☼ 12-1am (11 Sun)
☎ (01745) 812376
Bryn Bitter; guest beer Ⓗ
Multi-room 19th century pub with a public bar,
games room and two small lounges.
Described as the Bragdy'r Bryn brewery tap by
some (the brewery is just a short distance
away), the licensee and bar staff always have
time for a chat. Pictures of the area's past
adorn the walls, some railway related. Near to
the town's football ground, the pub attracts
sports fans. ⬠▲⊟(51)♣

Dyserth

New Inn

Waterfall Road, LL18 6ET (on B5119 near
waterfall) OS557995
☼ 12-11
☎ (01745) 570482
**Banks's Original, Bitter; Marston's Burton Bitter,
Pedigree; guest beer** Ⓗ
The New Inn is situated near the base of
Dyserth waterfall, a local tourist attraction.
Divided into three areas, including a recent
restaurant extension, meals are served
throughout, and the pub can cater for up to 70
diners. Photographs of old Dyserth adorn the
walls. A large outside drinking area is popular
in the summer. Four beers and a guest from
the Marston's portfolio give plenty of choice.
Guide dogs are welcome.
🏔❀◖◗⬠⊟(35, 36)P⬩

Glyndyfrdwy

Sun

LL21 9HG (on A5)
☼ 6-10.30; 12-2, 6-11 Sat & summer; 12-3, 6-11 Sun
☎ (01490) 430517
Banks's Original, Bitter; guest beer Ⓗ
Situated in Dee valley on the A5, the pub has
fine views from the front of the Berwyn

INDEPENDENT BREWERIES

Bryn Denbigh
Facer's Flint
Jolly Brewer Wrexham
Plassey Eyton

Range. It appears small from the outside but inside is quite spacious. A single bar serves three drinking areas; there is a separate dining area and games room. The interior mixes old wood beams with modern decor. The pub is new to serving cask beers but the enthusiastic licensee plans to delete keg products over time. Q✿❶▶≠⊞(X94)P⏚

Graianrhyd

Rose & Crown

Llanarmon Road, CH7 4QW (on B5430 off A5104)
🕑 4 (12 Fri-Sun)-11
☎ (01824) 780727 ⊕ theroseandcrownpub.co.uk
Flowers IPA; guest beers Ⓗ
Friendly, welcoming, traditional pub: winner of many CAMRA awards including local Pub of the Year 2006 and 2007. Popular with locals and walkers, it is split into two rooms, one with an open fire, the other a wood burner, served by a single bar. Two ever-changing guest beers are sourced from local breweries; real cider is occasionally on offer. The cheery landlord is justifiably proud of his excellent pub food and fine ales. ♨Q✿❶▶⎕●P⏚

Hendrerwydd

White Horse Inn

LL16 4LL (600m E of B5429, 1 mile S of Llandyrnog) OS121634
🕑 12-3, 6-11; closed Mon; 12-3.30 (closed eve) Sun
☎ (01824) 790218 ⊕ white-horse-inn.co.uk
Beer range varies Ⓗ
Fine old oak beamed building dating from the 16th-17th century with a whitewashed exterior, set in some of the prettiest scenery in Wales. Locals, tourists and walkers are welcomed in the snug with a log fire throughout winter. Good food is served ranging from bar snacks to an a la carte menu. There is a pool room and further dining areas – the restaurant is popular at weekends and booking is advised. ♨✿❶▶⎕⊞(76)●P

Llandyrnog

Golden Lion

LL16 4HG (on B5429)
🕑 3-11; 2-1am Fri & Sat; 2-11 Sun
☎ (01824) 790373
Thwaites Original; guest beer Ⓗ
A listed building, this village pub has a single bar serving two areas. The lounge has a real fire and there is a games area with jukebox. The regular beer is often complemented by a brew from the Facer's micro-brewery. The Golden Lion is linked to the nearby White Horse, where a further two real ales may be found. Parking can be difficult so consider using the 76 bus, linking Denbigh and Graigfechan, which passes the door. Last entry at weekends is 11.30pm. ♨⊞(76)⏚

White Horse (Ceffyl Gwyn)

LL16 4HG (on B5429) OS108652
🕑 12-3 (not Mon), 6-11
☎ (01824) 790582
Beer range varies Ⓗ
Next door to the Anglican church, this village pub is popular with diners. Served by a single

bar, the main dining area is to the rear and there are comfortable seats around the fireplace at the front. The walls display pictures and news cuttings about the local area. There may be background music but this is a quiet pub for a peaceful drink. The pub is linked to the nearby Golden Lion (see above). The 76 bus passes outside. ♨Q✿❶▶⎕(76)P⏚

Llangollen

Corn Mill

Dee Lane, LL20 8PN (off Castle Street) SJ214421
🕑 12-11 (10.30 Sun)
☎ (01978) 869555 ⊕ cornmill-llangollen.co.uk
Boddingtons Bitter; guest beers Ⓗ
Tasteful conversion of an 18th century flour mill, complete with water wheel. Inside, three split levels are divided into separate restaurant and bar areas; the decor features numerous wooden beams and pine flooring, with furniture to match. Outside, an extensive decked area over the mill race provides superb views of the river and restored steam railway station. Four guest beers come from local micro-breweries. Food is well prepared from an extensive, varied menu. Q✿❶▶ё≠⊞

Sun Inn

49 Regent Street, LL20 8HN (on A5 half mile E of town centre)
🕑 5-11; 3-2am Fri & Sat; 3-1am Sun
☎ (01978) 860079
Salopian Shropshire Gold; Thwaites Original; guest beers Ⓗ
Grade II listed corner pub with six real ales and a good range of continental beers. Coloured glass doors open into a large green-walled room with a slate floor, three real fires and school benches for seating. A stage area hosts an eclectic range of live music. At the rear of the bar is a small snug which leads to a covered courtyard for outdoor drinking. The pub may get busy when live music plays. ♨✿❶ёⒶ≠⊞⏚

Llangynhafal

Golden Lion Inn

LL16 4LN OS121634
🕑 closed Mon; 6 (4 Thu)-12.30am; 4-2am Fri; 12-2am Sat; 12-11.30 Sun
☎ (01824) 790451 ⊕ thegoldenlioninn.com
Holt Bitter; guest beer Ⓗ
At the foot of the Clwydian hills, the pub is close to Offa's Dyke path. A single bar serves two rooms: the bar with a pool table and juke box, and the lounge, leading to a dining area. The Holt's bitter is collected from the brewery by the landlord. This pub has become a regular in the Guide, offering a guest beer and a cider or perry according to the season. There is a campsite behind the pub. ♨✿≠❶▶ⒶⒶ⊞(76)●P⏛

Meliden

Miners Arms

23 Ffordd Talargoch, LL19 7TH (on A547) OS062809
🕑 11 (12 Sun)-11.30
☎ (01745) 852005

Marston's Burton Bitter, Pedigree; guest beers Ⓗ
Pleasantly refurbished with improved disabled access, the Miners Arms is a multi-room pub in the village centre. The small sports bar, which has a wide-screen TV, also acts as the official meeting place for the Royal Marines Association of North Wales. LS Lowry sketched the pub on a visit to the area in 1928; you can see the print on display. Pictures of old Meliden decorate the walls throughout. Guest beers are from the Marston's list. Guide dogs are allowed. ▲➤❀◑🖳(35, 36)P⬸⬻

Prestatyn

Royal Victoria
Sandy Lane, LL19 7SG (Near jct A547/B5120)
OS064831
🕗 11.30-11 (11.30 Thu; midnight Fri & Sat)
☎ (01745) 854670
Marston's Burton Bitter; John Smith's Bitter; guest beers Ⓗ
Large two room pub alongside the railway station and close to Prestatyn centre. Both rooms feature interesting brass wall lamps; look for the three ornamental elephants, too. The pub has keen darts and dominoes teams with a fine display of sports trophies in the bar to prove it. The beers come from the Admiral Taverns' portfolio. No food is available here. Near to Prestatyn beach, the pub is at the northern end of Offa's Dyke path. Guide dogs are allowed. ❀▲≒🖳♣⬸

Rhewl

Sun Inn
LL20 7YT (on B5103, follow signs from A542)
OS178449
🕗 12-2.30 (not Wed), 6-11; 12-11 Sun
☎ (01978) 861043
Beer range varies Ⓗ
This 14th-century former drover's cottage is a rural gem in delightful countryside overlooking the Dee valley. In addition to the splendid walks in the immediate vicinity, the Horseshoe Falls and the attractions of Llangollen are nearby. A central bar serves three separate rooms each with its own character and charm. Children are allowed in two of the rooms and dogs are also welcome. Excellent home cooked meals are highly recommended. ▲Q➤❀◑ 🖴▲♣P

Rhuddlan

Kings Head
High Street, LL18 2TH
🕗 9.30am-midnight
☎ (01745) 590345
Jennings Dark Mild; Marston's Burton Bitter; guest beer Ⓗ
Large town centre pub with three rooms: a small lounge for drinkers, a large restaurant with seating for 50 diners and a sports bar with separate access where darts and pool are played. There has been a pub on this site for hundreds of years but it was rebuilt in 1967. Nearby Rhuddlan Castle, built by Edward II, dominates the landscape. There are regular bus connections from Rhyl. Dogs are welcome.

Guest beers are from the Marston's list.
◑&▲🖳♣P⬸⬻

Rhyl

Crown Bard
Rhuddlan Road, LL18 2RL (on A525) OS024793
🕗 11.30-11 (12-3, 5-11 winter); 11.30-midnight Fri & Sat; 12-11 Sun
☎ (01745) 338465
Spitting Feathers Thirstquencher; guest beer Ⓗ
Large pub next to Clwyd Retail Park on the A525 road out of Rhyl. The large lounge is mainly used for dining, offering an extensive menu with plenty of vegetarian options. Off the lounge is a snug with a number of water jugs hanging from the ceiling. The public bar has its own entrance. The landlord is a supporter of local breweries with Spitting Feathers' Thirstquencher the regular beer and two guest beers including a mild in summer. Guide dogs are allowed. ▲❀◑ 🖴🖳P⬸⬻

Swan
13 Russell Road, LL18 3BS (Near parish church and main pedestrianised streets.)
🕗 11-11 Mon – Thur, 11-11:30 Fri & Sat; 12-10:30 Sun
☎ (01745) 336694
Thwaites Dark Mild, Original, Lancaster Bomber Ⓗ
The Swan is a small town centre pub. There are two areas; the lounge has a section dedicated to lunchtime diners. The bar caters for sports fans with dart board and pool table. The Swan has several teams in darts, dominoes and pool leagues. There is a wide-screen television for sports watching. Hanging on the walls of both rooms are photographs of Rhyl in days gone by. Dogs are allowed in the bar only. Guide dogs allowed in lounge.
◑🖴≒(Rhyl)🖳♣

Ruthin

Boar's Head
LL15 1HW
🕗 12-midnight (1am Fri & Sat)
☎ (01824) 703355
Marston's Burton Bitter; guest beer Ⓗ
Brightly lit, friendly, single bar, town centre pub. It has two drinking areas and a raised area with a pool table to the rear. The wide-screen TV mainly shows sport. Among the pictures on the wall are a number of local views. The guest beer is from the Marston's list. Ruthin is a historic market town with many heritage sites, including a former gaol. ❀&🖳(51)⬸

St Asaph

Plough
The Roe, LL17 0LU (on A525 off jct 27 of A55)
OS033745
🕗 12-11 (1am Fri & Sat; 10.30 Sun)
☎ (01745) 585080
Plassey Bitter; guest beers Ⓗ
St Asaph has a number of pubs that serve real ale, however the Plough specialises in stocking beers from local breweries. A central bar serves several drinking areas. The ground floor has a horseracing theme, with tables

WALES

named after racehorses. Above is the Plough restaurant and wine bar where diners can choose from the bar menu or full restaurant fare. ⚑🌸🕙🍴🔥🛆🚃(51, 53)**P**⚊

FLINTSHIRE
Babell

Black Lion
CH8 8PZ (off B5121)
🌣 6-11; 12-midnight Sat; 12-10.30 Sun
☎ (01352) 720239
Beer range varies Ⓗ
Old coaching inn on former drovers' route. Somewhat off the beaten track, in an isolated position but offering good views and well worth a visit. Specialising in local beers and local produce in the bar menu and a-la-carte restaurant. Note the ornate carving over the fireplace, which reputedly originated from the composer Liszt's house in Germany. The single guest beer is usually from a local microbrewey or Thwaites of Blackburn. ⚑🌸🕙**P**⚊

Cadole

Colomendy Arms
Village Road, CH7 5LL (off A494 Mold-Ruthin Road)
🌣 7 (6 Thu; 4 Fri; 12 Sat)-11; 12-11 Sun
☎ (01352) 810217
Beer range varies Ⓗ
Delightful, traditional village local on the edge of Loggerheads Country Park, This frequent CAMRA Local Pub of the Year winner is popular with families, walkers, cavers, runners and even well-behaved dogs. Friendly conversation is the main entertainment. The cosy, single bar has a roaring fire in winter. Five handpumps provide an ever changing range of ales (some more than once during a busy evening), many from local breweries. ⚑Q🌣🌸🚃🛆**P**

Cefn-y-Bedd

Ffrwd
Ffrwd Road, LL12 9TS (1 mile along B5102 from A541)
🌣 5-12.30am (may close winter Mon); 12.30-12.30am Sat; 12.30-11.30 Sun
☎ (01978) 757951
Beer range varies Ⓗ
The Ffrwd sits in an attractive wooded valley alongside the River Cegidog. It was built on top of a former pub that was buried when the bridge replaced the original ford across the river. Separate dining and bar areas are served by a central bar. The landlord-cum-chef can often be seen in the kitchen preparing the excellent home-cooked food. Up to three guest beers are available, often including quirky or rare ales. Lunches are available at weekends. ⚑🌸🕙🚃🍴🚃**P**⚊🍽

Cilcain

White Horse
CH7 5NN
🌣 12-3, 6.30-11; 12-11 Sat & Sun
☎ (01352) 740142
Banks's Bitter; guest beers Ⓗ

Situated at the northern foot of Moel Famau, the pub is popular with hill walkers using local access paths. A traditional village pub, the interior includes a lounge with four drinking areas and a small dining room plus a separate locals/public bar. It has copper topped tables and a good display of brass and bric-a-brac. Old beer engines, no longer in use, are on display still showing the original prices.
⚑Q🌸🕙🛆🍀

Halkyn

Blue Bell
Rhosesmor Road, CH8 8DL (on B5123) OS209123
🌣 5-11 (midnight Fri); 12-11 Sat & Sun
☎ (01352) 780309 🌐 bluebell.uk.eu.org
Blue Bell Bitter; guest beers Ⓗ
Situated on Halkyn Mountain with spectacular views, the pub is the focal point for organised local walks (see website for details). Offering a warm welcome to visitors, locals and their dogs, it runs community activities from singalongs to games' nights. Good food is home made using local produce and the beer range usually features local micro-brews alongside the house beer (brewed by Facer's). There is a choice of real cider and often a perry. Buses from Mold and Holywell pass nearby. ⚑🌸🕙🛆🚃(126)🍀🍺**P**

Llanasa

Red Lion
Llanasa Road, CH8 9NE OS105815
🌣 12-11 (midnight Sat; 10.30 Sun)
☎ (01745) 854291
Courage Directors; Webster's Yorkshire Bitter; guest beer Ⓗ
Popular two-bar inn in a conservation area at the centre of the village. The pub has open fires and a pool table off the public bar. Two regular beers are served with a guest at weekends. There is an outside seating area overlooking the duck pond with views of the surrounding hills. The restaurant is busy at weekends – prior booking is advisable.
⚑🌸🚃🕙🚃🛆🍀**P**⚊

Mold

Glasfryn
Raikes Lane, CH7 6LR (off A5119, follow sign to Theatr Clwyd)
🌣 11.30-11; 12-10.30 Sun
☎ (01352) 750500 🌐 glasfryn-mold.co.uk
Bryn Bitter; Flowers Original; Taylor Landlord; Thwaites Bitter; guest beer Ⓗ
The Glasfryn is situated in its own grounds near Theatr Clwyd. Converted to its present use in 1999 by Brunning and Price, the building was originally a residence for circuit judges attending the courts opposite. The spacious interior is decorated with old books, prints and posters. Food is served daily until 9.30pm. Three guest beers from independent breweries, often local micros, supplement the regular range. ⚑🌸🕙🛆**P**

Gold Cape
8 Wrexham Road, CH7 1ES (30m off Market Square)

✪ 9-midnight (1am Fri & Sat)
☎ (01352) 705920
Bryn Bitter; Marston's Burton Bitter; guest beers ⒣
Popular Wetherspoon's pub offering the best choice of cask ales in Mold town centre, now with the added attractions of electronic amusements and Sky TV screens. The Gold Cape is named after a Bronze Age find, unearthed by local workmen in 1831 – an impression of the cape stands in the foyer and a replica is on show in Mold Heritage Centre and Museum. ⌂❀◗➁➡❀⌐

Sandycroft

Bridge Inn

Chester Road, CH5 2QN (on B5129)
✪ 12-11 (11.30 Wed-Sat)
☎ (01244) 538806
Caledonian Deuchars IPA; Jennings Cumberland Ale; Shepherd Neame Spitfire ⒣
Bright and airy real ale oasis on the edge of the Deeside beer desert. Good value home cooked food is served and children are allowed in the family dining area. The pub is reached by a wooden footbridge from the car park and boasts a large beer garden. The open plan lounge is adorned with photographs of old Chester. ⌂❀➁◗➁♿➡P

Ysceifiog

Fox ☆

Ysceifiog Village Road, CH8 8NJ (signed from A541 Denbigh-Mold road) OS151715
✪ 6 (12 Sat)-11; 12-10.30 Sun summer; 6 (2 Sat)-11 (closed Wed); 2-10.30 Sun winter
☎ (01352) 720241
Beer range varies ⒣
Unspoilt by progress, the three-room Fox was built circa 1730 and named after Ignatius Fox, head of the local gentry. The small bar, frequented by most regulars, has water jugs hanging from the ceiling, hops over the bar and an unusual bench seat against the bar. The larger lounge is for meals and meetings. Dogs are allowed in the snug which is filled with local sporting memorabilia. Difficult to find, this pub is a gem and well worth seeking out. ⌂❀◗⊟P

WREXHAM
Bersham

Black Lion

L14 4HN (off B5099 near Bersham Heritage Centre)
✪ 12 (11.30 Fri & Sat)-2am; 12-1am Sun
☎ (01978) 365588 ⊕ blacklionpub.co.uk
Hydes Original Bitter, seasonal beers ⒣
Friendly pub with a long-serving landlord set on a hillside on the Clwyedog Industrial Trail, known by locals as the Hole in the Wall. A wood panelled bar serves two rooms, both with real fires in winter, and a games room. There is a play area in the garden and a new patio for summer drinking. An outdoor drinking area at the front is popular with walkers. Basic bar meals are available all day. ⌂⌂❀◗♿➡⌐

Cross Lanes

Cross Lanes Hotel (Kagan's Brasserie)

Bangor Road, Marchwiel, LL13 0TF (on A525)
✪ 11-midnight (11 Sun)
☎ (01978) 780555 ⊕ crosslaneshotel.co.uk
Plassey Bitter; guest beer ⒣
This upmarket hotel lounge bar in a pleasant rural setting is a rare local outlet for the local Plassey brewery. Served by a central bar, the drinking area comprises an airy, well lit and comfortably furnished front room along with a more rustic back room featuring slate floors, solid oak tables and a superb log fire. The adjoining dining area is decorated with old prints and photographs. Visitors should note the magnificent 17th-century oak panelling in the front hall. ⌂Q⌂❀➁◗♿♣P

Erbistock

Boat

LL13 0DL (at end of narrow lane signed from A539 between Ruabon and Overton)
✪ 12-11 (10.30 Sun)
☎ (01978) 780666
Tetley Bitter; guest beers ⒣
This Grade II listed inn is set in an idyllic location on the banks of the River Dee. A conservatory restaurant serving high quality food takes up a large part of the building, but drinkers should head for the small oak-beamed bar which oozes character and charm. Guest beers are often from local micros such as Weetwood or Hanby. On warmer days you can enjoy a pint at one of the outdoor tables while admiring the blissful riverside scene. ⌂Q❀◗P

Gresford

Griffin

Church Green, LL12 8RG (next to All Saints church)
✪ 4 -11.30 (11 Sun)
☎ (01978) 852231
Greenalls Bitter; guest beers ⒣
Welcoming community oriented village pub adjacent to the 15th-century All Saints church famous for its bells – one of the seven wonders of Wales. The walls of the main bar feature pictures of some of the 266 victims tragically killed in the Gresford mining disaster of 1934. Guest beers are usually from regional or small breweries. The friendly, long-serving landlady is an accomplished pianist and she occasionally provides musical entertainment. Q❀➡♣P

Pant-yr-Ochain

Old Wrexham Road, LL12 8TY (off A5156, follow signs to The Flash)
✪ 12-11 (10.30 Sun)
☎ (01978) 853525 ⊕ pantyrochain-gresford.co.uk
Flowers Original; Thwaites Original; Taylor Landlord; guest beers ⒣
Overlooking a small lake to the rear, this magnificent, converted manor house is approached via a long sweeping drive. Inside, the original rooms have been opened out into a large open plan area with a central bar and an abundance of nooks and crannies. Assorted

WALES

603

old wooden tables and chairs provide ample seating to enjoy the excellent food and real ales on offer. During the winter, there is often a pleasant smell of wood smoke emanating from the 16th-century inglenook fireplace. ♨Q❄❉◑&P

Holt

Peal O' Bells

12 Church Street, LL13 9JP (400m S of Holt-Farndon bridge)

✪ Closed Mon; 6-11 Tue; 12-11 Wed & Thu; 12-midnight Fri & Sat; 12-11 Sun

☎ (01829) 270411

Adnams Bittter; Marston's Pedigree; guest beer Ⓗ

Popular family-friendly village pub next to St Chads church on the English border. Good value home-cooked food is served in the restaurant area Wednesday-Sunday lunchtime and Thursday-Saturday evening (booking essential at weekends). The sizeable fully enclosed garden has a small play area and excellent views of the Dee Valley and Peckforton Hills. Real perry is on handpump. ♨❄◑&🖼─

Lavister

Nag's Head

Old Chester Road, LL12 8SN (on Old Chester-Wrexham road)

✪ 5.30-midnight; 12-2am Fri; 11.30-2am Sat; 12-midnight Sun

☎ (01244) 570486

Cains Bitter; Flowers IPA; guest beers Ⓗ

Large roadside pub with a small, welcoming lounge area with open fire. A central bar serves the public bar, with pool table, darts and Sky TV. A plaque on the wall proclaims that the first CAMRA members were signed up here. The lively clientele mixes locals and visitors. Food is available Friday to Sunday, with Sunday lunches always popular. The guest beers usually include at least one from a local micro. There is a large children's play area in the garden. ♨❄◑&🖼♣P

Minera

Tyn-y-Capel

Church Road, LL11 3DA (off B5426)

✪ 12-11 (midnight Sat); 12-10.30 Sun

☎ (01978) 757702 ⊕ tyn-y-capel.co.uk

Greene King Old Speckled Hen; guest beers Ⓗ

Former drovers' pub originally linked with the adjacent church. The attractive whitewashed exterior with sturdy stone-flanked windows and painted heraldic shields belies a modern interior. Step down to the bar and marvel at the stunning views of Esclusham Mountain across the valley. Up to five guest beers are on offer and fine cuisine is served in a separate restaurant. Occasional live music sessions are hosted. The pub is close to the Minera lead mines and the start of the Clywedog Valley heritage trail. Q🐾❄◑🖳♣P

Moss

Clayton Arms

Moss Hill, LL11 6ES OS307538

✪ 7 (4 Sat)-11; closed Tue & Wed; 12-10.30 Sun

☎ (01978) 756444

Beer range varies Ⓗ

Refurbished pub in Moss Valley, a local beauty spot and part of the Clywedog industrial trail. The pub is furnished with cosy armchairs and settees where you can warm yourself in front of a roaring log fire on a winter's night. The restaurant is a good place to enjoy Sunday lunch after a walk in Moss Valley. The single cask beer changes twice weekly and is usually an interesting choice from an independent brewery. ♨❄◑P

Pontfadog

Swan

LL20 7AR (on B4500)

✪ 12-2.30, 5.30-11; 11-11 Sat; 12-10.30 Sun

☎ (01691) 718273

Beer range varies Ⓗ

Pontfadog is a picturesque village nestling in the Ceriog Valley between Chirk and Glyn Ceriog. The pub's cosy bar is popular with locals and visitors who come for the convivial atmosphere and unspoilt character. The guest beer is usually from a regional brewery or smaller local micro such as Jolly Brewer. The restaurant serves good quality home cooked food. There are plans to offer accommodation in 2008. ♨🛏&A🖼♣P

Ruabon

Wynnstay Arms

High Street, LL14 6BL (on B5605)

✪ 11.30-11.30

☎ (01978) 822187

Robinson's Unicorn, seasonal beers Ⓗ

Imposing late 18th-century red brick coaching inn enlarged and remodelled in 1841 into the public house and hotel that exists today. The interior is split into many distinct rooms, each with its own character. The impressive library room is used mainly for dining. A separate function room licensed for civil weddings is available for hire. ♨❄🛏◑🖳≢♣P─

Summerhill

Crown Inn

Top Road, LL11 4SR (via Summerhill Rd, 1 mile from A483/A541 jct)

✪ 12-midnight

☎ (01978) 755788

Hydes Bitter, seasonal beers Ⓗ

Real ale drinkers receive a hearty welcome from the award-winning landlord. The pub has a central bar with a lounge to one side, and a public bar with a pool table on the other. A Hyde's metal anvil can be seen in the lounge, and a collection of mirrors featuring the locals decorates the wall in the bar. With stunning views of Alyn and Deeside, treat yourself to a well priced pint just ring the serving bell. ♨Q🐾◑🖳≢(Gwersyllt)🖼♣P─

Wrexham

Albion

1 Pen-y-Bryn, LL13 7HU (Off Ruabon road S of town centre)

☼ 7 (12 Thu-Sun)-midnight

☎ (01978) 364969

Lees Bitter H

Large Edwardian pub on the corner of Pen-y-Bryn. Inside, a central bar serves the large, comfortable lounge and the two more basic public rooms. There is a pool table in one and darts and pub games in the other. As befits a community pub with a large following, it runs teams in the local pool and poker leagues. The lounge has a small stage where live music plays at weekends. You can expect a warm welcome here. ⌂⊟≠(Wrexham Central)♣

Gredington Arms

Holt Road, Llan-y-Pwll, LL13 9SD (on A534 between Wrexham and Holt)

☼ 12-2.30, 5-11 (midnight Fri); closed Mon; 12-midnight Sat & Sun

☎ (01978) 661728 ⊕ gredingtonarms.co.uk

Hydes Bitter, seasonal beers H

Newly refurbished pub close to the Cheshire border with a comfortable lounge bar and an attractive dining area where good quality meals are served. Children are welcome in the restaurant area. Outside, the former stables has been converted into an additional bar serving the pleasant beer garden overlooking open countryside. An outdoor marble dance floor is used for functions and marquee events. ♿❀⊞P

Golden Lion Inn, Llangynhafal, Denbighshire, North-East Wales.

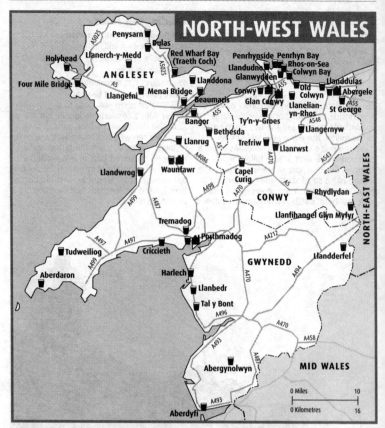

NORTH-WEST WALES

Authority areas covered: Anglesey UA, Conwy UA, Gwynedd UA

ANGLESEY/YNYS MÔN
Beaumaris

Olde Bulls Head Inn
Castle Street, LL58 8AA
✪ 11-11; 12-10.30 Sun
☎ (01248) 810329 ⊕ bullsheadinn.co.uk
Draught Bass; Hancock's HB; guest beer Ⓗ
Grade II listed building that was the original posting house of the borough. In 1645 General Mytton, a parliamentarian, commandeered the inn while his forces lay siege to the castle, which is a mere stone's throw away. The Royalists surrendered on 25th June 1646. Dr Samuel Johnson and Charles Dickens were famous guests and each bedroom is named after a Dickens character. The beamed bar has a large open fire. Parking is limited. ▲Q⇌P

Dulas

Pilot Boat Inn
LL70 9EX (on A5025)
✪ 11 (12 Sun)-11
☎ (01248) 410205
Robinson's Unicorn Ⓗ
Friendly, rural, family pub with a play area and converted double decker bus to keep children amused. Originally a cottage-type building, now much extended, the lounge features an unusual bar created from half a boat. The pub is much used by walkers; the coastal path passes through the car park. It is worth visiting Mynydd Bodafon for its spectacular views and Traeth Lligwy for the sands. Meals are served all day. Q❀❀◑▲♣P

Four Mile Bridge

Anchorage Hotel
LL65 3EZ (on B4545, just past bridge to Holy Island)
✪ 11 (12 Sun)-11
☎ (01407) 740168
Draught Bass; Taylor Landlord; Theakston XB; guest beer Ⓗ
This family-run hotel is situated on Holy Island close to Trearddur Bay. There is a large, comfortable lounge bar and a dining area serving a wide selection of meals all day. The hotel is close to some fine, sandy beaches and coastal walks. Its proximity to the A55 makes it a useful stopping off point for Holyhead Port. Q❀⇌◑▲⊟(4)P

Holyhead

79
79 Market Street, LL65 1VW
☯ 11-11; 12-10.30 Sun
☎ (01407) 763939
Beer range varies Ⓗ
Comfortable, recently refurbished town centre pub enjoying a good year round local trade. Beers are usually from the large regional breweries such as Brains (one of the few outlets for real ale in Holyhead). There are two bars, a pool room and a split level dining area. Good food prepared on the premises is served all day. Visit the new Celtic Gateway bridge and the ancient parish church at the start of the Anglesey Coastal Path. Q◑▬≉♣

Llanddona

Owain Glyndwr
Beaumaris, LL58 8UF (signed off B5109, Pentraeth-Beaumaris road)
☯ 12 (5 Mon)-midnight; winter hours vary
☎ (01248) 810710
Beer range varies Ⓗ
Originally cottages and a shop, this multi-room pub opened in 1981. It has a bar area, games room, lounge and dining room, and hosts live music every other Saturday. One guest beer is available in winter and two in summer, all from micro-breweries. Dogs are welcome in the drinking areas. Well worth a visit while on the island, the pub is in the centre of the village and close to the beach and Anglesey coastal path. ▲Q❀◑▬(53)♣P⅃

Llanerch-y-Medd

Twr Cyhelun Arms
Twr Cyheluh Street, LL71 8DB (on B5112)
☯ 7-11; 4-midnight Fri; 12-12.30am Sat; 12-11.30 Sun
☎ (01248) 470340
Lees Bitter, seasonal beers Ⓗ
Situated in the heart of the island, Twr Cyhelun means Holly Tower. This friendly local is well worth a visit. The pub has a main bar, snug, games room and a dining area with real fires creating a cosy, welcoming environment. Guest beers are supplied by JW Lees. Food is served all day at weekends. Llanerch-y-Medd is on a cycle route and near to Llyn Alaw. ▲Q❀◑▬(32)P

Llangefni

Railway Inn
48-50 High Street, LL77 7NA
☯ 4 (3 Thu & Fri)-11; 12-midnight Sat; 12-11 Sun
☎ (01248) 722166
Lees Bitter Ⓗ
Classic friendly small-town pub with a warm welcome, next to the old railway station, displaying old photographs of Llangefni. The main bar is hewn out of the stone wall. Near the centre of this county town, the pub is close to Oriel Mon (museum) where you can find out about the history of Anglesey and see Tunnicliffe's bird books and pictures, and the Dingle, a local wooded nature reserve. ▬(4)♣⅃

Menai Bridge

Auckland Arms
Water Street, LL59 5DD
☯ 5-midnight (2am Fri & Sat)
☎ (01248) 712545 ⊕ anglesey-hotel.co.uk
Greene King IPA, Old Speckled Hen; guest beers
Around 120 years old, the hotel is in a superb location, close to the pier and the strait. The busy bar, popular with students, has two pool tables and a range of pub games including a popular Monday quiz night. Open microphone night is Thursday. Food will soon be available with a new kitchen extension. There is an excellent patio and garden and the comfortable bed and breakfast accommodation is recommended. Check bar opening hours out of term time. ❀≌▬▦♣⅃

Tafarn y Bont (Bridge Inn)
Telford Road, LL59 5DT (on right as you come off suspension bridge)
☯ 11-midnight; 12-10.30 Sun
☎ (01248) 716888
Banks's Bitter; Marston's Pedigree Bitter; guest beers Ⓗ
Former mid 19th century shop and tea rooms, close to the famous bridge, now a brasserie style pub with an excellent restaurant. A beamed interior, log fires and numerous hideaway rooms give the pub an olde-worlde feel. Snowdonia is a short drive away and at nearby Caernarfon is the Welsh Highland Railway. ▲≿❀◑▲▬⅃

Victoria Hotel
Telford Bridge, LL59 5DR (between bridge and town centre)
☯ 11-11; 12-10.30 Sun
☎ (01248) 712309
Beer range varies Ⓗ
Situated 300 metres from the Menai Suspension Bridge, this 19 room hotel overlooks the Strait and affords delightful views from the garden and patio. It is licensed for weddings and has a spacious function room with widescreen HD TV for sports. Live music is a regular added attraction. There is easy access to Snowdonia and the Welsh Highland Railway from Caernarfon, now running to the foot of Snowdon, Rhyd Ddu and beyond. ≿❀≌◑▬&▲▦⅃

Penysarn

Bedol
LL69 9YR (just off A5025)
☯ 12 (2 winter Mon-Fri)-11; 12-11 Sat; 12-11 (2-10.30 winter) Sun
☎ (01407) 832590
Robinson's Ward's Bitter, Hartleys XB, seasonal beers Ⓗ
The Bedol (Horseshoe) was built in 1985 to serve a small village, but the regulars now come from a much wider area. A Robinson's tied house, it hosts regular live entertainment. Food is available all day, except midweek lunchtime in winter. Some of Anglesey's beautiful beaches and the newly opened coastal path are nearby. Q❀◑▬▲▦(62)♣P

Red Wharf Bay

Ship Inn

LL75 8RJ (off A5025 on Amlwch Road near Benllech)
☼ 11-11 (10.30 Sun)
☎ (01248) 852568 ⊕ shipinnredwharfbay.co.uk
Adnams Bitter; Brains SA; guest beers Ⓗ
Red Wharf Bay was once a busy port exporting coal and fertilizer in the 18th and 19th centuries. Previously known as the Quay, the Ship enjoys an excellent reputation for its bar and restaurant, with meals served all day, and gets busy with locals and visitors in the summer. The garden has panoramic views across the bay to south-east Anglesey. The resort town of Bennllech is two miles away. ▨Q▱❀◑▣ÅP⌐

CONWY
Abergele

Pen-y-Bont

Bridge Street, LL22 7HA OS947775
☼ 1 (12 Fri & Sat)-11; 12-10.30 Sun
☎ (01745) 833905
Brains Rev James; guest beers Ⓗ
A family owned and run free house, this one room pub is divided into two areas separated by a central bar. The lounge has a large screen TV showing major sporting events; the bar and games area has pool and darts. Two local pigeon clubs meet here three nights a week. The newly refurbished restaurant and letting rooms should now be up and running. Dogs and cyclists are always welcome.
❀♿Å≠▣(15, 12)♣P⌐

Capel Curig

Cobden's Hotel

Holyhead Road, LL24 0EE OS731576
☼ 11-11; 12-10.30 Sun
☎ (01690) 720243 ⊕ cobdens.co.uk
Tetley Bitter; Conwy Castle Bitter, seasonal beer Ⓗ
This 200 year old hotel is popular with walkers and climbers; at the rear is a fascinating bar area built into the side of an adjacent mountain. The 17-bedroom hotel has built up a good reputation for its hospitality and comfortable rooms, with a large lounge and comfortable restaurant. Lamb shank in Conwy Honey Fayre beer is one of the many excellent meals made with local produce. The Cobden's Ale house beer is brewed especially for the pub by Conwy. ▨Q❀⇌◑▣Å▣♣P

Colwyn Bay

Pen-y-Bryn

Pen-y-Bryn Road, Upper Colwyn Bay, LL29 6DD (top of King's Rd) OS842783
☼ 11.30-11; 12-10.30 Sun
☎ (01492) 533360 ⊕ penybryn-colwynbay.co.uk
Thwaites Original; guest beers Ⓗ
Open plan pub, popular with all ages, with old furniture, large bookcases and open fires in winter. The walls are decorated with old photographs and memorabilia from the local area. Panoramic views of Colwyn Bay and the Great Orme can be admired from the garden

and terrace. Excellent imaginative bar food is available from a menu that changes daily. Five guest beers are mainly from independent breweries. Local CAMRA Branch Pub of the Year 2006. ▨Q❀◑⅙▣♣P⌐

Wings Social Club

Station Square, LL29 (opp station) OS850791
☼ 11-3 (4 Fri), 7-11; 11-11 Sat; 12-4, 7-10.30 Sun
☎ (01492) 530682
Lees GB Mild, Bitter Ⓗ
Local CAMRA Club of the Year 2007, this popular social club is across the road from the resort's rail station and two minutes' walk from the main coast road bus services. A warm welcome is assured for visitors and their families. The bar area serves a large L-shaped lounge incorporating a small dance floor. The club holds a wedding licence and is popular for functions. There are separate rooms for billiards, pool, snooker, darts and TV. ≠▣♣

Conwy

Albion Vaults ☆

Uppergate Street, LL32 8RF OS780776
☼ 12-11
☎ (01492) 592740
Beer range varies Ⓗ
Originally two pubs, this traditional Victorian corner local was knocked into one in 1920. It is the only pub in the county of Conwy to feature in CAMRA's National Inventory of Historic Pub Interiors and is reputed to be haunted by a ghost called Bob. It has a quiet, secluded lounge with a large fireplace, a popular basic main bar with sports TV and real fire, and a pool/games room. Guest ales come from local breweries. Dogs are welcome.
▨▱❀Å≠▣♣⌐

Glanwydden

Queen's Head

LL31 9JP OS817804
☼ 11-3, 6-11 (10.30 Mon & Tue); 12-10.30 Sun
☎ (01492) 546570 ⊕ queensheadglanwydden.co.uk
Adnams Bitter; guest beers Ⓗ
Former wheelwright's cottage in the centre of the village run by the same landlord for more than 20 years. The olde-worlde pub atmosphere attracts locals and holidaymakers alike. The pub has been extended and attractively refurbished over the last year providing an additional dining area and an outside heated seating area. Quality food is served made with local Welsh produce. Guest beers come from Great Orme, Weetwood and Spitting Feathers. ▨Q❀⇌◑▣Å▣P⌐

Llanddulas

Dulas Arms

Abergele Road, LL22 8HP OS899783
☼ 12 (3 winter Mon)-11
☎ (01492) 515747
Lees Bitter, seasonal beer Ⓗ
Clearly visible from the A55, the ghoulish green exterior belies a cosy and welcoming interior. The large six room pub used to be known as the Railway when trains stopped here. The lounge leads to a snug, games

rooms, music-themed room with instruments on display, family room and upstairs restaurant with stunning views over the bay. A bluegrass music club meets on the last Friday of the month. A popular stop off for cyclists on the nearby coastal route 5.

🏚Q☞☺🏠◑🕮🖃(12, 15)♣P⅃

Llandudno

King's Head
Old Road, LL30 2NB (Next to Great Orme Tramway) OS778827
✪ 12-midnight (11 Sun)
☎ (01492) 877993
Greene King IPA, Abbot; guest beers ⊞
The 300-year-old King's Head is the oldest pub in Llandudno; it makes an ideal stop after walking on Great Orme or riding on Britain's only cable hauled tramway. The traditional split level bar is dominated by a large open fire. The sun-trap patio with its award winning flower display is a delightful place to watch the trams pass by. Excellent, high quality food is served in the grill restaurant.
🏚☞☺◑Å⊖🖃P

Llanelian-yn-Rhos

White Lion
LL29 8YA (off B583) OS863764
✪ 11.30-3, 6-midnight; closed Mon; 12-4, 6-11
☎ (01492) 515807 ∰ whitelioninn.co.uk
Marston's Burton Bitter, Pedigree; guest beer ⊞
Traditional 16th century inn next to St Elian's church in the hills above Old Colwyn. The slate flagstoned bar area has a real log fire, antique settles and large comfortable chairs. Stained glass decorates the tiny snug. The spacious restaurant has a collection of jugs hanging from the ceiling. Two white stone lions guard the door of this attractive family run inn which has been in the Guide for 16 years.
🏚Q☞☺◑ 🕮Å♣P

Llanfihangel Glyn Myfyr

Crown Inn
LL21 9UL (on B5105) OS992493
✪ 7-11; closed Mon; 12 (4 winter)-11 Sat & Sun
☎ (01490) 420209
Beer range varies ⊞
Delightful old inn, a rural gem beside the Afon Alwen. The unspoilt interior of the front bar with its slate floor area and open fire is warm and welcoming. Across the corridor is the games room with darts and TV. Monthly folk evenings are staged. Children are welcome in the pub and terraced gardens beside the river, where in summer bar meals are served. Permits are available for trout fishing. Beers come from small independent breweries at this regular CAMRA award winner.
🏚Q☺Å♣P

Llangernyw

Old Stag
LL22 8PP (A548 between Abergale and Llanrwst) OS875675
✪ 12-3, 6-11; 12-10.30 Sun
☎ (01745) 860213

Beer range varies ⊞
Early 17th century traditional inn located in the heart of the village of Llangernyw. The bar has two handpumps for guest beers, usually brewed in Wales, to accompany a varied menu of home-cooked food using local produce. There are several cosy rooms, some with open fires, filled with historic artefacts adorning the walls and ceilings. The car park is situated just up the way from this olde worlde country inn. 🏚Q☺◑▤♣P🖥

Llanrwst

New Inn
Denbigh Street, LL26 0LL OS798617
✪ 11-1am (2am Fri & Sat); 12-2am Sun
☎ (01492) 640467
Banks's Original; Marston's Burton Bitter; guest beer ⊞
Popular, traditional terraced town pub, winner of the local CAMRA branch seasonal award for autumn 2006. One bar serves a comfortably furnished narrow lounge and corner snug with open fire and TV. The games area has a pool table and jukebox. Smoking is permitted outside at the back of the pub, with a few picnic tables provided. This friendly pub appeals to all generations and you are assured of a warm welcome. Last entry is 11.30pm.
🏚☺Å⇌🖃♣

Pen-y-Bont
Bridge Street, LL26 0ET OS799615
✪ 11-11; 12-10.30 Sun
☎ (01492) 640202
Beer range varies ⊞
Picturesque 14th-century inn overlooking the 17th-century stone bridge that crosses the nearby Conwy river. This family run pub is full of character with its quaint rooms with low beams and stone floors. A central bar serving two frequently changing real ales from independent brewers separates the congenial public bar and the cosy lounge, both with welcoming real fires. The dining area at the rear has a family section and there is also a traditional games room.
🏚Q☞◑ 🕮Å⇌🖃♣P

Old Colwyn

Cuckoo
325-329 Abergele Road, LL29 9PF (on main Colwyn Bay to Abergele road) OS866784
✪ 10 (11 Sun)-11
☎ (01492) 514083
Coach House Dick Turpin; Conwy Celebration; guest beer ⊞
Formally known as Clwb y Gornel (Club on the Corner), the Cuckoo is aptly named with several cuckoo clocks greeting you as you enter. The main room has a wide screen TV and bar with three handpumps dispensing two regular ales and a guest. There is a smaller lounge and games room with pool table and dart board. Outside is a large covered and heated patio area. ☺🖫🖃(12)♣♠⅃

Red Lion
385 Abergele Road, LL29 9PL (on main Colwyn Bay to Abergele road) OS868783

✪ 5-11; 4-midnight Fri; 12-midnight Sat; 12-11 Sun
☎ (01492) 515042

Marston's Burton Bitter; guest beers Ⓗ

Ever popular local serving up to six guest beers from independent and local brewers including a regular guest mild. A genuine free house, it has won many local CAMRA awards including Pub of the Year 2007. The cosy L-shaped room is warmed by a real coal fire and features antique brewery mirrors and other memorabilia. The traditional public bar has a pool table, darts and TV. There is a patio area for warmer weather. ⚏Q✿❀▣☷(12)♣♨⚊

Sun Inn

383 Abergele Road, LL29 9PL (on main Colwyn Bay to Abergele road) OS868783
✪ 12-11 (midnight Fri & Sat); 12-11.30 Sun
☎ (01492) 517007

M&B Mild; Marston's Burton Bitter, Pedigree; guest beer Ⓗ

The only original pub building in Old Colwyn, dating from 1844. A typical beer drinker's local, the central bar serves a cosy lounge area with a welcoming real coal fire. CAMRA literature is displayed prominently on the top of the piano. There is also a side bar with TV and juke box. The large games/meeting room at the back has a dart board and pool table. Outside is a small patio area.
⚏Q✿❀▣☷(12)♣

Penrhyn Bay

Penrhyn Old Hall

LL30 3EE OS816815
✪ 12-3, 6-11; 12-3, 7-10.30 Sun
☎ (01492) 549888

Draught Bass; guest beer Ⓗ

This 16th-century hall has been in the Marsh family since 1963. The wood panelled Tudor bar serves the restaurant and lounge area. A large fireplace, with a stone dating back to 1590, conceals a priest hole and the adjacent staircase is reputed to be haunted. Good value meals are served daily in the restaurant, plus traditional three-course Sunday lunches. The hall has a nightclub and baronial hall with full-size skittle alley. ❀◑▲☷(12, 15)♣P

Penrhynside

Penrhyn Arms

Pendre Road, LL30 3BY (off B5115) OS814816
✪ 5.30 (5 Thu)-midnight; 12-1am Fri & Sat; 12-11 Sun
☎ (07780) 678927 ⊕ penrhynarms.com

Banks's Bitter; Marston's Pedigree; guest beers Ⓗ

Runner-up in CAMRA's national cider & perry Pub of the Year 2006, and a former local CAMRA pub of the year winner, this welcoming local pub is a real gem. The spacious L-shaped bar has pool, darts and a widescreen TV. Check the website for current beers and tasting notes. Framed pictures of notable drinkers and brewery memorabilia adorn the walls. There are real ciders and perries plus up to four guest beers including mild and winter ale on gravity at Christmas. ⚏❀◑▲☷♣♨⛾

Rhos-on-Sea

Toad

West Promenade, LL28 4BU OS847795
✪ 11-11.30 (10.30 Sun)
☎ (01492) 532726

Jennings Cumberland Ale; guest beers Ⓗ

Recently refurbished traditional pub with an upstairs bar overlooking the bay and a cosy restaurant serving quality food and famous Sunday lunches. Downstairs is a pool room and spacious front patio on the promenade. A weekly quiz is held on Monday evening and occasional music evenings are hosted. This attractive and popular pub offers a warm welcome to locals and visitors. It is available for private functions. ⚏❀◑☷(12)♣P⚊

Rhydlydan

Y Giler Arms

LL24 0LL OS892508
✪ 11 (12 winter)-2.30, 6 (6.30 winter)-11; 12-11 Sat; 12-10.30 (12-2.30, 6.30-11 winter) Sun
☎ (01690) 770612

Batham Mild, Best Bitter Ⓗ

Friendly country pub situated in six acres of grounds including a coarse fishing lake, small campsite and picturesque gardens beside the River Merddwr. Extensively refurbished by the owners, it has a comfortable lounge with large open stove, a public bar with open fire and a small pool room. The restaurant has lovely views over the lake. Children are welcome and there are seven letting bedrooms.
⚏Q✿⚲◑▣▲☷♣P⚊

St George

Kinmel Arms

LL22 9BP OS974758
✪ 12-3, 6.30-11; closed Mon; 12-10.30 Sun
☎ (01745) 832207 ⊕ thekinmelarms.co.uk

Thwaites Original; guest beers Ⓗ

Former coaching inn dating from the 17th century set on the hillside overlooking the sea. An L-shaped bar serves a large dining and drinking area with a real log fire in one corner and a spacious conservatory at the rear. Up to three guest beers, including a mild, come from independent breweries and there is a selection of Belgian beers. The pub has a reputation for good food and is a winner of numerous awards including local CAMRA Best Pub Food in 2006. ⚏Q✿⚲◑▣♿P

Trefriw

Old Ship/Yr Hen Long

LL27 0JH (on B5106) OS781632
✪ 12-3, 6-11; 12-11 Sat; 12-10.30 Sun
☎ (01492) 640013 ⊕ the-old-ship.co.uk

Banks's Bitter; Marston's Pedigree; guest beer Ⓗ

This former 16th-century customs house is now a busy village local. The small bar serves a cosy L-shaped lounge with an open fire and pictures of historical and nautical interest. The dining room has an inglenook. This genuine free house serves a range of guest beers and good home cooked food. A self catering holiday cottage is available. ⚏❀⚲◑▣☷(19)P

Ty'n-y-Groes

Groes Inn

LL32 8TN (on B5106) OS777740

☼ 12-3, 6.30-11; 6-11 Sat; 12-3, 6.30-10.30 Sun

☎ (01492) 650545 ⊕ groesinn.com

Great Orme Orme's Best; Tetley Burton Ale Ⓗ
The first licensed house in Wales, dating back to 1573, the Groes Inn has been owned by the Humphreys family for 21 years and the traditional interior retains ancient architectural features. In summer the flower-decked frontage and secluded gardens are a delight. Excellent food made with local produce is served in the bar or restaurant. The inn offers accommodation in comfortable bedroom suites or a luxury log cabin in the hills or a cottage in Conwy. ﴾Q✿▱◑❒(19)P

GWYNEDD
Aberdaron

Ship Hotel

LL53 8BE

☼ 11-11

☎ (01758) 760204 ⊕ theshiphotelaberdaron.co.uk

Beer range varies Ⓗ
The Ship is situated in the centre of the village of Aberdaron at the tip of the Llyn peninsula. You can be sure of a friendly welcome in the two bars, one with a games area. Excellent food made with locally sourced fresh ingredients is recommended. Two handpumps in summer and one in winter dispense local Welsh beer. The village has a bus service but check times first. ﴾⏚✿◑ ⊟↔▲❒♣

Aberdyfi

Penhelig Arms Hotel

Terrace Road, LL35 0LT (on A493)

☼ 11-midnight; 12-11 Sun

☎ (01654) 767215 ⊕ penheligarms.com

Hancock's HB; guest beers Ⓗ
Small friendly seaside town hotel by Penhelig harbour with superb views across the Dyfi estuary. The Fisherman's Bar is where locals and visitors congregate to enjoy traditional ales and good bar food. The restaurant is renowned for its fish dishes. The pub is close to Penhelig halt on the scenic Cambrian Coast Railway – don't forget to ask for the train to stop! ﴾Q▱◑▱↔(Penhelig Halt)P

Abergynolwyn

Railway Inn

LL36 9YN (on B4405)

☼ 12-midnight (11 Sun)

☎ (01654) 782279

Beer range varies Ⓗ
Friendly community local in the centre of the village not far from the Talyllyn Railway. You can still see the remains of the old incline that brought goods traffic down from the railway to the village. Excellent food is served and, following a refit in 2007, the range of beers will increase. The pub has stunning views of the surrounding hills and there is wonderful walking nearby. ﴾Q✿◑⊟↔(Talyllyn Railway)

Bangor

Black Bull/ Tarw Du

107 High Street, LL57 1NS

☼ 9-midnight (1am Fri & Sat); 10-midnight Sun

☎ (01248) 387900

Brains SA; Courage Directors; Greene King Abbot; Marston's Burton Bitter; guest beers Ⓗ
Wetherspoon's pub in a converted church and presbytery at the top of the high street. It has spacious drinking areas and outside the patio overlooks upper Bangor and the university. Popular with students, it is very busy during term time. Two draught ciders are regularly available. A lift is available for disabled access. ✿◑&↔♣

Boatyard

Garth Road, LL57 2SF (off old A5, follow pier signs)

☼ 11 (12 Sun)-11

☎ (01248) 362462

Marston's Burton Bitter; guest beers Ⓗ
Formerly the Union Garth, this large multi-roomed pub is in lower Bangor near Dickies Boatyard. Recently refurbished, each room is packed with local historic and horse racing pictures, brasses, wall plates and more. Part of the pub is now a well appointed restaurant. The garden overlooks sailing boats and the sea. Bangor Pier (a third of a mile long) is five minutes' walk away and well worth a visit. Two regularly changing guest beers are on offer. ﴾Q▱◑❒P↳

Harp Inn

80-82 High Street, LL57 1NS (along High St towards station)

☼ 11-1am; 12-10.30 Sun

☎ (01248) 361817

Greene King Abbot; Theakston HB; guest beers Ⓗ
One of the oldest pubs in Bangor, now owned by Scottish & Newcastle. Popular with students, it has a large open plan bar area with steps leading to a games room and a small snug to the side of the bar. Busy during term time, live music and karaoke night on Thursday can be noisy. Excellent value, good food served – hours may vary so ring to check. ﴾⏚◑▲↔♣↳

Tap & Spile

Garth Road, LL57 2SW (off old A5, follow pier signs)

☼ 12-11 (11.30 Tue, Fri & Sat)

☎ (01248) 370835

Beer range varies Ⓗ
Popular split level pub overlooking the renovated Victorian pier offering superb views of the Menai Straits. The pub has a back to basics feel with old wooden tables and chairs and several church pews, but the large screen TV and fruit machines can dominate. Food is served daily except Sunday evening. CAMRA Pub of the Year in 2004 and 2006. ◑♣

Bethesda

Douglas Arms Hotel ☆

London Road, LL57 3AY

☼ 6-11; 3.30-midnight Sat; 1-3, 7-11 Sun

☎ (01248) 600219

Marston's Burton Bitter, Pedigree; guest beer Ⓗ

WALES

This Grade II listed building features in CAMRA's national inventory. Built in 1820, it was an important coaching inn on the historic Telford post route from London to Holyhead. The four-room interior has not changed since the 1930s and includes a snug, lounges and a large tap room with a full sized snooker table. Bethesda, originally a town built on slate quarries, is convenient for buses to the Ogwen Valley and surrounding mountains. Q⊕▲⊠♣

Criccieth

Castle Inn
LL52 0RW
☼ 12-11
☎ (01766) 523515
Beer range varies ℍ
Traditional three-room pub just off the A497 Porthmadog to Pwllheli road, catering for locals and tourists alike. Three handpumps dispense an ever changing range of beer from regional and small breweries, as well as cider in summer. Well served by public transport, the Cambrian Coast railway station is less than 100 metres away. For enjoying a pint on a warm summer evening there is a small outdoor area. ▲❀❀◑⊕⊠▲⇌⊠♣♠

Harlech

Y Branwen Hotel
Ffordd Newydd, LL46 2UB (on A462 below Harlech Castle) OS583312
☼ 11-11
☎ (01766) 780477 ⊕ branwenhotel.co.uk
Beer range varies ℍ
Warm and welcoming family run hotel and bar overlooked by Harlech Castle. The hotel is named after a princess whose tales are found in a collection of Welsh myths known as Y Mabinogion. The popular and stylish bar has a wide range of cask ales as well as foreign beers. A large selection of wines and malt whiskies is also stocked. Ask for your favourite malt – they are sure to have it.
❀❀◑⊖▲⇌⊠(2, 38)♣P⌐

Llanbedr

Ty Mawr Hotel
LL45 2HH
☼ 11-11
☎ (01341) 241440
Worthington's Bitter; guest beers ℍ
Small country hotel set in its own grounds. The modern lounge bar has a slate flagged floor and cosy wood-burning stove. Unusual flying memorabilia reflect connections with the local airfield. French windows lead on to a verandah and landscaped terrace with outdoor seating. There is a beer festival held in a marquee on the lawn each year. Popular with locals, walkers and real ale enthusiasts, dogs and children are welcome. Meals are served all day. ▲❀❀◑⊖▲⇌P

Llandderfel

Bryntirion Inn
LL23 7RA (on B4401, 4 miles E of Bala)
☼ 11 (12 Sun)-11

☎ (01678) 530205
Jennings Cumberland Ale; guest beer ℍ
Old coaching inn in a rural setting with views to the River Dee. Off the pleasant public bar is a family room and there is a lounge where meals are served in a quiet environment. Bar snacks are also available. There is outdoor seating in the front car park; at the rear is a courtyard and a larger car park. Three bedrooms offer good value accommodation.
▲▲Q❀❀❀◑⊖⊕♣P

Llandwrog

Harp Inn/Ty'n Llan
LL54 5SY
☼ 12-11 (12-2, 6-11 closed Mon winter); 12-10.30 (12-3 winter) Sun
☎ (01286) 831071 ⊕ welcome.to/theharp
Beer range varies ℍ
Hidden on a back road to Dinas Dinlle and Caernarfon airport, this beautiful old stone inn boasts many cosy rooms and a resident parrot called Dylan. The ever-changing beers come from smaller breweries, with one pump in use in winter and two in summer. Legend says that there was tunnel from the cellar to the church, and in the churchyard look out for the pirate's grave. ▲▲☼❀❀◑⊖▲♣P

Llanrug

Glyntwrog
Caernarfon Road, LL55 4AN (on A4086)
☼ 11 (12 Sun)-midnight
☎ (01286) 671191
Greene King IPA; Wychwood Hobgoblin ℍ
This spacious local is situated just outside the village. It offers a games room, comfortable bar area and lounge, and a children's playground. Open all year round, it is handy for Llanberis, Padarn Lake, Snowdon Mountain Railway and the National Park. Meals are served lunchtime and evening every day. The pub is well served by buses. ❀◑▲⊠♣P⌐

Porthmadog

Spooner's Bar
Harbour Station, LL49 9NF
☼ 10-11; 12-10.30 Sun
☎ (01766) 516032 ⊕ festrail.co.uk
Beer range varies ℍ
An all year round mini beer festival – Spooner's has built its reputation on an ever changing range from small breweries, including the local Purple Moose. Situated in the terminus of the world famous Ffestiniog Railway, steam trains are outside the door most of the year. Food is served every lunchtime (Sunday lunches a speciality) but out of season only Thursday to Saturday in the evening. Q▲☼❀◑▲⇌⊠(1, X32)P

Tal y Bont

Abbeyfield Hotel
LL57 3UR (turn right at Penrhyn Castle)
☼ 12-3, 6.30-midnight; 12-midnight Sat & Sun
☎ (01248) 352219 ⊕ abbeyfieldhotel.co.uk
Great Orme Best, Three Feathers ℍ

Initially a converted 17th-century farmhouse, this is now a popular country hotel and pub, renowned for its restaurant and fine cuisine. The pub is a free house offering local bitter from Llandudno's Great Orme Brewery as well as occasional seasonal beers. The hotel, with eleven en-suite bedrooms, is ideally located for Snowdonia and the resorts of Anglesey.
🏛Q🍽🏨◑🚆♣P🅿

Tremadog

Golden Fleece

Market Square, LL49 9RB (on A487)
🕐 11-3, 6-11; 12.30-3, 6-10.30 Sun
☎ (01766) 512421
Draught Bass; Purple Moose Glaslyn; guest beer Ⓗ

Situated in the old market square, this former coaching inn is now a friendly local. Rock climbing and narrow gauge railways are nearby. It has a lounge bar and a snug which may occasionally be reserved for regulars. Outside there is a covered decked area with bench seats. Bar meals are good value and there is a bistro upstairs. 🏛Q🍽🏨◑🦽🚆

Tudweiliog

Lion Hotel

LL53 8ND (on B4417)
🕐 11-11 (12-2, 6-11 winter); 11.30-11 Sat; 11-10.30 (12-3 winter) Sun

☎ (01758) 770244
Beer range varies Ⓗ

Village pub on the glorious, quiet north coast of the Llyn Peninsula. The cliffs and beaches are a mile away by footpath, a little further by road. The origins of this friendly free house go back over 300 years. Up to four beers are served, depending on season, with Purple Moose a firm favourite. Accessible by no 8 bus from Pwllheli – but not in the evening. The pub is closed Monday lunchtime in winter.
Q🍽🏨◑🦽🚆P

Waunfawr

Snowdonia Parc

Beddgelert Road, LL55 4AQ
🕐 11-11; 11-10.30 Sun
☎ (01286) 650409 ⊕ snowdonia-parc.co.uk
Banks's Mansfield Dark Mild; Marston's Burton Bitter, Pedigree; guest beers Ⓗ

Home of the Snowdonia Brewery. Meals are served all day. There are children's play areas inside (separate from the bars) and outside. The large campsite gives a discount to CAMRA members. The pub adjoins the station on the Welsh Highland Railway; stop off here before going on to Rhyd Ddu (soon to be Beddgelert) on one of the most scenic sections of narrow gauge railway in Britain.
Q🍽◑🦽🛏🚂≠(Welsh Highland Railway) 🚌(54)♣P

Crown Inn, Llanfihangel Glyn Myfyr, Conwy, North-West Wales.

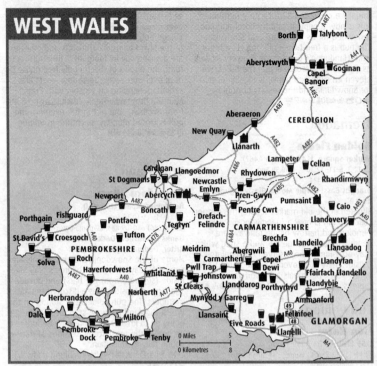

WEST WALES

Borth
Talybont
Aberystwyth
Capel Bangor
Goginan
Aberaeron
CEREDIGION
New Quay
Llanarth
Lampeter
Cellan
Cardigan
Llangoedmor
Rhydowen
Rhandirmwyn
St Dogmaels
Newcastle Emlyn
Newport
Abercych
Pren-Gwyn
Pumsaint
Caio
Boncath
Pentre Cwrt
Porthgain
Fishguard
Pontfaen
Drefach-Felindre
Llandovery
St David's
Croesgoch
Tegryn
CARMARTHENSHIRE
Tufton
Brechfa
Llandeilo
Langadog
PEMBROKESHIRE
Meidrim
Abergwili
Llandyfan
Solva
Roch
Carmarthen
Capel Dewi
Llandybie
Haverfordwest
Pwll Trap
Ffairfach Llandello
Whitland
Johnstown
Llanddarog
Porthyrhyd
Llandybie
Herbrandston
Narberth
St Clears
Mynydd y Garreg
Ammanford
Dale
Milton
Llansaint
Felinfoel
Pembroke Dock
Pembroke
Tenby
Five Roads
Llanelli
GLAMORGAN

0 Miles 5
0 Kilometres 8

Authority areas covered: Carmarthenshire UA, Ceredigion UA, Pembrokeshire UA

CARMARTHENSHIRE
Abergwili

Black Ox
High Street, SA31 2JB
🕐 12 (5 Mon)-midnight (1am Sat); 12-11 Sun
☎ (01267) 222458
Beer range varies Ⓗ
Welcoming village local that has gained a
well-deserved reputation for its excellent
home-cooked food. The bar is open plan but
has three small, distinct drinking areas. There
is a dining room where children are welcome
but meals are also served in the bar areas. The
former palace of the Bishop of St Davids now a
museum is nearby. ⊛◑🛏🌲P

Ammanford

Ammanford Hotel
Wernolau House,, 31 Pontamman Road
🕐 5.30 (1 Sat)-11; 12-10.30 Sun
☎ (01269) 592598
Beer range varies Ⓗ
Originally a colliery manager's house, this
pleasant hotel stands on the outskirts of the
town. It is set in five acres of landscaped
grounds and woodland. It was awarded
Carmarthenshire CAMRA Pub of the Year 2007
not only for the quality of its beer but also for
the warm welcome. Log fires burn in winter
and there is a large function room catering for
weddings and private events.
🏠Q⊛🚃◑🛏🅿P

Caio

Brunant Arms
SA19 8RD (approx 2 miles off A482)
🕐 12-3, 6-11 (1am Fri & Sat); 11-11 Sun
☎ (01558) 650483
Jacobi Light Ale, Original Bitter; guest beers Ⓗ
Traditional beamed pub dating from the 16th
century not far from the Dolau Cothi gold
mines. It is situated in the centre of the village
near the church where a legendary Welsh
wizard is buried and is popular with hikers and
pony-trekkers. Good food is served. The full
range of Jacobi beers is on offer, brewed just
down the road. 🏠◑P

Carmarthen

Queen's Hotel
Queen Street, SA71 1JR
🕐 11-11
☎ (01267) 231800
Draught Bass; guest beers Ⓗ

INDEPENDENT BREWERIES
Black Mountain Llangadog
Coles Llanddarog
Evan Evans Llandeilo
Felinfoel Felinfoel
Ffos y Ffyn Capel Dewi
Flock Brechfa
Gwynant Capel Bangor
Jacobi Pumsaint
Nags Head Abercych
Penlon Cottage Llanarth

Town centre pub near the county hall offices with a bar, lounge and small function room. The public bar is used by locals and has TV for sporting events. Bass is a regular beer complemented by up to two guest ales. The patio area nestles beneath the castle walls and is a suntrap during the summer months. Food is served daily with an option of buying two meals for the price of one. 🏠♿🚪⌐

Drefach Felindre

John y Gwas
SA44 5XG
🕐 2 (5 Mon)-11, 11-11 Fri-Sun
☎ (01559) 370469 ⊕ johnygwas.co.uk
Beer range varies Ⓗ
Traditional village pub with a rustic feel now under new management. A free house, it has two to three real ales on handpump. Home-cooked meals in the restaurant are recommended, with popular roasts on Sunday. The pub has a snug and a main bar with TV, pool table and jukebox. If you want to walk up a thirst, take one of the many woollen mill trails nearby and pop in for a pint – you can even bring your dog. 🏠🏵️◐P⌐

Felinfoel

Harry Watkins
2 Millfield Road, SA14 8HY (on A476)
🕐 12-11; closed Mon
☎ (01554) 776644
Banks's Bitter; Tomos Watkin OSB; guest beer Ⓗ
Renamed after a local rugby hero of yesteryear who features on the pub walls, the pub was originally called the Bear. The open plan split level family friendly pub has defined dining areas and a function room. The garden has a covered area for drinkers. Although there is no car park there is usually ample room on the road outside. Cycle and walking paths to the Swiss Valley Reservoir are nearby. ♿🏵️◐�' ⌐

Ffairfach

Torbay Inn
27 Heol Cennen, SA19 6UL
🕐 6 (11 Sat)-11; 12-10.30 Sun
☎ (01558) 823140
Beer range varies Ⓗ
Friendly pub and restaurant situated by a railway crossing on the Heart of Wales Line. The National Botanical Gardens and other attractions are nearby. The enthusiastic landlord is always happy to discuss beers. The pub is open plan and has a TV showing sporting events. 🏵️◐🚲≠P

Five Roads

Waun Wyllt Inn
Horeb Road, SA15 5AQ (off B3429 at Five Roads)
🕐 11-11
☎ (01269) 860209 ⊕ waunwyllt.com
Greene King Abbot Ale; guest beers Ⓗ
The Waun Wyllt Inn is set in the heart of the Carmarthenshire countryside. It was built in the 18th century and although recently refurbished retains many original features. The

inn was recently purchased by the Great Old Inns pub group and has become its flagship. It offers a warm welcome, good food and beer including a range of bottled real ales. 🏠Q🏵️🚪◐&ÅP

Johnstown

Friends Arms
Old Street Clears Road, SA31 3HH
🕐 11-11
☎ (01267) 234073
Tetley Bitter; guest beers Ⓗ
Lively and welcoming community local with a cosy, low-beamed bar. Adjoining a well-preserved toll house at the former western entry to Carmarthen, there has been a pub on this site for over 400 years. Home to the local carnival committee, regular quiz nights provide entertainment. An interesting selection of bottled beers is stocked. 🏠🏵️🚲🐾⌐

Llandeilo

Salutation
New Road, SA19 6DF
🕐 12-midnight (11 Sun)
☎ (01558) 823325
Greene King Abbot; Tomos Watkin Cwrw Braf, BB Ⓗ
Vibrant pub just away from the centre of town. The central bar serves both the lounge and public bar. A new bistro has been added at the rear of the building. Regular live music is hosted monthly – ring ahead for details. Major sporting events are screened in the bar. 🏠🏵️🍴&🚲⌐

White Horse
Rhosmaen Street, SA19 6EN
🕐 11-11; 12-10.30
☎ (01558) 822424
Evan Evans BB, Cwrw; guest beers Ⓗ
Grade II listed coaching inn dating from the 16th century. This multi-roomed pub is popular with all ages. There is a small outdoor drinking area to the front and a large car park to the rear with access to the pub down a short flight of steps. Regular buses from the town pass by. 🏵️🚲🐾⌐

Llandovery

Red Lion ☆
2 Market Square, SA20 0AA
🕐 5.30-10.30 Fri; 12-2, 7-11 Sat
☎ (01550) 720813
Beer range varies Ⓖ
You are assured of a warm welcome at this superb old pub which features in CAMRA's national inventory of historic interiors. The landlord is semi-retired hence the short opening hours. He is a mine of information about the town and its rugby team – note that Saturday lunchtime hours may vary depending on rugby fixtures. 🏠≠🚲

WALES

Llandybie

Ivy Bush

Church road, SA18 3HZ (100 yards from chruch in village centre)
🕙 12-11 mon ; 12-12 tues-fri ; 11-12 sat; 11-12
☎ (01269) 850272
Butty Bach Wye Valley; guest beer Ⓗ
The oldest pub in the village, this friendly local dates back nearly 300 years. It is close to the station on the Heart of Wales line. Popular for pub games and weekly quizzes, a large-screen TV shows sports. The E-shaped room is served by a single bar with comfortable seating. The guest beer changes regularly. ❀≠🖵(X13)♣

Llandyfan

Square & Compass

SA18 2UD (midway between Ammanford and Trap)
🕙 12 (1 Sat)-11 (4.30-10.30 Mon-Fri winter); 12-6 Sun
☎ (01269) 850402
Beer range varies Ⓗ
Originally the village blacksmith's, this 18th-century building was converted to a pub in the 1960s. Nestling on the western edge of the Brecon Beacons National Park, it offers magnificent panoramic views and plentiful walking opportunities. The pub has a wonderful rustic charm and is packed with yesteryear rural memorabilia. Three guest beers, one from a local brewery, are usually available. Q❀🌢◐♿🅰P

Llanelli

Lemon Tree

2 Prospect Place, SA15 3PT
🕙 12-11
☎ (01554) 775121
Brains Buckley's Best Bitter; Evan Evans BB; guest beer Ⓗ
Well established pub near the site of the former Buckley's Brewery. Popular with locals, it has a strong sports following. The interior, although open plan, is split level, creating different drinking areas. One guest beer is always available. Outside, a covered drinking area has lighting and patio heaters. ❀♣

Llangadog

Red Lion

Church Street, SA19 9AA
🕙 12-midnight
☎ (01550) 777357 ⊕ redlionllangadog.co.uk
Evan Evans Cwrw; guest beers Ⓗ
A recent refurbishment of this Grade II listed 16th-century coaching inn has taken it back to its origins. It was reputed to be a safe house for royalist soldiers during the civil war. Family friendly, it is full of character and atmosphere. Its excellent, fresh, locally produced food attracts locals and tourists alike. Guest beers include local Welsh ales as well as those from across the border. Car parking is through the arch. ♨❀💷◐♿🅰≠🖵P

Telegraph Inn

Station Road, SA19 9LS
🕙 4 (12 Sat)-midnight; 12-11 Sun
☎ (01550) 777727

Black Mountain Black 5; guest beers Ⓗ
On the edge of the village, the inn is next to the railway station on the spectacular Heart of Wales line. It is home to the Black Mountain Brewery which brews weekly. Built around 1830, the welcoming pub has a basic bar area and comfortable lounge. Food is served Wednesday to Saturday including takeaways. Curry night is Wednesday. Self-catering accommodation sleeps five.
♨❀🌢🅰≠🖵(280)P┗

LLansaint

King's Arms

13 Maes yr Eglwys, SA17 5JE (behind church)
🕙 12-2.30, 6-11 (closed Tue winter); 12-2.30, 6.30-10.30 Sun
☎ (01267) 267457
Brains Buckley's Best Bitter; guest beers Ⓗ
This friendly village local has been a pub for more than 200 years. Situated near an 11th-century church, it is reputedly built from stone recovered from the lost village of St Ishmaels. Music and poetry nights are held on the third Friday of the month. Good value home-cooked food is served. Carmarthen Bay Holiday Park is a few miles away. A past winner of CAMRA local Pub of the Year. ♨Q❀💷◐🅰♣P

Meidrim

New Inn

Drefach Road, SA33 5QN (signed off A40)
🕙 10-3, 6-midnight
☎ (01994) 231146 ⊕ the-newinn.co.uk
Brains Buckley's Best, Rev James; guest beer Ⓗ
The hub of the local community, staff and regulars at this 18th century pub in a delightful rural village offer a friendly welcome to visitors. The bar area has a cosy, traditional atmosphere, retaining the original stone walls and flagstone flooring. There is a French influence to the food served in the restaurant, though meals are made with local produce where possible. The pub runs darts teams and has a pool table. ❀💷◐♿🅰P┗

Mynydd y Garreg

Prince of Wales

SA17 4RP
🕙 7 (5 Sat)-11; 12-3 Sun
☎ (01554) 890522
Bullmastiff Brindle, Son of a Bitch; guest beers Ⓗ
This little gem of a pub is well worth seeking out, both for its beer range and its ambience. As well as the two regular Bullmastiff beers there are up to four rotating guest beers, usually from smaller breweries. The cosy single-room bar is packed with movie memorabilia and the small restaurant offers good, reasonably priced food. ♨Q❀◐P

Newcastle Emlyn

Bunch of Grapes

Bridge Street, SA38 9DU
🕙 12-11 (3 Sun)
☎ (01239) 711185
Courage Directors; guest beers Ⓗ

Superb town centre free house with original 17th-century wood beams and flooring run by Billy Brewer, the longest serving landlord in town. The open plan bar has photographs of local interest on the walls. Live music plays on Thursday evening. Excellent food is served in the restaurant. An unusual small but interesting indoor garden has a grapevine and advertising memorabilia. There is also a small enclosed garden at the rear and paved seating at the front adding a continental touch. ▲₩⊛◑♣P≗⌐

Pelican Inn
Sycamore Street, SA38 9AP
🕑 2.30 (12 Fri & Sat)-11.30
☎ (01239) 710606
Draught Bass; guest beer Ⓗ
Friendly local in the heart of the town. If you want to enjoy a decent pint while you watch the rugby, this is the place to be. It has an inviting open fire and there are plenty of cosy nooks for a quiet chat. The pub has Sky TV, a dartboard and pool table. ▲⊛🚲≗⌐

Pentre Cwrt

Plas Parke
Plas Parke Inn, SA44 5AX (on B4335 between Llandysul and Newcastle Emlyn)
🕑 4 (3 Fri-Sun)-11
☎ (01559) 362684
Draught Bass; guest beers Ⓗ
Friendly, family-run business popular with locals and visitors alike. It has two cosy bars and another area for a quiet drink. The restaurant offers good home-made meals with generous portions. In summer sheltered seating is provided in the garden under gazebos. Nearby is the 'Queen of Welsh rivers', the Teifi, where fishermen catch salmon and sewin (sea trout). It is also handy for the canoeing centre and the Teifi Valley narrow gauge railway two miles away at Henllan. ▲⊛◑▲🚲♣P

Pwll Trap

White Lion
St Clears, SA33 4AT
🕑 11-11; 12-10.30 Sun
☎ (01994) 230370
Worthington's Bitter; guest beers Ⓗ
Warm and comfortable pub full of olde worlde charm with a real fire in the pool room and beamed ceilings. It has a spacious restaurant annexe offering a good range of excellent food. Cask beers rotate regularly. Pool and darts are played and TV shown on a plasma screen. A range of events is organised including charity events and quizzes. On street parking is freely available. ▲🚲⊛◑🖰🚲♣♠≗⌐

Rhandirmwyn

Royal Oak
SA20 0NY
🕑 12-3 (2 winter), 6-11; 12-2, 7-10.30 Sun
☎ (01550) 760201 ⊕ rhandirmwyn.com
Beer range varies Ⓗ

Remote, stone-flagged pub with excellent views of the Towy Valley and close to the RSPB bird sanctuary. Originally built as a hunting lodge for the local landowner, it is now a focal point for community activities and popular with fans of outdoor pursuits. A good range of bottled beers and whiskies is stocked, and the good, wholesome food is recommended. ▲▲Q⊛🛏◑▲🚲♣P

St Clears

Corvus Hotel
Station Road, SA33 4BG
🕑 11-1am (2am Sat); 12-1am Sun
☎ (01994) 230965
Beer range varies Ⓗ
Warm and comfortable pub with an olde worlde feel due to the gas imitation coal fire, beams and dark wood interior. Bar snacks are available all day. Sky sports HD is shown on a 42in plasma screen. Regular entertainment is organised including singers, comedians and karaoke. The beer is well kept and rotated regularly, with a good selection of up to 10 bottled ales. On street parking is available. Q🚲◑🖰🚲🚲♣♠⌐

Whitland

Taf Hotel
SA34 0AP
🕑 11.30-11; 12-10.30 Sun
☎ (01994) 240356
Fuller's Chiswick; Greene King Old Speckled Hen Ⓗ
You are guaranteed a warm and friendly welcome from the landlord and landlady at this comfortable pub with a large restaurant annexe. A wide choice of excellent food is available alongside the frequently-changing beers. Pool and darts are played and Sky TV shows sport. A range of events is hosted each month from quizzes to curry nights. On-street parking is freely available. Q🚲⊛◑🖰▲🚲≈≗⌐

CEREDIGION
Aberaeron

Cadwgan
10 Market Street, SA46 0AU
🕑 12 (5 Mon)-midnight (1am Fri & Sat); 12-10.30 Sun
☎ (01545) 570149
Brains Bitter; guest beer Ⓗ
Close to the harbour in this charming regency town, this cosy pub caters to a generally mature clientele. It hosts meetings of various local societies either in the upstairs meeting room or in the single bar, where some fascinating photographs of bygone Aberaeron decorate the walls. The guest beer is selected from a wide range of mainly micro-breweries, though occasionally a second Brains beer may be on offer. ▲⊛◑▲🚲≗⌐

Aberystwyth

Downies Vaults
33 Eastgate, SY23 2AR
🕑 11-1, 7-1am (2am Fri); 11-2am Sat; 2-1am Sun

☎ (01970) 625446

Banks's Original, Bitter; ℗ Marston's Pedigree Ⓗ
Close to the beach and popular with students and townsfolk, the Downies, named after a bygone local worthy, is styled as a Victorian ale house. It is particularly busy when major sporting fixtures are shown on TV, with both rugby and soccer enthusiastically followed on the big screen. Note that the Banks' beers, though served by the now rare metered electric pump dispenser, are most definitely real ale. Opening hours may vary according to university term times. ⇌♣

Fountain Inn

Trefechan, SY23 1BE (S end of Trefechan Bridge)
✪ 12 (2.30 Mon-Fri Nov-Feb)-11.30
☎ (01970) 612430

Brains Dark, SA; guest beer Ⓗ
Close to the harbour in the old industrial (and brewing) quarter of town, this traditional two-bar local extends a friendly welcome with keen prices. The public bar accommodates a pool table while also providing ample drinking space. The cosier lounge has some fine local photographs and a small back room leads to the beer garden. The guest seasonal beer is often from the Brains range. Town buses stop outside, buses to outlying areas are a short walk away. ⊛◑⊟▲⇌♣⌐

Glengower Hotel

Victoria Terrace, SY23 2DH (N end of Promenade)
✪ 12-11
☎ (01970) 626191

Caledonian Deuchars IPA; Theakston Best Bitter; guest beer Ⓗ
Formerly best known as a student drinking haunt, this refurbished seafront hotel has broadened its appeal and offers a warm welcome to all. The outside seating area offers excellent views of the bay (though winter storms can be ferocious). Inside, the back of the pub is dominated by pool and big-screen sport leaving the front bar relatively undisturbed for sociable drinking. A guest beer (usually a fairly mainstream choice) is offered at busy times of year. ⊛⇌◑⇌⊟♣⌐

Hen Orsaf

Alexandra Road, SY23 1LN
✪ 9-midnight
☎ (01970) 636080

Courage Directors; Greene King Abbot; Marston's Pedigree; guest beers Ⓗ
This award-winning Wetherspoon's conversion of Aberystwyth's listed 1920s railway station is the town's largest and most central pub. The glass roofed former station concourse is now used as a beer patio. In an effort to boost guest beer sales, smaller casks are now in use to speed turnover and guarantee quality – two guests are usually available, increasing to four at busy times. Service can be slow at times, sometimes leading to queues at the bar. Q⊛◑&▲⇌⊟♣⌐

Ship & Castle

1 High Street, SY23 1JG (behind market hall)
✪ 2-midnight

Wye Valley Hereford Pale Ale; guest beers Ⓗ
Aber's jewel in the crown – this bare board ale house serves the widest range of real ales in the area to an eclectic mix of customers coming from near and far. A true free house and CAMRA Ceredigion Pub of the Year in 2007, it has five handpulls dispensing an ever-changing range of micro-brewers' beers, particularly from Wales and the borders. Irish music plays on Wednesday night. Beer festivals are held in spring and autumn with extra cider and perry also on offer. ▲⇌⊟♣●

Borth

Victoria Inn

High Street, SY24 5HZ
✪ 10.30-midnight (1am Fri & Sat); 11-midnight Sun
☎ (01970) 871417

Banks's Bitter; guest beer Ⓗ
This lovely beach-side hostelry with superb views over Cardigan Bay has an open plan bar and lounge area with a restaurant. Its fine ale and hearty food attract visitors and locals alike. Family-friendly, it has a children's activity table in the lounge. An interesting collection of ornamental brassware adds to the traditional ambience. The guest beer is sourced from a wide range of regional and smaller brewers. ⊛◑▲⇌⊟(510, 512)♣⌐

Capel Bangor

Tynllidiart Arms

SY23 3LR
✪ 11-3, 5-11.30; 11-11.30 Fri-Sun
☎ (01970) 880248

Gwynant Cwrw Gwynant; St Austell Tribute; Wye Valley Butty Bach; guest beers Ⓗ
This 300-year-old pub has five handpulls in use in summer and three in winter. At the front stands the 'world's smallest commerical brewery' (Guinness Book of Records) supplying limited quantities of Cwrw Gwynant to the pub only. Guest beers are usually from micros. Superb food is available in the restaurant upstairs as well as in the bar. An elevated decking area to the rear provides a quiet haven overlooking the Rheidol Valley, though traffic noise can be a problem at the front. ⋈⊛◑▲⊟(525, G3)P

Cardigan

Black Lion/Llew Du

High Street, SA43 1JW
✪ 11-11; 12-10.30 Sun
☎ (01239) 612532

Brains Rev James; Tomos Watkin OSB; Worthington's Bitter; guest beer Ⓗ
Historic coaching inn in a busy, characterful town. It dates back to the 12th century but the present buildings are 18th century. This friendly meeting place has a main drinking area, small panelled snug and a rear dining section. Good value food is available and four beers now feature, regularly including an interesting guest. ⌐⊟◑▲⊟♣

Grosvenor

SA43 1HY
✪ 11-late; 12-1am
☎ (01239) 613792

Greene King Old Speckled Hen; Worthington's Bitter Ⓗ

Attractive, friendly pub with views of the Teivi estuary from the bar and terrace. It is situated opposite Cardigan Castle which dates from 1169. The first recored Eisteddfod was held in the castle in 1176 to celebrate the completion of the building. Reasonably priced bar meals are available throughout the day in the bar and upstairs restaurant. ⊛◑&🖥♣🍴

Red Lion/Llew Coch
Pwllhai, SA43 1DB
✪ 11-11; 12-10.30 Sun
☎ (01239) 612482
Brains Buckley's Best Bitter; Greene King Old Speckled Hen Ⓗ
Homely local where Welsh is the first language. Visitors are made to feel most welcome. The main bar area is complemented by a smaller private lounge and a restaurant area. Live music is a regular feature here. Snacks are available at most times. Tucked away behind the bus station, this pub is well worth seeking out. ⊛◑▲🖥♣

Cellan

Fishers Arms
SA48 8HU (on B4343)
✪ 4.30-midnight; 12-11 Sat & Sun
☎ (01570) 422895
Tetley Bitter; guest beer Ⓗ
Situated close to the River Teifi, one of Wales' premier trout and salmon rivers, the Fishers dates from 1580 and was first granted a licence in 1891. The cosy main bar has an open fire and flagstone floor, fly rods and antique guns hang from the beamed ceiling. There is also a games room and restaurant. The guest beer is usually from a Welsh brewery. Occasional buses from Lampeter and Tregaron stop nearby. ⋘⊛◑▲🖥♣P

Goginan

Druid Inn
High Street, SY23 3NT
✪ 12-11; 12-10.30 Sun
☎ (01970) 880650
Banks's Bitter; Brains SA; guest beer Ⓗ
A past winner of CAMRA local Pub of the Year, this popular and welcoming village pub is the hub of village life and also enjoys a busy passing trade from A44 road users. Meals are served in the bar or busy restaurant. At quiet times ask to see the rock hewn cellar. Bwlch Nant-yr-Arian forestry centre and Llywernog mining museum are nearby. Well worth a visit if in the area. ⋗⊛�◑🖥(525, G3)♣P

Lampeter

King's Head
14 Bridge Street, SA48 7HG
✪ 11-11
☎ (01570) 422598
Beer range varies Ⓗ
Town centre pub popular with locals and students in this university town which has the oldest established rugby club in Wales. Although the pub is tied to Marston's, the new landlord offers two ever changing guest ales from a variety of small breweries. The pub has

a good reputation for food with special student meal deals. Quiz night is Thursday. ⋘🛏◑🖥&▲🖥♣P🍴

Llangoedmor

Penllwyndu
SA43 2LY (on B4570, 4 miles E of Cardigan) OS241458
✪ 3.30 (12 Sat)-11; 12-10.30 Sun
☎ (01239) 682533
Brains Buckley's Best Bitter; guest beers Ⓗ
Old-fashioned ale house standing on the crossroads where Cardigan's wrong-doers were hanged. The pub sign is worthy of close inspection. Cheerful and welcoming, the public bar has a slate floor and inglenook with wood-burning stove. Bar snacks are usually available and there is a restaurant area for more formal dining. In summer it is a treat to sit out in the garden and enjoy superb views of the Preseli Mountains. There are two guest beers in summer, one in winter, often from Cottage Brewery. ⋘⊛◑♣P

New Quay

Seahorse Inn
Uplands Square, SA45 9QH
✪ 11-midnight (1am Fri & Sat)
☎ (01545) 560736
Beer range varies Ⓗ
This town centre drinkers' local in a seaside resort is busy all year round. On the Dylan Thomas Trail, it is reputed to be the original for the Sailors Arms in Under Milk Wood. The cosy single bar features some sharp local cartoons. Live music plays on Saturday and Sunday evenings, quiz nights are occasionally hosted and there is an annual sloe gin competition. The real ales are drawn from a wide range of brewers large and small, often from Wales and south-west England. ⊛🖥(550, 551)♣🍴

Pren-gwyn

Gwarcefel Arms
SA44 4LU
✪ 12-midnight (1am Fri & Sat; 11 Sun)
☎ (01559) 362720
Beer range varies Ⓗ
Country pub situated at the junction of five roads. The main bar has an open fire with cosy seating and a games area for pool and darts. A separate bar serves the restaurant which caters for functions and parties as well as lunchtime and evening meals. The recommended specials menu changes frequently. Guest beers include ales from Brains, Tomos Watkin, Brecon and Cottage. ⋘⊛◑▲P

Rhydowen

Alltyrodyn Arms
SA44 4QB (at B4459/A475 crossroads)
✪ 3 (12 Sat)-midnight; closed Mon; 12-4 Sun
☎ (01545) 590319
Fuller's London Pride; guest beers Ⓗ
This gem in the countryside village of Rhydowen is well worth a visit. A friendly, family-run free house, the main bar has an

open fire and the pool room has a jukebox. The restaurant offers home-cooked food on Friday and Saturday evenings, and Sunday roasts. Occasional themed foreign food evenings are popular. There are usually three real ales on handpump and a mini beer festival is held in the summer. Dogs are welcome. ♨☸♣P

Talybont

White Lion/Llew Gwyn
SY24 5ER (7 miles N of Aberystwyth on A487)
☼ 11-1am (midnight Sun)
☎ (01970) 832245
Banks's Original, Bitter Ⓗ
Set on the village green, this friendly, family-run local is the hub of village life and a meeting place for groups ranging from young farmers to Welsh poets. The flagstoned public bar, with an alcove for a piano, has a fascinating display of local history and a TV turned on for news or sport. Across the corridor is a family/games room, and there is a cosy dining room at the rear. A covered area outside for smokers is planned.
♨👶☸🖛🌙➕🕹🚗♣P

PEMBROKESHIRE
Abercych

Nags Head
Abercych, Boncath, SA37 0HJ (on B4332)
☼ 11-3, 6-11.30; closed Mon; 12-10.30 Sun
☎ (01239) 841200
Nags Head Old Emrys; guest beers Ⓗ
Well restored old smithy with a beamed bar, riverside garden and children's play area. The bar area is furnished with collections of old medical instruments, railway memorabilia and clocks showing the time in various parts of the world. Space is also found for an extensive display of beer bottles. Old Emrys is no longer brewed on the premises. ☸🕹🌙P🖛

Boncath

Boncath Inn
SA37 0JN (on B4332)
☼ 11-11; 12-10.30 Sun
☎ (01239) 841241
Worthington's Bitter; guest beers Ⓗ
Attractive pub at the centre of village life, dating back to the 18th century. Several seating areas provide an intimate atmosphere. There is a pleasant restaurant serving home-cooked bar meals. A wealth of local history is displayed in old pictures and photographs. A beer festival is held on the August bank holiday weekend at Pembrokeshire CAMRA's Pub of the Year 2006.
♨☸🕹🚗➕♣P🖛

Croesgoch

Artramont Arms
SA62 5JP (on A487)
☼ 12-3, 6-11; 7-11 winter; 12-3, 7-10.30 Sun
☎ (01348) 831309
Brains SA; guest beer Ⓗ

A licensed premises since the 1700s, in the past this pub has also had a post office wing and sold petrol. A friendly village local, it has a large public bar, lounge with dining area and pleasant garden. Good food is available from an interesting and varied menu. ♨☸🕹🌙🖛

Dale

Griffin Inn
SA62 3RB
☼ 12-11 (12-3, 5-11 winter)
☎ (01646) 636227
Fuller's London Pride; guest beers Ⓗ
At the water's edge, close to the slipway, the Griffin is popular with visitors and locals alike. Some of the outside seats are right by the water. Inside, have some fun with the table skittles. The pub is ideally situated for walkers on the Pembrokeshire coastal path.
♨☸🕹🌙♣

Fishguard

Royal Oak Inn
Market Square, SA65 9HA
☼ 11-11; 12-10.30 Sun
☎ (01348) 872514
Beer range varies Ⓗ
Charming, friendly, comfortable pub with historic connections – the French forces landed here following the last invasion of mainland Britain in 1797. Some fascinating memorabilia from this period is on display. This pub is full of character with a public bar and pleasant garden. Home-cooked meals are served at affordable prices from a varied menu.
☸🕹🚗♣🖛

Haverfordwest

Fishguard Arms
7 Old Bridge, SA61 2EZ
☼ 10-1am (2am Sat)
☎ (01437) 768123
Brains Rev James, SA; guest beers Ⓗ
Comfortable, recently refurbished town centre pub with a lively atmosphere enhanced by a juke box. Live music plays on most weekends. The restaurant serves good home-cooked food. ☸🕹➡

Pembroke Yeoman
Hill Street, St Thomas Green, SA61 1QF
☼ 11-11; 12-3, 7-10.30 Sun
☎ (01437) 762500
Draught Bass; Flowers IPA; guest beers Ⓗ
Traditional local pub that attracts a wide range of customers. Conversation is the main entertainment at any time of the day. A meeting place for local organisations, it hosts a quiz night on Wednesday. Guest beers change regularly and are sourced from smaller brewers. Good food is served in generous portions. ♨🕹♣

Herbrandston

Taberna Inn
Milford Haven, SA73 0BP (3 miles W of Milford Haven)
☼ 12-midnight (1.30am Thu; 12.30am Fri-Sat)

☎ (01646) 693498
Beer range varies Ⓗ
Situated just off the Dale road three miles from Milford Haven. The atmosphere is pleasant and the locals are welcoming. It publishes its own good beer guide for all the guest ales it serves throughout the year.
Q✿❀◑ ⬤&P

Milton

Milton Brewery
SA70 8PH (on A477 to Pembroke Dock)
🕑 12-midnight (12-3, 4.30-11.30 winter); 12-3, 4.30-11 Sun
☎ (01646) 651202 ⊕ themiltonbrewery.com
Draught Bass; guest beers Ⓗ
Ivy covered pub just off the A477. This old brew pub ceased brewing in the early 1900s but there are plans to start brewing again using water from the well which is capped at present inside the pub. An extensive range of food is served. It has a large caravan park at the rear. ♨Q✿❀◑&AP⸍

Narberth

Angel Inn
High Street, SA67 7AS
🕑 11-3, 5-11; 7-10.30 Sun
☎ (01834) 860215
Brains Buckley's Best Bitter, Rev James; guest beers Ⓗ
Cosy, modernised town centre pub, popular for food. The lounge bar opens on to the split level dining area and there is a public bar for drinkers. Narberth Station on the Carmarthen Pembroke Dock Line is 20 mintues' walk from town. ♨Q✿❀◑⬤A⸍

Newport

Castle Hotel
Bridge Street, SA42 0TB
🕑 11-11; 12-10.30 Sun
☎ (01239) 820472
Wadworth 6X; Worthington's Bitter; guest beers Ⓗ
This friendly, popular local has an attractive bar with a real fire and a wealth of wood panelling. Food is served at all sessions in the extensive dining area. A large off-street car park is situated behind the hotel.
♨☎✿❀◑ AP⸍

Golden Lion
East Street, SA42 0SY (on A487)
🕑 12-midnight (11 Sun)
☎ (01239) 820321
Brains Rev James; Tomos Watkin OSB; guest beers Ⓗ
Another of Newport's sociable locals – this one is reputed to have a resident ghost. A number of internal walls have been removed to form a spacious bar area with distinct sections, thus retaining a cosy atmosphere. Car parking space is available on the opposite side of the road. ♨Q◑A⬤P⸍

Pembroke

Royal George Hotel
9 Northgate, SA71 4NR
🕑 11-12.30am (1am Fri & Sat)
☎ (01646) 682751
Banks's Original; guest beers Ⓗ
Pleasant cheery local on the old south quay, just on the edge of town. The building, situated directly below Pembroke Castle at what used to be the town's north gate, is part of the old town wall. The interior consists of one large, split-level, L-shaped room with a single bar. Current and future guest ales are listed on a blackboard by the bar.
⬤&⬟⬤♣P

Pembroke Dock

Flying Boat Inn
6 Queen Street, SA72 6JL (off route 9 to docks)
🕑 7am-12.30am; 12-10.30 Sun
☎ (01646) 682810
Beer range varies Ⓗ
This pub has a relaxed and friendly atmosphere. The bar with exposed stone and black beams displays memorabilia from the heyday of flying boats stationed at Pembroke Dock. Traditional pub games are played here including shove ha'penny. Sky Sports is shown on a wide screen TV. A winter beer festival is held in early December. ♨Q⬤⬟&⬟♣⬤

Station Inn
Hawkestone Road, SA72 6JL (in railway station building)
🕑 7-11 Mon; 11-3, 6-midnight (12.30am Fri & Sat); 12-3, 7-10.30 Sun
☎ (01646) 621255 ⊕ station-inn.com
Beer range varies Ⓗ
Housed in a Victorian railway station with the trains still running on the adjoining tracks, this town-centre pub is close to both the Irish ferry terminal and the coast path. It serves excellent value lunches and evening meals. Every Tuesday a new beer is on handpump. It holds a beer festival in June offering around 20 beers. Live music is performed on Saturday evening. Q◑&⬟⬟P

Pontfaen

Dyffryn Arms ☆
SA65 9SG (off B4313) OS027341
🕑 hours vary
☎ (01348) 881305
Draught Bass; Burton Ale Ⓖ
This bar resembles a 1920s front room where time has stood still. The landlady is in her eighties. The beer is still served by the jug through a sliding hatch. Conversation is the main form of entertainment and there is a superb, relaxed atmosphere in the pub. It lies in the heart of the Gwaun Valley between the Prselli mills and Fishguard. This establishment is at the the heart of nearly all local community activity. ♨Q✿A♣

Porthgain

Sloop Inn
SA62 5BN

✪ 11-11 (11.30-3, 6-11 winter); 12-4, 6-10.30 Sun
☎ (01348) 831449
Brains SA; Felinfoel Double Dragon; Worthington's Bitter Ⓗ
Sympathetically modernised old inn that has served both the locally-based fishing industry and the now-defunct quarrying industry. The pub displays quarrying and shipping artefacts as part of the decor. Holding hoppers on the stone can be seen on the opposite side of the harbour. Popular with both locals and visitors, it offers a good choice of beers and well-priced food. ⋒✿◑♣P⏚

Roch

Victoria Inn

SA62 6AW (on A487 St David's Road)
✪ 12-2.30am (10.30 Sun)
☎ (01437) 710426 ⊕ the-victoriainn.co.uk
Beer range varies Ⓗ
A little gem with views across St Brides Bay, this locals' pub offers a warm welcome to all. The inn was established in 1851 although some parts of the building date back to the 18th century. It has retained much of its old world charm with beamed ceilings and low doorways. Welsh food is a speciality and curry night is Friday. For those in a hurry there is a beer carry-out service. Occasional live music plays. ⋒Q✿✿⋈◑⏛&⏛P

St David's

Farmers Arms

12-14 Goat Street, SA62 6RF
✪ 11-11; 12-10.30 Sun
☎ (01437) 720328 ⊕ farmersstdavids.co.uk
Felinfoel Double Dragon; Flowers Original; Wadworth 6X; guest beers Ⓗ
Dating from the 19th century, this stone-built hostelry retains many original features. It is popular with local farmers and fishermen as well as tourists in the summer season. The pub serves an interesting range of good wholesome home-cooked food. Well worth a visit. Q◑▲P⏚

St Dogmaels

White Hart

Finch Street, SA43 3EA
✪ 10 (11 Sun)-11
☎ (01239) 612099
Felinfoel Double Dragon; Greene King IPA; guest beers Ⓗ
Cheery, small village pub with a good local following on the right hand side of the road when entering St Dogmaels from Cardigan. The guest beers change on a regular basis and are often from breweries not usually found in the area. Three guest ales are served in summer and two in winter. The landlord is a rugby enthusiast. Opening hours are extended in summer and the pub is a good place to stop off for walkers on the Pembrokeshire coast path. ⋒Q◑▲P⏚

Solva

Cambrian Inn

SA62 6UU (on A487)

✪ 11-11
☎ (01437) 721210
Tomos Watkin OSB; guest beers Ⓗ
Situated in a popular costal village, this sympathically restored local pub now serves real ales and good food. The bar area has been decorated with local crafts, creating a cosy atmosphere enjoyed by village residents and visitors alike. Q◑▲P⏚

Harbour Inn

SA62 6RF (on A487 adjoining harbour)
✪ 11-11; 12-10.30 Sun
☎ (01437) 720013
Brains Dark, SA; guest beers Ⓗ
This delightful seaside hostelry with a traditional atmosphere remains the same year after year. It serves as a base for many community activities and is very popular with locals who come to enjoy a quiet, relaxing pint. Camping facilities are close by for caravans and tents. ⋒Q✿✿⋈◑▲⏛P⏚

Tegryn

Butchers Arms

SA35 0BL
✪ 12-2 (not Mon), 6 (7 Mon)-11
☎ (01239) 698680
Beer range varies Ⓗ
Rural pub off the beaten track in a hard to find location, but on cycle route 47. It has been attractively refurbished with local slate on the walls and floor. It has a games room with a mobile skittle alley. A beer festival is held every July. ⋒Q✿⋈◑⏛♣P

Tenby

Hope & Anchor

St Julian Street, SA70 7AS
✪ 11-11; 12.30-10.30 Sun
☎ (01834) 842131
Brains Rev James; guest beers Ⓗ
Near the harbour and close to the beaches, the pub caters for locals and tourists alike. A range of bar snacks makes it an ideal place to take a break when walking to and from the beaches and harbour. It has a drinking and dining area outside. The medieval town walls can be seen nearby. ⋒✿◑▲⇌♣⏚

Tufton

Tufton Arms

Claberston Road, SA63 4TU
✪ 6-11; closed Sun
☎ (01437) 532692
Wye Valley Butty Bach; guest beers Ⓗ
A meeting place for the community, this locals' pub is the hub of a village where there are no other pubs or shops for two miles. Within easy reach of the Preseli Hills, it is a fine place to relax after a long walk. Bingo is held on the third Wednesday of the month and a beer festival on the first Friday in July. ⋒Q✿&P⏚

Scotland

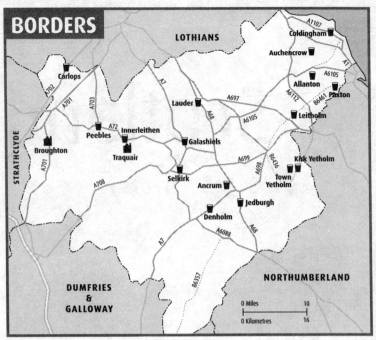

BORDERS

LOTHIANS

Coldingham

Auchencrow

Carlops

Allanton

Paxton

Lauder

Leitholm

Innerleithen

Peebles

Galashiels

Broughton

Traquair

Kirk Yetholm

Selkirk

Ancrum

Town Yetholm

Jedburgh

Denholm

STRATHCLYDE

DUMFRIES & GALLOWAY

NORTHUMBERLAND

0 Miles 10
0 Kilometres 16

Authority area covered: Scottish Borders UA

Allanton

Allanton Inn

TD11 3JZ
☼ 12-2 (not Mon & Tue), 6-11 (10.30 Wed; 11.30 Fri & Sat); 12-2, 6-11 Sun
☎ (01890) 818260 ⊕ allantoninn.co.uk
Beer range varies Ⓗ
Welcoming Borders coaching inn in a small village surrounded by rolling farmland. Hitching rings by the door are useful if you arrive by horse. The front rooms are for dining, with a good, varied menu on offer (booking recommended), while the back bar serves an interesting selection of up to three real ales. There are plans for an extension to the bar opening onto the lovely rear garden. Well-behaved dogs are welcome. The bar is closed Sunday evening and all day Monday in winter.
ᛗQ✿⌂✍◑⇔♣P

Ancrum

Cross Keys Inn

The Green, TD8 6XH (on B6400, off A68)
☼ 12 (6 Mon-Fri winter)-11 (midnight Thu-Sat; 1am Fri); 12.30-11 Sun
☎ (01835) 830344 ⊕ ancrumcrosskeys.co.uk
Beer range varies Ⓗ
Friendly village local with a bar that has changed little since 1908, retaining the original pine panelling through into the gantry. The bar has compact seating and tables made from old sewing machines. The spacious back lounge has been sympathetically refurbished and retains overhead tramlines from the former cellar. A good, varied menu is supplemented by daily specials. Beers are often from Broughton

Brewery. Children are welcome and dogs are also permitted in the bar.
ᛗQ✿⌂◑⇔&⇔♣P

Auchencrow

Craw Inn

TD14 5LS (signed from A1)
☼ 12-2.30, 6-11 (midnight Fri); 12- midnight Sat; 12.30-11 Sun
☎ (01890) 761253 ⊕ thecrawinn.co.uk
Beer range varies Ⓗ
Friendly village inn, circa 1680. The beamed bar has bench seating at one end and wooden tables, chairs and a church pew by the log-burning stove at the other. The two beers are usually from smaller breweries, and change regularly. The rear is divided into a lounge/dining area and restaurant, with traditional furniture giving a select feel. Local produce is used in many dishes on the wide-ranging menu. Children are welcome. A beer festival is held in November. ᛗQ✿⌂◑⇔♣P

Carlops

Allan Ramsay Hotel

Main Street, EH26 9NF
☼ 12-11 (1am Fri & Sat); 12.30-11 Sun
☎ (01968) 660258 ⊕ allanramsayhotel.co.uk
Caledonian Deuchars IPA; guest beer Ⓗ
Set in a small village beside the Pentland hills, the hotel dates from 1792. Several rooms have been knocked through into a single area,

retaining many original features including the fine stone fireplace. At one end is the restaurant, the bar is in the centre and a pool table occupies the far end. Tartan upholstery gives a Scottish feel. The bar is inlayed with pre-decimal pennies. Children and dogs are welcome and food is served all day Sunday and in the summer. ⚐❀⚲◀❶◗🍴♣P

Coldingham

Anchor Inn
School Road, TD14 5NS
☉ 12-midnight (may be earlier in winter)
☎ (01890) 771243
Beer range varies Ⓗ
Sympathetically renovated and extended, the wood-panelled bar is decorated with local photographs. The walls in the cosy, well-appointed lounge feature more photos along with a mirror recovered from the wreck of the Glenmire, which sank off St Abbs head in 1910. There is an attractive dining room at the rear. The menu is extensive and has a good vegetarian selection. Children are welcome in the lounge and dining room.
⚐Q❀◀❶▲🖵(235)♣

Denholm

Fox & Hounds Inn
Main Street, TD9 8NU
☉ 11-3, 5-midnight (1am Fri); 11-1am Sat; 12.30-midnight Sun
☎ (01450) 870247 ∰ foxandhoundsinndenholm.co.uk
Wylam Gold Tankard; guest beer Ⓗ
Village local, built in 1728, overlooking the village green. The main bar is light and retains the original beams with a real fire giving it a cosy feel in winter. Pictures and memorabilia decorate the walls. The rear lounge has a coffee house feel. The dining room is upstairs. In summer a courtyard is used for sheltered outdoor drinking, and is now the all year smoking area. Children are welcome until 8pm and dogs are also permitted.
⚐❀⚲◀❶ 🖵🖵♣⭘

Galashiels

Ladhope Inn
33 High Buckholmside, TD1 2HR (A7, half mile N of centre)
☉ 11-3, 5-11; 11-11 Wed; 11-midnight Thu-Sat; 12.30-midnight Sun
☎ (01896) 752446
Caledonian Deuchars IPA; guest beer Ⓗ
Comfortable, friendly local with a vibrant Borders atmosphere. Originating circa 1792, it has been altered considerably inside and now comprises a single room decorated with whisky jugs and a large inked map of the Galashiels area. A wee alcove has a golfing theme. Three flat-screen TVs ensure the pub is busy during sporting events. The guest beer is often from Hadrian & Border but changes regularly. Children and dogs are welcome.
❀▲🖵♣

Salmon Inn
54 Bank Street, TD1 1EP (opp Gardens)
☉ 11-11 (midnight Thu, 1am Fri & Sat); 12.30-11 Sun

☎ (01896) 752577
Caledonian Deuchars IPA; guest beers Ⓗ
Centrally situated by the fountain and gardens, this comfortable, friendly, single-room pub is split into two areas. Historic photographs of the Galashiels area decorate the walls. It can be very lively when sports events are shown on the flat screen TVs. The guest beer, often from a smaller brewery, changes regularly. Good, home-cooked meals are popular (no food on Sunday). Children are welcome at lunchtime. Dogs are also permitted. ❀◀❶▲🖵♣

Innerleithen

St Ronan's Hotel
High Street, EH44 6HF
☉ 11-midnight (12.45am Fri & Sat); 12-midnight Sun
☎ (01896) 831487
Beer range varies Ⓗ
This local village hotel takes its name from the local Saint who is also associated with a well. The functional public bar is long and thin and has a brick and wooden fireplace. There are two alcoves, one with seating, the other with a dartboard and a wide-angled photograph of the village. A further room has a pool table. Food is only served in the summer. A pick up service is available for Southern Upland Way walkers. Children and dogs are welcome.
⚐❀⚲◀❶▲🖵(62)♣P⬆

Traquair Arms Hotel
Traquair Road, EH44 6PD (B709, off A72)
☉ 11-11 (midnight Fri & Sat); 12-11.30 Sun
☎ (01896) 830229 ∰ traquair-arms-hotel.co.uk
Caledonian Deuchars IPA, 80; Traquair Bear Ale Ⓗ
Elegant 18th-century hotel in the scenic Tweed Valley. The comfortable lounge bar features a welcoming real fire in winter and a relaxing tropical fish tank. A bistro area and separate restaurant provide plenty of room for diners. Food is served all day at weekends. The bar is one of the few outlets for draft ales from Traquair House. Children are welcome.
⚐❀⚲◀❶▲🖵(62)P

Jedburgh

Spreadeagle Hotel
20 High Street, TD8 6AG
☉ 12-11 (midnight Fri & Sat); 12-11 Sun
☎ (01835) 862870 ∰ spreadeaglejedburgh.co.uk
Beer range varies Ⓗ
Georgian façaded old town hotel undergoing renovation by enthusiastic new owners. The functional public bar, entered through a fine half-glazed door, has wood panelled walls and an unusual blue tiled floor. It is furnished with wooden tables, chairs and stools. There is a further alcoved seating area and an additional room. The guest beer is often from Hadrian & Border or Wylam brewery. Dogs are welcome.
❀⚲🖲▲🖵♣P

Kirk Yetholm

Border Hotel
The Green, TD5 8PQ

SCOTLAND

✪ 11-midnight (1am Fri & Sat); 12-midnight Sun (closes 1 hour earlier in winter)
☎ (01573) 420237 ⊕ theborderhotel.com
Beer range varies Ⓗ
Built in 1750 as a coaching inn, the front was rebuilt following a fire in 2006. Situated at the end of the Pennine Way and on St Cuthbert's Way, it is popular with walkers. The wood-beamed bar has a practical feel, with stone-flagged floor and red vinyl banquette seating, decorated with photographs and horse brasses. A warren of small rooms lead off, with two snugs, a pool room and conservatory dining area. Dogs and children are welcome. The garden has a play area.
🏨✿🛏◑⑅👪🚃🅿︎⚓️

Lauder

Black Bull Hotel
Market Place, TD2 6SR
✪ 12-11 (midnight Sat); 12-2.30, 5-11 winter; 12-11 Sun
☎ (01578) 722208 ⊕ blackbull-lauder.com
Beer range varies Ⓗ
A changing range of beers supplied by Broughton Ales is on offer at this well-appointed old coaching inn. The small wood-panelled bar is adorned with artefacts and retains much of the character of yesteryear. Sporting and historical prints decorate the walls. Excellent food is served in various dining areas with main courses averaging around £9; favourites include Guinness and mushroom pie, fillet of salmon or breast of duck. Close to the Southern Upland Way, dogs and children are welcome.
Q✿🛏◑⑅👪🚃(29)⚓️🅿︎

Leitholm

Plough Hotel
Main Street, TD12 4JN
✪ 12-midnight (1am Fri & Sat)
☎ (01890) 840252
Hadrian & Border Farne Island Pale Ale; guest beers Ⓗ
Terraced pub dating from the 19th century on the main street of this quiet Borders village. The simple, plain interior is comfortably furnished and decorated with prints of local scenes. There is a separate dining room and small lounge. The real fire, in winter at least, and the resident golden retriever provide a welcoming and homely atmosphere. Children are permitted in the lounge and dogs too, provided they don't upset the retriever. No food is served on Monday.
🏨✿🛏◑⑅👪🅿︎⚓️🅿︎

Paxton

Cross Inn
TD15 1TE (off B6460)
✪ 11 (12.30am Sun)-3, 6.30-midnight (closed Mon)
☎ (01289) 386267
Beer range varies Ⓗ
Friendly village pub, circa 1870s, named after the recently restored old cross outside. The real ale is often from Wylam or Stewart Brewing. Recent refurbishment has given the wood-panelled bar room a brighter and more modern appearance. Although now more spacious, it retains an intimate feel. The appealing, extensive menu features home-cooked dishes made with locally sourced ingredients. Children are welcome but dogs are only permitted after 9pm. ✿◑⑅👪🚃⚓️🅿︎⚓️

Peebles

Bridge Inn
Portbrae, EH45 8AW
✪ 11 (12.30am Sun)-midnight
☎ (01721) 720589
Caledonian Deuchars IPA; Stewart Pentland IPA; Taylor Landlord; guest beer Ⓗ
Cheerful, welcoming single-room town-centre local, also known as the 'Trust'. The mosaic entrance floor shows it was once the Tweeddale Inn. The bright, comfortable bar is decorated with jugs, bottles, memorabilia of outdoor pursuits and photos of old Peebles. The Gents is superb, with well-maintained original Twyford Adamant urinals. A child free zone, but dogs are welcome. An outdoor heated patio area overlooks the river. Awarded CAMRA Borders Pub of the Year 2004-2006. The house beer is Atlas Three Sisters rebadged as Tweedside Ale.
✿👪🚃(62)⚓️⚓️

Selkirk

Heatherlie House Hotel
Heatherlie Park, TD7 5AL (half mile W of centre)
✪ 12-11 (midnight Fri & Sat); 12.30-midnight Sun
☎ (01750) 721200 ⊕ heatherlie.freeserve.co.uk
Beer range varies Ⓗ
Family run hotel in tranquil surroundings. Once a Victorian villa, it retains a stately air of grandeur with beautiful cornices and a magnificent hand-carved fireplace in the entrance depicting barn owls. The bar, which has a dining area, is comfortable and airy, with views through the large bay windows to the gardens. In winter the single real ale is often from Broughton or Caledonian. In summer a choice is available. Children are welcome until 8pm. 🏨✿🛏◑👪🚃🅿︎

Town Yetholm

Plough Hotel
High Street, TD5 8RF
✪ 11-midnight (1am Fri & Sat)
☎ (01573) 420215
Beer range varies Ⓗ
Friendly village local dating from 1710 set in idyllic surrounds near the end of the Pennine Way. The pleasant public bar has Tudor-style décor and a real fire. The functional games room has a pool table and video machine. There is also a small, tastefully decorated dining room. Horse brasses and memorabilia of the gypsy king and queen adorn the walls, along with the leek growers' memorial board. Children are welcome until 8.30pm and dogs are permitted. 🏨✿🛏◑⑅👪🚃👪⚓️🅿︎

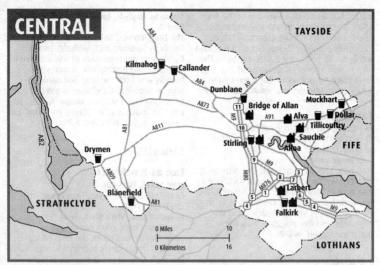

CENTRAL

Authority areas covered: Clackmannanshire UA, Falkirk UA, Stirling UA

Blanefield

Carbeth Inn

Stockiemuir Road, G63 9AY (on A809 N of Milngavie, near B821 jct)
🕐 11-11 (midnight Fri & Sat); 12.30-11 Sun
☎ (01360) 770 002
Beer range varies Ⓗ
Established in 1816, this country pub features in Walter Scott's novel Rob Roy and continues to be a popular inn for locals and visitors. Considerable amounts of wood, a flagstone floor and two stoves lend the interior much character. An ever-changing guest ale from the handpump complements the good food. Near to Mugdock Country Park, the West Highland Way and the Whangie (a hill providing views over Loch Lomond), it is frequented by walkers and bikers, and makes for a pleasant destination from Glasgow.
🚶🌳🕪&🚐(8)P⌐

Callander

Waverley Hotel

88-92 Main Street, FK17 8BD
🕐 11-midnight (1am Fri & Sat)
☎ (01877) 330245 🌐 thewaverleycallander.com
Beer range varies Ⓗ
Renowned for its quality and range of good ales, the Waverley also hosts two beer festivals each year in September and December. There may be up to four ales available, increasing to around eight including some from mainland Europe at the height of the season. Ideally sited for tourists, on the whisky trail in beautiful Perthshire, the pub is also well known for its good food using mainly local ingredients. Q🚶🕪Å♣

Dollar

Castle Campbell Hotel

11 Bridge Street, FK14 7DE
🕐 11-11.30 (1am Fri, midnight Sat); 12.30-11 Sun
☎ (01259) 742519 🌐 castle-campbell.co.uk

Caledonian Deuchars IPA; Harviestoun Bitter & Twisted Ⓗ
Pleasant hotel with a refurbished lounge bar and two further lounges, situated in the village of Dollar at the foot of the Ochil Hills. The historic Castle Campbell overlooks the village at the top of Dollar Glen and can be reached either by an excellent walk up the glen or via a steep road. The hotel is well presented with interesting wall decorations. A large range of whiskies is on offer in the lounge bar. Q🚶🕪Å🚐P⌐

Drymen

Winnock Hotel

The Square, G63 0BL
🕐 11-midnight (1am Fri & Sat); 12-midnight Sun
☎ (01360) 660 245 🌐 winnockhotel.com
Caledonian Deuchars IPA, 80 Ⓗ
Whitewashed hotel dating from 1702 occupying one side of the green in a picturesque village east of Loch Lomond. Updated by a recent refurbishment, the bar retains its wood beams, log fire and other original features. The lower lounge, finished in light oak panelling, provides comfortable seating. Bar food is available and the restaurant serves Scottish specialities. Live Scottish music is hosted on Friday night. It is well situated for those visiting Loch Lomond & Trossachs National Park or walking the West Highland Way. 🚶🌳🕪Å🚐P⌐

Dunblane

Dunblane Hotel

10 Stirling Road, FK15 9EP (opp railway station)
🕐 11-midnight (1am Fri & Sat)
☎ (01786) 822178
Greene King Abbot Ale; Taylor Landlord; guest beers Ⓗ
Situated next to the railway station, this is a popular stop off for those on their way home from work. The bar is comfortable and decorated with old brewery mirrors. The

lounge has an excellent view over the River Allan. A good range of national and micro beers is on offer – there are usually three frequently changing ales on tap, so it is always worth a visit just to try a different beer. The area is well known for golfing and this is an ideal place for golfers to stay overnight in small, cosy surroundings. ⊛☎◑◗⬛♿≉♣P

Tappit Hen
Kirk Street, FK15 0AL (opp cathedral)
🕓 11-11.45 (12.45am Fri & Sat); 12.30-11.30 Sun
☎ (01786) 825226
Beer range varies Ⓗ
Real pub, popular with locals and discerning drinkers, with a single bar room partitioned into smaller areas by the use of screens. The town, with an imposing Cathedral, is in an ideal position to visit Gleneagles and the Highlands. Just five minutes' walk from Dunblane station. ≉🖭♣

Falkirk

Behind the Wall
14 Melville Street, FK1 1HZ
🕓 11 (12 Sun)-midnight (1am Fri & Sat)
☎ (01324) 633338 ⊕ behindthewall.co.uk
Beer range varies Ⓗ
Established in 1985 and still managed by the original owners, Behind the Wall is a bar, restaurant and micro-brewery under one roof. The interior is a mix of traditional and contemporary, with a bistro-style restaurant area. Four guest ales are normally on offer. Beer from the Eglesbrech Brewing Company is kept under blanket pressure.
⊛◑≉(Falkirk Grahamston)🖭

Carron Works
Bank Street, FK1 1NB
🕓 9am-midnight (1am Fri & Sat)
☎ (01324) 673020
Beer range varies Ⓗ
Large, single room pub situated in an old cinema, with several seating areas at different levels. Up to six ales are available; the real cider is Weston's Old Rosie.
◑≉(Falkirk Grahamston)🖭♣

Wheatsheaf Inn
16 Baxters Wynd, FK1 1PF
🕓 11-11 (12.30am Sat); 12.30-11 Sun
☎ (01324) 623716
Caledonian Deuchars IPA; guest beers Ⓗ
A firm favourite with locals and real ale enthusiasts alike, this public house dates from the late 18th century and retains much of its character. The bar is wood panelled with a mix of features from the past. A regular winner of CAMRA's local branch Pub of the Year award, this is definitely one to visit. Two guest beers are usually available.
≉(Grahamston/Falkirk High)🖭

Kilmahog

Lade Inn
FK17 8HD (A84/A821 jct, 1 mile W of Callander)
🕓 12-11 (1am Fri & Sat); 12.30-11 Sun
☎ (01877) 330152 ⊕ theladeinn.com

Trossachs Waylade, Ladeback Ladeout; guest beer Ⓗ
The Lade Inn was purchased by the Parks family in Summer 2005 with the aim of building on the reputation of this well known local pub. The atmosphere is warm and friendly and both the food and drink are popular with locals and tourists alike. The three cask beers sold are unique to the Lade Inn. Live music is often played on Friday and Saturday nights. ⋈☎◑⬛♿P

Muckhart

Inn at Muckhart
Main Street, FK14 7JN
🕓 11-11 (midnight Fri & Sat); 12.30-11 Sun
☎ (01259) 781324
Devon Original, Thick Black, Pride Ⓗ
This atmospheric 200-year-old pub is conveniently located on the A91, which passes through lovely countryside and skirts the south side of the Ochil Hills, making it an ideal place for walkers or tourists to stop off for a meal or a drink. It sells the locally produced Devon Ales, brewed at its sister pub, the Mansfield Arms at Sauchie. A fine example of an old coaching inn operating as a pub and restaurant. ⋈⊛⋈◑♿▲P⬛♿⊟

Stirling

Birds & Bees
Easter Cornton Road, Causewayhead, FK9 5PB
🕓 11-11.45 (12.45am Fri & Sat); 12.30-11.45 Sun
☎ (01786) 463384 ⊕ thebirdsandthebees-stirling.com
Beer range varies Ⓗ
Located in a residential area, this converted farm building is popular with locals. Its decor reflects its semi-rural setting. Ample seating and parking make it a popular choice for a pub meal. The beer garden includes a large covered area and adjoining barbecue. Customers may also enjoy a game of petanque. There are always two ales on sale. ⋈⊛◑♿⬛P⬛♿

No 2 Baker Street
2 Baker Street, FK9 1BJ
🕓 11-midnight (1am Fri & Sat); 12.30-midnight Sun
☎ (01786) 448722
Beer range varies Ⓗ
Bustling, noisy pub, popular with local residents and students. It hosts live Scottish music on Wednesday, a 60s/70s disco every second Friday and a live music event once a month on Saturday. The interior is traditional with bare floorboards and paintings depicting local history on the walls. There are tables on the pavement outside for drinking alfresco.
⊛◑≉🖭

Portcullis Hotel
Castle Wynd, FK8 1EG
☼ 11.30 (12.30 Sun)-midnight
☎ (01786) 472290
Orkney Dark Island; guest beers ⊞
Situated close to Stirling Castle, the Portcullis is a popular pub with tourists and locals alike. Renowned for good food and fine ale, booking is advised for evening and weekend dining during the tourist season. Located in a former 18th-century grammar school, the building reflects the historic nature of its setting.
🏚Q❀⇙◑≉⊟P

Tillicoultry

Woolpack
1 Glassford Square, FK13 6AU (W end of town)
☼ 11-midnight (1am Fri & Sat); 12.30-midnight Sun
☎ (01259) 750332
Beer range varies ⊞
Old drovers' inn tucked away behind the village at the bottom of the Tillicoultry Glen which leads to the Ochil Hills. The pub has a number of small rooms with low ceilings creating a cosy atmosphere. This cheerful hostelry is popular with hill walkers in summer and gets busy at weekends. A blazing fire in the winter months helps to make this an ideal stop off after coming off the hill. Three handpumps dispense frequently changing ales and the bar stocks an excellent range of malt whiskies. No food is served on Monday.
Q◑⊟♣

Harviestoun Bitter & Twisted, brewed in Alva, Central.

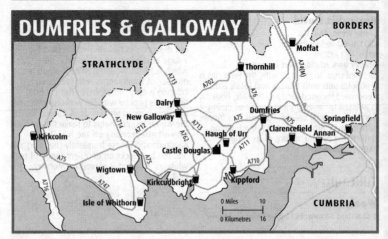

DUMFRIES & GALLOWAY

Authority area covered: Dumfries & Galloway UA

Annan

Bluebell Inn

10 High Street, DG12 6AG
⊕ 11-11 (midnight Thu-Sat); 12.30-11 Sun
☎ (01461) 202385
Caledonian Deuchars IPA; guest beer Ⓗ
Fine old coaching inn retaining original panelling and features from its time as a Gretna & District State Management Scheme house. Adjacent to the River Annan, it is easily identified by the large blue bell above the main entrance. This friendly pub offers a wide selection of beers from across the UK. It has pool, darts and large-screen TV. During the summer you can drink outside in the rear courtyard. ⚘Å≈⊟♣⌐

Clarencefield

Farmers Inn

Main Street, DG1 4NF (on B724)
⊕ 11-2.30, 6-11.30 (12.30am Fri); 12-12.30am Sat; 12.30-11.30 Sun
☎ (01387) 870675 ⊕ farmersinn.co.uk
Beer range varies Ⓗ
Late 16th-century coaching inn with a varied history. The current building opened in 1983 with the original bar area still in use. It was the post office and also housed the village's first telephone exchange. Robert Burns was a customer when he came on a visit to the Brow Well for health reasons. Nearby tourist attractions include the world's first savings bank at Ruthwell and the 8th-century Ruthwell Cross. ⚏≽⚘⇄⊕♿⊟♣P

Dalry

Clachan Inn

8-10 Main Street, DG7 3UW (on A713 in centre of village)
⊕ 11 (12 Sun)-midnight
☎ (01644) 430241 ⊕ clachaninn.com
Greene King Abbot; guest beer Ⓗ
The Clachan Inn is set in the picturesque village of St. John's Town of Dalry, which straddles the A713. The area has a growing reputation for country pursuits and walkers are particularly welcome at this stopping off point along the Southern Upland Way. A year round special walkers' rate is available for accommodation. The pub has a varied menu and prides itself on using local produce as much as possible. There are usually two real ales on tap. The bus service from Castle Douglas is limited. ⚏⚘⇄⊕⊟♿Å⊟♣P

Dumfries

Cavens Arms

20 Buccleuch Street, DG1 2AH
⊕ 11-11 (midnight Wed-Sat); 12.30-11 Sun
☎ (01387) 252896
Caledonian Deuchars IPA; Greene King Abbot Ale; guest beer Ⓗ
Lively town centre pub with a varied selection of beers on tap. Customers are encouraged to request beers that they would like to try and if they leave a contact number they are notified when the ales are available at the bar. A range of good value meals is served from 11.30am until 9.00pm every day except Monday (Sun from 12.30pm). There are occasional traditional music sessions and themed nights. Local CAMRA Pub of the Year in 2007.
⊕⇄(Dumfries)⊟

Coach & Horses

66 Whitesands, DG1 2RS
⊕ 11 (12.30 Sun)-11
☎ (01387) 265224
Draught Bass Ⓗ
Next door to the Tourist Information Centre on Whitesands in the town centre, this pub was extensively renovated in 2006. It now has a very pleasant, spacious bar area with a fabulous flagstone floor. The food menu includes a variety of excellent, freshly cooked dishes served in the upstairs dining room. Occasional music sessions are hosted. Car parking is nearby. Q⊕♿⇄⊟♣

INDEPENDENT BREWERIES

Sulwath Castle Douglas

New Bazaar

39 Whitesands, DG1 2RS

🕑 11-11 (midnight Thu-Sat); 12.30 – 11 Sun

☎ (01387) 268776 ⊕ newbazaardumfries.co.uk

Greene King Abbot Ale; Theakston XB; guest beer Ⓗ

The Bazaar is a former coaching inn beside the river Nith in the town centre with a pleasing Victorian gantry in the small, welcoming bar. The pub also has a cosy, quiet lounge with a warming coal fire in winter, and another room available for meetings. Ideally situated for local tourist attractions, there is car parking nearby. Popular with football fans on match days. ⚫≈🖥♣⏴

Robert the Bruce

81-83 Buccleuch Street, DG1 IDJ

🕑 11-midnight (1am Fri & Sat); 12.30-midnight Sun

☎ (01387) 270320

Caledonian Deuchars IPA; Strathaven Robert the Bruce; guest beer Ⓗ

Former 19th-century church, sympathetically converted for the Wetherspoon pub group in 2001. The pub has a relaxed, comfortable atmosphere and has established itself as a favourite meeting place in the town centre. It has an interesting mezzanine gallery above the spacious bar area. The Strathaven Brewery produces the house beer, Robert the Bruce. There is an outside smoking and seating area. ⚫🕻&≈🖥⏴

Haugh of Urr

Laurie Arms Hotel

11-13 Main Street, DG7 3YA (on B794, 1 Mile S of A75)

🕑 12-3, 5.30-midnight

☎ (01556) 660246

Beer range varies Ⓗ

Welcoming family-run pub and restaurant on the main street of a quiet village in the scenic valley of the River Urr. It is popular with locals and visitors for its range of well-kept ales and good food, often featuring local produce. Up to four real ales are available depending on the season, sourced mainly from independent breweries across Britain. Open fires set in local stone fireplaces feature in both main rooms. A beer garden is being re-established. ⚫Q🕻🖥♣P

Isle of Whithorn

Steampacket Inn

Harbour Row, DG8 8LL (A750)

🕑 11-11 (1am Fri; 12.30am Sat); hours vary in winter; 12-11 Sun

☎ (01988) 500334 ⊕ steampacketinn.com

Theakston XB; guest beers Ⓗ

Run by the same family for over 20 years, this pub sits on the quayside overlooking the harbour. It caters for an eclectic mix of locals, tourists and fishermen who come to enjoy the informal atmosphere. Meals, featuring local produce, can be enjoyed in the lounge bar or restaurant (booking is advised for summer weekend evenings). Real ale is served in both the lounge and public bar (10p per pint cheaper in the latter). The two guest ales are usually from the Houston brewery and the

north of England, although local Sulwath beers sometimes feature. ⚫Q🕻❄🖥🕻🖥(415)♣

Kippford

Anchor Hotel

DG5 4LN

🕑 11-3, 6-11 (midnight summer)

☎ (01556) 620205

Beer range varies Ⓗ

Situated on the main street in the heart of this popular sailing centre, this friendly inn has fine views over the Urr estuary. The varied menu includes meals made with local produce as well as good vegetarian options. One real ale is stocked throughout the year, more during the tourist season. Beers from Sulwath Brewery are usually available. There is an infrequent daytime bus service for using public transport. 🖥🕻▶🅰🖥P

Kirkcolm

Blue Peter Hotel

23 Main Street, DG9 0NL (A718 5 miles N of Stranraer)

🕑 6-11.30; 12-midnight Sat; 12.30-11.30 Sun

☎ (01776) 853221 ⊕ thebluepeterhotel.co.uk

Beer range varies Ⓗ

Family-owned hotel set in a beautiful area ideally situated for golfers, fishermen and bird watchers. Both lounge and public bars display beer memorabilia – look out for the model beer trucks and tankers. Rotating guest ales and a selection of over 70 malt whiskies are available. Good quality food is based on local produce. Red squirrels and other wildlife can be seen from the beer garden. Joint local CAMRA Pub of the Year 2006. A discount on accommodation is available to CAMRA members. ⚫Q🕻❄🖥🕻🖥&🅰🖥(408)P

Kirkcudbright

Masonic Arms

19 Castle Street, DG6 4JA

🕑 11 (12.30 Sun)-midnight

☎ (01557) 330517

Taylor Landlord; guest beer Ⓗ

This small, sociable bar is welcoming to both locals and visitors. The tables and bar fronts are made from old malt whisky casks from Islay's Bowmore Distillery. One real ale is available throughout the year with up to two more during the summer months. The Masonic also offers draught Budvar, a selection of 30 bottled beers from all over the world, and 100 malt whiskies. The town is very picturesque with a variety of tourist attractions. ⚫Q🅰🖥♣

Springfield

Queen's Head

Main Street, DG16 5EH

🕑 5 (12 Sat)-11 (mid Thu & Fri); 12.30-11 Sun

☎ (01461) 337173

Caledonian Deuchars IPA Ⓗ

This single-room village pub, although slightly off the beaten track, is actually little more than a stone's throw from Gretna, wedding

SCOTLAND

capital of the country. It is very close to the A74(M) and about a mile from Gretna Green railway station. Just one real ale is served in this friendly, unpretentious local. Note there is no lunchtime opening on weekdays.
❀₪(382)♣P

Thornhill

Buccleuch & Queensberry Hotel
112 Drumlanrig Street, DG3 5LU
🕐 11 – mid (1am Thu – Sat); 12.30 – mid Sun
☎ (01848) 330215 ⊕ buccleuchhotel.co.uk
Caledonian 80; guest beer Ⓗ
This friendly hotel, situated on the A76 in the middle of Thornhill, is popular with locals and visitors to the area. The solitary guest beer could be from anywhere in the UK. The food is always hearty – watch the blackboard for special dishes. The nearby Drumlanrig Castle is

worth a visit and regularly hosts special events. The area is an ideal location for country pursuits. ᴁQ♿🍴◖❶₪♣

Wigtown

Wigtown Ploughman
30 South Main Street, DG8 9HG
🕐 12-11.30 (1am Fri & Sat); 12-10.30 Sun
☎ (01988) 403236 ⊕ wigtownploughman.co.uk
Beer range varies Ⓗ
This friendly, family-run hotel is a prominent black and white building on the main square of Scotland's national book town. While the bar area is rather basic, dominated at one end by a pool table, the lounge and restaurant areas are more comfortable. One of the two guest ales offered is usually from the Houston brewery. ᴁ♿❀🍴◖❶₪(415)♣

Scottish Beers

Just as monks call their Lenten beers 'liquid bread', it's tempting to call traditional Scottish ales 'liquid porridge'. They are beers brewed for a cold climate, a country in which beer vies with whisky (uisge breatha – water of life) for nourishment and sustenance.

Brewers blend not only darker malts such as black and chocolate with paler grains, but also add oats, that staple of many foodstuffs in the country. In common with the farmer-brewers of the Low Countries and French Flanders in earlier centuries, domestic brewers in Scotland tended to use whatever grains, herbs and plants were available to make beer. The intriguing use of heather in the Fraoch range of ales recalls brewing practice in Scotland from bygone times.

Different

Traditionally, Scottish ales were brewed in a different manner to English ones. Before refrigeration, beer was fermented at ambient temperatures far lower than in England. As a result, not all the sugars turned to alcohol, producing rich, full-bodied ales. As hops had to be imported from England at considerable cost, they were used sparingly. The result was a style of beer markedly different to English ones: vinous, fruity, malty and with only a gentle hop bitterness.
Many of the new breed f ales produced by micro-brewers in Scotland tend to be paler and more bitter than used to be the norm. For the true taste of traditional Scottish ales you will have to sample the products of the likes of Belhaven, Broughton, Caledonian and Traquair.

Complexities

The language of Scottish beers is different, too. The equivalent to English mild is called Light (even when it is dark in colour), standard bitter is called Heavy premium bitter Export, while strong old ales and barley wines (now rare) are called Wee Heavies.
To add to the complexities of the language differences, many traditional beers incorporate the word Shilling in their names. A Light may be dubbed 60 Shilling, a Heavy 70 Shilling, an Export 80 Shilling, and a Wee Heavy 90 Shilling. The designations stem from a pre-decimalisation method of invoicing beer in Victorian times. The stronger the beer, the higher the number of shillings.
Until recent times, cask-conditioned beer in Scotland was served by air pressure. In the pub cellar a water engine, which looks exactly the same as a lavatory cistern but works in reverse, used water to produce air pressure that drove the beer to the bar. Sadly, these wonderful Victorian devices are rarely seen, and the Sassenach handpump and beer engine dominate the pub scene.

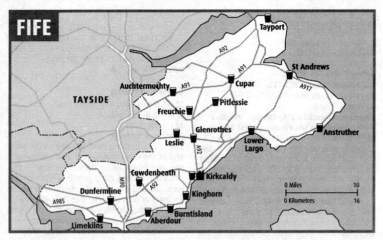

Authority area covered: Fife UA

Aberdour

Aberdour Hotel
38 High Street, KY3 0SW
🕓 4-11; 3-11.45pm Fri; 11-11.45pm Sun
☎ (01383) 860325 ⊕ aberdourhotel.com
Caledonian Deuchars IPA; guest beer Ⓗ
Small, friendly, family run hotel in this popular
town overlooking the Forth, handy for the golf
course and beaches. The hotel started life as a
coaching inn and the old stables remain at the
rear, converted into bedrooms. The cosy bar
has one handpump in use during winter, two
in spring and summer. Excellent meals are
available in the evening and at weekends
made with fresh local produce.
🛏🍽🕯✏🕓🐾🚃(7)P

Anstruther

Dreel Tavern
16 High Street, KY10 3DL
🕓 11 (12.30 Sun)-midnight
☎ (01334) 310727
Beer range varies Ⓗ
The Dreel is housed in an old stone building in
a fishing village on the Forth with traditional
crow step gables and pantile roof. The public
and lounge bars are separated by an open fire,
while the conservatory provides a pleasant
dining area. Local, freshly caught seafood
features on the menu. A past winner of Fife
CAMRA Pub Of The Year, three beers are
usually available.
🛏Q🍽🏮✏🕓🚃(X26, 95)🐾ᴸ

Auchtermuchty

Cycle Tavern
75 Burnside, KY14 7AJ
🕓 11-11; 12.30-midnight Sun
☎ (01337) 828326
Beer range varies Ⓗ
Friendly two-room pub in the town probably
best known as the birthplace of The
Proclaimers and home to Jimmy Shand. The
bar is popular with fans of outdoor pursuits
and has a pool table and large screen for sport.
The more comfortable lounge is busy at meal

times serving a good selection of keenly
priced home-made food. 🕓🔲🐾🚃🐾P ᴸ

Burntisland

Crown Tavern
17 Links Place, KY3 9DY
🕓 11 (12.30 Sun)-midnight
☎ (01592) 873697
Beer range varies Ⓗ
Two room, traditional small town pub with a
lively, spacious public bar and even larger
lounge with pool table. An attractive gantry,
wood panelling and splendid etched glass
windows create an old fashioned and relaxed
atmosphere. One beer is on handpump with a
second at weekends and busy times.
🔲🐾🚃(6, 7)🐾

Cowdenbeath

Crown Hotel
6 High Street, KY4 9NA
🕓 11 (12.30 Sun)-midnight
☎ (01383) 610540
Beer range varies Ⓗ
Spacious single room pub at the west end of
the High Street. This ex-mining town is
famous for being the home of the 'Blue Brazil'
(the local football team – so named,
sarcastically, for its ineptitude). The bar has a
raised, railed off pool area. The beer usually
comes from Scottish independents.
🏮✏🕓🐾🚃Pᴸ

Cupar

Golf Tavern
11 South Road, KY15 5JF (800 yds S of town over
railway bridge)
🕓 11-midnight (1am Fri & Sat); 12.20-11 Sun
☎ (01334) 654233
Beer range varies Ⓗ
Small, single storey terraced building just to
the south of town. The single room has a
modern interior with an L-shaped bar and a
friendly, comfortable atmosphere. Usually just
one beer is available during the week with

633

two at the weekend. Good, home-cooked lunches are served. Q◑&≠⊟

Dunfermline

Commercial Inn
13 Douglas Street, KY12 7EB
☺ 11-11 (midnight Fri & Sat); 12.30-11 Sun
☎ (01383) 733876
Caledonian Deuchars IPA; Courage Directors Bitter; Theakston Old Peculier; guest beer ⒣
Well known ale house attracting an eclectic clientele in a building that dates back to the 1820s. This cosy town centre pub is situated opposite the main post office off the High Street. The emphasis here is on conversation, with quiet background music. Good quality food and friendly service are assured. Eight ales are always available plus one cider. An extensive menu includes regular specials available from 11am. Fife CAMRA Pub Of The Year 2005 and 2006. ◑≠⊟♦

Freuchie

Albert Tavern
2 High Street, KY15 7EX (half km E of A92 Kirkcaldy to Dundee rd)
☺ 11-2, 5-11 (12-1am Fri & Sat); 12.30-11 Sun
☎ (07765) 169342
Beer range varies ⒣
Family friendly village local, reputedly a coaching inn when nearby Falkland Palace was a royal residence. An old photograph shows the property as a tavern some time in the 19th century. Both bar and lounge have beamed ceilings and the bar has wainscot panelling. The small upstairs restaurant seats 20. Three handpumps offer guest beers.
♨Q✿◑⊟

Glenrothes

Golden Acorn
1 North Street, KY7 5NA (next to to bus station)
☺ 11 (12.30 Sun)-midnight
☎ (01592) 751175
Caledonian Deuchars IPA; guest beer ⒣
Large JD Wetherspoon with hotel next to the main shopping centre in town. Scenes of days gone by in the local area decorate the various pillars. Real ale on four handpumps and an occasional cider are available, plus the usual Wetherspoon festivals and special offers. The house beer is from the local Fyfe Brewing Company. ⇆⇤◑&⊟♦P⌐

Kinghorn

Auld Hoose
6-8 Nethergate, KY3 9SY (down flight of steps off main street)
☺ 12 (11 Sat; 12.30 Sun)-midnight
☎ (01592) 891074 ⊕ theauldhoose.co.uk
Broughton Greenmantle Original; Caledonian Deuchars IPA; guest beers ⒣
Busy village local on a steep side street leading off the east end of Kinghorn main street. Popular with locals and visitors, it is handy for the station and Kinghorn beach. The main bar has a TV and pool table to keep sports fans happy and holds dominoes

competitions at the weekend. The lounge is quieter and more comfortable with a relaxed atmosphere. Two regular and two guest beers are sold from the three handpumps and one Scottish upright font on air pressure.
⇆◑⇤&≠⊟(6, 7)♣

Crown Tavern
55-57 High Street, KY3 9UW
☺ 11 (12.30 Sun)-midnight
☎ (01592) 890340
Beer range varies ⒣
Two room, bustling local situated to the west end of the main street. Two ever changing ales are dispensed by cheery bar staff. Attractive stained glass panels feature on the windows and the door. A collection of signed footballs adorns the bar. The TV in the bar shows football and horseracing; there is a pool table in another room. Beers always come from Scottish independents. ≠⊟(6, 7)♣

Ship Tavern
2 Bruce Street, KY3 9TJ (E end of main street)
☺ 12 (12.30 Sun)-midnight
☎ (01592) 890655
Caledonian Deuchars IPA; guest beer ⒣
One of the older buildings in Kinghorn, originally built as a house for Bible John who printed the first bibles in Scotland. The unobtrusive entrance door, facing the main road, opens into a fine timber-panelled interior with a long bar counter and ornate gantry. The small jug bar is probably one of the finest surviving traditional interiors in Fife. Two beers are usually available. A new attractively decorated dining area has been added to the rear. Check out the comfy chairs and TV in the outdoor smoking area.
♨◑&≠⊟(6, 7)⌐

Kirkcaldy

Harbour Bar
471-475 High Street, KY1 1JL (N end of High Street)
☺ 11-3, 5-midnight; 11-midnight Thu-Sat; 12.30-midnight Sun
☎ (01592) 264270 ⊕ fifebrewery.co.uk
Beer range varies ⒣
Situated on the ground floor of a tenement building, this unspoilt local has been described by regulars as a 'village local in the middle of town'. The recently refurbished public bar sports shipping prints depicting the town's maritime history while the lounge features model sailing ships in glass cases. Six handpumps sell up to 20 different beers each week from micros all over Britain, including those from Fyfe Brewery at the rear of the pub. A fine selection of malt whiskies is also available. Winner of many CAMRA awards including Scottish Pub Of The Year. ⊕⊟

Leslie

Burns Tavern
184 High Street, KY6 3DD (S side of main street)

✪ 12 (11 Fri & Sat)-midnight; 12.30-midnight Sun
☎ (01592) 741345
Taylor Landlord; guest beer Ⓗ
Typical Scottish two room main street local in a town once famous for paper making. The public bar is on two levels: the lower lively and friendly, the upper with large-screen TV and pool table, and football memorabilia on the walls. The lounge bar is quieter and more spacious. Pub quizzes are held on Wednesday and Thursday evenings and dominoes/darts/pool competitions on Sunday afternoon. A good honest community friendly local. Two beers are usually available.
🏚🍴🕮♿☐(X1, 201)♣↿

Limekilns

Ship Inn
Halkett's Hall, KY11 3HJ (on the promenade)
✪ 11-11 (midnight Fri & Sat); 12.30-11 Sun
☎ (01383) 872247
Beer range varies Ⓗ
Long established village pub on the north shore of the River Forth with superb views from well placed outdoor seats. With its single room interior, the bar area at one end can get very congested on Friday and Saturday evenings while the seating area is under used. Two ales from small independents are available throughout the year rising to three during summer and holiday periods. Good quality home cooked bar lunches have become more popular now that smoking is not permitted in the pub so it is advisable to book a table. ✿◖☐(73, 76)♣●

Lower Largo

Railway Inn
1 Station Wynd, KY6 6BU (under railway viaduct)
✪ 11 (12.30 Sun)-midnight
☎ (01333) 320239
Beer range varies Ⓗ
Small two room pub close to the picturesque harbour. The bar has a nautical theme, as well as photos of some of the last trains to pass over the viaduct overhead before the Beeching measures of the 60s. The beers usually rotate and may include Caledonian Deuchars, Fuller's London Pride, Orkney Dark Island and Taylor Landlord. Q◖♿☐↿

Pitlessie

Village Inn
Cupar Road, KY15 7SU
✪ 11-2, 5-midnight; 11-midnight Fri & Sat; 12.30-midnight Sun
☎ (01337) 830595
Beer range varies Ⓗ
A typical Scottish village pub from the outside, the public bar is a pleasant surprise featuring bare stonework and an open fire. It has the feel of a bothy with bare wooden tables for dining. Good restaurant standard food is available at all times. Several rooms, one with an old Raeburn cooker, provide space for families and pub games including pool. A cosy wee village local with the emphasis very much on conversation. 🏚Q🕭◖�°♿☐♣P↿

St Andrews

Aikmans Cellar Bar
32 Bell Street, KY16 9UK
✪ 6-midnight; 1-1am Thu-Sat
☎ (01334) 477425 ⊕ cellarbar.co.uk
Beer range varies Ⓗ
Basement lounge bar, in the Guide since 1987, selling a good selection of real ales together with a variety of continental bottled beers. The rolled copper bar top was salvaged from the White Star liner Oceanic (same shipping line as the Titanic). Opening hours outside term time can vary and the bar is closed most lunchtimes but cask ales are available on request in the Bistro upstairs. Regular music and occasional beer festivals are hosted (see website for details). ◖☐♣

Central Bar
77-79 Market Street, KY16 9NU
✪ 11-11.45 (1am Fri & Sat); 12.30-11.45 Sun
☎ (01334) 478296
Caledonian Deuchars IPA; Greene King Old Speckled Hen; Theakston Best Bitter, Old Peculier; guest beer Ⓗ
Student oriented town centre pub also popular with the locals. It has a Victorian-style island bar, large windows and ornate mirrors creating a late 19th-century feel. The only pub in town that serves food after 9pm, pavement tables are available, weather permitting. A good mix of students, local business folk and tourists make this an interesting, bustling hostelry. ✿◖☐♣

Whey Pat Tavern
2 Argyle Street, KY16 9EX
✪ 11-11.30 (11.45 Fri & Sat); 12.30-11.30 Sun
☎ (01334) 477740
Beer range varies Ⓗ
Town centre pub on a busy road junction just outside the old town walls. There has been a hostelry on this site for several centuries; it was taken over by Belhaven in 2002 but minimal changes were made. The front bar is L-shaped with a dart board and TV and there is an airy lounge/meeting room to the rear. A mixed clientele of all ages frequent this usually busy pub and there are three beers on handpump. ◖♿☐♣

Tayport

Bellrock Tavern
4-6 Dalgleish Street, DD6 9BB
✪ 11-midnight (1am Thu-Sat); 12.30-midnight Sun
☎ (01382) 552388
Caledonian Deuchars IPA; guest beer Ⓗ
Friendly small town local opposite the picturesque harbour with wonderful views across the Tay to Dundee and Broughty Ferry. The bar is on three levels, each with a mainly nautical theme, including old charts, photographs of ships and aircraft, old Dundee and the Tay Ferries. Good value home cooking is served at lunchtimes. One beer is on handpump with a second at busy times. Close to the Fife coastal path, this pub is well worth seeking out. Q�°✿☐♣↿

SCOTLAND

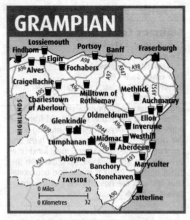

GRAMPIAN

Authority areas covered: Aberdeenshire UA, City of Aberdeen UA, Moray UA

Aberdeen

Camerons Inn (Mas)

6-8 Little Belmont Street, AB10 9JG
☼ 11-midnight (1am Fri & Sat); 12.30-11 Sun
☎ (01224) 644487
Caledonian Deuchars IPA; Greene King IPA, Abbot, Old Speckled Hen; Inveralmond Lia Fail; Orkney Dark Island Ⓗ
Part of Belhaven's ever-increasing Aberdeen empire, this ancient inn, listed in CAMRA's Scottish Inventory, is the longest serving outlet for real ale in Aberdeen. It boasts the most character-filled listed snug and bar in the city. The open plan, rear lounge bar is where meals are served daily and the quiz takes place on the first Monday of the month. The snug may close early evening mid week if there are no customers. Only three of the beers listed are available at any one time in both bars. ⌂◑⊟⇌♣⌐

Carriages

101 Crown Street, AB11 6HH (below Brentwood Hotel)
☼ 11-2.30 (not Sat), 4.30-midnight; 6-11 Sun
☎ (01224) 595440 ⊕ brentwood-hotel.co.uk
Caledonian Deuchars IPA; guest beers Ⓗ
Located in the basement of the Brentwood Hotel, just a few minutes from the bustle of Union Street, this is a comfortable pub with an atmosphere that goes beyond the typical hotel bar. With its 10 handpumps, the bar offers the widest selection of real ales in Aberdeen, and has earned a number of awards from the local CAMRA branch. The restaurant offers good food, and lunches are also served in the bar. The pub can get busy with business travellers from the hotel during the week, but is more relaxed at weekends. ⌂◑⇌P

Grill ☆

213 Union Street, AB11 6BA
☼ 10-midnight (1am Fri & Sat); 12.30-midnight Sun
☎ (01224) 573530 ⊕ thegrillaberdeen.co.uk
Caledonian 80; guest beers Ⓗ
Centrally located on Union Street with an exquisite interior dating back to a redesign in 1926, and remaining largely unchanged since

then, this is the only CAMRA National Inventory pub in the Aberdeen area. Traditions die hard in this pub – ladies have only been permitted since the Sex Discrimination Act of 1975, and Ladies' toilets only introduced in 1998. An extensive collection of malt whiskies is offered, including exotic items such as Japanese malts, and a variety of bar snacks is available. Situated across from the Music Hall, various types of musicians may be spotted during concert breaks. ⇌

Moorings

2 Trinity Quay, AB11 2AA
☼ 12-midnight (1am Fri & Sat); 12.30-midnight Sun
☎ (01224) 587602
Beer range varies Ⓗ
Pirates, mermaids, leather and deep sea anglerfish are just some of the features of this atmospheric, dark-panelled and dimly lit bar. A range of beers, predominantly from Scottish micro-breweries, rotates through five handpumps, with another pump for cider. Imported bottled beers and premium spirits are also available. The bar has an eclectic cast of regular customers who come to enjoy live bands at the weekend, or just to relax with the paper with the rock jukebox as background music. The bar supports an active darts team. Students and pirates benefit from special discounts. ⇌♣♠⊟

Old Blackfriars

52 Castle Street, AB11 5BB
☼ 11-midnight (1am Fri & Sat); 12.30-11 Sun
☎ (01224) 581922
Caledonian Deuchars IPA, 80; Greene King Abbot; Inveralmond Ossian's Ale; guest beer Ⓗ
Located on the Castlegate in the historic centre of the city, this is the local CAMRA Pub of the Year 2007, with several prior awards, set on two levels, with bars on both with unobtrusive background music, but no TV. Part of the Belhaven/Greene King empire, but maintaining an independent choice of guest beers, mainly featuring Scottish breweries. The pub has a reputation for good pub food. Quiz night first Tuesday of each month and occasional themed beer festivals are held, normally 4 times a year. ⌂◑⊟⇌(Aberdeen)

Prince of Wales

7 St Nicholas Lane, AB10 1HF
☼ 10-midnight (1am Fri & Sat); 12-midnight Sun
☎ (01224) 640597
Caledonian 80; Inveralmond Prince of Wales; Theakston Old Peculier; guest beers Ⓗ
Listed in CAMRA's Scottish Inventory, this is one of the oldest pubs in Aberdeen. This premier real ale pub has a traditional feel with a flagstone floor at the rear, carpeted lounge and possibly the longest bar in Aberdeen. Eight handpumps serve a selection of ales, with most Scottish micros and many English represented. Good value pub grub is available at lunchtime (only until 4pm on Sat & Sun), folk music plays on Sunday evening and

INDEPENDENT BREWERIES

Brewdog Fraserburgh
Hillside Lumphanan
Old Foreigner Glenkindie

Monday is quiz night. Winner of CAMRA City Pub on several occasions. Q◁⇌

Tilted Wig

55-56 Castle Street, AB11 5BA (opp Court House)
🌐 12-midnight (1am Fri & Sat); 12.30-11 Sun
☎ (01224) 583248
Caledonian Deuchars IPA; Courage Directors; Theakston XB; guest beer Ⓗ
Small city centre pub on the historic Castlegate, originally called the Lang or Saloon Bar, and in the 70s, the Welly Boot. The name comes from its proximity to the local Sheriff court. Food is served until 10pm every day. A large-screen TV shows sports, with an alternative screen in an area to the front of the pub. A quiz is held on the first Tuesday of the month and occasional live bands hosted on Saturday. ◁▶⇌

Under The Hammer

11 North Silver Street, AB10 1RJ (off Golden Square)
🌐 5 (4 Fri; 2 Sat)-midnight (1am Thu-Sat); 5-11 Sun
☎ (01224) 640253
Caledonian Deuchars IPA; Inveralmond Ossian's Ale; guest beer Ⓗ
Atmospheric, comfortable and inviting basement pub, next door to an auction house – hence the name. Works of art by local artists displayed on the walls are for sale if they take your fancy. Convenient for the Music Hall and His Majesty's Theatre. The large noticeboard has posters advertising forthcoming events in town. ⇌

Aboyne

Boat Inn

Charleston Road, AB34 5EL (N bank of River Dee next to Aboyne Bridge)
🌐 11-2.30, 5-11 (midnight Fri); 11-midnight Sat; 11-11 Sun
☎ (01339) 886137
Draught Bass; guest beers Ⓗ
Popular, riverside inn with food oriented lounge featuring a log-burning stove and spiral staircase leading to the upper dining area. Junior diners (and adults!) may request to see the model train, complete with sound effects, traverse the entire pub at picture-rail height upon completion of their meal. The local Rotary Club regularly meets here. Limited accommodation is provided in a self-catering flat. 🏚⊛🚃◁▶🕮🛏🅰♣P

Alves

Crooked Inn

Burghead Road, IV30 8UU
🌐 12-2, 5.30-11 (11.30 Fri; midnight Sat); closed Mon; 12.30-10.30 Sun
☎ (01343) 850646
Beer range varies Ⓗ
Tardis like labyrinth of a pub, low-roofed and full of clutter. Very much food led, it offers a weekend a la carte menu and an extensive selection at other times. Popular with families and RAF personnel from the nearby bases, it feels busy even with few customers. The two beers (only one in winter) tend to come from local micros. 🏚⊛◁▶🅰🚃(10, 315)P

Auchmacoy

Poachers Rest

Denhead, AB41 8JL (off A90 Ellon bypass, 2 miles E of Ellon)
🌐 11-2.30, 5-11 (midnight Thu & Fri); closed Mon; 11-midnight Sat; 12-11 Sun
☎ (01358) 722114
Inveralmond Thrappledouser Ⓗ
Situated in a pleasant rural location on the edge of a large country estate in what was once a General Merchant store, this is primarily a split level restaurant with a small bar at the top end. A limited range of bottled beer is available. In summer, parents can relax over a pleasant pint of ale while their children enjoy the bouncy castle outside in the play area. ⊛◁▶🕭P

Banchory

Douglas Arms Hotel

22 High Street, AB31 5SR
🌐 11-midnight (1am Fri & Sat)
☎ (01330) 822547 🌐 douglasarms.co.uk
Beer range varies Ⓗ
This small hotel with budget price accommodation has a public bar and lounge separated by a pool area. Now listed in CAMRA's Scottish Inventory, the bar is a classic Scottish long bar with vintage mirrors and etched windows on to the High Street. The lounge has a large fireplace and a Chesterfield suite, and there is another room to the rear leading to the recently installed south-facing decking – ideal for balmy summer afternoons and evenings.
🏚Q🛏⊛🚃◁▶🕭🕭🅰(201, 202)♣

Ravenswood Club (Royal British Legion)

25 Ramsay Road, AB31 5TS
🌐 11-2.30, 5-midnight (11 winter); 11 – midnight Fri & Sat; 11-11 Sun
☎ (01330) 822347 🌐 banchorylegion.com
Beer range varies Ⓗ
Large British Legion Club where CAMRA members and bearers of this Guide are welcome as guests. A comfortable lounge adjoins the pool and TV room; there is also a large function room much used by local clubs and societies. Darts and snooker are popular. Two handpumps provide the cheapest real ale in the area. The outdoor terrace offers fine views of the Deeside hills. ⊛🚃◁▶🕭🅰♣P

Banff

Ship Inn

8 Deveronside, AB45 1HP (on seafront near harbour)
🌐 11-midnight (12.30am Fri & Sat); 7-11 Wed & Sun
☎ (01261) 812620
Courage Directors Ⓗ
Wonderful time-warp bar, complete with its own slice of silver screen fame – it was the bar interior featured in Local Hero. Heavily decorated with nautical artefacts, a blocked carriage arch at the front hints at the pub's distant history. Both bar and lounge are wood-lined and have tremendous sea views overlooking Banff bay towards Macduff

SCOTLAND

although the windows are small. Very close to the baroque mansion of Duff House which is now home to one of Scotland's National Gallery collections. Golf and sailing are available close by. ♨Q⊟

Catterline

Creel Inn

AB39 2UL (on coast off A92, 5 miles S of Stonehaven) OS868781
✪ 12-3, 6-midnight (1am Fri & Sat); 12-midnight Sun
☎ (01569) 750254 ⊕ thecreelinn.co.uk
Beer range varies Ⓗ
Built in 1838, this compact village inn in a stunning clifftop location has gradually expanded into the neighbouring row of fisherman's cottages. A selection of more than 30 specialist bottled beers is available (mainly Belgian) and an extensive selection of whiskies. Locally caught seafood is a speciality – reservations are recommended. Nearby Crawton bird sanctuary and the St Cyrus national nature reserve are well worth visiting. Kinneff old church two miles away was the hiding place of the Scottish crown jewels for 10 years from 1651. ♨Q❀◑P⚟

Charleston of Aberlour

Mash Tun

8 Broomfield Square, AB38 9QP
✪ 11-11 (11.45 Thu & Sun; 12.30am Fri & Sat)
☎ (01340) 881771 ⊕ mashtun-aberlour.com
Beer range varies Ⓗ
Built in 1896 as the Station Bar, this unusual, round ended building has a light timber-bedecked interior. A pledge in the title deeds permitted a name change if the railway closed but with the instruction that it must revert to Station Bar if a train ever pulls up again outside! The Speyside Way runs past the door and patrons may drink their ales enjoying the view from the former station platform (weather permitting). Two beers are served during the tourist season and one in winter, mainly from local micros, especially Cairngorm. Q❀⇔◑⊟(336)

Craigellachie

Highlander Inn

10 Victoria Street, AB38 9SR (on A95, opp post office)
✪ 12-11 (12.30am Fri & Sat)
☎ (01340) 881446 ⊕ whiskyinn.com
Cairngorm Trade Winds; guest beers Ⓗ
Picturesque whisky and cask ale bar on the banks of the Spey and close to the Speyside Way with small, well furnished bars where customers can enjoy the atmosphere. Popular with visitors for fishing, walking and negotiating the Whisky Trail. CRAC (Craigellachie Real Ale Club) meets monthly where members discuss the choice of ales with the support of owners and staff.
◑♿⇌⊟♣●P⚟

Elgin

Muckle Cross

34 High Street, IV30 1BU
✪ 11-midnight (1am Fri & Sat); 12.30-11.45 Sun
☎ (01343) 559030
Greene King Abbot; guest beer Ⓗ
Typical small Wetherspoon's outlet converted from a bicycle repair shop, latterly a Halfords branch, on the High Street. A pleasant long room with ample seating and a long bar, it can get very busy, particularly at weekends. Five handpumps serve a wide range of beers, with particular focus on Scottish micro-breweries. The recently launched house beer Muckle Cross Ale is from Isle of Skye brewery. The pub also offers whiskies from 20 local distilleries. It opens at 9am for coffee and breakfast.
Q❀⇔◑⊟♣P⚟

Sunninghill Hotel

Hay Street, IV30 1NH
✪ 12-2.30, 5-11 (12.30am Fri & Sat)
☎ (01343) 547799 ⊕ sunninghillhotel.com
Beer range varies Ⓗ
Family run hotel set in its own grounds in a quiet residential area close to the town centre and railway station. A comfortable lounge includes a dining area with additional tables in the conservatory, making it a popular venue for families. There are four handpumps, serving a variety of beers and a large selection of whiskies. Outside seating is available on the patio. ❀⇔◑♿⇌⊟P

Thunderton House

Thunderton Place, IV30 1BG
✪ 10-11 (12.30am Fri & Sat); 12.30-11 Sun
☎ (01343) 554921 ⊕ thundertonhouse.co.uk
Caledonian Deuchars IPA; Courage Directors Ⓗ
This historic old townhouse can be traced back as far as the 11th century but most of the building dates back to the 17th century. Bonnie Prince Charlie stayed here in 1746 before the battle of Culloden and his ghost is still said to haunt the house. The bar has ample seating and a big screen TV for sports.
♉❀◑♿⇌⊟

Ellon

Station Hotel

Station Brae, AB41 9BD (W of village centre)
✪ 11-11 (11.45 Thu & Sat; 1am Fri)
☎ (01358) 720209
Beer range varies Ⓗ
Impressive Victorian hotel situated on what used to be the Buchan railway line – the energetic may still cycle here along the path from Aberdeen. The range of ales varies depending on availability, often coming from larger English breweries. Food is served throughout the public bar, lounge and restaurant. The hotel has excellent function facilities and a room available for private parties. Fishing and shooting can be arranged, golf course is next door and Haddo Country Park five miles away. ♉⇔◑⊟♿P

Tolbooth

21-23 Station Road, AB41 9AE
✪ 11-11 (midnight Thu; 12.30pm Fri & Sat); 12.30-11 Sun
☎ (01358) 721308
Greene King Abbot; guest beers Ⓗ
Large, comfortable pub that attracts a mature clientele close to the centre of town. It has

seating areas on split levels including a conservatory leading to an enclosed patio. The range of ales varies depending on availability, often coming from larger English breweries. A smaller attic bar is available for meetings. ✿&🖳(X50, 260)

Findhorn

Crown & Anchor Inn

44 Findhorn, IV36 3YF

🕐 12-11 (midnight Wed & Thu; 1am Fri & Sat); 12-11.30 Sun

☎ (01309) 690243 ⊕ crownandanchorinn.co.uk

Taylor Landlord; guest beer Ⓗ

Situated in a historic village, with glorious views over Findhorn Bay, this pub is a favourite with ornithologists, yachtsmen and local RAF personnel. The shop at the nearby world famous Findhorn Foundation is worth a visit for a selection of interesting organic beers from around the planet.

🏚✿🍴◑🕭🚶🖳(336)♣P⚊

Fochabers

Red Lion Tavern

65-67 High Street, IV32 7DU

🕐 12-midnight (12.30am Fri & Sat)

☎ (01343) 820455 ⊕ redlionfochabers.co.uk

Caledonian Deuchars IPA Ⓗ

Lively coaching inn with a modernised interior. Real ale is served in both the sport-dominated public bar and the quieter lounge and dining area. A sun lounge is at the back of building. Handy for the Speyside Way long distance path and fishing in the Spey. Baxter's Soup visitor centre is nearby.

✿🍴◑🕭🖳♣P⚊

Glenkindie

Glenkindie Arms Hotel

AB33 8SX (on A97 E of village)

🕐 12 (5 Mon-Fri winter)-11 (1am Fri; 11.45 Sat); 12-10.30 Sun

☎ (019756) 41288 ⊕ theglenkindiearmshotel.com

Beer range varies Ⓗ

Tiny 400-year-old former drovers' inn in a listed building known as The Lodge due to its former Masonic use, serving an extensive menu of good local produce. The Old Foreigner single-barrel brewery was launched in 2007 – the guest beer range may lessen once the brewery is in full swing, with the local brew complementing a range of malt whiskies and Belgian beers. The hotel stands on the Castle Trail between Kildrummy and Corgarff Castles and is close to the Lecht Ski Centre. Check winter opening hours before travelling.

🏚✿🍴◑P

Inverurie

Edwards

2 West High Street, AB51 3SA

🕐 10-1am; 12.30-midnight Sun

☎ (01467) 629788 ⊕ edwardsinverurie.co.uk

Beer range varies Ⓗ

Modern café bar converted from an old hotel several years ago, which has quickly became part of the town circuit. The upstairs function

room doubles as a disco at the weekend. Although light and modern, the decor has a hint of art-deco and there is a series of comfortable snugs to relax in while enjoying a snack and browsing the newspapers. ◑&🖛🖳

Lossiemouth

Skerry Brae Hotel

Stotfield Road, IV31 6QS

🕐 11-11 (12.30am Fri & Sat); 12 – 11 Sun

☎ (01343) 812040 ⊕ skerrybrae.co.uk

Beer range varies Ⓗ

Modern lounge bar in an old hotel building overlooking the Moray Firth and adjacent to the golf course. Very much a food based premises, it is popular with families, especially from the nearby RAF base (see the collection of squadron insignia on the bar wall). The range of up to three beers tends to come from Scottish micros. ✿🍴◑🖳(329)P

Maryculter

Old Mill Inn

South Deeside Road, AB12 5FX (B979/B9077 jct)

🕐 11 (12 Sun)-11

☎ (01224) 733212 ⊕ oldmillinn.co.uk

Caledonian Deuchars IPA; Draught Bass; Taylor Landlord Ⓗ

Privately owned and run small hotel dating from 1797, situated close to the banks of the River Dee in a rural location five miles west of the city. Beer is available in the lounge and restaurant. Numerous local golf courses are close by with salmon fishing on the adjacent river. Storybook Glen children's theme park, Drum Castle and Crathes Castle are all nearby attractions. ✿🍴◑🛆🖳(204)P⚊

Methlick

Kingscliff Sporting Lodge

AB41 7HQ (1 mile W of village on B9005 Methlick-Fyvie)

🕐 12-11 (midnight Fri & Sat); closed Mon & Tue

☎ (01651) 806375 ⊕ kingscliff.co.uk

Beer range varies Ⓗ

The Kingscliff is an award-winning sporting activity centre with its own pub open to all, offering good beer and local food. The beers are supplied by nearby Ardo Ales, with an excellent selection, usually from Scottish micro-brewers. Regular events and dinners such as Burns night are celebrated. If you are in a party of eight or more they will even drive you home within the local area. 🍴◑&P

Ythanview Hotel

Main Street, AB41 7DT

🕐 11-2.30, 5-11 (1am Fri); 11-12.30 Sat; 11-11 Sunday

☎ (01651) 806235 ⊕ ythanview.com

Beer range varies Ⓗ

Situated in the heart of the Ythan valley, this family-run establishment offers good food and beer. The public bar is at the rear; the welcoming restaurant has a real fire and serves good food made with local ingredients. Why not try the chicken curry – it is certainly a challenge. The owner, Jay, is a well known cricket enthusiast – the village has its own

SCOTLAND

cricket team, the MCC (Methlick Cricket Club).
♨🚗🍴◐ 🍽🛏🏓

Midmar

Midmar Inn

AB51 7LX (on B9119, 2 miles W of Echt)
🕐 5-11; 11-midnight Wed-Sat; 12.30-midnight Sun
☎ (01330) 860515
Beer range varies Ⓗ
Welcoming, small locals' bar which, despite
the paucity of adjacent housing, can be
especially busy at weekends and on
Thursday's ceilidh night. The reasonably-priced
menu is popular and booking, especially at
weekends, is advisable. A games room at the
back overlooks the grassy outside area.
Opening hours may vary seasonally. There are
plans to expand the premises in the future.
�◐🍽🚗(210)P↙

Milltown of Rothiemay

Forbes Arms Hotel

AB54 7LT
🕐 12-2.30 (not Mon & Tue), 5-11; 12.30-2.30, 5-10 Sun
☎ (01466) 711248
Beer range varies Ⓗ
Small family-run hotel in pleasant country
location with a public bar and separate dining
area. Fishing and shooting activities are
nearby. The local folk club are regular visitors.
🌳◐🍽🚗P

Oldmeldrum

Redgarth Hotel

Kirk Brae, AB51 0DJ (off A947 towards golf course)
🕐 11-2.30, 5-midnight; 12-2.30, 5-11 Sun
☎ (01651) 872353 ⊕ redgarth.com
Beer range varies Ⓗ /Ⓖ
Winner of local CAMRA Pub of the Year many
times, this is the premier pub in North
Aberdeenshire for real ale. Situated on the
outskirts of Oldmeldrum with fantastic views
of Bennachie, a warm welcome from the
friendly landlord is assured. The public bar and
restaurant are both in one open plan room;
the restaurant serves good pub food, often
locally sourced, and is busy most nights. The
pub is also frequented by many clubs and
committees and a private room is available on
request. Q🍴🌳og◐🍽🚗(305, 325)P↙

Portsoy

Boyne Hotel

2 North High Street, AB45 2PA
🕐 11-11 (midnight Fri & Sat)

☎ (01261) 842242 ⊕ boynehotel.co.uk
Beer range varies Ⓗ
Modern lounge bar in a traditional building in
the old, main square. It can be quite noisy,
especially at weekends. Just down the hill is
the picturesque, 17th-century harbour where
the annual Scottish Traditional Boat Festival is
held each July. 🍴◐ Å

Stonehaven

Marine Hotel

9-10 Shorehead, AB39 2JY (on harbour front)
🕐 11-midnight (1am Fri & Sat)
☎ (01569) 762155 ⊕ britnett-carver.co.uk/marine
Inveralmond Dunottar Ale; guest beers Ⓗ
This former Scottish CAMRA Pub of the Year,
featuring in CAMRA's Scottish Inventory, has
recently undergone major refurbishment and
renovation, but retains its traditional
character. The interior has a narrow wood-
lined bar and stone walled lounge area, with a
huge fireplace. The restaurant upstairs enjoys
magnificent views. A large range of
continental beers, especially Belgian, is
available bottled and draught. Customers may
drink outside on provided benches and tables.
♨🌳🍴◐ Å↙🍽

Ship Inn

5 Shorehead, AB39 2JY (on harbour front)
🕐 11-midnight (1am Fri & Sat)
☎ (01569) 762617 ⊕ shipinnstonehaven.com
Beer range varies Ⓗ
Small, narrow, wood-panelled inn with a
separate restaurant area. An antique mirror
from the former Devanha brewery in
Aberdeen features in the bar area. The low
walled patio area outside has magnificent
harbour views. Six guest rooms are available
and food is served all day at weekends.
🌳🍴◐ Å↙

Westhill

Shepherds Rest

10 Straik Road, AB32 6HF (Arnhall Business Park)
🕐 11 (12.30 Sun)-11
☎ (01224) 740208
Beer range varies Ⓗ
In a rural location, this kit-built pub was built
in 2000, and has recently been extended. Very
food oriented, it is busy with families at
weekends. The beers are mainly from the
Scottish & Newcastle range but often feature
an Isle of Skye ale. Accommodation is
provided in the adjacent Premier Travel Inn.
♨🌳◐🚗P↙

Recipe for Buttered Beer

Take a quart of more of Double Beere and put to it a good piece of fresh butter,
sugar candie an ounce, or liquerise in powder, or ginger grated, of each a
dramme, and if you would have it strong, put in as much long pepper and
Greynes, let it boyle in the quart in the maner as you burne wine, and who so will
drink it, let him drinke it hot as he may suffer. Some put in the yolke of an egge
or two towards the latter end, and so they make it more strength-full.

Thomas Cogan, The Haven of Health, 1584

HIGHLANDS & ISLANDS

SHETLAND

Baltasound
Brae
Wormadale
Scousburgh
LEWIS
Stornoway
WESTERN ISLES
Gairloch
Claddach
Kirkibost
NORTH UIST
Uig
Waternish
Carbost
Applecross
Lochcarron
SKYE
Sligachan
Plockton
Cluanie
Inverie
Fort Augustus
Glenfinnan
Birsay
Quoyloo
Stromness
ORKNEY
Onich
Glencoe
Melvich
Scourie
Ullapool
Dundonell
HIGHLAND
Fortrose
Munlochy
Drumnadrochit
Whitebridge
Roy Bridge
Fort William
Kinlochleven
Rosemarkie
Dornoch
Brora
Inverness
Cawdor
Boat of Garten
Aviemore
Kincraig
Newtonmore
GRAMPIAN
TAYSIDE

0 Miles 20
0 Kilometres 32

Authority areas covered: Highland UA, Orkney Islands UA, Shetland Islands UA, Western Isles UA

Applecross

Applecross Inn

Shore Street, IV54 8LR (on unclassified road off A896)
🕐 11-11.30 (midnight Fri); 12.30-11.30 Sun
☎ (01520) 744262 ⊕ applecross.uk.com
Beer range varies Ⓗ
Owned by the same family since 1989, the pub is spectacularly situated on the shore of the Applecross Peninsula, enjoying views of the Isles of Skye and Raasay. It is reached by a single track road over the highest vehicular ascent in Britain, or by a longer scenic route. Two handpumps dispense beer from the Isle of Skye Brewery; the food speciality is shellfish. It features regular ceilidhs and the area is ideal for climbing, walking and wildlife watching. ▲❀➮◑&⅄P⅄

Aviemore

Cairngorm Hotel

Grampian Road, PH22 1PE (Opposite train station)
🕐 11-midnight (1am Fri & Sat); 11.30-midnight Sun
☎ (01479) 810233 ⊕ cairngorm.com
Cairngorm Stag Ⓗ
The lounge bar of this 31-room privately owned hotel, though large, has a cosy feel, enhanced by two bay windows, distressed wooden furniture and a large coal effect fire. Though the trade is mainly holiday makers, it is very popular with locals, with a large-screen TV showing only sport. There is a Scottish theme throughout the hotel with tartan wall coverings and Scottish entertainment on many afternoons and evenings. ❀➮◑&⅄⇌❒P⅄

Old Bridge Inn

Dalfaber Road, PH22 1PU
🕐 11-midnight (1am Fri); 12.30-midnight Sun
☎ (01479) 811137 ⊕ oldbridgeinn.co.uk
Beer range varies Ⓗ
Busy pub, popular with outdoor enthusiasts, serving good quality food. Originally a cottage and now greatly enlarged, it lies on the road to the Strathspey Steam Railway, overlooking the River Spey on the opposite side of the road. One of the three handpumps usually serves a Scottish beer. Children are welcome and there is a modern bunkhouse attached accommodating 40. ▲Q❀➮◑&⅄⇌P⅄

Baltasound: Shetland

Baltasound Hotel

ZE2 9DS
🕐 12-2.30, 5-midnight (1am Fri & Sat); 12.30-2.30, 5-11 Sun
☎ (01957) 711334 ⊕ baltasound-hotel.shetland.co.uk
Valhalla White Wife, Simmer Dim, Auld Rock Ⓗ
The Baltasound – the most northerly hotel in Britain – is on the island of Unst, 70 miles and two ferry rides away from Lerwick, the capital of Shetland. It has 25 guest rooms. At midsummer there is almost perpetual daylight, known locally as 'Simmer Dim'. The Keen of Hamar nature reserve, home to some unique local species of flora, is within walking distance. ➮◑⊟&P

641

Boat of Garten

Boat Hotel
PH24 3BH
✪ 12-11 (1am Fri & Sat); 12.30-11 Sun
☎ (01479) 831258 ⊕ boathotel.co.uk
Beer range varies Ⓗ
This privately owned hotel is a haven for outdoor enthusiasts, situated close to the River Spey in the Cairngorm National Park, near the Strathspey Steam Railway, Boat of Garten Golf Course and the famous RSPB Osprey Centre at Loch Garten. Two handpumps in the Osprey Bar serve beers from the local Cairngorm Brewery. Bistro-style food is available and there is also a fine dining restaurant, The Capercaillie, accredited by EatScotland. Popular with locals, the small public bar has TV and a pool table.
Q✿☎⇔◑◐ ⬢ＡP

Brae: Shetland

Busta House Hotel
ZE2 9QN
✪ 11-11
☎ (01806) 522506 ⊕ bustahouse.com
Beer range varies Ⓗ
Elegant country mansion dating from 1588 with numerous later additions, lightly converted to a hotel, set in extensive gardens running down to the seashore. The hotel is allegedly haunted by the 18th century ghost of Barbara Pitcairn. Over 150 malt whiskies are available in the lounge. Near the centre of Shetland, it is a perfect base for exploring the islands. ⚏Q✿☎⇔◑◐P

Brora

Sutherland Inn
Fountain Square, KW9 6NX
✪ 11 (12.30 Sun)-midnight
☎ (01408) 621209
Beer range varies Ⓗ
Dating from 1853, this recently renamed inn (formerly the Sutherland Arms) has two bars, one with a welcoming open fire. A good range of food is served, including steaks and seafood, with vegetarians well catered for. In addition to beers from the Isle of Skye brewery, a wide range of whiskies is available. The lounge bar and restaurant feature an exhibition of local photography – the pictures available for purchase.
⚏Q☎✿☎⇔◑◐ ⬢Ａ⟲⇌￫

Carbost: Skye

Old Inn
IV47 8SR (A87 towards Dunvegan, A863 then B8009 to Carbost)
✪ 11-midnight; 12.30-11.30 Sun; open weekends only in winter
☎ (01478) 640205 ⊕ carbost.f9.co.uk
Beer range varies Ⓗ
On the edge of Loch Harport, The Old Inn enjoys splendid views of the Cuillin Hills. The simple interior, with stone walls and bare floors, reflects the relaxed atmosphere here. There are two handpumps – beers are rotated. Traditional, hearty pub food is served and

families are welcome. Meals and drinks can also be taken on the patio overlooking the loch. Live music plays at the weekend. Six en-suite rooms in the Lodge have sea views. There is also a 24 bed bunk house.
⚏Q☎✿☎⇔◑◐⬡Ｐ⟲⇌

Cawdor

Cawdor Tavern
The Lane, IV12 5XP
✪ 11-3, 5 -11 Oct-April; 11-11 (midnight Fri & Sat) summer; 12.30-11 Sun
☎ (01667) 404777 ⊕ cawdortavern.com
Beer range varies Ⓗ
At the heart of this conservation village, the pub is a short walk from the famous castle and within easy reach of Fort George and Culloden battlefield. Full of character, it has a large lounge bar, cosy public bar and 70-cover restaurant. Both bars are wood panelled with log fires, the public bar featuring a splendid antique mahogany bar and a ceiling covered in old maps. Owned by the same family that owns Atlas and Orkney Breweries, it features their beers. ⚏✿◑◐ ⬢⬡⟲P

Cladach Chireboist: North Uist

Westford Inn
HS6 5EP (5km NW of A867/A865 jct)
✪ 11 (4 Oct-Mar)-midnight (2am Thu-Sat); 12.30-midnight Sun
☎ (01876) 580653
Isle of Skye Red Cuillin Ⓗ
Popular with local fishermen and tourists, this slightly eccentric pub has a good old-fashioned atmosphere where a quick drink can turn into a ceilidh. A Georgian listed building on the edge of the Atlantic in a working crofting community with grazing highland cattle, it hosts live music, both traditional and modern. Home-cooked pub food is available late into the evening and the real fires are fuelled by peat from the pub's own peat cutting. Dogs are welcome.
⚏Q✿⇔◑◐ ⬢Ａ⇌⟲P

Cluanie

Cluanie Inn
IV63 7YW
✪ 11-midnight; 12.30-11 Sun
☎ (01320) 340238 ⊕ cluanieinn.com
Beer range varies Ⓗ

INDEPENDENT BREWERIES

An Teallach Dundonell
Atlas Kinlochleven
Black Isle Munlochy
Cairngorm Aviemore
Cuillin Sligachan
Far North Melvich
Glenfinnan Glenfinnan
Hebridean Stornoway
Highland Birsay
Isle of Skye Uig
Orkney Quoyloo
Valhalla Baltasound

Set in the remote valley of Glen Shiel, midway between Loch Ness and the Isle of Skye, the Cluanie Inn has been welcoming guests for over a century. A perfect base for exploring the spectacular hills and glens of the west Highlands, it offers excellent accommodation, including one room with an en-suite sauna. There is a single handpull in the bar, with ales supplied by the Isle of Skye Brewery, and an extensive range of malt whiskies.
🏰❀⇦🌙▶&P

Dornoch

Dornoch Castle Hotel

Castle Street, IV25 3SD
🕐 11-11; 12.30-11 Sun
☎ (01862) 810216 ⊕ dornochcastlehotel.com
Caledonian Deuchars IPA; guest beers Ⓗ
Good service is the order of the day at this 15th- century hotel set in beautiful walled gardens opposite Dornoch cathedral. The comfortable bar area has a large open fire, 15th-century stone walls and wooden floors creating a relaxed and informal atmosphere. Good food features Scottish Highland produce including seafood, venison and Aberdeen Angus beef. A beautiful beach and a world-famous golf course are only five minutes' walk from the hotel. 🏰❀⇦🌙▶&🍴▣&A🌂P⇘

Drumnadrochit

Benleva Hotel

IV63 6UH (signposted 435 yds from A82)
🕐 12-midnight (1am Fri; 11.45 Sat); 12.30-11 Sun; times vary winter
☎ (01456) 450080 ⊕ benleva.co.uk
Beer range varies Ⓗ/Ⓖ
Popular, friendly village inn catering for locals and visitors. A 400 year old former manse, the sweet chestnut outside was at one time a hanging tree. Four handpumps sell mainly Highland beers including Isle of Skye and occasional beer from the wood. Evening meals and lunches are available with a limited menu in winter. It hosts the Loch Ness Beer Festival in September, occasional quiz nights and traditional music. Local CAMRA pub of the year 2003 and 2005. 🏰Q❀⇦🌙▶▣&A🌂♣●P⇘

Fort Augustus

Lock Inn

Canalside, PH32 4AU
🕐 11-1am (12.30am Sat); 12-11 Sun
☎ (01320) 366302
Beer range varies Ⓗ
Located alongside the Caledonian Canal, one of Scotland's finest engineering wonders, the Lock Inn is in the centre of Fort Augustus in close proximity to Loch Ness and the Great Glen Way. The cosy bar is extremely busy, particularly in the summer months, and is popular with walkers, locals and passing visitors. Good food is served all day, every day; a single handpump offers a selection of guest beers. ❀🌙 A

Fort William

Grog & Gruel

66 High Street, PH33 6AE
🕐 12-11 (1am Thu-Sat); 5-11 Sun
☎ (01397) 705078 ⊕ grogandgruel.co.uk
Beer range varies Ⓗ
In the shadow of Britain's highest mountain, this bare-floored traditional ale house is owned by the same family as the Clachaig Inn in Glencoe. It keeps up to six predominantly Scottish beers in summer, fewer in winter, and hosts live music and beer festivals. It is busy with locals, outdoor enthusiasts and tourists. Home-cooked food is available in the upstairs dining room or from the limited bar menu. ❀🌙A⇌🚃

Nevisport Bar

Airds Crossing, High Street, PH33 6EJ
🕐 11-11.30 (1am Fri & Sat)
☎ (01397) 704921 ⊕ nevisport.com
Beer range varies Ⓗ
A collection of classic mountaineering photographs and outdoor gear adorns the walls in this informal lounge-style bar, giving an interesting insight into times gone by. Close to the Ben Nevis mountain range, the end of the West Highland Way and start of the Great Glen Way, this is a favourite meeting place for walkers, climbers and skiers. A large and warming log fire welcomes winter visitors. Mainly Scottish beers are served, often from Highlands and Islands breweries. 🏰🛏🌙&A⇌🚃⇘

Fortrose

Anderson

Union Street, IV10 8TD
🕐 4 (11.30 Sat)-11.30; 12.30-11.30 Sun
☎ (01381) 620236 ⊕ theanderson.co.uk
Beer range varies Ⓗ
Homely bar in a quiet seaside village, part of a nine bedroom hotel. Most of the structure dates from the the 1840s, although parts of the wine cellar are nearly 200 years older. The owners are an international beer writer and self confessed 'beer geek' and his wife, a New Orleans trained chef. Serving only independent brewery beers, this beer drinkers' mecca also offers 85 Belgian beers, earning it a prestigious UK award, plus 210 malts. The food is reasonably priced, high quality international cuisine.
🏰🛏❀⇦🌙▶▣&A♣●P

Gairloch

Old Inn

Flowerdale, IV21 2BD (opp harbour)
🕐 11-1am (11.45 Sat); 12-11.15 Sun
☎ (0800) 542 5444 ⊕ theoldinn.net
An Teallach Ale; Greene King Abbot; Isle of Skye Red Cuillin; guest beer Ⓗ
Traditional Highland coaching inn, overlooking Gairloch harbour, in a delightful riverside setting at the foot of the picturesque Flowerdale Glen. A regularly changing selection of six real ales, fewer in winter, is available to accompany the enticing menu of home-cooked Highland game and locally caught seafood. Loch Maree, the Beinn Eighe

Nature Reserve, Inverewe Gardens and the mountains of Torridon are all within easy reach, making this an ideal base for outdoor enthusiasts. Regular CAMRA Wester Ross Pub-of-the-Year. ♨️🚲♿🏠◑◐🍴🅿️

Glencoe

Clachaig Inn

PH49 4HX (half mile off A82 on old road to Glencoe) OSNN128567

✪ 11-11 (midnight Fri, 11.30 Sat); 12.30-11 Sun

☎ (01855) 811 252 🌐 glencoescotland.com

Beer range varies Ⓗ

Set amid wild mountain scenery in spectacular and historic Glencoe, the Clachaig attracts climbers, walkers and more adventurous tourists all year round. The large, stone-floored public bar, heated by iron stoves, offers basic seating, but there are more comfortable rooms including a family lounge. In the summer it is a wonderful place to enjoy a drink outdoors. There is an ever-changing selection of beers to enjoy, mostly from Scottish Highland and Island breweries, should you have to wait at busy times for the hearty, reasonably-priced food. Occasional beer festivals are held. ♨️🚲♿🏠◑◐🍴🅿️A

Inverie

Old Forge

PH41 4PL (100m from ferry terminal)

✪ 11am-midnight (1am Thu-Sat)

☎ (01678) 462267 🌐 theoldforge.co.uk

Beer range varies Ⓗ

The most remote pub in mainland Britain can be reached only by ferry from Malaig or a 15 mile hilly walk. In a spectacular setting on the shore of Loch Nevis it provides an ideal location for walking the rough bounds of Knoydart. Moorings welcome waterborne visitors. The two handpumps offer mainly Isle of Skye beers and food is served all day with specialities including locally caught seafood. The pub has an informal atmosphere, dress code being wellies, waterproofs and midge cream. The landlord can arrange local accommodation. ♨️Q❀◑◐A

Inverness

Blackfriars

93-95 Academy Street, IV1 1LU

✪ 11-11 (12.30am Fri & Sat); 12.30-11 Sun

☎ (01463) 233881 🌐 blackfriarshighlandpub.co.uk

Beer range varies Ⓗ

Across the road from the new Ironworks music venue, this traditional, spacious, one-room town centre pub has plenty of room to stand by the bar and ample seating in comfortable alcoves. Guest ales are split between English and Scottish breweries, with the Scottish beers often from Isle of Skye or Cairngorm. Good value meals are home-cooked Scottish fayre with daily specials. A music oriented pub, it features ceilidh, folk and country nights, with local bands often performing at weekends. ◑◐≠🍴

Clachnaharry Inn

17-19 High Street, Clachnaharry, IV3 8RB (A862 Beauly Road on outskirts of town)

✪ 11-11 (midnight Thu-Sat); 2.30-11.45 Sun

☎ (01463) 239806 🌐 clachnaharryinn.co.uk

Adnams Broadside; Caledonian 80; Greene King Abbot; Ⓗ **Isle of Skye Blaven;** Ⓖ **Orkney Dark Island; guest beer** Ⓗ

A wide selection of bar meals is served all day, every day, in this popular 17th-century coaching inn. The selection of up to 10 real ales regularly includes beers from Highlands & Islands breweries. Families are made welcome, and real log fires warm the cosy bars in winter. Both lounge and the recently extended patio provide fine views over the Caledonian Canal sea lock and Beauly Firth toward the distant Ben Wyvis. Regular local CAMRA Pub of the Year. ♨️Q❀◑◐🍴🛏️🅿️♿

Snowgoose

Stoneyfield, IV2 7PA (on A96)

✪ 11-11; 12.30-10.30 Sun

☎ (01463) 701921

Caledonian Deuchars IPA; Draught Bass Ⓗ

Recently extended, this traditional dining house supports a popular bar trade. Though situated next to a Holiday Inn and a Travelodge, most of the custom is still from the local area. A converted 1788 coach house, the main interior is one large L-shaped room but alcoves and log fires give it a more cosy and intimate feel. A wide variety of food is offered all day at reasonable prices. An extremely well run example of a Mitchell & Butler's Vintage Inn. ♨️Q❀◑◐♿🅿️♿

Kincraig

Suie Hotel

PH21 1NA

✪ 5-11 (1am Fri); 12-3, 5-1am Sat

☎ (01540) 651344 🌐 suiehotel.com

Cairngorm Trade Winds; Isle of Skye Red Cuillin Ⓗ

This cosy, wooden, self-contained extension to a seven-bedroom Victorian character hotel is run by only the second owner in its 103 year history. Popular with locals, hill walkers and skiers, it is situated just 200 metres from the River Spey and Loch Insh. The wood-floored bar features a large stove and open fire, and has an alcove with pool table and juke box. Traditional Scottish music plays occasionally. ♨️❀🏠🍴🅿️♿

Kinlochleven

Tailrace Inn

Riverside Road, PH50 4QH (on B863)

✪ 11-11.45 (12.45am Thu-Sat)

☎ (01855) 831777 🌐 tailraceinn.co.uk

Beer range varies Ⓗ

Surrounded by the Mamore mountains, the Tailrace lies midway between Ben Nevis and Glencoe on the West Highland Way. Two handpumps offer beer from the Atlas Brewery, just a short walk away. This modern inn serves food until 8pm in winter and 9pm in summer. Live music plays on Friday night in summer. An ideal base for outdoor enthusiasts and

close to the Ice Factor climbing centre.
🏮🍽️◐🕭♿🖾P

Lochcarron

Rockvilla Hotel
Main Street, IV54 8YB
🕓 11.30-2.30, 5-11; 12.30-2.30, 5-11 Sun
☎ (01520) 722379 🌐 rockvilla-hotel.co.uk
Beer range varies Ⓗ
The Rockvilla offers spectacular views of Loch Carron and the surrounding mountains. The comfortable rooms are complemented by an excellent restaurant, serving local and organic produce whenever possible. The bar has a large range of malt whiskies as well as three handpumps dispensing a wide selection of ales, mainly from the Isle of Skye Brewery. Regular live music and themed food nights take place throughout the year. Winter opening hours vary. Q🏮🍽️◐P

Newtonmore

Glen Hotel
Main Street, PH20 1DD
🕓 11 (12.30 Sun)-midnight
☎ (01540) 673203 🌐 theglenhotel.co.uk
Isle of Skye Glenbogle; guest beers Ⓗ
Built in 1900, this small hotel is in 'Monarch of the Glen' country and Cairngorms National Park. As well as a strong local trade it is also popular with walkers and tourists. This welcoming 10-room hotel has a large bar and dining rooms. The extensive menu includes vegetarian dishes. Holder of prestigious Eat Safe award. Check winter opening times.
🏮🍽️◐♿🖾🚃♣P⅄

Onich

Corran Inn
Nether Lochaber, PH33 6SE (by E terminal of Corran ferry, 200m from A82)
🕓 11-11 (1am Fri-Sat)
☎ (01855) 821235 🌐 corraninn.co.uk
Beer range varies Ⓗ
On the shores of Loch Linnhe, beside the Corran ferry slipway, this inn is just a few yards from the busy A82. Close to Glencoe and the Ben Nevis range of mountains, it makes an ideal base for exploring. Food is served all day in the traditional bar and guests planning long days on hill or glen can arrange early breakfasts and late evening meals. Beers are usually from local breweries. 🏮Q🏮🍽️◐🖾P

Plockton

Plockton Inn
Innes Street, IV52 8TW (50m from seafront)
🕓 11-midnight; 12.30-11 Sun
☎ (01599) 544222 🌐 plocktoninn.co.uk
Beer range varies Ⓗ
Popular family run inn, set in the heart of this beautiful West Highland village, in a sheltered bay of Loch Carron, close to the Isle of Skye. Surrounded by hills, it is a regular haunt for outdoor enthusiasts. Locally caught seafood takes pride of place on the menu served in bars and restaurant. All are welcome to join in the regular live traditional music sessions.
🏮Q🏮🍽️◐♿≈(Plockton)♣P

Rosemarkie

Plough Inn
48 High Street, IV10 8UF
🕓 11-midnight (1am Fri; 11.45 Sat); 12.30-11 Sun
☎ (01381) 620164
Beer range varies Ⓗ
Beautiful old pub in a pretty seaside village just 100 metres from the beach. It has a cosy wood panelled bar with an ancient marriage stone lintel (dated 1691) over the fireplace. A wide choice of beers are served from north of Scotland breweries including Orkney, Cairngorm, An Teallach and Hebridean. Food ranges from lunchtime bites to an a la carte menu featuring Black Isle produce such as lamb, beef and game. Booking is recommended. 🏮🍽️◐♿🖾♣P

Roy Bridge

Stronlossit Hotel
PH31 4AG
🕓 11-11.45 (1am Thu-Sat); 12.30-11.45 Sun
☎ (01397) 712253 🌐 stronlossit.co.uk
Cairngorm Trade Winds; guest beer Ⓗ
Traditional inn at the foot of the Nevis mountain range, an ideal base for outdoor activities or touring. Bar meals with local produce are available all day. The three handpumps dispense a selection of Scottish beers, often from the Highland Brewery, and occasional cider. Opening times vary in December and January. 🏮🍽️◐♿≈♣

Scourie

Scourie Hotel
IV27 4SX (on A894)
🕓 11-2.30, 5-11; 12-2.30, 6.30-10.30 Sun
☎ (01971) 502396 🌐 scourie-hotel.co.uk
Beer range varies Ⓗ
Popular with fishermen, this converted 1640 coaching inn overlooks Scourie Bay. The bar has a fishing theme with 1940s fishing nets as decoration. As well as the fixed bar menu, the hotel dining room serves high quality four-course meals featuring seafood with the menu changing daily. The four handpumps serve Scottish beer and one cider. Closed lunchtimes in winter. Q🏮🍽️◐♿🖾♣P⅄

Scousburgh: Shetland

Spiggie Hotel
ZE2 9JE (follow signs off A970)
🕓 12-2, 5-11 (midnight Fri & Sat)
☎ (01950) 460409 🌐 thespiggiehotel.co.uk
Beer range varies Ⓗ
Built as the original terminus of the Northern Isles Ferries, this small family-run country hotel is in an elevated location overlooking St Ninians Isle. The small bar has a stone floor and there is a separate restaurant serving good home-made food. Trout fishing on the Spiggie Loch (RSPB) can be arranged by the hotel. Q🏮🍽️◐P⅄

SCOTLAND

645

Stromness: Orkney

Ferry Inn

John Street, KW16 3AA (100m from ferry terminal)
🕒 9-midnight (1am Thu-Sat); 9.30-midnight Sun
☎ (01856) 850280 ⏺ ferryinn.com
Highland Scapa Special; Orkney Red MacGregor, Northern Light, seasonal beers; guest beers Ⓗ
A former temperance hotel, this is a welcome sight after the ferry crossing from Scrabster. Fitted out in mahogany, the bar resembles the interior of a schooner. It is popular with locals and visitors, particularly when the harbour is busy with divers who come to Orkney to explore the wrecks of Scapa Flow. Local folk musicians meet regularly. ❀🍴◑▲🖾

Stromness Hotel

15 Victoria Street, KW16 3AA
🕒 11 – 11 (1am Fri & Sat); 12 – 11 Sun
☎ (01856) 850298 ⏺ stromnesshotel.com
Highland Scapa Special; Orkney Red MacGregor, Dark Island, seasonal beers; guest beer Ⓗ
On the first floor of this imposing hotel you will find a large bar, the Hamnavoe Lounge, with windows and a small balcony overlooking the harbour. In winter a roaring fire and comfy settees welcome the visitor and during the season more space is given up to dining. Used as an Army HQ during WW11, it is well placed for visiting local world heritage sites. Annual jazz, blues and beer festivals are organised by the hotel throughout the year. 🛏❀🍴◑▲🖾P

Uig: Skye

Uig Hotel

IV51 9YE OS397634
🕒 12 (5 winter)-11.30; 12.30 (5 winter)-11 Sun; closed Jan
☎ (01470) 542205 ⏺ uighotel.com
Beer range varies Ⓗ
Attractive and imposing old coaching inn with spectacular views across Uig Bay to the ferry terminal for the Western Isles. The cosy lounge bar dispenses Isle of Skye beers from two handpulls in summer and one in winter. Meals are served in the bar and restaurant. The hotel keeps its own Highland cattle. Handy for a visit to the Isle of Skye Brewery.
🛏Q🍂❀🍴◑🖾P

Ullapool

Ferry Boat Inn

Shore Street, IV26 2UJ (on the waterfront)
🕒 11 (12.30 Sun)-11
☎ (01854) 612366 ⏺ ferryboat-inn.com
An Teallach Ale; Greene King Old Speckled Hen, seasonal beers; guest beer Ⓗ
Small, comfortable 18th-century inn, set in the middle of a row of whitewashed cottages on the Loch Broom waterfront, a short stroll from the Western Isles ferry terminal. A mixed clientele enjoys the informal atmosphere in this popular, old-fashioned bar, warmed by an open fire in winter, with panoramic views across the busy harbour towards Beinn Dearg and the Fannichs. Fresh local produce is served in the bar (all year) and restaurant (spring-late autumn). 🛏Q🍂🍴◑▲🖾⌐

Morefield Hotel

North Road, IV26 2TQ (off the A835 heading N from Ullapool) OSNH125947
🕒 12 (12.30 Sun)-11
☎ (01854) 612161 ⏺ morefieldmotel.co.uk
Beer range varies Ⓗ
Locally caught seafood is the speciality on the menu at this friendly and welcoming hostelry. Three ales are mainly from local Highland breweries. Landlord Tony organises the annual Ullapool Beer Festival, held at the Morefield in October. Comfortable motel accommodation provides an excellent base for discovering the surrounding area. Q❀🍴◑🍴&▲♣P⌐

Waternish: Skye

Stein Inn

Stein, IV55 8GA (N of Dunvegan on B886)
🕒 11-midnight (1am Fri, 12.30am Sat); 11.30-11 Sun; winter hours vary
☎ (01470) 592362 ⏺ steininn.co.uk
Isle of Skye Red Cuillin; guest beer Ⓗ
Family-run 18th century inn, the oldest on the Isle of Skye, located in a tiny fishing village on the shores of Loch Bay. Enjoy the warm fireside of a traditional Highland bar in winter or the loch-side beer garden in summer. The inn and garden afford fine views over the sea loch to Rubha Maol. Fresh seafood, landed at the nearby jetty, is served in season. Facilities for seafarers include council moorings, showers, food supplies (by arrangement) and message relay services.
🛏Q🍂❀🍴◑🖾&♣P⌐

Whitebridge

Whitebridge Hotel

IV2 6UN
🕒 11-11 Apr-Oct; 11-2.30, 5-11 Nov-Mar; 12.30-11 Sun
☎ (01456) 486413
Caledonian 80; guest beers Ⓗ
Built in 1899, this hotel is situated on an original military road through the foothills of the Monadhliath mountains. There is a classic Wade bridge nearby and the famous Falls of Foyers are within walking distance. The hotel has fishing rights on two local lochs. The attractive pitch pine panelled main bar has an alcove with pool table. The second handpump sells a variety of Scottish ales in summer. Most of the traditional pub food is home made.
Q❀🍴◑🖾🖾♣P

Wormadale: Shetland

Westings Inn

ZE2 9LJ (on A971, 2 miles past Tingwall airstrip) OS402464
🕒 12-3, 5-11 (12-midnight Fri & Sat)
☎ (01595) 840242 ⏺ westings.shetland.co.uk
Beer range varies Ⓗ
White painted inn in a stunning location near the summit of Wormadale Hill with marvellous sea views. This friendly inn offers a warm welcome to visitors, the locals always happy to entertain with a good story or two. Caravans are welcome and camping is available in the pub grounds.
Q🍂❀🍴◑🖾&♣P⌐

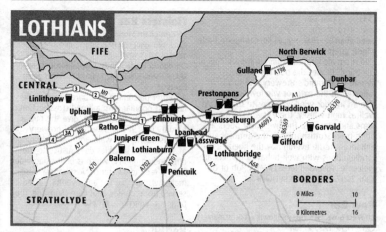

Authority areas covered: City of Edinburgh UA, East Lothian UA, Midlothian UA, West Lothian UA

Balerno

Malleny Arms
15 Main Street, EH14 7EQ
⚙ 11-midnight (11 Mon; 1am Fri & Sat); 12.30-11 Sun
☎ (0131) 449 7795
Caledonian Deuchars IPA Ⓗ
This one time hotel, also known as Honky Tonk, is situated in Balerno's pedestrian area. A vibrant community pub, it hosts weekly 'honky' pool competitions. Large screen TVs also make it popular on sporting occasions. Light wood floors and décor along with an area of comfy settees give a bright but homely feel. Dogs are welcome. ❀♣P

Dunbar

Volunteer Arms
17 Victoria Street, EH42 1HP (opp swimming pool)
⚙ 12-11(midnight Thu; 1am Fri & Sat); 12.30-midnight Sun
☎ (01368) 862278
Beer range varies Ⓗ
Overlooking Dunbar harbour, this is a friendly, traditional, locals' pub. The cosy panelled bar is decorated with lots of fishing and lifeboat oriented memorabilia. Upstairs is a restaurant serving an excellent menu with the emphasis on seafood. Food is served all day until 9.30pm. Live folk music is played every fortnight. Children are welcome until 8pm and dogs permitted after 9pm. Parasols on the patio provide shelter for smokers.
❀⊕Å⇌➡♣⌐

Edinburgh

Abbotsford Bar & Restaurant ☆
3 Rose Street, EH2 2PR
⚙ 11-11; 12.30-11 Sun
☎ (0131) 225 5276
Beer range varies Ⓐ
A traditional Scottish bar listed on CAMRA's national pub inventory. The magnificent island bar and gantry have been a fixture since 1902. The ornate plasterwork and corniced ceiling are highlighted by subdued lighting. Beers are often from micro-breweries. Evening meals are only served in the upstairs restaurant, but you may order beer with your meal from downstairs. Dogs are allowed in the bar after 3pm. Q⊕⇌(Waverley)➡

Barony Bar
81-85 Broughton Street, EH1 3RJ (E edge of New Town)
⚙ 11-midnight (1am Fri & Sat); 12.30-midnight Sun
☎ (0131) 558 2874
Caledonian Deuchars IPA, 80; Young's Bitter; guest beers Ⓗ
Characterful city pub, listed on the Scottish pub inventory due to its many fine internal features. Splendid tile work and stained wood are much in evidence while the bar and gantry are also noteworthy. Detailed cornices and a wooden floor add to the atmosphere of the L-shaped bar. Magnificent whisky mirrors adorn the walls. Food is served all day until 10pm (7pm Sun). ▲❀⊕&⇌(Waverley)➡♣

Bennets Bar
1 Maxwell Street, Morningside, EH10 5HT (S of centre)
⚙ 11-midnight (closed Sun)
☎ (0131) 447 1903
Greene King IPA; Inveralmond Ossian's Ale; guest beers Ⓐ
Couthy back-street boozer in the douce suburb of Morningside. The pub has been owned by the same family for generations. The decor appears to date back to at least the 1960s; the walls are adorned with photographs of old Edinburgh. Guest ales are generally from Scottish micros. Not a pub to visit with the kids. ❀

Blue Blazer
2 Spittal Street, EH3 9DX (SW side of centre)

SCOTLAND

☻ 11(12.30 Sun)-1am
☎ (0131) 229 5030
Caledonian Deuchars IPA, Ⓐ 80; Cairngorm Trade Winds; guest beers Ⓗ
Two room ale house nestling in the shadow of Edinburgh Castle. The pub was formerly owned by Bernard's Brewery and this is reflected in the exterior window screens and also an interior window opposite the bar. As well as malt whisky, there is a wide range of rums and brandies. The five guest beers are often from Scottish micros. The atmosphere is enhanced in the evening by the liberal use of candles. Dogs with well-behaved owners are welcome. Awarded local CAMRA Pub of the Year 2007. ≈(Haymarket)🖨♣

Bow Bar

80 West Bow, EH1 2HH (old town, off Grassmarket)
☻ 12-11.30; 12.30-11 Sun
☎ (0131) 226 7667 ⊕ bowbar.com
Belhaven 80/-; Caledonian Deuchars IPA; Taylor Landlord; guest beers Ⓐ
Classic Scottish one room ale house dedicated to traditional Scottish air pressure dispense and perpendicular drinking. The walls are festooned with original brewery mirrors and the superb gantry does justice to an award-winning selection of single malt whiskies. A map of the original 33 Scottish counties hangs above the fire place. Bar snacks are available at lunchtime. Awarded CAMRA Edinburgh Pub of the Year 2006. Dogs are welcome. Q≈(Waverley)🖨

Café Royal ☆

19 West Register Street, EH2 2AA (off E end of Princess St)
☻ 11-11(midnight Thu; 1am Fri & Sat); 12.30-11 Sun
☎ (0131) 556 1884 ⊕ thespiritgroup.com
Caledonian Deuchars IPA, 80; guest beers Ⓗ
One of the finest Victorian pub interiors in Scotland, listed on CAMRA's National Inventory dominated by an impressive oval island bar with ornate brass light fittings, and six magnificent ceramic tiled murals of innovators made by Doulton from pictures by John Eyre. The magnificent sporting windows of the Oyster bar were made by the same Edinburgh firm that supplied windows for the House of Lords. The Gents features an unusual hand basin. Meals are served all day. ◑≈(Waverley)🖨

Cask & Barrel

115 Broughton Street, EH1 3RZ (E of new town)
☻ 11-12.30am (1am Thu-Sat); 12.30-12.30am Sun
☎ (0131) 556 3132
Caledonian Deuchars IPA, 80; Draught Bass; Hadrian & Border Cowie; Harviestoun Bitter & Twisted; guest beers Ⓗ
Spacious and extremely busy ale house drawing a mainly local clientele of all ages, ranging from business people to football fans. The interior features an imposing horseshoe bar, bare floorboards, a splendid cornice and a collection of brewery mirrors. Old barrels act as tables for those who wish to stand up, or cannot find a seat. The guest beers, often from smaller Scottish breweries, come in a range of strengths. Sparklers can be removed on request. ❀◑♣≈(Waverley)🖨

Cloisters Bar

26 Brougham Street, EH3 9JH (SW edge of centre)
☻ 12-midnight (1am Fri & Sat); 12-midnight Sun
☎ (0131) 221 9997
Cairngorm Trade Winds; Caledonian Deuchars IPA; Greene King IPA; Taylor Landlord; guest beers Ⓗ
A former parsonage, this bare boarded ale house is popular with a broad cross section of drinkers. Large bench seats give the pub a friendly feel. A fine selection of brewery mirrors adorns the walls and the wide range of single malt whiskies does justice to the outstanding gantry, which is built using wood from a redundant church. A spiral staircase makes visiting the loo an adventure. Food is served from midday until 4pm (6pm Tue-Thu). Dogs are welcome. Q◑▤🖨

Dalriada

77 Promenade, Joppa, EH15 2EL (off Joppa Rd by St Philips church)
☻ 12-11 (midnight Fri & Sat); closed Mon Jan & Feb; 12-11 (10 winter) Sun
☎ (0131) 454 4500
Caledonian Deuchars IPA; guest beers Ⓗ
Located on the Portobello/Joppa promenade, where you can enjoy a pint and watch out for seals. The imposing entrance of this stone-built villa has an original tiled floor and fireplace. There are three bar areas with wooden flooring and furniture. The bar counter has a polished Italian granite top. An extensive snack menu is available 12-7 (not Mon). Children are welcome until 8pm. Dogs are also welcome on a lead and bowls of water provided. Live music plays on Friday and Saturday evenings and Sunday afternoon. 🚲❀≈(Brunstane Rd)🖨P↳

Halfway House

24 Fleshmarket Close, EH1 1BX (up steps opp. station's Market St entrance)
☻ 11-11.30 (1am Fri & Sat); 12.30-11.30 Sun
☎ (0131) 225 7101
Harviestoun Bitter & Twisted; guest beers Ⓗ
Cosy bar, full of character, hidden halfway down an old town 'close'. Old railway memorabilia and current timetables adorn the interior of this small, often busy, pub. Usually there are three interesting guest beers from smaller Scottish breweries. Card-carrying CAMRA members receive a discount on their first pint. Good quality, reasonably priced food is served all day. Opening hours may extend to 1am at busy times of the year. Dogs and children are welcome. ❀◑≈(Waverley)🖨♣↳

Homes Bar

102 Constitution Street, Leith, EH6 6AW
☻ 12-11 (midnight Thu-Sat); 12.30-11 Sun
☎ (0131) 553 7710
Beer range varies Ⓗ
Traditional one room, no frills, friendly public bar with wooden chairs and tables and a black and white lino tiled floor. The old-fashioned ambience is enhanced by the decor which features antique tin boxes, old beer bottles and miniature spirit bottles. An interesting range of real ales is served from five custom made handpumps. 🖨♣

Malt & Hops

45 The Shore, Leith, EH6 6QU
✪ 12-11 (midnight Wed & Thu; 1am Fri & Sat); 12.30-11 Sun
☎ (0131) 555 0083
Caledonian Deuchars IPA; Marston's Pedigree; Tetley Burton Ale; guest beers ⒣
One room public bar dating from 1749 in the heart of Leith's riverside restaurant district. Wood panelling gives an intimate feel with numerous mirrors, artefacts and a large oil painting adding interest. The superb collection of pump clips, many from now defunct breweries, indicates the ever-changing interesting range of guest beers served. No meals are served on Saturday or Sunday. Children are welcome until 6pm. Dogs are permitted. ♨❀◑🖵♣

Old Dock Bar

3-5 Dock Place, Leith, EH6 6LV
✪ 12-11 (1am Fri-Sat); 12.30-11 Sun
☎ (0131) 555 4474
Atlas Latitude; guest beers ⒣
Small, traditional bar adjoining a large restaurant, now home of the original eight-handpump bank from Todd's Tap. The building has been a bar since 1813 and claims to be Leith's oldest; its walls are decorated with maritime prints and photographs of old Leith. Conveniently situated for visitors to the Scottish Executive building and Ocean Terminal shopping centre, it offers good quality meals, with an Italian slant, served all day. ❀◑&🖵♣

Oxford Bar ☆

8 Young Street, EH2 4JB (New Town, off Charlotte Sq)
✪ 11-midnight (1am Thu-Sat); 12.30-11 Sun
☎ (0131) 539 7119 ⊕ oxfordbar.com
Caledonian Deuchars IPA; guest beers ⒣
Small, basic, vibrant New Town drinking shop decorated with Burns memorabilia. A favourite pub of Inspector Rebus and his creator Ian Rankin, it has also been the haunt of many other famous and infamous characters over the years – you never know who you might bump into. Why not visit the website and contribute a story. A real taste of New Town past, the bar is listed in CAMRA's national pub inventory. Simple bar snacks are available. Dogs are welcome. 🖵♣

Regent

2 Montrose Terrace, EH7 5OL (¾ mile E of centre)
✪ 11 (12.30 Sun)-1am
☎ (0131) 661 8198
Caledonian Deuchars IPA; guest beers ⒣
Large, comfortable tenement bar with two rooms (one music free), all on one level. Comfortable seating includes banquettes, leather sofas and armchairs. A new slant on pub games is the gymnastic pommel horse between the Ladies and Gents toilets. CAMRA LGBT group meet here on the 1st Monday of the month. Orkney Dark Island is often a guest beer. Bar snacks are available and dogs are welcome. 🖵

Stable Bar

Mortonhall Park, 30 Frogston Road East, EH16 6TJ (S edge of City)

✪ 11-midnight (11pm winter); 12.30-11 Sun
☎ (0131) 664 0773
Caledonian Deuchars IPA; Stewart Pentland IPA, Copper Cascade ⒣
A country pub in the city mind you don't knock down any Highland coos on the long driveway! The comfortable bar is dominated by a large stone chimney and fire place with a roaring log fire in winter. Food is served all day until 10pm (9pm winter). The plainer back room is primarily for diners. As befits a country pub, dogs are more than welcome, however arachnophobics beware! ♨❀◑▲🖵♣P

Standing Order

62-66 George Street, EH2 2LR
✪ 9am (12.30 Sun)-1am
☎ (0131) 225 4460
Caledonian Deuchars IPA, 80; guest beers ⒣
Built in 1879 to a Robert Adam design, once the head office of the British Linen Bank, the building was converted into a vast pub in 1997 by Wetherspoon. The main bar has a superb high ceiling and polished granite pillars. Smaller rooms lead off, one containing the old Chubb vault door. Despite its size it can be very busy at times, however it lacks atmosphere when quiet. Meals are served all day. Disabled access is via Rose Street entrance. Children are welcome until 8pm. ❀◑&≠(Waverley)🖵♦

Starbank Inn

64 Laverockbank Road, EH5 3BZ (foreshore near Newhaven)
✪ 11-11 (midnight Thu-Sat); 12.30-11 Sun
☎ (0131) 552 4141 ⊕ starbankinn.co.uk
Belhaven Sandy Hunter's Traditional Ale, 80/- Ale; Caledonian Deuchars IPA; Taylor Landlord; guest beers ⒣
Bright, airy, bare-boarded ale house, with a U-shaped layout extending into a conservatory dining area. The walls sport several rare brewery mirrors. Enjoy the superb views across the Firth to Fife. At least four interesting guest ales are usually available and the pub is proud not sell any keg ales. You can, however, try a pint of prawns with your beer! Children are welcome until 8.30pm. Dogs are also welcome if on a lead. Occasional jazz is played on Sundays. Q❀◑&🖵♣

Thomson's

182-184 Morrison Street, EH3 8EB (W edge of centre)
✪ 12-11.30 (midnight Thu-Sat); 4-11.30 Sun
☎ (0131) 228 5700 ⊕ thomsonsbar.co.uk
Caledonian Deuchars IPA; Taylor Landlord; guest beers Ⓐ
Modelled on the style of Glasgow architect Alexander 'Greek' Thomson, this award-winning pub is dedicated to traditional Scottish air pressure dispense. The superb, custom built gantry features mirrors inlaid with scenes from Greek mythology. The walls are a veritable history of Scottish brewing, with rare mirrors from long defunct Scottish breweries. Guest beers are often from Pictish, Hop Back or Atlas. Food is limited to pies only on Saturday and no food is served on Sunday. Dogs are welcome. Q❀◑≠(Haymarket)🖵

Winston's

20 Kirk Loan, Corstorphine, EH12 7HD (3 miles W of centre, off St Johns Road)

✪ 11-11.30 (midnight Thu-Sat); 12.30-11 Sun

☎ (0131) 539 7077

Caledonian Deuchars IPA, 80; guest beers Ⓗ

This comfortable lounge bar is situated in Corstorphine, just over a mile from Murrayfield stadium and not far from the zoo. The small, modern building houses a warm and welcoming active community pub, used by old and young alike (children are welcome until 3pm). The interior has golfing and rugby themes. Simple bar snacks are served all day and lunchtime meals feature wonderful home-made pies. Dogs are welcome.
🅼❀Ⓠ🖳♣🍺

Garvald

Garvald Inn

EH41 4LN

✪ 12-3, 5-11 (midnight Fri & Sat); closed Mon; 12.30-11 (5 winter) Sun

☎ (01620) 830311

Beer range varies Ⓗ

Family-run 18th-century pub located in a pretty conservation village by the Lammermuir Hills. The small bar is cosy and welcoming, with half-panelled walls, a crimson colour scheme and one exposed stone wall. Good food is served in both the bar and tiny dining room. The dinner menu is particularly impressive. Live music is played on the first Tuesday of the month. Children are welcome, with toys provided. Dogs are only welcome outside meal times. 🅼Ⓠ❀Ⓓ♣

Gifford

Goblin Ha' Hotel

Main Street, EH41 4QH

✪ 11-midnight (1am Fri & Sat); 11-11 Sun

☎ (01620) 810244 ⊕ goblinha.com

Caledonian Deuchars IPA; Hop Back Summer Lightning; guest beers Ⓗ

A long-established inn near the village green. With colourful decor and light stained wood, the focus is on food (served 11-9.30pm) in the smart contemporary lounge bar and conservatories, though an area is available for drinking. Non-diners may prefer the more rustic public bar, with its half-wood, half-stone walls. A games room leads off the bar. Children are welcome in the lounge areas until 8pm. Dogs are welcome in the bar. Live music is hosted on the third Friday of the month.
🅼Ⓠ❀🍴Ⓓ🖳🖨♣

Gullane

Old Clubhouse

East Links Road, EH31 2AF (W end of village, off A198)

✪ 11-11 (midnight Thu-Sat); 12.30-11 Sun

☎ (01620) 842008 ⊕ oldclubhouse.com

Caledonian Deuchars IPA; Taylor Landlord; guest beers Ⓐ

There's a colonial touch to this pub, which looks out over the golf links to the Lammermuir Hills. The half-panelled walls are adorned with historic memorabilia and stuffed animals. Caricature-style statuettes of the Marx Brothers and Laurel and Hardy look down from the gantry. Food features highly and is served all day. The extensive menu includes seafood, pasta, barbecue, curries, salads and burgers. Children are welcome until 8pm. Dogs are also permitted. 🅼❀Ⓓ🖳♿🖨🍺

Haddington

Tyneside Tavern

10 Poldrate, EH41 4DA (A6137, ⅓ mile S of centre)

✪ 11-11 (midnight Thu; 12.45am Fri & Sat); 12.30-midnight Sun

☎ (01620) 822221 ⊕ tynesidetavern.co.uk

Caledonian Deuchars IPA, 80; guest beer Ⓗ

Set close to the River Tyne near an old water mill, this community pub has a long, narrow bar that attracts a mixed clientele and is popular for watching televised sport. The lounge has been extended and serves mainly as a busy bistro at lunchtimes and evenings until 9pm. It has wooden floors and wood-topped tables with cast iron legs. Children are welcome until 8pm and dogs are also permitted. Guest beers are chosen from the S&N guest list. 🅼❀Ⓓ🍴♿🖳♣🍺

Juniper Green

Railway Inn

542 Lanark Road, EH14 5EL

✪ 11-11 (midnight Thu-Sat); 12.30-11 Sun

☎ (0131) 458 5395

Caledonian Deuchars IPA; Stewart Copper Cascade; Taylor Landlord Ⓗ

A strong community spirit exists within this well-appointed, single room lounge bar set in a late 1800s building. The decor is clean and attractive throughout; the bar counter is mahogany and a more modern gantry is designed to match. Pictures of the old Balerno branch line decorate the walls. The food is freshly cooked to a high standard. A secluded patio and garden are popular in summer. Not a pub to visit if you are wearing dirty overalls.
❀Ⓠ🖳🍺

Lasswade

Laird & Dog Hotel

5 High Street, EH18 1NA (on A768 near river)

✪ 11-11.30 (11.45 Thu; 12.30am Fri & Sat); 12.30-11.30 Sun

☎ (0131) 663 9219 ⊕ lairdanddog.btinternet.co.uk

Beer range varies Ⓗ

Comfortable village local catering for all tastes, from those who enjoy a quiet drink or meal to music-loving pool players. The two real ales are usually from smaller breweries. Food is available all day with a good menu, daily specials and cheaper bar snacks. Pictures and horse brasses decorate the bar and a real fire is surrounded by armchairs. Pictures and horse brasses decorate the bar, there is an unusual bottle-shaped well and a real fire surrounded by armchairs. Dogs and cats are welcome. Children are also welcome until 8pm.
🅼❀🛏Ⓓ♿🖳♣Ⓟ🍺

Linlithgow

Four Marys

65-67 High Street, EH49 7ED
🕐 11-11 (11.45 Thu-Sat); 12.30-11 Sun
☎ (01506) 842171
Belhaven 80/-, St Andrew's Ale; Caledonian Deuchars IPA; Greene King IPA; guest beers Ⓗ
Built around 1500 as a dwelling house, the pub was named after the four ladies-in-waiting of Mary, Queen of Scots, who was born in nearby Linlithgow Palace. The pub has seen several uses throughout the years; it was once a chemist's shop run by the Waldie family whose most famous member, David, established the anaesthetic properties of chloroform in 1847. Beer festivals are hosted in May and October when the handpumps are increased from eight to eighteen. ⓓ≠🖵🕯

Platform 3

1a High Street, EH49 7AB
🕐 10.30-midnight (1am Fri & Sat); 12.30-midnight Sun
☎ (01506) 847405
Caledonian Deuchars IPA; guest beers Ⓗ
Small, friendly pub on the railway station approach, originally the public bar of the hotel next door. It was purchased and renovated in 1998 as a pub in its own right. Note the interesting memorabilia displayed around the walls and look out for the train running above the bar. The guest ale, from either Cairngorm or Stewart, rotates on one pump. Live music is occasionally hosted. ≠🖵♣

Lothianbridge

Sun Inn

EH22 4TR (A7, near Newtongrange)
🕐 11 (12 Sun)-midnight
☎ (0131) 663 2456 ⊕ thesuninndalkeith.com
Caledonian Deuchars IPA; guest beer Ⓗ
Built circa 1870, the Sun is situated in the shadow of the impressive, currently disused, 23-span Waverley line viaduct. A friendly welcome is offered to both locals and travellers alike. The bar caters for drinkers and diners – food is served all day. Tastefully decorated throughout, a prominence of local art and a suspended model railway system add interest in the bar. An additional dining area overlooks the garden. Children and dogs are welcome. 🏨❀🍴ⓓ▲🖵P🕯

Lothianburn

Steading

118-120 Biggar Road, EH10 7DU (A702, just S of bypass)
🕐 11-midnight; 12.30-11 Sun
☎ (0131) 445 1128
Caledonian Deuchars IPA; Orkney Dark Island; Taylor Landlord; guest beer Ⓗ
The pub was converted from farm cottages and has distinct areas for drinkers and diners. The popular restaurant includes a large conservatory extension and food is served all day. A simple menu is available in the bar area. The outside drinking area has excellent views of the Pentland Hills and the pub is ideally placed for a relaxing pint after walking in the hills or visiting the nearby dry ski slope. Children and dogs are welcome. 🏨❀ⓓ🖵P

Musselburgh

Levenhall Arms

10 Ravensheugh Road, EH21 7PP (B1348, 1 mile E of centre)
🕐 12-11 (midnight Thu; 1am Fri & Sat); 12.30-midnight Sun
☎ (0131) 665 3220
Stewart Pentland IPA; guest beer Ⓗ
Three-room hostelry dating from 1830, popular with locals and race-goers. The lively, cheerfully decorated public bar is half timber panelled and carpeted. A smaller area leads off, with a dartboard and pictures of old local industries. The quieter lounge area has vinyl banquettes and tables for dining (food is served all day until 8pm). Dogs are welcome in the bar. Children are welcome until 8.30pm in lounge. Qⓓ🖵▲≠(Wallyford)🖵♣P🕯

Volunteer Arms (Staggs)

81 North High Street, EH21 6JE (behind Brunton Hall)
🕐 12-11 (11.30 Thu, midnight Fri & Sat); 1-11 Sun
☎ (0131) 665 9654
Caledonian Deuchars IPA; guest beers Ⓗ
Outstanding pub run by the same family since 1858. The bar and snug are traditional with a lino-tiled floor, dark wood panelling and mirrors from defunct local breweries. The superb gantry is topped with old casks. The snug has a nascent history collection featuring local breweries. The more modern lounge opens at the weekend. Three guest beers, often pale and hoppy, change regularly. Dogs are welcome in the bar, but don't bring the kids. Winner of CAMRA Lothian Pub of the Year 2007. ❀🖵🖵♣🕯

North Berwick

Nether Abbey Hotel

20 Dirleton Avenue, EH39 4BQ (on A198, ¾ mile W of town centre)
🕐 11-11 (midnight Thu; 1am Fri & Sat); 12.30-11 Sun
☎ (01620) 892802 ⊕ netherabbey.co.uk
Caledonian Deuchars IPA; guest beers Ⓐ
Comfortable, recently refurbished, family run hotel in a stone built villa. The ground floor is an open plan, split level room comprising a bar and two restaurant areas. It has a light and modern feel with pine and steel decor. The marble-topped bar counter has a row of modern chrome founts. The middle ones, with horizontally moving levers, dispense the real ales. Food is served all day in summer and at weekends. Children are welcome until 9pm. Dogs are also permitted. ❀🛏🍴ⓓ&▲≠🖵P🕯

Ship

7-9 Quality Street, EH39 4HJ
🕐 11-11 (midnight Thu-Sat); 12.30-11 Sun
☎ (01620) 890676
Caledonian Deuchars IPA; guest beers Ⓗ
Open plan bar, split into three areas by a glass partition and a twice pierced wall, with pine floorboards, a mahogany counter and a dark stained wooden gantry. Real ale is dispensed from founts, which look similar to those dispensing the keg beers, so look carefully at the pump clips. Popular for food, which is served until 3pm (4pm at weekends). Children are welcome until 8pm and dogs permitted.

SCOTLAND

Live music is hosted regularly on Saturday night. ⌂⊗◑Å⇌⊠♣⌐

Penicuick

Navaar
23 Bog Road, EH26 9BY (just W of centre)
🕐 12-1am (midnight Sun)
☎ (01968) 672693
Stewart Pentland IPA ⊞
A lively pub with a strong community spirit, situated in an old private house, circa 1870. The bar is open plan with a large log and coal fire. Pool and dominoes are played. The restaurant offers an extensive À la carte menu, serving meals all day. Snacks are available in the bar. A large patio and decked area is popular in summer. Dogs are welcome.
⌂⊗⌂◑⊠♣P⌐

Prestonpans

Prestoungrange Gothenburg ☆
227 High Street, EH32 9BE
🕐 11-11 (midnight Fri & Sat); 12.30-11 Sun
☎ (01875) 819922 ⊕ prestoungrange.org
Fowler's Gothenburg Porter, Prestonpans 80/-, Prestonpans IPA Ⓐ
Superbly refurbished Gothenburg pub, winner of the 2005 English Heritage pub refurbishment award and CAMRA Lothian Pub of the Year 2006. The ground floor comprises a micro-brewery, restaurant and public bar, which must be seen to be appreciated. Upstairs is a lounge/function room and meeting room with superb views over the Forth. The walls throughout are covered in murals, paintings and prints depicting past local life. Meals are served all day Sunday.

Children are welcome, but not in the bar.
⌂◑⊗&Å⊠P

Ratho

Bridge Inn
27 Baird Road, EH28 8RA (by canal)
🕐 11.30-11 (midnight Fri & Sat); 12.30-11 Sun
☎ (0131) 333 1320 ⊕ bridgeinn.com
Caledonian Deuchars IPA; guest beers ⊞
Food oriented old canal-side inn, with a modern extension. The older part, originally a farmhouse dating from around 1750, is used as a restaurant. The extension is a lounge bar/dining area with views over the canal where families are welcome. The original owner campaigned tirelessly for the restoration of the canal, part of the millennium link project. Regular cruises depart from the pub during the summer. Food is served all day until 9pm (8pm Sun). ⊗◑⊠♣P⌐

Uphall

Oatridge Hotel
2-4 East Main Street, EH52 5DA (jct A899/B8046)
🕐 11 (12.30 Sun)-midnight
☎ (01506) 856465
Beer range varies ⊞
Originally a 19th-century coaching inn, the hotel now serves the modern day traveller, as well as thirsty locals. Real ale is served in the public bar, where up to three ales are available. The bar has a stylish art deco feel and displays a collection of ceramic vessels that originally held refreshing liquids. Look out for the large etched mirror, depicting scenes of yesteryear. TV sports are popular at the weekend and pool is also played.
⊗⊭◑⊟⊠P

Half Way House, Edinburgh, Lothians.

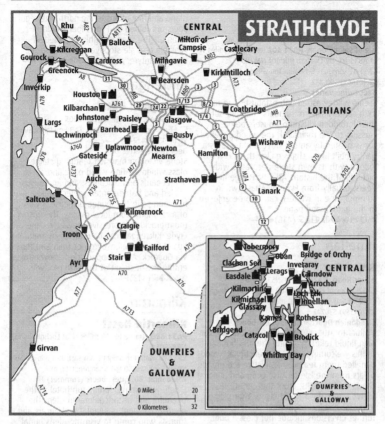

Authority areas covered: Argyll & Bute UA, Ayrshire UAs, City of Glasgow UA, Dunbartonshire UAs, Inverclyde UA, Lanarkshire UAs, Renfrewshire UAs

ARGYLL & BUTE
Arrochar

Village Inn

Shore Road, G83 7AX (on A814, S of A83 jct)
🕐 11-midnight (1am Fri & Sat); 12-midnight Sun
☎ (01301) 702 279 ⏚ maclay.com
Beer range varies Ⓗ

Attractive inn with impressive views near the head of Loch Long, set back among mature conifers. The bar room serves three ales, one usually from Fyne Ales. Food is available in the bar and garden at lunchtime, and in the evening in the restaurant. Close to the 'Arrochar Alps', it is popular with passing hill walkers, day trippers and tourists, as well as friendly locals and business people staying as guests. Tarbert/Arrochar rail station is a mile away. ⚏Q❀⇔⋈◑❶⊟ᗢ⏢P⌐

Bridge of Orchy

Bridge of Orchy Hotel

PA36 4AD (on A82 at N end of Glen Orchy)
NN298396
🕐 11-11 (midnight Fri & Sat); 12-11 Sun
☎ (01838) 400208 ⏚ scottish-selection.co.uk
Caledonian Deuchars IPA, 80; guest beers Ⓗ

The hub of the West Highland Way on the route northwards to Glencoe and Fort William. It has a railway station almost to itself and despite (or perhaps because of) its isolation, is popular with fishermen, hill walkers, climbers, canoeists and other outdoor types, some staying in the bunkhouse as an alternative to the hotel rooms. There are impressive views of the surrounding hills from the bar and lounge/restaurant to the rear. It may close for three weeks mid-winter, so ring to check. ⚏Q❀❀⇔⋈◑❶⊟ᗢP

Cardross

Coach House Inn

Main Road, G82 5JX OSNS347775
🕐 12-midnight (1am Fri & Sat)
☎ (01389) 841358
Caledonian Deuchars IPA; Fyne Piper's Gold; guest beer Ⓗ

Inviting village pub with a comfortable lounge with a real fire and sofas. Pool is played in a raised area of the smart bar. An ever-changing guest ale adds variety to the regular beers and the pub is known locally for good food. In the garden a tall fir tree allows in sun while deflecting summer showers. Its location close to Cardross rail station makes it ideal for a short trip out from Glasgow. ⚏❀⇔⋈◑❶⊟ᗢ⋈(216)P⌐

653

Clachan Seil

Tigh-an-Truish

Isle of Seil by Oban, PA34 4QZ (on B844 5 miles W of A816 jct, by Clachan Bridge) NM785197
✪ 11-11 summer; 5-11 Mon-Thu winter; 11-11 Sun
☎ (01852) 300 242
Beer range varies ⊞
Scenic whitewashed pub established in the 18th century where islanders changed out of their forbidden kilts into trousers before crossing to the mainland. The wood panelled bar is heated by an old stove and features a gantry built like a ship's galley.There is a cosy lounge with its own stove decorated with pictures of the historic Atlantic Bridge nearby. Beers, usually from Fyne or Atlas (two in summer, one in winter), can also be enjoyed in the garden and patio.
ᴁQ⍩ᔕⲀᔿ◖◗⏛Ⴑᕱ(418)♣Pⵎ

Innellan

Royal Bar

4 Pier Road, PA23 7TH OSNS153708
✪ 12-midnight (2am Fri & Sat) summer; 2-midnight (12-2am Sat) winter; 12.30-midnight Sun
☎ (01369) 830742
Caledonian Deuchars IPA; guest beers ⊞
Visitors to attractive yet ale-poor Dunoon can gain liquid relief by taking the 483 bus south to this welcoming local. The functional, wood-panelled room features distinctive red granite pillars from the isle of Ailsa Craig and nautical charts on the walls. From the bar are fine views across the Firth of Clyde. There is an impressive selection of malt whiskies and further diversions include hot pies, a pool table and a real fire. ᴁᕱ(483)

Inveraray

George Hotel

Main Street East, PA32 8TT
✪ 11 (12 Sun)-midnight
☎ (01499) 302111 ⊕ thegeorgehotel.co.uk
Caledonian Deuchars IPA; guest beers ⊞
Current CAMRA Argyll Pub of the Year, built in 1770 in the centre of a historic small town on the shore of Loch Fyne, owned by the same family since 1860. It has a small, lively public bar and a larger stone-walled and floored lounge with adjoining rooms. There is usually a guest beer from local Fyne Ales and sometimes beers from other micros are available. The food is of a high standard.
ᴁᔕ❄ᔿ◖◗⏛Ⴑᕱ(926, 976)**P**

Kames

Kames Hotel

PA21 2AR OSNR975714
✪ 12-1am (midnight winter); 12.30-midnight Sun
☎ (01700) 811489 ⊕ kames-hotel.com
Caledonian Deuchars IPA; Fyne Highlander ⊞
Located on the eastern edge of the most westerly peninsula of Cowal, the hotel is reached by a scenic highland drive. The long bar has several adjoining areas that are effectively separate rooms, with wood panelling and traditional decor. There are impressive views over the Kyles of Bute to the island and mountains to the north. The regular beers are joined by Fyne Piper's Gold in summer. The food is highly regarded. A valuable real ale stopover en-route to the ferry to Kintyre. ᴁQ⍩ᔕ❄ᔿ◖◗Ⴑᕱ♣♠Pⵎ

Kilcreggan

Kilcreggan Hotel

Argyll Road, G84 0JP OSNS238805
✪ 12-midnight (1am Fri & Sat); 12.30-midnight Sun
☎ (01436) 842243
Beer range varies ⊞
Stone Victorian mansion featuring stained glass windows, fine wood panelling, bargeboards and balconies, and an unusual gabled and battlemented tower. Four handpumps in the lounge dispense a variety of ales, many from local micros. The upstairs room provides impressive views over the Clyde. Kilcreggan can be reached by train and bus (813) via Helensburgh or train and ferry via Gourock. A Daytripper ticket allows travel enthusiasts a circuit of the Firth of Clyde.
❄ᔿ◖◗ᕱ(813)Pⵎ

Kilmartin

Kilmartin Hotel

PA31 8RQ (On A816, 10 miles N of Lochgilphead) NR835989
✪ 12 (5 winter)-midnight (1am Sat); 12-midnight Sun
☎ (01546) 510250 ⊕ kilmartin-hotel.com
Caledonian 80, guest beers (summer) ⊞
Small, welcoming, family-run hotel in the beautiful and historic Kilmartin Glen. The narrow bar room is popular with locals and tourists who come to visit the glens burial cairns, rock carvings and standing stones and the remains of the original fortress of the Scots at Dounadd. It serves a regular beer and at least one guest, often from a Scottish micro. Good home cooking is on offer lunchtimes and evenings. The games room has a pool table. Occasional traditional music sessions are hosted. Q❄ᔿ◖◗⏛Ⴑᕱ♣P

Kilmichael Glassary

Horseshoe Inn

Bridgend, PA31 8QA OSNR852928
✪ 5-11 (midnight Thu; 1am Fri); 12-1am Sat; 12-11 Sun
☎ (01546) 606369 ⊕ horshoeinn.biz
Caledonian Deuchars IPA; guest beers ⊞
Quiet pub converted from an old farmhouse in a small village nestling at the foot of a glen full of prehistoric significance. The public bar features pictures of local sites including

INDEPENDENT BREWERIES	
Arran	Brodick
Clockwork	Glasgow
Fyne	Cairndow
Houston	Houston
Islay	Bridgend
Isle of Mull	Tobermory
Kelburn	Barrhead
Oyster	Easdale
Strathaven	Strathaven
West	Glasgow
Windie Goat	Failford

Dunadd where early Celtic kings were crowned. To the rear is a games room and pool table. Meals can be taken in the stone walled lounge and separate dining room. The guest beers from the Houston Brewery are noted on a blackboard over the public bar. ♨Q❀⇔◑◐⊟⊡(423)P

Lerags

Barn

Cologin, PA34 4SE OSNM853260

☼ summer 12-11; winter 5-11 Mon & Fri, closed Tue-Thu, 12-11 Sat & Sun

☎ (01631) 564 618 ⊕ cologin.co.uk

Fyne Highlander, guest beers (summer) Ⓗ

A mile off the A 816, set in picturesque West Highland scenery, this converted farm building forms part of a small holiday chalet complex. Excellent food is very popular with holidaymakers using the accommodation. An additional guest beer is dispensed in summer. The outdoor seating in fine weather has views across the duck pond to the hills. Local musicians play regularly throughout the year. Q❀⇔◑P⅃

Loch Eck

Coylet Inn

PA23 8SG (on A815 at south end of Loch Eck) OSNS143885

☼ 11-11 (midnight Fri & Sat); 12.30-11 Sun

☎ (01369) 840426 ⊕ coylet-locheck.co.uk

Caledonian Deuchars IPA; Fyne Highlander; guest beers Ⓗ

Former coaching inn dating from 1650 in a magnificent highland setting on the shore of beautiful Loch Eck. The hotel has a small, cosy public bar and a restaurant. The latter enjoys a well-deserved reputation for good food made with high quality local produce. Boat hire and fishing permits can be obtained at the hotel. Those with a historical interest in their beer should note that this was one of the last Scottish pubs to replace water engines with handpumps. ♨❀⇔◑⊡P⅃

Oban

Lorne

Stevenson Street, PA34 5NA

☼ 12-1am (2am Fri & Sat); 12.30-2am Sun

☎ (01631) 570020

Caledonian Deuchars IPA; guest beers Ⓗ

The mustard coloured exterior of this smart, well-established locals' pub makes it easy to identify, set in a minor street just off the centre of town. The large room is mostly occupied by the island bar and high gantry - note the tall, twisted brass columns. The guest beer is usually from Fyne Ales and the food, made with local produce, is ever popular. The garden is protected from winds by a high cliff face. A convenient stop for visitors to Oban seeking refreshment. ❀◑Å⇌⊡⅃

Oban Inn

1 Stafford Street, PA34 5NJ

☼ 11 (12.30 Sun)-12.45am

☎ (01631) 562484

Caledonian 80; guest beers Ⓗ

Situated on the harbour front, this traditional bar is convenient for travellers using the ferries to the islands. Dating from 1790, the original Easdale slate and wood panelling is retained in the corner bar. The south-facing windows provide views down the harbour promenade, busy with shoppers and tourists. The theme here is the sea with maritime artefacts providing the decor and navy flags on the ceiling. A real ale is also available in the comfortable upstairs lounge in summer. ◑◐⊟⇌⊡

Rhu

Rhu Inn

49 Gareloch Road, G84 8LA (near village church)

☼ 11-midnight (1am Fri & Sat); 12.30-11 Sun

☎ (01436) 821048 ⊕ therhuinn.co.uk

Caledonian Deuchars IPA; guest beers Ⓗ

Originally a coaching inn dating from 1648, this friendly local is at the centre of the community. It has arguably the smallest bar in Strathclyde, featuring an impressive mahogany gantry, Tiffany-style windows and a flagstone floor. There is also a snug and larger lounge bar. The walls display pictures of past village life, giving an olde worlde feel. The regular beer is supported by a guest from Fyne Ales in the lounge. Live music plays at the weekend. ♨⇔◑⊟&⊡(813)♣P

Rothesay: Isle of Bute

Black Bull Inn

3 West Princes Street, PA20 9AF (on promenade opp. yacht marina)

☼ 11-11 (midnight Fri & Sat); 12.30-11 Sun

☎ (01700) 502366

Caledonian Deuchars IPA; guest beers Ⓗ

Friendly two-room 19th century seaside pub, sitting in the midst of the fading grandeur of a once busy Clyde resort. Handy for ferries to and from Wemyss Bay on the mainland and buses to all parts of the island, it is popular with locals and yachters moored at the marina opposite the pub's Albert Place entrance. In summer food is served all day, in winter lunchtimes only Mon-Thu, all day Fri-Sun. Steak sizzlers are a Friday and Saturday evening speciality. ◑◐⊟Å

AYRSHIRE & ARRAN
Auchentiber

Blair Tavern

KA13 7RR (A736/B778 jct)

☼ 11-3, 5-11; 11-11 Sat; 12.30-11 Sun

☎ (01294) 850237

Beer range varies Ⓗ

Opening as a public house in the late 19th century, this traditional inn is situated in a remote hamlet with few houses nearby. The emphasis here is on good food, making it well worth the journey to seek out this attractive hostelry. It has two rooms with traditional decor. The guest beers are usually from the Kelburn Brewery. Q◑◐⊡(X44)P

Ayr

Balgarth

9 Dunure Road, KA7 4HR (on A719 2 miles S of town centre)
✪ 11-10 (11 Fri & Sat)
☎ (01292) 442441
Beer range varies Ⓗ
Imposing red sandstone multi-room building set in its own grounds. Some areas are more akin to an up-market restaurant, while others cater for drinkers. The large gardens feature an excellent children's play area. At least one of the two beers offered is from one of the local Arran, Kelburn or Strathaven breweries. The opening times and beer range may be extended during the summer months.
⊛❶❺P

Geordie's Byre

103 Main Street, KA8 8BU
✪ 11-11 (midnight Thu-Sat); 12.30-11 Sun
☎ (01292) 264925
Caledonian Deuchars IPA; guest beers Ⓐ
The rather ordinary exterior belies a gem of a pub where the landlord and landlady have reigned supreme for over 30 years. Winner of numerous CAMRA awards (including joint branch winner 2006), both the public bar and lounge feature a wealth of memorabilia. Up to four guest ales are sourced from far and near; at least one is from a local micro. More than 100 malt whiskies and around 30 rums are also available. Several buses stop outside the front door. Q⊟≠(Newton-on-Ayr)⊟

Old Racecourse Hotel

2 Victoria Park, KA7 2TR (A719 1 mile S of Centre)
✪ 11 - midnight (12.30 Fri & Sat); 12.30 - 11 Sun
☎ (01292) 262873 ⊕ oldracecoursehotel.co.uk
Beer range varies Ⓗ
A refurbishment has resulted in a return to a multi-roomed design for this small, family run hotel. The lounge bar, whilst comfortable, is now rather small and dominated by a large flat-screen TV. However, drinkers are welcome to use the adjacent restaurant areas as overspill. Up to four changing guest ales are sourced from far and near. The racecourse in the title refers to a nearby former horse racing venue, now playing fields and a golf course. This hotel is an ideal base to visit the world renowned local golf courses, Burns Heritage Park and other delights of south Ayrshire. ⊛⋈❶⊟P

Wellington's Bar

17 Wellington Square, KA7 1EZ
✪ 11-12.30; 12.30-midnight Sun
☎ (01292) 262794
Beer range varies Ⓗ
A large Wellington boot advertises the location of this basement bar. Close to the seafront, court and local government offices, it is popular with tourists and office workers alike. The Wednesday evening quiz is a highlight and live music features at the weekend with bands on Saturday and an acoustic session on Sunday. One changing ale is often from the local Kelburn brewery but larger regional breweries also feature. Good value food is served daily until 6pm. ❶≠⊟

West Kirk

58A Sandgate, KA7 1BX
✪ 11-12.30am; 12.30-midnight Sun
☎ (01292) 880416 ⊕ jdwetherspoon.co.uk
Beer range varies Ⓗ
This Wetherspoon's conversion of a former church retains many of the original features – access to the toilets is via the pulpit. Up to six changing guest ales are offered with local micros usually well represented. Meals are available all day, from 9am for breakfast, and children are welcome until 6pm. The front patio drinking area has a shelter for smokers. The bus station is almost opposite.
⊛❶❺≠⊟⌐

Brodick: Isle of Arran

Brodick Bar

Alma Road, KA27 8BU
✪ 11-11 (midnight Fri & Sat); 3-11 winter; 5.30-11 Sun summer only
☎ (01770) 302169
Caledonian Deuchars IPA; guest beers Ⓟ
Long white building close to the post office with two bars on different levels. The lower area is used mainly as a restaurant, the top bar has more of a pub feel and is where the real ale is dispensed. The taps do not have pump clips - current beers are displayed on a blackboard. Good food is freshly cooked and features local produce. Q⊛❶⊟⊟

Ormidale Hotel

Knowe Road, KA27 8BY (off A841 at W end of village)
✪ 12-2.30 (not winter), 4.30-midnight; 12-midnight Sat & Sun
☎ (01770) 302293 ⊕ ormidale-hotel.co.uk
Arran Ale, Blonde; guest beers Ⓐ
Large red sandstone building set in seven acres of grounds with a small bar and large conservatory. Built in the 1850s as the holiday home of the artist Herring, it was converted to a hotel in 1935 by the present owner's grandfather. Regular and guest beers are served from tall fonts on the boat-shaped bar. Discos and folk sessions are held in the conservatory. Home-cooked meals are highly recommended. Accommodation is available in the summer only. Buses from Brodick pier pass close by. ⇙⊛❶⊟⊟♣P

Catacol: Isle of Arran

Catacol Bay Hotel

KA27 8HN
✪ 12-midnight (1am Thu-Sat); 11-midnight Sun
☎ (01770) 830231 ⊕ catacol.co.uk
Beer range varies Ⓗ
Former manse in its own grounds adjacent to the Twelve Apostles, a listed terrace of former estate workers' houses. The garden offers superb views over Kilbrannan Sound to Kintyre. Run by the same family since 1979, this hotel is an ideal base for exploring the north and west of Arran. Two guest ales are offered, one usually from the local Arran brewery. Bar meals are served daily with reduced prices for over 60s on Thursday lunchtime in winter and a renowned Sunday buffet lunch. ⇙⊛❶⊟⊟(324)♣P

Craigie

Craigie Inn

KA1 5LY (signed off B730)
⏰ 12-2, 5-midnight; 11-midnight Sat & Sun
☎ (01563) 860286 ⊕ craigieinn.com
Theakston XB; guest beer Ⓗ
A quiet retreat in a small village south of
Kilmarnock. It has an excellent reputation for
freshly cooked food made with local produce,
served in both the bar and restaurant. There is
also an outside seating area which is
extremely popular in summer. The guest beer
is usually from Strathaven Brewery. Live
acoustic music sessions feature on the third
Friday of the month. A function room is
available. The pub is not accessible by public
transport. ⚞Q☮⓪⑪&P

Failford

Failford Inn

KA5 5TF (B743 Mauchline-Ayr road)
⏰ 12-midnight (12.30am Fri & Sat); 12.30-midnight Sun
☎ (01292) 540117 ⊕ failfordinn.co.uk
Beer range varies Ⓗ
Country inn on the banks of the River Ayr with
low ceilings and an old tiled range. Both
restaurant and garden overlook the river.
Meals are prepared by the chef/owner with
an emphasis on freshly cooked local produce.
The inn is a good starting point for the River
Ayr Walk which passes through a dramatic
gorge. Home of the Windie Goat Brewery, one
of its beers is usually on handpump. Regular
beer festivals are held. Scottish CAMRA Pub of
the Year 2006. ⚞Q☮⓪⑪⓵⏛(43)⎸

Gateside

Gateside Inn

39 Main Road, KA15 2LF (on B777 1 mile E of
Beith)
⏰ 11-11 (midnight Fri & Sat); 12.30-11 Sun
☎ (01505) 503362 ⊕ thegatesideinn.co.uk
Greene King IPA; guest beer Ⓗ
Friendly village pub with a wide mix of
customers from all over the Garnock Valley,
which is otherwise a beer desert. The guest
beer is usually from a Scottish micro-brewery,
often Kelburn. The pub also stocks a wide
range of bottled beers and malts. Good food is
served all day in the bar and dining area. The
walls are adorned with old pictures of the
village. There is a patio for summer drinking.
Bus route 337 passes nearby and connects to
Glengarnock Station. ☮⓪⏛(337)♣P

Girvan

Royal Hotel

36 Montgomery Street, KA26 9HE
⏰ 11-12.30am; 12.30-midnight Sun
☎ (01465) 714203 ⊕ royalhotelgirvan.com
Beer range varies Ⓗ
Small hotel in a Clyde coast town which still
clings to fishing and tourist trades. The
traditional public bar attracts locals as well as
fishing, cycling and walking groups. The
world-renowned Turnberry golf course is five
miles away and the hotel is a good stopping
off point for travellers to and from Irish ferries.

The regular beer is from the Houston Brewery
with a summer-only guest beer from another
Scottish micro. A small but interesting range of
bottled beers is also stocked.
☮⚞⓪⓵⓵⎸⏛♣P

Kilmarnock

Brass & Granite

53 Grange Street, KA1 2DD
⏰ 11.30-midnight (1am Thu-Sat); 12.30-midnight Sun
☎ (01563) 523431
Beer range varies Ⓗ
Modern open-plan town centre pub situated in
a quiet street behind the post office, popular
with a varied mix of customers. Belgian fruit
beers are available on draught and a variety of
bottled beers are featured, with occasional
tastings held. There are several large screen
TVs, mostly used for sporting events. The pub
also has a good food selection, with some
speciality evenings. The pub quiz is Sunday
and Monday. Many bus routes pass close by.
⓪⎸⏛♣

Largs

Charlie Smith's

14 Gallowgate Street, KA30 8LX (On seafront A78,
close to pier)
⏰ 10 – midnight (1am Fri & Sat); 12.30 – midnight Sun
☎ (01475) 672250
Beer range varies Ⓗ
Friendly town centre pub situated at the
corner of the seafront and the Main Street,
opposite the ten-pin bowling alley, pier and
ferry terminal. A good place for catching (or
missing) the ferry to Cumbrae and, in summer,
the Waverley paddle steamer. Food available
all day. Live music at weekends. Apart from
ferry and steamer trips, Largs is home to two
fine golf courses and the Vikingar Centre.
⓪⓵⎸⏛♣

Saltcoats

Salt Cot

7 Hamilton Street, KA21 5DS
⏰ 10-11 (1am Thu-Sat); 10-1am Sun
☎ (01294) 465924
Greene King Abbot; guest beer Ⓗ
An excellent conversion of a former cinema by
Wetherspoon's, decorated with photos of the
cinema in its heyday and of old Saltcoats.
Children are allowed in one area and there is a
family menu. The pub's name comes from the
original cottages at the salt pans. Although
there are TVs in the bar area the sound is
never turned on. Q⓪⓵⎸⏛

Stair

Stair Inn

KA5 5HW (B730, 7 miles E of Ayr, 4 miles W of
Mauchline)
⏰ 12-11 (1am Fri & Sat); 12.30-11 Sun
☎ (01292) 591650 ⊕ stairinn.co.uk
Beer range varies Ⓗ
Family-run inn nestling at the foot of a glen on
the banks of the River Ayr. The bar, with an
open log fire, has bespoke handmade
furniture and the bedrooms are furnished in

similar style. Built around 1700, it serves a widespread area and is very close to the historic Stair Bridge. Houston beers are regulars and the food is highly recommended. The River Ayr Walk passes the pub but there is no public transport nearby. ♨Q❀✍◑& P

Troon

Ardneil Hotel

51 St Meddans Street, KA10 6NU
✪ 11-midnight (11 Sun)
☎ (01292) 311611
Caledonian Deuchars IPA; guest beer Ⓗ
Small family-run hotel close to Troon station, three municipal golf courses and the town centre. This smart bar offers three ales including two rotating guests. There is a popular quiz on Wednesday night and the pub hosts regular inter-pub pool competitions. The hotel is very popular with golfers from across Europe who take advantage of cheap flights into Prestwick Airport, four miles away. There is a large lawned beer garden and a heated, covered area for smokers.
❀✍◑≠⊟(14)P⌐

Bruce's Well

91 Portland Street, KA10 6QN
✪ 11 (12.30 Sun)-midnight
☎ (01292) 311429
Caledonian Deuchars IPA; guest beer Ⓗ
Friendly, spacious and comfortable lounge bar close to Troon town centre. Two ales are on offer including one from the Belhaven guest range. The bar shows regular live sport on the three plasma TVs and hosts live music at the end of every month. The bar has benefited from a new temperature-controlled cellar, situated next door. ≠⊟(14)

Harbour Bar

169 Templehill, KA10 6BH
✪ 11-12.30am; 12.30-midnight Sun
☎ (01292) 312668
Beer range varies Ⓗ
Two room bar close to the marina looking out over Troon's North Bay. Two ales tend to come from the Strathaven and Kelburn brewery ranges, with an occasional guest, and are competitively priced for the area. The bar has a nautical theme with a number of items on display from the former Ailsa shipyard that was sited down the road. Live music plays once a month in the lounge. A fine selection of malt whiskies and a good number of rums are on offer. ◑⊟&⊟♣P

Whiting Bay: Isle of Arran

Eden Lodge Hotel

KA27 8QH
✪ 12-midnight (1am Thu-Sat); 12.30-midnight Sun
☎ (01770) 700357 ⊕ edenlodgehotel.co.uk
Caledonian Deuchars IPA; guest beers Ⓗ
Bar Eden is a large, bright bar with superb views across the bay to Holy Island. Adjacent to the village's bowling green, this family run hotel, eight miles south of Brodick's ferry terminal, is an ideal base to take advantage of many local walks, including the spectacular Glenashdale Falls. Two changing guest ales

are offered. Home-cooked bar meals, featuring local produce, are available all day until 9pm (not lunchtime mid-week winter). ♨✍❀✍◑⊟⊟♣P

DUNBARTONSHIRE
Balloch

Tullie Inn

Balloch Road, G83 8SW (next to rail station)
✪ 11-midnight (1am Fri & Sat); 12-midnight Sun
☎ (01389) 752052 ⊕ tullieinnballoch.com
Caledonian Deuchars IPA; Theakston XB; guest beers Ⓗ
Established in 1895 and recently refurbished in a contemporary but comfortable style, the pub has a spacious split-level lounge with several distinct drinking areas. Four beers are usually available, including two from Fyne Ales, and the good food attracts locals and visitors. The large garden is an added attraction in summer. The pub is easy to reach from Glasgow by train. Loch Lomond and Trossachs National Park are near. ❀✍◑&▲≠⊟P⌐

Bearsden

Burnbrae

281 Milngavie Road, G61 3EA (on A81, near Mosshead road jct) OSNS554733
✪ 11-11.30 (Fri); 12.30-11.30 Sun
☎ (0141) 942 5951 ⊕ premierlodge.com
Courage Directors; Theakston Best Bitter; guest beers Ⓗ
Predominantly a food establishment, with a popular local following. Recently built with a mock farmhouse exterior, the use of reclaimed timber and brick has created a pleasant interior with a relaxed atmosphere. Two regular beers usually come from the regionals but the guest pump showcases smaller Scottish brewers' ales. Situated midway between Milngavie and Hillfoot railway stations, the site and depot of the Bennie Skyplane is just across the boundary with Milngavie. Various Roman ruins lie in the surrounding area. ♨❀✍◑&≠⊟P⌐

Kirkintilloch

Kirky Puffer

1-11 Townhead, G66 1NG
✪ 11 (12.30 Sun)-midnight
☎ (0141) 775 4140
Caledonian Deuchars IPA; Greene King Abbot; guest beers Ⓗ
Large Wetherspoon's, originally a police station, retaining some areas that used to be the cells. The major theme is the Forth & Clyde Canal, overlooked from two side rooms, with views of water traffic and the towpath. Pictures of old boats decorate the walls. A cosy alcove has settees and a coal-effect gas fire. Used by locals, cyclists, boaters and walkers from the nearby Roman Antonine Way, the pub is an easy bus ride from Glasgow. Q✍◑&⊟

Milngavie

Talbot Arms

30 Main Street, G62 6BU
⌚ 11-11 (midnight Thu & Sat, 1am Fri); 12.30-11 Sun
☎ (0141) 955 0981
Caledonian Deuchars IPA, 80; guest beers Ⓗ
Traditional corner pub with one large room with big-screen TVs at both ends, often showing football matches. Guest beers on three handpumps come from the regionals' lists, often featuring Caledonian's seasonal special. Milngavie is famous for its location at one end of the West Highland Way – the pub is a handy fuelling point for walkers heading north. Ask the locals for stories about Rob Roy McGregor's escapades in the vicinity.
◖Å⇌🚌♣⁵⁻

Milton of Campsie

Kincaid House Hotel

Birdston Road, G66 8BZ (signed on B757, 0.8km S of village) OSNS650759
⌚ 11-11.30 (1am Fri & Sat); 12.30-midnight Sun
☎ (0141) 776 2226 🌐kincaidhouse.com
Beer range varies Ⓗ
Genuine Scottish country house hotel reached by a long, winding, wooded driveway. The wood-panelled bar has horse brasses decorating the ceiling beams and a large Alloa Brewery mirror on the wall; the lounge area has a fireplace. The lengthy bar counter has two handpumps providing an ever-changing ale selection. There is also a child-safe garden and a conservatory restaurant. Food is served all day and is popular with locals. A handy stop-over for tourists and those walking Campsie Hills. ♨❀⇌◖◗♿🚌(175)♣P⁵⁻

GLASGOW
Glasgow

1901 Bar & Bistro

1534 Pollokshaws Road, G43 1RF (Haggs Road jct)
⌚ 11-11 (midnight Fri & Sat); 12.30-11 Sun
☎ (0141) 632 0161
Caledonian Deuchars IPA; Taylor Landlord; guest beers Ⓗ
As the name suggests, this bar opened in 1901, then called the Swan, and one of the original etched windows remains. A typical tenement bar with wooden floor and high ceiling, there is ample space to sit or stand at the bar. The lounge was reopened and converted into a bistro with a French influence, not surprising as owner Jacques is from across the Channel. The world famous Burrell Collection is in Pollok Park about a mile away.
◖◗♿⇌(Pollokshaws West/Shawlands)🚌(38)⁵⁻

Aragon

131 Byres Road, G12 8TT
⌚ 11-11 (midnight Fri & Sat); 12.30-11 Sun
☎ (0141) 339 3252
Caledonian Deuchars IPA; guest beers Ⓗ
Small, popular bar frequented by locals, city workers and staff and students from nearby Glasgow University in search of a retreat from the busy West End scene. The L-shaped bar's wooden fittings and assorted furniture, though not original, give the bar its own distinctive character. Large TV screens display the fantasy football league. Quiz night is Tuesday. Three guest beers come from small and medium sized brewers.
◖◗⊖(Hillhead/Kelvinhall)🚌(18, 18A)

Babbity Bowster

16-18 Blackfriars Street, Merchant City, G1 1PE (in paved section between High St and Walls St/ Albion St)
⌚ 11 (12.30 Sun)-midnight
☎ (0141) 552 5055 🌐babbity.com
Caledonian Deuchars IPA; guest beers Ⓟ
A unique establishment, attracting residents, locals, city workers and visitors to the city, it offers accommodation, an upstairs restaurant, beer garden and bar room. Watercolours and photographs decorate the walls. Two Scottish ales are dispensed plus a guest usually from south of the border. Traditional farmhouse ciders are also available. Good food served in the restaurant and bar is sourced from fresh local ingredients, with game and fish the specialities. In summer you can enjoy an outdoor barbecue and a game of boules.
♨Q❀⇌◖◗⇌⊖(Buchanan St)●P

Blackfriars

36 Bell Street, Merchant City, G1 1LG
⌚ 11 (12.30 Sun)-midnight
☎ (0141) 552 5924 🌐blackfriarsonline.co.uk
Courage Directors; Ⓗ **guest beers** Ⓟ
Cosmopolitan pub in the heart of the Good Community award-winning Merchant City district of Glasgow, currently CAMRA Glasgow Pub of the Year. Recently refurbished, it now has a quieter area plus disabled access/WC. Five pumps support mostly local micros, usually including Kelburn. Bottled and draught foreign beers are stocked plus traditional farmhouse ciders. Popular with locals, city workers, students and visitors, the pub hosts live jazz Sunday evening, comedy Thursday and a quiz on Monday. It can be hectic at the weekend. ◖◗♿⇌⊖(Buchanan St)●⁵⁻

Bon Accord

153 North Street, G3 7DA
⌚ 11-midnight; 12.30-11 Sun
☎ (0141) 248 4427 🌐thebonaccord.freeserve.co.uk
Caledonian Deuchars IPA; Marston's Pedigree; guest beers Ⓗ
One of the first pubs in town to bring back real ale to the city, the Bon Accord is now Glasgow's best known real ale pub. Up to 10 beers are available, together with farmhouse cider and a wide selection of bottled beers plus malt whiskies. The long bar adjoins a large split-level room with comfortable seating for dining – meals are served until 8pm. Live music often plays at weekends and there is a quiz on Wednesday.
◖◗♿⇌(Charing Cross/Anderston)♣●⁵⁻

Clockwork Beer Co.

1153-1155 Cathcart Road,, Mount Florida, G42 9BH (Kings Park Rd jct, by rail bridge)
⌚ 11-11 (midnight Thu-Sat); 12.30-11 Sun
☎ (0141) 649 0184
Caledonian Deuchars IPA; guest beers Ⓐ

SCOTLAND

Busy bar on Glasgow's south side situated near Hampden Park, Scotland's national football stadium. The large interior is split level with a five-barrel brewery opposite the bar, visible through a glass partition, and a spiral staircase leading to the upstairs room. A wide range of ales including seven guests and Clockwork's own regular beers and fruit beers, German and Belgian bottles and Weston's cider is dispensed. Bar meals are popular. A covered, heated area is provided for smokers.
🍴◖♿≑(Mount Florida)🚆(5, 34)✿P

Counting House

2 St Vincent Place, G1 2DH (on George Square)
🕐 9-midnight
☎ (0141) 225 0160
Cairngorm Wildcat; Caledonian Deuchars IPA, 80; Greene King Abbot; Marston's Pedigree; guest beers Ⓗ
In the heart of Glasgow, near Queen Street station, this Wetherspoon's conversion of a grand and ornate 1870s Bank of Scotland retains many original features, including the impressive central dome and fine sculptures. Photographs and paintings of Glasgow's past and personalities adorn the walls. The clientele includes office workers, students, shoppers and sightseers. A popular meeting place, it is seldom quiet, particularly during home international matches. Scottish breweries feature frequently and food is served all day. Children are welcome until 8pm.
Q◖♿≑(Queen St/Central)⊖(Buchanan St)

Crystal Palace

36 Jamaica Street, G1 4QD (100m S of Argyle St jct)
🕐 9-midnight
☎ (0141) 221 2624
Greene King Abbot; Marston's Pedigree; guest beers Ⓗ
Listed building close to Glasgow's Central Station, converted to a Wetherspoon's in 2000, with an expansive drinking hall on two floors, each with its own bar. Two sides of the building are made almost entirely of glass. A quieter, more relaxed drinking area is upstairs and there is a separate back room downstairs where children are welcome during the day. A wide choice of ales is available with both bars offering a different range. Popular with travellers, city workers and pre-clubbers.
Q🍴◖♿≑(Central)⊖(St Enoch)🚆🍺

Ingram Bar

136-138 Queen Street, G1 3BX
🕐 11 (12.30 Sun)-midnight
☎ (0141) 221 9330 ⊕ belhaven.co.uk
Caledonian Deuchars IPA; guest beers Ⓗ
Smart city bar, just off George Square, used by businessmen, office workers and visitors. The oval island bar sports three ales, including one from a local micro, and the gantry shelves display around 70 malt whiskies. A varied menu of home-made dishes is served throughout the day. Conversation is encouraged by a no sports policy. Note the 1953 newspaper dating from the day of opening and the stained glass panels which are the original windows.
◖≑(Queen St)⊖(Buchanan St)

Oran Mor

731 Great Western Road, G12 8XQ
🕐 11-1am (3am Fri & Sat); 12.30-1am Sun
☎ (0141) 357 6200
Caledonian Deuchars IPA; guest beers Ⓗ
Large multi-floored entertainment centre opened in 2004 in a converted church. The beers can be found at ground level round a stylish island bar with well designed decor retaining features of the old building. It has a night club in the basement; an auditorium and restaurant occupy the upper floors. Meals are served until 9pm, later in the dining area. Guest beers, often from Arran and Harviestoun, can be enjoyed at lunchtime with a play as well as a pie.
♿◖⊖(Hillhead)🚆(20, 18)

Phoenix

14-16 West George Street, G2 1HN
🕐 11-11 (midnight Fri & Sat); 12.30-10.30 Sun
☎ (0141) 353 6082
Greene King IPA; guest beers Ⓗ
Situated in Queen Street railway station precinct, the building housing the pub was originally a bank and the safe doors remain downstairs as an entrance to the toilets. In 2004 the Phoenix 'rose from the ashes' to become Glasgow's first no-smoking pub. It continues to provide a friendly welcome and a commitment to cask ales, also served on the upper floor (not always open). The frequently changing beer range often features Greene King and Inveralmond breweries.
◖♿≑(Queen St)⊖(Buchanan St)

Samuel Dows

69 – 71 Nithsdale Road, G41 2PZ
🕐 11-11 (midnight Fri & Sat); 12.30-11 Sun
☎ (0141) 423 0107
Caledonian Deuchars IPA; guest beers Ⓗ
Welcoming, traditional locals bar within a conservation area on the city's south side. Ample seating lines the varnished wood-trimmed walls. Note the gantry mirrors advertising Skol and Double Diamond. Live sport can be viewed throughout the bar on big screens. Food is served until 6pm daily. The lounge hosts live bands from Thursday to Saturday and a monthly Sunday acoustic session. Just under two miles from the city centre, it is easily accessed by rail and local buses.
◖♿≑(Pollokshields West/Queens Pk)🚆

State Bar

148 Holland Street, G2 4NG
🕐 11 (12.30 Sun)-midnight
☎ (0141) 332 2159
Caledonian Deuchars IPA, 80; Houston Killellan; Marston's Pedigree; guest beer Ⓗ
Theatrical memorabilia and photographs of old Glasgow adorn the walls of this popular city centre pub, just off Sauchiehall Street. Although dating from 1902, few of the original features remain. Customers include students and office workers attracted by the good value lunches. Its proximity to the Kings Theatre and Centre for Contemporary Arts makes it an ideal meeting place. The bar hosts blues bands on Tuesday and a comedy club on Saturday. Three guest beers are sourced from throughout the UK. ◖≑(Charing Cross)⊖(Cowcaddens)🚆

Station Bar

55 Port Dundas Road, G4 0HF
🕒 11-midnight; 12.30-11.45 Sun
☎ (0141) 332 3117
Caledonian Deuchars IPA; Greene King Abbot; guest beers Ⓗ

Traditional corner city bar, popular with locals, shoppers and workers in the area. The bar room has two big screen TVs for football and a large McEwans Pale Ale mirror. Behind the bar, art deco glass panels depict fire, police and ambulance services all based nearby and a steam engine in homage to the now gone station which gave the pub its name. There are two smaller, quieter areas away from the busy bar. Good lunches are served 12.30-3pm.
◖≢(Queen St)Ө(Cowcaddens/Buchanan St)⅃

Tennents

191 Byres Road, G12 8TN
🕒 11-11 (midnight Thu-Sat); 12.30-11 Sun
☎ (0141) 341 1021
Broughton Old Jock; Caledonian Deuchars IPA; Harviestoun Bitter & Twisted; Orkney Dark Island; Taylor Landlord; guest beers Ⓗ

Allegedly the last Scottish pub to allow women in after the law was changed, this large corner bar now welcomes a varied clientele. Students and academics from the university, shoppers escaping busy Byres Road, locals and visitors all enjoy the popular, good value food. Six regular and six guest ales come from well known breweries. The spacious room has a U-shaped counter with tall gantry, a raised corner with glass screening and several large TVs showing top sports events.
◖◗&Ө(Hillhead/Kelvinhall)⬚(18, 18A)

Three Judges

141 Dumbarton Road, G11 6PR
🕒 11-11 (midnight Fri; 11.45 Sat); 12.30-11 Sun
☎ (0141) 337 3055
Beer range varies Ⓐ

Traditional, award-winning, corner tenement pub in an increasingly gentrified district of Glasgow. The convivial L-shaped room has three distinct areas popular with a varied and interesting clientele. A raised corner gives views over bustling Partick Cross and is occupied on Sunday afternoon by a trad. jazz band. Eight regularly changing micro-brewery beers are available plus traditional farmhouse cider. The only food is occasional batches of 'real' pork pies from England. Customers may also bring their own food.
≢(Partick)Ө(Kelvinhall)●⅃

Toby Jug

97 Hope Street, G2 6XL
🕒 11-11 (midnight Thu-Sat); 12.30-midnight Sun
☎ (0141) 221 4159
Beer range varies Ⓗ

Busy city centre pub close to Central Station and on the route of numerous buses. Its location makes it popular with travellers and shoppers and as a meeting place for an evening out. Seating in the bar area is at high tables and in booths, and there is a quieter drinking area to the rear. Handpumps dispense four constantly changing real ales from Scotland and south of the border. The

pub can get busy at weekends when karaoke is in session.
◖&≢(Central/Queen St)Ө(Buchanan St/St Enoch)⬚⅃

LANARKSHIRE
Castlecary

Castlecary House Hotel

Castlecary Road, G68 0HD
🕒 11-11 (11.30 Thu-Sat); 12.30-midnight Sun
☎ (01324) 840233 ⊕ castlecaryhotel.com
Beer range varies Ⓗ

Situated on the site of one of the major forts on the Antonine Wall and close to the Forth and Clyde Canal walkway and cycle path, the Castlecary is known for good beer and fine food at reasonable prices. The interior has a cosy main bar with three adjoining areas, a traditional style lounge bar and a modern cocktail bar. Three beers are usually available and can be served in all areas. Two beer festivals are held a year.
▦⚲▣♨◖◗&⬚P⅃

Coatbridge

St Andrews Bar

37-38 Sunnyside Road, ML5 3DG
🕒 11-midnight (1am Fri & Sat); 12.30-midnight Sun
☎ (01236) 423 773 ⊕ standrewsbar.com
Beer range varies Ⓗ

Vibrant, traditional corner bar where locals enjoy conversation and offer a friendly welcome to visitors. A short walk from Sunnyside station and Summerlee Industrial Museum, the pub's popularity has increased following the introduction of real ale and a sensitive renovation. Most of the action occurs in the small bar room, where a wide range of malt whiskies is also available. An even smaller, quieter, cosy sitting-room serves those who seek relaxation – note the superb Campbell Hope & King mirror. ≢⅃

Hamilton

George Bar

18 Campbell Street, ML3 6AS
🕒 12 (11 Sat)-11.45 (1am Fri, 11.45 Sat); 12.30-11.45 Sun
☎ (01698) 424 225 ⊕ thegeorgebar.com
Beer range varies Ⓗ

Hosts Colin & Lynn have made the George a busy and popular bar since they took over in 1991. Recently refurbished by the staff, the bar room has drinks stands while the tables in alcoves soon fill up with locals enjoying the tasty home-cooked food. A pedestrianised pavement area with seating provides a café environment outside, with an awning to shelter from showers. Rail and bus stations are nearby. A frequent winner of Lanarkshire CAMRA Pub of the Year. ⊛◖&≢⬚⅃

Lanark

Horse & Jockey

56 High Street, ML11 7ES
🕒 11-11 (1am Fri; 11.45 Sat); 12.30-11 Sun
☎ (01555) 664 825

SCOTLAND

Beer range varies H
Locals' hostelry, welcoming to visitors, in the centre of a historic town. The pub gets its name from the racecourse which used to be at the edge of Lanark. It has a fairly small public bar and, along a low-ceilinged passageway, a separate room serves as a restaurant. The beers change frequently, usually supplied by micro-breweries, with Arran and Houston most often represented. New Lanark Village and Falls of Clyde are nearby. ⊄▶&⚭Ａ≠⊟(41)

Strathaven

Weavers
1-3 Green Street, ML10 6LT
✪ 5 (11 Mon)-midnight; 11-1am Fri & Sat; 7-1am Sun
Beer range varies H
This family-run pub is 2007 CAMRA Lanarkshire Pub of the Year. Formerly the Crown Hotel, it takes its name from the traditional trade of the town. The interior is decorated with pictures of Hollywood film stars, from Laurel & Hardy to the current governor of California. The beer range always includes something from the local Strathaven Ales, often Clydesdale IPA, present CAMRA Glasgow Beer of the Year, along with two guests. Note the restricted mid-week opening times. ⊟(13)

Wishaw

Wishaw Malt
62-66 Kirk Road, ML2 7BL
✪ 11-11 (1am Thu-Sat); 12.30-midnight Sun
☎ (01698) 358 806
Beer range varies H
Modern Wetherspoon's pub in the heart of the town. Its name comes from a local 19th-century distillery which produced the highly-regarded Clydesdale Single Malt. The spacious single room is divided into many areas and on different levels. Large windows overlook the activity on the main street. As well as local trade the pub attracts drinkers from all over the real ale starved county of Lanarkshire. ⊛⊄▶&≠⊟(240, 267)♠'⌐

RENFREWSHIRE
Barrhead

Cross Stobs Inn
4 Grahamston Road, G78 1NS (on B7712)
✪ 11-11 (midnight Thu; 1am Fri; 11.45 Sat); 12.30-11 Sun
☎ (0141) 881 1581
Kelburn Misty Law; guest beers H
Welcoming 18th-century coaching inn on the road to Paisley. The public bar has a real coal fire and retains much of its original charm with antique furniture and service bells. The lounge is spacious and leads to an enclosed rear garden. The front of the pub also has an outside drinking area. There is a pool room and a function suite available for hire. Children are welcome at lunchtime. Occasionally a second Kelburn beer is available. ⋒⊛⊄▶≠

Waterside Inn
Glasgow Road,, The Hurlet, G53 7TH (A736 near Hurlet)

✪ 11-11 (midnight Fri & Sat); 12.30-11 Sun
☎ (0141) 881 2822
Beer range varies H
Comfortable bar and restaurant near Levern Water. Although the emphasis is on food here, there is a cosy area around the real fire for those who only want to enjoy a relaxing drink. The restaurant holds themed nights with musical accompaniment. Local pictures adorning the walls add to the traditional ambience of the inn. The beer range is mostly from the Kelburn Brewery. ⋒⊛⊄▶&P

Busby

White Cart
61 East Kilbride Road, G76 8HX (on A726 100m SE of station)
✪ 11-11; 12.30-11 Sun
☎ (0141) 644 2711
Beer range varies H
The spacious interior is divided by large oak beams into several cosy nooks. The decor is from an earlier period featuring a grandfather clock, dressing tables and a host of bric-a-brac. Part of the stone walls are thought to be from the stables formerly on the site. Although the emphasis is on food, especially fish, recent refurbishment has created an area mainly for drinkers. Of the two beers one is always from the local Kelburn Brewery and the other from the Scottish Courage range. ⋒Q⊛⊄▶&⚭≠P

Gourock

Spinnaker Hotel
121 Albert Road, PA19 1BU
✪ 11-midnight (12.30am Thu, 1am Fri & Sat); 12.30-midnight Sun
☎ (01475) 633107 ⊕ spinnakerhotel.co.uk
Greene King Old Speckled Hen; Orkney Dark Island; guest beers H
Warm and friendly hotel, popular with locals and tourists alike, which constantly has three handpumps dispensing ale in the bar. It has wonderful views of the Firth of Clyde from the large bay windows and the patio tables outside are a good spot for watching the ships and submarines sailing up and down the river. Q⊛⇔⊄▶

Greenock

James Watt
80-92 Cathcart Road, PA15 1DD
✪ 11-11 (midnight Thu; 1am Fri & Sat); 12.30-midnight Sun
☎ (01475) 722640
Greene King Abbot; guest beers H
This easy to find town centre Wetherspoon's, near the Central train station, is a roomy pub with typical JDW trimmings. The outside patio is heated for cooler evenings. Inside is a partitioned area for families. Popular pub food is served all day. Guest beers come from local breweries as well as further afield. The disabled access is good. ⊛⊄▶&≠(Central)

Houston

Fox & Hounds
South Street, PA6 7EN

✪ 11-midnight (12.30am Fri & Sat); 12.30-midnight Sun
☎ (01505) 612448 ⊕ houston-brewing.co.uk/
fox_hound.htm

Houston Killellan, Peter's Well, Texas, Warlock Stout; guest beers ⓗ

Home of the Houston Brewing Co, this 17th-century coaching inn has a viewing window into the brewery from the lounge bar. The large and comfortable lounge is decorated with hunting memorabilia and paintings. The Stables bar has light wood decor with seating in large alcoves and has a pool table, large screen TV and fruit machine. Upstairs is the Huntsman's bar with two restaurants offering a la carte and bar menus. Food is served all day and a popular traditional Sunday roast. ◐⊕&P

Inverkip

Inverkip Hotel

Main Street, PA16 0AS (off A78 Greenock-Largs road)
✪ 11-11.30; 12.30-11.30 Sun
☎ (01475) 521478 ⊕ inverkip.co.uk

Caledonian Deuchars IPA; guest beers ⓗ

Set in the conservation village of Inverkip, this old coaching inn is handy for the ferries to the Western Isles. The hotel has an excellent restaurant which generally requires booking, even for Sunday lunch. Meals from the restaurant are also served in parts of the lounge. The public bar is quite lively and popular with locals. Q⇔◐⊕⊟⇌P

Johnstone

Coanes

26-28 High Street, PA5 8AH
✪ 11-11.30pm (midnight Fri & Sat); 12.30-11.30 Sun
☎ (01505) 322925

Caledonian Deuchars IPA; guest beers ⓗ

Town centre bar and lounge with a friendly atmosphere. The bar has fake beams; a raised area in the lounge doubles as a restaurant (food hours vary – phone to check). Seven real ales are on handpump including one from the Kelburn range. A regular front runner in local CAMRA Pub Of The Year. Q◐&⇌

Kilbarchan

Trust Inn

8 Low Barholm, PA10 2ET
✪ 11.45 (11 Fri & Sat)-11.30 (1am Fri & Sat); 11.45-11.30 Sun
☎ (01505) 702401

Caledonian Deuchars IPA; Tetley Bitter; guest beers ⓗ

Open and light single room village pub decorated in a modern style with a welcoming atmosphere and friendly staff, popular with a mixed clientele of all ages. A large screen shows sports and there is regular entertainment including bands and quizzes. Children are welcome. ◐&⊟(36)

Lochwinnoch

Brown Bull

33 Main Street, PA12 4AH
✪ 12-11 (midnight Fri, 11.45 Sat); 12.30-11 Sun

☎ (01505) 843250 ⊕ lochwinnoch.info/Business/
brownbull/

Caledonian Deuchars IPA; guest beers ⓗ

Traditional village inn with a friendly atmosphere and helpful staff, popular with locals and outdoor sports enthusiasts. Originally a coach house, the interior is a mix of bare stone and stained wood. Guest ales change regularly, offering a good range of beers from a wide choice of regional breweries. Food is served in the upstairs restaurant. ⋈◐⊕&

Newton Mearns

Osprey

Stewarton Road, G77 6NP
✪ 11 (12.30 Sun)-11
☎ (0141) 616 5071

Caledonian Deuchars IPA; guest beers ⓗ

Mitchell & Butler Vintage Inn with an olde worlde feel to the interior, with a mix of wood, brick and stone. Quiet, private areas as well as large open areas make the pub popular with drinkers and diners, including families. Three handpumps are in use. Food is served throughout the day until 10pm. Q❀◐&P

Paisley

Bull Inn ☆

7 New Street, PA1 1XU
✪ 12-midnight (1am Fri & Sat); 12.30-midnight Sun
☎ (0141) 849 0472 ⊕ maclay.com/MaclayInns.html

Caledonian Deuchars IPA; guest beers ⓗ

This popular, lively pub is the oldest in Paisley, built in 1901. An A-listed building on CAMRA's National Inventory, it has a most impressive interior rich in period detail. The gantry has its original whisky barrels, and there are three snugs at the rear ideal for holding meetings. Old pictures on the walls depict bygone Paisley and are well worth a browse. ⋟◐⇌(Gilmour St)

Gabriels

33-35 Gauze Street, PA1 1EX
✪ 11-midnight (1am Fri & Sat); 12.30-midnight Sun
☎ (0141) 887 8204

Beer range varies ⓗ

Popular town centre pub which always has two or three ales on handpump, usually including beers from Houston and Kelburn breweries. A large-screen TV shows all popular sporting fixtures. Good food is served daily and a separate function room is available for hire. Paisley Abbey is nearby. ◐⇌(Gilmour St)

Hamishes Hoose

Gilmour Street, PA3 3AP
✪ 11-11 (midnight Wed & Thu; 1am Fri & Sat); 12.30-11 Sun
☎ (0141) 561 7105 ⊕ hamisheshoose.com

Kelburn Dark Moor ⓗ

Spacious bar under Gilmour Street station. During the day the emphasis is on food, with families particularly welcome; in the evening there is live entertainment and karaoke nights. Note the pictures of old Paisley that adorn the walls and also a shawl made in the now defunct Paisley mill. There is a large

663

SCOTLAND

screen TV above the stage. The pub is usually crowded on Saturday lunchtimes when the local team, St Mirren, are at home. No food is served Sunday evening. ◖❶➤(Gilmour St)

Harvies Bar
86 Glasgow Road, PA1 3NU
✪ 11-11 (midnight Thu; 1am Fri & Sat); 12.30-midnight Sun
☎ (0141) 889 0911
Greene King Abbot; guest beers Ⓗ
Behind the well preserved exterior of this pub is a large, open plan bar room with a mezzanine overlooking the bar. There is a quieter, enclosed area for reading. Two plasma screens show sports and music videos with the volume turned down low. This well managed pub has gone through several ownerships and is presently thriving. ◖❶⛌⚊

Hogshead
45 High Street, PA1 2AH
✪ 11-midnight (1am Fri & Sat); 12.30-midnight Sun
☎ (0141) 840 4150
Beer range varies Ⓗ
In a central location near the university, this spacious, open plan pub has a split level interior featuring wood flooring and comfortable sofas, with large flat screen TVs, a dart board and pool table. Meals are served daily until 8pm. Music levels vary but the volume can get very loud at the weekend. There is usually one beer from the local Kelburn Brewery. ◖❶⛌➤(Gilmour St)

Last Post
2 County Square, PA1 1BN
✪ 11-midnight (1am Fri & Sat); 12.30-midnight Sun
☎ (0141) 849 6911
Caledonian Deuchars IPA; guest beers Ⓗ
Large town centre Wetherspoon's beside the railway station and two minutes' walk from

bus services. The ground floor is split level with a family dining area inside the main entrance and a balcony with tables. Six handpumps dispense a range of ales. The pub opens at 10am for breakfast.
Q◖❶⛌➤(Gilmour St)

Wee Howff
53 High Street, PA1 2AN
✪ 12-11 (1am Fri & Sat); closed Sun
☎ (0141) 889 2095
Caledonian Deuchars IPA; guest beers Ⓗ
Friendly pub with quaint old fashioned charm – the interior is intimate and cosy with soft lighting and wood panelled walls. The clientele is varied with a healthy mix of young and old. The atmosphere is particularly lively at the weekend, with a jukebox that is arguably the best in the area. Proprietor Danny Mcquigan was the first publican in Scotland to receive the Burton master cellarmanship award. ➤(Gilmour St)

Uplawmoor

Uplawmoor Hotel
66 Neilston Road, G78 4AF (off A736)
✪ 12-2.30, 5-11; 12-midnight Sun
☎ (01505) 850565 ⊕ uplawmoor.co.uk
Beer range varies Ⓗ
This village pub, part of the hotel, has a rustic and cosy interior with gentle lighting, red carpeting and wood panelling throughout. Bar meals are served all day and there is an award winning restaurant. Popular with locals as well as visitors, weekends are particularly lively. Two beers are usually available, one from the Houston seasonal range and the other from the Kelburn brewery. ❀⇔❶⛏⛌P

Uplawmoor Hotel, Uplawmoor, Renfrewshire, Strathclyde.

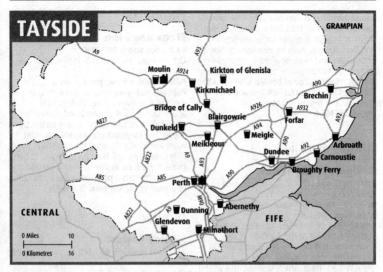

Authority areas covered: Angus UA, City of Dundee UA, Perth & Kinross UA

Abernethy

Crees Inn

Main Street, PH2 9LA
🕐 11-2.30, 5-11; 11-11 Sat & Sun
☎ (01738) 850714 ⊕ creesinn.co.uk
Beer range varies Ⓗ
Comfortable local free house in a quiet village. Timber panels and beams display an impressive collection of pump clips reflecting the varied beer range. Up to five ales are available with English ales predominating, plus a selection of 40 whiskies. Hops adorn the beams in the lounge seating area. A good selection of meals is available at lunchtime and evening made with fresh local produce. The village of Abernethy was once the southern Pictish capital of Scotland and has a Pictish watch tower (one of only two in Scotland) at its centre. Q✿✱⊲◑⅃⟁☒P

Arbroath

Corn Exchange

Market Place, DD11 1HR
🕐 11-midnight (1am Fri & Sat)
☎ (01241) 432430
Greene King Abbot; guest beer Ⓗ
Typical Wetherspoon conversion of a former corn exchange in the centre of Arbroath. The town is famous for the signing of the Declaration of Independence in 1320 and the delicious Arbroath smokie (smoked haddock). The pub can get very busy during weekend evenings but the large open plan bar room has several quieter areas. It opens at 9am for coffee. ◑⅃☒⟁

Lochlands Bar

14 Lochlands Street, DD11 3AB
🕐 11-midnight (1am Fri & Sat); 12.30-midnight Sun
☎ (01241) 873286
Beer range varies Ⓗ
Classic and busy street corner pub with strong sporting associations. The large public bar has a selection of sporting memorabilia adorning

the walls plus two large TVs that dominate when football matches (and some rugby games) are shown. For those customers not interested in sport there is a smaller, quieter lounge area. Three ales are always on tap. ⅃≷♣

Blairgowrie

Ericht Alehouse

13 Wellmeadow, PH10 6ND
🕐 1-11 (11.45pm Thu, 12.30am Fri & Sat); 1-11.30 Sun (times may vary)
☎ (01250) 872469
Beer range varies Ⓗ
Established in 1802, this friendly, traditional town centre pub has two seating areas split by a well stocked bar. The lounge area features a log-burning open fire. The range of up to six beers varies all the time, coming from Scottish and English breweries Inveralmond is a local favourite. Liefmans Frambozen is available on tap and there is a good selection of bottled beers. Although no food is available customers are welcome to take in their own. Weekends can be busy with occasional live music. ♨Q⅃☒⟁

Brechin

Caledonian Hotel

43-47 South Esk Street, DD9 6DZ (opp Caledonian Station)
🕐 5-11.30; 12-2.30, 5-midnight Fri; 11.30-1am Sat; 12.30-11 Sun; hours vary in summer
☎ (01356) 624345
Inveralmond Thrappledouser; guest beer Ⓗ
Extensively refurbished, the hotel has a large bar and separate function room/restaurant. It takes its name from the privately run railway

INDEPENDENT BREWERIES

Inveralmond Perth
Moulin Moulin

whose terminus is opposite. The Caledonian Railway closed in 1981 but now runs steam trains at regular intervals between Brechin and Dun stations, with connections to House of Dun. A guest beer, sourced by the landlord on his trips to Hampshire, is often available, as well as a large range of bottled beer including some Belgian beer. Live folk music on the last Friday of the month is popular.

🏛️Q❀🚲🌂🕽🍽️🚃♣

Bridge of Cally

Bridge of Cally Hotel
PH10 7JJ (6 miles N of Blairgowrie on A93)
☺ 11-11 (12.30am Fri-Sat); 12-11 Sun
☎ (01250) 886231 ⊕ bridgeofcallyhotel.com
Beer range varies Ⓗ

Situated beside the River Ardle in the heart of scenic Perthshire at the foothills of the Cairngorms and close to the Glen Shee Ski slopes, the hotel provides a practical and unfussy base from which to enjoy the widest range of local pastimes and attractions. The 63-mile Cateran Trail, Scotland's newest long distance walk, starts and finishes close to Blairgowrie. Bar food is available for most of the day, with the hotel restaurant offering more formal dining surroundings. Two regularly changing ales are available, with Houston beers often on tap.

🏛️Q🛏️❀🌂🕽🍽️🚃♣P

Broughty Ferry

Fisherman's Tavern Hotel
10-12 Fort Street, DD5 2AD (by lifeboat station)
☺ 11-midnight (1am Fri & Sat); 12.30-midnight Sun
☎ (01382) 775941 ⊕ fishermans-tavern-hotel.co.uk
Beer range varies Ⓗ

Long-standing guide entry maintaining its ever-changing range of ales, the widest variety in the city. Ales from local micro Inveralmond feature regularly. Originally three fishermen's cottages, now a small hotel, the atmosphere is cosy with low ceilings throughout the public, snug and lounge bars. The garden is popular during the summer and hosts an annual beer festival in aid of the RNLI. A quiz is held on the first Monday of the month; traditional music plays every Thursday.

🏛️Q❀🌂🕽🍽️🚃🚲🚃

Royal Arch
258 Queen Street, DD5 2DS (jct of Brook Street/Gray Street)
☺ 11-midnight; 12.30-11 Sun
☎ (01382) 779741 ⊕ royal-arch.co.uk
Caledonian Deuchars IPA; guest beer Ⓗ

Ornately refurbished street corner local with a cosy public bar, decorated with a collection of local memorabilia and sporting photos. Good bar meals are served in the adjacent lounge or outside at the pavement café in fair weather. The pub's name is thought to originate from a former masonic lodge nearby and not the Victoria arch (also long gone) shown in the hanging sign. Beers are from the Belhaven cask collection. 🕽🚃🚲🚃

Carnoustie

Stags Head Inn
61 Dundee Street, DD7 7PN
☺ 11-midnight (1am Fri & Sat); 12.30-midnight Sun
☎ (01241) 858777
Fuller s London Pride; guest beers Ⓗ

Popular local, very busy at weekends, to the west of the town centre. Golfers who appreciate a good pint will find succour here, especially now Carnoustie is back on the Open circuit. The large bar and lounge/function room are totally changed from the days when Billy Connolly drank here on TA camps at Barry (note the tribute in the form of a portrait and plaque). There is a pool room and patio to the rear next to the car park. ❀🚃♣P🚲

Dundee

Mickey Coyles
21-23 Old Hawkhill, DD1 5EU (by Hawkhill/West Port)
☺ 12-midnight
☎ (01382) 225871
Caledonian Deuchars IPA; guest beer Ⓗ

Long, split level bar popular with town and gown, just to the north of Dundee University campus. Formerly owned by Maclay's, now by Scottish & Newcastle, four ales are regularly on sale, usually including a mild. A popular place for meetings and club nights, football on the two TVs can dominate when big matches are on. Pub food here is good. Winner of local CAMRA Pub of the Year for Dundee in 2005 and 2006. 🕽🚃🚃

Phoenix
103 Nethergate, DD1 4DH (W of city centre)
☺ 11 (12.30 Sun)-midnight
☎ (01382) 200014
Caledonian Deuchars IPA; Taylor Landlord; guest beer Ⓗ

Busy pub near Dundee University and handy for the Rep Theatre and Contemporary Arts Centre. Four ales are regularly on sale. The decor is an eclectic mix of bric-a-brac and breweriana, with a gantry allegedly rescued from a demolished Cardiff bar, original metal pillars and snug alcoves. Good pub food is served up to 7pm. A comfortable, if rarely quiet, howff. 🕽🚃

Speedwell (Mennies) ☆
165-167 Perth Road, DD1 1AS (W of University and Art College)
☺ 11 (12.30 Sun)-midnight
☎ (01382) 667783
Beer range varies Ⓗ

Classic Edwardian pub with an L-shaped bar and two sitting rooms, featuring a fine moulded ceiling, etched glass dividing screens and mahogany gantry and dado panelling. Popularly known as Mennies after previous owners notably the famous Mrs Mennie. This unspoilt bar is listed in CAMRA's Inventory of Heritage Pubs. Two or three cask ales are available (Belhaven and Caledonian are regulars) as well as foreign keg and bottled beers alongside an array of malt whiskies. Q🚃

Dunkeld

Taybank

Tay Terrace, PH8 0AQ

☼ 11-11 (midnight Fri & Sat); 12-11 Sun

☎ (01350) 727340 ⊕ thetaybank.com

Inveralmond Ossian's Ale ⊞

Known as 'Scotland's musical meeting place', this is a haven for lovers of traditional Scottish and Irish music, often of a spontaneous nature. The small public bar is comfortable and full of character with an open fire and a large range of musical instruments including a piano. There is also a small music room where live events are regularly hosted. Ossian's is always on handpump plus a small selection of bottled beer. A good base for a variety of outdoor pursuits, the beer garden is located on the banks of the River Tay looking across toward Birnam Hill. ♨Q♿🐾✎◀◑➡🚆♣P🏃

Dunning

Kirkstyle Inn

Kirkstyle Square, PH2 0RR

☼ 11-2.30, 5-11 (midnight Fri); 11-midnight Sat; 12.30-11 Sun

☎ (01764) 684248

Beer range varies ⊞

Located in the centre of Dunning at the foothills of the Ochill range, dominated by the Norman steeple of St Serfs Church, the Kirkstyle is a traditional village inn circa 1760. It has a small public bar with wooden floor and wood burning stove where up to three ales are served (two in winter) – Harviestoun Bitter & Twisted and Caledonian Deuchars IPA are regulars. Adjacent to the bar is a small snug. There is a separate restaurant area and a room downstairs with pool table. ♨Q✎◀◑➡🚆

Forfar

Plough Inn

48 Market Street, DD8 3EW

☼ 11-midnight (1am Fri & Sat); 12.30-midnight Sun

☎ (01307) 469288 ⊕ ploughinnforfar.co.uk

Beer range varies ⊞

This is a traditional, street-corner, local lounge bar with up to three beers available and an emphasis on Scottish micros. It hosts frequent live music events along with an occasional beer festival. As well as traditional pub games there is foosball and backgammon. Food is served daily including high teas (12-2.30, 5-9). Remember that no visit to Forfar would be complete without trying one of the local delicacies – the legendary 'Forfar Bridie'. Good stopping off place for heading into the Angus Glens. 🐾◀◑♣

Glendevon

An Lochan Tormaukin

FK14 7JY

☼ 11 (12 Sun)-11

☎ (01259) 781252 ⊕ tormaukin.co.uk

Beer range varies ⊞

Originally an 18th-century drovers' inn, the Tormaukin (meaning 'hill of the mountain hare' in old Scots) is located in a peaceful setting surrounded by the Ochill hills. It is an ideal base for a variety of outdoor activities such as walking, fishing and golf. Up to three ales are available in the rear lounge, usually including one from Harviestoun. It has two comfortable lounge bars in natural timber and stone along with log fires. An extensive menu is on offer with traditional Scottish fare and international dishes. ♨Q♿🛏✎◀◑P

Kirkmichael

Strathardle Inn

PH10 7NS (on A924 Bridge of Cally to Pitlochry road)

☼ 12-2, 6-11 (11.30 Fri & Sat); times may vary

☎ (01250) 881224 ⊕ strathardleinn.co.uk

Beer range varies ⊞

The Strathardle is an old coaching inn on the route from Balmoral to Pitlochry dating back to the late 1700s it retains the original barn and stables. It has a 700 yard beat of the River Ardle, offering salmon and trout fishing, and is an excellent base for exploring central Scotland and the Southern Highlands. The Cateran Trail passes in front of the inn and the Cairngorms National Park is a few miles north. Up to three ales are available depending on the season with a strong commitment to Scottish micros. ♨Q♿🐾✎◀◑♣P

Kirkton of Glenisla

Glenisla Hotel

PH11 8PH (on B591 10 miles N of Alyth)

☼ 11-11 (midnight Sat) summer; 12-2.30, 6-11 winter; hours vary, phone to check

☎ (01575) 582223 ⊕ glenisla-hotel.com

Beer range varies ⊞

An oasis for thirsty and hungry travellers, this 17th-century coaching inn is also a centre for outdoor activities including walking, fishing, shooting and skiing. Now fully refurbished, the hotel welcomes visitors and locals in the cosy, oak beamed bar with its wood fire. Occasional traditional music sessions are held and various clubs meet in this social centre for Glen Isla. Dogs are welcome. ♨Q♿🛏✎◀◑🅰♣P🏃

Meigle

Belmont Arms

PH12 8TJ (on A927 between Newtyle and Meigle)

☼ 12-11.30 (midnight Sat); 12.30-midnight Sun

☎ (01828) 640232 ⊕ belmontarms.co.uk

Beer range varies ⊞

Small country hotel on a bend one and a half miles south of Meigle near the site of the old Alyth Junction Station. Ales are served in the comfortable lounge, but are also available in the small public bar – Inveralmond and Caledonian beers are regulars. There is a separate restaurant and an annexe for functions. Home-cooked meals are popular. Meigle has a small museum with a collection of Pictish stones and the grave of an alleged Pictish princess in the churchyard. ♨✎🛏◀◑🚆♿🚆🅰♣P🏃

SCOTLAND

Meikleour

Meikleour Hotel

PH2 6EB

🕓 11-3, 6-11 (midnight Fri); 11-midnight Sat; 12-11 Sun

☎ (01250) 883206 ⊕ meikleour-inn.co.uk

Beer range varies Ⓗ

Warm, welcoming country village inn. This is a popular venue for walkers and fishermen as well as those wanting a good meal or drink in a relaxing environment. The stone-flagged bar and comfortable lounge both offer two cask ales. The house beer, Lure of Meikleour, is brewed by Inveralmond. Nearby is the Meikleour Beech Hedge (100ft high and a third of a mile long), which was planted in 1745 and is recognised in the Guinness Book of Records as the tallest hedge in the world.

🏰Q❀✿🛏️♿🍴🅿

Milnathort

Village Inn

36 Westerloan, KY13 9Y4

🕓 2-11; 11-11.30 Fri & Sat; 12.30-11 Sun

☎ (01577) 863293

Greene King Abbot; Inveralmond Thrappledouser; Taylor Landlord; guest beer Ⓗ

Friendly pub at heart of village with low ceilings, exposed joists, stone walls and a log fire in the bar area. Although semi-open plan, there is a comfortable lounge area at one end. Unobtrusive pipe music adds to the relaxing atmosphere. The games room at the rear of the pub has a pool table. Nearby places of interest are the island castle on Loch Leven where Mary Queen of Scots was imprisoned and the RSPB site at Vane Farm. 🏰❀✿🍴♣

Moulin

Moulin Inn

11-13 Kirkmichael Road, PH16 5EH (NE of Pitlochry)

🕓 12-11 (11.45 Fri & Sat); 12-11.45 Sun

☎ (01796) 472196 ⊕ moulininn.co.uk

Moulin Light, Braveheart, Ale of Atholl, Old Remedial Ⓗ

This country inn is situated within the village square of Moulin, an ancient Scottish crossroads near Pitlochry, the 'gateway to the Highlands'. Extended and refurbished, it retains its original character and charm, furnished in traditional pub style with two log fires. A good choice of home-prepared local fare is served. The ales are provided by the small brewery in the old coach house behind the hotel. An ideal base for outdoor pursuits, there are a number of marked walks passing nearby. 🏰Q✿❀✿🍴♣🅿

Perth

Capital Asset

26 Tay Street, PH1 5LQ (on the banks of the River Tay)

🕓 11-11 (11.45 Thu, 12.30am Fri & Sat); 12.30-11.30 Sun

☎ (01738) 580457

Caledonian Deuchars IPA; Greene King Abbot; guest beer Ⓗ

A former TSB Bank building overlooking the River Tay and situated between the city's two road bridges, it was converted by Wetherspoon into a large, open plan lounge bar. The original high ceilings and ornate cornices have been retained along with the large 'safe'. A varying range of up to five ales is available along with a wide all day food menu. The pub is popular for pre-show refreshment for visitors to the nearby repertory theatre and modern concert hall. It gets very busy on weekend evenings.

♿❀✿♿

Cherrybank Inn

210 Glasgow Road,, PH2 0NA

🕓 11-11 (11.45 Sat),; 11-11.45 Sun

☎ (01738) 624349 ⊕ cherrybankinn.co.uk

Inveralmond Independence, Ossian's Ale; guest beer Ⓗ

This former drovers' inn is located on the western outskirts of Perth – a popular local, it is also ideal for travellers with comfortable accommodation in seven en-suite bedrooms. Thought to be one of the oldest public houses in Perth, it has a small public bar with two adjacent rooms. Lunches and evening meals are served in the well appointed lounge. Up to four real ales are available from Inveralmond and other Scottish micros. Q🛏️✿🍴🅿💷

Greyfriars

15 South Street, PH2 8PG

🕓 11-11 (11.45pm Fri & Sat); 3-11 Sun

☎ (01738) 633036 ⊕ greyfriarsbar.com

Beer range varies Ⓗ

Small but very popular city centre lounge bar. Good value lunches are served in the bar or in a small upstairs seated area. Up to four ales are available including the house beer Friars Tipple brewed by Inveralmond. 'More of a club without a membership', quotes the plaque above the bar; folk music is often hosted on Monday evening. The pub takes its name from the former Greyfriars monastery, gutted in 1559 by followers of John Knox and subsequently demolished. ✿≡

Northern Ireland
Channel Islands
Isle of Man

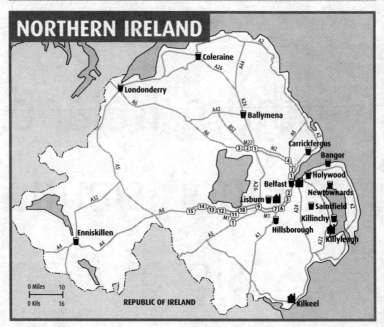

NORTHERN IRELAND

REPUBLIC OF IRELAND

0 Miles 10
0 Kils 16

Ballymena

Spinning Mill
17-21 Broughshane Street, BT43 6EB
⏰ 10-11 (midnight Thu; 1am Fri & Sat)
☎ (028) 2563 8985
Greene King Abbot; guest beer Ⓗ
Large Wetherspoon's pub spread over two floors with plenty of different spots to drink in. The interesting interior features unusual woodwork rescued from churches. The upstairs bar has three handpumps, downstairs there are five. Three large screens upstairs show music videos in the evening unless showing major sporting events. Alcohol is served from 11.30am (12.30am Sun). Fifteen minutes' walk from Ballymena rail/bus station. 🏨🏠🍴🕭♿🚋♣🚶♨

Bangor

Esplanade
12 Ballyhome Esplanade, BT20 5LZ (down Godfrey Avenue)
⏰ 11.30-11; 12.30-10 Sun
☎ (028) 9127 0954 🌐 esplanadebars.com
Whitewater Glen Ale; guest beer Ⓗ
First rate lounge and public bar situated on the coast at Ballyholme, about a mile and a half from the centre of Bangor. The public bar is known as Gillespie's Place and has three handpumps offering a combination of Whitewater and guest ales. The bar has three screens and along with the lounge can get very busy. There is an outside seating area with excellent views, particularly on a summer's day. Q🏠🍴♿🚋

Belfast

Botanic Inn
23-27 Malone Road, BT9 6RU

⏰ 11.30-1am
☎ (028) 9050 9740 🌐 botanicinns.com
Whitewater Belfast Ale Ⓗ
Large, bustling pub, a short walk from Queen's University, very popular with the student population. A number of screens show football and rugby matches – it gets very busy on match days. Good food is served daily. Live bands play on Monday and Friday. The ale pump is in the main part of the bar; order from the smaller public bar and it is a little cheaper. 🍴🕭♿

Bridge House
37-43 Bedford Street, BT2 4HF (opp. BBC building in Ormeau Avenue)
⏰ 10-midnight (1am Thu-Sat)
☎ (028) 9072 7890
Greene King Abbot; guest beer Ⓗ
Huge, busy Lloyds No 1 bar handy for the city centre. It has recently become even more popular with the introduction of large screens that show music videos and some sporting events. The bar generally attracts a young crowd and it tends to be packed, especially at the weekend. There are four handpumps downstairs offering a variety of guests. The upstairs bar is quieter, but doesn't serve ale. Alcohol is only served from 11.30am (12.30am Sun). 🚋🕭♿🚋(Gt Victoria St)♣🚶

Crown ☆
46 Great Victoria Street, BT2 7BA (opp Europa Hotel and Great Victoria Street station)
⏰ 11.30- midnight; 12.30-11 Sun
☎ (028) 9027 9901
Whitewater Belfast Ale; guest beer Ⓗ
Belfast's historic gem, possibly the UK's most ornate pub, is on CAMRA's National Inventory. Its much admired interior dates from the 1880s, and is unique in the city. It now has three handpumps, all dispensing Whitewater ales. Food is served in the bar and upstairs in

the Crown dining rooms. Conveniently situated close to the city centre, the pub tends to attract a lot of tourists and the ale is pricey, but it is a must see. ◑≉(Gt Victoria St)≞

John Hewitt

51 Donegal Street, BT1 2FH (100m from St Anne's Cathedral)
☼ 11.30 (12 Sat)-1am; Sun hours vary
☎ (028) 9023 3768 ⊕ thejohnhewitt.com
Hilden Ale; guest beer Ⓗ
The John Hewitt sits at the heart of Belfast's Cathedral Quarter, a hub for arts and music festivals. Run by the Unemployed Resource Centre, this is a pub with a very strong ethos, and a varied and friendly range of customers. No TV or jukebox here, just live music most nights. The layout is open plan with a large snug. Excellent food is served at lunchtime. A single handpump varies between Hilden and guest ales. ◑&≞

King's Head

829 Lisburn Road, BT9 7GY (opp Kings Hall at Balmoral)
☼ 12-1am (midnight Mon & Sun)
☎ (028) 9050 9950
Whitewater Belfast Ale Ⓗ
Large pub and restaurant opposite the King's Hall about three miles from the centre of Belfast. Downstairs has three distinct sections: dining area, public bar and cosy lounge. The ale is on two handpumps in the bar, usually Whitewater beers. The restaurant upstairs serves a variety of good food. Live music plays in the attached Live Lounge on Saturday nights. Easy to get to by train or bus.
❀◑ ⧉&≉(Balmoral)🚋P

Kitchen Bar

36-40 Victoria Square, BT1 4DY (access off Ann St via Upper Church St)
☼ 11.30-11.30 (midnight Mon; 1am Fri & Sat); 12-6 Sun
☎ (028) 9032 4901
Whitewater Belfast Ale; guest beer Ⓗ
A very different bar from the much missed Kitchen Bar, this new pub is bright, roomy and modern. Three large screens show sport and music videos. A jazz band plays on Monday evening and Thursday afternoon, a guitar player on Friday night. There is a disco on Saturday. Two handpumps serve Whitewater and guest ales. Access to the bar is restricted due to the construction of a new shopping centre. ◑≉(Central)

McHugh's

29-31 Queens Square, BT1 3FG (near Albert Clock)
☼ 12-1am (midnight Sun)
☎ (028) 9050 9999 ⊕ botanicinns.com
Whitewater Belfast Ale; guest beer Ⓗ
Modern pub and restaurant five minutes' walk from the city centre. The bar has two handpumps serving Whitewater ales; food is served in both the bar and upstairs restaurant. There is another room downstairs where live bands often play. A weekly quiz is held. Outside is a fine spot for drinking on a sunny day, with an excellent view of Customs House Square and the Albert Clock.
🏰◑&≉(Central)

Molly's Yard

1 College Green Mews, Botanic Avenue, BT7 1LW (behind Queen's University)
☼ 12-9 (9.30 Fri & Sat); closed Sun
☎ (028) 9032 2600
College Green Molly's Chocolate Stout, Headless Dog Ⓗ
Molly's Yard is in the heart of Belfast's bustling university area, housed in the restored stables of College Green House. Hilden Brewery's second restaurant, it first opened its doors in December 2005 and three months later won a best newcomers' award from the Restaurant Association of Ireland. The College Green ales here, at present still brewed at Hilden, are not available in any other restaurant in Belfast.
Q❀◑&≉(Botanic)🚋≞

Ryan's

116-118 Lisburn Road, BT9 6AH
☼ 11.30-1am; 12-midnight Sun
☎ (028) 9050 9850
Whitewater Belfast Ale Ⓗ
A new outlet for real ale. Ryan's is a corner pub situated on the Lisburn Road, a mile from the centre of Belfast. It has a modern interior, with several drinking areas. There is one handpump in the downstairs bar, and a restaurant upstairs. The patrons are generally students or sports fans, and the bar is always popular. Two quizzes are held every week and live matches are screened. ❀◑&≉(Botanic)

Carrickfergus

Central Bar

13-15 High Street, BT38 7AN (opp Carrickfergus Castle)
☼ 10-11 (midnight Thu-Sat)
☎ (028) 9335 7840
Beer range varies Ⓗ
Town centre Wetherspoon's pub overlooking the 12th-century Norman castle on the shore of Belfast Lough. The downstairs public bar is busy, the upstairs bar quieter – both serve Wetherspoon's standard beers and ciders as well as the usual good-value food (try the Ulster fry). Drinks can be enjoyed outside in a patio area overlooking the Lough. Although open at 10am every day alcohol is not served until 11.30am (12.30 Sun). Q❀◑⧉&≉🚋♿

Coleraine

Old Courthouse

Castlerock Road, BT51 3HP
☼ 10-11 (midnight Thu; 1am Fri & Sat)
☎ (028) 7032 5820
Beer range varies Ⓗ
Huge Wetherspoon's conversion a short walk from the River Bann. Formerly a county courthouse, it is now an outstanding pub with two floors: a single bar downstairs, a dining area upstairs. It serves a range of ales, Weston's cider and good value food. The patio

area is a fine spot to enjoy a drink when the weather is good. In common with other pubs in the chain, alcohol is not served until 11.30am and 12.30 on Sunday. ♨🛏️🏵️◑◗🍴

Enniskillen

Linen Hall

11-13 Townhall Street, BT74 7BD
✪ 10-11 (1am Fri & Sat)
☎ (028) 6634 0910
Beer range varies Ⓗ

Long, narrow Wetherspoon's pub in the centre of town near the bus station. It has four distinct areas: front entrance, bar, rear door, and family area at the back. The bar features five handpumps, one serving Weston's Old Rosie cider. There is background music from 5pm and a DJ plays on Friday night. Enniskillen is well worth a visit for the superb scenery. Alcohol is not served until 11.30am (12.30 Sunday). ♨🛏️🏵️◑◗♿🍴⤴️

Hillsborough

Hillside

21 Main Street, BT26 6AE
✪ 12-11.30 (1am Fri & Sat); 12-11 Sun
☎ (028) 9268 2765
Whitewater Belfast Ale; guest beers Ⓗ

One of the province's best real ale houses, this pub has changed ownership since the last Guide, and now has just three handpumps. Whitewater ales are the mainstay with occasional guests. Food is served in the bar, the refectory at the back and in the upstairs restaurant, open only on Friday and Saturday evenings. The bar also hosts a beer festival, usually in the summer. ♨Q🏵️◑◗🍴♿Ⓐ

Holywood

Dirty Duck Ale House

3 Kinnegar Road, BT18 9JW
✪ 11.30-midnight (1am Fri & Sat); 12.30-midnight Sun
☎ (028) 9059 6666
Beer range varies Ⓗ

This cheerful pub on the County Down side of Belfast Lough is a previous Northern Ireland CAMRA Pub of the Year. From the windows of the bar and upstairs restaurant you can enjoy superb views across the Lough. Four handpumps dispense a good range of beers. The pub hosts live music from Thursday to Sunday. Extra handpumps are installed for a late August beer festival held in a temporary covered bar outside. The pub has a Golf Society and a Tuesday night quiz. ♨🏵️◑◗♿⇌

Killinchy

Daft Eddy's

Sketrick Island, BT23 6QH (Whiterock Road 2 miles N of Killinchy)
✪ 11.30-11.30 (1am Fri); 12-10.30 Sun
☎ (028) 9754 1615
Whitewater Belfast Ale Ⓗ

A top flight dining and drinking experience in a picturesque location overlooking Whiterock Bay. The interior has a public bar, lounge and restaurant serving highly recommended food, especially the seafood. There is one

handpump offering a variety of ales from the Whitewater Brewery. A popular location despite the absence of public transport, this bar is well worth a visit, particularly in summer when you can relax outside and enjoy the superb views. Booking the restaurant is advisable. Q🏵️◑◗♿P

Lisburn

Tap Room

Hilden Brewery, Hilden, BT27 4TY (5 minutes' walk from Hilden railway halt)
✪ 11.30-2.30, 5.30-9; closed Monday; 12.30-3 Sun
☎ (028) 9266 3863
Hilden Molly Malone; guest beer Ⓗ

This is a licensed restaurant that belongs to Hilden Brewery. Ale is only served when it accompanies a meal. The Tap Room is adjacent to the brew house, in the grounds of the Scullion's Georgian manor. The brewery is about a 15 minute walk from the centre of Lisburn. It is such a good location that it often hosts business, social and music events, in particular, a very popular beer festival on August bank holiday. ♨Q🏵️◑◗♿⇌(Hilden)P

Tuesday Bell

Units 1 and 2 Lisburn Square, BT28 2TU (in shopping centre)
✪ 10-11 (1am Fri & Sat)
☎ (028) 9262 7390
Courage Directors; Greene King Abbot; guest beer Ⓗ

Large Wetherspoon's pub on two floors in the centre of Lisburn. The upper floor with its music and screens tends to attract a younger crowd than the quieter downstairs bar. The pub can be busy at lunchtimes and especially at the weekend. Although open for breakfast from 10am, alcohol is not served until 11.30am (12.30 Sunday). ◑◗♿⇌(Lisburn)⤴️

Londonderry

Diamond

23-24 The Diamond, BT48 6HP (centre of the walled city)
✪ 10-midnight (1am Fri & Sat)
☎ (028) 7127 2880
Beer range varies Ⓗ

Two storey Wetherspoon pub converted from a department store, with a bar on both floors and a children's room upstairs. The pub takes its name from the Diamond square inside the walled part of the 'Maiden City'. This part of the city is elevated and the pub has fine views towards the River Foyle. There is usually a good range of ales available; alcohol is served from 11.30am (12.30 Sunday). 🛏️◑◗♿⇌(Waterside)🍴⤴️

Ice Wharf

Strand Road, BT48 7AB
✪ 10-midnight (1am Thu-Sat)
☎ (028) 7127 6610
Greene King Abbot; guest beer Ⓗ

A short walk from Guildhall Square, this was Wetherspoon's first Lloyds No 1 in Northern Ireland. Formerly a hotel, it is now a large pub with a separate room for families. A selection of guest beers is usually available, with

Weston's cider on gravity tap. The Ice Wharf has gained a reputation for selling the cheapest ale in the province. In common with other Wetherspoon's, alcohol is served from 11.30am, 12.30 on Sunday. ⌖⟐⅃◧✦⌐

Newtownards

Spirit Merchant
54-56 Regent Street, BT23 4LP
🕐 10-11 (1am Fri & Sat); 10-midnight Sun
☎ (028) 9182 4270
Beer range varies ⊞
Large Wetherspoon's pub on the main street, formerly the Jolly Judge, busy and sometimes noisy. Keen pricing and music videos make this a popular venue with young people, particularly at weekends. Four handpumps offer Scottish ales as well as a range from the company's national list. Weston's Organic Draught Vintage and Old Rosie real ciders are available. Breakfast is available from 10am

every day, alcohol is not served until 11.30am (12.30 Sundays). ⌖⟐⅃◧P

Saintfield

White Horse
49 Main Street, BT24 7AB
🕐 11.30-11.30; 12-10.30 Sun
☎ (028) 9751 1143
Whitewater Mill Ale, Glen Ale, Knight Porter; guest beers ⊞
Very much a community pub, thronged with jolly locals, this pub has twice won Northern Ireland CAMRA Pub Of The Year. As befits a pub that finds favour with CAMRA members, it boasts five handpumps, usually with three Whitewater beers supplemented by guest ales. Owned by Whitewater Brewery, it also holds an annual beer festival in March. Food can be enjoyed in the downstairs restaurant, the bar, or in an elevated seating area above the bar. ♨⌖⟐⅃⌐

Old Courthouse, Coleraine, Northern Ireland.

673

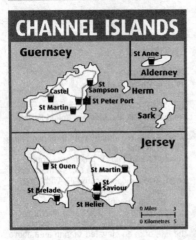

CHANNEL ISLANDS

ALDERNEY
St Anne

Georgian House Hotel
Victoria Street, GY9 3UF
🕐 10-12.30am; 10-3, 6.30-midnight (winter); 10-4 Sun
☎ (01481) 822471 ⊕ georgianhousealderney.com
Ringwood Best Bitter Ⓗ
Situated just up from the town church, this hotel extends a warm welcome to locals and visitors alike. There is a choice of areas to sit, from the front bar (where the handpump is situated) through to the dining room, the Orangery and outside in the sheltered sunny garden. Good food and a relaxed atmosphere awaits, making this a very pleasant way to while away the day. ❀⇔◑

GUERNSEY
Castel

Fleur du Jardin
Kings Mills, GY5 7JT
🕐 11.30-11.45
☎ (01481) 257996 ⊕ fleurdujardin.guernsey.net
Fuller's London Pride; Jersey Guernsey Sunbeam Ⓗ
Country pub with a good-sized, sheltered garden in an attractive rural setting. There are two bars: one small and cosy attached to the restaurant, the other larger, situated at the rear of the hotel. The menus in both the bar and the restaurant feature fresh local produce. This popular local can be busy at the weekend and throughout the summer. ⚑Q❀⇔◑P

Rockmount Hotel
Cobo, GY5 7HB
🕐 10-11.45 (12.45am Fri & Sat); 12-10.30 sun
☎ (01481) 256757
White Horse Wayland Smithy Ⓗ
This pub has two bars: a public to the rear of the building by the large car park and a lounge at the front by the road. With a warming fire in winter, it is a perfect place to retreat from the gales. A good range of food is served in the lounge. The pub is just across the road from a beautiful sandy beach. At the end of the day why not relax with a good pint and enjoy one of the island's best views of Guernsey's legendary sunsets. ⚑◑⇔P

St Martin

Ambassador Hotel
Route de Sausmarez, GY4 6SO
🕐 12-3, 6-11.45; 12-3.30 sun
☎ (01481) 238356 ⊕ ambassador.guernsey.net
White Horse Village Idiot Ⓗ
The hotel is situated just down from Sausmarez Manor. A delicious range of meals is available, either in the bar, the restaurant or the Old Guernsey Conservatory. There is also a patio area to the rear of the bar. The car park to the front is quite small and can be busy. The accommodation is good value. ⇔◑P

Captain's Hotel
La Fosse, GY4 6EF
🕐 11-11 Mon-Thu; 11-12 Fri-Sat; 12-4 sun
☎ (01481) 223890
Fullers London Pride Ⓗ
In a secluded location, down a country lane, this is a popular locals' pub with a lively, friendly atmosphere. There is a small area raised in front of the bar furnished with a sofa to make a 'comfy zone'. Meals can be eaten in the bar or in the newly refurbished bistro. A meat draw is held on Friday. There is a car park to the rear which can fill up quickly. ⇔◑P

St Peter Port

Cock & Bull
Lower Hauteville, GY1 1LL
🕐 11.30-2.30, 4-12.45am; 11.30-12.45am Fri & Sat; closed Sun
☎ (01481) 722660
Beer range varies Ⓗ
Popular pub, just up the hill from the town church. Five handpumps offer a changing range of different beers. Live music takes place on different nights of the week: it could be salsa, baroque or jazz on a Monday, Tuesday is open microphone and Irish plays on Thursday. Seating is on three levels and there is a large screen showing sporting events. A patio area is at the rear. ❀

Cornerstone Café
La Tour Beauregard, GY1 1LQ
🕐 10 (8am Thu & Fru)-12.45am; occasional Sun
☎ (01481) 713832 ⊕ cornerstoneguernsey.co.uk
Fuller's London Pride; Shepherd Neame Spitfire; White Horse Bitter Ⓗ
Situated across the road from the States Archives, the café has a small bar area to the front with bar stools, and further seating to the rear. The menu offers a wide range of hot and cold meals, served throughout the day. Regular quiz evenings are held. ◑

Randy Paddle
North Esplanade, GY1 2LQ
🕐 10-11.45 (12.45am Fri & Sat); closed Sun

☎ (01481) 725610
Fuller's London Pride; Wadworth 6X Ⓗ
Across the road from the harbour and next door to the tourist board, the pub is in an ideal position for a drink before a meal at one of the varied restaurants surrounding it. The bar has a nautical theme, and although small, makes good use of space, attracting a mixed crowd of regulars and visitors to the island.

Ship & Crown

North Esplanade, GY1 2NB (opp Crown Pier car park)
✪ 10-12.45am; 12-10 Sun
☎ (01481) 721368
Greene King Ruddles County; Marston's Pedigree; Shepherd Neame Spitfire Ⓗ
The pub has a nautical theme, with pictures of ships and a model of the 'Seven Seas', complete with tiny cannon balls, in a glass case. Situated across the road from the Victoria Pier (known locally as the Crown Pier), this busy pub attracts a varied clientele of all ages, both locals and tourists. Real cider or perry is available. Good quality bar meals including a daily changing range of specials are served in generous portions (no evening meals Fri & Sat). ◑▯♠

St Sampson

La Fontaine Inn

Vale Road, GY2 4DS
✪ 10-11.45; 12-3.30 (6 summer) Sun
☎ (01481) 247644
White Horse Wayland Smithy Ⓗ
Popular with the local community, the handpumps are located in the small public bar at the front. The L-shaped lounge has a bar at the end and a handy serving hatch halfway down the wall. Shove-ha'penny is played in the public bar and darts at the back of the lounge. A popular meat raffle is held on Friday. ❀Ⓖ♣P

JERSEY
St Brelade

Old Court House

Le Boulevard, St Aubin's Harbour, JE3 8AB
✪ 11-11
☎ (01534) 746433
Draught Bass; Skinner's Betty Stogs, seasonal beers; Wells Bombardier Ⓗ
Situated on the bulwarks of St Aubin's Harbour, the Old Court House is primarily a restaurant and hotel but drinkers are very welcome in the Granite Bar and conservatory. There is a very good bus service from St Helier and it is only a short walk over the hill to the Smugglers at Ouaisne. Q☎❀✍◑▯☜

Old Smugglers Inn

Le Mont du Ouaisne, JE3 8AW
✪ 11-11 (winter hours vary)
☎ (01534) 741510
Draught Bass; Greene King Abbot; Skinner's Betty Stogs, seasonal beers; Wells Bombardier; guest beers Ⓗ

Perched on the edge of Ouaisne Bay, the Smugglers has been the jewel in the crown of the Jersey real ale scene for many years. One of just a few free houses on the island, it is set on several levels within a row of granite fishermen's cottages dating back hundreds of years. Up to four real ales are usually available and mini beer festivals are held in autumn and spring. ♨Q◑▯

St Helier

Lamplighter

9 Mulcaster Street, JE2 3NJ
✪ 11-11
☎ (01534) 723119
Ringwood Best Bitter, Fortyniner, Ⓗ **Old Thumper;** Ⓖ **Skinner's Betty Stogs; Wells Bombardier;** Ⓗ **guest beers** Ⓖ
The Lamplighter is a traditional pub with a modern feel. The gas lamps that gave the pub its name remain, as does the origial antique pewter bar top. An excellent range of up to eight real ales are available, four served direct from the cask. The pub has been awarded CAMRA Pub of the Year 2006 and also a Beautiful Beer award by the BBPA. ◑▤

St Martin

Rozel

La Vallee de Rozel, JE3 6AJ
✪ 11-11
☎ (01534) 869801
Greene King Abbot; Ringwood Best Bitter; Wells Bombardier; guest beers Ⓗ
This charming little hostelry is tucked away in the north-west corner of the island. The pub has a delightful beer garden and there is also an excellent restaurant upstairs. Bar meals are available in both the public bar and snug, where there is a real fire in the winter months. The locals are very friendly if sometimes a little rumbustious! ♨Q❀◑ Ⓖ▤P

St Ouen

Moulin de Lecq

Le Mont de la Greve de Lecq, JE3 2DT
✪ 11-11
☎ (01534) 482818
Greene King Ruddles County, Abbot, Old Speckled Hen, Seasonal Beers; Wells Bombardier; guest beers Ⓗ
A rare free house on the island offering a range of real ales, the Moulin is a converted 17th-century watermill situated in the valley above the beach at Greve de Lecq. The waterwheel is still in place and the turning mechanism can be seen behind the bar. A welcome addition is the restaurant that has been added in a new but sympathetically constructed wing of the building. There is a children's playground and a large alfresco area. ♨Q❀◑▤♣P☜

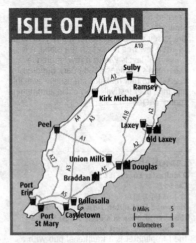

ISLE OF MAN

Ballasalla

Whitestone Inn

Station Road, IM9 2DD

🕐 12-11 (midnight Fri & Sat)

☎ (01624) 822334

Okells Mild, Bitter; guest beer Ⓗ

Former coaching inn extensively refurbished and extended in the last few years. Family friendly, the inn has a large dining area. A smaller room has its own bar plus pool table and TV screens. Barbecues are held in summer and live music hosted on most Saturday evenings. ⚘🍴ᘒ♿⇌(IMR)🚌♣P

Castletown

Castle Arms (Gluepot)

The Quay, IM9 1LP (between Castle Rushen and harbour)

🕐 12-11 (midnight Fri & Sat)

☎ (01624) 824673

Okells Bitter Ⓗ

Attractive, historic pub, also known as the Gluepot, next to the harbour and opposite Castle Rushen. The two small ground floor rooms have a seafaring theme, decorated with old nautical photographs and models. The patio is perfect on warm days for watching quayside activities and waterfront wildlife. ⚘Ɒ♿⇌(IMR)🚌

Sidings

Victoria Road, IM9 1EF (by station)

🕐 11.30-11 (midnight Fri & Sat)

☎ (01624) 823282

Bushy's Ruby Mild, Bitter; Castletown Bitter; guest beers Ⓗ

Close to the station, this is a popular destination for travellers on the historic steam railway. The bar has an impressive ornate wooden counter and offers an ever-changing variety of up to 10 cask ales, from Manx and UK breweries. There is a pool room. The secluded garden area is pleasant in summer. CAMRA Isle of Man Pub of the Year in 2003 and 2005. 🏠⚘Ɒ♿⇌(IMR)🚌♣–

Douglas

Albert Hotel

3 Chapel Row, IM1 2BJ (near indoor market)

🕐 10-11 (midnight Fri & Sat); 12-10.30 Sun

☎ (01624) 673632

Okells Mild, Bitter Ⓗ

In the centre of Douglas, this busy, traditional two-room pub has a central bar serving the spacious, wood-panelled lounge and smaller public bar. It also has a large games and TV room and a smaller snug area. The pub had its own house beer Jough (Manx Gaelic for beer) from Okells. Next to the bus station, this is an ideal starting or finishing point for real ale trips around the island. Q⚘⇌(IMR)🚌♣

Prospect

Prospect Hill, IM1 1ET

🕐 12-11 (11.30 Thu; midnight Fri); 6-midnight Sat; closed Sun

☎ (01624) 616773

Okells Bitter; guest beers Ⓗ

Spacious, stylish pub in the financial centre of Douglas, popular with office workers. The single-bar interior has a traditional feel with polished wood columns and carved shelving. Quiz night is Thursday. The guest beer comes from an island or UK brewery. There are picnic tables outside on the footpath in warmer weather. ⚘⇌(IMR)🚌

Queens Hotel

Queens Promenade, IM2 4NL (on seafront)

🕐 12-midnight (1am Fri & Sat)

☎ (01624) 674438

Okells Bitter; guest beers Ⓗ

Family-owned pub at the Onchan end of the promenade, popular with locals and tourists all year round. Though recently redecorated, this bright, cheery, open plan pub retains its olde worlde charm. With spectacular views over Douglas Bay, this is a perfect spot for summer drinking – there are picnic tables, awnings and heaters outside. The Douglas horse trams stop outside during the tourist season. Q👥⚘ⓓ♿⇌(IMR)🚌♣–

Rovers Return

11 Church Street, IM1 2AG (behind town hall)

🕐 12-11 (midnight Fri & Sat)

☎ (01624) 676459

Bushy's Ruby Mild, Bitter, seasonal beers; guest beers Ⓗ

This pub never stands still. As well as guest beers, an increasing range of bottled world beers are now available. However, the number of rooms in this multi-room pub remains at nine for the moment and (some) football fans will be pleased to note that the room dedicated to Blackburn Rovers FC remains unchanged. Live music staged most weekends draws the crowds in the evenings. 🏠⚘ⓓ⇌(IMR)🚌♣

Saddle Inn

Queen Street, IM1 1LH (on North Quay)

INDEPENDENT BREWERIES

Bushy's Braddan
Okells Douglas
Old Laxey Old Laxey

✪ 10-11 (midnight Fri & Sat); 12-10.30 summer; 12-4, 7-10.30 winter Sun
☎ (01624) 673161
Okells Mild, Bitter Ⓗ
Small pub set back from the main quayside full of olde worlde character. The beams are adorned with brewery logos. The lounge has a large-screen TV often showing horse racing, with bookmakers' cards provided by the pub. An increasingly rare stockist of Okells mild in the Douglas area. ▣≉(IMR)♣

Woodbourne Hotel
Alexander Drive, IM2 3QF
✪ 12 (2 Mon-Thu)-midnight
☎ (01624) 676754
Okells Mild, Bitter; guest beers Ⓗ
Friendly pub just outside the town centre. This is one of the last pubs on the island to have a gents' only bar (no longer strictly adhered to). Up to two guest ales are available alongside the regular Okells beers. This historic pub is reputed to have its own ghosts who occasionally put in an appearance. Q▣🖾

Kirk Michael

Mitre
IM6 1AJ
✪ 12-2.30 (not Mon), 5-11 (midnight Fri); 12-midnight Sat; 12-11 Sun
☎ (01624) 878244
Okells Bitter; guest beer Ⓗ
Recently refurbished, this cosy and welcoming two-room pub has lost none of its original charm. The homely lounge has photos and memorabilia of the TT from years gone by which fascinates the fans who flock here during the races. Good, home-cooked food is served. A large screen shows football in the bar and a weekly quiz is hosted. The extensive garden, a hidden gem at the back of the pub, has wonderful views to the hills.
🚶❀◑ ▣⚓🖾♣P⁻

Laxey

Bridge Inn
6 New Road, IM4 7BE
✪ 11.30-11 (midnight Fri & Sat)
☎ (01624) 862414
Bushy's Mild, Bitter Ⓗ
Popular community pub in the centre of the village near Laxey Glen gardens, home to the Poetry and Pints society. A wide-screen TV shows football and there is a pool table. The cellar was used as a morgue after the Snaefell mining disaster in 1897 in which 20 men perished. The inn is reputed to be haunted, with ghostly figures seen in the lounge.
🚶🛏❀≉(MER)🖾♣P

Queen's Hotel
New Road, IM4 7BP
✪ 12-11 (midnight Fri & Sat)
☎ (01624) 861195
Bushy's Ruby Mild, Bitter; guest beers Ⓗ
Busy one-room local on the edge of Laxey with comfortable button-back benches and an impressive array of pump clips. Numerous photos and pictures of the local area adorn every wall, mainly featuring motobikes and

riders including several of the late Joey Dunlop. Live music is hosted and barbecues held on summer weekends. The large porch with benches outside is perfect for watching the world go by, or even waiting for the bus to Douglas which stops outside.
❀🛏≉(MER)🖾(3)♣P⁻

Old Laxey

Shore Hotel
IM4 7DA
✪ 12-midnight; closed Mon winter
☎ (01624) 861509
Old Laxey Bosun Bitter Ⓗ
Cosy, renowned village brew pub next to the Laxey River. The large single room has a nautical theme, with faded fishing boat pictures and angling equipment and artefacts. There is a real fire in winter and plentiful outside seating in summer – an ideal spot to relax and watch the ducks while enjoying a pint of Bosun's. 🚶❀◑ 🖾P⁻

Peel

Creek Inn
Station Place, IM5 1AT (by harbour)
✪ 10-midnight
☎ (01624) 842216
Okells Bitter; guest bitter Ⓗ
Two-room pub situated on the harbour, close to Peel Castle, the House of Mananan and the famous Manx Kipper Factory. There is an ever increasing emphasis on real ale here and occasional beer festivals are held. A large-screen TV shows sports and one bar hosts local bands at the weekend. Food is served all day – try the local seafood. The patio over the road is an excellent place to watch the sun go down over the castle. ❀◑ 🖾P

Whitehouse Hotel
Tynwald Road, IM5 1LA
✪ 11-midnight
☎ (01624) 842252
Bushy's Bitter; Flowers Original; Okells Mild, Bitter; Taylor Landlord; guest beers Ⓗ
Popular, family-run, multi-roomed town pub which has remained largely unchanged since the 1930s, decorated with historic pictures of the local area. All rooms converge on a central bar. The 'Captain's Cabin' snug has its own bar. Local musicians meet informally most Saturday evenings to play Manx music. It's a staunch supporter of real ales over many years (note the many CAMRA awards adorning the walls), it also stocks over 120 malt whiskies.
🚶Q🛏❀▣🖾♣P

Port Erin

Bay Hotel
Shore Road, IM9 6HL
✪ 12-midnight (1am Fri & Sat)
☎ (01624) 832084
Bushy's Castletown Bitter, Manx Bitter, Old Bushy Tail, seasonal beers; guest beers Ⓗ
Welcoming pub with a friendly atmosphere and a traditional feel on the lower promenade next to Port Erin's beautiful beach. This large, established inn has an unspoiled interior with

timber floors. The lounge bar has plenty of seating for diners. Live music plays on Friday night. Five or more ales are usually available, as well as imported bottled beers and at least one real cider. A beer festival is held in August and September. ⌂⌇◑⊞⇌(IMR)♣⚲

Falcon's Nest Hotel
Station Road, IM9 6AF
◷ 11-midnight
☎ (01624) 834077 ⊕ falconsnesthotel.co.uk
Bushy's Bitter; Okells Bitter; guest beers ⊞
Family-run, seafront hotel with views over Port Erin Bay and the harbour. Real ale is served in the lounge, not the bar, due to the location of the cellar. The attractive lounge, with polished wood and stained glass, leads to the conservatory where you can enjoy panoramic views over the sea. A wide range of meals is available including the popular Sunday carvery served in the large restaurant. ⌂⇌◑⊞⇌(IMF)⊟P

Port St Mary

Albert Hotel
Athol Street, IM9 5DS (alongside bus terminal)
◷ 11.30-midnight (1am Fri & Sat); 12-midnight Sun
☎ (01624) 832118
Bushy's Ruby Mild, Old Bushy Tail; Okells Bitter; guest beers ⊞
Traditional free house with impressive views over the inner harbour and bay. A popular stop off for anglers returning from a fishing trip, the busy public bar has pool, darts and a juke box. The cosy lounge has a nautical theme; both bars have real fires. There is a small restaurant across the hallway and bar meals are available. Food and accommodation are highly recommended. ⌂⚘⇌◑⊞⊟P

Shore Hotel
Shore Road, Gansey, IM9 5LZ (on main Castletown-Port St Mary road) OS220689
◷ 12-midnight (1am Fri & Sat)
☎ (01624) 832269
Bushy's Bushy Tail; Okells Bitter; guest beer ⊞
Busy, friendly local which has grown in popularity in recent years, with good views of Carrick Rock and Bay. Traditional Manx ales along with a weekly guest beer are on dispense in the cosy bar. A large TV screen shows sport and there is a pool table. Good quality food is served in the restaurant prepared by the pub's award-winning chef – booking recommended. Themed food nights are popular, as well as Sunday lunches. Four B&B rooms are available. ⚘⇌◑⊞⊟♣P

Ramsey

Trafalgar Hotel
West Quay, IM8 1DW (E of harbour swing bridge)
◷ 11-11 (midnight Fri & Sat); 12-3, 8-11 Sun
☎ (01624) 814601
Cains Bitter; Okells Bitter; guest beers ⊞
Friendly, traditional harbourside free house, full of character. The 'Traf' is just a short walk from Parliament Square where you can get an unrivalled view of the races during TT and Manx Grand Prix weeks. A regular finalist for local CAMRA Pub of the Year, its no surprise that the pub can be very busy, particularly at the weekend. Guest ales are sourced from throughout the UK. ⇌(MER)⊟♣

Sulby

Ginger Hall Hotel
Ballamanagh Road, IM7 2HB (on A3 Ramsey-Kirk Michael road) OS394945
◷ 12-11.30 (1am Fri & Sat)
☎ (01624) 897231
Okells Mild, Bitter; guest beer ⊞
Traditional small village pub situated on a prominent corner on the TT course. The rear rooms have been refurbished but the bar remains unchanged with no gaming machines. The walls display many photos of TT riders and racing action going back over the years. There is a separate restaurant and accommodation is available in eight rooms. ⌂⚘⇌◑⊠▲⊟(5, 6)♣P

Sulby Glen Hotel
Main Road, IM7 2HR (Sulby crossroads, A3)
◷ 12-midnight (1am Fri & Sat); 12-11 Sun
☎ (01624) 897240
Bushy's Bitter; Okells Bitter; guest beers ⊞
Large multi-roomed pub on the famous Sulby Straight section of the TT course. Photographs of racers through the ages adorn the walls. The choice of real ales now includes Mild Rosie, a house beer from Bushy's named after the landlady. There is always something happening at the Sulby, from live bands and themed music nights to murder mysteries and pub outings. Excellent food is available from a varied menu. ⌂⌇⚘⇌◑⊞▲⊟♣⚲P↳

Union Mills

Railway Inn
Main Road, IM4 4NE
◷ 12 (11 Sun)-11
☎ (01624) 853006 ⊕ iomrailwayinn.com
Okells Mild, Bitter; guest beers ⊞
Independent, historic pub dating back to 1841. Frequented by a friendly crowd, this community pub at the centre of village life is now in the fifth generation of ownership by the same family. Located on the TT circuit, it is a spectacular place to watch the racing. Usually offering three guest ales, it was runner up local CAMRA Pub of the Year in 2006. Alas, a railway no longer serves this part of the island, but there is a regular bus service from Douglas. ⚘⊟P↳

Good health

A glass of bitter beer or pale ale, taken with the principal meal of the day, does more good and less harm than any medicine the physician can prescribe.
Dr Carpenter, 1750

The Breweries

How beer is brewed

Real ale is made by taking raw ingredients from the fields, the finest malting barley and hops, along with pure water from natural springs or the public supply, and carefully cultivated strains of brewers' yeast; in this exploded drawing by Trevor Hatchett of a classic British ale brewery, it is possible to follow the process that begins with raw grain and finishes with natural, living cask beer.

1. On the top floor, in the roof, are the tanks where pure water – called liquor by brewers – is stored. Soft water is not suited to ale brewing, and brewers will add such salts as gypsum and magnesium to replicate the hard, flinty waters of Burton-on-Trent, home of pale ale.

2. In the malt store, grain is weighed and kept until needed. The malt drops down a floor to the mills, which grind it into a coarse powder suitable for brewing. From the mills, the ground malt or grist is poured into the mash tuns along with heated liquor. During the mashing period, natural enzymes in the malt convert starches into fermentable malt sugars.

3. On the same floor as the conditioning tanks are the coppers, where after mashing, the wort is boiled with hops, which add aroma, flavour and bitterness.

4. At the end of the boil, the hopped wort is clarified in a vessel called the hop back on the ground floor. The clarified wort is pumped back to the malt store level where it is passed through a heat exchange unit. See 5.

5. The heat exchange unit cools the hopped wort prior to fermentation.

6. The fermenters are on the same floor as the mash tuns. The house yeast is blended or pitched with the wort. Yeast converts the malt sugars in the wort into alcohol and carbon dioxide. Excess yeast is skimmed off by funnels called parachutes.

7. Fermentation lasts for a week and the 'green' beer is then stored for a few days in conditioning tanks.

8. Finally, the fresh beer is run into casks on the ground floor, where additional hops for aroma and sugar to encourage a secondary fermentation may be added. The casks then leave for pubs, where the beer reaches maturity in the cellars.

How to use The Breweries section

Breweries are listed in alphabetical order. The independents (regional, smaller craft brewers and brew-pubs) are listed first, followed by the nationals, the globals and finally the major non-brewing pub groups. Within each brewery entry, beers are listed in increasing order of strength. Beers that are available for less than three months of the year are described as 'occasional' or 'seasonal' brews. Bottle-conditioned beers are also listed: these are beers that have not been pasteurised and contain live yeast, allowing them to continue to ferment and mature in the bottle as a draught real ale does in its cask.

Symbols

Ṵ A brew-pub: a pub that brews beer on the premises.

◆ CAMRA tasting notes, supplied by a trained CAMRA tasting panel. Beer descriptions that do not carry this symbol are based on more limited tastings or have been obtained from other sources.

Tasting notes are not provided for brew-pub beers that are available in fewer than five outlets, nor for other breweries' beers that are available for less than three months of the year.

🗖 A CAMRA Beer of the Year in 2006.

🖿 One of the 2007 CAMRA Beers of the Year, a finalist in the Champion Beer of Britain competition held during the Great British Beer Festival in London in August 2007, or the Champion Winter Beer of Britain competition held earlier in the year.

⊛ The brewery's beers can be acceptably served through a 'tight sparkler' attached to the nozzle of the beer pump, designed to give a thick collar of foam on the beer.

⊠ The brewery's beer should NOT be served through a tight sparkler. CAMRA is opposed to the growing tendency to serve southern-brewed beers with the aid of sparklers, which aerate the beer and tend to drive hop aroma and flavour into the head, altering the balance of the beer achieved in the brewery. When neither symbol is used it means the brewery in question has not stated a preference.

Abbreviations

OG stands for original gravity, the measure taken before fermentation of the level of 'fermentable material' (malt sugars and added sugars) in the brew. It is a rough indication of strength and is no longer used for duty purposes.

ABV stands for Alcohol by Volume, which is a more reliable measure of the percentage of alcohol in the finished beer. Many breweries now only disclose ABVs but the Guide lists OGs where available. Often the OG and the ABV of a beer are identical, ie 1035 and 3.5 per cent. If the ABV is higher than the OG, ie OG 1035, ABV 3.8, this indicates that the beer has been 'well attenuated' with most of the malt sugars turned into alcohol. If the ABV is lower than the OG, this means residual sugars have been left in the beer for fullness of body and flavour: this is rare but can apply to some milds or strong old ales, barley wines, and winter beers.

*The Breweries Section was correct at the time of going to press and every effort has been made to ensure that all cask-conditioned and bottle-conditioned beers are included.

The independents

❋Indicates a new brewery since the last edition; SIBA indicates a member of the Society of Independent Brewers; IFBB indicates a member of the Independent Family Brewers of Britain; EAB indicates a member of the East Anglian Brewers Co-operative.

1648 SIBA

1648 Brewing Co Ltd, Old Stables Brewery, Mill Lane, East Hoathly, East Sussex, BN8 6QB
Tel (01825) 840830
✉ brewmaster@1648brewing.co.uk
🌐 1648brewing.co.uk
Tours by arrangement

⊗ The 1648 brewery, set up an the old stable block at the King's Head pub in 2003, derives its name and some of the beer names from the time of the deposition of King Charles I. One pub is owned and more than 30 outlets are supplied. Seasonal beers: Three Threads (ABV 4.3%, Apr-Jul), Bee-Head (ABV 4.6%, May-Sep), Lammas Ale (ABV 4.2%, Jul-Oct), Armistice Ale (ABV 4.2%, Oct-Nov), Ginger Nol (ABV 4.7%, Oct-Mar), Winter Warrant (ABV 4.8%, Dec-Mar).

Original (OG 1040, ABV 3.9%)
Light, quaffable and easy drinking.

Signature (OG 1044, ABV 4.4%)
Light, crisp, medium hoppy clean beer with a bitter finish.

Saint George (OG 1045, ABV 4.5%)
Traditional English ale with a balanced malt and hop flavour.

3 Rivers SIBA

3 Rivers Brewing Ltd, Delta House, Greg Street, Reddish, Cheshire, SK5 7BS
Tel (0161) 477 3333
✉ contacts@3riversbrewing.co.uk
🌐 3riversbrewery.co.uk
Tours by arrangement

☺ 3 Rivers was launched in 2003. There is a members' club on site, a purpose-built tasting area for brewery tours and a classroom designed for brewing courses. More than 470 outlets are supplied. Seasonal beers: phone for details. Bottle-conditioned beers: Man IPA, Old Disreputable, Yummy Figgy Pudding.

GMT (ABV 3.8%)
Golden bitter with an underlying malt character supported by moderate hop bitterness and a light floral finish.

Harry Jacks (ABV 4.1%)
Tawny-coloured ale with a fruity character supplemented by hints of roast malt in the finish.

Manchester IPA (ABV 4.2%)
Light russet/amber colour with a refreshing biscuit-like flavour, supplemented by a complex citrus finish.

Fathers Favourite (ABV 4.2%)
Light amber-coloured ale with hints of coffee and caramel, complemented by a spicy hop character and a complex aroma.

Oxbow (ABV 4.5%)
Hoppy bitter; the initial dryness leads to a spicy character and citrus aftertaste.

Julie's Pride (ABV 5%)

Old Disreputable (ABV 5.2%)
Dark malty brew with distinctive coffee and chocolate hints and a lasting bitter finish.

Suitably Irish (ABV 6%)
Full-bodied black stout.

For Beechams Bar, St Helens:

Crystal Wheat (ABV 5%)
A spicy character with a floral aroma.

For Paradise Brewery Bar, Manchester:

Mild (OG 1036, ABV 3.6%)

Farmers Favourite (ABV 4%)

Dabbers (OG 1048, ABV 5%)

Nantwich Ale (ABV 5.6%)

Abbey Ales SIBA

Abbey Ales Ltd, Abbey Brewery, Camden Row, Bath, Somerset, BA1 5LB
Tel (01225) 444437
✉ enquiries@abbeyales.co.uk
🌐 abbeyales.co.uk
Tours by arrangement

⊗ Abbey Ales is the first and only brewery in Bath for nearly 50 years. It supplies more than 80 regular accounts within a 20-mile radius of Bath Abbey while selected wholesalers deliver beer nationally. One tied house, the Star Inn, Bath, is listed on CAMRA's National Inventory of heritage pubs. Seasonal beers: Bath Star (ABV 4.5%, spring), Chorister (ABV 4.5%, autumn), White Friar (ABV 5%), Black Friar (ABV 5.3%, winter), Twelfth Night (ABV 5%, Xmas).

Bellringer (OG 1042, ABV 4.2%) ◈
A notably hoppy ale, light to medium-bodied, clean-tasting, refreshingly dry, with a balancing sweetness. Citrus, pale malt aroma and dry, bitter finish.

Abbey Bells

Abbey Bells Brewery, 5 Main Road, Hirst Courtney, Selby, North Yorkshire, YO8 8QP
Tel 07940 726658
✉ enquiries@abbeybells.co.uk
🌐 abbeybells.co.uk
Tours by arrangement (for up to 12 persons only)

⊗ The brewery was launched in 2002 and has a 2.5-barrel plant with cellar tanks from the defunct Brigg Brewery and other parts from a dairy maker in Congleton. Some 30 outlets are supplied. Seasonal beers: Santa's Stocking Filler (ABV 4.5%), Black Satin (ABV 6.2%, winter).

Monday's Child (OG 1035, ABV 3.7%)
An easy-drinking session beer, made with Maris Otter malt and Goldings hops. Pale and refreshing.

Amber Neck Tie (OG 1040, ABV 4%)

Hoppy Daze (OG 1041, ABV 4.1%)
Similar in colour to Monday's Child, the beer is hopped with Target.

Cordelia's Gift (OG 1042, ABV 4.3%)
The combination of Pearl and chocolate malts and Fuggles hops imparts a flavour reminiscent of dandelion and burdock.

Leper Squint (OG 1045, ABV 4.5%)

Grease (OG 1045, ABV 4.6%)

1911 Celebration Ale (OG 1048, ABV 4.8%)

Original Bitter (OG 1050, ABV 5.1%)
Made from Pearl malt with a dash of crystal and flavoured with Goldings hops.

Abbeydale SIBA

Abbeydale Brewery Ltd, Unit 8 Aizlewood Road, Sheffield, South Yorkshire, S8 0YX
Tel (0114) 281 2712
✉ info@abbeydalebrewery.co.uk
⊕ abbeydalebrewery.co.uk

⊕ Abbeydale Brewery was set up in 1996 and now supplies more than 250 outlets. The brewery is noted for its pale, hoppy beers that are made with natural ingredients. It owns one pub, the Rising Sun at Nether Green. Seasonal beers: see website.

Matins (OG 1034.9, ABV 3.6%)
Pale and full flavoured; a hoppy session beer.

Brimstone (OG 1039, ABV 3.9%)

Moonshine (OG 1041.2, ABV 4.3%)
Pale premium beer balancing hints of sweetness and bitterness with full hop aroma.

Absolution (OG 1050, ABV 5.3%)
Strong, pale, sweetish beer.

Black Mass (OG 1065, ABV 6.66%)
Strong black stout, quite bitter and dry but full flavoured with a good hop aroma.

Last Rites (OG 1097, ABV 11%) ⬠
A pale, strong barley wine.

Acorn SIBA

Acorn Brewery of Barnsley Ltd, Unit 3 Mitchell Road, Aldham Industrial Estate, Wombwell, Barnsley, South Yorkshire, S73 8HA
Tel (01226) 270734
✉ acornbrewery@tiscali.co.uk
⊕ acornbrewery.net
Shop Mon-Fri 9am-5pm
Tours by arrangement

Acorn Brewery was set up in 2003 with a 10-barrel ex-Firkin plant. Expansion to a 20-barrel plant was completed in 2007 when demand outgrew capacity. All beers are produced using the original Barnsley Bitter yeast strains, dating back to the 1850s. The brewery currently has a 100 barrel a week capacity. Seasonal beers: see website.

Barnsley Bitter (OG 1038, ABV 3.8%) ⬛ ⬠ ◆
A complex aroma of malt and hops. A hint of chocolate with a fresh fruit and bitter taste.

Barnsley Gold (OG 1041.5, ABV 4.3%) ◆
Fruit in the aroma and taste. There is also a hoppy flavour throughout. A well-hopped, clean, dry finish.

Sovereign (OG 1044, ABV 4.4%) ◆
Well-balanced bitter with plenty of fruit and malt. Excellent mouthfeel.

Old Moor Porter (OG 1045, ABV 4.4%) ◆
A rich roast malt aroma with chocolate, cherry and liquorice flavours. A creamy mouthfeel leads to a dry finish.

IPA (OG 1047, ABV 5%) ◆
Full of hoppy and fruit aroma, a hoppy dry and fresh citrus fruit and bitter flavour that leads to a crisp citrus, hoppy finish.

Gorlovka Imperial Stout (OG 1058, ABV 6%) ◆
A deep malt and hoppy aroma with liquorice throughout. Roast, fruit and hops also carry through this full-bodied stout.

Adnams IFBB

Adnams plc, Sole Bay Brewery, East Green, Southwold, Suffolk, IP18 6JW
Tel (01502) 727200
✉ info@adnams.co.uk
⊕ adnams.co.uk
Shop 10am-6pm daily

⊗ The company was founded by George and Ernest Adnams in 1872, who were joined by the Loftus family in 1902; a member of each family is still an active director of the company. New fermenting vessels were installed in 2001, 2003 and 2005 to cope with demand while a new eco-friendly distribution centre has been opened in neighbouring Reydon. Real ale is available in all 82 pubs and there is national distribution to the free trade. Seasonal beers: Regatta (ABV 4.3%, summer), Fisherman (ABV 4.3%, winter), Old (ABV 4.1%, winter), Oyster Stout (ABV 4.3%, winter), Tally Ho (ABV 7%, Xmas ⬠).

Bitter (OG 1037, ABV 3.7%) ⬛ ⬛ ◆
Well-balanced but fairly dry session bitter, with a faintly sulphurous aroma and a long, bitter finish.

Explorer (OG 1042, ABV 4.3%) ◆
Brewed with American hops, hence the name. Citrus fruit in the mouth, with a long, sweet aftertaste.

Broadside (OG 1049, ABV 4.7%) ◆
The aroma and initial taste boom with prunes. Malt and sultanas with a trace of pepper in the mouth. The finish is long, turning drier.

Alcazar SIBA

⬧ **Sherwood Forest Brewing Co Ltd, Alcazar Brewery, 11-13 Church Street, Old Basford, Nottingham, NG6 0GA**
Tel (0115) 978 5155 / (0115) 978 2282
✉ alcazarbrewery@tiscali.co.uk
⊕ alcazarbrewery.co.uk
Tours by arrangement

⊗ Alcazar was established in 1999 and is located behind its brewery tap, the Fox & Crown. The brewery is full mash, 10 barrel brew length. Production is mainly for the Fox & Crown and other free houses within the Turnstone Taverns estate. The brewery shop has been expanded and sells a large range of continental and UK bottled ales. Seasonal beers: Maple Magic (ABV 5.5%, winter), Mocha Stout

(ABV 5%, spring), Black Fox Mild (ABV 3.9%, spring), Desert Fox (ABV 4.3%, summer), Bombay Castle IPA (ABV 6.5%, summer), Nottingham Nog (ABV 4.2%, winter).

Alcazar Ale (OG 1040, ABV 4%)
A session ale made with a blend of English and North American hops; pale, full-flavoured with a fruity aroma and finish.

New Dawn (OG 1045, ABV 4.5%)
Golden ale made with North American hops that give a unique fruity aroma and crisp, malty taste.

Foxtale Ale (OG 1050, ABV 4.9%)
A classic bitter, amber in colour with full malt flavour and a slight sweet edge.

Vixen's Vice (OG 1052, ABV 5.2%)
A pale, strong ale with a malt flavour balanced by a clean, crisp, hop taste.

Windjammer IPA (OG 1060, ABV 6%)
Traditional IPA brewed with five varieties of North American hops. Strong and hoppy.

Alehouse

◻ Alehouse Pub & Brewing Company Ltd, Verulam Brewery, Farmers Boy, 134 London Road, St Albans, Hertfordshire, AL1 1PQ
Tel 07725 138243
✉ contact@alehousebrewery.co.uk
⊕ alehousebrewery.co.uk
Tours by arrangement

⊗ Alehouse took over the Verulam Brewery in 2006 and continues to brew house beers for the Farmers Boy, to the original Verulam recipes, while producing beers under the Alehouse banner for the Lower Red Lion in St Albans and for distribution through High Spirits of Bedford.

Simplicity (ABV 3.6%)

Technician's Pale (OG 1040, ABV 4.3%)

Robust Porter (OG 1044, ABV 4.3%)

Butts Park Bitter (ABV 4.4%)

For Farmers Boy, St Albans:

Clipper IPA (OG 1039, ABV 4%)

Farmers Joy (OG 1043, ABV 4.5%)

Ales of Scilly SIBA

Ales of Scilly Brewery, 2b Porthmellon Industrial Estate, St Mary's, Isles of Scilly, TR21 0JY
Tel (01720) 423233
✉ mark@alesofscilly.co.uk
Tours by arrangement

Opened in 2001 as a two-barrel plant and expanded in 2004 to five barrels, Ales of Scilly is the most south-westerly brewery in Britain. Nine local pubs are supplied, with regular exports to mainland pubs and beer festivals. The brewery moved to new premises in March 2007. Seasonal ale: Old Bustard (ABV 4.2%). Bottle-conditioned beer: Scuppered (ABV 4.6%).

Natural Beauty (ABV 4.2%) ❧
Malt, hops and fruit aroma. This distinctly sweet, copper beer is full flavoured with a balance of malt and hops. Pleasant malty sweetness lingers in the finish, ending bitter.

Scuppered (ABV 4.6%) ❧
The aroma is of fruit and hops, leading to a rich, malty, creamy taste balanced by hops. An initial burst of sweetness is followed by an increasing bitterness on the tongue.

Allendale

Allendale Brew Co Ltd, Allen Mill, Allendale, Hexham, Northumberland, NE47 9EQ
Tel (01434) 618686
✉ info@allendalebrewco.co.uk
⊕ allendalebrewco.co.uk
Shop Mon-Sat 9am-5pm
Tours by arrangement

Allendale was set up in 2006 and is run by father and son team, Jim and Tom Hick. Their locally themed ales are on sale in nearby free houses and also in Newcastle, Durham and surrounding areas. Seasonal beers: Black Grouse Bitter (ABV 4%, Aug-Jan), Curlew's Return (ABV 4.2%, Feb-Jul). All beers are also available bottle-conditioned.

Best Bitter (OG 1037, ABV 3.8%)

Golden Plover (OG 1040, ABV 4%)

Wolf (OG 1060, ABV 5.5%)

All Gates

◻ All Gates Brewery Limited, The Old Brewery, Brewery Yard, off Wallgate, Wigan, WN1 1JU
Tel (01942) 234976
✉ information@allgatesbrewery.com
⊕ allgatesbrewery.com
Tours by arrangement

All Gates started brewing in 2006 in a Grade II listed building at the rear of Wigan Post Office. The building is an old tower brewery that has been lovingly restored, but with a new five-barrel plant. Seasonal beers: Randy Rudolph (ABV 5.2%, Dec), Hung, Drawn & Portered (ABV 5.2%).

Young Pretender (OG 1040, ABV 3.8%)

Napoleon's Retreat (OG 1041, ABV 3.9%)

Brightblade (OG 1042, ABV 4%)

Hasty Knoll (OG 1043, ABV 4.2%)

Bottoms Up (OG 1044, ABV 4.2%)

Twist & Stout (OG 1050, ABV 4.5%)

Reverend Ray (OG 1048, ABV 4.6%)

All Nations

See Worfield

Amber*

Amber Ales Ltd, PO Box 7277, Ripley, Derbyshire, DE5 4AP
Tel (01773) 512864
✉ info@amberales.co.uk
⊕ amberales.co.uk
Shop: Contact for opening hours
Tours by arrangement

Amber Ales began production in 2006 on a part-time basis at first, quickly progressing to full-time in 2007 due to strong local interest. Four seasonal beers are planned with a full bottle-conditioned range including an organic ale. Seasonal beers: Winter Ruby Ale (ABV 5.1%), Summer Blond.

Amber Pale (OG 1042, ABV 4.4%)

Original Black Stout (OG 1040, ABV 4%)
Silver award winner at SIBA East Midlands 2006.

Imperial Pale Ale (OG 1060, ABV 6.5%)

Anglo Dutch SIBA

Anglo Dutch Brewery, Unit 12 Saville Bridge Mill, Mill Street East, Dewsbury, West Yorkshire, WF12 9AF
Tel (01924) 457772
✉ anglodutchbrew@yahoo.co.uk
⊕ anglo-dutch-brewery.co.uk
Tours by arrangement

Paul Klos (Dutch) set up the brewery with Mike Field (Anglo), who also runs the Refreshment Rooms at Dewsbury Station. Most beers contain wheat except for Spike and Tabatha, which contain lager malt. A bottle-conditioned fruit beer range is also now available. Seasonal beers: Devil's Knell (ABV 4.8%, Jan), Wild Flower (ABV 4.2%, Sep).

Best Bitter (ABV 3.8%)

Kletswater (OG 1039, ABV 4%)
Pale-coloured beer with a hoppy nose and a good hop and citrus fruit flavour.

Mild Rabarber (ABV 4%) ◆
Light-coloured brown mild with a malty, fruity flavour and moderate hop character. Refreshing and light bodied.

Spike's on 't' Way (OG 1040.5, ABV 4.2%) ◆
Pale bitter with citrus/orange flavour and dry, fruity finish.

Spikus (OG 1040.5, ABV 4.2%)
Made with organic lager malt and New Zealand hops.

Ghost on the Rim (OG 1043, ABV 4.5%) ◆
Pale, dry and fruity.

Yorkshire Wit (ABV 4.5%)

At 't' Ghoul and Ghost (OG 1048, ABV 5.2%) ◆
Pale golden bitter with a strong citrus and hoppy aroma and flavour. The finish is long, dry, bitter and citrus.

Tabatha the Knackered (OG 1054, ABV 6%) ◆
Golden Belgian-style Tripel with a strong fruity, hoppy and bitter character. Powerful and warming, slightly thinnish, with a bitter, dry finish.

Anker

See page 837

An Teallach

An Teallach Ale Company Limited, Camusnagaul, Dundonnell, Garve, Ross-shire, IV23 2QT
Tel (01854) 633306
✉ ataleco1@yahoo.co.uk
Tours by arrangement

An Teallach was formed in 2001 by husband and wife team, David and Wilma Orr, on Wilma's family croft on the shores of Little Loch

Broom, Wester Ross. The business has grown steadily each year. 60 pubs are supplied. All beers are also available bottled.

Beinn Dearg Ale (OG 1038, ABV 3.8%) ◆
Sweetish, fruity beer but can vary while the brewery is still experimenting. Some malt and hop character.

An Teallach Ale (OG 1042, ABV 4.2%) ◆
A sweetish pint in the Scottish 80/- tradition. Malt and blackcurrant feature in the taste, which can also have a yeasty background.

Crofters Pale Ale (OG 1042, ABV 4.2%) ◆
A good quaffing golden ale with no strong flavours. Meaty, with yeast often to the fore.

Brew House Special (OG 1044, ABV 4.4%) ◆
A golden ale with some hoppy bitterness and often with yeast and sulphur background.

Kildonnon (OG 1044, ABV 4.4%) ◆
A straw-coloured golden ale with a hint of malt and hops. Fruit is prominent and it has a yeasty background.

Appleford

Appleford Brewery, Unit 14, Highlands Farm, High Road, Brightwell-cum-Sotwell, Wallingford, Oxfordshire, OX10 0QX
Tel (01235) 848055
✉ sales@applefordbrewery.co.uk
⊕ applefordbrewery.co.uk

Appleford Brewery opened in 2006 when two farm units were converted to house an eight-barrel plant. Deliveries are made nationally either via the brewery or wholesalers.

River Crossing (ABV 3.8%)

Power Station (ABV 4.2%)

Arbor*

Arbor Ales Ltd, The Old Tavern, Blackberry Hill, Stapleton, Bristol, BS16 1DB
Tel 07823 335392/07970 920627
✉ beer@arborales.co.uk
⊕ arborales.co.uk

Arbor Ales opened in March 2007 in the back of the Old Tavern pub using a 2.5-barrel brewery. Regular specials are also brewed.

Trendlewood Bitter (OG 1039, ABV 4%) ◆
Light, fruity and hoppy bitter.

Old Knobbley (OG 1044, ABV 4.5%) ◆
Brown, malty and complex best bitter.

Slumberjack (OG 1063, ABV 7%) ◆
Dark red and fruity.

Archers

Archers Brewery Ltd, Penzance Drive, Swindon, Wiltshire, SN5 7JL
Tel (01793) 879929/889453
✉ sales@archersbrewery.co.uk
⊕ archersbrewery.co.uk
Shop open Mon-Fri 9am-5pm
Tours by arrangement (on Weds at 6pm)

⊗ Archers Brewery was founded in 1979 and has continued to consolidate its position as one of the leading regional breweries in the south, with sales and distribution depots in

Swindon, Warrington and Cambridge. More than 3,000 trade outlets are supplied direct. Champion beer awards for IPA and Golden were achieved at festivals in 2006 to add to an International Brewing bronze in 2005. The company went into administration in May 2007 but continues to trade.

Dark Mild (OG 1034, ABV 3.4%)
Dark beer with a well-balanced hop character, malty roast flavour and rich aftertaste.

Village (OG 1035, ABV 3.6%) ◆
A dry, well-balanced beer with a full body for its gravity. Malty and fruity in the nose, then a fresh, hoppy flavour with balancing malt and a hoppy, fruity finish.

Pride (OG 1038, ABV 3.8%)
Blonde in colour, light and fresh.

Best Bitter (OG 1040, ABV 4%) ◆
Slightly sweeter and rounder than Village Bitter, with a malty, fruity aroma and pronounced bitter finish.

IPA (OG 1042, ABV 4.2%)
Pale golden, rich in citrus and grapefruit aroma and flavour with a crisp, bitter finish.

Golden (OG 1046, ABV 4.7%) ◆
A full-bodied, hoppy, straw-coloured brew with an underlying fruity sweetness. A gentle aroma, but a strong, distinctive bitter finish.

Special Bitter (OG 1047, ABV 4.7%)
Tawny coloured, full-flavoured and well-balanced.

Crystal Clear (OG 1050, ABV 5%)
Blonde, packed with hop aroma with a subtle, balanced finish.

Arkell's IFBB SIBA

Arkell's Brewery Ltd, Kingsdown Brewery, Upper Stratton, Swindon, Wiltshire, SN2 7RU
Tel (01793) 823026
✉ arkells@arkells.com
⊕ arkells.co.uk
Brewery merchandise can be purchased at reception
Tours by arrangement

⊗ Arkells Brewery was established in 1843 and is still run by the family. The brewery owns 103 pubs in Berkshire, Gloucestershire, Oxfordshire and Wiltshire. Seasonal beers: Summer Ale (ABV 4.2%), JRA (ABV 3.6%), Noel Ale (ABV 5.5%). Bees Organic Beer (ABV 4.5%) is suitable for vegetarians and vegans.

2B (OG 1032, ABV 3.2%) ◆
Light brown in colour, malty but with a smack of hops and an astringent aftertaste. It has good body for its strength.

3B (OG 1040, ABV 4%) ◆
A medium brown beer with a strong, sweetish malt/caramel flavour. The hops come through strongly in the aftertaste, which is lingering and dry.

Moonlight Ale (OG 1046, ABV 4.5%)

Kingsdown Ale (OG 1051, ABV 5%) ◆
A rich, deep russet-coloured beer, a stronger version of 3B. The malty/fruity aroma continues in the taste, which has a hint of pears. Hops come through in the aftertaste.

Arran SIBA

Arran Brewery Ltd, Cladach, Brodick, Isle of Arran, Strathclyde, KA27 8DE
Tel (01770) 302353
✉ info@arranbrewery.com
⊕ arranbrewery.com
Shop Mon-Sat 10am-5pm; Sun 12.30-5pm in summer, reduced hours in winter
Tours by arrangement

⊕ The brewery opened in 2000 with a 20-barrel plant. Production has increased to 200 barrels a week with additional bottling capability. 50 outlets are supplied. Bottle-conditioned occasional beer: Milestone (ABV 6%). Seasonal beers: Sunset (ABV 4.4%, Feb-Mar), Fireside (ABV 4.7%, Oct/Nov-Feb/Mar).

Ale (OG 1038, ABV 3.8%) ◆
An amber ale where the predominance of the hop produces a bitter beer with a subtle balancing sweetness of malt and an occasional hint of roast.

Dark (OG 1042, ABV 4.3%) ◆
A well-balanced malty beer with plenty of roast and hop in the taste and a dry, bitter finish.

Blonde (OG 1048, ABV 5%) ◆
A hoppy beer with substantial fruit balance. The taste is balanced and the finish increasingly bitter. An aromatic strong bitter that drinks below its weight.

Arrow

⋥ **Arrow Brewery, c/o Wine Vaults, 37 High Street, Kington, Herefordshire, HR5 3BJ**
Tel (01544) 230685
✉ deanewright@yahoo.co.uk

Former Bridge Street brewer Deane Wright has built his five-barrel brewery at the rear of the Wine Vaults and re-started brewing in 2005.

Bitter (OG 1042, ABV 4%)

Arundel SIBA

Arundel Brewery Ltd, Unit C7 Ford Airfield Industrial Estate, Ford, Arundel, West Sussex, BN18 0HY
Tel (01903) 733111
✉ arundelbrewery@dsl.pipex.com
⊕ arundelbrewery.co.uk
Off-sales available Mon-Fri 9am-5pm at brewery
Tours by arrangement

⊗ Founded in 1992, Arundel Brewery is the historic town's first brewery in more than 70 years. A range of occasional brands are available in selected months. Seasonal beers: Footslogger (ABV 4.4%, spring), Summer Daze (ABV 4.7%, summer), Black Beastie (ABV 4.9%, autumn).

Sussex Mild (OG 1037, ABV 3.7%) ◆
A dark mild. Strong chocolate and roast aromas, which lead to a bitter taste. The aftertaste is not powerful but the initial flavours remain in the dry and clean finish.

Castle (OG 1038, ABV 3.8%) ◆
A pale tawny beer with fruit and malt noticeable in the aroma. The flavour has a good balance of malt, fruit and hops, with a dry, hoppy finish.

Sussex Gold (OG 1042, ABV 4.2%) ♦
A golden-coloured best bitter with a strong floral hop aroma. The ale is clean-tasting and bitter for its strength, with a tangy citrus flavour. The initial hop and fruit die to a dry and bitter finish.

ASB (OG 1045, ABV 4.5%)
A special bitter with a complex roast malt flavour leading to a fruity, hoppy, bittersweet finish.

Stronghold (OG 1047, ABV 4.7%)
A smooth, full-flavoured premium bitter. A good balance of malt, fruit and hops comes through in this rich, chestnut-coloured beer.

Old Knucker (OG 1055, ABV 5.5%) ♦
A black coloured ale with a powerful bitter-sweet taste and a roasted burnt flavour coming at the end. Oily mouthfeel and a long, tangy, sweet aftertaste.

Ashover*

Ashover Brewery, 1 Butts Road, Ashover, Chesterfield, Derbyshire, S45 0EW
Tel (01246) 590888
✉ info@ashoverbrewery.co.uk
⊕ ashoverbrewery.co.uk
Tours by arrangement

⊠ Ashover Brewery was established in 2006 on a 3.5-barrel plant in the garage of the cottage next to the Old Poet's Corner pub. The brewery caters mainly for the pub but other local free houses and festivals are also supplied.

Light Rale (OG 1038, ABV 3.7%)

Poets Tipple (OG 1042, ABV 4.2%)

Butts Pale Ale (OG 1049, ABV 5%)

Aston Manor

Aston Manor Brewery Co Ltd, 173 Thimble Mill Lane, Aston, Birmingham, West Midlands, B7 5HS
Tel (0121) 328 4336
✉ sales@astonmanor.co.uk
⊕ astonmanor.co.uk

Aston Manor is the former owner of the Highgate Brewery in Walsall (qv). Its own plant concentrates on cider. Beer is bottled at Highgate but is not bottle-conditioned.

Atlantic

Atlantic Brewery, Treisaac Farm, Treisaac, Newquay, Cornwall, TR8 4DX
Tel 0870 042 1714
✉ contact@atlanticbrewery.com
⊕ atlanticbrewery.com

Atlantic started brewing in 2005. All beers are organic, Soil Association certified and suitable for vegetarians and vegans. It concentrates on bottle-conditioned beers: Gold (ABV 4.6%, summer), Blue (ABV 4.8%), Red (ABV 4.6%).

Atlas SIBA

Atlas Brewery, Sinclair Breweries Ltd, Lab Road, Kinlochleven, Argyll, PH50 4SG
Tel (01855) 831111
✉ info@atlasbrewery.com
⊕ atlasbrewery.com
Shop open office hours
Tours by arrangement

⊠ Founded in 2002, Atlas is a 20-barrel brewery in a 100 year-old listed Victorian industrial building on the banks of the River Leven. It merged in 2004 with Orkney (qv) and now forms part of Sinclair Breweries. Production remains at both sites. Around 150 outlets in Scotland are supplied direct and via wholesalers to the rest of Britain. Additional fermentation vessels were added in 2007 to increase weekly production capacity. Seasonal beers: Equinox (ABV 4.5%, spring), Wayfarer (ABV 4.4%, summer), Tempest (ABV 4.9%, autumn), Blizzard (ABV 4.7%, winter).

Latitude (OG 1036, ABV 3.6%) ♦
This golden ale has a light citrus taste with a hint of hops in the light, bitter finish.

Three Sisters (OG 1043, ABV 4.2%) ♦
Plenty of malt and summer fruits in the nose and taste, followed by a short, hoppy, bitter finish.

Nimbus (OG 1050, ABV 5%) ♦
A full-bodied golden beer using some wheat malt and three types of hops. Dry and fruity at the front, it becomes slightly astringent with lasting fruit and a pleasant, dry finish.

Atomic

Atomic Brewery, c/o Alexandra Arms, 72-73 James Street, Rugby, Warwickshire, CV21 2SL
Tel: (01788) 542170
✉ sales@atomicbrewery.com
⊕ atomicbrewery.com

⊠ Atomic Brewery started production in 2006 and is run by CAMRA members Keith Abbis and Nick Pugh. It is housed in one of the outbuildings of the Alexandra Arms in Rugby. Beer of the festival awards were won at two CAMRA festivals in 2006.

Strike (OG 1039, ABV 3.7%)

Fission (OG 1040, ABV 3.9%)

Fusion (OG 1042, ABV 4.1%)

Reactor (OG 1047, ABV 4.5%)

Power (OG 1049, ABV 4.8%)

Bomb (OG 1054, ABV 5.2%)

AVS

See Daleside

B&T SIBA EAB

B&T Brewery Ltd, The Brewery, Shefford, Bedfordshire, SG17 5DZ
Tel (01462) 815080
✉ brewery@banksandtaylor.com
⊕ banksandtaylor.com
Tours by arrangement

⊠ Banks & Taylor – now just B&T – was founded in 1982. It produces an extensive range of beers, including monthly special brews together with occasional beers: see website for details. Three pubs are owned. Bottle-conditioned beers: Shefford Bitter, Goalden Hatter, Black Dragon Mild, Edwin Taylor's Extra Stout, Dragonslayer, SOS, SOD, Autumn Porter, Fruit Bat, Hoppy Turkey.

Two Brewers (OG 1036, ABV 3.6%)
Hoppy, amber-brown session beer.

Shefford Bitter (OG 1038, ABV 3.8%)
A pleasant, predominantly hoppy session
beer with a bitter finish.

Shefford Dark Mild (OG 1038, ABV 3.8%) ❚ ◈
A dark beer with a well-balanced taste.
Sweetish, roast malt aftertaste.

Goalden Hatter (OG 1040, ABV 4%)

Black Dragon Mild (OG 1043, ABV 4.3%) ❚
Dark, rich in flavour, with a strong roast
barley finish.

Dragonslayer (OG 1045, ABV 4.5%) ◈
A straw-coloured beer, dry, malty and lightly
hopped.

Edwin Taylor's Extra Stout (OG 1045,
ABV 4.5%) ◈
A pleasant, bitter beer with a strong roast
malt flavour.

Fruit Bat (OG 1045, ABV 4.5%)
Raspberry flavoured, hoppy fruit beer.

Shefford Pale Ale/SPA (OG 1045, ABV 4.5%) ◈
A well-balanced beer with hop, fruit and malt
flavours. Dry, bitter aftertaste.

SOS (OG 1050, ABV 5%) ◈
A rich mixture of fruit, hops and malt is
present in the taste and aftertaste of this
beer. Predominantly hoppy aroma.

SOD (OG 1050, ABV 5%)
SOS with caramel added for colour, often sold
under house names.

Badger

See Hall & Woodhouse

Ballard's SIBA

Ballard's Brewery Ltd, The Old Sawmill,
Nyewood, Petersfield, Hants, GU31 5HA
Tel (01730) 821301/821362
✉ info@ballardsbrewery.org.uk
⊕ ballardsbrewery.org.uk
Shop Mon-Fri 8am-4pm
Tours by arrangement

⊠ Launched in 1980 by Carola Brown, one of
the founders of SIBA, at Cumbers Farm, Trotton,
Ballard's has been trading at Nyewood since
1988 and now supplies around 60 free trade
outlets. Seasonal beers: Trotton Bitter (ABV
3.6%, spring), Wheatsheaf (ABV 5%, summer),
On the Hop (ABV 4.5%, autumn), Old Bounder
Series (ABV over 9%, winter). Bottle-conditioned
beers: Old Bounder series, Best Bitter, Nyewood
Gold, Wassail and Kings Table (ABV 4.2%).

Midhurst Mild (OG 1034, ABV 3.5%)
Traditional dark mild, well-balanced,
refreshing, with a biscuity flavour.

Golden Bine (OG 1038, ABV 3.8%) ◈
Amber, clean-tasting bitter. A roast malt
aroma leads to a fruity, slightly sweet taste
and a dry finish.

Best Bitter (OG 1042, ABV 4.2%) ◈
A copper-coloured beer with a malty aroma.
A good balance of fruit and malt in the
flavour gives way to a dry, hoppy aftertaste.

Wild (ABV 4.7%)
A blend of Mild and Wassail.

Nyewood Gold (OG 1050, ABV 5%) ◈
Robust golden brown strong bitter, very
hoppy and fruity throughout, with a tasty
balanced finish.

Wassail (OG 1060, ABV 6%) ◈
A strong, full-bodied, tawny-red, fruity beer
with a predominance of malt throughout, but
also an underlying hoppiness.

Bank Top SIBA

Bank Top Brewery Ltd, The Pavilion, Ashworth
Lane, Bolton, Lancashire, BL1 8RA
Tel (01204) 595800
✉ john@banktopbrewery.com
⊕ banktopbrewery.com
Tours by arrangement

☺ Bank Top was established in 1995 by
John Feeney and has enjoyed gradual
expansion. It relocated in 2002 and in 2004
John formed a partnership with David
Sweeney, who will take over the business
in 2008 when John retires. The beers are
supplied to around 100 outlets locally and
throughout the north-west and Yorkshire.
Seasonal beers: Santa's Claws (ABV 5%,
Xmas), Leprechaun Stout (ABV 6%, Mar).
Bottle-conditioned beers: Leprechaun Stout,
Santa's Claws, Flat Cap, Pavilion Pale Ale,
Port O Call.

Bikes, Trikes and Beer (OG 1036, ABV 3.6%) ◈
A gold-coloured beer with a grainy
mouthfeel. Hoppy, fruity aroma with citrus,
hops and bitterness in taste and aftertaste.

Brydge Bitter (OG 1038, ABV 3.8%)

Game, Set and Match (OG 1038, ABV 3.8%)

Bad to the Bone (OG 1040, ABV 4%)

Dark Mild (OG 1040, ABV 4%) ◈
Dark brown beer with a malt and roast
aroma, rich mouthfeel and a complex taste,
including roast malt and toffee. Roast, hops
and bitterness in the finish.

Flat Cap (OG 1040, ABV 4%) ◈
Amber ale with a modest fruit aroma leading
to a beer with citrus fruit, malt and hops.
Good finish of fruit, malt and bitterness.

Gold Digger (OG 1040, ABV 4%) ◈
Golden coloured, with a citrus aroma,
grapefruit and a touch of spiciness on the
palate; a fresh, hoppy citrus finish.

Old Slapper (OG 1042, ABV 4.2%)

Samuel Crompton's Ale (OG 1042, ABV 4.2%) ◈
Amber beer with a fresh citrus-peel aroma.
Well-balanced with hops and a zesty
grapefruit flavour, and a hoppy, citrus finish.

Trotters Tipple (OG 1042, ABV 4.2%)

Volunteer Bitter (OG 1042, ABV 4.2%)

Pavilion Pale Ale (OG 1045, ABV 4.5%) ◈
A yellow beer with a citrus and hop aroma.
Big fruity flavour with a peppery hoppiness;
dry, bitter yet fruity finish.

Port O Call (OG 1050, ABV 5%)

Smokestack Lightnin' (OG 1050, ABV 5%)

For Strawbury Duck, Entwistle:

Strawberry Duck (OG 1042, ABV 4.2%)

Banks's

See Marston's in New national breweries section

Barearts

Barearts Brewery, 290-292 Rochdale Road, Todmorden, OL14 7PD
Tel (01706) 839305
⊕ barearts.com
Shop Fri 3-7pm; Sat 1-5pm; Sun 1-4pm

A four-barrel craft brewery that began production in 2005 and is owned by Kathryn and Trevor Cook. It is named after their gallery, which is dedicated to nude art work. The gallery has an off-licence that also sells 50 bottle-conditioned beers from other small breweries. The Cooks do not supply to pubs and only brew to order. They hope to expand into mail order via their website.

Barefoot

Barefoot Brewery, Unit 7, The Whitehouse Farm Centre, Stannington, Morpeth, Northumberland, NE61 6AW
Tel (01670) 789988
✉ barefootbeer@onetel.com

⊕ Barefoot was established on a 10-barrel plant in 2005. More than 50 outlets are supplied. There are plans to bottle the beers.

Barefoot (OG 1039, ABV 3.8%)
A dark copper session beer with an intense berry fruit flavour and a pleasant hint of chocolate.

Mellow Yellow (OG 1039, ABV 3.8%)
A pale wheat beer with pronounced grapefruit overtones.

Blackfoot (OG 1042, ABV 4.2%)
A smooth, easy-drinking stout with liquorice, chocolate and vanilla overtones and a rich mocha coffee in the aftertaste.

First Foot (OG 1042, ABV 4.2%)
A pale, golden, zesty ale with fragrant citrus notes.

Sole Beer (OG 1042, ABV 4.2%)
A light amber beer with subtle marmalade undertones and a crisp, hoppy finish.

Milk of Amnesia (OG 1044, ABV 4.5%)
Ruby-red, full-bodied ale with a delicate roasted toffee edge and a subtle but mellow, lingering hoppy finish.

SB (OG 1048, ABV 5%)
A strong pale ale with honeyed fruit aftertones and copious amounts of coriander.

Barge & Barrel

See Eastwood

Barngates SIBA

Barngates Brewery Ltd, Barngates, Ambleside, Cumbria, LA22 0NG
Tel (015394) 36575
✉ info@barngatesbrewery.co.uk

⊕ barngatesbrewery.co.uk
Tours by arrangement

☺ Barngates Brewery started brewing in 1997 and initially provided only the Drunken Duck Inn with its own beers. It now supplies more than 200 outlets throughout Cumbria, Lancashire, Northumberland and Yorkshire. Barngates doubled its production capacity in spring 2007 with a new plant. Seasonal beer: Chester's Strong & Ugly (ABV 5.2%)

Cat Nap (OG 1037, ABV 3.6%)
Pale, straw-coloured beer with a strong citrus hop aroma. Well-balanced bitterness leads to a long, dry finish. A fruity, zesty character throughout.

Cracker Ale (OG 1038, ABV 3.9%)
Copper-coloured with a subtle hoppy aroma, clean, smooth and refreshing, developing into a long bitter finish.

K9 Commemorative Ale (OG 1041, ABV 4%)
A light gold beer with a delicate grapefruit aroma and fresh, bitter, citrus flavour.

Pride of Westmorland (OG 1042, ABV 4.1%)
Ruby red with a berry fruit aroma and delicious malt and hop flavours. A polished, soft, bitter finish builds in the aftertaste.

Westmorland Gold (OG 1043, ABV 4.2%)
Golden ale with a distinct fruity and hoppy nose. Crisp with a lingering, bittersweet palate.

Tag Lag (OG 1044, ABV 4.4%) ✎
Light, golden bitter, citrus hints in the flavour with a slight dry finish.

Red Bull Terrier (OG 1048, ABV 4.8%)
A deep red tone and a complex hop nose are complemented by tangy fruit and malt flavours with a spicy aftertaste.

Barrowden SIBA

⛫ **Barrowden Brewing Company, c/o Exeter Arms, 28 Main Street, Barrowden, Rutland, LE15 8EQ**
Tel (01572) 747247
✉ info@exeterarms.com
⊕ exeterarms.com
Tours by arrangement

⊗ Set up in a barn behind the pub in 1998 by Peter Blencowe, the two-barrel plant was extended in 2001 with the addition of another fermenting vessel. Recipes are being formulated to broaden the range, including new seasonal beers, brewing for selected beer festivals and looking at exclusive outlets. Seasonal beers: Danny (ABV 4.5%, spring), Winter Hop (ABV 4.7%, winter), Attitude (ABV 6%, autumn).

Beach (OG 1038, ABV 3.8%)

Hop Gear (OG 1044, ABV 4.4%)

Bevin (OG 1045, ABV 4.5%)

Bartrams SIBA EAB

Bartrams Brewery, Rougham Estate, Ipswich Road (A14), Rougham, Suffolk, IP30 9LZ
Tel (01449) 737655/07768 062581
✉ marc@bartramsbrewery.co.uk

⊕ bartramsbrewery.co.uk
Shop Tue & Sat 12-6pm
Tours by arrangement

The brewery was set up in 1999. In 2005 the plant was moved to a building on Rougham Airfield, the site of Bartram's Brewery between 1894 and 1902 run by Captain Bill Bartram. His image graces the pump clips. Beers are available in a selection of local pubs and there is a large amount of trade through local farmers' markets. Marld, Beltane Braces and all porters and stouts are suitable for vegetarians and vegans. Seasonal beers: September Ale (ABV 7%), Xmas Holly Daze (ABV 5%), New Years Daze (ABV 5.2%), The Venerable Reed (ABV 5.6% – brewed for an annual medieval re-enactment on Rougham Airfield), Mother in Laws Tongue Tied (ABV 9%), Zodiac Beers range (ABV 4.2%).

Marld (ABV 3.4%)
A traditional mild. Spicy hops and malt with a hint of chocolate, slightly smoky with a light, roasted finish.

Rougham Ready (ABV 3.6%)
A light, crisp bitter, surprisingly full bodied for its strength.

Trial and Error (ABV 3.6%)
A full malty bitter, fruity with a lot of character.

Premier (ABV 3.7%)
A traditional quaffing ale, full-flavoured but light, dry and hoppy.

Little Green Man (ABV 3.8%)
A golden bitter with the peppery and delicate citrus tones of subtle coriander. Dry and bitter.

Red Queen (ABV 3.9%)
Typical IPA style, chocolate malt in the foreground while the resiny hop flavour lingers.

Grozet (ABV 4%)
Using Little Green Man as the base beer, gooseberries are added to give an appealing extra dimension.

Cats Whiskers (ABV 4%)
A straw-coloured beer with ginger and lemons added; a unique flavour experience.

Bees Knees (ABV 4.2%)
An amber beer with a floral aroma; honey softness on the palate leads to a crisp, bitter finish.

Catherine Bartram's IPA (ABV 4.3%)
A full-bodied malty IPA style; tangy hops lead the malt throughout and dominate the dry, hoppy aftertaste.

Jester Quick One (ABV 4.4%)
A sweet reddish bitter using fruity American Ahtanum hops.

Beltane Braces (ABV 4.5%)
Smooth and dark.

Coal Porter (ABV 4.5%)
Plenty of body in this ruby beer, supported by ample hops.

Stingo (ABV 4.5%)
A sweetish, fruity bitter with a hoppy nose. Light honey softens the bitter finish.

Beer Elsie Bub (ABV 4.8%)

Originally brewed for a Pagan wedding, this strong honey ale is now brewed all year round.

Captain Bill Bartram's Best Bitter (ABV 4.8%)
Modified from a 100-year old recipe, using full malt and traditional Kentish hops.

Captain's Stout (ABV 4.8%)
Biscuity dark malt leads to a lightly smoked aroma, plenty of roasted malt character, coffee notes and a whiff of smoke.

Cherry Stout (ABV 4.8%)
Sensuous hints of chocolate leads to a subtle suggestion of cherries.

Damson Stout (ABV 4.8%)
A robust, full-bodied stout with the chocolate and smoky aroma giving way to a lingering finish.

Trafalgar Squared (ABV 4.8%)
Brewed using malt grown a few miles from Nelson's birthplace and Goldings hops.

Suffolk 'n' Strong (ABV 5%)
A light, smooth and dangerously potable strong bitter, well-balanced malt and hops with an easy finish.

Comrade Bill Bartram's Egalitarian Anti-Imperialist Soviet Stout (ABV 6.9%)
A Russian stout by any other name, a luscious easy-drinking example of the style.

Barum SIBA

Barum Brewery Ltd, c/o Reform Inn, Pilton, Barnstaple, Devon, EX31 1PD
Tel (01271) 329994
✉ info@barumbrewery.co.uk
⊕ barumbrewery.co.uk
Tours by arrangement

Barum started brewing in 1996. Distribution is primarily within Devon. Seasonal beers: Gold (ABV 4%, summer), Barnstablaster (ABV 6.6%, winter).

Basil's Best (OG 1040, ABV 4%)

Original (OG 1044, ABV 4.4%)

Breakfast (OG 1050, ABV 5%)

Firing Squad (ABV 5.3%)

Bateman IFBB SIBA

George Bateman & Son Ltd, Salem Bridge Brewery, Wainfleet, Lincolnshire, PE24 4JE
Tel (01754) 880317
✉ enquiries@bateman.co.uk
⊕ bateman.co.uk
Shop 11.30am-3.30pm daily

⊛ Bateman's Brewery is an independent family-owned brewery established in 1874. A new brewhouse was opened in 2002. All but one of the 66 tied houses serve cask-conditioned beer. Seasonal beers: Middle Wicket (ABV 4.2%, Jan), Hooker (ABV 4.5%, Feb/Mar), Spring Goddess (ABV 4.2%, Apr/May), Miss Luscious (ABV 4.3%, Jun), Summer Swallow (ABV 3.9%, Jul-Aug), Victory Ale (ABV 5.9%, Sep-Oct), Miss Cheeky (ABV 4.2%, Nov), Rosey Nosey (ABV 4.9%, Dec).

Dark Mild (OG 1030, ABV 3%) ➘

Characteristic orchard fruit and roasted nut nose with hops evident. One of the classic mild ales, although the lasting bitter finish may not be entirely true to type; nevertheless, a ruby-black gem.

XB Bitter (OG 1037, ABV 3.7%) ◆
A mid-brown balanced session bitter with malt most obvious in the finish. The taste is dominated by the house style apple hop, which also leads the aroma.

Valiant (OG 1042, ABV 4.2%)
A delicious golden beer, clean, crisp and zesty.

Salem Porter (OG 1048, ABV 4.7%) ◆
A black and complex mix of chocolate, liquorice and cough elixir.

XXXB (OG 1048, ABV 4.8%) ◆
A brilliant blend of malt, hops and fruit on the nose with a bitter bite over the top of a faintly banana maltiness that stays the course. A russet-tan brown classic.

Bath Ales SIBA

Bath Ales Ltd, Units 3-7 Caxton Business Park, Tower Road North, Warmley, Bristol, BS30 8XN
Tel (0117) 947 4797
✉ hare@bathales.co.uk
⊕ bathales.com
Shop Mon-Fri 9am-5pm; Sat 9am-12pm
Tours by arrangement

⊗ Bath Ales started brewing in 1995 and moved in 1999 to new premises with a 15-barrel plant. The company now has a purpose-built site on the edge of east Bristol, and can brew 250 barrels a week. Around 350 outlets are supplied direct. Ten pubs are owned, all serving cask ale. Seasonal beers: Festivity (ABV 5% ✪), Rare Hare (ABV 5.2%). Bottled beers: Gem Bitter (ABV 4.8%), Festivity (ABV 5%), Wild Hare Organic (ABV 5%). Most beers are available for purchase from the website or shop.

SPA (OG 1037, ABV 3.7%) ▣ ◆
Gold/yellow colour, this is a light-bodied dry, bitter beer with a citrus hop aroma. Long malty, dry and bitter finish with some fruit.

Gem Bitter (OG 1041, ABV 4.1%) ▣ ◆
This well-balanced, medium-bodied bitter is malty (pale and crystal with caramel), fruity and hoppy throughout. Amber-coloured, it is dry and bitter at the end.

Barnstormer (OG 1047, ABV 4.5%) ◆
Malt, hops and fruit aroma with a faint hint of roast, with toffee sweetness. Dark brown, well balanced and smooth with a malty, bitter, dry finish.

Wild Hare (OG 1048, ABV 5%) ◆
Pale organic strong bitter. Toasted grapefruit aroma, hoppy/fruity taste developing into a long-lasting dry, fruity finish. Refreshing and clean on the palate.

Batham IFBB

Daniel Batham & Son Ltd, Delph Brewery, Delph Road, Brierley Hill, West Midlands, DY5 2TN
Tel (01384) 77229
✉ info@bathams.com
⊕ bathams.com

A classic Black Country small brewery established in 1877. Tim and Matthew Batham represent the fifth generation to run the company. The Vine, one of the Black Country's most famous pubs, is also the site of the brewery. The company has 10 tied houses and supplies around 30 other outlets. Batham's Bitter is delivered in 54-gallon hogsheads to meet demand. Seasonal beer: XXX (ABV 6.3%, Dec).

Mild Ale (OG 1036.5, ABV 3.5%) ◆
A fruity, dark brown mild with malty sweetness and a roast malt finish.

Best Bitter (OG 1043.5, ABV 4.3%) ▣ ◆
A pale yellow, fruity, sweetish bitter, with a dry, hoppy finish. A good, light, refreshing beer.

Battersea SIBA

Battersea Brewery Co Ltd, 43 Glycena Road, Battersea, London, SW11 5TP
Tel (020) 7978 7978
✉ enquiries@batterseabrewery.com
⊕ batterseabrewery.com

Battersea has been brewing since 2001. The beers are all sold locally and in south-east England to the free trade and pub chains. The beers are made from hops and malt sourced as close as possible to the brewery and no additives are used. Bottle-conditioned beer: Power Station Porter.

Pagoda (OG 1038, ABV 3.7%)
Pale amber ale with a citrus fruit and sweet malt character.

Bitter (OG 1040, ABV 4%) ◆
A well-balanced, easy-drinking, copper-coloured bitter; malt, apple and a slightly bitter hoppiness linger through to a short finish.

Power Station Porter (OG 1049, ABV 4.9%) ▣ ◆
Raisins and some citrus hops are present on nose, palate and finish of this ruby-black beer. The black roasted malt balances the sweetness and its bitter character lingers.

Battledown

Battledown Brewery llp, Keynsham Works, Keynsham Street, Cheltenham, Gloucestershire, GL52 6EJ
Tel (01242) 693409/07734 834104
✉ roland@battledownbrewery.com
⊕ battledownbrewery.com
Shop open Wed/Thu/Sat am
Tours by arrangement

⊗ Established in 2005 by Roland and Stephanie Elliott-Berry, Battledown operates from an old engineering works and started production with an eight-barrel plant. They supply around 50 outlets.

Saxon (OG 1038, ABV 3.8%)
Fresh and crisp with a hoppy finish.

Turncoat (OG 1046, ABV 4.5%)
A deep red and smooth porter with a hint of bitterness.

Brigand (OG 1048, ABV 4.7%)
Rich in malt with a hint of spice from Challenger hops.

Bazens' SIBA

Bazens' Brewery, Rees Bazen Brewing Co Ltd, Unit 6 Knoll Street Industrial Park, Knoll Street, Salford, Greater Manchester, M7 2BL
Tel (0161) 708 0247
✉ bazensbrewery@mac.com
⊕ bazensbrewery.co.uk
Tours by arrangement for CAMRA groups

Established in 2002, Bazens' moved to its present site in 2003, sharing plant and premises with Facer's Brewery (qv). Facer's has now relocated to Flintshire, North Wales.

Black Pig Mild (OG 1037, ABV 3.6%) 🍺 🗍 ◆
A dark brown beer with malt and fruit aromas. Roast, chocolate and fruit flavours, with an underlying bitterness, lead to a dry, malty and slightly smoky aftertaste.

Pacific Bitter (OG 1039, ABV 3.8%) ◆
Gold-coloured bitter with a fruity nose. Hops and citrus fruit dominate the taste and there is a bitter, hoppy finish.

Flatbac (OG 1042, ABV 4.2%)
Well-balanced, distinctive and refreshing blonde beer. A full hop character has pronounced citrus/floral notes.

Zebra Best Bitter (OG 1043, ABV 4.3%)
A complex premium bitter, loaded with full malt flavour and crisp fruity hop character.

Blue Bullet (OG 1045, ABV 4.5%) ◆
Yellow in colour, this golden ale has a fruity aroma. Hops, fruit and bitterness are in the taste and linger in the finish.

Knoll Street Porter (OG 1055, ABV 5.2%) 🗍 ◆
Dark brown beer with a chocolaty and malt aroma. Roast and chocolate malt, hops and fruit to taste, with a satisfying complex finish.

eXSB (OG 1055, ABV 5.5%)
Full-bodied traditional strong bitter. Hints of orange peel and fruit overlie complex malt flavours.

Beachy Head*

Beachy Head Brewing Co Ltd, Seven Sisters Sheep Centre, Birling Manor Farm, Birling Gap Road, East Dean, East Sussex, BN20 0AA
Tel (01323) 423906
✉ charlie@beachyhead.org.uk
⊕ beachyhead.org.uk

Beachy Head installed a 2.5-barrel brew plant at the end of 2006 and began producing bottle-conditioned beers early in 2007. Bottle-conditioned beers: Beachy Black (ABV 4.2%), Beachy Original (ABV 4.5%), Beachy Strong (ABV 5.2%).

Beartown SIBA

Beartown Brewery Ltd, Bromley House, Spindle Street, Congleton, Cheshire, CW12 3RH
Tel (01260) 299964
✉ headbrewer@beartownbrewery.co.uk
⊕ beartownbrewery.co.uk
Tours by arrangement

Congleton's links with brewing can be traced back to 1272. Two of its most senior officers at the time were Ale Taster and Bear Warden, hence the name of the brewery. Both the

brewery's Navigation in Stockport and the Beartown Tap have been named CAMRA regional pubs of the year. There are plans are to extend the tied estate to 15 outlets over the next two years. Beartown supplies 250 outlets and owns five pubs. A new 25-barrel plant has been installed. Seasonal beers: Blarney Bear (ABV 4.8%, Mar), St George's Bear (ABV 4.2%, Apr), Ambeardextrous (ABV 3.8%, May), Santa's Claws (ABV 4.5%, Dec), Pandamonium (ABV 4.8%), Wheat Bear (ABV 5%).

Bear Ass (OG 1040, ABV 4%) ◆
Dark ruby-red, malty bitter with good hop nose and fruity flavour with dry, bitter, astringent aftertaste.

Ginger Bear (OG 1040, ABV 4%) 🍺
The flavours from the malt and hops blend with the added bite from the root ginger to produce a quenching finish.

Kodiak Gold (OG 1040, ABV 4%) ◆
Hops and fruit dominate the taste of this crisp yellow bitter and these follow through to the dryish aftertaste. Biscuity malt also comes through on the aroma and taste.

Bearskinful (OG 1043, ABV 4.2%) ◆
Biscuity malt dominates the flavour of this amber best bitter. There are hops and a hint of sulphur on the aroma. A balance of malt and bitterness follow through to the aftertaste.

Bearly Literate (OG 1045, ABV 4.5%)

Polar Eclipse (OG 1048, ABV 4.8%) ◆
Classic black, dry and bitter stout, with roast flavours to the fore. Good hop on the nose following through the taste into a long dry finish.

Black Bear (OG 1050, ABV 5%) ◆
Advertised as a strong mild, this beer is rather bitter for the style. Bitter and malt flavours are balanced and there is also a good roast character along with a hint of liquorice. Aftertaste is short and reasonably dry.

Bruins Ruin (OG 1050, ABV 5%)

Beckstones SIBA

Beckstones Brewery, Upper Beckstones Mill, The Green, Millom, Cumbria, LA18 5HL
Tel (01229) 775294
✉ david@beckstonesbrewery.com

⊠ Beckstones started brewing in 2003 on the site of an 18th-century mill with its own water supply.

Leat (OG 1038, ABV 3.6%)
A floral, fruity, thirst quencher.

Black Dog Freddy Mild (OG 1038, ABV 3.8%)

Iron Town (OG 1040, ABV 3.8%)
A well-balanced, malt and hops session ale.

Beer O'Clock (OG 1040, ABV 3.9%)
A golden, hoppy beer.

Border Steeans (OG 1042, ABV 4.1%)
Scottish Borders style, bittersweet with berry fruit undertones.

Hematite (OG 1058, ABV 5.5%)
Smooth with full malt throughout.

Beer Engine SIBA

⌂ The Beer Engine, Newton St Cyres, Exeter,
Devon, EX5 5AX
Tel (01392) 851282
✉ info@thebeerengine.co.uk
⊕ thebeerengine.co.uk
Tours by arrangement

☺ The pub of the same name is situated next
to the Exeter and Barnstaple Tarka railway line.
Brewing started in 1983. The brewery is visible
behind glass downstairs in the pub. Eight
outlets are supplied regularly. Seasonal beer:
Whistlemas (ABV varies, winter).

Rail Ale (OG 1037, ABV 3.8%) ◈
A straw-coloured beer with a fruity aroma
and a sweet, fruity finish.

Piston Bitter (OG 1043, ABV 4.3%) ◈
A mid-brown, sweet-tasting beer with a
pleasant, bittersweet aftertaste.

Sleeper Heavy (OG 1052, ABV 5.4%) ◈
A red-coloured beer with a fruity, sweet taste
and a bitter finish.

Beeston*

Beeston Brewery Ltd, Fransham Road Farm,
Beeston, Norfolk, PE32 2LZ
Tel (01328) 700844/07768 742763
✉ mark_riches@tesco.net
⊕ beestonbrewery.co.uk
Tours by arrangement

⊗ The brewery was established in 2007 in an
old farm building using a five-barrel plant.
Brewing water comes from a dedicated
borehole and raw ingredients are sourced
locally whenever possible. Both cask beers are
also available bottle-conditioned.

Worth the Wait (OG 1041, ABV 4.2%)

On the Huh (OG 1048, ABV 5%)

Belhaven

See Greene King in New national breweries section

Bell's

Bell's Brewery & Merchants Ltd, The Workshop,
Lutterworth Road, Ullesthorpe, Leicestershire,
LE17 5DR
Tel (01455) 209940
✉ jon@bellsbrewery.co.uk
⊕ bellsbrewery.co.uk
Shop Mon-Sat 9.30am-5pm; Sun 10am-4pm
Tours by arrangement (Wed/Thur daytime only)

⊗ Bell's opened in 2004 and relocated from
Bitteswell to Ullesthorpe in 2005 to premises
within the Ullesthorpe Garden Centre complex. A
brewery shop and farm deli is located next to the
brewery selling all Bells' beers and up to 200
British bottle-conditioned beers along with cider,
Belgian beers and home-brewing equipment.
Seasonal beer: Yule Fuel (ABV 4.8%, Xmas). All
beers are also available bottle conditioned.

Wide Mouth Frog (OG 1038, ABV 3.8%)

Man in the Moon (OG 1039, ABV 3.9%)

Rainmaker (OG 1041, ABV 4.1%)

Smalley's Stout (OG 1042, ABV 4.2%)

Dreamcatcher (OG 1046, ABV 4.6%)

Vulcan Bomber (OG 1050, ABV 5%)

What The Duck (OG 1055, ABV 5.5%)

Belvoir SIBA

Belvoir Brewery Ltd, 6B Woodhill Industries,
Nottingham Lane, Old Dalby, Leicestershire,
LE14 3LX
Tel (01664) 823455
✉ colin@belvoirbrewery.co.uk
⊕ belvoirbrewery.co.uk
Tours occasionally by arrangement

⊗ Belvoir (pronounced 'beaver') Brewery
was set up in 1995 by former Shipstone's
brewer Colin Brown. Long-term expansion
has seen the introduction of a 20-barrel
plant that can produce 50 barrels a week.
Bottle-conditioned beers are now being
produced using in-house bottling equipment.
Up to 150 outlets are supplied. Seasonal
beers: Whipling Golden Bitter (ABV 3.6%,
spring/summer), Peacock's Glory (ABV 4.7%,
spring/summer), Old Dalby (ABV 5.1%,
winter). Bottle-conditioned beers: Star,
Beaver Bitter, Peacock's Glory, Old Dalby.

Star Mild (OG 1034, ABV 3.4%) ◈
Reddish/black in colour, this full-bodied and
well-balanced mild is both malty and hoppy
with hints of fruitiness leading to a long,
bittersweet finish.

Star Bitter (OG 1039, ABV 3.9%) ◈
Reminiscent of the long-extinct Shipstone's
Bitter, this mid-brown bitter lives up to its
name as it is bitter in taste but not
unpleasantly so.

Beaver Bitter (OG 1043, ABV 4.3%) ◈
A light brown bitter that starts malty in both
aroma and taste, but soon develops a hoppy
bitterness. Appreciably fruity.

Beowulf SIBA

Beowulf Brewing Co, Chasewater Country Park,
Pool Road, Brownhills, Staffordshire, WS8 7NL
Tel (01543) 454067
✉ beowulfbrewing@yahoo.co.uk
Tours by arrangement

Beowulf Brewing Company beers appear as
guest ales predominantly in the central region
but also across the country. The brewery's dark
beers have a particular reputation for
excellence. Seasonal beers: Hurricane (ABV 4%,
autumn), Glutlusty (ABV 4.5%, autumn),
Blizzard (ABV 5%, winter), Grendel's Winter Ale
(ABV 5.8%, winter), Wergild (ABV 4.3%,
spring/summer), Wuffa (ABV 4.4%,
spring/summer), Gold Work (ABV 5.1%,
spring/summer). Bottle-conditioned beer:
Dragon Smoke Stout (ABV 5.3%).

Beorma (OG 1038, ABV 3.9%) ◈
A pale session ale with a malty hint of fruit
giving way to a lingering bitterness.

Noble Bitter (OG 1039, ABV 4%) ◈
Golden with a sweet malty aroma. Malty
start becomes very hoppy then bitter, but not
an over-long finish.

Wiglaf (OG 1043, ABV 4.3%) ◆
A golden bitter, with a malty flavour married to a pleasing bitterness, with three hop varieties used.

Chasewater Bitter (OG 1043, ABV 4.4%) ◆
Golden bitter, hoppy throughout with citrus and hints of malt. Long mouth-watering, bitter finish.

Swordsman (OG 1045, ABV 4.5%) ◆
Pale gold, light fruity aroma, tangy hoppy flavour. Faintly hoppy finish.

Dark Raven (OG 1048, ABV 4.5%)

Dragon Smoke Stout (OG 1048, ABV 4.7%) ▢ ◆
Black and smoky, full of roast flavours and dark chocolate with a touch of fruit and hops, and a creamy head to add sweetness. Bitterness develops, supported by the roast bitterness.

Finn's Hall Porter (OG 1049, ABV 4.7%) ◆
Mint chocolate fumes laced with liquorice. Full roast flavours with fruit and toffee. Delicious hoppy finish with liquorice stick reminders, leading to a long nutty, dry astringency.

Heroes Bitter (OG 1046, ABV 4.7%) ◆
Gold colour, malt aroma, hoppy taste but sweetish finish.

Mercian Shine (OG 1048, ABV 5%) ◆
Amber to pale gold with a good bitter and hoppy start. Plenty of caramel and hops with background malt leading to a good bitter finish with caramel and hops lingering in the aftertaste.

Berrow SIBA

Berrow Brewery, Coast Road, Berrow, Burnham-on-Sea, Somerset, TA8 2QU
Tel (01278) 751345
Tours by arrangement

⊗ The brewery opened in 1982 and production is now around five barrels a week. It celebrated its silver jubilee in 2007. All the beers have won prizes at beer festivals. 15-20 outlets are supplied. Seasonal beers: Carnivale (ABV 4.7%, Oct-Nov), Christmas Ale (ABV 4.7%, Nov-Dec), Winter Sport (ABV 4.7%).

Best Bitter/4Bs (OG 1038, ABV 3.9%) ◆
A pleasant, pale brown session beer, with a fruity aroma, a malty, fruity flavour and bitterness in the palate and finish.

Berrow Porter (OG 1046, ABV 4.6%)
A ruby-coloured porter with a pronounced hop character.

Berrow Sport (OG 1047, ABV 4.7%)
A pale amber beer with a refreshing, distinctive taste.

Topsy Turvy (OG 1055, ABV 5.9%) ◆
A gold-coloured beer with an aroma of malt and hops. Well-balanced malt and hops taste is followed by a hoppy, bitter finish with some fruit notes.

Betwixt

Betwixt Beer Company, c/o Northern Brewing Ltd, Blakemere Brewery, Blakemere Craft Centre, Chester Road, Sandiway, Northwich,
Cheshire, CW8 2EB
Tel 07792 967414
✉ brewer@betwixtbeer.co.uk
⊕ betwixtbeer.co.uk

⊗ The company was created in 2005, based on the Wirral peninsula, 'Betwixt the Mersey and the Dee'. The brewery currently uses spare capacity at Northern Brewing (qv) in Cheshire but hopes to set up its own Wirral brewery in the near future. The beers are sold through farmers markets, festivals and in local pubs. Seasonal beer: BeWilder (ABV 4.3%, Sep-Nov). Bottle-conditioned beers: as for cask beer range including seasonal.

Dark Matter (OG 1046, ABV 4%)

Sunlight (OG 1043, ABV 4.3%)

Red Admiral (OG 1050, ABV 5%)

Big Lamp

Big Lamp Brewers, Grange Road, Newburn, Newcastle upon Tyne, NE15 8NL
Tel (0191) 267 1689
✉ admin@biglampbrewers.co.uk
⊕ biglampbrewers.co.uk
Tours by arrangement

⊛ Big Lamp started in 1982 and relocated in 1997 to a 55-barrel plant in a former water pumping station. It is the oldest micro-brewery in the north-east of England. 30 outlets are supplied and two pubs are owned. Seasonal/occasional beers: Keelman Brown (ABV 5.7%), Old Genie (ABV 7.4%), Blackout (ABV 11%).

Sunny Daze (OG 1037, ABV 3.7%)
A light coloured beer, well hopped with Styrian Goldings.

Bitter (OG 1039, ABV 3.9%) ◆
A clean-tasting tawny bitter, full of hops and malt. A hint of fruit, with a good hoppy finish.

Double M (OG 1043, ABV 4.3%)
Copper red in colour. A fruity mouth feel with slight traces of malt and a pleasant dry aftertaste.

Summerhill Stout (OG 1044, ABV 4.4%) ◆
A rich, tasty stout, dark in colour with a lasting rich roast character. Malty mouthfeel with a lingering finish.

Prince Bishop Ale (OG 1048, ABV 4.8%) ◆
A refreshing, easy-drinking bitter, golden in colour, full of fruit and hops. Strong bitterness with a spicy, dry finish.

Premium (OG 1052, ABV 5.2%) ◆
A well-balanced, flavoursome bitter with a big nose full of hops. The sweetness lasts into a mellow, dry finish.

Embers (OG 1055, ABV 5.5%)

Bitter End

▢ Bitter End Pub & Brewery, 15 Kirkgate, Cockermouth, Cumbria, CA13 9PJ
Tel (01900) 828993
✉ info@bitterend.co.uk
⊕ bitterend.co.uk
Tours by arrangement

The brewery opened in the back room of the Bitter End pub in 1995, using a one-barrel plant with former whisky casks as fermenters. The equipment was replaced in 2004 with a copper-clad, 2.5-barrel system imported from the U.S. Beer is available only at the pub.

Cockermouth Pride (OG 1038, ABV 3.8%)
A pale brown, malty bitter, fruity and sweet beer with a slight astringency in the finish.

Wheat Beer (ABV 4.1%)

Call Out (ABV 4.2%)
Brewed to raise funds for Cockermouth Rescue Team.

Czechumberland (ABV 4.5%)

Cuddy Lugs (ABV 4.7%) ◈
A malty aroma and sweet start quickly lead to lingering bitter flavours.

Skinner's Old Strong (ABV 5.5%)

Blackawton SIBA

Blackawton Brewery, Unit 7, Peninsula Park, Moorlands Trading Estate, Saltash, Cornwall, PL12 6LX
Tel (01752) 848777
✉ steve@blackawtonbrewery.eclipse.co.uk
⊕ blackawtonbrewery.com

⊗ Blackawton was once Devon's oldest operating brewery, but relocated to Cornwall in 2000 and ownership changed in 2004. Some 50 outlets are supplied. Seasonal beer: Winter Fuel (ABV 5%). Bottle-conditioned beers: Headstrong, Winter Fuel.

Original Bitter (OG 1037, ABV 3.8%)
A copper-coloured bitter; an ideal session beer with a fresh floral hop aroma.

Westcountry Gold (OG 1039, ABV 4.1%)
A light, golden, fresh-tasting summer beer with sweet malt flavours and delicate vanilla and fruit hints from Styrian Goldings hops.

44 Special (OG 1044, ABV 4.5%)
A premium, full-strength bitter that is rich and sweet with the aroma of ripe hops and fruit.

Peninsula Ale (OG 1046, ABV 4.6%)
A dark amber-coloured premium bitter with a hoppy, bitter finish.

Exhibition Ale (OG 1047, ABV 4.7%)

Headstrong (OG 1048, ABV 5.2%)
A deceptively smooth beer with a bitter malt taste.

Black Country

Black Country Ales, Old Bulls Head, 1 Redhall Road, Lower Gornal, Dudley, West Midlands, DY3 2NU
Tel (01384) 231616/07946 454150
✉ info@blackcountryales.co.uk
⊕ blackcountryales.co.uk
Tours by arrangement

The brewery was set up in 2004 by director Angus McMeeking and brewer Guy Perry from nearby Sarah Hughes (qv). The brewery uses a new plant situated in part of the pub's original tower brewery, dating from 1834, which had last

brewed in 1934. Oak vessels that were installed in 1900 have been refurbished and brought into production. One-off beers are produced for distributors. Seasonal beers: English Summer (ABV 4.5%), English Winter (ABV 5.5%).

Bradley's Finest Golden (OG 1040, ABV 4.2%)

Pig on the Wall (OG 1040, ABV 4.3%)

Fireside (OG 1047, ABV 5%)

Black Dog

Black Dog Brewery, Foulsyke Farm, Fylingdales, Whitby, North Yorkshire, YO22 4QL
Tel (0845) 301 2337
⊕ blackdogbrewery.co.uk

⊛ Black Dog started brewing in 1997 in the centre of Whitby, but closed in 2000. Beers under the Black Dog name were contract brewed by Hambleton. However, in 2006 Tony Bryars purchased the original Black Dog five-barrel plant, together with recipes, and re-established the brewery on his farm, using local spring water. Three regular beers are brewed plus other occasional beers from the original Black Dog portfolio.

Whitby Abbey Ale (ABV 3.8%)

Schooner (ABV 4.2%)

Rhatas (ABV 4.6%)

Blackdown

Blackdown Brewery Ltd, Unit C6, Dunkeswell Business Park, Honiton, Devon, EX14 4LE
Tel (01404) 890096
✉ info@blackdownbrewery.co.uk
⊕ blackdownbrewery.co.uk
Tours by arrangement

⊗ The brewery, established in 2002, is family-run and covers Devon, Dorset and Somerset. The brewery has recently been expanded to double its original brewing capacity. Some 180 outlets are supplied. Seasonal beers: Palm (ABV 4.2%), Honey (ABV 4.4%).

Devon's Pride (OG 1038, ABV 3.8%)

Gold (OG 1043, ABV 4.3%)

Dark Side (OG 1045, ABV 4.5%)

Premium (OG 1047, ABV 4.7%)

Blackfriars

Blackfriars Brewery Limited, Unit 4, Queens Road Business Centre, Great Yarmouth, Norfolk, NR30 3HT
Tel (01493) 850578
✉ w.russell4@ntlworld.com

⊗ The brewery was established in 2004 on a purpose-built five-barrel plant. Some 40 outlets are supplied. All beers are available in bottle-conditioned form.

Mild (ABV 3.4%) ◈
Sweet and malty in true Norfolk fashion. Red-hued with a gentle roast malt aroma. Stewed prunes and caramel lurk in the background as the finish lingers long and sweet.

Yarmouth Bitter (OG 1036, ABV 3.8%) ◈
A malt-dominated brew. Pale brown and

smooth drinking with a distinctly malty nose. A bittersweet fruitiness in the taste turns to an increasing bitterness to rival the malt character.

Sygnus Bitter Gold (OG 1044, ABV 4%) ◆
Hoppy golden ale with a grainy bitter feel. Malt mixes with a pear and pineapple backdrop to give depth and body. A long, lingering finish turns increasingly dry.

Whyte Angel (ABV 4.5%) ◆
Fragrant hoppy aroma leads to a strong bitter first taste. Golden hued with honey notes softening the dryness of the bitter hops. Gentle malt background throughout.

Maritime (ABV 5%) ◆ Copper-coloured, rich, heavy and malty brew. Vinous, fruitcake characteristics supplement the richness of taste. A muted hoppy bitterness can be detected in the long finish.

Old Habit (OG 1052, ABV 5.6%) ◆
Old-fashioned mix of roast, malt and plummy fruitiness. Smooth and aromatic with coffee notes and a heavy mouthfeel. Finish softens to a malty character.

Black Hole

Black Hole Brewery Ltd, Unit 63, Ground Floor, Imex Business Park, Shobnall Road, Burton upon Trent, Staffs, DE14 2AU
Tel (01283) 834060
✉ blackholebrewery@btconnect.com
⊕ blackholebrewery.co.uk
Tours by arrangement

Black Hole started in January 2007 in the old Ind Coope bottling stores.

Bitter (OG 1040, ABV 3.8%) ◆
Amber beer with a sweet caramel and hops aroma. Light taste, easy to drink, with a well-defined sharp hop taste and a bitter finish that is slightly dry.

Red Dwarf (OG 1044, ABV 4.4%)

No Escape (ABV 5.2%)

Black Isle SIBA

Black Isle Brewing Co Ltd, Old Allengrange, Munlochy, Ross-shire, IV8 8NZ
Tel (01463) 811871
✉ greatbeers@blackislebrewery.com
⊕ blackislebrewery.com
Shop open Mon-Sat 10am-6pm
Tours by arrangement

⊗ Black Isle Brewery was set up in 1998 in the heart of the Scottish Highlands and is the first dedicated organic brewery in Scotland. All beers have Soil Association certification, while the bottle-conditioned beers are certified by both the SA and the Vegetarian Society. The brewery plans to use its own spring water, grow and malt its own barley and feed the brewer's grains to its own stock. Some 35 outlets are supplied. Bottle-conditioned beers (all suitable for vegetarians and vegans): Wheat Beer (ABV 4.5%), Scotch Ale (ABV 4.5%), Porter (ABV 4.5%), Hibernator III, Goldeneye.

Yellowhammer (OG 1042, ABV 4%) ◆
A refreshing, hoppy golden ale with light hop and fruit throughout. A short, bitter finish with a yeasty background.

Red Kite (OG 1041, ABV 4.2%) ◆
Can vary but generally light malt on the nose and some fruit on the palate. Slight sweetness in the taste and a short, bitter finish.

Hibernator (ABV 4.5%)

Wagtail Porter (ABV 4.5%)

Black Mountain*

Black Mountain Brewery Ltd, Telegraph Inn, Station Road, Llangadog, Carmarthenshire, S19 9LS
Tel (01550) 777727
✉ khwrigley@aol.com
Tours by arrangement

☺ Black Mountain was established in 2006 on a four-barrel plant by Dave Porter in a converted garage behind the Telegraph Inn.

Black Five (ABV 4.1%)

Black Sheep SIBA

Black Sheep Brewery plc, Wellgarth, Masham, Ripon, North Yorkshire, HG4 4EN
Tel (01765) 689227
⊕ blacksheepbrewery.com
Shop 10am-5pm daily
Tours by arrangement

☺ Black Sheep was established 1992 by Paul Theakston, a member of Masham's famous brewing family, in the former Wellgarth Maltings. The company has enjoyed continued growth and now supplies a free trade of around 700 outlets, but owns no pubs. The brewery specialises in cask ale (70% of production). Occasional beer: Emmerdale Ale (ABV 4.2%).

Best Bitter (OG 1038, ABV 3.8%) ◆
A hoppy and fruity beer with strong bitter overtones, leading to a long, dry, bitter finish.

Ale (OG 1044, ABV 4.4%)
A premium bitter with robust fruit, malt and hops.

Riggwelter (OG 1059, ABV 5.9%) ◆
A fruity bitter, with complex underlying tastes and hints of liquorice and pear drops leading to a long, dry, bitter finish.

Blackwater

Blackwater Brewery, Brewers Wholesale, Unit 2b Gainsborough Trading Estate, Rufford Road, Stourbridge, West Midlands, DY9 7ND
✉ enquiries@thebrewerswholesale.co.uk
⊕ thebrewerswholesale.co.uk
Tel (01384) 374050

Beers contract brewed by Salopian Brewery (qv).

Blakemere

See Northern

Blanchfields SIBA

Blanchfields Brewing Co, Blanchfields Bar, 1 Southend Road, Rochford, Essex SS4 1HA
Tel (01702) 544015

✉ blanchfields@blanchfields.co.uk
⊕ blanchfields.co.uk
Tours by arrangement

⊗ The 2.5-barrel brewery was established in 1997 at the Bull in Fakenham, Norfolk. The brewery moved in 2003 to Rochford and in 2006 began sharing premises with the Star Beermaking Company in Steeple, Essex. The brewery has its own brewery tap, Blanchfields Bar, in Rochford. Around 30 outlets are supplied.

IPA Twist (OG 1036, ABV 3.6%)

Black Bull Mild (OG 1040, ABV 3.6%) ◈
Light malty airs introduce this red-coloured, traditional mild. A dry fruity maltiness gives a hint of cocoa. The finish fades quickly although roasted malt remains.

Golden Bull (OG 1045, ABV 4.2%)

Porter Bull (OG 1042, ABV 4.2%)

White Bull (OG 1044, ABV 4.4%)

Raging Bull Bitter (OG 1048, ABV 4.9%) ◈
Fruity strong ale with a perfumed aroma and a reasonably bitter finish.

Blencowe

See Barrowden

Blindmans SIBA

Blindmans Brewery Ltd, Talbot Farm, Leighton, Frome, Somerset, BA11 4PN
Tel (01749) 880038
✉ info@blindmansbrewery.co.uk
⊕ blindmansbrewery.co.uk
Tours by arrangement

Blindmans Brewery was established in 2002 with a five-barrel plant in a converted milking parlour. The brewery has its own exclusive water spring. In 2004 the brewery was bought by Paul Edney and Lloyd Chamberlain. Approximately 50 outlets are supplied. Seasonal beers: Eclipse (ABV 4.2%), Siberia (ABV 4.7%), Bah Humbug! (ABV 4.5%).

Buff (ABV 3.6%)
Amber-coloured, smooth session beer.

Golden Spring (ABV 4%)
Fresh and aromatic straw-coloured beer, brewed using selected lager malt.

Mine Beer (ABV 4.2%)
Full-bodied, copper-coloured, blended malt ale.

Icarus (ABV 4.5%)
Fruity, rich, mid-dark ruby ale.

Blue Anchor SIBA

⚲ Blue Anchor Inn, 50 Coinagehall Street, Helston, Cornwall, TR13 8EL
Tel (01326) 562821
✉ theblueanchor@btconnect.com
⊕ spingoales.com
Tours by arrangement

⊗ Dating back to the 15th century, this is the oldest brewery in Cornwall and was originally a monks' hospice. After the dissolution of the monasteries it became a tavern brewing its own uniquely flavoured beer called Spingo at the rear of the premises. Brewing has continued to this day and people travel from all over the world to sample the delights of this wonderful inn, untouched by time. Five outlets are supplied. Seasonal beers: Spingo Bragget (ABV 6.1%, April-Oct), Spingo Easter Special (ABV 7.6%), Spingo Christmas Special (ABV 7.6%). All draught beers are available in bottle conditioned form. Bragget is a recreation of a medieval beer style.

Spingo Jubilee/IPA (OG 1045, ABV 4.6%)

Spingo Middle (OG 1050, ABV 5.1%)
A copper-red beer with a fruity aroma, a hint of vanilla and a peppery note from the hops. The palate is nutty, with a fruit cake note. The complex bittersweet finish is fruity and dry.

Spingo Special (OG 1066, ABV 6.7%)
Darker than Middle with a pronounced earthy character on the nose balanced by rich fruit. Fruit and peppery hops dominate the mouth, followed by a finish with malt, fruit and hops.

Blue Bear*

Blue Bear Brewery Ltd, Unit 1 Open Barn Farm, Kempsey, Worcestershire, WR5 3LW
Tel (01905) 828258
⊕ bluebearbrewery.co.uk
Tours by arrangement (for 12 people or more)

⊗ Blue Bear started production in 2006 in an old potato store.

Wanderlust (OG 1036, ABV 3.8%)
A straw-coloured beer with a biscuity palate. Refreshingly hoppy with a floral finish.

Roar Spirit (OG 1040, ABV 4.2%)
An amber-coloured beer with a rounded, malted flavour and a spicy, blackcurrant aftertaste.

Fearless (OG 1042, ABV 4.4%)
Burnished gold in colour with caramel tones and delicate citrus notes.

White Bear (OG 1043, ABV 4.5%)
A golden premium ale with a fruit character that leaves a smooth mouth feel of citrus on the palate.

Blue Bell

Blue Bell Brewery, Sycamore House, Lapwater Lane, Holbeach St Marks, Lincolnshire, PE12 8EX
Tel (01406) 701000
✉ enquiries@bluebellbrewery.co.uk
⊕ bluebellbrewery.co.uk
Tours by arrangement

⊛ Alan and Emma Bell took over the Blue Bell Brewery in 2004 from original founder Mick Pilkington. The brewery operates as a separate business from the Blue Bell pub but the pub does act as the brewery tap. Some 40 outlets are supplied. Seasonal beer: Mild (ABV 3.6%).

Old Honesty (OG 1040, ABV 4.1%)

Old Gold (OG 1045, ABV 4.5%)

Old Fashioned (OG 1045, ABV 4.8%)

Old Comfort (OG 1050, ABV 5%)

For Blue Bell Inn, Whaplode St Catherine:

Ingledingle Ale (OG 1054, ABV 5.1%)

For Ivy Wall (Wetherspoons), Spalding:

Pain in the Glass (OG 1040, ABV 4.1%)

Blue Cow

◊ Blue Cow Inn and Brewery, 29 High Street, South Witham, Lincolnshire, NG33 5QB
Tel (01572) 768432
⊕ thebluecowinn.co.uk
Tours by arrangement

☺ Taken over in 2005, the brewery owners plan to develop the range of beers.

Best Bitter (OG 1039, ABV 3.8%)

Witham Wobbler (OG 1045, ABV 4.5%)

Blue Moon

◊ Blue Moon Brewery, Cock Inn, Watton Road, Barford, Norfolk, NR9 4AS
Tel (01603) 757646

The brewery supplies the Cock Inn and around 40 other free trade outlets. Seasonal beer: Moon Dance (ABV 4.7%, summer).

Easy Life (OG 1040, ABV 3.8%) ◄
A golden-hued brew with a complex character. A hoppy nose continues through to a hoppy, slightly astringent finish. Malt and caramel swirl in the background as lemon notes grow.

Sea of Tranquillity (OG 1042, ABV 4.2%) ◄
A dry, malty character gives depth to this copper-coloured best bitter. A blackcurrant start fades as a long, ever-sweetening finish develops.

Dark Side (OG 1048, ABV 4%)

Hingham High (OG 1050, ABV 5.2%) ▣ ◄
A beautifully-balanced strong malty ale. Mellow fruitiness jostles for attention with chocolate, hops and toffee. The long, strong finish is reminiscent of a good vintage port.

Milk of Amnesia (OG 1055, ABV 5.2%) ◄
A complex, mid-brown beer. The taste has a port-like note; cinnamon and ginger jostle with pepper and citrus as the flavours continue to hold up well.

Liquor Mortis (OG 1075, ABV 7.5%) ◄
A heavy blackcurrant signature introduces this dark brown barley wine. A mature roast beginning counter-balances the fruity sweetness that carries through to a long, filling finish.

Total Eclipse (ABV 9%)

Blythe SIBA

Blythe Brewery, Blythe House Farm, Lichfield Road, Hamstall Ridware, Rugeley, Staffordshire, WS15 3QQ
Tel 07773 747724
✉ info@blythebrewery.plus.com
⊕ blythebrewery.co.uk
Tours by arrangement

Robert Greenway started brewing in 2003 using a 2.5-barrel plant in a converted barn on a farm. As well as specials, seasonal beers are produced on a quarterly basis. Fifteen outlets are supplied. Seasonal beer: Old Horny (ABV 4.6%, Sep-Nov). Bottle-conditioned beers: as for cask beers listed below.

Bitter (OG 1040, ABV 4%) ◄
Amber with a full hoppy aroma and sweet

touch. Immediate full hoppy taste that develops into an intense hoppy, lingering finish.

Chase Bitter (OG 1044, ABV 4.4%) ◄
Copper to tawny coloured, with a fruit and hop start with caramel sweetness developing; lingering bitterness with a sweet edge.

Staffie (OG 1044, ABV 4.4%) ◄
Sweet hoppy and citrus flower aroma from this amber beer. Gentle bitter start expands to a fresh fruity tang before the hops demand attention in the long bitter finish.

Palmer's Poison (OG 1045, ABV 4.5%) ◄
Mid-brown with spicy tastes amid the fruit and hops. The hops develop but sweet caramel holds back the long hoppy taste.

BMG Brewing

BMG Brewing Ltd, c/o Tower Brewery, Old Water Tower, Walsitch Maltings, Glensyl Way, Burton upon Trent, Staffordshire, DE14 1LX
Tel (01283) 561330

Beers are contract brews by Tower Brewery for Beer My Guest distributors.

Bob's

Bob's Brewing Co Ltd, c/o Red Lion, 73 Dewsbury Road, Ossett, West Yorkshire, WF5 9NQ
Tel 07789 693597

☺ The brewery was founded in 2002 by Bob Hunter, formerly one of the partners in Ossett Brewery, in outbuildings behind the Red Lion pub. The beers are sold as 'Red Lion Ales'. Around 10 outlets are supplied.

White Lion (OG 1043, ABV 4.3%)
Pale, flowery, lager-style beer using American Cascade hops.

Yakima Pale Ale (OG 1045.5, ABV 4.5%)
A hoppy and bitter yellow beer that uses hops from the Yakima Valley in Washington State, U.S.

Chardonnayle (OG 1051.5, ABV 5.1%)
Complex, stylish strong pale ale with hints of lemongrass and fruits, with Willamette hops for aroma.

Boggart Hole Clough

Boggart Hole Clough Brewing Co, Unit 13 Brookside Works, Clough Road, Moston, Manchester, M9 4FP
Tel (0161) 277 9666
✉ boggartoffice@btconnect.com
⊕ boggart-brewery.co.uk

☺ The brewery was set up in 2001 next to Boggart Hole Clough Park. The site includes a workshop brewery where visitors can design and produce beers to their own specifications on a 2.5-barrel plant. Boggart Distribution was launched in 2003 and beers are now sold to more than 250 free houses throughout the country. Monthly specials are produced. Bottle-conditioned beer: Steaming Boggart.

Best Bitter (ABV 3.9%)
An easy-drinking, light-coloured session beer with a hoppy, bitter aftertaste.

Bog Eyed (ABV 4%)
A light-coloured session ale with pronounced hoppiness and aroma.

Dark Mild (ABV 4%)
A classic dark mild.

Standard Pioneer (ABV 4%)
A light-coloured session ale with lemon citrus taste and aroma.

Angel Hill (OG 1042, ABV 4.2%)
A premium, golden pale ale with an aromatic explosion of flavour.

Boggart Brew (OG 1043, ABV 4.3%)
A quaffable ruby-red beer.

Dark Side (OG 1044, ABV 4.4%)
A classic porter with a smooth roast finish and subtle hop aftertaste.

Sun Dial (OG 1047, ABV 4.7%)
A pale beer with a refreshing, fruity hop taste and aroma.

Waterloo Sunset (ABV 5%)
Traditional porter with an oak roast finish.

Borough Arms

◻ Borough Arms, 33 Earle Street, Crewe, Cheshire, CW1 2BG
Tel (01270) 254999

A two-barrel brewery opened in 2005 at the pub. Brewing takes place twice a month to supply the pub and occasionally to beer festivals.

Bitter End (ABV 3.9%)

Full Moon (ABV 4.4%)

Goldings (ABV 4.8%)

Bottle Brook

Bottle Brook Brewery, Church Street, Kilburn, Belper, Derbyshire, DE56 0LU
Tel (01332) 880051/07971 189915

Bottle Brook was established in 2005 using a 2.5-barrel plant on a tower gravity system. The traditional brewery uses only rare and unusual hop varieties. There are no permanent house beers, just a series of experimental ales. A cider-making plant is planned.

Meandering Mild (OG 1039, ABV 4.1%)

Full Moon (OG 1046, ABV 4.6%)

Kilburn Pale Ale (OG 1044, ABV 4.6%)

Midnight Mash (OG 1050, ABV 5.1%)

Obsession (OG 1053, ABV 5.4)

Shandybelly (OG 1053, ABV 5.6%)

Turpin (OG 1053, ABV 5.6%)

Black Bess (OG 1069, ABV 7.4%)

Highwaymans Folly (OG 1076, ABV 8.6%)

Bowland SIBA

Bowland Brewery, Bashall Town, Clitheroe, Lancashire, BB7 3LQ
Tel 07952 639465
✉ richardbakerbb@aol.com
⊕ bowlandbrewery.com
Tours by arrangement

Bowland started brewing in 2003 using a five-barrel plant. It increased capacity to a 30-barrel kit in 2006 and opened a visitor centre and shop. More than 100 outlets are supplied throughout the north-west. Small scale bottling began in 2005 and bottle-conditioned five-litre mini-casks were introduced in 2006. At least one new beer is brewed each month. Seasonal beers include: Golden Trough, Sorceress, Headless Peg and Sleigh Bell.

Sawley Tempted (OG 1038, ABV 3.7%)
A copper-coloured fruity session bitter with toffee in the mouth and a spicy finish.

Hunters Moon (OG 1039, ABV 3.7%)
A dark mild with chocolate and coffee flavours.

Bowland Gold (OG 1039, ABV 3.8%)
A hoppy golden bitter with intense grapefruit flavours.

Chipping Steamer (OG 1040, ABV 3.9%)
A mid-gold bitter with hints of orange and a slightly floral finish.

Oak (OG 1041, ABV 4%)

Hen Harrier (OG 1040, ABV 4%)
A pale gold bitter with soft citrus, peach and apricot flavours throughout.

Dragon (OG 1043, ABV 4.2%)
A golden bitter with rounded fruit in the mouth and a refreshing finish.

Bowman*

Bowman Ales Ltd, Wallops Wood, Sheardley Lane, Droxford, Hampshire, SO32 3QY
Tel (01489) 878110
✉ info@bowman-ales.com
⊕ bowman-ales.com
Tours by arrangement

⊠ Brewing started in 2006 on a 20-barrel brew plant in converted farm buildings. The brewery supplies more than 60 outlets within a 30 mile radius. Future plans include bottling and a range of unusual celebratory and occasional brews.

Swift One (OG 1038.5, ABV 3.8%)

Wallops Wood (OG 1040, ABV 4%)

Quiver Bitter (OG 1045, ABV 4.5%)

Box Steam

Box Steam Brewery, Oaks Farm, Rode Hill, Colerne, Wiltshire, SN14 8AR
Tel (01225) 858383
✉ enquiries@boxsteambrewery.com
⊕ boxsteambrewery.com
Tours by arrangement

⊠ The brewery was founded in 2004 using a steam-fired copper. The village of Box has associations with brewing and railways, since Isambard Kingdom Brunel constructed a tunnel through the village. Two pubs are owned and more than 20 outlets are supplied. Seasonal beer: Figgy Pudding (ABV 4.7%, winter).

Reverend Awdry's Ale (OG 1042, ABV 3.8%)

Tunnel Vision (OG 1044, ABV 4.2%)

Blind House (OG 1046, ABV 4.6%)

Bradfield

Bradfield Brewery, Watt House Farm, High Bradfield, Sheffield, South Yorkshire, S6 6LG
Tel (0114) 285 1118
✉ info@bradfieldbrewery.com
⊕ bradfieldbrewery.co.uk
Shop Mon-Fri 10am-5pm; Sat 10am-4pm; Sun 10am-2pm

☺ Bradfield Brewery is a family-run business, based on a working farm in the Peak District. Only the finest ingredients are used, along with pure Milstone Grit spring water from a borehole. More than 200 outlets are supplied. Seasonal beer: Farmers Belgian Blue (ABV 4.9%, Xmas). Bottle-conditioned beers: Farmers Pale Ale, Farmers Stout.

Farmers Bitter (OG 1039, ABV 3.9%)
A traditional copper-coloured malt ale with a floral aroma.

Farmers Blonde (OG 1041, ABV 4%)
Pale, blonde beer with citrus and summer fruits aromas.

Farmers Brown Cow (OG 1042.5, ABV 4.2%)
Deep chestnut-coloured ale with a smooth, creamy head. A citrus taste gives way to a long, dry finish.

Farmers Stout (OG 1045, ABV 4.5%)
A dark stout with roasted malts and flaked oats and a subtle, bitter hop character.

Farmers Pale Ale (OG 1049, ABV 5%)
A full-bodied pale ale with a powerful floral bouquet leaving a predominantly dry aftertaste.

Farmers Sixer (OG 1056, ABV 6%)
A strong, lager-type ale with a fruity, pleasant finish.

Brains IFBB

S A Brain & Co Ltd, Cardiff Brewery, PO Box 53, Crawshay Street, Cardiff, CF10 1SP
Tel (029) 2040 2060
✉ brains@sabrain.com
⊕ sabrain.com

☺ S A Brain began trading at the Old Brewery in Cardiff in 1882 when Samuel Arthur Brain and his uncle Joseph Benjamin Brain purchased a site founded in 1713. The company has remained in family ownership ever since. The full range of Brains ales is now produced at the company's Cardiff Brewery (formerly Hancock's), bought from Bass in 1999. The company owns 260 pubs, has a sizeable free trade and a wholesale estate of more than 3,000 accounts. Brains is the official sponsor of the Wales Rugby Union Team, Glamorgan County Cricket Club and the Football Association of Wales.

Dark (OG 1035.5, ABV 3.5%) 🍺 ▣ ◆
A tasty, classic dark brown mild, a mix of malt, roast, caramel with a background of hops. Bittersweet, mellow and with a lasting finish of malt and roast.

Bitter (OG 1036, ABV 3.7%) ◆
Amber coloured with a gentle aroma of malt and hops. Malt, hops and bitterness combine in an easy-drinking beer with a bitter finish.

Bread of Heaven (OG 1040, ABV 4%)
Traditional cask ale with a distinctive reddish hue and rich hop aroma, finely balanced by a fruity finish.

SA (OG 1042, ABV 4.2%) ◆
A mellow, full-bodied beer. Gentle malt and hop aroma leads to a malty, hop and fruit mix with a balancing bitterness.

SA Gold (OG 1047, ABV 4.7%) 🍺 ◆
A golden beer with a hoppy aroma. Well balanced with a zesty hop, malt, fruit and balancing bitterness; a similar satisfying finish.

Rev James (OG 1045.5, ABV 4.5%) ◆
A faint malt and fruit aroma with malt and fruit flavours in the taste, initially bittersweet. Bitterness balances the flavour and makes this an easy-drinking beer.

Brakspear

Brakspear Brewing Co, Eagle Maltings, The Crofts, Witney, Oxon, OX28 4DP
Tel (01993) 890800
✉ info@brakspear-beers.co.uk
⊕ brakspear-beers.co.uk
Shop merchandise available online
Tours by arrangement

Brakspear brewing came back to Oxfordshire in 2004 and has its own fermenting room within Wychwood Brewery (qv). The major development of the Wychwood site in 2004 saw the installation of the original Brakspear copper and fermenting vessels, including the famous 'double drop' fermenters. All the regular and seasonal beers are now brewed at Witney. Bottle-conditioned beers: Live Organic (ABV 4.5%), Triple (ABV 7.2%).

Bitter (OG 1035, ABV 3.4%)
A classic copper-coloured pale ale with a big hop resins, juicy malt and orange fruit aroma, intense hop bitterness in the mouth and finish, and a firm maltiness and tangy fruitiness throughout.

Special (OG 1045, ABV 4.3%)
Rich malt, hops and fruit aroma; biscuity malt and hop resins in the mouth; long bitter-sweet finish with orange fruit notes.

Brancaster EAB

⌂ **Brancaster Brewery, Jolly Sailors, Main Road, Brancaster Staithe, Norfolk, PE31 8BJ**
Tel (01485) 210314
✉ jayatjolly@aol.com
⊕ jolllysailors.co.uk

Brancaster opened in 2003 with a five-barrel plant squeezed into a converted ocean-going steel container adjacent to its own pub/restaurant. Occasional specials are produced. Both beers are also available bottle-conditioned.

IPA (ABV 3.7%)

Old Les (ABV 5%)

Brandon

Brandon Brewery, 76 High Street, Brandon, Suffolk, IP27 0AU
Tel (01842) 878496/07876 234689
✉ enquiries@brandonbrewery.co.uk
⊕ brandonbrewery.co.uk

Shop Mon-Sat 9am-5pm (please ring before visiting)
Tours by arrangement

⊠ Brandon started brewing in 2005 in the old dairy of a 15th-century cottage. Visitors are welcome and encouraged to sample from the beer shop. 60 outlets are supplied. The entire range of beers is also available bottle conditioned.

Breckland Gold (OG 1037, ABV 3.8%)
A combination of Goldings and Fuggles hops give a delicate, smooth, slightly spicy taste and a dry, lingering, malty finish.

Bitter (OG 1040, ABV 4%)
A full-bodied but balanced bitterness with pleasant floral and spicy notes and a gentle, hoppy, dry aftertaste.

Saxon Gold (ABV 4%)
A pale, golden beer with a subtle aroma of hops. The taste is a clean, crisp mix of spice and bitter fruits with a dry, hoppy finish.

Molly's Secret (ABV 4.1%)
A pale ale based on an old recipe.

Norfolk Poacher (ABV 4.1%)
A reddish amber beer. Full-bodied and malty with a hoppy, fruit flavour.

Royal Ginger (ABV 4.1%)
A refreshing summer ale with a distinctive mix of malt and hoppy spice, balanced with a gentle ginger flavour and finish.

Wee Drop of Mischief (ABV 4.2%)
An amber-coloured premium bitter. Gentle malt flavours give way to a delightful hop character and a dry, increasingly bitter aftertaste.

Gun Flint (OG 1041, ABV 4.2%)
Roasted malts are used to produce a malty, chocolate flavour. This combines well with spicy, citrus hops to give a dry, bittersweet, roasted malt finish.

Rusty Bucket (OG 1043, ABV 4.4%)
Based on a traditional best bitter brew, this beer is smooth on the palate with a soft and fruity flavour.

Slippery Jack (OG 1044, ABV 4.5%)
A dark brown stout. Complex but well-balanced flavours of roasted grain and hop bitterness. Dry with a lingering, pleasantly bitter finish.

Nappertandy (OG 1047, ABV 4.8%)
A reddish amber beer, full-bodied with a malty aroma. Crisp and spicy with an underlying citrus flavour and a dry, malty, bitter fruit finish.

Brandy Cask SIBA

⚲ Brandy Cask Pub & Brewery, 25 Bridge Street, Pershore, Worcestershire, WR10 1AJ
Tel (01386) 552602
Tours by arrangement

☺ Brewing started in 1995 in a refurbished bottle store in the garden of the pub. Brewery and pub now operate under one umbrella, with brewing carried out by the owner/landlord.

Whistling Joe (ABV 3.6%) ◈
A sweet, fruity, copper-coloured beer that has plenty of contrast in the aroma. A malty balance lingers but the aftertaste is not dry.

Brandy Snapper (ABV 4%) ◈
Golden brew with low alpha hops. Plenty of fruit and hop aroma leads to a rich taste in the mouth and a lingering aftertaste.

John Baker's Original (ABV 4.8%) ◈
A superb blend of flavours with roasted malt to the fore. The rich hoppy aroma is complemented by a complex aftertaste.

Ale Mary (ABV 4.8%) ◈
A rich malt and fruit aroma leads to an equally complex taste with no one flavour dominating. A dry finish.

Branscombe Vale SIBA

Branscombe Vale Brewery Ltd, Branscombe, Devon, EX12 3DP
Tel (01297) 680511
✉ branscombebrewery@yahoo.co.uk

⊠ The brewery was set up in 1992 by former dairy workers Paul Dimond and Graham Luxton in cowsheds owned by the National Trust. Paul and Graham converted the sheds and dug their own well. The NT built an extension for the brewery to ensure future growth. Branscombe Vale currently supplies 60 regular outlets. 2008 will see a further extension to enable a 25-barrel plant to be installed. Seasonal beers: Anniversary Ale (ABV 4.6%, Feb-Mar), Hells Belles (ABV 4.8%), Yo Ho Ho (ABV 6%, Xmas). Bottle-conditioned beer: Draymans.

Branoc (OG 1035, ABV 3.8%) ◈
Pale brown brew with a malt and fruit aroma and a hint of caramel. Malt and bitter taste with a dry, hoppy finish.

Draymans (OG 1040, ABV 4.2%)
A mid-brown beer with hop and caramel notes and a lingering finish.

BVB Own Label (OG 1046, ABV 4.6%) ◈
Reddy/brown-coloured beer with a fruity aroma and taste, and bitter/astringent finish.

Summa That (OG 1050, ABV 5%)
Light golden beer with a clean and refreshing taste and a long hoppy finish.

Breconshire SIBA

Breconshire Brewery Ltd, Ffrwdgrech Industrial Estate, Brecon, Powys, LD3 8LA
Tel (01874) 623731
✉ sales@breconshirebrewery.com
⊕ breconshirebrewery.com
Shop Mon-Fri 8.30am-4.30pm
Tours by arrangement

⊠ Breconshire Brewery was founded by Howard Marlow in 2002 as part of C H Marlow, a wholesaler and distributor of ales, beers, wines and spirits in the south Wales area for more than 30 years. The 10-barrel plant uses British Optic malts blended with a range of British whole hops. The beers are distributed throughout mid, south and west Wales and the west of England. Seasonal beers include: Winter Beacon (ABV 5.3%, Nov-Feb). Bottle-conditioned beers: Golden Valley, Brecknock Best, Red Dragon, Ramblers Ruin, Winter Beacon.

Brecon County Ale (OG 1037, ABV 3.7%) ◆
A traditional amber-coloured bitter. A clean
hoppy flavour, background malt and fruit,
with a good thirst-quenching bitterness.

Golden Valley (OG 1042, ABV 4.2%) ◆
Golden in colour with a welcoming aroma of
hops, malt and fruit. A balanced mix of these
flavours and moderate, building bitterness
lead to a satisfying, rounded finish.

Brecknock Best (OG 1045, ABV 4.5%)
A tawny-coloured traditional best bitter,
brewed with Bramling Cross and Pilot hops.
First brewed to mark the Brecknockshire
Agricultural Society's 250th Anniversary.

Red Dragon (OG 1047, ABV 4.7%)
A red-hued premium ale brewed with a
complex grist of Optic and wheat malts and a
blend of hedgerow hops.

Ramblers Ruin (OG 1050, ABV 5%) ◆
Dark amber, full-bodied with rich biscuity
malt and fruit flavours; background hops and
bitterness round off the beer.

Brentwood

**Brentwood Brewing Co Ltd, 372 Ongar Road,
Brentwood, Essex, CM15 9JH**
Tel (01277) 375760
✉ brentwoodbrewing@aol.com
⊕ brentwoodbrewing.co.uk
Tours by arrangement

⊗ Launched in the summer of 2006,
Brentwood has expanded to a five-barrel
plant and, with the addition of more
fermenting capacity, now brews up to three
times a week. Brentwood supplies more than
a dozen local outlets and distributes to pubs
and festivals throughout Britain. Seasonal
beers: Summer Virgin (ABV 4.5%), Volcano
(ABV 4.6%, winter).

Canary Beaver (OG 1038, ABV 3.8%)

Spooky Moon (OG 1040, ABV 3.8%) ◆
Well-balanced session bitter. The sweet
marmalade aroma hints at the citrus
bitterness to be found in the finish.

Best (OG 1042, ABV 4.2%)

Hope & Glory (OG 1046, ABV 4.5%)

Brewdog*

**Brewdog Ltd, Unit 1 Kessock Workshops,
Kessock Road, Fraserburgh, AB43 8UE**
Tel (01346) 519009
✉ info@brewdog.co.uk
⊕ brewdog.co.uk
Tours by arrangement

Brewdog was established in March 2007 by
James Watt and Martin Dickie in their quest to
revolutionise the Scottish brewery sector. Hop
Rocker Lager (ABV 5.5%) is suitable for
vegetarians.

Physics (OG 1050, ABV 5.2%)

Punk IPA (OG 1058, ABV 6.2%)

Thunder Dog (OG 1072.6, ABV 8%)

Paradox (OG 1072.6, ABV 8.5-11%)
Matured in whisky barrels.

Brewster's SIBA

**Brewster's Brewing Co Ltd, Burnside,
Turnpike Close, Grantham,
Lincolnshire, NG31 7XU**
Tel (01476) 566000
✉ sara@brewsters.co.uk
⊕ brewsters.co.uk
Tours by arrangement

⊗ Brewster is the old English term for a female
brewer and Sara Barton is a modern example.
Brewster's Brewery was set up in the heart of
the Vale of Belvoir in 1998 and moved in 2006
to its current premises. Beer is supplied to some
250 outlets throughout central England and
further afield via wholesalers. Seasonal beers:
see website. Bottle-conditioned beer: Vale Pale
Ale (ABV 4.5%).

Hophead (OG 1036, ABV 3.6%) ◆
This amber beer has a floral/hoppy character;
hops predominate throughout before finally
yielding to grapefruit in a slightly astringent
finish.

Marquis (OG 1038, ABV 3.8%) ◆
A well-balanced and refreshing session bitter
with maltiness and a dry, hoppy finish.

Daffys Elixir (OG 1042, ABV 4.2%)

Hop A Doodle Doo (OG 1043, ABV 4.3%)

Rutterkin (OG 1046, ABV 4.6%) ◆
A premium bitter with a golden appearance.
A zesty hop flavour from American Mount
Hood hops combines with a touch of malt
sweetness to give a rich, full-bodied beer.

Wicked Woman Range (OG 1048, ABV 4.8%)
(Varies seasonally)

Belly Dancer (OG 1050, ABV 5.2%) ◆
Well-balanced, ruby-red ale with a full-
bodied taste from crystal and roast malts,
with a subtle hop finish from Bramling Cross
and Fuggles.

Brew Wharf

⟁ Brew Wharf Co Ltd, Brew Wharf Yard, Stoney
Street, London, SE1 9AD
Tel (020) 7378 6601
✉ iain@brewwharf.com
⊕ brewwharf.com

Brew Wharf opened in 2005 and has a bar plus
a restaurant where dishes are matched with
beer. Seasonal beer: Rebel (ABV 5.4%, Nov-Apr).

Wharf Bitter (OG 1036, ABV 3.6%)

Wharf Best (OG 1041, ABV 4.2%)

Bricktop*

**Bricktop Brewery,
c/o Gate Hangs Well, Woodgate Road,
Stoke Prior,
Worcestershire, B60 4HG**
Tel (01527) 821957
✉ info@thegatehangswell.co.uk
⊕ thegatehangswell.co.uk

Beers are brewed at Weatheroak Brewery under
the Bricktop Brewery name exclusively for the
owner's pub, Gate Hangs Well in Stoke Prior.
See Weatheroak listing for beers list.

Bridestones*

Bridestones Brewing Co Ltd, The Brewery, c/o Smithy Farm, Blackshaw Head, Hebden Bridge, West Yorkshire, HX7 7JB
Tel (01422) 847104/846178
✉ dan@newdelight.freeserve.co.uk

⊕ Bridestones started brewing in 2006 and supplies some 25 outlets, including the brewer's own pub, the New Delight Inn at Jack Bridge. All beers are available bottled and are suitable for vegans. Seasonal beer: White Bride (ABV 4.3%, Xmas).

Bridesmaid (ABV 4%)

Bottleneck Bride (ABV 4.3%)

Burning Bridge (ABV 4.7%)

Bridge of Allan SIBA

Bridge of Allan Brewery, The Brewhouse, Queens Lane, Bridge of Allan, Stirlingshire, FK9 4NY
Tel (01786) 834555
✉ brewery@bridgeofallan.co.uk
Shop 12-5pm daily

Beer is now brewed by Traditional Scottish Ales at Stirling (qv). Bridge of Allan beer is, however, still available from the Brewhouse. The Brewhouse also showcases a range of Scottish bottled beers, which includes both bottle-conditioned and organic beers.

Bridgnorth

Bridgnorth Brewing Co Ltd, The Old Brewhouse, Kings Head Courtyard, Whitburn Street, Bridgnorth, Shropshire, WV16 4QN
Tel (01746) 762889
✉ info@bridgnorthbrewing.com
⊕ bridgnorthbrewing.com

Brewing started early in 2007 on a four-barrel plant. The brewery plans a real ale and wine bar called the King's Head Stable Bar, which will act as the brewery tap, behind the Kings Head pub. Seasonal ales are also available.

Apley Ale (ABV 3.9%)

Best Bitter (ABV 4.4%)

Bishop Percy (ABV 4.7%)

Old Mo (ABV 5.6%)

Brimstage

Brimstage Brewing Co, Home Farm, Brimstage, Wirral, CH63 6LY
Tel (0151) 342 1181/07870 968323
⊕ brimstagebrewery.com
Tours by arrangement (max of 20 people)

⊗ Brewing started in 2006 on a 10-barrel plant in a redundant farm dairy in the heart of the Wirral countryside. This is Wirral's first brewery since the closure of the Birkenhead Brewery in the late 1960s. Some 30 outlets are supplied.

Trappers Hat Bitter (ABV 3.8%)

Rhode Island Red Bitter (ABV 4%) ◆
Red, smooth and well-balanced malty beer with a good dry aftertaste. Some fruitiness in the taste.

Scarecrow (ABV 4.2%)

Oystercatcher (ABV 4.6%)

Briscoe's

Briscoe's Brewery, 16 Ash Grove, Otley, West Yorkshire, LS21 3EL
Tel (01943) 466515
✉ briscoe.brewery@virgin.net

The brewery was launched in 1998 by microbiologist/chemist Dr Paul Briscoe in the cellar of his house with a one-barrel brew length. Following a spell brewing on a larger scale at the back of a local pub, Dr Briscoe is currently producing occasional brews on his original plant. Seasonal beers: Rombalds Reviver (ABV 3.8%), Runner's Ruin (ABV 4.3%), Shane's Shamrock Stout (ABV 4.6%), Chevinbrau Pilsner-style lager (ABV 5.2%), Puddled and Barmy Ale (ABV 5.8%).

Burnsall Classic Bitter (OG 1040, ABV 4%)
A full-flavoured, reddish-coloured bitter with a good hop flavour.

Chevin Chaser (OG 1043, ABV 4.3%)
A refreshing, pale-coloured, all-malt bitter with a distinct hop finish.

Dalebottom Dark (OG 1043, ABV 4.3%)
A smooth and malty strong dark mild with a good hop character.

Badger Stone Bitter (OG 1044, ABV 4.4%)
A classic English bitter, packed with the flavour of malt and hops.

Three Peaks Ale (OG 1045, ABV 4.5%)
A strong, pale premium bitter brewed with only pale malt and traditional hops.

Otley Gold (OG 1043, ABV 4.6%)
A pale, fairly full-flavoured but soft beer brewed in the style of a lager.

Victorian Velvet (OG 1049, ABV 4.9%)
A malty, fruity and smooth copper-coloured special bitter. Small amounts are available bottle-conditioned from the brewery at Xmas.

Bristol Beer Factory

Bristol Brewing Co Ltd, t/a Bristol Beer Factory, Unit A, The Old Brewery, Durnford Street, Ashton, Bristol, BS3 2AW
Tel (0117) 902 6317
✉ enquiries@bristolbeerfactory.co.uk
⊕ bristolbeerfactory.co.uk
Tours by arrangement

The Beer Factory is a 10-barrel micro-brewery in a part of the former Ashton Gate Brewing Co, which closed in 1933. 50 outlets are supplied.

Red (OG 1038, ABV 3.8%)
Dark ale with slight roast barley taste, fruity aroma and ruby red tint.

No. 7 (OG 1042, ABV 4.2%) ◆
Mid brown, old-fashioned style, malty best bitter. Good body and mouthfeel, some apple-type fruit flavours, with a drying bitter and astringent finish.

Sunrise (OG 1044.5, ABV 4.4%) ◆
Light, gold-coloured best bitter, with a strong hoppy finish.

Milk Stout (OG 1059, ABV 4.5%) ◆
Dark creamy stout, reviving an old Bristol recipe. Black colour with a creamy mouthfeel.

Gold (OG 1048.5, ABV 5%) ✦
Full-bodied and strong-flavoured golden ale. Complex aroma of pineapple and unripe pale fruits with hints of butterscotch and pear drops. A dry and bitter beer.

Brothers

Brothers Brewing Co Ltd, No. 1 Park Lodge House, Bagots Park Estate, Abbots Bromley, Staffordshire, WS15 3ES
Tel (01283) 840417
✉ pam@brothersbrewing.co.uk
⊕ freedombeer.com
Tours by arrangement

No real ale. Established in 2005 by acquiring Freedom Brewery, Brothers Brewery specialises in lagers produced to the German Reinheitsgebot purity law. It currently produces three lagers. Freedom Organic is suitable for vegetarians and vegans. There are plans to produce cask beer. (See also Bünker). Beers: Freedom Organic Lager (ABV 4.8%), Freedom Pilsener (ABV 5%), Freedom Soho Red (ABV 5%).

Broughton SIBA

Broughton Ales Ltd, Broughton, Biggar, Peebles-shire, ML12 6HQ
Tel (01899) 830345
✉ beer@broughtonales.co.uk
⊕ broughtonales.co.uk
Shop Mon-Fri 8am-5pm
Tours by arrangement only

☺ Founded in 1979 in the Scottish Border country, Broughton Ales has been brewing cask beers for more than 25 years but more than 60% of production goes into bottle for sale in Britain and export markets. Seasonal beers: Summer Ale (ABV 3.6%), Winter Fire (ABV 4.2%), Scottish Oatmeal Stout (ABV 4.2%), The Ghillie (ABV 4.5%), Dr Johnson's Definitive (ABV 5%). All bottled beers are suitable for vegetarians and vegans.

The Reiver (OG 1038, ABV 3.8%)
A light-coloured session ale with a predominantly hoppy flavour and aroma on a background of fruity malt. The aftertaste is crisp and clean.

Clipper IPA (OG 1042, ABV 4.2%)
A light-coloured, crisp, hoppy beer with a clean aftertaste.

Bramling Cross (OG 1041, ABV 4.2)
A golden ale with a blend of malt and hop flavours followed by a hoppy aftertaste.

Merlin's Ale (OG 1041, ABV 4.2%) ✦
A well-hopped, fruity flavour is balanced by malt in the taste. The finish is bittersweet, light but dry.

Exciseman's 80/- (OG 1045, ABV 4.6%)
A traditional 80/- cask ale. A dark, malty brew. Full drinking with a good hop aftertaste.

Old Jock (OG 1070, ABV 6.7%) 🍾
Strong, sweetish and fruity in the finish.

Brown Cow

Brown Cow Brewery, Brown Cow Road, Barlow, Selby, North Yorkshire, YO8 8EH
Tel (01757) 618947

✉ susansimpson@browncowbrewery.co.uk
⊕ browncowbrewery.co.uk

Set up in 1997, the original 2.5-barrel plant was replaced by a five-barrel unit in 2002. Additional fermenting vessels were installed in 2006 and the current brew-length is about 15 barrels a week. In addition to the core beers, one-off recipes are brewed regularly. The beers are delivered throughout Yorkshire and to a small number of outlets in the south. Seasonal beers: Simpsons No. 4 (ABV 4.4%, Oct-Mar), 1049 Celebration Ale (ABV 5%, Oct-Mar).

Bitter (OG 1038, ABV 3.8%) ✦
A well-hopped traditional session bitter.

Celestial Light (OG 1039, ABV 4.1%)
A pale, triple hopped ale with a good level of bitterness. Citrus notes and a clean, fresh finish on the palate.

Captain Oates Dark Mild (OG 1044, ABV 4.5%)

For Malton Brewery:

After Dark Coffee Porter (OG 1052, ABV 5%)
Full-flavoured porter with complex mix of malts and subtle hint of coffee.

Auld Bob (OG 1062, ABV 6%)
Deep ruby strong ale with rich velvet finish.

Brunswick SIBA

Brunswick Brewery Ltd, 1 Railway Terrace, Derby, DE1 2RU
Tel (01332) 290677
✉ thebrunswickinn@yahoo.co.uk
Tours by arrangement

⊗ The Brunswick is a purpose-built tower brewery that started brewing in 1991. A viewing area allows pub users to watch production. Bought by Everards in 2002, it is now a tenancy supplying beers to local outlets and the Everard's estate. Seasonal beer: Rambo (ABV 7.3%, winter).

Mild (OG 1036, ABV 3.6%) ✦
A light-bodied, well-balanced Midlands dark mild with liquorice and hints of coffee on the nose and balanced fruit, caramel and roast in the taste.

Bitter (OG 1036, ABV 3.7%)
Brewed with a little crystal rye malt and flavoured with Styrian hops; a full bodied session bitter, malty with bitter undertones.

Triple Hop (OG 1038, ABV 4%) ✦
A pale gold colour and citrus hop bouquet promise sweetness but the hops deliver a firm, dry, lasting bitterness.

Second Brew (OG 1040, ABV 4%) ✦
This tawny best bitter, also known as The Usual, presents an aroma of sulphur and hops that continue throughout, accompanied by a striking bitterness and astringency.

Station Approach (OG 1048, ABV 4.7%)
Straw-coloured bitter with lingering hints of citrus, with a hoppy aftertaste.

Old Accidental (OG 1050, ABV 5%)
A well-balanced, malty beer leading to a bitter finish with warming aftertaste. A light, vinous floral hop has underlying malt notes.

Father Mike's Dark Rich Ruby (OG 1055, ABV 5.8%) ◈
A smooth, near black mild with a hint of red. Well-balanced and filled with sweet roast flavours that conceal its strength.

Black Sabbath (OG 1058, ABV 6%)

Bryn

Bragdy'r Bryn Cyfyngedig, Unit 2, Vale Park, Colomendy Industrial Estate, Denbigh, LL16 5TA
Tel (01745) 812266
✉ info@bragdyrbryn.co.uk
⊕ bragdyrbryn.co.uk

Bryn was launched in 2005 with financial assistance from the Welsh Assembly with a five-barrel plant. Some 40 outlets are supplied. Seasonal beers: Du Stout (ABV 4.2%), Golau (ABV 3.8%). Brewing currently suspended.

Bitter (OG 1039, ABV 4%) ◈
Full-flavoured bitter with a hoppy aroma leading to a refreshing hop flavour throughout. Good mouthfeel and satisfying finish. Sharp, clean-tasting and drinkable.

Special (OG 1044, ABV 4.5%) ◈
Fruity (blackcurrant) bitter premium beer with a hoppy aroma and a long, dry aftertaste.

Herald (OG 1060, ABV 6.2%) ◈
Classic IPA with citrus hop, bitterness and fruit coming through strongly in the flavour, leading to a long, dry, bitter aftertaste.

Bryncelyn

⌂ **Bryncelyn Brewery, Wern Fawr Inn, 47 Wern Road, Ystalyfera, Swansea, SA9 2LX**
Tel (01639) 843625
✉ bryncelynbrewery@aol.com
⊕ bryncelynbrewery.co.uk
Tours by arrangement

⊛ A one-quarter barrel brewery was opened in 1999 by William Hopton (owner) and Robert Scott (brewer). Capacity was increased to its present three-quarter barrel capacity in the same year. As the beer names imply, the owner is fond of Buddy Holly: Feb 59 commemorates the singer's death. Seasonal beers: Feb 59 (ABV 3.7%), Peggy's Brew (ABV 4.2%, Mar), May B Baby (ABV 4.5%, May), That Will Be the Sleigh (ABV 6.6%, Dec-Jan).

Holly Hop (ABV 3.9%) ◈
Pale amber with a hoppy aroma. A refreshing hoppy, fruity flavour with balancing bitterness; a similar lasting finish. A beer full of flavour for its gravity.

Buddy Marvellous (OG 1040, ABV 4%) ◈
Dark brown with an inviting aroma of malt, roast and fruit. A gentle bitterness mixes roast with malt, hops and fruit, giving a complex, satisfying and lasting finish.

Buddy's Delight (OG 1042, ABV 4.2%)

Cwrw Celyn (OG 1044, ABV 4.4%)

CHH (OG 1045, ABV 4.5%) ◈
A pale brown beer with hints of red malt and an inviting hop aroma, with fruit and bitterness adding to the flavour. The finish is clean and hoppy-bitter.

Oh Boy (OG 1045, ABV 4.5%) ◈
An inviting aroma of hops, fruit and malt, and a golden colour. The tasty mix of hops, fruit, bitterness and background malt ends with a long, hoppy, bitter aftertaste. Full-bodied and drinkable.

Rave On (OG 1050, ABV 5%)

Buddy Confusing (OG 1050, ABV 5%)

Bryson's

Morecambe Bay Wines & Spirits Co Ltd, Newgate Brewery, White Lund Industrial Estate, Morecambe, Lancashire, LA3 3PT
Tel (01524) 39481
✉ sales@baywines.co.uk
⊕ baywines.co.uk

Bryson's closed in Heysham in 2004 and moved to Morecambe. Morecambe Bay Wines & Spirits took over production in 2006.

Westmorland Bitter (ABV 3.6%)

Bitter (ABV 3.8%) ◈
Light-bodied, easy-drinking session ale.

Shifting Sands (ABV 3.8%) ◈
Well-balanced, gold-coloured bitter with firm malt notes and a hoppy aroma.

Hurricane (ABV 4.1%)

Barrows Bitter (ABV 4.2%) ◈
Full-flavoured, well-balanced golden bitter.

Buffy's SIBA EAB

Buffy's Brewery Ltd, Rectory Road, Tivetshall St Mary, Norwich, Norfolk, NR15 2DD
Tel (01379) 676523
✉ buffys@buffys.co.uk
⊕ buffys.co.uk

⊠ Buffy's was established in 1993. The brewing capacity is 45 barrels, but a move to bigger premises is in hand. The brewery has one pub, the Cherry Tree at Wicklewood, and there are plans to buy a second pub: the brewery will eventually move to these premises. Some 150 outlets are supplied. Beers are now available in five-litre mini-kegs. Seasonal beers: Sleigher (ABV 4.1%, Nov-Dec), Hollybeery (ABV 6% Dec), Festival 9X (ABV 9%, winter), Birthstone Bitters (ABV 4.2%, changes every month).

Norwich Terrier (OG 1036, ABV 3.6%) ◈
A fragrant peachy aroma introduces this refreshing, gold-coloured bitter. Strong bitter notes dominate throughout as hops mingle with grapefruit to produce a long, increasingly dry finish.

Bitter (OG 1039, ABV 3.9%) ◈
A pale brown beer with a distinctly hoppy nose and grainy feel. A combination of bitterness and hops gives a dry astringent feel to the beer. A long, vinous finish.

Lite Releaf (OG 1041.5, ABV 4.1%) ◈
Hop notes introduce a beer with a definitive dry, hoppy character. Malt fades quickly as the overall dryness develops to a lingering tartness.

Mild (OG 1042, ABV 4.2%) ▢ ◈
A complex brew, deep red with a smooth but grainy feel. Caramel and blackcurrant bolster

the heavy malt influence that is the main characteristic of this understated, deceptively strong mild.

Polly's Folly (OG 1043, ABV 4.3%) ◈
A mixture of hoppiness, citrus fruit and malt gives this well-balanced offering a lively, satisfying feel. Grapefruit creeps into the flavour towards the end as the overall character becomes biscuity dry.

Mucky Duck (OG 1044, ABV 4.5%)
Porter style beer. Slightly sweet but with a good bitter edge.

Hopleaf (OG 1044.5, ABV 4.5%) ◈
Clean tasting with a pronounced hoppy signature. The hop bouquet wanes slightly in the initial taste as malt combines with a sweet fruitiness to give greater depth. Consistent dry finish.

Norwegian Blue (OG 1049, ABV 4.9%) ◈
A gentle hoppy nose belies the rich warming character of the taste explosion. A complex, ever-changing mix of malt, hops, bitterness and fruit. A long, lingering, bittersweet ending.

Roger's Ruin (OG 1063, ABV 6.2%)
A warming, full-bodied, satisfying beer with a spicy kick. Deep copper in colour.

Bull Box

Bull Box Brewery, c/o 1 Brickyard Cottage, Fordham, Downham Market, Norfolk, PE38 0LW
Tel (01366) 385349/07920 163116
✉ bullboxinfo@msn.com

Bull Box Brewery was launched in 2006 and operates on a two-barrel plant based in Stradsett. There are plans for bottle-conditioned ales.

Bitter (ABV 4%)

Mid Life Crisis (ABV 4.5%)

Kerb Crawler (ABV 5.2%)

Bull Lane

▢ Bull Lane Brewing Co,
The Clarendon, 143 High Street East,
Sunderland, Tyne & Wear,
SR1 2BL
Tel (0191) 510 3200
✉ bulllanebrewingco@hotmail.co.uk
⊕ bull-lane-brewing.co.uk
Tours by arrangement

⊛ Sunderland's first brew-pub started production in 2005 in the Clarendon pub on a 2.5-barrel plant. Capacity has been increased twice and brewing now takes place twice a week. The beers are widely available in the Wearside area and are also available through Boggarts (qv).

Amber (OG 1036, ABV 3.6%)

Nowtsa Matta BB (OG 1037, ABV 3.7%)

Ryhope Tug (OG 1039, ABV 3.9%)

East End Light/EEL (OG 1040, ABV 4%)

Clary Brown (OG 1045, ABV 4.5%)

Jack's Flag (OG 1045, ABV 4.5%)

Nowtsa Matta XB (OG 1045, ABV 4.5%)

Sauce of the Niall (OG 1045, ABV 4.5%)

White Bull (OG 1048, ABV 4.8%)

Bull Terrier (OG 1050, ABV 5%)

Bullmastiff SIBA

Bullmastiff Brewery,
14 Bessemer Close, Leckwith,
Cardiff, CF11 8DL
Tel (029) 2066 5292

⊗ An award-winning small craft brewery run by brothers Bob and Paul Jenkins since 1987. The name stems from their love of the bullmastiff breed. They have no ambitions for expansion or owning any pubs, preferring to concentrate on quality control. 30 outlets are supplied.
Seasonal beers: Summer Moult (ABV 4.3%), Mogadog (ABV 10%, winter).

Welsh Gold (OG 1039, ABV 3.8%) ◈
A hoppy and fruity aroma leads into the same juicy blend of flavours. Bittersweet initially, an easy-drinking and refreshing beer.

Jack the Lad (OG 1041, ABV 4.1%)

Thoroughbred (OG 1046, ABV 4.5%) ◈
A good hop aroma leads to a hoppy flavour with accompanying fruit, malt and balancing bitterness. There is a quenching hoppy bitterness in the finish.

Welsh Red (OG 1048, ABV 4.8%)

Welsh Black (OG 1050, ABV 4.8%)

Brindle (OG 1050, ABV 5.1%) ◈
A full-bodied, flavoursome pale beer. Good hop aroma with a mix of malt, hops, fruit and bitterness in the taste. A lasting and satisfying finish.

Son of a Bitch (OG 1062, ABV 6%) ▣ ◈
A complex, warming amber ale with a tasty blend of hops, malt and fruit flavours, with increasing bitterness.

Bünker

Bünker Bar, 41 Earlham Street, Covent Garden,
London, WC2H 9LD
Tel (020) 7240 0606
✉ info@bunkerbar.com
⊕ bunkerbar.com

A micro-brewery producing Freedom lager — see entry for Brothers Brewing Co.

Buntingford SIBA

Buntingford Brewery Co Ltd, Greys Brewhouse,
Therfield Road, Royston, Hertfordshire, SG8 9NW
Tel (01763) 250749/07947 214058
✉ catherine@buntingford-brewery.co.uk
⊕ buntingford-brewery.co.uk
Tours by arrangement

Production started in 2005 using a 15-barrel plant capable of producing up to 45 barrels a week. Locally grown barley is used whenever possible, all floor malted by Warminster Maltings. The brewery is located on a conservation farm: all brewery waste liquids are treated in a reedbed and plans are in hand to make full use of green energy sources. Beers are delivered over a wide area. Occasional beers: Royston Red (ABV 4.8%), Grey Partridge (ABV 4%, autumn/winter), Night Owl Porter (ABV 4.2%).

Pargetters (ABV 3.7%)
A traditional style dark mild.

Challenger (ABV 3.8%)
Pale session beer with citrus hop flavours.

Royston Pale Ale (ABV 4.3%)
Golden best bitter.

Oatmeal Stout (ABV 4.4%)
A quaffing stout with oats and plenty of hop flavour.

Britannia (ABV 4.4%)
Light brown best bitter.

Silence (ABV 5.2%)
Lager malt and American hops combine with a strong citrus character.

Burford

(Formerly Windrush)
Burford Brewery, Downs Road, Witney, Oxfordshire, OX28 0SY
Tel (01993) 703333
✉ burfordbrewery@yahoo.co.uk

Husband and wife team Nigel and Susan Harrison started brewing in 2005 in a purpose-built unit on a small industrial park. A five-barrel plant is used. Local free houses and beer festivals are supplied. One regular beer is produced with plans to brew a summer ale.

Best Bitter (ABV 4.3%)

Burton Bridge SIBA

Burton Bridge Brewery Ltd, 24 Bridge Street, Burton upon Trent, Staffordshire, DE14 1SY
Tel (01283) 510573
✉ bbb@burtonbridgebrewery.fsnet.co.uk
⊕ burtonbridgebrewery.co.uk
Shop Bridge Inn 11.30am-2pm, 5-11pm
Tours by arrangement

⊛ Burton Bridge celebrated 25 years of success and steady growth in 2007 and is still owned by its founding partners, Bruce Wilkinson and Geoff Mumford. The brewery owns five pubs in the town, including its award-winning brewery tap. More than 300 outlets are supplied. An ever-changing range of seasonal/monthly beers is available. Bottle-conditioned beers: Burton Porter (ABV 4.5%), Empire Pale Ale (ABV 7.5%), Bramble Stout (ABV 5% ⬛), Tickle Brain (ABV 8%).

Golden Delicious (OG 1037, ABV 3.8%) ◗
A Burton classic, with sulphurous aroma, well-balanced hops and fruit, and a lingering, mouth-watering bitter finish and a hint of astringency.

XL Bitter (OG 1039, ABV 4%) ◗
A golden, malty bitter, with fruity and hoppy aromas. Hoppy and bitter finish with a characteristic astringent aftertaste.

Bridge Bitter (OG 1041, ABV 4.2%) ◗
Pale brown and hoppy with a hint of roast and caramel. Complex taste with hops just dominating to provide a lingering hoppy finish.

Burton Porter (OG 1044, ABV 4.5%) ◗
Amazingly red with a pure white head. Sweet caramel aroma with some hops. Fruity taste combining with liquorice and hops develop an astringent bitterness.

Stairway to Heaven (OG 1049, ABV 5%) ◗
Golden bitter. A perfectly balanced beer. The malty and hoppy start leads to a hoppy body with some astringency.

Top Dog Stout (OG 1049, ABV 5%) ◗
Black and rich with a roast and malty start. Fruity and abundant hops give a fruity, bitter finish with a mouth-watering edge.

Festival Ale (OG 1054, ABV 5.5%) ◗
Pale brown with a fruity aroma. Fruity start reminiscent of Xmas pudding ingredients; sweet fruity finish that develops to bitterness.

Thomas Sykes (OG 1095, ABV 10%) ⬛ ◗
Rich and warming, fruity, heady and hoppy. A true barley wine to be handled with caution.

Burtonwood

Thomas Hardy Burtonwood Ltd, Bold Lane, Burtonwood, Warrington, Cheshire, WA5 4PJ
Tel (01925) 220022
⊕ thomashardybrewery.co.uk
Tours by arrangement (for a charge)

Following the sale of 60% of its brewing operation to Thomas Hardy in 1998, Burtonwood sold the remaining 40% in 2004 to become solely a pub-owning group that was bought by Marston's (qv) in 2005. Burtonwood is now Thomas Hardy's only brewery, run by Peter Ward as a contract operation, principally for Scottish & Newcastle.

For S&N:

Webster's Green Label (OG 1032, ABV 3.2%)

Webster's Yorkshire Bitter (OG 1035, ABV 3.5%)

Bushy's SIBA

Mount Murray Brewing Co Ltd, Mount Murray Brewery, Mount Murray, Braddan, Isle of Man, IM4 1JE
Tel (01624) 661244
✉ bushys@manx.net
⊕ bushys.com
Tours by arrangement

⊛ Set up in 1986 as a brew-pub, Bushy's moved to its present site in 1990 when demand outgrew capacity. It owns four tied houses and the beers are also supplied to 25 other outlets. Bushy's goes one step further than the Manx Pure Beer Law, which permits only malt, hops, sugar and yeast, preferring the German Reinheitsgebot (Pure Beer Law) that excludes sugar. Seasonal beers are numerous – see website.

Castletown Bitter (OG 1035, ABV 3.5%)

Ruby (1874) Mild (OG 1035, ABV 3.5%)

Bitter (OG 1038, ABV 3.8%) ◗
An aroma full of pale malt and hops introduces a beautifully hoppy, bitter beer. Despite the predominant hop character, malt is also evident. Fresh and clean-tasting.

Old Bushy Tail (OG 1045, ABV 4.5%)

Piston Brew (OG 1045, ABV 4.5%)

Weiss Beer (OG 1040, ABV 4.5%)

Butcombe SIBA

Butcombe Brewery Ltd, Cox's Green, Wrington, Bristol, BS40 5PA
Tel (01934) 863963
✉ info@butcombe.com
⊕ butcombe.com
Shop Mon-Fri 9am-5pm; Sat 9am-12pm
Tours by arrangement

⊗ Established in 1978, Butcombe moved to a new purpose-built brewery in 2004. It supplies about 400 outlets and similar numbers via wholesalers and pub companies. Butcombe has an estate of 13 freehouses. Seasonal beer: Brunel IPA (ABV 5%, Oct-Mar).

Bitter (OG 1039, ABV 4%) ◈
Amber-coloured, malty and notably bitter beer, with subtle citrus notes. Hoppy, malty, citrus and a slight sulphur aroma, and a long, dry, bitter finish.

Blond (ABV 4.3%) ◈
Crisp, hoppy best bitter. Floral and fruity hops predominate, balanced by a slight sweetness, followed by a quenching finish.

Gold (OG 1047, ABV 4.7%) ◈
Aroma of pale malt, citrus hops and fruit. Medium bodied, well-balanced, with subtle pale malt, hops and bitterness. It is fruity, slightly sweet, with an abiding dryness.

Butler's SIBA

Butler's Brewery Co Ltd, The Brewery, Whittles Farm, Mapledurham, Oxfordshire, RG4 7UP
Tel (0118) 972 3201
✉ butlerbrew@aol.com
⊕ butlersbrewery.co.uk

⊗ The brewery was started by Mark and Sarah Butler in 2003. An old cart shed was converted into a brewery and a six-barrel plant was installed. A bottling plant is now operating and the brewery is concentrating on its bottle-conditioned range. Around 20 outlets are supplied. Bottle-conditioned beers: Whittles Bitter (ABV 5%), Old Specific (ABV 6%).

Oxfordshire Bitter (OG 1036.6, ABV 3.6%)

Butts SIBA

Butts Brewery Ltd, Northfield Farm, Wantage Road, Great Shefford, Hungerford, Berkshire, RG17 7BY
Tel (01488) 648133
✉ enquiries@buttsbrewery.com
⊕ buttsbrewery.com
Tours by arrangement

⊗ The brewery was set up in a converted Dutch barn in 1994. In 2002, the brewery took the decision to become dedicated to organic production: all the beers brewed use organic malted barley and organic hops when suitable varieties are available. All beers are certified by the Soil Association. Some 60 outlets are supplied. Bottle-conditioned beers: Blackguard, Barbus Barbus, Golden Brown, Le Butts.

Jester Organic (OG 1035, ABV 3.5%) ◈
A pale brown session bitter with a hoppy aroma and a hint of fruit. The taste balances malt, hops, fruit and bitterness with a hoppy aftertaste.

Traditional (OG 1040, ABV 4%) ◈
A pale brown bitter that is quite soft on the tongue, with hoppy citrus flavours accompanying a gentle, bittersweetness. A long, dry aftertaste is dominated by fruity hops.

Blackguard (OG 1045, ABV 4.5%) ▣ ◈
A porter with caramel, malt, roast and fruit dominating the aroma. The taste is a combination of sweet, malt and roast with caramel undertones and a hoppy finish.

Barbus Barbus (OG 1046, ABV 4.6%) ◈
Golden ale with a hoppy aroma and a hint of malt. Hops dominate taste and aftertaste, accompanied by fruitiness and bitterness, with a hint of balancing sweetness.

Golden Brown (OG 1050, ABV 5%) ◈
A golden brown ale with malt and caramel dominating the aroma. A malty, bittersweet taste lingers on into the subtle aftertaste.

Le Butts (OG 1050, ABV 5%)
Brewed with lager yeast and hops resulting in a crisp and refreshing European-style beer.

Cains SIBA

Cains Beer Co plc, Stanhope Street, Liverpool, Merseyside, L8 5XJ
Tel (0151) 709 8734
✉ info@cains.co.uk
⊕ cains.co.uk
Shop – Brewery Tap open during pub hours
Tours by arrangement

⊛ The Dusanj brothers, Ajmail and Sudarghara, bought the brewery in 2002, have invested heavily and won many awards for their beers. 12 pubs were owned, and in May 2007 Cains bought the Honeycombe Leisure pub company with 95 pubs (see Pub groups). Around 400 outlets are supplied. All of the beers are suitable for vegetarians and vegans. Seasonal beers: see website.

Dark Mild (OG 1034.5, ABV 3.2%) ◈
Sweetish, fruity mild with roast notes throughout and a dry aftertaste.

IPA (OG 1036, ABV 3.5%)

Traditional Bitter (OG 1041, ABV 4%) ◈
Blackcurrant fruit and malt dominate the aroma. A sweetish malty bitter with hints of roast and caramel. Hops come through in the dry, bitter aftertaste.

Formidable Ale (OG 1049, ABV 5%) ◈
A bitter and hoppy beer with a good dry aftertaste. Sharp, clean and dry.

2008 (OG 1049, ABV 5%)

Cairngorm SIBA

Cairngorm Brewery Co Ltd, Unit 12 Dalfaber Industrial Estate, Aviemore, Highlands, PH22 1ST
Tel (01479) 812222
✉ info@cairngormbrewery.com
⊕ cairngormbrewery.com

Shop Mon-Fri 9am-4.30pm (Online shop also available)
Tours by arrangement

⊕ The brewery has enjoyed much success since winning Champion Beer of Scotland in 2004 and 2005, and gold medals at GBBF in 2004 and 2005. Seven regular cask beers are produced along with a rolling programme of seasonal ales throughout the year. Expansion was completed in spring 2005 taking fermentation capacity to 90 barrels. The free trade is supplied as far as the central belt with national delivery via wholesalers. Seasonal beers (available for more than one month): White Lady (ABV 4.7%, spring), Blessed Thistle (ABV 4.5%, summer).

Stag (OG 1040, ABV 4.1%)
A drinkable best bitter with plenty of hop bitterness throughout. This tawny brew has some malt in the lingering bitter aftertaste.

Trade Winds (OG 1043, ABV 4.3%) 🍴 🖒
A massive citrus fruit, hop and elderflower nose leads to hints of grapefruit and apricot in the mouth. The exceptional bittersweetness in the taste lasts through the long, lingering aftertaste.

Black Gold (OG 1044, ABV 4.4%) 🍴
Worthy Championship-winning beer with many accolades. Roast malt dominates but the liquorice and blackcurrant in the taste and nose give it a background sweetness. Very long, dry, bitter finish.

Nessies Monster Mash (OG 1044, ABV 4.4%)
A good, traditional, English-type bitter with plenty of bitterness and light malt flavour. Lingering bitterness in the aftertaste with diminishing sweetness.

Cairngorm Gold (OG 1044, ABV 4.5%)

Sheepshaggers Gold (OG 1044, ABV 4.5%)
A golden amber brew with faint aromas and tastes of grapefruit and passion fruit. Some light bitterness in the otherwise sweet aftertaste.

Wildcat (OG 1049.5, ABV 5.1%)
A full-bodied strong bitter. Malt predominates but there is an underlying hop character through to the well-balanced aftertaste.

Caledonian

Caledonian Brewing Co Ltd, 42 Slateford Road, Edinburgh, EH11 1PH
Tel (0131) 337 1286
✉ info@caledonian-brewery.co.uk
⊕ caledonian-brewery.co.uk
Tours by arrangement

The brewery was founded by Lorimer and Clark in 1869 and was sold to Vaux of Sunderland in 1919. In 1987 the brewery was saved from closure by a management buy-out. The brewery site was purchased by Scottish & Newcastle in 2004 but is operated on its behalf by Caledonian, which still an independently owned company. A rolling programme of seasonal ales are also produced. S&N has axed McEwan's cask 80/- brewed at Caledonian. In 2006, CBC bought the Harviestoun Brewery (qv).

Deuchars IPA (OG 1039, ABV 3.8%)
Tasty and refreshing, pale golden session beer. Hops and fruit are evident and are

balanced by malt. The lingering aftertaste is bitter and hoppy.

80 (OG 1042, ABV 4.1%)
A predominantly malty, copper-coloured beer with hop and fruit. A Scottish heavy that lacks any complexity or significant hoppiness.

XPA (ABV 4.3%)

Callow Top

See Haywood Bad Ram

Cambridge Moonshine

Cambridge Moonshine Brewery, 28 Radegund Road, Cambridge, Cambridgeshire, CB1 3RS
Tel 07906 066794
✉ mark.watch@ntlworld.com

A micro-brewery established in 2004. A new 2.5-barrel plant was installed in 2006. Plans for the future are to move to larger premises. The brewery concentrates on supplying CAMRA beer festivals, with two outlets supplied direct. Bottle-conditioned beers: Porter (ABV 5.8%), Red Watch, Mulberry Whale.

Harvest Moon Mild (OG 1040, ABV 3.8%)

Mulberry Whale Bitter (OG 1040, ABV 4%)

Red Watch Blueberry Ale (OG 1042, ABV 4.4%)

Black Hole Stout (OG 1044, ABV 4.5%)

Pigs Ear Porter (OG 1048, ABV 4.7%)

Cambrinus SIBA

Cambrinus Craft Brewery, Home Farm, Knowsley Park, Knowsley, Merseyside, L34 4AQ
Tel (0151) 546 2226

⊗ Established in 1997, Cambrinus is housed in part of a former farm building on a private estate. It produces around 250 hectolitres a year on a five-barrel plant. Some 45 outlets are supplied on a regular basis in and around Lancashire, Cheshire and Cumbria. The brewery supply own label beer to Knowsley Safari Park in filtered bottle form. Seasonal beers: Bootstrap (ABV 4.5%, spring), Fruit Wheat Beer (summer), St Georges Ale (ABV 4.5%, Apr), Clogdance (ABV 3.6%, May), Solstice (ABV 3.8%, Jun), Honeywheat (ABV 3.7%, Jul), Dark Harvest (ABV 4%, autumn), Hearts of Oak (ABV 5%, Oct), Parkin (ABV 3.8%, Nov), Lamp Oil (ABV 4.5%, winter), Celebrance (ABV 5.5%, Christmas).

Herald (OG 1036, ABV 3.7%)
Light summer drinking bitter, pale and refreshing.

Yardstick (OG 1040, ABV 4%)
Mild, malty and lightly hopped.

Deliverance (OG 1040, ABV 4.2%)
Pale premium bitter.

Endurance (OG 1045, ABV 4.3%)
IPA-style, smooth and hoppy, fermented in oak.

Camerons

Camerons Brewery Ltd, Lion Brewery, Hartlepool, Co Durham, TS24 7QS

Tel (01429) 266666
✉ **martindutoy@cameronsbrewery.com**
⊕ **cameronsbrewery.com**
Shop Tue-Sun 10am-4pm
Tours by arrangement

☺ Founded in 1865, Camerons was bought in 2002 by Castle Eden brewery, which moved production to Hartlepool. In 2003 a 10-barrel micro-brewery, known as the Lion's Den, was commissioned in a separate building. This gives the company the capability of brewing small batches of guest beers and includes a bottling line. Around 60 pubs are owned, with six selling real ale. Seasonal beers: Spring Knights (ABV 4%), Summer Knights (ABV 4.2%), Autumn Knights (ABV 4.2%), Winter Royal Knights (ABV 5%).

Bitter (OG 1036, ABV 3.6%) ◆
A light bitter, but well-balanced, with hops and malt.

Strongarm (OG 1041, ABV 4%) ◆
A well-rounded, ruby-red ale with a distinctive, tight creamy head; initially fruity, but with a good balance of malt, hops and moderate bitterness.

Castle Eden Ale (OG 1043, ABV 4.2%) ◆
A light, creamy, malty sweet ale with fruit notes and a mellow dry bitterness in the finish.

Nimmos XXXX (OG 1045, ABV 4.4%) ◆
Light golden beer with a well-balanced character derived from English malt and Goldings hops.

For Scottish & Newcastle:

John Smith's Magnet (OG 1039.8, ABV 4%)

Canavans

Canavans Liverpool Brewery, Unit 29 Barclays Business Park, Wareing Road, Aintree, Liverpool, L9 7AU
Tel 07951 210972
Tours by arrangement

Canavans has been brewing since 2005 on a five-barrel plant. 10 outlets are supplied.

Two Churches Bitter (OG 1040, ABV 4.5%) ◆
Fairly bitter brown beer with balanced malt and hop flavours.

Dublin to Liverpool Stout (OG 1040, ABV 4.5%) ◆
Dry stout with a long, dry aftertaste. Sharp acidic bite leads to an intense roast flavour that follows through to the aftertaste.

Milligans Lager (OG 1042, ABV 4.7%)

Cannon Royall SIBA

⌂ **Cannon Royall Brewery Ltd, Fruiterer's Arms, Uphampton Lane, Ombersley, Worcestershire, WR9 0JW**
Tel (01905) 621161
✉ **info@cannonroyall.co.uk**
⊕ **cannonroyall.co.uk**
Tours by arrangement (CAMRA only)

Cannon Royall's first brew was in 1993 in a converted cider house behind the Fruiterer's Arms. It has increased capacity from five barrels to more than 16 a week. The brewery supplies a number of outlets throughout the Midlands. Seasonal beers are regularly produced. Bottle-conditioned beers: Fruiterers Mild, King's Shilling, Arrowhead Bitter and Muzzle Loader.

Fruiterer's Mild (OG 1037, ABV 3.7%) ◆
This black-hued brew has rich malty aromas that lead to a fruity mix of bitter hops and sweetness, and a short balanced aftertaste.

King's Shilling (OG 1038, ABV 3.8%) ◆
A golden bitter that packs a citrus hoppy punch throughout.

Arrowhead Bitter (OG 1039, ABV 3.9%) ◆
A powerful punch of hops attack the nose before the feast of bitterness. The memory of this golden brew fades too soon.

Muzzle Loader (OG 1042, ABV 4.2%) ◆
The lingering aftertaste bears witness to this amber liquid's agreeable balance of malt and hoppy flavours that is evident in the aroma and palate.

Arrowhead Extra (OG 1045, ABV 4.3%)
An intense hop aroma with some sweetness on the palate. The finish is long and bitter.

Captain Cook SIBA

⌂ **Captain Cook Brewery Ltd, White Swan, 1 West End, Stokesley, North Yorkshire, TS9 5BL**
Tel (01642) 710263
⊕ **thecaptaincookbrewery.co.uk**
Tours by arrangement

The 18th-century White Swan concentrated on promoting real ale for 10 years before taking on the challenge of becoming a brew-pub. The brewery, with a four-barrel plant, started operations in 1999 and was opened by White Swan regular James Cook on his 79th birthday. Seasonal beer: Black Porter (ABV 4.4%, autumn/winter).

Sunset (OG 1040, ABV 4%)
An extremely smooth light ale with a good balance of malt and hops.

Slipway (OG 1042, ABV 4%)
A light-coloured hoppy ale with bitterness coming through from Challenger hops. A full-flavoured ale with a smooth malt aftertaste.

Carter's*

⌂ **Carter's Brewery, White Hart Inn, White Hart Lane, Machen, CF83 8QQ**
Tel (01633) 441005
✉ **acarter@whitehartinn.wanadoo.co.uk**

Carter's started in 2002 on a 1.5-barrel plant and only brews for the pub and local beer festivals.

Last Bus (ABV 4%)

Machen Best (ABV 4.2%)

BFB (ABV 4.5%)

Tits Up (ABV 4.7%)

Castle Rock SIBA

Castle Rock Brewery, Queens Bridge Road, Nottingham, NG2 1NB
Tel (0115) 985 1615

✉ admin@castlerockbrewery.co.uk
⏣ castlerockbrewery.co.uk
Tours by arrangement

☺ Castle Rock has been brewing next door to
the Vat & Fiddle pub since 1998; the brewery is
a trading division of the Tynemill pub group.
Production now runs at around 80 barrels a week
and is distributed on a local and national basis. It
also supplies the Tynemill estate with its own
and reciprocated beers. A different beer with a
wildlife theme is brewed every month in
conjunction with the Nottingham Wildlife Trust.
Work to complete a brewery visitor centre should
be completed shortly. See website for up-to-date
details. Seasonal beers: Nottingham Dark Stout
(ABV 4.5%, winter), Snowhite (ABV 4.2%).
Bottle-conditioned beers: Elsie Mo, Hemlock.

Black Gold (OG 1035, ABV 3.5%)
Hints of caramel and fruit balanced by
bitterness in this dark mild.

Nottingham Gold (OG 1035, ABV 3.5%)
Full flavoured for its strength. A subtle toffee
sweetness quickly gives way to a crisp
dryness. Used as the house beer in many
Tynemill pubs.

Harvest Pale (OG 1037, ABV 3.8%) ▣ ▢
Assertive citrus hop bitterness with some
underlying sweetness leading to a refreshing
zesty finish.

Hemlock (OG 1040, ABV 4%)
Aromas of dried fruit enhance this well-
rounded, bittersweet session beer.

Elsie Mo (OG 1045, ABV 4.7%)
Blond beer with a subtle floral nose and
lemongrass freshness delivering a clean
finish.

Caythorpe SIBA

**Caythorpe Brewery Ltd, c/o Black Horse, 29 Main
Street, Caythorpe, Nottinghamshire, NG14 7ED**
Tel (0115) 966 4933/07913 434922
✉ caythorpebrewery@btinternet.com

Caythorpe was set up using a 2.5-barrel
brewery in a building at the rear of the Black
Horse pub in 1997. Ownership changed in 2005
but the brewery continues to produce its small
range of beers that have a big reputation in the
local area. Seasonal beers: Winter Light (ABV
3.6%, autumn/winter), One Swallow (ABV
3.6%, spring/summer).

Bitter (OG 1034.7, ABV 3.7%)

Dover Beck (OG 1037, ABV 4%)

Stout Fellow (OG 1038.6, ABV 4.2%)

Chalk Hill

Chalk Hill Brewery, Rosary Road, Norwich, NR1 4DA
Tel (01603) 477078
✉ chalkhillinns@ntlworld.com

Chalk Hill began production in 1993 on a 15-
barrel plant. It supplies local pubs and festivals.

Tap Bitter (OG 1036, ABV 3.6%) ◥
A pale brown brew with a gentle fruity nose.
Lightly flavoured with apple notes among a
malty support. Fading finish with a hint of
bitterness.

CHB (OG 1042, ABV 4.2%) ◥
A copper-coloured brew with a dominant
bitter flavour. Hops in the bouquet continue
through and give a dry, lingering aftertaste.
Background maltiness gives balance.

Gold (ABV 4.3%) ◥
A well-balanced golden ale. Malt, hops, citrus
notes and bitterness can all be found in
subtle amounts in both the aroma and taste.
Surprisingly long finish develops a slight
dryness.

Dreadnought (OG 1049, ABV 4.9%) ◥
A rich plummy fruitiness pervades the nose
and taste of this mid-brown strong bitter.
Malt joins with a caramel and roast
background to give depth. Sweetness outlasts
a quick finish.

Flintknapper's Mild (OG 1052, ABV 5%) ◥
Chocolate, stewed fruits, liquorice, hops and
malt can all be found in this rich, red-
coloured brew. The light malt nose belies the
variety of flavours.

Old Tackle (OG 1056, ABV 5.6%) ◥
Red hued with a blackcurrant bouquet, this
rich malty brew slowly subsides to a long
dryish end. Roast notes remain consistent.

Cheddar*

**J.R. Ham t/a Cheddar Ales, Winchester Farm,
Draycott Road, Cheddar, Somerset, BS27 3RP**
Tel (01934) 744193
✉ jem@cheddarales.co.uk
⏣ cheddarales.co.uk
Shop open Mon-Fri 8am-4pm; Sat-Sun 9am-2pm by
appointment
Tours by arrangement

⊗ Cheddar Ales is a 20-barrel brewery set up in
2007 by former Butcombe brewer Jeremy Ham.
The kit was sourced from a barn in Dublin,
where it had sat unused for six years. Some 40
outlets are supplied.

Best Bitter (OG 1040, ABV 4%) ◥
Noticeably bitter ale with hints of caramel
and an astringent finish.

Potholer (OG 1043.5, ABV 4.3%) ◥
Amber malty best bitter, biscuity aroma and
citrus in the mouth. Bitter fruit afterstaste.

Chiltern SIBA

**Chiltern Brewery, Nash Lee Road, Terrick,
Aylesbury, Buckinghamshire, HP17 0TQ**
Tel (01296) 613647
✉ info@chilternbrewery.co.uk
⏣ chilternbrewery.co.uk
Shop Mon-Sat 9am-5pm
Tours by arrangement every Saturday at noon and
weekdays for groups

Founded in 1980, the brewery is one of the first
dozen micro-breweries to have been
established in the country and is the oldest
independent brewery in the Chilterns. This
second generation family brewery produces a
broad range of beers with English ingredients.
Seasonal beers: Chiltern's Nut Brown Mild (ABV
3.9%, spring), Cobblestones (ABV 3.5%,
summer), Copper Beech (ABV 4.4%, autumn),
Glad Tidings (ABV 4.6%, winter). Bottle-

conditioned beers: Glad Tidings, Bodgers Barley Wine (ABV 8.5%).

Ale (OG 1037, ABV 3.7%) ◆
An amber, refreshing beer with a slight fruit aroma, leading to a good malt/bitter balance in the mouth. The aftertaste is bitter and dry.

Beechwood Bitter (OG 1043, ABV 4.3%) ◆
This pale brown beer has a balanced butterscotch/toffee aroma, with a slight hop note. The taste balances bitterness and sweetness, leading to a long bitter finish.

Three Hundreds Old Ale (OG 1049, ABV 4.9%) ◆
A complex, copper-coloured, old ale. The mixed fruit/caramel aroma leads to a balanced taste, with sweetness slightly dominating. The finish starts sweet and leads to a long-lasting bitterness.

Church End SIBA

Church End Brewery Ltd, 109 Ridge Lane, Nuneaton, Warwickshire, CV10 0RD
Tel (01827) 713080
✉ stuart@churchendbrewery.co.uk
⊕ churchendbrewery.co.uk
Shop during tap opening hours
Tours by arrangement

⊠ Stewart Elliot started brewing in 1994 in an old coffin shop in Shustoke. He moved to the present site and upgraded to a 10-barrel plant in 2001. The brewery tap was opened on the same site a year later. A portfolio of around 60 irregular beers are produced as well as many one-off specials, including fruit, herb and spice beers. Some 500 outlets are supplied. Seasonal beers: Without-a-Bix (ABV 4.2%), Pews Porter (ABV 4.5%), Old Pal (ABV 5.5%), Arthurs Wit (ABV 6%), Rest-in-Peace (ABV 7%). Bottle-conditioned beers: Nuns Ale (ABV 4.5%), Rugby Ale (ABV 5%), Arthurs Wit.

Poachers Pocket (ABV 3.5%)

Pheasant Plucker (ABV 3.7%)

Cuthberts (ABV 3.8%) ◆
A refreshing, hoppy beer, with hints of malt, fruit and caramel taste. Lingering bitter aftertaste.

Goat's Milk (ABV 3.8%)

Gravediggers Ale (ABV 3.8%) ◆
A premium mild. Black and red in colour, with a complex mix of chocolate and roast flavours, it is almost a light porter.

Hop Gun (ABV 4.1%)

What the Fox's Hat (ABV 4.2%) ◆
A beer with a malty aroma, and a hoppy and malty taste with some caramel flavour.

Pooh Bear (ABV 4.3%)

Vicar's Ruin (ABV 4.4%) ◆
A straw-coloured best bitter with an initially hoppy, bitter flavour, softening to a delicate malt finish.

Stout Coffin (ABV 4.6%)

Fallen Angel (ABV 5%)

For Cape of Good Hope, Warwick:

Two Llocks (ABV 4%)

City of Cambridge EAB

City of Cambridge Brewery Co Ltd, Ely Road, Chittering, Cambridge, CB5 9PH
Tel (01223) 864864
✉ sales@cambridge-brewery.co.uk
⊕ cambridge-brewery.co.uk

⊠ City of Cambridge opened in 1997 and moved to its present site in 2002. In addition to prizes for its cask beers, the brewery holds a conservation award for the introduction of native reed beds at its site to treat brewery water. Seasonal ales (subject to availability): Jet Black (ABV 3.7%), Bramling Traditional (ABV 5.5%), Drummer St Stout (ABV 4.5%), Mich'aelmas (ABV 4.6%), Holly Heaven (ABV 5.2%). All beers are available in bottle-conditioned form.

Boathouse Bitter (ABV 3.8%) ◆
Copper-brown and full-bodied session bitter, starting with impressive citrus and floral hop; grassy fruit notes are present with finally a gentle bitterness.

Rutherford IPA (ABV 3.8%) ◆
Satisfying session bitter with a soft hoppy, bittersweet balance and a light sulphury character. This amber brew ends dry and bitter with a light balance of malt and hops.

Hobson's Choice (ABV 4.1%) ◆
A highly drinkable, golden brew with a pronounced hop aroma and taste, and a fruity, bitter balance in the mouth, finishing dry.

Sunset Square (ABV 4.4%)
A blend of two best-selling beers to create a unique smooth flavour. A pleasing, golden colour, with a refreshing aftertaste.

Atom Splitter (ABV 4.7%) ◆
Robust copper-coloured strong bitter with a hop aroma and taste, and a distinct sulphury edge.

Darwin's Downfall (ABV 5%)
A blended, ruby-golden coloured beer. Hoppy with a fruity character and a refreshing citrus aftertaste.

Parkers Porter (ABV 5.3%) ◆
Impressive reddish brew with a defined roast character throughout, and a short, fruity, bittersweet palate.

Bramling Traditional (ABV 5.5%)
Made with Bramling Cross hops, fruity and delicious.

City of Stirling

See Traditional Scottish Ales

Clark's SIBA

HB Clark & Co (Successors) Ltd, Westgate Brewery, Wakefield, West Yorkshire, WF2 9SW
Tel (01924) 373328
✉ phillip.owen@hbclark.co.uk
⊕ hbclark.co.uk
Tours by arrangement

☺ Founded in 1906, Clark's recently celebrated its centenary. It ceased brewing during the 1960s/70s but resumed cask ale production in 1982 and now delivers to more than 170 outlets. Four pubs are owned, all serving cask ale. Seasonal beers: see website.

Classic Blonde (OG 1039, ABV 3.9%)
A light-coloured ale with a citrus and hoppy flavour, a distinctive grapefruit aroma and a dry finish.

No Angel (OG 1040, ABV 4%)
A bitter with a dry hop finish, well-balanced and full of flavour. Pale brown in colour with hints of fruit and hops.

Westgate Gold (OG 1042, ABV 4.2%)
A light-coloured, fruity beer with a full body and rich aroma.

Rams Revenge (OG 1046, ABV 4.6%) ◆
A rich, ruby-coloured premium ale, well-balanced with malt and hops, with a deep fruity taste and a dry hoppy aftertaste, with a pleasant hoppy aroma.

Clearwater SIBA

Clearwater Brewery, 2 Devon Units, Hatchmoor Industrial Estate, Torrington, Devon, EX38 7HP
Tel (01805) 625242
✉ brian@clearwaterbrewery.co.uk
Tours by arrangement

⊗ Clearwater took on the closed St Giles in the Wood brewery in 1999 and has steadily grown since. The brewery has a 10-12 barrel capacity and the owners plan to bottle their beers. Around 80 outlets are supplied. Seasonal/occasional beers: Ebony & Ivory (ABV 4.2%, winter), 1646 (ABV 4.8%). Bottle-conditioned beers: Cavalier Ale, Oliver's Nectar.

Village Pride (ABV 3.7%)

Cavalier Ale (OG 1041, ABV 4%) ◆
Mid-brown, full-bodied best bitter with a burnt, rich malt aroma and taste, leading to a bitter, well-rounded finish.

Torridge Best (OG 1044, ABV 4.4%)

Oliver's Nectar (OG 1051, ABV 5.2%)

Clockwork

⚑ Athol Sky Ltd t/a Clockwork Beer Company, 1153 Cathcart Road, Glasgow, G42 9HB
Tel (0141) 649 0184

⊗ Set up in 1997 by Robin Graham, Clockwork is a five-barrel brew plant in the middle of a bar. The beers are kept in cellar tanks where fermentation gases from the conditioning vessel blanket the beers on tap (but not under pressure). A wide range of ales, lagers and specials are produced. Most beers are naturally gassed while some, such as Lager and Gosch, are pressurised.

Amber (ABV 3.8%)

Autumn Ale (ABV 4.1%)

Red Alt (ABV 4.4%)

Ginger (ABV 5%)

Oregon (ABV 5.5%)

Coach House SIBA

Coach House Brewing Co Ltd, Wharf Street, Warrington, Cheshire, WA1 2DQ

Tel (01925) 232800
✉ info@coach-house-brewing.co.uk
⊕ coach-house-brewing.co.uk
Tours by arrangement for CAMRA groups

☺ The brewery was founded in 1991 by four ex-Greenall Whitley employees. In 1995 Coach House increased its brewing capacity to cope with growing demand and it now delivers to around 250 outlets throughout Britain, either from the brewery or via wholesalers. The brewery also brews a large number of one-off and special beers. Seasonal beers: Ostlers Summer Pale Ale (ABV 4%, summer), Squires Gold (ABV 4.2%, spring), Summer Sizzler (ABV 4.2%, summer), Countdown (ABV 4.7%, 6 Dec onwards), Taverners Autumn Ale (ABV 5%), Blunderbus Old Porter (ABV 5.5%, winter).

Coachman's Best Bitter (OG 1037, ABV 3.7%) ◆
A well-hopped, malty bitter, moderately fruity with a hint of sweetness and a peppery nose.

Gunpowder Mild (OG 1037, ABV 3.8%) ◆
Biscuity dark mild with a blackcurrant sweetness. Bitterness and fruit dominate with some hints of caramel and a slightly stronger roast flavour.

Honeypot Bitter (OG 1037, ABV 3.8%)

Farrier's Best Bitter (OG 1038, ABV 3.9%)

Dick Turpin (OG 1042, ABV 4.2%) ◆
Malty, hoppy pale brown beer with some initial sweetish flavours leading to a short, bitter aftertaste. Sold under other names as a pub house beer.

Flintlock Pale Ale (OG 1044, ABV 4.4%)

Innkeeper's Special Reserve (OG 1045, ABV 4.5%) ◆
A darkish, full-flavoured bitter. Quite fruity, with a strong, bitter aftertaste.

Postlethwaite (OG 1045, ABV 4.6%) ◆
Thin bitter with a short, dry aftertaste. Biscuity malt dominates.

Gingernut Premium (OG 1050, ABV 5%)

Posthorn Premium (OG 1050, ABV 5%) ▣ ◆
Dry golden bitter with a blackcurrant fruitiness and good hop flavours leading to a strong, dry finish. Well-balanced but slightly thin for its gravity.

For John Joule of Stone:

Old Knotty (ABV 3.6%)

Old Priory (ABV 4.4%)

Victory (ABV 5.2%)

Coastal*

Coastal Brewery, Unit 9B Cardrew Industrial Estate, Redruth, Cornwall, TR15 1SS
Tel 07875 405407
✉ coastalbrewery@tiscali.co.uk

Coastal was set up in 2006 on a five-barrel plant by Alan Hinde, former brewer for the Borough Arms in Crewe, Cheshire. A seasonal beer and monthly specials are planned.

Cascade (OG 1040, ABV 3.9%)

Handliner (OG 1041, ABV 4.1%)

Angelina (OG 1042, ABV 4.1%)

Golden Hinde (OG 1044, ABV 4.3%)

Cornish Gold (OG 1057, ABV 5.5%)

Cock & Hen*

Cock & Hen Brew Pub, 360 North End Road, Fulham, London, SW6 1LY
Tel (020) 7385 6021

⊗ The pub is part of the Capital Pub Co chain part owned by former Firkin brewpub founder David Bruce. There are plans to install brewing equipment in other pubs in the chain. The Cock & Hen has a four-barrel plant built by David Porter of Porter Brewing. Other beers will be added.

Bonovo (OG 1045, ABV 4.5%)
Dark and fruity with hop balance.

Coles

⇩ **Coles Family Brewery, White Hart Thatched Inn & Brewery, Llanddarog, Carmarthen, SA32 8NT**
Tel (01267) 275395
Tours by arrangement

Coles is based in an ancient inn built in 1371. Centuries ago beer was brewed on site, but brewing only started again in 1999. The brewery has its own water supply 320 feet below ground, free from pollution. Coles makes a large selection of cask ales due to a system that allows small-batch production. Two pubs are owned. Seasonal beers: Cwrw Nadolig (ABV 3%, Xmas), Summer Harvest (ABV 3.8%).

Nettle Ale (OG 1039, ABV 3.8%)

Amber Ale (OG 1042, ABV 4%)

Black Stag (OG 1042, ABV 4%)

Cwrw Betys Beetroot Ale (OG 1042, ABV 4%)

Liquorice Stout (OG 1042, ABV 4%)

Oaten Barley Stout (OG 1042, ABV 4%)

Roasted Barley Stout (OG 1042, ABV 4%)

Cwrw Llanddarog (OG 1043, ABV 4.1%)

Cwrw Blasus (OG 1044, ABV 4.3%)

Dewi Sant (OG 1045, ABV 4.4%)

College Green

College Green Brewery,
1 College Green Mews,
Botanic Avenue, Belfast, BT7 1LW
Tel (02890) 322600/(02892) 660800
✉ info@collegegreenbrewery.com
⊕ www.collegegreenbrewery.com
Tours by arrangement

☺ College Green was set up in 2005 by Owen Scullion as a sister brewery to Hilden Brewery. Located in Belfast's lively university area, College Green (the city's only brewery) is housed in a tiny 19th-century coach house and brews for Molly's Yard Restaurant in the adjoining stables building.

Molly's Chocolate Stout (OG 1042, ABV 4.2%)
A dark chocolate-coloured beer with a full-bodied character due to the use of whole malted oats. A small amount of pure cocoa is added to give added credence to the name.

Headless Dog (OG 1042, ABV 4.3%)
A bright amber ale, using Munich malt. The well-hopped beer is named after the mural of a headless dog at the front of the brewery.

Belfast Blonde (OG 1047, ABV 4.7%)
A natural blonde beer with a clean and refreshing character, derived from the use of lager malt along with a small proportion of maize.

Combe Martin

Combe Martin Brewery, 4 Springfield Terrace, High Street, Combe Martin, Devon, EX34 0EE
Tel (01271) 883507

Combe Martin started by making country wine, then moved on to beer and cider. It operates from the kitchen and backyard of the owner's house on a one-barrel plant. Five outlets are supplied direct.

Past Times (OG 1036, ABV 3.9%)

Hangman's Bitter (OG 1044, ABV 4.5%)

Shammick Ale (OG 1062, ABV 6.2%)

Concertina SIBA

⇩ **Concertina Brewery, 9a Dolcliffe Road, Mexborough, South Yorkshire, S64 9AZ**
Tel (01709) 580841
Tours by arrangement

The brewery started in 1992 in the cellar of a club once famous as the home of a long-gone concertina band. The plant produces up to eight barrels a week for the club and other occasional outlets. Other beers are brewed on a seasonal basis, including Room at the Inn at Xmas.

Club Bitter (ABV 3.9%) ✦
A fruity session bitter with a good bitter flavour.

Old Dark Attic (OG 1038, ABV 3.9%)
A dark brown beer with a fairly sweet, fruity taste.

One Eyed Jack (OG 1039, ABV 4%)
Fairly pale in colour with plenty of hop bitterness. Brewed with the same malt and hop combination as Bengal Tiger, but more of a session beer. Also badged as Mexborough Bitter.

Bengal Tiger (OG 1043, ABV 4.6%) ✦
Light amber ale with an aromatic hoppy nose followed by a combination of fruit and bitterness.

Dictators (OG 1044, ABV 4.7%)

Ariel Square Four (OG 1046, ABV 5.2%)

Coniston SIBA

Coniston Brewing Co Ltd, Coppermines Road, Coniston, Cumbria, LA21 8HL
Tel (01539) 441133
✉ sales@conistonbrewery.com
⊕ conistonbrewery.com
Shop (in Black Bull Inn) 10am-11pm
Tours by arrangement

☺ A 10-barrel brewery set up in 1995 behind the Black Bull inn, Coniston. It now brews 40 barrels a week and supplies 50 local outlets while the beers are distributed nationally by wholesalers. One pub is owned. Bottle-conditioned Coniston beers are brewed by Refresh UK using Hepworth's Horsham plant: Bluebird (ABV 4.2%), Bluebird XB (ABV 4.4%), Oldman Ale (ABV 4.8%).

Bluebird Bitter (OG 1036, ABV 3.6%) ◆
A yellow-gold, predominantly hoppy and fruity beer, well-balanced with some sweetness and a rising bitter finish.

Bluebird XB (OG 1040.5, ABV 4.2%) ◆
Well-balanced, hoppy and fruity golden bitter. Bitter-sweet in the mouth with dryness building.

Oldman Ale (OG 1040.5, ABV 4.2%) ◆
Delicious fruity, winey beer with a complex, well-balanced richness.

Quicksilver (OG 1044, ABV 4.3%)
A golden amber ale, smooth and fruity with malt and hop tones.

Blacksmiths Ale (OG 1047.5, ABV 5%)
A well-balanced strong bitter with hints of Xmas pudding.

Consett Ale Works

⌂ Consett Ale Works Ltd, Grey Horse, 115 Sherburn Terrace, Consett, Co Durham, DH8 6NE
Tel (01207) 502585
✉ jeffhind@aol.com
⊕ thegreyhorse.co.uk
Tours by arrangement

☺ The brewery opened in 2006 in the stables of a former coaching inn, the Grey Horse, Consett's oldest pub at 159 years old. Some 20 outlets are supplied direct.

Steel Town Bitter (ABV 3.8%)

White Hot (ABV 4%)

Cast Iron (ABV 4.1%)

Red Dust (ABV 4.5%)

Conwy

Conwy Brewery Ltd, Unit 3 Morfa Conwy Enterprise Park, Parc Caer Selon, Conwy, LL32 8FA
Tel (01492) 585287
✉ enquiries@conwybrewery.co.uk
⊕ conwybrewery.co.uk
Tours by arrangement

☺ Conwy started brewing in 2003 and was the first brewery in Conwy for at least 100 years. Due to steady growth they have recently moved premises. Around 50 outlets are supplied. All cask beers are also available bottle conditioned. Seasonal beers: Sun Dance/Dawns Haul (ABV 4%, summer), Telford Porter (ABV 5.6%, autumn), Hoppy Xmas/Nadolig Hopus (ABV 4.3%, Dec).

Castle Bitter/Cwrw Castell (OG 1037, ABV 3.8%) ◆
Malty session bitter with some toffee and caramel notes in the aroma and taste. Full, smooth mouthfeel leading to a satisfying hoppy finish.

Welsh Pride/Balchder Cymru (OG 1040, ABV 4%)

Celebration Ale (OG 1041, ABV 4.2%)

Honey Fayre/Cwrw Mêl (OG 1044, ABV 4.5%) ◆
Amber best bitter with hints of honey sweetness in the taste balanced by an increasingly hoppy, bitter finish. Slightly watery mouthfeel for a beer of this strength.

Special/Arbennig (OG 1043, ABV 4.5%) ◆
Rich, fruity and smooth dark bitter. Fruit dominates the aroma and leads into the flavour where malt is also prominent, as are some nuttiness and roasty hints. Dry aftertaste.

For Cobdens Hotel, Capel Curig:

Cobdens Hotel Bitter/Cwrw Gwesty Cobdens (OG 1040, ABV 4.1%)

Copper Dragon SIBA

Copper Dragon Brewery Ltd, Snaygill Industrial Estate, Keighley Road, Skipton, North Yorkshire, BD23 2QR
Tel (01756) 702130
✉ post@copperdragon.uk.com
⊕ copperdragon.uk.com
Shop Mon-Fri 11am-5pm; Sat 11am-2pm
Tours by arrangement

☺ Copper Dragon began brewing in 2003 and now brews 250 barrels a week, using German plant. The company supplies the free trade within a 100-mile radius of Skipton. The brewery is acquiring its own outlets in Lancashire and Yorkshire with plans to expand production. More than 1,200 outlets are supplied, with half as permanent stockists. There are plans in 2008 to double production on a new site.

Black Gold (OG 1036, ABV 3.7%) ◆
A dark ale with subtle fruit and dark malts on the nose. Quite bitter with roast coffee flavours and a long burnt and bitter finish.

Best Bitter (OG 1036, ABV 3.8%) ◆
A gently hoppy, fruity aroma leads to an aggressively bitter and hoppy taste, with a bitter finish.

Golden Pippin (OG 1037, ABV 3.9%) ⬚ ◆
This straw-coloured beer has an intense citrus aroma and flavour, characteristic of American Cascade hops. The dry, bitter astringency increases in the aftertaste.

Scotts 1816 (OG 1041, ABV 4.1%) ⬚ ◆
A well-balanced, full-bodied, copper-coloured premium bitter with a fruity, hoppy tropical fruit character. Bitterness increases in the finish to leave a dry, hoppy fruitiness.

Challenger IPA (OG 1042, ABV 4.4%) ◆
Amber-coloured, this is more of a best bitter than a traditional IPA, with a fruity hoppiness in the aroma and taste and a growing dry bitter finish.

Corvedale SIBA

⌂ Corvedale Brewery, Sun Inn, Corfton, Craven Arms, Shropshire, SY7 9DF
Tel (01584) 861239
✉ normanspride@aol.com
⊕ suninncorfton.co.uk
Tours by arrangement

☺ Brewing started in 1999 in a building behind

the pub. Landlord Norman Pearce is also the brewer and he uses only British malt and hops, with water from a local borehole. One pub is owned and 100 outlets are supplied. Seasonal beer: Teresa's Pride (ABV 4.6%, Jan). All beers are on sale in the pub in bottle-conditioned form and are suitable for vegetarians and vegans.

Katie's Pride (OG 1040, ABV 4.3%)

Norman's Pride (OG 1043, ABV 4.3%)
A golden amber beer with a refreshing, slightly hoppy taste and a bitter finish.

Secret Hop (OG 1045, ABV 4.5%)
A clear, ruby bitter with a smooth malty taste. Customers are invited to guess the hop!

Dark and Delicious (OG 1045, ABV 4.6%)
A dark ruby beer with hops on the aroma and palate, and a sweet aftertaste.

Cotleigh SIBA

Cotleigh Brewery Ltd, Ford Road, Wiveliscombe, Somerset, TA4 2RE
Tel (01984) 624086
✉ sales@cotleighbrewery.com
⊕ cotleighbrewery.co.uk
Shop 9am-4pm
Tours by arrangement for select CAMRA groups

⊗ Situated in the historic brewing town of Wiveliscombe, Cotleigh has become one of the most successful independent breweries in the West Country. The brewery, which started trading in 1979, is housed in specially converted premises with a modern plant capable of producing 165 barrels a week. 300 pubs and 100 retail outlets are supplied; the beers are also widely available through wholesalers. In 2005 a portfolio of six bottled beers was launched. Seasonal beers: Buzzard (ABV 4.8%, Oct-Mar), Buzzard Dark Ale (ABV 4.8%), Peregrine Porter (ABV 5%), Red Nose Reinbeer (ABV 5%, Sep-Dec).

Harrier Lite (OG 1035, ABV 3.5%)
A delicate floral and fruity aroma with a refreshing, sweet and slightly hopped finish.

Tawny Bitter (OG 1038, ABV 3.8%) ◆
Well-balanced, tawny-coloured bitter with plenty of malt and fruitiness on the nose, and malt to the fore in the taste, followed by hop fruit, developing to a satisfying bitter finish.

Cotleigh (OG 1040, ABV 4%)
Bright and golden-coloured. An explosion of flavours originating from American Cascade hops.

Golden Seahawk (OG 1042, ABV 4.2%) ◆
A gold, well-hopped premium bitter with a flowery hop aroma and fruity hop flavour, clean mouthfeel, leading to a dry, hoppy finish.

Barn Owl (OG 1045, ABV 4.5%) ◆
A pale to mid-brown beer with a good balance of malt and hops on the nose; a smooth, full-bodied taste where hops dominate, but balanced by malt, following through to the finish.

Cotswold

Cotswold Brewing Co Ltd, Foxholes Lane, Foscot, Oxfordshire, OX7 6RL
Tel (01608) 659631

✉ lager@cotswoldbrewingcompany.com
⊕ cotswoldbrewingcompany.com
Tours by arrangement

Cotswold Brewing Co is an independent producer of lager and speciality beers. The brewery was established in 2005 with the intention of supplying quality lagers to the local Cotswold market. Inspiration is drawn from continental Europe. The brewery is housed in an old Cotswold stone barn, part of a working farm estate. More than 45 outlets are supplied. Seasonal beer: Winter Lager (ABV 5.3%).

Three Point Eight Lager (OG 1035, ABV 3.8%)

Premium Lager (OG 1044, ABV 5%)

Cotswold Spring

Cotswold Spring Brewery Ltd, Dodington Ash, Chipping Sodbury, Gloucestershire, BS37 6RX
Tel (01454) 323088
✉ info@cotswoldbrewery.com
⊕ cotswoldbrewery.com
Shop Mon-Fri 9am-6pm; Sat 10am-1pm
Tours by arrangement

☺ Cotswold Spring opened in 2005 with a 10-barrel refurbished plant that produces beers brewed using only the finest malted barley, subtle blends of hops and natural Cotswold spring water. All the beers are fermented in traditional vessels using specialist strains of yeast. They contain no artificial preservatives, flavourings or colourings. Seasonal beers: Christmas Old Ale (ABV 5%), Codrington Old Ale (ABV 4.8%), Codrington Winter Royal (ABV 5%).

Old English Rose (OG 1040, ABV 4%) ◆
Beautifully balanced quaffing ale with delicate floral aroma and hints of tropical fruit. Bittersweet finish.

Codrington Codger (OG 1042, ABV 4.2%) ◆
Mid-brown best bitter with the emphasis on malt. Nutty character.

Codrington Royal (OG 1045, ABV 4.5%) ◆
Ruby in colour with dark, sweet malt. Fruity with a hint of dandelion and burdock.

Cottage SIBA

Cottage Brewing Co Ltd, The Old Cheese Dairy, Hornblotton Road, Lovington, Somerset, BA7 7PP
Tel (01963) 240551
Tours by arrangement

⊗ The brewery was established in 1993 in West Lydford and upgraded to a 10-barrel plant in 1994. The brewery moved to larger premises in 1996, doubling brewing capacity at the same time. In 2001, Cottage installed a 30-barrel plant. 1,500 outlets are supplied. The names of beers mostly follow a railway theme. Seasonal beers: Goldrush (ABV 5%), Santa's Steaming Ale (ABV 5.5%, Xmas). Norman's Conquest is also available bottle conditioned.

Southern Bitter (OG 1039, ABV 3.7%) ◆
Gold-coloured beer with malt and fruity hops on the nose. Malt and hops in the mouth with a long fruity, bitter finish.

Broadgauge Bitter (OG 1040, ABV 3.9%)
A light tawny-coloured session bitter with a floral aroma and a balanced bitter finish.

Champflower Ale (OG 1041, ABV 4.2%) ◈
Amber beer with a fruity hop aroma, full hop
taste and powerful bitter finish.

Somerset & Dorset Ale (OG 1044, ABV 4.4%)
A well-hopped, malty brew, with a deep red
colour.

Golden Arrow (OG 1043, ABV 4.5%) ◈
A hoppy golden bitter with a powerful floral
bouquet, a fruity, full-bodied taste and a
lingering dry, bitter finish.

Goldrush (OG 1051, ABV 5%)
A deep golden strong ale brewed with
Cascade hops.

Norman's Conquest (OG 1066, ABV 7%) ◈
A dark strong ale, with plenty of fruit in the
aroma and taste; rounded vinous, hoppy finish.

Country Life SIBA

**Country Life Brewery, The Big Sheep,
Abbotsham, Bideford, Devon, EX39 5AP
Tel (01237) 420808/07971 267790**
✉ simon@countrylifebrewery.co.uk
⊕ countrylifebrewery.co.uk
Shop open 7 days a week 12-4pm
Tours by arrangement

⊗ The brewery is based at the Big Sheep tourist
attraction that welcomes more than 100,000
visitors in the summer. The brewery offers a
beer show and free samples in the shop during
the peak season (Apr-Oct). A 15.5-barrel plant
was installed in 2005, making Country Life the
biggest brewery in north Devon. Bottling is now
carried out on site. Around 100 outlets are
supplied. All cask ales are also available in
bottle-conditioned form. Bottle-conditioned
beers: The 8%-er (ABV 8%), The 10%-er (ABV
10%), Devonshire Ten-der (ABV 10%).

Old Appledore (OG 1037, ABV 3.7%)

Lacey's Ale (OG 1042, ABV 4.2%)

Pot Wallop (OG 1044, ABV 4.4%)

Golden Pig (OG 1046, ABV 4.7%)

Country Bum (OG 1058, ABV 6%)

Cox & Holbrook EAB

**Cox & Holbrook, Manor Farm, Brettenham
Road, Buxhall, Suffolk, IP14 3DY
Tel (01449) 736323**
Tours by arrangement

First opened in 1997, the brewery concentrates
on producing a range of bitters, four of which
are available at any one time, along with more
specialised medium strength beers and milds.
There is also a strong emphasis on the
preservation and resurrection of rare and
traditional styles.

Crown Dark Mild (OG 1037, ABV 3.6%) ◈
Thin tasting at first but plenty of malt,
caramel and roast flavours burst through to
give a thoroughly satisfying beer.

Shelley Dark (OG 1036, ABV 3.6%)
Full-flavoured and satisfying.

Beyton Bitter (OG 1038, ABV 3.8%)
A traditional bitter, pale tawny in colour,
malty with Fuggles and Goldings hops.

Old Mill Bitter (OG 1038, ABV 3.8%)
Pale, hoppy and thirst quenching.

Bridge Road Bitter (OG 1043 ABV 4%)
Brewed exclusively for Grays Athletic FC. A
robust malty bitter with a full hop flavour.

Rattlesden Best Bitter (OG 1043, ABV 4%)
A slightly darker than average, full-bodied
and malty best bitter.

JT's Superlative (OG 1043, ABV 4.2%)
Full-flavoured, mid-range ale bordering on
amber in colour.

Goodcock's Winner (OG 1050, ABV 5%)
An amber ale, rather malty yet not too heavy,
with a sharp hop finish.

Ironoak Single Stout (OG 1051, ABV 5%)
Full-bodied with strong roast grain flavours
and plenty of hop bitterness plus a distinct
hint of oak.

Remus (OG 1051, ABV 5%)
An amber ale, soft on the palate with full
hop flavours but subdued bitterness.

Stormwatch (OG 1052, ABV 5%)
An unusual premium pale ale with a full,
slightly fruity flavour.

Stowmarket Porter (OG 1056, ABV 5%) ◈
Strong caramel flavour and lingering caramel
aftertaste, balanced by full malt and roast
flavours. The overall impression is of a very
sweet beer.

Uncle Stan Single Brown Stout (OG 1053,
ABV 5%)
Unusual soft malt and fruit flavours in a full
and satisfying bit of history.

East Anglian Pale Ale (OG 1059, ABV 6%)
Well-matured, pale beer with a strong
Goldings hops character.

Prentice Strong Dark Ale (OG 1083, ABV 8%)
A strong porter.

Crondall

**Crondall Brewing Co Ltd, Lower Old Park Farm,
Dora's Green Lane, Dora's Green, Nr Crondall,
Hampshire, GU10 5DX
Tel (01252) 319000**
✉ info@crondallbrewery.co.uk
⊕ crondallbrewery.co.uk
Shop Fri 3-7pm; Sat 10am-5pm

Crondall was established in 2005 using a 10-barrel
plant in a converted granary barn. The company
sells to the general public and to local free houses
in the area, and supplies around 75 outlets.
Seasonal beers include Easter Gold, Mr T's Wedding
Ale, Ghoulies, Rocket Fuel, Crondall's Stocking Filler.

Crondall's Best (ABV 4%) ◈
A modest bouquet and initially unassuming
bitter palate, leading to a satisfying dry, bitter
aftertaste.

Sober As A Judge (ABV 4%) ◈
A dark brown best bitter with a malty aroma.
Sharp flavour with some liquorice in the
taste. Short hoppy finish but predominantly
malty and slightly spicy.

Mitchell's Dream (ABV 4.5%)
A ruby-coloured, full-bodied beer with a
malty taste and a subtle hint of hops.

Cropton SIBA

⊽ The New Inn & Cropton Brewery, Woolcroft, Cropton, North Yorkshire, YO18 8HH
Tel (01751) 417330
✉ info@croptonbrewery.co.uk
⊕ croptonbrewery.com
Tours by arrangement

☺ Cropton was established in the cellars of the New Inn in 1984 on a five-barrel plant. This was extended in 1988, but by 1994 it had outgrown the cellar and a purpose-built brewery was installed behind the pub. A brand new state of the art brewery was opened in September 2006 that can produce 100 barrels per week. All the beers, with the exception of Haunting Hanks, are available bottle-conditioned and are suitable for vegetarians and vegans. Seasonal beer: Rudolph's Revenge (ABV 4.6%, winter).

Endeavour Ale (OG 1038, ABV 3.6%)
A light session ale, made with best quality hops, providing a refreshing drink with a delicate fruity aftertaste.

Two Pints (OG 1040, ABV 4%) ◈
A good, full-bodied bitter. Malt flavours initially dominate, with a touch of caramel, but the balancing hoppiness and residual sweetness come through.

Honey Gold (OG 1042, ABV 4.2%) ◈
A medium-bodied beer, ideal for summer drinking. Honey is apparent in both aroma and taste but does not overwhelm. Clean finish with a hint of hops.

Scoresby Stout (OG 1042, ABV 4.2%)

Balmy Mild (OG 1044, ABV 4.4%)

Uncle Sam's (OG 1046, ABV 4.4%)

Yorkshire Moors Bitter (OG 1046, ABV 4.6%)
A fine ruby beer brewed with Fuggles and Progress hops. A hoppy beer with a fruity aftertaste.

Monkmans Slaughter (OG 1060, ABV 6%) ◈
Rich tasting and warming; fruit and malt in the aroma and taste, with dark chocolate, caramel and autumn fruit notes. Subtle bitterness continues into the aftertaste.

Crouch Vale SIBA

Crouch Vale Brewery Ltd, 23 Haltwhistle Road, South Woodham Ferrers, Essex, CM3 5ZA
Tel (01245) 322744
✉ info@crouch-vale.co.uk
⊕ crouch-vale.co.uk
Shop Mon-Fri 8am-5pm
Tours by arrangement

☒ Founded in 1981 by two CAMRA enthusiasts, Crouch Vale is now well established as a major craft brewer in Essex, having moved to larger premises in 2006. The company is also a major wholesaler of cask ale from other independent breweries, which they supply to more than 100 outlets as well as beer festivals throughout the region. One tied house, the Queen's Head in Chelmsford, is owned. Seasonal beers: two beers are available each month, details on website.

Essex Boys Bitter (OG 1035, ABV 3.5%) ◈
Light-bodied pale bitter with a hoppy citrus aroma and a dry finish.

Blackwater Mild (OG 1037, ABV 3.7%) ◈
Dark, roasty and bitter with a dry finish.

Brewers Gold (OG 1040, ABV 4%) 🗇 ◈
Perfumed golden ale with a citrus fruit taste. Bitterness dominates more in the finish.

Crouch Best (OG 1040, ABV 4%) ◈
Dry, fruity bitter, with malt and hops. Well-balanced throughout.

Anchor Street Porter (OG 1049, ABV 4.9%) ◈
Roasty dark ale with a pleasing fresh hoppy character to the aroma. Coffee in the taste is balanced by dark fruits and a delicate sweetness.

Amarillo (OG 1050, ABV 5%)

Brewers Gold Extra (OG 1052, ABV 5.2%)

Crown & Wellington

⊽ Crown & Wellington Brewery, Hillsborough Hotel, 54-58 Langsett Road, Sheffield, South Yorkshire, S6 2UB
Tel (0114) 232 2100
Tours by arrangement

☒ The brewery was set up in 2001 with a five-barrel plant in the cellar of the hotel. It was sold to Edale Brewery in 2004 but is now back in private hands. Beers are currently only on sale at the hotel. All regular beers come under the Crown badge with seasonal and special ales labelled as Wellington.

HPA (OG 1039, ABV 3.9%)

Loxley Gold (OG 1045, ABV 4.5%)

Sam Berry's IPA (OG 1050, ABV 5%)

Stannington Stout (OG 1050, ABV 5%)

Cuckoo*

Cuckoo Ales, c/o FILO Brewing Co Ltd, First In Last Out, 14-15 High Street, Hastings, East Sussex, TN34 3EY
Tel 07817 589341
⊕ cuckooales.co.uk/

☒ Established in 2006 and sharing FILO Brewery equipment. Brewing is temporarily suspended but will restart again soon.

First Cuckoo (ABV 4.2%)
A well-hopped golden bitter.

Cuillin

Cuillin Brewery Ltd, Sligachan Hotel, Sligachan, Carbost, Isle of Skye, IV47 8SW
Tel (01478) 650204/07795 250808
✉ steve@cuillinbrewery.co.uk
⊕ cuillinbrewery.co.uk
Tours by arrangement

The brewery opened in 2004 and consists of a five-barrel plant that came from a Firkin pub. Four beers are produced and are available on the island and occasionally on the mainland. All beers are suitable for vegetarians and vegans. Seasonal beers: Black Face (Easter-Aug), Eagle Ale (Easter-Aug).

Skye Ale (ABV 4.1%)

Pinnacle (OG 1047, ABV 4.7%)

Cumbrian

Cumbrian Legendary Ales Ltd, Old Hall Brewery, Hawkshead, Cumbria, LA22 0QF
Tel (015394) 36436
✉ info@cumbrianlegendaryales.com
⊕ cumbrianlegendaryales.com

⊕ Old Hall Brewery and its 10-barrel brewhouse were established in 2006 in a renovated Tudor farmstead on the western shores of Esthwaite Water. Characters from Cumbrian folklore and legends give their names to each beer produced by brewer David Newham. 40 outlets are supplied.

Wicked Jimmy (OG 1037, ABV 3.6%)

King Dunmail (OG 1042, ABV 4.2%)

Buttermere Beauty (OG 1047, ABV 4.8%)

Claife Crier (OG 1048.5, ABV 5%)

Custom

Custom Beers Ltd, Little Burchetts Farm, Isaacs Lane, Haywards Heath, West Sussex, RH16 4RZ
Tel 07799 134188

Launched in 2005, Custom produces beers on request from its customers. Head brewer Peter Skinner encourages customers to suggest new options for flavour, names and design. The custom service is complemented by a regular premium range.

Centennial Pale Ale (ABV 3.7%)

Smooth Mild (ABV 3.8%)

Chinook Best Bitter (ABV 4.2%)

Cascade Special Bitter (ABV 4.8%)

Dark Roast Porter (ABV 5.5%)

Tomahawk Strong Ale (ABV 5.5%)

Cwmbran SIBA

Cwmbran Brewery, Gorse Cottage, Graig Road, Upper Cwmbran, Torfaen, NP44 5AS
Tel (01633) 485233
✉ cwmbran.brewery@btopenworld.com
⊕ cwmbranbrewery.co.uk

⊕ Cwmbran is a craft brewery on the slopes of Mynydd Maen in Upper Cwmbran in Gwent's eastern valley. Founded in 1994, it is sited alongside the brewer's cottage home. A mountain spring supplies the water used for brewing liquor. An extension to the brewery has increased both capacity and flexibility. Seasonal beers: Easter Bunny (ABV 4.5%), spring/summer — Drayman's Gold (ABV 4.2%), Golden Wheat (ABV 4.5%), Four Seasons (ABV 4.8%), Pink Panther (ABV 4.8%); autumn/winter — Plum Porter (ABV 4.8%); winter/Xmas -- Taff's Winter Ale (ABV 5.2%) Santa's Tipple (ABV 5.2%). Bottle-conditioned beer: Crow Valley Bitter.

Drayman's Choice (OG 1041, ABV 3.8%)

Pure Welsh (OG 1045, ABV 4.5%)

Blackcurrant Stout (OG 1050, ABV 4%)

Crow Valley Bitter (OG 1042, ABV 4.2%) ◆
Faint malt and hops aroma. Amber coloured with a clean taste of malt, hops and fruit

flavours. Bitterness builds with a lasting bitter finish.

Crow Valley Stout (OG 1048, ABV 4.2%)

Nut Brown Premium Ale (OG 1044, ABV 4.5%)

Full Malty (OG 1048, ABV 4.8%)

Gorse Porter (OG 1048, ABV 4.8%)

Daleside

Daleside Brewery Ltd, Camwal Road, Starbeck, Harrogate, North Yorkshire, HG1 4PT
Tel (01423) 880022
✉ enquiries@dalesidebrewery.plus.com
⊕ dalesidebrewery.com
Shop Mon-Fri 9am-4pm

⊕ Opened in 1991 in Harrogate with a 20-barrel plant, beer is now supplied to some 200 outlets locally, via wholesalers nationally and to the London area through SIBA's direct delivery scheme. Seasonal beers: see website.

Bitter (OG 1039, ABV 3.7%) ◆
Pale brown in colour, this well-balanced, hoppy beer is complemented by fruity bitterness and a hint of sweetness, leading to a long, bitter finish.

Blonde (OG 1040, ABV 3.9%) ◆
A pale golden beer with a predominantly hoppy aroma and taste, leading to a refreshing hoppy, bitter but short finish.

Special Bitter/Shrimper (OG 1043, ABV 4.1%)

Danelaw

Danelaw were not brewing at time of going to press but will re-start as soon as suitable premises are found.

Dark Star SIBA

Dark Star Brewing Co Ltd, Moonhill Farm, Ansty, Haywards Heath, West Sussex, RH17 5AH
Tel (01444) 412311
✉ info@darkstarbrewing.co.uk
⊕ darkstarbrewing.co.uk
Tours by arrangement

⊠ Dark Star started brewing in Brighton and moved operations to its current site in 2001. The brewery's range of beers is divided between permanent, seasonal and monthly specials. Around 70 outlets are supplied. Seasonal beers: English Pale Ale (ABV 4.5%, Jan-Feb), Sunburst (ABV 4.8%, Apr-Sep), Summer Meltdown (ABV 4.8%, Jun-Aug), Porter (ABV 5.5%, Oct-Dec), Critical Mass (ABV 7.8%, Xmas), Winter Meltdown (ABV 5%, Sep-Mar).

Hophead (OG 1040, ABV 3.8%) ⬡ ◆
A golden-coloured bitter with a fruity/hoppy aroma and a citrus/bitter taste and aftertaste. Flavours remain strong to the end.

Best Bitter (OG 1042, ABV 4%)
A slight malty flavour is complemented by East Kent Goldings hops.

Old Ale (ABV 4%)
A rich bronze colour with a malty caramel taste.

Espresso (OG 1041, ABV 4.2%)

Dark Star Original (OG 1052, ABV 5%) ◆
Dark, full-bodied ale with a roast malt aroma and a dry, bitter, stout-like finish.

Festival (OG 1051, ABV 5%)
A chestnut, bronze-coloured bitter with a smooth mouthfeel and freshness.

DarkTribe

DarkTribe Brewery, Dog & Gun, High Street, East Butterwick, Lincolnshire, DN17 3AJ
Tel (01724) 782324
✉ dixie@darktribe.co.uk
⊕ darktribe.co.uk
Tours by arrangement

☺ A small brewery was built during the summer of 1996 in a workshop at the bottom of his garden by Dave 'Dixie' Dean. In 2005 Dixie bought the Dog & Gun pub and moved the 2.5-barrel brewing equipment there. The beers generally follow a marine theme, recalling Dixie's days as an engineer in the Merchant Navy and his enthusiasm for sailing. Local outlets are supplied. Seasonal beers: Dixie's Midnight Runner (ABV 6.5%, Dec-Jan), Dark Destroyer (ABV 9.7%, Aug onwards), Daft Bat (ABV 4.9%, Halloween), Starburst (ABV 5.1%, Bonfire Night).

Dixie's Mild (ABV 3.6%)

Honey Mild (ABV 3.6%)

Full Ahead (ABV 3.8%) ◆
A malty smoothness is backed by a slightly fruity hop that gives a good bitterness to this amber-brown bitter.

Albacore (ABV 4%)

Red Duster (ABV 4%)

Red Rock (ABV 4.2%)

Sternwheeler (ABV 4.2%)

Bucket Hitch (ABV 4.4%)

Dixie's Bollards (ABV 4.5%)

Dr Griffin's Mermaid (ABV 4.5%)

Old Gaffer (ABV 4.5%)

Galleon (ABV 4.7%) ◆
A tasty, golden, smooth, full-bodied ale with fruity hops and consistent malt. The thirst-quenching bitterness lingers into a well-balanced finish.

Twin Screw (ABV 5.1%) ◆
A fruity, rose-hip tasting beer, red in colour. Good malt presence with a dry, hoppy bitterness coming through in the finish.

Darwin SIBA

Darwin Brewery Ltd, 63 Back Tatham Street, Sunderland, Tyne & Wear, SR1 2QE
Tel (0191) 514 4746
Email info@darwinbrewery.com
Website www.darwinbrewery.com
Tours by arrangement (including tasting at local venue)

☺ The Darwin Brewery first brewed in 1994 and expanded with the construction of its Wearside brewery in central Sunderland in 2002 after a move from the Hodges brewhouse in Crook, Co Durham. Darwin specialises in recreations of past beers and also produces trial beers from the Brewlab training and research unit at the University of Sunderland, and experiments in the production of novel and overseas styles for occasional production. Output from the brewery grew significantly in 2005. The brewery also produces the beers of the closed High Force Brewery in Teesdale. Seasonal beers: Richmond Ale (ABV 4.5%, summer/autumn), Saints Sinner (ABV 5%, autumn/winter). Bottle-conditioned beers: Richmond Ale (ABV 4.5%), Hammond's Porter (ABV 4.7%), Extinction Ale (ABV 8.2%), Hammond's Stingo (ABV 10%), Cauldron Snout, Forest XB.

Sunderland Best (OG 1041, ABV 3.9%)
A light and smooth-tasting session bitter, full of hop character and moderate bitterness. Amber malt provides a smooth body and creamy character.

Evolution Ale (OG 1041, ABV 4%)
A dark amber, full-bodied bitter with a malty flavour and a clean, bitter aftertaste.

Ghost Ale (OG 1041, ABV 4.1%)

Rolling Hitch (OG 1055, ABV 5.2%)

Hop Drop (OG 1054, ABV 5.3%)

Killer Bee (OG 1054, ABV 6%)
A strong but light ale matured with pure, organic honey produced from Darwin's own hives.

Extinction Ale (OG 1084, ABV 8.3%)

For High Force Hotel:

Forest XB (OG 1044, ABV 4.2%)

Cauldron Snout (OG 1056, ABV 5.6%)

De Koninck

See final entry in Independent breweries section

Dent SIBA

Dent Brewery Ltd, Hollins, Cowgill, Sedbergh, Cumbria, LA10 5TQ
Tel (015396) 25326
✉ paul@dentbrewery.co.uk
⊕ dentbrewery.co.uk

☺ A brewery set up in a converted barn in the picturesque Yorkshire Dales. Expansion has allowed the beer to be supplied throughout the country to some 50 free trade outlets. Monthly specials are produced, all at ABV 4.5%.

Bitter (OG 1035, ABV 3.7%) ◆
Fruity throughout and lightly hopped. This beer has a pervading earthiness. A short, bitter finish.

Aviator (OG 1039, ABV 4%) ◆
This medium-bodied amber ale is characterised by strong citrus and hoppy flavours that develop into a long bitter finish.

Rambrau (OG 1042, ABV 4.5%)
A cask-conditioned lager.

Ramsbottom Strong Ale (OG 1042, ABV 4.5%) ◆
This complex, mid-brown beer has a warming, dry, bitter finish to follow its unusual combination of roast, bitter, fruity and sweet flavours.

Kamikaze (OG 1047, ABV 5%) ◆
Hops and fruit dominate this full-bodied, golden, strong bitter, with a dry bitterness growing in the aftertaste.

T'Owd Tup (OG 1056, ABV 6%) ◆
A rich, full-flavoured, strong stout with a coffee aroma. The dominant roast character is balanced by a warming sweetness and a raisiny, fruitcake taste that linger on into the finish.

Derby SIBA

Derby Brewing Co Ltd,
Masons Place Business Park,
Nottingham Road, Derby, DE21 6AQ
Tel 07887 556788
✉ sales@derbybrewing.co.uk
⊕ derbybrewing.co.uk
Tours by arrangement

A purpose-built brewery, established 2004, in the varnish workshop of the old Masons Paintworks by owner/brewer Trevor Harris, former brewer at the Brunswick Inn, Derby. Seasonal beer: White Christmas (ABV 5.5%, Dec & Jun). Two new beers are brewed each month.

Triple Hop (OG 1041, ABV 4.1%)

Business As Usual (OG 1044, ABV 4.4%)

Dashingly Dark (OG 1045, ABV 4.5%)

Old Intentional (OG 1050, ABV 5%)

For the Babington Arms, Derby:

Penny's Porter (OG 1046, ABV 4.6%)

Taylor's Tipple (OG 1046, ABV 4.6%)

Derventio

Derventio Brewery Ltd, Trusley Brook Farm,
Trusley, Derbyshire, DE6 5JP
Tel 07816 878129
✉ enquiries@derventiobrewery.co.uk
⊕ derventiobrewery.co.uk
Tours by arrangement

⊠ Derventio Brewery was formed in 2005 although commercial brewing did not begin until 2007. There are plans to bottle the beers. 30 outlets are supplied. Seasonal beers: Aquilifer (ABV 3.8%), Et Tu Brutus? (ABV 4.5%).

Centurion (OG 1042, ABV 4.3%)

Venus (OG 1048, ABV 5%)

Derwent

Derwent Brewery Co, Units 2A/2B Station Road
Industrial Estate, Silloth, Cumbria CA7 4AG
Tel (016973) 31522
Tours by arrangement

⊕ Derwent was set up in 1996 in Cockermouth and moved to Silloth in 1998. Derwent supplies beers throughout the north of England, with outlets in Cheshire, Cumbria, Lancashire, Yorkshire and the North-east. It organises the Silloth Beer Festival every September and has supplied Carlisle State Bitter to the House of Commons, a beer that recreates one produced by the former state-owned Carlisle Brewery. Seasonal beers: Derwent Summer Rose (ABV 4.2%), Derwent Spring Time (ABV 4.3%),

Harvesters Ale (ABV 4.3%), Bill Monk (ABV 4.5%), Auld Kendal (ABV 5.7%, winter).

Carlisle State Bitter (OG 1037, ABV 3.7%) ◆
A light hoppy beer with underlying malt and fruit, and a dry, yeasty finish.

Parsons Pledge (OG 1040, ABV 4%)

Winters Gold (ABV 4.1%)

Hofbrau (ABV 4.2%)

W&M Kendal Pale Ale (OG 1044, ABV 4.4%) ◆
A sweet, fruity, hoppy beer with a bitter finish.

Derwent Rose

See Consett Ale Works

Devil's Dyke*

Devil's Dyke Brewery, Dyke's End, 8 Fair Green,
Reach, Cambridgeshire, CB25 0JD
Tel (01638) 743816/07875 273581
✉ martinfeehan@aol.com

⊠ The Dyke's End is off the village green at the end of a 7.5 mile long Anglo-Saxon earthwork. Established in late 2006, casks of ale were initially produced for the local pub and beer festivals. A 2.5-barrel plant was installed in summer 2007.

Bitter (OG 1036.8, ABV 3.8%)

No. 7 Pale Ale (OG 1039.7, ABV 4.1%)

No. 8 Ale (OG 1044, ABV 4.6%)

Devon

⌷ Devon Ales Ltd, Mansfield Arms, 7 Main
Street, Sauchie, Clackmannanshire, FK10 3JR
Tel (01259) 722020
✉ info@devonales.com
⊕ devonales.com
Tours by arrangement

⊕ Established in 1992 to produce high quality cask ales for the Mansfield Arms, Sauchie. A second pub, The Inn at Muckhart, was purchased in 1994.

Original (OG 1038, ABV 3.8%)

Thick Black (OG 1042, ABV 4.2%)

Pride (OG 1046, ABV 4.8%)

Digfield

Digfield Ales, North Lodge Farm, Barnwell,
Peterborough, Cambridgeshire, PE8 5RJ
Tel (01832) 293248

With equipment from the Cannon Brewery, Digfield Ales started brewing in 2005 as part of a farm diversification scheme. Digfield operates on a 7.5-barrel plant run by three partners. It supplies the local Barnwell pub, the Montagu Arms, as well as 20 other outlets.

Fools Nook (ABV 3.8%) ◆
The floral aroma, dominated by lavender and honey, belies the hoppy bitterness that comes through in the taste of this golden ale. A fruity balance lasts.

Barnwell Bitter (OG 1039, ABV 4%) ◆
A fruity, sulphurous aroma introduces a beer

in which sharp bitterness is balanced by dry, biscuity malt.

Shacklebush (ABV 4.5%) ◈
Dry tawny bitter with a roasty, astringent finish.

Mad Monk (ABV 4.7%) ◈
Fruity beer with bitter, earthy hops in evidence.

Dobbins & Jackson*

Dobbins & Jackson Newport Brewing Co Ltd,
Unit 9, Star Trading Estate,
Ponthir Road, Caerleon,
Nr Newport, NP18 1PQ
Tel (01633) 431233
✉ ale@dobbinsandjackson.co.uk
⊕ dobbinsandjackson.co.uk

⊜ Established in 2006 by brothers-in-law Kerry Dobbins and Richard Jackson, the brewery supplies local pubs in the Gwent area.

Newport Blonde (OG 1038, ABV 4%)

Usk Vale Best Bitter (ABV 4.2%)

Coaltrimmer (ABV 4.4%)

Newport Pale Ale (OG 1042, ABV 4.5%)

Doghouse SIBA

Doghouse Brewery, Scorrier, Redruth, Cornwall,
TR16 5BN
Tel (01209) 822022
✉ stevewillmott@btinternet.com
Tours by arrangement

⊗ Established in 2001, the five-barrel plant continues to brew in a former dog rescue kennel at Startrax Pets Hotel. The second-hand equipment was originally from the Fly & Firkin in Middlesbrough. Some 60 outlets are supplied. Seasonal beers: Staffi Stout (ABV 4.7%, Feb-Mar), Dingo Lager (ABV 5%, May-Oct), Christmas Tail/Winter's Tail (ABV 5.8%, Dec-Jan). Bottle-conditioned beers: all seasonal ales plus Biter, Dozey Dawg, Cornish Corgi, Bow Wow and Hot Dog Chilli Beer.

Wet Nose (OG 1038, ABV 3.8%)
A gold-coloured, quaffing bitter with plenty of hoppy bite in the aftertaste.

Retriever (OG 1039, ABV 3.9%)
A golden-coloured, easy-drinking beer.

Biter (OG 1040, ABV 4%)
A standard mid-brown bitter.

Snoozy Suzy (OG 1043, ABV 4.3%)
Copper-coloured, well hopped bitter.

Dozey Dawg (OG 1044, ABV 4.4%)
A light golden, refreshing beer.

Cornish Corgi (OG 1045, ABV 4.5%)
A golden premium ale brewed with Pilot hedgerow hops.

Seadog (OG 1046, ABV 4.6%)
Originally brewed to celebrate the 200th Anniversary of Nelson's victory and death at the Battle of Trafalgar.

Bow Wow (OG 1050, ABV 5%)
Dark ruby-coloured premium ale; well rounded maltiness gives way to a more bitter aftertaste.

Dolphin

◘ Dolphin Brewery Ltd, The Dolphin, 48 St Michael Street, Shrewsbury, Shropshire, SY1 2EZ
Tel (01743) 350419
✉ oz@icom-web.com

⊚ Dolphin was launched in 2000 and upgraded to a 4.5-barrel plant in 2001. In 2006 both the pub and brewery were taken over by present owner Mark Oseland. After pub alterations the brewery was re-opened with a new range of beers.

Dizzy Lizzy (OG 1040, ABV 4%)

Ollie Dog (OG 1040, ABV 4%)

George's Best (OG 1048, ABV 4.8%)

Donnington IFBB

Donnington Brewery, Stow-on-the-Wold,
Cheltenham, Gloucestershire, GL54 1EP
Tel (01451) 830603

⊗ Thomas Arkell bought a 13th-century watermill in 1827 and began brewing on the site in 1865; the waterwheel is still in use. Thomas' decendent Claude owned and ran the brewery until his death in 2007, supplying 15 tied houses and a small free trade. It has now passed to Claude's cousins, Peter and James of Arkells Brewery, Swindon (qv), who plan to continue brewing Donnington beers at this unique site.

BB (OG 1035, ABV 3.6%) ◈
A pleasant amber bitter with a slight hop aroma, a good balance of malt and hops in the mouth and a bitter aftertaste.

SBA (OG 1045, ABV 4.4%) ◈
Malt dominates over bitterness in the subtle flavour of this premium bitter, which has a hint of fruit and a dry malty finish.

Dorset SIBA

Dorset Brewing Co, Hope Square, Weymouth,
Dorset, DT4 8TR
Tel (01305) 777515
✉ info@dbcales.com
⊕ dbcales.com
Shop at Brewers Quay 10am-5.30pm daily
Tours by arrangement via Timewalk at Brewers Quay

The Dorset Brewing Company, formerly the Quay Brewery, is the most recent in a long succession of breweries in Hope Square. Brewing first started there in 1256 but in more recent times it was famous for being the home of the Devenish and Groves breweries. Brewing stopped in 1986 but restarted in 1996, when Giles Smeath set up Quay in part of the old brewery buildings. His beers are available in local Weymouth pubs and selected outlets throughout the South-west. Seasonal beers: Coastguard (ABV 4.1%, spring), Chesil (ABV 4.1%, summer ▣), Ammonite (ABV 3.8%, autumn), Silent Knight (ABV 5.9%, winter).

Weymouth Harbour Master (OG 1036, ABV 3.6%) ◈
Light, easy-drinking session beer. Well-balanced, with a long, bittersweet, citrus finish.

Weymouth Best Bitter (OG 1038, ABV 4%) ◈
Complex bitter ale with strong malt and fruit flavours despite its light gravity.

Weymouth JD 1742 (OG 1040, ABV 4.2%) ◈
Clean-tasting, easy-drinking bitter. Well balanced with lingering bitterness after moderate sweetness.

Steam Beer (OG 1043, ABV 4.5%) ◈
Citrus fruit and roasted malt dominate this complex best bitter, from the first aroma through to the long, lingering finish.

Jurassic (OG 1045, ABV 4.7%)
An organic premium bitter, pale golden colour; smooth with suggestions of honey underlying a complex hop palate.

Durdle Door (OG 1046, ABV 5%) ◈
A tawny hue and fruity aroma with a hint of pear drops and good malty undertone, joined by hops and a little roast malt in the taste. Lingering bittersweet finish.

Dow Bridge

Dow Bridge Brewery, 2-3 Rugby Road, Catthorpe, Leicestershire, LE17 6DA.
Tel (01788) 869121
✉ dowbridge.brewery@virgin.net
Tours by arrangement

⊗ Operational since 2002, recent building expansion has been completed. Traditional brewing methods, without the use of added sugars, adjuncts or additives, are adhered to. Beers are supplied to 138 outlets via the brewery's own distributor. All regular brews are also available bottle-conditioned. Beers are also contract brewed for Morgan Ales. Seasonal beers: Summer Light (ABV 3.6%), Porter (ABV 4.9%). Seasonal beers for Morgan Ales: Cuckoo Spit (ABV 4%), Xmas Cracker (ABV 4.5%).

Bonum Mild (OG 1035, ABV 3.5%) ◈
Complex dark brown, full-flavoured mild, with strong malt and roast flavours to the fore and continuing into the aftertaste, leading to a long, satisfying finish.

Acris (OG 1037, ABV 3.8%)

Ratae'd (OG 1042, ABV 4.3%) ◈
Tawny-coloured, bitter beer in which bitter and hop flavours dominate, to the detriment of balance, leading to a long, bitter and astringent aftertaste.

Fosse Ale (OG 1046, ABV 4.8%)

For Morgan Ales:

Churchill's Best (OG 1041, ABV 4.2%)

Olde Codger (OG 1042, ABV 4.4%)

Bishops Revenge (OG 1047, ABV 5%)

Downton

Downton Brewery Co Ltd, Unit 11 Batten Road, Downton Business Centre, Downton, Wiltshire, SP5 3HU
Tel (01722) 322890/(01725) 513313
✉ martins@downtonbrewery.com
⊕ downtonbrewery.com
Tours by arrangement

⊗ Downton was set up in 2003 with equipment leased from Hop Back (qv). The brewery has a 20-barrel brew length. A different monthly special is brewed every month as well as regular and seasonal beers. 20 outlets are supplied direct. Seasonal beers: Black Knight Bitter (ABV 4.1%, winter), German Pale Ale (ABV 4.2%, autumn), Polish Golden Ale (ABV 4.2%, spring/summer), Mad Hare (ABV 4.4%, Mar), Dark Delight (ABV 5.5%, autumn/winter). Bottle-conditioned beers: Chimera Dark Delight (ABV 6%), Chimera IPA (ABV 7%).

Quadhop (OG 1038, ABV 3.9%)

Elderquad (OG 1039, ABV 4%)

India Pale Ale (OG 1063, ABV 6.8%)

Driftwood

⚲ **Driftwood Brewery, Driftwood Spars Hotel, Trevaunance Cove, St Agnes, Cornwall, TR5 0RT**
Tel (01872) 552428/553323
✉ driftwoodspars@hotmail.com
⊕ driftwoodspars.com
Tours by arrangement

⊗ Brewing commenced in 2000 in this famous Cornish pub and hotel that dates back to 1660. The brewery is based in the former Flying Dutchman café across the road. The Old Horsebridge one-barrel plant has been replaced by a customised, five-barrel kit. Pale malt comes from Tuckers of Newton Abbot and the hops are Fuggles. The brewery has been under new ownership since April 2007.

Cuckoo Ale (OG 1045, ABV 4.5%)

Dunkery

Dunkery Ales Ltd, The Brewery, Edgcott Farmyard, Exford, Minehead, Somerset, TA24 7QG
Tel (01643) 831115
✉ enquiries@dunkeryales.co.uk/jimwinzer @hotmail.com
⊕ dunkeryales.co.uk
Tours by arrangement

⊗ Dunkery Ales opened in 2006 in a converted cattle shed. The brewery aims to brew several seasonal ales in the near future and there are also plans for expansion of production. Six outlets are supplied.

Ale (OG 1038, ABV 4%)

Dunn Plowman SIBA

⚲ **Dunn Plowman Brewery, Unit 1A, Arrow Court Industrial Estate, Hergest Road, Kington, Herefordshire, HR5 3ER**
Tel 07716 438288
✉ dunnplowman.brewery@talk21.com
Tours by arrangement

The brewery was established in 1987 as a brew-pub, moved to Leominster in 1992, to Kington in 1993 and to its present site in 2002. It is run by husband and wife team Steve and Gaye Dunn, who also run the Olde Tavern in Kington. The brewery also supplies several freehouses within a 50-mile radius. Bottle-conditioned beers: Old Jake Stout, Kyneton Ale (ABV 5%), Golden Haze Wheat Beer (ABV 5%), Crooked Furrow.

Brewhouse Bitter (OG 1037, ABV 3.8%)

Early Riser (OG 1039, ABV 4%)

Sting (OG 1040, ABV 4.2%)

Kingdom Bitter (OG 1043, ABV 4.5%)

Old Jake Stout (OG 1046, ABV 4.8%)

Dunner Artois (OG 1049, ABV 5%)

Shirehorse Ale (OG 1053, ABV 5.5%)

Railway Porter (OG 1056, ABV 5.7%)

Crooked Furrow (OG 1063, ABV 6.5%)

Durham SIBA

Durham Brewery Ltd, Unit 5a, Bowburn North Industrial Estate, Bowburn, Co Durham, DH6 5PF
Tel (0191) 377 1991
✉ gibbs@durham-brewery.co.uk
⊕ durham-brewery.co.uk
Shop open Mon-Fri 8am-4pm; Sat 9.30am-12.30pm
Tours by arrangement

Established in 1994, Durham now has a portfolio of around 20 beers plus a bottle-conditioned range. Bottles can be purchased via the online shop and an own label/special message service is available. Seasonal beers: Sunstroke (ABV 3.6%, summer), Frostbite (ABV 3.6%, winter). Bottle-conditioned beers: Cloister (ABV 4.5% ▣), Evensong, Black Abbot, Saint Cuthbert (ABV 6.5%), Silver Chalice (ABV 7.2%), Benedictus (ABV 8.4% ▣), Temptation (ABV 10%) ▢. All bottle-conditioned beers are suitable for vegans.

Gold (ABV 3.7%)

Green Goddess (ABV 3.8%)
English Goldings hops give a spicy, bitter flavour.

Magus (ABV 3.8%) ▣ ▢ ◆
Pale malt gives this brew its straw colour but the hops define its character, with a fruity aroma, a clean bitter mouthfeel, and a lingering dry, citrus-like finish.

Bonny Lass (ABV 3.9%)
Ruby coloured but with the flavour of a white beer.

White Gem (ABV 3.9%)

White Herald (ABV 3.9%)

Black Velvet (ABV 4%)
Black like a stout but with the strength of a porter. Traditional English hops balance rich liquorice and roast flavours.

White Gold (ABV 4%)
Pale and aromatic, mouth-filling and thirst-quenching with citrus aromas and flavours.

White Amarillo (ABV 4.1%)
Named after the predominant hop — Amarillo is a floral American variety. The addition of Goldings hops add a little more spice. The result is a deliciously fragrant session beer.

Bede's Gold (ABV 4.2%)

Keltic (ABV 4.2%)

White Velvet (ABV 4.2%) ◆
Smooth, golden bitter with a tangy hop and fruit taste. The aftertaste lingers with a pleasant fruitiness

Canny Lad (ABV 4.3%)
Rich, malty Scotch-type beer. Six malts make a complex body and ruby colour.

Dark Secret (ABV 4.3%)

White Crystal (ABV 4.3%)
Crystal is an aromatic American hop. The flavour is clean, spicy and refreshing.

Durham County (ABV 4.4%)

White Bullet (ABV 4.4%)

Prior's Gold (ABV 4.5%)

White Friar (ABV 4.5%)
A strong version of White Gold. All the aroma and rich grapefruit bitterness with a fuller body.

White Sapphire (ABV 4.5%)
Light and easy, aromatic and refreshing.

Bishop's Gold (ABV 4.6%)

Cuthberts Cross (ABV 4.7%)
Pale gold in colour but rich with grapefruit notes. This bitter is strong in alcohol and flavour, yet is thirst quenching.

White Bishop (ABV 4.8%)
A premium ale using lager malt. American fruity hops make this strong beer easy going and satisfying.

Evensong (ABV 5%)

Black Abbot (ABV 5.3%)

Magnificat (ABV 6.5%)

E&S Elland

See Elland

Eagles Bush

Eagles Bush Brewery, Salutation Inn, Ham, Berkeley, Gloucestershire, GL13 9QH
Tel (01453) 810284
✉ eaglesbushbeer@aol.com

The brewery moved to the Salutation in 2005 and brewing restarted in September that year. It was originally located at the Borough Arms, New Henry Street, Neath where it was first installed in 2004. The equipment used is a $^3/_4$-barrel full mash with two fermenters, all self-made. Beers are only available from the Salutation. Seasonal beer: Honey Buzzard (ABV 4.2%, summer).

Kestrel Bitter (ABV 3.7%)

Osprey Dark (ABV 3.9%)

Red Kite (ABV 4%)

Golden Eagle IPA (ABV 4.2%)

Goshawk (ABV 4.2%)

Earl Soham SIBA

Earl Soham Brewery, The Street, Earl Soham, Woodbridge, Suffolk, IP13 7RT
Tel (01728) 684097
✉ info@earlsohambrewery.co.uk
⊕ earlsohambrewery.co.uk
Shop is Village store next to brewery
Tours by arrangement

⊠ Earl Soham was set up behind the Victoria pub in 1984 and continued there until 2001 when the brewery moved 200 metres down the road. The Victoria and the Station in Framlingham both sell the beers on a regular basis and, when there is spare stock, it is supplied to local free houses and as many beer festivals as possible. 30 outlets are supplied and two pubs are owned. Seasonal beer: Jolabrugg (ABV 5%, Dec). Most of the beers are bottle conditioned for the shop next door and are only available there.

Gannet Mild (OG 1034, ABV 3.3%)
An unusual, full-tasting mild with a bitter finish and roast flavours that compete with underlying maltiness.

Victoria Bitter (OG 1037, ABV 3.6%) ◈
A light, fruity, amber session beer with a clean taste and a long, lingering hoppy aftertaste.

Sir Roger's Porter (OG 1040, ABV 4%) ◈
Very lively mouthfeel; well balanced sweet, bitter and malt flavours.

Albert Ale (OG 1045, ABV 4.4%)
Hops dominate every aspect of this beer, but especially the finish. A fruity, astringent beer.

Gold (OG 1052, ABV 5%)
A light, golden bitter with a pronounced hop aroma, contributing to the refreshing bitter aftertaste.

Eastwood

Mitchell Eastwood, Barge & Barrel, 10-20 Park Road, Elland, West Yorkshire, HX5 9HP
Tel 07949 148476
✉ eastwoodthebrewer@tiscali.co.uk
Tours by arrangement

⊕ The brewery, founded by John Eastwood at the Barge & Barrel pub, has a new brewer, Gary Mitchell. Some 50-70 outlets are supplied direct. Seasonal beers: Englands Glory (ABV 4%), Pach (ABV 4.2%), EPA (ABV 5%), Myrtles Temper (ABV 7%), Ginger Beer (ABV 4.2%), Mosquito (ABV 4.7%).

Best Bitter (ABV 4%) ◈
Creamy, yellow, hoppy bitter with hints of citrus fruits. Pleasantly strong bitter aftertaste.

Jollification (ABV 4%)
A copper-coloured session beer.

Eden (ABV 4.2%)
A pale, well-hopped session beer with a long citrus aftertaste.

Gold Award (ABV 4.4%) ◈
Complex copper-coloured beer with malt, roast and caramel flavours. It has a hoppy and bitter aftertaste.

Black Prince (ABV 5%) ◈
Creamy black, robustly flavoured stout. Dry with a predominantly roasted malt flavour. Soft and smooth with a clean finish.

Old Skool (ABV 5%)
A copper-coloured premium bitter.

Diablo (ABV 5.6%)
A dark porter.

726

Lilburne (ABV 5.7%)
Copper-coloured beer bursting with malt and hops.

Eccleshall

See Slater's

Edale

Edale Brewery Co, rear of Ruskin Villa, Hope Road, Edale, Derbyshire, S33 7ZE
Tel (01433) 670289
✉ info@edalebrewery.co.uk
⊕ edalebrewery.co.uk
Tours by arrangement

Edale started brewing in 2001 on a 2.5-barrel plant. It expanded by buying the Hillsborough Hotel in Sheffield, including the Crown Brewery in 2004, but that association ended in 2006 when the Hillsborough brewery changed hands (see Crown & Wellington). Richard Grimes brews on a part-time basis for local events – commercial brewing is suspended.

Kinder Right to Roam (OG 1039, ABV 3.9%)
Kinder Trespass (OG 1040, ABV 4%)
Backtor Bitter (OG 1042, ABV 4.2%)
Kinder Downfall (OG 1050, ABV 5%)
Kinder Stouter (OG 1050, ABV 5%)
Vincent Black (OG 1052, ABV 5.2%)
Ringing Roger (OG 1060, ABV 6%)

Edinburgh

See Greene King/Belhaven in New national breweries section

Eglesbrech

⚑ **Eglesbrech Brewing Co, Behind the Wall, 14 Melville Street, Falkirk, FK1 1HZ**
Tel (01324) 633338
✉ info@behindthewall.co.uk
⊕ behindthewall.co.uk
Tours by arrangement

The brewery is part of an extension to the Ale House in Falkirk. Occasional special beers are made and a Falkirk Wheel Ale is planned to tie in with the area's newest tourist attraction, the Canal Boat Lift. Three pubs are owned, one of which serves cask beer although using gas pressure.

Falkirk 400 (ABV 3.8%)
Golden Nectar (ABV 3.8%)
Antonine Ale (ABV 3.9%)
Cascade (ABV 4.1%)
Stones Ginger Beer (ABV 4.2%)
Alt Bier (ABV 4.4%)

Elgood's IFBB SIBA

Elgood & Sons Ltd, North Brink Brewery, Wisbech, Cambridgeshire, PE13 1LN
Tel (01945) 583160
✉ info@elgoods-brewery.co.uk

⊕ elgoods-brewery.co.uk
Shop May-Sep 11.30am-4.30pm
Tours by arrangement

⊠ The North Brink Brewery was established in 1795 and was one of the first classic Georgian breweries to be built outside London. In 1878 it came under the control of the Elgood family and is still run today as one of the few remaining independent family breweries, with the fifth generation of the family now helping to run the company. The beers go to 42 Elgood's pubs within a 50-mile radius of Wisbech and free trade outlets throughout East Anglia, while wholesalers distribute nationally. Elgood's has a visitor centre, offering a tour of the brewery and the magnificent gardens. Seasonal beers: see website.

Black Dog (OG 1036.8, ABV 3.6%) ⬡ ◈
Reddish black with liquorica, rounded by hints of roast malt and a growing dry bitterness.

Cambridge Bitter (OG 1037.8, ABV 3.8%) ⬡ ◈
Thirst-quenching, copper-coloured bitter with a distinct biscuity malt presence throughout and a drying, bitter finish.

Golden Newt (OG 1041.5, ABV 4.1%) ◈
Golden ale with floral citrus hop aroma and a satisfying soft hoppy palate ending with a spritzy bitterness.

Pageant Ale (OG 1043.8, ABV 4.3%) ◈
Gentle pale brown best bitter with a lingering light bitterness and peppery hops, well balanced by a touch of sweetness and flavours of malt, raisins and Demerara sugar.

Greyhound Strong Bitter (OG 1052.8, ABV 5.2%) ◈
Strong, copper-red bitter with a malty aroma and palate. The malt is joined by soft berry fruits in the mouth and they are eventually subsumed by a powerful dry bitterness.

Elland SIBA

Elland Brewery Ltd, Units 3-5, Heathfield Industrial Estate, Heathfield Street, Elland, West Yorkshire, HX5 9AE
Tel (01422) 377677
⊠ brewery@eandsbrewery.co.uk
⊕ eandsbrewery.co.uk
Tours by arrangement

☺ The brewery was originally formed as Eastwood & Sanders in 2002 by the amalgamation of the Barge & Barrel Brewery and West Yorkshire Brewery. The company was renamed Elland in 2006 to reinforce its links with the town of Elland. The brewery has a capacity to brew 50 barrels a week and offers more than 25 seasonal specials as well as a monthly Head Brewer's Reserve range of beers. More than 150 outlets are supplied.

Bargee (OG 1038, ABV 3.8%) ⬡ ◈
Amber, creamy session bitter. Fruity, hoppy aroma and taste complemented by a bitter edge in the finish.

Best Bitter (OG 1041, ABV 4%) ◈
Robust, creamy yellow bitter. A balance of fruit and hops on the nose anticipates a rush of fruit on the tongue. Tart, dry, bitter aftertaste.

Beyond the Pale (OG 1042, ABV 4.2%) ▣ ◈
Yellow-coloured, robust, creamy beer with ripe aromas of hops and fruit. Bitterness predominates in the mouth and leads to a dry, fruity and hoppy aftertaste.

Nettlethrasher (OG 1044, ABV 4.4%) ◈
Grainy amber-coloured beer. A rounded nose with some fragrant hops notes followed by a mellow nutty and fruity taste and a dry finish.

Goldrush (OG 1047, ABV 4.6%) ◈
Creamy golden ale. Aromatic, hoppy aroma, clean fresh fruity taste, followed by a powerful dry bitter aftertaste.

1872 Porter (OG 1065, ABV 6.5%) ▣ ⬡ ◈
Creamy, full-flavoured porter. Rich liquorice flavours with a hint of chocolate from the roast malt. A soft but satisfying aftertaste of bittersweet roast and malt.

IPA (OG 1065, ABV 6.5%)

Elmtree*

Elmtree Beers, The Stables, Mill Lane, Snetterton, Norfolk, NR16 2LQ
Tel 07939 549241
⊠ sales@elmtreebeers.co.uk
⊕ elmtreebeers.co.uk

Elmtree was established in early 2007. Its produces both cask and bottle conditioned beers.

Bitter (ABV 4.2%)

Dark Horse (ABV 5%)

Golden Pale Ale (ABV 5%)

Cooper's Tipple (ABV 6%)

Elveden EAB

Elveden Ales, The Courtyard, Elveden Estate, Elveden, Thetford, Norfolk, IP24 3TA
Tel (01842) 878922

Elveden is a five-barrel brewery based on the estate of Lord Iveagh, a member of the ennobled branch of the Guinness family. The brewery is run by Frances Moore, daughter of Brendan Moore at Iceni Brewery (qv) and produces three ales: Elveden Stout (ABV 5%) and Elveden Ale (ABV 5.2%), which are mainly bottled in stoneware bottles. The third is Charter Ale (ABV 10%) to mark the celebrations for the award of a Royal Charter for Harwich in 1604. The beer is available in cask and bottle-conditioned versions. The phone number listed is shared with Iceni. The majority of sales take place through their farm shop, adjacent to the brewery.

Empire

Empire Brewing, The Old Boiler House, Upper Mills, Slaithwaite, Huddersfield, West Yorkshire, HD7 7HA
Tel (01484) 847343/07966 592276
⊕ empirebrewing.com
Tours by arrangement

Empire Brewing was set up in a garage in 2004 by Russell Beverley with a five-barrel plant and relocated in 2006. All the beers are predominantly pale and hoppy. Beers are supplied to local free houses, CAMRA beer festivals and via specialist agencies. Seasonal beers: Jerusalem (ABV 4.5%), East India IPA (ABV 4.5%).

Golden Warrior (ABV 3.8%)
Pale bitter, quite fruity with a sherbet aftertaste, moderate bitterness.

Ensign (ABV 3.9%)
Pale, straw-coloured bitter made with lager malt, quite floral on the nose with a pine/lemon flavour.

Strikes Back (ABV 4%)
Pale golden bitter with a hoppy aroma and good hop and malt balance with a citrussy flavour, very light on the palate. Good session beer.

Valour (ABV 4.2%)

Longbow (ABV 4.3%)
Golden bitter with a well-balanced malt, floral citrus hop aroma. Spicy yet smooth tasting.

Crusader (ABV 5%)
Light coloured ale with distinctive pine/lemon citrus flavour, good hoppy nose with moderate bitterness.

Enville SIBA

Enville Ales Ltd, Enville Brewery, Cox Green, Hollies Lane, Enville, Stourbridge, West Midlands, DY7 5LG
Tel (01384) 873728
✉ **info@envilleales.com**
⊕ **envilleales.com**
Tours by arrangement for small groups only

Enville is based on a picturesque Victorian farm complex. Using the same water source as the original Village Brewery (closed in 1919), the beers also incorporate more than three tons of honey annually, and recipes passed down from the proprietor's great-great aunt. Seasonal beers: Gothic (ABV 5.2%, Oct-Mar), Phoenix IPA (ABV 4.8%, Apr-Sep).

Chainmaker Mild (OG 1037, ABV 3.6%)

Nailmaker Mild (OG 1041, ABV 4%)

White (OG 1041, ABV 4.2%) ◆
Yellow with a malt, hops and fruit aroma. Hoppy but sweet finish.

Saaz (OG 1042, ABV 4.2%) ◆
Golden lager-style beer. Lager bite but with more taste and lasting bitterness. The malty aroma is late arriving but the bitter finish, balanced by fruit and hops, compensates.

Ale (OG 1044, ABV 4.5%) ◆
Golden ale with a sweet, hoppy aroma. Sweet start when the honey kicks in, but a hoppy ending with a whisky and heather blend; thirst-quenching.

Porter (OG 1044, ABV 4.5%) ◆
Black with a creamy head and sulphurous aroma. Sweet and fruity start with touches of spice. Good balance between sweet and bitter, but hops dominate the finish.

Ginger (OG 1045, ABV 4.6%) ⬚ ◆
Golden bright with gently gingered tangs. A drinkable beer with no acute flavours but a satisfying aftertaste of sweet hoppiness.

Evan Evans

Wm Evan Evans, The New Brewery, 1 Rhosmaen Street, Llandeilo, Carmarthenshire, SA14 6LU
Tel (01558) 824455
✉ **info@evan-evans.com**
⊕ **evan-evans.com**
Shop open 10am-4pm daily
Tours by arrangement

⊕ Wm Evan Evans opened in 2004 using a modern, purpose-built brewery, with a 20-barrel brew length and integrated fermenting room. Ten pubs are owned and around 60 outlets are supplied direct. Seasonal beers: Fly Half (ABV 4%, Jan), Easter Ale (ABV 4%, Apr), Golden Hop (Jun-Jul), Harvest Home (ABV 4.3%, Aug), Full Cry (ABV 4.3%, Oct), Winter Glory (Nov), Bishops Revenge (ABV 4.2%, Nov), Santa's Tipple (ABV 4.4%, Dec).

BB (OG 1038, ABV 3.8%)

Cwrw (OG 1043, ABV 4.2%)

Warrior (OG 1043, ABV 4.6%)

Everards IFBB

Everards Brewery Ltd, Castle Acres, Enderby, near Narborough, Leicestershire, LE19 1BY
Tel (0116) 201 4100
✉ **mail@everards.co.uk**
⊕ **everards.co.uk**
Shop open Mon-Fri 10am-5pm; Sat 10am-4pm
Tours by arrangement for parties of 8-12

Established by William Everard in 1849, Everards brewery remains an independent family-owned brewery. Four core ales are brewed as well as a range of seasonal beers. Everards owns a pub estate of more than 160 tenanted houses throughout the Midlands.

Beacon Bitter (OG 1036, ABV 3.8%) ◆
Light, refreshing, well-balanced pale amber bitter in the Burton style.

Sunchaser Blonde (ABV 4%) ⬚ ◆
A golden brew with a sweet, lightly-hopped character. Some citrus notes to the fore in a quick finish that becomes increasingly bitter.

Tiger Best Bitter (OG 1041, ABV 4.2%) ◆
A mid-brown, well-balanced best bitter crafted for broad appeal, benefiting from a long, bitter-sweet finish.

Original (OG 1050, ABV 5.2%) ◆
Full-bodied, mid-brown strong bitter with a pleasant rich, grainy mouthfeel. Well-balanced flavours, with malt slightly to the fore, merging into a long, satisfying finish.

For Coors:

Stones Bitter (ABV 4.1%)

Exe Valley SIBA

Exe Valley Brewery, Silverton, Exeter, Devon, EX5 4HF
Tel (01392) 860406
✉ **exevalley@supanet.com**
⊕ **siba-southwest.co.uk/breweries/exevalley**
Tours by arrangement (charge made)

⊠ Exe Valley was established as Barron's

Brewery in 1984. Guy Sheppard, who joined the business in 1991, continues to run the company. The beers are all brewed traditionally, using spring water, Devon malt and English hops. Deliveries are made to some 60 pubs within a 40-mile radius of the brewery; the beers are also available nationally via wholesalers. Seasonal beers: Devon Summer (ABV 3.9%, Jun-Aug), Spring Beer (ABV 4.3%, Mar-May), Autumn Glory (ABV 4.5%, Sep-Nov), Devon Dawn (ABV 4.5%, Dec), Winter Glow (ABV 6%, Dec-Feb). Bottle-conditioned beer: Devon Glory.

Bitter (OG 1036, ABV 3.7%) ◄
Mid-brown bitter, pleasantly fruity with underlying malt through the aroma, taste and finish.

Barron's Hopsit (OG 1040, ABV 4.1%) ◄
Straw-coloured beer with strong hop aroma, hop and fruit flavour and a bitter hop finish.

Dob's Best Bitter (OG 1040, ABV 4.1%) ◄
Light brown bitter. Malt and fruit predominate in the aroma and taste with a dry, bitter, fruity finish.

Devon Glory (OG 1046, ABV 4.7%)
Mid-brown, fruity-tasting pint with a sweet, fruity finish.

Mr Sheppard's Crook (OG 1046, ABV 4.7%) ◄
Smooth, full-bodied, mid-brown beer with a malty-fruit nose and a sweetish palate leading to a bitter, dry finish.

Exeter Old Bitter (OG 1046, ABV 4.8%) ◄
Mid-brown old ale with a rich fruity taste and slightly earthy aroma and bitter finish.

Exmoor SIBA

Exmoor Ales Ltd, Golden Hill Brewery, Wiveliscombe, Somerset, TA4 2NY
Tel (01984) 623798
✉ info@exmoorales.co.uk
⊕ exmoorales.co.uk
Tours by arrangement

⊗ Somerset's largest brewery was founded in 1980 in the old Hancock's brewery, which closed in 1959. Around 250 outlets in the South-west are supplied and others nationwide via wholesalers and pub chains. Seasonal beers: Hound Dog (ABV 4%, Mar-May), Silver Stallion (ABV 4.3%, Jun-Jul), Wild Cat (ABV 4.4%, Sep-Nov), Exmas (ABV 5%, Nov-Dec).

Ale (OG 1039, ABV 3.8%) ◄
A pale to mid-brown, medium-bodied session bitter. A mixture of malt and hops in the aroma and taste lead to a hoppy, bitter aftertaste.

Fox (OG 1043, ABV 4.2%)
A mid-brown beer; the slight maltiness on the tongue is followed by a burst of hops with a lingering bittersweet aftertaste.

Gold (OG 1045, ABV 4.5%) ◄
A yellow/golden best bitter with a good balance of malt and fruity hop on the nose and the palate. The sweetness follows through an ultimately more bitter finish.

Hart (OG 1049, ABV 4.8%) ◄
A mid-to-dark brown beer with a mixture of malt and hops in the aroma. A rich, full-bodied malt and fruit flavour follows through to a clean, hoppy aftertaste.

Stag (OG 1050, ABV 5.2%) ◄
A pale brown beer, with a malty taste and aroma, and a bitter finish.

Beast (OG 1066, ABV 6.6%) ⌕
A dark beer brewed with chocolate and crystal malts.

Facer's SIBA

Facer's Flintshire Brewery, A8, Ashmount Enterprise Park, Aber Road, Flint, North Wales, CH6 5YL
Tel 07713 566370
✉ dave@facers.co.uk
⊕ facers.co.uk
Tours by arrangement for CAMRA groups only

Bragdy Sir y Fflint Facer's (Facer's Flintshire Brewery) is the only brewery in Flintshire, having moved west from Salford in 2006. Ex-Boddington's head brewer Dave Facer ran the brewery single-handed from its launch in 2003 until 2007, when the first employee was recruited. Around 40 outlets are supplied.

Clwyd Gold (OG 1034, ABV 3.5%)

Northern County (OG 1037, ABV 3.8%) ◄
Straw-coloured light bitter with a mouthwatering floral hop nose and taste. Some astringency in the long, dry, bitter finish.

Sunny Bitter (OG 1040, ABV 4.2%)

Dave's Hoppy Beer (OG 1041, ABV 4.3%)

Splendid Ale (OG 1041, ABV 4.3%)

Landslide (OG 1047, ABV 4.9%) ▣ ◄
Full-flavoured, complex premium bitter with tangy orange marmalade fruitiness in aroma and taste. Long-lasting hoppy flavours throughout.

Fallen Angel

Fallen Angel Micro-brewery, PO Box 95, Battle, East Sussex, TN33 0XF
Tel (01424) 777996
✉ custservice@fallenangelbrewery.com
⊕ fallenangelbrewery.com

The brewery was launched in 2004 by Tony Betts and his wife, who are first-time brewers. The one-barrel brewery makes bottle-conditioned beers supplied to farmers' markets and pubs. Cask ales are planned for festivals. Seasonal beers are produced. Bottle-conditioned beers: St Patricks Irish Stout (ABV 3.1%), Englishmans Nut Brown Ale (ABV 3.2%), Cowgirl Lite (ABV 3.6%), Lemon Weissbier (ABV 3.7%), Fire in the Hole Chilli Beer (ABV 3.9%), Hickory Switch Porter (ABV 4.3%), Caribbean Lime (ABV 5.3%), Angry Ox Bitter (ABV 5.3%)

Falstaff

Falstaff Brewery, 24 Society Place, Normanton, Derbyshire, DE23 6UH
Tel (01332) 342902
✉ info@falstaffbrewery.co.uk
⊕ falstaffbrewery.co.uk
Tours by arrangement

⊗ Attached to the Falstaff freehouse, the brewery dates from 1999 but was refurbished and re-opened in 2003 under new management and has recently doubled capacity to 10 barrels. Since 2005 Falstaff has also brewed themed monthly specials for the Babington Arms in Derby. More than 30 outlets are supplied.

Fist Full of Hops (OG 1044, ABV 4.5%)

Phoenix (OG 1047, ABV 4.7%) ◈
A smooth, tawny ale with fruit and hop, joined by plenty of malt in the mouth. A subtle sweetness produces a drinkable ale.

Smiling Assassin (OG 1050, ABV 5.2%)
A warm copper-coloured beer.

Good, the Bad and the Drunk (OG 1058, ABV 6.2%)

Famous Railway Tavern

♥ Famous Railway Tavern Brewing Co, 58 Station Road, Brightlingsea, Essex, CO7 0DT
Tel (01206) 302581
✉ famousrailway@yahoo.co.uk
⊕ geocities.com/famousrailway
Tours by arrangement

The brewery started life as a kitchen-sink affair in 1998 but Crouch Vale Brewery assisted the development and increased production. At the end of 2006 the brewery and pub were expanded and it is now able to brew up to 135 gallons of beer a week for the pub, other local pubs and beer festivals. Many of the beers are also available bottle-conditioned. Seasonal beers: Frog Ale (ABV 3.7%), Fireside Porter (ABV 4.4%), Nettle Ale (ABV 4.4%). Crab & Winkle Mild, Bladderwrack Stout, Nettle Ale and Fireside Porter are suitable for vegetarians and vegans.

Crab & Winkle Mild (ABV 3.7%) ◈
Fruity, dark mild with a full-bodied fruitiness balanced by a roasty bitterness and a delicate hop character.

Bladderwrack Stout (ABV 4.7%) ◈
Full-bodied black beer with a powerful roast bitter character complemented by an underlying fruity sweetness.

Farmer's Ales EAB

Farmer's Ales, Stable Brewery, Silver Street, Maldon, Essex, CM9 4QE
Tel (01621) 851000
✉ info@maldonbrewing.co.uk
⊕ maldonbrewing.co.uk
Shop open for beer sales at the brewery
Tours by arrangement for small parties only

Situated in a restored stable block behind the historic Blue Boar Hotel, the five-barrel brewery started in 2002 and continues to enjoy success in local pubs and beer festivals. An expansion of production is planned to meet increasing demand. The beers are available at the Blue Boar as well as in a number of local pubs. Other outlets are supplied through Crouch Vale Brewery. All cask beers are available in bottle-conditioned form from the brewery and other local shops.

Drop of Nelson's Blood (OG 1038, ABV 3.8%) ▣ ◈
Red-brown session beer, whose sweet, easy-drinking initial taste leads to a hoppier, more bitter finish.

Hotel Porter (OG 1041, ABV 4.1%) ◈
Milk chocolate, roasty dryness and a subtle geranium perfume are evident in the aroma and initial taste. An underlying rhubarb tartness leads to a dry, ash-like finish.

Pucks Folly (OG 1042, ABV 4.2%) ◈
Pleasant, light-bodied golden ale. Sweet melon dominates the aroma, with juicy malt more evident in the taste. Bitterness increases later but does not dominate the finish.

Golden Boar (OG 1050, ABV 5%) ◈
Strong golden ale with suggestions of lime marmalade throughout. A spicy hop character becomes more evident in the aftertaste.

Farnham*

♥ Farnham Brewery, Ball & Wicket, 104 Upper Hale Road, Farnham, Surrey, GU9 0PB
Tel (01252) 735278
✉ ballwick@ntlworld.com

⊗ The brewery opened in 2006 and supplies the Ball & Wicket pub as well as five other local outlets. Farnham also brews some beer for Archers of Swindon (qv). Seasonal beers include Wheat Spring Ale (ABV 4.2%).

Bishop Sumner (ABV 3.8%)

William Cobbett (ABV 4.5%)

Mike Hawthorn (ABV 5.3%)

Far North SIBA

♥ Far North Brewery, Melvich Hotel, Melvich, Thurso, Caithness, KW14 7YJ
Tel (01641) 531206
✉ farnorthbrewery@aol.com
Tours for hotel residents

⊗ The most northerly brew-pub in Britain. It originally produced just one cask a week for hotel guests working at Dounreay power station. Far North now has a two-barrel plant from Dark Star's original brewery in Brighton. One pub is owned and one other outlet is supplied.

Real Mackay (OG 1038, ABV 3.8%)

Split Stone Pale Ale (OG 1042, ABV 4.2%)

Fast Reactor (OG 1048, ABV 4.8%)

John O'Groats Dark Ale (OG 1048, ABV 4.8%)

John O'Groats Porter (OG 1048, ABV 4.8%)

John O'Groats Wheat (OG 1050, ABV 5%)

Edge of Darkness (OG 1065, ABV 7%)

Fat Cat

Fat Cat Brewing Co, Cider Shed, 98-100 Lawson Road, Norwich, NR3 4LF
Tel (01603) 788508/624364/07816 672397
✉ norfolkcottagebeers@tiscali.co.uk
⊕ fatcatbrewery.co.uk
Tours by arrangement

Fat Cat Brewery was founded by the owner of the Fat Cat free house in Norwich. Brewing started in 2005 at the Fat Cat's sister pub, the Shed, under the supervision and management of former Woodforde's owner Ray Ashworth. Five stock beers are brewed regularly, together with a range of seasonal and speciality beers.

Bitter (OG 1038, ABV 3.8%) ◀
Hop in the aroma is joined by a distinct bitterness in the initial taste. A low malt background is sustained while the hops subside and gentle citrus notes flower and fade.

Honey Cat (OG 1043, ABV 4.3%) ◀
An aroma and flavour dominated by honey with a solid hop background. A caramel note continues as the initial sweetness turns to a butterscotch character. Smooth but lacking depth.

Stout Cat (OG 1047, ABV 4.6%) ◀
Solid black, traditional stout. Heavy roast and malt notes throughout still allow hops to show through as the long finish turns to a dry, coffee-like bitterness.

Top Cat (OG 1048, ABV 4.8%) ◀
Superb balance of hops and sweet maltiness. Amber with a hop nose. Vanilla and citrus add depth to the hop and malt base. Surprisingly light on the tongue for its strength.

Marmalade Cat (OG 1055, ABV 5.5%) ◀
Pale brown old ale with a rich, hoppy fruitiness. A contrasting hoppiness builds as the finish develops an increasing bitterness.

Felinfoel SIBA

Felinfoel Brewery Co Ltd, Farmers Row, Felinfoel, Llanelli, Carmarthenshire, SA14 8LB
Tel (01554) 773357
✉ info@felinfoel-brewery.com
⊕ felinfoel-brewery.com
Shop 9am-4pm
Tours by arrangement

Founded in the 1830s, the company is still family-owned and is now the oldest brewery in Wales. The present buildings are Grade II* listed and were built in the 1870s. It supplies cask ale to half its 84 houses, though some use top pressure dispense, and to approximately 350 free trade outlets.

Best Bitter (OG 1038, ABV 3.8%) ◀
A balanced beer, with a low aroma. Bittersweet initially with an increasing moderate bitterness.

Cambrian Best Bitter (OG 1039, ABV 3.9%)

Stout (OG 1041, ABV 4.1%)

Double Dragon Ale (OG 1042, ABV 4.2%) ◀
This pale brown beer has a malty, fruity aroma. The taste is also malt and fruit with a background hop presence throughout. A malty and fruity finish.

Celtic Pride (OG 1043, ABV 4.3%)

Fellows, Morton & Clayton

Fellows, Morton & Clayton Brewhouse Co Ltd, 54 Canal Street, Nottingham, NG1 7EH
Tel (0115) 950 6795
✉ sales@fellowsmortonandclayton.co.uk
⊕ fellowsmortonandclayton.co.uk

Nottingham's first brew-pub since the 1940s, it was founded in 1980 as a Whitbread home-brew house but is now operated under a tenancy from Enterprise Inns (qv). The beers are brewed using malt extract. Clayton's

Original, a full mash beer, is brewed by Nottingham Brewery.

Fellows Bitter (OG 1039, ABV 3.8%)

Post Haste (OG 1048, ABV 4.5%)

Felstar EAB

Felstar Brewery, Felsted Vineyards, Crix Green, Felsted, Essex, CM6 3JT
Tel (01245) 361504/07973 315503
✉ sales@felstarbrewery.co.uk
⊕ felstarbrewery.co.uk
Shop 10am-dusk daily
Tours by arrangement

⊗ The Felstar Brewery opened in 2001 with a five-barrel plant based in the old bonded warehouse of the Felsted Vineyard. A small number of outlets are supplied. Seasonal beers: Rayne Forest (ABV 4%), Chick Chat (ABV 4.1%), Dark Wheat (ABV 5.4%), Xmas Ale (ABV 6%). All cask beers are available bottle conditioned plus Peckin' Order (ABV 5%), Lord Kulmbach (ABV 4.4%).

Felstar (OG 1036, ABV 3.4%)

Crix Gold (OG 1041, ABV 4%)

Shalford (OG 1042, ABV 4%)

Hopsin (OG 1048, ABV 4.6%)

Wheat (OG 1048, ABV 4.8%)

Good Knight (OG 1050, ABV 5%)

Lord Essex (OG 1056, ABV 5.4%)

Haunted Hen (OG 1062, ABV 6%)

Fen*

Fen Ales, The Beeches, Austendyke Road, Weston Hills, Spalding, Lincolnshire, PE12 6BZ
Tel (01406) 370345

⊗ Fen Ales was established in 2007 on an eight-barrel brewery. Some 10 outlets are supplied.

Red Fox (OG 1040, ABV 4%)

Fenland SIBA

Fenland Brewery Ltd, Unit 2, Fieldview, Cowbridge Hall Road, Little Downham, Ely, Cambridgeshire, CB6 2UQ
Tel (01353) 699966
✉ enquiries@elybeer.co.uk
⊕ elybeer.co.uk
Tours by arrangement

The brewery opened in 1997 in Chatteris, but moved to new premises on the Isle of Ely. Beers are supplied to more than 100 outlets. Seasonal beers: Amber Solstice (ABV 4.1%), Winter Warmer (ABV 5.5%). Bottle-conditioned beers: Doctors Orders, Sparkling Wit, Smokestack Lightning, Babylon Banks.

Paul's Pale Ale (ABV 3.6%)

Rabbit Poacher (ABV 3.8%)

St Audrey's Ale (ABV 3.9%)

Babylon Banks (ABV 4.1%)

Osier Cutter (ABV 4.2%)

Smokestack Lightning (ABV 4.2%)

Sparkling Wit (ABV 4.5%)

Raspberry Stout (ABV 4.6%)

Doctors Orders (ABV 5%)

Fernandes SIBA

Fernandes Brewery, 5 Avison Yard, Kirkgate, Wakefield, West Yorkshire, WF1 1UA
Tel (01924) 291709/369547
✉ fernandesbrewery@blueyonder.co.uk
⊕ fernandes-brewery.gowyld.com
Tours by arrangement

The brewery opened in 1997 and is housed in a 19th-century malthouse. It incorporates a home-brew shop and a brewery tap, which has won Wakefield CAMRA's Pub of the Year every year since 1999. One pub is owned and 10-15 outlets are supplied.

Malt Shovel Mild (OG 1038, ABV 3.8%)
A dark, full-bodied, malty mild with roast malt and chocolate flavours, leading to a lingering, dry, malty finish.

Triple O (OG 1041, ABV 3.9%)
A light, refreshing, hoppy session beer with a lingering fruity finish.

Ale to the Tsar (OG 1042, ABV 4.1%)
A pale, smooth, well-balanced beer with some sweetness leading to a nutty, malty and satisfying aftertaste.

Wakefield Pride (OG 1045, ABV 4.5%)
A light-coloured and full-bodied, clean-tasting malty beer with a good hop character leading to a dry, bitter finish.

Empress of India (OG 1058, ABV 6%)
A strong, light-coloured, malty beer with a complex bitter palate. Fruit and malt dominate the aftertaste.

Double Six (OG 1062, ABV 6%)
A powerful, dark and rich strong beer with an array of malt, roast malt and chocolate flavours and a strong, lasting malty finish, with some hoppiness.

Festival*

A.Forbes Ltd t/a Festival Brewery, Unit 17 Malmesbury Road, Kingsditch Trading Estate, Cheltenham, Gloucestershire, GL51 9PL
Tel (01242) 521444
✉ info@festivalbrewery.co.uk
⊕ festivalbrewery.co.uk
Tours by arrangement

Festival was established in March 2007 on a 10-barrel plant. Further beers are planned. The beer is available within a 50 mile radius of Cheltenham and through selected wholesalers. 40 outlets are supplied direct.

Bitter (OG 1036.8, ABV 3.8%)
A well-balanced and refreshing copper-coloured session beer with a full body and a fruity grapefruit zest followed by a long, deep finish.

Ffos y Ffin*

Ffos y Ffin Brewery, Capel Dewi, Carmarthen, SA32 8AG
Tel 07838 384868
✉ info@ffosyffinbrewery.co.uk

⊕ ffosyffinbrewery.co.uk
Tours by arrangement

⊠ Established in 2006, the brewery has its own well to provide brewing liquor. The processes used are traditional with no chemical or mechanical filtering. Around 25 outlets are supplied. All beers are bottle conditioned.

Dylans Choice (OG 1042, ABV 4.4%)

Three Arches (OG 1046, ABV 4.8%)

Towy Ale (OG 1048, ABV 5%)

Paxtons Pride (OG 1053, ABV 5.5%)

FILO SIBA

⌂ **FILO Brewing Co Ltd, First In Last Out, 14-15 High Street, Hastings, East Sussex, TN34 3EY**
Tel (01424) 425079
✉ mike@thefilo.co.uk
⊕ thefilo.co.uk
Tours by arrangement

⊠ FILO Brewery was first installed in 1985, using old milk tanks. The current owner, Mike Bigg, took over in 1988 and remains in control of the pub and brewery business. In 2000, the brewery went through a complete overhaul, although it remains a small, five-barrel craft brewery with the First In Last Out pub as the only outlet apart from beer festivals.

Crofters (ABV 4%)

Ginger Tom (ABV 4.4%)

Cardinal (ABV 4.4%)

Gold (ABV 4.8%)

Flock Inn

⌂ **The Flock Inn Brewery, Ty Mawr Country Hotel, Brechfa, Carmarthen, SA32 7RA**
Tel (01267) 202332
✉ info@wales-country-hotel.co.uk
⊕ flockinnbrewery.co.uk
Tours by arrangement

◎ Flock Inn opened in 2006. As well as a 2.5-barrel plant, the site also has a tap room and bar that are open Friday to Monday (please ring for times).

Bois Baaach (OG 1038, ABV 3.8%)

Tup of the Morning (OG 1039, ABV 4%)

Sheer Delight (OG 1042, ABV 4.2%)

Ewe-phoria (OG 1041, ABV 4.3%)

Ewe-reek-a! (OG 1045, ABV 4.5%)

Flowerpots*

Flowerpots Brewery, Cheriton, Alresford, Hampshire, SO24 0QQ
Tel (01962) 771534
Tours by arrangment

⊠ Flowerpots began production in 2006. CAMRA member Iain McIntosh is head brewer alongside the owner, Paul Tickner. Around 12 outlets are supplied direct.

Elder Ale (OG 1038, ABV 3.8%)

Bitter (OG 1038, ABV 3.8%) ◆
Dry, earthy hop flavours balanced by malt

and fruit. Good bitterness with an enticing hoppy aroma and a sharp, refreshing finish.

Goodens Gold (OG 1048, ABV 4.8%)

Font Valley

See Barefoot

Four Alls

⌂ Four Alls Brewery, Ovington, Richmond, Co Durham, DL11 7BP
Tel (01833) 627302
⊕ thefouralls-teesdale.co.uk
Tours by arrangement

The one-barrel brewery was launched in 2003 by John Stroud, one of the founders of Ales of Kent, using that name. In 2004 it became Four Alls, named after the pub where it is based, the only outlet except for two beers supplied yearly to Darlington beer festivals. Phone first to check if beer is available.

Bitter (OG 1035, ABV 3.6%)
A light-coloured beer using pale and crystal malts and hopped with Fuggles, Goldings and Styrian Goldings to give a lingering citrus bitterness.

Iggy Pop (OG 1036, ABV 3.6%)
A honey-coloured beer made from pale, crystal and wheat malts and hopped with First Gold and Goldings.

30 Shillings (OG 1039, ABV 3.8%)
A dark session ale made from pale, crystal and chocolate malts with First Gold and Fuggles hops.

Swift (OG 1038, ABV 3.8%)
A dark mild made with pale, crystal and chocolate malts. Hopped with Fuggles and Goldings to give a smooth, pleasant character.

Red Admiral (OG 1041, ABV 3.9%)
A deep red beer that uses pale and crystal malts and is hopped with Fuggles. A malty beer with flowery notes.

Smugglers Glory (OG 1048, ABV 4.8%)
A black beer made with pale, crystal and chocolate malts and roast barley. Hopped with Fuggles and Goldings, it is a stronger and more bitter version of Swift.

Fowler's

⌂ Fowler's Ales (Prestoungrange) Ltd also t/a Prestonpans Ales, 227-229 High Street, Prestonpans, East Lothian, EH32 9BE
Tel (01875) 819922
✉ craigallan@prestoungrange.org
⊕ prestoungrange.org/fowlers
Tours by arrangement

☺ Fowler's opened in 2004. The adjacent pub, the Prestoungrange Gothenburg, offers all the beers and the ales are also distributed to pubs in Edinburgh and the Lothians, and throughout Britain via Flying Firkin. Fowler's also offers brewsets (brewing courses). Seasonal beer: Winter Warmer (ABV 4.8%, Nov-Feb).

Prestonpans IPA (OG 1040, ABV 4.1%)

Prestonpans 80/- (OG 1041, ABV 4.2%)

Gothenburg Porter (OG 1043, ABV 4.4%)

Fox EAB

⌂ Fox Brewery, 22 Station Road, Heacham, Norfolk, PE31 7EX
Tel (01485) 570345
✉ info@foxbrewery.co.uk
⊕ foxbrewery.co.uk
Tours by arrangement

⊗ Based in a converted outbuilding of the Fox & Hounds, Fox brewery was established in 2002 and now supplies around 100 outlets as well as the pub. All the Branthill beers are brewed from barley grown on Branthill Farm and malted at Crisp's in Great Ryburgh. All cask beers are also available bottle conditioned. Seasonal beers: Nina's Mild (ABV 3.9%, spring/summer), Fresh as a Daisy (ABV 4.2%, autumn).

Branthill Best (OG 1037, ABV 3.8%)
Old-fashioned best bitter.

Heacham Gold (OG 1037, ABV 3.9%) ◆
A gentle beer with light citrus airs. A low but increasing bitterness is the major flavour as some initial sweet hoppiness quickly declines.

LJB (OG 1040, ABV 4%) ◆
A well-balanced malty brew with a hoppy, bitter background. Long finish holds up well, as a sultana-like fruitiness develops. Mid-brown with a slightly thin mouthfeel.

Red Knocker (OG 1043, ABV 4.2%)
Copper coloured and malty.

Branthill Norfolk Nectar (OG 1043, ABV 4.3%)
Slightly sweet. Brewed only with Maris Otter pale malt.

Cerberus Norfolk Stout (OG 1046, ABV 4.5%) ◆
A solid, creamy stout with a heavy chocolate and raisin character. Vanilla, grapefruit and melon add variety as the long, sustained ending develops increasing bitterness.

Branthill Pioneer (OG 1050, ABV 5%)
Malty, fresh aroma. Hops are present in the background.

Nelson's Blood (ABV 5.1%)
A liquor of beers. Red, full-bodied; made with Nelsons Blood Rum.

IPA (OG 1051, ABV 5.2%)
Based on a 19th-century recipe. Easy drinking for its strength.

Punt Gun (OG 1056, ABV 5.9%) ◆
A dark brown, malt-based brew with solid fruity overtones. A distinct roast aroma subsides in the flavour as a sweet prune character competes with the maltiness in the long ending.

Foxfield

⌂ Foxfield Brewery, Prince of Wales, Foxfield, Broughton in Furness, Cumbria, LA20 6BX
Tel (01229) 716238
✉ drink@princeofwalesfoxfield.co.uk
⊕ princeofwalesfoxfield.co.uk
Tours by arrangement

☺ Foxfield is a three-barrel plant in old stables attached to the Prince of Wales inn. A few other outlets are supplied. Tigertops in Wakefield is also owned. The beer range constantly changes

733

so the beers listed here may not necessarily be available. There are many occasional and seasonal beers. Dark Mild is suitable for vegetarians and vegans.

Sands (OG 1038, ABV 3.4%)
A pale, light, aromatic quaffing ale.

Fleur-de-Lys (OG 1038, ABV 3.6%)

Dark Mild (OG 1040, ABV 3.7%)

Brief Encounter (OG 1040, ABV 3.8%)
A fruity beer with a long, bitter finish.

Freedom

See Brothers

Freeminer SIBA

Freeminer Ltd, Whimsey Road, Steam Mills, Cinderford, Gloucestershire, GL14 3JA
Tel (01594) 827989
✉ sales@freeminer.com
⊕ freeminer.com

⊠ Founded in 1992, Freeminer — previously Freeminer Brewery — went into receivership in September 2006 and was bought by Peter Thomas. The brewery is now in the process of being developed and expanded. Bottle-conditioned beers: Deep Shaft Stout (ABV 6.2%), Trafalgar (ABV 6%), Waterloo (ABV 4.5%), Morrison's Best (ABV 6%, for Morrisons), Co-op Goldminer (ABV 5%, for Co-op). Bitter, Speculation and Back Street Heroes are also occasionally available bottle conditioned.

Bitter (OG 1038, ABV 4%) ✎
A light, hoppy session bitter with an intense hop aroma and a dry, hoppy finish.

Strip & At It (ABV 4%)

Back Street Heroes (ABV 4.8%)

Slaughter Porter (OG 1047, ABV 4.8%)

Speculation (OG 1046, ABV 4.8%) ✎
An aromatic, chestnut-brown, full-bodied beer with a smooth, well-balanced mix of malt and hops, and a predominantly hoppy aftertaste.

Frog Island SIBA

Frog Island Brewery, The Maltings, Westbridge, St James Road, Northampton, NN5 5HS
Tel (01604) 587772
✉ beer@frogislandbrewery.co.uk
⊕ frogislandbrewery.co.uk
Tours by arrangement to licensed trade only

⊠ Started in 1994 by home-brewer Bruce Littler and business partner Graham Cherry in a malt house built by the long-defunct Thomas Manning brewery, Frog Island expanded by doubling its brew length to 10 barrels in 1998. It specialises in beers with personalised bottle labels, available by mail order. Some 40 free trade outlets are supplied, with the beer occasionally available through other micro-brewers. Seasonal beers: Fuggled Frog (ABV 3.5%, May), Head in the Clouds (ABV 4.5%, Aug). Bottle-conditioned beers: Natterjack, Fire Bellied Toad, Croak & Stagger.

Best Bitter (OG 1040, ABV 3.8%) ✎

Blackcurrant and gooseberry enhance the full malty aroma with pineapple and papaya joining on the tongue. Bitterness develops in the fairly long Target/Fuggles finish.

Shoemaker (OG 1043, ABV 4.2%) ✎
An orangey aroma of fruity Cascade hops is balanced by malt. Citrus and hoppy bitterness last into a long, dry finish. Amber colour.

That Old Chestnut (OG 1044, ABV 4.4%)
A malty ale brewed with Maris Otter pale malt, with a hint of crystal and malted wheat, and coloured with roast barley. Target is the bittering hop with Cascade for aroma.

Natterjack (OG 1048, ABV 4.8%) ✎
Deceptively robust, golden and smooth. Fruit and hop aromas fight for dominance before the grainy astringency and floral palate give way to a long, dry aftertaste.

Fire Bellied Toad (OG 1050, ABV 5%) ✎
Amber-gold brew with an extraordinary long bitter/fruity finish. Huge malt and Phoenix hop flavours have a hint of apples.

Croak & Stagger (OG 1056, ABV 5.8%) ✎
The initial honey/fruit aroma is quickly overpowered by roast malt then bitter chocolate and pale malt sweetness on the tongue. Gentle, bittersweet finish.

Frog & Parrot

⊽ Frog & Parrot Brewhouse, 64 Division Street, Sheffield, South Yorkshire, S1 4GF
Tel (0114) 272 1280
✉ 7776@greeneking.co.uk
Tours by arrangement

Opened in 1982 by Whitbread, the brewers of Gold Label barley wine, to regain the title of World's Strongest Beer, Roger and Out weighed in at 16.9%. The strength has since been reduced to 12.5%, though the recipe, handed down by word of mouth, remains the same. The brewery underneath the pub is now Sheffield's oldest surviving brewery. Brewing is suspended at present.

Roger & Out (OG 1125, ABV 12.5%)

Front Street

Front Street Brewery, 45 Front Street, Binham, Fakenham, Norfolk, NR21 0AL
Tel (01328) 830297
✉ steve@frontstreetbrewery.co.uk
⊕ frontstreetbrewery.co.uk
Tours by arrangement

The brewery is based at the Chequers Inn and is probably Britain's smallest five-barrel plant. Brewing started in 2005 and three regular beers are produced as well as seasonal and occasional brews. Both cask and bottled beers are delivered to the free trade and retail outlets throughout East Anglia. Seasonal beers: China Gold (ABV 5%, winter), The Tsar (ABV 8.5%, winter). Bottle-conditioned beers: Callums Ale, Unity Strong, China Gold, The Tsar.

Binham Cheer (OG 1039, ABV 3.9%)

Callums Ale (OG 1043, ABV 4.3%)

Unity Strong (OG 1051, ABV 5%)

Fugelestou

Fugelestou Ales, Fulstow Brewery, Unit 13, Thames Street Business Complex, Thames Street, Louth, LN11 7AD
Office: 6 Northway, Fulstow, Lincolnshire, LN11 0XH
Tel (01507) 363642
✉ fulstow.brewery@virgin.net
⊕ fulstowbrewery.co.uk
Tours by arrangement

Fugelestou operates on a 2.5-barrel plant. Some 30 outlets are supplied and one-off brews are produced regularly. Seasonal ales: Sumerheade (ABV 4.7%), Autumn Village (ABV 4%), Xmas Spirit (ABV 5%), White Xmas (ABV 4.6%). Bottle-conditioned beers: Fulstow Common, Northway IPA, Sledge Hammer Stout.

Fulstow Common (OG 1038, ABV 3.8%)

Marsh Mild (OG 1039, ABV 3.8%)

Northway IPA (OG 1042, ABV 4.2%)

Pride of Fulstow (ABV 4.5%)

Sledge Hammer Stout (OG 1077, ABV 8%)

Fuller's IFBB SIBA

Fuller, Smith and Turner plc, Griffin Brewery, Chiswick Lane South, London, W4 2QB
Tel (020) 8996 2000
✉ fullers@fullers.co.uk
⊕ fullers.co.uk
Shop Mon-Fri 10am-6pm; Sat 10am-5pm
Tours by arrangement

⊗ Fuller, Smith & Turner's Griffin Brewery in Chiswick has stood on the same site for more than 350 years and direct descendants of the founding families are still involved in running the company. Fuller's has won the Champion Beer of Britain award five times in the 25 years the competition has been staged. In 2006 beer production was around 200,000 barrels of which London Pride took up a significant proportion. Both Chiswick Bitter and ESB have undergone a change to their dry hopping regime to improve consistency. At the end of 2005 Fuller's announced an agreed acquisition of Hampshire brewer George Gale. This added 111 tied outlets to produce a combined estate of 368. Fuller's stopped brewing at the Gale's Horndean site in 2006. The main Gales brands are now brewed at Chiswick. Some of Gale's seasonal beers are still brewed. Seasonal beers: Hock (ABV 3.5%) London Porter (5.4% 🍶 🗍), India Pale Ale (ABV 4.8%), Organic Honey Dew (ABV 4.3%,), Jack Frost (ABV 4.5%). Bottle-conditioned beers: 1845 (ABV 6.3% 🍶 🗍), Vintage Ale (ABV 8.5%), Prize Old Ale (ABV 9%, under the Gale's brand name).

Chiswick Bitter (OG 1034.5, ABV 3.5%) ✎
Pale brown, slightly bitter beer with malt and citrus overtones and a touch of sweetness. There is a pleasant dryness in the short aftertaste.

Discovery (ABV 3.9%) ✎
Hops balance the sweet maltiness in this dark gold, light-drinking beer. Citrus notes and pithy bitterness add a little complexity that lingers slightly in the aftertaste.

London Pride (OG 1040.5, ABV 4.1%) 🍶 🗍 ✎
A well-balanced pale brown best bitter with bitter orange notes, blending with the malt characteristics that build and remain in the finish, with a touch of dryness.

ESB (OG 1054, ABV 5.5%) 🗍 ✎
A wonderfully complex copper-coloured beer with malt, hops and marmalade throughout. The smooth rich mouthfeel leads to a dry sweet, bitter aftertaste that is warming and persistent.

Under the Gale's brand name:

Butser Bitter (OG 1034, ABV 3.4%)

HSB (OG 1050, ABV 4.8%) ✎
A full-bodied and bitter beer. Toffee aromas with an initial taste that is malty with dark fruits. Bitterness balances the sweetness with a bittersweet finish. Some background hoppiness.

Festival Mild (OG 1052, ABV 4.8%) 🗍
(when brewed by Gale's)

Full Mash

Full Mash Brewery, 17 Lower Park Street, Stapleford, Nottinghamshire, NG9 8EW
Tel (0115) 949 9262
✉ fullmashbrewery@yahoo.com

Full Mash started brewing in 2003 with a quarter-barrel plant. The brewery has now expanded to five barrels and, with the addition of extra fermenters, 20 barrels a week are now produced. Trade is expanding with four regular beers and a large production of one-off brews every month.

Whistlin' Dixie (OG 1040, ABV 3.9%)

Séance (OG 1041, ABV 4%)

Spiritualist (OG 1044, ABV 4.3%)

Apparition (OG 1046, ABV 4.5%)

Funfair

Funfair Brewing Co,
34 Spinney Road, Ilkeston,
Derbyshire, DE7 4LH
(Office Address)
Tel 07971 540186
✉ sales@funfairbrewingcompany.co.uk
⊕ funfairbrewingcompany.co.uk
Tours by arrangement

⊗ Funfair was launched in 2004 in Holbrook. The brewing equipment relocated to Ilkeston and in 2006 the brewery relocated again to its present site. There are plans for a bottling plant. Seasonal beers: Tiz the Season to be Jolly (ABV 5%), Xmas Cakewalk (ABV 6.5%).

Gallopers (OG 1038, ABV 3.8%)

Showman's Bitter (OG 1039, ABV 3.9%)

Waltzer (OG 1045, ABV 4.5%)

Brandy Snap (OG 1047, ABV 4.7%)

Dive Bomber (OG 1047, ABV 4.7%)

Dodgem (OG 1047, ABV 4.7%)

Ghost Train (OG 1050, ABV 5%)

Showman's IPA (OG 1050, ABV 5%)

Cakewalk (OG 1060, ABV 6%)

Fuzzy Duck

Fuzzy Duck Brewery, 18 Wood Street, Poulton Industrial Estate, Poulton-le-Fylde, Lancashire, FY6 8JY
Tel 07904 343729
✉ ben@fuzzyduckbrewery.co.uk
⊕ fuzzyduckbrewery.co.uk

⊕ Fuzzy Duck was started on a half-barrel plant at the owner's home in 2006. It relocated to an industrial unit and expanded capacity to eight barrels. There are plans to introduce a bottle-conditioned range of beers.

Feathers (OG 1040, ABV 4%)

Stout (OG 1042, ABV 4%)

Pheasant Plucker (OG 1044, ABV 4.2%)

Fyfe SIBA

Fyfe Brewing Company, 469 High Street, Kirkcaldy, Fife, KY1 2SN
Tel (01592) 646211
✉ fyfebrew@blueyonder.co.uk
⊕ fyfebrewery.co.uk
Tours by arrangement

⊕ Fyfe was established in an old sailmakers behind the Harbour Bar in 1995 on a 2.5-barrel plant. Most of the output is taken by the pub, the remainder being sold direct to around 20 local outlets, including a house beer for J D Wetherspoons in Glenrothes. Seasonal beer: Cauld Turkey (ABV 6%, winter but can be brewed on request all year round).

Rope of Sand (OG 1037, ABV 3.7%) ◥
A quenching bitter. Malt and fruit throughout, with a hoppy, bitter aftertaste.

Greengo (OG 1038, ABV 3.8%)
Golden coloured with a hoppy aroma and a citrus/bitter taste and aftertaste. Clean and refreshing.

Fidra (OG 1039, ABV 3.9%)
Straw-coloured with malt and hops on the nose. Medium bodied with a sweetish finish.

Auld Alliance (OG 1040, ABV 4%) ◥
A bitter beer with a lingering, dry, hoppy finish. Malt and hop, with fruit, are present throughout, fading in the finish.

Featherie (OG 1041, ABV 4.1%)
A light, refreshing, easy-drinking pale ale with a hoppy, lingering finish.

Lion Slayer (OG 1042, ABV 4.2%)
Amber-coloured ale with malt and fruit on the nose. Fruit predominates on the palate. A slightly dry finish.

Baffie (OG 1043, ABV 4.3%)
A pale coloured beer. Hops and fruit are evident and are balanced by malt throughout. A hoppy, bitter finish.

First Lyte (OG 1043, ABV 4.3%)
Clean tasting, light in colour with a good balance of malt and hops. Dry bitter finish.

Weiss Squad (OG 1045, ABV 4.5%)
Hoppy, bitter wheat beer with bags of citrus in the taste and finish.

Fyfe Fyre (OG 1048, ABV 4.8%)
Pale golden best bitter, full-bodied and balanced with malt, hops and fruit. Hoppy bitterness grows in an increasingly dry aftertaste.

Fyne SIBA

Fyne Ales, Achadunan, Cairndow, Argyll, PA26 8BJ
Tel (01499) 600238
✉ jonny@fyneales.com
⊕ fyneales.com
Tours by arrangement

⊕ Fyne Ales brewed for the first time on St Andrew's Day 2001. The 10-barrel plant was installed in a redundant milking parlour on a farm in Argyll. Around 200 outlets are supplied. Seasonal beers: Somerled (ABV 4%), Holly Daze (ABV 5%).

Piper's Gold (OG 1037.5, ABV 3.8%) ▤ ◥
Fresh, golden session ale. Well bittered but balanced with fruit and malt. Long, dry, bitter finish.

Maverick (OG 1040.5, ABV 4.2%) ◥
Smooth, nutty session beer with a sweet, fruity finish.

Vital Spark (OG 1042.5, ABV 4.4%)
A rich, dark beer that shows glints of red. The taste is clean and slightly sharp with a hint of blackcurrant.

Highlander (OG 1045.5, ABV 4.8%) ◥
Full-bodied, bittersweet ale with good dry hop finish. In the style of a heavy although the malt is less pronounced and the sweetness ebbs away to leave a bitter, hoppy finish.

Gale's

See Fuller's

Gargoyles

Gargoyles Brewery, Court Farm, Holcombe Village, Dawlish, Devon, EX7 0JT
Tel 07773 444501

Gargoyles Brewery was established in 2005. A honey beer is planned in the near future. Around 30 outlets are supplied. Seasonal beers: Summer Ale (ABV 3.8%), Humbug (ABV 5%, winter).

Best Bitter (ABV 4.2%)
An amber-coloured beer with a fresh, hoppy aftertaste.

Garton SIBA

Garton Brewery, Station House, Station Road, Garton on the Wolds, East Yorkshire, YO25 3EX
Tel (01377) 252340
✉ gartonbrewery@aol.com
Tours by arrangement

⊗ Garton was launched in 2001 and specialises in strong ales. Seasonal beer: Stunned Mullet (ABV 5%).

Old Buffer Mild (OG 1050, ABV 4.5%)
A dark mild of a type brewed around the time of the First World War.

Woldsman Bitter (OG 1048, ABV 4.5%) ◥
This refreshing bitter is gold in colour. The

full-bodied beer has a mix of hops and fruit balancing the sweetness. A dry, crisp finish.

Chocolate Frog Porter (ABV 8%)

Liquid Lobotomy Stout (OG 1080, ABV 8%)
Garston's flagship beer, its strength derived from grain without the aid of extracts and sugars.

Geltsdale*

Geltsdale Brewery Ltd, Unit 6, Old Brewery Yard, Craw Hall, Brampton, Cumbria, CA8 1TR
Tel (016977) 41541
✉ geltsdale@mac.com
⊕ geltsdalebrewery.com

☺ Geltsdale started brewing in 2006 and operates from a small unit housed in Brampton Old Brewery, dating back to 1785. The beers are all named after areas within Geltsdale.

Black Dub (OG 1036, ABV 3.6%)

King's Forest (OG 1038, ABV 3.8%)

Tarnmonath (OG 1040, ABV 4%)

Hell Beck (OG 1042, ABV 4.2%)

George Wright

See Wright

Glastonbury SIBA

Glastonbury Ales, 10 Wessex Park, Somerton Business Park, Somerton, Somerset, TA11 6SB
Tel (01458) 272244
✉ info@glastonburyales.com
Tours by arrangement

☒ Glastonbury Ales was established in 2002 on a five-barrel plant. In 2006 the brewery changed ownership. Seasonal beers: Ley Line (ABV 4.2%, Jan-Mar), Pomparles Porter (ABV 4.5%, Feb-Mar), Spring Loaded (ABV 4.2%, Mar-Apr), Pilton Pop (ABV 4.2%, May-Jun), Black as Yer 'At (ABV 4.3%, Sep-Nov), FMB (ABV 5%, Sep-Dec), Holy Thorn (ABV 4.2%, Nov-Jan), Excalibur (ABV 4%, Nov-May).

Mystery Tor (OG 1040, ABV 3.8%) ◗
A golden bitter with plenty of floral hop and fruit on the nose and palate, the sweetness giving way to a bitter hop finish. Full-bodied for a session bitter.

Lady of the Lake (OG 1042, ABV 4.2%) ◗
A full-bodied amber best bitter with plenty of hops to the fore balanced by a fruity malt flavour and a subtle hint of vanilla, leading to a clean, bitter hop aftertaste.

Hedgemonkey (OG 1048, ABV 4.6%)
A well-rounded deep amber bitter. Malty, rich and very hoppy.

Golden Chalice (OG 1048, ABV 4.8%)
Light and golden best bitter with a robust malt character.

Glenfinnan*

Glenfinnan Brewery Co Ltd, Sruth A Mhuilinn, Glenfinnan, PH37 4LT
✉ info@glenfinnanbrewery.co.uk
⊕ glenfinnanbrewery.co.uk

Glenfinnan officially opened in May 2007.

Light Ale (ABV 3.3%)

Gold Ale (ABV 4%)

Standard Ale (ABV 4.3%)

Glentworth SIBA

Glentworth Brewery, Glentworth House, Crossfield Lane, Skellow, Doncaster, South Yorkshire, DN6 8PL
Tel (01302) 725555

☺ The brewery was formed in 1996 and is housed in dairy buildings. The five-barrel plant supplies more than 80 pubs. Production is concentrated on mainly light-coloured, hoppy ales. Seasonal beers (brewed to order): Oasis (ABV 4.1%), Happy Hooker (ABV 4.3%), North Star (ABV 4.3%), Perle (ABV 4.4%), Dizzy Blonde (ABV 4.5%), Whispers (ABV 4.5%).

Lightyear (OG 1037, ABV 3.9%)

Globe*

▯ The Globe Brewpub, 144 High Street West, Glossop, Derbyshire, SK13 8HJ
Tel (01457) 852417

☒ Globe was established in May 2006 on a 2.5-barrel plant in an old stable behind the Globe pub. The beers are mainly for the pub but special one-off brews are produced for beer festivals.

Amber (ABV 3.8%)

Comet (ABV 4.3%)

Eclipse (ABV 4.3%)

Sirius (ABV 5.2%)

Goacher's

P&DJ Goacher, Unit 8, Tovil Green Business Park, Burial Ground Lane, Tovil, Maidstone, Kent, ME15 6TA
Tel (01622) 682112
⊕ goachers.com
Tours by arrangement

☒ A traditional brewery that uses only malt and Kentish hops for all its beers, Goacher's celebrated 21 years in the business in 2004. Phil and Debbie Goacher have concentrated on brewing good wholesome beers without gimmicks. Two tied houses and around 30 free trade outlets in the mid-Kent area are supplied. Special is brewed for sale under house names. Seasonal beer: Old 1066 (ABV 6.7%).

Real Mild Ale (OG 1033, ABV 3.4%)
A full-flavoured malty ale with background bitterness.

Fine Light Ale (OG 1036, ABV 3.7%) ◗
A pale, golden brown bitter with a strong, floral, hoppy aroma and aftertaste. A hoppy and moderately malty session beer.

Special/House Beer (OG 1037, ABV 3.8%)

Best Dark Ale (OG 1040, ABV 4.1%) ◗
A bitter beer, balanced by a moderate maltiness, with a complex aftertaste.

Crown Imperial Stout (OG 1044, ABV 4.5%)
A classic Irish-style stout with a clean palate

and satisfying aftertaste from Kent Fuggles hops.

Gold Star Strong Ale (OG 1050, ABV 5.1%) ◈
A strong pale ale brewed from 100% Maris Otter malt and East Kent Goldings hops.

Old/Maidstone Old Ale (OG 1066, ABV 6.7%)

Goddards SIBA

**Goddards Brewery Ltd,
Barnsley Farm, Bullen Road,
Ryde, Isle of Wight, PO33 1QF**
Tel (01983) 611011
✉ office@goddards-brewery.co.uk/andrew@goddards-brewery.co.uk (sales)
⊕ goddards-brewery.co.uk

Established on the Isle of Wight in 1993 and occupying 18th-century converted barns, the brewery supplies around 100 outlets. Seasonal beers: Duck's Folly (ABV 5%, early autumn), Iron Horse (ABV 4.8%, late autumn), Inspiration (ABV 5.2%), Winter Warmer (ABV 5.2%).

Ale of Wight (OG 1037, ABV 3.7%)
An aromatic, fresh and zesty pale beer.

Special Bitter (OG 1038.5, ABV 4%) ◈
Well-balanced session beer that maintains its flavour and bite with compelling drinkability.

Fuggle-Dee-Dum (OG 1048.5, ABV 4.8%) ◈
Brown-coloured strong ale with plenty of malt and hops.

Goff's SIBA

**Goff's Brewery Ltd,
9 Isbourne Way, Winchcombe,
Cheltenham,
Gloucestershire, GL54 5NS**
Tel (01242) 603383
✉ brewery@goffsbrewery.com
⊕ goffsbrewery.com

⊗ Goff's is a family concern that celebrated its 10th anniversary in 2004. Its ales are available regionally in more than 200 outlets and nationally through wholesalers. The addition of the seasonal Ales of the Round Table provides a range of 12 beers of which four or five are always available. Seasonal beers: see website.

Tournament (OG 1038, ABV 4%) ◈
Dark golden in colour, with a pleasant hop aroma. A clean, light and refreshing session bitter with a pleasant hop aftertaste.

Jouster (OG 1040, ABV 4%) ◈
A drinkable, tawny-coloured ale, with a light hoppiness in the aroma. It has a good balance of malt and bitterness in the mouth, underscored by fruitiness, with a clean, hoppy aftertaste.

White Knight (OG 1046, ABV 4.7%) ◈
A well-hopped bitter with a light colour and full-bodied taste. Bitterness predominates in the mouth and leads to a dry, hoppy aftertaste.

Black Knight (OG 1053, ABV 5.3%) ⏏ ◈
A dark, ruby-red tinted beer with a strong chocolate malt aroma. It has a smooth, dry, malty taste, with a subtle hoppiness, leading to a dry finish.

Golcar SIBA

**Golcar Brewery, Swallow Lane, Golcar,
Huddersfield, West Yorkshire, HD7 4HT**
Tel (01484) 644241/07970 267555
✉ golcarbrewery@btconnect.com
Tours by arrangement

⊕ Golcar started brewing in 2001 and production has increased from 2.4 barrels to five barrels a week. The brewery owns one pub, the Rose and Crown at Golcar, and supplies four other outlets in the local area.

Dark Mild (OG 1034, ABV 3.4%) ◈
Dark mild with a light roasted malt and liquorice taste. Smooth and satisfying.

Pennine Gold (OG 1038, ABV 3.8%)
A hoppy and fruity session beer.

Bitter (OG 1039, ABV 3.9%) ◈
Amber bitter with a hoppy, citrus taste, with fruity overtones and a bitter finish.

Weavers Delight (OG 1045, ABV 4.8%)
Malty best bitter with fruity overtones.

Winkle Warmer Porter (OG 1047, ABV 5%)
A robust all grain and malty working man's porter.

Goldfinch

◻ **Goldfinch Brewery, 47 High East Street,
Dorchester, Dorset, DT1 1HU**
Tel (01305) 264020
✉ info@goldfinchbrewery.com
⊕ goldfinchbrewery.com
Shop open 11am-11pm daily
Tours by arrangment

⊗ Goldfinch has been brewing since 1987 and is situated behind the Tom Brown public house. In 2006 the company was purchased by Oak Taverns. Eight outlets are supplied. Seasonal beer: Midnight Blinder (ABV 5%, Nov-Feb).

Tom Brown's (ABV 4%)

Flashman's Clout (ABV 4.5%)

Midnight Sun (ABV 4.5%)

Goose Eye SIBA

Goose Eye Brewery Ltd, Ingrow Bridge, South Street, Keighley, West Yorkshire, BD21 5AX
Tel (01535) 605807
✉ goose-eye@totalise.co.uk
⊕ goose-eye.co.uk

⊕ Goose Eye has been run by Jack and David Atkinson for the past 16 years. The brewery supplies 60-70 regular outlets, mainly in West and North Yorkshire, and Lancashire. The beers are also available through national wholesalers and pub chains. It produces an ever-expanding range of occasional beers, sometimes brewed to order, and is diversifying into wholesaling and bottled beers (filtered but not pasteurised). No-Eye Deer is often re-badged under house names.

Barm Pot Bitter (OG 1038, ABV 3.8%) ◈
The bitter hop and citrus flavours that dominate this amber session bitter are balanced by a malty base. The finish is increasingly dry and bitter.

Bronte Bitter (OG 1040, ABV 4%) ◈
A malty amber best bitter with bitterness increasing to give a lingering dry finish.

No-Eye Deer (OG 1040, ABV 4%) ◈
A faint fruity and malty aroma. Strong hoppy flavours and a long, bitter finish characterise this refreshing bitter.

Golden Goose (OG 1045, ABV 4.5%)
A straw-coloured beer light on the palate with a smooth and refreshing hoppy finish.

Wharfedale (OG 1045, ABV 4.5%) ◈
Malt and hops dominate the taste of this copper-coloured premium bitter. Bitterness comes through into the finish.

Over and Stout (OG 1052, ABV 5.2%) ◈
A full-bodied stout in which roast and caramel flavours dominate. Look also for tart fruit on the nose and an increasingly bitter, astringent finish.

Pommies Revenge (OG 1052, ABV 5.2%)
An extra strong, single malt bitter.

Grafton*

Grafton Brewing Co, Packet Inn, Bescoby Street, Retford, Nottinghamshire, DN22 6LJ
Tel (01909) 476121/07816 443581
✉ allbeers@oakclose.orangehome.co.uk
Shop open during licensing hours
Tours by arrangement

⊕ The 2.5-barrel brewery became operational in early 2007 and is housed in a converted stable block at the Packet Inn. The recipes for the re-named beers were purchased from Broadstone Brewery when that closed in 2006. 15 outlets are supplied. Seasonal beers: Snowmans Folly (ABV 4.1%, Nov-Jan), Yuel Fuel (ABV 4%, Nov-Jan).

Grafton Grog (OG 1040, ABV 4%)

Lady Catherine (OG 1044, ABV 4.5%)

Steam Packet (OG 1052, ABV 5.5%)

Grain*

Grain Brewery, South Farm, Tunbeck Road, Alburgh, Harleston, Norfolk, IP20 0BS
Tel (01986) 788884
✉ info@grainbrewery.co.uk
⊕ grainbrewery.co.uk
Shop open Mon-Sat 10am-5pm
Tours by arrangement

⊗ Grain Brewery was launched in 2006 by friends, Geoff Wright (former marketing manager at Adnams) and Phil Halls. The five-barrel brewery is located in a converted dairy on a farm in the Waveney Valley. 30 local outlets are supplied. Seasonal beer: Winter Spice (ABV 4.6%). Bottle-conditioned beers: Blackwood Stout, Ported Porter, Winter Spice, Alburgh Bitter (ABV 3.8%), Dark Oak (ABV 4%).

Oak (OG 1038, ABV 3.8%)
A well-balanced session beer, light amber in colour with a malty character and dry finish.

Blackwood Stout (OG 1048, ABV 5%)
A traditional black stout with burnt toast dryness and a hint of coffee.

Ported Porter (OG 1050, ABV 5.2%)
An old-style porter. Smooth and creamy, spiked with port to give it the flavour of dark berries.

Grainstore SIBA

Davis'es Brewing Co Ltd (Grainstore), Grainstore Brewery, Station Approach, Oakham, Rutland, LE15 6RE
Tel (01572) 770065 ✉ grainstorebry@aol.com
⊕ grainstorebrewery.com
Tours by arrangement

⊗ Grainstore, the smallest county's largest brewery, has been in production since 1995. The brewery's curious name comes from the fact that it was founded by Tony Davis and Mike Davies. After 30 years in the industry Tony decided to set up his own business after finding a derelict Victorian railway grainstore building. 80 outlets are supplied. Seasonal beers: Springtime (ABV 4.5%, Mar-May), Tupping Ale (ABV 4.5%, Sep-Oct), Three Kings (ABV 4.5%, Nov-Dec). Bottle-conditioned beer: Ten Fifty.

Rutland Panther (OG 1034, ABV 3.4%) ⬚ ◈
This superb reddish-black mild punches above its weight with malt and roast flavours combining to deliver a brew that can match the average stout for intensity of flavour.

Cooking Bitter (OG 1036, ABV 3.6%) ◈
Tawny-coloured beer with malt and hops on the nose and a pleasant grainy mouthfeel. Hops and fruit flavours combine to give a bitterness that continues into a long finish.

Triple B (OG 1042, ABV 4.2%) ◈
Initially hops dominate over malt in both the aroma and taste, but fruit is there, too. All three linger in varying degrees in the sweetish aftertaste of this brown brew.

Gold (OG 1045, ABV 4.5%)
A refreshing, light beer with a complex blend of mellow malt and sweetness, balanced against a subtle floral aroma and smooth bitterness.

Ten Fifty (OG 1050, ABV 5%) ◈
Full-bodied, mid-brown strong bitter with a hint of malt on the nose. Malt, hops and fruitiness coalesce in a well-balanced taste; bittersweet finish.

Rutland Beast (OG 1053, ABV 5.3%)
A strong beer, dark brown in colour. Well-balanced flavours blend together to produce a full-bodied drink.

Winter Nip (OG 1073, ABV 7.7%)
A true barley wine. A good balance of sweetness and bitterness meld together so that neither predominates over the other. Smooth and warming.

For Steamin' Billy Brewing Co (qv):

Country Bitter (OG 1036, ABV 3.6%)

Grand Prix Mild (OG 1036, ABV 3.6%)

Bitter (OG 1043, ABV 4.3%) ◈
Brown-coloured best bitter. Initial malt and hops aromas are superseded by fruit and hop taste and aftertaste, accompanied by a refreshing bitterness.

Skydiver (OG 1050, ABV 5%) ◈
Full-bodied, strong, mahogany-coloured beer in which an initial malty aroma is followed by a characteristic malty sweetness that is balanced by a hoppy bitterness.

Grand Union SIBA

Grand Union Brewery Co, 10 Aberglen Industrial Estate, Betam Road, Hayes, Middlesex, UB3 1SS
Tel (020) 8573 9888
✉ info@gubrewery.co.uk
⊕ gubrewery.co.uk
Tours groups by arrangement

⊗ Grand Union started brewing in 2002 with a 10-barrel plant that came from Mash and Air in Manchester. Direct deliveries are made to Greater London and surrounding counties and the beers are available through selected wholesalers. The single varietal One Hop series of beers uses hop varieties from around the world. Some 200 outlets are supplied. Seasonal beers: see website.

Bitter (OG 1036, ABV 3.7%) ◆
An amber-coloured bitter with citrus hop characteristics in the aroma and flavour, balanced by a trace of malt. The bitterness on the palate and aftertaste grows.

Gold (OG 1040, ABV 4.2%) ◆
Light, easy-drinking beer with grapefruit notes that pull through to the finish, leaving a lingering dry bitterness. Pleasant melon and peach aromas.

Liberty Blonde (OG 1041, ABV 4.2%) ◆
Citrussy yellow beer with some floral notes in the aroma and bittersweet kiwi fruit aftertaste.

English Wheat Beer (OG 1041, ABV 4.4%)

One Hop (OG 1043, ABV 4.5%) ◆
This yellow-coloured beer has hops and fruit on the nose and palate, giving way to a dominating bitterness in the finish.

Special (OG 1044, ABV 4.5%) ◆
Malt and floral hops dominate this well-balanced, pale brown beer, which has a lingering bitterness.

Stout (OG 1050, ABV 4.8%) ◆
Roasted malt notes coupled with apples and plums in the aroma. Baked apples are noticeable in the flavour, with a short, slightly bitter roast finish.

Honey Porter (OG 1050, ABV 4.9%) ◆
Caramelised fruit and honey on the nose and palate. The black malt character adds balance and bitterness that build in the aftertaste. Liquorice can sometimes be present.

Great Gable

◊ Great Gable Brewing Co Ltd, Wasdale Head Inn, Gosforth, Cumbria, CA20 1EX
Tel (019467) 26229
✉ info@greatgablebrewing.com
⊕ greatgablebrewing.com
Tours by arrangement

☺ Great Gable brewery is situated at the Wasdale Head Inn, which is at the head of the valley near England's highest mountains and deepest lake. The inn is the main outlet for the beers. Seasonal beers: Liar (ABV 3.4%, autumn/winter), Wry 'Nose (ABV 4%, spring/summer), Haycock (ABV 4.5%, autumn/winter). Bottle-conditioned beer: Yewbarrow.

Great Gable (OG 1035, ABV 3.7%)
Made from Thomas Fawcett's pale malt with a little dark crystal malt. High alpha Challenger hops for bittering and another hop for aroma.

Lingmell (ABV 4.1%)

Burnmoor Pale (OG 1040, ABV 4.2%)

Wasd'ale (OG 1042, ABV 4.4%)
Ruby in colour with a fine aftertaste.

Scawfell (OG 1046, ABV 4.8%)
Reminiscent of an old-fashioned ale, brewed with pale malt and a small amount of pale crystal. The hops are Bramling Cross.

Illgill IPA (OG 1048, ABV 5%)
A blend of pale malts, highly hopped with only aroma varieties.

Brown Tongue (OG 1050, ABV 5.2%)

Yewbarrow (OG 1054, ABV 5.5%)
A rich, dark, mellow, strong dark mild (some say stout) with an unusual fruit flavour.

Great Newsome*

Great Newsome Brewery Ltd, Great Newsome Farm, South Frodingham, Winestead, Hull, East Yorkshire, HU12 0NR
Tel (01964) 612201/07808 367386
✉ enquiries@greatnewsomebrewery.co.uk
⊕ greatnewsomebrewery.co.uk

⊕ Nestled in the Holderness countryside, Great Newsome began production in spring 2007, brewing in renovated farm buildings. Around 20 outlets are supplied. Bottles and polypins are planned in the near future.

Sleck Dust (OG 1036, ABV 3.8%)

Pricky Back (OG 1040, ABV 4.2%)

Great Oakley

Great Oakley Brewery, Bridge Farm, 11 Brooke Road, Great Oakley, Northamptonshire, NN18 8HG
Tel (01536) 744888
✉ sales@greatoakleybrewery.co.uk
⊕ greatoakleybrewery.co.uk
Tours by arrangement

The brewery is housed in converted stables on a former working farm. Partners Mike Evans and Phil Greenway started production in 2005 and supply more than 50 outlets, including the Malt Shovel Tavern, Northampton, which is the brewery tap. Seasonal beer: Wobbly Santa (ABV 4.8%, Xmas).

Welland Valley Mild (OG 1037, ABV 3.6%)

Wot's Occurring (OG 1040, ABV 3.9%)

Harpers (OG 1045, ABV 4.3%)

Gobble (OG 1047, ABV 4.5%)

Delapre Dark (OG 1046, ABV 4.6%)

Tailshaker (OG 1052, ABV 5%)

Great Orme

Great Orme Brewery Ltd, Nant y Cywarch, Glan Conwy, Conwy, LL28 5PP
Tel (01492) 580548

✉ info@greatormebrewery.co.uk
⊕ greatormebrewery.co.uk

◎ Great Orme is a five-barrel micro-brewery situated on a hillside in the Conwy Valley between Llandudno and Betws-y-Coed, with views of the Conwy Estuary and the Great Orme. Established in 2005, it is housed in a number of converted farm buildings. Around 50 outlets are supplied.

Welsh Mountain IPA (OG 1040, ABV 3.8%)

Welsh Black (OG 1042, ABV 4%)

Orme's Best (OG 1043, ABV 4.2%) ◈
Malty best bitter with a dry finish. Faint hop and fruit notes in aroma and taste, but malt dominates throughout.

Celtic Dragon (OG 1045, ABV 4.5%)

Three Feathers (OG 1051, ABV 5%)

Green Dragon

⬯ Green Dragon Brewery, Green Dragon, 29 Broad Street, Bungay, Suffolk, NR35 1EF
Tel (01986) 892681
Tours by arrangement

⊗ The Green Dragon pub was purchased from Brent Walker in 1991 and the buildings at the rear converted to a brewery. In 1994 the plant was expanded and moved into a converted barn across the car park. The doubling of capacity allowed the production of a larger range of ales, including seasonal and occasional brews. The beers are available at the pub and beer festivals. Seasonal beers: Mild (ABV 5%, autumn/winter), Wynnter Warmer (ABV 6.5%).

Chaucer Ale (OG 1037, ABV 3.7%)

Gold (OG 1045, ABV 4.4%)

Bridge Street Bitter (OG 1046, ABV 4.5%)

Strong Mild (ABV 5.4%)

Greene King

See New national breweries section

Greenfield

Greenfield Real Ale Brewery Ltd, Unit 8, Tanners Business Centre, Waterside Mill, Chew Valley Road, Greenfield, Saddleworth, Greater Manchester, OL3 7NH
Tel (01457) 879789
✉ office@greenfieldrealale.co.uk
⊕ greenfieldrealale.co.uk
Tours by arrangement (call 07813 176121)

◎ Greenfield was launched in 2002 by Peter Percival, former brewer at Saddleworth. Tony Harratt joined Peter in 2005 as a partner. They plan to expand the delivery area and look into the possibility of producing bottled beer. 70-80 outlets are supplied.

Black Five (OG 1040, ABV 4%)

Celebration (OG 1040, ABV 4%)

Dovestones Bitter (OG 1040, ABV 4%)

Bill O' Jacks (OG 1041, ABV 4.1%)

Delph Donkey (OG 1041, ABV 4.1%)

Castleshaw (OG 1041, ABV 4.2%)

Dobcross Bitter (OG 1041, ABV 4.2%)

Evening Glory (OG 1041, ABV 4.2%)

Ice Breaker (OG 1041, ABV 4.2%)

Pride of England (OG 1041, ABV 4.2%)

Uppermill Ale (OG 1041, ABV 4.2%)

Brassed Off (OG 1044, ABV 4.4%)

Friezeland Ale (OG 1044, ABV 4.4%)

Icicle (OG 1044, ABV 4.4%)

Indians Head (OG 1044, ABV 4.4%)

Longwood Thump (OG 1050, ABV 4.5%)

Rudolph's Tipple (OG 1050, ABV 5%)

Green Jack

Green Jack Brewing Co Ltd, 29 St Peters Street, Lowestoft, Suffolk, NR32 1QA
Tel (01502) 582711
⊕ greenjackbrewery.co.uk,
Tours by arrangement

⊗ Green Jack started brewing in 2003. 20 outlets are supplied and two pubs are owned. Seasonal ales: Honey Bunny (ABV 4%, spring), Summer Dream (ABV 4%), Lurcher (ABV 5.9%, winter).

Canary (OG 1038, ABV 3.8%)

Orange Wheat (OG 1042, ABV 4.2%) ⬚ ◈
Citrus notes dominate this deceptively interesting beer. Gold coloured with equal hints of hop and mandarin in the first impression. A dry bitterness develops as the fruit slowly fades.

Grasshopper (OG 1045, ABV 4.6%)

Gone Fishing (OG 1052, ABV 5.5%)

Ripper (OG 1074, ABV 8.5%) ▯

Raspberry Blower (OG 1074, ABV 8.5%)
Ripper with added raspberries, which impart a reddish colour and a strong, sweet flavour. Well balanced and not sugary.

Green Tye EAB

Green Tye Brewery, Green Tye, Much Hadham, Hertfordshire, SG10 6JP
Tel (01279) 841041
✉ info@gtbrewery.co.uk
⊕ gtbrewery.co.uk
Tours by arrangement for small groups

⊗ Established in 1999 at the back of the Prince of Wales pub on the edge of the Ash Valley. The local free trade is supplied as well as further afield via beer agencies and swaps with other micro-breweries. Most cask beers are also available bottle conditioned. Seasonal beers: Snowdrop (ABV 3.9%, spring), Mad Morris (ABV 4.2%, summer), Autumn Gold (ABV 4.2%, autumn), Conkerer (ABV 4.7%, conker season), Coal Porter (ABV 4.5%, winter).

Union Jack (OG 1036, ABV 3.6%)
A copper-coloured bitter, fruity with a citrus taste and a hoppy, citrus aroma, with a balanced, bitter finish.

East Anglian Gold (ABV 4.2%)

Wheelbarrow (OG 1044, ABV 4.3%)
Amber-coloured beer with a soft, fruity nose and taste. Gentle malt, with underlying hop bitterness, with a fruity and slightly dry finish.

XBF (OG 1042, ABV 4.3%)

Gribble

◘ Gribble Brewery Ltd, Gribble Inn, Oving, West Sussex, PO20 6BP
Tel 07813 321795
✉ gribblebeers@hotmail.co.uk
⊕ gribblebeers.co.uk

⊗ The Gribble Brewery is more than 25 years old. Until 2005 it was run as a managed house operation by Hall & Woodhouse (qv) but it is now an independent micro-brewery owned by Brian Elderfield, the previous manager. Brian and brewer Rob Cooper still brew K&B Mild for Hall & Woodhouse and will continue to brew and sell the full range of Gribble beers for the free trade. Seasonal beer: Wobbler (ABV 7.2%).

Slurping Stoat (ABV 3.8%)

Toff's Ale (ABV 4%)

Best Bitter (ABV 4.1%)

Reg's Tipple (ABV 5%)
Reg's Tipple was named after a customer from the early days of the brewery. It has a smooth nutty flavour with a pleasant afterbite.

Plucking Pheasant (ABV 5.2%)

Pig's Ear (ABV 5.8%)
A full-bodied old ale with a rich ruby-brown colour.

For Hall & Woodhouse:

K&B Mild Ale (ABV 3.5%) ◈
A truly dark mild with a toffee, roast malt character that is present throughout. Short aftertaste. Nothing like the old K&B Mild, but pleasant nonetheless.

Grindleton*

Grindleton Brewhouse Ltd, 12 Deanfield Way, Link 59 Business Park, Clitheroe, Lancashire, BB7 1QU
Tel 07713 687026
✉ enquiries@grindletonbrewhouse.co.uk
⊕ grindletonbrewhouse.co.uk
Tours by arrangement

Grindleton began brewing in February 2007 in Bolton-by-Bowland on a five-barrel plant and moved to larger premises in April 2007, increasing capacity to 30 barrels a week. An on-site retail shop is planned selling their own ales plus other UK and Continental bottled beers. They currently supply pubs in the Ribble valley and surrounding area.

Gradely Bitter (OG 1039, ABV 3.8%)

Ribble Rouser (OG 1039, ABV 3.8%)

Old Fecker (OG 1040.5, ABV 4%)

Farleys Dusk (OG 1055, ABV 5.5%)

Man Down (OG 1060, ABV 6%)

Gwynant

◘ Bragdy Gwynant, Tynllidiart Arms, Capel Bangor, Aberystwyth, Ceredigion, SY23 3LR
Tel (01970) 880248
Tours by arrangement

☺ Brewing started in 2004 in a building at the front of the pub, measuring just 4ft 6ins by 4ft, with a brew length of nine gallons. Beer is sold only in the pub and there are no plans for expansion. The brewery has now been recognised as the smallest commercial brewery by the Guinness Book of Records (certificate on display in the Tynllidiart Arms). The small scale of the plant means that beer may not always be available; however, additional beers may be brewed occasionally.

Cwrw Gwynant (OG 1044, ABV 4.2%)

Hadrian & Border SIBA

Alnwick Ales Ltd t/a Hadrian & Border Brewery, Unit 10 Hawick Crescent Industrial Estate, Newcastle upon Tyne, Tyne & Wear, NE6 1AS
Tel (0191) 276 5302
✉ border@rampart.freeserve.co.uk
⊕ Hadrian-border-brewery.co.uk
Tours by arrangement

Hadrian & Border is based at the former Four Rivers 20-barrel site in Newcastle. The company's brands are available from Glasgow to Yorkshire, and nationally through wholesalers. They are hard to find on Tyneside, though the Sir John Fitzgerald group (qv) stocks them from time to time. Approximately 100 outlets are supplied.

Vallum Bitter (OG 1034, ABV 3.6%)
A well-hopped, amber-coloured bitter with a distinctive dry, refreshing taste.

Gladiator (OG 1036, ABV 3.8%) ◈
Tawny-coloured bitter with plenty of malt in the aroma and palate, leading to a strong bitter finish.

Tyneside Blonde (OG 1037, ABV 3.9%)

Farne Island Pale Ale (OG 1038, ABV 4%) ◈
A copper-coloured bitter with a refreshing malt/hop balance.

Flotsam (OG 1038, ABV 4%)
Bronze coloured with a citrus bitterness and a distinctive floral aroma.

Legion Ale (OG 1040, ABV 4.2%) ◈
Well-balanced, amber-coloured beer, full bodied with good malt flavours. Well hopped with a long bitter finish.

Secret Kingdom (OG 1042, ABV 4.3%)
Dark, rich and full-bodied, slightly roasted with a malty palate ending with a pleasant bitterness.

Reiver's IPA (OG 1042, ABV 4.4%)
Dark golden bitter with a clean citrus palate and aroma with subtle malt flavours breaking through at the end.

Centurion Best Bitter (OG 1043, ABV 4.5%) ◈
Smooth, clean-tasting bitter with a distinct hop palate leading to a good bitter finish.

Halifax Steam

**Halifax Steam Brewing Co Ltd, The Conclave,
Southedge Works, Brighouse Road,
Hipperholme, Halifax, West Yorkshire, HX3 8EF
Tel 07974 544980**
✉ davidearnshaw@blueyonder.co.uk
● halifaxsteam.co.uk/myspace.com/
cockofthenorthbar

☺ Halifax Steam was established in 2001 on a
five-barrel plant and only supplies its own
brewery tap, the Cock o' the North, which is
adjacent to the brewery. 40 different rotating
beers are produced, four of which are
permanent. 12 Halifax Steam beers are
available in the tap at any one time, plus
occasional guests on a fair trade basis.

Jamaican Ginger (ABV 4%)

Uncle John (ABV 4.3%)

Luftkissenfahrzeug (ABV 4.6%) ◈
Pale beer brewed with a lager recipe, with a
good balance of flavours and slight bitter
aftertaste.

Cock o' the North (ABV 5%) ◈
Amber-coloured, grainy strong bitter,
predominately malty nose and taste, with a
dry and astringent finish.

Hall & Woodhouse IFBB

**Hall & Woodhouse Ltd, Blandford St Mary,
Blandford Forum, Dorset, DT11 9LS
Tel (01258) 452141**
✉ info@hall-woodhouse.co.uk
● hall-woodhouse.co.uk
Shop Mon-Sat 9am-6pm; Sun 11am-3pm
Tours by arrangement (Call 01258 452141 to book)

☒ Founded 1777, Hall & Woodhouse is an
independent family brewer, today run by the
fifth generation of the Woodhouse family. The
Badger logo was adopted in 1875. The
company moved from Ansty to its present site
in 1900 and a new brewery is planned on part
of the current site. Cask beer is sold in all 260
pubs. Seasonal beers: Hopping Hare (ABV 4.5%,
Feb-Apr), Stinger (ABV 4.5%, May-Jul), Fursty
Ferret (ABV 4.4%, Aug-Oct), Festive Feasant
(ABV 4.5%, Nov-Jan). Stinger is suitable for
vegetarians and vegans.

K&B Sussex Bitter (OG 1033, ABV 3.5%) ◈
A thin, malty session beer, with little of its
traditional hop bitterness. Mid-brown in
colour with a moderate bitterness that lasts
into a bitter, somewhat sharp finish.

Badger First Gold (OG 1040, ABV 4%)
A new beer that replaced Best Bitter in 2005.
Well-balanced bitterness plus hints of orange
and spice.

Tanglefoot (OG 1047, ABV 4.9%)
The beer was reformulated in 2004. The ABV
has been dropped from 5.1% to 4.9%, crystal
malt is now used and the beer is dry hopped
in cask with Goldings hops.

Hambleton SIBA

**Nick Stafford Hambleton Ales, Melmerby Green
Road, Melmerby, North Yorkshire, HG4 5NB
Tel (01765) 640108**
✉ sales@hambletonales.co.uk
● hambletonales.co.uk
Shop Mon-Fri 7.30am-5pm
Tours by arrangement

☺ Hambleton Ales was established in 1991 on
the banks of the River Swale in the heart of the
Vale of York. Expansion of the brewery in 2005
resulted in relocation to larger premises.
Brewing capacity has increased to 100 barrels a
week and a bottling line caters for micros and
larger brewers, handling more than 20 brands.
More than 100 outlets are supplied throughout
Yorkshire and the North-east. Five core brands
are produced along with an additional special
brew each month. The company also brew
beers under contract for the Village Brewer.

Bitter (ABV 3.8%)
A golden bitter with a good balance of malty
and refreshing citrus notes leading to a
mellow, tangy finish.

Goldfield (OG 1041, ABV 4.2%)
A light amber bitter with good hop character
and increasing dryness. A fine blend of malts
gives a smooth overall impression.

Stallion (OG 1041, ABV 4.2%) ◈
A premium bitter, moderately hoppy
throughout and richly balanced in malt and
fruit, developing a sound and robust
bitterness, with earthy hops drying the
aftertaste.

Stud (OG 1042.5, ABV 4.3%) ◈
A strongly bitter beer, with rich hop and fruit.
It ends dry and spicy.

Nightmare (OG 1050, ABV 5%) ◈
This impressively flavoured beer satisfies all
parts of the palate. Strong roast malts
dominate, but hoppiness rears out of this
complex blend.

For Village Brewer:

White Boar (OG 1037.5, ABV 3.8%) ◈
A light, flowery and fruity ale; crisp, clean
and refreshing, with a dry-hopped, powerful
but not aggressive bitter finish.

Bull (OG 1039, ABV 4%) ◈
A pale, full, fruity bitter, well hopped to give
a lingering bitterness.

Old Raby (OG 1045, ABV 4.8%) ◈
A full-bodied, smooth, rich-tasting dark ale. A
complex balance of malt, fruit character and
creamy caramel sweetness offsets the
bitterness.

Hammerpot

**Hammerpot Brewery Ltd, Unit 30, The Vinery,
Arundel Road, Poling, West Sussex, BN18 9PY
Tel (01903) 883338**
✉ info@hammerpot-brewery.co.uk
● hammerpot-brewery.co.uk
Tours by arrangement

☒ Hammerpot started brewing in 2005 and the
brew plant has recently been upgraded to a
five-barrel brew-length. The brewery supplies a
wide area between Portsmouth and Newhaven
and north to the M25. All cask beers are
available in bottle-conditioned form.

Martlet (OG 1035, ABV 3.5%)

Meteor (OG 1038, ABV 3.8%)

Red Hunter (OG 1046, ABV 4.3%)

Woodcote (OG 1047, ABV 4.5%)

Madgwick Gold (OG 1050, ABV 5%)

Hampshire SIBA

Hampshire Brewery Ltd, 6 Romsey Industrial Estate, Greatbridge Road, Romsey, Hampshire, SO51 0HR
Tel (01794) 830529
✉ online@hampshirebrewery.com
⊕ hampshirebrewery.com
Shop Mon-Fri 9am-4pm; Sat 10am-1pm
Tours by arrangement (for parties of 12-18)

⊗ Hampshire was founded in 1992 and merged with the Millennium Bottling Company in 2002. All the beers are also available in bottle-conditioned form. The brewery produces five core beers, 24 monthly specials at the rate of two a month, and four other seasonal beers over longer 3-4 month periods: see website for full details. 150 outlets are supplied. Seasonal beers: Pendragon (ABV 4.8%, Sep-Nov), King's Ransom (ABV 4.8%, Jun-Aug), 1066 (ABV 6%, Mar-May), Penny Black Porter (ABV 4.5%). The entire range of bottled beers is suitable for vegetarians and vegans.

King Alfred's (OG 1037, ABV 3.8%) ◆
A pale brown session beer featuring a malty aroma with some hops and fruit. Rather thin but well-balanced citrus taste with plenty of malt and a dry, bitter finish.

Strong's Best Bitter (OG 1037, ABV 3.8%) ◆
Named after the original Romsey Brewery, this tawny-coloured bitter is predominantly malty. An initially hoppy aroma gives way to an increasingly bitter finish.

Ironside (OG 1041, ABV 4.2%) ◆
A clean-tasting, flavoursome best bitter with a fruit and hops aroma. Hops are predominant but balanced by malt, fruit and a hint of sweetness. The finish is long and dry.

Lionheart (OG 1042, ABV 4.5%) ◆
This golden beer has a hoppy aroma with a sharp citrus flavour that builds into a dry, hoppy finish.

Pride of Romsey (OG 1050, ABV 5%) ◆
A strong citrus aroma leads to a beautifully-balanced mix of fruit and hops that continues to build in the aftertaste.

Hanby SIBA

Hanby Ales Ltd, Aston Park, Soulton Road, Wem, Shropshire, SY4 5SD
Tel (01939) 232432
✉ info@hanbyales.co.uk
⊕ hanbyales.co.uk
Tours by arrangement

⊗ Hanby was set up in 1988 by Jack Hanby following the closure of the Shrewsbury & Wem Brewery. The aim was to continue the 200 year-old tradition of brewing in the area. In 1990 the brewery moved to its present home and has been upgraded to 30-barrel production runs. Hanby supplies 300 outlets. Seasonal beer:

Green Admiral (ABV 4.5%, Sep-Oct). Bottled beers: Rainbow Chaser, Golden Honey, Nut Cracker, Cherry Bomb.

Drawwell Bitter (OG 1039, ABV 3.9%) ◆
A hoppy beer with excellent bitterness, both in taste and aftertaste. Beautiful amber colour.

Black Magic Mild (OG 1040, ABV 4%) ◆
A dark, reddish-brown mild, which is dry and bitter with a roast malt taste.

All Seasons (OG 1042, ABV 4.2%)
A light, hoppy bitter, well balanced and thirst quenching, brewed with a fine blend of Cascade and Fuggles hops.

Rainbow Chaser (OG 1043, ABV 4.3%)
A pale beer brewed with Styrian Goldings hops.

Cascade (OG 1045, ABV 4.4%)
A pale beer, brewed with Cascade hops, producing a clean crisp flavour and a hoppy finish.

Wem Special (OG 1044, ABV 4.4%)
A pale, straw-coloured, smooth, hoppy bitter.

Golden Honey (OG 1045, ABV 4.5%)
A beer made with the addition of Australian honey. Not over sweet.

Scorpio Porter (OG 1045, ABV 4.5%)
A dark porter with a complex palate introducing hints of coffee and chocolate, contrasting and complementing the background hoppiness.

Shropshire Stout (OG 1044, ABV 4.5%)
A full-bodied, rich ruby/black coloured stout. A blend of four malts produces a distinct chocolate malt dry flavour, with a mushroom-coloured head.

Premium (OG 1046, ABV 4.6%)
An amber-coloured beer that is sweeter and fruitier than most of the beers above. Slight malt and hop taste.

Old Wemian (OG 1049, ABV 4.9%)
Golden-brown colour with an aroma of malt and hops and a soft, malty palate.

Taverners (OG 1053, ABV 5.3%)
A smooth and fruity old ale, full of body.

Cherry Bomb (OG 1060, ABV 6%) ▣
A splendid rich and fruity beer with maraschino cherry flavour.

Joy Bringer (OG 1060, ABV 6%)
Deceptively strong beer with a distinct ginger flavour.

Nutcracker (OG 1060, ABV 6%)
Tawny beer with a fine blend of malt and hops.

Hardknott

⬓ **Hardknott Brewery t/a Woolpack Inn, Boot, Cumbria, CA19 1TH**
Tel (019467) 23230
✉ dave@woolpack.co.uk
⊕ woolpack.co.uk
Tours by arrangement

⊕ Hardknott Brewery opened in 2005 using a two-barrel plant. The beers are only available at the Woolpack.

Mildly Complex (ABV 3.2%)

Woolpacker (ABV 3.8%)

Wooliness (ABV 4%)

Lauters Lann (ABV 4.3%)

Tenacity (ABV 4.8%)

Hardys & Hansons IFBB

See Greene King in the
New national breweries section

Hart

⌂ Hart Brewery Ltd, Cartford Hotel, Cartford Lane,
Little Eccleston, Preston, Lancashire, PR3 0YP
Tel (01995) 671686
Tours by arrangement Tue-Thu evenings

☺ The brewery was founded in 1994 in a
small private garage in Preston. It moved to
its present site at the rear of the Cartford
Hotel in 1995. With a 10-barrel plant, Hart
now supplies around 150 outlets nationwide
and does swaps with other breweries.
Seasonal beers: Gold Beach (ABV 3.8%,
summer), Lord of the Glen (ABV 4%,
summer), Snowella (ABV 4.3%, winter), Bat
Out of Hell (ABV 4.5%, Halloween), Val
Addiction (ABV 4.8%, winter).

Dishie Debbie (OG 1040, ABV 4%)

Ice Maiden (OG 1040, ABV 4%) ◆
Hoppy, crisp, straw-coloured bitter with floral
notes and a dry finish.

Squirrels Hoard (OG 1040, ABV 4%)

Nemesis (OG 1045, ABV 4.5%)

Excalibur (OG 1050, ABV 5%)

Harveys IFBB

Harvey & Son (Lewes) Ltd, Bridge Wharf
Brewery, 6 Cliffe High Street, Lewes, East
Sussex, BN7 2AH
Tel (01273) 480209
✉ maj@harveys.org.uk
⊕ harveys.org.uk
Shop Mon-Sat 9.30am-4.45pm
Tours by arrangement (currently two year waiting list)

☒ Established in 1790, this independent family
brewery operates from the banks of the River Ouse
in Lewes. A major development in 1985 doubled
the brewhouse capacity and subsequent additional
fermenting capacity has seen production rise to
more than 38,000 barrels a year. Harveys supplies
real ale to all its 48 pubs and 450 free trade outlets
in Sussex and Kent. Seasonal beers: see website.
Bottle-conditioned beer: Le Coq's Imperial Extra
Double Stout (ABV 9% ⓒ).

Sussex XX Mild Ale (OG 1030, ABV 3%) ▣ ◆
A dark copper-brown colour. Roast malt
dominates the aroma and palate leading to a
sweet, caramel finish.

Hadlow Bitter (OG 1033, ABV 3.5%)
Formerly Sussex Pale Ale

Sussex Best Bitter (OG 1040, ABV 4%) ⓒ ◆
Full-bodied brown bitter. A hoppy aroma
leads to a good malt and hop balance, and a
dry aftertaste.

Armada Ale (OG 1045, ABV 4.5%) ◆
Hoppy amber best bitter. Well-balanced fruit and
hops dominate throughout with a fruity palate.

Harviestoun SIBA

Harviestoun Brewery Ltd, Alva Industrial Estate,
Alva, Clackmannanshire, FK12 5DQ
Tel (01259) 769100
✉ info@harviestoun-brewery.co.uk
⊕ harviestoun-brewery.co.uk
Shop Mon-Fri 9am-4.30pm

Harviestoun started in a barn in the village of
Dollar in 1985 with a five-barrel brew plant, but
now operate on a state-of-the-art 50-barrel
brewery seven miles from the original site. The
brewery supplies local outlets itself and
nationwide through wholesalers. It was bought
by Caledonian Brewing Co (qv) in 2006.
Seasonal beers: see website.

Bitter & Twisted (OG 1036, ABV 3.8%) ◆
Refreshingly hoppy beer with fruit
throughout. A bittersweet taste with a long
bitter finish. A golden session beer.

Celebration Ale (OG 1042, ABV 4.1%)
A new beer brewed to celebrate 20 years
brewing. 50/50 pale and wheat malts with
Amarillo, Brewers Gold and Fuggles hops.

Ptarmigan (OG 1047, ABV 4.5%) ◆
A well-balanced, bittersweet beer in which hops
and malt dominate. The blend of malt, hops and
fruit produces a clean, hoppy aftertaste.

Schiehallion (OG 1048, ABV 4.8%) ◆
A Scottish cask lager, brewed using a lager
yeast and Hersbrucker hops. A hoppy aroma,
with fruit and malt, leads to a malty, bitter
taste with floral hoppiness and a bitter finish.

Harwich Town* EAB

Harwich Town Brewing Co, Station Approach,
Harwich, Essex, CO12 3NA
Tel (01255) 551155
✉ info@harwichtown.co.uk
⊕ harwichtown.co.uk

☒ Brewing started in June 2007 on a five-barrel
plant. All beers are named after local landmarks
or worthies. Bottled beers are available from
the on-site shop (opening hours erratic - please
see website). Around 40 outlets are supplied
direct. All beers are also available bottle-
conditioned. Seasonal beers: Mayflower (ABV
4%, May-Jul), Redoubt Stout (ABV 4.4%,
winter), High Light (ABV 8%, winter).

Ha'Penny Mild (ABV 3.4%)

Leading Lights (ABV 3.8%)

Lighthouse Bitter (ABV 4.2%)

Station Porter (ABV 4.2%)

Hawkshead SIBA

Hawkshead Brewery Ltd, Mill Yard, Staveley,
Cumbria, LA8 9LR
Tel (01539) 822644
✉ info@hawksheadbrewery.co.uk
⊕ hawksheadbrewery.co.uk
Shop open 12-5pm daily
Tours by arrangement

Hawkshead Brewery, founded by former BBC journalist Alex Brodie, now has two working breweries in the heart of the Lake District. It began in 2002 on a seven-barrel plant at Hawkshead, which is now used for developing new beers, but is based mainly at its new purpose-built brewery and Beer Hall, opened in late 2006, at Staveley Mill on the River Kent. The Beer Hall is a showcase for real ale and includes a visitor centre, sampling room, beer shop and fully licensed bar with restaurant.

Bitter (OG 1037, ABV 3.7%) ◆
Well-balanced, thirst-quenching beer with fruit and hops aroma, leading to a lasting bitter finish.

UPA/Ulverston Pale Ale (OG 1041, ABV 4.1%)
A very pale ale, using three English hops.

Red/Best Bitter (OG 1042, ABV 4.2%)
A red ale; malty and spicy, with a long dry finish.

Lakeland Gold (OG 1043, ABV 4.4%) ◆
Fresh, well-balanced fruity, hoppy beer with a clean bitter aftertaste.

Brodie's Prime (OG 1048, ABV 4.9%) ◆
Complex, dark brown beer with plenty of malt, fruit and roast taste. Satisfying full body with clean finish.

Haywood Bad Ram

Haywood Bad Ram Brewery, Callow Top Holiday Park, Sandybrook, Ashbourne, Derbyshire, DE6 2AQ
Tel 07974 948427
✉ acphaywood@aol.com
⊕ callowtop.co.uk
Shop 9am-5pm (seasonal)
Tours by arrangement

The brewery is based in a converted barn. There are plans for a bottling plant to supply own label beers. One pub is owned (on site) and several other outlets are supplied. The brewery is not operational during the winter.

Dr Samuel Johnson (ABV 4.5%)

Bad Ram (ABV 5%)

Lone Soldier (ABV 5%)

Woggle Dance (ABV 5%)

Callow Top IPA (ABV 5.2%)

Headless*

▯ Headless Brewery, The Flowerpot, 19-25 King Street, Derby, Derbyshire, DE1 3DZ
Tel (01332) 204955

Headless was established in September 2007 on a 10-barrel plant. The beer list was not finalised at time of going to press.

Heart of Wales*

Heart of Wales Brewery, Stables Yard, Zion Street, Llanwrtyd Wells, Powys, LD5 4RD
Tel (01591) 610732
✉ Lindsay@heartofwalesbrewery.co.uk
⊕ heartofwalesbrewery.co.uk
Shop 10am-6pm daily
Tours by arrangement

The brewery was set up with a six-barrel plant in 2006 in old stables at the rear of the Neuadd Arms Hotel. Selected ales are conditioned in oak barrels prior to being casked. Seasonal brews are planned to celebrate local events such as the World Bogsnorkelling Championships. Bottle-conditioned beers are also planned.

Aur Cymru (ABV 3.8%)

Bitter (ABV 4.1%)

Welsh Black (ABV 4.4%)

Noble Eden Ale (ABV 4.6%)

Innstable (ABV 5.5%)

Hebridean SIBA

Hebridean Brewing Co, 18A Bells Road, Stornoway, Isle of Lewis, HS1 2RA
Tel (01851) 700123
✉ info@hebridean-brewery.co.uk
⊕ hebridean-brewery.co.uk
Shop open in summer months only
Tours by arrangement

The company was set up in 2001 on a steam powered plant with a 14-barrel brew length. A shop is attached to the brewery and the beers are also bottled (not bottle-conditioned). Seasonal beers are produced for Mods, Gaelic festivals that are the Scottish equivalent of the Welsh Eisteddfod.

Celtic Black Ale (OG 1036, ABV 3.9%)
A dark ale full of flavour, balancing an aromatic hop combined with a subtle bite and a pleasantly smooth caramel aftertaste.

Clansman Ale (OG 1036, ABV 3.9%)
A light Hebridean beer, brewed with Scottish malts and lightly hopped to give a subtle bittering.

Seaforth Ale (ABV 4.2%)
A golden beer in the continental style.

Islander Strong Premium Ale (OG 1044, ABV 4.8%) ◆
A malty, fruity strong bitter drinking dangerously below its ABV.

Berserker Export Pale Ale (OG 1068, ABV 7.5%)
Brewed using traditional methods and based on 19th-century recipes. Matured to develop a smooth, intricate flavour.

Hepworth SIBA

Hepworth & Co Brewers Ltd, The Beer Station, Railway Yard, Horsham, West Sussex, RH12 2NW
Tel (01403) 269696
✉ mail@hepworthbrewery.co.uk
⊕ hepworthbrewery.co.uk
Shop 9am-6pm
Tours by arrangement

Four workers from King & Barnes started the brewery in 2001, bottling beer only. In 2003 draught beer brewing was started with Sussex malt and hops. In 2004 an organic lager was introduced in bottle and on draught. 120 outlets are supplied. Seasonal beers: Prospect Organic Ale (ABV 4.5%, spring), Summer Ale (ABV 3.4%), Harvest Ale (ABV 4.5%, autumn), Old

Ale (ABV 4.8%, winter), Christmas Ale (ABV 7.5%), Super Horse (ABV 6.1%). Bottle-conditioned beers: Prospect Organic Ale, Xmas Ale. Prospect Organic Ale and Blonde Organic Lager are suitable for vegetarians and vegans.

Traditional Sussex Bitter (OG 1035, ABV 3.6%) ◆
A fine, clean-tasting amber session beer. A bitter beer with a pleasant fruity and hoppy aroma that leads to a crisp, tangy taste. A long, dry finish.

Pullman First Class Ale (OG 1041, ABV 4.2%) ◆
A sweet, nutty maltiness and fruitiness are balanced by hops and bitterness in this easy-drinking, pale brown best bitter. A subtle bitter aftertaste.

Iron Horse (OG 1048, ABV 4.8%) ◆
There's a fruity, toffee aroma to this light brown, full-bodied bitter. A citrus flavour balanced by caramel and malt leads to a clean, dry finish.

Hereward

Hereward Brewery, 50 Fleetwood, Ely, Cambridgeshire, CB6 1BH
Tel (01353) 666441
✉ michael.czarnobaj@ntlworld.com

A small home-based brewery launched in 2003 on a 10-gallon kit. The brewery supplies mainly beer festivals and also brews festival specials (brewed to order). Seasonal beer: Uncle Joe's Winter Ale (ABV 5%). The entire range of beers is now also available bottle conditioned.

Bitter (ABV 3.8%)

St Ethelreda's Golden Bitter (ABV 4%)

Porta Porter (ABV 4.2%)

Oatmeal Stout (ABV 4.5%)

Hesket Newmarket SIBA

Hesket Newmarket Brewery Ltd, Old Crown Barn, Back Green, Hesket Newmarket, Cumbria, CA7 8JG
Tel (016974) 78066
✉ brewer@hesketbrewery.co.uk
⊕ hesketbrewery.co.uk
Tours via the Old Crown Inn (016974) 78288

☺ The brewery was established in 1988 and was bought by a co-operative of villagers in 1999, anxious to preserve a community resource. It is now managed on their behalf by Mike Parker, ex-Stones head brewer. Most of the original recipes have been retained, all named after local fells except for Doris's 90th Birthday Ale. A 10-barrel plant was installed in 2004 followed by bottling on a small scale in late 2005. 30 regular outlets are supplied. Seasonal beer: Sharp Edge Autumn Ale (ABV 4.2%, Oct-Jan). Bottle-conditioned beers: Haystacks Refreshing Ale, Doris's 90th Birthday Ale, Sca Fell Blonde, Catbells Pale Ale, Old Carrock Strong Ale.

Great Cockup Porter (OG 1035, ABV 3%)
A refreshing, dark and chocolaty porter with a dry finish.

Blencathra Bitter (OG 1035, ABV 3.2%) ◆
A malty, tawny ale, mild and mellow for a bitter, with a dominant caramel flavour.

Skiddaw Special Bitter (OG 1035, ABV 3.6%)
An amber session beer, malty throughout, thin with a dryish finish.

Haystacks Refreshing Ale (OG 1037, ABV 3.7%)
A light, pale, refreshing beer with a zesty hop. Hint of grapefruit on the finish.

Doris's 90th Birthday Ale (OG 1045, ABV 4.3%) ◆
A full-bodied, nicely balanced malty beer with an increasing hop finish and butterscotch in the mouth.

Sca Fell Blonde (OG 1047, ABV 4.5%)
Pale with fruity hop notes. A good introduction to real ale for lager drinkers.

Catbells Pale Ale (OG 1050, ABV 5%) ◆
A powerful golden ale with a well-balanced malty bitterness, ending with a bitter and decidedly dry aftertaste.

Old Carrock Strong Ale (OG 1060, ABV 6%)
A dark red, powerful ale.

Hexhamshire SIBA

Hexhamshire Brewery, Leafields, Ordley, Hexham, Northumberland, NE46 1SX
Tel (01434) 606577
✉ ghb@hexhamshire.co.uk

☺ Hexhamshire was founded in 1992 in a converted cattle shed. The brewery has been operated by one of the founding partners and his family since 1997. Five beers are brewed regularly for the Dipton Mill pub and 40 other outlets are supplied.

Devil's Elbow (OG 1036, ABV 3.6%) ◆
Amber brew full of hops and fruit, leading to a bitter finish.

Shire Bitter (OG 1037, ABV 3.8%) ◆
A good balance of hops with fruity overtones, this amber beer makes an easy-drinking session bitter.

Devil's Water (OG 1041, ABV 4.1%) ◆
Copper-coloured best bitter, well-balanced with a slightly fruity, hoppy finish.

Whapweasel (OG 1048, ABV 4.8%) ◆
An interesting smooth, hoppy beer with a fruity flavour. Amber in colour, the bitter finish brings out the fruit and hops.

Old Humbug (OG 1055, ABV 5.5%)

Hidden SIBA

Hidden Brewery Ltd, Unit 1, Oakley Business Park, Wylye Road, Dinton, Salisbury, Wiltshire, SP3 5EU
Tel (01722) 716440
✉ sales@thehiddenbrewery.com
⊕ thehiddenbrewery.com
Tours by arrangement

Hidden Brewery was founded in 2003 by head brewer Gary Lumber and partner Michael Woodhouse. The brewery is named after its location, hidden away in the Wiltshire countryside. It supplies some 1,000 outlets and has a brewery tap, the Bell at Wylye. One other pub is owned. Seasonal beers: Hidden Spring (ABV 4.5%), Hidden Fantasy (ABV 4.6%), Hidden Depths (ABV 4.6%), Hidden Treasure (ABV 4.8%), Hidden Export (ABV 5.2%).

Strength (ABV 3.4%)
A copper-coloured session beer with a lingering bitterness and fruity aroma.

Pint (OG 1039, ABV 3.8%)
A clean-tasting, tangy bitter with good hop content, and a citrus fruit and malt balance. Dry finish, mid-brown in colour; light hop aroma.

Old Sarum (OG 1042, ABV 4.1%)
A well-balanced bitter with a complex combination of malts and hops. The aroma is floral and spicy, full-flavoured with a dry bitterness.

Potential (OG 1042, ABV 4.2%)
A full hop, traditional bitter with a balanced malty flavour. Clean tasting with slight citrus notes.

Quest (OG 1042, ABV 4.2%)
An amber-coloured bitter with a malt background, fruity aroma and a dry finish.

Pleasure (OG 1049, ABV 4.9%)
A deep golden coloured, strong, dry, traditional IPA with a hoppy finish.

Highgate SIBA

Highgate Brewery Ltd, Sandymount Road, Walsall, West Midlands, WS1 3AP
Tel (01922) 644453
info@highgatebrewery.com
highgatebrewery.com
Tours by arrangement

Built in 1898, Highgate was an independent brewery until 1938 when it was taken over by Mitchells & Butlers and subsequently became the smallest brewery in the Bass group. It was brought back into the independent sector in 1995 as the result of a management buy-out and was subsequently acquired by Aston Manor (qv) in 2000. Highgate has nine tied houses, six of which serve cask beer. In July 2007 Highgate was bought by Global Star, a pub group in Birmingham (see Pub groups section). Some 200 outlets are supplied. The company also has a contract to supply Mitchells & Butlers pubs as well as contract brewing for Smiles Brewery. Beer range liable to change. Seasonal beer: Old Ale (ABV 5.3%, winter).

Dark Mild (OG 1036.8, ABV 3.6%)
A dark brown Black Country mild with a good balance of malt and hops, and traces of roast flavour following a malty aroma.

Special Bitter (OG 1037.8, ABV 3.8%)

Davenports Bitter (OG 1040.8, ABV 4%)

Saddlers Best Bitter (OG 1043.8, ABV 4.3%)
A fruity, pale yellow bitter with a strong hop flavour and a light, refreshing bitter aftertaste.

Davenports Premium (OG 1046.8, ABV 4.6%)

For Coors:

M&B Mild (OG 1034.8, ABV 3.2%)

For Smiles:

Blonde (ABV 3.8%)

Best (ABV 4.1%)

Bristol IPA (ABV 4.4%)

Heritage (ABV 5.2%)

748

High House SIBA

High House Farm Brewery, Matfen, Newcastle upon Tyne, Tyne & Wear, NE20 0RG
Tel (01661) 886192
info@highhousefarmbrewery.co.uk
highhousefarmbrewery.co.uk
Shop open 10.30am-5pm daily except Wed
Tours by arrangement

The brewery was founded in 2003 by farmer Steven Urwin on his 200-acre family farm in Grade II listed converted farm buildings. The beers are named after the farm collie dogs, horse and cat. Some 200 outlets are supplied. A visitor centre, including shop, bar and café with function room, opened in 2006. Seasonal beers: Sundancer (ABV 3.6%, summer), Red Shep (ABV 4%, autumn/winter), Black Moss (ABV 4.3%, winter).

Auld Hemp (OG 1038, ABV 3.8%)
Tawny-coloured ale with malt and fruit flavours and a good bitter finish.

Nel's Best (OG 1041, ABV 4.2%)
Golden hoppy ale full of flavour with a clean bitter finish.

Matfen Magic (OG 1046.5, ABV 4.8%)
Well-hopped brown ale with a fruity aroma, malt and chocolate overtones with a rich, bitter finish.

Highland

Highland Brewing Co Ltd, Swannay Brewery, Swannay by Evie, Birsay, Orkney, KW17 2NP
Tel (01856) 721700
info@highlandbrewingcompany.co.uk
highlandbrewingcompany.co.uk
Tours by arrangement

Brewing began in 2006 and bigger plant was installed a year later. A visitor centre and café are planned. 80 outlets are supplied.

Orkney Best (OG 1038, ABV 3.6%)
A refreshing, light-bodied, low gravity golden beer bursting with hop and sweet malt flavours. The long, hoppy finish leaves a dry bitterness.

Dark Munro (OG 1040, ABV 4%)
The nose presents an intense roast hit which is followed by summer fruits and some frankfurter in the mouth. The strong roast malt continues into the aftertaste. A very drinkable stout.

Scapa Special (OG 1042, ABV 4.2%)
A good copy of a typical Lancashire bitter, full of bitterness and background hops, leaving your mouth tingling in the lingering aftertaste.

Saint Magnus Ale (OG 1045, ABV 4.5%)
A complex tawny bitter with a stunning balance of malt and hop, and some soft roast. Full-bodied and very drinkable.

Strong Northerley (OG 1055, ABV 5.5%)

Orkney Blast (OG 1058, ABV 6%)
A warming strong bitter/barley wine. A mushroom and woody aroma blossoms into a well-balanced smack of malt and hop in the taste.

Highlands & Islands

Now Sinclair Breweries, see Atlas and Orkney

Highwood SIBA

Highwood Brewery Ltd, Grimsby West, Birchin Way, Grimsby, Lincolnshire, DN31 2SG
Tel (01472) 255500
✉ tomwood@tom-wood.com
⊕ tom-wood.com

Highwood, best known under the Tom Wood brand name, started brewing in a converted Victorian granary on the family farm in 1995. The brew-length was increased from 10 barrels to 30 in 2001, using plant from Ash Vine brewery. In 2002, Highwood bought Conway's Licensed Trade Wholesalers. It now distributes most regional and national cask ales throughout Lincolnshire and Nottinghamshire. More than 300 outlets are supplied. Seasonal beers: see website.

Dark Mild (OG 1034, ABV 3.5%)

Best Bitter (OG 1034, ABV 3.5%) ◀
A good citrus, passion fruit hop dominates the nose and taste, with background malt. A lingering hoppy and bitter finish.

Shepherd's Delight (OG 1040, ABV 4%) ◀
Malt is the dominant taste in this amber brew, although the fruity hop bitterness complements it all the way.

Harvest Bitter (OG 1042, ABV 4.3%)
A well-balanced amber beer where the hops and bitterness just about outdo the malt.

Old Timber (OG 1043, ABV 4.5%) ◀
Hoppy on the nose, but featuring well-balanced malt and hops. A slight, lingering roast/coffee flavour develops, but this is generally a bitter, darkish brown beer.

Bomber County (OG 1046, ABV 4.8%) ◀
An earthy malt aroma but with a complex underlying mix of coffee, hops, caramel and apple fruit. The beer starts bitter and intensifies to the end.

Higson's

Higson's Brewery, Unit 21 Brunswick Business Park, Liverpool, L3 4BD
Tel (0151) 228 2309
⊕ higsonsbrewery.co.uk

The proud name of Higson's has been restored to Liverpool. The brewery was founded in 1780 and was taken over by Boddingtons in 1985. When Whitbread bought Boddingtons it closed the Liverpool site. The new company currently has its beers brewed by Mayflower (qv) but will transfer to its own site once brewing equipment has been installed.

Bitter (ABV 4.1%)

Hilden

Hilden Brewing Co, Hilden House, Hilden, Lisburn, Co Antrim, BT27 4TY
Tel (02892) 660800
✉ irishbeers@hildenbrewery.co.uk
⊕ hildenbrewery.co.uk
Tours by arrangement

☺ Hilden was established in 1981 and is Ireland's oldest independent brewery. Hilden supplies beer to a large number of pubs throughout the UK and there are plans to start bottling.

Ale (OG 1038, ABV 4%) ◀
An amber-coloured beer with an aroma of malt, hops and fruit. The balanced taste is slightly slanted towards hops, and hops are also prominent in the full, malty finish.

Silver (OG 1042, ABV 4.2%)
A pale ale, light and refreshing on the palate but with a satisfying mellow hop character derived from a judicious blend of aromatic Saaz hops.

Molly Malone (OG 1045, ABV 4.6%)
Dark ruby-red porter with complex flavours of hop bitterness and chocolate malt.

Scullion's Irish (OG 1045, ABV 4.6%)
A bright amber ale, initially smooth with a slight taste of honey that is balanced by a long, dry aftertaste that lingers on the palate.

Halt (OG 1058, ABV 6.1%)
A premium traditional Irish red ale with a malty, mild hop flavour. This special reserve derives its name from the local train stop, which was used to service the local linen mill.

Hill Island

Michael Griffin t/a Hill Island Brewery, Unit 7 Fowlers Yard, Back Silver Street, Durham, County Durham, DH1 3RA
Tel 07740 932584
✉ mike@hillisland.freeserve.co.uk
Shop most weekdays 10am-2pm (bulk purchasing only – ring first)
Tours by arrangement for groups of 10 or more

☺ Hill Island is a literal translation of Dunholme from which Durham is derived. The brewery began trading in 2002 and stands by the banks of the Wear in the heart of Durham City. Many of the beers produced have names reflecting local history and heritage. Brews can also be made exclusively for individual pubs. Around 40 outlets are supplied. Seasonal beers: Priory Summer Ale (ABV 3.5%), Festive Ale (ABV 4%), St Oswald's Xmas Ale (ABV 4.5%).

Peninsula Pint (OG 1036.5, ABV 3.7%)

Bitter (OG 1038, ABV 3.9%)

Dun Cow Bitter (OG 1039, ABV 4.2%)

Cathedral Ale (OG 1042, ABV 4.3%)

Griffin's Irish Stout (OG 1045, ABV 4.5%)

Hillside

Hillside Brewery Ltd, Hillside, Corse, Lumphanan, Aberdeenshire, AB31 4RY
Tel (01339) 883506
✉ brewery@hillsidecroft.eclipse.co.uk
⊕ hillsidecroft.eclipse.co.uk

Business consultant and home brewer Rob James established Hillside Brewery in 2005 and began selling his bottle-conditioned beers into local food outlets in early 2006. Bottle-conditioned beers: Brude (ABV 3.8%), Macbeth (ABV 4.2%). The bottled beers are suitable for vegetarians and vegans.

Broichan's (ABV 5.2%)

Hobden's

See Wessex

Hobsons SIBA

Hobsons Brewery & Co Ltd, Newhouse Farm, Tenbury Road, Cleobury Mortimer, Worcestershire, DY14 8RD
Tel (01299) 270837
✉ beer@hobsons-brewery.co.uk
⊕ hobsons-brewery.co.uk

⊗ Established in 1993 in a former sawmill, Hobsons relocated to a farm site with more space. Beers are supplied within a radius of 50 miles. The most recent addition is a new brewery adjoining the existing one, including a bottling plant. Hobsons also brews and bottles for the local tourist attraction, the Severn Valley Railway (Manor Ale, ABV 4.2%). Seasonal beers: Old Henry (ABV 5.2%, Sep-Apr), Steam No 9 (ABV 4.2%, Sep).

Mild (OG 1034, ABV 3.2%) 🍺 ◆
A classic mild. Complex layers of taste come from roasted malts that predominate and give lots of flavour.

Best Bitter (OG 1038.5, ABV 3.8%) ◆
A pale brown to amber, medium-bodied beer with strong hop character throughout. It is consequently bitter, but with malt discernible in the taste.

Town Crier (OG 1044, ABV 4.5%) 🍺
An elegant straw-coloured bitter. The hint of sweetness is complemented by subtle hop flavours, leading to a dry finish.

Hoggleys SIBA

Hoggleys Brewery, Unit 12 Litchborough Industrial Estate, Northampton Road, Litchborough, Northamptonshire, NN12 8JB
Tel (01604) 831762
✉ enquiries@hoggleys.co.uk
⊕ hoggleysbrewery.co.uk

⊗ Hoggleys was established in 2003 as a part-time brewery. It has now expanded to an eight-barrel plant, become full-time and moved to larger premises. All cask beers are also available bottle conditioned. 20 outlets are supplied. Solstice Stout and Mill Lane Mild are suitable for vegetarians as are all bottle-conditioned beers.

Mill Lane Mild (OG 1040, ABV 4%)
Brewed from mild, black and crystal malts and hopped with Challenger and Fuggles.

Kislingbury Bitter (OG 1042, ABV 4%)

Northamptonshire Bitter (OG 1044, ABV 4%)
A straw-coloured bitter brewed with pale malt only. The hops are Fuggles and Northdown, and the beer is late hopped with Fuggles for aroma.

Solstice Stout (OG 1050, ABV 5%)

Yuletide Ale (OG 1073, ABV 7.2%)

Hogs Back SIBA

Hogs Back Brewery Ltd, Manor Farm, The Street, Tongham, Surrey, GU10 1DE
Tel (01252) 783000
✉ info@hogsback.co.uk
⊕ hogsback.co.uk
Shop – see website
Tours by arrangement

⊗ This traditionally-styled brewery was established in 1992. Seasonal and commemorative ales are brewed throughout the year while the shop and visitors centre now sell more than 400 beers. Guided tours and tastings can be arranged; see website. More than 800 outlets are supplied. Seasonal beers: see website. Bottle-conditioned beers: TEA 🍺, BSA (ABV 4.5% 🗓), OTT (ABV 6%), Brewster's Bundle (ABV 7.4%), Wobble in a Bottle (ABV 7.5%), A over T (ABV 9% 🗓).

HBB/Hogs Back Bitter (ABV 3.7%) ◆
Aromatic session beer. Biscuity aroma with some hops and orange notes. Hoppy impact in the mouth with a long-lasting, well-balanced, dry, hoppy, bitter finish.

Legend (OG 1040, ABV 4%) ◆
Complex and drinkable, this golden-coloured beer contains both wheat and lager malts, and has a dry, malty and bitter taste that lingers.

TEA/Traditional English Ale (OG 1044, ABV 4.2%) ◆
A pale brown best bitter with both malt and hops on the nose. A well-rounded bitter flavour, balanced by fruit and some sweetness. Hoppy bitterness grows in the aftertaste.

Hop Garden Gold (OG 1048, ABV 4.6%) ◆
Pale golden best bitter, full bodied with an aroma of malt, hops and fruit. Citrus hop flavours are balanced by malt and fruit. Hoppy bitterness grows in a dry aftertaste with a hint of sweetness.

Holden's IFBB

Holden's Brewery Ltd, George Street, Woodsetton, Dudley, West Midlands, DY1 4LW
Tel (01902) 880051
✉ holdens.brewery@virgin.net
⊕ holdensbrewery.co.uk
Shop open Mon-Fri 9am-5pm
Tours by arrangement

☺ A family brewery going back four generations, Holden's began life as a brew-pub in the 1920s. The company continues to grow with 22 tied pubs and supplies around 70 other outlets.

Black Country Mild (OG 1037, ABV 3.7%) 🍺 ◆
A good, red/brown mild; a refreshing, light blend of roast malt, hops and fruit, dominated by malt throughout.

Black Country Bitter (OG 1039, ABV 3.9%) 🍺 🗓 ◆
A medium-bodied, golden ale; a light, well-balanced bitter with a subtle, dry, hoppy finish.

XB (OG 1042, ABV 4.1%) ◆
A sweeter, slightly fuller version of the Bitter. Sold in a number of outlets under different names.

Golden Glow (OG 1045, ABV 4.4%) 🍺 🗓
A pale golden beer with a subtle hop aroma plus gentle sweetness and a light hoppiness.

Special (OG 1052, ABV 5.1%) ◆
A sweet, malty, full-bodied amber ale with hops to balance in the taste and in the good, bittersweet finish.

Holland

**Holland Brewery, 5 Browns Flats, Brewery Street, Kimberley, Nottinghamshire, NG16 2JU
Tel (0115) 938 2685
✉ hollandbrew@btopenworld.com**

Len Holland, a keen home-brewer for 30 years, went commercial in 2000, in the shadow of now closed Hardys & Hansons. Seasonal beers: Holly Hop Gold (ABV 4.7%, Xmas), Dutch Courage (ABV 5%, winter), Glamour Puss (ABV 4.2%, spring), Blonde Belter (ABV 4.5%, summer).

Chocolate Clog (OG 1038, ABV 3.8%)

Golden Blond (OG 1040, ABV 4%)

Lipsmacker (OG 1040, ABV 4%)

Cloghopper (OG 1042, ABV 4.2%)

Double Dutch (OG 1045, ABV 4.5%)

Mad Jack Stout (OG 1045, ABV 4.5%)

Holt IFBB

**Joseph Holt Ltd, The Brewery, Empire Street, Cheetham, Manchester, M3 1JD
Tel (0161) 834 3285
⊕ joseph-holt.com**
Tours Saturday mornings only for groups of 10-15 (£10 donation to Christie Hospital/Holt Radium Institute)

The brewery was established in 1849 by Joseph Holt and his wife Catherine. It is still a family-run business in the hands of the great, great-grandson of the founder. Holt's supplies approximately 80 outlets as well as its own estate of 135 tied pubs. It still delivers beer to many of its tied houses in large 54-gallon hogsheads. A dedicated 30-barrel brew plant is used for seasonal beers: see website. Bottle-conditioned beer: Pioneer (ABV 5.2%).

Mild (OG 1033, ABV 3.2%) ◈
A dark brown/red beer with a fruity, malty nose. Roast, malt, fruit and hops in the taste, with strong bitterness for a mild, and a dry malt and hops finish.

Bitter (OG 1040, ABV 4%) ◈
Copper-coloured beer with malt and fruit in the aroma. Malt, hops and fruit in the taste with a very bitter and hoppy finish.

Hook Norton IFBB

**Hook Norton Brewery Co Ltd, The Brewery, Hook Norton, Banbury, Oxfordshire, OX15 5NY
Tel (01608) 737210
⊕ hooky.co.uk**
Shop open Mon-Fri 9am-5pm
Tours by arrangement

⊗ Hook Norton was founded in 1849 by John Harris, a farmer and maltster. The current premises were built in 1900 and Hook Norton is one of the finest examples of a Victorian tower brewery, with a 25hp steam engine for most of its motive power. The brewhouse has recently been expanded. Hook Norton owns 47 pubs and supplies approximately 300 free trade accounts. Seasonal beers: Double Stout (ABV 4.8%, Jan/Feb), 303AD (ABV 4%, Mar/Apr), Cotswold Lion (ABV 4.2%, May/Jun), Haymaker (ABV 5%, Jul/Aug), Flagship (ABV 5.3%, Sep/Oct), Twelve Days (ABV 5.5%, Nov/Dec).

Hooky Dark (OG 1033, ABV 3.2%) ⬚ ◈
A chestnut brown, easy-drinking mild. A complex malt and hop aroma give way to a well-balanced taste, leading to a long, hoppy finish that is unusual for a mild.

Hooky Bitter (OG 1036, ABV 3.6%) ◈
A classic golden session bitter. Hoppy and fruity aroma followed by a malt and hops taste and a continuing hoppy finish.

Hooky Gold (OG 1042, ABV 4.1%)
A golden, crisp beer with a citrus aroma and a fruity, rounded body.

Old Hooky (OG 1048, ABV 4.6%) ◈
A strong bitter, tawny in colour. A well-rounded fruity taste with a balanced bitter finish.

Hop Back SIBA

**Hop Back Brewery plc, Units 22-24, Batten Road Industrial Estate, Downton, Salisbury, Wiltshire, SP5 3HU
Tel (01725) 510986
✉ info@hopback.co.uk
⊕ hopback.co.uk**
Tours by arrangement

⊗ Started by John Gilbert in 1987 at the Wyndham Arms in Salisbury, the brewery has expanded steadily ever since. It went public via a Business Expansion Scheme in 1993 and has enjoyed rapid continued growth. Summer Lightning has won many awards. The brewery has 11 tied houses and also sells to some 500 other outlets. Seasonal beers are produced on a monthly basis. Bottle-conditioned beers: Summer Lightning ▣ ⬚, Taiphoon (ABV 4.2%), Crop Circle, Entire Stout. Entire Stout is suitable for vegans.

GFB/Gilbert's First Brew (OG 1035, ABV 3.5%) ◈
A golden beer, with a light, clean quality that makes it an ideal session ale. A hoppy aroma and taste lead to a good, dry finish.

Odyssey (OG 1040, ABV 4%)
A new, darker beer with a blend of four malts.

Crop Circle (OG 1041, ABV 4.2%) ◈
A refreshingly sharp and hoppy summer beer. Gold coloured with a slight citrus taste. The crisp, dry aftertaste lingers.

Entire Stout (OG 1043, ABV 4.5%) ⬚ ◈
A rich, dark stout with a strong roasted malt flavour and a long, sweet and malty aftertaste. A beer suitable for vegans. Also produced with ginger.

Summer Lightning (OG 1049, ABV 5%) ⬚ ◈
A pleasurable pale bitter with a good, fresh, hoppy aroma and a malty, hoppy flavour. Finely balanced, it has an intense bitterness leading to a long, dry finish.

Hopdaemon

**Hopdaemon Brewery Co Ltd, Unit 1 Parsonage Farm, Seed Road, Newnham, Kent, ME9 0NA
Tel (01795) 892078
✉ hopdaemon@supanet.com
⊕ hopdaemon.com**
Tonie Prins opened a 12-barrel plant in 2001 in Canterbury and within six months was supplying more than 30 pubs in the area, as

well as exclusive bottle-conditioned, own-label beers for London's British Museum, Southwark Cathedral, the Science Museum, and more recently for the Barbican and National Gallery. In 2005 the brewery moved to bigger premises in Newnham and some 100 outlets are now supplied. Bottle-conditioned beers: Skrimshander IPA, Green Daemon (ABV 5%), Leviathan, Barbican Beer (ABV 5%), British Museum Beer (ABV 5%), National Gallery Beer (ABV 4.5%).

Golden Braid (OG 1039, ABV 3.7%)

Incubus (OG 1041, ABV 4%)

Skrimshander IPA (OG 1045, ABV 4.5%)

Leviathan (OG 1057, ABV 6%)

Hopshackle*

Hopshackle Brewery Ltd, Unit F, Bentley Business Park, Blenheim Way, Northfields Industrial Estate, Market Deeping, Lincolnshire, PE6 8LD
Tel (01778) 348542
✉ **nigel@hopshacklebrewery.co.uk**
⊕ **hopshacklebrewery.co.uk**
Tours by arrangement

☺ Hopshackle was established in 2006 on a five-barrel brew plant. An expansion of the beer range and bottling are planned. Around 12 outlets are supplied.

Bitter (OG 1038, ABV 3.8%)

Special Bitter (OG 1040, ABV 4.3%)

Special No. 1 Bitter (OG 1049, ABV 5.2%)

Hopstar

Hopstar Brewery, c/o Black Horse, 72 Redearth Road, Darwen, Lancashire, BB3 2AF
Tel (01254) 873040
✉ **hopstar@theblackun.co.uk**

Hopstar first brewed in 2005 on a half-barrel plant and subsequently commissioned a 2.5-barrel kit. Two new fermenters were added in 2006 to double capacity due to demand.

Dizzy Danny Ale (ABV 3.8%)

Spinning Jenny (ABV 4%)

Smokey Joe's Black Beer (ABV 4%)

Hornbeam*

Hornbeam Brewery, 1-1c Grey Street, Denton, Manchester, M34 3RU
Tel (0161) 320 5627
✉ **kevin@hornbeambrewery.co.uk**
Tours by arrangement

☺ Hornbeam began brewing in July 2007 on an eight-barrel plant. Seasonal beers: Dark Domination Porter (ABV 6%), Malt Mountain Mild (ABV 3.2%), Winterlong Dark Bitter (ABV 4.7%, winter).

Hop Hornbeam Bitter (ABV 3.8%)

Top Hop (ABV 4.2%)

Black Coral Stout (ABV 4.5%)

Golden Wraith Pale Ale (ABV 5%)

Horseshoe*

♥ **Horseshoe Brewery/McLaughlin Brewhouse, The Horseshoe, 28 Heath Street, Hampstead, London, NW3 6TE**
Tel (020) 7431 7206
✉ **getlucky@thehorseshoehampstead.com**
⊕ **thehorseshoehampstead.com**

A micro-brewery built in July 2006 to honour the landlord's late grandfather, who owned Mac's Brewery in Rockhampton, Australia. More beers are planned as well as an expansion in the near future. At present they only supply their own pub, the Horseshoe.

McLaughlin Summer (ABV 3.6%)

McLaughlin Laurie Best Bitter (ABV 4.1%)

Hoskins Brothers

Hoskins Brothers Ales, The Ale Wagon, 27 Rutland Street, Leicester, LE1 1RE
Tel (0116) 262 3330
✉ **mail@alewagon.com**
⊕ **alewagon.co.uk**

Hoskins brothers are not currently brewing pending the building of a new brewery at the Ale Wagon in Leicester. Their beers are currently contract brewed at Tower Brewery, Burton upon Trent. See Tower for beer list.

Houston SIBA

Houston Brewing Co, South Street, Houston, Renfrewshire, PA6 7EN
Tel (01505) 612620
✉ **ale@houston-brewing.co.uk**
⊕ **houston-brewing.co.uk**
Shop open pub hours, every day
Tours by arrangement

A brewery attached to the Fox & Hounds pub and restaurant. Brewery tours include dinner and tastings. Gift packs and bottles are also available. 200 outlets are supplied. Seasonal beers: see website.

Killellan Bitter (OG 1037, ABV 3.7%) ✦
A light session ale, with a floral hop and fruity taste. The finish of this amber beer is dry and quenching.

Blonde Bombshell (OG 1040, ABV 4%)
A gold-coloured ale with a fresh hop aroma and rounded maltiness.

Black & Tan (ABV 4.2%)

Peter's Well (OG 1042, ABV 4.2%) ✦
Well-balanced fruity taste with sweet hop, leading to an increasingly bitter-sweet finish.

Texas (ABV 4.3%)

Tartan Terror (ABV 4.5%)

Warlock Stout (ABV 4.7%)

Howard Town

Howard Town Brewery Ltd, Hawkshead Mill, Hawkshead Lane, Hope Street, Glossop, Derbyshire, SK13 7SS
Tel (01457) 869800
✉ **beer@howardtownbrewery.co.uk**

⊕ **howardtownbrewery.co.uk**
Tours by arrangement

☺ Howard Town was established in 2005 by partners Tony Hulme and Les Dove, with their wives. More than 100 outlets are supplied. Seasonal beers: Snake Ale (ABV 4%, autumn), Robins Nest (ABV 5.2%, Xmas).

Bleaklow (OG 1040, ABV 3.8%)

Wrens Nest (OG 1043, ABV 4.2%)

Dinting Arches (OG 1045, ABV 4.5%)

Glotts Hop (OG 1049, ABV 5%)

Sarah Hughes

⌂ Sarah Hughes Brewery, Beacon Hotel, 129 Bilston Street, Sedgley, Dudley, West Midlands, DY3 1JE
Tel (01902) 883381
✉ andrew.brough@tiscali.co.uk
Tours by arrangement

A traditional Black Country tower brewery, established in 1921. The original grist case and rare open-topped copper add to the ambience of the Victorian brewhouse and give a unique character to the brews. Seasonal beers: Raucous (ABV 4.8%, summer), Rampur (ABV 5.2%, summer), Pale Bock (ABV 4.7%, autumn), Imperial Stout (ABV 7.3%, winter), 1921 (ABV 5.5%, Nov-Jan).

Pale Amber (OG 1038, ABV 4%)
A well-balanced beer, initially slightly sweet but with hops close behind.

Sedgley Surprise (OG 1048, ABV 5%) ◈
A bittersweet, medium-bodied, hoppy ale with some malt.

Dark Ruby (OG 1058, ABV 6%) 🍾 🗖 ◈
A dark ruby strong ale with a good balance of fruit and hops, leading to a pleasant, lingering hops and malt finish.

Humpty Dumpty

Humpty Dumpty Brewery, Church Road, Reedham, Norfolk, NR13 3TZ
Tel (01493) 701818
✉ sales@humptydumptybrewery.co.uk
⊕ humptydumptybrewery.co.uk
Shop 9am-5pm daily spring/summer, 12-5pm weekends autumn/winter
Tours by arrangement

⊗ Established in 1998, the 11-barrel brewery moved to its present site in 2001 and changed hands in 2006. The new owners continue to brew using local ingredients and have expanded the original range. The brewery shop sells the company's ales as well as a large range of Belgian beers, local ciders, wines and local produce. All beers are also available bottle conditioned. Seasonal beers vary from year to year.

Nord Atlantic (OG 1039, ABV 3.7%)
A mid brown session ale with strong roast malt character. Fruit flavours linger on the tongue, which then gives way to a dry hop finish.

Little Sharpie (OG 1040, ABV 3.8%) ◈
A delicate hoppy aroma is a forerunner to a sweet hoppy, lagerish flavour. A clean golden yellow bitter with a finish in which bitterness grows.

Ale (OG 1043, ABV 4.1%) ◈
Amber coloured with a hoppy nose and grainy feel. The balance is on the bitter side. Underlying sweetness fades to leave a long, dry finish.

Claud Hamilton (OG 1043, ABV 4.1%) ◈
A well-rounded, red-brown beer with a distinct hickory stick aroma. The roast malt base lingers as the bittersweet beginning fades into a light hoppy dryness.

Reedham Gold (OG 1044, ABV 4.2%)

Reedcutter (OG 1046, ABV 4.4%) ◈
A light, soft-flavoured beer with banana and toffee notes. A malted milk flavour in the first taste, and a shallow, sweetish, fruity follow through.

King John (OG 1046, ABV 4.5%)
A golden ale with soft, fruity undertones leading to a complex bittersweet finish.

Cheltenham Flyer (OG 1048, ABV 4.6%)
Clean, crisp, golden-coloured ale. Hints of malt at the start are soon overtaken by a refreshing dry hop bitterness.

Norfolk Nectar (OG 1048, ABV 4.6%)
Amber-coloured ale infused with local Reedham honey. A refreshing hop bitterness lingers on the palate leaving a slight honey and vanilla sweetness.

Iron Duke (OG 1048, ABV 4.6%)
Red in colour with a well-balanced hop.

Railway Sleeper (OG 1051, ABV 5%) ◈
Full-bodied tawny brew with a rich, fruity nature. A strong plummy character where sweetness and malt counterbalance the background bitterness. A quick, spicy, bitter finish.

Golden Gorse (OG 1054, ABV 5.4%)
A pale golden ale with a fruity sweetness on the nose that is quickly overtaken by Cascade hops, leaving a pleasant bitter aftertaste.

Porter (OG 1054, ABV 5.4%)
Traditional porter giving a full roast aroma with hints of liquorice on the tongue and a dry, bitter finish.

Hurns

See Tomos Watkin

Hydes IFBB

Hydes Brewery Ltd, 46 Moss Lane West, Manchester, M15 5PH
Tel (0161) 226 1317
✉ mail@hydesbrewery.com
⊕ hydesbrewery.com
Tours by arrangement (Mon-Thu 7pm)

Hydes has recently undergone major restructuring, moving from managed houses to tenancies. More than 200 outlets are supplied. The brewery is diversifying and has a growing number of pub restaurants and café bars. The company is now the biggest volume producer of cask beers in the North-west, with further expansion planned. Seasonal beers: Jumpin' Jack (ABV 4.7%, Jan-Feb), Vertigo (ABV 4.2%, Mar-Apr), Golden Brown (ABV 4.4%, May-Jun), Summertime Blue (ABV 4.1%, Jul-Aug), Thriller (ABV 4.5%, Sep-Oct), Atomic (ABV 4.9%, Nov-Dec).

Light Mild/1863 (OG 1033.5, ABV 3.5%) ◈
A lightly-hopped, amber-coloured session beer with a fresh lemon fruit taste and a short, dry finish. Sold as 1863 Bitter is some outlets.

Traditional Mild (OG 1033.5, ABV 3.5%) ◈
A mid-brown beer with malt and citrus fruits in the aroma and taste. Dry, malty aftertaste.

Owd Oak (OG 1033.5, ABV 3.5%) ◈
Dark brown/red in colour with a fruit and malt nose. Complex taste, including berry fruits, malt and a hint of chocolate. Satisfying aftertaste.

Original Bitter (OG 1036.5, ABV 3.8%) ⬚ ◈
Pale brown beer with a malty nose, malt and an earthy hoppiness in the taste, and a good bitterness through to the finish.

Jekyll's Gold Premium (OG 1042, ABV 4.3%) ◈
Pale gold in colour, with a fruity nose. A well-balanced beer with hops, fruit and malt in the taste and the bitter finish.

XXXX (OG 1070, ABV 6.8%)

For InBev UK:

Boddingtons Bitter (OG 1038, ABV 4.1%)

Iceni SIBA EAB

Iceni Brewery, 3 Foulden Road, Ickburgh, nr Mundford, Norfolk, IP26 5HB
Tel (01842) 878922
✉ icenibrewe@aol.com
⊕ icenibrewery.co.uk
Shop Mon-Fri 8.30am-5pm; Sat 9am-3pm
Tours by arrangement

▨ Iceni was launched in 1995 by Brendan Moore. The brewery has its own hop garden aimed at the many visitors who flock to the shop to buy the 28 different ales, stouts and lagers bottled on-site. 40 outlets are supplied as well as local farmers' markets and a tourist shop in nearby Thetford Forest. Special beers are brewed for festivals. Seasonal beer: Winter Lightning (ABV 5%). All cask ales are also bottle conditioned; there are many additional bottle-conditioned beers: see website.

Elveden Forest Gold (OG 1040, ABV 3.9%) ◈
Forest fruits on the nose give way to strong hop bitterness in the initial taste. Residual maltiness provides balance at first but is swamped by a long, dry, bitter finish.

Fine Soft Day (OG 1038, ABV 4%) ◈
The jam nose contrasts with the distinctly bitter character of this quick-finishing brew. Hops and malt can be found initially but soon subside.

Celtic Queen (OG 1038, ABV 4%) ◈
A golden brew with a light hoppy nose giving way to distinctly bitter characteristics throughout. A shallow mix of malt and hops adds some depth. A long, lingering finish.

Fen Tiger (OG 1040, ABV 4.2%)

It's A Grand Day (OG 1044, ABV 4.5%)

Raspberry Wheat (OG 1048, ABV 5%)

Men of Norfolk (OG 1060, ABV 6.2%) ◈
Chocolaty stout with roast overtones from initial aroma to strong finish. Malt and vine fruits counterbalance the initial roast character while a caramel undertone remains to the end.

Idle*

⬚ **The Idle Brewery, White Hart Inn, Main Street, West Stockwith, Nr Doncaster, South Yorkshire, DN10 4EY**
Tel (01427) 890176
✉ wcmoorecd@aol.com
Tours by arrangement

The brewery began production in early 2007 and is situated in an old cart shed barn at the back of the White Hart Inn. The beer list had not been finalised when the guide went to press.

Idle Landlord (ABV 4.2%)

Innis & Gunn

Innis & Gunn Brewing Co Ltd, PO Box 17246, Edinburgh, EH11 1YR
Tel (0131) 337 4420
✉ dougal.sharp@innisandgunn.com
⊕ innisandgunn.com

Innis & Gunn do not brew but an unnamed Scottish brewer produces one regular bottled (not bottle-conditioned) beer for the company, Oak Aged Beer (ABV 6.6%).

Inveralmond SIBA

Inveralmond Brewery Ltd, 1 Inveralmond Way, Inveralmond, Perth, PH1 3UQ
Tel (01738) 449448
✉ info@inveralmond-brewery.co.uk
⊕ inveralmond-brewery.co.uk

Established in 1997, Inveralmond was the first brewery in Perth for more than 30 years. The brewery has gone from strength to strength, with around 150 outlets supplied and wholesalers taking beers nationwide. In 2005 the brewery expanded ino the next door premises, more than doubling floor space and output. Seasonal ales: see website.

Independence (OG 1040, ABV 3.8%) ◈
A well-balanced Scottish ale with fruit and malt tones. Hop provides an increasing bitterness in the finish.

Ossian (OG 1042, ABV 4.1%) ◈
Well-balanced best bitter with a dry finish. This full-bodied amber ale is dominated by fruit and hop with a bittersweet character although excessive caramel can distract from this.

Thrappledouser (OG 1043, ABV 4.3%) ◈
A refreshing amber beer with reddish hues. The crisp, hoppy aroma is finely balanced with a tangy but quenching taste.

Lia Fail (OG 1048, ABV 4.7%) ▨ ◈
The Gaelic name means Stone of Destiny. A dark, robust, full-bodied beer with a deep malty taste. Smooth texture and balanced finish.

Islay

Islay Ales Company Ltd, The Brewery, Islay House Square, Bridgend, Isle of Islay, PA44 7NZ
Tel (01496) 810014

✉ info@islayales.com
⊕ islayales.com
Shop Mon-Sat 10.30am-5pm
Tours by arrangement

☺ Brewing started on a four-barrel plant in a converted tractor shed in 2004. The brewery shop is next door. Paul Hathaway, Paul Capper and Walter Schobert set up the brewery on an island more famous for its whisky, but it has quickly established itself as a must-see place for those visiting the eight working distilleries on the island. Four outlets are supplied. All the beers are available in bottle-conditioned form.

Finlaggan Ale (OG 1039, ABV 3.7%)

Black Rock Ale (OG 1040, ABV 4.2%)

Saligo Ale (OG 1044, ABV 4.4%)

Dun Hogs Head Ale (OG 1044, ABV 4.4%)

Angus OG Ale (OG 1046, ABV 4.5%)

Ardnave Ale (OG 1048, ABV 4.6%)

Nerabus Ale (OG 1048, ABV 4.8%)

Single Malt Ale (OG 1050, ABV 5%)

Isle of Arran

See Arran

Isle of Mull

Isle of Mull Brewing Co Ltd, Ledaig, Tobermory, Isle of Mull, Argyll, PA75 6NR
Tel (01688) 302830
✉ isleofmullbrewing@btinternet.com

Brewing started in 2005 using a five-barrel plant. Bottled beers are available but are not bottle conditioned.

Island Pale Ale (OG 1038, ABV 3.9%)

Galleon Gold (ABV 4.1%)

Royal Regiment of Scotland (ABV 4.1%)

McCaig's Folly (OG 1042, ABV 4.2%)

Terror of Tobermory (OG 1045, ABV 4.6%)

Isle of Purbeck

◻ **Isle of Purbeck Brewery, Manor Road, Studland, Dorset, BH19 3AU**
Tel (01929) 450227
Tours by arrangement

The 10-barrel brewing equipment from the former Poole Brewery has been installed in the grounds of the Bankes Arms Hotel that overlooks Studland Bay. There are plans to add new brews. 50 outlets are supplied. Seasonal beer: Thermal Cheer (ABV 4.8%, winter).

Fossil Fuel (OG 1040, ABV 4.1%)

Solar Power (OG 1043, ABV 4.3%)

Studland Bay Wrecked (OG 1044, ABV 4.5%)

IPA (OG 1047, ABV 4.8%)

Isle of Skye

Isle of Skye Brewing Co (Leann an Eilein) Ltd, The Pier, Uig, Isle of Skye, IV51 9XP
Tel (01470) 542477vinfo@skyebrewery.co.uk

⊕ skyebrewery.co.uk
Shop Mon-Sat 10am-6pm; Sun 12.30-4.30pm (Apr-Oct)
Tours by arrangement

☺ The Isle of Skye Brewery was established in 1995, the first commercial brewery in the Hebrides. Originally a 10-barrel plant, it was upgraded to 20-barrels in 2004. Fermenting capacity now stands at 80 barrels, with plans to further increase this and upgrade bottling facilities. Seasonal beers: see website. Bottle-conditioned beers: Misty Isle, Am Basteir (ABV 7%).

Young Pretender (OG 1039, ABV 4%) ◈
A full-bodied golden ale, predominantly hoppy and fruity. The bitterness in the mouth is also balanced by summer fruits and hops, continuing into the lingering bitter finish.

Red Cuillin (OG 1041, ABV 4.2%) ◈
A light, fruity nose with a hint of caramel leads to a full-bodied, malty flavour and a long, dry, bittersweet finish.

Hebridean Gold (OG 1041.5, ABV 4.3%) ◈
Oats are used to produce this delicious speciality beer. Nicely balanced, it has a refreshingly soft, fruity, bitter flavour. Thirst quenching and very drinkable.

Black Cuillin (OG 1044, ABV 4.5%) ◈
A complex, tasty brew worthy of its many awards. Full-bodied with a malty richness, malts do hold sway but there are plenty of hops and fruit to be discovered in its varied character. A truly delicious 'Scottish' old ale.

Blaven (OG 1047, ABV 5%) ◈
Sweetish amber ale with orange fruit notes. There is plenty of hop bitterness to balance the fruitiness. The malty aroma gives way to a bittersweet finish.

Cuillin Beast (OG 1061.5, ABV 7%) ▢ ◈
Sweet and fruity, and much more drinkable than the strength would suggest. Plenty of caramel throughout with a variety of fruit on the nose. A really good winter warmer.

Itchen Valley SIBA

Itchen Valley Brewery Ltd, Unit D Prospect Commercial Park, Prospect Road, Alresford, Hampshire, SO24 9QF
Tel (01962) 735111/736429
✉ info@itchenvalley.com
⊕ itchenvalley.com
Shop Mon-Fri 9am-5pm
Tours by arrangement

▨ Established more than 10 years ago, Itchen Valley moved to new premises in 2006 and now offers regular brewery tours, a gift shop and mini conferencing facilities. 300+ pubs are supplied, with wholesalers used for futher distribution. Seasonal beers: Green Jackets (ABV 4.5%), Watercress Line (ABV 4.2%), Father Christmas (ABV 5%), Rudolph (ABV 3.8%). Bottle-conditioned beers: as for cask range plus Wat Tyler (ABV 5%), Hambledon Honey (ABV 4.6%), Hambledon Elderflower (ABV 4.6%).

Godfathers (OG 1038, ABV 3.8%) ◈
A citrus hop character with a malty taste and a light body, leading to an increasingly dry, bitter finish. Pale brown in colour.

Fagin's (OG 1041, ABV 4.1%) ◈
Enjoyable copper-coloured best bitter with a
hint of crystal malt and a pleasant bitter
aftertaste.

Hampshire Rose (OG 1042, ABV 4.2%)
A golden amber ale. Fruit and hops dominate
the taste throughout, with a good mouth feel.

Winchester Ale (OG 1042, ABV 4.2%)

Pure Gold (OG 1046, ABV 4.6%) ◈
An aromatic, hoppy, golden bitter. Initial
grapefruit flavours lead to a dry, bitter finish.

Wat Tyler (OG 1048, ABV 4.8%)

Jacobi

**Jacobi Brewery of Caio, Penlanwen Farm,
Pumsaint, Carmarthenshire, SA19 8RR**
Tel (01558) 650605
✉ justin@jacobibrewery.co.uk
⊕ jacobibrewery.co.uk

⊗ Brewing started in 2006 on an eight-barrel
plant in a converted barn. Brewer Justin Jacobi
is also the owner of the Brunant Arms in Caio,
which is a regular outlet for the beers. The
brewery is located 50 yards from the Dolaucothi
mines where the Romans dug for gold. A visitor
centre and bottling line are planned.

Light Ale (OG 1040, ABV 3.8%)

Original (OG 1044, ABV 4%)

Dark Ale (OG 1052, ABV 5%)

Jarrow SIBA

◻ Jarrow Brewery, Robin Hood, Primrose Hill,
Jarrow, Tyne & Wear, NE32 5UB
Tel (0191) 483 6792
✉ jarrowbrewery@btconnect.com
⊕ jarrowbrewing.co.uk
Tours by arrangement

☺ Brewing started in 2002 and during the first
year the brewery won five CAMRA awards. Three
pubs are owned and around 150 outlets are
supplied. Brewing has also started at the Maltings
pub in South Shields to give the brewery a 100-
barrel a week capacity. Seasonal beers: Westoe
Netty (ABV 4.3%, Feb & Nov), Red Ellen (ABV
4.4%, Jan & Oct), Venerable Bede (ABV 4.5%, Jun-
Sep), Old Cornelius (ABV 4.8%, Mar & Dec).

Bitter (OG 1037.5, ABV 3.8%)
A light golden session bitter with a delicate
hop aroma and a lingering fruity finish.

Rivet Catcher (OG 1039, ABV 4%)
A light, smooth, satisfying gold bitter with
fruity hops on the tongue and nose.

Joblings Swinging Gibbet (OG 1041,
ABV 4.1%)
A copper-coloured, evenly balanced beer
with a good hop aroma and a fruity finish.

McConnells Irish Stout (OG 1045,
ABV 4.6%)

Westoe IPA (OG 1044.5, ABV 4.6%)

Jennings

See Marstons in New national breweries section

Jersey SIBA

**Jersey Brewery, Tregear House, Longueville
Road, St Saviour, Jersey, JE2 7WF**
Tel (01534) 508151
✉ paulhurley@victor-hugo-ltd.com
Tours by arrangement

Following the closure of the original brewery in
Ann Street in 2004, the Jersey Brewery is now
located in an old soft drinks factory using a 40-
barrel plant along with the eight-barrel plant
from the former Tipsy Toad Brewery. Most cask
beers are produced on the smaller plant,
though the bigger one, which usually produces
keg beer, can also be used for cask production.
Cask Special was first produced for the 2005
Jersey beer festival but, after receiving the Beer
of the Festival award, is now in regular
production. The other cask ale, Sunbeam, is
produced for the Guernsey market following the
closure of the Guernsey Brewery.

Guernsey Sunbeam (OG 1042, ABV 4.2%)

Jimmy's Bitter (OG 1042, ABV 4.2%)

Special (OG 1045, ABV 4.5%)

Horny Toad (OG 1050, ABV 5%)

Jollyboat

**Jollyboat Brewery (Bideford) Ltd, The Coach
House, Buttgarden Street, Bideford, Devon,
EX39 2AU**
Tel (01237) 424343

⊗ The brewery was established in 1995 by
Hugh Parry and his son, Simon. Jollyboat
currently supplies some 16 outlets. A Jollyboat
is a sailors' leave boat and all the beer names
have nautical connections.

Grenville's Renown (ABV 3.8%)

Freebooter (OG 1040, ABV 4%)

Mainbrace (OG 1041, ABV 4.2%) ◈
Pale brown brew with a rich fruity aroma and
a bitter taste and aftertaste.

Plunder (ABV 4.8%)

Contraband (ABV 5.8%)
An award-winning ale based on a Victorian
porter recipe.

Jolly Brewer

**Jolly Brewer, Kingston Villa, 27 Poplar Road,
Wrexham, LL13 7DG**
Tel (01978) 261884
✉ pene@jollybrewer.co.uk
⊕ jollybrewer.co.uk
Shop 9am-4.45pm daily
Tours by arrangement (small numbers only)

Penelope Coles has been brewing for the past
25 years. In 1993 she opened a craft brewing
shop, the Jolly Brewer, and a real ale off licence
was added later. She became a registered
brewer in order to sell her beer in the shop at
Stall 21, Butchers Market, Henblas Street,
Wrexham. The brew plant is based in her home
and around 15 gallons can be produced a day.
All beers are also available bottle-conditioned
and are suitable for vegetarians and vegans.

Benno's (OG 1040, ABV 4%)

Druid's Ale (OG 1040, ABV 4%)

Mathew's Mild (OG 1040, ABV 4%)

McGivern's Pale (OG 1040, ABV 4%)

Taid's Garden (OG 1040, ABV 4%)

Chwerw Cymru (OG 1045, ABV 4.5%)

Lucinda's Lager (OG 1045, ABV 4.5%)

Suzanne's Stout (OG 1045, ABV 4.5%)

Taffy's Tipple (OG 1050, ABV 5%)

Y Ddraig Goch (OG 1050, ABV 5%)

Tommy's (OG 1055, ABV 5.5%)

Penelope's Secret/Porter (OG 1060, ABV 6%)

Strange Brew (OG 1060, ABV 6%) ◆
Powerful, fruity, black lager-style beer. Dry, crisp, vinous and sharp with a sweetish aftertaste.

Juwards

Juwards Brewery, Unit 14 Tonedale Business Park, Wellington, Somerset, TA21 0AW

Ted Bishop started brewing in 1994 on a six-barrel brewplant. In 1999 a 10-barrel plant was bought to allow further expansion. Brewing ceased in 2001 but in 2005 Ted restarted on a part-time basis. Four firkins are brewed at a time, once or twice a week. All beer is sold through the Moor Beer Company to whom all enquiries should be directed. Seasonal beers: Winter Brew (ABV 4.3%), Stout (ABV 4.6%).

Bishops Special Mild (ABV 3.8%)

Bitter (ABV 3.8%)

Bishops Somerset Ale (ABV 4%)

Juwards (ABV 4%)

Amber (ABV 4.1%)

Premium (ABV 4.3%)

Kelburn SIBA

Kelburn Brewing Co Ltd, 10 Muriel Lane, Barrhead, East Renfrewshire, G78 1QB
Tel (0141) 881 2138
✉ info@kelburnbrewery.com
⊕ kelburnbrewery.com
Tours by arrangement

⊗ Kelburn is a family business established in 2002. In the first five years of business, the beers have won 22 awards. Beers are available bottled and in take-away polypins. Seasonal beers: Ca'Canny (ABV 5.2%, winter 🗓), Pivo Estivo (ABV 3.9%, summer).

Goldihops (OG 1038, ABV 3.8%) ◆
Well-hopped session ale with a fruity taste and a bitter finish.

Misty Law (ABV 4%)
A dry, hoppy amber ale with a long-lasting bitter finish.

Red Smiddy (OG 1040, ABV 4.1%) 🗓 ◆
This bittersweet ale predominantly features an intense citrus hop character that assaults the nose and continues into the flavour, balanced perfectly with fruity malt.

Dark Moor (OG 1044, ABV 4.5%)
A dark, fruity ale with undertones of liquorice and blackcurrant.

Cart Blanche (OG 1048, ABV 5%) ◆
A golden, full-bodied ale. The assault of fruit and hop camouflages the strength of this easy-drinking, malty ale.

Kelham Island SIBA

Kelham Island Brewery Ltd, Alma Street, Sheffield, South Yorkshire, S3 8SA
Tel (0114) 249 4804
✉ sales@kelhambrewery.co.uk
⊕ kelhambrewery.co.uk
Tours by arrangement

⊛ The brewery opened in 1990 behind the Fat Cat public house. Due to its success, the brewery moved to new purpose-built premises in 1999 (adjacent to the pub), with five times the capacity of the original brewery. The old building has been converted into a visitor centre. Five regular beers are brewed as well as monthly seasonal specials and more than 200 outlets are supplied.

Kelham Best Bitter (OG 1038, ABV 3.8%) ◆
A clean, characterful, crisp, pale brown beer. The nose and palate are dominated by refreshing hoppiness and fruitiness, which, with a good bitter dryness, lasts in the aftertaste.

Kelham Gold (OG 1038, ABV 3.8%)
A light golden ale, a hoppy nose and finish, a smooth drinking bitter.

Pride of Sheffield (OG 1040.5, ABV 4%)
A full-flavoured amber coloured bitter.

Easy Rider (OG 1041.8, ABV 4.3%) ◆
A pale, straw-coloured beer with a sweetish flavour and delicate hints of citrus fruits. A beer with hints of flavour rather than full-bodied.

Pale Rider (OG 1050, ABV 5.2%) ◆
A full-bodied, straw pale ale, with a good fruity aroma and a strong fruit and hop taste. Its well-balanced sweetness and bitterness continue in the finish.

Keltek SIBA

Keltek Brewery, Candela House, Cardrew Way, Redruth, Cornwall, TR15 1SS
Tel (01209) 313620
✉ sales@keltekbrewery.co.uk
⊕ keltekbrewery.co.uk
Shop Mon-Fri 8am-6pm

Keltek Brewery moved to Lostwithiel in 1999 and in 2006 moved again to Redruth and installed a new 100-barrel plant in addition to the original two-barrel plant, which is still used for specials and development. More than 200 outlets are supplied via wholesalers. Seasonal ales and custom beers are available. All cask ales are also available bottle conditioned.

4K Mild (OG 1038, ABV 3.8%)

Golden Lance (OG 1038, ABV 4%)

Kornish Nektar (OG 1042, ABV 4%)

Magik (OG 1042, ABV 4.2%) ◆
A rounded, well-balanced and complex beer.

Natural Magik (OG 1045, ABV 4.6%)

Grim Reaper (OG 1047, ABV 4.8%)

Mr Harvey's Golden Sunshine Ale (OG 1050, ABV 4.9%)

King (OG 1051, ABV 5.1%)

Kripple Dick (ABV 6%)

Uncle Stu's Famous Steak Pie Stout (ABV 6.5%)

Beheaded '76 (ABV 7.6%)

Kemptown SIBA

⚐ Kemptown Brewery Co Ltd, 33 Upper St James's Street, Brighton, East Sussex, BN2 1JN
Tel (01273) 699595
✉ bev@kemptownbrewery.co.uk
⊕ kemptownbrewery.co.uk
Tours by arrangement

⊗ Kemptown was established in 1989 and built in the tower tradition behind the Hand in Hand, which is possibly the smallest pub in England with its own brewery. It takes its name and logo from the former Charrington's Kemptown Brewery, 500 yards away, which closed in 1964. Three free trade outlets are supplied. Seasonal beer: Ho Bloody Ho (winter).

Black Moggy Mild (OG 1038, ABV 3.8%)

Bitter (OG 1040, ABV 4%)

Ye Olde Trout (OG 1045, ABV 4.5%)

Dragons Blood (OG 1043, ABV 5.2%)

Keswick

Keswick Brewing Co, The Old Brewery, Brewery Lane, Keswick, Cumbria, CA12 5BY
Tel (017687) 80700
✉ enquiries@keswickbrewery.co.uk
⊕ keswickbrewery.co.uk
Shop – call for details
Tours by arrangement

Phil and Sue Harrison set up their 10-barrel brewery in 2006. Around 30 outlets are supplied and the beers are always available in the Dog & Gun, Keswick, the Middle Ruddings Hotel, Braithwaite and the Royal Oak, Ambleside. Seasonal beers: Thirst Blood (ABV 6%), Thirst Noel (ABV 6%).

Thirst Pitch (OG 1038, ABV 3.8%)

Thirst Ascent (OG 1040, ABV 4%)

Thirst Run (OG 1042, ABV 4.2%)

Thirst Fall (OG 1049, ABV 5%)

Keynsham

Keynsham Brewing Co Ltd, Brookleaze, Stockwood Vale, Keynsham, Bristol, BS4 5DU
Tel (0117) 983 6373
✉ jonfirth@blueyonder.co.uk
⊕ keynshambrewery.co.uk
Tours by arrangement

⊗ Keynsham opened in 2005 on the site of a former 10-barrel brewery. The brewer is John Firth, a long-standing CAMRA member and a craft brewer for many years. A wide variety of hops and grains is used. Some 30 outlets are supplied. Seasonal beers are available quarterly.

Pixash (OG 1042, ABV 4.1%) ◆
Mahogany-coloured best bitter with distinct

dark forest fruit flavours from Bramling Cross hops.

Chewton (OG 1044, ABV 4.3%) ◆
Pale, refreshing best bitter with undertones of lime and green apples.

Somerdale Golden (OG 1047, ABV 4.5%) ◆
Interestingly floral best bitter with spicy aroma and flavours of peppery hops and citrus.

Stockwood Stout (OG 1053, ABV 5%) ◆
Dark and complex stout, smoky, roast and liquorice flavour with a hint of sourness and sweet dark fruits fading to bittersweet.

Keystone

Keystone Brewery, Old Carpenters Workshop, Berwick St Leonard, Salisbury, Wiltshire, SP3 5SN
Tel (01747) 820426
✉ info@keystonebrewery.co.uk
⊕ keystonebrewery.co.uk
Shop Mon-Fri 9am-5pm
Tours by arrangement

⊗ Keystone Brewery was set up in 2006 with a 10-barrel plant. The beers have low food miles to help support a sustainable local community. Around 70 outlets are supplied. Bottle-conditioned beers: Gold Standard, Large One.

Bed Rock (OG 1035, ABV 3.6%)

Gold Standard (OG 1039, ABV 4%)

Large One/Alasdair's 1st Brew (OG 1041, ABV 4.2%)

Cornerstone (OG 1047, ABV 4.8%)

King SIBA

W J King & Co (Brewers), 3-5 Jubilee Estate, Foundry Lane, Horsham, West Sussex, RH13 5UE
Tel (01403) 272102
✉ office@kingfamilybrewers.co.uk
⊕ kingfamilybrewers.co.uk
Shop Sat 10am-2pm
Tours by arrangement (limited to 15)

⊗ Launched in 2001 on a 20-barrel plant, the brewery had expanded to a capacity of 50 barrels a week by mid-2004. In 2004 premises next door were added to give more cellar space and to enable room to stock more bottle-conditioned beers. One pub is owned and approximately 200 regular and occasional outlets are supplied. Seasonal beers: Old Ale, (ABV 4.5%, winter), Summer Ale (ABV 4%), Merry Ale (ABV 6.5%, Xmas). Bottle-conditioned beers: Red River (ABV 5%), Old Ale, Cereal Thriller (ABV 6.3%), Five Generation (ABV 4.4%), Merry Ale, Mallard Ale (ABV 5%), Winter's Tale (ABV 4.8%). All the bottled beers are suitable for vegetarians.

Horsham Best Bitter (OG 1038, ABV 3.8%) ◆
A predominantly malty best bitter, brown in colour. The nutty flavours have some sweetness with a little bitterness that grows in the aftertaste.

Red River (OG 1048, ABV 4.8%) ◆
A full-flavoured, mid-brown beer. It is malty with some berry fruitiness in the aroma and taste. The finish is reasonably balanced with a sharp bitterness coming through.

Kings Head

⚲ Kings Head Brewery, Kings Head,
132 High Street, Bildeston, Ipswich,
Suffolk, IP7 7ED
Tel (01449) 741434
✉ enquiries@bildestonkingshead.co.uk
⊕ bildestonkingshead.co.uk
Tours by arrangement

Kings Head has been brewing since 1996 in the
old stables at the back of the pub. The plant has
approximately five barrels' capacity and brewing
takes place twice a week. The brewery stages a
beer festival in May (Late Spring Bank Holiday)
every year. Six other pubs and many beer
festivals are supplied. Seasonal beer: Dark Vader
(ABV 5.4%, winter). Bottle-conditioned beers:
Blondie, Apache, Crowdie and Dark Vader.

Not Strong Beer/NSB (OG 1030, ABV 2.8%)

Best Bitter (OG 1040, ABV 3.8%)

Blondie (OG 1041, ABV 4%)

First Gold (OG 1044, ABV 4.3%)

Apache (OG 1046, ABV 4.5%)

Crowdie (OG 1050, ABV 5%)

Kingstone

Kingstone Brewery, Kinsons Farm, Whitebrook,
Monmouth, NP25 4TX
Tel (01600) 860778
Tours by arrangement

Kingstone Brewery is located in the Wye Valley
where brewing began on a four-barrel plant in
2005. All beers are available in both cask and
bottle-conditioned forms.

Three Castles (ABV 3.8%)

Challenger (ABV 4%)

Gold (ABV 4%)

No. 1 Stout (ABV 4.4%)

Classic (ABV 4.5%)

Gatehouse (ABV 5.1%)

Humpty Dumpty's Downfall (ABV 5.2%)

Kinver

Kinver Brewery, Unit 2 Fairfield Drive, Kinver,
Staffordshire, DY7 6EW
Tel 07715 842679/07906 146777
✉ info@kinverbrewery.co.uk
⊕ kinverbrewery.co.uk
Tours by arrangement

Established in 2004 by two CAMRA members,
Kinver Brewery consists of a five-barrel plant,
producing three regular beers, seasonals and
one-off brews. Kinver brews up to three times a
week and supplies more than 30 pubs and
clubs throughout the Midlands, including two in
Kinver. Seasonal beers: Maybug (ABV 4.8%),
Over the Edge (ABV 7.6%, Nov-Mar).

Sunarise (OG 1039, ABV 4%)
A pale, hoppy session beer.

Edge (OG 1041, ABV 4.2%) ◆
Hoppy aroma from this copper-coloured ale,
which has a full hop taste with fruity and
flowery asides. Bitterness develops with a
great hoppy, lingering mouthfeel.

Pail Ale (OG 1044, ABV 4.4%) ◆
Gold with a hoppy aroma and malty
background. Citrus hops dominate but are
tempered with fruit for a bittersweet
balance. Astringent note at the end.

Dudley Bug (OG 1046, ABV 4.8%)
Golden and dry with a bitter finish.

Caveman (OG 1050, ABV 5%) ◆
Pale brown with a caramel start, sweet and
fruity middle, fruity finish becoming bitter
with satisfying astringency.

Khyber (OG 1054, ABV 5.8%)
Traditional strength imperial pale ale.

Lancaster

Lancaster Brewery Ltd, Unit 19 Lansil Industrial
Estate, Caton Road, Lancaster, LA1 3PQ
Tel (01524) 844610
⊕ lancasterbrewery.co.uk

Lancaster started brewing in 2005 and has a
12-barrel plant. The brewery plans to relocate
to a purpose-built site but remains dedicated to
staying in Lancaster. Seasonal beers: Borasic
(ABV 3.8%, Jan), Murry's Vanguard (ABV 3.8%,
Mar), Turner's Sunset (ABV 4.1%, Jun/Jul), Giant
Axe (ABV 4%, Aug), Kingmaker (ABV 4.8%,
summer), Good Will Ale (ABV 5%, Christmas).

Duchy (OG 1040, ABV 3.9%) ◆
Smooth-tasting bitter with a delicate
sweetness balanced by firm hop notes. A
sweet, hoppy finish.

Blonde (OG 1042, ABV 4.1%)

JSB (OG 1044, ABV 4.3%) ◆
Dry yet mellow-tasting bitter with a good
balance of malt and hops.

Flaming Nora (OG 1050, ABV 4.9%)

Langham

Langham Brewery, Old Granary, Langham Lane,
Lodsworth, West Sussex, GU28 9BU
Tel (01798) 860861
✉ office@langhambrewery.co.uk
⊕ langhambrewery.co.uk
Shop Tue & Sat 9am-5pm
Tours by arrangement

⊠ Langham Brewery opened in 2006 using a
10-barrel plant. It is owned by Steve Mansley
and James Berrow. 10 outlets are supplied.

Halfway to Heaven (OG 1035, ABV 3.5%)

Sundowner (OG 1041, ABV 4.2%)

Langton

Langton Brewery, Grange Farm, Welham Road,
Thorpe Langton, Leicestershire, LE16 7TU
Tel 07840 532826
⊕ thelangtonbrewery.co.uk

⊠ The Langton Brewery started in 1999 in
buildings behind the Bell Inn, East Langton. Due
to demand, the brewery relocated in 2005 to a
converted barn in Thorpe Langton, where a four-
barrel plant was installed. All beers are available
to take away in casks, polypins or bottles.

Around 20 outlets are supplied. Seasonal beers: Bankers Draught (ABV 4.2%), Prime Shank (ABV 4.4%), Boxer Heavyweight (ABV 5.2%).

Caudle Bitter (OG 1039, ABV 3.9%) ◈
Copper-coloured session bitter that is close to pale ale in style. Flavours are relatively well-balanced throughout with hops slightly to the fore.

Inclined Plane Bitter (OG 1042, ABV 4.2%)
A straw coloured bitter with a citrus nose and long, hoppy finish.

Bowler Strong Ale (ABV 4.8%)
A strong traditional ale with a deep red colour and a hoppy nose.

Larkins SIBA

Larkins Brewery Ltd, Larkins Farm, Hampkin Hill Road, Chiddingstone, Kent, TN8 7BB
Tel (01892) 870328
Tours by arrangement Nov-Feb

⊗ Larkins Brewery was founded in 1986 by the Dockerty family, who bought the Royal Tunbridge Wells Brewery. The company moved to Larkins Farm in 1987. Since then the production of three regular brews and Porter in the winter months has steadily increased. Larkins owns one pub, the Rock at Chiddingstone Hoath, and supplies around 70 free houses within a radius of 20 miles.

Traditional Ale (OG 1035, ABV 3.4%)
Tawny in colour, a full-tasting hoppy ale with plenty of character for its strength.

Chiddingstone (OG 1040, ABV 4%)
Named after the village where the brewery is based, Chiddingstone is a mid-strength, hoppy, fruity ale with a long, bittersweet aftertaste.

Best (OG 1045, ABV 4.4%) ◈
Full-bodied, slightly fruity and unusually bitter for its gravity.

Porter (OG 1052, ABV 5.2%) ◈
Each taste and smell of this potent black winter beer (Nov-Apr) reveals another facet of its character. An explosion of roasted malt, bitter and fruity flavours leaves a bittersweet aftertaste.

Leadmill

Leadmill Brewery Ltd, Unit 1 Park Hall Farm, Park Hall Road, Denby, Derbyshire, DE5 8PX
Tel (01332) 883577
✉ tlc@leadmill.net

⊗ Originally set up in a pig sty in Selston, the brewery moved to Denby in 2002 and now has a four-barrel plant. Its sister brewery, Bottle Brook (qv), sources rare and unusual hops to be incorporated into Leadmill recipes. Its brewery tap is the Old Oak Inn, two miles away. Seasonal beers: Jersey City (ABV 5%, autumn), Ginger Spice (ABV 5%, summer), Autumn Goddess (ABV 4.2%), Get Stuffed (ABV 6.7%, Xmas).

Mash Tun Bitter (OG 1036, ABV 3.6%)

Old Oak Bitter (OG 1037, ABV 3.8%)

Duchess (OG 1041, ABV 4.2%)

Old Mottled Cock (OG 1041, ABV 4.2%)

Dream Weaver (OG 1042, ABV 4.3%)

Frosted Hop (OG 1042, ABV 4.3%)

Strawberry Blonde (OG 1042, ABV 4.4%)

Rolling Thunder (OG 1043, ABV 4.5%)

Curly Blonde (OG 1044, ABV 4.6%)

Maple Porter (OG 1045, ABV 4.7%)

Snakeyes (OG 1045, ABV 4.8%)

Agent Orange (OG 1047, ABV 4.9%)

Born in the USA (OG 1048, ABV 5%)

Retribution (OG 1048, ABV 5%)

Rampage (OG 1050, ABV 5.1%)

B52 (OG 1050, ABV 5.2%)

Destitution (OG 1051, ABV 5.3%)

Ghostrider (OG 1052, ABV 5.4%)

Rack and Ruin (OG 1055, ABV 5.7%)

Beast (OG 1053, ABV 5.7%)

Nemesis (OG 1062, ABV 6.4%)

WMD (OG 1065, ABV 6.7%)

Leatherbritches SIBA

Leatherbritches Brewery, Bentley Brook Inn, Fenny Bentley, Derbyshire, DE6 1LF
Tel (01335) 864492/07976 279253
Tours by arrangement

⊛ The brewery was started by 'Steamin' Billy Allingham in the 1990s and is now owned and run by his brother, Edward. 100 outlets are supplied. The brewery has plans to expand and move to Ashbourne. Bottle-conditioned beers: Hairy Helmet, Bespoke, Porter (ABV 5.5%), Blue (ABV 9%).

Goldings (OG 1036, ABV 3.6%)
A light golden beer with a flowery hoppy aroma and a bitter finish.

Ginger Spice (OG 1036, ABV 3.8%)
A light, highly-hopped bitter with the added zest of Chinese stem ginger.

Ashbourne Ale (OG 1040, ABV 4%)
A pale bitter brewed with Goldings hops for a crisp lasting taste.

Belter (OG 1040, ABV 4.4%)
Maris Otter malt produces a pale but interesting beer.

Belt-n-Braces (OG 1040, ABV 4.4%)
Mid-brown, full-flavoured, dry-hopped bitter.

Dovedale (OG 1044, ABV 4.4%)
Copper-coloured.

Hairy Helmet (OG 1047, ABV 4.7%)
Pale bitter, well hopped but with a sweet finish.

Ginger Helmet (OG 1047, ABV 4.7%)
As above but with a hint of China's most astringent herb.

Bespoke (OG 1050, ABV 5%)
Full-bodied, well-rounded premium bitter.

Bentley Brook Bitter (OG 1050, ABV 5.2%)
Pale, dry and crisp.

Leek

Staffordshire Brewing Company Ltd t/a Leek Brewers Co, 12 Churnet Court, Cheddleton,

Staffordshire, ST13 7EF
Tel (01538) 361919
✉ leekbrewery@hotmail.com
Tours by arrangement

⊗ Brewing started in 2002 with a 4.5-barrel plant located behind the owner's house, before moving to the current site in 2004. All beers are available in bottle-conditioned form and are suitable for vegetarians. The brewery experiments with styles and ingredients, producing various 'one off' special beers during the year.

Staffordshire Gold (ABV 3.8%) ◆
Light, straw-coloured with a pleasing hoppy aroma and a hint of malt. Bitter finish from the hops, making it easily drunk and thirst-quenching.

Danebridge IPA (ABV 4.1%) ◆
Full fruit and hop aroma. Flowery hop start with a great bitter taste. Fabulous finish of hops and flowers.

Staffordshire Bitter (ABV 4.2%) ◆
Amber with a fruity aroma. Malty and hoppy start with the hoppy finish diminishing quickly.

Black Grouse (ABV 4.5%)

Hen Cloud (ABV 4.5%)

St Edwards (ABV 4.7%)

Rudyard Ruby (ABV 4.8%)

Double Sunset (ABV 5.2%)

Danebridge XXX (ABV 5.5%)

Cheddleton Steamer (ABV 6%)

Tittesworth Tipple (ABV 6.5%)

Lees IFBB

J W Lees & Co (Brewers) Ltd, Greengate Brewery, Middleton Junction, Manchester, M24 2AX
Tel (0161) 643 2487
✉ mail@jwlees.co.uk
⊕ jwlees.co.uk
Tours by arrangement

☺ Lees is a family-owned brewery founded in 1828 by John Lees and run by the sixth generation of the family. Brewing takes place in the 1876 brewhouse designed and built by John Willie Lees, the grandson of the founder. The brewhouse has been completely modernised in recent years to give greater flexibility. The company has a tied estate of around 170 pubs, mostly in North Manchester, with 30 in North Wales; all serve cask beer. Seasonal beers are brewed four times a year.

GB Mild (OG 1032, ABV 3.5%) ◆
Red-brown beer with malt and fruit aroma. Creamy mouthfeel with chocolate malt and fruit flavours and a malty finish.

Bitter (OG 1037, ABV 4%) ◆
Pale brown beer with a malty, hoppy aroma. Distinctive malty, dry flavour and aftertaste.

Moonraker (OG 1073, ABV 7.5%) ◆
A reddish-brown beer with a strong, malty, fruity aroma. The flavour is rich and sweet, with roast malt, and the finish is fruity yet dry. Available only in a handful of outlets.

Leith Hill

⌂ Leith Hill Brewery, c/o Plough Inn, Coldharbour, Surrey, RH5 6HD
Tel (01306) 711793
✉ theploughinn@btinternet.com
⊕ ploughinn.com
Tours by arrangement

⊗ Leith Hill was formed in 1996 using home-made equipment to produce nine-gallon brews in a room at the front of the pub. The brewery moved to converted storerooms at the rear of the Plough Inn in 2001 and increased capacity to 2.5-barrels in 2005. All beers brewed are sold only on the premises.

Hoppily Ever After (OG 1036, ABV 3.6%) ◆
Initially hoppy and citrussy with a sharp, hoppy/malty taste, slightly lacking in body. A hoppy, dry finish.

Crooked Furrow (OG 1040, ABV 4%) ◆
A tangy, bitter beer, with malt and some balancing hop flavours. Pale brown in colour with an earthy, malty aroma and a long, dry and bittersweet aftertaste.

Tallywhacker (OG 1048, ABV 4.8%)

Leyden SIBA

⌂ Leyden Brewing Ltd, Lord Raglan, Nangreaves, Bury, Greater Manchester, BL9 6SP
Tel (0161) 764 6680
Tours by arrangement

☺ The brewery was built by Brian Farnworth and started production in 1999. Additional fermenting vessels have been installed, allowing a maximum production of 12 barrels a week. One pub is owned and 30 outlets are supplied.

Balaclava (ABV 3.8%)

Black Pudding (ABV 3.8%)
A dark brown, creamy mild with a malty flavour, followed by a balanced finish.

Nanny Flyer (OG 1040, ABV 3.8%)
A drinkable session bitter with an initial dryness, and a hint of citrus, followed by a strong, malty finish.

Light Brigade (OG 1043, ABV 4.2%) ◆
Copper in colour with a citrus aroma. The flavour is a balance of malt, hops and fruit, with a bitter finish.

Forever Bury (ABV 4.5%)

Raglan Sleeve (OG 1047, ABV 4.6%) ◆
Dark red/brown beer with a hoppy aroma and a dry, roasty, hoppy taste and finish.

Crowning Glory (OG 1069, ABV 6.8%)
A surprisingly smooth-tasting beer for its strength, ideal for cold winter nights.

Lichfield

Lichfield Brewery Co Ltd, Upper St John Street, Lichfield, Staffordshire
✉ robsondavidb@hotmail.com
⊕ lichfieldbrewery.co.uk

Does not brew; beers mainly contracted by Blythe, Tower and Highgate breweries (qv).

Linfit

⎔ Linfit Brewery, Sair Inn, 139 Lane Top,
Linthwaite, Huddersfield, West Yorkshire, HD7 5SG
Tel (01484) 842370

⊛ A 19th-century brew-pub that started
brewing again in 1982, producing an impressive
range of ales for sale at the pub. The beer is
only available at the Sair Inn. English Guineas
Stout is suitable for vegetarians and vegans.

Bitter (OG 1035, ABV 3.7%) ◖
A refreshing session beer. A dry-hopped
aroma leads to a clean-tasting, hoppy
bitterness, then a long, bitter finish with a
hint of malt.

Gold Medal (OG 1040, ABV 4.2%)
Very pale and hoppy. Use of the new dwarf
variety of English hops, First Gold, gives an
aromatic and fruity character.

Swift (OG 1040, ABV 4.2%)
Pale and hoppy with a smooth mouthfeel
and a slightly malty finish.

Special (OG 1041, ABV 4.3%)
Dry-hopping provides the aroma for this rich
and mellow bitter, which has a very soft profile
and character: it fills the mouth with texture
rather than taste. Clean, rounded finish.

Autumn Gold (OG 1045, ABV 4.7%) ◖
Straw-coloured best bitter with hop and fruit
aromas, then the bittersweetness of autumn
fruit in the taste and the finish.

English Guineas Stout (OG 1050, ABV 5.3%) ◖
A fruity, roast aroma preludes a smooth,
roasted barley, chocolaty flavour that is bitter
but not too dry. Excellent appearance; good,
bitter finish.

Old Eli (OG 1050, ABV 5.3%)
A well-balanced premium bitter with a dry-
hop aroma and a fruity, bitter finish.

Leadboiler (OG 1060, ABV 6.6%) ◖
Powerful malt, hop and fruit in good balance
on the tongue, with a well-rounded
bittersweet finish.

Lion's Tail

⎔ Lion's Tail Brewery, Red Lion, High Street,
Cheswardine, Shropshire, TF9 2RS
Tel (01630) 661234
Email cheslion@btinternet.com

The building that houses the brewery was
purpose-built in 2005 and houses a 2.5-barrel
plant. Jon Morris and his wife have owned the
Red Lion pub since 1996. Seasonal beer:
Chesmas Bells (ABV 5.2%, Xmas).

Blooming Blonde (ABV 4.1%)

Lionbru (ABV 4.1%)

Chesbrewnette (ABV 4.5%)

Little Ale Cart

⎔ Little Ale Cart Brewing Co, c/o The
Wellington, 1 Henry Street, Sheffield, South
Yorkshire, S3 7EQ
Tel (0114) 249 2295

⊠ Brewing started in 2001, as Port Mahon, in a
purpose-built brewery behind the Cask & Cutler.
In 2007 the brewery and pub were taken over
and the names of both changed to Little Ale
Cart Brewing and the Wellington. The beer
range is yet to be established.

Little Valley

Little Valley Brewery Ltd, Turkey Lodge Farm,
New Road, Cragg Vale, Hebden Bridge, West
Yorkshire, HX7 5TT
Tel (01422) 883888
✉ info@littlevalleybrewery.co.uk
⊕ littlevalleybrewery.co.uk
Tours by arrangement

⊛ The brewery opened in 2005 and is based in
the Upper Calder Valley. The 10-barrel plant is
in a converted pig shed. All beers are organic
and approved by the Soil Association. Around
100 outlets are supplied. Seasonal beer: Moor
Ale (ABV 5.5%, autumn/winter). All cask beers
are also available in bottle-conditioned form
and have Vegan Society approval. Several beers
are also contract brewed in bottle-conditioned
form for Suma Wholefoods and sold under
different names on Suma labels.

Withens IPA (OG 1037, ABV 3.9%) ◖
Creamy, yellow-coloured, refreshingly light
IPA. Floral spicy hop aroma. Lightly flavoured
with hints of lemon and grapefruit. Clean,
bitter aftertaste.

Cragg Vale Bitter (OG 1039, ABV 4.2%) ◖
Grainy, amber-coloured session bitter. Light
on the palate. Delicate flavour of malt and
fruit with a bitter finish.

Hebden's Wheat (OG 1043, ABV 4.5%) ▣ ◖
A pale yellow, creamy, grainy wheat beer
with a good balance of bitterness and fruit
with a hint of sweetness. Lasting dry finish.

Stoodley Stout (OG 1044, ABV 4.8%) ◖
Dark red creamy stout with a rich roast aroma
and luscious fruity, chocolate, roast flavours.
Well balanced with a clean, bitter finish.

Tod's Blonde (OG 1045, ABV 5%) ◖
Bright yellow, grainy speciality beer with a
citrus hoppy start and a dry finish. Fruity with
a hint of spice. Similar in style to a Belgian
blonde beer.

Moor Ale (OG 1051, ABV 5.5%) ◖
Pale brown in colour with a full-bodied taste.
It has a strong malty nose and palate with
hints of heather and peat-smoked malt. Well
balanced with a bitter finish.

Litton

Litton Ale Brewery, Queens Arms,
Litton, North Yorkshire,
BD23 5QJ
Tel 07834 622632
⊕ yorkshirenet.co.uk/stayat/queensarms
Tours by arrangement

⊛ Brewing started in 2003 in a purpose-built
stone extension at the rear of the pub. Brewing
liquor is sourced from a spring that provides the
pub with its own water supply. The brew length
is three barrels and all production is in cask
form. More than 100 outlets are supplied.
Bottle-conditioned beers have been introduced.

Ale (OG 1038, ABV 3.8%) ◆
An easy-drinking, tawny-coloured traditional bitter with a good malt/hop balance and a dry finish.

Leading Light (OG 1038, ABV 3.8%) ◆
A long, bitter aftertaste follows a malty flavour with tart fruit and a rising hop bitterness in this light-coloured beer. Low aroma.

Gold Crest (OG 1039, ABV 3.9%)

Dark Star (OG 1040, ABV 4%) ◆
A smooth, creamy dark mild, full-bodied for its strength. The taste is quite bitter with roast coffee and tart dark fruit flavours, complemented by a bitter, roast finish.

Potts Beck (OG 1043, ABV 4.2%) ◆
Malt and hops fight for control in this copper-coloured best bitter with a fruity aroma.

Lizard

**Lizard Ales Ltd, Unit 2a
St Keverne Rural Workshops, St Keverne, Helston, Cornwall, TR12 6PE
Tel (01326) 281135**
✉ lizardales@msn.com

Launched in autumn 2004 by partners Richard Martin and Mark and Leonora Nattrass, Lizard Ales supplies some 25 regular outlets, mainly in west Cornwall. Bottle-conditioned beers: Kernow Gold (ABV 3.7%), Lizard Bitter, Frenchman's Creek Cornish Pale Ale, An Gof Strong Cornish Ale.

Helford River (1035, ABV 3.6%)

Bitter (OG 1041, ABV 4.2%)

Frenchman's Creek Cornish Pale Ale (OG 1042, ABV 4.6%)

An Gof Strong Cornish Ale (OG 1049.5, ABV 5.2%)

Loddon SIBA

**Loddon Brewery Ltd, Dunsden Green Farm, Church Lane, Dunsden, Oxfordshire, RG4 9QD
Tel (01189) 481111**
✉ loddonbrewery@aol.com
⊕ loddonbrewery.co.uk
Shop Mon-Fri 8am-5pm; Sat 9am-2pm
Tours by arrangement

Loddon was established in 2003 in a 240-year-old brick and flint barn that houses a 17-barrel brewery able to produce 70 barrels a week. 250 outlets are supplied. The brewery site was expanded in 2007 with future plans for a new fermenting room. Seasonal beers: Bloomin' Eck (ABV 4%, Feb-Mar), Flight of Fancy (ABV 4.2%, Apr-Aug), Russet (ABV 4.5%, Sep-Nov), Hocus Pocus (ABV 4.6%, Dec-Jan). Bottle-conditioned beer: Ferryman's Gold (ABV 4.8% 🍶). The brewery also produce monthly specials: see website.

Hoppit (OG 1035.5, ABV 3.5%) ◆
Hops dominate the aroma and taste of this drinkable, light-coloured session beer. A hint of malt and fruit accompanies and a pleasant bitterness carries through to the aftertaste.

Dragonfly (OG 1040, ABV 4%)

Hullabaloo (OG 1043.8, ABV 4.2%) ◆
A hint of banana in the initial taste develops into a balance of hops and malt in this well-rounded, medium-bodied tawny bitter with a bitter aftertaste.

Ferryman's Gold (OG 1044.8, ABV 4.4%) ◆
Golden coloured with a strong hoppy character throughout, accompanied by malt in the mouth.

Bamboozle (OG 1048.8, ABV 4.8%) ◆
Full-bodied and well-balanced golden ale. Distinctive bittersweet flavour with hop character to accompany.

Lovibonds

**Lovibonds Brewery Ltd, Rear of 19-21 Market Place, Henley-on-Thames, Oxon, RG9 2AA
Tel 07761 543987**
✉ info@lovibonds.com
⊕ lovibonds.com
Shop Fri & Sat 10am-6pm, Sun 11am-4pm
Tours by arrangement

⊠ Lovibonds Brewery was founded in 2005 and is named after Joseph William Lovibond, who invented the Tintometer to measure beer colour. In addition to cask conditioned ales, Lovibonds brews beers inspired by the traditions of other brewing nations. Around 50 outlets are supplied. Bottle-conditioned beers are planned.

Henley Bitter (OG 1035, ABV 3.4%)
An amber session bitter with a blend of roasted malts that gives a complex profile.

Henley Gold (OG 1046, ABV 4.6%)

Henley Dark (OG 1048, ABV 4.8%)

Lowes Arms

**⬠ Lowes Arms Brewery, Lowes Arms, 301 Hyde Road, Denton, Manchester, M34 3FF
Tel (0161) 336 3064**
✉ info@lowesarms.co.uk
⊕ lowesarms.co.uk
Tours by arrangement

☺ The brewery, known as The Lab, is located in the cellars of the Lowes Arms. It produces a range of beers named after local landmarks and sites of interest. The brewery is a 2.5-barrel system, but two new fermenting vessels have been added to enable The Lab to brew four times a week. There are plans to wholesale the beer. Brewing is currently suspended while a new brewer is sought.

Jet Amber (OG 1040, ABV 3.5%)
Brewed for the Stockport and Manchester Mild Challenge.

IPA (ABV 3.8%)

Frog Bog (OG 1040, ABV 3.9%)
A light, easy-drinking bitter with an orange aroma and a light hoppy taste.

Sweaty Clog (ABV 4%)

Wild Wood (OG 1043, ABV 4.1%)
A spicy session bitter with a malty and fruity aroma, and spicy hop taste.

Broomstairs (OG 1043, ABV 4.3%)
A dark best bitter with distinct roast flavours and a hoppy aftertaste.

Haughton Weave (OG 1043, ABV 4.5%)
Distinct tangerine aromas in this light-

coloured beer are followed by lots of bitterness and hoppy tastes in the mouth.

Loweswater

⌂ Loweswater Brewery, Kirkstile Inn, Loweswater, Cumbria, CA13 0RU
Tel (01900) 85219
✉ info@kirkstile.com
⊕ kirkstile.com
Tours by arrangement

Loweswater Brewery was re-established at the Kirkstile Inn in 2003 by head brewer Matt Webster. The brewery produces six barrels a week for the inn and local beer festivals. There are plans to increase the brewery capacity.

Melbreak Bitter (OG 1038, ABV 3.7%)
Pale bronze with a tangy fruit and hop resins aroma, and a long, bitter finish.

Rannerdale (OG 1042, ABV 4%)
A fruity beer made with Styrian Goldings hops.

Kirkstile Gold (OG 1042, ABV 4.3%)
Pale lager-style beer with masses of tropical fruit flavour. Brewed with German hops.

Grasmoor Dark Ale (OG 1043, ABV 4.3%)
Deep ruby red beer with chocolate malt on the aroma, and hop resins, roast malt and raisin fruit on the palate.

Ludlow

Ludlow Brewing Co Ltd, Kingsley Garage, 105 Corve Street, Ludlow, Shropshire, SY8 1DJ
Tel (01584) 873291
✉ gary@ludlowbrewingcompany.co.uk
⊕ theludlowbrewery.co.uk
Tours by arrangement

The brewery opened in 2006 in a building that was once a malthouse. Some 20 pubs are supplied within a 35-mile radius. Both beers are bottled on site for sale on the premises.

Gold (ABV 4.2%)

Boiling Well (ABV 4.7%)

Maclay

See Belhaven in New national breweries section

McMullen IFBB

McMullen & Sons Ltd, 26 Old Cross, Hertford, Hertfordshire, SG14 1RD
Tel (01992) 584911
✉ reception@mcmullens.co.uk
⊕ mcmullens.co.uk

McMullen, Hertfordshire's oldest independent brewery, has just celebrated 180 years of brewing. A new brewhouse opened in 2006, giving the company greater flexibility to produce its regular cask beers and up to eight seasonal beers a year. Cask ale is served in all 135 pubs, though many managed pubs use cask breathers on all cask beers, as do some tenanted houses.

AK (OG 1035, ABV 3.7%) ✦
A pleasant mix of malt and hops leads to a distinctive, dry aftertaste that isn't always as pronounced as it used to be.

Cask Ale (OG 1039, ABV 3.8%)

Country Bitter (OG 1042, ABV 4.3%) ✦
A full-bodied beer with a well-balanced mix of malt, hops and fruit throughout.

Magpie

Magpie Brewery, Unit 4 Ashling Court, Ashling Street, Nottingham, NG2 3JA
Tel 07738 762897
✉ info@magpiebrewery.com
⊕ magpiebrewery.com

⊛ Magpie is a six-barrel plant launched in 2006 by three friends. It is located a few feet from the perimeter of Meadow Lane Stadium, home of Notts County FC — the Magpies — from which the brewery name naturally derived. Seasonal beer: Dark Secret (ABV 3.7%, spring & autumn).

Fledgling (ABV 3.8%)
A golden, hoppy session beer.

Two 4 Joy (ABV 4.2%)
A traditional bitter with plenty of hops.

Early Bird (ABV 4.3%)
A very hoppy, mid-golden beer.

Thieving Rogue (ABV 4.5%)
A golden beer made entirely with pale malt but fewer hops.

Full Flight (ABV 4.8%)
A strong, dark winter beer.

Maldon

See Farmer's Ales

Mallard SIBA

Mallard Brewery, 15 Hartington Avenue, Carlton, Nottingham, NG4 3NR
Tel (0115) 952 1289
✉ phil@mallard-brewery.co.uk
⊕ mallard-brewery.co.uk
Tours by arrangement

⊠ Phil Mallard built and installed a two-barrel plant in a shed at his home and started brewing in 1995. The brewery is only nine square metres and contains a hot liquor tank, mash tun, copper, and three fermenters. Since 1995 production has risen from one barrel a week to between six or eight barrels, which is the plant's maximum. Around 12 outlets are supplied. Seasonal beers: Waddlers Mild (ABV 3.7%, spring), DA (ABV 5.8%, Jan-Mar), Quismas Quacker (ABV 6%, Dec), Owd Duck (ABV 4.8%, winter).

Duck 'n' Dive (OG 1039, ABV 3.7%)
A light, single-hopped beer made from the hedgerow hop, First Gold. A bitter beer with a hoppy nose, good bitterness on the palate and a dry finish.

Quacker Jack (OG 1040, ABV 4%)

Feather Light (OG 1040, ABV 4.1%)
A very pale lager-style bitter with a floral bouquet and sweetness on the palate. A light, hoppy session beer.

Duckling (OG 1041, ABV 4.2%) ⊡
A crisp refreshing bitter with a hint of honey and citrus flavour.

Webbed Wheat (OG 1043, ABV 4.3%)
A wheat beer with a fruity, hoppy nose and taste.

Spittin' Feathers (OG 1044, ABV 4.4%)
A mellow, ruby bitter with a complex malt flavour of chocolate, toffee and coffee, complemented with a full and fruity/hoppy aftertaste.

Drake (OG 1045, ABV 4.5%)
A full-bodied premium bitter, with malt and hops on the palate, and a fruity finish.

Friar Duck (OG 1050, ABV 5%)
A pale, full malt beer, hoppy with a hint of blackcurrant flavour.

Duck 'n' Disorderly (OG 1050, ABV 5%)

Malton

See Suddaby's

Malvern Hills SIBA

Malvern Hills Brewery Ltd, 15 West Malvern Road, Malvern, Worcestershire, WR14 4ND
Tel (01684) 560165
✉ beer@tiscali.co.uk
⊕ malvernhillsbrewery.co.uk
Tours by arrangement

Founded in 1997 in an old quarrying dynamite store, the brewery has gained some 40 regular outlets in the area and the Black Country. Flagship brew Black Pear is a multiple beer festival and CAMRA regional award winner. Seasonal beer: Dr Gully's Winter Ale (ABV 5.2%).

Red Earl (OG 1037, ABV 3.7%) ◆
A very light beer that does not overpower the senses. With a hint of apple fruit, it is ideal for slaking the thirst.

Feelgood (OG 1038, ABV 3.8%)

Moel Bryn (OG 1039, ABV 3.9%)

Swedish Nightingale (OG 1040, ABV 4%)

Worcestershire Whym (OG 1042, ABV 4.2%)

Priessnitz Plsen (OG 1043, ABV 4.3%) ▉ ◆
A mix of soft fruit and citrus give this straw-coloured brew its quaffability, making it ideal for quenching summer thirsts.

Black Pear (OG 1044, ABV 4.4%) ◆
A sharp citrus hoppiness is the main constituent of this golden brew that has a long, dry aftertaste.

Black Country Wobble (OG 1045, ABV 4.5%) ◆
A sharp, clean-tasting golden beer with an aroma of hops challenged by fruit and malt, which hold up well in the mouth. A bitter dryness grows as the contrasting sweetness subsides.

Mr Phoebus (OG 1047, ABV 4.7%)

Dr Gully's IPA (OG 1052, ABV 5.2%)

Mansfield

See Marston's in New national breweries section

Marble SIBA

⌷ **Marble Beers Ltd, 73 Rochdale Road, Manchester, M4 4HY**
Tel (0161) 819 2694
✉ thebrewers_marblebeers@msn.com
Tours by arrangement

Marble opened at the Marble Arch Inn in 1997 and produces organic and vegan beers. It is registered with the Soil Association and the Vegetarian Society. It has a five-barrel plant that operates at full capacity, producing six regular beers and a number of seasonal ales including Port Stout (ABV 4.7%, Xmas). Marble currently owns two pubs and supplies around 40 outlets. Bottle-conditioned beers: Ginger 6 (ABV 6%), Tawny No. 3 (ABV 5.7%), Chocolate, Lagonda IPA.

GSB/Gould Street Bitter (OG 1037.5, ABV 3.8%)
A pale, hoppy brew dominated by the flavour of Goldings hops and a slight fruitiness.

Manchester Bitter (OG 1042, ABV 4.2%) ◆
Yellow beer with a hoppy aroma. A balance of malt, hops and fruit on the palate, with a hoppy and bitter aftertaste.

JP Best (ABV 4.3%)
Pale tawny in colour. Hoppy with a good malt balance, assertively bitter.

Ginger Marble (OG 1045, ABV 4.5%)
Intense and complex. Full-bodied and fiery with a sharp, snappy bite.

Lagonda IPA (OG 1048, ABV 5%)
A golden, dry bitter. A quadruple addition of hops gives it depth and complexity.

Chocolate (ABV 5.5%)
A strong, stout-like ale.

Marches

Marches Brewing Co, The Old Hop Kiln, Claston Farm, Dormington, Hereford, Herefordshire, HR1 4EA
Tel (01584) 878999
✉ littlebeer@totalise.co.uk
Tours by arrangement

⊗ Brewing restarted at Marches in 2004. The brewery is now housed in two converted hop kilns with beer mostly brewed for the owner's shop in Ludlow, plus some 20 local outlets. Bottle-conditioned beers: Ludlow Gold, St Lawrence Ale.

Forever Autumn (ABV 4.2%)

Ludlow Gold (ABV 4.3%)

Dormington Gold (OG 1044, ABV 4.5%)
A light golden bitter brewed using First Gold hedgerow hops. It has an intense bitterness with a citrus zest.

St Lawrence Ale (ABV 4.5%)
A ruby premium bitter brewed with Boadicea hops.

Marston Moor

Marston Moor Brewery Ltd, PO Box 9, York, North Yorkshire, YO26 7XW
Tel (01423) 359641
✉ info@marstonmoorbrewery.co.uk
Tours by arrangement

⊚ Established in 1983 in Kirk Hammerton, the brewery had a re-investment programme in 2005, moving brewing operations to nearby Tockwith, where it shares the site with Rudgate

Brewery (qv). Two special beers are available each month, based either on an English Civil War theme or on rural England. Some 150 outlets are supplied.

Cromwell Pale (OG 1036, ABV 3.8%) ◈
A golden beer with hops and fruit in strong evidence on the nose. Bitterness as well as fruit and hops dominate the taste and long aftertaste.

Matchlock Mild (OG 1038, ABV 4%)

Mongrel (OG 1038, ABV 4%)

Brewers Pride (OG 1039, ABV 4.2%) ◈
A light but somewhat thin, fruity beer, with a hoppy, bitter aftertaste.

Fairfax Special (OG 1039, ABV 4.2%)

Merriemaker (OG 1042, ABV 4.5%)

Brewers Droop (OG 1045.5, ABV 5%)
A pale, robust ale with hops and fruit notes in prominence. A long, bitter aftertaste.

Marston's

See New national breweries section

Mash SIBA

⚲ Mash Ltd, 19-21 Great Portland Street, London, W1W 8QB
Tel (020) 7637 5555
⊕ mashrestaurantandbar.co.uk
Tours by arrangement

The micro-brewery is the centrepiece of the Mash bar and restaurant. The American-style brewery can be toured to inspect the process. The beers are not cask conditioned but are stored in cellar tanks using a CO2 system. Regular beer: Mash Wheat (ABV 5.2%). Other beers include a Blackcurrant Porter, Scotch, IPA, Peach, Extra Stout and Pils.

Masters*

Masters Brewery,
Unit 8 Greenham Business Park,
Wellington, Somerset, TA21 0LR
Tel (01823) 674444
⊠ info@mastersbrewery.co.uk
⊕ mastersbrewery.co.uk
Tours by arrangement

Master's plant was commissioned in 2006 and after extensive tests the first brew went on sale in the autumn of that year. Numerous upgrades to the brewery have been made since, with an additional fermenter added recently. There are plans to bottle. 15 outlets are supplied. Seasonal beer: Carnivale (ABV 4.3%).

Appley Ale (OG 1037, ABV 3.7%)

Spypost Bitter (OG 1040, ABV 4%)

Redball (OG 1041, ABV 4.1%)

Rockwell Tower (OG 1043, ABV 4.3%)

Whiteball (OG 1043, ABV 4.3%)

Thunderbridge (OG 1047, ABV 4.7%)

Monument (ABV 1050, ABV 5%)

Matthews SIBA

Matthews Brewing Co Ltd, Unit 7 Timsbury

Workshop Estate, Hayeswood Road, Timsbury, Bath, BA2 0HQ
Tel (01761) 472242
⊠ brewery@matthewsbrewing.co.uk
⊕ matthewsbrewing.co.uk
Tours by arrangement

Matthews Brewing was established in 2005 on a five-barrel plant by Stuart Matthews and Sue Appleby. The emphasis is on the use of traditional techniques and quality ingredients, such as floor-malted barley from the nearby Warminster Maltings. Around 60 outlets are supplied and the ales are distributed more widely by wholesalers. Seasonal beers: see website.

Brassknocker (OG 1037, ABV 3.8%) ▥ ◈
Well-flavoured pale, hoppy citrus bitter with underlying sweetness; dry, astringent finish.

Bob Wall (OG 1041, ABV 4.2%) ◈
Fruity best bitter; roasty hint with intense forest fruit and rich malt flavour continuing to a good balanced finish.

Mauldons SIBA EAB

Mauldons Ltd, Black Adder Brewery,
13 Churchfield Road, Sudbury,
Suffolk, CO10 2YA
Tel (01787) 311055
⊠ sims@mauldons.co.uk
⊕ mauldons.co.uk
Shop Mon-Fri 9.30am-4pm
Tours by arrangement

▨ The Mauldon family started brewing in Sudbury in 1795. The brewery with 26 pubs was bought by Greene King in the 1960s. The current business, established in 1982, was bought by Steve and Alison Sims -- both former employees of Adnams -- in 2000. They relocated to a new brewery in 2005, with a 30-barrel plant that has doubled production. Some 200 outlets are supplied. There is a rolling programme of seasonal beers: see website. Bottle-conditioned beers: Suffolk Pride, Bah Humbug (ABV 4.9%), Black Adder.

Micawber's Mild (OG 1035, ABV 3.5%) ◈
A smooth, dark, East Anglian mild, easy drinking despite its body.

Bitter (OG 1036, ABV 3.6%)
A traditional session bitter with a strong floral nose and lingering, bitter finish.

Moletrap Bitter (OG 1038, ABV 3.8%) ◈
A well-balanced session beer with a crisp, hoppy bitterness balancing sweet malt.

Pickwick (OG 1042, ABV 4.2%)
A best bitter with a rich, rounded malt flavour and ripe aromas of hops and fruit. A bittersweet finish.

Suffolk Pride (OG 1048, ABV 4.8%) ◈
A full-bodied, copper-coloured beer with a good balance of malt, hops and fruit in the taste.

Black Adder (OG 1053, ABV 5.3%) ◈
A grainy, roast mouthfeel. The tastebuds are almost overwhelmed by caramel, malt and vine fruit.

White Adder (OG 1053, ABV 5.3%) ◈
A pale brown, almost golden, strong ale. A warming, fruity flavour dominates and lingers into a dry, hoppy finish.

Suffolk Comfort (OG 1066, ABV 6.6%)
A powerful peppery Goldings aroma with malt notes. There is a rich balance of crystal malt and hops in the mouth with a long, malty finish.

Mayfields

Mayfields Brewery, Mayfields Farm, Bishop Frome, Herefordshire, WR6 5AS
Tel (01531) 640015
✉ themayfieldsbrewery@yahoo.co.uk
Tours by arrangement

Established in 2005, the Mayfields Brewery is based in an 18th-century hop kiln, located in the heart of one of England's major hop growing regions, the Frome Valley. Only Herefordshire hops are used, many of which are grown on the brewery's farm. The brewery also produces real cider and perry to complement its beer range. Around 25 outlets are supplied. Seasonal beers: Crusader (ABV 4.3%, St George's Day/Trafalgar Day), Conqueror (ABV 4.3%, winter).

Pioneer (ABV 3.9%)
Straw-coloured ale with a fruity finish.

Excalibur (ABV 4.1%)
Light in colour with a hoppy, bitter finish.

Naughty Nell's (ABV 4.2%)
Smooth, copper-coloured ale with a malty body and citrussy hop finish.

Aunty Myrtle's (ABV 5%)
Full bodied and fruity.

Mayflower

Mayflower Brewery, r/o Royal Oak Hotel, Standishgate, Wigan, WN1 1XL
Tel (01257) 400605
✉ info@mayflowerbrewery.co.uk
⊕ mayflowerbrewery.co.uk

Mayflower was established in 2001 in Standish and relocated to the Royal Oak Hotel in Wigan in 2004. The original vessels and casks are still used. The Royal Oak is supplied as well as a number of other outlets in and around Wigan. Seasonal beers: Oakey Cokey (ABV 8%, winter), Cuckoo Spit (ABV 4.4%, spring).

Black Diamond (OG 1033.5, ABV 3.4%)

Dark Oak (OG 1034, ABV 3.5%)

Myles Best Bitter (OG 1036, ABV 3.7%)

Light Oak (OG 1038, ABV 4%)

Special Branch (OG 1038, ABV 4%)

Premiership (ABV 4.1%)

Wigan Bier (OG 1039.5, ABV 4.2%)

Black Oak (ABV 5%)

Maypole

Maypole Brewery Ltd, North Laithes Farm, Wellow Road, Eakring, Newark, Nottinghamshire, NG22 0AN
Tel 07971 277598
✉ maypolebrewery@aol.com
⊕ maypolebrewery.co.uk

The brewery opened in 1995 in a converted 18th-century farm building. After changing hands in 2001 it was bought by the former head brewer in 2005. Increased demand has seen the installation of a fourth fermenting vessel. Maypole beers are always available at the Eight Jolly Brewers, Gainsborough, and at the Beehive Inn, Maplebeck. Seasonal beers can be ordered at any time for beer festivals. Seasonal beers: see website.

Mayfly Bitter (OG 1038, ABV 3.8%)

BXA (OG 1039, ABV 4%)

Mayfair (OG 1039, ABV 4.1%)

Maybee (OG 1040, ABV 4.3%)

Major Oak (OG 1042, ABV 4.4%)

Mae West/Wellow Gold (OG 1044, ABV 4.6%)

Mayhem (OG 1048, ABV 5%)

Meantime SIBA

Meantime Brewing Co Ltd, Greenwich Brewery, 2 Penhall Road, London, SE7 8RX
Tel (020) 8293 1111
✉ info@meantimebrewing.com
⊕ meantimebrewing.com

⊠ Meantime Brewing was established in 2000 and specialises in properly matured beers and brews traditional, unpasteurised Continental styles as well as innovative new flavours. One pub is owned in Greenwich. Bottle-conditioned beers: IPA (ABV 7.5%), Raspberry Grand Cru (ABV 6.5%), London Porter (ABV 6.5%), Wheat Grand Cru (ABV 6.3%), Coffee (ABV 6%), Chocolate (ABV 6.5%), Pale Ale (ABV 4.7%). Organic Pilsner (ABV 5.4%) is suitable for vegetarians and vegans.

Meesons

See Old Bog

Melbourn

Melbourn Bros Brewery, 22 All Saints Street, Stamford, Lincolnshire, PE9 2PA
Tel (01780) 752186
✉ info@melbournbrothers.co.uk
⊕ melbournbrothers.co.uk

A famous Stamford brewery that opened in 1825 and closed in 1974. It re-opened in 1994 and is owned by Samuel Smith of Tadcaster (qv). Melbourn brews spontaneously fermented fruit beers primarily for the American market but which can be ordered by the case in Britain by mail order. The beers are Apricot, Cherry and Strawberry (all ABV 3.4%). The brewery is open for tours Wednesday to Sunday 10am-4pm and there are open evenings for brewery tours, and beer and food tastings: prior booking essential.

Mersea Island

Mersea Island Brewery, Rewsalls Lane, East Mersea, Colchester, Essex, CO5 8SX
Tel (01206) 385900
✉ beer@merseawine.com
⊕ merseawine.com
Shop/café 11am-4pm daily, closed Tue
Tours by arrangement

The brewery started production at Mersea Island Vineyard in 2005, producing cask and bottle-conditioned beers. The beers are available from an on-site shop and also served in a café. Take-home sales in beer-in-a-box format is available. The brewery supplies a growing number of pubs and clubs on a guest beer basis as well as most local beer festivals.

Mud Mild (OG 1035, ABV 3.6%)
Dark from the use of black and chocolate malts. Fuggles hops add a distinctive flavour.

Yo Boy Bitter (OG 1038, ABV 3.8%) ◆
Very bitter pale ale with a subtle maltiness and a tinned strawberry aroma.

Skippers Bitter (OG 1047, ABV 4.8%) ◆
Full-bodied strong bitter, dominated by sweet berries and pear drops. The grassy aftertaste has hints of vanilla.

Monkeys (OG 1049, ABV 5.1%)
A porter with deep and lasting malt and hop flavours.

Mighty Oak SIBA

**Mighty Oak Brewing Co Ltd, 14b West Station Yard, Spital Road, Maldon, Essex, CM9 6TW
Tel (01621) 843713
✉ moakbrew@aol.com**
Tours by arrangement

⊗ Mighty Oak was formed in 1996 and moved in 2001 to Maldon, where capacity was increased to 67.5 barrels a week, increased again in 2006 to 85.2 barrels a week. Around 200 outlets are supplied plus a small number of wholesalers are used. Twelve monthly ales are brewed based on a theme; for 2007 there was a 007 theme including Honey Rider, From Russia and Goldfinger.

IPA (OG 1035.1, ABV 3.5%) ◆
Light-bodied session beer with a bitter finish following a sweeter, less forceful taste.

Oscar Wilde (OG 1039.5, ABV 3.7%) ⬚ ◆
Blackberry, chocolate and chicory dominate the aroma of this roasty dark mild. A dry, fruity aftertaste follows.

Maldon Gold (OG 1039.5, ABV 3.8%) ▦ ◆
A spicy hop aroma, balanced with citrus fruit leads to a taste in which lemon torte and mixed peel are dominant. Sharp sherbet and biscuit malt fade in the bitter finish.

Burntwood Bitter (OG 1041, ABV 4%) ◆
Unusually roasty bitter with a banana and nutmeg aroma. Grapefruit joins the sweeter flavours, which yield to a very bitter finish.

Simply The Best (OG 1044.1, ABV 4.4%) ◆
Full-flavoured best bitter in which fruity caramel is balanced with bitterness. The finish is drier, with the bitterness dominating.

English Oak (OG 1047.9, ABV 4.8%) ◆
Fruity, tawny beer with caramel and vanilla tones. Less bitter than in previous years, with reduced hop character.

Saxon Strong (OG 1063.6, ABV 6.5%)
A deep tawny ale with full-bodied fruity flavours alongside a complex malt character reminiscent of a barley wine.

Milestone

Milestone Brewing Co, Great North Road,

Cromwell, Newark, Nottinghamshire, NG23 6JE
Tel (01636) 822255
✉ info@milestonebrewery.co.uk
⊕ milestonebrewery.co.uk
Shop 9am-5pm daily
Tours by arrangement

⊛ The brewery has been in production since 2005 on a 12-barrel plant. It was founded by Kenneth and Frances Munro with head brewer Dean Penney. Around 150 outlets are supplied. Seasonal beers: Cool Amber (ABV 6%, May-Aug), Donner & Blitzed/Xmas Cracker (ABV 5.4%, Nov-Dec). Bottle-conditioned beers: Lions Pride, Black Pearl, Loxley Ale, Olde Home Wrecker, Donner & Blitzed, Raspberry Wheat Beer (ABV 5.6%).

Hoptimism (ABV 3.6%)

Lions Pride (ABV 3.8%)

Classic Dark Mild (ABV 4%)

Normanton IPA (ABV 4.1%)

Loxley Ale (ABV 4.2%)

Black Pearl (ABV 4.3%)

Crusader (ABV 4.4%)

Rich Ruby (ABV 4.5%)

Deliverance (ABV 4.6%)

Imperial Pale Ale (ABV 4.8%)

Olde Home Wrecker (ABV 4.9%)

Milk Street SIBA

**⚑ Milk Street Brewery Ltd (MSB Ltd), The Griffin, 25 Milk Street, Frome, Somerset, BA11 3DB
Tel (01373) 467766
✉ rjlyall@hotmail.com
⊕ milkstreet.5u.com**
Tours by arrangement

Milk Street was commissioned in 1999 and expanded capacity in 2006 to 25 barrels a week.

Funky Monkey (OG 1040, ABV 4%)
Copper-coloured summer ale boasting fruity flavours and aromas. A dry finish with developing bitterness and an undertone of citrus fruit.

Mermaid (OG 1041, ABV 4.1%)
Amber-coloured ale with a rich hop character on the nose, plenty of citrus fruit on the palate and a lasting bitter and hoppy finish.

Amarillo (OG 1043, ABV 4.3%)
Brewed with American hops to give the beer floral and spicy notes. Initially soft on the palate, the flavour develops to that of burnt oranges and a pleasant herbal taste.

Nick's (OG 1045, ABV 4.4%)
A malty best bitter with a rich nose of toffee and nuts, while the palate delivers plenty of rich chocolaty flavours. A dry finish with a slight sweetness.

Zig-Zag Stout (OG 1046, ABV 4.5%)
A dark ruby stout with characteristic roastiness and dryness with bitter chocolate and citrus fruit in the background.

Beer (OG 1049, ABV 5%)
A blonde beer with musky hoppiness and

citrus fruit on the nose, while more fruit surges through on the palate before the bittersweet finish.

Elderfizz (OG 1049, ABV 5%)
A golden yellow wheat beer with a prominent elderflower edge.

Millis

Millis Brewing Co Ltd, St Margaret's Farm, St Margaret's Road, South Darenth, Dartford, Kent, DA4 9LB
Tel (01322) 866233

⊛ John Millis started with a half-barrel plant at his home in Gravesend. Demand outstripped the facility and Millis moved in 2003 to a new site -- a former farm cold store -- with a 10-barrel plant. John now supplies around 40 outlets within a 50-mile radius. Seasonal beer: Winter Witch (ABV 4.8%).

Kentish Dark (OG 1035, ABV 3.5%)

Gravesend Guzzler (OG 1037, ABV 3.7%)

Oast Shovellers (OG 1039, ABV 3.9%)
A copper-coloured ale with a pale and crystal malt base, ending with a distinctive, clean finish.

Hopping Haze (OG 1041, ABV 4.1%)

Dartford Wobbler (OG 1043, ABV 4.3%)
A tawny-coloured, full-bodied best bitter with complex malt and hop flavours and a long, clean, slightly roasted finish.

Kentish Red Ale (OG 1043, ABV 4.3%)
A traditional red ale with complex malt, hops and fruit notes.

Millstone SIBA

Millstone Brewery Ltd, Unit 4, Vale Mill, Micklehurst Road, Mossley, OL5 9JL
Tel (01457) 835835
✉ info@millstonebrewery.co.uk
⊕ millstonebrewery.co.uk
Tours by arrangement

Established in 2003 by Nick Boughton and Jon Hunt, the brewery is located in an 18th-century textile mill. The eight-barrel plant produces a range of beers including five regular and eight seasonal/occasional beers. More than 50 outlets are supplied. Seasonal beers: see website. Bottle-conditioned beers: Three Shires Bitter, Windy Miller, Grain Storm, Millstone Edge, Autumn Leaves, True Grit.

Three Shires Bitter (OG 1040, ABV 4%) ◈
Yellow beer with hop and fruit aroma. Fresh citrus fruit, hops and bitterness in the taste and aftertaste.

Tiger Rut (OG 1040, ABV 4%)
A pale, hoppy ale with a distinctive citrus/grapefruit aroma.

Grain Storm (OG 1042, ABV 4.2%) ◈
Yellow/gold beer with a grainy mouthfeel and fresh fruit and hop aroma. Citrus peel and hops in the mouth, with a bitter finish.

Millwright (OG 1046, ABV 4.6%)
A pale gold premium bitter with a floral and spicy aroma, building on a crisp and refreshing taste.

True Grit (OG 1050, ABV 5%)
A well-hopped strong ale with a mellow bitterness.

Milton SIBA EAB

Milton Brewery Cambridge Ltd, 111 Cambridge Road, Milton, Cambridgeshire, CB24 6AT
Tel (01223) 226198
✉ enquiries@miltonbrewery.co.uk
⊕ miltonbrewery.co.uk
Tours by arrangement

⊗ The brewery has grown steadily since it was founded in 1999. More than 100 outlets are supplied around the Cambridge area and further afield through wholesalers. Three tied houses (Peterborough and London) are owned by an associated company, Individual Pubs Ltd. Regular seasonal beers are also brewed including Mammon (ABV 7%, Dec-Feb). Nero is suitable for vegetarians and vegans.

Minotaur (OG 1035, ABV 3.3%) ◈
Impressive full-flavoured, reddish-brown mild ale. Distinctly malty with a smoky roast layer and touches of liquorice. A delicate bittersweet balance becomes dry and bitter.

Jupiter (OG 1037, ABV 3.5%) ◈
A light malty aroma and a delicate hoppy palate lead to a bitter finish. A light barley sugar aroma and taste underpin this amber session bitter.

Neptune (OG 1039, ABV 3.8%) ◈
Delicious hop aromas introduce this well-balanced, nutty and refreshing copper-coloured ale. Good hoppy finish.

Pegasus (OG 1043, ABV 4.1%) ◈
Malty dark brown best bitter with a butterscotch aroma and taste. Hints of hops and fruit appear in the mouth and the malt/hop balance remains in the bitter ending.

Sparta (OG 1043, ABV 4.3%)

Nero (OG 1050, ABV 5%)

Cyclops (OG 1055, ABV 5.3%)
Deep copper-coloured ale, with a rich hoppy aroma and full body; fruit and malt notes develop in the finish.

Moles SIBA

Moles Brewery, Merlin Way, Bowerhill Trading Estate, Melksham, Wiltshire, SN12 6TJ
Tel (01225) 704734/708842
✉ sales@moles-cascade.co.uk
⊕ molesbrewery.com
Shop Mon-Fri 9am-5pm
Tours by arrangement

Moles was established in 1982. 13 pubs are owned, all serving cask beer. Around 150 outlets are supplied direct. Seasonal beers: Barleymole (ABV 4.2%, summer), Molegrip (ABV 4.3%, autumn), Holy Moley (ABV 4.7%, spring), Moel Moel (ABV 6%, winter), Mole Slayer (ABV 4.4%, St Georges Day).

Tap Bitter (OG 1035, ABV 3.5%)
A session bitter with a smooth, malty flavour and clean bitter finish.

Best Bitter (OG 1040, ABV 4%)
A well-balanced, amber-coloured bitter, clean, dry and malty with some bitterness, and delicate floral hop flavour.

769

Landlords Choice (OG 1045, ABV 4.5%)
A dark, strong, smooth porter, with a rich fruity palate and malty finish.

Molennium (OG 1045, ABV 4.5%)
There are fruit, caramel and malty overtones in the aroma of this deep amber-coloured ale, balanced by a pleasant bitterness in the taste.

Rucking Mole (OG 1045, ABV 4.5%)
A chestnut-coloured premium ale, fruity and malty with a smooth bitter finish.

Molecatcher (OG 1050, ABV 5%)
A copper-coloured ale with a delightfully spicy hop aroma and taste, and a long bitter finish.

Moonstone

♀ Moonstone Brewery
(Gem Taverns Ltd), Ministry of Ale,
9 Trafalgar Street, Burnley,
Lancashire, BB11 1TQ
Tel (01282) 830909
✉ meet@ministryofale.co.uk
⊕ moonstonebrewery.co.uk
Tours by arrangement

⊕ A small, 2.5-barrel brewery, based in the Ministry of Ale pub. Brewing started in 2001 and beer is only generally available in the pub. Seasonal beer: Red Jasper (ABV 6%, winter).

Black Star (OG 1037, ABV 3.4%)

Blue John (ABV 3.6%)

Tigers Eye (OG 1037, ABV 3.8%)

MPA (ABV 4%)

Darkish (OG 1042, ABV 4.2%)

Moor SIBA

Moor Beer Co, Whitley Farm, Ashcott,
Bridgwater, Somerset, TA7 9QW
Tel (01458) 210050
✉ arthur@moorbeer.co.uk
⊕ moorbeer.co.uk
Tours by arrangement

Moor Beer was started by Arthur and Annette Frampton in 1996 on their dairy farm. Brewing originally started on a five-barrel plant and was expanded in 2006 to 10 barrels. The brewery bottles on a limited scale and also runs a thriving wholesale business, supplying pubs and beer festivals. Seasonal beer: Santa Moors (ABV 4%). Bottle-conditioned beers: Old Freddy Walker, Peat Porter, Merlin's Magic.

Revival (ABV 3.8%)
An immensely hoppy and refreshing bitter.

Milly's (ABV 3.9%)
A dark mild with a smooth mouthfeel and a slightly roasty finish.

Merlin's Magic (OG 1044, ABV 4.3%) ◆
Dark amber-coloured, complex, full-bodied beer, with fruity notes.

Peat Porter (OG 1045, ABV 4.5%) ◆
Dark brown/black beer with an initially fruity taste leading to roast malt with a little bitterness. A slightly sweet malty finish.

Confidence (ABV 4.6%)
Premium bitter with a spicy hoppiness and rich malt profile.

Ported Peat Porter (ABV 4.7%)
Peat Porter with added Reserve Port.

Somerland Gold (OG 1052, ABV 5%)
Hoppy golden ale with hints of honey.

Old Freddy Walker (OG 1074, ABV 7.3%) ▣ ◆
Rich, dark, strong ale with a fruity complex taste, leaving a fruitcake finish.

Moorcock

Moorcock Brewing Co, 1F Hawes Rural Workshop Estate, Brunt Acres Road, Hawes, North Yorkshire, DL8 3UZ
Tel (01969) 666188
✉ info@moorcockbrewing.co.uk
⊕ moorcockbrewing.co.uk

The brewery was launched in 2005. The plant was originally located at the Moorcock inn in Garsdale, but has been moved five miles away to an industrial unit in Hawes. It supplies only the Moorcock.

Garsdale (ABV 3.2%)

OPA (ABV 3.8%)

Mescan's Porter (ABV 4.3%)

Hail Ale (ABV 4.8%)

1888 (ABV 5%)

Moorhouses SIBA

Moorhouses Brewery (Burnley) Ltd, The Brewery, Moorhouse Street, Burnley,
Lancashire, BB11 5EN
Tel (01282) 422864/416004
✉ info@moorhouses.co.uk
⊕ moorhouses.co.uk
Tours by arrangement

Established in 1865 as a drinks manufacturer, the brewery started producing cask-conditioned ale in 1978 and has achieved recognition by winning more international and CAMRA awards than any other brewery of its size. Two new additional 30-barrel fermenters were installed in 2004, taking production to 320 barrels a week maximum. The company owns six pubs, all serving cask-conditioned beer, and supplies some 250 free trade outlets. There is a selection of seasonal ales throughout the year: see website.

Black Cat (OG 1036, ABV 3.4%) ◆
A dark mild-style beer with delicate chocolate and coffee roast flavours and a crisp, bitter finish.

Premier Bitter (OG 1036, ABV 3.7%) ◆
A clean and satisfying bitter aftertaste rounds off this well-balanced hoppy, amber session bitter.

Pride of Pendle (OG 1040, ABV 4.1%) ◆
Well-balanced amber best bitter with a fresh initial hoppiness and a mellow, malt-driven body.

Blond Witch (OG 1045, ABV 4.5%) ◆
A pale coloured ale with a crisp, delicate fruit flavour. Dry and refreshing with a smooth hop finish.

Pendle Witches Brew (OG 1050, ABV 5.1%) ◆
Well-balanced, full-bodied, malty beer with a long, complex finish.

Mordue SIBA

Mordue Brewery, Units D1 & D2, Narvic Way, Tyne Tunnel Estate, North Shields, Tyne & Wear, NE29 7XJ
Tel (0191) 296 1879
✉ enquiries@morduebrewery.com
⊕ morduebrewery.com
Tours by arrangement

The original Mordue Brewery closed in 1879 and the name was revived in 1995. In 1998, a 20-barrel plant and a move to bigger premises allowed production to keep pace with demand. By 2005 the business had expanded to the point where another move became necessary. The beers are distributed nationally and 200 outlets are supplied direct. Seasonal beers: see website.

Five Bridge Bitter (OG 1038, ABV 3.8%) ◗
Crisp, golden beer with a good hint of hops. The bitterness carries on in the finish. A good session bitter.

Geordie Pride (OG 1042, ABV 4.2%) ◗
Well-balanced and hoppy copper-coloured ale with a long, bitter finish.

Workie Ticket (OG 1045, ABV 4.5%) ◗
Complex, tasty bitter with plenty of malt and hops and a long, satisfying, bitter finish.

Radgie Gadgie (OG 1048, ABV 4.8%) ◗
Strong, easy-drinking bitter with plenty of fruit and hops.

IPA (OG 1051, ABV 5.1%) ◗
Easy-drinking, golden ale with plenty of hops. The bitterness carries on into the finish.

Morton*

Morton Brewery, c/o 96 Brewood Road, Coven, Staffordshire, WV9 5EF
Tel 07988 069647
✉ mortonbrewery@aol.com
⊕ mortonbrewery.co.uk

Morton was established in January 2007 on a three-barrel plant by Gary and Angela Morton, both CAMRA members. Seasonal beers: Irish George (ABV 5%, Dec-Feb), Forever in Darkness (ABV 4%, Mar-May), Penkside Pale (ABV 3.6%, Jun-Aug), Gregory's Gold (ABV 4.4%, Sep-Nov).

Merry Mount (OG 1038, ABV 3.8%)

Jelly Roll (OG 1042, ABV 4.2%)

Scottish Maiden (OG 1046, ABV 4.6%)

Moulin

⌂ Moulin Hotel & Brewery, 2 Baledmund Road, Moulin, Pitlochry, Perthshire, PH16 5EL
Tel (01796) 472196
✉ enquiries@moulinhotel.co.uk
⊕ moulinhotel.co.uk
Shop 12-3pm daily
Tours by arrangement

☺ The brewery opened in 1995 to celebrate the Moulin Hotel's 300th anniversary. Two pubs are owned and four outlets are supplied. Bottle-conditioned beer: Ale of Atholl.

Light (OG 1036, ABV 3.7%) ◗
Thirst-quenching, straw-coloured session beer, with a light, hoppy, fruity balance, ending with a gentle, hoppy sweetness.

Braveheart (OG 1039, ABV 4%) ◗
An amber bitter, with a delicate balance of malt and fruit and a Scottish-style sweetness.

Ale of Atholl (OG 1043.5, ABV 4.5%) ◗
A reddish, quaffable, malty ale, with a solid body and a mellow finish.

Old Remedial (OG 1050.5, ABV 5.2%) ◗
A distinctive and satisfying dark brown old ale, with roast malt to the fore and tannin in a robust taste.

Nags Head

⌂ Nags Head Inn & Brewery, Abercych, Boncath, Pembrokeshire, SA37 0HJ
Tel (01239) 841200

Pub-brewery producing just one beer for its own customers and two other outlets.

Old Emrys (OG 1039, ABV 3.9%)

Nailsworth

Nailsworth Brewery Ltd, The Village Inn, Bath Road, Nailsworth, Gloucestershire, GL6 0HH
Tel (01453) 839343 / (07738) 178452
✉ jonk@nailsworth-brewery.co.uk
⊕ nailsworth-brewery.co.uk
Shop Mon-Sat 12-2pm
Tours by arrangement

The original Nailsworth Brewery closed in 1908. After a gap of 98 years, commercial brewing has returned in the form of a six-barrel micro-brewery. This is the brainchild of Messrs Hawes and Kemp, whose aim it is to make the town of Nailsworth once again synonymous with quality beer. They intend to supply the whole range of beers in bottle in the near future.

Dudbridge Donkey (ABV 3.6%)
A sweet and malty mild.

Artist's Ale (ABV 3.9%)
A light-coloured bitter full of citrus flavours.

Mayor's Bitter (ABV 4.2%)
A best bitter with malt textures complemented by a long-lasting taste of blackcurrant.

Vicar's Stout (ABV 4.5%)
A dark, rich, smoky stout.

Town Crier (ABV 4.7%)
A premium ale with delicate grassy and floral overtones.

Naylors

Naylor's Brewery, Units 1 & 2, Midland Mills, Station Road, Cross Hills, Keighley, West Yorkshire, BD20 7DT
Tel (01535) 637451
✉ info@naylorsbrewery.co.uk
⊕ naylorsbrewery.co.uk
Tours by arrangement

☺ Naylors started brewing early in 2005, based at the Old White Bear pub in Keighley. Expansion required a move to the current site in 2006 and the rebranding of the beers. Some 40 outlets are supplied.

Pinnacle Mild (ABV 3.4%) 🍺 ◆
Formerly Sparkey's Mild, this dark brown malty mild has rich roast flavours with chocolate and fruity undertones and a dryish bitter finish.

Pinnacle Pale Ale (ABV 3.6%)

Pinnacle Bitter (ABV ABV 3.9%)

Pinnacle Blonde (ABV 4.3%)

Pinnacle Porter (ABV 4.8%)

Nelson SIBA

Nelson Brewing Co UK Ltd, Unit 2, Building 64, The Historic Dockyard, Chatham, Kent, ME4 4TE
Tel (01634) 832828
✉ sales@nelsonbrewingcompany.co.uk
⊕ nelsonbrewingcompany.co.uk
Shop Mon-Fri 9am-4.30pm
Tours by arrangement

☺ Nelson started out in 1995 as the Flagship Brewery but changed its name in 2004. It was acquired by Piers MacDonald in 2006. The brewery is based in Chatham's preserved Georgian dockyard, where Nelson's flaship, HMS Victory, was built. All beers are also available bottle conditioned. Seasonal beers: Powder Monkey (ABV 4.4%, summer), Loose Cannon (ABV 4.4%, autumn), Shiver me' Timbers (ABV 4.5%, winter), Santa's Salvo (ABV 4.5%, Xmas).

Victory Dark Mild (OG 1036, ABV 3.5%)
A dark mild with smooth malt and hop flavour and roast aftertaste.

Rochester Bitter (OG 1038, ABV 3.7%)
A refreshing pale and hoppy bitter.

Pieces of Eight (OG 1039, ABV 3.8%)

Trafalgar Bitter (OG 1039, ABV 4.1%)
A light, easy-drinking ale with balanced malt and hop flavour and hints of honey and nuts to finish.

England Expects (OG 1041, ABV 4.2%)

Dogwatch Stout (OG 1044, ABV 4.5%)

Friggin in the Riggin (OG 1048, ABV 4.7%)
Drinkable premium bitter with smooth malt flavour and bittersweet aftertaste.

Nelson's Blood (OG 1062, ABV 6%)
Malty with mellow roast tones, slightly nutty and fruity.

Nethergate SIBA EAB

Nethergate Brewery Co Ltd, Growler Brewery, The Street, Pentlow, Essex, CO10 7JJ
Tel (01787) 283220
✉ orders@nethergate.co.uk
⊕ nethergatebrewery.co.uk

☒ Nethergate Brewery was established in 1986 at Clare, Suffolk. Production tripled in the 1990s, but the brewery was unable to meet demand and in 2005 moved four miles away to a new site to enable production to double. Some 400 outlets are supplied. Seasonal beers are brewed monthly and a bottling plant is now up and running.

IPA (OG 1036, ABV 3.5%) 🍺 ◆
This amber-coloured session bitter is clean, crisp and drinkable. Plenty of malt and hoppy

bitterness with some fruit are pleasing to the palate. Bitterness lingers in a long dry aftertaste.

Priory Mild (OG 1036, ABV 3.5%) ◆
Distinctive, full-flavoured, very dark mild. Pronounced lingering roast and dry hop aftertaste.

Umbel Ale (OG 1039, ABV 3.8%) ◆
Light-bodied bitter infused with coriander, which dominates throughout.

Three Point Nine (OG 1040, ABV 3.9%) ◆
Light tasting, sweetish and fruity session beer.

Suffolk County Best Bitter (OG 1041, ABV 4%) 🍺 ◆
Dry bitter, dominated by biscuity malt, bitter hops and an astringent roast character.

Augustinian Ale (OG 1046, ABV 4.5%) ◆
A pale, refreshing, complex best bitter. A fruity aroma leads to a bittersweet flavour and aftertaste with a predominance of citrus tones.

Old Growler (OG 1052, ABV 5%) ◆
Smooth, creamy porter, with roast grain supported by caramel and butterscotch, with some bubblegum character.

Umbel Magna (OG 1052, ABV 5%) 🍺 ◆
Old Growler infused with coriander, which dominates throughout.

Stour Valley Strong/SVS (OG 1063, ABV 6.2%)
A dark ruby red porter, brewed using a blend of amber, black and chocolate malts.

Newby Wyke SIBA

Newby Wyke Brewery, Willoughby Arms Cottages, Station Road, Little Bytham, Lincolnshire, NG33 4RA
Tel (01780) 411119
✉ newbywyke.brewery@btopenworld.com
⊕ newbywyke.co.uk
Tours by arrangement

☒ The brewery is named after a Hull trawler skippered by brewer Rob March's grandfather. After starting life in 1998 as a 2.5-barrel plant in a converted garage, growth has been steady and the brewery moved to premises behind the Willoughby Arms. Current brewing capacity is 50 barrels a week. Some 180 outlets are supplied. Seasonal beers: see website.

HMS Revenge (OG 1039, ABV 4.2%)
A single-hopped ale with floral undertones.

Red Squall (OG 1042, ABV 4.4%)
A full, rich red ale, full of fruit with a hoppy finish.

Bear Island (OG 1044, ABV 4.6%)
A blonde beer with a hoppy aroma and a crisp, dry citrus finish.

Black Squall Porter (OG 1044, ABV 4.6%)
A subtle taste of coffee and chocolate with a hoppy finish.

White Squall (OG 1045, ABV 4.8%)
A pale blonde ale with a full hop taste and a citrus finish.

Chesapeake (OG 1050, ABV 5.5%)
Strong, pale, complex hoppy ale.

For Nobody Inn, Grantham:
Grantham Gold (OG 1039, ABV 4.2%)

Newmans SIBA

T G Newman t/a Newmans Brewery, 107
Wemberham Lane, Yatton, Somerset, BS49 4BP
Tel (01934) 830638
✉ sales@newmansbrewery.com
⊕ newmansbrewery.com
Tours by arrangement

⊗ Newmans opened on the day England won
the Rugby World Cup in November 2003 and
has since expanded from a five-barrel to a 20-
barrel plant. The beer is sold locally and
nationwide to more than 250 outlets and the
company plans to introduce bottling. Seasonal
beer: Cave Bear Stout (ABV 4%).

Red Stag Bitter (OG 1039, ABV 3.6%) ◆
Dark red session ale, smooth, malty with soft
fruit accents; dry fruit finish.

Wolvers Ale (OG 1042, ABV 4.1%) ◆
Well-rounded best bitter with good body for
its strength. Initial sweetness with a fine
malt flavour is balanced by a slightly
astringent, hoppy finish.

Mendip Mammoth (OG 1044, ABV 4.3%)

Bite IPA (OG 1046, ABV 4.6%) ◆
Amber strong bitter with long hoppy finish.

Nobby's

Nobby's Brewery, 3 Pagent Court, Kettering,
Northants, NN15 6GR
Tel (01536) 521868
✉ info@nobbysbrewery.co.uk
⊕ nobbysbrewery.co.uk
Tours by arrangmnt

Paul 'Nobby' Mulliner started commercial brewing
in 2004 on a 2.5-barrel plant at the rear of the
Alexandra Arms in Kettering, which also serves as
the brewery tap. The plant has since been
enlarged to five barrels and further growth will
see a move to the Ward Arms at Guilsborough
with a 10-barrel plant in late 2007. The plant at
the Alex will continue brewing for the pub.
Seasonal beers: Santa's Secret (ABV 4.7%), Wet
Spell (ABV 4%), Dark Spell (ABV 4.2%).

Claridges Crystal (ABV 3.6%)

Best (OG 1039, ABV 3.8%)

Tressler XXX Mild (OG 1039, ABV 3.8%)

Monster Mash (OG 1045, ABV 4.3%)

Wild West (OG 1046, ABV 4.6%)

Brewhouse Special (ABV 4.8%)

Landlord (OG 1050, ABV 5%)

T'owd Navigation (ABV 6.1%)

Norfolk Cottage SIBA

Norfolk Cottage Brewing, 98-100 Lawson Road,
Norwich, Norfolk, NR3 4LF
Tel (01603) 788508/270520
✉ norfolkcottagebeers@tiscali.co.uk

Launched in 2004 by Ray Ashworth, founder of
Woodforde's, Norfolk Cottage undertakes
consultancy brewing and pilot brews for the Fat

Cat Brewing Co at the same address. One best
bitter is available to the trade plus bespoke ales
in small quantities to order. Three outlets are
supplied direct.

Best (OG 1042, ABV 4.1%)

North Cotswold SIBA

North Cotswold Brewery (Pilling Brewing
Company), Unit 3 Ditchford Farm, Stretton-on-
Fosse, Warwickshire, GL56 9RD
Tel (01608) 663947
✉ mail@northcotswoldbrewery.co.uk
⊕ northcotswoldbrewery.co.uk
Shop – please ring first
Tours by arrangement

◎ North Cotswold started in 1999 as a 2.5-
barrel plant, which was upgraded in 2000 to 10
barrels. A shop and visitor centre are on site.
Medieval beers are produced under contract,
using original recipes. The brewery also owns
the Happy Apple Cider Company, which
produces real cider and perry from orchards on
the estate of the farm. Around 150 outlets are
supplied. All ales are also available bottle
conditioned. Seasonal beers: Blitzen (ABV 6%,
Dec), Monarch IPA (ABV 10%, Aug-Sep), Mayfair
Mild (ABV 4.1%, May-Jun), Summer Solstice
(ABV 4.5%, Jul-Sep), Winter Solstice (ABV 4.5%,
Oct-Dec), Stour Stout (ABV 5%, Mar-Apr).

Pig Brook (OG 1038, ABV 3.8%)

Ditchford Ale (OG 1045, ABV 4.5%)

Hung, Drawn 'n' Portered (OG 1050, ABV 5%)

Northern SIBA

Northern Brewing Ltd,
**Blakemere Brewery, Blakemere Craft Centre,
Chester Road, Sandiway, Northwich,
Cheshire, CW8 2EB**
Tel (01606) 301000
✉ sales@norbrew.co.uk
⊕ norbrew.co.uk
Tours by arrangement

⊗ Northern first brewed in 2003 on a five-
barrel plant located in Runcorn. It relocated to a
larger unit at Blakemere Craft Centre in 2005. A
hospitality/bar area is available for brewery
tours. The beer names are Northern Soul
themed and at least two specials per month are
produced under both the 'Northern' and
'Blakemere' brand names.

All-Niter (ABV 3.8%) ◆
Full-bodied, pale bitter beer with caramel
overtones. Good hoppy nose and aftertaste.

Soul Rider (ABV 4%)

Soul Master (ABV 4.4%)

'45 (ABV 4.5%) ◆
Soft, light and malty pale brown beer. Fairly
sweet with fruit to the fore on the nose and
in the flavour. Hop flavour leads into the
aftertaste.

One-Der-Ful Wheat (ABV 4.7%)

Two Tone Special Stout (ABV 5%)

Soul Time (ABV 5%)

Flaming Embers (ABV 6%)

Northumberland

Northumberland Brewery Ltd, Accessory House, Barrington Road, Bedlington, Northumberland, NE22 7AP
Tel (01670) 822112
✉ dave@northumberlandbrewery.co.uk
⊕ northumberlandbrewery.co.uk
Tours by arrangement

⊛ The brewery has been in operation for 11 years using a 10-barrel brew plant. More than 400 outlets are supplied. Seasonal beers: Summer Gold (ABV 3.7%), Spring Gold (ABV 3.9%), Autumn Gold (ABV 4.1%), Winter Gold (ABV 4.5%), Blaydon Races (ABV 4%, Jun), Dracula's Soup (ABV 4.5%, Oct), Rudolph's Balls (ABV 4.5%, Dec). Bottle-conditioned beers: Gateshead Gold, Fog on the Tyne, Sheepdog, McCrory's Irish Stout, Northumbrian Bitter (ABV 4.1%), Bucking Fastard (ABV 4%), Cranky Flannen (ABV 4%).

Castles Bitter (ABV 3.8%)
A golden, full-flavoured beer with a hoppy aftertaste.

Holy Island (ABV 3.8%)

Byker Bitter (ABV 4%)

Highway Robbery (ABV 4%)

Fog on the Tyne (ABV 4.1%)

Ashington (ABV 4.2%)

Newcastle Pride (ABV 4.3%)

Sheepdog (ABV 4.7%)
An old-fashioned tawny beer, with fruit and malt throughout and a hoppy finish.

McCrory's Irish Stout (ABV 4.8%)

Gateshead Gold (ABV 5%)

Whitley Wobbler (ABV 5%)

North Wales* SIBA

North Wales Brewery, Tan-y-Mynydd, Moelfre, Abergele, Conwy, LL22 9RF
Tel 0800 083 4100
⊕ northwalesbrewery.net

⊠ North Wales started brewing in June 2007 on a plant transferred from Paradise Brewery's former home in Wrenbury. Brewer John Wood also produces Paradise beers at the 3 Rivers Brewery (qv) in Stockport. Cask and bottled beers are available at the Paradise Brewery Bar, located in Manchester Arndale's indoor food market (Mon-Sat 11-6, 8 Thu; Sun 11-4). Paradise beers are also bottle conditioned under the Old Creamery Brewery name.

Moelfre Mild (ABV 3.6%)

Bodelwyddan Bitter (ABV 4%)

North Yorkshire

North Yorkshire Brewing Co, Pinchinthorpe Hall, Guisborough, North Yorkshire, TS14 8HG
Tel (01287) 630200
✉ sales@nybrewery.com
⊕ nybrewery.co.uk
Shop 10am-5pm
Tours by arrangement

⊛ The brewery was founded in Middlesbrough

in 1989 and moved in 1998 to Pinchinthorpe Hall, a moated and listed medieval estate near Guisborough that has its own spring water. The site also includes a hotel, restaurant and bistro. More than 100 free trade outlets are supplied. A special monthly beer is produced together with four beers in the Cosmic range. All beers are organic and the range is also available bottle conditioned except for Mayhem and Xmas Herbert (ABV 4.4%).

Best (OG 1036, ABV 3.6%)
Clean tasting, well hopped, pale-coloured traditional bitter.

Golden Ginseng (ABV 3.6%)

Prior's Ale (OG 1036, ABV 3.6%) ◈
Light, refreshing and surprisingly full-flavoured for a pale, low gravity beer, with a complex, bittersweet mixture of malt, hops and fruit carrying through into the aftertaste.

Archbishop Lee's Ruby Ale (OG 1040, ABV 4%)
A full-bodied beer with a malty aroma and a balanced malt and hops taste, with vanilla notes.

Boro Best (OG 1040, ABV 4%)
Northern-style, full-bodied beer.

Crystal Tips (OG 1040, ABV 4%)

Love Muscle (OG 1040, ABV 4%)

Honey Bunny (OG 1042, ABV 4.2%)

Mayhem (ABV 4.3%)

Cereal Killer (OG 1045, ABV 4.5%)

Blond (ABV 4.6%)

Fools Gold (OG 1046, ABV 4.6%)
Hoppy, pale-coloured premium beer.

Golden Ale (OG 1046, ABV 4.6%) ◈
A well-hopped, lightly-malted, golden premium bitter, using Styrian Goldings and Goldings hops.

Flying Herbert (OG 1047, ABV 4.7%)
Full-flavoured premium bitter, smooth and well balanced.

Lord Lee's (OG 1047, ABV 4.7%) ◈
A refreshing, red/brown beer with a hoppy aroma. The flavour is a pleasant balance of roast malt and sweetness that predominates over hops. The malty, bitter finish develops slowly.

White Lady (OG 1047, ABV 4.7%)

Dizzy Dick (OG 1048, ABV 4.8%)

Rocket Fuel (OG 1050, ABV 5%)

Nottingham SIBA

⬚ Nottingham Brewing Co Ltd, Plough Inn, 17 St Peter's Street, Radford, Nottingham, NG7 3EN
Tel (0115) 9422649 / 07815 073447
✉ philip.darby@nottinghambrewery.com
⊕ nottinghambrewery.com
Tours by arrangement

⊠ Founded in 2001, the brewery produces beers in the style of the original Nottingham Brewery that closed in 1960. Owners Niven Balfour and Philip and Peter Darby have expanded the brewing plant and also bottle the beers. 60 outlets are supplied and one pub is owned.

Rock Ale Bitter Beer (OG 1038, ABV 3.8%) 🗍

Rock Ale Mild Beer (OG 1038, ABV 3.8%) 🗍

Legend (OG 1040, ABV 4%) 🗍

Extra Pale Ale (OG 1042, ABV 4.2%)

Dreadnought (OG 1046, ABV 4.5%)

Bullion (OG 1048, ABV 4.7%)

Sooty Stout (OG 1050, ABV 4.8%)

Supreme Bitter (OG 1055, ABV 5.2%)

For Fellows, Morton & Clayton Brewery:

Matthew Clayton's Original Strong Brew (ABV 4.4%)

For Wetherspoons:

Spoon & Arrow (OG 1047, ABV 4.7%)

Nutbrook*

Nutbrook Brewery, 6 Hallam Way, West Hallam, Derbyshire, DE7 6LA
Tel 0800 458 2460
✉ dean@nutbrookbrewery.com
⊕ nutbrookbrewery.com
Tours by arrangement

⊠ Nutbrook was established in January 2007 on a one-barrel brewery in the owner's garage. Beers are brewed to order for domestic and corporate clients, and customers can design their own recipes. All beers are also available bottle conditioned and a range of organic beers is planned.

Squirrel Bitter (OG 1043.2, ABV 4%)

Banter Bitter (OG 1040.9, ABV 4.5%)

Moor Bitter (OG 1043.2, ABV 4.8%)

O'Hanlon's SIBA

O'Hanlon's Brewing Co Ltd, Great Barton Farm, Whimple, Devon, EX5 2NY
Tel (01404) 822412
✉ info@ohanlons.co.uk
⊕ ohanlons.co.uk

⊠ Since moving to Whimple in 2000, O'Hanlon's has continued to expand to cope with ever increasing demand for its prize-winning beers. More than 100 outlets are regularly supplied, with wholesalers providing publicans nationwide with access to the cask products. A new bottling plant has increased production and enabled O'Hanlon's to contract bottle for several other breweries. Export sales also continue to grow with Thomas Hardy's Ale available in Canada, Chile, Denmark and Japan. Bottle-conditioned beers: Port Stout, Double Champion Wheat Beer, Royal Oak, Thomas Hardy's Ale.

Firefly (OG 1035, ABV 3.7%) ◆
Malty and fruity light bitter. Hints of orange in the taste.

Double Champion Wheat (OG 1037, ABV 4%) ◆
1999 and 2002 SIBA Champion Wheat Beer of Britain has a fine citrus taste.

Yellowhammer (OG 1041, ABV 4%) ◆
A well-balanced, smooth pale yellow beer

with a predominant hop and fruit nose and taste, leading to a dry, bitter finish.

Dry Stout (OG 1041, ABV 4.2%) ◆
A dark malty, well-balanced stout with a dry, bitter finish and plenty of roast and fruit flavours up front.

Original Port Stout (OG 1041, ABV 4.8%) 🗍 ◆
A black beer with roast malt in the aroma that remains in the taste but gives way to hoppy bitterness in the aftertaste.

Royal Oak (OG 1048, ABV 5%) ◆
Well-balanced copper-coloured beer with a strong fruit and malt aroma; a malty, fruity and sweet taste; and bitter aftertaste.

Thomas Hardy Ale (OG 1120, ABV 11.7%)
A tawny brown colour. Dark malts dominate with hints of sherry, treacle, molasses, toffee and port. The finish combines red wine, sherry and plenty of rich fruit.

Oakham SIBA EAB

Oakham Ales, Unit 2, Maxwell Road, Woodston Industrial Estate, Peterborough, PE2 7JB
Tel (01733) 370500
✉ info@oakhamales.com
⊕ oakhamales.com
Tours by arrangement

⊠ The brewery started in 1993 in Oakham, Rutland, and expanded to a 35-barrel plant from the original 10-barrel in 1998 after moving to Peterborough. This was the brewery's main brewhouse until 2006 when a new 70-barrel brewery was completed at Maxwell Road, designed to brew more than 700 barrels a week. Some 80 outlets are supplied and four pubs are owned. Several one-off specials are also brewed throughout the year. Seasonal beers: Inferno (ABV 4%, Jan-Feb), Asylum (ABV 4.5%, Mar-Apr), Mompesson's Gold (ABV 5%, May-Jun), Helter Skelter (ABV 4%, Jul-Aug), JHB Extra (ABV 4.2%, Sep-Oct), Gravity (ABV 5.1%, Nov-Dec).

Jeffrey Hudson Bitter/JHB (OG 1038, ABV 3.8%) ◆
An assault of aromatic citrus hop, a hoppy, fruity and grassy bittersweet palate and an uncompromising dry, bitter aftertaste characterise this impressive straw-coloured ale.

White Dwarf Wheat Beer (OG 1042, ABV 4.3%) 🗍 ◆
Straw-coloured hoppy brew with a powerful citrus hop aroma and a zesty hop bitterness, ending with a powerful dry bite.

Bishops Farewell (OG 1046, ABV 4.6%) 🗍 ◆
Intensely hoppy and full-bodied golden best bitter. Tropical fruit flavours provide a counterpoint to the grapefruit hoppy character. An abiding dryness develops.

Oakleaf SIBA

Oakleaf Brewing Co Ltd, Unit 7 Clarence Wharf Industrial Estate, Mumby Road, Gosport, Hampshire, PO12 1AJ
Tel (023) 9251 3222
✉ info@oakleafbrewing.co.uk
⊕ oakleafbrewing.co.uk
Shop Mon-Fri 9am-5pm, Sat 10am-1pm
Tours by arrangement

⊗ Ed Anderson set up Oakleaf with his father-in-law, Dave Pickersgill, in 2000. The brewery stands on the side of Portsmouth Harbour. Bottled beers are sold in the Victory Shop at the historic dockyard in Portsmouth. Some 150 outlets are supplied. Seasonal beers: Green Gold (ABV 4.3%, Sep), Reindeer's Delight (ABV 4.5%, Xmas), Piston Porter (ABV 4.6%, Oct/Nov), Stoker's Stout (ABV 5%, Jan-Feb), Blake's Heaven (ABV 7%, Dec). Bottle-conditioned beers: Oakleaf Bitter, Maypole Mild, Hole Hearted, I Can't Believe It's Not Bitter, Blake's Gosport Bitter, Heart of Oak (ABV 4.5%), Eichenblatt Bitte (ABV 5.4%), Reindeers Delight, Blake's Heaven.

Bitter (OG 1038, ABV 3.8%) ◈
A copper-coloured beer with a hoppy and fruity aroma, which leads to an intensely hoppy and bitter flavour, with balancing lemon and grapefruit and some malt. A long, dry finish.

Maypole Mild (OG 1040, ABV 3.8%) ◈
This dark mild has a full biscuity aroma. A lasting mix of flavours, roast and toffee lead to a slightly unexpected hoppiness. A roast, bitter finish.

Nuptu'ale (OG 1042, ABV 4.2%) ◈
A full-bodied pale ale, strongly hopped with an uncompromising bitterness. An intense hoppy, spicy, floral aroma leads to a complex hoppy taste. Well balanced with malt and citrus flavours.

Hole Hearted (OG 1048, ABV 4.7%) ▦ ◈
An amber-coloured strong bitter with strong floral hop and citrus notes in the aroma. These continue to dominate the flavour and lead to a long, bittersweet finish.

I Can't Believe It's Not Bitter (OG 1048, ABV 4.9%)
Cask conditioned lager.

Blake's Gosport Bitter (OG 1053, ABV 5.2%) ◈
Packed with berry fruits and roastiness, this is a complex strong bitter, with hoppy bitterness. Malt, roast and caramel are prevalent as sweetness builds to a vinous finish. Warming and spicy.

For Suthwyk Ales:

Bloomfields Bitter (ABV 3.8%) ◈
Pleasant, clean-tasting, pale brown bitter. Easy drinking and well balanced, brewed with ingredients grown on their farm.

Skew Sunshine Ale (ABV 4.6%) ◈
An amber-coloured beer. Initial hoppiness leads to a fruity taste and finish. A slightly cloying mouthfeel.

Liberation (ABV 4.2%)

Oakwell

Oakwell Brewery, PO Box 87, Pontefract Road, Barnsley, South Yorkshire, S71 1EZ
Tel (01226) 296161
✉ jstancill@oakwellbrewery.co.uk

⊛ Brewing started in 1997. Oakwell supplies some 30 outlets.

Old Tom Mild (ABV 3.4%) ◈
A dark brown session mild, with a fruit aroma and a subtle hint of roast. Crisp and refreshing with a sharp finish.

Barnsley Bitter (OG 1036, ABV 3.8%)

Odcombe

⎓ Odcombe Brewery, Masons Arms, 41 Lower Odcombe, Odcombe, Yeovil, Somerset, BA22 8TX
Tel (01935) 862591
✉ paula@masonsarmsodcombe.co.uk
⊕ masonsarmsodcombe.co.uk
Tours by arrangement

Odcombe Brewery opened in 2000 and closed a few years later. It re-opened in 2005 with assistance from Shepherd Neame. Brewing takes place every week and more beers and seasonal brews are planned.

No 1 (OG 1040, ABV 4%)

Spring (OG 1042, ABV 4.1%)

Offa's Dyke

Offa's Dyke Brewery Ltd, Chapel Lane, Trefonen, Oswestry, Shropshire, SY10 9DX
Tel (01691) 831680

Offa's Dyke was established in 2006 and changed hands early in 2007. New brewing equipment was being installed as the guide went to press.

Okells SIBA

Okell & Son Ltd, Kewaigue, Douglas, Isle of Man, IM2 1QG
Tel (01624) 699400
✉ mac@okells.co.uk
⊕ okells.co.uk
Tours by arrangement

⊛ Founded in 1874 by Dr Okell and formerly trading as Isle of Man Breweries, this is the main brewery on the island, having taken over and closed the rival Castletown Brewery in 1986. The brewery moved in 1994 to a new, purpose-built plant at Kewaigue to replace the Falcon Brewery in Douglas. All the beers are produced under the Manx Brewers' Act 1874 (permitted ingredients: water, malt, sugar and hops only). 36 of the company's 48 IoM pubs and four on the mainland sell cask beer and some 70 free trade outlets are also supplied. Seasonal beers: Spring Ram (ABV 4.2%), Autumn Dawn (ABV 4.2%), Summer Storm (ABV 4.2%), St Nick (ABV 4.5%), Aile (ABV 4.8%, winter), Castletown Bitter (ABV 4%), Olde Skipper (ABV 4.5%).

Mild (OG 1034, ABV 3.4%) ◈
A fine aroma of hops and crystal malt. Red-brown in colour, the beer has a full malt flavour with surprising bitter hop notes and a hint of blackcurrants and oranges.

Bitter (OG 1035, ABV 3.7%) ◈
A golden beer, malty and hoppy in aroma, with a hint of honey. Rich and malty on the tongue, it has a dry, malt and hop finish. A complex but rewarding beer.

Maclir (OG 1042, ABV 4.4%)
Beer with resiny hops and lemon fruit on the

aroma, banana and lemon in the mouth and a big, bitter finish, dominated by hops, juicy malt and citrus fruit.

Dr Okells IPA (OG 1044, ABV 4.5%)
An light-coloured beer with a full-bodied taste. The sweetness is offset by strong hopping that gives the beer an overall roundness with spicy lemon notes and a fine dry finish.

Old Bear

Old Bear Brewery, Unit 4b, Atlas Works, Pitt Street, Keighley, West Yorkshire, BD21 4YL
Tel (01535) 601222/07713 161224
✉ sales@oldbearbrewery.com
🌐 oldbearbrewery.co.uk
Tours by arrangement

☺ The brewery was founded in 1993 as a brew-pub at the Old White Bear in Crosshills. The brewery moved to Keighley in 2005 to a purpose-built unit to cater for increased production. The original 10-barrel plant was retained and there is now a one-barrel plant for specials. 60 outlets are supplied. All beers are also available bottle conditioned.

Bruin (OG 1035, ABV 3.5%)
A mix of three malts, one being dark chocolate, giving a soft bronze colour. The combination of English Fuggles and Goldings hops give a sharp blackcurrant aftertaste.

Estivator (OG 1037, ABV 3.8%)
A light golden ale with a smooth, creamy, sweet lemon taste followed by buttery smoothness leading to a bitter, hoppy aftertaste.

Original (OG 1039, ABV 3.9%) ✦
A refreshing and easy-to-drink bitter. The balance of malt and hops gives way to a short, dry, bitter aftertaste.

Black Mari'a (OG 1043, ABV 4.2%)
A jet black stout, smooth on the palate. Brewed with Maris Otter malt and roasted barley and a blend of two English hops producing a strong roast malt flavour with a fruity finish.

Yorkshire Day Ale (OG 1042, ABV 4.2%)
A copper-coloured traditional bitter, malty with nutty overtones with a bitter finish.

Honeypot (OG 1044, ABV 4.4%)
Straw-coloured beer enhanced with golden honey from Denholme Gate.

Goldilocks (OG 1047, ABV 4.5%) ✦
A fruity, straw-coloured golden ale, well-hopped and assertively bitter through to the finish.

Hibernator (OG 1055, ABV 5%)
A strong, dark ale, ruby red in colour with a powerful malt and light liquorice aroma.

Old Bog

▢ **Old Bog Brewery, Masons Arms, 2 Quarry School Place, Oxford, OX3 8LH**
Tel (01865) 764579
✉ theoldbog@hotmail.co.uk
🌐 masonsquarry.co.uk

Brewing started in 2005 on a one-barrel plant. At present Old Bog brews once a week. The beers, when available, are sold at the Masons Arms and

occasionally at beer festivals. A number of one-off brews appear throughout the year.

Quarry Gold (ABV 4%)

Wheat Beer (ABV 5%)

Quarry Wrecked (ABV 5.5%)

Old Cannon

▢ **Old Cannon Brewery Ltd, 86 Cannon Street, Bury St Edmunds, Suffolk, IP33 1JR**
Tel (01284) 768769
✉ drink@oldcannonbrewery.co.uk
🌐 oldcannonbrewery.co.uk
Tours by arrangement (small groups only)

⊠ The St Edmunds Head pub opened in 1845 with its own brewery. Brewing ceased in 1917, and Greene King closed the pub in 1995. It re-opened in 1999 complete with a unique state-of-the-art brewery housed in the bar area. 10 outlets are supplied. Seasonal beers: Blonde Bombshell (ABV 4.2%), Brass Monkey (ABV 4.6%).

Best Bitter (OG 1037, ABV 3.8%) ✦
Session bitter brewed using Styrian Goldings, giving a crisp grapefruit aroma and taste. Refreshing and full of flavour.

Gunner's Daughter (OG 1052, ABV 5.5%) ✦
A well-balanced strong ale with a complexity of hop, fruit, sweetness and bitterness in the flavour, and a lingering hoppy, bitter aftertaste.

Old Chimneys

Old Chimneys Brewery, The Street, Market Weston, Diss, Norfolk, IP22 2NZ
Tel (01359) 221411/(01359) 221013
Shop Fri 2-7pm, Sat 11am-2pm
Tours by arrangement

Old Chimneys opened in 1995 and moved to larger premises in a converted farm building in 2001. Despite the postal address, the brewery is in Suffolk. The beers produced are mostly named after endangered local species. Seasonal beers: Corncleavers Ale (ABV 4.3%, summer), Polecat Porter (ABV 4.2%, winter), Natterjack (ABV 5%, winter), Winter Cloving (ABV 6%, winter). All cask ales are available bottle conditioned plus Hairy Canary (ABV 4.2%), IPA (ABV 5.6%), Brimstone Lager (ABV 6.5%), Redshank (ABV 8.7%). In bottled form, Military Mild is known as Meadow Brown and bottled Good King Henry is marketed as Special Reserve and is stronger at ABV 11%; it is also bottle conditioned for two years before going on sale. All bottle-conditioned beers are suitable for vegetarians and all except Black Rat and Hairy Canary are suitable for vegans.

Military Mild (OG 1035, ABV 3.3%) ✦
A rich, dark mild with good body for its gravity. Sweetish toffee and light roast bitterness dominate, leading to a dry aftertaste.

Great Raft Bitter (OG 1040, ABV 4%)
Pale copper bitter bursting with fruit. Malt and hops add to the sweetish fruity flavour, which is rounded off with hoppy bitterness in the aftertaste.

Black Rat Stout (OG 1048, ABV 4.4%)

Golden Pheasant (ABV 4.5%)

Good King Henry (OG 1107, ABV 9%)

Old Cottage

Burton Old Cottage Beer Co Ltd, Unit 10, Eccleshall Business Park, Hawkins Lane, Burton upon Trent, Staffordshire, DE14 1PT
Tel 07909 931250
✉ jwsaville@tiscali.co.uk
⊕ oldcottagebeer.co.uk
Tours by arrangement

⊛ Old Cottage was originally installed in the old Heritage Brewery, once Everard's production plant in Burton. When the site was taken over, the brewery moved to a modern industrial unit. The brewery was sold in 2005 and 2006 saw heavy investment in new production and storage facilities by the new owners. Around 10 outlets are supplied. Seasonal beer: Snow Joke (ABV 5.2%, winter).

Pail Ale (OG 1040, ABV 3.8%)

Oak Ale (OG 1044, ABV 4%) ◆
Tawny, full-bodied bitter. A sweet start gives way to a slight roast taste with some caramel. A dry, hoppy finish.

Cottage IPA (OG 1047, ABV 4.4%)

Redwood (OG 1046, ABV 4.6%)

Cloughy's Clout (OG 1047, ABV 4.7%)

Stout (OG 1047, ABV 4.7%) ◆
Dense black but not heavy. Sweet with lots of caramel, hints of liquorice and a roast and bitter finish.

Pastiche (OG 1050, ABV 5.2%)

Halcyon Daze (OG 1050, ABV 5.3%) ◆
Tawny and creamy with touches of hop, fruit and malt aroma. Fruity taste and finish.

Oldershaw SIBA

Oldershaw Brewery, 12 Harrowby Hall Estate, Grantham, Lincolnshire, NG31 9HB
Tel (01476) 572135
✉ oldershawbrewery@btconnect.com
⊕ oldershawbrewery.com
Tours by arrangement

Experienced home-brewer Gary Oldershaw and his wife Diane set up the brewery at their home in 1997. Grantham's first brewery for 30 years, Oldershaw now supplies 60 local free houses. The Oldershaws have introduced small-scale bottling and sell bottle-conditioned beer direct from the brewery. Seasonal beers: Sunnydaze (ABV 4%, May-Aug), Yuletide (ABV 5.2%, Nov-Dec), Grantham Dark (ABV 3.6%), Alma's Brew (ABV 4.1%).

Mowbrays Mash (OG 1037, ABV 3.7%)

Harrowby Pale Ale (OG 1039, ABV 3.9%)

High Dyke (OG 1039, ABV 3.9%)
Golden and moderately bitter. A predominantly hoppy session beer.

OSB (OG 1040, ABV 4%)

Newton's Drop (OG 1041, ABV 4.1%) ◆
Balanced malt and hops but with a strong bitter, lingering taste in this mid-brown beer.

Caskade (OG 1042, ABV 4.2%)
Pale, golden beer brewed with American Cascade hops to give a distinctive floral, hoppy flavour and aroma, and a clean lasting finish.

Ahtanum Gold (OG 1043, ABV 4.3%)
A gold-coloured, fruity, hoppy beer balanced with some maltiness. Moderately bitter.

Grantham Stout (OG 1043, ABV 4.3%)
Dark brown and smooth with rich roast malt flavour, supported by some fruit and bitterness. A long, moderately dry finish.

Regal Blonde (OG 1043, ABV 4.4%) ◆
Straw-coloured, lager-style beer with a good malt/hop balance throughout; strong bitterness on the taste lingers.

Isaac's Gold (OG 1044, ABV 4.5%)

Old Boy (OG 1047, ABV 4.8%) ◆
A full-bodied amber ale, fruity and bitter with a hop/fruit aroma. The malt that backs the taste dies in the long finish.

Alchemy (OG 1052, ABV 5.3%)
A golden, premium hoppy beer brewed with First Gold hops.

Olde Swan

⌂ Olde Swan Brewery, 89 Halesowen Road, Netherton, Dudley, West Midlands, DY2 9PY
Tel (01384) 253075
Tours by arrangement

⊛ A famous brew-pub best known as 'Ma Pardoe's' after the matriarch who ruled it for years. The pub has been licensed since 1835 and the present brewery and pub were built in 1863. Brewing continued until 1988 and restarted in 2001. The plant brews primarily for the on-site pub with some beer available to the trade. Seasonal beer: Black Widow (ABV 6.7%, winter). Monthly specials are available together with various commemorative beers for sporting events. Bottle-conditioned beers are also available from the brewery tap.

Original (OG 1034, ABV 3.5%) ◆
Straw-coloured light mild, smooth but tangy, and sweetly refreshing with a faint hoppiness.

Dark Swan (OG 1041, ABV 4.2%) ◆
Smooth, sweet dark mild with late roast malt in the finish.

Entire (OG 1043, ABV 4.4%) ◆
Faintly hoppy, amber premium bitter with sweetness persistent throughout.

Bumble Hole Bitter (OG 1052, ABV 5.2%) ◆
Sweet, smooth amber ale with hints of astringency in the finish.

Old Foreigner*

⌂ Old Foreigner Brewery, Glenkindie Arms Hotel, Glenkindie, Aberdeenshire, AB33 8SX
Tel (01975) 641288
✉ eddie@theglenkindiearmshotel.com
⊕ theglenkindiearmshotel.com
Tours by arrangement

⊠ A one-barrel brew plant was installed in April 2007.

Gartly Nagger (ABV 4.2%)

Sentinel (ABV 4.4%)

Old Laxey

⌂ **Old Laxey Brewing Co Ltd, Shore Hotel Brew Pub, Old Laxey, Isle of Man, IM4 7DA**
Tel (01624) 863214
✉ shore@mcb.net
Tours by arrangement

Beer brewed on the Isle of Man is brewed to a strict Beer Purity Act. Additives are not permitted to extend shelf life, nor are chemicals allowed to assist with head retention. Most of Old Laxey's beer is sold through the Shore Hotel alongside the brewery.

Bosun Bitter (OG 1038, ABV 3.8%)
Crisp and fresh with a hoppy aftertaste.

Old Luxters SIBA

Old Luxters Farm Brewery, Hambleden, Henley-on-Thames, Oxfordshire, RG9 6JW
Tel (01491) 638330
✉ enquiries@chilternvalley.co.uk
⊕ chilternvalley.co.uk
Shop Mon-Fri 9am-6pm (5pm winter), Sat-Sun 11am-6pm (5pm winter)
Tours by arrangement

A traditional, full-mash, independent farm brewery established in 1990 and situated in a 17th-century barn alongside the Chiltern Valley vineyard. The craft brewery retails three cask ales through the brewery shop. The brewery is in Buckinghamshire despite the postal address. Old Windsor Gold (ABV 5%) and Old Windsor Dark Ale (ABV 5%) are brewed for the Royal Household farm shops (Balmoral, Sandringham, Windsor etc). They are believed to be the first micro-brewery to have been awarded a Royal warrant of appointment to the Queen. Fortnum & Mason Ale (ABV 5%) and several others are brewed under contract. Bottle-conditioned beers: Barn Ale (ABV 5.4%), Damson Ale (ABV 7%), Dark Roast Ale, Luxters Gold (ABV 5%), Winter Warmer (ABV 4.5%).

Barn Ale Bitter (OG 1038, ABV 4%)
A fruity, aromatic, fairly hoppy, bitter beer.

Barn Ale Special (OG 1042.5, ABV 4.5%) ◆
Predominantly malty, fruity and hoppy in taste and nose, and tawny/amber in colour. Fairly strong in flavour: the initial, sharp, malty and fruity taste leaves a dry, bittersweet, fruity aftertaste. It can be slightly sulphurous.

Dark Roast Ale (OG 1048, ABV 5%)
The use of chocolate and crystal malts give this ale a nutty, roasty bitter flavour.

Old Mill

Old Mill Brewery, Mill Street, Snaith, East Yorkshire, DN14 9HU
Tel (01405) 861813
✉ mail@oldmillbrewery.co.uk
⊕ oldmillbrewery.co.uk
Tours by arrangement to organisations and customers only

Old Mill is a craft brewery opened in 1983 in a 200-year-old former malt kiln and corn mill. The brew-length is 60 barrels. The brewery is building a tied estate, now standing at 19 houses. Beers can be found nationwide through wholesalers and around 80 free trade outlets are supplied direct. There is a rolling programme of seasonal beers (see website) and monthly specials.

Mild (OG 1034, ABV 3.4%) ◆
A satisfying roast malt flavour dominates this easy-drinking, quality dark mild.

Bitter (OG 1038.5, ABV 3.9%) ◆
A malty nose is carried through to the initial flavour. Bitterness runs throughout.

Old Curiosity (OG 1044.5, ABV 4.5%) ◆
Slightly sweet amber brew, malty to start with. Malt flavours all the way through.

Bullion (OG 1047.5, ABV 4.7%) ◆
The malty and hoppy aroma is followed by a neat mix of hop and fruit tastes within an enveloping maltiness. Dark brown/amber in colour.

Old Poets'

See Ashover

Old Spot

Old Spot Brewery Ltd, Manor Farm, Station Road, Cullingworth, Bradford, West Yorkshire, BD13 5HN
Tel (01525) 691144
✉ sales@oldspotbrewery.co.uk
⊕ oldspotbrewery.co.uk
Tours by arrangement

☺ Old Spot started brewing in 2005 and is named after a retired sheepdog on Manor Farm. The brewery targets the ever-changing guest ale market and creates new brews every 2-3 weeks, along with the stock beers. Around 25 outlets are supplied.

Ruby Lu (ABV 3.8%)

Dog's in't Barrel (ABV 4.5%)

Hunter Hill (ABV 5%)

Organic SIBA

Organic Brewhouse, Unit 1, Higher Bochym, Cury Cross Lanes, Helston, Cornwall, TR12 7AZ
Tel (01326) 241555
✉ orgbrewandy@tiscali.co.uk
⊕ theorganicbrewhouse.com
Tours by arrangement

⊗ Laid out as a mini 'tower' system, Organic's production has increased to six regular beers. It was established in 2000 and is dedicated to supplying exclusively organic beer, using its own source of natural mineral water. More than 20 local outlets are supplied regularly and the beers occasionally head north with wholesalers. Bottle-conditioned beers: Lizard Point, Serpentine, Black Rock, Wolf Rock. All beers are Soil Association certified and bottled beers are suitable for vegetarians.

Halzephron Gold (OG 1033, ABV 3.6%)

Lizard Point (OG 1036, ABV 4%)

Serpentine (OG 1042, ABV 4.5%)
A big malty nose, a bittersweet palate and a finish balanced by rich malt and tangy hops.

Black Rock (OG 1043, ABV 4.7%) ◈
Hop and apple aroma masked by complex roast overtones.

Wolf Rock (OG 1046, ABV 5%)

Charlie's Pride Lager (OG 1048, ABV 5.3%)

Orkney SIBA

Orkney Brewery, Sinclair Breweries Ltd, Quoyloo, Stromness, Orkney, KW16 3LT
Tel (01855) 831111
✉ info@orkneybrewery.co.uk
⊕ orkneybrewery.co.uk

⊛ Set up in 1988 in an old school building in the remote Orkney hamlet of Quayloo, the brewery was modernised in 1995. Capacity is now 120 barrels a week, all brewed along strict ecological lines from its own water supply. All waste water is treated through two lakes on the brewery's land, which in turn support fish and several dozen mallard ducks. There are plans for additional fermenting capacity and a visitor centre. Along with Atlas (qv), Orkney is part of Sinclair Breweries; the combined business distributes to some 350 outlets across Scotland and via wholesalers to the rest of Britain. Seasonal beer: White Christmas (ABV 5%, Dec).

Raven Ale (OG 1038, ABV 3.8%) ◈
A well-balanced, quaffable bitter. Malty fruitiness and bitter hops last through to the long, dry aftertaste.

Dragonhead Stout (OG 1040, ABV 4%) ◈
A strong, dark malt aroma flows into the taste in this superb Scottish stout. The roast malt continues to dominate the aftertaste, and blends with chocolate to develop a strong, dry finish.

Northern Light (OG 1040, ABV 4%) ◈
A straw-coloured beer, hoppy and refreshing. Fruity hop notes can develop a true lager nose. A late copper hop is intense without being cloying.

Red MacGregor (OG 1040, ABV 4%) ◈
Generally a well-balanced bitter, this tawny red ale has a powerful smack of fruit and a clean, fresh mouthfeel.

Dark Island (OG 1045, ABV 4.6%) ▦ ⬚ ◈
An excellent brew receiving many awards. The roast malt and chocolate character varies, making the beer hard to categorise as a stout or old ale. Generally a sweetish roast malt taste leads to a long-lasting roasted, slightly bitter, dry finish.

Skullsplitter (OG 1080, ABV 8.5%) ▦ ⬚ ◈
An intense velvet malt nose with hints of apple, prune and plum. The hoppy taste is balanced by satiny smooth malt with fruity spicy edges, leading to a long, dry finish with a hint of nut.

Ossett SIBA

Ossett Brewing Co Ltd, Kings Yard, Low Mill Road, Ossett, West Yorkshire, WF5 8ND
Tel (01924) 261333
✉ brewery@ossett-brewery.co.uk
⊕ ossett-brewery.co.uk
Shop Mon-Fri 9am-4.30pm
Tours by arrangement

⊛ Brewing began in 1998 and the company has gone from strength to strength. The brewery moved premises in 2005 — less than 50 metres — and now has a capacity of around 120 barrels a week. Ossett delivers between Newcastle and Peterborough and beer is also available through wholesalers. The brewery owns nine pubs. For a list of seasonal and special beers, see the website. Ossett Brewery purchased Riverhead Brewery Ltd in 2006.

Pale Gold (OG 1038, ABV 3.8%)
A light, refreshing pale ale with a light, hoppy aroma.

Black Bull Bitter (OG 1039, ABV 3.9%)
A dark, dry bitter.

Silver King (OG 1041, ABV 4.3%)
A lager-style beer with a crisp, dry flavour and citrus fruity aroma.

Fine Fettle (OG 1048, ABV 4.8%)
A strong yet refreshing pale ale with a crisp, clean flavour and citrus aroma.

Excelsior (OG 1051, ABV 5.2%)
A strong pale ale with a full, mellow flavour and a fresh, hoppy aroma with citrus/floral characteristics.

Otley

Otley Brewing Co Ltd, Units 42 & 43, Albion Industrial Estate, Cilfynydd, Pontypridd, Mid Glamorgan, CF37 4NX
Tel (01443) 480555
✉ info@otleybrewing.co.uk
⊕ otleybrewing.co.uk
Tours by arrangement

⊛ Otley Brewing was set up during the summer of 2005. The brew plant was originally from Moor Beer Co in Somerset. Seasonal beers: O-Garden (ABV 4.8%), O1 Dry Hop (ABV 4.2%), O-Ho-Ho (ABV 4.5%), Boss (ABV 4.4%), Amarill-O (ABV 4.3%), O-riginal (ABV 4.3%), O-lé (ABV 4%). Bottle-conditioned beers: O1, O8.

Dark O (OG 1036.8, ABV 3.8%)
A light, easy-drinking mild/stout with chocolate malt flavours and Fuggles hops.

O1 (OG 1038.8, ABV 4%) ▦ ◈
A pale golden beer with a hoppy aroma. The taste has hops, malt, fruit and a thirst-quenching bitterness. A satisfying finish completes this beer.

CO2 (OG 1040.7, ABV 4.2%)
Golden-brown in colour, fruity with heavy floral aromas from Cascade and Centennial hops.

OBB (OG 1043.6, ABV 4.5%)
A tawny-red coloured ale that is a gentle blend of pale, wheat and crystal malts bittered with Centennial hops and aromas from Mount Hood.

OG (OG 1052.3, ABV 5.4%)
A golden, honey-coloured ale, extremely smooth; steeped in Progress and Bramling Cross hops.

O8 (OG 1077.5, ABV 8%)
A pale and strong ale, deceptively smooth.

Otter SIBA

Otter Brewery Ltd, Mathayes, Luppitt, Honiton,

Devon, EX14 4SA
Tel (01404) 891285
✉ info@otterbrewery.com
⊕ otterbrewery.com
Tours by arrangement

⊗ Otter Brewery was set up in 1990 and has grown into one of the West Country's major producers of beers. The brewery is located in the Blackdown Hills, between Taunton and Honiton. An 80-barrel plant was commissioned in 2004 and has proved invaluable in supplying demand. The beers are made from the brewery's own springs and are delivered to more than 500 pubs across the south-west including the brewery's first pub, the Holt, in Honiton.

Bitter (OG 1036, ABV 3.6%) ◆
Well-balanced amber session bitter with a fruity nose and bitter taste and aftertaste.

Bright (OG 1039, ABV 4.3%) ◆
Pale yellow/golden ale with a strong fruit aroma, sweet fruity taste and a bittersweet finish.

Ale (OG 1043, ABV 4.5%) ◆
A full-bodied best bitter. A malty aroma predominates with a fruity taste and finish.

Head (OG 1054, ABV 5.8%)
Fruity aroma and taste with a pleasant bitter finish. Dark brown and full-bodied.

Oulton

Oulton Ales Ltd, Lake Lothing Brewery, Harbour Road, Oulton Broad, Lowestoft, Suffolk, NR32 3LZ
Tel (01502) 587905
⊕ oultonales.co.uk
Tours by arrangement

⊗ The brewery was expanded in 2005 to give a capacity of 30 barrels a week. 20 outlets are supplied as well as its own three pubs. Five of the brands are brewed throughout the year. Bottle-conditioned beers: Nautilus, Gone Fishing, Roaring Boy, Sunrise, Cormorant Porter.

Bitter (OG 1037, ABV 3.5%)

Mutford Mild (OG 1038, ABV 3.7%)

Beedazzled (OG 1040, ABV 4%)

Sunrise (OG 1040, ABV 4%)

Nautilus (OG 1042, ABV 4.2%)

Sunset (OG 1041, ABV 4.2%)

Wet and Windy (OG 1044, ABV 4.3%)

Windswept (OG 1044, ABV 4.5%) ◆
Fairly full-bodied with an intense elderflower aroma and flavour. Quite sweet but with a hint of bitterness, particularly in the finish.

Excelsior (OG 1045, ABV 4.6%)

Gone Fishing (OG 1049, ABV 5%) ◆
The initial taste is bitter but sweetness, tinged with roast and caramel, comes through. The aftertaste is sweet and lingers.

Cormorant Porter (OG 1050, ABV 5.2%) ◆
An initial rich, plummy fruitiness gives way to bittersweetness and a long, sweet aftertaste.

Keelhaul (OG 1060, ABV 6.5%)

Roaring Boy (OG 1075, ABV 8.5%) ◆
A solid, vinous brew with sultry fruit notes

lightening the heavy, brooding character. The finish is long and deep.

Outlaw

See Roosters

Owl

Owl Brewing Co Ltd, Unit 41, The Acorn Centre, Barry Street, Oldham, Lancashire, OL1 3NE
Tel 07889 631366
✉ gordon@owlbrew.co.uk/sid@sidsolutions. freeserve.co.uk
Shop: Ring for opening times
Tours by arrangement (max. 12)

☺ Brewing started at the Hope Inn, Oldham, in 2004. The brewery relocated to the Acorn Centre in 2006. The brewery concentrates on free trade supplies and has room for expansion. Beers are available in nine gallon firkins and 15-pint party pig carry-outs. Seasonal and special event ales are produced at least once every two months. Most beers are available bottle conditioned.

Snowbird (OG 1038, ABV 4.1%) ◆

OB Bitter (OG 1040, ABV 4.2%) ◆
An amber beer with some malt and fruit in the aroma. A tart fruitiness and some sweetness in the mouth, but the finish is dry and more bitter.

Russett (OG 1040, ABV 4.3%)

Dawnbreaker (OG 1041, ABV 4.4%)

Eventide (OG 1042, ABV 4.4%)

Raptor in Blue (OG 1050, ABV 5.4%)

Oxfordshire Ales

Bicester Beers & Minerals Ltd, 12 Pear Tree Farm Industrial Units, Bicester Road, Marsh Gibbon, Bicester, Oxfordshire, OX27 0GB
Tel (01869) 278765
✉ bicesterbeers@tiscali.co.uk
⊕ oxfordshireales.co.uk
Tours by arrangement

The company first brewed in 2005. The five-barrel plant was previously at Picks Brewery but has now been upgraded to a 10-barrel plant with the purchase of a larger copper. It supplies 50-60 outlets as well as several wholesalers. There are plans to produce seasonal beers and an organic beer.

Triple B (ABV 3.7%) ◆
This pale amber beer has a huge caramel aroma. The caramel diminishes in the initial taste, which changes to a fruit/bitter balance. This in turn leads to a long, refreshing, bitter aftertaste.

IPA (ABV 4.1%) ◆
An amber beer, the aroma is butterscotch/caramel, which carries on into the initial taste. The taste then becomes bitter with sweetish/malty overtones. There is a long, dry, bitter finish.

Marshmellow (ABV 4.7%) ◆
The slightly fruity aroma in this golden-amber beer leads to a hoppy but thin taste, with slight caramel notes. The aftertaste is short and bitter.

Oyster

Oyster Brewery, Ellenabeich Harbour, Isle of Seil, Oban, PA34 4RQ
Tel (01852) 300121
✉ gascoignea@tiscali.co.uk
⊕ oysterbrewery.com
Shop 9am-5pm daily
Tours by arrangement

⊛ The brewery was built in 2004 and came on stream in the spring of 2005. Head brewer Andy Gascoigne brought the state-of-the-art brewery north after first installing it in his pub in West Yorkshire. A bottling plant was installed in 2006.

Easd'ale (OG 1038, ABV 3.8%)
Golden smooth bitter with a dry aftertaste.

Thistle Tickler (OG 1040, ABV 4%)
Amber, fruity session bitter using Fuggles hops and Vienna malt.

Corryvreckan (OG 1044, ABV 4.4%)

Red Pearl (OG 1044, ABV 4.4%)
Traditional red-hued Scottish ale brewed with a blend of malts and roasted barley with First Gold hops. Toffeeish aftertaste.

Old Tosser (OG 1050, ABV 5%)
Strong dark ale brewed with roasted barley and American Cascade hops to give a rich, full-bodied character.

Grey Dogs (OG 1056, ABV 5.6%)

Palmer IFBB SIBA

JC & RH Palmer Ltd, The Old Brewery, West Bay Road, Bridport, Dorset, DT6 4JA
Tel (01308) 422396
✉ enquiries@palmersbrewery.com
⊕ palmersbrewery.com
Shop Mon-Sat 9am-6pm
Tours by arrangement (Please ring 01308 427500)

⊗ Palmers is Britain's only thatched brewery and dates from 1794. It is based in an idyllic location by the sea in west Dorset. The company is run by John and Cleeves Palmer, great-grandsons of Robert Henry and John Cleeves Palmer, who bought the brewery in 1896. Palmers enjoys sustained growth in real ale sales. Heavy investment is made in free trade ale dispense. 56 pubs are owned and a further 240 outlets are supplied.

Copper Ale (OG 1036, ABV 3.7%) ◈
Beautifully balanced, copper-coloured light bitter with a hoppy aroma.

Traditional Best Bitter IPA (OG 1040, ABV 4.2%) ◈
Hop aroma and bitterness stay in the background in this predominately malty best bitter, with some fruit on the aroma.

Dorset Gold (OG 1046, ABV 4.5%) ◈
More complex than many golden ales thanks to a pleasant banana and mango fruitiness on the aroma that carries on into the taste and aftertaste.

200 (OG 1052, ABV 5%) ◈
This is a big beer with a touch of caramel sweetness adding to a complex hoppy, fruit taste that lasts from the aroma well into the aftertaste.

Tally Ho! (OG 1057, ABV 5.5%) ◈
A complex dark old ale. Roast malts and treacle toffee on the palate lead in to a long, lingering finish with more than a hint of coffee.

Paradise

See North Wales

Parish

⌂ Parish Brewery Ltd, 6 Main Street, Burrough on the Hill, Leicestershire, LE14 2JQ
Tel (01664) 454801
Tours by arrangement

⊛ Parish began in 1983 in a 400-year-old building next to the Stag & Hounds pub. It moved to Somerby in 1990 before returning home four years ago. The 20-barrel brewery supplies local outlets, notably with bottle-conditioned Baz's Bonce Blower.

Mild (OG 1038, ABV 3.8%)

Special Bitter/PSB (OG 1040, ABV 4%)

Somerby Premium (OG 1041, ABV 4.2%)

Farm Gold (OG 1042, ABV 4.2%)

Burrough Bitter (OG 1048, ABV 4.8%)

Poachers Ale (OG 1060, ABV 6%)

Baz's Bonce Blower (OG 1120, ABV 12%)

Peak Ales SIBA

Peak Ales, Barn Brewery, Chatsworth, Bakewell, Derbyshire, DE45 1EX
Tel (01246) 583737
✉ info@peakales.co.uk
⊕ peakales.co.uk

Peak Ales opened in 2005 in converted, former derelict farm buildings on the Chatsworth estate, with the aid of a DEFRA Rural Enterprise Scheme grant, with support from trustees of Chatsworth Settlement. The brewery supplies local outlets and wholesalers for national distribution. Seasonal beer: Noggin Filler (ABV 5%, winter). Bottled beer: Gardener's Tap (ABV 5%, for Chatsworth Estate).

Swift Nick (OG 1037.5, ABV 3.8%) ▨ ◈
Traditional English session bitter with a slight fruit and hop aroma. Balanced flavours of malt and hops lead to a dry, bitter finish.

Dalesman (OG 1039, ABV 4%)

Bakewell Best Bitter (OG 1040.5, ABV 4.2%) ▨ ◈
Copper-coloured bitter with little aroma. Initial sweetness leads to a complex but balanced hop and malt flavour. Bitterness is present throughout, ending in a dry, fruity finish.

DPA (OG 1045, ABV 4.6%) ◈
Pale brown, easy-drinking best bitter with a slight malt and hop aroma. Initial sweetness gives way to a bitter finish.

Peakstones Rock

Peakstones Rock Brewery, Peakstones Farm, Cheadle Road, Alton, Staffordshire, ST10 4DH
Tel 07891 350908
✉ peakstones.rock@btinternet.com

⊕ peakstonesrockbreweryalton.co.uk

⊠ Peakstones Rock was established in 2005 on a purpose-built, five-barrel plant in an old farm building. A new fermentation vessel was installed in 2006 to keep up with demand for the beer. Around 40-50 outlets are supplied.

Nemesis (OG 1042, ABV 3.8%) ◕
Pale brown with a liquorice aroma; roast but not burnt. Pleasing lingering bitter finish.

Chained Oak (OG 1045, ABV 4.2%)

Alton Abbey (OG 1051, ABV 4.5%)

Black Hole (OG 1048, ABV 4.8%)

Oblivion (OG 1055, ABV 5.5%)

Penlon Cottage

Penlon Cottage Brewery, Pencae, Llanarth, Ceredigion, SA47 0QN
Tel (01545) 580022
✉ beer@penlon.biz
⊕ penlon.biz

Penlon opened in 2004 and is located on a working smallholding in the Ceredigion coastal region of West Wales. Hops and malting barley are part of a programme of self-sufficiency, with grain, yeast and beer fed to pigs, sheep and chickens on the holding. Only bottle-conditioned beers are brewed. Seasonal beers: Autumn Harvest (ABV 3.2%, Sep-Nov), Shepherds Delight Xmas Ale (ABV 5.6%). Bottle-conditioned beers: Lambs Gold Light Ale (ABV 3.2%), Tipsy Tup Pale Ale (ABV 3.8%), Heather Honey Ale (ABV 4.2%), Chocolate Stout (ABV 4.5%), Stock Ram Stout (ABV 4.6%), Twin Ram IPA (ABV 4.8%), Ewes Frolic Lager (ABV 5.2%), Premium Ale (ABV 5.2%), Ramnesia Strong Ale (ABV 5.6%). All beers are suitable for vegetarians and vegans.

Phoenix

Oak Brewing Co Ltd t/a Phoenix Brewery, Green Lane, Heywood, Greater Manchester, OL10 2EP
Tel (01706) 627009
✉ tony@phoenixbrewery.fsnet.co.uk

⊛ A company established as Oak Brewery in 1982 at Ellesmere Port, it moved in 1991 to the disused Phoenix Brewery and adopted the name. It now supplies 400-500 outlets with additional deliveries via wholesalers. Many seasonal beers are produced throughout the year. Restoration of the old brewery, built in 1897, is progressing well.

Bantam (OG 1035, ABV 3.5%) ◕
Light brown beer with a fruity aroma. Balance of malt, citrus fruit and hops in taste. Hoppy, bitter finish.

Navvy (OG 1039, ABV 3.8%) ◕
Amber beer with a citrus fruit and malt nose. Good balance of citrus fruit, malt and hops with bitterness coming through in the aftertaste.

Best Bitter (OG 1039, ABV 3.9%)

Monkeytown Mild (OG 1039, ABV 3.9%)

Arizona (OG 1040, ABV 4.1%) ◕
Yellow in colour with a fruity and hoppy aroma. A refreshing beer with citrus, hops and good bitterness, and a shortish dry aftertaste.

Pale Moonlight (OG 1042, ABV 4.2%)

Black Bee (OG 1045, ABV 4.5%)

White Monk (OG 1045, ABV 4.5%) ◕
Yellow beer with a citrus fruit aroma, plenty of fruit, hops and bitterness in the taste, and a hoppy, bitter finish.

Thirsty Moon (OG 1046, ABV 4.6%) ◕
Tawny beer with a fresh citrus aroma. Hoppy, fruity and malty with a dry, hoppy finish.

West Coast IPA (OG 1046, ABV 4.6%)

Double Gold (OG 1050, ABV 5%)

Wobbly Bob (OG 1060, ABV 6%) ◕
A red/brown beer with a malty, fruity aroma. Strongly malty and fruity in flavour and quite hoppy, with the sweetness yielding to a dryness in the aftertaste.

Pictish

Pictish Brewing Co Ltd, Unit 9 Canalside Industrial Estate, Rochdale, Greater Manchester, OL16 5LB
Tel (01706) 522227
✉ mail@pictish-brewing.co.uk
⊕ pictish-brewing.co.uk

⊛ The brewery was established in 2000 by Richard Sutton and supplies 60 free trade outlets in the north-west and west Yorkshire. Seasonal beers: see website.

Brewers Gold (OG 1038, ABV 3.8%) ▣ ◕
Yellow in colour, with a hoppy, fruity nose. Soft maltiness and a strong hop/citrus flavour lead to a dry, bitter finish.

Celtic Warrior (OG 1042, ABV 4.2%) ◕
Tawny beer with malt and hops dominant in aroma and taste. Good bitter finish.

Alchemists Ale (OG 1043, ABV 4.3%)

For Crown Inn, Bacup:

Crown IPA (OG 1050, ABV 5%)

Pilgrim SIBA

Pilgrim Brewery, 11 West Street, Reigate, Surrey, RH2 9BL
Tel (01737) 222651
✉ pilgrimbrewery@hotmail.com
⊕ pilgrim.co.uk

⊠ Pilgrim was set up in 1982 in Woldingham, Surrey and moved to Reigate in 1985. The original owner, Dave Roberts, is still in charge. Beers are sold mostly in the Surrey area: around 30 outlets. Seasonal beers: Autumnal (ABV 4.5%), Excalibur (ABV 4.5%, Easter), Crusader (ABV 4.9%, summer), Talisman (ABV 5%, winter), Pudding (ABV 5.3%, Xmas).

Surrey Bitter (OG 1037, ABV 3.7%) ◕
Pineapple, grapefruit and spicy aromas in this well-balanced beer. Initial biscuity maltiness with a hint of vanilla give way to a bitterness that becomes pronounced in a bittersweet finish.

Porter (OG 1040, ABV 4%) ◕
Black beer with a good balance of dark malts with hints of berry fruit. Roast character is

present throughout to give a bittersweet finish.

Progress (OG 1040, ABV 4%) ◈
A well-rounded, tawny-coloured bitter. Predominantly sweet and malty, with an underlying fruitiness and a hint of toffee. The flavour is well balanced with a subdued bitterness.

Pitfield

Pitfield Brewery, Unit 1 The Nurseries, London Road, Great Horkesley, Essex, CO6 4AJ
Tel 0845 833 1492
✉ sales@pitfieldbeershop.co.uk
⊕ pitfieldbeershop.co.uk
Tours by arrangement

⊠ After 24 years in London, Pitfield Brewery left the capital in 2006 and moved to new premises in Essex with its own vineyard. The beers are now sold at farmers' and organic markets in the south-east of England. Pitfield has started producing organic fruit wines. Cider and perry are also available. Seasonal beer: St George's Ale (ABV 4.3%). All beers are also available bottle conditioned except for SB Bitter and are organically produced to Soil Association standards and vegan friendly.

Dark Mild (OG 1036, ABV 3.4%)

Bitter (OG 1036, ABV 3.7%)

Lager (OG 1036, ABV 3.7%)

SB Bitter (OG 1036, ABV 3.7%)

Shoreditch Stout (OG 1038, ABV 4%) ◈
Chocolate and a raisin fruitiness on the nose lead to a fruity roast flavour and a sweetish finish with a little bitterness.

East Kent Goldings (OG 1040, ABV 4.2%) ◈
A dry, yellow beer with bitter notes throughout and a faint hint of honey on the palate.

Eco Warrior (OG 1043, ABV 4.5%) ◈
This pale golden beer has a hoppy, citrus aroma and flavour that is balanced by some sweetness and a developing bitterness.

Red Ale (OG 1046, ABV 4.8%)

1850 London Porter (OG 1048, ABV 5%)

N1 Wheat Beer (OG 1048, ABV 5%)

1837 India Pale Ale (OG 1065, ABV 7%)

1792 Imperial Stout (OG 1085, ABV 9.3%)

1896 Stock Ale (OG 1090, ABV 10%)

Plassey SIBA

Plassey Brewery, Eyton, Wrexham, LL13 0SP
Tel (01978) 781111/07050 327127
✉ plassey@globalnet.co.uk
⊕ plasseybrewery.co.uk
Shop open office hours
Tours by arrangement

The brewery was founded in 1985 on the 250-acre Plassey Estate, which also incorporates a touring caravan park, craft centres, a golf course, three licensed outlets for Plassey's ales, and a brewery shop. Some 30 free trade outlets are also supplied. Seasonal beers: Ruddy Rudolph (ABV 4.5%, Xmas), Lager (ABV 4%). Bottle-conditioned beer: Fusilier.

Welsh Border Exhibition Ale (OG 1036, ABV 3.5%)

Bitter (OG 1041, ABV 4%) ◈
Full-bodied and distinctive best bitter. Good balance of hops and fruit flavours with a lasting dry bitter aftertaste.

Offa's Dyke Ale (OG 1043, ABV 4.3%) ◈
Sweetish and fruity refreshing best bitter with caramel undertones. Some bitterness in the finish.

Owain Glyndwr's Ale (OG 1043, ABV 4.3%)

Fusilier (OG 1046, ABV 4.5%)

Cwrw Tudno (OG 1048, ABV 5%) ◈
A mellow, sweetish premium beer with classic Plassey flavours of fruit and hops.

Dragon's Breath (OG 1060, ABV 6%)
A fruity, strong bitter, smooth and quite sweet, though not cloying, with an intense, fruity aroma.

Poachers

Poachers Brewery, 439 Newark Road, North Hykeham, Lincolnshire, LN6 9SP
Tel (01522) 807404/07956 229638
⊕ poachersbrewery.co.uk
Tours by arrangement

Brewing started in 2001 on a five-barrel plant. In 2006 it was downsized to a 2.5-barrel plant and relocated by brewer George Batterbee at the rear of his house. Regular outlets are supplied throughout Lincolnshire and surrounding counties; outlets further afield are supplied via wholesalers. All the beers are also available bottle conditioned. Seasonal beer: Santas Come (ABV 6.5%, Xmas).

Trembling Rabbit (OG 1034, ABV 3.4%)
Rich, dark mild with a smooth malty flavour and a slightly bitter finish.

Shy Talk (OG 1037, ABV 3.7%)
Clean-tasting session beer, pale gold in colour; slightly bitter finish, dry hopped.

Poachers Pride (OG 1040, ABV 4%)
Amber bitter brewed using Cascade hops that produce a fine flavour and aroma that lingers.

Poachers Trail (OG 1042, ABV 4.2%) ◈
A flowery hop-nosed, mid-brown beer with a well-balanced but bitter taste that stays with the malt, becoming more apparent in the drying finish.

Billy Boy (OG 1044, ABV 4.4%)
A mid-brown beer hopped with Fuggles and Mount Hood.

Poachers Dick (OG 1045, ABV 4.5%)
Ruby-red bitter, smooth fruity flavour balanced by the bitterness of Goldings hops.

Black Crow Stout (OG 1045, ABV 4.5%)
Dry stout with burnt toffee and caramel flavour.

Jock's Trap (OG 1050, ABV 5%)
A strong, pale brown bitter; hoppy and well-balanced with a slightly dry fruit finish.

Trout Tickler (OG 1055, ABV 5.5%)
Ruby bitter with intense flavour and character, sweet undertones with a hint of chocolate.

Porter

Porter Brewing Co Ltd, Rossendale Brewery, Griffin Inn, 84 Hud Rake, Haslingden, Lancashire, BB4 5AF
Tel (01706) 214021
✉ dporter@porterbrewing.fsnet.co.uk
⊕ pbcbreweryinstallations.com
Tours by arrangement

⊗ Established in 1994, the company has two tied pubs and each sells a minimum of five cask beers. Seasonal beers: Timmy's Ginger Beer (ABV 4.2%, Mar-Aug), Stout (ABV 5.5%, Sep-Oct), Sleighed (ABV 6.5%, Dec-Jan), Celebration Ale (ABV 7.1%, Jul-Aug). All beers are suitable for vegetarians and vegans.

Floral Dance (OG 1035, ABV 3.6%)
Pale and fruity.

Bitter (OG 1037, ABV 3.8%) ◆
Unusually dark for a standard bitter, this beer has a dry and assertively bitter character that develops in the finish.

Railway Sleeper (OG 1040, ABV 4.2%)
Intensely bitter and hoppy.

Rossendale Ale (OG 1041, ABV 4.2%) ◆
A malty aroma leads to a complex, malt-dominated flavour supported by a dry, increasingly bitter finish.

Porter (OG 1050, ABV 5%)
A rich beer with a slightly sweet, malty start, counter-balanced with sharp bitterness and a noticeable roast barley dominance.

Sunshine (OG 1050, ABV 5.3%) ◆
A hoppy and bitter golden beer with a citrus character. The lingering finish is dry and spicy.

Port Mahon

See Little Ale Cart

Potbelly

**Potbelly Brewery Ltd,
25-31 Durban Road, Kettering,
Northamptonshire, NN16 0JA**
Tel (01536) 410818/07834 867825
✉ toni@potbelly-brewery.co.uk
⊕ potbelly-brewery.co.uk
Tours by arrangement

Potbelly started brewing in 2005 on a 10-barrel plant. Sawyers in Kettering acts as a brewery tap and some 200 other outlets across the country are supplied. Seasonal beers: Streaky (ABV 3.6%), Made in England (ABV 4.4%), Inner Daze (ABV 4.6%), Black Sun (ABV 5%), Jingle Bellies (ABV 5%).

Aisling (ABV 4%)

Beijing Black (ABV 4.4%)

Pigs Do Fly (ABV 4.4%)

Redwing (ABV 4.8%)

Crazy Daze (ABV 5.5%)

Potton SIBA

Potton Brewery Co Ltd, 10 Shannon Place, Potton, Bedfordshire, SG19 2SP
Tel (01767) 261042
✉ info@potton-brewery.co.uk
⊕ potton-brewery.co.uk
Shop 8.30am-5pm
Tours by arrangement

⊗ Set up by Clive Towner and Bob Hearson in 1998, it was Potton's first brewery since 1922. They expanded from 20 barrels a week to 50 in 2004. Some 150 outlets are supplied. Seasonal beers: Bunny Hops (ABV 4.1%, Mar-Apr), No-Ale (ABV 4.8%, Nov-Dec). Bottle-conditioned beers: Butlers Ale (ABV 4.3%), Shambles Bitter (for the National Trust, Wimpole Hall).

Shannon IPA (OG 1035, ABV 3.6%)
A well-balanced session bitter with good bitterness and fruity late-hop character.

Gold (OG 1040, ABV 4.1%)
Golden-coloured, refreshing beer with a spicy/citrus late-hop character.

Village Bike (OG 1042, ABV 4.3%) ▣ ▢
Classic English premium bitter, amber in colour, heavily late-hopped.

Shambles Bitter (OG 1043, ABV 4.3%)
A robust pale and heavily hopped beer with a subtle dry hop character imparted by Styrian Goldings.

Pride of Potton (OG 1057, ABV 6%) ◆
Impressive, robust amber ale with a malty aroma, malt and ripe fruit in the mouth, and a fading sweetness.

Princetown SIBA

Princetown Breweries Ltd, The Brewery, Station Road, Princetown, Dartmoor, Devon, PL20 6QX
Tel (01822) 890789
✉ ale@princetownbreweries.co.uk
⊕ princetownbreweries.co.uk

⊗ The highest brewery in England at 1,400 feet above sea level, it moved into a new purpose-built building in 2005 with equipment manufactured in Germany. The capacity is now 180 barrels a week with scope for further expansion. Established in 1994, local demand has allowed the brewery to expand production of its cask beers. Bottle-conditioned beer: Jail Ale.

Dartmoor IPA (OG 1039, ABV 4%) ◆
There is a flowery hop aroma and taste with a bitter aftertaste to this full-bodied, amber-coloured beer.

Jail Ale (OG 1047, ABV 4.8%) ◆
Hops and fruit predominate in the flavour of this mid-brown beer, which has a slightly sweet aftertaste.

Purity

Purity Brewing Co Ltd, The Brewery, Upper Spernall Farm, off Spernal Lane, Great Alne, Warwickshire, B49 6JF
Tel (01789) 488007
✉ sales@puritybrewing.com
⊕ puritybrewing.com
Shop Mon-Fri 8am-5pm
Tours by arrangement

⊕ Brewing began in 2005 in a purpose-designed plant housed in converted barns in the heart of Warwickshire. Capable of producing 60 barrels per week, the plant incorporates an environmentally-friendly effluent treatment system. The company supplies the free trade within a 50-mile radius and delivers to around 120 outlets.

Pure Gold (OG 1039.5, ABV 3.8%)

Pure Ubu (OG 1044.8, ABV 4.5%)

Purple Moose SIBA

Bragdy Mws Piws Cyf/Purple Moose Brewery Ltd, Madoc Street, Porthmadog, Gwynedd, LL49 9DB
Tel (01766) 515571
✉ beer@purplemoose.co.uk
⊕ purplemoose.co.uk
Shop Mon-Fri 9am-5pm
Tours by arrangement

A 10-barrel plant opened in 2005 by Lawrence Washington in a former saw mill and farmers' warehouse in the coastal town of Porthmadog. The names of the beers reflect local history and geography. The brewery now supplies around 100 outlets. Seasonal beers: X-Mws Llawen/Merry X-Moose (ABV 5%), Ochr Tywyll y Mws/Dark Side of the Moose (ABV 4.6%, Oct-Mar), Cwrw Dewi Da (ABV 4.5%), Cwrw'r Pasg/Easter Ale (ABV 3.9%). All beers are also available in bottle-conditioned form.

Cwrw Eryri/Snowdonia Ale (ABV 3.6%)

Cwrw Madog/Madog's Ale (OG 1037, ABV 3.7%) 🍺 ◆
Full-bodied session bitter. Malty nose and an initial nutty flavour but bitterness dominates. Well balanced and refreshing with a dry roastiness on the taste and a good dry finish.

Cwrw Glaslyn/Glaslyn Ale (OG 1041, ABV 4.2%) 🍺 ◆
Refreshing light and malty amber-coloured ale. Plenty of hop in the aroma and taste. Good smooth mouthfeel leading to a slightly chewy finish.

Quartz

Quartz Brewing Ltd, Archers, Alrewas Road, Kings Bromley, Staffordshire, DE13 7HW
Tel (01543) 473965
✉ info@quartzbrewing.co.uk
⊕ quartzbrewing.co.uk
Tours by arrangement

The brewery was set up on 2005 by Scott Barnett, a brewing engineer previously with Bass, and Julia Barnett, a master brewer from Carlsberg. The brewery produces three main brands plus seasonal specials throughout the year. Around 30 outlets are supplied. Bottles and mini-casks are planned for the future.

Blonde (OG 1038, ABV 3.8%) ◆
Light amber bitter, slightly sweet and fruity with a pleasant bitter finish and an astringent hint.

Crystal (OG 1040, ABV 4.2%) ◆
Copper with aromas of caramel and touches of hops and malt. Fruity tasting with a hedgerow bitterness and short hoppy finish.

Extra Blonde (OG 1042, ABV 4.4%)

Rainbow

♀ Rainbow Inn & Brewery, 73 Birmingham Road, Allesley Village, Coventry, West Midlands, CV5 9GT
Tel (02476) 402888
Tours by arrangement

⊕ Rainbow was launched in 1994. The current landlord, Jon Grote, took over in 2001. Output is through the pub although nine-gallon casks and polypins can be ordered for home use or beer festivals.

Piddlebrook (OG 1038, ABV 3.8%)

Ramsbury

Ramsbury Estates Ltd, Priory Farm, Axford, Marlborough, Wiltshire, SN8 2HA
Tel (01672) 520647/541407
✉ dgolding@ramsburyestates.com
⊕ ramsburybrewery.com
Tours by arrangement

Ramsbury started brewing in 2004. Ramsbury Estates is a farming company covering approximately 5,500 acres of the Marlborough Downs in Wiltshire. It grows malting barley for the brewing industry including Optic, which the brewery also uses. Additional fermenters have been purchased and contract bottling taken on. Some 90 outlets are supplied. Seasonal beer: Deerhunter (ABV 5%, winter).

Bitter (OG 1036, ABV 3.6%)
Amber-coloured beer with a smooth, delicate aroma and flavour.

Kennet Valley (OG 1040, ABV 4.1%)
A light amber, hoppy bitter with a long, dry finish.

Flintknapper (OG 1041, ABV 4.2%)
Rich amber in colour with a malty taste.

Gold (OG 1043, ABV 4.5%)
A rich golden-coloured beer with a light hoppy aroma and taste.

Ramsgate SIBA

Ramsgate Brewery Ltd, 1 Hornets Close, Pyson's Road Industrial Estate, Broadstairs, Kent, CT10 2YD
Tel (01843) 580037
✉ info@ramsgatebrewery.co.uk
⊕ ramsgatebrewery.co.uk
Shop Mon-Fri 9am-5pm
Tours by arrangement

⊠ Ramsgate was established in 2002 in a derelict sea-front restaurant and only uses locally grown hops. In 2006 the brewery moved to its current location, allowing for increased capacity and bottling. Within the brewery is possibly the smallest pub in the world, the Ram's Head, which can only accommodate three people standing. Bottle-conditioned beers: Gadds' No. 3 Kent Pale Ale, Gadds' Faithful Dogbolter Porter, Gadds' Well Hopped India Pale Ale (ABV 6.7%).

Gadds' No. 7 Bitter Ale (OG 1037, ABV 3.8%)
Satisfying session bitter using local Fuggles hops.

East Kent Pale Ale (OG 1041, ABV 4.1%)

Gadds' Seasider (OG 1042, ABV 4.3%)

Gadds' No. 5 Best Bitter Ale (OG 1043, ABV 4.4%)
Complex, easy-drinking best bitter using East Kent Goldings and Fuggles hops.

Gadds' No. 3 Kent Pale Ale (OG 1047, ABV 5%)
A light and refreshing, full-strength pale ale, brewed with locally-grown East Kent Goldings hops.

Gadds' Faithful Dogbolter Porter (OG 1054, ABV 5.6%)

Randalls SIBA

RW Randall Ltd, St Georges Esplanade, St Peter Port, Guernsey
Tel (01481) 720134

⊗ Randalls has been brewing since 1868 and was bought in 2006 by a group of private investors, headed by Ian Rogers, the founder of Wychwood Brewery. 18 pubs are owned, nine serving cask beer and a further 50 outlets are supplied. The brewery was due to move in September 2007 to larger premises with a new 20-barrel plant. Further beers are planned but no information was available at time of going to press.

Patois (OG 1045, ABV 4.5%)

For the Cock & Bull, Guernsey:

Sipping Bull (OG 1042, ABV 4.2%)

RCH SIBA

RCH Brewery, West Hewish, Weston-Super-Mare, Somerset, BS24 6RR
Tel (01934) 834447
✉ rchbrew@aol.com
⊕ rchbrewery.com
Shop Mon-Fri 8.30am-4pm

⊗ The brewery was originally installed in the early 1980s behind the Royal Clarence Hotel at Burnham-on-Sea. Since 1993 brewing has taken place in a former cider mill at West Hewish. A 30-barrel plant was installed in 2000. RCH supplies 75 outlets and the award-winning beers are available nationwide through its own wholesaling company, which also distributes beers from other small independent breweries. Seasonal beers: see website. Bottle-conditioned beers: Pitchfork, Old Slug Porter, Double Header, Firebox, Ale Mary (ABV 6%).

Hewish IPA (OG 1036, ABV 3.6%) ◆
Light, hoppy bitter with some malt and fruit, though slightly less fruit in the finish. Floral citrus hop aroma; pale/brown amber colour.

PG Steam (OG 1039, ABV 3.9%) ◆
Amber-coloured, medium-bodied with a floral hop aroma. Bitter citrus taste with a hint of sweetness.

Pitchfork (OG 1043, ABV 4.3%) ◆
Yellow, grapefruit-flavoured bitter bursting with citrus with underlying sweetness.

Old Slug Porter (OG 1046, ABV 4.5%) ◆
Chocolate, coffee, roast malt and hops with lots of body and dark fruits. A complex, rich beer, dark brown in colour.

East Street Cream (OG 1050, ABV 5%) ◆
Pale brown strong bitter. Flavours of roast malt and fruit with a bittersweet finish.

Double Header (OG 1053, ABV 5.3%) ◆
Light brown, full-bodied strong bitter. Beautifully balanced flavours of malt, hops and tropical fruits are followed by a long, bittersweet finish. Refreshing and easy drinking for its strength.

Firebox (OG 1060, ABV 6%) ◆
An aroma and taste of citrus hops and pale crystal malt are followed by a strong, complex, full-bodied, mid-brown beer with a well-balanced flavour of malt and hops.

Rebellion SIBA

Rebellion Beer Co, Marlow Brewery, Bencombe Farm, Marlow Bottom, Buckinghamshire, SL7 3LT
Tel (01628) 476594
✉ info@rebellionbeer.co.uk
⊕ rebellionbeer.co.uk
Shop Mon-Fri 8am-6pm; Sat 9am-6pm
Tours by arrangement (1st Tuesday of the month – £10)

⊗ Established in 1993, Rebellion has filled the void left when Wethereds ceased brewing in 1998 at Marlow. A steady growth in fortunes led to larger premises being sought and, following relocation in 1999, the brewery has gone from strength to strength and maximised output. Rebellion's nearby Three Horseshoes pub is the brewery tap. Rebellion Mild is exclusive to this pub. Around 200 other outlets are supplied. Seasonal beers: Overdraft Ale (ABV 4.3%, Jan-Feb), Blonde (ABV 4.3%, May-Sep), Roasted Nuts (ABV 4.6%, Nov-Jan), Zebedee (ABV 4.7%, Feb-May), Red (ABV 4.7%, Sep-Nov). Bottle-conditioned beer: White (ABV 4.5%).

Mild (OG 1035, ABV 3.5%)

IPA (OG 1039, ABV 3.7%) ◆
Copper-coloured bitter, sweet and malty, with resinous and red apple flavours. Caramel and fruit decline to leave a dry, bitter and malty finish.

Smuggler (OG 1042, ABV 4.1%) ◆
A red-brown beer, well-bodied and bitter with an uncompromisingly dry, bitter finish.

Mutiny (OG 1046, ABV 4.5%) ◆
Tawny in colour, this full-bodied best bitter is predominantly fruity and moderately bitter with crystal malt continuing to a dry finish.

Rectory SIBA

Rectory Ales Ltd, Streat Hill Farm, Streat Hill, Streat, Hassocks, East Sussex, BN6 8RP
Tel (01273) 890570
✉ rectoryales@hotmail.com
Tours by arrangement (Easter to Sep)

⊗ Rectory was founded in 1995 by the Rector of Plumpton, the Rev Godfrey Broster, to generate funds for the maintenance of his three parish churches. 107 parishioners are shareholders. The brewing capacity is now 20 barrels a week. All outlets are supplied from the brewery. Seasonal beer: Christmas Cheer (ABV 3.8%, Dec).

Rector's Bitter (OG 1040, ABV 4%)

Rector's Best Bitter (OG 1043, ABV 4.3%)

Rector's Strong Ale (OG 1050, ABV 5%)

787

Red Rock

**Red Rock Brewery Ltd,
Higher Humber Farm,
Bishopsteignton, Devon, TQ14 9TD**
Tel 07894 035094
✉ john@redrockbrewery.co.uk
⊕ redrockbrewery.co.uk
Shop Mon-Fri 9am-4pm (Phone for Sat-Sun hours)
Tours by arrangement

⊗ Red Rock first started brewing in 2006 with a
four-barrel plant. It is based in a converted barn
on a working farm using locally sourced malt,
English hops and the farm's own spring water.
All beers are also hand bottled and labelled.
Around 30 outlets are supplied.

Back Beach (OG 1038, ABV 3.8%)

Red Rock (OG 1041, ABV 4.2%)

Break Water (OG 1042, ABV 4.3%)

Dark Ness (OG 1045, ABV 4.6%)

Red Rose SIBA

**Red Rose Brewery,
Unit 4 Stanley Court,
Heys Lane Industrial Estate,
Great Harwood, Lancashire, BB6 7UR**
Tel (01254) 877373/883541
✉ beer@redrosebrewery.co.uk
⊕ redrosebrewery.co.uk
Tours by arrangement

⊛ Red Rose was launched in 2002 to supply
the Royal Hotel, Great Harwood. A 2.5-barrel
plant was installed but demand for the ales
outstripped capacity and the brewery
expanded. Further expansion in a new unit
in 2005 allowed production to grow further
and as a result the beers are available
nationwide. Seasonal beers: Blackpool Belle
Golden Age Ale (ABV 4%), Pissed Over
Pendle Halloween Ale (ABV 4.4%), 34th
Street Miracle Beer (ABV 4.9%), 65 Special
Celebration Ale (ABV 3.9%). Special beers
are available throughout the year.

Bowley Best (ABV 3.7%)
Darkish northern bitter. Malty yet sharp with
hoppy citrus finish.

Quaffing Ale (ABV 3.8%)

Treacle Miners Tipple (ABV 3.9%)

Felix (ABV 4.2%)
Dry, pale and remarkably hoppy with a keen
nose, yet rounded and smooth with a
lingering finish.

Old Ben (ABV 4.3%)
Pale, clean-tasting, crisp beer with a strong
hop presence and no sweetness.

**Lancashire & Yorkshire
Aleway/Steaming** (ABV 4.5%)
Copper-coloured, strong beer. Initially sweet
and malty, with a good hop aroma. Full and
fruity.

Older Empire (ABV 5.5%)

Care Taker of History (ABV 6%) ⬧
A dark, strong ale with a roast malt aroma.
The taste is complex, rich and warming. Well-
balanced and drinkable.

Red Shoot

⚑ Red Shoot Inn Brewery, Toms Lane, Linwood,
Ringwood, Hampshire, BH24 3QT
Tel (01425) 475792

The 2.5-barrel brewery, owned by Wadworth,
was commissioned in 1998. Tom's Tipple was
introduced in 1998 as a winter brew and is
now a permanent brand. Seasonal beers: Forest
Gold (ABV 3.8%, summer), Forest Grump (ABV
4.2%, winter).

Muddy Boot (ABV 4.2%)

Tom's Tipple (ABV 4.8%)

Red Squirrel

**Red Squirrel Brewery, 14b Mimram Road,
Hertford, SG14 1NN**
Tel (01992) 501100
✉ gary@redsquirrelbrewery.co.uk
⊕ redsquirrelbrewery.co.uk
Tours by arrangement

⊗ Red Squirrel started brewing in 2004 with a
10-barrel plant. Several seasonal beers are also
produced including Irish, Scottish and strong
American ales (produced to original recipes). 40
outlets are supplied.

Dark Ruby Mild (OG 1036, ABV 3.7%)

RSB (ABV 3.9%)

Conservation Bitter (OG 1040, ABV 4.1%)

Organic Blonde (ABV 4.1%)

Gold (OG 1041, ABV 4.2%)

London Porter (ABV 5%)

American IPA (ABV 5.4%)

Reepham

**Reepham Brewery, Unit 1, Collers Way,
Reepham, Norwich, NR10 4SW**
Tel (01603) 871091
Tours by arrangement

⊗ Reepham has completed more than 20 years
of continuous brewing in the same premises. A
beer in the style of Newcastle Brown Ale was
introduced (Tyne Brown), to show support for
the Tynesiders' brewery. S&P Best Bitter was
launched in 2005 to celebrate Norwich's
brewing heritage: the beer is named after
Steward & Patteson, bought and closed by
Watneys. Some 20 outlets are supplied. Bottle-
conditioned beer: Rapier Pale Ale.

Granary Bitter (OG 1038, ABV 3.5%) ⬧
A gold-coloured beer with a light hoppy
aroma followed by a malty sweetish flavour
with some smoke notes. A well-balanced
beer with a long, moderately hoppy
aftertaste.

S&P Best Bitter (OG 1038, ABV 3.7%)

Rapier Pale Ale (OG 1043, ABV 4.2%) ⬧
Complex, amber-coloured brew. Malt and
hops in the aroma metamorphose into a
distinctly hoppy first taste with smoky bitter
overtones. Long drawn-out bitter finale.

Velvet Sweet Stout (OG 1044, ABV 4.5%) ⬧
There is a heavy roast influence in aroma and

taste. A smoky malt feel produces a combination that is both creamy and well-defined. Fruit and hop indicate a subtle sweetness that soon fades to leave a growing dry bitterness.

Tyne Brown (OG 1046, ABV 4.6%) ◆
Marzipan and fruit cake overtones dominate this rich, malty brown ale. The aroma and taste are malty although a rising bitterness gives the finish a vinous quality.

St Agnes (OG 1047, ABV 4.8%) ◆
Smooth and creamy with bananas to the fore in aroma and taste. Smoky malt overtones subside as increasing bitterness dominates a gently receding finish.

Rhymney

Rhymney Brewery Ltd, Unit A2 Valley Enterprise Centre, Pant Industrial Estate, Dowlais, Merthyr Tydfil, CF48 2SR
Tel (01685) 722253
✉ marc@rhymneybreweryltd.com
⊕ rhymneybreweryltd.com
Shop Sat 10am-2pm
Tours by arrangement

Rhymney first brewed in 2005. The 75-hl plant, sourced from Canada, is capable of producing both cask and keg beers. Around 220 outlets are supplied.

Best (OG 1038, ABV 3.7%)

1905 Centenary Ale (OG 1040, ABV 3.9%)

Dark (OG 1044, ABV 4%)

Bevans Bitter (OG 1043, ABV 4.2%)

General Picton (OG 1044, ABV 4.3%)

Premier Lager (OG 1046, ABV 4.5%)

Bitter (OG 1044, ABV 4.5%)

Ridgeway SIBA

Ridgeway Brewing, Beer Counter Ltd, South Stoke, Oxfordshire, RG8 0JW
Tel (01491) 873474
✉ peter.scholey@beercounter.co.uk

Ridgeway was set up by ex-Brakspear head brewer Peter Scholey. It specialises in bottle-conditioned beers but equivalent cask beers are also available. At present Ridgeway beers are brewed by Peter using his own ingredients on a plant at Hepworth's of Horsham (qv) and occasionally elsewhere. All beers listed are available cask and bottle-conditioned. Six strong (ABV 6-9%) bottle-conditioned Christmas beers are produced annually, principally for export to the U.S.

Bitter (OG 1040, ABV 4%)

Organic Beer/ROB (OG 1043, ABV 4.3%)

Blue (OG 1049, ABV 5%)

Ivanhoe (OG 1050, ABV 5.2%)

IPA (OG 1055, ABV 5.5%)

For Coniston Brewing:

Coniston Bluebird (ABV 4.2%)

Coniston Old Man (ABV 4.8%)

Coniston XB (ABV 4.4%)

Ringwood IFBB SIBA

Ringwood Brewery Ltd, Christchurch Road, Ringwood, Hampshire, BH24 3AP
Tel (01425) 471177
✉ enq@ringwoodbrewery.co.uk
⊕ ringwoodbrewery.co.uk
Shop Mon-Fri 9.30am-5pm; Sat 9.30am-12pm
Tours by arrangement

⊗ Ringwood was bought in July 2007 for £19 million by Marston's which says it will maintain production in Hampshire. Some 750 outlets are supplied from the brewery and seven pubs are owned. A new 120-barrel fermenting vessel has recently been installed to allow for the increase in growth. Seasonal beers: Boondoggle (ABV 4%, summer), Bold Forester (ABV 4.2%, spring), Huffkin (ABV 4.4%, autumn), XXXX Porter (ABV 4.7%, winter). Bottle-conditioned beers: Bold Forester, Huffkin, Fortyniner, XXXX Porter.

Best Bitter (OG 1038, ABV 3.8%) ◆
Easy-drinking, predominantly malty session beer. A malty aroma leads to a malty taste with some toffee and hops to balance an underlying sweetness. A short malty and bitter finish.

Fortyniner (OG 1049, ABV 4.9%) ◆
A mid-brown beer. A fruity aroma with some malt leads to a sweet but well-balanced taste with malt, fruit and citrus hop flavours all present. The finish is bittersweet with some fruit.

Old Thumper (OG 1055, ABV 5.6%) ◆
A powerful mid-brown beer. A fruity aroma preludes a sweet, malty taste with soft fruit and caramel, which is not cloying and leads to a surprisingly bitter bittersweet aftertaste, with malt and hops.

Riverhead

⚲ **Riverhead Brewery Ltd, 2 Peel Street, Marsden, Huddersfield, West Yorkshire, HD7 6BR**
Tel (01484) 841270 (pub) /(01924) 261333 (brewery)
✉ brewery@ossett-brewery.co.uk
⊕ ossett-brewery.co.uk
Tours by arrangement (through Ossett Brewing Co)

☺ Riverhead is a brew-pub that opened in 1995 after conversion from an old grocery store. Ossett Brewing Co Ltd purchased the site in 2006 but run it as a separate brewery. Original recipes have been retained. Several beers are named after local reservoirs, with the height of the reservoir relating to the strength of the beer. Rotating beers: Deer Hill Porter (ABV 4%), Black Moss Stout (ABV 4.3%). Seasonal beers: Ruffled Feathers (ABV 4.5%, for Cuckoo Day), Eastergate Bitter (ABV 4.4%, Easter), Bandsman Bitter (ABV 3.8%, for Brass Band Competition), Jazz Bitter (ABV 4%, for Marsden Jazz Festival).

Sparth Mild (ABV 3.6%)

Butterley Bitter (OG 1038, ABV 3.8%) ◆
A dry, amber-coloured, hoppy session beer.

Wessenden Wheat (ABV 4%)

March Haigh (OG 1046, ABV 4.6%)
A smooth, rounded flavour is created by the complex selection of hops.

Redbrook Premium (ABV 5.5%)

Riverside

Riverside Brewery, Unit 1 Church Lane, Wainfleet, Lincolnshire, PE24 4BY
Tel (01754) 881288
⊕ wainfleet.info/shops/brewery-riverside.htm

Riverside started brewing in 2003, almost across the road from Bateman's, using a five-barrel plant. Owner John Dixon had not previously brewed but he was assisted by his father Ken, who had been head brewer at several breweries, including Bateman's. Eight barrels a week are produced for local trade, with some 15-20 outlets supplied. Seasonal beer: Dixon's Good Swill (ABV 5.8%, Nov-Dec).

Dixon's Major Bitter (OG 1038, ABV 3.9%)

Dixon's Light Brigade (OG 1038, ABV 3.9%)

Dixon's Desert Rat (OG 1048, ABV 4.8%)

John Roberts

See Three Tuns

Robinson's IFBB

Frederic Robinson Ltd, Unicorn Brewery, Stockport, Cheshire, SK1 1JJ
Tel (0161) 480 6571
✉ brewery@frederic-robinson.co.uk
⊕ frederic-robinson.com
Tours by arrangement

⊛ Robinson's has been brewing since 1865 and the business is still owned and run by the family. It has an estate of more than 500 pubs. Wards Bitter (ABV 4%) is brewed under contract. Seasonal beers: Dizzy Blonde (ABV 3.8%, Jun-Aug), Flash Harry (ABV 4.1%, Sep-Nov), Dark Horse (ABV 4.3%, Feb-Apr), Mr Scrooge's Humbug Bitter (ABV 4.4%, Dec).

Hatters (OG 1032, ABV 3.3%) ◆
A light mild with a malty, fruity aroma. Biscuity malt with some hop and fruit in the taste and finish. (A darkened version is available in a handful of outlets and badged Dark Mild.)

Old Stockport (OG 1034, ABV 3.5%) ◆
A beer with a refreshing taste of malt, hops and citrus fruit, a fruity aroma, and a short, dry finish.

Oldham Bitter (ABV 3.8%)

Hartleys XB (OG 1040, ABV 4%) ◆
An overly sweet and malty bitter with a bitter citrus peel fruitiness and a hint of liquorice in the finish.

Cumbria Way (OG 1040, ABV 4.1%)
A pronounced malt aroma with rich fruit notes. Rounded malt and hops in the mouth, long dry finish with citrus fruit notes. Brewed for the Hartley's estate in Cumbria.

Unicorn (OG 1041, ABV 4.2%) 🍺 ◆
Amber beer with a fruity aroma. Hoppy, bitter and fruity to taste, with a bitter finish.

Double Hop (OG 1050, ABV 5%) ◆
Pale brown beer with malt and fruit on the nose. Full hoppy taste with malt and fruit, leading to a hoppy, bitter finish.

Old Tom (OG 1079, ABV 8.5%) 🍺 🍾 ◆
A full-bodied, dark beer with malt, fruit and chocolate on the aroma. A complex range of flavours includes dark chocolate, full maltiness, port and fruits and lead to a long, bittersweet aftertaste.

Rockingham SIBA

Rockingham Ales, c/o 25 Wansford Road, Elton, Cambridgeshire, PE8 6RZ
Tel (01832) 280722
✉ brian@rockinghamales.co.uk
⊕ rockinghamales.co.uk

⊠ A part-time brewery established in 1997 that operates from a converted farm building near Blatherwycke, Northamptonshire (business address as above). The two-barrel plant produces a prolific range of beers and supplies half a dozen local outlets. The regular beers are brewed on a rota basis, with special beers brewed to order. Seasonal beers: Fineshade (ABV 3.8%, autumn), Sanity Clause (ABV 4.3%, Dec), Old Herbaceous (ABV 4.5%, winter).

Forest Gold (OG 1040, ABV 3.9%)
A hoppy blonde ale with citrus flavours. Well-balanced and clean finishing.

Hop Devil (OG 1040, ABV 3.9%)
Six hop varieties give this light amber ale a bitter start and spicy finish.

A1 Amber Ale (OG 1041, ABV 4%)
A hoppy session beer with fruit and blackcurrant undertones.

Saxon Cross (OG 1041, ABV 4.1%)
A golden-red ale with nut and coffee aromas. Citrus hop flavours predominate.

Fruits of the Forest (OG 1043, ABV 4.2%)
A multi-layered beer in which summer fruits and several spices compete with a big hop presence.

Dark Forest (OG 1050, ABV 5%)
A dark and complex beer, similar to a Belgian dubbel, with malty/smoky flavours that give way to a fruity bitter finish.

Rodham's

Rodham's Brewery, 74 Albion Street, Otley, West Yorkshire, LS21 1BZ
Tel (01943) 464530

Michael Rodham began brewing in 2005 on a one-barrel plant in the cellar of his house. Capacity has now increased to 1.5 barrels and plans are underway to start bottling. All beers produced are malt-only, using whole hops. Around 10 outlets are supplied.

Rubicon (OG 1039, ABV 4.1%)
Amber-coloured with a nutty, malt and light fruit taste. A dry, peppery and bitter aftertaste.

Wheat Beer (OG 1039, ABV 4.1%)
Naturally cloudy, sharp and refreshing.

Royale (OG 1042, ABV 4.4%)
A golden beer with a citrus, hoppy taste, underlying malt with a bitter finish.

Old Albion (OG 1048, ABV 5%)
Ruby black premium beer with a complex

mix of roasted malt, liquorice and tart fruit with a balancing bitterness.

Rooster's SIBA

Rooster's Brewing Co Ltd, Unit 3, Grimbald Park, Wetherby Road, Knaresborough, North Yorkshire, HG5 8LJ
Tel (01423) 865959
✉ sean@roosters.co.uk
⊕ roosters.co.uk
Tours by arrangement

☺ Rooster's Brewery was opened in 1993 by Sean and Alison Franklin. Its sister company, Outlaw Brewery Co, started in 1996. In 2001 the brewery relocated to larger premises at Knaresborough. Production is close to 80 barrels a week. Under the Rooster's label, Sean and Alison make six regular beers while Outlaw produces experimental beers. Around 500 outlets are supplied direct. Seasonal beers: Oyster Stout (ABV 4.7%, autumn), Nector (ABV 5.2%, autumn/winter).

Special (OG 1038, ABV 3.9%) ♦
Yellow in colour, a full-bodied, floral bitter with fruit and hop notes being carried over in to the long aftertaste. Hops and bitterness tend to increase in the finish.

Leghorn (OG 1042, ABV 4.3%)
A pale-coloured bitter with fruity aromas and a long finish.

YPA (OG 1042, ABV 4.3%)
A pale-coloured beer with pronounced raspberry and flower aromas.

Yankee (OG 1042, ABV 4.3%) ♦
A straw-coloured beer with a delicate, fruity aroma leading to a well-balanced taste of malt and hops with a slight evidence of sweetness, followed by a refreshing, fruity/bitter finish.

Hooligan (OG 1042, ABV 4.3%) ♦
Pale and aromatic bitter, with a citrus fruit aroma and hints of tangerine. The palate has pronounced fruit and hops with a hint of sweetness. Bitterness and hops linger in the aftertaste.

Cream (OG 1045, ABV 4.7%) ♦
A pale-coloured beer with a complex, floral bouquet leading to a well-balanced, refreshing taste. Fruit lasts throughout and into the aftertaste.

Rother Valley SIBA

Rother Valley Brewing Co, Gate Court Farm, Station Road, Northiam, East Sussex, TN31 6QT
Tel (01797) 253535
Tours by arrangement

Rother Valley was established in Northiam in 1993 with the brewhouse situated between hop fields and the oast house. Hops grown on the farm and from Sandhurst Hop Farm are used. Brewing is split between cask and an ever-increasing range of filtered bottled beers. Around 50 outlets are supplied. Seasonal beers: Summertime Blues (ABV 3.7%, summer), Copper Ale (ABV 4.1%), Holly Daze (ABV 4.2%, Christmas), Blues (ABV 5%, winter).

Smild (OG 1038, ABV 3.8%)

Level Best (OG 1040, ABV 4%) ♦

Full-bodied tawny session bitter with a malt and fruit aroma, malty taste and a dry, hoppy finish.

Hoppers Ale (OG 1044, ABV 4.4%)

Boadicea (OG 1046, ABV 4.6%)

Rudgate SIBA

Rudgate Brewery Ltd, 2 Centre Park, Marston Moor Business Park, Tockwith, York, YO26 7QF
Tel (01423) 358382
✉ sales@rudgate-beers.co.uk
⊕ rudgate-beers.co.uk

☺ Rudgate Brewery was founded in 1992 and is located in an old armoury building on a disused World War II airfield. It has a 15-barrel plant and four open fermenting vessels, producing more than 40 barrels a week. Around 300 outlets are supplied direct. Seasonal beers: Rudolphs Ruin (ABV 4.6%, Xmas), Crimble Ale (ABV 4.2%, Xmas). Other seasonal beers are produced on a monthly basis.

Viking (OG 1036, ABV 3.8%) ♦
An initially warming and malty, full-bodied beer, with hops and fruit lingering into the aftertaste.

Battleaxe (OG 1040, ABV 4.2%) ♦
A well-hopped bitter with slightly sweet initial taste and light bitterness. Complex fruit character gives a memorable aftertaste.

Ruby Mild (OG 1041, ABV 4.4%) 🍺
Nutty, rich ruby ale, stronger than usual for a mild.

Special (OG 1042, ABV 4.5%)

Well Blathered (OG 1046, ABV 5%)

Rugby

Rugby Brewing Co Ltd, Wood Farm Buildings, Coal Pit Lane, Willey, Monks Kirby, Rugby, Warwickshire, CV23 0SL
Tel 0845 0091626
⊕ rugbybrewingco.co.uk

Rugby started brewing in 2005 and is owned by the Pig Pub Company. All the beer names are connected to the town or Rugby Union football. The brewery has now relocated to new premises and is finalising specification of a custom-built 30-barrel plant.

1823 (ABV 3.5%)
A chocolate mild.

Twickers (ABV 3.7%)
A traditional Yorkshire bitter.

Webb Ellis (ABV 3.8%)
A straw-coloured, hoppy beer.

Victorious (ABV 4.2%)
A reddish-coloured bitter.

Sidestep (ABV 4.5%)
A full-flavoured, golden bitter.

No. 8 (ABV 5%)
A strong ale with a fruity note.

Winger IPA (ABV 5.2%)
A light IPA brewed with Fuggles hops.

Ryburn SIBA

◊ **Ryburn Brewery, Rams Head Inn, 26 Wakefield Road, Sowerby Bridge, West**

Yorkshire, HX6 2AZ
Tel (01422) 835413
✉ ryburnbrewery@talk21.com
Tours by arrangement

☺ The brewery was established in 1989 at Mill House, Sowerby Bridge, but has since been relocated to the company's sole tied house, the Rams Head. Some business is done with the local free trade but the main market for the brewery's products is via wholesalers, chiefly JD Wetherspoon.

Best Mild (OG 1033, ABV 3.3%)
A traditional northern-style mild with chocolate in evidence. Smooth, bitter aftertaste.

Best Bitter (OG 1038, ABV 3.8%) ◆
Amber-coloured, fresh, fruity session bitter. Lightly flavoured with a bitter aftertaste.

Numpty Bitter (OG 1044, ABV 4.2%) ◆
Pale brown beer with a sweeter, vinous flavour than Best Bitter.

Luddite (OG 1048, ABV 5%) ◆
Intensely flavoured black, creamy stout. Well balanced with strong chocolate, caramel and liquorice flavours tempered by sweetness.

Stabbers (OG 1052, ABV 5.2%) ◆
Pale brown, creamy, fruity, sweet and vinous bitter. Its drinkability belies its strength.

Saddleworth

⌂ Church Inn & Saddleworth Brewery, Church Lane, Uppermill, Oldham, Greater Manchester, OL3 6LW
Tel (01457) 820902/872415
Tours by arrangement

☺ Saddleworth started brewing in 1997 in a brewhouse that had been closed for around 120 years. Brewery and inn are set in a historic location at the top of a valley overlooking Saddleworth and next to St Chads Church, which dates from 1215. Seasonal beers: Ayrton's Ale (ABV 4.1%, Apr-May), Robyn's Bitter (ABV 4.6%, Nov-Dec), Christmas Carol (ABV 5%, Dec-Jan), Harvest Moon (ABV 4.1%, Aug-Sep), Bert Corner (ABV 4%, summer), Indya Pale Ale (ABV 4.1%, May-Jun).

Clog Dancer (ABV 3.6%)

Mild (ABV 3.8%)

More (ABV 3.8%)

St George's Bitter (ABV 4%)

Honey Smacker (ABV 4.1%)

Hop Smacker (ABV 4.1%)

Shaftbender (ABV 5.4%)

Saffron

Saffron Brewery, Unit 2, Pledgdon Hall Farm, Henham, Essex, CM22 6BJ
Tel (01279) 850923/07747 696901
✉ tb@saffronbrewery.co.uk
⊕ saffronbrewery.co.uk
Tours by arrangement

Founded in 2005, Saffron is situated near the historic East Anglian town of Saffron Walden, famous for its malting industry in the 18th century. The five-barrel plant, designed and

built on split-levels, started commercial production in 2006. Seasonal beers: Saffron Blonde (ABV 4.3%, Apr-Sep), EPA Extra (ABV 4.5%, Oct-May), Chestnut Grove (ABV 4.8%, Sep-Feb), Silent Night (ABV 5.2%, Oct-Feb), Henham Honey (ABV 4.6%, Mar-Oct), Endeavour (ABV 4.1%, Mar-Oct).

Muntjac (OG 1036, ABV 3.7%)
A copper-coloured session bitter with floral notes in the aroma. Pleasantly bitter in taste with plenty of hop character and slight sweetness.

EPA (OG 1038, ABV 3.9%)
A golden/straw-coloured ale with a subtle floral aroma with hints of blackcurrant spice.

Pledgdon Ale (OG 1042, ABV 4.3%)
An amber ale with a soft, mellow full flavour with hints of citrus and biscuit.

St Austell IFBB SIBA

St Austell Brewery Co Ltd, 63 Trevarthian Road, St Austell, Cornwall, PL25 4BY
Tel (01726) 74444
✉ info@staustellbrewery.co.uk
⊕ staustellbrewery.co.uk
Shop Mon-Fri 9am-5pm
Tours by arrangement

St Austell Brewery celebrated 150 years of brewing in 2001. Founded by Walter Hicks in 1851, the company is still family owned, with a powerful commitment to cask beer. Cask beer is available in all 160 licensed houses, as well as in the free trade throughout Cornwall, Devon and Somerset. A visitor centre offers guided tours and souvenirs from the brewery. Bottle-conditioned beers: Admiral's Ale (ABV 5%), Clouded Yellow (ABV 4.8%), Proper Job IPA (ABV 5.5%).

IPA (OG 1035, ABV 3.4%)
Copper/bronze in colour, the nose blossoms with fresh hops. The palate is clean and full-bodied with a hint of toffee caramel. The finish is short and crisp.

Tinners (OG 1038, ABV 3.7%) ◆
Golden beer with an appetising malt aroma and a good balance of malt and hops in the flavour. Lasting finish.

Dartmoor Best Bitter (OG 1039, ABV 3.9%)
A delicately hopped, golden bitter.

Black Prince (OG 1041, ABV 4%) ◆
Little aroma, but a strong, malty character. A caramel-sweetish flavour is followed by a good, lingering aftertaste that is sweet but with a fruity dryness.

Tribute (OG 1043, ABV 4.2%) ▣ ◆
Aroma of Oregon hops and malt with a trace of tangy ester. Refreshingly bittersweet with a balance of malt and hops. The finish is long, bitter and moderately dry with a hint of sweetness.

Proper Job IPA (ABV 4.5%)

Hicks Special Draught/HSD (OG 1052, ABV 5%) ◆
An aromatic, fruity, hoppy bitter that is initially sweet with an aftertaste of pronounced bitterness, but whose flavour is fully rounded.

St George's

St George's Brewery Ltd, Bush Lane, Callow End,
Worcester, WR2 4TF
Tel (01905) 831316
✉ andrewsankey@tiscali.co.uk
Tours by arrangement

⊠ The brewery was established in 1998 and
supplies local freehouses and wholesalers for
wider distribution. The five-barrel brewery
operates from the old village bakery. At least
two monthly specials are usually available.

Maiden's Saviour (OG 1037, ABV 3.7%)
Light and refreshing, brewed using traditional
English barley and hops.

Paragon Steam (OG 1040, ABV 4%)
Styled on California steam beer, this amber
thirst-quencher features a marked maize and
hop character.

St George Is Cross (OG 1042, ABV 4.2%)
A chocolate-brown bitter brewed using a
complex mixture of hops and a little honey,
resulting in a subtle, sweet flavour.

WPA/Worcestershire Premium Ale
(OG 1043, ABV 4.3%) ◆
Straw-coloured and medium-bodied with a
gentle fruity nose and a combination of
bitterness with malt on the palate and finish.

Charger (OG 1046, ABV 4.6%)
A light, golden bitter with a hoppy aroma
and a dry, bitter aftertaste.

St Judes*

St Judes Brewery, St Judes, 2 Cardigan Street,
Ipswich, Suffolk, IP1 3PF
Tel (01473) 413334
✉ gt6xxx@yahoo.co.uk
⊕ stjudesbrewery.co.uk
Shop Mon-Sat 10am-5pm; Sun 11am-5pm
Tours by arrangement

⊠ St Judes was established in late 2006 on a
seven-barrel plant in a converted coach house
hayloft. What began as a hobby has now taken
off and there are future plans for expansion.
Bottle-conditioned beer: Thaddeus Bitter.

Guest Fest (ABV 3.6%)

Ipswich Bright (ABV 3.8%)

Thaddeus Bitter (ABV 4.2%)

Coachmans Whip (ABV 4.9%)

St Peter's SIBA EAB

St Peter's Brewery Co Ltd, St Peter's Hall, St
Peter South Elmham, Suffolk, NR35 1NQ
Tel (01986) 782322
✉ beers@stpetersbrewery.co.uk
⊕ stpetersbrewery.co.uk
Shop Mon-Fri 9am-5pm; Sat-Sun 11am-5pm

⊠ St Peter's was launched in 1996 and
concentrates in the main on bottled beer (80%
of capacity) but has a rapidly increasing cask
market. Two pubs are owned and 75 outlets are
supplied. Seasonal beers: Ruby Red (ABV 4.3%),
Wheat Beer (ABV 4.7%), Summer Ale (ABV
6.5%), Winter Ale (ABV 6.5%), Cream Stout
(ABV 6.5%), Strong Ale (ABV 5.1%).

Mild (OG 1037, ABV 3.7%)
Sweetness balanced by bitter chocolate malt
to produce a rare but much sought after
traditional mild.

Best Bitter (OG 1038, ABV 3.7%) ◆
A complex but well-balanced hoppy brew. A
gentle hop nose introduces a singular
hoppiness with supporting malt notes and
underlying bitterness. Other flavours fade to
leave a long, dry, hoppy finish.

Organic Best (OG 1041, ABV 4.1%)
Hop and vanilla aroma. Hoppy and astringent
first taste remains constant. Initial fruit and
malt notes soon fade to leave a persistent
dry astringency.

Organic Ale (OG 1045, ABV 4.5%)
Soil Association standard, light malted barley
from Scotland, with organic Target hops
create a refreshing ale with a delicate
character.

Golden Ale (OG 1047, ABV 4.7%) ◆
Amber-coloured, full-bodied, robust ale. A
strong hop bouquet leads to a mix of malt
and hops combined with a dry, fruity
hoppiness. The malt quickly subsides, leaving
creamy bitterness.

Grapefruit Beer (OG 1047, ABV 4.7%) 🍺
Wheat Beer is the base for this refreshing,
zesty/pithy beer.

IPA (OG 1055, ABV 5.5%)
A full-bodied, highly hopped pale ale with a
zesty character.

Sadlers

See Windsor Castle

Salamander

Salamander Brewing Co Ltd,
22 Harry Street, Bradford,
West Yorkshire, BD4 9PH
Tel (01274) 652323
✉ salamanderbrewing@fsmail.net
⊕ salamanderbrewing.com
Tours by arrangement

⊠ Salamander first brewed in 2000 in a
former pork pie factory. Further expansion
during 2004 took the brewery to 40-barrel
capacity. There are direct deliveries to
more widespread areas such as Cumbria,
East Yorkshire and Lancashire in addition to
the established trade of about 100 outlets
throughout Lancashire, Manchester, North
Yorkshire and Derbyshire.

Mudpuppy (OG 1042, ABV 4.2%) ◆
A well-balanced, copper-coloured best bitter
with a fruity, hoppy nose and a bitter finish.

Golden Salamander (OG 1045, ABV 4.5%) ◆
Citrus hops characterise the aroma and taste
of this golden premium bitter, which has
malt undertones throughout. The aftertaste is
dry, hoppy and bitter.

Stout (OG 1045, ABV 4.5%) ◆
Rich roast malts dominate the smooth
coffee and chocolate flavour. Nicely
balanced. A dry, roast, bitter finish
develops over time.

Salopian SIBA

Salopian Brewing Co Ltd, 67 Mytton Oak Road, Shrewsbury, Shropshire, SY3 8UQ
Tel (01743) 248414
✉ enquiries@salopianbrewery.co.uk
⊕ salopianbrewery.co.uk
Tours by arrangement

⊚ The brewery was opened in 1995 in an old dairy on the outskirts of Shrewsbury. Owner Wilf Nelson has developed cask sales locally and nationally through wholesalers. Capacity has increased to 72 barrels. The brewery tap is the Bull in the Barne, Shrewsbury. Around 200 outlets are supplied.

Shropshire Gold (OG 1037, ABV 3.8%)

Abbey Gates (OG 1042, ABV 4.3%)

Hoptwister (OG 1044, ABV 4.5%)

Lemon Dream (OG 1043.5, ABV 4.5%) ●

Golden Thread (OG 1048, ABV 5%)

Saltaire

Saltaire Brewery Limited, Dockfield Road, Shipley, West Yorkshire, BD17 7AR
Tel (01274) 594959
✉ info@saltairebrewery.co.uk
⊕ saltairebrewery.co.uk
Tours by arrangement

⊚ Launched in 2006, Saltaire Brewery is a 20-barrel brewery based in a Victorian industrial building that formerly generated electricity for the local tram system. A mezzanine bar gives visitors views of the brewing plant and the chance to taste the beers. More than 300 pubs are supplied across West Yorkshire and the north of England.

Fuggles Bitter (OG 1036, ABV 3.8%)

Goldings Ale (OG 1040, ABV 4.2%)

XB (OG 1042, ABV 4.3%)

Cascade Pale Ale (OG 1047, ABV 4.8%)

Challenger Special (OG 1050, ABV 5.2%)

Sawbridgeworth

Sawbridgeworth Brewery, 81 London Road, Sawbridgeworth, Hertfordshire, CM21 9JJ
Tel (01279) 722313
✉ the.gate.pub@dial.pipex.com
⊕ the-gate-pub.co.uk
Tours by arrangement

The brewery was set up in 2000 by Tom and Gary Barnett at the back of the Gate pub. One pub is owned. Tom is a former professional footballer whose clubs included Crystal Palace. Special or one-off beers are occasionally brewed.

Selhurst Park Flyer (ABV 3.7%)

'erbert (ABV 3.8%)

Viking (ABV 3.8%)

Is It Yourself (ABV 4.2%)

Stout (ABV 4.3%)

Brooklands Express (ABV 4.6%)

Piledriver (ABV 5.3%)

Scattor Rock

Scattor Rock Brewery Ltd, Unit 5, Gidley's Meadow, Christow, Exeter, EX6 7QB
Tel (01647) 252120
⊕ scattorrockbrewery.com

The brewery was set up in 1998 on the edge of Dartmoor National Park and is named after a local landmark. The brewery has expanded its business and now supplies around 300 outlets on a regular basis. There is a monthly rotation of seasonal brews, with two or three available in addition to the regular beers at any one time.

Scatty Bitter (OG 1040, ABV 3.8%)

Teign Valley Tipple (OG 1042, ABV 4%)
A well-balanced, tawny-coloured beer with a hoppy aroma.

Tom Cobley (OG 1043, ABV 4.2%)
A refreshing, light brown session ale.

Devonian (OG 1045, ABV 4.5%)
A strong, fruity, light-coloured ale.

Golden Valley (OG 1046, ABV 4.6%)
A golden refreshing ale.

Valley Stomper (OG 1051, ABV 5%)
Light brown and deceptively drinkable.

Selby

Selby (Middlebrough) Brewery Ltd, 131 Millgate, Selby, North Yorkshire, YO8 3LL
Tel (01757) 702826

Not currently brewing but there are plans to restart.

Severn Vale

Severn Vale Brewing Co, Woodend Lane, Cam, Dursley, Gloucestershire, GL11 5HS
Tel (01453) 547550
✉ severnbrew@gmail.com
⊕ severnvalebrewing.co.uk
Shop Mon-Fri 10am-4pm; Sat 10am-12pm
Tours by arrangement

Severn Vale started brewing in 2005 in a redundant milking parlour using a new five-barrel plant. Some 50 outlets are supplied. Seasonal beer: Severn Sins (ABV 5.2%, Oct-Mar + beer festivals).

Vale Ale (OG 1039, ABV 3.8%)
Traditional bitter using four different hop varieties to flavour a quaffable session ale.

Dursley Steam Bitter (OG 1043, ABV 4.2%)
A refreshing, pale, hoppy beer.

Dance (OG 1046, ABV 4.5%)
Light and refreshing, straw-coloured best bitter.

Monumentale (OG 1047, ABV 4.6%)
Designed as a porter but not dissimilar to a strong mild. Dark and warming with plenty of hop aroma and flavour.

Shalford*

Shalford Brewery, 3 Broome Close Villas, Church End, Shalford, Essex, CM7 5EY
Tel (01371) 850925/07749 658512
✉ nigel@shalfordbrewery.co.uk
⊕ shalfordbrewery.co.uk

⊗ Shalford was set up in May 2007 on a five-barrel plant. The beer range was not finalised at time of going to press but will include traditional cask ales and bottle-conditioned beers.

Shardlow

Shardlow Brewing Co Ltd, The Old Brewery Stables, British Waterways Yard, Cavendish Bridge, Leicestershire, DE72 2HL
Tel (01332) 799188
Tours by arrangement

☺ On a site associated with brewing since 1819, Shardlow delivers to more than 100 outlets throughout the East Midlands. Due to increased sales, two new fermenters have been added. Reverend Eaton is named after a scion of the Eaton brewing family, Rector of Shardlow for 40 years. The brewery tap is the Blue Bell Inn at Melbourne, Derbyshire. Seasonal beers: Frostbite (ABV 5.5%), Stedmans Tipple (ABV 5.1%), Six Bells (ABV 6%). Bottle-conditioned beers: Special Bitter, Golden Hop, Narrow Boat, Reverend Eaton's Ale, Five Bells, Whistle Stop.

Chancellors Revenge (OG 1036, ABV 3.6%)
A light-coloured, refreshing, full-flavoured and well-hopped session bitter.

Cavendish Dark (OG 1037, ABV 3.7%)

Special Bitter (OG 1039, ABV 3.9%)
A well-balanced, amber-coloured, quaffable bitter.

Golden Hop (OG 1041, ABV 4.1%)

Kiln House (ABV 4.1%)

Narrow Boat (OG 1043, ABV 4.3%)
A pale amber bitter, with a short, crisp hoppy aftertaste.

Cavendish Bridge (ABV 4.5)

Cavendish Gold (ABV 4.5%)

Reverend Eaton (OG 1045, ABV 4.5%)
A smooth, medium-strong bitter, full of malt and hop flavours with a sweet aftertaste.

Mayfly (ABV 4.8%)

Five Bells (OG 1050, ABV 5%)

Whistlestop (OG 1050, ABV 5%)
Maris Otter pale malt and two hops produce this smooth and surprisingly strong pale beer.

Sharp's SIBA

Sharp's Brewery Ltd, Pityme Business Centre, Rock, Cornwall, PL27 6NU
Tel (01208) 862121
✉ enquiries@sharpsbrewery.co.uk
⊕ sharpsbrewery.co.uk
Shop 9am-5pm weekdays
Tours by arrangement

⊗ Sharp's Brewery was founded in 1994. Within 10 years the brewery had grown from producing 1,500 barrels annually to selling 25,000. Sharp's has no pubs and delivers beer to more than 1,000 outlets across the south of England. All beer is produced at the brewery in Rock and is delivered via temperature controlled depots in Cornwall, Bristol and Reading. Seasonal beer: Nadelik Lowen (ABV 4.8%). Bottle-conditioned beer: Chalky's Bite (ABV 6.8%).

Cornish Coaster (OG 1035.2, ABV 3.6%) ◈
A smooth, easy-drinking beer, golden in colour, with a fresh hop aroma and dry malt and hops in the mouth. The finish starts malty but becomes dry and hoppy.

Cornish Jack (OG 1037, ABV 3.8%)
Light candied fruit dominates the aroma, underpinned with fresh hop notes. The flavour is a delicate balance of light sweetness, fruity notes and fresh spicy hops. Subtle bitterness and dry fruit notes linger in the finish.

Doom Bar (OG 1038.5, ABV 4%) 🗇 ◈
Quaffing bitter with a faint flowery aroma and a moderately fruity, malty taste, although bitterness can mask other flavours. The finish is long but pleasantly bitter with some sweetness and dryness.

Eden Pure Ale (OG 1042, ABV 4.4%)
Hops dominate the aroma complemented by light fruit esters. In the mouth hops are again the centrepiece with a dry bitterness and a hint of malty sweetness. The finish is dry and hoppy.

Own (OG 1042.5, ABV 4.4%) ◈
A deep golden brown beer with a delicate hops and malt aroma, and dry malt and hops in the mouth. Like the other beers, its finish starts malty but turns dry and hoppy.

Atlantic IPA (OG 1045, ABV 4.8%)
Lightly sweet and fruity. The finish is sweet at first then becomes dry and lingering.

Special (OG 1048.5, ABV 5.2%) ◈
Deep golden brown with a fresh hop aroma. Dry malt and hops in the mouth; the finish is malty but becomes dry and hoppy.

Shaws

Shaws Brewery, The Old Stables, Park Road, Dukinfield, Greater Manchester, SK16 5LX
Tel (0161) 330 5471
✉ windfab@aol.com

☺ The brewery is housed in the stables of William Shaws Brewery, established in 1856 and closed by John Smiths in 1941. Brewing re-started in 2002 with a five-barrel plant. Beer is supplied to more than 30 local free trade outlets and beer festivals. Monthly guest beers are produced.

Best Bitter (OG 1038, ABV 4%)

Golden Globe (OG 1040, ABV 4.3%)

IPA (OG 1044, ABV 4.8%)

Sheffield* SIBA

Sheffield Brewery Co Ltd, Unit 111, J C Albyn Complex, Burton Road, Sheffield, S3 8BZ
Tel (0114) 272 7256
✉ sheffieldbrewery@btinternet.com
⊕ sheffieldbrewery.com

Sheffield began brewing in January 2007 in the former Blanco polish works. The brewery is part-owned by the landlord of the Gardeners Rest, Sheffield, where many of the beers are on sale. A seasonal range is planned.

Crucible Best (ABV 3.8%)
A complex bitter.

Five Rivers (ABV 3.8%)
A straw-coloured session ale with a hoppy aroma.

Blanco Blonde (ABV 4.2%)
A continental lager-style beer.

Seven Hills (ABV 4.2%)
A golden best bitter with an intense hoppy taste.

Spring Steel (ABV 4.6%)
A premium strength golden ale with a grapefruit aroma.

Top Forge (ABV 4.7%)
A powerful, malty, strong beer with an intense ruby colour.

Shepherd Neame IFBB

Shepherd Neame Ltd, 17 Court Street, Faversham, Kent, ME13 7AX
Tel (01795) 532206
✉ company@shepherdneame.co.uk
⊕ shepherdneame.co.uk
Shop Mon-Fri 11am-3pm
Tours by arrangement

Kent's major independent brewery is believed to be the oldest continuous brewer in the country (since 1698), but records show brewing began on the site as far back as the 12th century. The same water source is still used today and 1914 Russian teak mash tuns are still operational. A visitor centre and brewery shop are housed in a restored medieval hall. In 2004/5 investment increased production to more than 200,000 barrels a year. The company has 370 tied houses in the South-east, nearly all selling cask ale. More than 2,000 other outlets are also supplied. All Shepherd Neame ales use locally sourced ingredients. The cask beers are made with Kentish hops, local malted barley and water from the brewery's own artesian well. Seasonal beers: see website.

Master Brew Bitter (OG 1032, ABV 3.7%) ♦
A distinctive bitter, mid-brown in colour, with a hoppy aroma. Well-balanced, with a nicely aggressive bitter taste from its hops, it leaves a hoppy/bitter finish, tinged with sweetness.

Kent's Best Invicta Ale (OG 1036, ABV 4.1%)
An ambient bitter which merges the biscuity sweetness of English malt with the fruity, floral bitterness of locally grown hops.

Spitfire Premium Ale (OG 1039, ABV 4.5%)
A commemorative Battle of Britain brew for the RAF Benevolent Fund's appeal, now the brewery's flagship ale.

Bishops Finger (OG 1046, ABV 5%)
A cask-conditioned version of a famous bottled beer.

Sherborne

Sherborne Brewery Ltd, 257 Westbury, Sherborne, Dorset, DT9 3EH
Tel (01935) 812094
✉ stephen@walshg82.freeserve.co.uk
⊕ sherbornebrewery.co.uk

☺ Sherborne Brewery started in late 2005 on a 2.5-barrel plant. It moved in 2006 to new premises at the rear of the brewery's pub.

257 (OG 1039, ABV 3.9%)

Cheap Street (OG 1044, ABV 4.4%)

Sherwood Forest

See Alcazar

Shoes SIBA

⚲ **Shoes Brewery, Three Horseshoes Inn, Norton Canon, Hereford, HR4 7BH**
Tel (01544) 318375
Tours by arrangement

Landlord Frank Goodwin was a keen home brewer who decided in 1994 to brew on a commercial basis for his pub. The beers are brewed from malt extract and are normally only available at the Three Horseshoes. Each September Canon Bitter and Norton Ale are brewed with 'green' hops fresh from the harvest. Bottle-conditioned beers: Canon Bitter, Norton Ale, Farriers Ale.

Canon Bitter (OG 1038, ABV 3.6%)

Norton Ale (OG 1040, ABV 4.1%)

Peploe's Tipple (OG 1060, ABV 6%)

Farriers Ale (OG 1114, ABV 15%)

Shugborough

Shugborough Brewery, Shugborough Estate, Milford, Staffordshire, ST17 0XB
Tel (01782) 823447
Tours daily Mar-Oct

Brewing in the original brewhouse at Shugborough, home of the Earls of Lichfield, restarted in 1990 but a lack of expertise led to the brewery being a static museum piece until Titanic Brewery of Stoke-on-Trent (qv) began helping in 1996. Since then, the brewery has produced many one-off brews under Titanic's guidance. Ten outlets are supplied.

Miladys Fancy (OG 1048, ABV 4.6%)

Coachmans Tipple (OG 1049, ABV 4.7%)

Gardeners Retreat (OG 1049, ABV 4.7%)

Farmers Half (OG 1049, ABV 4.8%)

Butlers Revenge (OG 1053, ABV 4.9%)

Lordships Own (OG 1054, ABV 5%)

Sinclair

See Atlas and Orkney entries

Six Bells SIBA

⚲ **Six Bells Brewery, Church Street, Bishop's Castle, Shropshire, SY9 5AA**
Tel (01588) 638930
⊕ bishops-castle.co.uk/SixBells/brewery.htm
Tours by arrangement

⊠ Neville Richards – 'Big Nev' – started brewing in 1997 with a five-barrel plant and two fermenters. Alterations in 1999 included two more fermenters, a new grain store and mashing equipment. He supplies a number of customers both within the county and over the border in Wales. A new 12-barrel plant opened in April 2007. In addition to the core beer range, 12 monthly specials are produced.

Big Nev's (OG 1037, ABV 3.8%)
A pale, fairly hoppy bitter.

Goldings BB (OG 1041, ABV 4%)
Made entirely with Goldings hops; moderately hoppy with a distinctive aroma.

Cloud Nine (OG 1043, ABV 4.2%)
Pale amber-colour with a slight citrus finish.

Skinner's SIBA

Skinner's Brewing Co Ltd, Riverside, Newham Road, Truro, Cornwall, TR1 2DP
Tel (01872) 271885
✉ info@skinnersbrewery.com
⊕ skinnersbrewery.com
Shop Mon-Sat 10am-5pm
Tours by arrangement: (01872) 254689

⊠ Skinner's brewery was founded by Steve and Sarah Skinner in 1997. The brewery moved to bigger premises in 2003 and opened a brewery shop and visitor centre. Seasonal beers: Christmas Fairy (ABV 3.9%), Pennycomequick (ABV 4.5%), Davey Jones Knocker (ABV 5%), Skilliwidden (ABV 5.1%), Jingle Knocker (ABV 5.5%), Green Hop (ABV 4.2%), Hunny Bunny (ABV 4.5%), Ginger Tosser (ABV 3.8%).

Spriggan Ale (OG 1038, ABV 3.8%) ◈
A light golden, hoppy bitter. Well-balanced with a smooth bitter finish.

Betty Stogs (OG 1040, ABV 4%) ▣ ◈
Light hop perfume with underlying malt. Easy-drinking copper ale with balance of citrus hops, malt and bitterness, plus hint of sulphur. Bitter finish is slow to develop but long to fade.

Heligan Honey (OG 1040, ABV 4%)
A slightly sweet amber bitter, brewed with West Country malt and Heligan Garden honey.

Keel Over (OG 1041, ABV 4.2%)
A classic Cornish bitter, amber in colour, beautifully balanced with a smooth finish.

Cornish Knocker Ale (OG 1044, ABV 4.5%) ◈
Refreshing, golden beer full of life with hops all the way through. Flowery and fruity hops in the mouth and malt undertones, with a clean and lasting malty, bittersweet finish.

Figgy's Brew (OG 1044, ABV 4.5%) ◈
A classic, dark, premium-strength bitter. Full-flavoured with a smooth finish.

Cornish Blonde (OG 1048, ABV 5%)
A combination of wheat malt and English and American hops makes this light-coloured wheat beer deceptively easy to drink.

Slater's SIBA

Eccleshall Brewing Co Ltd, Slater's Brewery, St Albans Road, Stafford, Staffordshire, ST16 3DR
Tel (01785) 257976
✉ info@slatersales.co.uk
⊕ slatersales.co.uk
Tours by arrangement

⊛ The brewery was opened in 1995 and in 2006 moved to new, larger premises, resulting in a tripling of capacity. It has won numerous awards from CAMRA and supplies more than 850 outlets. One pub is owned, the George at Eccleshall, which serves as the brewery tap. Seasonal beers: Slater's Monkey Magic (ABV 3.4%, May); other seasonal beers are bi-annual.

Bitter (OG 1036, ABV 3.6%) ◈
Golden bitter with a hop and malt aroma. Bitterness develops to a long, pleasant astringency.

Original (OG 1040, ABV 4%) ◈
Malty aroma with sharper than normal bitterness. Bitterness gives way to a hoppy finish.

Top Totty (OG 1040, ABV 4%) ◈
Golden colour with a fruity aroma. Thin, hoppy start then hops develop to a fruit and hop finish and latent astringency.

Premium (OG 1044, ABV 4.4%) ◈
Pale brown with a caramel, malt and hop aroma. Complex hop and fruit with hints of roast develop into a bitter finish with a malty background.

Shining Knight (OG 1045, ABV 4.5%) ◈
No dominant flavours but hops and fruit combine in the bitter finish. A good session beer for its strength.

Supreme (OG 1047, ABV 4.7%) ◈
Amber with a fruitcake aroma. Fruity start and finish with developing bitterness.

Slaughterhouse SIBA

Slaughterhouse Brewery Ltd, Bridge Street, Warwick, CV34 5PD
Tel (01926) 490986
✉ enquiries@slaughterhousebrewery.com
⊕ slaughterhousebrewery.com
Tours by arrangement

Production began in 2003 on a four-barrel plant in a former slaughterhouse. Due to its success, beer production now consists mainly of Saddleback, supplemented by monthly special and seasonal beers. Around 30 outlets are supplied. The brewery premises are licensed for off-sales direct to the pubic and bottle-conditioned beers are also available. Seasonal beers: see website.

Saddleback Best Bitter (OG 1038, ABV 3.8%)
Amber-coloured session bitter with a distinctive Challenger hop flavour.

For the Waterman, Hatton:

Arkwright's Special Bitter (ABV 3.8%)

Smiles

See Highgate

Samuel Smith

Samuel Smith Old Brewery (Tadcaster), High Street, Tadcaster, North Yorkshire, LS24 9SB
Tel (01937) 832225

⊛ Although related to the nearby John Smith's, this fiercely independent, family-owned company is radically different. Tradition, quality and value are important, resulting in traditional brewing without any artificial additives, with real ale supplied in wooden casks, though nitrokeg has replaced cask beer in some pubs, especially in London. A range of bottled beers is produced, though they are not bottle conditioned. A filtered draught wheat beer is a recent addition. Some 200 pubs are owned.

Old Brewery Bitter/OBB (OG 1040, ABV 4%) ◆
Malt dominates the aroma, with an initial burst of malt, hops and fruit in the taste, which is sustained in the aftertaste.

Snowdonia SIBA

◘ Snowdonia Brewery, Snowdonia Parc
Brewpub & Campsite, Waunfawr, Caernarfon,
Gwynedd, LL55 4AQ
Tel (01286) 650409
✉ info@snowdonia-park.co.uk
⊕ snowdonia-park.co.uk

Snowdonia started brewing in 1998 in a two-barrel brewhouse. The brewing is now carried out by the new co-owner, Carmen Pierce. The beer is brewed solely for the Snowdonia Park pub and campsite.

Station Bitter (OG 1040, ABV 4%)

Snowdonia Gold (OG 1050, ABV 5%)

Welsh Highland Bitter (OG 1048, ABV 5%)

Somerset (Electric)

See Taunton

South Hams SIBA

South Hams Brewery Ltd, Stokeley Barton,
Stokenham, Kingsbridge, Devon, TQ7 2SE
Tel (01548) 581151
✉ info@southhamsbrewery.co.uk
⊕ southhamsbrewery.co.uk
Tours by arrangement

The brewery moved to its present site in 2003, with a 10-barrel plant and plenty of room to expand. It supplies more than 60 outlets in Plymouth and south Devon. Wholesalers are used to distribute to other areas. Two pubs are owned. Seasonal beers: Wild Blonde (ABV 4.4%), Hopnosis (ABV 4.5%), Porter (ABV 5%), Knickadroppa Glory (ABV 5.2%). Bottle-conditioned beers: Porter, Knickadroppa Glory, Eddystone, Devon Pride.

Devon Pride (OG 1039, ABV 3.8%)

XSB (OG 1043, ABV 4.2%) ◆
Amber nectar with a fruity nose and a bitter finish.

Sutton Comfort (OG 1045, ABV 4.5%) ◆
Hoppy-tasting, mid-brown beer with a bitter hop finish underscored by malt and fruit.

Eddystone (OG 1050, ABV 4.8%)

Southport

Southport Brewery, Unit 3,
Enterprise Business Park, Russell Road,
Southport, Merseyside, PR9 7RF
Tel (07748) 387652
✉ southportbrewery@fsmail.net

☺ The Southport brewery opened in 2004 as a 2.5-barrel plant and supplies around 30 pubs in the North-west. It also supplies the free trade via Boggart Brewery (qv). Seasonal beers: Old Shrimper (ABV 5.5%, Nov-Feb), Tower Mild (ABV 3.7%, May-Sep), National Hero (ABV 4%, Mar-Apr).

Sandgrounder Bitter (OG 1039.5, ABV 3.8%)
Pale, hoppy session bitter with a floral character.

Carousel (OG 1041.5, ABV 4%)
A refreshing, floral, hoppy best bitter.

Golden Sands (OG 1041.5, ABV 4%)
A golden-coloured, triple hopped bitter with citrus flavour.

Natterjack (OG 1043.5, ABV 4.3%)
A premium bitter with fruit notes and a hint of coffee.

For Southport Football Club:

Grandstand Gold (OG 1039.5, ABV 3.8%)
A gold-coloured bitter, available for all Saturday home matches.

Spectrum SIBA EAB

Spectrum Brewery, Unit 11 Wellington Road,
Tharston, Norwich, NR15 2PE
Tel 07949 254383
✉ info@spectrumbrewery.co.uk
⊕ spectrumbrewery.co.uk
Tours by arrangement

⊗ Proprietor and founder Andy Mitchell established Spectrum in 2002. The brewery moved premises in 2007 as well as increasing brew length and gaining organic certification for all beers. Seasonal beers: Spring Promise (ABV 4.5%, Jan-Feb), Autumn Beer (ABV 4.5%, Sep-Oct – names and formulations vary), Yule Fuel (ABV 7%). Most beers are also available bottled.

Light Fantastic (OG 1035.5, ABV 3.7%) ◆
A sulphurous nose introduces this refreshing bitter. The initial hoppy bitterness continues to a dry grapefruit finish that slowly becomes more astringent. Yellow hued with a grainy feel.

Dark Fantastic (OG 1041, ABV 3.8%)
A very dark red, malty mild.

Bezants (OG 1038, ABV 4%) ◆
A well-hopped, clean-tasting bitter. Some maltiness can be detected in both the aroma and taste, but hops dominate. A residual bitterness adds to a long aftertaste that ends in a lingering dryness.

42 (OG 1039.5, ABV 4.2%) ◆
Blackcurrant fruitiness vies for dominance with a strong malty base. Undercurrents of hops, caramel and bitterness give a woody feel to this pale brown brew.

Black Buffle (OG 1047, ABV 4.5%) ◆
Dark chocolate and liquorice hold sway in this deep red porter. The nose and taste are balanced by a noticeable hop presence although the finish attains a roasted coffee dryness.

XXXX (OG 1045.5, ABV 4.6%)
A deep copper strong bitter, first brewed for the proprietor's 40th birthday.

Wizzard (OG 1047.5, ABV 4.9%) ◆
Pale brown, smooth, easy-drinking ale. Initial golden syrup taste is reflected in the aroma. Underlying bitterness comes to the fore as the inherent maltiness subsides in a quick finish.

Old Stoatwobbler (OG 1064.5, ABV 6%) ◆
Complex brew with dark chocolate, morello cherry, raisin and banana vying for dominance alongside hops and malt. A black-coloured brew with a solid fruity nose, and a well-balanced finish.

Trip Hazard (OG 1061.5, ABV 6.5%) ◆
Exceptionally malty but easy-drinking for its strength. Rich fruity flavours dominate throughout, date and sultana to the fore. A growing bitterness in the finish.

Solstice Blinder (OG 1079, ABV 8.5%)
Strong IPA. Brewed twice a year, dry-hopped and left to mature (unfined) for at least three months before release in time for the solstices.

Spinning Dog SIBA

Spinning Dog Brewery, 88 St Owen Street, Hereford, HR1 2QD
Tel (01432) 342125
✉ jfkenyon@aol.com
⊕ spinningdogbrewery.co.uk
Tours by arrangement

The brewery was built in a room of the Victory in 2000 by Jim Kenyon, following the purchase of the pub. Initially only serving the pub, it has steadily grown from a four-barrel to a 10-barrel plant. In 2005 the brewery commissioned its own bottling plant, capable of producing 80 cases a day. It now supplies some 300 other outlets as well as selling bottle-conditioned beers via the internet. Seasonal beers: Mutleys Mongrel (ABV 3.9%), Harvest Moon (ABV 4.5%), Santa Paws (ABV 5.2%), Mutleys Sprinter (ABV 4.4%), Xmas Cheer (ABV 4.3%). Bottle-conditioned beers: Hereford Organic Bitter, Organic Oatmeal Stout, Mutleys Revenge.

Chase Your Tail (OG 1036, ABV 3.6%)
A good session beer with an abundance of hops and bitterness. Dry, with citrus aftertaste.

Hereford Organic Bitter (ABV 3.7%)
Light in colour with a distinctive fruitiness from start to finish.

Herefordshire Owd Bull (ABV 3.9%)

Hereford Cathedral Bitter (OG 1040, ABV 4%)
A crisp amber beer made with local hops, producing a well-rounded malt/hop bitterness throughout and a pleasing, lingering aftertaste.

Mutleys Dark (OG 1040, ABV 4%)
A dark, malty mild with a hint of bitterness and a touch of roast caramel. A smooth drinkable ale.

Herefordshire Light Ale (ABV 4%)
Brewed along the lines of the award-winning Mutleys Pitstop. Light and refreshing.

Top Dog (OG 1042, ABV 4.2%)
A hoppy beer with both malt and fruit flavours.

Organic Oatmeal Stout (OG 1044, ABV 4.4%)
The subtle blend of organic oats and barley along with New Zealand hops produce a complex mixture of flavours.

Celtic Gold (OG 1045, ABV 4.5%)

Mutleys Revenge (OG 1048, ABV 4.8%)
A strong, smooth, hoppy beer, amber in colour. Full-bodied with a dry, citrus aftertaste.

Mutts Nuts (OG 1050, ABV 5%)
A dark, strong ale, full bodied with a hint of a chocolate aftertaste.

Spire

Spire Brewery, Units 2-3, Gisborne Close, Ireland Business Park, Staveley, Chesterfield, Derbyshire, S43 3JT
Tel (01246) 476005
✉ info@spirebrewery.co.uk
⊕ spirebrewery.co.uk
Tours by arrangement

☺ The brewery was established in 2006 with a 10-barrel plant and adhere to the principles of the German Reinheitsgebot or Purity Law, using only malt, hops and yeast plus water, with no adjuncts added to the beers. Around 45 outlets are supplied. Seasonal beers: Spire Lite (ABV 2.9%, summer), 80/- Ale (ABV 4.3%, autumn), Winter Wonderland (ABV 6.1%, winter), Nocturne Porter (ABV 5.7%, Jan-Feb).

Encore (OG 1038, ABV 3.9%) ◆
Traditional amber session beer with a little malt and hop aroma. Balanced malt and roast flavours lead to a developing bitterness, ending with a long, malty finish.

Chesterfield Best Bitter (OG 1042, ABV 4.3%) ◆
Brown bitter with malt and fruit flavours and a hint of caramel and chocolate in the finish. There is a little bitterness in the aftertaste.

Land of Hop & Glory (OG 1044, ABV 4.5%) ◆
Clean, crisp golden ale. Grapefruit and lemon flavours develop and these complex citrus notes lead to a bitter, dry aftertaste.

Sgt Pepper Stout (OG 1053, ABV 5.5%) ◆
Full-flavoured stout brewed with ground black pepper. Liquorice and pepper flavours dominate this complex dark beer.

Britannia Cream Ale (OG 1061, ABV 6.4%) ◆
Strong golden ale with malt and caramel aroma and a pleasant smooth mouthfeel. Complex malt, fruit and hop flavours lead to a bittersweet aftertaste.

Spitting Feathers

Spitting Feathers Brewery, Common Farm, Waverton, Chester, CH3 7QT
Tel (01244) 332052
✉ info@spittingfeathers.org
⊕ spittingfeathers.org
Tours by arrangement

Spitting Feathers was established in 2005 at Common Farm on the outskirts of Chester. The brewery and visitors bar are in traditional sandstone buildings around a cobbled yard. Beehives provide honey for the brewery and spent grains are fed to livestock. Around 200 outlets are supplied. Seasonal beers: see website. Most beers are also available bottle conditioned and all bottled beers are suitable for vegetarians and vegans.

Farmhouse Ale (OG 1035, ABV 3.6%)

Thirstquencher (OG 1038, ABV 3.9%) 🍺 ◆
Powerful hop aroma leads into the taste.

Bitterness and a fruity citrus hop flavour fight for attention. A sharp, clean golden beer with a long, dry, bitter aftertaste.

Special Ale (OG 1041, ABV 4.2%) ◈
Complex tawny-coloured beer with a sharp, grainy mouthfeel. Malty with good hop coming through in the aroma and taste. Hints of nuttiness and a touch of acidity. Dry, astringent finish.

Old Wavertonian (OG 1043, ABV 4.4%) ◈
Creamy and smooth stout. Full-flavoured with coffee notes in aroma and taste. Roast and nut flavours throughout, leading to a hoppy, bitter finish.

Basket Case (OG 1046, ABV 4.8%) ◈
Reddish, complex beer. Sweetness and fruit dominate taste, offset by hops and bitterness that follow through into the aftertaste.

Springhead SIBA

Springhead Fine Ales Ltd, Old Great North Road, Sutton on Trent, Nottinghamshire, NG23 6QS
Tel (01636) 821000
✉ steve@springhead.co.uk
⊕ springhead.co.uk
Tours by arrangement

◎ Springhead Brewery opened in 1990 and moved to bigger premises three years later and, to meet increased demand, expanded to a 50-barrel plant in 2004. Some 500 outlets are supplied. Many of the beer names have a Civil War theme.

Surrender 1646 (OG 1038, ABV 3.6%)
A burnished, copper-coloured bitter with a good combination of malt and hops. Long dry finish.

Bitter (OG 1041, ABV 4%)
A clean-tasting, easy-drinking, hoppy beer.

Puritans Porter (OG 1041, ABV 4%) ▣
A porter, dark but not heavy. Smooth with a lingering finish of roasted barley.

Roundhead's Gold (OG 1042, ABV 4.2%)
Golden beer made with wild flower honey. Refreshing but not too sweet with the aroma of Saaz hops.

Rupert's Ruin (OG 1042, ABV 4.2%)
A coppery, complex beer with a fruity aroma and a long, malty aftertaste.

Goodrich Castle (OG 1044, ABV 4.4%)
Brewed following a 17th-century recipe using rosemary: a pale ale, light on the palate with a bitter finish and a delicate flavour.

Oliver's Army (OG 1044, ABV 4.4%)

Charlie's Angel (OG 1045, ABV 4.5%)

Sweet Lips (OG 1046, ABV 4.6%)
A light, smooth and refreshing beer with some grapefruit notes from American Cascade hops.

Leveller (OG 1047, ABV 4.8%)

Newark Castle Brown (OG 1049, ABV 5%)

Willy's Wheatbeer (OG 1051, ABV 5.3%)

Roaring Meg (OG 1052, ABV 5.5%)
Smooth and sweet with a dry finish and citrus honey aroma.

Cromwell's Hat (OG 1056, ABV 6%)

Stanway

Stanway Brewery, Stanway, Cheltenham, Gloucestershire, GL54 5PQ
Tel (01386) 584320
⊕ stanwaybrewery.co.uk

⊠ Stanway is a small brewery founded in 1993 with a five-barrel plant that confines its sales to the Cotswolds area (15 to 20 outlets). The brewery is the only known plant in the country to use wood-fired coppers for all its production. Seasonal beers: Morris-a-Leaping (ABV 3.9%, spring), Cotteswold Gold (ABV 3.9%, summer), Wizard (ABV 4%, autumn), Lords-a-Leaping (ABV 4.5%, Xmas).

Stanney Bitter (OG 1042, ABV 4.5%) ◈
A light, refreshing, amber-coloured beer, dominated by hops in the aroma, with a bitter taste and a hoppy, bitter finish.

Star

Star Beermaking Co, Mystique Too, Maldon Road, Steeple, Essex, CM0 7RT
Tel (07980) 530707
✉ jamesradams@tiscali.co.uk

⊠ Star was launched in 2006 and shares premises with Blanchfields Brewery (qv). It concentrates on supplying local free houses and festivals.

Gold Star (ABV 3.6%)

Starstruck (ABV 3.8%)

Pawn Star (ABV 4%)

SPA (ABV 4%)

Star Player (ABV 4%)

Old Coppernob (ABV 4.2%)

Sir Alec (ABV 4.2%)

Station House

Station House Brewery, Unit 1 Meadow Lane Industrial Estate, Meadow Lane, Ellesmere Port, Cheshire, CH65 4TY
Tel (0151) 356 3000
✉ enquire@stationhousebrewery.co.uk
⊕ stationhousebrewery.co.uk
Tours by arrangement

⊠ Station House opened in 2005 with a 5-7 barrel kit powered by electricity and propane gas. The beers are available in the free trade in the North-west and beyond. Occasional and seasonal beers are also brewed throughout the year. The brewery was due to move to new premises in the summer of 2007.

1'st Lite (ABV 3.8%) ◈
Light, hoppy bitter with clean lemon/grapefruit hop flavours and the trademark Station House bitterness and dry aftertaste. Clean and refreshing.

Lady o' the Stream (ABV 3.9%) ◈
Fruit dominates the aroma, leading into the characteristic brewery strong bitterness and lip-puckering aftertaste. Good hops throughout in this gold-coloured bitter.

4 a' that (ABV 4%)

Ode 2 Joy (ABV 4.1%) ◈
Clean, bitter beer in which citrus fruit dominates. Strong bitterness in flavour and an astringent, dry finish.

Buzzin' (ABV 4.3%) 🍷 ♦
Golden fruity bitter dominated by a honey sweetness. Good hop flavours in initital taste and a long, lasting dry finish.

3 Score (ABV 4.5%)

Steamin' Billy

Steamin' Billy Brewing Co Ltd, 5 The Oval, Oadby, Leicestershire, LE2 5JB
Tel (0116) 271 2616
✉ enquiries@steamin-billy.co.uk
⊕ steamin-billy.co.uk

☺ In spite of the name, Steamin' Billy doesn't brew and its beers are contracted to Grainstore (qv) in Oakham. Six outlets are supplied and three pubs are owned. The beers are named after the owners Jack Russell dog. Seasonal beers: Lazy Summer (ABV 4.5%), Spring Goldings (ABV 4.5%). Bottle-conditioned beers: Skydiver (ABV 5%), Steamin' Billy Bitter (ABV 4.3%). See Grainstore for regular beers.

Stewart

Stewart Brewing Ltd, 42 Dryden Road, Bilston Glen Industrial Estate, Loanhead, Midlothian, EH20 9LZ
Tel (0131) 440 2442
✉ steve.stewart@stewartbrewing.co.uk
⊕ stewartbrewing.co.uk

Stewart Brewing specialises in a variety of styles of premium cask ales, all made from natural ingredients. Beer for home can be purchased direct from the brewery for collection or delivery in the Edinburgh area.

Pentland IPA (OG 1041, ABV 4.1%) ♦
Delightfully refreshing hoppy IPA. Hops and fruit announce their presence on the nose and continue through the taste and lingering bitter aftertaste of this full-flavoured beer.

Copper Cascade (OG 1042, ABV 4.2%) ♦
A full-bodied tawny-coloured beer with a predominantly malty character. Fruit and Cascade hops give a bittersweet note with increasing bitterness in the aftertaste.

Edinburgh No.3 Premium Scotch Ale (OG 1043, ABV 4.3%) ♦
Traditional dark Scottish heavy. The pronounced malt character is part of a complex flavour profile, including fruit and hop. Initial sweetness leads into a dry, bitter, lingering finish.

80/- (OG 1044, ABV 4.4%)
Classic full-bodied, malty, bittersweet Scottish 80/-, with plenty of character.

Edinburgh Gold (OG 1048, ABV 4.8%) ♦
Full-bodied golden ale in the continental style. Plenty of hops are enjoyed throughout the drinking experience and give the beer a bitter profile balanced by the sweetness of fruit.

Stirling

See Traditional Scottish Ales

Stonehenge SIBA

Stonehenge Ales Ltd, The Old Mill, Mill Road, Netheravon, Salisbury, Wiltshire, SP4 9QB
Tel (01980) 670631
✉ stonehengeales@onetel.com
⊕ stonehengeales.co.uk
Tours by arrangement

⊗ The beers are brewed in a mill built in 1914, using the water power of the River Avon. The site was converted for brewing in 1984 and in 1994 the company was bought by Danish master brewer Stig Anker Anderson. More than 300 outlets in the south of England and several wholesalers are supplied. Seasonal beers: Sign of Spring (ABV 4.6%, Mar-May), Second-to-None (ABV 4.6%, summer), Old Smokey (ABV 5%, autumn), Rudolph (Xmas, ABV 5%).

Spire Ale (OG 1037, ABV 3.8%)
A light, golden, hoppy bitter.

Pigswill (OG 1040, ABV 4%)
A full-bodied beer, rich in hop aroma, with a warm amber colour.

Heel Stone (OG 1042, ABV 4.3%)
A crisp, clean, refreshing bitter, deep amber in colour, well balanced with a fruity blackcurrant nose.

Great Bustard (OG 1046, ABV 4.8%)
A strong, fruity, malty bitter.

Danish Dynamite (OG 1050, ABV 5%)
A strong, dry ale, slightly fruity with a well-balanced, bitter hop flavour.

Stonehouse*

Stonehouse Brewery, Stonehouse, Weston, Oswestry, Shropshire, SY10 9ES
Tel (01691) 676457
✉ info@stonehousebrewery.co.uk
⊕ stonehousebrewery.co.uk
Tours by arrangement

Stonehouse was established early in 2007 on a 15-barrel plant. Due to its location adjacent to the Cambrian railway line, the beer names (range not finalised as the Guide went to press) will all have a railway theme.

Station Bitter (ABV 3.9%)

Storm

Storm Brewing Co Ltd, 2 Waterside, Macclesfield, Cheshire, SK11 7HJ
Tel (01625) 431234
✉ thompsonhugh@talk21.com

Storm Brewing was founded in 1998 and operated from an old ICI boiler room until 2001 when the brewing operation moved to the current location, which until 1937 was a public house known as the Mechanics Arms. More than 60 outlets are supplied in Cheshire, Manchester and the Peak District. Seasonal beers: Summer Breeze (ABV 3.8%), Looks Like Rain Dear (ABV 4.8%, Xmas). All cask beers are also available in bottle-conditioned form.

Beauforts Ale (OG 1038, ABV 3.8%)
Golden brown, full-flavoured session bitter with a lingering hoppy taste.

Bitter Experience (OG 1040, ABV 4%)
A distinctive hop aroma draws you into this amber-coloured bitter. The palate has a mineral dryness that accentuates the crisp hop flavour and clean bitter finish.

Desert Storm (OG 1040, ABV 4%)
Amber-coloured beer with a smoky flavour of fruit and malt.

Twister (OG 1041, ABV 4%)
A light golden bitter with a smooth fruity hop aroma complemented by a subtle bitter aftertaste.

Bosley Cloud (OG 1041, ABV 4.1%) ◆
Dry, golden bitter with peppery hop notes throughout. Some initial sweetness and a mainly bitter aftertaste. Soft, well-balanced and quaffable.

Brainstorm (OG 1041, ABV 4.1%)
Light gold in colour and strong in citrus fruit flavours.

Ale Force (OG 1042, ABV 4.2%) ◆
Amber, smooth-tasting, complex beer that balances malt, hop and fruit on the taste, leading to a roasty, slightly sweet aftertaste.

Downpour (OG 1043, ABV 4.3%)
A combination of Pearl and lager malts produces this pale ale with a full, fruity flavour with a hint of apple and sightly hoppy aftertaste.

PGA (OG 1044, ABV 4.4%) ◆
Light, crisp, lager-style beer with a balance of malt, hops and fruit. Moderately bitter and slight dry aftertaste.

Tornado (OG 1044, ABV 4.4%) ◆
Fruity premium bitter with some graininess. Dry, satisfying finish.

Hurricane Hubert (OG 1045, ABV 4.5%)
A dark beer with a refreshing full, fruity hop aroma and a subtle bitter aftertaste.

Windgather (OG 1045, ABV 4.5%)
A gold-coloured beer with a distinctive crisp, fruity flavour right through to the aftertaste.

Storm Damage (OG 1047, ABV 4.7%)
A light-coloured, well-hopped and fruity beer balanced by a clean bitterness and smooth full palate.

Silk of Amnesia (OG 1047, ABV 4.7%) ◆
Smooth premium, easy-drinking bitter. Fruit and hops dominate throughout. Not too sweet, with a good lasting finish.

Typhoon (OG 1050, ABV 5%) ◆
Copper-coloured, smooth strong bitter. Roasty overtones and a hint of caramel and marzipan. Drinkable despite the gravity.

Stowey

Stowey Brewery, Old Cider House, 25 Castle Street, Nether Stowey, Somerset, TA5 1LN
Tel (01278) 732228
✉ info@stoweybrewery.co.uk
⊕ stoweybrewery.co.uk

⊗ Stowey was established in 2006 to provide real ale to the owner's guesthouse. Since then the brewery has expanded to supply three local pubs and now offers 'Brew your own Beer' breaks to guests. Seasonal beers include Nether Snowy (ABV 5%, Xmas).

Nether Ending (OG 1044, ABV 4.2%)

Nether Underestimate a Blonde (OG 1044, ABV 4.2%)

Strands*

Strands Brewery, Strands Hotel, Nether Wasdale, Cumbria, CA20 1ET
Tel (019467) 26237
✉ info@strandshotel.com
⊕ strandshotel.com
Tours by arrangement

⊛ Strands began brewing in February 2007. The first beer produced was called Errmmm...'as the owners couldn't think of a name for it. Seasonal beer: T'Errmmm-inator (ABV 5%, winter).

Errmmm... (OG 1042, ABV 3.8%)

Strangford Lough

Strangford Lough Brewing Co, 22 Shore Road, Killyleagh, Downpatrick, Northern Ireland, BT30 9UE
Tel (028) 4482 1461
✉ contact@slbc.ie
⊕ slbc.ie

Beers for the company are contract-brewed by an unknown brewery in England, though there are plans to build a plant in Northern Ireland. Bottle-conditioned beers: St Patrick's Best (ABV 3.8%), St Patrick's Gold (ABV 4.5%), St Patrick's Ale (ABV 6%), Barelegs Brew (ABV 4.5%), Legbiter (ABV 4.8%).

Strathaven

Strathaven Ales, Craigmill Brewery, Strathaven, ML10 6PB
Tel (01357) 520419
✉ info@strathavenales.co.uk
⊕ strathavenales.co.uk
Shop Mon-Fri 9am-5pm; phone at weekend
Tours by arrangement

⊗ Strathaven Ales is a 10-barrel brewery on the River Avon close to Strathaven and was converted from the remains of a 16th-century mill. The range is distributed throughout Scotland and the north of England. Seasonal beers: Duchess Anne (ABV 3.9%), Trumpeter (ABV 4.2%).

Clydesdale (OG 1048, ABV 3.8%)

Avondale (OG 1048, ABV 4%)

Old Mortality (OG 1046, ABV 4.2%)

Claverhouse (OG 1046, ABV 4.5%)

Stroud SIBA

Stroud Brewery Ltd, Unit 7 Phoenix Works, London Road, Thrupp, Stroud, Gloucestershire, GL5 2BU
Office: 141 Thrupp Lane, Thrupp, Stroud, Gloucestershire, GL5 2DQ
Tel 07891 995878
✉ greg@stroudbrewery.co.uk
⊕ stroudbrewery.co.uk
Tours by arrangement

⊗ Brewer Greg Pilley was a keen home-brewer since his university days, went on a Brewlab course and then assembled a five-barrel plant that came on stream in 2006. Around 25 outlets are supplied.

Tom Long (OG 1039, ABV 3.8%)

Redcoat (OG 1038, ABV 3.9%)

Budding (OG 1044, ABV 4.5%)

Five Valleys (OG 1049, ABV 5%)

Stumpy's

Stumpy's Brewery, Unit 5, Lycroft Farm, Park Lane, Upper Swanmore, Hampshire, SO32 2QQ
Tel (01329) 664902/07771 557378
✉ info@stumpysbrewery.com
⊕ stumpysbrewery.com
Tours by arrangement

Stumpy's is a five-barrel brewery that opened in 2004 in a converted hen house on a farm so remote than an Ordnance Survey map and reference (SU 588185) are essential to find it. Around 20 outlets are supplied. All cask ales are available bottled. Seasonal beer: Silent Night (ABV 5%, autumn/winter).

Dog Daze (OG 1040, ABV 3.8%) ◈
A light-tasting golden beer with a strong malty aroma. The taste is predominantly sweet rather than bitter; tastes rather thin and sweet and lacking in bitterness. A sweet malty finish.

Hop a Doodle Doo (OG 1040, ABV 4%)

Hot Dog (ABV 4.5%)

Old Ginger (ABV 4.5%)

Old Stumpy (OG 1045, ABV 4.5%) ◈
Grassy best bitter with a strong hoppy and fruity aroma. Some malt and bitterness in the flavour lead to a harsh finish.

Bo'sun's Call (ABV 5%)

Haven (OG 1050, ABV 5%)
A strong amber bitter.

Tumble Down (ABV 5%)

Suddaby's SIBA

Suddabys Ltd (Malton), Crown Hotel, 12 Wheelgate, Malton, North Yorkshire, YO17 7HP
Tel (01653) 692038
✉ enquiries@suddabys.co.uk
⊕ suddabys.co.uk

Suddabys is not currently brewing while a bigger site is sourced. The beers are contract brewed at Brown Cow (qv) and Cropton (qv).

Sulwath SIBA

Sulwath Brewers Ltd, The Brewery, 209 King Street, Castle Douglas, Dumfries & Galloway, DG7 1DT
Tel (01556) 504525
✉ allen@scottdavid98.freeserve.co.uk
⊕ sulwathbrewers.co.uk
Shop Mon-Sat 10am-4pm
Tours by arrangment

☺ Sulwath started brewing in 1995. The beers are supplied to markets as far away as Devon in the south and Aberdeen in the north. The brewery has a fully licensed brewery tap open 10am-4pm Mon-Sat. Cask ales are sold to around 100 outlets and four wholesalers. Seasonal beers: Rein Beer (ABV 4.5%, Nov-Dec), Tam O'Shanter (ABV 4.1%, Jan-Feb), Happy Hooker (ABV 4%, Feb), Woozy Wabbit

(ABV 5%, Mar-Apr), Hells Bells (ABV 4.5%, May-Jun), John Paul Jones (ABV 4%, Jul-Aug), Solway Mist (ABV 5.5%, May-Oct), Saltaire Cross (ABV 4.1%, Nov-Dec).

Cuil Hill (OG 1039, ABV 3.6%) ◈
Distinctively fruity session ale with malt and hop undertones. The taste is bittersweet with a long-lasting dry finish.

Black Galloway (OG 1046, ABV 4.4%)
A robust porter/stout that derives its colour from the abundance of Maris Otter barley and chocolate malts used in the brewing process.

Criffel (OG 1044, ABV 4.6%) ◈
Full-bodied beer with a distinctive bitterness. Fruit is to the fore of the taste with hop becoming increasingly dominant in the taste and finish.

Galloway Gold (OG 1049, ABV 5%) ◈
A cask-conditioned lager that will be too sweet for many despite being heavily hopped.

Knockendoch (OG 1047, ABV 5%) ◈
Dark, copper-coloured, reflecting a roast malt content, with bitterness from Challenger hops.

Summerskills SIBA

Summerskills Brewery, 15 Pomphlett Farm Industrial Estate, Broxton Drive, Billacombe, Plymouth, Devon, PL9 7BG
Tel (01752) 481283
✉ info@summerskills.co.uk
⊕ summerskills.co.uk

Originally established in a vineyard in 1983 at Bigbury-on-Sea, Summerskills moved to its present site in 1985 and has expanded since then. National distribution is carried out by wholesalers. 20 outlets are supplied by the brewery. Seasonal beers: Menacing Dennis (ABV 4.5%), Whistle Belly Vengeance (ABV 4.7%), Indiana's Bones (ABV 5.6%).

Cellar Vee (OG 1037, ABV 3.7%)

Hopscotch (OG 1042, ABV 4.1%)

Best Bitter (OG 1043, ABV 4.3%) ◈
A mid-brown beer, with plenty of malt and hops through the aroma, taste and finish. A good session beer.

Tamar (OG 1043, ABV 4.3%)
A tawny-coloured bitter with a fruity aroma and a hop taste and finish.

Summer Wine*

Summer Wine Brewery Ltd, Rock Cottage, 383 New Mill Road, Brockholes, Holmfirth, West Yorkshire, HD9 7AB
Tel (01484) 660597
✉ info@summerwinebrewery.co.uk
⊕ summerwinebrewery.co.uk

☺ Summer Wine started brewing in 2006 in the cellar of the home of owner James Farran, using a 10-gallon kit. The emphasis is on bottle-conditioned beers; the occasional cask beer is produced for the Star Inn, Huddersfield. The brewery plans to increase production of cask volumes when bigger premises are found. Seasonal beers: Black Jack Stout (ABV 4%),

Rudolph's Razzle (ABV 4.9%, Dec). Bottle-conditioned beers: Woodland Rogue (ABV 5.3%), Elbow Grease (ABV 4.7%), Aleshire (ABV 4.5%).

Surrey Hills SIBA

Surrey Hills Brewery Ltd, Old Scotland Farm, Staple Lane, Shere, Guildford, Surrey, GU5 9TE
Tel (01483) 212812
✉ info@surreyhills.co.uk
⊕ surreyhills.co.uk
Brewery open for beer sales Thu-Fri 12-2pm, 4-5pm; Sat 10am-12pm
Tours by arrangement

⊗ Surrey Hills started in 2005 and is based in an old milking parlour, hidden away down country lanes in the Surrey Hills. The beers are sold in around 40 local outlets – see website for up-to-date list. Seasonal beers (available for six months): Albury Ruby (ABV 4.6%, winter), Gilt Complex (ABV 4.6%, summer).

Ranmore Ale (ABV 3.8%) ⬛ ◆
A light session beer with bags of flavour. An earthy hoppy nose leads into citrus grapefruit and a hoppy taste, and a clean, bitter finish.

Shere Drop (ABV 4.2%) ⬛ ◆
Well-balanced and hoppy, with a pleasant citrus aroma and a noticeable fruitiness in the taste. The finish is dry, hoppy and bitter.

Suthwyk

Suthwyk Ales, Offwell Farm, Southwick, Fareham, Hampshire, PO17 6DX
Tel (02392) 325252
✉ mjbazeley@suthwykales.com
⊕ suthwykales.com/southwickbrewhouse.co.uk

Barley farmer Martin Bazeley does not brew himself. The beers are produced by Oakleaf Brewing (qv) in Gosport. The beers listed are also available in bottle-conditioned form and can be bought by mail order or from the shop and steam brewery museum, the Southwick Brewhouse.

Bloomfields (ABV 3.8%)

Liberation (ABV 4.2%)

Skew Sunshine Ale (ABV 4.6%)

Sutton

See South Hams

Swan on the Green

Swan on the Green Brewery, West Peckham, Maidstone, Kent, ME18 5JW
Tel (01622) 812271
✉ info@swan-on-the-green.co.uk
⊕ swan-on-the-green.co.uk
Tours by arrangement

⊗ The brewery was established in 2000 to produce handcrafted beers. Major developments have taken place to include lager production and standard British bitters. The beers are not filtered and no artificial ingredients are used. There are plans to expand the plant. One pub is owned and other outlets and beer festivals are occasionally supplied.

Fuggles Pale (OG 1037, ABV 3.6%)

A session bitter, traditionally hoppy, using local Fuggles hops.

Whooper (OG 1037, ABV 3.6%)
Straw coloured and lightly hopped with American Cascade for a subtle fruity aroma.

Trumpeter Best (OG 1041, ABV 4%)
A copper-coloured ale hopped with First Gold and Target.

Porter (OG 1045, ABV 4.5%)

Bewick (OG 1052, ABV 5.3%)
A heavyweight premium bitter hopped with Target for bite and softened with Kentish Goldings for aroma.

Swansea SIBA

⛁ **Swansea Brewing Co, Joiners Arms, 50 Bishopston Road, Bishopston, Swansea, SA3 3EJ**
Office: 74 Hawthorne Avenue, Uplands, Swansea, SA2 0LY
Tel (01792) 232658 brewery/(01792) 290197 office
✉ rorygowland@fsbdial.co.uk
Tours by arrangement

Opened in 1996, Swansea was the first commercial brewery in the area for almost 30 years and is the city's only brew-pub. It doubled its capacity within the first year and now produces four regular beers and occasional experimental ones. Four regular outlets are supplied along with other pubs in the South Wales area. Seasonal beers: St Teilo's Tipple (ABV 5.5%), Barland Strong (ABV 6%), Pwll Du XXXX (ABV 4.9%).

Deep Slade Dark (OG 1034, ABV 4%)

Bishopswood Bitter (OG 1038, ABV 4.3%) ◆
A delicate aroma of hops and malt in this pale brown colour. The taste is a balanced mix of hops and malt with a growing hoppy bitterness ending in a lasting bitter finish.

Three Cliffs Gold (OG 1042, ABV 4.7%) ◆
A golden beer with a hoppy and fruity aroma, a hoppy taste with fruit and malt, and a quenching bitterness. The pleasant finish has a good hop flavour and bitterness.

Original Wood (OG 1046, ABV 5.2%) ◆
A full-bodied, pale brown beer with an aroma of hops, fruit and malt. A complex blend of these flavours with a firm bitterness ends with increasing bitterness.

Tarka

Tarka Ales, Yelland Manor Farm, Yelland, Barnstaple, Devon, EX19 8SN
Tel (01837) 811030

A five-barrel plant was recommissioned after being mothballed in 2004. It is under new management with new beer recipes. Two pubs are supplied on a regular basis. Seasonal beer: Cockle Warmer (ABV 5.7%, Dec-Feb). Bottle-conditioned beers: Tom Noddy, Golden Pool, Black Hen (ABV 5.7%), Stock Ale (ABV 8%), Barley Wine (ABV 8.7%).

Tom Noddy (OG 1041, ABV 4.2%)
A dark ruby-coloured beer with a rich malt taste; dry in the mouth.

Golden Pool (OG 1042, ABV 4.3%)
A light, aromatic beer with strong hop character.

HW (OG 1048, ABV 4.9%)
A dark copper-coloured beer with a hint of roast barley.

Taunton

Taunton Brewing Co Ltd, c/o New Inn, Halse, Taunton, Somerset, TA4 3AF
Tel (01823) 432352
✉ colin1green@aol.com
⊕ newinnhalse.com
Tours by arrangement

⊠ Formerly Taunton Vale Brewery, established in 2003 in the cellar of the New Inn, Taunton Brewing Co took over in 2006, led by the former head brewer from Exmoor Ales. Around 45 outlets are supplied. Seasonal beer: Taunton Tinsel (ABV 4.5%, Xmas). Bottle-conditioned beer: Taunton Ale.

Ale (OG 1039.8, ABV 3.9%)

Timothy Taylor IFBB

Timothy Taylor & Co Ltd, Knowle Spring Brewery, Keighley, West Yorkshire, BD21 1AW
Tel (01535) 603139
⊕ timothy-taylor.co.uk

☺ Timothy Taylor is an independent family-owned company established in 1858. It moved to the site of the Knowle Spring in 1863. Its prize-winning ales, which use Pennine spring water, are served in all 27 of the brewery's pubs as well as more than 300 other outlets. In 2003 the brewery was given planning permission for a £1 million expansion programme that included a new brewhouse. Bottled beers are suitable for vegetarians and vegans.

Golden Best (OG 1033, ABV 3.5%) ◆
A clean-tasting and refreshing traditional Pennine light mild. A little fruit in the nose increases to complement the delicate hoppy taste. Background malt throughout.

Dark Mild (OG 1034, ABV 3.5%) ◆
Malt and caramel dominate the aroma and palate with hops and hints of fruit leading to a dry, bitter finish.

Best Bitter (OG 1038, ABV 4%) ◆
Hops and citrus fruit combine well with a nutty malt character in this drinkable bitter. Bitterness increases down the glass and lingers in the aftertaste.

Landlord (OG 1042, ABV 4.3%) ▣ ◆
An increasingly dry, hoppy, bitter finish complements the spicy, citrus character of this full-flavoured and well-balanced amber beer.

Ram Tam (OG 1043, ABV 4.3%)
A dark brown beer with red hints. Caramel dominates the aroma and leads to sweetish toffee and chocolate flavours. Increasingly dry and bitter finish.

Teignworthy SIBA

Teignworthy Brewery Ltd, The Maltings, Teign Road, Newton Abbot, Devon, TQ12 4AA
Tel (01626) 332066
✉ john@teignworthy.freeserve.co.uk
⊕ siba-southwest.co.uk/breweries/teignworthy/
Shop 10am-5pm weekdays at Tuckers Maltings
Tours available for trade customers only

Teignworthy Brewery was established in 1994 and is located in part of the historic Tuckers Maltings. The brewery is a 15-barrel plant and production is now up to 50 barrels a week, using malt from Tuckers. It supplies around 150 outlets in Devon and Somerset. Some of the beers are bottled on site and are available from the Tuckers Maltings shop and mail order. A large range of seasonal ales is available: see website. Bottle-conditioned beers: Reel Ale, Springtide, Old Moggie, Beachcomber, Martha's Mild (ABV 5.3%).

Reel Ale (OG 1039.5, ABV 4%) ◆
Clean, sharp-tasting bitter with lasting hoppiness; predominantly malty aroma.

Springtide (OG 1043.5, ABV 4.3%) ◆
An excellent, full and well-rounded, mid-brown beer with a dry, bitter taste and aftertaste.

Old Moggie (OG 1044.5, ABV 4.4%)
A golden, hoppy and fruity ale.

Beachcomber (OG 1045.5, ABV 4.5%) ◆
A pale brown beer with a light, refreshing fruit and hop nose, grapefruit taste and a dry, hoppy finish.

Teme Valley SIBA

⬓ **Teme Valley Brewery, The Talbot, Bromyard Road, Knightwick, Worcester, WR6 5PH**
Tel (01886) 821235
✉ enquiries@temevalleybrewery.co.uk
⊕ temevalleybrewery.co.uk
Tours by arrangement

☺ Teme Valley Brewery opened in 1997. In 2005, new investment enabled the brewery to expand to a 10-barrel brew-length. It maintains strong ties with local hop farming, using only Worcestershire-grown hops. Some 30 outlets are supplied. Seasonal beers: see website. Bottle-conditioned beers: This, That, Hop Nouvelle, Wotever Next? (ABV 5%), Heartwarmer (ABV 6%).

T'Other (OG 1035, ABV 3.5%) ◆
Refreshing amber offering with an abundance of flavour in the fruity aroma, followed by a short, dry bitterness.

This (OG 1037, ABV 3.7%) ◆
Dark gold brew with a mellow array of flavours in a malty balance.

That (OG 1041, ABV 4.1%) ◆
A rich fruity nose and a wide range of hoppy and malty flavours in this copper-coloured best bitter.

Theakston

T&R Theakston Ltd, The Brewery, Masham, Ripon, North Yorkshire, HG4 4YD
Tel (01765) 680000
✉ info@theakstons.co.uk
⊕ theakstons.co.uk
Tours by arrangement

After 20 years under the control of first Matthew Brown and then Scottish & Newcastle, Theakstons returned to the independent sector in 2003 when S&N sold the company back to the family, and it is now controlled by four Theakston brothers. The brewery is one of the oldest in Yorkshire, built in 1875 by the brothers' great-grandfather, Thomas Theakston, the son of the company's founder. The Theakston's range, with the exception of Best Bitter, is brewed in Masham but as a result of restraints on capacity the company has contracted S&N to brew Best Bitter at John Smith's in Tadcaster. In 2004 a new fermentation room was added to provide additional flexibility and capacity, and further capacity was added in 2006. Seasonal beers: Hogshead Bitter (ABV 4.1%), Lightfoot (ABV 4.1%), Grouse Beater (ABV 4.2%), Paradise Ale (ABV 4.2%), Cooper's Butt (ABV 4.3%), Masham Ale (ABV 6.5%).

Traditional Mild (OG 1035, ABV 3.5%) ◆
A rich and smooth mild ale with a creamy body and a rounded liquorice taste. Dark ruby/amber in colour, with a mix of malt and fruit on the nose, and a dry, hoppy aftertaste.

Best Bitter (ABV 3.8%)
A golden-coloured beer with a full flavour that lingers pleasantly on the palate.

Black Bull Bitter (OG 1037, ABV 3.9%) ◆
A distinctively hoppy aroma leads to a bitter, hoppy taste with some fruitiness and a short bitter finish. Rather thin.

XB (OG 1044, ABV 4.5%)
A sweet-tasting bitter with background fruit and spicy hop. Some caramel character gives this ale a malty dominance.

Old Peculier (OG 1057, ABV 5.6%) ◆
A full-bodied, dark brown, strong ale. Slightly malty but with hints of roast coffee and liquorice. A smooth caramel overlay and a complex fruitiness leads to a bitter chocolate finish.

Abraham Thompson

Abraham Thompson's Brewing Co, Flass Lane, Barrow-in-Furness, Cumbria, LA13 0AD
Tel 07708 191437
✉ abraham.thompson@btinternet.com

Abraham Thompson was set up in 2004 to return Barrow-brewed beers to local pubs. This was achieved in 2005 after an absence of more than 30 years following the demise of Case's Brewery in 1972. With a half-barrel plant, this nano-brewery has concentrated almost exclusively on dark beers, reflecting the tastes of the brewer. As a result of the small output, finding the beers outside the Low Furness area is difficult. The only frequent stockist is the Black Dog Inn between Dalton and Ireleth.

Dark Mild (ABV 3.5%)

Lickerish Stout (ABV 4%)
A black, full-bodied stout with heavy roast flavours and good bitterness.

Oatmeal Stout (ABV 4.5%)

Porter (ABV 4.8%)
A deep, dark porter with good body and a smooth chocolate finish.

Letargion (ABV 9%)
Black, bitter and heavily roast but still very drinkable. A meal in a glass.

John Thompson

◻ **John Thompson Inn & Brewery, Ingleby, Melbourne, Derbyshire, DE73 7HW**
Tel (01332) 852469
✉ nick_w_thompson@yahoo.co.uk
Tours by arrangement

John Thompson set up the brewery in 1977. The pub and brewery are now run by his son, Nick. Seasonal beers: Gold (ABV 4.5%, summer), Rich Porter (ABV 4.5%, winter), St Nicks (ABV 5%, Xmas).

JTS XXX (OG 1041, ABV 4.1%)

Porter (OG 1045, ABV 4.5%)

Thornbridge SIBA

Thornbridge Brewery, Thornbridge Hall, Ashford in the Water, Bakewell, Derbyshire, DE45 1NZ
Tel (01629) 641000
✉ info@thornbridgebrewery.co.uk
⊕ thornbridgebrewery.co.uk
Tours by arrangement

⊗ The first Thornbridge craft beers were produced in 2005 in the 10-barrel brewery, housed in the grounds of Thornbridge Hall. Around 75 outlets are supplied direct. There are plans to expand the brewery to meet increasing demand. Bottle-conditioned beers: Jaipur IPA, Saint Petersburg Imperial Russian Stout.

Wild Swan (OG 1035, ABV 3.5%) ◆
Light bodied, pale gold beer with subtle lemon and spice aroma. Citrus notes continue in the taste, leading to a bitter aftertaste.

Brother Rabbit (OG 1038, ABV 3.7%)
A straw-coloured beer with a crisp, hoppy aroma. A dry palate leads to a resinous finish with some bitterness.

Lord Marples (OG 1041, ABV 4%) ◆
Easy drinking, copper-coloured, fruity session beer. Malty, with a citrus finish and a long, bitter aftertaste.

Brock (OG 1040, ABV 4.1%) ◆
Dark, full-bodied stout with aroma and flavour of roast malt and treacle toffee. Aftertaste is dry and bitter but short.

Blackthorn Ale (OG 1044, ABV 4.4%) ◆
Clear golden ale with a slight aroma of floral hops. Well balanced flavours of hops, citrus and sweetness lead to a lingering fruit and hop aftertaste.

Kipling (OG 1050, ABV 5.2%) ◆
Golden pale bitter with aroma of grapefruit and passion fruit. Intense fruit flavours continue throughout, leading to a long, bitter aftertaste.

Jaipur IPA (OG 1055, ABV 5.9%) ▣ ◻ ◆
Complex, well-balanced IPA with a fine blend of citrus and other fruit flavours, mixed with a slight sweetness and ending with a lingering bitter finish.

Saint Petersburg (Imperial Russian

Stout) (OG 1073, ABV 7.7%) ◆
Full-bodied beer in the style of a Russian
Imperial Stout. A combination of coffee,
liquorice and roasted malt flavours give way
to a long, bittersweet finish.

Three B's

**Three B's Brewery, Laneside Works, Stockclough
Lane, Feniscowles, Blackburn, Lancashire, BB2 5JR
Tel (01254) 207686**
✉ info@threebsbrewery.co.uk
⊕ threebsbrewery.co.uk
Tours by arrangement

Robert Bell designed and began building his
two-barrel brewery in 1998 and in 1999 he
obtained premises in Blackburn to set up the
equipment and complete the project. It is now
a 10-barrel brewery. 20 outlets are supplied.
Seasonal beers: Weaver's Brew (ABV 4%),
Easter Gold (ABV 4.5%), Fettler's Choice (ABV
4.2%, summer), Autumn Gold (ABV 4.5%),
Santa's Skinful (ABV 4%, Xmas). Bottle
conditioned beers: Shuttle Ale, Doff Cocker,
Knocker Up, Tackler's Tipple.

Stoker's Slake (ABV 3.6%) ◆
Lightly roasted coffee flavours are in the
aroma and the initial taste. A well-rounded,
dark brown mild with dried fruit flavours in
the long finish.

Bobbin's Bitter (ABV 3.8%)
Warm aromas of malt, Goldings hops and
nuts; a full, fruity flavour with a light dry
finish.

Tackler's Tipple (ABV 4.3%)
A best bitter with full hop flavour, biscuit
tones on the tongue and a deep, dry finish. A
darker coloured ale with a fascinating blend
of hops and dark malt.

Doff Cocker (ABV 4.5%) ◆
Yellow with a hoppy aroma and initial taste
giving way to subtle malt notes and orchard
fruit flavours. Crisp, dry finish.

Pinch Noggin' (ABV 4.6%)
A luscious balance of malt, hops and fruit,
with a lively, colourful spicy aroma of citrus
fruit. A quenching golden beer.

Knocker Up (ABV 4.8%) ◆
A smooth, rich, creamy porter. The roast
flavour is foremost without dominating and is
balanced by fruit and hop notes.

Shuttle Ale (ABV 5.2%)
A strong pale ale, light in colour with a
balanced malt and hop flavour, a Goldings
hops aroma, a long dry finish and delicate
fruit notes.

Three Castles* SIBA

**Three Castles Brewery Ltd, Unit 12, Salisbury
Road Business Park, Pewsey, Wiltshire, SN9 5PZ
Tel (01672) 564433**
✉ sales@threecastlesbrewery.co.uk
Shop Mon-Fri 9am-4pm; Sat 9am-1pm
Tours by arrangement

⊠ Three Castles is an independent, family-run
brewery, established in 2006. Its location in the
Vale of Pewsey has inspired the names for its
range of ales. The brewery has invested in a

new six-barrel brew plant and there are already
plans for expansion, including a bottling facility.
Around 65 outlets are supplied.

Liddington Castle (OG 1035, ABV 3.5%)
A deep amber-coloured ale with a nutty
palate and pleasant bitterness.

Barbury Castle (OG 1039, ABV 3.9%)
A balanced, easy-drinking pale ale with a
hoppy, spicy palate.

Vale Ale (OG 1043, ABV 4.3%)
Golden-coloured with a fruity palate and
strong floral aroma.

Long Barrow (OG 1045, ABV 4.5%)
Copper-coloured with a spicy, nutty flavour
and a hoppy aftertaste.

Tanked Up (OG 1050, ABV 5%)
Copper-coloured strong ale.

Three Peaks*

**Three Peaks Brewery, 7 Craven Terrace, Settle,
North Yorkshire, BD24 9DB
Tel (01729) 822939**

⊠ Formed in 2006, Three Peaks is run by
husband and wife team Colin and Susan
Ashwell. The brewery is located in the cellar of
their home. One beer is brewed at present on
their 1.25-barrel plant but more are planned.

Pen-y-Ghent Bitter (OG 1040, ABV 3.8%)

Three Rivers

See 3 Rivers

Three Tuns SIBA

**John Roberts Brewing Co Ltd t/a Three Tuns
Brewery, 16 Market Square, Bishop's Castle,
Shropshire, SY9 5BN
Tel (01588) 638392**
✉ tunsbrewery@aol.co.uk
Tours by arrangement

⊠ Brewing started on the site more than 300
years ago. In the 1970s the Three Tuns was one of
only four brew-pubs left in the country. Nowadays
the brewery and Three Tuns pub are separate
businesses. Plans to increase the brew length are
in progress. Around 100 outlets are supplied.
Seasonal beer: Ginger (ABV 3.8%, summer).

Qu'offa's (OG 1036, ABV 3.4%)

Three 8 (OG 1042, ABV 3.8%)

XXX (OG 1046, ABV 4.3%) ◆
A pale, sweetish bitter with a light hop
aftertaste that has a honey finish.

Steamer (ABV 4.4%) ◆
A dark and well-roasted porter/stout with
coffee tastes and a hop finish.

Cleric's Cure (ABV 5%)
A pale beer with strong hopping to resemble
old IPAs.

Old Scrooge (ABV 6%)

Thwaites IFBB

**Daniel Thwaites plc, Star Brewery, PO Box 50,
Blackburn, Lancashire, BB1 5BU**

Tel (01254) 686868
✉ marketing@thwaites.co.uk
⊕ thwaites.co.uk
Tours by arrangement

☻ Thwaites celebrated its 200th anniversary in 2007 and is still controlled by the Yerburgh family, descendants of founder Daniel Thwaites. The bi-centenary celebrations saw the introduction of new seasonal beers inspired by the company's brewing heritage. Cask beer is available in around 60% of the company's 430 pubs but Dark Mild is hard to find. Seasonal beers are brewed for spring, autumn and Xmas.

Dark Mild (OG 1036, ABV 3.3%) ◆
A tasty traditional dark mild presenting a malty flavour with caramel notes and a slightly bitter finish.

Original (OG 1036, ABV 3.6%) ◆
Hop driven, yet well-balanced amber session bitter. Hops continue through to the long finish.

Thoroughbred Gold (OG 1040, ABV 4%)

Lancaster Bomber (OG 1044, ABV 4.4%) ◆
Well-balanced, copper-coloured best bitter with firm malt flavours, a fruity background and a long, dry finish.

For Carlsberg:

Ansells Mild (OG 1035, ABV 3.4%)

Tigertops SIBA

Tigertops Brewery, 22 Oaks Street, Flanshaw, Wakefield, West Yorkshire, WF2 9LN
Tel (01229) 716238/(01924) 897728
✉ tigertopsbrewery@hotmail.com

☻ Tigertops was established in 1995 by Stuart Johnson and his wife Lynda. They own the brewery as well as running the Foxfield brew-pub in Cumbria (qv) but Tigertops is run on their behalf by Barry Smith. Five outlets are supplied. Seasonal beers: Billy Bock (ABV 7.9%, Nov-Feb), May Bock (ABV 6.2%, May-Jun).

Axeman's Block (OG 1036, ABV 3.6%)
A malty beer with a good hop finish.

Dark Wheat Mild (OG 1036, ABV 3.6%)
An unusual mild made primarily with wheat malt.

Thor Bitter (OG 1038, ABV 3.8%)
A light, hoppy bitter.

Charles Town Best Bitter (ABV 4%)

Blanche de Newland (OG 1044, ABV 4.5%)
A cloudy Belgian-style wheat beer.

Ginger Fix (OG 1044, ABV 4.6%)
A mid-amber ginger beer.

White Max (OG 1044, ABV 4.6%)
A light, German-style wheat beer.

Uber Weiss (OG 1046, ABV 4.8%)
A dark, German-style wheat beer.

Big Ginger (OG 1058, ABV 6%)
A strong, amber ginger beer.

Tindall EAB

Tindall Ales Brewery, Toad Lane, Seething, Norfolk, NR35 2EQ
Tel (01508) 483844/07795 113163

✉ greenangela5@aol.com
Tours by arrangement

Tindall Ales opened in 1998 and and now only brews occasional seasonal ales.

Tipples EAB

Tipples Brewery, Unit 6, Damgate Lane Industrial Estate, Acle, Norwich, NR13 3DJ
Tel (01493) 741007
✉ brewery@tipplesbrewery.com
⊕ tipplesbrewery.com

☒ Tipples was established by Jason Tipple in 2004 on a six-barrel brew plant built by Porter Brewing Co. The brewery initially concentrated on the bottled market but cask ale production has since increased and there are plans for expansion on the existing site.

Longshore (OG 1036, ABV 3.6%) ▨ ◆
Yellow hued with a soft, peachy aroma and creamy mouthfeel. The initial fruity apricot flavour quickly subsides to a long, dry bitterness.

Ginger (ABV 3.8%) ◆
A spicy aroma introduces this well-balanced yellow-gold brew. Ginger dominates but does not overwhelm the supporting malty bitterness. Quick ginger nut finish.

Hanged Monk (ABV 4%) ◆
Heavy roast notes dominate throughout. The initial aroma and taste has a malt and dry, fruity bitterness to add depth and complexity. A long finish develops a distinct, pleasant sourness.

Lady Evelyn (OG 1041, ABV 4.1%) ◆
Straw-coloured with a gentle citrus aroma that belies a clean hop bitterness in the initial taste. Lemon citrus background adds some depth to a light, undemanding summer ale.

Redhead (OG 1042, ABV 4.2%) ◆
A mix of hop and malt in the nose carries through to a first taste of bitter hoppiness and background malt. Bitterness continues to dominate the long finish as a grapefruit dryness creeps in.

Lady Hamilton (ABV 4.3%) ◆
Mid-brown with a caramel toffee nose. Sweet and full-bodied with a lingering malty finish. Some dryness can be detected towards the end.

Jacks' Revenge (ABV 5.8%) ▨ ◆
An explosion of malt, chocolate, roast and plum pudding fruitiness. Full-bodied with a deep red hue and a strong solid finish that develops into a vinous fruitiness.

Tipsy Toad

See Jersey

Tirril SIBA

Tirril Brewery Ltd, Red House, Long Marton, Appleby-in-Westmorland, Cumbria, CA16 6BN
Tel (017683) 61846
✉ enquiries@tirrilbrewery.co.uk
⊕ tirrilbrewery.co.uk
Tours by arrangement

☻ Tirril Brewery was established in 1999 in an abandoned toilet block behind the Queen's Head in Tirril. Since then it has relocated to the

1823 gothic brewing rooms at Brougham Hall and is now at the Red House Barn in Long Marton beneath the Pennines. Capacity has grown from 2.25 barrels to 20 barrels over the years. More than 50 outlets are supplied and two pubs are owned. Seasonal beers: Graduate (ABV 4.6%, Dec), Balls Up (ABV 3.9%, summer).

John Bewsher's Best Bitter (OG 1038.5, ABV 3.8%)
A lightly-hopped, golden brown session beer, named after the landlord and brewer at the Queen's Head in the 1830s.

Brougham Ale (OG 1039, ABV 3.9%)
A gently hopped, amber bitter.

Charles Gough's Old Faithful (OG 1040, ABV 4%)
Pale gold, aromatic and well-hopped.

1823 (OG 1041, ABV 4.1%)
A full-bodied session bitter with a gentle bitterness.

Thomas Slee's Academy Ale (OG 1041.5, ABV 4.2%)
A dark, full-bodied, traditional rich and malty ale.

Titanic SIBA

Titanic Brewery Co Ltd, Unit 5, Callender Place, Burslem, Stoke-on-Trent, Staffordshire, ST6 1JL
Tel (01782) 823447
✉ titanic@titanicbrewery.co.uk
⊕ titanicbrewery.co.uk
Tours by arrangement

☺ Founded in 1985, the brewery is named in honour of Captain Smith who hailed from the Potteries and had the misfortune to captain the Titanic. A monthly seasonal beer provides the opportunity to offer distinctive beers of many styles, each with a link to the liner. Titanic supplies 300 free trade outlets throughout the country. The brewery has two tied houses. A 50-barrel brew plant was installed in 2005. Bottle-conditioned beer: Titanic Stout (ABV 4.5% 🍾 ⏹).

Steerage (OG 1036, ABV 3.5%) ◈
Straw-coloured bitter with a sulphurous nose, a fruity start, a well-hopped middle and a dry finish.

Mild (OG 1036, ABV 3.5%) ◈
Hints of fruit among the caramel aroma. Sweet start with roast and caramel mix giving way to hops. Good hoppy finish.

Lifeboat (OG 1040, ABV 4%) ◈
A fruity and malty beer, dark red with a fruity finish.

Iceberg (OG 1042, ABV 4.1%) ◈
Gold coloured, with a hoppy and fruity aroma leading to a fruity and hoppy taste with tones of honey and grass. Bitterness develops in the long finish.

Anchor Bitter (OG 1042, ABV 4.1%) ◈
Copper-coloured with a sulphurous aroma parting to reveal fruit and hops. A robust bitterness relaxes in to a long, dry, hoppy finish.

Stout (OG 1046, ABV 4.5%) ◈
Good and black! Full roast aroma with fruit and malt tones. Roast dominates with a bitter, fruity finish and mouth-watering liquorice flavours.

White Star (OG 1050, ABV 4.8%) ◈
Golden bitter with some hop and fruit aromas. Touches of honey and citrus begin the taste. Malty sweetness arrives but quickly gives way to a bitterness that lingers to perfection.

Captain Smith's Strong Ale (OG 1054, ABV 5.2%) ◈
Red with a hoppy aroma plus malt and a touch of sulphur. Fine balance of hop and caramel with roast and hints of malt and fruit. Sweet to start then a hoppy, bitter finish with a fruity layer.

Toll End

⎙ Toll End Brewery, c/o Waggon & Horses, 131 Toll End Road, Tipton, West Midlands, DY4 0ET
Tel 07903 725574
Tours by arrangement

⌧ The four-barrel brewery opened in 2004. With the exception of Phoebe's Ale, named after the brewer's daughter, all brews commemorate local landmarks, events and people. Toll End is brewing to full capacity and produces around 300 gallons a week. Four outlets are supplied. Several specials are also brewed throughout the year.

William Perry (OG 1043, ABV 4.3%)

Phoebe's Ale (PA) (OG 1044, ABV 4.4%)

Polly Stevens (OG 1044, ABV 4.4%)

Black Bridge (OG 1046, ABV 4.6%)

Tipton Pride (OG 1046, ABV 4.6%)

Power Station (OG 1049, ABV 4.9%)
Cask-conditioned lager.

Tollgate SIBA

Tollgate Brewery, Unit 8, Viking Business Centre, High Street, Woodville, Derbyshire, DE11 7EH
Tel (01283) 229194
✉ tollgatebrewery@tiscali.co.uk
Tours by arrangement

⌧ Tollgate, a six-barrel brewery that opened in 2005, is on the site of the old Brunt & Bucknall Brewery, which was bought and closed by Bass in 1927. Most beers are named after locally known landmarks. Mofre than 40 outlets are supplied. Seasonal beer: Woodville Winter Warmer (ABV 5.4%, Nov-Feb).

Woodville Pale (OG 1042, ABV 4%)

Wooden Box Bitter (OG 1045, ABV 4.3%)

Red Star IPA (OG 1047, ABV 4.5%)

Tollgate Light/TGL (OG 1047, ABV 4.5%)

Woodville Wonder (OG 1051, ABV 4.9%)

Topsham & Exminster

Topsham & Exminster Brewery, Lions Rest Industrial Estate, Exminster, Devon, EX6 8DZ
Tel (01392) 823013
⊕ topexe.co.uk
Tours by arrangement

The brewery was established in 2003 and is located in the Exminster Marshes, a popular bird sanctuary on the River Exe. The brew run is now 10 barrels and, while Ferryman is the regular beer, others occasionally appear in a few selected local pubs and clubs.

Ferryman (OG 1041, ABV 4.4%)

Tower SIBA

Tower Brewery, Old Water Tower, Walsitch Maltings, Glensyl Way, Burton upon Trent, Staffordshire, DE14 1LX
Tel (01283) 530695
✉ towerbrewery@aol.com
Tours by arrangement

Tower was established in 2001 by John Mills, previously the brewer at Burton Bridge, in a converted derelict water tower of Thomas Salt's maltings. The conversion was given a Civic Society award for the restoration of a Historic Industrial Building in 2001. Tower has 20 regular outlets. Seasonal beers: Sundowner (ABV 4%, May-Aug), Spring Equinox (ABV 4.6%, Mar-May), Autumn Equinox (ABV 4.6%, Sep-Nov), Winter Spirit (ABV 5%).

Thomas Salt's Bitter (OG 1038, ABV 3.8%)

Bitter (OG 1042, ABV 4.2%) ◈
Gold coloured with a malty, caramel and hoppy aroma. A full hop and fruit taste with the fruit lingering. A bitter and astringent finish.

Malty Towers (OG 1044, ABV 4.4%) ◈
Yellow with a malty aroma and a hint of tobacco. Strong hops give a long, dry, bitter finish with pleasant astringency.

Pale Ale (OG 1048, ABV 4.8%)

Tower of Strength (OG 1076, ABV 7.6%)

For Hoskins Brothers, Leicester:

Hob Best Mild (ABV 3.5%)

Brigadier Bitter (ABV 3.6%)

Hob Bitter (ABV 4%)

White Dolphin (ABV 4%)

Tom Kelly's Stout (ABV 4.2%)

EXS (ABV 5%)

Ginger Tom (ABV 5.2%)

Old Navigation Ale (ABV 7%)

Townes SIBA

⌂ **Townes Brewery, Speedwell Inn, Lowgates, Staveley, Chesterfield, Derbyshire, S43 3TT**
Tel (01246) 472252
✉ curly@townes48.wanadoo.co.uk
Tours by arrangement

⊗ Townes Brewery started in 1994 in an old bakery on the outskirts of Chesterfield using a five-barrel plant. It was the first brewery in the town for more than 40 years. In 1997, the Speedwell Inn at Staveley was bought and the plant was moved to the rear of the pub, becoming the first brew-pub in north Derbyshire in the 20th century. Seasonal beers: Stargazer (ABV 5.5%, winter), Sunshine (ABV 3.7%, summer). A monthly special is available under the Real Gone motif. Two seasonal milds are produced to increase interest in the style: Golden Bud (ABV 3.8%, summer) and Muffin Man (ABV 4.6%,

winter). Staveley Cross, IPA, Oatmeal Stout and Staveleyan are also available in bottle-conditioned form and are suitable for vegetarians and vegans.

Speedwell Bitter (OG 1039, ABV 3.9%) ◈
Well-balanced amber bitter with little aroma. Hints of caramel and hops lead to a bitterness developing in the long aftertaste.

Lockoford Best Bitter (ABV 4%)

Lowgate Light (OG 1041, ABV 4.1%)

Staveley Cross (OG 1043, ABV 4.3%) ◈
Amber-gold best bitter with a faint caramel aroma. Hoppy with bitterness present throughout, culminating in a long, dry, slightly astringent aftertaste.

IPA (OG 1045, ABV 4.5%) ◈
Well-crafted, flavoursome IPA of little aroma and a good bittersweet, balanced taste. This leads to a lingering aftertaste that is predominantly sweet with hoppy undertones.

Oatmeal Stout (OG 1047, ABV 4.7%)

Staveleyan (OG 1049, ABV 4.9%)

Townhouse

Townhouse Brewery, Units 1-4, Townhouse Studios, Townhouse Farm, Alsager Road, Audley, Staffordshire, ST7 8JQ
Tel 07976 209437/07812 035143
✉ j.nixon2@btinternet.com
Tours by arrangement

⊗ Townhouse was set up in 2002 with a 2.5-barrel plant. In 2004 the brewery scaled up to a five-barrels. Demand is growing rapidly and in early 2006 two additional fermenting vessels were added. Bottling is planned. Some 30 outlets are supplied.

Audley Bitter (OG 1038, ABV 3.8%)
A pale, well-balanced session bitter with a citrus hop character.

Flowerdew (OG 1039, ABV 4%) ◈
Golden with a wonderful floral aroma. Fabulous flavour of flowery hops delivering a hoppy bite and presenting a lingering taste of flowery citrus waves.

Dark Horse (OG 1042, ABV 4.3%)
A dark ruby ale with malt character and late hoppy finish.

A'dleyweisse (OG 1043, ABV 4.5%)
An English style wheat beer, full-bodied and golden with a strongly defined fruity hop character and a dry finish.

Audley Gold (OG 1043, ABV 4.5%) ◈
Straw colour with some hops on the aroma. An explosion of hops in the taste gives a perfect bitter effect, leaving a hoppy mouthfeel without too much astringency.

Barney's Stout (OG 1043, ABV 4.5%) ◈
Roast chocolate and toffee nose atop this black stout. Sweet start going bitter at the end, with roast throughout.

Armstrong Ale (OG 1045, ABV 4.8%)
A rich, fruity ruby red beer with a hoppy, dry finish.

Monument Ale (OG 1048, ABV 5%)
A copper-coloured, well-balanced strong ale with a pronounced malt character.

Traditional Scottish Ales*

Traditional Scottish Ales Ltd, Unit 7c Bandeath Industrial Estate, Stirling, FK7 7NP
Tel (01786) 817000
✉ brewery@traditionalscottishales.com

☺ A new company set up in 2005 to develop and market the Bridge of Allan, Stirling and Trossach's Craft Brewery products. The brewery is located in a former torpedo factory. A five-barrel plant is used for cask ales and a custom-built 20-barrel plant is dedicated to bottled products. More than 100 outlets are supplied. Bottle-conditioned beer: Brig O'Allan (ABV 4%). Ben Nevis, Glencoe Wild Oat Stout and Lomond Gold are organic and suitable for vegetarians and vegans.

Stirling Bitter (OG 1039, ABV 3.7%)

Ben Nevis Organic (OG 1042, ABV 4%) ◈
A traditional Scottish 80/-, with a distinctive roast and caramel character. Bittersweet fruit throughout provides the sweetness typical of a Scottish Heavy.

Stirling Brig (OG 1042, ABV 4.1%)

Bannockburn Ale (OG 1044, ABV 4.2%)

Glencoe Wild Oat Stout Organic (OG 1048, ABV 4.5%) ◈
A sweetish stout, surprisingly not dark in colour. Plenty of malt and roast balanced by fruit and finished with a hint of hop.

Wallace Monument (OG 1052, ABV 4.8%)

William Wallace (OG 1050, ABV 4.8%)

Lomond Gold Organic (OG 1054, ABV 5%) ◈
A malty, bittersweet golden ale with plenty of fruity hop character.

1488 (OG 1075, ABV 7%)

For Trossach's Craft Brewery:

Waylade (OG 1040, ABV 3.9%)

LadeBack (OG 1048, ABV 4.5%)

LadeOut (OG 1055, ABV 5.1%)

Traquair SIBA

Traquair House Brewery, Traquair House, Innerleithen, Peeblesshire, EH44 6PW
Tel (01896) 830323
✉ enquiries@traquair.co.uk
⊕ traquair.co.uk
Shop Easter-Oct 12-5pm daily (Jun-Aug 10.30am-5pm)
Tours by arrangement

The 18th-century brewhouse is based in one of the wings of the 1,000-year-old Traquair House, Scotland's oldest inhabited house. The brewhouse was rediscovered by the 20th Laird, the late Peter Maxwell Stuart, in 1965. He began brewing again using all the original equipment, which remained intact, despite having lain idle for more than 100 years. The brewery has been run by Peter's daughter, Catherine Maxwell Stuart, since his death in 1990. The Maxwell Stuarts are members of the Stuart clan, and the main Bear Gates will remain shut until a Stuart returns to the throne. All the beers are oak-fermented and 60 per cent of production is exported. Seasonal beers: Stuart Ale (ABV 4.5%, summer), Bear Ale (ABV 5%, winter).

Laird's Liquor (ABV 6%)

Traquair House Ale (ABV 7%)

Jacobite Ale (ABV 8%)

Tring SIBA

Tring Brewery Co Ltd, 81-82 Akeman Street, Tring, Hertfordshire, HP23 6AF
Tel (01442) 890721
✉ info@tringbrewery.co.uk
⊕ tringbrewery.co.uk
Shop Mon-Fri 9am-6pm; Sat 9am-12pm
Tours by arrangement (evenings only)

Founded in 1992, the Tring Brewery is based on a small industrial estate and brews 45 barrels a week. Most of the beers take their names from local myths and legends. In addition to the regular and seasonal ales, Tring brews a selection of monthly specials. There are plans to move the brewery to larger premises. Seasonal beers: Walter's Winter Ale (ABV 4%), Royal Poacher (ABV 4.1%), Fanny Ebbs Summer Ale (ABV 3.9%), Huck-Me-Buck (ABV 4.4%), Santa's Little Helper (ABV 4.8%).

Side Pocket for a Toad (OG 1035, ABV 3.6%)
Citrus notes from American Cascade hops balanced with a floral aroma and a crisp, dry finish in a straw-coloured ale.

Brock Bitter (ABV 3.7%)
A light brown session ale with hints of sweetness and caramel, gentle bitterness and a floral aroma from Styrian hops.

Mansion Mild (ABV 3.7%)
Smooth and creamy dark ruby mild with a fruity palate and gentle late hop.

Blonde (OG 1039, ABV 4%)
A refreshing blonde beer with a fruity palate, balanced with a lingering hop aroma.

Ridgeway (OG 1039, ABV 4%)
Balanced malt and hop flavours with a dry, flowery hop aftertaste.

Jack O'Legs (OG 1041, ABV 4.2%)
A combination of four types of malt and two types of aroma hops provide a copper-coloured premium ale with full fruit and a distinctive hoppy bitterness.

Tea Kettle Stout (OG 1047, ABV 4.7%)
Rich and complex traditional stout with a hint of liquorish and moderate bitterness.

Colley's Dog (OG 1051, ABV 5.2%)
Dark but not over-rich, strong yet drinkable, this premium ale has a long dry finish with overtones of malt and walnuts.

Death or Glory (ABV 7.2%)
A strong, dark, aromatic barley wine.

Triple fff SIBA

Triple fff Brewing Company Ltd, Magpie Works, Station Approach, Four Marks, Alton, Hampshire, GU34 5HN
Tel (01420) 561422
✉ sales-triplefbrewery@tiscali.co.uk
⊕ triplefff.com
Shop (please ring for opening hours)
Tours by arrangement

⊗ The brewery was founded in 1997 with a five-barrel plant. Ever increasing demand has culminated in a £¾ million investment in a new 50-barrel plant. The brewery have two of their own outlets, the Railway Arms in Alton and the White Lion in Aldershot, as well as supplying over 200 other outlets. One or two seasonal beers are offered to complement the regular range.

Alton's Pride (ABV 3.8%) ◄
Clean-tasting, golden brown session beer, full-bodied for its strength with an aroma of floral hops. An initial malty flavour fades as citrus notes and hoppiness take over, leading to a hoppy, bitter finish.

Pressed Rat & Warthog (ABV 3.8%) ◄
Complex hoppy and bitter ruby mild. Roast malt aroma with hints of blackcurrant and chocolate lead to a well-balanced flavour with roast, fruit and malt vying with the hoppy bitterness and a dry bitter finish.

Moondance (ABV 4.2%) ▯ ◄
A pale brown-coloured best bitter with an aromatic, citrus hop nose balanced by bitterness and a hint of sweetness in the mouth. Bitterness increases in the finish as the fruit declines.

Stairway (ABV 4.6%) ◄
An aroma of pale and crystal malts introduces this pale brown beer with a flavour of summer fruits. Well-balanced, with a dry, strong, hoppy finish. Predominantly bitter with some sweetness and malt.

Trossach's Craft

See Traditional Scottish Ales

Tryst

Tryst Brewery, Lorne Road, Larbert, Stirling, FK5 4AT
Tel (01324) 554000
✉ johnmcgarva@tinyworld.co.uk
⊕ trystbrewery.co.uk
Tours by arrangement

John McGarva, a member of Scottish Craft Brewers, started brewing in 2003 in an industrial unit near Larbert station. Around 30 outlets are supplied. All beers are also available bottle conditioned.

Brockville Dark (OG 1039, ABV 3.8%)

Brockville Pale (OG 1039, ABV 3.8%)

Festival Red (OG 1041, ABV 4%)

Buckled Wheel (OG 1043, ABV 4.2%)

Carronade IPA (OG 1043, ABV 4.2%) ▯

Zetland Wheatbier (OG 1046, ABV 4.5%)

Tunnel SIBA

Tunnel Brewery Ltd, Lord Nelson Inn, Birmingham Road, Ansley, Nuneaton, Warwickshire, CV10 9PQ
Tel (02476) 394888
✉ info@tunnelbrewery.co.uk
⊕ tunnelbrewery.co.uk
Shop open Sat & Sun mornings
Tours by arrangement

Bob Yates and Mike Walsh started brewing in 2005, taking the name from a rail tunnel that passes under the village. Pub and brewery are independent of one another but the beers are available in the pub as well as being supplied to more than 40 other outlets. Seasonal beers: See website. All beers are available bottle conditioned and are suitable for vegans.

Late Ott (OG 1040, ABV 4%)
Dark golden session bitter with a fruity nose and perfumed hop edge. The finish is dry and bitter.

Trade Winds (OG 1045, ABV 4.6%)
An aromatic, copper-coloured beer with an aroma of Cascade hops and a clean, crisp hint of citrus, followed by fruity malts and a dry finish full of scented hops.

Sweet Parish Ale (OG 1047, ABV 4.7%)
A reddish-amber, malty ale with a slight chocolate aroma enhanced by citrus notes. It becomes increasingly fruity as the English hops kick in. Smooth, gentle hop bitterness in the finish.

Nelsons Column (OG 1051, ABV 5.2%)
A ruby red, strong old English ale.

Turkey

▯ **Turkey Brewery, Turkey Inn, Goose Eye, Oakworth, Keighley, West Yorkshire, BD22 0PD**
Tel (01535) 681339
Tours by arrangement

⊛ Turkey is a purpose-built brewery with walls four feet thick, built into the hillside at the back of the pub. Some of the beers are named after local caves. Brewery trips are free, with a small donation to Upper Wharfdale Fell Rescue. Beer festivals are staged every May Bank Holiday.

Bitter (ABV 3.9%)

Black Shiver (ABV 4.3%)

Twickenham

Twickenham Fine Ales Ltd, Ryecroft Works, Edwin Road, Twickenham, Middlesex, TW2 6SP
Tel (020) 8241 1825
✉ info@twickenham-fine-ales.co.uk
⊕ twickenham-fine-ales.co.uk
Tours by arrangement

The 10-barrel brewery was set up in 2004 and was the first brewery in Twickenham since the 1920s. The brewery supplies around 200 pubs and clubs in west London and the surrounding counties. Seasonal beers: Summer Gold (ABV 4.1%), Spring Ale (ABV 4.3%), Autumn Blaze (ABV 4.4%), Strong & Dark (ABV 5.2%, winter).

Crane Sundancer (OG 1037, ABV 3.7%) ▯ ◄
Strong citrus hops dominate this light gold beer. Malt softens the bitter finish that is clean and slightly astringent.

Advantage Ale (OG 1040, ABV 4%) ◄
Smooth amber beer with citrus notes throughout. The aroma has a touch of spice that disappears; hops and malt give way to a dry, bitter finish.

Original (OG 1042, ABV 4.2%) ◄
Brown coloured with a toffee malt aroma heralds a sweet malt character in both the flavour and aftertaste, which is balanced by a mild hopppiness.

Naked Ladies (OG 1044, ABV 4.4%)

Daisy Cutter (OG 1061, ABV 6.1%)
A golden-coloured, strong ale with a fruity, citrus nose and flavour.

Tydd Steam*

Tydd Steam Brewery, Manor Barn, Kirkgate, Tydd Saint Giles, Cambridgeshire, PE13 5NE
Tel (01945) 871020/07932 726552
✉ tyddsteam@fsmail.net

Tydd Steam operates on a custom-built 5.5-barrel micro-brewery in an agricultural barn. The barn used to house two working farm steam engines, which have now been moved to the Museum of Lincolnshire Life. At time of going to press two regular brews were planned, Piston Bitter and Lubrication Ale.

Ufford

Ufford Ales Ltd, Ye Olde White Hart, Main Street, Ufford, Cambridgeshire, PE9 3BH
Tel (01780) 740250
✉ info@ufford-ales.co.uk
⊕ ufford-ales.co.uk
Tours by arrangement

⊠ Ufford Ales opened in 2005. It supplies seven regular outlets and the products are often found as guest beers in other local pubs. Due to demand, the brewery started operating full time in 2006 and there are plans to expand capacity. Seasonal beers: Red Clover (ABV 4.5%, summer/autumn), Setting Sun (ABV 5.2%, summer), Snow Storm (ABV 5.3%, winter). Bottle-conditioned beer: White Hart.

Idle Hour (OG 1040, ABV 3.9%) ◆
Amber-gold bitter with a light malty aroma. The malt is supported in the mouth by a gentle hoppy bite as the bitterness grows.

White Hart (ABV 3.8%)

Uley

Uley Brewery Ltd, The Old Brewery, 31 The Street, Uley, Gloucestershire, GL11 5TB
Tel (01453) 860120
✉ chas@uleybrewery.com
⊕ uleybrewery.com

⊠ Brewing at Uley began in 1833 as Price's Brewery. After a long gap, the premises were restored and Uley Brewery opened in 1985. It has its own spring water, which is used to mash with Tucker's Maris Otter malt and boiled with Herefordshire hops. Uley serves around 40 free trade outlets in the Cotswold area and is brewing to capacity.

Hogshead PA (OG 1030, ABV 3.5%) ◆
A pale-coloured, hoppy session bitter with a good hop aroma and a full flavour for its strength, ending in a bittersweet aftertaste.

Bitter (OG 1040, ABV 4%) ◆
A copper-coloured beer with hops and fruit in the aroma and a malty, fruity taste, underscored by a hoppy bitterness. The finish is dry, with a balance of hops and malt.

Laurie Lee's Bitter (OG 1045, ABV 4.5%)

Old Ric (OG 1045, ABV 4.5%) ◆
A full-flavoured, hoppy bitter with some fruitiness and a smooth, balanced finish. Distinctively copper-coloured, this is the house beer for the Old Spot Inn, Dursley.

Old Spot Prize Ale (OG 1050, ABV 5%) ▨ ◆
A distinctive full-bodied, red/brown ale with a fruity aroma, a malty, fruity taste, with a hoppy bitterness, and a strong, balanced aftertaste.

Pig's Ear Strong Beer (OG 1050, ABV 5%) ◆
A pale-coloured beer, deceptively strong. Notably bitter in flavour, with a hoppy, fruity aroma and a bitter finish.

Ulverston

Ulverston Brewing Co, Diamond Buildings, Pennington Lane, Lindal in Furness, Cumbria, LA12 0LA
Tel (01229) 584280/07840 192022
✉ info.ubc@tiscali.co.uk
⊕ ulverstonbrewingco.co.uk

☺ The brewery went into production in 2006, the first beers to be brewed in Ulverston since the closure of Hartleys in 1991. It is situated in a building which used to house the winding gear for the Lindal Moor Mining Company. Most of the beers are named using a Laurel and Hardy theme after Ulverston's most famouse son, Stan Laurel. 25 outlets are supplied.

Harvest Moon (OG 1039, ABV 3.9%)

Another Fine Mess (OG 1040, ABV 4%)

Laughing Gravy (OG 1040, ABV 4%)

Lonesome Pine (OG 1042, ABV 4.2%)

UXB (OG 1042, ABV 4.2%)

Stout Olive (OG 1042, ABV 4.3%)

Bad Medicine (OG 1059, ABV 6.3%)

Uncle Stuarts EAB

Uncle Stuarts Brewery, Antoma, Pack Lane, Lingwood, Norwich, Norfolk, NR13 4PD
Tel (01603) 211833/07732 012112
✉ stuartsbrewery@aol.com
⊕ unclestuartsbrewery.com
Tours by arrangement

The brewery started in 2002, selling bottle-conditioned beers and polypins direct to customers and by mail order. Since 2003, all the beers have also been available in nine-gallon casks. Seasonal beer: Xmas (ABV 7%).

Pack Lane (OG 1038, ABV 4%)

Excelsior (OG 1042, ABV 4.5%) ◆
Copper-coloured beer with a gentle hop aroma. Lightly flavoured with a good balance of hoppy bitterness countered by a vinous fruit base. Finish subsides to a bitter dryness.

Church View (OG 1050, ABV 4.7%)

Buckenham Woods (OG 1051, ABV 5.6%) ◆
Spicy with more than a hint of raisin and sultana. Heavy aroma translates into a richly-flavoured ale with a surprisingly light and creamy mouthfeel.

Union*

⚲ Union Brewery, Dartmoor Union, Fore Street, Holbeton, Devon, PL8 1NE
Tel (01752) 830288
✉ info@dartmoorunion.co.uk
⊕ dartmoorunion.co.uk

Union started brewing in 2007 on a three-barrel brew plant.

Union Pride (ABV 3.9%)

Union Jacks (ABV 4.5%)

Upper Agbrigg

See Holme Valley Ales

Vale SIBA

Vale Brewery Co,
Tramway Business Park,
Luggershall Road, Brill,
Buckinghamshire, HP18 9TY
Tel (01844) 239237
✉ info@valebrewery.co.uk
⊕ valebrewery.co.uk
Tours by arrangement

After many years working for large regional breweries and allied industries, brothers Mark and Phil Stevens opened a small, purpose-built brewery in Haddenham in 1994. The plant expanded several times and due to its success relocated to larger premises in 2007. Four pubs are owned, including brewery tap the Hop Pole in Aylesbury, and over 250 local outlets are supplied. Seasonal beers: Hadda's Spring Gold (ABV 4.6%), Hadda's Summer Glory (ABV 4%), Hadda's Autumn Ale (ABV 4.5%), Hadda's Winter Solstice (ABV 4.1%), Good King Senseless (ABV 5.2%). Bottle-conditioned beers: all regular cask beers. All are suitable for vegetarians and vegans.

Best Bitter (OG 1036, ABV 3.7%) ◆
This pale amber beer starts with a slight fruit aroma. This leads to a clean, bitter taste where hops and fruit dominate. The finish is long and bitter with a slight hop note.

Wychert Ale (OG 1038, ABV 3.9%)
A full-flavoured beer with nutty overtones.

Black Swan (OG 1038, ABV 3.9%)
A traditional ale, dark and smooth with an impressive full roast flavour that belies its strength.

VPA/Vale Pale Ale (ABV 4.2%)
An elegantly hopped golden amber ale. A strong hop flavour gives way to a dry, refreshing finish.

Black Beauty Porter (OG 1043, ABV 4.3%) ◆
A complex, black-coloured porter with little aroma and a thin, balanced bittersweet taste with roast flavours dominating. The finish is dry and bitter.

Edgar's Golden Ale (OG 1043, ABV 4.3%) ◆
A golden, hoppy best bitter with some sweetness and a dry, bittersweet finish. An unpretentious and well-crafted beer.

Special (OG 1046, ABV 4.5%)
Deep brown-coloured premium ale brewed with Maris Otter, crystal and chocolate malts blended with choicest hops.

Grumpling Premium Ale (OG 1046, ABV 4.6%)
Ruby premium ale with complex malt and hop flavours and a moorish smack.

Hadda's Headbanger (OG 1050, ABV 5%)

Vale of Glamorgan

Vale of Glamorgan Brewery Ltd, Unit 8a, Atlantic Trading Estate, Barry, Vale of Glamorgan, CF63 3RF
Tel (01446) 730757
✉ info@vogbrewery.co.uk
⊕ vogbrewery.co.uk
Tours by arrangement (Max 15 people)

⊛ Vale of Glamorgan Brewery started brewing in 2005 on a 10-barrel plant. More than 40 local outlets are supplied. Seasonal beer: Special VoG (ABV 4.8%, winter).

Oggy VoG (ABV 4%)

VoG No. 1 (OG 1039, ABV 4.2%)

Grog Y VoG (OG 1043, ABV 4.3%)

Valhalla

Valhalla Brewery, Shetland Refreshments Ltd, Baltasound, Unst, Shetland, ZE2 9DX
Tel (01957) 711658
✉ mail@valhallabrewery.co.uk
⊕ valhallabrewery.co.uk
Tours by arrangement

The brewery started production in 1997, set up by husband and wife team Sonny and Sylvia Priest. A bottling plant was installed in 1999. The Priests plan a new brewery/visitor centre within the next two years. One outlet is supplied direct.

White Wife (OG 1038, ABV 3.8%) ◆
Predominantly malty aroma with hop and fruit, which remain on the palate. The aftertaste is increasingly bitter.

Old Scatness (OG 1038, ABV 4%)
A light bitter, named after an archaeological dig at the south end of Shetland where early evidence of malting and brewing was found. One of the ingredients is an ancient strain of barley called Bere which used to be common in Shetland until the middle of the last century.

Simmer Dim (OG 1039, ABV 4%) ◆
A light golden ale, named after the long Shetland twilight. The sulphur features do not mask the fruits and hops of this well-balanced beer.

Auld Rock (OG 1043, ABV 4.5%) ◆
A full-bodied, dark Scottish-style best bitter, it has a rich malty nose but does not lack bitterness in the long dry finish.

Sjolmet Stout (OG 1048, ABV 5%) ◆
Full of malt and roast barley, especially in the taste. Smooth, creamy, fruity finish, not as dry as some stouts.

Ventnor SIBA

Ventnor Brewery Ltd, 119 High Street, Ventnor, Isle of Wight, PO38 1LY
Tel (01983) 856161
✉ sales@ventnorbrewery.co.uk
⊕ ventnorbrewery.co.uk
Shop Mon-Fri 9am-5pm; Sat 10.30am-1pm

Beer has been brewed on the site since 1840. The beers today are still made with St Boniface natural spring water that flows through the brewery. Ventnor has a 10-barrel plant and supplies pub chains, wholesalers and supermarkets nationwide. Seasonal beers: see website. Bottle-conditioned beer: Old Ruby Ale (ABV 4.7%). Hygeia Organic Ale is suitable for vegetarians and vegans.

Golden Bitter (OG 1040, ABV 4%)
Creamy, light bitter with hints of honey and gorse persisting through to the aftertaste.

Sunfire (OG 1043, ABV 4.3%) ◆
A generously and distinctively bittered amber beer that could be toned down if pulled through a sparkler.

Hippy High Ale (ABV 4.4%)
A light, hoppy beer brewed especially for Radio 1 DJ Rob Da Bank's first Bestival 2004 on the Isle of Wight.

Pistol Night (OG 1043, ABV 4.4%) ◆
Deceptive light, flowery, hoppy bitter with scents and flavours of early spring that continue through to a pleasant and satisfying finish.

Oyster Stout (OG 1045, ABV 4.5%) ◆
Rich, sugary, malty but watery dark brown beer.

Hygeia Organic Ale (OG 1046, ABV 4.6%) ◆
A malty but refreshing beer.

Wight Spirit (OG 1050, ABV 5%) ◆
Predominantly bitter, hoppy and fruity strong and very pale ale.

Sandrock Smoked Ale (OG 1056, ABV 5.6%)
A smoked beer created to commemorate the famous Sandrock Inn in Niton, tragically destroyed by fire in 1985. Brewed using peated malt and a combination of hops.

Village Brewer

See Hambleton

Wadworth IFBB

Wadworth & Co Ltd, Northgate Brewery, Devizes, Wiltshire, SN10 1JW
Tel (01380) 723361
✉ sales@wadworth.co.uk
⊕ wadworth.co.uk
Shop (reception) Mon-Fri 9am-5pm
Tours: Trade April-Oct; Public September
(by prior arrangement)

⊗ A market town brewery set up in 1885 by Henry Wadworth, it is one of few remaining producers to sell beer locally in oak casks; the brewery still employs a cooper. Though solidly traditional, with its own dray horses, it continues to invest in the future and to expand, producing up to 2,000 barrels a week to supply a wide-ranging free trade, around 300 outlets in the south of England, as well as its own 256 pubs. All tied houses serve cask beer. Wadworth also has a 2.5-barrel micro-brewery used for brewing trials, speciality brews and the production of cask mild. Seasonal beers: Old Father Timer (ABV 5.8%, Nov-Dec), Malt n' Hops (ABV 4.5%, Oct-Nov), Summersault (ABV 4%, May-Sep), Bishops Tipple (ABV 5.5%, winter).

Henry's Original IPA (OG 1035, ABV 3.6%)
A light copper bitter with a balanced flavour and long-lasting biscuity aftertaste.

6X (OG 1041, ABV 4.3%) ◆
Copper-coloured ale with a malty and fruity nose, and some balancing hop character. The flavour is similar, with some bitterness and a lingering malty, but bitter finish.

JCB (OG 1046 ABV 4.7%)
An amber ale with a rich, malty body, complex hop character and a hint of tropical fruit in the aroma and taste. A barley sugar sweetness blends with nutty malt and hop bitterness before a dry, biscuity, bitter finish.

Wagtail

Wagtail Brewery, New Barn Farm, Wilby Warrens, Old Buckenham, Norfolk, NR17 1PF
Tel (01953) 887133
✉ wagtailbrewery@btinternet.com
⊕ wagtailbrewery.com
Shop Sat 10am-5pm

Wagtail brewery went into full-time production in 2006. There are plans to make it the first brewery to be turbine powered. All cask-conditioned beers are also available bottle-conditioned and are suitable for vegetarians and vegans.

Best Bitter (ABV 4%)

Golden Ale (ABV 4%)

English Ale (ABV 4.5%)

Irish Ale (ABV 4.5%)

Ruby Ale (ABV 4.5%)

Stout (ABV 4.5%)

Wapping

⚲ **Wapping Beers Ltd, Baltic Fleet, 33A Wapping, Liverpool, Merseyside, L1 8DQ**
Tel (0151) 707 2242

☺ Established in 2002, Wapping has expanded by installing two additional fermenting vessels, increasing capacity by half. The brewery delivers to trade in the local area. Seasonal beer: Winter Ale (ABV 6.5%, Nov-Feb).

Bitter (OG 1036, ABV 3.6%)
Light, easy-drinking session beer with a good, bitter finish.

Bowsprit (OG 1036, ABV 3.6%) ◆
Dry, hoppy session beer with a satisfyingly dry, bitter aftertaste. Hint of fruitiness on the aroma.

Baltic Gold (OG 1039, ABV 3.9%) ◆
Hoppy golden ale with plenty of citrus hop flavour. Refreshing with good body and mouthfeel.

Summer Ale (OG 1042, ABV 4.2%) ◆
Refresing golden beer with floral hops dominating the nose and taste. Some fruit also on the aroma and in the taste. Good bitterness throughout, leading to a dry, bitter aftertaste.

Stout (OG 1050, ABV 5%) ◆
Classic dry roasty stout with strong bitterness balanced by fruit and hop flavours. The flavours follow through to a pleasantly dry finish.

Warcop

Warcop Country Ales, 9 Nellive Park, St Brides Wentlooge, Gwent, NP10 8SE
Tel (01633) 680058
✉ william.picton@tesco.net
⊕ warcopales.com

A small brewery based in a converted milking parlour. Cask ales are also available bottle conditioned. The beers are made on a cyclical basis, with five to six beers normally in stock at any one time: see website for full range. There is also a stock of four to eight bottled beers. Seasonal beers: see website.

Pit Shaft (ABV 3.4%)

Pitside (ABV 3.7%)

Pit Prop (ABV 3.8%) ◈
Fruit and roast aroma, dark brown in colour. A mixture of roast, malt, caramel and fruit in taste and aftertaste. The bitterness builds, adding to the character.

Black and Amber (ABV 4%)

Steeler's (ABV 4.2%)

Brokers (ABV 4.3%)

Cutters (ABV 4.4%)

Honeyed Stout (ABV 4.5%)

Printers (ABV 4.6%)

Forgers (ABV 4.8%)

Deep Pit (ABV 5%)

Blasters (ABV 5.4%)

Fulcrum (ABV 5.6%)

QE2 (ABV 6%)

Warrior

Warrior Brewing Co, 4 Old Matford House, Old Matford Lane, Alphington, Exeter, EX2 8XS
Tel (01392) 221451
✉ warrior@warrior.go-plus.net

James and Jude Warrior started brewing in 2004. James has been a professional actor for more than 30 years and has to suspend brewing from time to time when he is called away to work in the theatre or appear before the cameras. The brewery has a five-barrel plant and supplies around 12 outlets. Seasonal beer: Custer's Last Stand (ABV 6.8%, Dec-Feb).

Tomahawk (OG 1042, ABV 4%)
A full-bodied bitter with lots of hops.

Geronimo (OG 1049, ABV 4.9%)
A hoppy, refreshing amber bitter.

Crazy Horse (ABV 5%)
Pale gold in colour, dry and hoppy.

Warwickshire

Warwickshire Beer Co Ltd, The Brewery, Queen Street, Cubbington, Warwickshire, CV32 7NA
Tel (01926) 450747
✉ info@warwickshirebeer.co.uk
⊕ warwickshirebeer.co.uk
Shop Sat 8am-12pm (ring first)
Tours by arrangement

Warwickshire is a six-barrel brewery operating in a former village bakery since 1998. Brewing takes place four times a week and, in addition, some beer is produced under licence by Highgate Brewery. The cask beers are available in around 80 outlets as well as the brewery's two pubs. Seasonal beers: Xmas Bare (ABV 4.9%), Thunderbolt (ABV 8.5%). Bottle-conditioned beers: Best Bitter, Lady Godiva, Churchyard Bob, King Maker.

Shakespeare's County (OG 1034, ABV 3.4%)
A very light session ale.

Best Bitter (OG 1039, ABV 3.9%)
A golden brown session bitter flavoured with First Gold hops.

Lady Godiva (OG 1042, ABV 4.2%)
Blond, gentle, and full-bodied.

Falstaff (OG 1044, ABV 4.4%)
A mahogany-coloured bitter flavoured with Cascade and First Gold hops.

Golden Bear (OG 1049, ABV 4.9%)
Golden in colour with well-balanced bitterness and spicy/fruity notes.

Churchyard Bob (OG 1049, ABV 4.9%)

King Maker (OG 1055, ABV 5.5%)

Watermill

Watermill Brewing Co, Watermill Inn, Ings, nr Staveley, Kendal, Cumbria, LA8 9PY
Tel (01539) 821309
✉ doggiebeer@tiscali.co.uk
⊕ watermillinn.co.uk
Tours by arrangement

Watermill was established in 2006 in a purpose-built extension to the inn. The five-barrel plant and equipment were originally at the Hops Bar & Grill opposite Daytona International Speedway, U.S. The beers have a doggie theme; dogs are allowed in the main bar of the pub and usually get served with biscuits before their owners.

Collie Wobbles (ABV 3.9%)

A Bit'er Ruff (ABV 4.2%)

W'Ruff Night (ABV 5%)

Tomos Watkin SIBA

Hurns Brewing Company Ltd t/a Tomos Watkin, Unit 3, Century Park, Valley Way, Swansea Enterprise Park, Swansea, SA6 8RP
Tel (01792) 797300/797264
✉ beer@hurns.co.uk
⊕ hurnsbeer.co.uk
Shop Mon-Fri 9am-5pm
Tours by arrangement

Brewing started in 1995 in Llandeilo using a 10-barrel plant in converted garages. Tomos Watkin moved to bigger premises in Swansea in 2000 and the plant increased to a 50-barrel capacity. HBC Ltd was formed in 2002 when the Swansea Brewery was purchased from Tomos Watkin. Plans are under way to build a state-of-the-art, interactive visitor centre with shop and brewery tap. Some 100 outlets are supplied. Seasonal beers: Cwrw Ceridwen (ABV 4.2%, spring), Cwrw Haf (ABV 4.2%, summer ⬆), Owain Glyndwr (ABV 4.2%, autumn), Cwrw Santa (ABV 4.6%, winter).

Cwrw Braf (OG 1037, ABV 3.7%)

Brewery Bitter (OG 1041, ABV 4%) ◈
Dark amber with a malt and hop aroma. A
rounded blend of malt, hops and fruit with a
building bitterness.

Merlin Stout (OG 1043, ABV 4.2%) ▣ ◈
Dark brown with a malty and roast aroma.
Pleasing blend of malt, roast, caramel and
background hop flavour with a balancing
bitterness and a similar lasting finish. A
rounded and satisfying beer.

Old Style Bitter/OSB (OG 1046, ABV 4.5%) ◈
Amber-coloured with an inviting aroma of
hops and malt. Full bodied; hops, fruit, malt
and bitterness combine to give a balanced
flavour continuing into the finish.

Waveney

◊ Waveney Brewing Co, Queen's Head, Station
Road, Earsham, Norfolk, NR35 2TS
Tel (01986) 892623
✉ lyndahamps@aol.com

Established at the Queens Head in 2004, the
five-barrel brewery produces three beers,
regularly available at the pub along with free
trade outlets. Occasional beers are brewed and
there are plans to bottle beers. Seasonal beer:
Raging Bullace (ABV 5.1%, Dec-Jan), Sugar Ray
(ABV 4.4%, Mar-May).

East Coast Mild (OG 1037, ABV 3.8%) ◈
A traditional mild with distinctive roast malt
aroma and red-brown colouring. A sweet,
plummy malt beginning quickly fades as a
dry roasted bitterness begins to make its
presence felt.

Lightweight (OG 1039, ABV 3.9%) ◈
A gentle beer with a light but well-balanced
hop and malt character. A light body is reflected
in the quick, bitter finish. Golden hued with a
distinctive strawberry and cream nose.

Great White Hope (OG 1047, ABV 4.8%) ◈
A well-balanced golden brew with a dry,
bitter character. Grapefruit in both aroma and
taste gives depth and contrast. A long,
slightly hoppy ending lingers on.

Waylands*

Wayland's Brewery, 6 Marley Close,
Addlestone, Surrey, KT15 1AR
Tel 07956 531618
✉ s.wayland@ntlworld.com
⊕ waylandsbrewery.co.uk

⊗ Waylands was established in 2007 on a 2.5-
barrel plant and is a part-time venture at present.
Seasonal beers: Waylands Winter Warmer (ABV
4.6%), Staggering Santa (ABV 5.2%).

Olympic Gold (ABV 3.8%)

Addled Ale (ABV 4.3%)

Special FX (ABV 5.2%)

WC

WC Brewery, 3 Micklegate, Mickle Trafford,
Chester, CH2 4TF
✉ thegents@wcbrewery.com
⊕ wcbrewery.com

⊕ Founded in 2003 by Ian Williams and Steve Carr,
the WC Brewery is one of the smallest commercial
breweries in the country. The Gents generally brew
to order for local pubs and beer festivals. Seasonal
beers: B'Day (ABV 3.8%, Jun), Autumn's Platter
(ABV 4.3%), Yellow Snow (ABV 5.5%, Jan).

IPA Ale (ABV 3.8%)
A pale beer, heavily hopped for extra
bitterness and a lingering citrus finish.

Golden Cascade (ABV 4%)

Gypsy's Kiss (ABV 4.1%)
A copper-coloured ale brewed to produce a
well-balanced session bitter.

SBD (ABV 5%)
A premium ale; rich, fruity and deceptively strong.

Wear Valley

Wear Valley Brewery, The Grand, South Church
Road, Bishop Auckland, Co Durham, DL14 6DU
Tel 07810 751425
✉ mail@the-grand-hotel.co.uk
⊕ wear-valley-brewery.co.uk
Tours by arrangement

The brewery was established in 2005 on a four-
barrel plant situated at the rear of the Grand
Hotel. It was opened by the Bishop of Durham
and the first brew was named Bishop's Blessing
in his honour. Most of the beers are locally
themed. Seasonal beers: Weardale Wheat (ABV
4.3%, summer), Wear Wolf (ABV 4.3%, Oct),
Wear Three Kings (ABV 4.5%, Xmas). All beers
are suitable for vegetarians and vegans.

Weardale Bitter (OG 1037, ABV 3.7%)

Auckland Glory (OG 1038, ABV 3.8%)

Blue Gentian (OG 1040, ABV 4%)

Tindale Tipple (OG 1040, ABV 4%)

Weardale Blonde (OG 1040, ABV 4%)

Hamsterley Dark Ale (OG 1042, ABV 4.2%)

Auckland Ale (OG 1043, ABV 4.3%)

Hamsterley Gold (OG 1050, ABV 5%)

Weatheroak

Weatheroak Brewery Ltd,
Coach & Horses Inn, Weatheroak Hill,
Alvechurch, Birmingham, B48 7EA
Tel 07798 773894 (day)/
(0121) 445 4411 (eve)
✉ dave@weatheroakales.co.uk
⊕ weatheroakales.co.uk

⊕ The brewery was set up in 1997 in an outhouse
at the Coach & Horses. The first brew was produced
in 1998. A real ale off-licence has been opened in
nearby Alvechurch. Weatheroak supplies 40 outlets.
Seasonal beer: Miss Stout (ABV 4.7%, winter).

Light Oak (ABV 3.6%) ◈
This straw-coloured quaffing ale has lots of
hoppy notes on the tongue and nose, and a
fleetingly sweet aftertaste.

Ale (ABV 4.1%) ◈
The aroma is dominated by hops in this
golden-coloured brew. Hops also feature in
the mouth and there is a rapidly fading dry
aftertaste.

Redwood (ABV 4.7%) ◈
A rich tawny strong bitter with a short-lived sweet fruit and malt balance.

Keystone Hops (ABV 5%) ◈
A golden yellow beer that is surprisingly easy to quaff given the strength. Fruity hops are the dominant flavour without the commonly associated astringency.

**For Bricktop Brewery
(Gate Hangs Well, Woodgate):**

Scoop (ABV 3.7%)
A honey beer with a pleasing bitter flavour and slightly sweet aftertaste.

Duck and Cover (ABV 4.3%)

Winner Takes It All (ABV 4.6%)

Webbs

**Webbs Brewery Ltd, Unit 12, Cwm Small Business Centre, Cwm, Ebbw Vale, NP23 7TB
Tel (01495) 370026/07812 172413**
✉ info@webbsbrewery.co.uk
⊕ webbsbrewery.co.uk
Tours by arrangement

The brewery was set up in 2006 with a six-barrel plant. It is named after an old brewery in nearby Aberbeeg that was closed by Bass Charrington in 1969. Bottled beers are also produced with occasional bottle-conditioned beers.

Huntsman (ABV 3.8%)

Black Widow (ABV 4.5%)

Arachnaphobia (ABV 5.1%)

Weetwood

**Weetwood Ales Ltd, Weetwood Grange, Weetwood, Tarporley, Cheshire, CW6 0NQ
Tel (01829) 752377**
✉ sales@weetwoodales.co.uk
⊕ weetwoodales.co.uk

⊛ The brewery was set up at an equestrian centre in 1993. In 1998, the five-barrel plant was replaced by a 10-barrel kit. Around 200 regular customers are supplied.

Best Bitter (OG 1038.5, ABV 3.8%) ◈
Pale brown beer with an assertive bitterness and a lingering dry finish. Despite initial sweetness, peppery hops dominate throughout.

Cheshire Cat (ABV 4%) ◈
Pale, dry bitter with a spritzy lemon zest and a grapy aroma. Hoppy aroma leads through to the initial taste before fruitiness takes over. Smooth creamy mouthfeel and a short, dry finish.

Eastgate Ale (OG 1043.5, ABV 4.2%) ◈
Well-balanced and refreshing clean amber beer. Citrus fruit flavours predominate in the taste and there is a short, dry aftertaste.

Old Dog Bitter (OG 1045, ABV 4.5%) ◈
Robust, well-balanced amber beer with a slightly fruity aroma. Rich malt and fruit flavours are balanced by bitterness. Some sweetness and a hint of sulphur on nose and taste.

Ambush Ale (OG 1047.5, ABV 4.8%) ◈
Full-bodied malty, premium bitter with initial sweetness balanced by bitterness and

leading to a long-lasting dry finish. Blackberries and bitterness predominate alongside the hops.

Oasthouse Gold (OG 1050, ABV 5%) 🗇 ◈
Straw-coloured, crisp, full-bodied and fruity golden ale with a good dry finish.

Wellington

See Crown & Wellington

Wells & Young's

See New national breweries section

Welton's SIBA

**Welton's Brewery, 1 Mulberry Trading Estate, Foundry Lane, Horsham, West Sussex, RH13 5PX
Tel (01403) 242901/251873**
✉ sales@weltons.co.uk
⊕ weltons.co.uk
Tours by arrangement

Ray Welton moved his brewery to a factory unit in Horsham in 2003, which has given him space to expand. Around 400 outlets in the south-east are supplied.

Pride 'n' Joy (ABV 2.8%) ◈
A light brown bitter with a slight malty and hoppy aroma. Fruity with a pleasant hoppiness and some sweetness in the flavour, leading to a short malty finish.

Kid & Bard (OG 1036, ABV 3.5%) ◈
Some fruit and hops in the aroma lead to a well-balanced beer with hops dominating, but malt and fruit prevalent. Bitterness grows in to a pleasant hoppy, bitter finish.

Horsham Bitter (ABV 3.8%)

Sussex Pride (ABV 4%)

Old Cocky (OG 1043, ABV 4.3%)

Horsham Old (OG 1046, ABV 4.5%) ◈
Roast and toffee flavours predominate with some bitterness in this traditional old ale. Bittersweet with plenty of caramel and roast in a rather short finish.

Old Harry (OG 1051, ABV 5.2%)

Wensleydale

**Wensleydale Brewery Ltd, Manor Farm, Bellerby, Leyburn, North Yorkshire, DL8 5QH
Tel (01969) 622327**
✉ info@wensleydalebrewery.com
⊕ wensleydalebrewery.com
Tours by arrangement

⊠ Wensleydale Brewery (formerly Lidstone's) was set up in 2003 on a two-barrel plant in Yorkshire Dales National Park. A year later the brewery relocated to larger premises six miles away. In 2006 Wensleydale bought its second pub, the Three Horseshoes at Wensley. Most beers are available as bottle-conditioned ales. About 30 outlets are supplied.

Lidstone's Rowley Mild (OG 1037, ABV 3.2%) ◈
Chocolate and toffee aromas lead into what, for its strength, is an impressively rich and flavoursome taste. The finish is pleasantly bittersweet.

Forester's Session Bitter (OG 1038, ABV 3.7%) ◆
Intensely aromatic, straw-coloured ale offering a superb balance of malt and hops on the tongue.

Semer Water (OG 1041, ABV 4.1%)
Golden ale with a hint of banana on the nose. The taste is clean, crisp and hoppy, with grapefruit flavours also present.

Coverdale Gamekeeper (OG 1042, ABV 4.3%)
A light copper best bitter with a lingering aftertaste.

Aysgarth Falls (ABV 4.4%)
A thirst-quenching cloudy wheat beer with tart apple and banana fruit.

Black Dub Oat Stout (OG 1044, ABV 4.4%)
Black beer brimming with roasted chocolate taste and aroma.

Polly Peacham (ABV 4.4%)
A light Pilsner-type lager.

Coverdale Poacher IPA (OG 1049, ABV 5%) ◆
Citrus flavours dominate both aroma and taste in this pale, smooth, refreshing beer; the aftertaste is quite dry.

Hardraw Force Strong Ale (ABV 5.6%)
A well-balanced premium ale with a fine malty, hoppy character.

Barley Wine (ABV 8.5%)
A rich, complex, strong ale with a lingering bittersweet aftertaste.

Wentworth SIBA

Wentworth Brewery Ltd, Power House, Gun Park, Wentworth, South Yorkshire, S62 7TF
Tel (01226) 747070
✉ info@wentworth-brewery.co.uk
⊕ wentworth-brewery.co.uk
Tours by arrangement

Brewing started at Wentworth in 1999. In 2006 custom-built brewing kit was installed, increasing production to 30 barrels a day. More than 300 outlets are supplied.

Imperial Ale (OG 1038, ABV 3.8%)
A tawny, bitter beer with a floral nose. There is a slight hint of sweetness on the aftertaste.

WPA (OG 1039.5, ABV 4%) ◆
An extremely well hopped IPA-style beer that leads to some astringency. A very bitter beer.

Best Bitter (OG 1040, ABV 4.1%) ◆
A hoppy, bitter beer with hints of citrus fruits. A bitter taste dominates the aftertaste.

Bumble Beer (OG 1043, ABV 4.3%)
A pale golden beer, made with local honey, which gives it a unique and distinctive flavour throughout the year.

Black Zac (OG 1046, ABV 4.6%)
A mellow, dark ruby-red ale with chocolate and pale malts leading to a bitter taste, with a coffee finish.

Oatmeal Stout (OG 1050, ABV 4.8%) ◆
Black, smooth, with roast and chocolate malt and toffee overtones.

Rampant Gryphon (OG 1062, ABV 6.2%) ◆
A strong, well-balanced golden ale with hints of fruit and sweetness but which retains a hoppy character.

Weobley*

Weobley Organic Beers Ltd, Unit 6, Whitehill Park, Weobley, Herefordshire, HR4 8QE
Tel (01544) 319333

A brewery established in the same building as the now defunct Wild's Brewery, brewing two organic bottled beers on new equipment. The beers are based on the old Wild's recipes; Weobley's Blonde (ABV 5%), Weobley's Gold (ABV 5%).

Wessex SIBA

Wessex Brewery, Rye Hill Farm, Longbridge Deverill, Warminster, Wiltshire, BA12 7DE
Tel (01985) 844532
✉ wessexbrewery@tinyworld.co.uk
Tours by arrangement

⊗ The brewery went into production in 2001 as Hobden's Wessex Brewery and moved to a new building in 2004, at which time the name Wessex Brewery was adopted. 10 outlets are supplied by the brewery with all beers always available through wholesalers. Westbury Ales beers are also produced here.

Naughty Ferrets (OG 1035, ABV 3.5%)
A session bitter with full flavour. Tawny colour, spicy bitterness and citrus hop aroma.

Horningsham Pride (OG 1040, ABV 4%)
A pale, sweet, hoppy beer.

Crockerton Classic (OG 1041, ABV 4.1%)
A full-bodied, tawny, full-flavoured bitter; fruity and malty.

Kilmington Best (OG 1041, ABV 4.2%)
Sweet, hoppy bitter.

Deverill's Advocate (OG 1045, ABV 4.5%)

Warminster Warrior (OG 1045, ABV 4.5%)

Midnight Rambler (OG 1050, ABV 5%)

Russian Stoat (OG 1080, ABV 9%)

For Westbury Ales:

Amber Daze (OG 1038, ABV 3.8%)

Early Daze (OG 1040, ABV 4.1%)

Bitham Blonde (OG 1044, ABV 4.5%)

Midnight Mash (OG 1048, ABV 5%)

West Berkshire SIBA

West Berkshire Brewery Co Ltd, Old Bakery, Yattendon, Thatcham, Berkshire, RG18 0UE
Tel (01635) 202968 / 202638
✉ info@wbbrew.co.uk
⊕ wbbrew.co.uk
Shop Mon-Fri 10am-4pm; Sat 10am-1pm

The brewery, established in 1995, has since moved its main site to Yattendon. In 2006 the brewhouse was extended and a new plant installed, the original five-barrel plant at the Potkiln pub in Failsham has now closed. More than 100 outlets are supplied. One pub is owned, and the brewery hopes to acquire more to build a small estate. A monthly beer is also brewed. Seasonal beer: Spiced Porter (ABV 4.5%, Nov-Feb).

Old Father Thames (OG 1038, ABV 3.4%)
A traditional pale ale with a full flavour despite its low strength.

Mr Chubb's Lunchtime Bitter (OG 1040, ABV 3.7%) ◈
A malty session bitter. A malty caramel note dominates aroma and taste and is accompanied by a nutty bittersweetness and a hoppy aroma.

Maggs' Magnificent Mild (OG 1041, ABV 3.8%) ▣ ◈
Silky, full-bodied dark mild with a creamy head. Roast malt aroma is joined in the taste by caramel, sweetness and mild, fruity hoppiness. Aftertaste of roast malt with balancing bitterness.

Good Old Boy (OG 1043, ABV 4%) ◈
Well-rounded, tawny bitter with malt and hops dominating throughout and a balancing bitterness in the taste and aftertaste.

Dr Hexter's Wedding Ale (OG 1044, ABV 4.1%) ◈
Fruit and hops dominate the aroma and are joined in the bittersweet taste by a hint of malt. The aftertaste has a pleasant bitter hoppiness.

Full Circle (OG 1047, ABV 4.5%) ◈
A golden ale with a pleasing aroma and taste of bitter hops with a hint of malt. The aftertaste is hoppy and bitter with a rounding note of malt.

Dr Hexter's Healer (OG 1052, ABV 5%) ▣ ◈
Amber strong bitter with malt, caramel and hops in the aroma. The taste is a balance of malt, caramel, fruit, hops and bittersweetness. Caramel, fruit and bittersweetness dominate the aftertaste.

West Brewing

West Brewing Co Ltd, Binnie Place, Glasgow Green, Glasgow, G40 1AW
Tel (0141) 550 0135
✉ gordon@westbeer.com
⊕ westbeer.com
Tours by arrangement

West Brewing opened in 2006 and produces a full range of European-style beers. The two brewers are both German-trained in Munich and their copper-clad system, visible from the 300-seat bar and restaurant, is a fully-automated German one with an annual capacity of 1.5 million litres. Brewing is in strict accordance with the Reinheitsgebot, the German purity law, importing all malt, hops and yeast from Germany. Beers: Hefeweizen (ABV 4.9%); Munich-Style Helles (ABV 5%); St Mungo (ABV 4.9%); U-Bier (ABV 5.2%); Dunkel Hefeweizen (ABV 5.3%); Dunkel (ABV 4.9%).

Westbury

See Wessex

Westerham SIBA

Westerham Brewery Co Ltd, Grange Farm, Pootings Road, Crockham Hill, Edenbridge, Kent, TN8 6SA
Tel (01732) 864427
✉ sales@westerhambrewery.co.uk

⊕ westerhambrewery.co.uk
Shop Mon-Fri 9am-5pm
Tours by arrangement

The brewery was established in 2004 and restored a brewing tradition to Westerham that was lost when the Black Eagle Brewery was taken over by Ind Coope in 1959 and closed in 1965. Two of Black Eagle's yeast strains were deposited at the National Collection of Yeast Cultures and are used to recreate the true flavour of Westerham beers. The new brewery is based at the National Trust's Grange Farm in a former dairy and uses the same water supply as Black Eagle. Around 100 free trade outlets are supplied in Kent, Surrey and Sussex. Seasonal beers: General Wolfe Maple Ale (ABV 4.3%, autumn), God's Wallop Xmas Ale (ABV 4.3%), Puddledock Porter (ABV 4.3%, winter), Summer Perle (ABV 3.8%), Little Scotney Bitter (ABV 4.3%, summer). Bottle-conditioned beers: British Bulldog, William Wilberforce Freedom Ale (4.8%).

Finchcocks Original (OG 1036, ABV 3.5%)

Grasshopper Kentish Bitter (OG 1039, ABV 3.8%)

Black Eagle Special Pale Ale (OG 1039, ABV 3.8%)

British Bulldog (OG 1042, ABV 4.3%)

India Pale Ale (OG 1047, ABV 4.8%)

Sevenoaks Bitter 7X (OG 1046, ABV 4.8%)

Special Bitter Ale 1965 (OG 1048, ABV 4.9%)

WF6

WF6 Brewing Co, c/o 21 Rose Farm Approach, Altofts, West Yorkshire, WF6 2RZ
Tel 07876 141336/07767 351611
✉ r.d.turton@btinternet.com
⊕ wf6brewingcompany.co.uk

WF6 began brewing in 2004 with the brand name Birkwoods. The brewery is in a converted milking parlour. A custom-made five-barrel plant allows the brewery to produce a varying portfolio of seasonal beers, mostly at ABV 4.2%, that are supplied to distributors, pubs and festivals. Bottled beers are sold at farmers' markets.

Whalebone

♻ **Whalebone Brewery, 163 Wincolmlee, Hull, East Yorkshire, HU2 0PA**
Tel (01482) 226648
Tours by arrangement

The Whalebone pub, which dates from 1796, was bought by Hull CAMRA founding member Alex Craig in 2002. He opened the brewery the following year and his beers have names connected with the former whaling industry on the adjoining River Hull. Two or three outlets are supplied as well as the pub. Seasonal beers: Truelove Porter (ABV 4.7%), Joseph Allen (ABV 5%), Moby Dick (ABV 8%), Full Ship (ABV 8.4%).

Diana Mild (OG 1037, ABV 3.6%)

Neckoil Bitter (OG 1037, ABV 3.9%)

Wharfedale SIBA

Wharfedale Brewery Ltd, Coonlands Laithe, Hetton, Skipton, North Yorkshire, BD23 6LY

Tel (01756) 730555
✉ sales@follyale.com
🌐 follyale.com
Tours by arrangement

Opened in 2003 by the Duke of Kent, the brewery is based in an old hay barn within the Yorkshire Dales National Park. Water comes from its own 56 metres-deep borehole. Three beers are permanently available, plus two specials each month and are supplied to free houses and distributors throughout Yorkshire, Lancashire and the West Midlands. All beers are also available bottle conditioned. A range of monthly seasonals is also available.

Folly Ale (OG 1038, ABV 3.8%) ◈
A pale brown beer with crystal malt character throughout. Bitterness comes through in the taste and increases in the finish.

Executioner (OG 1046, ABV 4.5%) ◈
A complex reddish-brown ale, more akin to a strong mild than a best bitter. Malt and roast flavours combine with a vinous fruitiness, leading to a bitter finish.

Folly Gold (OG 1051, ABV 5%) ◈
A heavy, pale golden premium strong bitter with a fruity aroma and malty palate. The dry character extends into the finish.

Whim SIBA

Whim Ales Ltd, Whim Farm, Hartington, near Buxton, Derbyshire, SK17 0AX
Tel (01298) 84991

A brewery opened in 1993 in outbuildings at Whim Farm. Whim's beers are available in 50-70 outlets and the brewery's tied house, the Wilkes Head in Leek, Staffs. Some one-off brews are produced. Occasional/seasonal beers: Kaskade (ABV 4.3%, lager), Snow White (ABV 4.5%, wheat beer), Easter Special (ABV 4.8%), Stout Jenny (ABV 4.7%), Black Xmas (ABV 6.5%).

Arbor Light (OG 1035, ABV 3.6%)
Light-coloured bitter, sharp and clean with lots of hop character and a delicate light aroma.

Hartington Bitter (OG 1039, ABV 4%)
A light, golden-coloured, well-hopped session beer. A dry finish with a spicy, floral aroma.

Hartington IPA (OG 1045, ABV 4.5%)
Pale and light-coloured, smooth on the palate allowing malt to predominate. Slightly sweet finish combined with distinctive light hop bitterness. Well rounded.

White SIBA

White Brewing Co, 1066 Country Brewery, Pebsham Farm Industrial Estate, Pebsham Lane, Bexhill-on-Sea, East Sussex, TN40 2RZ
Tel (01424) 731066
✉ whitebrewing@fsbdial.co.uk
Tours by arrangement

The brewery was founded in 1995 to serve local free trade outlets and some wholesalers. White has expanded production threefold with the addition of seasonal and occasional beers. Around 30 outlets are supplied. Seasonal beers: White Gold (ABV 4.9%, summer), Chilly Willy (ABV 5.1%, winter), Old White Christmas (ABV 4%), Heart of Rother (spring).

1066 Country Bitter (OG 1040, ABV 4%)
Amber-gold in colour, a light, sweetish beer with good malt and hop balance, and a bitter, refreshing finish.

Dark (OG 1040, ABV 4%)

White Horse

White Horse Brewery Co Ltd, 3 White Horse Business Park, Ware Road, Stanford in the Vale, Oxfordshire, SN7 8NY
Tel (01367) 718700
🌐 whitehorsebrewery.com
Tours by arrangement

White Horse was founded on a modern industrial estate in 2004. The second-hand brewing plant was manufactured in Belgium and has a brew-length of 7.5 barrels. More than 100 outlets are supplied. Seasonal beers: Dragon Hill (ABV 4.2%), Flibbertigibbet (ABV 4.3%), Saracen (ABV 4.5%), Xmas Ale (ABV 4.8%).

Bitter (OG 1040, ABV 3.7%)

Village Idiot (OG 1043, ABV 4.1%)

Wayland Smithy (OG 1049, ABV 4.4%)

For Turf Tavern, Oxford:

Summer Ale (OG 1044, ABV 4.1%)

Guv'nor (OG 1066, ABV 6.5%)

White Star SIBA

White Star Brewery Ltd, The Brewery, Clewers Lane, Waltham Chase, Southampton, Hampshire, SO32 2LP
Tel (01489) 893926
✉ info@whitestarbrewery.com
Tours by arrangement

⊗ The brewery was set up in 2003 with a 10-barrel plant. The name comes from the White Star Shipping Line of Southampton, whose most famous liner was the Titanic. In 2006 the brewery moved to larger premises and now supplies more than 150 outlets. The core range of beers is available bottle conditioned. Seasonal beers: Frostbite (ABV 4.5%, Nov-Mar), Royal Standard (ABV 4.3%, May-Sep), Battleaxe (ABV 4.6%, May-Jun), Steamer (ABV 5%, Sep-Oct), Over the Moon (ABV 3.9%, Jul-Aug), Afrodizzysack (ABV 4.8%, Dec), Black Panther Stout (ABV 4.4%, Mar-Apr).

UXB (ABV 3.8%) ◈
Session bitter with little aroma and some hops and malt in the flavour and finish. Rather sulphurous throughout.

Crafty Shag (ABV 4.1%)
A Pilsner-style beer, brewed using German hops.

Majestic (ABV 4.2%) ◈
A Burton-style best bitter, sulphurous and sharp but with some malt and biscuit character. Quite bitter, becoming hoppy and increasingly astringent in the finish.

Dark Destroyer (ABV 4.7%)
Roasted malts produce a rich, dark ale blended with English hops. A good thirst quencher.

Starlight (ABV 5%) ◈
Gentle aroma in this hoppy strong bitter, with hints of toffee and fruit. A light body and a sharp finish.

Capstan (ABV 6%) ◆
A smooth, dark ale, with a spicy aroma of blackberries and blackcurrants. Strong fruit flavours dominate but with hops and malt providing some balance. The finish is bittersweet and vinous.

Whitewater

Whitewater Brewing Co, 40 Tullyframe Road, Kilkeel, Co Down, Northern Ireland, BT34 4RZ
Tel (028) 417 69449
✉ bernard@whitewaterbrewing.co.uk
⊕ whitewaterbrewing.co.uk
Tours by arrangement

⊛ Set up in 1996, Whitewater is now the biggest brewery in Northern Ireland. The brewery has a 15-barrel brew length and produces 14 different ales and a real lager. Currently, Whitewater supplies 15 outlets and owns one pub, the White Horse, Saintfield, Co. Down. Seasonal beers: Solstice Pale (ABV 4%, summer), Nut Brown (ABV 4%, winter), Snake Drive (ABV 4.3%, spring), Sanity Claus (ABV 4.5%, Xmas), Bee's Endeavour (ABV 4.8%, autumn).

Mill Ale (OG 1038, ABV 3.7%)
A golden-coloured, light ale.

Blond Lager (OG 1040, ABV 4%)

Glen Ale (OG 1043, ABV 4.2%)

Belfast Ale (OG 1046, ABV 4.5%)

Whitstable

Whitstable Brewery, Little Telpits Farm, Woodcock Lane, Grafty Green, Kent, ME17 2AY
Tel (01622) 851007
✉ whitstablebrewer@btconnect.com
⊕ whitstablebrewery.info
Tours by arrangement

Whitstable came about in 2003 when the Green family purchased the Swale and North Weald Brewery to supply their own outlets (a hotel and two restaurants) in Whitstable, and beer festival orders. In 2006 a new bar was opened in East Quay selling their own beers and other micros. Seasonal beer: Smack Ale (ABV 5.5%, winter).

Native Bitter (OG 1037, ABV 3.7%)

East India Pale Ale (OG 1040, ABV 4.1%)
A light, refreshing pale ale with floral hop aroma and bitterness that give a well-balanced flavour.

Oyster Stout (OG 1047, ABV 4.5%)
Rich and dry with deep chocolate and mocha flavours.

Bohemian (OG 1044, ABV 4.9%)
Dry-hopped, cask-conditioned lager.

Raspberry Wheat (OG 1049, ABV 5.2%)

Wheat Beer (OG 1049, ABV 5.2%)

Whittington's SIBA

Whittington's Brewery, Three Choirs Vineyards Ltd, Newent, Gloucestershire, GL18 1LS
Tel (01531) 890223
✉ info@whittingtonsbrewery.co.uk
⊕ whittingtonsbrewery.co.uk
Shop Tue-Sat 9am-8.30pm; Mon & Sun 9am-5pm
Tours by arrangement (for a charge)

⊠ Whittington's started in 2003 using a purpose-built five-barrel plant producing 20 barrels a week. Dick Whittington came from nearby Gloucester, hence the name and feline theme. All beers are bottled and available from the onsite shop, online and from local outlets. Seasonal beers: Summer Pale Ale (ABV 4%, May-Aug), Winters Tail (ABV 5.1%, Oct-Mar). Bottle-conditioned beer: Cats Whiskers.

Nine Lives (OG 1035, ABV 3.6%)

Cats Whiskers (OG 1041, ABV 4.2%)

Why Not

Why Not Brewery, 17 Cavalier Close, Thorpe St Andrew, Norwich, NR7 0TE
Tel (01603) 300786
✉ colin@thewhynotbrewery.co.uk
⊕ thewhynotbrewery.co.uk

Why Not opened in 2006 with equipment located in a shed and custom-made by Brendan Moore of Iceni Brewery. The brewery can produce up to 200 litres per brew. All cask beers are also available in bottle-conditioned form.

Wally's Revenge (OG 1040, ABV 4%) ◆
An overtly bitter beer with a hoppy background. The bitterness holds on to the end as an increasing astringent dryness develops.

Roundhead Porter (OG 1045, ABV 4.5%)

Cavalier Red (OG 1047, ABV 4.7%) ◆
Explosive fruity nose belies the gentleness of the taste. The summer fruit aroma dominates this red-gold brew. A sweet, fruity start disappears under a quick, bitter ending.

Chocolate Nutter (OG 1056, ABV 5.5%)

Wicked Hathern

Wicked Hathern Brewery Ltd, 17 Nixon Walk, East Leake, Leicestershire, LE12 6HL
Tel (01509) 559308
✉ soarhead@ntlworld.com
⊕ wicked-hathern.co.uk

Opened in 2000, the brewery generally supplies beer on a guest basis to many local pubs and beer festivals, and brews commissioned beers for special occasions. All beers are available bottled from selected off licences (see website) and from Hathern Stores. Special beers are brewed exclusively for Hathern Stores and Alexander Wines in Earlsdon. The brewery is not currently operating and the beers are being produced by the Wicked Hathern brewers at Shardlow Brewery. Seasonal beer: Gladstone Tidings (ABV 5.1%, Xmas).

WHB/Wicked Hathern Bitter (OG 1038, ABV 3.8%)
A light-tasting session bitter with a dry palate and good hop aroma.

Cockfighter (OG 1043, ABV 4.2%)
A copper-coloured beer with an aroma of fruit, creamy malt and hop resins.

Hawthorn Gold (OG 1045, ABV 4.5%)
A pale golden ale with delicate malt and spicy hop in the aroma. The taste is hoppy and mostly bitter but with good malt support and body. Dry, malt and hops aftertaste.

Derby Porter (OG 1048, ABV 4.8%)
A deep ruby porter with a creamy nose of lightly smoky, chocolaty, nutty dark malts.

Soar Head (OG 1048, ABV 4.8%) ◈
A dark ruby-coloured strong bitter with a cocktail of distinctive flavours.

For Albion, Bank:

Albion Special (OG 1041, ABV 4%)
A light, copper-coloured bitter with a nutty aroma and smoky malt taste, hops leading through.

For Harrington Arms, Thulston:

Earl of Harrington (OG 1041, ABV 4%)
A pale bitter with a pronounced maltiness offset by a delicate hop flavour.

Wickwar SIBA

Wickwar Brewing Co Ltd, Old Brewery, Station Road, Wickwar, Gloucestershire, GL12 8NB
Tel (0870) 777 5671
✉ bob@wickwarbrewing.co.uk
⊕ wickwarbrewing.co.uk
Shop Mon-Fri 10am-5pm; Sat 10am-4pm
(Tel 01453 299592)
Tours by arrangement

Wickwar was established in 1990 in the cooper's shop of the former Arnold Perrett Brewery and since 2004 its home has been the original early 19th-century brewery. In addition to supplying beers to some 350 outlets in the vicinity of the brewery, Wickwar also supplies Coors, Scottish & Newcastle, Waverley TBS and Wetherspoon. Seasonal beers: Premium Spring Ale (ABV 3.8%, Apr-May), Sunny Daze (ABV 4.2%, Jun-Aug), Xmas Cracker (ABV 4.2%, Dec), Autumnale (ABV 4.6%, Sep-Nov). Bottle-conditioned beers: Brand Oak Bitter and Old Arnold.

Coopers WPA (OG 1036.5, ABV 3.5%) ◈
Golden-coloured, this well-balanced beer is light and refreshing, with hops, citrus fruit, apple/pear flavour and notable pale malt character. Bitter, dry finish.

Brand Oak Bitter (BOB) (OG 1039, ABV 4%) ◈
Amber-coloured, this has a distinctive blend of hop, malt and apple/pear citrus fruits. The slightly sweet taste turns into a fine, dry bitterness, with a similar malty-lasting finish.

Cotswold Way (OG 1043, ABV 4.2%) ◈
Amber-coloured, it has a pleasant aroma of pale malt, hop and fruit. Good dry bitterness in the taste with some sweetness. Similar though less sweet in the finish, with good hop content.

Rite Flanker (ABV 4.3%)
Amber in colour with a big malt taste and fruit notes and a hoppy finish.

IKB (OG 1045, ABV 4.5%)
A ruby-red ale with a complex hop aroma and flavour derived from the use of three hop varieties. Flowery but well balanced.

Old Arnold (OG 1047, ABV 4.8%)
A full-flavoured and well-balanced ale with malt, hops and cherry fruit throughout. Amber/pale brown, it is slightly sweet with a long-lasting, malty, dry, fruity and increasingly bitter finish.

Mr Perretts Traditional Stout (OG 1059, ABV 5.9%) ◈
Aroma and taste of smoky chocolate malts and peppery hops. Dark fruits of black cherry and blackcurrant give hints of sweetness to the dry, quite bitter, slightly spicy, well-balanced taste.

Station Porter (OG 1062, ABV 6.1%) ◈
This is a rich, smooth, dark ruby-brown ale. Starts with roast malt; coffee, chocolate and dark fruit then develops a complex, spicy, bittersweet taste and a long roast finish.

Wild's

See Weobley

Williams SIBA

Williams Brothers Brewing Co/Heather Ale Ltd, New Alloa Brewery, Kelliebank, Alloa, FK10 1NT
Tel (01259) 725511
✉ fraoch@heatherale.co.uk
⊕ heatherale.co.uk
Tours by arrangement

Bruce and Scott Williams started brewing Heather Ale in the West Highlands in 1993. A range of indigenous, historical ales were added over the following 10 years. The brothers now have their own 40-barrel brewery and bottling line and produce a range of hoppy beers under the Williams Bros banner as well as continuing with the range of historical ales. Around 30 outlets are supplied. Seasonal beers: Ebulum (ABV 6.5%, winter), Alba (ABV 7.5%, winter).

Gold (OG 1040, ABV 3.9%)

Fraoch Heather Ale (OG 1041, ABV 4.1%) ⊡ ◈
The unique taste of heather flowers is noticeable in this beer. A fine floral aroma and spicy taste give character to this drinkable speciality beer.

Black (OG 1042, ABV 4.2%)

Roisin-Tayberry (OG 1042, ABV 4.2%)

Red (OG 1045, ABV 4.5%)

Grozet (OG 1047, ABV 5%)

Joker (OG 1047, ABV 5%)

Willy's SIBA

⊡ **Willy's Wine Bar Ltd, 17 High Cliff Road, Cleethorpes, Lincolnshire, DN35 8RQ**
Tel (01472) 602145
Tours by arrangement

The brewery opened in 1989 to provide beer for its two pubs in Grimsby and Cleethorpes. It has a five-barrel plant with maximum capacity of 15 barrels a week. The brewery can be viewed at any time from pub or street.

Original Bitter (OG 1038, ABV 3.8%) ◈
A light brown 'sea air' beer with a fruity, tangy hop on the nose and taste, giving a strong bitterness tempered by the underlying malt.

Burcom Bitter (OG 1044, ABV 4.2%) ◈
Sometimes known as Mariner's Gold, although the beer is dark ruby in colour. It is a smooth and creamy brew with a sweet chocolate-bar maltiness, giving way to an increasingly bitter finish.

Last Resort (OG 1044, ABV 4.3%)

Weiss Buoy (OG 1045, ABV 4.5%)
A cloudy wheat beer.

Coxswains Special (OG 1050, ABV 4.9%)

Old Groyne (OG 1060, ABV 6.2%) ◆
An initial sweet banana fruitiness blends with malt to give a vanilla quality to the taste and slightly bitter aftertaste. A copper-coloured beer reminiscent of a Belgian ale.

Winchester

Winchester Brewery Ltd, Unit 19 Longbridge Industrial Park, Floating Bridge Road, Southampton, Hampshire, SO14 3FL
Tel 07764 949157
✉ info@winchesterbrewery.com
⊕ winchesterbrewery.com

The brewery was launched in 2004 and was intended to be located in Winchester but problems with premises meant it is based in the heart of Southampton. Four regular beers are produced alongside a small but growing range of seasonals. Around 30 outlets are supplied. All cask ales are also available in bottle-conditioned form.

Best Bitter (OG 1038, ABV 3.7%)
An amber beer with strong hop flavours.

Summer '76 (OG 1045, ABV 3.7%)
A lightly-hopped golden ale.

West Window (OG 1048, ABV 4.5%)
A premium bitter with a unique hop blend.

Trusty Servant (OG 1052, ABV 4.7%)
A dark premium ale with a strong, hoppy flavour.

Swithun Gold (ABV 5%)

Windie Goat

◊ **Windie Goat Brewery, Failford Inn, Failford, South Ayrshire, KA5 5TF**
Tel (01292) 540117
✉ enquiries@windiegoatbrewery.co.uk
⊕ windiegoatbrewery.co.uk

☺ Established in 2006 in the old cellar of the Failford Inn, the brewery is named after an area of local woodland with the beer names derived from fishing pools in the River Ayr. Beer is supplied mainly to the inn and also to beer festivals on request. Further regular beers are planned.

Peden's Cove (ABV 3.5%)
A pale bitter, named after the area where Alexander Peden preached from.

Priest's Wheel (ABV 4.3%)
An amber ale with pale and crystal malt using three varieties of American hops.

The Dubh (ABV 4.6%)
A chocolate porter with a smooth, easy-drinking finish.

Windrush

See Burford

Windsor Castle

Windsor Castle Brewery Ltd t/a Sadler's Ales, 7 Stourbridge Road, Lye, West Midlands, DY9 7DG

Tel (01384) 897809/895230 (sales)
✉ enquiries@windsorcastlebrewery.com
⊕ windsorcastlebrewery.com
Shop 11am-11pm daily
Tours by arrangement

☺ Thomas Sadler founded the original brewery in 1900 adjacent to the Windsor Castle inn, Oldbury. Fourth generation brewers John and Chris Sadler re-opened the brewery in its new location in 2004. Around 250 outlets are supplied. Bottle-conditioned beers: Worcester Sorcerer, 1900, Thin Ice, IPA.

Jack's Ale (OG 1037, ABV 3.8%)
Light, hoppy beer with a crisp and zesty lemon undertone.

Mild (OG 1039, ABV 4%)

Worcester Sorcerer (OG 1043, ABV 4.3%)
Pale beer, light and refreshing yet smooth and fruity with hints of mint and lemon. Floral aroma and crisp bitterness combine to make a balanced and clean-tasting beer.

1900 (OG 1044, ABV 4.4%)
Dark malty bitter with a light hoppy aroma and a dry, lingering finish.

Thin Ice (OG 1045, ABV 4.5%)

IPA (OG 1048, ABV 4.8%)
Classic India Pale Ale, light, tangy and bitter with a distinctive refreshing aftertaste.

Winter's SIBA

Winter's Brewery, 8 Keelan Close, Norwich, NR6 6QZ
Tel (01603) 787820
✉ sales@wintersbrewery.com
⊕ wintersbrewery.com

☒ David Winter, who had previous award-winning success as brewer for both Woodforde's and Chalk Hill breweries, decided to set up on his own in 2001. He purchased the brewing plant from the now defunct Scott's Brewery in Lowestoft. The local free trade is supplied.

Mild (OG 1036.5, ABV 3.6%) ◆
A solid malty mild with roast overtones and well-balanced, bittersweet undercurrent. A slightly coarse mouthfeel adds to the overall character of an olde time mild.

Bitter (OG 1039.5, ABV 3.8%) ◆
A well-balanced amber bitter. Hops and malt are balanced by a crisp citrus fruitiness. A pleasant hoppy nose with a hint of grapefruit. Long, sustained, dry, grapefruit finish.

Golden (ABV 4.1%) ◆
Gentle hop airs introduce this golden ale. A hoppy bitterness pervades all aspects, although a banana/toffee flavour can be detected in the quick, sharp finish.

Revenge (OG 1047, ABV 4.7%) ◆
Blackcurrant notes give depth to the inherent maltiness of this pale brown beer. A bittersweet background becomes more pronounced as the fruitiness gently wanes.

Storm Force (OG 1053, ABV 5.3%) ◆
Rich and heavy with blackcurrant, sultanas and pepper vying with the more traditional malt and hop flavours. A long cloying finish loses both malt and hops.

Tempest (OG 1062, ABV 6.2%) 🎫 🔷
Malt is foremost in both aroma and initial taste. A heavy fruitiness overwhelms the background hops and bitterness. The sweetness remains constant as the malt dwindles.

Wissey Valley

Wissey Valley Brewery, Clover Club, Low Road, Wretton, Norfolk, PE33 9QN
Tel (01366) 500767
✉ info@wisseyvalleybrewery.com
🌐 wisseyvalleybrewery.com
Tours by arrangement

⊗ The brewery was launched in 2002 as Captain Grumpy and in 2003 moved to Stoke Ferry and was re-established as Wissey Valley. The brewery re-launched in 2006, moving to the neighbouring village of Wretton. Around 15 outlets are supplied direct as well as wholesalers and beer festivals. All beers are also available bottle conditioned.

Wild Widow Mild (OG 1035, ABV 3.6%)

Captain Grumpy's Best (OG 1039, ABV 3.9%)

Captain Grumpy's Busted Flush (OG 1045, ABV 4.5%)

Captain Grumpy's Golden Rivet (OG 1050, ABV 5%)

Khaki Sergeant (OG 1058, ABV 6.7%)

Wizard SIBA

Wizard Ales, Unit 4, Lundy View, Mullacott Cross Industrial Estate, Ilfracombe, Devon, EX34 8PY
Tel (01271) 865350
✉ mike@wizardales.co.uk
🌐 wizardales.co.uk
Tours by arrangement

⊗ Brewing started in 2003 on a 1.25-barrel plant, since upgraded to a five-barrel. The brewery moved from Warwickshire to Devon in 2007. Around 20 local outlets are supplied. Seasonal beer: Bah Humbug (ABV 5.8%, Xmas).

Apprentice (OG 1038, ABV 3.6%)

One For The Toad (OG 1041, ABV 4%)

Black Magic (OG 1040, ABV 4%)

Mother in Law (OG 1043, ABV 4.2%)

Sorcerer (OG 1044, ABV 4.3%)

White Witch (OG 1045, ABV 4.5%)

Bullfrog (OG 1047, ABV 4.8%)

Druid's Fluid (OG 1048, ABV 5%)

Wold Top SIBA

Wold Top Brewery, Hunmanby Grange, Wold Newton, Driffield, East Yorkshire, YO25 3HS
Tel (01723) 892222
✉ enquiries@woldtopbrewery.co.uk
🌐 woldtopbrewery.co.uk
Tours by arrangement (summer only)

Wold Top started brewing in 2002 in a converted granary on a farm. The brewery grows its own barley, uses its own water and would like to grow its own hops. A 10-barrel plant is used. One pub, the Falling Stone in Thwing, is owned. 300 outlets are served. All beers are also available in bottled form from off-licences and via mail order.

Bitter (OG 1037, ABV 3.7%)
Maris Otter pale malt and a small amount of crystal malt form the basis of the beer, with Northdown hops for aroma and bitterness.

Falling Stone (OG 1042, ABV 4.2%)
A full-bodied and well-rounded beer. The rich colour is produced by adding a small amount of chocolate malt to the mash, along with Maris Otter pale malt. Progress hops are used for aroma.

Mars Magic (OG 1044, ABV 4.6%)
Dark beer with red hue from the roast barley used. Progress hops are used for both bittering and aroma and give a well-balanced flavour with a hint of caramel.

Wold Gold (OG 1046, ABV 4.8%)
Light-coloured summer beer. Maris Otter, wheat and cara malts, along with Goldings and Styrian hops, make this very drinkable with a hint of spice.

Wolf

WBC (Norfolk) Ltd, t/a Wolf Brewery, Rookery Farm, Silver Street, Besthorpe, Attleborough, Norfolk, NR17 2LD
Tel (01953) 457775
✉ info@wolfbrewery.com
🌐 wolfbrewery.com
Tours by arrangement

The brewery was founded by Wolfe Witham in 1996 using a 20-barrel plant housed on the site of the old Gaymer's cider orchard. More than 200 outlets are supplied. Seasonal beer: Timber Wolf (ABV 5.8%, winter), Whistle (ABV 4.7%, spring), Santa Paws (ABV 4.5%), Grandma's Xmas Reserve (ABV 4.8%).

Edith Cavell (ABV 3.7%)

Golden Jackal (OG 1039, ABV 3.7%) 🔷
Flavoursome golden ale with a hoppy, citrus nose. Lemon notes enhance the dominant hop flavour that soars above a sweet malty background. Long-lasting with hops to the end.

Norfolk Lavender Honey (ABV 3.7%)

Wolf In Sheep's Clothing (OG 1039, ABV 3.7%) 🔷
A malty aroma with fruity undertones introduces this reddish-hued mild. Malt, with a bitter background that remains throughout, is the dominant flavour of this clean-tasting beer.

Bitter (OG 1041, ABV 3.9%) 🔷
Well-balanced mix of flavours. Hops blend with malt and bitterness in a grainy first impression. Some citrus notes in the background fade quickly.

Coyote Bitter (OG 1044, ABV 4.3%) 🔷
Citrus notes introduce this amber-coloured bitter. The first impression is of a distinctive mix of malt and bitterness with a dry hoppiness. The flavours are distinctive but none is initially dominant.

Straw Dog (ABV 4.5%) 🍺 🔷
Citrus fruits are the signature of this straw-

coloured brew. Grapefruit and lemon on the nose and taste swirls over other flavours. Hops and bitterness add depth and character.

Woild Moild (OG 1048, ABV 4.8%) ◆
Dark brown and creamy with overall roast-dominated flavour. Molasses and caramel add to the depth with more than a hint of sweetness also present. Finish somewhat more bitter and drier.

Granny Wouldn't Like It (OG 1049, ABV 4.8%) ◆
Well-rounded strong ale with a robust mix of malt and cherry fruitiness. The aroma matches the taste with the fruity malt character Ithroughout. A hoppy bitterness gives an understated contrast.

Wolverhampton & Dudley

See Marston's in the New national breweries section

Wood SIBA

Wood Brewery Ltd, Wistanstow, Craven Arms, Shropshire, SY7 8DG
Tel (01588) 672523
✉ mail@woodbrewery.co.uk
⊕ woodbrewery.co.uk
Tours by arrangement

The brewery opened in 1980 in buildings next to the Plough Inn, still the brewery's only tied house. Steady growth over the years included the acquisition of the Sam Powell Brewery and its beers in 1991. Production averages 70 barrels a week and around 200 outlets are supplied. Seasonal beers: Summerthat (ABV 3.9%, Jun-Aug), Woodcutter (ABV 4.2%, Sep-Nov), Hopping Mad (ABV 4.7%, Mar-May), Xmas Cracker (ABV 6%, Nov-Dec). A monthly beer is also brewed.

Quaff (ABV 3.7%)
A pale and refreshing light bitter with a clean, hoppy finish.

Craven Ale (ABV 3.8%)
An attractively coloured beer with a pleasant hop aroma and a refreshing taste.

Parish Bitter (OG 1040, ABV 4%) ◆
A blend of malt and hops with a bitter aftertaste. Pale brown in colour.

Special Bitter (OG 1042, ABV 4.2%) ◆
A tawny brown bitter with malt, hops and some fruitiness.

Pot O' Gold (OG 1044, ABV 4.4%)

Shropshire Lad (OG 1045, ABV 4.5%)
A strong, well-rounded bitter, drawing flavour from a fine blend of selected English malted barley and Fuggles and Golding hops.

Old Sam (OG 1047, ABV 4.6%)
A dark copper ale with a ripe, rounded flavour and hop bitterness.

Wonderful (OG 1048, ABV 4.8%) ◆
A mid-brown, fruity beer, with a roast and malt taste.

Tom Wood

See Highwood

Wooden Hand

Wooden Hand Brewery, Unit 3, Grampound Road Industrial Estate, Truro, Cornwall, TR2 4TB
Tel (01726) 884596
✉ sales@woodenhand.co.uk
⊕ woodenhand.co.uk

Wooden Hand was founded in 2004 by Anglo-Swedish businessman Rolf Munding, who also owns the Zatec Brewery in the Czech Republic. The brewery is named after the Black Hand of John Carew of Penwarne, in the parish of Mevagissey — Carew lost his hand in fighting at the siege of Ostend in the reign of Elizabeth I. The brewery operates on a 7.5-barrel plant and supplies around 40 outlets as well as supermarkets locally. A bottling line was installed in 2005, which also bottles for other breweries.

Pirates Gold (OG 1036, ABV 3.6%)
A golden bitter with complex grain and fruit and a deep, dry finish.

Black Pearl (OG 1039, ABV 4%)
A slightly tart, pale bitter with a tempting hop aroma and light fruit notes giving strong malt and hop flavours with a dry, tangy fruit finish.

Cornish Buccaneer (OG 1039, ABV 4.3%)
A golden coloured beer with great hop character. Full fruit in the mouth with good hop balance and a long, dry finish.

Cornish Mutiny (OG 1048, ABV 4.8%)
A dark, rich ale with a distinctive hoppy character.

Woodforde's SIBA

Woodforde's Norfolk Ales, Broadland Brewery, Woodbastwick, Norwich, NR13 6SW
Tel (01603) 720353
✉ info@woodfordes.co.uk
⊕ woodfordes.co.uk
Shop Mon-Fri 10.30am-4.30pm; Sat-Sun 11.30am-4.30pm (01603 722218)
Tours by arrangement (Tue & Thu evenings)

Founded in 1981 in Drayton, Woodforde's moved to Erpingham in 1982, and then moved again to a converted farm complex, with greatly increased production capacity, in 1989. A major expansion took place in 2001 to more than double production and included a new brewery shop and visitor centre. Woodforde's runs two tied houses with around 600 outlets supplied on a regular basis. Bottle-conditioned beers: Wherry Bitter, Sundew Ale, Nelson's Revenge ⬚, Admiral's Reserve, Norfolk Nog, Headcracker, Norfolk Nip.

Mardler's (OG 1035, ABV 3.5%) ◆
The gentle malt signature of the aroma and first taste subsides slowly to be replaced by a mix of sweetness and roast. Smooth drinking with an underlying fruitiness.

Wherry Best Bitter (OG 1037.4, ABV 3.8%) ⬚ ◆
Hoppy nose with a hint of sulphur. Similar taste as the hops are bolstered by a bittersweet fruitiness that continues to the end. Amber-coloured, easy-drinking brew.

Sundew Ale (OG 1039, ABV 4.1%)
A subtle golden beer, pale in colour and light on the palate with a distinct hoppy finish.

Nelson's Revenge (OG 1042.7, ABV 4.5%) 🍴 🍂
A glorious mix of vine fruit, malt and hops give a rich Xmas pudding feel. Malt begins in the nose and remains to the end. Sultana-like fruitiness blunts the hop background throughout.

Norfolk Nog (OG 1046.8, ABV 4.6%) 🍂
Well-balanced dark brown porter with a heavy roast malt character. Plenty of sweetness and caramel to add depth, countered by an underlying hoppy bitterness. Strong finish.

Admiral's Reserve (OG 1050, ABV 5%) 🍂
Light tasting for its strength but well balanced throughout. Malt and caramel on the nose and initial flavour with a growing hop influence. Quick finish with a gentle bitterness.

Headcracker (OG 1065.7, ABV 7%) 🍴 🍂
Surprisingly clean-tasting for a barley wine. A booming, plummy aroma buttressed with malt continues to become the dominant taste. A pleasant winey bitterness gives a counterpoint while a dry sultana plumminess provides a fitting finale.

Norfolk Nip (OG 1076, ABV 8.5%) 🍴
Dark mahogany in colour, this intensely flavoured beer has a stunning range of malts and hops enveloped by a warming balanced bitterness.

Woodlands SIBA

Woodlands Brewing Co, Unit 4-6, Creamery Industrial Estate, Station Road, Wrenbury, Cheshire, CW5 8EX
Tel (01270) 620101
✉ info@woodlandsbrewery.co.uk
🌐 woodlandsbrewery.co.uk
Shop 8am-5pm daily
Tours by arrangement

The brewery opened in 2004 with a five-barrel plant from the former Khean Brewery. The beers are brewed using water from a spring that surfaces on a nearby peat field at Woodlands Farm. There are plans to upgrade to a 10-barrel plant. 120 outlets are supplied. Bottle-conditioned beers: Woodlands Bitter, Oak Beauty, Midnight Stout, Gold Brew, IPA, Old Willow, Generals Tipple, Bees Knees.

Mild (OG 1035, ABV 3.5%)

Drummer (OG 1039, ABV 3.9%) 🍂
Clean, malty session bitter with lasting dry finish and increasing bitterness in the aftertaste.

Old Willow (OG 1041, ABV 4.1%)

Oak Beauty (OG 1042, ABV 4.2%) 🍂
Malty, sweetish copper-coloured bitter with toffee and caramel flavours. Long-lasting and satisfying bitter finish.

IPA (OG 1043, ABV 4.3%) 🍴 🍂
Pale, dry and very bitter beer with sharp initial tartness leading to a moderate fruitiness. Good citrus hop throughout but not strong enough for an IPA. Good dry aftertaste.

Midnight Stout (OG 1044, ABV 4.4%) 🍂
Classic creamy dry stout with roast flavours to the fore. Well-balanced with bitterness and good hops on the taste and a good dry, roasty aftertaste. Some sweetness.

Bitter (OG 1044, ABV 4.4%)

Bees Knees (OG 1045, ABV 4.5%)

Gold Brew (OG 1050, ABV 5%) 🍂
Strong malty nose with fruit and sweetness balanced in the flavour. Hint of caramel and a dry finish.

Generals Tipple (OG 1055, ABV 5.5%)

Worfield

🏠 Worfield Brewing Co,
All Nations Brewhouse,
Coalport Road, Madeley,
Shropshire, TF6 6DP
Tel (01746) 769606
✉ mike@worfieldbrew.fsbusiness.co.uk

☺ Worfield began brewing in 1993 at the Davenport Arms and moved to Bridgnorth in 1998. Following the reopening of the All Nations in Madeley, the brewery produced Dabley Ale for the pub and in 2004 relocated to the All Nations. Around 200 outlets are supplied. Seasonal beers: Winter Classic (ABV 4.5%, Jan), Spring Classic (ABV 4.5%, Mar), Summer Classic (ABV 4.5%, Jun), Autumn Classic (ABV 4.5%), Ironfounders (ABV 4.6%), Bedlam Strong Bitter (ABV 5.2%), Redneck (ABV 5.5%, Xmas).

Coalport Dodger Mild (OG 1034, ABV 3.5%)

Dabley Ale (OG 1039, ABV 3.8%)

OBJ (OG 1043, ABV 4.2%) 🍂
A light and sweet bitter; delicate flavour belies the strength.

Shropshire Pride (OG 1045, ABV 4.5%)

Dabley Gold (OG 1050, ABV 5%)

George Wright

George Wright Brewing Co, Unit 11, Diamond Business Park, Sandwash Close, Rainford, Merseyside, WA11 8LU
Tel (01744) 886686
✉ sales@georgewrightbrewing.co.uk
🌐 georgewrightbrewing.co.uk
Tours by arrangement

George Wright started production in 2003. The original 2.5-barrel plant was replaced by a five-barrel one, which has since been upgraded again to 25 barrels with production of 200 casks a week. Beers with Polish ingredients were introduced in 2006/7.

Drunken Duck (ABV 3.9%) 🍂
Fruity gold-coloured bitter beer with good hop and a dry aftertaste. Some acidity.

Longboat (ABV 3.9%) 🍴 🍂
Good hoppy bitter with grapefruit and an almost tart bitterness throughout. Some astringency in the aftertaste. Well-balanced, light and refreshing with a good mouthfeel and long, dry finish.

Midday Sun (ABV 4.2%)

Winter Sun (ABV 4.2%) 🍂
Thinnish bitter with strong fruit aroma. Hops and bitterness dominate the flavour along with caramel. Flavours follow through to a sharp finish.

Pipe Dream (ABV 4.3%) 🍴 🍂
Refreshing hoppy best bitter with a fruity

nose and grapefruit to the fore in the taste. Lasting dry, bitter finish.

Biale Orzel (ABV 4.4%)

Kings Shillin' (ABV 4.5%) ◈
Amber bitter with a hoppy aroma leading to a sharp, almost tart initial taste with citrus fruit notes. This full-flavoured malty beer has a good dry finish.

Cheeky Pheasant (ABV 4.7%)

Roman Black (ABV 4.8%)

Black Swan (ABV 3.8%)

Blue Moon (ABV 4.9%) ◈
Easy-drinking strong, gold-coloured beer. Good malt/bitter balance and well hopped.

Mochne Pivo (ABV 5.1%)

Icebreaker (ABV 5.5%)
A regular beer brewed at eight-weekly intervals

Wychwood SIBA

Wychwood Brewery Ltd, Eagle Maltings, The Crofts, Witney, Oxfordshire, OX28 4DP
Tel (01993) 890800
✉ info@wychwood.co.uk
⊕ wychwood.co.uk
Shop Sat 2-6pm
Tours by arrangement

Wychwood Brewery is located on the fringes of the ancient medieval forest, the Wychwood. The brewery was founded in 1983 on a site dating back to the 1800s, which was once the original maltings for the town's brewery. The brewery is now owned by Refresh UK, and the site also includes the Brakspear Brewery (qv). A range of seasonal beers is also produced, including the infamous Dog's Bollocks.

Hobgoblin (OG 1050, ABV 5%) ◈
Powerful, full-bodied, copper-red, well-balanced brew. Strong in roasted malt, with a moderate bitterness and a slight fruity character.

Wye Valley SIBA

Wye Valley Brewery, Stoke Lacy, Herefordshire, HR7 4HG
Tel (01885) 490505
✉ enquiries@wyevalleybrewery.co.uk
⊕ wyevalleybrewery.co.uk
Shop Mon-Fri 10am-4pm
Tours by arrangement

Wye Valley was founded in 1985 in Canon Pyon, Herefordshire. The following year it moved to an old stable block behind the Barrels pub in Hereford and 2002 saw another move to the former Symond's Cider site at Stoke Lacy, upping capacity to brew 80 barrels a day. Growth and investment continue with future plans to increase the tied estate from its current level of two and installing a bottling line. Bottle-conditioned beers: Butty Bach, Dorothy Goodbody's Golden Ale, Dorothy Goodbody's Wholesome Stout ⬚, Dorothy Goodbody's Country Ale (ABV 6%).

Bitter (OG 1037, ABV 3.7%) ◈
A beer whose aroma gives little hint of the bitter hoppiness that follows right through to the aftertaste.

HPA (OG 1040, ABV 4%) ◈
A pale, hoppy, malty brew with a hint of sweetness before a dry finish.

Dorothy Goodbody's Golden Ale (OG 1042, ABV 4.2%)
A light, gold-coloured ale with a malty sweetness and crisp bitterness.

Butty Bach (OG 1046, ABV 4.5%) ⬚ ⬚
A burnished gold, full-bodied premium ale.

Dorothy Goodbody's Wholesome Stout (OG 1046, ABV 4.6%) ⬚ ◈
A smooth and satisfying stout with a bitter edge to its roast flavours. The finish combines roast grain and malt.

Wylam SIBA

Wylam Brewery Ltd, South Houghton Farm, Heddon on the Wall, Northumberland, NE15 0EZ
Tel (01661) 853377
✉ admin@wylambrew.co.uk
⊕ wylambrew.co.uk
Tours by arrangement

Wylam started in 2000 on a 4.5-barrel plant, which increased to nine barrels in 2002. New premises and brew plant (20 barrels) were installed on the same site in 2006. The brewery delivers to more than 200 local outlets and beers are available through wholesalers around the country. Seasonal beers: Spring Thing (ABV 3.4%), Houblon Nouveau (ABV 4.2%, Oct), Legless Santa (ABV 4.6%, Dec).

Hedonist (OG 1038, ABV 3.8%)

Bitter (OG 1039, ABV 3.8%) ◈
A refreshing, copper-coloured, hoppy bitter with a clean, bitter finish.

Gold Tankard (OG 1040, ABV 4%) ◈
Fresh, clean flavour, full of hops. This golden ale has a hint of citrus in the finish.

Magic (OG 1042, ABV 4.2%) ◈
Light, crisp and refreshing. Floral and spicy with a good bitter finish.

Whistle Stop (OG 1046, ABV 4.4%)

Bohemia (OG 1046, ABV 4.6%) ⬚ ◈
Tawny in colour with a heady bouquet of malt and hops, and a deep finish of fruit.

Haugh (OG 1046, ABV 4.6%) ◈
A smooth velvet porter packed with flavour. Roast malt and a slight fruitiness provide a satisfying beer with a smooth finish.

Landlords Choice (OG 1046, ABV 4.6%)
A single malt pale bitter.

Rocket (OG 1048, ABV 5%)
A copper-coloured strong bitter.

Silver Ghost (OG 1050, ABV 5%)

Wyre Piddle

Wyre Piddle Brewery, Highgrove Farm, Peopleton, near Pershore, Worcestershire, WR10 2LF
Tel (01905) 841853

⊗ Wyre Piddle was established in 1992 in a

converted stable. It supplies around 200 pubs in the Midlands. The brewery relocated and upgraded its equipment in 1997 and has now moved again to Highgrove Farm. It also brews for Green Dragon, Malvern: Dragon's Downfall (ABV 3.9%), Dragon's Revenge (ABV 4%). For Severn Valley Railway: Royal Piddle (ABV 4.2%). Seasonal beers: Piddle in the Sun (ABV 5.2%, summer), Yule Piddle (ABV 4.5%, Xmas).

Piddle in the Hole (OG 1039, ABV 3.9%) ◆
Copper-coloured and quite dry, with lots of hops and fruitiness throughout.

Piddle in the Dark (ABV 4.5%)
A rich ruby-red bitter with a smooth flavour.

Piddle in the Wind (ABV 4.5%) ◆
This drink has a superb mix of flavours. A hoppy nose continues through to a lasting aftertaste, making it a good, all-round beer.

Piddle in the Snow (ABV 5.2%) ◆
A dry, strong taste all the way through draws your attention to the balance between malt and hops in the brew. A glorious way to end an evening's drinking.

Yates

Yates Brewery Ltd, Ghyll Farm, Westnewton, Wigton, Cumbria, CA7 3NX
Tel (016973) 21081
✉ enquiry@yatesbrewery.co.uk
⊕ yatesbrewery.co.uk
Tours by arrangement

Cumbria's oldest micro-brewery, established in 1986. The brewery was bought in 1998 by Graeme and Caroline Baxter, who had previously owned High Force Brewery in Teesdale. Deliveries are mainly to its Cumbrian stronghold and the A69 corridor as far as Hexham. A brewhouse and reed bed effluent system have been added on the same site. Around 40 outlets are supplied. Seasonal beers: Spring Fever (ABV 4.7%), Best Cellar (ABV 5.8%, Xmas), IPA (ABV 4.9%), Genius (ABV 4.1%), Solway Sunset (ABV 4.3%), Bees Knees (ABV 4.2%), Winter Fever (ABV 4%).

Bitter (OG 1035, ABV 3.7%) ◆
A well-balanced, full-bodied bitter, golden in colour with complex hop bitterness. Good aroma and distinctive flavour.

Fever Pitch (OG 1039, ABV 3.9%)
An extremely pale-coloured beer. Fully rounded, smooth, hoppy flavour, using lager malt and hops.

Sun Goddess (OG 1042, ABV 4.2%)
A lager-style cask beer, light and fruity with agreeable bitterness.

Yates' SIBA

**Yates' Brewery,
The Inn at St Lawrence,
Undercliff Drive, St Lawrence,
Isle of Wight, PO38 1XG**
Tel (01983) 731731
✉ info@yates-brewery.fsnet.co.uk
⊕ yates-brewery.co.uk
Tours by arrangement

Brewing started in 2000 on a five-barrel plant

at the Inn at St Lawrence. Yates' now has 40 regular outlets. All the draught beers are also available in bottle-conditioned form. Seasonal beer: Yule B Sorry (ABV 5.5%, Xmas), St Lawrence Ale (ABV 5%, Mar-Nov).

Bugle Best (OG 1039, ABV 3.8%)
A light, refreshing session bitter.

Undercliff Experience (OG 1040, ABV 4.1%)
An amber-copper ale with a bittersweet malt and hop taste with a dry lemon edge that dominates the bitter finish.

Blonde (OG 1045, ABV 4.5%)
A light beer with a fruity, citrus nose and a dry, hoppy finish.

Holy Joe (OG 1050, ABV 4.9%) ◆
Strongly bittered golden ale with pronounced spice and citrus character, and underlying light hint of malt.

Special Bitter/YSD (OG 1056, ABV 5.5%) ◆
Easy-drinking strong, amber ale with pronounced tart bitterness and a refreshing bite in the aftertaste.

Yeovil

Yeovil Ales, Unit 5, Bofors Park, Artillery Road, Lufton Trading Estate, Yeovil, Somerset, BA22 8YH
Tel (01935) 414888
✉ rob@yeovilales.com
⊕ yeovilales.com

Yeovil Ales was established in 2006 with an 18-barrel plant. The brewery supplies free trade pubs throughout the Yeovil district.

Glover's Glory (ABV 3.8%)

Star Gazer (ABV 4%)

Summerset (ABV 4.1%)

Yetman's

**Yetman's Brewery,
c/o 37 Norwich Road, Holt,
Norfolk, NR25 6SA**
Tel 07774 809016
✉ peter@yetmans.net
⊕ yetmans.net

⊗ A 2.5-barrel plant built by Moss Brew was installed in restored medieval barns in 2005. The brewery supplies local free trade outlets. Bottle-conditioned beers: Orange, Green.

Red (OG 1036, ABV 3.8%)

Orange (OG 1040, ABV 4.2%) ◆
A distinctly malty beer in both taste and aroma. Copper coloured with a sustained bitter edge that becomes slightly astringent in the long finish.

Green (OG 1044, ABV 4.8%)

Keep your Good Beer Guide up to date by visiting **www.camra.org.uk** Click on 'Good Beer Guide' then 'Updates to the GBG 2008', where you will find information about changes to breweries.

York SIBA

**York Brewery Co Ltd, 12 Toft Green,
York, North Yorkshire, YO1 6JT**
Tel (01904) 621162
✉ info@yorkbrew.co.uk
⊕ yorkbrew.co.uk
Shop Mon-Sat 12-6pm
Tours by arrangement (ring for daily tour times)

York started production in 1996, the first
brewery in the city for 40 years. It has a visitor
centre with bar and gift shop, and was
designed as a show brewery, with a gallery
above the 20-barrel plant and viewing panels
to fermentation and conditioning rooms. The
brewery owns several pubs and in 2006
additional space was acquired to increase
production capacity. More than 400 outlets are
supplied. Seasonal beers: see website.

Guzzler (OG 1036, ABV 3.6%) 🍺 ◆
Refreshing golden ale with dominant hop
and fruit flavours developing throughout.

Stonewall (OG 1038, ABV 3.8%) ◆
Balanced amber bitter where maltiness
underlines strong hop and fruit aromas
and flavours.

Decade (OG 1040, ABV 4.1%)
A light, hoppy beer to celebrate
10 years of brewing.

Wild Wheat (OG 1040, ABV 4.1%)

Yorkshire Terrier (OG 1041, ABV 4.2%) ◆
Refreshing and distinctive amber/gold brew
where fruit and hops dominate the aroma
and taste. Hoppy bitterness remains assertive
in the aftertaste.

R.I.P.

The following breweries have closed, gone
out of business, suspended operations or
merged with another company since the
2007 Guide was published:

**Bard's, Bidford-on-Avon, Warwickshire
Bathtub, Stithians, Cornwall
Broadstone, Retford, Nottinghamshire
Burrington, Burrington, Devon
Ceredigion, Ceredigion, West Wales
Cheriton, Cheriton, Hampshire
Evesham, Evesham, Worcestershire
Frankton Bagby, Church Lawford,
   Warwickshire
George & Dragon, Southend-on-Sea, Essex
Goodmanham, Goodmanham,
   East Yorkshire
Greenwood, Bradford, West Yorkshire
Holme Valley, Honley, West Yorkshire
Home County, Wickwar, Gloucestershire
McCowans, Edinburgh, Lothians
Thomas McGuinness, Rochdale,
   Greater Manchester
Peelwalls, Ayton, Borders
Ramsbottom, Ramsbottom,
   Greater Manchester
Redburn, Bardon Mill, Northumberland
Ring O' Bells, Launceston, Cornwall
Scarecrow, Arreton, Isle of Wight
Sidecar, Huddersfield, West Yorkshire
Trossach's Craft, Kilmahog, Central
Wild's, Weobley, Herefordshire**

Centurion's Ghost Ale (OG 1051,
ABV 5.4%) 🍺 🗆 ◆
Dark ruby in colour, full-tasting with mellow
roast malt character balanced by light
bitterness and autumn fruit flavours that
linger into the aftertaste.

Yorkshire Dales

**Yorkshire Dales Brewing Co Ltd,
Seata Barn, Elm Hill, Askrigg,
North Yorkshire, DL8 3HG**
Tel (01969) 622027/07818 035592
✉ rob@yorkshiredalesbrewery.com
⊕ yorkshiredalesbrewery.com

⊕ Situated in the heart of the Yorkshire
Dales, brewing started in 2005. Installation
of a new five-barrel plant and additional
fermenters at the converted milking
parlour have increased capacity to 20
barrels a week. Around 100 pubs are
supplied throughout the north of England.
A monthly special is always available.

Darrowby Dark (OG 1036, ABV 3.6%)
A mahogany mild with warming
complex malt flavours that give
a good mouthfeel.

Butter Tubs (OG 1037, ABV 3.7%)
A pale golden beer with a dry bitterness
complemented by a citrus flavour and aroma.

Herriot Country Ale (OG 1041, ABV 4%)
A straw-coloured pale ale with a good
flavour balance.

Gunnerside Gold (OG 1044, ABV 4.4%)
A golden beer with a distinct hop character.

Nappa Scar (OG 1048, ABV 4.8%)
A deep red chestnut-coloured best bitter
with a well-rounded malty flavour and a
fruity finish.

Whernside ESB (OG 1050, ABV 5.2%)
A strong, dark bitter, full-bodied with a
richness of flavours from the dark and
chocolate malts.

Young's

See Wells & Young's in
New national breweries section

Zerodegrees SIBA

**London: Zerodegrees Microbrewery, 29-31
Montpelier Vale, Blackheath, London, SE3 0TJ**
Tel (020) 8852 5619

**Bristol: Zerodegrees Microbrewery,
53 Colston Street, Bristol, BS1 5BA**
Tel (0117) 925 2706

**Reading: 9 Bridge Street, Reading,
Berkshire, RG1 2LR**
Tel (0118) 959 7959
✉ info@zerodegrees.co.uk
⊕ zerodegrees.co.uk
Tours by arrangement

Brewing started in 2000 in London and
incorporates a state-of-the-art, computer-
controlled German plant, producing
unfiltered and unfined ales and lagers,
served from tanks using air pressure (not

CO2). Four pubs are owned. All beers are suitable for vegetarians and vegans. All branches of Zerodegrees follow the same concept of beers with natural ingredients. There are regular seasonal specials including fruit beers.

Fruit Beer (OG 1040, ABV 4%)
The type of fruit used varies during the year.

Wheat Beer (OG 1045, ABV 4.2%) ◈
Refreshing wheat ale with spicy aroma; banana, vanilla and sweet flavours; dry, lasting finish.

Pale Ale (OG 1046, ABV 4.6%) ◈
American-style IPA with complex fruit aroma and peach flavours. Clean bitter finish with long aftertaste.

Black Lager (OG 1048, ABV 4.8%) ◈
Light, Eastern European-style black lager brewed with roasted malt. Refreshing coffee finish.

Pilsner (OG 1048, ABV 4.8%) ◈
Clean-tasting refreshing Pilsner with a malty aroma and taste, accompanied by delicate bitterness and citrus fruits.

FROM OVERSEAS

Anker

Brouwerij Het Anker, 49 Guido Gezellelaan, 2800 Mechelen, Belgium
Tel (0032) 15 28 71 47
✉ het.anker@pandora.be
⊕ hetanker.be

The Anchor Brewery has been in production since the 14th century. It was seriously damaged during the two world wars of the 20th century. It achieved fame from the 1960s when it introduced Gouden Carolus, a strong dark ale named after a coin from the reign of Emperor Charles V. The brewery was updated in the 1990s and the beer range extended. As with De Koninck below, the beer is served under pressure in Belgium but a cask version is on sale in selected outlets of the Wetherspoons chain of pubs.

Gouden Carolus Ambrio (ABV 8%)

De Koninck

Brouwerij De Koninck NV, 291 Mechelsesteenweg, 2018 Antwerp, Belgium
Tel (0032) 3 218 4048
✉ info@dekoninck.com
⊕ dekoninck.be

Legendary Belgian brewer of a classic pale ale, founded in 1833. In its home territory the beer is served under pressure but a cask-conditioned version is now available in Wetherspoon's pubs in Britain. The beer is sent in tankers to Shepherd Neame in Faversham (qv) where it is fined and racked into casks. It is called Ambrée in Britain but is known simply as De Koninck in Belgium.

Ambrée (ABV 5%)

FUTURE Breweries

The following new breweries have been notified to the Guide and should come on stream during 2007/2008:

**Brampton, Brampton, Derbyshire
Chequers, Little Gransden, Bedfordshire
Crown Inn, Little Staughton, Bedfordshire
Farmers Arms, Newton-in-Furness, Cumbria
Florence, SE24, London
Fox & Newt, Leeds, West Yorkshire
Green Mill, Rochdale, Gtr Manchester
Kilderkin, Impington, Cambridgeshire
Leeds, Leeds, West Yorkshire
Leeming Waters, Oxenhope, West Yorkshire
Phipps, Banbury, Oxfordshire
Plockton, Plockton, Highlands
Prospect, Standish, Gtr Manchester
Quercus, Churchstow, Devon
Ringmore, Teignmouth, Devon
Taddington, Blackwell, Derbyshire
Taylors, Egremont, Cumbria
Whitehaven, Croasdale, Cumbria
Wild Hop, Manfield, North Yorkshire
Wonky Dog, Brightlingsea, Essex**

Brewery organisations

There are three organisations mentioned in the Breweries section to which breweries can belong.

The Independent Family Brewers of Britain (IFBB) represents around 35 regional companies still owned by families. As many regional breweries closed in the 1990s, the IFBB represents the interests of the survivors, staging events such as the annual Cask Beer Week to emphasise the important role played by the independent sector.

The Society of Independent Brewers (SIBA) represents the growing number of small craft or micro brewers: some smaller regionals are also members. SIBA is an effective lobbying organisation and played a leading role in persuading the government to introduce Progressive Beer Duty. It has also campaigned to get large pub companies to take beers from small breweries and has had considerable success with Enterprise Inns, the biggest pubco.

The East Anglian Brewers' Co-operative (EAB) was the brainchild of Brendan Moore at Iceni Brewery. Finding it impossible to get their beers into pub companies and faced by the giant power of Greene King in the region, the co-op makes bulk deliveries to the genuine free trade and also sells beer at farmers' markets and specialist beer shops. EAB also buys malt and hops in bulk for its members, thus reducing costs.

New nationals

The rapid growth of Greene King and Marston's (the new name for Wolverhampton & Dudley Breweries) since 2000 has given them the status of national breweries. Wells & Young's has now joined their ranks: the group was formed when Young & Co of London closed its brewery in 2006 and all production was moved to Bedford. The new nationals do not match the size of the global brewers but they do reach most areas of Britain as a result of both their tied and free trade activities. Unlike the global producers or the old national brewers who disappeared in the 1990s, Greene King, Marstons and W&Y are committed to cask beer production. Greene King IPA is the biggest-selling standard cask beer in the country, Marston's Pedigree now outsells Draught Bass in the premium sector, and Wells Bombardier is one of the fastest-growing premium cask brands. There is a down-side to this progress: in some parts of the country, the choice of real ale is often confined to the products of Greene King and Marston's, and their continued expansion, seen in the takeovers of Belhaven, Hardys & Hansons, Jennings and Ridley's, is cause for concern for drinkers who cherish choice and diversity.

Greene King

Greene King plc, Westgate Brewery, Bury St Edmunds, Suffolk, IP33 1QT
Tel (01284) 763222
✉ solutions@greeneking.co.uk
⊕ greeneking.co.uk
Shop Mon-Sat 10-5, Sun 12-4
Tours 11am, 2pm and evening by arrangements

⊠ Greene King has been brewing in the market town of Bury St Edmunds since 1799. In the 1990s it bought the brands of the former Morland and Ruddles breweries and has given a massive promotion to Old Speckled Hen, which in bottled form is now the biggest ale brand in Britain. As a result of buying the former Morland pub estate, the company acquired a major presence in the Thames Valley region. But it has not confined itself to East Anglia or the Home Counties. Its tenanted and managed pubs, which include Old English Inns and Hungry Horse, total more than 2,100 while the assiduous development of its free trade sales, totalling more than 3,000 outlets, means its beers can be found as far from its home base as Wales and the north of England. In 2005 Greene King bought and rapidly closed Ridley's of Essex. Also in 2005, the company bought Belhaven of Dunbar in Scotland. Belhaven has a large pub estate that has enabled Greene King to build sales north of border. In 2006 the group bought Hardys & Hansons in Nottingham, taking its pub estate to close to 3,000. Seasonal beers: Rumpus (ABV 4.5%, Jan), Prospect (ABV 4.1%, May), Triumph Ale (ABV 4.3%, May), Ale Fresco (ABV 4.3%, Jun), Tolly Original (ABV 3.8%, Aug), Ruddles Orchard (ABV 4.2%, Sep), Old Bob (ABV 5.1%, Sep), Firewall (ABV 4.5%, Nov). Bottle-conditioned beer: Hen's Tooth (ABV 6.5% ⬛).

XX Mild (OG 1035, ABV 3%)

H&H Mild (OG 1035, ABV 3.1%)

IPA (OG 1036, ABV ⬥
A light, uncomplicated session bitter. Copper coloured with a subtle malty nose and just a hint of hops. A light bitter introduction with a sweetish, malty undertone give a refreshing, lemonade-type feel. A long, tapering finish turns drier and increases bitterness.

Ruddles Best Bitter (OG 1037, ABV 3.7%) ⬥
An amber/brown beer, strong on bitterness but with some initial sweetness, fruit and subtle, distinctive Bramling Cross hop. Dryness lingers in the aftertaste.

H&H Bitter (OG 1038, ABV 3.9%)

Morland Original Bitter (OG 1039, ABV 4%)

H&H Olde Trip (OG 1043, ABV 4.3%)

Ruddles County (OG 1048, ABV 4.3%) ⬥
Sweet, malty and bitter, with a dry and bitter aftertaste.

Old Speckled Hen (OG 1045, ABV 4.5%) ⬥
Smooth, malty and fruity, with a short finish. (The strength of the cask version was reduced from 5.2% in 2006.)

Abbot Ale (OG 1049, ABV 5%) ⬥
A full-bodied, distinctive beer with a bittersweet aftertaste.

Belhaven

Belhaven Brewing Co, Spott Road, Dunbar, East Lothian, EH42 1RS
Tel (01368) 862734
✉ info@belhaven.co.uk
⊕ belhaven.co.uk
Shop open during tours
Tours by arrangement

⊕ Belhaven is located in Dunbar, some 30 miles east of Edinburgh on the East Lothian coast. The company claimed to be the oldest independent brewery in Scotland but it lost that independence when Greene King bought it. Belhaven owns 275 tied pubs and has around 2,500 direct free trade accounts. Seasonal beers: Fruit Beer (ABV 4.6%, Jul), Fruity Partridge (ABV 5.2%, Dec).

60/- Ale (OG 1030, ABV 2.9%) ⬥
A fine but virtually unavailable example of a Scottish light. This bittersweet, reddish-brown beer is dominated by fruit and malt with a hint of roast and caramel, and increasing bitterness in the aftertaste.

70/- Ale (OG 1038, ABV 3.5%) ⬥
This pale brown beer has malt and fruit and some hop throughout, and is increasingly bittersweet in the aftertaste.

Sandy Hunter's Traditional Ale
(OG 1038, ABV 3.6%) ◆
A distinctive, medium-bodied beer. An aroma of malt and hops greets the nose. A hint of roast combines with the malt and hops to give a bittersweet taste and finish.

80/- Ale **(OG 1040, ABV 4.2%)** ◆
One of the last remaining original Scottish 80 Shillings, with malt the predominant flavour characteristic, though it is balanced by hop and fruit. Those used to hops as the leaders in a beer's taste may find this complex ale disconcerting.

St Andrew's Ale **(OG 1046, ABV 4.9%)**
A bittersweet beer with lots of body. The malt, fruit and roast mingle throughout with hints of hop and caramel.

For Maclay pub group (qv):

Signature **(OG 1038, ABV 3.8%)**
A pronounced malty note is followed by a digestive biscuit flavour. The beer has a late addition of Goldings and Styrian hops.

Kane's Amber Ale **(AV 4%)**
A hoppy aroma gives way to a malty yet slightly bitter flavour.

Wallace IPA **(ABV 4.5%)**
A classic IPA in both colour and style, with a long, dry finish.

Golden Scotch Ale **(ABV 5%)**
Brewed to an original Maclay's recipe, the emphasis is firmly on malt.

For Edinburgh Brewing Co:

Edinburgh Pale Ale **(ABV 3.4%)**

Marston's

Marston's plc, Marston's House, Wolverhampton WV1 4JT
Tel (01902) 711811
✉ **enquiries@marstons.co.uk**
⊕ **wdb.co.uk**

Marston's, formerly Wolverhampton & Dudley, has grown with spectacular speed in recent years. It became a 'super regional' in 1999 when it bought both Mansfield and Marston's breweries, though it quickly closed Mansfield. In 2005 it bought Jennings of Cockermouth and announced it would invest £250,000 in Cumbria to expand fermenting and cask racking capacity. In total, Marston's owns 2,537 pubs and supplies some 3,000 free trade pubs and clubs throughout the country. It no longer has a stake in Burtonwood Brewery (qv) but brews Burtonwood Bitter for the pub estate, which is owned by Marston's (see Pub groups). It added a further 70 pubs in March 2006 when it bought Celtic Inns for £43.6 million. In January 2007 it paid £155 million for the 158-strong Eldridge Pope pub estate.

Banks's & Hanson's

Banks's Brewery, Park Brewery, Wolverhampton, West Midlands, WV1 4NY
Contact details as above

Banks's was formed in 1890 by the amalgamation of three local companies.

Hanson's was acquired in 1943 but its Dudley brewery was closed in 1991. Hanson's beers are now brewed in Wolverhampton, though its pubs retain the Hanson's livery. Banks's Original, the biggest-selling brand, is a fine example of West Midlands mild ale but the name was changed to give it a more 'modern' image. Beers from the closed Mansfield Brewery are now brewed at Wolverhampton. Hanson's Mild has been discontinued.

Mansfield Dark Mild **(OG 1035, ABV 3.5%)**

Riding Bitter **(OG 1035, ABV 3.6%)**

Original **(OG 1036, ABV 3.5%)** ◆
An amber-coloured, well-balanced, refreshing session beer.

Bitter **(OG 1038, ABV 3.8%)** ◆
A pale brown bitter with a pleasant balance of hops and malt. Hops continue from the taste through to a bittersweet aftertaste.

Mansfield Cask Ale **(OG 1038, ABV 3.9%)**

For Burtonwood pub group:

Bitter **(OG 1036.8, ABV 3.7%)** ◆
A well-balanced, refreshing, malty bitter, with a good hoppiness. Fairly dry aftertaste.

Jennings

Jennings Bros plc, Castle Brewery, Cockermouth, Cumbria, CA13 9NE
Tel 0845 1297185
w jenningsbrewery.co.uk
Shop 9-5 Mon-Fri, 10-4 Sat, 10-4 Sun (Jul & Aug)
Tours by arrangement

⊕ Jennings Brewery was established as a family concern in 1828 in the village of Lorton. The company moved to its present location in 1874. Pure Lakeland water is still used for brewing, drawn from the brewery's own well, along with Maris Otter barley malt and Fuggles and Goldings hops. A distribution centre in Workington services the brewery's estate of 127 pubs and 350 free trade houses. Seasonal beers: Crag Rat (ABV 4.3%, Mar-Apr), Golden Host (ABV 4.3%, Mar-Apr), Redbreast (ABV 4.5%, Oct-Jan).

Dark Mild **(OG 1031, ABV 3.1%)** ◆
A well-balanced, dark brown mild with a malty aroma, strong roast taste, not over-sweet, with some hops and a slightly bitter finish.

Bitter **(OG 1035, ABV 3.5%)** ◆
A malty beer with a good mouthfeel that combines with roast flavour and a hoppy finish.

Cumberland Ale **(OG 1039, ABV 4%)** ◆
A light, creamy, hoppy beer with a dry aftertaste.

Cocker Hoop **(OG 1044, ABV 4.6%)** ◆
A rich, creamy, copper-coloured beer with raisiny maltiness balanced with a resiny hoppiness, with a developing bitterness towards the end.

Sneck Lifter **(OG 1051, ABV 5.1%)** ◆
A strong, dark brown ale with a complex balance of fruit, malt and roast flavours through to the finish.

Marstons

**Marston, Thompson & Evershed,
Marston's Brewery, Shobnall Road,
Burton upon Trent, Staffordshire,
DE14 2BW**
Tel (01283) 531131
⊕ wdb.co.uk

⊛ Marston's has been brewing cask beer in Burton since 1834 and the current site is the home of the only working 'Burton Union' fermenters, housed in rooms known collectively as the 'Cathedral of Brewing'. Burton Unions were developed in the 19th century to cleanse the new pale ales of yeast. Only Pedigree is fermented in the unions but yeast from the system is used to ferment the other beers.

Burton Bitter (OG 1037, ABV 3.8%) ◈
Overwhelming sulphurous aroma supports a scattering of hops and fruit with an easy-drinking sweetness. The taste develops from the sweet middle to a satisfyingly hoppy finish.

Pedigree (OG 1043, ABV 4.5%) ◈
Sweet beer with a slight sulphur aroma. Has the hoppy but sweet finish of a short session beer.

Old Empire (OG 1057, ABV 5.7%) ◈
Sulphur dominates the aroma over malt. Malty and sweet to start but developing bitterness with fruit and a touch of sweetness. A balanced aftertaste of hops and fruit leads to a lingering bitterness.

For InBev UK:

Draught Bass (OG 1043, ABV 4.4%) ◈
Pale brown with a fruity aroma and a hint of hops. Hoppy but sweet taste with malt, then a lingering hoppy bitterness.

Wells & Young's IFBB

**Wells & Young's Brewing Co,
Eagle Brewery, Havelock Street,
Bedford, MK40 4LU**
Tel (01234) 272766
✉ postmaster@wellsandyoungs.co.uk
⊕ wellsandyoungs.co.uk
Shop Mon-Thu 7.30am-10pm
Tours by arrangement

Wells & Young's was created in 2006 when Young's of Wandsworth, south London, announced it would close its brewery and transfer production to Bedford. The new company jointly owns the Eagle Brewery, which opened in 1976; the family has been brewing in Bedford since 1876. Wells & Young's has a combined sales team that has expanded sales of such key brands as Wells Bombardier, the fastest-growing premium cask beer in Britain, and Young's Bitter, the fastest-growing standard cask bitter. Wells and Young's runs separate pub estates: see Young's in Pub Companies section. In

January 2007, Scottish & Newcastle reached an agreement with W&Y to brew Courage beers at Bedford. A new company, Courage Brands Ltd, was created, with W&Y controlling 83% of the shares. The deal added a further 80,000 barrels a year at Bedford, taking volumes to more than 500,000 barrels and overtaking Greene King in size. The Courage beers will be aimed primarily at the free trade. Some Wells' beers are now available in Young's pubs and vice-versa. Wells owns 255 pubs and 230 serve cask beer. Seasonal beers: Wells Summer Solstice (ABV 4.1%, Jun), Wells Lock, Stock and Barrel (ABV 4.3%, Sep), Wells Banana Bread Beer (ABV 5.4%, Jan/Jun), Wells Winter Cheer (ABV 5.5%, Nov-Dec). Bottle-conditioned beers: Young's Special London Ale (ABV 6.4% G), Young's Champion Live Ale (ABV 5%).

Eagle IPA (OG 1035, ABV 3.6%) ◈
A refreshing, amber session bitter with pronounced citrus hop aroma and palate, faint malt in the mouth, and a lasting dry, bitter finish.

Young's Bitter (OG 1036, ABV 3.7%) ⬡ ◈
Citrus hops on the nose linger into the palate where the bitterness grows, but the overall character of this pleasant amber bitter is balanced by maltiness that was not so noticeable in the Wandsworth version.

Wells Bombardier (OG 1042, ABV 4.3%) ◈
Gentle citrus hop is balanced by traces of malt in the mouth, and this pale brown best bitter ends with a lasting dryness. Sulphur often dominates the aroma, particularly with younger casks.

Young's Special (OG 1044, ABV 4.5%) ◈
A malty, slightly sweet pale brown beer with lemon fruitiness and a bitterness that lingers. Some hoppiness on the palate and aftertaste.

Young's Waggledance (OG 1052, ABV 5%)

Young's Winter Warmer (OG 1055, ABV 5%) ⬡ ◈
Dark roasted malt is noticeable throughout this smooth, sweetish, ruby-black-brown beer with raisin and caramel notes in both flavour and aftertaste. The aroma can be slightly perfumed.

For Courage Brands:

Courage Best Bitter (OG 1038.3, ABV 4%)

Courage Directors Bitter (OG 1045.5, ABV 4.8%)

Keep your Good Beer Guide up to date by visiting www.camra.org.uk Click on 'Good Beer Guide' then 'Updates to the GBG 2008', where you will find information about changes to breweries.

Global giants

Eight out of ten pints of beer brewed in Britain come from the international groups listed below. Most of these huge companies have little or no interest in cask beer. Increasingly, their real ale brands are produced for them by smaller regional brewers.

Anheuser-Busch UK

**Anheuser-Busch UK, Thames Link House, 1 Church Road, Richmond, Surrey, TW9 2QW
Tel (020) 8332 2302**

The company brews 'American' Budweiser at the Stag Brewery, Lower Richmond Road, Mortlake, London SW14 7ET, the former Watney's plant, which is now run as a joint operation with Scottish & Newcastle (qv). Budweiser in bottle, can and keg is brewed from rice (listed first on the label), malt and hops, with planks of wood – the famous beechwood chips – used to clarify the beer. Not to be confused with the classic Czech lager, Budweiser Budvar.

Carlsberg UK

**Carlsberg Brewing Ltd, PO Box 142, The Brewery, Leeds, West Yorkshire, LS1 1QG
Tel (0113) 259 4594
⊕ carlsberg.co.uk/carlsberg.com**

Tetley, the historic Leeds brewery with its open Yorkshire Square fermenters, now answers to the name of Carlsberg UK: Carlsberg-Tetley was unceremoniously dumped in 2004. A wholly-owned subsidiary of Carlsberg Breweries of Copenhagen, Denmark, Carlsberg is an international lager giant. In Britain its lagers are brewed at a dedicated plant in Northampton, while Tetley in Leeds produces ales and some Carlsberg products. Some 140,000 barrels are produced annually. Tetley's cask brands receive little or no promotional support outside Yorkshire, most advertising being reserved for the nitro-keg version of Tetley's Bitter.

Tetley's Dark Mild (OG 1031, ABV 3.2%) ◈
A reddish, mid-brown beer with a light malt and caramel aroma. A well-balanced taste of malt and caramel follows, with good bitterness and a satisfying finish.

Tetley's Mild (OG 1034, ABV 3.3%) ◈
A mid-brown beer with a light malt and caramel aroma. A well-balanced taste of malt and caramel follows, with good bitterness and a satisfying finish.

Ansells Best Bitter (OG 1035, ABV 3.7%)

Tetley's Cask Bitter (OG 1035, ABV 3.7%) ◈
A variable, amber-coloured light, dry bitter with a slight malt and hop aroma, leading to a moderate bitterness with a hint of fruit, ending with a dry and bitter finish.

Tetley's Imperial (ABV 4.3%)

Draught Burton Ale (OG 1047, ABV 4.8%) ◈
A beer with hops, fruit and malt present throughout, and a lingering complex aftertaste, but lacking some hoppiness compared to its Burton original. Carlsberg also brews Greenalls Bitter (ABV 3.8%) for former Greenalls pubs supplied by wholesalers. Greenalls Mild has been discontinued.

Coors

**Coors Brewers Ltd, 137 High Street, Burton upon Trent, Staffs, DE14 1JZ.
Tel (01283) 511000
⊕ coorsbrewers.com**

Coors of Colorado established itself in Europe in 2002 by buying part of the former Bass brewing empire, when Interbrew (now InBev) was instructed by the British government to divest itself of some of its interests in Bass. Coors owns several cask ale brands. It brews 110,000 barrels of cask beer a year (under licensing arrangements with other brewers) and also provides a further 50,000 barrels of cask beer from other breweries.

M&B Mild (OG 1034, ABV 3.2%)
Brewed under licence by Highgate Brewery, Walsall.

Stones Bitter (OG 1041, ABV 4.1%)
Brewed for Coors by Everards.

Hancock's HB (OG 1038, ABV 3.6%) ◈
A pale brown, slightly malty beer whose initial sweetness is balanced by bitterness but lacks a noticeable finish. A consistent if inoffensive Welsh beer brewed for Coors by Brains.

Worthington's Bitter (OG 1038, ABV 3.6%)
A pale brown bitter of thin and unremarkable character.

M&B Brew XI (OG 1039.5, ABV 3.8%)
A sweet, malty beer with a hoppy, bitter aftertaste, brewed under licence by Brains.

Worthington's White Shield (ABV 5.6%) ⬚ ◈
Bottle-conditioned. Fruity aroma with malt touches. Fruity start with hops but the fruit lasts to a classic bitter finish.

White Shield Brewery

**Horninglow Street, Burton upon Trent, Staffs, DE14 1YQ
Tel 0845 6000598
⊕ coorsvisitorcentre.com**
Shop (in Museum of Brewing) 9.30-4.30
Tours by arrangement

The White Shield Brewery – formerly the Museum Brewing Co – based in the Museum of Brewing, is part of Coors. Confusingly, while it brews White Shield, the beer is now a Coors brand (see above). The brewery opened in 1994 and recreates some of the older Bass beers that had been discontinued. The brewery dates from 1920 with some equipment going back to 1840. It has a maximum capacity of 60 barrels a week. Production is divided 50:50 between cask and bottled beers.

Imperial Stout and No 1 Barley Wine are now brewed on an occasional basis and in bottle only, though draught versions are supplied to CAMRA festivals when supplies are available.

Worthington's St Modwen (OG 1038, ABV 4.2%) ◈
Hop and malt aroma. Delicate taste of hops and orange. Flowery citrus fruity finish.

Brewery Tap (OG 1042, ABV 4.5%)

Worthington E (OG 1044, ABV 4.8%)

Czar's Imperial Stout (OG 1078, ABV 8%) ◈
A library of tastes, from a full roast, liquorice beginning, dark toffee, brown sugar, molasses, Christmas pudding, rum, dark chocolate to name but a few. Fruit emerges, blackberry changing to blackcurrant jam, then liquorice root.

No 1 Barley Wine (OG 1105, ABV 10.5%) ▭ ◈
Unbelievably fruity! Thick and chewy, with fruit and sugar going in to an amazing complex of bitter, fruity tastes. Brewed in summer and fermented in casks for 12 months.

Guinness

Guinness closed its London brewery in 2005. All Guinness keg and bottled products on sale in Britain are now brewed in Dublin.

InBev UK

InBev UK Ltd, Porter Tun House,
500 Capability Green,
Luton, Beds, LU1 3LS
Tel (01582) 391166
✉ **name.surname@interbrew.co.uk**
⊕ **inbev.com**

A wholly-owned subsidiary of InBev of Belgium and Brazil. Interbrew of Belgium became the world's biggest brewer in 2004 when it merged with Brazil's leading producer, Ambev, leapfrogging Anheuser-Busch in the production stakes. Its international name is now InBev and it is a major player in the European market with such lager brands as Stella Artois and Jupiler, and internationally with Labatt and Molson of Canada. It has some interest in ale brewing with the cask- and bottle-conditioned wheat beer, Hoegaarden, and the Abbey beer Leffe. It has a ruthless track record of closing plants and disposing of brands. In the summer of 2000 it bought both Bass's and Whitbread's brewing operations, giving it a 32 per cent market share. The British government told Interbrew to dispose of parts of the Bass brewing group, which were bought by Coors (qv). Draught Bass has declined to around 100,000 barrels a year: it once sold more than two million barrels a year, but was sidelined by the Bass empire. It is now brewed under licence by Marston's (see New Nationals section). Only 30 per cent of draught Boddingtons is now in cask form and this is brewed under licence by Hydes of Manchester (qv Independent breweries section).

Scottish & Newcastle

Scottish & Newcastle UK,
2-4 Broadway Park,
South Gyle Broadway,
Edinburgh, EH12 9JZ
Tel (0131) 528 1000
⊕ **scottish-newcastle.com**

Scottish & Newcastle UK is Britain's biggest brewing group with close to 30 per cent of the market. S&N joined the ranks of the global brewers in 2000 when it bought Brasseries Kronenbourg and Alken Maes from the French group Danone; Kronenbourg is the biggest French beer brand and is exported internationally. Alken Maes is a major Belgian group that produces lagers, the Grimbergen abbey beer range and Morte Subite lambic beers. The group also has extensive brewing interests in Russia and the Baltic States through a consortium, BBH, formed with Carlsberg. BBH owns the biggest brewery in Russia, Baltika. S&N also has brewing interests in China, India, Greece, Finland, Vietnam and Portugal. The group has focused on Kronenbourg and its Baltic operations to such an extent that a major rationalisation of its brewing operations in Britain was announced in 2004, with the closure of both the Fountain and Tyne breweries in Edinburgh and Tyneside respectively. Scottish & Newcastle was formed in 1960, a merger between Scottish Brewers (Younger and McEwan) and Newcastle Breweries. In 1995 it bought Courage from its Australian owners, Foster's. Since the merger that formed Scottish Courage, the group has rationalised by closing its breweries in Nottingham, Halifax and the historic Courage (George's) Brewery in Bristol. The remaining beers were transferred to John Smith's in Tadcaster. It bought the financially stricken Bulmer's Cider group, which included the Beer Seller wholesalers, now part of WaverleyTBS. In 2003, S&N sold the Theakston's Brewery in Yorkshire back to the original family (see Theakston's entry in Independent breweries section) but still brews some of the beers at John Smith's. In February 2004, S&N entered into an arrangement with the Caledonian brewery in Edinburgh that gave S&N a 30% stake in Caledonian and 100% control of the brewery's assets (see Caledonian in the Independents). S&N's sole Scottish cask beer, McEwan's 80/-, has been axed. S&N also owns a leased pub estate: see Pub Groups. The Courage brands are now brewed by Wells & Young's and owned by a new company, Courage Brands Ltd (see New national breweries section).

Berkshire

Berkshire Brewery,
Imperial Way, Reading,
Berkshire, RG2 0PN
Tel (0118) 922 2988

No cask beer.

Federation

Federation Brewery,
Lancaster Road,
Dunston, Gateshead,
Tyne & Wear, NE11 9JR

The former co-operative brewery run by workingmen's clubs. S&N transferred production to Dunston when it closed its Tyneside plant in 2004 and bought Federation. 'Newcastle' Brown Ale is now brewed in Gateshead. No cask beer.

Royal

Royal Brewery,
201 Denmark Road,
Manchester, M15 6LD
Tel (0161) 220 4371

Massive brewery in Manchester capable of producing 1.3 million barrels of beer a year. No cask beer.

John Smith's

John Smith's Brewery, Tadcaster, North
Yorkshire, LS24 9SA
Tel (01937) 832091
⊕ **scottish-newcastle.com**
Tours by arrangement

The brewery was built in 1879 by a relative of Samuel Smith (qv). John Smith's became part of the Courage group in 1970. Major expansion has taken place, with 11 new fermenting vessels installed. Traditional Yorkshire Square fermenters have been replaced by conical vessels.

John Smith's Bitter (OG 1035.8, ABV 3.8%) ◤
A copper-coloured beer, well-balanced but with no dominating features. It has a short hoppy finish.

For Theakston's of Masham (qv):

Theakston Best Bitter (OG 1038, ABV 3.8%)
S&N also runs the Stag Brewery in Mortlake, London, as a joint venture with Anheuser-Busch (qv).

Three breweries change hands

There's a cynical view in the Good Beer Guide office that just before each edition goes to press a major announcement will be made about the future of a brewery. In the late summer of 2007, new records were set when three breweries changed hands.

The most significant was the takeover of the Ringwood Brewery in Hampshire by national giant Marston's. Ringwood started life in 1978 as the tiniest of micros in an old bakery, but under the guidance of first Peter Austin and then David Welsh grew to become a major regional force, brewing some 33,000 barrels a year.

In July 2007, Marston's paid £19 million for Ringwood. The deal involves a highly modern brewery in Ringwood, seven pubs and even a vineyard in France. Marston's met local CAMRA officials and said it would maintain production at Ringwood and would also keep the brewery's brands in production. The group's role at Jennings in Cumbria – major investment and greater availability of the brands – suggests it will be true to its word. CAMRA's concerns are that the takeover will trigger a further round of takeovers in the affluent south, with Greene King in particular anxious to match Marston's presence in the area, and in the longer term Marston's Pedigree swamping Ringwood's beers.

Archers of Swindon, a sizeable player in the free trade, went into administration in 2007 and in July was taken over by a local businessman, John Williams. Mr Williams has no previous experience of the brewing industry but is convinced he can build the fortunes of a company with some 2,000 free trade accounts and depots in Cambridge, Swindon and Warrington.

The historic Highgate Brewery in Walsall was acquired in July by Global Star Leisure, a previously unknown pub group. Highgate was once part of Mitchells & Butlers of Birmingham, which in turn became part of the Bass group. For most of its history, Highgate produced only mild and stronger dark ales, but, following a management buy-out from Bass, the product range has expanded. Until the Global Star takeover, Highgate was owned latterly by the Aston Manor group, which makes cider and sells bottled beers produced in Walsall. Global Star will continue to supply Aston Manor and will make Highgate beers available in its own pub estate.

Pub groups

Pubs groups or 'pubcos' (pub companies) dominate beer retailing in Britain but, with the exception of Wetherspoons, tend not to brand their outlets. The global brewers – with the exception of S&N – have disengaged from running pubs, preferring to sell beer to the pub groups. As a result of the deep discounts demanded by the pubcos, most sell beers mainly from the globals, thus restricting drinkers' choice, and forming a barrier to regional and micro-breweries. The market is dominated by three giant pub companies: Enterprise, which acquired the Unique chain; Mitchells & Butlers (the former Bass managed pubs); and Punch, which merged with Pubmaster and in 2005 bought Avebury Taverns and the Spirit Group, making it the biggest in the country. The national pub groups act like supermarkets: buying heavily-discounted national brands in large volumes and selling them at inflated prices. However, as a result of a Direct Delivery Scheme developed by the Society of Independent Brewers (SIBA), a number of pubcos, including Admiral Taverns, Enterprise, New Century and Punch, now stock beers from micro-breweries in selected outlets. Nevertheless, as this section shows, there is a depressing tendency for many pubcos to take their beers mainly or exclusively from the global brewers, with a devastating impact on drinkers' choice. There are some independent companies that are committed to cask beer: *after a company's name indicates it's an independent pub group that focuses on cask.

Admiral

Admiral Taverns, Penn House, 30 High Street, Rickmansworth, Herts, WD3 1EP
Tel (01923) 726300
✉ info@admiraltaverns.co.uk
⊕ admiraltaverns.com

Admiral was formed in 2004 and has rapidly become a major player in the pubco market, with many of its pubs bought from Enterprise, Globe and Punch. It doubled the size of its estate to 1,670 in 2007 when it bought 869 pubs from Punch. Its main beer suppliers are Carlsberg, Coors, InBev and S&N.

Bar

Bar Group, Eden House, Enterprise Way, Edenbridge, Kent, TN8 6HF.
Tel (01732) 866588
✉ info@thebargroup.com
⊕ thebargroup.com

The group runs 30 managed pubs in South-east England, under such names as Wishing Well and Bok.

Barracuda

Barracuda Group Ltd, Lunar House, Globe Park, Fieldhouse Lane, Marlow, Bucks, SL7 1LW
Tel (0845) 345 2528
✉ info@barracudagroup.co.uk
⊕ barracudagroup.co.uk

Barracuda was formed in 2000 and runs 181 managed outlets. The main pub brands in Barracuda are the 20-strong Smith & Jones chain, Varsity student bars and 44 Juniper Inns. It takes its main cask beers from Adnams, Coors, Greene King, InBev, and S&N.

Barter

Barter Inns, 132 Gypsy Hill, London, SE19 1PW
Tel (020) 8670 7001.
✉ barterinns@aol.com

Barter was formed in 1993 and operates in South-east England with 25 managed pubs. It takes beer from InBev and S&N, but its best-selling beer is Fuller's London Pride.

Bold

Bold Pub Company, Unit 13, Bold Business Centre, Sutton, St Helens, Merseyside, WA9 4TX
Tel (01925) 228999

Bold was set up in 2003 and operates in the North-west and Wales. It has 30 managed pubs and runs 16 of them as community locals under the Value Inns name. It takes its beers mainly from Coors and Carlsberg.

Botanic Inns

Botanic Inns Ltd, 261-263 Ormeau Road, Belfast, North Ireland, BT7 3GG
Tel (0289) 0509 700

Botanic runs nine bars, two hotels and two off-licences. It takes cask beer from unspecified suppliers.

Brakspear

W H Brakspear & Sons plc, Bull Courtyard, Bell Street, Henley-on-Thames, Oxon, RG9 2BA.
Tel (01491) 570200
✉ information@brakspear.co.uk
⊕ brakspear.co.uk

Brakspear is a pub company that emerged from the ashes of the Henley brewery. It sold the beer brands to Refresh UK: see Brakspear in Independent Breweries section. In December 2006, the pub company was bought for £106 million by London-based J T Davies. The combined estate numbers 150 pubs and most – but not all — of these will be re-branded as Brakspear. The pubs will sell Brakspear cask beers but not exclusively: where pubs trade in other independent brewers' areas, such as Harvey's, they will take beers from those producers.

Brunning & Price*

Brunning & Price, Yew Tree Farm Buildings, Saighton, Chester, CH3 6EG.
Tel (01244) 333100
⊕ brunningandprice.co.uk

Brunning & Price runs 12 managed pubs in the North-west. The company is committed to cask beer; its managers and tenants are free to choose their beers but are encouraged to support independents and micros. Customers may find Hydes, Ossett, Robinsons, Rooster and Phoenix and the company says 'You won't find keg or smoothflow bitters in any of our pubs'. See website for the company's beer page.

Bulldog

Bulldog Pubs Co, 6 Bridge Street, Boston, Lincolnshire, PE21 8QF
Tel (01205) 355522
✉ kevin.charity@bpcgroup.co.uk
⊕ bpcgroup.com

Formed in 1996, Bulldog runs 16 pubs in the Midlands and East Anglia.

Burtonwood

Burtonwood plc, Bold Lane, Burtonwood, Warrington, WA5 4PJ
Tel (01925) 225131
✉ seyles@burtonwood.co.uk
⊕ burtonwood.co.uk

Burtonwood's 480 pubs, the majority of which are traditional tenancies, were sold to Wolverhampton & Dudley Breweries (now Marston's) in 2005. The brewery is owned by Thomas Hardy Burtonwood but Burtonwood Bitter is now brewed by Marston's. Fewer than half the Burtonwood pubs stock cask beer but the number is expected to increase under Marston's ownership.

Cains*

Cains Beer Co, Stanhope Street, Liverpool, L8 5XJ
Tel (0151) 709 8734
✉ info@cains.co.uk ⊕ cains.co.uk

In May 2007 the owners of Robert Cain (qv) bought Honeycombe Leisure for £37 million, with finance from the Bank of Scotland. The pub company owns 109 outlets in the North-west and has an annual turnover of £65 million. The pubs will concentrate on beers – including cask ales – from Cains brewery.

Caledonian Heritable

Caledonian Heritable, 4 Hope Street, Edinburgh, EH2 4DB.
Tel (0131) 220 5511
✉ ga@caleyheritable.co.uk
⊕ caley-heritable.co.uk

A group with 292 pubs, all in Scotland. Beers come mainly from S&N, but the best-selling ale is Caledonian Deuchars IPA.

Camelot

Camelot Inns & Taverns, 22 Bancroft, Hitchin, Hertfordshire, SG5 1JS
Tel (01462) 455188
✉ mikek@camelotinns.fsnet.co.uk

Formed in 1993, Camelot runs 12 managed pubs in Hertfordshire and North-east London.

Candu

Candu Entertainment, Bloxham Mill, Barford Road, Bloxham, Oxfordshire, OX15 4FF.
Tel 0870 8385800
✉ admin@candu.com
⊕ candu.com

Formed in 2005, Candu has 40 managed pubs with limited interest in cask beer.

Capital*

Capital Pub Co, 1 Relton Mews, London SW7 1ET
Tel (020) 7589 4888
✉ enquiries@capitalpubcompany.com
⊕ capitalpubcompany.com

Formed in 2000 by veteran pub owner David Bruce of Firkin brewpub fame, Capital runs 26 managed pubs in London. The company is funded through the Enterprise Investment programme, which allows small investors to back companies. Most of the pubs in the estate, which includes the Anglesea Arms in SW7, serve cask beer from independent brewers.

Cascade

Cascade Public House Management, 5 Merlin Way, Bowerhill, Melksham, Wiltshire, SN12 6TJ
Tel (01225) 704734)
✉ cascade@blueyonder.co.uk

Formed in 1993, Cascade runs 14 managed pubs in South-west England.

Catmere

Catmere Group, Bridge House, Station Road, Scunthorpe, Lincolnshire, DN15 6PY
Tel (01724) 861703

Catmere owns 10 pubs in Leicestershire and Lincolnshire. Five serve cask beer from both national and regional brewers.

CCT Group

CCT Group/Jack Beard, 76 Mitcham Road, Tooting, London, SW17 9NG.
Tel (020) 8767 8967
✉ admin@jackbeards.co.uk

A South-east based company with 40 managed pubs operating under the Jack Beards name. Beer is supplied by S&N and Greene King.

Chapman

Chapman Group, Syon House, High Street, Angmering, West Sussex, BN16 4AG.
Tel (01903) 856744
✉ vicki@thechapmansgroup.co.uk
⊕ thechapmansgroup.co.uk

Formed in 1978, Chapman runs 44 pubs in southern England and Gloucestershire. Its main beer supplies come from S&N but it also sells cask beers from Harvey's of Lewes.

Churchill

Churchill Taverns Group, Avon House, Tithe Barn Road, Wellingborough, Northamptonshire, NN8 1DH
Tel (01933) 222110
✉ frwpjm@churchilltaverns.freeserve.co.uk

Formed in 1997, Churchill runs 17 managed pubs in Cambridgeshire, other parts of East Anglia, and Northamptonshire.

CI Hospitality

CI Hospitality, 19 Royal Square, St Helier,
Jersey, JE2 4WA
Tel (01534) 764000
⊕ indulgence.co.uk

CI Hospitality is the trading name of Citann, part of
CI Traders, which bought the Ann Street Brewery
in 2002, now known as Jersey Brewery (qv). The
group runs 81 pubs in the Channel Islands, which
sell beer from its own brewery and Coors.

Clark

Clark Pub Co, 6a Western Corner,
Edinburgh, EH12 5PY
Tel (0131) 466 7190
✉ info@clarkpubco.co.uk
⊕ clarkpubs.com

Formed in 1997, Clark runs four pubs in Scotland.

County Estate

County Estate Management, 79 New Cavendish
Street, London W1G 6XB
Tel (020) 7436 2080
✉ mail@countyestate.co.uk
⊕ countyestate.co.uk

County Estate runs 640 pubs nationwide. It
works hand-in-glove with Pubfolio (qv) on pub
acquisitions. It takes beers from Carlsberg, Coors,
InBev, Marstons and S&N, and has its own
supply company. Many houses serve cask beer.

Daisychain

Daisychain Inns, Chesterton Way,
Eastwood Trading Estate, Rotherham,
South Yorkshire, S65 1ST
Tel (01709) 820073

Daisychain operates 90 pubs across the
Midlands, north of England, Wales and Scotland
and also acts as a holding company for other
pub operators. It takes beers from Coors, InBev
and S&N.

JT Davies

See Brakspear.

Davy's Wine Bars

Davy & Co, 59-63 Bermondsey Street, London,
SE1 3XF
Tel (020) 7407 9670
✉ info@davy.co.uk
⊕ davy.co.uk

Wine merchants and shippers since 1870, Davy
has been opening wine bars and restaurants in
the London area since 1965. Its Davy's Old
Wallop (ABV 4.8%) is believed to be Courage
Directors. The company runs some 45 outlets,
including a few pubs.

Dorbiere

Dorbiere Public Houses, Unit 3, Stainburn Road,
Openshaw, Manchester, M11 2ER.
Tel (0161) 438 4060.
✉ robin.gray@LWC-drinks.co.uk

Dorbiere is part of LWC, a major drinks
wholesaling group. It runs 40 managed pubs in
the North of England. It takes beers from InBev
and S&N and has only a marginal interest in
cask beer.

Dukedom

Dukedom Leisure, Blenheim House, Falcon
Court, Preston Farm Industrial Estate, Stockton-
on-Tees, TS18 3TD.
Tel (01642) 704930
✉ enquiries@dukedom.co.uk

Dukedom runs 32 managed pubs and
nightclubs in North-east England.

Eldridge Pope

The 158-strong estate was bought by Marston's
in January 2007 for £155 million.

Elizabeth Inns

Elizabeth Inns, Merchant House, 33 Fore Street,
Ipswich, Suffolk, IP4 1JL
Tel (01473) 217458
✉ info@elizabethholdings.co.uk
⊕ elizabethhotels.co.uk

The company runs 45 pubs in East Anglia, many
bought from national brewers. Some pubs are
tied to InBev. Other suppliers are Adnams,
Greene King and Nethergate.

English Inns*

English Inns, 5 Mill Meadow, Langford,
Bedfordshire, SG18 9UR
Tel (01462) 701750
✉ burlisoninns@aol.com

Formely Burlison Inns, English owns seven pubs
in Bedfordshire, Cambridgeshire, Hertfordshire
and Warwickshire. Its main cask beer supplier is
Everards and it also takes beers from B&T, City
of Cambridge, Nethergate, and Tring.

Enterprise Inns

Enterprise Inns plc, 3 Monkspath Hall Road,
Solihull, West Midlands, B90 4SJ
Tel (0121) 733 7700
✉ enquiries@enterpriseinns.plc.uk
⊕ enterpriseinns.com

Formed in 1991 with an initial acquisition of
372 pubs from Bass, the company has grown
rapidly and is now Britain's second biggest pub
group. In 2002 it bought the former Whitbread
tenanted pub estate known as Laurel Inns, and
it has consolidated its position by adding the
Unique pub estate from Nomura. Enterprise
previously purchased pubs from John Labatt
Retail, Discovery Inns, Gibbs Mew, Mayfair
Taverns, Century Inns (Tap & Spile), and
Swallow Inns. Enterprise added to this number
by buying 439 former Whitbread pubs, and
then in 2001 bought 432 managed houses from
Scottish & Newcastle. Its current estate
numbers 7,000 and it has a war chest of £100
million for further acquisitions. A range of cask
beers from all the major brewers, as well as
many of the regionals and some micros through
the SIBA Direct Delivery Scheme, is available.

Festival Inns

Festival Inns, PO Box 12288, Loanhead, Midlothian, EH20 9YF
Tel (0131) 440 3290
✉ headoffice@festival-inns.co.uk
⊕ festival-inns.co.uk

Festival Inns was founded in 1997 and now has 26 pubs in Scotland. The main beer suppliers are Carlsberg, InBev and Greene King.

Fitzgerald*

Sir John Fitzgerald Ltd, Cafe Royal Buildings, 8 Nelson Street, Newcastle upon Tyne, NE1 5AW
Tel (0191) 232 0664
⊕ sjf.co.uk

Long-established, family-owned property and pubs company. Its pubs convey a free house image, most offering a good choice of cask beers, including guest ales from smaller craft breweries. The 28 pubs are mainly in the North-east but there are also outlets in Edinburgh, Harrogate and London.

G1

G1 Group, 62 Virginia Street, Glasgow, G1 1DA.
Tel (0141) 552 4494
✉ info@1group.co.uk
⊕ g1group.co.uk

G1 owns 37 managed pubs in Scotland in Aberdeen, Dundee, Edinburgh, Glasgow and Perth. The main beer supplier is S&N.

Global Star

Global Star, Empire House, New Street, Smethwick, Birmingham, B66 2AJ.
Tel (0121) 555 7001

Global Star owns some 100 pubs. In July 2007 it bought Highgate Brewery.

Globe

Globe Pub Company, c/o Scottish & Newcastle Pub Enterprises, 2-4 Broadway Park, South Gyle Broadway, Edinburgh, EH12 9JZ.
Tel (0131) 528 2700
⊕ pub-enterprises.co.uk

Globe owns leasehold pubs bought by Robert Tchenguiz, owner of Laurel (qv), through his R20 investment company. Ten pubs are leased through S&N Pub Enterprises (qv). Not surprisingly the beer is supplied by S&N.

Gray*

Gray & Sons (Chelmsford) Ltd, Rignals Lane, Galleywood, Chelmsford, Essex, CM2 8RE
Tel (01245) 475181
✉ enquiries@grayandsons.co.uk
⊕ grayandsons.co.uk

Former Chelmsford brewery that ceased production in 1974 and which now supplies its 49 tied and tenanted houses in Essex with a choice of cask beers from Adnams, Greene King and Mighty Oak. The tenants are also free to choose from a monthly guest list that features at least 10 different ales.

Great British Pub Co

Great British Pub Company, Redhill House, Hope Street, Salthey, Cheshire, CH4 8BU
Tel (01244) 678780
✉ info@gbpubco.co.uk

Formed in 1998, the company runs an estate of 35 managed pubs in Yorkshire.

Head of Steam*

Head of Steam Ltd, Manesty, Leazes Lane, Hexham, Northumberland, NE46 3AE.
Tel (01434) 607393
✉ tony@theheadofsteam.co.uk
⊕ theheadofsteam.com

Founded by CAMRA activist Tony Brookes, Head of Steam has pubs based on railway station concourses at Huddersfield, Newcastle-on-Tyne and Liverpool. All the outlets serve a wide range of cask beers and they stage regular beer festivals.

Heavitree

Heavitree Brewing, Trood Lane, Matford, Exeter, EX2 8YP Tel (01392) 217733

A West Country brewery, established in 1790, which gave up production in 1970 to concentrate on running pubs. The current estate, which is mainly confined to Devon, stands at 102. The pubs are tied to beers from Coors and InBev.

Herald Inns

Herald Inns and Bars, Sagar House, Eccleston, Chorley, Lancashire, PR7 5SH
Tel (01257) 452452
⊕ branniganbars.com

Herald runs 41 managed pubs and bars nationwide, including the Brannigans bar chain. The range of suppliers is wide and includes Arkells and Wells & Young's, as well as Anheuser-Busch, InBev and S&N.

Heritage

Heritage Pub Co, Donnington House, Riverside Road, Pride Park, Derby, DE24 8HY
Tel (01332) 384808
✉ firsttname@heritagepubs.com

Heritage runs 65 tenanted pubs in the East Midlands. Its main suppliers are Greene King and InBev. Its best-selling cask beer is Marston's Pedigree.

Honeycombe

See Cains.

Inns & Leisure

Inns & Leisure, 20-24 Leicester Road, Preston, Lancashire, PR1 1PP.
Tel (01772) 252917
✉ innsleisure@btconnect.com
⊕ innsandleisure.co.uk

Inns & Leisure, formed in 1970, runs 28 pubs in Cumbria, Lancashire and Yorkshire. Beer is supplied by S&N.

Interpub

Interpub, c/o the Stag, Hawthorn Lane, Burnham Beeches, Buckinghamshire, SL2 3TA.
Tel (01753) 647603
✉ office@interpub.co.uk
⊕ interpub.co.uk

Formed in 1996, Interpub runs 14 pubs in London, Cornwall and Scotland.

Kingdom

Kingdom Taverns, Dean House, 191 Nicol Street, Kirkcaldy, Fife, KY1 1PF
Tel (01592) 200033

Formed in 1972, Kingdom has a pub estate of 38 in Scotland. Major beer suppliers are InBev and S&N.

Laurel

Laurel Pub Co, Porter Tun House, 500 Capability Green, Luton, Bedfordshire, LU1 3LS
Tel 07002 528735
⊕ laurelpubco.com

Laurel was created in 2001 from the Whitbread pub estate. Laurel sold the tenanted pubs to Enterprise Inns (qv) a year later, but kept the managed houses, including the Hogshead chain. They have been re-branded Hogs Head and no longer specialise in cask beer. Other brand names include Litten Tree and Slug & Lettuce. The company was bought in 2005 by Robert Tchenguiz, who then added the Yates's estate of 149 pubs for £202 million. See also Globe. Main suppliers are Coors, Diageo, InBev and S&N.

Lionheart

Lionheart Inns, Porter Black Holdings, 7 Market Street, Newton Abbot, Devon, TQ12 2RJ
Tel (01626) 882000
✉ admin@lionheartinns.co.uk
⊕ lionheartinns.co.uk

Lionheart runs 33 managed pubs throughout the country.

London Town

London Town, 7 Cowley Street, London, SW1P 3NB.
Tel (020) 7799 3911
✉ pubs@londontowngroup.co.uk
⊕ londontowngroup.co.uk

The group operates 225 pubs acquired from the Petchey group (qv).

Maclay*

Maclay Group plc, The e-Centre, Cooperage Way Business Village, Alloa, FK10 3LP
Tel (01259) 272 087
⊕ maclay.com

Maclay, founded in 1830, stopped brewing in 1999. It owns 23 managed pubs in Scotland and supplies them with cask ales under the Maclay name brewed by Belhaven (qv). It also serves Caledonian Deuchars IPA.

McManus

McManus Taverns, Kingsthorpe Road, Northampton, NN2 6HT
Tel (01604) 713601
✉ enquiry@mcmanuspub.co.uk
⊕ mcmanuspub.co.uk

McManus was formed in 1970 with 22 pubs in the East Midlands; half serve cask beer mainly from S&N and Wadworth.

Market Town Taverns*

Market Town Taverns, 6 Green Dragon Yard, Knaresborough, North Yorkshire, HG5 8AU.
Tel (01423) 866100
✉ offfice@markettaverns.co.uk
⊕ markettowntaverns.co.uk

Run by CAMRA member Ian Fozard, the group owns eight pubs in North and West Yorkshire. It concentrates on beers from independent and micro-breweries, including Black Sheep and Timothy Taylor.

Massive

Massive Pub Co, Central House, 124 High Street, Hampton Hill, Middlesex, TW12 1NS
Tel (020) 8977 0633
⊕ massivepub.com

Formed in 1993, Massive owns 68 bars in London, Surrey and Hampshire.

Mentor

Mentor Inns, 20B Chancellor Street, London, W6 9RN.
Tel 0870 111 822
⊕ mentorinns.co.uk

Mentor runs 32 leased and tenanted pubs.

Mercury

Mercury Management (UK) Ltd, Mercury House, 19-20 Amber Business Village, Amington, Tamworth, Staffordshire, B77 4RP
Tel (01827) 62345
✉ headoffice@mercurymanagement.co.uk
⊕ mercurymanagement.co.uk

Mercury Management is the result of a 1999 buy-out of Mercury Taverns. It has slimmed down its estate from 45 pubs to 16.

Mitchells & Butlers

Mitchells & Butlers plc, 27 Fleet Street, Birmingham, B3 1JP   Tel 0870 609 3000
✉ communications@mbplc.com
⊕ mbplc.com

M&B owns some 1,800 pubs, bars and restaurants. Its brands include Ember Inns, Goose, Harvester, Nicholson's, O'Neill's, Toby Carvery and Vintage Inns. Some of the pubs serve cask beer and Ember also holds mini-beer festivals. Most pubs stock Draught Bass and also offer a choice of cask beers from Coors and some regional breweries. Ember specialises in regional brewers' beers. Robert Tchenguiz of Laurel has attempted to buy M&B and in May 2007 the two groups discussed a possible joint venture.

Mitchells*

Mitchells Hotels, 11 Moor Lane, Lancaster, LA2 6AZ
Tel (01524) 596000
✉ sales@mitchellspubs.co.uk
⊕ mitchellsoflancaster.co.uk

Mitchells stopped brewing in 1999 and now runs 60 pubs in North-west England. Its leading cask beer brand, Lancaster Bomber, is leased to Thwaites of Blackburn (qv). The pubs take cask beers from Everards, Moorhouses and Thwaites.

Morrells

Morrells of Oxford, with 132 pubs, was bought by Greene King in 2002.

New Century

New Century Inns, Belasis Business Centre, Billingham, TS23 4EA
Tel (01642) 343415
✉ NCI@newcenturyinns.co.uk
⊕ newcentury inns.co.uk

Formed in 1999, New Century owns 48 pubs in Yorkshire and the North-east. Its main beer suppliers are Coors, InBev and S&N.

Noble House

Noble House, 580 Ipswich Road, Slough, Berks, SL1 4EQ.
Tel (01753) 515250
✉ mail@noblehouseleisure.com
⊕ noblehouseonline.net

Noble House has retreated from owning pubs to concentrate on oriental-style bars and restaurants plus the Arbuckles American diner chain.

Novus

Novus Leisure, Vernon House, 40 Shaftesbury Avenue, London, W1D 7ER.
Tel (020) 7434 0030
✉ info@novusleisure.com
⊕ novusleisure.com

Novus has 32 managed pubs. The group's Tiger Tiger pubs serve cask beer.

Orchid

Orchid Pub Group, Park Mill, Burndell Lane, Park Street, St Albans, Hertfordshire, AL2 2HB.
Tel (01727) 871 100
⊕ orchidgroup.co.uk

Orchid runs 305 managed pubs under such names as Jim Thompson, Country Carvery and Bar Room Bar. 290 of the outlets were bought from Punch in 2006.

Passionate

Passionate Pub Co, Belasis Business Centre, Billingham, TS23 4EA
Tel (01642) 345639
✉ postmaster@passionatepub.co.uk
⊕ passionatepub.co.uk

In spite of sharing the same address, Passionate and New Century (qv) are separate companies that 'work alongside' one another. Passionate was founded in 1999 and runs 30 pubs in the North-west, East Midlands and East Anglia. Beers are sourced via Enterprise Inns and include Caledonian Deuchars IPA.

Pathfinder

Pathfinder Pubs was the managed pubs division of Wolverhampton & Dudley Breweries, but is now branded as Marston's.

Peach

Peach Pub Co, Leadenporch House, New Street, Deddington, Oxfordshire, OX15 0SP.
✉ info@peachpubs.com ⊕ peachpubs.com

Peach operates six pubs in Oxford, Milton Keynes, Stratford-on-Avon, Warwick and Witney.

Peninsula

Peninsula Inns, Peninsula House, Castle Circus, Torquay, Devon, TQ2 5QQ
Tel (01803) 200960
✉ office@peninsula.co.uk
⊕ peninsulainns.co.uk

Peninsula has 28 managed pubs in the South-west. It takes its beer supplies from Coors and S&N but some pubs offer Sharp's Doom Bar.

Petchey

Petchey Group, Exchange House, 13-14 Clements Court, Clements Lane, Ilford, Essex, IG1 2QY.
Tel (0208) 252 8000

Petchey runs 90 leased and tenanted pubs.

Pub Estate

Pub Estate Co Ltd, Blenheim House, Foxhole Road, Ackhurst Park, Chorley, Lancashire, PR7 1NY
Tel (01257) 238800
✉ info@pub-estate.co.uk
⊕ pub-estate.co.uk

A company established with the purchase of 230 pubs from Scottish & Newcastle, it currently has 510 pubs nationwide. The pubs offer beers from Carlsberg, Coors, InBev, Carlsberg and S&N.

Pubs 'n'Bars

Pubs 'n' Bars, Sandwood House, 10-12 Weir Road, London, SW12 0NA
Tel (020) 8228 4800

Formed in 1990, the group owns 66 pubs within the M25, Wales and the West Country.

Pub People*

Pub People Co, Morewood House, Broadmeadows Business Park, South Normanton, Alfreton, Derbyshire, DE55 3NA
Tel (01773) 510863 ⊕ pubpeople.com

The company has 72 managed pubs based in the Midlands and the North-east. Its main suppliers are Carlsberg, Coors, InBev and S&N but some pubs offer ales from Castle Rock and Greene King, with regular micro-brewed beers from the likes of Acorn and Milestone.

843

Pub Support

Pub Support Co, Unit 13, Bold Business Centre, Sutton, St Helens, Merseyside, WA9 4TX
Tel (01925) 228999

Pub Support has the same management as Bold (qv) but operates its own outlets. It has 40 managed pubs and they are supplied by S&N.

Pubfolio

Pubfolio, Wiltshire Drive, Trowbridge, Wilts, BN4 0TT
Tel (01225) 763171 ⊕ pubfolio.co.uk

Pubfolio grew out of the Innspired pub company, the former tied estate of Ushers of Trowbridge. The pubs were taken over by Punch and then sold to Pubfolio, which works closely with County Estate (qv) on tenant recruitment. Pubfolio has 540 tenanted pubs and takes its supplies from Carlsberg, Coors, InBev and Marstons.

Punch Group

Punch Taverns, Jubilee House, Second Avenue, Burton upon Trent, Staffordshire, DE14 2WF
Tel (01283) 501600
✉ firstname.lastname@punchpubs.co.uk
⊕ punchtaverns.com

Punch was formed in 1998 with the purchase of the Bass leased pub estate. In 1999, Punch, with the backing of Bass, bought Allied Domecq's pub estate. It sold 550 former managed houses to Bass, now Mitchells & Butlers (qv). In 2004, Punch merged with Pubmaster, creating an estate of more than 8,000 pubs. In December it leapfrogged Enterprise (qv) and became Britain's biggest pubco when it bought the Spirit Group of managed outlets for £2.7 billion. It also acquired Avebury Taverns. The group now owns 9,300 pubs though some of the recent acquisitions that are not suitable for conversion to tenancy or lease will be disposed of. It trades under such brand names as Chef & Brewer, John Barras and Qs. Punch claims its lessees are free to take guest beers, but brewers who supply the group are closely monitored and have to offer substantial discounts to be accepted. The main suppliers of beer are Carlsberg, Coors, Greene King, InBev and S&N, with guest ales from a number of regionals, including Adnams. It takes some micro-brewed beers via the SIBA Direct Delivery Scheme.

Pyramid

Pyramid Pub Co Ltd, Suite H3, Steam Mill Business Centre, Steam Mill Street, Chester, CH3 5AN
Tel (01244) 321171
✉ admin@pyramidpub.co.uk
⊕ pyramidpub.co.uk

Pyramid manages 410 tenanted pubs. It was formerly known as Paramount and bought its estate from Royal Bank of Scotland. The pub estate is widely spread, mainly in towns and cities in the North-west, North-east, Midlands and Wales. Beers are supplied by InBev, S&N and Marstons. Banks's is the leading cask ale.

Randalls

Randalls Jersey Ltd, PO Box 43, Clare Street, St Helier, Jersey, JE4 8NZ
Tel (01534) 836700
✉ lequesne@randalls.je
⊕ randallsjersey.com

A brewery that ceased production in 1992. It now runs 58 pubs on Jersey selling beers from InBev and S&N as well as the Jersey Brewery. Not to be confused with Randalls of Guernsey (see Independent breweries section).

Regent Inns

Regent Inns plc, 77 Muswell Hill, London, N10 3PJ
Tel (020) 8375 3000
✉ info@regent-inns.plc.uk
⊕ regentinns.co.uk

Founded in 1980, Regent owns 71 managed bars in London and the Home Counties under such names as Bar Risa, Jongleurs and Walkabout. The company has contracts with Coors, InBev and S&N.

Rosemount

Rosemount Taverns, 5 Fitzroy Place, Glasgow, G3 7RH.
Tel (0141) 221 7799
⊕ rosemounttaverns.co.uk

Rosemount operates 48 leased pubs.

Sarumdale

Sarumdale, 102 London Road, Burgess Hill, West Sussex, RH15 8NB
Tel (01444) 243573

Sarumdale runs 23 managed pubs in the Brighton area.

S&N Pub Enterprises

Scottish & Newcastle Pub Enterprises, 2-4 Broadway Park, South Gyle Broadway, Edinburgh, EH12 9JZ
Tel (0131) 528 2700
⊕ pub-enterprises.co.uk

The pub-owning arm of global brewer S&N, it has 1,170 leased pubs throughout Britain and also operates a further 470 pubs on behalf of Globe (qv). It is developing river and canalside pubs through the Waterside Pub Co, a joint venture with British Waterways. Unsurprisingly, S&NPE takes its beer supplies from the parent company and its other subsidiary, WaverleyTBS. A regular cask beer is Theakston Best Bitter.

Sovereign

Sovereign Inns, 65 King Richard's Road, Leicester, LE3 5QG
Tel (0116) 262 8828

Sovereign runs 33 tenanted, managed and leased pubs.

Tadcaster

Tadcaster Pub Co, Commer Group Ltd, Commer House, Station Road, Tadcaster, North Yorkshire, LS24 9JF

Tel (01937) 835020
✉ info@tadpubco.uk
⊕ tadpubco.co.uk

The company has 57 pubs in the North-east. Beers are supplied by Carlsberg, Coors, InBev and S&N.

Tattershall

Tattershall Castle Group,
Regus House, Windmill Hill Business Park,
Whitehill Way, Swindon,
Wilts, SN5 6QR
Tel (01793) 441429
⊕ tattershallcastlegroup.com

Tattershall was created when the Spirit Group, now part of Punch (qv), sold 178 managed city-centre pubs for £177 million in 2005. Tattershall is backed by the private equity group Alchemy Partners, and has such brands as Rat & Parrot, Bar 38 and Henry's in the group. Pubs and bars are owned throughout Britain but the main concentration is in London and the South-east. The main beer supplier is S&N.

Taverna Inns

Taverna Inns, Marquis of Granby, Main Street,
Hoveringham, Nottinghamshire, NG14 7JR
Tel (0115) 966 5566
✉ tavernainns@freuk.com

Formed in 1990, Taverna owns 30 pubs in the Midlands, Lincolnshire and NE England.

Thorley Taverns

Thorley Taverns, Old Police Station,
60 Gladstone Road, Broadstairs,
Kent, CT10 2HZ
Tel (01843) 602010
✉ ho@thorleytaverns.com
⊕ thorleytaverns.com

Founded in 1971, Thorley operates 36 managed pubs in Kent and London. Beers are supplied by S&N.

Trust Inns

Trust Inns, Blenheim House, Ackhurst Park,
Foxhole Road, Chorley, Lancs, PR7 1NY
Tel (01257) 238800
✉ info@trustinns.co.uk
⊕ trustinns.co.uk

Trust Inns runs 510 pubs throughout Britain. The main beer suppliers are Carlsberg and S&N.

Tynemill*

Tynemill Ltd, 2nd Floor, Victoria Hotel,
Dovecote Lane, Beeston, Nottingham, NG9 1JG
Tel (0115) 925 3333
⊕ tynemill.co.uk

Founded by former CAMRA chairman Chris Holmes, Tynemill has been established in the East Midlands for more than 20 years, and now owns 17 pubs. It has a 'pubs for everyone' philosophy, avoiding trends and gimmicks, and concentrating on quality cask ales and food in good surroundings, including public bars where space permits. It sells more than 1,500 different cask ales a year. Managers have complete autonomy on guest beers they sell. Tynemill is now the sole owner of the Castle Rock Brewery in Nottingham (qv). Regional and micro-brewers make up the bulk of Tynemill's products.

Ultimate Leisure

Ultimate Leisure, 26 Mosley Street, Newcastle
upon Tyne, NE1 1DF
Tel (0191) 261 8800
✉ enquiries@ultimateleisure
⊕ ultimateleisure.com

Ultimate, a North-east based bar operator, expanded into Northern England and Northern Ireland in 2005. Its venues are branded Coyote Wild, Blue Bambu and Chase and, not surprisingly, have little or no interest in cask.

Union

Union was the tenanted and leased pub estate of Wolverhamtpon & Dudley Breweries. The group is now called Marston's (qv) and the 1,750 pubs come under the title of Martston's Pub Co.

Wellington

Wellington Pub Co,
c/o Criterion Asset Management Ltd,
Beechwood Place, Thames Business Park,
Wenman Road, Thame,
Oxfordshire, OX9 3XA
Tel (01844) 262200
⊕ criterionasset.co.uk

A private company running 840 leased pubs nationwide. It is chaired by Hugh Osmond, founder of Pizza Express.

Wetherspoon*

J D Wetherspoon plc, Wetherspoon House,
Reeds Crescent, Central Park, Watford,
Hertfordshire, WD11 1QH
Tel (01923) 477777
✉ customersservices@jdwetherspoon.co.uk
⊕ jdwetherspoon.co.uk

Wetherspoon is a vigorous and independent pub retailer that currently owns 675 managed pubs. No music is played in any of the pubs and food is served all day. Each pub stocks regional ales from the likes of Cains, Fuller's, Greene King and Marstons, plus at least two guest beers. There are usually two beer festivals a year, one in the spring, the other in the autumn, at which up to 30 micro-breweries are stocked over a four-day period. The group also owns the Lloyds No 1 chain.

Wharfedale

Wharfedale Taverns Ltd,
Highcliffe Court, Greenfold Lane,
Wetherby, West Yorkshire, LS22 6RG
Tel (01937) 580805
✉ post@wharfedaletaverns.co.uk
⊕ wharfedaletaverns.co.uk

A company set up in 1993, it currently owns 30 pubs, mainly in the north. The main beers come from Carlsberg; guest beers are from the Tapster's Choice range.

845

Whitbread

Whitbread Court,
PO Box 77, Dunstable,
Bedforshire, LU5 5XG
Tel (01582) 424200
⊕ whitbread.com

Once a mighty power in the world of brewing and pub retailing, 670 managed pubs are all that are left of the empire. They operate under such banners as Beefeater, Brewers Fayre, Out & Out and TGI Friday's. Beers are supplied by InBev.

Wigan

Wigan Pub Co, Grimes Arcade,
22-24 King Street,
Wigan, WN1 1BS
Tel (01942) 823980
✉ enquiries@yesteryearpubco.co.uk
⊕ yesterydearpubco.co.uk

Wigan, formerly Yesteryear, operates 31 managed pubs in North-west England and is expanding its estate. The main beer supplier is S&N.

Young's

Young & Co's Brewery plc, Riverside House,
26 Osiers Road, London, SW18 4JD.
Tel (020) 8875 7000
✉ sales@youngs.co.uk
⊕ youngs.co.uk

There is no brewery any more: Young's closed its historic Wandsworth plant in 2006 when it created Wells & Young's with Charles Wells of Bedford (see W&Y in New national breweries section). It owns some 210 pubs in London and the Home Counties.

Zelgrain

Zelgrain, PO Box 85, Brighton,
East Sussex, BN1 6YT
Tel (01273) 550000
✉ info@zelnet.com
⊕ zelnet.com

Zelgrain was formed in 1995 and operates 31 managed pubs in South-east England. Beers are supplied by S&N and WaverleyTBS.

*This list does not include brewers with tied estates. See the breweries section.

All hands to the pumps

British beer is unique and so are the methods used for serving it. The best-known English system, the beer engine operated by a handpump on the pub bar, arrived early in the 19th century. It coincided with and was prompted by the decline of the publican brewer and the rise of commercial companies that began to dominate the supply of beer to public houses. In order to sell more beer, commercial brewers and publicans looked for faster and less labour-intensive methods of serving beer.

In *The Brewing Industry in England, 1700-1830,* Peter Mathias records that 'most beer had to be stored in butts in the publicans' cellars for the technical reason that it needed an even and fairly low temperature, even where convenience and restricted space behind the bar did not enforce it. This meant, equally inevitably, continuous journeying to and from the cellars by the potboys to fill up jugs from the spigots: a waste of time for the customer and of labour and trade for the publican. Drawing up beer from the cellar at the pull of a handle at the bar at once increased the speed of sale and cut the wage bill.'

The first attempt at a system for raising beer from cellar to bar was patented by Joseph Bramah in 1797. But his system – using heavy boxes of sand that pressed down on storage vessels holding the beer – was so elaborate that it was never used. But his idea encouraged others to develop simpler systems. Mathias writes: 'One of the few technical devices of importance to come into the public house since the publican stopped brewing his own beer was the beer engine. It was, from the first, a simple manually operated pump, incorporating no advances in hydraulic knowledge or engineering skill, similar in design to many pumps used at sea, yet perfectly adapted to its function in the public house.'

By 1801, John Chadwell of Blackfriars, London, was registered as a 'beer-engine maker' and soon afterwards Thomas Rowntree in the same area described himself as a 'maker of a double-acting beer-machine'. By the 1820s, beer engine services had become standard throughout most of urban England and Gaskell & Chambers in the Midlands had become the leading manufacturer, employing more than 700 people in their Birmingham works alone.

The Beers Index

More than 3,000 beers are listed in this index. They refer to the beers in bold type in The Breweries section (beers in regular production) and so therefore do not include seasonal, special or occasional beers that may be mentioned elsewhere in the text. Also omitted are beers that are easy to identify, because they are simply named after the brewery and the beer style (e.g. Brakspear Bitter, Exmoor Ale, Titanic Stout, Bateman Dark Mild, Rebellion IPA, etc.).

Auckland Ale Wear Valley 817
Auckland Glory Wear Valley 817
Audley Bitter Townhouse 810
Audley Gold Townhouse 810
Augustinian Ale Nethergate 772
Auld Alliance Fyfe 736
Auld Bob Malton (Brown Cow) 705
Auld Hemp High House 748
Auld Rock Valhalla 814
Aunty Myrtle's Mayfields 767
Aur Cymru Heart of Wales 746
Autumn Ale Clockwork 714
Autumn Gold Linfit 762
Aviator Dent 721
Avondale Strathaven 802
Axeman's Block Tigertops 808
Aysgarth Falls Wensleydale 819

B

B52 Leadmill 760
Babylon Banks Fenland 731
Back Beach Red Rock 788
Back Street Heroes Freeminer 734
Backtor Bitter Edale 726
Bad Medicine Ulverston 813
Bad Ram Haywood Bad Ram 746
Bad to the Bone Bank Top 689
Badger First Gold Hall & Woodhouse 743
Badger Stone Bitter Briscoe's 704
Baffie Fyfe 736
Bakewell Best Bitter Peak Ales 782
Balaclava Leyden 761
Balchder Cymru Conwy 716
Balmy Mild Cropton 719
Baltic Gold Wapping 815
Bamboozle Loddon 763
Bannockburn Ale Traditional Scottish Ales 811
Bantam Phoenix 783
Banter Bitter Nutbrook 775
Barbury Castle Three Castles 807
Barbus Barbus Butts 709
Bargee Elland 727
Barley Wine Wensleydale 819
Barm Pot Bitter Goose Eye 738
Barn Ale Bitter Old Luxters 779
Barn Ale Special Old Luxters 779
Barn Owl Cotleigh 717
Barney's Stout Townhouse 810
Barnsley Bitter Acorn 684
  Oakwell 776
Barnsley Gold Acorn 684
Barnstormer Bath Ales 692
Barnwell Bitter Digfield 722
Barron's Hopsit Exe Valley 729
Barrows Bitter Bryson's 706
Basil's Best Barum 691
Basket Case Spitting Feathers 800
Battleaxe Rudgate 791
Baz's Bonce Blower Parish 782
BB Donnington 723
  Evan Evans 728
Beach Barrowden 690
Beachcomber Teignworthy 805
Beacon Bitter Everards 728
Bear Ass Beartown 693
Bear Island Newby Wyke 772
Bearly Literate Beartown 693
Bearskinful Beartown 693
Beast Exmoor 729
  Leadmill 760

Beauforts Ale Storm 801
Beaver Bitter Belvoir 694
Bed Rock Keystone 758
Bede's Gold Durham 725
Beechwood Bitter Chiltern 713
Beedazzled Oulton 781
Beer Milk Street 768
Beer Elsie Bub Bartrams 691
Beer O'Clock Beckstones 693
Bees Knees Bartrams 691
  Woodlands 827
Beheaded '76 Keltek 758
Beijing Black Potbelly 785
Beinn Dearg Ale An Teallach 686
Belfast Ale Whitewater 822
Belfast Blonde College Green 715
Bellringer Abbey Ales 683
Belly Dancer Brewster's 703
Belt-n-Braces Leatherbritches 760
Beltane Braces Bartrams 691
Belter Leatherbritches 760
Ben Nevis Organic Traditional Scottish Ales 811
Bengal Tiger Concertina 715
Benno's Jolly Brewer 756
Bentley Brook Bitter Leatherbritches 760
Beorma Beowulf 694
Berserker Export Pale Ale Hebridean 746
Bespoke Leatherbritches 760
Best Dark Ale Goacher's 737
Betty Stogs Skinner's 797
Bevans Bitter Rhymney 789
Bevin Barrowden 690
Bewick Swan on the Green 804
Beyond the Pale Elland 727
Beyton Bitter Cox & Holbrook 718
Bezants Spectrum 798
BFB Carter's 711
Biale Orzel George Wright 828
Big Ginger Tigertops 808
Big Nev's Six Bells 797
Bikes, Trikes and Beer Bank Top 689
Bill O' Jacks Greenfield 741
Billy Boy Poachers 784
Binham Cheer Front Street 734
Bishop Percy Bridgnorth 704
Bishop Sumner Farnham 730
Bishop's Gold Durham 725
Bishops Farewell Oakham 775
Bishops Finger Shepherd Neame 796
Bishops Revenge
  Morgan Ales (Dow Bridge) 724
Bishops Somerset Ale Juwards 757
Bishops Special Mild Juwards 757
Bishopswood Bitter Swansea 804
A Bit'er Ruff Watermill 816
Bite IPA Newmans 773
Biter Doghouse 723
Bitham Blonde Westbury Ales (Wessex) 819
Bitter & Twisted Harviestoun 745
Bitter End Borough Arms 700
Bitter Experience Storm 801
Black Williams 823
Black & Tan Houston 752
Black Abbot Durham 725
Black Adder Mauldons 766
Black and Amber Warcop 816
Black Bear Beartown 693
Black Beauty Porter Vale 814
Black Bee Phoenix 783
Black Bess Bottle Brook 700

Black Bridge Toll End *809*
Black Buffle Spectrum *798*
Black Bull Bitter Ossett *780*
 Theakston *806*
Black Bull Mild Blanchfields *698*
Black Cat Moorhouses *770*
Black Coral Stout Hornbeam *752*
Black Country Bitter Holden's *750*
Black Country Mild Holden's *750*
Black Country Wobble Malvern Hills *765*
Black Crow Stout Poachers *784*
Black Cuillin Isle of Skye *755*
Black Diamond Mayflower *767*
Black Dog Elgood's *727*
Black Dog Freddy Mild Beckstones *693*
Black Dragon Mild B&T *689*
Black Dub Geltsdale *737*
Black Dub Oat Stout Wensleydale *819*
Black Eagle Special Pale Ale Westerham *820*
Black Five Black Mountain *697*
 Greenfield *741*
Black Galloway Sulwath *803*
Black Gold Cairngorm *710*
 Castle Rock *712*
 Copper Dragon *716*
Black Grouse Leek *761*
Black Hole Peakstones Rock *783*
Black Hole Stout Cambridge Moonshine *710*
Black Knight Goff's *738*
Black Lager Zerodegrees *831*
Black Magic Wizard *825*
Black Magic Mild Hanby *744*
Black Mari'a Old Bear *777*
Black Mass Abbeydale *684*
Black Moggy Mild Kemptown *758*
Black Oak Mayflower *767*
Black Pear Malvern Hills *765*
Black Pearl Milestone *768*
 Wooden Hand *826*
Black Pig Mild Bazens' *693*
Black Prince Eastwood *726*
 St Austell *792*
Black Pudding Leyden *761*
Black Rat Stout Old Chimneys *777*
Black Rock Organic *780*
Black Rock Ale Islay *755*
Black Sabbath Brunswick *706*
Black Shiver Turkey *812*
Black Squall Porter Newby Wyke *772*
Black Stag Coles *715*
Black Star Moonstone *770*
 Vale *814*
Black Velvet Durham *725*
Black Widow Webbs *818*
Black Zac Wentworth *819*
Blackcurrant Stout Cwmbran *720*
Blackfoot Barefoot *690*
Blackguard Butts *709*
Blacksmiths Ale Coniston *716*
Blackthorn Ale Thornbridge *806*
Blackwater Mild Crouch Vale *719*
Blackwood Stout Grain *739*
Bladderwrack Stout
 Famous Railway Tavern *730*
Blake's Gosport Bitter Oakleaf *776*
Blanche de Newland Tigertops *808*
Blanco Blonde Sheffield *796*
Blasters Warcop *816*
Blaven Isle of Skye *755*

Bleaklow Howard Town *753*
Blencathra Bitter Hesket Newmarket *747*
Blind House Box Steam *700*
Blond Butcombe *709*
 North Yorkshire *774*
Blond Lager Whitewater *822*
Blond Witch Moorhouses *770*
Blonde Arran *687*
 Daleside *720*
 Lancaster *759*
 Quartz *786*
 Smiles (Highgate) *748*
 Tring *811*
 Yates' *829*
Blonde Bombshell Houston *752*
Blondie Kings Head *759*
Bloomfields Bitter Suthwyk Ales (Oakleaf) *776*
Blooming Blonde Lion's Tail *762*
Blue Ridgeway *789*
Blue Bullet Bazens' *693*
Blue Gentian Wear Valley *817*
Blue John Moonstone *770*
Blue Moon George Wright *828*
Bluebird Bitter Coniston *716*
Bluebird XB Coniston *716*
Bo'sun's Call Stumpy's *803*
Boadicea Rother Valley *791*
Boathouse Bitter City of Cambridge *713*
BOB Wickwar *823*
Bob Wall Matthews *766*
Bobbin's Bitter Three B's *807*
Boddingtons Bitter InBev UK (Hydes) *754*
Bodelwyddan Bitter North Wales *774*
Bog Eyed Boggart Hole Clough *700*
Boggart Brew Boggart Hole Clough *700*
Bohemia Wylam *828*
Bohemian Whitstable *822*
Boiling Well Ludlow *764*
Bois Baaach Flock Inn *732*
Bomb Atomic *688*
Bomber County Highwood *749*
Bonny Lass Durham *725*
Bonovo Cock & Hen *715*
Bonum Mild Dow Bridge *724*
Border Steeans Beckstones *693*
Born in the USA Leadmill *760*
Boro Best North Yorkshire *774*
Bosley Cloud Storm *802*
Bosun Bitter Old Laxey *779*
Bottleneck Bride Bridestones *704*
Bottoms Up All Gates *685*
Bow Wow Doghouse *723*
Bowler Strong Ale Langton *760*
Bowley Best Red Rose *788*
Bowsprit Wapping *815*
Bradley's Finest Golden Black Country *696*
Brainstorm Storm *802*
Bramling Cross Broughton *705*
Bramling Traditional City of Cambridge *713*
Brand Oak Bitter Wickwar *823*
Brandy Snap Funfair *735*
Brandy Snapper Brandy Cask *702*
Branoc Branscombe Vale *702*
Branthill Best Fox *733*
Branthill Norfolk Nectar Fox *733*
Branthill Pioneer Fox *733*
Brassed Off Greenfield *741*
Brassknocker Matthews *766*
Braveheart Moulin *771*
Bread of Heaven Brains *701*

Break Water Red Rock 788
Breakfast Barum 691
Breckland Gold Brandon 702
Brecknock Best Breconshire 703
Brecon County Ale Breconshire 703
Brew House Special An Teallach 686
Brewers Droop Marston Moor 766
Brewers Gold Crouch Vale 719
    Pictish 783
Brewers Gold Extra Crouch Vale 719
Brewers Pride Marston Moor 766
Brewery Bitter Tomos Watkin 817
Brewery Tap White Shield (Coors) 836
Brewhouse Bitter Dunn Plowman 724
Brewhouse Special Nobby's 773
Bridesmaid Bridestones 704
Bridge Bitter Burton Bridge 708
Bridge Road Bitter Cox & Holbrook 718
Bridge Street Bitter Green Dragon 741
Brief Encounter Foxfield 734
Brigadier Bitter Hoskins Brothers (Tower) 810
Brigand Battledown 692
Bright Otter 781
Brightblade All Gates 685
Brimstone Abbeydale 684
Brindle Bullmastiff 707
Bristol IPA Smiles (Highgate) 748
Britannia Buntingford 708
Britannia Cream Ale Spire 799
British Bulldog Westerham 820
Broadgauge Bitter Cottage 717
Broadside Adnams 684
Brock Thornbridge 806
Brock Bitter Tring 811
Brockville Dark Tryst 812
Brockville Pale Tryst 812
Brodie's Prime Hawkshead 746
Broichan's Hillside 749
Brokers Warcop 816
Bronte Bitter Goose Eye 738
Brooklands Express Sawbridgeworth 794
Broomstairs Lowes Arms 763
Brother Rabbit Thornbridge 806
Brougham Ale Tirril 809
Brown Tongue Great Gable 740
Bruin Old Bear 777
Bruins Ruin Beartown 693
Brydge Bitter Bank Top 689
Buckenham Woods Uncle Stuarts 813
Bucket Hitch DarkTribe 721
Buckled Wheel Tryst 812
Budding Stroud 803
Buddy Confusing Bryncelyn 706
Buddy Marvellous Bryncelyn 706
Buddy's Delight Bryncelyn 706
Buff Blindmans 698
Bugle Best Yates' 829
Bull Village Brewer (Hambleton) 743
Bull Terrier Bull Lane 707
Bullfrog Wizard 825
Bullion Nottingham 775
    Old Mill 779
Bumble Beer Wentworth 819
Bumble Hole Bitter Olde Swan 778
Burcom Bitter Willy's 823
Burning Bridge Bridestones 704
Burnmoor Pale Great Gable 740
Burnsall Classic Bitter Briscoe's 704
Burntwood Bitter Mighty Oak 768
Burrough Bitter Parish 782

Burton Bitter Marston's 834
Burton Porter Burton Bridge 708
Burtonwood Bitter Marston's 833
Business As Usual Derby 722
Butlers Revenge Shugborough 796
Butser Bitter Gale's (Fuller's) 735
Butter Tubs Yorkshire Dales 830
Butterley Bitter Riverhead 789
Buttermere Beauty Cumbrian 720
Butts Pale Ale Ashover 688
Butts Park Bitter Alehouse 685
Butty Bach Wye Valley 828
Buzzin' Station House 801
BVB Own Label Branscombe Vale 702
BXA Maypole 767
Byker Bitter Northumberland 774

C

Cakewalk Funfair 735
Call Out Bitter End 696
Callow Top IPA Haywood Bad Ram 746
Callums Ale Front Street 734
Cambrian Best Bitter Felinfoel 731
Cambridge Bitter Elgood's 727
Canary Green Jack 741
Canary Beaver Brentwood 703
Canny Lad Durham 725
Canon Bitter Shoes 796
Capstan White Star 822
Captain Bill Bartram's Best Bitter
    Bartrams 691
Captain Grumpy's Best Wissey Valley 825
Captain Grumpy's Busted Flush
    Wissey Valley 825
Captain Grumpy's Golden Rivet
    Wissey Valley 825
Captain Oates Dark Mild Brown Cow 705
Captain Smith's Strong Ale Titanic 809
Captain's Stout Bartrams 691
Cardinal FILO 732
Care Taker of History Red Rose 788
Carlisle State Bitter Derwent 722
Carousel Southport 798
Carronade IPA Tryst 812
Cart Blanche Kelburn 757
Cascade Coastal 714
    Eglesbrech 726
    Hanby 744
Cascade Pale Ale Saltaire 794
Cascade Special Bitter Custom 720
Caskade Oldershaw 778
Cast Iron Consett Ale Works 716
Castle Arundel 687
Castle Bitter Conwy 716
Castle Eden Ale Camerons 711
Castles Bitter Northumberland 774
Castleshaw Greenfield 741
Castletown Bitter Bushy's 708
Cat Nap Barngates 690
Catbells Pale Ale Hesket Newmarket 747
Cathedral Ale Hill Island 749
Catherine Bartram's IPA Bartrams 691
Cats Whiskers Bartrams 691
    Whittington's 822
Caudle Bitter Langton 760
Cauldron Snout Darwin 721
Cavalier Ale Clearwater 714
Cavalier Red Why Not 822
Caveman Kinver 759
Cavendish Bridge Shardlow 795

Craven Ale Wood 826
Crazy Daze Potbelly 785
Crazy Horse Warrior 816
Cream Rooster's 791
Criffel Sulwath 803
Crix Gold Felstar 731
Croak & Stagger Frog Island 734
Crockerton Classic Wessex 819
Crofters FILO 732
Crofters Pale Ale An Teallach 686
Cromwell Pale Marston Moor 766
Cromwell's Hat Springhead 800
Crondall's Best Crondall 718
Crooked Furrow Dunn Plowman 725
Leith Hill 761
Crop Circle Hop Back 751
Crouch Best Crouch Vale 719
Crow Valley Bitter Cwmbran 720
Crow Valley Stout Cwmbran 720
Crowdie Kings Head 759
Crown Dark Mild Cox & Holbrook 718
Crown Imperial Stout Goacher's 737
Crown IPA Pictish 783
Crowning Glory Leyden 761
Crucible Best Sheffield 795
Crusader Empire 728
Milestone 768
Crystal Quartz 786
Crystal Clear Archers 687
Crystal Tips North Yorkshire 774
Crystal Wheat 3 Rivers 683
Cuckoo Ale Driftwood 724
Cuddy Lugs Bitter End 696
Cuil Hill Sulwath 803
Cuillin Beast Isle of Skye 755
Cumberland Ale Jennings (Marston's) 833
Cumbria Way Robinson's 790
Curly Blonde Leadmill 760
Cuthberts Church End 713
Cuthberts Cross Durham 725
Cutters Warcop 816
Cwrw Evan Evans 728
Cwrw Betys Beetroot Ale Coles 715
Cwrw Blasus Coles 715
Cwrw Braf Tomos Watkin 817
Cwrw Castell Conwy 716
Cwrw Celyn Bryncelyn 706
Cwrw Eryri Purple Moose 786
Cwrw Glaslyn Purple Moose 786
Cwrw Gwesty Cobdens Conwy 716
Cwrw Gwynant Gwynant 742
Cwrw Llanddarog Coles 715
Cwrw Madog Purple Moose 786
Cwrw Mêl Conwy 716
Cwrw Tudno Plassey 784
Cyclops Milton 769
Czar's Imperial Stout White Shield (Coors) 836
Czechumberland Bitter End 696

D

Dabbers 3 Rivers 683
Dabley Ale Worfield 827
Dabley Gold Worfield 827
Daffys Elixir Brewster's 703
Daisy Cutter Twickenham 813
Dalebottom Dark Briscoe's 704
Dalesman Peak Ales 782
Damson Stout Bartrams 691
Dance Severn Vale 794

Danebridge IPA Leek 761
Danebridge XXX Leek 761
Danish Dynamite Stonehenge 801
Dark and Delicious Corvedale 717
Dark Destroyer White Star 821
Dark Fantastic Spectrum 798
Dark Forest Rockingham 790
Dark Horse Elmtree 727
Townhouse 810
Dark Island Orkney 780
Dark Matter Betwixt 695
Dark Moor Kelburn 757
Dark Munro Highland 748
Dark Ness Red Rock 788
Dark O Otley 780
Dark Oak Mayflower 767
Dark Raven Beowulf 695
Dark Roast Ale Old Luxters 779
Dark Roast Porter Custom 720
Dark Ruby Sarah Hughes 753
Dark Ruby Mild Red Squirrel 788
Dark Secret Durham 725
Dark Side Blackdown 696
Blue Moon 699
Boggart Hole Clough 700
Dark Star Litton 763
Dark Swan Olde Swan 778
Dark Wheat Mild Tigertops 808
Darkish Moonstone 770
Darrowby Dark Yorkshire Dales 830
Dartford Wobbler Millis 769
Dartmoor Best Bitter St Austell 792
Dartmoor IPA Princetown 785
Darwin's Downfall City of Cambridge 713
Dashingly Dark Derby 722
Dave's Hoppy Beer Facer's 729
Davenports Bitter Highgate 748
Davenports Premium Highgate 748
Dawnbreaker Owl 781
Death or Glory Tring 811
Decade York 830
Deep Pit Warcop 816
Deep Slade Dark Swansea 804
Delapre Dark Great Oakley 740
Deliverance Cambrinus 710
Milestone 768
Delph Donkey Greenfield 741
Derby Porter Wicked Hathern 823
Desert Storm Storm 802
Destitution Leadmill 760
Deuchars IPA Caledonian 710
Deverill's Advocate Wessex 819
Devil's Elbow Hexhamshire 747
Devil's Water Hexhamshire 747
Devon Glory Exe Valley 729
Devon Pride South Hams 798
Devon's Pride Blackdown 696
Devonian Scattor Rock 794
Dewi Sant Coles 715
Diablo Eastwood 726
Diana Mild Whalebone 820
Dick Turpin Coach House 714
Dictators Concertina 715
Dinting Arches Howard Town 753
Discovery Fuller's 735
Dishie Debbie Hart 745
Ditchford Ale North Cotswold 773
Dive Bomber Funfair 735
Dixie's Bollards DarkTribe 721
Dixie's Mild DarkTribe 721

ESB Fuller's 735
Espresso Dark Star 720
Essex Boys Bitter Crouch Vale 719
Estivator Old Bear 777
Evening Glory Greenfield 741
Evensong Durham 725
Eventide Owl 781
Evolution Ale Darwin 721
Ewe-phoria Flock Inn 732
Ewe-reek-a! Flock Inn 732
Excalibur Hart 745
   Mayfields 767
Excelsior Ossett 780
   Oulton 781
   Uncle Stuarts 813
Exciseman's 80/- Broughton 705
Executioner Wharfedale 821
Exeter Old Bitter Exe Valley 729
Exhibition Ale Blackawton 696
Explorer Adnams 684
EXS Hoskins Brothers (Tower) 810
eXSB Bazens' 693
Extinction Ale Darwin 721
Extra Blonde Quartz 786
Extra Pale Ale Nottingham 775

F

Fagin's Itchen Valley 756
Fairfax Special Marston Moor 766
Falkirk 400 Eglesbrech 726
Fallen Angel Church End 713
Falling Stone Wold Top 825
Falstaff Warwickshire 816
Farleys Dusk Grindleton 742
Farm Gold Parish 782
Farmers Bitter Bradfield 701
Farmers Blonde Bradfield 701
Farmers Brown Cow Bradfield 701
Farmers Favourite 3 Rivers 683
Farmers Half Shugborough 796
Farmers Joy Alehouse 685
Farmers Pale Ale Bradfield 701
Farmers Sixer Bradfield 701
Farmers Stout Bradfield 701
Farmhouse Ale Spitting Feathers 799
Farne Island Pale Ale Hadrian & Border 742
Farrier's Best Bitter Coach House 714
Farriers Ale Shoes 796
Fast Reactor Far North 730
Father Mike's Dark Rich Ruby Brunswick 706
Fathers Favourite 3 Rivers 683
Fearless Blue Bear 698
Feather Light Mallard 764
Featherie Fyfe 736
Feathers Fuzzy Duck 736
Feelgood Malvern Hills 765
Felix Red Rose 788
Fellows Bitter Fellows, Morton & Clayton 731
Fen Tiger Iceni 754
Ferryman Topsham & Exminster 810
Ferryman's Gold Loddon 763
Festival Dark Star 721
Festival Ale Burton Bridge 708
Festival Mild Gale's (Fuller's) 735
Festival Red Tryst 812
Fever Pitch Yates 829
Fidra Fyfe 736
Figgy's Brew Skinner's 797
Finchcocks Original Westerham 820
Fine Fettle Ossett 780

Fine Light Ale Goacher's 737
Fine Soft Day Iceni 754
Finlaggan Ale Islay 755
Finn's Hall Porter Beowulf 695
Fire Bellied Toad Frog Island 734
Firebox RCH 787
Firefly O'Hanlon's 775
Fireside Black Country 696
Firing Squad Barum 691
First Cuckoo Cuckoo 719
First Foot Barefoot 690
First Gold Kings Head 759
First Lyte Fyfe 736
Fission Atomic 688
Fist Full of Hops Falstaff 730
Five Bells Shardlow 795
Five Bridge Bitter Mordue 771
Five Rivers Sheffield 796
Five Valleys Stroud 803
Flaming Embers Northern 773
Flaming Nora Lancaster 759
Flashman's Clout Goldfinch 738
Flat Cap Bank Top 689
Flatbac Bazens' 693
Fledgling Magpie 764
Fleur-de-Lys Foxfield 734
Flintknapper Ramsbury 786
Flintknapper's Mild Chalk Hill 712
Flintlock Pale Ale Coach House 714
Floral Dance Porter 785
Flotsam Hadrian & Border 742
Flowerdew Townhouse 810
Flying Herbert North Yorkshire 774
Fog on the Tyne Northumberland 774
Folly Ale Wharfedale 821
Folly Gold Wharfedale 821
Fools Gold North Yorkshire 774
Fools Nook Digfield 722
Forest Gold Rockingham 790
Forest XB Darwin 721
Forester's Session Bitter Wensleydale 819
Forever Autumn Marches 765
Forever Bury Leyden 761
Forgers Warcop 816
Formidable Ale Cains 709
Fortyniner Ringwood 789
Fosse Ale Dow Bridge 724
Fossil Fuel Isle of Purbeck 755
Fox Exmoor 729
Foxtale Ale Alcazar 685
Fraoch Heather Ale Williams 823
Freebooter Jollyboat 756
Frenchman's Creek Cornish Pale Ale Lizard 763
Friar Duck Mallard 764
Friezeland Ale Greenfield 741
Friggin in the Riggin Nelson 772
Frog Bog Lowes Arms 763
Frosted Hop Leadmill 760
Fruit Bat B&T 689
Fruit Beer Zerodegrees 831
Fruiterer's Mild Cannon Royall 711
Fruits of the Forest Rockingham 790
Fuggle-Dee-Dum Goddards 738
Fuggles Bitter Saltaire 794
Fuggles Pale Swan on the Green 804
Fulcrum Warcop 816
Full Ahead DarkTribe 721
Full Circle West Berkshire 820
Full Flight Magpie 764
Full Malty Cwmbran 720

Goldings Borough Arms *700*
    Leatherbritches *760*
Goldings Ale Saltaire *794*
Goldings BB Six Bells *797*
Goldrush Cottage *718*
    Elland *727*
Gone Fishing Green Jack *741*
    Oulton *781*
Good King Henry Old Chimneys *778*
Good Knight Felstar *731*
Good Old Boy West Berkshire *820*
Good, the Bad and the Drunk Falstaff *730*
Goodcock's Winner Cox & Holbrook *718*
Goodens Gold Flowerpots *733*
Goodrich Castle Springhead *800*
Gorlovka Imperial Stout Acorn *684*
Gorse Porter Cwmbran *720*
Goshawk Eagles Bush *725*
Gothenburg Porter Fowler's *733*
Gouden Carolus Ambrio Anker *831*
Gould Street Bitter Marble *765*
Gradely Bitter Grindleton *742*
Grain Storm Millstone *769*
Granary Bitter Reepham *788*
Grand Prix Mild Steamin' Billy
    (Grainstore) *739*
Grandstand Gold Southport *798*
Granny Wouldn't Like It Wolf *826*
Grantham Gold Newby Wyke *773*
Grantham Stout Oldershaw *778*
Grapefruit Beer St Peter's *793*
Grasmoor Dark Ale Loweswater *764*
Grasshopper Green Jack *741*
Grasshopper Kentish Bitter Westerham *820*
Gravediggers Ale Church End *713*
Gravesend Guzzler Millis *769*
Grease Abbey Bells *684*
Great Bustard Stonehenge *801*
Great Cockup Porter Hesket Newmarket *747*
Great Raft Bitter Old Chimneys *777*
Great White Hope Waveney *817*
Green Yetman's *829*
Green Goddess Durham *725*
Greengo Fyfe *736*
Grenville's Renown Jollyboat *756*
Grey Dogs Oyster *782*
Greyhound Strong Bitter Elgood's *727*
Griffin's Irish Stout Hill Island *749*
Grim Reaper Keltek *757*
Grog Grafton *739*
Grog Y VoG Vale of Glamorgan *814*
Grozet Bartrams *691*
    Williams *823*
Grumpling Premium Ale Vale *814*
GSB Marble *765*
Guernsey Sunbeam Jersey *756*
Guest Fest St Judes *793*
Gun Flint Brandon *702*
Gunner's Daughter Old Cannon *777*
Gunnerside Gold Yorkshire Dales *830*
Gunpowder Mild Coach House *714*
Guv'nor White Horse *821*
Guzzler York *830*
Gypsy's Kiss WC *817*

H

H&H Bitter Greene King *832*
H&H Mild Greene King *832*
H&H Olde Trip Greene King *832*
Ha'Penny Mild Harwich Town *745*

Hadda's Headbanger Vale *814*
Hadlow Bitter Harveys *745*
Hail Ale Moorcock *770*
Hairy Helmet Leatherbritches *760*
Halcyon Daze Old Cottage *778*
Halfway to Heaven Langham *759*
Halt Hilden *749*
Halzephron Gold Organic *779*
Hampshire Rose Itchen Valley *756*
Hamsterley Dark Ale Wear Valley *817*
Hamsterley Gold Wear Valley *817*
Hancock's HB Coors (Brains) *835*
Handliner Coastal *714*
Hanged Monk Tipples *808*
Hangman's Bitter Combe Martin *715*
Hardraw Force Strong Ale
    Wensleydale *819*
Harpers Great Oakley *740*
Harrier Lite Cotleigh *717*
Harrowby Pale Ale Oldershaw *778*
Harry Jacks 3 Rivers *683*
Hart Exmoor *729*
Hartington Bitter Whim *821*
Hartington IPA Whim *821*
Hartleys XB Robinson's *790*
Harvest Bitter Highwood *749*
Harvest Moon Ulverston *813*
Harvest Moon Mild Cambridge Moonshine *710*
Harvest Pale Castle Rock *712*
Hasty Knoll All Gates *685*
Hatters Robinson's *790*
Haugh Wylam *828*
Haughton Weave Lowes Arms *763*
Haunted Hen Felstar *731*
Haven Stumpy's *803*
Hawthorn Gold Wicked Hathern *822*
Haystacks Refreshing Ale
    Hesket Newmarket *747*
HBB Hogs Back *750*
Heacham Gold Fox *733*
Head Otter *781*
Headcracker Woodforde's *827*
Headless Dog College Green *715*
Headstrong Blackawton *696*
Hebden's Wheat Little Valley *762*
Hebridean Gold Isle of Skye *755*
Hedgemonkey Glastonbury *737*
Hedonist Wylam *828*
Heel Stone Stonehenge *801*
Helford River Lizard *763*
Heligan Honey Skinner's *797*
Hell Beck Geltsdale *737*
Hematite Beckstones *693*
Hemlock Castle Rock *712*
Hen Cloud Leek *761*
Hen Harrier Bowland *700*
Henley Bitter Lovibonds *763*
Henley Dark Lovibonds *763*
Henley Gold Lovibonds *763*
Henry's Original IPA Wadworth *815*
Herald Bryn *706*
    Cambrinus *710*
Hereford Cathedral Bitter Spinning Dog *799*
Hereford Organic Bitter Spinning Dog *799*
Herefordshire Light Ale Spinning Dog *799*
Herefordshire Owd Bull Spinning Dog *799*
Heritage Smiles (Highgate) *748*
Heroes Bitter Beowulf *695*
Herriot Country Ale Yorkshire Dales *830*
Hewish IPA RCH *787*

I

J

Lion Slayer Fyfe 736
Lionbru Lion's Tail 762
Lionheart Hampshire 744
Lions Pride Milestone 768
Lipsmacker Holland 751
Liquid Lobotomy Stout Garton 737
Liquor Mortis Blue Moon 699
Liquorice Stout Coles 715
Lite Releaf Buffy's 706
Little Green Man Bartrams 691
Little Sharpie Humpty Dumpty 753
Lizard Point Organic 779
LJB Fox 733
Lockoford Best Bitter Townes 810
Lomond Gold Organic
    Traditional Scottish Ales 811
London Porter Red Squirrel 788
London Pride Fuller's 735
Lone Soldier Haywood Bad Ram 746
Lonesome Pine Ulverston 813
Long Barrow Three Castles 807
Longboat George Wright 827
Longbow Empire 728
Longshore Tipples 808
Longwood Thump Greenfield 741
Lord Essex Felstar 731
Lord Lee's North Yorkshire 774
Lord Marples Thornbridge 806
Lordships Own Shugborough 796
Love Muscle North Yorkshire 774
Lowgate Light Townes 810
Loxley Ale Milestone 768
Loxley Gold Crown & Wellington 719
Lucinda's Lager Jolly Brewer 757
Luddite Ryburn 792
Ludlow Gold Marches 765
Luftkissenfahrzeug Halifax Steam 743

M

M&B Brew XI Coors (Brains) 835
M&B Mild Coors (Highgate) 835
Machen Best Carter's 711
Maclir Okells 776
Mad Jack Stout Holland 751
Mad Monk Digfield 723
Madgwick Gold Hammerpot 744
Madog's Ale Purple Moose 786
Mae West Maypole 767
Maggs' Magnificent Mild West Berkshire 820
Magic Wylam 828
Magik Keltek 757
Magnificat Durham 725
Magus Durham 725
Maiden's Saviour St George's 793
Maidstone Old Ale Goacher's 738
Mainbrace Jollyboat 756
Majestic White Star 821
Major Oak Maypole 767
Maldon Gold Mighty Oak 768
Malt Shovel Mild Fernandes 732
Malty Towers Tower 810
Man Down Grindleton 742
Man in the Moon Bell's 694
Manchester Bitter Marble 765
Manchester IPA 3 Rivers 683
Mansfield Cask Ale Marston's 833
Mansfield Dark Mild Marston's 833
Mansion Mild Tring 811
Maple Porter Leadmill 760
March Haigh Riverhead 789

Mardler's Woodforde's 826
Maritime Blackfriars 697
Marld Bartrams 691
Marmalade Cat Fat Cat 731
Marquis Brewster's 703
Mars Magic Wold Top 825
Marsh Mild Fugelestou 735
Marshmellow Oxfordshire Ales 781
Martlet Hammerpot 743
Mash Tun Bitter Leadmill 760
Master Brew Bitter Shepherd Neame 796
Matchlock Mild Marston Moor 766
Matfen Magic High House 748
Mathew's Mild Jolly Brewer 757
Matins Abbeydale 684
Matthew Clayton's Original Strong Brew
    Fellows, Morton & Clayton
    (Nottingham) 775
Maverick Fyne 736
Maybee Maypole 767
Mayfair Maypole 767
Mayfly Shardlow 795
Mayfly Bitter Maypole 767
Mayhem Maypole 767
    North Yorkshire 774
Mayor's Bitter Nailsworth 771
Maypole Mild Oakleaf 776
McCaig's Folly Isle of Mull 755
McConnells Irish Stout Jarrow 756
McCrory's Irish Stout Northumberland 774
McGivern's Pale Jolly Brewer 757
McLaughlin Laurie Best Bitter Horseshoe 752
McLaughlin Summer Horseshoe 752
Meandering Mild Bottle Brook 700
Melbreak Bitter Loweswater 764
Mellow Yellow Barefoot 690
Men of Norfolk Iceni 754
Mendip Mammoth Newmans 773
Mercian Shine Beowulf 695
Merlin Stout Tomos Watkin 817
Merlin's Ale Broughton 705
Merlin's Magic Moor 770
Mermaid Milk Street 768
Merriemaker Marston Moor 766
Merry Mount Morton 771
Mescan's Porter Moorcock 770
Meteor Hammerpot 744
Micawber's Mild Mauldons 766
Mid Life Crisis Bull Box 707
Midday Sun George Wright 827
Midhurst Mild Ballard's 689
Midnight Mash Bottle Brook 700
    Westbury Ales (Wessex) 819
Midnight Rambler Wessex 819
Midnight Stout Woodlands 827
Midnight Sun Goldfinch 738
Mike Hawthorn Farnham 730
Miladys Fancy Shugborough 796
Mild Rabarber Anglo Dutch 686
Mildly Complex Hardknott 745
Military Mild Old Chimneys 777
Milk of Amnesia Barefoot 690
    Blue Moon 699
Milk Stout Bristol Beer Factory 704
Mill Ale Whitewater 822
Mill Lane Mild Hoggleys 750
Milligans Lager Canavans 711
Millwright Millstone 769
Milly's Moor 770
Mine Beer Blindmans 698

Minotaur Milton 769
Misty Law Kelburn 757
Mitchell's Dream Crondall 718
Mochne Pivo George Wright 828
Moel Bryn Malvern Hills 765
Moelfre Mild North Wales 774
Molecatcher Moles 770
Molennium Moles 770
Moletrap Bitter Mauldons 766
Molly Malone Hilden 749
Molly's Chocolate Stout College Green 715
Molly's Secret Brandon 702
Monday's Child Abbey Bells 683
Mongrel Marston Moor 766
Monkeys Mersea Island 768
Monkeytown Mild Phoenix 783
Monkmans Slaughter Cropton 719
Monster Mash Nobby's 773
Monument Masters 766
Monument Ale Townhouse 810
Monumentale Severn Vale 794
Moondance Triple fff 812
Moonlight Ale Arkell's 687
Moonraker Lees 761
Moonshine Abbeydale 684
Moor Ale Little Valley 762
Moor Bitter Nutbrook 775
More Saddleworth 792
Morland Original Bitter Greene King 832
Mother in Law Wizard 825
Mowbrays Mash Oldershaw 778
MPA Moonstone 770
Mr Chubb's Lunchtime Bitter West Berkshire 820
Mr Harvey's Golden Sunshine Ale Keltek 758
Mr Perretts Traditional Stout Wickwar 823
Mr Phoebus Malvern Hills 765
Mr Sheppard's Crook Exe Valley 729
Mucky Duck Buffy's 707
Mud Mild Mersea Island 768
Muddy Boot Red Shoot 788
Mudpuppy Salamander 793
Mulberry Whale Bitter
  Cambridge Moonshine 710
Muntjac Saffron 792
Mutford Mild Oulton 781
Mutiny Rebellion 787
Mutleys Dark Spinning Dog 799
Mutleys Revenge Spinning Dog 799
Mutts Nuts Spinning Dog 799
Muzzle Loader Cannon Royall 711
Myles Best Bitter Mayflower 767
Mystery Tor Glastonbury 737

N

N1 Wheat Beer Pitfield 784
Nailmaker Mild Enville 728
Naked Ladies Twickenham 813
Nanny Flyer Leyden 761
Nantwich Ale 3 Rivers 683
Napoleon's Retreat All Gates 685
Nappertandy Brandon 702
Narrow Boat Shardlow 795
Native Ale Whitstable 822
Natterjack Frog Island 734
  Southport 798
Natural Beauty Ales of Scilly 685
Natural Magik Keltek 757
Naughty Ferrets Wessex 819
Naughty Nell's Mayfields 767

Nautilus Oulton 781
Navvy Phoenix 783
Neckoil Bitter Whalebone 820
Nel's Best High House 748
Nelson's Blood Fox 733
  Nelson 772
Nelson's Revenge Woodforde's 827
Nelsons Column Tunnel 812
Nemesis Hart 745
Nemesis Leadmill 760
  Peakstones Rock 783
Neptune Milton 769
Nerabus Ale Islay 755
Nero Milton 769
Nessies Monster Mash Cairngorm 710
Nether Ending Stowey 802
Nether Underestimate a Blonde
  Stowey 802
Nettle Ale Coles 715
Nettlethrasher Elland 727
New Dawn Alcazar 685
Newark Castle Brown Springhead 800
Newcastle Pride Northumberland 774
Newport Blonde Dobbins & Jackson 723
Newport Pale Ale Dobbins & Jackson 723
Newton's Drop Oldershaw 778
Nick's Milk Street 768
Nightmare Hambleton 743
Nimbus Atlas 688
Nimmos XXXX Camerons 711
Nine Lives Whittington's 822
No Angel Clark's 714
No Escape Black Hole 697
No-Eye Deer Goose Eye 739
Noble Bitter Beowulf 694
Noble Eden Ale Heart of Wales 746
Nord Atlantic Humpty Dumpty 753
Norfolk Lavender Honey Wolf 825
Norfolk Nectar Humpty Dumpty 753
Norfolk Nip Woodforde's 827
Norfolk Nog Woodforde's 827
Norfolk Poacher Brandon 702
Norman's Conquest Cottage 718
Norman's Pride Corvedale 717
Normanton IPA Milestone 768
Northamptonshire Bitter Hoggleys 750
Northern County Facer's 729
Northern Light Orkney 780
Northway IPA Fugelestou 735
Norton Ale Shoes 796
Norwegian Blue Buffy's 707
Norwich Terrier Buffy's 706
Not Strong Beer Kings Head 759
Nottingham Gold Castle Rock 712
Nowtsa Matta BB Bull Lane 707
Nowtsa Matta XB Bull Lane 707
NSB Kings Head 759
No 1 Odcombe 776
No 1 Barley Wine White Shield
  (Coors) 836
No. 1 Stout Kingstone 759
No. 7 Bristol Beer Factory 704
No. 7 Pale Ale Devil's Dyke 722
No. 8 Rugby 791
No. 8 Ale Devil's Dyke 722
Numpty Bitter Ryburn 792
Nuptu'ale Oakleaf 776
Nut Brown Premium Ale Cwmbran 720
Nutcracker Hanby 744
Nyewood Gold Ballard's 689

Original Bitter Abbey Bells 684
Blackawton 696
Hydes 754
Willy's 823
Original Black Stout Amber 686
Original Port Stout O'Hanlon's 775
Original Wood Swansea 804
Orkney Best Highland 748
Orkney Blast Highland 748
Orme's Best Great Orme 741
OSB Oldershaw 778
Tomos Watkin 817
Oscar Wilde Mighty Oak 768
Osier Cutter Fenland 731
Osprey Dark Eagles Bush 725
Ossian Inveralmond 754
Otley Gold Briscoe's 704
Over and Stout Goose Eye 739
Owain Glyndwr's Ale Plassey 784
Owd Oak Hydes 754
Own Sharp's 795
Oxbow 3 Rivers 683
Oxfordshire Bitter Butler's 709
Oyster Stout Ventnor 815
Whitstable 822
Oystercatcher Brimstage 704

P

PA Toll End 809
Pacific Bitter Bazens' 693
Pack Lane Uncle Stuarts 813
Pageant Ale Elgood's 727
Pagoda Battersea 692
Pail Ale Kinver 759
Old Cottage 778
Pain in the Glass Blue Bell 698
Pale Amber Sarah Hughes 753
Pale Gold Ossett 780
Pale Moonlight Phoenix 783
Pale Rider Kelham Island 757
Palmer's Poison Blythe 699
Paradox Brewdog 703
Paragon Steam St George's 793
Pargetters Buntingford 708
Parish Bitter Wood 826
Parkers Porter City of Cambridge 713
Parsons Pledge Derwent 722
Past Times Combe Martin 715
Pastiche Old Cottage 778
Patois Randalls 787
Paul's Pale Ale Fenland 731
Pavilion Pale Ale Bank Top 689
Pawn Star Star 800
Paxtons Pride Ffos y Ffin 732
Peat Porter Moor 770
Peden's Cove Windie Goat 824
Pedigree Marston's 834
Pegasus Milton 769
Pen-y-Ghent Bitter Three Peaks 807
Pendle Witches Brew Moorhouses 770
Penelope's Secret Jolly Brewer 757
Peninsula Ale Blackawton 696
Peninsula Pint Hill Island 749
Pennine Gold Golcar 739
Penny's Porter Derby 722
Pentland IPA Stewart 801
Peploe's Tipple Shoes 796
Peter's Well Houston 752
PG Steam RCH 787
PGA Storm 802

Pheasant Plucker Church End 713
Fuzzy Duck 736
Phoebe's Ale Toll End 809
Phoenix Falstaff 730
Physics Brewdog 703
Pickwick Mauldons 766
Piddle in the Dark Wyre Piddle 829
Piddle in the Hole Wyre Piddle 829
Piddle in the Snow Wyre Piddle 829
Piddle in the Wind Wyre Piddle 829
Piddlebrook Rainbow 786
Pieces of Eight Nelson 772
Pig Brook North Cotswold 773
Pig on the Wall Black Country 696
Pig's Ear Gribble 742
Pig's Ear Strong Beer Uley 813
Pigs Do Fly Potbelly 785
Pigs Ear Porter Cambridge Moonshine 710
Pigswill Stonehenge 801
Piledriver Sawbridgeworth 794
Pilsner Zerodegrees 831
Pinch Noggin' Three B's 807
Pinnacle Cuillin 719
Pinnacle Bitter Naylors 772
Pinnacle Blonde Naylors 772
Pinnacle Mild Naylors 772
Pinnacle Pale Ale Naylors 772
Pinnacle Porter Naylors 772
Pint Hidden 748
Pioneer Mayfields 767
Pipe Dream George Wright 827
Piper's Gold Fyne 736
Pirates Gold Wooden Hand 826
Pistol Night Ventnor 815
Piston Bitter Beer Engine 694
Piston Brew Bushy's 709
Pit Prop Warcop 816
Pit Shaft Warcop 816
Pitchfork RCH 787
Pitside Warcop 816
Pixash Keynsham 758
Pleasure Hidden 748
Pledgdon Ale Saffron 792
Plucking Pheasant Gribble 742
Plunder Jollyboat 756
Poachers Ale Parish 782
Poachers Dick Poachers 784
Poachers Pocket Church End 713
Poachers Pride Poachers 784
Poachers Trail Poachers 784
Poets Tipple Ashover 688
Polar Eclipse Beartown 693
Polly Peacham Wensleydale 819
Polly Stevens Toll End 809
Polly's Folly Buffy's 707
Pommies Revenge Goose Eye 739
Pooh Bear Church End 713
Port O Call Bank Top 689
Porta Porter Hereward 747
Ported Peat Porter Moor 770
Ported Porter Grain 739
Porter Bull Blanchfields 698
Post Haste Fellows, Morton & Clayton 731
Posthorn Premium Coach House 714
Postlethwaite Coach House 714
Pot O' Gold Wood 826
Pot Wallop Country Life 718
Potential Hidden 748
Potholer Cheddar 712
Potts Beck Litton 763

Reedcutter Humpty Dumpty 753
Reedham Gold Humpty Dumpty 753
Reel Ale Teignworthy 805
Reg's Tipple Gribble 742
Regal Blonde Oldershaw 778
The Reiver Broughton 705
Reiver's IPA Hadrian & Border 742
Remus Cox & Holbrook 718
Retribution Leadmill 760
Retriever Doghouse 723
Rev James Brains 701
Revenge Winter's 824
Reverend Awdry's Ale Box Steam 700
Reverend Eaton Shardlow 795
Reverend Ray All Gates 685
Revival Moor 770
Rhatas Black Dog 696
Rhode Island Red Bitter Brimstage 704
Ribble Rouser Grindleton 742
Rich Ruby Milestone 768
Ridgeway Tring 811
Riding Bitter Marston's 833
Riggwelter Black Sheep 697
Ringing Roger Edale 726
Ripper Green Jack 741
Rite Flanker Wickwar 823
River Crossing Appleford 686
Rivet Catcher Jarrow 756
Roar Spirit Blue Bear 698
Roaring Boy Oulton 781
Roaring Meg Springhead 800
Roasted Barley Stout Coles 715
ROB Ridgeway 789
Robust Porter Alehouse 685
Rochester Bitter Nelson 772
Rock Ale Bitter Beer Nottingham 775
Rock Ale Mild Beer Nottingham 775
Rocket Wylam 828
Rocket Fuel North Yorkshire 774
Rockwell Tower Masters 766
Roger & Out Frog & Parrot 734
Roger's Ruin Buffy's 707
Roisin-Tayberry Williams 823
Rolling Hitch Darwin 721
Rolling Thunder Leadmill 760
Roman Black George Wright 828
Rope of Sand Fyfe 736
Rossendale Ale Porter 785
Rougham Ready Bartrams 691
Roundhead Porter Why Not 822
Roundhead's Gold Springhead 800
Royal Ginger Brandon 702
Royal Oak O'Hanlon's 775
Royal Regiment of Scotland Isle of Mull 755
Royale Rodham's 790
Royston Pale Ale Buntingford 708
RSB Red Squirrel 788
Rubicon Rodham's 790
Ruby (1874) Mild Bushy's 708
Ruby Ale Wagtail 815
Ruby Lu Old Spot 779
Ruby Mild Rudgate 791
Rucking Mole Moles 770
Ruddles Best Bitter Greene King 832
Ruddles County Greene King 832
Rudolph's Tipple Greenfield 741
Rudyard Ruby Leek 761
Rupert's Ruin Springhead 800
Russett Owl 781
Russian Stoat Wessex 819

Rusty Bucket Brandon 702
Rutherford IPA City of Cambridge 713
Rutland Beast Grainstore 739
Rutland Panther Grainstore 739
Rutterkin Brewster's 703
Ryhope Tug Bull Lane 707

S

S&P Best Bitter Reepham 788
SA Brains 701
SA Gold Brains 701
Saaz Enville 728
Saddleback Best Bitter Slaughterhouse 797
Saddlers Best Bitter Highgate 748
St Agnes Reepham 789
St Andrew's Ale Belhaven (Greene King) 833
St Audrey's Ale Fenland 731
St Edwards Leek 761
St Ethelreda's Golden Bitter Hereward 747
Saint George 1648 683
St George Is Cross St George's 793
St George's Bitter Saddleworth 792
St Lawrence Ale Marches 765
Saint Magnus Ale Highland 748
Saint Petersburg Thornbridge 806
Salem Porter Bateman 692
Saligo Ale Islay 755
Sam Berry's IPA Crown & Wellington 719
Samuel Crompton's Ale Bank Top 689
Sandgrounder Bitter Southport 798
Sandrock Smoked Ale Ventnor 815
Sands Foxfield 734
Sandy Hunter's Traditional Ale
    Belhaven (Greene King) 833
Sauce of the Niall Bull Lane 707
Sawley Tempted Bowland 700
Saxon Battledown 692
Saxon Cross Rockingham 790
Saxon Gold Brandon 702
Saxon Strong Mighty Oak 768
SB Barefoot 690
SB Bitter Pitfield 784
SBA Donnington 723
SBD WC 817
Sca Fell Blonde Hesket Newmarket 747
Scapa Special Highland 748
Scarecrow Brimstage 704
Scatty Bitter Scattor Rock 794
Scawfell Great Gable 740
Schiehallion Harviestoun 745
Schooner Black Dog 696
Scoop Bricktop Brewery (Weatheroak) 818
Scoresby Stout Cropton 719
Scorpio Porter Hanby 744
Scottish Maiden Morton 771
Scotts 1816 Copper Dragon 716
Scullion's Irish Hilden 749
Scuppered Ales of Scilly 685
Sea of Tranquillity Blue Moon 699
Seadog Doghouse 723
Seaforth Ale Hebridean 746
Séance Full Mash 735
Second Brew Brunswick 705
Secret Hop Corvedale 717
Secret Kingdom Hadrian & Border 742
Sedgley Surprise Sarah Hughes 753
Selhurst Park Flyer Sawbridgeworth 794
Semer Water Wensleydale 819
Sentinel Old Foreigner 778
Serpentine Organic 779

Stabbers Ryburn *792*
Staffie Blythe *699*
Staffordshire Bitter Leek *761*
Staffordshire Gold Leek *761*
Stag Cairngorm *710*
   Exmoor *729*
Stairway Triple fff *812*
Stairway to Heaven Burton Bridge *708*
Stallion Hambleton *743*
Standard Ale Glenfinnan *737*
Standard Pioneer Boggart Hole Clough *700*
Stanney Bitter Stanway *800*
Stannington Stout Crown & Wellington *719*
Star Bitter Belvoir *694*
Star Gazer Yeovil *829*
Star Mild Belvoir *694*
Star Player Star *800*
Starlight White Star *821*
Starstruck Star *800*
Station Approach Brunswick *705*
Station Bitter Snowdonia *798*
   Stonehouse *801*
Station Porter Harwich Town *745*
   Wickwar *823*
Staveley Cross Townes *810*
Staveleyan Townes *810*
Steam Beer Dorset *724*
Steam Packet Grafton *739*
Steamer Three Tuns *807*
Steaming Red Rose *788*
Steel Town Bitter Consett Ale Works *716*
Steeler's Warcop *816*
Steerage Titanic *809*
Sternwheeler DarkTribe *721*
Sting Dunn Plowman *725*
Stingo Bartrams *691*
Stirling Bitter Traditional Scottish Ales *811*
Stirling Brig Traditional Scottish Ales *811*
Stockwood Stout Keynsham *758*
Stoker's Slake Three B's *807*
Stones Bitter Coors (Everards) *835*
Stones Ginger Beer Eglesbrech *726*
Stonewall York *830*
Stoodley Stout Little Valley *762*
Storm Damage Storm *802*
Storm Force Winter's *824*
Stormwatch Cox & Holbrook *718*
Stour Valley Strong Nethergate *772*
Stout Cat Fat Cat *731*
Stout Coffin Church End *713*
Stout Fellow Caythorpe *712*
Stout Olive Ulverston *813*
Stowmarket Porter Cox & Holbrook *718*
Strange Brew Jolly Brewer *757*
Straw Dog Wolf *825*
Strawberry Blonde Leadmill *760*
Strawberry Duck Bank Top *690*
Strength Hidden *748*
Strike Atomic *688*
Strikes Back Empire *728*
Strip & At It Freeminer *734*
Strong Mild Green Dragon *741*
Strong Northerley Highland *748*
Strong's Best Bitter Hampshire *744*
Strongarm Camerons *711*
Stronghold Arundel *688*
Stud Hambleton *743*
Studland Bay Wrecked Isle of Purbeck *755*
Suffolk 'n' Strong Bartrams *691*
Suffolk Comfort Mauldons *767*

Suffolk County Best Bitter Nethergate *772*
Suffolk Pride Mauldons *766*
Suitably Irish 3 Rivers *683*
Summa That Branscombe Vale *702*
Summer '76 Winchester *824*
Summer Ale Wapping *815*
   White Horse *821*
Summer Lightning Hop Back *751*
Summerhill Stout Big Lamp *695*
Summerset Yeovil *829*
Sun Dial Boggart Hole Clough *700*
Sun Goddess Yates *829*
Sunarise Kinver *759*
Sunchaser Blonde Everards *728*
Sunderland Best Darwin *721*
Sundew Ale Woodforde's *826*
Sundowner Langham *759*
Sunfire Ventnor *815*
Sunlight Betwixt *695*
Sunny Bitter Facer's *729*
Sunny Daze Big Lamp *695*
Sunrise Bristol Beer Factory *704*
   Oulton *781*
Sunset Captain Cook *711*
   Oulton *781*
Sunset Square City of Cambridge *713*
Sunshine Porter *785*
Supreme Bitter Nottingham *775*
Supreme Slater's *797*
Surrender 1646 Springhead *800*
Surrey Bitter Pilgrim *783*
Sussex Best Bitter Harveys *745*
Sussex Gold Arundel *688*
Sussex Mild Arundel *687*
Sussex Pride Welton's *818*
Sussex XX Mild Ale Harveys *745*
Sutton Comfort South Hams *798*
Suzanne's Stout Jolly Brewer *757*
SVS Nethergate *772*
Sweaty Clog Lowes Arms *763*
Swedish Nightingale Malvern Hills *765*
Sweet Lips Springhead *800*
Sweet Parish Ale Tunnel *812*
Swift Four Alls *733*
   Linfit *762*
Swift Nick Peak Ales *782*
Swift One Bowman *700*
Swithun Gold Winchester *824*
Swordsman Beowulf *695*
Sygnus Bitter Gold Blackfriars *697*

T

T'Other Teme Valley *805*
T'owd Navigation Nobby's *773*
T'Owd Tup Dent *722*
Tabatha the Knackered Anglo Dutch *686*
Tackler's Tipple Three B's *807*
Taffy's Tipple Jolly Brewer *757*
Tag Lag Barngates *690*
Taid's Garden Jolly Brewer *757*
Tailshaker Great Oakley *740*
Tally Ho! Palmer *782*
Tallywhacker Leith Hill *761*
Tamar Summerskills *803*
Tanglefoot Hall & Woodhouse *743*
Tanked Up Three Castles *807*
Tap Bitter Chalk Hill *712*
   Moles *769*
Tarnmonath Geltsdale *737*
Tartan Terror Houston *752*

U

Uber Weiss Tigertops 808
Ulverston Pale Ale Hawkshead 746
Umbel Ale Nethergate 772
Umbel Magna Nethergate 772
Uncle John Halifax Steam 743
Uncle Sam's Cropton 719
Uncle Stan Single Brown Stout
  Cox & Holbrook 718
Uncle Stu's Famous Steak Pie Stout
  Keltek 758
Undercliff Experience Yates' 829
Unicorn Robinson's 790
Union Jack Green Tye 741
Unity Strong Front Street 734
UPA Hawkshead 746
Uppermill Ale Greenfield 741
Usk Vale Best Bitter Dobbins & Jackson 723
UXB Ulverston 813
  White Star 821

V

Vale Ale Severn Vale 794
  Three Castles 807
Valiant Bateman 692
Valley Stomper Scattor Rock 794
Vallum Bitter Hadrian & Border 742
Valour Empire 728
Velvet Sweet Stout Reepham 788
Venus Derventio 722
Vicar's Ruin Church End 713
Vicar's Stout Nailsworth 771
Victoria Bitter Earl Soham 726
Victorian Velvet Briscoe's 704
Victorious Rugby 791
Victory John Joule (Coach House) 714
Victory Dark Mild Nelson 772
Viking Rudgate 791
  Sawbridgeworth 794
Village Archers 687
Village Bike Potton 785
Village Idiot White Horse 821
Village Pride Clearwater 714
Vincent Black Edale 726
Vital Spark Fyne 736
Vixen's Vice Alcazar 685
VoG No. 1 Vale of Glamorgan 814
Volunteer Bitter Bank Top 689
VPA Vale 814
Vulcan Bomber Bell's 694

W

W&M Kendal Pale Ale Derwent 722
W'Ruff Night Watermill 816
Waggledance Wells & Young's 834
Wagtail Porter Black Isle 697
Wakefield Pride Fernandes 732
Wallace IPA Belhaven (Greene King) 833
Wallace Monument Traditional Scottish Ales 811
Wallops Wood Bowman 700
Wally's Revenge Why Not 822
Waltzer Funfair 735
Wanderlust Blue Bear 698
Warlock Stout Houston 752
Warminster Warrior Wessex 819
Warrior Evan Evans 728
Wasd'ale Great Gable 740
Wassail Ballard's 689

Wat Tyler Itchen Valley 756
Waterloo Sunset Boggart Hole Clough 700
Waylade Trossach's Craft Brewery
  (Traditional Scottish Ales) 811
Wayland Smithy White Horse 821
Weardale Bitter Wear Valley 817
Weardale Blonde Wear Valley 817
Weavers Delight Golcar 738
Webb Ellis Rugby 791
Webbed Wheat Mallard 765
Webster's Green Label
  S&N (Burtonwood) 708
Webster's Yorkshire Bitter
  S&N (Burtonwood) 708
Wee Drop of Mischief Brandon 702
Weiss Beer Bushy's 709
Weiss Buoy Willy's 824
Weiss Squad Fyfe 736
Well Blathered Rudgate 791
Welland Valley Mild Great Oakley 740
Wellow Gold Maypole 767
Wells Bombardier Wells & Young's 834
Welsh Black Bullmastiff 707
  Great Orme 741
  Heart of Wales 746
Welsh Border Exhibition Ale Plassey 784
Welsh Gold Bullmastiff 707
Welsh Highland Bitter Snowdonia 798
Welsh Mountain IPA Great Orme 741
Welsh Pride Conwy 716
Welsh Red Bullmastiff 707
Wem Special Hanby 744
Wessenden Wheat Riverhead 789
West Coast IPA Phoenix 783
West Window Winchester 824
Westcountry Gold Blackawton 696
Westgate Gold Clark's 714
Westmorland Bitter Bryson's 706
Westmorland Gold Barngates 690
Westoe IPA Jarrow 756
Wet and Windy Oulton 781
Wet Nose Doghouse 723
Weymouth Best Bitter Dorset 724
Weymouth Harbour Master Dorset 723
Weymouth JD 1742 Dorset 724
Whapweasel Hexhamshire 747
Wharf Best Brew Wharf 703
Wharf Bitter Brew Wharf 703
Wharfedale Goose Eye 739
What The Duck Bell's 694
What the Fox's Hat Church End 713
WHB Wicked Hathern 822
Wheelbarrow Green Tye 742
Whernside ESB Yorkshire Dales 830
Whistle Stop Wylam 828
Whistlestop Shardlow 795
Whistlin' Dixie Full Mash 735
Whistling Joe Brandy Cask 702
Whitby Abbey Ale Black Dog 696
White Enville 728
White Adder Mauldons 766
White Amarillo Durham 725
White Bear Blue Bear 698
White Bishop Durham 725
White Boar Village Brewer (Hambleton) 743
White Bull Blanchfields 698
  Bull Lane 707
White Bullet Durham 725
White Crystal Durham 725

CAMRA's National Inventory
of Pub Interiors of Outstanding Historic Interest

The NATIONAL INVENTORY is CAMRA's pioneering effort to identify and help protect the most important historic pub interiors in the country. It has been part of the Campaign's mission for the past 35 years to not only save real ale but also Britain's rich heritage of pubs.

National Inventory Part One

Part One emphasises intactness. It lists pubs whose interiors have remained largely unaltered since before World War Two and also fully-intact post-war interiors completed before 1977 (either as part of purpose-built pubs or as exemplary refurbishment schemes).

ENGLAND

Buckinghamshire

West Wycombe: Swan

Cambridgeshire

Peterborough: Hand & Heart

Cheshire

Alpraham: Travellers Rest
Barthomley: White Lion
Bollington: Holly Bush
Gawsworth: Harrington Arms
Macclesfield: Castle
Scholar Green: Bleeding Wolf

Cornwall

Falmouth: Seven Stars

Cumbria

Broughton Mills: Blacksmiths Arms
Carlisle: Cumberland Inn

Derbyshire

Derby: Old Dolphin
Elton: Duke of York
Kirk Ireton: Barley Mow
Wardlow Mires: Three Stags' Heads

Devon

Drewsteignton: Drewe Arms
Luppitt: Luppitt Inn
Topsham: Bridge Inn

Dorset

Pamphill: Vine
Worth Matravers: Square & Compass

Durham

Billy Row: Dun Cow
Durham City: Shakespeare; Victoria

Essex

Mill Green (Ingatestone): Viper

Gloucestershire & Bristol

Ampney St Peter: Red Lion Inn
Bristol: (centre) King's Head
Purton: Berkeley Arms
Willsbridge: Queen's Head

Hampshire

Steep: Harrow

Herefordshire

Leintwardine: Sun Inn
Leysters: Duke of York

Kent

Ightham Common: Old House
Snargate: Red Lion

Lancashire

Great Harwood: Victoria
Preston: Black Horse
Stacksteads: Commercial

Leicestershire

Whitwick: Three Horseshoes

Greater London

Central London: (Hatton Garden, EC1) Old Mitre; (Smithfield, EC1) Hand & Shears; (Bloomsbury, WC1) Duke of York; (Holborn, WC1) Cittie of York
East London: (Dagenham) Eastbrook; (Ilford) Doctor Johnson
North London: (Harringay, N4) Salisbury; (Crouch End, N8) Queen's Hotel; (Tottenham, N17) Beehive
North West London: (Eastcote) Case is Altered; (Harrow) Castle; (South Kenton) Windermere
South East London: (Kennington, SE11) Old Red Lion
South West London: (West Brompton, SW10) Fox & Pheasant
West London: (Soho, W1) Argyll Arms; (Hammersmith, W6) Hope & Anchor; (Kensington, W8) Windsor Castle; (West Ealing, W13) Forester

Greater Manchester

Altrincham: Railway
Ashton-under-Lyne: March Hare
Chorlton on Medlock: Mawson
Eccles: Grapes; Lamb; Royal Oak; Stanley Arms
Farnworth: Shakespeare
Gorton: Plough
Heaton Norris: Nursery Inn
Manchester: (centre) Briton's Protection, Circus Tavern, Hare & Hounds, Peveril of the Peak

Rochdale: Cemetery Hotel
Salford: Coach & Horses
Stockport: Alexandra; Arden Arms; Swan with Two Necks
Westhoughton: White Lion

Merseyside

Birkenhead: Stork Hotel
Liverpool: (centre) Nook, Peter Kavanagh's, Philharmonic, Vines; (Walton) Prince Arthur
Lydiate: Scotch Piper
Waterloo: Volunteer Canteen

Norfolk

Warham: Three Horseshoes

Northumberland

Berwick upon Tweed: Free Trade
Netherton: Star Inn

Nottinghamshire

Nottingham: (centre) Olde Trip to Jerusalem; (Sherwood) Five Ways

Oxfordshire

Steventon: North Star
Stoke Lyne: Peyton Arms

Shropshire

Selattyn: Cross Keys
Shrewsbury: Loggerheads

Somerset

Bath: Long Acre Tavern, Old Green Tree; Star
Faulkland: Tucker's Grave Inn
Midsomer Norton: White Hart
Witham Friary: Seymour Arms

Staffordshire

Rugeley: Red Lion
Tunstall: Vine

Suffolk

Brent Eleigh: Cock
Bury St Edmunds: Nutshell
Ipswich: Margaret Catchpole
Laxfield: King's Head ('Low House')

Sussex (East)

Hadlow Down: New Inn

Sussex (West)

Haywards Heath: Golden Eagle
The Haven: Blue Ship

Tyne & Wear

Newcastle upon Tyne: (centre) Crown Posada; (Byker) Cumberland Arms

Warwickshire

Rugby: Peacock

West Midlands

Birmingham: (Digbeth) Anchor, Market Tavern, White Swan, Woodman; (Handsworth) Red Lion; (Nechells) Villa Tavern; (Small Heath) Samson & Lion; (Sparkbrook) Marlborough; (Stirchley) British Oak
Bloxwich: Romping Cat; Turf Tavern
Coventry: Black Horse
Dudley: Shakespeare
Oldbury: Waggon & Horses
Rushall: Manor Arms
Sedgley: Beacon Hotel
Wednesfield: Vine

Wiltshire

Easton Royal: Bruce Arms
Salisbury: Haunch of Venison

Worcestershire

Bretforton: Fleece
Clent: Bell & Cross
Defford: Cider House ('Monkey House')

Yorkshire (East)

Hull: (centre) Olde Black Boy, Olde White Harte

Yorkshire (North)

Beck Hole: Birch Hall Inn
Boroughbridge: Three Horse Shoes
Harrogate: Gardeners Arms
York: Blue Bell; Golden Ball; Swan

Yorkshire (South)

Barnburgh: Coach & Horses
Doncaster: Plough
Sheffield: (centre) Bath Hotel

Yorkshire (West)

Bradford: (centre) Cock & Bottle, New Beehive
Halifax: Three Pigeons
Leeds: (centre) Adelphi, Whitelock's; (Burley) Cardigan Arms, Rising Sun; (Hunslet) Garden Gate; (Lower Wortley) Beech

WALES

Mid Wales

Llanfihangel-yng-Ngwynfa: Goat
Llanidloes: Crown & Anchor
Welshpool: Grapes

North East Wales

Ysceifiog: Fox

North West Wales

Bethesda: Douglas Arms
Conwy: Albion Hotel

West Wales

Llandovery: Red Lion Inn
Pontfaen: Dyffryn Arms

SCOTLAND

Dumfries & Galloway

Stranraer: Grapes

Fife

Kincardine: Railway Tavern
Leslie: Auld Hoose

Grampian

Aberdeen: (centre) Grill
Craigellachie: Fiddichside Inn

The Lothians

Edinburgh: (centre) Abbotsford, Bennet's Bar, H P Mather's Bar, Oxford Bar; Rutherford's; (Newington) Leslie's Bar
West Calder: Railway

Strathclyde

Glasgow: (centre) Horseshoe Bar, Laurieston Bar, Old Toll Bar, Steps Bar; (Shettleston) Portland Arms, Railway Tavern
Larkhall: Village Tavern
Lochgilphead: Commercial ('The Comm')
Paisley: Bull
Renton: Central Bar

Tayside

Dundee: Clep; Frew's Bar; Speedwell Bar; Tay Bridge Bar

NORTHERN IRELAND

County Antrim

Ballycastle: Boyd's; House of McDonnell
Ballyeaston: Carmichael's
Bushmills: Bush House

County Armagh

Camlough: Carragher's
Portadown: Mandeville Arms (McConville's)

Belfast

Belfast: (centre) Crown; (west) Fort Bar (Gilmartin's)

County Fermanagh

Irvinestown: Central Bar

County Londonderry

Limavady: Owen's Bar

National Inventory Part Two

Part Two lists pub interiors which, although altered, have exceptional rooms or features of national historic importance. We also include (in italics) a number of outstanding pub-type rooms in other kinds of establishment, such as hotel bars.

ENGLAND

Bedfordshire

Broom: Cock
Luton: Painters Arms

Berkshire

Aldworth: Bell

Cumbria

Bassenthwaite Lake: Pheasant
Bootle: King's Head
Carlisle: Redfern

Devon

South Zeal: Oxenham Arms

Durham

Barningham: Millbank Arms

Gloucestershire & Bristol

Duntisbourne Abbots: Five Mile House

Hertfordshire

Bishop's Stortford: Nag's Head

Kent

Cowden Pound: Queen's Arms

Greater London

Central London: (Blackfriars, EC4) Black Friar; (Holborn, EC4) Olde Cheshire Cheese; (Holborn, WC1) Princess Louise; (Covent Garden, WC2) Salisbury
East London: (Newham, E6) Boleyn
South East London: (Southwark, SE1) George Inn; (Herne Hill, SE24) Half Moon

South West London: (St James's, SW1) Red Lion; (Battersea, SW11) Falcon; (Tooting, SW17) King's Head
West London: (Fitzrovia, W1) Tottenham; (Soho, W1) Dog & Duck; (Maida Vale, W9) Prince Alfred, Warrington Hotel; (Notting Hill, W11) Elgin Arms

Greater Manchester

Manchester: (centre) Marble Arch, Mr Thomas's
Stalybridge: *Railway Station Buffet*
Stockport: Queen's Head

Merseyside

Liverpool: (centre) Crown, Lion

Northumberland

Blyth: King's Head

Nottinghamshire

Arnold: Vale Hotel
West Bridgford: Test Match Hotel

Shropshire

Edgerley: Royal Hill

Somerset

Huish Episcopi: Rose & Crown ('Eli's')

Sussex (East)

Brighton: King & Queen
Hastings: Havelock

Tyne & Wear

Gateshead: Central Hotel
South Shields: Stag's Head
Sunderland: Dun Cow, Mountain Daisy

West Midlands

Birmingham: (Aston) Bartons Arms; (Hockley) Rose Villa Tavern; (Northfield) Black Horse
Netherton: Old Swan ('Ma Pardoe's')
Smethwick: Waterloo Hotel
Upper Gornal: Britannia

Worcestershire

Hanley Castle: Three Kings

Yorkshire (East)

Beverley: White Horse Inn ('Nellie's')
Bridlington: *Railway Station Buffet*
Hull: (centre) White Hart

Yorkshire (North)

Middlesbrough: (centre) Zetland Hotel
Settle: Royal Oak

Yorkshire (South)

Sheffield: (Carbrook) Stumble Inn

Yorkshire (West)

Heath: King's Arms

WALES
Glamorgan

Cardiff: (centre) Golden Cross

Mid-Wales

Rhayader: *Lion Royal Hotel*

SCOTLAND
Borders

Oxton: *Tower Hotel*

Fife

Kirkcaldy: Feuars Arms

The Lothians

Edinburgh: (centre) Cafe Royal, Kenilworth
Leith: Central Bar
Prestonpans: Prestoungrange Gothenburg

NORTHERN IRELAND

County Fermanagh

Enniskillen: Blake's Bar

Cittie of Yorke, Holborn, London WC1.

Readers' Recommendations

Suggestions for pubs to be included or excluded

All pubs are surveyed by local branches of the Campaign for Real Ale. If you would like to comment on a pub already featured, or on any you think should be featured, please fill in the form below (or copy it), and send it to the address indicated. Your views will be passed on to the branch concerned. Please mark your envelope with the county where the pub is, which will help us to sort the suggestion efficiently.

Pub name:

Address:

Reason for recommendation/criticism:

Pub name:

Address:

Reason for recommendation/criticism:

Pub name:

Address:

Reason for recommendation/criticism:

Your name and address:

Pub name:

Address:

Reason for recommendation/criticism:

Pub name:

Address:

Reason for recommendation/criticism:

Pub name:

Address:

Reason for recommendation/criticism:

Pub name:

Address:

Reason for recommendation/criticism:

Your name and address:

Please send to: (Name of county) Section, Good Beer Guide,
230 Hatfield Road, St Albans, Hertfordshire AL1 4LW

Books for Beer Lovers

CAMRA Books, the publishing arm of the Campaign for Real Ale, is the leading publisher of books on beer and pubs. Key titles include:

300 Beers To Try Before You Die

ROGER PROTZ

300 beers from around the world, handpicked by award-winning journalist, author and broadcaster Roger Protz to try before you die! A comprehensive portfolio of top beers from the smallest microbreweries in the United States to family-run British breweries and the world's largest brands. This book is indispensable for both beer novices and aficionados.

£14.99   ISBN 978 1 85249 213 7

An Appetite For Ale

FIONA BECKETT/WILL BECKETT

A beer and food revolution is under way in Britain and award-winning food writer Fiona Beckett and her publican son, Will, have joined forces to write the first cookbook to explore this exciting new food phenomenon that celebrates beer as a culinary tour de force. This ground-breaking collection of simple and approachable recipes has been specially created to show the versatility and fantastic flavour that ale has to offer. With sections on Snacks, Spreads and Dips, Soups, Pasta and Risotto, Seafood, Chicken and other Birds, Meat Feasts, Spicy Foods, Bread and Cheese and Sweet Treats it provides countless ideas for using beer from around the world. With an open mind, a bottle opener and a well-stocked larder, this exciting book will allow you to enjoy real food, real ale and real flavour.

£19.99   ISBN 978 1 85249 234 2

Beer, Bed & Breakfast

JILL ADAM & SUSAN NOWAK

A unique and comprehensive guide to more than 500 of the UK's real ale pubs that also offer great accommodation, from tiny inns with a couple of rooms upstairs to luxury gastro-pubs with country-house style bedrooms. All entries include contact details, type and extent of accommodation, beers served, meal types and times, and an easy-to-understand price guide to help plan your budget. This year why not stay somewhere with a comfortable bed, a decent breakfast and a well-kept pint of beer, providing a home from home wherever you are in the country.

£14.99   ISBN 978 1 85249 230 4

Good Beer Guide Prague & The Czech Republic

EVAN RAIL

This fully updated and expanded version of a collectible classic is the first new edition to be produced by CAMRA for 10 years! It is the definitive guide for visitors to the Czech Republic and compulsory reading for fans of great beer, featuring more than 100 Czech breweries, 400 different beers and over 100 great places to try them. It includes listings of brewery-hotels and regional attractions for planning complete vacations outside of the capital, sections on historical background, how to get there and what to expect, as well as detailed descriptions of the 12 most common Czech beer styles.

£12.99   ISBN 978 1 85249 233 5

Beer Lover's Guide to Cricket

ROGER PROTZ

There are many books about cricket and many on beer, but this is the first book to bring the two subjects together. Leading beer writer and cricket enthusiast Roger Protz has visited the major grounds of all the First Class counties and gives in-depth profiles of them – their history, museums, and memorabilia, plus listings of the best real ale pubs to visit within easy reach of each ground and details of the cask ales available. This fully illustrated book also features individual sections on the birth of the modern game of cricket and the history of each featured ground, making it an essential purchase for any cricket fan.

£16.99   ISBN 978 1 85249 227 4

Good Bottled Beer Guide

JEFF EVANS

This award-winning book is the bible for all aficionados of real ale in a bottle. It is a comprehensive guide to the huge number of beers now available in supermarkets, off-licences and via the internet in the UK, from bitters and milds to wheat beers, stouts, porters, fruit beers and barley wines. This fully updated and expanded sixth edition profiles nearly 800 bottle-conditioned beers with tasting notes, ingredients and brewery details.

£10.99   ISBN 978 1 85249 226 7

Good Beer Guide Germany

STEVE THOMAS

The first ever comprehensive region-by-region guide to Germany's brewers, beer and outlets. Includes more than 1,200 breweries, 1,000 brewery taps and 7,200 beers. Complete with useful travel information on how to get there, informative essays on German beer and brewing plus beer festival listings.

£16.99   ISBN 978 1 85249 219 9

The Book of Beer Knowledge

JEFF EVANS

A unique collection of entertaining trivia and essential wisdom, this is the perfect gift for beer lovers everywhere. Fully revised and updated it includes more than 200 entries covering everything from the fictional 'celebrity landlords' of soap pubs to the harsh facts detailing the world's biggest brewers; from bizarre beer names to the serious subject of fermentation.

£9.99   ISBN 978 1 85249 198 7

Order these and other CAMRA books online at **www.camra.org.uk/books**, ask at your local bookstore, or contact: **CAMRA, 230 Hatfield Road, St Albans, AL1 4LW**. Telephone **01727 867201**

An offer for CAMRA members
GOOD BEER GUIDE
Annual Subscription

Being a CAMRA member brings many benefits, not least a big discount on the *Good Beer Guide*. Now you can take advantage of an even bigger discount on the Guide by taking out an annual subscription.

Simply fill in the form below and the Direct Debit form opposite (photocopies will do if you don't want to spoil your book), and send them to CAMRA at the usual St Albans address.

You will then receive the *Good Beer Guide* automatically every year. It will be posted to you before the official publication date and before any other postal sales are processed.

You won't have to bother with filling in cheques every year and you will receive the book at a lower price than other CAMRA members (for instance, the 2007 Guide was sold to annual subscribers at only £9.50).

So sign up now and be sure of receiving your copy early every year.

Note: This offer is open only to CAMRA members and is only available through using a Direct Debit instruction to a UK bank. This offer applies to the 2008 *Good Beer Guide* onwards.

Name

CAMRA Membership No.

Address and Postcode

I wish to purchase the *Good Beer Guide* annually by Direct Debit and I have completed the Direct Debit instructions to my bank which are enclosed.

Signature   Date

Instruction to your Bank or Building Society to pay by Direct Debit

CAMPAIGN FOR REAL ALE

Please fill in the form and send to: Campaign for Real Ale Ltd. 230 Hatfield Road, St. Albans, Herts. AL1 4LW

Name and full postal address of your Bank or Building Society

To The Manager _____ Bank or Building Society

Address _____

_____

_____ Postcode _____

Name (s) of Account Holder (s)

_____

Bank or Building Society account number

Branch Sort Code

Reference Number

Banks and Building Societies may not accept Direct Debit Instructions for some types of account

DIRECT Debit

Originator's Identification Number

| 9 | 2 | 6 | 1 | 2 | 9 |

FOR CAMRA OFFICIAL USE ONLY
This is not part of the instruction to your Bank or Building Society

Membership Number

Name

Postcode

Instruction to your Bank or Building Society

Please pay CAMRA Direct Debits from the account detailed on this instruction subject to the safeguards assured by the Direct Debit Guarantee. I understand that this instruction may remain with CAMRA and, if so, will be passed electronically to my Bank/Building Society

Signature(s) _____

Date _____

✂ detached and retained this section

This Guarantee should be detached and retained by the payer.

DIRECT Debit

The Direct Debit Guarantee

- This Guarantee is offered by all Banks and Building Societies that take part in the Direct Debit Scheme. The efficiency and security of the Scheme is monitored and protected by your own Bank or Building Society.

- If the amounts to be paid or the payment dates change CAMRA will notify you 10 working days in advance of your account being debited or as otherwise agreed.

- If an error is made by CAMRA or your Bank or Building Society, you are guaranteed a full and immediate refund from your branch of the amount paid.

- You can cancel a Direct Debit at any time by writing to your Bank or Building Society. Please also send a copy of your letter to us.

It takes all sorts to campaign for real ale

Join by Direct Debit and get three months' membership FREE!

www.camra.org.uk/joinus

CAMRA, the Campaign for Real Ale, is an independent, not-for-profit, volunteer-led consumer organisation. We actively campaign for full pints and longer licensing hours as well as protecting the local pub and lobbying government to champion pub-goers' rights.

CAMRA has 87,000 members from all ages and backgrounds, brought together by a common belief in the issues that CAMRA deals with and their love of good quality British beer. From just £20 a year, that's less than a pint a month, you can join CAMRA and enjoy the following benefits:

- A monthly newspaper informing you about beer and pub news and detailing events and beer festivals around the country.
- Free or reduced entry to over 140 national, regional and local beer festivals.
- Money off many of our publications including the Good Beer Guide.
- Access to a members' only section of our national website, www.camra.org.uk, which gives up-to-the-minute news stories and includes a special offer section with regular features saving money on beer and trips away.
- The opportunity to campaign to save pubs under threat of closure, for pubs to be open when people want to drink and a reduction in beer duty that will help Britain's brewing industry survive.

Do you feel passionately about your pint? Then why not join CAMRA?

Just fill in the application form below (or a photocopy of it) and the Direct Debit form on the previous page to receive three months' membership free AND a discounted membership rate! If you wish to join... but do not want to pay by Direct Debit, please fill in the form and send a cheque, payable to CAMRA, to: CAMRA, 230 Hatfield Road, St Albans, Hertfordshire AL1 4LW.

Please tick appropriate box. DD = Direct Debit. Rates are for UK and EU residents only.

Single membership	DD £20	Non DD £22
Joint membership	DD £25	Non DD £27
Single concessionary membership	DD £11	Non DD £13
Joint concessionary membership	DD £14	Non DD £16

■ Concessionary membership available to under 26s and over 60s. Please note that both members must be eligible for the membership rate. ■ Life membership information available on request.

If you join by Direct Debit you will receive three months' membership extra free!

Title	Surname	
Forename (s)		
Address		
		Postcode
Date of Birth	E-mail address	
Signature		

Partners details if required

Title	Surname	
Date of Birth	E-mail address	

☐ Please tick here if you would like to receive occasional e-mails from CAMRA, (at no point will your details be released to a third party).

Find out more about CAMRA at www.camra.org.uk